Encyclopedia of California's Catholic Heritage

1769-1999

Fray Junípero Serra

1713/1784

A drawing by Jena Kavin
for the Grabhorn Press.

Encyclopedia of California's Catholic Heritage

1769-1999

by
Msgr. Francis J. Weber

SAINT FRANCIS HISTORICAL SOCIETY
and
THE ARTHUR H. CLARK COMPANY
Mission Hills, California   Spokane, Washington
2001

The author gratefully acknowledges the dedicated interest of
Daniel Donohue
and the generous support of
the Dan Murphy Foundation
in the publication of this book.

Library of Congress Catalog Card Number 00-045758
ISBN-0-9678477-1-0

Copies may be secured from
Saint Francis Historical Society
15151 San Fernando Mission Blvd
Mission Hills, CA 91345
and
The Arthur H. Clark Co.
P.O. Box 14707
Spokane, WA 99214
800-842-9286

Library of Congress Cataloging-in-Publication Data

Weber, Francis J.
Encyclopedia of California's Catholic heritage, 1769–1999 / by Francis J. Weber. p. cm.
Includes index.
    1. Catholic Church—California—History—17th century—Encyclopedias. 2. California—Church history—17th century—Encyclopedias. 3. Catholic Church—California—History—18th century—Encyclopedias. 4. California—Church history—18th century—Encyclopedias. 5. Catholic Church—California—History—19th century—Encyclopedias. 6. California—Church history—19th century—Encyclopedias. I. Title.

BX1415.C2 W415 2000
282'.794'09—dc21

                                                                                00-045758

Contents

PREFACE

California has experienced everything in recent years—riots, floods, droughts, fires, earthquakes and even killer bees. Yet, the Golden State is still the garden spot of old planet earth. One often recalls and affirms what Fray Junípero Serra said: "In California is my life and there, God willing, I hope to die."

Truly, California is a state of superlatives. Twelve percent of the nation's residents live in California, an area that boasts of 64,500 millionaires, 57 percent of them women! Well over 56 percent of the state's population own their own homes and 90 percent have at least one car.

Despite the rape, mayhem, robbery and murder, California is still *El Dorado* to refugees from boredom, poverty, stagnation and despotism. A favored statistic, quoted for the benefit of easterners, is that Blue Canyon, California, is the snowiest town in the country with a mean average of 243.2 inches.

However decadent it may appear to outsiders—weakened by unemployment and inflation, demoralized by crime, deluded by cultists, corrupted by pornographers, debased by junk bond dealers, decimated by psychopaths and pillaged by rioters—California remains a never–never land of riches, fame and freedom to millions around the world. Despite pockets of poverty, Californians are fabulously wealthy in other ways.

In a booster pamphlet issued in 1886 by the Illinois Association, one reads that "in this grand country, we have the tallest mountains, the biggest trees, the crookedest railroads, the driest rivers, the loveliest flowers, the smoothest ocean, the finest fruits, the mildest lives, the softest breezes, the brightest skies and the most genial sunshine to be found anywhere else in North America." The pamphlet goes on to say that "we welcome those sojourning in a 'City of Angels' where their hearts will be irrigated by living waters from the perennial fountains of health, happiness and longevity."

Angelenos are used to being misunderstood. The November 22, 1943 issue of *Life* carried a feature story about California's southland which stated that "Los Angeles is the damnedest place in all the world," a comment typical of eastern cynics.

Realistically, Los Angeles is the most interesting metropolis in all the world. In altitude, it ranges from 5,049 feet in Tujunga (which is higher than all but a few mountains east of the Mississippi) to below sea level at Terminal Island. Los Angeles is divided by both a river and a mountain range. It is the only major city in the country large enough to have forest fires within its limits! It boasts of snow–clad mountains and sunshine beaches at the same time, with a 40 degree difference in temperature in a single day. Los Angeles completely surrounds full–fledged municipalities and unincorporated county areas.

There has always been a strange loyalty to the rhythmic flow of life in California. Perhaps that was best expressed by a youngster who, when asked where she came from, answered, "I was born in California at the age of six."

At the outset of the new millennium, almost nine million Catholics look back on their heritage as part of the great California saga. Catholicism in the Golden State was begun, developed and then sustained by immigrants from mostly Catholic countries who brought their faith to the Pacific Slope and then passed that precious jewel to new generations.

For those who might consider the term "encyclopedia" a bit pretentious for a work of this kind, perhaps an explanation is in order. In the case of most encyclopedias, a panel of scholars spends long months drawing up exhaustive lists of topics which cover all the major phases of a particular subject. Then qualified experts are chosen to actually write the individual entries, and finally, somebody is chosen to edit the entries into a uniform style. It's a process that can and often does occupy many years.

Less frequently, an individual will take on himself the task of both selecting the topics and writing the entries. A good example would be Dan L. Thrapp's four volume *Encyclopedia of Frontier History* (Glendale, 1988–1994) in which the compiler personally delineated "the lives and deeds of 4,500 key players in the discovery and development of Western America."

Several close friends and historical scholars, aware that I had been researching and writing in this field for forty plus years, contended that I was uniquely qualified to compile this book. Apart from the validity of that contention, this encyclopedia does provide a unique opportunity for codifiying and perpetuating a portion of the work that has occupied my time for so many years.

Candidates for inclusion in this encyclopedia include people of either sex and any race: white, red, black, brown or yellow who merited attention through the significance of their deeds or who were in some other way related to the evolving drama of California's Catholic heritage. While only a couple are candidates for sainthood, most of them surely qualify as pioneers, heroes, innovators and role models.

For the most part, entries are presented alphabetically under nine major headings, one each for the California missions, hierarchy, laity, clergymen, friars, religious, ecclesial foundations, memoirs and topical subjects.

Careful use of the Index is crucial for those wishing to make the fullest use of this work because many names and/or events for which there are no formal entries will be found in the Index. In the section on memoirs, the entries are listed chronologically by date of occurrence.

Even in a collection of over 1,600 entries, it was physically impossible to mention and discuss every worthy candidate or all the vital topics. Possibly a future edition of this book or maybe even a wholly new compilation will occupy the time of some enterprising researcher of another age who can update what is here presented.

After he compiled his monumental four volumes on *The Missions and Missionaries of California,* Father Zephyrin Engelhardt embarked on a series of books about the individual missions. He was motivated by the scriptural injunction: "Gather up the fragments, lest they be lost." Those subsequent sixteen volumes took on a life of their own and even today they occupy the shelves of any serious student or *aficionado* of that chain of missionary foundations along California's *El Camino Real.*

John Tracy Ellis often recalled attending the funeral of his predecessor, Msgr. Peter Guilday, the paramount historian for the Catholic Church in the United States. As the casket was being lowered into its earthly tomb, Ellis overheard a little old lady say: "What a shame that so much history is being interred in that coffin."

Hopefully, this book will forestall a similar comment when my own frail remains are carted off to the local boneyard. Or, to quote my dear friend, Doyce B. Nunis, "Weber never had an unpublished thought."

It is a pleasure here to acknowledge the assistance of Gladys Posakony who read and corrected the galleys and Terry Ruscin who designed the beautiful jacket.

I. The California Missions
1. Individual Missions

San Diego de Alcalá (1769)

FIRST LINK IN THE ROSARY OF MISSIONS

The earliest of the Upper California missions, dedicated to Saint Didacus of Alcalá, dates from 1769 and has been located near the city which bears its name since 1774. San Diego de Alcalá had its ups and downs like all the missions but it probably reached the zenith of its prosperity in 1797. Stretching over an expanse of 50,000 acres, the mission property accommodated its largest number of Indians and formed a vital link in the overall spiritual success along *El Camino Real*.

Within the mission's confines was developed one of the first irrigation systems in the western United States covering almost eight miles up the San Diego River. A dam, with a large aqueduct lined with tiles resting on cobblestones, proved extremely important to the far away mission farmlands.

When secularization came, the fortunes of the first link in the Franciscan chain of missions declined rapidly. The property was sold in 1846, and shortly thereafter, Father Vicente Oliva was forced to relinquish his post to Santiago Arguello. The American flag flew over the mission during the years when a contingent of union soliders occupied it as a fort in the early 1850s. What few parts were left of the historic buildings after the army's retirement were shaken down by the earthquake of 1860.

At the turn of the century Father Anthony Ubach utilized some of the ruins for an Indian School and brought the Sisters of Saint Joseph to San Diego to staff the institution. After Ubach's death, however, the children were moved to Banning where they studied in another school, this one under the patronage of Saint Boniface. Bishop John J. Cantwell asked the Sisters of Nazareth to take charge in 1924, and within a few years the nuns erected a home for children known as "Nazareth House." In the years after 1930, the bishop spearheaded plans to restore the mission along its original lines. Several walls, buttresses and arches of the earlier structure were salvaged and used as foundations for the restored edifice. The rebuilt mission was re–dedicated in 1931. On February 2, 1941, Bishop Charles Francis Buddy elevated the mission to parochial status and in 1954 the old church was once again put into actual use.

The restored Mission of San Diego de Alcalá has attracted comment from various sources. One authority noted that the early missionaries "created a type of Spanish colonial architecture which alone belongs to California and is nowhere better exemplified than in Mission San Diego de Alcalá." The graveyard is probably the oldest one used by colonizers in California. Several adobe and burnt crosses mark the tombs of countless hundreds of Indians who died during the mission period—along with their spiritual mentors, the Franciscan friars. Erected to introduce Christianity and its culture to a whole new people, Mission San Diego de Alcalá stands today a noble relic of a great era!

SAN DIEGO'S MYTHICAL TUNNEL—1919

Hillaire Belloc once rather harshly observed, "Almost all the historical work worth doing at the present moment in the English language is the work of shovelling off heaps of rubbish inherited from the immediate past." Though the general emphasis on truth and accuracy has improved considerably in the last half century, Belloc's dictum was well taken, at least as far as certain of his contemporary writers on the California scene were concerned.

In 1919, for example, the author of an interesting book on mission architecture attracted considerable attention by calling attention to the "underground passages" reportedly used by the friars "as a means of escape in case they were besieged" by hostile natives. One of these alleged subterranean tunnels was located at Mission San Diego. It was, according to the writer, a "passage of very ingenious arrangement leading, perhaps, from some room in the mission to the well at the foot of the hill." The imaginative writer noted that the entrance to the passageway "has never been sought for and it has for the most part fallen in, as can be found by exploring from the well." Though obviously basing his knowledge of the tunnel on secondary, verbal accounts, the author further recorded that "the passage led underground from the well, opening into the sides several yards below the level of the grade." Such an arrangement allowed the *padres* to "go and fetch water without being seen by a hostile band of Indians. Across the well, the passage continued some distance further and made an exit in the group of palm trees, planted by the Fathers."

Despite this detailed explanation and description, there is absolutely no evidence that such a tunnel ever existed outside the mind of Prent Duel, the creative author. Nor is there any indication of underground passageways at the other California missions. Father Zephyrin Engelhardt, the historian of the missions, states that "in the whole mass of available documents no mention whatever is made that a tunnel was built, nor is there the faintest allusion that anything of the kind was ever contemplated."

It is true, as Duel observed, that the mission at an early date was destroyed, but his allegation that several of the friars escaped by this means (i.e., the tunnel) is not factually founded, for during the 1775 uprising, one of the friars was killed and the other most assuredly had neither the time nor inclination to go "underground." It should also be noted that any tunnel would have been unearthed in 1847–48 when the United States troops quartered at the mission excavated a cistern in which to store fresh water for their domestic needs.

The story of San Diego's mythical tunnel is hardly a novelty. Many prevarications have circulated about the old missions, some of them quite silly, others vicious and made–to–order and still others gleaned from the cursory reading of and listening to fiction.

A MISSION REDEDICATED—1931

On September 13, 1931, ceremonies were held at San Diego to mark the rededication of California's first mission. Reproduced here are the highlights from the sermon delivered on that historic occasion by Bishop John J. Mitty of Salt Lake City.

During the latter half of the eighteenth century . . . here on the golden shores of the Pacific Ocean, a few hundred Spanish soldiers and a few score Franciscan *padres* were carving a new empire out of the wilderness; were opening up a country whose riches and resources would astound the world; were laying the foundations of civilization in California and bringing the blessings of religion to this western coast.

From San Diego in the South to Sonoma in the North, the greyrobed sons of St. Francis walked from mission to mission, tracing out the path that is now known as *El Camino Real*, The King's Highway.

Along its path the Kings of Spain sent their emissaries to claim and possess the land, to develop its natural resources, to enroll its inhabitants as the subjects of Spain, to train them in the arts of industry and to fit them for civilization. Along this same road the Eternal King of ages sent His missionaries to extend the Kingdom of Heaven, to develop its spiritual resources, to enroll its inhabitants as subjects of the Kingdom of God, to train them in the way of salvation and to fit them for eternity.

California was an empire to be gained for Christ; Christ was to be its King; the Franciscan *Padres* were to be His soldiers. They were to claim this empire in His name; they were to possess it for Him, not by earthly means, but by living Christ–like lives, by practicing the Christ–like virtues of charity, poverty and sacrifice.

No soil seemed more unpromising; no race seemed more unconquerable. But inspired by the love of God and zeal for souls, armed with the commission of the Apostles and of the Vicar of Christ, the humble, zealous Franciscan, Fray Junípero Serra, erected the Cross of Christ and began his labors for the extension of Christ's Kingdom here in California.

By the ministry of Junípero Serra, this mission of San Diego became the first tabernacle of God among men in California. By the ministry of Junípero Serra here in San Diego, Christ was brought to the Indians of California, and they were brought to Christ. By the ministry of Junípero Serra, this spot became the very cradle of Christianity in the West.

The disciple is not above the master; and the lives of the Franciscan missionaries in the history of the California missions were to be a counterpart of the life of Christ and the history of His Church. Hard toil, incessant labor, constant sacrifice were the portion of Christ and His Church. They were the portion, likewise, of the missionaries in California.

The conquest of souls was the reward of the California missionaries. The envy and hatred of men brought Christ along the way of the Cross to His Crucifixion on Calvary. Time and again in history, the Church has had her Good Friday and walked along the sorrowful way of the Cross to Crucifixion at the hands of her enemies.

So too, through the envy and hatred of men, the missions of California had their Good Friday and were crucified for Christ. But Christ's Good Friday had its Easter Sunday; His Crucifixion had its Resurrection. And time and again down the ages the defeat of the Church has been turned into victory; her seeming death was but the prelude to a stronger and more active life. So, too, the California missions, after their Good Friday and their Crucifixion, are having their Resurrection.

Today San Diego mission has its resurrection in the dedication of this mission Church. The simple dedication ceremony of the first humble mission in the presence of a few soldiers and Indians, by Fray Junipero Serra on that July in 1769, is renewed today with all the splendor of Church ritual.

We may well bare our heads and bend our knees for we stand on sacred ground. This is a holy spot; it has been sanctified by the prayers and labors of heroic men of God.

San Carlos del Rio Carmelo (1770)

GOLDEN STATE'S OLDEST LIBRARY—1770

The re–assembled collection of mission tomes at San Carlos Borromeo del Río Carmelo, the oldest extant library in California, has been described as "one of the most truly precious restorations of our Spanish colonial era." Earliest of the titles brought to Monterey, in 1770 by Fray Junípero Serra were shipped by sea from Baja California, where they had been gathered by the friars from the various holdings of the already–established peninsular missions.

The wide range of subject matter exhibited in the various titles underscores the need in provincial times for books both professional in nature and utilitarian in purpose. Some dealt with scripture, theology and homiletics, while others touched on history, music, medicine, geography, agriculture and architecture.

A close examination of the annual inventories reveals that the collection at Carmel had grown to fifty volumes by 1784. Sixteen years later, there were at least 300 titles and, by 1834, the number had expanded to 405. During the tenure of Fray Junípero Serra at San Carlos, the books were arranged by size in sectional redwood cases built especially to accommodate the small but functional library.

The collection became the only one among the missions formally catalogued during the administration of Fray Fermín Lasuén. Sometime between June, 1798, and June, 1803, the Cantabrian friar classified the books in a fashion analagous to the one used at his Apostolic College of San Fernando in Mexico City. Lasuén's system was quite simple. A field about an inch square was painted with white lead at the top of the spine. Catalogue marks followed the Latin sequence, the case number in Roman numerals and the book number in Arabic. Both were inscribed in black India ink. There were four sections in the library, one each for 4to, 8vo, 12mo and smaller volumes.

Sometime after the departure of the last resident priest from Carmel, the few remaining books from the mission library were taken to the Sherman Rose adobe in nearby Monterey. Subsequently they were moved to the various parochial dwellings attached to the *presidio* chapel.

The markings on the spines of the books facilitated their identification and, in the 1930s, a search was initiated for missing titles. Sixty–seven books from the mission era were discovered in the attic and library of Santa Cruz Rectory. The shelves at San Juan Bautista yielded another eight. A private collection of 177 was retrieved and various others were located from scattered places.

Of the 458 volumes assembled by Father James Culleton in 1933, 143 bore the Carmel mission accession number. Most recent addition to the library was a collection of sixteen titles which, since 1842, had formed part of the *Bibliotheca Montereyensis–Angelorum Dioeceseos.* In 1949, the library was returned to the mission and placed in the restored room originally designed for that purpose.

Presently, there are 579 volumes in the Carmel Mission Library, 261 of which have been identified as belonging to San Carlos between 1771 and 1842. The collection is displayed in four specifically built cases fashioned after original designs by Harry Downie. A fifth cabinet houses part of the William E.P. Hartnell Library, once the largest private book collection in California.

JOURNALIST VISITS CARMEL MISSION—1879

During his sojourn in Monterey, Robert Louis Stevenson was engaged as a journalist by the *Monterey Californian.* Experts suggest that he wrote (but didn't sign) fourteen articles between October 7th and December 23rd, 1879. Nellie Van de Grift Sanchez pointed out that "perhaps nothing about the place interested him more deeply than the old mission of San Carlos Borromeo," the burial place of Fray Junipero Serra.

Once a year, on San Carlos Day (November 4th), the entire population of the area travelled to the Old Mission. In 1879, RLS was among the visitors. He found the church fast falling into ruins. Nothing of the roof remained, except for a few rafters.

Stevenson attended the Mass that year and then joined in the *merienda* (lunch) under the trees, during which vast quantities of *tamales, enchiladas* and other distinctive Hispanic foods were distributed to friends and strangers, Catholics and Protestants. Stevenson was greatly moved. He described the scene in "The Old Pacific Capital," which first appeared in *Fraser's Magazine* in London and was later included in the work *Across the Plains,* which has been published separately and as part of *The Amateur Emigrant:*

> Only one day in the year, the day before Guy Fawkes, the *padre* drives over the hill from Monterey; the little sacristy, which is the only covered portion of the church, is filled with seats and decorated for the service.
>
> The Indians troop together, their bright dresses contrasting with their dark and melancholy faces; and there,

among a crowd of somewhat unsympathetic holiday makers, you may hear God served under perhaps more touching circumstances than in any other temple under heaven.

An Indian, stone blind and about eighty years of age, conducts the singing; and other Indians compose the choir; yet they have the Gregorian music at their finger ends, and pronounce the Latin so correctly that I could follow the meaning as they sang.

I have never seen faces more vividly lit up with joy than the faces of these Indian singers. It was to them not only the worship of God, nor an act by which they recalled and commemorated better days, but was besides an exercise of culture, where all they knew of art and letters was united and expressed.

And it made a man's heart sorry for the good fathers of yore, who had taught them to dig and to reap, to read and to sing, who had given them European Mass books which they still preserve and study in their cottages, and who had now passed away from all authority and influence in that land—to be succeeded by greedy land thieves and sacrilegious pistolshots. So ugly a thing our Anglo–Protestantism may appear beside the doings of the Society of Jesus.

Robert Louis Stevenson ended this essay, signed "The Monterey Barbarian," on November 11, 1879, thusly:

A fine old church, a fine old race, both brutally neglected; a survival, a memory and a ruin. The United States Mint can coin many million more dollar pieces, but not make a single Indian; and when Carmel Church is in the dust, not all the wealth of all the States and Territories can replace what has been lost.

No man's word can move the Indians from the ruin that awaits them, but the church? How, my dear Bronson, if you and I put together our little mites and, through the columns of your paper, sought upon all hands to interest others in this useful work of protection?

I feel sure that the money would be forthcoming before long; and the future little ones of Monterey would clap their hands to see the old Church, and learn by the sight of it more history than even Mr. Graves and all his successors can manage to teach them out of history books.

RESTORATION AT CARMEL – 1884

Though San Carlos Borromeo suffered almost total destruction in the years after its abandonment, it is today one of the best restored of the California missions. Founded on June 3, 1770, the mission's church and compound were built gradually over the next forty–six years. The present church, the sixth in the order of time, was finished in 1797 and the quadrangle was closed in 1815.

In 1834, the mission was secularized and twelve years later it was sold. From 1846 to 1933, there was no resident priest there. President James Buchanan adjudicated ecclesial ownership of the church and nine acres of land in 1859. In the meantime, tiles had been carried off and most of the adobe buildings had melted back into the ground. The roofless stone church fell into decay and animals sought shelter within its walls. Gradually, statues, paintings and other furnishings disappeared. San Carlos Borromeo became a cathedral in the wilderness.

In 1882, Father Angelo Casanova, the pastor at nearby Monterey, began the work of restoration. An astute man, Casanova foresaw that the opening of the Del Monte Hotel would insure a future for the entire peninsula.

The historic church was renovated in 1884 with funds raised by Casanova from personal friends and local inhabitants. Casanova's roof had a considerably higher pitch than the original one, a factor that was later rectified. The church stood alone until 1914, surrounded by the stumps of adobe walls in the compound. Excellent sketches, drawings and photographs had been made over the years and these made accurate restoration a realistic possibility.

Father Ramon Mestres restored the section of the north wing protruding from the church tower in 1924. Within it was placed Jo Mora's elaborate bronze and travertine sarcophagus honoring Fray Junípero Serra. Mestres also built a rectory (still extant but used as a museum) near the cemetery.

In 1931, Father Philip Scher built Serra–Crespi Hall, to the south of the church along what was the south section of the west wing of the original quadrangle. In 1953, the hall was moved to its present location to the rear of the church. It was also in 1931 that Harry Downie began his monumental work at Carmel. A skilled cabinet-maker, Downie was without a peer in California for his knowledge of mission buildings and their restoration.

Downie continued adding to the north wing begun by Mestres, extending it to the present Serra room by 1932 and completing it in 1941. Moreover he removed Casanova's roof and restored its original pitch. In 1942, he began building the south side of the quadrangle piecemeal between 1950 and 1955, and these wings became the parochial school.

The gap in the east wing between the rectory and the original *padres'* quarters was filled in to serve as a small chapel in 1948. All the buildings in the quadrangle were built atop the original foundations and externally their form followed as closely as possible the original structures. The convent was located beyond the quadrangle parallel to the west wing.

The sanctuary floor had been renovated by Downie in 1943 when the graves of the friars were opened and identified. The reredos and altar were built by Downie personally. An extension to the east wing was later used as the living quarters for the Bishop of Monterey. The room built between the convent and the hall is known as the Munras Memorial.

Many artifacts, paintings, statues and other items belonging to the Old Mission were recovered through the course of the years. Interiorly, the north wing, which is used mostly for exhibits, is one of the finest museums in California. A number of authentic mission rooms have been restored, including Serra's cell and the original mission library.

Carmel Mission has been a parish since 1931. It became a basilica in 1960 and later was consecrated. Today San Carlos Borromeo continues to serve as the flagship of the missions scattered along *El Camino Real.*

EASTERN PILGRIM AT CARMEL—1913

The popular writer, Redfern Mason, wrote a most fascinating essay for the December 20, 1913 issue of *The Monitor* under the title: "I Came to Stay." It outlines what he called "the Record of an Eastern Pilgrim's Coming to California."

The first time I ever heard Mass in California was on the first Sunday of last year. It was at the old mission church of San Carlos de Monterey. We had come into Monterey the night before, and found the old town sleeping in the moonlight while the surf smote the beach with the sound of thunder.

Mason said that he would "never forget the first Mass in the old Spanish church. The deep window embrasures, the walls which threw shadows that reminded me of the paintings of Murillo, the dark-eyed celebrant at the altar thrilled me."

I had come to the ends of the earth and here was the same august sacrifice and with that reflection there came a strange, delightful feeling that here, at least, the kindlier oldness which cradles one to sentiment had not been obliterated by the rush of commerce as it is in New York and New England.

We had come from New York State, two families of us, to find a land where the climate was equable and men and women could live a quiet life, content to be poor, if need be, so long as they did the work which lay nearest their heart.

The feelings that I had at that first Mass, with the figure of the Blessed Virgin smiling upon me, and the genial California sunshine shining through the stained glass of the windows was that, after many years wanderings, in the Old World and the New, I had found a land which I could call home and love better than any other, better than my native England, though her name is music to me and ever will be, better than France, though Gallic culture rejoices heart, better even than Italy, though the verse of Horace and the music of Palestrina are a delight to me still and will continue to be so, I think, as long as I live.

Eighteen months among the pines of Carmel and a quarter of a year in the Western Metropolis have bound me to California by ties which though delicate as the tendrils of the ivy, are as strong as steel.

When I was a schoolboy, I used to read of California. Those were the times when "The Luck of Roaring Camp" and "The Idyll of Poker Flat" were a new page in literature. Men like Bret Harte and Mark Twain had so prepared my mind for this new domain beyond the mountains that I never for a moment felt a stranger here as, for example, I have felt in bleak thoroughfares of New York City.

I will register my conviction that, for a man with ideals, willingness to work, and none too plentiful a stock of this world's goods, California is the most blessed spot on God's earth.

If you have anything to give the people and it is worth while they will give you full credit. But, if you say you can do a thing, they will call your bluff immediately. If you can do what you say, it will be well for you; if you cannot, they will mark you down as a 'make-believe.'

Those words were spoken to me by Bishop (Edward) Hanna and they are true California gospel. When men meet for the first time, there is a sharp interrogative glance. The Western eye sees clearly and the one thing which the Western man will not put up with is pretense.

In very truth I think of this territory to the west of the Rockies as the Promised Land of American art and letters. It is no accidental circumstance that outdoor theatres are springing up all over the State.

The Old Spanish *padres*, those heroes in russet, struck the fundamental note when they determined that California should be a Catholic State. Their work still goes on and it is leaving the whole of California. The influence is to be felt in our latest as in our earliest writers. It vibrates in Bret Harte; it is present more deeply than they know it perhaps in the poems of George Sterling and the prose of Mary Austin.

FOOTPATH OF THE PADRES—1915

Though it was written many years ago, *California Padres and Their Missions* still ranks prominently among the books about the Golden State's *El Camino Real.* Charles Francis Saunders was not only an historian, but a naturalist as well. A keen observer and an inveterate hiker, Saunders was especially intrigued by the trail that Fray Junipero Serra and his Indian neophytes took to the top of Carmel Hill and down to Monterey. Here is what he wrote in 1915:

San Carlos Borromeo Mission

Here at the hilltop, there branches dimly from the high road a footpath which you may follow the rest of the way to Carmel, through idyllic ways now beneath the pines and now across grassy glades where wildflowers twinkle. Through a rift in the woods you can see now and again the blue of the sea, and the breeze brings you the complaint of the distant surf. I would have liked mightily to think this trail I trod was the very path of the Padres, worn by their faithful feet as they traveled to and from Monterey.

Though it is among Carmel's best kept secrets, the Mission Trail Park remains much the same today as it did when described by Charles Francis Saunders.

Across Rio Road from San Carlos Borromeo Mission, one can see a rustic wooden gate that leads into the little–known park. A brochure about the park describes it as "the last remaining example of the natural flora of the Carmel area. Stately Monterey pines, oaks and a pure stand of toyon dominate the northern reaches of the park, while a dense stand of willow shrouds the low lying flood plain to the south. During any season of the year, displays of native grasses, trees, shrubs and wildflowers can be viewed as one hikes along the five miles of trails within the park boundaries. Each new season announces the coming of subtle alterations in the character of the park's vegetation and provides new color displays for the avid or casual hiker."

Among the designated paths are Serra's Trail, Flanders Trail, Mesa Trail, Doolittle Trail and Willow Trail covering the fifteen acres of unspoiled beauty. At the summit of the trails is a sweeping panoramic view encompassing the dome of the Mission, the majestic coastline of Point Lobos Reserve and the foothills in the distance.

The Flanders mansion is located in the park. Built in 1924 by Paul Flanders, the mansion adjoins a meadow which was used as a grazing field for the family's horses. At the end of the Flanders property is the Lester Rowntree Memorial Arboretum which is maintained by the California Native Plant Society. There visitors can see numerous specimens of native flora.

The city fathers of Carmel–by–the–Sea purchased the Flanders property in 1971 and shortly thereafter the Mission Trail Park Consortium was established by local inhabitants. Future plans call for planting more native shrubs and flowers in the arboretum to extend the meadow area. Drinking fountains, picnic facilities and expanded parking areas made the park more accessible to visitors.

SERRA'S SARCOPHAGUS AT CARMEL—1922

The sarcophagus of Fray Junípero Serra, at Mission San Carlos Borromeo, is a synthesis of the early Catholic history in the far–away province of California. Designed by the noted Catalan sculptor, Joseph A. Mora, it depicts Serra lying in state, with his close associates, Crespí, López and Lasuén, Serra's successor as President of the Missions, grouped around the main body of the sarcophagus.

The *dramatis personae* of the Alta California conquest are represented as Spanish soldiers, Franciscans, Indians in their native state, and the neophytes as they are Christianized appear in the vertical panels. At the side of the handsome art–form, is a medallion of Carlos, King of Spain, and of the pope who gave the friars their authority in matters of local development. Seven low flat bas–reliefs in bronze picture the historical events in California, such as the first Mass, the first baptism and the miracle of the ship, San Antonio, in San Diego Bay. Also portrayed is the Indian uprising at the first of the Franciscan missionary foundations. The Spanish coat–of–arms, with the Franciscan cord denoting the order, is shown interwoven with a garland of California poppies at the foot.

The whole creation is executed in bronze and California travertine marble, and is original as well as beautiful in its thought and execution. Critics agree that it is among the finest of Mora's artistic masterpieces. It is entirely appropriate that the monument should be erected in Carmel, for to Serra that was the most beloved of all the missions. His home was there, and there he died. His body now rests under the pavement on the Gospel side of the mission church.

An account of the Mora sarcophagus, published in the *Catholic News* of New York, on July 29, 1922, states that "now, nearly two hundred years later, it is 'Hail, Junípero Serra!' He has exemplified the mystic paradox of the grain of mustard seed of his Master's parable, that was cast into the earth, and died, so that from it might spring a mighty tree."

> He humbled himself—and now he is exalted. He made himself least–and now he is among the foremost. At his birthplace the King of Spain lately unveiled a monument and dedicated a plaza to Mallorca's great son. The mighty commonwealth of the New World, the cornerstone of whose civilization he helped to lay in the western wilderness a few years ago officially celebrated his two–hundredth anniversary.
>
> The most successful drama ever written and produced in the West spreads his name and glory through the effective suggestion of theatrical appeal among the people of the land. To his lonely grave, in the Mission San Carlos de Carmelo, which for generations remained unknown, yearly go thousands of pilgrims in homage to his memory.

There, in the fall of 1922, was dedicated "the memorial which perpetuates the fame and honor which now belong to Fray Junípero Serra, to whom fame and honor meant nothing. Yet, it is well that fame and honor should be his just because he did not seek these things but sought only the Kingdom of God."

GOOD FRIDAY IN MISSIONARY TIMES—1930s

Religious pageantry has always played an important part in the Catholic prayerstyle. From the earliest centuries, the life of Christ has been portrayed in a manner understandable to local cultures. California was no exception. Francisco Palo described how, on Good Friday, the founder of the California Missions, Fray Junípero Serra, "used to preach in the morning on the Passion, and in the afternoon the Descent from the Cross was represented with the greatest vividness by means of a lifelike figure which he had ordered made for the purpose and which had hinges."

He handled the subject in his sermon with the greatest devotion and tenderness. The body of Our Lord was placed in a casket and then used in the procession of the Holy Burial.

It was afterward placed upon an altar which he had prepared for this purpose and at night another procession was made in honor of Our Lady of Solitude, and then the day finished with a special sermon on the subject.

The traditions associated with the Good Friday liturgy in missionary times were re–instated at San Carlos Borromeo in the early 1930s by Harry Downie, the legendary and colorful curator. The pageantry was captured in print by the late Edith Webb: "On Good Friday, 1935, this writer witnessed from the choir loft of the church of San Carlos del Carmelo, the celebration of the 'Descent from the Cross' as it had been observed by Fr. Serra and his fellow priests . . . a ceremony that is rarely performed in California. It was a never–to–be forgotten experience:"

> The great doors of the church were closed. Sunlight came filtering through the colored glass of the small windows, set high in the church walls, catching up here and there some figure or detail in the old paintings hanging there. A curtain of purple velvet concealed the altar.
>
> Ranged in front of this screen was the Calvary Group, a large Crucifix, a statue of Our Lady of Sorrows, and one of St. John, the Evangelist. Six lighted candles, three at each side of the group, shone like stars through the gloom of the sanctuary. These candles, together with those carried by the acolytes in the procession that slowly made the Way of the Cross along the side aisles of the church, and the mellow sunlight from the windows furnished the only illumination of the darkened interior.

The ceremony was of three hours duration and throughout that period there came through the door that opened upon the bell chamber the soft but insistent and far–carrying cooing of many white pigeons who made their nests in the bell tower.

The priests celebrating the Mass were black–robed, the acolytes, the choristers, and the worshippers were all from the little community of today, but, if one has really learned to concentrate it is not difficult to brush such tangibles from the scene and people it with the mission *padres* and the dusky neophytes of long ago.

Picturing the Indians kneeling on the tiled floor, or standing, as the celebration demanded, this watcher wondered if they were as startled as she was, when, at the proper moment in the ceremony, the nails were drawn from the hands and feet of the lifelike, life–size figure of the Christ on the cross, and the arms allowed slowly to fall to its sides.

Then, gently, carefully the figure was taken down, the knees bending as if it were a human form. Following the custom established by Fr. Serra, this act was performed as the procession making the Way of the Cross reached the thirteenth Station.

At the fourteenth Station, commemorating the burial of Christ, the figure was carried out the front door of the church, around the plaza and back into the Mortuary chapel, the choir singing the "Reproaches" even as the Indian neophytes did in mission days.

Indeed, that was pageantry at its best and who can measure the impression it made on the minds of the Indians?

spent the rest of his life. For obvious reasons, the buttons lost their relevance.

The French government, having no use for the buttons, sold them to King Henri Christophe of Haiti. His Black Majesty was one of the leaders in the successful negro uprising, aided considerably by yellow fever, that forced the French from the western part of the Island of Haiti, which the French had dominated for over a century and a half.

Since the people of Haiti spoke French, Henri Christophe thought the buttons would add a measure of elegance to his soldiers. Then as now, brass buttons, medals and similar insignia that can be worn conspicuously seem to be, next to weapons and food, one of the essential requirements of any military or naval force.

Before the buttons arrived, however, the army revolted against the ruthless and cruel monarch and Henri I terminated his earthly existence with a silver bullet into his heart. With no market for the buttons, the captain of the ship bringing them to Haiti sailed on to the Pacific Coast, where he traded them for furs. They were popular items among the natives and today can be found as far north as Oregon.

The Franciscans at San Carlos Borromeo Mission bought some of the buttons and used them on the clothes of the Indian neophytes, possibly giving them as rewards for exceptionally good behavior.

All of which proves that there is an explanation behind every historical puzzle, provided one is inclined and equipped to look beyond the buttonhole!

CARMEL'S MYSTERIOUS BUTTONS

Historians thrive on challenges. Perhaps that's why the puzzle as to how buttons from the soldiers in Napoleon's army found their way to Carmel proved so fascinating. The buttons in question are about an inch in diameter. Around their edges are the words *"Je remais de mes cendres"* (I am born again from my ashes). In the center is the image of a bird, probably the legendary phoenix.

According to ancient stories, the phoenix came once in every 500 years from Arabia to Egypt and built a funeral pyre in the Temple of the Sun. Fanning the pyre with its wings, the pyre burst into flames. The bird was consumed in the fire, but soon rose from its ashes with renewed life.

A little research revealed that Napoleon ordered the buttons for his soldiers upon his return from exile on the Isle of Elba. They were intended to signify the emperor's new life and vigor. Unfortunately, a hundred days later, Napoleon was defeated at Waterloo. He was sent again to exile, this time at Saint Helena, where he

THE BIBLICAL GARDEN

During his first pilgrimage to the tomb of Fray Junípero Serra at San Carlos Borromeo Mission, the late James Francis Cardinal McIntyre was driven to nearby Carmel–by–the–Sea, where he visited the "Biblical Garden" designed by Butler Sturtevant and made possible through the generosity of Mrs. George Beardsley.

Among the cardinal's papers is a pamphlet describing the attractive garden where the various plants, shrubs, trees and flowers mentioned in Sacred Scripture were flourishing. Each item was carefully marked and explained. Among the trees were a Cedar of Lebanon (referred to several times in the Bible as a symbol of grandeur and might), the Fig (an important tree for its shade and fruit), the Olive (essential for its fruit and oil) and the Tamarisk (a hardy tree used as a windbreak along the coastal areas).

Other trees were the Myrtle (a symbol of peace and joy), the Myrrh (used for perfumes and embalming), the Citron (representing God's gift of fruit) and Box tree (a hardy evergreen used for decorative purposes). Among the shrubs in the Biblical Garden were the Bulrush or Papyrus (used for weaving baskets and making paper), the Giant Reed (useful as measuring rods), the Acanthus (common in architectural designs) and the Vine (the official emblem of the nation).

Herbs were often mentioned by the inspired writers. Among these at Carmel–by–the–Sea were the Mint (valued for its use in condiments), the Anise (used for seasoning), the Cumin (used as a spice in bread) and Rue (a bitter–tasting medicinal plant).

Probably the most attractive part of the Biblical Garden were its flowers. As visitors will testify, the Holy Land abounds in wildflowers, many of which grow also in California which has a similar climate. As happens in California, when the rainy season comes, seeds and bulbs dormant during the dry months spring to life again and cover the hillsides and valleys with brilliant flowers.

The more common wildflowers found in Palestine are lupines, daisies, marigolds, larkspurs, violets, salvia, nigella, mallow and morning glories. There are also abundant bulbs such as anemone, ranunculus, narcissus, crocus, hyacinth, tulip, iris and star–of–Bethlehem, all of which grow profusely after the spring rains.

The term "rose", translated from the Hebrew, means bulblike. Botanists generally believe it to be the narcissus or tulip. The Rose of Sharon is thought to be the crocus or the amaryllis distinctive to the plain of Sharon.

Many biblical scholars believe that the anemone can be identified with the lily of the field. (The white Madonna lily so often painted into pictures of the Madonna and Child was introduced into Palestine after the time of Christ.) Wildflowers are frequently referred to in the Bible as "flowers of the field". In Luke 2, 27, Jesus called wildflowers "lilies of the field."

Throughout the Biblical Garden, each of the trees, shrubs and herbs is described along with the pertinent scriptural verse. For example, attached to the Cedar of Lebanon is the quotation from Psalm 92: "The righteous shall flourish like the palm tree; he shall grow like a cedar of Lebanon." Cardinal McIntyre was city–bred. To him the Biblical Garden provided a whole new glimpse into the magnificence of God's glory.

THE DOWNIE MEMORIAL

During his long and colorful life, Harry Downie became a legendary figure. His restoration work on California's missions earned him a unique place in the Golden State's historical annals. Shortly after his demise, on March 10, 1980, Richard Joseph Menn, one of Downie's closest associates and successor, began planning a memorial to the venerable "Sir Harry of Carmel."

A modest adobe structure, shaded by a cork tree in the garden area of San Carlos Borromeo Mission, was designated the "Downie Museum." It is well worth a reflective visit. There are three separate sections or "galleries" in the museum. The first is lined with glass cases in which are exhibited artifacts and photographs showing a chronological overview of the mission's history.

The Indian baskets, shell necklaces and other utility items shown there were used by the natives who lived in the area prior to the arrival of Fray Junípero Serra and his companions in 1770. Also displayed are a number of mementos related to the establishment of San Carlos Borromeo Mission. Items associated with the various periods of mission development are also featured, along with views portraying the decline brought on by secularization.

The second gallery is devoted to the "restoration" of San Carlos, for which Harry Downie gained renown in architectural circles. An array of Downie memorabilia brings into focus the dedication which this truly remarkable man exhibited in his almost half century at Carmel.

A cabinet–maker by trade, Harry's childhood notebooks indicate an early interest in the missions. Just above the notebooks is a wooden statue which Downie carved as a boy. To the right and left are the tools which he used throughout his career, some of them dating to the past century.

A portion of the numerous awards, citations and decorations bestowed on Harry are also displayed. Though no other person associated with the California missions received as many public commendations as did Harry Downie, he was never very impressed by such recognitions. His work was his reward.

In the third gallery is a replica of Downie's workshop. The tools of his trade scattered on the wooden table evoke memories of Harry fashioning a hinge, fixing a statue, carving a pediment or painting a reredos. Harry's wide–brimmed hat hangs on a hook, together with his tattered "Sunday" suit and an old umbrella. Next to the cluttered desk is an easel on which is Downie's drawing for the reconstruction of the retable for Carmel Mission Basilica's altar.

The adobe housing the museum had formerly contained a photographic exhibit. Having planned to bring the structure into conformity with the basilica's exterior, Harry would have approved of the workmanship that went into his memorial.

Early in life, Harry Downie thought about becoming a Jesuit brother. But, as he once told this writer, "I carved better than I prayed, so the Lord told me to get busy and fix up His missions." He did—and did well. And how fitting there's a museum which tells the story of this marvelous man and his dedication to *El Camino Real.*

SAN ANTONIO DE PADUA (1771)

When the expeditionary soldiers led by Gaspar de Portola camped in the beautiful oak–covered valley bordering the foothills of the Santa Lucia Mountains in 1769, their attention was caught immediately by the scenic grandeur of that peaceful region. The area was called *Los Robles* (Oak Trees) a term now associated with a city fifty miles to the south.

In the words of Fray Francisco Palou, "The ardent zeal for the conversion of the gentiles which ever burned in the heart of the venerable Fray Junípero Serra, gave him no rest, nor permitted him to delay founding a third mission for which Viceroy Marqués de Croix had already selected the name as early as November, 1770." Actual foundation of San Antonio de Padua, among the first institutions in the hemisphere erected to that saint's honor, dates from July 14th, 1771. Within ten years almost a thousand Indians were attached to the thriving San Antonio, the largest number of neophytes contained at any one of the mission chain.

Installation of the intricate series of aqueducts in the next decade increased the material fortunes of the mission considerably, so that by 1830 the entire valley was one giant vineyard stretching as far as the eye could see. The downfall of the mission was swift and by 1843 the whole compound was a mass of ruins. Between 1844 and 1852 there was no resident priest. Father Dorotéo Ambrís, ordained by Bishop Garcia Diego y Moreno, labored there for thirty years, doing what he could to carry on the noble traditions of earlier decades. After 1882 neighboring ranchers carried off the tiles and other usable materials and soon the barren adobe walls began to disintegrate. In 1903, the California Historic Landmarks League took steps to restore the church and certain other parts of the mission. The 1906 earthquake set restoration attempts back considerably, but progress continued on a small scale through the following years, due mostly to private incentive.

In 1928 John B. MacGinley, Bishop of Monterey–Fresno, entrusted the mission to the Franciscan friars and from 1948 onwards the restoration proceeded with some consistency. Impetus to the work was gained from the realization that San Antonio, alone among its sister–missions, was still surrounded by the same primitive environment that so appealed to its founders.

Bishop Aloysius J. Willinger, C.Ss.R., of Monterey–Fresno spearheaded an ambitious attempt to complete the work and give San Antonio a measure of its former dignity. With a generous grant from the Hearst Foundation, the work was supervised by Harry Downie, prominent authority on mission restoration. Adobe bricks were replaced and rough timbers hewn and cut to size until the original structure had been reproduced down to the smallest detail, an exact replica of the former establishment.

A colorful re–dedication ceremony was scheduled for June 4, 1950, to mark completion of the project. The bell announcing the dedication was recast from the only two American–made bells in the mission system, fashioned by Paul Revere in Boston and hanging for many years at San Gabriel.

Located twenty–seven miles from King City, San Antonio de Padua today is the most "typical" of all the missions. And, as one author has pointed out, "In the story of this chain of missions a heartening fact comes shiningly forward, a light in a dark, indifferent world, a world that, once the gleam is seen, is neither so dark nor so indifferent as was supposed."

THE NATIVES AT MISSION SAN ANTONIO— 1814

The *respuesta* to the Spanish government from San Antonio de Padua de los Robles, dated February 26, 1814, reveals a great deal about the natives attached to the third of the California missionary foundations. Written in the hand of Fray Pedro Cabot and countersigned by Fray Juan Bautista Sancho, the report indicated that the natives of San Antonio used two distinct languages, though most understood Spanish fairly well and could speak it with some fluency.

Concerning their past, the neophytes had neither writers nor documents, neither of paper or bark. Their writing was reduced to a few strokes made on the ground. Instead of numbers, they used knots in a thread or cord, or notches on a stick. Pity was their most outstanding virtue. From that proceeded the charity practiced among both men and women. Compassion was more natural to the feminine sex. It was always a source of wonderment to the missionaries how they endured their sufferings and illnesses without complaint.

As for their pre–Christian religious practices, the Indians at San Antonio never engaged in idolatry. In their pagan state, they returned one good deed for another and they pardoned injuries and affronts, though with some repugnance. In their pagan state, they married and divorced with ease. In order to marry, nothing was required beyond consent to live with another. Verbal bargains were more often than not disregarded. A few

SAN ANTONIO DE PADUA MISSION

engaged in polygamy. Unchastity appeared to be their greatest vice, laziness their natural inclination. They were a people so crude and so clever that each of the friars had to sharpen his ingenuity to avoid the consequences of not paying careful attention to even the most ordinary of tasks.

The natives were much inclined to music. They played the violin, cello, flute, trumpet, drum and other instruments supplied by the friars. They retained a flute of their own from the days of paganism which was played like the dulcet. They also had a stringed instrument which resembled a wooden bow to which they would attach an animal sinew. They sang many songs at their dances, singing in variable pitches and tones. They performed Spanish pieces to perfection and easily learned every kind of song taught them, whether in plain or figured music. The natives had their own choir at San Antonio which provided the chant for liturgical celebrations. All possessed clear and sonorous voices.

Their ideas about eternity were transient and superficial. They understood little about eternal glory, though they accepted Catholic doctrine willingly and with docility. They were attracted to religious pageantry and attended sacred functions with great respect and eagerness. The friars reported that both the sick and the well received the sacraments with devotion and recollection.

The work of the missionaries among the Indians in the Santa Lucia Mountains was highly successful. By the end of 1813, 3,731 had been baptized and 1,074 were living at the mission. That year saw the harvesting of 4,528 bushels of wheat, barley, corn, beans and peas.

A MISSIONARY OUTPOST AT MID–CENTURY—1877

An unidentified visitor to San Antonio de Padua described that one–time thriving missionary outpost in an article published by the San Jose *Pioneer,* on January 27, 1877:

> The Mission buildings were then (1849) in good order with buildings on three sides of the square. To the left of the church looking south were the rooms of the Indians. Behind the Mission was the garden with the adobe walls covered with tiles to protect them from the weather.
>
> The vineyard of several acres had a good adobe wall around it, tiled like that of the garden, and had a small adobe house, with a red tiled roof, inside the enclosure.
>
> Some of the vines were six inches or more in diameter. The vineyard and garden could be irrigated from the small stream, behind the Mission, but the plain in front, when the Mission was in full charge of the priests, was irrigated from a ditch that tapped San Antonio River some two miles above, on the way to Milpitas.

Part of this ditch was dug in solid rock. There used to be a grist mill at the Mission, although it was not in use when I was there. There were a good many people living at the Mission itself, but not very many on ranches, which were wide apart—Maurico Soberanes at the Ojetos, and Joaquin Soto at Piojo ranch, they being the principal landowners around.

An Indian named Ygnacio Pastor was living on a small ranch at the Milpitas since swelled into a 11–league ranch. At that time there was more travel through the Mission of San Antonio than at present.

Most of the travel was on horseback through the Release Canyon, the carts of the native Californians with wooden axles and wooden wheels, generally passing by way of the Mission to their ranches, turning off to the right on passing the Questa, and coming in behind the Mission, instead of going to the Jolon first, as they do at present.

There were not many ranches then on the left or southwest bank of the Salinas River from Buena Vista to the mouth of the Release Canyon by the *Arroyo Seco* — *Santiago Estrada* at *Buena Vista*, Malarin and Lugo's being the only ones between Buena Vista and Soledad.

The road was shorter then than now, a large bottom having afterward been swept away by a flood. Richardson's house, on the Coches, was to the left near the Salinas River. There was no house then where Palacio afterwards kept a store, and no one living in Release Canyon, but there were plenty of deer and bear.

At that time a wagon or cart could not pass up the canyon, there being only a horse–trail. The first wagon road was made by hunters to send their game to the San Francisco market. We saw two bears on our trip and for several years afterwards one could rarely go through the canyon without seeing a grizzly.

Most of the Sonorans, on their way to and from the mine, passed through Release Canyon. It was a shorter road, had better grass, wood and water, good camping ground and plenty of game.

Thus appeared Mission San Antonio de Padua in mid–century.

RESTORATION AT SAN ANTONIO MISSION

Few people are aware of the work undertaken by the California Historic Landmarks League just after the turn of the century. One of their more extensive projects was that of restoring parts of San Antonio Mission, situated in a beautiful valley of the Santa Lucia Mountains. The following account of the work is excerpted from an unidentified newspaper clipping in the Chancery Archives, Archdiocese of Los Angeles, dated May 28, 1904.

Commercialism in its mad rush passed San Antonio Mission by and today it stands apparently as left when the last *padre,* discouraged and disheartened, ceased his labors and the last Indian reluctantly deserted its fast crumbling walls. Located twenty–six miles from the nearest railroad, difficulties apparently impossible to overcome presented themselves when restoration was first suggested.

But Californians are blind to obstacles. San Antonio Mission must be restored, and with this determination backed by boundless enthusiasm (and little money), the Landmarks League began work, with the result that the most satisfactory progress has already been made.

A committee from the League visited the mission in July, 1902, for the purpose of ascertaining the condition of the ruins and the probable cost of restoration. Architects took accurate measurements and made drawings of the buildings. Plans were later adopted in compliance with the by–laws of the organization. They were approved by an advisory committee, thus insuring intelligent restoration and dismodernization. The lumber problem was solved when it was discovered that a small saw mill was located on the coast twenty miles from the mission. From the mill a reasonable figure was submitted and order placed.

On the thirteenth day of June, 1903, the Feast of Saint Anthony was celebrated at the old mission. From a radius of thirty miles gathered the inhabitants, some two hundred in all, included in the number being the last descendants of the San Antonio Mission Indians. When those assembled within the ruined walls of the old mission were informed of the work contemplated by the League, the response was prompt. A number voluntarily donated a week's labor, while others offered the use of teams. And what is still more gratifying, the promises are being fulfilled.

The League is attempting at the present time to restore the chapel only, no small task. This structure is 184 feet in length by about forty in width, outside measurement. The great adobe walls are six feet in thickness below the corbel, and five feet above it. Not only has the roof entirely disappeared, but the rains of many winters left great yawning gaps in the side walls. All the old roof timbers were unsound and had to be removed.

On the fifth day of September of last year, the work commenced. An old well near by, formerly used by the mission, was cleaned out and the water problem solved. Tons of debris, the accumulation of years, were first removed from the chapel's interior. Attention was then directed toward filling in the great breaches in the adobe walls. Old adobes, taken from the ruins in the vicinity, are being used at San Antonio. This saves expense and the walls, when completed, will compare favorably, in strength and durability, with the original.

When work ceased on November 21, the entire west wall of the chapel had been restored, the east wall nearly completed and thirty feet of the roof frame in place. Between six and seven thousand adobes have already been used in patching the walls.

It was indeed a noble beginning.

San Gabriel (1771)

SOUTHLAND'S OLDEST CRUCIFIX

The crucifix above the tabernacle of the high altar at San Gabriel Mission has the distinction of being the oldest portrayal of the crucifixion in the Archdiocese of Los Angeles. Mention is made of the historic crucifix in San Gabriel's earliest inventory which was compiled on December 31, 1773. At that time the mission was located on the Rio Hondo River, at present–day San Gabriel Boulevard at Lincoln Avenue.

In November of 1775, when the mission was moved to its present location, the crucifix was among the few items preserved for use in the projected new church.

When the mission was struck by the devastating earthquake of December, 1812, the crucifix was severely damaged. In a report written later that month, Friars Jose de Miguel and Joe M. Zalvidea mentioned that "the holy crucifix" on the high altar was "broken into pieces."

Because of the reverence exhibited for this particular depiction of the Lord, the friars had it carefully restored. An inventory drawn up the following year reports that the "repaired" crucifix was back in service on the altar.

A minute examination of the wooden polychromed and elaborately–carved and painted crucifix reveals a hairline break in the left arm of the *corpus*. There are other almost undetectable indications of repair. The crucifix, although following the general pattern as to style, is a combination of unusual characteristics. More sensitive than most others, it is also more emotional in feeling.

The face has an open mouth and eyes rolled back, portraying the agonizing Christ in the depths of suffering and anguish. To the peoples of those times, the torn tendons and shredded flesh convey the agony of the Savior. The work is consistent with the later Baroque type sculpture and carving common in mid 18th century Mexico. Though it lacks the extravagant twisting and turning of the more theatrical crucifixes of the period, some of those qualities are retained, as for example, the treatment of the elaborately gathered and tied loin cloth.

Christ's figure is realized as a superb, beautiful figure in nearly perfect proportions, and the body is virtually unblemished. That in direct contrast to the unrestrained and often brutal expression that is more in the Mexican and Spanish emotional tradition.

The representation of Our Lord is prior to His death, and though the *corpus* hangs from the arms of the cross, there is little feeling of surging weight. The figure itself is principally of carved wood, with gesso for minor details, while the loin cloth is a combination of wood carving, gesso dipped cloth and gesso. The cross to which the *corpus* is attached is of rusticated wood of a later date.

There is a monochrome character in the near ivory–white of the corpus. Unfortunately it has been somewhat destroyed and obscured by a later repainting. The hair and beard are a warm brown color, the few bruises and the wound in the side are a dull red. The crown of thorns is made of woven cord.

WATER FOR SAN GABRIEL—1776

During the summer of 1950, a grading crew preparing an athletic field for San Gabriel Mission High School, near the intersection of Broadway and Santa Anita streets, unearthed pieces of red tile and parts of hand–molded clay pipe. The scraper had, in fact, bit into the ancient two and a half inch pipe aqueduct that carried water from El Molino Viejo (near the site of the Huntington Hotel) to San Gabriel Mission.

Similar remnants of an old pipe line had been found in the area about ten years earlier between the mission cemetery and the cloister. The 1950 discovery is believed to have connected with that water line.

Thomas Workman Temple II and priests from the Old Mission dug to a depth of three feet with shovels. There they unearthed the aqueduct, with its base still intact. The mill, believed to have been the source of supply for this line, was constructed in 1816, under the supervision of Fray Jose Zalvidea, the gentle friar known as the "Franciscan Johnny Appleseed."

Constructed of solid masonry, the aged mill still stands on Old Mill Road, just west of San Marino. It is now operated by the California Historical Society as its southland headquarters.

Bed of the aqueduct consists of large boulders and rocks beneath a lime base. A handmade tile pipe was laid over the lime, then covered with still another layer of lime. Resting atop the whole aqueduct and its base were pieces of what appeared to be roofing tile from the Old Mission. Tile on the top strata of the aqueduct is composed of pieces salvaged when the mission roof was destroyed by an earthquake in the early 1800s. Individual links of the clay pipe aqueduct showed distinct signs of having been molded by hand.

Finger impressions are visible around the joints where workman had sized them so they would fit together snugly. Evidence of hand and finger impressions were also found on the inside of the pipe.

Sections of both the aqueduct and the pipe were salvaged and placed on exhibit in the museum at San Gabriel Mission. Their intricate design continues to intrigue those knowledgable about early waterworks.

Discovery of a slight curve in the line indicate that the pipe led to the tannery of the mission. Water from the pipe is thought to have been used both for drinking and agricultural purposes as well as in the tanning process.

Fray Pedro Font was the first to mention the *acequia* (ditch) by means of which water was provided for San Gabriel Mission. This he did in his diary entry for January 5, 1776, where he noted that the ditch "dominates all the fields near the Mission site, and renders them apt for planting grain. Hence it is that the land near the village is cultivated."

The subsequent improvement and enlargement of those waterways made it possible for San Gabriel to become one of the most productive agricultural centers in the chain of missions. The 1950 discovery provided one more piece of evidence for the genius of earlier generations.

JEDEDIAH SMITH ARRIVES AT SAN GABRIEL —1826

Jedediah Smith (1799–1831) was one of those "splendid wayfarers" who exemplified the Manifest Destiny of the vigorous young nation whence he came. A restless, adventure–seeker, he was endowed with that physical energy, fondness for life and detachment from locality that fitted him so well to cope with a Titanic Nature.

Smith led a party of fifteen adventurers to California, in 1816, arriving at Mission San Gabriel on November 27. The first of the overland American trappers known to have reached the Pacific Coast, Smith and his confreres were portrayed by Herbert Eugene Bolton as "a gaudily decorated, buckskin clad, full armored host of uncouth mien, pushing keelboats, cinching smelly saddle girths, loading pack horses, wading knee deep to set beaver traps in the mountain stream, stalking the grizzly or the hostile Indian, or spinning flabbergasting yarns and singing unprintable songs around the campfire."

After the long journey through the dreary desert wastelands, San Gabriel, with its fertile lands and bounteous hospitality probably impressed Smith and his companions as the Promised Land. Harrison Rogers, the Calvinist diarist with the party, noted that everyone at the mission appeared friendly and treated them well, "although they are Catholics by profession."

The party's arrival at San Gabriel, with their beaver skins and many traps, created a sensation among the Indian population. The friars extended a generous welcome, supplying the Americans with beef, cornmeal and wine, along with sixty–four yards of cloth to replace their tattered shirts. During their two months at San Gabriel, the Americans must have proven to be a great burden for the mission and Fray Francisco Sánchez, the resident friar. The Indians regarded their ill–behaved guests as "heathens, despite the protestations that they possessed Christianity in its purity." When the governor eventually ordered the Smith party to leave the territory, the routine of daily life at the mission gradually returned to normal.

Although the modesty of his disposition, the isolated nature of his travels, the absence of strong backing or governmental support and the loss of his papers by fire militated against the proper remembrance of his accomplishments, Smith's reputation as a forerunner of the American pioneers is now firmly ensconced in historical annals, thanks mostly to Harrison Rogers. The New York–born Smith, a man of intelligence, character, education and leadership, was one of the Western world's most outstanding "pathfinders." He and his party, the first white men to cross the High Sierras, deserve to be remembered in the Catholic heritage of California, for theirs was the initial procession which streamed into the Golden State to inaugurate the modern era.

Unwearied by trials and undaunted by opposition, Jedediah Smith had those qualities that make for greatness. His premature death, at thirty–two, cut short what most surely would have been an even more remarkable litany of achievements along *El Camino Real.*

ARTIST SKETCHES SAN GABRIEL—1836

German–born Ferdinand Deppe, a naturalist of considerable prominence, was an agent for the Acapulco mercantile house of Henry Virmonde. He is best remembered in California for his artistic rendition of San Gabriel Mission. Deppe visited the mission in 1828, and while there made a sketch of the *Corpus Christi* procession. Four years later, he transferred that scene to canvas.

On a subsequent visit to Santa Barbara, in 1836, Deppe sold the painting to Daniel Hill, a Yankee pioneer. Several decades later, the Hill family entrusted the canvas to the friars. Alexander Taylor noted that the painting was photographed by Edward Vischer in 1866, and indeed many of the details in Deppe's work are evident in Vischer's view portraying San Gabriel in 1842.

The first public recognition of Deppe's masterpiece came in 1952, when the late Edith Webb used a black and white reproduction of the scene for the end papers of her book on *Indian Life at the Old Missions.*

The only known painting of any California mission done before the secularization decrees of 1834 ended the period, the canvas portrays San Gabriel at the zenith of its material and spiritual prosperity. The Sierra Madre range of mountains with snowcapped San Antonio (or Mount Baldy) can be seen in the background. Fray Jose Sánchez, the *Presidente* of the California Missions, is portrayed in the lower lefthand portion of the canvas discussing business with James Scott, a Yankee supercargo from Boston. Two Indians stand behind the friar.

To the right, the celebrated *mayordomo*, Claudio Lopez, talks to an Indian neophyte in front of a brush hut. The nearby date palm was blown down in a windstorm in 1891. In the left background are the habitations of the neophytes and the open *zanja* that conveyed domestic water from Wilson Lake to the mission.

As was the case in many of his paintings, Deppe incorporates lots of action into the canvas. An Indian vaquero is coaxing a reluctant steer, while his friend is about to hit the animal's rump with a big stick. On the other side are the *zanja*, guard house and complete mission quadrangle. As Fray Sánchez and a procession of acolytes are carrying the Blessed Sacrament, soldiers are preparing to shoot the mission cannon in salute, a common practice in provincial times.

The stylized mission church has ten buttresses and the original symmetrical openings, as well as the belfry erected in 1815 to replace the one ruined by earthquake three years earlier. The historic and colorful 36 1/2 by 27 1/2 inch painting was restored to its pristine beauty at the Huntington Library in the 1960s and is now on permanent display in the Santa Barbara Mission Archives.

MEMORIES OF SAN GABRIEL MISSION—1846

Alfred Robinson (1807–1895) is credited with writing "the first English book on California to be written by a resident of the province." His treatise, published at New York in 1846, tells about his visit to San Gabriel, the "pride" of the missions.

> It was Saturday evening and as we approached the buildings of the Mission, the chapel bells tolled the hour for prayer. Hundreds of Indians were kneeling upon the ground, and as the tolling ceased, they slowly rose to retire, and a merry peal announced the coming of the Sabbath.
>
> The director of San Gabriel was Father Jose Sánchez, who for many years had controlled the establishment which, through his management, had advanced to its present flourishing condition. Possessing a kind, generous and lively disposition, he had acquired, in consequence, a multitude of friends, who constantly flocked around him; whilst through his liberality the needy wanderer, of whatever nation or creed, found a home and protection in the Mission.
>
> In the morning, at six o'clock, we went to the church where the priest had already commenced the service of the Mass. The imposing ceremony, glittering ornaments

and illuminated walls, were well adapted to captivate the simple mind of the Indian, and I could not but admire the apparent devotion of the multitude, who seemed absorbed, heart and soul, in the scene before them. The solemn music of the Mass was well selected, and the Indian voices accorded harmoniously with the flutes and violins that accompanied them. . .

> There are several extensive gardens attached to this Mission, where may be found oranges, citrons, limes, apples, pears, peaches, pomegranates, figs and grapes in abundance. From the latter they make yearly from four to six hundred barrels of wine, and two hundred of brandy; the sale of which produces an income of more than twelve thousand dollars.
>
> The storehouse and granaries are kept well supplied, and the corridor in the square is usually heaped up with piles of hides and tallow. Besides the resources of the vineyard, the Mission derives considerable revenue from the sale of grain; and the weekly slaughter of cattle produces a sufficient sum for clothing and supporting the Indians.
>
> The two *ranchos* of St. Bernardino and Sta. Anita are included in the possessions of the Mission; the former of these has been assigned by the *padres* for the sole purpose of domesticating cattle, and is located some leagues distant, in a secluded valley among the mountains; the latter is for cultivation, and is one of the fairy spots to be met with so often in California. On the declivity of a hill is erected a *molino*, or gristmill, surrounded with fruit trees and flowers.
>
> A beautiful lake lies calm and unruffled in front, and all around fresh streams are gushing from the earth, and scattering their waters in every direction. It would be a magnificent spot for a summer retreat, and much reminded me of many of the beautiful locations to be met with in the vicinity of Boston.

While his writings show "here and there the personal and political prejudices of the author," the account easily ranks among "the most valuable works in existence for the life and history of the period." Robinson's narrative "gives a circumstantial account of all the missions as he found them of the state of the country, and of the family life and amusements of the Californians."

Robinson "wrote about the *padres* with a Yankee humor that is frequently delightful." It should be noted, however, that he "became a Catholic because a Spanish lady (Ana Maria de la Guerra) would not have otherwise consented to marry him." Unquestionably, Baptism did not entirely cleanse him of "anti–Catholicism."

THE BULL AND BEAR FIGHTS AT SAN GABRIEL—1856

The descriptive journal compiled by Henry Miller to accompany his artistic sketches of the California missions reveal a keen eye for detail. His comments about the environs of San Gabriel are especially fascinating. He referred to the third of California's historic foundations as having degenerated by his time (1856) into a haunt for "notorious cattle thieves." In those post–mission years, he reported that murders were committed frequently "often as the result of the *fandangos* which are given almost every night, breaking up in a row and a stabbing or shooting affair."

Miller noted that the church was well–preserved, but that the other buildings were "dilapidated or totally in ruins." His sharp eye for detail allowed for the observation that the "long hedges of prickly pears" near the buildings were thriving because of an advanced form of grafting. The artist's description of a local "sport" is of special interest. "When I returned to the Mission, I was informed that a bull and bear fight would come off there today, which I resolved to witness:"

> There were two bears penned up, a she–bear and her cub, which had been caught by the lasso by some natives. I took my stand in some ruins close by the spot selected for the sport, with the intention of making a sketch.
>
> Being about 200 persons assembled, the large brown bear was dragged out by rope and also a bull, who was ferocious enough. The two animals were now chained close together, besides being governed by several horsemen with lassos which were attached to the feet of the animals.
>
> After the bear had made several grabs at the bull's nose, which drew blood, the bull caught him on his horns, threw him up and gored him to death after the bear had fallen to the ground.
>
> The roaring and yelling of the crowd was horrible. Horsemen galloped to and fro, raising dark dust clouds, regarding nothing, trampling down children, and the horses rearing and kicking. It was a very pandemonium.
>
> After the dead bear had been removed, the other one was dragged out, who was smaller than the former. He showed but little fight, making a noise like a young calf and, having been fastened by a chain to the horns of the bull, the latter after awhile tossed him up, twirling him round in the air like a playball, let him fall and buried his horns into him.

Mr. Miller then noted that "the sport being over, I bought the large bear for $3, which I skinned properly, preparing the same with an arsenical sopam with the intention of stuffing it at some future period." The roving artist concluded his remarks on the San Gabriel of post–missionary times by observing that when he returned to the mission itself, two murders had just been committed.

A young man named Evertson, who resides here, quarrelled with an Englishman named Mitchell while gambling. Mitchell threw a rock at the other party when the latter drew his revolver killing Mitchell. He was examined by a justice of the peace and discharged. And then, as if by footnote, Miller recalled also that a poor Indian was stabbed mortally today!

San Gabriel in the late 1850s was obviously an unhealthy place for bears, Englishmen and Indians!

SAN GABRIEL TO AN OUTSIDER—1859

Louis John Xantus de Vasey (1825–1895) came to California in 1857, as a collector of specimens in all the branches of natural history for the Smithsonian Institution. His observations of Mission San Gabriel are extracted from a letter to his mother, published at Budapest in 1859.

> The cloister and parish house are built of massive carved stones and are very elegant. In the outhouses about 140 Indian families live, all of whom speak, read, and write Spanish. Besides this they are engaged in such trades as blacksmith, carpenter, saddler, carver, shoemaker, etc., in neatly equipped shops, supplying their own needs and those of the mission.
>
> The married couples have separate little houses built of dried clay with shingle roofs and consisting of a living room, a bedroom and a kitchen. The single ones all live in a big house, two in a bedroom, having a common dining room. The girls are occupied with sewing, weaving, and washing, and live in an entirely separate house.
>
> The garden, which contains about 500 acres, is fenced all around by adobe walls six feet high and two thick, alongside of which a ditch six feet deep and six feet wide runs all around and outside of this, such a dreadful and thick cactus fence, so full of thorns that even a porcupine would stick himself if he attempted to break through it. The garden itself will arouse wonder and admiration in those to whom the useful, the beautiful and the comfortable are of interest. It is square, cut through by two main roads.
>
> In the center is an enormous pool (200 feet in diameter) built of carved stones. The water is let in and out of this from a nearby stream by way of stone–lined and well–kept ditches, which run in every direction through the garden. This pool, besides being used for breeding and raising thousands of rare fish, is also used for irrigating the garden.
>
> The roads are planted with giant orange trees, which all the year round are filled with so much fine fruit that their limbs bend down under them, and form such beautiful rows that the sun can hardly send its rays through them to the road. One quarter is left strictly to cultivation of the grape which produces such heavy harvests, that yearly the mission sells 500 barrels of wine, not figuring the amount consumed there.
>
> Another quarter contains vegetables, corn, rye, and potatoes, the third sugar cane, and the fourth banana plants, almond, pomegranate and fig trees which are trimmed to the same height as the adobe wall. This garden is under the supervision of a separate department and the men work in it in shifts.

The Mission Play

Besides all this the mission owns 2,000 horses and mules and 5,000 head of cattle, pastured on ten square miles of the mission property, under the care of cowboys and horsemen. The pasture being good both summer and winter, the sheep and shepherds are always in the mountains, except the working heads.

The Indians (or as the monks call them 'converted lambs') share in the work and benefit alike. Out of the surplus which is sold yearly, part is spent on repairs, part on clothing, groceries, etc.

The observations of Louis John Xantus de Vasey have a false ring about them, written as they were in the dreary days of the postmission era. One is almost inclined to believe that the Hungarian naturalist gleaned his comments from existing accounts of an earlier period, though such a theory still must be proven by some enterprising student of Californiana.

THE MISSION PLAY

The rise and fall of the old California missions was the central theme around which John Steven McGroarty wrote one of the most fascinating productions of all time. Since 1912, the Mission Play has been rendered periodically at San Gabriel. Over the years thousands of people have journeyed across the country to witness it, including such outstanding personages as Vice President Thomas Marshall.

In former times, whenever the play was enacted, it attracted a large company of highly talented professional actors. The viewers were people of distinction, quite accustomed to the ultimate in thespian productions.

Act one opens on the shore of San Diego Bay in 1769. Portrayed in this scene are Fray Junípero Serra, a corporal and three soldiers anxiously awaiting the long–overdue supply ship from Mexico. Soon, Gaspar de Portola, the first *comandante–gobernador* of California returns from Monterey to report his inability to find the elusive port. While the half–starved group waits for the ship, a few Indians approach with a baby and ask Serra to baptize the infant. Just as suddenly as they arrived, the natives grab the child from the friar's arms and dash back into the wilds.

When the food supply is completely depleted, Portola orders a withdrawal to Mexico—only to be confronted by Serra's pleadings for one additional day. Early the next morning, a "miracle" occurs when, on the distant horizon, can be seen the sail of the relief ship with adequate provisions to permanize the San Diego establishment.

The Second Act begins fifteen years later at San Carlos Mission in Carmel at the height of its prosperity. All the neighboring Indians have been Christianized and plans for their religious, educational and industrial training are moving along with great rapidity. Reports of the progress at the other missions are read out by a party of actors after a procession during which historic old songs associated with early mission days are sung by a chorus.

At intermission time, visitors toured the authentic replicas of the twenty–one missions prepared by Ida L. McGroarty from actual floor plans of the existing foundations.

The next act contains an anachronistic and unhistorical scene depicting *comandante* Rivera attempting to abduct Anita, a young half–Indian and half–Spanish maiden. Also introduced in this act is a fiesta scene with dancing, song and music and poetry of the earlier days in California.

In the final scene, portrayed at San Juan Capistrano, the mission is shown, in the decay and ruin of its last years. The Indians have been driven out and scattered and the *padres* forced to flee. The scene opens with Joséfa Yorba making a pilgrimage from her *rancho* to the distant mission before whose altar her ancestors had knelt in devotion. As she prepares to leave, several natives carry in the body of an old friar who made them promise, before his death, to inter him in the mission sanctuary beside his confreres. Destitute though they are, the Indians bury with the *padre* his gold chalice, the last remnant of more prosperous days.

The play ends with Joséfa bemoaning the lost glory of the missions and their banishment from the California scene. The curtain rings down on the hopeful note that one day the missions will again resume their earlier grandeur.

SAN GABRIEL'S BICENTENNIAL—1971

The bicentennial *of La Mision del Santo Principe el Arcangel San Gabriel de los Temblores,* the northernmost of the four Indian frontier establishments under the military jurisdiction of San Diego, afforded an appropriate occasion for hastily recalling the colorful montage into which the fourth of California's missionary outposts figures so prominently.

Surely it is a marvel, in the history of the modern world, that the relatively small nation of Spain, most of whose blood and treasure were already committed to the European theater, could embark upon and actually succeed, with a handful of men, in taking possession of the Caribbean archipelago and, from that base, to diffuse Iberian religion, culture, law and language to more than half the population of the two American continents.

In the overall Spanish policy of converting, civilizing and exploiting the Indians, no single priority outranked that of Christianizing the native races. The colonizers felt that the New World's inhabitants could become desirable and integrated subjects only through acceptance of the discipline which religion imparts to civilized life. For that reason, "wherever the Spanish conqueror or adventurer penetrated, there also penetrated the servant of God."

A favorite retort to charges, voiced as recently as the 1960 presidential campaign, about the alleged "foreign" character of Catholicism, is the gentle, but persuasive reminder that, in California and elsewhere, "the altar is older than the hearth." The Church's liturgy was first enacted in 1542, only a short half–century after the initial voyage by Genoa's "Admiral of the Ocean Sea."

Man's history in California, as well as in all the Spanish colonies, can hardly be told, and surely not understood, apart from its ecclesiastical context. The interlocking directorate of Church and state, welded in place by the *Patronato Real de las Indias,* forged a long, if not always compatible marriage between things human and affairs divine.

Paradoxically, it was the disastrous failure of the Jesuit missionary enterprise, in Florida, together with the subsequent transfer of the Society's activities to Mexico, in 1572, that foreshadowed the first serious attempts to colonize the Californias. Though visitations to that "thorny heap of stones and the pathless, waterless rock, rising between two oceans" are chronicled in 1535, effective penetration of peninsular California can be reckoned only with the foundation of *Nuestra Señora de Loreto,* in 1697. The entire program for that treacherously dangerous endeavor, mapped out and financed exclusively by the Jesuits, was one of spiritual orientation. Indians were invited and encouraged to learn about "the Catholic religion, the Spanish language, and the rudiments of the white man's way of life." Despite a few isolated outbursts of human opposition and the natural obstacles of plagues, pests and epidemics, the fifty–nine "Black Robes" who toiled in Baja California inaugurated a chain of eighteen missions, extending from Cape San Lucas at the southernmost tip of the peninsula, to within 300 miles of the present international boundary. By imparting a knowledge of God and diffusing a familiarity with such manual arts as cultivating the soil and raising livestock, the Jesuits managed to put solidly in place the cornerstone of a viable civilization in the relatively short period of their incumbency. Hubert Howe Bancroft, no lover of anything Catholic, believed that "had the Jesuits been left alone, it is doubtful whether the Spanish American provinces would have revolted so soon, for they were devoted servants of the crown, and had great influence with all classes."

For reasons still open to further interpretation by historians, the government replaced the Society of Jesus, in 1767, with Franciscan missionaries from the Apostolic College of San Fernando, near Mexico City. Providentially chosen to supervise and coordinate the new priestly contingency was Fray Junípero Serra, a Mallorcan, who had previously labored in the Sierra Gorda region to Mexico.

Some few months after assuming their pastoral duties on the peninsula, the friars learned of the government's plans to push the Spanish frontier further northward. Since the time of Sebastián Viscaíno, missionaries had hoped to see permanent foundations in such distant places as San Diego and Monterey. When Madrid officials finally concluded that occupation of Alta California was no longer a matter of strategic military indifference, "the passion of the Church gladly allied itself with the purpose of the State."

The long–contemplated colonization thrust was formally launched, in 1769, by Gaspár de Portolá, who was to oversee the expedition of extending "religion among the pagans who live to the north."

If Spanish troops were the key whereby the royal court manifested its concern for California, the missionaries were the masterkey. No single friar more adequately personified the characteristics associated with that monumental challenge than Fray Junípero Serra. Willingly and eagerly, he and his confreres volunteered for the thankless, dangerous and yet pivotal role of transforming and elevating a whole race from the darkness of heathenism.

In the course of the subsequent seventy–nine years, Serra and his 142 collaborators expended 2,269 man–years, each averaging sixteen years of service, to bring into the Christian fold and the ambit of Hispanic civilization nearly 100,000 aborigines. This they did while attending to the spiritual needs of the conquering Spaniards and Mexicans in the *presidios, pueblos* and *ranchos.*

The overall missionary achievement was, in certain respects, nothing less than colossal. Agriculture, pasturalism, horticulture and gardening were among the major trades introduced and developed, as was a modicum of foreign exchange. The Franciscans "brought to Alta California a new set of economic activities. They created a new California. And though the mission structure disappeared with secularization, the land it had transformed continued to bear its marks."

San Gabriel Mission, now well into a third century of service, is among the most typical of those historic adobes that have dotted California's skyline since provincial times. Though its primary function was spiritual, San Gabriel, like all its sister–foundations, performed the parallel service of raising the Indians to a standard of European civilization. To acquit itself of that duty, San Gabriel became a massive industrial school, its spinning and weaving room, carpenter and blacksmith shop, tannery, winepress, orchards, fields and irrigation ditches placing it among "the most flourishing of the California missions."

The religious, moral, social and industrial accomplishments at San Gabriel explain how California's mission complex could challenge "the result of any other system of control of dependent people developed in the field of modern colonization." Indeed, they "were such as to justify the plans of the wise statesmen who hitherto devised it, and to gladden the hearts of the pious men who devoted their lives to its execution."

Whether it be viewed as a monument to the achievements of an adventurous and heroic group of friars, an outpost of Christianity upon a barbarous frontier or an interesting example of architectural adaptation, San Gabriel, known at the height of its prosperity, not inaptly, as "The Pride of the Missions," stood, on the threshold of bicentennial, as a mute monitor of all that is best in California. It has been suggested that a bystander break off a piece from one of the century–old adobe walls:

> Crumble it to dust between your thoughtless fingers. Then place this dust in the open palm of your hand and hold it out so that the wind from the sea will blow it away forever. Only the dust of a crumbling adobe brick from a crumbling Mission wall, you say with an idle shrug. Yes, but a trifle more. The dust you held so carelessly in your open hand was the dust of an empire, if you had only understood—the glory of an ancient, heroic, race. And the wind which blew it so utterly away? Ah, that was the wind which men call time.

MADONNA AT SAN GABRIEL STOLEN—1977

During the month of June, 1977, someone crept into the sanctuary of the mission church at San Gabriel, cut the historic canvas depiction of Our Lady of Sorrows from its wrought–iron frame, and then fled with one of California's most treasured madonnas.

Though nothing is known about the painting prior to its arrival at San Diego aboard the pilot ship, *San Jose,* in 1770, it was presumably one of the gifts bestowed by the king on what was to become the fourth of the California missions. The painting at once achieved a prominence, however, which surely was not intended or foreseen by its 17th century artist in faraway Spain.

In his life of Fray Junípero Serra, Francisco Palou relates how the two friars selected to begin the work of conversion at San Gabriel were enroute there with their guards, in August of 1770, when they were set upon by "a great multitude of savages" anxious to discourage the foundation. Hoping to avoid any open conflict, one of the missionaries unrolled the canvas painting of Our Lady of Sorrows and placed it on view before the Indians. Overcome by the sight of the beautiful image, they put aside their bows and arrows and approached the Marian depiction with token gifts.

The account goes on to say that "the sight of the image of Our Lady transformed the savages around San Gabriel Mission so that they made frequent visits to the Fathers, not knowing how else to express their satisfaction for having come to stay in their country." One can readily appreciate the esteem held for the painting of Our Lady in subsequent years by those attached to San

Gabriel Mission. For 172 years, the depiction was prominently displayed at the mission.

It was actually a very simple portrait of Mary, with her hands clasped together and her sorrowful eyes turned upward. Atop the long oval face was the faint touch of an aureole. It was well–modelled, with good flesh tones. From the texture of the canvas and technique of the artist, the *Dolorosa* was an example of a characteristic type of devotional painting common in 17th century Spain.

Jack Smith, popular columnist for the Los Angeles *Times,* answering an appeal from a writer, journeyed to San Gabriel Mission and then wrote an essay for the October 27, 1977 issue of the paper in which he said the one who stole the painting was obviously a person without faith. He described how "the frame from which Our Lady Of Sorrows had been nipped stood behind the statue and the altar, on which six polychrome wood statues of saints, including San Gabriel the Archangel himself, stood in two awesome rows, one above the other, looking down on the desecrated sanctuary.

"The thief must have waited for a moment like this, when he was alone in the church. Then—zip—he had cut Our Lady out and stuffed her under his coat, perhaps, and hurriedly ran down the nave to the door, not looking up, I would think, at the 17 saints who roosted along the walls, dark with antiquity and perhaps with rage."

Smith concluded his essay by observing that he "didn't think a man with even a glimmer of religious experience could have walked the gauntlet of all those saints and into the sunlight of the garden, past all those graves and flowers, with a stolen Mother of God in his hands, and not have faltered."

Happily, after an absence of fourteen years, the historic canvas depiction of Our Lady of Sorrows was re–enthroned at San Gabriel Mission on Thursday, August 22, 1991. It was fitted back into its wrought iron frame by Father Gary Smith, the pastor of the Old Mission in ceremonies attended by hundreds of parishioners.

The culprit was apprehended early in 1990 by agents from the Federal Bureau of Investigation. Among the hundreds of art objects and antiquarian books discovered in the home of William March Witherell was *La Dolorosa.* The return of the historic depiction coincided with the 220th anniversary of the establishment of San Gabriel Mission. A local newspaper reporter captured local sentiments well when he observed that "the return of *La Dolorosa* made this year's celebration the happiest of them all."

THE MISSION REOPENS

The eulogies pronounced over San Gabriel Mission after the disastrous earthquake of October, 1987, were premature. Several years later the fourth of the frontier establishments along California's *El Camino Real* resumed its role as the "pride" of the California missions.

Visitors found much about the venerable church to capture their interest, not the least of which was the magnificently restored altar reredos which is surely the jewel of the reopened house–of–worship.

According to art historian, Norman Neuerburg, it was fabricated in Mexico City at the shop of Jose Maria Uriarte about 1810 at the cost of 1500 *pesos.* Shipped to Alta California in twenty cases, it was assembled on the spot prior to the earthquake of 1812. Interestingly enough, it was not damaged in that temblor, though several of the statues fell and were broken. In subsequent years, it was repeatedly repainted and shellacked so that little could be seen of its original beauty.

With the removal of all the accumulated over–painting, the reredos now appears in its pristine colors. Especially beautiful are the panels with urns of flowers on the lower level, flanking the altar table. It is an outstanding example of the neo–classical style popular in Mexico and California during the early 19th century.

The six original statues, together with the crucifix, which had also suffered from damage and tasteless repainting, have been cleaned, repaired and restored to reflect the high quality associated with the artistic work of the colonial era.

Five of the statues (Immaculate Conception, the Archangel Gabriel and Saints Francis, Anthony and Joachim) had arrived in 1791 and one (Saint Dominic) was sent three years later. The depictions of Saints Anthony, Francis and Dominic were damaged in the 1812 earthquake, along with the statue of Saint Joseph.

Originally, there were eleven statues in the sanctuary, six on the main reredos and five on the no–longer extant side panels. Atop the main altar was the Archangel Gabriel, situated in the center above the image of the Immaculate Conception, between Saints Francis and Dominic.

Saints Joseph and Anthony were probably above these. On the side altar reredos was a portrayal of Our Lady of Guadalupe, flanked by statues of Saints Joachim and Anna, the latter of which disappeared in the last century.

On the opposite panel were statues of Saints Bonaventure, Thomas Aquinas (now at San Juan Capistrano Mission) and Vincent Ferrer (now at the old Plaza Church of *Nuestra Senora de los Angeles).* The statues have been shifted about in recent years and the present configuration is the one shown in the earliest photographs.

During the Spanish era, ten main altar reredoes were sent to California, but only those at San Gabriel, Mission Dolores and San Buenaventura survive. The one at San Gabriel is closest to its original dimensions. Lamentably, it is the sole testimony of the church's original interior appearance during mission times.

The exquisite restorative work was executed at the South Coast Fine Arts Conservation Center in Santa Barbara, where many of the paintings at nearby San Fernando Mission have been cleaned and re–backed.

Now re–roofed and retrofitted, the historic church at San Gabriel Mission is once again back on the list of necessary places to visit in California's southland.

THE BELLS OF SAN GABRIEL

The infinitude of natural beauty that adorns the Golden State irresistibly stirs the poetic sense. In no country of the world does the very spirit of poesy breathe over the face of the land as in California. Indeed, poetry in California is as inevitable as fruits and flowers —it is in the very air and soil. There is an inspiring sweep to the Californian landscape—a mighty cascading of green–forested mountainside spreading to the golden valleys; a towering splendor, as of the sublime old giant redwoods, and an infinitely fragile beauty, as of delicate little wind–shaken flowers starring the meadows or dancing at the feet of those same great swaying trees in whose heaven–touching tops the wind plays like an organ.

From the earliest recorded moments California has given poetic inspiration to men. The state's very name has its sources in a legend wherein the land of gold was seen as a mystic isle of undreamt wonders lost in a magic sea. No poet has ever surpassed Charles Warren Stoddard in picturing California as the garden spot of God.

His classic "The Bells of San Gabriel" is considered among the great poetic accomplishments of all time.

Thine was the corn and the wine,
The blood of the grape that nourished;
The blossom and fruit of the vine
That was heralded far away.
These were thy gifts; and thine.
When the vine and fig tree flourished,
The promise of peace or of glad increase
Forever and ever and aye.
What then wert thou, and what are now?
Answer me, O, I pray!
And every note of every bell
Sang Gabriel! rang Gabriel!

In the tower that is left the tale to tell
Of Gabriel, the Archangel.
Where are they now, O bells?
Where are the fruits o' the mission?
Garnered where no one dwells,
Shepherd and flock are fled.
O'er the Lord's vineyard swells
The tide that fell with perdition
Sounded their doom and fashioned their tomb
And buried them with the dead.
What then wert thou, and what are now?
The answer is still unsaid.
And every note of every bell
Sang Gabriel! rang Gabriel!
In the tower that is left the tale to tell
Of Gabriel, the Archangel.
Seed o' the corn was thine –
Body of Him thus broken
And mingled with blood o' the vine
The bread and the wine of life;
Out of the good sunshine
They were given to thee as a token,
The body of Him, and the blood of Him,
When the gifts of God were rife.
What then were thou, and what are now?
After the weary strife?
And every note of every bell
Sang Gabriel! rang Gabriel!
In the tower that is left the tale to tell
Of Gabriel, the Archangel.
Oil of the olive was thine:
Flood of the wine–press flowing:
Blood o' the Christ was the wine –
Blood o' the Lamb that was slain.
Thy gifts were fat o' the kine
Forever coming and going hills –
Far over the hills, the thousand
Their lowing a soft refrain.
What then were thou, and what are now?
Answer me, once again!
And every note of every bell
Sang Gabriel! rang Gabriel!
In the tower that is left the tale to tell
Of Gabriel, the Archangel.
Where are they now, O tower !
The locusts and wild honey?
Where is the sacred dower
That the bride of Christ was given?
Gone to the wielders of power,
The misers and minters of money;
Gone for the greed that is their creed –
And these in the land have thriven.
What then wert thou, and what are now,
And wherefore hast thou striven?
And every note of every bell
Sang Gabriel! rang Gabriel!
In the tower that is left the tale to tell
Of Gabriel, the Archangel.

SAN LUIS OBISPO (1772)

CATHOLICITY IN THE VALLEY OF THE BEARS—1774

The Mission of San Luis Obispo, fifth of the frontier outposts established along El *Camino Real* by Fray Junípero Serra, was located among the Chumash Indians, on a slight rise between Arroyo de San Luis and Arroyo de la Huerta (Garden Creek). It belongs to the glory of that foundation, dedicated to the sainted Bishop of Toulouse, that the first white child baptized within the confines of Alta California, Juan José Garcia, was born on November 11, 1774, at San Luis Obispo.

Dr. Paul H. Kocher, Professor Emeritus of English and Humanities at Stanford University, has gathered the story of the spiritual longings, defeats and triumphs of those attached to San Luis Obispo in a ninety–five page historical monograph. Issued to commemorate the mission's bicentennial, the generously–illustrated paper–bound book, produced by Blake Printing and Publishing, Inc., is the first substantial study made of Catholic activities in that area of the vineyard since 1933, when Father Zephyrin Engelhardt published his work on *Mission San Luis Obispo in the Valley of the Bears.*

The personages and events at San Luis Obispo are fairly typical of the happenings at other California missions. At that particular outpost, the Indian population reached its high point of 961, in 1805, with an annual average of forty–five baptisms and twenty–five marriages. The Franciscans served at San Luis Obispo until 1842, and the departure of Fray Ramon Abella. He was replaced by Father José Miguel Gómez, a priest attached to the newly–created Diocese of Both Californias.

In modern times, the physical surroundings of the mission have been admirably enhanced. Over 40,000 tourists visit the historic foundation each year from every state in the union and a host of foreign countries as well. The secret ingredient that made possible the foundation and sustenance of Mission San Luis Obispo and its sister establishments along the Pacific Slope was spelled out years ago by no less than Rudyard Kipling. In one of his stories, he graphically depicted the life of a missionary:

> Do you know what life at a mission outpost means? Try to imagine a loneliness exceeding that of the smallest station to which the Government has ever sent you—isolation that weighs upon the waking eyelids and drives you by force into the labors of the day.
>
> There is no post, there is no one of your own color to speak to you, there are no roads; there is, indeed, food to keep you alive, but it is not pleasant to eat; and whatever good or beauty or interest there is in your life must come from yourself and the grace that may be planted in you.
>
> You must be infinitely kind and patient, and above all, clear–sighted, for you deal with the simplicity of childhood, the experience of man, and the subtlety of the savage. If to the cure of souls you add that of bodies, your task will be all the more difficult.
>
> As the day wears on and the impetus of the morning dies away, there will come upon you an overwhelming sense of the uselessness of your toil. This must be striven against, and the only spur in your side will be the belief that you are playing against the devil for the living soul.
>
> It is a great and joyous belief; but he who can hold it unwavering for four and twenty consecutive hours must be blessed with an abundantly strong physique and equable nerves.

THE OLDEST OF THE TEXTILE ARTS

Among the observations recorded in his diary, Fray Pedro Font noted how the natives at San Luis Obispo made *coritas* (basketwork) "of much diversity in the designs, and of any shape that is asked of them, even *sombreros.*" An observer of later times, Charles Fletcher Lummis, founder of the Southwest Museum, noted that basket making is the oldest of the textile arts, the far beginning of all the vast industry with which millions of looms are humming today. Primitive man braided and pleated and wove twigs and grasses and fibers for baskets before he began weaving garments, long before.

It is an older art than pottery and more universal—for the obvious reason of the greater adaptability to the vicissitudes of the average primitive environments. The basket–maker has thrived in the tropics and in the Arctic Circle since the beginning of recorded time. As with all primitive workmanship, the ancient basket everywhere was beautiful in its degree and kind. It is beyond reasonable question that the American Indians lead the field.

In some localities, as in California, Oregon and Nevada, were made the most beautiful and most perfect baskets ever turned out by mankind. Rather, she made them, for basketry in America was mostly done by women. One talented Indian woman, Dat–so–la–le of the Wasin tribe (the decimated Washoes) made baskets which sold at $1,500 each. They were true works of art;

and of the most exquisite fineness—thirty stitches to the inch. Their shape and decoration were of classic proportions.

Mr. Lummis reported that he possessed a Mesa Grande basket with a rattlesnake beginning at the first stitch and winding symmetrically through the pattern up to the rim; the rattles as perfectly depicted in the stitch as our best pen–and–ink artist could ever do it.

Basketry was probably the only art in which the natives of California displayed outstanding skill. The productions of the natives far excel those of any other peoples in color, design and symmetry. Each of the many patterns used by the Indians was skillfully worked out. Human figures, hills, valleys and scenes from nature were also employed. Sometimes small mosaics were utilized for purposes of diversity. It was an industry cultivated by the women who were quite ingenious in weaving grass, sumac, splints, rushes, cedar, tule, yucca stems, kelp thread, willow roots and sea plants. The finished product varied in size and shape from flat, basin–shaped coiled weave bowls to large pointed cones which were used when digging for roots, picking berries or gathering acorns.

Louis Choris recorded that the Indians near San Francisco and to the south made charming vessels and vase–shaped baskets, capable of holding water. He noted that they knew how to give them graceful forms and pleasing designs. They often ornamented their works with bits of shell and feathers.

Basketry as it developed in California displayed patience, beauty, symmetry and a keen sense of design. It was a highly symbolic means of expression, an art medium of considerable importance. Kurt Baer has observed that these people "could not have been as stupid as the early chroniclers" reported.

MURILLO AT SAN LUIS OBISPO—1934

Some of the most exquisite religious portrayals ever done bear the signature of Bartolome Esteban Murillo (1617–1682), the Spanish born artist who epitomized the "golden age" of Spanish baroque. Characterized by softness, splendor, harmony of color and spiritual feeling, Murillo's renditions of the Madonna are considered without peer in the artistic world. The brilliant coloring and preference for beauty earned for the artist a wide following among the common people.

In its edition for September 27, 1934, the Los Angeles *Examiner* reported that "an oil painting *Madonna Con Niño Velado,* believed to have been done by Murillo in 1630, has been placed in the museum of Mission San Luis, Obispo de Tolosa."

The article acknowledged that the painting was "a subject of controversy among art critics of the world as to whether or not it is an authentic Murillo." Plans were afoot to have it "tested and examined by a representative of the Metropolitan Art Museum of New York" who was coming to catalogue the other artistic and historic items in the mission museum.

The painting did indeed exhibit considerable internal evidence linking it to Murillo. For example, the background figures appear to have the same spontaneity of composition, lightness of movement and clarity of purpose that are distinctive in other Murillo works.

According to Father John Harnett, the pastor of San Luis Obispo, the painting came into his possession three years earlier "when he heard the death bed confession of the late A. Iken of Bakersfield." One of Iken's ancestors, an officer in the English army, "came across the painting in a huckster's shop on a side street in Barcelona while he was stationed in Spain during the war period of the 18th century." The shopkeeper claimed that "the painting had been stolen from a Spanish cathedral during an earlier period of conflict."

Iken's ancestor carried the painting back to England where "it was handed down from generation to generation. When Iken moved to Bakersfield, he brought the painting with him."

In 1874, an art critic in England "first declared that the Madonna was an original Murillo." Since that time opinion has been divided. In any event, there was a consensus among all the experts who examined the painting that it was executed sometime in the early 1680s, shortly before Murillo died as a result of injuries suffered in a scaffolding mishap.

For a time, the painting was loaned to a museum in Monterey by Father John Harnett. During that time, several art critics contended that the *Madonna Con Niño Velado* was indeed an authentic Murillo painting. The colorful painting portrays Mary and the Child surrounded by crowned saints. The crowns, according to one interpretation, indicate a miracle performed before the portrayal was executed, or at least prior to its completion.

In a "Letter to the Editor" of the *Examiner,* a few days later, Margaret Jackson noted that "if the *Madonna Con Niño Velado* is indeed authentic, then San Luis Obispo Mission shares with the Cathedral in Guadalajara the rare honor of housing a work by the universally popular interpreter of the Immaculate Conception."

SAN FRANCISCO OR MISSION DOLORES (1776)

A FAMED CAMPO SANTO—1777

In the quiet and peaceful graveyard of Mission San Francisco de Asís (or Dolores) can be found the richest memories of California's picturesque and romantic beginnings. The cemetery is of historical interest for both its antiquity and its famous "residents."

The first burial took place at California's sixth missionary foundation on March 4, 1777, when Francisca, the nine year old daughter of Spanish soldier Joaquin Alvarez was laid to rest "in the Church of the Mission." The initial Indian interment, recorded only as "Pedro," took place on October 29th of the same year. The register book indicates that the youngster had fallen into a copper kettle full of hot water.

The present *campo santo* or cemetery dates from October 2, 1781, when the first interment was made "in the cemetery attached to the Church of this Mission." Between 1777 and October 24, 1834, no fewer than 5,351 entries are recorded in the two volume *Registro de Difuntos*. Though the earliest wooden grave markers have disintegrated, many have been replaced with stone or metallic slabs.

On March 28, 1830, the earthly remains of Luís Antonio Argüéllo, the first Governor of Alta California under Mexico, were interred. He was joined, nineteen years later, by Francisco de Haro, the initial *alcalde* for San Francisco. Another famous personage in the *campo santo* is William Alexander Leidesdorff, the first black pioneer in San Francisco, who died on May 18, 1848.

A host of other historic names can be found on the markers, including Francisco Guerrero, José Noe, Francisco Sanchez and José Bernal. The cemetery has world–wide representation, with MacNamara from England, Renault from France, Murtha from New Brunswick, Steward from Scotland, Carmichael from Australia, Brunnel from Canada, Urbano from Portugal, Kramer from Germany and Ruffino from Italy.

A statue of Kateri Tekakwitha, the Mohawk Indian maiden, stands guard over the unmarked graves of some 5,000 red–skinned natives from the Pacific Slope. Etched onto the marble portrayal are the words: "In prayerful memory of our faithful Indians."

Among the collection of homespun verses on the various markers is one that's typical of many:

> My bones that moulder in silent dust
> My soul to Heaven has fled to find my
> Father, mother, brothers and sisters there
> To rest with them in sight of God.
> So farewell, dear brothers and sisters,
> We all shall meet again.

Today, a marble depiction of Fray Junípero Serra overlooks the *campo santo* at Mission San Francisco de Asís, waiting ever–so–patiently for the day when California's pioneers will walk forth from their tombs. What a fascinating collection of stories will be exchanged on that great occasion!

MARTYRDOM OF "SAINT" PETER THE ALEUT —1815

During October of 1980, the Synod of Bishops for the Russian Orthodox Church Outside of Russia heard an appeal from the faithful for the canonization of Peter the Aleut. The synod resolved that inasmuch as Peter had suffered martyrdom, his "memory should be celebrated" each year "on the same day as that of the Venerable Herman of Alaska."

The action by Metropolitan Philaret and the other prelates of the Russian Orthodox Church Abroad allows for an interesting but questionable presumption of historical evidence. Writing in the January issue of *Orthodox Life,* 1981, a bimonthly publication by the Brotherhood of St. Job of Pochaev, Marina D. Ilyin endeavored to present "the historical background" behind the synodal decree.

She identified Peter Tchounagnak as "an Aleut Indian converted to Orthodoxy in the late 18th or early 19th century by Russian Orthodox missionaries. He departed this life in San Francisco, California, on Sept. 8, 1815, martyred for refusing to become Roman Catholic at the hands of Padre (José Ramon) Abella at Dolores Mission."

The writer goes on to state that "an account by one of Peter's fellow prisoners was found among the notes of . . . Simeon Yanovsky," the governor at Sitka. In that 1865 report, it is related how the Spaniards had taken fourteen Aleuts captive, and how the " Jesuits had tortured one Aleut to death, trying to force them all to accept the Catholic faith." Peter's fingers were allegedly severed, causing him to die from loss of blood.

(Perhaps it should also be mentioned that the original Yanovsky account does not mention Mission Dolores, rather a place "on the coast of California near Mission San Pedro.")

Though there appears to be *no* other source for this "martyrdom," Marina Ilyin endorses Peter the Aleut as "the first Orthodox martyr on American soil." In his monumental *History of California*, Hubert Howe Bancroft discusses the illegal arrival of the Aleut hunters aboard the Russian vessel, *Ilmen,* and how they were obliged "to work for their rations like Spanish prisoners."

Bancroft, no lover of the Church, dismisses in a footnote the report that "one Aleut who refused to become a Catholic died from ill–treatment received from the *padre* at San Francisco." The whole incident just doesn't make historical sense. There were *no* Jesuits in Alta California at that time, Father Abella was regarded by his contemporaries as "one of the best missionaries in the entire territory" and there is no verbal or recorded account of Peter's burial in the register books at Mission Dolores. And why does Marina Ilyin take it upon herself to change the place of martyrdom?

Peter's "sainthood" is not so much in question as is his martyrdom." The responsible historian would have to conclude, from the paucity of evidence, that Peter Tchounagnak has an acute identity crisis.

(After reading a draft of this essay, one expert in orthodox history ventures the opinion that the Russian Church Outside of Russia was motivated by efforts to portray itself as the only authentic voice for "holy Russia." Actually, such a move does more to lessen that claim, for the plenitude of available candidates for canonization makes creation of phantom ones unrealistic.)

GRAVEYARD AT MISSION DOLORES—1870s

In the late 1870s Benjamin F. Taylor visited San Francisco. He later published his reflections in a book entitled *Between the Gates.* Taylor was especially enamored with the cemetery at Mission Dolores (San Francisco de Asis). Here are some of his observations about the historic burial grounds.

The graveyard of a hundred–and–one years adjoins the church. You pass under the cross that surmounts the gate, and are in the city of the houses that shall last till doomsday. The earth is rich with the uncounted dead. You tread upon them in the alleyways.

There are hundreds and then hundreds. Nameless Indians with their heads to the rising sun lie here by bands and tribes. The old sexton unearths them sometimes wrapped in the hides of wild cattle for shrouds. Soldiers of the blue and the scarlet, English, American, Russian, Spanish, Mexican have bidden farewell to the big wars, and gone into camp together.

Descendants of Spanish willows vainly weep over yew and English hawthorn are ever 'wearing of the green.' Trees in everlasting bud and bloom give Christmas roses, and bouquets for June. The ivy's glossy leaves caress the graves. How rich and rank they grow!

Let us hope the dead have gained the crown, for behold, the crosses they have left behind. And still they come! There goes the sexton with his spade. The place is full of angels, altars, lambs, tombs, urns and shrines, in wood washed blank of letter and device, in marble and in granite.

You stand by the grave of the first Spanish Governor of California, and you read: '*Aqui yacen restos De Capitan Don Louis Antonio Argüéllo, Primero Gobernador del Alta California.*' He lies in the sacristy of the old church, the granite chamber where they kept chalices and censers for frankincense and wine; a right stout lodging, and time–proof as the globe.

Reading monument after monument, you feel as if in a foreign land. The names are no household words of ours. Here is a slab bearing the name, James Sullivan, the Yankee Sullivan of whom the world has heard, and the words, who died by the hands of the V.C. 1856. That V.C. is graven upon other marbles here, and means Vigilance Committee, and revives the memory of wild and lawless times. Following the name are these significant words: 'In Thy mercy Thou shalt destroy mine enemies!'

At last, beside the old adobe wall, the sexton shows an unsuspected grave, no slab nor mound nor coverlet of grass. Beside it is another, with turf subsided like a tired wave. It is surrounded by a bleached and sagging fence of pickets. Over these two graves a small historic war has been waged.

Within six months after the Signing of the Declaration they had two funerals; an Indian and a Spaniard were buried here. Now, which was buried first? One has one grave, and one the other—and which the honor of the first inhabitant? Over what trifles will even wise men fight! The name and story of each had fallen out of human speech and memory as long ago as gray–haired men were in their swaddling bands. What matters who or when? The poet Montgomery wrote the epitaph for the broad world's men: 'There lived a Man.'

As you turn to leave the place, the marble figure of a suppliant woman with lifted hands and sad and sightless eyes turned heavenward, impresses you like a spoken word. So are these all beneath the sod, all but the lifted hands. Speechless, helpless, front–face to Heaven, here they lie and wait. God save the world!

Let us go out at the time–stained gate, and into the ever–flowing tides of living creatures. We had almost forgotten the glad sun and the crystal air, and even the roses the sexton gathered from some graves to give us, seemed to shed a sad, funereal fragrance, as of crape, and the vexed and troubled earth that, for the graves they make within it, has little rest.

As he made his way to catch the streetcar on Valencia Street, the author said that "if a man meant to make a compact sentence unburdened with adverbs, he could say, California is a country where the places are all saints and the people are all sinners!"

MISSION DOLORES (SAN FRANCISCO) IN 1882.

In 1882, D. Appleton & Co., a New York publishing house, issued a series of impressions about *The Mission Churches of California* by Francisco L. Ortega. The description of Mission Dolores, in San Francisco, is of particular interest and is here presented in digested form.

All that now remains of the Mission of San Francisco is the Mission Church, standing at the end of Sixteenth Street. Between the church and Valencia Street still stand buildings which belong to the early mission times. On the right side of Sixteenth, a block and a half distant from Valencia Street is a long boarded building, some fifty–three feet in length, with small glass windows, and just beyond that an old adobe structure, with a rough stone foundation; its windows are now boarded up, and to the doors lead rickety stairs. Adjoining this is a modern frame building, and then again a low adobe dwelling with a tiled roof. Opposite these houses, on the other side of the street, are two houses of adobe, curiously faced with boards.

The church faces the road, looking due south. It is gabled roofed and painted white, and neath the eaves hang three bells. Beneath this, running the length of the building, is a projecting beam, from which rise five rounded pillars. The gateway is arched and is between four more pillars, which rise out from a balustrade. A long double storied building runs westward, which is inhabited by the priests, and adjoining is a new stone church, which was completed last February. On the other end of the old church, is the mission graveyard, protected by a wooden railing, from which hangs a poster, warning visitors not to pluck the flowers.

The entrance to the church is through two swinging doorways which creak miserably with every passing wind. Within, the church looks gloomy and deserted, though it is seldom that it is long empty, for not an hour of the day passes but what some child or woman comes within the Sanctuary, and kneeling, says her prayers before the primitive altar.

On the right hand side of the church in a deep embrasure is a modern door which connects the church with the priest's house, and nigh this is a narrow, dark–stained stairway leading to a gallery which runs the entire breadth of the church. In the southern wall is a small window furnished with seats cut out of the adobe and well–worn from constant use. Before the windows hang three ropes by which the bells are tolled. On the right is a modern paneled door, now screwed up. The gallery is divided into two parts by a wooden railing, and just above where it commences, on the right side, is a huge cupboard, now given over to the spiders for the weaving of their webs. A narrow strip of well–worn carpeting runs down the gallery.

Returning to the body of the church, nearby the entrance, and on both the right and left walls are niches where is placed some broken crockery containing holy water. On the left wall is a confessional box, close to a door, which gives admission to the graveyard. On the right wall, and stretching some thirty feet in length, and extending to the rafters, is a wooden screen covered with a canvas, on which are depicted scenes in the life of our Savior. On the farther side of the screen and high up on the wall, is a quaint fashioned window. Some seven feet from the window, and not quite reaching the eaves, is an altar, dedicated to three saints belonging to the Franciscan Order.

The top of this altar is broken, and at one time on each end of the beam stood two vases, but that on the extreme left is gone. Four wooden pillars painted in gold, support the topmost beam and on wooden gold colored projections stand the three saints. The middle saint has lost its right arm. The faces are well carved and full of character. On the altar proper are no ornaments. The table is covered with a shabby red–colored cloth. Supports that hold the table are painted in gold, and in red and blue.

On the opposite side of the church is a similarly fashioned altar. An arch spans the building, which rises just before the principal altar, and within the span is another confessional box, adjoining which commences the railing. Half hidden in the deep wall on the left is a doorway, which opens on the outside on to a portico, and on the left side is the sacristy. The carpet within the railing is well worn, and that on the three steps leading to the altar is very fragile. The back of the altar is elaborately decorated with figures of numerous saints and pictures. Two modern vases containing flowers, the gift of young children, give to the altar a fresher appearance and look sadly strange amidst the faded grandeur.

Before the altar railing the boards have given way, as if weakened by the constant kneeling of the devout. On the left–hand side of the altar is an unused organ. The ceiling is raftered and painted in triangles of red, white and blue.

Services are still held in the church, notwithstanding that the more pretentious structure adjoins it. At nine o'clock every Sunday morning Mass is celebrated for the young children and afterwards Sunday School is held.

IMPRESSIONS FOR *SUNSET* MAGAZINE — 1902

In mid–1902, Sarah Henry visited Mission San Francisco de Asis. She later recorded her impressions of that famous frontier outpost for *Sunset* Magazine. The following is excerpted from that essay.

A San Franciscan standing before the low tile–roofed chapel of the Mission Dolores has somewhat the feeling of the man who finds himself in a dark corner of the attic before the cradle in which he once slept. Both wonder if they were ever small enough to find room in so small a thing.

The chapel is fairly well preserved. In its best days this mission lacked the architectural beauty of many of the other missions. There were no arches, no arcades, no towers, no buttresses, no ornamental facades. The severity of outline is relieved only by four columns flanking the entrance and the niches where hang the bells.

As usual the building formed a quadrangle. Opposite the chapel was the "mansion house," which stood on the present Sixteenth Street The two were connected by long, low buildings, at front and rear, the one at the front used as a residence by the priests, with rooms for overseers and travelers; the other probably was where the young Indian girls were kept under the guardianship of Indian matrons. Here also were small workshops, schoolrooms and storerooms.

The part of this wing which remains was rebuilt and made two stories high in the days of Father Carroll, the first English–speaking priest of the parish after the Franciscans. The front of the chapel is practically unchanged except for a thick coating of whitewash; but about 1864 it was found necessary to board up the sides of the church in order to make it safe to hold services there. This was in the time of Father Prendergast who succeeded Father Carroll.

In order to do this work men were obliged to cut away the beams which projected about midway of the south wall and which had served as a support for the tiling and a sort of second roof, which was a way these early builders had of protecting adobe walls on the exposed side. Other changes made at that time were wood flooring where adobe had served before, and a small balcony at the rear.

The interior decoration, however, was left undisturbed, and today shows the pains the pious fathers took with even their plainest sanctuaries. The uncovered, rough–hewn rafters, which rest on heavy, adzed supports, are painted in diamond–shaped patterns, the dull red, yellow, blue and white giving an effective touch of color against the monotonous gray of the adobe walls.

On the north wall is an immense symbolic painting on canvas, the work of Spanish artists, representing the religious mysteries. This was part of the original decoration, and the difficulty of early transportation is shown by the canvas being in small pieces, carefully matched in hanging. The painting is in excellent condition, except for holes in the lower part where mischievous youngsters have been at work with pocket–knives.

Two side altars support images of saints; on one side a group of Franciscans, on the other a group with Saint Charles Borromeo as the central figure. In the sanctuary the decoration is quite elaborate and in a good state of preservation. The entire end of the chapel is a mass of carving painted in a dull reddish color with much gilt. Five empty niches show where images formerly stood, and which were probably removed for safety as time weakened their supports.

A plain, inartistic wooden altar, painted white is clearly of comparatively recent date. it covers the original altar and was erected because the predella was too low for the priest to be seen by the people sitting in the back of the church.

TWO SURVIVORS OF MISSION DOLORES— 1909

In a 1909 issue of the San Francisco Sunday *Call*,

Ashleigh B. Simpson tells about a visit with Raymundo Miramontes and Pablo Vasquez, "two survivors of the great days of Mission Dolores." Miramontes had been an altar server at Mission Dolores in the days when the Spaniards knelt alongside the Indians at Holy Mass; Vasquez was the son of a man who had served for many years as *majordomo* of the mission.

In spite of their graying hair and failing eyesight, the two old comrades were able to relate a host of fascinating stories about the early days of missionary life in and around San Francisco de Asís. Miramontes and Vasquez were the only ones still living of those who had trod the ground of Mission Dolores when the bells described by Bret Harte sounded the knell of sacred music. They were the last who could recall the Masses offered at the elaborate altar by friars, Miguel Muro and José Real.

In their youth, San Francisco was only a phantom, a dream of the future. To the west of Mission Dolores lay nothing but barren, rolling hills and the ocean; to the south the Indians tilled the soil and herded the cattle under the direction of the friars. Sand dunes lay between the mission and the *presidio* toward the north and to the east the waters of San Francisco bay lapped gently in tides that washed over the sites of future buildings and thoroughfares.

The hills, later hidden by thousands of homes and streets, stifled with the congestion of traffic, were open country when Raymundo and Pablo played their youthful games around the walls of Mission Dolores.

The writer told about "the light that crossed the faces of the two lifelong comrades" as they dwelt in memory upon the familiar scenes which played such an important part in the history of early California. Vasquez remembered that the home of the resident friars, next to the church, directly adjoined the place of his own birth. He was able to identify mentally the location of the blacksmith shop, the weaving room and the pottery kilns.

He pointed out the source of the aqueduct near Precita and described how it flowed down Dolores Street and then meandered easterly toward the bay. Miramontes and Vasquez told how, in the days of their youth, the valleys of the coast range and the soils of the San Joaquin were wild and crossed only by the trails of animals.

They recalled the bull fights that "once stirred the dust before Dolores until all there was of San Francisco lay hidden in the cloud, and the meager populace choked and coughed as it cheered the brave matadors in the fierce encounter."

It must have been a thrilling experience to talk with and record the memories of those men who were still alive with the priceless memories of early California. They had known San Francisco before the first creeping cluster of houses appeared in the sand dunes as an omen of the huddled thousands who would conquer the seven hills. They remembered the area before the progress of a great nation had stamped out the work of the friars and razed the mud houses to dust, leaving nothing but the mission itself for the generations to come.

A MISSION REACHES 160TH ANNIVERSARY—1936

The 160th anniversary of Mission San Francisco de Asis (or Dolores) was observed on October 4, 1936. In his lengthy sermon for that occasion, Father Thomas N. O'Kane outlined the history of the famed missionary outpost and its pivotal part in the overall program of Hispanic penetration.

> The whole theory of Spanish colonization, as well as the faith which was the drive of the pioneers, was founded upon the recognition of the necessity of religion. (Viceroy Antonio) Bucareli, in his letter to Fray (Junípero) Serra, commanding the founding of our city wrote: "The first object of the expedition is to conduct troops for the protection of the missions which it is decided to establish at the port of San Francisco.

> Nothing is of such importance as the accomplishment of this for the subsequent plans . . . that those establishments aid one another." Hence it was that religion entered this region with (Gaspár de) Portolá· and by the hands of Fray (Francisco) Palou raised its standard on the rim of our western hills. One hundred and sixty years ago, it took this spot for its dwelling and from here sent forth the power which first remade our land.

> From here the *presidio* was founded. Here grew up the command which was to be the center of our civilization for nigh sixty years. In the little church beside us first went forth the notions basic in our culture—the dignity of human personality, made in the image and likeness of God and redeemed by His most precious blood—the sanctity of the family and the irrevocable nature of the union that binds man and wife in the august kingdom of the home—the notion of the divine origin of the authority of the state and the debt of strict obedience which the citizens owe it.

> It was in the shadow of the Old Mission, where day after day the bloodless representation of the Sacrifice of Calvary was enacted and His Body broken for the life of the world, that there grew up the first of our arts and our sciences.

> Agriculture, commerce, industry, letters, music and painting—all had their origins here. It was here that Saint Thomas Diocesan Seminary was established as the beginning of the tremendous influence which our colleges for training priests continue to exercise on our culture today.

> It was energy derived from here that founded, close to eighty years ago, the Roman Catholic Orphan Asylum and Free School Association as the beginning of that wide arid intricate system of charity which is now at the service of San Francisco.

> It was on this very spot that Father Flavian (Fontaine) built the first unit of that vast system of parochial schools which the Catholic Church maintains at tremendous expense for those citizens of San Francisco who wish to give their children their rightful heritage.

> And it was from here that the three earliest of our churches—the Church of Saint Francis on Vallejo Streets, the Church of Saint Patrick on Mission Street and the Church of Saint Mary on California Street, had their rise.

> The better parts of San Francisco, its beliefs and morals, its structure of government and pattern of civilization, all have come from the past. If there be anything properly the merit of this generation, we must remember that it is ours only because we live by the travail of the generations which have preceded us. It is their heritage which fructifies in our hands.

SAN JUAN CAPISTRANO (1776)

SWALLOWS AT SAN JUAN CAPISTRANO—1777

Each year, on the Feast of Saint Joseph, the quaint little town of San Juan Capistrano becomes the center of national attention for, on that day, hundreds of eager visitors gather to await the "miracle of the birds," the return of the swallows to the old mission. The cheery little harbingers of spring are cream–headed, grey–breasted, red–rumped cliff swallows, known technically and scientifically as *Petrochelidon pyrrhonta*. They are a warrior–type bird whose migratory fields cover the wide expanse between Alaska and Argentina.

The legend of the annual arrival of "*Las Golondrinas*" on Saint Joseph's Day is deeply imbedded in tradition. According to one account, the first migration took place on March 19, 1777, when "an old Indian, leaning heavily on his staff of gnarled olive wood, paused a moment to rest beside the courtyard wall before continuing to the chapel. His attention was attracted to a half–dozen small birds, skimming the walls and darting with the swiftness of light over the mission patio. Such birds he had never seen before. The backs were a rich purplish black, a spot of white marked their foreheads and their throats and breasts were dove–gray. Suddenly, as though their inspection of the mission was complete, they rose into the air and disappeared in the direction of the sea. Mass was scarcely over when the birds returned, bringing with them thousands of their kind. Without a moment's delay they settled on the mission, the walls and old olive trees and straightway set to work building their mud nests under the eaves of the mission.

"Summer passed and autumn came, and then about October 21st, a restlessness was noticed among the swallows. There was much chattering and preening of feathers. At the dawn of October 23rd, the feast day of Saint John, for whom the mission was named, the mission Fathers and Indians were awakened by a great rustling of wings. They rushed out in time to see the swallows rise into the air, as one, and, swinging into perfect formation, head for the sea. No sooner had the swallows left their mud nests, than the swifts moved in. All winter the swifts held sway, and then came the morning of March 19th in another year. Out of the mists of the sea came the swallows, 3,000 strong. The swifts were discovered and a battle royal followed. The swifts were driven out and the swallows took up residence again for another happy season."

The number of swallows returning to the mission in recent years has been gradually diminishing. Pesticides are slowly killing off insects in southern Orange County and this factor alone helps to account for the fewer number of birds at Capistrano. It might also be noted that many of the swallows have taken refuge in nearby irrigation tunnels where the food supply is more abundant and the tourists less exuberant.

Legends die hard and traditions have a way of lingering on. Undoubtedly there will be swallows in Capistrano as long as the town has a Chamber of Commerce for the annual migration of "*Las Golondrinas*" has been a "miracle" to the commercial life of local inhabitants, and that, in itself, will guarantee its permanence.

EARTHQUAKE AT SAN JUAN CAPISTRANO— 1812

Apparently earthquakes have always been characteristic occurrences in California. So familiar are these temblors that residents rarely pay them any attention. Today, construction codes allow for "earthquake ordinances" which have, to a considerable extent, insulated the largest buildings against this phenomenon of nature.

Such was not always the case, however, for little was known in mission days about the principles of stress and strain. Over the years, several temblors have wrought considerable damage to mission buildings, the latest being that at Santa Barbara on June 29, 1925, which toppled the church towers and weakened the entire structure. Probably the worst tragedy along these lines was the earthquake of 1812 which brought down the new church of masonry at San Juan Capistrano. Notations in the local registers state that the edifice collapsed "during the first Mass on the 8th of December, 1812," and that "two days later, thirty–nine bodies taken out of the ruins were buried in the cemetery."

Early tradition fills in many of the details. At the offertory of the Mass, the worshippers could feel the earth shaking and see the walls and roof rocking back and forth. One jolt broke loose the domes in the rear of the church and the walls fell inward. The celebrant of the Mass, Fray José Barona, motioned the people to move quickly into the sanctuary. A few attempted to get out through an exit on the west side of the building but the weight of the walls had broken the door jams. The tower fell northwest bringing down with it the roof of the nave as far as the transept, making escape through the west door the only possibility.

As soon as the shocks subsided, rescue workers went into the rubble to search out bodies. Two days after the disaster, a woman was found in the debris still alive. She recovered from the ordeal and lived on for many years at the mission to tell visitors about the dreadful incident. Great as the tragedy was, it could have been much worse for, as Fray José Señan noted, "if the disaster had occurred at the time of the High Mass, instead of during the first Mass . . . scarcely any neophytes would have been left at San Juan Capistrano."

Before its destruction, the church was among the most magnificent of all California's early mission foundations. Even today, standing in ruins, its carved pilasters, capitals, doorways, arches and keystones retain their artistic embellishments. Indeed, the life of the church was short—only six years and three months. An entry in the annals tells of its erection, noting that it was "built by its neophytes at the expense of their application and labor. It is all of lime, with the vaults of the same material, and with a transept. It was begun on the 2nd day of February in the year 1797 . . . and was blessed on the evening of the 7th of September in the year 1806."

Experts have ventured several opinions as to why the church collapsed while neighboring buildings weathered the earthquake with little damage. One theory revolves around the possibility that an earlier jolt in 1800 cracked some of the walls which were not later reinforced. It is known that the master builder, Isidor Aguilar, died before the church's completion and the friars themselves had to finish the work.

RANCHOS OF SAN JUAN CAPISTRANO—1819

The *ranchos* attached to the California missions were envisioned by the *Recopilación de Leyes* as land tracts suitable for grazing cattle. Areas were generally chosen where flat land and adequate water were readily available.

The herds at San Juan Capistrano Mission numbered 140,000 cattle and 16,000 sheep by 1819, the year of the highest livestock census. The herds were cared for by *vaqueros* or cowboys at a number of *ranchos* in what is now Orange County.

Rancho Las Bolsas (the pockets) became a part of the great Nieto grant at a very early date. Only the southwesterly portion of the *Santiago de Santa Ana* was occupied by mission cattle as the northerly portion was possessed by José Antonio Yorba and his family before 1800 .

Ranchos San Joaquin and *Cienega de las Ranas* remained within the mission domain until the late 1830s, when José Andres Sepulveda, son of a mission administrator, occupied and joined the lands to form the single *Rancho San Joaquin. Rancho Cerro de Santiago*, after secularization, became *Rancho Lomas de Santiago* of

Teodocio Yorba. Yorba was a son of the first owner of the great *Santa Ana Rancho*. The Lomas and San Joaquin *ranchos* later became part of the Irvine Ranch.

Rancho Cañada de los Alisos in the 1840s passed into the hands of José Antonio Serrano and Leandro Serrano, a former *majordomo* at San Luis Rey Mission. El Toro Marine base is located on this *rancho* today.

Rancho Yuguilli, named after an Indian *rancheria* of early times, became simply *Rancho Niguel*. It was first occupied by Juan Avila, then Domingo Yorba. Later purchased by C. B. Rawson, it was sold to Louis Moulton and Jean Pierre Daguerre in the 1890s for sheep grazing.

Rancho San Mateo, later called *Losa Desechos*, passed into the hands of Felipe Pico, a nephew of the infamous governor. Today the city of San Clemente is situated on this former mission *rancho. Rancho Boca de Playa* (the mouth of the beach) is now Capistrano Beach. On this *rancho* was the Hide House of the mission—where hides and tallow were stored to await passing ships bearing supplies for the mission in exchange for the "leather dollar," as the hides were called in *rancho* days.

Rancho Agua Caliente, situated at the top of the *Arroyo Agua Caliente,* later became San Juan Hot Springs and was known for its nitre water even in mission times. This *rancho* is now bisected by the Ortega Highway.

There were also three *potreros* or pastures attached to San Juan Capistrano. These small ranches, totaling about 1,167.74 acres, were incorporated into the Cleveland National Forest in 1907 by President Theodore Roosevelt.

The *Ranchos Las Flores, Cerro de Trabuco* and *Mission Vieja* in the 1870s became part of the great *Santa Margarita Rancho. Rancho San Onofre y Santa Margarita* was originally part of San Luis Rey Mission, near Oceanside. When the Pico family took control of this *rancho*, they added to it the *Asistencia of Las Flores*, known as the *Ranchito Las Flores*.

This brief outline of a single mission gives some indication of the land needed to graze the cattle needed for sustenance.

CAPISTRANO'S GOLDEN ALTAR

The old missions have long been regarded as the most characteristic works of man to be found in the Golden State. Of all the twenty–one such establishments, San Juan Capistrano, established in the year of American independence, has long enjoyed the special distinction of being the "Lordliest of California's Missions." The adobe structure forming the east side of the mission quadrangle at Capistrano is the oldest building in California, and the only one hallowed by the presence of Fray Junípero Serra, founder of the California Missions.

Since 1922, this so–called "Serra Church" has housed one of the most ornate altar pieces ever assembled along the Pacific Slope. The decision to install that historic work of art at Capistrano was a most appropriate gesture which elicited the unequivocal endorsement of contemporary architects.

The exact date of the altar and reredos is not certain, though they are surely "several centuries old." Bishop Thomas J. Conaty acquired the elaborately carved artistic gem from Barcelona, about 1906. It was the prelate's ambition to install it as the centerpiece of the Cathedral of Our Lady of Guadalupe, which he envisioned as the new mother–church for the Diocese of Monterey–Los Angeles. Conaty's dreams for the massive new church never materialized and the dismantled altar pieces remained in their original packing crates for almost fifteen years in the basement of the rectory at Saint Vibiana's Cathedral.

In 1920, Father St. John O'Sullivan asked Bishop John J. Cantwell if the altar and its appurtenances could be reassembled in the "Serra Church" at San Juan Capistrano, which had been in ruins since 1866. "Judging that the restored church would be the most fitting place in the diocese for it," the bishop readily consented and the altar subsequently became the "crowning joy" of Father O'Sullivan's restoration program. The intricate task of fitting the several hundred pieces of hand–carved Spanish cedar into place, entrusted to the experienced southland architect, Arthur B. Benson, was a slow and painstaking process which consumed the greater part of eighteen months.

The walls of the sanctuary were heightened to accommodate the massive retable. So artistically were the altar and retable assembled that one knowledgeable visitor recorded that "by design or accident, they fit the place perfectly, their complexity contrasting the simplicity of the provincial surroundings."

In addition to a number of structural alterations, it was necessary to replace three statues which had mysteriously disappeared from the original baroque reredos. The eminent Mexican artist, Fray Francisco España, was commissioned to carve depictions of Saints Francis and Clare. He also fashioned, for the central niche, the handsome image of San Juan Capistrano with unfurled banner.

From the semi–darkness of the long nave, the richly carved "Golden Altar," with its winged–heads of cherubim glimmering in the natural light from a narrow horizontal window above the sanctuary, recalls the day, in 1778, when the "Serra Church" first took its place among the historic buildings of the American West. Mission San Juan Capistrano is "one of the monuments of our faith and one of the sources of our pride in our religion and our civilization."

JUANEÑOS FINALLY RECOGNIZED—1993

The Juaneños are a part of the Shoshonean Indians evangelized by the Franciscans at San Juan Capistrano Mission. They are prominent in the early annals of that and other frontier posts along *El Camino Real*.

Occupying the area between the related Gabrielinos and Luiseños, the lands of the Juaneños extended approximately from the coast about Los Alisos Creek northeastward to Santiago Park, the southern extension of the Sierra Santa Ana, thence southeastward, passing the uppermost reaches of San Juan Creek and Arroyo Mateo, and southwestward to the sea between Arroyo San Onofre and Las Pulgas Cañon, in the present Orange and San Diego counties.

It was among the Juaneños that Fray Geronimo Boscana conducted his missionary work between 1814 and 1826, Boscana's famous memoir, *Chinigchinich* is regarded as the most intensive and best written account of the customs and religion of any group of California Indians in early times.

But a strange fate fell to the Juaneños in the post mission era. In 1850, bureaucrats made a list of all the native American tribes in the country and, for some unknown reason, the Juaneños were omitted. It was as if they never existed and no subsequent appeal by local leaders had any effect.

Since the 1850s, the Juaneños people have battled in the courts, in the pages of history books and in the halls of the State Legislature for redress. Yet, nothing was ever done, at least officially.

What a regrettable mistake! The history of the Juaneños goes back at least 10,000 years, during which time they lived in the canyons, on the beaches and alongside the hills of Southern California. In later times, the tribe occupied a coastal area stretching from what is now Huntington Beach to the north, Oceanside to the south and inland to Cleveland National Forest, Lake Elsinore and Corona. Yet, officially they never existed.

The Juaneños were a friendly people who lived in villages loosely organized into family units. They were in great evidence among the white peoples who settled and developed that area of California in provincial times.

After the mission era, the Juaneños tribe lived in a village of Acjackemen at the fork of what is now San Juan and Trabuco creeks. Though their members moved freely in the greater area, they kept their identity and preserved many of their customs and beliefs.

Happily there is a pleasant ending to this unfortunate page of history. Late in 1993, after 140 years of struggle, the California State Legislature finally recognized the Juaneño Band of Mission Indians as the original tribe of Orange County. At last, the Juaneños were accorded their rightful place in the annals of America's native peoples.

One observer who witnessed the reconciliation ceremonies at San Juan Capistrano Mission observed that "this recognition changes nothing, and yet it changes everything. We are now given back our birthright. Like Job in the Old Testament, we have received from the Lord our rightful heritage." Though it gives no retroactive satisfaction to earlier generations, the recognition of the Juaneños is applauded by all peoples of good will. What is right is always right!

SWALLOWS AND SAINT JOSEPH

The return of California's cliff swallows (*petrochelidon pyrrhonata*) to their breeding grounds at and/or near San Juan Capistrano Mission has become famous in song and story, due primarily to their reportedly punctual return on March 19th. The ability of swallows to find their way about successfully has been recognized for a long time. For example, Pliny wrote that occasionally a Roman racehorse owner would take swallows with him to the races. The birds stained with the colors of the winning horses, were released to carry news of the victories back to his friends at home.

Fabius Pictor recorded that when a certain Roman garrison was besieged by the Ligurians, swallows were sneaked out of the city and taken to the army advancing to aid the garrison. When released the birds would return to the surrounded city with knotted strings tied to their feet. The number of knots indicated the days before relief could be expected.

Dr. William H. Mayhew of the University of California gives four major requirements for a successful cliff swallow colony: (a) an open area for foraging air–borne insects, (b) a vertical object (preferably with an overhang) for nest attachment, (c) a supply of mud for nests and (d) some smooth–surfaced fresh water for drinking.

Cliff swallows are widely distributed in the western hemisphere. They spend their winter in Argentina and southern Brazil, but return each spring to North America. Although they do not nest in desert areas, their migratory route in the western United States takes them across one of the most inhospitable desert areas in the world.

Being diurnal birds, they feed almost exclusively on flying insects and they are unable to survive in regions where it is so cold that no such insects are available. The groups of insects normally fed upon by cliff swallows do not become active until air temperature reaches approximately 70 or above. As soon as warm weather returns to the Pacific coastal area, large concentrations of cliff swallows move from the Imperial Valley into such places as San Juan Capistrano.

Nest building starts shortly after their arrival and requires from one to two weeks. The nest is built by both members of the pair, each bird carrying small pellets of mud from a nearby source. The pellets are painstakingly added one at a time.

Although both parents stay in the nest during the night, only the female incubates the eggs. This process lasts from fifteen to sixteen days. Once the young hatch, they remain in the nest for three weeks before attempting to fly. Mortality rate is rather high in this species. About a 50 percent mortality occurs between one year and the next. Very few of them live for more than four or five years.

The considerable reduction of cliff swallows in recent years has been due to dry weather cycles, insecticides, removal of nesting sites and the like. Biologists still know relatively little about the tiny birds which navigate over tremendous expanses of sea and land, from one continent to another, without the aid of compass or sextant.

But, to residents of San Juan Capistrano, the annual coming of the cliff swallows is somehow connected with Saint Joseph, whose feastday is celebrated on March 19th.

Santa Clara de Asis (1777)

THE "MOST BEAUTIFUL CHURCH" IN CALIFORNIA—1784

On May 15, 1784, just a few short months before his death, the venerable Fray Junípero Serra, President of the California missions, journeyed to Santa Clara for the dedication of "the most beautiful church yet erected" along *El Camino Real*. The account of that ceremony, recorded on page 100 of the *Libro de Bautismos*, is rich in its detail:

> On the fifth Sunday after Easter, which throughout the entire Franciscan Order is dedicated to the Feast of the Dedication of the Basilica and Papal Chapel on the Hill of Heaven in Assisi where the sacred body of our Seraphic Father Saint Francis rests, there was held and celebrated in this Mission of Santa Clara, our Seraphic Mother, the dedication and inauguration of the new church. The start of this church and the laying of the foundation stone is described on page 59 of this record book. The church walls are a *vara* and a half thick of adobe bricks placed on a foundation of stones and strengthened by buttresses yet another *vara* in breadth.

> The inside height is eight *varas* of free space. The inside length is forty *varas* and a half and the width nine. There is besides a sacristy which abuts from the forepart of the sanctuary; it is of the same height and with the same thickness of walls as the church. The length of the sacristy corresponds to the width of the church, and it is six *varas* broad.

> Then there is the portico of the church which measures five *varas* and so lengthens the building as far as the roof is concerned.

> The roof of the church and sacristy is flat and composed of beams laid on corbels with boarding of alerche wood, commonly called redwood. On the top of that is a layer of adobes, which are covered with thatching to throw off the rains. The corbels project beyond the side walls and with them the roof thatching so as to protect these walls from the rains which ordinarily are heavy.

> The doors—both the main doorway and the side or cloister entrance—each have double doors. Some are of cedar wood and the others of alerche, and both are provided with locks. The sacristy likewise has two doors of alerche wood. These are single doors, and each has its lock.

Santa Clara de Asis Mission

This church, besides, is calcimined both inside and out. Besides this, the front of the exterior is neatly painted in various colors, and in the interior there is a painted border, with a border below, all around the walls. So too with the sanctuary both above and below, and a large part of the ceiling has similar designs. The floor is all paved with adobe bricks.

It was inaugurated and dedicated on the said feast day in this way:

First Vespers for the feast were sung on Saturday, May 15, 1784. The Reverend Father President of these missions, Fray Junípero Serra, was vested as celebrant with alb, stole and cope. As his assistants were the Reverend Fathers Preachers Fray Francisco Palóu and Fray Thomás de la Peña, the former from the Mission of San Francisco, our Seraphic Father, and the latter from this Mission of Santa Clara. He is the only minister here because just four days before, the Reverend Father Preacher Fray Joseph Antonio de Murguia, the principal promoter of the beautiful temple, died. Blessed be God.

When everything was in readiness for the ceremonies—acolytes, cross bearer, torchbearers and everything else—the key of the said church was handed over to Don Pedro Fages, Lieutenant Colonel of the Royal Armies, Military Governor, head of Government of both Californias as patron of ceremonies—a post he was happy to fulfill. At his side was the Lieutenant and Commandant of the Presidio of San Francisco, Don Joseph Joaquin Moraga. Thus gathered in a body and in order of our rank, we went to the main door of the said church which was still shut. And thus we began, carried out and finished the blessing of the said church according to the formula of the Roman Ritual, amid the ringing of bells and continual gun shots from the troops, which added to the solemnity of the occasion. The little guns of the mission were likewise fired. We concluded with a solemn Te Deum Laudamus and so ended the functions of that afternoon.

On the following day, namely the said Sunday and the 16th of the said month, the inauguration of the said holy temple was held with the holy Sacrifice of the Mass. The Reverend Father President sang the said principal Mass and delivered a sermon at it. He called upon his hearers to give glory to God because of the new temple. As a culmination to the functions and celebrations, at the end of the Mass he administered Confirmation with all possible solemnity.

MISSION BECOMES UNIVERSITY

Of all the California missions, only Santa Clara has the distinction of having become the site of a modern university. Founded in 1777 as the eighth in the chain of frontier outposts along *El Camino Real*, Santa Clara was also destined to evolve into the titular head of the Jesuit apostolate in the far west.

Alta California was not a field of Jesuit missionary activity prior to 1849. Such early pioneers as William Hartnell saw the advantage of such a ministry noting that he would be "very glad to see 20 or 30 Jesuits come to the area."

It was due mostly to an energetic Italian priest, Father Michael Accolti, that the Society of Jesus finally came to regard the Pacific Slope as a worthwhile investment for their clerical personnel. Accolti was busily corresponding with friends in San Francisco about the feasibility of bringing Jesuits from Oregon to provide spiritual and educational assistance to California's Catholics.

The Administrator for the vacant Diocese of Both Californias, Fray José Maria de Jesus González Rúbio, appealed for one or two Jesuits who would be willing to raise the necessary funds for inaugurating an educational apostolate in his vast jurisdiction. Accolti and a fellow missionary, John Nobili, arrived in California during December of 1849. Fearing that San Francisco was not well suited for a college, they initially favored San Jose but that area too proved unsatisfactory.

Shortly after Bishop Joseph Sadoc Alemany arrived as the new Ordinary for the Diocese of Monterey, the Dominican prelate met with Father Nobili and formally offered the Jesuits the old Franciscan mission at Santa Clara. With an optimism that one could only qualify as audacious, John Nobili committed himself and the Society of Jesus to accept Santa Clara Mission as the site for their envisioned educational work. On March 4, 1851, Alemany officially signed a document appointing the Jesuit pastor of Santa Clara and administrator of "all belonging to the mission."

It was in May, 1851, that Nobili first opened the doors of the mission as a schoolhouse. The decaying adobe buildings, described as "wretched" by the bishop, were to signal the beginning of a new era for both the Jesuits and the Church in California.

The gold rush was still in its heyday and the last friar, Jose Maria del Refugio Suarez de Real, had only recently departed for Mexico and a wholly new apostolate was thrust upon an institution that for almost three quarters of a century had served as a missionary foundation. By the time Santa Clara Mission celebrated its bicentennial, there were 7,020 students enrolled on, the university campus. California's first institution of higher learning had successfully accommodated itself to the ever–changing needs of a growing Church and society.

Catholic education had come of age in the far west. And, not surprising, the Society of Jesus had been the instigators.

SAN BUENAVENTURA (1782)

MISSION BELLS THAT NEVER RANG

Among the many items on exhibit in the Historical Museum at San Buenaventura Mission, none is more fascinating than the two wooden bells, now badly deteriorated, which have mystified visitors and experts alike for several generations.

Early in 1995, Max R. Kurillo and E. M. Tuttle, using the findings of a half century of science, history and hundreds of hours of original research, decided to publish their findings about the only two full–sized wooden bells in the world. That fascinating, 110 page book was released at Los Angeles by the Bordon Publishing Company under the title, *The Mission Bells that Never Rang*.

The bells had received public attention for many years. When President Theodore Roosevelt visited San Buenaventura Mission in 1903, the *Daily Free Press* reported that "he climbed the stairway built in the tower, went out into the cupola, rang the old wooden bells and climbed down again."

While there are many other references to the bells in the historical annals, none offered any clue to their origin or date. They have remained unique and so mysterious as to almost defy the imagination. Kurillo and Tuttle have determined that both of the bells (there was originally a third one, now long lost) were made of mahogany, possibly from trees growing on Santa Catalina Island.

The bells were carved in two halves and joined together by wood butterfly fasteners outside and metal plates inside. The alignment and fitting of the bell halves was so masterfully done that casual observers would think that they were carved from single blocks of wood.

They were obviously carved by a master craftsman with a knowledge of furniture making. Though fabricated from mahogany, their pegs were made of redwood. There are no carvings, lettering or engraving that would provide any hint as to their origin.

Available photographic evidence indicates that the wooden bells hung in the upper tier of the mission tower continuously from about 1861 until at least 1907, probably even until the mid 1920s. The authors enumerate the more credible theories about the origin of the bells. Possibly, they were intended to replace the original bells destroyed by the 1812 earthquake, or maybe they were put in place as a decoy to protect the real bells from being stolen by the pirate Hippolyte Bouchard in 1818.

Another popular contention is that the bells were used annually from noon on Holy Thursday until Holy Saturday, when metallic bells were prohibited. The practice of silencing bells on those days perdured until modern times.

Finally, the most logical theory is that the bells were carved and hung in the tower simply to fit spaces where metallic bells once hung. There is a wooden replica at La Purisima that was fabricated for that purpose in the 1930s.

After examining all the evidence in great detail, Kurillo and Tuttle present their own conclusion that the bells were carved in 1861 or 1862 at the behest of Father Juan Comapla, for the purpose of filling the niches in the top level of the cupola, thus placing logic ahead of fantasy. In any event, theirs is a most scholarly treatise about two historical objects that, since the turn of the century, have been "inspiring awe and wonder in those who view them."

"LA ASUMPTA" PERMANENTLY ENSHRINED —1952

The name bestowed on San Buenaventura Mission's "daughter parish" is deeply embedded in the area's history. *La Asumcion de Nuestra Señora* or *La Asumpta* was the patronage proclaimed by the friars when Gaspar de Portolá's expedition first arrived, on August 15, 1769.

In bestowing the title of Our Lady's Assumption, the Spanish *padres* followed the ancient custom of naming an area for the saint whose feast falls on the day the first Mass is celebrated. "*La Asumcion de Nuestra Señora*" was an appellation that remained with the Indian village which grew up on the site until 1782, when Fray Junípero Serra founded San Buenaventura Mission. That historic establishment was named for the third superior of the Franciscan Order.

In 1943, when plans for another parish in the City of San Buenaventura were first discussed, the original name was suggested by Father Daniel Hurley, the pastor of the Old Mission. The idea was happily endorsed by Archbishop John J. Cantwell.

Ground–breaking ceremonies at the ten acre plot on Telegraph Road were held a decade later, on July 28, 1952. The first mass was offered in the unfinished edifice the following October 12th. As a means of permanently recalling the patronage of Our Lady's Assumption, it was decided to enshrine a scene of the historic 1769 event in a clay mural which would be mounted on the outside the church.

Millard Sheets, a world famous artist and head of the Fine Arts Department at Scripps College, Claremont, conceived the unique clay tile mural. It was an unusual concept inasmuch as it marked the first time an artist

San Buenaventura Mission

was able to create and paint a design with frost free glazes on a clay tile base.

And that was necessary as a means of insuring that the mural would withstand the rigors of weathering, while still retaining the brightness of the original colors. Richard and Alice Petterson were entrusted with developing an occult formula which resulted in a high–fired porcelain glaze. It was necessary for them to mix sixty gallons of the solution for the project.

From Millard Sheets' original drawing, his assistants executed the tile mural on huge panel easels designed especially for the project. The glazes were applied to 9 x 9 quarry tile made of California clays by the Jordan Manufacturing Company of Corona.

Unique new combinations of rare metallic oxides, such as chromium, tin, vanadium, triconium, cobalt, gold and silver resulted in the lovely, glowing colors. From the ninety–four colors used, there were over a thousand distinct shades.

The actual firing required constant care for a total of 212 hours. Firing temperatures reached 2200 F, sufficient to give the tile the greatest durability of any mural technique ever devised. Completed on April 12, 1954, the unique mural immortalizes the association of Our Lady's Assumption with the beautiful and historic City of San Buenaventura.

A PRECIOUS ADDITION AT SAN BUENAVENTURA—1978

The use of lights (candles) as an adjunct worship goes back to the beginning of the Church, and even farther. Among the Jews, their use had long been looked upon as appropriate in connection with public homage to Almighty God. And, fittingly enough, candlesticks, the supportive receptacles for these lights, typify Christ and His Church, the "light of the world and the dispeller of darkness."

San Buenaventura Mission acquired a beautiful and historic silver candlestick which was used for the first time on Holy Saturday, 1978. The provenance of this artistic masterpiece is indeed impressive. It was one of six candlesticks commissioned by King Louis XIII and presented to Notre Dame Cathedral in thanksgiving for the making of Our Lady's Assumption a feastday for the kingdom, on February 10, 1638.

It reposed on the high altar of the famed Parisian church until the early days of the French Revolution. Fortunately, at that time, it was hidden away from the despoilers, who melted down most of the other precious ornaments in the cathedral. The candlestick was among the few pre–Revolutionary items restored in April, 1802. It was plainly visible in an etching made of Napoleon's coronation, on December 2, 1804.

For unknown reasons, the candlestick fell into private hands during the reign of the "Citizen King," Louis Philippe (1773–1850). It was brought to the United States from Manchester, near the turn of the century, and for many years belonged to descendants of Oliver Cromwell, who lived in Colorado.

In 1959, Mr. James Pendelton, an antique dealer in Hollywood, purchased the candlestick and presented it as a personal gift to Msgr. John J. Devlin. Throughout the remaining years of the monsignor's life, the handsome and artistic candlestick was used in the sanctuary of Saint Victor's Church in West Hollywood.

Following the monsignor's death, on April 6, 1977, the candlestick was dismantled and thoroughly cleaned by Mr. P. L. Lesch, a talented silversmith. It now bears the engraved inscription:

> Presented to San Buenaventura Mission
> from the Estate of Msgr. John J. Devlin
> (1898–1977)

The revered candlestick, cast in honor of Our Lady's Assumption, has an historical relevance to San Buenaventura Mission too, for it was on that feastday, in 1769, that the friars Juan Crespi and Francisco Gomez offered the first Holy Mass in the area where, thirteen years later, the ninth and last of Fray Junípero Serra's frontier outposts would be established.

A magnificent piece of workmanship, the forty–nine

inch high candlestick, with its ovular pricket on top, weighs fifty–one pounds. Its graceful lines blend perfectly with the Gothic architecture of Notre Dame. The long shaft is supported by a three–clawed base, its panels decorated with three cherubic angels, reminiscent of Our Lady's bodily assumption into heaven.

OUR LADY OF ANGELS AT SAN BUENAVENTURA—1979

In mid–August of 1979, a beautiful fibreglass statue of Our Lady of the Angels was set into the niche above the side entranceway to the historic church at San Buenaventura Mission. Devotion to Our Lady of the Angels has been associated with California's southland since July 31, 1769, when the Gaspár de Portolá expedition crossed an *arroyo* of muddy water and camped a little further on in a wide clearing.

Fray Juan Crespi, the diarist for the expedition, recorded that the following day was to be set aside "to celebrate the jubilee of Our Lady of *Los Angeles de Porciúncula.* " The next morning, on the Vigil of the feast, the expeditionary force continued its journey and came through a pass between two hills into a broad valley abounding in poplar and alder trees. After travelling another few leagues, the Spaniards camped along a river which they appropriately named "in honor of *Nuestra Señora de los Angeles de Porciúncula,*" a title derived from the day's sanctorial cycle.

When Felipe de Neve decided to set up a town on the site, he incorporated the religious title of the river and the popular appellation of Assisi's chapel in the name and the result was *El Pueblo de Nuestra Señora de los Angeles de Porciúncula.* Fray Juan Crespi's familiarity with the term Porciúncula grew out of the *toties quoties* indulgence gained at the Franciscan churches on August 1st and 2nd, as well as the devotion to Our Lady of the Angels prevalent in the *Convento de San Bernardino* at Petra.

The Marian patronage in that Franciscan church can easily be traced to the small village at the base of the steep mountainous town of Assisi in Italy. There the small community of *Santa Maria degli Angeli* (near present day Perugia) developed around the monastery where Francis Bernardone is said to have received his vocation to the ministry on February 24, 1208.

The humble friar lived there on a tiny plot of land alongside a chapel supposedly erected by the hermits from the Valley of Josaphat in the fourth century. As early as 516, the chapel was known as "Our Lady of the Valley of Josaphat" or "Our Lady of the Angels." Porciúncula, the commonly used term for the chapel, was a favorite of Saint Francis who regarded his small quarters as the "little portion" assigned to him by Divine Providence.

In as much as no depiction of Our Lady of the Angels could be found at San Buenaventura Mission, it was decided to honor the Mother of the Savior with a statue reminiscent of her historic "angelic" role. The talented craftsman, Fred Rolla, was commissioned to cast the statue in fibreglass, so as to sustain outside weathering. He, in turn, entrusted the actual fabrication of the thirty–seven inch high statue to the Demetz Family Studios, at Ortesei, a colorful mountain village in Northern Italy.

The complicated procedure used in executing the statue involved a number of stages: First of all, a model was sculptured by hand in plasterine; then latex was used to make a negative mold. Next, plaster–of–paris was smeared over rubber to reinforce and hold the form in place. Finally, liquid fibreglass was poured into the rubber negative mold. When the statue was properly cured and polished, it was painted by the artist.

The beautiful statue, with its three cherubic figurines at the base, was sent by train to Genoa, then across the Atlantic and through the Panama Canal aboard the merchant ship *Hong Kong.*

TWO HUNDRED YEARS AT SAN BUENAVENTURA—1984

On Sunday, March 28th 1984, San Buenaventura Mission observed the bicentennial of its founding by Fray Junípero Serra. It was a gala occasion, widely covered by local and national news media.

Fifty years earlier, when the Old Mission celebrated its sesquicentennial, the Los Angeles *Times* sent its most popular "staff representative" to record the events. And chances were slim that the prosaic coverage of John Steven McGroarty would be "outreported" a half century later.

> From the mists of the past and the dust of long–forgotten trails, the soul of the old California that used to be was reborn in San Buenaventura.
>
> It is almost 400 years now since the first white men, sailing on a voyage of discovery in the caravels of Juan Rodriguez Cabrillo saw the place. And it is 150 years since the renowned Fray Junípero Serra stopped on his wandering way to found the mission here.
>
> And so it is a far cry back to the beginning of the beautiful modern city which is the San Buenaventura of today. A full century has passed, and half of another, since the cornerstone of this civilization was laid, which is a long time as time goes in the life of man.
>
> There is not a living soul left now that breathed the breath of life when San Buenaventura uttered its first articulate cry. Only the hills that were there and the sea that was there remain.
>
> The first roof that was reared has long since crumbled. The first cross that was planted went the way of dust many and many a year ago.
>
> Happily, though, time does not forget the things that

it loves to remember. And Ventura, perhaps more than any other community of our modern California clings with affection to its memories and keeps deep in its heart the treasure of a golden heritage. And to all that, it gave today a full expression.

There was much pomp and color in the ceremonies that marked the founding of the Old Mission and the city itself. Yet, under the panoply of the splendor of it all, there was something deeper—the voice of a soul that still endures.

It is when you climb the road from the San Fernando Valley and come to the Calabasas Hills that you enter old California. From there on to San Luis Obispo you journey with the spirits of the past. The voices of adventurers speak to you from the breakers of the sea.

Spanish speech greets you as you pass, silent adobe walls speak their haunted memories. The noise and clamor of a crazy world is left behind. The mask that San Buenaventura puts on is easily penetrated. You have but to be an hour with them to know how deeply Spanish they are still at heart.

All charm, all beauty and high romance is not yet fled from the world. And this is what we knew who participated in the celebration of the sesquicentennial of San Buenaventura.

It was on a high hill that rises above the Old Mission and the city that the ceremonies were held. The same hill upon which the wandering sons of St. Francis reared their first cross. It is a hill from which you can look down upon a panorama of land and sea not rivaled elsewhere in all the world.

The sky above it today was flawless. There was not even a speck of a cloud to fleck the endless expanse of the heavens' turquoise blue. Across the channel lay the purple isles upon one of which Cabrillo sleeps waiting the sound of Gabriel's horn.

Hospitality ran riot and boundless. Nobody had anything to sell. It was open house and open heart from rise to set of sun. The generous past lived again. The old days lent their heartbeats to the new. It was a gorgeous and a happy day.

SANTA BARBARA (1786)

"QUEEN" OF THE MISSIONS

In a number of his sixteen books about the individual California missions, Father Zephyrin Engelhardt applied his own surnames to the frontier outposts established along *El Camino Real*.

Examples would be San Gabriel (the "Pride of the Missions"), San Luis Rey (the "King of the Missions"), San Juan Capistrano (the "Jewel of the Missions") and San Carlos Borromeo (the "Father of the Missions"). But he saved the queenly title for his own Santa Barbara Mission, a distinction it truly deserved.

In his treatise on *Santa Barbara Mission* (San Francisco, 1923), Engelhardt openly admits that he himself stands sponsor for the book's surname, "Queen of the Missions." He went on to explain how "Queen" came to be applied to Santa Barbara Mission. "The saint herself, after whom this mission was named, lays no claim to royalty; she never ruled over a temporal principality. No, it is not the name of Santa Barbara that gives the clue to the title; it is the appearance, the local setting of the Mission that suggested it."

The Franciscan chronicler goes on to say that "Santa Barbara is the Queen among the Missions because it is raised up, as it were, on a throne and from its prominent position high above the beautiful city that lies below in the valley, it appears to hold sway over all the surroundings in an attitude of queenly dignity.

"In the olden days, during the time in which the events told in this history took place, Santa Barbara Mission was Queen in a more pronounced sense, perhaps, than she is today. Some of the old people tell us that her stately towers loomed up beyond all else that was here; that for miles around the Mission attracted the eye and compelled it to gaze in mute and reverent admiration. Those who lived in the valley looked up to the Mission daily and silently paid their homage to the Queen that ruled their little city."

According to Engelhardt, even in the 1920s Santa Barbara was still Queen. "Though the aged building is now surrounded by many beautiful homes, built up at the cost of fortunes and in the same Spanish style of architecture, and though some of these grand new structures are set up higher on the hills than the Mission itself; with all their splendor they form but the retinue of 'Her Royal Majesty' whose reign began more than a hundred years ago."

Engelhardt encouraged readers to examine the views of the mission and its surroundings for justification of the queenly title. "The building itself is not only set up in a commanding position, it is a structure of grand proportions: the ponderous weight of wall and arch and tower breathe a strength easily associated with royalty; the grace in proportion of lines, the harmony in the blending of soft colors suggest the beauty becoming to a fair Queen."

Santa Barbara Mission

And the colorful surroundings! "Nature has built a court such as no genius of man could fashion for a queen. The mountains towards the rear rise up like a protecting barrier; rock–ribbed and lofty, they form the outworks and battlements for the royal palace."

He concludes by noting that "such a panorama of ocean and mountain, of hill and dale, of garden and meadows and wooded slopes of green, all resting peacefully under skies of perpetual spring, and suffused the year round with gentle rays of golden sunshine! It is a realm that any ruler would be proud to own."

FAITH, HOPE AND CHARITY

During Santa Barbara's disastrous earthquake of June 29, 1925, the three stone figures of Faith, Hope and Charity, perched on the gable of the Old Mission's facade, fell to the pavement below and were broken into numerous pieces. Cut from native sandstone by Chumash neophytes under the supervision of an expert stone carver, they were a curious mixture of classical and Baroque postures, ideals and technical crudity.

Kurt Baer described the remnants in 1955: The most intact of the figures is the standing one, probably *Hope*. Its arms, which originally were separately carved and then cemented into the sockets, are missing. The head is characteristically archaic, its stiff, yet half–smile reminiscent of both early Greek and early Gothic sculpture. The tunic of the figure is Greek in style.

The remains of the figure *Faith*, with its right hand over the heart, is more in the nature of a relief. The top of the head is missing, as is the lower left arm, where evidence of a fastening bolt remains. The lower portion, containing the crudely–carved feet, is in several fragments.

What remains of *Charity* are the two lower sections, the most interesting being the trunk. Here a robed woman holds a "cuddling" infant in her left arm. The lower portion of the sculpture is the draped legs, the fluttering robe vaguely reminiscent of the lower drapery of the Nike of Samothrace.

In his book on the *Painting and Sculpture at Mission Santa Barbara*, Kurt Baer goes on to note that the central figure is a little under five feet in height; each of the others vary from three to four feet. The slight traces of coloring which indicate that the imitation of antique sculpture was carried out to the logical extreme.

A statewide campaign to raise funds for restoration was mounted and within two years most of the Old Mission had been refurbished. During the rebuilding, artisans crafted new figures to replace *Faith, Hope and Charity*. The broken pieces of the earlier statues were consigned to a storeroom where they remained for the next forty years.

Recognizing that the earlier statues were among the few examples of monument stone sculpture fashioned by native Californians, Dr. Norman Neuerburg suggested that the remnants be consigned to the South Coast Fine Arts Conservation Center for restoration. Carol Kenyon and others at the Center are among a handful of craftsmen working to reverse the ravages of time, nature and human carelessness on highly prized works of art. In an article for a recent issue of the *Santa Barbara* magazine, Hilary Cole Klein tells how craftsmen at the Center combine conservation techniques with a knowledge of art history, chemistry, painting and sculpture to erase the effects of dampness, heat or destruction.

In the case of *Faith, Hope and Charity,* the work was superbly done. Visitors to Santa Barbara Mission will probably find it hard to realize that those important relics, now totally restored, were once little more than a jumble of broken pieces.

RESTORATION AT SANTA BARBARA

Of all the California missions, only Santa Barbara has never been abandoned. Although the Franciscans have lived there until the present day, there have been many changes over the years since 1786. The following comments are based on two extensive interviews views with the late Father Maynard Geiger in 1974.

Physical development at Santa Barbara Mission reached its zenith in 1833, when the second tower was added to the church. At that time, the compound consisted of two quadrangles and a long building to the west, a guard house, a *majordomo's* house and a Christian village of 252 homes.

Three of the interior corridors had colonnades of brick while the exterior arcade consisted of stone from which the church was also erected. About 1812, a roof with tile supported by wooden poles over the front wing was built forming an open second story. The cemetery with its stone wall was located to the right of the church. The main water works and irrigation system were to the rear, side and front of the church.

There were many changes between 1848 and 1887. The Indian village disappeared after 1856 chiefly through the sale and robbery of roof tiles. Visitors recalled that the foundations were still visible in the last decades of the nineteenth century. The guardhouse, though in somewhat ruinous condition, was still recognizable in 1865. In 1887 the remaining portions of the *majordomo's* and tanner's house were torn down. All the buildings of the second quadrangle and the north wing of the first quadrangle, as well as the long building, disappeared after 1852.

The water works, though in partial ruins, remained until the 1960s. Until 1897 all that remained of the original mission compound was the church, the front and west wing of the first quadrangle. Renovations were made in the interior of the church in 1873 and new roofing replaced the old.

The upper open story of the front wing in the original quadrangle was renovated and enlarged between the years 1856 and 1870, becoming a closed story with living rooms. The area closest to the church was dedicated to the use of the apostolic college, which began functioning in 1854.

The second section to the west was brought in line with its eastern counterpart when a boarding college opened at the mission in 1868. In 1890 a room of stone and wood was built behind the church for a winery. After 1927, that room was used as a sacristy.

In 1897 the west wing of the original quadrangle at Santa Barbara Mission was completely altered to serve as Saint Anthony's Seminary which opened in 1896. The adobe wall on the cloister side and the walls between the adjoining rooms were preserved and incorporated into the new building of frame and plaster. This was again renovated in 1917 and almost completely redone in 1958.

The original pillars of 1800 were taken down in 1927 and replaced. In 1905, an L–shaped stone and concrete building about 100 feet in length and about 30 feet wide was added to the west end of the front wing. It was three and a half stories high owing to the sloping of the ground towards the west.

The principal damage caused by the earthquake of 1925 was to the church and the front wing erected between 1820 and 1905. By 1927 the entire interior of the church had been renovated as well as its adjoining sacristy built in 1820.

The right tower had to be taken down entirely as well as a part of the church's facade. These were repaired with the same stones used in 1820. Finally, the church was re–roofed.

The second story of the front wing built between 1856 and 1870 of adobe walls in some places covered with boards with a shingle roof and dormer windows, had to be torn down entirely. It was rebuilt with reinforced concrete supported by shafts running through the stone and adobe walls of the first floor deep into the ground.

The front section of this roof had been tiled in 1888. Changes were made in the number of rooms. The west wing which had disappeared a few years after 1850 and which through many years was replaced by a wooden shed, now became a two story building of frame and stucco, thus restoring the original quadrangle.

In 1950, because of deterioration caused by chemical action in the concrete, cracks and fissures appeared in the towers and facade. They had to be taken down and rebuilt completely. Deep foundations were laid and the towers and facade were anchored to the walls of the church of 1820. The new structure was of reinforced concrete and faced with Santa Maria limestone, the proportions and appearance remaining the same as the church of 1820.

In 1956 a major building program was undertaken at the mission, when two large quadrangles were added to the mission and the west wing of the original quadrangle substantially altered. In this process the second quadrangle which had been begun in 1796 and finished prior to 1833, was restored this time in two stories rather than one. To the west of this north quadrangle, a third was built to serve as a chapel, auditorium and lounge. This covered the ground where formerly the long wing of early mission days existed.

DEDICATION OF CHURCH AT MISSION SANTA BARBARA—1820

Through the centuries, churches have served the faithful as houses of prayer, galleries of art and incentives to devotion. From the earliest times, Catholic ceremonial has adorned the dedication of a church with solemnity and reverence. The formal blessing of a mission church in provincial California was an event of singular importance. On September 13, 1820, Fray Francisco Suñer described the colorful pageantry surrounding the dedication of the church at Mission Santa Barbara:

> Three religious missionaries of as many other Missions of New California, came to honor the occasion and to assist us, namely Fray José Señan, Vicar Forane to the Bishop of Sonora, Fray Luis Martinez of Mission San Luis Obispo and Fray Gerónimo Boscana of Mission San Juan Capistrano.
>
> Neither the missionary of Santa Inés nor the one from San Fernando, though both of neighboring foundations, could come because they were

alone at their respective posts. Nevertheless, they did allow some of their neophytes to come with their musicians and dancers, whom our *alcaldes* had invited.

> The dedication took place on September 10th of this year 1820. With his retinue, the Colonel of the Military and Governor of this Province came from Monterey at our invitation. Although he had been asked to come for September 7th, the vigil of Our Lady's Nativity, he did not arrive until the 9th.
>
> The ceremony then began on the appointed day, the feast of Mary's name. In the afternoon, the *Presidente* and the other priests, the Governor, the Captain and commander of the nearby *Presidio,* José de la Guerra y Noriega, with all his troops and officers, Narciso Fabregat, lieutenant of the auxiliary troops of Mazatlan and a great number of people from all stations and conditions gathered for the event.
>
> The *Te Deum* was intoned, whereupon Compline was chanted with great solemnity by the *Presidente,* amid the great illumination of all the altars, especially that of the titular, Santa Barbara. Then, in succession, candles were lighted on the housetops, the corridors and the tower. Flags of many colors danced in the winds.
>
> Immediately, the musicians passed through the corridors, where they played for about two hours. Meanwhile, rockets, serpents, firecrackers and the like were fired. All this was repeated on the two following nights.
>
> On Sunday the Feast of Our Lady's Nativity, after the merry ringing of the bells, Solemn High Mass was sung by Fray Gerónimo Boscana, during which liturgy the *Presidente* preached.
>
> On the following day, the coffins of the deceased religious were taken from their tombs and placed in the center of the church, whereupon a solemn vigil was chanted for their repose. With this the liturgical functions were terminated.
>
> Immediately after going out, the soldiers, cavalry as well as infantry, continued the festivities commenced on the preceding day, while the Indians had their dances and other diversions.
>
> Food, drink and shelter were given to all who asked for or needed them. To accommodate all with whatever they required, the Mission had at its disposal two houses of the whites, besides the barracks which did not prove sufficient.
>
> A man was appointed to serve the wine and brandy. Since the number of people was so large (there were 1,132 Indians alone at Santa Barbara at the time), the whole event cost considerably, but the expenses were well spent. It was a lively, continuous and pure blessing to the Lord and from the Lord.

"BULL MOOSE" VISITS SANTA BARBARA MISSION—1903

When President Theodore Roosevelt visited Santa Barbara Mission, on May 9, 1903, he complimented the friars "for preserving the memorials of an older civilization." The Chief Executive's train stopped at Depot Road in Montecito at 11 o'clock in the morning, where he was greeted by a committee of local citizenry.

The carriages carrying the President and other dignitaries then proceeded into the city via the Eucalyptus Road. Unfortunately, it was a hazy day and the view of the offshore islands was impeded. After a formal greeting by Mayor George Edwards, the presidential party made its way to the Old Mission where Father Ludger Glauber formally welcomed Mr. Roosevelt and conducted him through the premises.

According to the local press reports, "the President took a keen and reverent delight in viewing the chambers, the chapel, the altar and the quaint relics. He visited the graveyard where the early mission fathers sleep."

Helen Starry Adams was present when the "Bull Moose" arrived at the Old Mission and she reported on the incident in an essay later published in *The Brown Book of Boston.*

> During President Roosevelt's recent visit to the Pacific coast, he tarried for two enchanted hours at Santa Barbara. While he was standing within the deep shadows of the entrance to the old mission with a grave, black–robed *padre* on one side, and a time–scarred burial vault on the other, the ubiquitous camera fastened a quick, flitting, superbly unconscious pose of the 'strenuous' and the spiritual, for the interested gaze of loyal Americans.
>
> President and priest. A ruler and a recluse; a dreamer and a dynamo!
>
> This dear, kindly old town of Santa Barbara, nestling so peacefully in the vine–tangled valley of southern California is one of the most unique and lovable spots in our good land.

Later, Miss Adams sent a copy of her remarks to the President and, though she said very little about his actual visit, her observations greatly influenced the Chief Executive's later decision about "reserving" part of the area for the benefit of future generations. She had noted for example, that "in the old, old days, long before the mad inrush of gold–crazed 'barbarians,' the grave, astute Franciscan Fathers, roaming over the state seeking out eligible sites for churchly habitations, located the old mission of Santa Barbara on a beautiful slope overlooking both the town and sea.

"It was," she observed, "the quaintest corner of the quaint old town—a rare bit of eighteenth century placidity left, wondering, at the heart of the twentieth. In those fair, far–off days when California was more remote from the heart of the world's activities than the isles of the sea, the scattered missions of the Franciscan Brotherhood were serene centers of prosperity."

> Each churchly establishment was a shut–in, peaceful cosmos with broad, fertile acres billowing away to the purple horizon; and countless herds of sleek cattle browsed on a thousand hills, faithfully cared for by obedient and industrious Indian converts.

RESCUE OF SANTA BARBARA MISSION—1925

Charles F. Lummis once said that "to the world at large, the name of Santa Barbara means chiefly (if not exclusively) a grey old Landmark of the beginnings of California—a mighty Monument to historic pioneering, a venerable Teacher that has done more to influence the architecture of California homes and business blocks today than all the architectural traditions of England, New England, France and Italy together.

"To the world 'Santa Barbara' means the old Mission there, founded in 1786 in a wilderness, and a focus of civilization ever since." With that sentiment in mind, Lummis joined with a committee of seventy–five people "to undertake, as a patriotic trusteeship, the raising of a fund to rehabilitate" the Queen of the Missions which had been severely damaged in the earthquake of June 29, 1925.

Lummis was asked to compile a small leaflet explaining the project of restoring "our foremost monument of California romance." Here, in part, is what the non–Catholic Lummis had to say:

> If the Franciscan Missions hadn't homesteaded California for Spain, 156 years ago, who would be here today?
>
> Certainly not you and I! California, Oregon and Washington would be part of British Columbia and probably called 'New Albion,' as Drake named it in 1579. The United States had twenty million people, and Missouri was the extreme westerly state, when patriotic Tom Benton, its first senator, sent his son–in–law, Fremont, across the 2,200 miles of the Great American Desert to take California for us, and unroll our map to the Pacific.
>
> The greatest asset of California is romance—and in that romance, the Old Missions are the foremost factor. The romance of Gold in California, seventy–five years ago, revolutionized the money markets of the world; the Gold Rush of the Argonauts was the most Homeric era that our land and blood have ever known—but where are its bones today?
>
> Of the million visitors to California less than one percent visit the scenes immortalized by Bret Harte and Mark Twain; eighty percent visit at least some of the Old Missions. More travelers every year make pilgrim-

age to the one Mission of Santa Barbara than to all the mines and Mother Lodes that gave California its name of Golden State.

The President of the Los Angeles Chamber of Commerce said at San Fernando Mission's Candle Day, to an audience of seven thousand people: 'We realize that the Old Missions are our greatest asset; worth more in dollars and cents to Southern California than our Oranges, our Oil—even our Climate!'

Historically, ten years from now it would be less of a disaster to California if every skyscraper in it had been destroyed, than if this Queen of the Missions crumbled back to dust or was replaced by a modern Cathedral. We can build a million skyscrapers—we can't build one Old Mission!

On the pledge that Santa Barbara Mission shall be rehabilitated as a landmark, with all its romance and beauty and historic appeal—and not rebuilt or modernized or substituted–this fund is sought.

To save that monument of faith and art and romance is not only a privilege to those who know reverence, but a distinct investment to those who understand even the rudiments of business.

HOLY WEEK AT MISSION SANTA BARBARA— 1860

William H. Brewer, who came to California in 1860, as the chief field director of the Josiah Dwight Whitney Geological Survey Expedition, kept a daily record of his personal observations in the form of letters written to friends in the east. The "sober and industrious" recollections of the 14,000–mile sojourn by road and trail, across the breadth and length of the state, is especially useful for its descriptions of the people, conditions and early history of the area.

Brewer's keen and accurate observations, coupled with his sound conclusions, make the published version of his diary a very readable and valuable commentary on the California of that period. Brewer spent part of Holy Week, in 1861, at Santa Barbara, where the *padres* gave their inquiring visitor much information on the mission's past history. On April 4, Brewer described the religious setting in one of his many letters:

The whole week was a week of festival, but I was in town only the last three days. Friday I was in camp most of the day, but there was the ceremony 'lying in the sepulchre,' 'washing of feet,' etc. The town seemed like a true Sabbath day. Among the true Catholics, men are not allowed to ride horseback—formerly policemen prevented any from so riding on Good Friday—and but few horsemen are seen now.

On the afternoon of Good Friday, Brewer visited the Church of Our Lady of Sorrows, noting that "the altar

was trimmed off with a profusion of flowers around the sepulchre, tapers were burning, the windows were partially darkened, and a few of the devout were praying to their favorite saints." Later, at the mission, he noticed that the windows there too were "darkened by thick curtains and the many candles at the altar did not light up the obscurity. Many Indians were about. Within, a number of Indian women were kneeling before a shrine; one would lead off with the prayers and all join in the responses. Their pensive voices, the darkened vast interior, the pictures and images obscurely seen in the dim light, the tapers of the altar, the echoes of their voices, the only sounds breaking the stillness, produced an effect I can easily conceive most touching to the imagination of the worshippers. Some of the Indian girls and half–breeds were quite pretty, but the majority were decidedly ugly."

Next morning, Holy Saturday, again found us at the mission. This time the curtains were removed from the altar, and more ceremonies were gone through with than I can detail, but they differed very materially from the ceremonies at Munich on a similar occasion. The music was the best I have heard in California. It began with an instrumental gallopade (I think from Norma), decidedly lively and undevotional in its effects and associations. But other parts were more appropriate. . . . At the unveiling of the altar, two lovely little girls dressed as angels, with large white swan wings upon their shoulders, one at each side of the altar, looked most lovely. They stood there as watching angels during the ceremonies.

Not the least interesting to me were the costumes. Standing, kneeling, sitting over the floor were people of many races. Here was a genuine American; in the side aisle kneels a genuine Irishman, his wife by his side; near him some Germans; in the short pew by the wall, I recognize some acquaintances, French Catholics, also an Italian. But the majority of the congregation are Spanish Californians.

Black eyes twinkle beneath the shawls drawn over the heads of the females and glossy hair peeps out also, and the responses show sets of teeth that would make an American belle die with envy should she see them. A few bonnets and 'flats' tell of American or foreign women mingled with the crowd. Here is a group of Indians, the women neatly conforming to the Spanish dress, only their calico dresses are of even brighter colors—all are dressed in holiday clothes. Here is a man with a Parisian rig; there one with a regular Mexican costume, buttons down the sides of his pants; beside him is an Indian with fancy moccasins and gay leggings; behind me in the vestibule, looking on with curiosity, are two Chinamen. No place but California can produce such groups.

The honest and meticulous observations of William Brewer became a notable addition to the state's scientific exploration. Beyond that, as a picture of the overall

California scene in the 1860s, "there is not to be found in print anything to compare with this series of letters, written on the spot, by a highly educated man of broad sympathies trained in the art of observing, and blessed with a delightfully whimsical humor."

QUEEN ELIZABETH AT SANTA BARBARA MISSION—1983

Since 1875, when the Arlington Hotel was built at Santa Barbara, tourism has been that city's major "industry." The trend accelerated with the coming of the railroad in 1887 and developed still more with the appearance of the first automobiles at the turn of the century.

Some journeyed to Santa Barbara for their health, others for pleasure, vacation or business, while still others remained to enrich the area, developing its resources and adding their knowledge, skills and experience to local betterment. Because of its colorful history and picturesque location, Santa Barbara Mission has been an attraction of primary interest. The Franciscans have provided guides since 1885 and, in modern times, upwards of 150,000 guests affix their names to the register books annually at the Old Mission.

The celebrated visit to Santa Barbara of Her Royal Majesty, Queen Elizabeth II of Great Britain, came just a century after the first member of the English royal family was greeted at the Old Mission. Princess Louise, the daughter of Queen Victoria and wife of the Canadian Governor General, was welcomed to Santa Barbara Mission at Christmas time, 1882. She was also the first woman allowed to enter the cloistered gardens.

(At that time, Canon Law allowed only one category of women, the wives of actual rulers of countries or governors of states, to enter the cloistered area of a monastery. Prior to 1965, only nine woman had qualified for that privilege, including Mrs. Benjamin Harrison, Queen Elizabeth of Belgium, Marta de Rios (wife of Chile's President), Mrs. John Bricker (wife of the Governor of Ohio), Mrs. Harry Kelly (wife of the Governor of Michigan), Mrs. Earl Warren, Mrs. Goodwin Knight and Mrs. Edmund Brown (wives of governors of California).

There have been numerous royal visitors at the "Queen" of the California missions. King Albert, his wife and Prince Leopold came on Sunday, the 12th of October, 1919. Mass was celebrated for their convenience by Father Julius Gliebe who fittingly spoke in his homily on "Christian kingship.'

On April 24, 1891, President Benjamin Harrison stopped briefly at the Old Mission. Father Maynard Geiger recorded that the *House Chronicle* simply stated that the President "in company with Mr. Wanamaker, Postmaster General, and Secretary Rusk, paid a visit to our mission." President William McKinley's visit to Santa Barbara Mission a decade later was a gala affair. There was a grand parade in his honor, complete with a "chariot of roses" containing 15,000 pink Duchess roses.

Two years afterwards, President Theodore Roosevelt journeyed to Santa Barbara Mission. The Chief Executive congratulated the people of the Channel City for "perpetuating the memorials of an old civilization." The press reported that "the President took a keen and reverent delight in viewing the chambers, the chapel, the altar and the quaint relics." And "he visited the graveyard where the early mission fathers sleep."

The queen's visit to California in 1983 was rich in historical significance. Possession of California was taken in the name of Queen Elizabeth I by Francis Drake who remained in his "New Albion" for thirty–six days. After his return to England, Drake was knighted by the queen.

Four centuries have come and gone.

SANTA BARBARA AND HER MISSION

The story of Santa Barbara is that of a pagan noblewoman who became a Christian martyr and then gave her name to one of California's most important missions. Though little if any historical knowledge exists about Santa Barbara, she is thought to have been born in Heliopolis, "the city in the sun," on the east branch of the Nile, within travelling distance of Alexandria.

The Roman martyrology for December 4th has this to say: "At Nicomedia, there took place the martyrdom of Saint Barbara, Virgin and Martyr, who in the persecution of Emperor Maximin, after having suffered a long imprisonment, was incinerated with torches, had her breasts cut off and, after other unspeakable tortures, secured the crown of martyrdom by decapitation."

There is no value here in recalling the "legendary" Santa Barbara except to say that in that context her story reads like a page from the *Arabian Nights*, or a fairy tale from Grimm, or princesses in towers, cruel fathers and evil genies. Despite the paucity of details about her real life, Santa Barbara remains one of the most popular saints in Christendom. She is the patroness of armorers and gunsmith, of firearms and fortifications. And she is traditionally invoked against thunder and lightning.

Santa Barbara has long been a favorite of artists and she frequently appears in depictions of the enthroned Madonna. The most celebrated example is Raphael's Madonna di San Sisto wherein Barbara, in a violet robe with blue and yellow full sleeves, gazes in worship at Mary. For some unknown reason, the monks of Saint

Sixtus consented in 1754, to sell this superb depiction to Augustus III, King of Poland. That painting has since been known in Polish annals as "the glory of Dresden."

In the many other devotional portrayals of Santa Barbara, she carries the sword and palm which are associated with martyrdom. Guidebooks claim that the Church of all Saints in Rome has a reliquary containing Santa Barbara's severed head. And there is a church bearing her Patronage close to the Eternal City's Piazza Farnese.

While Santa Barbara is Spanish only in the translation of her name, she was exceedingly popular among the Hispanics who brought the Christian faith to Alta California in the years after 1769. Many churches in Mexico were named for her and she was the Patroness of the military.

Her name was bestowed upon the channel by Sebastian Vizcaíno in 1602 and upon the *presidio* established in 1782. Four years later, on her feastday, the tenth of the California missions was founded under her patronage. There is a statue of Santa Barbara in the *presidio* church, along with a large oil portrayal of the saint painted by the famed artist Jose de Alcibar in 1785.

The statue of Santa Barbara at the Old Mission was brought to the Channel City in 1791. Later a stone replica was carved by an Indian for placement in a niche in the gable of the church facade.

Though Santa Barbara's name no longer appears on the universal calendar, her influence remains indelibly imprinted on the fabric of California's religious heritage. All of which recalls Richard Cardinal Cushing's comment about the dropping of another saint from the sanctoral cycle: "Maybe she's no longer in heaven, but surely someone there is answering her mail."

MEMORIES OF MISSION SANTA BARBARA

Thousands of visitors tour Santa Barbara each year, each coming away with a lasting impression of the "Queen of the Missions." One such tourist, Irvin S. Cobb, subsequently recorded his memories in a book entitled *Roughing It De Luxe.*

There is something wonderfully impressive about the first trip to any of those old gray churches; everything about it is eloquent with memories of that older civilization which this Western Country knew long before the Celt and the Anglo–Saxon breeds came over the Divide and down the Pacific Slope, filled with their lust for gold and lands, craving ever more power and more territory over which to float the Stars and Stripes.

There is one Mission which in itself, it seemed to me, is almost worth a trip across the continent to see— the one at Santa Barbara. It is up the side of a gentle foothill, with the mountains of the Coast Range behind. Down below the roofs and spires of a brisk little city show through green clumpage, and still farther beyond, the blue waters of the Pacific may be seen.

Parts of this 'Mission are comparatively new; there are retouchings and restorations that date back only sixty or seventy years; but most of it speaks to you of an earlier century than this and an earlier race than the one that now peoples the land.

You pass through walls of solid masonry that are sixteen feet thick and pierced by narrow passages; you climb winding stairs to a squat tower where sundry cracked brazen bells swing by withes of ancient rawhide from great, worm–gnawed, hand–riven beams; you walk through the Mission burying–ground, past crumbly old family vaults with half–obliterated names and titles and dates upon their ovenlike fronts, and you wander at will among sunken individual graves under the palms and pepper trees.

Most convincing of all to me were the stone–flagged steps at the door of the church itself, for they are all worn down like the teeth of an old horse—in places they are almost worn in two. Better than any guidebook patter of facts and figures—better than the bells and the graves and the hand–made beams—these steps convey to the mind a sense of age.

You stand and look at them, and you see the tally of vanished generations—the heavy boot of the conquistador; the sandaled feet of an old *padre*, the high heel of a dainty Spanish–born lady; the bare, horny sole of the Indian convert—each of them taking its tiny toll out of stone and mortar—each of them wearing away its infinitesimal mite—until through years and years the firm stone was scored away and channeled out and left as it is now, with curves in it and deep hollows.

LA PURÍSIMA (1787)

"MOST DESOLATE RUIN OF ALL"—1882

A portrayal of how civilization first came to the West Coast is illustrated in a picturesque, quiet valley not far north of Santa Barbara, on the 960 acres comprising the grounds of California's eleventh missionary foundation. Described by Helen Hunt Jackson as "the most desolate ruin of all," *La Purísima Concepción de la Santísima Virgen Maria* has since become the "Williamsburg of the West," one of the most thoroughly and attractively rebuilt of the California missions.

The historic outpost was established in 1787, as part of a trinity of missions designed to Christianize the numerous Indians living in the coastal area beside the Santa Barbara Channel. Before long the *padres* and their Chumash neophytes had transformed the fertile fields into numerous walled gardens, groves of olive trees and broad vineyards.

Following the disastrous earthquake of 1812, the mission was moved from its initial location to the present site. It thrived in the more protected surroundings until the late 1830s, when secularization brought an end to the California missionary enterprise.

By the end of the century, all of the remaining ruins and most of the land had drifted into private ownership. Only the church itself and a few acres remained under ecclesial control. It was that site which confronted Helen Hunt Jackson when she visited the "desolate ruin" in 1882. Mrs. Jackson was understandably shaken that so great a symbol of California's heritage had fallen on such horrendous times.

Efforts to rebuild the famous Franciscan establishment were begun in the depression years by the Civilian Conservation Corps in what became the most massive restoration program every undertaken on a California mission. Some 110,000 handmade adobe bricks were used in rebuilding tile monastery roof tiles and 10,000 floor pieces were 32,000 alone. Other structures reconstructed in subsequent years under Federal or State auspices included shops and soldiers' quarters, infirmary and dormitory.

Extreme attention to detail marked every aspect of the restoration. The forging of hardware and the hand–carving of wooden furniture was as carefully executed to resemble that used by the early *padres* and their Indian charges.

Mexican longhorn cattle, similar to those kept in Baja California, were brought in to roam the fields, as were sheep and goats. Burros were trained to turn the wheels in the olive and grist mills. A few choice palomino and pinto horses, once the pride of the Californians, were also acquired.

Today, the Mission of La Purisima Concepción, described 1905 by *The Tidings* as "the only monument in America that stands evidence that the belief in the Immaculate Conception was long held before it was defined as a dogma by Pius IX," depicts life as it was under Spanish rule with more realism than any other of California's restored missions

A MEMOIR OF MISSION DAYS—1935

Señora Josefa Malo de Jansenns was born at La Purisima Concepción Mission on May 31, 1855. Her father, an emigrant from Ecuador, had come to California with Fray Jose Gonzalez Rubio, secretary to Bishop Francisco Garcia Diego. In the December 8, 1935 issue of the Los Angeles *Times Sunday Magazine*, she gave a first person glimpse of California as it had been eighty years earlier.

There were many claims and misunderstandings about the mission lands during the chaos of secularization and Pio Pico gave a patch of land known as Santa Rita to my father. This belonged to Purisima Mission. Father had many cattle grazing there as the mission herds by this time had disappeared.

The mission itself had been sold to Juan Temple and it was purchased from him by my father who took his family there to live. There I was born, the youngest of eight children.

Father Juan Comapla baptized me. He was from San Luis Obispo Mission. Purisima had no resident missionary from about 1836, but was attended from Santa Ines Mission. I also remember very well jolly Padre Juan Basso and Padre Joaquin Bot, who taught me Spanish.

On the eighth of December, the feast and founding date of the mission, there was a gala celebration at the mission. First, a Mass would be held in the morning and the musicians would get out the old mission violin, viola, drum and triangle and accompany the singers.

There were also two pipe organs with bellows which were turned with a crank, and these, too, were called into use on fiesta days. The singers were Margarita Rosa and Fernando Liberado. The latter is known to this day as "being the last of the Purisima Indians who was 111 years of age upon his death." His age was a little exaggerated, as he was perhaps little more than 80–odd, but it is said that he was paid to say that he was older.

When the mission property was sold, thirteen acres were reserved around the mission for ecclesiastical use. There was quite a garden in those days, and nasturtiums, marigolds and the malva real, a little tree with wide leaves and small blooms, grew in profusion.

In front of the mission, I also remember the long adobe house in which the Indians lived, as well as the

La Purisima Concepcion Mission

three *pilas* or reservoirs. There were all a different size, but only the middle one remains today, the others having been buried with the dust of years.

The pepper trees which still shade the mission ruins used to shelter the garden of which I spoke, in the days of our residence there. The mission orchard was noted for its fine pears, and the early settlers of the valley, for miles around, used to send to the orchard for this delicious fruit.

We also had rodeos at the mission when the Picos and Cotas, Carrillos, de la Guerras and Danas, Ybarras and Ruizes all came and we had much fun. I used to trap quail in the long tub with a covered, curved roof which resembled a vault. This also stood at some distance from the mission and was used in the early days by the *padres* for bathing purposes.

I remember the coming of Bishop Amat to the mission. He usually came just at evening time and the Indians would kneel in the corridor to kiss his ring. One day he came for confirmation and all the children of the surrounding *ranchos* for many miles were brought for the ceremony. It is pleasant to think over these things and to know that the beauty shall again be restored. l hope we may see (the restoration at work at La Purisima) all complete.

LA PURÌSIMA CONCEPCION

The most beautiful and symbolic of her many titles proclaims that Mary "in the first instant of her conception, by a singular privilege and grace granted by God, in view of the merits of Jesus Christ, the Savior of the human race, was preserved exempt from all stain of original sin." Though it was only officially defined in the decree *Ineffabilis Deus,* issued in 1854, the tradition of honoring Mary under that title dates at least to the eighth century when the devotion was already accepted in large segments of the Latin Church. The devotion has a long and honored history in the New World. On November 8, 1760, the Immaculate Conception was declared principal patroness of all the possessions of the Crown of Spain.

The old California mission located at Lompoc stands as an impressive monument to the widespread belief of Catholics in the Blessed Mother's Immaculate Conception. Sixty–seven years before the official declaration at Rome, the eleventh in the Golden State's rosary of missions was established under the patronage of *Purisima Concepcion de la Santísima Virgen Maria.* Inauguration of the mission actually took place on December 8, 1787, a holy day in the liturgical calendar, since 1708.

The foundation preceded by fifty–nine years the action of the nation's hierarchy at the Sixth Provincial Council of Baltimore, whereby Pope Pius IX was asked to ratify their choice of the Blessed Virgin, under her appellation of the Immaculate Conception, as the national patroness. The pontiff's subsequent approval bestowed "most willingly," gave the United States the distinction of being the first nation to have Mary, "conceived without sin," as its heavenly protectoress.

When Fray Fermín Francisco de Lasuén wrote the title page for the baptismal register of Purísima Concepcion, in 1787, he described the new foundation as the "Mission of the Most Pure Conception of the Most Holy Virgin Mary, Mother of God and Our Lady." In keeping with this devotion, the first Indian baptized, in *articulo mortis*, was named Francisco de la Concepción.

The almost verbatim use of Lasuén's phrase, "conceived without original sin at the first moment of her natural existence," by Pius IX in his infallible definition of the Immaculate Conception gives California reason for taking pride in the orthodoxy of its early missionaries. There is at least one entry, in August of 1825, where Fray Márcos Antonio de Vitoria allowed his enthusiasm to spell out the title in its fullest form: *En la Iglesia de esta Mision de la Purísima Inmaculada Concepción de Maria Santísima Nuestra Señora, Madre de Dios. . .*

Though devoted to the Immaculate Conception for over six centuries, the friars normally exercised great care in their terminology and this explains their preference for the term *"Purísima"* over that of *"Inmaculada,"* which was sanctioned only after the official proclamation. Devotion of the early *padres* to Our Lady, and in particular to her Immaculate Conception, is one more example of the rich heritage those pioneers imprinted on a previously uncharted land and people.

A MISSION GOES TO SEA—1943

In the midst of the perilous days of World War II on the evening of August 25, 1943, the oil tanker S.S. Mission Purísima was launched at Sausalito, California, "to do her part towards preserving forever the privilege to live in California, to live in America, under the sacred banner of the Stars and Stripes." The U.S. Maritime Commission's tanker was the first of a fleet "bearing the name of a patron saint given years ago to the shrines of this state, which have merited the reverent study of a thousand historians in books that shall be read . . . for a thousand years to come."

Fortuitously, the mission for which the twenty–fifth of the Marinship Corporation's vessels was named, had itself been re–dedicated, after decades of abandonment, on December 7, 1941, "a day of treachery, a day of grave menace to our national honor, to our national existence."

Selection of the eleventh in the chain of missionary foundations to be the initial one of the twenty–eight ships designated for a California mission or *asistencia* was indeed appropriate for "La Purísima, meaning 'Most Pure, is the name given to the Virgin Mother of God, the purest creature that ever existed."

In a benediction delivered at the launching of the S.S. Mission Purísima, Father Augustine Hobrecht sent the vessel on her way with the fervent prayer that she would help to preserve, for the world at large, that same Christian civilization which Fray Junípero Serra first planted on California shores so many years earlier.

As the noble ship, built to carry the life–blood and energy for the nation's floating fortresses of defense, slipped into the sea, the attentive onlooker could visualize a man of prophetic vision, clad in the humble robe of a Franciscan friar, standing near that very spot a century and a half earlier. Expressing his admiration for the broad ad and magnificent harbor, Fray Junípero Serra predicted the rise of a large and populous city and then, gazing out over the western horizon, the first *Presidente* of the California Missions noted that "we have come to the land's end, to the rim of the western world; to go further we must have ships!"

According to records of the Maritime Administration, all the mission tankers had uniform characteristics: 523'6" length; 68' beam; 29' 11" draft; 141 knots speed; 16,582 deadweight and 10,558 gross tons.

During the relatively short period of its active service, the S.S. Mission Purísima was operated under lease from the government by the Deconhil Shipping Company. In April Of 1946, the vessel was laid up in the National Defense Reserve Fleet at California's Suisun Bay. It was withdrawn and delivered to the Navy in October of 1947.

The ship was returned to the Reserve Fleet in May of I955, this time at the Olympia, Washington site, where it remained approximately one year. It was transferred back to the Maritime Administration, in late 1957, and laid up in the Suisun Bay Reserve Fleet where it remains today. At latest count, six of the Mission tankers still were anchored with the 1,000 ships scattered in this nation's half–dozen reserve fleets.

This first of the Mission tankers, like the institution whose name it bears, has become a relic of another age, symbolizing the accomplishments of a generation to whom contemporary society owes an unredeemable debt.

SHOWPLACE OF THE MISSIONS

Lompoc's handsome Mission La Purísima Concepcion is the " showplace" of *El Camino Real,* although it is one of the two California missions not under ecclesiastical jurisdiction.

In 1883 all the lands of the mission, with the exception of the ground occupied by the ruined church and cemetery were sold by Bishop Francis Mora to Eduardo de la Cuesta. The living quarters were used for some years as ranch headquarters and for shops and stores. After a fire which partially destroyed the building, sometime around 1900, it was abandoned. The Union Oil Company bought the ranch in 1903, and two years later deeded it to the Landmarks Club on the provision that the latter group would give $1,500 toward restoration. Since no money was available, the ruins reverted to the Oil Company.

When the Federal Government set up the Civil Conservation Corps in the early 1930's as part of the National Park Service the "deed of gift, titles to the church ruins and the monastery ruins were transferred to the county by the Catholic Church and the Union Oil Company, respectively, and the County of Santa Barbara and the State of California jointly purchased additional land, making a total of 507 acres." In its entirety, the area was then deeded to the State of California, Division of State Parks, and given the appropriate name of La Purísima Mission State Historical Monument. The State Park Commission then requested the National Park Service to establish a C.C.C. camp on the premises to undertake restoration in cooperation with the Division of State Parks.

When Bishop John J. Cantwell relinquished the Church's claim to the historic site, the prelate insisted that if any religious services ever be held at the mission, they be under Catholic auspices. Traditionally since that time, Holy Mass is offered at La Purísima in mid–May when the City of Lompoc hosts over a thousand people at the annual fiesta.

Today's tourists may be unaware that the restored mission near Lompoc is not the original foundation of 1787, nor is it even in the original location. The mission of Fray Fermin de Lasuén is three miles away, largely ignored and forgotten by all except a few enthusiasts. The earlier mission was established near the *Rio de Santa Rosa* in December of 1787. Little has been recorded of its first years but it is known that a new church was dedicated in 1802, and from all indications the establishment prospered for at least another decade. Near the end of 1812, "an extraordinary and horrible earthquake" entirely destroyed the church and over a hundred of the Indian dwellings. The inclement weather that followed prevented immediate repair. Viewing the extensive damage, the *padres* concluded that relocating the mission would be preferable to rebuilding. Their petition to this effect was sent to the *presidente* and governor on March 11, 1813.

Noting in their appeal–that what "God, like a Father, chastises and afflicts with one hand, and with the other He helps and supports," the missionaries suggested that "*Los Berros*" on the other side of the river would be a splendid site for the new foundation. The plan was approved and building operations were set in motion in the plain north of the Santa Rosa River. Salvageable materials were moved from the destroyed edifice, as were many of the actual building elements, such as tiles and doorsteads.

With the inauguration of the new mission, the already collapsed ruins of the original establishment fell into quick obscurity and today only one or two pillars indicate its existence. But, in the words of Zephyrin Engelhardt, the earlier ruins should be regarded "as a hallowed spot, worthy of much more veneration than the heap of adobe on the north side of the *Rio Santa Ines*."

SANTA CRUZ (1791)

PICTURESQUE SANTA CRUZ

Of all the twenty–one missionary outposts established along *El Camino Real,* none surpassed in beauty the natural setting of Santa Cruz. Climatically and topographically, it was the best located of all the missions in either Baja or Alta California. Fray Juan Crespi, the conscientious chronicler for the Portola Expedition, noted in October, 1769, that just across the San Lorenzo River and the Santa Cruz creek, not far from the sea, was an area abounding in good pasture, a variety of herbs and rose bushes in great plenitude.

Fray Francisco Palou spoke even more enthusiastically about the location, noting that the banks of the river "were covered with sycamore, cottonwood and willow trees." He also mentioned the nearby palo *Colorado* (redwood) forest. Palou reckoned that the place was "fit not only for a town, but for a city, without wanting any of the necessary things." He went on to enumerate the "good land, water, pasture, wood and timber just within reach and in great abundance," all of which would provide an ideal resource for a permanent foundation.

The actual spot chosen by the friars for Santa Cruz Mission was a level spot, exposed to the unobstructed rays of the sun, only a short distance from the flowering canyons, rushing river and wooded slopes. The friars would have been hard put to find a more delightful place. Fray Fermin Francisco de Lasuén was delighted with the location and reported that he found the site quite as excellent as all the descriptions he had heard.

One historian imagined that he could see the friars "standing on the hill, looking down upon the San Lorenzo River, lined with a great variety of deciduous trees, flowing through the small, lovely valley towards the west, or gazing towards the deep blue Bay of Monterey, on the opposite side of which the San Carlos Mission and *presidio* were situated and admiring the glorious sunsets over the Pacific Ocean."

Things really haven't changed much in that area even today. It is still much untouched by the desecrating hand of civilization. Soft purple shades cover the mountains and gentle fogs gather over the bay–chased away only by a brilliant sun which leaves the waters blue and sparkling.

Besides the scenic beauty and salubrious climate, the friars found abundant forests close at hand, containing redwoods that were readily split and sawed for use in their buildings. And the nearby hills contained lime rock and easily–worked chalk rock. It wasn't necessary to bring in construction materials from long distances.

Those fortunate enough to have lived and worked at Santa Cruz Mission were greeted with the beauty and aroma of flowering shrubs, of mountain lilac and wild azalea, of manzanita and madrone, covered with white flowers in spring and red berries in winter. Also growing profusely in the area were Toyon berries, the real Christmas berries of California.

As was the case with all the missions, the history of the founding, maintenance and abandonment of Santa Cruz Mission followed the natural law of bloom, growth and decay. It was once again a story of high hopes and endeavors, of bold undertakings and accomplishments and unselfish devotion. But nowhere did that pageant unfold in more natural beauty.

QUAKE DESTROYS SANTA CRUZ—1857

The day of January 1, 1857 began badly and grew worse as the hours passed. There were several moderate earthquakes soon after midnight that disturbed the sleep of those living at and around Santa Cruz. At dawn another tremor–probably 5 or 6 on the Richter Scale of magnitude, although there were no such instruments then to measure such events, sharply jolted the area and awakened everyone.

It was followed by another strong earthquake, with about the same magnitude, at sunrise. But the worst was yet to come. At 8:24 that morning, subsurface layers near what is today Parkfield suddenly collapsed under the enormous stresses to which they had long been subjected.

The land on opposite sides of the fractured rock zone lunged forward, the western side toward San Francisco, the eastern toward the Mexican border. The surface ruptured and, like a rip propagating in a sheet of canvas moved high speed toward the southwest. This great tear in the earth's crust did not stop until somewhere around San Bernardino, more than 225 miles away. It was one of the largest earthquakes ever to have happened in California.

Scientists estimate its magnitude on a par with the 1906 quake that devastated San Francisco. The damage to buildings in the area was extensive, especially adobe structures. The tremor crumbled the front wall of the mission building proper, which had already passed through the earthquake in 1840, when the tower at one front corner had fallen. A few days later a rather severe "after–shock" further weakened the remaining structures at Santa Cruz.

Thirty eight days after the first shock, the southwest corner of the old edifice fell at three o'clock in the morning with a crash that awakened people for many miles around. Father Benito Capdevilla, the priest in charge, immediately launched plans for rebuilding and on July 5th of that year, Bishop Thaddeus Amat laid the cornerstone of the new church.

(In 1931, a smaller replica of the mission church and rooms for the *padres* dwelling were erected on ground adjoining the former compound. That is the structure now seen by visitors to the area).

What makes the 1857 earthquake of interest is the fact that it was the last large earthquake to have occurred on the southern segment of the San Andreas Fault. Since that day so many years ago, there has been no movement on this segment of the San Andreas. And yet stress has been accumulating all along several hundred miles of the fault.

Sooner or later, all of the stress that is now stored in the southern segment of the San Andreas will be released. Scientists feel that the 1857 quake could recur anywhere from fifty to 350 years. Generally there is a time span of 160 years between successive spasms. But that 160 year average is only a statistical figure and actually, another tremor approximating that of 1857 could happen anytime.

NUESTRA SEÑORA DE LA SOLEDAD (1791)

NUESTRA SEÑORA DE LA SOLEDAD—1904

The thirteenth of the California missions, dedicated to *Maria Santísima Nuestra Señora de la Soledad*, was established by Fray Fermín Francisco de Lasuén, in the fall of 1791. Situated on the plain at the base of somber foothills enclosing the Salinas Valley, the missionary outpost flourished until its abandonment in 1862. George Wharton James visited La Soledad, in 1904, and left his impressions for readers of subsequent generations.

The ruins of Soledad are about four miles from the station of the Southern Pacific of that name. The church itself is at the southwest corner of a mass of ruins. These are all of adobe, though the foundations are of rough rock. Flint pebbles have been mixed with the adobe of the church walls. They were originally about three feet thick and plastered. A little of the plaster remains.

In 1904 there was but one circular arch remaining on all the ruins; everything else has fallen in. The roof fell in thirty years ago. At the eastern end, where the arch is, there are three or four rotten beams still in place; and on the south side of the ruins, where one line of corridors ran, a few poles are still in place. Heaps of ruined tiles lie here and there, just as they fell when the supporting poles rotted and gave way.

Over the entrance of the church–the ruins of which now bring sadness to the hearts of all who care–is a niche in which a statue of Our Lady of Solitude–La Soledad–used to stand.

Methinks that if the ghosts of things that were exist, surely a weeping ghost of the Lady of Solitude haunts these deserted and forlorn ruins. Weep! weep on! for the church of Our Lady of Solitude. It is entirely in ruins. The adobe walls are rapidly melting away. For years it has stood exposed to the weather, nothing whatever being done to preserve it.

It is roofless and unprotected. The winds howl around it , the rains beat upon it, the fierce sun shines upon it, and all do their part to aid in its more speedy dissolution.

It is not demolition; that could better be borne than this heartless abandonment, this careless indifference, this hateful casting aside of a once noble building, dedicated to high, blessed purposes, sanctified by the earnest labors of devoted men.

It seems as if the building itself felt its desertion, though smiling fields of wheat and barley surround it. Nay, these evidences of material prosperity so close at hand only serve to accentuate the devastation of the old Mission.

The foundation named for Our Lady of Solitude was indeed, as stated by Alfred Robinson, "the gloomiest, bleakest, and most abject–looking spot in all California."

SAN JOSE (1797)

A LOST TRIBE OF MISSION SAN JOSE

The Ohlone Indians were a gentle race, according to the records of the mission founders. They were industrious and anxious to learn, somewhat skin to the Aztecs whose wits were always as sharp as their tomahawks. They embraced Christianity readily, and the entire Indian colony eventually became neophytes at Mission San Jose. "They attended the services and the Masses, the *padres'* schools, and worked with the priests on the roads, the gardens and the farms. They learned industry from the white man, and applied it in a way that to this day is one of the wonders of California–the remarkable old gardens that have been famed and filmed all over the world."

An article in the Oakland *Tribune, in* November, 1916, stated that "the Ohlones and the priests labored shoulder to shoulder to implant civilization on a new land, and carry the word of the white man afar into strange places." They paved the path of the *padres* in Alameda county, lightening the work of the friars who came to be their friends and guides. The San Francisco *Monitor* testified that "they assisted in the building of the church, the planting of the Mission gardens (which later became Palmdale, the famous estate of the late Henry Lachman), and built the road to Alvarado, then the landing place of the boats that the *padres* used to carry their supplies from other parts of the new land they were struggling to civilize."

Little is known of the Ohlones in modern times. One by one they were called to the God they had learned to worship. Today there are few descendants of the friars' pupils and helpers to sustain their traditions. One of the few associations with the tribe is the cemetery at Mission San Jose, with its unmarked graves for several thousand neophytes. Initially blessed by Fray Magín Catalá, on July 8, 1809, the historic burial grounds were gradually forgotten and overgrown with weeds. Sometimes an old settler would speak of the "road that runs by the old Indian burying ground" and, if one was curious, would add that "a lot of Indians were buried there a long time ago." Over the years, the "rain, the wind, and the plow" had leveled the consecrated mounds that once hallowed over the resting places of the humble Indian pioneers. The cemetery, unmarked and unknown, ultimately passed into the hands of a farmer who was about to turn it into grazing land, when Mrs. C. L. Stephens, a prominent Alameda county resident, became interested in its history and decided to stop what she called this "impending sacrilege."

She obtained the aid of George Donovan and was able to prove that the farmer had no legitimate claim to the land. Inasmuch as the descendants of the original tribe were all dead themselves, Mrs. Stephens succeeded in having the cemetery turned over to the care of the Archbishop of San Francisco. The re–dedication services were a wonderful spectacle. One account stated that "priests from the mission, attired in the ancient robes of the *padres*, including one that had been worn by Fray Serra, said the rites over the consecrated ground, and a magnificent monument, donated by Mrs. Stephens, and commemorating the tribesmen," was formally erected and blessed. The restoration of the burial grounds was, in a measure, the payment of a debt modern California owed this little–known tribe of Indians, but only one woman realized the indebtedness and she alone paid for it.

HOSTELRY AT SAN JOSE MISSION—1840s

For almost eight decades, the Franciscan missions were the only places in California where the public could find accommodations comparable to wayside inns. Hence it comes as no surprise that when the need for such places arose, the old missions were occasionally turned into hostelries. What happened at San Jose Mission is a typical story of these makeshift hostelries, and the same fate overtook several other of the once–flourishing missionary establishments.

Founded in 1797, about fifteen miles north of the *pueblo* bearing the same name, San Jose was for two generations one of the most important agricultural missions in California. For almost forty years, it continued to grow and prosper.

By 1846, however, the decade after secularization, San Jose was little more than a silent memory of what it had been in the past. With the departure of the *padres*, San Jose's neophytes gradually drifted away. Its cattle were sold or stolen, its land lay abandoned and its irrigation system began disintegrating.

With the exception of the church and the two story adobe dwelling, the mission buildings were a menacing ruin. Where, a few years earlier, the traveler had met with a kindly welcome, all that could be found was a makeshift meal and a corner on the filthy and flea–infested floor. Such was the picture in September of 1846.

Later that year, Walter Colton and Robert Semple wrote an editorial urging newly arrived American immigrants to move into the San Jose Mission's buildings, settle on its lands and otherwise make themselves at home.

The "recent arrivals" mentioned in the advertisement

took the exhortation literally and proceeded to follow the recommendations of Colton and Semple. They proceeded to make free with the mission property. By the spring of 1847, George Harlan, his family and numerous other immigrants were camped out in the allegedly ownerless and abandoned San Jose Mission. One observer of those days noted that he "strolled out into the courtyard to see how my horse had been provided for, when I was agreeably surprised at finding assembled there a group of fresh– looking Yankee girls, chatting and jesting together. They must have come across the mountains."

A trading store was set up in one of the mission buildings where goods were sold at a profit of at least eight hundred percent. Gambling and other shady activities took whatever loose change customers happened to have left after making their purchases. Guests were at liberty to seek repose on a pile of straw in what had once been the *padres'* stable. It must be recorded that the straw was not second hand, and was therefore reasonably clean.

The fact that some of the other missions escaped this fate is due to two all–important considerations. The first had to do with the mission's location with respect to the principal roads. About a dozen of the missions were located on these early arterial highways. The second factor was that of proprietorship. By the time that the American immigrants began to settle in California, all but the missions of San Francisco de Asis and Santa Clara had been sold or rented to private individuals and were being held by their new owners.

San Jose was among those missions not so fortunate.

LUTHER BELL RECALLS SAN JOSÉ MISSION— 1906

Located in the Alameda foothills, San José Mission has been aptly called the "cradle of Northern California." Built in the summer of 1797, when the great Pacific was an unfathomed mystery, it has survived the ravages of time in name only.

Luther Bell visited the site in 1906. There he found a little town nestled among the foothills and sheltered from the winds by the mighty Mission peak. His reflections of the once–proud institution appeared in *The Monitor* for June 30th:

It was noon when I reached the inn. The cool of the rambling old adobe was grateful after the dust of the highway. Then I wandered out in the shade of the fig trees, past the little gate that led to the mission gardens.

Beneath an aged fig, pensively contemplating the valley that lay below us, bathed in the quiet sunlight, I found the genial *padre*. Yes, he was only too happy to show the visitor what remained of the past. And so we two visited the Mission of San Jose.

We walked up the highway bordered with flaming poppies and bright roses. We halted on the stone steps that had been worn smooth by the feet of many penitents and then from the tower of the little chapel came forth the chimes. We listened.

The notes that fell from the three bronzes above us, he said, were like those that called the people of the settlement to worship century ago. With reverent words, he showed the eight oil paintings of the saints that were all but hidden in the gloom of the broken sunlight. The old baptismal font of beaten copper, the waters of which have blest the heads of many, had been used that self–same day.

The *padre* stopped for a moment to offer a silent prayer and then led me past the kneeling worshippers to the vestry, where the old and faded raiments of the stout–hearted friars were stored. He brought out from its cabinet the time–stained silver and then, without a word, we walked again into the gardens and down to the old warehouse.

Past swathes of sweet–scented hay and piles of grain, we went to where the casks of rare old wines kept company with the dust and cobwebs of bygone years. The vintage will soon be sold, it is said, and the proceeds given to the mission's restoration.

But it was in the graveyard adjoining that my friend loved to wander. We walked the narrow way surrounded by the bramble–grown graves of the *padres* and their Indian converts. Time in its flight had overthrown many of the stones, but the mounds bore roses whose perfume told only of the fragrant summer and not of the musty past and the mound from which they draw their life.

We stopped at length in the prolific gardens filled with fruits. There on a seat beneath an olive tree, just a hundred and ten years old, the Father told me of the mission life.

While admitting that the account given by the priest sounded dull and unentertaining when translated into English, Mr. Bell proceeded to recall the historical background of San Jose Mission. He noted that the mission was "built in the form of a quadrangle. In the year 1825, it was at its zenith and over 75,000 herd of stock grazed in the miles of pasture. Thirty–three hundred Indians were fed and sheltered within its walls at that time and the choir at each service consisted of thirty musicians."

But like its sister–foundations, San Jose Mission "and its romance have passed into history." Visitors to the site are shown only a crumbling, low structure, a chest of gorgeous vestments faded with age and a few other remnants that give mute testimony to this one–time Christian bastion in Northern California.

SAN JUAN BAUTISTA (1797)

THE BARRELLED ORGAN AT SAN JUAN BAUTISTA—1793

Just prior to his departure from San Diego, in December, 1793 the famous English sea captain, George Vancouver, generously presented to Fermin Francisco de Lasuen the resident missionary, a "handsome barreled organ which, notwithstanding the vicissitudes of climate, was still in complete order and repair." Constructed at London, in 1735, the fascinating "music box" was initially intended, according to Father Zephyrin Engelhardt, "to entertain rude British sailors" who, he said, "the world over were not known for piety in word or music."

Portable as it was, the organ was apparently moved about between the missions rather extensively. In 1829, Fray Felipe Arroyo de la Cuesta reported that his Mission of San Juan Bautista had received an *"organo de 3 cilindros,"* very probably the Vancouver organ. The imposing instrument, still at San Juan Bautista, is over five feet in height, two feet in width and a foot and a half in depth. The wooden case is fashioned in Gothic design. Each of the two front panels bear five ornamental wooden pipes.

All of the seventeen wooden and twenty–nine metal pipes located inside engage when the crank is turned. There are ten tunes on each of the three cylinders. Engelhardt reported that "the unholy titles of its music clearly indicated that it was not intended for church services." Among the titles, enumerated on the side of the case are Go to the Devil, Spanish Waltz, College Hornpipe and Lady Campbell's Reel.

The term "barrel" organ derives from the wooden cylinder with its series of brass staples, which is mounted horizontally. As the crank turns the cylinder, the staples activate a mechanism which opens the pallets, allowing wind from the bellows to enter the pipes. The instrument resembles the hand organ popularized in later times by street merchants. Very likely, the organ was utilized primarily for entertainment purposes. Concerning this type of instrument, George Wharton James wrote: "with what feelings one of the sainted *padres,* after a peculiarly trying day with his aboriginal children, would put in this barrel, and while his lips said holy things, his hand instinctively grinded out with vigor the first piece on the list."

There is a charming legend about Fray Felipe Arroyo de la Cuesta and his barreled organ. We are told that "the first language of this *padre* was a little music box which he would load on the back of a sturdy mule, and carry to some far–away Indian settlement; there he would set it up in some prominent place and rapidly turn the crank. When the Indians first heard the strange noises they fell on their faces with fear, but as the music continued, their fear left them and they began to enjoy the sweet sounds, ending by slowly approaching and gathering about the *padre,* listening to the wonderful songs with delight. Then Padre Arroyo, just at the right moment, always turning the crank, would reload the mule and, like the Pied Piper of Hamlin, wend his way back to the mission, all the Indians following after.

On another occasion, the Vancouver organ was credited with saving San Juan Bautista Mission from a group of un–Christianized Tulare Indians:

> Fray de la Cuesta hastily dragged out the organ, and began furiously grinding away at the crank. The blare of music first puzzled, and than delighted the raiders, who then peacefully came in to the mission which they had intended to destroy.

Barrelled Organ at San Juan Bautista

VISITOR AT SAN JUAN BAUTISTA—1844

William Maxwell Wood (1809–1850) visited California late in 1844, as surgeon aboard the United States man–of–war *Savannah*. Upon returning to Philadelphia five years later, Wood published his carefully recorded observations as *Wandering Sketches of People and Things in South America, Polynesia, California and Other Places.*

Most of his remarks concern the manners and customs of the people whom he met enroute, especially those whose hospitality he had enjoyed. Nowhere is the "pleasing style" of the 386–page treatise more obvious than in the author's account of his visit to Mission San Juan Bautista, where he was received "with great urbanity and cordiality."

Wood described how, "before the revolution, the chief, indeed the only seats of civilization in California were the Catholic Missions. These, with their various buildings, formed small villages, and controlled and directed the Indians within their influence. The ecclesiastics of the missions, with the semi–converted Indians for laborers, were the only cultivators of the soil; and beneath their care, and in their vicinity, orchards and gardens beautified the wilderness; and their doors were always opened to the accommodation of any wayfarer in this lonely land."

Every attempt was made to accommodate the needs of the distinguished visitor who seems to have been impressed with the "great mirth and good humor of the *padres.*" Wood's description of the liturgical activities at the mission are especially interesting.

> The harp, and guitar, which had played so important a part in the dances, were now played in a gallery at one end of the church, as a sacred choir. The padre was arrayed in handsome pontifical robes, the handkerchief [cowl] had been removed from his head, and a circlet of long gray hair fell down upon his shoulders. His fine person, face, and costume, associated with his present functions, were fitted to inspire veneration and it was difficult to realize that this was the same person with whom we had associated in the hilarity of the dinner table.
>
> As he passed down the body of the church, sprinkling holy water on either hand, he, in a kind and paternal manner, directed a special supply upon us, as though he considered it a courtesy to his heretical guests.

Though a Puritan, Wood took every precaution against inserting his personal feelings into his recorded observations, stating that "in this narrative of our– stay at the mission of San Juan, my object has been to paint the manner and customs of the time and place. If anything appears in the habits of our clerical host, inconsistent with our own notions of propriety, it should be measured by the different circumstances of education. In the performance of what he had been taught to be his clerical duties, Fray [José Antonio] Anzar was scrupulously rigid."

The author even made allowances for what he regarded as "violations" of the Lord's Day. He noted that "it was part of his [Anzar's] religion to consider the Sabbath as a day of festival. But a little while ago it was the custom for Protestant clergymen to mingle in the dance, and, in some parts of Europe is so still. The more rigid ideas of communities of the United States, and the progress of temperance reformation are things of modern times and it is scarcely just to apply our principles of judgment to a secluded *padre* in California, fifty years behind the age in more cultivated communities."

These and other utterances of William Maxwell Wood categorize that early visitor to California as a man of considerable "tolerance" in an era not generally known for such broad–minded gestures.

A "SANCTIFIED SHRINE" IS VISITED—1884

In late July, 1884, an anonymous young man set out to visit "the scenes of his boyhood, a place in the mountains thirty miles below Monterey, at the headwaters of the Carmel River." He later wrote an account of that journey which is here reproduced from the San Jose *Herald.*

> We traveled in a one horse vehicle, and the first day of our journey took us to the quaint old town of San Juan. After our horse had been cared for, and our supper served, we walked out to the old Catholic Mission and wondered at its ancient tumbledown adobe walls, and from its peculiar surroundings became anxious to know something of its history.
>
> At the entrance way was a large gate, which was locked, and on it hung a notice saying in substance that anyone desiring to visit the Mission could do so for the consideration of one dollar, which would be used in repairing the church which is at present sadly in need of funds.
>
> We then knocked at the door of the Father's study, and upon his answering the bell, made him acquainted with the object of our He is a gentlemanly, modest, unassuming, mild–mannered man, and without inquiring we saw upon the door, "Rev. V(alentine) Closa."
>
> He took us to the entrance and unlocked the swinging gates; and we all three, with uncovered heads, walked into the ancient cathedral that has stood there for nearly one hundred years. There was something supernatural about this place of worship; everything was as still as death, nothing being heard but our footfall on the bare thick floor.
>
> We stood struck with awe for a moment in this tomb–like place as we gazed at the further end of the

building at the snow white altars, and the ancient statuary, made grim and death–like by the dimly lighted wax candle, which cast sepulchral shadows on the wall, while a noiseless bat flew with sudden fright behind the blood stained image of Christ at the sound of our voices.

On either side of the walls hung numerous beautiful oil paintings, the Father saying that they were painted many years ago, in Mexico. At the entrance way was the baptismal font, which was a relic most surprising to look at. It is made of a large stone, chiseled out after the fashion of the mortar trowels made by the ancient aborigines.

At this font, seven thousand people were baptized. As we passed on we approached the 'gospel side ' and standing there for a moment, the Father reverently pointed to a slab near the altar, saying that directly under it Father Estevan Tapis was buried 70 years ago, he being the founder of the Mission.

Going to a drawer nearby he took from it some clothing, which he said he had just lately taken from the dead Father's dress. It was made of heavy woolen goods, and although it had been in the tomb for 70 years, seemed as strong as ever.

The Father also said that the hair and beard of the priest looked as natural as ever and the bones though well preserved were disjointed with the exception of the skull.

Out of this drawer the Father took some ancient vestments which must excite the admiration of all who have ever seen them. It is thought to have been made in Mexico many years ago, but still retains its lustre as though it were made yesterday.

The Father then showed us some music books written and made by Father Tapis; the books were made of sheepskin and covered with rawhide clasped with iron clasps. The music was written by hand and so arranged by dots and colors that each voice in the choir was enabled to carry the tune in his respective tones.

By this time it had almost grown dark and the Father led us from the old church to the graveyard. It is situated on the eastern side of the Mission and overlooks the San Jose Valley.

The two visitors offered to pay the priest, but he declined. He did say, however, that if they had "any Catholic friends who would like to aid the old Mission tell them I am working hard to make some needed repairs and anything they may offer will be most thankfully received."

SAN JUAN BAUTISTA MISSION—1902

One of the most interesting commentaries on the California missions was that written by Redfern Mason, in mid–1920, for a southland newspaper. The following excerpts pertain to San Juan Bautista:

Recently it was my self–imposed task to make a pilgrimage to the Mission of San Juan Bautista and through that monument of the historic past to catch glimpses of the aborigines as they lived when they were under the guardianship of the Franciscan *padres*.

It was an object lesson in Christian providence. The Franciscans came from Spain, worked among the Indians of Mexico and then made their way north to California. They were fired with the purpose of spreading the gospel of their Master. That was their sole motive. Under the paternal discipline of the *padres*, the Redskins achieved a measure of civilization unequaled by any other indigenous people in America.

San Juan Bautista is an eloquent witness to the old times when the Indian could look upon the face of nature with joy in his heart. Its dilapidation is a token of the miserable part which the American successors of the *padres* have played in the melancholy drama.

The tiles of the old mission gleam like copper in the sunlight. We strolled through the long ambulatory, with its solid arches built of bricks that were made by the Indians. The wooden tower, in the debased taste that mars most restorations, is the only jarring note.

The *padres* were not only spiritual leaders of their flock. They cared for their bodily needs as well. Here is a wool–comber and here a branding iron. When Dana visited the coast in the years immediately preceding the discovery of gold in California, he found the mission *padres* great herders of cattle and intelligent men of affairs.

But do not imagine that they made fortunes for themselves. The reverse is the case. The missionaries and the Indians shared alike in all that was produced. When the missionaries came to San Juan it was a wilderness. But gradually they taught the Indians the art of making bricks, the fashioning of stone and the shaping of timbers. And finding that the aborigines had a simple art of their own, they encouraged them to use it to the glory of God. The walls about the chancel still bear the marks of the ruddy floral ornamentations in which the Redskins delighted. Those of the present day mission priests who love and understand the Indians cherish these relics.

Once a year Mass is said in the ruined mission, usually at Pentecost, and that is the time when old people long for a return to the decorous order of long ago. Will it ever come? Will the Mission San Juan Bautista be restored to its primitive glory? Will the cowled Franciscans return ?

It was by sheer mischance that "Ramona" was not written in San Juan. Brother Regan, who runs the stage and is the depository of all the lore of the countryside, told me about it. Helen Hunt Jackson came here to write her novel. She wanted to live in the Governor's house, which adjoins the hotel, but the caretaker thought the authoress had slighted her in some way and would not let her have it.

I question whether any mission is more interesting than San Juan. So many things in it speak of the past, that we seemed nearer to those old Californias than we do in most of the missions. The ruin is great, it is true; but it is local and the main walls of the fabric are still stout.

SAN MIGUEL (1797)

MURDER AT SAN MIGUEL–1848

What has been described as "the most atrocious murder ever committed in California" occurred at San Miguel Mission in 1848. The details of the event were recalled ninety–three years later in the columns of the Santa Maria *Free Advertiser.*

In December of 1848, a party of former sailors, deserters from a ship lying at Monterey, stopped at San Miguel where they were entertained by William Reed and his family. (Reed and Petronillo Rios had illegally purchased the mission from Governor Pio Pico).

Unhappily, in the course of conversation with the strangers, Reed made known that he had in his possession a large sum of gold, obtained from the sale of a flock of sheep.

The villains left San Miguel, ostensibly for the purpose of continuing their journey southward. They went no further than Santa Margarita, however. After dark, they returned and murdered all the unsuspecting occupants of the ex–mission. One of the killers grabbed a child and struck its head against a pillar, leaving a blood–stained wall which for years reminded visitors of the horrible incident.

Dragging the corpses of the dead into one room, they made a heap of them, and then fled with the gold and whatever other valuables they could find in the living quarters. The victims were Mr. Reed, his infant son, his wife Maria Antonia, her unborn child, her brother Jose Ramon, a midwife Josefa Olivera and five other members of the family.

The five murderers were pursued by a force of men from Santa Barbara and overtaken on the coast near the Ortega ranch. One of the killers was shot and killed and another jumped to his death from a cliff. The other three were captured and taken to Santa Barbara. Governor R.B. Mason was notified and asked for instructions. Mason wrote that "great credit is due to . .. the citizens of Santa Barbara for promptness and energy and perseverance in pursuing and apprehending that band of outlaws who have been committing such horrid acts of barbarity through the country."

In a subsequent report, the governor noted that he had instructed a local official "that if the evidence were clear and positive, and the sentence of the jury were death, he might cause it to be executed without referring the case to me." He explained that such a course of action "is absolutely necessary, as there are no jails or prisons in the country where a criminal can be safely secured."

No further details are available, but the villains were accordingly put to death for their crimes at Santa Barbara on December 28, 1848. When relating the event in 1931, "Rocky" Dana said that the murder of the Reed family at San Miguel was one of the worst tragedies this section of the country ever experienced. "Although only eleven years old at the time, the constant fear of the murderers made such an indelible impression on my mind that I never forgot the incident."

He recalled that several of his relatives happened to stop at San Miguel some years after the murders. They told him that the blood– stained pillar was still plainly visible, a memorial to the sad events of 1848.

MISSION SAN MIGUEL—1889

Early in 1889, after visiting the sixteenth of the California missions, Charles F. Wilcox permanized his observations in an article for *Ave Maria* entitled: "A Halt at the Mission of San Miguel." The essay, reproduced in condensed form, is one of the few memoirs of that historic missionary foundation.

On a bright Sunday morning in early February, returning from the Hot Springs of El Paso de Robles, we approached the old California mission of San Miguel Archangel. Driving over the crest of a slight eminence, we saw the long lofty white structure of the church, surmounted by its red tile roof, a distant bed of bright color in the green landscape of river bottom and rolling hills.

The great new bell, disdaining the society of its ancient fellows hanging near, rings for ten o'clock Mass, so we hastened to enter the side door of the old Church; and, kneeling among a few modern pews, upon the old flat brick floor, and joining a small congregation of farmers and *rancheros*, we assisted at the Holy Sacrifice. The Spanish pastor, Father Mut, was the celebrant, and preached, in a quaint but pleasant manner, a practical sermon on the gospel of the day. The English tongue, spoken by a Spaniard takes on a certain dignity and softness, decidedly foreign but delightful to the ear.

San Miguel ... was always, I believe, rather a poor mission; certainly what little grandeur there ever was has long since departed. The entire structure was of adobe and tiles. The exterior walls ... have mostly crumbled away; in some parts their line cannot now be traced.

The Church itself is in good repair. The American congregation having been too poor to attempt any work of restoration, we have everything, inside and out, much as the Franciscans had created it when Mexico secularized all the California missions. Over the main altar is a statue of the patron, the glorious Archangel Michael, holding in the left hand a sword and in the right the scales.

On the side altar stands an ancient painted wooden

image of St. Joseph carrying in his arms the Infant Son. The frescoing of the thick and lofty side walls and beamed ceiling is in distemper, executed in soft tints, rose–color, blue, grey, and a pale green predominating; the drawing is skillful, and the adaptation of colors very harmonious.

Moldings, carvings, screens, pillars, and all sorts of projecting or lamentation being impossible from the materials at hand, the flat wall surfaces are relieved by a drawing of a lofty Corinthian colonnade, supporting an elaborate balustrade, with painted awnings stretched from fluted pillar to pillar. The main altar–piece, filling up the end wall behind the altar on either side of the large statue, contains emblems of the Crucifixion, two small statues of Franciscan saints, and other religious works; it is surmounted in the center by an eye looking from a radiant cloud, and at each upper corner by a large Easter verse with roses.

The buildings originally occupied by the Fathers are in good preservation; and the long arcade in front, with its heavy square columns, low circular arches brick floor and tiled roof, is all intact. Here lives the resident priest, cheerfully giving his life to the obscure and arduous care of this post and three or four outlying chapels of his parish. In his announcements, before the gospel, he stated that on one Sunday before Easter he should be absent at Los Angeles, the episcopal seat. The draft of invigoration to be taken then must refresh him for a long, dry and arduous season to follow.

Many other original structures of the Mission are still standing. Long, narrow buildings now roofless and without partitions, others again divided into many rooms, surround the inner court–a space of more than an acre; everywhere appear a multitude of arched door-ways, pillars built of thin, flat bricks, once supporting veranda roofs, and great hewn beams, and piles of fallen walls. We come into the inner court through the main entrance way, just wide enough for the passage of a cart; the ground underfoot is worn concave by the multitude of footsteps that have trod it. An irrigating ditch once brought water, taken out of the river at a point some ten miles higher up its course; and in a fertile valley not far distant flourished a generous orchard.

After an inspection all too brief, we returned, through the sunny, exhilarating atmosphere, to the modern comforts of Paso Robles Hotel.

SAN FERNANDO, REY DE ESPAÑA (1797)

ROOTS OF SAN FERNANDO—1769

The Los Encinos State Historical Monument commemorates the location of the first encounter that European explorers had with the San Fernando Valley area. Fray Juan Crespi records that on August 5, 1769, Gaspár de Portola and his sixty–three companions traveled over the Santa Monica mountains through Sepulveda canyon and entered the vicinity of Ventura and Balboa boulevards.

"We saw a very pleasant and spacious valley. We descended to it and stopped close to the watering place, which is a very large pool. Near it we found a large village of heathen, very friendly and docile. They offered us their seeds in baskets and other things made of rushes ... we gave to this plain the name of Valley of *Santa Catalina de Bononia de los Encinos.*"

The following day was Sunday and Fray Juan Crespi offered Holy Mass and blessed the ground. After the Liturgy was completed, the friar acknowledged "receiving innumerable visits from heathen who came to see us from different parts."

Encino was considered among the possible sites for San Fernando Mission. When Fray Fermín Francisco de Lasuen visited the site, in 1797, he felt the water supply was inadequate for the envisioned agricultural needs. With the selection of a site some miles north for the mission, Francisco Reyes, the *alcalde* for *El Pueblo de Nuestra Señora de los Angeles,* moved to Encino and assumed title of the adjoining acreage.

Following the tenure of Reyes, three Indians were associated with the grant–remembered only as Ramon, Francisco and Rogue. The *rancho* was then known as *Encino Providencia.* In 1845, they sold out to Vicente de la Ossa.

Four years later, de la Ossa erected an adobe *hacienda,* probably the first such building in the southwestern part of the San Fernando Valley. Vicente, his wife Rita and their fourteen children lived there for several years. The adobe has nine rooms, one of which was set aside for use as a chapel. Visiting friars frequently offered Holy Mass there.

The title to the 4,410 acre ranch was confirmed in mid 1862 and, shortly thereafter Rita conveyed ownership to James Thompson, her son–in–law. In 1872, Thompson sold the *rancho* to Eugene Garnier, a prominent local Frenchman, and he it was who built the two story limestone house that stands near the adobe. He also walled up the spring and lake areas.

Garnier also improved the adobe by installing wooden floors, tongue and groove wainscoting and kerosene lamps. He further built an Inn across the roadway in a cove. Inasmuch as the *rancho* was a popular stopping place for travelers, Garnier also made an arrangement whereby the Inn became a regular stop on the Butterfield Stage Line.

In subsequent years, the *rancho* passed into the hands of Gaston Oxacart, Simon Gless and Domingo Amestoy. With Amestoy's death, in 1900, an Estate Company was set up. The properties remained in the Amestoy family for almost fifty years. About 1916, Encino became fashionable for residential and business development.

The Native Daughters of the Golden West designated the original adobe an Historical Monument in 1937. The Encino Historical Committee was established, in 1945, and four years later, the five acre Los Encinos State Historical Monument was formally acquired by the State of California.

As part of the Catholic observance for the nation's bicentennial, Timothy Cardinal Manning offered the Eucharistic Liturgy at Los Encinos State Historical Monument on July 15, 1976, and later prayed in the room used so many years earlier as a chapel at the *rancho.*

A MYSTERY BELL—1796

Among the treasures at Mission San Fernando is a bronze bell suspended by rawhide thongs from a beam along a porchway outside the chapel. Discovery of the bell is attributed to Mrs. Alice Harriman who unearthed it in an orange grove on the Camulos Rancho in 1920 .After spending many months trying to decipher the bell's inscription (written in a forgotten Slavonic language), Mrs. Harriman finally succeeded in unraveling the words:

In the Year 1796, in the month of January, this bell was cast on the Island of Kodiak by the blessing of Archimandrite Joseph, during the sojourn of Alexander Baranof.

Just how the bell found its way to California is something of a mystery. It is known that Alexander Baranof changed his headquarters from Kodiak to Sitka in 1805. Very possibly be took the bell with him to his new assignment. When the Russian Count, Nicolai Rezanof, visited Sitka and found the people there starving, be loaded his ship with materials useful to the California missions and proceeded to San Francisco hoping to exchange his goods for food. Tradition has it that at this time the bell came into the possession of José Dario Argüello who, in turn, brought it to Santa Barbara in 1806. Sometime before his appointment as Governor of

Baja California in 1815, Argüello entrusted the bell to Mission San Fernando, at that time part of the military jurisdiction of Santa Barbara.

There are other theories about the bell's peregrination to California. One explanation associates the trek to the Golden State with a settlement of people on Santa Rosa Island. Another opinion places it at Fort Ross where Captain John A. Sutter purchased it for later resale to Mission San Fernando. In any event, the bell was highly valued by the inhabitants of San Fernando. When the mission was falling into ruin in the 1860, the prized possession was moved to the Del Valle *rancho* and buried there to save it from vandals.

After its discovery by Mrs. Harriman, the famed bell was taken to the *Asistencia de Nuestra Señora de los Angeles* and from there to the Los Angeles Orphanage. It was finally located and re–identified through the efforts of Marie T. Walsh who returned it to the restored Mission of San Fernando in 1948. The small bell weighs only a hundred pounds. It has a crown top, bands of ornamentation, and fancy Russian scrollwork resembling lace. Though badly cracked, it still has a delightful tone.

One mission authority says that this bell's importance lies in its being a connecting link in the circling of the globe by Catholicism. The Greek–Russian from the north connects with the Spanish of the south—the meeting of two heritages, both Christian, in a world hitherto enslaved in the darkness of paganism.

SOME MISSIONARY SIDELIGHTS—1798

A number of interesting items about missionary life in early California can be gleaned from the old register books in which baptisms, marriages, confirmations and deaths are recorded. San Fernando's *Libro Primero de Difuntos,* or burial journal, can be taken as a typical example.

The first interment in Christian times *at Achois Comihabit* took place seven months after the founding of Mission San Fernando, on April 7, 1798, when Fray Francisco Dumetz consigned to the earth the remains of José Antonio. A check of the baptismal register indicates that this neophyte was the twenty–third native christened at San Fernando.

Though there are 2,425 notices of death in the burial register, not all those neophytes were buried in the mission cemetery proper. The natives, for example, baptized in *articulo mortis,* were usually interred in the remote areas where they died. Customarily, a cross was placed on their grave to distinguish them from pagan resting places. Despite its relatively small size, there were well over 2,000 natives interred in the cemetery between 1798 and 1852. The lack of headstones or markers in the early years helps to explain how so many bodies could be buried in so small an area.

An old tradition suggests that there was at one time a charnel house at San Fernando. Supposedly, at stated intervals, bones were disinterred and deposited in sepulchral chambers in order to conserve space. Though there is no evidence to substantiate the use of a charnel house, there is little doubt that tombs were used for multiple interments. Such a practice was possible since the remains were rarely enclosed in coffins but wrapped in mats and lowered directly into the ground. Laboratory analysis of the soil gives no indication of any decomposition chemicals.

Though the cemetery itself was primarily envisioned for Indians, a fair number of Spaniards and others were buried there over the decades. The first of these *gente de razón,* or non–Indians, was Roque Cota, husband of Juana Maria Verdugo, who was interred on September 30, 1798. The last recorded burial in the mission registers was that of an un–named child of Mexican parents, entombed on April 7, 1852 by Amable Petithomme a Picpus Father from the Sandwich Islands.

There are five priests buried at San Fernando, at least one of whom, Fray José de Miguel (1761–1813), is interred within the sanctuary of the church. One source reports that in March of 1905, "considerable excitement was caused by the actions of the parish priest of San Fernando, a Frenchman named LeBelleguy, of venerable appearance and gentle manners. . . . He exhumed the bodies of the Franciscan friars who had been buried in the church and reburied them."

The tiny cemetery continued to serve the Catholics of the area until 1917. On February 9 of that year, notices were posted that no more interments would be allowed on the grounds "which have served first the mission folks and then the Mexican population of this section for a great many years."

Whenever the information was available, the friars listed both the Christian and pagan names of the decedent, the name of his tribe and/or village, along with his occupation, place of origin and death, date of burial, sacraments received, circumstances of demise and officiating priest. Surprisingly few "sudden" deaths are recorded. Natives rarely succumbed of snake bite, from encounters with wild animals or as a result of accident. Most died of age or some debilitating illness. Indications are that the natives normally buried their dead the day after demise.

A FAMOUS VIA CRUCIS – 1800s

Probably the most outstanding example of all Indian art in California, and possibly in the whole United States, is the set of Stations of the Cross painted at San Fernando about 1805–07, by the Indian neophyte, Juan Antonio. One authority has noted that "these paintings are unique in the field of American Indian art as influenced by the Spanish Franciscan missionaries. Crude though they are in every respect, they nevertheless represent a phase in mission Indian endeavor that is almost forgotten."

The artist, known by oldtimers as *El Indio de la Via Crucis,* undoubtedly used a series of black and white woodcuts illustrating various religions tomes as his models; however, it is clearly evident that he placed his own interpretation on the pictures, especially in his use of color schemes and arrangement of characters. The features of the persons are a curious mixture of Biblical imagery and the contemporary. This is especially pronounced in the faces of the soldiers, whose expressions, with their trim moustaches, border on the comic.

According to one view of the artistic style, the paintings bear considerable resemblance in pose and perspective to that blend of savagery and civilization common to Assyrian and Egyptian depictions. Though they represent a wide range of incongruities, the stations reveal the depth of sympathy, passion and pity inherent in the neophyte mind. The crucifixion scene surpasses the others and is easily the most realistic, pathetic and strangely attractive of them all.

Originally uniform in size, measuring some 32 by 52 inches, the paintings were executed on patched pieces of durable sail cloth, possibly salvaged from the ship of William Shaler, a trader who visited California in 1803–05. The pigmentation used has been the source of confusion insofar as several early commentators thought it was obtained from crushed flowers. Such a substance, however, could not have withstood the long years of exposure which the stations subsequently endured. Most authorities are inclined to agree that all the colors used were derived from mineral or earth sources. The artist probably ground certain of the pigments himself, while using others imported from Mexico and Spain. Fortunately, he was able to secure linseed oil, which proved to be a substantial medium.

As pieces of art, the paintings are highly prized. One authority, recognizing them as "the most outstanding example of Indian art in California," placed a monetary value of $1,500,000 on the fourteen paintings in 1936. Despite their prominence among students of art the stations have a long and rather unhappy history. Removed from San Fernando in the 1850s, they were stored a number of years at the old Plaza Church in Los Angeles. By the time of the World's Columbian Exposition in 1890, the paintings had all but rotted on their original stretchers. Fortunately, before being shipped to Chicago for exhibition in the California Building, they were trimmed, cleaned and mounted on new wooden panels. After their return to Los Angeles, the stations were put away in the basement of Saint Vibiana's Cathedral and later loaned to Mission San Gabriel, where they were eventually placed along an outside corridor. Here for some twenty years, they were buffeted by wind, sun and dust and subjected to the dampness of rain and fog.

In recent years, these "most celebrated of the Indian paintings on canvas" have received better attention, though at least one of the stations has faded beyond recognition, a sad fate for the most remarkable and imaginative examples of neophyte Indian art in the Californias." Those who gaze at these unique paintings "cannot fail to read the whole heart history of that noble nation – and read it more truly than ever he could by the word of any writer or historian.

ISABELLE VILLEGAS REMEMBERS—1837

One of the more interesting historical memoranda relating to California's provincial era is that of Isabelle Villegas, who recalls episodes in the history of San Fernando Mission between 1797 and 1825. The original manuscript, now on deposit at the Southwest Museum, was initially published in *The Masterkey,* January, 1946, with annotations by the late Mark Harrington.

It was in 1837 that my grandmother with her parents first came to San Fernando. She was then six years of age and saw the San Fernando Mission in all its glory with beautiful orchards and gardens surrounding it and the wide plain in front of it covered with large herds of cattle and sheep. San Fernando was far–famed for its immense riches, being at this time accredited the most prosperous of all the missions.

Her father, Don Pedro Lopez, held the position of majordomo at the San Fernando Mission. There were two thousand Indians living at the mission alone, besides several tribes living in the hills and mountains. The Indians were divided into four groups or *rancherias,* each under an *alcalde,* or foreman, who was responsible to the *majordomo.*

San Fernando was widely famous for its "Fiestas, but the greatest of the year was on May 30th, San Fernando or Saint Ferdinand's Day." People from of all southern California gathered at San Fernando on this day to taste the first fruits of the year.

This day was begun by attending Mass—all attended, from the *majordomo* to its lowliest Indian. Following the Mass was a great feast or banquet. The table was spread between two long rows of immense pomegranate trees in the orchard at the rear of the old church.

In the afternoon of this fiesta day such sports as horseracing, a rodeo, in which the best riders took part,

was enjoyed; but the main event of the afternoon was a bull–fight held in the plaza in front of the old church. In the evening songs and dancing (dances were solos and duet dancing), and then everyone joined in, thus ending the gay fiesta.

The Indians held special fiestas of their own; the greatest of these was the anniversary of the death of an Indian chief. Indians came to San Fernando from what at that time were great distances. Whole tribes would make the yearly pilgrimage, some coming from Tehachapi, and others as far as San Jacinto. Those tribes known as the Mission Indians were the Tujungas, El Encino, and El Escorpion, and, of course, those who lived in the mission proper. The feature of the fiesta was a dance in which all the members of the different tribes joined. A large image of the Indian chief was erected, around which a fire was built. As the dancers moved in a circle about the image, they cast into the fire some personal belongings of their dead. The music to the dance was the wailing and weeping of the dancers themselves.

My grandmother remained at the mission until 1846; she then moved to Los Angeles and did not return until 1853, when she came as the bride of Don Geronimo Lopez. It was a sad sight that greeted her on her return The mission she had known to be so wealthy and beautiful no longer remained, but in its place were broken, shattered buildings, poorly cultivated orchards, and but a few cattle and sheep. There was no longer a resident priest, and even the Indians, with the exception of a very few who remained as servants to the owner, had gone away.

In concluding her recollections about Mission San Fernando, the author recalled that "it was with great joy that my grandparents looked back to those days!" Those who read her memoir can surely understand why.

GOLD DISCOVERED AT SAN FERNANDO – 1842

In a description of Mission San Fernando written in 1842, Eugene Duflot de Mofras mentions several of the neighboring *ranchos,* among then San Francisquito where, he notes, gold was discovered that very year. The *rancho,* then occupied by the Del Valle family, was so productive that "by May the gold region had been found to extend two leagues and the dirt, with a scanty supply of water, was paying two dollars per day to each man engaged in mining."

The San Fernando Mission district then "bears the distinction of having supplied the world with the first California gold, six years before James W. Marshall on January 24, 1848, found the glittering nuggets in Sutter's mill–race near the South Branch of the American River."

Actual discovery is credited to William Francis

Lopez on March 9, 1842. Pulling up a cluster of onions, Lopez noticed yellow particles on the stems which he reasoned to be the precious substance. The first parcel of gold dust was sent to Philadelphia by Abel Stearns and consisted of 18.34 ounces at a value of $344.75 or $19 per ounce. The historic discovery had its Christian baptism exactly one year later when Fray Blas Ordaz from Mission San Fernando celebrated a High Mass at the site in the presence of a great gathering of people. Excitement abounded for the next four years, but with the development of the Mother Lode country in 1849, interest in the small San Fernando deposits abated and soon died out altogether.

As far as the missionaries were concerned, the discovery of gold in California brought more problems than comforts for it opened the floodgates to one of the largest migratory movements in the nation's history. To Picpus Bishop Desiré Maigret, Vicar Apostolic of the Sandwich Islands, gold meant that "California is going to be an important country. Everybody is going thither. Soon there will be over a million inhabitants. The clergy of California have written to me that I should come to their rescue."

There were those who believed that the *padres* hid away great quantities of the precious metal for their private use. Theodore T. Johnson's treatise accounted for "the rigid silence as to the existence of gold in the country, maintained for more than a century (!)" by charging that the missionaries realized that "the day of their supremacy and influence in California had gone by never to return" and were planning well for the years ahead.

One visitor to Mission San Fernando in 1904 saw huge gaping holes in the soil within the church itself. Even before the main altar were vestiges of a disappointed prospector. Father Zephyrin Engelhardt found similar excavations at Mission Soledad "not withstanding that the last Franciscan was said to have died there at the foot of the altar from starvation!" Even today people are occasionally seen digging in the area on the theory of "where gold has been—gold should be!"

It certainly seems historically significant that California's two greatest treasures, its Catholic Heritage and its golden reserves, should have been so closely aligned to the old mission chain. In any event, California has a double debt to *El Camino Real,* especially that part of the King's Highway passing through San Fernando!

THE GARDENS AT SAN FERNANDO MISSION —1846

In many of the early promotional books and articles about Southern California, the central image of the area was its astonishing landscape. The rich soil and favorable climate helped the southland to evolve into an unfenced garden for magnificent exotic plants.

There was much to sustain that portrayal. The abounding palms, citrus, eucalyptus and pepper trees seem indigenous. Southern California was an earthly paradise where anything would grow and thrive. Interestingly, the image so cleverly circulated by propagandists is sustained in the many public and private gardens of Southern California. The Edenlike mystique survives, especially at such places as San Fernando Mission.

The grounds at the Old Mission convey a sense of permanence and beauty that no building or monument could portray. They confirm and epitomize the fabled landscape celebrated in books and portrayed on television. There is considerable more to the accolades than idle rhetoric. By the early 1800s the *huerta* or garden at San Fernando had already become a center of agricultural productivity and ornamental delight. Plant novelties brought from the Pacific ports of Latin America and Asia flourished alongside native plants and Mediterranean introductions imported from Spain by the early Mallorcan friars.

When Edwin Bryant visited San Fernando Mission in 1846, he recorded his impressions of that outpost along *El Camino Real in* these words:

> There are two extensive gardens, surrounded by high walls; and a stroll through them is a most delightful contrast from the usually uncultivated landscape we have been travelling through for so long a time. Here were brought together most of the fruits and many of the plants of the temperate and tropical climates.
>
> Although not the season of flowers (January), still the roses were in bloom. Oranges, lemons, figs, and olives hung upon the trees, and the blood–red tuna, or prickly pear, looked very tempting.

Throughout Southern California, the land soon began to resemble what Bryant had seen at San Fernando Mission. In what later became an asphalt jungle, portions of Southern California as a garden still endure. Thousands view personally and millions see on television the annual Rose Parade where the flower–covered caravan of floats exhibit anew the brilliance of the southland's garden. The colorful and scenic garden paradise at San Fernando is still in evidence. The vision of Edwin Bryant is alive amidst a blanket of colors and flavors.

At least one of every kind of tree that adorned the mission in provincial times can be seen at San Fernando. The pathways and buildings are framed by boxwood offshoots from the royal palace at Palma de Mallorca. Walkways of crushed rock are bordered with lush green lawns, colorful flowers and manicured shrubbery.

Indeed San Fernando Mission is regarded as one of the most attractive and yet authentic windows to California's past. Those walking through its gardens, gazing at its building and looking at its displays truly have a glimpse of paradise.

TOPOGRAPHICAL REPORT–1853

In the Military Appropriations Act of March 3, 1853, the United States Congress directed that explorations and surveys be made "to ascertain the most practical and economical route for a railroad from the Mississippi River to the Pacific Ocean." Under orders from the Secretary of War, Lieutenant Robert Stockton Williamson, a twenty–nine year old graduate of West Point Academy then attached to the Topographical Engineer Corps, was commissioned "to examine the passes of the Sierra Nevada leading from the San Joaquin and Tulare Valleys."

Lieutenant Williamson and his party, arrived during the late fall of 1853, and proceeded to carefully explore the area and chart their discoveries for the War Department. Williamson's survey was subsequently published as the "Report of Explorations in California for Railroad Routes." It appeared in *Explorations and Surveys for a Railroad Route to the Pacific* Volume V (Washington, 1853).

The graphic description provided in the Williamson report on Mission San Fernando is a valuable and often overlooked source on the physical status of that missionary outpost in the early 1850s. That portrayal, here reproduced in summary form, indicates that the Williamson party had camped a few miles north of the mission

> Soon after leaving our camp, under the fig trees, we found that we were entering a widely extended valley, with a nearly level surface, without trees or verdure, and bounded on all sides by distant mountains. On turning the point of a hill, we suddenly came in sight of the Mission buildings, which, with the surrounding gardens, stood isolated in the seemingly desert plain, and produced a most beautiful effect.
>
> The gardens were enclosed by walls but the graceful palms rose above them all, and groves of olive, lemon and orange trees could be seen within. Outside the walls, the surface was barren and gravelly, and the fertility within is the result of irrigation.
>
> The building presents an imposing appearance, having a long portico formed by a colonnade, with twenty arches, built of brick, or adobe, plastered and whitewashed. The floor is paved with tiles, and a pleasant promenade in front of the edifice is thus afforded.
>
> The remains of a large fountain, with a circular basin ten feet or more in diameter, was directly in front of the main entrance, and gave an indication of the splendor of

the establishment in former days. The grape is cultivated here, and we purchased a quantity of a very pleasant red wine, similar to claret.

> Several men were employed in filling a large still with the fermented pulp and skins of grapes, from which the juice had been pressed, with the intention of distilling brandy from it.

Thus did San Fernando Mission appear to visitors in the decade after the last resident priest had departed.

WELLS FARGO AT SAN FERNANDO—1858

Among the more popular exhibits at San Fernando Mission is a halfsize stagecoach model bearing the traditional markings of the Wells Fargo & Company which provided mail and passenger service from the Mississippi River to the Pacific Coast for over half a century.

Wells Fargo used stagecoaches from its earliest days until 1918. At first it contracted with independent companies to carry its mail, express and treasure shipments throughout California. Later, Wells Fargo financially backed the development of the first transcontinental stagecoach venture, the Overland Mail Company.

By 1866, Wells Fargo operated the largest staging enterprise in the west. Its stagecoaches ran between Cisco, California and North Platte, Nebraska, the railheads of the transcontinental railroad. The coaches used by Wells Fargo were built by Abbot–Downing Company of Concord, New Hampshire, and were the finest vehicles available. They were constructed of the very best wood, leather and metal, and could transport nine passengers inside and as many more on the roof.

The scale stagecoach on exhibit at San Fernando Mission was handcarved in balsa wood by Oscar Joe Montagno, Jr. It faithfully illustrates the details of a Concord Stage, including the suspension system called thoroughbraces which gave the coach its unique ride.

The westernmost rooms of the convento at San Fernando Mission, cut off from the rest of the building, originally served as a hospice or inn for travelers along *El Camino Real.* Later the area became a station on the Butterfield line between San Francisco and Los Angeles.

John Butterfield, the guiding force for the Overland Mail Company, also served as Vice President of the American Express Company which was founded in 1850 by Henry Wells and William G. Fargo. Wells Fargo and American Express controlled the Overland Mail Company and acted for Butterfield in California. In later years, the interests of Butterfield and Wells Fargo were consolidated in many areas of the west.

Not much is known about the station at San Fernando Mission. One of the few insights into its operation was provided by Waterman L. Ormsby (1834–1908) who kept a diary of a trip he made by the stage during the final months of 1858.

Arriving at San Fernando Mission on October 8th of that year, he wrote the following description as part of an essay that appeared in the New York *Herald* for November 19, 1858.

> Our first change was nine miles from Los Angeles. Fifteen miles further, we changed at the old Spanish mission of San Fernando, which is marked on Colton's map. It was built for the Indians and consists of a number of low ranches; the remains indicate that it was once a fine adobe building, with large pillars in front and a fine belfry and fountain.
>
> A niche in the centre of the building contains a fine piece of old statuary. Part of the building is now used as a stable for the company's horses; and the only inhabitants we saw were a few Indian women, washing in a little brook which gurgles by, who giggled in high glee as we passed with our beautiful team of six white horses— two more than our usual allowance, in consideration of a heavy canyon and pass which lay in our route.

RESTORATION AT SAN FERNANDO—1865

There were several attempts, some of them abortive, to restore the Old Mission at San Fernando. As early as 1865, a journalist reported that the *convento* had been "newly repaired."

The Landmarks Club was especially active in restorative efforts at San Fernando, thought by many to be the most typical of all the missions. With the support of other civic–minded organizations, the club financed repair of the *convento* in time for the mission's centennial in 1897. In addition to completely re–roofing the building, a temporary covering was placed over the church to forestall further deterioration from wind and rain.

The workshops connecting the abandoned church and the *convento* had long been in ruins and, by 1904, an observer noted that "there is little in the ruin of this Mission to tell its early story of peace and prosperity." In 1908, the Missionary Sons of the Immaculate Heart of Mary were placed in charge of the parish in nearby San Fernando. During their tenure, sometime after 1912, several rooms in the *convento* were restored by the exiled Archbishop of Oaxaca, Eulogio Gillow y Zavala, who tried unsuccessfully to inaugurate therein a seminary for clerical students expelled from Mexico.

In 1916, a "Candle Sale" raised funds for strengthening the walls and replacing the central portion of the temporary church roof. The relief was only temporary, however, for in 1918 a visitor recorded that "San Fer-

nando, one of the oldest missions, is being used as a hay barn. It is a plain old place, simple even to severity in its designs, but it is one of the best examples of mission architecture known."

Considerable restoration was done on the *convento* by the Oblates of Mary Immaculate in the years after 1923. The earlier, non–authentic roof was replaced and several rooms re–opened. In the October 1929 issue of their community magazine was this observation: "The columns of the cloister have been replaced, a new foundation has been placed under the rear wall of the *convento*, while five long steel anchors have been inserted to hold it in place. Along the street front an adobe wall has been built, the porter's lodge has been restored, and an entirely new roof has taken the place of the old one of patchwork that covered the venerable monument."

Father Charles Burns, who looked after the old Mission from 1938 to 1944, launched an extensive program to further restore the *convento* and the church. Under the supervision of Dr. Mark Harrington, curator of the Southwest Museum, the arches of the *convento* as well as the interior corridor were rebuilt.

Many of the side walls were strengthened and several rooms plastered and painted. Period furniture was added and doors hung throughout the edifice. All replacements, whether hinges, door latches, bolts, keys or nails were exact reproductions from originals unearthed at the scene. The church was refurbished and a replica altar placed in the sanctuary. Just one day short of the mission's 144th birthday, September 7, 1941, Mass was celebrated in the church for the first time since 1874.

Between 1945 and 1947, Harrington restored the old kitchen, the belfry (with its original *Ave Maria Purisima* bell), the majordomo's house and the sacristy.

After War World II, the tower was rebuilt and the mission bells once again hoisted into place. In 1947, with funds from the Hearst Foundation, Father Augustine O'Dea began the final stage of the restoration program which included rebuilding the ruins of the Indian workshops originally connecting the *convento* and the church. The walls were erected atop the earlier foundation stones "since some of the adobe bricks still show the handmarks of the people that fashioned them."

The work was executed with great precision and handmade adobe bricks were used throughout the structure. In addition to the buildings themselves, considerable time was spent landscaping the courtyards and placing in the plaza a colorful replica of the original water fountain.

PEAFOWL AT MISSION HILLS—1874

In a questionnaire circulated among 1,500 recent

tourists at San Fernando Mission, 72 percent identified the peafowl as the most attractive and interesting feature associated with the seventeenth of the frontier outposts along California's *El Camino Real.*

Though the present colony is of fairly recent origin at Mission Hills, there is a century old tradition about peafowl at the mission. Claude Bain visited the area in 1874 and recorded seeing "several beautiful peacocks allegedly brought to the west coast from India." He was right about their origin. The peafowl is the national bird of India and the colorful birds abound in the city parks and country estates of that nation and neighboring Sri Lanka.

There are several species of peafowl in other areas. Those found in Burma, Malaysia and Java are smaller and distinguished by a slightly different coloration. In ancient times, the peacock was carried from India to other parts of the civilized world as a great treasure. Holy Scripture tells that every three years during the reign of King Solomon there "came the navy of Tarshish, bringing gold and silver, ivory, apes and peacocks." (I Kings, 10:22)

Peacocks are mentioned in a play by Aristophanes written in Greece during the fourth century before Christ. Pliny speaks of peacocks being common in the Rome of his day. And, in classical mythology, the bird is the favorite of Hera.

The birds have never freely rendered themselves to domestication. Happily they are no longer considered a delicacy for the table. In the days of chivalry, one of the most solemn oaths was that taken "on the peacock."

Available evidence indicates that peafowl were first brought to the United States in the early 1800s. According to Mrs. Anita Baldwin, daughter of the legendary E. J. (Lucky) Baldwin, a party of sportsmen from England visited her father's estate in 1867. Knowing their host loved hunting, they invited him to join them on a safari to India. There Mr. Baldwin became fascinated by peafowl and brought back a pair to California. Claire Charles subsequently recalled that there were once as many as a thousand of the birds roaming freely on Baldwin's property.

The rather large peafowl family in Palos Verdes dates to 1916, when Frank Valderlip purchased the 16,000 acres that later became Palos Verdes Estates. Anita Baldwin reportedly gave Valderlip nine peafowl for his home overlooking Portuguese Bend. Most of the peafowl in California are descended from the Baldwin strain. The somewhat frail birds have thrived in the mild Palos Verdes climate since they cannot tolerate changeable weather.

Peafowl are among the showiest of all birds because of their great size and the beauty of their feathers. Males have a metallic, greenish–blue neck and breast, pur-plish–blue underparts and long greenish feathers brilliantly marked with bold spots that resemble eyes. They often spread their feathers into gorgeous fans as they parade slowly and majestically in front of the females. The females or peahens are smaller, less vividly colored and have no train.

Peafowl nest in the thick brush and spend their waking hours roosting in trees or feeding on snails, frogs and insects, as well as on grain, juicy grasses and bulbs. Their dark–green coloration gives them great protective value in the midst of tropical foliage.

VISIT TO SAN FERNANDO—1875

Early in 1982, Donna R.M. Adams presented a transcript of a letter to the Archival Center written by Douglas A. Joy. Addressed to his brother, the letter describes a visit to San Fernando Mission on July 9, 1875

Joy and his companions had camped "under two very large olive trees." In the nearby orchard were "palm, orange, lemon, fig and all kinds of tropical trees, but unfortunately they are not bearing ripe fruit at the present." He went on to say that "the old mission which is just outside the camp is a very peculiar and tumbledown looking place. All the buildings are what I believe they call adobe, that is, they are built of mud bricks." Joy and his friends managed to get into the church, although it was locked, by climbing up into the belfry where the chimes are and then walking into the place where the choir used to sing."

> The altar still remains in good condition and has on it the crucifix and a statue of one of the saints. There is a looking glass on the left side of the altar, and one of the workman said there had been one on the other side, but it had been stolen by some visitor.

> The pulpit is fastened to the left hand wall somewhat in advance of the chancel and there is a winding stair leading up to it very much in I the same way as it is on the fashionable churches of today in New York. There are no seats in the church, and when one of the fellows said, 'where has my little dog gone?', it echoed from the walls as if we were in some cavern.

> An old Indian sweeps out the church every Sunday, but no services are ever held there now. The outside is much worn and washed away, but it has stood wonderfully well considering it is built entirely of mud and is 88 years old. There is an old Indian here who is 105 years old, and lie says he helped to build it.

> The main building is built of the same material and has a long veranda which is paved with brick and the covering of which is supported by large brick pillars arched at the top. The bricks were made by the Indians and look in color and structure like one of our own bricks, but only half as thick and twice as wide.

> The veranda looks out into a most beautiful garden

in which are the remains of two old fountains. One of them is in a good state of preservation, but the other only has the basin left. They are both built of the kind of brick before mentioned, but has been cemented over and must have been very beautiful when first built.

Like I suppose all the various houses about here, the old mission possesses a haunted room. It is said that an old monk died there under very suspicious circumstances, and that ever after that anyone sleeping there would be visited by him.

You would be surprised to see the size the cactus grows here. Some of them are at least twenty feet high and are grown so thickly together that no man or animal can possibly get through them. They bear a kind of fruit called the prickly pear and are said to be very palatable when ripe. The flowers and green fruit are on them now, but nothing seems to be ripe about here at this season.

Joy examined the geological formations of the nearby hills, but saw nothing which was especially interesting He did, however, obtain "an excellent view of the San Fernando Valley and surrounding mountain from the top of one of the hills, which the American reading indicated to be 800 feet above camp, which is itself considerably above the level of the plain." He acknowledged that it was "a very beautiful valley and must be much more so in the winter time when it is all green with grass and grain."

PROBLEMS AT MISSION SAN FERNANDO— 1905

On March 13, 1905, a writer for the Los Angeles *Times* reported an "almost incredible state of affairs, whereby the existence is threatened of one of the oldest and most interesting of the ancient Franciscan missions." The account related how the mission had Ida narrow escape from being completely destroyed by fire" built in one of its rooms by squatters. It seems as if a huge conflagration had begun in one of the little fireplaces, at the end of the *convento* building. "In a short time some of the Mexicans discovered volumes of smoke issuing from the cracks of the casements, and bursting into the room found it black with smoke, and the flames reaching out to gobble whatever was within their reach. Prompt action saved the buildings from destruction."

According to the newspaper report, "the sacred old pile of adobe and heavy–hewed timbers, whose walls are redolent with the memories of historic incidents reaching out through the long stretch of a full century past, has been captured, as if a Russian fortress, by colonies of Buddhistic Japanese who live and cook in it, taking complete possession, while other sections are used as shelters for the gangs of not overclean laborers and camps of wholly indifferent Americans." The indignant reporter continued: "Just think of the desecration! The worship of orientals before the shrine of Nirvana, and the practice of their heathenistic rites in the cloisters which were reared under the shadow of the cross, and on whose walls erstwhile were hung the crucifix and the ewers of holy water."

Surely the seventeenth of California's missions had "fallen into hard times, and the more the present situation is investigated the worse appears." The historic foundation stood uncared for, in 1905, "a prey for vandals," overrun by camps of men to whom the old walls and their traditions were meaningless. The report noted that "the beautiful olive orchards, planted by the grey–habited *padres* of another century, are being hewed down and chopped into cordwood; the walls of the various structures are being allowed to crumble and fall, for want of a caretaker, and the campers who have taken possession of the long cloisters have laid ruthless hands on the ancient doors and frames, because, forsooth, they make such easy and convenient firewood."

Piles of firewood which were lying on the old brick floors ready to be offered up on the soup fires of the cooks, were actually pieces which had been parts of the old mission itself, and which had been hewn out and placed in that sacred edifice years before the ruthless hands which destroyed them were in existence. The essay went on to state that "Mexicans have been removing the adobes in the walls for use in shacks and shelters set up in town. The rear portion of the mission itself has been allowed to crumble and stand unroofed, an inviting subject for the play [of] the elements. The rain of yesterday did the old pile almost incalculable damage. Underneath the long series of archways the laborers on the Huntington lands, which surround the church property, have found a shelter for their various implements. Piles of old harness, a winnowing machine, a reaper, and other such farming machinery stood there yesterday, while about them were groups of men. passing the time in idle talk and ribald jest and story."

At one end of the patio, an enterprising local resident had even set up a barbershop, which was doing a thriving business among the standers–by. The essay for the *Times* concluded by asking whether "these old landmarks [are] to be allowed to sink into hopeless ruin, hurried on by the vandalism of transient campers, nesting hobos and careless ranch hands. There is crying need of preservation work at old San Fernando Mission."

DESPOLIATION AT SAN FERNANDO—1915

The seventeenth of California's missions, dedicated to San Fernando, Rey de España, stands just beyond the shadows of the Sierra Madre Mountains, overlooking a splendid broad valley, known in the annals as *Santa Catalina de los Encinos*. Fray Fermín Francisco de Lasuén's missionary foundation was destined to become the mother church of a valley that, by 1970, had become the eighth largest of the nation's urban markets, accounting for 78 percent of the population gain in Los Angeles over the preceding dozen years. More people resided in the 235 square mile bowl of twenty–two valley towns than inhabited eleven of the country's states.

The prominence of San Fernando and its missionary establishment was not without its bleak days. During the period of its abandonment, the historic foundation suffered both natural and man–induced despoliation. An account appearing in the Los Angeles Sunday *Times*, February 14, 1915, tells how the graves in the sanctuary of the church were defiled by "vandals in search of the holy treasures that were buried in the bosoms of the dead monks."

A visitor to San Fernando discovered a great hole "where the floor of the old sacristy has been firm and smooth to the feet of pilgrims for a century." The opening led "into the depths that were consecrated as the resting place for the *padres* that died" in the service of the mission. Who the ghouls were, when they came and why they operated as they did, are unanswered queries. It is also unknown what they secured as they tunneled through the precious depths, but it is practically certain that they were searching the graves of the priests of old.

The report noted that "the freshly dug tunnel begins in the sacristy, a small room to the right of the altar space in the lofty chapel. it darts straight down for twelve feet, roots around in a series of prying offshoots, and then continues under the heavy walls, toward the spot just outside the chapel and close to the altar where burial ground for the priests might have been chosen."

From a fragment of paper found in the depths of the tunnel, "it appears probable that a chart may have been the guide of the ghouls in the midnight labor, as legends abound of great treasures that were in the hands of the *padres,* and that the treasures were buried close to the altar because people of the Catholic faith would not dare to loot there." Apparently, the intruders were familiar with the ground "for they sought the sacristy for their operations. In their exploration they withdrew at least five tons of earth and stowed it behind a concealing ruin. The tunnel extends seventy–five feet through the very heart of the ground chosen for God. It swerves under the altar and then rushes to a tell–tale end twenty feet beyond the altar walls where a cave–in gave the alarm that the mad moles had been at work."

Had the vandals violated the tombs in daylight, the flocks of doves winging above the sagging roof beams would have given alarm, but "at midnight, only the spirit of decency is on watch. So there was no one to shame away the ghouls who came like witches armed with picks, and tunneled into the grave beds of the old padres and searched among the helpless bones."

MOTION PICTURES AT SAN FERNANDO—1915

For over eighty–five years, San Fernando Mission has been a favorite location for the entertainment industry. Innumerable motion pictures and television programs have been filmed in the peaceful surroundings of California's seventeenth mission.

The first known motion picture was filmed at San Fernando Mission during 1915. Entitled "Captain Courtesy," it was produced by Bosworth Inc in association with the Oliver Morosco Photoplay Company. The feature length production was distributed by Paramount Pictures Corporation.

According to the copyright entry preserved at the American Film Institute, the subtitle for the film was "A Story of the Mexican Occupation of California, 1840–1846." It was first reissued in early 1919 by Jesse L. Lasky.

Edward Childs Carpenter wrote the story on which the five reel romance was based at Philadelphia in 1906. One of the early commentators wrote that "the story had a Robert Louis Stevenson suggestion, with its atmosphere of fighting, hair breadth escapes, daring horsemen and vigorous incidents throughout."

The basic plot was described in an issue of the *Motion Picture News* for April 10, 1915: "A young American whose parents have been murdered by a band of robbers swears to have vengeance. He becomes an outlaw of a most unusual sort. He robs only Mexicans, and gives his plunder to Americans who have been robbed. When the Californians decide on real resistance, he becomes a captain of the Rifleman. There is a fine love story with Eleanor, an orphan, who lives with the old priest, Father Reinaldo.

The role of Captain Courtesy was played by Dustin Farnum and one reviewer of the film noted that those who have seen Farnum "in his previous screen successes will realize what a fortunate choice was made in assigning him the leading role in this powerful story of the frontier." Winifred Kingston was equally pleasing as Eleanor, the plucky heroine. Father Reinaldo was played with much feeling by Herbert Standing. Courtenay Foote had the role of the renegade American, and Carl Von Schiller was the energetic Mexican leader.

The many fine settings of the picture create an atmosphere of surprising realism, at the same time giving great beauty to the scenes. One of the most spectacular scenes occurs when Captain Courtesy rides his horse into the church and takes a daring leap through a high window.

Lois Weber, who directed the film, was careful to utilize the parts of San Fernando Mission most easily recognized by those who had visited the historic Southern California landmark. We are told in one advertisement that "the interior of the Mission, with its inlaid floor, massive doors and ancient stairway, is particularly striking."

The New York *Dramatic Mirror* for April 24, 1915 described the film as "a whooping melodrama plus a marvelous lot of scenery . . . put on by a director and cast that entered fully into the spirit of the moment." The review notes that "the director did not stint himself in the use of pretty locations. Their single interior was the mission which for reality and correct settings might have been a still extant sample of Spanish architecture with the roof removed for better lighting effects."

Clifford H. Pengburn, a film critic of that era, said that "the picture is one of the finest of recent productions!"

SAN FERNANDO MISSION IN 1917

In early 1917, Bostonian Larry Hoar toured Southern California. A few months later, the *Overland Monthly* (founded by Bret Harte in 1868) published "The Mission San Fernando, Rey de Espagno" in which Hoar recorded his impressions of the 17th establishment along *El Camino Real.*

Hoar was greatly enamored with "this Land of the Golden West, this California—a place that seems to be outside the pale of endless heartaches and strife and money–mad hurry, a place clothed in soul–quieting peace." One day, while motoring "along turtle fashion slowly and alone—through broadcircled, splendidly groomed San Fernando Valley," Hoar caught sight of "a distant, many–arched gleam of white shimmering through the trees."

He had found "a fascinating array of old adobe structures; some great, some small and all more or less crumbled by the relentless hand of Time." To his delight, Hoar learned that he had "discovered" the "famous, though rather unfrequented, Mission San Fernando, Rey de Espagno, founded in 1797 by Fray (Fermin Francisco de) Lasuén." Hoar left his car "beside a quaint, three–basined fountain which was built by the Mission *padres* decades ago and marks the center of what is said to have been a very fine old garden."

From a vantage point on an elevated stone, he looked about. "Skirting the whole place could be traced irregular fragments of the great wall that, a century ago, protected ten, possibly only eight, acres of the richest Church land in the entire chain of missions that linked San Diego to San Francisco."

He was interested in "two imposing structures—the monastery and the church–both of which, though picturesquely ravaged by time, still survived the great circle of ruins about them." Hoar rightly reckoned that "San Fernando Mission is, perhaps, the most satisfactory relic of the early California missions in the original completeness and until the past months almost untouched state of its decay."

The wide, white–arched monastery corridors that first caught Hoar's attention "have remained stolidly indifferent to the insults of the years, and assume grotesque superiority toward the present day embellishments." The entire mission, or what remained of it, was guarded by "a sort of self– appointed doorman," a soft–eyed, shabbily garbed idler watching out for the buildings and helping visitors to find their way through the ruins.

The church, then under reconstruction by the Landmarks Club, was "a tall, rectangular pile, pleasingly disguised by the trees through" which the visitor had first seen it. It was indeed a romantic sight. Scaffolded and laddered, cement pillared and newly bricked, daringly excavated at bottom and glaringly roofed at the top.

Hoar looked at the sacristy (which "looked rather like a shelled dugout–so tunneled and tumbled and pillaged by numberless treasure seekers"), walked through the graveyard (which was "sad, unkept") and examined some partially–opened vaults in the central part of the church. Hoar left San Fernando Mission wishing only that he had "seen the grand old ruin" earlier, before "the too transient splendor of its picturesqueness had passed."

RESTORATION OF THE MISSION—1918

The rebuilding of earthquake–damaged Mission San Fernando recalls attempts made, in 1918, by Gavin McNabb, non–Catholic proponent of a statewide campaign to restore and preserve all the California missions, many of which had already fallen into ruins. McNabb's views were spelled out in an article he wrote for the San Francisco *Chronicle:*

> The care of the Mission churches—those monuments to the spiritual and picturesque origin of California— should appeal to every Western heart.
>
> California is the only great territory that founded civilization by the cross and not by the sword. The same month and year that the Liberty Bell, on the Atlantic, rang out the birth of a Nation at war for freedom, the Mission bells of San Francisco, on the shore of the ocean named for peace, chimed in religious tones, for the Prince of Peace.
>
> At the same time was founded San Francisco, named for the saint, whose love and tenderness for all living things have sweetened all earthly existence.
>
> Does it occur to many that, while California is

young, as measured by population, she is old in history? When Britain was mostly marsh and forest; when Elizabeth, perhaps the greatest ruler that womankind has given to the world, sat on a throne; when Shakespeare was forming our language in matchless power and beauty, Drake, the genius ruffian of the seas, sailed here.

How interesting to speculate on what a different world this might have been had Drake discovered San Francisco Bay! Curtains of fog hung across the Golden Gate. The fierce rover passed unseeing. The Almighty had another destiny for these shores.

California has enjoyed three great periods of romance. The *padres*, from distant Spain, brought religions and knowledge. Their spiritual wanderings sanctified the soil and gave to our places names sweet to the tongue to utter. Their hospitable establishments were founded a day's horseback ride apart.

The traveler found there food and shelter without charge. Thus originated that splendid hospitality that together with its charity, characterized the West and made its greatest fame.

Before the Mission period ended and long succeeding it, here lived and ruled the Spanish dons, who measured their ranches by the league rather than by the acre, whose cattle ranged a thousand hills, whose life was quaint and patriarchial.

They shared their bounty with the stranger without price. Their generosity was so great that it was their undoing. They passed away, less from their faults than from their virtues.

Then came the discovery of gold, and with it the argonauts. There is an alluring enchantment about the search for gold in its native condition that appeals to men's imagination and romance far beyond and superior to its pursuit in the avenues of commerce.

The world's most adventurous and chivalrous assembled here. The best contended with the best for the prizes of the soil. In this land of almost fabulous riches and supreme beauty these giants founded a mighty race and the great State of California.

It is the duty of this race never to forget the tender and beautiful things that make Western history. Of these, none is more attractive or rich in sentiment and poetry than the Mission church, founded by those noble enthusiasts, the Franciscan Fathers of long ago.

HENRY HUNTINGTON "DOES THE RIGHT THING"—1922

The story of the *Libro de Difuntos de la Mision del Señor San Fernando* has already been told. However, through the kindness of Dr. Carey Bliss, Curator of Rare Manuscripts at the Huntington Library, copies of correspondence between Father Zephyrin Engelhardt and Henry E. Huntington have been discovered which shed further light on this fascinating chapter in California's Catholic heritage.

When Hubert Howe Bancroft examined the register books of Mission San Fernando, in 1874, the *Libro de Difuntos* was already missing. A concerted attempt by Thomas Savage to locate the volume three years later was unsuccessful. Father Engelhardt later reported that he had discovered the *registro* "among the relics which the heirs of Andrés Pico had placed in the Coronel Room of the Chamber of Commerce, in Los Angeles." The Franciscan chronicler examined the volume and copied out several large segments for his files.

A decade later, when wishing to verify his earlier transcriptions, Engelhardt was told that the volume had been taken out of the collection by the Pico heirs and sold. The elusive book passed through several hands before ultimately coming into the possession of Mr. Huntington, who was totally unaware of its background.

As soon as he heard that the volume was among the treasures amassed by Huntington, Father Engelhardt approached George Watson Cole and Edward Ayer, two confidants of the famed book collector, both of whom felt that Mr. Huntington "would do the right thing."

On December 4, 1922, Engelhardt wrote to Henry Huntington, appraising him of the book's provenance. In his three page letter, the friar pointed out that the "Mission Registers of the Catholic Church are regarded as Church property in the strict sense. They can never be sold nor given away. They can be alienated only by theft or robbery." He said that the volumes were considered "sacred and precious" partly because "the honor of persons and families is frequently bound up with these Registers in the keeping of the Church Authorities."

Engelhardt concluded by saying that he would be "exceedingly glad" if he could report to Bishop John J. Cantwell "that Mr. Huntington had done not only the right thing, but the noble and generous thing, and that ere long the Register would be returned to [the] Bishop's Archives, as the right place for it."

The ever–gracious and public–minded Huntington hastily responded with assurances that he would "take pleasure in returning . . . the book of the San Fernando Mission." He also promised to look into the identity of the vender from whom the fugitive register book had been purchased.

At the time, Mr. Huntington's books were still packed in some 700 boxes awaiting completion of the new library building at San Marino, and it was another three years before the *Libro de Difuntos* was confided to the Diocese of Los Angeles–San Diego.

The whole incident is recalled here because, as Father Engelhardt later wrote, "it is but fair and just that Mr. Huntington receive due credit for restoring the priceless Burial Register without demanding any compensation."

FANCIFUL LEGENDS ABOUT SAN FERNANDO —1927

Legends about gold and fortune have long been associated with Mission San Fernando. One such fanciful tale appeared in the Kansas City *Times* (of all places!), for May 21, 1927:

The Pacific rainbow comes down in Pacoima Canyon, back in the mountains east of San Fernando Mission, in California. It is not a mere pot of gold that is suspended from it, but a whole chest full of the yellow metal, beaten into the form of plates and platters from altar and dining service. By some it is said that the chest contains gold valued at a million dollars.

Pacoima Canyon is wild and rugged but men have time and again tried to find the treasure. Aided by a map on a tanned sheepskin, sketched with a hot metal point by a San Fernando *padre* himself, the seekers for the chest have been unable to find it. If tradition is true history this elusive chest contains the largest assortment of gold plates and platters ever beaten into form by the Indian smiths of any of the missions in the Californias, either below or above the Mexican boundary line.

From the rear doorway of the convento one can see across fifteen miles to the spot in the Sierra Madre Mountains where gold is said to have been discovered in California before the discovery at Sutter's mill, in 1849.

Rojerio Rocha, gold and silversmith at the San Fernando mission, who sang and played a violin and led the choir of many Indian voices, not only helped beat the plates and platters of yellow metal into form for the altar, refectory and dining room. He was also one of the trusted party which stole out from the mission one night and hid the golden utensils in Pacoima Canyon, where white men could not and cannot find it.

The hiding was done when word came that the United States soldiers were marching down the San Fernando Valley. The alarm was that they were coming to take possession of the mission and seize all of the material wealth it contained. But there was nothing in this alarm.

Rocha, a stalwart Indian, straight as an arrow and strong as a giant, worked in metals, iron, silver and gold, at the mission smiths for many years. At his forge he could fashion a window bar of iron, point a plow or with a blowpipe and hammer turn a silver piece of Spanish eight into a finger ring or bracelet for an Indian maiden, as readily as he could beat a lump of gold into a plate or platter.

With just as much skill too, he turned lumps and bars of silver into bridle bits, chains, rosettes, stirrups and spurs and similar decorative trifles with which to ornament the saddle horses of the Spaniards.

A tract of about three acres three miles east of the mission on Pacoima Creek was given to Rocha in an allotment of lands to the Indians by Governor Pico. There an adobe home was built for the Rocha family but they were not to live there in peace for long.

Land–greedy adventurers began driving the Indians from their little farms and one day these despoilers came riding up to the Rocha door. When the father of the Indian family remonstrated with the white invaders, he was bound with rope and dragged to Pacoima Creek, the stream then being in high flood.

A long rope was tied to the Indian and the other end was fastened to a sycamore tree. He was pushed into the turbulent stream and left there to drown. But Rocha did not drown. He drifted down stream the full length of the rope, and the waters swirled him to the bank. After clinging there all night, the Indian freed himself and went to find his family.

But the wife and children were not in the house where Rocha had left them. Not only were they gone but all else the house contained, which was not much. They and their meager home outfit had been loaded into a wagon, taken out on a lonesome country road, and left to shift for themselves as best they might. That night it rained and in the rain shivered the unsheltered, hungry family. Rocha's wife, sickly to begin with, died from exposure at the roadside where the white men had made them outcasts.

Rojerio Rocha never forgot nor forgave this wrong that had been perpetrated on his family and himself. His faith in Americans, which had come through the gentler treatment of his mission friends, had been outraged and destroyed.

Rocha knew the location of the gold mine from which the supply was obtained for making the plates and platters for the altar and dining table.

A short time before his death in 1904, when Rocha was nearly 100 years old, he told an Indian friend that he would reveal the secret place of the mission mine if a deed could be so drawn that no white man could ever obtain possession. But the deed was never drawn.

A few weeks before Rocha died he took from his old wooden chest a piece of tanned sheepskin with tracings of lines, arrows and crosses on it. The skin, he told one of his Indian friends, was a map showing location of the buried golden plates hastily gathered up by the mission fathers and sent off in the. night to be hidden from enemy invaders. It was said that in his later years Rocha was the only living person who knew where the treasure was hidden and he would not tell. His hate for the white men because of the wrong they had done him and his family burned within him to the last.

After Rocha died, the Indian friend to whom he had given the sheepskin map delivered it to some white men for a price with the further stipulation that he was to share in the distribution when the gold plates were discovered.

The white men made a long and careful study of the tracings, the arrows and the crosses, to interpret them into definite directions and locations. The arrows unmistakably pointed east from the mission to the distant Pacoima canyon, one of the wildest in Southern California. From there the arrows directed the way up Pacoima Creek for a mile, and there a cross marked a sycamore tree on the map. Across the creek from the sycamore, the map directed the way to a flat stone in the mountain side.

Watchmen were stationed up and down the canyon and the digging began with the utmost secrecy. As the sheepskin map instructed, a shaft twenty feet was dug. But the chest of gold was not at the bottom of it. The map pointed from the bottom of the shaft toward the west and the men dug in that direction.

As the search went on a tunnel was opened up and hopes surged higher and higher. But failure was the only reward. The sheepskin map still is in existence, but now held more as a curiosity than as a guide to hidden treasure.

VISIT TO SAN FERNANDO MISSION – 1930

In the February, 1930 issue of *Touring Topics,* J. E. Pleasants recalled "A Fourth of July at San Fernando in 1856." He had been one of the "Party of school–boys who were, with their teachers, invited to spend a week" at the Old Mission as guests of General Andres Pico.

The outing began with a rodeo "which was a source of great entertainment to all the boys for we were allowed to take part in it as far as our skill permitted. We were all furnished with gentle saddle horses and had great sport in helping the ranch *vaqueros."* According to Pleasants, "San Fernando Mission was then in good condition. It was one of the largest of the southern missions and the buildings were on a large scale and very imposing."

Pleasants recalled that the "south side of the (main) building is the ruin still standing. In the patio were still to be seen the large cauldrons set in masonry which had been used for drying out tallow in the mission days. The tan vats for curing hides were here also, as well as the old fountain which was set in a pool constructed of masonry. The fountain was the gathering place for the pigeons of the ranch, and many wild birds which came during the hot summer days.

> Our rooms were the guest rooms of the convento, or monastery, and we had the full benefit of the early matin songs of the wild birds–a cheerful awakening for a long busy day on the open range with the *vaqueros* who were rounding up the cattle.

The orchards and vineyards of the mission, including the gardens, must have totaled almost one hundred acres. In fact, seventy–six acres were confirmed to the Church by the United States Land Commission.

General Pico used the buildings as a residence and maintained a large stock ranch on what had been mission lands before secularization. He lived in a luxurious style and had a large household of trained servants, chiefly Indians. Like the grandee that he was, he entertained lavishly.

His silver and china table service made a brilliant display. His house hold furnishings were plain, but massive and luxurious. The plain old mission furniture was retained but many an expensive and more ornate piece had been added.

The general's "table afforded an ample style of living; the dinners consisted of five to six courses–all of the far– famed California Spanish cookery, which no nation–not even the French, has ever excelled. . . "

"At the mid–day and evening meals, and on the *veranda* in the evening, we were delightfully entertained by native musicians who played on three stringed instruments then mostly in vogue–the harp, violin and guitar.... After the noon dinner, all work was suspended for the customary two hour *siesta.* The cool rooms of the thick–walled adobe afforded a refreshing change from the July sunshine of the open plains."

Pleasants was impressed by dawn at San Fernando. "The rugged peaks of the Sierra Tujunga slowly emerged from the shadows of night, tinted rose and purple; and as the stars faded from sight, a band of clouds behind them turned to rose, then to gold, and the whole plain and the old mission buildings were flooded with a transparent golden light."

The youngster's memories of that week lasted a lifetime. In concluding his memoir of that event so many years earlier, he said: "Whatever may be the doubts as to the Pico title to the mission lands, I must say that the General took good care of the buildings and the orchards during his occupancy, and he surely knew how to entertain his friends and his pupils."

THE FRANCISCANS AT MISSION SAN FERNANDO—1938

Like all its sister establishments on New Spain's frontier, the Mission of San Fernando, Rey de España, was "a commonwealth between walls, a little world in itself set down amid a savage universe, a citadel of civilization within whose adobe walls religion and learning and human mercy could make head against the outer barbarism." Gradually, with the passage of time, a host of interesting stories and anecdotes about San Fernando Mission are emerging from the misty shadows of forgotten sources. One fascinating episode concerns the "almost return" of the Franciscans in the years immediately preceding World War 11.

Late in 1938, Archbishop John J. Cantwell was approached by John Steven McGroarty about the feasibility of entrusting the seventeenth of the missionary establishments to the friars. Wanting to revive his popular *Mission Play,* McGroarty offered to build a theater at San Fernando, where the world–famous production could be staged again in its historic setting. The long–time poet laureate for California agreed to direct and control the overall operation during his lifetime, allowing all the profits to benefit the friars and their work at San Fernando. He felt that the proximity of the mission to Los Angeles would ensure reasonably good patronage for the play.

Archbishop Cantwell was amenable to the idea, especially if the Franciscans would agree to cede their claims to the church in Camarillo to the archdiocese. They had inherited Saint Mary Magdalen Church from the lately deceased Juan Camarillo and Cantwell was anxious to advance that private chapel to parochial status if he could acquire its title.

On November 4, Fathers Augustine Hobrecht and Maynard Geiger met with the archbishop and Mr. McGroarty to discuss the question of San Fernando Mission. It was a cordial encounter during which the many advantages of the friars returning to their once prosperous missionary foundation were carefully examined. Father Maynard Geiger recorded in his diary that "personally, as I see the matter, I do not think the proposition will go through with the Provincial and the definitorium. Fr. Augustine who has imagination enough to see the benefits, is in favor of the substantial idea with modifications." But the Franciscan historian doubted whether other key members of his order shared Hobrecht's breadth of view.

Geiger's natural instincts were quite accurate, for when the proposal came before the provincial, Father Ildephonse Moser the Germanic friar "proved to be uninterested" and didn't bother giving any serious thought to acquiring what he considered to be just "another pile of adobes." It is interesting to speculate as to what eventual purpose the friars would have put San Fernando had they accepted its charge. Very likely it would have housed one or another of the seminary branches which were located later at Santa Barbara and San Luis Rey.

There are no official records about the overtures to the Franciscans concerning Mission San Fernando and like so many of the historical happenings associated with California's Catholic heritage, the passage of time has rather effectively blotted out most of the significant details. The only positive evidence is a singular entry in the multi–volume personal diary of the celebrated Franciscan historian, Father Maynard Geiger.

S.S. MISSION SAN FERNANDO—1941

In the midst of the perilous days of World War II, on the evening of November 25, 1943, the oil tanker S.S. Mission San Fernando ",as launched at Sausalito, California "to do her part towards preserving forever the privilege to live in California and America under the sacred banner of the Stars and Stripes."

The U.S. Maritime Commission's tanker was the first "bearing the name of a patron saint given years ago to the shrines of this state, which have merited the reverent study of a thousand historians in books that shall be read ...for a thousand years to come."

Providentially, the mission for which the thirty–first of the Marinship Corporation's vessels was named, had itself been re–dedicated, after decades of abandonment, on September 7th, 1941, just three months prior to that "day of treachery, a day of grave menace to our national honor, to our national existence."

As the noble ship, built to carry the life–blood and energy for the nation's floating fortresses of defense, slipped into the sea, the attentive onlooker could visualize a man of prophetic vision, clad in the humble robe of a Franciscan friar, standing near that very spot a century and a half earlier.

Expressing his admiration for the broad and magnificent harbor, Fray Junípero Serra predicted the rise of a large and populous state and then, gazing out over the western horizon, the first *Presidente* of the California Missions noted that "we have come to the land's end, to the rim of the western world; to go further we must have ships!"

According to records of the Maritime Administration, all the mission tankers had uniform characteristics: 523' 6" length; 68' beam; 29' 11" draft; 14 1/2 knots speed; 16,582 deadweight and 10,558 gross tons.

During the relatively short period of its active service, the S.S. Mission San Fernando was operated under lease from the government by the Deconhil Shipping Company. Eventually, the vessel was laid up in the National Defense Reserve Fleet at California's Suisun Bay. it was withdrawn and delivered to the Navy in October of 1947.

The ship, known in maritime annals as U.S.M.C. #1274, was ultimately consigned to the Reserve Fleet, at the Olympia, Washington site, where it remained. It was transferred back to the Maritime Administration in late 1957.

The Mission tankers, like the institutions whose names became relics of another age, symbolized the accomplishments of a generation to whom contemporary society owes an unredeemable debt.

THE BICENTENNIAL BELL— 1976

On October 25, 198 1, Bishop John J. Ward blessed the newly hung Bicentennial Bell at San Fernando Mission to commemorate the 200th birthday of *El Pueblo de Nuestra Señora de los Angeles*. Bells have played a vital part in the human drama from the very earliest days of recorded history. They have tolled births, deaths and marriages; they have announced wars, truces and plagues; they have heralded ceremonies, plays and games and they have counted out minutes, hours and days.

A medieval legend held that the bell was "invented" in Nola, in the Campania, Italy and that Saint Paulinus of Nola was responsible for its adoption into the church. Christians have always had a close association with bells. Saint Gregory of Tours noted, in 585, that bells were struck, shaken and pulled to awaken monks, a practice that has perdured into contemporary times.

Later, it was customary to commemorate historic events with the erection of a new bell. America's independence, for example, was ushered in by the ringing of bells. The "Liberty Bell" become a cherished symbol of the nation's heritage.

The first bell heard in Alta California was the one rung during Holy Mass offered on these shores in 1542. Since that time millions of bells have rung up and down the broad sunlit valleys of California.

A special bell at San Fernando to commemorate the birthday of Los Angeles is highly appropriate, for the mission is the only one of California's historic outposts located within the confines of the one–time *Pueblo de Nuestra Señora de los Angeles*. (A thirty–five bell carillon, one of seven in the Golden State, was installed at San Fernando Mission in the 1970s. Between 10 a.m. and 6 p.m. it plays the ancient melody *"Cantico de Alba"* every hour).

The bell erected for the bicentennial is quite old. It was hung at the *Rancho Cañada Largo,* near San Buenaventura Mission, shortly after the arrival of the Canet family in 1873. In more recent times it was mounted on a circular device in a small wooden tower, just outside the central ranchhouse.

When the Canet family trust finally sold the ranch a few years ago, Reni Pezzi gave the bell to San Fernando in memory of her late mother, Marie Louise Canet. It was her intention that the historic bell one day be associated with a California mission. San Fernando was an ideal setting, for the Sentous family (Marie Louise Canet was a Sentous) had been pioneers in Los Angeles. There is still a Sentous Street just west of the Los Angeles Convention Center.

The Bicentennial Bell, its damaged clapper removed for safety reasons, will long recall the 200th birthday of Los Angeles. Perhaps it can be blessed again when today's grand–children began celebration for the city's tricentennial.

INDIAN BASKETS AT SAN FERNANDO—1980s

The name "Marie Walsh" is well known in local historical circles. Her first book, *The Mission of the Passes*, published by the Times–Mirror Press in 1930, occasioned a personal commendation from Eugenio Cardinal

Pacelli, late Pope Pius XII. Then four years later, Marie wrote her classical treatise on *The Mission Bells of California* and that interesting volume is still the recognized authority in the field.

In subsequent decades, Miss Walsh was active as a journalist and publicist. She was a close friend of the famed and fugitive Archbishop Francisco Orozco y Jimenez of Guadalajara who spent many years of his exile in Southern California. Marie's assistance to the archbishop and her concern for the plight of the Mexicans persecuted by their hostile government was officially chronicled by Pope Pius XI who awarded her the *Pro Pontifice* medal in 1933.

In 1949, Marie married Mark Harrington (1882–1971), a prominent anthropologist, who was curator of the Southwest Museum. The couple lived in an adobe house Mark erected on Memory Park Avenue, just across the street from San Fernando Mission.

Mark had been director of the restoration for the Old Mission in the 1940s, working closely with Father Augustine O'Dea. He had earlier restored the Andres Pico adobe which is now the headquarters for the San Fernando Valley Historical Society.

During his many years as an internationally–known Indianologist, Mark Harrington gathered an outstanding collection of Indian baskets from tribes scattered across the nation. In mid 1981, Marie generously agreed to present the collection to San Fernando Mission, in honor of her late husband. The twenty–one baskets are publicly displayed in two cases, alongside the other fifty–four baskets associated with the Old Mission.

Louise Maynard, an expert in basketry at the Southwest Museum, carefully examined and identified each of the specimens, providing a short description as to origin, design and material. There are several superb examples of Indian craftsmanship in the collection. One Pima basket, for example, has a clearly recognizable figure of the diamond–back rattler.

Another comes from the Seneca Indians of New York State, a branch of the Iroquois nations. A utility basket with a fringe of corn husks, it resembles baskets fashioned by the Hopis of Arizona. Probably the most distinctive is a Navajo wedding basket. It has the sacred rattlesnake design with an opening so that the soul may depart and not be snatched up by evil spirits.

Later, Marie Walsh Harrington presented a rare Chumash basket to the Historical Museum of the Archival Center. Of all the Indian baskets, those made by the Chumash are the most exquisite and sought after.

BELLS AND GONGS AT SAN FERNANDO—1986

In a review of Marie Walsh's book, *The Mission Bells of California* (San Francisco, 1934), a reporter for the New York *Times* referred to the authoress as "the

Bell Lady of *El Camino Real,*" a title she retained throughout her long and interesting writing career. Though Marie write other volumes and hundreds of essays in succeeding years, her book on *The Mission Bells of California* remained the centerfold of her works and the one which brought her the most acclaim.

With Marie's death in 1986, her own personal collection of miniature bells was bequeathed to the Historical Museum of the Archival Center, at San Fernando Mission. That fascinating collection is now open to tourists and surely it is worth a trip to Mission Hills. The collection was begun in the early 1920s, when Marie made her first trek to all the California missions. It was her intention to have replicas of the bells from each of the twenty–one historic foundations.

Apparently, the major portion of the collection was sold or otherwise discarded years ago. Indications are that there were as many as several hundred bells at one time. Only forty–six remain. There are several very distinctive "call" bells, some of them marked with the name of a particular mission. Also in evidence are a number of miniature variations of the bell standards inaugurated along California's highways by Harriet Rebecca Piper Forbes.

There are segments of what was once a string of twenty–one bells called "Father Serra's Rosary." At an earlier date, several of the parts were either dismantled or broken apart, leaving only a portion of the original number. Fray Junípero Serra is portrayed on several of the "call" bells. It would appear that there were variations of this bell, possibly cast in the same molds, with only the name of the sponsoring mission altered.

An elaborately mounted bell, dated 1915, and apparently purchased at the Panama Exposition, has a California grizzly bear walking atop a triangular mounting. Chiseled into one side of the bell are the words: "1769 *El Camino Real.*" Another bell, suspended from a wooden cradle, has a handwritten inscription beneath the base which indicates that it was acquired from a Capuchin friar at San Juan Capistrano Mission on October 31, 1929. Then there is a bell from San Gabriel Mission fixed atop a curved ink drying apparatus. Beneath and around the base of the bell is a raised depiction of the rosary.

A miniature reproduction of the Liberty Bell was seemingly distributed in 1936 as a promotional gimmick by the Liberty Dairy Company, 277 Tehama Street, Douglas, Arizona. There is a variation of the same theme on another bell, probably indicating the existence of a whole set of similar miniatures. The famed Mission Inn is represented by several of the smaller bells, each one cast to resemble an original on display or otherwise associated with Riverside's famed resort. (Marie was married there years later)

One of the most fascinating items in the collection is a "crucifix bell" which carries an inscription around its base: "Remember the Missions." It was purchased at San Carlos Borromeo in 1935. California is not the only area represented by the bells. One charming little "tinkerbell" is obviously from China, another has an inscription "Prince Matchabelli," and a third carries the etched wording "1878 Saignelegier."

One of the largest collections of small or miniature bells is that amassed some years ago by Mr. and Mrs. A. C. Meyer of Saint Louis. In a booklet about that notable collection, Irene Leher says that "a California woman who had a collection of one thousand bells" had aroused Mr. Meyer's interest in gathering bells. That woman was Marie Walsh (later Mrs. M. R. Harrington). Very likely, many of Marie's bells found their way into the Meyer Collection.

STOLEN PAINTINGS RETURNED—1989

The principle in Moral Theology that says *"res clamat domino"* (a thing cries out for its legitimate owner) came to mind in early May of 1991, when Special Agent Thomas F. Dowd informed us that the Federal Bureau of Investigation had located two paintings purloined from San Fernando Mission over a decade ago.

In his letter, Mr. Dowd explained that, on August 16, 1989, "two books by Benjamin Franklin valued at $50,000 and $10,000 respectively were stolen from the Van Pelt Library at the University of Pennsylvania. Investigation revealed that the books were taken by someone representing himself as 'Greg Williams'."

This Greg Williams, later identified as William March Witherell of San Gabriel, California, "was arrested by the Federal Bureau of Investigation on January 5, 1990 and was charged with interstate transportation of stolen property." Among the hundreds of price–less books and religious objects found when authorities searched Witherell's home were two oil paintings that had long been missing from San Fernando Mission, together with the famed rendition of Our Lady of Sorrows stolen fourteen years earlier from San Gabriel Mission.

Digging back into the files, correspondence was unearthed about the robbery that occurred in the fall of 1981, along with the police report and an article that appeared in *The Sun and Breeze* for October 7, 1981:

Historical paintings valued at $10,000 were stolen from the San Fernando Mission in the 15100 block of San Fernando Mission Boulevard in Mission Hills, September 20, police said.

Police report the bandits forced open a side iron door, gaining entry to the church convento, and removed two historical paintings, both of the Madonna, and each worth $5,000.

Police further report that the paintings were last seen on the morning of the 20th hanging on the inner walls of the locked room of the convento, but when church administrators returned about 4:30 that afternoon, they found the iron gate open, the lock on the floor in the middle of the room and the two paintings missing.

Further research by the F.B.I. indicated that Witherell had been arrested on July 20, 1977, for the theft of a painting and several books from Santa Ines Mission in Solvang. Happily, those items were recovered at the scene.

The objects found in the Witherell home, which included numerous other books and artifacts that probably belonged to one or another of the California missions, were transported to Philadelphia where they were used in evidence along with the two items from the Van Pelt Library, for the trial of the perpetrator. The paintings arrived back in Mission Hills on September 24th, 1991 and, after they were professionally restored and cleaned, they were rehung in the room which they adorned for so many years.

One is a 16th century oil painting of the Annunciation which is identified only as belonging to the "School of Correggio"; the other an 18th century oil depiction of "Hagar and the Angel". Also returned with the paintings were five other items, including a wooden sculpture of "Madonna and Child" and two brass candlesticks.

Whatever else might be said about the man who quietly slipped the paintings over the wall at San Fernando Mission so many years ago, he surely must be acknowledged as a man of exquisite taste. The paintings he took were among the finest then belonging to the Old Mission. He never attempted to sell them, but kept them for his own enjoyment.

Should he ever return to Mission Hills, he will find the two paintings back in their place, this time alarmed and firmly anchored into place. They've already traveled extensively, probably more than the artists who painted them in the 16th century.

SHIPSTAD COLLECTION AT SAN FERNANDO— 1990s

For almost fifty years, the Shipstad name has been associated with one of the most exquisite and artistic Madonna collections ever assembled. The ceramic statues were eventually presented to San Fernando Mission for permanent exhibition. Minnesota–born Lula Anna Shipstad (1907–1990), whose name was legendary in the world of Catholic charities, spent many years gathering her collection which she exhibited publicly no fewer than forty times.

Twenty–four of the Madonnas were designed and fired by the late Clarise Harvey (d.1978), a long– time resident of Encino. Though not a Catholic, Ms. Harvey's interest in symbolism and detail makes her renditions both accurate and beautiful. Each of the Madonnas was envisioned to represent either countries or themes. With the exception of Our Lady of Chavez Ravine, the Madonna of Baseball, all the statues are one–of–a–kind.

The charming statue of Our Lady of Japan has a cherry blossom halo and an obi with two folds at the back denoting Mary's ancestry in the royal house of King David. The African Madonna and Child stands apart from the others inasmuch as it is the only one made of terra cotta. In the statue of Our Lady of China, Mary is portrayed in authentic Chinese garments.

Perhaps the most colorful statue in the collection is the Belgian Madonna, Our Lady of Leopoldville. Mary is depicted carrying a basket, with the infant Jesus safely tucked away in the fold of her broad sash.

The portrayal of the Immaculate Heart of Mary has Our Lady seated with the Child in her lap. Twelve jewels and an equal number of peaks, representing the apostles, form the halo. The contrast between the violet bisque dress and the yellow scarf add technical interest as well as beauty. In the statue of Our Lady of the Prairies, the notion of thanksgiving is featured. This depiction has a captivating simplicity that eloquently expresses the American spirit of gratitude. Mary holds a sheaf of grains and at her feet are other symbols of the harvest.

Under the patronage of Our Lady of Ethiopia, the Blessed Lady is pictured with outstretched arms, the blue one representing god the Father and the white one portraying God the Son. The dove is Holy Spirit. Finally, the Holy Trinity is shown placing a crown on Mary's head.

The artist's great interest in the missionary work of the Catholic Church is evident in her portrayal of Mary, Queen of the Apostles. The Blessed Mother is holding the Infant Jesus against a backdrop of lattice work, attended on each side by an apostle. The evangelical theme is further evident in the statue of Our Lady, Queen of the Missions. The cross–topped world rests in Mary's hands and, at her feet, are replicas of the various missionary areas–India's Tai Majal, Africa's grass hut, Japan's Fujiyama and America's desert cactus. Symbolically, Mary is crushing the head of the serpent.

And there are more. Of all the many Madonna collections on exhibit around the country, none surpasses the artistic works gathered by Mrs. Edwin Shipstad and now displayed at San Fernando Mission.

GOD'S ACTUAL GRACES

The working of God's actual graces never fail to amaze His people. A most interesting parochial program could be staged by asking a dozen or so converts to relate how they were led to the Church. More often than not, their stories provide insight into the marvelous workings of the Godhead.

Several years ago, a lady from New Brunswick wrote to "the priest at San Fernando Mission" with this tale of her first association with the Church–and her eventual reception of Baptism.

> Four of us visited your mission during Easter week on a trek sponsored by the Native American Society. I had never before been inside a Catholic Church and I was utterly fascinated by the simplicity and beauty of the altar and its furnishings.
>
> The red sanctuary lamp fascinated me and I decided to investigate what it was and what it signified. When I got back home, I called a Catholic friend (who didn't know the answer), but she put me in touch with a priest.
>
> Over the next few months I entered the RCIA program, learned about the Church and was received into the local Catholic community. It was the high point of my life and I cherish my newly found faith. And it all started at your mission.

Imagine how a sanctuary candle at San Fernando Mission proved to be the instrumental for bringing someone into the Catholic Church! But that lady's experience is not unique. People can be and often are impressed by other "accidentals" of the Church–the vestments, the candles, the flowers, the music, the liturgy and, hopefully, even the homilies preached at Holy Mass.

A few years before the American Revolution, John Adams happened into a Catholic church in Philadelphia. He recounted his impression in a letter to his wife, Abigail:

> This afternoon, led by curiosity and good company, I strolled away to mother church, or rather grandmother church. I mean the Romish chapel . . . The entertainment was to me most awful and affecting . . . their Pater nosters and ave Marias; their holy water; their crossing themselves perpetually . . . their bowing, kneelings and genuflections before the altar. The dress of the priest was rich white lace. His pulpit was velvet and gold.
>
> The altar piece was very rich, little images and crucifixes about; wax candles lighted up. But how shall I describe the picture of our Saviour in a frame of marble over the altar, at full length, upon the cross in the agonies, and the blood dropping and streaming from his wounds! ... and the assembly chanted most sweetly and exquisitely. Here is everything which can lay hold of the eye, ear and imagination . . . I wonder how Luther ever broke the spell.

While Adams was anything but sympathetic towards Catholicism, the "entertainment" of the Mass, he wrote, "can charm and bewitch the ignorant." He could not deny the evidence of his senses. He, himself, by no means a "simple and ignorant" critic, had clearly been captivated. Nor was he the last Protestant to be struck by the beauty of the Catholic liturgy.

Though John Adams died a Protestant, there are countless others who began their trek toward Rome precisely because they were entranced by the beauty of our worship and the adornment of our churches. Surely that can only be good .

SAN FERNANDO MISSION—NEVER A PARISH

San Fernando Mission is one of the few California missions that has never functioned as a canonical parish. There were several attempts to bestow a parochial title to the Old Mission, but each one proved ineffectual.

On August 9, 1834, for example, Governor Jose Figueroa issued a decree confiscating the California missions. Shortly thereafter, according to Father Zephyrin Engelhardt, San Fernando Mission was made "a parish of the second class" by legislative edict.

The Franciscans, however, never recognized the action, "since they would not allow themselves to be called parish priests." In as much as it wasn't within the power of the government to create parishes, the action by the civil realm had no canonical force.

Fray Blas Ordaz, the last Franciscan to serve as residential priest at San Fernando Mission, left in 1847. In the years immediately following, the spiritual needs of the few people living in the area were cared for by priests from the Plaza Church of *Nuestra Señora de los Angeles*. The last entries in the register books are dated 1852. Extant evidence indicates that Father Peter Verdaguer offered the last Mass at the Old Mission in 1874.

The town of San Fernando sprang up about two miles east of the Old Mission as a stop for the Southern Pacific Railroad. In 1902, Bishop George T. Montgomery established the Parish of Saint Ferdinand and appointed Father James. E. Burns as pastor. During the early months of his tenure, Father Burns made the Old Mission his headquarters. Within a short while, however, he erected a frame church on Pico Street. Not long afterwards, he took up residence in a house close to the church.

In 1903, Father Antonio Le Bellegay became pastor at San Fernando. And it was during his time that property was purchased for a church at Newhall. Bellegay remained until 1906, when he retired to France.

The ailing Father James S. O'Neill then came to San Fernando, on the condition that his appointment would be temporary. Between 1908 and 1912, the parish was administered by the Missionary Sons of the Immaculate Heart of Mary (Claretians). In 1912, Bishop Thomas J. Conaty asked Father Gerald Bergan to assume the pastorate of Saint Ferdinand and it was he who purchased the residence at 719 South Brand Boulevard. Father Bergan remained until 1919.

Father James B. Roure served as pastor from 1918 until 1922 and, during his time, he did research which resulted in a fifteen page monograph on the *History of Mission San Fernando* which was directed primarily at arousing interest in the mission as a tourist center.

In 1923, Bishop John J. Cantwell suggested to the Oblates of Mary Immaculate that they assume charge of the parish of Saint Ferdinand which, at that time, included most of the San Fernando Valley, together with Palmdale in the Mojave desert. Cantwell also requested the Oblates to take on the responsibility of looking after the Old Mission which was then in almost total ruins, except for the *convento*. Having recently been expelled from their foundations in Mexico, the Oblates agreed to the bishop's proposal and, on August 2, 1923, they took canonical possession of Saint Ferdinand's Parish.

SANTOS AT SAN FERNANDO MISSION

One of the most fascinating exhibits at San Fernando Mission is a collection of carved images of the saints or *santos* which were popular in the southwest and, to a lesser extent, in California.

The colonists, isolated as they were from Mexico City, the main source of European supplies, brought with them from Spain the craft of wood carving, a skill in which they often excelled. With their crude tools, they carved *vigas,* corbels, doors, chests, chairs and other furnishings for the missions and *pueblos*. They were especially adept at carving images of the saints. As often as not, they used pieces of soft cottonwood or pine.

When an image was ready for painting, it was covered with a mixture of glue made from horses' hoofs and gesso, burned or calcined gypsum, or a mixture of piñon gum with gesso. Then the artist painted the surface with colorful mineral paints.

Throughout the missions and in other early adobes and outside areas, there were numerous tiny niches hollowed out of the walls to accommodate the images of the saints. Most frequently, the image was a *Santo Niño*, the Holy Child, gaily dressed with silks, ribbons, laces and paper flowers. In addition to the *Santo Niño,* the patron of the family, there were nearly a hundred other *santos*.

Another common rendition was the crucifix. The *Cristo* also appears in other forms, as at Gethsemane, or as a child in the arms of Saint Joseph, Saint Anthony, *Nuestra Señora de Carmel* and others.

Santo Niño de Atocbe was also popular. He was generally seated on a chair, with a cape around his shoulders and a flat–crowned, broad–rimmed, black hat on his head. The *Santo Niño de Prague* was gaudily attired with his right hand raised in benediction. Next in frequency to the image of the Holy Child is that of *Nuestra Santisima,* the Blessed Mother. She is represented in many different ways; as *Nuestra Señora del Rosario* or under her titles of Mercy, Light, Sorrows, Pilar and Guadalupe. Probably the most common is *Nuestra Señora de Dolores* or *Mater Dolorosa*.

The artists were also fond of using more obscure Spanish saints or personages from the Old Testament. Moses is often portrayed, dressed in an oriental garb with a staff and crawling serpent. Often the saint can be identified by habit or dress. San Cristobal, for example, always has his garments tucked up over his knees.

Interestingly enough, many of the *santos* have lost an arm or hand because they were broken off and thrown out to calm a storm or repel a demon. They were sometimes burned to make "holy ashes" for anointing.

Some of the sixteen *santos* in the collection at San Fernando actually predate the mission era and were probably brought to Alta California from Latin America. The four mounted apostles are antique Gothic wood carvings, either from Germany or Austria (c. 1475). Though most of the *santos* are somewhat crude in workmanship, they exude a charm and simplicity bespeaking the depth of the Catholic faith in earlier generations.

ARTISTIC RESTORATION AT THE OLD MISSION

The costly and extensive repair work done on the convento building at San Fernando Mission, following the disastrous earthquake of 1971, was more structural than artistic. Inasmuch as the primary consideration then was functional preservation, the challenge of restoring the building's artistic embellishments was left for another time.

Shortly after the establishment *of Los Padrinos de la Mision de San Fernando,* early in 1986, founders William Hannon and Frank Modugno suggested that high priority be given to restoring the *convento's* traditional ornamentation.

There is evidence that from a very early time the front of the *convento,* in the vicinity of the main portal, presented an ornate appearance, due to painted imitations of stone and brick trimmings in the Mooresque manner. Indications of this type of decorative treatment are not discernible in the early sketches or photographs of the mission, nor is such ornamentation described in written records, factors which make the subject all the more fascinating.

Throughout the interior of the building, the impression is given that indigenous decorators were encouraged to portray the familiar figures of their everyday lives. In other words, the walls of the building became a kaleidoscope of primitive Indian lore.

In one area of the *gran sala*, for example, a wall space approximately 6 by 4 feet was occupied by a distemper painting on plaster showing human figures of Indians engaged in activities beneath trees or vines which seem to be bearing fruit. Another of the paintings portrayed an Indian hunting deer with a bow and arrow. Over the frame of a doorway, an igneous ball (perhaps the sun) surmounted the extended radiation.

At some undetermined date, the murals were overlaid by whitewash and a design showing European influence (although executed with primitive techniques) was superimposed. Elaborately painted wall decorations around the doors and on the walls of the convento were partly uncovered and restored under the direction of the late M. R. Harrington in the 1940s. Frank Gutierrez and Jean L'Empereur were the artists.

Following the structural reinforcement of the early 1970s, four massive antique Roman arches were installed in the *convento*, an addition that resulted in the painting out of the Harrington murals. Fortunately, there are photographs from the earlier years which could be used to reproduce the elaborate details of those designs.

Now, *Los Padrinos* were anxious to restore the interior of the *convento* to its earlier, more representative state. Dr. Norman Neuerburg, Professor Emeritus of Art at California State University, Dominguez Hills, was retained to carry out this project. Dr. Neuerburg had been associated with restorative work at San Fernando for forty–five years, as a young boy, student, professor and now restorative artist.

Work began in the Governor's Room, early in November of 1987. The first stage of bringing alive the long–forgotten murals took some months. Later, plans were drawn up for continuing the artistic embellishments in other rooms of the *convento*.

SAN FERNANDO, REY DE ESPAÑA MISSION

The seventeenth of the California missions has a noble history. Its natural beauty was described by G. M. Waseurtz: "The nearer one approaches to San Fernando, the more bold becomes the scenery. The hilly, steep ridges which separated the gold plains from those of San Fernando were really romantic. Steep broken rocks, green flower–clothed hills tufted with mountain oak, and brooks lined with salix gave a softness to the landscape which was enchanting. The river at the gold places was very shallow, and not always plentifully supplied with water, though encouragement was held out for the

gold–washer to obtain it out of the sand of the gulches of the river by turning the river, as they called it. That means leading off the stream to another channel. The willow and oaks were plentiful in this neighborhood and first rate for turning."

The early natives at San Fernando were especially adept in the handling of iron. According to one early commentator, the ancient priests stood in their blacksmith shops, before the flaming forge and made the anvil ring and the sparks spring out with a lively to zest as any smith of the present day. From their shops were turned out clever bear traps that enabled them to protect the mission herds from all wild beasts. Hammers, flatirons, scissors, pulleys, plowshares, scales for measuring gold and scales for measuring rations–all of these and many more are still left as their well–preserved relics.

San Fernando was famous also for the inlaying of iron with silver; an art employed principally in the decoration of bits and bridles. The effect of these shining decorations upon a horse, prancing madly in the sunshine, and with every toss of his head sending out myriad of scintillations, can be imagined, when, on a gala day, many young *caballeros* and *señoritas* were gathered together for a good time and a display.

Father Juan Caballeria reported that "this section of the country is still devoted to vinegrowing, and a large annual output of wine is still made. The early fathers took the lead and tons and tons of the finest wine were turned out from their great winery. San Fernando, being in close proximity, was famous also for brandy making, *aguardiente,* literally fire–water, as it was then called." The priests also noted that "the Indians were especially interested in the building of houses and assisted in all possible ways for the convenience and strength of the mission buildings and the comfort of the houses occupied by the *padres.*

"They felled great trees on the mountains and brought them down for rafters; they readily took up the trade of stone cutter from their familiarity in making stone mortars and vessels in earlier days, and it is quite likely that the ease and perfection with which they did cement work that, in Southern California, at any rate, they were readily trained by their previously having used *asphaltum* so successfully in their own work. The cement work in the mission buildings themselves is of such a remarkably durable character as to outwear even the stones which it holds in place. It is harder than flint, and this, too, after the lapse of more than one hundred and thirty years. The trade of coppersmith was not unknown to them. The copper bowls which they made were handsomely decorated and finished with most perfect *repousse* around the tops. These were used on the altars and in the niches of the churches for holy water.

The priestly commentator also observed that the

women converts performed extremely useful tasks for the mission enterprise. "Under the guidance of the friars they became the weavers and menders of the mission, and were very skillful in this work. They were led most readily from their knowledge of basketry and its intricacy of patterns to the making of Mexican drawn work. In this they displayed all that rare and unusual talent of symbolization found in savage art, which, as refined and chastened by their Christian teaching into the finest of all fine service cloths for priest, chapel and altar."

Noting that all their work was "filled with a perfect meaning and symbolism," Father Caballeria concluded by saying that "it was indeed their catechism well learned and emblazoned upon the work of hand, heart and brain" that characterized their talented productions.

SYMBOLOGY OF THE ALTAR FURNISHINGS

One of the most precious relics of statuary still preserved in California is the depiction of San Fernando (1198–1252) a life–size replica sent to the area by the King of Spain in memory of his revered predecessor. The 125 pound statue, carved from a single piece of wood, occupied the place of eminence in the chapel at San Fernando Mission from the earliest days of the institution's foundation.

When plans were made to install the Ezcaray altar furnishings in the sanctuary of the Old Mission, Richard Merin decided that the focal point of the restored reredos would be the historic statue of Saint Ferdinand after whom the seventeenth of the missions along *El Camino Real* was named.

In Spanish artistic circles, renditions of the Holy Trinity were fairly common in the 16th century. San Fernando is portrayed as being welcomed into heaven by God the Father (to his left), God the Son (to his right) and God the Holy Spirit, represented by a dove at the pinacle of the reredos. An angel holds a heavenly crown on a pillow. The entire scene is overshadowed by a baldachino whose tassels recall the seven sacraments, as well as the gifts of the Holy Spirit. The rays emanating from the statue are reminiscent of the glory associated with eternal bliss.

At the right of the upper panel of the reredos is a statue of Saint Philip Neri, the titular patron of the chapel at Ezcaray where these altar furnishings were originally erected in the early 1600s. On the opposite panel is a kneeling statue of Saint Dominic who holds a wooden rosary which brought about a wholly new dimension of devotion to Mary, the Mother of the Savior.

Below, Blessed Junípero Serra holds a copy of his celebrated *Marian Novena* in his right hand and a missionary crucifix in the other. Around his neck is a cross

of Caravaca in which was customarily housed a relic of Ramon Lull. Saint Mary Magdalen, long a highly revered devotional figure in Spain, is attired in the sack-cloth traditionally associated with repentant sinners.

There are three printed scenes on the reredos. The one above the tabernacle is a farm scene in Zaragoza, while the one to the right is the tree at which the figure of Our Lady of the Pillar was found. The opposite panel portrays the havoc of a storm toppling a tree, thus revealing the statue of Our Lady which had been hidden for fear of desecration.

Above the tabernacle, *Nuestra Señora del Pilar* stands atop a marble stand as she appeared to Saint James, the Apostle. It was under his title that Our Lady was honored as patroness of the Spanish monarchy. Immediately in front of the statue is a relic of San Fernando, displayed in a handsome metallic reliquary. Beneath the tabernacle ledge is one of the "throne" angels which is constantly chanting the *Te Deum*. A massive wooden triptych has been fitted into the Gospel side of the reredos. It depicts the four evangelists, surrounded by a wooden replica of Our Lady of Guadalupe.

The impressive silver door concealing the specially–fabricated tabernacle is adorned with a scene of the Lamb of God. It is surrounded by seven letters representing the seals of the Apocalypse which will be opened when Christ returns for the final judgement. On a wooden plaque at the center of the altar of repose are the Latin words of consecration.

RESTORATION OF SAINT FERDINAND

One of the most historic relics of wooden statuary still preserved in California is the depiction of San Fernando (1198–1252) a life–size replica sent to California by the King of Spain in memory of his noble predecessor.

The handsomely executed likeness of the Iberian peninsula's third king is mentioned in the inventory of March 12, 1849, which states that "there is also a statue in grand style of San Fernando on a wooden bracket and in colored garments" among the mission's holdings,

In subsequent years, after the abandonment of the church and its gradual deterioration from the elements, the statue was moved to a pedestal at the right of the altar in the temporary chapel located near the end of the *convento* building. With the erection of Saint Ferdinand's Church, in the nearby village of San Fernando, the statue was given primatial status among the trilogy of saints adorning the reredos of the central altar.

After the restoration of the church at Mission San Fernando, in 1941, the hand–carved, polychrome statue was returned and displayed on an extended ledge, directly above the main altar of sacrifice. During the devastating earthquake which shook the north end of the triangular–shaped San Fernando Valley, on February 9, 1971, "the historic statue of Saint Ferdinand pulled away from its moorings and careened through the air, striking the altar with a force strong enough to splinter the wooden *mensa.* "

The delicate project of restoring the 15th century work of art was entrusted to Fred Rolla, one of the nation's leading restorative experts. He carefully sifted the rubble and was able to locate and identify twenty–seven pieces of the disfigured statue. The sixty–five year old artist deftly glued and cemented each of the remnants with dowels, then filled, leafed and painted them. Crevices were leveled with gesso and wood putty. Once the various parts of the twelve–color theme had been properly retouched, a flat varnish was applied over the whole surface. After eight days of intensive effort, the talented Rolla had restored the statue's integrity in an almost unbelievable exhibit of artistic craftsmanship.

When the new church at California's seventeenth mission was opened to the public, the be–crowned statue of Saint Ferdinand, arrayed in the colorful garments of his kingly office, sceptre in hand, resumed its rightful place of prominence in the institution bearing the name and patronage of San Fernando, Rey de España.

THE MADONNA ROOM

Marian devotion is intricately linked to the old missions along *El Camino Real.* The earliest works–of–art in California were statues and paintings of Mary, some of which are still in place at one or another of the historic foundations.

From 1492 onwards, devotion to Mary has been expressed in the New World in a remarkably diverse manner. Even today in Mexico, for example, almost every village has its own Madonna tailored to local customs, needs and expressions.

In an effort to capture and portray the universality of devotions associated with Our Lady, a *Madonna Room* was opened at San Fernando Mission and therein the Blessed Mother is exhibited in a cross section of her many titles. Interestingly enough, the exhibit is housed in a room never before open to the public. Thought to have been the mission's *carcel* or prison, the room has been totally refurbished in memory of Eugenie Hannon.

Presently there are three major collections in the Madonna Room–those gathered over the years by Lula Anna Shipstad (44 statues), E. Jean Hill (43 statues and 8 plaques) and Anita Watson (11 statues and 33 plaques).

In addition to the core collections, there are numerous other statues, plaques, paintings and depictions from a host of sources. Among the most spectacular are a cloisonné reproduction of Murillo's Assumption (belonged to J. Francis Cardinal McIntyre), an original tin *Refugio* (brought to California by Bishop Francisco Garcia Diego), a mother–of–pearl Nativity Scene (estate of Msgr. Robert E. Brennan) and a large marble reproduction of Michelangelo's *Pieta* carved in 1499. The walls are adorned with several paintings of Our Lady, including one of the Madonna of Guadalupe which has been at San Fernando Mission since the 1790s.

The famous artist Pattarino is represented by several of his ceramic masterpieces which are now highly sought–after by collectors.

Among the works by local artists are three kiln–cast depictions of Our Lady made by Betsy Brown in the late 1950s.

There is also a sampling of the philatelic portrayals of Mary that have appeared on stamps issued by the United States Postal Service since 1968. In an adjoining case is a collection of colorful vellum cards onto which classic depictions of Mary have been attached.

The elaborate rosary is an oversized version originally manufactured from alabaster as an adornment for a large statue. Over the years the rosary has been separated from its original setting. There are numerous panels or plaques in the Anita Watson Collection, most of them originating in Europe during the earliest years of this century. Outstanding in that collection is a hand–executed wooden Madonna with the face of Mary and the infant carved in ivory.

Hanging on the eastern wall is a hand–fabricated and framed cutout of the *Hail Mary* in its entirety. It dates from the late 19th century and likely originated in Austria. The *petit point* portrayal of The Madonna of the Chair is a copy of the famous painting by Raphael in the Pitti Palace in Florence. It was embroidered by the late Mary Moore of Hollywood.

Viewing the portrayals of the Blessed Mother at San Fernando Mission is enhanced by various musical renditions of the Ave *Maria* which are played as background music. Initial reaction to the new exhibit has been extremely favorable. Youngsters from the Los Angeles Unified School District are especially fascinated.

SAN LUIS, REY DE FRANCIA (1798)

"KING OF THE MISSIONS"

The eighteenth of the California missions, named for ng Saint Louis IX of France (1215–1270), was located in the Santa Margarita Valley, an elliptical plain about ten miles long from east to west, and bounded on the sides and at the lower end by smooth green hills. Once among the richest and most populous of the early Franciscan establishments, San Luis Rey boasted a splendid church, the most elaborate in its design and architecture as any of the mission structures.

At the time of its completion, in 1815, the church was an exceedingly grand and imposing edifice. Its walls were partly of adobe and partly of sun–burned bricks and cement, and were nearly five feet thick. The interior was remarkable for its space and for the grace and symmetry of all its parts. A huge tower ran up by its side upon which was a belfry containing eight bells, each marked "South Boston, 1799!"

A visitor to San Luis Rey, in 1867, recalled that the walls of the church were profusely decorated and hung with fine pictures. He was told by a local resident that "only a few years before the altar was a gem of artistic excellence, many of its decorations being of the purest gold and silver, while the external and internal pediments all bore unmistakable evidences of art in the minuteness of their design and ornamentation."

Upon returning to the mission a few years later, however, the same visitor noted that "the tower had fallen and crumbled, and the beautiful bells had disappeared." Even then, while falling into decay, "this old mission presents lingering evidences of pretentiousness. Up to 1849 there was not a break in the noble structure, although it had been abandoned in 1883–4."

He further noted the curious manner in which the chancel's floor had been undermined by persons searching for buried treasure. The place was then "tenanted only by two great white owls, but in the sunny angles of the exterior and in the tiles of the roof were swarms of bees and colonies of swallows. These or some other agents had carried to the ledges above the belfry the seeds of the cactus and the sage which are growing there."

The ravages of time and abandonment rapidly reduced the "King of the Missions" and its stately church, once the grandest upon the coast, into a mass of tottering ruins. Only in another generation would that proud outpost on the Spanish frontier be restored to its former regal grandeur. George Watson Cole stated, in 1910, that "the old missions are certainly the most characteristic works of man to be found in California. The early history of the State while under Spanish domination is so intimately associated with them that no more appropriate and artistic decorations can be placed on the walls of its educational institutions, libraries, public buildings and homes than the beautiful views of them that can so easily be procured in some of the various forms that have" been passed down the annals concerning the state's earliest foundations.

RESTORATION AT SAN LUIS REY

San Luis Rey was one of the later missions, founded only in 1798. Between that year and 1834 it grew into the largest of the frontier establishments along *El Camino Real.* The mission was the work of one man, Fray Antonio Peyri. A visitor to San Luis Rey in the early 1840s recalled that "the buildings . . . are the most beautiful, the most regular and the most solid in whole California." There was nothing like it then along the Pacific Slope.

Besides the church, finished in 1815, Peyri built a huge quadrangle which was already substantially finished by 1804, though the building program continued until 1813. Only in 1879 were the finishing touches put on the church in the form of a dome and a lantern.

When the remains of the mission were measured by Zephyrin Engelhardt in 1904, it was found that the buildings had covered an area of over six acres. The mission had a frontage of 600 feet from east to west, while extending back 450 feet.

The buildings were fashioned of adobe and one story in height. The facade of the church was of brick, as were the arcades. Above the single story was a flat roof bordered by a parapet. The interior arcades numbered eighty–eight. The church was cruciform in style.

The Franciscans served at San Luis Rey until 1846. There is no record of any priest living there in later times until 1892, when the friars returned to the mission where they remain today. By the time of their return, there was little left. Even the church was in partial decay. Several rows of brick arches stood, but all the living quarters and the workshops had fallen back into the adobe dust of the earth.

Father Joseph O'Keefe began the task of rebuilding at San Luis Rey. He restored about a fourth of the original quadrangle. The remaining adobe ruins were leveled and the ground put to agricultural use. The long row of arches along the west end of the property were left in place. They were incorporated into the restored buildings in modern times.

In 1926, a section of the tower fell during the night. It was repaired during the same year. In the 1930s, the east wing of Peyri's quadrangle was rebuilt. Between 1948 and 1950, the friars completed the quadrangle. At that time, the grounds were beautified and a fountain erected in front of the mission. Excavations were made of the early guard house and of the gardens and waterworks across the road during the 1950s. These later have now been restored to a great extent.

Today San Luis, Rey de Francia, reigns once again as the "King of the California Missions." Visitors can identify with the comments made by Auguste Bernard Duhaut–Cilly who visited the mission in 1817:

This edifice, very beautifully modeled and supported by its numerous pillars, has the aspect of a palace. The green valley in which the building is situated extends further than the eye can see to the north, where the fine landscape terminates on the summit of high mountains.

SANTA INES (1804)

MISSION OF THE PASSES

In 1798, Fray Fermin Francisco de Lasuén dispatched a military party with instructions to locate a suitable site for a mission midway between Santa Barbara and La Purísima Concepción. The chaplain for that expedition was Fray Estevan Tapis. Some years later, on September 17, 1804, Tapis blessed the ground and raised the cross for what was to be the nineteenth of the California missions on a *ranchería* known to the Indians as Alajulapu, three miles east of present–day Buellton.

Santa Ines Mission was ideally situated in a valley inhabited by natives who maintained contact with the more unfriendly Tulare tribes. It was the hope of Tapis that converts at Santa Ines would carry Christianity to the pagans of the eastern *sierras*. On the very day Santa Ines Mission was founded, Tapis baptized twenty–seven children of the local natives. Before leaving, he appointed Friars José Antonio Calzada and Romualdo Gutierrez to care for the newest establishment along *El Camino Real*.

By the close of that first year, there were 122 Indian neophytes at Santa Ines and, by the beginning of 1806, there were 570 natives associated with the Old Mission. From 1804 to 1812, an extensive building program was carried on. The walls of the church, habitations for the *padres*, dwellings for the soldiers and their families, adobe homes for the Indian converts, warehouses, granaries and other structures were erected.

On December 21, 1812, much of the work was undone by an earthquake that rendered the church unsafe and left numerous other buildings in shambles. The following year, a long structure was erected to serve as a church, but it wasn't until 1817 that the present church was completed. Dedicated on July 4th, its interior was modeled after the one at Santa Barbara Mission.

Beginning in 1810, when Mexico's revolt against Spain commenced, Santa Ines, in common with the other missions, received no further aid from the mother country and was compelled not only to support itself but to provide food, clothing and money for the garrison at Santa Barbara. The Santa Ines Indians objected to being forced to work for the idle soldiers and their resentment flared into rebellion on February 21, 1824. That uprising extended to Santa Barbara and La Purísima.

The Indians set fire to many buildings at Santa Ines but when it appeared that the flames would destroy the church, their anger subsided and they helped to save the edifice. All the workshops, barracks and habitations of the guards were destroyed. Then the revolting natives fled to the Tulares.

During the years prior to 1834, the *padres* fought to keep the mission afloat under the oppression of successive civil administrators. The final blow came in 1836, when the newly–appointed Governor, Mariano Chico, arrived unexpectedly at Santa Ines. He determined to entrust the mission to a civil commissioner, in the person of José Maria Ramirez. By 1839, conditions were deplorable.

Though matters temporarily improved during the tenure of Governor Manuel Micheltorena, the "Mission of the Passes" never again functioned in its envisioned role. Rather, it was to become a cherished monument to the ideals and accomplishments of missionary zeal along the Pacific Slope.

LAY PARTICIPATION AT SANTA INES—1874

A report written on March 8, 1814, by Fray Francisco Xavier Uría noted that the Indians at Santa Inés, in the pagan state, "neither knew nor used any other musical instruments than a wooden tube which resembled the flute, opened at both ends, which produced a buzzing sound disagreeable to the ears." He went on to say that after being exposed to the civilizing influence of the missions, they became "fond of music, learning it easily by memory."

The Franciscan chronicler gives a description of how the Indians were taught to sing at divine services, one of the earliest efforts of "participation of the laity in California annals."

> The singers were men who had been chosen in their boyhood, and carefully trained for their good voices. Of course, they were taught reading and writing.
>
> They would sing the Gregorian Chant in the choir loft or gallery in the rear of the church. Access to it was through a little room on the ground floor next to the church facing the inner court or patio . . . During the few– years when the seminary existed at the mission, 1844–1850, the seminarians recited the Divine Office with the Fathers in this gallery.
>
> The Indian singers would sing the *Introitus* and all other portions of the High Mass as found in the Graduals or large music sheets and books having the parts in square notes. Vespers were also sung from the *Vesperale*. Even much later, when but few of the singers survived, whenever there would be a High Mass the Gregorian or Plain Chant was sung.
>
> Instrumental music was played by the band, not as accompaniment, but when the singing terminated in places. Violin, violoncello, bassviolo and even a triangle constituted the musical outfit.

The chief singers at Mission Santa Ines were Louis Anasoyu as bass, and Venancio Lamlawinat as contralto.

During Holy Week all the singing and the ceremonies were observed. The *Mandatum,* during which the officiating priest would, in the sanctuary, wash the feet of some old Indian men, was carried out musically by the Indian choir. A violin would indicate the right tone or note. Everything was practiced with the missionary beforehand.

The first Indians of the Mission were such as had belonged to Mission Santa Barbara, but were natives of the Santa Ines district. When the mission was started, those who wished could leave Santa Barbara Mission and join Santa Ines. It was a great help to the Fathers, because these neophytes would introduce the customs they had learned at the older mission. In matters musical, they followed the older mission choir. They were especially enthusiastic about Father [Fermin] Lasuen, the Superior of all the Missions, who would stay at Santa Barbara at times. He must have been a great musician in church music, for the neophytes at Santa Ines many years later would a–rain mention *"Dehunto Padre Lashuen"* as authority on anything concerning their singing.

On great feasts, and also on Sundays, the rosary would be recited in the evening. The choir would sing in Spanish or Latin the *Pater Noster, Ave Maria,* the *Gloria Patri,* and the mystery, whereupon the missionary or later the secular priests would recite in Spanish the Hail Mary ten times with the people. A litany would also be recited or sung.

The *Viene El Alba* would be sung after the prayers at daybreak, as the name implies – "The Dawn is coming."

The *alcalde* would go around the village and call out: *A Misa! A Misa!* In this way also other services were announced.

Thus the Indians during the Mission period enjoyed happy times. It was a pity that they were not allowed to continue to live in that manner always. They had to yield to white greed: Satan himself must have envied the neophytes.

FERNANDITO OF SANTA INES—1850s

Much of the early history of the Franciscan missions, as well as the customs of the aboriginal population, have come from the lips of the old Christianized Indians, the *hijos de la misión* One such person was Fernandito of Santa Ines.

Fernandito was not a California Indian, save by adoption, but a native of Latin America. Born of an Ecuadorian father and a Peruvian mother, he was brought to Santa Ines in the 1850s. By that time, the mission was in a declining state. A hundred or so of its Indians were living nearby in what was known as Zanja Cota. There Fernandito found a congenial home for over sixty years.

Many of the natives with whom he associated were old enough to have been the mission's first neophytes. From them Fernandito learned much about life as lived in early California both during the golden age and the *tiempo de vandalismo* that succeeded secularization. He possessed an astute mind, intellectual sanity and tenacious memory, all of which contributed to his value as a witness of the happenings of those pioneering days at Santa Ines.

The Franciscan chronicler, Father Zephyrin Engelhardt, interviewed Fernandito several times and acknowledged his indebtedness to the kindly old Indian for enlightenment on several historical puzzles. Visitors to Solvang would find Fernandito sitting on his easy chair in the mission's south corridor, enhaloed in cigarette smoke. As he spoke to the fascinated listeners, chewed stubs and burnt tobacco were scattered in all directions.

Fernandito never married. Once he apparently lost his heart to an attractive Mexican girl. He gave her $50 to buy a trousseau, whereupon she pocketed the money and ran off with another man. Fernandito was a quaint little figure, spare of body, gray bearded and featured. He was obviously more Latin than Indian. He spoke in a whisper, as if for emphasis. He tolerated no interruptions.

In his later years, Fernandito occupied a little two room cabin of his own construction under the hill in front of the mission. The local priest allowed him to till a bit of land on which he raised corn, tomatoes and chili peppers.

His innate gentility and fund of information made Fernandito a fascinating attraction to tourists as well as historians. Charles Francis Saunders once came to Santa Ines for an interview. He recounted to Saunders the old California lifestyle and how it was a pleasant adventure. Altogether lovely in his memory was the ancient countryside unmarred as yet by the inroads of commercialism. In the early spring, he said, the landscape "looked as though covered with a woolen carpet woven with flowers of different shapes and colors laid down over the hills and valleys."

People were not in a hurry then and they were all friendly; there was plenty for everybody; every man's house was open to visitors and never was there any thought of being paid for a night's lodging. The tomb of the Peruvian native can be seen at Calvary Cemetery in Santa Barbara, scaled with a marble slab which reads:

Fernandito Cardenas
Died February 7, 1919
R.I.P.

HARDSHIPS AT SANTA INES MISSION – 1904

A measure of the hardships associated with the priestly ministry in early California can be seen in a letter sent on August 6, 1913 to Bishop Thomas J. Conaty by the pastor of Santa Ines Mission, Father Alexander Buckler (1885–1930).

Padre Alejandro, as he was known throughout the diocese, had arrived at Santa Ines in 1904. He noted that "there was absolutely nothing here when I came, except 2 bedsteads and a few chairs, not even a cook stove, not a single towel or sheet." While he had already stabilized and restored the existing buildings, there was still much to do. The "fences around the property are and have been in bad shape. The old posts, put down 20 years ago, are rotten. I have patched up things as good as I could, but can't do any more. The cemetery fence especially needs attention."

And he went on to note that "the wooden casing in the well is rotten. Squirrels drop in and die there and the water stinks. The windmill itself needs repairing; it is in operation since 1905 and the life of a windmill is from 8 to 10 years."

The priest felt also that "the outbuildings, blown down in 1905 and rebuilt in 1906 should carry some fire insurance. There is now a town near the Mission and there have been 2 fires within the last 6 months, one of them could have resulted in great damage to the Mission, except for timely help. As it was, a good part of the rubble north of (the) cemetery burned; if the Danes had not worked like beavers, all the wooden sheds and contents would have been destroyed."

And "the choir floor in the church is unsafe; someone is liable to fall through; a hard pine floor should be put over the old rotten one; it should not cost so very much–the space to be covered is about 20 x 30. The last item mentioned in his letter had to do with plumbing. "I would appreciate very much to have some toilets and a bath room in the Mission. Things are very disagreeable as they are and extremely unpleasant in winter or during the night."

Father Buckler was a man of aristocratic birth, reared in culture and refinement. It must have pained him to admit that "I miss the bath room greatly and I don't hesitate to tell you that I haven't taken a bath in 5 years or more. On account of the distances considerable pipe would be needed and I don't think this work, including cesspool etc. could be done for less than $500."

Had it not been an exceptionally dry year, Buckler said "I might do a few of these things myself; I am however absolutely unable and in all truth I haven't $15 to call my own." Padre Alejandro concluded his appeal to the Bishop in these words: "I submit this report to your kind consideration and whatever you can do for me and this Old Mission shall be highly appreciated. You have been good to this equally romantic and historic landmark so far, very good indeed, and, if possible, kindly help us again–for the last time I am sure."

Of the venerable pastor of Santa Ines, John Steven McGroarty said that he built "his own monument in the remembering heart of God, who knows and sees all things. The life of a man so generous, so charitable, so forgiving and so good constitutes a monument greater than any that can be builded of bronze or hewn of stone."

SAN RAFAEL (1817)

THE PENULTIMATE MISSION–SAN RAFAEL

Ceremonies marking the 150th anniversary of Mission San Rafael were concluded with a Mass concelebrated by Archbishop Joseph T. McGucken of San Francisco and the pastors of all the California missions. San Rafael, known as the "hospital mission," was established in order to remove ailing neophytes of Mission Dolores to a climate warmer than that of "the gusty and foggy peninsula of the sand dunes."

Since the whole purpose of the experimental foundation was to ascertain whether the Indians "would find better health and less mortality" in the more favorable surroundings, the new establishment was fittingly placed under the spiritual patronage of San Rafael, "that most glorious prince, whose name signifies the healing of God." The penultimate of California's twenty–one missions was located at a site recommended by Gabriel Moraga "in the lee of Mount Tamalpais... beneath a line of rolling, tawny hills, crowned here and there with live oaks." Dedication ceremonies were conducted on December 14, 1817.

During its earliest years the foundation was an *asistencia* of Mission Dolores. Fray Luis Gil erected a combination chapel, hospital and monastery at San Rafael, but there was no resident friar assigned there until 1823. In the latter year, San Rafael was raised to full mission status, thus becoming the only one of the five *asistencias* to achieve autonomy.

The mission seems to have prospered and when Otto von Kotzebue stopped there, in 1824, he spoke enthusiastically about the area's natural advantages. Indications are that the mission reached its maximum efficiency in 1828, when the Indian population numbered 1,140.

The foundation which "entered the mission family almost as an interloper" was among the first to be secularized, in 1834. Disintegration of the buildings set in quickly and by the time of Eugene Duflot de Mofras' visit, in 1841, the mission was mostly in ruins. Deterioration continued and, in the 1860s, it was recorded that "of all the California missions, San Rafael Arcangel, has been the most completely obliterated." Since 1870, only the spirit of Mission San Rafael remains for in that year the last of the original buildings were removed to make room for a parish church.

Even without its mission, the area retained the atmosphere of earlier times. One writer came to the site in 1915, and noted that "in the midst of a garden of magnolias and palms, apricot and orange trees, fragrant beds of roses, lilies and violets, and glowing banks of geraniums, a Catholic Church lifts its cross–tipped spire, and holds an open door to the devout." The visitor, obviously a non–Catholic, continued.

Though my worshipping of God is after the way which Rome calls heresy, I hoped it was not an intrusion to step inside and bow my spirit for a moment in silent prayer. It was a lofty interior, rather splendid, in fact, with pictures and decorations, and statues with candles burning before them; and the sunlight streaming through stained–glass windows gave a certain pure joyousness to the place, more to my mood just then than any sermon could have been.

SAN FRANCISCO DE SOLANO (SONOMA) (1823)

SAN FRANCISCO SOLANO

"Like the slow, sweet music of bells in a *companario* telling the Angelus at twilight, comes the memory of the peaceful, happy life at Mission San Francisco de Solano, commonly referred to as Sonoma Mission." The last and most northerly of California's twenty–one missionary foundations, inaugurated on July 4, 1823 by Fray José Altimira, was the only one established under Mexican rule.

The Franciscan chronicler records that the sterility of the soil and severity of the climate at Mission Dolores along with the prospect of numerous conversions, gave Father Altimira "sufficient reasons for removing his neophytes to a locality north of San Rafael." Selection of Sonoma's Valley of the Moon was providential indeed. One visitor to the mission, in 1827, observed that there were few happier sites than the one "bounded on the north by the mountains and hills, on the south by the bay, and everywhere watered and crossed by streams of fresh water."

Though its life was barely a dozen years in duration, the mission operated successfully until the time of its secularization, having the unusual distinction of harboring its largest number of Indians during the last five years. Hubert Howe Bancroft estimated that thirty–eight different tribes were represented at Sonoma during its short existence.

In the years after secularization, the once–proud structure suffered considerable physical deterioration. What remained of the abandoned mission was sold by Archbishop Joseph Sadoc Alemany in 1881 to Solomon Shocken who utilized the buildings for storage purposes. In 1903, the California Landmarks League purchased the ruined edifice with funds collected by William Randolph Hearst's San Francisco *Examiner*. Purpose of the League was to demonstrate "that Californians, while alive to the material advantages of their soil and climate, do not neglect those higher spiritual and esthetic considerations that make life less selfish and better worth living." Title was subsequently given to the State of California and, in 1922, the partially restored mission complex was opened as Sonoma Mission State Park.

"Although the mission bell no longer calls the Indians to worship in the Valley of Sonoma, and scarcely a brick remains of the original adobe walls which had crumbled to almost irreparable ruin, there is a spirit about this pioneer northernmost mission that never can be erased. The *padres* have left us an everlasting example of physical endurance, of spiritual zeal, of sincerity and sympathy that is peculiar to the beginnings of California, that is unique in the world's colonial history."

THE "SLEEPY HOLLOW OF CALIFORNIA"—1873

According to Benjamin Cummings Truman, "there is no town, not even Monterey itself, that has kept so much of the character of the old days," than Sonoma, "the Sleepy Hollow of California." The versatile journalist's account of his visit there, in 1867, was recorded in a series of newspaper articles appearing in the Los Angeles *Star*, during his editorship, between 1873 and 1877,

"On a corner street of the *plaza* close to the old barracks there is a structure so crazy in appearance, so jumbled in architectural style, that one has to walk clear round it and view it from all sides before he can see its reason for being. Viewed directly from the front. it appears to be a saloon, with a ruined bell–tower rising from somewhere behind it, and with a tiled shed extending out along the street."

Not until it is viewed from the rear "does one appreciate that he is looking at one of the California missions. It is in truth San Francisco Solano Mission, last holy place built by the heroic fathers in their campaign for the salvation of the California Indians, almost the first to be allowed to fall into ruin." According to Truman, it was "not so much the fact that it is ruined, either, that shocks the sensibilities of the student of California history, as the manner of the ruins."

A search through "the strange old structure" revealed that the church proper was "being employed as a storehouse for straw and partly as an overflow room for the liquors and empty bottles of the saloon building that has been erected against its front wall, while the tiled cloister, where the friars lived, is a chicken house at one end and 2 wagon shed at the other." Truman noted that the church itself was "in pretty good condition. The roof holds tight; hence the straw. Founded later than the other missions, and at a time when pastoral California was learning some of the arts of life, it was made to be finished in lath and plaster, and the plaster still holds."

"It has not the architectural beauty of some of the more pretentious southern missions, for San Francisco Solano was a comparatively poor mission, but it has a simple charm and beauty of its own." The perceptive journalist recorded that "at the back there is a tiny gallery with a beautiful, old window, this end forming a little nook of quaint and alluring charm—charm which is not entirely spoiled by the fact that the gallery now holds beer cases. The opposite wall, where the high altar stood in the old days, is perfectly plain except for a niche at either side and is piled high with straw."

"It is the cloister which is in most need of attention and repair. Its uses have been mentioned. At the end which serves as a wagon shed, a part of the roof has fallen in, spilling the tiles to the ground. It is one proof of the loneliness of old Sonoma that these tiles lie as they fell, untouched by relic hunters."

"The interior woodwork has long since disappeared, to be replaced by the perches and boxes of the hens. A little doorway through which the Franciscans crept to Mass in the early dawn now lets the feathered flock out and in. The bell was taken down with the cross when the place was abandoned for Christian worship, and the ruin of its tower still surmounts that strange structure—a deserted church, a saloon, a barn and a henhouse, all in one."

Truman wondered if "this singular" end was typical of the career of San Francisco Solano, the latest and "most unlucky of all the communities of the Franciscans." It was founded, he noted, as "the last expiring effort in that zealous campaign inaugurated by the heroic Serra for the conversion of the California Indians to the true faith."

I. The California Missions
2. Missions in General

MISSIONS IN GENERAL

SKETCHES OF THE MISSION ERA

The lack of graphic illustrations depicting the missions during their early history, the period of their greatest magnificence, helps to account for the undeniable fact that the system "was instituted, nurtured, and grew to its highest prosperity almost unknown to the outside world." As one might expect, before the days of photography, the first pictures of the missions were book illustrations, reproduced from sketches made by visiting artists. One of the earliest visitors to depict the missions was John Sykes (1773–1858), an English–born master's mate attached to the expedition of Captain George Vancouver. In addition to his "Log of the Proceedings of His Majesty's Sloop Discovery," Sykes is known to have made at least sixty–nine sepia wash drawings during the historic voyage. The value of the Monterey scenes is heightened by the fact that Sykes was allowed to sketch whatever he pleased, without any restrictions from local officials.

At the conclusion of the voyage, the twenty–two year old naval agent turned over his journal and drawings to Captain George Vancouver as part of the permanent record. Shortly thereafter, Vancouver engaged William Alexander to complete the Sykes work and those of others made during the expedition. Of the twenty–two watercolors based on the works of Sykes by the talented draughtsman, fourteen actually appeared as illustrations in the account of the 65,000 mile journey published, in 1798, as *A Voyage of Discovery to the North Pacific Ocean, and Round the World.*

The carefully engraved plate of San Carlos Borromeo, measuring 61 by 9 inches, was chronologically the earliest depiction of a California mission to find its way into print. It was likely made early in November, 1793, during Vancouver's third and most productive visit to the area. The scene of San Carlos, dominated by the massive cross, placed by Fray Junípero Serra in the courtyard, represents the mission before the erection of the permanent buildings. In the distance can be seen the foundations of Serra's envisioned church, still three years short of completion.

This "first view we have of any of the mission buildings" has been reproduced a number of times since the publication of Vancouver's three–volume work. It appeared in *Land of Sunshine* for April, 1896, and, most recently, was among the forty plates in the artistic book of Jeanne Van Nostrand, *A Pictorial and Narrative History of Monterey, Adobe Capital of California, 1770–1847.*

Though most of the Sykes' sketches are housed in the Bancroft Library at the Berkeley campus of the University of California, the original of "The Mission of St. Carlos near Monterrey" [*sic*] is one of the three still on file at the Hydographer's Office of the Admiralty, in London. William Alexander's watercolor copy is displayed at the Newberry Library, in Chicago. Though Divine Providence decreed a special historical significance to the works of John Sykes, the artistic talents of the English seaman are, in themselves, well worth commendation.

ROYAL PATRONAGE OF THE CHURCH

In the history of Spanish America, no one feature is of greater interest and perhaps of more lasting importance than the *Real Patronato de las Indias.* Certainly the Royal Patronage of the Indies was influential in forming the pattern of ecclesiastical affairs in those areas subject to the Spanish crown.

The concession of patronal rights arose from the desire of the popes to recognize publicly the generosity of the Church's benefactors. It was a practice rooted in canonical law, in medieval custom and in Germanic legislation. As centuries passed, patronage became more common and, for this reason, was found in the crusades and in other happenings of the Middle Ages.

Basically, the *Real Patronato de las Indias* was a concession granted by the popes to Spanish monarchs empowering them to take over the obligations of providing for the temporal maintenance of religious activities in the New World, the Philippines and other Spanish possessions in the Far East. It must be pointed out that these duties were not neglected. Philip II, for example, sent to the Indies 2,682 religious and 376 clerics. Nor was the king negligent in providing material support to the churches and missions.

Based on terms contained in the papal bull, *Universalis Ecclesiae* of 1508, the *Patronato Real* granted privileges as well as duties and it was the royal insistence on the former that brought about difficulties. Insofar as the New World was concerned, the union of Church and state in Spain was entirely too close. Civil officials were not always men of judgment and singleness of purpose. It has never been desirable to have ecclesiastical dignitaries dependent upon either civil or military rule.

Among the royal privileges was that of granting formal permission for the erection of each and every collegiate or prelatial church in the New World. The king was also allowed to "present" names of bishops prior to the pope's convocation of papal consistories. Nominations to lesser ecclesiastical offices and benefices were made by royal presentation to the ordinaries concerned. In this way, the king had it within his power to nominate the holders of ecclesiastical positions of all kinds, from archbishops to sacristans. This system, whatever its advantageous merits may have been, threatened to enslave the Church and, ultimately did so in many provinces of the Americas.

If there was one thing in subsequent centuries that leaders of the new Latin American states agreed upon, it was their succession to the privileges of the *Real Patronato de las Indias* as an integral part of the sovereignty transferred from the crown to the new republics. So it was that California's *Junta de Fomento* (1825–1827) proposed a plan "for the better government of the Californias" calling for two lieutenant–governors, one for each of the Californias, to exercise the powers of the *Patronato*.

It can be readily seen how the Church in many areas was thus virtually absorbed in and became part of governmental machinery. In one form or another, and in varying degrees, this "heresy," persisting ever since in some Latin American nations, has clouded and vexed the relations of the Church and State to the present. Fortunately, many of the more dangerous aspects of the *Patronato* have been modified by concordats with the Holy See. With due recognition of the benefits of Royal Patronage, it was always, but more especially after 1700, a grave source of potential and often active danger to the liberty of the Church

TRADES AND CRAFTS AT THE MISSIONS

Early in 1902, E. T. Mills wrote a long and interesting article for the *Scientific American* magazine in which he spoke about the "trades and crafts in the Old Missions" of California. The following observations are taken from that essay.

Looking back at the work accomplished by the fathers of the old Spanish missions, one is deeply impressed with the extensive and rapid progress that they made as well as by the wide learning which they were enabled to transmit to the races about them.

The wilderness was conquered in weeks. Great trees were torn from the mountain tops to aid in building spacious halls and corridors which have withstood the tide of more than a hundred years. Agriculture and mining flourished side by side with manufacture and trades of all descriptions and kinds.

Religious and other training was speedily introduced. An unlettered, unenlightened, foreign people were subdued and taught all the arts of the enlightened, well–schooled people of European countries. And all of

this was done in a miraculously short period of time. More than that, the work accomplished by these pioneers of western civilization, as shown by the relics from their workshops now in existence, is of superior quality to that which may be found in many factories of the present day.

Each priest that came to this country was a master mechanic; he knew something of all trades and much of many. He taught the Indians and as soon as one became proficient, he in turn communicated his knowledge to others. By so doing there was spread among the people the greatest amount of learning in the shortest space of time. The Indians, like the Chinese, were apt in imitation. They picked up the trades easily, and were flattered into perfect workmanship by becoming so soon the instructors of their fellows.

This time has been called "the Golden Age of California." Then everyone was busy, and yet no one was overworked. Labor began usually at 5 a.m., after the morning *Angelus* and breakfast. Rest coming at 11 a.m., when the noon meal was served, continued until 2 p.m.

Everyone was allowed complete relaxation during this period. From 2 to 5 work was resumed; then supper, often eaten in the open air, and after the evening *Angelus* there was time for recreation, for dancing and games, until 7:30 p.m., when all retired within the mission to peaceful and well–protected slumbers.

The mission buildings themselves constituted the whole city. They were the fortress, the church, the state, the school and the seat of all industrial learning and technical training. They were built in a rectangular form enclosing a square or *cuardo*, or great square court of the mission, where the workman and his tools could be safe from theft and invasion.

Later there were houses built for the trades people and their work on the outside. The ruins of these are still remaining in some places ruined gristmills and old tanneries, which are picturesque features of these ancient times and furnish additional pages to the history of the occupations of the age.

Each mission was expected to be able not only to carry on all trades, but also to manufacture the tools with which that trade was carried on. To a certain extent tools were brought from Spain and Mexico, yet in the main the missions were self–sustaining and provided every article for their own consumption and use. They were, moreover, especially renowned for certain trades and famous for certain articles manufactured.

CARDINALS AND THE CALIFORNIA MISSIONS

The satirical remark heard in recent years that the College of Cardinals is "a proof of life after death" is perhaps truer than one might imagine, especially when weighed against the spiritual influence of its varied membership. The Golden State exemplifies that concept. Two of the first three missionary foundations envisioned for Alta California were named for members of the Sacred College by the Inspector General of New Spain, José de Gálvez.

The mission of San Carlos del Puerto de Monterey, founded on June 3, 1770, bore the name of King Charles III's patron, Charles Borromeo (1538–1584). Appointed to the Sacred College at the age of twenty–two, by Pope Pius IV, Charles was entrusted with the civil administration of the papal states. He subsequently received episcopal ordination and, in the years after 1560, took the initiative in ecclesial reform at Milan. He founded seminaries, organized monasteries, inaugurated elementary schools for the poor, established relief centers for the destitute, solved labor disputes and opened medical dispensaries. The towering figure of the counter–Reformation was canonized in 1610.

Though envisioned among the first foundations for Alta California by José de Gálvez, the mission dedicated to the sainted–Cardinal Bonaventura Fidanza (1221–1274) was the ninth and last of the establishments inaugurated by Fray Junípero Serra. Founded on March 31, 1782, at the site of an Indian village called *La Asunción de Nuestra Señora*, the mission was christened in honor of *Glorioso Cardenal y Doctor Seráfico, San Buenaventura*.

Bonaventure belonged to that long list of learned men, brave saints and pious leaders who made the thirteenth the greatest of the Christian centuries. It was during his tenure as Superior General of the Friars Minor, that Bonaventure introduced the custom of reciting the *Angelus*. The story is told that when Pope Clement IV sent envoys to inform Friar Bonaventure of his elevation to the Sacred College, the Seraphic Doctor was washing dishes in the monastery kitchen. He refused to receive the Red Hat until he had finished that task. Serra is reported to have said, in reference to the delay in canonizing Saint Bonaventure as well as founding Mission San Buenaventura, that "the longer it took, the more solemnly did we celebrate it."

Cardinal–Saints Charles Borromeo and Bonaventure Fidanza, both of whom are now remembered in California by cities bearing apocopated forms of their names (Carmel and Ventura), are but two prominent members of a collegial body that truly forms the "hinges" on which the door of the whole Church rests and finds its support. Such is really not surprising for in his constitution for the Sacred College, issued on December 3, 1586, Pope Sixtus V said that "their life and conduct should provide an example to others, their utterances, their answers, their opinions and advice should be considered by all Christians as rules for right thinking and good living."

EDITH WEBB RETURNS

A book described by Kurt Baer as "the one comprehensive work of its kind" re–issued by the University of Nebraska Press is Edith Webb's classic study of *Indian Life at the Old Missions*. If it is rare that a study merits republication, especially after thirty years, then this book is an exception. In his appraisal of the first edition, Arthur Woodward predicted that the Webb to me will "never be equaled." That statement can now be regarded as prophetic.

Though not born in California, Edith Buckland Webb (1877–1959) came from an old western family. Her father was fond of recalling his distinction as the first white child born in San Joaquin County. Shortly after coming west, Edith visited Mission Dolores, where her grandmother had resided during secularization days. A photograph of Edith and her infant son in front of the church was the first in a series of scenes about the California missions captured on film by her husband, Hugh Pascal Webb.

Hugh later augmented his income as a school teacher by selling postcards and larger photographs, many of them hand–tinted by his wife. Today those that remain are a charming souvenir of an almost lost art.

Edith gradually perfected her artistic talents and later turned to painting on canvas. Then she conceived the notion of a series of mission paintings as they existed in halcyon days. Wanting to have her renditions as historically accurate as possible, she began researching the many facets of mission development.

Edith's scholarly interests soon overtook her artistic inclinations and she began gathering materials for a book about the Indians and their missions. She read everything available, amassing dozens of notebooks and photographs, many of which were taken by her husband.

During those years, Edith met William M. Connelly who had concocted a plan to fashion miniatures of the missions. She and her son collaborated in constructing a replica of San Diego Mission which was publicly exhibited in the garden of the Ambassador Hotel in Los Angeles.

Meanwhile, Edith continued visiting the various missions, always eager to verify and expand upon the data she had so carefully collected. Early in 1950 she made the acquaintance of Warren F. Lewis, a Hollywood publisher. He was impressed with her work and offered to publish her book as soon as she could complete the historical narrative.

The appearance of *Indian Life at the Old Missions* was widely heralded in historical circles. Father Maynard J. Geiger commended the volume and noted that "it is authentic throughout. I want it on my shelf and I recommend it unqualifiedly to others." He gave her the ultimate accolade by saying that "there is no other book

Morning Sun lemon crate label

even approaching it." It was indeed a handsome and informative volume. Edith Webb became the first person to attempt a definitive study of the Mission Indians, how and where they lived, what they ate and did, how they worshipped and worked, their amusements, arts and crafts. She introduced her book with several brief and concisely written chapters covering the Spanish heritage of California and the founding of a typical mission.

In 1979, Mrs. Webb's heirs graciously presented her tremendously valuable collection of research materials to the Santa Barbara Mission Archives.

MISSIONS ON ORANGE BOXES

During the seventy years between the 1800s and the mid 1950s, millions of colorful paper labels were used by California citrus growers to identify and advertise the wooden boxes of oranges they shipped throughout the United States. Those labels provide a social history, a history of commercial art and a history of California business. They are of increasing interest to collectors because of their attractive designs and interesting subject matter.

Oranges were first grown in California during the late 1700s. Their cultivation gradually increased as the population grew and as new areas were found which had sat-

isfactory soil and climate. For the first eighty years of orange cultivation, Southern California had no easy way to communicate with the rest of the country; oranges were grown mainly for local consumption.

The construction of the Southern Pacific and Santa Fe railroads in the late 1870s linked Southern California to the rest of the continent. This provided an eastern market for the fruit and led to a rapid influx of new settlers who recognized the agricultural promise of the state. Many settled in rural areas and planted orange groves.

The early growers were presented with problems that had never been faced on this scale before—how to pack, ship, identify and advertise a perishable product for customers who lived thousands of miles away. The brightly–colored label proved to be a key ingredient in the solution of this problem.

A great deal of experimentation took place in the early years to develop and label a satisfactory shipping container. A rectangular box that could be easily handled and efficiently packed in railroad cars was developed.

The first boxes were labeled by branded trademarks or stenciled images. The earliest surviving labels are small circular paper images about six inches in diameter. They were quickly superseded by large paper labels about 11" by 10" pasted on the ends of rectangular boxes. The dimensions of those orange box labels did not change for the next seventy years.

Because the early citrus growers were interested in the Spanish–Mexican culture in which they found themselves, they encouraged such artists as Felix Martini and Othello Michetti to utilize the California missions in their labels. Thus it came about that mission buildings and scenes of early mission life became the subject of many early labels. San Fernando Mission, for example, was portrayed by the Fernando Fruit Growers Association for many years. And A.B. Chapman utilized several views of San Gabriel Mission on the oranges he grew and shipped from the San Gabriel Valley.

More often than not, one or another mission became identified with a particular grower's oranges, a relationship that frequently enhanced the market for California's citrus produce. During the period of label use, an estimated 8,000 distinct designs were used on over two billion boxes of oranges. And few were more distinctive or attractive than those embodying mission themes.

Today, few of the original labels survive, except in government and industry trademark and pattern files. They are valuable because they personify a graphic form of American commercial art—the elegant small poster.

A MIRACULOUS MISSION DOLL

On December 19, 1902, Bishop George Montgomery wrote a letter of introduction for Harrie Rebecca Piper Forbes to the clergy of the Diocese of Monterey–Los Angeles. Therein he characterized the popular writer as "a most excellent and well–known lady" who had long been active in efforts to preserve the California missions.

Two of Mrs. Forbes' books, *California Missions and Landmarks* and *Mission Tales in the Days of the Dons*, were generally well received among historians. A reviewer of the latter volume said that these romantic sketches are "of unusual interest because they are derived from facts, stories and reminiscences told to the author by early pioneers."

One of Mrs. Forbes' lesser known essays appeared in the June 24, 1932 issue of *The Free Advertiser*, a weekly newspaper published by Elwin E. Mussell at Santa Maria, California. It related the details of a visit to San Luis Obispo Mission. Harrie had journeyed to the Valley of the Bears to see "the miraculous image of the *Santissimo Bambino*," hoping that its "power of healing might perhaps be extended even to the ungodly."

Recalling that the original *Santissimo Bambino d'Ara Coeli*, which is in Rome, is made available only on the Feast of the Epiphany, Mrs. Forbes assumed that the depiction at San Luis Obispo was likewise kept in the inner sacristy.

She managed to locate a priest and together they "wandered through the old mission, musing amidst the repaired ruins of this, the fifth of the Franciscan chapels that were established in California during the latter part of the eighteenth and the beginning of the nineteenth century."

According to a local legend, "a barefoot friar in coarse gray garb had lovingly carved" the statue "in imitation of the famed miraculous *Santissimo Bambino* sculptured in the sacred olive wood of Gethsemane by a holy Franciscan of the fifteenth century . .. and carried by him to Rome and placed in the Santa Maria in Ara Coeli."

"We paused before the altar and were told that the two splendid brass candle–sticks were votive offerings from a happy, proud mother, a woman of Vancouver, who had once dared to carry away the *Santissimo Bambino* of San Luis Obispo." The *Bambino* had not been stolen as a crime by the poor and distressed woman, but in the sincere belief that the healing influence of the sacred image would somehow intervene with the divine power and make her whole.

It was later returned, neatly packed in folds of silk, together with the two brass candlesticks as a votive offering. Another lady repeated the alienation. A year or so later, she returned bearing in one arm a child of her own and in the other the *Bambino*. This time "the image was heavily jeweled by the proud mother and replaced in the arms of the virginal figure in the chapel."

In the chapel of the *Presepio* (a word that literally means "manger"), Mrs. Forbes came upon a pastoral scene representing the birth of Jesus. She observed that it was carefully staged and laboriously explained to scores of children ranging in age from 5 to 10 years who have been trained for many weeks to proclaim from an improvised platform opposite the chapel the import of the scene.

Mrs. Forbes was deeply moved by the *Santissimo Bambino* of San Luis Obispo and when she sent her essay to *The Free Advertiser*, she asked that it be headlined to read: "The Miraculous Mission Doll. San Luis Obispo has mysterious Child Image which, twice stolen by women, is believed to have strange influence over the stork."

NAMING THE CALIFORNIA MISSIONS

The naming of the Alta California missions has traditionally been credited to José de Galvez (1729–1787), the great jurist and statesman who was *Visitador General* of New Spain. On September 24, 1768, two months before Galvez is known to have first met Fray Junípero Serra, the *Visitador* provided the patronage for the envisioned missions, along with an explanation for his choices.

There are cogent reasons for believing, however, that the actual names originated with Serra himself, although no correspondence or documentary evidence to that effect has yet been discovered. The sustaining rationale for such a viewpoint is couched within the Franciscan Church of San Bernardino, at Petra, once regarded as "the pearl of all the churches in the Province" of Mallorca.

Located on the southeastern edge of the city, in the oldest part of Petra, the church stands within a block of the home on *Calle Baracar* where Serra was born. The Renaissance structure, dating from 1677, has a slender tower of Moorish design. Romanesque in its interior, the church is richly and elegantly ornamented.

During Serra's boyhood, there was a Franciscan convent adjacent to San Bernardino. The sixteen friars attached to that house operated a thriving primary school, something of an intellectual oasis in the agricultural plain of Mallorca. Serra studied Latin, mathematics, reading, writing and oral music at the school. And it was there he received the inspiration to associate himself with the spiritual endeavors of the friars. Each day, following classes, the youthful student would stop to pray before one of the chapels in San Bernardino.

That daily practice, one might conjecture, provided the key for naming the missions that Serra would one day establish along *El Camino Real* in faraway Alta California. There are five chapels along either side of the church, each with a baroque gilded altar, containing paintings and statues of excellent quality and appeal.

Compare, if you will, the patronage of those chapels with the names ultimately bestowed on the missions: There were chapels dedicated to Santa Clara, San Antonio de Padua, San Juan Bautista, San Francisco Solano, San Buenaventura, San Miguel, San Gabriel, San Rafael, San Diego de Alcala and San Francisco de Asis.

And in other areas of the church were statues of *Nuestra Señora de Los Angeles* and *Nuestra Señora de Belén* or *"La Conquistadora,"* both of which Marian titles also found their way to the Pacific Slope. The saints to which those chapels and shrines were dedicated were names as familiar to Serra as were those of his family and friends.

It seems hardly coincidental that José de Galvez could have come up with an identical list of patrons, the more so when one recalls the thousands of saints from which he had to draw. Rather, he must have contacted Serra, by letter or personal emissary, before issuing his famous letter of September 24, 1768.

WEIGHTS AND MEASURES IN PROVINCIAL TIME

One encounters considerable variations in concepts of weight and measures when reading through the documents and printed sources of early California. This is especially true in private land grants and in the agricultural statistics of the missionary foundations. The basic units of measurement used in the province originated in Mexico and Spain and their history is characteristic of those two countries.

Though standardization was attempted, it was based on natural objects or personal traits: seeds, tree trunks, river beds and such unbelievable things as the length of the king's foot, hand and forearm or the spread of his royal hand and width of his thumb. Certain of the units used in Spain later spread to other countries. The *troy* weights, for example, were subsequently used throughout Europe and the name continues even to the present. The *vara* of Burgos came to be known in most parts of the Spanish and Portuguese empires.

There is a three–fold difference between current standards and those of earlier times; first, in the greater exactness of present units of measure; secondly, in the national and international basis of the units and thirdly, in the constant checking of local units with the standard.

The fluctuation and variations of the California measures were due, in great part, to the *vara* which was allowed to "float" in different areas of the Hispanic world. The friars in Alta California were constantly troubled by these variations. Fray Junípero Serra, for example, complained in 1775 about the difference between the quantity of goods purchased from the same drafts at San Blas and at Monterrey. Things were so confused by 1833, that the council of the *pueblo* at Monterey suggested that merchants adopt their own system of weights and measures.

On June 25, 1844, the council for *El Pueblo de Nuestra Señora de los Angeles* issued a regulation specifying the inner and outer dimensions of the half *fanega* measure. Attempts in the 1830s and 1840s to introduce and enforce the use of standards were mostly futile. No absolute system could be decided upon and hence none could be enforced.

The *vara* was probably the most widely accepted unit because of the measure etched on the staffs of the *alcalde* offices. Originally measuring 32.99 inches in Alta California, it had been adjusted to 33.372 by the years after 1855. The *vara* was used in California to determine the length of the cordel in land measurement and in measuring the size of churches and public buildings. It is worth recalling that the variation in practice helps to explain the differences in testimony, and in the reports of travelers and explorers as to the English equivalents of the various units.

Those who presently throw up their arms about the possible adoption in the United States of the metric system can consider themselves fortunate not to have lived a century and a half ago in California.

ECONOMICS AT THE CALIFORNIA MISSIONS

Hispanic California provides a unique opportunity for scrutinizing the Spanish conquest of the New World. In the short span of sixty–one years, the area experienced almost all of the vexations that occurred over centuries in other parts of Spanish America.

Within a relatively short time span, California passed from a struggling frontier bastion to virtual economic (in 1810) and then political (in 1821) independence. While the area's political independence was not appreciably influenced by domestic events, its economic independence was made possible, in large part, by the missions,

The ordained role of the missions as frontier institutions for the Christianization and Hispanicization of native peoples implied the gathering of Indians into communities. That, in turn, demanded a viable economic base for support.

The twenty–one establishments founded along *El Camino Real* by Fray Junípero Serra and his successors closely approximated the ideal of the mission as a frontier institution. In their dual role of service to Church and State, the missions became the dynamo of Hispanic California.

Not alone did the missions score exceedingly high in their primary and implied functions, but they also shouldered a host of burdens never envisioned by their founders. Their ability, for example, to support the military and much of the civilian establishment went far beyond reasonable expectations.

Oh, quite naturally, there was friction between the friars and their civil counterparts, mostly because the missionaries hesitated to deprive the Indians in favor of the military. Yet it is a testimony to the basic goodwill of both sides that such differences were generally resolved in an amicable fashion. Unlike the English colonies, Spanish presence in California was not prompted by economic motives, but by a combination of religious zeal and defensive strategy. Given the incidental interest of Crown and missionary in solvency, the economic achievements of the California missions are all the more remarkable.

The mission system approached its ideal in the 1820s. At the same time, those forces which ultimately brought it thundering down were gathering impetus. Outside liberal influences in Spain and Mexico eventually judged the system incompatible with the notion of equality, liberty and justice. The friars probably never realized that the very mercantilistic restrictions against which they chafed were among the strongest forces binding together the mission system.

Free trade, which the missionaries espoused in their dealings with foreigners, was an integral part of that new liberalism which rode the wake of the French Revolution. It gradually lessened and finally severed economic ties with Mexico and, in so doing, attracted outsiders who determined to see California linked to a wholly new system. And so a remarkable era came to a rather unpleasant conclusion.

THE MISSION SPOONS

Over the years, the historic twenty–one missions founded along *El Camino Real* by Fray Junípero Serra and his Franciscan companions have furnished silver craftsmen a rich source for commemorative souvenir spoons. There are, for example, three spoons honoring the *Presidente* of the missions. Made by the Watson–Newell Company, the handles have full figures of *Padre* Serra at the tip, with wreaths circling his head. Etched in the bowls are scenes of San Carlos Borromeo, Santa Barbara and San Gabriel Missions.

R. Wallace and Sons have two spoons with etched scenes of San Diego Mission, each one featuring palms. One also has a California Grizzly bear in relief at the crown. Another bear scene is portrayed by the Shepard Company on a spoon having an engraved view of San Francisco de Solano Mission in the bowl.

Two of the Shepard spoons feature San Carlos Borromeo Mission with either engraved or etched scenes in the bowls. One has a twisted handle with a round ball at the tip, the other has a plain handle. A third spoon, also featuring Carmel Mission, is made by Payne and Barker. It shows a fish in the lower half of the handle, with a netting and shell–shaped tip.

A beautifully–etched scene of San Francisco de Asís Mission is impressed on a spoon manufactured by the Joseph Mayer Company. The word "California" is lettered on the handle and ends with the state seal at the tip. The *Asistencia de Nuestra Señora de los Angeles* is also featured on one of the spoons. It has a curved handle with an orange and enameled green leaf at the corner.

R. Wallace and Sons have a spoon with an engraved scene in the bowl of Santa Cruz Mission. Its handle is patterned in roses and leaves. San Gabriel Mission is featured on at least four spoons. Two of them have twisted handles with bears at the tip. Another one, manufactured by Montgomery Brothers, shows an angel in relief at the crown, with the "City of Angels" written above the angel. The Payne and Barker Company has a spoon with an etched scene of San Luis Obispo Mission in the bowl and the Gorham firm issues one with a plain outlined handle and fluted tip.

Probably Santa Barbara is the most commonly portrayed of all the missions, with at least six classic spoons bearing scenes of that historic foundation. One shows a bunch of goldenrod with stems forming the handle, another has the state seal at the tip and "California" lettered down the handle. A third one has the head of an Indian chief on its handle.

R. Wallace and Sons has a Santa Barbara spoon with a flowered handle. And the handle of the one issued by Payne and Barker bears poppies in relief from tip to bowl. The ninth and last of Fray Junípero Serra's missionary foundations, San Buenaventura, is represented by several spoons. One, manufactured by the Dutch American Company bears a rendition of the mission in cameo on both the tip and bowl.

These spoons and others too numerous to mention are symbols of California's rich heritage. Spoonlore is just one other way of demonstrating the Golden State's unique place in the family of American commonwealths.

MISSION CATTLE BRANDS

In the early days of the west, brands were romantically referred to as the cattleman's coat-of-arms, the heraldry of the range or the nomenclature of the prairies. Although the practice of branding is as old as civilization, branding, as we know it today, is associated almost entirely with the west. Brands and branding irons are part of the tradition associated first and foremost with the cattle industry.

Placing livestock under a brand is figuratively putting them under lock and key. The unlawful change or working over of a brand constituted an offense that simply was not tolerated. Branding of farm animals included cattle, horses, mules, sheep, hogs and even fowl. Turkeys were often branded with a miniature iron having a lettered outline of sharp points which, when dipped in indelible ink, punctures the skin along the wing bone.

Wineries also fashioned branding irons similar to those used on livestock, but in smaller proportion, to identify their casks. Even loggers had a private mark for their product as it drifted down the rivers.

Brands are intriguing, resembling as they do the hieroglyphics of past civilizations. Many irons show a lively imagination, creative ability and artistic talent. The experts tell us that not a few originated with a bad dream or poor liquor.

Because each of the California missions had its own herd of cattle, it became necessary for the friars to utilize the branding iron as a means of identification. Though they are almost forgotten today, the brands marking the huge herds owned by the missions were once familiar to everyone. The brands, earliest in California, were derived from figures, letters and the customary calligraphic flourish at the end of a signature called a rubric.

Scrutiny often reveals their relationship to the title of the mission. For example, the "T" used at San Gabriel Mission referred to the Spanish word *terremoto* which means earthquake. The horses and mules used by the soldiers attached to California's four *presidios* during the Spanish period were also marked with similar brands that indicated the order in which the *presidios* were founded.

A careful reading of Zephyrin Engelhardt's books on *The Missions and Missionaries of California* reveals much about the use of the branding iron in provincial times. The Franciscan chronicler also related how earmarks corroborated ownership. Ears could be slit, notched, punched, tattooed and clipped and sometimes tagged with metal markers.

In 1967, Frank J. Thomas compiled a book on *Mission Cattle Brands* which reproduces samples of the brands used at the *presidios* and missions. It is a colorful book printed on Kozo paper by an Adana press.

Time passes by, pioneers move on and practices gradually change, but the branding iron lingers to symbolize what was once the hallmark of America's proud frontier.

CALIFORNIA MISSIONS AND ROMANCES

Among the many women authors who have written about the California missions, none stands taller than Cora Baggerly Older(1873–1968), the talented lady behind *California Missions and Their Romances*.

While a student at Syracuse University, in her home state of New York, Cora journeyed to Sacramento in the spring of 1893, and there met Fremont Older, then managing editor of the San Francisco *Bulletin*. Shortly thereafter, Cora took up an active role in the crusading career of her famous husband. She followed him, in 1918, to William Randolph Hearst's San Francisco *Call*, and while there began to work on the biography of the publisher's father, Senator George Hearst.

In 1915, Cora launched the first volume of her famous diary which would eventually span half a century in fifty-one volumes. The diaries were subsequently placed on deposit at the Bancroft Library, University of California, Berkeley. Throughout her husband's career, Cora wrote book reviews, conducted interviews with celebrated personages, reported on society figures and inaugurated what would later be called "investigative journalism." Meanwhile she wrote widely for such prominent journals as *McClures*.

Her first novel appeared in 1903 and thereafter her writings received national recognition. *Love Stories of Old California*, in 1940, carried with it an introduction by Gertrude Atherton. In 1961, at the age of eighty-six, she wrote *San Francisco, Magic City* which Carl Sandburg called "one of the best books ever done about an American city."

Mrs. Older's *California Missions and Their Romances,* published by Coward–McCann in 1938, was an interesting book, written in the popular vein and effectively illustrated. Printed at the Van Rees Press in New York, the 314 page book was dedicated to Father John A. Leal, of San Jose Mission, "in appreciation of his patient criticism."

Herbert Eugene Bolton said that this book "will be a cherished companion for visitors to the missions, and a well of information for all who delight in their lore." He pointed out that Mrs. Older's emphasis was "on mission life, the comedy and tragedy, joy and sorrow, toil and merrymaking, religious fervor and worldliness, which filled the days at the missions and their neighbor establishments."

In the Preface, R. L. Duffus said that "the *padres* shine like the saints of old compared with those who came after them. He went on to say he could "almost hear the murmur of prayers, chanted by priests broken by rheumatism, hardship and fasting, but rarely broken in spirit."

During the final years of her long and eventful life, Mrs. Older lived at a ranch in Woodhills, overlooking the Santa Clara Valley. She remained active in social and civic affairs, entertaining visiting celebrities as she had done in earlier days. She died at Los Gatos on September 26,1968.

In a rather insignificant tribute to Cora Baggerly Older, one writer said this: "Mrs. Older was at least two generations ahead of her contemporaries. Endowed with a superabundance of literary talent, she used it well. Her writings are a credit to her gender, a benefaction to her state and a dowry for the missions. She was a grand old lady whose shadow falls broad in the afternoon of California's daytime."

WILL SPARKS AND THE MISSIONS

Will Sparks (1867–1937) was nationally known for his jewel–like paintings of the California missions. Through the genius of his palette, the historic establishments become symphonies in color. Painter, etcher, muralist and illustrator, Will Sparks was born in Saint Louis, Missouri on February 7, 1862. and there obtained his early education. His name is still remembered in that area with great pride.

After medical training and classes in anatomy, Sparks decided to pursue a career in art. He took advance courses in France and, while in Paris, he supported himself as an anatomical illustrator for the famed Louis Pasteur. He returned to the United States and during an exhibit at the Saint Louis Expo, in 1886, he met Samuel Clemens whose vivid descriptions of California convinced Sparks to move west.

He spent several years working for newspapers in Central California, settling finally in San Francisco, where he joined the staff of the *Evening Call* as a writer–illustrator. Widely recognized for his rare ability in anatomy, Sparks taught that subject at the University of California's medical school. It was during those years that he assisted in the founding of the Del Monte Art Gallery.

Always introspective and literary, Sparks was early on inspired by California's vivid and dramatic historical background which he poetized in his many land and sea scapes. The artist portrayed the grandeur of the mountains, the great towering forests and the never–ending distances as few other artists before or after. Authorities estimate that he painted over 3,000 such oils.

Enthralled with the missions, the poet was a frequent traveler along *El Camino Real.* The disintegration of those once thriving institutions impressed him deeply. In a splendid sequence, ranging from elaborate saracenic domes and arches to the stark simplicity of primitive chapels, he painted them in twilight, in moonlight and in the darker nocturnes from which their Moorish outlines loom mysteriously.

Shortly after the artist's death at San Francisco, on March 30, 1937, Albert G. Haskell approached Mrs. Adolph B. Spreckels with the proposal that her collection of Sparks' mission paintings be reproduced in book–form. With her hearty support, he engaged the proprietor of the Otto Press to print the book which was released under the title *A Rosary of California's Early Spanish Missions for the Indians on El Camino Real.*

The attractive thirty–two page monograph contained twenty–five color renditions, each described with an historical resume by the compiler. The missions are arranged in sequence so that the traveler can follow from one mission to another, San Diego to Sonoma.

Advertised as "the most complete collection of the California Missions ever printed in four colors," the publication was an instant success and was re–issued in several editions. Now a collector's item, the Haskell monograph confirmed the already–accepted reputation of Will Sparks, whom the outstanding authority, Edan Milton Hughes, reckoned as "one of California's most important artists."

ARE THE OLD MISSIONS HAUNTED?

One is often asked whether the old California missions were haunted. Certainly there are many such stories that cling to the crumbling old walls. According to an article by Andy Hamilton in the March 28, 1937 issue of the Los Angeles *Times Sunday Magazine,* "almost all our old Spanish churches have a spook or two."

At San Diego, for example, descendants of the early Indians still believe that the spirit of California's first martyred friar, Luis Jayme, visits the Old Mission on dark nights. Many bear witness that the gray–robed vision can be seen, with lighted candle and cross in hand, moving about the ruins of the old church.

To the north, at the *asistencia* of San Antonio de Pala, there lingers a weird story of an Indian curse among the native American families living near Warner's Hot Springs. It seems that when the Indians were told by the courts to evacuate their ancestral lands, they left behind a curse on the future owners. Since that time, the Warner Ranch has changed hands many times. Each owner there has fallen victim to injury, grief, bankruptcy or death!

San Juan Capistrano abounds in uncanny tales. There's supposed to be a mysterious flame that illumines the night there, showing the way to buried treasure. Charles Francis Saunders told about an *espanto* or ghost who resembled a priest dressed in a long black cassock.

John Steven McGroarty related how voices and footsteps were heard in the basement of the Mission Playhouse at San Gabriel. On one occasion, an elderly carpenter was frightened by hundreds of feet tramping across the stage at midnight.

San Fernando Mission offers a strange tale of a wooden chest of gold and three grinning skeletons. That account tells about two cowhands hunting up the canyon of the Simi one day for stray steers. Unexpectedly, they chanced upon the ruins of an old house. Naturally curious, they peeked inside. And there, they saw a heavy wooden chest guarded by three bleached skeletons. Juan, the younger brother, was thoroughly terrified and wanted to leave. But Pedro, the elder, was greedy. He stepped across the skeletons and snatched a few gold coins from the chest.

That was the beginning of bad luck for Pedro. Enroute home, he fell from his horse, broke his back and lived out his life a cripple. He is supposed to have spent his remaining years searching for the golden chest so as to return the coins.

And then there is the story of Fray Francisco Uria and his four cats at San Buenaventura. A strange relationship grew up between the priest and his cats. All five ate together at the same table, walked through the grounds together and slept in the same bed. When the friar died, in 1834, the four cats solemnly marched into the church. Leaping to the rope of the bell, they swung it back and forth, tolling out the mournful message that the *padre* was dead. It is said that on stormy nights, if one listens carefully, he can still hear the meows of the four cats.

(Don't tell anyone that the friar actually died in Santa Barbara—it'll ruin the story!)

GREAT PARDON OF PORTIUNCULA

Inasmuch as *El Pueblo de Nuestra Señora de los Angeles* acquired its name from *El Rio de Portiúncula,* it seems appropriate to dwell upon the origin of that title as it appears in the Franciscan liturgical calendar for August 2nd. At the foot of the mountain on which the Italian town of Assisi is situated, hermits from Palestine built a tiny chapel or oratory in the first centuries of the Christian era. The oratory and a small plot of land was given to Saint Benedict in the sixth century.

The name Portiúncula or "little portion" derived from the transfer of this small parcel of property. The tiny church was called Saint Mary of the Angels and the inhabitants of Assisi often went there to pray.

When Saint Francis renounced the world, his first goal was that of restoring this sanctuary which, by that time, had become somewhat dilapidated. Many extraordinary favors were granted to him in the little church. The Blessed Mother designated the chapel as the cradle of his order. Here, likewise, she implored for him the great indulgence by which the Portiuncula chapel became famous throughout Christendom.

A special impulse led Francis to visit the church one night. There he saw Our Lord and His Blessed Mother surrounded by a great host of angels. Filled with astonishment, he prostrated himself on the ground in prayer. Then he heard the voice of the Lord urging him to ask for a special favor. After a few moments of reflection, Francis implored the grace of full pardon for all people who, being contrite and having confessed their sins, would visit the church.

Thereupon the Lord said to Francis: "It is a great favor that you request, but it will be granted to you. Go to My Vicar on earth and ask him, in My name, to grant this indulgence." Francis obeyed and hurried off to see Pope Honorius III. The Holy Father readily granted the petition, but with the restriction that the indulgence could be gained only once each year. The second of August was designated, since that was the anniversary of the little church's dedication.

At the Pope's command, Francis preached the extraordinary indulgence at the Portiúncula before a great concourse of people. From that time onwards, the Portiúncula indulgence became the annual goal of innumerable pilgrims.

A large basilica was subsequently built over the little chapel, thus allowing the sanctuary to be preserved in its original condition. In later times, the Popes have extended the indulgence to all Franciscan churches.

The Feast of the Portiúncula was being anticipated, in

1769, when the Gaspár de Portolá expedition came through a pass between two hills into a broad valley abounding in poplar and alder trees. They traveled on for about twenty miles and camped along a river appropriately named in honor of the Portiúncula. And that's how the name of Assisi's church of Saint Mary of the Angels came to grace the town established adjacent to *El Rio Portiúncula*.

SAINTS OF THE OLD MISSIONS

Saints of the California Missions is the name of a colorful book prepared by Dr. Norman Neuerburg for Bellerophon. Therein are enumerated each of the twenty–one mission patrons, along with biographical sketches and places where paintings and statues of the saints can be found.

San Diego de Alcalá (c. 1400–1463) became the patron of the bay which bears his name in 1602. Fray Junípero Serra placed the first of California's missions under his patronage in 1769.

San Carlos Borromeo (1538–1584) was chosen as patron for the mission at Carmel as a gesture of honor to Carlos III, King of Spain. The statue of the saint atop the high altar was sent there in 1791.

San Antonio de Padua (1195–1231) was chosen patron of the third mission which Fray Junípero Serra founded, this one in the Valley of the Oaks, 1771. After Christ and the Virgin Mary, his was the most popular devotion in Hispanic California.

The patronage of the archangel Gabriel was conferred on the fourth of the missions by Viceroy Carlos Francisco de Croix. Represented widely throughout Alta California both in sculpture and painting, San Gabriel is remembered primarily for his role as an announcer of glad tidings.

San Luis, Obispo de Tolosa (1274–1297) was canonized in 1317. His patronage of California's fifth mission is celebrated by a painting attributed to Jose de Paez which can be traced from 1774.

Mission Dolores was named for Saint Francis of Assisi (1182–1226). Established in the year of American Independence, that Hispanic outpost became the nucleus for the great city of San Francisco. Of the many depictions of the Franciscan patron along *El Camino Real*, the one at San Fernando Mission is the most famous.

The patronage of San Juan de Capistrano (1385–1456) was bestowed on the seventh of California's missions by Viceroy Antonio de Bucareli. The painting of the saint commissioned by Fray Junípero Serra, in 1775, now hangs in the new church at San Juan Capistrano.

Santa Clara de Asis (1194–1253) was chosen as patroness for the eighth mission by Viceroy Antonio

Bucareli. The colorfully attired statue of the saint was lost in the 1926 fire. There is an 18th century Mexican painting of Saint Clare at Santa Barbara Mission.

San Buenaventura (1221–1274) served as Minister General of the Franciscans and later as Cardinal Bishop of Albano. He is remembered at the mission bearing his name by a statue mounted on the reredos behind the main altar.

The mission dedicated to Santa Barbara was founded on her feastday in 1786. According to inventory records, her statue atop and to the rear of the altar was brought to California in 1791.

La Purísima was the first of the missions dedicated to Mary, the Mother of the Savior. Founded in 1787, the mission commemorates Our Lady's Immaculate Concepcion. The portrayal of *La Purísima Concepcion* at the eleventh of the missions probably belongs to the period after the 1800s.

Santa Cruz was named for the Holy Cross. Its nomenclature can be traced to the Portola Expedition of 1769. That tragic event in Our Lord's life is recalled by a painting from the *Via Crucis* by Indian neophytes at San Fernando Mission.

Nuestra Señora Dolorosisima de la Soledad was the patronage bestowed on the twelfth of the missions. The original 18th century statue of Our Lady of Solitude is now in the Presidio Chapel at Monterey. It is attired in a weathered black cope formerly used at Benediction of the Blessed Sacrament.

San Jose Mission was named for the foster father of Jesus. His image was found at all the missions whether in sculpture or painting. Numerous early examples survive, many of them showing the often–crowned Joseph carrying the Infant Jesus.

San Juan Bautista, patron of the 15th mission, is represented by an 18th century Mexican painting of the Baptism of Christ in the River Jordan. Most of the missions had similar depictions in their baptistries.

San Miguel Mission, named for the celebrated archangel, was founded in 1797 by Fray Fermín Francisco de Lasuen. There are many paintings or carved images of this saint at the other missions. He is immortalized at his own foundation by an 18th century Mexican painting.

San Fernando, Rey de España (1198–1252), is among the states more popular saints. The statue enshrined over the main altar, dating from 1808, was severely damaged in the earthquake of 1971, but has since been totally restored. Pope John Paul II knelt before that statue in 1987.

Viceroy Marquis de Branciforte chose Saint Louis, King of France (1215–1270) as patron of the eighteenth mission. The statue of San Luis Rey, enshrined over the main altar, was sent to the mission from Mexico in 1808.

The patronage of Santa Ines (Agnes) was given to the

19th of the California missions by Fray Esteván Tapis in 1804. There is a painting of Santa Ines, executed by the renown Andres Lopez in 1803 and sent to Alta California by ship several years later.

San Rafael was the last of the archangels honored with patronage of a California mission. Founded as an *asistencia*, San Rafael was raised to mission status in 1823. The painting mentioned in the 1818 inventory is now hanging in the replica structure.

The mission dedicated to San Francisco Solano (1549–1610) was established in 1823 at the site of Sonoma. The 19th century wooden statue of Saint Francis Solanus on the side altar at Mission Dolores is probably the one which came with the reredos in 1810.

There are several other colorful portrayals in the Neuerburg volume. One is a statue of San Gabriel which has been perched atop the main altar of his mission since 1891. On the book's back cover is a painting of the archangel Raphael which was executed by a neophyte at Santa Ines Mission in the early 19th century.

On the inside back cover is an engraving of Blessed Junípero Serra taken from Palou's *Relación Histórica*, in 1787. There are no actual portraits of Serra painted or sketched during his lifetime.

Saints of the California Missions is indeed a beautiful and accurate account of those celestial figures who have been looking after the historic foundations along *El Camino Real* since 1769.

Palms at San Fernando Mission

MISSIONARIES INTRODUCED PALM TREES

In an exhibit for the Olympics Arts Festival, Robert J. Fitzpatrick reflected on the love affair that Los Angeles had long had with its favorite tree, the palm: "Between the sprawling reality and the fantastic myth of L.A., the palm assumes a role less as botanical specimen than as made–to–order public relations icon. It has become indispensable in the charade, embroidered over a century, that Southern California has played as the world's last shot at Paradise on Earth. Los Angeles has become Oz—a land that can scarcely exist without illusion. And the palm is its enduring totem."

Indeed, the ubiquitous palm tree has become the trademark of Southern California's skyline. There are probably in excess of 100,000 of them lining streets, shading parks and beautifying homes in and around Los Angeles alone. Though not indigenous to the area, the palm trees of Southern California have become as native to the area as the European settlers who sank their roots here in the years after 1769.

The spindly Mexican fan is the most widely representative of the palm family planted in Southern California. Plentiful from the coast to the desert, they grow to more than 100 feet, their dead leaves adhering to their trunks, forming thick petticoats of thatch. These and other members of the palm family were first introduced by Spanish missionaries in the late 1700s and planted extensively a century later by land promoters. The plantings of E. J. Baldwin on his Rancho Santa Anita survive today on the grounds of the Los Angeles State and County Arboretum.

Aficionados point out that the palm is very traditional plant material for Los Angeles. They show up in lots of places, indeed they are very democratic, being found in the barrios, in Beverly Hills and South Central. In this Mediterranean climate, palms explode. Some of them grow nine feet a year. They put out forty to fifty fronds annually and if they aren't trimmed periodically, they become infested with rats. One of the trees, which measured 121 feet when last checked, is considered to be the tallest palm in the continental United States.

The systematic planting of palms in the one–time *Pueblo de Nuestra Señora de los Angeles*, took place in the year before the 1932 Olympics. According to a newspaper report at the time: "One of the main objectives of the street tree–planting program is to show thousands of Olympic Games visitors who will assemble here during the summer of 1932 that local citizens value civic beauty." Palms were encouraged in business sections because they didn't obstruct vision.

Interest waned after the Olympics and then, during the 1950s, the palm was rediscovered with a vengeance. Landscapers tried bizarre things like strapping palms to the blank facades of high–rise buildings and punching holes in overhangs to allow a palm's leafy head to poke through.

The return of the Olympics to Los Angeles, in 1984, created a new interest. As a pre–Olympic boost, the gateway to Los Angeles International Airport was spruced up with hundreds of palms, as was Pershing Square in the downtown area. In a commentary written for the Olympics Arts Festival, a local journalist note that "if God had not created the palm tree, it would have been necessary for Los Angeles to invent it."

TREES AT THE MISSIONS

The variety of trees found in and around Los Angeles, nearly 1,000 species, is perhaps unmatched by any other area of equal size in all the world. This phenomenon is due to the area's long and colorful history of horticulture dating back to the days of the Spanish missions.

Early friars, many of whom came from the Province of Catalonia, an area of similar climate, took full advantage of the diverse climatic zones in California—ranging from desert and alpine areas inland to frost–free, nearly tropical coastal areas—to plant and nurture a host of non–native tree species.

In 1984, a group of distinguished horticulturists and botanists began a program of identifying trees in the area. Then, four years later, Donald R. Hodel expanded upon their findings to produce his treatise on 167 *Exceptional Trees of Los Angeles*, a book published by the California Arboretum Foundation. The enumerated trees were evaluated according to age, historical or cultural value, esthetic quality, endemic status, location, rarity, size and spread of branches.

The two giant star pines that spread majestically over the garden area at San Buenaventura Mission date back to the 1890s—maybe even earlier. Native to Norfolk Island, a penal colony cast of Australia, the star pine is a distinctive and formal tree characterized by its pyramidal shape and uniform layers of whorled branches appearing as spokes on a horizontally set wheel. Whorls of young branches at the top are star–shaped, hence the name.

The Guadalupe palm trees at San Fernando Mission are native to Mexico and northern Central America. Their botanical name, *braehea edulis*, honors the noted

16th century Dutch astronomer, Tycho Brahe, who first recorded the palm on Guadalupe Island, off the western coast of Baja California.

The floss–silk trees at San Fernando Mission, introduced by Clarese Kroll in 1982 from the Huntington Library, are often referred to as "the single most spectacular flowering trees in the United States." Silk trees are natives of southern Brazil and Argentina and are called *samohu* by local Indians. They are truly breathtaking in the late summer when their bare branches are covered completely with pink flowers and green fruit.

Though it might be stretching the definition of "tree" slightly, the *vitis vinifera* at San Gabriel Mission is a remnant of the first vineyard planted in Alta California by the missionaries in the early 19th century.

Hodel affirms that San Gabriel Mission "played an important role in the introduction of exotic plants into California." In fact, their nurseries were the only source of plants for the early settlers.

The Spanish *padres* introduced the first lemons, limes, oranges, figs, olives, pecans, dates, apples, pears, pomegranates, plums, grapes and bananas to California, in addition to many ornamentals and other flowering plants, including the California pepper trees from South America.

A group of Moreton Bay fig trees dating to the 1870s is located in *El Pueblo de los Angeles* State Historic park, just across from the Old Plaza Church of *Nuestra Señora de los Angeles*. Those fig trees are native to Queensland and northern New South Wales in Australia. Specimens are noted for their massive, buttressed trunks which spread out for many feet from their trunks.

EUCHARISTIC DEVOTION IN 1771

Fray Junípero Serra's devotion to the Holy Eucharist was one of the Franciscan missionary's outstanding trademarks. The following is excerpted and digested from an address delivered over the Vatican Radio, in 1952, by Father Eric O'Brien, Vice Postulator for the Serra Cause.

Landing at Vera Cruz in Mexico, Fray Junípero Serra carried no provisions for his bodily needs to sustain him in the walk to the Capital. He was anxious only to reach some place each night where he could offer Mass next morning. When he reached his new home, the College of San Fernando in Mexico City, he first went into Church to greet his Lord. During his months in the College where he was trained for missionary work, he would remain in prayer before the Blessed Sacrament from midnight until time for Mass.

When he was sent to work among the Indians of the Sierra Gorda, he found that not one of them had ever made his Easter duty. But he soon saw to it that they became regular communicants. And when the feast of *Corpus Christi* came around, he had the procession wend its way through his mountain village of Jalpan, to stop for Benediction at the altars he had shown the Indians how to decorate. He called such a procession "an act of faith that fills the land with blessings" and with his kindly understanding of the Indian mind he made the Blessed Sacrament the high romance of their rustic lives.

Once he was so effective in cleaning up the local evils that someone poisoned the wine he used at Mass. When he drank the Precious Blood, he collapsed at the altar. They carried him to the sacristy, and someone offered him a glassful of a remedy that their own primitive medicine had devised. Though he had lost the power of speech Serra pushed the glass away and waited patiently to see what God would do about his case. He lived.

Fray Junípero Serra lived and died a poor man, but he was greedy for golden vessels to enshrine the Lord of Glory. Thus, when he was *Presidente* of the Missions of New California, he asked the viceroy to donate a monstrance for the new Mission of San Francisco and he added that he would be glad to pay for it with his own blood. In acknowledging the gift, the friar wrote "When the Divine Lord passes in procession across the fields, the very breezes will be glad, as such public proof is given to heaven and earth that the Christian Faith has reached so far."

From the very beginnings of Alta California, the Feast of *Corpus Christi* was observed by Serra and others with all possible solemnity. Thus he was delighted, in 1771, when ten new missionaries arrived from Mexico just in time to share that celebration. His sermon that day voiced his holy joy. And with a humble sort of bragging, he wrote the Viceroy of New Spain that the ceremonies on the beach at Monterey rivaled those of the capital itself.

In early California, when a priest went on sick-call, the King of Glory came in procession with a canopy, and the priest was dressed in special vestments. Junípero Serra had worked hard to obtain all that was needed for such ceremonies. But when his own time came, he declined the honor of having the Blessed Sacrament brought to him. All his life, he had tried with all his might, to meet his God halfway. So now he rose from his deathbed and walked to the church alone. Kneeling in the sanctuary, he led in singing the *Tantum Ergo* before Christ came to him for that last time. Then he returned to his little room and spent the entire day in silent, prayerful recollection.

In our mechanical age, many priests die suddenly without the opportunity for Viaticum. Serra received his last Communion there in the frontier mission he had

built, before the tearful eyes of his Indian converts. Surely it was in loving recompense for the special care this holy priest had always given to his sacramental Lord.

LEGEND DEBUNKED

Legends die hard, especially when they appeal to the imagination. An example would be the notion that "the trip from one mission to another was made between sun-up and sun-down and on foot." One often reads how the friars walked from one mission to another, but nothing could be further from the truth. Yet, despite all the evidence to the contrary, the "Johnnie-Walkers" of *El Camino Real* have received accolades for feats they never performed.

Except on very extraordinary occasions, Fray Junípero Serra rode horseback or by mule on his California journeys, as did the other 141 missionaries who brought the Gospel to California. That was true even on short trips for sick calls or visits to nearby *presidios*. The plain fact is that by Spanish and military law, the friars were strictly forbidden to leave their missions without a military guard and the guards always rode horseback.

When the *Presidente* of the California missions wanted to make a visitation or administer confirmation, he had to wait until a special military escort was available to accompany him. Fray Francisco Palou explicitly stated that in early California, it was physically impossible to travel from mission to mission on foot because of the distances involved and the uncertain reaction of the unchristianized Indians who lived between the missions. Even after more missions had been established and the distances between them had become shorter, there is no record of a friar ever making such a dangerous trip on foot.

So, how did this exotic and unrealistic legend of the "walking missionaries" of California take root in literature? First of all, there was the Franciscan rule that directed friars not to travel on horseback except in case of infirmity or manifest necessity.

In California, the "manifest necessity" was almost always present because of the extreme distances, the danger of hostile natives and the ill-health or advanced age of many missionaries. It is also a fact of history that the friars rarely left the missions to which they were assigned. When they did so, they needed to "hitch a ride" with a caravan or a group of soldiers.

Serra made walking journeys in Mexico, but never in California, where conditions were entirely different. Even in a place like Santa Barbara, where the Spanish *presidio*-town was just a mile and a half from the mission, the friars rode horseback when going to offer Holy

Mass. Fray Junípero Serra once described how a mule threw him when leaving Santa Clara and, on another occasion, he told about his rescue by Indians along the Santa Barbara channel when waves almost engulfed him when, riding along the beach, he had become hemmed in between the high cliffs and the sea.

The legend of the "walking friars" then has no historical basis. Spanish military law, the nature of the Indians, the terrain and the "manifest necessity" expressed in the Franciscan rule precluded the possibility of early missionaries walking from mission to mission even in the era of their fullest development. So, if you hear or read the contrary, set the record straight.

MISSION FURNITURE

Though the term has long been associated with the twenty–one outposts along California's *El Camino Real*, most "mission furniture" has only a titular relationship to the missions around which it developed.

Mission furniture, whose style proved exceedingly popular, was built primarily with the idea of comfort and durability. Its plain, straight lines reflected designs which could be effected with a minimum of tools. Nails and screws were never used and the oaken pin or mortise and tenon joint were the only methods utilized for holding the parts together. That method, the acme of joint construction, was used in all pieces comprising what was referred to as "cloister styles." Very little upholstering was used and, when it was, strips of goat or cowhide were interlaced and securely lashed to the backs and seats of the chairs.

Construction–wise, the furniture proved to be as sturdy as it was functional. The front and back rails of all settees, chairs and rockers were tenoned on the ends, each tenon passing into a mortise in its respective position. Holes were bored in the post passing through the tenon at its intersection with the mortise. Straight grained oak pins were then covered with glue and driven snugly into the holes.

The posts were fastened into the arms in a similar manner. Every joint receiving the least strain was fitted with this mortise and tenon pinned construction. In addition, the best hide stock glue was used to insure maximum strength.

On rocking chairs, the rockers were fastened to the posts by a lock pin joint which effectively prevented their working loose or squeaking. Thus assembled, rockers and other "mission furniture" lasted many years.

Cushion work, where it was used, utilized crucible springs which were anchored to a steel bar frame fastened to a hard wooden box, the same size as the seat. The springs were covered with heavy ducking, over which was placed a pad of felted hair about two inches thick. The hair prevented the springs from working through the upholstery and making ridges.

Next came the padding of high grade cotton which filled the cushion and made it soft and luxurious. Heavy muslin was placed over the entire seat to hold each layer and section in place until the leather could be drawn taut and securely fastened to the frame.

Though neither historically nor technically "mission furniture," this style has become so identified with the establishments along the California coastline that efforts to otherwise designate it have proven futile.

Early this century, the Lyon–McKinney–Smith Company issued an informative thirty–two page booklet entitled *Views and History of the California Missions and Mission Furniture as Exemplified in Cloister Styles.*

That monograph was based on Jesse S. Hildrup's *The Missions of California and the Old Southwest,* published by A. C. McGlurg. The photographs were provided by the O. Newman Company of Los Angeles. Furniture featured in the monograph, manufactured by the Grand Rapids Bookcase and Chair Company, was distributed by Lyon–McKinney–Smith from their store on South Hill Street.

Advertised as "furniture that endures," the products adhered to the company's motto of being "not the cheapest—but more value, dollar for dollar." From that company came most of the pieces now identified as "mission furniture."

THE MISSION PAKS

In earlier years the Christmas holidays were incomplete until some generous relative or friend would send a "Mission Pak," crammed with beautiful and tasty oranges, apples, nuts and cheeses. And, to make matters even better, everything tasted as good as it looked.

At a recent paper fair, a tiny pamphlet emerged telling about "the Romance of Mission Paks from California." It is worth recalling here because of its identification with the frontier outposts established by the Franciscans along *El Camino Real.*

Readers were first told how "in the deep, fertile, seaside valleys of California, the *padres* established the early missions. Long days of sunshine and nights of mothering warmth provide ideal growing conditions for wonderful fruits and nuts . . . unequalled in all the world.

From these verdant valleys, our Mission Folk select the very finest of tree–ripened fruits, picked at the precise moment of full flavor. These are rushed to our workrooms, to be assembled with the artistry of rich satin ribbons and colorful gift wrappings into festive Mission Paks . . . individually made by hand just for you."

Though undated, the pamphlet recalls that it had been "over 40 years since the First Mission Paks brought Holiday joy to happy recipients . . . a deep sense of satisfaction to thoughtful givers." After selection by "experts whose standards are uncompromising," every item in the Mission Pak was separately wrapped to insure its safe transport to consumers the world over. The pamphlet then describes some of the contents.

Avocados date from 1519. They were widely cultivated in tropical America. About 1900, the avocado was introduced in the United States. By 1910, California "began giving the avocado its true distinction and today Mission Pak presents this delicious delicacy at its finest, to garnish a cooling salad or to serve on the half shell in a wide variety of ways."

The romantic history of oranges goes back to the 12th century. "It was about 1565 that Spanish colonists introduced oranges in the United States. In 1769, with the founding of the first of the Franciscan Missions by Fray Junípero Serra, large plantings of this healthful fruit were started. Today, California oranges must measure up to strict state standards. Nowhere else is fruit quality so rigidly supervised."

And then there are figs, "the oldest known fruit. Fossils have been found in rock strata laid down 25 millions years ago Asia, the Orient and even the Arctic. Figs nourished people from the earliest recorded history." They were regarded as a "brain food" that fostered thinking power. "Today the sweet, soft–seed varieties grown only in California are a favorite fruit—abundant in natural sugars for quick energy and rich in vitamins and minerals essential for good health."

Finally came the dates. "The date palm is probably the oldest cultivated tree known to man. Directions for its culture are recorded on sun–baked bricks made over 5,000 years ago. California's first date palms were planted by the Mission Fathers."

Recipients long remembered the Mission Paks and their generous providers, mostly because "The Mission Folk" guaranteed their customers "a deep sense of satisfaction with their purchase." And, indeed, they achieved that goal.

CHRISTMAS IN THE MISSIONS

Christmas came to California with the Europeans. The Spanish colonizers were Catholic and they eagerly introduced their feasts and customs to the area. Perhaps none of those appealed to the Mission Indians more than the celebration of Christmas Eve, *La Noche Buena*.

It was on this great occasion that the friars staged *La Pastorela*, a dramatic portrayal of the birth of Christ. Churchmen of earlier ages frequently used religious themes as a means of inculcating faith and reverence among their people. Following midnight Mass, the Indians stood eagerly on tiptoe as the local *padre* returned to the sanctuary with something hidden in his arms. He placed it behind a curtained arbor in front of the church. The *Niño* was in its place in the crib and *La Pastorela* would commence.

The actors in the play marched into the staging area, each in character and costume. First came the angel Gabriel in blue garb with a long wand; then other angels in white garments and finally the shepherds, among whom was the clown Bartolo about whom the *Pastorela* revolves.

After the age–old *Adeste Fideles* was sung, the angel Gabriel advanced, and in language taken from the Gospel narrative, announced the birth of *El Niño Salvador*. He explained to his listeners that God had sent a marvelous star to illuminate the Infant Savior's birthplace. But *El Diablo*, the devil, was not so easily silenced. Masked and with a fiery fork, he darted this way and that as he objected to anything being done for humankind, arguing that since the sin of Adam and Eve all peoples belonged to him. There could be no hope and no redemption.

The audience listened attentively, as if their fate would be decided then and there. The children shrank from him as he grimaced and darted to and fro as if to impale some of them upon his trident. Bartolo, the shepherd clown, mimicked him and tried to make fun of his every action and word. But this was just a comic interlude. Then Gabriel took up the argument again. He proclaimed that there is indeed hope for mankind, since God sent His Son to redeem the world.

He explained how those who repent may be saved, and he held a cross out before him as the symbol of hope and a promise of redemption. The hermit–shepherd who had wavered when the devil spoke is now convinced and he fell to his knees before the cross. The devil made fun of his kneeling down and Bartolo poked fun of the devil. Gabriel stepped before the devil and made him unwillingly kneel before the cross. The choir broke out in a song of victory.

As Gabriel walked away, he pointed to the sky and all beheld the wondrous star. As he walked the star descended over the veiled manger. The veil is removed and the people could see *El Niño* with Mary and Joseph. Thus is formed the tableau, with the infant in the center of the scene. Then all brought their gifts to *El Niño* and the Indians re–enacted the scene that took place at Bethlehem so many centuries earlier.

There are numerous variations to this simple portrayal, but the overall theme remains the same. The friars knew the value of the Christmas drama and encouraged its annual enactment as an integral part of celebrations honoring the Infant Jesus.

FRANCISCANS AT MISSION INN

When Frank Miller began the "Mission Inn" in Riverside in 1902, he adopted Saint Francis of Assisi (1182–1226) as the "patron" of his famous hostelry. Given Miller's love for the California missions, the selection of "Everybody's Saint" came as no great surprise.

Saint Francis appears on the Mission Inn escutcheon at the left of a shield adorned with bells and crosses, while at the right is Fray Junípero Serra, the founder and first *Presidente* of the missions. At the base, an Indian gazes upward at the bell and cross.

Over the succeeding years, Miller gathered one of the most complete collections of Franciscana ever amassed. He scoured the world looking for items associated with or related to Francis of Assisi. In 1945, Allis Miller Hutchings compiled a thirty–six page booklet which she released under the title *Franciscana,* in which are mentioned all the items at Riverside's Mission Inn related to Francis.

Among the 222 entries enumerated and described in her treatise is a bronze Latin aureole cross from the Church of Saint Mary of the Angels at Portiúncula, located just down the mountain from Assisi. Attached to the cross, presented by a priest attached to the church, are these words: "St. Francis, shivering in his cell in the depths of winter, a demon whispers to him suggestions of ease and luxury; he repels the temptation by going out and rolling himself in the snow on a heap of thorns."

There are many paintings at the Mission Inn related to Francis, such as his "Admonishing the Ants," the "Virgin Mary with Francis and Anthony," "Francis Holding a Crucifix" and the "Marriage of Saint Francis to Lady Poverty."

There are numerous other artistic renditions, like a reproduction of Giotto's "Preaching to the Birds," Benouville's "Francis Blessing Assisi" and Olivier's "Exhortation to the Fishes." And there is a framed sketch of the famous "Christmas Message" which is often seen during the Nativity season on greeting cards. Other items related to Francis of Assisi would be a silver plaque of the Saint with the Crucified Christ mounted on a marble base, an embroidered Cardinal's crest (probably belonging to Saint Bonaventure) and several wrought–iron candlesticks with the traditional Franciscan skull and cross bones.

Among the old books are volumes containing portrayals of Francis receiving the stigmata, kneeling outside Assisi's walls, feeding the birds and animals and embracing the Virgin Mary.

The book collection also has many volumes about Francis, such as the *Little Flowers of St. Francis, Princess Poverty, De Re Franciscana, God's Troubadour* and *The Larks of Umbria.*

There are many silver medals, some of them issued to mark various Franciscan anniversaries down through the centuries. A favorite scene is Francis holding a crucifix, the Christ Child or some depiction of the Blessed Mother.

Photographs and postcards abound in the collection as do statues and figurines. The chapel is yet another story and many of its furnishings are still in evidence for those who visit what has become Riverside's most famous tourist attraction.

LAS GOLONDRINAS

Each year, on the Feast of Saint Joseph, the picturesque city of San Juan Capistrano becomes the center of national attention for, on that day, hundreds of eager visitors gather to await the "miracle of the birds," the return of the swallows to the Old Mission.

The cheery little harbingers of spring are cream–headed, grey–breasted, red–rumped cliff swallows, known technically and scientifically as *Detrochelidon luniforms.* They are a warrior–type bird whose migratory fields cover the wide expanse between Alaska and Argentina.

The ability of swallows to find their way about successfully has been recognized for a long time. For example, Pliny wrote that occasionally a Roman racehorse owner would take swallows with him to the races. The birds stained with the colors of the winning horses, were released to carry news of the victories back to his friends at home.

Fabius Pictor recorded that when a certain Roman garrison was besieged by the Ligurians, swallows were sneaked out of the city and taken to the army advancing to aid the garrison. When released the birds would return to the surrounded city with knotted strings tied to their feet. The number of knots indicated the days before relief could be expected.

The legend of the annual arrival of "*Las Golondrinas*" at Capistrano on Saint Joseph's Day is deeply imbedded in tradition. According to one account, the first migration took place on March 19, 1777, when "an old Indian, leaning heavily on his staff of gnarled olive wood, paused a moment to rest beside the courtyard wall before continuing to the chapel."

His attention was attracted to a half–dozen small birds, skimming the walls and darting with the swiftness of light over the mission patio. Such birds he had never seen before. The backs were a rich purplish black, a spot of white marked their foreheads and their throats and breasts were dove–gray. Suddenly, as though their inspection of the mission was complete, they rose into the air and disappeared in the direction of the sea.

Mass was scarcely over when the birds returned,

bringing with them thousands of their kind. Without a moment's delay they settled on the mission, the walls and old olive trees and straightway set to work building their mud nests under the eaves of the mission. Summer passed and autumn came, and then about October 21st, a restlessness was noticed among the swallows. There was much chattering and preening of feathers.

At the dawn of October 23rd, the feast day of San Juan Capistrano, for whom the mission was named, the friars and Indians were awakened by a great rustling of wings. They rushed out in time to see the swallows rise into the air, as one, and, swinging into perfect formation, head for the sea. No sooner had the swallows left their mud nests, than the swifts moved in.

All winter the swifts held sway, and then came the morning of March 19th in another year. Out of the mists of the sea came the swallows, 3,000 strong. The swifts were discovered and a battle royal followed. Gradually, the swifts were driven out and the swallows took up residence again for another happy season.

The considerable reduction of cliff swallows in recent years has been due to dry weather cycles, insecticides, removal of nesting sites and the like. Biologists still know relatively little about the tiny birds which navigate over tremendous expanses of sea and land, from one continent to another, without the aid of compass or sextant.

Legends die hard and traditions have a way of lingering on. Undoubtedly there will be swallows in Capistrano as long as the town has a Chamber of Commerce for the annual migration of "*Las Golondrinas*" has been a "miracle" to the local inhabitants, and that, in itself, will guarantee its permanence.

METATES Y MANOS

Among the common household implements found along *El Camino Real*, the *metate* and *mano* milling tool is, perhaps, the most important. Of all their possessions, none tells more about the culture of the native Americans attached to the California missions.

The use of the *metate* and *mano*, coupled with a knowledge of wild seed–plants, provided a generous food yield for the relatively large native population of California. For upwards of 10,000 years, grinding tools have been used in California and elsewhere in the New World to pulverize plant seeds into meal which, when mixed with water, was made into cakes and breads.

Along the Pacific Slope, as well as in the Southwestern regions of what is now the United States, grinding tools were referred to as *metates* and *manos*. From earliest times, these tools have been the characteristic implements of tribes whose principal subsistence was gained by collecting and gathering wild plant foods and products as opposed to those who lived off the hunting of animals.

Both the economies of hunting and plant–collecting have one important factor in common: they required their practitioners to move about almost continuously as game traveled from one feeding area to another or as the seasons changed from one harvest to a second. The *metate* and *mano* is essentially one implement made up of two parts: the lower member is called the *metate* which forms a base or anvil upon which the smaller *mano* is manually moved back and forth so as to produce an abrading and pulverizing action.

Together the *metate* and *mano* form a hand–powered machine for milling grain, thus serving the same purpose as the water or oxen–powered mill stones used by Europeans to make flour from wheat. *Metate* is a corruption of the old Aztec name for the nether grinding tool called *metlatl*. Actually the term is little changed from the original Mexican word in widespread use today. The corresponding *mano* tool, referred to as a *metlapil* by the Aztecs, literally means "son of metate." Both tools were common implements in Mexico at the time of the conquest by Spain.

The Spaniards adopted the *metate–mano* grinders, keeping the modified Aztec terms for the stationary *metate* and applying a Spanish term, *mano* (hand) for its upper, hand–held grinder. In a certain way, the *metate–mano* tool has come to symbolize the union of the Old with the New World cultures which was expressed so harmoniously in contemporary Mexico.

The large, stationary member of the *metate–mano* grinding tool set was usually fashioned from a block of sandstone or porous lava rock. The grainy texture of the stone provided a sandpaper effect when the *mano* was rubbed across the *metate*. The block of stone was quarried from a rock outcrop or a suitable boulder from an *arroyo* bed. Manufacture of the implement was performed by flaking with a sharp–edged stone hammer to fashion a rectangular or oval shaped block. Further modification consisted of pecking with a stone hammer and grinding to remove high spots and smooth sharp edges.

LINCOLN FREED THE MISSIONS!

Familiar to every American is the story of Abraham Lincoln's vow to free the slaves. As a young farmer of nineteen years old, Lincoln was hired to float a cargo down the Mississippi River on a flatboat. There he saw black men, women and children being sold into slavery, like so many cattle. That human parade of misery went straight to the heart of the tall, awkward and sensitive Lincoln. "Someday," he muttered to a companion, "I'm going to set those slaves free."

Every school child knows that Lincoln attained his objective on September 22, 1862, when he issued his famous "Emancipation Proclamation" that freed the blacks in the south. And now—for the rest of the story. Six months after his decree for the slaves went into effect, Lincoln issued a series of proclamations which "freed" nine of the California missions, thereby confirming their ownership by the Catholic Church.

The first attempt to alienate the missions occurred in 1813, when the Spanish Cortes passed legislation directing that all missions established ten years or longer were to be "secularized" and entrusted to the spiritual care of the local diocesan clergy. Though not implemented at the time, the legislation was re–enacted six years later and promulgated in New Spain in January of 1821. By that time the process was irreversible.

Following Mexico's independence, things got progressively worse until 1831 when a formalized plan for secularization was published in California. Between 1834 and 1837, all the missions, together with their property and lands, were distributed in accordance with a plan that provided for the appointment of administrators by the governor. Those friars who stayed at their post were to function only as chaplains.

Governor Pio Pico ultimately prevailed upon the Assembly to pass further legislation whereby the land at the missions would be sold or rented. He and his brother, Andres, purchased several of the missions, including San Fernando.

Shortly after California was admitted into the union, in 1848, the land titles were found to be hopelessly embroiled in bureaucratic technicalities. In 1851, Congress passed a bill to "ascertain and settle private land claims" for California.

On February 19, 1853, Bishop Joseph Sadoc Alemany filed a claim before the United States Board of Land Commissioners asking that the graveyards, quadrangle of buildings, enclosed gardens, orchards and vineyards attached to the missions be returned to ecclesial ownership. When the Church's claims were finally adjudicated, documentation was referred to the president for final approval. Abraham Lincoln's signature appears on the patents for Santa Ines, San Diego, San Buenaventura, San Fernando, San Antonio, San Francisco Solano, Santa Barbara, San Luis Rey and San Juan Capistrano Missions.

Some of those original patents are still around and they confirm that Abraham Lincoln truly did "free" the missions.

FUNERALS IN MISSIONS TIMES

Hidden away in the deepest recesses of the Bancroft Library, at the Berkeley campus of the University of California, is a 265 page manuscript containing the memoirs of Antonio Francisco Coronel (1817–1895).

In 1929, Nellie van der Grift Sanchez translated large excerpts of the memoirs which she published under the title "Things Past" in the September issue of *Touring Topics*. Included therein are samplings of Coronel's observations about "sports, dances, diversions and other domestic and social customs of old California."

Coronel was a creditable observer. He served at various times as a judge, county assessor, a member of the common council, state treasurer and mayor of Los Angeles. He was "visitor" of the southern missions under Governor Manuel Micheltorena. Of special interest to Catholics was Coronel's description of burial procedures as they were practiced in the mid 1830s and early 1840s:

When a person dies, no matter what his means were, the first thing that was done was to provide as a shroud a habit of Saint Francis, and if it were possible, to procure an old habit of the Franciscan missionaries, its merit was so much the greater.

From the time that the patient entered the last agony the habit was placed on top of the blanket, in the faith that it would gain for him more indulgences. Relatives and friends were in the house or nearby—always a great number of them. Prayers were kept up constantly, even before death.

A short time after the death of the person the habit was put on him. He was laid on the floor and a stone was placed at his head, with four candles.

From that moment the whole population, with few exceptions, were obliged to visit the body, to keep watch, and to take part in the prayers which were continued at short intervals until he was given burial. These prayers were also accompanied by sad *alabados* sung in chorus, which alone were sufficient to cause great melancholy.

For the purpose of conducting the body to the cemetery, the first thing done was to place it upon a table covered with a black cloth. It was carried by four men, who were relieved by others from time to time.

The priest went before with his lay brothers, making stops in order to sing responses for the soul of the deceased. Once arrived at the church, a Mass, "the body present," was sung or recited. When the Mass and other prayers were concluded, the body was taken to the cemetery in the same order.

When the cemetery was reached, the body was placed in the coffin, which up to that time had been carried behind empty. The *padre* recited the last prayers, and the body was placed in the grave.

As it was obligatory according to custom for the principal mourners to go to the funeral, as well as all the families of the place (including women and children) there was much weeping and moaning.

When the head of a family died, even those living in distant parts were obliged to attend his funeral, and there were times when the body was kept waiting for them two or three days without burial.

When young girls died, whatever might be the age, they were dressed in white and a palm and crown of flowers was placed with them. If it were an infant or young child, then a festival was held; there was dancing, eating, and drinking, rockets, and gun firing—in testimony of their faith that the soul of that little one went straight to heaven.

The little dead person was dressed like an angel, or the saint bearing his name, according to the wishes of the parents and godparents. If it were a little girl, the body was dressed like an image of the virgin or of some female saint.

ARTIST RECORDS THE CALIFORNIA MISSIONS

In 1875, Henry Chapman Ford (1828–1894) came to California. Already a widely acclaimed landscape painter, Ford became enamored with the California missions. In San Francisco, Ford first sketched Mission Dolores. There he met Edward Vischer who may have suggested the project of pictorially recording the missions as they existed in those days.

Later that year, Ford and his wife opened a studio in Santa Barbara. His reputation must have preceded him and he was soon a part of the Channel City's innermost circles, becoming the first artist to establish himself in the area.

During the ensuing years, Ford painted most of the missions. He journeyed throughout the state and, as often as possible, he stayed overnight at the missions, making pencil sketches and keeping careful notes. Ford was also adept at watercolors and etchings. Many of his drawings are preserved locally in the Southwest Museum and the Mission Inn in Riverside. Most of the major western galleries have one or more of his works.

In 1883, Ford went to New York to prepare the copper plates for his monumental *Etchings of the Franciscan Missions of California.* It was a part of his attempt to preserve in pictorial form the fast disappearing remnants of the California missions.

About 1888, Ford began gathering materials for a serious study of the missions. Between then and 1893, he completed a handwritten manuscript which, had it been published, would have been the first large scale book on the missions, antedating the works of George Wharton James and Zephyrin Engelhardt.

After Ford's death, on February 26, 1894, his manuscript was put aside, then forgotten, later sold and finally rediscovered at Grass Valley in 1984. Dr. Norman Neuerburg acquired the manuscript and, after editing and annotating the text, prepared a major portion for publication. *An Artist Records the California Missions* was released by the Book Club of California.

Unveiled to the public at a gala reception in the *convento* of San Fernando Mission, the 100 page book was printed by Patrick Reagh and bound by Bela and Mariana Blau in a limited edition of 450 copies. The colorful cloth used for the binding incorporates a pattern used for the wallpapers and decorations popular along *El Camino Real.*

Ford's comments on the individual missions and his reflections on the Indians are superb. He is one of the many Protestants who were in the front line of those eager to appreciate and preserve the missions.

His writings are totally free of the anti–Popish bias so typical of 19th century America. Mrs. Harrison Gray Otis, a close friend of the artist, in an article on "The Old Missions" speaks highly of Ford's work and then remarks that "Puritanism commends the work accomplished by those early Mission Fathers, and comes here to sow and to reap in the soil which they prepared and which they made ready for the larger and grander life of this century . . . there is no page in the past history of California that is more eloquent of sacrifice, of patient and devoted endeavor, than these old missions supply."

A STUDY OF THE SPANISH MISSIONS

The California Outlook for April, 1917, announces and appraises the "Revolution in Russia." On page twenty–one of that monthly magazine is another feature story commenting on the Fifth Annual Faculty research lecture delivered at the University of California by Dr. Herbert Eugene Bolton.

In that address, the distinguished Professor of American History released the results of his original investigation on "the Mission as a Frontier Institution in the Spanish–American Colonies."

Professor Bolton told how Spain, while still a relatively small nation, with only about 60 percent more inhabitants than at that time (1917) dwelt in California, performed the marvelous exploit of establishing her language, her Church, her lineage and her civilization in over two–thirds of the two American continents.

He pointed out that there were then tenfold as many Spanish–Americans as there were Spaniards in Spain during the days of the conquest. Bolton's lecture was given in accordance with a custom whereby the Academic Senate annually honored a faculty member who had distinguished himself in scholarly pursuits.

"Little has been said," declared Dr. Bolton, "of the missions in their relation to the general Spanish colonial policy of which they were an integral and important part. Father Engelhardt's books are a notable exception, but his view is confined closely to California, whereas the mission, in the Spanish colonies, was an almost universal establishment" in the New World.

Bolton said that "some fifty million people in America today (1917) are tinged with Spanish blood, still speak the Spanish language, still worship at the altar set up by the Catholic kings, still live under laws essentially Spanish and still possess a culture largely inherited from a Spain which at the time . . . had less than a million inhabitants." The non–Catholic Bolton noted that those results were an index of the vigor and virility of Spain's frontier forces and they should give pause to those who speak glibly about that nation's role as a colonizing agency.

Students of the future were encouraged to reflect on the importance of the missions in the Spanish system and how they constituted a primary frontier influence, with great political as well as religious significance. But the missions were basically religious establishments. Designedly, they were also political and civilizing agencies of a very positive sort and, as such, they formed a vital feature of Spain's pioneering system. Their primary work was that of spreading the faith. "To doubt this," Bolton noted, "is to confess complete ignorance of the great mass of unmistakable proofs of the religious zeal and devotion of the majority of the missionaries."

As viewed by the government, the role of the missionaries was to Christianize and at the same time to aid in extending, holding and civilizing the frontier. By going among the outlying tribes, the friars were often most useful as diplomatic agents. And Spanish policy looked to the civilizing of the Indian as well to the holding of the frontier. Discipline and the elements of civilization were imparted in the missions through religious instruction, through industrial routine, and, among the more advanced natives, even through instruction in arts and letters.

One occasionally wonders if certain current historians have ever read Professor Bolton's masterful essay on the role of the missions. His classical essay, later published in the *American Historical Review*, remains eighty years later a keystone to understanding what the missions were all about.

PIOUS FUND OF THE CALIFORNIAS

Nowhere is Spanish benevolence toward the savages of America more clearly evident than in the history of the Pious Fund of the Californias, a sum of money raised wholly from charitable persons interested in the conversion and civilization of the Indians of California. Missions for these natives were founded by Spanish and Mexican Catholics much as chairs in universities are established today. The yearly allowance for a missionary's support was $350 and the benefactor of a mission gave $10,000 to provide that amount perpetually.

The whole Indian population from Cape San Lucas in peninsular California to San Francisco in the north was brought to Christian civilization by priests supported by revenues from the Fund. It speaks well for the general integrity of the Spanish Government that the principal of the Pious Fund remained practically intact when its dominion in Mexico ended.

At the time Father Juan Mariá Salvatierra, S.J., obtained permission from the civil officials to establish a chain of missions in Baja California, he was told that no governmental funds would be available for the venture and that all the necessary financial backing would have to be raised from private sources. Salvatierra accepted those terms and began soliciting money for his adventurous undertaking.

Within the next thirty years, fourteen missions had been started, five or six of them endowed by the Marqués of Villapuénte. In 1764 the Duchess of Gandia left her vast estate to the California missions and two years later Joséfa Arguellas willed the Fund over half a million. The Pious Fund was administered as a separate trust by the Society of Jesus until 1767, when the Jesuits were banished from Mexico by King Charles III, at which time a royal administrator for the Fund was named. Revenues were applied for the next three decades to paying salaries of the Franciscan and Dominican missionaries who had replaced the Society of Jesus.

During the invasion of Spain by Napoleon, the finances of the country were thrown into hopeless confusion and the revenues of the Pious Fund suffered a common fate. Nonetheless, the obligation of applying the revenues to mission uses was recognized by both the Spanish and Mexican governments until 1842. In that year, the trust was appropriated by the Santa Anna regime and incorporated into the national treasury.

Such was the condition of affairs when Bishop Francisco Garcia Diego y Moreno was named to the newly created Diocese of Both Californias in 1840. While the justice of handing over the money was admitted, the Mexican Treasury found itself unable to pay the bishop his agreed–upon income in the years after 1842. The amount of something over $800,000 was reckoned as due the church at the time California came into the Union. An award by the Mixed Claims Commission in 1875 decided that half this amount should be paid to the bishops of Alta California and the other half to Church officials in Baja California.

Payments were made annually for thirteen years and then discontinued. In 1902 the United States and Mexico submitted the question to the Permanent Court of Arbitration at the Hague, the first international controversy submitted to that tribunal. On October 4th an award was made favoring the United States claim on behalf of the

California bishops. By the new decision, the Mexican Government was obliged to pay the sum of $1,420,682.67 to extinguish annuities accruing between 1869 and 1902. A further stipulation placed an annual obligation of $43,050.99 to be paid perpetually. Mexico made three payments until 1914.

EL CAMINO REAL EN NUEVA CALIFORNIA

The original purpose of the "King's Highway" was to consolidate the royal dominions, further commerce and propagate religion. While it is true that "nothing served the public interest more than good roads, nothing was given less attention," at least in the New World, and the actual route of the highways grew up from trial and error, rarely from design. The earliest *Camino Real* in California was the route taken by Gaspar de Portolá from San Diego to San Francisco in 1769. This twisting, turning and rambling road did not remain fixed, however, and many adjustments were made as easier paths became evident. Normally the highway followed the natural course of the valleys avoiding, when possible any upward climbs.

Anza's "open and continuous" road from San Gabriel to San Diego and the "regular road" from San Gabriel to Monterey remained more or less unchanged during Serra's lifetime and today that route is the one most closely associated with California's missionary endeavors. Even though *El Camino Real* was, in places, only a foot–path, soldiers and travelers rarely wandered off course; parties traveling in opposite directions would always meet one another enroute. In the years after Serra's death, as missions were established at a distance from earlier pathways, the King's Highway was gradually altered to accommodate the new foundations, a factor which accounts for the discrepancies about the original road's actual location.

In his monumental volumes on *The Life and Times of Fray Junípero Serra*, Father Maynard J. Geiger traces in great detail the course of *El Camino Real* as it was known to Serra. Had the venerable *Presidente* wanted to travel from San Buenaventura to San Gabriel, for example, he would have set out from Ventura and passed over the broad alluvial plain watered by the Santa Clara River to the base of the Conejo Grade. There, the road winds upward and, remaining on a somewhat elevated terrain through the hills of Ventura and Los Angeles, continues to San Fernando.

For twenty–seven miles through Newbury Park, Thousand Oaks, Agoura and Calabasas, the trail continues eventually leading to the *Rio Porciuncula* as it turns around Griffith Park Mountain through Burbank and Glendale to San Fernando Boulevard into East Los Angeles. Where San Fernando Boulevard ends, the path crosses in the direction of the county hospital and Lincoln Park toward Alhambra and then on to San Gabriel. Before 1776 the road ran directly east and southeast since the original mission was located along the northern folds of the Montebello Hills.

Today, markers are placed along certain portions of the King's Highway to indicate the path used by California's early pioneers. And if one can abstract from the noise and confusion, the steel and concrete of twentieth century freeways, he might recall that beautiful poem of John Steven McGroarty, "Dreamers of God" which even now has significance:

> Here are their footprints in the desert sands
> that time still treasures from its wreck and loss,
> And here is memory of their tireless hands—
> The gray–robed wanderers of the Cross.
> The sea remembers and the hills still know
> The olden trails their sandaled footsteps trod
> Who swung Christ's fragrant censers long ago
> And wrought in beauty as they dreamed of God.

MEDICINE IN PROVINCIAL TIMES

There were all kinds of medical problems in missionary California. Battle casualities and accidental wounds coupled with the natural scourges of pneumonia, scurvy, consumption, typhoid, smallpox and cholera presented serious obstacles to the work of the friars. Despite it all, the spirit of Francis of Assisi was evident in those hectic days. "If any of the brethren should fall ill, the other shall serve him as they would wish to be served themselves."

Treatment was frequently crude and primitive. On one occasion Fray Junípero Serra ordered the same poultice applied to his lame leg as was used on mules— with astonishing results! Medical care progressed so rapidly that on his deathbed, Serra had the services of a naval surgeon, Juan Garcia. The Indians had their healers, most of whom were frauds. Surprisingly enough though, many of the native remedies were successful and the Indians exhibited a remarkable facility with such difficult problems as the setting of bones.

California's first resident physician was the Frenchman, Pedro Prat, who came in 1769. A zealous person, Prat contracted a debilitating brain disorder at Monterey and succumbed at Guadalajara in mid 1771.

While medical practices in California were highly undeveloped, it must be remembered that the entire profession was only then coming into its own. One author states, with apparent amazement, that "at the time of the founding of the Mission of San Diego the science of surgery had only recently been separated from the trade of barber."

A hospital was established at San Gabriel early in the mission period and by 1810 had more than 300 patients. The *Asistencia de San Rafael* was founded primarily as a health resort for those Indians unable to tolerate the coolness of San Francisco's climate. Where mission–hospitals existed they were made of thick adobe walls, white–washed, with red tile floors and roofs and running water. Not all the foundations had hospitals but Governor Manuel Victoria stated in 1813 that "in all the missions there is an apothecary shop."

Probably the "first original contribution ever offered by a resident of California in the field of medicine" was a paper written by Frey Vicente Francisco de Sarría in 1830, on the morals and method of caesarian section.

Fray Ramon Olbes reported from Santa Barbara in 1813 that "we missionary Fathers are careful, as far as possible, that the Mission lacks nothing in the way of medicine." There still exists leather–bound volumes on medicine in several of the old mission libraries. Fray Luis Martinez noted in 1814 that "I have a little book of medicines, and am guided by it in order to apply some kind of remedy, as there is such a dearth of drugs in the country. . . ."

The missionaries were not as adept physicians of the body as they were of the soul but, in times of urgent need and in default of a physician, they did a tolerably good job of improvising in a field totally foreign to their education.

SECULARIZATION OF THE MISSIONS

Secularization was a process fully recognized in Spanish and Mexican law and was among the ultimate objectives of California's missionaries who wanted to see their natives spiritually and materially self–sufficient. By nature, however, it is a slow process—and in California it was forced on the Indians prematurely by a government less concerned with their spiritual welfare than their material exploitation.

On September 13, 1813, the Cortes in Spain passed a law which stated that all missions in the dominions established for ten years and longer were to be handed over by the religious orders to the care of the secular clergy. At that time, King Ferdinand, a prisoner of Napoleon, was unable to oppose the legislation. Upon his subsequent release in 1814, he abrogated all the acts of the Cortes.

Six years later, however, the liberal element was again in political control and this time the king was constrained to validate the reenacted 1813 legislation. Thus the decree of September 13, 1813, again held the force

of law and was subsequently published in Mexico in January of 1821. A conservative reaction in 1823 brought still a new government to power and again the act of secularization was annulled. But by this time, however, Mexico was an independent nation and the law of 1813, as promulgated in 1821, remained in effect.

The missions of California actually felt the impact of secularization in 1825. José María Echeandia, then governor, was inclined to yield to the desires of native Californians for distributing mission lands. Fray Vicente de Sarria, *Comisario–Prefecto* of the Missions, was among those who refused to take the oath to the new Mexican Government. He was placed under arrest but no action was taken against him for fear of a reprisal from the Indians. Fray Narciso Durán, *Presidente* of the Missions, agreed to refrain from any action prejudicial to the new Mexican Government, but even he would go no further than that.

Governor Echeandía has been described accurately enough as "anti–Franciscan," but he apparently saw no way of saving things in California without allowing the Spanish–born missionaries to remain. He went so far as to refuse several requests from the *padres* for visas to leave the area. Though José Figueroa was appointed governor in May of 1832, Echeandía remained and on November 18, 1832, issued an order implementing his earlier decree for secularizing the mission system. Only the arrival of Figueroa in 1833 prevented its execution.

Although he thought that any drastic attempt to proceed with secularization immediately ill–advised, Figueroa did publish an order on July 15, 1833, by virtue of which the gradual release of the Indians from the jurisdiction of the missions would be achieved. The results of the experiment were not overly impressive but, in spite of his recommendations, the government was anxious to proceed with more advanced measures. Both the Franciscan superiors, Narciso Durán and Francisco Garcia Diego, were convinced that such actions were impractical and premature and they spared no effort in making their views known.

On August 17, 1833, legislation was passed by the Mexican Congress providing for the secularization of all the missions. By the terms of the loosely–worded directive the missions were to be placed under the care of the secular clergy (of which there were none in California)! Supplementary legislation came on April 16, 1834, directing that all the missions in Mexican territory were to be converted into parish churches. One week later, José María Hijar was commissioned to take over all properties belonging to the missions.

A procedural decree was promulgated by Governor Figueroa on August 9th, and from the publication of this decree to the raising of the American Flag at Monterey on July 7, 1846, nearly twelve years passed. The interval saw the complete ruin of the mission system by spoliation and injustice—all the result of an ill–timed "liberation" of the Indians by a group of men whose prime motivation was personal gain.

THE MISSION REGISTER BOOKS

The register books used by the friars in the California missions have been described as "the mine in which the scholar must delve in order to bring up the true story of California and the Church." Upon the establishment of each new missionary foundation, the Apostolic College of San Fernando, in Mexico City, would provide six blank folio volumes into which were recorded baptisms, confirmations, marriages, deaths, patents and *padrones*.

The volumes were uniformly bound in limp Spanish calf, measuring 12 1/2 by 8 1/2 inches of excellent quality paper, and fastened with rawhide claspstrings. A special type of carbon ink was used and, except for occasional areas of faded and indecipheral writing, the script remains generally quite legible. The pages of heavy, laid paper are numbered exclusive of the title and final leaves.

Normally, a margin of an inch or more was allowed on the left side of each page for insertion of the cumulative serial number, the names of persons concerned, chronological status of entry and tribe (or *gente de razón*). The rest of the page was devoted to recording the official entries, dates, places, family names, sex, nationality, legitimacy, age, parents and signature of priestly officiant. With the secularization of the mission system, in the mid 1830s, a number of the register books were lost, confiscated and destroyed. Father Joseph W. Gleason recalled, in 1904, seeing "some of the quaintly bound tomes put up for sale at a book auction in San Francisco."

The same writer testified that "the books of the Northern Missions are scattered. Those of Santa Clara are still on the ground. The original records of Mission Dolores and Mission San Jose were taken from those two parishes and placed for safety by Archbishop [Patrick] Riordan in the Cathedral Archives."

As for the others, Father Gleason reported that "the most important of the original sources in the south are intact, namely, the Carmelo manuscripts, now in the archives of the Monterey parish, and the annals of the Santa Barbara Mission." In more recent times, most of the extant registers have been restored to ecclesial control. The historic volumes "are considered diocesan and parish property rather than Franciscan since the data they contain refers to pastoral activity in places which have since become parishes."

The lacuna is still unfilled. For example, the original registers at Mission San Diego were burned in the conflagration of 1775; the volumes pertaining to San Luis Rey

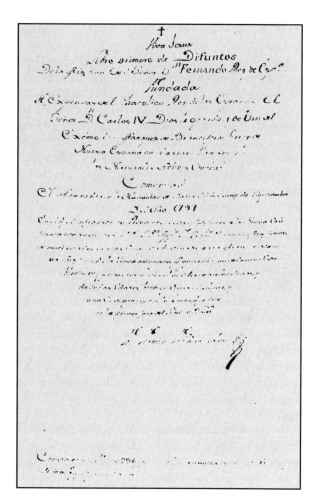

Register Book from San Fernando Mission

have been lost since 1847 and the burial record of Soledad is still missing after many years of diligent searching. That any of the old volumes are still in existence is a wonder. One early commentator noted that some of the documents from San Fernando and Zacatecas "were actually used by the Mexican soldiery to make gun wads!"

The late Jacob N. Bowman compiled an interesting study, in 1961, on "The Parochial Books of the California Missions" wherein he located and described all the known registers, accounting for eighty–two statistical volumes in which are recorded 89,124 Baptisms, 25,348 Marriages and 65,848 Deaths. For a host of valid reasons, he allowed for an error ratio of about three–tenths of one percent in those figures, which extended to 1834. Because of their peculiar interest to genealogists, the old mission registers have received a disproportionate amount of attention over the years. Yet apart from their valuable purpose in that area, the old tomes also confirm the adage that "each dead hand relinquishes a light, each living hand carries it on."

DOGS AND CATS IN THE OLD MISSIONS

There were domestic animals representing almost every category at the California missions, most familiar of which were dogs and cats, the trusted companions of all generations. Remains of dogs, unearthed in ancient cemeteries on Santa Cruz Island, indicate their existence in California centuries prior to the arrival of the white man.

Native canines, together with sheep dogs brought to California by the Spaniards or traders, had become a numerous and curious breed by 1834, when Richard Henry Dana recorded his impressions of the beach at San Diego:

> . . . I ought, perhaps, to except the dogs, for they were an important part of our settlement. Some of the first vessels brought dogs out with them, who, for convenience, were left ashore, and there multiplied, until they came to be a great people. When I was on the beach, the average number was about forty. . . . The father of the colony, old Sachem, so called from the ship in which he was brought out, died while I was there, full of years, and was honorably buried. . . .

> A smaller dog, belonging to us, once attacked a coyote, and was considerably worsted, and might, perhaps, have been killed, had we not come to his assistance.

> We had, however, one dog which gave them a good deal of trouble and many hard runs. He was a fine, tall fellow, and united strength and agility better than any dog I have ever seen. He was born at the Islands, his father being an English mastiff and his mother a greyhound. He had the high head, long legs, narrow body, and springing gait of the latter, and the heavy jaw, thick jowls and strong forequarters of the mastiff.

> When he was brought to San Diego an English sailor said that he looked, about the face, like the Duke of Wellington, whom he had once seen at the tower; and indeed, there was something about him which resembled the portraits of the duke. From this time he was christened "Welly" and became the favorite and bully of the beach. He always led the dogs by several yards in the chase, and killed two coyotes at different times in single combats.

> We often had fine sport with these fellows. A quick, sharp bark from a coyote, and in an instant every dog was at the height of his speed. A few minutes made up for an unfair start, and gave each dog his right place. Welly, at the head, seemed almost to skim over the bushes, and after him came Fanny, Feliciana, Childers, and the other fleet ones, the spaniels and terriers; and then behind, followed the heavy corps, bulldogs, etc., for we had every breed. . . .

Such were the dogs that helped guard the drying adobes and *ladrillos*, the fields and orchards, and the horses, cattle and sheep. That they were highly valued by the *vaqueros* and herdsmen is readily gathered from Dana's account, for, as Edith Webb has noted, "the live stock, especially the young, were preyed upon by coyotes, mountain lions, and other wild animals which prowled about the pastures."

Cats are mentioned in the annals as early as 1775–1776, when Fray Pedro Font, diarist for the Anza Expedition, was asked by the missionaries at Carmel "to deliver on their way down the coast, two cats to each of the missions of San Gabriel and San Diego." There was an urgent need for felines, inasmuch as both the missions and the surrounding countryside were infested with mice. The friars recognized the imperialistic nature of cats and cut holes in the massive wooden doors to allow their honored guests the privilege of passing, unencumbered, throughout the buildings.

That there were dogs and cats during provincial days in California comes as no real surprise to that vast majority of people who could hardly imagine even heaven without the affection and comfort of those treasured little creatures.

CANDLE–MAKING IN THE PROVINCIAL ERA

By necessity, the early California Missions aimed at becoming self–sustaining institutions. With some few exceptions, they were able to provide all the basic needs of daily life. An obvious example of provincial ingenuity was the art of candle–making. A good percentage of tallow or animal fat was annually set aside for making the innumerable candles needed to illuminate the various shops and other rooms within the dark, generally windowless adobe mission buildings.

The candle shop, among the busiest places at the different missions, utilized the services of both men and women. Production of tallow also served a quasi–liturgical function. Although beeswax was normally used for the altars, tallow candles were utilized for lighting the church and other buildings on great feastdays.

There were two ways of producing the pungent–smelling tallow or suet candles. One consisted of carefully immersing and reimmersing the wicks into a sticky bath of tallow and allowing them to harden on the arms of a dipping wheel. Another method commonly used consisted of a rack suspended from the ceiling and holding a dozen candle wicks over a caldron of heated tallow. It was repeatedly dipped into the adhesive mixture and then allowed to harden. When the candles had been fully formed, they were hung from rafters until completely dried into shape.

The latter and more efficient method was described in the excellent book, *Indian Life at the Old Missions*. The tallow from eight or ten beef cattle "was rendered, strained in a burlap sack and put away until the cool weather would set in. Then candle making would be put into operation. The candle wicks which were cut off about sixteen inches long, were hung on a cross stick, or sticks and the ends brought together to the length of eight inches and about three inches apart.

"The tallow was heated to a lukewarm degree. Then the dipping would begin and kept up until you would get the candle size you would prefer." The wicks "run through the bottom of the molds and knots tied at the bottom to keep the tallow from running out of the molds. A vessel of water was used to cool them off, and in removing them from the molds we would cut off the knot at the bottom and raise out the candles. The molds would then be ready for another batch."

The abundant use made of tallow candles is further evidence of the competency inherent in the overall missionary enterprise. It was a primitive, but absolutely necessary art and one which greatly enhanced the lives of a people only recently advanced from the aboriginal state.

RELIGIOUS FREEDOM IN PROVINCIAL CALIFORNIA

Though Christian tradition has constantly proclaimed that man's response to God must be free, practically every age has witnessed a distortion of the Catholic attitude towards some aspect of the delicate question of religious freedom.

Richard Henry Dana, for example, in speaking about those wishing to take up residence in Provincial California, implied that conversion to the Catholic Faith was a necessary requisite imposed by Church officials. He stated that among Americans and Englishmen it was understood that "a man must leave his conscience at Cape Horn" enroute to California. The Franciscan chronicler, Father Zephyrin Engelhardt, took exception to that insinuation by noting that "what Dana here styles conscience, with those adventurous immigrants were rather hazy religion opinions, views or notions, which it cost them very little to lay aside when it suited their purpose. Scarcely any of them could be said to have had convictions on the subject of religion, otherwise they would not have parted with them so readily."

Spanish and Mexican law did not regard rights derived from the natural law as totally unencumbered privileges. Hence there was no hesitation in applying restrictions to such rights as ownership which carried with it the qualifying limitation that titles could only be registered to Catholics. Before the American occupation, the civil law was frequently more severe than the ecclesiastical about such matters as marriage. Alfred Robinson recalled how his friend, Henry D. Fitch, became enamored with a young lass whom he wanted to marry if he could prevail upon the *presidio* chaplain to

perform the ceremony without the necessary stipulation of becoming a citizen. Since it was an edict of the governor, however, "that no foreigner should marry in the country without his special license," Fitch outmaneuvered officials by taking his fiancée to Valparaiso, where the nuptials were apparently performed without further incident.

It is undeniably true that many foreigners, upon arriving in California, did embrace the Catholic Faith, especially when contemplating matrimony. This they often did for less than noble motives, inasmuch as most Spanish and Mexican damsels would, under no consideration, "join a 'heretic' or a white 'heathen' in wedlock." Eugene Duflot de Mofras also testified that the young ladies of California were inflexible on the subject of religion. Nonetheless, what moral suasion may have been exerted in the Catholic atmosphere of provincial days certainly lacked any semblance of sanction in ecclesiastical law.

The first Bishop of Both Californias, Francisco Garcia Diego y Moreno, insisted that Catholics observe the canonical precepts of their religious commitment. At the same time, the prelate respected the conscience of non–Catholics by allowing them to be married before their respective consuls. "Out of consideration for the laws and Religion of the land," the bishop did think that such ceremonies should be performed privately in order not to disedify the piety of the faithful.

Regulations governing the Sacrament of Matrimony for Catholics were generally respected by civil authorities in the early years of American influence. So it was that Governor Richard B. Mason issued directives that "no *alcalde*, nor any other civil authority, [may] perform the ceremony of marriage in any case, when one of the parties is a member of the Catholic Church in California."

What abuses there were, and their number appears considerably inflated, occurred when insincere persons compromised their consciences merely to satisfy a legal code which attached the note of "Catholicity" as a necessary condition for validly engaging in certain public transactions. Available evidence indicates that the Christian tradition respecting man's inalienable responsibility toward his own religious practices was maintained in a noble fashion by the Catholic Church in Provincial California.

THE MISSION *TEJAS*

Among the distinctive features of mission architecture are the vari–shaded, red roof tiles, a handiwork the neophyte Indians of California perfected at San Antonio in the years after 1779. The quality of mission tiles var-

Tiles for mission contruction

ied with the clays of the different localities. Some specimens were soft and irregular while others were fine examples of craftsmanship.

The clay from which the *tejas* or roof tiles were made was soaked in pits until it was sufficiently soft. It was then mixed with sand or other materials to prevent cracking and excessive shrinking in the drying and firing process. As the art of tile–making was refined, the Indians learned the advantages of adding "grog" to clay in order to reduce shrinkage. This material reacted somewhat like the coarse aggregate in concrete.

There were two molds for the roofing tiles; one was a shallow wooden frame without top or bottom, slightly larger than the size envisioned for the finished product. This form was wider at one end than at the other. Typical measurements would have been 22" in length, 15" in width on the wide end and 11 ½" on the narrow end. A thickness of about one inch was considered desirable. The tapering semicylindrical mold which gave the finished tile the necessary curvature, was customarily fashioned out of solid wood with a handle on the larger end.

The mixed clay was placed on the sand–coated forms and worked and patted down with the hands until the desired pattern was filled out. After scraping off the surplus clay, the form was lifted away. If the clay had achieved the needed rigidity, it would not collapse.

There is no evidence to sustain the theory that the "Indians molded the roof tiles on their naked thighs," as was often thought. In any event, when the tiles were fully dried, they were stacked vertically to be fired. The kiln was made of adobe bricks laid up in square form. The wooden fuel was used to raise the temperature to about 1,800 Fahrenheit, where it was maintained for thirty–six hours. None of the original mission kilns survive intact today, though the ruins of a fairly complete one was unearthed several years ago at San Luis Rey. The multi–shaded, handmade *tejas*, or roof tiles, in their varying shapes and sizes gave the roofs of the old missions that uneven look that so effectively suited the thick adobe walls beneath them.

Development of roofing–tiles was only one of the many contributions made by the mission system to the civilizing process in California. Perhaps it was a realization of this that prompted one writer to note, as long ago as 1913, that "every Californian as he turns the pages of the early history of his State feels at times that he can hear the echo of the *Angelus* bell of the missions that are dead and gone."

HOLY WEEK IN THE CALIFORNIA MISSIONS

The routine of daily life at the missions was brightened with the color, pomp and solemnity of religious pageantry. Especially impressive were the liturgical ceremonies of Holy Week. Encarnación Piñedo records that on Thursday, for example, "a solemn Mass was chanted, the Indians joining in the responses, and at the end of the Mass, the clergy and acolytes, robed in their richest vestments and carrying crosses and lighted candles on poles, and the people in gala attire, formed a procession which reverently issuing from the church, escorted the Holy Sacrament around the plaza and back to the sanctuary, where it was deposited with every manifestation of deepest devotion. During the ceremonies solemn hymns and psalms were chanted and prayers were offered to the divine Redeemer, while incense was constantly burned."

In the afternoon, "the oldest Indians in the *rancheria* were crowned with flowers brought to the church, where they were seated on benches prepared for the occasion. The priest in his alb, and carrying a white towel and a pitcher of water scented with bay leaves, then washed their feet and wiped them, after which he ascended to the pulpit and preached the sermon on true Christian humility and brotherhood, typified by the ceremony just performed."

On Good Friday, Fray Junípero Serra "used to preach in the morning on the Passion, and in the afternoon the Descent from the Cross was represented with the greatest vividness by means of a lifelike figure which he had ordered made for the purpose and which had hinges. He handled the subject in his sermon with the greatest devotion and tenderness. The figure of Our Lord was placed in a casket and then used in the procession of the Holy Burial. It was afterward placed upon an altar which he had prepared for this purpose and at night another procession was made in honor of Our Lady of Solitude, and then the day finished with a special sermon on the subject."

In the afternoon, the *Via Crucis* was recited. Three men enveloped in vestments of white linen carried a heavy crucifix from one station to another.

A *tenebrae* or darkness service took place on Wednesday, Thursday and Friday evenings, so named "from the act of extinguishing one–by–one fourteen of the fifteen lighted candles on the *Tenebrae* candlestick. This rite occurred after the singing of the Lamentations by the Indian choristers. The tune to which these mournful lines were sung is considered 'the saddest melody within the whole range of music.' After the fourteen candles had been extinguished, and during the chanting of the *Benedictus*, the six candles on the altar were also put out. The shutters were closed and curtains drawn across the windows. The fifteenth candle was next removed and placed upon the altar. The church became quite dark. And then, following the recitation of the psalm *Miserere*, there came a terrifying noise caused by the striking together of wooden clappers accompanied by a creaking, clacking, grinding, and clanking sound produced by the whirling around and around, or the shaking of the wooden *matracas* (ratchets or rattles), symbolizing the confusion of nature at the time of Christ's death."

Early on Holy Saturday "came the ceremonies of the blessing of the salt, the new fire, the baptismal water to be used in the ensuing year, as well as the paschal candle, the litany and the Mass being chanted by the Indian singers." The "chastising of Judas Iscariot" also took place on Saturday. "An effigy was constructed, dressed in man's clothing and strung up on a yardarm set in the mission plaza. It was then shot at, stoned, spat upon, reviled and beaten with sticks."

Finally, in anticipation of Easter, the church bells, silent since Thursday were rung joyously. Statues and paintings were divested of their purple wrappings and the curtain concealing the altar, once more resplendent with flowers, gleaming silver candlesticks, and unveiled statues, was drawn aside."

Through provincial times the neophytes responded to the colorful and solemn ceremonies of Holy Week accompanied, as they were, by music and song ranging from the saddest to the most joyous known to man, as only unsophisticated peoples can respond, and the impressions received through participation in those ceremonies was most enduring.

MISSIONARIES AND THE LANGUAGE BARRIER

That California's early Spanish friars were able to overcome the obstacle of twenty–one linguistic families is adduced as an additional proof of the kind treatment the Indians received at the hands of the missionaries. There was scarcely one mission whose neophyte population used the same language. The fact that one–fourth of all the separate lingual dialects in North America were found in California led a noted ethnologist to classify the region as one with "the greatest aboriginal linguistic diversity in the world."

Besides the great multiplicity of language and inter–lingual dialects most of the commonly used terminology proved wholly inadequate to convey the philosophical concepts of the Christian religion. There were no words for anything that could not be seen, heard, touched, tasted or smelled.

The possibility of a missionary achieving fluency in even one of the many languages or dialects was complicated by the fact that most of the friars were at least middle–aged, far beyond the stage of rapid assimilation of foreign terms and expressions. While civil officials encouraged the Franciscans to learn the native tongues, as late as 1795, the king obliged the missionaries to teach Spanish to the neophytes, forbidding them, as far as possible, "to use their native language."

Yet there was no uniform practice among the friars. The younger and more zealous, perhaps recalling Saint Augustine's observation that "men would prefer to be alone with their dogs than with a stranger whose language they do not understand," made heroic efforts to gain facility in the native tongues.

Fray Francisco Palóu recorded that immediately after their arrival at Monterey, the missionaries "dedicated themselves with the greatest care to learning from the children the language of those rude people." Such was the practice of Fray Junípero Serra who, we are told, tried to win the favor of the natives by learning to talk with them in their own language. Fortunately, "with the Spaniard's innate ability to gesticulate and the uncommon vivacity and significance of the Indian's gestures, the difficulty of speech was lessened."

Fray Felipe Arroyo de la Cuésta was another who applied himself most assiduously to learning the respective languages. His *Vocabulary or Phrase Book of the Mutsun Language of Alta California* was published under the auspices of the Smithsonian Institution, in 1862.

Other missionaries concentrated on teaching the Spanish language to the Indians, especially the children. "The comparative facility of Castillian enabled the Indians to learn it well enough to serve as the interpreters." It was also found that the Spanish tongue forged a bond of unity between the inhabitants of the various California missions.

Even in such places as San Buenaventura, where one elderly friar was reported as never speaking "to the natives in any other language than his own," the Indians understood quickly what was said, "especially when it served their own convenience or interest." The apostolic spirit evident in their attempts to learn native languages and to elevate the Indians to higher linguistic accomplishments is a further example of the size and significance of the Franciscan contribution to the Pacific Slope.

CASADOS Y VELADOS

According to the 17th–century writer, Sir William Davenant, custom is an unwritten law by which the people keep even kings in awe. In canonical usage, the term stands for a right or law introduced by repeated behavior of a community with the consent of the legislator. One of the most colorful of California's early ecclesiastical customs is recalled in the annals as the *Casados y Velados.* It was described by Friederich Gerstaeker, author of *Kalifornian's Gold,* who visited San Francisco's Mission Dolores in 1849:

> In the Church I saw about that time the marriage of a young girl of a Mission with a Californian from Los Angeles. There is here a strange custom, according to which the young couple during the ceremony, and whilst they are still kneeling before the altar, are tied together with ropes and covered with a large cloth.

The "strange custom" observed by the German novelist, widespread in Spanish and Mexican California, indicated that the couple had complied with the canonical legislation concerning the seasons of the year during which matrimonial promises could be exchanged with special solemnization.

Use of the ribbons (or ropes) and veil was allowed only for marriages at which the Nuptial Blessing was bestowed. Such a benediction was not given to a woman entering her second marriage, nor was it imparted during Lent and Advent and certain other specified days. If for some valid reason the couple could not be married at Mass or during the "open" season, the Nuptial Blessing was liturgically supplied later, at which time the partners were "canonically veiled."

While the tying with ribbons and veiling was an extra–rubrical ceremony, it was more than the "pretty custom in vogue among Mexicans in California" spoken of by one writer. Indeed, the practice is quite probably an outgrowth of the *Velatio Nuptialis* found in the old Leonine Sacramentary. Saint Isidore of Seville likened the ceremony to the Roman conception of matrimony as the veiling of the woman for the special behoof of her spouse.

During the reading of the actual blessing, just before reception of Holy Communion, a yoke of gauze, trimmed with brightly colored ribbons (*jugale*), was stretched over the couple so as to hide them. From that time onwards, the newly wedded pair were known as *Casados y Velados* and the veil was retained as a certificate that they had been married at Mass or that the Nuptial Blessing had subsequently been given.

The colorful practice, no longer observed in California, carried with it considerable symbolic meaning, typifying as it did the inseparable union of the Divine word with human nature and of Christ with the Church.

INTERMARRIAGE ON THE SPANISH FRONTIER

Judged within the context of its earliest religious and secular history, California has an impressive heritage in the area of racial relations. One outstanding aspect of this attitude revolves around the thorny question of intermarriage in mission times.

The mixture of races had been extensive during the seven centuries of Moorish occupation in Spain. The honest and inborn respect for dark–skinned peoples exhibited in the mother country endowed the earliest of the New World's Iberian civilizers with a tradition of tolerance sadly lacking in their Anglo–Saxon counterparts. In his classic work, *Politica Indiana*, Juan de Solórzano noted that intermarriage between Spaniards and Indians was an approved method of contributing to "the population, growth and retention of these provinces" and "furthering the desired unity and conformity among Indians and Spaniards."

In California, marriage between the *gente de razón* and the natives "figured among the subsidiary means fostered by the fathers to assimilate the Indians to the Christian, civilized Spaniards." Mindful that a person's dignity arises from the praise of truth, not from blood, Fray Junípero Serra, in a report to Antonio Maria de Bucareli, asked "a bounty for those, be they soldiers or not, who enter the state of marriage with girls of that far-away country, new Christian converts." The Franciscan friar felt that anyone who married after that fashion should be allowed to stay permanently attached to his wife's mission, without being removed to another and that he should be given an animal for his own use. After a year or so working on the Mission farm, the man also rated, in Serra's opinion, two cows and a mule from the royal herd as well as a parcel of land for his own personal use.

In anticipation of Pius XII's dictum that one who prefers people of any particular race over another "perverts an order of the world planned and created by God," José de Gálvez favored giving Spaniards or pure *mestizos* who married converted Indian women, a double share of land. The Visitator General wished, however, to forbid matrimonial entanglements between the natives and the other castes of contemporary times, figuring as he did that such unions might demoralize the Indian spouses.

Father Zephyrin Engelhardt, the Franciscan chronicler, stated "that down to the year 1800 as many as twenty–nine neophyte girls or women had married white men, which was a large percentage considering the small white population, for many of the soldiers brought their wives along from Mexico."

Spain's early representatives of Church and State developed an overall colonial policy equaled in humanitarian principles by that of no other country. In the matter of inter–racial marriage, the program "looked to the preservation of the natives, and to their elevation to at least a limited citizenship" in the royal realm. Such a policy served to reaffirm the Church's unwavering proclamation about "the unity and solidarity of the human race, according to which all men are children of the same Father, redeemed by the same Blood of Christ, destined for the same heaven and endowed with the same inalienable rights."

THE CALIFORNIA MISSIONS ON POSTCARDS

As an accepted part of western culture, pictorial postcards are a normal outgrowth of an accelerated society. Now in their second century of service, these colorful message–bearers seem just as relevant to the interplanetary age as leisurely letters were to stagecoach days.

Since postcards reflect the tastes, interests and sentiments of the areas where they originate, it is easy to see why California mission scenes have been among the favorite postcard adornments for well over half a century. Probably no other medium so vividly portrays the provincial era. One authority claims that picture postcards are all the more valuable, as a record of local history, since they bear "a somewhat similar relation to the place represented as does its local newspaper." In 1910, George Watson Cole reported, "The most familiar form in which the old missions are presented to the eye at the present time is perhaps the post card." Even a cursory glance at the volume of productions from the various publishing houses lends credence to that assertion.

The largest western publisher of postcards was Edward H. Mitchell of San Francisco. His firm issued about 4,000 different scenes between 1898 and 1915, including thirty–two postcards depicting fourteen of the California missions. In addition to an alternate series published on yellow or canary colored paper, Mitchell printed many cards distributed by other California specialty houses.

The Detroit Publishing Company, originally known as the Photochrome Company, issued postcards from 1898 until 1919. Experts generally agree that the output of this firm was by far the most important in the American postcard field. It has been estimated that approximately 15,000 different cards were published in their "photostint" process, 700 of which fell into the category of art and humor. An unspecified number of their twenty–nine views of twelve missions were printed in Switzerland.

Twelve views of five missions and one *asistencia* were published by Cardinell–Vincent Company of Oakland. This firm was an outgrowth of Britton and Rey, early San Francisco lithographers. M. Rieder of Los

Postcard view of the Old Mission (1797), Mission San Jose, made by the Western Card Company, Reedley, California.

Angeles disseminated the greatest variety of mission specimens, representing all but San José. Among his 181 depictions are the only known views of Santa Ysabel and San Pascual. Published at several places, mostly in Germany, the center of the postcard industry, the Rieder line was purchased by George 0. Restall about 1909.

There were 132 postcards distributed by the Oscar Newman Company of Los Angeles and San Francisco. Their depictions of eighteen missions and two *capillas* were made in Germany prior to World War I and later in the United States. Adam Clark Vroman of Pasadena circulated thirty–six replica colored prints of the missions. In addition to scenes of eighteen different missions and one *capilla* was an outstanding postcard–map of *El Camino Real*, reproduced from the original used in the census of 1890.

Twenty different mission scenes were among the forty–four postcards published by the Paul C. Koeber Company of New York City. Included among the four scenes of *asistencias* is a rare view of Santa Margarita. The L. R. Severn firm of Los Angeles issued twenty–two views of six missions and two *capillas* on postcards printed in Germany. In later years their business was merged with Woods Publishers of Los Angeles and Leipzig.

The Pacific Novelty Company of San Francisco distributed fourteen views of seven missions and one *capilla*. Another Bay Area firm, Richard Behrendt, cir-

culated mission postcards between 1905 and 1909. N. H. Reed of Santa Barbara had a variety of 800 different California scenes. Among his photographic postcards were about 200 views of the missions, mostly of the one at Santa Barbara. The Adolph Seilige Publishing Company of St. Louis offered nineteen views of four missions, while the Benham Indian Trading Company of Los Angeles made available fourteen views of four missions. The Ghirardellis Milk Chocolate Company's set of fifteen missions was never sold commercially.

No period in human annals has been devoid of a medium to express its own particular beauty and fascination. When seen in their proper historical perspective, mission postcards can be said to express the tone of California's provincial atmosphere far more effectively than many other of the less ephemeral survivals of the era.

TOYPURINA THE TEMPTRESS

The story of "Toypurina the Temptress" is a true account of a remarkable Indian woman. It is gleaned from a manuscript of Thomas Workman Temple II, who ferreted out the details in Mexico City's Archives of the Indies.

Toypurina, simultaneousIy a sorceress, medicine woman, and witch exerted a power over her tribesmen of the San Gabriel area scarcely paralleled in the colonial period. It was at the instigation of this twenty–three year old savagely attractive beauty that a band of warriors crawled over the adobe parapet of Mission San Gabriel on the "first night of the new moon," October 25, 1785, for the express purpose of killing those responsible for trespassing upon the land of their forefathers and despoiling their tribal domain. Fortunately, the Spaniards had been warned by one of the guards who overheard the natives planning the revolt in their native Gabrieliño dialect.

The assault was quickly put down and Toypurina was captured a few days later. On January 3, 1786, a formal hearing was held and Toypurina and her companions were interrogated at considerable length. The investigation revealed that it was Toypurina's artful wizardry that persuaded the braves of six *rancherias,* including her own of Japchivet, to enter the nefarious plot. At the conclusion of the trial, Toypurina was exiled "to the mission most distant from San Gabriel, where she might settle, become married and be free from the vengeance demanded by the Gabrieliños."

Officially, the account closes under the date of December 14, 1787, and were it not for subsequent research, the record of the only Indian woman to have plotted the destruction of a mission would be complete. But there is a sequel, and a happy one at that. Further study brings to light that Toypurina was "exiled" to Mission San Carlos Borromeo and there, after learning the *doctrina* and embracing the Faith as Regina Teipurina, on July 26, 1789 she married Manuel Montero, a Spanish soldier. The Governor of California, Pedro Fages, came to act as sponsor—that same Fages—who had known the lovely bride as the wildest and most feared temptress in all of Alta California.

The couple lived out their life at Mission San Luis Obispo and their four children were born and raised into the Faith Toypurina had once so bitterly assailed. Toypurina died an exemplary Christian at Mission San Juan Bautista on May 22, 1799, and was buried the following day in the mission's *Campo Santo.*

Probably in all of California annals, there is no more outstanding victory of the Holy Cross than the conversion of Toypurina, a native temptress brought forth from the darkness of evil, rebellion, and paganism to the knowledge, love, and service of the one true God.

BASKET–WEAVING AND THE CALIFORNIA MISSIONS

Though the Indians of the Pacific Slope were not known for their handicrafts, they did excel in the production of colorful baskets. As a matter of fact, with the possible exception of the canoes of the Canaliños, basketry was probably the only art in which the natives on the west coast displayed outstanding skill. One authority admits that the baskets produced by the California Indians "far excel those of any other people in fineness of weaving and beauty of decoration."

Basketry decoration was an ancient art with the natives. Each of the multitudinous patterns was skillfully worked out and each had its own symbolic significance. Among the Mono Indians, for example, the diamondback rattlesnake design was common. Human figures, hills, valleys, and scenes from nature were also employed. Sometimes small mosaics were applied to the baskets to create a more diversified pattern. The so–called "trinket" baskets were even more gayly decorated. Tiny beads and bright feathers from the head of the woodpecker, the breast of the wild canary, or the teal duck were often lavishly utilized in adorning the baskets.

The industry was cultivated by the women who were quite ingenious in weaving grass, sumac, splints, rushes, cedar, tule, yucca stems, kelp thread, willow roots, and sea plants into mats and baskets. Their finished product varied in sizes and shapes from flat, basin–shaped coiled weave bowls to the large pointed cones which the women carried on their back when digging for roots, picking berries, or gathering acorns. The multiple purpose of the finished products was underscored by the diarist, Miguel Costanso, who noted that each of the "thousand forms and graceful patterns was geared to the particular use they were made to serve."

Tools of the weaver were her adroit fingers, a stone knife, and a bone awl. Fingernails were used as a gauge, and teeth for nippers. The pliable baskets, some of which had lids, were woven (rather than coiled) from vegetable fibres on a warp of willow strips. By adding pitch or some other resinous substance such as asphaltum, baskets were made waterproof. They could then be utilized for such purposes as cooking, trapping fish, and carrying water; moreover, basket–work was employed in fences, houses, shields, and for harvesting.

Though many of the American Indians exhibited some proficiency in the art, the "California Indians are now generally regarded as the most skillful basketmakers among the primitive peoples of the entire world." One early visitor, Louis Choris, observed that the Indians of the missions to the south of San Francisco, particularly near Santa Barbara, made charming vessels and vase–shaped baskets, capable of holding water. They knew how to give them graceful forms and how to introduce pleasing designs into the fabric. They ornamented their works with bits of shell and feathers.

Indian basketry was a skill that displayed patience, beauty, symmetry and a keen sense of design. It was a highly symbolic means of expression, an art medium of considerable importance to students of California Indians. Any in–depth research of the basket–making abilities of the natives inclines one to agree with Kurt Baer that these people "could not have been as stupid as the early chroniclers" reported.

APOSTOLIC COLLEGE OF SAN FERNANDO

Mexico's apostolic colleges were established during one of those revivals of evangelical fervor to which the sons of Saint Francis are periodically subject. These foundations, independent from one another, were an innovation in the Order.

Drawing their recruits from all the Spanish provinces and subject to none, they were directly answerable to the Commissary General of the Indies. Each was governed by a guardian, elected for three years, with the assistance of his discretory. They were made up of friars who pledged to serve ten years in the missions.

San Fernando, the Apostolic College in Mexico City to which Fray Junípero Serra belonged, was located in his time at the western edge of Mexico City. With fields and orchards stretching north and west, the church and monastery had been founded as a hospice by the friars of Santa Cruz de Querétaro. Blessed on May 29, 1731, the foundation was then in the *barrio* or neighborhood of Necaltitlan.

Three years after its establishment as a hospice, San Fernando was elevated to the status of apostolic college. Its first superior was Fray Diego de Alcántara who had come from Querétaro for that specific purpose.

The cornerstone of the large church and monastery was laid on October 19, 1735, by the bishop elect of Durango. By the time of Serra's arrival, the edifice must have been nearly finished, though it was not dedicated for another two decades. Almost a city block long, the splendid church was the largest in Mexico City, with the exception of the Metropolitan Cathedral. It is cruciform in style, with its single tower to the left, and has a vaulted roof and cupola. There are no pillars within.

Today the sturdily–built church with its facade and tower faced with dark *tezontle* stone and the gray *canteria*, so common in other Mexican churches, public buildings and private residences of an earlier day is somewhat somber in appearance. To the left of San Fernando's church was the large monastery or college, two storied and plain in appearance. The edifice housed several cloisters of varied proportions. From their monastery on the second floor, the friars had a partial view of the many towers of the capital's churches to the south, as well as of the fields encircling the city to the west and north.

To the far west, a distance of about four miles, lay the heights of Chapultepec whose western slopes gradually rose into a higher range of hills and mountains. Fifty miles to the east loomed the snow clad volcanoes, Popocatepetl and Ixtacchiuatl.

The church was always dear to Fray Junípero Serra. The churrigueresque altars, glowing with gold, had just been installed. Their gaudy splendor had a tropical brilliance of which the friars tired in time and substituted simple classic altars. In recent years, replicas of the older altars have been erected and set in place.

Serra's first impression of San Fernando, however, was not of the symmetry of its architecture, but the harmony of its prayers. He was pleased and a note of optimism struck his soul. He said to a companion: "We can indeed consider as well employed our journey here from so far away . . . if only to gain the happiness of being members of a community which so slowly and devoutly fulfills the obligation of the Divine Office."

CROSS, SWORD AND GOLD PAN

In 1931, a collection of historical essays and ballads were published in the pages of *Touring Topics* (later *Westways*), the official publication for the Automobile Club of Southern California. The purpose of the series was "to portray visually outstanding and decisive episodes in the development of the Southwest."

There were twelve colorful scenes painted by Carl Oscar Borg and one by Millard Sheets in the series, each of them described in an historical narrative by Herbert Eugene Bolton. In 1936, the Primavera Press published the series in book form under the title *Cross, Sword and Gold Pan*. Each of the hundred copies was signed by the contributing artists and historian.

The copy of this now rare book at the Archival Center for the Archdiocese of Los Angeles has a centerfold illustration of "the Founding of Los Angeles in 1781," wherein the masterful Millard Sheets apocryphally portrays the governor, friars and settlers crossing into the valley adjacent to the Rio Portiuncula. A ballad by John Russell McCarthy captures the sentiment of the occasion.

Father Eusebio Francisco Kino occupies center stage in the portrayal about the "Coming of the Cattle" to the Southwest. The famed Jesuit missionary is depicted overlooking and directing all aspects of the moment. Bolton believed that Kino "deserves remembrance as founder of the stock industry." In one hand, he is carrying the Bible; in the other, a branding iron. "Where his churches arise, famine fled. He transformed his neophytes from nomads to a people of a settled life."

In Bolton's view, Kino symbolized the whole of the Jesuit apostolate. The Society of Jesus "came primarily to save souls. Incidentally, they spread the elements of European civilization." The work which Kino did as a ranchman or stockman would, alone, stamp him as an unusual genius. "From the small outfit supplied him from the older missions, within fifteen years he established the beginnings of ranching in the rolling valleys of the southwest."

Kino is not alone among the heroes featured in this marvelous book. Several of the full–cover paintings depict other outstanding episodes in the exploration and settlement of the west and the role played in that outreach by the Franciscans, most of them from faraway Spain. The " founding of San Diego Mission," for example, is vividly portrayed. Bolton explains how Fray "Junipero Serra, superior of the new missions to be founded," would become "one of America's most famous pioneers." Serra is shown preaching at the first Mass offered on July 1, 1769.

In the portrayal of "Anza Crossing the Sand Dunes," Fray Francisco Garces accompanies the trailblazer, carrying aloft the pictorial banner of Our Lady and the Christ Child that became famous among the Indians. In all of these historical depictions, the cross shares equal billing with the sword.

In the colorful scene of Jedediah Smith arriving at San Gabriel Mission in 1826, the first of the American trappers to reach California overland is welcomed by a friar who offers him a small rosary. It is a scene reminiscent of all that was good about the spiritual impact of the European way of–life brought to the native Americans.

If one were to look for a half dozen of the most attractive reflections about the "conquest" of California, *Cross, Sword and Gold Pan* would surely be among the chief contenders.

BAJA CALIFORNIA APOSTOLATE

After a recent lecture about Fray Junípero Serra and his accomplishments for the Lord in Alta California, a lady asked a question for which there is no easy answer: "Whatever happened in and to the area the friars left behind when Serra journeyed northward in 1769?" Some quick research found that among the better descriptions of conditions in contemporary Baja California, few would surpass that given by Godfrey Poage in his biography of Father Henry Vetter, the "Magic Padre."

Poage points out that except for the small towns near the California–Arizona border, the peninsula remains today mostly as it was known to Fray Junípero Serra and his priestly collaborators, an area sparsely marked by civilization. The satellite pictures one sees on television portray the area as a slender, misshapen finger of land dangling from the southwestern corner of the North American continent.

The peninsula extends some 800 miles from the United States border to well below the Tropic of Cancer, a region of tumbled mountains, yawning chasms, desert plains and lonely beaches. There are no fenced and cultivated lands, no ribbons of concrete highway nor mirrors of rivers and lakes. It is a huge area, twice the length of Florida and a hundred miles longer than Italy. Bounded on one side by a gulf and on the other by the sea, it has upwards of a thousand miles of lonely Pacific shoreline on the west.

The early missionaries used to say that Baja California was unlike any place on earth. The Gulf of California separates it from Mexico, to which it is related both by language and politics. It is separated from the United States by an arbitrary line drawn from Yuma straight west to the Pacific Ocean. Below that hundred and fifty mile border, fixed at the end of the Mexican–American War, lie 55,000 square miles of almost untouched wilderness. "Desolate" would be a very accurate word for describing the area.

Most of the world's wilderness areas have remained so because they are inaccessible. But Baja remains a wilderness because of its indomitable stubbornness, a built–in resistance to the impact of civilization. For more than four centuries people have attempted to subdue that area and exploit its resources. But despite it all the land clings to its primitive state. Visitors to the area note that everywhere there are signs of this resistance: adobe walls blasted by abrasive winds, abandoned missions, roads that lead nowhere, bleached bones, forgotten mines and wrecked machinery.

First came the Spanish conquistadors, avidly searching for pearls and gold. Then came the Jesuits, Franciscans and Dominicans who tried to elevate the aborigines with plow and catechism. Then followed a motley procession of adventurers, buccaneers, speculators, miners and treasure hunters. There is something about a barren country that inspires the belief that it contains hidden riches, waiting only to be uncovered by a blow of a pick or the ding of a geiger counter.

Poage summarizes the question and answers the initial query. "Whatever happened in and to the area the friars left behind when they journeyed northward in 1769?" in rather succinct terms: "Most of it remains as it was a thousand years ago."

But that will all change within the next few decades. The miracle of water will transform Peninsular California and make of it a paradise. Then perhaps we will be able to see what it was about the area that has so attracted the interest of the outside world.

PENINSULAR CALIFORNIA FOUNDATIONS

Fray Junípero Serra and fifteen of his Franciscan confreres arrived in Peninsular California in April, 1768, to replace the Society of Jesus in their missionary foundations. On August 12th, when the friars were entrusted with the temporalities of the missions, the *Presidente* was asked to submit a detailed report to Don Jose de Gálvez.

The Mallorcan–born friar gathered the necessary data, which he sent from the Presidio of Santa Ana, on November 3, 1768. Annexed to his statistical survey were the following remarks from the *Presidente*:

The soldiers belonging to the garrison of the *Presidio*, the crew and commanding officers of the ships, the Spanish citizens and settlers who live in some missions, especially in the parish of the *Presidio* of Santa Ana and its neighborhood, whose population is growing rapidly now on account of the measures taken by the Most Illustrious Inspector General, are to be found in another statistical account, prepared separately and taken from the special census ordered by the decrees of His Illustrious Lordship.

The *rancherias* mentioned in these statistics and in the census, from where they are taken, are not established in determined spots, nor have they fixed dwellings in the various districts of the missions to which they belong. They wander off into the mountains. The only exceptions are those belonging to *Nuestra Señora de Guadalupe* which are true *rancherias* and form little towns and also one belonging to San Francisco Xavier.

Name of the Mission	Number of Rancherias	Marriages	Their children	Widowers and Widows	Their children	Single persons	Their children	Orphans	Total of souls
San Jose del Cavo .	1	13	29	5	4	7	—	—	71
Santiago	1	41	62	12	3	18	—	1	178
Nuestra Señora del Pilar, called Todos Santos	1	13	17	17	9	12	—	2	83
La Pasión.	8	120	139	36	20	13	—	10	458
San Luis Gonzaga .	3	83	92	16	10	1	—	3	288
San Francisco Xavier Biaunda	4	117	227	11	7	1	—	2	482
Loreto	1	20	32	12	10	—	—	5	99
San José Comondu	1	95	119	9	6	—	—	6	330
La Purisima Concepción	1	51	38	5	5	—	—	2	152
Nuestra Señora de Guadalupe	5	128	225	26	25	—	—	12	544
Santa Rosalia Melexé	1	63	91	10	10	—	—	8	245
San Ignacio	7	196	208	54	23	—	—	33	710
Santa Gertrudis . . .	8	377	392	92	50	—	—	63	1,360
San Francisco de Borja	7	441	390	58	60	229	7	14	1,640
Santa Maria	4	146	77	19	9	118	—	—	509
Total	53	1,904	2,138	382	254	399	7	161	7,149

In conclusion, since the census was taken and the reports were made out by the apostolic missionaries who now take care of the missions, the *rancherías* are becoming organized towns with formal civilized life. In addition, the two Missions of La Pasión and San Luis Gonzaga were incorporated with the nearest mission, Nuestra Señora del Pilar, whose lands are as fertile as their lands were barren. These very useful changes as well as others commanded by the Most Illustrious Lord will be noticed in the statistics and reports for the next year.

Fray Junípero Serra concluded by listing the number of Spaniards, settlers and Indians not included in his earlier statistics:

Statistics taken from the census returns gathered by the Reverend Fathers in obedience to the decree of the Most Illustrious Lord Don Jose de Gálvez, member of His Majesty's Council and Cabinet. In it are given the number of Spaniards and settlers, and that of the Indians living in this peninsula and other provinces.

Castes	Marriages	Their children	Widowers and Widows	Their children	Single persons	Orphans	Total of souls
Spaniards and Settlers	98	220	17	24	59	4	520 [422]
Indians	40	85	2	1	49	2	219 [179]
Total	138	305	19	25	108	6	739 [601]

Serra noted that

Among the ninety–eight families of Spanish and of settlers are included forty–two soldiers, the number comprising the garrison of the *presidio*; and the two hundred and nineteen Indians come from the coast of Sonora and Sinaloa; they came to this peninsula as servants and workmen in the missions and *presidios* here.

Some of the married men listed above have their families on the other coast.

MISSION MUSIC IN PROVINCIAL TIMES

Nowhere has the influence of sacred music been more striking than in missionary fields. It was with "psalms, hymns and spiritual canticles, singing and making melody in heart to the Lord" that the Franciscan friars introduced Christianity to California. At the time of the white man's penetration to the Pacific Slope, the natives idea of music was noise with harmony. Nonetheless, the California Indians were not totally devoid of musical talent. Their innate abilities budded when the missionaries introduced melodious songs and perfected instruments.

With their sonorous voices and sharp ears, the neophytes quickly learned to chant the liturgical services. Before long they could play, from note, the violin, bass viola, flute and guitar. The missionary report from San Gabriel, in 1814, states that "as Christians they have learned how to play our instruments, the wind and the string. Some of the neophytes exhibit a lively interest and fondness for the new instruments, and prefer them to their own."

The earliest musical selections taught to the Indians were congregational hymns. Men, women and children were encouraged to sing the *Alabado* (Song of Divine Praise), the *Cantico del Alba* (Morning Song) and the *Salve Regina* (Hail holy queen). Certain prayers were changed to a simple psalm tone; often antiphonally with the *padre*, a couple of singers or even little children taking one part, and the congregation responding. In addition to certain litanies, the neophytes also learned some of simpler Spanish *alabanzas* embodying the commandments, sacraments and other religious teachings.

Father Zephyrin Engelhardt, the mission chronicler, reported that the Indians "became so used to the prayers and hymns, and they were so firmly grounded by practice on the doctrinal and moral points of religion, that even after half a century, when no priests had appeared among the descendants of the Mission Indians away from the cities and *ranchos,* they recited all that their fathers and mothers had learned and practiced. Hence it was that they preserved the priceless treasure of Christian Faith, even when, for lack of guidance and moral support, they lapsed into a wild life." Throughout the provincial era, music quickened the activity of the entire mission day. At San Juan Capistrano, for example, upon awakening, the neophytes would throw open their windows to the sun, and the Morning Hymn to Mary would echo from every adobe: *Ya viene al alba* (Now breaks the glowing dawn).

Father Owen da Silva stated that "from the morning bell, *El Alba*, to the Poor Souls Bell, at night, the daily routine was regulated by musical tones. . . . It is said that even the animals in the field understood the various calls" of the bells. The smallest children were also musically involved. While their parents and older brothers and sisters were performing their daily tasks, the youngsters assembled in the mission patio for catechism. There the *padre* would urge them to sing some hymn or ditty. At times they were taken into the church to sing their solos before the Blessed Sacrament.

Truly then, music became a valuable instrument by which the Indians found their way to the Kingdom of God. And what happy times not only for the little ones but also for the Indians in general; the nearest thing to Utopia that a primitive people have ever experienced! As one old native was heard to say: "The Indians during the Mission period had happy times, it was a pity they were not allowed to continue to live in that manner always."

MUSIC AT THE MISSIONS

Many as yet unplumbed chapters in California history lie waiting for musicologists at the libraries of the University of California at Berkeley and the Santa Barbara Mission Archives. Several researchers have called attention to the largely unexamined collection of California music on deposit in the Stanford Library's Bender Room, much of it given to Mrs. Leland Stanford in the late 1800s by Father Angelo Casanova, then the pastor at Monterey.

Bringing those musical treasures to the public will surely prove exciting. Music played a paramount role in the early European settlements along California's *El Camino Real*. Up and down the coast, in all the missions, music occupied a unique place in religious and social life. The Indians were readily attracted to the Church's melodious hymns and chants. They were carefully trained by the friars to sing the sacred chant, to play in bands and to otherwise participate in the Church's liturgical activities.

There are several colorful contemporary descriptions of these musical involvements. One writer told about a "rag–tag choir and band" playing the Marseillaise (learned by ear from a barrel organ), another recalled Jose el Cantor conducting 400 neophytes in the *Miserere* at the funeral of Governor Jose Arrillaga at Mission Soledad.

Fray Felipe Arroyo de la Cuesta, one of the many missionaries who actively championed musical involvement by the Indians, travelled around the vast environs of his mission using a barrel organ to entice participation in religious services. There was a flourishing musical life based on sacred music imported from Spain, South and Central America and undoubtedly also composed in California. Relics of that era's accomplishments exist transcribed in the early 1800s on the water–stained parchment scores now reposing at Stanford and other research centers.

Much of the music written or arranged for the neophyte choirs like Masses and motets, was written in easy, short–phrased homophonic style by Fray Narciso Duran, California's first prominent composer. He and other friars used notched sticks or knotted ropes to count time. Often they utilized notes of different colors to indicate the variation of tones. The appearance of such devices indicates that the friars simplified the traditional notations, using a combination of old style writing and contemporary notes, with a dash of color.

The music believed to have been composed in California was clearly influenced by the 17th and 18th century music from Europe and Latin America. It was tonal, permeated with plain chant, though harmonized, conveying its free rhythm. The early California repertory was touched strongly by the major works from the Mexican cathedrals by Padilla (from Puebla), Lienas (Bogota), Hidalgo (La Plata), Zurnaya (Mexico City) and Jose Nunes Garcia, the first major black composer of the Americas.

This is only a short glimpse of what is chronicled in the Stanford collection. Some enterprising students must one day delve more deeply into California's earliest musical history covering the years between 1760 and 1840.

MISSION CHORAL MUSIC

The libraries of the Santa Barbara Mission Archives, the Archival Center at Mission Hills, Stanford University (Bender Room) and the University of California, Berkeley, are the main depositories of original musical manuscripts related to the frontier outposts established along California's *El Camino Real* in the years 1769–1823.

Of special interest to historians is material relating to the choral music and trained choirs used by the Franciscan to enhance the liturgical ceremonies at the California missions. During the earliest years, most of the Church–related music in the area was congregational. As is still the case in most parochial churches in California, the neophytes learned to sing the common hymns in unison, such as the *Alabado* (Song of Divine Praise), the *Cantico del Alba* (Morning Prayer), the *Salve Regina* and others.

Later, choirs and orchestras were developed. The most intelligent, docile and musically talented young boys were recruited and they learned to read music and play a number of musical instruments.

Several of the friars had been accomplished musicians in their native Spain. Fray Jose Señan reported that the natives at San Buenaventura Mission were "quite eager to sing and play on the instruments, string as well as wind, and they easily learn by ear and sight."

Another friar, Felipe Arroyo de la Cuesta, described the neophytes at San Juan Bautista Mission as being "fond of music and song. They learn anything with ease and can even play their pagan tunes on our instruments."

Fray Narciso Duran sent some of his converts to Santa Clara, where Fray Jose Viader successfully taught them the basics. "The results," as Duran noted, "exceeded my fondest hope; and once music was somewhat underway . . . the sacred functions were carried out with a fitness more than mediocre." Since Duran realized that most of the friars lacked the background for teaching music, he devised a simplified musical notation system and certain other strategies that facilitated the procedure.

He decided to use only one clef rather than treble, tenor and bass clefs. He employed a six line staff instead of the usual five, all of which made the notes look clear and uncomplicated. Duran also adopted the use of colored notes to distinguish the soprano, alto, tenor and bass parts of three and four–part music. Hence the tenor part, for example, could easily be followed even when it roamed above the notes of the alto.

The ingenious friar also simplified the long and often complicated Sequences in the chants. For instance, he set all the Introits to the well–known melody of the sixth tone. The Graduals and Offertories he omitted entirely and, to create a stronger sense of standard tones, Duran devised a way to have the instruments accompany the singers with the vocal line.

Admittedly, some of his procedures violated tradition, but Duran knew by experience that his system worked and it worked fairly well. While later critics frowned on the concept of instrumental accompaniment for mission choirs, listeners reported that the music was pleasant and harmonious, with the human voice always remaining the primary and dominant element.

In her superb booklet, *Gloria Dei. The Story Of California Mission Music*, Sister Mary Dominic Ray wrote that "over the years, the practical, down–to–earth musical methods of the missionaries resulted in a level of musical accomplishment that was adequate at worst and surprisingly beautiful at best."

THE MISSION ORCHESTRAS

The Spanish friars in California, like their seraphic founder, were troubadours of God. That many Indians were influenced by the musical talents of the missionaries is noted by Fray Francisco Garcés who related that after his campfire singing "their shoutings and dancings and chaffings then ceased, and everything remained in profound silence."

Instrumental accompaniment was used to keep singers on pitch and to enhance the tonal quality of choral endeavors. In the absence of organs, which did not exist in mission times, the customary instruments were the violin, viola, violincello, base viol, flute, trumpet, horns, bandola, guitar, drums and triangle.

Apparently only stringed instruments and flutes were allowed in the church proper with perhaps a drum or triangle to maintain the beat. Otto von Kotzebue visited Mission San Francisco in 1816 and described a choir singing to the accompaniment of a violincello, violin and two flutes. By 1827, the orchestra at that mission had grown to eight violins, two bass viols and two drums.

Another visitor to California, Harrison Rogers, recalled that at Mission San Gabriel the orchestra was composed of two violins, one bass viol, a trumpet and a triangle. After listening to a lengthy concert, the stalwart Calvinist concluded that the Indians made "tolerably good music."

Besides contributing to the solemnity of liturgical celebrations, the missions orchestras added considerably to the life and happiness of the Indian villages. They also provided music for weddings and dances of the *gente de razón*. The more accomplished orchestras even went on tour. At the dedication of the church at Mission Santa Barbara, in 1820, for example, the bands of Santa Ines and San Fernando pooled their talents with the local musicians, "playing with a will for about two continuous hours."

Many of the musical instruments were fashioned at the missions. One flute was actually made from the barrel of an old gun. Such locally manufactured items obviously lacked the quality of those imported from Spain and Mexico.

Alfred Robinson complained that occasionally the musical selections played were inappropriate for Church. Another writer conjectured that the *padres* may have tolerated those lively tunes for a definite purpose. "After all," he says, "his neophytes were like little children, and he may have considered this a laudable way to hold their attention and interest during the long devotions."

Still another commentator recorded an amusing encounter, in 1851, at Mission Santa Cruz. After the religious rites were concluded, the church choir changed into a street band. Their instruments consisted of a brass and kettle drum, two violins, a triangle and a banjo. The performers, all Indians, appeared to have suffered in some recent encounter; "for every head was more or less damaged, the eyes, foreheads, noses and cheeks, being badly battered and patched; doubtless a reverent, but certainly not a reverend choir."

The late John Steven McGroarty once observed that "the most exquisite of all the gifts the Mission Fathers brought, save the boon of Christianity, was music." Such was indeed a most integral aspect in lifting the California aborigines "out of spiritual darkness into the great white light of God."

MISSIONARY CHORISTERS

That plainsong which made up the greater portion of the music used in the old missions was adapted, in large measure, from the Gregorian chant of the 18th century and had only a slight variation from that used in contemporary Spain and Mexico.

The gifted Fray Narciso Duran fashioned many parts of the Mass to uniform rhythm; hence, common melodies for Introits, Graduals and Communions made is possible to have sung Masses with greater frequency. Robert Louis Stevenson visited Mission San Carlos Borromeo at Carmel in 1879 and noted:

> The Indians troop together, their bright dresses contrasting with their dark and melancholy faces; and there among a crowd of somewhat unsympathetic holiday makers, you may hear God served with perhaps more touching circumstances than in any other temple under heaven.
>
> An Indian, stone blind and about eighty years of age, conducts the singing; other Indians compose the choir; yet they have the Gregorian music at their finger ends, and pronounce the Latin so correctly that I could follow the meaning as they sang. The pronunciation was odd and nasal, the singing hurried and staccato. In *saecula saeculo–ho–horum*, they went, with a vigorous aspirate to every additional syllable. I have never seen faces more vividly lit up with joy than the faces of these Indian singers. It was to them not only the worship of God, nor an act by which they recalled better days, but was besides an exercise of culture, where all they knew of art and letters was united and expressed.
>
> And it made a man's heart sorry for the good Fathers of yore, who had taught them to dig and to reap, to read and to sing—who had given them European massbooks, which they still preserve and study in their cottages, and who had now passed away from all authority and influence in that land — to be succeeded by greedy thieves and sacrilegious pistol shots.

Much of the music used at the missions was composed by the *padres* themselves. The few extant music books reveal a number of two and four part hymns and Masses. "Structurally they are simple. The two part music is usually sung in thirds. The four part compositions are homophonic."

Indian music was written on one staff of four or six lines with notes in bold squares and diamonds with and without tails, corresponding to present–day half, quarter and eighth notes. If there were two or more parts singing simultaneously, each group's notes would be executed in a different color and all each singer had to do was follow his assigned color. Violins and flutes sometimes accompanied the music and on great feastdays the whole mission orchestra might be used.

Another eye–witness, Alfred Robinson, reports his impressions of mission music at San Gabriel where he attended Holy Mass one day in 1829:

> At six o'clock we went to the church where the priest had already commenced the service of the Mass. The

imposing ceremony, the glittering ornaments, and illuminated walls were well adapted to captivate the simple mind of the Indian and I could not but admire the apparent devotion of the multitude, who seemed absorbed, heart and soul, in the scene before them.

The solemn music of the Mass was well–selected, and the Indian voices accorded harmoniously with the flutes and violins that accompanied them. On retiring from the church, the musicians stationed themselves at a private door of the building, whence issued the Reverend Father whom they escorted to his quarters; where they remained for half an hour, performing waltzes and marches until some trifling present was distributed among them, when they returned to their homes.

Today, the Indians' voices are stilled, but "their old and humble music scores remain for us to quicken again with life, with mystic spell and deep devotion."

MISSION PRAYER AND SONG BOARD

One of the truly significant and unique items associated with any of the California missions is the "Prayer and Song Board" found among the treasures in the National Anthropological Archives in Washington, D.C.

Earliest mention of the board can be traced to the 1860 *Annual Report* for the Smithsonian Institution wherein a catechism is referred to as being copied from a wooden tablet used by the missionaries to instruct the Indians at Church. By 1973, when it was borrowed for an international exhibition on "California: The Golden Quest," the wooden tablet had been studied extensively.

The board consists of a single piece of sawed or split, carved and smoothed wood measuring 16–1/8 x 8–1/4 inches. Its vertical, rectangular form displays a semicircular crest. Shaped to accommodate a standard sheet of paper, the wood is juniper or incense cedar, both of which are from trees found in nine of the western United States, including the Santa Lucia mountains of California.

Each side of the board supports a piece of flax, laid paper with words and music written in two colors of ink. A most unfortunate accession mark reading "1082. Ethnology" cannot be removed. Reminiscent of the altar cards prominent in Catholic churches until recent times, the first sheet of the prayer is divided by ruled lines into three sections. Red lettering accentuates titles and directives.

One whole section is devoted to the *Asperges* which was sung by the priest and choir alternately prior to chanted Masses. The second page contains the Acts of Faith, Hope and Charity (in Spanish and the Salinan dialect) which the neophytes recited or sung prior to liturgical functions. The card was obviously intended as a mnemonic device whereby the new converts could read (if they hadn't already memorized) their prayers.

Records at the National Anthropological Archives clearly associated the prayer and song board with San Antonio Mission. Material analysis points to Spanish paper, colonial inks and local wood. The board was probably crafted at the mission and is stylistically appropriate to the early 1800s.

Written at the top of one side of the board are the names of Friars Miguel Pieras and Buenaventura Sitjer, both of whom served at San Antonio Mission at various times. The musical skills brought to San Antonio by another friar, Juan Bautista Sancho, may have contributed to the fabrication of the board although, it must be noted, the words and music were typical of the times.

In a recent essay for the *Southern California Quarterly,* Richard Ahlborn noted that "the board's significance extends from a rare historical object indicative of California mission Hispanization to an artifact of anthropological interest." Of special relevance is the board's construction from local and imported materials, its documentation of European musical traditions and linguistic skills, and its function as an educational tool.

Similar devices were known to have existed in mission times. In the case of San Antonio Mission, the Prayer and Song Board personified the Church's primary role of teaching the Gospels and administering the Sacraments.

SONGS OF THE CALIFORNIA MISSIONS

In March of 1951, Father Owen da Silva directed the Padre Choristers of Santa Barbara Mission in a series of recordings. The unique album, consisting of two ten inch records (four sides, 78 r.p.m.) was entitled *Songs of the California Missions* and was produced by R.C.A. Victor.

The album presented a cross section of California's earliest music: the *Sanctus* and *Benedictus* of the highly popular *Misa Cataluña,* the Morning and Evening hymns of the missions, the *Ave Maria* in Spanish, together with four other selections. For the production of the album the ranks of the internationally known Padre Choristers were augmented by their Franciscan brethren at San Luis Rey Mission.

It came as no surprise that the album was received enthusiastically from the very outset. Its popularity with tourists led to its distribution beyond the mainland of the United States. The records were heard in Rome, on the Isle of Mallorca, in London and Mexico and in parts of South America and Australia.

The reviews of the *Songs of the California Missions* are an indication of the album's acceptance within and without the music world. Following is a sampling of the comments made by experts in the field. Alexander Fried, writing in the San Francisco *Examiner,* said it was "a very warm and charming blend of religious, historic and musical interest. . . . Technically first rate. . . . The Padre Choristers of Santa Barbara sing the music with flawless gentle tone and sincerity."

In the Los Angeles *Examiner,* Patterson Green wrote that it is "a fascinating album of music. . . . charmingly sung under Father da Silva's experienced direction. . . . The album is interesting for its content and important as a document of California history."

In the Channel City's *News–Press* are these comments: "Santa Barbara's famed Padre Choristers of the Old Mission have greatly enriched the literature of recorded choral music. . . . unique, both in form and in musical excellence. . . . Excellent for their melodious and rhythmic qualities, impressive for their solemn simplicity . . . Those who have heard the *padres* need not be reminded of their skill in phrasing and harmonics. It is sufficient to say the records find them at their best."

Aileen Campbell, in *The Monitor,* wrote: "The music is rendered by the Padre Choristers with great warmth and simplicity. Their style is notable for its happily unforced tone and refinement of phrasing. . . . the records were actually produced by RCA Victor and are technically perfect."

In the *Catholic Educator,* John C. Selner said: "Father Owen captures a very fine spirit for these recordings. Those who are interested in the nostalgic saga of missionary achievements in California will find their reveries enhanced greatly by the sound of the Padres' songs in this album." In *The Americas* it was reported that *"Songs of the California Missions,"* an album of records which revive the music that the Spanish *padres* taught their Indian charges during the mission period, is believed to be a 'first' in Spanish American history. . . . The music is authentically interpreted by Father Owen da Silva, who here directs the internationally known Padre Choristers of Mission Santa Barbara. . . . Music critics have been superlative in their praise, acclaiming *Songs of the California Missions* a contribution to art, culture, to Franciscana and Californiana."

Today, original copies of *Songs of the California Missions* are a collector's item, highly sought after by music enthusiasts and those interested in the growth and development of Fray Junipero Serra's missions along *El Camino Real.*

THE *BULA CRUZADA*

The *Bula Cruzada* was a papal document containing privileges, indults and favors granted to the Kings of Spain as an aid in their wars against the Moslems. It was called *Cruzada* because of its similarity to the indults given to the soldiers engaged in the crusades—campaigns for the recovery of the Holy Land. (The term *Cruzada* was derived from the red or purple cross which, as a mark of their holy purpose, the soldiers wore upon their right shoulder.)

The privileges outlined in the *Bula Cruzada* were first granted to the Spaniards as early as 1089 by Pope Urban II on behalf of the warriors fighting for the recovery of Tarrangona. Among its other privileges, the bull dispensed from the law of abstinence. By that provision, a person was exempted from the ecclesial law forbidding the use of fleshmeat and other animal food, such as eggs, milk and cheese, at certain seasons and on specified days (Friday).

The privileges were printed on a paper leaflet which, with the passage of years, came to be known as a *bula* or bull. In California, the *bulas* could be obtained from the governor's secretary or his representative and were valid for one year only. After expiration, the certificate had to be renewed.

There was a small stipend charged for the *bula* and it was this feature that gave rise to the mistaken notion that *bulas* were simply "pay offs." (The offering or stipend was about two *reales* or a quarter and the poor, the infirm and the Indians were all exempted from paying the stipend.) A number of writers also had the erroneous impression that the *bulas* allowed the recipients to sin— or that they forgave past sins. That concept was reflected in the pages of Hubert Howe Bancroft's *History of California.*

Another feature of the *Bula Cruzada* was the fact that it was granted not in favor of the Church. Rather, it was given to the Spanish kings and they, in turn, sub–delegated and dispensed the system. All stipends went to the national treasury, not the Church. With the withdrawal of subjection to the kings of Spain, California forfeited the privileges which the popes had granted through the *Bula Cruzada.* From that time onward, dispensations had to come from the internal forum.

Following are excerpts from *La Bula de la Santa Cruzada* for the years 1818–1819:

> Whereas our Most Holy Father, Pius VII, by means of his brief, has deigned to extend for nine years the Apostolic Indult so that all the faithful of both sexes and of either the secular or ecclesial state, who reside in these dominions and islands, may eat wholesome fleshmeats, eggs and other animal food (but observing the fast) on Lenten days and other days of abstinence during the year. . . .
>
> Therefore you, N.N., who have contributed the alms of two silver *reales* . . . may eat wholesome fleshmeat, eggs and other animal food on Lenten days and other days of abstinence for the next term of two years, with the exception only of Ash Wednesday, the Fridays of Lent. . . .

CALIFORNIA'S MISSION BELLS

Henry Wadsworth Longfellow's observation that "bells are the voice of the Church" is surely true along the Pacific Slope. In California they are the revered symbols of the past and hold an honored place in local lore. The first bells in Alta California were brought from the peninsular foundations. At least three of the old bells that once called Indians to prayer and devotions in Jesuit churches in Baja California or Mexico are still hanging in belfries of Alta California. The entire day's activity of prayer, work and devotion at the missions was regulated by bells. In addition they proclaimed religious festivals, greeted distinguished guests, hailed national holidays, added merriment to weddings and bespoke sorrow at funerals.

There was a large variety of sizes and qualities in the many bells of the California scene. Generally, the largest bell was used to call the Indians to prayer and devotions, while the smallest one sounded the signal for work, meals and rest. Three or more bells normally hung on a cross–bar, in the Church tower, bell wall or *espadaña*. Another one hung near the corporal's quarters and still another close to the friar's living room.

Some of the bells played themselves out in the faithful performance of their musical calling. Others sustained injury during a convulsion of nature. Some found an unmarked resting place. The story of *The Mission Bells of California*, factually and interestingly related in 1934, by Marie T. Walsh, is worthy of a revised and expanded edition. A wholly new generation of Californians is fascinated by the intriguing background of mission bells.

One has hardly to scratch the surface to see how "the story of the bell is full of romantic instances, and many a chapter in history has been rung in and out by the mission bells." Alice J. Stevens has captured the theme of the mission bells most beautifully:

> From rafters old, in the mission tower,
>   Swing the bells.
> Tales of the past, at evening hour,
>   Their music tells.
> They clang and crash with brazen voice,
>   And seem to say,
> "For love and hope we now rejoice,
>   A wedding day."
> Again they wail a mournful part,
>   While Mass is said,
> A mother bends with breaking heart
>   Above her dead.
> Anon they whisper soft and low
>   At vesper hour,
> Soothe all our sorrows and our woe,
>   By magic power.
> We hear the anthems that were sung,

EL CAMINO REAL BELL

> To dry sad tears,
> While from the tower those bells have rung,
>   A hundred years.
> Like cherished friends of other times,
>   Those bells to me.
> The clanging of their broken chimes,
>   Sweet melody.

AN UNPUBLISHED MANUSCRIPT

One of the most famous unpublished books about California, a volume tentatively entitled *Bells of Camino Real,* was researched and written by Alice Harriman during the early years of this century. Very little is known about Mrs. Harriman, beyond the fact that she operated a small publishing house "of fine books" at 542 Fifth Avenue, in New York City prior to 1915.

She subsequently moved to California and took up residence at 633 West 15th Street in downtown Los Angeles. There she spent many years on two contemplated books, *Bells and their Overtones* and *Bells of Camino Real.*

The Archival Center at Mission Hills has two original letters from Mrs. Harriman, one written June 10, 1917 and the other October 6, 1921, both seeking information from Dr. A. H. Nichols of Boston about bells. Mrs. Harriman apparently knew the late Marie Walsh because there are copies of three letters to her among the Harrington papers, all of them relating to the origin of Russian bells along the Pacific Slope.

And it would seem that Miss Walsh was aware of the unpublished manuscript because on two occasions she relates incidents told to Harriman in her own book, *The Mission Bells of California,* which was released in 1934 by the Harr Wagner Publishing Company of San Francisco.

Mrs. Harriman completed her manuscript on the *Bells of Camino Real* just a day or so before her death in 1925. According to Phil Townsend Hanna, the treatise "was the result of months upon months of study at the various missions." Hanna told how "Mrs. Harriman had delved deeply into mission records, interviewing Indians and the *padres* and searching the archives of public institutions in her quest for pertinent materials." He said she "left no stone unturned to tell the full and complete story of the mission bells."

David Starr Jordan, President emeritus of Stanford University, was also familiar with Mrs. Harriman's work and agreed to write a foreword to the book. Therein he told about the labor and love "devoted to her self–imposed task."

After Mrs. Harriman's death, a committee of her friends undertook to secure publication of the fascinating work. Unfortunately, in the words of Hanna, "publishers everywhere turned it down." When Hanna learned of the manuscript's availability, he offered to serialize three chapters in *Touring Topics,* a magazine for motorists sponsored by the Automobile Club of Southern California.

Hanna noted, in an editorial aside, that the willingness of officials at the Auto Club to run the essays was "hardly to be regarded as evidence of their superior wisdom, but rather of the abysmal stupidity of publishers in general." He ventured the view that "here unless yours truly is greatly mistaken, are three fragments of a great story, and this publication is glad to give the work an audience."

The trilogy of installments in *Touring Topics* were entitled "The First Bell Rung In California" (July, 1929), "Bells of Ramona's Country" (August, 1929) and "The *Miserere* of San Luis Rey" (September, 1929). Excerpts from other chapters appeared in the Los Angeles *Times* and *Out West* Magazine.

It was also in 1929 that Mrs. Harriman's poetic remembrance of *The Bells of Santa Ysabel* appeared in pamphlet form. On the title page is a notation that "her

new book, *Bells of Camino Real,* will be published next spring." Finally, there is an eleven page typescript of an essay on the "Lost Bells of the Missions" at the Archival Center. That too appears to have been a chapter in the never–published *Bells of Camino Real.*

CALIFORNIA MISSION GARDENS

Of the twenty–one missions established along California's El Camino Real, seventeen have gardens stretching back to the beginnings of the Provincial Era. While many have some irrigated sections, most of the missions abound in water–sensible plants such as ceanothus which, once taking root, can survive on practically no water at all.

Among such survivors of earlier times is an oleander pruned as a tree, now more than a century old, which still blooms in summer at San Juan Bautista Mission. At Santa Clara Mission is a row of graceful 160 year old olive trees and at San Antonio is an equally venerable olive tree with neatly rounded canopy.

Nine of the missions have the widest variety of plants with water needs suited to California's climate. At San Diego, for example, arid climate plants combine in lush, colorful groupings. Under the shade of pepper trees, aloe sends up orange candle–like bloom spikes behind hedges of yellow–flowered euryops.

At San Luis Rey Mission, water–conserving bottlebrush, palms, oleanders and strawberry tree grow in the enclosed garden east of the church. In the old Sunken Garden, paths edged with ice plant and sea lavender curve past olive and pepper trees. Plants native to arid, temperate and semi–temperate climates are abundant at San Juan Capistrano Mission. Bougainvillea and a majestic century–old pepper tree grow against a backdrop of ruins and a Moorish–style fountain in the entry garden.

In the rear of the quadrangle at San Gabriel Mission are two olive trees that were planted in 1860. Grapevines covering a trellis along the garden's west side were started from cuttings planted a century earlier. At San Fernando Mission are one or two fruit trees from every variety that originally grew at the mission. These include pomegranate, olive, citrus, plum and fig.

In the enclosed cloister garden at Santa Barbara Mission is a Moreton Bay fig, a native of Australia, which was planted in 1860. Fences in the parking area are festooned with bougainvillea, cassias, honeysuckle and trumpet vine.

The garden at La Purisima contains a wide variety of plants used by the friars and Indians for food, fiber and medicinal purposes. Grapevines and pomegranate, fig and pepper trees were developed from grafts, buds and cuttings taken from plants at the other missions. There are over eighty species now.

More than 200 kinds of plants thrive in the gardens at San Carlos Borromeo Mission, many of them able to withstand extreme types of weather and climatic conditions, including the brutally cold coastal winds. Probably the most typical is "Mamam Cochet," an eighty year old tree rose planted a half century ago by Harry Downie with cuttings from San Juan Bautista. In the courtyard of San Francisco Solano is a small bed of native plants, including *lupines, manzanita* and *ceanothus*. Along a back fence is a 135 year old prickly pear cactus mound almost twenty feet tall, with fat, gnarled trunks and spiny beaver–tail pads.

Those wishing to take a lesson in landscaping for a water–sensible future need look no further than the California missions, whose early friars were adept at using plants and flowers to beautify this Rim of Christendom.

TOBACCO AND THE INDIANS

The use of tobacco in mission days is an established fact and it has been estimated that from eight to twelve bundles of *Manojos de Tabaco* (leaf tobacco) arrived annually from Mexico City. These dried leaves were crushed in a mortar and smoked by the Indians in their pipes or rolled into *cigarritos*.

Tobacco was frequently given by the *padres* as a reward for good behavior or for exceptional work, and, although the natives were fond of smoking, they apparently did so in moderation. Duflot de Mofras claims that tobacco was cultivated at several of the missions but, if so, the yield was never great for the dry climate was not conducive to good quality. In the 1870s a method was developed to effectively cure tobacco for local usage.

Only once in the first six decades of the mission era was the use of tobacco associated with a friar and even that connection is not clear. This happened in 1828 when George Cosme, the gate–keeper at Mission San Buenaventura, noted that Fray José Altimira took with him to Santa Barbara "a little box of cigars." Generally, however, early friars had no concern for tobacco since as neither food nor drink, they viewed it as a luxury unbecoming to their vow of poverty.

Sometimes ground–tobacco was sent to the missions in the form of snuff. Fray José Señan was known to have used it and the venerable old *Presidente* admitted without apology, that "our noses are yearning for snuff, of which none has been sent since 1810." Austrians, Germans, Italians and Spaniards of those days were notorious snuff consumers and, with them, it was nothing short of a national custom. Professors and students from Europe claimed that snuff was good for weak eyes. It was often used as a cure for those suffering from catarrh and head colds, a common malady among the friars. The damp mission cells aggravated sinus conditions and made the use of snuff more a matter of practicality than of pleasure.

Leaf–tobacco was frequently used to attract the natives. Fray Juan Crespi relates an early meeting with a tribe near present day Los Angeles noting that "some of the old men were smoking pipes . . . and they puffed at us three mouthfuls of smoke. We gave them a little tobacco and glass beads and they went away well pleased."

By 1800 in California "the largest item of royal revenue was that produced by the sale of tobacco. The net proceeds from cigars, cigarettes and snuff in the last years of the century amounted to $8,000. In 1790, for instance, 7,751 packages of cigars, 71,323 packages of cigarettes and thirteen pounds of snuff were consumed."

Current controversies notwithstanding, had the question of "side effects" been raised in mission times, the issue probably would have been dismissed by the typical Indian observation that "it is better to smoke here than hereafter!"

MISSION VINEYARDS

Vineyards were in full bloom as early as 1767 in at least three of the missions in Peninsular California. Though vines may have been brought northward to San Diego in 1769, there is reason to believe that Fray Pablo de Mugártegui made the first successful planting only in 1779 at San Juan Capistrano. Since the vines needed three or four years to mature into self–supporting stalks, it was probably 1783 or 1784 before wine–making achieved any measure of stability in Alta California.

It was not long after that, however, before viniculture was well on the way to becoming the most valuable of California's industries and the progress "was due to the friars and the Indians, who were the only industrious hands in the country." To the early Spanish settlers, wine had a nutritional, medicinal, social and religious value and that explains why Cortes introduced Spanish vines into the New World in 1542. There were occasional fluctuations in the mother–country's policy, however, and Alexander Humboldt noted in 1811 that the viceroy had been instructed "to root out all the vines in the northern provinces because the merchants of Cadiz complained of a diminution in the consumption of Spanish wines."

"Mission grape" was a large reddish–black berry full of tasty juice. Before 1833 it was the only variety of grape produced in California, although wine was procured from other wild fruits as soon as the natives mastered the technique of fermentation and distillation.

The favorable climate and fertile soil of Southern California accounts for the region's leadership in wine and raisin production. In the early years the best wines came from Missions San Gabriel, Santa Barbara, San Diego, San Buenaventura and San Juan Capistrano. In 1830 Alfred Robinson recorded that the vineyards at San Gabriel "make yearly from four to six hundred barrels of wine, and two hundred of brandy; the sale of which produces an income of more than twelve thousand dollars."

Three years later, Fray Narciso Duran, speaking of San Gabriel's *Viña Madre* (Mother Vineyard), observed that "the best wines which I have found in the various missions are those of San Gabriel." In his letter to Governor José Figueroa, Duran described the four types of mission vintage:

> There are two kinds of red wine. One is dry, but very good for the table; the other is sweet, resembling the juice pressed from the blackberries and so rather unpleasant. There are also two kinds of white wine. One of them is from pure grapes without fermenting—I mean from pure grape juice without fermenting it with the skins of the pressed grapes. This produces the white wine. The other of the same juice is fermented with a quantity of grape brandy. These two make a most delicious drink for the dessert.

Though wine was produced at most of the missions, the size of the vineyards varied considerably, ranging from 170 acres at San Gabriel to one acre at Santa Clara. Wine–making was a highly specialized skill. As described by Hubert Howe Bancroft, "suitable ground was selected, and a *desvan*, or platform, placed thereon. This was covered with clean hides, and the grapes piled upon it. Some well–washed Indians, having on only a *zapata* (loin cloth), the hair carefully tied up and hand covered with cloth wherewith to wipe away the perspiration, each having a stick to steady himself withal, were put to treading out the grape juice, which was caught in *coras*, or in leathern bags. These were emptied into a large wooden tub, where the liquid was kept two or three months, under cover of the grape skins to ferment. Such as did not flow off was put into wooden presses, and the juice into cooper jars, and covered with a kind of hat. Through two or three inserted tubes, heat was conveyed to the mass to aid evaporation and condensation. These jars served as a still for brandy. For white wine the first juice only was taken and stored."

Colonel Agoston Harazthy, whom one authority calls "the most important figure in after–mission–day grape culture and wine making," stated in 1858 that the mode of wine making had changed little even in his time.

The fermentation process was done in two ways. "The one, where the mist is put to ferment without the skins, and the other where it is fermented with the skins.

With the first method the wine is clear like water, keeps better, and by nature does not have many defects. . . . Where it is fermented with the skins the wine is more golden, has more strength. . . ."

CROPS IN PROVINCIAL TIMES

Though food supplies were brought from Baja California by the early missionaries, it was foreseen that after a five–year period, with industry and the careful husbanding of seeds, the frontier outposts would evolve into self–supporting institutions.

As soon as they had introduced the staple commodities of beans, corn, and wheat, the *padres* turned their attention to the wide variety of other delicacies now associated with California's provincial era. At the same time, the Indians were encouraged to domesticate the vast natural gardens of fruits, berries, wild vegetables, roots, acorns, nuts and edible seeds already prolific in the area.

Almost immediately after inaugurating a missionary foundation, slips and saplings were planted in the fertile soil. Within a relatively short while, vegetables, medicinal herbs and flowers were flourishing in the propitious climate of Alta California. As early as 1776, Fray Pedro Font described the vegetable garden at San Carlos Borromeo as consisting of "beds of cauliflower, lettuce, artichokes, and other vegetables and herbs than which there were no better in Mexico."

In his visits to the various mission orchards in 1792–1793, Captain George Vancouver observed flourishing crops of pears, apricots, apples, pears and figs. Auguste Bernard Duhaut–Cilly stopped at Mission San Luis Rey, in 1827, and related how the "two well planted gardens furnish an abundance of vegetables and fruits of all kinds."

Jean Francois de Galaup, Comte de Laperouse, reported that the "gardens of the Governor and the missions were filled with an infinity of culinary plants." He went on to note that his seamen "never had a greater abundance of vegetables in any part of the world." At Mission Dolores, Georg Heinrich, Freiherr von Langsdorff, told of seeing asparagus, cabbage and several sorts of salad, onions and potatoes. Certain sheltered areas also produced peas, beans and Turkish corn (maize).

Some of the missions specialized in particular crops. Chili peppers, melons, pumpkins, gourds for drinking cups and herbs were, for example, the specialties at Mission Santa Cruz. Pepper, olive and pomegranate trees were cultivated at San Luis Obispo. That mission also boasted the first cruciform grape arbor in California.

Mission San Gabriel, according to Alfred Robinson, had several extensive gardens with copious "oranges, citrons, limes, apples, pears, peaches, pomegranates, figs and grapes in abundance." The inventory of 1834 enumerated 2,333 fruit trees in nine orchards!

The *padres* personally superintended the work in the fields until proper persons were found or trained to act as overseers. In subsequent years, the general management of agricultural pursuits devolved upon the *mayordomo*, chief coordinator of mission activities.

HERBS, PLANTS AND ROOTS IN PROVINCIAL TIMES

The California Indians were familiar with the medicinal value of many herbs, plants and roots. One of the early missionaries wrote from Mission San Carlos, for example, that a native there knew "a root, a remedy against blood dysentery. The root is beaten to a powder and this is given with a little water. Some have been cured and highly praise the remedy."

Father Doroteo Ambris, the last resident priest at San Antonio, once compiled a list of oral remedies used by the Indians at his mission. For relieving the effects of consumption, the natives would boil leaves of rosemary in red wine until two–thirds of the mixture had evaporated. The residue would be drunk twice daily. Dysentery was counteracted by a strong tea solution made from the threads of the outside fibre of coconuts. Eating a dozen hazel nuts before retiring was an effective cure for excessive urine.

The root of wild peonies was chewed for such illnesses as colds, dyspepsia and poison oak paralysis. For ordinary aches and pains, the oiled leaves of prickly pears were applied. Tea made from pine tree needles or blossoms of elder trees was a common antidote for headache relief. Pure lemon juice taken after the morning meal was considered effective against inflammatory rheumatism.

The swallows weed (*yerba de la golondrina*) was a favorite for coughs, dropsy, jaundice, and poison bites. A cup of boiled milk with sage, taken before retiring, warded off insomnia.

There is no denying that "some California plants were practically drug stores." For instance, the red shand (*adenostema*) supplied a cure for cramps, snake–bites, sores and lockjaw. And a concoction from this plant was used for chills and fever and as a tonic, while from the twigs they made a purgative and a vomitive. The manzanita supplied a remedy for poison oak, bronchitis and other ailments. One writer has noted that there is a touch of humor in the fact that from the mistletoe the Indians made a remedy for saddle–sores on horses.

Dr. Cephas L. Bard once observed that the California Indians furnished three extremely valuable vegetable additions to *Pharmacopoeia*. "One, the Eriodyction Glutinosum, growing profusely in our foothills, was used by them in the infections of the respiratory tract, and its worth was so appreciated by the missionaries as to be named *Yerba Santa*, or Holy Plant. The second, the *Rhamnus purshiana* (the buckthorn) gathered now for the market in the upper portions of the State, is found scattered through the timbered mountains of Southern California. It was used as a laxative, and on account of the constipating effect of an acorn diet, was doubtless in active demand. The third, *Grindelia robusta* (gum weed), was used in the treatment of pulmonary troubles, and externally in poisoning from poison oak, and in various skin diseases."

The missionaries made medicine available to the Indians, but as Fray Ramon Abella recorded: "The greatest favor that can be offered the sick and his relatives is not to force him to take anything, because they say force makes the sick die."

FOOD WITH A MISSION

In an article for *Country Home*, Lisa Kingsley tells how "with spade in one hand and a holy book in the other, Franciscan fathers preached Catholicism, cookery and agricultural revolution to California's American Indian population." The faraway land that the Spanish rulers envisioned as providing monetary wealth for the empire, eventually yielded a harvest far richer than thousands of doubloons.

The material success in raising beef and cultivating wheat, corn, grapes, olives, citrus and a host of other fruits and vegetables focused attention on California's ability to produce some of the world's best food.

The indigenous cuisine born of the fusion of Spanish, Mexican and native cultures was fresh, earthy and healthy. It was destined to develop through the years into a distinctly American entity.

Agriculture was unknown to the natives of Alta California prior to the arrival of the friars. The peoples lived on a seasonally determined diet of nuts, roots, berries, salmon and acorn. The friars were the first to put the spade to California soil. Their arrival was a major transition, for it signaled the replacement of the acorn culture with the corn culture.

The fruits, grapes, vegetables, chilies, chocolate, beans, corn and wheat brought by the Franciscans was a welcome change for the natives who were attracted to the European diet. During the earliest years of European presence, it took more than sunshine and faith to make the land burst forth with its produce. During those first, lean years, the Indians were encouraged to bring in their own dried nuts, berries, game, grasses and roots to supplement the new food supply.

The food provided for breakfast was a homegrown cereal such as barley (*atole*), bolted tortilla flour with cream, and fresh fruit from the gardens. Neophytes baked loaves of bread in large outdoor ovens. Generally, the women tended the gardens and fields which yielded wheat, dates, oranges, lemons, legumes, corn, pumpkins, onions, vegetables of every stripe, together with grapes which were eaten fresh or made into wine.

The men spent much of their day tending cattle, tanning leather, operating olive presses, erecting buildings and making repairs. They were ready for the noon meal which was the largest of the day.

It included meat and *legume* stew, greens, tortillas along with fruit and cheese for desert. The tough range beef was doused with sauces made from the several dozen varieties of chilies. Ms. Kingsley observes that "the spirited growth of the converts and the expansion of the *padres*' experience mirrored the burgeoning of the fruits of the mission garden."

When Fray Pedro Font visited San Carlos Borromeo Mission in 1776, the year of American Independence, he observed its lovely garden laid out in a square and bordered with flowers. He reported that the cauliflower, lettuce, artichokes and other vegetables and herbs tasted "better than any in Mexico."

A JESUIT VIEWS RESTORATION

The road to civilization in California "is paved with the bones of those who died that others might live. Christianity is not a bloody religion, but it is one through which trails the crimson thread of blood. Its Leader, though called a King, was withal a suffering King — His crown was a crown of thorns and His throne was the hard, rough wood of the Cross."

In an article appearing in T*he Indian Sentinel,* for October, 1921, Father David P. McAstocker praised the "very laudable" program for refurbishing the Franciscan Missions, noting that it was "but meet and just that *El Camino Real*, the beginnings of Catholicity and of civilization in the State should be restored and preserved for the edification of future generations."

Decrying the fact that "most people" of his time saw "nothing else but the secular or material side of restoring the missions, the Jesuit writer pointed out that it would be vain to take on the task "without a soul to actuate" it. Father McAstocker said that "the soul of the old Missions is the ideal that was behind the men who built them —the motor power of their actions."

He rejected "the grossness in vision of the present generation" which so often measures greatness by the height of the Woolworth Building, success according to financial worth and advances in civilization by achievements in electricity, aeronautics and science. Father McAstocker reminded his readers that "the Missions speak of Halcyon days in Arcady before the white man came and invaded the hallowed spot and scattered the native over the land."

He called on the citizenry to exploit that "indefinable aroma of old Spain that hovers about the Missions," an aroma which "takes us back to another age—a golden. age of peace, prosperity and concord, when knighthood was in flower, when the laws of God were more universally respected and the native knew that his highest ideals were realized in submitting himself to lawful authority."

For those who had forgotten, Father McAstocker recalled that "it was self–denial, the labors, the sweat and the blood of the old Franciscan Fathers that in former years brought the Mission Indians back from paganism. This was their sole ideal—the sole motive for erecting the Missions—to minister to the souls of the Indians of California."

The Jesuit writer concluded his observations by observing that we who desire to see the old missions restored, must ever keep this objective in view. The missions are not ends in themselves, but means towards an end—towards helping spiritually the mission Indians. We have that sacred trust from the Franciscan *Padres*, and we must not fail. It is our bounden duty to carry on —to assist these souls in preserving the faith bequeathed to them by Fr. Junípero and his early companions."

WHAT TRUE RESTORATION ENTAILS

During the years that Father Thomas K. Gorman edited *The Tidings*, he delighted in stirring the waters of controversy in his weekly *El Rodeo* columns. On April 14, 1931, just prior to the announcement that Gorman would be named first Bishop of Reno, he dropped one of his bombshells:

"We hope that the processes of artificially and prematurely aging beams and adobe walls will not be generally adopted in Mission restoration." His comments were directed at San Diego where restorers were about to complete the first phase of restoration. When he heard that the pastor at San Juan Capistrano Mission, Father St. John O'Sullivan, was furious at his remarks, Gorman invited him to submit a rebuttal which appeared in *The Tidings* for May 15th.

O'Sullivan took particular exception to the sentence which stated that "fake antiques are an abomination" and "buildings should not be aged prematurely even to satisfy the cravings of tourists for pseudo–antiquity." The priest contended that "restored portions of the missions should be made to harmonize with their surroundings" and not be allowed to "stick out like a sore thumb" to the offense of observing eyes.

Though he admitted that visitors wanted "to see genuine antiques," he felt that they "are justly offended, on grounds of good taste, when they note that an old mission is disfigured by having a new portion In all the glory of its newness, abutting upon it. The average tourist," he noted, "has a keen appreciation of a piece of restoration that is well done, and hates sham just as much as anyone else."

O'Sullivan said that San Juan Capistrano Mission "was once a beautiful example of the architect's and builder's art. Like the cathedrals in the ages of faith, the builders contributed their full share to the merit of the structure. It stood here for many decades, mostly abandoned and almost unprotected. Vandals came and disfigured it, by tearing down the arches, taking off the roof tiles, ripping up the floors in search of fabled treasures and by a thousand other modes of attack."

The priest then asked: "What kind of a restorer would I be if I ordered the workmen to erect perfect arches in a first–class workmanlike manner, smooth of surface, sharp of edge and all shining to the heavens like a white celluloid collar on an otherwise picturesquely attired" mannequin? "Restoration," he said, "is not by any means the same as building anew. It is utterly different. In new work, you may choose any style of architecture you please, but in restoration, since your problem is to fill in a part that has been torn away from the general structure, you are limited in what you may appropriately do by the character of the part that remains."

Father O'Sullivan pointed out that "the object of harmonization is not to fool anybody, it is to avoid giving offense to the eye when it is necessary to tamper with a beautiful object." He admitted that "it is too bad these things have to be touched at all, but it seems to be a case of either doing the best you can to preserve them, or let them disappear entirely."

O'Sullivan was among those who felt that "the old mission texture, masses, lines and color are inimitable. Where these still exist, they should be preserved. Where they do not, and it is necessary to fill in what is missing, these parts should be made to harmonize as well as possible with their surroundings and not clash with them."

Himself a degreed historian, Father Gorman knew better. But, as he said in a subsequent letter to O'Sullivan, "we both won: You made your point and I picked up thirty five new subscribers from mission lovers."

MISSION RESTORATION

Restoration of the California missions has been an on–going process since late in the last century. This was possible because between 1834 and 1882 writers, photographers and artists recorded what they saw and knew about the missions of that period.

Photographic records of men like George Vancouver and A.L. Reed, pen sketches of H.M.T. Powell, William Hutton, William J. Miller, Edward Vischer and Henry Chapman Ford; surveys and plats made by the United States Government; the writings of Helen Hunt Jackson and George Wharton James, Zephyrin Engelhardt, Edith Webb and others enabled architects and engineers of modern times to recreate and restore the historic foundations along *El Camino Real* in a substantially authentic manner.

In 1834, the care of temporalities was removed from the friars and entrusted to lay administrators. From that time onwards, decay and destruction ensued. As the Indians wandered away, the once flourishing missions gradually faded from the scene.

The first steps taken to preserve what was left of the missions was initiated by Bishop Joseph Sadoc Alemany in 1852, when he petitioned the United States Government through the Private Land Grant Commission to recognize as ecclesial property those specified sections of the mission holdings always recognized as such by the laws of Spain and Mexico.

Witnesses were called in who testified that in earlier times the churches, dwellings of the *padres*, cemeteries, orchards, vineyards and certain waterworks were traditionally regarded as ecclesial property. Eventually, those claims were adjudicated as valid by the United States with the result that under the administrations of Presidents James Buchanan, Abraham Lincoln and Ulysses Grant, the buildings and certain lands of the missions were returned to Alemany as the incumbent of the bishopric of Monterey.

Today, the twenty–one California missions are located in the two archdioceses and ten dioceses comprising the jurisdiction of the Catholic Church in California. Only four of the missions are still under the care of the friars, namely Santa Barbara, San Luis Rey (since 1892) San Antonio (1928) and San Miguel (1928) Two are owned by the State of California (Purisima and Sonoma) and the others are administered by various local church authorities. Except for *Nuestra Señora de la Soledad*, all the missions under ecclesial care are currently used for worship and/or educational purposes.

With the subsequent expansion and development of California and the founding of new cities and population centers, some of the missions remained mostly unused and exposed to decay and deterioration. These would include San Diego, San Luis Rey, San Fernando, Purisima, San Miguel, San Antonio, San Carlos, San Jose and San Rafael.

There were other problems too that contributed to the disintegration of the missions. Squatters occupied most of the sites and the litigation to expel them was costly; tiles had been removed from roofs and that caused many of the adobe walls to crumble and, finally rain, wind and the burrowing of animals brought on further destruction. While much was written in prose and poetry, little was done effectively by propagandists to forestall the ravages of time, neglect and weathering.

RESTORATION AT THE OTHER MISSIONS

Restoration is an ongoing project at most of the California missions. The following overview of this uncoordinated and somewhat haphazard program could easily be developed into a full–sized and certainly useful book.

Before 1930, *San Diego* Mission was a shambles of ugly decay. All that remained were the outlines of the adobe church, its facade and small portions of the side wall. Only the church structure was restored in the following years. In 1950, the ambulatory and front wall of the main wing was put in place with funds from the Hearst Restoration Fund.

San Juan Capistrano preserves the only building at any of the missions which dates back to the time of Fray Junípero Serra (1779). Though somewhat lengthened and heightened, it is still used as a chapel. The large stone church of 1806 was thoroughly destroyed by the earthquake of 1812 and remains in ruin as "California's Melrose Abbey." The south, east and north wings of the great quadrangle were restored, the arcades remaining in their original condition. The north wing served as the parish school and convent. Much of this work was done during the pastorate of Father St. John O'Sullivan (1910–1933).

Only the stone and brick church remain at *San Gabriel*, together with a partial section of the front wing of the original quadrangle with its pillars and the tile floor of the east wing. Some changes in the church were made in 1886 and general renovations were made in 1938. The church was severely damaged in the 1988 earthquake. The most recognizable feature at *San Fernando* is the *convento* with its arcade and arches. It was re–roofed for the mission's centennial in 1897. The workshops connecting the abandoned church and the *convento* had become a huge ruins. Re–roofed in 1916 the church was finally restored in 1941 (and the adjacent bell tower in 1946). It was destroyed in the earthquake of 1971 and rebuilt in replica four years later. In 1949, the shops and the south wing of the original quadrangle

were restored under the supervision of Mark Harrington and Father Augustine O'Dea.

Only the church is still extant at *San Buenaventura*. Interior renovation took place in 1957 when the wooden floor was removed and the original tiles unveiled. The massive boards were taken off the ceiling and the original beams were revealed. Thus the artificial modernization effected in 1848–1895 was corrected. A portion of the original sacristy was also rebuilt in 1957.

Santa Ines Mission was severely damaged by the flood of 1911. The campanile fell and considerable damage was done to the church and living quarters. The campanile was later restored in concrete. The second story on the front wing was added in 1948 and today only the church and the greater portion of the front wing of the quadrangle survive from early times.

When the restoration began at *Purisima Concepcion* in 1933, the mission was a desolate ruin. A few pillars and weathered adobe walls of the living quarters survived, with trees and grass growing among them. No remains of the church existed. The restored convento, the barracks and workshops, the church and the cemetery were re–dedicated on the morning of Pearl Harbor. The restoration was done under the direction of the United States Government, with the assistance of CCC workers. The greatest exactitude was employed to insure authentic restoration in what is now a State Park.

The church and the front wing of the original quadrangle remain at *San Luis Obispo*. Exterior and interior renovation took place in 1948, with the aid of the Hearst Restoration Fund.

San Miguel Mission was entrusted to the Franciscans in 1948. Only the church and a part of the front wing remained, the latter in a dilapidated condition. A new roof was placed on the church and the front wing was once again made livable. Between 1933 and 1939, the greater part of the original quadrangle was restored, as well as the front adobe wall. The whole plant was re–dedicated in 1938. The roof of the church was retiled in 1939 and an adobe wall placed around the cemetery. In more recent times another adobe wall was erected around acreage south of the mission. Later a T–shaped building was located to the south of the original quadrangle.

By 1904, most of the adobe buildings at *San Antonio* had crumbled back to the earth. Only a few pillars and arches of the front corridor remained. The church stood, but its roof was severely damaged. The replacing of the roof by the Native Sons of the Golden West, in 1904, preserved the walls of the church from further decay. In the early 1950s, the church was totally restored. The original quadrangle and some buildings to the east of the church were rebuilt by the friars themselves.

Until the middle of this century at *Nuestra Señora de*

la Soledad there were only clusters of adobe walls surrounded by a bean field. Restoration of the church and a few rooms was undertaken by the Native Daughters of the Golden West in 1955. Since then several more rooms have been added, but only a small fraction of the original mission has been put back in place.

Restoration at *San Juan Bautista* dates from 1949. The church still stands as does the front wing of the original quadrangle. The inappropriate tower erected in the last century was removed. The church had been damaged in the earthquake of 1906. In the 1970s, the three naves were restored to the church.

Nothing at all remains at *Santa Cruz*. A miniature replica of the early mission was built near the original site in 1933. Only the church and the historic cemetery remain at *San Francisco* or *Mission Dolores*. What was left of the original church at *Santa Clara* was burned in 1926. The present church is modeled along the lines of the earlier building. With regard to the quadrangle, three adobes remain and are incorporated into the present buildings of the adjacent Jesuit University.

Only the south wing of the original quadrangle remains at *San Jose*. The replica church, erected in 1984, is one of the most beautiful and authentic houses–of–worship in California. At *San Rafael* the original mission and church have entirely disappeared. A replica of the earlier mission church was erected in 1949 with funds from the Hearst Foundation.

The mission property at *San Francisco Solano* (Sonoma), consisting of a small church and the front wing of a quadrangle, were sold by Archbishop Alemany in 1881. The State of California effected the initial restoration in 1912–1914. Continued work occurred in 1943 and, at that time, the church of 1840 and the front wing of the quadrangle were restored.

THE MISSION PROPERTIES

One of the most treasured documents of a California mission is the patent whereby Church ownership is confirmed by the United States government. The one for San Fernando Mission, dated May 31, 1862, is signed by Abraham Lincoln. During the Mexican–American war, the administration of President James Polk followed a policy whereby the Church's claims to the property of the missions was generally presumed.

On March 22, 1847, General Stephen Watts Kearny, Military Governor of California, issued a proclamation directing that "the houses, grounds, gardens, vineyards, etc. around" the missions "shall remain under the charge of the Catholic priests." That policy was abandoned with cessation of the hostilities and, by the time the peace treaty was finally ratified, on March 10, 1848, the claims

of the Catholic Church were no longer given any special privilege or protection.

If the Church wanted to pursue its claims, it would need to avail itself of the proper judicial tribunals just like any other corporation or citizen. There would be no special preference for ecclesial claims.

One of the first tasks confronting Joseph Sadoc Alemany as he arrived to take up his position as Bishop of Monterey in 1850, was that of pursuing the claim of the Church to the Mission properties of earlier times. He would contend that "the Churches, Church edifices, stores, cemeteries, orchards and vineyards with aqueducts should be considered the property of the Church."

On March 3 1851, the 31st Congress passed legislation known as the California Land Act, whereby the burden of proof would fall to those who claimed title under the earlier Spanish or Mexican regimes. A board of three commissioners was established to receive evidence, take testimony, review the law and render decisions upon the claims. In compliance with that procedure, Alemany employed attorneys Eugene Casserly and John Doyle to argue the case for the Church. The attorneys based the bishop's claim upon his being incorporated under California law as Bishop of Monterey and, as such, the local head of the Catholic Church.

Casserly and Doyle further argued that Spanish and Mexican law recognized the right of the Church to hold property, as did common law, the canon law of the Church, the legislation of the Baltimore Councils and the priests assembled in local synod.

At each of the twenty–one missions the bishop claimed the church, graveyard, quadrangle of buildings, enclosed gardens, orchards and vineyards. The bishop's petition challenged pretensions of those claiming the lands under previous "illegitimate" sales.

After hearing testimony from numerous parties, Alpheus Felch, former governor and senator from Michigan, rendered a decision based on his extensive research of the evidence. He stated that "the claim of the Bishop was not so much for a grant of land, as for a recognition of the right of the Church to the premises."

He concluded that "these concurrent proofs bring us irresistibly to the conclusion that before the Treaty of Guadalupe Hidalgo, these possessions were solemnly dedicated to the use of the Church, and the property withdrawn from commerce." Such an interest, he said, "is protected by the provisions of the treaty, and must be held inviolable under our laws."

It was indeed a fascinating case in which Bishop Joseph Sadoc Alemany claimed no special privilege, but only the judicial vindication of the Church's rights. The successful prosecution of his claim established a strong precedent for the recognition of the Church's property rights as a corporate institution within American jurisprudence.

THE CALIFORNIA MISSIONS

Title	Founded	Patented	President
1. San Diego de Alcala	1769	May 23, 1862	Abraham Lincoln
2. San Carlos Borromeo	1770	October 19, 1859	James Buchanan
3. San Antonio de Padua	1771	May 31, 1862	Abraham Lincoln
4. San Gabriel Archangel	1771	November 19, 1859	James Buchanan
5. San Luis Obispo	1772	September 2, 1859	James Buchanan
6. San Francisco de Asis	1776	March 3, 1858	James Buchanan
7. San Juan Capistrano	1776	March 18, 1865	Abraham Lincoln
8. Santa Clara de Asis	1777	March 3, 1858	James Buchanan
9. San Buenaventura	1782	May 23, 1862	Abraham Lincoln
10. Santa Barbara	1786	March 18, 1865	Abraham Lincoln
11. La Purisima Concepcion	1787	January 24, 1874	Ulysses S. Grant
12. Santa Cruz	1791	September 2, 1859	James Buchanan
13. Nuestra Señora de la Soledad	1791	November 19, 1859	James Buchanan
14. San Jose	1797	March 3, 1858	James Buchanan
15. San Juan Bautista	1797	November 19, 1859	James Buchanan
16. San Miguel Arcangel	1797	September 2, 1859	James Buchanan
17. San Fernando, Rey de España	1797	May 31, 1862	Abraham Lincoln
18. San Luis, Rey de Francia	1798	March 18, 1865	Abraham Lincoln
19. Santa Ines	1804	May 23, 1862	Abraham Lincoln
20. San Rafael Arcangel	1817	October 19, 1859	James Buchanan
21. San Francisco Solano	1823	May 31, 1861	Abraham Lincoln

CALIFORNIA MISSION ARCHITECTURE

The missions were self–sustaining units whose very purpose demanded space for the numerous activities—social, religious, agricultural, and industrial—that took place within their precincts. In addition to living–quarters for the two *padres*, warehouses, storehouses, workshops and dwellings for the Indians were needed. It can be seen, therefore, that the mission's architecture had to be along lines at once functional and protective. A distinctive style, known as "California Mission," characterizes that great era of history as an outstanding contribution to American culture.

Most of the missions, following the same general architectural pattern, were designed to enclose an open–air patio. Normally the church was located at the northeast corner of a quadrangle and was the most imposing part of the overall structure. Decorative work had to be imported, either from Spain or Mexico. Over the years a remarkably varied collection of sculpture and painting accumulated in most of the missions, some of it quite artistic.

Mission architecture, though related both to Spanish Colonial in Mexico and to the Spanish of the mother–country was, in comparison with either, unpolished. Of necessity, the California version was a more sturdy design, generally built around wood plastered with clay. Where wood was scarce, sun–dried bricks were used. That simplicity is the distinctive charm of the missions is explained by the almost total absence of experienced architects and surface decorators on the scene. The lack or ornamentation is more than compensated for by the frankness of proportions forced on the *padres* by the limitations of material.

Simple columns and pediments bespeak Moorish, Spanish–Roman and Renaissance motifs although the overall style leans more toward the neo–classic than the Baroque. Rexford Newcomb lists the characteristics of what he calls the "mission style:" (1) massive walls and buttresses, (2) arcaded corridors and arches on piers, (3) curved pediment gables, (4) terraced bell towers, (5) pierced *campanarios*, (6) patios with fountains, (7) wide, projecting eaves and (8) low pitched, red–tiled roofs.

Living quarters for the *padres* were usually located adjacent to the church in a *convento* building while the two remaining sides of the quadrangle were given over to shops, rooms for unmarried native girls (*monjerio*) and storehouses. As a rule the exterior corridor running the length of the buildings under an extended roof was supported either by square pillars or the familiar round arched colonnades. When possible the grounds were landscaped with plants, fountains and pathways depending on the locale and the supply of water.

Originally, the construction of the missions was entirely in the hands of the *padres*, but in later years the viceroys provided mechanics, masons, carpenters, and others to assist in the work. These skills were taught, in turn, to the natives.

Burial grounds were usually to the north of the church and usually a separate doorway opened out in that direction. High walls around the cemetery divided the space between clergy and laity.

> Perhaps no architectural style in history has created so much with so little; so much that is still ennobling with so little good material to work with; so much that is warm and touching in its beautiful simplicity with so little creative experience to fall back on. Perhaps more than anything else, the priceless intrinsic that the *padres* put into their buildings was the very one that prompted them to venture into the wilderness in the first place. That ingredient was Faith.

ARCHITECTURAL CLASSIC

Though it was published two generations ago, Rexford Newcomb's book on *The Old Mission Churches and Historic Houses of California* remains one of the great classics of Western Americana. When they can be found, copies sell for five or six times their initial cost.

Rexford Newcomb (1886–1968), the distinguished Professor of Architectural History at the University of Illinois, first journeyed to the Pacific Slope in 1912, where he befriended Father Zephyrin Engelhardt and others associated with the history and care of the California Missions. He was astounded to discover that "little or no serious work had heretofore been spent on the architectural expression of that interesting politicosocial movement which resulted from Spanish occupation of the southwestern United States."

Engelhardt encouraged Newcomb to make accurate and detailed drawings, sketches and photographs of the existing missions and/or their ruins. Newcomb enlisted Messrs. Putnam and Valentine of Los Angeles to assist him with their photographic talents.

Newcomb's initial study about the "Architecture of the California Missions" appeared in the 1914 *Annual* for the Historical Society of Southern California. It was expanded and retitled a year later for the *Notre Dame Quarterly.* Those two essays were widely acclaimed in both historical and architectural circles. The following year, the text, along with numerous illustrations, was released in book form under the title *The Franciscan Mission Architecture of Alta California* by the Architectural Book Publishing Company of New York. It was reprinted by Dover Publications in 1973.

According to reviews dating back to the 1916 edition,

Newcomb was remarkably successful in gathering "a well–rounded series that reflected the original spirit and detail of the early buildings" of California. In a real sense, Newcomb rediscovered the mission style.

Since many of the missions were built along similar plans and others had since been destroyed, Newcomb selected the typical and most profound examples of the various styles, featuring scaled drawings of doorways, gates, windows, fountains, chimneys, a baptistry, fireplaces, laundry basins, niches, transepts, mouldings, gables, patios and roofs that characterized the Franciscan foundations.

The drawings and photographs in his book were useful for their many suggestions of how mission architecture could be applied to modern works in similar surroundings as well as for their reflections on the land and culture from which they came. In 1915, at the behest of the J. B. Lippincott Company of Philadelphia, Newcomb expanded his earlier works into T*he Old Mission Churches and Historic Houses of California,* a 379 page tome with 217 illustrations and numerous measured drawings.

A review of Newcomb's classic work, written for the *Catholic Historical Review,* describes this lucid, well–illustrated and informative text as "a bibliographical pilgrimage to shrines, the ruins of which recall, as nothing else can, that political and religious movement of the eighteenth century which brought the Pacific coast for the first time in contact with European civilization."

While Newcomb is perhaps best remembered for his work on the California missions, his talents weren't restricted to that area. His book on *The Spanish House for America,* for example, was an encyclopedic work of tremendous proportions. Many are the architectural commentators of the California missions, but Rexford Newcomb exceeded them all.

DECORATIONS OF THE MISSIONS

The Indians, artisans from Mexico, passing foreigners and even the friars themselves all contributed to the decoration of the missions in California, though exactly in what measure may never be known. With a few exceptions, almost all the motifs derived from the neoclassical style which was at its height during the period of the most intensive mission construction and decoration.

California, in contrast to New Mexico which remained frozen in time artistically, was remarkably up–to–date in its fashions, in spite of being on the fringes of the then civilized world. The version used in California is infinitely more colorful, not to say naive, than the more sober white and gold decreed by the Academy of San Carlos in Mexico City and followed in such major centers as Puebla and Guadalajara.

If anything, it seems closer to what happened in Spain itself where an abundance of colorful marbles used in wealthy churches inspired imitation in more humble structures. This modification of Mexican taste is probably due to the Spanish origin of the missionaries.

The writer, Norman Neuerburg, feels that the precise artistic contribution of the Franciscan missionaries to California is difficult to appraise. As multi–talented as the friars surely were, few had any special artistic bent or talent. Most likely, their contribution was mainly advisory, extending to the specifying of the overall lay-out for the individual foundations.

Since most of them were Spanish born, they modified Mexican fashions with their own experience in the mother country. Some of the friars made occasional sketches for church decoration, but it is doubtful that much of the actual work was done by them personally. One notable exception was the talented Fray José Maria de Jesús González Rúbio, the only missionary whose artistic activity can be positively documented.

During the decade that González Rúbio spent at San Jose Mission, he painted a curtain for midnight Mass on Christmas Eve that covered the entire front of the church. The friar also did a "*monumentum*" or set of scenery to be placed in front of the altar of repose on Holy Thursday. There is a sketch of that opus in the Bancroft Library. Another of his creations was a funeral catafalque decorated with sixteen skeletons Fray González Rúbio also made two tunics for the statue of Jesus, one of which survived to be photographed by George Wharton James in 1905.

Whether the work of Fray González Rúbio and others add up to a California style is difficult to say, especially without further study of neoclassical decoration in the village and country churches of Mexico. Neuerburg did feel, however, that even now a good case could be made for a special California variant, if not an independent style as such.

ARTISTIC RENDITION OF THE MISSIONS

Among the most celebrated published works relating to the historic foundations of Fray Junipero Serra and his collaborators along *El Camino Real* must be Henry Chapman Ford's *Etchings of the Franciscan Missions of California*. The twenty–four proof–etchings, measuring 17 x 22 inches on their mounts, were enclosed in a portfolio of two–tone linen. The prints, each signed by the artist, include duplicate views of Missions Santa Barbara and San Carlos Borromeo, together with a depiction of the abandoned ruins of the first La Purísima Concepción. The handsome opus was printed, in 1883, at New York's Studio Press, in a limited edition of fifty sets.

The fifty–two year old New York–born artist had first visited the missions by covered wagon, in 1880–1881, and during that trek had made careful photographs which he later enlarged for use as models. From the very outset, Ford intended to produce the most elaborate work yet published on the subject. Upon completion of the oil portrayals, Mr. Ford journeyed to New York, where he personally supervised their transferal to copper plates. The freedom, delicacy and strength of the completed scenes amply testify to his success.

The publication of Ford's monumental opus was widely–heralded. Archbishop Joseph Sadoc Alemany of San Francisco, recalling his own first tour of the missions, in 1851, found "the execution by Mr. Ford accurate." The Dominican prelate went on to say that the artist deserved "the special gratitude of the State of California for his zeal in preserving the glorious memories of the Pioneers of its Christian civilization." Another foremost authority on the early missionary foundations, Father Joachim Adam, wrote from Los Angeles that he had carefully examined the etchings and considered them "not only exquisite as a work of art, but also a faithful representation" of Provincial California.

A reviewer for the Los Angeles *Times* labeled the Ford etchings "an invaluable addition to the history of these earliest monuments of civilization in California" and hoped that folios would find their way into "every library and public institution of the State."

Newspapers from around the nation joined the chorus of praise. The Washington *National Republican* said that Ford's "work perpetuates on copper about the only interesting ruins to be seen in America." A writer in the Cleveland *Leader* called the etchings "not only beautiful and interesting as works of art" but also depictions of "great historical value." The Chicago *Times* ranked the portfolio as "one of the finest specimens of the 'art preservative' which has appeared in this country."

In its "Exposition Notes," the New Orleans *Time Democrat* declared that Ford's masterpiece showed "marked artistic talent, and admirable technique and perfect familiarity with the graver and acid bath." In Chicago's *Present Age*, Enoch Root wrote that the reproduction of the missions, from canvas to copper plates, demonstrated that the artist's "skill with the needle point equals his power in the use of the brush." Another prominent artist, Norton Bush of San Francisco, happily endorsed the etchings "as being works of art of an exceedingly interesting character," while the Protestant Rector of Christ Church, Bridgeport, Connecticut, went even further and proclaimed them "the most ambitious work of the kind ever produced by an American."

When, in 1961, many of the surviving sets were found to be soiled and battered, Mr. William A. Edwards made available his remarkably clean portfolio for reproduction purposes to the Santa Barbara Historical Society. To the original twenty–four etchings, another dozen scenes, covering a variety of subjects, were added by Edward Selden Spaulding for his volume of Ford's *Etchings of California.*

Mr. Ford continued his interest in the missions and subsequently painted a number of other scenes, some of them in watercolor. At the time of his death, in 1894, the artist was busily working on a history of the early missionary foundations. A few of his isolated notes were published by the *California Historical Society Quarterly, in 1961.*

The assertion, by the San Francisco *Bulletin,* that the Ford portrayals would never be equaled "in truthfulness and artistic presentation," undoubtedly helped to sustain and augment the initial selling price of $50. The etchings have multiplied in value thirty–five times(!) in the past ninety years and a portfolio was offered for sale by Warren Howell at $1,750! Even a four page *Prospectus for the Etchings of the Franciscan Missions of California* was sold by Glen Dawson, in August, 1974, for $200!

Henry Chapman Ford's fascination for and reproduction of the California missions rank the artist among the truly great benefactors of Western Americana.

SUNDIALS AT THE MISSIONS

The Indians of Provincial California had no calendars, but calculated the passage of months according to the moon and the hours according to the sun. Their careful daily routine of rest, work and play was regulated by the sounding of a bell at different times by the bell–ringer who, in turn, took his signal from the shadows cast upon the mission sundial.

In view of their mode of life in the open, the sundial was time–teller for the Indians. Their concept of time and its passage went little beyond the position of the sun in the sky as recorded by *una maestra de Sol.*

Transfering the shadows of trees and other objects to those cast by the gnomon of the sundial was well within the mentality of the Indians. In all probability, that device was among the most effective wedges used by the missionaries in opening the minds of the primitive California peoples to the European way–of–life.

Strangely enough, there is very little written about the mechanical form of time–keeping in the literature on the missions. The 1771 invoices from Missions San Diego, San Carlos Borromeo and San Antonio contain requests for sundials at those frontier establishments. The one ultimately secured for San Antonio was later described as *un relojito de Sol con su agula y caja* (a sundial with its gnomon and case). Since each foundation had its own latitude, the dials had to be specially made for the individual missions.

The quiet but relentless immutability of the sundials was an invitation to ornamentation, even in its crudest expressions. Some of the mission dials were quite picturesque. Carved in the stone face of the sundial at Santa Cruz, for example was the inscription: "*Como la Sombra Huye la Hora*" (Like a shadow the hour creeps by).

The sundial unearthed at San Carlos Borromeo, in the 1920s, was a large flat stone, on which were outlined a host of figures. Around the dial, carved in stone, were objects indicating the various duties performed by the neophytes at the hour marked by the shadow on the gnomon.

There were portrayals of kneeling Indians, indicating the time for prayer, and others partaking of food at breakfast, dinner and supper. In addition, there were shepherds looking after the sheep, workers laboring in the shops and farmers caring for the fields.

At San Juan Capistrano, the dial used by Father Jose Mut was the long end of the ridge pole that extended beyond the eaves of the building now used as a souvenir shop. Between 1866 and 1886, that structure had a simple gable end. The dial, of course, was not a horizontal one. Father Mut used it as a timing device for the village children attending his school.

In the museum room at Mission San Luis Obispo is a broken fragment of a dial that once surmounted a column similar to those upon which the corridor roof rests. It formerly stood in front of the priest's dwelling. A traveler sketched this dial in the early 1850s and H.M.T. Powell later wrote a very accurate description of it.

"TIME" AND THE CALIFORNIA MISSIONS

The eminent Dominican theologian, A.D. Sertillanges, has observed that "he who knows the value of time always has enough; not being able to lengthen it, he intensifies its value; and first of all he does nothing to shorten it. Time, like gold, has thickness: a solid medal, well struck and pure in line, has more value than the thin leaf from the gold–beater's hammer."

The careful allotment of time was an integral part of the system used by the Franciscans in the California missions. This was a natural outgrowth of the rules and regulations observed by the friars in their own seraphic way–of–life. For the Indians, the sundial was an ideal device for telling time. The aboriginal concept of measuring the hours was limited to their observance of the sun and the shadows cast at various parts of the day. Sundials, effective as they were, had very obvious deficiencies. Their construction demanded precise knowledge of the local latitude, a factor which was frequently difficult to ascertain. Since they were functional only when the sun was shining, the devices were useless inside, at night or on overcast days.

It seems quite certain that each mission had its clock. Fray Junípero Serra had an alarm clock and in the first annual report from Santa Clara, a notation was made of a wooden clock with little bells which counted the hours and quarter hours. It was noted in another early report that "the months they calculate according to the moon, and the hours according to the sun. They have never used a calendar. However, the new Christians regulate themselves by the clock of the mission; and for timing their own rest, meals and work, we sound the bell."

In 1776, Juan Bautista de Ánza recalled that he had arrived at Mission San Luis Obispo "just as it was striking half past eleven." The inventories of Missions San Francisco Solano, Santa Barbara and Santa Cruz all enumerate *un relox de sala*, a parlor clock. W. Barclay Stephens believes that while the form of the ordinary clocks at the missions cannot be definitely determined, from the standpoint of applicability, suitability and location, a striking hanging clock was the probable form common in provincial times.

Fray Arroyo de la Cuesta is credited with assembling the first clock in California, at San Juan Bautista. Frederick William Beechey reported, in 1826, that the friar "had constructed a water clock which communicated with a bell by his bedside, and which by being arranged at night could be made to give an alarm at any stated hour." With the possible exception of a wooden movement at Santa Barbara, not a single one of the existing clocks can be authoritatively declared as having existed in mission days.

The existence of clocks at the missions has often been discounted. Yet, as Edith Webb has observed, "The *padres* had known nothing but the strict routine of the Rule of their Order since their earliest days of training. It is unreasonable then to think that they would have gone or been sent to a far–distant and unknown field without the necessary means for marking the hours. And, with the reports of early explorers before them, they would have known that our California's days were not all of unmixed sunshine. The sundial, man's first timepiece, would not serve every day. Therefore, clocks were a necessity."

CLOCKS AT THE OLD MISSIONS

The invention and development of the first mechanical clocks dates back to 1300, with the first such timepieces being used to regulate the *horarium* or schedule of daily activities in monasteries. The initial mechanical clocks used a rope wound around a cylinder. A weight on the free end of the rope was allowed to slowly fall, using the force of gravity to unwind. As it fell, it rotated the dial of the clock past a stationary hand which registered the hour.

Later the dial was fixed in position and the hand

rotated. Since those early, crudely–made clocks were five or ten minutes off each day, they were reset every morning in reference to a sundial.

The monks of England developed a high degree of expertise in clock making. Automatic alarms were added to warn the bell ringer to toll the curfew each night and alert the friars to other special events. In 1320, Fray Richard of Wallingford started assembling a complex astronomical clock that took thirty years to complete. Two centuries later, the clock was still running quite accurately.

In Italy, the birthplace of the Renaissance, history's first public, mechanical, bell–striking clock was installed in the Catholic church of San Gottardo, Milan, in 1335. This innovation was subsequently adopted by hundreds of churches throughout Europe.

In the latter part of the 15th century, the mechanical clock played a pivotal role in Jesuit efforts to convert the Chinese. In 1601, Father Matteo Ricci gave the emperor two mechanical clocks, explaining that they were products of Catholic ingenuity. His Majesty was immensely impressed.

In 1504, Peter Henlein developed the spring–wound clock, a revolutionary invention that allowed clocks to become portable. Between 1550 and 1650, thousands of clocks were made in the German–speaking parts of the Holy Roman Empire. In 1657, Christian Huygens, a Dutch mathematician, invented the pendulum clock and once again revolutionized clockmaking. The pendulum kept time by using the natural swing of a weight attached to the end of a rod swinging in a fixed arc.

It seems certain that each of the California missions had at least one timepiece, in addition to the traditional sundial. Aside from the need of an accurate timepiece to regulate the activities of the local community, the friars themselves needed a means for fulfilling their Franciscan Rule.

The friars would never have come to such a distant area without the necessary means for counting the passage of the hours. And, with the reports of early explorers before them, they would have known that the California weather was not all sunshine.

Fray Junípero Serra had an alarm clock at San Carlos Borromeo Mission in 1774. And it is known that the friars at Santa Clara had a wooden clock with little bells or chimes for striking the hours. An *informe* of 1777 stated that "the new Christians regulate themselves by the clock of the mission; for timing their rest, meals and work, they sound the bell."

Inventories at the missions of San Francisco Solano, Santa Barbara and Santa Cruz all list "*un relox de sala*" (a parlor clock). In the museum at Santa Barbara Mission are the works of an old wooden clock which, in all probability, is all that remains of the one mentioned above.

EDUCATION AT THE MISSIONS

In dealing with education in Mission times, it must be remembered that the "Franciscans came to California not as schoolmen but as apostles." Nonetheless, William E. North has observed that "educators they undoubtedly were, if by education we mean character formation and an endeavor to fit one for the role he is to play in life."

Instructing the natives in the rudiments of the Catholic Faith always presented a challenge to the missionaries. Many of the abstract teachings of Catholicism could not be expressed in native language. Often the simple minds of the Indians experienced great difficulty in grasping even single philosophical concepts. Hence it was that the friars utilized the system their predecessors found so useful in the New World, the *Doctrina*. The missionaries would have the Indians recite, until they knew it by heart, the Sign of the Cross, Our Father, Hail Mary, Creed; Acts of Faith, Hope and Charity; the *Confiteor*, Ten Commandments, Six Precepts, Seven Sacraments, the Necessary Points of Faith and the Four Last Things.

Known throughout Latin America as the *Doctrina Cristiana* this summary of the Deposit of Faith was required of the Indians before they were admitted to baptism. It was recited each day prior to Holy Mass and again in the evening before retiring. With a minimum of effort, even the dullest Indian gradually absorbed the basic groundwork of Catholicism in a relatively short time. Although the local dialect was occasionally employed, Spanish was mostly used in the learning process since it was a uniform language and could be taught throughout California, an area with a multitude of local dialects. Not only did the natives quickly assimilate the basic rudiments of the new language but they profited from the unifying effect it had on the separate tribes.

Isolating and explaining some aspects of the teaching, Sunday sermons normally centered about the *Doctrina*. In the early years, sermons were translated into the local dialect by an interpreter. Later the missionaries mastered the Indian tongues and were able to converse in their own languages. As the *Doctrina* was intended primarily for adults, a special type of catechetical instructions was used for the youngsters. "In the morning, as soon as the grown people shall have gone their way . . . the Fathers give instructions to the boys and girls who are five years old and more." In order to demonstrate more graphically the truths of the *Doctrina*, pictures and statues were placed in the corridors, living quarters and around the mission compound of Our Lord, the Blessed Mother, the saints and various mysteries of the Faith.

Another supplement used in religious instruction of the natives was a series of religious dramas based on the liturgical cycle. The Christmas season was especially appealing in this regard and the story of Bethlehem was portrayed as vividly as possible with the natives themselves acting out the various parts.

The daily schedule of religion, work, and play was designed to keep the neophytes busy from dawn to dusk. While it was the most important part of their daily duties, religious instruction was only one aspect of that mission culture upon which foundation "men of a later day have reared the structure of history, the cornerstone of California art, literature and sentiment."

I. The California Missions
3. Memoirs, Reflections, Impressions, Observations, Descriptions and Commentaries

THE *PASTORELA*—1780s

There was probably no California mission where, on Christmas Eve, the scene of the Nativity was not re–created, for the *padres* were followers of Francis of Assisi and it was that gentle saint who, with the permission of Pope Honorius III, popularized the custom of representing the manger of Bethlehem. The following account of the *Pastorela* is taken from the superb account of the late Edith Webb:

The celebration began with the illumination of the mission buildings, the lighting of bonfires, and the firing of rockets. The bells rang merrily calling the neophytes, the soldiers of the guard, the *mayordomos* and their families to the church, and, on this night of nights, "*la nocha buena,*" there were few laggards. From the choir loft came the clear, melodious voices of the Indians, their singing mingling with the sweet, haunting music of flutes, violins, bass–viols, and trumpets rendering the old hymns and chants taught them by the *padres.* Then the *padre* celebrant sang the Midnight Mass and closed with the injunction—"*Ite Missa est!*"

Immediately there came strains of lively music from the loft, announcing the beginning of the long–awaited drama, the *Pastorela,* or Nativity play, perhaps that one composed by Fr. Florencio Ibañez of Mission La Soledad. Then through the great, wide–flung doors of the church came the procession of actors, the Indians and others within the church crowding along the side walls and facing the center aisle the better to view the enactment.

Accounts differ somewhat as to some of the characters represented in the play, but always there were the Archangel Gabriel, Satan, or *El Diablo,* the shepherd of Bethlehem, a hermit, a clownlike fellow, and a number of girls representing angels. The archangel was clothed in a blue garment bespangled with gilt stars, a larger star being fastened with wire above his forehead. *El Diablo* wore a flaming red costume and carried a rod tipped with red paint to simulate heat. The hermit with long white beard was clad in nondescript apparel and carried a tattered missal and sin chastening lash. The shepherd, clothed in sheepskins with wool side out, carried a crook. The girls were dressed in white and had veil–like head coverings, each being adorned with a star. Bartolo, the clown, had no real part in the play, his sole purpose being to amuse the onlookers, especially the children.

The story of their performance is partially drawn from the Bible, and commences with the angel's appearance to the shepherds, his account of the birth of our Saviour, and exhortation to them to repair to the scene of the manger. Lucifer appears among them and endeavors to prevent the prosecution of their journey. His influence and temptations are about to succeed when Gabriel again appears and frustrates their effect. A dialogue is then carried on of considerable length relative to the attributes of the Deity, which ends in the submission of Satan. The whole is interspersed with songs and incidents that seem better adapted to the stage than the church.

In the final act of the play, Gabriel leads the shepherd, the others following, to a covered platform erected just outside the altar rail, and, drawing aside the covering, discloses a manger, or crib, in which an image of the Child has been placed. On one side of the crib is a small statue of the Virgin Mary and, on the other, one of Saint Joseph. The *Padre* then invites the spectators to come forward and view the *Niño Santo* in the manger. The bells in the belfry ring out merrily and the drama is ended.

IMPRESSIONS OF THE CALIFORNIA MISSIONS—1792–1793

Captain George Vancouver (1758–1798) was an "intelligent and honest British sailor, a good representative of a good class of explorers and writers, plain of speech, and a reliable witness on matters which fell under his personal observation." In his description of California and the four missions he visited, Vancouver endeavored to be fair in describing what he saw, and even for what he thought faulty, he made due allowance.

The central theme of the California settlements by the time of Vancouver's visits was to spread the Christian faith among the Indians. Vancouver recognized that motive, and his descriptions of the missions show his interest and admiration for their spiritual accomplishments as well as their physical layouts. In his narrative, the English navigator spoke of the conduct of the fathers as mild and kind–hearted and as never failing to attach to their interests the affection of the natives.

The British seaman was impressed by the magnitude, architecture and internal decorations of the mission churches. He noted that the comforts the friars might have provided in their own humble habitations, seemed to have been totally sacrificed to the accomplishment of worthy places of prayer. Though he regarded the California natives as "certainly a race of the most miserable beings possessing the faculties of human reason" he had ever seen, Vancouver was impressed by the manner in which the uniform, mild disposition of this religious order (the Franciscans) had never failed to attract the loyalties of the neophytes.

Throughout the mission system, the natives were well fed, better clothed than the Indians of the neighborhood, were kept clean, instructed, and had every necessary care taken of them. Vancouver was fascinated by the various trades taught at Mission Dolores. He observed how "one large room was occupied by manufacturers of a coarse sort of blanketing, made from the wool produced in the neighborhood. The looms, though rudely wrought, were tolerably well contrived, and had been made by the Indians, under the immediate direction and superintendence of the fathers; who, by the same assiduity, had carried the manufacture thus far into effect. The produce resulting from their manufactory is wholly applied to clothing of the converted Indians." Vancouver further noted that he had seen "some of the cloth," which was by no means despicable; and had it received the advantage of fulling, would have been a very decent sort of clothing." He also observed that, besides manufacturing the wool, the natives were also instructed in a variety of necessary, useful and beneficial employments.

Though not himself a Catholic and unfamiliar with the Spanish language, Vancouver's views of California and its missions are remarkably accurate. According to one commentator his account remains "superior to any of its kind, and constitutes the chiefest source of authority of that period."

CALIFORNIA MISSION LIFE—1792–1793

Archibald Menzies (1754–1842) was the Scot surgeon and naturalist who accompanied George Vancouver to California, in 1792–1793. His purpose on the voyage was "to investigate the whole of natural history of the countries visited. . . ." Those parts of Menzies' observations pertaining to California, now in the British museum, were translated by Alice Eastwood and published in 1924.

The Menzies narrative closely resembles that of Vancouver, though the latter dwells more extensively on details. For the most part, Menzies gives a fair appraisal of attempts by the friars to spread the Christian faith among the natives. Menzies spoke approvingly of the manner in which the Indians assimilated the trades and mannerisms of civilized society, noting that "these are the happy effects of religious persuasions when conducted on the rational plans of industry and supplying of necessary wants, and when inculcated by the mild influence of such exemplary Fathers."

The contentment of the natives greatly impressed Menzies, who expressed himself as having "no doubt but they will be induced to continue in pursuing that quiet industrious line of life which so easily gratifies all their wants and comforts." Along with Vancouver, Menzies' admiration for the motives of the missionaries, evident in his descriptions of their establishments, "show his interest and admiration for their spiritual accomplishments as well as their physical layouts." Menzies carefully recorded his impressions of Indian life at Missions Dolores, Santa Clara, San Carlos and Santa Barbara. A number of his observations are worth recalling at some length.

> The painful constancy with which these abstemious Fathers maintain the religious observances of the Church of Rome in this distant region is a great proof of their indefatigable zeal and uncommon fortitude, for notwithstanding the inconveniences and sufferings to which they are here daily exposed, they go patiently on encountering every difficulty with a manly perseverance and overcoming every obstacle by a noble principle of enthusiastic zeal and inward conviction of the importance of the object they pursue, in converting these poor savages from that pagan state of darkness in which they have hitherto roamed at large in the forests, to the enlightened paths of the Christian religion and the practical knowledge of useful arts.

> Surely a system of civilization conducted upon such humane and exemplary principles can never fail of attaining its end, even in a political view, by securing to the state in process of time a number of valuable and industrious subjects, reared up in the paths of virtue and morality under the mild auspices of those worthy Fathers, whose religious austerities must daily impress on their minds a lasting conviction of the exalted objects they pursue and whose little plans of industry, so easy and natural, renders their manner of living less precarious and consequently more comfortable and happy than in their roving state. Thus influenced, these proselytes act the part of grateful and affectionate children and gradually become useful members of the community, so that we cannot sufficiently applaud the persevering zeal of their humane conductors through a process so tedious and difficult.

OBSERVATIONS OF A REAR ADMIRAL—1826

Frederick William Beechey (1796–1856) arrived in the harbor of San Francisco, on November 6, 1826, with his impressive ship, H.M. Blossom. The London–born geographer was among the several dozen noteworthy foreign visitors to California in provincial times. His carefully recorded notes of that sojourn were published in 1831, as a *Narrative of a Voyage to the Pacific and Bering's Strait to Cooperate with the Polar Expeditions.*

The mission Indians claimed a large share of the English rear admiral's attention and, though "he was not blind to either the faults or excellences of the system or of the friars who had it in charge," Beechey's descriptions are generally fair and "even that which sounds unfavorable, if interpreted by the circumstances of Mexican missrule and settlers' misrepresentations, will be found to speak well for the missionaries and their efforts."

Beechey affirmed that "the worthy and benevolent priests of the mission devote almost the whole of their time to the duties of the establishment, and have a fatherly regard for those placed under them who are obedient and diligent; and too much praise cannot be bestowed on them, considering that they have relinquished many of the enjoyments of life, and have embraced a voluntary exile in a distant and barbarous country." He further observed that the kindness of the *padres* was of such a nature that, in some of the missions, the converts were so "attached to them that I have heard them declare they would go with them if they were obliged to quit the country."

Beechey recognized the importance of the missions to California and felt that "the government cannot be too careful to promote their welfare, as the prosperity of the country in a great measure is dependent upon them, and must continue to be so until settlers from the mother country can be induced to resort thither." The rear admiral expressed reservations about certain aspects of the missionary program which he thought "not calculated to raise the colony to any great prosperity." On the other hand, Beechey shrewdly reckoned that "neglect of the missions would not long precede the ruin of the *presidios*, and of the whole district."

Beechey correctly captured the underlying theme of the system by noting that "the object of the missions is to convert as many of the wild Indians as possible, and to train them up within the walls of the establishment in the exercise of a good life, and of some trade, so that they may in time be able to provide for themselves and become useful members of civilized society."

The English seaman's impartiality was not impaired by his Protestant background. He exhibited, for example, no hesitation in stating that the Indian converts "lead a far better life in the missions than in their forests, where they are in the state of nudity, and are frequently obliged to depend solely upon wild acorns for their subsistence."

While the account of Frederick William Beechey's visit to California "added little to our knowledge of the country that could not have been gathered from the published accounts of his predecessors," the narrative "is important for the accurate and detailed description" of that area's inhabitants. The supreme accolade of the Beechey account came from Hubert Howe Bancroft, who recorded that the "observations published in the voyager's narrative were perhaps more evenly accurate and satisfactory than those of any preceding navigator."

WILLIAM HEATH DAVIS VIEWS THE MISSIONS—1831

William Heath Davis (1822–1909) first visited California when the missions were still rather prosperous and populous. He subsequently witnessed the upheaval of the provincial period and inauguration of a whole new breed of westerners, thus coming to know first-hand many of the vexations rained on the mission system as it began to crumble. The thoroughly readable account of *Life in Pastoral California*, which Davis penned, won for him the respect of his countrymen in a manner unparalleled in the literature of the west.

Davis viewed the priests of the various missions as decidedly "superior men in point of talent, education, morals and executive ability." To him the *padres* seemed to be entirely disinterested, their aim and ambition being to develop the country, and civilize and Christianize the Indians, for which purpose the missions were established. "They worked zealously and untiringly in this behalf, and to them must be given the credit for what advancement in civilization, intelligence, industry, good habits and good morals pertained to the country at that day, when they laid the foundation of the present civilization and development of the country." Though he considered the Mexican friars "as a class inferior to their predecessors," Davis felt that even they "were a fine body of men of superior character" who "accomplished a vast deal of good" in California. As an honest, genial, industrious and successful mercantilist himself, Davis regarded the *padres* as "first class merchants," testifying that in their dealings on behalf of the neophytes, "they exhibited good judgment in their selections, so much so that it was a pleasure to deal with them."

The Honolulu–born observer was especially enamored with Fray González Rubio, one of the most renowned missionaries in California's annals. Rubio "was a noble man, a true Christian, very much respected and beloved by all who knew him." According to Davis, who felt drawn to Rubio "as by a lodestone," the gentle friar was greatly honored and loved by his people who designated him as "The Saint on Earth."

Throughout his *Seventy–Five Years in California*, Davis spoke of the *padres* as the "original pioneers of California, beyond all others." He stated that "They have left behind them, as mementoes of their zeal and industry in the work in which they were engaged, the Missions they built and conducted, besides other evidences, less tangible, of their influence for the welfare of the people of California and the whole world."

William Heath Davis was an active and vital participant in the day and generation of which he has written so well and convincingly. He wrote extensively, concerning the *padres* and their simple but untiring mission life. There was something prophetic in his observation: "When this State, imperial in its dimensions, shall have grown to an empire itself, great will be the interest as to what were its beginnings, and as to what manner of men they, were who founded it." Davis went a long way to help record that saga.

RUSSIAN ORTHODOX PRIEST TOURS MISSIONS—1836

One of the most intriguing visitors to provincial California, one about whom very little evidence can be unearthed, was the Reverend John Veniaminov

(1797–1879), a Russian Orthodox priest, the "Enlightener of the Aleuts." What little information is available concerning the Russian cleric is excerpted from a typed transcript of his diary, in the Bancroft Library, at the Berkeley campus of the University of California.

The diary, entitled *Travel Journey of the Priest John Veniaminov, kept at the time of his trip to California and back from July 1 to October 13, 1836,* is exceedingly interesting for it lacks evidence of friction between the Spanish–speaking and the Russians. Nor are there any allusions to ill feeling on the other side or hint about the impending withdrawal of the Russians from California five years later.

Veniaminov arrived in Alaska, in 1823. He journeyed to California thirteen years later, visiting Missions San Rafael, San Jose, Santa Clara and San Francisco. He was greatly impressed with Fray José Maria González Rubio, whom he described as the best educated and most kind of all his confraternity in California. At all the missions he was courteously and kindly received and hospitably entertained. He speaks of the uniform respect, and honor accorded him. Very likely the Franciscan *padres* who so graciously welcomed the schismatic priest never learned that he died as a Metropolitan of Moscow!

Veniaminov recorded in his diary that "all the missions are constructed very uniformly, namely: The main building called MISSION is a large quadrangle one–story building, having a courtyard in the center, built of unburnt bricks and covered with tile. One side is set apart for the church, the other for the *padre*, and the remaining ones are either storerooms or shops. Alongside extend several buildings of the same material for the Indians, for the married and single ones separately."

Four years after his leaving California, Veniaminov became the first Bishop of Alaska and during his administration there, the first Catholic priests were readmitted to Russian America. George 0. Schanzer conjectures as to "whether the friendly reception accorded the Russian visitor by the *padres* of California had something to do with the possible decision of the later Metropolitan of Moscow to receive the Jesuits in the territory then under his jurisdiction."

The prelate was advanced to an archbishopric in 1850, and seventeen years later was called to the highest dignity of the Russian Orthodox Church, as Metropolitan of Moscow. A scholar in his own right, with no less than six books catalogued by the Library of Congress, Father Veniaminov wrote on such subjects as the Aleut language, customs and history; meteorology, geography and natural history; grammar of the native peoples and religious instruction. He is referred to in the original *Catholic Encyclopedia* as "the most authoritative Russian writer on Alaska and the most distinguished of her Russian ecclesiastics."

The generally overlooked visit of John Veniaminov

was an instance of peaceful relations whose record belies totally the concept about an early nineteenth–century "cold war" on the Pacific Coast.

IMPRESSIONS OF A NEPHEW OF MOTHER SETON—1838

Charles Wilkes (1798–1877) commanded the first United States Exploring Expedition, which arrived in California, in 1838. While the New York–born observer "developed no personal enthusiasm for the province," he did succeed "in learning much about the social and economic life of the people; and in getting an insight, especially valuable to his government in later years, into the political conditions of the province."

The main object of Wilkes' scientific expedition was "to examine, survey and gather information about California and the great bay of San Francisco." His report was published in five volumes by C. Sherman of Philadelphia in 1844, as *Narrative of the United States Exploring Expedition During the Years 1838, 1839, 1840, 1841, 1842.*

Wilkes recorded a good deal of information about the California missions, most of it appearing in the fifth volume of his extensive report. He noted that "fortunately for the country the *padres* and rulers of the missions were men well adapted for their calling: good managers, sincere Christians. They exerted a salutary influence over all in any way connected with them, practicing at the same time the proper virtues of their calling in order more effectually to inculcate them upon others." He further observed that "during the management of the Spanish priests, everything was judiciously conducted: the Indians were well dressed, well fed and happy. . . . Each mission formed a body politic of itself . . . and everything went on prosperously."

Wilkes described how "at the missions the manufacture of various coarse articles had been introduced as a step in the education of the neophytes. Among these were blankets and wearing apparel to supply all the Indians. . . ." Unfortunately, however, by the time of his arrival on the California scene, the missionary foundations were well into their period of decline. Wilkes recorded that "the missions are no more what they once were, the pride of the *padres*, and the seat of the wealth and prosperity of the country. Moreover, this state of things has left the whole community destitute of any religious observance. . . ."

With the change of sovereignty in California, Wilkes pointed out that "the country was deprived of the religious establishments upon which its society and good order were founded. Anarchy, confusion began to reign, and the want of authority was everywhere felt. Some of the missions were deserted; the property which had been amassed in them was dissipated, and the Indians turned out to seek their native wilds."

Though he was a nephew of Mother Elizabeth Ann Seton, Wilkes did not share her belief in or sympathy for the Catholic Faith. In a number of passages can be found remarks which are, to say the least, uncomplimentary and misleading. Obviously much of Wilkes' displeasure about mission life as it existed in the early 1840s was a reaction to the lack of influence then exerted by the friars, many of whom were Mexican–born. He regarded most of them as "inferior to the old Spaniards, neither possessing their intelligence, their skill in governing, their correct principles, nor their dignity in deportment. . . ." The fact is that the few remaining friars, totally deprived of their earlier authority, were accommodated as mere "guests" at the missions, whose only official function was that of caring for the spiritual needs of the community.

The generally pessimistic observations of Charles Wilkes are valuable, insofar as they testify to the effect exerted on the California missions and the Indians committed to their care. Any truly objective analysis of Spain's missionary endeavors must incorporate a contrast between the peaceful life of the earlier decades with the utter chaos that reigned after conferral of "freedom" on the Indians.

MARIANO GUALADUPE VALLEJO MEMOIRS—(BEFORE 1840)

Mariano Guadalupe Vallejo (1806–1890), a patriarchal figure in early California wrote his reflections of "ranch and missions" days in Alta California. Here is a portion of his colorful memoir.

I have often been asked about the old Mission and ranch gardens. They were, I think, more extensive, and contained a greater variety of trees and plants, than most persons imagine. The Franciscans in Alta California began to cultivate the soil as soon as they landed. The first grapevines were brought from Lower California in 1769, and were soon planted at all the Missions—except Dolores, where the climate was not suitable. Before the year 1800 the orchards at the Missions contained apples, pears, peaches, apricots, plums, cherries, figs, olives, oranges, pomegranates.

At San Diego and San Buenaventura Missions there were also sugar canes, date palms, plantains, bananas, and citrons. There were orchards and vineyards in California sufficient to supply all the wants of the people. I remember that at the Mission San Jose we had many varieties of seedling fruits which have now been lost to cultivation.

Of pears we had four sorts, one ripening in early summer, one in late summer, and two in autumn and winter. One of them was as large as a Bartlett, but there are no trees of it left now. The apples, grown from seed, ripened at different seasons, and there were seedling peaches, both early and late.

An interesting and popular fruit was that of the Nopal, or prickly pear. This fruit, called tuna, grew on the great hedges which protected part of the Mission orchards and were twenty feet high and ten or twelve feet thick. Those who know how to eat a tuna, peeling it so as to escape the tiny thorns on the skin, find it delicious.

The Missions had avenues of fig, olive, and other trees about the buildings, besides the orchards. In later times American squatters and campers often cut down these trees for firewood, or built fires against the trunks, which killed them. Several hundred large and valuable olive trees at the San Diego Mission were killed in this way.

The old orchards were pruned and cultivated with much care, and the paths were swept by the Indians, but after the sequestration of the Mission property they were neglected and ran wild. The olivemills and wine–presses were destroyed, and cattle were pastured in the once fruitful groves.

The flower gardens were gay with roses, chiefly a pink and very fragrant sort from Mexico, called by us the Castilian rose, and still seen in a few old gardens. Besides roses, we had pinks, sweet–peas, hollyhocks, nasturtiums which had been brought from Mexico, and white lilies.

The vegetable gardens contained peas, beans, beets, lentils, onions, carrots, red peppers, corn, potatoes, squashes, cucumbers, and melons. A fine quality of tobacco was cultivated and cured by the Indians. Hemp and flax were grown to some extent. A fine large cane, a native of Mexico, was planted, and the joints found useful as spools in the blanket factory, and for many domestic purposes. The young shoots of this cane were sometimes cooked for food. Other kinds of plants were grown in the old gardens, but these are all that I can remember.

No class of American citizens is more loyal than the Spanish Californians, but we shall always be especially proud of the traditions and memories of the long pastoral age before 1840. Indeed, our social life still tends to keep alive a spirit of love for the simple, homely, outdoor life of our Spanish ancestors on this coast, and we try, as best we may, to honor the founders of our ancient families, and the saints and heroes of our history since the days when Father Junípero planted the cross at Monterey!

A FRENCHMAN RECALLS THE MISSIONS— 1841

Eugene Duflot de Mofras (1810–1884) was an attache at the French Embassy in Madrid. He came to the Pacific West in order to ascertain, independently of a political point of view, what advantage might be offered to his nation's commerce and navigation by mercantile expeditions and the establishment of trading posts.

"It would be difficult to find a more complete account of any comparatively unknown country" than that penned by Duflot de Mofras after his visit to California in 1841. Certainly the French–born "gentleman of learning and culture left one of the most valuable records of the mission system."

It is commonly thought that Duflot de Mofras was an advance agent of the Government of Louis Philippe who, like leaders in England and the United States, "cherished ambitions to acquire California." In any event, the talented Frenchman was the most important representative of a foreign power to visit the area since the close of the Spanish regime.

Duflot de Mofras probably saw most of the missions personally on his tour. His observations of the friars, about whom he invariably speaks in a reverential tone, are contained in *Exploration du Territoire de l'Oregon, des Californies et de la Mer Vermeille*, two tomes published under the auspices of the French government in 1844. The volume was "the only early illustrated work on the Pacific Coast comparable in beauty to the *Voyage Pittoresque* of Choris or to Litke's account of the Russian survey of the northwest coast." Critics classify it as "superior to any issued within that decade" and there is no doubt that the account "gave more historical information than any other book of the time."

Concerning the activities of the missionaries, Duflot de Mofras was astonished "to see with what scanty resources they have achieved amazing results." He was especially impressed with the paternal relationship between the friars and the natives, which he felt was "not unlike that of a father and son." In his attempts to give a complete description of the country, the French diplomat familiarized himself with the principal works that had been published on the subject. Reading the observations of his predecessors, Duflot de Mofras was unable to comprehend how certain of the foreign visitors were able "to slander the Spanish clergy, from whom they have received the most generous hospitality." He categorized such comments as "indeed deplorable."

Regarding two of the more prominent narratives, Duflot de Mofras noted that "with typical English coldness, Captain [Frederick William] Beechey and Mr. [Alexander] Forbes, men imbued with the intolerance of Protestantism, are inclined to ridicule and cast insinuations on the activities of the Fathers." He noted, however, that facts "clearly disprove their contentions."

The French visitor himself fell victim to inaccurate reporting on several occasions, though he seems to have done so in good faith. For example, his exaggerated estimates of mission wealth, especially at San Gabriel, obviously based on reports from unfriendly territorial officials, caused considerable amazement when published. Generally, however, the observations of Eugene

Duflot de Mofras were a fair appraisal of the mission system which, by the time of his visit in 1841, was a relic of another era. The classic account, now 125 years old, remains "the most thorough history of California, both political and physical, that had been ever condensed into one work."

A JOURNALIST ON THE MISSIONS—1846-1847

Possibly the most detailed and reliable of all the overland journals is that written by Edwin Bryant (1805–1869), a Massachusetts–born newspaper editor who toured California in 1846–47. Nearly half the narrative is devoted to a day–by–day account of Bryant's trek from Independence to the mouth of the American River. San Francisco's one–time *alcalde* recorded his observations in the journalistic style of which he was a master.

Bryant's book was released, in 1848, by D. Appleton & Company under the title, *What I Saw in California: Being the Journal of a Tour, by the Emigrant Route and South Pass of the Rocky Mountains, Across the Continent of North America, the Great Desert Basin, and through California*. The 455–page tome, regarded as a classic description of pre–gold rush California, found its way in many a miner's kit. The unquestionably well–written account of a typical Overland journey subsequently became a prime authority on California's discovery period.

If Edwin Bryant's observations of the missions are not overly sympathetic, perhaps a measure of the blame can be attributed to his failure to understand the purpose of the overall spiritual conquest. It must also be remembered that his visit took place well after the most flourishing years of the Franciscan dominance. To Bryant, the Indians were "naturally filthy and careless" with very limited understanding. While acknowledging that "in the small arts they are not deficient in ideas of imitation," he decried their lack of inventive talents, maintaining that their true character is revengeful, timid and treacherous. He noted that the Indians were weak and invigorous "whether from the continual use of the sweathouse, or from their filthiness, or the little ventilation in their habitations." Spasms and rheumatics were the obvious consequences of such customs.

The greatest scourge for the Indians during Bryant's time was the European–imported plague of venereal disease, a factor to which the New England journalist attributed "the enormous difference between the births and deaths." He credited the missionaries with doing "all in their power to prevent this, with respect to the catechumens situated near them." In the spiritual realm, Bryant noted that "the religion of the Californians is the Roman Catholic, and like the people of all Roman Catholic countries, they appear to be devotedly attached to the forms of their religion." Though he spoke unfavorably of the "paganish grafts upon the laws, formalities, and ceremonies," he conceded that "these probably do not materially affect the system."

The weakest parts of Edwin Bryant's observations are those relating to the California missions whose function he failed to grasp and the Indians whose dignity he refused to acknowledge. As is frequently the case with "topical" books, timing contributed immeasurably to the popularity of Bryant's work. The volume appeared just in time to titilate the gold rushers, and a factor that accounted for much of the grass–roots acclaim for the volume.

AN ENGLISHMAN'S REFLECTIONS—1847

The narrative of Sir George Simpson (1792–1860) is "a model record of travels by an exceedingly able man and a keen observer." According to his biographer, the Scottish–born official of the British government came to California to "give special attention to the commercial interests of the time. . . ." That he had a sharp eye for business is obvious from his observations about Mexico's financial indebtedness to Great Britain. One chronicler pictured Simpson as believing "that it was not only possible but most desirable for England to take the country [California] in part payment of the debt."

Simpson was an important visitor, inasmuch as his position with the Hudson Bay Company gave him jurisdiction over all the British territory and claims west of the Great Lakes. The account of his travels was notably influenced by the work of Alexander Forbes, whose published work he carefully read and annotated enroute to the West Coast.

In his *Narrative of a Journey Round the World*, published at London, in 1847, Sir George devotes about 150 pages to California. "The crisp sentences rarely even corrected, betray a trained mind, endowed with a clarity of vision." Inasmuch as the British traveler regarded the work of the friars in California as "a show, in which the puppets cease to dance when the wire–pullers were withdrawn," it is understandable that his "criticism of the mission system is severe."

For the Jesuits and their efforts in the peninsula, Simpson was somewhat generous in his appraisal. After all, said he, it was they who "had covered the sterile rocks of Lower California with the monuments, agricultural and architectural and economical, of their patience and aptitude, not only leaving to their successors apposite models and tolerable workmen, but also bequeathing to them the invaluable lesson that nothing was impossible to energy and perseverance." The zeal, patience and talent Simpson attributed to the Society of Jesus, he withheld from their Franciscan counterparts in Alta California—whom be credited only with a longing "to eclipse the renown of their hated predecessors."

At the time of his visit, in 1841–1842, "priests, cattle, savages and dwellings had all vanished" and the missions presented a picture of ruin, decay and failure. From this Simpson concluded that Catholicism was nothing more than "an external religion" which had not prepared the natives for their eventual freedom.

Speaking of the sad plight of the "emancipated" natives, Simpson observed that they "no sooner became their own masters than they showed that their steadiness and industry had been the result of external control rather than of internal principle. . . . This miserable failure, if not actually desired by the priests, must at least have been anticipated by them as the legitimate fruit of a discipline, which whether necessarily or not, regarded the natives as children."

Simpson did reserve a few kind comments about the intellectual activities of the *padres*, noting that "it was, in fact, chiefly by means of books that the missionaries had contrived to overcome all the difficulties of their isolated position, from the preparing of the adobes to the decorating of churches, from the constructing of the plow to the baking of the bread, from the shearing of the sheep to the fulling of the web. But, in addition to their ingenuity in planning, they toiled more diligently than any of their unwilling assistants in the actual execution of their various labors, striving at the same time to render their drudgery morally available as an example.

While it is hardly true, as Hubert Howe Bancroft stated, that the Simpson volume shows "no strong prejudices, indulging in neither abuse nor flattery," that same historian is accurate in saying that "this English visitor describes in a most charming style his own experience and impressions of what he saw, introducing here and there, with a pleasing disregard of order, sketches of the country's history, conditions, prospects, people and institutions."

One might only have wished, in retrospect, that Simpson could have read more widely about the aims, conditions and achievements of the California mission system before setting down his own observations in print.

THE JONES REPORT ON THE MISSIONS—1849

William Carey Jones, a son–in–law of Senator Thomas Hart Benson, came to California, in the fall of 1849, as a confidential agent of the United States government. A lawyer skilled in the complicated intricacies of Spanish colonial titles, Jones had been instructed to give "particular attention to the extensive tracts of land covered by what are known as missions."

The report which Jones ultimately submitted

"showed a definitely friendly attitude towards Californians and helped to lay the basis for tolerance and understanding in meeting the claims of those who were in possession of the land of California." His observations were published, in 1851, as a *Report of the Secretary of the Interior, Communicating a Copy of the Report of William Carey Jones, Special Agent to examine the Subject of Land Titles in California.* Issued as an excerpt from Document No. 18, for the first session of the 31st Congress, the 136–page treatise, now a rare collector's item, contained many historical documents and a lengthy list of private grants in California, as recorded in the archives then at Monterey.

Robert Ernest Cowan noted that the literature on the history of land claims was extremely voluminous, and included much early local history otherwise inaccessible. "Remarkable in scope and detail, as well as being a model of clarity and direct writing," the Jones report was a landmark in the history of land titles. W. W. Robinson noted how it "had its effect on the legislation Congress passed, and its liberal viewpoint found continuing expression in later court rulings upon the ownership of California land."

As for mission–held land, the report said that "the missionaries (in California) had never any other rights than to the occupation and use of the lands for the purpose of the missions and at the pleasure of the government. That is shown by the history and principles of their foundation, by the laws in relation to them, by the constant practice of the government towards them, and by the rules of the Franciscan order which forbid its members to possess property."

Each of the missions was given special attention. For example, that of Nuestra Señora, de la Soledad, figured into the report thusly:

> The said mission, according to the information of the presiding minister, Francisco Xavier, is situated in 36 1/2° of latitude, at the extremity of the plain of Monterey. On the west it is bounded by the mission of San Carlos. From north to south, from the district called *Laguna de los Palos* to that of Cholar, three and a half leagues distant, there are two sheep ranges, and two leagues further a third, with the permission of the mission of San Carlos, which is to the north, and the cattle of which on this line, to the east, mingle with those of this mission. To the east of this line are the cattle and horses, which are branded and marked as in the margin. It is bounded by the farm of San Benito, belonging to the mission of San Antonio, distant nine leagues from south to north, the soil of which is very barren, and affords pasture only when there are copious rains.

> The two mountains which form this district or range are barren and impracticable. It has only some small outlets, by which the cattle can go to Tulares, in a northeast direction. The river Monterey crosses the entire district, and its waters only serve for the use of the cattle,

on account of its not being capable of being dammed, owing to its depth. On the southeast there is a stream, at the distance of three leagues, which runs from west to east until it unites with the river Monterey, which is dammed, for the purpose of irrigation, until June or July, when it becomes dry. There are some drains of little consequence.

> There are no trees, except elms, alders, and willows, in the river bottoms. On the skirts of the mountain there are some knotty oaks and live oaks, without other timber, for the want of which they have constructed their out–houses and dams with timber from the pine groves of Monterey.

William Carey Jones was indeed a notable contributor to the California scene!

CONGREGATIONALIST MINISTER VIEWS THE MISSIONS—1850

Walter Colton (1797–1851), the first Protestant minister to live in California, was a naval chaplain who later served as *alcalde* of Monterey. The annals testify that Colton, a Congregationalist, was "an earnest, kind–hearted, and sensible man, whose official and private record in California was a most excellent one."

The diary of this co–founder of the *Californian*, the area's first American newspaper, is considered to be "possibly the most important of the original narratives for the vital period of transition from Mexican to American rule." Dr. Colton's "entertaining and informative" journal was published, in 1850, by the A.S. Barnes and Company as *Three Years in California.* The 456–page treatise subsequently appeared in several editions and titles including *The Land of Gold* and *California Diary.*

Colton regarded the missions in California as "the most prominent features in her history." He looked upon the friars as "men of unwearied zeal and heroic action; their enterprise, fortitude, and unshaken purpose might rouse all the slumbering strings of the religious minstrel." His insight enabled Colton to understand how the friars contemplated the conversion of the untutored natives as an extension of the same system which, half a century earlier, had achieved signal triumph on the peninsula and throughout the northern provinces of Mexico.

Colton accurately described the manner in which the California missions formed a religious cordon about the entire extent of the coast, reared as they were at intervals of twelve or fourteen leagues in valleys opening on the sea.

With an admiration characteristic of his religious vocation, Dr. Colton depicted the physical structure of the individual missions, the church, living quarters, storehouses, workshops, fields, forests, streams, orchards, cattle "and above all, a faith that could scoop up whole tribes of savages, dazzling them with the symbols of religion, and impressing them with the conviction that submission to the *padres* was obedience to God." To Colton, "California, though seemingly young, is piled with the wrecks of the past; around the stately ruins flits the shadow of the *padre;* his warm welcome to streaming guests still lingers in the hall; and the loud mirth of the festive crowds still echoes in the darkened arches." Even though his association with the missions came after their dominance, he conceded that "their localities will serve as important guides to emigrants in quest of lands adapted to pasturage and agriculture, and their statistics will show, to some extent, the productive forces of the soil."

Colton's estimate of mission "wealth," apparently based on the spurious figures of Mariano Guadalupe Vallejo, is grossly exaggerated and not at all in agreement with any of the sources. There is every reason to believe that the Vermont–born minister was honestly deceived about the purported holdings of the missions. With this one reservation, the Colton narrative can be classified among those giving an excellent picture of the times.

WOMAN RECALLS VISIT TO MISSIONS—1856

After touring the California missions in 1856, Mrs. E. Williams wrote her reflections for the April, 1863 issue of *The Hesperian*. A portion of that memoir is here presented, courtesy of the Huntington Library in San Marino.

Scattered up and down our rapidly–growing and prosperous state, like monuments of an epoch already past, stand the rudely–built yet picturesque and attractive edifices known as missions. These consist generally of a church substantially built of adobes and plastered, of a peculiar but not ungraceful style of architecture, and various out buildings, which were to subserve the different purposes of barns, granaries, or dwellings for those attached to the mission, and a greater or less extent of land brought into a condition capable of supplying most of the necessities and many of the luxuries of life.

These missions, from their attractive situations, have often become centres for towns—and, in many cases, the *pueblos* or villages formed by the settlement of the Spanish soldiers attached to the garrison of the mission, who married native women and became permanent residents, have become the germs even of cities.

Such is, for instance, Los Angeles—in the garden region of our state—the seeds of whose prosperity were sown by the grape culture introduced by the mission fathers, and whose flocks and herds, covering hill and valley and rapidly increasing in that genial and fruitful clime, were mainly due to the enterprise and energy of men who, in the seventeenth and eighteenth centuries, worked not for themselves but for the world—which

has inherited their labors and reaped the fruit of the seed that they sowed and the trees that they planted.

Among all the missions, for picturesque and so to speak tropical beauty, we should indicate that of San Fernando, about twelve miles from Los Angeles, as preeminent. A widely extended valley, with nearly a level surface, bounded by distant ranges of mountains, at first presents itself; these mountains have a peculiarly barren look, but this defect is almost compensated for by the various and beautiful shades of color they assume—blue, brown and purple contrasting finely with the clear, transparent skies, and with the even surface of the valley.

The road is bordered by a low growth of shrubbery and cactus. On turning the point of a hill, you come suddenly upon the mission buildings, which, with their surrounding gardens, stand seemingly isolated in the midst of a desert plain, and produce a most beautiful effect. The gardens were enclosed by walls, but the graceful palm rose above them, and groves of olive, lemon and orange trees could be seen within.

Outside the walls, the surface was barren and gravelly, and the fertility within was the result of irrigation. The building presented an imposing appearance, having a long portico formed by a colonnade with twenty arches built of brick or adobe plastered and whitewashed.

The floor is paved with tiles, and a pleasant promenade in front of the edifice is afforded. In the days of the prosperity of the mission, a large fountain, with a circular basin ten feet or more in diameter, rose directly in front of the main building. This fountain is now in ruins; its beautiful jet no longer refreshes the palm trees, and is blown back upon the flowers.

A great variety of tropical fruits still exist there, bearing testimony to the skillful horticulture and industry of the community; and, though the forms of the men who reared the colonnade and planted these trees, and sought refreshment and relaxation in these walks from the cares of business, or from the labors of their mission, have long since passed away, their memory still survives in the breath of the orange blossoms, in the melancholy and sweetness of the palm—the tree of the desert, the tree of the solitary—communing more with the heavens than the earth, disdaining to spread its branches near the soil, but lifting up in the blue air, far above our heads, its flowers and its fruit.

TOUR OF THE CALIFORNIA MISSIONS—1856

One of the most attractive and informative books printed at The Grabhorn Press is the *Account of a Tour of the California Missions, 1856*, issued in a limited edition of 375 copies by the Book Club of California, in 1952. The handsomely bound and boxed fifty–nine page book, released under the editorship of Edith M. Coulter and Eleanor A. Bancroft, contains a descriptive journal and nineteen pencil–drawing reproductions of the missions by Henry Miller. The journal and drawings are part of thirty–seven pictures on file in the Bancroft Library, at the Berkeley campus of the University of California. An earlier publication appeared as *California Towns From the Original Drawings*, in 1947.

Very little is known about the person of Henry Miller. Obviously an educated man, with a keen eye for detail, his journal reveals first–hand familiarity with the West Indies, Latin America and Mexico. It was only the recent discovery of a manuscript describing the wanderings of the artist from San Francisco to San Diego that identified the Henry Miller mentioned in Benjamin Hayes' diary as the executor of the unsigned drawings. Miller was, in his own words, a "diffident man," a trait that accounts for the anonymity of his sketches and journal.

According to Benjamin Hayes, Miller originally intended to paint the missions on a large scale as part of a complete panorama of California for exhibition in the Eastern States and Europe. Feeling himself too illiterate for such a task, he limited the scope of his work to only that which he considered "remarkable and peculiar in this state."

The artist traveled through "all the southern counties, rendered dangerous by banditti and ferocious animals of the forest," until his "little fund of money was exhausted by the enormous rates which a traveler has to pay." He then endeavored to offset expenses by making sketches for those he met along the way, an expediency that compelled him to observe the "strictest economy." Miller's drawings are historically valuable, constituting as they do the earliest attempt to depict the missions in series form. They accurately portray the establishments twenty–three years after secularization before deterioration had become too marked.

The fact that the journal is more descriptive than interpretative makes it impossible to ascertain Miller's personal reaction to the overall missionary enterprise. Fortunately, Miller's works found their way into the vast collection of Hubert Howe Bancroft where they were preserved for future generations. Although he admitted "having not the slightest pretentions to literary capacities," the journal and depictions of the hitherto little–known artist entitle Henry Miller to a place of honor in the Golden State's historical heritage.

PRIEST EXPLAINS THE MISSION SYSTEM—1870s

Time has woven a web of romantic interest around that period of California history known as the missionary era. The following observations were originally prepared by Father Juan Caballeria:

The success of the missionary fathers was largely due to the system employed by them to bring the Indians within Christianizing influence. It may be safely asserted that no other system, either ancient or modern, can compare results with that of the *padres* in bringing a degraded, savage people to a remarkable degree of civilization in a brief period of time.

(The system) was the result of long years of experience in dealing with savage tribes. Spain was old in the work of colonization when Fray Junípero Serra, the beloved apostle of Christianity, consented to accept the arduous mission of Christianizing the Indians of Alta California.

At the time of the colonization of California by Spain, the question of a system under which the missionary work should be conducted was an important one. It was the subject of much discussion and some dissension. Three systems had been employed in the various colonies of South America and Mexico, and each had advocates, defending one and condemning the others as worthless or impracticable.

The advocates of the system of "civilization by imitation" contended that the Indian should be left free to accept or reject civilization, never doubting that, once the matter was properly presented, the Indian would not fail to appreciate its advantages, and the superior way of living would prove so attractive he would, by 'imitation,' follow in the pathway of his white neighbor. The Indian was to be left free to follow his inclination in all matters. He was to be permitted to enter the places of religious worship and the homes of the white man, and by every means kindness could devise be encouraged to embrace civilization. This was clearly a humanitarian view of the subject. It is apparent that those who advocated the system knew little of the nature of the Indian. Those who are familiar with the Indian and his abhorrence to the restraints of civilization and disinclination to labor will appreciate the hopelessness of this method.

Another system called the "new system" met with much favor. On the outside it seems practicable, and an easy way of solving the difficulty. This, like the first, provided that the Indian should be left practically unrestrained and undisturbed in his native haunts, but settlements of whites were to be located in his immediate vicinity. These white men were to endeavor by example and kindness to stimulate in the Indian a desire for work and advancement. It was reasoned that this could be accomplished through gifts of agricultural implements, food and clothing, until the Indian, becoming accustomed to the necessities of the white man, and having the fullest opportunity for observing them, would in time follow their example, become self–supporting and gradually civilized. This seemed like a most excellent idea, and it met with so much favor that it was put in operation at Yuma and on the Colorado River.

The result was that so long as the gifts continued the Indians were friendly and were profuse in promises which they never fulfilled; but when the supplies became scarce the Indians rose up and treacherously massacred the missionaries and settlers in the most fiendish and cold–blooded manner.

The plan finally adopted was the one favored by the *padres* in charge of the work known as the "old system." The method employed was to first familiarize the

Indian with the mission and to overcome his natural timidity. This was accomplished by general kindness, aided by gifts of food and clothing, of which the Indians were very proud. It was only when confidence was established that the so called "harsh" methods were invoked, and they consisted principally in restraining the Indian, or depriving him of his liberty, confining him within the mission enclosure until such a time as he was considered sufficiently trustworthy, when he was by degrees allowed more freedom.

In the meantime, the *padres* undertook to teach him Christianity and the various arts of civilization. In some cases there may have been unnecessary severity and abuses—no system is free from them—and there is no question but that corporal punishment was sometimes resorted to but it stopped short of cruelty or in the taking of life. In that respect the system of the *padres* was in advance of the usual "civilizing process."

The enlightened twentieth century furnishes an example in those who look on a "dead Indian" as the only "good Indian," but the mission system could point with pride to some very live Indians.

The ruins of the missions today mutely testify to the thoroughness of the system and the faith of the *padres* in the work they had undertaken. When it is considered that these missions were built almost entirely by the hands of a people not one generation removed from savagery, they are nothing short of a marvel, and in a less enlightened age would have been deemed a miracle.

OAK VISITS THE MISSIONS—1874

Henry Lebbeus Oak (1844–1905) came to California in 1866, and took a position as clerk in charge of a grain warehouse in Petaluma. He later taught briefly at the Napa Collegiate Institute and then joined the staff of the San Francisco *Occident*.

In 1869, Oak became associated with Hubert Howe Bancroft's library in San Francisco, where he labored for eighteen years. While there he spent much of his time writing and editing at least ten of the thirty–nine volumes that comprised *The Works of Hubert Howe Bancroft*.

Unhappily, the role of Oak in that monumental undertaking was never adequately acknowledged by Bancroft, a factor which deeply embittered his long–time New England collaborator. In any event, Oak was invited, in 1874, to accompany Bancroft and his daughter, Kate, on a tour of the California missions. Oak readily accepted the opportunity of retracing the steps of the *padres* along *El Camino Real*.

Fortunately, Oak kept a journal of that journey wherein he carefully recorded his observations. The manuscript subsequently found its way to the Southwest Museum. It has been edited by Ruth Frey Axe, Edwin H. Carpenter and Norman Neuerburg as Volume XI in the *Frederick Webb Hodge* series.

Extending from February 18 to March 15, 1874, the diary is more scholarly and less imaginative than the one kept by Bancroft on the same journey. Oak made fairly accurate sketches of the missions, interviewed priests and others living in and around the historic foundations and inventoried what old register books he was able to personally examine.

Going by sea to San Diego, the trio then worked their way northward, through the "desolate and dreary region" around San Luis Rey, and on to San Juan Capistrano. They journeyed to Los Angeles and then through the "best orange orchards in California" to San Gabriel. Oak noted that though the church at San Fernando had not been used for many years, it "seemed to be in tolerably good preservation."

He found the buildings at San Buenaventura "still in comparatively good condition," noting that "both the Church and most of the court buildings (were) being still occupied." At San Buenaventura, Oak met Bishop Thaddeus Amat who was making a pastoral visitation. He quoted the Vincentian prelate as saying that "most of the mission archives were sent to the College of San Fernando at Mexico City." Amat also recalled having "seen some documents on the subject in Seville, Spain."

Further north, Santa Barbara Mission, "unlike all the others" they had seen, was "kept in perfect repair without the slightest sign of decay." And he found Santa Ines, as Bishop Amat had warned, "used for the storage of hay which has been several times set on fire by malicious persons." All told, Oak visited ten missions, interviewing such prominent personages as Benjamin Hayes Cornelius Cole, Alfred Robinson, Andres Pico, B.D. Wilson, J.J. Warner, Agustin Olvera and a host of other outstanding California pioneers.

Surely it must have been an exciting twenty–seven days!

SEÑORA EULALIA DESCRIBES THE *MONJE-RIOS*—1877

Señora Eulalia Pérez de Guillen, thought by some to have been "the oldest woman ever to have lived," was born at the Royal Presidio of Loreto, in Baja California, in 1768. The ancient Indian died at San Gabriel on June 8, 1878 at the advanced age of 110 years. Eulalia had a remarkable background. Twice married, she was at San Juan Capistrano when the 1812 earthquake leveled the church. She was attending Mass at the time, although she managed to squeeze out through a side entrance of the church, and a short while later, gave birth to a healthy daughter, one of her many children.

In subsequent years, Eulalia went to Mission San Gabriel, where, as one of the three women in California with culinary training, she served as housekeeper to Friars José Sanchez and Jose de Zalvidea. Besides overlooking the cutting of garments for those attached to the mission, Señora Eulalia had charge of the soap house, the wine presses, and the olive grinders.

On December 10, 1877, Señora Eulalia was interviewed by Thomas Savage, a historian in the employ of Hubert Howe Bancroft. One of the interview's highlights was Eulalia's description of the *monjerios* or nunneries, a vital part of the overall mission system. Married Indians lived in small villages clustered around the mission compound. The younger children were lodged there with their parents. For the single natives, however, there were special lodgings, one for women and another for men. Little girls were brought to the *monjerio* at the age of seven or eight and were reared there until ready for marriage.

The nunnery was under the care of an Indian matron and each night the doors were locked and the keys hidden away. A blind native stood guard and would call out the name of each young girl as she entered. That the young women were locked in their quarters at night is quite understandable to those conversant with Spanish customs and practices.

In the morning the girls attended Mass where they heard an explanation of the Faith (*doctrina*) in their own dialect and afterwards went to the cookhouse for breakfast. The meal consisted of *champurrado* (chocolate made with corn meal gruel), with bread and sweets on festival days. On other days *pozole* (barley and beans boiled together) and meat formed the menu.

After breakfast, each young girl went to her assigned task—weaving, housework, sewing, or the like. Those doing housework would bring up one or two carts of refreshments (water and vinegar with sugar) to the Indians laboring in the fields. All work stopped about eleven o'clock and everyone assembled at the cookhouse at noon to eat *pozole* made with meat and vegetables. At one o'clock they returned to their work. The day's activities stopped at sundown when all gathered again at the cookhouse for supper of gruel with meat. Each brought her own dish which was filled with generous helpings.

Such was the practice at San Gabriel, described by Señora Eulalia Perez de Guillen, the venerable centenarian whose longevity was advertised around the world as due to the "healthful climate and orderly living of the far western prairies."

AN EARLY VIEW OF THE MISSIONS—1880

Charles H. Robinson's account of "The Early Catholic Missions of California" was based on personal observations and extensive interviews with native Americans and European colonizers. His essay is here excerpted from *The Catholic World* XXXII (October, 1880).

In the light of recent modern history, which relates the subjugation of nations through the bloodiest contests, sending the victims of national greed into the next world unshriven, it would be manifestly improper and unjust to urge against the Church the important part her priests took in the Spanish conquests.

No apology now is necessary on behalf of the Church for perfecting her mission of carrying the 'glad tidings' to the uttermost parts of the earth, and availing herself of the favorable opportunities afforded by the Spaniards to accomplish the purpose she has always been destined to effect—to wit, the conversion of the unbelievers.

The dream of the soldier was the acquisition of gold and the hope of reward or preferment from the king he served; his motives were human, transitory, and related to the present only, while to the priest occurred the promises of Christ—the world was to be redeemed and an earthly kingdom, a church militant, established; visions of future glory existed in his mind.

Under the leadership of Friar Junípero Serra, whose name is pronounced with reverence in California, the conversion of Upper, or what is now the State of, California was effected.

The civilization and development of California was the desired object of the Spanish king, and he was urged to accomplish his designs, more particularly because the marvelous conditions of climate and soil of the country were such that its agricultural resources and productions must be incalculable.

It was to become the seat of an immense population and of a highly civilized and prosperous people; these would form the nucleus of an empire of great power, which would exercise a controlling influence over the whole coast bordering upon the Pacific Ocean.

The Franciscans were entrusted with the establishment of a civilization which, when compared with that generally inaugurated by civil or military power, was singularly adapted to endure for ages and provide for every contingency that might arise in human affairs. A long line of missions gives evidence of a perfect system of homogeneous *pueblos*, frequently differing in rank, but always the same in kind and in organization.

The missions were built up from a uniform basis, perfectly resembling each other in all their features and emancipated from the irregularities and uncertainties which deform more modern communes. All this was the work of the priest, who knew how to mould the temporal affairs of mankind in perfect shape by the addition of the leaven of religion.

The reign of the church had brought peace and contentment upon the land; the hills teemed with cattle, the soil was cultivated and its resources developed to a greater extent every year. The management and discipline were simple and patriarchal, and so wisely conceived that no exceptions or disorders could possibly occur.

In sixty years of labor the missionaries of California had planted twenty-one prosperous missions upon a line of seven hundred miles from San Diego north to the latitude of Sonoma. More than thirty thousand Indian converts were lodged in the mission establishments and taught a variety of useful arts, besides receiving religious instruction.

SOME THOUGHTS ON THE MISSIONS—1892

An unsigned article on "The Missions," published in the Los Angeles *Times* for October 21, 1892, credited the Franciscans with being "the pioneers of religion and civilization on the Pacific Coast." The California missions "were something more than Catholic churches; — they were the first centers of civilization, and, as the friars gradually drew the wild tribes under religious influence and instructed them in useful callings, the sacred pilings came to be centers of settlement and industry."

Noting how the neophytes "were required to manifest a change of heart by their works as well as by faith," the author noted how "they tilled the fields, planted and tended the vineyards and orchards, and performed all sorts of manual service for their religious teachers."

Under the direction of Fray Junípero Serra and his Franciscan collaborators, "the country was explored, surveys made, and here in this wild uncultivated" area the friars erected the substructure of a whole new way of life for an aboriginal people within a few short decades. The work progressed "until a chain of establishments was planted extending about seven hundred miles along the coast, from San Diego to Sonoma, none being more than thirty miles inland, nor more than an easy day's journey on horseback apart."

The missionary foundations were "all constructed upon the same general plan, the style of architecture being of the semi–Moorish type, which prevails in all the Spanish provinces. The materials were mostly gathered within a few miles of the establishments, and the Fathers, with a few skilled mechanics who accompanied them to the country, directed the labor of the Indians."

The foundations "were mostly built of adobe (sun–dried brick of large dimensions) though, for the more pretentious, stone and kiln–burned brick were used. . . . The staunch construction of these mission buildings enabled them to defy the envious tooth of time remarkably well."

The daily routine followed was uniform throughout the missions: "At sunrise they all arose and repaired to the church, where, after morning prayers, they assisted at Mass, which occupied about an hour; thence they went to breakfast and afterward to their respective employments. At noon they returned to the Mission and spent two hours for dinner and rest, thence to work again until *Angelus*, when all betook themselves to church again for evening devotions.

"After supper they amused themselves in various games, sports and dances until bedtime, when the unmarried of both sexes were locked in their separate apartments until morning." Their diet "consisted of good beef and mutton, with vegetables, wheaten cakes, puddings and porridges. The married Indians lived in small huts grouped around the Mission and about two hundred yards from it. Some of their dwellings were made of adobe and others were conical in shape and of rough poles thatched with grass. A tract of about fifteen miles square was attached to each mission, which was used for cultivation and pasturage."

True enough, as the anonymous author pointed out, "the history of the missions is therefore the history of the civil no less than the religious development of California from a condition of barbarism, and is fraught with the deepest interest."

TRUMAN'S COMMENTARY ON THE MISSIONS —1892

According to one local author, "of all the pioneer journalists here, it is probable" that none has surpassed Benjamin Cummings Truman (1835–1916) "in brilliancy and genial, kindly touch." The widely–traveled, much–published, highly–esteemed Truman wrote and published a number of promotional items on or about Los Angeles and the advantages of taking up residence in California's southland.

Truman also wrote extensively about the missions and a collection of his writings appeared in 1978 as *The Observations of Benjamin Cummings Truman on El Camino Real*. The following essay, written in 1892 for the New York *Times*, was not in the above mentioned compilation:

One hundred and twenty–one years ago, on the 15th of May, Juan Crespi, a Friar of the Order of St. Francis, accompanied by twenty–six soldiers, three packers, and four or five Indian servants, arrived at San Diego, Cal., with the purpose of establishing a permanent mission, converting the savages, and introducing the arts of civilization and those purposes were not only solemnly and religiously, but commercially and successfully carried out.

The settlement was permanent, but it was not made so without the encountering of disturbing elements, and, in two or three other cases, loss of life was involved. Fray Juan Crespi's name as founder, however, gives way historically to Fray Junípero Serra, who arrived at San Diego July 1, 1769, and who at once formally founded the first mission in California at what is now known as Old San Diego.

As I have stated, this mission was permanent, and others soon followed, until nearly all of the great villages bordering on the Pacific, where there were harbors or roadsteads, were marked by mission churches and commercial structures from San Diego to San Francisco, and new California, as it was then called, took its place as one of the occupied provinces of the Spanish Empire.

Since then the remote, poor, insignificant, thinly–settled, and almost unknown province has become rich, influential, and populous, and is today one of the most noted states in the American aggregation, its prodigality of soil and its equability of temperature (west of the Sierra Nevada Mountains) being unsurpassed by any other section of country in the world, although these pioneers had not, of course, the remotest conception of the superstructure that was to arise majestically on their unpretentious foundation.

The only original record accessible of the first settlement of California is that briefly presented in the life of Junípero Serra, by his friend, Francisco Palou, who wrote it at the Mission of San Francisco in 1785, but his biographer, whose attention was fixed chiefly on the pious labors and seraphic character of his hero, leaves the searcher of these curious–looking old volumes of worn–out Spanish manuscript in almost complete ignorance of many of the particulars of the adventures by land and sea, and of the conduct of the Indians upon the first appearance of the missionaries.

There is one thing certain; Serra and his brother friars did their work well, as they understood it, and their missions continued to gain converts, herds of cattle, horses and sheep, and wealth for forty–five years, after which, under the influence of the Mexican rebellion, they declined, until at last, in 1835 after an existence of sixty–six years, they were secularized, the property placed in the hands of civil officers, and the friars were deprived of power to control.

And thus ended in California a great system or combination of commerce and agriculture and religion, the result of which, whatever good may have been derived therefrom, was to leave the Indians in a worse state than that in which they were found by the missionaries, as they afterward abandoned their habit of regular industry and began to die off very rapidly, until there are not now two thousand of the ten times that number fifty years ago left, and most of these at present live away from the whites in a condition little better than that of the coyote."

THE MISSION INDIANS—1902

In response to an inquiry from the editor of *Saint Michael's Almanac*, Father B. Florian Hahn, a long–time missionary among the Indians of California, submitted the following report in mid 1902.

The California Indians have dwindled down to about 5,000 souls of whom one half may be Christians, the rest being neglected and living in the old pagan way.

There are still Catholic Mission Indians in many places, although their settlements are small and insignificant. The counties of San Diego, Riverside and San Bernardino harbor the greatest number of these remnants of the Mission Indians.

The government of the United States has established fourteen day schools and two boarding–schools for them. In these schools the children are taught Protestant prayers, Protestant Bible and Protestant religion. Preachers visit these schools or the teachers who are all Protestant with the exception of a few employees at the boardings schools, teach them.

Thus the Catholic Indian families still true to their religion, will see their children return home Protestants.

There are two Catholic boarding schools in California, one at San Diego and one at Banning. In these two schools two hundred boys and girls are educated, receiving a common school education and an industrial training. The schools are maintained by the Bureau of Catholic Indian Missions.

Justice and gratitude permits me to mention here the charity of Mother Katherine Drexel's Sisters of the Blessed Sacrament who in a special manner aided the mission work in California. It was her zeal for the salvation of the Mission Indians that furnished the means of establishing and building the Banning school and providing annually for part of the funds necessary for its maintenance.

The Mission Indians of today are almost civilized. The men understand well how to take care of orchards and they are working for the American population and are also cultivating some land of their own. Thus they are self–supporting.

The old women are expert basket makers and the young women and girls are first–rate help in kitchen and house. Generally speaking, the Mission Indians are making their living honestly.

As to morals, I must say that I found the best Indians among those who had nothing or little to do with the white population. The Indian gets his liquor from the white man, and again it is the white man who wrongs the Indian by seduction.

However, there are good men and women, and sincere and intelligent Mission Indians in the barren and God–forsaken California Indian reservations. Many mistakes could be prevented by the Government, but the officials do not trouble themselves more than is absolutely necessary. They are for their salaries first, second and last.

The annual feasts with nightly dances are the worst feature in the Mission Indian's life. Of course, as the women dance with women and the men only with men, the dancing in itself is not wrong. On the contrary, it is even more chaste than the modern round dances.

However, the promiscuous meeting of Whites, Mexicans and Indians is objectionable. In fact, the social condition of the Indian is unsatisfactory.

The Mission Indians are a religious people. They are Catholic in their hearts. There are chapels and houses of worship everywhere. The cross and rosary, the pictures of the saints and the crucifix are in their homes, on their persons and upon their cemeteries.

They will approach the sacraments, and they will call the *padre* when sick and in danger of death. Their will is good; they desire to be followers of Christ and, I

Indians of California—The Miwok in Ceremonial dress, Sonora, California, 1858-1860.

am sure, had they not been so awfully neglected, many of them would be better Christians and the various missionary perversions brought on by well–paid Protestant missionaries would be less numerous.

The Catholics of the United States owe it to God and to their Church to contribute to their home missions, and mission schools.

MISSIONARY SYSTEM IN CALIFORNIA—1903

Father Zephyrin Engelhardt, the famed Franciscan chronicler of the California Missions, often wrote for journals and magazines under the pen name of *"Esperanza."* One such article, published in *The Monitor* for June 20, 1903, tells about the "Early Franciscan Missionary System in California." The following is digested from that treatise.

The system employed by the Franciscans in civilizing and Christianizing the natives was the same under which the Jesuits successfully conducted the missions in Paraguay, Sonora and Baja California until 1767, and under which the friars managed the missions of Texas and Mexico nearly a century before they arrived in California.

These men certainly knew from experience what means would best further the noble object of making Christians and citizens of the Indians on the coast. It stands to reason that they would choose the best and quickest method for that purpose, and the one most adapted to their pupils.

We, who live more than a century later, must acknowledge that to this day no better system has been discovered. If there existed any other means to make even passably good citizens out of the American Indians, let alone Christians, then surely the Government of the United States would not have adopted the old mission system in all its essential features, and applied it in dealing with the natives on their reservations.

The missionary system consisted in this: that the Fathers first endeavored to gain the good will of the natives through kindness, and by means of gifts, of food, clothing, trinkets, etc. Thereupon they persuaded the savages to abandon the squalor and want of the desert and mountain camps, and to make their home with the missionaries, who would provide for their corporal and spiritual needs.

Here they were instructed in the most essential doctrines of Christianity and, if willing, baptized. There was no intention to have them pass the time in idleness, since the plan was to make citizens and good Christians of them.

Therefore, suitable work was allotted to satisfy the demands of the community and to lead all to provide for themselves later on. Hence all trades and arts were taught that might be of use to them should they be capable and desirous of competing with their white neighbors.

As the savages never took kindly to much work, only so much was imposed as the community wants demanded, not more than six or seven hours daily. Moreover, there were so many holidays that the Indians cannot be said to have worked five days in the week, rather much less.

While it flourished, the Indian community was like a great family of which the missionary was the father and protector. Peace and contentment reigned; for the missionary sought only the interest of his red children, without regard to his personal comfort, and unmindful to profit to a number of hungry relatives nor friends to gratify or to enrich. His family was composed of many hundreds, sometimes thousands of natives, good, bad and indifferent.

That in a nutshell was the mission system. It was the old patriarchal family revived. To call it slavery as unscrupulous writers do, is evidence of a warped mind!

KNOWLAND'S MEMOIR ON MISSIONS—1908

Joseph Russell Knowland (1873–1955), long time editor of the *Oakland Tribune* was a supporter of research on California history and a public figure who served in the United States Congress (1904–1906). In April of 1908, non–Catholic Knowland wrote an essay for *The Architect and Engineer* magazine on "The California Missions." Here are some extracts:

The remains of the old Franciscan missions recall a most important historic period, arousing interest in the fascinating story of the establishment of the twenty–one missions, stretching from San Diego in the south to Sonoma in the north. The Franciscan missionaries were the original pioneers of California, sowing the first seeds of civilization and establishing the first permanent settlements. It was in the year 1769, at San Diego, that the first mission was established, located in such proximity that a traveler could start on foot from San Diego and nightly enjoy the hospitality of a different mission until Sonoma was reached.

Of the original twenty–one mission establishments,

but two have entirely disappeared—San Rafael Arcangel and Santa Cruz. Of the remaining nineteen, all but five are in a fair state of preservation, and portions of at least four of these five can be saved.

Crumbling walls mark the spot where Soledad mission once stood, and in a few more years all trace of this mission will be obliterated. San Diego, the mother mission, is in a poor state of preservation, little remaining but the front wall of the chapel. La Purisima Conception, five miles from the town of Lompoc, in Santa Barbara county, was fast reaching a state of disintegration when restoration would be impossible, but fortunately the property was turned over to the Landmarks Club of Southern California, which organization, under the leadership of Mr. Charles F. Lummis, is exerting every effort to raise funds for its preservation.

San Francisco Solano (Sonoma) mission was purchased in 1903 with a portion of the Landmarks Fund raised by the San Francisco *Examiner* with the assistance of the California Historic Landmarks League and other patriotic bodies. In 1905 the California Legislature passed an act providing for the acquisition, preservation and protection of the Sonoma mission property, which was turned over to the State without cost.

One of the most beautiful and less frequently visited missions is located in Monterey county, twenty–six miles from King City. This is mission San Antonio de Padua, a most picturesque ruin. It was formerly one of the most extensive of the mission establishments. For years it was neglected with no one to stay the hand of the vandal. The mission stands alone, its crumbling walls and deserted buildings appearing as if untouched since the departure of the *padres* and neophytes years ago.

At San Luis Rey, the church is in a good state of preservation, but the picturesque arches, of which there were originally thirty–two, ornamented with latticed railings, are year by year crumbling. At San Juan Capistrano, the great chapel was years ago destroyed by an earthquake, but a number of other buildings, safeguarded by the Southern California Landmarks Club, remain.

San Gabriel mission, ten miles from the city of Los Angeles, is in use, services being regularly held within the walls of the old structure. Twenty miles north of Los Angeles stand the remaining buildings belonging to San Fernando Rey. The chapel was re–roofed by the Landmarks Club. Santa Barbara and San Buenaventura missions are in an excellent condition of preservation. This is likewise the case with Santa Ines mission in Santa Barbara county.

The two missions of San Luis Obispo and San Juan Bautista, located respectively in the counties of San Luis Obispo and San Benito, have been to a certain degree disfigured by the erection of modern church steeples. The recent earthquake did considerable damage to San Juan Bautista.

While the exterior of Santa Clara mission is quite modern, painstaking effort has been put forth to have the interior of the modern chapel conform to the old. This is particularly true of the decorated ceiling above the sanctuary, each board in the old ceiling having been carefully taken down, numbered, and later made use of in the new church.

The mission a few miles from the old town of Monterey, San Carlos Borromeo, has been restored with a peaked shingle roof destroying, to a great extent, the original beauty of this structure. Little remains of Mission San Jose, in Alameda county. The old mission San Miguel is most interesting, its interior still showing the decorations made by the Indians. San Francisco de Asis (Dolores) mission, in San Francisco, withstood the earthquake and conflagration of 1906, the modern church adjoining suffering great damage.

These old missions should be preserved. Over one hundred years have come and gone since the passing of the mission system, and each year Californians are becoming more impressed with the importance of preserving these reminders of the days of Spanish rule and monuments to those self–sacrificing *padres* who labored unceasingly for the betterment of the Indians, facing the greatest difficulties, enduring hardships, and in many instances sacrificing their lives."

ARTHUR BENTON ON THE MISSIONS—1919

Arthur Burnett Benton, a well–known Southern California writer, belonged to the American Institute of Architects Committee on Historic Landmarks and War Memorials. His twenty–six page treatise on "The California Mission and Its Influence Upon Pacific Coast Architecture," published originally in the *West Coast Magazine*, was subsequently issued in book form.

Benton's observations on the missionary enterprise in California are worth recalling, even after the passage of half a century. In an article published by the San Diego *Union*, July 20, 1919, he noted, for example, that the early friars were "men remarkable for some of the best attributes of mankind. Courage—that is common to all civilized and to many savage races. Piety—that was a leading characteristic of most of the explorers and colonizers of America. Humanity—that most God–like of human attainments, and its rarest. And is it not to this last that we must look for a logical explanation of the success that differentiated this colonial undertaking from the failures" of other Spanish, French and English expeditions?

The prominent southland architect placed "Fray Serra and his coadjutors so far ahead in their altruism of the prevailing cruelties and bigotries of their age as to rank them on a parity with the advanced exponents of humanitarianism of this age." Regarding the Franciscan attitude toward the neophytes, Benton observed that their feelings toward them "were not inspired by an uneducated enthusiasm but were the result of genuine conviction and affection, and to the end of Serra's life his great — almost his sole ambition continued to be the conversion and enlightenment of the Gentiles."

Benton further pointed out that "in any just comparison of the history of the pioneer period of California with that of other beginnings of states and commonwealths in the United States, contemporaneous in time, it becomes evident that in their dealing with the native Indians, the Franciscan missionaries were more humane, their motives more unselfish, and their system of education in agricultural and industrial schools vastly superior to the practices and ideals of most of the new settlements anywhere throughout the country."

Noting that "while the permanent prosperity of the California colonies was the result of the wise and humane policy pursued by the Franciscan fathers toward the native inhabitants," it was the courage and the devotion of Fray Junípero Serra to his great ideal, the conquest of the souls to Christianity, which prevented the abandonment of the San Diego settlement within a few months of its occupation.

"That which avarice and political ambition had so often failed to bring to successful fruition in enterprises of like nature in other places in America was here accomplished by simple faith and heroic personal endeavor. The prominent Southern California observer also called attention to the fact that "it is to the honor of the soldiers of the cross that to that emblem rather than to the royal banner of Spain is due the praise and glory of the perseverance of the attempt to colonize" the Californias!

LUMMIS SPEAKS ABOUT THE MISSIONS— 1928

Charles Fletcher Lummis (1859–1928) was once described by the eminent Franciscan historian, Father Maynard J. Geiger, as "the enthusiastic propagandist of the brighter side of the Spanish conquest." Though a non–Catholic, Lummis was a man of keen observation and broad Christian sympathies. A lifetime of research and study had convinced him that there was "nothing whatever, east of New Mexico, to compare for a moment with these wonderful monuments which the Franciscans built in the wilderness."

An editorial in the *Daily Catholic Tribune* for November 28, 1928, quoted Lummis as saying that "the Mission system (in California) was the most just, humane and equitable system ever devised for the treatment of an aboriginal people."

The long–time editor of *Land of Sunshine* and *Out West* magazines noted that "the history and impregnable fact is disquieting to thoughtful Americans that in 54 years Spain (Spanish missionaries) had converted about 100,000 of these Indians from savagery to Christianity, had built 21 costly and beautiful temples for them to worship in, had given them [grade] schools and industrial schools, in a far greater number than they have today after 54 years of American rule, had taught them a religion and language to which 99 per cent "of them are still devoted, had taught them to build good houses, to be good carpenters, masons, plasterers, blacksmiths, soapmakers, tanners, shoemakers, cooks, bricklayers, spinners, weavers, saddlers, shepherds, cowboys, vineyardists, fruitgrowers, millers, wagon–makers and so on."

In another related passage, Lummis wrote that "in all the Spanish occupation of California, I cannot discover that it ever once happened that an Indian was driven off his land." A decided change came with the Mexican flag. American rule likewise has much to answer for, as the U.S. Senate report No. 74, January 23, 1888, acknowledges, when it says

> The history of the Mission Indians for a century may be written in four words, conversion, civilization, neglect, outrage. The conversion and civilization were the work of the Mission Fathers previous to our acquisition of California; the neglect and outrage have been mainly our own.

To Lummis, the missions were worth more money, were a greater asset to Southern California, than our oil, our oranges, even our climate! It was this conviction that motivated his establishment of the Landmarks Club, in 1893, as a means of restoring the historic monuments.

Father St. John O'Sullivan noted that after 1895, Lummis "threw himself into the work of saving these precious monuments from complete destruction." Over the years, the Landmarks Club actually supervised the reconstruction of more than an acre of roofs and a half mile of walls! Early in 1902, the editor of *The Monitor* remarked that "Mr. Lummis through the columns of his magazine and elsewhere has been the fearless upholder of religious toleration, the staunch defender of the down–trodden and oppressed of every clime."

He concluded by noting that Lummis stood "out boldly against the desecration and abandonment of the venerable buildings reared by the old *padres*."

CHRISTMAS ESSAY ON THE MISSIONS—1934

A Christmas issue of *The Monitor* summarizes John Steven McGroarty's description of Mission life and its achievements beautifully and in a manner well worth recalling in abbreviated form, a half century later.

In the crazy–mad hurry and scurry of today it will ease the heart and soothe a jangled nerve to open the dusty doorways of the past and look in on those who lived and toiled and had their being in the old missions of California before the day of evil befell them.

At 5 o'clock in the morning the mission was astir.

The priests rose early and slipped their feet into their sandals and hastened to the chapel to say Mass. The corporal and his six soldiers, a mighty military establishment, tumbled out of their quarters, grudgingly perhaps, after the manner of rough men of war. They too must join in the prayers.

Then from within and without the great, gray adobe walls, the neophytes, men, women, children and all, came to kneel and ask God's blessings on the new day. After the Mass, the monks retired to the dining room to partake, standing and in silence, of their breakfast of bread and coffee.

Now, everybody, priests and all, turn to the day's task, some to the wide, far–flung fields, others to shop and mill, and others still to tend the herds and flocks.

There was the sound of anvils ringing and the quaint chant of harvest songs from the fields. The women were at the looms or sewing. At eleven o'clock the bells summoned the workers to their midday meal, which consisted of simple but wholesome fare.

Looking in where the Franciscans are dining, we find one of their number reading to the others from some pious book. After the meal there were prayers again in the chapel and the recitation of a psalm, then an hour or so for recreation or *siesta*.

The afternoon was spent in toil again until six o'clock, which was the supper hour. This meal concluded, there was recreation once more for all but the monks, who had still their tasks of teaching Spanish, music and Christian doctrine to those who were fitted for or in need of such instruction.

At nine o'clock the day was done—a day spent in prayer and toil–the stars gleamed above the Mission towers, enfolding it and its happy people in peace and dreams.

This was the usual daily routine, but life at the Mission was not permitted to become monotonous. There were great feast days—many of them, indeed—when the whole community gave itself over to some religious celebration, followed by play and sport, horseracing, feats of strength and endurance, games and every kind of innocent pleasure.

The result of this system on the Indians was little short of marvelous. From the degraded "diggers" without law or morals to guide them, they grew into the stature of civilized beings.

This was the dream of Junípero Serra, a dream which reached splendid proportions. Within the sheltering walls of those vast establishments there were as many as thirty thousand Christianized Indians at one time, leading not only wholesome Christian lives, but following, as well, all the occupations of artisans known to those days.

The California Missions
2. Non-Mission Foundations

THE OLD PLAZA CHURCH—1784

There were five *asistencias*, or assistant missions, established along *El Camino Real* between 1784 and 1818. The first and most famous of these foundations is that of *Nuestra Señora de los Angeles*, around which eventually, grew up the nation's largest city dedicated to the Mother of God.

The small Church of Our Lady of the Angels, in the plaza area of downtown Los Angeles, has always been and will undoubtedly continue to be the "city's first and principal landmark." Though until recently, the church was masquerading behind the Victorian facade, it can be referred to as "our most notable building of the Spanish period." The old Plaza church differed from the other *asistencias* insofar as it was never intended as an independent mission but rather as a *pueblo* or parochial center, destined to achieve eventual autonomy.

Early annals indicate that a crude adobe *capilla* was erected about 1784, near the corner of Buena Vista Street and Bellevue Avenue (the intersection of present-day Sunset Boulevard and North Broadway). Completed in 1789, it somewhat resembled the chapel of the hospital of the old mission at San Gabriel. A petition was made for a new edifice in 1810, and four years later Fray Luis Gil revealed plans to lay the first stone on the fifteenth of August, the *pueblo's* titular feastday. Unfortunately, the half-completed structure located "in the vicinity of Aliso Street and the River" was destroyed by the flooding *Rio Porciúncula* in 1815.

In 1818, Governor Pablo Vicente de Sola recommended that a new site be chosen on higher ground, close to the place where the 1784 structure had been located. The present *Iglesia de Nuestra Señora de los Angeles* dates from 1822 when Father Mariano Payéras spearheaded a drive to raise funds from the previously established missions. On December 8th, the church "conceived in brandy, roofed by a pirate, and dedicated to the Holy Mother of God," was formally set aside as a place for divine worship.

Completion of the edifice did not bring about its independence from San Gabriel, for even after 1822, "Los Angeles was still regarded as an *asistencia,* not as a parish." Priestly ministrations in the *pueblo* were taken care of by *padres* from the nearby mission until the appointment of the first chaplain in 1832.

As the oldest church in Los Angeles, the "Placita" has been an integral part of the city's growth. Harris Newmark was fond of recalling the 1850s when the bells "ringing at six in the morning and at eight in the evening, served as a curfew to regulate the daily activities of the town. . . .

In 1859 the *Iglesia de Nuestra Señora de los Angeles* became the pro-Cathedral of the Diocese of Monterey-Los Angeles when Bishop Thaddeus Amat moved his residence from Santa Barbara to the southland. For a decade and a half the relics of Saint Vibiana, patroness of the diocese, were enthroned in the church until the erection and consecration of a cathedral in her honor in 1876.

The *asistencia*, never artistically outstanding, has profited little from its numerous restorations. "Lacking good written history, the building has suffered in the literary realm as well as the historical. Repeated remodelings eventually robbed the building of its 'Spanish' appearance, and when this disappeared the interest of the writer, the architect and the historian waned. Not being a 'mission,' it was relegated to the sideline as the ever-present tourist came to California to see missions . . . and not Victorianized *pueblo* churches of the Spanish colonial period." Today, however, the future of the plaza church seems assured for its most recent restoration has proceeded on the principle that the little church was an altogether unique creation of the late mission period—and should be made to look that way again.

SANTA MARGARITA *ASISTENCIA*—1787

Several assistant-missions or *asistencias* were set up as branches or extensions of fully established and flourishing missions at various times. Although there were no resident priests at these foundations, services were conducted at periodic intervals as the need arose.

One of these establishments is hidden away on a private ranch about a mile due west of the town of Santa Margarita in the Diocese of Fresno. The stone and mortar walls are the ruins of the almost forgotten *Asistencia de Santa Margarita de Cortona*, one of California's four major assistant-missions Now protected from the rains by a long corrugated iron barn, the foundation, about ten miles north of Mission San Luis Obispo, once served as a *rancho* and relief station for that mission and its other close neighbor, San Miguel.

It is conjectured that the *asistencia* was built about 1787, although there are no extant records to substantiate the details. One of the first descriptions was that of Alfred Robinson in 1830:

> We reached '*El Rancho de Santa Rita*' a place used for the cultivation of grain, where on an eminence that overlooked the grounds, an extensive building was erected. It was divided into storerooms for different kinds of grain, and apartments for the accommodation of the *mayordomo*, servants, and wayfarers. At one end was a chapel, and snug lodging rooms for the priest, who, I was informed, frequently passed some weeks at the place during the time of harvest; and the holy friars of the two missions occasionally met there to acknowledge to each other their sins.

Huge pieces of sandstone, mortar and tile went into the construction of the 120-foot long building. Walls three feet thick still stand at intervals of thirty feet from one another. Only the beamed ceilings have collapsed with the passage of time. The exquisitely designed interior arches indicate skillful planning. Probably a large concentration of Indians in the area accounts for the *asistencia*. The generous water supply of the Santa Margarita River was alluded to by Don Juan Bautista de Anza in March of 1776, when he passed through there on his way to the San Francisco peninsula.

Title to the *asistencia* passed into the hands of the Estrada family in 1841, shortly after the death there of Fray Luis Gil y Taboada. At that time there were 17,000 acres attached to the ranch, much of it along the rich bottom of the Salinas River. Joaquin Estrada made little attempt to cultivate or otherwise use the land. Martin Murphy of Santa Clara took over the ranch in 1860, and during his long tenure and that of his son, the Southern Pacific Railroad laid its tracks paralleling *El Camino Real*. A town grew up to serve the needs of construction crews for the many tunnels down the Cuesta Pass to San Luis Obispo.

Besides the *asistencia*, three adobe buildings are still standing, the main residence, the *hacienda* and a pump house. All are within a few hundred yards of the *asistencia* on property privately owned.

Today "hay is stored and fed through the window openings to cattle and horses having stalls and mangers beneath a shed that extends the whole length of the building." All of which seems a little unfitting to a one-time mission outpost!

PICTURESQUE PALA — 1810

The picturesque *Asistencia San Antonio de Pala*, located in a narrow valley about twenty miles from San Luis Rey Mission at the base of Palomar Mountain, has been aptly described as "the most interesting of all the chapels in the mission chain."

First mention of Pala, a place of abundant water, appears in the annual report of San Luis Rey Mission for 1810, wherein Fray Antonio Peyri recorded building a granary at *Rancho de Pala*. Six years later, a chapel was constructed there, and within a year or two about a thousand converts were gathered to till the soil and recite the *doctrina*. By 1818, a town was beginning to take shape, and three years later, Fray Mariano Payeras noted that nothing was lacking at Pala for a mission, save the assignment of a resident friar.

The *asistencia* prospered and, in 1827, José Maria Echeandía reported that San Luis Rey Mission "has a station called San Antonio de Pala with a church, dwellings and granaries and with a few fields where wheat, corn, beans, garbanzos and other leguminous plants are grown." San Antonio was sold, along with

San Luis Rey Mission, on November 14, 1845, to Jose A Cot and Jose A. Pico in a transaction subsequently nullified by the United States Land Commission.

San Antonio was envisioned as part of an elaborate plan to create a chain of inland missions for those Indians who couldn't be reached by the existing coastal foundations. Its remote location protected Pala during those tumultuous years when secularization brought on the demise of the mission system in California, with the consequent collapse of physical structures.

Although much of the quadrangle was ravaged, the chapel and west wing remained standing. The faithful Indians remaining in the village kept the chapel in repair and often neighboring priests came to Pala for the administration of the sacraments.

When the chapel was severely damaged by earthquake, in 1899, the Landmarks Club helped the Indians to rebuild. Further damage occurred when flood waters demolished the *campanile* or bell tower, but once again the local inhabitants opted to begin anew.

The most ambitious restoration program was inaugurated by Father Januarius Carillo, in 1954. Under his direction, the Indians made adobe bricks from the soil of Pala Valley, cut cedar logs from nearby Palomar Mountain and rebuilt the quadrangle. Faith is contagious and people of all religious persuasions from San Diego county began to share in Father Carillo's dream of a refurbished San Antonio de Pala. The work was brought to a successful climax in 1959.

Today San Antonio de Pala is the only one of the California missionary establishments still serving the spiritual needs of an exclusively Indian population, the Palatinguas, who were relocated from Warner's Ranch by the United States government.

A PALA MEMOIR — 1913

Late in 1913, Father Peter Wallischeck, Franciscan superior at San Luis Rey Mission, wrote a memoir about the *asistencia* of San Antonio de Pala. This abbreviated account is taken from a transcript at the Archival Center, Archdiocese of Los Angeles.

Pala Mission, as it is now generally called, though it was never a mission properly speaking, is situated about twenty miles east of San Luis Rey in a very fertile valley. Low mountains surround this valley forming, as it were, a frame for the beautiful landscape.

In the mission days a great number of Indians lived in this valley. In order to Christianize them, and to provide better for their spiritual wants, it was considered expedient to build a church for them. Fr. Antonio Peyri, the superior of Mission San Luis Rey, therefore, decided that an "*asistencia*"—that is to say, a chapel with a visiting *padre*—should be erected at Pala.

The Tower at San Antonio de Pala

Work on the church and residence was commenced in 1816, and the church placed under the patronage of St. Anthony of Padua, the Wonderworker of the world, as Charles Warren Stoddard called this saint. There is one feature that is unique in the construction of this church or chapel. The belfry or *campanile* is entirely separated from the main building. Two large mission bells are suspended in the openings, the sound of which is carried to a great distance, calling the Indians for divine service.

This mission, like the mother–mission, San Luis Rey, was prosperous from the beginning. Two years had hardly elapsed when the Baptismal Records showed a thousand names enrolled.

Fr. Peyri did not only have the spiritual welfare of his children at Pala at heart, he also provided for their material prosperity. Seeing that some system of irrigation was imperative, he designed and constructed an aqueduct, or waterditch, which even now elicits the admiration of our modern surveyors. They admit that no better route could have been chosen.

The act of "secularization" also sounded the death–knell of the Pala *asistencia*. With the confiscation of the mission property and the departure of the *padre*, the Indian was without the necessary means of support, and without a friend and father, poverty and disease soon decimated their number, so that but few long survived this dreadful blow.

In 1902, the government of the United States decided to remove the Indians from Warner's Ranch to some other locality. Much was done to select a proper place. Finally some property at Pala was purchased for this purpose. The poor Indians were loath to leave their old homes: the place where their fathers and forefathers had lived and died, the place where their mortal remains

were buried. Many preferred death to a change of homes. The sad and sorrowful transportation took place in the spring of 1903.

Many a tear was shed, when the Indians bid a sad and last farewell to the graves of their ancestors; for the Indians retain a sacred memory for their deceased friends and relatives. Owing to the efforts of Right Rev. Thomas J. Conaty, D.D., Bishop of Monterey–Los Angeles, the old chapel was partly restored and rededicated. Of late years the Rev. George Doyle, the present pastor of Pala Indian Reservation, has done much to improve both the interior and exterior of this old and venerable " *asistencia*," the daughter of San Luis Rey.

IMPRESSIONS OF PALA — 1932

San Antonio de Pala is the only missionary foundation along California's *El Camino Real* where native Americans are still very much in evidence. In 1932, Harry Carr visited the *asistencia* and then recorded his impressions for a column in the Los Angeles *Times*.

> That night I slept in the spare room in the *padre's* house. It had little windows that were like tiny tunnels through the six–foot adobe walls. The *padre* was stirring around when I woke. For once, Renigo Lugo, the sacristan who is also the policeman, had neglected to ring the bells for early Mass. So the *padre* and I climbed up the adobe steps of the old campanile and rang them ourselves—old, old mellowed bells, made in Spain.
>
> By the laws of his religion, a priest must go empty and unfed to celebrate Mass; but the *padre* had prepared a breakfast for me—eggs from Renigo's flock, thick brown wheat bread, honey from the sage blossoms, and coffee.

Then I went into the little church while he said Mass. It is a quaint and lovely place, founded by Fray Antonio Peyri on June 18, 1816. It belonged to the establishment of the San Luis Rey Mission and now has a thousand Indians. Most of the present congregation are grandchildren of the Indians who built the church. Before that their ancestors had lived here in the Pala for at least a thousand years—probably longer.

The church is a long, low building with a great door. The walls and low ceilings are of adobe and whitewashed. Under the whitewash can still be seen the gaudy decorations painted by the first neophytes. The altar is very simple, with its cloth of white and decorated with wild flowers picked on the hills by the Indian women.

Flanking the altar are the sacred images—a life–sized San Luis carved out of wood and a life–sized figure of the Virgin, San Antonio and San Dominic, both with hair mustaches glued on their wooden faces.

The congregation filed in. Agatha Yarger, whose grandmother was a girl at the old mission, played the organ. The choir consisted of five Indian women and five boys. The violinist was a slender, wistful young Indian whose shirt–sleeves were held up by a pair of flaming pink garters.

After that—hungry as wolves, for it didn't seem polite for me to eat again while the *padre* still had another Mass to say—we drove in the car to Rincon. They had just had a *fiesta* and the leaves were wilting on the *ramadas* they had erected.

Mass was in a tiny little wooden church; there were just eleven sad old Indians present; but it impressed me that the same Mass that the *padre* sang was being sung at that moment amid the gorgeousness of Saint Peter's in Rome. Then we went to a *rancho* and gorged ourselves with food.

By evening things had begun to happen. In preparation for the *fiesta,* the Indians had spent days building *ramadas* of cottonwood limbs and leaves. We ate in one of them—chicken served with Mexican chili. The *ramadas* were built around a great open patio. At one side of the patio was the schoolhouse in which the young Indians were jazz–dancing to the music of an orchestra—a fiddle, a drum, and a guitar.

When the thick, mysterious darkness of the mountain settled over the patio, old Albanez Scala lit a bonfire and they played *peon.* This is one of the oldest known games in the world. It has been played for uncounted centuries in Pala.

ASISTENCIA SANTA YSABEL — 1818

Far in the back country, about sixty miles from San Diego, in the deep peace of a mountain valley, is a lonely outpost of Provincial California, the site of the *Asistencia Santa Ysabel.* (The present church of Santa Isabel dates only from 1924.)

There is evidence that Fray Fernando Martin blessed the site for a *capilla* at Canada de Santa Ysabel on September 20, 1818, and soon thereafter erected a temporary chapel. On February 2, 1819, Fray Vicente Sarria noted that "in the place called Santa Isabel, toward the Sierra, they count a goodly number of baptized souls . . . I asked the governor for permission to formally erect a chapel there."

Permission was eventually granted, and "by 1822 a chapel had been built at Santa Isabel, and there were also several houses, a granary, and a graveyard with 450 neophytes at this branch settlement, which proved a great aid in keeping the gentiles quiet."

A report of May 7, 1839, recorded that the natives at Santa Ysabel "have their fields on which they cultivate wheat, barley, corn, beans, horsebeans, peas, and other seeds for their maintenance, besides keeping two vineyards and orchards and their horses." As early as 1836, however, the "corrosion of mountain weather began to inch into the foundation of the lovely chapel and other buildings." Within a decade, the chapel was in complete ruins and the mud houses no longer habitable. A contemporary account, written in 1899, described the ruins with the observation that "leveled by time and washed by winter rains, the adobe walls of the church have sunk into indistinguishable heaps of earth which vaguely define the outlines of the ancient edifice."

Nonetheless, "all the natives from the coast to the Sierras around Santa Ysabel were eventually won for Christ, and of all the Indians still living in San Diego county, those who survived the eviction from the mission and its stations through the greed of unscrupulous fortune hunters have, generally speaking, themselves or their descendents remained not only the most numerous but also the most religious and moral."

Although frequently referred to as a "mission," Santa Ysabel was only an *asistencia,* although Father Zephyrin Engelhardt admits that it "lacked only a resident priest to make it a mission." Those visiting the region today will find that nothing remains of the original buildings (uncovered and identified in 1963 by scholars from the University of California) save outlines of the structure, faintly visible under the pasture grass."

EARLY WORSHIP AT SAN FRANCISCO'S *PRESIDIO*—1776

The site for the *presidio* of San Francisco, selected by Juan Bautista de Anza on March 28, 1776, was dedicated on the following September 17th, feast of the Stigmata of Saint Francis. The entire *presidio,* including the chapel, was constructed from a crude palisade of wood from the gnarled California Live Oak which dotted surrounding hills.

Though they would have preferred adobe, the Spanish managed to provide a reasonable facsimile of the frontier settlements which existed throughout North America during the 18th and 19th centuries. The finished product resembled a wooden Anglo outpost more than the Hispanic version found elsewhere in Alta California and the borderlands. The layout of the compound, with its open central *plaza* and its quarters huddled against the defense work, was very much in the traditional fashion. As was the case in the other *presidios*, the chapel dominated the entire complex. Indeed the tiny house of worship was the first structure built, thereby underscoring the official importance of worship in the *presidio's* social order.

The first chapel was not long–lived. Hubert Howe Bancroft reported that by 1792, "none of the structures were those originally built." Very likely it was never intended to be more than a temporary shelter. Early visitors to San Francisco were not impressed by the *presidio*. In his account, George Vancouver portrayed the image of an ill–constructed, poorly–situated establishment. Georg Heinrich, Freiherr von Langsdorff, skipper of a Russian ship, contended that the *presidio* resembled little more than a German farmstead.

A second chapel was severely damaged by earthquake in 1808 and, two years later, the governor reported that storms and floods had completely destroyed an adobe edifice. In 1817, Camille de Roquefeuil mentioned that he attended Mass in a great hall since the post chapel had burned. The temporary religious facility offered somewhat better surroundings than the remainder of the installation since "it was white–washed and neatly kept, had an altar in pretty good taste, some pictures and benches on the sides."

Benjamin Morrell visited the *presidio* in 1825, and he described it as comprising only about 120 houses and a church. The next year, Captain William Beechey spoke of the chapel and the governor's houses as being distinguished only by their whitewash. After 1836, no regular troops were stationed there and, by 1840, the adobe chapel was in ruins.

In 1854, Colonel J. K. F. Mansfield dismissed the *presidio* as "miserable adoby (*sic*) buildings, the leavings of the Mexican government." Another observer felt it was "a disgrace and an eyesore to the community. . . ." Precisely at what time the chapel was taken or fell down is not recorded. It is known that a new chapel was added in the fall of 1862, but that too had a rather short existence.

The contemporary chapel at the *presidio* of San Francisco is a fairly recent edifice and bears no resemblance to any of its predecessors. Perhaps at some future time, a facsimile chapel can be built, based on sketches, descriptions and approximations of earlier buildings.

MONTEREY'S *CAPILLA REAL*—1770

La Capilla del Real Presidio, the provincial era's most important church in a political sense, regained a measure of its earlier prominence, on December 14, 1967, when it was canonically raised to the status of "cathedral" for the newly proclaimed Diocese of Monterey. The *presidio* at Monterey, one of the four headquarter–sites for perma-

Monterey's Capilla Real

nent military garrisons along the Pacific Slope, had its own *capilla* or chapel "erected for the benefit of the governor, the officers and soldiers of the *presidio* and their families."

In the initial foundation, located "along the shore of the beach . . . not far away from where the packet–boats anchor," an arbor of boughs served as the proto–chapel of the *presidio*. The formal establishment, on June 3, 1770, was placed under the spiritual patronage of San Carlos Borromeo.

Permanent buildings were soon under construction and the pioneers built a chapel of palings to serve as a makeshift house–of–worship. Readied for use, on July 14, 1770, during the first weeks at Monterey, the original buildings did double duty as both *presidio* and church.

Manuel Estévan Rúiz, one of the master masons sent to California after 1790 to teach whites and Indians trades and skills useful to the colony, supervised the construction of the sandstone church, which he situated on the south side of the *plaza* as part of the twelve–foot wall enclosing the entire compound. To the left of the church was an adobe building for the friars.

Completed in 1794, by Indian laborers, the *capilla* was blessed, on January 25, 1795, by Fray Fermín Francisco de Lasuén. The first infant baptized therein was Paula Madelena, on February 10th. An early description of the *capilla* is contained in an official report to Viceroy Antonio Maria Bucareli, dated November 29, 1773, by Captain Pedro Fages:

> In the wing of the *presidio* on the south side facing the base is an *adobe* church whose foundations are of stone set in mortar. These foundations extend two quarters above the surface and are a *vara* and a half in width. Upon these foundations rise the walls five fourths in thickness. The church is fifteen *varas* long, seven *varas* wide and seven *varas* high. Twenty hewn beams each a palm in width and ten *varas* in length have an overlay of cane and upon this rests the roof which is flat. This has a cover of lime. The roof has four spouts to carry off the rain water.

The present *capilla* never actually functioned as a mission church, inasmuch as Fray Junípero Serra relocated Mission San Carlos Borromeo, at Carmel, in August, 1771. In 1855, the chapel was enlarged and, three years later, the transept, with its elaborately carved doors, was added. The ornate facade, completed in 1796, remains almost as erected, although the pyramidal roof upon the tower was added, in 1893.

San Carlos enjoyed the distinction of being a pro–cathedral, in 1851–1853,when Bishop Joseph Sadoc Alemany resided at Monterey and frequently pontificated at liturgical functions in the historic edifice. "The old structure has passed through many vicissitudes and has witnessed many stirring events, and, although the old *presidio* of which it was originally a part has

practically disappeared, the church stands as staunch and firm today as in its earlier years."

SANTA BARBARA'S ROYAL *PRESIDIO*—1782

The fourth and last *presidio* in Hispanic California was that founded at Santa Barbara on April 21, 1782, seven years before George Washington took his oath as President of the United States. From this *presidio*, about one fourth of Alta California was governed. Its territory extended from San Fernando Mission to the farthest confines of La Purísima Concepción Mission at the Santa Maria River.

The commander of the *presidio* was responsible to the governor and viceroy for the security, peace and prosperity of the area committed to his care. Jose Francisco Ortega was the first to exercise authority there.

Fray Junípero Serra was present for the establishment of the *presidio*. He had just come north from San Buenaventura Mission which was founded on March 31st. Santa Barbara *Presidio* was part of a well–planned program for the development of a large section of Alta California. It was a pivotal link too, for Serra himself had pointed out that if the Indians in the area ever combined their forces, coastal California would be cut in two. The Channel islands remained the missing link in a unified California until, with the founding of the *presidio,* California became politically, militarily and spiritually integrated.

Though it was also Serra's intention to establish Santa Barbara Mission in 1782, the actual founding of that institution was delayed for four years, until December 4, 1786. Governor Felipe de Neve determined the exact locale of the *presidio*. Its axis was the present juncture of Santa Barbara and Cañon Perdido streets, less than a mile away from the native village of Siujtu where the *mesa* and the ocean meet.

In the Spanish settlement were the commander, two ensigns, three sergeants, two corporals and nine Christian Indians. Some of the soldiers were married and these brought along their wives and children. Their exact number is not known. Probably there were not more than a hundred altogether.

Ortega built the initial *presidio*, largely in a log cabin style as a frontier fort. He brought water through an aqueduct system from Mission Creek, introduced domestic animals and planted the first grainfields. He even succeeded in having the pagan Indians of the neighborhood help build the *presidio* through kind treatment and bestowal of gifts.

The second and permanent buildings were erected by Felipe de Goycochea between 1784 and 1802. Those are the ones earmarked for eventual restoration. The chapel was located in the middle of the north wall and faced South. The building to the west was designed for the chaplain. The chapel was formally dedicated on December 12, 1797. The chapel walls were still in existence in 1853, when J. N. Alden, an American, made a painting of the remains.

PRESIDIO CHAPEL AT SANTA BARBARA—1782

The recent completion of the *presidio* chapel at Santa Barbara brought back memories of the years between 1782 and 1855 when the earlier edifices served the spiritual needs of the Channel City's military and then parochial population. Founded by Fray Junípero Serra on "the edge of a grove of oaks apart from the beach and the Indian village," the Royal Presidio of Santa Barbara was the final link in a chain of military fortresses built by the Spanish along the coast of Alta California. In fact, it was also the last permanent *presidio* in the western world.

The actual inauguration took place on April 21, 1782, when Fray Junípero Serra offered Holy Mass and then chanted the *alabado*. Francisco Palou noted that the following day soldiers "began to hew wood to build a chapel." The permanent house–of–worship, envisioned by the military personnel as the most imposing and prominent structure in the compound, was formally dedicated on the Feast of Our Lady of Guadalupe in 1797.

That building served the religious needs of the area until 1806, when an earthquake cracked its walls and rendered the structure unsafe. A subsequent storm almost totally destroyed what was left of the chapel.

Since there is no evidence that a new chapel was erected, one can presume that the existing edifice was repaired and continued in operation until the 1812 earthquake. Early the following year, Fray Jose Señan notified the Bishop of Sonora that the entire *presidio* was in danger of collapsing.

A temporary chapel built of wood and covered with tile was ready for occupancy in March of 1813. The painting of this chapel by James N. Alden depicts it in the same place as in the 1798 drawing by Felipe de Goycochea. By the time that José Antonio de la Guerra arrived in Santa Barbara in 1815, a commentator observed that the chapel was "the pride of the Spanish forces in California." In 1831, a resident chaplain in the person of Father Antonio Menendez was in charge of the *capilla*.

This chapel served the town to July of 1854, when Our Lady of Sorrows Church was built at what is now State and Figueroa streets. It was obliterated by the earthquake of Fort Tejon in 1855. In the painting by Lieutenant Alden, the main entrance to the chapel has a single arched door with a square window above and two windows along the side wall. From a crossbeam hung two small bells held by uprights located in the area facing the facade.

Following a thorough search of the area in the 1960s, the original foundations were discovered and marked. The Santa Barbara Trust for Historic Preservation purchased the site and, in 1972, title was transferred to the State of California.

In the reconstruction of the chapel, the Alden watercolor served as a guide for the chapel's external appearance. Excavations supplied the actual dimensions of its floor plan and a few scattered documents provided supplementary clues.

SYMBOLISM OF SANTA BARBARA *PRESIDIO*

Miniature books testify to the printer's skill in cutting, casting and setting tiny type and in providing suitable paper for the special ink required to avoid clogging the midget–sized letters. Though the artistic tomes are often dismissed as typographical curiosities, miniature books frequently have an independent value based on the nature of their subject matter. Such is the case with Father Francis F. Guest's 1 3/4 by 2–inch work on *The Symbolism of the Santa Barbara Presidio*.

The Franciscan historian endeavored to depict the *presidio*, the final link in the mighty chain of conquest forged by a long line of heroic Iberian soldiers, as uniquely symbolic of the culture and civilization associated with Spain's expansionary activities in the New World. In looking beyond the glitter and the glamor, the muskets and *mantillas*, the flags, the fiestas and the dances traditionally predicated of the *presidio*, Father Guest saw the primary symbolism of the last permanent institution of its kind in the far–flung empire as revolving around the trifold notes of unity, peace and justice.

In its role as a symbol of unity, the Santa Barbara Presidio forged a durable bond between the northern and southern areas of California. During the Mexican and American periods, when sectional interests occasionally threatened to divide California, integrity was somehow maintained and, "historically speaking, the symbol of that unity is the Santa Barbara Presidio." Although the *presidio* served as a fortress, "the purpose of the soldiers was to keep the peace." The natives were frequently reminded of Spanish intentions "to live with them in love and friendship, to defend them against their enemies, and to teach them to know and love God." Finally, the *presidio* symbolized justice, for Indians accused of various crimes and offenses were taken out of the jurisdiction of the missionaries and tried in military court. Because the defendants were often so barbarous, ignorant, simple and primitive, the application of penalties was diminished to a great extent. The author reserved special words of praise for the project of restoring the *presidio's* chapel which he envisioned "will stand as a tribute not only to Christianity, not only to Spanish culture and Spanish traditions, but to unity, peace and justice."

In addition to subject matter, the technical perfection and manual dexterity evident in the production of this miniature book demands special commendation. It was printed in a limited edition of 500 copies by Grant Dahlstrom of Pasadena and hand–bound in attractive leather at the studios of Bela Blau. One hundred copies are numbered and signed. Literary excellence, historical relevancy and artistic craftsmanship, taken separately, are incentives enough to purchase a book. When a single volume unites all three of those qualities, one has a real treasure indeed!

THE *ESTANCIAS* OF PROVINCIAL CALIFORNIA

As the neophyte population of Provincial California increased, it became necessary to remove the flocks and herds from the immediate vicinity of the missions where land was needed for cultivating crop of various kinds. "Thus it was that the mission *ranchos* came into existence. The first of those ranches or *estancias* was established in 1774, when the *padres* at San Diego opened a corral for horses and mares at nearby Rancho San Luis.

Best known of the *estancias* were San Bernardino, Santa Gertrudis, San Marcos and Las Flores. There were scores of others dotting the landscape from San Diego to San Francisco de Solano (Sonoma), some of them located at a considerable distance from the parent mission.

One of the most famous of California's cattle ranches was that of San Pedro, attached to Mission San Luis Rey. From a commanding knoll overlooking the blue Pacific, Alfred Robinson described in great detail how its gardens were "cultivated by the Indians, for their own personal benefit." Fray Antonio Peyri noted on December 22, 1827, that "Rancho San Pedro, known as Las Flores . . . has a house, granaries and a chapel." Two decades later, William B. Emory related that his expedition encamped near Las Flores which, by then, was like a "deserted mission."

At Mission San Francisco de Asís, one of the most pressing needs was tillable land to offset the inadequate acreage in the area of Lake Dolores. As a result, in 1785, Fray Francisco Palóu established Rancho San Pedro y San Pablo about fourteen miles southeast of the mission for that purpose. The chapel, a storehouse and two other undesignated rooms are first mentioned in the annual report of Mission San Francisco for 1786, where they are referred to as "*la nueva labor de San Pedro y San Pablo.*" The *padres* subsequently declared that without the agricultural outpost of San Pedro y San Pablo, they could not have provided for their neophytes and the maintenance of the parent foundation. The adobe building, occasionally referred to in the annals as San Mateo,

was demolished after sustaining serious damage in the temblors of 1868.

The number of *estancias* varied from one mission to another, depending on local needs. San Gabriel is known to have had from twelve to fifteen *ranchos*, the most distant one being San Gorgonio (Beaumont). Generally, adobe quarters were provided at those outposts for the majordomo and Indian workers attached to the *estancias.* Many of the ranch houses were quite picturesque, such as the one at Paso del Robles.

When the distance from the mission was too great for the proper attendance at religious services, a chapel was built in connection with the ranch buildings for the benefit of resident neophytes. Since the mission ranches themselves eventually fell into private hands, most of the *capillas* were alienated and later abandoned. Wheat, beans and corn were grown at the *estancias*. At San Bernardino, stock raising was also engaged in. The annals indicate that there were 600 Indians working in the grain fields at La Puente in 1816. At San Miguel (Cieneguitas), a *rancho* of Santa Barbara Mission, there existed a whole village of Indians. There was an adobe chapel, cottages and well–cultivated little orchards of fruit trees there.

THE *ESTANCIA* OF COSTA MESA—1817

Though there is no documented evidence of Holy Mass having been offered there, the Diego Sepulveda adobe in Costa Mesa certainly dates back to mission times and, for that reason alone, it deserves consideration. Now known as State Historical Landmark #227, the historic *estancia* was given to the City of Costa Mesa by the Segerstrom family in 1962. It comprises five acres and a rambling ranch house that had been both sheltered and concealed by its adobe walls for many years. An additional five acres were purchased by the city.

At some unknown time in the early 1800s, the area was used for grazing cattle from San Juan Capistrano Mission. There are references in early missionary correspondence to a mission station located on the banks of the Santa Ana River and to fields in that locale cultivated by natives attached to the Old Mission.

Possibly as early as 1817, but surely between 1820 and 1823, a small adobe was erected with a tar and tule roof for the herdsmen who looked after the cattle and cared for the crops in the adjacent fields. Several large "mission bricks" of that first adobe were found in the east and south walls of the present structure.

Several years ago, the bones of a mastodon were uncovered in an excavation on the bluff. For untold generations, the site was part of the Indian village known as "Lukup." Many artifacts have been found, as well as graves of several local Canaliño Indians.

After secularization, the property seems to have been recognized as belonging to the Rancho Santa Ana, which was granted to Pablo Grijalva and, in 1810, to his son–in–law Antonio Yorba. In a later subdivision, the adobe passed into the possession of Diego Sepulveda.

The structure probably took on its present shape when Sepulveda lived there. It was then one of three adobes on the lower river, as depicted on a map of 1868. Undoubtedly it owes its preservation to being incorporated into a rambling ranch house that was sheltered and protected by its thick walls.

From Diego Sepulveda, who was at one time *alcalde* for *El Pueblo de Nuestra Señora de Los Angeles*, the property passed to Gabe Allen, a colorful character who, in his later years, became a Los Angeles County supervisor. He and his brother Jesse occupied the home for seventeen years.

As late as 1868, the adobe appears on a map now hanging in the east room of the adobe as the "House of Diego Sepulveda." Later, it became the property of the Adams family for whom the street on which it now stands was named. It appears on subsequent maps as the "Derby Ranch." It was presented by the Segerstroms "as a memorial to the early settlers of what is now Costa Mesa."

A fire destroyed part of the framed west portion of the ranch house on the night of November 25, 1961. Fortunately the original adobe was mostly undamaged. Reconstruction was completed early the following year, at which time a fountain and flagpole were erected bearing plaques about the history and present use of the adobe. The restored adobe, a window into California's colorful past, was officially dedicated as a historical monument on August 28, 1966.

SAN BERNARDINO DE SIENA—1810 (1819)

A feeling of tender reverence unconsciously associates itself with thoughts of the old Missions of California. Imagination rehabilitates the ruined walls and recalls from the vanished past the gray–robed *padres*—most of them saintly souls—who, offering their lives on the altar of their faith, firmly planted the cross of Christianity in the new land. Again the fertile fields are tilled by dark–skinned natives, and as the vesper bells chime softly the evening call to prayer, they flock to the mission to receive the paternal priestly blessing, then benediction and to sleep and silence—a silence now long broken. The hands that laboriously toiled day–by–day to upbuild the walls, the hearts that beat high with hopes and aspirations for the future, have long been dust. That which they built in the fullness of their faith outlasted the hands of the builders, but only to fall at last into decay and ruin; and amidst the desolation again may be read the world–old lesson of the mutability of earthly things; the passing of all human hopes, ambitions, loves and fears.

Something of this spirit hovers around the restored *estancia* of San Bernardino de Siena. Though frequently referred to as an "*asistencia*," San Bernardino was never anything more than an *estancia* or cattle ranch. It had no permanent chapel and could not, in the words of Zephyrin Engelhardt, "compare with the Asistencia of San Antonio de Pala, or even with that of Las Flores."

Father Juan Caballeria, author of the *History of San Bernardino Valley From the Padres to the Pioneers* (San Bernardino, 1892), recalls seeing a record at San Gabriel showing when and where the name San Bernardino had been assigned to the valley and in which reference was made to the *capilla* or chapel there. The account "described how Fr. (Francisco) Dumetz founded a *capilla* on the Guachama *rancheria* on May 20, 1810, under the invocation of San Bernardino de Siena."

The initial site was visited from time–to–time by the friars from San Gabriel, who would celebrate Mass for the Indians living in the district. It doesn't appear likely that any station was actually established at San Bernardino or any buildings erected in the early years. The earthquake of 1812 so alienated the surrounding tribes as to cause postponement of further development in the immediate area.

In 1819, several miles east of the original site, "at the request of the unchristianized Indians of the place they call Guachama and which we call San Bernardino, on the road to the Colorado . . . we began the introduction of cattle raising and farming, in order to induce the natives to become Christians." In succeeding years, several adobe structures were erected for the local Cahuilla and Serrano neophytes caring for the olive and fruit trees, grape vines and assorted vegetable plantings in the area. Later, herds of cattle were brought in and fattened on the rich wild grass.

Mariano Payeras reported, in 1820, the presence of a storehouse, planted fields and quarters for a missionary, along with a temporary chapel at San Bernardino. In the register book at San Gabriel is a notation that Carlos Garcia was baptized in the San Bernardino Valley, in 1821.

New buildings were erected some distance to the east, in 1830, on present–day Barton Hill. Unfortunately, four years later, non–Christian Indians attacked the outpost, stole the ornaments and sacred furnishings of the chapel and despoiled the grain in the storehouse. In December they returned and slew fourteen neophytes. As put by one local resident, "after this there was no more mission." The foundation figured in plans put forth, at various times, for a chain of inland missions envisioned by the friars. That phase of development never materialized.

The remnants of the *estancia* passed into private hands, in 1842, with its purchase by José del Carmen Lugo. During the 1850s the buildings were successively occupied by Mormons, used as a school and operated as a furniture factory. Dr. Benjamin Barton acquired title to the *estancia*, in 1857. Earliest attempts at restoration date to 1925, when the ruins were deeded to San Bernardino County. Over the following dozen years, the *capilla* was eventually rebuilt, along with the other buildings at the site and today the San Bernardino *estancia*, located west of Redlands, is a worthwhile tourist attraction.

CAPILLA VERSUS FREEWAY (SANTA GERTRUDIS)—1808

In addition to the missions and assistant missions established during provincial days, there were a number of chapels or *capillas* set up at strategic places to facilitate missionary activities.

Santa Gertrudis was a temporary chapel erected about 1793 for the Indian community at the entrance to Casitas Pass, seven miles north of Mission San Buenaventura. The chapel served as an outpost of San Buenaventura and substituted for the mother mission when it "was abandoned for three weeks and three days" due to severe damage inflicted by the earthquake of 1812. Indians in the area built small willow–thatched huts around the adobe chapel and the settlement there became known as *casitas*, which means "Little House." (The settlement was located near the present junction of the Ojai Road and the highway leading through Foster Park in Casitas Pass.)

Last mention of the Capilla de Santa Gertrudis in the official mission registers was made in 1857, when a second earthquake weakened the roof of the mission and forced the *padres* to temporarily transfer their religious services to the tiny chapel. It is not known how long the adobe chapel remained in service, although there is evidence that it was still being used as late as 1868. Certainly the adobe was in poor repair by the 1880s, for, as one account stated, Santa Gertrudis "was in ruins, its adobe cracked by time and weather, its tile roof sagging, but its small rooms could be seen. Nearby were its tuna cactus and its fig tree. The mission garden, which was across the road, had only seven old pear trees still standing."

Rancho Cañada Larga, on which the chapel remnants were located, also contains segments of a standing aqueduct with a covered water–trough. The buttressed waterway formerly extended the entire distance from the Ventura River to a settling basin at San Buenaventura Mission. The tile aqueduct irrigated the mission gardens and orchards until 1861–1862, when portions of the masonry were destroyed by floods and landslides.

The 8,000 acre *rancho*, presently owned by descendants of Edward Canet, was later criss–crossed by the new Ventura–Ojai freeway and thus will begin a new chapter in its long and fascinating history.

CALIFORNIA'S TWENTY–SECOND MISSION

Many have written much and spoken often about Fray Junípero Serra and that heroic band of missionaries who introduced Christianity along the Pacific Slope. But none has told the story more effectively, none has spoken more eloquently, none has reached so vast an audience as did John Steven McGroarty, California's Poet Laureate.

Undeniably one of the truest friends of the *padres* and their missions, McGroarty was a native of Pennsylvania. A lifelong fidelity to Christian and American ideals, his greatest legacy to California was the Franciscan spirit which pervaded his literary masterpieces.

With chaste and unrestrained art, the one–time Congressman, journalist, author, teacher and lawyer dramatized the beauty, romance and faith that was Spanish and the unequaled charity that was Franciscan in early California. The Mission Play, his supreme and most successful effort in a long career of letters, was repeated 3,200 times before an estimated audience of two and a half million people.

Though McGroarty's contributions on or about provincial life in California have long been recognized, very little is recorded concerning his attempt to establish, for his own century, a missionary outpost patterned after those of the Franciscan friars. McGroarty had long harbored plans for erecting the "twenty–second" Franciscan mission in a glen at the foot of the Verdugos. Developer N. V. Hartranft set aside an acre of Oak Grove Park as the site of the proposed foundation and announced plans for the structure in the Tujunga *Record–Ledger*, in 1923.

In its tenth anniversary edition, the newspaper proclaimed that "the plan of the author of the Mission Play to add a new Franciscan mission to the great chain that was founded by Fray Junípero Serra and his gray–robed priests and to build it this summer at Tujunga may be properly classed as a non–sectarian project, for men and women of all creeds and faiths are rallying to his aid with offers of assistance." The account went on to state that "the ceremonies attending its founding will be a reproduction of the great and colorful pageants that marked the founding of the old missions in the days of the Spanish occupation. This pageant will form in the hills above the mission, and not only will it be in plain view of the thousands of people gathering below, but the acoustics of the hills will make the music and the words of consecration service audible throughout the great concourse."

For unknown reasons, the high hopes and elaborate plans for San Juan Evangelista, once envisioned as the capstone of the California missions, never materialized. Had things gone differently, the entire economical, cultural and social climate of the Valley very likely would have been changed, no doubt for the better.

It is a tragedy that the McGroarty mission remained unbuilt for "no man has caught the spirit of California from the beginning of the coming of the Spanish *padres* down to the present time and gathered it together into one continuous golden thread such as this great man has done."

THE "GHOST MISSION" OF CALIFORNIA

Situated not far from the boundary where the old Jalama Rancho ends and the *Rancho La Punta de la Concepcion* begins, roughly twenty–nine miles from Las Cruces, are the ruins of what many old–timers called "the lost mission of San Francisquito." Early in 1935, Kenneth Crist and several companions decided to locate the ruins. He wrote about his findings in the Los Angeles *Times Sunday Magazine* for April 14th.

Since the various accounts were so vague about the exact location of the ruins on the 16,000 acre Jalama Rancho, Crist employed Mack Rodman to act as guide. Rodman's father had been the manager of the *rancho* and young Mack had been riding over its wind–swept hills since childhood. After driving their car around an infinite succession of curves, they arrived at an oak studded area used as a picnic grounds. There they left the auto behind and followed Rodman across a meandering stream once called Tinta Creek.

Several more hours they continued before they viewed the first trace of ruins, the remnant of what was probably an elaborate garden area. An adobe wall still stood, balanced precariously upon an undercut bank. Further up the creek stood the remains of an old dam. Toward the adjacent hillside was the skeleton of an ancient aqueduct. Rodman noted that the "mission buildings, all that is left of them, are four miles to the west.

Later they came across a well–preserved wine vat: Square of mixed stone and tile buried to fifteen feet, with a circular reservoir almost as deep and nine feet in diameter. Its walls, two or three feet thick, were similar to those comprising the reservoir at Santa Ines, like the sides of the spring house at La Purisima Concepcion.

Thick bush robed the scene, but fragments of adobe buildings covering an area of some eighty–five by a hundred feet could be traced with ease, while broken roofing tile was scattered like so many sea shells upon the beach.

There also were remains of stone foundation walls, carefully laid, and worn tiers of steps trod a century earlier by the Franciscan missionaries as they began their liturgical chants. Crist noted that "here, when California was in youth, there was the tall trooping of candles, the solemnity of Gregorian chants and the lifting of bright brown eyes in mingled hope and expectation."

Evidence indicated that a great fire had swept over the land. By the time Crist and his companions reached the area, California's elfin forest had re–carpeted the cooked earth and reclaimed it as its own. In his account, Crist said that "things are today as they were before the Franciscans came, save for the wine vat, the stone, the adobe walls weeping away to the soil, and, in the flat below, some scrawny pear trees now dead."

By some weird process known only to nature, the vines that once bore grapes have retreated from the thirsty hillside to find pasture closer to the waters of the stream. The so–called "ghost mission" was likely one of the numerous *estancias* or mission ranches that once dotted California's skyline. Whatever its precise function, local residents still maintain that on clear nights they can hear its tolling bells counting away the hours.

FORGOTTEN MISSIONARY ESTABLISHMENTS

Most accounts of the mission era reckon the number of its ecclesiastical foundations at twenty–one; but the enumeration omits entirely a whole host of establishments considered at one time or another integral units along *El Camino Real.*

Two quasi–missions, for example, were founded in October of 1780 in present–day Imperial County along the Colorado River. Purísima Concepción and San Pedro y San Pablo del Vado de Bicuñer were actually *pueblo*–churches used both by soldiers and Indians, an arrangement which eventually proved impractical.

A dozen or more *capillas* or chapels were founded at various times beginning in 1785 with the locating of San Pedro y San Pablo in San Mateo County. The year 1793 saw the addition of the chapels dedicated to Santa Gertrudis at Casitas Springs and San Mateo in the county bearing its name. The Capilla de San Marcos on the further side of San Marcos Pass dates from 1817.

In 1824 Fray José Zalvidea erected a small chapel in Kern County dedicated to the patron of earthquakes, San Emigdio. Riverside's Capilla Santa Catalina at Temecula came four years later. No date is available for the chapel of San Francisco at Warner's Ranch in San Diego County, although the one at present–day Camp Pendleton, known as Santa Margarita y Las Flores, was begun in 1835. The Capilla San Pascual on the Tejon Ranch in Kern County dates from November, 1843.

On the grounds of the old San Bernardino Rancho is the restored *estancia* or *rancho* chapel founded on May 20, 1810, by Fray Francisco Dumetz. Originally started as a *rancho* of Mission San Gabriel, San Bernardino was to have been converted into a mission to serve as an approach to the more distant internal regions of California. The *capilla* has been restored along with other buildings at the site and is now a worthwhile tourist attraction.

The *presidios* or forts erected in California were not looked upon as mission stations for they had a purpose all their own. Though the realm was obligated to provide chaplains at the *presidios*, this was rarely done and the nearest mission usually had to care for the spiritual needs of those attached to the forts. Each of the four major *presidios* had its own *capilla* where the *padres* functioned while attending the garrison. Chapels were originally located at San Diego (1769), Monterey (1770), San Francisco (1776) and Santa Barbara (1782).

An *asistencia* was "a mission on a small scale with all the requisites for a mission, and with Divine service held regularly on days of obligation, except that it lacked a resident priest." Of the five *asistencias* functioning in Provincial California, only one, that of San Rafael, ever achieved full mission–status.

Nineteen miles east of Mission San Luis Rey is the Asistencia de San Antonio de Pala. Founded in 1816 by Father Antonio Peyri, it is still serving the Indians along the border of Riverside County. Two years later the nearby Asistencia Santa Ysabel was established by Fray Fernando Martin.

Most famous of all the assistant–missions is that of Nuestra Señora de Los Angeles. Established as an extension of Mission San Gabriel on December 8, 1822, by Father Mariano Payeras, the small little "plaza church" continues to serve as a parochial structure although its original designs have been altered several times.

Other edifices in California date from the early pioneering years but none has the romantic aura of these missionary establishments. And for those wishing to "avoid the crowd" the foundations mentioned above are a good beginning.

CALIFORNIA'S UNBUILT MISSIONS

By offering the natives food, clothing and a general improvement in their living conditions, the missionaries quickly won the loyalty of the Indians and were soon able to teach them the basic elements of a higher civilization. However, the unchristianized natives of the interior regions, clinging to their Stone Age practices, provided a constant menace to the missions and many friars thought this danger could be alleviated only by a new chain of missionary foundations extending into the central area of what is now the State of California.

A fundamental principal of the whole missionary program was a realization that the mission itself was a merely temporary frontier institution, designed to introduce the Faith. Nonetheless, Fray Mariano Payeras noted in 1818 that "the backward condition of the California neophytes, and the lack of secular priests, have prolonged the existence of the older missions here."

As early as 1814, Fray José Señan had proposed establishing outposts in the Tulare Valley for "the poor natives of that region are very deserving of this favor." His plea was repeated a few years later by Fray Payeras who wanted to sow "the germ of a new seed of Christianity which will produce for the Church a new plant." The *Presidente* thought that it was "necessary in the Valley of the Tulares to form another chain of missions and *presidios* . . . and in the intervening territory some dwelling houses for a *padre* and some soldiers or settlers."

Later dispatches from Payeras indicate that a system of establishments further to the south paralleling the coast chain would have been useful as sources of supply for further expansion.

Interest in opening new missions was undoubtedly stimulated by the adoption in 1813 of the Decree of Secularization, which stated that those foundations in existence more than ten years "shall be immediately turned over to the respective ordinaries.

Fray Narciso Duran was in full sympathy with Payeras and repeated the sentiments of his predecessor by noting that there was no further need of "introducing" the Faith along the coast. In his opinion, the introduction of the secular clergy in the older establishments was greatly to be desired. Duran reported in 1826 that "the first step to be taken for the future prosperity of the Territory should be the foundation of a new chain of missions and *presidios* to the east . . . ." In 1830 he appealed for additional priests, whose presence would "then let a new chain of missions and *presidios* be established along the coast range of mountains."

Revolution in Mexico and the lukewarmness of the new government towards missions and missionaries thwarted any effort in this direction, however, and Duran wrote his superiors at San Fernando in Mexico City that "if the Mexican Republic had been bred in peace . . . California at this date might have a new chain of missions in the very heart of paganism with scarcely any expense to the Government, for the requisites to found them could have been obtained from the old establishments."

I. The California Missions
5. Native Americans

EUROPEAN IMPACT ON THE CALIFORNIA INDIANS

In a carefully documented essay appearing in the April, 1985 issue of *The Americas,* Dr. Harry Kelsey notes that at the time of European penetration into Alta California, visitors found the native Americans there to be poor and the country sparsely settled. Guestimates placed the population in 1769 at somewhere between 135,000 and 350,000.

The natives lived in semi–permanent villages of brush shelters and huts. Primarily hunters and gatherers, their social groups were fragmented by complex language differences. Though naturally suspicious of strangers, they were attracted to the culture brought by the newcomers.

In most cases, the missionaries found the native Americans eager for conversion. Dr. Kelsey pointed out that sophisticates tended to view the Indians as ignorant and brutish, kindly people considered them warm and friendly and soldiers regarded them as fierce and hostile. In fact, they were all of those things and none of them, much like people everywhere.

Contact with Europeans had tragic results for the Indians. Soldiers, sailors and settlers introduced syphilis and other diseases. While social contacts may have accelerated the infant mortality rate, there is also evidence to indicate that the native population was in a decline that predated the arrival of the outsiders.

In Alta California, the friars used the same methods employed with great efficiency in the Sierra Gorda regions of Central Mexico. When food supplies were meagre, the natives would return to the wilderness and forage for themselves. As conditions improved, these absences became less frequent, though the average native spent about two months annually with unchristianized Indians away from the mission.

The Indians adhered to a rigidly ordered regimen at the missions, each day beginning with prayer and recitation of the *doctrina.* Meals of *pozole* and *atole* were provided, along with meats, fruits and vegetables when available. Father Maynard Geiger figured that the Indians at Santa Barbara Mission consumed an average of eight pounds of food each day.

Though the children generally adapted easily to the new program, many adult neophytes never fully embraced Christianity. In 1830, Fray Narciso Duran wrote that even though the natives at San Jose Mission "are baptized voluntarily, they easily tire and change . . . because their character is fickle and childlike."

As mission Indians began adjusting to the new practices, they took to living in permanent abodes, ate regular meals, learned to care for their youngsters, abandoned intramural fights, raised crops, cared for livestock, learned new arts and crafts and began mixing with settlers in the *pueblos, presidios* and *ranchos.*

Believing that the neophytes were as yet unready to compete with the general population, the friars felt, in the 1830s, that release of the Indians from the missions was still premature. In fact, when the natives actually did leave, they quickly lost their property and became virtual slaves in the *pueblos* and *ranchos.*

Despite the obvious shortcomings of a system that attempted to mould the Indian population into a societal unit in a relatively short period of time, the impact on the natives was total and irreversible. Dr. Kelsey concludes his study by saying that "the inescapable judgement of history is that the missions protected the Indians from total extermination and prepared them to participate in a Europeanized society."

THE MISSIONS AND CORPOREAL PUNISHMENT

Corporeal chastisements figured prominently among the pedagogical inducements used by the early California missionaries and, while punishment in any form is not a pleasant subject, the story of the mission Indians would be neither complete nor true without its mention. The attitude of the friars toward corporeal punishment can only be properly understood when viewed within the context of their overall relationship as "guardians" of the natives. This *loco parentis* role was well stated, in 1773, when the Viceregal Council of War and Exchequer declared that the missionaries were to have charge of the baptized Indians "just as the father of a family has charge of his house and the education and correction of his children."

Recognizing the principle of those days, that a friar was to deal with an Indian "as a tender and prudent father," one can easily grasp Fray Junípero Serra's defense of corporeal punishment as being "in complete harmony with the natural law concerning the education of children." The excesses of later decades underscores Serra's wisdom in asking for and receiving governmental assurances that "no chastisement or ill–treatment shall be inflicted on any of them . . . without consulting the missionary father."

Fray Estévan Tápis explained the manner in which punishments were meted out by noting that an offender is once warned of his offense and then given a chance to amend. If he repeats the act, "he experiences the chastisement of the lash or the stocks. If this is insufficient, as is the case with some, seeing that a warning is useless, he is made to feel the shackles, which he wears for three days while he is kept at work. The same practice is observed with those who are caught in concubinage. With those who steal something of value, or who fight with the danger of doing harm, this order is not observed; for these are first chastised and then made to abhor theft or exhorted to keep the peace. It has been noticed that this is the successful way of maintaining public and private tranquility."

The punishments themselves were calculated to cause smarting pain and embarrassing ignominy, rather than long protracted privation or abiding injury. Included were whipping, the stocks (fixed and portable) and irons. Less often, diminished rations and imprisonment were used. By far the most common correction was whipping. The lash, a generally mild and moderate chastisement, is the first one mentioned in available lists of punishments. Fray Fermín Lasuén used that punishment only as a last resort and, "no matter how serious and great the crime, they [the Indians] are never sentenced to more than twenty–five strokes with such a lash as will not draw blood or cause notable contusion."

Another missionary, Fray Estéven Tápis described the chastisements inflicted as quite in keeping with the judgment with which parents punish their own children. He went on to explain that "we have begotten the neophytes for Christianity by means of our labors for them, and by means of Baptism in which they received the life of grace. We rear them by means of the Sacraments and by means of the instruction in the maxims of Christian morals. We therefore use the authority which Almighty God concedes to parents for the education of their children, now exhorting, now rebuking, now also chastising when necessity demands it."

Corporeal punishment, relatively unfamiliar in modern life, was not so exclusive in provincial times. The use of the lash, the stocks and the shackles, for example, were implements of punishment even among civilized people in many parts of the world in those days. Inasmuch as the whole question of bodily chastisements continues to be a disputed matter among psychiatrists and psychologists, this writer can only note that most of the criticism leveled at the friars in early California on the question of corporeal punishment came from those who reproached them for their "excessive tolerance and lenience" rather than for their severity.

PUNISHMENT OF THE INDIANS

Every vocation, trade and profession has its handbook or manual which outlines the norms observed by members in pursuit of their objectives. Such was surely true of the early missionaries in California. In their case, it was a thick volume compiled by the Bishop of Quito, Alonso de la Peña Montenegro (1596–1687) entitled *Itinerario para Parrochos de Indias*.

Compiled around 1668, the massive tome, one of the first treatises on human rights, encompassed a moral code that covered almost every facet of missionization. There was a copy of the *Itinerario* at every foundation along California's *El Camino Real*. The one at San Fernando, which later belonged to the *Bibliotheca Montereyensis Angelorum Dioceseos*, was printed by Juan Bautista Verdussen at Antwerp in 1726.

Fray Junípero Serra's copy of the *Itinerario*, which he acquired shortly after its publication in 1754, is still preserved at San Juan Capistrano. It bears the friar's signature, along with an inscription which recalls his almost–appointment to San Sabba in Texas.

This book is vitally important for a balanced appreciation of how Serra and his Franciscan collaborators treated the Indians. The *Itinerario* occupied a place second only to the Bible for the friars. Each of its prescriptions was followed scrupulously and violations were considered gravely sinful.

The *Itinerario* touched upon a wide variety of topics, including what and how priests should teach the Indians, the necessity of learning local dialects and the methodology of catechization. The *Itinerario* was exceedingly specific about the question of punishment. The Indians were only to be "verbally admonished" and in a way that reflected "more the love of a father than the imperiousness of a judge."

As to whether priests could "beat and inflict punishments on the Indians, in order to prevent sins," the priest is reminded that "punishment belongs to judges and prelates and the priest is neither." And even though the priest "has jurisdiction in the court of conscience . . . , he has none in the civil courts." The author of the *Itinerario* tells readers that the Council of Lima orders that "no priest shall punish the Indians" without the authorization of his bishop (and there was no bishop in California until fifty–six years after Serra's death!) In another context, "the priest who governs the Indians" is told "not to punish their wrongdoings but report them" to the civil authorities.

In still another part of the book, the teaching of Juan de Solorzano is invoked to the effect that "it is inadvisable to use arms, soldiers and war machines to introduce the gospel to the infidels." Further, "enforced baptisms shall be considered null and void" as is commonly stated by theologians and stipulated in the canonical precepts of Francisco Suarez.

Finally, the *Itinerario* points out that "just as the apostles were poor, humble, suffering fishermen," having neither staffs nor money, their successors can most effectively "harvest souls if they come armed only with virtue and confidence in God's pity and mercy." For well over 700 pages, the *Itinerario* spells out and regulates every conceivable relationship between the missionaries and their potential converts. Would that the detractors of the friars take the time to check the sources!

INDIAN DEATH RATE IN CALIFORNIA

One hears a lot these days about the dramatic upsurge in the death rate among the Indians of Alta California after the arrival of the missionaries, almost as if to suggest a sinister plot by the friars serving in the area.

Soldiers, sailors and settlers were the real culprits who spread disease wherever they went in the New World. Precisely when this started in the Californias is a moot question, but likely the earliest expeditions left those hidden reminders behind. Interestingly enough, none of the earliest accounts speaks of Indian families with more than two or three children. Father Jacob Baegert noted in 1752 that in peninsular California, "two or three children are a great burden."

It seems likely that the Jesuit missionaries in the eighteenth century were dealing with a native population already on the decline and a native family in which few youngsters survived the diseases of childhood. Baegert attributes the rapid decline of the Indian population in Baja California between 1700 and 1752 to "sickness and rebellion." He later opined that abortion and parental neglect accounted for the low rate of live births, as well as the high infant mortality rate. Likewise, he said that poor diet, inadequate attention to the ill and outright killing of infirm people contributed heavily to the decline of the adult population.

During the earliest years of European presence in Alta California, the Indian population also declined at an alarming rate. Disease took a huge toll. There were recurring epidemics of smallpox, measles and dysentery, but the greatest killer of all was syphilis, a disease passed on to children. Three out of four children succumbed the first or second year.

Very few studies of the mission population changes have been based on the original records. Researchers have relied on copies and summaries of the originals, or doubtfully valid estimates, guesses and assumptions by anthropologists.

The works of Sherburne Cook have not withstood the scrutiny of subsequent research. In a later study, he reduced considerably his earlier totals and finally concluded that the infant mortality rate in Alta California was "no worse than in other comparable societies in the eighteenth and nineteenth centuries." Francis Guest has suggested that a study of the death rate in Europe for the same period of time might well cast a wholly new dimension on what transpired in faraway California.

Neither is it possible to state with certainty whether the Indian population at the missions declined at a greater or a lesser rate than among the unconverted Indians, for whom there is no available evidence and who accounted for at least three quarters of the Indian population during mission days. Also, it must be remembered that the friars often came across or were called to administer the Sacrament of Extreme Unction to people already *in extremis* (the point of dying), a factor that would inflate the normal death rate in proportion to baptized Christians.

The Indian population of Alta California did begin declining dramatically after 1769, mostly through disease. But there were other reasons for that phenomenon, many of them not thoroughly understood then or now.

This much is certain—*if* the Indian population of Alta California declined faster than that of other areas and *if* the death rate of neophytes was higher than that of the non–mission Indians, the paramount cause can likely be assigned to such diseases as already mentioned. Yet, this is not something for which the missionaries (Fray Junípero Serra or anyone else) can be blamed. There is no recorded case of any friar serving in the area between those crucial years 1769–1840 ever having suffered or died from any of those diseases.

NEW EVIDENCE ABOUT INDIAN DEATH RATE

The story of the past is forever being updated and re–interpreted. History will never stay written as long as scholars are unearthing fresh evidence and re–evaluating the old. An example at hand is the traditional explanation given for the accelerated death rate among native Americans in the years after European penetration. Not alone have statistics been misused and exaggerated, but discoveries in medical science are providing wholly new and convincing theories.

Historians have long realized that European diseases took a heavy toll on American Indians. But now, recent studies demonstrate how at least one mid–western tribe, the Omahas, were ravaged by a totally different source.

Karl Reinhard, an anthropologist at the University of Nebraska, has examined the chemical contents of skeletons exhumed forty years ago from Omaha tribal graves. More than half were found to be heavily laced with lead, a substance known to have decimated ancient Romans. Unlike such other tribes as the Sioux and Pawnee, the Omahas had more extensive contacts with Europeans from whom they obtained lead in trade for a variety of uses.

By the early 19th century, the Omahas had become the first gunsmiths of the Plains. They avidly bartered for lead with which to make musket balls. Artifacts found at the grave sites also suggest that traders supplied the Indians with such items as wine bottles and food tins sealed with lead solder. Additionally, some skeletal remains showed signs of lead–based paint on their faces.

Once ingested, lead is absorbed into the bones and does not readily dissipate. Depending on the quantities and the age of those exposed, lead can cause retardation, developmental problems and even death. In the case of the Omaha skeletons, twenty–two of the remains exhibited lead in dangerous to lethal quantities ranging from eighty to 400 parts per million. The skeleton of one child measured 1,000 parts per million.

The skeletons in question were buried between 1780 and 1820 in northwestern Nebraska. During that time frame, the population of the Omahas began to dwindle from about 1,700 until it leveled out at about 300.

Previously, tribal historians had blamed the decline on epidemics spread by white traders and settlers, a fate that is known to have befallen most other tribes in the New World. But, according to Reinhard's studies, the chemical analysis conducted with mass spectrometers and other high–tech gear, showed surprisingly little evidence of infectious diseases on the Omaha skeletons.

Whether lead poisoning affected other tribes of the period is unknown and probably would not have been discovered in the case of the Omahas had it not been for an unusual resolution of a long custody fight for the skeletal remains. What happened to the Omahas could have happened elsewhere. In their case, history has now spoken through science. Reinhard said that "the findings have implications for the broader population as well . . . . Here we have a culture that almost went extinct because of the toxic elements they were coming into contact with."

Could something like that have occurred in California? Surely such a discovery would keep a whole new generation of historians off the streets.

WHERE DID THE MISSION INDIANS GO?

Historians are frequently asked, "what ever happened to the Christian Indians in the years after secularization of the California missions," a question that especially fascinates genealogists. A few of the neophytes reverted to the wilderness and their aboriginal way of life. That number was small, however, because California had changed dramatically and there were relatively few areas still isolated from European contact and influence.

As the year 1833 approached, much of the mission population consisted of natives who had been born and raised at the missions. And the *ranchos* owned by Spanish, Mexican and (soon) American landholders controlled most of the native environment. In other words, most of the neophytes were no longer participants in a hunter–gatherer culture. And, because of the *ranchos*, there was less and less room for such a culture to survive.

Many of the Christianized Indians remained as long as they could at the missions, in spite of the economic changes introduced by the new managerial system.

Eventually, they either died or drifted either to Hispanic settlements or *ranchos*. A small percentage of the Indians engaged in such civilian enterprises as farming and ranching, occupations they had learned while still attached to the once–thriving missions.

Finally, there were those who assimilated and became part of the *gente de razon* by intermarriage with Spanish, Mexican and later American colonists. As occurred earlier, when Indians married members of the military detachments, they acquired a social standing superior to that enjoyed by the other neophytes. Since many of the soldiers received governmental land grants upon completion of their services, their Indian spouses also shared in whatever social and economic advantages accrued to property holders.

It is interesting to note that many of the soldiers in California already had high percentages of Indian blood in their veins, a factor not emphasized (and sometimes vociferously denied) because of the social pressures then prevalent in Mexican society.

Since a large percentage of the soldiers who married Indian wives found it inexpedient to identify with native American customs and practices, most of them made it a practice to avoid counting or otherwise considering their offspring as "Indians." The children of those "mixed" marriages generally tended to marry non–Indians, probably because their contact and association with other natives was minimal.

However considered, America's western "melting pot" certainly included a goodly percentage of California Indians, something untrue along the eastern seaboard, where marriage with natives was not encouraged and often forbidden. Descendants of these "mixed marriages" are generously represented in today's general population though, more often than not, they have completely lost their native American identity. This assimilation continued well into the American period. One immediately recalls the Indian wife of Hugo Reid about whom the Los Angeles *Star* published "Letters on the Los Angeles County Indians" in 1852.

Guestimates put the number of people with Indian ancestry living along the Pacific Slope as fairly large in the 1990s. Many Americans look to Europe, Asia, Africa or Latin America for their roots. But residents of the Golden State might be among those privileged enough to find their family tree grafted to one of California's ancient "red" woods.

CIMARRONES — THE "RUNAWAY" INDIANS

The writer of a recent anthropological study dealing with the Tuhuvitan Indians of Southern California criticized the attitude of the early missionaries toward the *cimarrones*, those Christianized natives who "escaped" from the jurisdiction of the local mission. Among other things, the report expressed disapproval of the policy whereby the Indians, once baptized, "were not free to leave the missions except for brief periods (and then only when properly licensed)."

The relationship of the Franciscans to the Indians, however, was neither so severe nor unreasoned as certain observers indicate. For California, as elsewhere in the Church's long history, a particular missionary program can only be fairly appraised within the context of existing circumstances, many of which change considerably from one century to another.

The aboriginals along the Pacific Slope were never coerced into accepting Christianity and, in fact, the greater majority were not converted in mission times. "Once however, an Indian accepted his new mode of life, he was not considered free to reject it." It is true that "while adjuring the use of force in effecting the initial conversion of the natives, the Fathers had no qualms about bringing it to bear to keep the Indians at the mission, once baptized." According to the reasoning of the friars, reception of Baptism by an Indian was an irrevocable manifestation of religious conviction. As such it had a binding obligation subject to the normal sanctions of any other type of public contract. One scholar also notes that the missionaries further "felt that a 'traitor' who forsook the Christian ranks was likely to be hostile and dangerous both to the Church and to the Spanish state."

On those relatively few occasions when an Indian ran away or failed to come back after his monthly excursion, other Christian neophytes were sent after him. "On being returned he was reproached for failing to be at divine services on Sunday or holy day. He was warned that if he repeated the transgression he would be chastised. If he transgressed a second time, he was put in stocks or given the lash. In certain cases even this was insufficient to effect a reform. Then he was placed in shackles and at the same time given work to do."

The precise extent to which the *padres* violated the "freedom" of their charges obviously depends on the interpretation attached to the overall *loco parentis* role. As legal guardians of the natives, the friars believed that "they were acting for the Indians' own good, as we do today when we invoke the law and its enforcement to constrain the young to remain in school up to a certain age."

In any event, the sympathy, kindness, patience and forbearance exhibited by the missionaries was plainly obvious to even such critical persons as Alexander Forbes, who reflected a consensus opinion that the *padres* consistently evidenced "excellent motives and most benevolent and Christian–like intentions" towards the California natives.

BLACK LEGEND FOREVER REFUTED

It is not at all uncommon to hear the contention that the Spaniards in Provincial California "forced the Indians into the missions where they were coerced into conversion." Such a translocation of the Indians, so the thesis goes, created an antipathy which "found an outlet in apostasy, fugitivism and physical resistance."

Father Francis A. Guest, the distinguished Franciscan historian and director of the Santa Barbara Mission Archives, wrote a superb refutation of this whole contention for the *Southern California Quarterly*. Guest contends that the issue of "forced conversions" originated with the late Sherburne F. Cook, who served as Professor of Physiology at the University of California from 1928 to 1963.

In the course of his academic career, Cook did extensive research in the history of California's Indians, particularly with reference to disease and population. Cook's four–part study on *The Conflict Between the California Indian and White Civilization*, published in 1943, states that "although the baptism of Indian converts was voluntary under Junípero Serra, Francisco Palou and Fermín Francisco de Lasuén, it became a common practice, especially after 1800, for the Spanish to force the Indians into the missions" where they necessarily became Christians.

To "prove" his thesis, Cook had recourse to both Spanish and non–Spanish sources. Unfortunately, as Guest so carefully documents, Cook "takes liberties with a number of the fundamental principles of historical methodology." In his seventy–seven page study, Guest points out that "there is abundant evidence that the missionaries notwithstanding the confusing difficulties that arose, endeavored faithfully to follow" the policy inaugurated by Serra at the outset of the California enterprise.

Quoting no fewer than 224 sources, the Franciscan historian concludes that "in the history of Alta California there is no valid or reliable documentation which proves that a governor, *presidio* commander or missionary sent an armed party of soldiers or missionized Indians into the wilderness to force non–Christian Indians to be reduced in a mission in violation" of the *Recopilacion de leyes de los reinos de las Indias*.

The importance of the Guest study cannot be overemphasized. Cook's writings are still quoted extensively and his students continue propagating their mentor's errors. For the first time, a scholar of national prominence has clearly proven how, in Cook's dealings with historical sources, he mistranslates, misreads and misunderstands documentation, omits significant matter from various passages, takes words and sentences out of context, assumes conclusions he needs to prove, relies on questionable testimony, fails to put sources into their proper context and uses selected evidence.

Guest does not accuse Dr. Cook of bias. "It would seem that he formulated his thesis first and then sought evidence with which to support it. Putting the cart before the horse led him into untenable positions. And it contributed generously to the development of the Black Legend."

SOME UNASKED QUESTIONS ABOUT THE MISSIONS

The seemingly endless discussions about the impact of the California missions on the Indians have left some crucial questions unasked. For example, what happened to the more than half of the area's natives who were not assimilated into the mission system? Did their descendants prosper in later years? Did they have a lesser death and disease rate than their Christian counterparts? Since these peoples were not "contaminated" by the friars, did they continue to live in their aboriginal paradise?

There are no death or other records for the non–mission Indians, so no definitive statements can be made as to precisely how they were or were not affected by Europeans. But all the available evidence indicates that, if anything, the non–missionized Indians died even more rapidly than the others. No pockets of "untouched" Indians have been discovered.

The end result then was virtually identical for both the Christianized and the non–Christianized Indians. They all experienced a higher death rate which rapidly decimated their once considerable numbers. It would be factually wrong to say or intimate that the negative factors discernible at the missions affected only these peoples living within their confines.

Given the explorative patterns of the time, penetration and colonization by the European or at least by some outside force was inevitable for California in the 1760s or soon thereafter. Aboriginal peoples even then were an endangered species. And the results of mixing of peoples has been fairly consistent everywhere through the ages—when a lower culture meets a higher culture, the lower culture is demoralized.

There is no way that the disease factor and all the other related effects of colonization could have been avoided in California. Even though statistics can be over or under estimated and possibly mis–evaluated, their basic thrust remains fairly consistent.

The missionaries knew history. Though they didn't understand how or why, they pretty much anticipated what would happen in California and that probably explains why they were not overly surprised when the death rate began its sharp rise upwards. They concentrated their energies on doing what they could to alleviate or ameliorate a bad situation. Fray Junípero Serra for

example did everything he could to keep the military from having direct contact with the Indians.

The friars didn't volunteer for the California apostolate because they wanted to participate in the destruction of its peoples. They came to Christianize what they sensed was an inevitable trend.

The Franciscans in 1769 and all missionaries in every age were obsessed with adding a supernatural dimension to the quest for expanding the world's frontiers. Theirs was a *spiritual* conquest, totally motivated by other–worldly incentives. The presence of the friars in California can only be explained in spiritual terminology. No other explanation makes any sense for men bound by vows of poverty, chastity and obedience.

What happened to the Indians in California would have occurred had there been no missions. That's why the missions should be portrayed not as an element of destruction, but a force for spiritual betterment.

For about a third of the California natives between 1769 and 1840, the mission system made available whatever advantages European civilization had to offer. But infinitely more important, the missions provided what the friars believed to be the all important and saving message of Christianity.

Those who responded affirmatively, and only those, became members of a spiritual kingdom, a kingdom of truth and life, a kingdom of holiness and grace, a kingdom of justice, love and peace.

SHOULD THEY HAVE BEEN CATECHIZED?

There are not a few contemporary anthropologists and ethnologists who ask if the California Indians should have been evangelized. Whether it is a valid question or not, once asked it needs to be answered.

Actually, the question is anything but new. It was first posed shortly after the fall of Tenochtitlan, the Aztec Capital, on August 13, 1531. Were the Indians of the New World rational or human beings? Were they capable and worthy of becoming and living as Christians? Obviously, the question had enormous practical implications. If the natives were not rational, then they possessed no human rights and could be treated like animals, with no property claims or governmental obligations.

Bishop Julian Garces intervened and placed the whole matter before Pope Paul III. In 1537, the Holy Father issued his classic declaration *Sublimis Deus*, wherein he stated unequivocally that native peoples throughout the world were to be considered rational, capable and worthy of the Christian faith. And, as humans, they were to be included among the beneficiaries of Christ's mandate.

This complicated but interesting subject is well

treated by the distinguished Jesuit historian, Father Ernest J. Burrus, in his forty–eight books about the history of Colonial Mexico and the American Southwest. Burrus carefully notes that all groups of peoples everywhere, excepting only some small inaccessible islands and jungle enclaves, have, since before the dawn of history, undergone mutual influence through contact with others.

The earliest recorded materials about the city–states of Mesopotamia, the Biblical peoples, the Greeks and Romans of classical times, the barbarian invaders (and their European victims), the Renaissance and Golden Ages of Italy, Spain, France and England and elsewhere clearly show that none ever developed in isolation.

Even Greece, which was long thought to be the only possible exception to the rule that all peoples progressed through reciprocal influence, has now been found to be the recipient of Egyptian literature and philosophy.

When the Spaniards came to California, the area's natives had long lived in relative isolation, with the exception of some occasional crews seeking shelter and a few supplies through barter. With Pope Paul III's declaration in mind, the Hispanic missionaries considered the native peoples of California capable, worthy and in need of hearing about the Christian faith. Those who contend that nothing in the Indian way–of–life should ever have been disturbed, close their eyes to the story of humankind and its progress since before records were kept.

In a changing world, even in the seventeenth and eighteenth century pace, no portion of the Spanish American dominions could be kept forever in hermetical isolation. The natives were destined to change for better or worse. The missionaries strove to assist them in changing for the better.

Whether it be evangelizing, civilizing or aculturizing, "sharing" is now and always has been the name of God's game here on planet earth.

PLIGHT OF MISSION INDIANS

The sad plight of California's "Mission Indians" during the years following secularization has been graphically described in lengthy reports from such reputable authorities as Benjamin D. Wilson (1853), John G. Ames (1873), Charles A. Wetmore (1875), William Vandever (1876), Charles C. Painter (1887) and Helen Hunt Jackson (1883).

The account of Mrs. Jackson was especially provocative, including as it did a moving plea for whatever atonement was then possible for the long–suffering natives along the Pacific Slope. All of the observers professed admiration for what the early missionaries had

accomplished on behalf of the natives. Indeed, as late as 1901, Constance Goddard Du Bois wrote that "the seed the early Spanish friars planted still bears fruit."

She went on to describe those places "where no priest has visited for many, many years." In such locales, the Indians "still have their little church, an adobe hut, or one of boughs; the altar is decked with a few poor ornaments, and candles set in tin cans for candlesticks. The men enter with covered heads, and the people kneel on the earth floor.

"One better educated than the rest or with a better memory for the Spanish liturgy will say the prayers, and the people make the responses as reverently as at a cathedral service. The simple faith which rears that humble altar should commend itself to any professed Christian, by whatever name he chooses to be called."

Writing for the Office of the Indian Rights Association, a Protestant–oriented group in Philadelphia, Miss Du Bois decried the fact that "the unfortunate divisions among professed Christians make it possible for many worthy people to remain blind to the beauty of religion unless it speaks through the formulae most acceptable to themselves."

Such individuals, she maintained, "cannot see the forms of Catholicism without burning with zeal to uproot them. I am no Catholic, but I have seldom seen anything more sincere than the devout religious worship among these poor neglected people. They cherish as their most precious possession, the only good gift left to them of those the early fathers gave them."

The Reverend George Wharton James, a Protestant minister, argued that had "they been left in the hands of the Mission fathers, the Indians would slowly but surely have progressed to racial manhood. Given over to their own tender mercies, they have been hurried down the incline smeared by white men with every known form of slippery evil, in order that their destruction might be the more rapid and complete."

James went on to say that "until we are able, nationally, to cleanse our own skirts from the blood of these trustful, weak, helpless aborigines, let us not insult the memory of the Mission fathers. . . .

Whatever may be said about the missionary program of the Franciscans, one is forced to agree with Charles C. Painter that "no chapter in the sad and shameful history of our dealings with the Indians is more disgraceful than that" which followed discontinuance of the mission system in Alta California.

NEW ATTACK ON THE MISSIONS

Early in 1995, the University of New Mexico Press published a book by Robert H. Jackson and Edward

Castillo entitled *Indians, Franciscans, and Spanish Colonization*. Because this book is a vicious attack on the whole concept of missionization, a few cautionary observations seem appropriate.

Bernard Baruch was fond of observing that "everyone is entitled to an opinion, but no one is entitled to be wrong with the facts." In that vein, this writer finds no fault with the authors of this book for having a negative view about the impact of the California missions on native Americans. But he does strongly object to their invention, misuse and distortion of evidence. Their book is riddled with factual errancy. Even the essay on sources is flawed. For example, the register books for San Buenaventura, La Purisima and Santa Ines are not in the Santa Barbara Mission Archives, nor have they ever been! The last time I looked at Bancroft's *History of California*, there were seven volumes, not six (p. 169).

The book purports to offer "an interpretation of the history of the Alta California missions that draws upon a long and contentious literature. " But it doesn't. The bibliography, though lengthy, has enormous gaps of basic sources that would have answered or at least shed considerable light on many complaints made or suggested by the authors. The eighteen citations to their own works could have been omitted in favor of equally or probably more substantial studies by Maynard Geiger, Francis Guest, Clement Meighan and Michael Mathes. The authors claim to have "drawn on previously unused sources," yet this reviewer finds nothing in the book, beyond unsubstantiated generalizations, that is either new or revealing.

Potential readers need to be alerted that Jackson and Castillo are practitioners of what is often called "pyramiding." A dubious, misleading or otherwise unsubstantiated statement is made or alleged by the author who later, in another context quotes himself. Blatant examples occur in Chapter One where Jackson quotes Jackson no fewer than six times in the first fifteen footnotes. Another form of this practice comes about when statements attributed to recognized authorities like Hubert Howe Bancroft are really quotations from third parties. Finally, they reproduce charts and figures based on the research of others as proof for their own convoluted and often unrelated theories. (The chart in page 182 looks most impressive until one notices that grand old wiggle-word, "estimate.")

While admitting that many question Sherburne Cook's findings, specifically the results of his initial research in the late 1930s and 1940s at both the popular and professional level, the authors, nonetheless, anchor much of their study to Cook's findings which he himself discounted near the end of his life.

Jackson and Castillo violate basic historical methodology by equating folklore with fact, legend with truth

and oral with evidential history. Much of their work is anchored to preposterous stories by such discredited sources as Lorenzo Asisara, who claimed to recall Fray Ramon Olbes examining the reproductive organs of an Indian woman believed to be sterile and then made her stand in front of the mission church with a small wooden doll!

The mission system was not without its flaws and there are those who honestly disagree with the whole rationale of missionization. But critics need to attack the system for what it was, not what they make it out to be. Distorting the facts, misinterpreting the evidence and validating fourth–hand oral tradition is not a scholarly, honest or fair way of proceeding.

If this book were a spaceship, mission control would have shut it down halfway through the first chapter. Not alone are the facts askew and often plainly manufactured and/or wrong, the basic design is flawed. There is quite enough available about the shortcomings of the mission system without creating more. "No one is entitled to be wrong with the facts."

REVISIONISTS OR DETRACTORS?

Several recent studies have emphasized the negative aspects of the California Missions to the virtual exclusion of the positive. Such approaches represent an affront to the historical narrative as it actually unfolded.

An example is the suggestion that, had the Franciscans remained in their Mallorcan monasteries, the native peoples along the Pacific Slope would still be living in their pristine state, with their culture intact. Such a theory is hardly viable. Once contact was made by outsiders, the colonization of California became inevitable. The friars were not unmindful of history. They voluntarily became a part of the process in order to Christianize and cushion what they foresaw would be a cultural shock of major proportions.

Another misleading assumption implies that the Indians in California were living in some sort of idyllic lifestyle, akin to that in Eden, prior to the arrival of the white man. Such a "myth" is even more misleading than the one it seeks to debunk. Portraying Indian culture as only slightly less attractive than that of ancient Greece is nothing short of preposterous.

The contention that life in the missions provided natives with an inadequate or unpalatable diet was simply untrue. Those writers who maintain that the Indian neophytes objected to the food provided by the missions or found it unappealing is hardly convincing for, in their natural state, they were accustomed to consuming anything that was edible.

Had the missions been "concentration camps," as

charged by writers long on theory and short on history, then one could ask, why did 80,000 natives freely adopt the Christian way–of–life? If indeed, the mission system was repressive, how does one explain how such friars as Antonio Peyri at San Luis Rey Mission, presided over a community of 3,000 Indians with only a handful of poorly trained and inadequately armed soldiers?

Then there are those who hint that discovery and colonization in Alta California was unique, something without parallel in human annals. Not so. The story of colonization is the story of humanity. The only difference is that the process in Alta California was extremely well–documented, thus providing a before, during and after scenario often lacking in the other areas.

And the "spanking" of the Indians gets grossly exaggerated. Few critics bother to point out that flogging was then the standard punishment in both the American and English navies. Spanking was an acceptable practice in Hispanic society and it should be remembered that the Spaniards were as harsh on themselves as they were on the natives. Nor do we often hear that "spanking" was more repugnant to the friars than it was to contemporary observers.

Finally, the accelerated death rate in California after discovery gets blown out of context. Parallel and even worse statistics have been recorded in other places. An example would be the Hawaiian Islands after the arrival of the American Methodists. Post colonization death rates have escalated in all areas where a higher culture confronts a lower one.

If, then, certain writers distort the role of the missions in California and, if their criticism goes undocumented, why do the press and learned journals continue to publish their articles? Perhaps we are witnessing the emergence from the closet of an anti–Spanish bias, together with an anti–Catholic prejudice that has long hovered beneath the surface in California.

HOW EARLY INDIANS WERE NOURISHED

The early missionaries along the Pacific Slope were careful observers of the Indians to whom they brought the news of salvation. One of the friars, writing to a nephew in Italy, made some very interesting comments about the eating habits of the aboriginal Californians.

The area's hills and valleys, the desert and the ocean, produced hundreds of edible plants, animals and sea foods whereby the native population lived and prospered. Among the animals hunted and eaten were coyotes, squirrels, badgers, antelope, wood rats, gophers, raccoon, skunks, wildcats and rabbits. Deer were stalked by Indians in disguise. The skin of a deer's head was stuffed with grass and then placed over the hunter's head. Holding an arrow in his teeth and other shafts in reserve, he stalked the feeding deer, carefully imitating the motions of the grazing animal until he was close enough to strike.

Occasionally, deer and other larger animals were driven into long nets woven out of stout cordage made from the tough fibers of the wild hemp plant. All snakes (except rattlers), lizards, large locusts and grasshoppers were considered choice tidbits for the family larder. Such fowl as hawks, small crows, blackbirds, quail and doves were also part of the daily fare.

Along the coast, sea–otters, seals, sea–lions and whales were the principal food source. The Indians consumed enormous quantities of abalones, mussels, clams, sea–urchins and chitons.

The sea–otters, hunted from plank canoes or tule–rafts, were harpooned or shot with bow and arrow. Seals and sea–lions were slain at night with clubs or rocks. Grounded whales were rare but highly prized delicacies. The many varieties of fish were caught in nets, harpooned with circular shell hooks made from abalone and mussels or with devices fashioned from wood or bone. Fishing lines were made of milkweed, wild hemp, yucca fiber, or sea grass. Shellfish, gathered from rocks or dug from the sand were eaten fresh, cooked or dried and smoked for future use.

Though there was little if any agriculture in pre–Christian California, the natives lived fairly well on the natural products of the land. Women and children were adept at gathering up seeds, berries, roots and plants; the men and boys were expert fishers and hunters. Rocky reefs and still lagoons along the ocean were searched for edible shellfish and other products of the sea.

To the California Indians, the acorn was the staff of life. There are some fifteen species of oaks in the state, not all of which were considered edible. The most highly esteemed were the black oak, live oak and canyon oak. Acorns were gathered in the fall, spread out to dry and then stored away in large baskets. When needed, the acorns were shucked and the dried meats pounded in stone mortars until reduced to a fine meal or flour. Water was added until the bitter tannin was leached out.

Hundreds of plants were used. Piñon seeds, juniper seeds and the seeds of wild grasses were gathered. Many of these were first toasted with hot rocks in flat baskets before ground into flour.

PASTIMES OF THE CALIFORNIA INDIANS

California's early missionaries were very lenient with regard to the forms of recreation permitted among the Christian neophytes, allowing them to retain many of the games and pastimes they had enjoyed in their savage state. As long as Christian decency and modesty were observed, the Franciscans were not at all rigid or puritanical. Youth, ever ingenious, will always discover new games or new variations of older ideas.

The various visitors to the missions describe several versions of a game called "school." One Indian would conceal a little stick or a small piece of bone in his hand, while the opponent would guess in which hand the object was to be found. It was a favorite form of gambling, for which the Indians were notorious. Another of their "parlor" games resembled "straws." Two men would sit opposite one another. One would throw a handful of sticks into the air, while his friend would attempt to guess whether the number of sticks was odd or even. At the side of each player was the scorekeeper.

Then there was a game which followed the principle on which "hoop–la" is based. A visitor to Mission San Luis Rey explained it in some detail. There were two players to a team. One would send a ring, made of tule and about three inches in diameter, whirling through the air. During its flight, the other partner would throw two slender sticks about four feet long from the opposite direction. The object was to pierce the ring with the thin poles. Points varied according as one or two poles went through the ring. Even if the team failed to make a "bulls–eye," they could still score points if the ring fell on one or both of the sticks. When the points were tallied, the opposing team enjoyed its opportunity to score. The game lasted for a number of innings or serves until a determined quantity of points had been reached.

Besides these simpler games, the Indians also engaged in sports. Alfred Robinson described a ballgame at Santa Barbara which took place after Sunday liturgy. He sat in front of the door of his dwelling which faced a large square wherein the Indians would gather for their games. He observed that small groups of natives were scattered, here and there, engaged in animated and even angry conversation. Upon inquiry, he learned that they were adjusting the boundary lines for the afternoon's ballgame. The game resembled baseball, using a small ball made of hard wood. They were adept at hitting it some two or three hundred yards before it struck the ground. Robinson noted that there were some several hundred natives involved in the game which lasted for three or four hours.

California's Indians were also adept at a game resembling hockey. They would range themselves in two opposing parties, everyone armed with a curved stick. The goal was to drive a wooden ball to a goal, while the opposing team tried to block the action. Both men and women engaged in the sport. It often involved a certain amount of diplomacy, on the part of the friars, for the women were generally accused of cheating, especially when their men counterparts were winning. All of which suggests that the Christianization and civilization program utilized by the friars in early California was anything but an "all work and no play" kind of existence.

THE INDIANS AND THEIR PROPERTY

Originally, absolute title to land in the territory of California was vested in the king. There was no individual ownership during Spanish times but only usufructuary titles of various grades. This policy continued in effect for more than two hundred years after the first conquest of Mexico. The realm's *actual* possessions were restricted to the grounds on which the *presidios* stood and such adjoining lands as were necessary for royal administration of civil matters.

Under this program, the natives were recognized as the owners of whatever land was needed for their subsistence. Although it was foreseen that as their civilizing process advanced, the neophytes would need less acreage for this purpose, Spanish colonial law specifically stated "that the Indians have a *right* to as much land as they need for their habitations, for tillage, and for the pasturage of their flocks." Note should be taken, however, that there never was any title or deed given to the Indians, and it was on this legal technicality that the holdings were later expropriated and sold to private parties.

While it was understood that the mission lands belonged to the Indians, they were not the owners in the true or legal sense. "The system was merely that the government refrained from granting to anyone else such lands as were needed by the neophytes." The amount of land held in trust for the Indians by the missionaries was limited. For example, in 1784, Governor Pedro Fages approved a grant to Manuel Nieto (Santa Gertrudis or Los Nietos) of 300,000 acres, more land than was held by many single missions.

Provisions were made for settlement of white people. Each new *pueblo* was to have lands, to the extent of four leagues, always without prejudice to the rights of the Indians and, therefore, a goodly distance from existing Indian missions or *rancherias*. Part of the missionary program was geared to preparing the neophytes to take individual possession of those lands previously held in common and in trust by the mission establishments. It was envisioned that once the natives had reached the proper stage of development only that area actually occupied by church buildings, the cemetery, orchard, vineyard and aqueduct would remain under ecclesiastical ownership. As a matter of fact, only those sections were adjudicated to the Church by the United States Government in the 1860s.

A close examination of Spanish law and early California annals led Father Zephyrin Engelhardt to the conclusion that the charge against the *padres* claiming all land from one extremity of the territory to the other, and making the bounds of one mission from those of another, in order to exclude any white settlers, must have proceeded from willful ignorance or from unreasoning bigotry.

TAKE NO PITY ON NATIVE AMERICANS

In his superb new book, *Days of Obligation*, Richard Rodriguez argues that "the first Americans were not hapless victims; their descendants are refining and redefining the European legacy." Himself a native American, Rodriguez points out that five hundred years after Christopher Columbus set foot in the Americas, Indians are alive and growing in numbers from the tip of South America to the Arctic Circle.

In what Rodriguez calls "the European version of history," the Indian is supposed to have died—been slaughtered by the *conquistador*, or lost his soul to the *padres* or died of disease. The native American has become the mascot for the international ecology movement. The industrial countries romanticize Indians who no longer exist, while ignoring the ones who do, those who are poised to chop down the rain forest, for example, or the Indians who refuse to practice birth control.

Early in 1992, a man with a German surname declared that year to be one of "mourning." He suggested that there be no celebration of the 500th anniversary of Columbus' voyage. That man didn't know much about history and even less about sociology.

Though history testifies that many Indians died of diseases contracted from their association with Europeans, how does one account for the tens of millions of Indians who are alive today? Rodriguez is *mestizo*, of mixed Spanish and Indian blood. He noted that he was alive because of his ancestral mother's interest in the Europeans, their way of life and their standards of living.

"Oh, the poor Indian!" The white lament is that the Indians lost their souls when the Europeans arrived, lost their Gods, their virtues, their innocence. Yet, in 1992, it is Europe that has lost its God. The religion of Spain—Roman Catholicism—is now centered in the Latin Americas.

Rodriguez suggests that people take no pity on native Americans in 1992 or after. "Spanish is an Indian language now. The capital of the Spanish–speaking world is Mexico City, not Madrid."

And, if the paleface continues to romanticize the dead Indian, there remains also a fear of the live Indian. The trouble with those who criticize Columbus too much is that they assume he and his fellow Europeans alone decided the history of the Americas and that the Indians were only helpless bystanders.

Not so. Today, the Americas are alive with Indians. In Peru, the Shining Path Maoists are descendants of the Incas; in the Guatemalan mountains, the Indians are evangelical Protestants. Both are headed north. They are coming to secular United States to convert us!

Residents of the southland need only look around. The Indian is alive and thriving! "He communtes between his Mexican village and his job in downtown Los Angeles, she is a nanny in San Diego." And the Indian Virgin Mary, Our Lady of Guadalupe, is the Patroness of the Americas. Keep in mind that Mary appeared first on this continent to a native American, not to a European.

The story of Christopher Columbus or, rather, what his presence unleashed, is far from being told. What is a mere 500 years? Who can predict how the final chapter will be written? Stay tuned!

pg. 204 is blank

II. Hierarchy
1. In General

CALIFORNIA'S EPISCOPAL ROOTS

Development of episcopal authority in California is in no way connected with nor descended from the ecclesial organization set up in the eastern part of the nation when John Carroll was ordained to the episcopate by Charles Walmsley, the Vicar Apostolic of England's Western District.

Nor did the extensive French influence of Francis Montmorency Laval and his successors at Quebec have any causal relation with the jurisdiction conferred upon Francisco Garcia Diego y Moreno, O.F.M., when he was named to the Diocese of Both Californias.

There had been several attempts to exercise episcopal prerogatives in California prior to formal action by the Holy See in 1840. As early as 1775, Bishop Antonio Marcarulla of Durango claimed that the area fell under his aegis on the shaky assumption that all unassigned territories canonically belonged to the nearest established jurisdiction. The Marcarulla contention was rejected outright by Fray Junípero Serra, as was the less convincing assertion of the Bishop of Guadalajara who felt that Alta California rightfully belonged to his diocese as a normal appendage to the area over which he exercised authority.

Durango was closer to Alta California than Guadalajara, but the means of communication were less satisfactory. For this reason, the holy oils used in California were sent each year from Guadalajara aboard ships sailing from San Blas. In any event, documentary evidence of episcopal jurisdiction being exercised in California can be traced only from May 7, 1779, when Pope Pius VI issued the bull *Innumera divinae* erecting the Diocese of Sonora, an area then encompassing Sinaloa, Sonora and the two Californias.

As a suffragan of Mexico City, Bishop Antonio de los Reyes, O.F.M., and his successors had the canonical responsibility of watching out for the spiritual needs of California, an obligation satisfied by delegating the Franciscan superior in the missions to function as Vicar Forane of Sonora.

In 1836, the Republic of Mexico initiated action to have an independent diocesan curia established for Baja and Alta California. On April 27, 1840, Pope Gregory XVI removed that extensive area from adherence to Sonora and gave it canonical autonomy as the Diocese of Both Californias. Boundaries of the new jurisdiction were the Colorado River in the east, the 42º of north latitude (Oregon line), the Pacific Ocean and the tip of peninsular California.

The first incumbent, Fray Francisco Garcia Diego, lived only a few years and, after his death, the Holy See allowed the orphaned diocese to remain vacant under the supervision of a vicar. On November 20, 1849, the title of the original jurisdiction was changed to Monterey and several years afterwards, peninsular California reverted to the Metropolitan Province of Mexico City.

During the first dozen years of its existence, the California diocese was a suffragan of Mexico City. However, the change of sovereignty necessitated a reorganization of ecclesial boundaries and, early in 1853, Bishop Joseph Sadoc Alemany was informed that the Diocese of Monterey had been removed from its former metropolitan province.

On the following July 29th, acting on the advice of the First Plenary Council of Baltimore, the Holy See erected a separate province in California "to provide for the orderly administration and welfare of souls." With this action, Alta California was divided into two jurisdictions, the Archdiocese of San Francisco and the suffragan Diocese of Monterey.

Those parts of the archdiocese which later became separate Sees were Sacramento (1886), Salt Lake City (1891), Reno (1931), Oakland (1962), Santa Rosa (1962), Stockton (1962) and San Jose (1981). The southern jurisdiction of Monterey (later Monterey–Los Angeles) remained intact until 1922, when it was split into the Dioceses of Monterey–Fresno and Los Angeles–San Diego.

In 1936, California received its second province when Los Angeles was advanced to archiepiscopal rank and given as its suffragans the Sees of Monterey–Fresno, San Diego and Tucson. The Diocese of Monterey–Fresno was divided in 1967 and, nine years later, the Diocese of Orange was established. The Diocese of San Bernardino dates from 1978.

And so it is that within a little less than a century and a half, the original ecclesial authority grew from a single unit into a dozen, providing California with the distinction of being the only state in the union with two metropolitan districts. The Church in California had come of age!

A CARDINAL IN SAN FRANCISCO?

If magnificent cathedrals were the criterion for cardinalatial sees, the Archdiocese of San Francisco would surely qualify as the prime candidate on the American scene.

The first connection of San Francisco with the College of Cardinals can be traced to 1864, when Father

Herbert Vaughan (1832–1903) visited the Bay Area. This interesting cleric went on to become Cardinal Archbishop of Westminster.

On October 15, 1902, a half century before the distinction actually came to California, a world–wide news agency reported that the favorable decision handed down by the International Court of Arbitration concerning the Pious Fund of the Californias was a sweeping victory for San Francisco's Archbishop Patrick W. Riordan. It would make him, according to the story, "a prominent figure when the question of the next cardinal for the United States comes up."

Some years later, there was speculation that Archbishop Edward J. Hanna might be named to the cardinalate. In a letter to Bishop John J. Cantwell, dated June 3, 1929, Donato Cardinal Sbaretti admitted that he would be pleased "if the announcement made by Prince Pignatelli, concerning Archbishop Hanna, be true." Ceretti feared, however, "that a new hat will not be conferred in America before one of the four will be hanged on the roof of the cathedral." By that he meant that it would be unlikely that, with a limitation of seventy cardinals worldwide, that a fifth would be allocated to the United States.

Sharetti concluded this fascinating commentary on a positive note: "Anyhow, let us hope that sometime the announcement be verified." No further correspondence on the matter has been located.

During his triumphant visit to San Francisco, following dismissal by President Harry S. Truman, General Douglas MacArthur was heard to say: "if I were the Pope, my first act would be to name Archbishop (John J.) Mitty a cardinal. I can think of no one more qualified for that distinction."

During a journey to Rome, in 1973, Archbishop Joseph T. McGucken was asked if he envisioned a red hat in San Francisco's future. His answer was well worth recalling: "Nothing would please me more than to anticipate that honor for 'the city.' But, realistically, San Francisco is a city with a golden past and a chromium future." He went on to say that "as the role of cardinals takes on greater significance, membership in the Sacred College will be restricted to massive population centers. Increasingly, the red hat will be given, not to the person, but to the area."

The rumor mills, however, began churning again in 1979. In a column for the San Francisco *Progress*, Jack Rosenbaum led off with the following "rumor in inner Catholic circles:"

> Archbishop John Quinn will be elevated to Cardinal, but not in San Francisco. Step one: Timothy Cardinal Manning of Los Angeles, the word goes, will be transferred to Rome to assume the duties of ailing American Cardinal John Wright. Step two: Archbishop Quinn will move to L.A., then receive the red hat.

The following year, Herb Caen joined in the speculation. In the *Vista* section of his newspaper, for May 4, he noted: "If Archbishop John Quinn becomes a cardinal next year, and that's the rumor, he may have to leave 'heaven,' his word for San Francisco. Los Angeles already has a cardinal, and one red hat per state seems to be unwritten law."

A distinguished elder churchman of the American hierarchy once said that "San Francisco is the Baltimore of the west." That means that the archbishopric of San Francisco has a "premier status" in the western Church. By that measuring rod, there may yet be a red hat one day hanging in Saint Mary's Cathedral!

THE CALIFORNIA CARDINALATE

A faint thread of purple moire or watered–silk in California's Catholic heritage can be traced to September 17, 1875. In a letter to his cousin, Luigi Cardinal Amat, the Right Reverend Thaddeus Amat, Bishop of Monterey–Los Angeles, expressed his happiness about Pius IX's elevation of New York's Archbishop John McCloskey to the cardinalate, noting that "someday, possibly within a century, that honor will come to Los Angeles." The Vincentian prelate went on to say that "when I asked the Holy Father to move [my] episcopal *sedes*, it was from a contention that Los Angeles would one day rank among the great cities of the republic and even the world." Bishop Amat concluded by observing that he was planning "a cathedral fit for an eminent Cardinal!"

The Golden State was honored, in the latter part of 1887, with a visit by James Cardinal Gibbons, the ranking dignitary of the Catholic Church in the United States. After a brief stop in San Francisco, the prelate proceeded to the southland. The first cardinalatial visitation to the City of Our Lady of the Angels began with a liturgical ceremony at Saint Vibiana's Cathedral and an official greeting by the Right Reverend Francis Mora, Bishop of Monterey–Los Angeles.

In responding, His Eminence of Baltimore observed that the growth and progress of the Pacific Coast far exceeded his "wildest expectations." The prelate went on to say that "the glory of your State after all lies not so much in your climate and soil, but your prosperity consists in your manhood, intelligence and the zeal and earnestness which the American people bring to every enterprise they undertake." The Cardinal's biographer later wrote that the presence of Gibbons in the far west "aroused a great deal of interest and enthusiasm among the Catholic people of those regions. It was their first glimpse of a prince of the Church, and their pride in playing host to a member of the College of Cardinals was heightened when they observed the generally friendly manner in which their non–Catholic friends and neighbors greeted the visitor."

The cardinalatial dignity ultimately came to the Golden State in 1953, with Pope Pius XII's bestowal of the red hat on James Francis McIntyre, Archbishop of Los Angeles. The nation's twelfth cardinal was welcomed by the Catholic populace of the southland, in Amat's "cathedral fit for an eminent Cardinal," on January 21, 1953.

The distinction was renewed two Popes and twenty years later by Pope Paul VI's elevation of Archbishop Timothy Manning, as America's twenty–eighth member of the Sacred College.

Los Angeles, one of the nine cities in the continental United States honored with the cardinalate over a span of ninety–eight years, enjoyed the further distinction of being one of the five ecclesial jurisdications in all the world possessing two living cardinals at one time.

Pope John Paul II's appointment of Archbishop Roger M. Mahony to the cardinalate on May 29, 1991, confirms a precedent and renews a commitment to the spiritual well–being of the faithful in Southern California.

Cardinals are commonly referred to as "brothers of the Pope," a terminology especially apt for the Shepherd of God's People in Southern California. There is much that binds the City of *Nuestra Señora de los Angeles* to the See of Peter.

EPISCOPAL LINEAGE

Apostolic succession has always been a distinctive mark of the Roman Catholic Church. By it is meant the authoritative and unbroken succession of the mission and powers conferred by Jesus Christ on Saint Peter and the apostles and through them to the present Vicar of Christ and the college of bishops.

The actual tracing of episcopal lineage is a fascinating saga that has intrigued and occupied historians and genealogists for many centuries. Charles Bransom, a young scholar from Brandon, Florida, completed a study of the American hierarchy that was published by the United States Catholic Conference.

Among the interesting discoveries unearthed by Bransom is the fact that 91.2% of all the bishops alive in the world today can trace their episcopal orders to Scipione Rebiba, named Auxiliary Bishop of Chieti in 1541. Knowing who Rebiba was might prove interesting, especially here in Los Angeles.

Scipione Rebiba was born at San Marco di Novara di Sicilia (Messina) on February 3, 1504. His earliest studies were made at Palermo. After ordination to the priesthood, Rebiba became affiliated with the cardinalatial family of Giovanni Pietro Carafa who named him archpriest of Chieti.

On March 13, 1541, Father Rebiba was appointed to the titular See of Amicle and made Auxiliary Bishop of Chieti. The date of his episcopal ordination is not recorded, though it surely occurred about mid 1541.

Since the diaries of the pontifical master of ceremonies are missing for 1541 and 1542, there is no extant evidence as to Rebiba's consecrator. Very likely it was Cardinal Carafa.

In any event, Carafa dispatched Rebiba to Naples in 1549 as his vicar and, two years later, Rebiba became Ordinary of Mottola in Puglia. When Carafa succeeded to the Chair of Peter as Paul IV in 1555, Rebiba accompanied him to the Eternal City as Governor of Rome. Later in 1555, Rebiba himself was named a cardinal. He became Archbishop of Pisa in 1556 and later served as papal legate to Phillip II in Flanders. In 1558, he served a similar mission to Ferdinand I.

When accusations were leveled at the cardinal for abuses that allegedly occurred during his years with Carafa, Pope Pius IV had Rebiba imprisoned in the Castel Sant'angelo. After extended hearings, Rebiba was cleared of all charges and restored to full freedom.

The cardinal resigned his archbishopric at Pisa in 1560. Later Pius IV named him Patriarch of Constantinople and, during the reign of Paul V, Rebiba became a member of the Roman Inquisition. Described in the chronicles as a "man learned in doctrine and practiced in virtue," Rebiba was appointed Bishop of Albano by Gregory XIII and subsequently he served as Bishop of Sabina. These were honorary but important positions in the Church of those years.

When Cardinal Rebiba died at Rome on July 23, 1577, he was buried in the church of San Silvestrio al Quirinale. He was indeed a colorful prelate who left an impression on the Church that is felt universally over 400 years after his earthly demise.

AMERICAN LINEAL DESCENT

It is highly appropriate that the two Auxiliary Bishops of Los Angeles were consecrated during the octave of the American hierarchy's bicentennial. They were among a minority of prelates who can trace their episcopal lineage back to John Carroll, the former Jesuit who was appointed as the nation's proto bishop by Pope Pius VI.

Bishops Stephen Blaire and Sylvester Ryan take their place among the less than three dozen living United States bishops who enjoy the distinction of being descended from Carroll. Among that exclusive number are three American cardinals: William Baum (Major Penitentiary), Bernard Law (Boston) and Roger Mahony.

According to the genealogist for the American hierarchy, it all began twelve consecrations ago in the premier See of Baltimore. This is how it unfolds:

JOHN CARROLL was consecrated first Bishop of Baltimore August 15, 1790 in Lulworth Castle, Dorset, England, by Charles Walmesley, O.S.B., Titular Bishop of Ramatha, assisted by Father Charles Plowden and Father James Porter.

JEAN LOUIS ANNE MADELAIN LEFEBVRE de CHEVERUS was consecrated Bishop of Boston on November 1, 1810 in the Pro–cathedral of Saint Peter, Baltimore, by John Carroll, Archbishop of Baltimore, assisted by Leonard Neale, Titular Bishop of Gortyna and Michael Francis Egan, Bishop of Philadelphia.

AMBROSE MARECHAL was consecrated Archbishop of Baltimore on December 14, 1817 in the Pro–cathedral of Saint Peter, Baltimore, by Jean Louis Anne Madelain Lefebvre de Cheverus, Bishop of Boston, assisted by John Connolly, Bishop of New York and Father Louis de Barth of Philadelphia.

JOHN DUBOIS was consecrated Bishop of New York on October 29, 1826 in the Cathedral of the Assumption, Baltimore, by Ambrose Marechal, Archbishop of Baltimore, assisted by Henry Conwell, Bishop of Philadelphia and Father John Power of New York.

JOHN JOSEPH HUGHES was consecrated Bishop of Basilinopolis and Coadjutor Bishop of New York on January 7, 1838 in the Cathedral of Saint Patrick on Mott Street, New York, by John Dubois, Bishop of New York, assisted by Benedict Joseph Fenwick, Bishop of Boston and Francis Patrick Kenrick, Titutlar Bishop of Arathia.

JOHN McCLOSKEY was consecrated Titular Bishop of Axieri and Coadjutor of New York on March 10, 1844 in the Cathedral of Saint Patrick on Mott Street, New York, by John Joseph Hughes, Bishop of New York, assisted by Benedict Joseph Fenwick, Bishop of Boston and Richard Vincent Whelan, Bishop of Richmond.

MICHAEL AUGUSTINE CORRIGAN was consecrated Bishop of Newark on May 4, 1873 in the Pro–cathedral of Saint Patrick, Newark, by John McCloskey, Archbishop of New York, assisted by John Loughlin, Bishop of Brooklyn and William George McCloskey, Bishop of Louisville.

JOHN MURPHY FARLEY was consecrated Titular Bishop of Zeugma and Auxiliary of New York on December 21, 1895 in the Cathedral of Saint Patrick, New York, by Michael Augustine Corrigan, Archbishop of New York, assisted by Charles Edward McDonnell, Bishop of Brooklyn and Henry Gabriels, Bishop of Ogdensburg.

PATRICK JOSEPH HAYES was consecrated Titular Bishop of Thagaste and Auxiliary of New York on October 28, 1914 in the Cathedral of Saint Patrick, New York, by John Cardinal Farley, Archbishop of New York, assisted by Henry Gabriels, Bishop of Ogdensburg and Thomas Francis Cusack, Bishop of Albany.

JOHN JOSEPH MITTY was consecrated Bishop of Salt Lake on September 8, 1926 in the Cathedral of Saint Patrick, New York, by Patrick Cardinal Hayes, Archbishop of New York, assisted by John Joseph Dunn, Titular Bishop of Camuliana and Daniel Joseph Curley, Bishop of Syracuse.

HUGH ALOYSIUS DONOHOE was consecrated Titular Bishop of Taium and Auxiliary of San Francisco on October 7, 1947 in the cathedral of Saint Mary, San Francisco, by John Joseph Mitty, Archbishop of San Francisco, assisted by James Joseph Sweeney, Bishop of Honolulu and Thomas Arthur Connolly, Titular Bishop of Sita. And, finally,

ROGER MICHAEL MAHONY was consecrated Titular Bishop of Tamascani and Auxiliary of Fresno on March 19, 1975 in the Fresno Convention Center by Hugh Aloysius Donohoe, Bishop of Fresno, assisted by William Robert Johnson, Titular Bishop of Blera and John Stephen Cummins, Titular Bishop of Lambaesis.

TITULAR SEES — LOS ANGELES

A titular see is an ecclesial area where Catholicism once flourished, but has since declined for one reason or another. Titles to those dormant sees have been traditionally bestowed on prelates who serve as auxiliary or coadjutors to residential bishops. The *Annuario Pontificio* lists more than 1,500 such places, located principally in Asia Minor, Palestine, Syria and Africa.

Over the years, a number of titular sees have been associated with the Archbishops of Los Angeles, a linkage that is historically significant and worth investigating.

Before his transfer to Los Angeles in 1948, James Francis Cardinal McIntyre (1886–1979) served as titular Bishop of Cyrene (1940–1946), an area in Libya whose episcopal lineage can be traced to the 15th century. Cyrene was the most important of the five ancient cities called the Pentapolis in Northern Africa. It was a bishopric during the Crusaders' occupation and formed part of the Ottoman Empire from the 16th century.

Then, on July 20, 1946, McIntyre was advanced to the archiepiscopal coadjutorship of New York as titular of Paltus, a title revived and subsequently bestowed in 1902. McIntyre was the proto occupant to receive it as a titular archbishopric. Paltus, an ancient see in Syria Prima, is listed as #801 in the *Index Sedium Titularum* published by the Vatican Polyglot Press in 1933. Very little is known about the early history of that see.

Timothy Cardinal Manning (1909–1989) initially served as titular Bishop of Lesvi, when he was named Auxiliary Bishop of Los Angeles in 1946. That area was first given as titular see in 1908 and, since early 1998, has been occupied by Juan Maria Leonard Villasmil of Venezuela. The former see of Lesvi was in Algeria, near Setif, along the River Savav. Last of the residential ordinaries of that diocese was Bishop Vadius who was exiled by King Huneric in 484.

In 1969, Manning was appointed Coadjutor of Los Angeles and titular Archbishop of Capri, the first ever to occupy that once prominent see in a titular capacity. Interestingly, the title was subsequently held by William J. Levada (1983–1986) who later became Archbishop of San Francisco. Capri was a long–time residential episcopate which functioned until June 27, 1818, when it was suppressed and its territory united to Sorrento. The last residential Bishop of Capri was Nicola Saverio Gamboni who later became Patriarch of Venice.

Roger Cardinal Mahony also occupied a titular see during the years he served as Auxiliary Bishop of Fresno (1975–1980). Mahony's titular see was Tamascani, one of the many dioceses in Asia Minor which once was suffragan to the Patriarchate of Constantinople and Antioch. Most recently, it has been given to Gabino Zavala of Los Angeles.

Three other residential bishops of the southland jurisdiction also held titular sees, namely Francis Mora (Mosnopolis, 1873–1876 and Hierapolis, 1896–1905), George T. Montgomery (Tmui, 1894–1896 and Auxum, 1903–1907) and Thomas J. Conaty (Samos, 1901–1903).

CALIFORNIA'S TITULAR SEES

Among the many uses of the term "ancient" by ecclesial historians is one associated with those centers of Christendom that were once thriving centers of Catholicity, but have since become only monuments to an earlier age. Such areas, known as "titular" sees, are mostly cities of Northern Africa, the Middle East or Spain that had to be abandoned because of schism or Islamic rule. The *Annuario Pontificio* devotes 233 pages to enumerating titular sees.

Because of the proliferation of retired and auxiliary bishops in the last quarter century, the Holy See has had to increase the number of titular sees. In July of 1995, the Vatican announced establishment of twelve new titular sees named for former jurisdictions in the United States. Until that time, only Bardstown, Kentucky enjoyed that status. Most of the ones in the United States

are areas which ceased to be active see cities simply because of a decision to merge dioceses or transfer diocesan headquarters to another city.

Histories of diocesan and titular sees are often complex. The See of Monterey in California, for example, established on November 20, 1849, became the Diocese of Monterey–Los Angeles in 1859 and Monterey–Fresno in 1922. On December 15, 1967, the original title was restored when the Diocese of Monterey–Fresno was divided. "In California" was added to distinguish the diocese from that of Monterey in Mexico.

Among the dozen new titular sees is Grass Valley, California, erected in 1868 and transferred to Sacramento in May of 1886. The history of the state's first titular see is both interesting and amusing.

When, on March 3, 1868, the Vicariate Apostolic of Marysville was elevated by Rome to the status of a diocese, the Roman decree directed that the title and episcopal seat was to be in Grass Valley. Bishop Eugene O'Connell (1815–1891) was obviously not consulted about the change and his letters to Roman authorities over the next few years reveal why he opposed and resented the change.

He told the Prefect of the Sacred Congregation of Propaganda Fide that "Marysville much more deserves the dignity (of having its named used) than the town called Grass Valley. Truly the transfer from the city of Marysville to Grass Valley is going from the greater to the lesser in every sense."

In another letter, written on July 31, 1870, O'Connell had the temerity to sign himself "Bishop of Marysville" and it was yet three more years before he could bring himself to acknowledging his status as Bishop of Grass Valley. O'Connell was so irritated by the new title that he adamantly refused to take possession of the newly–designated Saint Peter's Cathedral in Grass Valley. He wrote to a friend in Ireland that his installation had not yet occurred and he intended to wait until "the final translation of my remains" takes place, at which time "the change will no longer be a fiction of law."

O'Connell's metropolitan, Archbishop Joseph Sadoc Alemany of San Francisco, wisely took no action and allowed O'Connell to remain in Marysville. He was probably more amused than upset at his suffragan's intransigence. Like most ecclesial squabbles, the matter eventually resolved itself, though not before O'Connell indignantly complained to Rome that the Apostolic Bull erecting Grass Valley had been erroneously directed to "Daniel" rather than "Eugene" O'Connell.

AUXILIARY BISHOPS

Very little research has been done over the years

about the history and role of "auxiliary" bishops. According to the new Code of Canon Law, an "auxiliary" is appointed without the right of succession to a residential bishop. His rights, duties and privileges are delineated in the bull issued by the Holy See at the time of appointment.

Though they participate fully in the plenitude of priesthood, "auxiliary" bishops lack what Canon Law calls "jurisdiction." They may exercise their office only in conjunction with and at the direction of the residential bishop. It is understood, however, that what an "auxiliary" bishop is able and willing to do should not be delegated to someone else.

At the time of his appointment, an "auxiliary" bishop is assigned to a titular diocese, generally in a place in the Near or Middle East where the Church flourished in earlier centuries. Interestingly, the appointee may not visit that area without authorization from Rome.

Since Vatican Council II, "auxiliary" bishops have a deliberative vote in ecumenical gatherings. Their role in regional episcopal conferences is determined by local legislation. In the United States, they have a vote in all matters except those touching on finances.

Prior to Vatican Council II, the function of an "auxiliary" ceased with the death or transfer of the residential bishop to whom he was assigned. Presently, "auxiliary" bishops are named to the see itself and retain their office during vacancies.

Auxiliary Bishops of Los Angeles

Prelate	Years	Titular See
1. Joseph T. McGucken	1941–1955	Sanavus
2. Timothy Manning	1946–1967	Lesvi
3. Alden J. Bell	1956–1962	Rhodopolis
4. John J. Ward	1963–	Bria
5. Joseph P. Dougherty	1969–1970	Altino
6. William R. Johnson	1971–1976	Biera
7. Juan A. Arzube	1971–1993	Civitate
8. Thaddeus Shubsda	1977–1982.	Trau
9. Manuel D. Moreno	1977–1982	Tamagrista
10. Donald W. Montrose	1983–1985	Vescovio
11. William J. Levada	1983–1986	Capri
12. Carl A. Fisher	1987–1993	Tlos
13. Armando X. Ochoa	1987–1996	Sitifi
14. G. Patrick Ziemann	1987–1991	Obba
15. Sylvester D. Ryan	1990–1992	Remesiana
16. Stephen E. Blaire	1990–1998	Lamzella
17. Joseph M. Sartoris	1994	Oliva
18. Thomas J. Curry	1994	Ceanannus Mor
19. Gabino Zavala	1994	Tamascani
20. Gerald Wilkerson	1998	Vincennes

The appointment of "auxiliary" bishops is not of ancient origin, though some of the early commentators

point out that Linus and Cletus were referred to in the annals as "vicars" or "auxiliaries" to Peter at Rome.

From the 14th to the 19th centuries, "auxiliary" bishops were fairly common in Spain, Poland, Germany and pre–Reformation England. The first "auxiliary" named for the United States was Sylvester Horton Rosecrans who received episcopal ordination as titular of Pompey and auxiliary of Cincinnati on March 25, 1862. It was almost thirty years later when John Brady was named "auxiliary" of Boston.

California's proto "auxiliary" was Bishop Denis J. O'Connell who was assigned to San Francisco in 1908. He served there until 1912, when he was transferred to the residential bishopric of Richmond.

The practice of naming "auxiliary" bishops in the Archdiocese of Los Angeles dates from 1941 and the appointment of Joseph T. McGucken to the titular see of Sanavus. Since then, there have been a total of twenty "auxiliaries" assigned to the southland jurisdiction.

As of this date, there are more than ninety "auxiliary" bishops in the United States. The country with the next largest number is Poland (58), followed by Germany (41). Italy has twenty–eight, with Brazil and Spain with twenty–four each. There are 553 "auxiliary" bishops worldwide, with the six countries mentioned accounting for 48 percent of the total number.

In what Gregory Baum described as a "truly parliamentary speech," Auxiliary Bishop Gerald McDevitt of Philadelphia addressed the conciliar fathers of Vatican Council II on November 13, 1963, scolding them for using the term "merely" when referring to titular bishops, especially those serving as "auxiliaries." He convinced his listeners that it was an important issue which touched the very nature of the episcopacy.

According to current practice, an "auxiliary" may be requested when the diocesan or residential bishop cannot adequately fulfill all his episcopal duties as the good of souls demands. The two most common reasons given are the "vast extent" and/or the "great number" of Catholics in the particular jurisdiction.

In the Archdiocese of Los Angeles, the largest ecclesial district in the United States, Roger Cardinal Mahony wanted each of the five pastoral regions to be presided over by an "auxiliary" bishop.

EPISCOPAL ORDINATIONS AT CATHEDRAL

Saint Vibiana's Cathedral was a silent but persistent witness to the ecclesial growth and development of Southern California since 1876. A myriad of significant events have taken place within its historic walls, including a long series of ordinations to the episcopacy.

The first such ceremony took place on August 24,

1924, when Stephen Peter Alencastre (1876–1940) received the fullness of the priesthood. A member of the Picpus Fathers (The Society of the Sacred Hearts of Jesus and Mary), the Madeira–born cleric had been named Coadjutor Vicar Apostolic of the Sandwich Islands.

Two years later, on October 17, 1926, John Joseph Maiztegui–Besoitaiturria (1878–1943) was consecrated titular Bishop of Tanais and Vicar Apostolic of Darien. The Claretian prelate later served as Metropolitan Archbishop of Panama.

The first native Californian raised to the episcopate in Saint Vibiana's Cathedral was Thomas Kiely Gorman (1892–1980). Named to the newly–created Diocese of Reno, the former editor of *The Tidings* was advanced to the bishopric on July 22, 1931. He subsequently served as Coadjutor and Residential Bishop of Dallas–Fort Worth.

With the passage of another three years, Robert Emmet Lucey (1891–1977) was named to the episcopate by Pope Pius XI. The first native of Los Angeles to wear the mitre, he was ordained on May 1, 1934, as Bishop of Amarillo. Between 1941 and 1969, Lucey was Metropolitan Archbishop of San Antonio.

Joseph T. McGucken (1902–1983), designated Auxiliary Bishop of Los Angeles, was advanced to the titular See of Sanavus on March 19, 1941. He subsequently functioned as Apostolic Administrator of Monterey–Fresno, Coadjutor and Residential Bishop of Sacramento and Archbishop of San Francisco. McGucken had been baptized at the cathedral.

Timothy Manning (1909–1989) became the youngest priest named to the Golden State's hierarchy with his ordination as Auxiliary Bishop of Los Angeles, on October 15, 1946. Twenty–one years later, he was transferred to the Diocese of Fresno. He returned to Los Angeles as Coadjutor Archbishop in 1969, and succeeded to that See the following year. He was named to the Sacred College of Cardinals in 1973.

The first rector of the Cathedral named to the episcopate during his tenure at Saint Vibiana's was Alden J. Bell (1904–1982). He was advanced to the titular See of Rhodopolis as Auxiliary Bishop of Los Angeles on June 4, 1956. Six years later he became Bishop of Sacramento.

The fifteenth Californian and the fourth native Angelino to share in the fullness of the priestly office was John J. Ward (b. 1920). He was consecrated titular Bishop of Bria and Auxiliary of Los Angeles on the Feast of Our Lady of Guadalupe, 1963,

Two priests were elevated to the bishopric as Auxiliaries of Los Angeles on March 25, 1971: William R. Johnson (1918–1986) and Juan A. Arzube (b. 1918). In 1976, Bishop Johnson became proto Bishop of Orange. The second dual episcopal ordination at Saint Vibiana's occurred on February 19, 1977, when Thaddeus Shub-

sda (1925–1991) and Manuel Moreno (b. 1930) became Auxiliaries to the Archbishop of Los Angeles.

"AT THEIR PRESENCE THE EARTH HATH TREMBLED"

It is perhaps significant that one of the Holy Father's public announcement about the two new auxiliary bishops for the Archdiocese of Los Angeles occurred at the very moment when the area was being rocked and shattered by one of the most disastrous earthquakes ever recorded in the Golden State.

The first "dual" appointment in California's ecclesiastical annals brought to the episcopal ministry two prelates richly gifted with pastoral experience, administrative expertise and balanced thought—men abundantly endowed to share the burdens of caring for the spiritual destinies of 44 percent of the state's total Catholic population. Though comprising only one of California's nine ecclesiastical jurisdictions, the 1,707,605 People of God living in Santa Barbara, Ventura, Los Angeles and Orange Counties had a proud heritage upon which to build the southland's future. The "Most Beautiful Diocese in America" was well described by John Steven McGroarty, who noted that:

> Its mountain peaks, its hills, its valleys, its cities and towns, its rivers and lakes and harbors bear to this day the holy names of the saints of Christ's Church. Its episcopal see bears the name of Our Lady of the Angels. It has had more than one saint of its own who but wait the authority of the Church that they may be so revered; it has the record of miracles that also but wait the seal of authority upon them.
>
> The blood of martyrs is upon it, it has known bitter persecution and suffering, it has felt the thrill of glory and the sting of shame, but it has never lost the faith; and today it lifts its head from the dust of the past to greet new altar lights that crowd the old King's Highway like stars in the night of a summer sky.
>
> Within this marvelous principality of the Church, set in the golden heart of California, a man might spend his whole life, yet never satiate his soul with its beauty.

The bi–centennial of Catholic colonization, observed at nearby *La Mision del Santo Príncipe el Arcangel San Gabriel de los Temblores,* on September 8, 1971, focused attention on the results of the apostolate begun in the area by Fray Junípero Serra and his evangelical co–workers.

The Archdiocese of Los Angeles stood at the threshold of a promising new era, the Catholics in California's southland, united with their episcopal shepherds and ever mindful that "fidelity to Christ cannot be separated from faithfulness to His Church," recalled the prophetically realistic words of Friederich von Schlegel:

I regard the Catholic Church as the greatest historical authority on earth. From her seat on the seven hills she has watched the development of history of the past nineteen centuries; she has seen the rise and fall of nations and has lived as an eye–witness to record their deeds. Rome alone understands their history and writes their epitaph, herself ever young.

BISHOPS BONDED TO ANCIENT TITLES

Titular sees are ancient dioceses that no longer have residential bishops. Some were founded by the Apostles themselves and in them the Church flourished perhaps for many centuries, only to be destroyed by persecutions, Mohammedanism or even schism. The Church wishes to perpetuate the historic prestige of these citadels of Catholicism by assigning them to bishops who are not ordinaries of dioceses. They are therefore known as "titular bishoprics."

Since the time of Pope Leo X, the Holy See has allowed for the creation of titular bishops to serve in the capacity of auxiliaries in order to lighten the burdens of certain residential ordinaries. However, since no bishop can be consecrated licitly without a title to a diocese, papal legislation provides for the naming of these prelates to former canonically erected jurisdictions which have long since been suppressed for one reason or another.

Titular bishops are impeded from exercising pontifical functions in their dioceses and normally the Holy Father, through the Sacred Congregation of Propaganda Fide, reserves actual jurisdiction in those areas to himself.

But if the titular bishop should discover, at any time, a large number of clergy and laity in his see lacking proper ecclesiastical administration, he can take up his duties there at which time he automatically becomes a residential bishop. There is no historical record that such an action has been taken for many centuries.

Bishop Sylvester Ryan was named to the titular ordinary of Remesiana, in Dacia Mediterranea. It is known that Justinian rebuilt and fortified the area in the 5th century. Today, renamed Bela Palanka, it serves as a railway junction between Nich and Pirot in Servia.

Remesiana, a suffragan diocese in the Metropolitan District of Sardica, the capital of Bulgaria, belonged to the Patriarchate of Rome. Two of its outstanding bishops were Saint Nicetus and Diogenianus, the later of whom was prominent in the Robber Synod of Ephesus in 449. The see was probably suppressed in the late 6th century. Occupying the See of Remesiana since 1983 has been the Most Reverend Jacquez Fihey (b. 1931), who directed the Military Ordinariate in France from his offices in Paris.

Bishop Blaire was given the titular See of Lamzella, a part of the African province of Numidia. It was situated west of Carthage and south of Hippo, where Saint Augustine lived.

The once flourishing Christian outpost, ravaged by schism, persecution and invasion, was eventually abandoned and then fell into the category formerly known as *in partibus infidelium*, a terminology modified by the Holy See in 1982. Jean–Louie Plouffe (b. 1940), the auxiliary Bishop and Vicar General of the Archdiocese of Sault Sainte Marie, has occupied the titular See of Lamzella since 1986.

The *Annuario Pontificio* lists more than 1,500 such titular sees, located principally in ancient Asia Minor, Palestine, Syria and Africa.

METROPOLITAN PROVINCE IN CALIFORNIA

The establishment of Los Angeles as a metropolitan jurisdiction, in 1936, was a news event of national importance. For the first time, the sixteenth of the nation's archdioceses received lead coverage in the columns of *Time* magazine: "His Holiness Pope Plus XI turned from the contemplation of troubled Spain to accord honor in the New World to a city" named for *Nuestra Señora de los Angeles*.

Los Angeles was only the second archdiocese created in the United States in the twentieth century. The distinction had not been bestowed since San Antonio became a metropolitan province in 1926. Separated from the province of San Francisco and, encompassing the Dioceses of Monterey–Fresno, San Diego and Tucson, the new jurisdiction accorded California the unique distinction of being the only state with two metropolitan districts.

The Holy Father placed the new province "under the supervision of brawny, sixty–one year old John Cantwell," for eighteen years Bishop of Monterey–Los Angeles (1917–1922) and Los Angeles–San Diego (1922–1936). In its story about Los Angeles, the magazine rejoiced that "a major U.S. playground was belatedly recognized as a major province of the Church."

Southern California was reported as being "historically dear to Rome. In 1769, Franciscan Fray Junípero Serra with seventy–five Spanish soldiers and a gang of Mexican muleteers journeyed 900 miles overland from Lower California to the Pacific, which they reached at the sand–spit of San Diego."

Early in August, the expeditionary force "forded a shallow river among sunburnt hills, discovering a village of unpromising heathens, named it for the feast day of Our Lady of the Angels and pushed on. A few years later the glory of God was attested by Franciscan missions in these towns and for 1,000 miles along the Pacific Coast."

The account went on to say that "vastly different from these labors have been those of Los Angeles' new Archbishop. Last week's promotion signalized the phenomenal increase of Catholic population in the Los Angeles area since Churchman Cantwell was installed as Bishop in 1917." The appointment, according to *Time* magazine, rewarded Cantwell "for distinguished moral service to the Church. Having his diocesan offices in Los Angeles' busy Petroleum Securities Building," the new archbishop "was accustomed to rubbing elbows with bankers, brokers and cinemagnates."

Though characterized as the "gentlest of speakers," the archbishop "still has the brogue of Southern Ireland, where he was born in 1874 and ordained in 1899. His present cathedral is musty St. Vibiana's in the grubbiest part of Los Angeles." The account also acknowledged that "before his elevation last week he had planned a magnificent new Cathedral in the swanky Wilshire section, but he changed his mind [and] decided to use the new cathedral money for a seminary."

The article concluded by alluding to Cantwell's "private quarters on fashionable Fremont Place, where his sister keeps his house and a dog keeps him company." A photograph also accompanied the presentation. Credited to Paul Dorsey, it portrayed Cantwell writing a sermon at his desk in the Chancery Office.

WEST'S FIRST CHOR–BISHOPS

The first conferral of the ecclesial distinction of Chor–Bishop in Los Angeles occurred in 1978, when Monsignors John Chedid and Kenneth O'Brien were invested with that office by the Most Reverend Francis M. Zayek of Saint Maron, New York. Chor–Bishop is an honorary title dating back to the second century. The term itself is derived from the Greek "chora" or country, a designation associated with priests who provided spiritual ministrations to people residing in rural areas.

Their counterparts in the city areas were known as urban bishops (*antistites urbani*) but like the Chor–Bishops, they lacked the power of ordaining others, a privilege always reserved to those bearing the marks of apostolic succession. The Synod of Antioch (341 A.D.) resolved the issue even further by emphasizing the dependence of the Chor–Bishops on the nearest residential ordinary in communion with the Holy See. Even in those early times, great care was taken in the matter of holy orders and how and when they were conferred.

After the eighth century, the office of Chor–Bishop or country pastor disappeared totally in the Latin Church, but remained in other Rites (Alexandrine, Anti-

ochene, Byzantine, Chaldean and Armenian), as well as in certain of the so–called "minor" Rites. Today, the title Chor–Bishop in the Eastern Rites is conferred *honoris causa* and is roughly equivalent to the Latin Rite position of Protonotary Apostolic, the highest of the ranks of monsignors.

The Chor–Bishop has no added jurisdiction over persons or things, but he may wear certain signs and symbols reserved for bishops, such as the mitre, ring and pectoral cross. He may also use a crozier when celebrating Holy Mass and administering the sacraments. The pectoral cross in the Eastern Rites is not necessarily a sign of the episcopal office. Oriental Rite Bishops use a *panagia* (medallion of the Blessed Mother), richly decorated with gold and gems and hanging on a golden chain. Chor–Bishops and other dignitaries who are only priests wear a golden cross or a chain.

In 1978, there were only eight Chor–Bishops in the forty–six parishes then comprising a Catholic population of 30,000 in the United States. The directories for that year indicate that sixty–five priests were serving the spiritual needs of the nation's Maronite peoples. Both of the Los Angeles priests named Chor–Bishops had long exercised bi–ritual faculties, a privilege which allowed them to offer the Liturgy in both the Roman and Maronite Rites.

The Maronite Antiochene Church is one of Christendom's oldest. Saint Peter, the first pope, personally established the Church at Antioch and served for many years there as bishop before moving on to Rome. The Diocese of Saint Maron, Brooklyn, was begun as an Exarchy on January 10, 1966 and then was advanced by Pope Paul VI to the status of Eparchy on November 29, 1971. The installation of the Chor–Bishops took place in the Church of Our Lady of Mount Lebanon, Los Angeles, on November 12, 1978. It was indeed an historic occasion for the west coast.

TOMBS OF SOUTHLAND BISHOPS

What the Church in Los Angeles has become is due in great measure to the stature of its leadership in earlier generations. For that reason, it is fitting occasionally that we recall those who have walked before us along *El Camino Real*.

One could visit the tombs of all the nine deceased bishops/archbishops who have shepherded the Church at Los Angeles by journeying to three places: Calvary Mausoleum and cemetery (Los Angeles), Santa Barbara Mission (Santa Barbara) and Holy Cross Mausoleum (Colma).

The first of California's bishops, Francisco Garcia Diego (1785–1846) is buried in a vault beneath the sanc-

Tomb of Bishop Francisco Garcia Diego

tuary of the church at Santa Barbara Mission. The colorful monument designed by Eduardo Tresquerras is the most elaborate of any used for the state's subsequent prelates.

Archbishop Joseph Sadoc Alemany (1814–1888), who presided over the Diocese of Monterey during the years 1850–1853, died at Valencia, Spain and was interred in a chapel of Vich's *Iglesia de Santo Domingo*. His remains were removed to the chapel of Colma's Holy Cross Mausoleum early in 1965.

Bishop Thaddeus Amat (1811–1878), who served the Diocese of Monterey and later the Diocese of Monterey–Los Angeles for a quarter century, beginning in 1853, died in Los Angeles and was entombed in the vault of Saint Vibiana's Cathedral. His *restos* remained there until 1962, when they were transferred to the Episcopal Vault at Calvary Mausoleum.

The fourth bishop of California's southland, Francis Mora (1827–1905), served the Diocese of Monterey–Los Angeles in several capacities. He was Coadjutor (1873–1878) and Ordinary (1878–1896). Following his resignation due to poor health, Bishop Mora

retired to Spain. He died at Sarria and was buried in the tiny cemetery of that Barcelona suburb. In 1962, his remains were removed to Los Angeles and reinterred at Calvary Mausoleum.

The Most Reverend George Montgomery (1847–1907) was named Coadjutor Bishop of Monterey–Los Angeles in 1894. He succeeded in 1896 and headed the southland jurisdiction until 1903, when he became Coadjutor Archbishop of San Francisco. Following his sudden death after emergency surgery, the archbishop was buried at Holy Cross Cemetery, Colma. His remains were moved into the new mausoleum shortly after its completion.

Thomas J. Conaty (1847–1915) was Bishop of Monterey–Los Angeles for a dozen years beginning in 1903. A former Rector of The Catholic University of America, the prelate died in the seaside town of Coronado and was buried in a receiving vault at Calvary Cemetery, Los Angeles. His remains were moved to the mausoleum in July, 1936.

Archbishop John J. Cantwell (1874–1947) had a trilogy of titles during his thirty year tenure: Bishop of Monterey–Los Angeles (1917–1922), Bishop of Los Angeles–San Diego (1922–1936) and Archbishop of Los Angeles (1936–1947). He succumbed at Los Angeles and was interred in the Episcopal Vault at Calvary Mausoleum.

James Francis Cardinal McIntyre (1886–1979) was Archbishop of Los Angeles from 1948 to 1970. He lived on for nine years after his retirement. He is interred with four of his predecessors in the Episcopal Vault at Calvary Mausoleum.

Timothy Cardinal Manning (1909–1989) served as Archbishop of Los Angeles from 1970 to 1985. He is buried among his clerical confreres in the priests plot at Calvary Cemetery in Los Angeles.

After visiting a graveyard where many of his Dominican confreres were buried, the great theologian, A. D. Sertillanges, wrote: "Let us not be like those people who always seem to be pallbearers at the funeral of the past. Let us utilize, by living, the qualities of the dead."

NATIVE BORN BISHOPS

Sacred Scripture exhorts us to "remember our prelates, who spoke the word of God." In California, the hierarchy has included bishops from Ireland, Spain, Mexico and Canada. The Emerald Isle has contributed the largest number of prelates to actually serve in the state (ten), but California itself has numerous of its native sons presented with mitre and crozier.

The first Californian raised to the episcopate was

Peter J. Muldoon. Born at Columbia on October 10, 1863, Muldoon was consecrated Auxiliary Bishop of Chicago in 1901, and seven years later became the Ordinary of Rockford. Rumored by many newspapers as a possible successor to Archbishop Patrick W. Riordan in 1914, Muldoon later refused an appointment to Monterey–Los Angeles and died at Rockford in 1927. Thomas O'Shea was the first San Franciscan "imposed upon" by the Holy See. O'Shea was twenty–three years old at the time of his ordination as a Marist Father in 1893. He became Coadjutor Archbishop of Wellington in 1913 and succeeded to that See in 1935.

The distinction of being the first Californian to become a bishop within the state belongs to Robert J. Armstrong, also a native of the Bay City. Consecrated as Ordinary of Sacramento on March 12, 1929, the highly esteemed prelate commandeered the destinies of the Church on the Gold Dust Trails for almost three decades. Pasadena claims Thomas K. Gorman. Ordained in 1917 at the age of twenty–five, the articulate editor of *The Tidings* was consecrated Bishop of Reno, July 22, 1931. He was sent as coadjutor to the Diocese of Dallas–Fort Worth in 1952, and became its chief shepherd two years later. An earlier tie with the Lone Star State developed in 1934 when Los Angeles–born Robert E. Lucey was named Bishop of Amarillo. In 1941 he moved up to San Antonio, the second Californian to occupy a metropolitan province.

Born at the end of the century, Thomas A. Connolly was consecrated Auxiliary Bishop of his native San Francisco on August 24, 1939. After a decade of service there, he was named Coadjutor of Seattle in 1948. A year after his succession in 1951, he became a metropolitan when the new Province of Seattle was created. The youngest man named to the purple from California was William Charles Quinn, C.M. Born at Savannah, Quinn was consecrated Vicar Apostolic of Yukiang, China on October 3, 1940. Imprisoned by the communists and later exiled to the United States, Bishop Quinn taught for some years at Saint Thomas Seminary in Denver. He died on Formosa, March 12, 1960.

Archbishop Joseph T. McGucken claims Los Angeles as his birthplace. Born on March 13, 1902, he studied for the priesthood in Rome and was ordained in the Eternal City in 1928. He served as Auxiliary of Los Angeles, Apostolic Administrator of Monterey–Fresno, Coadjutor and later Ordinary of Sacramento, and finally, Archbishop of San Francisco.

Honolulu's Bishop James J. Sweeney was born in San Francisco on June 19, 1898, ordained June 20, 1925, and consecrated July 25, 1941. No California diocese had ever been given for its chief shepherd a man born within its own territorial confines, although it might be mentioned that at the time of Hugh A. Donohoe's birth

in the Bay City in 1905, the future See of Stockton was still part of the larger Archdiocese of San Francisco.

Two other San Franciscans were elevated to the bishopric within as many years: James T. O'Dowd on June 29, 1948, and Merlin J. Guilfoyle on September 21, 1950. The next Californian to wear the mitre was Harry A. Clinch. Born at San Rafael in 1908, he was consecrated Auxiliary Bishop of Monterey–Fresno on February 27, 1957. Thomas Collins was born in San Francisco on January 13, 1915. A member of Maryknoll, he was consecrated Titular Bishop of Sufetula and Vicar Apostolic of Pando on March 7, 1961. John J. Ward was named Titular Bishop of Bria; he was consecrated Auxiliary Bishop of Los Angeles on December 12, 1963. Another Californian elected to the episcopate is William Joseph Moran. He was consecrated as Auxiliary to the Military Ordinariate on December 13, 1965.

And so it can be seen that of the state's first sixteen native–born prelates, four were archbishops and twelve bishops. Three were members of religious communities, thirteen belonged to the secular clergy. Nine were born in San Francisco, four in Los Angeles, and another three in other parts of the Golden State. The average age at the time of consecration was forty–one, and the average number of years ordained at time of consecration was fifteen.

CONFERRAL OF A CROZIER

The crozier has been among the principal insignia associated with the episcopal office since the fifth century. Though usually made of a metallic substance, plated with gold or silver, the shepherd's "stick" is occasionally fashioned from wood in elaborately carved designs.

Symbolic of the Good Shepherd and indicative of temporal power and spiritual jurisdiction, the crozier is one of the ecclesiastical ornaments conferred on bishops at their episcopal ordination. As the principal consecrator hands it to the new prelate, he says:

> Take the staff as a sign of the shepherd's office, and watch over all the flock to which the Holy Spirit has assigned you as bishop to govern the Church of God.

At his episcopal ordination to the titular See of Blera, Bishop–elect William R. Johnson was presented with the historic crozier used by the Right Reverend Thaddeus Amat during the quarter century that prelate watched over the spiritual destinies of the People of God in the Diocese of Monterey–Los Angeles.

The brightly–polished, four–part silver pastoral staff, permanently displayed in the Historical Museum of the Chancery Archives, Archdiocese of Los Angeles, was "rolled" during the early 1850s, at Barcelona, Spain. The threads connecting the joints of the crozier were added by Bishop Thomas J. Conaty, who used the staff frequently during his episcopal tenure in Southern California.

As a symbol of authority and jurisdiction, the conferral of the crozier spells out the bishop's obligation "to correct vices, stimulate piety, administer punishments and thus to rule and govern with a gentleness tempered with severity."

Probably no discourse on the symbolism of the apostolic sceptre surpasses the crude eloquence of an early missionary who thus lectured his newly–installed ordinary:

> Now this crozier is a symbol of episcopal power and lordship; and, consequently, of the obedience we owe you, and which we solemnly pledge ourselves here and now to observe. But it also has lessons for Your Lordship.
>
> In the first place, though the crozier has a hook on top, to catch hold of the sheep that stray from the flock, it is while in your hands a straight pole. That means, if you will let me say it, that a bishop's ways with his people are to be straight–forward. The pole with its crook means to you that you have the sacred obligation of correcting and attracting, while letting the law rule.

The priest then went on to explain some of the difficulties which the shepherd in a missionary district has to meet, problems which he obviously knew much more intimately than did his recently–arrived ordinary. He concluded his observations by saying:

> Now, Bishop, don't hesitate to use the lower end of the crozier, which is intended to chastise those of your flock who disobey and need correction.

As if to emphasize this last obligation, the venerable priest pointed out that the lower end of the crozier had a sharp point and "that is to poke you in the ribs, to remind you of your duty."

PARALLEL PATTERNS: JAMES FRANCIS CARDINAL McINTYRE

FRANCISCO GARCIA DIEGO Y MORENO, our first Ordinary, nominated to the episcopate in 1840, considered the most important accomplishment of his tenure the erection of a seminary on land adjacent to Mission Santa Ines.

JAMES FRANCIS CARDINAL McINTYRE, the eighth Ordinary, nominated to the episcopte in 1940, considered a most important accomplishment of his tenure the erection of a seminary on land adjacent to Mission San Fernando.

JOSE SADOC ALEMANY Y CONILL, our second Ordinary, was a highly respected and outspoken metropolitan archbishop at the First Council of the Vatican.

JAMES FRANCIS CARDINAL McINTYRE, the eighth Ordinary, was a highly respected and outspoken metropolitan archbishop at the Second Council of the Vatican.

TADEO AMAT Y BRUSI, our third Ordinary, a recognized authority on collegial infallibility, had never set foot on California soil before his arrival as residential bishop.

JAMES FRANCIS CARDINAL McINTYRE, the eighth Ordinary, a recognized authority on papal infallibility, had never set foot on California soil before his arrival as residential bishop.

FRANCISCO MORA Y BORRELL, our fourth Ordinary, ordained at Santa Barbara on March 19th lost his mother at the age of ten and was raised by an aunt.

JAMES FRANCIS CARDINAL McINTYRE, the eighth Ordinary, installed at Los Angeles on March 19th, lost his mother at the age of ten and was raised by an aunt.

GEORGE THOMAS MONTGOMERY, our fifth Ordinary, first native American to govern the diocese, functioned for some years as a coadjutor archbishop but never succeeded the residential prelate.

JAMES FRANCIS CARDINAL McINTYRE, the eighth Ordinary, first papal prince to govern the diocese, functioned for some years as a coadjutor archbishop but never succeeded the residential prelate.

THOMAS JAMES CONATY, our sixth Ordinary, fifty-four years old at the time of his episcopal appointment, was known for his championship of Catholic education through his position as Rector of The Catholic University of America.

JAMES FRANCIS CARDINAL McINTYRE, the eighth Ordinary, fifty-four years old at the time of his episcopal appointment, is known for his championship of Catholic education through his erection of 206 schools.

JOHN JOSEPH CANTWELL, our seventh Ordinary, named archbishop in 1936 was Vicar General of a large archdiocese before coming to Los Angeles.

JAMES FRANCIS CARDINAL McINTYRE, the eighth Ordinary, named domestic prelate in 1936, was Vicar General of a large archdiocese before coming to Los Angeles.

PARALLEL PATTERNS: JOSEPH T. McGUCKEN

In the first 108 years of its existence (1853–1961), the Archdiocese of San Francisco had only four archbishops, each of whom, in his own way, left an indelible stamp on California's Catholic Heritage. To compare the fifth ordinary with his predecessors serves only to affirm Newman's dictum that "every event of this world is a type of those that follow, history proceeding forward as a circle ever enlarging."

JOSEPH SADOC ALEMANY, Spanish-born first Archbishop of San Francisco, spoke fluent English. He represented the Bay City at the First Vatican Council. At one time he exercised ecclesiastical jurisdiction over all of present-day California.

JOSEPH THOMAS McGUCKEN, American-born fifth Archbishop of San Francisco, spoke fluent Spanish. He represented the Bay, City at the Second Vatican Council. At various times he exercised ecclesiastical jurisdiction in all of present day California.

PATRICK WILLIAM RIORDAN, San Francisco's second ordinary, took his theological studies at the American College (Louvain). He was present at the opening of St. Mary's Cathedral in 1887.

JOSEPH THOMAS McGUCKEN, San Francisco's fifth ordinary, took his theological studies at the American College (Rome). He was present at the closing of St. Mary's Cathedral in 1962.

EDWARD JOSEPH HANNA, the Bay City's third residential archbishop, ordained by the Viceregent of Rome in 1885, had episcopal lineal descent from Raphael Cardinal Merry del Val. He served for some years as an auxiliary bishop before becoming metropolitan of San Francisco.

JOHN JOSEPH MITTY, fourth Archbishop of the City by the Golden Gate, received a doctorate from Rome's Major Pontifical Seminary. He served as Suffragan Bishop of Salt Lake before his promotion to the metropolitan see of San Francisco.

JOSEPH THOMAS MCGUCKEN, the Bay City's fifth residential archbishop, ordained by the Viceregent of Rome in 1928, had episcopal lineal descent from Raphael Cardinal Merry del Val. He served for some years as an auxiliary bishop before becoming metropolitan of San Francisco.

JOSEPH THOMAS MCGUCKEN, fifth Archbishop of the City by the Golden Gate, received a doctorate from Rome's Urban College of Propaganda Fide. He served as Suffragan Bishop of Sacramento before his promotion to the metropolitan seat of San Francisco in 1962.

PARALLEL PATTERNS — TIMOTHY CARDINAL MANNING

In the first 135 years of its curial existence (1840–1975), the Church in Southern California had eight Ordinaries, each of whom left an memorable imprint on the area's Catholic heritage. Timothy Cardinal Manning's incumbency had much in common with his hierarchical forebears.

FRANCISCO GARCIA DIEGO, the proto Bishop for the Diocese of Both Californias, was the oldest priest ever named to serve in the episcopacy for the Golden State.

JOSEPH SADOC ALEMANY, the first Metropolitan for the People of God in California, was

CARDINAL TIMOTHY MANNING, the ninth Ordinary for the Archdiocese of Los Angeles, was the youngest priest ever named to serve in the episcopacy for the Golden State.

CARDINAL TIMOTHY MANNING, the ninth Metropolitan for the People of God in Southern

thirty-six years old when advanced to the episcopate. He participated at Vatican Council I.

THADDEUS AMAT, the third Pastor for the Church in California's southland, prepared for the ministry by studying in Rome. He was named bishop by Pope Pius IX and moved to Los Angeles in 1859.

FRANCIS MORA, the fourth residential bishop for Southern California, served as coadjutor under his predecessor and lived, during his incumbency, at Saint Vibiana's Cathedral.

GEORGE MONTGOMERY, the fifth Ordinary for the Los Angeles jurisdiction, served as an Ordinary outside his original See before returning as Coadjutor Archbishop.

THOMAS JAMES CONATY, the sixth Chief Shepherd, was born in Eire and served as a titular Bishop and Rector of The Catholic University of America before becoming residential Ordinary of Los Angeles.

JOHN JOSEPH CANTWELL, the seventh Ordinary, served as Vicar General for San Francisco before becoming Archbishop of Los Angeles.

JAMES FRANCIS MCINTYRE, the eighth Ordinary, was named to the titular archiepiscopal See of Paltus as reported by the New York *Times*, on March 11, 1946.

California, was thirty-six years old when advanced to the episcopate. He attended Vatican Council II.

CARDINAL TIMOTHY MANNING, the ninth Pastor for the Church in California's southland, prepared for the ministry by studying in Rome. He was named Bishop by Pope Pius XII and returned to Los Angeles, in 1969.

CARDINAL TIMOTHY MANNING, the ninth residential bishop for Los Angeles, served as coadjutor under his predecessor and lived during his incumbency, at Saint Vibiana's Cathedral.

CARDINAL TIMOTHY MANNING, the ninth Archbishop for the Los Angeles jurisdiction, served as an Ordinary outside his original See before returning as Coadjutor Archbishop.

CARDINAL TIMOTHY MANNING, the ninth Chief Shepherd, was born in Eire and served as a titular Bishop and trustee for The Catholic University of America before becoming residential Ordinary of Los Angeles.

CARDINAL TIMOTHY MANNING, the ninth incumbent, served as Vicar General for Los Angeles, before becoming Archbishop of Los Angeles.

CARDINAL TIMOTHY MANNING, the ninth Ordinary, was named to the titular piscopal See of Lesvi as reported by the New York *Times*, on March 11, 1946.

II. Hierarchy
2. Individual Bishops

✛RICHARD ACKERMAN (1903–1992)

Through his involvement in the missionary apostolate, Richard Ackerman endeavored to impress upon Catholics that no baptized person is completely excluded from the task of preaching. It is binding on all men and women, children and adults, each in his proper manner, each according to the conditions of his life, each within the framework of the Church.

Richard was born at Pittsburgh, on August 30, 1903, the son of John and Josephine (Richard) Ackerman. He studied at Duquesne University prior to beginning his studies for the priesthood at the Holy Ghost Novitiate, in Connecticut. Richard took final vows with the Holy Ghost Fathers on April 18, 1926. He was ordained to the priesthood on August 28, 1926, at Norwalk, Connecticut. He subsequently did graduate work at the University of Fribourg and the State University, Ann Arbor, Michigan.

Father Ackerman's earliest years in the ministry were engaged in teaching philosophy at Saint Mary's Seminary, Norwalk. He was appointed Assistant National Director for the Holy Childhood in 1929. Ackerman later held field pastoral assignments at Saint Benedict the Moor Parish, Pittsburgh and Saint Mary's Parish, Detroit. In 1940, he returned to Pittsburgh as National Director for the Pontifical Association of the Holy Childhood.

In the next sixteen years, Father Ackerman directed nationwide campaigns aimed at forming in the hearts of Catholic youth a desire to participate in the missionary apostolate of the Church at home and abroad. Ackerman's long incumbency with the Holy Childhood gave spiritual rebirth to many thousands of infants in the Orient and elsewhere. That he did by awakening the missionary spirit among the Catholic youngsters of the United States.

Pope Pius XII named Father Ackerman to the titular See of Lares and Auxiliary Bishop of San Diego on April 6, 1956. On the following May 22, Ackerman became the fifth native of Pittsburgh raised to the fullness of the priesthood. During his years in San Diego, Bishop Ackerman served as Pastor of Holy Trinity Parish, El Cajon, from 1956 to 1957, and diocesan Vicar General from 1956 to 1960. On April 6, 1960, the prelate was transferred to Kentucky as the seventh Bishop of Covington, a 17,286 square mile jurisdiction comprising some 100,000 Catholics.

At the parochial, diocesan and national levels, Richard Ackerman has embodied the contention of a contemporary theologian that "Christ did not entrust His Gospel to the Church to have her jealously guard it underground or preserve it in the secrecy of archives."

The bishop retired in 1978 and succumbed on November 18, 1992.

✛JOSEPH SADOC ALEMANY (1814–1888)

A. MEXICAN SOJOURN—1852

After attending the First Plenary Council of Baltimore, in the spring of 1852, Bishop Joseph Sadoc Alemany journeyed to Mexico City, where he hoped to bring about a favorable settlement of the long–contested legal case regarding the Pious Fund of the Californias.

Through the courtesy of Francis P. Clark of the University of Notre Dame, the Chancery Archives for the Archdiocese of Los Angeles acquired a copy of the *New York Freeman's Journal and Catholic Register* for January 22, 1853, in which the prelate records his personal impressions of the Church in Mexico.

Writing from San Francisco, on November 10, 1852, the bishop noted that "unhappily for the cause of truth, prejudice, national, political, and religious, as the case may be," some travelers were wont to give accounts which misrepresent the countries in which they sojourn. Having found Mexico "considerably misrepresented," he had decided to record his observations for the Catholic populace of the United States.

At Acapulco, Alemany could not help noticing and admiring "the disinterested charity of the people of that place. It was shortly after the wreck of the ill–fated steamer *North America*, which occurred a short distance below that city, and by which some hundreds were subjected to great hardships both by sickness and want. Over and above what the inhabitants of the place had done to alleviate the distress of the sufferers, I found the pastor of the place had converted his own house into a hospital for all indiscriminately—and himself supporting them, and attending to all their wants personally, with untiring patience day and night."

About the Mexican clergy, Alemany said he was "happy to be able to bear testimony" that they were as a whole pious, deeply learned and industrious. He was especially impressed by the Archbishop of Mexico City, whom he considered to be "a model for holy apostolic prelates." Alemany said that he was "a man of most profound learning, untiring industry, and most disinterested charity. He rises at half–past two o'clock every morning—goes through his private devotions, prayers, meditations, and then offers up the Holy Sacrifice, and gives his whole time thenceforward, not to indolence or recreation, but to the multiplicity of business which the duties of his immense archdiocese impose upon him."

"The people of Mexico are remarkable for strong faith and devoted attachment to the Holy See. In these respects they compare favorably with what we know of the Irish people. The public and striking proofs of this are seen in the grandeur of their ecclesiastical edifices, and their liberal endowments. Indeed, their Churches for size, style and magnificence, would do credit to the oldest capitals of Europe. Whereas their private dwellings are sufficiently comfortable, with which they are contented, they do not consider anything too costly or too rich for the holy temple of the Great King, and particularly in those things that are more immediately connected with the Holy Sacrament of the altar."

The Bishop of Monterey noted that the Mexican people were "good and pious, and would soon become even more happy and prosperous, but for those few who are so ambitious of gaining power." He said that "it must ever be to the immortal credit of Mexico and the influences and principles that operated in her mission, that whereas in other places the Indians have been ruined, exterminated, there she has raised them to what they are, saved them to Christianity and society."

Alemany felt there was a shortage of bishops in Mexico. "For over nine millions of souls spread over that vast extent of territory, only nine dioceses, and some of those generally long vacant, and owing to the much concern with which Government charges itself about such matters may be so far long enough. A vacancy occurring in the ordinary way may continue for years, but the creation of a new diocese is the work of a generation."

The Spanish–born prelate went on to say that "owing to this the few zealous and worthy Bishops that are, are oppressed with duty, and find it, in consequence, impossible to visit the more distant parts of their districts as often as might be desirable, and hence must ensue to those neglected localities very great spiritual privation." Alemany continued with the prayer that God might "increase the number of the Mexican prelates, and long preserve the faith of that Catholic people."

practice the catholic apostolate precepts of poverty, chastity and obedience."

One especially forceful anecdote told about the Dominican prelate was related in Baltimore's *Catholic Mirror*, for August 21, 1875. It recalled those days when it was "a crime punishable with fine and imprisonment for anyone to wear the religious habit:"

> In 1867, he left California to attend the centenary celebration of the martyrdom of Saints Peter and Paul at Rome. On his way thither he visited his native country, but mindful of the intolerance which in his youth had caused him to fly as an exile to Rome, and contrasting it with the freedom of his adopted country, before crossing the frontiers of Spain he laid aside his episcopal attire and clothed himself again in the habit of his Order.

> The officials were astounded, remonstrated and told him he could not enter or travel in Spain attired in the religious habit. Still concealing his episcopal rank, he drew forth his American passport, and claimed the right of an American citizen to be free from such interference.

> Thus did he silently but effectually protest against such intolerant laws; and his progress through the towns and cities of Spain, attired in the habit of his Order, eloquently proclaimed the contrast between the false liberalism in European countries and the national liberty of these United States of America.

Archbishop Alemany was a "Christian witness" long before the term and the practice became popular. The name of the Dominican prelate is indeed, as the *Catholic Mirror* so eloquently put it, a monument to the "cradle days" of California's faith.

✛JOSEPH SADOC ALEMANY (1814–1888)

B. ALEMANY TRAVELS *INCOMMUNICADO*—1851

The first of California's archbishops was an outstanding person in many ways. A "gentle" man in every respect, he was anything but hesitant about speaking out on issues which he felt hindered or discolored Catholic expression. In mid–1851, for example, he had publicly rebuked Spain and its officialdom for avoiding their missionary responsibilities to the universal apostolate: "Oh, how uncatholic thou wert, when in a raving fit of impiety, thou didst exclaustrate those holy cloisters! How uncatholic that hour in which thou didst refuse admission into thy dominions of the noble catholic work of the Propagation of the Faith for fear that thy own poor should suffer from it!"

At that time, Alemany called on his homeland to "blot out those black stains from thy history! Efface them from the pages of history for they give lie to thy name of Catholic. Let the world know that thou art no longer ashamed to admit into thy precincts men who

✛JOSEPH SADOC ALEMANY (1814–1888)

C. PASTORAL ON CIVIL WAR—1861

Officially, California was neutral during the Civil War. But the thousands of southerners who had participated in the Gold Rush scramble quite naturally retained their earlier sympathies and openly supported a program of secession.

Union sympathizers, certainly a majority of the state's population, varied considerably in their devotion to the Lincoln government. While there were ardent crusaders for the northern cause, such as the Unitarian Minister, Thomas Starr King, most of the pro–Union group was decidedly lukewarm in its attitude. The leading voice for moderation throughout the difficult years was San Francisco's Archbishop, Joseph Sadoc Alemany. On February 22, 1861, the Dominican prelate issued a pastoral letter asking his flock to avoid any participation in secessionist movements. He viewed such moves in the same light as divorce and duelling, "The sacred bond . . . never to be severed, is ruthlessly violated."

Alemany unhesitatingly denounced the "deadly contest by which men laying claim to Christianity and refined manners, but acting as the red men of the forest, whose mental eye has never yet seen the least glimpse of civilization divest themselves of all sense of duties which they may owe to kindred or to society, and sacrifice, perhaps forever, the honor and welfare of parents, wife or children; while they place themselves in the most imminent danger of sending their soul into endless misery." Noting that "God alone can avert the evils that our sins may have provoked," he pleaded for recourse to the Almighty that "He may grant us the blessings of a true and lasting peace."

Among those overlooking the archbishop's pleas for restraint was Thomas Brady, editor of *The Monitor*. Deploring the apparent blundering of Lincoln's military attempts, Brady publicly voiced the personal view (*The Monitor* at that time was privately owned) that Lincoln was seeking to overthrow the state's rights and the personal liberties. Brady's opinions were highly unpopular and one complainant, writing under the name "Irish American," making it quite clear in an open letter to the *Daily Evening Bulletin* that "*The Monitor* did not speak for the Catholic Church," urged the archbishop to "define the positions which these journals bear to the Catholic Church."

Alemany responded the following day by releasing a statement to the effect that "as some journals of this state, alleging in their justification the tone and sentiments of certain so–called periodicals and journals, have assailed and misrepresented the principles of the Catholic Church, I deem it my duty to disavow any responsibility for articles and statements without her sanction and approval, and to state that the periodicals and journals alluded to not only have not this sanction, but are not always faithful exponents of the doctrines and wishes of the Catholic Church which in this diocese has no official organ." Happily, *The Monitor's* editor heeded the advice of the archbishop and somewhat moderated his attitudes.

Though Archbishop Alemany very probably had strong personal views on the conflict, he felt that "it is not our province to allude to the causes which may have brought our country . . . to the very eve of so many evils; but our only desire is to request you all to raise up your most fervent prayers to the God of all nations, that he may vouchsafe to grant us peace, harmony and brotherly love."

✝JOSEPH SADOC ALEMANY (1814–1888)

D. Retirement of an Archbishop—1883

Prior to Vatican Council II and its recognition of "the increasing burden of age," there were no provisions for episcopal retirement. In fact, relatively few American prelates petitioned for retirement and even fewer succeeded in putting aside their pastoral staffs. San Francisco's Joseph Sadoc Alemany (1814–1888), California's initial archbishop, was also the first to ask Roman officials for permission to resign—though he won approval only after sixteen years and a mountain of correspondence.

The Dominican prelate made overtures, as early as 1868, about the appointment of a coadjutor archbishop, whose presence in San Francisco would allow his own resignation. That suggestion was blocked, however, "by the expressed opinion of some of the American bishops that he should remain at the helm for some time more."

Alemany renewed his attempts to have a coadjutor named for San Francisco in 1876. The archbishop's biographer hints that a paramount reason for Rome's unfavorable reaction to the petition was his success in managing the finances of his growing archdiocese. The Spanish–born prelate's desire to step down were apparently widely known. An article in the Portland *Catholic Sentinel*, August 29, 1878, stated that everyone "knows that the Most Reverend Archbishop has been for many years seeking to retire from the active management of this vast and rapidly growing field of missionary enterprise."

The long and involved negotiations for an episcopal collaborator reached a happy conclusion, on June 18, 1883, with the appointment of Father Patrick W. Riordan as Coadjutor Archbishop of San Francisco. As soon as Riordan had been safely ensconced in the Bay City, Alemany again bombarded Rome to "let me resign and retire to some convent of my order." Giovanni Cardinal Simeoni thought such a move was "inopportune," but promised that "the time is not far off when you will be able to lay down the burdens of the rule."

Finally, on July 10, 1884, the archbishop asked the pope directly "to free me from the episcopal office which I have tried to fulfill for thirty–four years." On the following February 4, *The Monitor* announced that Pope Leo XIII had "acceded to his request." And so it came about that Joseph Sadoc Alemany anticipated the practice of a future generation by resigning from "the episcopal office which he had accepted only under obedience."

His departure was not without regret by the people for and among whom he had labored for so many years. A Congregational newspaper in San Francisco, *The Pacific*, stated that "the Archbishop has well earned all the rewards he has received. He has been efficient and laborious. In particular, he has administered the finances of his charge, as well as his own, with diligence, economy and safety. Modest in deportment and small in person, he has been always at his post and done the work of a giant. We hope he may live long and enjoy a green old age, amid the scenes of his earliest memories. . . ."

✝JOSEPH SADOC ALEMANY (1814–1888)

E. A VISIT TO VALENCIA—1887

When the Most Reverend Joseph Sadoc Alemany retired from the Archbishopric of San Francisco, he returned to his native Spain, where he spent the final three years of his life. Father Alexander De Campos (d. 1905) visited the Dominican prelate and wrote the following account of that encounter which appeared in the *New York Freemans' Journal and Catholic Register*, for September 10, 1887.

> I had long made up my mind to pay a visit to the venerable Archbishop J. S. Alemany, O.P. Not knowing where to find him, I crossed once more the Spanish frontier, and at Gerona I inquired about the great benefactor of California Catholics. There I was told that very likely the dear and beloved prelate was to be found at Barcelona.
>
> Southwards I went and inquired at the Cathedral, longing to hear news from His Grace. There the canons could not give me any information, but thought a priest living a quarter of a mile, the confessor of some Dominican Sisters, could tell me all I wanted to know about the dear archbishop's new abode.
>
> After examining the cathedral and episcopal palace, I took the direction given, where it was my good fortune to find the priest who gave me all the information I wanted. Without loss of time I took the train to Valencia, where I arrived the next morning.
>
> At once I inquired my way towards Maldronado street, and after leaving the depot, turned to the left, crossed a few narrow and long streets, and at last knocked at a second floor door of a modest, simple and quiet narrow house, No. 46.
>
> A sickly–looking priest, wearing the well–known habit of St. Dominic, opened the door, and I saw at once I could not be understood by him in Spanish, for the holy priest was French. So I spoke in French, and learned that our dear Archbishop was in the church of Our Lady of the Pilar, near by, saying Mass.
>
> There I went, and in a short time His Grace got through and I followed him to the vestry, where he could not believe his eyes on seeing me so unexpectedly. He expressed his surprise and joy to see in that far land one he was so well acquainted with in San Francisco.
>
> As for myself I could not express fully my feelings of joy on beholding once more the well–known features of the pioneer of Catholics in California. The good Archbishop felt glad indeed and he told me afterwards I was the first one who went to see him as a visitor from a land he cannot forget. Again, as we were talking in Eng-

lish, I noticed a peculiar pleasure in His Grace who stated he had not spoken it since he left America.

> I had the pleasure to walk through Valencia with His Grace as a companion, for there a bishop could not think of going out doors without another priest to escort him, and this usage seemed to grieve Archbishop Alemany, for he complained of it as an attack upon the freedom and the liberty he was used to here in California.
>
> There, in the city of the Virgin, the aged prelate is respected and loved as he was here, and it did me good to witness through the streets, as he passed along, the people, old and young coming out doors, to kneel down, join their hands and implore the archbishop's blessing.
>
> They know His Grace there by the name of 'Bishop of California.' I noticed that he had not grown any older and keeps up his kind and gentle manners we admired here so much during all those long years that he presided over the archdiocese of San Francisco.
>
> With him I went to the church of Our Lady of the Pilar, and there said Mass on the High Altar of the old Dominican church, a large building with a few side altars ornamented with nicely carved wood, all gilt. His Grace usually says Mass on the altar of the Blessed Virgin, a nice chapel, the first on the left side entering the main door of the building, and beautifully adorned by the Valencian people, who profess special devotion for the *Nuestra Señora*. His Grace is trying to build up a convent there, where of old the Dominicans had so many.
>
> I parted with the good archbishop after receiving his blessing, and his regards and good wishes to all in California.

✝JOSEPH SADOC ALEMANY (1814–1888)

F. IN THE IMAGE OF CHRIST—1904

Though much has been written over the years about San Francisco's first Archbishop, Joseph Sadoc Alemany, seldom has the sterling personality of the Dominican prelate emerged in proper relief. That Alemany was highly respected by those who knew him best is obvious from an observation of the Irish historian, Hugh Quigley, who noted that "there is not perhaps, in the Church, a bishop, save 'John of Tuam,' more generally beloved by his priests than the Archbishop of San Francisco." Possibly the most penetrating portrayal of California's first metropolitan was contained within a larger historical treatise appearing in the San Francisco *Monitor*, for January 23, 1904:

> Archbishop Alemany, whose personality served to inspire both priests and people to their best efforts was a character not often met in life. He had the pride not only of the Spaniard but of the Catalonian. But coupled with the spirit of the *caballero* was the humility of the saint. He was considered one of the finest horsemen of early

Mass offered at Vich for exhumation of Archbishop Joseph S. Alemany

California. He was a king in the saddle, and only the breaking of his leg on one occasion led him to give up his favorite mode of travel.

Always small, he was ever erect even in his latest day, and age never seemed to take away the briskness of his step. With his hands tucked in his sleeves, in a fashion of his own, he was a familiar sight as, pensively unmindful of anything but his thoughts, he walked with the step of a cadet through the crowded thoroughfares.

Then, too, at the old Cathedral when he would enter his confessional, the children would line up on either side, in order that they might individually get that kind word he knew so well how to give.

He followed a beautiful old custom still observed in Spanish countries. On Holy Thursday afternoon with towel and basin he used to wash the feet of twelve altar boys, in imitation of the Savior's action at the Last Supper. This would take place in a space set apart in the middle aisle of the old cathedral and the edifice was always crowded.

His visitation of the distant parts of the diocese was always looked forward to with joy by the congregation, for the spirit of love seemed to exude from him.

One unconsciously wonders if this biographical pen–sketch is not precisely what Giovanni Cardinal Montini had in mind when he traced a good bishop's influence to its source—"the image of the Father and the image of Christ."

✛JOSEPH SADOC ALEMANY (1814–1888)

G. RETURN OF THE ARCHBISHOP—1964

The return of Archbishop Joseph Sadoc Alemany's body to San Francisco was the culmination of over two years' negotiations with the Spanish Government and the realization of efforts begun over forty years ago. California's first archbishop died at Valencia, Spain, on April 14, 1888, and was buried four days later in a vault beneath the Blessed Sacrament Chapel of the *Iglesia de Santo Domingo* in Vich. The first concerted attempt to remove Alemany's remains back to San Francisco seems to have taken place in the spring of 1921, when a formal petition was submitted to the cathedral chapter of Vich by Archbishop Edward J. Hanna. Apparently the proposal was given some attention, but the response was unfavorable, since "after consulting with our chapter, the Alamany family and others, we find ourselves unanimously opposed to transfering the archbishop from the humble city where he is interred."

Thirteen years later, another attempt was initiated by the Very, Reverend James B. Connolly, Dominican Provincial of Holy Name Province, to have Alemany re–interred beneath the Chapel of the new College of Saint Albert the Great at the Dominican House of Studies in Oakland. This second set of negotiations was thwarted by the Spanish Civil War, and by the time hostilities were over, there was such confusion about the actual site of the tomb that the matter was indefinitely postponed. The grave was later rediscovered and authenticated by Antonio Alamany but the grand nephew of the archbishop expressed his family's wishes that their illustrious ancestor not be moved to California.

A third overture was made by Jaime Ensenat who was anxious that an exposition be staged in San Francisco of "the many souvenirs and personal objects of the archbishop" but this time there was intervention by the Bishop of Vich "because of the rather faint possibility of a process for the Congregation of Rites."

There the matter rested until the summer of 1962 when this writer visited Barcelona seeking archival data on the ecclesiastical history of Southern California. At that time, the question of the removal was again brought up. Antonio Alamany still remembered quite vividly his grand uncle's funeral in 1888, and was extremely receptive to our suggestions. Both Antonio and his son, attended the Mass celebrated at Sarria when Bishop Francisco Mora y Borrell was disinterred; both were eventually won over to the logic of bringing the archbishop back to his California jurisdiction. At long last, it seemed as if the state's first metropolitan would return.

The matter was subsequently brought to the attention of Archbishop Joseph T. McGucken of San Francisco and the Bay City's prelate wholeheartedly endorsed the plan and appointed this writer his agent for the removal. Because of the delicate relationship existing between the Church and State in Spain, the negotiations dragged on for over two years until late November of 1964, when formal approval was obtained from the *Ayuntamiento de Vich* and the Most Reverend Ramon Masnou Boixeda, Bishop of Vich.

With the return of Alemany's body to San Francisco, after an absence of eighty years, the Golden State once again had within its confines the earthly remains of all its episcopal prelates, those giants who reared the superstructure of California's Catholic Heritage.

✝JOSEPH SADOC ALEMANY (1814–1888)

H. TRIBUTE TO A FOREBEAR—1975

The visit to California of Archbishop Joseph Sadoc Alemany's great grand nephew in 1975, afforded an ideal opportunity for recalling the spiritual legacy of that noble Dominican prelate. Jose Alamany (the spelling altered in accord with modern Catalan usage), his wife and son had journeyed to the West Coast from their ancestral home at Vich, Spain, to see those places associated with their distinguished forebear.

It was just ten years previously that the Alamany family consented to and participated in the complicated negotiations which resulted in returning the arch-

bishop's remains to San Francisco. Jose's father, Antonio (d. 1969), who was present for Archbishop Alemany's funeral at Vich, in 1888, lived on to personally supervise the disinterment of the Dominican prelate, seventy–seven years later!

The "heart and affection" that California's first archbishop left in San Francisco was once again united to his earthly remains on February 6, 1965. Spain's ambassador, California's governor and San Francisco's mayor came in tribute of the humble Iberian friar. Then, after a public observance to honor one who was an architect of its greatness, the Catholics of the "city" hurriedly moved ahead, ever anxious to achieve the destiny envisioned by Alemany and other pioneers.

And then, after the passage of another decade, Jose Alamany and his family came to retrace the archbishop's steps along *El Camino Real*. They visited his tomb, prayed in his two cathedrals and greeted his Dominican communities. They toured a library, traveled over a highway and walked through a school named in his memory. They saw the documents he wrote, the books he read and the missions he restored. They talked with his successors at Monterey, San Francisco and Los Angeles, a bishop, an archbishop and a cardinal.

The Alamanys returned to Catalonia, surely impressed with the esteem their ancestor occupied in the historical montage of the Far West. Truly he was one "whose personality served to inspire both priests and people to their best efforts."

While others were drawn to Gold–Rush California by the glittering nuggets, Joseph Sadoc Alemany came to carry the cross. That he bore it well is amply attested by the historical annals.

✝JOSEPH SADOC ALEMANY (1814–1888)

I. MEMORIES OF AN HISTORICAL DAY

On February 6, 1965, "the heart and affection that California's first archbishop, Joseph Sadoc Alemany, left in San Francisco were once again united to his earthly remains. The gentle Dominican friar had returned to his people, eight long decades after a tearful departure in 1885.

A truly historical atmosphere marked the occasion. The mitre placed on Alemany's head at the time of his consecration in Rome, on June 30, 1850, rested atop the prelate's African mahogany casket, as if to signify the uninterrupted succession of episcopal jurisdiction in the universal Church. No less significant was the decision to hold the funeral obsequies in old Saint Mary's Church, which Alemany himself built and personally dedicated to Our Lady on Christmas Day in 1854. During the twenty–four hours that the archbishop's remains lay in state, the little brick church once again became Saint Mary's Cathedral, the proud Mother–Church of the Archdiocese of San Francisco.

The ceremonies had special meaning to three men attending the Mass. For Charles Kendrick, 88 year old San Francisco industrialist, it marked the return of the "frail and faltering" prelate who confirmed him in that very church in 1884. By their presence, two other men, the Right Reverend Harold Collins, Vicar Forane for San Francisco, and Harry Downie, restorer of California's missions, won the distinction of having attended funeral services for all of the Bay City's metropolitans, a remarkable fact when one recalls that prior to 1961, 108 years of episcopal tenure were shared by San Francisco's four archbishops.

There were no false eulogies during the observances, for, as Father John B. McGloin pointed out in his splendid sermon, "Alemany would never have approved of idle boasting." What was said by Archbishop Joseph T. McGucken and Marqués Merry del Val is part of the record. If the Church and State of California is proud of its pioneer prelate, it is a pride based on solid accomplishments. Every aspect of the Bay City's tribute to Alemany was eminently fitting. The seminary choir, the multi–phased representation of religious and secular clergy, the trek along Alemany Boulevard, the participation of San Francisco's civic officials, the presence of the consular corps and the colorful array of Papal Knights and Knights of Columbus all contributed to an occasion unique in California annals.

Archbishop Alemany's successors were well represented at the Mass. Of the seventeen prelates attached to the area formerly designated as the Diocese of Monterey, six bishops journeyed to San Francisco to pay their respects to the modern–day "founder" of California Catholicism. On the very day of the funeral services in San Francisco, fortuitous coincidence saw the issuance, by the California Historical Society, of a translation of Archbishop Alemany's long–lost diary, unearthed in the family's Barcelona residence in the fall of 1962.

A most appropriate conclusion to the two–day observance was an expression of gratitude, in Alemany's native language, by the then Archbishop of San Francisco to the Spanish Ambassador. Fittingly enough, although Archbishop McGucken was the first native Californian to occupy the See of San Francisco, he was also the only one of Alemany's successors to speak the Spanish language—and he did so with a grace that obviously pleased Marques Merry del Val.

The curtain then descended on the final chapter in the life of Joseph Sadoc Alemany.

✦THADDEUS AMAT (1811–1878)

A. Bishop Amat—Practitioner Of Virtues

Poverty is one of the virtues that glistens most prominently in the life of Thaddeus Amat, the long–time (1853–1878) Bishop of Monterey–Los Angeles. As a youth, the Vincentian prelate was ill–fed, poorly–clothed and inadequately housed. Very likely, he didn't know it!

Few families in Catalonia, a hundred and fifty years ago, were well–provided for, at least if civilization be measured by the number of indoor toilets, automobiles, radios and television sets adorning one's life–style.

Young Amat ate the scanty rations of the time; side–meat and greens in the spring, side–meat and beans in winter. He probably never heard of *filet mignon* or *crêpes suzette* and he wouldn't have known what to do with a finger bowl. He was ill–fed, but didn't know it!

He wore the home–spun clothes of the country. His trousers bagged at the knees and sagged in the seat; his coat fit nowhere but at the shoulders. He wore a suit as long as it would hold together and then, with the assistance of a few patches, wore it on until its eventual dissolution. He was poorly–clothed, but didn't know it!

Thaddeus Amat knew the rigors of a winter in Northern Spain. The house didn't properly keep out the snow and icy winds. He read by the light of a blazing log and wrote with a stick of charcoal. He slept in an attic room where the wind howled through chinks in the walls and snow filtered in upon his patched and tattered coverlet. He was inadequately–housed, but didn't know it!

Times have changed in Spain—as well they should have. But along with that, the atmosphere has become cluttered with all matter of sludge. The difference between the poor of Amat's time and those of today is not so much gauged by the material as by the spiritual. In former times, the poor didn't know or even suspect they were inferior to anyone. Thaddeus Amat lived in an era when religion "informed" the lives of the rich and poor alike. To his family, Christ provided all the wealth they ever wanted or could acquire.

In today's luxury–based civilization, Christians must once again endeavor to cultivate that sublime indifference to poverty and wealth that animated the Peoples of God in earlier times. This writer suspects that would be the theme of his sermon if Bishop Thaddeus Amat were once again to mount the pulpit, in the now abandoned Cathedral of Saint Vibiana, which he built.

Just imagine, Amat and the people of his time were born and reared in a society which saw them ill–fed, poorly–clothed and inadequately housed—and they didn't even know it!

✛THADDEUS AMAT (1811–1878)

B. Two "Reluctant Prelates"—1852

Thaddeus Amat, the Vincentian Bishop of Monterey–Los Angeles (1854–1878) had the good fortune of knowing personally John Nepomucene Neumann, C.Ss.R., who was beatified by the Holy Father on October 13, 1963. Their relationship dated back to 1852 when America's first professed Redemptorist succeeded Francis Patrick Kenrick as Bishop of Philadelphia. Father Amat had already served for some years under Kenrick as rector of Saint Charles Seminary and was retained in that position by the new Ordinary.

The kindly bishop–elect requested Amat to come to Baltimore for his consecration and to participate in the solemn ceremonies which took place in the nation's premier see on March 28, 1852. At the conclusion of the events, it was Father Amat's privilege to escort the new bishop back to Philadelphia, where the townspeople had arranged for an enthusiastic welcome for their new shepherd. Not infrequently during the ensuing months, Amat accompanied the tireless prelate on his visitations around the huge diocese, preaching, confirming and hearing confessions. Their journeys were on horseback, canal boat, railroad and afoot.

Neumann learned to rely heavily on Amat, and when the First Plenary Council of Baltimore convened in May of 1852, he followed his predecessor's example in asking Amat to go along as his private theologian. Here it was that the young Vincentian was proposed as a possible successor to Bishop Joseph Sadoc Alemany of the Diocese of Monterey in California. It would have taken a far less perceptive man than John Neumann to realize that his seminary rector would eventually be "promoted out" of Philadelphia; nevertheless, he actively interceded on behalf of Father Amat in the latter's desperate pleas to evade the appointment—but to no avail!

There is no documentation of any dealings between the two prelates after 1854, although we do know that Amat visited Neumann on his way to California the next year. The premature death of Bishop Neumann on January 5, 1860, was noted by Amat as a "loss for America, a gain for heaven."

The two bishops had much in common. Both were born in 1811, and their careers paralleled in many ways. Neumann and Amat were Europeans, one from Bavaria, the other from Catalonia. Both later became naturalized American citizens. The religious life attracted both men, one before ordination, the other after. Neither of the two missionaries had any time for leisure. Neumann took up his duties at Philadelphia when it was the largest diocese in America and proceeded to organize the first parochial school system in the United States. His California confrere assumed charge of a diocese where thousands of newly–arrived immigrants "found their misery where they expected to find plenty of gold."

Both Neumann and Amat had been "reluctant prelates," for both men had tearfully begged to be relieved of their episcopal appointments. Pius IX was forced personally to order the two candidates to acquiesce. Just how far the parallel goes we cannot know, for the Church reserves the honors of the altar for a selected few.

✛THADDEUS AMAT (1811–1878)

C. A Giant in the Wilderness—1853

Thaddeus Amat (1811–1878) epitomizes those pioneer prelates whose breadth of experience and depth of perception are reflected today in the flourishing condition of the Catholic Church in California. Named to the bishopric, on July 29, 1853, the Barcelona–born Vincentian was entrusted with the gigantic task of guiding ecclesial activities over the 75,984 square mile area then comprising the Diocese of Monterey.

The problems faced by the prelate are evident from many sources. In a letter of appeal to the missionary colleges of Ireland, for example, written shortly after his arrival in California, Amat pleaded for priests to serve the spiritual needs of the "many thousands of Gold Seekers from every nation, who found misery where they expected to make a fortune." He pointed out that his sixteen priests were unable to care for the 78,000 Indians in the diocese, a third of whom were Catholics. "Living still in a savage state they are deprived of all education, and so poor, that they have hardly clothes to cover them." Nevertheless, Amat noted, "these poor Indians might all be gained to religion, if there were any missionaries to visit them."

The bishop observed that "we have some very striking proofs of the admirable effects which the faith would produce in their hearts. Many of those Indians who are enlightened by the light of the true faith, have undertaken journeys of three hundred, and even six hundred miles, to be able to see the priest before their death, and to receive the last Sacraments."

The notable development of Catholic life under his direction reflects a measure of Amat's administrative competency. The vigor and enthusiastic energy of his younger days, coupled with the resources latent in his strong personality, figured prominently in Amat's successful efforts to bring the missionary diocese out of the near–chaos in which he found it, to that of an efficiently organized ecclesiastical jurisdiction.

The Spanish–born prelate brought to the United States and California an academic background that few ecclesiastics in the young republic of that period could match. Perhaps nowhere are Amat's talents more obvious than in his solicitude for Catholic education. In a pastoral letter, written in 1869, the prelate reminded the faithful of the Diocese of Monterey–Los Angeles of the serious obliga-

Bishop Thaddeus Amat, C.M. A painting by Faustine Adam y Tous, 1873.

tion that parents had to watch over their children and diligently see and assiduously labor to secure for them a thorough Catholic education. Amat's zeal in promoting education spoke for itself. When he arrived, there was but one struggling college; when he died, in 1878, there were two colleges, six academies, nine parochial schools and five orphanages, an impressive total for a diocese that boasted barely 34,000 Catholics.

The charm of Amat's character, his deep but unostentatious piety and outward dignity, would have ennobled human nature in any profession, but they dignified it with a peculiar grace in the person of this Catholic bishop. His quick–tempered disposition in no way diminished Amat's effectiveness among the people of Southern California, who esteemed the prelate's "sweet simplicity and extreme goodness of heart." Thaddeus Amat was looked upon and respected as a plain and humble man, a well–disciplined priest, and a shepherd of deep personal convictions.

✝THADDEUS AMAT (1811–1878)

D. BISHOP KNEW THE SAINTS—1870S

If one were to accept the notion of "sanctity by asso-

ciation," the name of Bishop Thaddeus Amat would long ago have been enrolled on the roster of saints. Amat was a close friend and companion of Bishop John Neumann (canonized in 1977). He served as Neumann's theologian at the First Plenary Council of Baltimore, as well as his rector for Saint Charles Seminary, Philadelphia.

Amat was also a personal acquaintance of Archbishop Anthony Claret (canonized in 1950). The two prelates were collaborators at Vatican Council I and it was Claret's influence that made it possible to bring the Immaculate Heart Sisters from Olot to California in 1871.

During the final years of his preparation for the ministry, young Thaddeus Amat also knew Sister Catherine Laboure (canonized in 1947), the Daughter of Charity to whom Our Lady appeared in 1830.

When Amat arrived as a seminarian at Saint Lazare, the entire city of Paris was agog at what had occurred in the chapel of the Motherhouse for the Daughters a few years earlier.

It all began on the Feast of Saint Vincent de Paul in 1830. Sister Catherine had been summoned from her sleep by a little child who said the Blessed Mother wanted to see her in the chapel. She hurriedly dressed and accompanied the child. In the chapel, Catherine knelt in prayer and at precisely midnight, the Blessed Mother appeared—sitting in the chair of the Father Director. Catherine was told that God had a special mission for her, one that would entail much suffering. She was told that the details would be given later. On November 27th, Our Lady appeared again, this time holding a globe in her hands. Surrounding the virgin were the following letters in gold: "0 Mary conceived without sin, pray for us who have recourse to Thee." Catherine was told to have a medal struck after that model. Those wearing the medal would be assured of great and abundant graces. And so began the story of Our Lady of the Miraculous Medal.

Amat, the youthful Catalan seminarian, was anxious to know more about the apparitions and during his sojourn in Paris, he journeyed twice to the hospice at Enghien, where Sister Catherine Laboure worked with patients, cared for the poultry yard and acted as portress. Shortly after his ordination to the priesthood by the Most Reverend Hyacinthe Louise de Quelen, Archbishop of Paris, Father Amat received that prelate's approval and encouragement to bring the miraculous medals to America.

Early in 1855, while enroute back to the United States, following his episcopal ordination, Bishop Amat visited Enghien and there sought the prayers of Catherine Laboure for his expanded apostolate in California. Though there is no extant correspondence between Sister Catherine Laboure and Bishop Thaddeus Amat, it is known that the Vincentian prelate visited Enghien a final time in August of 1859.

✝THADDEUS AMAT (1811–1878)

E. FINAL CHAPTER FOR SOUTHLAND PRELATE

Perhaps the most significant chapter in the life of the Right Reverend Thaddeus Amat, C.M., Bishop of Monterey–Los Angeles (1854–1878), can only be written a century after his death. This postscript helps to rank his as one of the most remarkable stories in the nation's ecclesial annals.

Late in 1962, Cardinal James Francis McIntyre directed that Amat's remains be removed from their vault beneath Saint Vibiana's Cathedral, and re–interred at Calvary Mausoleum, with other members of the California hierarchy. Upon opening the casket, it was discovered that the features of the prelate were completely intact and easily recognizable. No external evidence of decomposition was present, except for a slight darkening of the facial tissues. Despite the obvious dismay of the witnesses, no public disclosure was made. A thorough investigation was conducted and the available evidence was carefully examined so as to place the phenomenon in its proper perspective.

The deceased bishop had been vested in full pontificals and placed in a specially–designed metallic casket. The mortician took the precaution of placing ice around the outer case for the better preservation of the remains. It appeared that the tomb had remained unopened for the next eighty–four years. The seals were intact.

The cause of death usually has some influence on the rate of decomposition, since the process of *algor mortis* can be accelerated or retarded by the suddenness of expiration. In Amat's case, the actual death was unexpected, for none of the deceased prelate's close friends had any idea that his end was so nearly at hand.

Nonetheless, the bishop had been in such poor health during the six years preceding his demise, that he asked for and received a coadjutor to assist in governing the vast diocese. Amat suffered several minor strokes, as evidenced by the fact that his memory was severely impaired on occasion. Whether the actual cause was heart failure or " generalized debility," as recorded on the health department's certificate, the actual death was "sudden" and that factor likely helped to retard, if only briefly, the process of *algor mortis.*

Experts maintain that clothing, acting as an insulating agent for preventing loss of body heat, can also alter the rapidity of decomposition. However, that explanation offers no help in answering this particular question, since the various vestments placed on Amat's remains were only put there some hours after death, when the process of algor mortis was already well–advanced.

Obesity also affects decomposition rates. Though Bishop Amat was not greatly overweight, contemporary pictures indicate that his poundage exceeded the average for a man of his relatively short stature. Doctor William Jones noted that Amat "was quite corpulent," a description that fits well with Bernard Ullathorne's observation that the bishop was "a little man, with broad shoulders and a broad compact head, like that of the first Napoleon." Obese persons have a tendency to decompose more quickly because of the higher content of bodily moisture and greater heat retention. Amat's body gave no indication of dehydration or mummification. Such a phenomenon occurs only when a body is interred in extremely dry soil, where the temperature remains consistently above or below the level at which bacterial activity takes place.

Inasmuch as it indicates some alteration of the natural laws, bodily incorruption after death has been occasionally looked upon as a supporting, though not a conclusive sign of personal holiness.

When the remains were exhumed for a second time, on May 22, 1996, at Calvary mausoleum, they had deteriorated markedly and gave no reason for any further consideration.

✝THADDEUS AMAT (1811–1878)

F. HISTORY REPEATS ITSELF

It was 1870, and Bishop Amat had journeyed with the two other California prelates to Rome, where he played a pivotal role in the deliberations on papal infallibility. Chroniclers say that no American at the council was more respected, and few were more plain–speaking than the Bishop of Monterey–Los Angeles.

And then, on June 28, 1991, a bright and sunny summer morning, a century and twenty years later, the first native son of that tiny diocese on the rim of Christendom walked into the same Basilica, fully robed as a cardinal "prince" of the Catholic Church. Indeed it was a scene that sent shivers up the spines of the several hundred pilgrims from Los Angeles who had come to witness this historic event. And, amidst a solemn and meaningful pageantry, the memory bank of historians tilted first one way, then another.

The ever–relentless flow of time comes to a standstill in Rome, the city of the Caesars, the city of the popes. Yesterday, today and tomorrow blend into a singular radiance that can only be defined as eternity. Thomas Babington Macauley, a contemporary of Bishop Amat, was neither a Catholic nor a friend of the Church. But he was a realist and once he wrote "there is not, and there never was on this earth, a work of human policy so well deserving of examination as the Roman Catholic Church."

"The history of that Church," he said, "joins together the two great ages of human civilization. No other institution is left standing which carries the mind back to the times when the smoke of sacrifice rose from the Pantheon, and when camels, leopards and tigers bounded in the Flavian Amphitheatre."

He reckoned that "the proudest royal houses are but of yesterday, when compared with the line of the Supreme Pontiffs. That line we trace back in an unbroken series from the pope who crowned Napoleon in the 19th century, to the pope who crowned Pepin in the 8th; and far beyond the time of Pepin the august dynasty extends, till it is lost in the twilight of fable."

Macauley's words echoed between Bernini's Colonnade when Pope John Paul II approached the altar. Though written 100 years earlier, they tell how, "the papacy remains, not in decay, but full of life and useful vigor. The Catholic Church is still sending forth to the farthest ends of the world missionaries as zealous as those who landed on Kent with Augustin.

"The number of her children is greater than in any former age. Her spiritual ascendency extends over the vast countries which lie between the plains of the Missouri and Cape Horn . . . Nor do we see any signs which indicate that the term of her long dominion is approaching. She saw the commencement of all the governments and of all the ecclesiastical establishments that now exist . . . and we feel no assurance that she is not destined to see the end of them all."

✛FERDINAND CARDINAL ANTONELLI (1897–1993)

In what was the first serious activity on the part of Roman authorities for the cause of Fray Junípero Serra, Father Ferdinand Antonelli, relator general for the Sacred Congregation of Rites, visited California during the fall months of 1948.

While Antonelli's visit had other implications, the trek along *El Camino Real* provided him with a first hand view of the area where Serra had lived and worked between 1769 and 1784. A scholarly Italian, Father Antonelli had been attached to the Sacred Congregation for eighteen years, ranking just below the Cardinal Prefect. His personal interest in Serra had great significance for the cause.

While in the northern area of the state, Antonelli visited extensively with Dr. Herbert Eugene Bolton who had long been an advocate for beatifying Serra. It was Bolton, a non–Catholic, who helped the Vatican official "to know the ambient" in which Serra labored.

Following Antonelli's visit, diocesan court sessions were inaugurated. They were concerned with interrogating members of California families whose forebears had known or worked with Serra. There was still considerable verbal tradition alive, even 164 years after Serra's demise. With the conclusion of the various hearings, some 7,500 pages of documentation were sent to Rome, where Antonelli inaugurated the long and tedious chore of beginning the next phase in the Serra Cause.

During his sojourn in the United States, Father Antonelli also travelled in the east where he acquainted himself with the geographical and historical environments in which two other candidates, Mother Elizabeth Seton and Kateri Tekakwitha worked for the Lord.

Antonelli, a Franciscan and a specialist in ecclesial history and archeology, took up his first position at the Vatican in the 1930s. In addition to his curial tasks, he served four terms as rector for the Pontifical *Antonianum Atheneum* through the 1950s. Antonelli later became an archbishop and in that capacity served as a *peritus* at Vatican Council II, where he contributed to many conciliar documents, including the one on the Sacred Liturgy.

Afterwards, Antonelli became secretary for the Congregation of Rites and, in 1969, was named secretary of the new Congregation for Sainthood Causes. In all those posts, the archbishop worked closely with the Serra Cause.

Antonelli retired in 1973 and, in that same year, was named a member of the Sacred College of Cardinals. He published extensive works on saints' causes and liturgical reform, and edited several specialized dictionaries and encyclopedias. His scholarship was recognized in both the ecclesial and civil forums.

By the time of his demise, on July 12, 1993, the ninety–six year old Ferdinand Cardinal Antonelli was the eldest member of the College of Cardinals. Throughout his long life, His Eminence retained a personal devotion to Fray Junipero Serra, the founder and *Presidente* of the California missions.

Many years ago, the late Father Maynard J. Geiger displayed a letter he had received from Antonelli in which the then archbishop spoke forcibly about Serra. Among other things, he said that "Fray Junípero Serra exemplified all that's good and worthy of our holy founder, Francis. Most assuredly he will one day be canonized. Of that, there is no doubt. In the meanwhile, we pray that Serra's example will be followed by those of our own generation. They could not have a better role model."

✛ROBERT ARMSTRONG (1884–1957)

If it be true that only the humble deserve to rule, then Robert Armstrong (1884–1957), by his simplicity and humility of heart, was admirably fitted for the bishopric of Sacramento, a position he occupied for over a quarter– century. The son of William and Margaret (Ryan) Armstrong received his education, in Spokane, at Gonzaga High School and University. His preparation for the ministry was made at Montreal's Grand Seminaire, under the direction of the Sulpician Fathers. He was ordained for the Diocese of Seattle, in 1910.

During his earliest years in the priesthood, Father Armstrong worked as a curate at Our Lady of Lourdes Church, in Spokane. In 1914 be was sent to Yakima as pastor of the newly organized parochial unit of Saint Paul. There he erected a church, rectory and school. To his parishioners, "Father Bob" achieved an enviable reputation as "a magnetic and dynamic personality, a man's man, a builder, humble, zealous, a friend of the poor; in short an ideal priest."

Shortly after the death of Bishop Patrick Keane in 1928, Pope Pius XI appointed Father Armstrong to the shepherdless Diocese of Sacramento. He was consecrated on March 12, 1929, in Seattle's Cathedral of Saint James. Throughout the twenty–eight years Bishop Armstrong guided the spiritual destinies of the 53,400 square mile diocese, he built more churches, schools and other religious edifices than had been erected in the entire previous history of the Sacramento jurisdiction.

In addition to opening twenty–two chapels and thirty–one mission stations, the bishop increased the number of parishes from fifty–two to seventy–nine. Erection of twenty–six schools advanced the total enrollment of pupils in the diocesan educational system from 3,000 to 11,500. Early in 1930, Bishop Armstrong inaugurated a newspaper to succeed the privately owned *Catholic Herald* which had ceased publication the previous December. Indeed, the record shows that ecclesial activities in the Diocese of Sacramento "increased and grew far beyond the most grandiose dreams of the most exacting administrator."

And yet, Robert John Armstrong is not remembered so much for his statistically outstanding accomplishments as he is for the human qualities of charity, patience and humility. "He was revered by his people as a very human and kind man, one who gave himself without measure." Clearly, the San Francisco–born bishop "was no ordinary prelate. His was an unusually lovable and colorful character. Rugged in physique and generous of heart, he loved the grandeur of the high mountains and the growing things in his garden, as he shunned everything pretentious and artificial."

Though always in demand as an orator along the Gold Dust Trails, Armstrong's listeners attested that "the ornament of his speech was not in the false colors of rhetoric, but rather in the simplicity of ripened wisdom." Even when measured against the more critical yardstick of a later generation, the most exacting observer can recognize "that in Bishop Armstrong there was no contradiction between his wonderful good humor and love of sports and his deep reverence for both the priesthood and his office" as a successor of the apostles.

✛JUAN ARZUBE (b. 1918)

Juan Arzube was born in the picturesque seaport city of Guayaquil, on June 1, 1918. His earliest education was acquired at the Christian Brothers foundation in those Ecuadorian surroundings. In 1927, Juan was taken to England for further schooling. There he studied at Saint George's in Weybridge, and Saint Joseph's in Beulah Hills, completing his first two years of secondary education at Cardinal Vaughan School, in London.

Following the family's return to Ecuador, in 1932, Juan enrolled at Quito's Colegio San Gabriel. He completed his preparatory courses at the Colegio Vicente Rocafuerte, in Guayaquil, where he received his Bachelor of Arts degree in philosophy.

In 1937, wishing to round out his Latin sensitivity and English sternness Juan applied to and was accepted as a graduate student at Rensselaer Polytechnic Institute, at Troy, New York. After four years of intensive work, he returned to Guayaquil with a highly–coveted degree in civil engineering. Hoping to launch out into some other phase of engineering, Juan returned to New York, where he planned to further augment his study. When employment opportunities beckoned to California, in 1944, he came to Los Angeles, to take up work at a correspondence school, monitoring English lessons and translating materials into his native tongue.

Juan's lifestyle was radically altered by a retreat he made at Malibu, in 1945. Having strayed from the sacraments, he made his reconciliation with great diligence and fervor. From that time onwards, Juan began to feel a lack of fulfillment. God had entrusted him with special gifts, which he wanted to utilize in the most effective manner possible. Those sentiments became more pronounced after his religious experience at Malibu.

In the fall of 1947, Juan entered the preparatory seminary for accelerated courses in Latin and Greek. The following September, he enrolled at Saint John's Seminary, Camarillo, as a divinity student for the Archdiocese of Los Angeles.

Juan was ordained on May 4, 1954, by James Francis Cardinal McIntyre. The young priest's initial assignment was the curacy of Saint Agnes Church, in downtown Los Angeles. After three years of feverish activity, Father Arzube was transferred to the predominantly Mexican–American community comprising Resurrection Parish.

In late 1960, Father Arzube moved to the south central part of Los Angeles as assistant pastor of Ascension Parish. His apostolic endeavors in that busy metropolitan area lasted until October 1963, when Cardinal McIntyre named him to El Monte's Nativity Parish. There he supervised erection of the handsome shrine of Our Lady of Guadalupe, a mission church of which he was the canonical administrator, in 1968. It was while serving the People of God in that capacity that the priest was named to the episcopacy as titular bishop of Civitate and auxiliary to the metropolitan Archbishop of Los Angeles.

The first native of Ecuador ever to serve in the United States hierarchy received episcopal ordination on March 25, 1971. He was subsequently named Pastor of Saint Alphonsus Parish, in east Los Angeles.

Over the next twenty–two years, Bishop Juan served on various committees for the National Conference of Catholic Bishops and the United States Catholic Conference. He attended several episcopal gatherings in Latin America, including the one marking the 25th anniversary of CELAM which convened in Rio de Janeiro in 1980. The bishop has received numerous citations such as the John Anson Ford Human Relations Award, the Mexican–American opportunity Foundation's Humanitarian Award and the CHD's Empowerment Award.

With the division of the Archdiocese into five geographical units in 1986, Bishop Arzube was asked to preside over the San Gabriel Region as the personal representative of Roger Cardinal Mahony. At the time of his appointment to the bishopric, Juan Arzube chose as his episcopal motto the meaningful words *Hagase Tu Voluntad*. His ministry has since come to be identified with those beautiful words of the Lord's Prayer.

After serving under Roger Cardinal Mahony as Regional Bishop for the San Gabriel Valley, Arzube retired on June 1, 1993.

✢FREDERIC BARAGA (1797–1868)

San Fernando Mission was established along California's *Camino Real* on September 8, 1797. That same year there was born, in faraway Slovenia, Frederic Baraga who would be remembered in the annals as the "Apostle to the Chippewa."

Ordained priest in 1823, Father Baraga spent the first years of his ministry in what would become Yugoslavia. At the urging of the Leopoldine Foreign Missionary Society, Father Baraga came to the United States in 1830. The youthful priest affiliated himself with a Bishop Edward Fenwick who was then responsible for a huge expanse of territory comprising all or part of eight midwestern states.

Part of that area had been evangelized by French Jesuits who came in the 17th century and who suffered untold hardships and cruelties. Some, like Isaac Jogues and Jean de Brebeuf, were even martyred and later became canonized saints. After the War of 1812, Bishop Fenwick was eager to continue the missionary outreach inaugurated by the Jesuits.

Baraga was entrusted with caring for the spiritual needs of northern Michigan and there he worked with the Ottawa Indians in the Arbre Croche Mission, near present–day Harbor Springs, Michigan. Those formative years were marked by striking successes and it was there that Baraga developed the pattern for his labors among the native Americans in missions founded at Grand River (1833), La Pointe and Fond–du–Lac (1835) and L'Anse (1843).

BISHOP FREDERIC BARAGA (1797-1868)

His pattern of evangelization began with construction of a small church and included catechesis of converts, emphasis on the sacramental life of the Church and acceptance of Christian morality. He insisted on extending that notion also to the trappers and Indian agents who moved among his peoples.

Baraga was a model missionary in a tractless wilderness. He considered it vitally important to personally visit his widely–scattered parishioners, bringing them the sacraments as well as food and medicine. Often his missionary journeys were made in the dead of winter, over land and through deep drifts of snow or across frozen lakes where gale force winds threatened to freeze the blood in his veins. With Mass vestments, blankets and provisions strapped to a pack on his back, Father Baraga covered as many as forty miles in a day, walking on snowshoes and sleeping in the open.

In July of 1853, Michigan's Upper peninsula became a Vicariate Apostolic and Pope Plus IX named Baraga its first bishop. Between 1856 and 1860, the region enjoyed spectacular growth and the Holy See established the Diocese of Sault Ste. Marie (later Marquette).

As the first resident bishop, Baraga wore himself out and, by 1880, his health began to fail. He died in the early weeks of 1868, penniless and with only two priests at his side. His remains are buried in the Cathedral at Marquette.

The Slovenian pioneer, a close friend of Bishop Thaddeus Amat of Monterey–Los Angeles, was an exemplary missionary. Early in 1834, he revealed the terrible deprivation and loneliness which he suffered when he wrote: "Were it not for the ardent desire and fond hope I cherish that some unhappy soul will be saved, nothing in this world could induce me to remain here."

✝ANGELO BARBISOTTI (1904–1972)

Angelo Barbisotti was a latter–day missionary whose ministry for souls was exercised on four continents. He was born at Osio Sotto, in the Italian Diocese of Bergamo, on October 31, 1904. Two years after his entry into the Novitiate of the Verona Fathers, Angelo made his religious profession at Venegono, Milan. Following his ordination to the priesthood, in 1928, Father Barbisotti went to the British Isles for intensive studies in English.

From 1931 to 1947, Father Barbisotti resided in Bahr–el–Gebel, in Southern Sudan, where he taught in the seminary of Okaru. During those years he also engaged in missionary work among the Lotuko and Madi tribes of British Equatorial Africa. In 1947, Father Barbisotti came to America to formulate plans for establishing a United States province for the Verona Fathers.

He was appointed pastor at the *Asistencia of San Antonio de Pala*, on December 15, 1948.

Father Barbisotti spent five years at the picturesque *asistencia* toiling among the descendants of California's earliest converts to Christianity. Pala is the only one of the missionary establishments still serving the needs of an exclusively Indian population. In May, 1953, Father Barbisotti was recalled to Italy and the following September he became Provincial of the Verona Fathers in England.

Pope Pius XII appointed Barbisotti to the Vicariate Apostolic of Esmeraldas, a mission territory in Ecuador, on December 14, 1957. He received episcopal ordination as titular Bishop of Cauno, on March 2, 1958. At the time of its creation, the vicariate comprised 115,000 Catholics, most of them living in rural areas around the port town of Esmeraldas. The five churches and ten mission stations in the area were served by less than a dozen priests.

By 1961, Bishop Barbisotti could report the establishment of six schools, a high school and four vocational centers, with a total enrollment of 1,300 students. There were by then eighteen Verona Fathers, twenty–five Sisters and five Brothers working in the area. In addition, the prelate was able to secure the services of three Lay Mission Helpers from the Archdiocese of Los Angeles.

Angelo Barbisotti shared not only the name and birthplace of John XXIII, but his tireless energy as well. He once reported baptizing, in a single day, 204 persons! The one–time Pastor at Pala died at Limones, Esmeraldas, on September 16, 1972, while travelling to dedicate his latest chapel to the glory of God.

✝FLOYD LAWRENCE BEGIN (1902–1977)

In a letter sent to the People of God at Cleveland, on April 22, 1948, Pope Pius XII reflected on the unique number of priests from that jurisdiction who had or were serving in the American hierarchy. Among those native sons of Cleveland was Floyd Lawrence Begin, who was to be the proto–Bishop for the Diocese of Oakland. Born on February 5, 1902, Floyd was the eldest of Peter and Stella (McFarland) Begin's seven children.

After completing his elementary education at the parochial school of Saint Columbkille and Saint Thomas, Floyd entered Loyola High School in 1916, but transferred to the newly established Cathedral Latin School the following year. Always a sports enthusiast, he earned letters in baseball and basketball and was student manager of the football team at Cathedral. Young Mr. Begin was among that institution's first graduating class in 1920.

Floyd began his studies for the priesthood that same year and following some preliminary work at Saint John's Cathedral College, he was sent for further studies to the North American College in Rome. There he earned doctorates in philosophy and theology. Begin was ordained for the Diocese of Cleveland, on July 31, 1927, by Bishop Ignatius Dubowski, a colorful refuge prelate who had suffered for the Faith under the communists in the Ukraine.

After a brief visit with his parents, Father Begin returned to the Eternal City as Assistant to the Rector of the North American College and while serving in that position, he completed work for a doctorate in Canon Law at the Pontifical College of the Apollinaris. Soon after coming back to the United States, in 1930, Father Begin was named secretary to Bishop Joseph Schrembs and Vice Chancellor for the Diocese of Cleveland.

In later years, Father Begin also served as Chaplain of Rosemary Home for Crippled Children and Vicar General for Religious Men and Women. He was created a papal chamberlain to Pope Pius XI, in 1934, and a domestic prelate two years afterwards. In 1935, Begin supervised the details resulting in the VIIth National Eucharistic Congress which was convened at Cleveland in September. During his tenure as *Officialis*, he reorganized the operations of the matrimonial–tribunal on a larger and more efficient scale.

On March 22, 1947, Monsignor Begin was appointed to the titular bishopric of Sala and Auxiliary of Cleveland. He received episcopal ordination from Bishop Edward F. Hoban on the following May 1st. Among the co–consecrators for that ceremony was the then Auxiliary Bishop Joseph T. McGucken of Los Angeles, alongside whom Begin would later serve in the Metropolitan Province of San Francisco.

In 1949, Bishop Begin was named Pastor of Saint Agnes Parish in mid–Cleveland. In addition to many physical improvements on the monumental stone Romanesque church, the bishop introduced numerous parochial innovations. He also found time to engage in many civic and community projects, such as neighborhood renewal.

Bishop Begin was transferred to the newly–created Diocese of Oakland on February 21, 1962. He was installed by the Apostolic Delegate on April 28th. At the time of its creation, the Diocese of Oakland encompassed the two counties of Alameda and Contra Costa. The seventy–four parishes in the 1,467 square mile jurisdiction were served by 296 priests, sixty–nine brothers and 792 Religious Women. There were approximately 362,669 faithful in the diocese, of whom 67,509 were enrolled in Catholic schools.

Bishop Begin's work in Oakland during those formative years covered a wide range of apostolic activities, including the foundation of the *Catholic Voice*, on May 10, 1963. The prelate attended all the sessions of Vatican Council II and later diligently implemented the various conciliar decrees throughout his diocese. He was consistent and outspoken in attempts at seeking social justice for minority peoples.

The proto Bishop of Oakland returned his soul to Almighty God on the 26th of April, 1977.

✣ALDEN JOHN BELL (1904–1982)

Alden John Bell was born in Peterborough, Ontario, Canada, on July 11, 1904, the son of Henry and Catherine (Galvin) Bell. He received his earliest education at Orillia, Ontario. Following a brief sojourn in Ohio, the family moved to Southern California in 1918, where Alden enrolled at Sacred Heart School in Los Angeles. After his father's death, the youngster sold newspapers at the foot of Angels Flight to help support his mother and six brothers.

He later worked for four years as an office boy for the Pacific Telephone Company. At night he took classes at Polytechnic High School in commercial drawing and mechanics. In 1922, Alden became a clerical aspirant for the Diocese of Monterey–Los Angeles. His preparation for the priesthood was made at Saint Joseph's Seminary, Mountain View, and Saint Patrick's Seminary, Menlo

Bishop Alden Bell

Park. He was ordained by Bishop John J. Cantwell on May 14, 1932.

Father Bell's first assignment was to a curacy at Saint Elizabeth's Parish, in Altadena. Later he served in a similar capacity at Cathedral Chapel Parish, in Los Angeles. In 1937, Father Bell was sent to The Catholic University of America for graduate studies. After acquiring a Master of Science degree in Social Work, he returned to Los Angeles where he was assigned to the staff of the Catholic Welfare Bureau.

During World War II, Father Bell served as a military chaplain for the Fifth Air Force in New Guinea, the Philippines, Okinawa, Japan and other areas of the Pacific Theatre. He retired from the armed forces as a lieutenant colonel.

Upon his return to California's southland, Father Bell resumed his earlier position with the Catholic Welfare Bureau. He was twice honored by Pope Pius XII. In 1950, the Holy Father named Bell a papal chamberlain and, five years later, a domestic prelate. In 1953, Monsignor Bell was appointed Rector of Saint Vibiana's Cathedral. The following year, he became Director of Charities for the Archdiocese of Los Angeles.

On April 11, 1956, Monsignor Bell was named to the titular See of Rhodopolis and Auxiliary Bishop of Los Angeles. He was ordained to the episcopate the following June 4th by James Francis Cardinal McIntyre, at the seventh such ceremony performed in Saint Vibiana's Cathedral. Bishop Bell was also entrusted with the office of Chancellor. He continued as Rector of the Cathedral and during his years there supervised several renovation projects for that venerable edifice, as well as Our Lady's Chapel on Flower Street.

Pope John XXIII transferred Bishop Bell to the residential See of Sacramento, on March 30, 1962. He was installed in Blessed Sacrament Cathedral on May 15th. The years at Sacramento were busy ones. Within the first decade, he had established three parishes, opened four elementary schools, constructed three parochial high schools and encouraged religious to undertake two more. Bishop Bell also established during that time a diocesan Liturgical Commission, an office for Continuing Education for priests, a Commission for Ecumenical Affairs and a separate department for the Confraternity of Christian Doctrine. He retired in 1979 and died on August 28, 1982.

In every capacity he was called upon to fill California's only Canadian–born bishop proved a worthy successor to such ecclesial pioneers as Eugene O'Connell, Patrick Manogue, Thomas Grace, Patrick Keane, Robert Armstrong and Joseph T. McGucken.

✚JOHN LOUIS BOEYNAEMS, SS.CC. (1857–1926)

In mid April, 1903, Archbishop George T. Montgomery received a dispatch from Rome announcing that the Reverend Libert Hubert John Louis Boeynaems, a Picpus Father, had been named Vicar Apostolic of the Sandwich Islands. The cable suggested that the titular bishop–elect of Zeugma be ordained to the episcopacy at San Francisco, at the earliest possible opportunity.

The forty–six year old priest entrusted with the new office was a native of Antwerp, the son of John and Leopoldina (Van Opstol) Boeynaems. He had studied in his native city with the Jesuits and later at the Petit Seminaire, Mechlin.

Following graduate courses at the University of Louvain, Boeynaems entered the Mother House of the Sacred Heart or Picpus Fathers, at Paris. He was professed in that community on May 10, 1877. Ordained at Louvain on September 11, 1881, by Bishop Charles Andre Anthonis, Boeynaems was sent immediately to the Sandwich Islands, where he spent the next fourteen years exercising the ministry on the Island of Kauai.

In April, 1895, Father Boeynaems was placed in charge of the Wailuku Mission. There he built several chapels and repaired a number of other places of worship. Described as "a sturdy man with distinguished bearing," the young priest was known by his people as a genial man, "extremely kind in manner and considerate."

Late in 1902, Bishop Gulstan Ropert named Boeynaems Pro–Vicar and Administrator of the vicariate. And with Ropert's death a few months later, Pope Leo XIII elevated Boeynaems to the vacancy. The episcopal ordination in San Francisco attracted considerable attention in both the civic and religious communities. Archbishop Patrick W. Riordan and Bishop Thomas Grace assisted at the ceremony, as did a large contingency of the local clergy. The historic ties between California and the Sandwich Islands were welded even closer on that historic occasion.

Bishop Boeynaems returned to his post in early fall and there continued the apostolic work so long associated with the Sacred Heart Fathers. The prelate constructed many new churches, a school for boys, several recreational facilities and a magnificent building for the Knights of Columbus. He was especially interested in the Kalihi Orphanage which he founded and placed under the patronage of Saint Anthony.

Though a conservative man opposed to changes and innovations, the bishop exhibited a deep understanding and appreciation for the growing needs of the Church in the islands. He was instrumental in establishing the Catholic Instruction League in 1923. That group of lay catechists circulated along the slums and suburbs teaching catechism to those unable to attend Catholic schools.

The Belgian–born prelate died at Honolulu, on May 13, 1926. His remains were interred with those of his predecessors at the Catholic Cemetery on King Street.

✝JUAN BAUTISTA BRIGNOLE (f. 1840s)

In the spring of 1849, a certain Juan Bautista Brignole arrived at San Francisco, styling himself Bishop, Apostolic Legate *urbis et orbis*, Superior General, Reformer of the Catholic Religion, and of the Regular and Monastic Orders in the Mexican Republic and adjacent countries. Brignole's lack of credentials, strange vestments and weird actions provoked considerable discussion among the local populace. The administrator for the vacant Diocese of Both Californias, Father José María de Jesús González Rubio, wrote Governor Richard B. Mason, on May 28, 1849, telling him that "more than a month ago there arrived at the Port of San Francisco, an individual calling himself, Juan Bautista Brignole. . .

González Rubio noted that "he had already" started to exercise his jurisdiction by issuing in writing the secularization of two Religious, Fathers (Paulino) Romani and (Alexander) Branchi" who had arrived from Mexico a short while earlier. The perplexed friar observed that the "Bishop and Pontifical Legate" appeared without a retinue, "in a garb so foreign to his exalted station that the first time he visited the Father Minister of San Francisco, he came wrapped up in a blue serape, saying that his luggage had been stolen." Father González Rubio contended that "a personage of such high rank never travels alone," and that in any civilized country, it would be relatively easy to ask public assistance in recovering stolen property.

The so–called legate had not attempted to exact from the administrator "and the rest of the Clergy the honor and deference due him" and González Rubio wondered if that conduct in itself did not appear suspicious.

The administrator entreated the governor "to make a careful investigation of the origin and true character of the likes of Señor Brignole, and if he by means of authentic Bulls or other genuine documents can prove that he is Bishop, Legate, Reformer etc. . . . I may forthwith order all the Clergy and Catholics of this country to render every honor, consideration and obedience due to so high a personage." On the other hand, Father González Rubio said that "if Brignole could not prove his mission as he should, or . . . shows that he is some fool or imposter, then it would be wise for the governor to have him deported, so as to avoid disrupting public order".

Secretary of State Henry W. Halleck answered the administrator's letter on August 10, 1849, thanking him for the "information on the arrival of an imposter . . . who falsely referred to himself as bishop." According to Halleck, Brignole had earlier been arraigned before the *alcalde* in one of the northern Districts under the charge of being an imposter. He had apparently dropped out of sight and was supposed either to have left the country, or to have thrown off his assumed character of bishop.

When word of Brignole's antics reached Europe, early the following year, Archbishop Pierre Dominique Marcellin Raphael Bonamie, C.SS.CC., alerted Rome that "a pseudo *apostolic nuncio*" had been travelling secretly in California, claiming authorization to conduct negotiations in important political and ecclesiastical affairs. On April 15, 1850, officials at Propaganda Fide informed Archbishop Samuel Eccleston of Baltimore about California's "pseudo *apostolic nuncio*." The Cardinal Prefect denied that any such visitor had been sent and advised Eccleston to so inform the bishop–elect of Monterey, Father Charles Pius Montgomery.

The imposter very likely borrowed the family name of Cardinal Giacomo Luigi Brignole, the President of the Roman Branch of the Lyons *Société de la Propagation de la Foi*. He vanished from the California scene almost as mysteriously as he had appeared. Who Brignole was, what he hoped to do and where he went are, as yet, among the unanswered questions of California's Catholic heritage.

✝CHARLES FRANCIS BUDDY (1887–1966)

The twenty–nine year episcopate of Charles Francis Buddy is an impressive monument to that prelate's courage and zeal. Higher education, seminary training, convert crusades, immigrant solicitude, literary ventures—all these were assembled to put the Church in the Diocese of San Diego prominently and progressively ahead of most other sees in the network of jurisdictions that blanket the United States.

Charles Buddy, one of seven youngsters of Charles A. and Annie F. Buddy, was born, on October 4, 1887, at Saint Joseph, Missouri. Upon graduation from Saint Mary's College, in Kansas, he began his clerical studies at Rome's North American College. He was ordained, in the Basilica of Saint John Lateran, on September 19, 1914. Father Buddy returned to the Diocese of Saint Joseph where he immersed himself in the manifold duties of parochial life. He organized Saint Augustine's parish and soon became "a priest of widespread popularity." In 1917, Father Buddy was named diocesan–chancellor and secretary to Bishop Maurice F. Burke. During his years as rector of Saint Joseph's Cathedral, Father Buddy achieved fame "for his plan of feeding, clothing and providing medical care for the unemployed and their dependents through the depression years."

Father Buddy's familiarity with California dated from 1922, when he ventured westward with the "thought that a few months in the delightful climate of California" would be advantageous to his then delicate health. When, in 1936, the Holy See fashioned a new diocese from the southernmost counties of the earlier jurisdiction of Los Angeles–San Diego, Pope Pius XI named Father Buddy to the bishopric of San Diego. He was consecrated on December 21.

Bishop Buddy "nursed the new jurisdiction in its weak and tender years; he tended its growth; he met and overcame the difficulties incident to development; he accepted the challenge presented by the constant influx of new communicants from other states. And he met it successfully." Under his competent direction, the Diocese of San Diego grew from 80,000 Catholics to 300,000, from eighty–seven priests to 472 and from fifty–one parishes to 166. Parochial schools were multiplied, education developed at all levels and societies, clubs and associations promoted during a most crucial period of growth in California's southland. Though relieved of much responsibility by the appointment of a coadjutor in 1963, Bishop Buddy continued his feverish schedule as Chief Shepherd of his flock. Death claimed the tireless prelate at Banning on March 6, 1966, where he had gone to conduct a day of recollection.

Whether it was as preacher, theologian, educator, author or administrator, Charles Francis Buddy embodied the best of those qualities Americans have come to associate with their episcopal leaders. In addition, however, Bishop Buddy had that restless, impulsive and generous personality characteristic of those who accomplish great things for God and man . As noted in the prophetic words uttered at his funeral: "We may safely predict that the memory of Bishop Buddy will live as a great churchman and as a champion in a chapter of salvation history in California."

✝ JOHN J. CANTWELL (1874–1947)

A. SOUTHLAND CHURCHMAN

Twice in its history, the Archdiocese of San Francisco has provided California's southland with a shepherd and twice that favor as been repaid. One of the prelates given by the Bay City to the City of the Angels was John Joseph Cantwell, whose thirty–year episcopate has yet to be matched in years of actual service.

John Cantwell was one of seven California prelates from the Emerald Isle. Born in Limerick, he was baptized in Saint Michael's Church on December 7, 1874, the only one of Patrick and Ellen Cantwell's ten children not initiated into the Mystical Body at the ancestral city of Fethard. Sent at the age of six to the Patrician Monastery National School and later to the nearby Classical Academy, young Cantwell began early to prepare for the clerical life he was to share with three of his brothers in the Archdiocese of San Francisco. From Fethard, John went to Sacred Heart College in Limerick near the home of his grandparents on George Street.

The future bishop entered Saint Patrick's College at Thurles, one of Ireland's renowned missionary seminaries in 1892, and spent the following seven years preparing for his ordination. He was raised to the priesthood on June 18, 1899, at the hands of Robert Browne, Bishop of Cloyne in the 19th century Cathedral of the Assumption.

Soon after his ordination, Father Cantwell arrived in San Francisco and served for the next five years at Saint Joseph's Church in Berkeley. An enthusiastic promoter of educational activities, he helped to organize the Newman Club at the University of California and taught classics at Saint Joseph's Presentation Convent. In 1905 he became secretary to Archbishop Patrick W. Riordan and nine years later was promoted to Vicar General under Archbishop Edward J. Hanna. He was named to the long vacant Diocese of Monterey–Los Angeles in 1917, after having refused an appointment to Salt Lake City some years earlier. The staggering problems facing the young bishop on his arrival in Los Angeles were manifold; but he took as his yardstick the sage advice of his longtime friend, Father Peter C. Yorke:

> Don't start by building a cathedral . . . get the little ones to love Christ . . . concentrate on Christian education of the youth and you will be a great success in the eyes of the Lord.

During an episcopate that stretched over three full decades, Cantwell saw his original diocese divided twice, first in 1922 when the Monterey–Fresno area was detached and again in 1936 when San Diego became a distinct ecclesiastical jurisdiction. In the latter year, Los Angeles became a Metropolitan See thus making California the only state in the Union with two separate provinces. Honors from the Church, the state and numerous private institutions were bestowed on the archbishop over the year but probably the most significant of them all was the awarding of the Golden Rose of Tepeyac in 1931. This presentation, made by the Canons of the Basilica of Our Lady of Guadalupe in Mexico City, hearkened back almost a century when California's first bishop, Francisco Garcia Diego y Moreno, was consecrated in that historic basilica.

By the time of his death on October 30, 1947, Archbishop Cantwell had developed a bustling sprawling diocese of a few churches and schools into one of the major provinces in the nation. An archdiocese and two diocese are his monument—or as the archbishop himself so nobly stated it,

> . . . here and hereafter our contributions to the great cause may be our lasting monument after we are gone.

We live, we give, we die. Years, decades after we leave this earthly sphere of endeavor, the [deeds] will stand, noble, vigorous, everlasting . . .

✛JOHN J. CANTWELL (1874–1947)

B. CANTWELL AND CATHOLIC CHARITIES—1919

Believing as he did that "the work of Catholic charity in any diocese takes first place among our responsibilities," Bishop John J. Cantwell totally reorganized and coordinated diocesan activities along those lines by establishing, in 1919, the Associated Catholic Charities.

Under the supervision of Father William E. Corr, existing facilities were brought under the jurisdiction of a central office. Included among the earliest of the far–flung operations of the association were seven orphanages, two settlement houses, a preventorium, an infant home, two clinics, two homes for the aged and a day nursery. New departments were subsequently inaugurated for child and family welfare, correctional service and immigrant needs.

Bishop Cantwell succinctly outlined his concept of the Associated Catholic Charities as that of coordinating the work of all Catholic charitable organizations and institutions, modernizing and increasing the efficiency of existing facilities, promoting needed additional works, guiding and encouraging benefactions, establishing a liaison with other public agencies and gathering sociological information useful for rendering even more efficient the operation of Catholic activities.

Within two years after its establishment, the association reported cash expenditures for its vast programs totaling $140,178.71. That figure, impressive as it was, excluded entirely the donated services of thirty–six physicians, twenty–five lawyers, fifteen volunteer workers and nurses and twenty child case–workers.

By 1923, thirty–seven professionally–trained persons were employed to direct and supervise twenty–eight institutions throughout the diocese, including several boarding schools for dependent children, a correctional school for wayward girls, a maternity hospital, two homes for unemployed ladies and one for men, two salvage shops, three community hospitals and two branch offices, all in addition to those agencies already functioning under the Bureau's aegis.

Cantwell's uncanny ability for utilizing the talents of his priests was nowhere more evident than in the field of charitable work. The naming of Father Robert Emmet Lucey as diocesan Director of Charities in 1921, for example, brought to that office a young priest intensely attuned to the work of promoting such causes as those favoring labor and racial equality. During his tenure, Lucey became a brilliant and respected exponent of the principles of social justice.

With the appointment of Lucey to the Bishopric of Amarillo, Texas, in 1934, his long–time assistant, Father Thomas O'Dwyer, succeeded to the directorship. This unassuming, Irish–born priest became, over the ensuing decades, something of a legend for his tireless dedication to the social needs of the area's Catholic populace.

In the years before such campaigns were popular, Father O'Dwyer asserted the essential rights each and every person enjoys in the societal structure. The workingman's claim for the necessities of life was a theme often repeated by O'Dwyer who, as early as 1930, pointed out the duty "to sponsor and support in every way possible legislation that will secure the workman his fundamental right to a living wage, adequate protection against industrial hazards and an income that will provide properly for old age." The structural realignment of the Associated Catholic Charities, in 1921, as the Bureau of Catholic Charities and again, in 1926, when it became the Catholic Welfare Bureau, is additional evidence of concern for the needy.

Branches of the Bureau were established at Pasadena, Santa Barbara, San Pedro, Long Beach, Glendale and Alhambra–San Gabriel. Bishop Cantwell envisioned the Associated Catholic Charities and its successors as that arm of the Church whose role was to have "a voice strong enough, and a tongue eloquent enough to bespeak the needs of those people who cannot declare their own wants."

✛JOHN J. CANTWELL (1874–1947)

C. BISHOP CHAMPIONED MEXICAN IMMIGRANTS—1921

As a body, priests in the United States have traditionally functioned as "champions" of their people. In addition to caring for their spiritual needs, they have defended their civil rights, watched over their education and helped improve their working conditions.

There have been rare occasions, however, when sacerdotal zeal and dedication for what they felt was best for their parishes got out–of–focus. After all, as human beings, they share the same weaknesses that affect their people.

The first native Californian ordained for the Old Diocese of Monterey–Los Angeles fell into that trap during the 1920s, when thousands of persecuted Mexican Catholics began arriving in the southland seeking a new life in less hostile surroundings. His parish, one of the more affluent in the diocese, was among the first to experience those demographical changes that occurred in most other major cities of the United States.

As more and more of his parishioners began moving westward, the pastor panicked. His anxiety became vocal and often manifested itself in unfortunate reflections about the lack of enthusiasm among the newcomers for parochial activities and financial support.

Very likely, the priest would have been appalled had someone suggested that his attitude gave the outward appearances of being racist or discriminatory. As one observer of the contemporary scene put it, he momentarily "lost touch with the reality of change."

In any event, when the situation was brought to the attention of Bishop John J. Cantwell, the southland prelate wasted no time putting the record straight. If ever Cantwell despised anything, it was injustice. He made that point forcefully in an address to a meeting of the NAACP in 1921.

Cantwell rarely wrote directly to his priests, preferring instead to deal with them personally or through his chancellor. In this case, he made an exception and, on May 24, 1928, he wrote a stinging letter to the priest in question. He began by saying that he had received a long intervention from certain families living in his parish. They "alleged in their petition that you spoke in opprobious terms of the Mexican people; that instead of receiving kindness from the shepherd of the flock, they were treated with contumely."

While recognizing and sympathizing with the cleric's frail health, the bishop said that "henceforth I expect that you will show to your people every possible kindness, and particularly to the Mexican people." He suggested that the priest was "entirely out of sympathy with the mind of the Holy Father in his recent Encyclical Letter, in which he held before the people of the world the heroic conduct" of the Mexican hierarchy, priests, religious and laity.

He went on to point out that "many Mexicans who have come among us have given up their homes, their businesses and their farms rather" than yield to tyranny. They suffered themselves to be driven out for Christ's Name's sake. The prelate concluded by saying that "to treat these people harshly is unpriestly."

Happily, there is evidence that the priest accepted the rebuke of his bishop and, in fact, spent his remaining twenty–one years at the parish as a model pastor of souls.

Modern sociologists are looking for evidence of how the Church in Southern California dealt with the influx of Mexican Americans in the 1920s. This incident addresses that subject insofar as it exemplifies the policy of the local bishop.

✛JOHN J. CANTWELL (18 74–1947)

D. CANTWELL RECALLS EARTHQUAKE—1933

The so–called "Long Beach earthquake" of March 10, 1933 was not especially strong, but because it occurred in one of the most highly developed areas of the state, it is regarded as one of the major disasters in California history, ranking second only to the 1906 quake in its destructive effect. The epicenter was offshore, about three miles southwest of Newport Beach. The earthquake was significant not only for the extent of its damage and loss of life (118 persons), but also because it focused attention on the inadequacy of some types of construction, especially that used in many school buildings.

According to reports printed in *The Tidings,* forty–two Catholic institutions were severely damaged at an estimated loss of one million dollars. Catholics from all over the United States opened their hearts and purses to the needs of the Diocese of Los Angeles–San Diego.

In a letter written on March 16th, to his priest brother James, Chancellor for the Archdiocese of San Francisco, Bishop John J. Cantwell graphically described the earthquake and its effect on Southern California.

> The many aftershocks following the big earthquake at 5:55 o'clock on Friday seem to be discontinuing. Though I had experience of the tremendous earthquake in San Francisco, our own one here was in one sense more terrifying.

> We were asleep when the big earthquake of San Francisco took place and when we awoke and had come to our full senses, we only experienced the end of the shock. With this one in Los Angeles, we had the full benefit from the time that the lights became dim and the shock commenced and continued, for I suppose, twenty seconds. The water in the fish pond was violently agitated and came right out on the walks.

The bishop went on to say that "I visited Whittier and found that the school will be closed for repairs that will take three weeks. Otherwise things are fairly good in Whittier. The whole town of Artesia is practically destroyed. The furnishings of the church are all gone but the walls are intact.

> The church in Los Alamitos is a total wreck. I think Compton, which is getting the least help and the least advertising, suffered the most. I feel sorry for these people because they are largely very poor.

> The public schools are all closed, and *The Times* this morning demands an investigation as to why public schools fall more readily than other buildings. Saint Matthew's School, in a report received today from Long Beach, will have to be torn down. It was built, you remember by Father (Thomas) Morris, and I suppose cheaply.

> Saint Anthony's, as you will see from *The Tidings,* is a fearful ruin. Unfortunately, there is a debt of $140,000. The hospital in Long Beach is gone forever. I think the sisters will rebuild. They have no debt. The other hospitals in the town have been seriously injured but can carry on.

Huntington Park is in very bad condition and the new brick house in which the Sisters live is really crooked. And so it goes with all the towns south of Redondo. Father (William) Stewart only lost a chimney (but) he cannot shut the doors in the house which, of course, means that the house is a little out of plumb.

Cantwell worried about the Cathedral rectory, noting that "the upper walls are leaning out. It is not condemned but the sooner I get a house there the better. The priests are really afraid to sleep on the third floor and I cannot blame them."

The bishop concluded by explaining to his brother that a Jesuit seismographer at Santa Clara "told me a surprising thing, that your Saint Joseph's Seminary is built directly over a Fault. A certain portion of the Fault around Los Gatos . . . moves at the rate of eighteen inches a year." Little could Cantwell have imagined that fifty–six years later, the seminary in question would be destroyed by another earthquake.

✢JOHN J. CANTWELL (1874–1947)

E. MEXICAN HIERARCHY APPLAUDS CANTWELL—1937

In 1937, the "Church of God in Mexico" paid public homage to Pope Plus XI on the 80th anniversary of "his glorious existence." People in each of the nation's thirty–two ecclesial districts pledged prayers and works of mercy for the Holy Father. In a beautifully–calligraphed book, printed in a limited press run of 500 copies, were enumerated no fewer than 31,560,481 spiritual pledges.

As a recognition of their esteem for the Most Reverend John J. Cantwell, the Mexican hierarchy invited the Archbishop of Los Angeles to participate in their tribute to the Holy Father. Cantwell, the only non–Mexican to share in the spiritual bouquet, submitted a list of 390,220 pledges. In his message, Cantwell took "great pleasure" in offering to His Holiness "this spiritual bouquet composed of the Communions, Holy Masses, prayers and sacrifices from the large number of Mexican people under my jurisdiction in this State of California which is on the confines of the Republic of Mexico."

Included in the book was an historical outline of the archdiocese as it had evolved from the Diocese of Both Californias, created in 1840 by Pope Gregory XVI. The compilation says much about Cantwell and the dedication of the Church in the area to peoples of Mexican origin. The account begins by pointing out that Cantwell had been named an Assistant at the Papal Throne on September 20, 1929 "at the request of the hierarchy of Mexico in recognition of his pastoral care and solicitude for the Mexican people under his care."

In the Archdiocese of Los Angeles which then con-

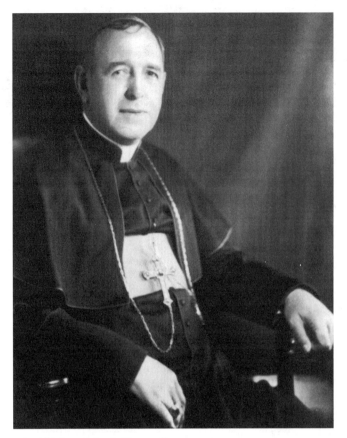

Archbishop John J. Cantwell

sisted of 177 parishes, 81 mission churches, and 571 priests, there were over 200,000 Mexicans. It goes on to say that "since the great influx of Mexicans into Southern California, the chancery records show that over $800,000 has been spent by the diocese in the erection of mission churches and schools for their exclusive use, and in the establishment of social action and recreational centers, as well as for care of various kinds extended to them through the Catholic Welfare Bureau.

There were built from diocesan funds, over 50 churches in those districts where the Mexican people colonized. Several communities of sisters and a large number of priests were brought into the diocese to care for them.

The archbishop has always manifested lively sympathy for the Mexican people and a great admiration for their spirit of faith and their loyalty to the church. He has insisted that the American priests learn the Spanish language in order to be of greater assistance to them.

He has also given great impetus by his encouragement to the organizations of Catholic societies among the Mexican people, so that at present there exists in the archdiocese a very large Holy Name Society, the Knights of Columbus, the *Union Mutualista de San Jose*, the A.C.J.M. and the A.C.F.M.

Under the sponsorship of the Archbishop there is also a weekly Catholic radio hour in Spanish for the benefit of the Mexican people. His zeal for the spiritual and material welfare of the Mexican people in this district was recognized by the chapter of the Basilica of Our Lady of Guadalupe in Mexico City, which chapter graciously awarded him the Golden Rose of Tepeyac.

This account, written by Msgr. Agustin de la Cueva of Mexico City, was an honest or unsolicited appraisal of Cantwell and the work of the Church in Southern California for the Mexican Americans then living in the area.

✠JOHN J. CANTWELL (1874–1947)

F. ARCHBISHOP CANTWELL—A CARDINAL?—1937

The first recorded hint that Roman officials were considering appointment of a cardinal for Los Angeles came in mid 1937, during an interview with Father Maurice Sheehy, a professor of theology at the Catholic University of America. Dr. Sheehy had journeyed to California where he was a house guest at 564 East Claremont Street in Pasadena. While there, the nationally prominent theologian consented to be interviewed by James Warnack of the Los Angeles *Times*.

When asked if Archbishop John J. Cantwell of Los Angeles was a candidate for the Sacred College of Cardinals, Sheehy said that "if the work being done by the archbishop were as well known in Rome as it should be, there would be no honor too high for him." Queried as to when and how Pope Pius XI would learn of the prelate's spiritual influence in the area, Sheehy answered "when the people of this section devote half as much precious breath to exploiting their spiritual and cultural progress as they now devote to climate and motion pictures."

Dr. Sheehy went on to observe that he knew of "no place on earth that has made such gigantic strides religiously and educationally, within the last fifteen years, as has Southern California. The records speak for themselves."

"Certainly Rome recognized, to no small extent, California's spiritual advancement, and Archbishop Cantwell's part in that progress when the Church broke a precedent in establishing two archdioceses in one state."

"It is the old story of a prophet being more honored abroad than at home. The eastern bishops recognize Archbishop Cantwell as one of the greatest spiritual leaders in America, past or present." Sheehy felt that "another cardinal or two, perhaps in the Middle West and the Western States, would not be out of place in American life. In fact, we should have them. According to Catholic population, I might say we deserve them."

He noted that the Catholic population of the world was approximately 300,000,000. In the United States there were roughly 22,000,000. "The Church has seventy–two cardinals, with only four in America, these being the Archbishops of Boston, Chicago, Philadelphia and New York." Father Sheehy noted, for the record, that "the conferral of the cardinalcy on Archbishop Cantwell would add nothing to his jurisdiction or duties, except to make him one of the electors of a future Pope."

The intriguing interview even had ecumenical overtones for it took place in the home of Sheehy's long–time friend, H.R. Worrall, a deacon in the First Congregational Church of Pasadena.

While it was another fifteen years before the Archbishop of Los Angeles was named to the Sacred College of Cardinals, the remarks of Dr. Sheehy must be regarded as more than the casual observations of an interested bystander. Sheehy had been professor of religion and director of the survey council at the Catholic University of America since 1927. And he went on to become the first priest ever to hold the position of admiral in the United States Navy.

Sheehy was obviously testing the ecclesial waters of California. It will be interesting one day to discover for whom and why.

✠JOHN J. CANTWELL (1874–1947)

G. CANTWELL AND MEXICO—1941

In an article written for the N.C.W.C. News Service and published in the nation's Catholic newspapers on October 24, 1941, Bishop John Mark Gannon described the *Dia de la Raza* which commemorated the crowning of the Virgin of Guadalupe at Mexico City.

"It was as colorful, as beautiful and particularly as devout a ceremony as I have ever seen in any Catholic edifice in any part of the world. I am still under the spell of that impressive observance." Gannon noted that "particular honors were given Archbishop Cantwell of Los Angeles, who pontificated at the high Mass. There was no lack of appreciation for this outstanding American prelate who had been an ardent friend of the very numerous Mexicans within his archdiocese with the beautiful Spanish name."

Cantwell "led an impressive group of priests and lay people to the celebration from the United States. The coadjutor Archbishop of Morelia preached an eloquent sermon" for the occasion. The writer tells how he met about thirty Mexican priests, all in lay clothing. He observed that "the California priests, who were numerous, were in clerical garb, including clerical collars. This was a concession of the government in honor of Archbishop Cantwell's wish."

"The presence of Archbishop Cantwell and the pilgrims who accompanied him was particularly appreciated. Seemingly His Excellency already was widely known for the splendid pastoral care and the sincere and practical measures he has taken in his archdiocese for the Mexican people who are part of it.

"His coming was accepted as a gracious gesture, and I think everyone was impressed most deeply. Almost a hundred priests accompanied the archbishop, together with many laymen, in a special Pullman train." Gannon noted that "the Mexico City secular press widely reported and editorialized on the arrival and printed His Excellency's remarks in full text."

He went on to say that "I think many Mexican Catholics have knowledge particularly of the ceremonies attended by 75,000 Catholics, four years ago in which Archbishop Cantwell presided at the formal crowning of a statue of Our Lady of Guadalupe in Los Angeles.

"Many also know that last June, in furtherance of the movement for the spiritual uniting of the Catholics in the Americas, the archbishop presided at the exercises for the laying of the cornerstone of the new Sanctuary of Our Lady of Guadalupe in his archdiocese." In concluding his mentioning of Cantwell, Gannon noted that "this prelate of the United States is coming to be known as a particular friend of the neighboring Mexican Catholics."

After returning to the United States, Archbishop Cantwell issued several statements about his trip to the Mexican capital. He predicted that "in the days to come Mexico and the Church in Mexico will outshine their older glories." Noting that his journey was the culmination "of a hope of twenty years," Cantwell went on record that "the Mexican government, from the highest official to the lowest, gave to us and to our people a generous welcome."

In retrospect, it can be said that much of the "new spirit of toleration" spoken about by Gannon can be credited to the Archbishop of Los Angeles who had finally realized his dream of one day kneeling before the Virgin of Guadalupe, where the first bishop of Both Californias had been consecrated in 1840.

✛JOHN J. CANTWELL (1874–1947)

H. THE SILENT SPECTATOR—1967

The consistent pattern of historical development discernible in California's Catholic heritage affirms the human insight of Christ's parable about one man sowing, another watering and a third reaping. Installation of Bishop Timothy Manning in the Diocese of Fresno graphically illustrated that unchanging truism.

As the People of God approached the time of spiritual harvest, the historically–minded individual might well have glanced back to another December day, forty–five years earlier, when the seed of ecclesiastical autonomy was first planted in the diocese known thereafter as Monterey–Fresno. Such a backward insight would have revealed the many personalities who had a share in the responsibility for nurturing the seed that brought forth the bountiful blessings of a later generation's Catholicism.

One name, however, towers above all others, so much so that one half expected the unmistakable figure of that tall, erect churchman to emerge from the shadows of Saint John's Cathedral on December 15, certainly in spirit, if not in fact.

Though long since departed from the scenes of his earthly endeavors, the imprint of John Joseph Cantwell remains indelibly embossed on the Church in Central California. It was he who brought about its juridical formation; governed it in the earliest years of its existence; proposed its initial ordinary; guided it as part of his metropolitan province and arranged for its administration in days of tribulation. That the hand of the prelate still influences the destinies of the Church in Central California can hardly be disputed –for it was the archbishop's protege who gathered the harvest first sown by his Irish–born predecessor almost half a century earlier.

Archbishop Cantwell knew and lived by the Scriptures. Had it been possible for him to counsel the one who was to localize the authority of Pope Paul VI, in the Diocese of Fresno, he most assuredly would have recalled the advice etched onto the pages of Holy Writ by another Paul to an equally favored disciple:

> Timothy, guard most carefully your divine commission. Avoid the Godless mixture of contradictory notions which is falsely known as "knowledge"– some have followed it and lost the faith. Go now and grace be with you

✛JOHN J. CANTWELL (1874–1947)

I. ANNIVERSARY FOR AN ARCHBISHOP—1972

October 30, 1972 marked the twenty–fifth anniversary of the death of the southland's first archbishop. The Most Reverend John Joseph Cantwell succumbed in 1947, after serving the People of God for thirty years— first as Bishop of Monterey–Los Angeles (1917–1922), then Bishop of Los Angeles–San Diego (1922–1936) and finally as Archbishop of Los Angeles (1936–1947)

Though the people of a new era probably associate him mostly with the high school bearing his name, John J. Cantwell left his mark, and a prominent one at that, in the Catholic annals of California's southland. In fact, he was a pioneer whose stature contrasts favorably with the Golden State's great missionary founders. The prelate's accomplishments were as spiritually profitable to the faithful of his day as they are statistically phenomenal to those of a succeeding generation. The archbishop was a far–sighted man whose programs envisioned the time when, in fulfillment of the prediction made early in his tenure, "Los Angeles will be the second largest city in the United States." His instinctive qualities of leadership, augmented by efficient organization, careful planning and gentle persuasion were a rallying point for the creative talent in that elite corps of highly competent subordinates which he fashioned into his official family.

An austere man in his personal habits, the Irish–born prelate had no private life, few friends and fewer still who knew him intimately. Nonetheless, he was as acquainted with the astute idiom of business, the calculated phrases of diplomacy and the tangy vernacular of the people as he was with the sonorous Latin of the *Roman Missal.*

He brought to Southern California "those habits of ordered industry and that keenness of vision so necessary for the bishop of a town of such growth and such importance as Los Angeles." Though there was an imperious atmosphere about his demeanor, the archbishop's rise to ecclesiastical prominence was clearly the result of "a talent for hard work, steadiness of purpose and a deftness in the handling of matters requiring poise and a judicial attitude."

The formidable array of achievements initiated, encouraged and endorsed during the Cantwell years were further implemented and expanded by the two men he singled out to shepherd California's People of God in another era. Those prelates, one the Archbishop of San Francisco, the other the Archbishop of Los Angeles, effectively projected the influence of their mentor well beyond the half century mark.

As noted in Cantwell's biography, by his long–time friend and collaborator, the archbishop "was a worthy successor to the prelates who preceded him. He piloted the Church of Los Angeles from a frontier rim of the Christian world to the edge of greatness in the family of American jurisdictions." ✛

✛JOHN J. CANTWELL (1874–1947)

J. THE CANTWELL DOCUMENTS—1991

Father John J. Cantwell, Vicar General for the Archdiocese of San Francisco, received a special delivery letter from Washington, D.C., and marked in bold type: "Personal and Confidential." Inside was another, smaller envelope on which were printed these words: "The contents of this letter may not be divulged until the day so indicated. Violation of these directives is reserved to the Holy Father."

The letter itself read thusly: "I am instructed to inform you that the Holy Father has deigned to appoint you to the vacant Bishopric of Monterey–Los Angeles. After conferring with Archbishop Hanna, kindly notify this office about the person of your consecrator and the date of the ceremony." Thus began the thirty year episcopal tenure of John J. Cantwell as Bishop of Monterey–Los Angeles (1917–1922), Bishop of Los Angeles–San Diego (1922–1936) and Archbishop of Los Angeles (1936–1947).

Happily for his biographer and others interested in the records of the past, Cantwell left behind a long and fascinating paper trail about his administration of the Church in Southern California. The documents themselves were gathered from a myriad of sources in the years since 1962, when James Francis Cardinal McIntyre established a canonical archives for the Archdiocese of Los Angeles. Since 1981 they have been housed at the Archival Center, erected adjacent to San Fernando Mission in Mission Hills.

Prior to 1984, the Cantwell documents remained arranged, but uncatalogued. In that year, through a providential concurrence of circumstances, Sister Miriam Ann Cunningham, C.S.C. (1916–1987) became associated with the Archival Center. After her demise, she was succeeded by Sister Mary Rose Cunningham, C.S.C. her blood sister. Based on the format used successively by Anthony Debevec and Finbar Kenneally, O.F.M., at the Academy of American Franciscan History, Sister Mary Rose continued the challenging task of cataloging the papers of the Cantwell era.

In November of 1991, the Saint Francis Historical Society published the first of the two volumes entitled a *Calendar of Documents and Related Historical Materials in the Archival Center, Archdiocese of Los Angeles, for the Most Reverend John Joseph Cantwell.* The calendar which contains a lengthy biographical sketch of Cantwell's episcopate was published with a grant from the Dan Murphy Foundation.

Volume One contains 3840 entries from the years 1918 to 1935. Each document is assigned a code number and described as to correspondents, date, language, pagination, place of origin and contents. The next volume extended the coverage from 1936 to 1947. It also contained references to an additional 3671 entries, together with an index to all the Cantwell letters and documents.

A reviewer of the earlier–published calendar for the Conaty era noted that it was appropriate that "the first catalogue of its kind for the American Church had come from Los Angeles which has been pioneering in this work for the last thirty years."

✤GILBERT ESPINOSA CHAVEZ (b. 1932)

The first Mexican–American bishop in modern times to serve on the west coast was born, reared and educated entirely within the confines of the four county Diocese of San Diego. Gilbert Espinoza Chavez was born in Ontario, California, on May 9, 1932, the son of Margarito and Ramona (Espinoza) Chavez. His father was a farm worker who supported his family by harvesting fruits and vegetables in San Bernardino County.

Gilbert studied for the priesthood at both Saint Francis and Immaculate Heart Seminary. He was ordained by Bishop Charles F. Buddy, on the Feast of Saint Joseph, 1960. Father Chavez subsequently took various courses in philosophy and psychology at the University of California, Riverside. He taught geometry and algebra for two years at Aquinas High School, San Bernardino, and served as chaplain at the State Rehabilitation Center for Drug Addicts, Norco, for four years.

At various times Father Chavez also engaged in pastoral work at Our Lady of Guadalupe (Riverside) and Sacred Heart (Redlands). In 1969, he became administrator of Saint Anne's Parish, San Diego, and, six months afterwards, pastor of the same parish.

Two years later, he was appointed pastor of Our Lady of Mount Carmel, in San Ysidro, a parish adjacent to the international boundary. His pastoral ministrations in that difficult assignment were recognized by Pope Paul VI, who conferred the title of monsignor on Father Chavez, in 1972.

Early in 1974, Msgr. Chavez was designated Episcopal Vicar for the more than 300,000 Spanish–speaking Catholics residing in the 36,000 square mile San Diego jurisdiction. Recognized in all his various assignments as "a churchman of exceptional qualities," Msgr. Chavez was characterized as one who places love above force, humility over ambition, humor before sadness and gratitude ahead of indifference.

Msgr. Chavez became the fifth American of Hispanic heritage to serve in the United States hierarchy on April 16, 1974, with his appointment to the titular See of Magarmel. Shortly after his episcopal ordination as Auxiliary Bishop of San Diego, Chavez was installed as pastor of Our Lady of Guadalupe Parish, in San Bernardino. His presence in the northern part of the diocese was envisioned as a "means of touching and enriching the lives of thousands of Mexican–American people and deepening their love for Christ."

The Hispanic heritage of the California episcopate is as old as the hierarchy itself. The proto–bishop, Fray Francisco Garcia Diego y Moreno, was Mexican–born and his three successors were Spanish–born. Bishop Gilbert Chavez continues the apostolate of those noble forebears by exercising a ministry endowed with charity and wisdom and crowned with courtesy and kindness.

Like his famed counterparts of an earlier era, he sought to cast out the idols of inequality and service in order to demonstrate to yet another generation of believers that Christ's universal vision is color–blind.

✤HARRY ANSELM CLINCH (b. 1908)

Historical origins for the Diocese of Monterey can be traced to November 20, 1849, when Pope Pius IX transferred the title and seat formerly associated with the Diocese of Both Californias to Monterey. The residential bishopric at Monterey existed until 1859, when Bishop Thaddeus Amat received authorization to transfer his headquarters to Los Angeles. From that time onwards (until 1922), the southland jurisdiction was known as Monterey–Los Angeles.

The man destined by God to return the bishopric to Monterey was born at San Anselmo, California, on October 27, 1908, the son of Harry and Mary (McLaughlin) Clinch, natives of New York City. In 1915, Harry Anselm Clinch moved with his family from San Francisco to Fresno, where he completed his secondary education at the local public schools. In 1925, he was accepted by Bishop John MacGinley as a clerical candidate for the Diocese of Monterey–Fresno

Harry entered Saint Benedict's Seminary in Kansas, with a grant from the Students Endowment Fund established by the Catholic Church Extension Society. He later attended Saint Joseph's College (Mountain View) and Saint Patrick's Seminary (Menlo Park). He was ordained to the priesthood on June 6, 1936, by Bishop Philip G. Scher.

During his early years in the ministry, Father Clinch engaged in pastoral work at a number of places and, in 1940, he became editor for the *Central California Register*, a position he occupied for eight years. In 1946, Father Clinch was given a pastorate at Clovis. Two years later, with his retirement from journalistic endeavors, he became pastor of Saint Mary's Parish in Taft. There he directed the building of a new church, rectory, hall, convent and school.

Pope Pius XII conferred the title of Domestic Prelate on Father Clinch in September, 1952. Eighteen months afterwards, Msgr. Clinch became Dean of Bakersfield, Kern and Inyo counties. Among the other assignments filled by Msgr. Clinch during those years were those of director for the Propagation of the Faith (1936–1948), organizer of the C.Y.O. (1939–1940), chaplain for Saint Agnes Hospital (1942–1946) and founder–director of Camp Santa Teresita, the diocesan young peoples' mountain summer camp.

Msgr. Clinch became the thirteenth native Californian elevated to the bishopric on December 5, 1956, when he was named to the titular See of Badiae. He received episcopal ordination the following February 27th, at Fresno's Shrine of Saint Therese, where he had served the first parish Mass in 1919. In addition to serving as the proto–auxiliary for the 43,714 square mile Diocese of Monterey–Fresno, Bishop Clinch also functioned as pastor of Carmel's historic Mission Basilica from 1958 to 1967.

With the dismemberment of the Central California jurisdiction of Monterey– Fresno, in 1967, the Holy See decided to reconstitute an episcopal seat at the one–time state capital. Bishop Harry Clinch was named first (and third) Ordinary of Monterey, a diocese encompassing the coast counties of Santa Cruz, San Benito, San Luis Obispo and Monterey.

After an interim of 108 years, Harry Anselm Clinch returned the bishopric to the Cathedral of San Carlos. Though reduced to only 8,475 square miles, the area once again had a successor to Joseph Sadoc Alemany and Thaddeus Amat.

Clinch served as Bishop of Monterey until his retirement on January 19, 1982.

✝THOMAS PATRICK COLLINS, M.M. (1915–1973)

Thomas Patrick Collins was born within the shadows of Mission San Francisco de Asís or Dolores, on January 13, 1915, the son of Thomas and Molly (Norton) Collins. He attended Sacred Heart School in San Francisco and then entered the Maryknoll Minor Seminary at Los Altos.

Collins completed his education for the ministry at the Maryknoll Motherhouse in Ossining, New York. He was a member of the first group of deacons ordained to the priesthood by the Auxiliary Bishop of New York, the Most Reverend J. Francis A. McIntyre, on June 21, 1942. Shortly thereafter, Father Collins was appointed to missionary work in Latin America. His was the first party of Maryknollers assigned to Bolivia. There he labored for eighteen years.

On November 15, 1960, Pope John XXIII named Father Collins Titular Bishop of Sufetula and Vicar Apostolic of Pando, a tropical jungle region in north-eastern Bolivia. He thus became the second United States bishop to head a see in that nation. The Vicariate Apostolic of Pando then comprised a 40,000 square mile area, about the size of Kentucky, in the "Green Hell" region of Bolivia. The bishop–elect came home to San Francisco, where he was advanced to episcopal orders on March 7, 1961, by the Most Reverend Hugh A. Donohoe, Auxiliary of San Francisco.

Bishop Collins returned to Bolivia, where he spent the next seven years in attempts to update and modern-ize the backward peoples of his vicariate. It was largely through Bishop Collins' influence that the United States and Bolivian governments agreed to build a hospital at Riberata and to place that facility under contract to the vicariate. The medical services were vitally important too. Though the people of that area had plenty of natural food available, they were plagued with anemia caused by a combination of weather and intestinal parasites.

The prelate was also able to open a professional school, where young ladies could learn typing, cooking and dressmaking. Generally, however, education back-fired—insofar as those fortunate enough to have school-ing often moved out of the area to Cochabamba or Brazil or Argentina. The role of a spiritual shepherd in such areas is fraught with medical complications and on December 6, 1968, Bishop Collins was forced to resign his position because of failing health.

During the final years of his life, Bishop Collins lived with the Maryknoll Fathers at Mountain View, Califor-nia, and at Saint Theresa's Residence, in New York State. Quietly, on December 7, 1973, the one–time Vicar Apostolic of Pando closed his rich and varied life. Though a Californian in birth and in death, Thomas Patrick Collins belonged not to his native state or his country of allegiance but to another continent, where he generously and willingly poured out his life's blood for the cause of Christ.

✝THOMAS J. CONATY (1847–1915)

A. ECUMENISM AND A SOUTHLAND BISHOP

To Bishop Thomas J. Conaty, prejudice was "the meanest of sentiments, especially when it caused bitter-ness and hate towards those who differ in religion." The prelate's earliest ecumenical statements were couched in terms of civic responsibility. He firmly believed that "Church and party do not weaken the bonds of a com-mon citizenship, nor allow any lines to be drawn in devotion to the country, when her life is in danger." The prelate pointed out to a meeting of the Chamber of Com-merce, that Americans form a united brotherhood cemented together "upon the battlefield where creeds and races merged in one common act of devotion to a common country."

Such expressions were symptomatic of Bishop Conaty's ecumenical outlook for, as he told a predomi-nantly non–Catholic audience, in 1895: "The altar I kneel at and the altar you kneel at are common founda-tions of our individual goodness." Personally a man of strong convictions, the bishop allowed "no room for belief in indifference as to the form of a man's religion." In his opinion, Catholics "should be apostles of truth everywhere under the inspiration of our grand old Church, to whom Christ has given the mission to redeem mankind." At the same time, Conaty defended a man's right to strive for truth within the framework of his own environment. "Let us understand one another's motive, and judge of it honestly from one another's work."

As Bishop of Monterey–Los Angeles, Conaty removed the "denominational requirement" from Catholic charitable institutions by insisting on the "absolute respect for the religious rights of all." While such overtures did not go uncriticized, the prelate recalled that Catholics and non–Catholics, having a common interest in the community had to learn to live with religious as well as political differences. Though he frequently expressed the personal wish that "all men believed religiously as I do," he went on to say that "I find no fault with the man who conscientiously differs with me, and I bid him God's blessing."

With such convictions it is not surprising that the Los Angeles *Times* believed that "few Catholic clergymen in America have broader reputations than Bishop Conaty, who stands as the embodiment of religious zeal and patriotic love." Sentiments such as these increased with the passage of years as is evident from many sources. John Steven McGroarty, for example, observed that wherever he went, "among people of all classes, and all creeds, ministers of other denominations, in the meeting houses of a hundred sects, in the synagogues and on the open highways, among those who know or seek no temple whatever," he heard the prelate's name spoken always with admiration and respect.

Conaty had no reluctance about championing his own views, especially regarding the obligations of his episcopal office. And yet, a measure of the esteem with which those views were accepted by the general populace was noted by one observer of the southland scene who stated that "he does not hesitate to express himself freely upon a point and will surely do a very great amount of good in this state. He is respected and beloved by all our citizens, without regard to their religious affiliations."

No man in contemporary Los Angeles was more generally loved than Bishop Thomas Conaty and his reputation among non–Catholics was unique for those troubled times. His involvement in ecumenical activities was already established by the time he arrived in California. In 1894, he addressed a conference of the Unitarian Church and, a decade later, *The Tidings* reported that the "Right Rev. Bishop Conaty is in great demand as a lecturer before our most enlightened non–Catholic clubs and associations." In his appearances before such assemblies, the prelate dwelt on those tenets held in common by all Christians. He was especially fond of speaking about patriotism and continually reminded his hearers that, while good men and women make good citizens, law alone could not bring about virtue.

One of his collaborators recalled that the bishop's voice "was always raised to defend human rights, to uphold love of country, to demand fair treatment of all." He sympathized with the legitimate sentiments and aspirations of all races. Charles C. Conroy, who edited the diocesan newspaper through most of the Conaty years, felt that "no man better understood the value of the right to worship God according to the dictates of one's conscience—a right which is ours in this country, and which we prize as the best of our possessions. To him religious intolerance, and, indeed any sort of intolerance, was a thing to be "abhorred." At all times, Bishop Thomas J. Conaty "stood squarely on his principles, prepared to deal with his fellowman only upon the basis of justice, integrity and truth."

✛THOMAS J. CONATY (1847–1915)

B. PROMINENT CATHOLIC CATECHIST—1898

Though he anticipated Vatican Council II by over sixty years, the Reverend Thomas F. Conaty (1847–1915) felt strongly that the "catechumenate should be properly instructed in the mystery of salvation and in the practice of gospel morality." Father Conaty's interest in the teaching apostolate was evident throughout the many years of his priestly ministry. It was during his pastorate of Sacred Heart Parish, in Worcester, that the Irish–born cleric launched the *Catholic School and Home Magazine*.

That endeavor, which was originally envisioned as a parochial bulletin, was so successful that it was enlarged to literary status in March of 1892, and was soon being circulated throughout the New England area. It was described as "an excellent little publication whose good work has won commendation from the highest church dignitaries."

After his appointment to the rectorship of The Catholic University of America, Conaty related, in a letter to Archbishop Michael Corrigan, on May 8, 1898, that "while in parish work I had an advanced class of children under my personal direction, engaged in studying the Life of Christ from the New Testament narrative. The lessons appeared monthly in the little Magazine which I published and afterwards were issued as Leaflets and circulated among our schools, academies and convents." Conaty went on to say that "I have completed the series since I came to the University, led to it by the demand of many who followed the courses as they appeared. I have been frequently solicited to publish the series in manual form in the hope that it would supply to some extent at least a want in our school text books." The volume was released, in its *New Testament Studies* series, by Benziger Brothers, in 1898, under the title *The Principal Events in the Life of Our Lord*.

The future Bishop of Monterey–Los Angeles explained in the Introduction to the book that "in present-

Bishop Thomas Conaty's home
at 717 Burlington Avenue

ing to the public a manual of New Testament Studies, the author offers to Catholic teachers and parents the results of special work, in a city parish, among the older children who met with him regularly to study the life of our divine Saviour, as told in the Holy Gospels." Conaty stated that the book was "prompted by the encyclical on the study of the Holy Scriptures, in which our Holy Father Leo XIII, encourages clergy and people to a greater love for the word of God, wherein they are to find the image of Christ." He further noted that the 254–page book was his personal response to the desire "that our Catholic children should be taught how to study the Gospels, and thus see in the written word of God the beauty of the life of Him who came as a Child to Bethlehem that He might become a Saviour at Calvary."

The methodology of Conaty's presentation consisted of memory texts, moral thoughts and questions with answers. It began with a series of preliminary lessons on the Bible proper—its nature and authority. Though the work went into several editions, copies are now something of a rarity. The one in the library, at the Archival Center in Mission Hills, may well be the only extant copy on the West Coast.

Father Conaty's book was representative of a vital phase in the history of catechetical development. It exemplified to contemporaries his basic conviction that the whole Catholic educational movement is unalterably cemented to the same purpose for which the Church exists, namely, "to establish the Kingdom of God in the lives of men."

✛THOMAS J. CONATY (1847–1915)

C. 717 SOUTH BURLINGTON—1903

Shortly after his arrival in California's southland as Bishop of Monterey–Los Angeles, Thomas J. Conaty purchased a stately Victorian home at 717 South Burlington Avenue in downtown Los Angeles. The escrow papers were dated December 3, 1903.

The home, located in one of the most fashionable residential sections of the growing city, replaced the earlier episcopal residence at Second and Main streets, adjacent to Saint Vibiana's Cathedral. Surrounding the home were graceful palm trees, flower gardens and rolling lawns. A second, smaller building on the property was used to house the bishop's domestic staff.

There were sixteen rooms in the two–story frame house. It was a landmark building, featured in several early histories of the city as a perfect example of Victorian architecture.

Many distinguished ecclesial figures visited the historic home, including Pietro Cardinal Fumasoni–Biondi who came in 1922 as a papal legate for the reconsecration of the cathedral; John Cardinal Farley and Patrick Cardinal Hays of New York and Archbishops Patrick Riordan and Edward Hanna of San Francisco.

Conaty's successor, Bishop John J. Cantwell, lived in the house until 1928, when he was able to acquire the King Gillette mansion at 100 Fremont Place in the Wilshire district. For some years after the bishop's departure, the home served the Church in a myriad of ways. During World War II it was rented out for dwelling purposes in the shelter shortage.

In 1951, Archbishop J. Francis A. McIntyre designated the house as the central offices for the Saint Vincent de Paul Society. The historic edifice was formally re–dedicated by the archbishop and nearly 200 Vincentians from all parts of the four county archdiocese. McIntyre said that he was "most pleased with the redecoration and rebuilding program undertaken by the society to transform the historic building into fresh, bright and adequate offices."

Msgr. James Dolan, Spiritual Director for the Saint Vincent de Paul Society, reported that there had long been a need for larger quarters for the society away from congested downtown streets of Los Angeles, "where society members can meet to discuss problems and gain advice concerning such matters as county welfare, aid to children and assistance to the aged."

During its years as service to the Saint Vincent de Paul Society, the home was also used as the executive headquarters for the Catholic Summer Camps and Catholic Scouting program. The one–time episcopal residence served as the flagship of the Saint Vincent de Paul Society for some years, until the new Catholic Charities complex was erected on Ninth Street, east of the Chancery Office.

During its final years, the building was used for occasional meetings and for storage. With the changing pattern of the neighborhood, the once stately home finally fell victim to progress and was torn down. Few other buildings served the Church longer and with greater distinction than the stately home at 717 South Burlington Avenue.

✝THOMAS J. CONATY (1847–1915)

D. DEFENDER OF THE INDIANS—1904

Shortly after his appointment to the Diocese of Monterey–Los Angeles, Bishop Thomas J. Conaty was received at the White House by President Theodore Roosevelt. Their conversation centered around the Indians of California and their treatment by government officials. The Chief Executive asked Conaty to submit a written memorandum on the matter. This the prelate did in May of 1904.

Conaty reported that there were about 4,000 Catholic Indians in his Southern California jurisdiction. He singled out three aspects worthy of attention, the first of which was marriage. Invalid (and illegal) unions were common and the bishop felt that "it would be wise to urge upon the agents the advisability of recommending that all Indians belonging to any Church have their marriage performed by the clergymen in charge of their Church or Chapel, as many of them, especially the

Catholics, realize the conscience obligation as to the sacramental character of the contract."

Another source of anxiety was the liquor policy which, at that time, was very ineffective "inasmuch as the Indian policeman is apt to be afraid of his fellows in the stringent enforcement of any required regulation." Conaty thought that the "wholesale fear of jail would act as a repressing influence upon the Indian and the fear of the penitentiary would hinder the Mexicans and the Whites from invading the reservations with their wagons of liquor."

The third and most vexing difficulty which bothered the bishop arose from the undefined tenure of land among the Indians. When California was ceded to the United States, treaty provisions recognized inhabitants of the area, including Indians, as citizens of the Republic of Mexico with the privilege of emigrating there if they did so within a two year period. Those remaining in California would enter the United States under the same conditions previously enjoyed under Mexican rule. Hence the Indians became *ipso facto* citizens of the United States though in many cases they were totally unaware of their legal status. This lack of knowledge often resulted in loss of holdings to unscrupulous white men. To remedy the evil and to save at least some of the land for the Indians, Congress reserved 85,000 acres in Southern California for the natives, empowering the President to have surveys made prior to erection of reservations. The total area thus set aside consisted of between three and four hundred thousand acres, eighty percent of which was mountainous or desert.

The land remained subject to Congressional litigation since the area exceeded that originally allocated. This last factor resulted in an almost constant molestation of the Indians by government officials. In addition, the small amount of arable land made it difficult for some of the reservations to give sufficient returns to the Indians for their industry in cultivation.

Bishop Conaty told the President that the appointment of honest agents would go far to remedy this situation. He urged Roosevelt "to consider the policy of appointing the agent from some section of the state as remote as possible from the reservations, so he will not be subjected so much to the influence of white people in the vicinity." The prelate also suggested that the government "send a good, reliable, unprejudiced inspector to make a thorough investigation" of the area. "He should be instructed to consult, not only with the agent, but with the Indians, priests, and ministers, as well as with those of us who have general charge of the spiritual affairs of the Indians."

Throughout his California episcopate, Bishop Conaty remained an outspoken champion for Indian interests and on more than one occasion he took their problems to the highest personage in the land, the President of the United States.

✚THOMAS J, CONATY (1847–1915)

E. REFLECTIONS ON BISHOPRIC—1907

The public addresses of the Right Reverend Thomas J. Bishop of Monterey–Los Angeles have long been regarded among the classical utterances of the American hierarchy. His "Reflections on the Bishopric," delivered at San Francisco, on January 10, 1907, are typical of the prelate's mastery of subject, prose and delivery.

The bishop of our modern life has the fight to wage, the same cross to bear, the same difficulties to contend with as the bishops of all ages. He is the follower of his Divine Master, the apostolic messenger of His Gospel, and while going about doing good he must also bear the burden of the cross. Our American conditions bring their special difficulties and our present age its special demands. The bishop in his diocese is the High Priest, the leader of the people, the spokesman of the Divine Saviour, the father of his priests, the guardian of authority and unity, the center of the link that binds the jurisdiction of the diocese to the great and mighty apostolic commission. He, indeed, must be prepared to meet the conditions, to preach the Gospel, to stand for the truth and defend the people against error and evil. Wealth, the comforts of life, contempt of restraint, the indulgence of self, the desire for independence of all spiritual obligations, add to our difficulties; yet we know that the ideal Christian life remains the same, that the cross of Calvary is the only means of salvation, that the Gospel of Christ is the form of life and the salvation of nations as well as individuals. The duty that lies before us is to fearlessly preach the old truths, to adopt the means best suited to adapt them to conditions, to know our age and work to guide it, to reach the hearts of the people, and to lead their souls to Christ. The bishop in our modern life is called to lead his clergy and people in the way of God, in piety, in knowledge and in truth.

Success in life is to be estimated by the efforts made for God in the midst of all difficulties of life. No man is truly great who is not truly good. The love of God is the source of all true greatness and union with God is the soul of character. To sanctify oneself, to keep aloof the banner of Christian principle, to maintain the fight to the end and never allow the standards to be lowered, to be an apostle of the truth, to stand for the divine things, to work for the adjustment of things human to the divine order, to seek to establish and maintain the Kingdom of God in the lives of men, to pray and work for the restoration of all things in Christ is, indeed, the apostolic spirit. To have lived according to such ideals and to have been rewarded in one's life by victories give warrant in attributing to a man the elements of true greatness.

✚THOMAS J. CONATY (1847–1915)

F. JOAN OF ARC—1910

Whether it was in the pulpit or in the public forum,

Bishop Thomas J. Conaty (1847–1915) was looked upon by Catholics and non–Catholics of his time as a shepherd of souls, a conscience for the Church and a spokesman for the commonwealth.

One of Conaty's long–standing prayers was answered on April 18, 1909, when sixty–five French bishops and 40,000 pilgrims gathered in Saint Peter's Basilica to hear Pope Pius X beatify Joan of Arc. The Bishop of Monterey–Los Angeles gave several lectures about Joan of Arc in the southland, one in Hollywood on April 25, 1910 and another at the Newman Club. Several of his homilies on the "shepherd maiden of Domremy" were published in *The Tidings*.

Early in 1910, John Steven McGroarty, who was then editor of the *West Coast Magazine*, asked Conaty to write an extensive essay on Blessed Joan of Arc for the March issue of his journal. In his classic style, Bishop Conaty portrayed Joan as a "striking illustration of the reward which finally comes to those who in simplicity of heart and earnestness of purpose are faithful to that duty to which they feel God has called them."

The prelate felt that the recent beatification was "evidence of that broad–minded impartiality of the Church which makes no distinction in her recognition of sanctity, whether in the simplicity of an unlettered shepherd or in the intellect of a doctor of the Church." He pointed out that "the humble fishermen who became apostles, the sinners who became saints, the martyrs who shed their blood for religion are in the same family with the kings and popes who have given glory to God by their imitation of Christ."

And while Conaty felt that "the life of Joan of Arc presents magnificent opportunities for study of character," he also noted that "one must look for the source of her greatness beyond anything found in the natural resources with which God had blessed her." In his masterful presentation, the Bishop of Monterey–Los Angeles said that "the story of Joan of Arc is full of simple, childlike faith, as well as womanly virtue and soldier–like bravery. Her childhood was one of piety and happiness, her home that of a good Christian, and innocence as well as industry characterized her life."

The bishop told about "her voices" and how she commanded the English forces besieging Orleans. Her first act, after the hostilities, "was to visit the Cathedral of the Holy Rood to give thanks to God for the blessing of victory."

Never one to dodge a thorny issue, Bishop Conaty explained the relation of the Catholic Church to the trial, condemnation and death of this "remarkable girl" and how the sentence was pronounced in the presence of a cardinal who just happened to be an uncle of the English monarch. In 1455, Pope Callistus III ordered a full and complete review of the case at Notre Dame in Paris. It was there that the earlier verdict was annulled and Joan of Arc was proclaimed innocent of all charges.

The bishop concluded his nine page essay by saying that "in all we know of the world's great ones, we can find no parallel for the Maid of Domremy. Whether as a saint or a nation–maker, Joan's place in world history is assured." Then he quoted Mark Twain: "she was a beautiful, simple and lovable character. She is pure from all spot or stain of baseness and always she was a girl. She is easily and by far the most extraordinary person the human race has produced."

✛THOMAS J. CONATY (1847–1915)

G. ENDORSEMENT OF COCA COLA—1910

Thomas J. Conaty had long been active in the temperance movement by the time he arrived in California as Bishop of Monterey–Los Angeles. He first gained national attention by his eloquent talks at gatherings advocating total abstinence as the most effective way of combating alcoholism.

It came then as no surprise that in a letter written in 1910, the bishop advised a correspondent in the east that "abstinence is the best route for you to follow." He then suggested, in place of alcohol, "the great national temperance beverage."

A lot of research went into determining what Conaty meant by "the great national temperance beverage." Recently the mystery was solved with the discovery that the Coca–Cola company had introduced that theme into its advertising in 1906.

The endorsement of Coca–Cola by such temperance leaders as Conaty help to explain how that beverage went on to become the best–known trademarked product in all the world. Ironically, that status was achieved as the result of a blunder. In May of 1886, an Atlanta chemist, John Styth Pemberton, brought a jug of sweet, sticky syrup to a local pharmacy for a taste test.

The operator of the soda fountain followed Pemberton's suggestion and mixed the syrup with ice and plain water. Later, he accidentally put carbonated water into the glasses—and Coca–Cola was born.

It was Pemberton's partner and bookkeeper, Frank M. Robinson, who suggested the name Coca–Cola. Shortly thereafter, the two words were cast into the flowing script that is now recognized everywhere.

The trademark "Coca–Cola" was recorded with the United States Patent and Trademark Office in 1893. (The more familiar term "Coke" was only registered in 1945.) In 1916 the unique contour bottle was designed by the Root Glass Company of Terre Haute, Indiana. It too was eventually given a trademark registration, a distinction accorded few other "packages."

By 1891, Asa G. Candler had acquired complete ownership of Coca–Cola. Within four years, his merchandising genius had helped to expand distribution of the drink to every state in the union. A candy merchant, Joseph A. Biedenharn, became the first person to bottle Coca–Cola, using syrup shipped from Atlanta. His 1894 innovation created a marketing concept that led to an even wider consumption of the beverage.

Coca–Cola has been a part of people's lives for over a century. Today Coca–Cola branded products are asked for more than 371 million times a day, in eighty languages and in more than 155 countries. Interestingly, the beverage is sold in more countries than belong to the United Nations.

Fortune magazine reported recently that Coca–Cola is so powerful that it is virtually off the charts. "It is both the best known and most esteemed brand in America." Unquestionably, a portion of that phenomenal success can be attributed to temperance leaders like Bishop Thomas J. Conaty who, eighty years ago, provided a huge market for what was then "the great national temperance beverage."

✛THOMAS ARTHUR CONNOLLY (1899–1991)

The introduction to the new ceremonial for ordination states that "the title of bishop arises not from his rank but from his duty and it is the part of a bishop to serve rather than to rule."

Thomas Arthur Connolly was the third native San Franciscan entrusted with that title. He was born on October 5, 1899, the son of Thomas and Catherine (Gilsenan) Connolly. Thomas received his elementary education in the schools of the Bay Area and, in September, 1915, entered Saint Patrick's Seminary, Menlo Park, as a clerical candidate for the Archdiocese of San Francisco.

Following his ordination to the priesthood, on June 11, 1926, Father Connolly engaged in parochial work for four years at Star of the Sea Parish, Sausalito. In September, 1930, he enrolled in the School of Canon Law at The Catholic University of America. As a partial requirement for his doctoral degree, the San Francisco priest wrote an historical synopsis and commentary on the initial chapter of Title XIV, in the fourth book of the *Codex Juris Canonicis*. The brilliant dissertation, dealing with the ordinances and prescriptions governing appeals in contentious (civil) causes, was published as No. 79 in the Canon Law Studies for The Catholic University of America.

Shortly after returning to California, Father Connolly was appointed secretary to Archbishop Edward J. Hanna. Three years later, he was advanced to the office of Chancellor for the Archdiocese of San Francisco by the Most Reverend John J. Mitty. Over the years, Father Connolly also served at various parochial assignments, including Saint Rose, in Santa Rosa, and Saint Cecilia and Saint Mary's Cathedral, both in San Francisco.

On July 23, 1936, Pope Pius XI named Father Connolly a domestic prelate. Two years later, Monsignor Connolly represented the Archdiocese of San Francisco at the Eucharistic Congress in Budapest. Connolly was designated Titular Bishop of Sila and Auxiliary of San Francisco, on June 10, 1939. He received episcopal ordination on August 24th.

With the passage of another nine years, Bishop Connolly was named Coadjutor of Seattle. Following the death of the Most Reverend Gerald M. Shaughnessy, S.M., on May 18, 1950, Connolly became the fifth Ordinary for the Washington jurisdiction. In June, 1951, Pope Pius XII created a new ecclesiastical province for the northwestern area of the nation and elevated Seattle to archiepiscopal status. Included in the new metropolitan district were the Dioceses of Spokane, Yakima and Juneau, together with the Vicariate Apostolic of Alaska.

Late in 1974, Archbishop Connolly asked the Holy See for permission to put aside the burdens of the 24,834 square mile jurisdiction, a request granted early in 1975, by Pope Paul VI. He lived on until 1991.

Throughout his long episcopal tenure, Thomas Arthur Connolly personified that part of the *Directory on the Pastoral Ministry of Bishops* which states that "the bishop should above all understand the mentality, customs, conditions, dangers and prejudices of the individuals and groups to whom he speaks" and for whom he toils. That he consistently did in order to enable the People of God "to draw water joyfully from the springs of salvation and the treasury of sacred doctrine."

✚JOHN STEPHEN CUMMINS (b. 1928)

John Stephen Cummins, the 21st native Californian raised to the episcopal rank, was born at Oakland, on March 3, 1928, the son of Michael and Mary (Connolly) Cummins. John received his early education at Saint Augustine's School in Oakland. He later declared an interest in the priesthood and was enrolled in Saint Joseph's College, Mountain View.

Upon completion of theological courses at Saint Patrick's Seminary, John was ordained to the priesthood by Bishop Hugh A. Donohoe, Auxiliary of San Francisco, on January 24, 1953. During the initial years of his priestly ministry, Father Cummins served as curate at Mission Dolores Basilica. From 1953 to 1957, he was also Chaplain to the Catholic students at San Francisco State College.

In 1957, Father Cummins was appointed to the teaching staff at Bishop O'Dowd High School, Oakland, a position he occupied for five years. He simultaneously cared for the spiritualities of Catholic enrollees at nearby Mills College. Concomitant with his teaching apostolate, Father Cummins was active as a member of the Roman Catholic Baptist Dialogue of the Bishops Committee on Interreligious and Ecumenical Affairs. He also found time to take graduate courses in history at the Berkeley campus of the University of California.

With the dismemberment of the Archdiocese of San Francisco, in 1962, Father Cummins became Chancellor for the newly–created Diocese of Oakland. In that position, he was in charge of personnel relationships and the daily activities of the curial office. He also coordinated the Social Justice and Ecumenical Commissions and looked after the diocesan insurance program. On July 27, 1963, he was made a Domestic Prelate by Pope Paul VI.

Monsignor Cummins continued as Chancellor for the Diocese of Oakland until 1971, when he became Executive Director for the recently–formed California Catholic Conference. In that capacity, Cummins helped channel the functions of the Conference into three areas: (1) liaison with state departments and with the Legislature, (2) information to Catholic associations and organizations, to other state conferences and to the United States Catholic Conference and (3) coordination of interdiocesan activities in the areas of education, welfare and related items.

On February 12, 1974, Pope Paul VI named Msgr. Cummins to the titular See of Lambesi as Auxiliary Bishop of Sacramento. He received episcopal ordination in that city's Memorial Auditorium on May 16th, an occasion described as "one of the truly historic days in the life of the Sacramento Church." Bishop Cummins served the People of God along the Gold Dust trails for three years before assuming his present position as the second Bishop of Oakland.

In the various capacities of his priestly and episcopal role, Bishop Cummins has demonstrated that he is wholly a product of the atmosphere engendered by Vatican Council II. That, in itself, speaks volumes for his ongoing contribution to California's Catholic heritage.

✚HUGH ALOYSIUS DONOHUE (1905–1987)

Bishop Hugh Aloysius Donohoe (1905–1987) was a convinced believer and firm practitioner of the view that "in exercising their office of Father and Pastor, Bishops should stand in the midst of their people as those who serve." One of ten children born to Patrick and Frances (Brogan) Donohoe, on June 28, 1905, Hugh attended Saint Anthony and Saint Paul elementary schools in San Francisco. His priestly studies were made at Saint Patrick's Seminary, Menlo Park.

Ordained by Archbishop Edward J. Hanna, on June 14, 1930, Father Donohoe was appointed to the faculty of Saint Joseph's College, Mountain View. Two years later he was sent to The Catholic University of America, where he earned a doctorate in Sociology. Upon returning to San

Francisco, Father Donohoe became Professor of Industrial Ethics at Saint Patrick's Seminary. He remained on the faculty at Menlo Park from 1936 to 1942.

In the latter year, he became editor of *The Monitor*, the Catholic newspaper for the Archdiocese of San Francisco. It was during his five year tenure as editor that Father Donohoe founded the Association of Catholic Trade Unionists. Donohoe's concern for labor relations is a natural outgrowth of his conviction that the Christian message must be presented in a manner responsive to the difficulties and questions by which people are burdened and troubled.

Father Donohoe was made a Domestic Prelate on June 13, 1947. Two months afterwards, Pope Pius XII named him to the titular See of Taium and Auxiliary Bishop of San Francisco. His episcopal ordination took place on the Feast of the Holy Rosary. Early the following year, Bishop Donohoe was named Pastor of Saint Mary's Cathedral. From 1956 to 1962, he was Vicar General of San Francisco. Following the death of Archbishop John J. Mitty, Donohoe served as Administrator for the vacant See.

On February 21, 1962, Bishop Donohoe was appointed to the newly–created Diocese of Stockton. The 9,247 square mile jurisdiction comprised the two counties of San Joaquin and Stanislaus (from the Archdiocese of San Francisco) and the three counties of Calaveras, Tuolumne and Mono (from the Diocese of Sacramento). There were 83,654 Catholics in the Stockton diocese.

The San Francisco–born prelate was transferred to Central California as Bishop of Fresno, on August 27, 1969. He was installed, again on the Feast of the Holy Rosary, by Archbishop Luigi Raimondi the Apostolic Delegate.

An outspoken proponent of Catholic principles on labor matters throughout his episcopate, Bishop Donohoe believed strongly that "justice, equity and charity are essential elements in every labor contract." He vigorously supported Catholic participation in campaigns for justice. It was within that context that he endorsed such moves as Cesar Chavez's quest for a "secret ballot" in the settlement of the farm labor dispute.

As a man of fearless honesty, one who remained intolerant only of duplicity and pretense, Hugh Aloysius Donohoe nonetheless epitomized the motto chosen for his episcopal seal, "in all things charity."

✝JOSEPH P. DOUGHERTY (1905–1970)

Every Christ–like man casts a lengthy shadow as he crosses center stage. Whatever be his accomplishments, the People of God instinctively proclaimed, with his passing, that "a prophet has been among them." Those fortunate enough to have known Bishop Joseph P.

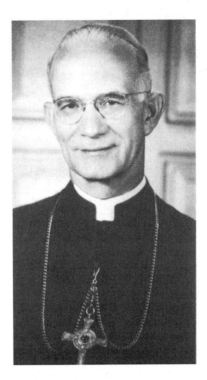

Bishop Joseph Dougherty

Dougherty during his brief sojourn in Southern California were deeply impressed by the very unusual spirituality and charm of a man steeped in the priestly traditions of piety and sanctity. His sudden death, almost exactly nineteen years after his appointment to the bishopric, deprived the Church of a dedicated apostle, a devoted pastor, an exemplary priest and a holy man.

The sixty–five year old prelate was reared and educated in the Pacific Northwest. During the earliest years of his ministry, he taught at Saint Edward's Seminary, in Kenmore, Washington. From 1934 onwards, he served as Vice Chancellor, and later Chancellor, for the colorful Bishop Gerald Shaughnessy in the Diocese of Seattle.

His "most attractive and consoling" years were those between 1948 and 1951, when, as Pastor of Saint Edward's Church in Seattle, he enjoyed the intimate dealings with the faithful, the identification with all their joys and sorrows, care of the sick and poor, instruction of little children, preparation of converts, pardon and guidance in the Sacrament of Penance and the seeking of wayward sheep.

On July 9, 1951, just a month after creation of the Diocese of Yakima, Pope Pius XII asked Monsignor Dougherty to take up the pastoral staff in that six–county, 17,787 square–mile jurisdiction.

The Kansas–born bishop's vision of diocesan life anticipated many features of the post–conciliar era. From the very outset, he entreated Yakima's 36,000 Catholics to be sensitive of their "responsibility to be personally involved in the Church's effort to bring Christ to the world" in which they lived.

During his eighteen year episcopate, Bishop Dougherty strongly championed basic human rights throughout South Central Washington. He decried the fact that "thousands of our American citizen migrants whether of Mexican ancestry or Negroes are forced into a form of economic slavery which is far worse than I would call in comparison with the benign slavery of pre–Civil war days." He appealed for open housing, provided Spanish–speaking priests for migrants, organized *Centro Catolico* aid for Mexican–American flood victims and launched a Spanish radio program for those unable to otherwise fulfill their religious obligations.

Eighteen parishes were erected between 1951 and 1969. The Catholic educational program was greatly expanded as were the facilities of the Confraternity of Christian Doctrine. Teaching personnel was doubled while the Newman Apostolate was launched and a diocesan newspaper founded.

The renewal and revolt, progress and chaos, reform and revolution, awareness and reaction, insight and confusion sweeping the country had reverberations even in the tiny Christian community at Yakima. Recognizing the advantages that a younger man would have in meeting the "multitude of onerous and unattractive tasks" involved in administering a diocese, Bishop Dougherty stepped aside on February 5, 1969.

Though never fully recovered from a near–fatal heart seizure and several subsequent cardiac ailments, the bishop felt that he was "too young to retire completely and not old enough to sit and wait for death." Those were the sentiments that prompted him to request Pope Paul VI for the unprecedented favor of returning to pastoral work at the parochial level.

The pontiff agreed and, on April 16, 1969, assigned the titular Bishop of Altimo as auxiliary to the Archdiocese of Los Angeles. The final phase of his priesthood began with Bishop Dougherty's appointment to the pastorate of Saint Alphonsus Church on June 28th.

Though the prelate devoted the major portion of his last year to parochial activities, he took an active interest in his role as archdiocesan Vicar for Christian Education and in the fulfillment of the many confirmation engagements he was given throughout the southland.

Bishop Dougherty's contagious spirituality and optimistic outlook made him a favorite guest at the archdiocesan seminaries. Perhaps those endearing qualities are nowhere more obvious than in one of his baccalaureate sermons which subsequently appeared in the *Congressional Record:*

> . . . even though the world may fear the future of the atomic age, you need not do so, because your knowledge of the truth and your desire to seek it always will make you free to face the realities of life on earth as you go forward to the eternal destiny for which you were created and redeemed.

✦ROLAND PIERRE DUMAINE (b. 1921)

Roland Pierre DuMaine was born at Paducah, in the beautiful bluegrass state of Kentucky, on August 2, 1931, the only son of Nolan and Eula (Burch) DuMaine. His early education was acquired at Saint Mary's Academy, an outstanding school operated by the Sisters of Charity of Nazareth at Paducah. Mr. DuMaine, who was in the produce business, brought the family west in 1942 and young Pierre was enrolled in parochial schools at Holy Family in Glendale and Saint Vincent de Paul in San Francisco.

In 1945, Pierre entered Saint Joseph's Seminary, Mountain View, as a clerical candidate for the Archdiocese of San Francisco. Upon completion of his theological studies at Saint Patrick's Seminary, Menlo Park, he was ordained to the priesthood on June 15, 1957, by Bishop Hugh A. Donohoe, in Saint Mary's Cathedral.

Father DuMaine returned to Glendale, where he offered his first solemn Mass in Holy Family Church. A long–time friend and pastor, Msgr. Michael Galvin, *officialis* for the Archdiocese of Los Angeles, served as archpriest. Archbishop John J. Mitty assigned the new priest to Immaculate Heart of Mary Parish, where he served as curate for one year. In 1958, Father DuMaine continued his studies at The Catholic University of America, in Washington, D.C., as a doctoral, candidate for the Department of Education. Following the bestowal of his degree, Father DuMaine was honored by being invited to join the faculty of the university. There he remained for two years teaching a number of graduate courses in comparative education and pedagogical history.

In 1963, Father DuMaine returned to the Pacific Slope and the teaching staff of Serra High School, in San Mateo. Two years later, he was named Assistant Superintendent of Schools for the Archdiocese of San Francisco. The subsequent years were busy ones. In 1968, Father DuMaine became Director of Educational Television. Six years later he was advanced to the superintendency of schools.

DuMaine served the church nationally and locally with admirable devotion and distinction. He was on the board of directors and is a past president of the Catholic Television Network. In addition he was a member of the accrediting commission for secondary schools of the Western Association of Schools and Colleges. For a number of years, Father DuMaine was on the educational committee of the United States Catholic Conference, as well as the President's National Advisory Council on the Education of Disadvantaged Children.

On July 28,1972, at the behest of Archbishop Joseph T. McGucken, Father DuMaine was named a Prelate of Honor by Pope Paul VI. In 1975, he received a Danforth Fellowship to the National Academy for School Executives.

On April 28, 1978, the Apostolic Delegate to the United States announced that Monsignor DuMaine had been named Auxiliary to the Archbishop of San Francisco and titular Bishop of Sarda. At that time, Archbishop John Quinn praised the appointment, saying that it provided "a new opportunity for service to the Church and the people the Church serves" in the one hundred and fifty–three parishes in Marin, San Francisco, San Mateo and Santa Clara counties.

DuMaine received episcopal ordination, together with Francis A. Quinn, the first in the new Saint Mary's Cathedral, on the Feast of Saint Peter and Paul, June 29, 1978, an event witnessed by over 3,000 people.

On January 27, 1981, DuMaine was appointed proto Bishop of San José in California, an area encompassing Santa Clara county. He retired in 2000.

✛ROBERT J. DWYER (1908–1976)

One of the longest associations between *The Tidings* and any of its writers was that enjoyed by the late Archbishop Robert J. Dwyer (1908–1976). He wrote a column for the newspaper between 1952 and 1976 and a survey in the fall before his death revealed that he was the paper's best read writer.

Though he possessed a doctorate in history from The Catholic University of America, young Father Dwyer spent most of his priestly life associated with the Catholic press. He was first named editor of Utah's *Intermountain Catholic* in 1934 and during those years he not only presided over the affairs of the newspaper, but composed editorials and book reviews, invented a column called "Intermountain Daybook" and wrote a goodly portion of the local news stories.

After a stint at graduate school in Washington, he returned to Salt Lake City and was restored to the editorship in 1937. He received other appointments but again returned to the paper, by now *The Register*, in 1950.

Msgr. Dwyer was visiting at Saint Victor's Church in West Hollywood, in the spring of 1952, when word arrived that Pope Pius XII had appointed him Bishop of Reno. If anything, the promotion quickened the flow of printer's ink in his veins.

Dwyer's weekly columns, which appeared for forty–one years, were printed in many papers throughout the United States. His literary presence on the pages of the Catholic press during more than 2,100 weeks had a vitality and brightness unparalleled in America's ecclesial annals.

In 1967, Dwyer, now the Archbishop of Portland in Oregon, became chairman of the *National Catholic Register* and the *Twin Circle*. Seven years later, the then retired prelate took over the editorship of *The Register*, assuming responsibility for editorials and administrative duties in addition to the syndicated weekly columns.

The archbishop was fond of recalling the words of Pope Leo XIII: "My predecessors chose to bless the swords of the Crusaders: I would prefer to bless the pens of Catholic journalists." Surely those words epitomize the incalculable value of the press as a modern arm of the Church. Dwyer felt that there would always be a place for the priest in the field of Catholic journalism. He noted that "the clergy here is not abdicating its responsibility, but sensibly sharing it."

He pointed out that the Catholic press remains "the standard means of forming an alert and intelligent laity, of raising Catholic literary ideals, and of presenting the Catholic viewpoint in a positive manner, not merely as an antidote for error but as something in itself of infinite worth."

It has been remarked, unkindly, that most Catholic papers deal with dreary diocesan drivel. In part this is true, yet there is an importance in such trivia which can never be overestimated, for it is the stuff of the daily life of the Church, the anguish and the effort of those countless obscure souls who make up the kingdom.

Dwyer was a realist. He looked upon journalism as a "dreadful vocation—unhonored, unsung, poorly paid, permitting no interruptions for vacations and recreation, open to criticism of the most rabid and uncomprehending sort." Yet, though this is true, Dwyer felt that "for him who has printer's ink on his fingers, by birth or by exposure, there is nothing else in life, on the natural level, that answers half so well.

"There is a joy in journalism which more than compensates for the listed sorrows; there is a sense of dedication which trails the trivia through clouds of glory."

✛SAMUEL ECCLESTON (1801–1851)

Papers recently unearthed by Father Harry B. Morrison shed a new light on the role of Baltimore's Archbishop Samuel Eccleston (1801–1851) in providing for the orphaned Diocese of Both Californias in the latter years of the 1840s.

On March 16, 1848, Edward H. Harrison, Quartermaster of the New York Volunteers, wrote from San Francisco to Fielding Lucas asking his friend to bring the needs of California's Catholics to the attention of his archbishop. While admitting that he was "ignorant of the relative positions of the Church in the United States and that in Mexico," he pointed out that "in former times, each of the missions was under the control of a priest sent from Mexico." Those "good men" had been forced to return to Mexico and "it is now some years since this took place and those buildings once so clean and pretty in their simplicity are becoming fast a mass of ruins."

Shortly thereafter, Eccleston received other interventions from Jonathan D. Stevenson and Joseph Warren Revere, both of whom felt that "the missions buildings are of great value although many of them are in ruins and might be easily repaired." Revere felt that "this state of things calls for prompt action on the part of the Church."

Eccleston discussed the matter with the Bishop of Philadelphia, expressing his concern that the Church's property in California might fall into unfriendly hands. He was adamant that anyone appointed "should, if practicable, speak the English language and have a previous understanding with our Government."

Eccleston wondered if it might be advisable to send to California someone like Bishop John Timon of Buffalo who was "a man of business and understands those wild regions." After gathering additional information from other bishops, Eccleston went to Washington to lobby for the Church's interest in California. There, Secretary of State James Buchanan advised the sending of a "commission" to the area.

In a letter to a friend, Eccleston reported that "Buchanan agrees with us that, in the present unorganized state of the country, we cannot act too promptly and too prudently." When the name of Bishop John Odin was "floated" by Eccleston, the Galveston prelate reported back that his jurisdiction in Galveston did not include California and that he had quite enough challenges at the moment.

Eccleston felt that whoever was eventually sent to California should be an American, a viewpoint that was passed along to officials in Rome. When Father Charles Pius Montgomery refused appointment to the Diocese of Monterey, Eccleston recommended another Dominican, Joseph Sadoc Alemany, a native of Spain, but a naturalized citizen of the United States. Alemany received the Holy Father's approval and was consecrated in Rome on June 30, 1850.

Acting in his role as the "premier" of the American hierarchy, Eccleston deserves much of the credit for addressing and eventually solving the needs of the orphaned Church in California. Through his involvement, the protection of the Church's property along the Pacific Slope would eventually be decided by American legal processes.

As the paper trail of Eccleston and others finally begins to surface, historians will be able to add a wholly new dimension to ecclesial activities along California's *El Camino Real*. The final chapter will only be written on Judgment Day.

✢DIOMEDE CARDINAL FALCONIO (1842–1917)

In May of 1903, the Apostolic Delegate to the United States, Archbishop Diomede Falconio (1842–1917),

came to Los Angeles for the dedication of Saint Joseph's Church. His days in California's southland were filled with a myriad of religious and civic commitments. The address delivered by Isidore Dockweiler, on behalf of the Catholic laity, was among the more notable of the week's events.

If it be alone remembered that Your Excellency occupies the highest ecclesiastical position in the Catholic Church in these United States, which numbers twelve millions of adherents, and which is the greatest religious body in our country, it will readily be conceded by even our separated brethren that a fitting welcome should be extended to you; but when, one born and educated a Catholic and believing as such, and therefore necessarily more appreciative of your exalted office as the personal representative of the pope, and the greatest pope known to several centuries, is called upon to speak on behalf of his fellow Catholics, he must needs do so with a consciousness of the insufficiency of his own words, to adequately express the sentiments of our hearts and minds, and the sense of pleasure and happiness that we tonight enjoy.

Monsignor Falconio, we bid you a sincere, and most cordial, and thrice hearty welcome. We are indeed proud to have you in our midst. We appreciate your effort and your kindness in travelling thousands of miles to bless a new and splendid temple recently erected in our city, and dedicated to the service of the God of nations.

This is the first time that our southland has been honored by the presence of an Apostolic Delegate and we realize the special appropriateness of your presence; for, while you are the representative of our Holy Father, you were long since enrolled as a member of the Franciscan order and a humble follower of the great St. Francis, whose devoted and intrepid sons more than a century ago first christianized and civilized California and built upon our coast a chain of missions, the remains of which are even now the wonder and admiration of a grateful people.

And again, it must be noted as more than a mere coincidence that in his solicitude for our welfare the Holy Father should have been pleased to select Your Excellency as his representative in our land, since many years ago, when but a lowly Franciscan friar, you were pleased to adopt American ideals of government and secure the coveted prize of American citizenship.

It need hardly be mentioned that, in the natural order, an American citizen, whether such by birth or adoption, has a stronger claim upon our personal affection and interest than one of foreign allegiance.

Therefore we congratulate you, as one of our own, upon attaining the ecclesiastical dignity and office you now enjoy and the duties which you so ably and wisely discharge.

It is indeed an exalted honor and distinguished privilege to be the personal and direct Ambassador of that Grand Old Man, known to the world as Leo XIII, who now sits by Tiber's shore, and, as we believe, by divine right, controls the religious destinies of two hundred million human beings; who, though past his ninety–third year, and frail of body, yet possesses a mind endowed with such intellectual power and brilliancy as to challenge the admiration of the civilized world, irrespective of religious, political or racial difference, and whose spotless and noble character is reverenced and exalted by Catholic and non–Catholic alike.

We entreat your excellency to accept the assurances of our high regard and warmest affection, and we would charge you to convey to His Holiness, Leo XIII, our unchangeable sentiments of unswerving loyalty, heartfelt devotion and undying fealty to the Chair of Peter.

✝JOSEPH ANTHONY FERRARIO (b. 1926)

As a suffragan see in the Province of San Francisco, the multiracial and multi–ethnic Diocese of Honolulu shares a prominent place in California's Catholic annals. An event occurred there on January 13, 1978, which was unique for that island paradise. That was the day scheduled for the episcopal ordination of an auxiliary bishop to serve the diverse and complex area of Hawaii.

Joseph Anthony Ferrario was born at Scranton, Pennsylvania, on March 3, 1926, the second son of Angelo and Angelina Ferrario. His earliest education was acquired in the local public schools.

Following the usual preparatory courses, Joseph entered Saint Charles Seminary at Baltimore and, a few years later, joined the Sulpician Fathers. Completing his theology at The Catholic University of America, he was ordained at Scranton on May 19, 1951. Father Ferrario's first teaching assignment was in the Archdiocese of San Francisco, where he was appointed to the faculty of Saint Joseph's Seminary, Mountain View. He remained there from 1951 to 1957.

Ferrario, known among his peers as a quiet but energetic priest, was transferred, in 1957, to Saint Stephen's Seminary, in Hawaii. A decade later he was incardinated in the Diocese of Honolulu.

During his early years in the islands, Father Ferrario served in a number of capacities, including seminary professor, director of the Catholic Youth Organization, chairman of the diocesan Liturgy Commission and president of the Priests Senate.

The zealous cleric also spearheaded "Project Hawaii," the first drive ever held in Hawaii to raise funds for diocesan development. He also managed the vocation program for the Honolulu jurisdiction. Ferrario also functioned as secretary to Bishop John J. Scanlan and Pastor of Holy Trinity Parish. He was subsequently entrusted with the pastorate of Saint Anthony's, Kailua.

Late in 1977, Pope Paul VI named Ferrario to the titular see of Cuse, and Auxiliary Bishop of the 200,000 Catholics attached to the Diocese of Honolulu. The ordi-

nation ceremony was held under bright skies in the openness of the Neal Blaisdell Center, Honolulu. It was the first such rite performed in the 151 years of Catholic presence in Hawaii.

The leaf of the breadfruit tree dominated the scene of the ordination as if to bring alive the idea of life and the continuance of the people through the transferal of episcopal power from the consecrators to the new prelate.

Bishop Ferrario has been described as a person who is "a sound, sensible and sensitive human being who will do his best to serve his people, his Church and his God." In his homily at the ordination Mass, Cardinal Timothy Manning touched upon those same qualities, noting that "the torch is today passed to a whole new generation of leaders in this kingdom of the sea."

He retired on October 12, 1993.

✝CARL A. FISHER (1945–1993)

Throughout the annals of humankind, the story of emerging peoples has been consistently linked to a handful of leaders graced with generous portions of courage, talent and charisma. Carl A. Fisher was one of those favored individuals whose statue will stand tall alongside Booker T. Washington, Thurgood Marshall and Martin Luther King if ever there is an Afro–American Hall of Fame.

Born black, Catholic and poor to Peter and Evelyn Fisher, the fourth of twelve children, at Pascagoula, Mississippi, Carl Fisher early on set out to prove that the American dream was still alive and not restricted to his white, Protestant and rich contemporaries. He attended Saint Peter the Apostle School on the Gulf of Mexico, just a few miles from the Alabama border. At fourteen, he enrolled at Epiphany Apostolic School in Newburgh, New York.

After graduation in 1963, he entered Mary Immaculate, the Novitiate for the Josephite Fathers. Upon completing his theological studies at Saint Joseph's Seminary, the Oblate College and the Washington Theological Coalition, he was ordained on June 2, 1973.

Father Fisher served as curate at Incarnation Parish in Washington, D.C. (1973–1975) and Saint Veronica's in Baltimore (1975–1982) before assuming a four year pastorate at Saint Francis Xavier, America's oldest Afro–Catholic parish. According to the *Baltimore Sun*, attendance skyrocketed, due to the "exuberant and energetic style" of Fisher's preaching.

On December 23, 1986, Pope John Paul II named the youthful Fisher to the titular See of Tlos and Auxiliary Bishop of Los Angeles. He was the third Josephite and the eleventh African American appointed to the American hierarchy. Consecrated on February 23, 1987, Fisher was installed as Episcopal Vicar of the San Pedro

Region on November 8th. On the day of his arrival in the area, a reporter noted that the prelate "was richly blessed by his God with innumerable virtues and attributes."

Fisher fitted well into the incredible ethnic diversity and blend of his people. It was indeed a vibrant network of Catholics—four deaneries, sixty–five parishes, fifty–three elementary schools, ten high schools and three hospitals. The details of Fisher's whirlwind ministry in the San Pedro Region must await a future historian. Surely no other area in California or elsewhere was served more diligently and prayerfully by its shepherd.

At the time of his premature death from cancer, Carl Fisher was still the youngest bishop in California. He fell asleep in the Lord at Lakewood, in the presence of Roger Cardinal Mahony and other close friends, on September 2, 1993. On the day of his funeral, an elderly lady in the cathedral parking lot told how the bishop had personally validated her marriage, buried her son, confirmed her niece and baptized her great granddaughter—four generations of ministry crammed into six and a half years!

Anyone can tell us how to live, but only the exceptional person can teach us how to die. Tucked away in a huge box of papers which the bishop personally dispatched to the Archival Center just a week before he died, was a recorded telephone conservation which the dying prelate had with the Holy Father in Denver on August 15th. He concluded with these cheerful words! "Goodbye, Holy Father, I will see you in heaven."

Only statisticians are impressed by longevity. Heroes rarely live long, but they always live well. Carl Anthony Fisher was one of California's heroes, a rare distinction indeed for a Catholic priest!

✛PIETRO CARDINAL FUMASONI–BIONDI (1872–1960)

It was early in 1924, that Monsignor Patrick Harnett, speaking on behalf of the People of God, welcomed to California's southland, the Most Reverend Pietro Fumasoni–Biondi (1872–1960), Apostolic Delegate to the United States. Noting that "ours is not the language of diplomacy but the language of hearts overflowing with love," the Vicar General for the Diocese of Monterey–Los Angeles reflected on "the young and vigorous Church in the United States:"

> It is not in a spirit of self–glorification that we speak of the Church in the United States as a very important portion of the Vineyard of the Lord. If we must refer to it, it is because we wish to emphasize the importance of him who represents the Holy Father in its government.
>
> There has not been, I dare say, in the history of the Church, a country in which the Catholic cause has so progressed in so short a time, as in these United States.

> A little over a hundred years ago, the Catholics in this country were numbered by thousands; today, they are numbered by millions. We are proud to state that our American flag floats today over Catholics as devoted to the Holy See as any Catholics on earth.
>
> This devotedness is not a matter of sentimentality; it is a matter founded on strong religious convictions. We are convinced that Christ is God. We are convinced that He founded a Church. We know that He appointed Peter to be its head. We know that to him as to Peter was given in its fullness the power of loosing and binding. We know that the Sovereign Pontiff is Peter's successor. We know that he like Peter is the Vicar of Christ and the Father of the Faithful. We know that to him as to Peter was given the care of the lambs and the sheep of Christ's fold. We know that like Peter, he it is who is to confirm his brethren in the faith.
>
> We know that it is through him we are enabled to escape the pitfalls of error and to know with absolute certainty what we have to believe and what we have to do to save our souls.
>
> No wonder, then, that we are devoted to the See of Peter and its august occupant. No wonder that we are not ashamed of professing our loyalty and devotion to him.
>
> God has wonderfully blessed the people of these United States. He has copiously showered upon us His blessings. That temporal prosperity has been ours none will deny. That we have used the material goods bestowed on us to promote God's glory we are vain enough to imagine.
>
> Our churches, our schools for primary and secondary education, our colleges and universities, our hospitals and orphanages, our homes for the aged and insane, and other charitable institutions dot the land.
>
> It is not only in the Eastern States that evidences of our Faith are found. Here in the land hallowed by the footsteps of the saintly Spanish Franciscans and with Catholic traditions the most ennobling, are to be seen evidences of a spirit of self–sacrifice and of devotion to the Catholic cause.
>
> In the territory comprised in the cathedral parish of this city forty years ago, there are today sixty parishes, for the most part well equipped and self–sustaining.
>
> Our Catholic institutions owe their existence to the generosity of our people and stand as monuments to the love of the people for that God who has so generously bestowed His gifts upon them.
>
> Have we in our thought of promoting God's glory forgotten the needs of the Vicar of Christ? The Holy See, doubtless, realizes that in these latter years her revenue for the most part has been supplied by American Catholics, a people as loyal and devoted as ever championed the Catholic cause.

✛FRANCIS JAMES FUREY (1905–1979)

Francis James Furey (1905–1979) was born in Summit Hill, Pennsylvania, the son of John F. and Anna

(O'Donnell) Furey. He received his earliest education in the public system of Coaldale and graduated from that town's Catholic High School.

Beginning his clerical studies at Saint Charles Seminary, Overbrook, Francis was later sent to Rome's Pontifical Seminary, where he successfully completed work for doctorates in both philosophy and theology. He was ordained on March 15, 1930, by Basilio Cardinal Pompilj, Vicar General to Pope Pius XI. Soon after arriving back on Philadelphia, Father Furey was appointed Secretary to Cardinal Dennis Dougherty, a position he held for six years. In 1936, he was made President of Immaculata College and, ten years later, Rector of Saint Charles Seminary.

On becoming rector, Father Furey was honored by Pope Pius XII with the title of Domestic Prelate. During his years at Overbrook, Msgr. Furey was also Professor of Pastoral Theology, Homiletics and Liturgy. In 1958, Furey was named Pastor of Saint Helena's Parish, Philadelphia. Two years later, Pope John XXIII advanced him to the titular Bishopric of Temnus, as Auxiliary to Cardinal John F. O'Hara.

Msgr. Furey received episcopal ordination on December 22, 1960, and a few months afterwards was appointed Vicar General and Director of the Catholic Charities Appeal. In 1962, he was selected by Pope John XXIII to serve on the administrative tribunal of Vatican Council II.

Bishop Furey was named Coadjutor of San Diego on July 21, 1963 and Apostolic Administrator on September 12th. At the time of his installation, there were 350,000 Catholics in the 36,000 square mile jurisdiction. Bishop Furey became Ordinary of San Diego on March 6, 1966, with the demise of the Most Reverend Charles F. Buddy. His episcopate was characterized by spiritual renewal, liturgical reform, social advances and educational improvements.

Active in promoting ecumenical and civic projects, Bishop Furey was a founder of the local urban coalition. By his openness, balance and even–tempered reaction to proposals and problems, he invited initiative and candor from both clergy and laity. Though he found the Diocese of San Diego in severe financial straits, Bishop Furey was able to bring about erection of sixteen churches, seven schools and six convents.

In mid 1969, Furey was transferred to the Archbishopric of San Antonio. He was installed in San Fernando Cathedral, on August 6th. At the time of his move to the southwest, one acquaintance observed that Texas "was the only place big enough to measure up to his expectations."

As the Archbishop of San Antonio reflected on his years along the Pacific Slope, he likely recalls the words spoken at his departure by Governor Ronald Reagan: "As the second Bishop of San Diego, you have earned a lasting place in our history and heritage."

✚FRANCISCO GARCIA DIEGO Y MORENO (1785 –1846)

A. AN EPISCOPAL OVERVIEW

A partial explanation for the relative paucity of details about the initial member of California's hierarchy, Fray Francisco García Diego y Moreno, a good man too long forgotten, can be found in the fact that "when he died in 1846, the whole mission structure collapsed and buried him in its dust." Born in 1785, at the *Hacienda de la Daga*, a few miles from the Mexican village of Lagos, off the roadway to San Luís Potosí, Francisco Garcia Diego came from a well–established and socially–prominent family, long active in ecclesial and civil affairs.

Garcia Diego first came to California, in 1832, as Commissary Prefect of the Zacatecan Franciscans, a small band of friars from the Apostolic College of *Nuestra Señora de Guadalupe*, to whom a portion of the already founded missions had been entrusted by governmental mandate. After a number of faithful missionary years at Santa Clara, Fray Francisco Garcia Diego returned to Mexico City seeking authorization for a structural overhaul of the mission system to meet post–secularization needs and stresses.

He came back, late in 1841, as the first bishop of the newly–created Diocese of Both Californias. During his brief episcopal tenure, the prelate governed the infant church and its twenty priests from headquarters at Mission Santa Barbara. That "the bishop was poor and that his episcopate was but a series of frustrations, no one can deny." Upon his premature death, on April 30, 1846, no less a personage than Anastásio Carrillo stated that "Divine Providence has taken from us a good man, a just soul."

Sir George Simpson reported that the inhabitants of Santa Barbara initially derived considerable encouragement from the appointment of a bishop, an attitude possibly based on the widely accepted assumption that the prelate had made some arrangement with the Mexican Government for a partial restoration of the missions. Few other contemporary writers reflected such optimism, however Angustias de la Guerra Ord, for example, doubted that the area needed a bishop. Her biographer felt that Garcia Diego "was unfitted to overcome the difficulties he faced without priests or money," inasmuch as his only base of popular support was Santa Barbara and "rarely did the discouraged man leave his home."

Eugene Duflot de Mofras shared that opinion and predicted, in 1841, that "the influence of the bishop will not be widespread; his advanced age and his Mexican education will not permit him to take part in any spiritual conquests, nor augment the imposing foundations that are the glory of the Spanish Fathers."

Obviously the ill feelings harbored by such *paisanos*,

or Californians, as Mariano Guadalupe Vallejo, for Mexican immigrants explains much of the personal antipathy for Garcia Diego. The bishop would surely have fared better if his cradle had stood in Spain rather than in Mexico!

Francisco Garcia Diego y Moreno gave every indication of having been a very humble and pious man, unworldly, unselfish and well versed in the ecclesiastical disciplines. While he may not have been the strong character that the stormy years indeed required, "it is doubtful if any man could have been a great leader in the troublous times" of his episcopacy. The bishop was destined, like Saint Francis of Assisi, to taste the stigma of anticlericalism then pervading turbulent, revolutionary Mexico. Suffering not unto blood, his natural death was hastened by the unfulfilled promises of greedy men who governed California in the name of "God and Liberty."

✢FRANCISCO GARCIA DIEGO Y MORENO (1785–1846)

B. A 125TH ANNIVERSARY

October 4, 1965, marked the 125th anniversary of the consecration, at Mexico's National Shrine of Our Lady of Guadalupe, of Fray Francisco García Diego y Moreno, first Bishop of Both Californias.

The son of Francisco Diego and Ana María Moreno was born at Lagos in the central part of Mexico on September 17, 1785, only a short year after the death of Father Junípero Serra, in whose footsteps he was destined to follow. At the age of ten, Francisco entered the conciliar seminary at Guadalajara, and from there he advanced to the Franciscan College of Our Lady of Guadalupe. He was ordained to the priesthood on November 14, 1808.

In 1831 when the Mexican Government ordered the Apostolic College at Zacatecas to supply friars in California, Father Garcia Diego was *Comisaro–Prefecto* of his community, in which position he had charge of all missionary activities. After examining the various aspects of the new apostolate, Garcia Diego and nine companions set out for California late in 1832. The Zacatecan friars were entrusted with the southern branch of the mission chain begun at San Diego in 1769.

With the subsequent collapse of the mission system, a new form of ecclesiastical administration was drawn up for California and at the request of the Republic of Mexico, Pope Gregory XVI named Father Garcia Diego Bishop of Both Californias on April 27, 1840. One chronicler speaks of the bishop's arrival in his See City, noting that "the whole population of the place turned out to pay homage to this first Bishop of California. All was bustle; men and women and children hastening to the

Bishop Francisco Garcio Diego

beach, banners flying, drums beating, and soldiers marching." Though San Diego had been designated as his official residence, the prelate soon found it expedient to move northward to Santa Barbara where he "was received with enthusiasm by the inhabitants."

The post–mission years were difficult ones for the Church in California. As the bishop himself pointed out in 1843: "Divine worship is scantily maintained, and the missionaries are decreasing for want of substitution . . . . Instead of being able to support and civilize the natives, they are obligated to beg their subsistence, bewail the oppression of the neophytes and the annihilation of the settlements they founded."

"In many ways Garcia Diego's episcopate was a period of frustration. He had come to witness the deathbed scene of the mission system which passed away in successive gasps of agony. The bishop's pleas for restoration of the Society of Jesus, use of the Pious Fund of the Californias, and means to make a canonical visitation went unheeded by a government which had earlier pledged to make "all suitable arrangements that the new prelate may not lack the proper support necessary in order to cover the expenses and maintain the decorum of episcopal dignity. . . .''

We are told that 'large piles of stones were heaped up in several places for laying the foundations'' of the bishop's envisioned residence, cathedral and monastery, but, as Alfred Robinson observed, "they will undoubtedly remain for some years, as monuments of the frailty of human speculation.'' Though his death on April 30, 1846 preceded the hoisting of the American flag at Monterey by some days, the tireless friar–bishop had nurtured the seed of Christianity which another generation would reap in a bountiful harvest.

✛FRANCISCO GARCIA DIEGO Y MORENO (1785–1846)

C. *REQUIESCAT IN PACE!*

One of the most interesting historical items at Mission Santa Barbara is the artistic monument erected to mark the tomb of Fray Francisco Garcia Diego y Moreno, first Bishop of Both Californias. Located at right angles to the reredos which it adjoins, the monument adorns the wall of the Epistle–side of the sanctuary. Though it is five feet, three inches wide and seven feet, ten inches in height, the colorful piece of art work is usually overlooked by the casual visitor.

The facade of the monument is executed in wooden paneling painted to resemble marble. The capitals of the smooth semi–engaged pillars are carved imitations of Ionic volutes. A pinkish color scheme is broken only by the light blue pediment and the imitation green marble surrounding the medallion.

At the base of the monument is a rectangular marker containing the prelate's obituary. Translated into English, it reads "Here lies the most reverend and illustrious Fray Francisco Garcia Diego y Moreno, first Bishop of this Diocese of Both Californias, who departed life on the 30th of April, 1846." Directly above the central marker is a circular reproduction of the bishop's coat–of–arms. In the central portion of the episcopal shield is the crowned Madonna and Child, commonly known as the *Mater Amabilis* This particular depiction, obviously based on the *Refugio* of Jose Alzibar, clearly reflects the Raphaelean influence. A rather crudely painted border encloses the field with the words: "*F. Franciscus Garcia Diego Prim. Epis. Californ.*"

Atop the seal is the traditional episcopal hat from which descend the six tassels associated with residential bishops. In the apex of the facade is a "precious" mitre, and beneath that, an oversized chalice, symbolizing the priesthood.

The neo–classic influence is obvious in both the sculpture and architecture of the tomb. One authority has noted the marked similarity of the monument to the *entradas* and niches designed by Francisco Eduardo Tresguerras. This famous Mexican architect's style is plainly discernible in a church at Aguas Calientes which Fray Francisco Garcia Diego planned in the strict neo–classical form before coming to California. The monument was made shortly after the prelate's death, possibly by the same artist who designed the elaborate altar for the bishop.

It was erroneously conjectured by some that the actual vault extended into the wall. However, in November of 1912, the tomb was located exactly in the corner of the sanctuary on the epistle–side of the altar. When the vault was opened, the coffin was found standing in the middle of the grave, leaving about six or eight inches space on either side and more space on the ends; it was covered with velvet of purple color and having some crosses, and the name of the Rt. Rev. Bishop on the cover being formed of brass or copper nails with large heads. The coffin was found in good, well preserved condition.

The artistically finished monument marking the tomb of California's first bishop is the most elaborate of any used for the state's subsequent prelates. The paradox is that Francisco Garcia Diego y Moreno was the poorest of them all!

✛DANIEL JAMES GERCKE (1874–1964)

The personage of Daniel James Gercke (1874–1964), longtime Bishop of Tucson, formerly a suffragan diocese within the Metropolitan Province of Los Angeles, embodies all the traits one might have expected in an ecclesial pioneer. Highlights from his eulogy, preached by the then Auxiliary Bishop of Los Angeles, Timothy Manning, are here reproduced:

> Death has come for the archbishop. In the 89th year of his age; in the 63rd year of his priesthood and in the 41st year of his episcopate, on March 19, 1964, Daniel J. Gercke, recent Bishop of Tucson, then Titular Archbishop of Cotyaeum, passed out of this world and entered into eternity.
>
> In fancy we like to think of the dear archbishop met at the entrance of Paradise and companioned to the Most High Priest by those "Soldiers of the Faith" whose seeding he watered and harvested in this recovered wilderness.
>
> Archbishop Lamy will be there, who, one hundred years ago entered Tucson for the first time to claim it for the jurisdiction of Santa Fe; Archbishop Salpointe, first Vicar Apostolic of the Arizona territory, who resigned from Santa Fe to return here to Tucson and to lie buried in its cathedral.
>
> In that company surely would be found Fray Francisco de Porras, first Franciscan missionary among the Hopi Indians; Father Kino and Fr. Salvatierra, intrepid

Jesuits pioneering north from Sonora, sanctifying with their foot–falls the rich earth of Arizona; Fray Francisco Garces, apostle of San Xavier del Bac, lovely cradle of the faith in the desert.

Daniel Gercke was of their company and their kindred. Somehow, he was the termination of the apostolic age of the faith which they began and, at the same time, the architect of the new Church of Arizona wedded to the 20th and nuclear century.

We pay tribute to his glorious priesthood, vested in a measure of earthly clay, conditioned by the environment of the womb, the home, the seminary, that bore him, and flashing in brilliance in the things that best expressed that priesthood.

His mold was German–Irish; from the one came the methodical, unvarying, humorless precision which was so invaluable in the organization, husbanding and building up of a diocese; from the other, the warmth of heart that intimated the furnace of an ancient faith, the patriotism indigent at the fortunes of his forebears at the hands of their oppressors.

From blending of both strains, as is so often the case, the mission was largely to the Spanish–speaking. Three times he returned to them in the Philippines and for forty years in the southland he would be their champion, their confidant, their shepherd.

There was in him that element which is of the essence of all great apostleship. It was of Abraham, of the Apostles, of Paul, of all the soldiers of the Cross. It is a departure from the land, kindred, attachment, and going into the unknown armed only with unswerving faith and never looking back. This was what he brought to Arizona.

A translation from Philadelphia to the West was not then the promotion it might connote today. It was an uprooting, a testing, an exile, a plunge into the unknown, a dedication—an act of faith. It was grandly done, irrevocably done, holily done by Archbishop Gercke.

The result of all testing in the crucible of faith is fruitfulness. For Abraham it was a progeny, more numerous than the stars in the sky above, countless as the grains of sand below. For this prelate it shall be the statistics of growth in population, in parishes, in schools, in priests and religious, in divisions of diocese, in the totality of which will be reflected the paternal image of his generating priesthood.

Such is the tribute of our farewell. May the earth rest gently on his ashes.

✣JAMES CARDINAL GIBBONS (1834–1921)

The visit to Los Angeles, in October, 1887, of James Cardinal Gibbons, the ranking dignitary of the Catholic Church in the United States created "great interest not only among Catholics, but among all classes in the city." After a brief stop in San Francisco, the cardinal proceeded to the southland, where he received an elaborate reception. Members of a special delegation journeyed by train to Newhall to meet the distinguished head of the Church in America and escort him to Los Angeles.

The first cardinalatial visitation to the city of Our Lady of the Angels began with a liturgical ceremony at Saint Vibiana's Cathedral, where the prelate was officially greeted by the Right Reverend Francis Mora, Bishop of Monterey–Los Angeles. At the public reception, attended by well over 4,000 persons, R. F. del Valle welcomed the cardinal to California not only as a prince of the Church but as one who had aided in perpetuating the very principles upon which the government was founded.

Mayor William H. Workman noted in his address, "The distinguished and eminent ecclesiastical dignitary whose presence was the signal for this demonstration tonight, is admittedly entitled to universal admiration and respect." The city's chief executive went on to say that the cardinal's devotion to his country's institutions, his solicitation, often and ably expressed, to keep the administration of public affairs pure and free from all taint, have served to direct attention to needed reforms and have stamped Cardinal Gibbons as one of the most thoughtful and needed citizens of the republic.

Stephen Mallory White, the Lieutenant Governor, concluded the official welcoming ceremonies by observing that there had not been among all those who have greeted him in other places a heartier welcome from intelligent brain and honest soul than he received in Los Angeles.

In responding to the enthusiastic greetings, the cardinal observed that the growth and progress of the Pacific Coast far exceeded his mildest expectations. After pointing out some of the more attractive qualities of the area, His Eminence stated, "The glory of your State after all lies not so much in your climate and soil, but your prosperity consists of your manhood, intelligence and the zeal and earnestness which the American people bring to every enterprise they undertake."

An interesting insight is gleaned from the report of a journalist from the Los Angeles *Tribune*, who interviewed the prelate at Saint Vincent's College. He recorded that were it "not for the awe inspired by his office and his great intelligence one would almost be tempted to call him a good fellow, so absolutely is he devoid of hauteur or chilling capacity."

Though visibly exhausted from the long trek to Portland, where he had invested Archbishop William H. Gross with the pallium, Baltimore's cardinal lost none of that dynamic charm which characterized his role as leader of American Catholicism for so many decades. His interviewer noted: "In the small frame and chiseled features of the cardinal shone that power which is recognized by the term of intellectuality." The *Tribune's* reporter further observed that "in addition to the mental fire imbuing his countenance, there is that far better force of benevolence in his kindly mouth and gentle blue eyes."

The cardinal's biographer later observed that the visit of Gibbons to the far west "aroused a great deal of interest and enthusiasm among the Catholic people of those regions. It was their first glimpse of a prince of the Church, and their pride in playing host to a member of the College of Cardinals was heightened when they observed the generally friendly manner in which their non–Catholic friends and neighbors greeted the visitor."

✛ EULOGIO GREGORIO GILLOW Y ZAVALZA (1841–1922)

One of the most interesting chapters in the long history of California's seventeenth mission revolves about the presence at San Fernando of the Most Reverend Eulogio Gregorio Gillow y Zavalza (1841–1922), the exiled Archbishop of Oaxaca. A native of Puebla de los Angeles, Gillow studied in England, Belgium and Rome. After ordination, he returned to Rome for further studies prior to entering the Holy See's diplomatic corps.

He attended Vatican Council I as a *peritus* for the Bishop of Oaxaca. Later Gillow returned to Mexico and became active in efforts to establish a rail system for the country. In 1887, he became Bishop (and later Archbishop) of Oaxaca.

Archbishop Gillow was early on recognized as a leader of the Mexican hierarchy. General Porfirio Diaz was so enamored with the prelate that he proposed to Roman authorities that Gillow be named the first Mexican cardinal. In 1913, during the persecution of Venustiano Carranza, the archbishop was exiled to the United States. He lived for a while in San Antonio and it was from there, on September 12, 1915, that he wrote to the Bishop of Monterey–Los Angeles with a most interesting suggestion.

He prefaced his remarks by pointing out that Fray Junípero Serra had "begun his missions in the Villa Alta, one of the principal parishes of the Archbishopric of Oaxaca, continuing them in several districts of the same, until he decided to come to California."

Based on that earlier connection between Oaxaca and California, Gillow asked if the *convento* and surrounding grounds at San Fernando could be restored and utilized for establishing a school to train several dozen teenage boys and older men in agricultural pursuits. The students would cultivate and maintain the orchards, farmlands and flower gardens as part of their projects. Gillow also wanted to set up a printing office where

leaflets and books could be issued in defense of the beseiged Church in Mexico.

Gillow's final proposal was the most ambitious of them all. He wanted to oversee the construction of a railroad from San Diego to peninsular California. With better communications, he could then inaugurate a catechetical program for the inhabitants of that area who had little or no instruction about their faith. The institution at San Fernando would be staffed by qualified secular and/or regular priests chosen by the archbishop and approved by the Bishop of Monterey–Los Angeles. If and when the need for the school would cease, the property would revert to the local Church.

There is no extant reply to Gillow's letter, probably because Bishop Thomas J. Conaty died just six days after the letter was posted. Whatever response there was originated with the diocesan administrator.

Gillow managed to raise enough seed money for the project to begin and, with $500 allocated by the Catholic Church Extension Society, he was able to start restoring several of the *convento* rooms. Unfortunately, there is no record about which ones were utilized.

Apparently the Diocese of Monterey–Los Angeles expected Gillow to pay a modest rent for the facilities at San Fernando because on at least two occasions there are indications that the archbishop defaulted in his quarterly payments. Precisely how far the restorative and educative program continued is unknown. Archbishop Gillow returned to Oaxaca early in 1921 and died there the following year.

✛ JOSEPH GILMORE (1893–1962)

On April 2, 1962, just as Catholics in San Francisco were completing preparations for installing their new archbishop, the massive toll bell at Saint Mary's Cathedral began its ominous peal, a sign of movement in the turnstile of heaven.

Father John F. Carvlin had been summoned from the cathedral to bring the holy oils to a private dining room on the mezzanine floor of the Fairmont Hotel. In those days, prior to the Heimlich method, the Bishop of Helena Montana, was dying of asphyxia.

Born to John Joseph and Mary Teresa (Hanrahan) Gilmore on March 22, 1893, Joseph Gilmore was brought by his parents to Anaconda in 1898. He was educated at Saint Joseph's College in Dubuque and later entered the Urban College of Propaganda Fide in Rome as a clerical candidate for the Diocese of Helena.

Ordained on July 25, 1915, by Basilio Cardinal Pompilj, Father Gilmore was appointed to the faculty of Mount Saint Charles College where he served with great distinction until 1919. The young priest then engaged in pastoral work in the massive Diocese of Helena and, in 1927, he was appointed Chancellor and assistant to Bishop Ralph L. Hayes.

Later, when Hayes was named Rector of the North American College, Pope Plus XII selected Father Gilmore to succeed him as the Bishop of Helena. He was consecrated on February 19, 1936, by Archbishop Amleto Cicognani, the Apostolic Delegate to the United States.

In addition to serving longer than any of his predecessors, Bishop Gilmore occupied several positions in the National Catholic Welfare Conference. He was chairman of the Department of Immigration, adviser of the National Confraternity of Christian Doctrine and a member of N.C.W.C.'s administrative board.

A long–time friend of Archbishop Joseph T. McGucken, Gilmore had journeyed to California with Bishop William Condon of Great Falls to attend McGucken's installation as Archbishop of San Francisco. It was during a private dinner honoring McGucken, in the California Room of the Fairmont Hotel, that Bishop Gilmore suddenly slumped forward on the table. Two waiters rushed to his assistance, but he was unconscious and obviously near death.

Archbishop Egidio Vagnozzi, the Apostolic Delegate, gave absolution to the dying prelate. The sacrament of Extreme Unction was administered when Father Carvlin arrived from the cathedral with the holy oils.

Dr. Gunther Nashelsky was summoned to the scene and officially pronounced the bishop dead. "It appeared to be a heart attack" according to Nashelsky. The actual cause of death was later made known by Coroner Henry Turkel, when an autopsy determined that death was accidental and not, as had originally been assumed, due to heart failure.

Archbishop McGucken accompanied his friend's remains back to Helena and there participated in the final obsequies for the highly loved Bishop of Helena. He was eulogized by McGucken as "a gentle shepherd who quietly moved among his flock in the robes of high priest." McGucken went on to say that "it was characteristic of his generous temperament that Bishop Gilmore was on a mission of friendship when he was summoned to Eternal Life."

✛JOSEPH SARSFIELD GLASS, C.M. (1874–1926)

A. BISHOP OF SALT LAKE CITY

Joseph Sarsfield Glass was born, in Bushnell, Illinois on March 13, 1874. James and Mary Kelly Glass brought their young son to the City of the Angels in 1887 and enrolled him at Saint Vincent's College, then recently located in its new building on Grand Avenue.

After some years at Saint Mary's Seminary in Per-

ryville, Missouri, Glass returned to Los Angeles in 1896 and took his place again at Saint Vincent's College, this time as a member of the Vincentian faculty. He was ordained to the priesthood the following summer by Bishop George T. Montgomery of Monterey–Los Angeles. The young priest was then sent to Rome for advanced theological studies and in 1899 received his doctorate in Sacred Theology. Upon coming back to the United States, Father Glass taught moral theology and acted as director of students at Perryville for two years before arriving in Los Angeles as President of Saint Vincent's College.

During his administration, the college was expanded several times and soon achieved a reputation as the leading educational institution in the entire southwest. When the Congregation of the Mission withdrew from the college in 1911, Father Glass remained in Los Angeles as Pastor of Saint Vincent's Church. There he reorganized the parish school on a free–basis in some of the old college buildings. Early in 1915, plans were afoot to name Father Glass Auxiliary Bishop of Salt Lake to assist the aged Lawrence Scanlan. The incumbent died, however, before the appointment could be processed and Pope Benedict XV then assigned Glass Ordinary of Salt Lake on June 1, 1915.

Archbishop Edward J. Hanna of San Francisco performed the consecration ceremonies in Saint Vincent's Church on August 24, 1915, the first such event in Los Angeles since the crozier was handed to Francis Mora in 1873. 1,300 persons crammed the church to pay tribute to "one of the best known and popular citizens of Los Angeles." It was no idle rhetoric that prompted Bishop Thomas J. Conaty to say that "as a teacher and president of Saint Vincent's College, he has been identified with the educational life of the diocese, and as pastor of Saint Vincent's parish he has been one of the city's prominent rectors."

Bishop Glass's diocese was a missionary area even as late as 1915 and yet the industrious prelate was able "to leave behind monuments that tell of his zeal, of his power, of his intelligence." During World War I, Bishop Glass was one of the four episcopal directors of the National Catholic War Council, and concerning his activity in those years, it is said that "his knowledge of the world, his sympathy with men were large factors in the unparalleled success that attend the efforts," of the N.C.W.C.

✛JOSEPH SARSFIELD GLASS, C.M. (1874–1926)

B. JOSEPH S. GLASS COLLECTION

A substantial portion of what once constituted the private art collection of the late Bishop Joseph Sarsfield Glass (1874–1926) has been placed on permanent exhibit at San Fernando Mission.

The Glass family were prominent Los Angeles pioneers. After his ordination as a priest for the Congregation of the Mission, Father Joseph Glass served many years at Saint Vincent's College and was that institution's president when it closed in 1911. During his subsequent tenure as Pastor of Saint Vincent's parish, Father Glass became a close friend of Edward Laurence and Carrie Estelle Doheny and it was through his ministrations that Mrs. Doheny entered the Catholic Church on October 25, 1918.

Glass was a longtime patron of the arts, an interest developed during his years of study in Rome from 1897 to 1899 and while on a trip through Spain in 1913 to survey ecclesial architecture. In 1915, Father Glass was appointed Bishop of Salt Lake City. During his decade there, the Dohenys provided for many of his temporalities, including a Pierce Arrow automobile.

The Dohenys also financed a collection of statuary and some forty paintings which Glass purchased in Europe during 1924 and 1925. In addition to what became the "Collection of the Madeleine," which is presently housed in the Pastoral Center at Salt Lake City, the Dohenys encouraged Bishop Glass to acquire a smaller but no less exquisite number of paintings and art works for his own personal use.

This latter collection was eventually bequeathed to the bishop's sister, Mary Glass Pope, who lived in Saint Martin of Tours Parish in Brentwood, California. Soon after the completion of a new parochial church, Mrs. Pope arranged with Father Augustine Murray to have the paintings and certain other art items installed in the church, where they remained for the next quarter century.

In mid 1988, the Glass Collection was removed from the church and, by virtue of an agreement between Msgr. Lawrence O'Leary and Mrs. Leona Pope, it was given to San Fernando Mission. The largest of the dozen paintings, affectionately referred to by Bishop Glass as "the Lady of the House," is an early 17th century portrayal of the Immaculate Conception attributed to Jusepe Ribera.

The oil painting of Christ Crucified, the work of the Hungarian artist, Neogrady, is dated 1712. It has been placed on exhibit in the Grand Sala of the mission's *convento* building. Two other 17th century oils depict the Death of Saint Joseph and Saint John the Evangelist. The latter is encased in a handsome Dutch frame.

Five of the smaller paintings are hung in Cantwell Hall. The subjects of those artistic masterpieces are the *Pieta*, God the Father, the Temptation of Saint Anthony, the Massacre of the Innocents and Saint John the Divine. Other paintings in the collection are a 17th century rendition of Nefratiti, an 18th century Adoration of the Magi and a Florentine depiction with Saints Jerome and Catherine of Siena.

Finally, atop the doorway leading into the Archival Center is a small reproduction of Luca Della Robbia's 15th century *Cantoria* or choir balcony in the Cathedral of Florence. This four paneled diorama, enclosed in a gold–leafed wooden frame, probably dates from the turn of the 20th century. Seeing the treasures of the Joseph S. Glass Collection is just another of the many compelling reasons for scheduling a visit to San Fernando Mission.

✤THOMAS KIELY GORMAN (1892–1980)

On June 23, 1967, a Californian with "Nevada gold in his episcopal ring, Irish blood in his veins and printer's scissors on his coat–of–arms" observed the golden anniversary of his ordination to the priesthood. Thomas Kiely Gorman (1892–1980) was born to John Joseph and Elizabeth Gorman. He acquired his early education at the Academy of the Holy Names in his native Pasadena. At the end of the tenth grade he entered Pomona High School. His preparation for the ministry was done at Saint Patrick's Seminary in Menlo Park and Saint Mary's Seminary in Baltimore.

After being ordained to the priesthood by Bishop Daniel F. Feehan of Fall River, Father Gorman continued his studies at The Catholic University of America,

Bishop Thomas J. Gorman

where he obtained a licentiate in Canon Law. He then returned to California's southland and engaged in pastoral work at Santa Clara Church in Oxnard and Saint Vibiana's Cathedral in Los Angeles. In 1922, Bishop John J. Cantwell sent the young priest to the University of Louvain. There he completed his studies for a doctorate in history by writing a brilliant thesis about the influence of the United States on the Belgian Revolution of 1789–1790.

Upon his return to Los Angeles, Father Gorman was named editor of *The Tidings*. "He brought to the newspaper journalistic experience based on sound scholarship, charity and a spirit of Western initiative." As editor, Father Gorman's "aim was that no week should pass wherein he could not point to some technical improvement or the accession of some new educational feature." In the five years of his tenure with *The Tidings*, Gorman "tilted with bigots, nailed attacks, and dealt with the pressing news stories of an era which encompassed persecution in Mexico, gangsterism at home, Ku Klux Klanism, the Hoover–Smith presidential campaign—and steady diocesan growth."

Early in 1931, the Holy See detached all the territory within the State of Nevada from the Dioceses of Sacramento and Salt Lake and created a new ecclesiastical jurisdiction at Reno. On April 24, Father Gorman was named Bishop of the newly–erected diocese. "Immediately, with sustained and amazing energy, like the fence riders of the old West, he ranged his vast, lonely diocese, spurring the labor of the Church, building schools, parishes, stimulating the works of charity and education."

In subsequent years the prelate continued his interest in Catholic journalism. He served, for example, as assistant episcopal chairman, and later for six years as chairman of the Press Department of the National Catholic Welfare Conference. In more recent times, he was episcopal chairman of the N.C.W.C.'s Bureau of Information.

On February 1, 1952, Bishop Gorman was named Coadjutor of Dallas, a diocesan seat to which he succeeded on August 19, 1954. In Texas, the prelate maintained his tireless pace, placing special emphasis on the apostolate of Catholic education. Repeatedly he called for a strong religious educational program through the school, on the platform and in the pulpit to help restore man's confidence in God. Throughout a priesthood spanning half a century in California, Nevada and Texas, Bishop Gorman exhibited deep interest and concern in the development of the Confraternity of Christian Doctrine for the care of Catholic youngsters attending public schools. He also actively championed the programs of the Councils of Catholic Men and Women. In the midst of his many duties, the prelate

found time for the intellectual apostolate. He wrote the story of *Seventy–Five Years of Catholic Life in Nevada* (1935) and established two diocesan newspapers, the *Nevada Register* and the *Texas Catholic*.

Catholics in the Golden State proudly recalled the many accomplishments of the Bishop of Dallas–Fort Worth on the fiftieth anniversary of that day when he first uttered those words later emblazoned on his episcopal coat–of–arms: "*Agni Agnos Numerare*" . . ., "May I always tell the sheep about the glories of their Shepherd."

✛THOMAS GRACE (1842–1921)

Thomas Grace was an "intrepid Irishman" who "consecrated his life wholly to the glory of God and the maintenance and spread of Christianity on these western shores." Shortly after his ordination at All Hallows in 1867, the twenty–six year old priest left for California "not to seek an earthly fortune, but to win souls for Christ." The young Irishman served at a number of posts in the Vicariate of Marysville and the Diocese of Grass Valley. He was "a universal favorite among his people" because, as one contemporary noted, any one could see "that he has not the slightest leaven of selfishness in his nature."

"As a simple priest, in charge of various missions in the mining towns for twenty–nine years, he showed the energy and capacity for hard work which resulted in organizing many parishes, building churches and bringing many converts into the fold." One chronicler of those days has recorded that "it was no easy task to stick to the simple duties of a parish priest in communities of those rugged and lonely mining districts, where men in their desire to acquire worldly riches were impatient of the restraints imposed by religion." The same writer goes on to say that "it was a sign of a certain nobility of character for a man of his high ideals and personal endowments to humbly submit to the trials which the missionary life entailed, where labor was unending and where results were oftentimes discouraging and heart–breaking, the reward frequently being hunger, thirst, poverty and privation."

Among Father Grace's more successful pastorates was that of Carson City where he built Saint Theresa's Church in 1870. Three years later he was placed in charge of the cathedral at Marysville. He was subsequently sent to Sacramento to occupy a similar post. The Wexford–born priest "was beloved by all who knew him and was esteemed as a great priest and citizen by all who came in touch with his activities." One author felt that "there was never a more popular clergyman . . . on the Pacific Coast than Thomas Grace. When it was rumored that his name was prominent among those submitted for the episcopal dignity, a noted writer stated that if Grace were named to the bishopric, "he will adorn it by his many virtues."

With the death of Bishop Patrick Manogue in 1895, Father Grace became administrator of the diocese and just a year later was made ordinary of the Sacramento jurisdiction by Pope Leo XIII. In his new position, "the dauntless prelate showed energy and capacity for hard work which had characterized him as a humble missionary along the gold dust trails."

After a priestly life of fifty–four years, twenty–five of them as Bishop of Sacramento, Thomas Grace passed to his eternal reward on December 27, 1921. At the time of his funeral, it was said that "the secret of his calm, gentle character, his constant and unostentatious character . . . was deep down in his religious soul."

According to the *Catholic Herald*, "Rich and poor, old and young, the strong and weak men, women and children, of all races and conditions in life—Catholics, Jew, Protestant, agnostic and pagan—united in a final act of homage to the memory of a truly great and good man, who laboured so unobtrusively for the betterment of mankind, and by precept and example expounded the doctrine of Christian kindness and charity." With the death of Bishop Grace, the great romance of the golden days of California, came to an end.

✠MERLIN JOSEPH GUILFOYLE (1908–1981)

Merlin Joseph Guilfoyle (1908–1981) was born in San Francisco, the son of John and Teresa (Bassity) Guilfoyle. His earliest education was acquired at Saint James School under the tutelage of the Brothers of Mary. Attending Saint Joseph's College, Mountain View, and Saint Patrick's Seminary, Menlo Park, he was ordained to the priesthood by Archbishop John J. Mitty on June 10, 1933, in Saint Mary's Cathedral..

Father Guilfoyle was appointed curate at Saint Theresa, Oakland. In 1935, he was sent to The Catholic University of America for graduate courses in Canon Law. As part of the requirements for his doctorate, he wrote a masterful dissertation on *Custom. An Historical Synopsis and Commentary.*

Upon his return to San Francisco, Father Guilfoyle engaged in pastoral work at Saint Finn Barr, Saint Anne and Saint Mary's Cathedral. For two years he was administrator for the national church of the Yugoslavs. In addition to his teaching assignments at Presentation High School, the Novitiate for the Sisters of Presentation, Saint Joseph's Hospital of Nursing and the San Francisco College for Women, Father Guilfoyle was associated for many years with the archdiocesan matri-

monial tribunal as *Officialis*. He was chaplain and co–founder of the Saint Thomas More Society. On July 17, 1949, Father Guilfoyle was named a Domestic Prelate by Pope Pius XII.

Just a year later, Msgr. Guilfoyle was appointed to the titular See of Bulla. He became the seventh native of San Francisco ordained to the episcopate on September 21, 1950. Soon thereafter, the prelate was entrusted with the pastorate of Mission Dolores Basilica.

Bishop Guilfoyle served as Military Vicar of the Armed Forces, a position in which he exercised jurisdiction over chaplains and military personnel attached to bases in California, Utah and Nevada. He was also Vicar General for the Archdiocese of San Francisco from 1962 to 1969. Guilfoyle's influence was considerably expanded in 1969, when Pope Paul VI named him to the residential See of Stockton, a diocese in Central California comprising 10,023 square miles and encompassing Alpine, Calaveras, Mono, San Joaquin, Stanislaus and Tuolumne counties.

During the two decades that Guilfoyle served as Auxiliary Bishop of San Francisco, he wrote over a thousand weekly articles for *The Monitor*. His columns were subsequently published in book form under the titles *San Francisco, No Mean City* (1945), *California, State of Grace* (1959) and *Of Thee I Sing* (1962). His articles also appeared in such prestigious journals as *The Jurist*. The prelate's last publication was *The Little "0"*. (Stockton, 1972), a series of poetic reflections about his extensive travels to the four corners of the world.

A versifier in his own right, Bishop Merlin Guilfoyle's mastery of words recalls a remark by John Henry Newman: "The Church herself is the most sacred and august of poets. Poetry . . . is a method of relieving the over–burdened mind; it is a channel through which emotion finds expression, and that a safe, regulated expression."

If it is true, as Thomas Merton once said, that "no Christian poetry worthy of the name has been written by anyone who was not in some degree a contemplative," then Bishop Merlin Guilfoyle qualifies for a stall at Gethsemane monastery.

✠EDWARD J. HANNA (1860–1944)

A. THE SCHOLAR AND THE MAN

Shortly after the episcopal ordination of Edward J. Hanna (1860–1944), a long–time acquaintance of the prelate was asked to write an essay for *The Monitor* about the newly–appointed Auxiliary Bishop of San Francisco.

Redfern Mason's response, appearing in the Christmas issue for 1912, was aptly entitled: "Bishop Hanna:

The Scholar and the Man." He assured the readers of the Bay City's newspaper that the Holy Spirit had provided a truly worthy associate shepherd for the Church of San Francisco.

Mason said that Bishop Hanna had "the kind of head one loves to see on the shoulders of a friend. His look is the look that puts heart into the poor fellow who is down; he is genial, affable, winning, without so much as a hint of that condescension which sets the spirit of a sensitive person on edge." At the same time, the New York born prelate was known as "a man of huge learning, doctor of divinity by a double sanction–by dint of patient, long–continued study and by the grace of Almighty God."

In Mason's opinion, it was the "very bigness of the man" that made him so companionable, so graciously humble. "If he knows much, he is also aware that the greatest intellect is only comparable to a pitcher which has descended some little way into the well of divine truth and brought forth a few priceless drops." Noting that "it is not only among the Italian laborers that the good father and bishop is welcomed." Mason went on to say that he was "received with open mix wherever he goes." Mr. Mason had lived for a dozen or so years in Rochester and there he "knew no one so intimately linked with all kinds and conditions of humanity" as was Hanna. "His gift for remembering names and faces" was extraordinary. His mind must have been an archive of biographies, each precisely labeled and docketed, like so many questions in a scholastic *Summa*.

According to Mason, Bishop Hanna believed "that Catholics should be well trained mentally; that Catholics should rise in the professions and succeed in business because they have thoroughly mastered the craft they have set their mind to." He pointed out that while "it is true that the Catholic Church is the Church of the poor, the Church to which the broken in spirit may turn with the assuredness of finding comfort; it is also the Church in whose possession is the sole philosophy that remains unshaken throughout the ages."

Mason observed that to Bishop Edward J. Hanna, "the Catholic Church is home, truth, peace. His belief and confidence in her are glorious." The people of San Francisco would find Hanna "delighted with all that tends to make the worship of God beautiful, whether it be the building of churches, worthy of their august purpose, the preservation of the glorious tradition of the California missions, anything, in a word, that will help make the worshipper feel, as he enters a Catholic church, 'This is none other than the House of God.' "

The famed writer concluded his essay on Hanna by saying that the new prelate "is a man in whose society you cannot pass an hour without coming away improved in mind and refreshed in spirit. He is interested in every-thing, but most of all in humanity, and that, in particular, on the side which brings us nearest to our Maker."

✝EDWARD J. HANNA (1860–1944)

B. CATHOLIC SCHOOL IN A DEMOCRACY

Edward J. Hanna (1860–1944) was not only a great churchman, but also an outstanding leader in civic affairs. The ability and profound scholarship of the respected Archbishop of San Francisco was also recognized by the heads of state and nations, who called upon him in times of crisis.

The archbishop accentuated the liberal trend of his churchmanship by the leading part he took in all the great movements of his time. A noteworthy example was his championship of Catholic education and its growth within the framework of American democracy. In a discourse delivered at the opening of The Catholic Educational Convention, in 1918, the prelate characterized the ideal democracy as that which ultimately depends "upon the developed sense of personal responsibility in each individual making up the nation." Where "the people really rule," said the archbishop, "religion must ever be a directing, energizing power, and if we hope for such a democracy in the future, the Church which represents religion, and bears unto the world the message and the power of Christ, will ever be democracy's greatest bulwark."

The need of transmitting such lofty ideals to the emerging generations was a paramount concern in Hanna's plan for preserving true democracy. The archbishop envisioned the Catholic school system as the framework in which students can learn the great moral sanctions of the law. Therein they will become familiar with the counsels of Christ, and from His lips take their rule of life. They will find that man, made in God's image, is of more worth than all the earth's possessions. There they will learn about love and mercy seasoned with justice. In the Catholic educational program, youngsters will be taught to sacrifice personal interests for the higher things of the Spirit and to recognize the higher code taught by Christ whereby men are ruled by moral force, not by armed power. They will search out the mystery of man's weakness by learning God's way of strength, they will know the power of humble prayer, and the moral strength that flows from the heavenly Sacraments. They will be trained for self– conquest and thereby achieve greatness by becoming humble in mind and heart.

Archbishop Hanna portrayed religion, the great foundation–stone of democracy, as an absolutely essential quality for the betterment of the masses. Through such commitments came the opportunity to fashion minds

Archbishop Edward J. Hanna

and hearts towards everlasting things. For that reason, "more efficacious than the crash of cannon and the clang of arms will be the Christian teacher, at whose feet we can learn the answer to the questions that vex our age; more efficacious than embattled militarism will be the Christian School wherein the children of our great Republic will learn that there is a God in Heaven to whose behests they must bow, and before whose judgment seat they must stand."

✠EDWARD J. HANNA (1860–1944)

C. THE N.C.W.C.

The National Catholic Welfare Conference was an association of this country's bishops which served as a central agency for organizing and coordinating the Church's efforts in carrying out its apostolate in the United States. If and when a history of the N.C.W.C. is written, considerable credit for the agency's early success must be given to the sterling leadership of the Most Reverend Edward J. Hanna (1860–1944). In his long-time role as episcopal chairman of the administrative council, the Archbishop of San Francisco frequently

spoke and acted officially both for the board and the conference as a whole.

Among the many problems confronted by Archbishop Hanna were such matters as the distribution of sacramental wine during prohibition days; accommodations for Catholic worship in Federal parks; tariff schedules on church articles; cooperation with government officials in religious census work; regulation of broadcasting stations and use of the mails for obscene and immoral purposes.

One concrete example of Hanna's influence on the national level was his leadership of the effective opposition to the Reed–Curtis Federalization of Education Bill. In a statement issued by the San Francisco metropolitan, attention was focused on the problems that would ensue if the nation's school system were immersed into the caldron of partisan politics. On the international scene, Archbishop Hanna, as chief spokesman for the N.C.W.C.'s administrative council, personally advised the President and other United States officials of the Catholic attitude to such questions as universal disarmament and world peace. The archbishop called upon President Calvin Coolidge, in May of 1926, concerning the unhappy status of the Church in Mexico. He also issued a blistering statement deploring the insults heaped on Catholics by the Calles Government. Hanna followed up the protest with a number of N.C.W.C. pamphlets on "The Religious Crisis in Mexico." In December of 1926, the committee gave widespread circulation to the *Pastoral Letter of the Catholic Episcopate of the United States on the Religious Situation in Mexico.*

During his years with the executive board, the Bay City's prelate rarely missed the bi–annual meetings of the administrative committee, even though each entailed a round trip of 6,000 long and tedious railroad miles to Washington. The San Francisco prelate also traveled abroad several times for the N.C.W.C. In 1928, be was given the honor of preaching at the opening of the 29th International Eucharistic Congress at Sydney, as the official representative of the American hierarchy and the Catholics of the United States.

Archbishop Hanna was a staunch advocate of increased cooperation between the Catholic clergy and laity in the country. "If we are to act," said the prelate, "as a great body in the United States, then there must be unity of action as well as unity of spirit." Attention was drawn again to the usefulness of the N.C.W.C. when the archbishop noted the necessity of uniting "in one great body, with the ideals of Jesus Christ before us and the ideals of our mighty country beckoning us on."

Charles A. McMahon, editor of the N.C.W.C.'s official publications, said in later years that in the history of the National Catholic Welfare Conference, "There stands out the vitalizing leadership of one of the

Church's great prelates, one of the country's patriotic and worthy citizens, one of humanity's conscientious benefactors—His Grace, Archbishop Hanna of San Francisco!"

✢EDWARD J. HANNA (1860–1944)

D. GENIUS FOR FRIENDSHIP

San Francisco's third archbishop is the subject of a study released under the auspices of the Rochester City Library. In his "Archbishop Hanna, Rochesterian," Robert F. McNamara sketches the highlights of the Bay City's beloved prelate.

Hanna studied for the priesthood in Rome where he attended classes at the Athenaeum of the Urban College. The strict discipline, frugal meals and intellectual challenge of the Eternal City sharpened the youngster's talents and won for him the coveted appointment to debate before Leo XIII and twenty–two cardinals. Father Francis Satolli, one of Hanna's professors, was deeply impressed by his student's accomplishments and the two began a long personal friendship that eventually saw them both raised to the episcopate, the one a prominent archbishop, the other an eminent cardinal. Another of Hanna's mentors was Denis J. O'Connell, Rector of the North American College, a highly influential agent for various members of the American hierarchy.

Edward Hanna was ordained in the Basilica of Saint John Lateran on May 30, 1885, by Archbishop Guilio Lenti, Viceregent of Rome. At O'Connell's request, the youthful Rochesterian was allowed by Bishop Bernard McQuaid to continue his studies in Rome as assistant to Professor Satolli. Upon returning to the United States, Hanna taught Classics at Saint Andrew's Seminary and, in 1893, moved to the new Saint Bernard's Seminary as Professor of Dogmatic Theology.

His religious devotion, his theological knowledge, his skill with people, and his encouraging personality combined to recommend Edward Hanna for advancement in the Church. That he would even make an able bishop was the conviction not only of his lay friends but also of his ordinary.

Hanna's name first appeared among the *episcopabili* in 1905, and two years later he was placed on the *terna* of Archbishop Patrick W. Riordan as a possible auxiliary of San Francisco. Both McQuaid of Rochester and Gibbons of Baltimore joined in commending Hanna to Propaganda Fide but the Congregation had other plans and eventually Hanna's old friend, Denis J. O'Connell, went to San Francisco.

When Father Hanna observed his silver jubilee in 1910, the Rochester *Union and Advertiser* called him "one of the best known Catholic clergymen in this section of the country." Bishop McQuaid never doubted that his protege would one day go west and before he died he told a nun: "My boy will go to San Francisco and he will later be made Archbishop, so all is well. The gilded edge of every cross is resignation to the divine will."

With the transfer of O'Connell to Richmond in 1912, Archbishop Riordan again petitioned Rome for assistance and, on October 21, Hanna was named Titular Bishop of Titiopolis and Auxiliary of San Francisco. His episcopal consecration took place in Saint Patrick's Cathedral at Rochester on December 4th, and on that festive occasion he was presented with the amethyst ring McQuaid had specifically put aside for his "boy." It came as no surprise in 1915, when Hanna succeeded Riordan as the Metropolitan of the Church in California and almost immediately the new archbishop set out to win the hearts and souls of his people. So well did he succeed that the University of California named him a "Friend of Mankind" in 1931.

Whether it was as labor arbitrator, housing administrator, or welfare and relief, Hanna was always a shepherd to his people. He set up or expanded 120 parishes in his two decades and devoted much of his energy to Catholic education. When the beloved old prelate's health began to fail in 1932, he was given a coadjutor. Three years later he resigned his archbishopric and returned to Rome to spend the final decade of his useful life as a humble resident of the Villa San Francesco.

On July 10, 1944, a few weeks after the fall of Rome to the allies, the Titular Archbishop of Gortyna passed quietly to his reward. One of the Bay City's leading Protestant ministers noted that Hanna had "made San Francisco a better place in which to live, by his spiritual and civic leadership. He was a truly great man. He had a genius for friendship and comfort among all kinds of people, rich and poor, educated and uneducated."

✢JEREMIAH JAMES HARTY (1853–1927)

Jeremiah James Harty, the son of Irish immigrants Andrew and Julia (Murphy) Harty, was born at Saint Louis, Missouri, on November 5, 1853. He studied for the priesthood with the Congregation of the Mission at Cape Girardeau.

Ordained April 28, 1878, Father Harty devoted the first quarter century of his priestly life to the pastoral ministry in and around the city of his birth. In 1902, his name was on the terna for auxiliary of Saint Louis. In mid 1903, when Coadjutor Archbishop George T. Montgomery of San Francisco turned down the appointment to the Metropolitan District of Manila, the Holy See gave the nod to Harty. Appointed June 6th, he was consecrated at Rome on the Feast of Our Lady's Assumption by Francesco Cardinal Satolli.

Enroute to the Philippines, Archbishop Harty stopped in Washington for a visit with President Theodore Roosevelt. There he was assured of United States support in his work, especially the difficult monetary challenges that resulted from the change of sovereignty. Harty's work was hampered at the very outset by his ignorance of Spanish and the several native languages then prevalent in the area. There were major ecclesial problems, too, chief of which was the Anglipayan schism rampant among the poorer classes of Catholics.

There was widespread Protestant proselytization in the islandic jurisdiction. Matters were further complicated by the long–simmering Friar's controversy that was still largely unresolved. And there were the complications arising from the abolition of the *Patronato Real* by the Holy See.

The titles to hospitals operated jointly by the government and the Church were unilaterally claimed by the new civil regime, something which Harty totally rejected. There were expensive lawsuits pending regarding ecclesial properties previously seized by the schismatics. "Chaos" was an appropriate word to describe the archbishopric of Manila in those times. In spite of these and other obstacles, Archbishop Harty reorganized seminaries, rebuilt churches and established schools in his efforts to stabilize the problem–ridden area.

Following a serious bout with illness, Harty was transferred to Omaha, Nebraska in May of 1916. There he erected thirteen parishes and nine parochial schools, established an education board, organized Catholic Charities and aided in the establishment of Boys Town.

Ill health continued to plague the archbishop. In 1923, he had a severe attack of influenza which subsequently developed into tuberculosis. Two years later, with the approval of the Apostolic Delegate, Harty entrusted the administration of the diocese to Bishop Francis Beckman. After a brief stint in Tucson, the archbishop came to Los Angeles, where he took up residence with his long–time friend, Father Clement Molony, founding pastor of Saint Agnes parish.

Archbishop Harty died on October 29, 1927. His funeral was conducted by Bishop John B. MacGinley of Monterey–Fresno who had worked with him in the Philippines. Following the services, the prelate's remains were shipped to Omaha for final interment.

✠DUANE G. HUNT (1884–1960)

During the golden years of radio, a young priest in the Diocese of Salt Lake launched a program over Station KSL that quickly gained national stature and wide acclaim. Duane G. Hunt (1884–1960) was born and raised in a thoroughly—even militantly Protestant atmosphere. It was while studying at Cornell College, a Methodist sponsored institution, that the young man first read and was influenced by James Cardinal Gibbon's book, *Faith of Our Fathers.*

Hunt was eventually received into the Church and not long thereafter he began his studies for the priesthood as a clerical candidate for the Diocese of Salt Lake. He was ordained in 1920. Always a forceful homilist, Father Hunt began his radio apostolate, in 1927, over Station KSL. Within a few years the program was "boosted" onto the national airways. Over a million homes tuned into the program every Sunday night.

People scattered over the vast region from the Missouri River to the Pacific and from Salt Lake City to the northernmost Canadian settlements became "fans" of the Hunt presentations. Except for Father Charles Coughlin and the Catholic Hour, no other ecclesial program reached so many listeners. In the western part of the nation, Father Hunt personified Catholicism and its mission to the world.

It was a varied congregation too. Listeners were from farming areas, remote villages, densely–populated cities; they were members of every conceivable religious persuasion. Their only common trait was the dictum that "Sunday would not be Sunday without Monsignor Hunt."

The priest was a master of technique. His early experience as coach of the debating teams at college served him well. Gifted with an incisive voice, Hunt's delivery at the microphone was an invaluable asset. He spoke clearly, rarely slurring even a syllable. That's not to minimize the effort involved. Hunt spent long hours writing, revising, weighing and balancing his presentations. He was always conscious that he was only a spokesman for the Lord. But it was important that he perform that role well.

His sermons were almost invariably based on the intellectual appeal of the Church to those who are already Christian. Frequently, he didn't even so much as mention Catholicism, but confined himself to a logical discussion of religious problems. He usually concluded by showing how the true solution could be found only in the "one, holy, Catholic and apostolic Church."

Interestingly enough, KSL was owned and operated by the Latter Day Saints. Their cooperation and encouragement over the years was due, at least in large degree, to a desire for keeping a million dials tuned to their frequency.

Because of his national stature, it came as no surprise that Msgr. Hunt was chosen to become the fifth Bishop of Salt Lake, in 1937. In subsequent times, pastoral duties prevented him from being more than casually involved in the radio apostolate.

Yet, for thousands of people, nationwide, the name of Duane G. Hunt is permanently etched onto the dial of KSL Salt Lake City.

✠FRANCIS T. HURLEY (b. 1927)

The appointment of Monsignor Francis T. Hurley (b. 1927) to the titular bishopric of Daimlaig fulfilled a prediction, made in 1962, by the eminent historian of the American Church, John Tracy Ellis: "The question is not whether the Hurley brothers will be bishops, but rather, when!"

The bishop's brother, Mark, already the Ordinary of Santa Rosa, previously served as Auxiliary of San Francisco. It had happened only seven times before that brothers became members of the American hierarchy. The first family so honored was that of Matthew and Elizabeth Foley. Their son, Thomas Patrick (1822–1879), served a decade as titular Bishop of Pergamum, during which time he was coadjutor and administrator of Chicago. Nine years after Thomas's death, his brother, John Samuel (1833–1918), began a three–decade tenure as Bishop of Detroit. Quebec–born brothers Augustin M. Blanchet (1797–1887) and Francis N. Blanchet (1795–1883), shared a total of seventy-eight years in the American hierarchy.

The first brothers to serve as archbishops in the United States were the Kenricks. Francis Patrick (1796–1863) and Peter Richard (1806–1896) are generally ranked among the most outstanding prelates in the country's ecclesiastical annals, the one at Philadelphia and Baltimore, the other at Saint Louis. Peter Richard is one of five American prelates to have celebrated his golden episcopal jubilee.

John W. Shanahan (1846–1916) had the unusual distinction of succeeding, after an interval of thirteen years, his older brother, Jeremiah F. (1834–1886), in the Diocese of Harrisburg. The two sons of Edmond and Mary Lenihan were the only brother members of the American hierarchy born in different countries. Thomas (1844–1901), Bishop of Cheyenne, was a native of Ireland, while his younger brother, Mathias (1854–1943), Bishop of Great Falls, was born in the United States.

Two of the offspring of Charles and Ellen O'Connor became bishops. Michael (1810–1872) was the first (and second) Bishop of Pittsburgh, while his brother, James (1823–1885), served as Vicar Apostolic of Nebraska and, later, as Bishop of Omaha. Michael resigned, in 1860, joined the Society of Jesus, and spent the final dozen years of his life in the classroom. Both Coleman F. Carroll of Miami (1905–1977) and Howard J. Carroll (1902–1960) of Altoona–Johnstown, were elevated to the bishopric by Amleto Giovanni Cicognani, long–time Apostolic Delegate to the United States.

With the consecration of Monsignor Francis Hurley as Auxiliary and Apostolic Administrator of Juneau, the San Francisco–born Hurleys became the first episcopal brothers to jointly serve in the American hierarchy since 1960. Generally speaking, historians are "backward–looking prophets." But there are grounds for wondering if the unusual distinction that came to the Hurley family might be the first in a chain of events that one day could equal or surpass the noble traditions heretofore associated only with the Kenricks!

✠MARK HURLEY (b. 1919)

The installation of Bishop Mark Hurley, at Santa Rosa, on January 14, 1970, called to mind the timely words penned a quarter–century earlier by Henry L. Walsh, the eminent Jesuit historian of the Mother Lode:

> Nobility is the only virtue, according to Juvenal. The province in which the bishops of Northern California ruled had been endowed by nature with primeval trappings of nobility: nobility was reflected in her snow– crowned mountains, in the majestic sweep of her towering forests, in the regal dignity of her mighty redwoods, in the queenly grace of her lakes and rivers, and the imperial munificence of her hills of gold.
>
> The fortunate pioneers who first cast their gaze upon this bounteous wonderland fell in love with her from the start, they marveled and grew proud of her, and in turn she imparted to them some of her own stately character, exemplified in that boundless hospitality which gained for her the reputation of unselfish hostess to the world.
>
> There is an air of nobility in the spirit of her people, whose prayer, "Give me men to match my mountains," is to be seen today carved deep on the walls of her Capitol, even as it is indelibly engraved in the hearts of her loyal sons and daughters.
>
> And there is an air of nobility in the bishops who were chosen by the Vicar of Christ to rule over her spiritual destinies. Each and every one of them lived up to St. Paul's requirements, being especially noted for apostolic zeal, for extraordinary charity and self–sacrifice, and for unswerving faithfulness to the duties of his episcopal office.
>
> Though the curtain has long since descended on that "most bewildering extravaganza" of modern American history, perhaps the greatest scene was still to come. Northern California preserved the scenic grandeur of her gigantic mountains and myriad hills. Age has not dimmed the glory of her colossal forests nor dispelled the enchantment of her perennial streams. More importantly, the elements of that substantial and honorable character generated in the lives and deeds of the pioneers, are in evidence today, possibly more than ever before.

The kindly souls who loved their fellowmen, the brave pioneers who defended justice at the risk of their lives and the provident men who strove to make Northern California a proud commonwealth have their counterparts in the Catholics who populate the six counties comprising the Diocese of Santa Rosa. Bishop Hurley had a keen appreciation for the noble traditions associated with the Church in Northern California. The example of his valiant predecessors was to exert considerable influence in the future activities of the San Francisco–born prelate, as he became the shepherd of the 11,711 square mile jurisdiction at Santa Rosa.

While reaping the spiritual harvest of earlier decades, the Bishop of Santa Rosa, cut from the fabric of Vatican II, directed his gaze at a new age by planting deep in the hearts of his people those vigorous roots of Eternal Truth which alone assure the continuance of God's message for generations not yet born. In that role, he mirrored the gentleness of Joseph Sadoc Alemany, the patience of Eugene O'Connell, the sympathy of Patrick Manogue, the simplicity of Thomas Grace, the kindness of Robert Armstrong, the tenacity of Joseph T. McGucken and the industry of Leo T. Maher.

Bishop Hurley served at Santa Rosa until his retirement on April 15, 1986. Subsequently he filled positions on several Roman congregations.

✠WILLIAM R. JOHNSON (1918–1986)

The priestly life of Bishop William R. Johnson (1918–1986) mirrored the growth and development of Catholic charities in the United States in the post World War II era. He was born in Tonopah, Nevada, on November 19, 1918, the son of Jorgen and Marie (O'Connell) Johnson.

The family moved to Los Angeles in the early 1920s in the hopes that the milder climate would restore Jorgen's failing health. Young William enrolled at Saint Ignatius School, where he received his elementary education from the Dominican Sisters of Mission San Jose. William entered Los Angeles College in 1932, as a clerical aspirant for the Diocese of Los Angeles–San Diego. Upon completion of his theological courses at Saint John's Seminary, Camarillo, Johnson was ordained to the priesthood by Archbishop John J. Cantwell, on May 28, 1944.

After serving several years in the parochial ministry, Father Johnson was sent to The Catholic University of America, where he obtained a Master's degree in Social Work. He was named Assistant Director of the Catholic Welfare Bureau in 1948. With the appointment of Msgr. Alden J. Bell to the bishopric, in 1956, Johnson advanced to the directorship of the Bureau. Four years later, he was elected to the Board of Directors for the National Conference of Catholic Charities and, in 1964, president of that body.

On January 15, 1960, Pope John XXIII bestowed the title of papal chamberlain upon Father Johnson. Five years later, he was promoted to the domestic prelacy. During his years as director, Msgr. Johnson inaugurated new divisions of Catholic Social Service and Catholic Community Service. A new charities building at 1400 West Ninth Street was erected under Johnson's guidance in the early 1960s.

Between 1962 and 1968, Msgr. Johnson also served as pastor of the inner–city parish of Holy Name. He was transferred to American Martyrs in 1968 and, in 1970, he became Parochial Vicar for Saint Vibiana's Cathedral.

Early in 1971, Pope Paul VI appointed Msgr. Johnson to the titular See of Blera and Auxiliary for the Archdiocese of Los Angeles. He received episcopal ordination on March 25, at the hands of Archbishop Timothy Manning. Fittingly enough, he chose for his motto the words *Caritas Christi*. At the ceremonies of his consecration, Johnson was presented with the historic crozier or shepherd's stick used by Bishop Thaddeus Amat during the quarter century that Vincentian pioneer watched over the spiritual destinies of the People of God in the Diocese of Monterey–Los Angeles.

In April 0f 1973, Bishop Johnson visited the far–flung outposts in New Guinea, New Ireland and Africa operated by the Lay Mission Helpers of Los Angeles. Later that summer, the prelate was named Episcopal Vicar for Charities and for the Black Community in the four county archdiocese.

With the erection of a diocesan seat at Orange, on June 18, 1976, Bishop Johnson became the first Ordinary of the forty–two parishes comprising that jurisdiction.

Bishop Johnson's whole priestly life was involved in the ministry of charity. The congenial, thorough–going priest served the needy at all levels—diocesan, community, state and national.

✠PATRICK JOSEPH KEANE (1872–1928)

With the death of Bishop Thomas Grace of Sacramento, on December 27, 1921, the great romance of California's golden days came to an end. The curtain had fallen on the final act of the most extraordinary ecclesial extravaganza in American history. Yet, though the glory of that glamorous era is a thing of the past, those elements of a more substantial and honorable character remained in the lives and deeds of the pioneers and were recognized in those who followed in their footsteps. Among the principle heirs and benefactors of that noble heritage was Patrick Joseph Keane, who had been called to walk beside Bishop Grace in his declining years.

Patrick Joseph Keane was born at Ballybunion, County Kerry, Ireland, on January 6, 1872, the son of Jeremiah and Mary (Kissane) Keane. He studied for the ministry at Saint Michael's College, Listowell and Saint Patrick's College, Carlow. His final years were spent at the Theological College, for The Catholic University of America. Following in the path of his distinguished uncle, Father Patrick O'Kane (1841–1926), one of the most colorful Irish–born priests ever to serve along the Gold Dust Trails, young Keane decided to align himself with the Church in California and, on June 20, 1895, he was ordained priest for the Archdiocese of San Francisco.

Upon the youthful cleric's arrival in the Bay City, Archbishop Patrick W. Riordan appointed Father Keane curate at Saint Patrick's Church, on Mission Street. In 1905, Father Keane was advanced to the pastorship of Saint Francis Church, in Oakland, where he served the People of God for the following fifteen years.

Pope Pius XI appointed Keane auxiliary to the aged Bishop Thomas Grace of Sacramento, on September 10, 1920. He received episcopal ordination on December 4th, at the hands of San Francisco's Archbishop Edward J. Hanna. On March 17, 1922, shortly after the death of Grace, Bishop Keane was named Ordinary of Sacramento, a position he filled with admirable zeal for the following six years. Keane's most notable contribution to the diocese, besides his spiritual leadership, was the extension of the school system to the north and south sections of Sacramento. The beloved prelate also sponsored the erection of Mater Misericordiae Hospital and the remodeling and updating of Sacramento's historic old cathedral.

By the time death claimed the spiritual shepherd of Sacramento, on September 1, 1928, it could be said of him, as it was of his predecessors, that he "had planted deep in the hearts of the Western youth the vigorous roots of Eternal Truth."

✠JAMES EDWARD KEARNEY (1884–1977)

The fifth Bishop of Salt Lake, James Edward Kearney (1884–1977), was born on October 28, 1884, at Red Oak, Iowa. At the age of two, the youngster was brought by his parents, William and Rosina (O'Doherty) Kearney, to New York City, where his playground became the old Grand Central Station. After obtaining a teaching credential, James taught briefly at Public School No. 25. Then he entered Saint Joseph's Seminary, Dunwoodie, as a clerical aspirant for the Archdiocese of New York. He was ordained to the priesthood on September 19, 1908, by Auxiliary Bishop Thomas F. Cusack.

Father Kearney was sent to The Catholic University of America, where he earned a licentiate in Sacred Theology. His first pastoral assignment was to Saint Cecilia's Church, a position he occupied for nineteen years. In addition to teaching at Cathedral College, the energetic curate directed the large parochial school that served the Catholic populace of the area.

In 1928, Cardinal Patrick Hayes asked Father Kearney to establish a new parish, under the patronage of

Saint Francis Xavier, in the Bronx. At the same time, he was placed in charge of the parochial school system for the entire borough. With the advancement of another New Yorker, John J. Mitty, to the coadjutor archbishopric of San Francisco, Pope Pius XI asked Father Kearney to become Bishop of Salt Lake. He received episcopal ordination at Saint Patrick's Cathedral on his birthday, in 1932. At the time of his transferal to the west, Cardinal Hayes noted that "Catholic New York suffers a great loss, with no small regret, by the call of (Father Kearney) to the larger apostolate of a Missionary Bishop."

The Diocese of Salt Lake comprised 84,900 square miles, with a Catholic population of 14,084 scattered through the vast territory in cities, mining camps and farms. With meager funds, bolstered by his own tireless energy, Bishop Kearney tackled the problem of developing churches, schools and other progressive programs for the far–flung jurisdiction. He came to know the Mormons well. His sincerity and forthrightness soon won for the prelate the respect and friendship of the entire state.

During his five years in the Mormon capital, Bishop Kearney became a familiar face to the twenty–two priests serving the thirteen parishes in the Diocese of Salt Lake. On July 31, 1937, Bishop Kearney was recalled to New York State as Ordinary for the twelve county Diocese of Rochester. There he continued his priestly apostolate until his retirement, in 1965, and appointment to the titular See of Tubicara.

Throughout his long service to the People of God, James Edward Kearney came to personify the ideal of "true giving of self" which the poet James Russell Lowell put on the lips of Christ:

> Not what we give, but what we share
> For the gift, without the giver, is bare.
> Who gives himself with his alms feeds three
> Himself, his hungering neighbor and Me.

✠BERNARD HERMAN KOECKEMANN (1828–1892)

While historians often give the impression of knowing everything about their specialty, they are constantly stumbling across new discoveries that further expand the boundaries of their expertise.

Recently, for example, while reading the excellent new treatise on the *Ordination of U.S. Catholic Bishops 1790–1989* by Charles Bransom, this writer came across the previously unknown episcopal ordination of Bernard Herman Koeckemann that occurred in San Francisco on August 21, 1881. It took a while to search out the details of this event which now becomes another chapter in California's Catholic heritage.

Bernard Koeckemann was born at Osteven, Germany

on January 10, 1828. At the age of fourteen he was sent to the "Gymnasium" of Munster. Studious and mentally well–endowed, Bernard achieved a brilliant record in classical studies. His mastery of Latin, Greek, Hebrew and French was such that he won exemption from the traditional oral exams.

Later he journeyed to Belgium where he entered the Congregation of the Sacred Hearts (Picpus Fathers). After completing the usual novitiate, he made his final profession on April 11, 1851, taking the religious name of Herman. Upon completion of his theological studies, Koeckemann was sent to the Sandwich Isles (Hawaiian Islands), where he arrived on November 13, 1854. He was ordained priest on May 31, 1862 and for some years he looked after the English speaking members of the local church.

In 1850, the Superior General of the Picpus Fathers, worried about the declining health of Bishop Louis Maigret, petitioned the Holy See to appoint Father Koeckemann coadjutor vicar apostolic. Pope Plus IX acquiesced and had the papal bulls dispatched to Honolulu. The bishop–elect journeyed to San Francisco and there received Episcopal ordination at the hands of Archbishop Joseph Sadoc Alemany in Saint Mary's Cathedral. Assisting in the ceremonies were Bishops Eugene O'Connell and Timoleon Raimondi. Koeckemann was entrusted with the titular See of Olba as he assumed his duties as Coadjutor Vicar Apostolic.

According to documents in the Picpus Archives, Bishop Koeckemann was directed "only to interfere in the administration of the vicariate as far as the actual incumbent willed and allowed it." However, prompted by the latter's occasional feeble–mindedness and ill health, Koeckemann gradually assumed full control of the vicariate. Within a year, Bishop Maigret succumbed and, in the words of Reginald Yzendoorn, was reverently "interred behind the throne which during thirty–five years he had adorned with his many virtues."

After becoming vicar, Koeckemann was not satisfied with simply overseeing his flock. He continued to work zealously in the vineyard, teaching catechism, visiting the sick, assisting the poor, hearing confessions and performing all the other duties associated with the pastoral ministry.

Maintaining a close relationship with Archbishop Alemany, he asked for and received several priests from San Francisco to assist in Hawaii. The religious education of Catholic youth became Bishop Koeckemann's first priority and he established numerous schools and catechetical centers throughout his islandic vicariate.

On February 18, 1892, the prelate suffered a paralytic stroke and he died four days later. Governmental recognition of his demise was observed by the closing of all government offices and the lowering of the consular colors during his funeral.

✝JOHN BAPTIST LAMY (1814–1888)

Probably one of the nation's most celebrated churchmen was John Baptist Lamy (1814–1888), a prime civilizer of the southwest frontier. His presence was felt from the Rocky Mountains across New Mexico, Colorado and Arizona into old Mexico. Lamy (1814–1888) was a native of the Diocese of Clermont, France. He was ordained in 1838, and subsequently did pastoral work there before coming to Cincinnati and Louisville.

In 1850, Lamy was appointed the first Vicar Apostolic of New Mexico and ordained to the titular bishopric of Agathonice. After laboring in that vast missionary district for three years, Lamy was transferred to the newly–erected Diocese of Santa Fe. When Santa Fe was advanced to metropolitan status, in 1875, Lamy was made archbishop, a position he held until his retirement a decade later.

The literary world first heard of Lamy in Willa Cather's *Death Comes for the Archbishop*, where he was fictionalized as Bishop Latour. More recently, Paul Horgan's classical treatise on *Lamy of Sante Fe* has been a best seller.

At the invitation of Bishop Thaddeus Amat, Lamy visited Southern California, early in 1864. It seems as if Amat was influential in transactions inaugurated to have the Jesuits return to the historic San Xavier del Bac Mission, founded by the legendary Jesuit, Eusebius Kino.

With the hope of meeting officials of the Society of Jesus at Los Angeles, Lamy and Father J. M. Coudert, the pastor of Albuquerque, set out on the long and difficult trip to the Pacific Slope late in 1863. It was a tortuous journey. They suffered from cold in the higher altitudes and one night the two travelers were nearly killed by the noxious air released by live coals inside their tent. Another time their feet were almost frozen. Once their horses were nearly stolen and that would have meant death on the desert.

On Christmas Eve, the two priests offered Holy Mass in a miner's cabin, high on a wintry mountain of granite. The next day, Bishop Lamy wrote that "we were able to celebrate the Holy Sacrifice, attended by twenty or twenty–five people kneeling on earth covered with nighttime's snow." They moved ahead, stopping briefly at Fort Mojave and then crossing the Colorado River by ferry into California. Finally, they reached San Bernardino, where they were welcomed by a ".Mr. Quinn," a longtime Irish friend. Quinn extended every hospitality and then saw to it that Lamy and Coudert continued to Los Angeles in the relative comfort of a stagecoach. It was indeed a luxurious ride by comparison to weeks in the saddle.

At Los Angeles, they were greeted by Bishop Amat, who showed them the whole of Southern California, including San Gabriel Mission with its great groves of orange and lemon trees, which were heavily laden with scented flowers and ripened fruit. For the missionary bishop, Los Angeles was a place of ease, the air then pure, the light clear and the land beguiling. Lamy remained for eight happy days with Bishop Amat. The Bishop of Monterey–Los Angeles was able to report that two Jesuits had already departed for Tucson—the harbingers of a return to the missionary apostolate interrupted by the expulsion of the Society of Jesus from New Spain, in 1767.

Returning to San Bernardino, the two travelers were again entertained by Quinn and with his help they stocked all equipment for their long sojourn through the desert wilderness.

How much of the future was planned during those eight days in Los Angeles when southwest and west momentarily joined forces is a matter of pure conjecture. A rerun of the conversations between Amat and Lamy will be a featured attraction in heaven!

✢LOUIS LOOTENS (1827–1898)

Though mentioned sparsely in the annals of the American Catholic Church, Louis Lootens (1827–1898) deserves a larger chunk of recognition by his spiritual heirs in Northern California and Idaho. Born on the Feast of Saint Patrick, at Bruges in Belgium, the son of Charles and Catherine (Beijaert) Lootens studied for the priesthood in Paris where he befriended a young Lazarist priest, Father Thaddeus Amat.

Ordained on June 14, 1851 by Bishop Modeste Demers of Vancouver Island, Father Lootens spent the first years of his ministry in pastoral work in and around Victoria. Plagued during his earliest years by poor health, Lootens journeyed to California, where he was eventually incardinated in the Archdiocese of San Francisco by the Dominican prelate, Joseph Sadoc Alemany.

On June 29, 1857, Father Lootens was entrusted with the extensive area that included La Grange, Mariposa and Hornitos. About a year later, he was transferred to Sonora. In addition to Saint Raphaels, Father Lootens looked after Saint Vincent's Church in Petaluma and the attached orphanage which then had forty–six young boys under the tutelage of Sister Francis McEnnis.

According to a contemporary account, Lootens, "being artistic as well as practical, set out many of the trees and shrubs that today (1871) add to the beauty of St. Vincent's." During the first part of his tenure, Father Lootens devoted a great portion of attention to his vast parish and those who remembered him testified to the love and admiration directed towards him by the people of San Rafael. That the work of Father Lootens was also appreciated by Archbishop Alemany is evidenced by the prelate's recommendation in 1864 that Lootens be advanced to the bishopric.

In a letter written on February 2, 1867, Nicholas French noted that "during the past two years the Reverend Father Lootens has completed the additional school rooms and dormitories, capable of accommodating 140 boys. The farm, which measures about 300 acres, has been fenced all around, and divided into fields and gardens. The children have been supported, clothed and educated by the Reverend Director with the limited means at his disposal and, in addition, he has raised up a church in the institution capable of seating a congregation of 300 without using in its construction one cent of the orphans' fund."

A remarkably able administrator, Father Lootens even succeeded in getting a substantial appropriation from the state legislature for the "Roman Catholic Orphan Asylum located at Las Gallinas near San Rafael." The ambitious program at Saint Vincent's was aimed at giving as much academic education as possible to the youngsters during their primary years after which they were "farmed out" to local families.

In June of 1866, Father Lootens journeyed briefly to Oregon and British Columbia for a visit. Shortly after his return, Lootens was informed that Pope Pius IX had named him the first Vicar Apostolic of Idaho and Montana.

On August 9, 1868, Father Lootens was ordained to the titular See of Castabala in Old Saint Mary's Cathedral by Archbishop Alemany, assisted by Bishops Thaddeus Amat of Monterey–Los Angeles and Eugene O'Connell of Grass Valley. From that moment onwards, the Church in Idaho was wedded to California by a spiritual kinship that was confirmed as recently as 1989 with the appointment of Bishop Tod David Brown.

The narrative of Louis Lootens as Vicar Apostolic of Idaho and Montana (1868–1876) belongs in another context. Several years after attending Vatican Council I, Bishop Lootens retired for reasons of health and returned to Victoria, Vancouver Island where, on January 10, 1898, he returned his noble soul to the Lord.

✢ROBERT EMMET LUCEY (1891–1977)

In the philosophy of Archbishop Robert Emmet Lucey (1891–1977), the nature and worth of man "must be analyzed in the school of religion, not in the school of natural sciences." This nationally–known pioneer of the underprivileged, who lived to celebrate the golden jubilee of his ordination to the priesthood, was the first resident of Los Angeles and the fifth native Californian raised to the episcopate.

Robert Emmet Lucey, one of three sons of John Joseph and Mary Nettle Lucey, was born on March 16, 1891. He received his primary education at Sacred Heart School and later took courses at Saint Vincent's College.

Archbishop Robert E. Lucey

real Christian cannot go along with the world on every point. There are times when he has to take a stand against prevailing customs and popular prejudices."

In 1941, Bishop Lucey was promoted to the Metropolitan See of San Antonio. There be continued his campaign for equal social and economic rights for the underprivileged. President Lyndon B. Johnson recalled Lucey's "writing me and quarreling and fussing and just doing everything that he could to try to help do something for people who were picking pecans in San Antonio for eight cents an hour."

The archbishop was highly respected in the area of social welfare. As Executive Chairman of the Bishop's Committee for the Spanish–speaking, he championed the rights of Mexican Americans. He served on a five–man team named by President Harry S. Truman to study the problems of migratory workers and was later appointed by President Johnson to membership on the National Advisory Council for the War on Poverty. He was also Co–Chairman of the National Inter–Religious Council against Poverty. San Antonio's archbishop will be remembered for his many contributions, not the least of which was calling attention of the American people to the fact that the Catholic Church "preaches in season and out of season a social philosophy founded on religious principles; it proclaims the surpassing dignity of men and reveals the basis of human rights."

He entered Saint Patrick's Seminary at Menlo Park as a clerical student for the Diocese of Monterey–Los Angeles in 1907. Five years later, the young seminarian was sent by Bishop Thomas J. Conaty to Rome's North American College. He was ordained in the Eternal City's Church of Saint Apollinaris by the Latin Patriarch of Constantinople, Archbishop Giuseppe Cepetelli.

Upon returning to the southland, Father Lucey served as curate at Saint Vibiana's Cathedral and Immaculate Heart Church. He became administrator of Saint Paul's in 1917, on the death of his brother, Father John Lucey. Four years later he was made Diocesan Director of Charities by Bishop John J. Cantwell. Father Lucey served five years at Saint Kevin's Church in Los Angeles, and, in 1929, was sent to Long Beach as Pastor of Saint Anthony's Church. Almost from the beginning of his priesthood, Father Lucey was active in welfare work and promotion of causes favoring labor and racial equality. Everywhere he was known as a brilliant exponent of the principles of social justice.

In February of 1934, Pope Pius XI named Father Lucey to the Bishopric of Amarillo. It came as no surprise that the long outspoken critic of racial discrimination set out at once to desegregate the Catholic school system in the Texas Panhandle. Though he did encounter some opposition, the prelate observed, "The

✛JEAN–MARIE CARDINAL LUSTIGER (b. 1926)

According to Jean–Marie Cardinal Lustiger, "the role which Christians have in today's culture is that of witnessing the transcendent goal of humankind." This was the basic thrust of his message to the Pacific School of Religion at Berkeley on July 8, 1989. Two days earlier, the Archbishop of Paris visited the Historical Museum of the Archival Center, at Mission Hills, as part of a tour of the Archdiocese of Los Angeles.

Lustiger was born in Paris on September 17, 1926 of Polish–Jewish parents who emigrated to France after World War I. His mother was among those who died at Auschwitz in 1943. Converted to the Catholic faith in mid 1940, Lustiger became active in the Young Christian student movement during his university days. He was ordained a priest for the Archdiocese of Paris on April 17, 1954.

He served as pastor of a parish in Paris before being named Bishop of Orleans on December 8, 1979. By the time of his appointment to the Archbishopric of Paris, two years later, Lustiger was widely recognized as one of the Church's most forceful proponents of the true meaning of faith.

Shortly after being elevated to the College of Cardinals, Lustiger published his *Dare to Live*, a collection of addresses, articles and responses to interviews. Therein he pointed out that "the wish to love has to be learned and sustained. To want to live means to learn what life is all about." In another book, *Dare to Believe*, Lustiger proclaimed that "the future of the Church lies in allowing ourselves to be embraced and inspired by the living Christ."

The cardinal's exultant faith is all the more dramatic because it originated in a teenage convert from Judaism who continued to esteem his roots in the Old Testament while expressing a profound belief in the New Testament.

In print and in person, the Archbishop of Paris leaves an indelible impression on the faithful, the doubting and the disaffected. No encounter with this intense man and his vibrant personality could be casual. "Christianity concerns the whole of life," according to Lustiger who mixes freely the fire and brimstone of the Old Testament with the loving and caring concern of the New Testament.

Another of the cardinal's books, *The Choice of God*, confronted the anticlerical, secular world of Paris intellectuals and went on to become a primary nonfiction best–seller in France. His writings are a favorite of the Parisian newspapers and few issues fail to mention his name.

Since his appointment to the historic See of Paris, Lustiger has attracted worldwide attention because of his unusual background. He neither seeks nor evades the limelight as he asserts the Church's presence. That he has attracted wide attention in Europe and the United States is attested by the responsive chord struck in a supportive article in the magazine section of the New York *Times* entitled "A Most Special Cardinal."

✛JOHN B. MACGINLEY (1871–1969)

The pages of California's history were momentarily fanned backwards on Saturday, October 25, 1969, at the Carmelite Monastery of Our Lady and Saint Therese, for the funeral of a prelate long absent from the field of his apostolic labors. Seventy–four people, one each for the years of his priesthood, gathered in the small monastery chapel at Carmel, to pay their final respects to the earthly remains of Bishop John Bernard MacGinley, at whose invitation the cloistered nuns began that foundation in May, 1925.

The one–time Bishop of Monterey–Fresno was born on August 19, 1871 in the scenic little Irish town of Killybegs, in the extreme southwest corner of Donegal. He was the son of a school teacher, one of three brothers who responded to the priestly vocation. During his earliest years in the ministry, Father MacGinley served in the Archdiocese of Philadelphia, first as curate at Our Lady of the Holy Rosary Church and, later, as Professor of

Classics and Moral Theology at Saint Charles Seminary. In 1903, Father MacGinley was among four priests who accompanied Bishop Dennis Dougherty to the Philippines. At Vigan, MacGinley was rector of the seminary for the Diocese of Nueva Segovia. A few years later, he was recalled to Philadelphia and the pastorate of Saint Charles Church.

Early in 1910, at the insistence of Pope Pius X, Father MacGinley returned to the Philippines, this time as Bishop of Nueva Caceres to look after the spiritual needs of that jurisdiction's 600,000 Catholics. It was while attending the installation of Daniel Gercke as Bishop Tucson that MacGinley first made the acquaintance of John J. Cantwell. Shortly thereafter, the Bishop of Los Angeles–San Diego asked the Holy See to name MacGinley to the recently formed Diocese of Monterey–Fresno.

Pope Pius XI acquiesced and, on March 24, 1924, it was announced that John B. MacGinley was to be Central California's first residential bishop. He was canonically installed by Dennis Cardinal Dougherty on July 31. The subsequent eight years were hectic ones. Churches were erected, schools built, parishes established and a whole litany of facilities opened and programs inaugurated to serve the Catholic populace in the 45,000 square mile jurisdiction.

When his services were no longer needed, Bishop MacGinley, like Longfellow's Arab, folded his tent and quietly stole away, leaving behind a noble "tradition of zeal and holiness." Official retirement provided the bishop with an opportunity for the contemplative life he had always so earnestly cherished. After thirty–seven years of active priestly work, he began the second phase of his ministry, another thirty–seven years, devoted exclusively to prayer and contemplation. The book of life was closed where it had opened, at Bruach na Mara, on October 18, 1969. By that time, the ninety–eight year old prelate, last of the appointees of Pius X, had become the world's oldest bishop and, at fifty–nine years, the longest consecrated.

When the Carmelite Monastery of Our Lady and Saint Therese was built, Bishop MacGinley asked that he might one day be entombed within the confines of the chapel. That privilege was fulfilled when Harry Downie and this writer helped to lower his handsome wooden casket to its final resting place.

John Bernard MacGinley did not believe that the joy of being a priest rested on a better definition of the priesthood, nor on the experience of its effectiveness, but rather on the total trust which he placed in the Lord who called him to a participation in the ministry. He affirmed on many occasions Saint Paul's dictum: "I know whom I have believed, and I am certain that He is able to guard the trust committed to me until the day of His return."

✤JOSEPH MADERA (b. 1927)

Born at San Francisco, on November 27, 1927, Joseph Madera was raised in Mexico. He studied vocal music for four years, along with all the regular high school subjects. In 1942, the fifteen year old Joseph was accepted as a clerical aspirant by the Missionaries of the Holy Spirit, a community founded in 1914 to provide the Church "with good spiritual directors."

Joseph followed in the footsteps of two uncles who had been Missionaries of the Holy Spirit. After completing his studies at Puebla, he was ordained to the priesthood on June 15, 1957 by Archbishop Luigi Raimondi, Apostolic Delegate to Mexico.

During the earliest years of his priestly ministry, Father Madera taught Latin and Mathematics and was choral director at his *alma mater*. He also ministered to the local residents attached to the motherhouse. In 1960, Father Madera returned to California as associate pastor of Christ the King Parish (now Our Lady of Guadalupe) in Oxnard. He also served in other capacities, such as chaplain to migrant workers and professor of pastoral Spanish at Saint John's Seminary, Camarillo.

Madera was advanced to the pastorate at Oxnard in 1970 and for the next six years worked tirelessly at implementing all the directives of Vatican Council II among the 1,628 Catholic families there. Among his many accomplishments at Oxnard was the establishment of an Hispanic radio program known throughout the county as *La Hora Catolica*. He also organized twenty–five adult religion education centers and inaugurated a host of innovative projects for teenagers.

In an interview with a local newspaper, Father Madera expressed his view that a healthy parish is one that has as its thrust the meeting of basic, deep spiritual needs of the people. His program worked too. On a pastoral visitation to Oxnard, in March of 1974, Cardinal Timothy Manning told the parishioners at Our Lady of Guadalupe that "you have expressed a joy, faith and unity I've seen nowhere else in the Archdiocese of Los Angeles."

Upon completion of his term of office at Oxnard, Father Madera was retained in California, this time to fill the need for priests in the Diocese of Fresno. He was named to the dual pastorate of Saint Lucy (Fowler) and Saint Katherine (Del Rey) and it was there that he received news of his appointment as Coadjutor Bishop of Fresno.

The bishop returned to Fowler, on February 24, 1980, to make his profession of faith. This he did to demonstrate "recognition to those communities who had been supportive" of his ministry. He was ordained to the bishopric in Selland Arena on March 4th. Bishop Madera was already known throughout Fresno, Inyo, Kern, King, Madera, Mariposa, Merced and Tulare counties for his zealous pastoral work among the Hispanic peoples.

Though Spanish–speaking peoples constitute about half the Catholic population in the Diocese of Fresno, Madera made it clear that he planned to be a bishop for all the 325,000 Catholics in the 35,239 square mile Central California jurisdiction. Currently the eleventh bishop of Mexican–American background serving in the American hierarchy, Bishop Madera is only the second member of his community to be advanced to episcopal status.

On May 28, 1991, Bishop Madera was appointed to the titular See of Orte and named auxiliary for the Archdiocese of Military Services.

✤LEO T. MAHER (1915–1991)

The third Bishop of San Diego was among the more prolific of the Golden State's hierarchy. And a goodly percentage of his writings on such topics as the "Role of Women," the "Task of the Catholic Press," "Worship and Sacrifice" and the "Unborn Child" appeared nationally in the columns of Our Sunday Visitor. And it was Bishop Leo T. Maher who suggested that Fray Junípero Serra "could well become the saint of ecology" for his work in the "development and preservation of natural beauty in California "

Leo T. Maher was born at Mount Union, Iowa, on July 1, 1915, the son of Thomas and Mary (Teberg) Maher. It was during his elementary school days that the Maher family came to California. His studies for the ministry commenced at Saint Joseph's College, in Mountain View. Upon completion of his theological courses at Saint Patrick's Seminary, Menlo Park, Maher was ordained to the priesthood by the Most Reverend John J. Mitty, on December 18, 1943.

During his earliest priestly years, Father Maher engaged in pastoral activities in several Bay City curacies. He was named Secretary to Archbishop Mitty in 1947, a position he occupied for almost two decades. Father Maher was created a monsignor by Pope Pius XII, on November 5, 1954 and, two years later, he became chancellor for the Archdiocese of San Francisco.

With the creation of an autonomous ecclesial jurisdiction for the six northernmost counties of the archdiocese in 1962, Msgr. Maher was named proto Bishop of Santa Rosa. He received episcopal ordination on April 5th from the Apostolic Delegate to the United States, Archbishop Egidio Vagnozzi. In the seven years that Bishop Maher presided over the spiritual destinies of Santa Rosa, he created nine parishes, erected ten churches, built three high schools, twelve rectories, four grammar schools, three convents and two parochial halls.

Upon his transferal to the Diocese of San Diego, in

July of 1969, Bishop Maher expressed his goals as those of helping "people develop self–reliance and to convert helplessness, self–distrust and conscious incapacity into courage, power and initiative." During the first decade of his apostolate in San Diego, Bishop Maher streamlined the school system, updated liturgical practices, established minority representation and convened a diocesan synod.

An outspoken defender and advocate for minority rights, Maher's 1974 pastoral on "Women in the New World" was widely heralded and praised. It was republished in such influential journals as the Vatican's *Osservatore Romano*. Therein the prelate pointed out that "from its beginning the Church of Christ has claimed for women the restoration of her original dignity and her emancipation from cultural inequities and the stigma of inferiority imposed in the past."

Maher was an active participant in the conciliar deliberations of Vatican Council II. While there he noted that "one could divide bishops into three types. First, those who made things happen; secondly, those who watched things happen, and, thirdly, those who wondered what happened." Bishop Leo T. Maher himself obviously fitted into the first category. Throughout his episcopate he demonstrated in a forceful manner, his love and dynamic concern for all persons.

✙ROGER CARDINAL MAHONY (b. 1936)

A. NEW BISHOP FOR CENTRAL CALIFORNIA

On Wednesday, March 19th, 1975, the fourth native of Los Angeles and the twenty–third Californian was ordained to the episcopacy as Auxiliary Bishop for the eight county Diocese of Fresno. Homilist for the ceremony was Timothy Cardinal Manning, with whom the new prelate's path had been entwined for almost thirty years. It was in the pages of *The Tidings* for October 18, 1946, that their relationship began. That issue, describing Mannings's consecration as Auxiliary Bishop of Los Angeles, carried a picture of ten year old Roger and his twin brother, Louis.

Thirteen years later, Bishop Manning conferred the minor orders of Lector and Porter on Mr. Mahony and, the following year, those of Acolyte and Exorcist. In 1967, when Bishop Manning was named to the Diocese of Fresno, Msgr. Mahony served as chief liaison between the new Ordinary and retiring Bishop Aloysius J. Willinger.

Roger Michael Mahony was born to Victor James and Loretta Marie (Baron) Mahony, on February 27, 1936. His entire elementary training was acquired at Saint Charles School, in North Hollywood, where he fell under the pastoral tutelage of Msgr. Harry Meade.

In 1950, Roger entered Los Angeles College, the preparatory seminary for the Archdiocese of Los Angeles. He was among the initial enrollees at San Fernando's Queen of Angels Seminary, in 1954. Upon completing his collegiate courses at Saint John's Seminary, Camarillo, Roger asked for and received incardination as a clerical aspirant for the Diocese of Monterey–Fresno.

Roger received priestly ordination at the hands of the Most Reverend Aloysius J. Willinger on May 1, 1962. A few days later, he was assigned to a curacy at Saint John's Cathedral, Fresno. In the following fall, Bishop Willinger asked Father Mahony to take further studies at the National Catholic School of Social Justice, in Washington, D.C.

Soon after returning to Central California, in 1964, Father Mahony was named diocesan Director for Catholic Charities and Social Service, an assignment he held for six years. In September, 1964, he became Administrator (and later Pastor) of Saint Genevieve's Parish, Fresno.

Among the other positions occupied by the tireless priest during the late 1960s were Executive Director for both the Catholic Welfare Bureau and the Infant of Prague Adoption Service, as well as Chaplain of the diocesan Saint Vincent de Paul Society. He also found time to teach during those years at Fresno State University and Coalinga College.

Long interested in the apostolate to Hispanic peoples, Father Mahony served a term on the Board of Directors for the West Coast Regional Office of the Bishops' Committee for the Spanish–Speaking. He was also active as Secretary for the United States Catholic Bishops Ad Hoc Committee on Farm Labor.

There was time for civil responsibilities too. Father Mahony was affiliated with the Fresno County Economic Opportunities Commission, the Alcoholic Rehabilitation Committee, the United Crusade, the Community Workshop, the Urban Coalition and the Fresno Redevelopment Agency. It was recognition of those manifold duties that prompted the Junior Chamber of Commerce to proclaim Father Mahony "Young Man of the Year" for 1967. It was also in that year that he was named an Honorary Chaplain to His Holiness.

In 1970, shortly after the transferal of the Most Reverend Hugh A. Donohoe to Fresno, Msgr. Mahony was appointed diocesan chancellor, a position he continued to hold as the titular Bishop of Tamascani. He became Pastor of Saint John's Cathedral on May 1, 1973.

✙ROGER CARDINAL MAHONY (b. 1936)

B. RECEPTION OF THE PALLIUM

Shortly after their installation, metropolitan archbishops petition the Holy Father for the pallium, the official insignia of their office. Bestowed on the Feast of Sts. Peter and Paul, the pallium signifies the "plentitude of jurisdiction" which the petitioner shares with the Holy Father in his designated ecclesial province.

On June 29, 1986, Archbishop Roger Mahony became the fourth ordinary of Los Angeles to receive the pallium. For the first time, this "fullness of the episcopal office" was bestowed directly on the recipient. Archbishops Cantwell, McIntyre and Manning received the pallium through couriers and local ceremonials.

Surely the most singularly unique of the prelatial garments, the pallium is a circular band of white wool worn exclusively by metropolitan archbishops on certain specified days while performing the liturgical duties of their office.

Just when and where the pallium initially became an ecclesial garment is unclear, although a Roman tradition associates it with Saint Peter's mantle, the long–recognized symbol of the papal office. In any event, the pallium was introduced as a liturgical badge for the Vicar of Christ in imitation of its counterpart in the Eastern Church, the pontifical *omorphorion*.

The practice of requiring metropolitans to submit a request for the pallium, along with a written pledge of their fidelity to the Holy See, has served to affirm the dependence of all episcopal authority on Christendom's Chief Pastor. Ancient versions of the pallium, preserved in the treasuries of European cathedrals, indicate that it was somewhat longer in earlier centuries than it is today. Even the manner of wearing it differed, depending on local traditions or on the directions spelled out in the bull of bestowal.

The present–day style of the pallium, dating from the 10th century, is that of a narrow scarf, worn about the neck with its appendages hanging downward over the breast and back. The only ornamentation are the six crosses over the breast, on the back, on each shoulder and at each of the two ends of the twelve inch pendant extentions which are themselves weighted down with lead and covered with black silk.

Three gold pins, fastened on the left shoulder, at the back and on the breast allow the pallium to retain its form while being worn over the chasuble. The "precious pins" of Cardinal McIntyre's pallium were removed and attached to the pallium bestowed on his successor. Symbolic as it is of the responsibility vested in the chief bishop of an ecclesial province, the pallium's bestowal is an outward manifestation of the special relationship existing between metropolitans and the Supreme Pontiff who alone can wear the insignia at all times and places.

There are thirty one Roman and two Eastern provinces in the United States, each of whose metropolitan archbishops is entitled to wear the pallium. Bestowal of that insignia in Rome was the final stage of ceremonies begun when Archbishop Mahony was installed as Chief Shepherd of the largest archdiocese in the United States.

There is a somber and realistic tone to the conferral of the pallium, inasmuch as tradition dictates that the pallium be entombed with the archbishop—as a reminder that all ecclesial authority derives from and is ultimately dissolved in God Himself.

Roger Cardinal Mahony

✦ROGER CARDINAL MAHONY (b. 1936)

C. Symbolism of Installation

The bonding of the new archbishop to the Church of Los Angeles in 1985 was symbolically manifested by a trinity of historical memorabilia relating to Catholicism along *El Camino Real.* The items in question are a cathedra, a cross and a crozier.

The *cathedra* (in former times called a throne) is the chair from which a bishop comments on the scriptural readings. Initially a piece of furniture in the Roman emperor's palace, it became a seat of distinction for orators and judges and finally a symbol of their office.

Gradually adopted into Christian worship services, the *cathedra* was placed in the vertex of the apse, raised above the priests' seats which adjoined it on both sides. The church where it was placed came to be known as the "cathedral" or bishop's house–of–worship. The chair which was used by Archbishop Roger Mahony during the presentation of the papal bulls at Mission Hills was the one in which John J. Cantwell was seated at Saint Vibiana's Cathedral in 1917 as Bishop of Monterey–Los Angeles.

Handsomely–carved from native California woods, the chair served as the official *cathedra* until 1924, when the cathedral was renovated and enlarged. Beneath the diocesan coat–of–arms is a strip for the official motto.

Then, the following day, when the archbishop entered his cathedral for the first time, he was presented with a mosaic cross bearing a depiction of the four Roman basilicas. Encased within the tiny sepulchre of the cross is a relic of the Venerable Fray Junípero Serra, the great pathfinder of the Church in the Californias.

Finally, there is the crozier. Historically this pastoral staff has been looked upon as one of the principal insignia associated with the episcopal office. Though usually made of a metallic substance, plated with gold or silver, the shepherd's "stick" has more recently been fashioned from wood in elaborately–carved designs.

The pastoral staff presented by the papal *pro–nuncio* to Archbishop Mahony embodies a long and rich association with the Church in Southern California. Joaquin Amat had it "rolled" in Barcelona for presentation to his uncle who came to the Pacific Slope as Bishop of Monterey in 1854. Bishop Thaddeus Amat carried the crozier to the far corners of his huge diocese during the quarter century of his episcopate. The brightly–polished, four–part silver pastoral staff was mentioned in several newspaper accounts describing the consecration of Saint Vibiana's Cathedral on April 30, 1876.

When Bishop Thomas J. Conaty came to the diocese in 1903, he had threads added to the connecting joints for greater facility in transporting the bulky staff. Likely it was the only crozier Conaty used during his years as Bishop of Monterey–Los Angeles. After Conaty's time, the crozier was put aside until the late 1950s, when then Auxiliary Bishop Joseph T. McGucken brought it to San Fernando Mission. There it was displayed and inaccurately labeled as "a missionary's walking staff."

In 1971, the crozier, by now a treasured item in the Historical Museum attached to the Archival Center, was utilized once again at the cathedral, this time for the episcopal ordination of William R. Johnson as titular Bishop of Blera and Auxiliary of Los Angeles.

The ancient tradition of using historically symbolic instruments in the Church's liturgy is a superb example of how gracefully and meaningfully the old blends with the new in the worship of God.

✠TIMOTHY CARDINAL MANNING (1909–1989)

A. THE *PRESIDENTE* AND THE CARDINAL

In the fall of 1928, a young Irish seminarian put aside the love of parents, comforts of home and the pride of life to follow Christ along California's *El Camino Real.* Without knowing it, Timothy Manning was repeating a similar scene that occurred, almost two centuries earlier, when a youthful Fray Junípero Serra traded the familiar haunts of his boyhood for the uncertainties of a far–away apostolate in the New World.

In the personages of those two islandic pioneers, the *Presidente* from Mallorca and the Cardinal from Eire, the Church was born, reared and brought to term along the Pacific Slope. Though Junípero Serra and Timothy Manning differed in generation, heritage and language, they shared a determination of projecting the priestly ideals of service to a needy people in a distant land.

It was Fray Junípero who first spelled out that mentality in a letter written on August 20, 1749, asking a priest friend at Petra to inform the elder Serras about his departure for the missions. The sentiments of that letter founded a Christian civilization in one era and are bringing it to fulfillment in another.

> I am writing this letter in farewell. The day fixed upon is unknown to me, but the trunks containing our baggage are locked and strapped and they say that after two, three, or possibly four days, the ship will sail.
>
> I want to ask you again to do me the favor of consoling my parents, who, I know, are going through a great sorrow.
>
> I wish I could give them some of the happiness that is mine; and I feel that they would urge me to go ahead and never turn back.
>
> Tell them that the dignity of an apostolic preacher, especially when united with the active ministry, is the highest vocation they could have wished me to follow.
>
> After all, considering their advanced age, their life is mostly spent. Their remaining days are obviously short and if they compare those days with eternity, they will see that it is no more than an instant. This being the case, it is very important, and according to God's will, that they do not depend on what little help I might be to them were I to remain behind. By so doing they will merit greatly from Almighty God. And if we are not to see each other again in this world, they may rest assured that we will all be united forever in eternal glory. Tell them how badly I feel at not being able to stay longer and make them happy by my presence. And yet, they know full well that first things come first; and our first duty is to do the will of God. Nothing else but that love has led me to leave them. And, if I, for the love of God and with the help of His grace, can muster the courage to leave, might I not suggest that they also, for the love of God, can be content to forego the happiness of my presence.
>
> Let them listen attentively to the advice of their confessor; and they will see that God has truly entered their home. By practicing holy patience and resignation to the Divine Will, they will possess and attain eternal life.
>
> They should hold no one but Our Lord God and Him alone responsible for the separation. They will find out how sweet His yoke can be, that what they now consider

Timothy Cardinal Manning

and endure as a great sorrow will be turned into a lasting joy. As a matter of fact, nothing in life should cause us sorrow. Our clear duty is to conform ourselves to His will and thus prepare well for death. Beyond this, nothing else matters.

Happy are they who have a son a priest—however bad and sinful—who every day in the Holy Sacrifice of the Mass prays for them as best he can and very often offers exclusively for them his Mass so that the Lord will send them help and the necessities of life; that He may grant them grace of patience in their trials, and finally, at the proper time, a happy death in God's holy grace.

If I succeed in being a good priest and missionary these prayers of mine will be all the more powerful and my parents will be the first to profit by them. And the same is to be said regarding the rest of my family.

I well remember that, while assisting my father when he had taken severely ill, sometime back, he said to me: "Son what I am most anxious about is that you be a good religious." Well, father, rest assured that I keep your words always before me, just as if I hear them from your mouth at this very moment. But bear in mind that it is to become a good religious that I have undertaken this voyage.

You must not feel badly that I am doing your will, which is, at this time, the will of God. As for my mother, I know full well that she has never missed offering up her prayers for me to God for that same purpose, that I

be a good priest. No wonder then that God hearing your prayers, has directed me in this way. Rest assured then with the way in which God has allowed things to work out.

Let us bless God who loves and cares for us all. May the Lord bring us all together in eternal glory and keep us all for many years.

✠ TIMOTHY CARDINAL MANNING (1909–1989)

B. *NOVA ET VETERA*

How appropriate it was that the Coadjutor Archbishop of Los Angeles chose to inaugurate the final phase of his Southern California apostolate on the feast of her whose title the jurisdiction bears. The day took on an added historical dimension, inasmuch as August 2, 1969 marked the 200th anniversary of the initial Christian penetration to the region named for Our Lady of the Angels.

To that spacious valley, abounding in cottonwoods and alders, among which ran a beautiful river, came a new shepherd to fulfill the papal mandate given a century earlier by another pontiff: "Where others are drawn by gold, you must go to carry the cross."

Archbishop Timothy Manning was no stranger. Trained in the noble traditions of the Cantwell years, seasoned in the expansionary complexities of the McIntyre archiepiscopate and steeped in the spirit of Vatican II, he was ready to make his own distinctive imprint on the pilgrim Church in the Archdiocese of Los Angeles.

He was, in fact as in title, a *pontifex maximus*, a bridge–builder. His was the formidable challenge of relating the magnificent accomplishments of two hundred years to the even greater forward strides envisioned for the dawning decade of the inter–planetary age.

The task was staggering in its proportions. Though only one of California's nine ecclesiastical divisions, the Archdiocese of Los Angeles accounted for 44% of the Catholic population in an "empire–state" whose economy ranked it sixth among world powers. Had it then been a separate nation, California's gross product would have been exceeded only by the United States, the Soviet Union, the Federal Republic of Germany, the United Kingdom and France. Per capita income in the Golden State surpassed that of any country, including the United States, while, in manufacturing, California vied with Japan for fifth place in the Free World.

The total value of its import–export trade outranked a hundred nations. It was more populous than 111 countries and larger in size than ninety–two. It had more telephones than any country except the United States and ranked only behind the United States, France and England in the number of motor vehicles. While these and many other impressive statistics testified to the future potentialities of California, they also clearly indicated that the apostolate begun by Fray Juan Crespi and his Franciscan confreres was far from completed.

Contemporary society craved, as perhaps never before, a renewal of that vibrant Christian awareness which motivated the early missionaries to plant the cross in this frontier–outpost of the Spanish realm. It was a noble challenge. Seldom in the Church's long history had there been so many favorable opportunities for expanding the message of Christ. Rarely had that message been more needed.

The People of God in the counties of Santa Barbara, Ventura, Los Angeles and Orange were fortunate in being given, in that privileged hour, a coadjutor archbishop bearing those dual biblical symbols of a rock and a river, one standing for stability and solidity, the other for advancement and challenge.

As he took up the banner of Our Lady of the Angels, first unfurled just a few steps from Saint Vibiana's Cathedral exactly two centuries earlier, Archbishop Timothy Manning had the assurances of sentiments similar to those uttered by J. Wiseman Macdonald on behalf of the faithful in the Diocese of Monterey–Los Angeles at the arrival of Thomas J. Conaty, in 1903:

> With you our Bishop, as engineer, we want to say that no matter what may be the speed of the train, how rough the road or heavy the grade, you can always look back from the engine with the certainty of seeing the green flag on the last coach waving the encouraging signal that every car is still with you and that the couplings riveted by the faith we have in Mother Church and you have securely held the train intact. We are always behind you; priests and laity.

✛TIMOTHY CARDINAL MANNING (1909–1989)

c. His Eminence of Los Angeles

The passing of Timothy Cardinal Manning left a spiritual vacuum in the Lord's vineyard that will not soon be filled. No churchman ever served California longer, knew its area better or loved its people more. He imparted a wholly new dimension to the concept of servanthood.

In the days and years ahead, writers will scramble to appraise the "Manning Era" and its place on the scale of spiritual accomplishments. Above all else, they will find that Timothy Manning was a wise and spiritual leader. He may not have been the most informed or imaginative of churchmen, but he understood himself and his people far better than most of his episcopal contemporaries.

Scholars will conclude that the sum of his rather nor-

mal parts add up to an exceptional figure. Manning's keen sense of ecclesial vision enabled him to correctly gauge the potential of God's people. The man was the monument; the monument was the Church.

His unobtrusive style of leadership was one of quiet persuasion and personal example. He once confided a preference for letting others take the well–charted super highways. "I prefer the backroads and alleyways where simple people like my own parents lived and worked out their salvation."

Manning verbalized his non–directive style a decade earlier in a homily preached over the founder of the Irish Christian Brothers: "The full measure of a man is to be found, not in his good works or his great achievements, but rather in the new colors and textures that come alive in other peoples because of him."

Unlike other giants in the post–Vatican Church, Cardinal Manning will be longer remembered for what he said than for what he did. Through his long ministry, stretching from 1934 to 1989, his God–given charisma shone brightest in the pulpit, on the podium and from the printed page.

Those who want to know him best must read his *Days of Change, Years of Challenge* and *Times of Tension, Moments of Grace,* the two volumes containing his major homilies, addresses and talks.

Therein one can understand how, more than any of his predecessors, Timothy Manning passed through fifty–five years of priestly ministry mostly untouched by critics, his reputation growing ever more prominent with the passage of time. An uncommon man made from common parts, he became the American Church's most eloquent mouthpiece in a time of institutional confusion and personal bewilderment.

People pay too much attention to college degrees, public acclaim and positions of prominence; they tend to be overawed by the listings in *Who's Who,* by prizes, travels and distinctions; they pay too much heed to organizational charts, paper–flow and human efficiency; they overly concern themselves with the shortfalls, mistakes and blemishes of their leadership.

Himself a gifted orator, a talented writer and a degreed canonist, Timothy Manning epitomized a totally different approach, one that paralleled and extolled the relationship of Jesus with His apostles. Though sometimes described as passive and unresponsive, Timothy Manning was acutely aware of problems, hurts and challenges. But in many cases, he simply chose to overlook them or delegate their solution to others. He was student enough of history to realize that the passage of time has always been the most effective cure for most wounds.

The cardinal's humble grave at Calvary Cemetery had been marked for many years with a simple stone bearing only his crest of office. By choice he elected to rest alongside his fellow levites. The only preference he sought in this life or the next was spiritual.

The flock he shepherded, the people he loved and the archdiocese he left behind must be forever grateful to God for sharing with them this singularly–gifted high priest. May we all strive to rest in his peace!

✤PATRICK MANOGUE (1831–1895)

California's "Gold Rush Bishop" is the subject of a volume written by the former editor of the *Central California Register*, Floyd Anderson. The treatise was the first full–sized edition published on a member of the state's hierarchy. Aimed principally for young readers, the narrative unfolds around the intriguing personality of Patrick Manogue, the second and last Bishop of Grass Valley. Born in County Kilkenny on the Emerald Isle, Manogue (1831–1895) is but one of a host of Irish–born priests who have been and still are as familiar to the California scene as the missions, whose *padres* they succeeded.

Patrick Manogue's career in California started out as a gold miner in the Mother Lode region. Forced to postpone his studies for the priesthood for economic reasons, he set out for Moore's Flat, Nevada County, to prospect for gold. His eventual success there enabled him to answer the call of Archbishop Joseph Sadoc Alemany to study for the Archdiocese of San Francisco. Ordained at Paris in 1861, Father Manogue returned immediately to his adopted home and was given the pastorate at Virginia City in the newly created Vicariate of Marysville, an area including most of the present–day State of Nevada. His annual reports over the next twenty years are filed at the Paris offices of *Propagation de la Foi* and reveal the many–sided genius of Patrick Manogue's fascinating personality.

Father Manogue's pastorate at Virginia City earned him great acclaim. Within two years he had begun a school and an orphanage. His educational endeavors resulted in the first institutions of learning in Nevada. By 1875 two churches were under way and construction was coming along slowly on Saint Mary's Hospital. Named Titular Bishop of Ceramus by Pius IX, Manogue was consecrated on January 16, 1881. Three years later he succeeded Eugene O'Connell as Bishop of Grass Valley. Realizing the growth pattern within his diocese, Manogue asked for and received permission to transfer the seat of his jurisdiction to Sacramento, the state's capital.

The sermon preached at Bishop Manogue's consecration sums up the sentiments of his contemporaries and while the words came from the lips of the famous Indian priest, Father James Bouchard, S.J., they could have been uttered by anyone there present.

I congratulate Bishop Manogue on his promotion to the dignity of a Bishop in the One, Holy, Catholic and Apostolic Church, and I congratulate the Venerable Archbishop and Bishops of the Province on the accession of Bishop Manogue, than whom there is none more worthy of the position which he has been called to occupy among you.

Anecdotes about the witty bishop are copious. Once chided by Bishop O'Connell for neglecting to preface his signature with the cross customarily used by bishops before their names, Manogue reportedly observed that "he had long been of the opinion that one cross in a diocese was amply sufficient." Manogue was ecumenical in an age when that spirit was decidedly not in vogue. He was welcome in the homes of peoples of all religious beliefs and persuasions. This attitude was all the more attractive in a man whose own radiant faith was contagious, one who had no hesitation in saying at a public reception in his honor, "I thought if I could become a good priest of the Church I would be the happiest man in the world."

The impressive career of California's "Gold Rush Bishop" came to a close on February 27, 1895, and several days later he was laid to rest in a simple tomb "out in the graveyard among my priests." It is no idle flattery to second Anderson's estimation that "the thriving Diocese of Sacramento today is a living testimonial to the foreseeing wisdom of Bishop Manogue." For to him belongs the title of the "most typically Californian of all prelates," a lasting tribute to a native of the Emerald Isle!

✤LUIS MARIA MARTINEZ (1881–1956)

When plans were being made for the dedication of Saint John's Seminary, the honor of celebrating the Pontifical Mass was reserved for the Archbishop of Mexico City. It was an altogether fitting choice for the roots of California are firmly anchored to the Hispanic era.

In retrospect, there were reasons other than the obvious ones why Archbishop Luis Maria Martinez (1881–1956) should have been chosen to inaugurate the seminary for what would become the largest archdiocese in the United States. Besides its academic and other functions, a seminary is a place where clerical aspirants learn how to acquire and help others acquire sanctity. In fact that role is what distinguishes a seminary from any other college or university.

Archbishop Martinez's contemporaries recognized him as a master of the ascetical life. Already, in 1940, he had written twenty–nine books on spiritual topics, volumes that were later published in 175 editions in five languages.

Those who knew him or read his books would not have been surprised that in 1980, the cause for sainthood on behalf of Archbishop Luis Maria Martinez was introduced at Mexico City. If and when that cause is favorably completed, Martinez would become the thirtieth saint in Mexico's history.

Martinez was born in the state of Michoacan on June 9, 1881. When the future archbishop was ten years old, he was enrolled in the seminary at Morelia. He was an outstanding student, noted for his intelligence and memory. He completed his studies for the priesthood before he was twenty years old. Being too young for ordination, he had to wait four and a half years to become a priest.

After his ordination, on November 20, 1904, Father Martinez was named prefect at the diocesan seminary and there he remained for thirty–two years, becoming rector in 1919. When the institution was seized and closed by the government and its students evicted, it was Martinez who watched over the dramatically new life–style forced upon the scattered seminarians.

In 1923, Martinez became Auxiliary Bishop of Morelia and fourteen years later he was advanced to the archbishopric of Mexico City which, even then, was perhaps the most populous in the world. Shortly thereafter, the Holy See entrusted Martinez with the delicate negotiations with the government on Church–State relations. These continued for a decade and were concluded successfully with the appointment of an apostolic delegate.

Archbishop Martinez held the first synod for Mexico City in 1945, restored the cathedral, refurbished the basilica of Our Lady of Guadalupe and visited every parish in the gigantic jurisdiction. More than that, "he was for everyone the presence of Christ, the Good Shepherd."

By 1945, the Mexican Church had passed through the most difficult moments of its history. Archbishop Martinez was credited with having gained the good will and friendship of those who governed Mexico; with having avoided further shedding of blood and with having opened new horizons for the Catholics of Mexico.

In 1950, Pope Pius XII proposed bestowing a red hat on Mexico City. To no one's surprise, Martinez politely declined the honor. Given the political circumstances of the country, he did not consider the time was yet opportune for Mexico to have its first cardinal.

The inscription on his tomb, in the crypt of Mexico City's Cathedral of the Assumption describes Martinez as the "great peacemaker of our homeland, most brilliant speaker of the Holy Word, joyful giver of himself for his children." It notes that "in death he is mourned by his bride the Church."

Possibly by the time Saint John's Seminary celebrates its hundredth year of existence, the man who offered its dedicatory Mass will have been acknowledged by the Church as among the *beati*!

✝JOHN JOSEPH McCORT (1860–1936)

The name of Bishop John Joseph McCort (1860–1936) is irrevocably associated with the Catholic Church in Southern California, though for "grave and urgent reasons" he never actually exercised his priestly prerogatives on the West Coast. McCort studied for the ministry at Saint Charles Seminary, Overbrook. His intellectual talents were such that after his ordination, on October 14, 1883, he was appointed to the seminary faculty. During the ensuing years he ably fulfilled every duty assigned him, lending distinction and inspiration by the force of his example and the charm of his personality.

In 1889, Father McCort was named Pastor of Our Mother of Sorrows Church, in Philadelphia, where, through his untiring and unselfish endeavors, he rebuilt the parochial church, convent and school. In addition to opening a day nursery, he was responsible for the erection of Misericordia Hospital. The high standard of proficiency reached and maintained by the parish school alone bespeaks the character of the faith that motivated McCort's life and work as a shepherd of his flock.

Pope Pius X designated Father McCort a Domestic Prelate, in 1910, and shortly thereafter he became Vicar General of Philadelphia. Two years later he was named to the titular see of Azotus and Auxiliary to the aging Archbishop Edmond F. Prendergast.

On June 27, 1916, the Los Angeles Evening *Herald* reported that "according to press dispatches from Rome," Bishop McCort had been asked to fill the episcopal vacancy in the Diocese of Monterey–Los Angeles. The transfer of McCort to California's southland never materialized, however, for the Archbishop of Philadelphia cabled the Holy Father with a plea that the appointment of his auxiliary be rescinded.

The man ultimately filling the position, Bishop John J. Cantwell, later chided McCort for his reluctance to journey west and advised him to "come out and see Hollywood while you are still young, so that you may learn what you missed when you preferred Altoona to the City of (Our Lady of) the Angels."

Bishop McCort remained in Philadelphia an additional four years, during which time he was associated prominently with every social and Catholic endeavor that marked the unprecedented advance of the Church in the archdiocese. In 1920, McCort was appointed Coadjutor Bishop of Altoona and within a few months he became that jurisdiction's residential ordinary. He presided wisely and discreetly over the diocese during the years of both its greatest development and its most perplexing problems. Laying the broad and deep foundation for future growth of an abiding Catholic faith in the diocese, Bishop McCort inaugurated a vast building program which included erection of the handsome Blessed Sacrament Cathedral.

Death claimed the "almost" Bishop of Monterey–Los Angeles, on April 21, 1936, after a priestly service of fifty–two years. Though circumstances militated against his transferal to the west, the personal concern of Bishop John J. McCort for the maintenance of his spiritual children proved him to be the ideal Catholic man of affairs.

✝NORMAN F. MCFARLAND (b. 1922)

The Diocese of Reno was established, in 1931, to encompass the entire State of Nevada. Its first and fourth Chief Shepherds were Californians by birth and temperament. Norman F. McFarland was born in Martinez, on February 21, 1922, the son of Francis and Agnes (Kotchevar) McFarland. He attended the public schools in Martinez prior to entering Saint Joseph's College, Mountain View, as a clerical candidate for the Archdiocese of San Francisco.

Upon completion of his theological courses at Saint Patrick's Seminary, Menlo Park, Norman was ordained to the priesthood by Archbishop John J. Mitty on June 15, 1946. Father McFarland served as associate pastor at Saint Andrew's Parish, in Oakland, before entering The Catholic University of America as a graduate student in Canon Law. His thesis for the doctorate, a 132 page historical synopsis and commentary on *Religious Vocation. Its Juridic Concept*, was published at Washington, in 1953. Therein Father McFarland formulated the terminology still used when he stated that the religious state was "one whose members officially represent the Church both in the life of perfection and in the various fields of education, charity and other apostolic activities."

In subsequent years, Father McFarland occupied several positions in the Matrimonial Tribunal for the Archdiocese of San Francisco. From 1951 to 1958, he was professor of Moral Theology at San Francisco College for Women. He also served as chaplain for the Cosmas–Damian Guild of Catholic Pharmacists.

On June 5, 1970, Pope Paul VI named McFarland Titular Bishop of Bida and Auxiliary of San Francisco. The twentieth native Californian elevated to the episcopacy, he received ordination on September 8th from Archbishop Joseph T. McGucken. Meanwhile, he had been entrusted with the pastorate of Mission San Francisco de Asis (or Dolores), the sixth of the historic Fran-ciscan foundations in Alta California. The prelate was also named Vicar for Finance a post in which he oversaw and guided the temporalities attached to the Archdiocese of San Francisco.

On November 16, 1974, the Holy Father appointed Bishop McFarland Apostolic Administrator for the Diocese of Reno. In that delicate and difficult task, McFarland exhibited his native tendency to understand and practice the principles of collegiality and subsidiarity. Pope Paul VI named McFarland residential Ordinary early in 1976. The State of Nevada was still very much a missionary frontier, whose Catholic population was scattered among forty parishes and thirty–five mission stations. Covering a territory of 110,829 square miles, the Diocese of Reno was the largest geographical jurisdiction in the continental United States.

Outside Reno and Las Vegas, with their tinsel trimmings and round–the–clock casinos the diocese is comprised of isolated, tiny communities separated by interminable stretches of desert and mountain ranges.

The ministry of souls in Nevada was indeed challenging. It was a unique apostolate within the American Church where priests and religious experience demanded of isolation and loneliness quite as severe as those endured by the earliest missionaries to the west coast.

After serving for a decade at Reno, McFarland was appointed to the Diocese of Orange. His retirement was accepted by the Holy See in mid–1998.

✝JAMES FRANCIS CARDINAL MCINTYRE (1886–1979)

A. NEW ARCHBISHOP FOR LOS ANGELES

The transfer of the Most Reverend J. Francis A. McIntyre from New York to Los Angeles, early in 1948, elicited widespread comment in the Catholic press. The following observations appeared from the pen of Patrick Scanlan, editor of the Brooklyn *Tablet*, for February 21, 1948:

> That His Excellency, Archbishop McIntyre, will be missed in Catholic New York is a foregone conclusion. He has been an intimate part of it for many years. Very few Catholic events of note have been held on which he did not have a direct or indirect influence.
>
> His friends among the laity will miss him sorely, for he has been the sympathetic counselor and friend–in–need of thousands. Because of the many meetings he has dignified by his presence, the programs he has suggested or cooperated with, and the various associations he has had with so many in all walks of life, he has earned the title of a truly democratic gentleman.
>
> In the minds of all thoughtful men, a Catholic bishop is expected to be a representative person. His appoint-

ment is a matter of public concern and common interest—for a Catholic bishop is the local symbol of the mystical and religious unity of his flock.

It is the office of the bishop to protect the common interests of religion, to maintain the deposit of Faith, to preserve the simple, concrete truths of our ancient and Catholic Christianity, to protect that real and humble creed by which, through Christ, men walk with God.

Archbishop McIntyre has put these ideals into practice. He has been a conscientious priest of sound spirituality and apostolic simplicity, a hard worker who never allowed the clock to interfere with his endeavor, an organizer with extensive business and administrative experience.

In his long and successful career it can be said that he never catered to anything as much as he did to his duties, for he performed every task with honest objectivity, always including the personal equation, but never permitting it to sway his conclusions from the straight line of truth.

Day in and day out, year in and year out, from his ordination day until the present, the new Archbishop of Los Angeles has always and everywhere been the churchman. Having chosen the Lord for his inheritance, he desired no other and possessed no other.

The tasks incident to his vocation have always engrossed his time and attention. Beyond these, there appeared nothing that has ostensibly caught his interest. A man so completely absorbed in the cause of religion can not but be a true shepherd of souls. And such unquestionably he is.

His chief concern will be, as it always has been, to promote the well–being of religion, of the flock committed to his keeping, of the cause to which he is assigned. Few priests have spent themselves more tirelessly, more enthusiastically and more undividedly for the spiritual perfection of the people placed under their charge.

The many friends of the new Archbishop of Los Angeles—and *The Tablet* has always been among his friends—congratulate him upon the signal honor the Holy Father has conferred upon him and trust that his years and administration in the great archdiocese in the West will be both happy and fruitful.

✝JAMES FRANCIS CARDINAL MCINTYRE (1886–1979)

B. CARDINAL AND UFOS

Nothing intrigues people more than UFOs and/or Flying Saucers which dart in and out of contemporary annals. Even churchmen occasionally figure into such scenarios. Over the years, we have received several requests for information about the late James Francis Cardinal McIntyre and his purported involvement in an incident that originally occurred in 1947.

James Francis Cardinal McIntyre

The story is spelled out in a book by Charles Berlitz and William L. Moore, entitled *The Roswell Incident*. Therein it is stated that on the evening of July 2, 1947, "what appeared to be a flying saucer passed over Roswell heading northwest at a high rate of speed." It was struck by a lighting bolt and suffered severe onboard damage. It managed to stay airborne long enough to get over the mountains before crashing violently in an area west of Socorro known as the Plains of San Agustin.

Military officials quickly sequestered the wreckage and removed it into a security facility at Edwards Air Force Base. Only top governmental personnel were allowed to view or study the wreckage.

In April of 1954, Meade Layne, Director of the Borderland Research Associates, received a letter from Gerald Light of Los Angeles who said that he had spent some forty–eight hours at Edwards Air Force Base in the company of three other men, Franklin Allen of the Hearst newspaper chain, Edwin Nourse of the Brookings Institute and Bishop MacIntyre (sic) of Los Angeles.

Here is what he reported: "We were allowed to enter the restricted area . . . During my two days visit, I saw five separate and distinct types of aircraft being studied and handled by our air force officials with the assistance and permission of The Etherians! I have no words to express my reactions."

According to Light, President Eisenhower had been spirited over to Muroc one night during a visit to Palm Springs. He felt that Ike would eventually "go directly to the people via radio and television" about the incident. Subsequently, Senator Barry Goldwater got involved in the story. While enroute to California, in the early 1960s he stopped at Wright–Patterson and inquired about the "Blue Room" where the UFO artifacts, photographs and exhibits were stored.

When later asked about the matter, Goldwater did not deny it, rather he said that he could not "believe that we are the only planet that has life on it." (We have a copy of that letter at the Archival Center.)

Apart from the details of the purported crash and its cover–up, was Cardinal McIntyre ever personally involved? We know that he visited Edwards Air Force Base several times, once in November of 1956, when he confirmed about fifty military people.

Was he there during the week of April 12–16, 1954, as alleged by Gerald Light? Not according to entries in his *Standard Daily Journal*. It was Holy Week and the cardinal was busy with office appointments at the Chancery and liturgical ceremonies at the Cathedral.

After searching through all of McIntyre's papers, there is no evidence that would lend the slightest credence to the story of Gerald Light. Evidence can often be interpreted in diverse ways, but lack of evidence lends only to conjecture.

✠JAMES FRANCIS CARDINAL McINTYRE (1886–1979)

C. CATHOLIC AND/OR CHRISTIAN

The late James Francis Cardinal McIntyre once received an indignant letter from a lady who faulted him for using the term "Christian" in referring to the faithful. She insisted on being called "Catholic."

In his response, His Eminence of Los Angeles agreed that the terms were not always interchangeable, but gently pointed out that the term "Christian" was older than "Catholic." Then he quoted an ancient letter by Diognetus, a "follower of the apostles." In simple, lucid and graceful language, Diognetus told what the term "Christian" meant in the mid 2nd century:

Christians are indistinguishable from other people either by nationality, language or customs. They do not inhabit separate cities of their own, or speak a strange dialect, or follow some outlandish way of life. Their teaching is not based upon reveries inspired by the curiosity of men.

Unlike some others, they champion no purely human

doctrine. With regard to dress, food and manner of life in general, they follow the customs of whatever city they happen to be living in, whether it is Greek or foreign.

And yet there is something extraordinary about their lives. They live in their own countries as though they were only passing through. They play their full role as citizens, but labor under all the disabilities of aliens. Any country can be their homeland, but for them, their homeland, wherever it may be, is a foreign country.

Like others, they marry and have children, but they do not expose them. They share their meals, but not their wives. They live in the flesh, but they are not governed by the desires of the flesh. They pass their days upon earth, but they are citizens of heaven. Obedient to the laws, they yet live on a level that transcends the law.

Christians love everyone, but all people persecute them. Condemned because they are not understood, they are put to death, but raised to life again. They live in poverty, but enrich many; they are totally destitute, but possess an abundance of everything. They suffer dishonor, but that is their glory. They are defamed, but vindicated.

A blessing is their answer to abuse, deference their response to insult. For the good they do they receive the punishment of malefactors, but even then they rejoice as though receiving the gift of life. They are attacked by the Jews as aliens, they are persecuted by the Greeks, yet no one can explain the reason for this hatred.

To speak in general terms, we may say that the Christian is to the world what the soul is to the body. As the soul is present in every part of the body, while remaining distinct from it, so Christians are found in all the cities of the world, but cannot be identified with the world.

As the visible body contains the invisible soul, so Christians are seen living in the world, but their religious life remains unseen. The body hates the soul and wars against it, not because of any injury the soul has done it, but because of the restriction the soul places on its pleasures.

Similarly, the world hates the Christians, not because they have done it any wrong, but because they are opposed to its enjoyments.

Christians love those who hate them just as the soul loves the body and all its members despite the body's hatred. It is by the soul, enclosed within the body, that the body is held together, and similarly, it is by the Christians, detained in the world as in a prison, that the world is held together. The soul, though immortal, has a mortal dwelling place; and Christians also live for a time amidst perishable things, while awaiting the freedom from change and decay that will be theirs in heaven. As the soul benefits from the deprivation of food and drink, so Christians flourish under persecution. Such is the Christian's lofty and divinely appointed function, from which they are not permitted to excuse themselves.

✛JAMES FRANCIS CARDINAL MCINTYRE (1886–1979)

D. GOLDEN SACERDOTAL JUBILEE

"Youth" is a state of mind, rather than a time of life. It is a temper of the will, a quality of the imagination, a vigor of the emotions. The "young" man, no matter his chronological age, is one whose courage overshadows his timidity, whose appetite for adventure rules out his love of ease. No one grows old by merely living a specified number of years, for the aging process is evident only when people abandon their willingness to adjust the scope of their ideals.

As he prepared to observe the fiftieth anniversary of priestly ordination, James Francis Cardinal McIntyre, apart from his eighty–six years, was a "young" man in his thoughts, aspirations and demeanor. Though officially and canonically "retired," the ageless prelate had altered only the immediate objective of his personal service to God and His people. Formerly he served the faithful on the archdiocesan level, now he concentrated on those within the parish where he resided.

Quite probably, the obligations of no office in all the world are so minutely spelled out as those of the cardinalate. The select bishops chosen by the pope for membership in the Sacred College receive a 485 page treatise outlining the duties, restrictions and privileges "*de cardinalis.*"

One provision not anticipated by Roman canonists, however, was that of retirement, an almost unknown term in the ecclesiastical terminology of pre–Vatican II days. Only with the Church's twenty–first ecumenical council were formal provisions made whereby elderly prelates were "invited" to submit their resignations. The Archbishop of Los Angeles was the first American in the College of Cardinals to retire from active duty. After providing for his orderly succession by the appointment of a coadjutor, James Francis Cardinal McIntyre asked Pope Paul VI for permission to put aside his burdensome duties as the southland's second metropolitan archbishop.

That the New York–born prelate found himself in a unique status, one without precedent, is quite in keeping with the adventuresome character of the man who ventured west for the first time, in 1948, to take up the pastoral staff of the world's fastest growing archdiocese. This he did at an age when his contemporaries were anticipating the well–earned rest associated with a lifetime of active labor.

Though resigned from the administrative board of the United States Catholic Conference, the cardinal retained and intended to exercise, by virtue of his episcopal ordination, his membership in the semi–annual meetings of the American hierarchy and the annual convocations of the California Conference of Catholic Bishops.

In retirement, the cardinal continued to reside in his small, modest quarters adjacent to Saint Basil's Church near downtown Los Angeles. He neither had a "rocking–chair" nor any plans to acquire one. Though the orientation of his life had radically changed, his days were as crowded as ever with concern for the spiritual welfare of others. Cardinal McIntyre cherished the privilege of living in parochial surroundings as he did for the quarter–century he worked in New York as priest, bishop and archbishop. The opportunity of moving into a rectory presented itself only a few years earlier when facilities were provided for that purpose at the new Saint Basil's. Before that time, circumstances compelled the cardinal to live in the more commodious, but isolated home of his predecessor in Fremont Place.

The eighty–six year old prelate was hardly considered "retired" by conventional standards. His daily *horarium* was crammed, in fact, with the normal demands associated with the parish ministry. He rose early and was in the sacristy vested for Mass at 7:30 a.m. Unless impeded by other commitments, the cardinal offered an English public Mass at 8:30 on Sundays and holydays. Whenever possible, he used the option of concelebrating with one of the other priests assigned in residence at the church. On weekdays, His Eminence, dressed in a plain black cassock, spent several hours hearing confessions during the scheduled Masses. He enjoyed the pastoral role of greeting the parishioners and visitors arriving and leaving the handsome Wilshire Boulevard church.

The cardinal received his first "post–retirement" convert into the Church on May 23, 1970. "It was a happy day," recalled the tall, slender prelate, "for I was also able to confer on him the Sacrament of Confirmation."

His appointment book did not, in any way, resemble that of a "retired" archbishop. The cardinal's thirty years as an active and provocative participant in proceedings of the National Catholic Welfare Conference partially accounted for the steady stream of cardinals, archbishops, bishops and priests who came by his Kingsley Drive residence for counsel and advice. Though he had no secretarial staff, the cardinal responded personally to as much of his extensive correspondence as possible. The literal "avalanche" of good wishes following his retirement indicated the esteem felt for the cardinal by the 1,727, 161 Catholics whom he served for twenty two hectic years as Archbishop of Los Angeles. The cardinal devoted a considerable amount of time to an oral history program whereby material was recorded and preserved for an eventual biographer. All his public and personal correspondence and official papers were consigned to and accessioned in the archdiocesan Chancery Archives.

Those who visited the cardinal during this "epilogue" of his service to the Church in the United States were impressed by the ease with which he bridged the last of his many transitions in a long and productive life. "To retire from a position of authority is one thing," said Cardinal McIntyre, "but to abdicate the care and concern of souls is something a priestly conscience could never endure."

✢JAMES FRANCIS CARDINAL MCINTYRE (1886–1979)

E. A RECORD IN AMERICAN HIERARCHY

On May 21, 1974, Cardinal James Francis McIntyre observed the fifty–third anniversary of his sacerdotal ordination. And that's a long time for one who was already thirty–five years old when he reached the priesthood. The retired Archbishop of Los Angeles had been a member of the Sacred College of Cardinals for twenty–one years, a record surpassed only by James Gibbons of Baltimore (35), William O'Connell of Boston (33) and Dennis Dougherty of Philadelphia (30).

Six months earlier, Cardinal McIntyre exceeded the longevity of His Eminence of Baltimore (Gibbons died at 87) to become the oldest American ever to have served in the College of Cardinals. And, strangely enough, longevity did not run in the McIntyre family. His mother died at thirty–six, his father at fifty–six. A brother, John McIntyre, succumbed in 1948, at the age of sixty.

It was, in fact, the circumstances of his home life that temporarily delayed McIntyre's long–time inclinations toward the priestly ministry. Like the nation's first bishop, John Carroll of Baltimore, J. Francis A. McIntyre came from a Gaelic parentage who had the good sense to seek their fortunes in America rather than in France or England.

He worked in the business world to support an invalid father, until his death in 1915. At the age of twenty–nine, "Frank" McIntyre was an acknowledged expert on the stock market and a key executive in a prominent brokerage firm. With the termination of his familial responsibilities, McIntyre was faced with the severest decision of his life.

Though he probably knew nothing of it at the time, another New Yorker of Irish parentage had faced a similar decision, just a hundred years earlier. John McCloskey's father had died, an attractive position awaited in a brokerage firm and the "good life" was there for the taking. Fortunately, John McCloskey and Frank McIntyre opted for the Church. Both eventually achieved membership in the Sacred College, McCloskey as the nation's first cardinal, McIntyre as its twelfth. There was nearly a century and a lot of history between those two "eminent" men, but they shared the one ideal that characterizes all great personages—service to others.

McIntyre's years as priest, auxiliary bishop and coadjutor archbishop of New York, as well as his twenty–two years as Chief Shepherd for God's People at Los Angeles were carefully studied and appraised by his biographer. But that's not to say that His Eminence went into hibernation in 1970, when he officially put aside the spiritual responsibilities for the 1,727,161 Catholics in the Archdiocese of Los Angeles. Quite the contrary. The intervening years were crammed with activities. Though the orientation of his life changed considerably, his days were as crowded as ever with concern for the spiritual welfare of others.

In the busy Wilshire Boulevard parish of Saint Basil's, where he resided with six other priests, the cardinal offered the liturgy, heard confessions, instructed potential converts and engaged in whatever else called for priestly attention. The most joyful event of his post–administrative years was the appointment of his successor to the cardinalate, in 1973. Archbishop Timothy Manning's promotion to the Sacred College gave the Archdiocese of Los Angeles the distinction of being among only five centers of Catholicity ever honored with two cardinals simultaneously.

Archbishop Fulton J. Sheen once credited McIntyre with being "the greatest spiritual inspiration of my life, not because of what he told me about the priesthood but because of the way he has lived it." The famed preacher went on to say that "he is the kind of priest the Mother of Christ loved most of all because he so resembles her Divine Son."

✢JAMES FRANCIS CARDINAL MCINTYRE (1996–1979)

F. EULOGY FOR HIS EMINENCE

Just as the red light of the setting sun surpasses in beauty and grandeur the first golden gleams of morning, so the man of character who has worked unfailingly throughout a long life goes down like the sun into a quiet and splendid death; his work follows him, and, at the same time, remains to inspire those who stay behind.

James Francis Cardinal McIntyre was such a man. Indeed, those who knew him best could describe the longtime Archbishop of Los Angeles as everybody's cardinal, in much the same sense that Francis of Assisi was everybody's saint. There was no formality in his presence. The sincerity of his person, even when circumstances demanded severity, bespoke a man principled enough to have opponents, but Christlike enough to have no enemies.

Though ecclesial protocol accorded him princely privileges, the second Archbishop of Los Angeles, like the apostle whose name he bore, preferred to be known only as "James, the servant of God and of Our Lord Jesus Christ." He was, in further similarity to his scriptural forebear, a man of traditional demeanor. And yet, while unmistakenly identified with the best features of the pre–Vatican II era the elasticity of his thoughts catapulted James Francis McIntyre a decade ahead of his episcopal confreres in such vitally contemporary pursuits as lay missionary work, inner–city renewal, qualitative educational expansion, clerical recruiting and training, radio and television communications—to mention but a few.

At an age when the average man contemplates the solace of a well–earned retirement, James Francis McIntyre accepted the reins of leadership in an area destined for growth pains unparalleled in United States Catholic annals. That the New York–born prelate successfully met the challenge is already part of the record. The hundreds of churches, schools and charitable organizations initiated and the scores of existing facilities and programs refurbished give witness to an episcopate based on the fundamental primacy of justice and parental rights.

The archbishop's years in Southern California were not without their vexations and often must he have recalled the brutally frank observation of Saint John Chrysostom who spoke of the episcopacy as "the target for every tongue." The same orator noted that "if the bishop is grave and austere, they put it down to priestly pride; if he is democratic and unassuming, they call it sacerdotal hypocrisy; if he is free–handed and generous, they accuse him of squandering the patrimony of the poor; if he is frugal and saving, he is another example of clerical avarice."

Divine Providence decreed that by the time James Francis McIntyre reached the end of an extended earthly sojourn his most notable accomplishments on behalf of God's People, expressed more in deeds than in words, were largely unknown by a generation born and reared after the years of the cardinal's most outstanding innovations. yet only the short–sighted will forget that the substance, not the style, of apostolic work is the yardstick by which a shepherd's place is determined in the montage of a nation's Catholic story.

The stage of his life was darkened before the curtain fell, inasmuch as McIntyre's final months were heavily burdened by the ailments of advanced age.

Epitomized years ago by Archbishop Fulton J. Sheen as "a human idealist and a divine realist," James Francis McIntyre was a man of fantastic energy whose personality bubbled over with simplicity, frankness and dedication. In the midst of his most trying days, he called this writer's attention to words penned seventy–five years ago by another prelate, himself destined for the cardinalate:

> The public man, whether churchman or layman, who has never committed an error of judgement, or who was never betrayed into any moral delinquency, will hardly ever be credited with any great words or deeds worthy of being transmitted to posterity.

As the "elder statesman of the American hierarchy" passed from the southland scene, to become part of the country's Catholic heritage, one was reminded of an observation in the Journal of Jules Renard to the effect that "the reward of great men is that, long after they have died, one is not quite sure that they are dead!"

✝PAUL CARDINAL MEOUCHI (1894–1975)

Paul Cardinal Meouchi, the Maronite Patriarch of Antioch, spent eight of the "happiest years" in his life at Los Angeles as Pastor of the Church of Our Lady of Mount Lebanon. Born in Jezzine, Syria, on April 1, 1894, young Paul made his clerical studies at the Collège de la Sagesse, the Urban College of Propaganda Fide and the Pontifical Gregorian University. He was ordained in the Eternal City, on December 7, 1917.

Father Meouchi engaged in pastoral work among Maronite Catholics in Indiana and Connecticut, from 1922 to 1926. In the latter year, he was invited to Los Angeles by Bishop John J. Cantwell, where he assumed the pastorate of the southland's Maronite community. During his tenure, Father Meouchi erected a church and hall, reminiscent of oriental design, for the Parish of Our Lady of Mount Lebanon. His commanding facility in English, Spanish, Italian, French, Arabic, Hebrew, Greek, Latin and Aramaic greatly enhanced Father Meouchi's apostolate among a wide spectrum of the local Catholic populace.

On April 29, 1934, Pope Pius XI named Meouchi to the historic archiepiscopate of Tyre, on the eastern shores of the Mediterranean Sea, near the birthplace of Christianity. In 1955, he succeeded Anthony Peter Arida as Patriarch of Antioch and all the East. Meouchi was highly influential in that troubled area of the world where he was relied upon for his political wisdom as well as his religious and moral beliefs. In order "to show the world that the Lebanese nation is one single and united family," the patriarch took the initiative in preventing a breakdown in relations between Christians and Moslems in Lebanon following the Suez crisis, by bringing leaders together at his patriarchal seat in Bkerke.

At the time, there had been talk of serious outbreaks of civil and communal strife in the wake of reports that Moslem extremists in Lebanon had smuggled in from Syria large quantities of arms and explosives made in Russia. The conference helped avoid a repetition, in Lebanon, of the anti–Christian incidents which took place in Aleppo, Syria, three weeks earlier, when Moslem terrorists completely gutted three schools and looted two Catholic churches.

Representing as he did the oldest of the Uniate patriarchates, Paul Meouchi received many marks of affection from Rome. In 1959, Pope John XXIII personally bestowed the pallium on Meouchi, the first time such a distinction had been conferred on a Maronite patriarch since the 13th century. Six years later, Meouchi was elevated to the College of Cardinals by Pope Paul VI.

Throughout the years, Cardinal Meouchi retained a great affection for Los Angeles. It was at his suggestion, for example, that the President of Lebanon presented the late Archbishop John J. Cantwell with a gold medal in recognition of the kindness bestowed upon the Maronite people by the Southern California Catholic community. His Beatitude, Paul Cardinal Meouchi, the Maronite Patriarch of Antioch, is firmly ensconced in the best of California's Catholic traditions.

✢RAPHAEL CARDINAL MERRY DEL VAL (1865–1930)

Among the truly cherished mementos in the Historical Museum of the Chancery Archives is a personally inscribed photograph of Raphael Cardinal Merry del Val (1865–1930), one of the most outstanding churchmen of modern times.

The inscription beneath the photograph is fraught with historical implications. And it all began at Saint Cuthbert's College (Ushaw), where Joseph Scott studied as a youngster. One of the part–time teachers there was Raphael Merry del Val, the son of Spain's Ambassador to Great Britain. Scott, the student, and Merry del Val, the tutor, forged a friendship that endured for a lifetime.

Merry del Val didn't remain long at Ushaw. At the instigation of Pope Leo XIII, he was brought to Rome, where he continued his studies for the priesthood at the *Pontificia Accademia*. In 1887, he was sent to represent the Holy See at Queen Victoria's golden jubilee. Though not yet ordained a priest, Merry del Val was made a monsignor on that occasion.

Merry del Val's subsequent priestly life ranks among the most extraordinary in church annals—ordained priest (1888), appointed Apostolic Delegate to Canada (1897), designated President of the Academy for Noble Ecclesiastics (1899), named archbishop (1900), elected secretary of the papal conclave (1903), created cardinal and Secretary of State (1903) and later made archpriest of Saint Peters and Secretary of the Holy Office.

During those years, Joseph Scott also became prominent in another part of the world. His name in the legal circles of faraway Los Angeles went on to become almost legendary. In 1905, one of Scott's close friends, Ernest K. Foster, made a journey to Rome and, armed with a letter of introduction from Scott, called on Cardinal Merry del Val.

He was received in the ornate quarters of the Secretariate of State on February 8, 1905. It was a cordial encounter and Foster recalled to a reporter that Merry del Val was "a man of commanding presence with wonderfully keen, expressive eyes, master of almost every living language." As he was leaving, the Cardinal asked Mr. Foster to take 'with him a portrait for Joseph Scott. His Eminence inscribed it with the words: "To my old friend and pupil, Joseph Scott, with every best wish and blessing."

Mr. Scott obviously cherished the photograph and, at the suggestion of Bishop Thomas J. Conaty, had it reproduced in *The Tidings* for June 2, 1905. For many years, the photograph hung in the Scott home in Pasadena. Over two decades ago, while visiting with Mr. Scott and his grandson, Alfonso (now a priest of the Archdiocese of Los Angeles), this writer expressed an interest in the photograph. A few months after the demise of this fine gentleman, Judge A. A. Scott confided the precious photograph to my care. It has since been given a permanent home in the Historical Museum of the Archival Center, Archdiocese of Los Angeles.

✢JOSEF CARDINAL MINDSZENTY (1892–1975)

It happens only rarely that one meets or otherwise encounters a truly saintly person here on planet earth. One of those times occurred on June 13, 1974, when Josef Cardinal Mindszenty toured the archdiocesan archival facilities which were then located at the Chancery Office on 9th Street.

We had arranged an elaborate pictorial and documentary exhibit featuring accounts of his trial, imprisonment and subsequent exile. Never having seen most of the items, His Eminence of Esztergom was fascinated by the wide coverage given to him in the religious and secular news media.

The eighty–two year old former Primate of Hungary was accompanied by his secretary, Msgr. Tibor Meszaros, who had himself been a prisoner of communist oppression for eight years. It was Meszaros who graciously sent to the Historical Museum the faded scarlet zucchetto which Mindszenty wore during his fifteen years of forced incarceration as a refugee of the United States Legation at Budapest.

The cardinal had a busy schedule in the southland. He was the honored guest for a testimonial dinner at the Century Plaza Hotel, the celebration of "Captive Nations" day and at liturgies celebrated at Blessed

Sacrament and Saint Stephen's churches in Los Angeles and at Saint Michael Priory in Orange. Though his physical suffering was over by 1974, Mindszenty was then enduring what he later called "the heaviest cross of my life," that of stepping aside as primate and archbishop at the request of Pope Paul VI.

After the cardinal's tour of the United States was completed, he returned to Europe and was asked by the Holy Father to reside in Vienna for the remaining months of his life. He died there in 1975 and was buried in Saint Laszlo Church in Mariazell.

Now all of this is here recalled because early in May of 1991, Josef Cardinal Mindszenty's remains were returned to Esztergom, where they were interred alongside his predecessors in that city's hilltop cathedral. Father Hermann Joseph Rettig, the Norbertine pastor of Saint Stephen's Church, was among the 90,000 people who attended the open–air funeral Mass on the Cathedral lawns overlooking the Danube River. Also present was a delegation of Sacred Heart Sisters from Los Angeles who have accepted the challenge of returning the Gospel message to post–Communist Hungary.

Though diplomatic protocol denied any ecclesial recognition for his lifelong campaign on behalf of human freedom, Cardinal Mindszenty is emerging from the pages of history as perhaps the most loved and respected churchman of this century. Opilio Cardinal Rossi, the Holy Father's delegate for the ceremonies in Esztergom, described Mindszenty as an "outstanding man of God" who had returned to his homeland "no longer as the vanquished, but as the victor."

Father Rettig said something that was overlooked or at least unreported in the newspaper accounts of that memorable day of May 4th. The remains of Josef Cardinal Mindszenty were found to be incorrupt, sixteen years after his death! The cardinal's zucchetto remains one of the most precious mementos at the Historical Museum of the Archival Center. Indeed, it may one day become a relic!

✟JOHN JOSEPH MITTY (1884–1961)

A. *VIVERE, CHRISTUS EST*

San Francisco's fourth metropolitan archbishop was a prelate of the old school. He grew into the office as a trail–blazer in the hostile atmosphere of Utah and he never really lost that gruffness in sophisticated San Francisco. Nonetheless, beneath an outwardly aloof personality beat the heart of a great churchman, one for whom the *mens ecclesiae*, or mind of the Church, was a guiding principle.

John Joseph Mitty was born in the Greenwich Village section of New York City on January 20, 1884.

Orphaned at fourteen, he was educated at De La Salle Institute and Manhattan College before entering Saint Joseph's Seminary at Dunwoodie in 1901. After a stint at The Catholic University of America, Father Mitty returned to Dunwoodie where he taught for some years prior to becoming a chaplain in the armed forces during World War I. He was consecrated Bishop of Salt Lake on September 8, 1926 by Patrick Cardinal Hayes. In 1935, three years after his appointment to San Francisco as coadjutor, he succeeded the retired Edward J. Hanna to become the state's fourth residential archbishop.

The New York–born prelate quickly acclimatized himself to the west. He once noted that "I feel that I have made no sacrifice in exchanging the sidewalks of New York for *El Camino Real* and that I have by far the best of the bargain in trading Hell's Gate for the Golden Gate." The archbishop was fond of reminding easterners that California was the "State of Grace" with a litany of places dedicated to the Blessed Sacrament (Sacramento), the Holy Cross (Santa Cruz), the Virgin Mary (Los Angeles) and the saints (San Francisco, Santa Barbara, San Miguel, *etc.*).

Indeed, Archbishop Mitty had an almost unmatched devotion to his adopted state. As far as he was concerned, the City of San Francisco was "enthralling, alluring, delightful, charming, colorful, beautiful, enchanting, captivating, exciting, picturesque, distinguished, and unique." To Mitty, the inscription on the capitol building at Sacramento, "Give me men to match my mountains," meant an intensified vocation program which he fostered ceaselessly throughout the archdiocese. Certainly the eight bishops and 700 priests he consecrated and ordained are a monument to his success in that endeavor. If the archbishop had one regret, it was that he could not claim California as his own by reason of birth. He set out early to remedy that defect in others by securing for his jurisdiction a predominantly native–born clergy. Within a quarter century, seventy–five percent of San Francisco's priests were westerners.

Vocations were, by no means, the prelate's only concern. By the time of his golden jubilee in 1956, Archbishop Mitty had guided to completion 451 major building projects in the Bay area. In less than two decades the archbishop had seen the formation of sixty–five new parishes. Though partially incapacitated during the last years of his life, the archbishop remained the alert shepherd of his jurisdiction until his death at Menlo Park on October 15, 1961.

Traditionally, bishops outline their spiritual ideals in a short but descriptive Latin phrase placed on their episcopal coat–of–arms. That chosen by John J. Mitty was *Vivere, Christus est*, For me, to live is Christ! The late Bishop Duane Hunt used that phrase when speaking of his predecessor some years ago:

In the far west, there is the harbinger, Garcia Diego Moreno; the pioneer, Joseph Alemany; the builder, Patrick Riordan; those figures of singular sweetness, George Montgomery and Edward Hanna. Beyond them, more shadowy perhaps, the suffragans of the past, Eugene O'Connell, Patrick Manogue, Thomas Grace, Patrick Keane, Lawrence Scanlan, Joseph Glass. And presiding over all, as the Patron Saint of this See by the Golden Gate, the Poor Little Man of Assisi. On his lips, as an echo from heaven, gently sound the words: "For me, to live is Christ!"

✢JOHN JOSEPH MITTY (1884–1961)

B. MITTY AND MACARTHUR JOIN FORCES

An interesting article in a Brooklyn newspaper, *Il Crociato,* for May 30, 1942, revealed the close personal friendship between Archbishop John J. Mitty (1884–1961) of San Francisco and General Douglas MacArthur (1880–1964), the commander of Pacific Forces in World War II.

The origin of their relationship can be traced to the years 1919 through 1922, when the youthful Father Mitty was Catholic Chaplain at the United States Military Academy at West Point. General MacArthur was Superintendent at West Point during those years and, in that capacity, took an active part in encouraging the spiritual development of the enrollees.

Mitty later served as Pastor of Saint Luke's Church in New York City and, in 1926, was named Bishop of Salt Lake City. This writer recalls seeing, in the Chancery Archives for the Archdiocese of San Francisco, a letter from MacArthur congratulating Mitty upon his appointment to the American hierarchy. The New York–born prelate moved on to the Bay Area, in 1932, as coadjutor archbishop. With the resignation of the Most Reverend Edward J. Hanna, in 1935, Mitty became Metropolitan Archbishop of San Francisco.

Because of his previous service as Chaplain in the United States Army (1917–1919), Archbishop Mitty was a logical choice to serve as California State Chaplain for the American Legion. In that role, Mitty was extremely active in the "Pledge Victory Campaign" during the early days of World War II, noting that "this is an all–out war that calls for sacrifice from every American man, woman and child."

The archbishop further observed that "Pearl Harbor stunned America. But Pearl Harbor united America as it never was united before. Under the banner of freedom we must and shall remain united. We shall sink our differences in one firm resolve to win this war. United we shall labor and battle to victory. The basis of our unity is our American way of living. Our forefathers bled and died to win and defend our liberties of worship, of speech, of the press, of assembly. In Europe and Asia sinister forces have banded together to deprive all mankind of these fundamental liberties, America is battling again for human liberty. There can be no peace until human freedom is secure."

Echoing the sentiments and words of his long–time friend, General Douglas MacArthur, the archbishop concluded by telling the people of California that "this is our war, yours and mine. You and I must make sacrifices to win. Every bond and stamp is a blow struck for our American way of life. Every bond and stamp is our answer to Pearl Harbor and Bataan."

The reference to "Bataan" was surely prompted by Mitty's reflection on MacArthur, the famed war–hero who once said his proudest title was that of "Hero of Bataan."

✢JOHN JOSEPH MITTY (1884–1961)

C. GREETINGS FROM THE ARCHBISHOP

On behalf of the ecclesiastical provinces of the West, the Most Reverend John J. Mitty (1884–1961) delivered an address of welcome to the newly–named Archbishop of Los Angeles, J. Francis A. McIntyre, on March 19, 1948. In terms of "historical awareness," it was a classical presentation of California's Catholic heritage.

You come to a land dotted with places dedicated to Our Savior, His Blessed Mother, the angels and saints. You come to a land sanctified by the sacrifices of Franciscan missionaries who, starting with Junípero Serra, blazed the trail of *El Camino Real* from San Diego to Sonoma.

By their labors for the Indians in the 21 missions of the State, they made *El Camino Real* not only the Highway of the King of Spain, but the Highway of Christ the King.

You come to a land sanctified for over a century after the appointment of the first bishop, Garcia Diego, by the labors and sacrifices of devoted bishops, priests and religious men and women who gave themselves to the upbuilding of the Kingdom of Christ in our western land.

You will be the first to recall the words of Christ, 'For in this is the saying true: that it is one that soweth, and it is another that reapeth. I have sent you to reap that in which you did not labor: others have labored and you have entered into their labors.' But the work of building up the Kingdom of Christ is unending—and you have come to sow what another shall reap.

In the last eight years California has seen an unparalleled population growth of three million. We now number over ten million inhabitants, and they are continuing to come from the East and Midwest in tens of thousands every month. We now rank in population second to the State of New York—but it is only a matter of a few years when California will outstrip New York.

There is much work to be done for this seething population of many racial strains. It will require prayer, labor and sacrifice by bishops, priests, religious and laity, working with courage and in harmony to build the Kingdom of Christ strong and lasting.

Saint John in the Apocalypse was commanded to address messages to seven bishops of Asia Minor, whom he calls the 'Angels' of their respective cities. It happens that we too on this western seaboard number seven such 'Angels'—Seattle, Portland, Sacramento, San Francisco, Monterey, Los Angeles and San Diego. We are happy to welcome Archbishop McIntyre to his place in the ranks of the seven as the 'Angel of the Church of Los Angeles.'

My dear archbishop, you have come into another portion of the Vineyard of the Lord. Here, by divine Providence, your lot is cast. You will have the loyalty and devotion of your clergy, religious and laity. You will have the cooperation of your brother bishops. You will have the patronage of Our Lady of the Angels. You will have the benediction of the Great High Priest.

✛GEORGE T. MONTGOMERY (1847–1907)

A. Harbinger of Modern Social Thought

The years immediately preceding the issuance, by Pope Leo XIII, of the famous encyclical, *On the Condition of Labor (Rerum Novarum)*, in 1891, were foreboding times in California. A series of economic recessions, brought on in part by heavy speculation in mining stocks and the replacement of native workers by cheap imported labor, created an atmosphere akin to class warfare. The ostentatious wealth of certain San Francisco "capitalists" further antagonized working men, almost to the point of no return. Employers blatantly exhibited little or no hesitation in procuring workers at the lowest wages, for the longest hours, amid the hardest conditions which competition and unemployment could force the workers to accept.

It was in the context of those perilous times that the Bishop of Monterey–Los Angeles, a man "deservedly beloved by all classes of people," wrote an open letter to the American workingman. He advocated the placement of the labor cause on a religious pedestal, arguing that since capital possessed "undue purchasing power" in courts and legislatures, the worker's only hope of securing justice lay in honest, conscientious and representative public servants. Montgomery observed that so long "as gold can buy votes and legislation, the laboring man will be the victim of capital and gold will have that power wherever religious principles do not form and control man's consciences."

The southland prelate did not hesitate to involve himself personally in the delicate issues of income taxes, municipal socialism and nationalization of the railroads,

convinced as he was that if "the respective rights and duties of labor and capital are to be ever properly defined, it must be upon the principles which religion lays down." Throughout his relatively short public life as priest, bishop and archbishop, George T. Montgomery (1847–1907) showed himself to be "a friend of the friendless; a help to the helpless; an inspirational guide and friend to all."

The prelate endeared himself "by his good works, which were not performed with the robes of divinity about him, but with the humility of the gentle Nazarene, whose teachings he so faithfully followed and endeavored to inculcate in the minds and hearts of others." His whole life was an elongation of the Sermon on the Mount. "He served God by service to his fellow–men, nor asked whether they belonged to his church or believed his creed. In the broadest sense, the world was his country; to do good was his religion."

It was noted by a San Francisco newspaper, at the time of the archbishop's death, that "in preaching and teaching, he did not fill the mind with fear and awe, but inspired the heart with love. He hated cant, rant and all manner of hypocrisy. Truth from his lips prevailed with double sway, for all who heard knew that he was in earnest." Archbishop George T. Montgomery's zeal, piety, talents and scholarship explain how and why he is referred to as California's Catholic harbinger of modern social thought.

✛GEORGE T. MONTGOMERY (1847–1907)

B. Church Bells

The ringing of church bells on Sunday mornings is frequently a source of annoyance to those who feel that resting on the Sabbath is a prerogative that Almighty God wishes to share with his creatures. In response to several complaints received at the turn of the century, Bishop George T. Montgomery wrote the following letter to the Los Angeles *Herald* on September 1, 1900:

> From time to time there has appeared in the press the expression of dissatisfaction on the part of some people with the ringing of church bells on the mornings of Sundays, which is charged as useless if not a nuisance. I suppose the Catholic churches are the greatest offenders; and, as representing them, I beg leave to say a few words through your excellent paper in explanation and in defense of that custom.
>
> I am sure that there is nobody in the city that desires less to be a nuisance to neighbors than do the Catholic people. The first bell rung in any of our churches on Sunday morning is at 5:30, except on Christmas. That first bell, as well as that of 12 noon and 6 p.m., is called the *"Angelus"* bell and the meaning of it is to remind our people in the first conscious moments of the morning and during the day of that great fundamental doctrine of the

Christian religion known as the Incarnation when the Angel was sent by God to announce to the Blessed Virgin Mary that the Savior of man was to be born into the world, and that she was selected to be His mother.

There are prayers which Catholics recite at the ringing of that bell, nearly the whole of which are taken from the New Testament and bearing directly on that great mystery of Christian faith. There are many who honestly disbelieve in the divinity of Jesus Christ, but who at the same time believe that the human race owes more to Him than to any other person that ever lived on earth.

This *Angelus* bell is one of the ways in which we Catholic people make a profession of our Faith in Him and of our great gratitude to Him for what He has done for mankind.

I think that most people admit that religion is beneficial to society, and we all know that there are many agencies at work in human nature to weaken that influence; and I believe that fair–minded men will concede that whatever tends to preserve religious principles among men is a benefit. Therefore I believe it would be a great mistake to insist upon the suppression of the *Angelus* bell.

When rung at other times, it is to serve the purpose of notifying the people of the hour of service. Now we know that it is a great convenience to those who attend our churches. But about the inconvenience to others, I believe it is the experience of almost everyone that when we are accustomed to a regular ringing of church bells, or almost any other regular noise, it ceases to be the nuisance that some would like to make it. The street cars in this city and in most other cities run until 1 o'clock and, so accustomed do we become to the noise the cars make, that I believe few people notice it.

I think that as noisy a place as is in this city from the street cars is Second Street between Main and Los Angeles and so accustomed have we become to the noise that I believe if the cars should stop at 11 o'clock instead of 1 o'clock we should notice the stopping more than the continuance of the noise.

There is no record of how Bishop Montgomery's plea was received but it is known that Saint Vibiana's master bell continued on pealing out its daily message.

✝GEORGE T. MONTGOMERY (1847–1907)

C. *EL CAMINO REAL*

Shortly after the turn of the century, it was proposed that a road be constructed between the southern and northern extremities of California. The envisioned route would follow, as closely as possible, the King's Highway or *El Camino Real* used by the early Franciscan missionaries.

Early in December, 1902, Bishop George T. Montgomery dwelt on that theme in an address to the Los Angeles Ebell Club. In his remarks, the prelate did not speak of the material side of the project, but voiced the spiritual ideal underlying life at the missions.

There are so many views of the old missions, said the bishop, "but it seems to me that from any standpoint they are interesting." In his talk, he outlined the points in history not familiar to those who see the missions merely as monuments of the past.

The establishment of that chain of missions is one of the most remarkable things in the world's history. In those days there were few means of travel, and the very coming to these shores of the Franciscan friars was a hardship which we can hardly conceive, and only a supreme principle could sustain a man through what the mission friars passed.

Everyone knows that selfishness is the sin of the age, but there is no epoch of history that can equal the mission period, and I believe it is something that should be cherished by everyone, regardless of his religion, the perpetuation of a pathetic story of usefulness.

They worked through the hardships of their chosen life without thought of reward, and a man who knows told me the other day that to build one mission today, such as one of those built by the early mission fathers, even with all the mechanical devices of this period, would cost $150,000. And they erected twenty–one of these monuments of unselfishness. When we look at their ruins we see evidences of a work gigantic.

The mission friar was the architect, the carpenter and the mason. He gathered about him the native and taught him what he knew, and after much coaxing and teaching, secured his cooperation.

Smithies, tanneries and other branches of industry were established and the natives were taught to manufacture for themselves and others. If we take into consideration the materials and tools at their disposal, the things they wrought were simply marvelous.

The day is coming when a dispassionate view will be taken of these missions. I do not care to canonize the Franciscan frairs. They had their faults the same as other men, but they came here and worked unselfishly and gave to the world something phenomenal, which, if we take into consideration the body, the soul and the mind, I do not believe any other nation can duplicate, and I think the least we can do is to preserve these old missions.

Bishop Montgomery concluded his address by explaining secularization and how that process brought on the end of the mission era in Alta California. The guests were then treated to an exhibition of the arts and crafts of some local Indians.

✝GEORGE T. MONTGOMERY (1847–1907)

D. EVERYONE'S ARCHBISHOP

The appointment of Bishop George T. Montgomery (1847–1907) to the coadjutorship of San Francisco, in 1902, was widely applauded by Catholics as well as non–Catholics in the Bay Area. That he should return to

Archbishop George Montgomery

in the hearts of thousands."

The return of Montgomery to San Francisco was as regretfully felt in the southland as it was welcomed in the Bay Area. One newspaper observed that the prelate's "place in Los Angeles and in the hearts of all sorts and conditions of men may not be filled; but, nevertheless, we welcome the fact that he has been preferred to a still more important post, where his devotion to humanity and his sound liberal judgement may wield a still wider influence." Continuing, the writer noted that "Los Angeles will not forget her friend nor the lesson that Bishop Montgomery has ably demonstrated to this community, the greatest thing in the world, and Christ's single law—'Love One Another.'"

The Kentucky–born prelate's premature death was mourned throughout the western part of the nation. Truly, the Church in America, and more particularly in California, had "lost a man, a leader of the people, a father of the faithful, a High Priest, an Onias, a good and virtuous man who prayed for all the people." Such sentiments evoke the symbolic definition of the bishopric given by Fulton J. Sheen: "The bishop of a diocese must be like a rock and like a river—two biblical symbols, one indicating stability and solidity, the other movement, freshness and challenge."

✢GEORGE T. MONTGOMERY (1847–1907)

E. Public Aid to Catholic Schools

That the precarious financial plight presently faced by the Catholic school system is not a phenomenon peculiar to the present era can be seen in the tone of an article published, in the fall of 1903, by George T. Montgomery, Coadjutor Archbishop of San Francisco. Writing for *Dominicana*, a Catholic periodical issued monthly at San Francisco, the prelate called on public officials to widen their concept of the means used in communicating the basics of education.

Montgomery felt that a working plan could be found whereby the state could "profit by all the religious forces in it, and yet not compromise the principle of withholding state aid for the teaching of religion." He called on the state to avoid making a monopoly of education "to the extent of exacting that public money be paid for secular instruction in those schools only where secular instruction is given."

The archbishop had no objection to state officials prescribing the curriculum or examining teachers. He pledged that "those who really believed in dogmatic revealed religion would build schools at their own expense and would offer to the school board's teachers whose qualifications to teach the secular branches desired could be passed upon by the State." Inasmuch as religion and education are the two great factors consti-

the archdiocese for which he was ordained was fitting enough, inasmuch as Montgomery had always "been prominently identified with every important reformatory or charitable movement in San Francisco."

The welcome accorded the archbishop upon his accession was enthusiastic, joyful and sincere. "The bright record of his amiable prudence, priestly zeal, manly courage and sympathetic charity during his administration in Los Angeles has augmented the confidence of the clergy and the faithful of the archdiocese. Nine years of absence has but enhanced the interest of his friends in his past and future." *Dominicana's* editor went on to note that "the people of San Francisco, for so many years familiar with the sterling qualities of mind and soul that have endeared him to all, especially rejoice in his providential appointment to a position of responsibility that will secure to them the prudent counsel of priest, father and friend."

Described by one non–Catholic writer as an "enlightened progressive and thoroughly American" prelate, Montgomery was always "enthusiastically sympathetic with those who are ignorant of the Church's teachings." At the same time the archbishop "has ably, faithfully and intelligently combated error, and successfully destroyed unreasonable prejudices against our religion that existed tuting the character of society, the widely respected prelate pointed out the need for harmonious relationship between educators and churchmen at every level. He reminded his readers that "of all the dispositions and habits which lead to political prosperity, religion and morality are indispensable supports."

Montgomery recalled that "the State rests upon religion," noting that "the Declaration of Independence acknowledges a personal God, the God of nations, ruling over them with a beneficent providence, and appeals to Him to vindicate by victory the justice of revolt from the mother country. And when victory came," he observed, "our forefathers acknowledged God as having answered their prayer."

As one of Western America's most vociferous ecclesial leaders Montgomery called upon other Christian bodies to recognize "the necessity of taking this logical common sense and true view of the matter as a means of self– preservation, and of making common cause with us, instead of depending upon the haphazard reading of a chapter of the Bible in the schools, half the time by those who do not believe in its sacred character."

Though he has been dead for almost a century, George Thomas Montgomery would be no stranger to the contemporary scene. Glancing backward at the activities of earlier churchmen along *El Camino Real*, one ponders the veracity of Goethe's statement: "All truly wise thoughts have been thought already thousands of times!"

✛GEORGE T. MONTGOMERY (1847–1907)

F. WELCOME TO KNIGHTS OF COLUMBUS

In addition to his many other talents, Archbishop George T. Montgomery was a master of the English language. That ability is nowhere more evident than in his address of welcome to the National Conclave of the Knights of Columbus which met at Los Angeles in early June, 1905. The prelate began by asking to be excused "for adverting briefly to some matters of local interest" which, he said, were not "foreign to the organization itself nor to the purposes of the convention."

> Though we are young as a state, nevertheless there are Catholic traditions connected with our history that every true citizen of California feels proud of, irrespective of race or religion.

> Though we feel that we are today in complete accord and in touch with all that our older sister states of this great nation prize and enjoy, we have had besides an heroic age that can never be forgotten and whose history supplies the loftiest ideals and ambitions possible to men.

> It is a pleasing reminiscence to which we may call your attention that whilst our political and national forefathers on the Atlantic sea–coast were yet in training for—and finally actually engaged in this revolutionary conflict with the Mother Country, which, at the price of

much blood and treasure, won for us our nationality, there was here on the Pacific slope, a small but valiant army of soldiers of the Cross engaged in a bloodless conflict—preparing better than they knew—and laying the foundation of this great State of California.

> Their heroism none deny. The examples of unselfishness, of complete self abnegation, of practical self–sacrifice which these pioneers left behind them, will, for noble souls, ever remain as among the most precious and cherished of our traditions.

> The superficial student and the hasty tourist, absorbed with the thought and the aspect of our commercial and material greatness, might readily undervalue these things, and consider that the work of those pioneers had forever perished, and without leaving any appreciable results behind them

> The spirit that animated the old Spanish Franciscan *padres* was, of course, as all the world knows, a burning zeal to convey the light of the Gospel to His children whom God had placed here.

> In one sense their work might seem to some to have left no visible evidence. The few Indians remaining within our borders have been mostly driven back into the mountain fastnesses and I suppose are destined to pass away. Indeed, they serve now, too often, as mere objects of curiosity But most of these, whilst speaking still their own native Indian dialects, speak besides the language of the missioners and they say their prayers in that sweet Spanish tongue.

> Some of the most wonderful structures on the continent—and the old Missions still stand to bear testimony to the heroic labors of the missionaries—and even though they too may in time pass away, their memory is embalmed in our language and shall remain as long as that language be spoken or written.

> And what means much for you, Knights of Columbus, and what tells you of the real spirit that wrought here for civilization is this fact, that from San Diego to Sacramento, in the names of our old missions, in the names of our towns and cities, in the names of our mountains and rivers, in the names of our very streets, you may recite the Litany of the Saints and make an act of faith in the chief doctrines of the Christian religion.

> You are standing on hallowed ground, hallowed by the footprints, the labors and the lives surrendered, of a band of apostolic men, of men who brought here the faith that you profess, of men who, in all things, believed as you believe: that God must be in all things and over all things.

✛GEORGE T. MONTGOMERY (1847–1907)

G. EARTHQUAKE OF 1906

Shortly after the Bay Area's disastrous earthquake and fire in 1906, the editor of the *New San Francisco Magazine* asked Coadjutor Archbishop George T. Montgomery (1847–1907) to write about the "Losses of One Religious Denomination."

In the July issue of the journal "born amidst the embers of a stricken city," the archbishop began his observations by emphasizing that "had we suffered from earthquake only, not one family would have been driven from the city." While not wanting "to minimize the shock," Montgomery felt it necessary to correct "some unjust inferences" in certain eastern newspapers about the cause of San Francisco's destruction. Fire was the major culprit.

He noted that "the pictures in some illustrated papers" about "the effect of the earthquake on wooden buildings is entirely misleading." Scarcely one such building "was seriously damaged, unless from faulty and almost criminal construction, or from foundations absolutely rotten."

Montgomery had nothing but praise for the civil, military, state and federal authorities. "Our police and our fire departments did all that men could do under the circumstances." And while the city was still burning, "the mayor appointed a committee of fifty citizens from among the best people in the city, to consider with him the ways and means of keeping order and preserving life and property, in the meantime ministering as far as possible to those in need."

The committee performed its appointed tasks "in a manner beyond all praise, under the most trying conditions that were ever thrust suddenly upon a body of men." State and federal authorities "worked for the common good in a most unselfish manner," giving to the entire population "that confidence and feeling of security that is without parallel, and accounts for the absence of anything to be reasonably criticized under the conditions. As common sufferers with others in the disaster of fire and earthquake, we share their faith and courage which purposes to rebuild our city—stronger and better and nobler in every way."

The archbishop was a realist. "We are not blind," he said, "to the awful catastrophe that has befallen us, nor to the fact that the future has labor, privation and sacrifice in store for us all. But most of our people are either descendants of the old pioneers or have imbibed their noble spirit and they will continue to emulate the traditions of the city and state. With others of our fellow citizens, we hope that in the reconstruction and resurrection of San Francisco, those who represent us and legislate for us will look not merely to the material growth and beauty of our city, but to its higher interest—the purity of its citizens and its civic life."

Montgomery called for "widening our streets, strengthening our buildings and perfecting our water supply," but he also said that "the character of those who enjoy these—this is the most important." Being a shrewd man, the prelate said that "to specify further would carry me beyond the limits allotted to me, but our 'City Fathers' know what we mean and what we want. May they grant it to us!"

In his report about the devastating earthquake and fire of 1906, Archbishop T. Montgomery told the people of San Francisco that, as a corporate body, the Catholic Church has suffered a loss relatively greater, probably, than any other body of our citizens."

> We had a laudable pride in our churches, schools, academies, colleges, hospitals, homes for the aged and young, kindergartens and day homes. All of these lying within the area of the burned district are gone.

The prelate noted that in the fire district we lost twelve churches and residences for the clergy (to nearly every one of which was attached a parochial school for boys and girls), while twelve parishes with their parochial equipment were absolutely wiped out of existence: "Within that same district we lost by fire two well known colleges—the Sacred Heart College, conducted by the Christian Brothers, and the College of St. Ignatius, conducted by the Jesuit Fathers; three convent schools for the higher education of girls and young ladies; St. Mary's Hospital and Home for the Aged, the Mary Help Hospital for women and children and three Day Homes under the Sisters of the Holy Family whose special work is to care for and teach children whose mothers engage in work during the day."

Also lost was "the old Youths' Directory, occupied by a community of nuns, whose work is to gratuitously nurse the sick poor; the new Youths' Directory, whose purpose is to take neglected boys from the street, irrespective of class or creed."

The archbishop emphasized that "all of these institutions were lost by fire. We examined the matter most rigidly and know that with one or two exceptions the total damage was by fire and, of those exceptions, the damage by earthquake was insignificant: In the unburned part of the city, we have twenty churches. Of these, two have been practically destroyed by earthquake, while three others were considerably damaged but can be repaired. One school was somewhat injured, the others suffering either no damage at all or being only slightly affected."

Montgomery noted that "the greatest loss outside the city was at St. Patrick's Seminary at Menlo Park, the repairing of which will entail a great expense." Two churches outside the city were lost by earthquake, one in San Jose and one in Tomales. "Contrary to popular opinion," Montgomery observed, "there was little damage done in California outside the Archdiocese of San Francisco, except in Pajaro Valley, Salinas and Hollister, showing that the real area of the earthquake was not relatively of great extent."

When asked what Catholics of the archdiocese had done in face of this catastrophe, Montgomery said that "the priests and the nuns followed the people from their burning homes into the parks and squares, the *presidio* and the beach, where many are now gathered into camps."

On the first Sunday following the conflagration, "the priests held services for their scattered and bereaved flocks and both priests and nuns moved about them constantly, encouraging and assisting them in every way in their power and in perfect cooperation with the organizations so kindly taking their care in hand." Inspired by the faith and courage of their pastors, which Montgomery felt was "one of the best assets of San Francisco at this moment," many of the people "are even now returning, and there are many rude evidences of a growing population in the devastated section."

✠GEORGE T. MONTGOMERY (1847–1907)

H. FAREWELL TO THE COADJUTOR

On January 10, 1907, the Coadjutor Archbishop of San Francisco, George T. Montgomery, went home to God. Rarely has the passing of a California prelate elicited such widespread sorrow and grief. When Bishop Thomas J. Conaty stepped into the pulpit to preach the funeral oration, civic and religious figures listened attentively to the discourse about the man they all had loved.

> In the presence of a beloved one dead, sorrow chills the heart and makes the voice tremble with emotion. Earthquake and fire have done a great work of mighty devastation and ruin in this great city of San Francisco. The day of terror and anxiety seemed over, but before the full dawn of the new day the blow is struck which takes from you the one who held all your hearts in his.
>
> You have lost a man, a leader of the people, a father of the faithful, a High Priest, a good and virtuous man who prayed for all the people. Simple as a child, strong as a man, Christ–like as a priest, a man of broad humanity and deep sympathies, an ideal bishop, mighty as a Cedar of Lebanon, a faithful shepherd, a martyr to duty.
>
> Great and good men never wholly die. Their influence remains, their names and deeds are inspirations, the memory of them is our richest possession.
>
> Yesterday he was leading us, cheering us with word and smile; today his voice is stilled in death. Like a good shepherd he gave his life for his sheep, like a brave soldier he fell on the field of battle with his face to the foe.
>
> From his Kentucky home and its school, to Saint Charles College and Saint Mary's Seminary and the priesthood, the years are marked with devotion to the vocation to which in the sincerity of his heart he knew God had called him. The paths along which he passed are all marked with the simplicity, earnestness and devotedness of a supernatural life.
>
> The bishop of our modern life has the same fight to wage, the same cross to bear, the same difficulties to contend with as the bishops of all ages. He is the follower of his Divine Master, the apostolic messenger of His Gospel and while going about doing good he must also bear the burden of the cross.
>
> The bishop in his diocese is the High Priest, the leader of the people, the spokesman of the Divine Saviour, the father of his priests, the guardian of authority and unity, the center of that link that binds the jurisdiction of the diocese to the great and mighty apostolic commission.
>
> Wealth, the comforts of life, contempt of restraint, indulgence of self, the desire for independence of all spiritual obligations, add to our difficulties.
>
> Archbishop Montgomery was peculiarly fitted for apostolic work. He was a man of the people, the most democratic of men, ready to meet them, earnest in expressing his views on what was best, impressing everyone with his sincerity which became the more effective because of his devotedness to the best community ideals.
>
> He labored to sanctify every class but none attracted him more than the humble ones of his flock. He was gentleness itself and humility and kindness and with all there was in him an heroism which never hesitated at the call of duty to make long journeys, to preach, to lecture, to hear confessions, to administer the sacraments.
>
> Archbishop Montgomery was a man of prayer and obedience and the sacred priesthood in its highest form was a second nature to him. The secret of his success was in his fidelity to that vocation . . . in preaching Jesus Christ . . . and the beauty of his priestly and episcopal character shines out upon us from his deathbed.

✠FRANCIS MORA (1827–1905)

A. VISITOR TO MANRESA

Much of the spirituality evident in the life of Bishop Francis Mora can be attributed to a religious experience he had shortly before leaving his native Spain for the United States. It was the practice at Vich's Seminary of San Joachim for clerical students to visit Manresa and there to make the thirty day Spiritual Exercises composed by Ignatius Loyola.

The youthful Mora set out on his journey to Manresa in late 1853. Like Ignatius before him, he stopped enroute for several days at the Benedictine Monastery of *Nuestra Señora de Montserrat*. Upon his arrival at Manresa, Mora further imitated Ignatius by spending his first days serving the poor in the local hospital, performing acts of penance and writing down the inspirations received after periods of meditation.

The young seminarian found the atmosphere at Manresa highly conducive to prayer. Located on the left bank of the Cardoner River, the ancient city had long been a favorite retreat for those seeking solitude and introspection. The local Jesuit spiritual director assigned Mora a room in the residence normally reserved for members of the Society of Jesus—only a few steps from that solitary precinct frequented by Ignatius.

Each morning, it was possible for Mora to see the rocky peaks of Montserrat in the distance. Then as now, the influence of the "Black Madonna" of Montserrat pierced the innermost recesses of Manresa. Early every day, Mora would spend several hours in the tiny cave which, by then, had been turned into a chapel. He later attended Mass and the chanting of the Hours in the adjacent church dedicated to Saint Ignatius.

During his month–long retreat, Mora also visited the other places of devotion in Manresa—the collegiate Basilica of Saint Mary, the church of Saint Peter, the hermitage of Saint Paul and two other nearby shrines to Our Lady. He also retraced the roads leading in and out of the city, along which were the "terminal crosses" and smaller shrines dedicated to the Virgin Mary. Ignatius often trod those areas making the *Via Crucis.*

Francis Mora reflected carefully on the rich lessons of the Spiritual Exercises, especially those relating to the Holy Trinity and the real presence of Jesus in the Holy Eucharist. He was especially struck by the so–called "extraordinary revelation" which came to Ignatius in December of 1522.

His sojourn at Manresa was indeed a high watermark in Mora's spiritual life. How better could one prepare for the active ministry of souls! Solemnly approved in 1548, the Spiritual Exercises were, in the words of Pope Paul III, "full of piety and sanctity" and "very useful for the edification and spiritual profit of the faithful."

It was a rejuvenated and fortified Francis Mora who regretfully left Manresa for one last visit to his native Gurb. Then on to a whole new life of priestly service along *El Camino Real.*

✣ FRANCIS MORA (1827–1905)

B. AN ECUMENICAL PRELATE

Shortly after the assassination of President Kennedy, a well–known Baptist writer observed: "Two Johns, one on the Tiber and one on the Potomac, have in different ways compelled some people to re–examine their attitude towards the Catholic Church and others to think seriously about it for the first time."

One vitally important aspect of that renewed awareness in Catholicism grows out of the ecumenical movement, the desire of the world for Christian unity. Though concern for a united Christendom is as old as the controversies which originally tore asunder the family of Christ, Catholic thought on the subject reached the stage of codification only with Vatican Council II.

From then onwards, according to one reliable source, "no Christian who is animated by the charity of Christ can look upon his separated brethren as strangers or enemies. He must avoid all that can hurt and widen the trench that separates us. He must rid himself of historical and psychological prejudices."

The Decree on Ecumenism directs Catholics "to acquire a more adequate understanding of . . . their own history, spiritual and liturgical life, their religious psychology and cultural background." That exhortation calls to mind the atmosphere that existed in Los Angeles, shortly before the turn of the century. The heroic attitude of the Right Reverend Francis Mora (1827–1905), Bishop of Monterey–Los Angeles, is a marvelous example of the ecumenical gestures that Catholics in California's southland made towards patching the breech that had ripped apart the Christian family.

The Spanish–born prelate was a favorite target of the American Protective Association and was referred to by APA officials as "that damn old foreigner at Second and Main." While the bishop never hesitated to fight for essentials, he never engaged in useless polemics, preferring as he said, to pray "that God may bless them and give them the light to enter into His fold." When his broken health could no longer withstand the burden of persecution, Mora handed over the reins of the diocese to stronger hands, but before entering his lonely retirement, the bishop had this advice for his people about their dealings with non–Catholics:

> Give them always good example, for although of different religions, yet they are your brethren. Our creator is theirs. The sunshine and day fall alike on the field of Catholic and non–Catholic.
>
> God wishes the salvation of all. Be kind and considerate to your non–Catholic acquaintances, and let no animosity ever exist between you; have confidence in them. Such has been my endeavor always and I request you to do the same. I have never mentioned the name Protestant in the pulpit—they are my separated brethren.

By esteeming what was good in other Christian sects, Mora did not in any way minimize the uniqueness of Catholic teaching. He would have been the last to affirm what he knew to be false, but, at the same time, the prelate recognized that much of Protestantism is good, mirroring as it does the stone from which it was hewn.

The Catholic pioneers of this country rejected from the very outset the European concept of *cujus regio, ejus religio,* and to their foresight can be credited the gradual evolution of the climate which prompted a Catholic, Henry Brownson, in 1889, to tell a Congress of Laymen at Baltimore that "separation from the Church is no longer equivalent to outlawry, or privation of fire and water." All of which adds to the suspicion that a detailed study of Catholic ecumenical involvement in the United

States would demonstrate that the Church in the United States is a full sixty years ahead of parallel movements on the continent. Surely it was in California.

✛FRANCIS MORA (1827–1905)

C. THE BISHOP'S COACH

One of the most interesting mementos displayed in the Historical Museum attached to the Archival Center for the Archdiocese of Los Angeles is a model of the stagecoach given to and used by the Right Reverend Francis Mora, Bishop of Monterey–Los Angeles by the legendary Phineas T. Banning (1830–1885).

Historians can testify that the early stage coaches used in Southern California were seldom the freshly–painted concords drawn by six spirited horses and driven by a perfect reinsman. Passengers were carted about in those pioneering times by converted army ambulances, mud wagons or stages. The only common denominator was the motive power of horses or mules.

Horace Bell described a ride he took in October of 1852 from the landing at San Pedro to *El Pueblo de Nuestra Señora de Los Angeles*: "At San Pedro we found two stages of the old army ambulance pattern, to which were being harnessed as vicious a looking herd of broncho mules as ever kicked the brains out of a *gringo*."

> Finally the stages were ready and we were invited to get in. A sailor–looking fellow, who seemed to be at least half–seas–over, sat on the driver's seat and held the lines together in both hands, while two savage–looking Mexicans, mounted on horses which would have vied with the famous steed of Mazeppa, stood with lassoes tightly drawn on the leading mules to guide center, while two others stood in flanking position with their *riatas* ready to be used as whips to urge the animals forward.
>
> When all hands were seated, (Phineas) Banning, the operator of the line, offered to each of the passengers an ominous black bottle, remarking. 'Gentlemen, there is no water between here and Los Angeles!'
>
> '*Suelto carajo!*' shouts the Mexican *major–domo* and sure enough it was let loose and away we went. Of all the rattling of harnesses, kicking, bucking, pulling, lashing and swearing, the twelve broncho mules, the two half–drunk sailor drivers, and the six Mexican conductors with their chief, the major–domo, they did the most.

In December of 1854, Phineas Banning, hoping to gain publicity and financing for an improved roadway to the north, drove a concord stage and nine passengers over the treacherous San Fernando range. Fortunately he and his passengers emerged safely.

Bishop Francis Mora

The model of Bishop Mora's stage is a fairly good miniature reproduction, complete with the prelate's coat–of–arms. Though it bears the designation, *Obispado de Ambas Californias*, the original coach was built only in 1854 by the Abbott, Downing Company of Concord, New Hampshire.

It was later used by the California Stage Company on its overland routes. There was room for ten passengers inside, with others on top alongside the driver who handled the reins for the horses. It is not known whatever became of Mora's historic vehicle. Perhaps one day it will emerge from the shadows of an old country barn. Until then, the little model will serve to recall the chief means of transportation used in an earlier day by the Bishop of Monterey–Los Angeles.

✛FRANCIS MORA (1827–1905)

D. LOST NAPKIN RING

A research tour to Europe in 1961–62 unearthed many fascinating items pertaining to "California's Catholic Heritage." Certainly none has more historical significance than the napkin ring of the Right Reverend Francis Mora, Bishop of Monterey–Los Angeles from

1878 to 1896. The discovery of the bishop's long–lost grave and location of his relatives is a story in itself and has already received adequate attention. Needless to say, by the time the Mora residence in Sarriá was finally located, we fully expected to find there a goodly number of objects belonging to the southland's fourth bishop.

Such was not the case. Not even a picture of their distinguished relative graced the walls of the immaculate little home. Everything had been destroyed by the communists in 1937—everything, that is, but a tiny napkin ring bearing the inscription "Bishop Mora." Having no obvious religious connotation, this one object escaped the eyes of the red inspectors during their many visits to Graus 12. Covered as it was by tarnish, the officials failed to recognize even its material value and pitched it aside as they systematically burned all the religious articles.

Finding this memento was all the more significant, since the bishop undoubtedly brought it as a remembrance from California when he retired to Catalonia in 1896. When it was explained to the four grand nieces and one grandnephew that a museum was being opened for such objects in Los Angeles, they generously allowed its return to California. Worn by years of constant use, the napkin ring bears resemblance to those manufactured at Watsonville. The state's early silver mines were mostly in the deposits east of the main crest of the Sierra Nevada and south of Lake Tahoe but much of the actual fashioning of items took place in the Pajaro Valley where Mora was once pastor and where he returned frequently after his consecration.

The Mora family related that the bishop's crozier had been bequeathed to the monks at Montserrat. A personal visit to the monastery revealed that the staff had been destroyed when the communists melted down the shrine's precious articles in the late 1930s. The abbot remembered the crozier quite vividly.

Considerable sufferings were heaped on the Mora family during those dark days of Spain's history. A second grandnephew, a priest, was captured by the communist secret police, tortured and killed before the very eyes of his brother and sisters. His crime—administering the sacraments to a dying man!

With very little in the way of personal belongings, the family was not able to supply much factual data on their prelatial ancestor. But it was education enough to move among them for a short time and to observe the truly Catholic atmosphere of this typical Catalan family. If future studies bear us out, Bishop Francis Mora will be seen to personify the traditional qualities that Catalonia leaves on its native sons, traits which the present–day Mora family has in great abundance.

Quite obviously, it was disappointing to observe the paucity of materials and information pertaining to the bishop, but reflecting on the words spoken by Archbishop George T. Montgomery about Mora in 1906, perhaps too much had been expected:

> Mora was a bishop in the days when a bishop was obliged to do zealous work without luxuries. It was very different from being a bishop now. Then the episcopal luxuries in this part of the country had not been invented.

✢ WILLIAM JOSEPH MORAN (1906–1996)

The conciliar Fathers of Vatican Council II stated that "in the bishop, our Lord Jesus Christ is among us. In a word, it is the communication of the fullness as the one supreme priesthood of Christ Himself, now appropriated to the bishop, which must occupy our attention, our admiration and our exultation."

William Joseph Moran, the sixteenth native–born Californian elevated to the bishopric, was born on January 15, 1906, the son of Dominick and Winifred (Miskel) Moran. After receiving his primary education in the local schools of the Bay Area, William enrolled at Saint Joseph's College, Mountain View, as a clerical aspirant for the Archdiocese of San Francisco. In 1925, he began the final phase of his preparations for the priesthood at Saint Patrick's Seminary, Menlo Park.

Following his ordination by Archbishop Edward J. Hanna, on June 20, 1931, Father Moran was appointed to the curacy of Saint Charles Church, San Carlos. At other times the young priest also served the People of God at Saint Leo's, Oakland, and Saint Edward's, San Francisco. He became a chaplain in the United States Army, on August 7, 1933.

During his many years of active military duty, Father Moran looked after the spiritual needs of troops at many posts in the United States and overseas. He served as Division Chaplain for the Tenth Mountain Division and Command Chaplain for the United States Fifth Army, Italy, during much of World War II.

The San Francisco–born priest participated in the Algerian–French Morocco, Tunisian, Rome–Arno, North Appenines, Po Valley and Naples–Foggia campaigns. He earned numerous citations for outstanding service during his military career, among which were the Bronze Star, the American Defense medal and the World War II victory medal. He was made a Commander in the Order of the Crown of Italy, in 1945.

On November 1, 1958, Father Moran was advanced to the position of Deputy Chief of Chaplains for the United States Army. On the following May 14th, the Senate confirmed his nomination to the rank of Brigadier General by President Dwight D. Eisenhower. Pope John XXIII made Father Moran a Domestic Prelate, on September 12, 1959. General Moran was named by Pope Paul VI to the titular Bishopric of Centuria, as Auxiliary to the Military Vicar of the United States Armed Forces, on September 15, 1965.

Assisting Francis Cardinal Spellman at Moran's episcopal ordination, on December 13, 1965, was Archbishop Joseph T. McGucken of San Francisco. Also raised to the bishopric at that ceremony was the Most Reverend Terence J. Cooke, who later succeeded Spellman as Ordinary of the Armed Forces. For his consecration, held in Saint Patrick's Cathedral, New York, Bishop Moran wore the white vestments used by Eugenio Pacelli (later Pope Pius XII) when he received episcopal orders a half century earlier.

On February 1, 1966, Bishop Moran retired from the United States Army to take up his duties at the Military Ordinariate in New York. During the interval from December 13th, 1965 to February 1, 1966, the prelate became the first American bishop to be on active duty in the Armed Forces.

The "grandeur" of the bishopric bestowed upon William Joseph Moran and others confounds us, for God alone is its cause. Yet, as the conciliar Fathers stated, "it is a grandeur which exacts reverence and which no one can despise with impunity. Let us recognize Christ in the bishop and let us praise the Lord."

✛PETER JAMES MULDOON (1863–1927)

Peter James Muldoon (1863–1927), "one of the leaders of the American social apostolate in the early twentieth century," was the first native Californian to serve in the American hierarchy. The son of John and Catherine (Coughlin) Muldoon was born at Columbia, in Tuolumne County, on October 10, 1863. He studied in the public schools of Stockton prior to entering Saint Mary's College, near Lebanon, Kentucky, in 1877. There the enviable scholastic record he achieved speaks for the talents and industry he applied to the mastery of the college curriculum.

Peter pursued his theological studies at Saint Mary's Seminary, Baltimore, as a clerical student for the Archdiocese of Chicago. He was ordained December 18, 1886, by Bishop John Loughlin of Brooklyn. Upon his return to the Windy City, Father Muldoon was made curate at Saint Pius Church. In 1888, he became Chancellor for the Archdiocese of Chicago and secretary to Archbishop Patrick Feehan. He was entrusted with the pastorate of Saint Charles Borromeo Church, in 1895. Pope Leo XIII appointed Father Muldoon to the titular See of Tamasus, in 1901, and on July 25, he was raised to the episcopate, as Auxiliary Bishop of Chicago, by Sebastian Cardinal Martinelli.

In 1908, twelve of the eighteen counties in the Archdiocese of Chicago were dismembered and formed into the ecclesiastical jurisdiction of Rockford. On September 28, Muldoon was named the initial shepherd of the 50,000 Catholics comprising the seventy–five parishes in the new Diocese of Rockford.

Bishop Muldoon's administrative abilities were widely recognized and when, in 1917, candidates were being sought for the vacant Diocese of Monterey–Los Angeles, the name of California–born Muldoon was prominently mentioned. He had earlier been considered among the possible successors to San Francisco's Archbishop Patrick W. Riordan. The Holy See did, in fact, ask Bishop Muldoon to take up the episcopal reins at Los Angeles, but the prelate rather strongly expressed himself against returning to the West Coast. According to his biographer, "it is easy to question Peter Muldoon's wisdom and foresight, as well as that of his advisers, in their belief that he should remain in Rockford."

Public announcement of Muldoon's determination to remain in Illinois, released from the Apostolic Delegation, saddened the people of Monterey–Los Angeles as much as it encouraged those of Rockford for Southern California needed a man of Bishop Muldoon's ability to look after its growing numbers.

The remaining years of the prelate's life were active ones. He achieved considerable prominence as the initial episcopal Chairman for the National Catholic War Council, where his talents were exceedingly well utilized.

The final months of Muldoon's life were filled with a struggle against illness, and the end came for him at Rockford on October 8, 1927. Among the many tributes published by the press, perhaps none better characterized the prelate's career than that of Joseph S. Reiner:

> Bishop Muldoon stood out among the clergy for his heroic willingness to sacrifice himself to bring Catholic principles of charity and justice to bear on social and economic problems. The laboring classes, in particular, have lost a staunch friend.

PATRICK CARDINAL O'BOYLE (1896–1987)

A. An Infamous Day—1945

In April of 1983, Patrick Cardinal O'Boyle, by then the retired Archbishop of Washington, D.C., was interviewed at his home on Warren Street about an incident that occurred many years earlier.

The day was July 28, 1945, a date that burned itself into New Yorkers' memories with almost the same vividness as Pearl Harbor. Msgr. Patrick O'Boyle was then director of the Catholic Relief Services which functioned out of offices located on the 79th floor of the Empire State Building.

On that cold, rainy and foggy Saturday morning,

O'Boyle was making his way to work when, suddenly, he heard a thunderous noise. He looked up to see the tower of the Empire State Building, several blocks away, emerge from the mist as a bank of orange flames poured down the north face to the street below. It was several moments later, after arriving at the site, that O'Boyle learned that a twelve ton Army Air Force B–25 bomber, traveling from Bedford Field to Newark Airport, had slammed into the world's tallest building.

There was pandemonium at the entranceway. O'Boyle rushed in and was able to accompany firemen and a medical team by elevator to the 67th floor. From there they had to rush up the remaining twelve stories of stairs on foot. There were flames and smoke everywhere. An engine and part of a landing gear had plunged through an elevator shaft into the sub–basement. Eight hundred gallons of flaming gasoline poured down the stairways and halls as far as the 75th floor.

Unhappily, O'Boyle's hasty calculations proved correct. The bomber had smashed directly into the offices of Catholic Relief Services. He found the bodies of his two secretaries and eight others incinerated almost beyond recognition. All told, there were fourteen deaths and twenty–six injuries.

Catherine O'Connor was among the survivors. She and a handful of others had made their way to a small room on the 33rd Street side of the floor. Though weak from inhaling pitch–black smoke, they lived to recount the horrible event. O'Connor recalled that "the plane exploded within the building. There were five or six seconds—I was tottering on my feet trying to keep my balance—and three–quarters of the office was instantaneously consumed in a sheet of flame."

What makes this story memorable to Californians is the fact that when O'Boyle arrived at his office, he found that Auxiliary Bishop J. Francis A. McIntyre was already at the scene anointing the dead. When asked how he happened to arrive so quickly, on a normally slow–paced Saturday morning, McIntyre said that he had felt "inspired" to take a stroll in the vicinity (which he rarely did). He had the holy oils only because he had forgotten to replace them after a sick call the previous day.

O'Boyle never believed that McIntyre's presence was a fortuitous occurrence. He recalled that "I was devastated at seeing my friends and fellow workers lying there dead on the floor of my office. I doubt if I could have administered the sacraments myself. God sent McIntyre there that day because He knew that little Patrick just wasn't up to the job."

PATRICK CARDINAL O'BOYLE (1896–1987)

B. DEMISE OF A CARDINAL—1987

With the death of Patrick Cardinal O'Boyle, on August 10, 1987, the final chapter of the "Spellman Era"

in the country's ecclesial history came to a close. He was the last of the churchmen whose lineage stretched back to the days of New York dominance over the nation's hierarchy.

Cardinal O'Boyle had many links to Los Angeles. He had been a classmate of J. Francis A. McIntyre at Dunwoodie and was ordained alongside him in Saint Patrick's Cathedral, on May 21, 1921. During the early decades of their ministry, the two young priests spent their holidays with McIntyre's cousins in New York. They were both closely associated with the multi–faceted charitable outreach of the Church in the Empire State.

Patrick Aloysius O'Boyle was born in Scranton, on July 18, 1896. After graduation from what is now the University of Scranton, he enrolled at Saint Joseph's Seminary as a clerical aspirant for the Archdiocese of New York. Young Father O'Boyle's zeal for the poor inspired Cardinal Hayes to appoint him to a succession of responsibilities in the welfare apostolate. In 1941, he was named a papal chamberlain by Pope Pius XII and, three years later, he was made a domestic prelate. During that period, he served as assistant director of Catholic Charities in the New York archdiocese and afterwards became director of the Mission of the Immaculate Virgin at Mount Loretto, a home and school for dependent children. In 1943, he was appointed director of War Relief Services for the National Catholic Welfare Conference.

Designated executive director for New York's Catholic Charities in 1946, he also served as a consultor to Francis Cardinal Spellman. A year later, on November 29, 1947, he was named Archbishop of the newly–created Archdiocese of Washington, D.C. and Chancellor of The Catholic University of America.

When he arrived in the nations' capital, the tremendous growth that would challenge the new Ordinary was already under way. In less than twenty years, the Catholic population in the Washington area would more than double, and the school enrollment would nearly triple. To meet these pressing needs, O'Boyle launched a program for establishing forty new parishes and erecting more than 300 churches, convents, schools and rectories.

As he forged ahead with needed construction, O'Boyle sought to alleviate the challenge of social evils and racial discrimination. In a series of pastoral letters, O'Boyle emphasized that "those who deny a neighbor solely on the basis of race the opportunity to buy a house, enjoy equal education and job opportunities are in effect denying those rights to Christ Himself." President Harry S. Truman came to his house one day to thank him for integrating the district's Catholic school system.

O'Boyle served the Church at the national level as Chairman of the Administrative Board of the National

Catholic Welfare Conference. Becoming a cardinal only served to quicken his pace. He was fond of saying that "the certain road to peace is living the social Gospel of Christ."

It was easy to see why the only two American classmates to become Cardinals were such close friends. They shared a predilection for the poor and downtrodden. Or, as O'Boyle once stated to this writer in an interview: "Frank (Cardinal McIntyre) and I were fighting for human rights before it was fashionable."

✝DENIS J. O'CONNELL (1849–1927)

Denis J. O'Connell, the one-time Auxiliary Bishop of San Francisco, played an important role in the history of the Catholic Church in the United States during the forty years from 1885 to 1925. Denis was born on January 24, 1849, the son of Michael and Bridget O'Connell. His preparation for the ministry was made at Saint Charles College, Ellicott City, Maryland and the North American College, Rome.

The Irish-born O'Connell was ordained to the priesthood on May 26, 1877, by Raffaele Cardinal Monaco La Valletta. His earliest years in the apostolate were spent doing pastoral work in the Diocese of Richmond. He took an active part in the preparation and execution of the decrees for the Third Plenary Council of Baltimore.

From 1885 to 1895, Father O'Connell was Rector of the North American College. In those years, he also served the bishops and priests of the United States as contact and liaison with the Vatican. Upon his resignation of the rectorship, Father O'Connell became Vicar of Santa Maria in Trastevere. At the request of the American hierarchy, Father O'Connell returned to the academic world, in 1903, as the third Rector for The Catholic University of America, a post he occupied for the full five-year term. While at Washington, O'Connell helped to realize significant advances for the university. At the conclusion of his tenure, he left the institution improved from both the economic and academic point-of-view.

Father O'Connell was named to the Titular See of Sebaste, on December 16, 1907, and on the following May 3rd was advanced to episcopal orders by James Cardinal Gibbons, Archbishop of Baltimore. At the time of his episcopal ordination, O'Connell was described by the press as "the most widely known priest in the United States." Certainly that was true if one were to abide by the extant sources.

In December, 1908, Archbishop Patrick W. Riordan petitioned Rome to name O'Connell Auxiliary of San Francisco. When the appointment was finally approved by the Holy Father, O'Connell became a neighbor to Bishop Thomas J. Conaty in Los Angeles, who had preceded him by six years into the Metropolitan Province of San Francisco. Bishop O'Connell's tenure in California was relatively short. On January 19, 1912, he was transferred to the Diocese of Richmond. On that occasion, Archbishop Riordan wrote to Cardinal Gibbons:

> To me his appointment brings not only joy but sorrow. We have lived so happily together these three years, and he is so agreeable and genial all the time, that it will be difficult to find one to replace him.

With O'Connell's installation as the seventh Bishop of Richmond, he returned to the scenes of his first missionary labors. He was welcomed by Cardinal Gibbons as "an enlightened churchman" and a "patriotic citizen who will take an active interest in the welfare and prosperity of the Commonwealth." Bishop O'Connell served the People of God at Richmond until ill health forced his retirement, on January 15, 1926. At that time, he was advanced to the titular Archbishopric of Marianne.

O'Connell lived on at Richmond until January 1, 1927, when death ended his varied and colorful career. Truly could it be said by his biographer that the archbishop adorned the altar with his faith and piety and the pulpit with his solid eloquence.

✝EUGENE O'CONNELL (1815–1891)

A. ECHOES OF ERIN

No single nation has contributed as much to the growth of the Church in California as Ireland; yet much of the story of that nation's sons and daughters who were the Golden State's pioneers has been left to die in silence, perhaps for simple neglect of scholarship or scholars, perhaps in the thought that the Spanish missions adequately accounted for the foundation and prosperity of California Catholicism.

Eugene O'Connell was enlisted for the California apostolate by the new Bishop of Monterey, Joseph Sadoc Alemany, in 1850. He was, at the time, a professor at All Hallows College in Dublin. During his first sojourn in the west, O'Connell was superior of the seminary at Santa Ines and later rector of the smaller institution at Mission Dolores in San Francisco. He was consecrated Titular Bishop of Flaviopolis on February 6, 1861. His vicariate of Marysville was raised to diocesan status in 1868 under the title of Grass Valley.

Upon O'Connell's retirement in 1884, his coadjutor, Patrick Manogue, became Bishop of Grass Valley. A native of Kilkenny, the "Gold Rush Bishop" was the catalyzing agent of the Church in the Mother Lode Country. Besides a magnificent cathedral, several churches, convents and schools, Manogue was successful in having the seat of his jurisdiction moved to Sacramento where it remains today. The third incumbent of the See was Thomas Grace. Born August 2, 1841, Grace was twenty-six years old at the time of his ordination. His uncanny administrative abilities brought him to the attention of Archbishop Francis Satolli, the Apostolic Delegate, who recommended his appointment to the vacant Diocese of Sacramento.

The first nationally–known prelate appointed to California was Thomas J. Conaty. His attachment with the Total Abstinence Movement, rectorship of The Catholic University of America, and presidency of the National Catholic Educational Association gave that native of County Cavan a remarkably varied background for his position in Monterey–Los Angeles. Already consecrated as titular of Samos, Bishop Conaty served the California Church from 1903 until 1915. Denis J. O'Connell was also a former Rector of The Catholic University of America and previous to that had served as first Rector of the North American College in Rome. Designated Auxiliary of San Francisco, he was consecrated May 3, 1908, by James Cardinal Gibbons, his great mentor. He became Bishop of Richmond in 1912, and upon his retirement twelve years later was advanced to the titular archiepiscopal See of Mariamne.

Only a handful of prelates of the American hierarchy have lived to celebrate their golden episcopal jubilees. That number includes Bishop John B. MacGinley. Elected to *Nueva Caceres* in 1910, MacGinley came to California as the first Bishop of Monterey–Fresno in 1924. Ill–health forced his retirement eight years later, and after that time the Titular Bishop of Croae lived quietly at Killybegs.

Of the state's Irish–born prelates, John J. Cantwell served as a metropolitan archbishop. A native of Limerick, Cantwell was only eighteen years ordained when named to the Diocese of Monterey–Los Angeles in 1917. There he supervised the erection of the Monterey–Fresno jurisdiction in 1922, and fourteen years later saw his own jurisdiction made an archbishopric. His episcopate of thirty years was the longest of any of his predecessors.

The fourth Bishop of Sacramento, like that diocese's earlier three prelates, was born on the Emerald Isle. He was made Auxiliary in 1920, and a year after the death of Thomas Grace in 1921, Patrick J. Keane was named Ordinary. He died prematurely after only six years as Bishop of Sacramento. Another of the Irish prelates was Timothy Manning, Auxiliary Bishop of Los Angeles. Ordained on July 16, 1934, Manning was named Titular of Lesvi twelve years later at the age of thirty–five, becoming one of the youngest members of the Church's worldwide hierarchy. He later became a cardinal after being named Archbishop of Los Angeles.

Since 1597, when the first Irish priest, Father Richard Arthur, came to America as pastor of Saint Augustine's in Florida, the Irish heritage in American Catholicism has been written in capital letters. And California was no exception!

✦EUGENE O'CONNELL (1815–1891)

B. THE BISHOP WRITES HOME—1861

The correspondence of the Right Reverend Eugene O'Connell (1815–1891), Irish–born Vicar Apostolic of Marysville and later Bishop of Grass Valley, is something of a classic in the annals of Western American Catholicism. On May 27, 1861, the one–time theology professor dispatched the following letter to a former colleague at Dublin's All Hallows College:

I should have written to each of you, in particular, on account of the singular claims which you have individually upon me, but you will be satisfied with this installment of a vast debt which I owe you, when I assure you that the interval which I have sought for penning this is disturbed a good deal by heat and flies, how lucid soever it may be in other respects. What with flies and mosquitoes by day, and rats and mosquitoes by night, the sinner has got to suffer not a little, in and about Marysville. How is every one of you? I hope quite as well as I could wish. Father Bernard Morris stops with me here at Marysville and, between Father Richard Blake and myself, attends Smartsville, Oroville, Longbar, Cherokee Flat and Timbuctoo (a literal fact), places from thirty to forty miles and upwards distant from this city. Between Marysville and Sacramento there is a magnificent river formed by the influx of the Feather and the Yuba, two very large streams. Steamers ply every day between these two cities and take about seven hours to reach either one of them. I have twelve counties confided to my care and depending on six priests, one or two of whom is "caving in" (as the American miners say) from too much pressure of duty. Father Michael O'Reilly, strong and robust as he was, is a good deal shattered; so is Father Morris, who is at present collecting funds in order to build a new house for us. As yet we have none but a wretched shanty infested with flies during the day and with rats during the night, but it can't be helped. The Roman Pontiff is the cause of all this, and His Holiness is suffering more himself than are we, so we can't complain. It is a shame for me not to send you money from this golden country, but as yet I haven't got even a quasi–domicile, hardly a simple habitation, and if we tax the people too much and too soon it would never do.

But why is this city of 6,000 souls, one–third of whom are Catholic, called Marysville? Not from Our Lady, as I fondly supposed, but from the following circumstance, which involves a case of conscience, likely to prove interesting to the professor of moral theology. The lady who gave her name to Marysville is still living, and she is called Mrs. Mary Covillaud. Her present consort (I won't call him husband yet awhile, lest I should suppose the question, or prejudice the case) is a French Catholic and Freemason of the first class, and contracted matrimony with her as well as he could before the year 1854, i.e., before the extension to California of Benedict XIV's declaration in the case of marriages between Protestants and Catholics in Holland.

Bishop Eugene O'Connell

Now it is time to tell you to what religion Mrs. Covillaud, or Mrs. Johnson (her first husband's name) belonged, before and after her union with her present consort. (Her maiden name was Mary Murphy and she came to California with the Donner party in 1847.) She was a Baptist, and then became a Mormon. She then married a man from Boston, named Johnson (who owned a *rancho* just below Marysville), whose religious system is a perfect mystery to her. She got divorced from him, although he is still living in the Sandwich Islands, like Lamech with only two wives. Mrs. Johnson, or Covillaud, as the case may be, is satisfied with one husband (if indeed he can be recognized as such), first, on account of the probable ligamen with the first worthy, and secondly, because the contract with the second and present man was "*coram Magistratu Civili*" before the year 1854, in which year the Holy See communicated validity to marriages between Catholics and Protestants in California, the same as in Holland. The crowning and last circumstance in this matrimonial drama is the conversion of Mrs. Covillaud, or Johnson, to Catholicity a few months ago. Now, my dearly beloved brethren — and I can say this from my heart— if the lady in question has any qualms of conscience about her present union with Monsieur Covillaud, what is her director to do or to say? If she be disquieted, the evil and scandal would be very great indeed, and many a marriage would be unhinged and unsettled if parties

were aware that the Council of Trent was published in, and affects, all California; yet Archbishop Alemany insists that Marysville, Downieville, Jacksonville and all the rest were outside the sphere of California missions which extended only to Sacramento. Consult if you please, with each other and Doctor O'Reilly, and send me your decision of this perplexing case.

✦EUGENE O'CONNELL (1815–1891)

c. FINAL DAYS OF A HOLY MAN—1884

On February 29, 1884, after almost a quarter century as Vicar Apostolic of Marysville and Bishop of Grass Valley, the Right Reverend Eugene O'Connell (1815–1891) "laid down his arms and devoted the remainder of his life to prayer for the success of the great enterprise he had begun."

Retirement did not come easy to the Irish–born prelate and, several years after putting aside his mitre, he asked Bishop Francis Mora if there might be a chaplaincy available in the Diocese of Monterey–Los Angeles for an elderly priest "still desiring to remain in harness." Mora replied enthusiastically that the Sisters of the Immaculate Heart of Mary would welcome O'Connell's services at their motherhouse, on West Pico Boulevard. So it was that the Titular Bishop of Joppa took up residence at the Los Angeles convent in quarters furnished modestly by the ever–generous Gertrude Ponet.

The Sisters were congratulated for obtaining, as their chaplain, "one whose sanctity is a household word, one whose prudent counsel will be your safeguard, one whose zeal is unbounded, one who will not grow weary in God's service until he has thoroughly imbued others with that love of God and Christian charity which characterize himself."

The last years of Bishop O'Connell's life were as busy as any he ever spent along the Gold Dust Trails. He offered daily Mass, heard confessions, cared for the infirm, taught the youngsters, instructed the novices and counseled the professed nuns on a schedule that would have exhausted a more robust man. His lectures to the novices were "filled with unction" as he strove to impress upon them the beauty and joyousness, as well as the sacrificial nature of the life to which they were aspiring and the importance of fulfilling the obligations which such a life entailed.

Bishop O'Connell died "in harness," as he had wanted, on December 4, 1891. He was buried in a humble grave over which the Sisters had planned to extend the sanctuary so that the altar would rest atop his venerable remains. The foundations were built, but financial circumstances prevented completion. On November 16,

1910, the prelate's remains were transferred to old Calvary Cemetery where they were interred in the circle reserved for priests. Several decades later, they were removed again, this time to the newly opened Calvary Cemetery, on Whittier Boulevard.

Eugene O'Connell's life recalls Saint John Chrysostom's sermon on the priesthood: "The spiritual shepherd must be a generous soul, so as not to lose courage or to despair over the salvation of those straying from the true fold. . . . He who attends to his own perfection profits himself alone; but the benefit of the pastoral office extends to the whole people. One who distributes alms to the needy or otherwise defends the oppressed benefits his neighbor to some extent; but these corporal benefits are as much less than the spiritual benefits conferred by the priest as the body is inferior to the soul. Rightly then our Lord says that caring for the flock was a proof of love for himself."

The historian of the Church in the Mother Lode has written that "if scrupulous devotion to duty and solid virtue are signs of holiness, then there is all the reason in the world to look upon Bishop O'Connell as a holy man."

✛EUGENE O'CONNELL (1815–1891)

D. RETURN OF THE BISHOP—1982

One afternoon in the early autumn of 1850, Father Eugene O'Connell (1815–1891), a brilliant young professor of Moral Theology, invited a visitor to address his students at Dublin's All Hallows College. Bishop Joseph Sadoc Alemany, enroute to California after receiving episcopal ordination at Rome for the Diocese of Monterey, briefly told the small group of students about the need for priests along the Pacific Slope. It must have been an appealing presentation, for the professor himself signed up for a term of service.

When O'Connell arrived at San Francisco, in June of 1851, he was immediately assigned to Santa Ines Mission, where a handful of clerical candidates were studying their way through theology. At Bishop Alemany's suggestion, O'Connell moved the seminary to Mission Dolores, in San Francisco, shortly thereafter. At the same time, O'Connell was entrusted with the pastorate of the "American Church" of Saint Francis of Assisi, in North Beach.

In May, 1854, Father O'Connell returned to Dublin and the quiet seminary routine of All Hallows College. Six years later, his peace of mind was shattered forever when he was named Vicar Apostolic of Marysville.

His twenty–three year episcopate was as strenuous as any in California's annals. The vicariate (later the Diocese of Grass Valley) embraced all of Northern California and, for full measure, spilled over the Sierras to include the northern half of Nevada.

It became his responsibility to provide spiritual guidance and sustenance for a constantly shifting, forever changing Catholic populace. The prelate's letters to his friend, Bartholomew Woodlock, portray O'Connell as an immensely human, utterly devoted servant of his people. The record of O'Connell's years has been related in great detail by Msgr. John Dwyer in his book *Condemned to the Mines*. It was a tenure that lasted until the prelate's retirement, in 1884.

Several years after putting aside his crozier, Bishop O'Connell asked for and was given the chaplaincy for the Sisters of the Immaculate Heart of Mary at their motherhouse in the Pico Heights area of Los Angeles.

Those final years were happy ones for O'Connell. Living in modest quarters, the titular Bishop of Joppa offered daily Mass, heard confessions, taught youngsters, instructed the novices and counseled the professed sisters on a schedule that would have exhausted a more robust man.

The bishop died on December 4, 1891. On November 16, 1910, the prelate's remains were transferred to old Calvary Cemetery. Then, eleven years later, the prelate was moved again, this time to the newly–opened Calvary Cemetery on Whittier Boulevard. His tomb was marked by a simple marble slab which read "Rt. Rev. Eugene O'Connell, 1815–1891."

In life and death, it is appropriate that a shepherd be with his flock. And so, on April 6, 1982, Bishop O'Connell began his final journey along the Gold Dust Trails to the episcopal vault in Sacramento. May his shadow long fall over Northern California.

✛JAMES O'DOWD (1907–1950)

Though he died at the relatively young age of forty–two, Bishop James O'Dowd of San Francisco was already "renowned throughout the country for his comprehensive knowledge in the field of education." The son of Maurice and Margaret O'Dowd was born in the Richmond District of San Francisco on August 4, 1907. He attended Star of the Sea School before entering the archdiocesan minor seminary at Mountain View. Upon completion of his theological studies at Saint Patrick's Seminary, young O'Dowd was ordained to the priesthood, on June 4, 1932.

After a brief tenure as curate at Saint Lawrence O'Toole Parish in Oakland, Father O'Dowd was sent to The Catholic University of America for further studies in the field of education. He acquired a doctorate in that discipline, in 1935, and, shortly thereafter, returned to the Bay Area as assistant superintendent of schools for the Archdiocese of San Francisco. Six years later he succeeded to the superintendency. In that post Father O'Dowd "won the admiration and respect of all engaged in the work of Christian teaching by his untiring efforts constantly to promote the cause of Catholic education throughout the archdiocese."

During the hectic years that followed, Father O'Dowd gained a reputation for "exceptional kindness, good humor, sympathetic and personal friendliness" in his dealings with the area's various civil and religious officials in the educational field. At different times, he was chairman for California of the Secondary School Department, National Educational Association, member of the San Francisco Coordinating Council for Youth Welfare, member of the Teacher Training Committee for the California Board of Education, to mention but a few of his burdensome tasks.

Though he was in frequent contact with men in high official positions, Father O'Dowd never lost the common touch. "His complete naturalness, his sincerity and his genuine humility charmed the lowliest as well as the mightiest." His appointment, by Pope Pius XII, to the Titular See of Cea, was warmly applauded by the clergy and laity of the Bay Area. He was consecrated Auxiliary Bishop of San Francisco, in Saint Mary's Cathedral, on June 29, 1948. Whether it was fulfilling his duties as archdiocesan consultor, director of education or pastor of Mission Dolores, Bishop O'Dowd spent himself unsparingly in promoting the welfare of God's people.

The prelate's sudden death, on February 4, 1950, from injuries sustained in an auto–train accident at Suisun, took from the scene one of California's most promising churchmen. And yet, no truly good man ever fully dies. "Like a star which has become extinct but whose light lingers on for generations to gladden the eyes of man, so too, this holy bishop . . . will linger as a light in our memories and in the annals of the Church" of California.

✝THOMAS O'SHEA, S.M. (1870–1954)

Thomas O'Shea, the first San Franciscan named to the bishopric, was born on March 13, 1870. His was to be a life of conveying to others what the early Spanish missionaries brought to the Pacific Slope. Edmund and Joan O'Shea took their young son to New Zealand, where he began his preparation for the priesthood at Saint Patrick's College, Wellington. He subsequently continued his clerical studies at Saint Mary's Seminary, Napier.

On February 10, 1891, Thomas entered the Society of Mary. He was sent to Washington, D.C. and there, on August 15, 1892, he took his final vows in the commu-

nity. After his ordination to the priesthood, on December 3, 1893, Father O'Shea became a faculty member at Saint Mary's Seminary, Napier. Between 1897 and 1913, he engaged in pastoral work in the Archdiocese of Wellington, for which jurisdiction he was appointed Vicar General, in 1907. On May 19, 1913, Pope Pius X named Father O'Shea titular Archbishop of Gortyna and Coadjutor for Wellington. He was advanced to episcopal orders on August 17th.

The Archdiocese of Wellington, then comprising an area of 34,000 square miles, was somewhat larger than Ireland. It had been created an archiepiscopal seat in 1887, and, at the time of O'Shea's appointment, was inhabited mostly by Catholic emigrants from Ireland.

The new archbishop was a handsome and charming figure whose very demeanor bespoke warmth and sincerity. The People of God in Wellington saw in him not alone the representative of Catholic faith and discipline, but also a gentleman, a scholar and a patriot—ever ready to do his part in the development of the community. In all the phases of his varied ministry, O'Shea's love of Christian charity was an active force for harmony between individuals, classes and denominations.

During the twenty–two years he served as Coadjutor Archbishop, Thomas O'Shea came to know every major village in the far–flung New Zealand jurisdiction. His ministerial labor, civic service and community presence were all illumined by the power of his magnetic personality. Few expansionary projects were launched without his stamp of approval.

On January 3, 1935, Archbishop O'Shea became Ordinary of Wellington and for the ensuing nineteen years he continued his priestly apostolate among the Islands of the Western Pacific. The veteran Marist prelate died on May 9, 1954, fulfilling his wish and prayer of "going home to God" during the Marian Year proclaimed by Pope Pius XII.

Throughout his life, the archbishop retained a deep and abiding affection for his native San Francisco. He was fond of recalling that his own missionary ideals derived from reading about and admiring the wonderful accomplishments of Fray Junípero Serra and his confreres along *El Camino Real*.

✝EUGENIO CARDINAL PACELLI (1876–1958)

Pope Pius XII was the first occupant of the papal throne ever to have visited the United States. The then Eugenio Cardinal Pacelli arrived by ocean liner in New York on October 8, 1936.

In order to satisfy his "desire, cherished for a long time, to see with my own eyes this country and to feel the pulsation of its life and labors," the then Papal Secretary of State set out on a tour which stretched 16,000 miles and allowed him to meet seventy–nine bishops and visit twelve of the nation's sixteen ecclesial provinces.

The cardinal arrived at Mills Field in San Francisco on October 27th, aboard his chartered United Airlines Boeing Transport. He was taken to Archbishop John J. Mitty's home at 1000 Fulton Street, where he met with the other bishops of the province, as well as with local clergy.

The next morning, he offered Holy Mass and preached a short homily at Saint Mary's Cathedral. He was then driven to the nearly–completed Oakland Bay Bridge, the largest of its kind anywhere. After blessing this "newest wonder of the world," His Eminence visited the faculty and students of Saint Patrick's Seminary, Menlo Park.

California's southland was not on the original itinerary, but the Auxiliary Bishop of Boston, Francis J. Spellman, explained that "the future of the west centers around Los Angeles" which had just been created a metropolitan province. Pacelli, Spellman, Count Enrico Galeazzi and the other three members of the party left San Francisco at 4 o'clock for Los Angeles. They were greeted at the Burbank Airport by Archbishop John J. Cantwell and taken to 100 Fremont Place for a reception and dinner with local dignitaries.

Early next day, after offering Holy Mass in the chapel of the archbishop's home, the cardinal was given a whirlwind tour of the city, during which he visited Saint Vincent's Church (Los Angeles), Saint Andrew's Church (Pasadena) and Saint Elizabeth's Church (Altadena).

At the latter church, His Eminence was given a full canonical reception by Father William Corr. According to a local account, after "walking down the main aisle between lines of resplendent choir boys, the cardinal went immediately to the altar as a hymn of greeting was sung." After another brief prayer, Cardinal Pacelli ascended the predella and, without speaking, imparted a blessing. Leaving the sanctuary, he was led to the front pew where he greeted Countess Mary Young Moore.

Until recent times, a marble plaque recalled that historic day with this simple inscription: "Commemorating the visit of Cardinal Pacelli, to the late Father Corr and us, October 29, 1936." By early afternoon, the cardinal had completed his "informal visit to the archdiocese" and was escorted back to the airport. After walking to his plane between a double line of the Bellarmine–Jefferson guards, Pacelli left for Boulder City.

The trip to the west coast culminated a tour during which the Papal Secretary of State charmed his way around the country, making thousands of friends, speaking with a multitude of clergy and laity and exuding goodwill for the Church. A writer for *The Tidings* characterized the journey as "one of the most remarkable tours ever undertaken by a dignitary visiting this country." Three years later, Pacelli became Pope Plus XII.

✛LUIS PETTINELLI (1855–1935)

Luis Pettinelli was born at Metilica, Italy, on September 28, 1855. He began his studies for the priesthood at the Seminary of Fabriano, where he excelled in the philosophical and theological sciences. On December 30, 1876, Pettinelli affiliated himself with the *Seminario dei Ss. Pietro e Paolo per le Missioni Estere*, which had been founded by Pope Pius IX two years earlier as the missionary arm of the Italian clergy.

Following his ordination, on May 22, 1880, Father Pettinelli was sent as a missionary to Albania. In 1883, he was re–assigned, this time to far–away California. During his twelve years in San Francisco, Father Pettinelli was attached to Saint Teresa's Church, at 18th and Tennessee Streets. There he served as curate and pastor.

In addition to his normal parochial duties, Father Pettinelli was a popular confessor and spiritual advisor to the local clergy. He was also a close and trusted confidant to Archbishop Patrick W. Riordan.

When Pope Leo XIII entrusted the spiritual apostolate in Baja California to the Pontifical Seminary of Sts. Peter and Paul, on November 8, 1895, Father Pettinelli was named Superior of the peninsula. Pettinelli and several priests journeyed to their new assignment which, at that time, encompassed a Catholic population numbering about 40,000 souls.

Throughout his tenure as "Superior of the Mission of Baja California," Father Pettinelli remained vitally concerned about the interests of the Church in San Francisco, maintaining a frequent correspondence with the archbishop and other priest friends. During a return visit in 1900, Pettinelli was warmly received by the local Catholic populace. He reported that he was assisted by eight priests in the vast area which had been served earlier by a Vicariate Apostolic.

He mentioned the wonderful apostolic work being done by the Ladies Society of the Sacred Heart for the Poor, an organization he had established to further the educational and cultural needs of his people. He was also successful in raising funds to erect a large school where peninsular youngsters could secure "an education equal to the academies" in Alta California. The priest spoke enthusiastically about the natural qualities of the area, noting that "if rains were more abundant the country would be rich. The ground contains much mineral but comparatively little mining is done on account of lack of capital."

In 1905, a serious eye affliction forced Father Pettinelli to seek medical attention in Rome. Though he underwent a successful operation, his sight deteriorated further and on August 14, 1908, he resigned his post. Pettinelli spent the final years of his life in his native town of Metilica, where he succumbed on August 10, 1935.

Though little is recorded about the apostolic work done by Father Pettinelli in Baja California, it is known that he was among the most outstanding of the sixteen priests who toiled for souls in that vast area between 1895 and 1919.

✤JOSE MARIA PRECIADO Y NIEVA, C.M.F. (1886–1963)

The era of the Spanish missionaries in the New World extended well into the 1900s. Jose Maria Preciado y Nieva, a native of Cadreita, Navarre, was born on September 23, 1886. He studied for the priesthood with the Claretians at Alagon and Vich and, on August 15, 1904, took his final vows in the Congregation of the Sons of the Immaculate Heart of Mary. Ordained June 24, 1912, Father Preciado was sent to Mexico as the founding rector of a new seminary opened by his community. He was forced to flee to the United States, the following year, and between 1914 and 1921, he served as curate in Southern California's parish of *Nuestra Señora de Los Angeles*.

In 1921, Father Preciado began a two–year tenure as pastor of San Gabriel Mission, during which time he made a number of important additions and improvements to the parochial plant. He was subsequently transferred to the Diocese of San Antonio as pastor of Immaculate Heart of Mary Church and, later, San Fernando Cathedral. During his years in Texas, Father Preciado was also associated, in a professorial role, with Saint Mary's University.

On February 26, 1934, Pope Pius XI named Preciado to the Titular See of Teges. He was consecrated Vicar Apostolic of Darien, on the Isthmus of Panama, on May 31, 1934. The prominence of Darien, one of the oldest ecclesiastical seats on the American continent, had dwindled since the completion of the Panama Canal. It had been reduced to vicariate status, on November 29, 1925.

Anticipating the spirit of Vatican Council II, Bishop Preciado devoted himself wholeheartedly to those who had strayed in any way from the path of truth or who were ignorant of the gospel of Christ and His saving mercy. During the twenty–one years Preciado cared for the spiritual needs of Darien, the Claretian prelate built some sixty chapels and mission stations, as well as Colon's Immaculate Conception Cathedral in an area extending from the Atlantic to the Pacific, and scattered through the 400 San Blas Islands.

The bishop pioneered the use of airplanes in his missionary apostolate to the Cholo, Kuna and Chocoe Indians living in the rugged Panamanian terrain. More than 10,000 of the 25,000 Kuna Indians were converted during Preciado's episcopate. Forced to resign his position, in 1955, because of ill health, the bishop spent his final years in Los Angeles. He died August 13, 1963, and was entombed, at his own request, among his people at Panama City. The apostolic life of Jose Maria Preciado was a fulfillment of the stated goal of bishops: "that all people may walk in goodness and justice and truth."

✤CHARLES WILLIAM QUINN, C.M. (1905–1960)

Contemporary youngsters continue to be inspired by the zealous priest, strengthened by the holy priest, challenged by the imaginative priest and reassured by the democratic priest. Charles William Quinn occupied a prominent position among that select corps of priestly exemplars. Born on December 16, 1905, to Patrick and Catherine (Roundtree) Quinn, Charles was baptized at Mission San Gabriel by Father Jose Preciado, later the Vicar Apostolic of Darien.

He studied at Saint Vincent's School, in Los Angeles, prior to entering the Congregation of the Mission's preparatory seminary, at Cape Girardeau, in 1919. Upon completion of his ecclesiastical studies, Charles was ordained to the priesthood by Bishop John J. Cantwell, on October 11, 1931.

Father Quinn then went to Rome for an advanced degree in theology from the *Colegio Angelico*. In 1933, he was sent as a missionary to China's Vicariate Apostolic of Yukiang, in Kiangsi Province. Two years later, he became Vicar General of Yukiang and, on May 28, 1940, was named Vicar Apostolic and titular bishop of Halicarnasus. At the time of his episcopal ordination, on October 30, 1940, Charles Quinn was the youngest bishop in China.

The bishop was mindful of Saint Augustine's advice that "the man who is able to escape the horrors of invasion, but who does not flee because he will not forsake the ministry of Christ, without which men can neither become nor live as Christians, wins a greater reward for his charity than the one who flees for his own sake."

For that reason, the Vincentian prelate chose to remain with his people during the dark days of World War II. Prior to the arrival of the Japanese troops, the bishop was influential in hiding and subsequently evacuating nineteen of the Jimmy Doolittle flyers who had parachuted into the area.

Following the hostilities, Pope Pius XII advanced Yukiang to diocesan status. The relatively peaceful atmosphere of the region disappeared, however, as the menace of communism spread to the internal parts of China, in 1949. The bishop was placed under house–arrest as the Reds gradually curtailed and then forbade altogether religious freedom. He was eventually subjected to a mob trial, followed by a "formal" court proceeding in which the death penalty was sought. The final verdict, a jail sentence, was commuted "because of the leniency of the communist government" and, in mid–1951, Bishop Quinn was expelled from the Chinese mainland.

The prelate returned to the United States and lived for a while at Saint Thomas Seminary, in Denver. He resumed his missionary work in Taiwan, in 1955, and died at Kaohsiung, on March 12, 1960.

Though denied the privilege of martyrdom, the California–born Vincentian prelate was fond of recalling the prayer that his fellow bishop, Francis X. Ford, uttered shortly before his death in a communist prison:

> Grant us, Lord, to be the doorstep by which the multitudes may come to worship Thee. And if, in the saving of their souls, we are ground underfoot and spat upon and worn out, at least we shall have served Thee in some small way in helping pagan souls; we shall have become the King's Highway.

✛FRANCIS ANTHONY QUINN (b. 1921)

Francis Anthony Quinn was born at Los Angeles, on September 11, 1921, the younger son of Frank and Anne (Chierici) Quinn. The senior Quinn was superintendent of Scully Brothers Glove Factory. After her husband's premature death, in 1927, Anne began a quarter century stint as seamstress for a shirt manufacturer to support herself and her two sons.

According to Anne, Francis was "very quiet and studious as a child." He carried newspapers for the Napa *Register* and sold subscriptions to the *Saturday Evening Post*. Francis attended Saint John's Parochial School at Napa and then, at the age of fourteen, entered Saint Joseph's Seminary at Mountain View as a clerical aspirant for the Archdiocese of San Francisco.

Upon completion of his theological courses at Saint Patrick Seminary, Menlo Park, Francis was ordained to the priesthood on June 15, 1946, by Archbishop John J. Mitty. The young priest was sent to The Catholic University of America where he earned a Master's Degree in education. After returning to the Pacific Slope, Father Quinn was assigned to Serra High School, San Mateo, where he taught for three years.

Between 1950 and 1955, he was on the faculty of Sacred Heart High School in San Francisco. In the latter year, he became associate superintendent of schools for the archdiocese, a position he held until 1962. Shortly after receiving his doctorate from the University of California at Berkeley, Father Quinn became editor of *The Monitor* and for the succeeding decade he guided the editorial policy of the historic Bay Area newspaper.

A talented writer, Father Quinn had penned a column for *The Monitor* since February, 1952, entitled "The Faith In You." He later co–authored a four volume *Complete Group Guidance for Catholic High Schools* and was on the drafting committee for the booklet "As One Who Serves."

Quinn served in several other roles during that time, including Secretary of the Roman Catholic Welfare Corporation and Commission Chairman for the Western Education Association. He was named Director of Radio and TV in 1962. Quinn was also designated a monsignor in that year. In 1970, Quinn became Pastor of Saint Gabriel's Parish and a member of the archdiocesan Board of Consultors. He served as President of the Priests Senate in 1973–1974 and the following year was President of the Region XI Conference of Priests Senates.

On April 28, 1978, Pope Paul VI named Quinn titular Bishop of Numana and Auxiliary of San Francisco. He received episcopal ordination on June 29th. At that time, he described the "work of bishops," as that of giving "leadership and cooperating with all resources of the community in bringing as many people as possible to God and to His healing, reconciliation and love."

Early in 1980, Bishop Quinn was appointed the seventh Ordinary of the ninety–one parishes comprising the Diocese of Sacramento. He was installed on February 18th, giving as his priority the role of making "God known to as many people as possible." He served in Sacramento until his retirement in 1993.

✛JOHN RAPHAEL QUINN (b. 1929)

John Raphael Quinn, the first native of the Diocese of San Diego named to the bishopric, began his episcopal ministry with the gentle, humble spirit of Fray Junípero Serra. Born at Riverside, on March 28, 1929, the son of Raphael and Elizabeth (Carroll) Quinn, John received his earliest education at Saint Francis de Sales school in his native city.

He began his studies for the ministry at Sacred Heart Preparatory Seminary, Watertown, Wisconsin. Later he moved to Southern California and entered Saint Francis Seminary as a clerical aspirant for the Diocese of San Diego. Bishop Charles F. Buddy subsequently sent him to Rome, where he completed his courses in philosophy and theology at the North American College and the Gregorian University.

John was ordained to the priesthood on July 19, 1953, by Archbishop Ettore Cunial, the vicegerent of Rome. Upon his return to the southland, Father Quinn was assigned as curate to Saint George Parish, Ontario, California. Between 1955 and 1962, Quinn served as Professor of Dogmatic Theology at Immaculate Heart Seminary, El Cajon. In the latter year he was named President of Saint Francis College Seminary and, two years later, Rector of Immaculate Heart Seminary.

Pope Paul VI appointed Quinn to the titular See of Thisiduo and Auxiliary Bishop of San Diego on October 21, 1967. He received episcopal ordination from Archbishop Luigi Raimondi, the Apostolic Delegate, on the Feast of Our Lady of Guadalupe. The ceremony was the first of its kind in which the English liturgy was used.

During his relatively short episcopal tenure in California's second largest city, Bishop Quinn served in the dual role as Vicar General and Pastor of Saint Therese Church. In 1971, he was named a consultor to the Sacred Congregation for the Clergy, at Rome. Later that same year, he was appointed to the vacant Diocese of Oklahoma City–Tulsa, thus becoming the youngest prelate in the United States to head a residential bishopric.

The new ordinary's earliest months in Oklahoma were hectic ones. He spoke out strongly against abortion, endorsed the lettuce boycott, protested the escalation of bombing in Vietnam and wrote a pastoral letter on prison reform.

Quinn served the 115,000 Catholics in the statewide, 70,100 square mile jurisdiction for just a year, before being advanced to archbishop as the metropolitan for the newly proclaimed Province of Oklahoma City. Fittingly, the formation of the forty–six farmland counties into an archdiocese came in the centenary year of Catholicity in the state.

Early in 1977, Quinn was transferred back to California as the sixth Archbishop of San Francisco. He was installed in the 2,325 square mile jurisdiction on April 26th. One of his earliest priorities in San Francisco was the relocation and opening to scholars of the Chancery Archives.

On November 15, 1977, Archbishop Quinn was elected President of the National Conference of Catholic Bishops, the first time such a prominent and influential post had ever been conferred upon a westerner.

Archbishop Quinn was described by one reporter as being a "middle–road churchman, open to trends of research, desirous of frank communication and yet a letter–of–the law man in ecclesiology."

The archbishop remained at his post until his early retirement in 1995. Later he wrote a controversial book book on papal primacy.

✠HENRIQUE JOSE REED DA SILVA (1854–1930)

Henrique Jose Reed da Silva was born, at Lisbon, on January 19, 1854, the son of Sebastiao Jose and Elisa Maria (Reed) da Silva. His studies for the priesthood were made locally and he was ordained, in 1880, for service in the Patriarchiate of Lisbon.

Pope Leo XIII named Father da Silva to the titular see of Philadelphia, on March 17, 1884. He received episcopal ordination on the following May 4, as coadjutor to the Archbishop of Goa. Shortly after the Concordat of 1886, between the Holy See and Portugal, da Silva was transferred to the restructured Diocese of Sao Tome de Meliapor, in the East Indies.

The prelate unleashed a stream of apostolic activity among the 30,000 Catholics on the Coromandel Coast. His was the arduous task of gathering the broken shreds of the historic old diocese, putting them together and rendering it once again the thing of beauty it had been in earlier times.

Among the works inaugurated by the "princely" Dom Henrique was that of reforming the seminary which he re–populated with clerical candidates from Portugal and other European countries. He opened a convent of European Nuns at Saint Thomas and another of Indian Sisters at Mylapur. Da Silva's "courtly manners and noble bearing" endeared him to all stratas of society. He received enthusiastic support for his project of replacing the old cathedral with a magnificent new edifice over the tomb of Saint Thomas. He was also successful in establishing the *Catholic Register*, a weekly newspaper circulated throughout his diocese.

Political intrigues were considerable, however, and when, in 1897, "he incurred the ill–will of certain parties connected with the churches situated in other dioceses, and when he found the accusations brought against him accepted with demur in Europe, he resigned and retired to Portugal, as titular Bishop of Trajanopolis."

In 1906, the bishop traveled to the United States, where he spent some months as a house guest of San Francisco's affable Archbishop Patrick W. Riordan. Following the sudden death of Coadjutor Archbishop George T. Montgomery, on January 10, 1907, da Silva "substituted in the function of auxiliary" until the Holy Father could provide for the appointment of a successor.

The Lisbon–born prelate gave lectures and looked after the spiritual needs of the vast Portuguese colony living in the archdiocese, besides conferring the Sacrament of Confirmation wherever else required. After Bishop Denis J. O'Connell's arrival in the Bay City as auxiliary, da Silva resided for a while with the McLoughlin family of San Jose. Between 1911 and 1924, the bishop served in the Archdiocese of Boston as pastor of the Portuguese parish of Saint Anthony, in Lowell. He subsequently returned to Lisbon, where he died on October 6, 1930

Because of royal lineage (he was reportedly a nephew of King Carlos I), Bishop da Silva was entombed in the Pantheon with the crowned heads of the Portuguese nation. Though his sojourn in the Golden State was brief, the name of Henrique Jose Reed da Silva deserves its place among the Church's early pioneers along the Pacific Slope.

✢JUSTIN RIGALI (b. 1935)

The Roman Curia, the agency which the Pope uses to fulfill his divine mandate, was given its basic form by Sixtus V, in 1588. It was updated by Pope Benedict XV, in 1917, and formally incorporated into the Code of Canon Law. In order to insure that the offices and central agencies of the Catholic Church exhibit a truly universal character, the fathers of Vatican Council II suggested that the curia be "reorganized and better adapted to the needs of the times, and of various regions and rites." One vital aspect of that renewal was internationalization, whereby the clerical personnel assigned to the Vatican would "be drawn more widely from various geographical areas of the Church."

It was partially as a result of the curial *aggiornamento* that a priest from the Archdiocese of Los Angeles, Father Justin Rigali, came to occupy the highest post in the Roman curia ever bestowed upon a Californian. Since 1966, the forty–year–old cleric has been one of approximately 175 priests attached to the Vatican diplomatic service, generally considered to be the most important organ of the Holy See in the field of international relations.

Born in Los Angeles, on April 19, 1935, the son of Henry and Frances (White), Rigali studied at Holy Cross School prior to entering, in 1949, the archdiocesan preparatory seminary, then located at 241 South Detroit Street, in the Hancock Park area of the city. He was ordained to the priesthood by James Cardinal Francis McIntyre, on April 25, 1961, at Saint Vibiana's Cathedral. Following a brief tenure as curate at Ascension Church in Los Angeles and Saint Raymond's Church in Downey, Father Rigali was selected for graduate studies at Rome's Pontifical Gregorian University. In 1964, shortly after completing his thesis on *The Law of Tutela—An Historical and Juridical Study,* Father Rigali was awarded a doctorate in Canon Law.

In response to a request for a priest from Los Angeles to work in the papal diplomatic corps, Cardinal McIntyre asked Father Rigali if he would care to attach himself to the Vatican Secretariat of State. There he took further courses at the Piazza Minerva's Pontifical Ecclesiastical Academy prior to his formal induction into the Holy See's far–flung diplomatic mission. Father Rigali's initial appointment came, in 1966, when he was named secretary of the Apostolic Nunciature in the island–nation of Madagascar. He served at Tananarive for four years. On July 11, 1967, he was given the rank of monsignor and named a chaplain of His Holiness, Pope Paul VI.

Early in 1970, Monsignor Rigali was called back to Rome and the directorship of the English language section of the Secretariat of State. Among his chief duties in that post was providing the Holy Father with simultaneous translations of conversations and speeches on private and public occasions. When Msgr. Rigali was not with the pope, he performed his other duties under the direction of Archbishop Giovanni Benelli, at the secretariat's offices, on the third loggia of the Apostolic Palace. Along with fourteen other American priests, he lived at Villa Stritch, a residence maintained in the Eternal City by the American hierarchy for priests attached to the curia.

Monsignor Rigali traveled with Pope Paul on his nine nation visit to Asia, in November, 1970, where he functioned as the Holy Father's chief language assistant for the predominantly English–speaking journey. He had previously accompanied the pontiff on the trek to Pisa's National Eucharistic Congress.

Service in the Roman Curia is not an overly attractive assignment for the average priest. Living on a meager salary, isolated from the consolations of parochial work, an ocean away from family, friends, classmates and confreres carries with it a number of personal privations, most of which are unknown and unappreciated by the majority of American clerics.

Yet the priesthood encompasses a diversity of ministries. Whatever he does, be it dispensing the sacraments, preaching the gospel, teaching in the classroom, administering a parish or working at some insignificant position, the priest retains his sacramental imprint. Everything he does is "informed" by his priesthood and that is the reason why there really can't be such a person as a hyphenated priest.

Rigali was named a titular archbishop on 1985 and, nine years later, he was appointed to the Metropolitan See of Saint Louis.

✢PATRICK W. RIORDAN (1841–1914)

A. Bay City's "Great" Archbishop

The Church has been able in every age and at every turn of her varied fortunes to win to her cause the services of great men. And certainly when the final chapter of California's noble Catholic heritage is written, among the great names of which the Church in America is proud will stand the name of Patrick William Riordan, second Archbishop of San Francisco.

Born at Chatam, New Brunswick, on August 27, 1841, son of Matthew Riordan and Mary Dunne, Patrick received his earliest education in and around Chicago. He studied at Saint Mary of the Lake Seminary in Illinois and in 1856 entered the University of Notre Dame. Leaving South Bend in 1858, the young seminarian was among the dozen students making up the first class of the North American College in Rome, but owing to ill health, he was forced to transfer to the University of Louvain. Riordan was ordained by Engelbert Cardinal Sterecks on June 10, 1865 at Mechlin, Belguim.

Upon his return to Chicago, Father Riordan taught at Saint Mary's Seminary for several years and from 1868 onwards was pastor at Woodstock and Joliet before assuming his final parochial assignment at Saint James in Chicago. There he built a magnificent church and engaged in a wide variety of activities for the next twelve years. When his former classmate at Louvain, John Lancaster Spalding, Bishop of Peoria, turned down the appointment as Coadjutor of San Francisco, the choice fell to Father Riordan. Elected to the Titular See of Cabasa on July 17, 1883, he was consecrated September 16th, by Archbishop Patrick Feehan of Chicago.

With the resignation of Joseph Sadoc Alemany, O.P., Patrick Riordan became San Francisco's second archbishop and lived on to divide equally with his predecessor sixty–one years as shepherd of the metropolitan jurisdiction. As the years passed, the prophetic words of Spalding, spoken at Riordan's consecration, achieved their fullest meaning.

> I feel in my heart that he will do a great work for God. God will uphold him and use his abilities, augmented by his enthusiastic zeal, to accomplish a great work, and will crown his earnest efforts with the benisons of peace and joy everlasting.

Details of internal organization first occupied Riordan's attention. Then a new cathedral, a splendid seminary, numerous churches, schools, convents and hospitals rose up to become landmarks in the archdiocese. In the words of Father Peter C. Yorke, "whatever he did, he did in a princely fashion, and he did it without display." One distinctive feature of Riordan's episcopate was his effort to bring clergy and laity into a closer contact.

Knowing that large parishes tend to keep priests and people apart, the archbishop subdivided existing units as rapidly as circumstances allowed. If it is true today in California that a noticeable camaraderie exists between clergy and laity, the credit belongs to Patrick W. Riordan.

Whether it was rebuilding a ruined city after the 1906 earthquake and fire, bringing to a settlement the long–contested Pious Fund case, or helping to remove state taxation from churches, Riordan remained, first and foremost, a priest and father to his people.

Archbishop Riordan was one of the most distinguished prelates of the Church, one whose splendid personality made him conspicuous in all ranks of men. Eminent as a scholar, he ranked among the most eloquent of speakers. Brilliant as a conversationalist, brimming with native Irish wit, he was withal a man of such simplicity of manner that the lowliest of people found him most accessible.

It is true enough the Church's success in California has been due to the devotion, faith and example of her laity. But strength without leadership is impotent. Archbishop Riordan provided that quality and he did it in an era when anything less would have been catastrophic.

✤PATRICK W. RIORDAN (1841–1914)

B. ARCHBISHOP BREAKS THE PRECEDENT

Archbishop Patrick W. Riordan (1841–1914) has the distinction of being the first successful plaintiff to appear before the permanent international peace tribunal at The Hague. It was Riordan who brought to the Hague the celebrated Pious Fund case, a series of legal proceedings which had stretched over the last decades of the 19th century.

The final decision of the Court was in favor of the archbishop. It was a precedent–shaking triumph which the prelate hoped would encourage others to bring their claims to the tribunal. The San Francisco *Examiner* echoed the sentiments of the nation by noting that "the decision of the International Court of Arbitration at The Hague is regarded as a sweeping victory for Archbishop Riordan."

The prelate arrived in New York on November 28, 1902, aboard the *Celtic*. He was described by the local press as looking the "picture of health." They went on to say that he "walked with a springy step, his shoulders well back." The informal interview given by Riordan on that occasion is worth recalling, at least in part.

> It has been a victory for us and I rejoice greatly for this fund will make possible an extension of the educational and religious work in California. But it is not only for the sake of the Church that I rejoice. It is because this case forms a precedent in such matters.
>
> I mean by this that in my opinion all matters of minor importance can be settled by arbitration. Nations will not hereafter go to war except for grave causes. All minor matters, such as money claims, boundary disputes ... can be settled. In most cases they probably will be. I think the peace conference will accomplish much and the Czar (of Russia), in urging the value of such conferences, deserves all praise.
>
> But in grave international complications, I doubt much if the people of the world have as yet reached the state of civilization where it would be possible to settle

them by arbitration. Nations will not—at least now—be willing to submit matters of great national importance to a board of five men.

It seems reasonable now, however, to believe that the permanent peace conference will become one of the great and useful institutions of the world. Distinguished authorities on international law are convinced of the validity of its decisions.

In our case the United States and Mexico were the first to appeal to its rulings and the United States has the honor of the first victory.

It was only a few days before our claim was so referred that I understand a member of the permanent tribunal expressed the opinion to an English colleague that it would never be called upon to exercise its functions.

Many people in the United States, judging by the press, believed then that this tribunal would never have anything before it. But all opinions on these lines were set at naught when the United States broke the ice and gave the tribunal its first case.

President (Theodore) Roosevelt thus gave proof to the world of the possibilities of such a tribunal. It is an example that is bound to be followed by others nations.

And so it was. The court continued to function and, in 1945, was incorporated into the framework of the United Nations. It still hears cases and has become a strong force in international legal circles.

✝PATRICK W. RIORDAN (1841–1914)

C. HIS EXCELLENCY OF SAN FRANCISCO

Speaking editorially about San Francisco's Archbishop Patrick W. Riordan, *Dominicana* pointed out to its readers, in July of 1903, that the prelate's administration "during the past twenty years, bears the impress of a phenomenal personal activity and is a record of remarkably brilliant achievements."

Coming to the archdiocese with an experience gained in a school where the amenities of life, as well as the humanities, were taught in their highest excellence, "with a well disciplined mind and admirable graciousness of manner," Archbishop Riordan displayed a self–control and equipoise under many trying circumstances that instantly made him conspicuous as "an examplar of virtue, a model of knightly courtesy and a possessor of qualities of character that commanded universal reverence."

Fully alive as he was to the interests and future welfare of the Church and school, the archbishop identified himself with every movement to strengthen the foundations of religion, adding materially to their permanence and endurance. Actuated by the loftiest motives, recognizing the potent influence on society of great, good and noble souls, he strenuously directed his energies to the development of the perfectly balanced Christian character. Toward that end he made a most liberal provision for the popular enlightenment by founding and encouraging educational institutions throughout the archdiocese confident that they would practically illustrate, in the lives of future citizens of the state, the highest principles of religion.

Riordan never doubted that the career of the educated Christian would fulfill the expectations of those self–sacrificing teachers whose greatest consolation was the knowledge that the spiritual culture of their students had kept pace with their mental and physical development and that social and political relations had been founded upon impregnable virtue.

Conspicuous as he always was in the vigor of his intellectual force, Archbishop Riordan stood in the front rank as a leader in questions of intense concern to the Church. His active participation in matters of local significance, his untiring work for the good of young and old, his instant comprehension of the greatest opportunities, his faithful concentration of energy in the accomplishment of the highest good are familiar characteristics to students of California's Catholic heritage. In 1902, when the International Court of Arbitration at The Hague delivered its historic verdict concerning the Pious Fund of the Californias, a reporter for the San Francisco *Examiner* wrote that the court's decision "will make him a prominent figure when the question of the next cardinal for the United States comes up."

Alas, the honor, when it came, in 1911, went to New York and Boston. And yet, those familiar with the archbishop's activities can hardly help but feel that no churchman in United States Catholic annals was ever more princely than Patrick W. Riordan. No one would ever have borne the distinction more gracefully than His Excellency of San Francisco! One has only to read the biographical treatise by Monsignor James P. Gaffey to see why Archbishop Riordan still ranks at the head of the list for the California hierarchy!

✝JOHN BAPTISTE SALPOINTE (1825–1898)

If and when the integrated and complete history of the Catholic Church in Arizona is written, the name of John Baptiste Salpointe (1825–1898) will occupy a place of unique importance. The French–born missionary, coming to the west eight years after his ordination, served as Vicar General of the Diocese of Santa Fe between 1859 and 1868. He was named to the newly–established Vicariate Apostolic of Arizona on September 25, 1868, and on the following June 20th received episcopal ordination as the titular Bishop of Dorlaeum.

It was an enormous vicariate, encompassing the whole of Arizona, plus that section of New Mexico known as the Mesilla Valley, together with the counties of Grant, Doña Ana and Paso (Texas).

Bishop Salpointe served as Vicar Apostolic until February 1885, when, in accordance with an appointment made the previous April, he became coadjutor Archbishop of Sante Fe. The next month he received the pallium and confirmation as residential ordinary. There he worked until January, 1894. He spent the final years of his life in Tucson, where he died on July 15, 1898.

During his years in the southwest, Salpointe wrote several lengthy reports to the Paris office for the Society of the Propagation of the Faith, some of which were published in the *Annales de la Propagation de la Foi*. As he neared the end of his ministry, the aged prelate revised and considerably enlarged his earlier reports in narrative form in order "to place before the general reader an account of those interesting events of which people at present have little more than a vague tradition."

Early in 1893, Archbishop Salpointe journeyed to Los Angeles in an effort to find a printer for his book. It was the Bishop of Monterey–Los Angeles, Right Reverend Francis Mora, who suggested that Salpointe entrust the work to Father B. Florian Hahn. Hahn was then the director of Saint Boniface Indian School, at Banning, a Catholic boarding institution founded "to build up religion in the hearts" of youngsters with Indian ancestry.

Saint Boniface possessed sophisticated printing facilities on which the youthful Indians had already demonstrated their mastery and skill.

The archbishop visited Banning and personally discussed his proposed book with Father Hahn. It was agreed that the manuscript would be completed within a calendar year after its arrival at Saint Boniface.

The Arizona *Daily Star* announced the finished tome in its issue of July 28, 1897:

> It will be pleasing to those interested in the early history of this region to learn that the archbishop is now and has been for many months engaged in the preparation of a book on the early Catholic missionaries and the founding of the missions, the christening of the valleys, and the mountains, and thus perpetuating the names of the saints in this region, in the names of our valleys and mountains. The publication will be one of much value for its authenticity and historical research.

The book was completed in the spring of 1898, and the manuscript sent to Banning. The finished tome was ready by the end of the year, not, however, before the death of the archbishop. It was released as *Soldiers of the Cross: Notes on the Ecclesiastical History of New Mexico, Arizona and Colorado.*

It was indeed a valuable treatise for those interested in southwest history. And it won for its author the title "Historian of the Kingdom." Though now outdated and obsolete, the book evoked a newspaper editorial that rightly stated: "With the death of this man, the Right Reverend J.B. Salpointe, there passes away one of the most important figures in all the early history of Arizona."

✛JOHN JOSEPH SCANLAN (1906–1997)

That John Joseph Scanlan, (1906–1997) a priest from the Archdiocese of San Francisco, became the residential bishop for the "Paradise of the Pacific" is only the continuance of a relationship which dates back to the 1840s. John was born at Saint Anne's Hill, County Cork, the son of Peter and Katherine (Coleman) Scanlan. He studied with the Christian Brothers at North Monastery, in his native city. Later, he entered the National University of Ireland, at Dublin. His preparation for the priesthood was made at All Hallows College, where he was ordained on June 22, 1930, by Bishop John Norton of Bathurst.

Father Scanlan came to San Francisco that same year and served briefly at Saint Patrick's (San Jose) and Saint Joseph's (Berkeley). From 1931 to 1937, he was curate at Saint Brigid's in San Francisco. While engaging in pastoral work at Saint Therese's in Oakland (1937–1843), Father Scanlan took graduate studies at the Berkelely campus of the University of California. He subsequently taught in several of the local high schools and served as director for the archdiocesan Holy Name Society.

In 1950, Archbishop John J. Mitty appointed Scanlan founding Pastor of Saint Thomas More Parish. The Irish–born priest's first services were conducted in a carpet store provided by a generous Methodist businessman. That experience likely influenced the prelate's subsequent interest in the ecumenical activities inaugurated by him and other bishops at Vatican Council II.

On July 8, 1954, Pope Pius XII named Father Scanlan to the titular See of Cenae and Auxiliary Bishop of Honolulu. He received episcopal ordination on the following September 21st. Late in 1967, during the final illness of Bishop James J. Sweeney, Scanlan was appointed Apostolic Administrator for the diocese. He became residential ordinary early the following year.

The Diocese of Honolulu, a complex group of eight large volcanic islands (and 114 minor ones) with differing ethnic and racial structures, is co–terminus with the State of Hawaii, the fiftieth and most recent addition to the American commonwealth. Since its admission to the Union, on August 21, 1959, the area has become the cultural focal point of the Pacific. It is the first overseas and second noncontiguous state. Though separated from the mainland by 2,397 miles, the Diocese of Honolulu is canonically attached to the Metropolitan District of San Francisco.

The Catholic population represents one of the most diversified of any ecclesial area in the world. The native Hawaiians, Polynesian in origin, are intermarried with other groups. And there are large colonies of Japanese, Portuguese, Philippine, Puerto Rican, Chinese, Samoan, Vietnamese and Caucasians living peacefully in multi–racial neighborhoods. The growth and change in islandic life in the years since World War II have brought tremendous changes to the placid way–of–life which confronted Captain James Cook when he first visited the Sandwich Islands in 1778.

Sacred Heart missionaries from Hawaii came to California in the mid 1840s. It is indeed appropriate that the ties existing between the Golden and Aloha states should remain so close as the decades and centuries roll on.

✢LAWRENCE SCANLAN (1843–1915)

A. UTAH'S PIONEER PRELATE

Cardinal Gibbons once said that "the life of a missionary priest is never written, nor can it be. He has no Boswell. His biographer may recount the churches he erected, the schools he founded, the works of religion and charity he inaugurated and fostered, the sermons he preached, the children he catechized, the converts he received into the fold and this is already a great deal, but it only touches upon the surface of that devoted life. There is no memoir of his private daily life of usefulness and of his sacred and confidential relations with his flock— all this is hidden with Christ in God, and is registered only by His recording angel."

Such a man was Father Lawrence Scanlan who arrived in California in 1868, newly ordained for the Archdiocese of San Francisco. The Irish born priest was assigned as curate of Saint Patrick's Church. His next appointment was Saint Mary's Cathedral, and there the parishioners remembered him in later years as "a most devout and faithful priest," one truly conscious of their daily needs. After a few hectic years at the silver mining village at Pioche in the hills of southeastern Nevada, where Father Scanlan built a small church in honor of his patron saint, Archbishop Joseph Sadoc Alemany named Scanlan Pastor of Saint Vincent's Church in Petaluma.

That very year, however, according to his own account, "I took charge of the Church of Saint Mary Magdalene, which was then the only church and Catholic institution in the Territory of Utah. . . ." The parish at Salt Lake gave Father Scanlan the dubious dis-

Bishop Lawrence Scanlan

tinction of being pastor of the largest geographical region in the United States.

Contemporary estimates placed the number of Catholics in the Utah Territory at approximately 800 (out of a total population of 87,000) and of that number, perhaps ninety lived at Salt Lake City. Nonetheless, in 1875, Scanlan was able to open Saint Mary's Academy in the very stronghold of Mormonism, and a short while later Holy Cross Hospital was established in an old remodeled residence.

Although somewhat reserved in his attitude to the Mormons, Scanlan once "referred with no little feeling to [Brigham] Young's personal benevolence toward him and his fellow Catholics when the Church was struggling to obtain a footing in Utah."

Life in the mining camps of the area had its lighter moments. One day the priest was stopped on the street by a seedy–looking chap with a red and bulbous nose. The man asked for a dime, and the generous Scanlan responded by giving him twenty–five cents, saying: "Now promise me you won't get drunk on this." The tramp thanked him and replied: "Drunk on twenty–five cents! I promise you I won't. Why, Reverend Sir, it would take ninety–nine cents of a dollar to make me drunk."

When Saint Mary Magdalene's Cathedral was completed in the summer of 1909, James Cardinal Gibbons journeyed from the Premier See of Baltimore to dedicate the half–million dollar monument to Utah Catholicity. Appointed vicar forane in 1880, Scanlan assumed charge over the entire Utah mission. Six years later, when the Holy See erected a Vicariate Apostolic encompassing Utah and eastern Nevada, Lawrence Scanlan was named Titular Bishop of Larundun. When the vicariate was advanced to diocesan status in January of 1891, Scanlan became the first Bishop of Salt Lake.

When the pioneering prelate died on May 10, 1915, it was said that "the secret of a man's inspiration is hidden in his heart. If we study the life of Bishop Scanlan we can discover the secret of his inspiration—the life of Christ was one of sacrifice— and so was his."

✚LAWRENCE SCANLAN (1843–1915)

B. AN ECUMENICAL ENCOUNTER—1879

To Father Lawrence Scanlan (1843–1915) ecumenism may have been more a necessity than a virtue; nonetheless, this Irishborn missionary learned many decades ago that the enthusiasm non–Catholics have for their religious convictions is a factor not worthy of indiscriminate condemnation.

The 85,000 square mile Utah parish entrusted to Father Scanlan in 1873 represented the largest ecclesiastical unit in the United States. Out of a total population of 87,000, only a handful of the residents were Catholic. Throughout his many years as missionary, and later Bishop of Salt Lake, Scanlan made it a point to cultivate amicable relations with individual Mormons. There were times, of course, when he opened his well reserved batteries upon the Mormon citadel, but generally even then Scanlan rarely allowed his remarks to go beyond the walls of his own small church.

In 1879, the Mormon authorities of Saint George asked Father Scanlan to hold services in their tabernacle at Silver Reef. We are told by one chronicler: "He accepted, and as the services were to be on Sunday, the regular Sunday services—*Missa cantata* and sermon—formed the program of the day. A choir was needed, and as the tabernacle choir of the place did not know Latin, it was thought that the singing of the *Kyrie Eleison, Gloria* and *Credo* could not be carried out. The leader of the choir asked for Catholic music, and being given 'Peter's Mass,' in two weeks his choir knew the Mass and could sing it in Latin.

"On the third Sunday of May High Mass was sung in the tabernacle. Before the services Father Scanlan explained the meaning of the vestments used at Mass, and at the Gospel preached a logical and eloquent sermon, taking, for his text, 'True adorers of God shall adore Him in spirit and truth.' Careful to give no offense

and to respect the belief of his hearers, nearly all of whom were Mormons, he won for himself the esteem and good will of all."

So highly respected was the good natured priest that when he was named Vicar Apostolic in 1886, one local newspaper reporter admitted that Scanlan's apostolic work, performed under the most adverse circumstances amid a hostile people deserved recognition. The Mormon journalist went on to note that the new vicar had ridden thousands of miles and many times had deprived himself of necessities that others might be benefited thereby. A year later, commenting on Scanlan's consecration, the same newspaper observed, about the prelate's titular Asiatic see: "it is a jolly combination, this union of Asia and Utah, and one quite familiar to the minds of those posted on local affairs; but in the present instance, happily, the joinder is for decency and not the reverse."

It has been observed that "Mr. Young and his successor in the presidency, indeed all of the Mormon officials, were ever friendly to the Catholic priest, and Bishop Scanlan has many times in conversation gratefully referred to this repeated manifestation of generous feeling towards himself and his predecessors." The writer of the above then asked the question: "To what are we to attribute this exceptional treatment?" Perhaps the answer can be found in Vatican Council II's decree on ecumenism, the outline of which was surely in the daily activities of Lawrence Scanlan:

> Almost everyone, though in different ways, longs that there may be one visible Church of God, a Church universal and sent forth to the whole world that the world may be converted to the gospel and so be saved, to the glory of God.

✚PHILIP SCHER (1880–1953)

Philip Scher was born in 1880 "of a people strong in Catholic Faith and ardent in missionary spirit." He was educated for the priesthood at the Pontifical College of Josephinum in Ohio, and the Urban College of Propaganda Fide in Rome. The Illinois–born seminarian was ordained by Pietro Cardinal Respighi on June 6, 1904. After a brief period as professor at the Josephinum, the young priest came to the west where his work in the Diocese of Monterey–Los Angeles over the next three decades "equipped him with an intimate knowledge of the problems of the Church in Central California and a deep understanding and sympathy for the trials and difficulties of its missionary clergy."

Father Scher was named Bishop of Monterey–Fresno in 1933, to succeed the Most Reverend John B. MacGinley, and, although "in few dioceses was the picture so dismal as in the jurisdiction of the new bishop," he was able to organize "a system of interparochial catechetical centers and brought missionary sisters from many states to establish a program of religious instruction worthy of envy by many greater dioceses."

Though illness plagued the prelate in his final years, he "carried burdens and suffered torture that would have overcome the spirit of any one less than an apostle." As was noted at his funeral, in January of 1953, Bishop Scher's sufferings of nearly seven years "in the chains of paralysis did not for a moment distract him from his continuous prayer . . ."

An interesting letter unearthed in the archives of the Bureau of Catholic Indian Missions tells much about the zeal of Philip Scher. It was written on September 1, 1922, from Bakersfield:

> The Indians have been a source of worry for me ever since I came to Bakersfield, four years ago, and I knew nothing was being done for them. I found they were in No Man's Land or were not being attended by any priest. I went to Los Angeles in January and to solve this difficulty, I volunteered to take charge of the Indians, as I speak Spanish.
>
> Bishop Cantwell, who is, as you know, devoted to the Indians, gladly accepted my offer. This done, I learned that a wind storm last Christmas eve had unroofed the chapel, and the walls of adobe, being exposed to storms, soon crumbled so that the building became a total wreck. In spring I went up to inspect it. I found a trunk with everything needed for Mass. There was a fine gold chalice that no Indian, however poverty-stricken, would think of taking and selling.
>
> Since then I try to go every two or three weeks to say Mass and to give instructions to adults. Miss Streeter teaches the children. We gather clothes and distribute them. I had just made my first visit there when a Protestant woman phoned me, asking whether the Catholics were doing anything for the spiritual welfare of the Indians for if not, they, the Protestants, were prepared to undertake the work. I discovered that they had already sounded the Indians, who replied, "We are Catholics, and are proud of it."
>
> I was there again last Wednesday. In another week or two, most of the men will be in, after the fruit-picking season. I will get them together here, camp with them a week, have daily Mass and instructions for young and old, and, in the evening, night prayers and instructions. During the day, we shall try to rebuild the chapel. I wish to get all ready for the Sacraments and have the new bishop bless the church and give Confirmation.
>
> Last year I opened in Bakersfield a combination school and chapel for the Mexicans. In June we closed school with seventy-five and expect greater success the coming year. . . . While I am in Bakersfield you need not worry about the religious care of the Indians. These poor people who have been so cruelly scattered plan to return and settle about the chapel if they can get their lands back. They have kept the Faith and love it.

✛FULTON J. SHEEN (1895–1979)

In March of 1945, Archbishop John J. Mitty (1884–1961) asked the Secretary General of the National Catholic Welfare Conference what position the Catholic Church should take regarding the United Nations Conference on International Organizations which was scheduled to convene in San Francisco during the following month.

Though he was known as one of more unconventional figures within the American hierarchy, Mitty had an innate sense of what was demanded of his role as the host archbishop. The sixty-one year old Mitty felt that the occasion needed careful attention and he set out to provide it.

Mitty wanted some sort of religious service either before or during the conference. It was finally decided that a Pontifical High Mass would be celebrated on Sunday, April 29th in Saint Mary's Cathedral at which the colorful Bishop Duane Hunt of Salt Lake City would preach.

Then, Mitty arranged for a "mass meeting" at the San Francisco Civic Auditorium where no less a personage than Msgr. Fulton J. Sheen (1895–1979) was engaged to speak on "The Moral Basis of Peace." Even in his pre-television days, Sheen had a huge following for his dynamic and eloquent preaching. Since 1930, this "microphone of God" had captivated millions of Americans on the weekly "Catholic Hour."

Ever the brilliant popularizer of Catholic philosophy, Sheen presented the overflow audience with his own "five personal amendments" to the Dumbarton Oaks proposals. His talk was treated by the press and public as a formal ecclesial proclamation which, in fact, it was not.

Sheen insisted that a sound moral basis for world peace could only be obtained through creation of an International Bill of Rights, justice as the foundation of peace, U.N. membership for all "law abiding states" (neutrals and former enemies) and a charter that allowed the United Nations to revise unjust treaties.

In good Catholic tradition, Sheen defended the notions of a juridic World Court and a free Poland. In all this he reiterated, in his own spellbinding manner, the National Catholic Welfare Conference's position that the Big Five needed to exhibit purity of motives on each of those points. Although Sheen was technically correct in saying that his was not a formal Catholic position, yet, for anyone who cared it might well have been for that is how it was interpreted by the delegates.

Interestingly, the rumor mill circulated the notion that Pope Pius XII was not overly pleased that Sheen even gave the talk which had apparently not been cleared with the Vatican Secretariate of State. For its part, the National Catholic Welfare Conference was pleased with Mitty and Sheen because they had offered to participate in what was the highly delicate and diplomatically–sensitive gathering and had accurately verbalized objectives long–held by the American hierarchy.

Sheen's address and Mitty's other endeavors were looked upon by experts as among the most valuable contributions of the Catholic Church to the United Nations.

✦THADDEUS SHUBSDA (1925–1991)

Thaddeus Anthony Shubsda was born in Los Angeles, on April 2, 1925, the son of Julius and Mary (Jelski) Shubsda. He attended public schools until 1936, when he enrolled at Our Lady of Lourdes, then under the direction of the Presentation Sisters. Upon graduation from Verdugo Hills High School in Tujunga, in 1939, "Ted" entered Los Angeles College, the preparatory seminary for the Archdiocese of Los Angeles.

Ordained on April 26, 1950, by James Francis Cardinal McIntyre, Father Shubsda offered his first Holy Mass at Our Lady of Bright Mount Parish. After serving as curate at San Antonio de Padua and Saint Vibiana's Cathedral, he was appointed to the Matrimonial Tribunal, where he worked from 1964 to 1968. He was made a monsignor in 1965 by Pope Paul VI.

In 1968, Msgr. Shubsda was named Associate Director of the Propagation of the Faith and, in that capacity, he worked closely with the Holy Childhood Association and the Lay Mission Helpers. For thirty years, Shubsda served as Spiritual director for the Catholic Labor Institute, a group of laymen dedicated to promulgating and teaching the social doctrine of the Church.

Monsignor Shubsda was entrusted with the Parish of Saint Paul in 1971, a position he occupied until 1982. He was appointed Auxiliary Bishop of Los Angeles in 1977 and ordained to the episcopate on February 19th as titular of Trau.

On July 1, 1982, Bishop Thaddeus Shubsda was installed as the fourth Ordinary for the Diocese of Monterey and thereafter carried the message of Christ throughout that 8,475 square mile jurisdiction.

When asked to give his concept of priesthood, back in 1977, Bishop Shubsda replied that it provided him "with a unique opportunity of bringing God's influence, teaching and grace into the lives of people. It is a singular dedication to the service of others."

During the final decade of his life, Bishop Shubsda was active in many aspects of the ministry. His most rewarding experience was that of concelebrating Holy Mass with Pope John Paul II, on the steps of Saint Peter's Basilica, for the beatification of Fray Junípero Serra.

Shubsda returned his princely soul to the Lord on the forty–first anniversary of his ordination. What was said of Blessed Junipero Serra after his demise can be repeated 216 years later: "Looking upon the sorrow caused us by his death, we believe that our hearts should be cheered by the thought that he is now enjoying the sight of the eternal God."

✦PHILLIP FRANCIS STRALING (b. 1933)

The twenty–seventh native Californian named to the episcopate is Phillip Francis Straling. Born to Sylvester and Florence (Robinson) Straling, on April 25, 1933, Phillip was raised in a wholly Catholic atmosphere. As a youngster, he attended daily Mass at Our Lady of Guadalupe Church in the predominantly Hispanic–speaking area of San Bernardino.

During the 1930s, the Stralings owned and operated a poultry farm just outside the city. Later they managed the Oregon Hotel, a rooming house used mostly by local railroad officials. In 1945, the family moved to Colton, where Phillip, his brother, George and two sisters, Mary and Frances, took part in the many parochial activities of Immaculate Conception Parish.

At Newman High School in Fontana, Phillip played on the football team and was active in the Knights of Columbus youth organization known as the Squires. It was during those years that he decided to study for the priesthood. He entered Saint Francis Seminary in 1951 as a candidate for the Diocese of San Diego. While there, and later at Immaculate Heart Seminary, Phillip spent his summer working at Saint Bernardine's Hospital in his native city.

Ordained to the priesthood on March 19, 1959 by Bishop Charles Francis Buddy, Father Straling's first assignment was to Saint George's Parish, Ontario. A short while later, he was named to the administrative staff of Saint John's Academy, where he taught electronics and supervised the athletic program. He was curate at Saint Therese Church, San Diego, between 1960 and 1963. For the next decade, Straling was full–time diocesan chaplain of the Newman Apostolate, as well as campus pastor at San Diego State.

Never one to waste time, he taught at University High School and took graduate courses at the University of San Diego and San Diego State, receiving a Master of Science Degree in Counseling. Later he participated in sessions at the San Antonio based Mexican–American Cultural Center and Rome's Pastoral Institute. In 1972, Bishop Leo T. Maher named Straling director of the diocesan synod, a position in which he was to "facilitate" the drafting of new procedural guidelines in keeping with the suggestions of Vatican Council II. Over the next three years, he traveled over 45,000 miles around the diocese, eliciting grassroots participation from priests, sisters and laity in various synodal programs for renewal.

Father Straling's return to Holy Rosary Church as pastor, in April, 1976, was something of a personal satisfaction. It was there that his parents had been married and there that he had been baptized. And it was a relationship that would be further enhanced a few years later when that church became the first Cathedral for the Diocese of San Bernardino.

Straling was an innovative pastor. In the parochial school, for example, he started a program to make the children aware of the lifestyle, culture and needs of the Third World. In addition to serving as Episcopal Vicar and dean for San Bernardino, Father Straling was elected by his peers as president of the Priests' Senate, a position he occupied from 1976 to 1978.

On July 18, 1978, it was announced that Father Straling had been named by Pope Paul VI to serve as proto Bishop for the newly created Diocese of San Bernardino, a 27,047 square mile district comprising the five deaneries of Ontario, Palm Springs, Riverside, San Bernardino and Victorville. According to a source quoted in the Southern Cross, Straling's selection exemplified an effort by the Church to extend its influence through increased contacts with the community, as well as involvement with socially relevant issues.

Straling received episcopal ordination from the hands of Cardinal Timothy Manning on November 6th. Over 2,700 people crowded into Riverside's Raincross Square to witness the ceremonial inauguration of California's eleventh ecclesial district by the Apostolic Delegate to the United States Archbishop Jean Jadot. Bishop Straling subsequently served as the first Bishop of Reno.

✢JAMES JOSEPH SWEENEY (1898–1968)

James Joseph Sweeney was born in San Francisco, on June 19, 1898, the son of John Joseph and Catherine (McCarrick) Sweeney. He studied for the ministry at Saint Patrick's Seminary, Menlo Park, and was ordained to the priesthood on June 20, 1925, by Archbishop Edward J. Hanna.

In the years between 1925 and 1941, Father Sweeney engaged in pastoral work at various parishes in the Archdiocese of San Francisco. Everywhere he was remembered for his kind and benevolent disposition. On May 20, 1941, Pope Pius XII appointed Father Sweeney to the newly–created Diocese of Honolulu. The ninth native–born Californian named to the bishopric received episcopal ordination on the following June 25th.

The apostolate entrusted to Bishop Sweeney comprised all the Hawaiian Islands, plus the equatorial isles of Palmyra, Washington, Fanning and Christmas. The Catholic population of 85,392 was then being served by seventy–six priests, 253 Sisters and seventy–one brothers. Historically, the diocese can be traced to 1826, when

Pope Leo XII erected the Prefecturate Apostolic of the Sandwich Islands, which he confided to the Congregation of the Sacred Hearts or Picpus Fathers. The area was advanced to vicariate status in 1844.

The 6,449 square mile cluster of islands just within the northern tropic were annexed to the United States in 1898. From that time onwards, the capital was fixed at Honolulu, on the island of Oahu.

Bishop Sweeney was installed as the proto Bishop of Honolulu in the Cathedral of Our Lady of Peace, on September 10, 1941, just a few months before the outbreak of hostilities that inaugurated World War II. During his episcopal tenure, Bishop Sweeney worked diligently to create an indigenous clergy for the diocese. He founded and later expanded Saint Stephen's Seminary, at Kaneohe.

To the ever–increasing number of diocesan priests, Sweeney also added Maryknoll, Marist, Marianist and Sulpician clergymen, many of whom were of Chinese, Japanese and Filipino ancestry. The first native Hawaiian priest became chancellor in 1954.

Bishop Sweeney was also responsible for a phenomenal expansion of the Catholic school system in the scenic Pacific isles. By 1963, the eleven high and twenty–eight elementary schools enrolled more than 40 percent of Hawaii's Catholic youngsters. A diocesan unit of Catholic Charities was established, as well as a host of lay organizations. The fourth San Franciscan to wear the mitre, Bishop Sweeney served at his post until March, 1968, when ill health brought about his retirement. He succumbed shortly thereafter in Saint Mary's Hospital, in his native city.

Bishop Sweeney was eulogized as a "modern–day pioneer for Christ in a faraway apostolate." He was truly that and more.

HERBERT CARDINAL VAUGHAN (1832–1903)

Some of the most vivid accounts of California's early recorded history originated from the diaries and logs of visitors. One such narrative was penned by Father Herbert Vaughan, founder of the Mill Hill Fathers and later Cardinal Archbishop of Westminster.

Herbert Vaughan disembarked at San Francisco on February 1, 1864. The young English–born priest, son of a staunch pre–Reformation Catholic, had come to California to beg funds from the "gold–mad prospectors" to finance an English–speaking religious society for the foreign missions. Despite the "frigid politeness" with which Father Vaughan was received by Joseph Sadoc Alemany, the Archbishop of San Francisco, the future prelate came away from the Bay City filled with respect and admiration for the Dominican archbishop.

In an article subsequently written for the *Dublin*

Review, Father Vaughan described in detail the pitiful circumstances of the archbishop, a man he epitomized as "the city on the hill, the candle placed high upon the candlestick."

> Go, then, up California Street, turn round the cathedral of St. Mary's, and you will enter a miserable, dingy little house. This is the residence of the Archbishop of San Francisco and his clergy, who live with him in a community. To the left are a number of little yards, and the back windows of the houses in which the Chinamen are swarming. Broken pots and pans, old doors, and a yellow compost, window–frames, faggots, remnants of used fireworks, sides of pig glazed and varnished, long strings of meat – God only knows what meat—hanging long to dry, dog kennels, dead cats, dirty linen in heaps, and white and blue cottons drying on lines or lying on rubbish—such is the view to the left.
>
> The odours which exhale from it, who shall describe? A spark would probably set the whole of these premises in a conflagration; and one is tempted to think that even a fire would be a blessing.
>
> To the right, adjoining the cathedral, is the yard where the Catholic boys come out to play, and in this yard stands a little iron or zinc cottage containing two rooms. This is where the archbishop lives, one is his bedroom, the other his office, where secretaries are at work all day.
>
> No man is more poorly lodged in the whole city; and no man preaches the spirit of evangelical poverty, a detachment in the midst of this money–worshipping city, like the Spanish Dominican Archbishop of San Francisco. From ten to one every morning and for two or three hours every evening, his Grace, arrayed in his common white habit, and with his green cord and pectoral cross, receives all who come to consult him, to beg of him, to converse with him, be they who they may—emigrants, servants, merchants, the afflicted, the ruined, the unfortunate.
>
> The example of such a life of disinterested zeal, holy simplicity and poverty, has told upon the inhabitants of San Francisco with an irresistible power. It has been one of the Catholic influences experienced by the Church on the population.

It was Vaughan's belief that Alemany was the motivating force behind the Church's gradually "assimilating into herself the strange mass of the California population." The English cleric felt that under the archbishop's direction, the priests and religious of San Francisco were executing their commission as faithfully as was done "when Peter entered Rome, or Augustine Kent, or Xavier Asia, or Solano the wilds of South America." Concluding his remarks, the future Archbishop of Westminster stated that "Catholicity is in the ascendant, the sects are in the decline, and the battle is between paganism with a mythology of dollars, and the Church of God with her precepts of self–denial and her promises of eternal life."

✛PETER VERDAGUER (1835 –1911)

Father Peter Verdaguer or, *El Padre Pedro*, as he was known to his people, was born at San Pedro de Torello in Catalonia on December 10, 1835. His seminary education, begun at Vich and Barcelona, was completed at Cape Girardeau, Missouri. He was ordained in San Francisco by Bishop Thaddeus Amat for the Diocese of Monterey–Los Angeles on December 12, 1862. The young priest's initial assignment took him to Agua Mansa, where he labored for four years. In 1867, he worked among the 5,000 Cahuilla and Paiute Indians of San Bernardino County.

Bishop Francis Mora brought Father Verdaguer to Los Angeles and the pastorate of the old Plaza church in 1878 and there the Indian missionary quickly won the hearts of the people attached to the Asistencia of Our Lady of the Angels.

In 1889, at the centenary celebration of the nation's oldest ecclesiastical jurisdiction at Baltimore, Archbishop Francis Janssens of New Orleans and his suffragans held a meeting concerning the long vacant Vicariate Apostolic of Brownsville, Texas. Janssens requested Bishop Mora of Monterey–Los Angeles to submit a *terna* of candidates for the Texas jurisdiction. When Mora's vicar general, Father Joachim Adam, declined the position, Father Verdaguer, the second name on the list, was selected. Pope Leo XIII formalized the appointment on July 25, 1 1890, by naming Verdaguer to the titular See of Aulona. The proud and generous parishioners at the *Iglesia de Nuestra Señora de los Angeles* made it financially possible for their pastor to return to Spain for his consecration which took place at Barcelona's ancient Cathedral of Saint Eulalia on November 9, 1890.

Conditions in the Texas vicariate were primitive. Bishop Verdaguer spent three full months of every year traveling among his people dispensing the sacraments. The prelate was fond of telling how, as he approached a mission, a mounted group of cowboys would come out to meet him. A procession would be formed, and when the group was about two miles away from the village, the cowboys would begin to fire their pistols to let people know that the bishop was approaching.

Though there were 100,000 Catholics in his 22,391 square mile vicariate, Bishop Verdaguer had to make numerous appeals for financial assistance to sustain his far–flung jurisdiction. Several of these "begging tours" brought him back to California where he spelled out the needs of Catholics in the extreme southeastern part of Texas.

The prelate was always well received in Los Angeles. Customarily he would acknowledge the generosity of the people by an open letter to *The Tidings*. One letter, rather typical of the others, related his return to Colton, the Agua Mansa of his time. Verdaguer mentioned with sadness discovering only "small piles of adobe and brick rocks, the only marks left of my most dear church and house" which he had erected between 1863 and 1867. The bishop was easily recognized by the residents and the kindly old vicar agreed to preach for them once again, this time in the new church built just outside Colton. So great was the crowd that there was not room for all who came.

Leaving Colton, Verdaguer traveled to Banning and enroute confessed, "many things came to my memory passing that road on the train which I had passed over hundreds of times on horseback when going to say Mass at San Timoteo Canyon, San Jacinto, Cahuilla Valley or on sick calls to all those places."

The letter goes on to tell of his arrival at Banning's Industrial School of Saint Boniface. It must have been a happy event for the Indians to visit with the bishop whom they had not seen for a quarter of a century. The small frame church was jammed the following Sunday when Verdaguer "spoke to them about Our Lady of Guadalupe, the special patroness of the Indians."

Though he was separated from his beloved California during the last twenty–one years of his apostolate, the vicar remained in the memories of the many people whom he had served. Even today, the name of "Father Peter" evokes sentiments of esteem among the city's older generation.

Bishop Verdaguer was plagued with ill health in his final years, though he rarely allowed it to interfere with his duties. In October of 1911, against his physician's advice, he set out on a confirmation tour through the widely scattered mission stations of his vicariate. He never returned, for on the 26th, while enroute by train to Mercedes, from Santa Maria, Texas, Bishop Verdaguer gave back his valiant soul to God.

JEAN MARIE RODRIGUE CARDINAL VIL-LENUEVE (1883–1947)

Statisticians may be interested in knowing that James Francis Cardinal McIntyre was not the first Prince of the Church to die in Los Angeles. That distinction belongs to Jean Marie Rodrigue Cardinal Villenueve, Archbishop of Quebec, who succumbed at Ramona Convent on January 17, 1947.

Born the son of a humble shoemaker at Montreal, on November 2, 1883, Jean Marie joined the Oblates of Mary Immaculate in 1901. After his ordination in 1907, he served as his community's master of novices from 1920 to 1930. Following several years as the proto–bishop of Gravelbourg, Saskatchewan, he was named Archbishop of Quebec, the mother–see of Canada, in the final days of 1931 by Pope Pius XI.

Villenueve launched a broad program of Catholic Action in his area. Active in social movements, especially labor and colonization, he built a new seminary and was instrumental in raising the standards of Catholic education in Canada. He supported his country's participation in World War II, despite wide opposition from the French–speaking populace. He was created a cardinal in 1933.

His Eminence of Quebec was a personal friend of both Pius XI and Pius XII. He also had a close relationship with Winston Churchill and Franklin D. Roosevelt and often served as his country's unofficial representative to other world leaders.

The widely–traveled prelate made his first plane trip in 1944, when he flew overseas to visit Canadian troops serving in Britain, France and Italy. He became enthusiastic about that mode of travel and thereafter often made use of air passage. After the war, Villenueve raised his voice on behalf of stricken Poland and warned about the dangers of communism. He became a champion of the corporalist society as advocated in the papal social encyclicals.

When informed of the cardinal's illness, Archbishop John J. Cantwell visited the ailing Villenueve at Ramona Convent. After receiving news of the cardinal's demise, Cantwell issued a statement which read:

> We of Los Angeles extend our most heartfelt sympathies to the Church in Canada on the occasion of the death of its princely cardinal. In the short days he was among us, he already had symbolized the holiness and dignity of the Church by his gracious presence. We thank God that in His Providence , He called this holy man to his eternal reward from this city of Our Lady of the Angels.

Some 350 school children gathered at All Souls Church in Alhambra to assist at a Requiem Mass offered by Father Peter Hanrahan. His Eminence of Quebec was eulogized as a "pioneer churchman whose imprint was deeply imbedded throughout Canada." The cardinal's remains were then flown to Quebec, where thousands of people jammed into the cathedral for the final obsequies, including W. L. Mackenzie King, the prime minister.

Flags throughout the city and on government buildings were lowered to half mast in memory of the cardinal. Night radio programs were cancelled in favor of special tributes in memory of Villenueve. It was a remarkable show of affection for a man who was popular among peoples of all creeds. James Cardinal McGuigan, Archbishop of Toronto, portrayed Villenueve as "a man of brilliant intellectual gifts, of great personal charm and of the most profound religious character."

✝JOHN J. WARD (b. 1920)

A. SILVER EPISCOPAL ANNIVERSARY

There are certain characteristics endemic to the Southern California landscape: the Dodgers, Disneyland, Forest Lawn, Hollywood and Bishop John J. Ward. Somehow the area wouldn't be the same without them.

As their name implies, the Wards were professional and hereditary bards and their family is perpetuated at Lettermacaward near Glenties. Irish annals indicate that several members of the family achieved fame in their homeland. Among others, Malisa MacAward was Bishop of Clonfert and Hugh Macanward was professor of Theology in the Irish College at Louvain.

The Ward family was also prominently represented in the American struggle for Independence. Records show that Major Edward and Captain James Ward, both born in Ireland, were outstanding patriots in the army of George Washington. John Ward, Bishop of Leavenworth, was descended from a collateral branch of the family.

Born September 28, 1920. the son of Hugh J. and Mary (McHugh) Ward, John attended Holy Cross School and Los Angeles College, before entering Saint John's Seminary in 1940. The last of the priests ordained by Archbishop John J. Cantwell, young Father Ward served as assistant or lived in residence at Saint Vibiana's Cathedral, Saint Hilary (Pico Rivera), Transfiguration, Holy Spirit, Saint Thomas and Saint Ambrose. He also served a brief stint as procurator for Saint John's Seminary and during his time at Camarillo was instrumental in building the rectory for Saint Mary Magdalen's parish.

In 1950, he was sent to study Canon Law at the The Catholic University of America and afterwards was assigned to the archdiocesan matrimonial tribunal. For the next decade, he acted as notary, secretary and vice officialis. He was made a Papal Chamberlain in 1960 by Pope John XXIII.

In October of 1963, Msgr. Ward was informed by the Apostolic Delegate that he had been named Auxiliary Bishop of Los Angeles. His episcopal consecration was conferred by James Francis Cardinal McIntyre on the Feast of Our Lady of Guadalupe.

Ward, the first graduate of Saint John's Seminary raised to the episcopacy, was the fifteenth Californian and the fourth native Angelino to wear the mitre. His was the eighth to take place in Saint Vibiana's Cathedral.

During the next quarter century, Bishop Ward held many positions in the archdiocese. He served as Vicar General, Chancellor, Vicar for Religious, Vicar for Liturgy, Director of the Campaign for Human Development, Spiritual Director for the Saint Vincent de Paul Society and Director for the Cardinal McIntyre Fund for Charity. In 1986, Bishop Ward became Episcopal Vicar for the Region of Our Lady of the Angels.

He carried the shepherd's staff along *El Camino Real* for more years than any other of California's auxiliaries and longer than all but a handful of prelates in the state's ecclesial annals. The imprint of his anointing hand at Confirmation is born by more people than any other bishop in California, with the exception of Timothy Cardinal Manning.

Counting the number of churches, chapels, schools, convents, and halls bearing his episcopal blessing would challenge the most modern of computers. For many years, Ward was the sole auxiliary in what was then the four county archdiocese.

What is perhaps most edifying about his quarter century of service in the nation's largest and busiest ecclesial jurisdiction is the fact that Bishop Ward retained an active role in the parochial ministry. Over and above the obligations of his episcopal office, he remained, by choice, at the pastoral helm of a parish as an involved pastor of souls.

In the evenings and on weekends, parishioners at Saint Timothy's saw their pastor baptizing, hearing confessions, witnessing marriages, preaching, conducting inquiry classes, anointing the sick and caring for the needy. He was anything but an absentee pastor. Bishop

Bishop John J. Ward

Ward's love for his native city and its inhabitants is legendary and he served the local commonwealth in a host of positions. Among the many civic offices held over the years, probably the most rewarding was his long tenure on the board of *El Pueblo de Los Angeles State Historic Park*, a position he filled for both Mayors Sam Yorty and Tom Bradley.

The term "churchman" is one used sparingly. It's a title that has to be earned, it cannot be conferred. It signifies a person who towers above his contemporaries, one who personifies the ideals of the Christian commitment. John J. Ward, longtime and beloved Auxiliary Bishop of Los Angeles, is one of those select persons, a churchman par excellence.

✢JOHN J. WARD (b. 1920)

B. Historical Update

History doesn't stay written very long. New discoveries keep publishers busy issuing revised and updated editions. The wise and prudent writer avoids the use of "definitive" when compiling biographical studies or historical essays. The ultimate story of humankind won't be known until judgement day.

The late Archbishop John J. Mitty of San Francisco, who was never known to scatter around idle compliments, once commended an historical treatise by Father John B. McGloin with these words: "It'll do till something better comes along." Actually that was a rather astute observation.

An example of the ongoing study and revising of the historical record would be the episcopal lineage of Auxiliary Bishop John J. Ward. In 1963, shortly after his episcopal ordination, the bishop asked this writer to compile a list of his apostolic succession, a task that took several months of heavy–duty research. The finalized document, which was submitted to the then recognized authorities in the field, scholars like Joseph B. Code and Francis P. Leipzig, traced Ward's lineage back thirty–six generations, to Pope Gregory XI in 1380. It was a formidable document.

But, alas, now the carefully researched chart has crumbled, due to the recent findings of a new scholar in the field, Charles Bransom who, together with Joseph Sauget, has unearthed evidence hitherto unknown. The apostolic succession to 1666 is correct. But subsequent studies reveal the previously unknown fact that Paluzzo Altieri degli Albertoni was not consecrated by Alexander VII in 1666, but by Ulderico Carpegna. Alexander VII became ill on the morning of the ceremony and was replaced, at the last moment, by Carpegna according to a contemporary account published in the *Gazette de France*.

(There was a parallel occurrence in more recent times. On October 5, 1953, when Walter P. Kellenberg and Edward Dargin were consecrated Auxiliary Bishops of New York, Francis Cardinal Spellman was scheduled as principal consecrator. Shortly before the ceremony, Spellman became indisposed and was replaced by James Francis Cardinal McIntyre of Los Angeles.)

In any event, the succession prior to 1666 must be traced through Carpegna, not Alexander VII. Thus configured, one can only proceed back to 1541, and the consecration of the elusive Scipione Rebiba. It is hypothesized that Rebiba was consecrated by Gianpietro Carafa (later Pope Paul IV), but there is no proof since the diaries of the pontifical masters of ceremonies for 1541 are missing.

What this all means is that the apostolic succession of Bishop John J. Ward can be traced only to 1541, not 1380 as previously indicated. Of course, were one to follow historical "hunches," namely that Rebiba was consecrated by Carafa and Carafa by his uncle, Oliviero, all of which is very logical, he could move back another 147 years to 1452 and Leone Cortese. Unfortunately, historians must favor facts over logic.

Historians, even when writing about such lofty matters as faith and morals, have no valid claim to the infallibility entrusted to the Bishop of Rome and his successors. Nor are historians embarrassed when new discoveries surface to contradict their earlier conclusions. We have not here a perfect science, only one which struggles to do its best with whatever evidence is available.

✢ALOYSIUS J. WILLINGER, C.SS.R. (1886–1973)

The esteemed Jesuit historian, Henry L. Walsh, once observed that "there is an air of nobility in the bishops who were chosen by the Vicar of Christ to rule over California's spiritual destinies. Each and every one of them lived up to St. Paul's requirements, being especially noted for apostolic zeal, for extraordinary charity and self–sacrifice, and for unswerving faithfulness to the duties of his episcopal office." Such an appellation surely applies to Aloysius Joseph Willinger, who looked after the spiritual interests of the People of God in the Diocese of Monterey–Fresno during those tumultuous years between 1946 and 1967.

On July 2, 1911, six years after joining the Redemptorists, the twenty–five year old Willinger was ordained to the priesthood. During most of the ensuing eighteen years he served as a missionary in the Province of San Juan, Puerto Rico, where he was affectionately known as "Padre Luis."

In mid–1929, Father Willinger was named Chief Shepherd at Ponce, a diocese comprising a Catholic population of 774,379. He was advanced to the bishopric on October

28, in Brooklyn's Church of our Lady of Perpetual Help. Among the tireless prelate's activities was the establishment of the Confraternity of Christian Doctrine, for which he prepared and published a highly useful and scholarly Spanish catechism. One observer recalled that Bishop Willinger's thirty years "in the Island of Enchantment were like strands of a net hauling innumerable souls into the rich port of divine grace and peace."

In 1946, Willinger was recalled to the mainland and named Coadjutor Bishop and Apostolic Administrator of the Diocese of Monterey–Fresno, a 43,000 square mile jurisdiction in Central California. There he plunged into the work of building to give present and future Catholics of the diocese a chance to reap the harvest of a sturdy and enduring faith.

With the death of Bishop Philip G. Scher, in January, 1953, Willinger became residential ordinary of the twelve county diocese. He moved through the vast geographical area, expanding educational facilities, building hospitals, organizing C.C.D. centers and establishing lay organizations. His most prized foundation was a preparatory seminary. Throughout his years at Fresno, the Baltimore–born prelate exhibited a special concern for the spiritual and material plight of the large numbers of Mexican–Americans living in the San Joaquin Valley. It was his personal concern that brought about formation of the Guadalupana Society to serve their needs.

The two decades of his service to the People of God in the Diocese on Monterey–Fresno were statistically impressive. Fifty parishes, six high schools, twenty–nine elementary schools and two hospitals were added to serve the Catholic population which, by 1967, was approaching the half million mark. Shortly after returning from the final session of Vatican Council II, Bishop Willinger complied with the conciliar invitation about retirement and, in 1967, was named Titular Bishop of Tiguala. Four years later, on May 24, 1971, the retired Redemptorist prelate observed the sixtieth anniversary of his priestly ordination.

Aloysius Willinger was an episcopal realist—if ever there was one. He recognized that neither bishop nor priest has any basic significance apart from Christ's spirit in the fulfillment of the Church's mission.

KAROL CARDINAL WOJTYLA (b. 1920)

Karol Wojtyla is no stranger to the City of *Nuestra Señora de los Angeles*. Twenty–four years ago, during the United States bicentennial, the then Archbishop of Cracow spent several days in California southland. On August 29, 1976, Cardinal Wojtyla was the principal concelebrant at a Mass offered to commemorate the golden jubilee of Our Lady of the Bright Mount parish.

In his remarks for that occasion, His Eminence recalled how the Polish community had been founded shortly after the turn of the century by Father Jakub Organisciak, pointing out the enormous importance of parochial life in the spiritual well–being of Catholic families. The following day, Cardinal Wojtyla was given an extensive motor tour of the southland which included a visit to Saint Vibiana's Cathedral and Marineland of the Pacific, the world's largest Oceanarium.

During his sojourn to Griffith Park Observatory and Planetarium, in the Hollywood Hills, Cardinal Wojtyla was immensely impressed by the large monument to Father Nicolaus Copernicus (1473–1543), the priest–astronomer who had studied classics and mathematics at Cracow.

Having heard about Jan Styka's portrayal of "The Crucifixion" and wanting to see what is rightly considered the world's most tremendous dramatic religious rendition, Woltyla asked especially that Forest Lawn Memorial Park be placed on his itinerary. Officials there explained to His Eminence how Ignace Paderewski, the Polish musician and statesman, first conceived the notion of capturing on canvas an oil depiction of Christ's sacrifice on the cross.

Jan Styka (1858–1925) took up the idea and made its realization the culminating artistic experience of his life. Since 1951, the rendition of "The Crucifixion" has been admired by millions of people. His Eminence of Cracow was fascinated by the exhibit containing Jan Styka's palette, especially blessed for the project by Pope Leo XIII. A charming picture of Wojtyla is now displayed in the adjoining museum.

Monsignors Thaddeus Shubsda (later Bishop of Monterey) and August Moretti, together with Fathers Jacek Przygoda and Zbigniew Olbrys accompanied the Polish cardinal to several other local sites of spiritual and historical significance during the brief visit which was an extension of a pilgrimage to the International Eucharistic Congress in Philadelphia. That Southern California made a deep impression on Cardinal Wojtyla is obvious from a letter which Pope John Paul II sent to Cardinal Timothy Manning on November 20, 1980, wherein he stated that "it is always a joy to recall my own visit to Los Angeles. How impressed I was by the many monuments to the faith that were planted there and elsewhere along *El Camino Real* by Fray Junípero Serra and his Franciscan collaborators."

The Holy Father went on to say that "it is my hope that this religious tradition of Los Angeles will remain a source of pride and challenge for all the sons and daughters of your city, for all who live within her hospitable boundaries and for all who are chosen to serve her common good." In concluding his personally–signed letter, sent on the occasion of the city's bicentennial, the Pontiff said that "in manifesting my deep interest in the destiny of the entire people whom you serve, I commend your city to the protection of Our Lady of the Angels, and I ask for all its inhabitants the bountiful blessings of God our Father."

✣DOMINIC TANG YEE–MING (1908–1995)

One of the great heroes of the "Silent Church," Archbishop Dominic Tang Yee–Ming, has a claim to inclusion in California's Catholic heritage. The exiled Archbishop of Canton lived in San Francisco during the final months of his life.

Born in Hong Kong on May 13, 1908, the youngest son of Francis Tang Kok and Lucy Lam Ding studied for the priesthood at Saint Joseph Seminary, Macau, and later in Spain as a candidate for the Society of Jesus. Ordained at Shanghai in 1941, the youthful Jesuit spent his earliest priestly years teaching at Catholic colleges and secondary schools. During World War II, Tang was involved in various pursuits, many of them related to the Welfare Relief Association and other organizations established to care for the local Catholic populace.

In November of 1950, Tang was asked if he would serve as Apostolic Administrator for the Diocese of Canton. He was told by his Jesuit superiors that others had refused the appointment from Pope Plus XII, but that he should accept. Tang was consecrated on February 13, 1951. The communist government refused to allow American Bishop, James E. Walsh of Maryknoll, to journey from Shanghai for the ceremony.

Conditions worsened for the Church in China during the Korean War, 1950–1952. A propaganda campaign ensued which encouraged local inhabitants to "Resist America, Help Korea, Protect our Homes and Defend our Country." Officials wanted all outside influences, including the Church, to leave. Among other things, Tang was accused of undermining the government's land reform programs.

The remarkable story of Tang's activities during those tumultuous years in China are told in his memoirs which were published in 1987 under the title *How Inscrutable His Ways!* That book went through three editions and is still available from Condor Production Limited of Hong Kong.

In his memoirs, the bishop recalled the effectiveness of the Legion of Mary during those dark years on the Chinese mainland. Especially was the Legion active in Peking, Canton and Shanghai where Catholics were for-

Bishop Dominic Tang Yee-Ming

bidden to practice their faith publicly. The prelate recalled how the Patriotic Reform Church was established as a counter force to those priests remaining loyal to the Vatican. His many interrogations are catalogued, as well as the causes for his eventual incarceration.

Tang was imprisoned for twenty–two years and it was only in 1980 that he was allowed to journey to Hong Kong for treatment of cancer. The following year he went to Rome where he was enthusiastically welcomed by Pope John Paul II who advanced him to the rank of archbishop of Guangzhou (Canton).

The Holy Father later exempted Tang from the obligation of retiring, allowing him to remain as the shepherd of the Church at Canton. In a letter to Tang, dated May 14, 1991, the Holy Father commended him for his "most courageous witnessing to Jesus Christ." He could only "regard the course of his long and arduous life with similar feelings of fraternal congratulations."

Archbishop Tang took up residence in San Francisco early in 1995 and, on June 27th, while visiting Ignatius Cardinal Kung, Tang died at Stamford, Connecticut, of pneumonia. He was interred at the mission cemetery in San Jose.

III. Laity

ITALIANS IN CALIFORNIA

In very few regions of the United States have Italian activities been so important and successful as on the west coast. From the very earliest explorations up to the present time, Italians as individuals and as a group have consistently shared in the work and sacrifices which made possible the constant growth of the Pacific Coast.

The first Italian to anchor in California waters was probably Captain Allesandro Malaspina, who in the years 1786–1788, made a controversial scientific voyage around the world in the service of Spain. A valiant navigator of Florentine origin, Malaspina (1754–1809) is given recognition for having explored the Pacific Coast in great detail. His reflections were published in 1885. Juan B. Bonifacio was the first Italian colonist. He landed at Monterey, in 1822, where he secured work as a hide and tallow stevedore. Bonifacio became a naturalized Mexican citizen and raised a large family.

The earliest full description of California and its inhabitants written by an Italian, was that of Paolo Emilio Botta, a physician aboard a French vessel commanded by Auguste Duhaut–Cilly. Another early Italian description of California and Oregon was the vivid account of the missionary, Louis Rossi, entitled *Six ans en Amérique Californie et Oregon*, published at Paris, in 1863. Leonardo Barbieri was a highly–talented artist who painted portraits of members attending the state constitutional convention, in 1849. Barbieri's paintings hang in the Monterey Customs House.

King Victor Emmanuel II appointed Leonetto Cipriani the first Sardinian Consul, at San Francisco, in 1850. He it was, in later years, who supposedly offered President Abraham Lincoln a plan to kidnap Confederate General Pierre Beauregard. In 1859, Cipriani's successor, Federico Biesta, inaugurated *L'Eco della Patria*, the first Italian newspaper west of the Mississippi. Biesta estimated that there were 6,000 Italians in California by the 1850s. He remarked that "the Italian population is one of the best, most active and hard–working in California. Strong, industrious, and accustomed to suffering and toil, our nationals tend to their own affairs without taking part in those regrettable disorders that the heterogeneous people of the state give vent to from time to time." He went on to say that "generally, whether in San Francisco or in the interior, the Italians thrive and prosper in their businesses, and there is probably not a village in all California in which Italian business is not well represented, just as there is not a mining district where companies of Italian miners are not noted for their good conduct, their fraternal harmony, and for the energy which they bring to their work."

One of the most successful of the Gold Rush arrivals was Domenico Ghirardelli, who traveled through the Mother Lode mining towns selling chocolate and hard candy. His heirs long continued to operate the Ghirardelli Chocolate Company. Californians especially would endorse the words of President Calvin Coolidge that "Italians have immensely contributed and are still contributing with their skill, with their love for liberty, with their genius for science, arts and humanitarian deeds, to make this country what she is today."

CATHOLIC FOUNDERS OF LOS ANGELES

Romanticists are wont to think that the *Pueblo de Nuestra Señora de los Angeles* was settled by Spanish grandees and *caballeros*, sophisticated descendants of the *conquistadores*. A close look at the record reveals, however, that the original founders or *pobladores* were a motley lot, there was not a full–blooded white family among them, but they were pioneer stock, and, with three exceptions, they stayed and built the town we know today as Los Angeles.

When plans were completed for the envisioned *pueblo*, Fernando de Rivera y Moncada journeyed to Mexico to recruit settlers for the town. There, after a whole year of persuading, he succeeded in interesting only twelve families, or forty–six people and, of that number, only eleven families, or forty–four people, actually made the trek.

The outfitting of the settlers took place at Alamos, a small town on the Mexican mainland not far from the Gulf of California. Seven of the families enlisted at Rosario, three at Sinaloa, and one at Alamos. The small group, accompanied by an army contingent, set out for their new home on February 2, 1781. Though it is not widely known or emphasized, the overwhelming majority of the founders of the *Pueblo de Nuestra Señora de Los Angeles* were Catholics of Negro racial strain.

Of those forty–four *pobladores* ultimately arriving at the projected site, the only people of unmixed Caucasian race in the whole community were two Spanish men. The settlers, who represented a mixture of Indian and Negro with here and there a trace of Spanish, can be broken down into four racial strains:

3 Indian families	8 people
2 Indian–Caucasian families	8 people
4 Negro families	15 people
2 Negro–Caucasian families	13 people

Intermarriage among the Latin American natives and Europeans produced a multitude of castes. Children of an Indian mother (in an Indian–Caucasian union) are considered *mestizos*; whereas those of a Negro mother (in a Negro–Indian union) are classified as *mulattos*. By this enumeration, the forty– four founders of Los Angeles were:

Caucasian	2
Indian	16
Negro	26

Using the hyphenated system for the children of all mixed marriages, the classification would be:

Caucasian	2
Indian	12
Indian–Caucasian	4
Negro	17
Negro–Indian	9

If these statistics prove nothing else, at least they dispel the notion that there were any "blue–blooded Spanish Dons among the Catholics who pioneered the City of Our Lady of the Angels. Quite the contrary is the case for there were more Blacks among the founders of Los Angeles than any other racial group, and a realization of this factor, useful for the social historian confirms that these noble *pobladores* "sprang from hardy stock, and the blood of true pioneers coursed through their veins."

EMERGENCE OF THE CATHOLIC LAYMEN

Visitors to the west often express dismay about the impersonal cordiality existing in the Golden State between clergy and laity. Indeed, the laymen has long since "emerged" in California to take his place as a vital part of the apostolic endeavor. The role of the layman was the subject of a sermon preached by Bishop Thomas J. Conaty at Saint Vibiana's Cathedral on February 10, 1907, to representatives of the American Federation of Catholic Societies.

The Southern California prelate reminded his listeners that throughout history, "the union of the clergy and the laity had been the upbuilding of Christianity and the spreading of the Gospel of Christ." At the same time, he took cognizance of the perils inherent in an indifferent laity such as England had in the Tudor days and France in the pre–Revolution era. While he was no apologist for the crusades, Conaty observed that those who engaged in these campaigns manifested an admirable zeal and love "in answering the appeals of Peter the Hermit and Saint Bernard. . . ."

"An intelligent knowledge of religion, an earnest devotion to truth, a love for the Church and its doctrine, and a willingness on all occasions to teach the truth, is demanded from all our people." The bishop strongly felt the need for a renewal of "the spirit of the ages of Faith, the feeling of a divine calling to be not only members of the Church but also partners and cooperators in every work of the Church."

Conaty spoke of charity and education, of reformation and relief work, and observed that the Catholic layman is called to those activities of religious endeavor just as much as he is to more ordinary Church duties. "The Catholic layman should be found practicing and defending the domestic virtues, an unflinching enemy to divorce, living his life so that all men would find him without fear or reproach; he should be intelligently informed upon principles of government, loyal to the State, incapable of dishonesty and untruthfulness and filled with devotion to civic responsibility." Dwelling upon the obligations of Catholics as loyal citizens, he noted that Catholics should always be model members of society, expressing in their public life the character and goodness of their holy Faith.

Professional men, in Conaty's opinion, should always realize the force of the eternal precepts and the spirit of eternal justice "and should be models of faith, intelligence and probity." Referring to the work done on the national level, the bishop commended the generosity whereby the Church had developed its magnificent cathedral, churches, schools and institutions to answer the demands of mercy and charity.

In a strong plea supporting the Federation of Catholic Societies, the Bishop of Monterey–Los Angeles stressed its effort "to inspire zeal in the work of religion." He urged his congregation to centralize and unify the efforts of the organizations into one well–defined desire to serve the Church, to be its faithful ally in all the works of religion and charity to unite with the good men of all creeds against the evils threatening its very foundations.

Concluding his observations, the prelate said that "the battle cry is for God and country, for home and for the individual, against evil in every form for Christ and His Church, for faith and virtue. The inspiring motive guiding our life work should be to conquer the world for Christ."

MARTIN AGUIRRE (1858–1929)

Martin Aguirre (1858–1929) was one of the last of the old–time California sheriffs. Playing a significant part in the days when Los Angeles was a sleepy little adobe town, he lived on to occupy center stage when the same city became known for its skyscrapers, automobiles and entertainment industry.

In an essay for the *Quarterly of the Historical Society of Southern California*, Margaret Romer said that "the story of Martin Aguirre's life is a Western thriller that sounds, in spots, like fiction, but is actually true."

Born in San Diego, the son of Jose Antonio and Rosario (Eustudillo) Aguirre, Martin grew up within a family who had extensive land holdings between Santa Ana and San Diego, as well as in the San Jacinto area. After his mother's death, Martin moved to the *Pueblo de*

Nuestra Señora de Los Angeles, where he lived with his cousins, the Wolfskills. He subsequently graduated from Saint Vincent's College when that institution was the only one of its kind in the southland.

Martin's earliest employment was as foreman in the Wolfskill Orange Packing Company There, he did everything from picking and crating oranges to selling them at the public market. According to a description in the Los Angeles *Herald* for February 26, 1929, Martin "was not a very large man, but had a fine physique, muscles like iron. He was always very neatly dressed and conducted himself with the manners of a born gentlemen, a credit to his Catholic faith."

In 1885, Martin Aguirre was elected sheriff of Los Angeles County, a position in which he was entrusted with preserving order. Harry Carr recalled that "he had the fighting courage of a bull terrier, the tender sympathies of a lady and a soul unblemished by dishonor." Governor Henry T. Gage named Aguirre warden of San Quentin Penitentiary in 1899. There, under the most unfavorable circumstances, he straightened out the discipline by being strict, but unwaveringly fair.

Returning to Los Angeles a few years later, Martin again affiliated himself with the sheriff's department as Chief Criminal Deputy. He took up permanent residence in a suite of the old Baker Hotel on Main Street. During the flood of the Los Angeles River, in 1886, Aguirre became a local hero by personally riding along Center Street warning inhabitants to abandon their homes. Time and time again, he rode into the roaring flood waters, bringing out survivors. He was credited with saving nineteen lives.

Martin never married. He loved people, enjoyed visiting with them and was a frequent and welcome guest in the homes of his many friends and relatives. He was honorary "uncle" to more youngsters than any of his contemporaries.

In the shadow of the office where he worked for so many years, the one–time constable sheriff and warden died on February 25, 1929. In its story about 'the last old sheriff,' one local paper spoke extensively of how "deeds of valor" marked the "life of this veteran officer who had served the city since adobe days".

The funeral for one of California's most colorful peace officers was held at the Plaza Church of Our Lady of the Angels which Martin had attended most of his life. His body was interred at Calvary Cemetery.

JUAN ALVAREZ (b. 1740)

The desertion of Juan Alvarez from San Gabriel Mission is the story of one man's rebellion against hunger, and his flight into unknown dangers to escape its ener-vating pangs. The account of that event was related by the late Thomas Workman Temple who discovered the original description by José Francisco de Ortega in the *Archivo General de la Nacion*, in Mexico City.

Juan Alvarez was a native of Raun on the Yaqui River, just across the Gulf of California. He had enlisted as a soldier in 1770, at the Royal Presidio of Loreto. Pedro Fages appointed the youthful and robust recruit as a guard at San Gabriel Mission and he was present for the foundation of that mission on September 8, 1771. Those early days at San Gabriel were times of privation, hardship and sacrifice for those attached to the military *presidios* in Alta California.

According to his own testimony, Juan Alvarez was impelled to desert because he was receiving only four ounces of beans as a daily ration, together with one *almud* of corn every nine days. He claimed that those scanty rations weren't enough for him to maintain himself. At dawn on October 1, 1772, Juan stole quietly away from his post. Afoot and unarmed, save for a lance and his leather jacket, Juan made his way from San Gabriel Mission to San Fernando de Velicata, thus covering some 450 miles of forbidding and hostile Indian country.

He followed the first traces of *El Camino Real*, travelling mostly at night to avoid the Indians and soldier couriers. Cleverly he detoured around San Diego Mission to keep from alerting the sentinels there. He stuck to the coast as for as *Bahia de Todos Santos*, subsisting on clams, mussels and the like. More than once he feasted on small abalones pried from the rocks at low tide.

As steep cliffs and estuaries drove him inland from the sea he had to resort to his snares, with little success at best, and the few *arroyos* with running water that cut across his trail furnished their share of berries, cress and wild celery. By the time of his arrival at San Fernando de Velicata, Juan resembled a scarecrow. His gray eyes were glazed with exhaustion, his lips cracked and swollen and a thick shock of black hair and beard covered his dusty, sun–tanned face.

The welcome received by Juan was anything but cordial. He was questioned for long hours and then finally brought to trial for desertion. He was sentenced to six months imprisonment and then ordered back to San Gabriel. The deserter's reputation was later restored. He was wounded during the Indian uprising at San Diego in 1775. The annals relate that in 1790, nearing fifty years of age, Juan was married and living as a *vaquero* at the *Pueblo de Nuestra Señora de los Angeles*.

The desertion of Juan Alvarez is an unheralded escapade of daring and fortitude, unequaled by any other royal soldier in the early annals of Nueva California.

MARIANA ANDRADA (1832–1902)

One of the greatest delusions in the long history of California was perpetrated by Mariana Andrada (1832–1902), a woman of unusual charm and ability. The Mexican–born Mariana claimed to be the widow of the notorious bandit, Joaquin Murrieta, whose escapades along the Gold Rush Trails made him something of a folk hero among the Spanish–speaking population of the Far West.

Mariana claimed to be in contact with the spirit of the deceased Franciscan, Magín Catalá, the famous "Holy Man of Santa Clara." Speaking in the friar's name, she foretold the end of the world and the destruction of all those who refused to accept her preaching. In his published book on the "Prophetess of the Cantua," Raymund F. Wood describes how Mariana's machinations were looked upon in official ecclesiastical circles.

The predominantly "Catholic" overtones of Mariana Andrada's preaching eventually attracted the notice of *The Monitor*, weekly newspaper for the Archdiocese of San Francisco. To a report reprinted from the Fresno *Expositor*, *The Monitor*'s editor stated that if anybody believes in such stories, it only proves the adage which says, "The fools are not all dead yet." Archbishop Joseph Sadoc Alemany apparently read the account and, on May 30, the Dominican expressed himself with devastating thoroughness on the questioned bogus preachers, erroneous predictions and the anomalous position of women preachers. He labeled the whole affair of Mariana Andrada's prophecies as "a fraud, an imposition, and a witchcraft." The archbishop thought it would be desirable for the poor woman to retire to some private place and prepare for a happy death, and thus get rid of false prophets and false practices.

Recalling the Pauline injunction about a woman's role as preacher, Alemany said that it "agrees perfectly with the designs of the Son of God who, although He loved His Blessed Mother more than He ever did, or ever will, love any other of His creatures, yet He did not commission her to preach or to exercise any of the functions of the sacred ministry; but He conferred those offices upon men, who were to be ordained with due powers by the Sacrament of Holy Orders."

The prelate recalled the observation of a theologian who noted that "from the beginning of the world, among the followers of the true religion, never has a woman performed the offices of priesthood, neither Eve nor any of her daughters." For if the function of the priesthood "had been confided to women, to no one should the priestly offices have been entrusted with greater reason than to Mary, upon whom so great an honor was conferred that she was chosen to conceive in her chaste womb the Lord of all things, the God of Heaven, the Son of God."

In view of these remarks, said Archbishop Alemany, "the woman of the San Joaquin mountains ought to take the hint of the Apostle and be ashamed to do what was not confided even to the Mother of God." The strongly–worded exhortation of San Francisco's archbishop seems to have effectively dissipated the influence of Mariana who thereafter gradually withdrew from the public scene. She lived on for some years, until April 12, 1902, when she was killed by the *California Limited*, at a crossing near Kingston.

So died, and so was buried, Mariana Andrada, erstwhile "Prophetess of the Cantua," and self–styled "widow of Joaquin Murietta." No hint of her former claims to fame appeared in the newspaper account of her death. Only an old Mexican woman, probably drunk and partly deranged, instantly killed by a transcontinental train—a sad ending for a woman who once proclaimed herself as the sole salvation of the world!

JUAN BAUTISTA DE ANZA (1735–1788)

Early in 1963, a startling discovery of momentous historical significance was made within the *Catedral de Nuestra Señora de la Asuncion*, in the dusty town of Arizpe, Sonora, Mexico. While making repairs to the floor of the 317 year old cathedral, workmen uncovered the long–lost tomb of Juan Bautista de Anza (1735–c. 1788), founder of the *presidio* and city of San Francisco.

Anza, one of the giants of California's history, was commissioned by Viceroy Antonio Maria Bucareli to develop a plan for opening a land route from northern Sonora to San Gabriel. With thirty men, he and Fray Francisco Garces journeyed across the Colorado desert to the California missions.

In 1775, Juan Bautista de Anza led a party of 240 people, including women and children with cattle and supplies to establish the *presidio* and mission of San Francisco. It was a 1,500 mile trek which changed the whole direction of California's development. Anza was later Military Governor of the Internal Provinces of the West, a territory covering northern Mexico, Arizona, New Mexico, Baja and Alta California. He governed from the town of Arizpe (a name meaning "stinging red ants"). He died there at fifty–three.

There is no extant record of his funeral ceremonies. It was known only that he was interred in the cathedral, an edifice begun in 1646 and finished a century later by Carlos de Rojas, a priest whose name is carved over the central doorway.

The tomb located by workers in 1963 was under the floor of the nave, in an area customarily reserved for the burial of persons of rank. University of California experts sent by Governor Edmund Brown confirmed that the narrow, unmarked coffin contained the skeleton of Juan Bautista de Anza, still clothed in its blue and scarlet military uniform.

Professor Theodore McCown and other anthropologists confirmed that the skeleton satisfied all the necessary requirements. Not only was it attired in the contemporary military uniform, but nearby were two insignia of the Third Order of Saint Francis, a lay brotherhood to which Anza belonged. There was also a remnant of a scapular and rosary on the bony chest area. And around the waist was a cord worn by members of the Third Order, a smaller version of the one used by professed friars.

The church and village have remained practically unchanged in the last hundred years. From a fortress frontier capital of Hispanic North America, it has slid down to a cattle town of 1500 people.

Father Antonio Magallanes, the dark haired priest in charge of the cathedral, said that "the discovery of the mortal remains of this son of the Church is an important event in our peaceful lives. The Church does not need quality for it has the quality of Christ. But this discovery has the added quality of history. It has given us realization that from our humble town came great leaders.

"From here came the *caballero*, Captain Juan Bautista de Anza. He led his colonists—brave with discovery and with their faith firm in our Savior—to found the great San Francisco to the north."

GABRIEL ANTONIO (1750–1890)

Gabriel Antonio, an Indian attached to Mission San Carlos Borromeo enjoys the distinction of being the longest–lived California native on record. In his pre–Christian days, Gabriel lived in the San Jose Creek area. For a while he was married simultaneously to two sisters who bore him four children.

Gabriel claimed to have been present at the arrival of Gaspar de Portolá's expedition at Monterey, in 1769. He remained at Monterey and Carmel, probably carrying stone and mixing mortar during the construction phase of that missionary outpost. In subsequent decades, he was a *vaquero* on the mission's several *ranchos*.

The 607th entry in the Baptismal Register of San Carlos Borromeo Mission carries Father Junípero Serra's notice about Gabriel's christening:

On the seventh of February, 1780 in the church of this Mission of San Carlos de Monterey, I baptized solemnly a male adult of about thirty years or a little more, son of Homobono José named in the preceding entry and the mother who until today was a gentile and was baptized this same day.

He was from the *rancheria* de Ichentra *alias* San José and I gave for his name Gabriel Antonio. His god-father was the master blacksmith Fernando Chamoro of this mission.

Gabriel remained at Carmel until the mid–1850s, when he moved to the Salinas area, finding employment on a host of *ranchos*. His final years of active work were with the family of W. J. Johnson. A newspaper account, published in 1889, reported that the aging Indian had forgotten nearly all the training received at the mission. "The habits and associations of his early savage life survive all he learned," it said.

Gabriel died at the county hospital, in Salinas, on March 16, 1890, at the advanced age of about 140 years old! Though debilitated by bodily ailments and failing memory, the San Francisco *Chronicle* stated, on October 18, 1903, that Gabriel "lived and died a faithful and exemplary Christian." At the behest of Harry Downie, Curator of San Carlos Borromeo Mission, Gabriel Antonio's remains were exhumed, in the early 1960s, and reburied with his ancestors and descendants in the ancient cemetery adjoining Carmel Mission Basilica.

The story of Gabriel recalls a poem written many years ago by John Steven McGroarty:

Green is the way to Monterey,
And once, upon a wandering day,
With breath of mist and flash of sky
My feet were where the green ways lie;
My soul unleashed, my heart at play,
Upon the road to Monterey.

All in the morning's golden glow
I came by holy Carmelo
Where whispers still its silvery stream
Like voices from an ancient dream
And through the haunted silence beat
The long–hushed tread of sandaled feet

Dream–wrapped in memory's mystic spell
I rang the rusted Mission bell,
And called to hill and vale and sea
To give again their dead to me—
The gray–robed priests, the altar lights,
The hosts of dark–eyed neophytes.

ANTONIA (1807–1828)

The conciliar Fathers of Vatican Council II, in the first ever document setting forth official teaching on the lay apostolate, noted that "by performing their ordinary work according to God's will," the laity most assuredly "make progress in the holiness" characteristic of God's people. Though only hinted at in conciliar decrees prior to the 1960s, the notion of the "lay apostolate" has existed in the Church since the days of our Lord in Jerusalem. It is reflected in many of the early patristic writings.

Fray Junípero Serra and the pioneer missionaries who labored along *El Camino Real* were keenly aware of the sanctity inherent in their neophytes. In many of the entries made by the friars in the register books, there is mention of outstanding virtue. An example is that of a neophyte who was born, reared and died at Santa Cruz Mission. She became a role model for her contemporaries and she retains that distinction today. According to entry #1364, Antonia, the two day old daughter of Proyecto and Fabiana was baptized by Fray Andres Quintana on April 4, 1807.

Her whole life was spent within a few miles of the Old Mission and it was there, on April 26, 1821, that she married Severo Usculti de la Ra. de Churissaca. Fray Luis Gil, who witnessed the exchange of vows, noted that "the ceremony was performed at a Mass attended by all the Indian populace." There were two children born to the couple: one in May of 1824 (Maria Magdalena) and the other in April of 1827 (Angela del Ssmo Sacramento).

It was also in 1827 that Santa Cruz became a port–of–entry by order of the President and Congress of the Mexican Republic, an action that permitted foreign vessels to stop there for trading purposes. During the ensuing months, the area's Indians were ravaged by several European diseases, including a virulent strain of measles which devastated the local population.

Antonia responded to the call for volunteers to look after the infirm and eventually she too contracted the dread disease. The *Libro de Difuntos* indicates that she "died of an acute measles with severe chills." When the youthful Antonia was interred in the cemetery at Santa Cruz on April 26, 1828, Fray Luis Gil noted that "as a single person as well as in her married state, she gave splendid testimony of her faith not with extraordinary actions, but fulfilling with exactitude her duties as a virgin and later as a married woman.

"Always modest and quiet, she did not like crowds and mundane diversions but constantly and promptly performed the works assigned to her. She was a young woman who fulfilled the obligations of her state with perfection doing the ordinary and common tasks as best she could for the love of God. She became too good for this world and so she passed to a better life. Such Christians do not die, they are reborn. She received with fervor the sacraments of Penance, Holy Eucharist and Extreme Unction during the three days of her illness and fever."

According to Harry Kelsey, Mead Fellow at the Huntington Library, Antonia, "certainly seems to have lived a saintly life, if the testimony of the *padre* is any guide."

ALPHONSE ANTZCAK (b. 1922)

In 1989, Alphonse Antczak wrote the traditional "30" across his last editorial for *The Tidings*. His long and distinguished career in the public service of the Church faded into retirement.

Born on August 3, 1922, to Frank and Adela (Garcia) Antczak, young Alphonse attended Assumption School in the Polish corridor of Detroit, an institution operated by the Felician Sisters.

Al's father, a native of Poznan, Poland, came to the United States via Ellis Island. His mother, displaced from her home in Central Mexico by revolutionary turmoil, walked across the Rio Grande with her parents, brothers and sisters. A cousin is today the town physician in Jesus Maria, their birthplace in Aguascalientes.

The future editor was brought to Los Angeles in 1931, settling in San Antonio de Padua parish in Boyle Heights. His pastor was Msgr. Leroy Callahan who did much work for Archbishop Cantwell in the growing Mexican parishes of the eastside. After graduation from Loyola High School, Al enrolled as an English major at Loyola University. There he became a protege of the legendary Father Vincent Lloyd–Russell. Al joined the staff of *The Loyolan* and served twice as editor of that college newspaper, before and after World War II.

In 1943, Al enlisted in the United States Army Air Corps, first as a cadet and subsequently as a radio operator. He was on detached service with the Coast Guard for a time to learn airborne LORAN, then a secret navigational system.

Upon his return to Loyola after the war, Al resumed writing for *The Loyolan*. Msgr. Thomas McCarthy, editor of *The Tidings*, was impressed by several of Al's articles about wartime experiences in India and China and offered him a position with the archdiocesan newspaper. On the Monday after his graduation, Al was assigned to a desk at *The Tidings* which was then located at Jefferson and Figueroa Streets. From January of 1947, the imprint of Alphonse Antczak was on no fewer than 2200 weekly issues of *The Tidings*.

During the ensuing forty–two years, Al has witnessed and written about myriads of topics touching upon the Archdiocese of Los Angeles, including the five great western migrations—European displaced persons (late 1940s), easterners (1950s), Cuban refugees (1959), Asian boat people (mid 1970s) and the Central Americans (1980s). He has moved among these new peoples as friend, advocate and chronicler.

In August of 1973, Al became the sixteenth editor of *The Tidings*. During the next sixteen years he continued and expanded the policies of California's oldest Catholic newspaper. He has served as editor longer than any other person in the paper's one hundred plus year history.

During the Antczak years, *The Tidings* operated in the black and continued to help subsidize such projects as the construction of the Education Building, the Catholic Charities headquarters and Santa Marta Hospital. Substantial annual grants were also distributed to numerous inner city parishes during the tenure of post World War II editors, including Antczak.

During the Antczak years *The Tidings* won awards for reporting, editorials and layout. Among those citations, none pleased the editor more than the one given for the paper's editorial support of farm workers at Rancho Sespe in Ventura County.

The personages interviewed by Al over the years reads like a *Who's Who:* They include John Kennedy, General Vernon Walters, President Ramon Magsaysay, King Hussein, Dr. Thomas Dooley, Josef Cardinal Mindszenty, Prime Minister Itzakh Rabin and Karol Cardinal Wojtyla (now Pope John Paul II).

Al has also served as a Los Angeles correspondent for the Catholic News Service and the US Information Agency. His stories for the latter were published in Eastern and Western Europe, Latin America, Asia and particularly, Africa. During these busy years, Al and his wife, Helen, lived quietly in a modest home near San Gabriel Mission. Among their eight PIMA children (Polish–Irish–Mexican–American) is Sister Mary Catherine, director of novices for the Dominican Sisters of Mission San Jose.

During four archbishoprics, Alphonse Antczak was a primary witness and faithful chronicler of the life of the Church in Southern California. He verbalized his role as that of reporting the works of God's people fulfilling their spiritual destiny.

He was for his generation what Matthew, Mark, Luke and John were for theirs. In scriptural terminology, he was an evangelist *par excellence,* an embodiment of the conciliar notion of ecclesial service in California's southland.

MARIA FELICIANA ARBALLO Y GUTIERREZ (ff. 1770s)

The first woman to emerge as an individual in the Far West was Maria Feliciana Arballo y Gutierrez, referred to in the annals as the "merry widow of the Anza colonizing expedition." Little is known about Doña Feliciana's origins. At the youthful age of thirteen, she had married an equally young soldier of the Spanish empire.

Maria and Lieutenant Arballo had two daughters, Tomasa and Eustaquia.

"Dazzled by the promises of the viceroy," the Arballos were among those responding favorably to the invitation issued by Captain Juan Bautista deAnza to accompany his second expedition to Alta California, in 1775–1776. Suddenly, just before their departure, Lieutenant Arballo died. Undaunted, his widow and her two children decided to continue the trek, against the advice of Fray Pedro Font, the official chaplain and chronicler.

Maria and her two daughters were among the 240 men, women and children who left from Culiacan in Sinaloa, on the Mexican mainland. The expedition set out on September 30th. During the long, dangerous, sizzling hot and then freezing cold journey, the widow Arballo delighted and encouraged her fellow colonists, much to the annoyance of Pedro Font.

In his diary, the chaplain complained several times about the "somewhat discordant" and "very bold widow who came with the expedition." He was especially upset at her singing during a *fandango* in the Christmas season. She "sang some verses which were not at all nice," according to Font and, what was worse, she was "applauded and cheered by all the crowd." The next morning at Mass, the friar told his sleepy listeners that "instead of thanking God for having arrived with their lives . . . it appeared that they were making such festivities in honor of the Devil."

Captain Anza later intervened on behalf of Feliciana, explaining that she was a morale builder. (The *fandango* had been celebrated following the safe return of scouts feared lost in a mountain pass). The captain was then lectured on the evils of drinking and dancing. The friar later noted in his diary that his over–reaction may have been occasioned by the "flux" which "kept me very much prostrated."

Doña Feliciana and her two daughters never reached their destination, the shore of San Francisco bay. When the party arrived at San Gabriel Mission, she caused a minor sensation. A young soldier, Juan Francisco López, who had come to California with Fray Junípero Serra, persuaded the lovely widow to remain at San Gabriel as his wife. They were married by Fray Francisco Garces.

Even Pedro Font approved and joined in the week–long *fiesta* that ensued. Doña Feliciana served for a while as overseer for the young girls in the mission's *monjorio* or dormitory. From "the healthy parent tree grew many, flowering branches," according to Susanna Bryant Dakin. Eustaquia married Jose Maria Pico and one of her sons, Pio, became governor of California. One of their grand–daughters, Trinidad Ortega y de la Guerra, was so beautiful that she was known as *"La Primavera."* Modern–day "Spring" Street in Los Angeles is named after her.

In one of her books, Cora Miranda Older wrote that "no woman has so greatly endowed California's beauty and art as this singing, dancing, laughing Maria Feliciana Arballo y Gutierrez who deserted the Anza expedition at San Gabriel to become the wife of Juan Francisco López."

LUIS ANTONIO ARGUELLO (1784–1830)

According to one commentator on the Golden State's history, "The Arguellos of early times and their descendants have been accounted among the first families of California." One member of that outstanding pioneering clan, Luis Antonio, became the first native Californian to serve as governor. This son of Jose Dario Arguello and Maria Ignacio Moraga was born at the *Presidio* of San Francisco on June 21, 1784. Practically his whole life was spent in the military service he first entered in 1799.

Though known as "a dashing soldier, a reckless rider, a gay and handsome *caballero*," Arguello was an eager servant of his country and as *comandante* of San Francisco he became one of the foremost military officers of the province." By 1821, Arguello had also earned a reputation as explorer and it was he who named the Feather River, conferring on that body of water the title of *El Rio de las Plunias*.

The young military officer emerged as a political leader during the early months of Mexican independence. When he took formal possession of the governor's office on November 22, 1822, as "*Jefe Politico*," Spanish rule in California was at an end. During his tenure, Don Luis opened the ports of California to foreigners, thus encouraging trading and commercial relations which greatly enhanced the local economy. Arguello was among the first government officials to welcome settlers to the Pacific coast from the United States.

The governor maintained a close personal friendship with the missionaries though he was not always able to placate them in such matters as taxation. It was out of deference to the friars that he placed a prohibition against the importation of books and papers detrimental to the interests of the Catholic Church. This action he took to protect that faith "which alone leads to the salvation of our souls."

It fell to Arguello to supervise *pueblos*, repair roads, support troops, aid schools and control the Indians. Though he performed these duties well and, in addition, made numerous useful innovations, his regime was never more than provisional, filling in the time until Mexico could appoint a permanent governor for California. The end of Luis Arguello's term, in 1825, marked the conclusion of the so–called "Romantic Period" in Alta California, for the subsequent quarter century was one of constant turmoil, revolution and war.

Despite the fact that Arguello's "sense of justice and fair play and, above all, his election as governor turned many of the less idealistic Californians against him," even his most outspoken critics admitted that he was an honest, able, kind and friendly man. Probably the greatest tragedy of this first "*hijo del pais*" to rule California was that he lived a hundred years too soon. "Colonial California was no place for individuality and independence. Yet his achievement can be rated second to none, and his regime is the one great bright spot in the turbulent history of California under Mexico."

ELIZABETH ARMER (1851–1905)

Elizabeth Armer was born in Sydney, Australia, on April 30, 1851. As a youngster, she accompanied her parents to San Francisco. Following her mother's death, she was raised by Mr. and Mrs. Richard Tobin, a prominent Bay Area family.

Shortly after her eighteenth birthday, Elizabeth went to see Archbishop Joseph Sadoc Alemany about the possibility of entering a Carmelite community in the east. While encouraging her to think about religious life, the kindly Dominican prelate pointed out that there was much work to do at the local level.

At the behest of the archbishop and Father John J. Prendergast, Elizabeth and another young women moved into a rented flat on Pine Street in November, 1872. They were exhorted to devote their time to alleviating the needs of the poor and educating the minds of the young. The two dedicated women launched a program of social relief work that would eventually touch thousands of lives. Each day, Elizabeth and her friend visited the homes of the poor. They found countless cases of pitiful human misery, many of them the direct result of excessive drinking.

They worked long hours and endured endless vexations. Sleep was neglected and food was minimized. Elizabeth's companion fell ill and had to abandon the work. For a while, Mrs. Tobin assisted Elizabeth, her name and status a shield for her foster daughter. In April, 1873, another dedicated young lady, Ellen O'Connor, joined Elizabeth. Gradually, others came and within a few years half a dozen were engaged in laboring among the poor, ignorant and often depressing people of downtown San Francisco.

The archbishop was deeply impressed by the work of the ladies. At his request they began taking care of working mothers in their flat on Pine Street. Following a quasi–novitiate at Benecia's Dominican convent, Archbishop Alemany allowed the ladies to pronounce vows on March 19, 1880. The Holy Family Sisters were a reality and Elizabeth Armer was Mother Dolores.

At the time, the archbishop explained that the mission in her care was always "to be in the home and family, visiting the poor, teaching religion to children, or caring for the children who, without you, would have no care." By the time of Elizabeth's demise, on August 2, 1905, the Sisters had begun their practice of travelling away from their convents to hold classes wherever they could, a custom that began when pastors outside the city asked for assistance.

There still remain areas in the southwest where Holy Family Sisters dispense a kind of "chuck–wagon" Christianity, gathering groups of children together in rural areas where there is no church. They are a familiar sight in cities as well, in urban centers, from Texas to Hawaii, where they go from one school to another during the day, teaching on released time, sometimes to large assemblies.

Since 1959, the headquarters for the Holy Family Sisters has been located at Fremont, California, on land once a part of San Jose Mission. There, in a real way, they are continuing the work began by the missionaries in the provincial era.

DUCHESS D'AVEIRO D'ARCOS Y MAQUEDA (1630–1715)

One of the most influential figures of the late 17th and early 18th centuries was the Duchess d'Aveiro d'Arcos y Maqueda (1630–1715), a woman known for her wealth, influence and piety. The duchess exercised considerable influence at the courts of Madrid, Lisbon and Rome. And she was equally well–received at the headquarters of many religious Orders.

Maria de Guadalupe de Lencestre, as she was known early in life, was the eldest daughter of Jorge de Lencestre and Ana Henriques de Cardenas. She was born on January 11, 1630 in Azeitão, Portugal. By birth a Portuguese of the highest nobility, Maria was also descended from the famous English adventurer, John of Gaunt. She became the sixth Duchess of Aveiro on October 20, 1679.

The duchess was a person of many talents. With her considerable ability, she could read Portuguese, Spanish, French, Italian and Latin. She even had some facility with German, though her only extant writings are in Portuguese. She is also credited with being a painter of some distinction.

In 1665, the duchess married the Spanish duke of Arcos. Thereafter, she resided in and around Madrid. Her husband died in 1693 and the duchess lived on until 1715. She lies buried in the celebrated shrine of Guadalupe in the mountains of Estremadura, Spain. For nearly half a century, the duchess assisted missionaries and encouraged them to write numerous reports and personal letters which despite the ravages of time, still constitute a vast fund of historic, geographic, ethnologic and other scientific data.

She sent missionaries across the oceans, built and maintained seminaries and financed the publishing of learned books on mathematics, theology and natural sciences. Her home in Madrid became the information center for the foreign apostolic work of missionaries from every country of Europe and of the mission areas themselves.

"Mother of the Missions" was not an empty but a well–deserved title. The duchess summed up her ambition in life when she said, in one of her letters, that she hoped to build as many Catholic churches as Elizabeth of England had destroyed or confiscated. One of those who wrote to the duchess frequently from his post in peninsular California was Father Eusebio Kino, the Jesuit missionary described by John Gilmary Shea as "the greatest missionary who laboured in North America."

In 1922, a large portion of the correspondence addressed to the duchess from Kino and others working in Baja California came into the possession of Maggs Brothers, dealers in fine and rare books, prints and autographs. The London–based firm issued a special catalogue (#432) which featured Kino's "discoveries and explorations in California" in a series of thirty–three autograph letters written between 1680 and 1687

At the request of Dr. Herbert Eugene Bolton of Berkeley, the materials offered by Maggs were purchased by the Huntington Library of San Marino for $18,750 or $235 per page. Several years later, Bolton was able to acquire a second lot of the correspondence formerly belonging to the duchess.

FRANK M. BALFOUR (1856–1915)

A glance at the relatively short life of Frank W. Balfour (1856–1915) reveals a man who arose, in a period of only fifteen years, from practical obscurity to widespread esteem as one of Southern California's foremost public figures. Originating in London and educated at Saint Edmund's College, Balfour completed his studies at La Belle, France. Following a short apprenticeship in Hanover Square's Electrical Institute, the young Englishman journeyed to Canada, where he embroiled himself in the perilous speculations of cattle raising.

Local annals record Balfour's name among the thousands of immigrants wandering westward, in the 1880s.

Soon after his arrival in Southern California, "it became the good fortune of the then young city of Pomona to claim and thereafter hold his allegiance as a citizen." Balfour's loyal, energetic and patriotic qualities soon acclimatized themselves to new surroundings and numerous positions of public and private trust were bestowed upon him.

While employed for the firm of James Taylor and Company, Balfour helped to survey much of present–day Pomona, as well as several neighboring towns. His personality forged a vital relationship with the municipal affairs of Pomona and it was his honor, along with fourteen others, to draft that city's charter. Balfour subsequently chaired Pomona's Board of Health and directed its Chamber of Commerce. For several years, before his association with the Southern California Edison Company, Balfour functioned as the city's postmaster.

Apparently it was a rare day that did not see him engaged in some piece of committee work for the betterment of industrial, fraternal, social or political conditions of his fellowmen. Balfour was active in the Knights of Columbus, the Elks, the Fraternal Brotherhood and the Catholic Foresters.

One contemporary observer noted that "the memory of his life, fragrant with nobility of character and rich in achievement, is a solace and an inspiration to all who knew him." Bishop Thomas J. Conaty felt that "the beauty of Frank Balfour's character . . . sprang from his faith in God, his conscience was enlightened by the teachings of his Church and his heart was strengthened by the grace of its sacraments."

In a moving tribute before the Newman Club of Los Angeles, J. Vincent Hannon described Balfour as a most conspicuous figure in his community, as a loving, dutiful husband and father. But first and foremost, Frank W. Balfour was "a practical Catholic. He realized that the Divine Founder of the Church left in the sacraments the means of grace and strength to enable mortal man to live the life of rectitude that would lead him safely to his destined land."

JUAN LORENZO BRUNO BANDINI (1800–1859)

In addition to being a rancher, miner and merchant, Juan Lorenzo Bruno Bandini (1800–1859) probably knew or was related to more of California's early families than any other person. He is best remembered for his political activities, though they formed only a minor part of his career.

A native of Arica, Peru, Juan Lorenzo was characterized by Harris Newmark as "a gentleman typically Californian, warm–hearted, genial and social . . . one who possessed many very estimable qualities which endeared him to all who came within the kindly influence of his nature."

During his early years in California, Bandini lived in San Diego. He moved to *El Pueblo de Nuestra Señora de los Angeles* in 1837, after being appointed administrator of San Gabriel Mission. Soon thereafter, he petitioned for and was granted the *ranchos* of Jurupa and Rincon located along the Santa Ana River. A few years later, he resigned his position at San Gabriel and devoted his efforts to ranching. He was also active in a lumbering enterprise in the San Bernardino Mountains.

When those pursuits eventually proved unsuccessful, Bandini returned to Los Angeles and, in 1843, became a partner in a merchandise business with Abel Stearns, who had married his daugher, Arcadia. In 1844, he served as *sindico* for the city. In the summer of 1845, Juan Lorenzo decided to invest in the copper mines of Peninsular California. There he petitioned Governor Pio Pico for the lands of ex–misson *Nuestra Señora de Guadalupe de Frontera,* about seventy miles south of San Diego.

This once prosperous and impressive foundation had been established by a Dominican friar in 1834. An Indian rebellion had brought about closing of the mission and since that time the fertile valley bad been abandoned.

Bandini constructed his ranch house and corrals, planted orchards, set out vineyards, erected carpenter and blacksmith shops and filled the narrow valley with cattle. In order to facilitate the bringing of supplies and workers to the mines and ranch, Bandini opened the first wagon road into La Frontera, incurring great expenses. This industry on his part furthered the development of that section of Baja California.

During the 1850s Juan Lorenzo suffered the buffetings of misfortune created by the war and gold rush, Indians and outlaws, filibusters and, most deadly of all, the constantly changing political situation in Mexico. Long plagued with poor health, Juan Lorenzo died at Los Angeles on November 4, 1859, His "large and impressive" funeral was conducted by Father Blas Raho at the Old Plaza Church of Our Lady of the Angels, followed by interment in Calvary Cemetery.

Bandini's will, covering four sheets of paper and tied together with a bit of blue cord, sheds considerable light on his Christian demeanor. It was concluded with these words: "I sincerely implore my children to continue in the respect they should have toward religion as Christians, the love that they must have amongst themselves as brothers, that they must avoid all kinds of disputes, that they behave as gentlemen towards all, not to forget that as citizens they have certain obligations to their country."

PHILIP LAURENCE BANNAN (b. 1873)

The man who founded and long guided the Pacific Gear and Tool Works was an outstanding Catholic, a respected citizen and a trusted friend who contributed mightily to the mechanical history of California. Philip Laurence Bannan was born on February 26, 1873, at San Francisco. He went to Columbia Grammar School and then, as was customary in those days, he entered apprenticeship in the Van Drake Machine Works.

In 1892, Philip enlisted in the California National Guard where he was assigned to Company "B," First Infantry. He served there with distinction and was discharged with the rank of sergeant in 1901. The previous year he attained the rank of captain in Company "C" of the First Regiment, League of the Cross Cadets. On April 22nd of that year, he was presented with a sword by fellow members for his tireless devotion to the League and its objectives.

It was also in 1900 that Philip married Teresa Kelly. The uniting of the Bannan and Kelly families elicited the following observation: "Two family systems far removed from each other both geographically and by time, yet similar in achievement, are the Rothchilds of Europe and the Mitsuis of Japan."

The Bannan household on Bartlett Street near 23rd could have been a model for others. There were never any histrionics, no display of nerves; no outbreaks of temper. Philip and Teresa taught their ten children habits of studiousness, gave them every opportunity for development and saw them all through college.

Early in life, Philip became a machinist and rather soon thereafter he decided to make that work his permanent vocation. Eventually he became foreman, then partner and finally owner of the business. During the devastating fire that swept San Francisco after the earthquake, he managed to save only a small drill press. Yet, Philip always felt that the 1906 tragedy was a blessing in disguise. "After the fire," he said, "the realization came that an act of God or of nature can wipe out all the efforts of a human being." From that time onward, Philip always had his priorities straight.

Immediately, he began anew. In the first carload of machinery arriving at San Francisco there came the tools necessary to start again. The business thrived and Philip was subsequently able to establish plants in Seattle and Los Angeles, thereby laying the foundation for his family—opportunity and outlet for his sons and associates.

In 1939, Philip L. Bannan was feted on the occasion of the fiftieth anniversary of entry into business with a public tribute by San Francisco's leading figures. A memorial book was printed for the occasion by Samuel P. Johnston, Edwin E. Wachtler and Joseph Duries. Mayor Angelo J. Rossi noted that "a city does not grow by itself; it grows and becomes great through the character and industry and ability of its citizens. To establish, develop and expand an industry so that it serves business throughout all the Western States, to provide through the years employment, to spread the good name of San Francisco throughout the west, and all these things through the efforts of one man is an accomplishment" worthy of special note.

ELLEN CATHERINE BARRETT (1922–1965)

Though it came into history as "the most outlandish place in the world," the peninsula of Baja California is surely destined one day to be among the garden spots of planet earth.

The title of "Her Ladyship of Baja California" rightfully belongs to Ellen Catherine Barrett (1922–1965), whose monumental works of research and scholarship stimulated a whole new generation of peninsular enthusiasts. A native of Ilene, Minnesota, the first of four daughters born to Anthony and Lucille Barrett, Ellen received her earliest education at Immaculate Conception School, Watertown, South Dakota. Upon graduating from that city's secondary facility, she entered Saint Catherine's College, in Saint Paul, Minnesota.

Shortly after receiving her Bachelor's degree in Library Science, Miss Barrett joined her family in Redondo Beach, California. She became affiliated with the Los Angeles Public Library system, in 1945, and served in the children's section at various branch libraries. During most of her twenty years at the L.A.P.L., Miss Barrett worked in the Genealogy and Local History Department. A prodigious researcher, Ellen compiled numerous "house bibliographies" of the library's genealogical holdings, many of which have become standard reference tools for those attached to the staff.

She also sponsored many public and private exhibits and displays of rare books, early manuscripts, heraldic art and fine bindings. Interested also in geology and mineralogy, Ellen was instrumental in the organization of the South Bay Lapidary and Mineral Society. Paramount among Miss Barrett's many interests was that "thorny heap of stones" known in historical annals as Baja California. She traveled extensively in the peninsula, from the tip of Cape San Lucas to the American border.

In 1956, after seven years of exhaustive research, Miss Barrett published the initial volume of her monumental *Baja California 1737–1976. A Bibliography of Historical, Geographical and Scientific Literature Relating to the Peninsula of Baja California and to the Adjacent Islands in the Gulf of California and the Pacific Ocean.* Therein she enumerated, described and often located 2,873 books, pamphlets and periodicals on what had hitherto been a barren bibliographical area. Printed by Paul Bailey at Westernlore Press for Bennett and Marshall, the book was widely praised by reviewers and won a coveted "award for fine topography coupled with excellence of content."

The second volume of Miss Barrett's bibliography, published posthumously under the watchful eye of her sister, Mary, expanded the earlier coverage to 4,838 items. Included in the latter book was an exceedingly useful chronological index for the whole treatise. Though Ellen Barrett's interests were not restricted to Baja California, it is there that she made her greatest contribution and earned her most lasting acclaim. Her bibliographical works are indeed a "monument more lasting than bronze."

Despite the fact that her last years were plagued by illness, Ellen continued her practice of attending daily Mass whenever possible. She once remarked to this writer that her faith had been strengthened and perfected in the crucible of suffering. Ellen Catherine Barrett became an outstanding Catholic laywoman in her relatively short lifespan. Surely future generations of scholars will be indebted to "Her Ladyship of Baja California" for her contributions to the commonweal.

ROGER BAUDIER (1893–1960)

The reputation of Roger Baudier (1893–1960) among this country's Catholic historians has long been held in high esteem. Born and raised in New Orleans, Baudier's writings about the Church in that area of the Lord's vineyard are as interesting as they are informative.

Baudier's magnum opus was his classic book about *The Catholic Church in Louisiana,* wherein he brought together and arranged an overwhelming number of facts from long–forgotten manuscripts, ecclesial registers, civil records, books, periodicals and newspapers. In a review of Baudier's book, Michael J. Curley noted that "if all the dioceses in America had the ground equally well prepared, the longsought day when the writers of American Church history will give us a general history of the Church in the United States would be immeasurably hastened."

Only recently did this writer discover that there was a California chapter to Roger Baudier's busy life. The following observations are taken from an unpublished manuscript by Dr. Charles Nolan, archivist for the Archdiocese of New Orleans.

Baudier first came to California in the summer of 1909 as a clerical candidate at Saint Anthony's College in Santa Barbara. He quickly adapted to the regimented life there and later recalled his seminary years as generally pleasant ones.

A gifted student, Roger sang in the choir, played the cello in the seminary band and became proficient in his writing skills. The German Franciscans created a demanding, stern but not oppressive atmosphere for study, prayer and play. The youthful Creole, a superior student, remained at Saint Anthony's until 1913, when he decided against pursuing a priestly vocation. He left Santa Barbara with a sound liberal arts and religious education that provided the foundation for his future literary, journalistic and historical endeavors.

After a brief stint in New Orleans, Baudier returned to California where he joined the teaching staff at Saint Francis Orphanage Asylum in Watsonville, a position he occupied for five years. His professional duties spanned all grade levels and subjects. He taught spelling, composition, reading, grammar, arithmetic, geography, history and catechism to grades two through eight.

In 1918, Roger joined the armed forces and was initially attached to the Presidio in San Francisco. By the time he was ready for combat in Europe, World War I was over. And, unhappily in the meantime, the orphanage administration had changed and there was no place for him at Watsonville. He returned to New Orleans where he married Mary Mabel Demarest and began his family.

Throughout his life, Baudier retained a great affection for the Franciscans and he often spoke with respect about the sound education he had received from them. He was later instrumental in having a statue of a friar included in a piece of art designed by Angela Gregory for the Union Station in New Orleans. He saw that opportunity as a means of partially repaying "the Franciscans for what they have done for me principally, my education."

Beyond his formal education, Baudier also absorbed a bit of the Franciscan spirit. He had no interest in accumulating earthly treasures and a close friend once said that "he did not work for money. He had a faith in the future. He just wanted enough to see that his family was taken care of and a little left over to help other family members in need."

HENRY WARD BEECHER (1813–1887)

The Reverend Henry Ward Beecher (1813–1887) was one of the most powerful and convincing speakers of the nation. From the pulpit of Plymouth Congregational Church, Beecher championed a host of reforms, including temperance and related measures. He was an outspoken proponent of women's suffrage.

Beecher was not a theologian in any sense and his influence rested on a total abstinence from credal logic. A popular lecturer and after–dinner speaker, he was forever perpetrating indiscretions in speech, to the delight of his enemies and the discomfort of his friends.

In June of 1878, at the behest of Tom Maguire, the "Napoleon of the Stage," Dr. Beecher came to California, where he gave a series of lectures. The editor of *The Monitor*, who considered himself "no admirer of Mr. Beecher," did feel obliged to reproduce several of Beecher's observations for his readership. The editor noted that "to us it seems that his parting words enunciated a truth well worthy of the most serious consideration, and we would be glad if those to whom they were addressed would ponder on them and fully realize their meaning."

He went on to say that Beecher's words "were not spoken lightly, but in all seriousness, and it would seem as if he desired that these, his last utterances, should make an indelible impression." Here is what the popular speaker and religious leader said:

> May I say that among the virtues for which California is conspicuous, I have not learned that church–going is the most eminent. May I whisper to you that which has been whispered to me: that the leading men and most active men of California don't care about religion and that the leaders of the East all wilt away when they come to the atmosphere of California.
>
> Now it is not part of my professional doctrine that I am about to develop; I leave the whole relations of religion to the future and the superior world out of the question; but this I say, no property is safe and no city is safe unless somewhere or other there is an educated conscience among the common people.
>
> You cannot afford to say to the great mass of men in whose hands are your mansions, your funds, banks and stores, you cannot afford to say to them, substantially: 'There is no God to think about, no future you need to dread, and no duties the priest of the Church need teach you.'
>
> I tell you unless there is a conscience, unless men are instructed in equity, in justice, in relation to right and wrong, in relation to property, and in all the fruits of civilization, unless the voting men are instructed somewhere and somehow in these things, you are standing where Sodom and Gomorrah stood; and if there should come up flames from beneath to burn your dwellings, you may thank yourselves for it.
>
> You have neglected the means of instruction of the conscience of the common people, and if there were nothing else than mutual insurance and property insurance, I say you must reconsider such an example, build churches, procure moral teachers, train in sound and moral instruction the great mass of men, and their conscience will be your shield and will supplant the torch of passion.

The editor of *The Monitor* pointed out to his readers that "this is Catholic doctrine." And so for at least once, Henry Ward Beecher was in perfect accord with the teaching of Peter, the Prince of the Apostles.

KATHERINE BELL (1844–1926)

Katherine Bell, the daughter of Nicholas A Den, was fond of recalling that she arrived on the scene when California was in the pastoral phase of its development. Shortly after her birth, the Mexican flag was lowered over the Pacific Slope and in its place was hoisted the banner of the stars and stripes.

Born in one of Santa Barbara's old adobes, on July 22, 1844, Katherine grew into womanhood in the Channel City. There she married and raised her family and there she died on June 9, 1926, within the sound of the very bells that rang out the day of her birth.

She was part of the life known only to the pioneers. Her education came not alone from books, but also from her association with those who directed the forces of the state and who, in a short half century, brought California from a wilderness into a prominent position among the galaxy of states.

According to the Santa Barbara *Daily News*, Katherine "was recognized as an authority on the history of Santa Barbara County and its early–day families." That same account went on to say that "probably no other person knew the history of the county and of its early families as did Mrs. Bell, who was reared in an atmosphere created by its traditions and, as a child, absorbed its history and romance."

Katherine played a unique role in the gradual development of the area. "Her active mind and her unusual literary genius made her a most interesting writer and companion." The eminent California historian, Zoeth S. Eldredge, was known to consult frequently with Mrs. Bell about the events and dates associated with the early days of Santa Barbara.

Katherine's husband, John, was a prominent landowner in the area. He was a native of Tahiti, where his father operated a large sugar plantation. While Herman Melville was writing *Moby Dick*, he met the Bells and later devoted a chapter to Katherine in which he recalled that once, "taking a pensive afternoon stroll along one of the many bridle–paths which wind among the shady groves in the neighborhood of Taloo, I was startled by a sunny apparition. It was that of a beautiful young Englishwoman, charmingly dressed, and mounted upon a spirited little white pony: she was the wife of Mr. Bell (happy dog!), the proprietor of the sugar plantation." He concluded by characterizing Katherine as "the most beautiful white woman I ever saw in Polynesia."

During her busy lifetime, Katherine wrote often for the Santa Barbara *Morning Press* and *The Grizzly Bear*, the official organ for the Native Sons and Native Daughters of the Golden West. In those essays she described the events of her time in a charming style that endeared her to all of California.

In 1931, the Bell family published Katherine's "Reminiscences of Old Santa Barbara" under the title *Swinging the Censer*. This they did "not only as an affectionate tribute to her memory, but also as a contribution to the historical archives of California." Her chapter on "A Miraculous Saint's Adventure" is a classical portrayal of Francis of Assisi.

Katherine Bell belonged to the generation that inspired Mark Twain, Francis Bret Harte and other writers who brought renown to California. As Charles S. Storke observed, Kate never made a profession of literature "but her recollections attracted attention among those who appreciated good writing."

HILAIRE BELLOC (1870–1953)

The recent acquisition by Boston College of the library and papers of the late Hilaire Belloc (1870–1953) recalls the association that outstanding man of letters had with California. Belloc was born of a French father and an English mother. He studied under John Henry Newman, served in the French artillery and published more than 150 books in such varied fields as history, warfare, economics, satire, racialism, apologetics and topography.

A journalist for fifty years, he was widely traveled in Europe, North America and Africa. He was considered the most prominent Catholic layman in England during the first half of this century. The *Encyclopedia Britannica* refers to him as "one of the masters of modern English prose, a good poet . . . a deeply interesting literary personality, (and) among the most versatile of English writers."

Belloc was also a contributor to the Boston *Pilot*, where his byline appeared as recently as 1980, when the paper published his examination of Puritanism in its centennial number. As a young man, Belloc made two visits to California. In fact, on June 15, 1896, he married, while at Napa, Elodie Hogan. Father Maurice Slattery was the priestly witness for the nuptials.

His second son, Hilary, settled in San Francisco and wed a distant cousin, Hope Barnett, there. According to a local paper, Hilary died in San Francisco on October 12, 1977, at the age of seventy–four.

During one of his sojourns to the Pacific Coast, Belloc had a long visit with Father John Moclair. In later years, the two became close friends and exchanged numerous letters. The extensive Belloc materials now at Boston College include hundreds of boxes, filing cabinets and 10,000 volumes which span more than half a century in the life of the famed poet, essayist, historian and apologist.

Among the correspondence are letters to and from George Bernard Shaw, H.G. Wells, Arnold Bennett, Msgr. Ronald Knox, Frank and Maisie Sheed, W.B. Yeats, John Galsworthy, Desire Cardinal Mercier, David Lloyd–George and other luminaries in the worlds of politics, literature and the Church.

Of special interest in this category is a fair copy (a neat and exact version of a corrected manuscript) of Belloc's Path to Rome in his own hand. Also included are his verses in rough copy, drawings, a film script, several "meditative pieces," and a 10,000 word autobiography that has never been published.

Miscellaneous papers include Belloc's parliamentary speeches, family photographs, diaries and engagement books (1891–1939), original source materials, drawings by his children, catalogues of books and the like. As soon as the vast assortment of materials has been properly readied for research, scholars will begin poring over the fascinating life of Hilaire Belloc. And when that time comes, California will surely be a beneficiary of the process.

ALBERT MAURICE BENDER (1866–1941)

A prominent member of Ireland's diplomat corps recalled that Albert Maurice Bender (1866–1941) "always had his hand in his pocket to help needy friends. No struggling artist whoever approached him was left unaided." Such generosity explains why, in later years, very few of Bender's purchases of pictures, sculpture, books or manuscripts were made solely on the grounds of merit. The young son of Philip Bender and Augusta Bremer sailed into the San Francisco Bay, in 1883, where he began his climb to financial independence as a messenger for an insurance firm.

In his adopted country Bender gained a reputation for unfailingly esteeming everything even remotely related to Saint Patrick's Isle. Each year, on the 17th of March, he would gather a host of friends—artists, poets and musicians for a "birthday" party, explaining that "in our youth St. Patrick and I were cronies in Dublin and we agreed to share birthdays." The occasion for Bender was as good as any for bestowing hospitality to his many friends.

Bender's natural business ability and personal charm led him quickly along the road to success. He could easily have amassed a considerable fortune had he been less inclined to philanthropy. He devoted a major portion of his time, enthusiasm and income to a variety of religious, cultural and civic activities. Few citizens exercised a broader influence or were more closely identified with a greater number of the Bay City's constructive enterprises. There was hardly "any San Francisco organization devoted to artistic or scholarly or humanitarian ends that did not have his enthusiastic and generous support."

The "Patron Saint of the City's Artists," as Bender was "canonized" by the San Francisco *Examiner*, was "endlessly generous in his support and encouragement of writers and makers of books." A desire to share with others his interest in the masterpieces of book production led him to present important collections of fine printings, bindings, manuscripts and rare editions to such institutions as Mills College, San Francisco Public Library, Stanford University, the Library of Congress and the University of California. Bender also founded and equipped the Anne Bremer Memorial Library and the Robinson Jeffers Collection at Occidental College. Dublin's National Museum has a "Bender Room" completely devoted to items presented by its San Francisco benefactor.

The personal element was always evident in Bender's manifold collections. One contemporary observed that "in all fields of art, it is the producer rather than the product that mainly interests him." George West paid the ultimate tribute to the Irish–born philanthropist by noting that Albert Maurice Bender was that rare patron who stood always "modest and generous in the presence of another's achievements." Such would be virtuous in any man, but overly so in one with a true understanding of what it means to be creative.

JOHN JOSEPH BERGIN (1859–1912)

John Joseph Bergin (1859–1912) was "an ideal Catholic gentleman, and a figure that stood out most prominently for real worth" in the annals of California's southland. A native of Talladega, Alabama, John was one of seven youngsters born to John Albert Bergin and Mary Elizabeth Cameron. At the age of eleven, he accompanied his parents to Texas, where he learned the delicate trade of cutting, finishing, lettering and sculpturing marble and granite. The business he set up at Cleburne was an outgrowth of his widely recognized artistic talents.

Bergin journeyed westward, in 1886, as an associate of a soap manufacturing concern operated by an uncle. In 1891, he acquired full ownership of the Los Angeles Soap Company, a firm that subsequently developed into the largest west of the Mississippi River. While conservative in his business judgment, Bergin was progressive to the needs of his trade. His factory was the first industrial or commercial enterprise in Southern California to use steam–machinery.

Bergin "was one of those who believed in Catholic men devoting themselves to Catholic endeavor." From his earliest days in California, he played a pivotal role in the activities of the Young Men's Institute. He was also involved in the establishment of the Newman Club, and when the Knights of Columbus was organized, he became a charter member.

As a citizen, Bergin "fully appreciated his duties and was never too busy to discharge its attendant functions," and although "much occupied and constantly engrossed in matters" involving grave responsibilities, he nevertheless found time to faithfully execute such commissions as various civic, commercial, and fraternal organizations from time to time called upon him to attend to."

Bergin devoted a number of years to the Chamber of Commerce and the Merchants and Manufacturers Association. Generous man that he was, he also served Bishop Thomas J. Conaty as a director of the Tidings Publishing Company. In the performance of these various functions, Isidore Dockweiler recalled that Bergin "was genial and always interesting and at all times evidenced an intense interest in the advancement and success of his own people."

As a Catholic, John Bergin "always was a practical son of Holy Church, tenacious in his religious beliefs and unafraid to publicly put them in practice, and glad at all times to bear his burden in the support of the Church and its charities." In a tribute presented to his widow, Julia Frances Bergin, the membership of the Newman Club most appropriately referred to John Bergin "as a man, good and true, of repute unblemished and character unsullied."

RICHARD KEYS BIGGS (1866–1962)

Many priests like to think they were "liturgically aware" thirty–five years ago, at a time when congregational participation was considerably less than popular with the general Catholic populace. At Saint Brendan Church, for example, Father Thomas F. Fogarty and Bob Mitchell introduced community chanting of *tenebrae* (in English!) in the late 1940s, much to the chagrin of many neighboring pastors, clergy and laity. And it must have been successful too, for the church was packed, a major feat for Holy Week even then.

One of the most *avantgarde* champions of that "new feeling" for the liturgy was Richard Keys Biggs, for over thirty years the organist–choirmaster at Blessed Sacrament Church in Hollywood. A favorite activity of young seminarians in those days was a bus trip to hear Father Cornelius J. McCoy chant a Solemn High Mass with Dr. Biggs at the organ and his wife, Lucienne, leading the choir.

Those who watched, listened to and knew Richard Keys Biggs could only be captivated by his ability to play the four–decked console at Blessed Sacrament, all the while massaging the pedals of the giant organ with the ease of a logger. He liked to tell how his public career began almost by accident. One day, while attending the Presbyterian Church in Glendale, Ohio, the organist collapsed during the service. Twelve year old Biggs jumped onto the bench and continued the accompaniment without interruption.

His musical pedigree was indeed impressive and included the Cincinnati College of Music, the University of Michigan and Westminster Cathedral Choral School in England. By age twenty–two, Biggs had published his first organ composition. In the early teens of the century, he began touring the nation giving recitals. In 1915, he visited thirty–five states and was featured soloist at the San Diego Exposition and the San Francisco World's Fair. He made the first organ recording ever for Victor the following year.

Subsequently, he was organist and choirmaster at Saint Luke's Episcopal Church in Brooklyn, music director at the Madison Avenue Temple and teacher in the public and private schools of New York City.

Richard served his country in World War I and while in France met Lucienne Gourdon who would become his wife and the mother of his eleven children. He was received into the Catholic Church while on duty in Brittany. After the war, Richard studied musicology at the Abbey of Solesmes and it was there that he acquired his love and mastery of Gregorian Chant and the Church's liturgy.

While residing in Montreal, Richard learned that the position of organist at Blessed Sacrament Church in Hollywood was open. In 1928, he took the position and this began the California phase of his busy life. The talents of Richard Keys Biggs were not restricted to Hollywood. He trained and directed choirs in Westwood and Alhambra, even finding time to inaugurate choral groups at Loyola University, Mount Saint Mary's, Marymount and Immaculate Heart colleges. Biggs wrote numerous compositions, including fifteen Masses. Probably one of his most widely acclaimed Masses was that dedicated to Fray Junípero Serra (1937), whom Biggs called the "Pioneer of the Faith and Builder of the Civilization in California."

By the time of his demise in 1962, Richard Key Biggs had been honored by his country (Victory Medal–United States Navy), commended by his Church (*Pro Ecclesia et Pontifice* medal–Pope Plus XII) and acclaimed by his profession (Doctorate in Laws–Loyola University).

WINIFRED BLACK (1863–1936)

Relatively few people alive today will recall that "Annie Laurie," the beloved newspaper columnist for the San Francisco *Examiner*, was a Catholic and an outstanding one at that.

Born Winifred Black at Chilton, Wisconsin in 1863, she had printer's ink in her blood. Her earliest journalistic pursuits were accomplished as a member of the staff for the Chicago *Tribune*.

During her long career, Winifred covered national political conventions, the Washington disarmament conference and the peace negotiations at Paris. She was among the first reporters to reach Galveston after the disastrous floods in that coastal city.

In 1906, while riding on a streetcar in Denver, she saw a newspaper headline announcing the "destruction" of San Francisco. She burst into tears and hurried to her office. There she found a telegram from William Randolph Hearst. It contained only one word: "GO."

After coming to the West Coast and marrying Charles Bonfils, Winifred began writing under her by–line "Annie Laurie." With that pseudonym, she became one of the greatest crusaders of her day. The poor, oppressed and helpless invariably found her a true friend and champion. The cause of the suffering and needy always elicited her sympathy and assistance. She organized the first community Christmas tree in the Bay Area; took up the cause of the lepers of Molokai and exposed the wretched conditions of child labor in the cotton mills of the south.

In a rare glimpse into her personal life, Winifred once wrote: "I am not a sob sister or a specialty writer. I'm just a plain, practical, all–around newspaperwoman. That's my profession and that is my pride. I'd rather smell the printer's ink and hear the thundering presses than attend the greatest of operas."

In addition to her numerous newspaper commitments, "Annie Laurie" wrote several books. One of the most memorable was *The Little Boy* (1895) which told the story of her son who had drowned while swimming at Carmel. She also published a collection of stories under the title *Roses and Rain*.

Annie Laurie's career ended at her simple home beside the Golden Gate on May 25, 1936. She died as she would have wanted, still turning out a daily column for the Hearst newspapers. Mayor Angelo J. Rossi appointed a committee to arrange formal civic honors for "one of the city's most distinguished citizens." A public service was held in the rotunda of San Francisco's City Hall. Around the bier were thousands of flowers from people in all walks of life. The Municipal Orchestra provided the music.

Flags were lowered to half–staff over municipal buildings and the city mourned "the loss of a beloved daughter." According to one newspaper account, "it was a beautifully simple service, with friendship and love as the theme of each speaker."

In his eulogy, the mayor said that "the pen of Annie

Laurie had never been dipped in hatred or bitterness, except when turned on injustice or cruelty. Faithful, kindly, loving and benevolent, she was justly looked upon as one of the most outstanding women ever to have graced the life of our great city."

Her funeral liturgy was held the next day at Saint Mary's Cathedral. Msgr. Charles A. Ramm, a lifelong friend, celebrated the Mass and preached the homily. Annie Laurie was interred at Holy Cross Cemetery alongside her two sons.

JOHN J. BODKIN (1841–1918)

John J. Bodkin, the eleventh of fifteen children, was born at Tuam, County Galway, Ireland, on November 25, 1841. He came to the United States in 1867, and took a teaching position at Saint Genevieve, Missouri. In 1869, he moved to Texas where he taught in "the first Catholic school in the City of Dallas, the school being conducted in the pastoral residence, a small four room cottage." Shortly thereafter he married Marian O'Brennan in the Cathedral at Saint Louis. It was during his years in Texas that Bodkin edited the *Dallas Free Press*.

Bodkin came to the Golden State in July of 1875, and the next year was followed by his wife and two children, Elizabeth and Thomas. The family first took up residence in San Gabriel. In subsequent years Bodkin lived and taught in public schools in that city and various parts of Los Angeles County. The next five Bodkin children were born in California. During his early years on the west coast, Bodkin traveled in the interest of securing subscriptions and advertising for the *California Catholic*. When financial conditions forced the newspaper into bankruptcy, Bodkin resumed his teaching career in the Los Angeles County Public School system.

Early in 1898, the Right Reverend George T. Montgomery, Bishop of Monterey–Los Angeles, asked Bodkin to become associated with *The Tidings*, offering to personally underwrite his investment in that struggling journal. Bodkin complied and by the end of the year had purchased full control of the paper from its founder, Patrick W. Croake. Before the passage of many months, the new editor had enlarged the paper and the number of its readers was "greater and its influence wider than any other weekly paper published in this section." There was nothing pretentious about the journal in those years. It was "put to bed" and printed in a small press room in the basement of the Y.M.C.A. at Second and Broadway.

Bodkin was keenly aware that "the support which a newspaper receives determines its quality" and he took considerable care to emphasize that *The Tidings* was not a political sheet nor a partisan organ, for "while the editor has his own political convictions, and pronounced ones at that, he does not consider the columns of *The Tidings* the place to ventilate them." It was Bodkin's opinion that "the chief value of a Catholic paper lies in its treatment of local topics," and he resisted several suggestions about enlarging the journal, feeling that "its small size is one of the chief recommendations of *The Tidings*.'

Late in 1904, Bishop Thomas J. Conaty purchased the paper as the official Catholic Publication of the Diocese of Monterey–Los Angeles. As his final issue drew near, Bodkin remarked with justifiable pride that "there is not a city in the country where Catholics and their religion are more respected or where the entire secular press is more favorably disposed towards our people." After his retirement from journalism, Bodkin devoted full attention to the religious goods store which he had opened in December of 1899. When death finally claimed the pioneering editor, on January 25, 1918, one of his contemporaries noted:

> There have been wiser and abler men in the world than our old–time confrere, John Bodkin, but there have been few more sincere, when embarked on a worthy cause!

HERBERT EUGENE BOLTON (1870–1953)

A. HISTORIAN OF BORDERLANDS

Herbert Eugene Bolton, the Historian of the Borderlands, "became one of the most productive scholars of the century and the ablest interpreter of the essential unity of the peoples of the American nations." From the very day of his birth in Wilton, Wisconsin, on July 20, 1870, Herbert Bolton had attachments to California. He never tired of telling about his ancestor, Charles (alias Black Bart), reportedly the most publicized highwayman of Gold Rush Days.

Bolton came to California in 1909, to accept a professorship at Stanford. Two years later he transferred to the University of California at Berkeley where, in and out of retirement, he remained until 1944. From 1916 onwards, he was Curator and Director of the Bancroft Library. In addition to the thirty volumes and scores of learned articles and papers written in his decades at Berkeley, Bolton's legendary lectures on the "History of the Americas" attracted more than a thousand students bi–weekly for over a quarter century.

Bolton viewed the whole Western Hemisphere as having a common trend of development. The syllabus for his seminar came to be known as "The Bible," and in it Bolton outlined the factors common to all regions of the hemisphere, such as explorations, conquest, planting of western culture, colonial growth, and the international rivalries which eventually led to wars for independence. This idea of unity in the midst of the diversity in the

American continent was formalized in Bolton's famous essay, delivered at Toronto in 1932 on "The Epic of Greater America." Never politically minded, however, Bolton was not a Pan Americanist and his students represent today the most disinterested and permanent aspects of this nation's Good Neighbor Policy.

Aside from his chosen field of history, Herbert Eugene Bolton made important contributions to anthropology, sociology, cartography and to the general knowledge of America. One authority has rightly noted that "an appreciable part of our present historical knowledge of North America, west of the 100th meridian and south of the 40th parallel, is available because of discoveries, translations and publications directly resulting from the work of Herbert Eugene Bolton."

Though he remained a Methodist throughout his life, many of Bolton's writings contributed immeasurably to the appreciation of the Catholic Church's role in the early development of the southwest. Archbishop Edward J. Hanna of San Francisco once told Berkeley's famous historian: "Bolton, you darned old heretic, if I should say as good things about the Catholics as you do, nobody would believe me." To this Bolton replied, "Right you are, archbishop, they would think you prejudiced."

Among Bolton's many writings is a four volume set of Palou's *Relacion Historica,* the best biography of Junípero Serra done prior to the 1950s. It was also Bolton's privilege to be among the three–member committee that arranged to place Serra's statue in the national capitol's Hall of Fame. In later years, the Berkeley historian served on the Historical Commission for the beatification cause of California's Grey Ox.

On January 30, 1953, the Dean of American Historians, full of years, achievements, honors and service went home to God. To his students who remain to perpetuate the Bolton approach to history, Samuel Eliot Morison said: "A historical career can be a great adventure, and not in ideas alone; witness the life of Bolton, a man who wrote history that sings to the heart while it informs the understanding."

HERBERT EUGENE BOLTON (1870–1953)

B. Gentleman Scholar

Dr. Herbert Eugene Bolton (1870–1953), longtime chairman of the History Department at the University of California, Berkeley, was not a Catholic. But he did more than any other person, then and now, to popularize the work of the Franciscan missionaries in California.

He was truly a remarkable man, eminent as archaeologist, well–known as an ethnologist and distinguished as an explorer and cartographer. A writer in the November,

1928 issue of *Touring Topics* referred to Bolton as one "to whom America is more indebted, perhaps, than any other man, for his labors unlocking the hidden history of the southwest."

Initially drawn to the study of law, Bolton made the acquaintance of the legendary Frederick J. Turner and from that moment onwards turned his attention to the southwest and west. Where others found only interminable miles, Bolton discovered an enchanted kingdom.

In the borderlands of Texas, Dr. Bolton retraced the journeys of the Spanish missionaries as they blazed the trails of Christian civilization and carried the culture of Europe in their "splendid wayfaring." He saw the pageantry of it all and he witnessed the buried centuries stir and come to life again with miraculous vividness. Here was a land awaiting a necromancer for its recovered yesterdays.

Bolton searched the archives of the New World for the countless documents, official papers, personal records and diaries dating back more than 200 years. "My quest has been as romantic as the search for the Golden Fleece," he once admitted. And he wasn't far wrong.

Bolton lived with the *padres* in crumbling monasteries and in remote mountain villages, poring over diaries found in closets and attics that had not seen the light of day for a hundred years. Finishing with Eusebio Kino and others, Bolton turned his energies westward, where he chronicled, in his four volume *New California*, the history of the Spanish province and its missions. Somehow, he managed to find time to serve first as curator and then as director of the Bancroft Library.

Bolton paved the way for future historians and that is perhaps even more important than the litany of books he wrote or edited. Throughout his long career, he was always the critical scholar, the gentle teacher and the patient innovator. He said it right, he said it well. The initials H. E. B. came to be regarded as the *nil obstat* for western Americana scholarship.

Never an apologist, Bolton believed that the feats of the pioneers stood on their own merits. He didn't try to popularize such people as Fray Junípero Serra or Fray Juan Crespi—he merely recorded their accomplishments. Nothing else was necessary. Those trained by Bolton at Stanford and Berkeley formed the most vigorous group of historians in the country's annals. The writings of the so–called "Bolton School" will remain always a tribute to this man of genius.

The historical accuracy of Bolton's writings and explorations has stood the test of the decades. In an era of revisionist historians, the name of Herbert Eugene Bolton stands tall. He was, after all, the first and greatest of the revisionists. When once asked if he thought

Bolton would oneday become a Catholic, Archbishop Edward J. Hanna said: "I hope not. He does more outside the Church to vindicate the work of the missionaries than he could ever do within. I have no doubts that God made special provisions for the likes of Herbert Eugene Bolton."

CHESLEY K. BONESTELL (1888–1986)

During his long lifetime, Chesley K. Bonestell (1888–1986) was considered one of the world's greatest space artists. He was also an architect and astronomer whose paintings of the California missions are in a class all by themselves.

In the 1940s, Bonestell illustrated science fiction novels and crafted precision scale drawings based on his imagination and.the best scientific information available. In addition to his impressions of outer space, Mr. Bonestell left his imprint on the Monterey Peninsula through his design of the road system of Del Monte Forest, in 1916, and on many buildings in the San Francisco Bay area.

He chose the color scheme and the original gold curtain for the War Memorial Opera House in San Francisco where the United Nations was organized. His considerable design talents are memorialized in such national edifices as the Supreme Court building (Washington, D.C.), the Chrysler Building (New York City) and the Plymouth Rock Memorial (Massachusetts).

Among the projects on which Bonestell was an architect are the buildings at the California Institute of Technology in Pasadena and the Golden Gate Bridge, for which he made perspective drawings of the inner–workings. In 1938, Bonestell came to Hollywood where he began work in the motion picture industry as a matte artist, producing backgrounds and special effects. Among the pictures he worked on are "Citizen Kane," "War of the Worlds," "The Hunchback of Notre Dame" and "When Worlds Collide."

During the 1940s, he began devoting full time to space art, illustrating magazine articles, advertisements and books. He collaborated with scientist Wernher von Braun and Willy Ley.

Bonestell provided both the public and science with some of the first images of the solar system. He received numerous awards for his work and, in 1986, had the distinction of having asteroid #317–9 named after himself.

But Bonestell was not confined to the stars. He had a lifelong interest in the California missions. He worked up a series of paintings showing the missions as they were thought to have appeared in the days of their greatest glory. In 1974, his paintings were published by Chronicle Books of San Francisco. Entitled *The Golden Era of the Missions 1769–1834*, the text was written by Paul Johnson.

Johnson tells how Bonestell developed the graphic evidence of earlier artists, some of it written and some of it on–site visual evidence. From construction logs, or *fabricas*, came dimensions, material specifications and quantities and even a few plot plans.

Further descriptive clues were provided by the journals of ships' captains, overland travelers and early settlers. On–site archaeological evidence—foundations, cemeteries, handcraft detritus—and structural members in the restored buildings provided further supportive data. From these varied resources, Bonestell developed his graphic interpretations. Once finished, he checked his paintings with such authorities as Harry Downie of Carmel.

As an artist who specialized in creating scenes of the unknown from scraps of the known, a specialty light years away from the California missions, Bonestell came up with a remarkable collection of interpretative paintings.

JOHN EDWARD BOREIN (1872–1945)

Among the treasures at the Archival Center, Archdiocese of Los Angeles, is the book press that once belonged to Ed Borein (1872–1945) the "Cow–puncher artist" whose portrayals of western scenes have become classics. (John) Edward Borein was born on October 21,1872, at San Leandro, California, a "cow town" then located on the main trail between the South and the stockyards of Emeryville.

From his earliest years, Borein was fascinated by the colorful parade of longhorn steers, sombreroed *vaqueros* and skittering steeds that daily moved through his area. The youthful artist spent long hours sketching those colorful scenes. After leaving San Leandro, in 1893, Borein found work at various ranches as he drifted southward, leaving a trail of sketches on assorted bunkhouse walls and in numerous personal notebooks. His journey through Mexico gave him an acquaintance with all facets of ranching.

For some years, Borein worked in the Bay Area as staff artist for the San Francisco *Call*. Later he went to New York, where he met and befriended such personages as Charles Russell, Will Rogers and Teddy Roosevelt. It was in New York that Ed Borein gained full stature as an artist. One of his mentors, Edwin Emerson, noted that "for every horse this artist has drawn or painted, he has ridden a hundred; and for every long–horned steer depicted by him he has punched, or roped or branded a thousand. When he draws the picture of a saddle or a bridle or a lasso, he knows, more inti-

John Edward Borein

mately than any other artist could, just what he is draw-ing, knows, for he himself, in his day, has made saddles and bridles and lassoes with his own hands."

Borein made a good living illustrating ads for Stetson Hats, Pierce–Arrow autombiles and other national prod-ucts. The poster advertising the first Calgary Stampede, in 1912, is considered among Borein's most noteworthy works.

Borein returned to the west in 1919. He married Lucille Maxwell and established his home in Santa Bar-bara. His studio in *El Paseo* became a haunt for famous people and a refuge for struggling artists. During his res-idency in the Channel City, Borein became a close friend of Father Zephyrin Engelhardt (1851–1934), the "Dean" of California mission historians. Nine of Engel-hardt's volumes are enhanced by the etchings of Ed Bor-ein. Of Borein's four etched views of Santa Barbara Mission, the 1921 version is probably the best, inasmuch as it captures most perfectly the majestic lines of the old buildings.

In 1971, (John) Edward Borein was posthumously elected to the Hall of Westerners at Cowboy Hall of

Fame in Oklahoma City. That distinction was indeed appropriate in view of the artist's remark of forty years earlier that "I will leave only an accurate history of the West, nothing else but that. If anything isn't authentic, just right, I won't put it in any of my work."

The Borein press in the Historical Museum of the Archival Center was purchased from the artist's estate by Colonel Edmund Sayer in 1953. Following Sayer's demise it passed to an heir who subsequently sold it to a "Mr. Gross." Whitney Genns, a respected bookdealer in Santa Barbara, bought the press in 1963 and he, in turn, passed it on to John Swingle. It was the late Peg Christ-ian who entrusted it to the Archival Center in March of 1984.

ETHEL BOSSERT (f.f. 1930s–1980s)

The Feast of Our Lady of the Angels in the year of the Lord, 1986, richly deserves to be remembered by the Catholics of Southern California. For on that day, Ethel Bossert closed out a sixty year career of uninterrupted service to the Church of Los Angeles, a record unparalleled in the Golden State's religious annals.

A private person to the very last of her days in the Chancery Office, Ethel confided very little for the public record. This much we know—that she was born in Los Angeles, at the old Clara Barton Hospital. She and her brother attended elementary school in Ocean Park.

Her first contact with the Catholic Church came during her teen years as a student at Saint Mary's Commercial School in Boyle Heights. Shortly after her conversion, Ethel became a member of the first class at Conaty (Catholic Girls) High School. In 1926, after completing her education at Venice High, Ethel took a "temporary" position with Steve Sullivan, who was spearheading the drive to raise funds for Los Angeles College, the preparatory seminary for the Diocese of Los Angeles–San Diego.

She was assigned a desk in the chancery, which was then located in the Higgins Building, at 108 West Second Street, across from Saint Vibiana's Cathedral. When the drive was finished, Bishop John J. Cantwell invited Ethel to join Mary Sinclair and Pat Powers on the permanent curial staff. Though she worked at numerous tasks in the next six decades, Ethel was associated mostly with the chancellors of the diocese, including such outstanding churchmen as Bernard J. Dolan, Joseph T McGucken, Alden J. Bell and Benjamin G. Hawkes.

In the spring of 1932, when the diocesan offices were relocated, Ethel took up her work on the seventh floor of the then new Petroleum Securities Building, on West Olympic Boulevard at Figueroa. She recalls the ever-gracious Carrie Estelle Doheny insisting that she and Mary Sinclair take their meals with the staff of the Doheny Oil Company on another floor of the building.

The chancery was relocated in August of 1951, this time to 1531 West Ninth Street and there Ethel rounded out her service to the Archdiocese of Los Angeles. She alone has the distinction of having worked for all four of the southland's archbishops!

While researching an article for the golden jubilee of the archdiocese, we noticed that the earliest letters relating to that epochal event bear the initial "b," an indication that they were typed by Ethel Bossert who, in 1936, had already logged ten years of service to God's people!

Though her mark remains on tens of thousands of letters, reports, memoranda and journals, Ethel always preferred to work behind the scenes. Only once did she emerge from the shadows, and that time by obedience. It was January, 1929, and she appeared with Bishop Cantwell in a photograph published in the Los Angeles *Times*. The late Monsignor John J. Devlin, for whom Ethel worked in her earliest days at the chancery, once remarked that she was "the most professional, qualified and loyal person" he had known in all his long and distinguished ministry.

That testimony, made a quarter century earlier, was echoed by Cardinal Timothy Manning who said that "for half a century and a decade more, Ethel Bossert served the Church in Los Angeles in a manner unique among its hand-maidens. She was intimate to all the doings that were transacted at the headquarters of the Church. In that capacity she preserved a confidentiality that made her a treasured person. No one's light will ever shine brighter."

ELIZABETH BOUMAN (1843–1901)

If the accomplishments of so relatively few of California's religious women are recorded in the public annals, it is because the very nature of their sacred calling longs for the anonymity proclaimed in the Gospels. Occasionally, however, the force of circumstances penetrates that cloak of secrecy. One such case was that of Sister Elizabeth of Saint Celestine, whose fame was established long before she entered the darkened corridors of religious life.

Elizabeth Bouman was born at Amsterdam, Holland on November 3, 1843. Her mother was descended from the famous family which numbered among its members the saintly Clement Mary Hoffbauer. In 1849, the young girl was brought by her parents to the Pacific Coast via Cape Horn. After a brief respite in San Francisco, the Boumans settled in the quiet and picturesque town of Marysville.

Two decades later, Elizabeth married Charles T. Carvalho, a former officer for the United States Diplomatic Corps. Charles was a well-known and respected Chinese interpreter who had spent many years at Consulates in Hong Kong and Canton. Interestingly enough, Charles was a direct descendant of Sebastian Joseph Carvalho, the Marques of Pombal, Prime Minister of Portugal, the great archenemy of the Jesuits.

During the decade of their married life, the Carvalhos had a large family, three of whom lived to adulthood. Elizabeth endeavored to instill her children with a truly virtuous Christian lifestyle, one patterned after her patroness, Saint Elizabeth of Hungary. Amelia, the eldest of the children, joined the Presentation Sisters and lived until 1882. Her two brothers became Jesuits and were prominent in the educational apostolate for the Society of Jesus. Charles taught at Santa Clara College during his brief priestly career before his death in 1881. Xavier, the longest-lived of the Carvalho children, taught for many years at Saint Ignatius College, San Francisco.

A fervent and practical Catholic, Elizabeth Carvalho

became one of the first zealous members of the Ladies Sodality, an organization established by Father Marashi. Following the demise of her husband, on January 29, 1870, Elizabeth petitioned for admittance into religious life. Commenting about this phase of her life, a journalist observed that "this valiant woman entered among God's hidden saints by becoming a Sister of Notre Dame." Her final twenty years formed the capstone of her busy and useful life.

Sister Elizabeth of Saint Celestine succumbed at the College of Notre Dame, Marysville, on September 11, 1901. It was reported by a local newspaper that she crowned "a selfless life, by a serene and saintly death." Archbishop Patrick W. Riordan paid Sister Elizabeth the greatest compliment when he noted, at her passing, that she had "indeed succeeded to and passed on the traditions of holiness inherited from the Hoffbauer."

MARIA ELIZABETH BOYLE (1847–1933)

Maria Elizabeth Boyle was born in New Orleans on March 18, 1847. After the premature death of her mother, Maria lived with an aunt while her father journeyed to Los Angeles. In later life, Maria recounted how, as she was nearing her eighth birthday, Andrew made arrangements for his daughter and her aunt to come to Southern California.

"How well I remember that journey. We sailed from New Orleans and across the Gulf of Mexico. Then we crossed the Isthmus where the Panama canal now is, in a covered wagon similar to those used to cross the plains of this country. On the Pacific side we embarked on the famous old sailing ship, the *Sierra Nevada*, and sailed up the coast to California in a journey that took well over a month."

In an interview later given to a southland newspaper, Maria told how "her father purchased acreage east of the Los Angeles River in the vicinity of what is now Boyle avenue and East Fourth Street. "Along the river, on both banks, were luxuriant vineyards of the famous Mission grapes, planted by the *padres* who settled this country two centuries before. These were later destroyed when buildings were erected."

Maria Elizabeth Boyle attended the school then operated by the Daughters of Charity at Macy and Alameda streets. During the week she stayed with her aunt, who lived at Alameda and Aliso streets because the journey from her home to the school was "too hard to make daily."

At that time, "there were no bridges over the river and you could only cross where it was shallow enough to ford." One Christmas, Maria recalled, "daddy and I were to go to my aunt's for dinner. That Christmas eve we had

a torrential rain and the river was so swollen in the morning that we could not get across. "So father sent word to my aunt by one of our Indians who swam the raging stream with the message and then swam back with a goodly portion of the Christmas dinner tied on a large, light board."

Later, Andrew Boyle was among those instrumental in getting the first bridge built over the river. The old Macy street bridge was covered and allowed people to cross in inclement weather.

Maria liked to tell about "the religious processions of early days, when priests marched around the Plaza on saints' days, bearing aloft the sacred images, followed by altar boys and worshippers of the old Plaza church." She also told of the fiestas held in the same place, when music, dancing, feasting and love–making held sway.

In one of the first "society weddings" in Los Angeles, Maria married William H. Workman in 1867. Then a rising young business man of the city, William had been a member of the historic "California Grays," home guards of the Civil War. He later served as Mayor of Los Angeles in 1887 and 1888. Maria recalled how she was courted. "He took me horse–back riding on Sundays, to the old San Gabriel Mission, which was an all–day outing in those days. And during our rides, he told me the things girls have been hearing from their beaux since Eve's time."

Maria Workman lived a long life during which she witnessed the growth of Los Angeles from a little Spanish–speaking pueblo into a great world metropolis. She died on October 14, 1933.

MARY BOYLE (1885–1964)

Mary Boyle deserves a place among those whose total lives were devoted to the service of the Church in California. Because her life was so hidden, this will probably be the only memorial she will ever have.

Born to James and Mary (Hurley) Boyle at Saint Louis, Missouri, Mary was baptized at Saint Malachy's Church by Father C. Ziegler on September 27, 1885. In November of 1917, shortly after coming to the west coast and just a month before the arrival of the newly–appointed Bishop of Monterey–Los Angeles, Mary became the housekeeper at the old episcopal residence at 717 South Burlington Avenue.

She continued in that position when the residence was moved to the King Gillette Mansion at #100 Fremont Place in 1927. For almost a half century, forty–seven years to be exact, Mary Boyle looked after the episcopal residence and those who lived there. Whether it was a banquet for thirty–five visitors or a simple breakfast for the archbishop, Mary was always the gracious and efficient host who made guests and residents alike feel at home.

Mary catered especially to seminarians and her oatmeal cookies were a favorite with several generations of seminarians who came to serve Holy Mass each day in the archbishop's chapel. There was always a modest gift for the servers at Christmas–time and more often than not it was something she had been given by the archbishop. She was fond of "recycling," to the extent that there was nothing left of her earthly possessions when her life was over.

To Archbishop John J. Cantwell, Mary Boyle was as important to the operations of the archdiocese as the Vicar General. He once wrote on her birthday card: "To Mary, one of the brightest treasures of the local Church. I thank the Lord every day for your selfless service and dedication." On those rare days when there was no liturgy offered in the chapel at Fremont Place, Mary would take the Wilshire bus to La Brea and then walk south three blocks to Cathedral Chapel for the 6:30 a.m. Mass.

When I visited her in 1964 at Santa Teresita Hospital in Duarte, shortly after her leg had been amputated, she showed me an envelope which contained her "most valued possession." It was a note on monogrammed stationery which read: "Thank you, Mary, for your gracious care of this humble pilgrim." It was signed "Eugenio Cardinal Pacelli." The future Pope Plus XII had been a house guest at Fremont Place in October, 1936.

Miss Boyle was proud of her calling. She had business cards printed with her name and the words "Archbishop's Housekeeper" embossed in bold letters. To her, housekeeping was a ministry and she performed it well.

In his reflections, Timothy Cardinal Manning said that "God is not so concerned about what a person does for a living, but how well she or he does it." By that yardstick, Mary Boyle was an outstanding, even heroic practitioner of virtue. She did everything well because, to her, "housekeeping was a vocation of service for the Lord."

James Francis Cardinal McIntyre was with Mary when she died at Santa Teresita Hospital on October 24, 1964. Her funeral was conducted at Cathedral Chapel. In his homily, Msgr. Benjamin G. Hawkes said that "Mary resembled her namesake in Holy Scripture–always busy about the needs of others, little concerned for her own comfort."

JACOB N. BOWMAN (1875–1968)

One of the great benefactors of California mission studies is Jacob N. Bowman (1875–1968), a singular type of scholar and author whose contributions are still very much in demand. Born on May 4, 1875, in a log cabin near Greenville, Ohio, he graduated from Heidelberg College at Tiffin and completed his studies in Germany, the mecca of most of the ambitious students of his generation.

He sat at the feet of famous historians at the Universities of Heidelberg, Leipzig and Berlin. His doctoral dissertationon "The Protestant Interest in Cromwell's Foreign Policy" brought him a fellowship in the Royal Historical Society of Great Britain.

Shortly after the turn of the century, Dr. Bowman associated himself with the Pacific Coast as professor of European and Medieval history at the Universities of California and Washington. A professional free–lance writer, historian of the state archives at Sacramento, Bowman's chief interest was the Bancroft Library and scholars today find a rich harvest of printed, typed and manuscript studies on file there.

In 1957, Bowman made an etymological study of "The Names of the California Missions" for the *Quarterly* of the Historical Society of Southern California. The next year he published his findings on "The Resident neophytes (*Existentes*) of the California Missions, 1769–1834."

Then, two years later, there was Bowman's work on "The Comenzada Dates of the California Missions," followed by his highly informative analysis on "The Number of California Indians Baptized During the Mission Period." The next year, Bowman catalogued "The Parochial Books of the California Missions." This was an excellent article which also located the various *registros* used on California's frontier.

His last two publications on the subject were "The Birthdays of the California Missions" and "The Names of the California Missions" both of which studies revealed many hitherto unknown factors about the outposts along California's *El Camino Real*.

Though he was not a Catholic, Dr. Bowman had a very deep understanding of the Church's role and objectives among the native peoples of California. His writings are a lasting tribute to the spiritual accomplishments in what was then the Rim of Christendom.

In a letter to this writer, Dr. Bowman said that "I always love studying about the missions because they reflect so intimately the love held by the friars for their people." Alert to the very end of his ninety–three years, Bowman was ever ready to assist younger scholars with his wide knowledge. To them and others he remains a symbol of diligence, steadfastness and devotion to a field in which he was a master.

One of Bowman's last honors was the bestowal of the Centennial Award "for distinguished achievements and notable service" to the University of California at Berkeley. It was an appropriate recognition because with his passing, the last eyewitness to the group of scholars who were originally responsible for the acquisition and development of the Bancroft Library was removed from the scene.

JOSEPH BREEN (1888–1965)

With the passing of Joseph Breen, on December 5, 1965, several newspapers around the world reported the death of Hollywood's long–time movie "censor." Though he was an acknowledged journalist, story–teller, dramatist, one who could see ideas, actions, and words in terms of the screen, Breen was certainly not, in any sense, a "censor," for no one did more than he to keep the motion picture screen free. Throughout his years as director of the Motion Picture Association of America's Production Code, Breen's chief "aim was to persuade producers to keep off the screen material which might lower the moral level of the spectators."

Joseph Ignatius Breen, "the conscience of Hollywood," was born in Philadelphia on October 14, 1888. After graduating from Saint Joseph's College in his native city, the young journalist joined the staff of Philadelphia's *North American* newspaper. He served in Europe as a foreign correspondent in World War I. The "gruff, hearty and jovial" journalist was arrested by the Bolsheviks in Hungary and sentenced to death, a verdict set aside only through the intervention of the United States Department of State.

Breen subsequently became involved in the Irish Rebellion. He sent back numerous articles to his paper championing the Emerald Isle's freedom. On one occasion, he was captured by the British, loaded on a boat, and "unceremoniously dumped on the French shore."

In 1926, at the invitation of George Cardinal Mundelein, Joseph Breen became press relations director for the International Eucharistic Congress in Chicago. He later held a similar position for the Windy City's World Fair.

Will H. Hays, President of the Motion Picture Producers and Distributors of America, brought Breen to Hollywood in 1931. The "Hays Moral Code" had just been formally adopted by the eight leading motion picture companies. A bureau known as the Motion Picture Producers, Inc., was set up in Hollywood to put into force the principles spelled out in the code by its author, Father Daniel A. Lord, S.J. In 1934, Breen became Production Code Administrator, a position he held for the next twenty years. Breen's "toughness in administering the tenets of the Code was almost legendary" and "more than any single individual he shaped the moral stature of

the American motion picture" during his years in Hollywood.

Deeply devoted to his wife, Mary, and their six children, Breen "was outraged by any film which had anything that his children shouldn't see. . . . He thought in terms of family and therein lay his strength and potency." Pope Pius XI named Joseph Breen a Knight Commander of the Order of Saint Gregory the Great in 1938, as a mark of esteem for the campaigner's valuable assistance to the Legion of Decency, during that organization's formative years.

Further recognition of the contributions made by "the man who put teeth in the Motion Picture Association of America's Production Code" was evidenced in 1954 when he was given a special award by the Academy of Motion Picture Arts and Sciences. That Joseph Breen was successful during his two decades in the world's motion picture capital is beyond controversy, for it was the golden era for Hollywood. Those were the "Breen years."

PATRICK BREEN (f. 1828–1868)

Patrick Breen, known in the annals as "a man of more than ordinary intelligence," was one whose life furnishes a rare type of the pioneer Californian. It was shortly after arriving in Southwold, near Toronto, that the Carlow–born emigrant met and married Margaret Bulger, with whom he journeyed to the midwestern area of the United States.

In 1846, the Breen family cast an anxious glance at the possibility of moving to the far west. The predominate reason for his choice of California was Patrick's "desire to live in a Catholic culture, since he believed a full Catholic life was necessary for himself and for his young family." Three wagon loads of Breens, including seven children and "an ample supply of beef " set out on what eventually became one of the most hazardous journeys ever recorded. They joined the party of George Donner on a route that took them around the southern end of the Great Salt Lake, through Washoe country to the Sierra Nevada and into California.

With some dozen other families, the Breens shared the tragic weeks from October 31, 1846 to March 4, 1847, during which thirty–nine of the original eighty–seven members died of starvation and exposure. During a series of exceedingly severe snow storms, most of the cattle strayed and perished, thus forcing additional hardships on the already beleaguered travellers. So extensive was the plight of the Donner party that they were compelled "to eat the bodies of the dead" before relief came in mid–February. While admitting that "most of them ate human flesh," one prominent historian concludes that "they did right; it was the necessity, not the act, that was deplorable." By the time a rescue party located his family, Patrick Breen was a walking skeleton and his children were at the point of death.

With an intuition that the Donner party was making history, Patrick kept a diary for the period, carefully noting weather conditions, snow falls, storm intensity, wind velocity and temperature readings. That diary has become a classic, one which Hubert Howe Bancroft classified among "the most highly prized treasures" of Western Americana. It was written on eight sheets of letter paper and folded to make a book of thirty–two pages of which twenty–nine were actually utilized. Breen gave the manuscript to George McKinstray at Sutter's Fort, in 1848, who in turn, entrusted it to Bancroft. Parts of it were first published in 1847. After their arrival in California, the Breens lived temporarily at Mission San Jose before settling permanently in the San Juan Valley where the "Catholic atmosphere, the friendliness of the *padres* and native Californians about the mission were the deciding factors." In subsequent years, the Breens came to be known as honest, hard–working people. The "dignified patriarch with blue eyes and Irish brogue" served as a supervisor, school trustee and postmaster for Monterey County.

Patrick died during the smallpox epidemic of 1868. He and the other members of his family were buried just southwest of Mission San Juan Bautista. The monuments marking their graves recall a significant family of pioneers.

DAVID COLBRETH BRODERICK (1820–1859)

David Colbreth Broderick (1820–1859) was an outstanding public servant who, in the true American spirit, "sought place, position, and power that he might fearlessly advocate man's natural rights." He was born in Washington, D.C., where his father, a stonecutter, had emigrated from Leinster to assist in repairing the damage inflicted on the old Senate Chambers during the War of 1812.

The youngster's limited education was acquired in New York. After learning his father's trade, David opened a saloon where thirsty politicians frequently assembled to discuss state questions. Even in his youth, Broderick's "conversational powers led captive all with whom he came in contact."

David announced as a candidate for the Thirtieth Congress, in 1846, but was defeated, mostly because of the wide–spread bigotry in his constituency towards those of Irish–Catholic descent. Three years later, Broderick "determined to boldly abandon the chronic feuds and complications which beset him" to seek "in a virgin land, and amid a new and adventurous people, that coveted position" unobtainable in New York.

During his first years in California, Broderick engaged in smelting and assaying gold. He was a delegate to the constitutional convention of 1849, and served in the State Senate from 1850 to 1851. At the time of his election to the United States Senate on the Democratic ticket, in March of 1857, Broderick was warmly welcomed back to Washington "where his talents were highly esteemed and his principles were of the most disinterested quality."

Broderick was exceedingly active and conscientious about his senatorial duties. From the very outset of his short tenure, he loomed as a formidable political force on the national level. President James Buchanan credited Broderick with being the chief roadblock of the Lecompton measure as well as the refusal of Senator Stephen A. Douglas to compromise on the English bill.

Broderick was esteemed by such diverse personages as Abraham Lincoln and Jefferson Davis. Like those two great figures, the California legislator was a man of principle who championed various causes irrespective of political expediency. Even his unfortunate death, at the hands of David S. Terry, Chief Justice of California's Supreme Court, was the result of Broderick's refusal to deviate from personal convictions.

Senator Broderick was, according to one commentator, "the first and last from the Empire State of the Pacific Coast who truly represented the chivalric heraldry of the race from which he sprang." George Wilkes, editor of the *National Police Gazette*, said of David Colbreth Broderick: "As in life, no other voice so rang its trumpet blast upon the ear of free men, so in death its echoes will reverberate amid our mountains and valleys, until truth and valor cease to appeal to the human heart."

LUIGI BRUSATORI (1885–1942)

Luigi Brusatori (1885–1942) was one of California's most outstanding (though unknown) artists. The centennial of his birth was fittingly observed in both Italy and the United States.

Luigi was the tenth of the children born to Santino and Savina Brusatori. His father was cobbler, dentist and doctor for the village of San Antonio on the outskirts of Lonate Pozzolo in the old Papal States.

He began to sketch while still a youngster. At the age of fifteen, Luigi went to the neighboring town of Busto Arsizie to work as a hod–carrier. While employed there on a job, he became fascinated with a group of artists painting frescos inside the church. He felt inspired by them and decided to get some formal education in art. Later he qualified for the Reggia Academy in Milano.

In 1902, at the age of seventeen, Luigi Brusatori painted his first fresco in the church of San Marcario near Milano. From that day until his death, he never felt that his work was completed or successful until the local priest blessed it.

Luigi married Ida Castellana in 1908. Within three years their three children were born. The youthful artist found himself with a growing family and little means by which to support it. Brusatori's great dream was to build a home for his family. And it was that goal that led him to seek employment in the United States. For the next decade he worked hard in California to achieve his dream.

Brusatori painted a number of churches in the Bay Area. One of the best examples of his work is in Our Lady of Guadalupe Church located over the Broadway Tunnel in San Francisco. Virtually the entire church is covered with his paintings, including the ceiling. One observer said that "the faces of the angels were modeled after members of the children's choir."

After finishing that commission, Brusatori painted Saint Francis of Assisi Church on Vallejo Street. Although many of his works have since been painted over, two remain, one on either side of the altar. One scene depicts Francis receiving the stigmata, while the other portrays his death.

Luigi's fame spread rapidly as he was called on to paint not only churches, but other buildings as well. At one time, his works could be found in the Old Palace Cafe on Ellis Street, a theatre in Watsonville, a mausoleum in San Pablo, as well as Sacred Heart Church in Red Bluff and Saint John in Fresno. What may have been his greatest work was done in the Church of Santa Clara in Oxnard. Unfortunately, it was covered over after a fire damaged the church in 1972.

Brusatori was commissioned to paint the official portrait of John J. Cantwell when he was named to the bishopric of Monterey–Los Angeles in 1917. Cantwell was so pleased that he paid the artist $400 and recommended him for other work in Southern California. The muralist had a brother, Ambrose, who also lived in the Bay Area. Before he died, Ambrose recorded a number of anecdotes about Luigi in an oral history interview which is now preserved at the University of San Francisco.

With his payment of $5,000 for the work he did at Oxnard, Luigi was able to return to Italy and build his dream house. For the rest of his life he remained at San Antonio. He died in 1942.

PETER H. BURNETT (1807–1895)

No less an authority than Orestes Brownson noted that through Peter H. Burnett "California has made a more glorious contribution to the Union than all the gold of her mines, for the truth is more precious than gold, yea than fine gold!"

Born in Nashville, Tennessee, in 1807, Burnett was already a successful lawyer and editor by the time he brought his family to Oregon in 1843. In his new surroundings he was no less assiduous and soon became a respected legislator and later a judge. Among those attracted to California by "gold fever" in 1848, Burnett and the two–thirds of Oregon's male population migrated again, this time to the state where he was to achieve fame even beyond his expectations.

Burnett participated actively as a member of the Legislative Assembly of San Francisco and justice of the territorial court system. On November 13, 1849, he was elected first American Governor of California, though the state was not admitted to the Union until the following year. Although he cut short his term of office by resigning in 1851, Burnett continued to serve the commonwealth and was in later years appointed to the state's supreme court.

Peter Burnett was not born a Catholic and it was only after his arrival in Oregon that be realized that "this was the Church claiming to be the only true Church." He learned that "to love her was glory, to revile her was shame." Burnett's calm and methodical investigation of Catholic doctrine culminated in his baptism at Oregon City, on June 7, 1846, by Father Peter De Vos, S.J. He later published an account of his conversion under the title *The Path Which Led a Protestant Lawyer to the Catholic Church*, a book one reviewer described as "a noble homage to his new Faith."

Despite the fact that nine tenths of the people of Oregon were at that time opposed to his religion, California's first American governor stated that he "had no reason for the change from a popular to an unpopular religion but the simple love of truth." Even though he "did not hanker after it," Burnett never avoided opposition. Once convinced of his Faith, he "was able and prepared to bear the censure even of the wise and good." Hubert Howe Bancroft maintains that his fidelity brought about his early retirement from the governorship, noting that it was "in consequence of his conversion to the Catholic faith . . . that he resigned his office in 1851." Whether that be true or not, Burnett did not leave his post an embittered man but stated, that "should an unfortunate crisis ever arise my limited fortune and fame, and my life, will be at her [California's] disposal."

As author of several fascinating books, Peter Burnett remained active in his declining years and it was said that while he resided in Sacramento "there was no more frequent worshipper than the governor . . ." If the accusation be trite that "the Catholic Church has never been noted for overpublicizing her more distinguished sons," let this not be said of Peter H. Burnett. He was, as the title of one of his books indicates, "An Old Pioneer." But he was more than that—he was a man of destiny. Catholics, Protestant and Jews all owe much of their California heritage to this first American Governor of the State!

FRITZ B. BURNS (1899–1979)

At some future date, when historians begin arranging the "credits" for the "Catholic Story of California," the name of Fritz B. Burns will be featured on the marquee in block letters. Born in Minneapolis on October 9, 1899, Fritz attended the University of Minnesota and the Wharton School of Finance and Commerce at the University of Pennsylvania. During those days, he shrewdly concluded that California would be the nation's focal point for the rest of the twentieth century.

As so it was that after serving as an infantry lieutenant in World War I, Fritz Burns came west and settled in Los Angeles, where he began work in the development and sale of Southern California real estate. One of Mr. Burns' earliest projects was centered in the San Fernando Valley. He visited the Old Mission and thereafter became supportive of programs to restore the "fountainhead of Christianity" to its original dimensions. His interest in what later became Panorama City was clearly an outgrowth of his love for the seventeenth of California's missionary outposts.

The development of the Westchester area of Los Angeles occupied a major portion of Mr. Burns' attention in later years. And while engaged in that project, Fritz played an important role in the emerging Loyola University for which he later became a regent and principal benefactor. Westchester subsequently became one of Southern California's most attractive suburban communities, notable for its fine residential, commercial and industrial facilities.

The Burns imprint was felt in many other areas of the state, as well as in Hawaii, where industrial parks and residential communities began to appear in the years after World War II. Burns served as president, director and general partner in numerous land and investment companies, including Fritz Burns and Associates. He also found time to organize and serve as president for the National Association of Home Builders.

Burns always gave much of the credit for his success to his wife, the former Gladys Guadalupe Carson, a descendant of Juan Jose Dominguez, who had come to Alta California with Gaspar de Portola in 1769. Gladys, active in a multitude of charitable endeavors, was awarded the *Pro Ecclesia et Pontifice* medal by Pope John XXIII in 1960.

Burns and his wife took a leadership and supportive role on behalf of Sant Anne's Maternity Hospital, contributing the wing housing the hospital's delivery room. They provided funding for equipping the entire suite in the new hospital in 1955. Wherever there was some charitable need—there was Fritz Burns! He was a longtime director for the Saint Vincent de Paul Society and the Archbishop's Fund for Charity. And he was intimately associated with the outreach programs sponsored by the Knights of the Sovereign Military Order of Malta.

Mr. Burns died at his home in Hancock Park on February 19, 1979. At his funeral obsequies, held at Saint Basil's Church, Cardinal Manning said that "Fritz Burns was a unique blessing given by God to Southern California. His charitable programs touched the lives of countless people and he asked nothing in return."

The benefactions of Fritz Burns have and are reaching far beyond his simple grave through the foundation which he established while still alive. But that's a wholly different chapter.

JUAN RODRIQUEZ CABRILLO

The discovery in 1972 of what was thought to be an insignificant rock gathering dust in a museum back room may actually be the headstone of California's earliest European explorer, Juan Rodriguez Cabrillo, the highly–esteemed Catholic *conquistador*. According to a curator at the Lowie Museum of Anthropology on the Berkeley campus of the University of California, the foot long chunk of sandstone was picked up on Santa Rosa Island near Santa Barbara in 1901.

Bearing the carved initials "JR" and a stick figure of a man, the stone slab may have marked the last resting place of the great navigator who helped lead the Spanish conquest in 1521 of the fabulous city of Tenochtitlan.

Cabrillo began his historic voyage to Alta California in 1542, a journey from which he would not return. On November 23, he was injured by a fall on San Miguel Island and died the following January 3rd. Little is known of where he was buried. Piecing together bits of evidence from a wide variety of sources, historians have generally been inclined to the view that he succumbed on San Miguel Island and was buried there.

When a collector from the then new Lowie Museum picked up the stone on Santa Rosa Island, he had little reason for suspecting the implications of his discovery. For many years nothing happened. In 1956, Professor Robert F. Heizer compiled and published some reports on the earlier discoveries. Included in the old reports were photographs and descriptions of the peculiarly marked stone.

After the passage of another sixteen years, it occurred

to Heizer that the letters "JR" may have referred to Cabrillo's first and second names, Juan Rodriguez. Heizer checked with other early accounts and investigated further ramifications of the markings.

Reviewing records of the Cabrillo Voyage, Heizer found the descriptions of geographical locations so vague, and names of Indian villages so inconsistent, that he decided Cabrillo could have died on Santa Rosa Island rather than close by San Miguel. As for the letters "JR," Spanish historians confirmed to Heizer that use of just the first two initials was common in 16th century Spain, and the writing style that joined the letters on the stone into one figure was also typical.

The crudity of the carving also indicated that it was done by an inexperienced stone worker—such as a Spanish sailor hurriedly recruited to fashion a marker for his commander's grave. One final footnote . . . the latest historical research by such competent scholars as W. Michael Mathes and Harry Kelsey indicates that Joao Rodrigues Cabrilho or Juan Rodriguez Cabrillo was not really Portuguese, but Spanish.

According to this theory, Cabrillo probably concealed his real nationality to avoid persecution and to gain position. It is known that he served the Spanish crown for over two decades without their being a single mention during his life–time that he was Portuguese.

And if the stone at the Lowie Museum is authentic, it is significant that no letter "C" appears thereon. The monogram "JR" is in conformity with Castilian and not Portuguese usage in the sixteenth century.

ADOLFO CAMARILLO (1864–1959)

On Wednesday afternoon, the 10th of December, 1959, the flag atop the Ventura County Courthouse was lowered to half–mast in tribute to Don Adolfo Camarillo, whose death at Saint John's Hospital brought to a close the career of a man whose long life had spanned one of the most spectacular periods of world history. The genius of his life was this, that he helped to make history in a way that benefitted not only himself but his fellow men as well.

The Camarillos have been associated with California's history and growth since early mission days. Adolfo's father, Juan, immigrated to California from Mexico City in 1834, making the hazardous voyage from the Mexican capital on the *Natalia*, the vessel used by Napoleon in his escape from Elba a few years earlier.

After Juan Camarillo's death in 1880, Adolfo, then only sixteen, assumed control and management of the vast family holdings, known as the *Rancho Calleguas*, one of the largest estates in California and one of the few under continual ownership since the Mexican era in Cal-

ifornia. The land was originally an old Spanish grant by the Mexican Government to José Ruiz and its title was confirmed by the United States in 1862. During the seventy–eight years he managed the ranch, Adolfo witnessed one of the nation's greatest land development programs. He gradually converted the vast cattle ranch into an extensive farming area. In addition to barley and corn, Mr. Camarillo introduced lima beans to the valley in 1890, and today Ventura County is the largest producer of that commodity in the world.

With the erection of the Oxnard Air Force Base on his property, Adolfo saw the traveling time to Los Angeles reduced from twelve hours in 1880 to five minutes in 1958. From his half–century old ranch house, he saw two barriers broken, one of speed, the other of time. The oxcart was replaced by the F–89—all in one lifetime, all on his own property! During his years as "Patriarch of Ventura County" Adolfo Camarillo's interests were not restricted to ranching. He was active in many business and fraternal affairs. For many years he was parish captain of the Serra Laymen's Retreat League. His membership in the Knights of Columbus dated back fifty–six years when he was installed as Grand Knight of the Oxnard Council by the late Joseph Scott.

Among the Camarillo benefactions is Saint Mary Magdalen's Church, built in 1901, as a memorial chapel to Juan and Martina Camarillo who are entombed beneath the altar. It became the official Catholic Church in Camarillo when that town was raised to parochial status in 1940.

In 1952 Pope Pius XII named Adolfo a Knight of Saint Gregory in recognition of his many services to church and community. The years that followed only served to increase the zeal of this man for God and country, and with Adolfo's death at the age of ninety–five, another brilliant chapter in the history of California was brought to an end.

JUAN CAMARILLO (1812–1880)

Juan E. Camarillo was a fervent Catholic gentleman whose liberality in public and private works of charity are deeply imbedded in the traditions of Southern California. He was born in an adobe ranch house on the Camarillo acreage near what later became Ventura Avenue and Main Street, just west of San Buenaventura Mission, on April 10, 1867.

The eldest son of Juan and Martina (Hernandez) Camarillo, Juan took his secondary courses at the *Colegio Franciscano* in Santa Barbara. He later studied under the Lazarist Fathers in Los Angeles, where he graduated from Saint Vincent's College in 1887. Juan never married. For many years he lived with his mother at San Buenaventura. There he engaged in the general mercantile business. In subsequent times he resided at the Casa Camarillo, the Victorian home erected by his brother, Adolfo, in 1892.

Juan travelled extensively throughout the world and everywhere he carried with him the best traditions of pioneer Californians. He visited the Holy Land for the first time in 1906. During the following three decades, Juan journeyed to Italy, Spain, France, Greece, Egypt and Latin America. He was a keen observer of all the sacred shrines, ancient ruins and art treasures abounding in those faraway places.

On July 31, 1905, Juan and a select group of other Americans were received in a private papal audience at the Vatican. The *solideo* or zucchetto which Pope Pius X presented to Mr. Camarillo on that occasion is now displayed in the Historical Museum at San Buenaventura Mission. Also exhibited there is a picture of the audience, the first photograph ever taken of a Pope with a visiting group of dignitaries.

Early in 1916, Juan travelled to Hawaii for a visit with the Right Reverend Libert Boeynaems, Vicar Apostolic, who introduced him to the local clergy. He subsequently wrote an informative article for *The Tidings* on "The Church in Hawaii." Several other of Camarillo's essays were published by that newspaper, including one in Spanish, on February 18, 1927, describing his visit to Alhambra, Toledo and Madrid.

The artifacts collected by Juan during his many world travels were housed for many years in a special museum wing, adjacent to Saint Mary Magdalen Church, in Camarillo. Through the kindness of Msgr. John Hughes, the collection was moved to San Buenaventura Mission, where it has been on permanent display since 1976.

The benefactions of Juan Camarillo are legendary. On March 3, 1927, at a meeting of the Board of Trustees for the Roman Catholic Junior Seminary, Juan announced his intention of giving one hundred acres of choice land to the Diocese of Monterey–Los Angeles for the erection of a senior seminary, to be named after his patron saint. At the time of his demise, Juan willed the family chapel, Saint Mary Magdalen, to the Order of Friars Minor. The Franciscans agreed with diocesan authorities to exchange the chapel and it has ever since served as the parish church for the town (now city) of Camarillo.

Mr. Camarillo was almost a compulsive benefactor when it came to youngsters. In some parts of South America, "Juan's Day" became an annual holiday eagerly anticipated by the little ones. His generosity was publicly recognized on July 27, 1927, when Pope Pius X1 enrolled Juan Camarillo in the Equestrian Order of Knights of Pope Saint Sylvester, the first time that distinction was bestowed in the United States.

On August 24, 1936, Juan was laid to rest in the burial vaults of the beautiful church he had built as a house of God and memorial to his departed forebears in 1911. The news account reported that "the church and all the sightly hill on which it stands was crowded with those who had come from far and near to pay their respects." One reporter noted that "for himself and for his family it was a tribute richly deserved." The eulogy was preached by Archbishop John J. Cantwell who spoke "feelingly on the honorable Catholic life" of Juan Camarillo and his well–earned niche in the story of California's religious and social heritage.

JUAN E. CAMARILLO (1867–1936)

There was a Camarillo with Hernando Cortés as the great *conquistador* traveled from Spain to the New World, in 1518. Among the descendants of America's proto–Camarillo was Juan, born at Mexico City, on May 27th, 1812, the son of Luis and Maria (Rodriguez) Camarillo. Though he had learned the art of tailoring, a trade affording a comfortable living in those days, Juan was no less adventurous than his illustrious predecessor.

Having heard of José Maria Hijar's colonization

Juan E. Camarillo (1867-1936)

plans for the faraway Province of California, Juan joined the group of more than 200 volunteer colonists who gathered at the Mexican capital in 1834. It was an elite assemblage of mostly professional people. An observer noted that they were "far superior as a class to any before sent out as settlers to California." Upon arriving at San Diego, after a thirty day sea voyage from San Blas aboard the *Natalia*, Juan Camarillo and several others of the original contingency continued overland to Santa Barbara. During his early years in California, Juan earned his living by trading and selling merchandise between San Francisco and San Diego. As soon as he had accumulated sufficient capital, he opened a store in Santa Barbara, at the corner of what is now State and Cañon Perdido Streets.

Juan met the lovely Martina Hernández in 1840 and, on the following April 13th, the couple was married at Mission Santa Barbara in the presence of Fray Narciso Durán. Theirs was a happy marriage eventually blessed with fourteen youngsters. Always an active participant in community affairs, Juan served as a member of the *ayuntamiento* in Santa Barbara. In 1857, he moved his family to San Buenaventura and took up residence in an adobe at Main Street and Ventura Avenue. Juan was a member of the Board of Trustees when Ventura was incorporated as a city in 1866.

In 1875, Juan liquidated his real estate assets and purchased from Gabriel Ruíz the title to *Rancho Calleguas*. The ranch was an old Spanish land grant conveyed to José Ruíz in 1847. On September 17, 1862, the United States confirmed the title to the son of the original grantee. Initially the property was used as a cattle and sheep ranch, but gradually the aspects of a farm emerged and, by 1880, about 1,500 acres were under cultivation in corn and barley. Extensive rodeos and social affairs were staged on the vast acreage during the "cattle days" of California's history. The present City of Camarillo dates from the 1880s and the building of the Ventura section of the Southern Pacific Railroad. The name was assigned to the station by railway officials in memory of Juan.

By the time of Juan Camarillo's demise, on December 4, 1880, only half of his children were still alive. Martina, who outlived her husband by eighteen years, remained at the family home in Ventura for the remainder of her life. Succeeding generations of the Camarillos intermarried with the Peraltas and Ortegas, thus uniting three of the oldest and largest families in early California. Juan was a lifelong, practicing Catholic who reared his family according to strict Christian principles. He was one of California's foremost pioneers—one whose name lives on as a tribute to his achievements.

LEO ANTONIO CARILLO (1880–1961)

Leo Antonio Carillo (1880–1961), the last of California's great *caballeros*, was more than a superb actor, entertainer, narrator of a romantic past, American patriot and public servant. He was Leo the incomparable, the Maker of a Legend. It was a touching, sentimental, fabulous and nostalgic legend anchored to the eternal values of the human heart.

Descended from a man who accompanied Fray Junípero Serra to Alta California, Leo was the great–grandson of a California governor and the grandson of a prominent judge. His grandmother owned the large *rancho* where the city of Riverside now stands. In his veins flowed not only the blood of Spain and Mexico, but that of other pioneers who found their way to this fabled land.

In his boyhood, Leo was the prankster and mimic in a family whose father was the first mayor of Santa Monica and whose eldest son became an eminent civil engineer. While always the actor, Leo embodied the heritage of the Spanish dons.

Known to 53 million television viewers as Pancho, the sidekick of the Cisco Kid, Leo was an outspoken, reminiscing, story–telling personification of early California. He probably had a closer connection to that history and knew it better than any other person.

Leo spent his boyhood in Santa Monica and by the time he returned to live beside a sycamore–shaded street in the 1930s, he was an acknowledged and respected Broadway actor and matinee idol.

With the assistance of Ed Ainsworth, Leo told the story of his family and his own life in a charming book, *The California I Love*, which was published by Prentice–Hall. Therein he relived his successful and fascinating career on stage, screen and radio. In the pages of his book are scores of tales about a vanished culture and the early Hispanic days in California. Especially interesting is his personal account of how he got to San Francisco in his teens. While working there as an apprentice cartoonist on the old *Examiner*, he got a chance in vaudeville. His reflections come to life in a perfection of the story–teller's art, combining humor, pathos and the nostalgic recall of a gaudy era.

The boy from Santa Monica soon became a favorite on the old vaudeville circuit. From there he went on to Broadway to gain fame and fortune as the lead in "Lombardi, Ltd." and other hit plays. The years between 1915 and 1930 were heady ones indeed for Leo Carillo.

"In my family," he recalled, "I never needed the Arabian Nights. We had our own. It was compounded of the mighty saga of priests, leather–jacketed soldiers, grizzly bear hunters, *vaqueros* on horses swift as the wind, ropers who flung a *reata* with the precision of rifle fire, *grandees* of the *rancheros* and dancing girls with castanets who sang the siren songs of California to the tune of a Spanish guitar in a jasmine–scented patio."

Leo personified a whole era in Southern California and his memoir of those days was his most important bequest to the state which he loved so deeply and respected so profoundly. Leo Carillo stood with one foot in the proud past of Hispanic California, and the other in a different California, growing, expanding, changing so quickly that it had all but lost touch with its roots. Loving both past and present, he was a child of the first and an indispensable part of the second.

CARLOS ANTONIO CARRILLO (1783–1852)

Carlos Antonio Carrillo (1783–1852) is remembered as a man whose "genial disposition left him no superiors in the entire province in the matter of generosity and popularity." The Santa Barbara–born Carrillo held numerous important positions during his life of public service, including that of titular governor, in 1837–1838. Undoubtedly his most lasting contributions were made during the term he served as California's representative in the Mexican Congress.

As an ardent champion for the missionary endeavors of the friars, Carrillo seized every available opportunity to thwart the efforts towards secularization then prevalent in legislative circles. One of Carrillo's most forceful addresses was delivered, on September 15, 1831, to the Chamber of Deputies. One chronicler described how that speech "developed into a veritable panegyric which, though richly deserved, must have appeared a strange novelty, whereas, among the bawling young Californians, denunciation of the friars had been the fashion."

Copies of that address, known as the *Exposicón dirigada á la Camara de Diputados del Congreso de la Union por el Sr. Carlos Antonio Carrillo. Diputado por la Alta California* were subsequently distributed at Mexico City by C. Alejandro Valdés. The sixteen–page opus, measuring eighteen centimeters high and fifteen wide, is now exceedingly rare. The one at Berkeley is considered "one of the rarest treasures of the Bancroft Library."

Six hundred and fifty imprints of this "first production of a native Californian printed in book form," translated and edited by Herbert Ingram Priestley, were published, in 1938, by John Henry Nash of San Francisco. Included in that edition is a long and enlightening introduction on the significance of Carrillo's sentiments about the missions.

Carrillo's address provoked favorable response and, on May 25, 1832, the Mexican Congress enacted legislation in substantially the form he envisioned. The law provided that properties of the Pious Fund of the Californias were to be leased, rather than sold, for terms not exceeding seven years. Proceeds from these transactions were to be deposited in the public treasury and used exclusively for the missions.

Successful as he was in initiating legislation favorable to the work of the friars, Carrillo's two years in Mexico "proved to be of passing conservating influence in an historic process which moved inevitably toward liberalism, the disintegration of Mexico, and the regime of the Yankee in California." Nonetheless, his tireless interventions stand as "a memorial to the efforts of Carrillo and his associates—to save the Pious Fund for its original purposes when in the 1830s proposals were rife for government seizure of the revenues and properties."

It remained for another generation and the judgment of a higher tribunal to determine the ultimate fate of the Pious Fund. A cursory study of this fascinating case, however, reveals the legal expertise of Carlos Antonio Carrillo, a "Defender of the Faith in California."

HARRY CARR (1878–1936)

For over forty years, Harry Carr was an outstanding figure in the southland's journalistic world. Flags flew at half staff on the tower of the Los Angeles *Times* building when word of his demise was announced on January 9, 1936.

Born in Tipton, Iowa, in 1878, Harry settled in Los Angeles when the city numbered only 20,000 people. He became a reporter for the *Times* in 1897 and soon rose to the highest levels of his profession. In 1924, Carr began writing "The Lancer," a column of pungent, personal comment that was read locally and nationally by syndication.

John Steven McGroarty was not overspeaking when he remembered Carr as "the most thorough newspaperman I have ever known, and I have known the best during a lifetime of association with them." Carr authored scores of magazine articles on a myriad of subjects along with three books. His volume on *Los Angeles. City of Dreams* (New York, 1935) was a superb "journalistic rendition of the wondrous growth, picturesque beauty and tropic charm" of a truly unique metropolis.

Carr's career was permeated by journalistic honors, many won during his years as a correspondent in Europe during World War I. In 1934, he received a Pulitzer Prize honorable mention for his writings. A fellow journalist described Carr's "supreme ability as a writer," noting that "whatever he had to do, even though it were a task others would regard as trivial, he gave it the best that was in him. I have known him to make a report of a ladies' aid quilting party the star story of the morning's paper."

In another tribute, written by Julian Johnson, Carr

was praised for his account of the San Francisco earthquake: "It was the greatest piece of reporting that I can remember in my whole newspaper career," he said. "I never found anything so graphic and so simple in any account of a great disaster."

Though he was not professedly a Roman Catholic, Harry Carr probably knew more about the Church than any other writer on the local scene. Whenever an ecclesial event needed coverage, the task fell to Harry and he always did well. The day after his funeral and internment at Rosedale Cemetery, Harry's friends gathered at the Old Plaza Church of Our Lady of the Angels for a Requiem High Mass offered by Father Victor Marin, C.M.F.

Father Francis J. Caffrey of San Juan Bautista Mission delivered the eulogy in which he reflected on Carr's love and affection towards the poor and unfortunate, the homeless and destitute, the outcast and forgotten members of the local citizenry.

The Vice Consul for Mexico, Ernesto Romero, then said that we have lost a great benefactor in Harry Carr. "He was a friend of Mexico and its people when Mexico needed a friend. He was an unofficial ambassador of good will between his country and ours. His death is a loss we can hardly realize to Mexico and its citizens."

The writer's favorite musical selections were played by an orchestra and they included *Sobre Las Olas, Cuatro Milpas, El Nido de Amor* and *Ya va Cayendo.* The memorial service was closed with a chanted rendition of the rosary. The program was broadcast by station KMTR. The microphone was draped with a black wreath and a black–rimmed picture of Carr bearing the Hispanic farewell: *Vaya con Dios!*

It was "thirty" for a well–loved and respected journalist, a man who made a difference, a writer who cared. As one little lady noted—"he made us feel proud of our heritage."

GEORGE HENRY CARSON (1829–1901)

George Henry Carson, short and sturdy in appearance, was a shrewd business man who left an indelible mark on Southern California. His name still adorns the city founded on part of his extensive ranch holdings. Born in New Jordan, New York, on March 23, 1829, George, the eldest son of John C. and Sophia Cady Carson, was destined to be a considerable influence on the California skyline.

In 1841, the Carson family began moving west, settling for awhile on a farm in Illinois. George enlisted as a drummer boy in Company F, Seventh Regiment of the Illinois Volunteers. Later he became a bugler and regular soldier in active service, positions he held throughout the War with Mexico. Following his discharge, young Carson joined Chapman's Rangers and served in the campaign to suppress a Navajo uprising.

George spent several years as a merchandiser in Texas and New Mexico, a trade in which he managed to accumulate a considerable amount of money. In 1852, he went to Mexico and there engaged in the cattle trade. Early the following year, he drove a herd of sheep to Southern California. Later he spent time working as a carpenter.

George Carson become active in local politics and was elected to the Los Angeles City Council. Subsequently he served as Public Administrator and, in that capacity, he got to know Manuel Dominguez. While serving as Public Administrator, George also involved himself in construction work and is credited with having erected the first brick building in Los Angeles in what was known as the Childs Block.

After marrying Maria Victoria Dominguez on July 30, 1857, George worked in the hardware business for a few years before moving his family to *Rancho San Pedro*, where he became chief assistant to the elder Dominguez. George brought his considerable managerial acumen to the *rancho* and, during his tenure, the Dominguez holdings grew and stabilized. Grain and dairy farming were added to the *rancho* and George devised a method for shipping grain and wool to eastern markets.

Following the death of Manuel Dominguez, George Carson supervised the management of the lands inherited by his wife. His was the principal guiding hand in protecting the interests of the other Dominguez daughters.

George, a firm disciplinarian, controlled his own family of fifteen children in every respect. After the allotment of tracts to his offspring in 1885, George and Victoria built a large two story house for their family on a slight incline just north of the original Dominguez homesite.

In later years, George Carson also took a special interest in improving the strains of dairy cattle and sheep. He also raised thoroughbred horses and developed some of the best trotting and carriage stock in Los Angeles county.

George Henry Carson died at his home on November 20, 1901, at the age of seventy–two. His passing was given full coverage by the local press. The funeral was an elaborate ceremony with a long procession to Saint Vibiana's Cathedral and then on to Calvary cemetery.

For George Henry Carson, the Catholic faith was a "given." His whole life was anchored to the Church. He once confided to Bishop Francis Mora that he "never made a decision without first praying for divine guidance."

CHRISTOPHER (KIT) CARSON (1809–1869)

According to the historian, Hubert Howe Bancroft, Christopher (Kit) Carson (1809–1868), the famed American trapper, scout and Indian agent, was a small, wiry man of undoubted bravery and skill in all that pertained to his profession, comparatively quiet in manner and somewhat less garrulous and boastful than many of the frontiersmen.

Carson guided Stephen Kearny's army of the west across the Colorado desert. And he was the official messenger who carried the first news about the acquisition of California to the other states. Charles L. Camp considered Carson "a man of great energy and decision of character, alert, poised, calm in danger, and among the keenest, shrewdest and bravest of experienced frontiersmen."

No small amount of Kit Carson's fame is due to his exploits in California. The romantic and stirring interest which surrounds his name was first aroused when his overland and California adventures were chronicled in the writings of Fremont and Emory for whom he acted as guide and scout across the uncharted west.

His far western journey took place in 1829–30, when he came to California as a junior member of Ewing Young's band of beaver trappers. The party traversed that part of the Golden State later serviced by the Santa Fe Railroad. The twenty–two men in Young's party arrived in the environs of San Jose Mission in August. They were illegally setting traps along the Sacramento River when approached by the mission *alcalde* who asked their assistance in rounding up some fugitive Indians.

The trappers diplomatically agreed to help the *alcalde*, hoping thereby to win favor with local officials in selling their ill–gotten pelts. Young directed Kit Carson to lead an expedition of eleven trappers and fifteen mission neophytes in pursuit. With characteristic efficiency, Carson succeeded in locating and returning the fugitives.

Upon arriving at San Jose, the twenty year old Carson noted in his diary that "we were well received by the missionaries." (Carson mistakenly refers to the mission as "San Rafael" rather than San Jose.) In any event, Carson and his friends profited handsomely for their services to San Jose Mission. Through the intervention of the friars, Jose Asero, captain of a trading vessel anchored at Monterey, agreed to purchase Young's complete stock of furs.

A writer in the San Francisco *Call* stated that Kit Carson regularly travelled for some six hours from the Sacramento River to the San Jose region to court a Mexican girl named Teresita. All went well until an attack on the mission by renegade Indians disclosed the presence of the American trappers in the valley and brought an end to Kit's love affair. That incident is not mentioned in the autobiography that Carson later dictated to Dewitt Clinton Peter. Yet it could have been true, inasmuch as all the external evidence fits into place.

There was nothing in the youthful Carson's appearance to betoken the future place in American history he would achieve as a skilled pathfinder and fearless Indian fighter. But most of his life was still ahead of him in 1829–30.

THOMAS CASSIDY (b. 1917)

During the busiest days of the Christmas and Easter seasons most who call San Fernando Mission for the liturgical schedule are greeted with a burst of music from Tchaikovsky's Concerto #1 in B flat minor followed by the announcement: "This is Thomas Cassidy for the San Fernando Mission. Masses here at the Old Mission will be offered . . ."

One lady wrote to say that she "was so pleased to hear that impressive voice again. For over forty years I listened every evening to Mr. Cassidy as he broadcast the Gas Hour over KFAC. How good it is to hear him again."

And though retired from KFAC for some years, Tom continued his active lifestyle. He was a regular lector on Sundays as well as often during the week and he performed whatever other duties might arise at the Old Mission. When he attended Mass "among the troops" with his wife, Tom's trained voice soared above the others, giving a professional and melodious tone to the communal singing.

Born at Valparaiso, Indiana, on November 4, 1917, Tom was raised in the Allen County Orphan Home in Fort Wayne. Later he lived at Pixley Relief Home where he attended the local public schools. Because it was the depression era, there wasn't time for the luxury of schooling beyond the eighth grade.

After coming to California in September of 1932, Tom began acting in motion pictures with such movie personalities as James Cagney, Madge Evans, Frankie Darrow and Sydney Miller.

He worked for a while in the experimental department of Douglas Aircraft before launching his own business repairing speedometers and tachometers. It was while toiling in the latter position that he won a four year scholarship to the Los Angeles Conservatory of Music. From there he moved on to the Puck School of Acting where he had the rare opportunity of studying with the legendary thespian, Guy Bates Post.

Tom's fascination with the Catholic Church dated from his teen years. When he and his fiancée, Dorothy Logan, were making plans to be married, they both took instructions and were received into the Catholic fold, a decision which turned around his entire life.

During those years, Tom became an active member of the Catholic Theatre Guild and appeared in their annual plays which were staged at the old Wilshire Ebell Theatre.

Gifted with exceptional lingual ability, Cassidy became proficient in most of the European languages. He also studied music and voice, utilizing every opportunity of incorporating those skills into his acting career. His flawless pronunciation of difficult musical scores and titles gained for him the title of radio's "linguistic gymnast."

After a number of friends suggested that he enter the field of broadcasting, Tom won a competition to audition at NBC. At that time, the networks ran a "farm system" and Tom's option was picked up by KIDO in Boise, where he became staff announcer.

In May of 1943, he signed on with the Idaho radio station and, because of his background, he was entrusted with handling all their musical programming. It was while announcing a weekly concert of the Gowan Field Band that Cassidy began his parallel career of interviewing. His first guest was Lord Halifax, the famous British statesman.

When the Cassidys were expecting the first of their three children, they moved back to Los Angeles and Tom began his long and distinguished career with KFAC as emcee of the "Evening Concert."

Tom planned and announced that popular series from December 16, 1943 until his retirement on February of 1987, probably the longest such stint in American broadcasting history.

His nightly programs consistently ranked fourth or fifth in popularity among all the then current radio and TV shows. The station mailed out 40,000 programs every month to listeners.

In an interview with the Los Angeles *Times*, in February of 1957, Tom said that the greatest response ever provoked by one of his programs was for a concert of liturgical music that included fifty–four minutes of uninterrupted Gregorian Chants from St. Pierre des Solesmes.

During his 43 years as host for the Southern California Gas Company, Tom also wore other hats, all of which endeared him to such music lovers as Timothy Cardinal Manning, a long time admirer.

From March, 1965 to July, 1976, Tom did a daily program called "Luncheon at the Music Center," following a format suggested by Jeanette MacDonald. At the Pavilion Restaurant, Tom interviewed hundreds of celebrities, including André Kostelanetz, Bob Hope, Maureen O'Hara, Arthur Rubenstein, Princess Irene of Greece, Walter Pidgeon and Arthur Fiedler.

He was also busy at the Hollywood Bowl where he announced the Sunday Night Concerts intermittently from 1944 to 1968. And he emceed the Hollywood Bowl radio broadcasts from 1952 to 1974, as well as those emanating from the Los Angeles Philharmonic Auditorium, 1947–1973. His one hour daily program of "Musical Masterpieces" was a fixture for nineteen years.

Tom's home in Sepulveda is crammed with awards and citations, none more esteemed than the "Golden Mike—Pioneer Broadcasters" award which he received at a testimonial dinner in 1970.

Cassidy's retirement years are busy ones. Since 1959, he has spent a day every week at the Air Museum in Chino, building instrument panels for restored planes. He has been active at the Old Mission, planning liturgical and musical presentations for Christmas and Holy Week.

He is now collaborating with Dr. Gloria Ricci Lothrop on an autobiographical volume which will encompass the history of music broadcasting during the last half century.

JULIO CESAR (b. 1824)

Julio Cesar, a Luiseño Indian, was born at San Luis Rey in 1824. After residing at the Old Mission for many years, he moved to Tres Pinos in San Benito County, where, in 1878, he was interviewed by Hubert Howe Bancroft. The original manuscript, written in Spanish at Cesar's dictation, was later translated by Nellie Van de Grift Sanchez for the November, 1930, issue of *Touring Topics*. The following remarks are excerpted from that vivid and intimate memoir.

> When I first entered the mission to take service, they employed me to sing in the choir in the sung masses. The administrator of the mission was Don Pio Pico. When he left, soon after I entered, the administrator was Don Jose Antonio Estudillo, who was followed by Don Jose Joaquin Ortega, who in turn was succeeded by Don Juan Maria Marron.

> When I began to serve there were still a great many Indians at the mission and it was very rich. At that time it had the following *ranchos*—Rancho San Mateo and Las Flores. At the last named, there was a sort of little Indian town, with a small chapel where the *padre* said mass for the Indians every eight days.

> Santa Margarita had a large orchard, immense fields of wheat, corn and other grain, besides cattle; San Juan, cattle *rancho*; Pala, which had a large orchard, the same as Santa Margarita, besides a corner set off for planting beans and corn.

> Don Jose Joaquin Ortega, during his administration, appropriated to himself nearly all the mission cattle, but did not take any of its land. It was said that Señor Ortega left the mission stripped bare, making an end of everything, even to the plates and cups.

When Señor Ortega was administrator, I was a good–sized boy and worked in the fields, serving as a stirrup boy. I went everywhere with him, except when there was a sung mass, when I had to go and sing. For my services I received no pay but my food and clothing. I was taught music at the mission by an Indian teacher called Domingo.

The system which had been observed by the father ministers was continued by Señor Pico. There was a nunnery for the single girls, and a department for the bachelors. I was in the department of bachelors during the administration of Pico. During the time of the missions, neophytes were prohibited from riding horseback; the only ones permitted to do this were the *alcaldes*, corporals and *vaqueros*.

When Señor Marron took charge of the mission nearly all the cattle had disappeared. The Indians no longer served at the mission, although some of them were still there. Afterwards, in the time of the Americans, what was left of the cattle was divided among the Indians at Pala, but nothing came to me because I had left there in 1849, for the gold placers in the north, and never returned to San Luis Rey Mission.

I knew Father Zalvidea and served him as chorister. He was a very good man, but was already very ill. In order to overcome the devil he constantly flogged himself, wore hair–cloth, drove nails into his feet and, in short, tormented himself in the cruelest manner.

At one time I was in Baja California, perhaps for six years, at the Camp of San Rafael, working and traveling around for the greater part of that time. We went there to take out gold, but did not accomplish anything because of the lack of water in that barren country.

I am now living in this town of Tres Pinos, poor, as I always have been; but there is no lack of food or drink for I am always willing to work, and people are kind to me and favor me by giving me work enough to earn some *reales*.

JOSEPH CHAPMAN (1785–1849)

"Among all the earliest pioneers of California, there was no more attractive character, no more popular mid shipman than Joseph Chapman (1785–1849), the Yankee!" The Boston–born seaman came to the west coast from the Sandwich Islands, where he had been pressed into service by Hippolyte Bouchard, the famous pirate. Chapman was second in command of Bouchard's *Santa Rosa* during the invasion of 1818. Fortunately for California, Chapman was captured and imprisoned at Monterey.

That his seizure was indeed a stroke of good luck is obvious for he "brought with him to California a dignity and a skill in manual crafts unknown before his arrival." After his release from prison, Chapman journeyed to Santa Ines where he made his first contact with the Fran-

ciscan missionaries. He was baptized on June 22, 1824, by Fray Jose Senan at San Buenaventura. Later in the year, on November 3rd, he married Maria Guadalupe Ortega, thus bringing about "the first of a happy procession of international marriages between the adventurous immigrants and the gentle cultured daughters of old California."

According to one contemporary, Chapman was a "jack of all trades, and naturally a very ingenious man." At Mission San Gabriel he built a grist mill for the *padres* and superintended blacksmithing and other branches of mechanism. Chapman was a great favorite of the friars, especially José Sanchez who "declared it a marvel that one so long in the darkness of Baptist faith could give such an example of true Catholic piety to old Christians. . . ."

While at San Gabriel, Chapman constructed the first ship ever built in California (if one excludes the raft launched at Fort Ross by the Russians.) The immense boat was assembled at the mission with timbers hewn in the mountains. As the time drew near for the launch, the vessel was taken to pieces and great carts were prepared for its overland transportation to the water. Alfred Robinson recorded that it "was a schooner of about sixty tons that had been entirely framed at San Gabriel and fitted for subsequent completion at San Pedro. . . . She was called *Guadalupe* in honor of the patron saint of Mexico."

"José Huero" (Blond Joe) made his residence for some years in the *Pueblo de Nuestra Señora de los Angeles* and "with mission lore and mission shoots Chapman planted four thousand grapevines at Los Angeles between 1824 and 1826 to become the first American grower of record in California."

During the latter part of his life, Chapman lived at Santa Barbara, where the *friars* gave him the old hide–house on the beach atop what is now called Burton Mound. There he died on January 9, 1849, having brought credit to Americans through his upright actions at all times. His remains were placed in the cemetery of Santa Barbara Mission by Fray Gonzalez Rubio.

In his lifetime, the Yankee carpenter–blacksmith "had seen the downfall of the Spanish power, the disintegration of the missions, the debauchment and death of the Indians, the defeat of the Mexicans by the Americans; and he had seen his youngsters, at first timid about their American blood, proud to call themselves Americans after 1846!"

CESAR CHAVEZ (1927–1993)

Once described by Robert Kennedy as "one of the heroic figures of our time," Cesar Chavez (1927–1993) was a man whose life was deeply rooted in his Catholic faith and its social teachings. Everything he did was underpinned by the Gospel of Jesus Christ.

He was born March 21, 1927, in the small desert town of Yuma, a modest area whose small farmers daily battled dust and drought. At the age of ten, he and his family were forced out of Arizona and into the "Grapes of Wrath" era of California as a migrant worker.

Living in tents and labor camps during his pre–teen years, Chavez never finished high school. He once said that he had "passed through" sixty–five different grade schools. During World War II, Chavez served in the United States Navy. He met his wife in the 1950s while working in the fields.

Between 1952 and 1962, Chavez was active in the voter registration movement and, in the early 1960s, he helped to establish the National Farm Workers Association (later the United Farm Workers) which, at one time, numbered over 100,000 members. Chavez began *la huelta* (the strike) in 1965, when the NFWA joined an AFL–CIO affiliate striking against grape growers in Delano, California. For the first time, this man referred to by *Newsweek* magazine as "a secular saint" made Americans aware of the dreadful plight of men and women who labored so tirelessly to put food on the nation's tables.

In 1968, Chavez began the first of his celebrated twenty–five day fasts to dramatize "the pain and suffering" of farm workers. And it was a victory indeed, two years later, when the grape growers finally signed with the NFWA.

Roger Cardinal Mahony observed that "no farm worker ever affected the fields and the corporate board-rooms of agriculture" as did Cesar Chavez. Graced with an intense faith, Chavez insisted on following the path of non–violent resistance in his movement.

Fittingly, when it was all over, Chavez' funeral was conducted beneath a tented "church" at Forty Acres, the site of the United Farm Workers first headquarters. Thousands of friends gathered to hear Chavez eulogized as "a true prophet" who waged a relentless fight to promote the dignity of the farmworkers and their families.

The Archbishop of Los Angeles recalled how Chavez had "battled against decades–old unjust systems to ensure the farmworkers' basic rights to a living wage, to safe working conditions, to decent housing, to health care and to their children's education."

They were all there to praise Cesar one last time. Ethel Kennedy, Congressman Joseph Kennedy, former Governor Jerry Brown, the Reverend Jesse Jackson, Mickey Kantor, Corita King and countless others paid their respects as he lay in a plain pine coffin built by his brother. Everyone walked the three miles that symbolized the long pathway trod by Chavez over earlier years.

Cesar Chavez was a unique person who played a special role in United States Hispanic history. Saints come in many stripes, but they traditionally share two characteristics: they live simply and they make others uneasy. Cesar Chavez did both and his name will not soon be forgotten.

NANITA VERDUGO CHEVOYA (1808–1916)

An eyewitness to the building of the *Asistencia de Nuestra Señora de los Angeles* was still very much alive well into the 1900s, almost a century after that noble edifice was completed by Fray Mariano Payeras.

Antonia Verdugo Chevoya was born on February 13, 1808, at Santa Barbara. "Nanita's" parents brought her to the *Pueblo de Nuestra Señora de los Angeles* by stagecoach shortly after her birth. The Verdugos first built an adobe dwelling in the old Spanish quarter, north of the *Plaza*, and there Nanita spent a busy and fascinating childhood.

She was fond of recalling how she passed through the *Plaza* area with her father and watched workmen building the historic Church. She remembered vividly how a flood destroyed the half finished edifice in 1815, and how it was another eight years before the present church was finally dedicated, on August 15, 1822.

The Verdugo family was well known in Alta California. Antonia's mother, Lugarda Romero, was a beautiful Spanish belle who came to the New World in 1800. Shortly thereafter she married Julio Verdugo. Julio was the heir to both the Verdugo name and the family's vast land holdings. A shrewd man in his own right, Julio went on to become the largest land owner in Los Angeles county during the 1850s.

His magnificent Rancho San Rafael, with its 114,000 acres, encompassed much of the area later known as Glendale, Tropico, Eagle Rock, Highland Park and Garvanza. The Rancho San Rafael, one of the few real Spanish land grants, had been bestowed upon José María Verdugo by Governor Pedro Fages, in the name of the king, on October 20, 1784

Before she reached womanhood, Antonia and her parents, with their eight sons and two daughters, moved to Verdugo Canyon, just north of present–day Glendale, to a home nestled close against the foothills. In subsequent times, that charming home was familiar to all Californians as the *Casa Verdugo*.

Fray Francisco Sanchez of San Gabriel Mission officiated at Antonia's marriage to Pedro Chevoya, a wealthy sheep and land owner. It was a gala event. A three day *fiesta* was held at the *Casa Verdugo* where guests enjoyed dancing, banquets and bull fights. Theirs was a happy marriage. Antonia's only daughter gave to her parents six grandchildren and eleven great grand-children, all of whom were raised at the family home-stead.

As late as 1915, when Antonia was interviewed by a reporter for the Los Angeles *Times*, she still had the wine–colored silk dress and mantilla worn at her wed-ding. By the time of her demise, a year later, Antonia Verdugo Chevoya was the Golden State's oldest native, a distinction she intensely enjoyed. To the very end, she was alert and aware of her imprint on California's Catholic heritage.

OZRO WILLIAM CHILDS (1824–1890)

A. BIOGRAPHICAL SKETCH

Ozro William Childs (1824–1890) , one of eight chil-dren born to Jacob and Sarah Richardson Childs, was an asthmatic who journeyed west for his health in 1850. Initially, the youthful Childs sought his future in the gold mines near Sacramento. Later he lived for a while in San Francisco, but the prevailing cold winds there induced him to seek the milder climate of Southern Cal-ifornia.

In Los Angeles, Childs and a partner set up a shop and began manufacturing various articles of tin ware. Gradually, the business branched out to include gro-ceries and other household provisions. Childs was a nat-ural business man and before long his firm was among the leading ones in the city.

Mr. Childs purchased a large tract of land to the east of Main Street, where he developed fruit orchards and groves of walnut and chestnut trees. He also grew orna-mental trees and shrubs in his nursery from seeds imported from Latin America and Europe.

Bishop Thaddeus Amat was a frequent visitor to the Childs orchards and, in 1859, the Vincentian prelate asked Ozro for a parcel of land bounded by 6th, Broad-way, 7th and Hills streets as a site for the contemplated Saint Vincent's College. Mr. Childs, a onetime teacher, responded most favorably.

In 1860, Ozro married Emeline Huber. The Childs' home was located on Main Street, just south of 10th. There, the first four of their ten children were born. In a later home, several blocks away, Ozro built the first ten-nis court in Los Angeles.

Emeline Childs made her own mark on the city of Los Angeles in the way she named various streets. Hope is the only one still surviving of her Faith (now Flower), Hope and Charity (now Grand Avenue) streets.

In 1881, Childs built the Grand Opera House which brought to Los Angeles one of the finest theatres in all of America. The building, which seated nearly 1,800 peo-ple, gave the people of the city a welcome dose of cul-ture and delight. Mr. Childs was also one of the founders of the University of Southern California for which he contributed part of the land. He was an organizer of the Farmers & Merchants National Bank, as well as Presi-dent of the Los Angeles Electric Company.

Though born and raised a Protestant, Mr. Childs never was active in that religion. For many years, he was a "cultural" Catholic, insofar as his close friendship and association with the Catholic leadership of Los Angeles often incline people to presume he was a member of that persuasion. Early in 1880s, Ozro joined his wife in the Church and during the final decade of his life, he became an avid believer. Though prevented by his asth-matic condition from attending Mass with any fre-quency, he often received the sacraments at home.

After a life full of satisfying accomplishments. Ozro W. Childs fell asleep in the Lord on April 17, 1 1890. Father Joachim Adam, Vicar General for the Diocese of Monterey–Los Angeles, officiated at the funeral Mass which was celebrated at Saint Vibiana's Cathedral.

OZRO WILLIAM CHILDS (1824–1890)

B. LOS ANGELES BENEFACTOR

Pope Gregory I once said of the Catholic layman: "He that has talent, let him hide it not; he that has abun-dance, let him hasten to generosity; he that has art and skill, let him do his best to share the use and utility thereof with his neighbor."

Ozro William Childs was born at Sutton in Caledonia County, Vermont, on June 3, 1824. His early years were devoted to the teaching profession and learning the trade of tinsmith. Along with thousands of others, Childs was drawn to California in 1850, "partly with the hope of bettering his fortune, partly from a desire to find a milder climate." When he did not find his fortune in the Mother Lode, Childs moved southward to the *Pueblo de Nuestra Señora de los Angeles*. In 1856 he went into the nursery business where he became the undisputed "pio-neer nurseryman and florist of the southern portion of the state."

In 1860 Childs married Emaline Huber, a young lady just arrived in California from her birthplace in Louisville, Kentucky. Mrs. Childs lived well into the 20th century and became a dominating and respected force in the city's social life. When Los Angeles real estate values began their ascent in the mid–1880s, Childs subdivided his vast acreage and became one of the largest property holders in the city. His benefactions to the Catholic Church came at a time when the strug-gling Diocese of Monterey–Los Angeles was in dire financial straits. In 1866 he provided a nine–acre tract of land (the entire block bounded by Sixth, Broadway, Seventh and Hill Streets) for the relocation of Saint Vincent College. Three years later he donated property on the west side of Main Street, a little north of Sixth, for the proposed new Cathedral of Saint Vibiana. Cornerstone ceremonies were held at the site but the church was eventually located some blocks further north.

Childs was a founder of the University of Southern California, which at the time of its establishment, was controlled and managed by the Methodist Episcopal Church. The original deed of trust for the university was executed on July 29, 1879, by Childs, John G. Downey, and Isaias W. Hellman. Mr. Childs also made possible the erection of the Grand Opera House in 1884, and was influential in bringing to the City of the Angels the finest theatre productions then in America. Sometime in 1884 Childs joined his wife and ten children in the Church and during the last six years of his life was an outstanding proponent of Catholicism in the southland. He was buried from St. Vibiana's Cathedral on April 19, 1890, a man well–respected by both the clerical and civil officials of the city.

During his lifetime, Childs had seen Los Angeles grow from a small Mexican *pueblo* of adobe buildings to a city of magnificent residences and business structures. He had watched his area of the state develop from a thinly populated sheep range to a country dotted with cities and prosperous farms. Ozro William Childs "could feel a just pride in the thought that he had contributed in no inconsiderable degree in producing this transformation."

BRYAN JAMES CLINCH (1842–1906)

All too occasionally, one comes across an historian who can do something beyond recalling the deeds of others. Bryan James Clinch was one such person. Born in Ireland, Clinch (1842–1906) studied at the University of Dublin. He came around the Horn to San Francisco in 1867. Though he wanted to become a fullfledged historian, his architectural talents found expression in renovating and designing churches.

In 1868, Clinch was chosen to renovate the chapel at Santa Clara Mission which had been severely damaged by an earthquake. His work there won for the young Irishman a secure place in the architectural circles of Northern California. In the mid 1870s, Clinch was asked to submit designs for the new church envisioned for San Jose. It was the beginning of what became a Cathedral.

Clinch was familiar with the plans that Bramante, Raphael and Michelangelo had for the 16th century Basilica of Saint Peter in Rome. His concept for San Jose called for a Renaissance design emphasizing roundness and a compact cross design. Father Nicholas Con-

giato, the Jesuit pastor, enthusiastically endorsed the plan and was able to convince Archbishop Joseph Sadoc Alemany to approve the stark classical boldness that characterized the design.

The cornerstone for Clinch's church was set in place by the archbishop on March 19, 1876 and a year later, on April 22nd, the church was formally dedicated. People marvelled at Clinch's church as it took its place among the high rises of a predominantly agriculture community. The 12,000 people of San Jose believed as much in themselves as they did in the grand plans of the architect. There would never be anything quite like it in all of California.

Saint Joseph's Cathedral in San Jose remains the state's outstanding example of a strictly classical Greek Cross design. The recent renovation of that historic and magnificent edifice confirms the skill and genius of Bryan James Clinch.

Clinch continued his architectural work in other areas. He and his partner designed more than thirty Catholic churches, among them the Cathedral of the Blessed Sacrament (Sacramento) and Saint Peter's (San Francisco).

Somehow, amidst all his architectural tasks, Clinch found time to compile two volumes on *California and Its Missions. Their History to the Treaty of Guadalupe Hidalgo*. Published by the Whitaker and Ray Company of San Francisco, the work "epitomizes the principal events in a most satisfactory manner," according to a review by P. A. Kinsley. Tragically, a fire at the printers burned all but a few advance copies of the work. The library at the Archival Center has one of the few extant sets of Clinch's volumes.

In April of 1906, Clinch completed and delivered a manuscript on the history of the mission and church of Santa Clara to another printer. The earthquake and fire destroyed that incipient book and seriously injured Clinch himself. He was taken by boat to Oakland where he died at Providence Hospital a few weeks later. The historical accomplishments of Bryan James Clinch live on in the shelves of libraries and in the beautifully restored Cathedral of Saint Joseph in San Jose.

CHRISTOPHER COLUMBUS (1451–1506)

Christopher Columbus was the visionary and adventurer who brought together two worlds and changed the course of history. A man of courage, faith and resolve, he occupies a special place in our country's collective memory.

Over the years, the Knights of Columbus have directed many plaudits to their patron, none quite as significant or worth recalling as the one marking the 500th anniversary of discovery. The Knights fittingly chose 1992 to enter their first float in the annual Tournament of Roses Parade held in Pasadena, California. Their entry was appropriately named "Voyage of Discovery."

The float depicted Christopher Columbus and his flagship, the *Santa Maria*, in keeping with the parade's theme and the Order's observance of Columbus' arrival in the Americas. Four Knights and one Columbian Squire portrayed members of Columbus' crew while riding on the float. They were Joseph Cervetto, Vincent Ordonez, John Shea, James Dale and Kohn Paia.

Upwards of 1.5 million people lined the parade route in Pasadena to view the colorful event. In addition, the parade had a television viewing audience numbering 300 million throughout the world via live telecast facilities, including those of Univision, the Spanish–language network.

The spectacular float was an impressive scale replica of the *Santa Maria*, lead ship of Columbus' flotilla, its details remarkably accurate to the last detail. Designed by Fiesta Parade Floats, Inc., winner of many awards in earlier parades, the replica was portrayed as gently rocking over an ocean of colorful roses and dendrobium orchids.

Parchment scrolls of manuscript maps, portolan sea charts and copperplate engravings intertwined through imaginary water, creating a bold and dramatic floral presentation. On waves of roses and blue iris, the *Santa Maria* was craftfully recreated with a glossy covering of palm bark, with detail area of gold and bronze chrysanthemums. There were also off–white canvas sails of rolled oats with emblems of red carnations that billowed in the California breeze.

Scrolls of ironed cornhusks were crisply edged with gold chrysanthemums. Pennants, flags and the coats of arms were portrayed by an array of materials—carnations, gladioli, dendrobium petals, yellow button mums, sinuata statice, pearl onions and imported seeds. Preparations for the float stretched over several months and thousands of volunteer hours before the ship actually set sail on the parade route. The "launching" was presided over by State Deputy Paul Pryor.

The float measured fifty–five feet long, eighteen feet wide and thirty–four feet high. An on–board sound system provided background music and hydraulic devices compressed the float so it could pass beneath highway overpasses. All kinds of state–of–the–art mechanics were used to make the ship "sea–worthy." The California State Council sold Quincentennial pins and held fund raisers to help finance the $150,000 needed to design and construct the float. It was easily the most elaborate and popular public display in the long history of the Knights of Columbus.

JOSEPH CONCANNON (1928–1978)

Though he lacked any formal viticultural training, Joseph Concannon (1928–1978) was widely recognized for his technical expertise among the world's grape–growing scientists. A third generation wine maker, Concannon's family roots reached as deeply into the Livermore Valley as his grape vines. Those roots were so firmly implanted that when a projected freeway attempted to bisect his vineyard, he suggested a more practical alternate route that by–passed his property and saved the state $8 million!

Born at Livermore, Joseph attended Saint Michael's and the local high school prior to enrolling at Notre Dame University. Graduating in 1949, he served in the United States Air Force for two years during the Korean conflict. Upon his return to California, Joseph joined the family business which his grandfather began in 1883, at the behest of Archbishop Joseph Sadoc Alemany. In 1965, Joseph assumed managerial direction of the Concannon Vineyards.

Dedicated to improving techniques in viticulture, Joseph placed research high on his priority list. In addition to teaching the fundamentals of his trade at the UCLA Extension, he set aside three acres which students from the university could utilize for experimental purposes.

Known as the Wine Industry's "quiet giant," Joseph devoted most of his time to watching over the vineyards, improving marketing procedures and otherwise directing the century–old enterprise. With the ever–growing competition of larger companies, quality became of utmost importance.

In 1961, the tiny Concannon winery turned out a varietal Petite Sirah, based on an unheard–of, unheralded filler grape that was fine for rounding and finishing generic Burgundy. Today there are almost as many Petite Sirahs as Cabernet Sauvignons and Zinfandels.

Concannon served the commonweal too. He was President of the Livermore Public School Board and Chairman of its water district. He worked for the Diocese of Oakland as a member of the Charities and Education boards. And he was active in a host of parochial affairs. At the professional level, Mr. Concannon was a director of the Wine Institute and a member of the Enology Committee for the University of California at Davis.

Nathan Chroman, a professor at the University of California, wrote that Concannon was "as easy to like as his wines." He never oversold or over–promoted his wines. His reputation for honesty and competence was a by–word in the industry.

Concannon had a sense of humor too. Commenting once on California's "oaked" wines, he said: "I can't understand these oak lovers. If I liked the taste of wood, I would chew a toothpick."

A devout Catholic, Concannon liked to recall that his family had provided light and sweet altar wines for almost a century. In every section of the United States and in more than thirty countries, Concannon wine is still used at daily Mass. Joseph Concannon packed into a relatively short life accomplishments worthy of the traditions launched on California soil by other outstanding pioneers.

PETER THOMAS CONMY (1901–1996)

Not only does the Archdiocese of Los Angeles have the largest number of Catholics in the nation, it also has an archival facility which has been described by the State Librarian for California as the finest "of its sort in the United States." The holdings at Mission Hills were dramatically expanded in mid 1995 by the acquisition of the massive Peter T. Conmy Collection of materials relating to the history of the Catholic Church in Northern California.

Born at San Francisco July 8, 1901, the son of Thomas Cherry Conmy and Mary Henrietta (Richter), Peter made his initial studies in the local public schools. During the subsequent years, he established a distinguished educational pedigree, with degrees from the University of California, Stanford University and the University of San Francisco in Library Science, education, history and law.

From 1926 to 1943, Dr. Conmy was a certified teacher in the San Francisco Public School system, as well as debate coach, counselor and evening school administrator. On November 1, 1943, he was appointed Librarian for the City of Oakland, a position he held for over a quarter century. Upon his retirement in 1969, Conmy was named historian for the City of Oakland.

On July 11, 1928 Peter married Emiliette Constance Storti at Saint Francis of Assisi Church in San Francisco. His two children were raised at the family home on North Ardmore in Piedmont.

A lifelong member of the Knights of Columbus, Peter served as Grand Knight for two terms. He was named a Knight of Saint Gregory by Pope Paul VI in 1964 and a Knight of Malta in 1976. Conmy occupied many frater-

nal roles, including historiographer for the Order of Alhambra, official historian for the Native Sons of the Golden West, the Young Men's Institute, the Serra Club, the BPOE and the Rotary Club.

A prolific author, Peter wrote on practically every aspect of California Catholic life. In a series of brochures issued by the Native Sons of the Golden West, he composed essays on such luminaries as Stephen Mallory White, Fray Junípero Serra, Philip Augustine Roach and Romauldo Pacheco.

His encyclopedic 433 page tome, *Seventy Years of Service, 1902–1972*, a history of the Knights of Columbus in California, is without peer and, a quarter century after its appearance, is still hailed for its distinctive style and informative content. At the request of Bishop Floyd L. Begin, Peter spent several years preparing a history for the Diocese of Oakland, a superb example of historiography.

In mid–1995, plans were drawn up whereby Dr. Conmy, still active at ninety–four years of age, entrusted his vast collection of historical notes, writings, books and ephemera to the care of the Archival Center for the Archdiocese of Los Angeles. The actual transfer took place on July 6, when two large truckloads of books and files arrived in Mission Hills, California.

In addition to 120 boxes of books on practically every aspect of California history and the Catholic Church in the northland, the archival materials consist of eight large file cabinets. Twenty–five of the drawers contain clippings, brochures, handwritten notes, manuscripts, newspapers and related items arranged in a coded sequence. There are also two drawers of parochial materials, three drawers of items relating to the Knights of Columbus, one each for the Native Sons of the Golden West and the *Grizzly Bear*, and four devoted to miscellaneous ledgers and scrapbooks.

Dr. Conmy's materials, filed in an elaborately numbered code system, can be easily located by referring to eight drawers of alphabetically arranged filing cards. The acquisition of the Peter T. Conmy Collection by the Archival Center considerably expanded the data base of the Archival Center and made the archdiocesan facility a truly state wide resource for the story of the Catholic Church in the Golden State.

CHARLES CLIFFORD CONROY (1881–1953)

Eulogized as an internationally known scientist, historian, educator, Charles Clifford Conroy was "a man unique in his generation. . . one who was versed to an incomparable degree in the fields of theoretical knowledge," yet remaining "untainted by any spirit of mechanism or materialism."

Charles Conroy (1881–1953) was on the faculty of old Saint Vincent's College in Los Angeles when that noble institution forever closed its doors in 1911. Two years later, following his marriage to Agnes T. Hayes, Conroy was named Editor of *The Tidings* by Bishop Thomas J. Conaty, a post he held for the next thirteen years. In 1909 he was elected a member of the *Societe Scientifique* and, in 1912, a Fellow of the Royal Astronomical Society of London. Several of his learned articles were published, one on Innocent III and another on the Reformation. His book reviews were always in demand as were his personal observations on local history.

Conroy was a faculty member of Los Angeles College, the minor seminary in the southland, for seven years and from there he went to Loyola University where he became Chairman of the Department of History. He lived in Southern California during the episcopate of five bishops, one of whom ruled the Church for thirty years. Although history was foremost among Conroy's interests, his accomplishments in the areas of astronomy, meteorology and seismology were widely known. A paper on the 1933 Long Beach earthquake earned him a fellowship in the American Association for the Advancement of Science.

A gentle man as well as a gentleman, Conroy was decidedly outspoken on certain matters. He believed, for instance, that "the Church in this country was in danger of gradual conversion into a mere organ of social welfare, to the detriment of its fundamental object of divine worship." An entertaining speaker of wide repute, Conroy enjoyed telling about the youngster who wrote in his essay on early Church history, "there was a widespread movement in the 18th and 19th centuries called Latitude–in–Arianism."

Greatest of Conroy's written works was *The Centennial, 1840–1940* published to commemorate the establishment of the hierarchy in California. What little was recorded of ecclesiastical activities in Southern California prior to 1960 can be traced to that highly informative book. It will be forever lamented that Doctor Conroy's premature death cut short his contemplated history of Catholicism in California, for he had that rare knowledge of the Church that only a personal association with most of the "transitional priests" could give. He knew them all—and they knew him!

His incredible range of knowledge, tremendous patience for detail and an amazingly vivid memory were his qualities as an historian; but it was as a Christian that he excelled in those sublime virtues of simplicity, humility and courage. At home, in rectory, chancery, classroom, newspaper office and even in dusty old archives, Conroy was thought of as a member of everything "Catholic" in California. His life could almost be described as that of a "churchman," for to him nothing else had any importance.

To tell "California's Catholic Heritage" without mentioning Charles Clifford Conroy would be ingratitude at its height. He was, to quote a close friend, a "peerless Christian gentleman, a man to whom we shall look as a legendary figure by reason of the gifts with which God had endowed him."

PEDRO DE CORDOBA (1881–1950)

Monsignor Fulton J. Sheen once referred to Pedro de Cordoba (1881–1950) as having been "gifted with an angelic voice for his work of looking after that portion of God's flock unable to leave their homes for Sunday Mass."

Born in New York City, Pedro studied theater arts in school, while working nights and weekends as a stage hand on Broadway. He made his debut in 1902 with E. H. Southern in "If I Were a King." The reviewers enthusiastically hailed him as "an up–and–coming thespian."

Pedro came to Hollywood in 1935 and, shortly thereafter, appeared in several major films, including "The Keys of the Kingdom," "The Mark of Zorro" and "Captain Blood." There he became affiliated with the Catholic Family Theater and starred in such dramatizations as "The Lost Mines of the *Padres*" which emphasized the role of the Church in the work of evangelization.

Known for the dignity and grandeur of his voice, Pedro participated annually in the series of Holy Week broadcasts of "The Living God." That series attracted national attention and was commended by *Time* magazine for its spiritual values.

Perhaps Pedro de Cordoba is best remembered for his role as Fray Junípero Serra in John Steven McGroarty's "Mission Play" at San Gabriel. Surely that portrayal was esteemed by Pedro above all others for he personally regarded Serra as one of the "truly important personages in American Church annals."

During the many years of his involvement in the entertainment industry, Pedro served in many public positions, including that of President of the Catholic Actors Guild. In 1944, the Sodalities in the Archdiocese of Los Angeles, which represented all the Catholic high schools and colleges, selected Pedro de Cordoba as the "outstanding personality of the year" for his "inspirational characterizations in radio and movies." When Pedro was presented with the statuette of Our Lady in the Ball Room of the Biltmore Hotel, on February 11th Mary Lanigan Healy told her readers in *The Tidings* that Pedro had been awarded the first of Hollywood's "spiritual Oscars."

Pedro, his wife Eleanor and their six children lived at 112 South Wilton Place for many years. Shortly after Father Thomas Fogarty took up his pastorate at Saint Brendan's Church, Pedro suggested that the parish inaugurate a weekly Mass via radio. The Mitchell Boy Choir would provide the chant. The program, the first of its kind in the west, became an instant success. As narrator for the weekly series, Pedro became known to hundreds of thousands of shut–ins unable to attend Mass in their own churches.

The highly–respected veteran of stage and screen died on Sunday morning, September 17, 1950, while preparing for his weekly broadcast of Holy Mass. It was as if he had written the script himself. Pedro's funeral was conducted at Blessed Sacrament Church in Hollywood and there he was eulogized by James Francis Cardinal McIntyre as "the gentle voice of Christ in an industry so often forgetful of its obligations to God and society."

The committal prayers recited at Holy Cross Cemetery were broadcast the following Sunday as a prelude to the weekly radio Mass. Few people then or later had a larger funeral audience than Pedro de Cordoba.

DEAN CORNWELL (1892–1960)

Aside from its extensive collection of books, the Los Angeles Public Library has long been known for its exquisite "Pageant of California History in Mural Paintings," the work of Dean Cornwell (1892–1960).

Born in Louisville, Cornwell began drawing as a child and by eighteen he was a member of the staff for the Louisville *Herald*. In 1911, he moved to Chicago where he found work in the art department of the Chicago *Tribune*.

In 1915, Cornwell relocated in New York City where he became a pupil of Harvey Dunn. There he achieved success as an illustrator for such national magazines as *Redbook* and *Cosmopolitan*.

Cornwell exhibited some of his works in Los Angeles in the mid 1920s and, in 1927, he accepted a commission to paint a series of murals in the Los Angeles Public Library building, a challenge that stretched over five years. Later, Cornwell did murals for the Lincoln Memorial Shrine in Redlands. By the time of his demise in New York City on December 3, 1960, his name was prominently enshrined among the outstanding muralists of the American west.

Rupert Hughes contends that "Los Angeles chose Dean Cornwell to illuminate the Library with figures symbolizing the great builders of the Sunset Realm. He collected them into wonderfully–ordered groups, as into a heaven, where they muse on the past, serene in their immortality."

According to the artist himself, the mural paintings were executed in the manner of an Oriental block, or a fifteenth century tapestry, suggesting epoch–making events rather than portraying actual happenings . . . Men, women and children, fruits and flowers, birds and beasts, juxtaposed, moving clockwise and chronologically in colorful pageant, the whole an ordered pattern, comparable in tempo only with the printed pages of the history of this glowing and romantic country."

Cornwell selected four great epochs for the principal walls, flanking them with two sets of allegories carried out on the four double–faced piers supporting the dome. The whole was brought into a rhythmical scheme consistent with the symmetry of the building's architecture. Color values were purposely kept in a restrained key, harmonizing with the many–colored, mosaic–like ceiling decoration. The subjects for the main paintings, measuring 40 by 40 feet, including lunettes, are the Founding of Los Angeles–1781, the Discovery Era, the Mission Era and the Americanization of California.

Dominating the founding scene is a banner of Our Lady of Guadalupe, portrayed above the Holy Father reading a royal proclamation to a group of native Americans. Kneeling before the pontiff is Fray Junípero Serra.

A docked ship personifies the discovery scene which features a group of native Americans offering gifts to the Spanish friars as they disembark on California land for the first time. The mission era depicts three friars discussing plans for the frontier outposts they were planning to erect along California's *El Camino Real*. Finally, in the Americanization scene, the various nationalities of gold seekers and other immigrants are shown as they began replacing the Indians as the predominate population in the Golden State.

The eight smaller panels, measuring 12 by 19 feet, are symbolic presentations of the beginning of arts and industries in California, together with the conquering of the elements. In each of these panels, the Franciscans are featured as the protectors and spokesmen for the Indians.

Recently restored after suffering extensive smoke damage, the murals of Dean Cornwell are still a major attraction of the Los Angeles Public Library.

ANTONIO F. CORONEL (1817–1894)

The name of Antonio F. Coronel (1817–1894) is prominently associated with the early history of the *Pueblo de Nuestra Señora de los Angeles*. Probably no other individual occupied more positions of public trust than the Mexican–born merchant, rancher and educator who first came to California in 1834.

During his sixty years in the southland, Coronel actively participated in the transitional phase of the area's history. He not only witnessed the gradual development of its resources and the remarkable expansion of its interests, but he also contributed much thereto "by his sagacity, enterprise and thorough familiarity with local conditions."

His training in medicine, which Coronel never utilized in California, admirably qualified him for the various positions of trust which he occupied. The popular, clever and sprightly pioneer served as justice of the peace, member of the city council and county assessor.

Coronel's name was well known throughout California. He was state treasurer for several years as well as a member of the legislature. He established the first Department of Public Works, at Los Angeles, and was the city's mayor from 1851 to 1853. During his tenure in the latter office, he encouraged the citizenry to gather in the Plaza, where, at the sound of a gong, they would vote on matters by raising their hands.

Through his association with the old Franciscan friars, Coronel, a devout Catholic, became a staunch champion of the defenseless Mission Indians of Southern California, addressing countless interventions on their behalf to federal, state and local officials. He also gave most generously of his time whenever the *padres* sought his advice in business matters.

Coronel deeply appreciated the need for preserving the evidences of the Golden State's early heritage. He helped to organize the Historical Society of Southern California and was the one most responsible for the centennial celebration of Fray Junípero Serra's death. Antonio's close friendship with Helen Hunt Jackson was gratefully acknowledged by that versatile writer in her historical works.

During the course of many years, Coronel gradually gathered "the largest and most valuable collection of historical materials relating to this section and to this coast in the country." After Coronel's death, his wife, Mariana, presented the extensive collection to the city. It was publicly displayed in the Chamber of Commerce Building, until 1912, when it was transferred to the Los Angeles County Museum of History, Science and Art. The Coronel Collection can still be viewed at the museum by appointment. Catalogued as #A.110.58, the vast assortment of documents, paintings, photographs, costuming and other historical memorabilia forms a vital link with the transitional years of California's heritage.

Coronel was essentially a man of and for the people. For his generous aid to public and private enterprises, Los Angeles is much indebted.

MIGUEL COSTANSO (d. 1811)

Miguel Costanso has been described as the "indispensable man" among those pioneers who opened up California as an outpost of the Spanish Empire in 1769. Though officially listed in the army rosters as an engineer, Costanso accompanied the Pedro Fages expedition to California as a cosmographer. His instructions were to draw maps and plans of the ports and other places of importance discovered and occupied by the explorers.

The Pacific Slope's first engineer, architect, surveyor and city planner was, according to one commentator, responsible more than anyone, save Fray Junípero Serra, for the successful development of the California we know today. Even in our time, Costanso's map of California and the Bay of San Francisco is looked upon as a masterpiece of cartography.

On July 14, 1769, Costanso accompanied Gaspar de Portola, Fages, two priests and the twenty–seven soldiers, muleteers and Christian Indians on their trek from San Diego to Monterey. It was Costanso's business to lay out the royal *presidio* and mission—an assignment which ultimately he performed with singular success. Costanso was a careful and methodical recordkeeper. With the utmost precision he noted dates and places, characteristics of Indians, future mission sites, earthquakes, etc. His diary between July 14, 1769, and January 24, 1770, is a classic in California literature.

That diary has a history all its own. Published in 1770 as *Diario Histórico de los viages de Mar y Tierra hechos al norte de la California*, this first book relating exclusively to California gave a complete account of the Portola expedition to Monterey. This tome was rigidly suppressed, however, by the Spanish government which feared that its information would be useful to navigators of other nationalities. Fortunately, it was later republished in London.

Costanso exhibited a wide variety of talents. He envisioned the *pueblo* of San Diego, laid out the *presidio* at Monterey and suggested many ideas for the future *pueblos* and *presidios* of California. He was no visionary dreamer, but a practical engineer with ideas and plans. To him this vast expanse of land presented a challenging but golden opportunity for colonizing.

He was among the first to advocate "opening" California to outsiders. This he veiled under the guise of releasing the military from the "perpetual and involuntary celibacy" to which they were submitted in the early years. In 1794, he advised Viceroy Branciforte that the fortification of California would be most effectively achieved by enlarging even further the Spanish settlements then beginning to dot the landscape. Such could be done through introduction of commercial enterprises.

Costanso continued as an engineer in the viceregal government at Mexico City. His name appears in the annals for the last time at Vera Cruz in 1802. The eminent director of the Southwest Museum, Carl S. Dentzel, once remarked, "The magic of today's Golden State was first conjured by Miguel Costanso, engineer, cosmographer, surveyor, architect, city–planner, economist, sociologist and organizer of the ideas which have given to many the golden opportunity Costanso saw and so successfully worked for as California's first modern man."

NATHANIEL CURRIER (1813–1888) AND JAMES MERRITT IVES (1824–1895)

Nathaniel Currier (1813–1888) and James Merritt Ives (1824–1895) served as printmakers to the American people for over half a century. Offering affordable art to the masses, their hand–colored lithographs made them the largest and most successful print publishers of the 19th century. They outsold and outlasted all their competition.

Religion was an exceptionally potent factor in those days and a large number of Currier and Ives religious prints were made to order, while others were copied from European paintings. The Archival Center's one lithograph, from the Estelle Doheny Collection, is #69 and is entitled "The Sacred Tomb of The Redeemer." Hand–colored and printed on woven paper with margins, it is considerably time–stained, yet is still a precious remnant.

During seventy–five years, Currier and Ives printed more than 7,000 different images and, of these, only forty–two related to California. Though that number may appear insignificant, it far exceeded all other contemporary pictorial depictions of life west of the Mississippi. The major market for Currier and Ives was on the east coast, where the fascination with California started when James Marshall discovered gold in the South Fork of the American River in 1848. That event motivated Currier to publish the first California print, and the firm went on to issue fourteen different California scenes between 1849 and 1851.

Their *View of California*, described as "a fine early view of San Francisco," was probably the most important of their works. It illustrated the gold rush, focusing on the foibles and follies of the Argonauts who left friends and family to head west where discovering and mining of gold was portrayed as easy as plucking apples from trees.

Other satirical characterizations included *California Seeking the Elephant*, *Grand Patent India–Rubber, Air Line Railway to California* and *The Independent Gold Hunter on His Way to California*. The latter featured a well–dressed man walking along a road, carrying several pieces of gold–mining equipment including a shovel and set of scales, link sausages, a mess of fish and a kettle. Behind him is a sign reading "To St. Louis 350 miles. To California 1700 miles."

With the end of the Civil War, America again focused attention on California. Currier and Ives capitalized on this phenomenon and the firm entered its second phase of California printmaking. The earlier lithographs had mocked the rush to California, but now the transcontinental railway could swiftly and safely transport the "new pioneers" to the California coast.

The prints published after 1866 extolled the virtues, the beauty and the opportunity in California. Even mining for gold was pictured in a different light; the laborers in the 1871 lithograph *Gold Mining in California* are diligently working on their claims. That scene showed miners panning, sluicing and using a hydraulic hose to harvest gold, a scene that probably never occurred in real life. Many of the Currier and Ives California prints were obviously based on second–hand accounts.

Experts attributed a large part of their business success to the selection of lithograph subjects. Early on, Currier and Ives recognized the popularity of California prints and they quickly realized that retail sales were enhanced by using the word "California" in a print title.

By the time the doors of Currier and Ives were closed in 1907, the firm had left an indelible mark on 19th century California, from satirical cartoons of the 1850s to the "picture postcards" of the 1870s. Theirs was an American success story.

HENRY DALTON (1803–1884)

Henry Dalton has been characterized as a rash, bold, impulsive, energetic, ambitious, talented and courageous man who left an indelible mark on the local history of Upper San Gabriel Valley. In the course of his nearly eighty–one years, Dalton fled from the tedious routine of a London apprenticeship to Latin America and finally to California, where he owned and operated one of the most progressive *ranchos* in the southland.

Dalton left England at seventeen for Peru, where he worked for two decades as an English merchant. He arrived at San Pedro in October, 1843, aboard the little Mexican brig *Soledad*. His first quest in California centered around hides and tallow, land and gold. Initially, Dalton engaged in mercantilistic endeavors in Los Angeles, followed by several incursions into real estate. He later acquired the *Rancho Azusa* which he operated for many years.

Born and raised a member of the Church of England, Dalton embraced Catholicism and was baptized at San Gabriel Mission, on July 3, 1847. His sponsor was the prominent Hugo Reid. At the age of forty–three, Henry fell in love with the beautiful fourteen year old daughter of Agustin Zamorano. He married María Guadalupe Zamorano at San Gabriel Mission on July 14, 1847. Together the happy couple raised seven children.

A fearless innovator and promoter of forward–looking ideas, Dalton made and lost several fortunes.

Though primarily a man of business, he was active in the political life of Southern California. The prominence of Dalton was highlighted by such witnesses as James A. Forbes, who said that he was "the most important British citizen residing in Southern California in the 1840s." Indeed Dalton's lifestyle sheds light on significant aspects of the southland in the years between 1843 and 1884. And fortunately for posterity, the English–born Dalton left copious records.

A prolific writer, Dalton began keeping copies of his vast correspondence after 1841. At the Henry E. Huntington Library, in San Marino, there are fifty–one bound volumes of letters, 1,309 business papers and 1,123 pieces of correspondence. The story of Henry Dalton's life unfolds a tale of ceaseless ambition. His death on January 21, 1884, brought down the curtain on a pioneer whose example accelerated the end of the grazing era and the beginning of a new agricultural period for California's southland.

How appropriate that his biography, recently written by Sheldon G. Jackson for the Western Frontiersmen Series, was published under the umbrella of Azusa Pacific College, which occupies land once owned by Henry Dalton.

WILLIAM GOODWIN DANA (1797–1858)

William Goodwin Dana, a "gentleman whose unbounded liberality and hospitality were known throughout California," had a New England heritage, having been born in Boston on May 5, 1797. After a number of years at sea, the cousin of the man who authored *Two Years Before the Mast* came to California in 1825, and established himself in the trading business at Santa Barbara.

Shortly after his arrival in the Channel City, Dana became interested in the Catholic Faith. On July 29, 1827, he was baptized at San Diego by Father Antonio Menendez, the Dominican Chaplain of the *presidio*. Dana returned to Santa Barbara and applied for naturalization papers, which he received the following year. With these legal complications satisfied, "Don Guillermo" married Josefa Carrillo, daughter of the socially–prominent one–time governor.

In 1829, Dana began work on a schooner which he needed in his trading business along the coast. The ship, subsequently launched as *La Fama* (later *Santa Barbara*), merited for its designer the privilege of being among the first American to build a ship on the coast of California. Dana's accomplishments were more extensive, however, than ship–building. The annals refer to him as appraiser, captain of the port, *alcalde* of Santa Barbara, and, in the American period, prefect and county

treasurer. He was also listed as a trader, soapmaker, physician, and architect, and for a time as the holder of a special license for sea–otter hunting.

Though he held public office on several occasions, Dana was not politically–minded and managed to avoid entangling himself with his father–in–law's activities. Despite his lack of interest, he was elected to the senate in 1849, but there is no evidence that he ever accepted the office.

Dana became "one of the greatest landowners of California" as grantee of the 38,000 acre Rancho Nipomo in San Luis Obispo County where he established his permanent residence from 1839 onwards. For many years his home was among the few habitations between Santa Barbara and San Luis Obispo. In addition to his business dealings at the ranch, such activities as fiestas, bull fights, the sport of the cock–pit, and the other pastimes indulged in by Californians were in evidence on the Nipomo.

In 1847, the Dana home was designated by Governor Stephen W. Kearny as the central station for the mail route between San Francisco and San Diego. The two couriers one from each city, met and exchanged mail sacks, thus providing California with a bi–monthly mail service.

Thomas Oliver Larkin regarded Dana as a man "of greater influence than any other foreigner of the Santa Barbara region" and spoke of him as "a man of wealth and much respectability of character and honest intentions, well versed in general information of the day; much looked up to by the poorer people and of influence with them."

According to the register books at San Luis Obispo "Don Guillermo" died on February 12, 1858, leaving behind twelve children (nine others died in infancy) to carry on the name and tradition of the Dana family. The name of William Goodwin Dana, a native of New England, is written on the pages of our history as a worthy adopted son of California.

DOROTHY DAY (1897–1980)

It is not generally known that Dorothy Day (1897–1980), that extraordinary Christian woman of the twentieth century, lived in California through her childhood years. During a visit to the Bay Area, in November of 1971, the little lady who cherished and lived among America's poor, related her early experiences to Palma Trentacoste.

Dorothy's father had been a journalist in New York City. He moved his family first to Berkeley and then to Oakland's Idora Park district. He took the ferry boat to work each day in San Francisco. She recalled that on the early morning of April 18, 1906, "the chimney came down. I was in bed. We took refugees in. We shared food and clothes with all. It was a wonderful experience of true charity."

During her 1971 interview, she flipped through a big, shabby address book which never left her hands. She reeled off facts and figures that ranged from the 1920s, through the 30s, 40s, 50s and 60s. Her voice was described as "flat as a midwest farm wife."

Typically, Dorothy's clothes were right out of the Catholic Worker barrel. Clean, shapeless, cotton garments. A farm wife's housedress, eyeglasses on a string, a wool knit cap and nondescript shoes. Phone calls from all over California interrupted the interview. Cesar Chavez called from the valley. Catholic workers called for advice from New York where they were putting their paper to press.

A further delay occurred when Dorothy stopped for half an hour and did a telephone interview with Radio Station KPFA in Berkeley. Television Station KQED called about taping. Joan Baez called. A bouquet of tiny garnet roses was delivered from Podesta Baldocchi.

An admirer had lent Dorothy a white, four door Mercedes Benz for her stay. Her volunteer driver laughed as he told of the places he had driven his distinguished guest in the magnificient vehicle. The itinerary featured all of the Bay Area's poverty pockets.

One of the stops was Our Lady of Guadalupe Church, on Broadway, over the tunnel. There Dorothy and her long–time friend, Father Donald C. McDonnell, prayed the rosary. Some elderly Hispanic ladies joined in. The driver recalled that when they prayed "Deliver us from the fires of hell," he could "feel the fire."

Dorothy left the following day and continued her apostolate to the nation's poor for another decade. Throughout those years she occupied a central role in the formation of Catholic values regarding social action and concern about the forgotten and oppressed. The philosophy which formed the *Catholic Worker* movement has been described as "unifying religious hope and social betterment by advocating radical social reconstruction based on the Gospel."

And much of that philosophy owes its origin to the influences of the years Dorothy Day spent in California. And, even in death, she speaks to contemporary Catholics through her writings, as a journalist, and through the half–century–old newspaper she helped found, the *Catholic Worker*.

EDWIN DEAKIN (1838–1923)

While it is true that interest in the paintings of the California missions is predominantly historical, yet the crumbling condition of many of the structures and their unusual style of architecture lend them an air of the picturesque that is wholly wanting in many other scenes selected to convey Western America's grandeur and beauty. One of the half dozen outstanding artists who used the old Franciscan foundations as outlets for his artistic talent was Edwin Deakin (1838–1923). This English–born pioneer arrived in San Francisco in 1870, determined to place on canvas a series of paintings representing all the original missions.

Deakin's fascination with the missions dates to his earliest days in the Golden State, and San Francisco de Asis was probably his first California subject. Thus, the already well–known painter began what one writer called "the task of transmitting to future generations these notable old structures in all their timeworn beauty." While he shared with his contemporaries a great enthusiasm and talent for landscape scenes, Deakin "developed a special vein of his own in picturesque, romantic paintings of the California missions." His portrayal of the historic edifices in this style allowed Deakin to conjure up the nostalgic and sentimental visions deeply imbedded in popular imaginations. Without this "picturesque approach, his paintings may well have remained only historical curiosities."

Deakin was a careful observer, and on his journeys around the state he made numerous sketches of the missions, always with a mind to opening the eyes of Californians to the urgency of preserving the old landmarks. The artist completed two series of oil paintings depicting the missions. A third series of smaller scenes was executed on a fine grade of English watercolor paper.

A book of his reproductions was issued at Berkeley in 1900. The modest publication, entitled *The Twenty–One Missions of California*, consists of a representative grouping of a small black and white half–tones. There are obvious similarities in Deakin's works. In most cases the mission in question is portrayed against a natural setting in very vivid colors. The trails of fog and mist, one of Deakin's favorite motifs, is a trademark of the Turneresque school of painters to which he belonged.

Many of the artist's sketches are in the Howard Willoughby Collection at the Oakland Art Museum as are a number of his original oil works. One complete series of the Deakin paintings has been on exhibition in the galleries of the Los Angeles County Museum of Natural History for over thirty years.

That Deakin performed an invaluable service to historians is unquestionable. One writer noted that he did for the missions "what no other man has done, what no one else can hope to do." He portrayed those once–proud institutions in the years before the ravages of time and neglect took their terrible toll. "The story of Edwin Deakin's struggles and sacrifices to perpetuate these missions before the destroying hand of time and the vandalism of generations of robbers and abuse had utterly obliterated them" is as noble as any in the realm of arts and letters.

NICHOLAS DEN (1812–1862)

The "emerging" Santa Barbara of the 1850s passed through a decade of economic, social, religious and institutional confusion, all of which tended to bring out the baser qualities in many of that town's citizens. It was during this period of "cynical liberalism" that Nicholas Den came upon the scene as an ardent champion of ecclesiastical rights.

The Irish–born medical student had earlier left his native land for Nova Scotia "with an unblemished character, which I trust, shall ever uphold, no matter what lands and casualties the Almighty may send me. . . ." He subsequently journeyed to Boston where he shipped as supercargo on the American bark *Kent* for the west coast. Reaching California in 1836, the twenty–four year old Hibernian was heartened by the kindly reception accorded him and decided to make his home in the pastoral atmosphere of Santa Barbara.

Not long after his arrival, *Don Nicolas* began courting Rosa Antonia Hill, the daughter of a prominent Santa Barbara businessman. Their subsequent marriage was a most happy one even though neither spoke the other's language for a long while after their wedding at Santa Ines Mission.

Apparently Den never received his medical degree for we are told that he "did not practice or pose as a physician beyond treating friends and members of his own family." The ten children were brought up on the *Rancho Dos Pueblos*, a 16,000 acre land grant seventeen miles north of town. In 1845, four years after his naturalization, Den served a brief term as *alcalde*, or mayor, of Santa Barbara.

"A lover of the pastoral existence such as the *ranchos* assured," much of Den's time was spent raising cattle for their hides, which he shipped to markets in Boston. In all his activities, the Irish doctor best served the Church, and after he and his father–in–law, Daniel Hill rented Santa Barbara Mission from Governor Pio Pico in 1845, Den maintained a consistent attitude of defense for the historic old foundation.

Nicholas Augustus Den, "an intelligent, educated and accomplished gentleman," died at Santa Barbara on March 3, 1862. The friars rewarded his many years of faithful service by having his remains interred in the mission cemetery. Authors of California's early days took cognizance of Den's noble qualities. One noted that "Don Nicolas became a very prominent citizen of Santa Barbara, held several public offices, was a man of the highest reputation, and left an enviable record of service to his state and community. . . His honesty and generous nature gained him many friends, while his great influence was ever exerted for the betterment of those around him." The praise was not idle flattery, for California's Catholics can be grateful to this devoted, well–bred foreigner, more sympathetic in his understanding than many of its native leaders.

RICHARD SOMERSET DEN (1821–1895)

Richard Somerset Den, "a typical Irish gentleman of the old school," was one of five children born of a well–established and respected aristocratic family in Garandara, County Kilkenny, in 1821. Shortly after receiving his medical degree at Dublin in August of 1842, the Lord Mayor of London, Sir John Pirie, appointed Den surgeon of a Scottish ship bound for Melbourne and India.

Den altered his plans after disembarking at Mazatlan, where he heard that his brother, Nicholas, had settled in Santa Barbara. The young medic changed his course and arrived in the Channel City soon thereafter. With his coming, California received the first foreign physician possessing a medical degree.

The itinerant physician went to Los Angeles in 1842, "to perform some difficult surgical operations." He was so successful that the residents induced him to become "the first doctor to establish a regular medical practice in the *pueblo*." By 1845, Den had a quasi–hospital in operation to care for the smallpox victims of Los Angeles. "He engineered a piece of state legislation which returned two percent of the fines and the sales of smuggled goods confiscated at San Pedro for the support of his free hospital." During the hostilities of 1846–47, Dr. Den was a familiar sight in both camps where he served the injured soldiers without any recompense whatsoever.

In 1848, "*Don Ricardo*," as he was known to his friends, led a prospecting party north to Sullivan's diggings, near the present Angel's Camp, Calaveras County. The gold nuggets were neither as large nor as plentiful as the physician had expected and he abandoned the Mother Lode country for San Francisco, where, in 1850, he and six others founded the Society of California Pioneers,

Between 1854 and 1866, Den looked after his ranch of San Marcos near Santa Barbara. In the latter year he returned to Los Angeles and once again became active in the medical profession. That he was highly respected is attested to by those who felt that *despues de Dios, Doctor Doti Ricardo* (after God, comes Doctor Richard).

Den attended Holy Mass daily at the Plaza Church of Our Lady of the Angels. He would then go immediately to the Convent of the Daughters of Charity to examine and treat any infirm nuns or orphaned children. Afterwards he would make himself available to the general public. One contemporary commentator ventured the remark, "Old Dr. Den will be remembered not only with esteem, but with affection. He was seldom seen except on horseback, in which fashion he visited his patients and was, all in all, somewhat a man of mystery. He rode a magnificent coal–black charger, and was himself always dressed in black. He wore, too, a black felt hat and beneath the hat clustered a mass of wavy hair as white as snow. In addition to all this, his standing collar was so high that he was compelled to hold his head erect, and, as if to offset the immaculate linen, he tied around the collar a large black scarf. Thus attired and seated on his richly caparisoned horse, Dr. Den appeared always dignified and even imposing."

Though *Don Ricardo* was at all times dressed as though he were going to a wedding, he never attended his own but remained a bachelor until his death on July, 22, 1895. At the time of his funeral in Saint Vibiana's Cathedral, the local press noted that "Dr. Den was always a practical Catholic. He was deeply interested in the progress of the Church as well as various educational institutions connected with it, and a liberal patron of charitable institutions."

Richard Somerset Den, the first foreign physician to establish a medical practice in California, was buried at the very hill–top from which a half century earlier, he had first looked down upon the infant *Pueblo de Nuestra Señora de los Angeles.*

THOMAS DOAK (c. 1787–c. 1848)

It needs to be recorded in Catholic annals that the distinction of being "the first American to settle officially in California" belongs to Thomas Doak, a Yankee tar, hailing from Massachusetts. Very little is known about this interesting man. Professor John A. Schutz of the University of Southern California says that the Doak family was originally from Marblehead and spread across Massachusetts after 1690. Thomas may have been born in Dracut or Northfield, but probably not in Boston."

A Thomas Doak married Betsey in Dracut in 1813, when she was twenty–three. A child or two came in Northfield before her death on June 23, 1816. Thomas, in sorrow, could have left Northfield at the death of his wife and sailed for California. In any event, Thomas Doak arrived at Monterey, in 1816, aboard the *Albatross.* Though likely descended from Huguenots, he became aquainted almost immediately with the priests at Carmel.

After taking instructions, he was baptized at San Carlos Borromeo, as Felipe Santiago. Two years later, the twenty–nine year old Doak married Maria Lugarda, the daughter of Mariano Castro. Shortly after the ceremony, Doak, who was a carpenter by trade, was entrusted with the task of painting and decorating the church at San Juan Bautista Mission.

Doak usually signed his work as "Felipe Santiago Doc." It isn't clear precisely why he preferred this abbreviated surname. In fact, the form has long confused chroniclers. Doak received only board and lodging in return for his work. Charles Francis Saunders conjectured that "perhaps to that waif of the sea, with the memory of existence in a windjammer's forecastle still fresh upon him, life in a Mission may have been in itself return enough."

Rexford Newcomb wrote that Thomas Doak's use of quality paint "is attested by the remains of the color still extant." The distinguished architectural historian felt that there was abundant evidence to suggest that Doak was not an outstanding artist.

A careful scrutiny of the annals does not reveal much about the easterner. There's a note in William H. Cunningham's *Log of the Courier* that Doak accompanied the captain on his visit to *Nuestra Señora de la Soledad,* in early August of 1826. It is also known that in 1832, Doak took up residence at Monterey. He later lived for some years at Santa Cruz and it was there that two of his children were born. He had business at San Jose too, where he engaged in selling lumber.

Alexander Taylor recorded that Doak died sometime before 1848. He mentioned that the Doaks had six children. Possibly several of them grew to adulthood in the east. One of the few contemporary references to Doak states that the "American carpenter [had] a fair standing in the community." Future researchers will surely discover additional details about this Catholic pioneer.

DOCAS

Like all peoples everywhere, those who attended public schools in California at the turn of the century long recalled the lessons they learned and the textbooks they studied. One book that stands out more vividly than others is *Docas, The Indian Boy at Santa Clara,* which was published at Boston by the D.C. Heath Company in 1899.

The textbook has an interesting background. Initially written as a thesis in history under the direction of Dr. Mary Sheldon Barnes, it was envisioned "as reading material for the children in the University School connected with the Department of Education at the Leland Stanford Junior University."

The author, Genevra Sisson Snedden, noticing the "never–failing delight with which those children welcomed each new installment," decided to arrange the stories into a format that would have a larger audience. Research for the book was far more extensive than for most others of its kind. In addition to an impressive bibliography, the author conducted extensive personal interviews and consulted numerous unpublished manuscripts in her quest for accuracy.

The book is about Indians, those "who lived near the Pacific Ocean before our grandfathers were born, and before we Americans came west and settled the country." It tells the story of Docas, a native Californian who lived in a *rancheria* near San Francisco Bay where his father was the local chieftain. Docas was about seven years old when the stories began unfolding.

Docas's first encounter with the colonizers occurred when he met Fray Thomas de la Peña, about 1778. After some lengthy discussions, the friar invited Docas and his friends to take up residence at the newly–established Santa Clara Mission. The following chapters are concerned with life at the mission: building projects—schooling and catechizing—farming and ranching. A wholly new way–of–life was gradually unveiled before Docas and he found himself happily immersed in meeting its challenges.

In May of 1784, Fray Junípero Serra came to Santa Clara Mission to dedicate the new church. Docas and his friends were especially happy to meet the man who introduced Christianity to the Pacific Slope. The friar personally thanked Docas for singing in the choir and then, as he turned to leave, he said: "Love God, my son."

The rest of the book relates the later life of Docas and his final years with Don Secundini Robles. We are told that this native Californian who lived his life as a small boy at the Indian *ranchería*, as a larger boy and man at the Mission, and as an old man with his wife, children and grandchildren was a contented and happy person in every way.

Was Docas a real person—or was he the creation of the storyteller? Because the author was well–acquainted with the folklore and traditions of the native Californians, one can reasonably presume that if Docas were not real, he at least epitomized the people of his time. Can this historical novel adapted for children be regarded a valid portrayal of Indian life at the California mission? The answer must be "yes," if one attributes any credence to the author's preface which clearly states that these "stories tell about things that actually happened to Indian children long ago in California, so they are what you call true stories, not made–up ones."

ISIDORE BERNARD DOCKWEILER (1867–1947)

"Throughout his entire life," Isidore Bernard Dockweiler was known as a man who "never deviated a hair's breadth from his responsibility as a devout and uncompromising son of the Church. Born on December 28, 1867, in the family home, located at the southwest corner of First and Fort Streets (now Broadway), Isidore was one of the three sons of Henry Dockweiler and Margaretha Sugg.

During his early school days, young Dockweiler acted as "train bearer" for Bishop Francis Mora at pontifical ceremonies in Saint Vibiana's Cathedral. In later years the prelate offered to send *"pequeño* Ysidro," whom he had personally baptized, to Rome, should the lad decide to study for the priesthood.

Isidore attended Saint Vincent's College, where he received a commercial diploma in June of 1883. He then began work as a salesman in Joseph Mesmer's Queen Boot and Shoe Store in the old United States Hotel Building on North Main Street. In August of 1885, he returned to Saint Vincent's and two years later was awarded that institution's first Bachelor of Arts degree.

Soon after leaving school, Isidore was given a position in the law firm of Anderson, Fitzgerald and Anderson. There he "read law" and by October 4, 1889, was proficient enough to qualify for the California State Bar. Subsequently, he was also admitted to practice in Arizona and Nevada, as well as before the United States Supreme Court, where he argued several important railroad cases.

On June 30, 1891, Isidore married Gertrude Reeve (1870–1937) in San Francisco at Saint Mary's Cathedral. Of the eleven children born to the Dockweilers, five of the eight boys followed their father into the legal profession. One became a United States Congressman and later District Attorney for Los Angeles County; another, an admiral in the Navy; still another, a municipal and later superior court judge. Henry and Frederick remained active in the Dockweiler law firm, the former having served many years in the United States Diplomatic Service.

Though responsibilities to his large family ruled out a political career, Mr. Dockweiler was an active member of the Democratic Party. Against his protest, and while absent from the convention floor, he was nominated for lieutenant governor of California in 1902. (He received a plurality of votes but lost the election on a legal technicality.) He was delegate several times to Democratic National conventions, and from 1916 to 1932, was the party's California member on the National Committee. His name appeared on the ballot as a presidential elector on a number of occasions. When he refused an appointment as Assistant Secretary of the Treasury in 1913, President Woodrow Wilson named the California jurist to the Board of Indian Commissioners.

On the local scene, Dockweiler served in a variety of positions. He was a member of the Board of Library Commissioners, Chairman of the Los Angeles County Housing Authority and, on the state level, a trustee of the Normal School at San Diego, and a member of the California State Park Commission. After his death, a grateful state named the beach park between Playa del Rey and Redondo in Dockweiler's name.

It was largely through Dockweiler's efforts that the statue of Fray Junípero Serra was placed in Statuary Hall in the nation's capital in 1932. On that occasion, as principal speaker, Isidore credited the grey–robed friar with being "our country's first civilizer," a man justly standing "for the edification of future generations, among the immortals of our nation."

Mother Frances Cabrini was an occasional visitor to Dockweiler's legal office. The family recalls how Isidore referred to the humble little nun as a "veritable saint" many years before she formally received that designation from the Holy See. It was a source of great happiness to Isidore Dockweiler that, in 1939, he became the first native son of Southern California to complete fifty years of continuous law practice in the state. Several years earlier, he had been created a Knight of Saint Gregory by Pope Pius XI.

The seventy–nine year old jurist closed his busy life at Saint Vincent's Hospital in Los Angeles on February 6, 1947. His eulogy, preached by Bishop Timothy Manning, captured the image of a man who judged all things by religious standards:

> There was no conflict in his loyalties, there was no distortion in his obligations. No man could point the accusing finger at any page of his life's history. He was verily that blending of parent, priest and patriot, the Christian gentleman which it is the unique distinction of the Catholic Church to reproduce.

CARRIE ESTELLE DOHENY

Known as a woman "of vivid personality and irresistible charm," Mrs. Edward L. Doheny was endowed with that buoyant vitality, quick mind and grasp of practical affairs discernible only in personalities deeply etched in the chronicles of history.

Carrie Estelle Betzold was born in Philadelphia on the Feast of Our Lady of the Angels, August 2, 1875. After spending her earliest years in Marshalltown, Iowa, Carrie came to Los Angeles in 1897. With her marriage at Albuquerque to Edward L. Doheny, on August 22, 1900, she rose, as only a rarely gifted woman could have done, to the opportunities now open to her as the wife of a man of wealth. During the years of her wedded life, Carrie Doheny traveled widely with her husband. "She

reached the high noon of her long life" on October 25, 1918, when Bishop Joseph S. Glass of Salt Lake received her into the Catholic Church in New York's Saint Patrick's Cathedral.

In 1930, when Mr. Doheny's health began to fail, the couple settled down to a quieter life at their home in Chester Place, a park–like estate near the corner of Adams Boulevard and Figueroa Street in Los Angeles. Mrs. Doheny carried on her husband's philanthropic activities after his death. Among other institutions benefitting from her generosity were the Los Angeles Orphanage, the Orthopedic and Children's Hospital, Saint Vincent's Seminary and the Vincentian House of Studies in Washington, D.C. In 1956, she erected a five–story building to house the constantly expanding Estelle Doheny Eye Foundation of Saint Vincent's Hospital. In 1940, in memory of her late husband, Mrs. Doheny erected a magnificent library at Camarillo, adjacent to Saint John's Seminary. The top floor of the edifice was set aside for the extensive rare books, manuscripts and works of art know throughout the world as the "Estelle Doheny Collection."

Besides the Carrie Estelle Doheny Foundation, established in 1949 for the advancement of education, medicine, religion and science, Mrs. Doheny engaged in countless personal charities, unknown, unheralded and unappreciated. Recognition of her many charitable activities came on June 29, 1939, when Pope Pius XII conferred upon Mrs. Doheny the title of papal countess, the first such bestowal of pontifical nobility ever granted in southern California. Some years later she was named "Woman of the Year" by the Los Angeles *Times*.

Though she was forced to spend the last seventeen years of her life in a world dimmed by the affliciton of

Carrie Estelle Doheny

glaucoma, Carrie Doheny remained a "vital, magnetic woman whose sparkling brown eyes and radiant smile were the outward expression of a warm and generous heart." With the death of Mrs. Doheny on October 30, 1958, it could truly be said, "Her true riches were not the material wealth which was forced upon her, but the eternal, unchanging treasures of fortitude, wisdom, unselfish devotion to those she loved, and a radiant joy in serving God with her whole heart."

EDWARD LAURENCE DOHENY (1856–1929)

A. OIL DEVELOPER

It was once said of Edward L. Doheny, "In a future day when the complete story of the winning of the west is set down by some historian, his name will stand out in bold letters as a rugged personality whose outstanding achievements were marked by the unostentatious manner in which he lived and the scores of real friendships he found time to form during a busy and eventful career that is well worthy of emulation."

Edward was born at Fond du Lac, Wisconsin, on August 10, 1856, the son of Patrick and Eleanor Doheny. Upon graduating from the local high school in 1872, he went to work for the Federal Government as a public surveyor in Kansas, the Indian territories and New Mexico. He prospected for gold in many areas of the west and southwest before arriving in 1890, at San Bernardino, where he and Charles A. Canfield formed the Pacific Gold & Silver Extracting Company.

The story is told how Doheny was sitting one day in front of his Los Angeles hotel when he spotted a wagon coming down the street loaded with a dark, tar–like earthen material. A closer inspection revealed it to be "brea" a substance used for fuel in the local ice plant. Doheny contacted Canfield and the two set out to exploit this newly discovered "black gold." Though unable to lease *El Rancho de la Brea*, the prospectors sunk a shaft at the corner of Second and Glendale Boulevard. Their primitive methods brought in the initial gusher on November 4, 1892, the first of Doheny's eighty–one wells in Los Angeles. It was for him the beginning of "one of the most picturesque and profitable careers that industry ever produced."

In 1897, Edward L. Doheny began acquiring lands adjacent to the Santa Fe Railway in present day Fullerton, near the south slope of Puente Hills. Soon thereafter, he branched out to the San Joaquin Valley area west of Bakersfield. He purchased a block of land in the Coalinga fields in 1909, and organized for its development the American Petroleum Company. The holdings were later expanded by formation of the American Oil Fields Company and the Midway Petroleum Company.

After some years in Mexico, where he brought in the greatest gusher in history, Doheny came back to California in 1916, to form the Pan American Petroleum Company composed of land in Maricopa, and the Casmalia district.

With all his success, Doheny's life was not without its tragedies. His only son died in 1929, and five years earlier the "Dean of Western Oil Producers" was indicted for supposedly offering a bribe to Albert B. Fall, the Secretary of the Interior. Although declared innocent by two successive juries, the shadow of "Teapot Dome" remained a shadow the rest of Doheny's life.

The oil magnate's benefactions to Southern California were manifold. With the encouragement of his wife, Carrie Estelle, whom he married in 1900, Edward Doheny built Saint Vincent's Church, the library at the University of Southern California, and, according to one journalist "it was largely through his cooperation and benefactions that the extensive program to construct a $5,000,000 plant for Loyola University achieved success." Death came on September 8, 1935 to Edward Laurence Doheny, empire builder, philanthropist, and member of that host of trailblazers which followed the Argonauts into the Western frontiers and took up the work where those rugged pathfinders left off.

EDWARD LAURENCE DOHENY (1856–1935)

B. DOHENY PAPERS

When the Estelle Doheny Collection was closed out in 1986–1987, a fairly larger quantity of documents, letters and related materials amassed by Mrs. Doheny during her lifetime was entrusted for safekeeping and research purposes to the Archival Center, Archdiocese of Los Angeles. Those materials have been catalogued and are now available to qualified scholars.

The largest single quantity of correspondence is from or to Msgr. William J. Doheny (1898–1982), a Holy Cross priest attached to the Sacred Roman Rota. Stretching from 1940 to 1958, the 395 letters deal with a variety of topics, not the least of which was "Cousin Billy's" supposed relationship with Mr. Doheny. There are also eight letters from Eugenio Cardinal Pacelli (later Pope Plus XII) and Msgr. Giovanni Baptiste Montini (later Pope Paul VI) thanking Mrs. Doheny for her many benefactions to the charitable activities of the Holy See.

In an attempt to gather a representative collection of contemporary correspondence, Mrs. Doheny acquired the letters of two prominent personages of the early 1930s. She had known both of these men socially or through her husband's business dealings.

The larger of the collections belonged to a San Fran-

Santa Sabina Shrine at Forest Lawn
tomb of Edward L. Doheny, Jr.

cisco lawyer, Franklin Lane (1864–1921), who had
served as Secretary of the Interior during the Woodrow
Wilson administration. The 269 Lane letters deal predominantly with water and land conservation.

The other comprised ninety–two letters written to
Clarence Walker Barron (1855–1928), a New England
journalist associated with the Boston *Transcript*. Those
letters from the editor of *Barron's Financial Weekly*
relate mostly to the Wall Street scene.

The only letters pertaining directly to the legendary
Edward Laurence Doheny (1856–1935) are those in
which his wife reported on incidents that occurred while
Mr. Doheny was prospecting for oil in Ebano, Mexico.
She also speaks therein about the alterations made to
their mansion, the installation of street lights (which she
deplored) and the purchase of their first automobiles.
For some reason, Mr. Doheny had filed all those letters
in a paper box which became intermingled among other
items in the Estelle Doheny Collection.

This overall collection of Doheny papers will probably be more remembered for what it lacks than what it
contains. Those hoping that they would provide a window to Edward L's early days in the west will be greatly
disappointed. Unfortunately, the major portion of correspondence, personal and business papers and private
memoirs relating to the long and interesting career of
Mr. Doheny are no longer extant. Nor will they ever be.

This writer was told by the late Lucille V. Miller,
longtime personal secretary to Carrie Estelle Doheny,
that on the very day of Mr. Doheny's funeral, his widow
and her sister, Daisy Anderson, personally burned all the
papers in the basement furnaces at #8 Chester Place.

According to Miss Miller, who was an eye–witness to
the conflagration, Mrs. Doheny felt that "destroying all
the evidence, favorable and otherwise, would forever
ring down the curtain on the alleged and never proven
misdoings of her husband in the Teapot Dome affair."
Indeed it was a chapter in her life she wanted to forget.

In retrospect, burning the papers has proven to be the
single most disastrous decision she ever made. If it is
true that nothing wrong could thereafter be proven
against Mr. Doheny, it is equally true, because all the
evidence is gone, that nothing positive can be verified.
Destroying evidence invariably causes more problems
than it solves.

EDWARD LAURENCE DOHENY, JR. (1893–1929)

Few visitors to Forest Lawn Memorial Park in Glendale are aware of the name, significance and origin of
the "Temple of Santa Sabina" which is located at the
first summit of Cathedral Drive, just behind the Great
Mausoleum. Though the marble sarcophagus is
unmarked, in accordance with the wishes of the family,
it serves as the tomb of Edward Laurence Doheny, Jr.
(1893–1929), one of Southern California's truly legendary personages.

Shortly after Doheny's sudden demise, on February 16, 1929, Dr. Hubert Eaton, the founder and developer of Forest Lawn, suggested that an historic altar furnishing which he had recently acquired be utilized as a memorial for the Doheny family. The altar and baldacchino, designed and executed by the Italian sculptor, Poscetti, was originally assembled for the Basilica of Santa Sabina, regarded then and now among the Eternal City's oldest and most historic churches.

The church itself, dating back to the 5th century, was erected in memory of Sabina, the wife of the convert, Valentinus, whose name was added to the Roman Martyrology in the year 126 A.D. Built on the lower hills of the Aventine, the church is only a short distance from Saint Pauls.

The altar stood for many centuries in the basilica and many of Rome's great cardinals, archbishops and other prelates offered Holy Mass there. Others were interred in that locale, including several of the popes. Early in this century, probably in 1918, during a period of restoration, the altar was removed from its position and offered for sale. According to records at Forest Lawn, Professor Armando Vene, Italy's Royal Superintendent of Fine Arts, was entrusted with removing the altar pieces and later reassembling them at Glendale.

The "Temple of Santa Sabina," as it is known today, is regarded as a perfect example of early Romanesque architecture. It includes rare marbles from Italy, Africa and Asia. Four polished granite columns rise thirty-three feet to an elaborate marble cornice, with a double colonnade of smaller columns supporting an octagonal dome and turret surmounted by a cross.

In the Art Guide of Forest Lawn Memorial Parks, one can read how the altar is executed in superb marbles. Designs in exquisite Venetian mosaics decorate the front and back panels, while in the side panels are niches containing fine bas-reliefs, separated by delicate, twisted miniature columns.

The magnificent candlesticks that formerly stood beside the altar in the Basilica of Santa Sabina can be seen in the Memorial Terrace of the Great Mausoleum. In themselves, they are artistic masterpieces. Interestingly enough, the spot once occupied by the "Temple of Santa Sabina" in the Roman basilica of that name remains totally vacant even today—possibly a recognition that no work of art could match the earlier marble altar and furnishings.

The unique memorial erected by the Doheny family sixty years ago remains one of the most outstanding of the many artistic embellishments at Forest Lawn Memorial Park. The utilization of great works of art as monuments for the dead is a centuries-old practice that developed late in Southern California. Indeed it is a highly appropriate manner of recalling peoples of earlier generations.

PETER DONAHUE (1826–1885) AND JAMES DONAHUE (1859–1890)

Peter Donahue was a penniless immigrant who became an outstanding capitalist and railroad builder. Born at Glasgow in 1826, he was brought by his parents to the United States a decade later. His first position was that of a machinist.

In 1847, he was hired by the Peruvian Government as an engineer on that country's first steam boat. He and his brother came to California from New York shortly after the discovery of gold. Peter opened a blacksmith shop which later evolved into the Union Iron Foundry. In 1852, he launched San Francisco's first gas plant and, a while afterwards, he obtained a contract to supply street lighting for the downtown district.

Subsequently, Peter engaged in shipbuilding and in 1861 started the Omnibus Railroad Company. The following year he acquired controlling interest in the San Jose Railroad. A man of numerous talents, Peter also built California's first cast iron printing press. His San Francisco Gas Company was the forerunner of Pacific Gas and Electric. His railroad became the Northwestern Pacific.

When Peter died in 1885, his son, James (1859–1890), inherited the railroad interests. The young Donahue, a personable individual, also made a lasting contribution to the growth of California. James grew up in the family home on San Francisco's Rincon Hill. He attended Saint Ignatius College. Following his graduation from Santa Clara, he went to Stony Hurst in England to complete his education.

Returning to the United States, James took over his father's business interests and continued to develop railroads in northwest California, extending lines east to Sonoma and north to Ukiah. In 1884, James married Belle Wallace, the daughter of the famous west coast lawyer, William T. Wallace. (Wallace served both as superior judge in San Francisco and chief justice of California). On her maternal side, Belle was also a granddaughter of Peter H. Burnett, California's first governor.

In his role as supervisor for the railroads, James had to travel extensively over the lines. He contracted a bronchial infection on one of those trips which eventually brought on his premature demise. He died on March 3, 1890, at the Palace Hotel in San Francisco. Though he was only thirty-one years old, James Donahue outlived both his children, Mary and Peter.

There is a monument in San Francisco, erected by provision of James' will, to his father, Peter Donahue. The memorial to this fine Catholic family stands at the corner of Bush, Battery and Market streets.

DANIEL JOSEPH DONOHUE

Daniel Joseph Donohue was born on July 30, 1919, at Jersey City, the son of Daniel Joseph and Julia (Walter) Donohue. Along with the other two Donohue children, Eugene and Rosemary, Daniel studied at Saint Aloysius Grammar School which was staffed by the Sisters of Charity of Emmitsburg.

Entering the city's Jesuit–operated Saint Peter's Preparatory School in 1937, he completed his secondary education at Graymoor. Daniel then joined the Franciscan Friars of the Atonement as a postulant.

He was sent to the community's monastery in Washington, D.C. There he studied philosophy at The Catholic University of America, along with the other disciplines associated with the ministry inaugurated by the famed ecumenist, Father Paul Watson.

Daniel's father, a pediatrician and specialist in internal medicine, was a benefactor of Brother Mathias Barrett, a highly–respected and colorful member of the Order of Saint John of God.

With the expiration of his temporary vows as a Franciscan, Daniel affiliated himself with the Hospitaller Brothers of Saint John of God at their foundation in Los Angeles. He journeyed to the west coast in 1940 and it was there that he spent the remainder of his life.

In 1947, Daniel took solemn vows as a Brother of Saint John of God. He was attached to the community's motherhouse, located on West Adams Boulevard. With the exception of his years of graduate study at Mount Saint Mary's College, Brother Daniel spent most of his years at the motherhouse and at Rancho San Antonio.

Because his father had known and studied at Fordham University with Francis J. Spellman, who later became Archbishop of New York, Daniel was personally acquainted with many members of the American hierarchy, including Archbishop J. Francis A. McIntyre of Los Angeles. In 1950, when Daniel expressed a desire to study for the priesthood, Archbishop McIntyre suggested that he become a clerical candidate for the Diocese of San Diego.

While waiting for his dispensation, Daniel worked briefly for United States Steel Corporation in their newly–formed psychological screening program, an experience that served him well in later life.

In 1951, Daniel was accepted at Immaculate Heart of Mary Seminary in San Diego. By a strange but surely providential twist of circumstances, Daniel was assigned temporarily as a special assistant to the Most Reverend Charles Francis Buddy, Bishop of San Diego.

As time progressed, there was less and less time for study and more and more allotted to coordinating the multitudinous activities of Bishop Buddy. Daniel took up residence at the episcopal place and became, in fact if not in title, aide–de–camp to the bishop.

The almost three years in that capacity proved to be the most interesting of Daniel's life. That Buddy's reputation as the *prima donna* of the American hierarchy was amply deserved is confirmed by all who knew or worked with him. Daniel travelled with the bishop, looked after his house, arranged his appointments and acted as intermediary with clergy and laity.

While accompanying Buddy on his last *ad limina* visit to Rome, Cardinal Spellman suggested to Daniel that his position in San Diego was ambivalent and needed redirection.

After a ten day retreat and considerable thought, prayer and consultation, Daniel concurred that his vocation would find its maximum fulfillment outside the priestly ministry.

Daniel had known Bernardine Murphy since 1940, when she came regularly to visit the Brothers at their residence in Los Angeles. On several occasions, he had advised her about benefactions to charitable organizations.

Their relationship grew closer in the months after he left San Diego and, on January 16, 1954, they were married at a ceremony witnessed by James Francis Cardinal McIntyre in the archiepiscopal chapel in Fremont Place.

A few years later, Daniel and Bernardine purchased the Villa San Giuseppe on Waverly Drive, an old mansion formerly owned by car–magnate Earle C. Anthony, owner of KFI radio station.

In 1957, the Donohues established the Dan Murphy Foundation, a charitable trust funded by the Murphy fortune which had been accumulated from various sources, including California Portland Cement.

With first Bernardine and later Daniel Donohue as chairman of the Board, the Dan Murphy Foundation has been active in supporting charities, mostly those associated with the universal apostolate of the Roman Catholic Church.

After Bernardine's sudden and unexpected death, on March 5, 1968, Daniel continued the traditions of charity inaugurated by his wife. Personally and through his position as chair of the Dan Murphy Foundation, he has been one of the most generous benefactors of the Holy See and the local Church

BARTHOLOMEW DOWLING (c. 1820–1863)

The name of Bartholomew Dowling is not outstanding in the anthologies of literature pertaining to the American occupation in California; yet this Irish poet deserves to have his name remembered for he may yet emerge as a "bright light" in an otherwise darkened period of literary development.

Dowling was born in Listowel, County Kerry, Ireland, in the early 1820s. He is known to have arrived in California about 1852 among that horde of men seeking their fortunes along the Gold Dust Trails. Not finding his riches in mining, Dowling retired to the seclusion of Crucita Valley in the Contra Costa Hills, where he built a small home and settled down to farming. During his years on the ranch and later in San Francisco, Dowling was employed as a staff writer for *The Monitor*, and in 1856, P. J. Thomas induced him to join the paper as a full–time editor.

Undoubtedly the chief reason for his obscurity was the practice he followed of not signing his work. Even his commercial poems usually appeared anonymously or under the *nom de plume* of "Hard Knocks" or "Southern." Favorite of Dowling's signature was "Masque." The *California Pioneer* carried many of his writings. "Reminiscences of the Mines" depicts the California of Gold Rush Days in dramatically graphic fashion. Of all his poems appearing in the *Ballad Poetry of Ireland* only one bears his true name.

Until the publication of *Forgotten Pioneers* by Thomas F. Prendergast in 1942, the only sketch of Dowling's life was that in a volume entitled *Irish Poets and Novelists*. Therein is printed a brief biography "by a gentleman who for more than twenty years enjoyed the personal friendship of the deceased poet." Dowling's heroic ballad "The Brigade of Fontenoy" came out in 1889, in the little volume *A Chaplet of Verse by California Catholic Writers*. The *Irish Monthly* picked it up and ranked its author among the "brilliant galaxy of gifted young Irishmen who threw themselves and their fortunes into an inspiring national movement.

Very little is known about the poet's education, although it was said that 'he was versed in the Latin and several of the modern languages," a fact made obvious by his writings. Dowling's translation of Beranger's poems was published at San Francisco and his facility with the German language made the English version of the poems an instant success. Like many poets, Dowling was something of a romanticist. He avoided, as much as possible, the public life of San Francisco, preferring instead to read his books and jot down personal observations for later editorials. Although his personal opinions were sometimes expressed in *The Monitor* and in other publications, Dowling had no special attraction to politics and kept out of the public eye whenever possible.

Dowling's death was brought about by an accident late in 1863. His remains were laid to rest at Calvary Cemetery where a handsome monument, erected by his brother, "marks his grave and perpetuates his name." Perhaps the simple Irish Faith that inspired Dowling's life is nowhere more evident than in his translation of Theodor Körner's "Prayer During Battle."

Father, I call to Thee!

Roaring around me the cannons storm;
Like a shroud their lightnings enwrap my form.

Guide of the battles, I call to Thee:

Father! To–day be a guide to me.

JOHN G. DOWNEY (1827–1894)

In 1860 Ireland saw two of its sons achieve prominence on the Pacific Coast: on September 26th, Eugene O'Connell was elected to the Titular See of Flaviopolis and named Vicar Apostolic of Marysville, and on January 14th, John G. Downey was installed as the seventh Governor of the State of California. John Gatley Downey was a native of Roscommon who came to America in 1840, at the age of fourteen. He learned the trade of pharmacy in Maryland and immigrated to California with the fortune seekers of the 1850s, carrying only $10 and a gold watch in his pocket. Soon thereafter he opened a pharmacy in Los Angeles and married Doña Marie Jesús Giurado.

Always enthusiastic about his adopted home, Downey published a monograph describing the attractions of the southland and earned for himself the reputation of originating the "boom campaigns" of Southern California. In 1859 Downey was elected lieutenant governor on the Lecompton Democratic ticket and within a few weeks succeeded to the chief executive's chair when the incumbent, Milton S. Lathan, was named by the legislature to represent California in the United States Senate.

Downey was "a man of keen intellect, kindly sympathies and courage . . . for in shaping California's destiny in his day he was confronted with problems of a state moulting from the frontier stage into a well–ordered, self–confident commonwealth." It was during his term in Sacramento that the cornerstone of the state capitol was laid on May 15, 1861, and although he only occupied office for three years, Downey with his supporters managed to keep the state on the side of the Union during the Civil War while, at the same time, avoiding political entanglement wherever that was possible.

In his "retirement years" Downey campaigned to connect Los Angeles with the east by rail, realizing as he did that the future of the city depended upon bringing the railroad into the southland. After winning over the powerful Collis P. Huntington, Downey was given the honor of driving a golden spike near Lang Station to commemorate the linking of east and west. The railroad also brought tragedy to Downey for in January of 1883, the train in which he and his wife were traveling ran wild on a grade in the Tehachapi Mountains and plunged to the bottom of a canyon killing Mrs. Downey and severely injuring the former governor.

An extremely wealthy man, Downey was known for his benefactions both in and out of the Catholic Church. He gave land for the site of the University of Southern California, helped to finance the early foundations of the Daughters of Charity and spearheaded the founding of the city's public library system. He was a close friend of Bishop Thaddeus Amat and a collaborator in many of the prelate's programs. The Downey influence still remains. His name is attached to a city; that of his sister, Annie, (married by Bishop Amat to Peter Donohoe) graces the present City of Anaheim.

Downey's administration as governor was universally commended. As a private citizen, and one to whose enterprise and liberality is largely due the prosperity of Southern California, he is no less widely esteemed.

HARRY DOWNIE (1903–1980)

A. Farewell Reflections

One can hardly speak of Harry Downie (1903–1980) without recalling the adage that "the Church is far too important to be left to the care of the clergy." Those who knew and loved this great "restorer" of the missions have no hesitation in according him the unique title of "high priest" of California's laity.

Historians write about, politicians legislate for and administrators look after the remnants of the once proud mission chain. But it was Harry who "restored" and breathed a new life into those distinctive foundations that dot California's skyline. His contribution can only be properly appreciated within the context of architectural history.

The concept conveyed by the English term "restoration" is one which remained largely foreign to Spain and her possessions. In fact, the very word *restoración* did not even appear in most Spanish dictionaries until fairly recent times. The record indicates that no Spanish–speaking person in California ever possessed the notion implied by the English word "restoration" with respect to the missions.

Prior to Harry's time, a mission building was never "restored," but rather "improved" or, even worse, "modernized." Hence it was that so many of those precious edifices were grotesquely "improved" by obviously well–intentioned priests and laymen.

Though the theory of "restoration" was first introduced in California by Father Joseph O'Keefe at Santa Barbara and San Luis Rey, it was Harry Downie who pioneered and popularized the practice of "restoring" the historic mission period style. The work of this truly innovative pioneer began in 1931, when he first arrived at San Carlos Borromeo. Starting with nothing more than his skills at cabinetmaking, Harry "restored" Carmel Mission to its pristine position as a showpiece of mission architecture.

Like the original Franciscan founders and builders, Harry made his mark on other missions too—Santa Clara, San Luis Rey, San Juan Bautista, San Antonio, San Buenaventura, San Fernando, Nuestra Señora de la Soledad, San Miguel and San Francisco. His advice was sought and followed at other missions too, including Santa Cruz, Santa Ines, San Juan Capistrano, La Purisima Concepcion and Santa Barbara.

The small adobe home which he built for and then shared with his beloved Mabel gradually became something of a museum—crammed with awards, honors and a host of historic mementos, books and documents from the provincial era. Truly generous man that he was, Harry eventually decided to perpetuate these treasures and heirlooms by building an archival facility at his beloved Carmel Mission Basilica.

Harry's monuments are twenty–one in number, stretching from San Diego to San Rafael. His notion of "restoration" is now a commonly–accepted norm in architectural and historical circles. His name ranks, in recognition, with Serra, Palou and Lasuén.

Harry has gone to heaven now—there to meet and compare notes with his beloved Father Maynard Geiger, O.F.M. But watch closely and you can still see him at almost any point along California's *El Camino Real*.

HARRY DOWNIE (1903 –1980)

B. Legendary Restorer

Rarely does it happen that a man becomes a part of history in his own lifetime, but one such 'living legend' is Harry Downie, who belongs as much to the mission era of California's past as he does to the 1960s.

Born in 1903, a third generation San Franciscan, Harry grew up in the atmosphere of the early *padres*. His boyhood days were spent around Mission San Francisco de Asis (Dolores) where he learned the trade of a cabinet–maker. Harry's days at Carmel date from 1931, when he "stopped by" to help Father Philip Scher (later Bishop of Monterey–Fresno) raise interest in Junípero Serra's central missionary establishment. He remained there and created what Monsignor John Tracy Ellis called the "most attractive ecclesiastical museum in the United States."

Starting out with practically nothing, Downie made Mission San Carlos de Borromeo into a showpiece of mission architecture. To do this he became a stonemason, blacksmith, architect, electrician and plumber. Downie's efforts were not restricted to Carmel. After a disastrous fire in 1936, he restored the main altar and statuettes at Mission Santa Clara and acted as consultant for the overall project at the "University Mission." He has also rebuilt Missions San Luis Obispo, San Antonio, San Juan Bautista and parts of Soledad, while acting as adviser on projects at Missions Santa Cruz, Santa Ines, San Juan Capistrano, San Fernando, and La Purísima Concepción. Later he was associated with the *Asistencia de Nuestra Señora de Los Angeles*, the plaza church at Los Angeles.

Harry's knowledge of obscure mission lore more than often authenticated hitherto doubtful discoveries. Where the written sources fail, Downie took over, for "the *padres* were more concerned with building for the future than leaving behind footnotes for posterity." He went about his work like a paleontologist piecing together a few scattered bones to form a giant dinosaur. His "bones" were old church records, building reports, photographs and an uncanny instinct. His research took him as far away as Mexico City and gave him the ability "to think like a mission *padre*."

For four decades this humble resident of Carmel, California was "the" expert on mission architecture and restoration. Through his dedicated efforts, the state's rosary of missionary establishments was preserved and rebuilt for future generations.

Downie's scholarly labors merited him the honor of being an official collaborator on the cause of Junípero Serra. As a deputy of Bishop Aloysius J. Willinger, C.Ss.R., Harry supervised the opening of Serra's tomb in 1943, and helped to prepare the report for the Sacred Congregation of Rites. He was one of two laymen allowed to actually touch the bones of the "Grey Ox."

JOHN THOMAS DOYLE (1819–1906)

A. PIOUS FUND LAWYER

When John Thomas Doyle arrived in California to practice law in the early 1850s, he launched a career that would see him become "one of the great leaders of his profession." Today his name is prominently connected with some of the most important litigation in the state's history.

A native of New York, Doyle graduated from Columbia Law School in 1838, and practiced in the east some ten or twelve years. In 1851 he was hired by Cornelius Vanderbilt to manage an investment company in Nicaragua trying to finance a canal across the isthmus. Anticipating the failure of that project, Doyle moved on to California, where he entered once again into his chosen profession, remaining active for the next half century.

Although he will be mostly remembered for his association with the famous Pious Fund of the Californias, "Doyle's celebrated cases are too numerous to mention." His intimate knowledge of Spanish, French, Italian and German and his command of international and civil law established him as an authority in great demand. One outstanding historian said of Doyle that he "has been since the early days of this state, a very conspicuous and reputable jurist; recognized not only as among the ablest lawyers on the coast, but one who can be depended on to maintain the honor and dignity of the

bar, and withal a scholar of rare culture and refinement." Attention to civic duties was one of Doyle's hallmarks. A member of the first Board of Regents for the University of California and the Board of Commissioners of Transportation, he was also known at Menlo Park as an expert on viticulture for his experiments to develop a disease–resistant type of grapevine.

Doyle was an exemplary Catholic and he used his talents to promote any interests vital to the Church. He published an edition of Palou's *Noticias* in Spanish and wrote several long and captivating articles on the early history of California's missions.

Always the indefatigable worker, Doyle somehow managed to find leisure to read and study, and "in literature he had a keen appreciation for the best and his superb library was a repository of varied lore. He took delight in Shakespeare, and had collected many famous editions of the master's works as well as Horace and Don Quixote."

While it is true that he was often formidably antagonistic in his legal career, he lived a very simple life in the seclusion of his vineyards and companionship of his family. "He never sought public office, but, when the general welfare could be served, he willingly placed his talents at the disposal of the commonwealth." Doyle's writings display a rare emotion and sentimentality that is difficult to reconcile with a man known to be aggressive and irascible in his legal capacity. But his obvious religious convictions and strikingly human characteristics are quite understandable and in full accord with Doyle's acknowledged persuasions.

When John Thomas Doyle went home to God on December 23, 1906, at the age of eighty–seven, he left behind a noble record as churchman, statesman, public servant, a record that California's Catholic Heritage is proud to recall.

JOHN THOMAS DOYLE (1819–1906)

B. SHERMAN CORRESPONDENCE

Through the kind intervention of a friend, we were given access to a letter written by General William Tecumseh Sherman. It sheds considerable light on the views commonly held about the Catholic Church a century ago. The letter, written from the headquarters of the United States Army in Washington, D.C., on April 26, 1881, was addressed to John Thomas Doyle, a prominent San Francisco attorney and legal counsel to Archbishop Patrick W. Riordan.

In a casual reference to his wife, Ellen, the general noted that she was "as well as possible but claims all the privileges of age." She "will not distress herself about politics or society but is absolutely more Catholic than the pope, and according to my notions is a devout Irish Catholic—far more Catholic than any Roman ever professed to be."

As for his son, Thomas, who would later become a Jesuit priest, the general said that he had been "transferred to an establishment in Maryland near Frederick." Since Christmas, he had been "immured in his prison or cloister." Like most of those holding higher ranks in the military of his time, General Sherman was non–Catholic and anti–clerical. That state of mind is evident in several places of the four page letter. Here's an example:

"When I contemplate that this Earth was designed to feed and maintain a mixed class of men, women and children I cannot but think it sinful against notion that any man should ignore this fact and dedicate himself to any religious sentiment." Sherman went on to tell Doyle: "I cannot change my notion, and I suppose he (Thomas) still thinks he is serving his God by his course of action, but proceeding in opposite directions. Instead of coming nearer, we are growing further and further apart . . . I regard him as dead, as lost, a young good life thrown away."

The general then refers to the recently deceased priest in Saint Louis who happened to be the one "who in my opinion was most instrumental in leading Tom astray. Now he is dead, Tom's life is wasted and I am left without anyone to take up the thread where I leave off."

Sherman was a fair man, however. In a biography of *General Sherman's Son,* the author notes that though the general was not a Catholic, "he agreed that all their children should be raised in the faith of their mother. He felt a sincere respect toward priests and welcomed them into his home. As a military commander, he always saw to it that a Catholic chaplain was with his troops. Several Catholic bishops—such as Purcell, Ryan and Cardinal McCloskey of New York—were his friends. A profound appreciation of the necessity and value of religion was an essential note of the Sherman tradition."

The general, who was baptized on his deathbed, never was able to accept the notion of Thomas becoming a priest. He once referred to his son as "some sort of a Catholic divine" who should have taken an active "part in the great future of America." In fact, Father Thomas Ewing Sherman did just that. His stormy career as an apologist demonstrated that he was indeed his father's son and when the story of Catholic involvement in social questions and ecumenical relations is finally chronicled, the name of Father Sherman will occupy a prominent place.

JOHN P. DUNN (1852–1906)

John P. Dunn (1852–1906) was a responsive Christian whose religious convictions made him kind and charitable toward those with whom he associated. Practically all of Dunn's adult life was spent in public service. Though forced by circumstances to live in Sacramento and San Francisco, this dedicated layman slipped down to his orange grove at Duarte whenever his public duties permitted.

John was brought by his parents to the United States while only a few months old. The Irish–born youngster, reared and educated in his adoped homeland, completed formal schooling at Cornell University. Soon after coming to California, in 1875, John married May Mahoney, a union blessed by four children, Walter, May, John and Theresa.

In 1879 Dunn was elected Auditor of the City and County of San Francisco, an office he won by campaigning "for the purity of the government" in fiscal matters. It was in that role that Dunn gained state–wide notoriety for his refusal to sanction the payment of exhorbitant gas bills incurred under a dubiously legal contract signed by his predecessor. The bitterly contested case was ultimately appealed to the Supreme Court, where earlier rulings favoring the City of San Francisco were sustained.

During the eight years following 1881, while serving as State Controller, Dunn acquired the reputation of being the "Watchdog of the Treasury" for his measures aimed at curbing the irresponsible and indiscriminate use of governmental funds. It was also as Controller that John Dunn exposed the Dan Burns gang and thereby compiled one of the most exciting chapters in California's political history. Accusations of graft in the awarding of public contracts resulted in several indictments on charges of fraud.

In subsequent years, Dunn served as Secretary of the Citizens' Defense Association and Chairman of the Committee entrusted with framing a new charter for the City of San Francisco. Later he was appointed Registrar of the Bay City's United States Land Office by President Grover Cleveland. Though he was considered a powerful Democratic candidate for governor, a serious heart ailment forced Dunn's retirement from public office, in 1900. He returned to his home in California's southland, where he spent his remaining years as manager of the Duarte–Monrovia Fruit Exchange.

John P. Dunn, an outstanding Catholic enthusiast, was always alert to furthering the interests of the commonweal. "He was as impressive an example of a public man true to the people and to his duty as an official as could be recalled in the political history of this State." Well should he be memorialized as a man of unusual sincerity and goodness, of perfect fidelity to the public trust, of splendid loyalty to his friends and a remarkable kindliness and generosity to all with whom he associated.

WILL DURANT (1885–1981)

Time magazine conferred the ultimate honor upon Will Durant (1885–1981) when it described him as the "Biographer of Mankind." Indeed he was that and more—he signed one of his last letters as "another lover of Christ."

A graduate of Saint Peter's College, Massachusetts–born Durant studied at Seton Hall Divinity School. Shortly after leaving the seminary, the young philosopher drifted away from the Church. In later years, Durant used to claim that his estrangement from the Church was all Spinoza's fault. Having read *Ethics*, he had allowed himself to be overly influenced by the 17th century pantheist.

In January of 1912, Will was formally excommunicated by Bishop John J. O'Connor of Newark. The *Evening News* reported on that occasion that "no Catholic should henceforth associate with him in any avoidable way." The following year, Will met Ida Kaufman, whom he referred to as "Ariel" after the imp in Shakespeare's "The Tempest." The two were married soon thereafter, a union that lasted for sixty–eight years.

Though trained as a philosopher, Durant spent most of his life writing *The Story of Civilization*, an eleven volume series that propelled the author into almost all the world's major libraries and research centers. The masterful series, written in collaboration with Ariel, chronicled 10,000 years and sold more than two million copies. Volume Ten on "Rousseau and Revolution" won the coveted Pulitzer Prize.

Though Will remained outside the Catholic fold, he had a love and affection for the Church which surfaced in his later writings. He admitted, for example, in *The Lessons of History*, published in 1968, that "even the skeptical historian develops a humble respect for religion, since he sees it functioning and seemingly indispensable, in every land and age."

In another place, he noted that "Catholicism survives because it appeals to imagination, hope and the senses; because its mythology consoles and brightens the lives of the poor; and because the commanded fertility of the faithful slowly regains the lands lost to the Reformation."

Interestingly enough, though Durant was one of the few persons explicitly excommunicated in the history of the American Church, he was on exceedingly cordial terms with James Francis Cardinal McIntyre, the Archbishop of Los Angeles. On one occasion, at a private luncheon for the Durants at The Townhouse, His Eminence publicly acknowledged that Durant was his "favorite historian."

Over the years, Durant also remained in contact with a number of Jesuits, including Father Herbert Ryan, the step–son of his sister, Ethel. It was Father Ryan who rec- onciled the famed historian to the Church prior to his death, on November 7, 1981.

"Civilization," Durant once observed, "is a stream with banks." Most historians, he thought, concentrate on the stream, "which is sometimes filled with blood from people killing, stealing, shouting." Durant was devoted to what happened on the banks. There, "unnoticed, people build homes, make love, raise children, sing songs, write poetry, whittle statues" or write about it all.

JIMMY DURANTE (1893–1980)

The long career of Jimmy Durante, pianist, comedian, singer, actor and dancer, touched saloons, speakeasies, vaudeville, motion pictures, radio and television. His life was a capsulized history of 20th century show business.

James Francis Durante was born on Catherine Street, New York City, on February 10, 1893, the youngest child of Barthelmeo and Rosea (Millino) Durante. His earliest performing role was that of playing the piano at Diamond Tony's Saloon on Coney Island. In 1916, "Ragtime Jimmy" organized a five piece novelty band for the Club Alamo in Harlem and, in 1923, he opened a speakeasy called the Club Durante over a garage in New York City. It was also in that year that he married the former Jeanne Olsen.

The man with the huge nose, gravelly voice and cyclone personality joined with Eddie Jackson and Lou Clayton to crash into vaudeville at *Loew's State* and *The Palace*. They stayed at the top ever after. In 1928, Durante and his act were on Broadway in Florenz Ziegfeld's "Show Girl" and a year later Ben Hecht and Charles MacArthur wrote a screenplay for them called "Roadhouse Nights."

Durante accepted his first single comedy role in the Cole Porter musical, "The New Yorker," in 1930, and that was followed by a trip to Hollywood, where he went under contract to MGM. His first film for MGM was "Get Rich Quick Wallingford" and then came "The Phantom President," "The Cuban," "Her Cardboard Lover" and many more.

Jimmy returned to New York in 1934 to star in a musical "Strike Me Pink" with Ethel Merman. His wife Jeanne died, in 1943, and later that year his career was re–kindled with a booking at the Copacabana in New York City.

In 1950, Durante moved from network radio to television with the "Colgate Hour" and the "Texaco Star Theatre." Once again, the man referred to by Billy Rose as "the greatest American clown" broke all the records.

His words of farewell, "Goodnite, Mrs. Calabash, wherever you are" (a sentimental reference to his deceased wife, Jeanne) brought more inquiries by wire, mail and telephone than any single words ever delivered by a performer.

The hectic schedule continued, with nightclub appearances in New York, Boston, Miami, Philadelphia, New Orleans, Chicago and Las Vegas. In 1960, Jimmy married Marjorie Little and, two years later, adopted a baby girl, Cecilia Alicia. He suffered the first in a series of strokes that finally ended his career in 1972. His final appearance was fittingly made at the Waldorf–Astoria Hotel where he haltingly did one last rendition of "Inka Dinka Doo." Throughout his eighty–six years, Jimmy was a man of deep faith in God. A lifelong Catholic, he was known far and wide for his many benefactions and services to the Church. Probably the best description of the "Great Schnozzola" was that penned by his official biographer some years ago: "In a bad world, Jimmy stayed good."

ALBRECHT DÜRER (1471–1528)

In the closing chapter of Jane Campbell Hutchison's new biography of Albrecht Dürer (1471–1518), the 16th century master is credited with being "the most thorougly celebrated artist who ever lived." Indeed, the legendary figure who first brought the Renaissance to Germany, revolutionized European art. He was a master draftsman, print maker and painter, an intrepid traveler, a chronicler of his time, a humanist and writer, a teacher and theoretician. Dürer was also a paradigm of piety and virtue.

Born at Nuremberg, the sophisticated city–state at the center of the Holy Roman Empire, Dürer benefited from Nuremberg's progressive educational system and from its role as the center of humanist thought and ideals, most of which he either ignored or Christianized.

As one of only three surviving children of the eighteen born to his parents, Albrecht was imbued with a sense of uniqueness that served him well in later life. He studied the art of goldsmithing, drawing and engraving. Much later he perfected the technique of making woodcuts.

By 1505, he was famous. His art was revered and imitated by engravers, painters and even ceramic designers. His graphic work included a series on the Life of Mary, as well as illustrations of penitential self–flagellation. By the 19th century, Dürer was an international celebrity. His house became a shrine, festivals were staged in his memory and he was the subject of dramas. The proliferation of souvenirs ranged from jewelry to pastries.

Over the centuries, Dürer was frequently accused of being a Protestant because of his interest in the teachings of Martin Luther and the former monk's approach to liturgy. Historians point out, however, that Dürer died two years before the Augsburg Confession.

This most consistently admired of all Western artists is remembered at Mission Hills by two stained glass windows on the north elevation of the building housing the Archival Center. Patterned after Dürer's woodcuts, the panels were likely fashioned at Cologne. Dating from the era of stained glass revival, they are correct to the finest details, with no attempts made to improve upon Dürer's designs.

The panels are exceedingly well preserved. Though severely warped or bent, due to insufficient temperature control of their wooden kiln, the circular windows are in otherwise excellent condition. Encased in frames, with a diamond background fashioned by the talented Isabel Piczek, the panels now have red borders which enhance the contrast of the colors in the interior design.

The upper panel, depicting the Coronation of Mary as Queen of Heaven, exhibits a later style of Dürer, probably dating from about 1511. A departure from his earlier renaissance style, the scene shows indications of the German baroque. The lower panel is a copy of Dürer's renowned Virgin and Infant receiving the homage of Saints Joseph, John the Baptist, Anthony, Jerome, Paul and Catherine. Executed between 1497 and 1500, it exhibits the keen sense of artistic detail that was characteristic of Dürer.

Donor of the windows was the late Robert H. Schafhausen of Encino. He had acquired them from a relative who had been the German Consul in Ottawa. Earlier they had belonged to Father Johannes Ritten, a parish priest in the town of Dillendorf.

JOSE LORENZO DE ESPARZA

The first recorded marriage of white people in California took place a whole year before the celebrated alarm was sounded about the British approach to Concord by the "midnight ride" of Paul Revere and William Dawes. The incident must be related within the context of Fray Junípero Serra's report to Antonio Maria de Bucareli y Ursua, submitted at Mexico City, on March 13, 1773, wherein the Franciscan *Presidente* requested authorization to import carpenters "equipped with the tools of their trade" to Missions San Carlos and San Gabriel. Serra suggested that craftsmen be enlisted at Guadalajara, so as more easily to transport "all of their equipment" to far–away California. Bucareli formally approved the request on May 6th.

Fray Junípero subsequently traveled to Guadalajara and there recruited that small band of adventurers who accompanied him as the initial "colonizers" to Alta California. Among that first nonmilitary contingency of Spaniards venturing northward were two storekeepers, three master carpenters, three blacksmith and a surgeon.

Before their departure, José Lorenzo de Esparza, one of the newly–signed carpenters, made known to Serra his intentions to marry Maria Josefa Davila, the orphaned sister of a fellow artisan. The *Presidente* happily agreed to inaugurate the usual pre–marital investigation at Guadalajara. After presenting their witnesses, the couple plighted their troth in one of the local churches and then immediately joined the cavalcade to California.

Though the *Santiago*, with its ninety–eight passengers and crew, was bound for Monterey, it was forced by contrary winds to put in at San Diego, on March 13, 1774, where a goodly percentage of those aboard decided to continue their journey by land. It was at San Gabriel, after a six–day trek through heavy rains and sloggy mud, that Serra was able to fulfill his promise of witnessing the marriage contract entered into by the *novios*.

At the third of California's frontier outposts, in the little log cabin chapel at *La Misión Vieja*, Fray Junípero dispensed with two of the banns, and witnessed the first exchange of matrimonial vows by "whites" in California. Among those present and participating in the ceremony, on April 19, 1774, was Juan José Rodriguez, one of the soldiers from Juan Bautista de Anza's expedition from Sonora and Conrado de Toledo, the young man who acted as page for Fray Junípero Serra.

Unfortunately, the couple bore no offspring by which to extend and perpetuate their family name through subsequent generations. Yet the distinction of being the first whites joined in holy matrimony in California forever belongs to José Lorenzo de Esparza and Maria Josefa Davila.

JUAN EVANGELISTA (1758–1778)

A) CELEBRATED INDIAN CONVERT

One of the most celebrated of California's early Indian converts was Juan Evangelista, the neophyte who accompanied Fray Junípero Serra to Mexico City,   in 1772–1773. Born about 1758, Juan Evangelista was baptized at Mission San Carlos by Serra on March 19, 1771

When the *Presidente* decided to make the long journey to the capital for an interview with the viceroy, Juan Evangelista volunteered to accompany the friar. Fray Francisco Palóu later wrote that he was of great assistance and "won the attention of all, both along the road and in Mexico City." Serra reported that Juan Evangelista saw "what California might be some day if Euro-

Fray Junipero Serra and Evangelista

peans continued to live" in the area. The new sights, strange faces and novel customs, together with houses, monasteries, churches and the like must have been an immeasurable contrast to the crude adobe structures the Indian knew in his native land.

The *Presidente* envisioned that Juan Evangelista's experiences would serve as an object lesson for the neophyte population in Alta California. When the Spaniards had first arrived, the Indians were puzzled to see men and mules, but no women. That many looked upon the foreigners as offspring of she–mules is understandable, since white women came to the area only after 1781. Serra used that as an argument to convince the Viceroy about the need of sending married colonists to California. The *Presidente* subsequently wrote that the youth's experiences convinced him that "we did not come here in search of riches, but to work for their happiness." While in Mexico City, the California neophyte caught the attention of Viceroy Antonio Maria Bucareli, who looked upon him as the first fruit of the spiritual conquest.

Both Juan Evangelista and Serra were so ill with the fever at Guadalajara that they were anointed. The *Presi-*

dente worried that in the event of his companion's demise, his kinfolk would never believe that death had occurred from natural causes. Fortunately, both recovered and were able to continue their trek. Fray Junípero saw to it that Juan Evangelista was confirmed at the capital. He became the first Indian of Alta California so honored when, on August 4, 1773, he received the sacrament in the chapel of the archiepiscopal palace, at the hands of the Most Reverend Alonso Nuñez de Haro y Peralta.

By the time of his arrival back at Carmel, Juan Evangelista had become a personage of considerable stature among his countrymen. He had observed how the *gente de razon* lived in large cities amid culture and conveniences. He had seen and talked with the viceroy and the archbishop and many of his experiences he could hardly communicate to the Carmeleños. On September 8, 1774, Juan Evangelista sent a cache of sardines to the Viceroy in his own name and in the name of the entire Indian population that inhabited the region of Monterey. The gift was a subject of conversation for many years in Mexico City.

Juan married Tomasa Maria of the *ranchería* of Ichxenta, at San Carlos Borromeo, on December 2, 1775. The twenty–year old neophyte contracted measles, in mid 1778, and died at Carmel. His death followed by only nine days that of his wife. Fray Junípero's gentle companion had become a member of the Third Order of Saint Francis and was interred in the Franciscan habit, the first native Californian accorded that privilege.

JUAN EVANGELISTA (c. 1758–1778)

B) VISIT TO MEXICO CITY

The first native Californian to visit Mexico City was Juan Evangelista (c. 1758–1778). When Juan was a youngster of fifteen years old, he accompanied Fray Junípero Serra to the *Distrito Federal* where the *Presidente* made his celebrated plea for a bill of rights on behalf of the Indians. Though he left no memoir of that journey, it is easy enough to reconstruct the Mexico City of the eighteenth century and how it appeared to Juan Evangelista.

The city stretched over four square miles. The majority of its streets were paved with cobblestones. The numerous canals running through the city were crossed by small stone bridges. The city was surrounded by three lakes, San Cristobal, Texcoco and Chalco, with small forests of pine, cypress, ash and poplar in the immediate vicinity. Fields, gardens and orchards spread over the outlying countryside.

Then and now, most of the buildings were constructed on piles. They were mostly built of stone, although adobe was fairly common in the poorer districts. Many of the buildings of that era are still in evidence today. At the center of the city was the magnificent cathedral and viceregal palace, both fronting on the *plaza* or *zocalo*. The cathedral, begun in 1573 and dedicated in 1656, was still unfinished in 1773 and its towers were only completed two decades later.

The viceregal palace surely impressed Juan Evangelista. One of the largest buildings in New Spain, it covered an entire city block. Inside were the apartments for the viceroy and his family together with numerous offices. Paintings, drawings and maps of the period portray two remarkable aqueducts that supplied the city with water. In addition to governmental buildings, church–related foundations and private homes, a series of public fountains fed off the aqueducts.

The dense population made Mexico City a place of noise, confusion, clamor, filth and debris. Heaps of refuse, human and animal excrement and knee–deep mud were everywhere. The waters of the public fountains were used for both drinking and washing. There was relatively little disease.

Colonial Mexico, with its churches, chapels, monasteries, convents, asylums and educational institutions was an American Rome. The capital was the center for many religious orders whose activities extended throughout New Spain. An endless variety of flowers were on sale everywhere, along with silks, brocades, silver and gold braids, linen goods and cloth, velvet wearing apparel, fans, clocks, toys, glass and earthenware, tobacco, sweets, preserves, biscuits, fruits and the like.

The streets were used for many purposes other than transportation, making it difficult to move about. Horses and mules were tied to posts, cows and pigs picked their way through garbage and hundreds of dogs roamed loose seeking nourishment. Ordinances had been issued, but were mostly unobserved. Indeed Mexico City had its squalor as well as its splendor. Yet many places in Europe could match both. Filth was a problem in all major cities of that time. It was only with arrival of Viceroy Revilla Gigedo that real reforms were instituted and enforced.

Juan Evangelista had much to see and learn in Mexico City. It was a rare opportunity to see another civilization more complicated than his own. What fun he must have had in telling his friends about Mexico City when he returned to Carmel.

ALPHEUS FELCH (1804–1896)

Throughout the annals of history, some of the Church's greatest benefactors have been non–Catholics. An example on the California scene would be Alpheus

Felch (1804–1896) who served as President of the Board of Land Commissioners from 1853 to 1856.

Born in Limerick, York County, Maine, Alpheus studied at Phillips Exeter Academy and Bowdoin College where he majored in jurisprudence. After a brief stint in the Michigan House of Representatives, Felch was named associate justice of his state's Supreme Court. He was elected Governor of Michigan in 1842, and later served a term in the United States Senate.

On March 3, 1851, members of the Thirty–first Congress passed The California Land Act which provided a judicial procedure for claimants to adjudicate private land titles in the state. The three commissioners appointed by President Millard Fillmore were to receive evidence, take testimony, review the law and render decisions upon claims.

Among the many cases brought before the commission was that initiated by Bishop Joseph Sadoc Alemany, whereby the Church wanted its claims to the Old Missions validated by the United States Government. Alemany's lawyers eloquently contended that Spanish and Mexican law recognized the right of the Church to hold property, as did common law, canon law, the Councils of Baltimore and local priestly synods. At each of the missions, the bishop asked for patents to the church, graveyard, quadrangle of buildings, enclosed gardens, orchards and vineyards.

Though the case was copiously documented with examples of Spanish, Mexican and California legislation, the commissioners relied heavily on the testimony of such prominent witnesses as William E. P. Hartnell, James Alexander Forbes, Pablo de la Guerra and numerous priests. Once the commissioners reached their decision, the task of drafting the response fell to Alpheus Felch. For several months he engaged in personal research of ecclesial law in order to clarify in his own mind the nature of the Church's claim to hold property.

On December 18, 1855, Felch rendered his decision confirming to Joseph Sadoc Alemany the lands at the missions, including the churches, buildings, cemeteries, gardens, orchards and vineyards as claimed. Felch had no hesitation about confirming the titles based on his satisfaction that the grant was genuine, that its ownership had been proven and that all the other necessary conditions had been satisfied.

Noting that "the claim of the bishop was not so much for a grant of land, as for a recognition of the right of the Church to the premises." Felch concluded that "these concurrent proofs bring us irresistibly to the conclusion that before the Treaty of Guadalupe Hidalgo, these possessions in question were solemnly dedicated to the use of the Church, and the property withdrawn from commerce."

Felch's lengthy twenty–two page decision was printed by O'Meara and Painter from their Press at 132 Clay Street in San Francisco. That publication is now among the Golden States' rarest imprints. His decision has been sustained over the years since 1855. He was a "benefactor" of the Church, not because he ruled in its favor, but because he resisted strong pressures to do otherwise.

MARIA ANTONIA FIELD (1885–1962)

The doña, Maria Antonia Field (1885–1961), was once described as "a very lovely lady—aristocratic, gracious and filled with the largess that was traditional in her family." Maria Antonia was born in the family home of her mother, known as *La Granja* (today the Casa Munras Hotel) in Monterey, on December 5, 1885. She was baptized in the old Presidio Chapel of San Carlos Borromeo by the fabled Father Angelo Casanova.

A fourth generation resident of California, she lived most of her life in a Spanish style mansion overlooking two small lakes and the Fort Ord hills called Villa Munras. The Munras family, long associated with the diplomatic service of Spain, originated in Catalonia. Esteban Carlos Munras came from Barcelona in 1816. In California he received several extensive land grants and went on to purchase other lands in what is present–day Soledad.

Another well–known *rancho* which became part of the Munras holdings was *Laguna Seca*, a lovely countryside area abounding in wild game. It was there that Pope John Paul II offered Holy Mass in September of 1987.

During her life, Maria Antonia made numerous trips to Europe and there, fittingly enough, she was welcomed by the exiled King Alfonso XIII who was then living in Rome's Grand Hotel. While there, Maria Antonia was invested with the "Royal Order of Isabella the Catholic," a distinction which gave her the privilege of being referred to as a "*doña*."

Maria Antonia Field was a generous and faithful supporter of Harry Downie and his efforts to restore San Carlos Borromeo Mission in Carmel. Many of her personal belongings are on display in a special exhibit at the Old Mission.

In 1914, Maria Antonia's *Chimes of Mission Bells* was published by the Philopolis Press of San Francisco. That seventy–nine page monograph has been described as "a truthful outline of the heroic and chivalrous Mission days." Then, in 1942, Maria Antonia wrote her Brief Sketch of *De Anza's Expeditions to California and of Father Andres Quintana's Martyrdom*, a sixteen page pamphlet based on a paper she had delivered at the Catholic Study Class in San Francisco. A brochure about the festival days of California was released by the Cloister Press, in 1948, as *Copa de Oro*.

Finally, Maria Antonia published her memoirs under the title *Where Castilian Roses Bloom*. "A picture of the life and times of one of California's pioneer Spanish families," the book was printed in an edition of 500 copies at San Francisco in 1954. It bore the imprint of the Grabhorn Press.

In his Foreword to that volume, Aurelio M. Espinosa of Stanford University describes her reflections as "an authentic historical document" which he felt gave a valuable insight into "the family life of the Spanish families of gentle background who founded the Golden State and influenced its development."

JAMES W. FIFIELD (1899–1977)

During his thirty–two years as Pastor of the First Congregational Church of Los Angeles, Dr. James W. Fifield, Jr. (1899–1977) became one of the truly significant figures in American Protestantism.

Born in Chicago, he studied at Oberlin College, the University of Chicago and the Chicago Theological Seminary. Ordained a Congregationalist minister in 1924, Dr. Fifield served at various pastorates before coming to Los Angeles in 1934. Bishop John J. Cantwell encouraged Fifield to accept the pastorate of the First Congregational Church and the two religious leaders forged a friendship that lasted for many years.

By 1942, the impressive Gothic church on Commonwealth Avenue had become the largest Congregational fellowship in the world, with 4,317 registered members and over 20,000 parishioners. In 1959, Fifield established The Freedom Club movement which rapidly spread nationwide. His radio programs were aired over 600 stations and his television appearances were featured on forty channels around the country.

In addition to numerous books, Dr. Fifield wrote a weekly column for the Los Angeles *Times* which, in syndication format, reached over eight and a half million readers. By the 1950s, Fifield was easily the most outstanding Protestant leader in Southern California.

In the mid 1940s, Dr. Fifield joined Archbishop Cantwell and Rabbi Edgar Magnin of the Wilshire Temple in establishing an "inter-faith Council" which was recognized citywide by local religious and civic officials. It was a forerunner to the Interreligious Council that became popular twenty years later.

Frank Weber owned and operated the Ritz Plumbing Service. A longtime friend of Dr. Fifield, he assisted in the management of the Fifield Manors which were established for the benefit of elderly parishioners and retirees. And so it came about that Dr. Fifield was invited to young Weber's priestly ordination at Saint Vibiana's Cathedral on April 30, 1959. His presence was a rare ecumenical gesture that was publicly acknowledged by James Francis Cardinal McIntyre.

Dr. Fifield lived on Fremont Place, in a home that backed up against the old King Gillette Mansion where Cardinal McIntyre resided from 1948 to 1969. The two churchmen could often be seen taking an evening stroll, discussing the many problems then facing the area's ecclesial leaders.

On the occasion of Fifield's thirtieth anniversary as Pastor of the First Congregational Church, Cardinal McIntyre said that Fifield's "long service has been a very commendable contribution to our fair city, particularly since it has been expended in the promotion of freedom under God and the preservation of the fundamental American principles of liberty in conscience." His Eminence of Los Angeles concluded by congratulating Dr. Fifield "upon the stalwart leadership he has given to his congregation, and the splendid qualities of his ministry on behalf of our beloved city."

Though he officially retired in 1966, Dr. Fifield continued writing his column in the Los Angeles *Times* and looking after his many other religious interests in the area.

When the definitive story of Protestantism in Los Angeles is written, the name of Dr. James W. Fifield Jr., will appear in capital letters. When he died, Timothy Cardinal Manning said that Fifield had been a unique blessing to this city. He prayed that "others would rise in his shadow!"

HENRY DELANO FITCH (1799–1849)

One of early California's most colorful romances surrounds a bell hanging in the campanile of the *Asistencia de Nuestra Señora de los Angeles*. Captain Henry Delano Fitch (1799–1849) came to the West, in 1826, on a trade mission. While his ship was docked at San Diego, the Massachusetts–born seaman fell in love with Josefa Carrillo, daughter of a prominent California family.

Several years later, after his reception into the Church by Father Antonio Menéndez, Fitch asked Doña Josefa to become his wife. Governor José Echeandia, a secret admirer of the young Carrillo maiden, forbade the marriage on the grounds that Captain Fitch was barred from a marital commitment by reason of his citizenship. The couple secretly fled to Valparaiso, where they were married in a quiet ceremony on July 3, 1829. Nothing of this kind had ever happened on the local scene, and Fitch's action caused a sensation in California's "true blooded Spanish circles."

When Fitch returned to California, he was arrested for kidnapping and ordered to stand canonical trial at San Gabriel. He was charged with being invalidly married and possessing a wedding certificate on which neither the name of the church nor the designation of the city appeared. Happily for Fitch, Fray José Sánchez, acting by deputization from the Bishop of Sonora, ruled, on December 28, 1830, that the wedding was valid, but illicit thus "the impending illegitimacy of their child was averted." In reparation for the scandal caused, however, Fitch was given, in addition to his canonical penance, the obligation of providing "a bell of at least fifty pounds in weight" for the church of *Nuestra Señora de los Angeles.*

Henry Delano Fitch is remembered in the annals as "one of the earliest, most prominent, and most popular of the early pioneers; straight–forward in his dealings, generous in disposition, frank and cheerful in manner." One of his relatives, Clarice Garland, incorporated the fulfillment of the captain's penance in a delightful novel "which loses nothing in interest for being historically correct and morally clean:"

> Captain Fitch sailed to Boston and brought a wedding–bell gift which, on his return to California, he presented to President José Sanchez in gratitude for the Judge's *pronunciamento* in vindication of his honor and the restoration of his wife and child to him. This bell yet chimes out the vindication of the American and calls the faithful to worship in the adobe church opposite the *plaza* in Los Angeles.

Little did Captain Fitch dream that five hundred thousand Americans would follow in his footsteps during three quarters of a century later and occupy the City of the Angels. And the captain's bell from Boston may have sounded a mystic summons to eastern dwellers from the restless Atlantic to the shore of the great Pacific.

EDWARD HAROLD FITZGERALD (1815–1860)

Edward Harold Fitzgerald was born on December 23, 1815, in Morristown, Pennsylvania. He entered the United States Army in 1839, an enlistee from Virginia. Fitzgerald served in the Seminole War in Florida until 1841, when he conducted a band of Indians to the "Western frontier of Arkansas." He was stationed in the Cherokee Nation until 1846.

With the outbreak of the war with Mexico, Fitzgerald's battalion joined the American forces in Texas. In 1847, Fitzgerald was assigned to the troops commanded by General Winfield Scott. Reportedly the first of the invading troops to land at Vera Cruz, Fitzgerald received his commission of Brevet–Major for "conspicuous gallantry" during the attack on the Chapultepec Palace.

After the hostilities, Fitzgerald entered the First Dragoons and was posted on the Pacific Coast. There he served between 1849 and the time of his demise. He was supply officer at Fort Mason and, in 1851, during the disturbances at Warners Ranch, he organized a volunteer company to defend San Diego against the natives.

On January 9, 1860, Fitzgerald died of tuberculosis at the Sisters' Hospital in Los Angeles. When announcing his funeral, a local southland newspaper reported that a squadron of First Dragoons from Fort Tejon "performed the march, a distance of over 100 miles, in the unusually short time of thirty–one hours, including all stoppages, over bad roads and during a snowstorm in the mountains," to attend his final obsequies.

The Los Angeles *Star* for January 12th noted that "the mortal remains of Major Fitzgerald were conveyed to their lasting resting place, in the Catholic Cemetery of this city. The large assemblage of citizens who attended on the melancholy occasion, proved the esteem in which the deceased gentleman was held in this community; there were at least 2,000 persons, the stores along the line of procession were closed. A good man and a brave soldier was taken from us; our citizens mourned the loss, and by their presence testified their respect for the departed."

The newspaper account went on to state that "the body was conveyed to the Church, where the services were celebrated by the Very Rev. Father (Blas) Raho. . . After service, "the procession was re–formed, and marched to the cemetery, where Father Raho closed the religious services; the body was committed to the earth; the Dragoons fired the salute, and the gallant soldier and true Christian was left in his lone home."

And, there is a sequel to the story. When old Calvary Cemetery was closed, in 1926, the Brevet–Major's remains were ordered transferred to the National Cemetery in the San Francisco *presidio*. Fitzgerald's old monument was repaired and its shaft re–attached. It stands today over the grave, close by monuments to Generals Evan Miles and Henry Haskell.

ROBERT MULLINS FITZGERALD (1858–1934)

Robert Mullins Fitzgerald has aptly been described by Peter Conmy as "one of California's most noted lawyers, a citizen of sterling qualities and a strong leader of the Native Sons of the Golden West." Fitzgerald, the son of Edward and Catherine (Mullins) Fitzgerald, was born in San Francisco on January 7, 1858. Shortly thereafter, the family moved to Sonoma County and young Robert's early education was acquired at a district school in adjacent Marin.

After interrupting his schooling to look after family

obligations (his father had died unexpectedly), Fitzgerald resumed his education at Berkeley High. He graduated from the Hasting's College of Law in 1883. Fitzgerald practiced law in Oakland for several years and then he moved to San Francisco where, in 1895, he entered into partnership with Carl Hewes Abbott.

In 1902, it was Fitzgerald's happy choice to marry Laura Crellin, the daughter of a pioneer Alameda County family. It was a blissful marriage, blessed with two daughters and a son, all of them reared in the shadow of the law.

Following the devastating earthquake and fire of 1906, the firm of Fitzgerald, Abbott and Beardsley moved back to Oakland, where it became one of the most prestigious law offices in Alameda County. Few notable cases were filed in those years without one or the others of those firm named as legal consultants.

An ardent Democrat, Fitzgerald served as delegate to a number of his party's National Conventions. He was a member of the resolutions committee, in 1928, when Alfred A. Smith was nominated as the first Catholic to seek the presidency. He was also busy at the local level, serving for a long time on the governing board for the Department of Public Works. For many years he was also Vice President of Oakland's Central Bank. In that role he was influential in assisting the urban development of Oakland.

When a new Parlor for the Native Sons of the Golden West was established at Oakland, in 1885, Robert M. Fitzgerald was the logical choice to be president. In subsequent years, he was a fixture at most every local and statewide gathering of the Native Sons. In 1914, Fitzgerald was chosen President of the California State Bar Association. While in that position, he was successful in having former President William Howard Taft address the California Bar.

Fitzgerald died at his home in Oakland on January 3, 1934. Monsignor Charles A. Ramm eulogized his life–long friend as "an aristocratic pioneer with the common touch." And so he surely was. Truly Robert Mullins Fitzgerald was among the best of the early pioneers, a man who richly deserves to be remembered for his contributions to California's Catholic heritage.

LOUIS FLECKENSTEIN (1866–1943)

A man who died a half century earlier was among the "stars" at the XXV California International Antiquarian Book Fair in 1992. Louis Fleckenstein's portfolio of photographs about the California missions was the featured item by one of the prominent exhibitors.

Fleckenstein's family owned a brewery and grocery. He began his career as a painter but switched to photography in the mid 1890s. In 1904, he organized the Salon Club of America which evolved into the American Federation of Photographic Societies, an umbrella for a large number of local camera clubs

Coming to California in 1907, Fleckenstein (1866–1943) lived in and around the Eagle Rock area for some years. He later served as an art commissioner for the City of Long Beach. In the February, 1912 issue of *Photo Era*, Fleckenstein reflected on "What the Camera Records in Los Angeles." It was a penetrating essay, part of which is reproduced here as one of the early observations about the city dedicated to *Nuestra Señora de los Angeles.*

Nature has lavished upon this region all its florid treasures and everywhere are flowers of infinite variety and marvelous growth. They fill up the parkways bordering the streets, hedge about the well–kept, spacious lawns, entwine themselves about the trunks of shade trees, creep over and conceal fences and frequently envelop the sides and even the roofs of homes.

The wide–spreading palms express a feeling of contentment and security; the graceful and feathery pepper trees, peacefulness and rest. Bright sunshine and blue skies are our daily portions, yet so tempered by genial and refreshing sea–breezes that discomfort is rarely felt. It all seems artificial—a dream, too good to last—and only time will efface that impression.

By and by one becomes accustomed to it all—ceases to wonder at geranium plants climbing over a twelve foot fence; fuchsias growing to the size of trees; the hydrangea blossoms showing every hue of the rainbow, the castorbean the roosting–place of the barnyard flock and rose vines, wisteria, heliotrope, begonia and bougainvellaeas creeping over and concealing entire houses in a bewildering mass of fragrant blossoms.

They are with us constantly—summer and winter—beautiful pictures always, and therefore very likely to be kept on the waiting list and neglected. Most camerists have learned the futility of attempting to portray scenes depending alone on beauty of coloring; provided, of course, that photography in its present stage is the aim sought.

The old Mission Church (at the plaza), with its yellow plastered walls, patched and cracked, and its little triangular court, dotted here and there with gossiping groups of Mexican women and children standing in the shade of the great palms, presents an interesting picture on a Sunday morning.

At this time, also, the outside walk and the plaza opposite present an animated appearance, this being the congregating place of all Spanish–speaking races in the city. Their dark, swarthy faces, flowery–hued garb and prodigious *sombreros*—in some cases more hat than man—afford material for interesting studies."

On and on the one–time Death Valley miner wrote. In conclusion, he stated the obvious by observing that Los Angeles is "an ideal place for camera observation."

ARTHUR FLEISCHMANN (1896–1990)

The eminent sculptor, Arthur Fleischman (1896–1990) was renowned for his use of modern and unusual materials. He pioneered the use of Perspex as a sculptural medium in spite of early opposition and prejudice.

Born in Bratislava, Fleischman lived most of his life in London. He studied medicine in Budapest and Prague and was licensed and qualified as a practicing physician. Early in life, however, Fleischman became interested in art and was awarded a scholarship to the Master School of Sculpture in Vienna. After travelling to Italy and France, he returned to Vienna where he developed his skills in ceramics.

In 1948, Fleischmann took up permanent residence in London and there he lived in the St. John's Wood studio that once belonged to Sir George Frampton, the Victorian sculptor. The contents of Fleischmann's home, according to a newspaper account, conveyed the presence of greatness: "His humanism, his passionate attachment to people and the things of the classical life, were probably the secret of his exceptional and fruitful career."

It was while the artist was residing in London that he completed portrait busts of Pope Pius XII, John XXIII, Paul VI and John Paul II. Fleischmann had the distinction of being the only artist ever to have sculptured four popes from life.

Paramount to all Fleischmann's work was his devotion to the Catholic faith. The created a huge risen Christ from sheet aluminum for the Vatican Pavilion at the Brussel's World Exhibition in 1958 as well as devotional statues in many churches in England and on the continent. Fleischmann's portraits of popes and presidents, his dancing figures and his abstract sculptures can be seen and admired in collections and public places all over the world. His work was reproduced on thousands of commemorative medals minted over many years.

Today, Fleischmann is chiefly remembered for his bronzes of Pope Gregory the Great, Pope John XXIII, Paul VI (in the Scots College) and John Paul II (in the Venerable English College.)

Those who knew Fleischmann closely realized that his charming courtesy and great humility sprang from his deep faith and reverential love for the Church. Pope Paul VI and Cardinal Bea were his close and long–time personal friends.

In 1970 Arthur and his wife, Joy, came to Los Angeles where they met and visited with James Francis Cardinal McIntyre. At that time, Fleischmann was commissioned to do a bust portrayal of His Eminence of Los Angeles and that work–of–art is exhibited on the loggia of the Edward Laurence Doheny Library at Saint John's Seminary in Camarillo.

In February of 1992, two of Fleischmann's bronze pieces were presented to the Historical Museum attached to the Archival Center in Mission Hills. One is a bust of Dominique Fleischmann when he was a small boy and the other a depiction of Fleischmann's wife, Joy.

Arthur Fleischmann was indeed an extraordinary man—a sculptor, painter, artist and medical doctor. But above and beyond it all, he was a staunch and loyal Catholic whose faith was reflected on all his artistic masterpieces.

When he died at the venerable age of ninety–three, while visiting in Tenerife, the local newspaper, after describing Fleischmann's many accomplishments, concluded with the observation that "his devotion to the Catholic faith was central to his work." That was the ultimate compliment.

CATALINA FLORES (c. 1785–1902)

Catalina Flores continued her usual routine of activities until the very day of her death, late in 1902, at the remarkable age of 117. She had lived under the shadows of San Gabriel Mission for more than ninety years. Born in the vast wilderness domain of the northwest about 1785, while the Continental Congress was holding its sessions in Philadelphia, Catalina was four years old when George Washington was first elected President of the United States.

La Madre de la Misión, as Señora Flores was affectionately known by the Hispanic peoples of Southern California, likely lived her earliest years in a frontier hunting camp on the Columbia River. According to the San Francisco *Monitor*, in a story dated January 10, 1903, Catalina was "of that admixture of Spanish and Indian blood which has given to the world a race that counts three–score–and–ten as middle life, and which furnishes some of the most noted instances of human longevity."

She early married M. Flores, an adventurous Frenchman who had pushed on beyond the most remote of the Hudson Bay Company's posts. He later became affiliated with the Franciscan friars in San Francisco. Catalina had many stories concerning her childhood in the then unknown vastness of Astoria. They were memories of substance—stories of the *padres*, of painted Indians and brave hunters.

Whether the arrival of New England colonists, in 1810, or the establishment of the American Pacific Fur Company brought about the discontinuance of the little French colony was uncertain. In any event, Catalina migrated, with her husband, to the luxurious civilization of Spanish life in Southern California.

Evidence indicates that she arrived at San Gabriel, in

1812, at which time Catalina was twenty–seven years old. It is part of the mission lore that she was among the most skillful needlewomen of the community and that she wrought many of the most beautiful ornamentations of the edifice to which she was the last living witness. According to T*he Monitor* report, in later years Catalina "gloried in the radiant colorings of her basketry, and delighted to show it to the tourists from the big hotels, who count a day at the old mission town as one of the features of a Southern California tour." Even in those days, San Gabriel Mission remained a little circle of quiet, as yet undisturbed by the boisterous ocean of commercial and industrial activity which had inundated the new Southwest.

The death of Señora Catalina Flores marked the passing of the Spanish peoples and the supremacy of the Anglo–Saxon. The impressive funeral scene for *La Madre de la Misión* was described by an eyewitness:

> From before the altar of the old church, with its candles casting their shimmering reflection upon the silver mountings of the American–made coffin, we watched them bear the Mother of the Mission to the grave hard by. To north and east and west rose the Sierra Madre mountains, range above range. The purple shadows followed one another along their slopes, and the sun of the afternoon glinted on the eternal snow wrapping the crest of San Antonio.
>
> There, in the presence of the immaculate hills, that had stood while race chased race from under their lea, they laid their oldest human neighbor. She had outstripped the mortal span by half a century, but earth had claimed its tardy child.

FERDINAND FOCH (1852–1929)

Historians rank Ferdinand Foch among the great military geniuses of all time. Even his contemporaries hailed the French leader as "the world's greatest soldier since the days of Napoleon." Born at Tarbes, not far from present–day Lourdes, on October 2, 1851, Foch was educated at the Jesuit College of Saint Clement, at Metz. His brother subsequently entered the Society of Jesus and became a prominent preacher.

Foch was commissioned as an artillery officer, in 1873. In the following years, he occupied numerous positions of importance in military circles. In 1896, he was appointed Professor at the War College. Foch's ardent Catholicism held back his promotion for many years but, in 1907, the anti–clerical Premier, George Clemenceau, made him director of the *Ecole Superieure de Guerre.*

During the early stages of World War I, Foch was in charge of the 20th Corps at Nancy. Later, he commanded the 9th Army at the Marne. In 1917, he became Chief of Staff and President of the Allied Board of Strategy. The following year, Foch became *generalissimo* of the Allied armies in Europe and Marshal of France. He it was who dictated the armistice terms to the German delegation at Compiegne. Marshal Foch was a perfect exemplar of the Catholic soldier. He was a man of unaffected piety and deep faith in God. His special devotion to the Blessed Sacrament was perhaps his outstanding characteristic.

Following the war, the Marshal made a tour of the United States. He was welcomed by Joseph Scott who said that "We, in America, where the Church has had far better opportunity to live and thrive, than it has had in certain periods of French history, ought to profit by the stirring exhibition of the great Marshal."

On December 4, 1921, Foch was welcomed in Los Angeles by a large delegation of civic and religious leaders. He went immediately to Saint Vibiana's Cathedral "to pray for a just and lasting peace." He was greeted there by a huge throng of people waving French and American flags. Bishop John J. Cantwell saluted the Marshal and offered a Solemn Pontifical Mass for his party. Following the liturgical ceremonies, the Bishop of Monterey–Los Angeles told the prominent visitor that "you have modestly shown that religion and personal piety do not weaken and debase, but elevate and ennoble; that religion and obedience and true patriotism are not incompatible."

The simplicity and strength of Foch's Catholic faith charmed his hosts in Southern California. In his welcome, the editorial writer of one newspaper said that "you, by your courage, by your greatness, by your simple faith have won the love of thousands."

Marshal Foch lived on until February 14, 1929. He is interred in the *Invalides,* where even today he is remembered mostly for his plain and unpretentious Catholic faith.

HENRY CHAPMAN FORD (1828–1894)

A. A MISSION PAINTER

The skillful and clever artistic work of Henry Chapman Ford (1828–1894) forms an important adjunct to the overall history of the California Mission system. Though he was born in New York, Ford received his early training in Europe where he stayed three years studying in the ateliers of different masters.

Ford's first commercial art work dates from his tour of duty in the United States Army. While on military assignments, the artist kept careful sketches, which he subsequently submitted to an illustrated newspaper in New York City. In the fall of 1862, Ford went to

Henry Chapman Ford's depiction of San Fernando Mission

Chicago and opened that city's first landscape studio. So highly appreciated was his work that he was asked to serve a term as president of Chicago's old Academy of Design.

Shortly after the disastrous fire that swept the Windy City in 1871, Ford moved to California where, after a brief sojourn in the Bay Area, he took up permanent residence at Santa Barbara near the old mission. In 1880–1881 he toured the California missions, making at each foundation a series of studies in oil. Twenty–four of those masterful productions were published in a limited edition of fifty copies at New York in 1883. It was also about this time that the artist painted a set of mission scenes for an elderly lady living in Boston. After the publication of his *Etchings of the Franciscan Missions of California*, Ford turned to watercolors, and, in that medium executed a wholly different series of paintings.

A set of these watercolor productions was displayed at the Columbian Exposition in 1893. That particular collection was subsequently purchased by Mrs. Leland Stanford and is now housed at the university bearing her family name. At the earnest behest of N. H. Reed, Henry Ford authorized a selection of his works for postcard reproduction at Santa Barbara. These items have since become the most prized of Reed's 200 California scenes.

It was Ford's intention to preserve, in some pictorial form, the interesting remnants of the labors of the Franciscan Fathers, who overcame apparently insuperable obstacles in the successful establishment of twenty–one missions among the wild tribes scattered along the coast of California. The artist found "these monuments of the self–sacrificing zeal of the brotherhood . . . fast yielding to the corroding action of the elements, and, where towns have grown up about them, a spirit of alteration has sprung up which has left but slight traces of their original appearances."

At the time of his death, Ford was working on a history of the missions. A few of the artist's isolated notes were published by the California Historical Society in 1924, and, in 1961 thirty–six of his etchings from the collection of William A. Edwards were reproduced by the Santa Barbara Historical Association. Beyond their unchallenged artistic worth, the paintings and etchings of Henry Chapman Ford rank among the best records that remain to us of our mission buildings in the period of their neglect and decay.

HENRY CHAPMAN FORD (1828–1894)

B. FORD ON EXHIBITION

Through a happy confluence of circumstances, the Archival Center for the Archdiocese of Los Angeles acquired a complete set of Henry Chapman Ford's etchings of the California missions. The twenty–four etchings, measuring 17 by 22 inches on their mounts, were printed at New York's Studio Press in 1883. Limited to an edition of fifty sets, each print was signed by the artist. There are duplicate views of Missions Santa Barbara and San Carlos Borromeo, together with a depiction of the abandoned ruins of La Purisima Concepcion.

The New York–born artist first visited the missions by covered wagon, in 1880–1881, and during that trek made careful photographs which he later enlarged for use as models. From the very outset, Ford intended to produce the most elaborate work yet published on the subject.

Upon completion of the oil portrayals, Mr. Ford journeyed to New York, where he personally supervised their transferral to copperplates. The freedom, delicacy and strength of the completed scenes amply testify to his success.

The publication of Ford's monumental opus was widely–heralded. Archbishop Joseph Sadoc Alemany of San Francisco, recalling his own first tour of the missions, in 1851, found "the execution by Mr. Ford accurate." The Dominican prelate went on to say that the artist deserved "the special gratitude of the State of California for his zeal in preserving the glorious memories of the Pioneers of its Christian civilization." Another foremost authority on the early missionary foundations, Father Joachim Adam, wrote from Los Angeles that he had carefully examined the etchings and considered "them not only exquisite as a work of art, but also a faithful representation" of Provincial California.

A reviewer for the Los Angeles Times labelled the Ford etchings "an invaluable addition to the history of these earliest monuments of civilization in California" and hoped that folios would find their way into "every library and public institution of the State."

Newspapers from around the nation joined the chorus of praise. The Washington National Republican said that Ford's "work perpetuates on copper about the only interesting ruins to be seen in America." A writer in the Cleveland Leader called the etchings "not only beautiful and interesting as works of art" but also depictions of "great historical value." The Chicago Times ranked the portfolio as "one of the finest specimens of the 'art preservative' which has appeared in this country."

In its "Exposition Notes," the New Orleans Times Democrat declared that Ford's masterpiece showed "marked artistic talent, and admirable technique and perfect familiarity with the graver and acid bath." In Chicago's Present Age, Enoch Root wrote that the reproduction of the missions, from canvas to copper plates, demonstrated that the artist's "skill with the needle point equals his power in the use of the brush." Another prominent artist, Norton Bush of San Francisco happily endorsed the etchings "as being works of art of an exceedingly interesting character," while the Protestant Rector of Christ Church, Bridgeport, Connecticut, went ever further and proclaimed them "the most ambitious work of the kind ever produced by an American."

Henry Chapman Ford's fascination for and reproduction of the California missions rank the artist among the truly great benefactors of Western Americana.

HENRY CHAPMAN FORD (1929–1994)

C. On the Paper Trail

Everything in God's universe has its own story. *Where* it came from, *how* it got there, *who* was its donor or owner—all of these are ingredients in ascertaining the "history" of a particular item. Historians need only one thing to unravel these questions and others: a paper trail. If an item has one, its story can eventually be told. Perhaps an example would be useful.

During the last week in July of 1989, the director for the Center of Development in Ministry at Saint Mary of the Lake Seminary, Mundelein, asked about the beautifully framed set of scenes depicting the California missions that adorned the hallways of his building.

It didn't take long to determine that they were etchings, the work of Henry Chapman Ford. The twenty–four prints, measuring 17x 22 inches on their mounts, were sets that were printed in 1883.

When the director heard how valuable the etchings were (a set had recently sold for $10,000), she wondered *where* the exquisite prints came from, *how* did they get there and *who* was the donor. It was a challenging query that involved considerable research.

The first clue on the "paper trail" was found in the "California State Library–San Francisco Newspaper Index" where an entry for "Mundelein" told about the archbishop's visit to San Francisco in the early days of 1922, enroute home from Hawaii. Presuming that he would have also visited Los Angeles, I checked *The Tidings* and discovered, in the issue of February 14th, that Mundelein had indeed journeyed to Los Angeles "on the last stretch of his first trip west of Chicago." Mundelein was the house guest of Bishop John J. Cantwell. Chicago's archbishop was enamored with the California missions, several of which he personally visited while in the southland. He was especialy intrigued by several of Henry Chapman Ford's etchings which were hanging in a corridor of the rectory at Saint Vibiana's Cathedral. He asked if it would be possible to acquire a set for his new seminary. Dr. Charles Conroy eventually found a set of the etchings at a local bookstore and had them shipped to Chicago.

And here, the paper trail shifts to the archives. On May 21, 1922, Mundelein wrote to Bishop Cantwell saying that "the signed proof etchings of the Missions arrived in good time and in fine conditions. . . ."

He went on to say that he appreciated the etchings "both for their artistic value, but more so for the pleasant memories they bring me of a most enjoyable stay in your great and still growing city of the sunset land."

The archbishop expressed his interest in keeping "the etchings together hung in one or two corridors, so as to keep the continuity." He told Cantwell that the "next time you pass through and visit the seminary, you will find them in place telling the Chicago clergy of a sister church that was glorious and full of promise in its birth, but seems even more promising in its present–day development.

So, in response to an idle inquiry, an archivist hit the paper trail and found the story of *where* the etchings came from, *how* they got to the seminary and *who* was their donor.

JOHN FORD (1895–1973)

It was the view of President Richard M. Nixon that "in the history of American films, no name shines more brightly than that of John Ford." Born in Portland, Maine, Sean O'Feeney was the youngest of thirteen children. He followed an older brother to Hollywood, changed his name to Ford, and served an apprenticeship as stuntman, grip, cameraman and finally director.

He was abruptly thrust into the front ranks of his profession, in 1924, with "The Iron Horse." That film, like so many of his other great classics, was imbued with the subtlety, richness and complexity of a great poet. Some of his early movies, like "The Informer" (1935) and "How Green Was My Valley" (1941) paralleled a rising social consciousness in depression America and a growing general awareness of the film as a work of art.

John Ford flourished when movies were very popular and when they openly celebrated or at least hoped for, a shared community of feeling. The characteristics of a Ford production included the breathtaking sense of location, leading actors and a strong stock company. During the "Ford Era," others made films, John directed "classics." It was for filming the battle of Midway Island, in 1942, and gathering evidence for use at the Nuremberg Trials, that won him the rank of rear admiral in the United States Navy.

Within his films, Ford was able to provide a world in which a moral choice was meaningful, though not easy. It was in that atmosphere of morality that Mr. Ford lived, always a devout Catholic who took particular pride in his long marriage to an Irish sweetheart, Mary McBryde Smith. Ford did not know the meaning of hypocrisy. He remained an imposing figure of exceptional simplicity, even after a career that won him four Oscars and all the plaudits of his own profession.

Orson Welles was once asked which of the American movie directors most appealed to him. "The old masters," he replied, "by which I mean John Ford, John Ford and John Ford." No less a film personage than Ingrid Bergman pronounced Ford "the best director in the world." The title went uncontested. After a career that spanned six decades and nearly 200 films, the seventy–eight year old director died, full of honor and recognition, at his home in Palm Desert, on August 31, 1973

In his eulogy, Timothy Cardinal Manning referred to Ford as "the incomparable master of his trade." Indeed, his overriding, obsolete and heroic testament is a single line from one of his finest westerns: "When the legend becomes a fact, print the legend." The uncritical worship of great men may be a prelude to national self–delusion. But constant debunking can lead to an equally pernicious fiction—that no man is better than his society. That was a notion that Ford disputed in every scene of every film.

EUPHEMIA "EFFIE" CHARLTON FORTUNE (1885–1969)

To grasp a measure of Effie Fortune's greatness as an artist, one need only to go to Kansas City, look up the Cathedral of the Immaculate Conception, and there contemplate the vast mosaic which fills the space above the high altar. Euphemia Charlton Fortune (1885–1969) a native of Sausalito, studied at Edinburgh College of Art in Scotland and Saint John's Wood School of Art in London. After returning to her native California in 1905, she completed her training at Mark Hopkins under Arthur Mathews.

Early in her career, Effie concentrated on portrait paintings. Unfortunately, the Fortune family home was dynamited during the disaster of 1906, destroying many of her earliest works. Miss Fortune then turned to landscape and harbor scenes and these brought her international acclaim. She lived and worked in Europe during three periods between 1897 and 1927.

In California, her energies were divided between her studio home on Hyde Street in San Francisco and the Monterey Peninsula, where she exhibited at the Del Monte Art Gallery. Among collectors, her work was highly coveted. She was one of the first artists to introduce the bright palette of impressionism to California. Effie's work during those years has every right to rank along with the finest of the school of Cezanne, splendid in its conception and glorious in its finality. Had she chosen to remain a landscape painter, an artist who happened to be a Catholic, her name would be known everywhere.

But Effie had other aspirations and, in 1928, she founded the Monterey Guild, thereafter dedicating herself to ecclesial art. She abandoned easel painting for the liturgical arts and with other artists decorated over thirty Catholic churches across the country. Slowly her work gained recognition, though she came early to the realization that the Catholic artist, like the pioneer or prophet, is a fool to look for honor in his native country.

Effie decorated the chapel at Judge Memorial High School in Salt Lake City and later she designed the tabernacle for Saint Thomas Aquinas Cathedral. Others of her works remain in the chapels of the Dominican College at San Rafael and Providence Hospital, Oakland. A long–time favorite of Archbishop Edwin V. O'Hara of Kansas City, Effie was awarded the papal medal *"Pro Ecclesia et Pontifice"* in November of 1955. One commentator noted on that occasion that "it was not merely because she is an artist who happens to be a Catholic that this recognition came to her, but because she is an artist who had dedicated her life and talent to the praise of God through her art."

In a column on "Effie" for the *Catholic Sentinel*, the late Archbishop Robert Dwyer said that "here is one of the very few artists of our time who belongs to the main tradition of the Church as Mother of the Arts. Here is a woman gifted to an extraordinary degree as a painter and as a designer, at the zenith of her powers. Here is a valiant champion of Catholic idealism and artistic integrity, to whom the Church in America is deeply and permanently indebted."

The final decade of Effie's life was spent in retirement. One writer said that "for those who have known her through the years . . . she has provided, along with her genius, something of the salt that gives savor to life."

JOHN FILMORE FRANCIS (1850–1903)

"A career which elevates one's own self and at the same time reaches out and helps to raise those with whom one comes in contact has an influence so widespread as to be immeasurable. To the City of Los Angeles has been given such a character in the late John F. Francis."

Very little is known about the early life of John Filmore Francis (1850–1903) beyond the fact that his earliest years were spent mostly in Europe. A native of Clinton, Iowa, Francis was fascinated by military life, and, at the age of sixteen he enlisted in the Kansas Volunteer Cavalry where he had many thrilling experiences in the Indian campaign on the Western Kansas frontier in 1867. Afterwards "he spent several years adventuring over the plains and mountains of Wyoming, Colorado and California, obtaining a rich fund of information, so that by the time he came of age he was in possession of valuable ideas regarding this great country."

Shortly after coming to the west coast, Mr. Francis married the socially prominent Maria de los Reyes, the last of the direct descendants of the Dominguez family. Contemporary accounts speak of Francis as one whose personal qualities endeared him to every level of society. An able conversationalist with keen powers of observation, the jurist was acknowledged as discreet, adroit and considerate of the feelings of his fellowmen. Harrison

Gray Otis portrayed Francis as "essentially a good citizen and never a self–seeker." The publisher of the Los Angeles *Times* remarked that Francis "repeatedly declined to stand for public office, but as a private citizen in the civic ranks, never was there a better soldier." In 1897, he was president of *La Fiesta de los Angeles* and as such was largely instrumental in securing the success of that function, which formed so important a part of the social life of the city.

John Francis was converted to the Catholic Faith in 1891, largely through the influence of Father Joachim Adam, Vicar General of the Diocese of Monterey–Los Angeles. Even before adopting Catholicism, however, Francis was a man of deep religious feeling. On May 25, 1899, John Francis and several other outstanding Catholic laymen of the southland established the Newman Club whose avowed purpose was (and is) "the advancement of religious toleration in accordance with the Constitution of the United States; the expression of members' sentiments on matters of interest to Catholics and promotion of social intercourse among its members."

At the time of his death in Los Angeles on July 4, 1903, Francis was eulogized by *The Tidings* as "a good husband, a kind neighbor, an upright citizen, but above all, he was a good Catholic." It is recorded in the annals that Saint Vibiana's Cathedral could not hold the people who gathered to pay to the noble life of John F. Francis their last tribute of respect. Bishop J. Conaty characterized him as a man whose "life was a constant sermon of the value of the Catholic Faith," and one whose "greatness was his goodness."

JOHN CHARLES FREMONT (1813–1890)

One of the more intriguing examples of bigotry on file at the Archival Center, Archdiocese of Los Angeles, is a brochure entitled "The Romish Influence: Fremont a Catholic!" Circulated by Robert M. DeWitt, the sixteen page monograph figured prominently in Fremont's loss of the presidential election in 1856.

John Charles Fremont (1813–1890) needs little introduction to Californians. He came west with Kit Carson in 1843 and stayed on to become an important figure in bringing the state into the Federal Union. His *Report of the Exploring Expedition to Oregon and North California* (1845) is classical American adventure.

Fremont was a colorful individual in many other ways. His term as military governor ended with a charge of mutiny. Though a court martial in Washington found him guilty, he was pardoned by President James Polk. Fremont was adept at playing to the galleries and the public adored his defiant style. He later served in the United States Senate and became a national political figure.

In 1856, Fremont ran for the presidency on the ticket of the new anti–slavery Republican Party. It was then that he was falsely charged with being a Roman Catholic, an accusation that wouldn't go away.

For a dozen or so years, the Native Americans and Know–Nothings had been injecting the religious issue into nearly every major election. The campaign of 1856 was especially vitriolic. While the chief issue was "bleeding Kansas," the Know–Nothing element succeeded in further enlivening matters by accusing John Fremont of being a "bloody Catholic." Fremont appears to have ignored the charge. Horace Greeley, editor of the New York *Tribune*, declared that whether or not Fremont was a Catholic made little difference as far as voters were concerned, a statement hotly debated in retrospect.

The fact that Fremont's biographer, John Bigelow, went out of his way to prove that Fremont was a communicant in the Protestant Episcopal Church indicates that the religious issue was indeed a factor in the outcome. The American Party, who had nominated Millard Fillmore as its candidate, mounted a campaign of bigotry, slander and fear. Certain of their opponents in the Democratic Party, whose candidate was James Buchanan, allowed a report to be circulated claiming that Fremont was a Jesuit!

Actually the simplest inquiry would have ascertained Fremont's Episcopalian affiliations in his youth and his almost total lack of church connections in maturity, although he had his children baptized in the Anglican faith. Misstatements concerning Fremont's religion long survived the campaign. On October 13, 1928, his granddaughter, Juliet Fremont Hull, found it necessary to publicly correct erroneous assertions along these lines made in the New York *World*.

Fremont has the distinction of being the only non–Catholic in American history whose "catholicity" cost him a national election. Or, as one chronicler put it, "he may have been rightly defeated, but it was surely for the wrong reason."

JOHN T. GAFFEY (1859–1935)

When John T. Gaffey, the "father of the Los Angeles harbor," died at *La Rambla* in San Pedro, on January 9, 1935, he was eulogized in the columns of the Los Angeles *Examiner* as "a first citizen of California." Born in Galway, Ireland in 1859, John was brought "around the Horn" to California by his parents, Thomas and Anne (Tracy) Gaffey. He married Arcadia Bandini in 1887.

Besides serving as editor for the Santa Cruz *Herald* (1879–1880), Gaffey was under sheriff of Santa Cruz County (1880–1881), deputy clerk for the California Supreme Court (1882–1886), member of the State Board of Equalization (1886–1890) city councilman for Los Angeles (1893), editor of the Los Angeles *Herald* (1893–1894) and collector of customs (1896–1900).

He was also active in real estate development and promoted many crucial projects in the southland's financial district. A Democrat, he was a spokesman for the state party for nearly forty years. He served as a delegate to the second California constitutional convention (1890) and was one of FDR's presidential electors in 1932. Although offered ambassadorial posts by Presidents Grover Cleveland and Woodrow Wilson, Gaffey spurned all political appointments, preferring to remain on the sidelines. Intensely active in mining interests, Gaffey had extensive real estate holdings in Mexico, some in partnership with Senator George Hearst.

In addition to his many business and political involvements, Gaffey was an assiduous student of early California and Mexican history. He translated many works and memoirs from Spanish and gave a number of valuable manuscripts to the Bancroft Library at the University of California, Berkeley. His personal library was ranked second only to that of Henry Huntington.

Gaffey's most notable public achievement was his successful campaign for the harbor at San Pedro which he made with his intimate friend, Senator Stephen M. White. A charter member of the California Club, Gaffey was also its most brilliant and fascinating enthusiast.

Few people had a better claim to the title of "pioneer" than did John Gaffey. The illustrious Irishman left his mark socially, politically and constructively in numerous fields of endeavor, as well as in the promotion of many useful enterprises.

Known as a deeply religious man, Gaffey's funeral services were held in the chapel of his estate by Father James McLaughlin, pastor of Mary, Star of the Sea Church, an old and dear friend. He was interred in the family plot at the valley churchyard in Watsonville. Otherman Stevens wrote that "When John Gaffey was placed in his tomb, there was buried with him and lost to this world a unique storehouse of knowledge about gringo life in Southern California."

To write about John Gaffey is like trying to write an obituary of Ariel. The facts of his life can only be sketched in outline form.

Today, John Gaffey is primarily remembered in San Pedro for Gaffey Canyon and Gaffey Street. But, as long as ships sail in and out of the Port of Los Angeles, Gaffey will be saluted by Southern Californians.

JEAN FRANCOIS DE LA GALAUP, COMTE DE LA PEROUSE (1741–1788)

The four volume set (plus Atlas) of *Voyage de la Perouse Autour du Monde* in the Archival Center recalls the bond of friendship which Jean Francois de la Galaup, Comte de la Perouse (1741–1788) forged between France and California. On the evening of September 14, 1786, two French ships, *La Boussole* and *L'Astrobe* entered Monterey Bay bearing the first foreign contingency to visit California after Spanish occupation.

Officially commissioned by King Louis XVI to expand geographical knowledge by searching out such areas as the Northwest Passage, the Comte de la Perouse was equally intent on appraising the commercial and political potentialities of the whole Pacific area.

By his own admission, Galaup and his party were received at San Carlos Borromeo Mission "like lords of the parish making their first entry into their estates." The friars exhibited little reticence in discussing their activities and Galaup recorded that "the monks by their answers to our questions, left us in ignorance of nothing concerning the regime of this kind of religious community."

Though Galaup had nothing to say against the character of the missionaries, his general reaction to the Franciscan *modus agendi* was predominantly unfavorable. While testifying to the high purpose of the friars, he "thought they erred in attempting to enforce a disciplined life upon a wild people, whose self–reliance, he felt, suffered from the mission system."

Despite his critical attitude about certain features of mission life, Galaup expressed his sincere admiration for the missionaries themselves, noting that they were firmly convinced of their approach to an admittedly difficult problem.

Though he was only in Monterey for ten days, his recorded observations of that short span contain generally accurate and comprehensive information concerning the climate, geography, resources, Indians and government of the area. In the style common to his contemporaries, Galaup gave voice to his sentiments instead of suppressing them.

In 1797, the careful and extensive journals of Jean Francois de la Galaup were gathered into four volumes and published at Paris, under the editorship of M.L.A. Milet–Mureau. There were later translated into English, German, Swedish, Danish, Dutch, Italian and Russian. One hundred and sixty–one years after the pioneer navigator visited the area, in September of 1947, a bronze plaque was formally dedicated at San Carlos Borromeo Mission in memory of Jean Francois de la Galaup, Comte de la Perouse.

Father Pierre Arvin preached the homily at a Mass prior to the unveiling, stressing the community of interest which united Galaup and Fray Fermín Francisco de Lasuén. One represented the old world of his day, the other the new world, but they shared ideals of service to humanity, each in his own way.

Bishop Aloysius Willinger accepted the plaque on behalf of the mission, paying tribute to the humanitarian, courageous and patriotic qualities of the distinguished Frenchman, which the bishop said were worthy of esteem and imitation by people of later times. Willinger also recalled that France had been the first foreign power to extend the hand of friendship and help to the infant American nation in its struggle for independence.

JOHN A. T. GALVIN (b. 1908)

John A. T. Galvin was born in 1908, in a very poor Australian family. An exceptional student John won academic honors at Saint Virgil's Christian Brothers School on Barrack Street. The youthful Galvin gained local prominence when, at the age of twelve, he was awarded the coveted Royal Humane Society medal for heroically rescuing a childhood friend from drowning.

Leaving school three years later, John journeyed to Melbourne where he became a messenger runner at 15 shillings a week. He augmented that meager income by selling newspapers. In 1930, John went to work for the advertising firm of Gordon and Gotch. It was while employed there that he chanced to meet Stanley Smith, with whom he was later to amass a fortune of well beyond $300 million.

Galvin and Smith then moved on to Hong Kong, where John became a journalist for the United Press. It was while in that capacity that he journeyed into the mountains for an interview with a tough guerrilla leader, named Mao Tse–Tung.

During World War II, Galvin worked for the British Ministry of Information in India and Burma. Later, after becoming an executive officer in the Hong Kong government, John and Stanley Smith became involved in the operation of several commercial companies. Several years afterwards, the two men went to Malaya and bought an iron mine. They organized a steamship line to expedite delivery of the ore and that venture set them on their march to eventual wealth.

Galvin, his wife, Eileen, and their five children came to California in 1952 and took up residence in Woodside, a suburb just south of San Francisco. There the family became active in a raft of social and religious activities. John was referred to by a local newspaper as an "ardent churchman" interested in all manner of community projects.

Later, the Galvins moved to the 35,000 acre *Rancho San Fernando* in the Santa Ynez Valley. Their home became something of a showplace and the United States equestrian team trained there for the 1960 Olympics.

Since the mid 1960s, the Galvins have resided in the Sandyford area of Ireland.

Among his many benefactions to society are the series of volumes that Mr. Galvin has financed and published *in tandem* with Warren Howell of San Francisco. Among the more prominent of these magnificiently printed tomes is the long–lost narrative by Fray Vicente de Santa Maria about the first survey of San Francisco Bay aboard the *San Carlos* in 1771. Earlier Galvin had published Fray Francisco Garces' journal as *A Record of Travels in Arizona and California 1775–1776*. A Spanish translation of that work was released in 1968 by the *Universidad Nacional Autonoma de Mexico*.

As one would suspect, all of the Galvin books have been quality publications, most of them printed at the fine press of Lawton and Alfred Kennedy in San Francisco. The measure of a man is his perspective of history. By that yardstick, John Galvin fares exceedingly well in the annals.

RAFAEL GONZALEZ (1797–c.1880)

Rafael Gonzalez (1797–c.1880), a native of Santa Barbara, served as a *soldado de cuera* (leather–jacket soldier) at the Santa Barbara Presidio during most of the Spanish and Mexican period of California's history. After retiring from military service, Rafael was chosen as *alcalde* of the Santa Barbara *ayuntamiento* or community council and later was lay administrator at two of the missions.

Known as "a truthful, honest man," Gonzalez was interviewed by Thomas Savage in 1878. His memoir is important because of his involvement in "an unusually high percentage of the critical happenings" of the period.

The very fact that he was so involved is an indication of his character. His superiors used him when a person of proven responsibility, courage, initiative and intelligence was needed to perform a task. Like most of the soldiers at the time, Rafael was illiterate. Had he been able to write, a prerequisite for higher rank, he very likely would have been promoted to be an officer.

The Gonzalez memoir is "the only narrative recording the recollections of a soldier concerning his experiences as a *soldado de cuera* at the Santa Barbara Royal Presidio." Beyond a few reports and letters from officers, there is no other first–hand record of daily life at the *presidio*. The Savage interview, translated by Jarrell C. Jackman and edited by Richard S. Whitehead, has been published as *A Spanish Soldier in the Royal Presidio of Santa Barbara* by Bellerophan Books.

The narrative is enhanced considerably by extensive notes and elaborations of the events mentioned as recorded by such other authorities as Hubert Howe Bancroft and Theodore H. Hittell. Considering that Gonzalez was eighty–one years old when interviewed, his memory was remarkably accurate. Interestingly, the narrative records nothing that occurred after he was forty–five years old—perhaps because he grew tired of being interrogated.

A typical sampling of the Gonzalez memoir might be that describing his tenure at San Buenaventura Mission:

> I think it was in May, 1838, that Governor Alvarado appointed me administrator of San Buenaventura Mission, an office that I held for three or four years.
>
> Fray Buenaventura Fortuny was Father Minister. The friar was a very old man, tall, thin, white Catalan and a very likeable fellow. I never had any disagreement with him. He always treated me well, and I looked after and helped him with the greatest care.
>
> I received the Mission in good condition, and I kept it that way until the day I handed it over without anything missing from the inventory. During my administration I had delivered supplies of seeds, by the Governor's orders, to the artillerymen of Santa Barbara. The mission was never paid for those seeds, at least in my time.
>
> A neighbor was loaned fifty heifers for two or three years, and at the end of that time, he returned them. In 1845, 1 was again *alcalde* of Santa Barbara.

Thomas Savage, the interviewer, noted that Gonzalez was "in feeble health . . . he talks in a disconnected manner, and is much given to repetition. . . ."

MAMIE GOULET ABBOTT (1855–1930)

Mamie Goulet (Abbott) arrived at Santa Ines Mission on September 21, 1904. The twenty–three year old maiden, the niece of Father Alexander Buckler (1855–1930), had come to assist her German–born uncle in his task of caring for one of California's historic landmarks.

For two decades, this young lady, whom Father Zephyrin Engelhardt once called the "brave heroine of Mission Santa Ines," kept a faithful diary of her life at the Old Mission. During his many visits to Santa Ines, Father Engelhardt often consulted the diary, observing that it was "so graphic and touchingly beautiful that I would print it as it was."

The Franciscan chronicler's advice was eventually followed, in 1951, with the publication of *Santa Ines Hermosa. The Journal of the Padre's Niece*. And, in the autumn of 1962, portions of Mamie Goulet's diary were reprinted in *Noticias*, the journal issued by the Santa Barbara Historical Society. A few extracts from that version recall the day of March 7, 1911, when the mission was almost lost to posterity.

> The winter rains, most of which came in February and March, reached a total of 40.05 inches. The ruinous storm

started on February 25th, and for twelve days and nights it rained incessantly. The total precipitation for the storm was 8.51 inches. For the most part, the rain fell gently and soaked well into the ground, but, to the detriment of the Mission, it also soaked into the adobe walls.

These were tense days as we kept vigil. *Padre* (Buckler), decked in rubber coat, hat and boots, myself, in a heavy coat and rubber overshoes, would walk around the premises to view the destruction and sadly anticipate further devastation. When night came we were afraid to go to bed for fear that the whole building would crumble and bury us alive.

One by one the huge six by six buttresses supporting the walls of the chapel were crumbling and slithering into huge piles of mud, leaving gaping cavities in the thick walls. By the end of the storm, four buttresses had been reduced to heaps of adobe mud, three on the north side and one on the south side of the chapel. The abutment at the end of the colonnade also collapsed.

On the twelfth day of the storm, the rain came down in such torrents and the wind was so terrific that *Padre* was worried for the safety of the chapel.

The roof was in bad condition and the lower part of the north wall so water–soaked it looked as if it, too, would collapse.

At the hour of five *Padre* came in to take a short respite from the vigil. We were standing in the middle of the living room trying to decide what to do, when we heard prolonged rumblings followed by a heavy thud that seemed to shake the whole building and the tinkling of bells. The bell tower had fallen forward leaving the bells protruding here and there among the heap of bricks and soft adobe.

When the weather had cleared and we viewed the destruction all around us, we were the most forlorn, dejected and disheartened individuals one could conceive, and walked about as in a daze.

The bishop (Thomas J. Conaty) advised *Padre* to proceed with the rebuilding and restoring of the Mission, and to send all his bills for the work and materials to the Chancery office. Subsequently, the contract for the restoration was given and the work was finished in the early part of the following year.

The Mission, now, with its clean white–washed bell tower and outside walls, its repaired arches outlined in brick–red, its weather softened tiled roof, together with its majestic silhouette against a background of evergreen mountains and blue sky, was taking on some of its former grandeur and dignity. The story of the restoration will ever be a proud chapter in the history of Santa Ines Mission.

LEWIS A. GRANT (1853–1904)

It has been rightly observed that the man "who remains steadfast to his honest convictions whether religious or otherwise, and when giving expression to them does so in a manner not offensive, always earns and receives the respect and confidence of his dissenting neighbors and separated brethren and quite frequently wins their unstinted admiration." Lewis A. Grant (1853–1904) certainly ranks among those select California pioneers worthy of such an apellation.

Born of Scottish parents, far from the theatre of his manhood's achievment, the son of Archibald Grant and Anne McDonald was one of nine children raised in a respected family long esteemed for its prominence in Williamstown, Ontario. Young Grant spent his boyhood on the family farm "under an influence which early instilled in his heart the lessons of a Christian and a noble life that ever after clung to him through all his struggles and triumphs."

The Canadian–born trailblazer launched his business career in a general merchandising firm, in Lancaster. He moved on to Colorado, in 1880, where, with his brothers Angus and Richard, he contracted to extend the transcontinental lines of the Atlantic and Pacific Railroad west from Albuquerque. Grant transferred the headquarters of his firm to Los Angeles, in 1886, and from then onwards figured prominently in the construction of practically every important railroad artery in Southern California, New Mexico and Oregon.

Though a Republican by political persuasion, Grant disavowed partisanship in local matters, preferring to follow the promptings of good citizenship in upbuilding the community in which he lived. In addition to serving as a director of the Los Angeles National Bank and a commissioner for the City Water Company, Lewis Grant occupied the presidency of The Tidings Publishing Company. He was a charter member of the Newman Club and the Knights of Columbus. As the area's first Grand Knight, Grant displayed an enthusiasm and loyalty which endeared him to its membership. On June 23, 1891, Grant married Harriet M. McPherson. From that happy union came two youngsters, Anna Clarissa and Gertrude Mary, both of whom gained recognition as outstanding Southern California pioneers.

Local newspaper accounts reporting the death of Grant, in 1904, stated that his demise had "robbed the community of a distinguished citizen, a self–made man, who appreciated the sunny south and its people and loved to lend his strong hand and willing heart to its growth and accomplishment." Though an outstandingly respected figure in the civic, industrial and social affairs of Los Angeles, Lewis Grant's memory is actually enshrined for more lofty reasons. He was a lifelong witness to the Christian concepts embodied in his Catholic faith. Isidore Dockweiler recalled that Grant "never faltered in the faith, notwithstanding the kaleidoscopic changes of Western mountain, plain and desert, peopled by all sorts of grades and conditions of humanity with far more of the atheist and agnostic in composition than of the believer."

GRIFFITH J. GRIFFITH (1850–1919)

Often times people are remembered for the wrong reasons. Surely that is true for Colonel Griffith J. Griffith. In September of 1903, Griffith shot his wife, Christina, because he thought she was trying to poison him so she could turn over all his holdings to the Catholic Church!

Actually, when he was sober, Griffith was a fairly decent man. Residents of Los Angeles have every reason to be grateful to him because on December 16, 1896, he deeded 3,105 acres of land to the city for the purposes of a park.

That "Christmas gift," as he once called it, is now the largest park in the United States surrounded by an urban environment. Griffith Park certainly established the donor's immortality, at least in human annals. Yet, he is most remembered for shooting his wife.

Griffith was a Welsh immigrant who made his fortune in mining and real estate. His magnanimous gesture was one he often referred to as philanthropic. Others thought differently. Boyle Workman, for one, suspected that Griffith made the donation to avoid taxes. Another account claimed that Griffith got rid of the property because of a curse placed on it by a member of the family who originally owned the huge *Rancho Los Feliz.*

Major Horace Bell was slightly more prosaic. Describing Griffith as a man who carried himself as if he were the Prince of Wales, Bell wrote that "when this grand personage was seen on our streets with his long coat buttoned from top to bottom, head erect and eyes disdaining to look upon the earth, the humble Angelenos could hardly be blamed for mistaking him for royalty."

Griffith had purchased about half the old *Rancho Los Feliz* for $50,000. He stocked it with sheep, hogs, horses and cows. Disaster struck a few years later when a flood swept away trees, pastures, brush and livestock. At the time of his demise, Griffith left a trust fund to the City of Los Angeles to be used for civic and cultural additions to the park. He wrote that "public parks are a safety valve of great cities and should be made accessible and attractive, where neither race, creed nor color should be excluded. Crime and degeneracy can best be battled by pleasurable grounds."

Funds generated from the trust were used to maintain the park. Other portions of the funds were also allocated for erection of the Greek Theatre in 1930 and the famed observatory in 1935. But what about poor Christina (Mesmer) Griffith? She was the daughter of a wealthy hotel owner. Her husband, described by Jack Smith as "a toad of a man," accused her of infidelities and conspiring against him with the pope." She was guilty of neither.

Griffith employed the legendary Earl Rogers as his attorney. It was a superb choice because of the almost one hundred murder cases he pleaded, only one defendant was hanged. Anyway, Rogers concocted a defense that claimed that Christina was on her knees confessing while Griffith held a gun at her temple. "She moved her head just as he fired, and he shot her eye out."

The celebrated criminal attorney, claiming "alcoholic insanity" on the part of his client, got Griffith off with only two years at San Quentin. And Griffith only served about half that sentence before being paroled. Griffith's sojourn at San Quentin was a blessing in disguise. "Prison helped me," he said, "it don't help most" people. He appeared to have emerged from confinement a changed man. Certainly he was no less remembered for his experience behind bars.

JOSE DE LA GUERRA (1779–1858)

A. ILLUSTRIOUS PIONEER

José De la Guerra y Noriega (1779–1858) was an illustrious pioneer who, in all the epochs of his multi–phased activities, proved himself full of religious piety and Christian virtue. The panegyric delivered by Fray González Rúbio for California's "*Gran Capitan*," reproduced here in abbreviated form, reveals how De la Guerra's profound love and reverence for God "formed his character and became eventually the fertile principle, the support and perfection of all the acts of his long and well adjusted life."

Through many event–filled years, "he always showed himself the perfect model of a discreet young man, cultured, affable, devout, retired, resolute in the fulfillment of his duties, charitable towards the poor, obedient to his elders, considerate to his equals, kind toward his inferiors, and above all, most religious and pious without offense to anyone, and thereby pleasing to everybody."

De la Guerra was portrayed "as a model for parents by reason of his tenderness and vigilance; for upright citizens because of his patriotism and loyalty; for soldiers by reason of his bravery and his constant sacrifice; for rulers because of his prudence and solicitude; for public officials because of his uprightness and affability; for good Christians because of his great piety and unalterable patience in afflictions; for good Catholics because of his ardent zeal in propagating and preserving divine cult; and finally, for all honest men by reason of the constant tenor of his regulated life."

He was one of those rare individuals whose religious piety induced him to embrace a military career! If his heart "had sought after the pleasures, the distractions, and entertainments of life, he would never have left the beautiful cities, the brilliant society and the abundance of Mexico for the privations of the wilderness and wretched settlements of Indians, which was all that California had to offer at the end of the last and the beginning of the present century." If his soul had permitted itself to be dazzled by the love of riches, he would not have left in Spain his right of primogeniture with his endowments and education and the abundant resources which he enjoyed in the home of his uncle from whom he could have well acquired for himself a vast fortune.

"The noble soul of Señor Noriega, his energy and sagacity, his ruddy youth, his martial ardor and the powerful emulation of his companions–in–arms would have readily raised him to the highest ranks in military service, not in California but in Mexico or Europe; but he laid aside all this and promptly betook himself to California."

In the far–away frontier of California, José De la Guerra was attracted by "the interest of religion, the extension of Christianity, the spreading of Catholic cult, the destruction of paganism and its horrors, the erection of temples and altars to the true God, the civilization of innumerable barbarous tribes; in fine, the noble glory of planting and sustaining on these lonely shores the standard of the Cross, that Jesus Christ might be known, honored, and adored by these new settlements."

Whether at Monterey, San Diego or Santa Barbara, José De la Guerra "was ever vigilant for the proper discipline, the morals, and subsistence of the troops. He did not tolerate fatigue, be it in restraining the barbarians, in subduing the gentiles, in training and pacifying the neophytes, in constructing churches and other edifices or in the better adjustment and government of this province."

He distinguished himself in every way. He was the first at work; in privations the one to suffer most; in differences, the best arbiter; in matters of counsel, most prudent; in dangers, the most vigilant his conduct, he was the most exact, pious and exemplary."

JOSE DE LA GUERRA (1779–1858)

B. *EL GRAN CAPITAN*

The appearance of Joseph Thompson's *El Gran Capitan* deserves to be chronicled high among this era's significant contributions to the ecclesiastical annals of California. Written by his great–grandson, a Franciscan, this intimate historical biography of José De la Guerra presents its subject "as an example worthy of imitation by all persons who would live a long, useful and pious life."

Don José De la Guerra, known among his contemporaries as "*El Capitan*," sprang from "a race that founded empires, and that had been cradled amidst Castile's vast stretches of silence and solitude where the blood of Celt and Iberian had mingled to form a proud and unconquered race." Born on March 6, 1779, in Spain, José came to California while still very young. In later decades he played a pivotal role in mission history as an "exemplary Catholic, irreproachable *caballero*, and gallant officer in the forces of the Spanish crown."

De la Guerra's decision to be a soldier came early in life and seems to have been motivated by a zeal to spread the Catholic faith. He chose California as the land of his destiny for he saw himself as an instrumental cause in extending Christian civilization to a barbarous people. One source characterized De la Guerra as one who "did not hesitate for the sake of participating in so great an enterprise to sacrifice his interests, health, his comfort and even his life." Coming to Monterey in 1801, De la Guerra served in various capacities before being sent to Santa Barbara as *comandante*. It was in the Channel City that he sank his roots and did his greatest work.

Resigning his military office at Santa Barbara after twenty–four years of service, De la Guerra spent the years after 1829 living quietly with his family. His benefactions extended widely to persons of all classes and he was daily observed at Holy Mass and other religious functions.

Referring to himself as "a Catholic by the grace of God, a lover of humanity and loyal to the monarch to whom I have sworn obedience," De la Guerra was not overly receptive to the new United States Government, but he prudently avoided any occasions of friction and continued to be, as one authority notes, "perhaps the most influential and talented person throughout California."

Always "*El Justo*" to the friars at Santa Barbara, De la Guerra was spoken of as "the consoler of the poor and aided to give a religious cast to the people." Father González Rubio found it difficult to describe "even by abridgement how much he accomplished, how much he labored during extensive years, cooperating with the missionaries in order to uphold in this land the Catholic religion, the territory's peace, its civilization and progress . . . ."

At his death on February 11, 1858, the whole of Santa Barbara turned out to pay their respects to the "patriarch." Bishop Thaddeus Amat sang the Requiem Mass and afterwards read the absolution over a catafalque covered with a ten–line stanza of sorrow from the students at Santa Ines. With his passing, the end of an era was noted. "None of the pioneers . . . exerted for so long a period so wide and good an influence as Captain De la Guerra."

PABLO ANDRES ANTONIO MARIA SATURNINO DE LA GUERRA (1819–1874)

Pablo Andrés Antonio Maria Saturnino de la Guerra

(1819–1874) has long been classified, in California's historical annals, as "one of the outstanding citizens of the state." Born at Santa Barbara, the son of José Antonio de la Guerra, Pablo was educated in Mexico. He returned to California, in 1838, and for the remainder of his life served in a host of official and semi–official positions.

He was Collector of Customs, at Monterey, a member of the first Constitutional Convention, state senator for several terms, *alcalde* for Santa Barbara, acting Lieutenant Governor, United States Marshal and judge of the first Judicial District. As a politician, Pablo trimmed his sails adroitly to catch the breeze of popularity, yet he was regarded by Hubert Howe Bancroft as "a man of good ability and education; of gentlemanly manners. . . " With the exception of his father, Pablo was by far the most prominent of the Guerra family.

Pablo's marriage to Josefa Moreno, in 1847, united two of the area's oldest families. Their union was blessed by six daughters and a son. It was at Pablo's home, the famous *Casa de la Guerra*, that Richard Henry Dana witnessed (and immortalized in print) the nuptials between Maria Anna de la Guerra and Alfred Robinson. The quaint description of that Santa Barbara scene is even yet widely read in *Two Years Before the Mast*.

Among Pablo de la Guerra's chief concerns was the small Franciscan community at Santa Barbara. His esteem for the friars was expressed in a statement submitted to Rome during the difficulties experienced with Bishop Thaddeus Amat. Pablo wrote that the friars "have lived and are living a life entirely cloistered and monastic, dedicating themselves to prayer, study, corporal works of mercy and the assistance to the sick who frequently seek their help. I know and certify that Franciscan poverty among them is not merely nominal but real and positive for at various times I ate casually with them and their refectory is indeed a true place of abstinence."

At the demise of Pablo de la Guerra, a man highly esteemed by the local community, on February 5, 1874, he was accorded the privilege of being interred in the crypt beneath the sanctuary of Mission Santa Barbara. In 1911, when the crypt was opened and renovated, the remains of Pablo were found in a metal coffin. The face of the deceased could be seen through a glass opening at the head of the casket.

Personally, Pablo de la Guerra possessed a high sense of honor, great dignity of bearing and a marked consideration of others. Courteous to all, his friends were many, and his influence great. From every point of view, Pablo de la Guerra fulfilled the requirements of a "thoroughbred" layman outlined by John Henry Newman:

I want a laity, not arrogant, not rash in speech, not disputatious, but men who know their religion, who enter into it, who know just where they stand, who know what they hold, and what they do not, who know their creed so well that they can give an account of it, who know so much of history that they can defend it. I want an intelligent, well–instructed laity.

WILLIAM HAMILL (1819–1866)

William Hamill was known in journalistic circles as a finished scholar, one possessed of an extensive and accurate knowledge of general and classical literature. Born in County Antrim, Ireland, in 1819, young Hamill studied at Maynooth, where he gained the distinction of being the youngest man ever graduated from that institution. Later he attended Dublin University "but abandoned the religious career to enter the struggles of his country."

Shortly after completing his formal education, Hamill served a brief stint as an administrator in the Irish School System. The reputation of the youthful patriot was firmly established in the years immediately following his launching of the Glasgow *Free Press*.

After being "imprisoned and exiled for patriotic activity in his native land," Hamill came to California in 1851, where he invested in mines and real estate, from which he realized a comfortable fortune. Three years later he took an active part in establishing the *Catholic Standard* at San Francisco.

Father Eugene O'Connell, in a letter written during June of 1853, remarked that "William Hamill, formerly of Maynooth, is the teacher of the Bishop's English School." He also noted that "Mr. Hamill's salary is $60 a month in consideration of his acting as sexton to the Church." It is also reported in the annals of San Francisco that in mid–August of 1855, Hamill organized a Catholic school in the basement of Saint Mary's Church with 313 students.

That same year Hamill became principal of the Bay City's Union Street School. A writer noted some years later, "Perhaps the most conclusive proof of his competency and devotion is found in the fact that the members of the first class which was immediately under his charge, since grown to manhood, have ever loved him with a filial tenderness. . . ."

It was while teaching at the archdiocesan seminary, then located at Mission Dolores, that William Hamill drew up plans for a weekly Catholic newspaper for San Francisco. He formed a partnership with James Marks and Patrick J. Thomas and, on March 6, 1858, the first issue of *The Monitor* appeared from the Press of Marks, Thomas and Company. Hamill supplied two–thirds of the capital and edited the paper in its early days.

A man of many talents, Hamill was responsible for setting up the series of night schools in the Bay area for those unable to complete their education in the normal manner. As his civic responsibilities increased, he gradually turned over much of his editorial work to the talented Bartholomew Dowling. The final years of the journalist's life were spent in Mexico, where he had considerable financial investments. He returned to San Francisco in 1866, and died on May 28th, of consumption. This "good friend to the early missionary priests" was a California pioneer "endowed with an intellect of a very keen order, rendered by judicious and careful culture, and possessed of a graceful simplicity and charming geniality of manner."

G. ALLAN HANCOCK (1875–1965)

Few of those who grew up in the Hancock Park area of Los Angeles know much about the man for whom the area is named. G. Allan Hancock (1875–1965) was a person whose colorful and diverse career as businessman, scientist and philanthropist began humbly on his family's farm. The son of 49ers, Major Henry Hancock and Ida Haraszthy, Allan was born at San Francisco, the only heir to a family fortune derived from what was then the Rancho La Brea.

The elder Hancock was a land investor and surveyor in the area which now encompasses most of Hollywood and the Wilshire District of Los Angeles, including the legendary Miracle Mile. After his father's early death in 1883, Allen turned part of the family's hay, barley and oats farm into a productive enterprise and subdivided the rest. The Hancock name graces every property deed recorded in that region.

He gave considerable acreage to the University of Southern California. In 1926, he donated the site at Third and Detroit Streets to the Diocese of Los Angeles–San Diego for the erection of a minor seminary.

Earlier, Mr. Hancock had granted the Los Angeles County Museum exclusive rights to excavate fossils from Rancho La Brea Tar Pits. In 1916, he gave to the county the twenty–three acres surrounding the pits, together with his family home, specifying that the property was to be used as a public park and that no fee could ever be charged for admission.

In 1963, the grateful county supervisors unveiled a bust of Captain G. Allan Hancock at the site. At the time, Kenneth Hahn noted that the people of Los Angeles were "deeply indebted to this great American who not only has benefitted many fine colleges and universities to assure the education of youth, but has also provided this beautiful park perpetually dedicated to the good of all citizens."

Throughout his long career, Hancock continuously earned new fame from a growing list of interests—from farmer to oil and gas prospector, producer and distributor, banker, subdivider, manufacturer, merchant mariner, ship owner, railroader, aviator, explorer, educator and musician. Hancock acquired the title of "captain" in the late 1920s when he became one of the few men licensed by the Merchant Marine to master any ship of any tonnage on any ocean in the world.

Captain Hancock was also known as a pioneer in ocean photography. He established the Allan Hancock Foundation for Scientific Research on the USC campus in 1941, and with it offered the services of his 198 foot marine vessel, *Valero III*. That ship was later replaced with an even more modern cruiser. Through his foundation, Hancock provided millions of dollars for research. Among the many projects he financed was the sea expedition in which Otis Barton descended 4500 feet in Hancock's benthoscope to explore the depths of the oceans.

The captain was buried at services conducted at Saint Vibiana's Cathedral by James Francis Cardinal McIntyre. He was interred at Calvary Mausoleum in the family vault. No name is more deeply imprinted on the southland than that of G. Allan Hancock. And no one ever provided more generously for his Church, country, friends and family than the man eulogized by Cardinal McIntyre as a "catalyst for kindness and charity."

JAMES ALLEN HARDIE (1823–1876)

James Allen Hardie (1823–1876) was a "plain, frugal and remarkably industrious" career–soldier who found his way into the Catholic Church while serving at his military post in California. The eldest of eight children born to Allen and Caroline (Cox) Hardie, James studied at Western collegiate Institute, Pittsburgh College and Poughkeepsie Collegiate School prior to his appointment, in 1839, to West Point Military Academy.

During his years at the Academy, James was a quiet, diligent and studious youth, popular with his professors and esteemed by his fellow cadets. Shortly after his graduation, he returned to West Point as assistant professor of geography, history and ethics. In 1846, Hardie came to California as chief military assistant to Colonel Jonathan D. Stevenson. His position "was both arduous and delicate, having to deal with turbulent volunteers, anxious for the field and impatient at the restraints of garrison life, with discontented and sullen natives, and adventurers of all sorts from the United States."

Fears of a nation rising against the American occupation "were constant and well–founded, and served to keep the commanding officers in a constant state of watchfulness and anxiety, both with regard to the inhabitants, that they might not take the troops by surprise, and the troops, that they might always be ready to march or fight." It was while visiting Oregon to solicit recruits that Major Hardie "became an open convert to the Roman Catholic religion, towards which he had long been tending, and within whose communion he remained, as devoted, sincere, and useful a member as its laity ever contained, till the day of his death." He was baptized at Mission Dolores, in mid–1848.

Hardie's embracing of Catholicism "did not occur till he had thoroughly satisfied the demands of his mind and conscience as to the wisdom and righteousness of the step, and he entered it so fully prepared and persuaded, that the mental peace and happiness that it brought him were never thereafter marred by a doubt or regret."

Hardie's biographer states that "it is probable that among the influences that contributed to the bringing in of General Hardie to the Catholic fold was his personal experience and observation of the piety, zeal and devotion of the missionary priests who had been for so many decades laborers and even martyrs among the Indian tribes of the Northwest." As for the California missionary establishments, the same writer noted that "the silent voice of those interesting remains of the . . . early missionaries no doubt induced him to study a subject of which he knew before."

Upon his return to San Francisco, Hardie "set about the erection of a place of worship for the use of that church, and in one day succeeded in collecting $3,000, upon which sum the first Catholic church in San Francisco was erected in 1848." Hardie married Margaret Hunter, in 1851, a union blessed by eight children. In the years after his departure from California, Hardie advanced within the military ranks, until early 1863, when he was named judge advocate general of the Army of the Potomac. At the time of his demise, Hardie was a Brigadier General.

In 1877, the year after his death, the Assistant Adjutant General of the United States, Thomas M. Vincent, outlined the major accomplishments of his New York–born confrere in an introduction to the anonymously–edited seventy–nine page *Memoir of James Allen Hardie, Inspector General, United States Army*. A measure of General Hardie's philosophy of life can be seen in his reflections on death, contained in a letter to a close friend:

> . . . if Christianity amounts to a "row of pins," why shouldn't we want to go to a place where we are better off than we are here, when we have got through our task here?

ALEXANDER FRANCIS HARMER (1852–1925)

There were no professional artists in Alta California during the Spanish–Mexican period. Several foreign illustrators were in and out of the area, but it was only in the 1840s and 1850s that artists began arriving on the scene. Alexander Francis Harmer (1850–1925) was among the select number of artists who journeyed to the area in later times and few artists or illustrators have portrayed the California missions as ably as he did.

Born in Newark, New Jersey, Harmer first came to California as a member of Company B First United States Cavalry. A "young man of fine promise," he was discharged from military service in 1874. Harmer returned east where he found employment as an assistant in a photographic gallery. Later he was admitted to the Philadelphia Academy of Fine Arts. In 1881, he re–entered the army and served in several field expeditions organized to pursue the Apaches.

All during those campaigns, Harmer's pencil was busy recording events upon the trail. His experiences among the Apaches during those hectic times furnished him with a wealth of material which he later incorporated in watercolor, pen and ink sketches and large oil paintings.

In the 1880s, Harmer's life began paralleling that of Frederick Remington who was a few years younger than Harmer. After his service in the army, which lasted this time until 1883, Harmer followed Remington to the west. Between 1880 and 1900, his artistic work was devoted almost exclusively to the portrayal of Indian life.

Harmer made several tours of the California missions, pausing at each outpost to sketch and paint. One of his first commissions came from Mrs. Juan Forster who asked him to paint a large canvas rendition of San Luis Rey Mission. In 1893, after a sojourn in Mexico, Harmer returned to California where he married Felicidad A. Abadie, the daughter of a distinguished Santa Barbara family. From that marriage there were seven children.

In his later years, Harmer concentrated on depicting scenes from the area's Spanish–Mexican days. In the early 1900s, at the request of Father Zephyrin Engelhardt, Harmer did numerous sketches of Indian life at the California missions to illustrate the friar's books about the religious outposts along *El Camino Real*.

Charles Fletcher Lummis, the enthusiastic champion for the restoration of the missions, encouraged Harmer to perpetuate the earlier days through his art. This the artist did in hundreds of sketches for contemporary periodicals, including *Land of Sunshine* and *Out West*. In the 1960s, Whitney T. Genns, a prominent bookdealer in Santa Barbara, issued a portfolio of fifty–six *California Missions Engravings* by Harmer, most of which had appeared earlier in the Engelhardt volumes.

Harmer was also an excellent landscape and marine artist. He went on boating trips to the Channel Islands and his paintings of scenes on islands like Santa Cruz are highly prized.

Lummis said that "no other painter has given so much attention to California of the old times, and for that matter, no other painter knew the subject one–half so well." To Harmer's technical skill, which was far beyond the ordinary, is added "the rare distinction of accuracy beyond that of anyone else who has presented like objects." Mr. Lummis knew "of no one else, with half his talent as an artist."

MARIE WALSH HARRINGTON (1907–1986)

The person of Marie Walsh Harrington (1907–1986), the matriarch of the San Fernando Valley, is a woman whose name is indelibly inscribed on the walls of the Old Mission, as well as on the bibliographical rolls of Western America. A native of Santa Monica, Marie was by profession a journalist. Her first book, *The Mission of the Passes*, occasioned a personal commendation from Eugenio Cardinal Pacelli who became Pope Pius XII in 1939.

To this day, her subsequent book on *The Mission Bells of California* remains the standard authority on a subject that continues to fascinate readers all over the world. During years that stretched from the depression to the space age, Marie's byline appeared above a veritable litany of essays in magazines, journals and newspapers throughout the west. She was the official biographer for the Hearst newspapers in Los Angeles.

Her last and probably best book was about the man she married, a personal account of the life and career of Mark Raymond Harrington, published in 1985 by the Great Basin Press. Marie knew Mark for many years before they were married. She once said that the first time she met him, she knew that they would oneday marry! She quickly added: "Oh, I didn't tell him then, I just got in line." She became the fourth Mrs. Harrington in 1949.

There were many facets of Marie's life that were absolutely fascinating. One relates to her close relationship with Archbishop Francisco Orozco y Jimenez, the famed and fugitive Archbishop of Guadalajara, who spent several years of his exile during the Mexican persecutions hidden away in her home. Marie's assistance to the archbishop and her concern for the plight of Mexican Catholics persecuted by a hostile government was officially acknowledged by Pope Pius XI who awarded her the *Pro Pontifice et Ecclesia* medal in 1933.

In the early 1980s, shortly after the Archival Center for the archdiocese was opened at San Fernando Mission, Marie founded *Las Damas Archivistas,* a group of docents who conduct tours of the Historical Museum and perform other duties of vital importance. It was at Marie's insistence that California's Catholic Treasury was written as a guide to the Historical Museum of the Archival Center. The members of *Las Damas Archivistas* use that text as a handbook for learning about the artifacts on display.

For many decades, San Fernando Mission was the focal point of Marie's life. In mid 1981, she presented the Old Mission with twenty–one Indian baskets that had belonged to her late husband. They are on permanent exhibit in one of the rooms of the mission, just across the way from her longtime home.

Those who worked with Marie will always recall her as a determined, forceful (one might even say stubborn) person, one who outlived many of her doctors and defied the rest. When she was told that she had only a few months to live, she simply shrugged her shoulders and said: "We'll see about that." She lived another four years.

Marie Harrington epitomized in her person all that was best in mission history and lore. Were her own biography ever written, it would read like the chapters from one of her many books and articles—pages of the past, alive in the present, as a guide for the future.

MARK R. HARRINGTON (1882–1971)

Not far from the old mission at San Fernando stands the handsome adobe home of Dr. Mark R. Harrington, and there, on a street appropriately named "Memory Park Avenue," one of California's most faithful old–timers looked back on a life filled with loyal service to the cause of the American Indians.

Mark R. Harrington was born at Ann Arbor, Michigan, on July 6, 1882, the son of Mark and Rose Smith Harrington. His education in anthropology and archeology was obtained at Columbia University of Michigan. By the time he was seventeen, young Harrington was already publishing articles on Indian lore. A partial listing of his writings, completed only to 1959, reveals that he authored 301 articles in various scientific journals and nine complete volumes over the six decades on subjects covering a wide spectrum of interest.

His background in archeology and anthropology included connections with the American Museum of Natural History, the Peabody Museum at Harvard, the University of Pennsylvania Museum of the American Indian. It was while doing research for the Museum of the American Indian in 1924, that Harrington discovered the pre–historic *pueblo* remains in Noapa Valley, Nevada. He also established scientifically that the area around California's Borax and Little Lakes was peopled thousands of years ago,

Harrington became Curator of the Southwest Museum in 1928, and for the next thirty–six years the "genial, hardworking, thorough scientist" saw that institution become one of the most important centers of Indian culture in the Western Hemisphere. In 1956 the award of Doctor Of Humanities was bestowed on Harrington in recognition of his tests with Carbon 14, in which he proved that man occupied certain areas of Nevada 23,800 years ago, thus doubling the then known age of man in America!

Always a staunch ally of the Church, Harrington was the moving force behind restoration efforts at Mission San Fernando in the 1930s and 1940s. In 1954 he published *The Story of San Fernando Mission* wherein the fascinating tale of California's seventeenth mission is graphically related. Assuming the title of Curator Emeritus, Harrington retired from active work at the Southwest Museum in 1964. Then, in his adobe home, among the relics of Provincial California, the kindly old gentleman began work on his last volume about the Iroquois Indians of New York State.

One of Harrington's books tells its readers "How To Build a California Adobe." It was written in 1948, shortly after he moved into the adobe home he personally erected for his wife, the former Marie T. Walsh, herself a noted authority on early California. Removed from the hectic life of a busy museum, Harrington continued to live "in the hearts of West as the kindly, grand old man of Los Angeles Corral."

BRET HARTE (1829–1902)

During the 1840s, that same California which gave to America and the world material wealth in such abundance, was also destined to endow the literary realm with a poetry of the finest vein. Bret Harte (1829–1902) was among those who adorned the land of his adoption with immortal descriptions of its beauties and romance. It is unfortunate that Harte, long numbered along the nation's great literary geniuses, is not generally remembered as a poet for his writings in verse deserve to be ranked with the finest in the land.

The Catholic theme, inevitable in California poetry, resounds in much of Bret Harte's poetry. The romance of the country is so interwoven with the history of religion on the Pacific Coast, so glamored over with the soft music of far–off Mass bells and the perfumed aroma of incense as to be inescapable.

Though he didn't always comprehend the various nuances of Catholic belief, Harte atoned for that deficiency in his beautiful poem, "The *Angelus*," which the literary world regards among the most accomplished tributes ever written. It was composed at Mission Dolores, in 1868.

> Bells of the Past, whose long–forgotten music
>   Still fills the wide expanse.
> Tinging the sober twilight of the Present
>   With color of romance!
> I hear your call, and see the sun–descending
>   On rock and wave and sand.
> As down the coast the Mission voices, blending,
>   Girdle the heathen land.
> Within the circle of your incantation
>   No blight nor mildew falls;
> Nor fierce unrest, nor lust, nor low ambition
>   Passes those airy walls.
> Borne on the swell of your long waves receding
>   I touch the farther Past;
> I see the dying glow of Spanish glory.
>   The sunset dream and last!
>
> Before me rise the dome–shaped Mission towers;
>   The white Presidio;
> The swart commander in his leathern jerkin,
>   The priest in stole of snow.
> Once more I see Portola's cross uplifting
>   Above the setting sun;
> And past the headland, northward, slowly drifting
>   The freighted galleon.
> 0, solemn bells; whose consecrated masses
>   Recall the faith of old –
> 0, tinkling bells that lulled with twilight music
>   The spiritual fold;
> Your voices break and falter in the darkness;
>   Break–, falter and are still:
> And veiled and mystic, like the Host descending
>   The sun sinks from the hill.

Harte's love for the romance and legendary lore of California are captured in such memorable poems as his "The Miracle of Junípero," "Concepción De Argüello" and "Friar Pedro's Ride." The famed writer testified by these and other of his works "that to live in California is to breathe, to see, to feel, poetry at every turn."

WILLIAM E. P. HARTNELL (1799–1854)

The pages of California's history abound with the names of prominent Catholic laymen, many of whom made a lasting impression in their contemporary society. Among these noble pioneers was William E.P. Hartnell (1798–1854), whom one writer aptly described as "A California Patriarch."

Don Guillermo Eduardo Hartnell arrived in the Port of Monterey in 1822 as salesman for Begg and Company, a London firm engaged in trading machinery and manufactured goods for hides and tallow. Settling down at Monterey and opening the first mercantile house in the area, Hartnell set out on his interesting and fascinating career. He became a Catholic in 1824, receiving baptism at San Carlos Borromeo on October 13th. The next year he married Teresa de la Guerra, daughter of the *comandante* at Santa Barbara. Always greatly interested in intellectual pursuits, Hartnell operated several small schools at various times in and about Monterey. In 1851 he graciously put his house at the disposal of the Dominican Sisters whom Archbishop Joseph Sadoc Alemany brought to California to begin the Catholic educational system.

Governor Juan Bautista Alvarado named Hartnell *Visitador General* of the Missions in 1839, a position in which the gentle Englishman encountered many problems. Complaints from maltreated Indians, requests for non–payment of loans and food shortages were routine vexations. By nature a peace loving man, Hartnell found his new position discouraging and one which caused him considerable anxiety. But evidence of his strong faith is easy enough to find. For example, his courtesy to the downtrodden *padres,* whose position at the missions was, at best, ambiguous, is reflected in his *Diario.* He never omitted "consulting the wishes of the *padres*" because their views of affairs would be to the "spiritual as well as the temporal advantages of the missions."

In 1840 Hartnell relinquished his position as *Visitador General.* Three years later he was asked by Bishop Francisco Garcia Diego y Moreno to collect tithes throughout the Diocese of Both Californias. His efforts in that delicate task were somewhat successful in the central part of California, but ran into stiff opposition in the San Francisco jurisdiction of General Mariano Vallejo who would not "subject himself to an Indian bishop." Hartnell seems to have shared the common view regarding the missionaries, most of whom, by that time, were Mexican–born. Californians respected greatly the old Spanish friars, but after Mexico's Independence, when the Franciscans from Zacatecas came to the missions, their seemingly inferior education and, in rare cases, their low morals were a cause of discontent among many people.

Bishop Garcia Diego's tithing program was something less than successful, and in 1844 Hartnell resigned to become Customs Collector at the Port of Monterey. He served in a number of other official capacities, the last being the drawing up of the State Constitution of 1849. His career ended on February 2, 1854, at his *rancho* in Alisal.

That his religion played an active part in his life is reflected in Hartnell's last will and testament, which was as much an act of faith as it was a disposition of effects.

> In the name of the Most Holy Trinity, Father, Son and Holy Ghost, I William Edward Hartnell . . . declare that it is my desire to live and die in the bosom of the Holy, Catholic, Apostolic, Roman Church, and I beg that when God is pleased to call me out of this world, my burial may be conducted in as simple a manner as possible and without any unnecessary pomp.

Hartnell played an active part in early California history. He adopted its language, its customs and most important of all, its religion, to become a California Patriarch!

MARY LANIGAN HEALY (1908–1990)

Mary Lanigan Healy, a long–time columnist of *The Tidings,* died on July 8th 1990, at Saint Elizabeth's Convalescent Hospital in North Hollywood.

Mrs. Healy's byline "Among Us" appeared in the columns of the archdiocesan newspaper from 1939 until her retirement in 1974.

Born December 28, 1908, at Tucumcari, New Mexico, the daughter of of James and Daisy Ann (Brown) Lanigan, Mary studied at local schools prior to entering Saint Theresa College, Winona. Later she earned a Masters degree at the University of Southern California and then worked for five years at the Catholic Welfare Bureau.

Mary joined Raymond Healy in holy wedlock at Saint Dominic's Church in Eagle Rock and the nine Healy children were reared and educated in that neighborhood. Later the family lived in Saint Paul (Los Angeles) and Incarnation parishes (Glendale).

Mary Healy joined the staff of *The Tidings* in 1939 and a whole generation of Catholic readers in California's southland came to know her dedication to every facet of parochial and archdiocesan life. She was aptly described as "everybody's mother, sister and friend." A Catholic social function wasn't complete until it was mentioned in "Among Us."

While her column easily became the most popular and widely read feature of *The Tidings*, Mary also wrote for a host of other Catholic and secular publications. Most of the pamphlets emanating from the Confraternity of Christian Doctrine office bore her signature or at least her influence.

In 1947, McMullen Books published Mary's book, *Spots and Wrinkles*, a compilation of her essays for *The Tidings*. A reviewer noted that few parents "have the command over the situation of life, the Christian forbearance or the happy power of expression of a Mrs. Healy."

In 1948, Mary won the Family Catholic Action Award which was conferred by the National Catholic

Conference on Family Life. She continued an active pace as a popular speaker on the local and national level.

During her final months, Mary was hospitalized. Just a few days before her own demise, she attended the funeral of her eldest son, Tim. To the last she epitomized the scriptural role of motherhood to her own children and to her twenty grandchildren and three great grandchildren.

Buried from Saint Robert Bellarmine Church in Burbank, Mary was interred alongside her husband in San Fernando Mission Cemetery. To her file in *The Tidings* was affixed the journalistic device of "30".

WILLIAM RANDOLPH HEARST (1863–1951)

William Randolph Hearst (1863–1951) was a man who did everything in superlatives. His efforts to restore the California missions was just one of his many associations with the Catholic Church.

Early in his career, "Citizen" Hearst recognized aviation as a coming revolutionizer of international travel. His enthusiasm about the 1927 flight of Charles Lindbergh to Paris was typical of a man who sought to have America first in everything.

He offered to sponsor the transoceanic flight of Clarence Chamberlain and Charles Levine and, later, he got involved in a proposal by aviators Lloyd Bertaud and J. B. Hill for a flight from the United States to Rome. The Bertaud trip was the brainchild of Philip Payne, the airminded managing editor of the New York *Daily Mirror*. Payne envisioned it as a promotional scoop to gather more readers for the Hearst newspapers and, in that vein, it was a most successful idea. The aeroplane chosen for the flight was *Old Glory*, an innovative experimental ship that had been certified as air–worthy and safe by officials of the United States government.

In July of 1927, the Right Reverend John J. Cantwell, Bishop of Los Angeles–San Diego, was asked to compose a letter to the Holy Father which would be taken on the Bertaud flight and then personally delivered to Pope Pius XI. A copy of the letter, whose code number is 5531 AD C–1927, is on file at the Archival Center. It reads as follows:

> Through the courtesy of Mr. William Randolph Hearst, and the heroic flight of Mr. Bertaud, we, living on the shores of the Pacific Coast of the United States of America, are able to greet your Holiness in this unique manner.
>
> The rapid development of aeronautics is bringing the nations of the earth closer together, and thus helps to the realization of that peace and concord among nations which is dear to your paternal heart. The airship is becoming a messenger of peace to nations that heretofore immense distances kept apart as strangers.

> We beg your Holiness to accept a small token of our affection, and ask you to bestow upon your children on the shores of the Pacific your Apostolic Blessing.

The Tidings reported to its readers on August 19th that there were two other letters, one from Mayor George E. Cryer and the other from Buzzi Gradenigo, the Italian Vice Consul for Los Angeles. In the latter missive, addressed to Benito Mussolini, the consul reported that "twenty thousand of your countrymen entrust to *Old Glory* their greetings for Italy and the head of the Italian Government."

Future researchers will look in vain for Cantwell's letter in the Vatican Archives, for it never reached its destination, nor did the other two messages from local southland officials. *Old Glory* took off from Old Orchard, Maine and, unfortunately, was lost at sea with its three occupants. Hearst financed a search for survivors but no wreckage was ever sighted.

ISAIAS W. HELLMAN (1842–1920)

The cordiality presently existing between the Catholic and Jewish communities in Southern California has deep roots that frequently confront readers who page through the historical annals.

The personages of Francis Mora (1827–1905) and Isaias W. Hellman (1842–1910) come immediately to mind. Those two Los Angeles pioneers practiced ecumenism decades before the word was even coined.

When the seventeen year old, Bavarian–born Hellman arrived in Los Angeles, he found a city with a population of 4,000 people, of which three–fourths were Mexicans and Indians. He began clerking for the sum of $20 per month and slept under the counter of the store where he was employed.

Shortly thereafter, he met Father Francis Mora who came into the store one day to purchase some clothing. The two became close friends and Mora offered to help Hellman learn Spanish and perfect his English. It was a relationship that subsequently profited both the Church and the Synagogue. Hellman subsequently became a prominent merchant, banker and developer, while Mora went on to become the Bishop of Monterey–Los Angeles.

According to Hellman's executor, "the friendship formed then lasted throughout the lifetime of that eminent divine and Mr. Hellman from his youth continued to be the counselor and adviser on all financial matters pertaining to the welfare of the Church in Los Angeles."

Hellman was involved in practically every innovative activity that touched the southland. He was among those who brought the railroad to Los Angeles, he helped to organize the Farmers and Merchants Bank and he was instrumental in founding the University of Southern California. During his years as President of the Congregation of B'nai B'rith (now Wilshire Boulevard Temple), Hellman often sought out the advice of Father Mora. It was Mora who encouraged Hellman in his efforts to build a permanent structure for Jewish worship.

Hellman was truly an outstanding man. In one account it is noted that "from the time the city of Los Angeles was a frontier village to the present day of its marvelous progress, he was in the foreground of the chief enterprises undertaken in the work of development."

During the 1880s, the Diocese of Monterey–Los Angeles was in desperate financial straits. In 1887, Mr. Hellman came up with a proposal for selling the valuable parcel of property on which the Old Plaza Church was located. Hellman envisioned the site as ideal for commercial development.

Mora and his Vicar General, Father Joaquin Adam, favored the transaction, but because of opposition from the pastor and other influential parties, the sale was never consummated. Hellman, nonetheless, continued his interest in assisting the diocese and on numerous occasions he utilized his credit standing to guarantee Bishop Mora's notes. On February 23, 1911, some months after Hellman's death, Bishop John J. Cantwell wrote a lengthy letter outlining the many areas in which Hellman's kindness and generosity had benefited the Diocese of Monterey–Los Angeles.

At the head of Hellman's bequests in his last will and testament was a gift of $25,000 to the Catholic Orphan Asylum of Los Angeles. It was the last in a long series of benefactions stretching over the years between 1859 and 1920.

PATRICK HENRY (1876–1959)

Patrick Henry has long been acknowledged as one of the most colorful personages associated with the Church in Southern California. His influence lives on in the pages of *The Tidings*, where he labored to further the ideals and objectives of the journalistic apostolate.

Born January 29, 1876 in County Sligo, Ireland, Pat worked for a time as a bookkeeper in England. And it was there that he married Carrie Smith on October 1, 1902, a union blessed with five children. Early in the century, the Henrys moved to Canada. In 1908, Pat became a regular contributor to the *Northwest Review* and, eleven years later, its editor. The Winnipeg newspaper served an area extending from Ontario to the Pacific and from the United States boundary to the north Pole. Pat once speculated that he had seven–tenths of a reader for every one hundred square miles of territory.

Shortly after coming to Los Angeles, Mr. Henry founded the *Irish Review*, wherein he expounded his belief that the rights of small nations should be proclaimed "in words of thunder." The newspaper lasted for only thirteen issues.

Pat first became associated with *The Tidings* in 1924, when he joined the staff of the southland's Catholic newspaper as a "stringer." In his earliest days, he travelled the length and breadth of the diocese, gleaning material for special editions. With his ever–present pipe and never–faltering Celtic humor, the veteran journalist developed an identity with the Catholic reading public unparalleled to that time. His fascinating and unique essays and stories touched practically every phase of the Christian lifestyle.

Pat Henry wore many hats during his career under six editors at *The Tidings*. He wrote a weekly column About People featuring interviews with visiting dignitaries and local personalities. His contributions to *We Hear from Ireland*, which appeared under the name Sean O'Rahilly, lent strong support to the movement for the Emerald Isle's independence.

One of Pat's most popular series, published in the fall of 1945, was devoted to his "memories" of earlier days in the City of *Nuestra Señora de los Angeles*. Therein the indomitable journalist chronicled the growth of Catholic life in Southern California as recorded in former issues of *The Tidings*. During his thirty–five years with the newspaper, Pat saw the circulation increase from 2,500 to 90,000. But all the while, numbers never impressed him so much as quality. To the very end, he wrote his articles and essays in longhand, careful always about detail and accuracy.

When this unpretentious and humble man died, in 1959, he was credited by James Francis Cardinal McIntyre with being among the "major architects" of the Catholic "image" for the Church in California's southland. Through his many years at *The Tidings*, Patrick Henry strove to further the objectives of Catholic journalism. He believed, as Pope John XXIII did after him, that "one of the most effective ways to serve God, to reach into the home, to achieve understanding, is precisely the Catholic press."

DANIEL A. HILL (1797–1865)

There is a lot of history inscribed on the tombstones in the cemetery of Santa Barbara Mission. An example would be the marker for Daniel A. Hill which is still quite legible after 120 years.

The tombstone reads:

In memory of Daniel A. Hill, a native of Billerica, Mass., and a resident of California since 1823, who died at this place the 25th of January,1865. Aged 68 years. For we are as water thrown upon the earth which cannot be gathered again. But his death was in Christ, the Blessed Redeemer of Man.

Miss S. R. Skerry of Vendome, Boston, visited the Old Mission some years go. After seeing the marker for Daniel Hill, she wrote to the friars asking more information about her fellow statesman. In his response, Father F. George Carr said that he had consulted the death register of the Old Mission for the year 1865 and had discovered the following facts:

> The entries are all in long hand, written in Spanish by the resident priest here at the Mission at that time. According to this authentic and reliable document, Daniel Hill had died on the 20th of January, 1865. And he was buried on January 21st of the same year.

He went on to point out that "just next to the tombstone of Daniel A. Hill is a smaller tombstone which reads as follows: 'In memory of Thomas F., son of Rafael and Daniel Hill. Died July 22, 1862." Father Carr suggested that "Rafael" on the marker was evidently incorrect and should have been "Rafaela" (Ortega).

Daniel Hill was a very prominent personage in the early history of Southern California. He was born in 1797 and came to California in 1823, in command of a vessel called the "Rebecca," which was engaged in trade with the Sandwich Islands. His father's name was Job Hill, and his mother's maiden name was Susan Blanchard. They were of Presbyterian antecedents.

According to an early mugbook, he was a man of varied accomplishments—carpenter, stone–mason, soap maker and farmer, as occasion required. He first engaged in merchandising, his place of business being near the Old Mission. "He also acted as superintendent for the *padres* in some of their farming and building operations; his varied mechanical ability being in demand with them. He built several houses in the vicinity of the Clock–House, some of which have been removed to make way for State Street. A portion of one, the house in which the Carillo family lives, is a sample of his work done fifty years since. These were the first houses built in Santa Barbara that had wooden floors."

Hill's wife belonged to the famous Ortega and Olivera families. Rafaela Louisa married Daniel about 1826. Her parents were the socially prominent Jose Vicente Ortega and Maria Estefana Olivera. Daniel Hill was closely connected with the history of the Old Mission. In 1845, he and his son–in–law, Nicholas A. Den, offered to rent Santa Barbara Mission for an annual fee of $1,200.

According to an entry in the *Registro de Bautismos* at the *presidio* church of Santa Barbara, Fray Antonio Ripoll baptized Daniel Hill on January 29, 1825. The sponsor was Antonio Cota.

The first permanent resident of America to live in Santa Barbara, Daniel A. Hill is only one of the many prominent personages in the necropolis of Santa Barbara Mission.

CHARLES HUBBARD

In 1835, Captain Charles Hubbard was commissioned to remove the last remaining twenty Indians from San Nicolas, one of the channel islands off the Southern California coast, about seventy–five miles northwest of Los Angeles. Just as the captain was leaving the island, one of the young native women dashed back to the village for her infant, inadvertently left in the confusion.

During her absence, a storm arose and Hubbard was forced to sail for San Pedro. Though he had every intention of returning, the captain later lost his ship at sea and was unable to carry out his plans. The twenty–five year old widow was not forgotten in succeeding years, and in 1850, Fray Gonzalez Rubio of Santa Barbara sent two searching parties to San Nicolas, but neither was able to unearth any evidence of life on the island. In 1852, Captain George Nidever and a crew of natives stopped at San Nicolas to hunt seagull eggs. During their visit, they came across several tracks of small human feet on the wet sand. Nidever returned to the island in July of the following year. Near the top of a ridge where the footprints had earlier been discovered, the captain saw a dark object in motion, the long–lost woman of San Nicolas! From a distance she "resembled a large bird, dressed in a garment made of bird's skins and feathers. Her yellow–brown hair lay matted on her head. As the men drew closer, she was seen to be about fifty years of age, a strong and active woman of medium height. A closer examination revealed that she was wearing clothes fashioned from the skin of a shag."

Apparently the infant for which she had returned to the native village eighteen years earlier had died. When the crew went back to the mainland, the woman was taken to Captain Nidever's home, where she lived out the final weeks of her life. Though there was no one left in Santa Barbara who could speak her language, the Indian woman seemed quite happy and content in her new surroundings, taking great delight in the novel clothes and food of her new habitat.

Seven weeks after her arrival, she became critically ill, probably as a result of eating too much fruit. Fray Francisco Sanchez was summoned to administer conditional baptism, giving her the Christian name "Juana Maria. When she died in October 1853, the neophyte was buried with all possible solemnity, in the mission cemetery.

The location of her grave has been lost but a bronze

plaque was placed on the mission tower by the Daughters of the American Revolution in 1928 to commemorate "this resourceful, valiant and self–contained woman who had no one to talk to in eighteen years and survived." Though she could hardly appreciate its significance, Juana Maria's baskets, grass bottles and birdskin dresses were sent to Rome where today they may be seen in the Lateran Museum—a tribute to "The Lone Woman of San Nicolas Island."

WILLIAM J. HYNES (1842–1915)

Judge William J. Hynes was known as "a strong friend and a good man, a faithful Catholic, and man of integrity who loved his country as he loved his God." Hynes was born at Kilkee, County Clare, Ireland, on March 31, 1842. His widowed mother brought the family to the United States, in 1848, and settled in Springfield, Massachusetts.

Young William learned the printing trade after finishing school. In 1867, he enrolled at the Columbia University School of Law at Washington and gained admission to the bar three years later. The youthful lawyer opened an office in Little Rock, Arkansas, and, in 1872, was elected to the 43rd Congress as a member at large on the Greeley ticket.

Hynes had little inclination for politics, however, and after a term in the House of Representatives, he resumed his law practice in Chicago "where he acquired a reputation for his success in handling cases of national note." During his years in the Windy City, Hynes represented that city's railway, the beef trust and other important corporations. Throughout his life, he was prominently identified with the Irish national movement and, in this endeavor, as in others, his integrity won him the sincere respect of those with whom he came in contact.

It was his custom, after becoming a judge, to bring his wife, the former Jennie M. Way, to California each summer for a vacation. In 1910, he established a permanent residence in Los Angeles. Hynes was regarded as "a man who loved the truth, who loved his religion, and was always faithful to its precepts." He became deeply involved in the Church's charitable works and was most generous with his time and resources to the Saint Vincent de Paul Society and kindred southland organizations. In short, Hynes was "devoted to all the Church stands for in the home and in society, and he sought to realize the best ideals of the Catholic and the citizen."

Upon the judge's passing, on April 3, 1915, Bishop Thomas J. Conaty recalled that the Irish–born jurist "was firm in his convictions, fearless in his advocacy of what he believed to be true and right. He had an abiding faith, a love for the Sacraments, and a wholesome fear of God which led him to true wisdom." The Bishop of Monterey–Los Angeles said that Hynes "loved his fellowmen for God's sake, and his life was filled with the strongest of friendships. No man was more ready to sacrifice even his life for a friend; and we know that it was his anxiety to defend a friend whom he believed to have been wronged that led him to overtax his strength and perhaps hasten his death. His friend appealed to him, and the last great legal effort of his life was made in defending this friend before the highest court of the United States."

WILLIAM BROWN IDE (1796–1852)

In one of his letters, Archbishop Joseph Sadoc Alemany made a passing reference to our "esteemed former President," with whom the Dominican prelate appeared to have a cordial relationship. The identity of this individual has long evaded scholars.

On January 7, 1994, the mystery was providentially solved on the shelves of the Argonaut Book Shop in San Francisco. There, surfaced a small book entitled *William B. Ide. The President of California.*

It was indeed a rare book, one which appears in only a few bibliographies. Written by George Kirov, the thirty–seven page volume was printed by George H. Moore for the California State Printing Office in 1935.

Following the title page is a "resolution" by the state senate declaring that whereas "William Brown Ide, one of the most distinguished of California's pioneers, who was the president of the California Republic, has gone down in history practically unknown, unheralded and unsung," the Secretary of State had ordered that enough copies of Kirov's books he printed "to supply the members of the Legislature" and other state agencies.

Who was Ide, what did he do and when was he President? It would appear, from Kirov's book, that William Brown Ide was born at Rutland, Massachusetts on March 28, 1796, the son of parents who came to the New World from England just a decade after the arrival of the *Mayflower.*

As a youngster, he worked with his father at the carpenters' trade and, while looking for commissions, he met and married Susan G. Haskell. There were six children born to the couple. Coming to California by prairie schooner from New Hampshire in 1845, Ide and his family settled in present–day Tehama County, where his adobe is part of a state Historic Park near Red Bluff.

Early on, Ide befriended Peter Lassen and, for some months, his family took up residence in Lassen's *rancho.* In 1847, William Ide bought his own 7,000 acre ranch. Ide became a leader in the Bear Flag revolt which eventually resulted in the establishment of the short–lived (June 10–July 9, 1846) Republic of California. After the twenty–four patriots hoisted their flag at Sonoma, Ide was proclaimed President of California.

During his brief tenure as the area's only president, William Ide was praised for his "marvelous statesmanship and true American ideals." He became something of a folk hero to his countrymen. Ide was later present when the American flag was raised at Los Angeles on August 13, 1846. In subsequent years, he became a surveyor, miner, county treasurer and judge.

Late in 1852, like the mighty oak of the surrounding countryside cut down by greedy hands, William Ide was struck with small pox. After a week of sickness, the only president of California died at Monroeville at the age of fifty–six years.

Ide was buried beside the Colusa County courthouse, beneath a spreading oak tree, on a graceful knoll, in a pioneer village of the dead, in an unmarked grave.

IGNACIO DE JERUSALEM (1710–1769)

During the summer months of 1992, Dr. Craig Russell, Professor of Music at California Polytechnic State University, San Luis Obispo, made an interesting discovery while working at the archdiocesan Archival Center. In several uncatalogued folders containing the performance parts of three Masses, Russell identified at least two as being the works of Ignacio de Jerusalem, the renowned Chapel Master at Mexico City's cathedral. The scores are in Jerusalem's own hand, signed and dated. One is the *Mass in D* (completed in 1763) and the other is *Mass in F* (dated 1768).

There is a reasonable indication that the third Mass, the *Polychoral Mass in D* also was composed by Ignacio de Jerusalm. Russell's supposition is reinforced by the similarities in paper type and orthography that link the physical features of the latter manuscript to its companions.

The paper stock is indentical for all three works. The sheets are in an oblong format measuring 23 x 31 c.m., with ten staves per page. All the sheets have the same general texture and feel, and several of the watermarks recur in each work. Given the common paper stock, the overlap of scribal efforts between Masses and the similarities in notational procedures for all three works, it is clear that the three Masses were prepared in one location at roughly the same time.

Ignacio de Jerusalem y Stella was born at Leece, Italy, in 1710. After occupying a post as violinist in Cadiz, he journeyed to the New World in 1742, as director of the *Teatro de Coliseo* in Mexico City. Mention is made in the Cathedral's Capitular Acts that he was "very intelligent regarding everything musical, in composition and in counterpoint—of which he is the only one who understands it."

A further notation indicates that "with respect to his nimble dexterity on the violin and great musical expertise, he is the only composer that here in this city or even in Spain played violin in the orchestra. Ignacio de Jerusalem was appointed *maestro de capilia* by the Archbishop of Mexico City, even though he was regarded by the local board of examiners as being too *avant–garde* for the position. In his new role, Ignacio de Jerusalem churned out hundreds of substantive compositions in the ensuing years. These are found today in Mexico City, Puebla, Morelia, Guatemala, Cuenca and California. The Masses, Latin psalms and responsorials are particularly significant.

Though regarded by certain ecclesial authorities as having a "lax and and neglectful attitude toward his duties," the same critics judged his music "to be of the same high calibre as the European composers active at the time."

Ignacio de Jerusalem died in 1769, the very year that Fray Junípero Serra established the first of the California missions. It is highly likely that Serra and Ignacio had known one another during the years 1750–1759. Surely it is appropriate that the surviving concerted Masses from the California Mission Period were those written by a musical acquaintance of Serra.

According to Dr. Russell, the music identified at the Archival Center rebuts the view that California was a cultural backwater. It is time, he says, "to add Ignacio de Jerusalem to the names of Willam Billings and Andrew Law as major artists in our early cultural history."

HELEN HUNT JACKSON (1831–1885)

A. H.H. IN CALIFORNIA

Through the good offices of the Chacon Trust, the Archival Center was recently able to acquire a unique scrapbook entitled "H.H. in California. The Century Papers. Ramona." According to an imprint on the cover, the scrapbook is Volume XX of the "California Illustrated" series.

Prepared in March of 1897 by members of the Pasadena Loan Association "for Exhibition Space in the Chamber of Commerce," the 14 1/4 x 19 inch scrapbook contains "the Century Papers commemorative of Helen Jackson (1831–1885) as a contributor." Included in the scrapbook are copies of essays written by Mrs. Jackson for the then prominent and highly–respected journal, *The Century Illustrated Monthly Magazine*. The articles, illustrated by Henry Sandham, were later reprinted by several presses, including the Frontier Publishing Company of Cajon.

Helen Hunt Jackson's
Ramona Haunts

Helen Hunt Jackson, or "H.H." as she was known to her many thousands of readers, was described by one contemporary journal as "the most brilliant, impetuous and thoroughly individual woman of her time—one whose very temperament seemed mingled of sunshine and fire. . . . She is already being portrayed simply as a conventional Sunday school saint."

Helen Marie Fiske, the daughter of Nathan Wiley and Deborah (Vinal) Fiske, was born at Amherst, Maine, on October 18, 1831. She was reared in the strict Calvanistic traditions of her parents. Helen was a child of uncommon versatility and vivacity. She married Edward Hunt, an officer in the United States Army, in 1851. After his premature death, "H.H." began her writing career, publishing mostly in the columns of the *Nation* magazine.

In May of 1872, she journeyed to California and three years later married again, this time to William Jackson. Soon thereafter, she became interested in the sad plight of the native Americans to whom she dedicated the remaining years of her literary life.

Upon receiving an appointment from the United States government to study the conditions and needs of the California "Mission Indians" in connection with Abbott Kinney, Helen visited nearly all the tribes scattered along the Pacific Slope. Her report explored the history of the early Spanish missions whose story of enthusiasm and picturesqueness won her heart.

Jackson's famous novel *Ramona* was first published in the *Christian Union* in 1884. Its later appearance in book form enshrined "H.H" among the major authors of her time.

The handwritten "Table of Contents" in the scrapbook indicate that there were either more pages in the book or, possibly, another whole book into which were interleaved pages from *Ramona*. Also included in the original scrapbook(s) were pages relating to Father Anthony Ubach, the inspiration for the " Father Gaspara" in Hunt's *Ramona*, along with pages devoted to Santa Catalina Island and Saint Catherine of Alexandria.

Items such as this scrapbook give ample evidence that there are still many historical treasures yet to be found in the attics and closets of California. Each one of these discoveries adds considerably to the overall knowledge of earlier years along *El Camino Real*.

HELEN HUNT JACKSON (1831–1885)

B. REFLECTIONS ON LOS ANGELES

An admiring stranger from Colorado Springs arrived in *El Pueblo de Nuestra Señora de los Angeles* on December 30, 1881. The following month, a local newspaper reported that "*The Century*, better known as *Scribner's Monthly*, has sent out the well–known authoress Mrs. Jackson to Southern California to write up our old missions."

Helen Hunt Jackson (1831–1885) had come to "South" California for a definite purpose. Ruth Haisley Hampton told how "she had won the commission to study and write about the deplorable condition of the former Mission Indians."

Before launching her work, Mrs. Jackson took time to reflect on the unexpected attractions of the City named for Our Lady of the Angels. In her ebullient style, she described the astonishing area in an essay for *The Century* which appeared in December of 1883 under the title "Echoes of the City of the Angels."

Therein she related how "Mexican women, their

heads wrapped in black shawls, and their bright eyes peering out between the close–gathered folds, glide about everywhere; the soft Spanish speech is continually heard; long–robed priests hurry to and fro; and at each dawn, ancient jangling bells from the Church of the Lady of the Angels ring out the night and in the day." As Mrs. Jackson trod the city's plank walkways, she noted evidence of activity on all sides and her pen portrayed Los Angeles as a prosperous city with "busy thoroughfares, blocks of fine stone buildings, hotels, shops," all growing daily.

Indeed, 1882 was an important year for Los Angeles. Among other outstanding "modernizations" was the installation of the first telephone and the adoption of the electric light. (Quite naturally, the gas company frowned on electric lights, maintaining that they contributed to blindness, were hard on ladies' complexions and attracted bugs!)

As she moved about Los Angeles and its environs, Mrs. Jackson was enchanted with the gaily–colored windmills on every side, tall windbreaks of eucalyptus trees, picturesque sheep herds, orchards, ranches and the variety of irrigation systems. There was little that escaped Mrs. Jackson and, although astonished at the area's productivity, she was captivated by its colorful atmosphere, the simple–hearted, joyous people, their dwellings, customs and charm.

Her honestly–reported conversations with the area's leading residents reveal their hearts, as have few other writings. She was especially enamored with Antonio Coronel and his wife, Mariana.

From her lodgings at the Kimball Mansion, Mrs. Jackson told how "the bells from the Old Plaza Church ring out their call to worship at all hours of the day, while idle boys and still idler men are to be seen basking on the fountain's stone rim." Today the reflections of Helen Hunt Jackson on "El Pueblo" are highly esteemed by students of the city's life during the gallant nineties. Picturesque it was, but realistic too.

Mrs. Jackson portrayed Los Angeles on the verge of its reaching out to the sea and into the air. Though she captured well the atmosphere of the 1880s, she also envisioned the developments of succeeding decades.

GEORGE WHARTON JAMES (1858–1923)

George Wharton James was once aptly described (by a priest, no less) as "that most Catholic non–Catholic admirer of the missions and friend of the Indians." Born at Saint Oggs, Gainsborough, England, on September 27, 1858, the son of John and Ann (Wharton) James, George came to the United States in 1880. He settled in Nevada and for seven years functioned as a Methodist minister.

Mr. James first visited California in the mid 1880s and shortly thereafter developed a fascination for Western Americana literature. In subsequent years, he gathered notes for a lecture series that embraced sketches, criticisms and selections from California authors.

From 1890, James devoted full time to the platform. He traveled from coast–to–coast on the Chautauqua Circuit for the Brooks Humane Fund. Capitalizing on his considerable talents as a preacher, James captivated lucrative audiences throughout the nation. Employing modern equipment of slides, projectors and screens, he was also careful to have his appearances announced by striking posters and sumptuous brochures.

Later he published his *Syllabus of a Course of Lectures on California and Its Spirit*, containing outlines of nineteen lectures with appended reading lists. In 1912, James prepared a series of seven essays for *Out West* magazine on "The Historical Elements of California Literature." During those years, he was also a regular contributor to *Arena, Indoors and Out* and a host of other monthly publications. For a while he was literary editor for the Oakland *Tribune* and managing editor for the California *Indian Herald*.

The author of numerous books, including his classic two volume work on the *Wonders of the Colorado Desert*, George Wharton James was hailed by *The Monitor*, Catholic newspaper for the Archdiocese of San Francisco, in 1907, as "a commanding figure in the Western literary world." The stature of James was early acknowledged by Father Zephyrin Engelhardt, the renowned Franciscan chronicler. He once referred to James' book *In and Out of the Old Missions Of California* (Boston, 1905) as "by far the most trustworthy popular description of the twenty–one missions."

James wrote several other books on those historical foundations along *El Camino Real*, among them *Old Missions and Mission Indians of California* (Los Angeles, 1895), *Picturesque Pala* (Pasadena, 1916) *The Old Franciscan Missions of California* (Boston, 1925) and a pictorial opuscule published by Fred Harvey at Kansas City. In 1913, James provided the notes for and published a complete English edition of Fray Francisco Palou's *Life and Apostolic Labors of Father Junípero Serra*. It was a 338 page version of the *Relación Histórica*, translated by C. Scott Williams.

He lived quietly in Pasadena with his wife, Emma (Farnsworth) and daughter. The James home became the literary Mecca of Southern California where, according to the San Jose *Mercury*, "celebrities of the East and West" found a "hearty welcome and generous entertainment."

George Wharton James died at Saint Helena, California, on November 8, 1923. Though inactive as a Methodist in his later years, James practiced a sturdy Christian idealism, much reminiscent of the Catholic faith he so long admired and respected.

PAULINE JARICOT (1799–1862)

The early bishops of California are uniformly on record with crediting a woman for underwriting most of the missionary work in their areas from the 1850s onwards. The woman in question was not a wealthy duchess, a royal patron or an influential religious personality. She was a penniless French maiden who lived a most unpretentious life. Her name was Pauline Jaricot.

Very little is known about Pauline. Yet, by a fortunate stroke of Divine Providence, I happened across her tomb on September 30th 1995. She is interred in front of the Madeleine chapel in the historic 12th century church of Saint Nizier, in Lyons France.

Born on July 22, 1799, young Pauline took a perpetual vow of virginity on Christmas Day of 1816. The next year she founded the Union of Prayers in Reparation of the Sacred Heart, an organization for servant girls. From that group, she first solicited contributions to the foreign missions. In 1820, she formed an association to aid the Society of Foreign Missions of Paris. Each member was asked to recite a decade of the rosary daily, to circulate good books and distribute articles of piety. Later she established a home for working girls, promoted the Association of the Holy Childhood and engaged in other apostolic works for women of all classes.

Pauline's main concern and preoccupation, however, was to help the foreign missions through the alms and prayers of the faithful. In 1822, she joined her efforts to those of Angelo Inglesi, Vicar General of New Orleans, under the title of the Society for the Propagation of the Faith, then known as the Saint Francis Xavier Society.

Pauline Jaricot is the acknowledged "founder" of the Society for the Propagation of the Faith (1822) which began funding missionary activity all over the world, especially in the western part of the United States.

Pauline's fund raising techniques were unique at the time. It was a simple system whereby a promoter found ten persons to contribute a penny a week. Those funds were turned over to another person in charge of ten promoters and so on. In 1822, the Society collected $4,000 in this fashion. It is known that Pauline was very much influenced and motivated in her work as almoner of the missions by the parish priest of Ars, Pere Jean–Marie Baptiste Vianney. For reasons known only to God, Pauline Jaricot never entered religious life, but remained at her humble work until January 9, 1862, when she returned her magnificent soul to the Lord.

In 1930, her cause for beatification was introduced by the Archdiocese of Lyons and, on February 25, 1963, the Sacred Congregation of Rites declared that she had practiced virtue to a heroic degree. She now bears the title "venerable."

Though her tomb is totally unadorned, there are numerous handwritten notes taped everywhere acknowledging her intercessory assistance for a host of spiritual favors. She is obviously remembered and esteemed by the local populace.

The archives for the Archdiocese of Los Angeles are crammed with requests and responses from the Society for the Propagation of the Faith. Letters attached to those petitions tell much about the needs and goals of the Church in California during the 1850s, 1860s and 1870s. And it all began with Pauline Jaricot–a venerable lady indeed!

ROBINSON JEFFERS (1887–1962)

No writer on any aspect of Californiana can consider his or her work complete without at least a reference to Robinson Jeffers (1887–1962) because, to quote Alexander Jackson, "Jeffers and California are inseparable."

Born in Pittsburgh, Jeffers traveled widely in Europe until his family settled in Pasadena in 1903. He entered Occidental College and later studied medicine at the University of Southern California and forestry at the University of Washington. Those two subjects greatly affected the imagery of his poetry. In 1916, Jeffers and his wife, Una, moved to Carmel, where he found his own way and discovered a meaningful setting for his poetry in the surrounding region.

Jeffers was often judged irreligious, even blasphemous. His "Dear Judas, " for example, was banned in Boston. And a review in *The Monitor* of San Francisco of "Road Stallion," in 1926, styled it a "Pagan Horror from Carmel–by–the–Sea." Interestingly, others, just as orthodox, deemed Jeffers possibly America's most religious poet in this century.

In any event, in 1934 Jeffers was asked by Sister Mary James Power to write a few paragraphs about his religious beliefs for a thesis she was preparing at Fordham University, a work that was published four years later by Sheed and Ward as *Poets at Prayer*. Jeffers not only responded but wrote at length, an unusual if not unprecedented courtesy. The letter sent to Sister Mary James is included in *The Selected Letters of Robinson Jeffers, (1897–1962)* which was issued by the Johns Hopkins Press in 1968.

After apologizing for the delay in his response, Jeffers said that "as to my religious attitudes—you know it is sort of a tradition in this country not to talk about religion for fear of offending—I am still a little subject to tradition, and rather dislike stating my attitudes, except in the course of a poem."

Jeffers revealed himself as a pantheist who believed that "the universe is one being, all its parts are different expressions of the same energy, and they are all in communication with each other, influencing each other, therefore parts of one organic whole." He went on to expand on the notion. But, to our interest in this context, he believed "that it is our privilege and felicity to love God for his beauty, without claiming or expecting love from him. We are not important to him, but he to us. I think that one may contribute (ever so slightly) to the beauty of things by making one's life and surroundings beautiful, so far as one's power reaches. This includes moral beauty, one of the qualities of humanity, though it does not appear elsewhere in the universe."

Jeffers concluded saying: "there is nothing here that has not been more feelingly expressed in my verses; but I thought that a plain question deserves a plain answer."

Later, his friend, Blanche Matthias, asked Jeffers if she could have a copy of the letter "to show others that the dark words sometimes cast by the religious community were mostly unfounded." Jeffers readily agreed. That letter, given some years ago to the Gleeson Library at the University of San Francisco, was published as a keepsake by Father William Monihan and others in January of 1987 to commemorate the centenary of Robinson Jeffers' birth.

RYOZO FUSO KADO (1890–1982)

Ryozo Fuso Kado has been designated as "the greatest builder of Catholic shrines in the West and perhaps in the whole country." Most of his eighty–one years have been spent "gathering up boulders overlooked by others and squeezing and stretching them to fit like jigsaw–puzzle pieces to create dells, grottoes, shrines and artificial waterfalls that look like nature's work."

Ryozo Fuso Kado

R. F. Kado was born at the base of Mount Fuji in Japan to a devout Buddhist family of tea growers. He later became a Methodist and, after coming to the United States in 1911, entered the Catholic Church. Kado's wife and two children subsequently followed him into the "one true religion whose truth is eternal." Shortly after his arrival in America, Kado apprenticed himself to Chotaro Nishimura, an internationally recognized stone craftsman. "Mr. Nishi," as he was known, had designed part of the Imperial Garden in Tokyo and the Presidential Gardens in Mexico City.

In later years, Kado earned his own reputation as an architectural gardener, winning plaudits also for developing and propagating the Epiphyllum, or flowering cactus, a highly popular parasitic shade plant. Mr. Kado lived an exciting and often troubled life. His thriving nursery business was closed at the outbreak of World War II, when he and his family were forcibly sent with other Southern California Japanese–Americans to the Manzanar Relocation Center, a mile–square internment camp in the desert east of the Sierra Nevada.

Following a short interval in New York after the war, Kado and his family returned to California, in 1946, penniless, but anxious to begin anew. "After all," he stated, "where else in the whole world would we have the chance to start again?"

The eighty shrines and grottoes erected at sixty–five Catholic churches, cemeteries, schools, hospitals and homes during his lifetime have earned for Mr. Kado the reputation of being "the country's busiest rock–garden builder." Most ambitious of his undertakings, according to an article in the *Saturday Evening Post*, one he started, in 1946, on a barren hill overlooking Holy Cross in Cemetery in the southern section of Los Angeles. Completed in 1969, it is an eye–filling spread of gardens surrounded by a massive 400–foot rock wall out of which arises a thirty–foot high grotto. Within the wall, the three shrines of Our Lady of Lourdes, Saint Ann and Saint Joseph, blend together 700 tons of ornamental rocks so ingeniously that they resemble a giant out–cropping of natural serpentine. "This is Kado's art with rocks, making them look as though they had always been there."

Over twenty replicas of the Lourdes grotto, the first built for the cloistered Carmelites in Alhambra, have convinced Mr. Kado that rocks have character and are loaded with life and rhythm. R. F. Kado was a happy man, working at his chosen vocation. He expressed in stone and flowers the Faith he found so many years ago. He dedicated himself to the task of building shrines "so that people who pass by and stop to say a prayer, may reach up their hearts to God in a much–troubled world, and thereby gain solace and consolation."

JOSEPH F. KANE (1894–1948)

Were there a list of California's Catholic heroes, the name of Battalion Chief Joseph F. Kane (1894–1948) would surely rate a prominent place. He gave his life in the service of others. For well over a quarter century, Joseph Kane was a fire fighter who loved his profession. As one newspaper put it, "through his ability and his many sterling qualities he gained a well–merited place in the chief's rank and he was respected and beloved by every officer and member of the force."

Kane joined the San Francisco Fire Department in 1922, and, five years later, he won promotion to lieutenant. He became captain of Number 12 engine at 115 Drumm Street, in 1938.

In 1943, Kane scored top honor in the battalion chief's competitive examination and moved to Number Two district as chief. There Kane gained the respect of his men. He was known for never sending a fireman on a mission that he himself was not willing to attempt.

Kane's last fire started in a battery charging room of the three story United Automotive Supply Building, at 1414 Van Ness Avenue. The first alarm was pulled at 10 a.m., as billowing clouds of smoke erupted skyward from paint, lacquer and acetone–fed flames. Local newspapers described the conflagration as "one of the most stubborn fires in recent years."

For well over four hours, fifty pieces of equipment and 150 fire fighters doggedly battled to extinguish the four–alarm blaze. Over a dozen injuries were sustained by department personnel.

Kane was leading a group of his men into the second floor to battle flames when he was overcome by smoke. Dragged to a fire escape twenty feet above the street, he was given emergency oxygen treatment by Dr. J.C. Geiger. After being anointed by Father Donnell Walsh, the chief was taken to Central Emergency Hospital. He died as the ambulance sped past Saint Mary's Cathedral.

A contingency of 700 firemen, in their trim blue uniforms and white gloves, gathered at the cathedral to pay their final respects on May 18, 1948. Archbishop John J. Mitty and a host of public officials joined Mary Kane and her three sons to eulogize and pray for a "fireman's fireman."

In a release to the press, Chief Edward P. Walsh said that "Joe lived and died a man, and it is men like him who have made the San Francisco Fire Department what it is. His memory will live long among us as a guiding star toward greater achievement. Stricken in the prime of his life, while fighting a stubborn fire, he died a hero's death, and for this we honor him."

The popular San Francisco columnist, Val King, was a witness to the fire and later he wrote that "last Saturday morning the realities were elemental: a dangerous, raging fire which challenged the courage of strong and brave men. The men were there, with plenty of courage; but the priests were there with them. Chief Kane died a hero's death, but there was more to it than that; every Catholic from the Pope down to the newest baptized infant could hope for nothing better than the assurance of the Last Sacraments as Chief Kane received them."

YOUSUF KARSH (b. 1908–)

James Francis Cardinal McIntyre was among the celebrated personages captured on film by Yousuf Karsh, the famous photographer whose portraits of world leaders are without parallel in the twentieth century.

Born in Mardin, Armenia, on December 23, 1908, Yousuf Karsh grew up under the horrors of the Armenian massacre. He came to Canada in 1924 and a dozen years later opened his studios at Ottawa. In 1939, Karsh married Solange Gauthier of Tours and it was through her contacts with the Little Theatre that brought the photographer to the attention of Canada's Governor General.

From the very beginning of his career, Karsh possessed a unique ability of capturing on film the stuff of fame. He was justifiably called the "last of the great heroic portrait photographers" for, more than any other of his contemporaries, he helped shape the way the Western World remembered people of importance.

There are over 50,000 images in the Karsh archive of famous people. Though most of his portraits suggest meticulous planning and lighting, the portraitist insisted that he went into each sitting without preconceptions.

A selection of Karsh portrayals was published under the title *Faces of Destiny* and that volume established Karsh as an international figure in his own right. Among the notable world leaders captured by Karsh on film were Winston Churchill, King George, Pope Pius XII, Dwight Eisenhower, Ernest Hemingway, Queen Elizabeth and Pope John XXIII.

The story of his encounter with Winston Churchill tells much about the Karsh style. It was hastily staged during a two minute sitting at the Canadian Parliament building. Churchill was in a testy mood and when the photographer asked him to remove his cigar, the Prime Minister simply glared. Karsh stepped up and grabbed the cigar out of his mouth. Churchill's angry reaction, caught on film, is now a classic portrayal that has appeared in hundreds of books.

Karsh portraits have appeared in publications all over the world and Karsh himself has been the subject of many articles. His work is represented in the permanent collections of the Museum of Modern Art and the Metropolitan Museum of Art in New York City, the Art Institute of Chicago and other leading museums.

It was said that throughout the long life of the Canadian photographer, when historians needed to reach out for an understanding of great people, they used Karsh portraits. He magically transformed the human face into legend.

Instinctively, Karsh consistently captured the perfect and unique attitude of his subjects—the natural carriage of the head and body, the sensitive planning of the background, the illuminating gestures and the marvelous expressivity of the hands. Characteristic of Karsh portraits is the superb modelling of features achieved by the subtleties of lighting, so that the subject appeared to have his or her own luminosity rather than ordinary light and shadow.

Clare Booth Luce, the person who insisted that James Francis Cardinal McIntyre be filmed by Karsh, arranged (and paid for) the sitting in New York City. Probably that portrayal of His Eminence of Los Angeles was reproduced more than all the others combined.

DENIS KEARNEY (1847–1907)

A considerable amount of ink has flowed concerning Denis Kearney (1847–1907), the self–styled "people's dictator," and the extent of his influence on the political atmosphere of pre–1900 California. The Irish–born sailor arrived on the scene in 1868. He married four years later and took up residence in San Francisco, where he engaged in the freight–draying business.

Kearney's politically ambitious temperament was favorably complimented by a voluble oratory and compelling vigor. In the fall of 1877, he succeeded in uniting several disparate and ineffective groups into the Workingmen's Party of California. Among the organization's stated aims was that of uniting "workers and labor sympathizers into one political party against the encroachments of Capital."

Kearney's movement, based on the popular and widespread unrest of the time, achieved considerable initial results. The party successfully sponsored several members to the state legislature, as well as the mayor of San Francisco and a number of smaller municipal office holders. The self–educated, industrious and frugal Kearney unhesitatingly exhorted his listeners "to wrest the government from the hands of the rich and place it in those of the people." Contemporary literature depicted Kearney "as a hotheaded anarchist who played upon the coarsest impulses of the rabble." Yet, as John Walton Caughey has pointed out, Kearney, "for all his vocal advocacy of terrorist measures . . . precipitated no riot and produced no actual violence; his incendiary talk was but a means of promoting political action."

So widespread was the party's political influence, in its earliest days, that by 1878, Denis Kearney "was the most feared single individual on the Pacific Coast." Among the measures advocated by the Workingmen's Party of California were the eight–hour day, compulsory education, statewide schools, banking reform, tax restructure and direct election of senators.

Kearney's popularity eroded almost as rapidly as it began, when many of his followers and a considerable portion of his platform were absorbed into the Democratic Party. He retired from politics in 1884, and devoted the last two decades of his life to a quiet existence in the San Joaquin Valley. Henry George characterized Denis Kearney "as the burning reflection of a hot resentment felt by the people trapped by the machine politics of a monopolist state." Though he may well have been a noisy, overly confident and discontented demagogue, Denis Kearney did, in his own manner, what few others would have dared, staunchly pioneering a movement that was most important in the overall history of American labor.

HELEN WEBER KENNEDY (1889–1983)

When historians get around to telling the definitive story of California's pioneer women, the name of Helen Weber Kennedy (1889–1983), granddaughter of Stockton founder Captain Charles M. Weber, will be spelled out in block letters. An active Catholic pioneer well into her nineties, Mrs. Kennedy was a fellow of the Gleeson Library at the University of San Francisco, a trustee for the California Historical Society, a director of the California Heritage Council and an honorary trustee of the Haggin Museum in Stockton.

Helen served on the Council for the Friends of the Bancroft Library, where Captain Charles M. Weber's papers are housed. Those documents have been the source material for several invaluable printed books which Helen supported financially. She also represented San Joaquin County on the board of the California Heritage Council. Helen sponsored a number of publications at the University of the Pacific, in addition to being a charter member of the Book Club of California.

Long interested in the San Francisco Garden Club, she was its president during much of World War II and was later co–author, with Mrs. Robert Allen Kinzie, Jr., of *Vignettes of Old San Jose Gardens*.

Born at San Jose, Helen Weber attended Saint Agnes School in Stockton, then matriculated from Notre Dame in San Jose. In 1913 she became one of the first woman graduates in agriculture from the University of California at Berkeley. A member of the Alpha Phi sorority, it was her intention to carry on the family ranching tradition.

In 1915, Helen married Gerald Driscoll Kennedy, a native San Francisco banker. They took up residence in the Bay Area for a number of years before moving back to Stockton. During that time, Gerald and Helen had four daughters, Helen, Katherine, Moura and Geraldine.

The Kennedys lived in the ancestral home, which by then had been moved several hundred feet back from the Calaveras River which ran close to the south side of the house and away from West Lane which had become a major thoroughfare. The home was restored along its earlier architectural lines. In the landscaping plans, Thomas Church created a Victorian garden emphasizing the beautiful valley oaks so prized by residents of the area.

In a tribute to Helen, written as a preface for a book about her grandfather, Albert Shumate said that Helen was "not only a very gracious lady, but was active in preserving the historical heritage of California." She carefully looked after the family papers, furniture and memorabilia.

After Helen's demise, in accordance with her directives, the family home and two acres of land were bequeathed to the Helen Weber Kennedy Charitable Trust which was charged with maintaining a museum featuring farming life. The Trust endorsed a proposal from the San Joaquin County Historical Society which operated the local museum. Accordingly, a wing was added to the existing building and three rooms from "Helen Oaks" were reproduced within.

Throughout her long and productive life, Helen Weber Kennedy upheld the noble traditions established by her illustrious grandfather. She became in her own right an integral part of the "American Adventure," which Charles M. Weber began at Stockton on November 4, 1841.

At her funeral services, conducted in Stockton's Cathedral of the Annunciation, it was said that Helen Weber Kennedy "always epitomized what was best in her Church and in the country. She never allowed for anything less."

ROSE KENNEDY

America's grand old dowager, Rose Kennedy, celebrated her hundredth birthday in the summer of 1990 at the family estate in Hyannisport, Massachusetts. Born the daughter of John and Mary (Hannon) Fitzgerald, Rose was a graduate of Sacred Heart College in Manhattanville. Her father, the famous "Honey Fitz," had been Mayor of Boston and a veteran member of the House of Representatives.

Rose married Joseph Kennedy in 1914. An importer of Scotch whiskey, Kennedy later gained worldwide notoriety as a leading figure in the reorganization and codification of procedures for the nation's stock exchange system. After serving as Franklin D. Roosevelt's ambassador to England, Mr. Kennedy came to Hollywood where he purchased and operated the FBO Studios (later RKO). Throughout her husband's long and distinguished public career, Rose was a stalwart and active companion.

When Mr. Kennedy acted as a special representative of the United States Government at the coronation of Pope Pius XII in 1939, Rose insisted on taking all nine children to the event. Edward, the youngest, received his first Communion from the Holy Father. In 1942, Rose Kennedy received the *Pro Ecclesia et Pontifice* medal from Pope Plus XII and nine years later she was given the title Papal Countess in recognition of her "exemplary motherhood and charitable works."

Mrs. Kennedy was the first woman recipient of the Catholic Youth Organization's Champion Award in 1954, for her work with young people. Throughout her event–filled life, Rose has been especially attentive in caring for neglected children and promoting the education of exceptional and handicapped youngsters.

Through her efforts and encouragement, the Kennedy family has supported a dozen major institutions, many of them established in honor of her son, Lt. Joseph Kennedy Jr., who died during World War II.

Mrs. Kennedy knew James Francis Cardinal McIntyre from his days in New York. In fact, her entire family attended his episcopal ordination in Saint Patrick's Cathedral on January 8, 1941. In 1958, at the invitation of Cardinal McIntyre, Mrs. Kennedy journeyed to Los Angeles as a guest lecturer for the archdiocesan Council of Catholic Women. She spoke on her experiences as "An Ambassador's Wife at the Court of Saint James's."

It was during her visit that Cardinal McIntyre suggested the possibility of opening in the archdiocese a center for treatment of handicapped children. Mrs. Kennedy promised to present the proposal to directors of the Joseph P. Kennedy Jr. Memorial Foundation. Eventually, the foundation allocated $914,000 for the purpose and a one story building was erected adjacent to Saint John's Hospital in Santa Monica. The Kennedy Child Center was formally dedicated on March 18, 1962.

The avowed purpose of the new facility was that of providing out–patient services for mentally retarded, brain–damaged and emotionally–disturbed children. The task of operating the center was entrusted to the Sisters of Charity of Leavenworth.

During subsequent years, Rose Kennedy quietly used her influence in other outreach programs around the country. Yet she suffered immensely during that time. Within an eight year span, she saw her husband die and two of her sons assassinated. She credits her fortitude during those events to the belief that "God never gives a cross to bear larger than we can carry."

In an interview with *Parade* magazine, Rose said she had "always believed that God wants us to be happy. He doesn't want us to be sad," she said. "Birds sing after a storm. Why shouldn't we?" In 1974, Mrs. Kennedy gathered her thoughts into a manuscript which was published later that year under the title *Times to Remember*. It was a moving and inspirational book wherein the matriarch of the Kennedy clan spoke candidly about the incidents in life that shaped her positive outlook.

Rose Kennedy always managed to remain above politics and beyond controversy. Probably Cardinal McIntyre put it best a quarter century ago when he noted, that "Rose Kennedy is one of those rare scripture–like women whose imprint is on nothing, but whose influence is everywhere."

EDWARD J. LEBRETON (1852–1910)

The mail delivery of September 16, 1904, brought an offer to Bishop Thomas J. Conaty, as casual as it was monumental. After outlining the charitable work already accomplished by the Little Sisters of the Poor in San Francisco, Edward J. LeBreton asked the Southern California prelate if he would be "disposed to invite this religious community to start a house in Los Angeles." If so, LeBreton offered to purchase a seven or eight acre site and build quarters thereon where the nuns could accommodate 200 elderly patients.

Bishop Conaty did not know LeBreton personally. Had he inquired in the Bay Area, however, he would have found that Edward J. LeBreton was recognized among his contemporaries as "a man of irreproachable character and saintly life" and "a man of God who loved his religion and faithfully followed its precepts."

Edward Joseph LeBreton was born of French parentage in Folsom, California, in 1852. He had been educated in France and Germany and, by the time he was advanced to the presidency of the French Savings Bank in San Francisco, he had reached "the honorable distinction of being a successful man of affairs and by his industry and integrity he had accumulated a fortune."

LeBreton had been associated with the apostolic endeavors of the Little Sisters of the Poor since their arrival at San Francisco, in 1901. One of the nuns reported that at their initial meeting LeBreton said: "You will find in me a friend and a protector as often as you will choose to have recourse to my assistance or my advice in your needs." In addition to financial assistance, LeBreton visited the Home for the Aged Poor every Wednesday and Saturday, where he performed the most menial tasks. Frequently he would send elderly

patients on a day's outing in his private carriage. Such activities were a natural outgrowth of his philosophy that "to give one's money is little, but to give oneself is better."

The prospect of introducing the Sisters in the Diocese of Monterey–Los Angeles was most appealing to Bishop Conaty, and he arranged to meet with Mr. LeBreton in San Francisco, in October of 1904. After making some preliminary arrangements, the Little Sisters of the Poor arrived early in 1905, and immediately took up their apostolate among the elderly citizens of all races and creeds. LeBreton acquired property on East First Street and construction was soon underway for permanent quarters. A four–story red–brick building was ready in mid–1907, and Bishop Conaty dedicated the handsome American colonial structure on March 25, 1908. LeBreton absorbed the total cost of the institution which amounted to over $400,000.

In the following years, the generous San Francisco benefactor frequently visited the Sisters. A newspaper account recalled "how edifying it was to see this man of affairs, this successful businessman moving among the old people in the homes which he had built for them, sharing their simple meal, always delighted to wait on them at table." When asked by the nuns if they could display his portrait in the foyer, LeBreton replied that some sort of religious picture would more properly express their gratitude for his assistance.

The Bishop of Monterey–Los Angeles felt that "the humility and simplicity of his life and the repugnance to publicity, mark a nobility of character which is worthy of admiration." With Edward Joseph LeBreton's death at San Francisco's Home for the Aged Poor, on March 19, 1910, the Church in California lost a noble son; the poor, a princely benefactor; and the state, a most worthy citizen."

SHANE LESLIE (1886–1971)

In 1958, the late Sir Shane Leslie (1886–1971) visited California. The renowned poet, novelist and historian recorded his impressions of that journey which subsequently appeared in *The Tablet* of London, on June 14th.

> What of the future of this Queen of the Pacific which overflows into a new parish every month, which engulfs suburbs, of which Hollywood is only a garish pinpoint? Population is rising into millions as the oil–wealth is poured steadily out of the depths. It needs a staff of Monsignori and a Chancery savouring of Big Business to keep check of the flood. Immigrants, if religion they have, traditionalize in the old religion. But what is interesting to learn is that in the third generation the Italians and Mexicans are returning to the Church.

It is history in the states how the Italians and Mexicans who first arrived under the banners of Garibaldi and Juarez, long professed anti–clericalism, to the distress of Irish–born bishops. But the Italians are now the leading Latin strain in America. Their success is attributed to their industry and sobriety. They excel in banking, as the Medici excelled before them, and are acquiring the wealth and social positions that other peoples have forfeited by leisurely and less sober attitudes of life.

Los Angeles resembles an immense mining camp at which the luxuries of civilization have arrived before the natural riches have been pumped out of the earth. Amid the many square miles of prefabricated chalet and garish bungalow rise but few tall and settled buildings. The Dohenys of oil fame are responsible for the one magnificent church, as rich with marble as a Roman basilica. But society is not yet set, and classes are still unclassified. Los Angeles will find no order or society or civilization except what the Church can give her. San Francisco has been ecclesiastically and socially settled before and above Los Angeles, or at least considers herself so. Both are racing each other for the future. California is streaked with Spanish Catholic terminology—every town and district grew up around a mission; the missions of the Franciscans founded by Fray Junípero Serra. Their memory is a relief from the sordid artificiality of Hollywood, the scrambling crowds of immigrants, the endless tearing up and rebuilding of houses, the mileage of used cars for sale, the interpenetration of thousands of new ones at full speed all day and most of the night, for the whole plain lies set during the dark hours like an immense rivière of electrically sparking diamonds, rubies, emeralds—mile upon mile as far as the horizon.

Down in Carmel I reached the original mission of Fray Junípero, with chapel and reredos restored together with his tomb, a fine piece of recumbent statuary, with three Franciscans graven life–size in loving vigil. Hard by is the cell in which he was laid to die, so bare, so Christlike, so unAmerican. Churches and cathedrals, ecclesiastics and all the religious Orders may follow to this land, but no–one can take from simple Fray Junípero the title of Apostle of California.

The sense of peace and finality reigns about this humble spot as nowhere else in this mighty and super–wealthy state. Here time, or at least history, stands humbly still—as they stand nowhere else save in the presence of the giant trees in the California hills. How insignificant seem Kew, and even the English oak giants, in comparison with trees that stood in their array and waved gentle welcome at the very first Christmas of Nazareth. God was their Forester. So in spite of the gruesome rush for wealth and the sordid industry of wringing the oily wealth of dead seas out of the entrails of the earth, there are sacred moments and sacred scenes to be enjoyed in California.

RUFUS A. LOCKWOOD (1811–1857)

Rufus A. Lockwood was a colorful, controversial member of the California bar. He had an eye for publicity and was never far from the center of San Francisco's political and social life.

Born in 1811 at Stamford, Connecticut, Jonathan Jessup studied at Yale before entering the service of the United States Navy in 1830. He appears to have deserted during a cruise in the Caribbean. Probably because of that indiscretion, Jonathan adopted his mother's maiden name and then changed his first name as well. Thereafter he was Rufus A. Lockwood. With any name, he would have been remembered in the historical annals.

Rufus worked his way to Chicago and then on to Indianapolis, where he taught school and began the study of law. In 1834, he was admitted to practice before the Indiana Supreme Court. His first case in Lafayette was argued so well that he received a rare commendation from the judge. The following year he defended a client in a sensational murder trial, winning an acquittal after talking nine straight hours. His colleagues enthusiastically pronounced it the best jury speech over made!

In subsequent years Lockwood went broke. Discouraged, he journeyed to Mexico and there studied Hispanic jurisprudence. He returned to New Orleans and then enlisted for a stint in the United States Army. Ever the wanderer, he went back to Indiana and resumed his legal career. In 1849, Lockwood decided to take up residence in California. He left his wife and children behind as he set out to prospect for gold.

He sold his law books and devoted his energy to studying medicine during the long voyage around the Horn. The "awkward bear of a man" never prescribed a pill or picked up a shovel.

For a while he lived at San Jose Mission. But he soon tired of those surroundings and moved on to San Francisco where he became one of the most respected lawyers in the state. One reporter referred to him during that time as "an old lion at play." Tall, husky and ungainly, Rufus was a truly brilliant man. His propensity for alcohol and his fondness for gambling were the major flaws in his otherwise upright character. He was a man everyone liked, blemishes and all,

Rufus affiliated himself with Edmund Randolph and Frank Tillford and that trio of legal minds represented a formidable force in the juridical circles of San Francisco. The evidence indicates that they lost few if any major court skirmishes.

In 1853, Lockwood sent for his family to join him in San Francisco. But for unknown reasons, he set out shortly thereafter for Australia. Upon his return, Lockwood embraced the Catholic faith, probably at the behest of Archbishop Joseph Sadoc Alemany, an old friend. It was during a voyage to Havana in 1857 that the forty–six year old Rufus A. Lockwood died at sea when his ship went down in a terrible storm. Interestingly, his wife was rescued and lived on for many years in California.

Lockwood was an unpredictable social rebel who cared naught for money or position. His propensity for disappearing periodically has made it difficult to learn much about him from the public record. What little remains confirms that he was a fascinating person in many ways.

EDWARD LOUSTAUNAU (1914–1993)

Edward Loustaunau (1914–1993), the great–great–great–great grandson of Juan Bautista de Anza, died of cancer at his home in Riverside, California, on August 2, 1993. Among his many outstanding distinctions was that of posing for the granite statue of his illustrious ancestor that stands at Newman Park in Riverside.

Juan Bautista de Anza (1735–1788) was born in Mexico of Spanish parents. He became captain of the *presidio* at Tubac (1760) south of present–day Tucson. He was later asked by Viceroy Antonio Bucareli to develop a plan for opening a land route from northern Sonora to San Gabriel.

With thirty–four men, including the legendary Fray Francisco Garces, Anza made the difficult journey across the Colorado desert in the early weeks of 1774. They made it to San Gabriel Mission and, from there, to Monterey and back to Tubac.

In September of 1775, Anza traveled a route further to the south, through Nogales and Tubac to Tucson and then into California. That time, he led a party of 240 people, including women and children with cattle and supplies, to establish a *presidio* and mission at San Francisco. That 1,500 mile journey, begun on September 29, 1775, was brought to conclusion when his second in command, Jose Moraga, founded the *presidio* on July 27th, 1776. After Anza returned to Mexico, he served as Governor of New Mexico (1777–1788).

The largest state park in California, Anza–Borrego, is named for Juan Bautista de Anza. Established in 1933, it is a desert recreation area southwest of Coachella, on the edge of the Colorado desert, in San Diego county. The term *borrego* refers to the bighorn sheep which ranged there.

Edward John Loustaunau was a lifelong resident of Riverside. Graduating from Polytechnic High School in 1932, he was a teletype repairman and a mobile phone foreman at Pacific Bell Telephone Company for forty years. A member of Saint Francis de Sales parish in Riverside, Loustaunau was an active member of the Knights of Columbus and served as a downtown advisory member for the area's first baseball league. His ser-

vice to the commonwealth touched many organizations, including the Citrus Belt Golf Association.

Throughout his life, Loustaunau took an active interest in his family history. He rode in parades and played the role of Juan Bautista de Anza in the Riverside Centennial in 1970. He involved his wife, Ellen, and their five daughters, eighteen grandchildren and eleven great-grandchildren in these activities, always carefully explaining his family's long and prestigious involvement in civic and religious affairs.

While still a youngster, Edward was interviewed by Herbert Eugene Bolton who edited the thirteen diaries of Juan Bautista de Anza for publication by the University of California in 1930. Loustaunau knew a lot about his ancestor's life, much of it related to him by Bolton. He learned, for example, that the Anza diaries are not a biography of the man, but deal only with one brief episode of his eventful life.

Bolton had discovered that before going to California, Anza had an interesting career as a soldier on the Sonora border. After the California phase of his life, Anza had won considerable fame as a diplomat, administrator and Indian fighter.

Visiting with Loustaunau was always interesting. He had studied history well and it was obvious from his fascinating conversation about his ancestor and other early pioneers in California.

CHARLES F. LUMMIS (1859–1928)

A. NEWMAN CLUB ADDRESS

A local newspaper stated at the turn of the century, that "Mr. Charles F. Lummis is everywhere recognized as specially qualified to discuss the rights and wrongs of the red man and his treatment by the white people of this continent." The account went on to say that "no man in the United States claims a more accurate practical knowledge of the subject than he. He is familiar with the Indian, his needs and the history of his experience, from the time of Columbus to the present."

In November, 1900, Lummis was asked to speak before the Newman Club of Los Angeles on the Indian question. In his address, he contrasted the treatment of the aborigines under the Spanish Catholic system, with the policy pursued by the "superior" Anglo–Saxon prior to the establishment of the republic. The following brief resume of the talk, taken from *The Monitor*, December 8, 1900, was transcribed by a listener:

> Mr. Lummis pictured the early attempts of the Spanish missionaries and viceroys to civilize the 'red' man, and told how, in 1539, one year before the great English bible was printed, there was printed in Mexico a cathechism in the Aztec language, for the benefit of the

Aztec Indians. He contended that all the efforts of the early Spanish colonists were to win the affections and confidence of the Indian, by continually trying to better his condition, and not by allowing politics or unscrupulous 'trustees' to get control of the affairs of the various tribes.

He blamed the present Indian Bureau for ignorance and neglect of the fundamental principles of education, and contended that if our system were subjected to a radical reformation on the lines of the Spanish mission school, that we should have no scandals to hide and no dire failures to record.

He said that it was marvelous to think that by our so–called higher methods of civilization we are slowly but surely exterminating the Indian, while by a continuation of the system founded by the Spanish methods, the Indians throughout Mexico and the other South American countries were holding their own.

He severely arraigned Maj. Pratt and the government school at Carlisle, Pa., as the refinement of cruelty in educating children to forget their parents, and teaching the sons and daughters of the Indians to grow up impudent and worthless to the people to whom they owed their existence.

He took pains to express himself as not being an advocate of Catholic schools as such, but he believed that the Catholic schools should be supported simply because they are good schools.

He stated that he had come from generations of pure Methodist stock and yet he had to admit that he had yet to find a Catholic school devoted to Indian education that was not of salutary and permanent benefit to the Indians.

He reminded the club that the government appropriation had now entirely ceased, and in consequence thousands of Indian children will be dependent on the charity of the friends of common humanity for support and education and he therefore urged the members of the club to help in such a worthy cause.

CHARLES F. LUMMIS (1859–1928)

B. TRIBUTE TO AN EDITOR

In an essay for *Donahoe's Magazine* just after the turn of the century, Charles Fletcher Lummis (1859–1928) was referred to as the "greatest living American author." He was indeed the pioneer in a department of historical literature of surpassing interest, a traveler and explorer whose researches added materially to the knowledge of the Spanish conquerors and of the races they brought under subjection, an editor whose fearless views on all topics made him the terror of counterfeit philanthropists and sham humanitarians.

The brave Franciscan missionaries who "won this bare, brown land to Christ" at the price of incredible dangers, hardships and sufferings found an admirer, a eulogist and a historian who did them ample justice after the lapse of many generations. And that was not, by any means, the greatest of Mr. Lummis' contributions to the cause of historic truth. He aroused the West to the necessity of preserving the landmarks of a European civilization which were almost a century old—when the Pilgrim Fathers landed at Plymouth Rock. In his own words, he produced a new history of the United States, a real history, one which looked beyond the thin fringe of the Atlantic seaboard, one which realized that the history of the country began in the Great Southwest.

The Landmarks Club, organized primarily to preserve and restore the old mission buildings of California, was founded by him. He taught the people of the Pacific Slope, through his publications, the necessity and duty of preserving those monuments of a brave and successful attempt to uplift the degraded aborigines. Lummis had nothing but words of condemnation for the prevailing system of Indian education. To him it was the "refinement of brutality, cruelty and ignorance," a system which snatches children from their homes and forces them to forego their names, their speech and their manners." "When a man comes to me," he once said, "and tells me that a child could better be taught by a politician, who is rewarded by a government place in an Indian school, than by a Sister of Charity, he had better bring along his fire escape with him."

In his magazines *Land of Sunshine* and *Out West*, Lummis performed a work of incalculable value for students of American history. He published translations of Spanish documents bearing upon the early colonization of the country. One of the most valuable in that series was the diary of Fray Junípero Serra, founder and first *Presidente* of the California missions.

By the time Lummis had completed his life work, the history of North America needed to be rewritten. The blood–thirsty bush–whackers, Indian killers and dare devil *conquistadores* of Prescott and the New England school of "arm–chair historians" had to take into account a race of soldier pioneers, who inaugurated "the most just, humane and equitable system of treatment of the Indians ever devised." Spaniards no longer appeared as butchers bent upon the extermination of the native races, but civilizers who meted out to natives a larger measure of justice than has ever been accorded to Indians falling within the sphere of Anglo–Saxon influence.

And it took a non–Catholic to set the record straight!

CHARLES F. LUMMIS (1859–1928)

C. CRUSADER IN CORDUROY

Charles Fletcher Lummis (1859–1928), the enthusiastic propagandist of the brighter side of the Spanish conquest, walked to California in order "to learn more of the country and its people than railroad travel could ever teach; to have the physical joy which only the confirmed pedestrian knows; to have the mental awakening of new sights, and experiences; and to get, in this enjoyable fashion, to my new home."

In 1894, a decade after his arrival in Los Angeles, Lummis became editor for the *Land of Sunshine*, which he guided with singular diligence and ingenuity. The volumes of that publication, along with those of its successor *Out West*, abound in translated Spanish documents, scholarly treatises on early colonization, folk music, Indian lore, missionary activity as well as articles of general interest and short stories. His own monthly column, "That Which is Written," remains a superb commentary on books and essays issued during the fourteen years of his editorship.

It was also in 1894 that Lummis began work on El Alisal, now a state monument housing the headquarters of the Historical Society of Southern California. That historic edifice became, in addition to his home, a southland rendezvous for famed artists, authors, poets, thespians, scientists and statesmen.

In his multi–faceted role of historian, conservationist and archaeologist, Lummis founded the Landmarks Club, organized the Sequoia League and established the Southwest Museum, all of which were geared towards preserving and portraying the religion, heritage, art, industry and traditions of Western American aborigines.

His twenty–two books and numerous penetrating articles forced the armchair scholars to rewrite the pioneer period of American history, particularly those chapters bearing upon the lives and deeds of the early Spanish explorers. One of his most fascinating books, the *Birch Bark Poems*, was a mini–volume collection of youthful verse printed on real birch bark. Lummis personally gathered, cut to size, printed and stitched the twelve–page book which eventually sold over 14,000 copies.

The Harvard–trained Yankee was appointed City Librarian for Los Angeles, in 1905, and during his tenure in that post Lummis' experience, vision and energy literally revolutionized the whole concept of collecting and circulating the printed word.

Though a Methodist by religious persuasion, Charles Lummis openly pushed for the beatification of Fray Junípero Serra. No less a Catholic spokesman than Joseph Scott characterized "the plunky little editor of the *Land of Sunshine*" as a man "to whom Catholics of the land owe a debt of gratitude they can never expect to pay."

In an editorial aside, on February 8, 1902, a writer for *The Tidings*, Catholic newspaper for the Diocese of Monterey–Los Angeles, saluted "the brilliant thinker" who had proven himself to be a "fearless upholder of religious toleration, the staunch defender of the downtrodden and oppressed of every clime."

Indeed that he was—and far more.

J. WISEMAN MACDONALD (1866–1942)

J. Wiseman Macdonald, "a man of broad sympathies, of fine intellect and high ideals," was born at Mazomanie, Wisconsin, on January 17, 1866, the son of Allan and Eleanor (Wiseman) Macdonald. Descended from the Macdonald's of Clanranald, in the Western Highlands of Scotland, James received his education in the land of his ancestors and at the Grant School, in Lancashire. By the time of his return to the United States, the young man was steeped in the best traditions of a family that had been solidly Catholic for over a thousand years.

Admitted to the bar before the California Supreme Court, in 1892, J. Wiseman Macdonald was a lawyer by instinct as well as training. Early in his long legal career, he "gained wide recognition as a lawyer of fine natural ability, supplemented by an education in the law, extensive and comprehensive." In addition to his busy legal practice Macdonald lectured on corporation law for many years at the University of Southern California. He served two terms as trustee for the Los Angeles Bar Association. Throughout his life he had "an active and energetic interest in all civic affairs," serving, at various times as Director of the Bank of Italy and the Hibernian Savings Bank of Los Angeles as well as President of the Dimond Estate Company of San Francisco.

During the twenty–two years Macdonald occupied the presidency of the Saint Vincent de Paul Society, he won an abiding place in the hearts of the poor and downtrodden in California's southland. It was Macdonald's long and tireless dedication to charitable activities which brought him the papal knighthood from Pius XI, in February, 1924. That recognition, the first such ever accorded in California, was bestowed as a reward for faithful and devoted service to the Church and religion.

His charitable involvements were accelerated after the premature death of his wife, Jane (Boland) Macdonald, in 1919. From his suite of offices in the Higgins Building, Macdonald employed his manifold talents to further Catholic activities with utmost fidelity and rare ability. Macdonald's "very manner, his expression, his countenance, his reasonings, the tact with which he approached difficult situations, the keen light that he threw on abstruse subjects, his eloquent familiarity with the Spanish tongue, were the qualities that made success in his profession, and he had them at his command. His appearance in courts of the land was always such as to command respect."

Possibly the most outstanding ecclesiastical honor given to the well–known jurist was his selection as keynote speaker for the public reception held, on December 6, 1936, at the elevation of Los Angeles to the status of metropolitan archiepiscopate. The death of J. Wiseman Macdonald, on November 21, 1942, deprived the People of God in Southern California of a distinguished and eminent lawyer, a sympathetic friend of the poor and a high–toned Catholic gentleman.

LORETTA MAHONY (1906–1995)

Biographers place great emphasis on the role that parents have in the ecclesial vocations of their children. Surely that is reflected in the lives of the southland's bishops. A prime example would be that of Patrick and Ellen (O'Donnell) Cantwell. Of their ten children who survived, no fewer than five entered either the priesthood or the religious life. John Cantwell was Archbishop of Los Angeles for thirty years.

Some day, when historians begin looking back over the ministry of Roger Cardinal Mahony, they will surely focus on the influence of his parents, particularly that of Loretta, his mother.

Columnists rarely hear from satisfied readers. Most of their correspondence comes from those who write (or call) to point out errors, disagree with viewpoints or complain about emphasis. One of the attractive qualities of Loretta Marie Mahony was that she knew how to affirm people. Every year, she sent this writer a Christmas card. In the one for 1988, she said that "I do enjoy the articles that you have in *The Tidings*. And may the New Year be a good one for you."

The late Father Victor E. Roden, rector of Los Angeles College, often recalled that when Loretta delivered Roger to the preparatory seminary in 1950, she told him: "I have twins, but you can only have one of them." Not surprisingly, Loretta was proud of her priest son and she didn't hesitate to speak her mind on that subject. When young Father Mahony was ordained a bishop in 1975, she wrote to Cardinal Manning: "My family and I wish to express gratitude and appreciation of the honor of bishop given to Roger. I know that with your help and guidance, he will be able to accept the greater responsibilities of this new office . . . my cup runneth over." In his own hand, Cardinal Manning thanked Loretta "for giving Roger to the Church. We all knew he was episcopal material. The only issue was 'when.' God bless him. We are all richer for his being with us."

Shortly after Roger's return to Los Angeles as archbishop, Loretta phoned the Archival Center and wanted to know if we would like to have the scrapbooks she had compiled over the years. She admitted that she had fallen behind. "I couldn't keep up with him."

When I discreetly asked if she had cleared the idea of giving the albums to the archives with "himself," she replied: "Well, they're mine and I can do with them as I please." I offered to pick them up, but she insisted on delivering them personally. I'll stop and see Victor while in the neighborhood." (Her husband is buried at San Fernando Mission Cemetery.)

Not since Ellen Cantwell spent her final years in Los Angeles has the archdiocese had a "first mother." Loretta Mahony filled that position with dignity, poise and grace, preferring to keep in the background at her modest home in Saint Norbert's Parish in Orange. Loretta appeared pleased but unimpressed when informed that she qualified for a place in the *Guiness Book of World Records* as being the "only woman in American history to witness her son elevated to the cardinalate."

As mentioned by Msgr. James Peterson in his funeral homily at Saint Charles Church in North Hollywood, Loretta was not overly awed with ecclesial pomp. An example was her demeanor while in Rome for the cardinalatial investiture where she insisted on attending all the long and physically exhausting ceremonies. When asked how she was bearing up with it all, she said: "Quite honestly, my feet are killing me."

Though anything but a pretentious person, Loretta could hold her own. The late Helen Scott Ziemann liked to recount the time she and her son were attending a ballgame in Peter O'Malley's box at Dodgers Stadium. In introducing herself, Mrs. Ziemann proclaimed to bystanders that "My son is a bishop." When it was her turn, the little lady at the end of the row replied: "How nice, my son is a cardinal."

Historians of another generation will undoubtedly have much to say about the archiepiscopal tenure of Roger Cardinal Mahony. But this much is certain: His mother was one fine lady!

MARIANO MALARIN (d. 1895)

Mariano Malarín was a pioneer Catholic layman whose life spanned two cultures in California. During his colorful career, he successfully met the formidable challenges of adapting to the new American lifestyle.

Born to Juan and Josefa (Estrada) Malarín, Mariano began and completed most of his schooling in Peru. He returned to California upon his father's death in 1849, and assumed charge of the family's holdings. As Malarín became materially prosperous in his legal, business and ranching endeavors, he was always mindful of the needs and aspirations that others less astute than himself experienced.

He served the commonweal in Monterey County as judge and supervisor and, in 1859, Malarín served the first of his two terms as a member of the California State Assembly. During his years in the legislature, Malarín sponsored a number of useful and innovative programs. He was resolutely opposed to a resolution suggesting that the United States seize part of Nicaragua for a transit route.

Farsighted man that he was, Malarín also favored railroad development and was a supporter of the ambitious (but unrealized) plan put forth by the Sacramento Valley Railroad for extending its lines. In 1859, Mariano married the beautiful and popular daughter of Francisco Perez Pacheco, Isidora. Pacheco was a rancher who owned vast properties in Central California.

The magnificent wedding took place in the old *presidio* chapel at Monterey, San Carlos Borromeo, on October 25th. The couple was blessed with two daughters.

In addition to watching over the extensive holdings inherited by his wife, Mariano became a distinguished member of the San Jose bar. He also served as founding President of the San Jose Safe Deposit Bank, which was later sold to the Bank of Italy.

Things didn't always go smoothly for Mariano Malarín. There were, for example, many difficulties in maintaining the boundaries of his land, a factor which forced him into complicated legal battles and claims in Federal courts.

The Pacheco–Malarín land had numerous orchards, vineyards and olive trees. It was later dedicated exclusively to raising herds of cattle and sheep. Mariano was a careful businessman during a time when that ability was necessary for survival.

When Mariano died, on April 28, 1895, he was buried in the Catholic cemetery at Santa Clara. The death notices, referring to him as a "capitalist and banker," were complimentary. His importance is indicated by obituaries in the San Francisco *Call* and the Sacramento *Union*.

In 1891, Mariano Malarín dictated the "history of his life" to one of Hubert Howe Bancroft's agents. That transcription has recently been edited and annotated by Dr. Albert Shumate of San Francisco and published in monograph form by the California History Center at De Anza College. In his preface to Malarín's reflections, Dr. Shumate notes that "few Californios met with such notable success" in moving from one culture to another as did Mariano Malarín.

ALEJANDRO MALASPINA (1754–1810)

Though descended from noble blood on all four grandparental sides, Alejandro Malaspina (1754–1810) ultimately suffered the cruelest of fates, that of dying in total obscurity. He lost his military rank, his reputation and his freedom.

Malaspina was born in Mulazzo, in the Duchy of Parma, a city in modern Italy which was then under the protection of the Spanish crown. On November 18, 1774, he entered military service and was assigned to the Naval Department at Cadiz, where he rapidly rose to prominence.

By the time of his visit to the far west, Malaspina had a distinguished record as a naval officer. He had taken part in several naval engagements with the British during the War for American independence

On July 30, 1978, Malaspina left Cadiz as commander of a scientific expedition of exploration and discovery, the last of its kind under the aegis of Carlos III, who had died the previous year. After protracted months in northern waters, Malaspina sailed south aboard the *Descubierta* and *Atrevida* to California, stopping at Monterey on September 12, 1791, for rest and relaxation.

Malaspina and his crew visited San Carlos Borromeo Mission where his biographer states that "they took delight in learned conversation with these soldiers of Christ." Members of the expedition portrayed Fray Fermin Francisco de Lasuen as enthusiastic about their collections of natural history. The friar dispatched neophytes to gather appropriate botanical specimens, collect Indian artifacts and provide information on a variety of subjects of interest to the visitors.

The officers praised Lasuen as a man of intelligence, exemplary in conduct and doctrine, with uncommonly good manners. He was described as affable, humble and "religiously abundant" in his hospitality. Alejandro Malaspina vigorously defended the mission system, arguing that certain foreign authors had confused the system with its abuses and ignored its primary objectives, thereby painting it as horrible and oppressive.

He pointed out that the Spaniards, without the slightest shedding of blood, had brought an end to a thousand local wars that were destroying the Indians and had provided them with the beginnings of a sound social life. They had taught them a pure and holy religion, provided them with safe and healthful food and fostered in them such respect that the friars could traverse, all alone and without a guard, the forty to fifty leagues inhabited by neighboring nations. The fact that unconverted Indians came daily to the missions and *presidios* in search of work and food was looked upon by Malaspina as a tribute to the Spanish method.

After returning to Spain, Malaspina fell victim to a sinister political conspiracy. He was tried, convicted and sent to jail in 1796, where he lived until 1802 when he was released and banished from the empire. Officially, Malaspina had become a non–person and the fruits of his scientific labors were nearly lost completely.

In 1914, a portion of his journal was discovered and printed in the *California Historical Society Quarterly* and, in 1960, the monumental tome on *Malaspina in California* by Donald C. Cutter was published by John Howell Books. Finally, after almost two centuries of oblivion, Alejandro Malaspina was restored to his rightful place in California annals.

JOHN B. MANNIX (1843–1913)

John B. Mannix (1843–1913) can be classified as "a type of that class of Catholic layman which is all too few in numbers; a man who never shirked the responsibilities that came from Catholic duty, while at the same time he was tender and considerate of the beliefs of all sincere men, whatever might have been their religious affiliations."

The young Irish lad, a native of Ballybunion, in County Kerry, immigrated to the United States, in 1854, fortified with a deep and abiding sympathy for the poor and down–trodden, and with a tenacious and dedicated determination always to stand defiantly, if necessary, for the cause of liberty. Educated in the public schools of Delaware, Ohio, John continued his studies at Ohio Wesleyan University and the Cincinnati Law School. He served as legal counsel in the Buckeye State between 1866 and 1888.

Throughout his career, Mannix was, to quote a contemporary account, a "striking example to refute the common acceptation of distrust that the lawyer cannot be honest, inasmuch as the very atmosphere in which he lived breathed the spirit of wholesome integrity and square dealing." From May 15, 1873, when he married the talented author and poet, Mary E. Walsh, "his heart was first in the bosom of his family where every Catholic man rests his highest hopes of earthly consolation in the discharge of his duty."

Mannix brought his wife and seven children to San Diego, in 1888, where he became actively identified with the civic and cultural interests of the community. He was first president of the Ancient Order of Hibernians, a charter member and first Grand Knight of the San Diego Council of the Knights of Columbus and, in 1908, the president of the San Diego County Bar Association. In all these posts, Mannix was acknowledged as a scholarly man "interested in all that concerned the Church as well as the community in which he lived." Though personally lacking the advantages of a Catholic education, Mannix untiringly campaigned for "the need of it particularly in this country to stem the tide of infidelity and to strengthen the faith of our children."

The daily life of the southland lawyer spoke loudly and eloquently of the consolation derived from living in harmony with the principles of his religion. He stood for all those finer and more delicate sentiments that portray the character of a real gentleman. The late Joseph Scott, in an address delivered during August of 1913, eulogized John B. Mannix for having the quiet, unpretentious bearing that goes with the man of sincere conviction—the man who cares but little for the world's applause or its confirmation, provided his own conscience is satisfied. Here was a man who "recognized the stern and rigorous duties of a child of God and of the strict accountability which every man must realize for himself when he passes into the presence of the Searcher of all hearts."

GUGLIELMO MARCONI (1874–1937)

Guglielmo Marconi was born at Bologna, on April 25, 1874, the son of an Italian father and an Irish mother. His accomplishments were destined to revolutionize the scientific world. Early in 1895, Marconi began experiments with electromagnetic waves and succeeded in establishing communications over distances ranging upwards of a mile.

The following July 2nd, he was given a patent in England for a system of transmitting and receiving messages by wireless telegraphy, thus heralding in a new age of communication. In 1909, Marconi won the Nobel Prize in Physics. He later received the Prince Albert Medal from the Royal Society of Arts.

Marconi's experiments with "short waves" began during World War I, in an attempt to devise a directive system of wireless telegraphy for military purposes. Outstanding scientist that he was, Marconi found time for other pursuits. He was a plenipotentiary delegate to the Peace Conference in Paris and later served as President of the Pontifical Academy of Sciences. He was nominated to the Italian Senate by the King and created a Marchese, in 1929. Marconi visited the United States as a member of the Italian War Mission to the American Government. He died at Rome, on July 20, 1937.

Early in 1939, the San Francisco *Call–Bulletin* called for a popular subscription to raise funds for a monument honoring the inventor of the wireless. Mayor Angelo J. Rossi agreed to serve as honorary President of a Citizens Committee organized for that objective.

The completed monument, erected on the northern face of Telegraph Hill, was dedicated with considerable fanfare on September 9, 1939. Pope Pius XII sent personal greetings for the occasion, expressing the prayerful hope that "this magnificent memorial may serve to enshrine in the hearts of all peoples the memory of one whose gifts to humanity and to the advancement of its welfare were little short of miraculous."

The Holy Father saw the erection of the memorial as "a very striking and symbolical refutation of the contention of those who, in their attempts to disprove the existence of a Divine Intelligence, would have the world believe that Religion and Science are diametrically opposed." In a cover letter, Luigi Cardinal Maglione scribed Marconi as "a devout Catholic and a renowned scientist." The papal Secretary of State noted that Marconi's "sturdy faith in Almighty God found courage and strength for the pursuance of his efforts to harness, for the benefit of humankind, some of the God–given forces of the Universe." His Eminence concluded his letter with the observation that Marconi's "astounding success has, indeed, made possible a happier, better life for his fellow beings and, at the same time, has brought greater honor and glory to his Divine Creator." California had indeed honored a worthy and God–fearing man.

JACQUES MARITAIN (1882–1973)

Jacques Maritain (1882–1973), the great Catholic philosopher and international luminary of the 20th century, first travelled to the United States in 1933. He later wrote his reflections about visiting Saint Ann's Chapel at Palo Alto, where he was impressed with the artistic depictions of the famous Andre Giraud.

> What struck me first, upon entering the mystery of the chapel was a sense of all–pervading life and vividness; and, then, the mastery with which the frankness and the power of affirmation of color is tuned to the infinite delicacy and sweetness of the nuances of light.
>
> On your left, all along one of the sides of the chapel, are the stations of the Cross, a series of large pictures which advance, so to speak, in tiers; for the wall is composed of oblique segments that overlap one another, each one of which is lighted by a particular aperture.
>
> On your right are the windows—a continuum of light which constitutes the whole other side of the chapel. . . . It is impossible to describe the melodious variety of forms, the fluid harmony of lines and the fineness, the tenderness of the hues and embroidery of light of which their glory is made.
>
> The windows of the Palo Alto church are consecrated to the teachings of Jesus: The first to the parables, the second to the Sermon on the Mount, the third to the instructions to the disciples and the announcement of persecutions, the fourth to the last teachings, before and after the Resurrection, and to the symbolic gestures of the Mass.
>
> I remember especially the hieratic gravity of this last window—and the grace and joy of the images in the parable of the wise and foolish virgins; or in that of the lily of the valley more splendidly dressed than Solomon; and the spirited, so sweet and so alive grandeur of the scene of the Sermon on the Mount; and some translucid sporadic faces which seem mirrors of mystical love.
>
> An extraordinary generosity animates the art of Andre Girard, and appears in a striking manner in the entire decoration of the church of Palo Alto. This generosity is nourished by faith and intelligence, an assiduous meditation on the Gospels, and a contemplative pondering over the things he paints.
>
> With the human and divine mysteries of the stations of the Cross he has lived for long years, trying indefatigably to translate them into an appropriate imagery. Never perhaps has he represented them with so power-ful a rhythm and so fascinating a pictorial eloquence as in the chapel of Palo Alto.
>
> Both in the stations of the Cross and in the windows one feels the rare and invaluable conjunction of genuine religious inspiration and genuine artistic mastery.
>
> After leaving this church, one keeps on dreaming of it, and remains under the spell of the emotion it has awakened; and one thinks that despite all the difficulties of our times, the eternal possibilities of sacred art are still alive, depending no longer on the well–established resources and unity of the collective mind but on the personal effort and insight of some heroically disinterested artists.

Some years after Jacques Maritain visited Palo Alto, his reflections were printed in monograph form by the Pied Piper Press. The booklet was illustrated with original serigraphs by Andre Giraud.

PATRICK HENRY McCARTHY (1863–1933)

Characterized as an "invincible dictator of the industrial world,"Patrick Henry McCarthy (1863–1933) was the unrivalled leader of the strongest, most powerful and best governed labor organization in the United States. A tall, husky man with a flowing moustache, McCarthy ruled San Francisco's Building Trades Council from 1898 to 1922. The B.T.C. was, at that time, acknowledged as organized labor's strongest contingent in the country's premier union city.

Born in Ireland's County Limerick, McCarthy began life as a carpenter, apprenticed to a prosperous builder, James McCormack. His first strike was against a Catholic Church under construction. After a stint in Chicago, McCarthy moved to Saint Louis, where he organized the United Brotherhood of Carpenters and Joiners of America. That group was destined to develop into a body of skilled mechanics with national influence.

Arriving in San Francisco in 1866, McCarthy and a group of construction workers challenged small contractors for higher wages. So great was his clout that he was able to close down any projects which failed to meet his demands.

By the turn of the century, McCarthy had organized more than fifty disparate locals into a centralized, disciplined Building Trades Council. Among the first demands was that of an eight hour day. The closed shop became an impregnable reality in the San Francisco building trades.

"P.H." and his assistants traveled up and down California organizing BTCs from San Bernardino to Eureka. Everywhere, McCarthy promised to give the best work for the pay, and he delivered on that promise. The fire and earthquake of 1906 further solidified McCarthy's unions who signed up workers to begin replacing the

28,000 structures destroyed by temblors, fire and dynamite. McCarthy recommended "No Greed, Small Profits and Plenty of Western Patriotism" in the BTCs weekly journal.

In 1907, McCarthy entered politics and that eventually proved to be his greatest mistake. Two years later he became the first labor leader elected a mayor of a major American city. He openly pledged to make San Francisco "the Paris of America," a slogan misunderstood in many circles. ("P.H." explained the slogan as his wish that "a resurgent San Francisco should quickly take its legitimate place once more among the truly great cities of the world.")

McCarthy was not as adept a politician as he had been a union leader and he was forced to step down after a single term as Mayor of San Francisco. He continued to serve the BTC, however, until 1922. Because, in later years, McCarthy kept his membership from striking, correctly reasoning that strikes would lead to open shops, the work force angrily repudiated him. The resilient McCarthy then became a stalwart Republican and a real estate developer.

He remained a force on the labor scene until his death in 1933. And in his final years, McCarthy devoted more time to ecclesial affairs. He remained a close friend of Archbishop Edward J. Hanna.

NORMAN A. McDONALD (1833–1912)

With the demise of Norman A. McDonald (1833–1912), the Church militant in Southern California lost a member whose faith was "the inspiration of a long life of honesty, integrity and usefulness." Of Scottish descent, McDonald was born and reared in Canada. He inherited good morals from his parents and learned from them the habits of economy, industry, promptness and truthfulness which characterized all his activities.

Journeying to California in 1849, McDonald was among the first of the adventurers seeking their fortunes in the gold fields. On February 6, 1871, he married Catherine Redmond, daughter of a prominent pioneering family.

Led by climatic as well as vocational considerations to cast his lot in the southern part of the state, McDonald eventually settled in Los Angeles. From that time onward, the area's history is closely interwoven with his life story. For many years he was among the southland's most influential citizens, active in the Pioneer's Society, the Knights of Columbus and the Saint Vincent de Paul Society.

During much of his life McDonald was associated with the railroad industry. He supervised the building of the Los Angeles Independent Railroad running between the city and the harbor at Wilmington. After completing this first railway in Southern California, McDonald continued as general overseer for the line until the advent of the Southern Pacific which he subsequently served for twenty years as roadmaster.

McDonald foresaw a marvelous future for the city at a time when there were few indications of its coming prosperity. For his close identification with the religious, civil and social life of Los Angeles, he earned a reputation for his sterling character traits, unswerving integrity and honesty of purpose. The clear and penetrating judgment of the Canadian–born railroader was obvious in his keen, intelligent eyes and dignified demeanor. Evidence abounds that Norman A. McDonald was widely esteemed for that strong mental and moral timber which, more than any other agency, contributed its telling strokes toward California's supremacy.

Typically McDonald died "in the harness of charity." With the passing of that deeply devout Catholic layman, a local newspaper observed that Los Angeles had "lost a pioneer citizen whose work and ability to conduct large enterprise did much for the upbuilding of the city."

GARRET McENERNEY (1865–1942)

Garret McEnerney (1865–1942), the long–time Dean of the California Bar, was truly a significant figure in American history, one who changed for better the society in which he lived. Born of Irish parents at Napa, the son of John and Margaret McEnerney was educated at Saint Mary's College. After some years with the firm of Spencer and Henning, he launched his legal career at San Francisco in 1886.

While still a relatively young man, McEnerney achieved an extraordinary reputation in his chosen profession. In 1889, he entered partnership with Dennis Spencer. He later practiced with George Maxwell and, in the years after 1895, he became an esteemed lawyer for the business giants of his time.

The period of McEnerney's life stretching from the end of the Civil War to the outset of World War II marked a dramatic development in California and the nation economically, socially and politically. And McEnerney was an integral part of it all. His early prominence is attested by his appointment as a regent for the University of California in 1901, a position the socially conservative counselor occupied until his demise.

McEnerney's long and rewarding career was marked by many notable distinctions. For example, following the 1906 destruction by fire of legal documents in San Francisco, McEnerney was commissioned to draft legislation to accommodate that unfortunate event. The subsequent McEnerney Act is still in use. Courage, alertness, endurance, friendliness and diplomatic informality are among the descriptive terms applied to McEnerney. At the height of his career, he was widely acknowledged as a "quasi–public institution."

Though an astonishingly quiet and shy person, McEnerney was a singularly gracious man. Born the same year as the indomitable Father Peter C. Yorke, their careers paralleled each other in the development of city, state and region.

In 1902, he was named counsel for the United States in presenting before the Permanent Court of Arbitration claims against Mexico—the first such case presented at The Hague. During the ensuing forty years, McEnerney's devoted service to three successive Archbishops of San Francisco won him a coveted place of honor in California's ecclesial annals.

Though he was married twice, the first time to Elizabeth Hogan (d. 1900) and later to Genevieve Green (d. 1941), McEnerney left no offspring. His will was remarkable for its charitable provisions.

Over the years, the distinguished jurist built and retained one of the finest private law libraries in the nation. Today his name is perpetuated by the Garret W. McEnerney Law Library at Boalt Hall, University of California, at Berkeley. Truly Garret W. McEnerney fulfilled the American dream of spiritual identity, material success and personal advancement which Irish immigrants sought for their children. As his biographer has noted, " the greatest beauty of this personal story is that the central figure achieved success by the always comfortable engagement of talent in an open society which, though it demanded talent, also allowed it to spring freely from a natural source."

JOHN STEVEN McGROARTY (1862–1944)

A. POET LAUREATE

Of John Steven McGroarty, it was said that no man has caught the spirit of California from the beginning of the coming of the Spanish *padres* down to the present time and gathered it together into one continuous golden thread such as this great man has done. "His sense of the religious basis of the original settlement of our state not only illumined his writings about that portion of her history, but ran down through his appreciation of modern–day California."

Named Poet Laureate of the Golden State on May 15, 1933, McGroarty later represented his adopted commonwealth in the United States Congress as a representative from the eleventh congressional district. His column in the Los Angeles *Times*, appearing under the title "From the Green Verdugo Hills," was published for over forty years and won for McGroarty a place in almost every home in the southland. A man of endless talents, the Pennsylvania–born author and poet spent his early years in teaching, journalism and politics. Although licensed to practice law in Pennsylvania and Montana, McGroarty spent his life in California and it was there he won his fame.

Though he wrote a number of books, both prose and poetry, the name of John Steven McGroarty will best be remembered for his famous Mission Play, a production seen by almost 2,000,000 spectators, most of them non–Catholics, including President Calvin Coolidge and William Butler Yeats, the famous English poet

The idea of the play came from Frank Miller, founder of the Mission Inn in Riverside. Miller, himself a Quaker, wanted McGroarty to write a Nativity Play which could be shown each Christmas season at Riverside. The completed production told the story of the bringing and founding of Christian civilization to the Western shores of America. After Vice President Thomas R. Marshall saw the play, he remarked to McGroarty, "Some men may write a history, dry as dust; some may produce a drama, full of fire but wholly false; but it has been given to you to blend historic accuracy with dramatic power, and thus both to please and instruct mankind."

In addition to his books on California lore,

John Steven McGroarty

McGroarty served as editor for some years of *The West Coast Magazine* and his contributions to that journal are a valuable part of California's Catholic Heritage. This great pioneer, born just a month after Lincoln's Emancipation Proclamation, went home to God on the eve of his 82nd birthday, August 7, 1944. The night before he died, the gentle poet answered a query about his health in the lines of his last poem:

When I have had my little day
My chance at toil, my fling at play,
  And in the starry silence fall
  With broken staff against the wall,
May someone pass, God grant, that way,
And, as he bends above me say:

Goodnight, dear comrade, sleep you well,
Deep are the daisies where you fell,
  I fold your empty hand that shared
  Their little all with them that feared
Beside you in the rain and sun—
Goodnight, your little day is done.

JOHN STEVEN McGROARTY (1862–1944)

B. GIFTED REPORTER

The role of a responsible newspaper is among the most vital functions of society. There is a dignity which is its grandeur; the sincerity which is its truth; the thoroughness which is its massive substance; the sterling principle which is its force; the virtue which is its purity; the scholarship, mind, humor, taste, versatile aptitude of simulation and beautiful grace of method which are its powerful and delightful faculties and attributes. All these qualities abounded in the journalistic accomplishments of John Steven McGroarty (1862–1944).

A glowing tribute to McGroarty, delivered on the occasion of his retirement from the United States House of Representatives, by John E. King, editor of the Hemet *News*, is worthy of recalling for another generation:

> We think of John Steven McGroarty as a many-sided genius, of kaleidoscopic changes of mood and tempo. We view his success in the varied lines of his endeavor as editor, as poet, as dramatist, as historian, as statesman, and yet the horizons of each blend as harmoniously as do the colors of the iris. Running through them all are the lines of the patriot and the gentleman as gleams of golden light.

> We newspaper folk think of John Steven McGroarty first as the gifted reporter, giving the lights and shadows of human life, bereft of the barbs of unkindness, unfairness, envy. Ever he was radiating smiles and joy, and no heart was hurt by the poison of bitterness. We think of him as the master of poetic beauty, as evidenced by the lays of his adopted California, "down the middle of the

world." We think of him as the father of the movement to restore the missions, and of his efforts to give later generations the place in history that belongs to Junípero Serra.

> We think of him as author and director of the Mission Play, as friend and comforter to the Indian, as almoner to the weak and weary of every race and clime, as friend and guide to the oppressed and the downtrodden. We think of his work in the halls of Congress; of his efforts for the silent masses of the downcast and discouraged, too often without a friend in the courts of the mighty. In all his varied labors he has given the strength of a great enthusiasm, the charm of a great idealism. From his endeavors has come little of material wealth, but in the hearts of his countrymen there is the gold of love and esteem, of sincere appreciation.

> I have often lingered in fancy upon the idea of that strange, diversified, wonderful procession—here the dazzling visage of Wattersen, there the woeful face of Medill, here the glorious eyes of Dana, there the sparkling loveliness of Bryant and Prentice—which moves through the chambers of a memory across the storied stage of journalism.

> The thought is endless in its suggestion and fascinating in its charm. How often in the chimney–corner of life shall we—whose privilege it has been to rejoice in the works of this great journalist, and whose happiness it is to cluster around him in love and admiration—conjure up and muse upon his manifold virtues as we have seen them in the exemplification of his genius. The ruddy countenance, the twinkling gray eyes, the silver hair, the kind smile, the hearty voice, the old–time courtesy of manner—how tenderly will they be remembered! How dearly are they prized!

JOHN STEVEN McGROARTY (1862–1944)

C. YOUTHFUL OLD MAN

In August, 1943, after his own entry into the Ancient and Honorable Order of Octogenarians, John Steven McGroarty recorded some personal reflections about being "alive and well, free from aches or pains, busy with the day's work, still fit to earn a living, and no fault to find with the way fate had dealt with me." Though the world of those days was in "an age of feverish excitement that assaults man both in body and in mind with relentless cruelty, tearing his nervous system apart, blasting his mental and physical structure, hurrying him to an untimely end, leaving him mere junk to be picked up by the chief of all scrap gatherers—the undertaker," the state's poet laureate found many valid and weighty reasons to be appreciative and grateful to the "giver of Life."

He recalled that his long life had been after all, "a pleasant road that had more of joy than sorrow in it, more of laughter than tears." Though admitting that he had "blundered often and often lost my way," McGroarty looked upon that as "the story of most other men, and not either particularly or exclusively mine."

At eighty–one, McGroarty had strong ideas on the question of growing old. "The notion persists," he said, "That, like the age of man's body, the age of his mind and soul is measured by years. Nothing could be farther from the truth. Many of the oldest minds in the world, of which by no means the least number are to be found in the United States, have not yet reached their thirtieth birthday. They are fixed and set as to every conceivable question. They have definitely decided everything. That which they do not know—and what an infinity it is!—is not worth knowing, and indeed should not be known at all. Minds and temperaments such as these have reached advanced old age, not of course as measured in terms of years, but in fact. This explains many of the follies of those young persons who are not youthful and who probably never will be. Their recurring birthdays measure change only, not growth."

McGroarty went on to explain that "the open, alert, vigorous and well–disciplined mind bent upon the achievement of high ideals in practical fashion, facing new facts and new problems as the passing years reveal them, always willing to change a point of view or to alter a policy if new facts and new conditions so warrant, is youthful by nature no matter how many years may have passed over it. The mounting years find it growing no older but keeping itself youthful, and manifesting that youth in a hundred ways."

After all, he noted, "the plain fact is that the world's best's work is now being done, and always has been done, by men of youthful and forward–facing minds, no matter how many years of time may have passed over their heads and brought age to their physical frames." Those men "may have the likelihood of many years before them or they may have but few; nevertheless, the quality of youthfulness, of eager pursuit of wise and justified progress, is the same in them all. Unhappily one may be young without being youthful, but happily one may be old without being aged."

McGroarty's parting advice was: "Try to be youthful young man. . . . Try to keep youthful old man. . . . Above all else, do not ever forget that years of bodily life are no measure of intellectual age and capacity. To forge a fixed and arbitrary rule in terms of years as the limit of a man's usefulness or human service, would only be to behead a large portion of the world's intellectual and moral leadership and thereby to impoverish mankind."

JOSEPH McKENNA (1843–1926)

The third Catholic and second Californian to serve on the United States Supreme Court was Joseph McKenna (1843–1926), an astute State legislator of sharp political prudence. McKenna's earliest years in the Golden State were spent at Benicia, where his father opened a bakery in 1855. After graduating from Benicia Collegiate Institute, Joseph was admitted to the Bar and opened a law practice at Fairfield.

In the summer of 1865, McKenna was elected District Attorney for Solano County, a position which he occupied with distinction for the following decade. He served as a Republican member of the State Assembly in 1875–1876. The youthful politician was nominated for the House of Representatives in 1876, as a candidate for the Third Congressional District. He lost the election by less than a thousand votes. Joseph married Armanda Bornemann in 1879, a union blessed with three girls and a boy. During the forty–five years of their wedded life, the strikingly handsome Armanda was the constant confidante of her husband.

Mr. McKenna was elected to the Forty–Ninth Congress in 1884. His four year tenure as a Washington legislator was described by one commentator as "unblemished and conservative." President Benjamin Harrison appointed McKenna to the Circuit Bench in 1892. Five years later, President William McKinley selected Judge McKenna Attorney General of the United States, an appointment which Archbishop John Ireland attributed to the Chief Executive's gratitude for Catholic support in his bid for the presidency.

Known to the Department of Justice as a hard–working and exacting administrator, McKenna served as Attorney General only two years. In 1898, he was named Associate Justice of the Supreme court. During the ensuing twenty–seven years, McKenna championed the plight of the depressed and fulfilled what he believed was "the most serious duty of this court," that of protecting the liberties of those who looked to the Constitution for freedom from duress.

In his 650 written opinions, Justice McKenna evidenced loyal and fraternal responsibility to the principles of justice. He was reasonably favorable to organized labor and rather nationalistic in his concept of federal power.

McKenna was a lifelong and devout Roman Catholic. His biographer reports that the jurist "followed the ceremonies and liturgy with intelligence and discrimination, and as he walked home he usually expressed a critical estimate of the sermon". On the occasion of his retirement from the Court, in 1925, Chief Justice William Howard Taft praised McKenna in these words:

> Your pride in the Court, its high tradition and its courage has made deep impression on us who have enjoyed the benefit of your greater experience, example and *esprit de corps*. Your fraternal nature, your loyalty

toward each of us, your tenderness in times of strain and stress endear you to us and make us feel deeply sensible of our loss.

JOSEPH MESMER (1855–1947)

In the commercial and industrial history of Los Angeles, as well as in the record of its civil progress and development, the name of Joseph Mesmer occupies a prominent place. The son of Katherine Forst and Louis Mesmer was born in Tippecanoe, Ohio, on November 3, 1855. His parents brought their young son to California by steamer via the Isthmus of Panama, eventually settling in Los Angeles.

It was said of the youthful Mesmer by one chronicler that during the years that his parents conducted the United States Hotel he was known by, and knew more people than any other person in the city. In his boyhood days, while roaming around the country or delivering bread to customers, Mr. Mesmer traveled over almost every yard of territory now within the confines of this city. He could at that time speak the Spanish language as fluently as a native born. Shortly after his graduation from Saint Vincent's College, Joseph was sent to Europe, where he completed his education at Strasbourg. Upon returning to California's southland, Mesmer spent several years helping his father complete work on the new cathedral for the Diocese of Monterey–Los Angeles.

On March 22, 1879, Joseph married Rose Elizabeth Bouchard. This first wedding solemnized in Saint Vibiana's was witnessed by Bishop Francis Mora, a long-time friend of the Mesmer family. In 1878, Mesmer opened the Queen Boot and Shoe Store on North Main Street. When the city's thoroughfares were eventually paved and the need for boots to cope with the dust and mud eliminated, the name of the establishment was changed to the Queen Shoe Store. Mesmer disposed of his interests in 1906, and the following year gained control of the Saint Louise Fire Brick and Clay Company.

Though business affairs occupied much of his time, Joseph Mesmer was active in politics. He was a Democratic party leader and served for a while as president of the Jackson Club, the largest political organization of its kind in the state. He was one of the freeholders who drafted the city charter for Los Angeles, and subsequently held positions on the City, State, and Federal Planning Commissions and the Metropolitan Water District of Southern California.

Mesmer's appellation as the "Father of the Los Angeles Civic Center" was well deserved for, of his many contributions to the development of Los Angeles, the most important was his sponsorship of the plan to buy Downey Block, which was located at the northwest corner of Temple and Main Streets. He was also a leader in raising money to purchase the property which was then turned over to the government for use as a Federal building. This outstanding Catholic layman and advisor to five southland bishops was "a man of strong character, keen and alert mentality, broad in views and wide in sympathies, sincere and straight forward in all his relations with his fellow men."

HELENA MODJESKA (1840–1909)

Shortly before her death at Newport Beach, on April 8, 1909, the great stage actress, Helena Modjeska, whispered to those around her bed: "I hope that heaven is as beautiful as California." Now there was a discerning woman!

Born at Cracow, on October 12, 1840, Helena Opid demonstrated a natural beauty and innate talent that augured well for the theatre. Early on she learned how to play the piano and converse in several languages. Soon after eloping with Gustave Modrzejewski (a name she later shortened to Modjeska), Helena made her stage debut. Within a few short years, her reputation had spread throughout Poland and much of Europe.

Because of her questionable marital status, Helena was shunned by society. The people who admired and acclaimed her on stage ignored her socially. It was during those years that Helena began finding consolation in her Catholic faith.

She later married Count Karol Chlapowsk and emigrated to the United States, where she quickly gained theatrical prominence in a second career. Helena was acknowledged as one of the country's leading ladies of the stage. For many years, her thespian counterpart was Maurice Barrymore. She became the god–mother for his three children, Lionel, Ethel and John. In her autobiography, Ethel credits the conversion of the entire Barrymore family to the devout and personal faith of Helena Modjeska.

As a youngster, Helena had been an unwanted child. Though raised a Catholic, Helena's memories of her loveless home gave her a special predilection for the plight of young women.

Wherever she traveled, Helena would visit the local Catholic shelters for unwed mothers and talk with the young girls. She tried to give them the inspiration to believe that they, too, could change their lives for the better. She also donated considerable amounts of money to support projects for adoption of children.

America's "renowned tragedienne" gave her final performance, the sleepwalking scene from Macbeth, at a benefit for victims of the earthquake that leveled Messina, Sicily, in 1908. Tears flowed as the thin and frail Modjeska played her last role and played it well. Though the audience applauded for almost thirty minutes, she was too ill to acknowledge the acclaim.

When she died early the following year, Helena was mourned by many people, especially the scores of unwed mothers for whom her strong faith served as an inspiration. Countless youngsters born in those years were christened "Helen" for Madame Modjeska.

One of Helena's oldest friends and most enthusiastic fans was the Right Reverend Thomas J. Conaty, Bishop of Monterey–Los Angeles. He had first seen her perform at San Francisco where she starred in the French tragedy *Adrienne Lecouvreur*. In his tribute to Madame Modjeska, the prelate recalled that she "loved to portray truth and virtue and to act it not only on the stage, but better still, in her own life." He said that she will always remain "as one of the best examples of art wedded to truth and virtue."

WILLIAM R. MOLONY (1879–1976)

Shortly after the turn of the century, a young graduate of the Medical Department of the University of California attached his name to a small office on the second floor of a rooming house at Fifth and Broadway. He lived on to treat great grandchildren of those patients and, by the time of his demise, was the oldest practicing physician in Los Angeles.

William R. Molony was born on March 1, 1879, the son of Richard Molony and Catherine Fermessy, at 35 Vine Street (now Central Avenue). He was baptized a few days later in the old Plaza Church of Our Lady of the Angels. He was in the first class of the parochial school opened by the Sisters of the Immaculate Heart of Mary at the cathedral in 1886. The octogenarian vividly recalled the many times he served Holy Mass for Bishop Francis Mora during his years at Saint Vibiana's.

Young Molony subsequently studied at the University of Denver. It was there that he met Leona Egerer. They were married in Denver's Cathedral of the Immaculate Conception on July 3, 1897. The five youngsters born from that bond grew to eleven grandchildren and twenty–two great grandchildren. After finishing his studies at the College of Medicine of the University of Southern California, Molony took his internship at the California Hospital. In 1901, he became resident physician at Idyllwild Sanitarium. In 1905, Doctor Molony was one of three resident physicians given charge of the Department of Anatomy at his *alma mater*. He served as Director of the Anatomical Laboratory until that facility was absorbed as the Los Angeles Department of the College of Medicine by the expanding University of California in 1911.

Later he returned to the College of Dentistry of the University of Southern California as Professor of Anatomy and Associate Clinical Professor of Medicine in charge of forensic jurisprudence. Despite his manifold duties, the doctor had been engaged in private practice without interruption since 1901. Prior to 1905, when he purchased a Saint Louis one cylinder automobile, he made his house calls by streetcar (during the daytime) and by bicycle (after midnight when the railway closed down).

In later years, when his office was in the Mason Building, the doctor was frequently visited by Mother Cabrini whom he remembered as "a woman of saintly appearance, very humble, with a pleasant face and appealing eyes."

Though he never sought nor held political office, Dr. Molony was an active supporter of his party over the years. He was known personally by every governor since 1913, when Hiram Johnson appointed him to the California Board of Medical Examiners, a post he held for twenty–seven years, many of them as president. Molony was one of those rapidly vanishing "general practitioners." With the exception of the eye, ear, nose and throat men, when he first began medicine, there was not a single "specialist" in the city and every doctor, by necessity, was surgeon, family physician and specialist simultaneously.

Dr. Molony served as president of the County Medical Association and for twelve years as a member of the American Medical Association's House of Delegates. He took an active part in the battle against subsidized medicine in the early New Deal days and later when similar proposals were suggested by Governor Earl Warren for California. In 1942, Molony became president of the Catholic Medical Association and was three years president of the A.M.A.

Although later sharing office space with his physician son, Dr. Molony never had an assistant. Among the 3,300 babies he has delivered were the three Cremins brothers, all of whom became priests in the Archdiocese of Los Angeles. Molony was a familiar figure in Catholic organizations. He joined the Newman Club in 1905, and later served a term as its president. He was active in the Ancient Order of Hibernians and became the oldest charter–member of Los Angeles Council 621 of the Knights of Columbus.

Of all his charitable contacts through the years, the doctor cherished most his long–time association with the Little Sisters of the Poor. The venerable physician spent his Wednesdays at 2700 East First Street, dispensing medical advise to the "oldsters" cared for in Saint Anne's Home for the Aged.

JOHN JOSEPH MONTGOMERY (1858–1911)

A. FIRST FLYER ON WINGS

In 1883, Edison's electric light was only four years old, the photograph six, and the telephone eight. Men who experimented with controlled flights were objects of ridicule and so it happened that John Joseph Montgomery made the "first flight on wings without headlines or fanfare of any kind." The son of California's famous Zachariah Montgomery, Assistant United States Attorney General in the Cleveland administration, John was a cousin of the Right Reverend George T. Montgomery, first native–born Bishop of Monterey-Los Angeles.

Even as a youth, Montgomery was fascinated by the possibility of air travel and he spent long hours analyzing the flight of seagulls in San Francisco Bay. Later, he studied physics at Santa Clara College, and, following his graduation from Saint Ignatius College in 1880, Montgomery built and tested several ornithopters in his primitive workshop facilities. Six years before the widely heralded flight of Otto Lillienthal near Berlin in 1891, Montgomery constructed and had ready for use the world's initial air–supported glider.

Early on an August morning in 1883, John and his brother James loaded a newly constructed glider on a wagon and covered it with hay so as to attract no attention. On the crest of a gently sloping hill on Otay Mesa, just south of San Diego, the two brothers waited for the right moment. When a breeze finally came up, James grabbed hold of a forty–foot tow rope, and the glider, with John Montgomery aboard, soared to an altitude of thirty feet, for about an eighth of a mile, 603 feet toward the ocean.

It was an epochal day for John Joseph Montgomery had made the first *successful* attempt to fly a heavier–than–air ship, seventeen years before the Wright Brothers made their initial glider flight and twenty years prior to the powered flight on December 17, 1903, at Kitty Hawk.

In the following two years, Montgomery built three more gliders to demonstrate his theory, now an accepted principle, that a curved wing section is essential to flight. He later originated the tandem monoplane type of craft which formed the basis for the aerodromes of Samuel Pierpont Langley. In 1897, Montgomery was named Assistant Professor of Physics at Santa Clara and given a workshop in the basement of the college. There he built a glider or "aeroplane" named the *Santa Clara*. When that glider, piloted by Daniel John Maloney, was pulled up to 4,000 feet by a hot air balloon, on April 29, 1905, it set a world record by remaining aloft for twenty–two minutes.

Other aeroplanes were built and demonstrated at exhibitions in the years prior to the San Francisco earthquake. In Montgomery's own words, "the earthquake wrought such disaster that I had to turn my attention to other subjects and let the aeroplanes rest for a time!"

Montgomery was killed in a test flight on October 31, 1911, in Evergreen Valley when his single wing glider stalled in take–off and nosed over. During the two previous weeks, he and his companion, Joseph Vierra, had made fifty–five successful flights in the plane to which Montgomery had planned to attach a power–driven engine. Unfortunately, many of John Montgomery's effects, along with his pioneer glider, were washed into San Diego Bay when the Otay Dam burst in 1916, demolishing the Montgomery ranch buildings. And so it is that this First Man to Fly (so declared by the Austrian Flying Technical Society in 1910) remains known only to aeronautical historians.

JOHN JOSEPH MONTGOMERY (1858–1911)

B. BLESSING REFUSED

The spectacular flight of John Montgomery's ash-wood tandem–wing aeroplane, on April 29, 1905, was hailed by the press as "one of the most notable achievements of the present scientific age," Christened the *Santa Clara* in honor of the Jesuit college where Professor Montgomery had constructed "the strange bird–like machine," the ship elicited from Alexander Graham Bell the observation that "all subsequent attempts in aviation must begin with the Montgomery machine."

Fifteen hundred anxious spectators gathered for the exhibition flight which was scheduled as the major event of the traditional "President's Day" at the college. Among those especially invited to watch Daniel J. Maloney, become "the first man to fly maneuvered flight" in air was John Montgomery's half–cousin, the Coadjutor Archbishop of San Francisco. At precisely eleven o'clock, when preparations for the flight had been completed and the balloon which was to launch the aeroplane on its flight was inflated, Father Robert McKenna, with a number of other priests and vested attendants, walked to the center of the field to bless the novel machine.

The flight was a stunning success. The ship was hoisted to an altitude of 4,000 feet by Frank Hamilton's giant balloon and then released. Momentarily the *Santa Clara* paused motionless and then the "frail assemblage of rods, wire ribs and oiled muslin" began a demonstration of its capabilities. According to an eye–witness account of the fifteen–minute flight,

> The aeronaut directed his course straight against the wind and proceeded, in an all but level plane, for over three hundred yards, He then turned, the wings forming an angle of forty–five degrees, and dashing back with

frightening speed, he succeeded by the same manipulation of the wings to turn again and to move downwards. This process was, apparently without effort, repeated several times, before the courageous pilot made up his mind to alight.

The final descent was perhaps the most marvelous feature of the flight. He was about 1,500 feet above the Santa Clara Mill, with lumber piles and telegraph wires and trees beneath. The field of his own choosing lay at a great angle from him; but that was nothing. By the aid of the wind he mounted several yards, and turning made a great dive for the field. Like a meteor he shot through the air, and such was the velocity of the descent that had it not been checked, it would have ended in ruinous disaster for both aeronaut and aeroplane!

By a simple turn of the wings, however, the speed was checked and by a second dive and turn the aeronaut alighted with such ease and grace, that no one could imagine, had he not witnessed it, that the man had, but a moment before, a velocity of over a hundred feet per second.

Years later, Robert Ripley revealed in his famous "Believe it Or Not" series that Archbishop George T. Montgomery refused the invitation to bless the aeroplane on the grounds that "it could some day become a source of frightful war bombing!" It was apparently this apprehension that influenced Father McKenna to add the petition that "Archbishop Montgomery's fears of disaster by warplanes to the human race might not be realized."

While John Montgomery's biographer asserts that the prelate's reluctance to bless the machine may have been a "deliberate courtesy to the local Jesuit Fathers," the fact remains that the archbishop was the first to speculate on the unhappy consequences that did indeed occur, in later times, when weapons of war took to the air.

ZACHARIAH MONTGOMERY (1825–1900)

A. BIOGRAPHICAL SKETCH

Zachariah Montgomery was born on March 6, 1825, near Bardstown in Nelson County, Kentucky, a descendant of colonists who came to America seeking religious freedom with Lord Baltimore. He studied at Saint Mary's College in Marion County, Kentucky and later at Saint Joseph's in Bardstown, where he received a Master of Arts degree in 1849. The following year, young Montgomery was formally admitted to the bar.

In legal circles, Montgomery was known as a man who "gave to his work that earnest, zealous and persistent effort which characterized all his undertakings, and with which his natural ability and strength of intellect rendered him so formidable at the bar . . ."

With borrowed capital, Montgomery set out in July of 1850, for Sacramento. His first two years in the Golden State were spent in mining camps but in 1852, he moved to Shasta and resumed the practice of law. A short while later he formed a partnership with the widely known Francis L. Aud at Marysville. Two years after the death of his first wife, Helen Frances Graham, Zachariah was appointed District Attorney for Sutter County, where he soon acquired a reputation as an "able, vigorous prosecutor, though always just and fair in his practice." On April 28, 1857, he married Ellen Evoy and with her as his companion reared eight children.

As a candidate on the Democratic ticket Montgomery was elected to the State Assembly in 1860, where he expressed vigorous opposition to the mounting pressures which eventually brought on the Civil War. During the conflict itself Zachariah showed deep sympathy for the Confederate cause. In 1864 he temporarily retired from law to take up journalism in Oakland. He established the *Occidental* at San Francisco, a weekly paper that first appeared on October 29, 1864. "It was an independent journal, devoted largely to the publication of the news and discussion of the topics of the day but in the main its editorial columns were given to the subject of public education." The paper ceased publication in 1868.

Montgomery returned to his legal profession in 1868, and some years later moved to San Diego where he founded the *Family's Defender*, a "journal devoted almost exclusively to the subject of education, strongly and vigorously opposing the public school system of education, and advocating in its stead a system based on parental authority and control."

Despite his outspoken views, Montgomery was named Assistant Attorney General of the United States in 1885, by President Grover Cleveland, a post to which he came highly qualified. Zachariah Montgomery spent the final years of his life in Los Angeles where, among other pursuits , he acted as legal counsel for his nephew, the Right Reverend George T. Montgomery, Bishop of Monterey–Los Angeles.

Concerning his religious convictions, it was known that Montgomery was a life–long and ardent member of the Catholic Church. He was deeply conversant with its teachings, and realizing, the Catholic belief in all its followers, his faith was as strong and firm as conviction itself." Death came to the noted jurist on September 3,

1900. At his funeral, held in Saint Vibiana's Cathedral, Father Joseph Barron said:

> He was of the heroic school, endowed with giant stature that towered aloft above his fellow men. In trials and troubles and amid the battles and general warfare of an unusually active, life he maintained that steady adherence to principle which was his supreme satisfaction during life and his crowning consolation at his death.

ZACHARIAH MONTGOMERY (1825–1900)

B. DROPS FROM POISON PEN

Though he was widely known for a multitude of accomplishments, Zachariah Montgomery (1825–1900) is especially remembered for his views on education, which he spelled out in a booklet entitled *Drops from the Poison Fountain* (Oakland, 1878). Therein Montgomery cited statistics from the United States Census Bureau to prove that "vice and crime had grown in this country in direct proportion to the growth and development of our public school system."

Montgomery's platform really was quite basic. He held that parents having the ability to do so, are bound by the natural law not only to feed and clothe but to educate their own children. He emphasized that while "every parent or guardian [is] entitled to have his or her child or ward educated at public expense," the choice of school and teacher should be left to the parents' discretion, provided only that adequate standards are maintained. Montgomery further believed that only in those cases where this cannot be done should the public come to the parents' assistance by supplying means necessary for a good practical education. Zachariah's proposals placed emphasis on parentalism, leaving out altogether denominationalism. He thought that "no religious instruction which may be given in any school should be at public expense" nor subject to the supervision of state examiners.

For over forty years Montgomery fought the school question "on a strictly parental and non–denominational basis" and during most of that time he was beating down the false notions, both of Catholics and non–Catholics, that he was fighting to get money for Catholic schools. In Montgomery's plan, "the whole business of education and training the young should, like other professions, be open to private enterprise and free competition." He did not ask for an endorsement by the hierarchy of his proposals, pointing out that "when it comes to so shaping the laws, as to remove all legal barriers standing in the way of the faithful discharge of that great duty, that is the work of the layman."

Surprisingly enough, Montgomery did receive encouragment from twenty–five American bishops (and Henry Edward Cardinal Manning) though His Eminence thought that "the priest or bishop who undertakes the two jobs of running the Church and the state, is in great danger of spoiling them both.") The overall program was enthusiastically discussed at a public meeting held in San Francisco on October 7, 1879, at which the state superintendent of education presided. There was even considerable support of the plan from non–Catholic sources. Montgomery's views were more widely diffused after 1881, when he founded the *Family's Defender* at Oakland, a "journal devoted almost exclusively, to the subject of education, and advocating in its stead a system based on parental authority and control."

Throughout his long campaign, Montgomery made it clear that he bitterly opposed the *pro–rata* division of public school funds earlier suggested by Archbishop John Hughes of New York. It was a highly interesting though unsuccessful proposal that Zachariah Montgomery brought to the public's attention. When one bears novel proposals such as these discussed at modern educational meetings, he might recall the man who gave impetus to such ideas in years when they were highly unappreciated.

ZACHARIAH MONTGOMERY (1825–1900)

C. FAMILY'S DEFENDER

Zachariah Montgomery (1825–1900) was widely known in California for his views about education. In the fall of 1864, he established the *Occidental* newspaper in San Francisco as "an independent journal devoted largely to the publication of the topics of the day but in the main its editorial columns were given to the subject of public education." The quest for educational betterment was a consistent theme throughout Montgomery's life. Several of his books and a host of pamphlets were devoted exclusively to the parental role in the pedagogical process.

Montgomery's most lasting contribution to the literary realm was the journal he founded and edited through four years of existence. The prospectus for *The Family's Defender Magazine and Educational Review* described the publication as one given "to miscellaneous topics, but most especially to an exposure of the crying evils resulting from the unjust, extravagant and anti–parental features of the public school system now prevailing throughout the United States." In the initial issue of the journal, released in January, 1881, Zachariah Montgomery informed readers that *The Family's Defender* had been "established for the special purpose of fighting for educational reform."

The Kentucky–born editor pledged to approach the

school question from a parental standpoint, maintaining the equal rights of all before the law, without regard to political or religious differences, upon principles which are sanctioned by the leading churchmen of every religious denomination." Published successively at Oakland, San Diego and Fruitland, the journal perdured for twenty–four issues. Though originally a monthly publication, it was adjusted to quarterly status with Volume II, in 1882.

The circulation extended "to about every State in the American Union." Yet, by the end of 1882, Montgomery noted that "success in extending our circulation has not been commensurate with our desires, nor with the importance of the principles we are seeking to promulgate." At the same time, however, the editor assured his readers that *The Family's Defender* would continue, quoting one correspondent who had written that "heaven, with all its artillery, is on our side." Though advertised as "an independent, non–partisan, non–sectarian monthly magazine and educational review," Zachariah Montgomery claimed that the journal consistently "received the most unqualified indorsement *(sic)* of every Roman Catholic bishop and archbishop who has expressed an opinion on the subject."

It was a reluctant editor who announced that *The Family's Defender* would be discontinued with the issue of October–November–December, 1884, not as "a matter of choice, but simply a matter of necessity." Mr. Montgomery concluded his journal with the "proud consolation of knowing that during its four years of existence it has never had occasion to lower its colors, or turn its back to its foes." Thus was born, nurtured and succumbed a unique literary excursion into a sacrosanct realm of California's educational process.

MARY YOUNG MOORE (1882–1971)

The title of papal countess, an ancient one in the Church, was abrogated by Pope Paul VI in the 1970s. One of the two women to bear that designation in California's southland was Mary Young Moore. Born in Immaculate Conception parish in Los Angeles on November 7, 1882, the daughter of Robert B. and Mary C. (Wilson)Young , Mary was raised in the south central area of the city.

Miss Young studied at the old Immaculate Heart College and was later active in the National Conference of Catholic Charities where she befriended Father William Corr. She was a member of the Academy of Political Sciences and the Catholic Women's Club in the 1930s.

In October of 1940, on the recommendation of Archbishop John J. Cantwell, Mrs. Moore was awarded the *Pro Ecclesia et Pontifice* medal by the Holy Father. In

1946, she was made a Dame of the Holy Sepulchre and, four years later, a papal countess upon the request of Archbishop Francis J. Spellman of New York.

Mrs. Moore lived in a home at Hoover and Olympic in Los Angeles. Later, she purchased property at Figueroa and 7th street which subsequently became the headquarters of Barker Brothers Department Store. There is no archival evidence as to when she married her husband W. T. Moore. A heavy–set woman of regal bearing, she later moved to Altadena, where she became a parishioner of Msgr. Corr. Mrs. Moore was the principal benefactor for the magnificent Marian shrine modeled after that of Our Lady of Lourdes in France.

In a history of Saint Elizabeth Parish in Altadena, the late Msgr. Robert Brennan felt that it was "not out of place to pay special tribute to Countess Mary Young Moore for her unassuming yet constant and munificent offerings to the parish over many years."

Brennan goes on to say that "the convent itself was erected as a personal memorial to her mother and grandmother." He concluded by saying that "now that she has passed from the local scene Countess Mary Young Moore is still very much alive, and it is well to be mindful of her and to pray that her goodness to us will receive its blessed reward." Mrs. Moore's charities were not restricted to Altadena. She also assisted Msgr. Bernard Dolan of Long Beach by donating the property (or the cost of it) for Saint Anthony's School.

While it is not clear where Mrs. Moore's wealth originated, most of it probably came from oil. She owned a gasoline station across the street from Saint Elizabeth's Church in Altadena and, when she died, the station was willed to the parish. At some unrecorded date, Mrs. Moore, by then a widow, moved to New York, where she became a confidant of Francis Cardinal Spellman. She appears to have been a shrewd business woman and reportedly owned a considerable amount of real estate in the Empire State.

Mrs. Moore died at the advanced age of eighty–eight on October 23, 1971. Terence Cardinal Cooke of New York was the principal celebrant of her Requiem Mass which was offered at Saint Philip's Church in Pasadena. Always a shy woman, Countess Moore's charities were as unheralded as they were manifold. She is remembered chiefly today by students at Moore Catholic High School in Staten Island, New York.

THOMAS D. MOTT (1830–1904)

Those who worked side–by–side with Thomas D. Mott during his many years of service to Southern California referred to the New York–born pioneer as the "Father of Modern Los Angeles." Mott's sojourn in the business world began at the age of fourteen, when he launched his career as a clerk in one of Schuylerville's small merchandise stores. Since the youngster's natural aptitude and ambition led him to look for a more inviting field, he came to California in the early days of the Gold Rush era, by way of the Isthmus of Panama.

After acquiring working capital by laboring in the mines, Mott went into business for himself at Stockton. At twenty–one the young adventurer successfully planned and put into operation a ferry system over the San Joaquin River, a project that eventually turned into a highly lucrative investment.

In 1852, Thomas Mott moved to the southland where, nine years later, he married Ascencion Sepulveda, the daughter of one of the Golden State's most prominent citizens. With his "natural gift of organization and an ambition to master men and affairs," Mott entered the political arena in Los Angeles, first as a Democrat and later, when his party turned to silver, a Republican. He was elected first county clerk in 1863, and served in that capacity for three consecutive terms. During that particular period, the office included the duties subsequently performed by the county recorder and auditor.

Mott fought in the state legislature for construction of a rail line over the Tehachapi and through Soledad Canyon. His efforts are credited as principally instrumental in bringing the Southern Pacific to Southern California, a strong factor in the early development of Los Angeles. The indefatigable pioneer was also one of the organizers of the Los Angeles Chamber of Commerce. In 1886, he built the first large business block south of First Street in the City of Our Lady of the Angels.

In later life, Thomas Mott was "won by the beauty of Catholic worship" and "humbly knelt as a suppliant for its rites and blessings," thus joining his wife, four sons, and daughter in the Faith. One well–known writer recorded of Mott: "No man anywhere ever possessed a more radiant and charming personality. All through his life he had been noted for his unerring manliness, his irreproachable rectitude, his liberality and his love of home."

At the time of Thomas Mott's death in February of 1904, Bishop Thomas J. Conaty of the Diocese of Monterey–Los Angeles noted that "all regarded him as every inch a man whom all were proud to know and whose friendship it was a privilege to possess." Even a cursory glance at the life of this man inclines one to agree, "By her rich and varied resources California has drawn to her unshackled energies the sons of many states and countries." These pioneers, "while promoting their personal interests, at the same time advanced the welfare of their adopted state and have been found on the side of progress and justice in every cause."

ANNIE McGEOGHEGAN MURPHY (d. 1902)

Few women in California's Catholic heritage have played a more conspicuous role socially and philanthropically than Annie Murphy. Her entire life was devoted to helping others less gifted and favored than herself. And she did it all with a grace and dignity worthy of the saints.

A native of New York, Annie McGeoghegan emigrated to the west in the mid 1800s. Her subsequent marriage to Bernard D. Murphy united two persons totally dedicated to personifying the Gospel message of justice and charity. From her earliest days on the Pacific Coast, Annie was noted for her charitable enterprises. Her purse was always open to the needy and no woman was ever more loved by those whom she befriended.

The Rancho *Pastoria de las Barregas*, where the Murphys resided, was legendary far and wide for its hospitality. It was customary to feed dozens of poor people daily and Mrs Murphy was never so happy as when doing something for others. No family in California was more widely respected or favorably regarded than the Murphys, of which Annie was the most generally known and universally beloved member.

It comes as no undeserved praise to report that the greatest portion of Annie Murphy's life was spent in devising ways to make others happy and comfortable. And, in that pursuit, she became a living portrayal of Christianity.

According to one newspaper account, "her womanly tact; her social eminence; her gentle nature; her numberless and unheralded charities, all endeared her to an ever increasing number of devoted friends." In her later years, Annie gave much of her time and attention to the Catholic Ladies' Aid Society. Her gifts to the Church were unlimited and she was long remembered for all that is best in womanhood.

Annie's demise, on February 18, 1902, saddened the entire State of California. The inhabitants of San Jose were especially affected for no lady in that city's history ever enjoyed a wider circle of admirers. Considering her many accomplishments, one is not surprised that Annie's funeral was the largest and most imposing ever recorded for Santa Clara County. People from all parts of the state were present, the morning trains bringing in large delegations from San Francisco and other places.

It can be said that no California woman in the pre 1900s more completely ingratiated herself in the hearts of those who appreciate womanly sweetness, purity and worth than did Annie Murphy. And perhaps that's why one commentator noted, at her passing, that "death indeed in this instance has chosen a shining mark!"

DANIEL MURPHY (1855–1939)

The man for whom Daniel Murphy High School is named was " an eminent citizen, a man who in the days of his strength was a leader in public affairs, whose advice in critical circumstances was eagerly sought and always respected." Born in the farming community of Hazelton, Pennsylvania, on September 20, 1855, the son of Thomas Murphy and Anne Rafter spent his early years as a developer of oil interests throughout the expanses of Oklahoma. In the late 1870s, after becoming interested in railroading, young Murphy came to California as an employee of the Southern Pacific.

Murphy belonged to a generation of men whose rugged individualism contributed mightily to the growth of American civilization. Gifted with physical strength, rare intelligence and common sense, he faced and surmounted the problems that confront every pioneer. Descended as he was from a people acquainted with poverty and self denial, Daniel launched his business career with a courageous heart and mighty vision. At Needles, which he helped to develop as a townsite, Murphy established a mercantile house, opened a bank, provided domestic and commercial utilities and inaugurated a chain of refrigerating plants for the Santa Fe Railroad.

Shortly after the turn of the century, Murphy expanded his business interests to Los Angeles, where he engaged in petroleum and cement production, and participated in organizing the Brea Canyon Oil company. He was also among the founders of El Segundo's Standard Oil refinery, in 1911. During World War I, Murphy lent his talents to the inauguration of the Los Angeles Shipbuilding and Dry Dock Company.

A notice in the diocesan newspaper, for May 18, 1906, records that "Mr. Dan Murphy has lately returned from a visit to Needles and the theatre of his old and new mining interests. If there is anything in which the Irish–American shows superior quality it is in procuring gold and silver out of the earth, and Dan is no mean hand at that."

Daniel Murphy never allowed temporal success to diminish his reliance on Almighty God. Tried as he was in the furnace of affliction, the poor, the widow and the orphan never appealed to him in vain. He served as a trustee for the diocesan seminary and a board member for the Catholic Welfare Bureau as well as the Convent of the Good Shepherd. His heart was as big as his noble frame, and social organizations like the Red Cross, Travelers' Aid and Community Chest rarely looked his way without results. Bishop John J. Cantwell noted that Daniel Murphy "made the recipient of his bounty doubly happy because he always gave with pleasure and not with reluctance."

The stage of his life was darkened before the curtain fell, inasmuch as Murphy's final years were heavily burdened by the ailments of advancing age. On September 14, 1939, just a year and a half after the death of his wife, Antoinette, the eighty–three year old pioneer passed away quietly at his stately home, 2076 West Adams Boulevard. "A mighty oak had fallen by the wayside and Los Angeles mourned an eminent citizen."

MARTIN MURPHY (1807–1884)

The career of Martin Murphy (1807–1884) illustrates what an enterprising man could achieve in his life–span as a citizen of California. Young Martin journeyed to Canada from his native Wexford, in 1828. Three years later, he married Mary Bolger in Quebec's French cathedral. After another decade, the Murphys moved to Missouri.

"With renewed hopes of the benefits of religion, educational opportunity and agricultural success " Martin and his family emigrated to California in 1844, and settled in Sacramento. He purchased the *Rancho de Ernesto*, along the Consumnes River where, in June, 1846, the Bear Flag Revolt was initiated. Murphy's daughter Elizabeth was the proto–youngster born of emigrant parents in California.

The first wheat ever grown in the Sacramento Valley was raised on the Murphy ranch. Despite the allurements of quick wealth, the Irish–born pioneer preferred to remain on his ranch and took no part in the gold rush or its resulting speculation. In 1850, Murphy moved to the rich agricultural valley of the Santa Clara River where, for almost four decades, he utilized the experience of his varied life and natural talents to building a new community in California. He subsequently acquired large tracts of land in the central portion of the state, southward to San Luis Obispo.

Martin obtained definitive title to the *Rancho Pastoria de las Borregas*, a 4,000 acre tract of land bordering San Francisco Bay, in 1860. It was on that extensive ranch that the city of Sunnyvale was projected. His astute business acumen, combined with precision, honesty and prudent management eventually enabled Martin Murphy to become the largest individual land owner and cattle raiser on the central coast.

A longtime friend of Bishop Joseph Sadoc Alemany, Murphy contributed generously to the development of the Catholic Church in the post–mission years. The Dominican prelate often stopped at the Murphy residence, where special quarters were always reserved as the "Bishop's Room." Though himself a man of little book–learning Murphy appreciated the value of and need for educational opportunities. He played a significant role in establishing the Jesuit College of Santa Clara and was among those financially responsible for opening an academy for girls by the Sisters of Notre Dame de Namur, in San Jose.

By the time of his demise, on October 20, 1884, Santa Clara's most respected, widely–known and oldest citizen had earned an honored place in the annals of the local and regional community. Martin Murphy was aptly eulogized as "strict but not over–harsh in business matters, liberal but not unobtrusive in charities, warm as a friend, generous as a foe, and prompt in all things."

MARTIN MURPHY, SR. (d. 1865)

Martin Murphy Sr. was one of California's earliest pioneers. None of those pathfinders was more universally respected, affectionately remembered or widely known. His name stands as a synonym for generous hospitality in a country where that term had its origin.

A native of Ireland, nurtured on Wexford's historic soil, Martin imbibed a love for his fatherland which characterized his lifestyle to the end of his days. In 1820, Martin, his wife Mary and their children resolved to emigrate to the Canadian colonies. Disposing of their leasehold, they embarked for the New World, reaching Quebec near the end of the year.

Martin was able to purchase land in the Township of Frampton, thirty miles from the quaint old town that gave its name to the province. The long cold winters, with their mountainous snow–drifts and chilling winds, together with the countless inconveniences of frontier life were borne with cheerful Christian patience. The Martin home became the center to which all newcomers from Eire turned while seeking a haven for themselves. Soon their village became a virtual Ireland–in–exile.

In 1840, Martin and his family bade farewell to his friends and set out for Missouri. There they made their home in Holt County, then part of the Platte Purchase area. They found the soil fertile, the climate mild and the way–of– life pleasant. Unfortunately the malarial fevers common to the area prevailed and Mrs. Murphy succumbed to the dread disease on June 9, 1841

Not long afterwards, a Catholic missionary told Martin about California which he portrayed as a land of health, where almost endless summers reigned. It was quite enough to convince the Murphys about a third and final move. The family and a group of friends began their westward trek on May 6, 1844, reaching the Pacific coast in November of that same year.

The toils and dangers of their journey were considerable. Deep rivers had to be forded, roads made passable and natives placated. The difficulties of the route were augmented by the lateness of the season. Snow had fallen when they reached the Yuba and further progress was exceedingly treacherous.

The Murphys eventually settled in the Santa Clara Valley. There Martin found the glorious realization of his hopes in a soil of rare fertility and a climate of equable proportions.

His home at the *Ojo de Agua de la Coche* became known by all who travelled along *El Camino Real*. His generous hospitality was shared by the distinguished men of all nations who held the reins of leadership in the state. Clergymen, soldiers, statesmen and authors loved to linger there. In 1854, Martin erected a commodious chapel on the San Martin Ranch where the Catholic families of the neighboring regions could fulfill their religious commitments.

To the end of his life, Martin Murphy never faltered in the performance of his religious and social obligations. He personally attended to business and real estate dealings in the areas under his care. He succumbed on March 16, 1865. Martin Murphy preferred to live in the prayers not the praises of those who knew him. He was his own almoner. He broke bread with the needy and the orphan. He shrank from public applause and press notoriety and loved his peaceful surroundings.

His life in word and deed inculcated strict obedience to the commands of God and a faithful compliance with the laws of the land.

ERNEST ETIENNE NARJOT DE FRANCEVILLE (1826–1898)

Ernest Etienne Narjot de Franceville (1826–1898), described by his biographer as a "versatile genius," captured on canvas scenes that entitle him to a prominent place among the early painters of California. Narjot came from a family of artists. Both his father, Philippe Pierre, and his mother, Madelaine Garnier, were accomplished painters as were several of his cousins. Retracing the footsteps of those among whom he was raised, young Ernest began his education at a Parisian school known for the excellency of its graduates in art.

The French–born artist came to San Francisco in 1849. In the decades that followed, no man on the Pacific Coast "made a stronger attempt to truthfully depict the country life and habits of the people" in portraits, landscapes and frescoes.

One of Narjot's best portraits was that of Joseph Sadoc Alemany, the Dominican Archbishop of San Francisco, which he completed in 1878. The story behind that painting is interesting, inasmuch as it illustrates the prelate's humility and the artist's patience. The archbishop consistently "shunned portraiture of any kind" and while Narjot and Alemany were close friends, it was only by a carefully planned strategy that the artist succeeded in capturing the features of his elusive subject on canvas.

"Fortunately, Narjot had keen powers of observation, and on various occasions when the archbishop officiated, he made it his custom to be present." Albert Dressler further relates that in this manner Narjot was able to photograph Alemany's likeness upon his memory and then translate it faithfully to canvas.

The finished oil portrait was raffled off for a benefit accruing to old Saint Mary's Church. Winner of the drawing was the aunt of Frances M. Molera who placed the prized art object in the chapel of her home, at 2055 Sacramento Street. When this writer visited Miss Molera, on May 14, 1963, she related that Alemany's successor, Archbishop Patrick W. Riordan, occasionally offered Holy Mass there during his years in the Bay City. In 1965, the painting was given to the Holy Family Sisters, a community of which Archbishop Alemany was a co–founder. It presently hangs in the novitiate house at Mission San Jose, California.

Narjot's portrait of Alemany, aside from its artistic worth, is the only contemporary likeness of the archbishop and, as such, it has served as the basis for all subsequent depictions of San Francisco's well–beloved prelate.

The final years of Narjot's life were spent with his wife, Santos Ortiz and their three children, in almost total obscurity. Narjot had contracted a permanent eye infection while decorating the tomb of Leland Stanford. His accomplishments were further overshadowed when many of his works were destroyed in the fire of 1906.

The spirit of a master painter's work can never be completely obliterated, however, even though it rests for a time in oblivion. Fittingly enough, the painting for which Narjot received the least recompense, that of Archbishop Joseph Sadoc Alemany, remains the one for which he is most generally remembered. That portrait embodies, perhaps more than all his others, Narjot's "strong instinct of the picturesque, when combined with life and movement."

JOSE MARIA NARVAEZ (1771–1840)

Though Jose Maria Narvaez (1771–1840) was a memorable figure in New World annals, very little is recorded about this Spanish–born map maker and naval pioneer. In addition to a few references to Narvaez in the de la Guerra papers at Santa Barbara Mission, there was a solitary pamphlet published at Vancouver in 1941 about the *Pilot Commander Don Jose Maria Narvaez.*

Born in Leon, Jose Maria joined the Spanish Navy at the tender age of ten. In 1788, already an assistant pilot, Narvaez sailed from La Paz aboard the freighter *San Carlos* to explore the Pacific coast. Later, while commanding the schooner *Santa Gertrudis*, he explored the Straits of Juan de Fuca and mapped out sites for possible ports. On the return voyage, he was influential in capturing the British sloop, *Princes Royal.*

Narvaez established a Spanish settlement in Nutka Sound, mapped the Bay of Good Hope, discovered the archipelago of San Juan and the channel known as Rosario (Puget Sound). He made numerous maps, some of which were subsequently used by George Vancouver and Alejandro Malaspina. Narvaez rose to the rank of lieutenant and travelled the coast of the Californias in command of the brig *San Carlos.*

After the independence of Mexico, Narvaez became a provincial representative of the Patriotic Society of Guadalajara and a strong supporter of the new government, even though he was of Spanish origin. In 1822, he was asked to accompany Canon Agustin Fernandez de San Vicente to Monterey to establish a new government in Alta California. They arrived at Monterey on September 26th. On March 9, 1823, Narvaez was placed in charge of the 10th Naval Department of San Blas, a position which he occupied during a period of great internal conflict in the new republic.

Probably the most important of the maps executed by Narvaez is the one of 1822 whereupon he listed the population of each mission and *pueblo* of Alta California. In that map he charted the Indian *rancherias* and divided the area into four districts, with rather arbitrary boundaries. That important document now resides in The Library of Congress.

From all indications, Narvaez was an extremely skilled cartographer. With remarkable accuracy, he corrected many of the errors and omissions that had crept into earlier maps.

On August 22, 1828, Narvaez became a commercial captain. He commanded the schooner *Dorotea* on which Jose le la Guerra sailed to Santa Barbara with a set of new regulations for the governance of Alta California.

In 1831, Narvaez arrived back in San Blas aboard the *Maria Ester* from what appears to have been his last voyage to Alta California. Shortly thereafter, with more than fifty years of naval service, Narvaez retired and established his residence in Guadalajara. He died there at the age of sixty–nine, leaving a wife and seven children. (Jose Lopez Portillo, a great, great grandson, later became President of Mexico.)

The late Herbert Eugene Bolton had people like Jose Maria Narvaez in mind when he observed: "What a tragedy that we must wait until heaven to learn about so many of our great California pioneers!"

JOHN HENRY NASH (1871–1947)

A. FRIEND OF ARCHBISHOP

One of Archbishop Edward J. Hanna's closest friends was John Henry Nash (1871–1947), a Canadian–born typographer who moved to the Bay Area in 1895, to begin a tradition of fine printing that lasted for half a century.

In 1916, Nash established his own firm and from it lavishly designed and elegantly produced books for direct sale in limited editions. His works were all done in a grandly impressive style which even today are avidly sought by collectors.

Perhaps Nash's finest work was his edition of *The Divine Comedy* which consumed six years of his time. The beauty of the completed work testifies to the success of his insistence on details. Nash spent the years 1906–1909 in New York City. It was there that he first met the young Father Edward J. Hanna, then a professor at Saint Bernard's Seminary, Rochester. When Hanna came to San Francisco, the two renewed their acquaintance.

The archbishop was frequently a house guest at the Nash residence. One of the noted printer's most beautiful broadsides is an invitation "to join with His Grace in invoking the divine benediction upon the new home of John Henry Nash in the Contra Costa Hills of California."

Nash collectors have numerous other works commissioned by or presented to the archbishop. A particularly lovely book in this category is *The Great Archbishop* which reprinted a silver jubilee tribute from the October 17, 1908 issue of *The Monitor*.

One of the rarer broadsides, dated April 17, 1929, is an invitation to a luncheon at the Palace Hotel where Archbishop Hanna was to speak to the San Francisco Club of Printing House Craftsmen on "The Vatican Library." In his rather lengthy text, Nash points out that "most laymen, their experience of libraries confined to the withdrawal of novels and other popular books, do not understand the importance of libraries and library work in the scheme of civilization and culture.

"It is in libraries that all printed things of permanent value are jealously preserved against the gnawing tooth of time. A library is a 'Domesday Book' of many volumes recording the intellectual and spiritual title–deeds of mankind. Librarians are the learned clerks of the registry office. They are the trustees of the treasure administering their trust for the benefit of all humanity."

Nash recalled that he had visited the Vatican Library and examined some of its real treasures. He said that he had left "with a mind enriched and an ambition to do better work than before." He went on to observe that "The Vatican Library's contribution through the centuries to the promotion of scholarship is a fascinating story that few can tell as admirably as Archbishop Hanna." He told how the archbishop had lived and studied in Rome, enjoying the exceptional opportunities of becoming acquainted with the library's splendid collection of printed books and manuscripts.

Cardinal Achille Ratti was librarian in those days. He was better known in San Francisco as Pope Pius XI. "It adds to the interest of Archbishop Hanna's forthcoming

John Henry Nash

address that he is privileged to call His Holiness a friend." The printer ended his invitation by saying that he regarded Hanna as "a great American, a great San Franciscan" whose readiness to speak to all groups of people "is characteristic of his attitude toward all people of high ideals."

Throughout another decade, the two kindred souls of Hanna and Nash continued to make their mark on San Francisco, the one from the pulpit, the other from his press.

JOHN HENRY NASH (1871–1947)

B. SOCIAL RECONSTRUCTION

The Archival Center for the Archdiocese of Los Angeles has a formidable collection of books, broadsides and other ephemera printed in San Francisco by the late John Henry Nash (1871–1947). Nash was renowned as a printer of fine books. He is especially remembered in typographical circles for his masterful formats, the technical perfection of his workmanship and the completeness of his detail.

The Nash imprint is recognized as synonymous with quality. He was a sound and able craftsman who patiently strove for perfection and one who came closer to that goal than any other printer of his generation.

It was perhaps in the creation of his broadsides, made more frequently "for the joy of doing," that Nash allowed himself the greatest latitude and in those lovely specimens of his art, his personality found its fullest expression. Those "lesser pieces" are now quite scarce, even though they are little known to the general public because of their limited circulation.

The collection at the Archival Center encompasses those books and broadsides from the Estelle Doheny Collection with a Californiana theme, together with several dozen others acquired over the years from other sources. Nash's artistically–designed borders and decorative plates, often the work of Frederick Coyle, are the Nash trademark. He used them lavishly to enhance the work of poets, artists and authors.

Nash himself was an outstanding individual, once described as tolerant but stubborn, self–assertive but humble and ostentatious but simple. He was a man of outspoken likes and dislikes who personified the observation of Stanley Morrison that "the fine printer begins where the careful printer leaves off."

Whether he was printing beautiful books, promotional broadsides, decorating Christmas cards or elaborate announcements, Nash sought always to distinguish his work by the careful use of superlatives.

Among the Nash treasures at the Archival Center is *A Tribute to Mr Edward Laurence Doheny*, a eulogistic memorial written by Bishop Francis Clement Kelley of Oklahoma City–Tulsa in 1935. Housed in the same slipcase is *A Sermon of His Excellency, Most Reverend John J Cantwell, D.D.* which was preached at the Requiem Mass offered for Mr. Doheny in Saint Vincent's Church, Los Angeles on September 11, 1935.

Both of these beautifully printed and elaborately bound books were printed exclusively for Carrie Estelle Doheny. Neither is listed in *A Catalogue of Books Printed by John Henry Nash*, compiled by Nell O'Day in 1937. Possibly they are unique.

Though Nash was not a Catholic, one couldn't sense that from his work on behalf of churchmen and other Catholic figures in the Bay Area. In 1935, for example, he printed a lovely book on *The Great Archbishop* which contained the "Evening Service upon the Twenty-Fifth Anniversary of the Consecration of Most Rev. Patrick W. Riordan, Archbishop of San Francisco." There were only one hundred copies, two of which are at the Archival Center.

Fully a fourth of his other books and broadsides had a Catholic theme. Archbishop Edward J. Hanna publicly acknowledged that service to the Church when he personally presided at an open house at Nash's home in San Francisco.

JOHN HENRY NASH (1871–1947)

C. PROMINENT PRINTER

In addition to being the premier printer of California,

Canadian–born John Henry Nash (1871–1947) was an imaginative and forceful influence among the civic and religious leaders of San Francisco.

An example of Nash's literary talent is the promotional broadside in double spread which he composed and printed to raise funds for Newman Hall at the University of California in Berkeley.

Nash encouraged university alumni and others to pledge their support for what he envisioned would bring about "the Social Reconstruction of the United States and the restoration of Jesus Christ, King of Universal Society." He then went on to speak about the "vision" he had in these words: "Already it is predicted that the East Bay area will become one of the greatest metropolitan areas in the world. Berkeley rates as the cultural and educational center of the West."

In 1939, 'The Golden Gate International Exposition, the Pageant of the Pacific' will draw visitors from all parts of the world.

"So it happens that the land hallowed by Junípero Serra and his noble band is coming in for its own once more and the spirits of the *padres* are looking down from their heavenly outposts for another 'Pageant,' THE PAGEANT OF ETERNITY."

A wave of destructive philosophy is sweeping over the world—the culture of the ages is disappearing—a united front is needed to meet this peril.

Newman Hall the Catholic student center at the great University of California proposes a plan worthy of the Church it represents, a Church stretching back verily to the time of Jesus Christ, her Divine Founder; unbroken in her history of achievement, the greatest the world has ever known in art, in learning, in culture, in everything that makes life worth living.

It seems we are living the Thirteenth Century over again and may expect a RENAISSANCE—in art, in liturgy, in preaching, in music, in studies, in social, political and civil life—such as the Church effected in that period which a prominent historian calls 'the greatest of centuries.'

The plan is educational and aims to bring Catholic scholars to us from any part of the world as visiting professors and lecturers. It is the pooling or concentration of our intellectual forces, representing the highest scholarship in every department of knowledge and putting that scholarship at the service of the largest number of people.

Truth will shine again in its full beauty when this plan is carried out and men will be drawn back to a realization of true values. The stabilization of society, badly shattered by the forces of error, will be once more restored.

In his concluding remarks, Nash called upon "all lovers of the truth and of the finer things of life" to actively promote the drive for Newman Hall at the university of California:

America and its institutions are at stake—the threat to civilization can be met by the Catholic Church alone, the guarantor of man's liberties and of human rights. Our plan is an investment in social security.

What he cogently couched in prose, Nash even more masterfully expressed in typography. His craftfully–designed and skillfully–printed broadside is surely the most beautiful such promotional publication in California annals.

Though broadsides have become collectible in recent years, none is more highly–prized as the one composed, designed and printed by John Henry Nash to announce and promote Newman Hall at Berkeley.

ALEX NAVARRO (1890–1968)

The late Archbishop John J. Cantwell was forever lecturing his priests on the values of punctuality, once bragging that he "had never been late to a religious function." But, if that were true, the real credit belonged to Alex Navarro, Cantwell's faithful and always prompt chauffeur.

Alex was born on February 26, 1890, at Luna in the Philippines, Province of La Union, in northern Luzon. After studying at the Jesuit High School, he joined the United States Navy in 1906. Following his discharge, Alex took up residence in San Francisco where he worked as a vendor for the railroad, a waiter at Carmel and a photographer in his own studio.

During World War I, Alex became affiliated with the Merchant Marines and served for the duration of the hostilities. His ship was used almost exclusively for transporting prisoners to and from Siberia.

After the war, Alex went to work for Father James Cantwell who had succeeded his brother in the curial offices of San Francisco's Archbishop Edward J. Hanna. In 1922, Father James suggested that Alex move to Los Angeles and enter the employ of his brother, John, who had been named Bishop of Monterey–Los Angeles. Alex followed that advice and was placed in charge of transportation at the episcopal residence, then located at 717 South Burlington Avenue. Because Cantwell never drove, he became the official chauffeur for the bishop's many travels.

The diocese was vast in those days, stretching from Monterey to the Mexican border. Alex knew every parish and was often on tour with the bishop for several weeks at a time.

In 1928, Alex returned to the Philippines, where he married Leonor Bautista on August 4th. After a brief stint living in the bishop's carriage house, Alex and his wife moved to Saint Thomas parish. When he subsequently decided to purchase a house, he found that there was a restrictive covenant against Orientals. Father

Joseph T. McGucken, later Archbishop of San Francisco, made it possible for Alex to buy the home.

There were three children in the Navarro family—Mary, who became a pharmacist, and Alexis and Leonor who are college professors and members of the Immaculate Heart Community.

Cantwell, who became archbishop in 1936, rarely appeared at any function without Alex. Possibly the most distinguished passenger ever to ride in the prelate's car was Eugenio Cardinal Pacelli, Vatican Secretary of State, who visited Los Angeles in 1936. It was Alex who taught the young Father Timothy Manning to drive. And it was he who looked after the two Irish hunting dogs, Finn and Rosie, who travelled many places with Cantwell and his sister, Nellie.

The Navarros were an integral part of the episcopal household, even after its relocation to 100 Fremont Place. Leonor cared for the altar linens and albs, and the three girls were often busy at other chores around the house.

Following Cantwell's death in 1947, Alex continued working at Fremont Place under Archbishop J. Francis A. McIntyre. He retired in 1955, after thirty–three years of dedicated service.

When Alex died on April 25, 1968, Bishop Manning presided at his funeral services and Msgr. Benjamin G. Hawkes delivered the homily. He was buried from Saint Thomas Church and interred at Calvary Cemetery. Throughout his long "ministry" for the Diocese of Monterey–Los Angeles, the Diocese of Los Angeles–San Diego and the Archdiocese of Los Angeles, Alex Navarro was always the "professional" who considered his position a distinguished mark of service to God's Church. And, indeed, it was!

THOMAS ATWILL NEAL (1907–1983)

On the Feast of Our Lady's Visitation, a memorial Mass was offered at San Fernando Mission for Thomas Atwill Neal (1907–1983), one of Southern California's most respected booksellers. A graduate of Loyola University, Tom entered the trade in 1925, as an employee of C.C. Parker, the then acknowledged "Dean of American booksellers."

He later hung his shingle at the Hollywood Book Store and, finally, on Saint Valentine's Day in 1933, Tom joined the staff of Dawson's Book Shop, where he became a revered fixture for the next half century. Probably no other person in the area's history appraised, priced or sold a greater quantity of books. The tiny, pencilled code–letters T.A.N. indicated that numerous volumes passed through his hands a half dozen times or more.

Thomas Atwill Neal was a rarity among booksellers—in that he read what he sold. Very few scholars (and surely no dealers!) in the southland were better read in the classics. Tom was rightly regarded as a walking concordance. And he was a practitioner of the written word too. One of Tom's most elusive books is the one he wrote about *Saint Vibiana's Los Angeles Cathedral 1876–1950*, of which only fifty copies were printed by William Cheney.

A goodly number of the almost five hundred catalogues issued by Dawson's were compiled (and often illustrated) by T.A.N. Tom also authored six outstanding miniature books, including *Sixth & Figueroa*, his reflections of four decades among the bookstalls.

One day in the late 1930s, San Francisco's Archbishop Edward J. Hanna paid one of his visits to Dawson's. Always enamored by Tom's knowledge of books, the archbishop suggested that he write a column for *The Tidings*. Not so long afterwards, Tom received a deadline schedule from the editor of the Catholic weekly. That marked the beginning of "Books and Backgrounds," wherein Tom attempted "to showcase the facts about some of the forgotten classics."

An accomplished "pop artist" (those are his words), Tom frequently added his own illustrations to letters, bills of sale, paper sacks and broadsides. He was equally gifted as a versifier and his poetic observations found their way into a wide variety of publications.

Just a few weeks before his death at Saint Vincent's Hospital, Tom's autobiography appeared as Volume XIV in the *Los Angeles Miscellany* series. Entitled *Farewell My Book,* it is a delightful portrayal of a well–spent lifetime in Los Angeles.

Tom noted how his appreciation for books had ripened into an intense letterpress love. He pointed out that "the effects of the miracles of Johann Gutenberg are still with us, and are as deep and clear as the impressions of his editions."

If so many of his patrons and friends loved Tom, it was because he lived what he preached, said what he felt and read what he sold. Proud of his faith, he rarely missed daily Mass at Saint Basil's or other neighboring churches. If he was proud of anything it was that he had a cousin who was a priest (Msgr. William Atwill).

The *liber vitae* or book of life for Tom is impressive. His routine was simple and plain, hardly the kind historians are accustomed to write about. And yet, there are likely few among his contemporaries who were not spiritually uplifted by their having known Thomas Atwill Neal.

FELIPE DE NEVE (1727–1784)

Felipe de Neve (1727–1784), the first residential governor, shares with Fray Junípero Serra, the title of "founder" of Alta California. The descendant of an old and distinguished Andalusian family, Felipe de Neve was a highly intelligent and immensely effective civil official whose five–year governorship witnessed remarkable progress in conciliating the "vast heathendom" comprising the Spanish settlement along the Pacific slope.

He arrived in Vera Cruz, in November, 1764, and for the first decade of his service in New Spain, Felipe de Neve functioned as Sergeant Major of Provincial Cavalry at Querétaro. In March, 1775, he was made *Gobernador de California* with residence in Loreto, moving northward to Monterey early in 1777.

From that time onwards when California gained political autonomy as a full–fledged province, its proto governor successfully coped with a whole range of perplexing problems, some of which threatened the very continuance of Spain's last colonization thrust in the New World.

He updated the fundamental law by which the area was governed, oversaw the foundation of *pueblos* at San Jose and *Nuestra Señora de los Angeles*, imported colonizers from various parts of Mexico, consolidated the supply lines, restructured the financial underbase, fortified the *presidios* and augmented their military personnel. Neve had legitimately achieved, by the time of his demise, a reputation as one of Spain's most accomplished administrators.

A study of the endless feuds with Fray Junípero Serra, the governor's "historic antagonist," reveals the unusual abilities and inborn talents common to both men. Their basic disagreements emanated from a diverse interpretation of the *Patronato Real* as it applied to the California scene.

Neve, indoctrinated with the then–popular concept of regalism felt that he, as the King's deputy, should maintain an active role in policy decisions affecting the missionary foundations. Fray Junípero Serra, on the other hand, vehemently defended the friars against any such outside encroachment in their spiritual pursuits among the natives.

The Franciscan *Presidente* caused the governor untold anguish because of his insistence on operating independently on the civil realm. Though time had eroded much of their significance, the long series of controversies that characterized the Neve–Serra relationship polarized the two factions for the inevitable confrontation that was to occur in later decades. After leaving his position in California, Felipe de Neve was Commandant Inspector of the *Provincias Internas*. On August 21, 1784, by then a brigadier general, the talented governor died at the *Hacienda de Nuestra, Señora de Carmen del Peñablanca*, Nueva Vizcaya.

Though he disagreed with a host of Serra's administrative procedures, Neve had great regard for the overall Franciscan apostolate in California. In one report, he praised the manner in which the friars "have brought to those establishments that state of progress they enjoy today (1783), compared to which there are no other missions like theirs in all these provinces. They have made fertile and fecund a portion of land which they found uncultivated wastes." Despite the wretched state of his health Governor Felipe de Neve managed to etch out for himself a distinguished place among the historical personages of New Spain.

JOHN FRANCIS NEYLAN (1885–1960)

John Francis Neylan (1885–1960) was born into the prosperous family of John and Margaret (Rinn) Neylan, whose wealth had been earned in the pharmaceutical business. He attended Seton Hall and then came west to recover his health after a football injury. Shortly after marrying Gertrude Wiseman of Sacramento, in 1911, Neylan became associated with Fremont Older at the San Francisco *Bulletin*. He also took an active role in the campaign that brought Hiram Johnson to the governor's office.

Governor Johnson named Neylan head of the Board of Control, the chief financial agency of the state government. The youthful journalist reorganized operations, launched new ventures and cleaned up scandalous and shady financial practices. During his tenure, Neylan drove so many rascals out of government that Governor Johnson once jokingly complained that Neylan was running the state government by putting all its officials in jail.

With the succession of William Stephens to the governorship, Neylan moved to San Francisco—there to become a lawyer. He studied jurisprudence at night and was awarded his license in 1916.

Becoming publisher of William Randolph Hearst's San Francisco *Call* in 1919, Neylan subsequently assumed control of political policy for all the west coast newspapers flying the Hearst standard. In his "spare time," Neylan became a strong force in local, state and national progressive politics.

By 1929, Neylan was recognized in San Francisco as the "Czar" of the city's political leaders. In fact, his greater power was the influence he exerted over Hearst and the far–flung Hearst empire. Neylan, like San Francisco itself, was an exception to Irish–American models. He exercised dominating influence in several fields simultaneously. He came to the helm of progressive politics with little opposition and practically no fanfare.

Neylan's political philosophy was simple enough—he wanted to maintain a political and economic balance of power in urban society and this he endeavored to do within the context of law and ethics. Throughout his most active "political" years, Neylan's record in private legal practice remained enviable. He never lost a jury trial and only once did he forfeit an important legal encounter.

Neylan was one of a handful of advisers who could confront and/or turn around the often irascible Hearst. Though both men were generally progressive in conviction, they frequently disagreed over details. Nonetheless, Neylan was usually able to convince Hearst of his views, at least as they affected California.

Though he was surely an Irish reformer in the 1920s, John Francis Neylan was the antithesis of a machine politician. His technique was that of combining press, politics and law into a workable strategy. Furthermore, the combined quality of his family life, religious commitment (and golf score!) suggest that, taken together, politics, law and journalism ranked only a distant second in his order of priorities.

RICHARD NIXON (1913–1994)

Those who watched Richard Nixon's funeral on television, heard it by radio or read about it in the newspaper were moved by the remarks of President Bill Clinton, who urged that "the day of judging President Nixon on anything less than his entire life and career has come to a close."

In that context, an editorial in *Time Magazine*, on whose cover Nixon appeared no fewer than fifty–six times, declared unequivocally that Nixon would "emerge as the most important figure of the postwar era." There is ample evidence to corroborate that statement.

Richard M. Nixon was always kind, cordial and even generous to the Catholic Church, many of whose ideals and programs he supported. James Francis Cardinal McIntyre referred to him as "an old and dear friend" and Timothy Cardinal Manning exhibited a deep respect for Nixon whom he visited several times when the former President was near death from phlebitis at Scripps Memorial Hospital in La Jolla.

In the Archival Center is a copy of a substantial personal check which Nixon gave for the support of the archdiocesan school system, along with numerous letters to the archbishops of Los Angeles over many years. The name of Richard M. Nixon appeared many times in the pages of *The Tidings*. One such story, called to this writer's attention by long–time columnist Charles (Chuck) Johnson, appeared in the issue of November 15, 1968.

It seems that in the fall of 1933, when Richard Nixon was a second stringer with the Whittier "Poets," Loyola University's "Lion Gladiators " engaged Whittier in a football game which resulted in a 21–0 victory for Loyola.

Wallace Newman, the head coach at Whittier College from 1929 to 1951, said that "Dick played tackle and played it well. But the kid was just too light. Weeks would go by and he wouldn't play a minute, but he'd hardly ever miss a practice, and he worked hard. He was wonderful for morale, because he'd sit there and cheer the rest of the guys, and tell them how well they played."

"Chief" Newman went on to say that "to sit on the bench four years isn't easy. I always figured, especially in the case of Dick Nixon (who excelled in everything else), that kids like that have more guts than the first string football heroes." In addition to warming the bench for Whittier's "Poets," Nixon was the college's student–body president and an honor student all four years (B+ average).

Father Karl Von der Ahe, a Jesuit at Loyola University, remembered the Richard Nixon of those days. When he tied for debating honors at Loyola High School in 1929, Von der Ahe won the runoff, a victory that catapulted the future Jesuit into regional competition in the Hearst Oratorical Contest.

In the quarter finals, he encountered and eliminated Dick Nixon of Whittier High School. Nixon's oration for that occasion was entitled "Our Privileges Under the Constitution," suggesting that even then schoolboy Dick Nixon was interested in government.

When he appeared on the campus of Loyola University, during his candidacy for president of the United States in 1960, Nixon publicly alluded to his debating loss to Father Von der Ahe.

Bernard Baruch once observed that "everyone stumbles, but only the brave get up and start over." Maybe that's why RMN was characterized by the Wall Street Journal as "Mr. Comeback."

ANGELO NOCE (1847–1922)

Angelo Noce (1847–1922.), an Italian American from California, was the man chiefly instrumental in having a national holiday set aside each year to honor Christopher Columbus.

Columbus was not much acclaimed in Anglo America until the eighteenth century. Gradually, the whole tenor began changing and, as Noble Wilford has noted, Columbus, after George Washington, became the republic's "most exalted hero."

His popularity was evidenced by the number of towns, schools and places named in his honor, including the national capital which was designated the District of Columbia. Columbus had provided the way of escape from Old World tyranny. Mythology found the perfect hero from a distant past, one seemingly free of any taint from association with the European colonial powers.

As far as can be determined, the first major celebration honoring Columbus was observed in 1792, the three hun-

dredth anniversary of discovery, in New York City when the patriotic society of St. Tammany, also known as the Columbian Order, solemnized the event. In San Francisco, as in New York, the Columbus Day festival testified to the growth of the city's Italian population. The first "Discovery Day" occurred there on October 17, 1869.

Born in Genoa, Angelo Noce came to the United States with his parents in 1850. After a brief sojourn in the east, his family journeyed to California with others interested in the gold discoveries.

In 1863, Angelo entered Saint Mary's College and later moved on to Santa Clara. Upon his graduation, he was employed as a typesetter. He later recalled that he had "worked on the principal journals of the west, both as journeyman and foreman."

In 1876, Noce inaugurated his campaign to have a national holiday each year in recognition of his hero, Christopher Columbus. The Jesuit historian, Gerald McKevitt, believes that the movement became popular because it was a secular substitute for the religious *feste* of Italy. Columbus represented an ethnic hero and a welcome surrogate for the saints who had served to unify their communities in the New World while, at the same time, being a figure commanding respect from all Americans. Noce's fellow Italians were especially supportive of his efforts because the Genoese explorer symbolized the harmony existing between the Italian and American cultures.

In 1882, Noce moved to Denver and there ran for public office. He served as county assessor, constable, deputy sheriff and court translator, as well as working for eight years as clerk in the Colorado Legislature.

Noce, his wife and six children remained active in the campaign to have a national observance for Columbus and he was especially pleased when President Benjamin Harrison issued a proclamation in 1892 calling for "a general holiday for the people of the United States." In subsequent years, the Knights of Columbus took up the torch because it provided a unique opportunity for demonstrating Catholic patriotism and loyalty. It called to mind, in their view, a "sacred event, the Catholic baptism of the country."

Though he died before the holiday became nationally sanctioned, Noce saw it adopted as a state observance in thirty–five of the country's commonwealths. Though others share in the credit for that development, Angelo Noce retains his title in the annals as "the Father of Columbus Day."

JOSE NORMAN (1909)

One of Southern California's most active and colorful Catholic laymen, a multi–talented individual conversant in three tongues and accomplished in a host of professional roles, was once a "shoot–him–on–sight" target of Fidel Castro's henchmen in Communist Cuba. Later, Jose Norman placed that "distinction" at the top of his impressive *curriculum vitae*. Jose and his family went to Cuba, in 1949, to manage a 450 acre parcel of land that his wife, the grand–daughter of patriot Calixto Garcia Iñiguez, had inherited in the foothills of the Sierra Maestra region of Oriente Province. There, by introducing new agricultural methods and offering work to many otherwise unemployed mountain folk, he was able to convert a portion of the dense, tropical jungle into a thriving coffee plantation.

In Havana, Jose also delved into a myriad of other pursuits. He was a columnist for the Havana *Post* and its rival, the *Times*, as well as a principal music arranger for CMQ–TVstudios, one of Latin America's most modernly–equipped radio and television stations. In June of 1958, during the guerilla skirmishes preceding the Castro takeover, communist agitators harassed local land owners and eventually provoked the looting and burning of the Norman home and its adjacent plantation buildings. When Jose appealed for redress, he was assured that the structures would be restored. A lengthy interview ensued with the Castro High Command during which Jose was offered (and flatly refused!) the directorship of chemical warfare. When his attitude toward the revolutionary ideology remained adamant, Jose, his wife and son, were imprisoned and falsely accused of murder.

Politically, Jose was in a dilemma. He had already been arrested by the Batista regime for allegedly possessing unauthorized weapons. (For the record, Jose admitted that the Batista government did bring a measure of prosperity to the Caribbean nation. He also amusingly noted that Castro did something for his predecessor that even the Church could not do—"made him a saint by comparison.")

Jose's entry into politics was more accidental than premeditated. He already was, by temperament, training and reputation, a well–known classical pianist, composer and orchestra leader in his native England where he introduced the rumba, in 1930. His *Cuban Pete*, which Art Linkletter ranks as "one of the most popular rumbas ever written," became Desi Arnaz's signature tune for many years and inspired a film by the same title at Universal Pictures.

Norman's staunch Catholicism and outspoken political views made him a *persona non grata* in Cuba. With his life and those of his family in the balance, Jose fled to the United States, in 1960. He had vowed, while in prison, to dedicate the remainder of his days to telling the world about the atrocities of Cuban misrule, Church oppression and the contagious effect such a movement would surely have on other American countries.

Referred to by *Time* as Castro's "most publicized confiscation victim," Jose relentlessly toured the United States, the Caribbean and Central and Latin America explaining the chaos which communists prepared for the Free World. He appeared on practically all the television "talk–shows," including those of Joe Pine, Louis Lomax and George Putnam. For a number of years his daily column was syndicated in newspapers around the country.

Known as the "Paul Revere of the Cuban crisis," Jose Norman won wide acclaim for publicly disclosing the location and number of the island's thirty Russian–built missile bases prior to the announcement by President John F. Kennedy.

Though he doubted if Castro was initially a Soviet Puppet, Norman said that the Cuban revolutionary's affiliation with the Marxist cause was long–ago confided to the members of a select group of guerrilla rebels living near Bayamo. Jose regretted the sympathy given to Castro by certain churchmen in the early days, but he felt that their positions were more a reaction to the existing Batista regime than an endorsement of the aims and purposes of the "infidel" Castro.

An outspoken member of the West Hollywood community, Jose once startled his fellow parishioners, at Saint Victor's Church, by jumping up, in an unguarded moment, to challenge what he considered to be the "fuzzy" thinking of the Sunday homilist. He later apologetically confided to Danny Thomas, who was ushering at that Mass, that wounds inflicted for one's faith heal slowly.

JOSHUA ABRAHAM NORTON (1818–1880)

In a letter to Archbishop James Gibbons of Baltimore, written late in 1879, Joseph Sadoc Alemany asked "when will you pay a visit to this beautiful Pacific?" The Dominican prelate went on to say that "we have everything in San Francisco, even an emperor."

The archbishop was referring to the legendary Joshua Abraham Norton (1818–1880), remembered affectionately in California's annals as Norton 1, Emperor of the United States and Protector of Mexico. Norton first came to San Francisco during the gold rush winter of 1849. Having sold his father's business in North Africa, he brought with him a small fortune which he began investing in real estate.

Within a short time, the London–born Norton became one of the new merchant kings of sand–swept, ship–crowded San Francisco. Eventually, however, he lost everything in a wild scheme to corner the west coast rice market. In the process of becoming a pauper, he seems also to have lost his mind.

At this juncture of his life, Norton issued a proclamation which read: "At the peremptory request and desire of a large majority of the citizens of the United States, I, Joshua Norton . . . declare myself Emperor of these United States." Norton remained attentive enough to endow himself with powers and privileges that included issuance of his own money (promissory notes) and governance of the nation. And San Franciscans went along with him. Restaurants vied for his patronage, clothiers competed for his business and theatres sought his presence.

In addition to enjoying lifetime passes on the Southern Pacific and on several steamship lines, the emperor was accorded the privilege of "reviewing" the troops at San Francisco's *presidio* and the cadets at the University of California.

To finance his royal lifestyle, Emperor Norton levied moderate taxes on certain local businesses. His currency was accepted almost everywhere and is today highly sought after by collectors. On formal occasions, he wore a plumed hat, a quasi–military uniform with epaulettes and a sword. The emperor was generally accompanied by his royal dogs, Bummer and Lazarus.

His Majesty was a benevolent ruler. He preached tolerance and once stopped a race riot by reciting the Lord's Prayer aloud to an audience. He strongly favored public work projects and advocated bridges linking San Francisco to Marin and Oakland. He campaigned for well–lighted streets, an illuminated Christmas tree for youngsters in Union Square and for licensing of velocipedes (which he rode with great dexterity).

Norton dispatched a royal communication to Abraham Lincoln, suggesting that the Chief Executive marry the recently widowed Queen Victoria. The President responded graciously, promising to give the proposal his careful consideration. Tactfully, Mr. Lincoln made no mention of Mary Todd.

Whenever the emperor appeared at Saint Mary's Cathedral, he was treated with honor and respect by Archbishop Alemany and his clergy. And why not? Mark Twain's "likeable lunatic" was unique in North America. "In what other city," asked Robert Louis Stevenson, "would a harmless madman who supposed himself Emperor of the two Americas have been so fostered and encouraged? By honoring him, the city honored its own taste for fantasy and frivolity. San Francisco, after all, was founded on the madness of gold and sustained by the madness of silver."

MYLES P. O'CONNOR

Archbishop Patrick W. Riordan characterized Myles P. O'Connor as a man whose "chief aim in life was to benefit his fellow" human beings. The San Francisco prelate went on to say the jurist "felt that the large fortune which had come to him was given in trust, and he strove to administer that trust according to the dictate's of a clear Christian conscience and the commandments of God."

Born in Abbyleiux, Queen County, Ireland, on May 8, 1823, O'Connor was taken to England as a baby and then on to the United States when still in his teens. In 1842, he began the study of law in the office of Major A. Wright, an outstanding legal authority of the time. Later he took formal courses under the Jesuits at Saint Louis. It was while practicing law that O'Connor was lured by the discovery of gold to California. He followed the stream of humanity westward, crossing the plains with a mule team by the Carson route. After his arrival, in August, 1849, he located in Nevada County, where he pursued his legal career while engaging in mining interests. He was a man of great ability and strength of character. His sincerity and honesty soon won for O'Connor an important and influential place in the community as a spokesman and representative.

In 1859–1860, O'Connor ran for and won a seat in the state Assembly as a "Douglas Democrat." He subsequently served two terms in the senate and nine years as a Justice of the Peace. His public life was particularly remarkable for its sterling uprightness and unbounded philanthropy.

Always an exceedingly generous man, O'Connor built the memorial chapel at the sanitarium operated by the Sisters of Notre Dame in San Jose. He also provided funds for the sanitarium bearing his name, which was completed, in 1889, at a cost of half a million dollars.

Following his marriage to Armanda Butler, in 1868, the Judge lived in a beautiful residence at the corner of Second and Reed streets in San Francisco. He later gave that handsome home to the Notre Dame Sisters who used it as the central building for their orphanage known as Notre Dame Institute.

At the death of Judge O'Connor, on June 9, 1909, the San Jose *Mercury* said that "the whole state of California has sustained a loss, which will long be felt as irreparable by those who have benefited by his many benefactions and by everyone who has seen his humane hand outstretched." The funeral of the eminent jurist demonstrated the great honor, the deep respect, the tender love, the intense sorrow and the sincere sentiments of a people who cherished one who generously and sympathetically ministered to the alleviation of his suffering fellowmen.

Judge Myles P. O'Connor personified the spirit of Vatican Council II, for he regarded his material possessions "not merely as his own but also as common property in the sense that they should accrue to the benefit of not only himself but of others" as well.

JASPAR O'FARRELL (1817–1875)

Jaspar O'Farrell (1817–1875), "a cultured gentleman with a reputation for kindness, geniality and good humor," was the civil engineer who laid out and set the boundaries for San Francisco. The Wexford–born "lace–curtain Irishman" came to the Bay Area in the early 1840s, and soon thereafter had accumulated considerable wealth and reputation by virtue of his urban surveys. In 1846, Jaspar married the daughter of Patrick McChristian. He subsequently became a cattle rancher and served for a while in the upper house of the state legislature. The annals testify that "he was honest; he was an intellectual; he was an engineer. In a rural California short on skilled men, Don Gaspar was thrice–blessed."

This "first typical Californian," whose family name still graces one of San Francisco's prominent streets, was sharply criticized for "laying Market Street out on a bias so that the streets to the south of it do not intersect with the old cross–streets to the north." O'Farrell's plan was posthumously defended by an editorial in the San Francisco *Examiner*, March 13, 1935, which explained that Market Street was envisioned as the city's axis, the "magnificent central thoroughfare" from which other streets radiate.

> Market Street ranks among the great thoroughfares of the world. It is broader than Broadway, but serves the same central purpose that New York thoroughfare serves. It is a street which should be honored, for it will ever be the "Main Stem" of San Francisco, the trunk of the city tree from which other streets spring as branches or foliage. The street is the most vital part of San Francisco.

Thomas F. Prendergast discovered among O'Farrell's papers an unpublished manuscript which he apparently had intended as an introduction to a book on Irish settlers in the San Francisco area. In part it read:

> California, at the present time, gives but an idea and has but a faint resemblance to what it was when the good missionary priests of San Francisco, the *rancheros* and Indians were its sole occupants and lords of the soil. Then we looked out and beheld nature in its most lovely, wild and attractive forms—a wild expanse of undulating, rich and well–watered plains and valleys, unfenced, untilled, groves and noble forests, oak, pine and cedars, yet unculled by the settlers, and numerous herds of cattle and horses, little removed from the wild state of nature, the only living objects evidencing men's proximity.

> Sixteen years have elapsed, and we look again, behold the change. A landscape checkered with smiling farms, homesteads and villas, and dotted with cities, towns and villages, busy with the hum of industry. The missionary is still here in no way differing with his predecessor of old in courageous self–denial and devotion to holy Church; but that it is, for the most part, the souls of white men and not Indians he is solicitous. The latter as well as the old *rancheros* have nearly disappeared. California is in full possession of the white man, and embraced within the mighty area of his civilization.

While Jaspar O'Farrell recorded the price of progress, his own story is that of a pioneer who considered the overall investment, though steep, a wise one indeed.

DENIS J. OLIVER (1823–1886)

One prominent early California historian declared that Denis J. Oliver was "one of the most successful, as well as the most accomplished, Irish gentlemen on the Pacific coast, or on the continent." He went on to say that "by this statement we don't mean to assert that he is the richest man, or a great statesman, or a famous general. He is what is far more creditable——a good Christian, a good citizen and an honest man, who is an honor to the land which gave him birth, as well as to the race to which he belongs."

Of Norman descent, Oliver was born in Galway, the home of ancient nobility, in 1823. He came to the United States and, in 1840, married Mary McGlynn, described as a lady of the highest qualities of mind and heart. In 1849, Mr. Oliver journeyed to California around the Horn on the American clipper ship, *South Carolina*, Along with John A. McGlynn and William F. White, he opened a business in a tent at Montgomery and Sacramento streets.

Three decades later, William White recalled Oliver as "a fine, handsome, gentlemanly young fellow . . . who by close attention to his mercantile pursuits, became wealthy, retired from active business, traveled the world over twice." The disastrous fire of May 4, 1851, originated in his paint store on Clay Street. Undaunted, Oliver began over again and by the early 1860s was importing paints, oils and glass from a place of business on Washington Street. He later turned to speculation in land and accumulated a considerable fortune.

For his many services and benefactions to religion, Denis Oliver was knighted by Pope Pius IX. It was a fitting honor since the first Oliver who landed in England, 800 years earlier, had been knighted by William the Conqueror. Two of Oliver's ten children, Mary Agnes and Joseph, had the great distinction of receiving their first Communion from the Holy Father personally. And Pio Nono also granted the Oliver family the privilege of having a private Oratory in their home.

In 1869, Bishop Eugene O'Connell presented a 350 pound block of silver to the Pope on behalf of Mr. Oliver. The gift was so heavy that it had to be carried into the audience chamber by six men. It was out of that brick that medals were struck to commemorate Vatican Council I.

A man of cultured tastes, a lover of art and beauty, Denis J. Oliver was buried from Saint Mary's Cathedral on May 14, 1886. His eulogy was preached by Archbishop Patrick W. Riordan. An early chronicler appraised Mr. Oliver well when he noted that his "innate modesty and repugnance to anything savoring of praise precludes us from any further allusion to his worth as a citizen and high qualifications as a gentleman."

AGUSTIN OLVERA (d. 1877)

Agustin Olvera, for whom the famed Olvera Street in the *Plaza* area of Los Angeles was named, was a youngster from Mexico City who came to Alta California in 1834 with the Hijar and Padres Expedition. Very little is known about Olvera's early life, though his subsequent accomplishments indicate that he had a rather extensive education. An uncle, Ignacio Coronel, had been a well–known teacher in Mexico.

The youthful Olvera lived with his uncle on the Corralitos Ranch, in Santa Cruz County, until 1839, when he decided to take up his permanent residence in Southern California. In 1842, Governor Juan B. Alvarado named Olvera commissioner for the lands then comprising San Juan Capistrano Mission and, the following year, he was advanced to the position of Justice of the Peace.

On May 23, 1842, Agustin married Concepcion Zefferina Arguello and that union was blessed by five children. Unhappily, Concepcion died just a decade later. Agustin subsequently married Refugio Ortega, the widow of Edward Stokes.

In 1847, Olvera represented Governor Pio Pico at the signing of the Treaty of Cahuenga, an agreement that ended the fighting in California during the Mexican War. The treaty was confirmed at Guadalupe–Hidalgo on February 2, 1848. Following ratification of the latter treaty, Olvera was asked by the governor to supervise transferral of California to American officials, a diplomatic task that he performed with characteristic dignity.

Two *ranchos* were granted to Olvera in 1845 and the titles to both were subsequently confirmed by the United States Land Commission. Olvera later acquired the large Tujunga Rancho. Olvera was among the first to accept American citizenship. He was admitted to the bar and became a prominent local lawyer. In 1846, Governor Bennet Riley appointed him justice of the Peace for Los Angeles, a position he had held earlier during the Mexican regime.

On April 1, 1850, Olvera was named first Judge for Los Angeles County. That was an important position insofar as Olvera was called upon to decide cases and set precedents in a host of private matters and appeal cases. Olvera was also director of the Court of Sessions. When the State Legislature created the original counties, it placed their control and management under the Court of Sessions. Hence Olvera was also the proto chief executive officer for Los Angeles county.

A prominent Catholic layman, Olvera was active in many ecclesial affairs. An article in the *Weekly Star* for June 5, 1858, tells how his residence was decorated for the festival of *Corpus Christi,* an annual event in which many of the local citizenry participated. Agustin Olvera lived in California fourteen years as a Mexican citizen and twenty–nine years as an American. He was widely recognized as a man whose public trust was beyond question.

He died in 1877 and the name of his home, which originally faced the *Plaza de Nuestra Señora de los Angeles,* later was given to the street leading north from the *plaza.*

JAMES O'MEARA (1865–1903)

In a description of early pioneering life, James O'Meara (1865–1903) once noted, "Biographical sketches of the adventurers and intrepid spirits who explored the vast wilderness and broad deserts which now constitute the States and Territories of the Pacific . . . are befitting subjects for presentation to people. . . ." Certainly no less can be said about those pioneers who took the next faltering step in helping to bring permanent structures to those same areas.

Timothy O'Meara and Mary Saxton gave their son, James, the best education that the country afforded in order to prepare him for one of the learned professions. However, having had a taste for literature from his boyhood, instead of preparing himself for the bar, the pulpit or dissecting room, the young gentlemen took the press as his choice. In his early teens he was an apprentice in a newspaper office. After learning the trade of typesetting, he became a protege of Fernando Wood, who achieved a national reputation as a speaker, writer and shrewd politician between 1840 and 1860.

O'Meara's own qualities as an orator were impressive enough to win him a seat in the New York legislature but the fascination of a new life around the Horn impelled him to leave home and a promising career in New York for the West. The youthful journalist arrived in California in 1849. On the West Coast he wrote for the San Francisco *Times* and *Transcript*. His book, *Gwin and Broderick*, brought him national fame, describing as it did the fascinating senatorial election of 1856.

In 1857, James O'Meara went to Portland where he

became editor of the *Democratic Standard*. Two years later he purchased the Oregon *Sentinel*, which he edited until his pro–Southern views on the slavery issue ultimately brought bankruptcy to the paper. The outspoken journalist subsequently published the Southern Oregon *Gazette*, which, according to the annuals, "was so denunciatory of the government that it was denied the privilege of the United States mails." Despite his controversial views, O'Meara had many admirers and shortly after marrying Fanny Davidson in Salem, James narrowly missed being elected to the United States Senate.

O'Meara engaged in other journalistic activities in Oregon. He published the paper at Jacksonville for a while, and his articles on various topics of western interest continued to appear in eastern periodicals. The O'Meara family returned to the Bay City in 1876, and James resumed his trade, this time as editor of the San Francisco *Examiner*. His love for the stage resulted in an extremely interesting series of articles entitled "Recollections of the Stage by an Old Playgoer," which was published each Sunday in San Francisco papers.

While his political views were unacceptable in certain areas, James O'Meara never lost the esteem of the nation's literary giants. He retained, for example, his close friendship with Edgar Allan Poe, at whose home he frequently spent an evening. Such outstanding publications as the *Overland Monthly*, the *Californian* and the *Argonaut* carried scores of O'Meara's articles over the years and his sketches and editorials in the San Francisco papers were models in their way of graphic description, and easy, elegant composition.

The noted Irish chronicler, Hugh Quigley, observed, "Literature, taste and genius are above the influence of party, or should be so, and from Mr. O'Meara's style of writing, and the elegance and facility with which he writes, we are sure that he deserves high rank in the journalistic profession."

HELENA OPID (1840–1909)

Though born "a child of adversity," Helena Opid (1840–1909) "rose from the ranks of the humble, from the walks of poverty, to a position where the critical and cultural judgment and scholarship of two continents was proud to do her honor." Helena's parents were poor and her childhood was one continual struggle for the bare necessities. At twenty–one, Helena married Gustav Modrzejewski and that same year, 1861, the young bride made her professional stage debut in Cracow, capital of Poland.

Three years after losing her husband, Helena married again, this time Count Karol Bozenta Chlapowski. By then she was the leading actress of her country, famous for her interpretations of Shakespeare, Schiller, Goethe, and Moliere. In her stage life, Helena played more than 200 characters. She was, as one writer noted, "unusually sensitive, endowed with a passionate temperament, sometimes stormy and almost fierce."

In 1876, when the atmosphere of their Russian–dominated homeland became oppressive, the count and his wife agreed to financially sponsor and accompany a community of Polish exiles to Anaheim. The venture, not overly successful, was subsequently referred to as "the smallest and most short–lived of the California utopian communities."

Motivated chiefly by the desire to speak the great Shakespeare's lines in his native tongue, Helena re–entered the theatrical world in 1877 at San Francisco. There her role in *Adrienne Lecouveur* won the Polish actress instantaneous acclaim on the American stage. It was also in the Bay City that Helena adopted the Americanized "Modjeska," a shortened form of her deceased first husband's family name. Her success at San Francisco was followed by a starring tour throughout the United States. Once again she played those great scenes which had first brought her fame.

Though Madame Modjeska was an intense Catholic, she "never lost the friendship of the world which had little knowledge of her religion and less use for its principles." The famous actress loved her adopted land, and her home at Bay Island near Newport became a center for the great names of the entertainment world. Each year, at the close of her season's entertainment she traveled as fast as the trains could take her to Southern California.

In her *Memories and Impressions*, published the year after her death, Madame Modjeska glanced backward over past glories; "My thoughts are often united with the images of the glamorous moments of my stage life, yet no regret, no bitterness, disturbs my mind, but gratitude for all I received from God and man."

The life of the well–known Polish performer is of interest not only because of her ability as an actress, but because of her outstanding personality and love for humanity. Many critics regarded her the world's greatest tragedienne. Certainly her life demonstrated what can be accomplished despite poverty and discouragement. Thomas J. Conaty, the Bishop of Monterey–Los Angeles, recalled that this great lady of the stage "loved to portray, truth and virtue and to act it not only on the stage, but, better still, in her own life, and she stands today as one of the best examples of art wedded to truth and virtue."

FRANCISCO PEREZ PACHECO (1790–1860)

Until recently, a relatively unknown California pioneer, Francisco Perez Pacheco (1790–1960) was, in fact, a person of considerable influence and accomplishment during provincial times. He arrived in Alta California aboard the *Cleopatra* on May 7, 1820, accompanied by his wife Feliciana and their two children.

A master shipwright and artisan in the King's service, Francisco determined early in his life to overcome whatever obstacles might prevent him from becoming a leading personage. He was eminently successful.

Pacheco held several civil positions in those years. Commissioned *alferez* in 1824, he became *comandante* of the home guard five years later as well as a rural judge. In 1833 he was treasurer of Monterey and later alderman. The first of Pacheco's many real estate transactions occurred in 1825, when he acquired a town–lot in Monterey. Eight years later, he succeeded in securing a *rancho* grant near San Juan Bautista Mission, just east of present–day Gilroy.

From modest beginnings, Pacheco went on to become the wealthiest *ranchero* in Monterey county. And, in all his business dealings, the Guadalajara–born land merchant was scrupulously honest and fair, something that cannot be said for some of his contemporaries.

Following the 1850s, Pacheco's wealth allowed him to survive the complicated litigations concerning disputed land titles and claims. His own property was ultimately confirmed by the United States Federal Courts. A dignified gentleman of quiet strength and intelligence, Francisco Pacheco possessed one of the few libraries in early California. His holdings consisted of many *periodicos empastados*, along with a wide selection of volumes on Mexican history.

Unrelated to the well–known Governor Romualdo Pacheco or the Pacheco families of Contra Costa, Santa Clara and Marin counties, Francisco's name is permanently enshrined geographically on the Pacheco Pass, one of the few routes between the coast and California's great Central Valley. Though his life in California commenced in a humble manner, Francisco and his wife, a descendant of an Aztec chieftain, worked hard and attained great material success and personal prestige in the land of their adoption.

Pacheco's relationship with the clergy was always on the most cordial terms. He was a close friend of Archbishop Joseph S. Alemany of San Francisco. In February of 1856, he accompanied the pastor of Monterey to San Carlos Borromeo Mission, where a futile attempt was made to locate the grave of Fray Junípero Serra. In the same year, Pacheco assumed the major portion of the expenses involved in renovating and enlarging the Royal Presidio Chapel of San Carlos at Monterey. The annals consistently refer to Pacheco as "a liberal benefactor of the Catholic Church."

When the highly respected and venerable Pacheco died, in March, 1860, his remains were interred in the family crypt at the Royal Presidio Chapel. A plaque to the Pacheco family can still be seen just outside the sanctuary.

ANDREW PANSINI (1891–1958)

Los Angeles may well be the only major city in the world with more parking lots than churches. And it was there that Andrew Pansini (1891–1958) launched a wholly new concept of providing for cars in downtown areas of crowded cities.

In a fascinating book entitled *It All Started With a Nickel*, one can read the intimate story of a successful family business that revolutionized the skyline of Los Angeles, as well as every other major metropolitan center. Born in the Adriatic seacoast town of Molferta, Andrew Pansini entered the cobbler's trade where he is remembered for inventing the "ringing heel," a brass bell device implanted into the shoes of Italian women.

He emigrated to the United States in 1907 and found employment in Bloomfield, New Jersey. While there he met and married Mary Catherine Hoffman on April 15, 1915. The Pansinis came to Los Angeles the following year, with eleven cents between them.

Andrew opened a taxi service and then branched out to a fruit stand at 9th and Broadway. One day he got the inspiration of charging drivers for parking their cars on off–street vacant lots. He correctly foresaw that the 95,654 automobiles then in Los Angeles county would soon become a serious logistic problem.

Pansini leased a lot at 4th and Olive Streets, thus launching the Savoy Auto Parks, named for the ruling family of his native Italy. It was 1917 and over the next three years he began the Los Angeles tradition of knocking down obsolete buildings in favor of parking lots.

In the subsequent quarter century, Pansini purchased and demolished eighty–five buildings, prompting one newspaper to warn its readers: "Look out for Andrew Pansini or he'll be wrecking the whole of Los Angeles." Actually, he did considerably more than that by providing facilities that allowed the city to achieve its growth potential. Before long, the ubiquitous Savoy Auto Park sign, with its red, white and green circle, became a local trademark. At the beginning of the depression, there were ninety Savoy parking lots in Los Angeles.

In 1932, Pansini managed traffic control for the 10th Olympic Games in Los Angeles. He was later commended by civic officals for parking "in excess of 70,000 cars in approximately six weeks without a complaint of any character."

A decade later, Pansini reached out to San Francisco, where he opened the Union Square Garage, then advertised as the world's largest underground parking facility. He was especially pleased when the city designated the garage for use as a bomb shelter that could comfortably accommodate 30,000 people in times of disaster.

Since 1924, the Pansinis had lived in a home on the old San Antonio Rancho, alongside the Rio Hondo River. In 1949, they donated their fourteen acre estate to the Congregation of the Mission for what became Saint Vincent's

Preparatory Seminary. A lifelong and practicing Catholic, Mr. Pansini was active in a host of philanthropic activities on the local scene. In 1953, he and his wife accompanied Archbishop J. Francis A. McIntyre to Rome for his investiture in the Sacred College of Cardinals.

It All Started With a Nickel is a fascinating and folksy account of an enterprising parking baron. It is crammed with successes and failures, romances and tragedies. Told by the daughter who witnessed it all, it's a story that could only have unfolded in Los Angeles where all things are possible and most are probable.

JAMES OHIO PATTIE (1804–c. 1850)

James Ohio Pattie was an adventurer who came to the west, in 1828. After serving a term in prison for trapping without governmental authorization, he acquired permission from civil officials to visit the missions and to innoculate the natives against smallpox with a "rare serum" he supposedly brought from Kentucky.

There is an air of mystery about Pattie's shenanigans on the tour which, he claimed, took him to sixteen missions where he allegedly vaccinated 22,000 Indians. Apart from his own testimony, there is no evidence that he actually ever visited any of the old foundations. The peculiar combination of facts, legends and misinformation which Pattie crammed into his journal was dismissed by Father Zephyrin Engelhardt, the Franciscan chronicler, as one "wholesale" prevarication.

The authoritative Henry Raup Wagner was more generous in his view, holding that "probably in the main the story can be accepted as true, due allowance being made for the lapse of time." Pattie was not highly regarded by Hubert Howe Bancroft who characterized him as "a self–conceited and quick–tempered boy, with a freedom of speech often amounting to insolence, and unlimited ability to make himself disagreeable."

Throughout the text of his journal, Pattie exhibited an antagonistic attitude towards the overall missionary program, though he did feel kindly disposed to many of the individual *padres* whom he met on his journeys. In all fairness, it should be noted that a goodly portion of the narrative was substantially altered by the Reverend Timothy Flint who edited into the journal a considerable amount of sentiment and romance prior to its publication.

Pattie's literary laurels are as impressive as they are inconsistent. Robert Glass Cleland spoke highly of the account, observing that "American literature has not yet produced a tale of adventure equal to his simple narrative." Andrew F. Rolle was less exuberant in his appraisal of this "first printed narrative of an overland journey to California" which he looked upon as "a mine

of often unreliable but always fascinating information." Another authority claims that the itinerant vaccinator's narrative "remains the epic of the mountain men, perhaps more truly representing their attitudes, their experiences, and their adventures than any other book which has appeared on the subject."

A recent study of the original missions records by Rosemary K. Valle, published by the *Southern California Quarterly*, confirms the "doubts about Pattie's veracity." The author concludes her scientific article by observing that "Pattie's account of the epidemic and the vaccination episode is just another 'tall tale.'" Unquestionably, Pattie's written observations, published at Cincinnati in 1831, have "an assured place in frontier literature" though they must be classified as "semi–fiction" rather than history.

GREGORY PECK (b. 1916)

Veteran Hollywood personality Gregory Peck, one of the most likeable actors of the century, received many citations during his long career including two Oscars and numerous other Best Actor Awards. For over half a century, Peck starred in no fewer than thirty–three films, among them T*he Snows of Kilimanjaro, The Guns of Navarone, Old Gringo, Moby Dick* and *Days of Glory.*

Eldred Gregory Peck, known among his peers as "the liberal conscience of the American cinema," was born at La Jolla, California, on April 5, 1916. He made an impressive Broadway debut in 1941. The tall, upright and handsome actor found himself as a popular romantic leading man from the start of his screen career. Likeable, honest and believable, he proved an ideal hero in a series of memorable dramas.

Peck married Veronique, a journalist, in 1953. Their two children, Tony and Cecilia, also became active in the entertainment field. Their family was often held up as modular for their fellow Americans. The popular actor was active in many charitable and political causes, as well as serving as President of the Academy of Motion Picture Arts and Sciences in the years 1967 through 1970.

Among Peck's most notable pictures were T*he Keys of the Kingdom* (1945), *Twelve O'Clock High* (1950), *The Man in the Gray Flannel Suit* (1957) and *MacArthur* (1978). His role in *To Kill a Mockingbird* won him his first Oscar in 1963.

On October 29, 1955, Peck received the Lifetime Achievement Award from Catholics in Media Associates, an award granted "to recognize people in the entertainment industry who have, by their work, made clearer the Word of God." In his charming remarks for that occasion, Peck paid tribute to his grandmother, Catherine Ashe, from Country Kerry, Ireland. He felt that she "would smile if she were here today."

Peck recalled his days as a student at Saint John's Military Academy, where he once served Mass for Bishop John J. Cantwell. After the ceremonies, the prelate greeted the youthful Peck and pronounced his performance as "well done."

Peck said that over the succeeding years, he had received many favorable accolades for his roles, but the one from the Bishop of Los Angeles–San Diego "meant the most." That casual remark, uttered sixty–seven years earlier, inspired Gregory Peck to seek out a life of service to others "by pretending to be someone else." Few succeeded so well.

Peck was especially pleased that Cantwell's successor, Roger Cardinal Mahony, had capped his career in the Motion Picture Industry by once again pronouncing his work as "well done." The hand–written remarks of Peck on that occasion, scribbled with a felt pen on a page from a legal pad, are a treasured relic at the Archival Center for the Archdiocese of Los Angeles in Mission Hills. In a news account about Peck's receiving the award, he was referred to as "an actor, a producer, an industry leader, a citizen and remarkable human being who not only embodies—in his life and in his work—the highest ethical standards, but who has always expressed them with magnificent artistry."

JOHN C. PELTON (b. 1826)

John C. Pelton regarded religion as "the keystone of the arch on which, in every age, past and present, has rested and still rests the foundations of the institutions of all civilization and human society in general." It was the famous professor's hope that "a small, still, unimportant voice, like all important truth, may yet find a permanent lodgment in the minds of present and future educators" which inspired his address on "Education: Its True Motives and Methods," before the Newman Club of Los Angeles, on October 28, 1902.

A half century after organizing the first free public school in California, Pelton spoke out about the lack of religious and moral training that had pervaded the educational system by the turn of the century. In decrying the evaporation of the "sacred fires" and the "holy altars" of moral training from the schoolhouses, Pelton could foresee the possibility of "intellectual giants and immoral imbeciles."

He reminded Californians that "when God is ignored, forgotten, left out of heart and mind, though the sum of intellectuality therein may have reached its zenith, he is seen soon to decline, and goes down amid the dark waves of a darker oblivion." Those teachers failing to look beyond the classroom and the limits of mortal life fall infinitely short in the performance of that momentous duty which devolves upon them and which they alone can perform.

The supernatural values advocated by Pelton endangered no particular creed or code of morals, for he associated the term religion with "the right culture and development of that instinctive, innate sentiment of devotion, of worship, of fear, of reverence for something higher and better than self, which is found everywhere and in all ages—a principle in human nature, that sentiment which discloses itself in the infantile speech of humanity, that which distinguished man from brute, aye, that worshipful sentiment found in the first lisp of all speech, of all languages, of all tribes, peoples and nations, historic and pre–historic."

Indifference about that vital aspect of educating the nation's youth was a luxury which the professor could not tolerate. His identification of "religion" and morality with the foundation of human happiness forced him to conclude that any learning process totally lacking spiritual concepts would produce a generation of heartless infidels.

Pelton emphatically affirmed that religion had an important place in the state schools:

> I do believe, with all my heart, that anything should be taught in State, parish or private schools, which tends to make people wise and better, and the foundation of the State more secure and firm.

The pioneer educator, in quoting numerous authorities to substantiate his views, most of them non–Catholic, observed that "in the hands of the Protestant world chiefly rests the future destiny of our state's educational institutions." In his concluding remarks to the Newman Club, Professor Pelton quoted Daniel Webster: "In what age, by what sect, when, where, by whom, has religious truth been excluded from the education of youth? Nowhere, never. Everywhere and at all times it has been regarded as essential. It is of the essence, the vitality of useful instruction."

JUAN PEREZ (d. 1775)

Juan Perez (d. 1775), the foremost maritime figure in the early settlement of Alta California, was a remarkable Spanish naval officer whose exploits form an integral part of the area's early annals.

The mariner's birthplace is known from a letter written by Fray Junípero Serra wherein he refers to Perez as "our countryman from the banks of Palma." He joined the Spanish naval service and ultimately rose to the rank of *Alférez Graduado de Frigata*. Perez served for a number of years on the Manila galleon run as pilot or master.

In his later years he admitted to having "spent a great deal of time in China and the Philippines."

Captain Perez was in charge of the *San Antonio*, also known as *El Principe,* during the move into Alta California during 1769. He rendered exceptional service and survived the rigors of the initial voyage of California settlement. The first Spanish naval officer to enter both San Diego and Monterey harbors during the late eighteenth century, Perez's dedicated service on the extreme rim of Spain's farflung empire is a chapter well worth recalling.

Perez and other sailors who maintained the perilous lifeline by sea between San Blas and the new settlements held positions of greatest importance, a distinction marked by various honors. There is a harbor named *El Puerto de Juan Perez* on the inner side (east) of Queen Charlotte Island, off the coast of British Columbia.

The mariner's reputation as a dependable and competent sailing master was built strongly on his service as a sea–born supply and message carrier along one of the most treacherous coasts in the Spanish dominions. The ships and equipment available to Perez and his sailors were ill–suited for the arduous tasks. It is remarkable indeed that vessels of the type used were able to sustain the California settlements during the struggling years of their infancy.

Mallorcan influence was profound in the early period of California settlement. An abnormally large number of Mallorcans were active there. Among the friars sharing the Perez's birthright were Serra, Ripoll, Jaime, Crespi, Palou, Pieras and the Cabots. They were a tightly–knit group on a distant frontier. Serra and the other friars praised Perez in their letters to religious superiors and the viceroy. More than once Serra spoke about "our friend, Don Juan Perez."

The captain was in charge of the ship that returned Fray Junípero Serra from his historic journey to Mexico City in 1774. It was an important trek for Perez because it was his last great voyage as commanding officer. Late the following year, Juan Perez left Monterey for the last time. On November 1, 1775, the old sailor succumbed and was buried at sea, almost within sight of the port which had been the locale of much of his service.

Life at sea in the California supply service and along the Pacific Coast was, at best, rigorous and demanding. It is to Captain Perez' enduring credit that he continued his efforts to serve his monarch until the final beckoning overtook him. He "died in harness" as part of Spain's last major effort at colonization on the Pacific Coast of North America.

JAMES PHELAN (1819–1892)

James Phelan (1819–1892), a native of Eire, was a forty–niner who shrewdly found his *El Dorado* in supplying the needs of the Argonauts who thronged to San Francisco and the gold fields. After arriving in the United States with his parents, James was educated in New York's public schools. There he became thoroughly Americanzed and a staunch supporter and believer in the customs of his adopted country.

He opened general stores in Philadelphia, New Orleans and Cincinnati. In those early days he was described as a man "of sturdy frame, hale and vigorous in mind and body." According to Hubert Howe Bancroft, "James Phelan was engaged in trade at Cincinnati when the gold fever induced him to transfer his general merchandise to San Francisco." Phelan himself wrote that it was after reading about the discovery of gold in a published report by Thomas O. Larkin, that he thought about going west.

The long sea journey to San Francisco almost resulted in Phelan's death. While crossing the Isthmus of Panama, he was stricken with the dreaded Chagres fever. Only after a lengthy convalescence did he arrive in San Francisco during August of 1849. There he established a store with his brother, Michael, under the name of J. & M. Phelan. Though the firm was burned out in the fire of 1851, it rose Phoenix–like from the ashes and achieved great success in subsequent years.

In 1855, James journeyed east to Brooklyn, to claim his bride, Miss Agnes Kelly, a cousin of the well–known Irish politician, publicist and poet, William J. Corbett.

The Phelans were married at old Saint Mary's Cathedral in May of 1859 by Archbishop Joseph Sadoc Alemany. Their three children were born on the attractive 3½ acre spread near Mission Dolores, property described as "charmingly laid out and planted with a variety of trees."

Phelan continued in business until about 1869. Thereafter he devoted his talents to banking and real estate. In 1870, he helped to organize the First National Bank and, later the Western Fire and Marine Insurance Company. And he was also active in plans to build the Panama Canal through his organization of the American Contracting and Dredging Company. The impressive Phelan Building, erected in 1881–1882, was long considered "among the prominent edifices of Market Street."

In 1892, James Phelan succumbed. His remains are interred in the family mausoleum at Holy Cross Cemetery, San Mateo County. "By all who knew him, he was acknowledged as one of the most enterprising of our California pioneers, and one to whom the state was indebted for much of its early prosperity."

Shortly before his death, Phelan wrote his autobiography which was published by his son, James Duvall Phelan, as an appendix to the log of Sterling B. F. Clark, in 1929. In his foreword to that book, entitled *How*

Many Miles from St. Jo?, James Duvall noted that "many people tended to consider the gold rush as an event disassociated from the individuals who participated in it." Such a claim could not be made by anyone who knew James Phelan.

JAMES DUVAL PHELAN (1861–1930)

The Western Americana bibliographer, Robert Ernest Cowan, characterized the prominent San Franciscan, James Duval Phelan, as "the ablest Californian of his generation." Indeed, he was that—and much more. James was born in the Bay City, on April 20, 1861, the son of James and Agnes (Kelly) Phelan. From his parentage, he inherited the finest traits and abilities of Irish ancestry. His father, a native of Eire, was a forty–niner who shrewdly found his *El Dorado* in supplying the needs of the Argonauts who thronged to San Francisco and the gold fields.

Young James' systematic and thorough education was acquired at Saint Ignatius School and College, where he received his Bachelor's degree in 1881. He then studied law for a time at the University of California, at Berkeley, but after touring Europe, decided to enter his father's banking business. Subsequently, he pursued his legal courses and ultimately received a doctorate.

James' first public service was that of Vice President of the California Commission to the Chicago World's Fair, in 1893. At the urging of Fremont Older, editor of the San Francisco *Bulletin*, Phelan entered the race for mayor of San Francisco, in 1896. During his three terms as mayor, stretching from 1897 to 1902, Phelan played Pericles to an Athenic San Francisco. He banished the political bosses from City Hall and set about to beautify the city. In the face of stubborn opposition, he secured a new charter for San Francisco.

In 1906, at the personal behest of Theodore Roosevelt, Mr. Phelan served as President of Relief and Red Cross Funds that were raised for the victims of San Francisco's disastrous earthquake and fire. Phelan was elected to the United States Senate in 1915, where he served with distinction for six years. He went down to political death as a supporter of the Versailles Treaty that was so despised by the American Irish.

In his later years, Phelan engaged in a host of diplomatic missions, both domestic and foreign, for the government. In all his public roles, the affable Phelan exhibited the amenities of an extensive cultural and social awareness. James Duval Phelan died at his country estate, Villa Montalvo, Saratoga, in Santa Clara County, on August 7,1930.

Though he was associated with politics during much of his life, Phelan was not so much a politician as he was a statesman. His every thought and action was strongly entrenched in and expressive of the Catholic faith that pervaded the whole of his personality. An easy and graceful speaker, with a wide knowledge of art and music, Phelan was both a distinguished patron of the classics and a generous benefactor of the poor and downtrodden. Though formal and dignified, James Duval Phelan was, nevertheless, greatly loved by all the citizenry. His life of dedicated service is deeply engraved in the annals of California. Therein is abundantly expressed that finest attribute which throughout his years had been his creed—*noblesse oblige!*

PIO DE JESUS PICO (1801–1894)

Probably no other personage in western annals reaped as much disrepute and ill will as did Pio de Jesus Pico, the last of the Mexicans to hold the office of governor in Alta California. Born May 5, 1801, within the shadows of San Gabriel Mission, Pio was the son of Jose Maria Pico of Mazatlan and Estaquia Lopez. Very little is known about the youngster's boyhood.

Pio spent the greater part of his early life in San Diego where he engaged in mercantilistic pursuits. Much of his time was given to horse racing and gambling. Hubert Howe Bancroft recorded that "he introduced the use of ox–horns with false wooden bottoms" to disguise the quantity of liquor sold to drinkers.

Amassing fabulous wealth, Pico owned many large tracts of land, including the *ranchos* of Santa Margarita, Las Flores and Paso de Bartolo, all of which he ultimately lost through default of mortgage payments. His most beautiful holding was *El Ranchito* with its thirty–three room mansion. It was reportedly the largest adobe and the first two story house of its day. Pico served briefly as governor in 1832 following the ouster of Manuel Victoria. During his second term, in 1845–1846, after the departure of Manuel Micheltorena, he established his administration in Los Angeles, but was unable to control the northern area of the state.

During his tenure, Pico was lavish in disposing of land grants, especially those relating to the California missions. Though a nominal Catholic, neither he or his brother Andres was a friend of the Church. Father Zephyrin Engelhardt explained in in great detail how Pico "in disregard of all moral and religious principles, and of the catechism which he boasted he had learned by heart, began to sell the missions on May 4, 1846."

Pico effectively "wiped out the famous schools of civilization, of mechanical arts, agriculture and of stock raising, which the zealous Franciscan Fathers, amid indescribable hardships and difficulties, had established" for the Indians. After the Americans assumed administrative control of California, Pico was exiled to

Mexico. He returned in 1848 and spent the rest of his long life in and around *El Pueblo de Nuestra Señora de los Angeles.*

The Pico House in downtown Los Angeles was erected by the former governor in 1870 as a luxurious three–story Romanesque building. It has since become the cornerstone of the historic park around the old Plaza Church. During his residency at *El Ranchito* with his bride, Pico's home was the scene of great hospitality of numerous friends and the display of lavish riches. His home on the bank of the *Rio San Gabriel* had few equals in California.

Pico lived to the venerable age of ninety–three. He died in poverty at the home of a friend in Los Angeles. His remains, buried initially in Old Calvary Cemetery on North Broadway, were later moved by Walter Temple.

Living almost the entire century, Pio Pico's story affords an excellent glimpse of California life during that romantic but turbulent period when the west was catching up with the rest of the world. The epitaph of Pio Pico was perhaps best phrased by a youngster who concluded her paper about the one–time governor with these words: "He was not a very nice man."

ISABEL AND EDITH PICZEK

Isabel and Edith Piczek, two of the most outstanding ecclesial artists of contemporary times, are motivated by the realization that their art speaks a message for all humankind. From their modest and unobtrusive studios in the Echo Park district of Los Angeles, the Hungarian–born sisters have produced some of the finest murals, mosaics and stained glass in America.

The Piczeks inherited their talent from their father, an art professor of considerable renown in one of Hungary's leading universities. They completed their training in the School of Fine Arts in Budapest.

Shortly after the Communists took over their homeland, the sisters escaped to Vienna. Later, they literally painted their way across war–torn Europe, finally arriving in Rome at the outset of the 1950 Holy Year. In the Eternal City, Isabel and Edith won the celebrated Galleria di Roma prize and were commissioned to create a 377 square foot fresco mural at the Pontifical Biblical Institute, an unheard of distinction for women.

At the invitation of the Canadian hierarchy, the sisters set up studios in Hamilton and Toronto. Then, in 1955, they came to the United States where their first commission was a 2,880 foot mural for the cathedral at Reno.

Since 1958, the Piczeks have lived and worked in Los Angeles at their Construction Art Center. Their artistic masterpieces adorn almost two hundred churches, convents and public buildings on three continents and seven countries.

Probably the most celebrated of their many works are the stained glass windows, murals and mosaics at Guardian Angel Cathedral in Las Vegas. Within walking distance from the Strip, on Desert Inn Road, is the masterful ten–year project "Toward the Total Christ."

Locally, the Piczek art can be seen at Saint Philip Church (Pasadena), Saint Mary Magdalen (Camarillo), Saint Victor (West Hollywood), Saint Bridget of Sweden (Van Nuys), Saint Catherine Laboure (Torrance) and Our Lady of the Assumption (San Buenaventura). Their talents have a decided ecumenical attraction too. The Air Force Chapel at Nellis Air Base, Messiah Baptist Church and B'nai David Synagogue in Los Angeles are perhaps the three finest examples of their outreach, award–winning art.

Isabel and Edith describe their "aesthetic partnership" in terms of a "mystical realism" which they look upon as part of the modern visual and spiritual revolution in ecclesial art. The unassuming sisters see their vocation as a "cultural and religious mission." They feel

Piczek's depiction of Our Lady of the Angels

compelled to be "always moving forward," concerned as they are that the old ways will disappear or trap those who insist on a piety not in keeping with the times.

Believing that much of modern art has a de–humanizing effect, the Piczek sisters portray the destiny of humankind in forms of glass, paint and tile, while acknowledging that the "real artwork" is implanted on the soul of the observer.

And that's a philosophy almost as beautiful and attractive as their art work.

CECILIA PLUMMER

History is where one finds it. Someone recently wrote to ask: What is the origin of Plummer Park in Hollywood? The answer to that query forms an interesting link in California's Catholic heritage.

Plummer Park is located in what was once the vast Rancho La Brea, an area that stretched over some 4,432 acres. The *rancho* was created by a grant from the Mexican Government in 1828. In the mid 1860s, Major Henry Hancock purchased most of the *rancho*. A decade later, the United States made the first surveys in the area and, not long thereafter, the Plummer farm family acquired that land bounded by present–day Santa Monica Boulevard, Gardner Street, Sunset Boulevard and La Brea Avenue.

About 1878, Cecilia Plummer built the Audubon House. That edifice was a typical ranch adobe of the period, very similar to others in the southland. In Cecilia's garden were Castilian roses and pepper trees, fairly rare items in those times.

Wine and brandy were made on the premises; vegetables, fruits, flowers and dairy products were raised and sold to people throughout Los Angeles. There were large pits where meat, chicken, geese and wild game were barbecued. The ranch became a mecca for distant travelers and many noteworthy persons, including Helen Hunt Jackson.

On August 16, 1882, Father Peter Verdaguer witnessed the marriage of Eugene Plummer and Maria Amparo Lamoraux at the Plaza Church of *Nuestra Señora de Los Angeles*. Subsequently, Eugenio and his bride moved into the family homestead and began raising their children.

The members of the Plummer family were talented in music and household arts. Perhaps their finest trait was the ability to act as hosts and hostesses. From 1880 to 1900 the ranch was known as the Pioneer Fiesta Center. "Don Eugenio" Plummer appears to have been a rather poor business man and eventually he lost title to the land. In 1937, the last remaining acres were put to public auction as part of bankruptcy proceedings.

The County of Los Angeles eventually purchased the property and named it Plummer Park. The family was allowed to remain there in residence and Eugenio lived on there until his death on May 19, 1943, at the age of ninety. Soon afterwards a series of smaller buildings on the acreage were razed to make room for a community center which became an important link in the cultural life of Hollywood and adjoining areas.

Recreational facilities were later added and, in 1950, an auditorium was built and appropriately named Fiesta Hall by the Los Angeles Board of Supervisors. No other park in the county system has a longer and more interesting heritage than the one developed on what was once the Plummer *rancho*. For a long time after the park fell under the county's direction, the "Days of the Dons" were relived in a *fiesta* of Spanish songs and dances held in the rose garden by the Friends of Plummer Park, a group established by Anthony Lorenz in 1945, to honor the pioneers of earlier ages. The story of Plummer Park is told in a charming memoir, *Señor Plummer. The Life and Laughter of an Old–Californian* which was published at Hollywood by Murray & Gee in 1943.

WIKTOR PODOSKI (1901–1970)

One of the most striking, distinctive and memorable portrayals of Fray Junípero Serra is a woodcut engraving executed by the talented Wiktor Podoski (1901–1970). It was used to illustrate an article by J. George Szeptycki in *Polish Americans in California, 1817–1977*.

Podoski was among a dynamic group of young artists who began exhibiting innovative wood engravings in the galleries of Warsaw, Poland, in the 1920s. Art lovers were immediately captivated by their stylized works.

Prominent museums found it fashionable to include Polish prints in their collections and yearly international exhibitions of wood engravings became major cultural events on a world–wide scale. Wiktor Podoski played a doubly prominent role in this movement: first, as a talented wood engraver, and second, as its theoretician and art critic, equipped with a keen, analytical mind.

Podoski felt that because of the uniqueness of this almost unexplored medium, wood engravers should not only register visual reality, but rather use it as a point of departure in their quest for personalized graphic concepts. As time went on, Podoski developed a highly personalized style in his graphic concepts. One of his students, Stefan Mrozewski, became world famous as a result of his own unique artistic productions, and this factor did not in any way diminish Podoski's position in the field of artistic achievement.

Podoski's "California period" extended roughly from 1950 until his death and constituted the peak of the artist's activity. In those years, he produced a series of dazzlingly rich, nearly abstract forms, textures and patterns, constituting a sort of twilight zone between recognizable reality and a brilliant interpretation of this reality in graphic language.

The artist's still life compositions, usually engraved in small formats, represent the ultimate in artistic discipline, ingenuity and sophistication. The portrayal of Fray Junípero Serra would be an outstanding example. After the conception of an artistic idea, Podoski thought about it for a time. He would then sketch it loosely in pencil, indicating the general layout and relative values.

Next, he would render the sketch in black ink on white paper, with more details, where, for the first time, approximate effects of a wood engraving became discernible. Finally, when all the details were refined to his complete satisfaction, Podoski transferred the composition to a wood block, at which time he was ready to start cutting.

Podoski's process of evolution, from the initial notion to the final shape, often extended over several weeks or more. In some cases, several months were needed to satisfy the artist. Between each of these steps, Podoski spent many hours in libraries and bookstores reading and completing his collection of rare books on art and facsimile reproductions of the great masterpieces.

Unhappily, many of Podoski's early block and prints were lost or destroyed during the Warsaw insurrection of 1944. But what survived testifies eloquently to the talent of this fine Catholic artist.

LEO POLITI (1908–1996)

A. BLESSING OF ANIMALS'

The historic *Bendición de los Animales* can be traced back to the 4th century and Saint Anthony the Abbot. That ancient ceremony has been performed in *El Pueblo de Nuestra Señora de los Angeles* since the 1780s, in grateful recognition of the animal kingdom's tremendous services to humankind.

Year after year, the people of Olvera Street have recreated this tradition on Holy Saturday. The animals are assembled at the north entrance to the Street. Garlands of flowers adorn cows, donkeys and horses. Smaller animals gladly find their cages or leashes draped with ribbons, bows, flowers and handmade decorations.

About a decade ago, at the behest of the Filippa Pollia Foundation it was decided to enshrine an artistic portayal of the "Blessing of the Animals" at the entrance to the Eugene Biscailuz Building, just east of the cross on Olvera Street. Providentially chosen to depict the colorful scene was Leo Politi, the foremost interpreter of the city's heritage, an artist whose books for children have become a classical part of America's educational process.

Blessed on April 4, 1978 by Timothy Cardinal Man-

ning, the "Blessing of the Animals" mural speaks of a simple, trusting faith that reflects a link and reliance between God and His creatures in everyday life. That relationship was manifested, as the mural portrays, in man's invocation of God's blessings upon the animals that helped him in daily life by their work, devotion, cheerfulness and loyalty.

The mural also shows how reliance on Providence and human initiative founded Los Angeles. Admitting to being "sort of a naive primitive with a childlike style," Leo explained how the figures in the mural convey gentleness, sensitivity and simplicity.

Physically and in spirit, Leo Politi lived at the authentic heart of old Los Angeles. His home was within range of the night hum of the freeway, not far from the four level interchange. Despite the traffic, congestion and rush about him, Leo maintained an inner tranquility of spirit. In the mural is the blind harp player and the tall violinist, both of whom performed on Olvera Street. The baby in the basket is one that Leo once saw in the arms of her mother sitting on a bench across the street.

In a column for the Los Angeles *Times*, Jack Smith recalled how the people in Politi's mural looked gentle, innocent, serene. "The white–haired man playing a violin, the young woman with a dog in her arms, the children leading their pets, the priest sprinkling the animals with holy water. It seemed sadly ironic that this peaceful scene could have been painted in the same century as Pablo Picasso's 'Guernica,' with its people and animals perishing in horror." Smith went on to say that "there are those who would say Politi's mural is not real—that there is no gentleness, innocence, serenity or beauty left. But of course there are such things. They are in the eye of the beholder, and Leo Politi is our beholder."

A reporter covering the dedication of the mural doubted if the Biscailuz Building was constructed, like Notre Dame, to last for centuries. "But if it does, people may look at Politi's mural a thousand years from now and see that there were gentle people once upon a time in Los Angeles, or anyway there was a Leo Politi."

LEO POLITI (1908–1996)

B. CHILDREN'S ILLUSTRATOR

Leo Politi was not only among the nation's premier author illustrators, he was a folk–hero to generations of youngsters who grew up with his books and were nurtured with his gentle but persuasive love for the simple joys of life. For half a century, Leo deftly blended the old and the new into a colorful pageantry, depicting early California history and describing the great wealth of tradition brought to these shores by Spanish, Mexican, Italian and Chinese peoples who adopted California as their home of choice in the New World.

Born at Fresno, in 1908, Leo returned with his family to their native village of Broni, in Northern Italy. There he first developed an interest in artistically portraying the warmth of familial relationships.

At fifteen, Leo won a national scholarship to the University of Art and Decoration in the Royal Palace of Monza, near Milan. It was during the ensuing years that his sketches were recognized and extolled. His first illustrated book, one which he had never seen and which doesn't even bear his name, was an Italian text for deaf-mute children.

Upon graduation as a *Maestro d'Arte*, Leo taught art and augmented his income by textile and tapestry designing. In 1930, he returned to the United States and shortly thereafter took up permanent residence in Los Angeles. Eight years later he married Helen Fontes.

Leo Politi's literary career began with *Little Pancho*, a children's story he wrote and illustrated for Viking Press in 1938. That volume was the first in a long series of volumes he either composed himself or illustrated for others.

Over the years, Leo won practically every award and prize offered in his discipline. In 1949, *Song of the Swallows* earned the prestigious Caldecott Medal from the American Library Association for the nation's most distinguished picture book. *Moy Moy*, a book about Chinese-Americans in Los Angeles, won Politi further acclaim, this time for a truly "significant contribution to the field of illustration." Others of his prizes included the Regina Medal from the Catholic Library Association which was bestowed for Politi's "continued distinguished contributions to childrens books."

Besides excelling in painting, sculpture and design, Leo studied architecture and utilized its principles in his work. His books about Los Angeles became classics and elicited from such authorities as Carl Dentzel the comment that Politi "has done the most to call attention to the need to preserve the grace and heritage" of our city.

Foremost among Leo's broadsides is that portraying the youthful Fray Junípero Serra which he did for the Serra Bicentennial Commission in 1984. With the touch of a master artisan, he captured the spirit of optimism and love that characterized the life of California's religious pioneer.

Leo was stooped, his face craggy and weathered, his eyes large and luminous behind thick lenses. But he was full of wonder, like the little children in his pictures. He radiated great warmth and quiet humor. He was an

indigenous part of California's landscape who will never die or be diminished in the hearts and souls of his public. One of Politi's oldest friends and most ardent admirers, Timothy Cardinal Manning, contended that "the artistic genius of Leo Politi is his gift of being able to penetrate the heart of a child and to reproduce in his works the innocence and loveliness of those who reflect the Kingdom of God."

VICTOR PONET (1836–1914)

"On the roll of those incomparable citizens who laid the well-grounded foundation of the city of Los Angeles, California, the name of Victor Ponet is outstanding." Born at Lemburg, Belgium on March 9, 1836, Ponet spent the early years of his life at the trade of cabinet-making in Paris. He came to the United States in 1865, and, two years later, attracted by the lure of the Pacific, Ponet journeyed to California by way of the Isthmus of Panama.

When Victor Ponet arrived in Los Angeles in 1869, the city had only 4,500 inhabitants. He set up a business on North Main Street and in the ensuing years his liberality in the handling and improving of his various properties contributed much to the material development and civil prosperity of Los Angeles.

Throughout his career, Ponet was known as a man "actuated by purest motives, with an integrity and honesty of purpose" that was never questioned. "He was in the most significant degree the architect of his own fortunes, and in his progressive career, his activities concerned not only his individual success but also the well-being of the community at large."

The site of the Ponet residence in those early years was at the junction of present-day Pico Boulevard and Alvarado Street. Fiesta Park, bounded by Pico, Grand, Twelfth and Hope Streets, later became known as "Ponet Square," and on this property Victor erected one of the city's first apartment buildings.

Ponet was widely known as an exceedingly charitable man. In later years, after moving to Sherman, the West Hollywood of our time, he deeded a parcel of land to the Diocese of Monterey-Los Angeles and built there, for his employees, a church which later was raised to parochial status under the patronage of Saint Victor. A personally inscribed photograph and message from Pope Saint Pius X to Victor Ponet hangs in the sacristy of the recently erected successor to Ponet's little frame church.

In his role as a broad-minded, liberal and public spirited citizen, Ponet was a moving force in organizing the Los Angeles Chamber of Commerce. He also served for a few years as president of the German-American Savings Bank which he had helped to establish at the turn of the century. Victor Ponet was the unofficial representative of the Belgian Consular Corps in Los Angeles, and on May 20, 1896, was signally honored when the King of the Belgians conferred upon him the knightly title of *Chevalier de L'Ordre de Leopold* in recognition of services to his mother–country.

As he gazed back over a long life, which he shared with Ellen (Manning) Ponet, Victor's gratification rested in the knowledge that he had been a vital force in the development of a great city. It could be said of this western pioneer, at his death on February 7, 1914, that "in his person was reflected the fine character and progressive citizenship of those men of foreign birth whose careers are so imperishably described in all the histories of Southern California."

PEDRO PRAT (d. 1772)

"The medical history of California goes back to the cradle of the new Spanish province, the sword, the cross and the scalpel proceeding hand in hand. . . ." Though there may well have been physicians with Juan Rodriguez Cabrillo, in 1542, and Sebastian Vizcaino in 1602, Pedro Prat was the first doctor actually to practice the profession in California.

While his family name was a common one in Catalonia, the best evidence available about this hard–wrought man who held the rank of Captain in the Royal Spanish Army, is that he was either of French birth or extraction. To all intents and purposes, however, he was probably as much a Spaniard as were the people with whom he cast his lot when he arrived from Baja California at San Diego.

Prat came to the latter city with Gaspar de Portola and Fray Junípero Serra in 1769, and, almost immediately after his arrival, was hard at work treating victims of the scurvy then decimating the tiny community. As could be expected of a graduate from the University of Barcelona, Dr. Prat was also a skilled botanist. When his scant supply of medicines was depleted, he gathered quantities of green mustard leaves, wild horseradish, and water cress, and from these raw elements, he concocted an effective remedy for his patients.

Even though he himself fell victim to the dread scurvy, brought on by lack of fresh vegetables and fruit and an extensive diet of salt meats, the indefatigable physician continued treating the afflicted in his tent hospital at the *Punta de los Muertos*.

After laboring unceasingly at San Diego for nearly a year, Prat accompanied Junípero Serra to Monterey, where he spent additional months caring for the sick. According to Francisco Palou, "the surgeon performed his office with the highest extremes of benevolence.

Indeed, according to reports of all who composed the expedition, he had no equal."

The tremendous physical strain of his many medical activities at Monterey soon had their effect on the *presidio's* first surgeon general. In mid 1771, "his mind had been so harassed by the harrowing experiences at San Diego that he became demented." In June the authorities deemed it wise to send the stricken doctor to Guadalajara for hospitalization. Soon after his arrival there, on the ship *El Principe*, the "skilled surgeon of the royal armies of His Majesty" quietly gave up his noble soul.

The physician's charity and efficiency in California were "officially reported to Madrid" where even today the name of Pedro Prat is held in high repute in medical circles. California's pioneers were deeply indebted to this generous man, for "had it not been for the presence of Pedro Prat, it is probable that the projected province would have miscarried and never withstood the travail of its birth."

LUIGI PROVIDENZA (1894–1981)

Luigi Providenza was born in the small and ancient city of Chiavari, by the waters of the Gulf of Genoa, on January 29, 1894. After spending his childhood among his native people, Luigi began a career working in the shipyards. An ardent follower of Luigi Sturzo, he became secretary of the local *Partito Popolare*.

Anxious to be away from the violent political strife and hatreds of postwar Italy, Luigi and his wife, Augusta, came to the United States in 1921. He first worked for *L'Unione*, an Italian Catholic newspaper published in San Francisco.

As the tall, upright and impressive Providenza moved around the Golden State, he was appalled by the fact that upwards of 90% of the Italian Catholic immigrants had abandoned their faith commitment. After many months of intensive soul searching and prayer, Luigi developed the idea of a Catholic apostolate aimed specifically at peoples of Italian origin.

In 1924, he established the Italian Catholic Federation, a group whose sole purpose was that of bringing Italian– Americans back to the active practice of Catholicism. The first meeting of the ICF took place in San Francisco's Church of the Immaculate Conception. Luigi was fond of recalling that there were twelve "disciples" at that inaugural gathering.

Because so many influential Italians refused to cooperate with his work, Luigi realized that the ICF would need a strong yet flexible structure. At that juncture, he enlisted the talented Father Albert Bandini to draft the organizational format. At first, the work was arduous but Luigi was persistent. He was a charismatic orator and along with Father Bandini, he travelled over the state spreading the message and forming new branches.

Luigi somehow arranged to squeeze other obligations into his busy schedule. He became business manager for the *Central California Register* in 1937 and during his decade with that newspaper increased the circulation by 250%

After 1948, Luigi devoted his whole time to the Italian Catholic Federation. By the time of his demise, the Federation numbered 28,000 members in California, Indiana, Illinois, Nevada and Wisconsin.

Luigi received all manner of awards and distinctions over the years. In 1963, he was initiated into the papal knighthood of Saint Gregory and, fifteen years later, the Order of Malta presented him with its highest medal of honor, the Cross of Valor.

At the time of his death, on February 7, 1981, Bishop John S. Cummins said that "what Luigi gave to his people was identity and pride of heritage, and he did it in such a way that it was astonishingly successful. . . . We are grateful for what his life was among us."

MANUEL QUIXANO (d. 1825)

One of the commentators on medical practices in early California has noted that "so closely allied were the cross, the sword and the scalpel during the Spanish, Mexican and early American phases of California history, that it is impossible to give a survey of the latter without including the events that moulded the former."

Manuel Quixano proves that contention. A native of Leon, Spain, he studied and mastered the techniques of his profession at the Royal Medical University of Madrid. Shortly after receiving his license to practice, the youthful physician offered his services to the Spanish armed forces. After almost a quarter century, Dr. Quixano was assigned to a contingency of troops destined for military duties in New Spain.

In 1807, Dr. Quixano arrived in California as the ninth and last of the Spanish surgeons general to serve in that far–away province. He was stationed at the *presidio* of Monterey, where his medical expertise proved to be of invaluable benefit for seventeen years. Among the doctor's first duties was that of being an official witness for Governor Jose Arrillaga, on August 10, 1809, when the governor took the oath of allegiance to King Ferdinand VII.

In 1815, Dr. Quixano made an official tour of the missions for the Spanish Crown, during which he carefully recorded and commented on the medical practices then being observed in those foundations. It is recorded that "in every mission he was treated with respect due to his rank, but especially due to his ability and benevolence."

It was Dr. Quixano who performed the "first recorded autopsy in California," in October, 1812. At the request of the governor, he journeyed to Mission Santa Cruz, where he exhumed the remains of Fray Andrés Quintana for a careful medical analysis. The Franciscan had died earlier under suspicious circumstances and Dr. Quixano determined that the friar had indeed been slain "in a most cruel manner." By 1822, Quixano had risen to the rank of captain in the army. In that year, he retired from military service rather than swear an oath of fidelity to the Mexican regime in California. After relinquishing his commission, Dr. Quixano retired to private practice on the Monterey peninsula, where he labored until his death, in 1825.

Upon his retirement, Quixano was presented with the office chair that he and his predecessors as surgeons general had used at Monterey. That chair, a mahogany box containing his medical instruments and the scales he used for weighing drugs are now on display at Mission San Carlos Borromeo.

Known throughout his life for his devout faith and allegiance to the Catholic faith, Dr. Quixano was an exemplary Catholic. His great granddaughter, Maria Antonia Fields, in an address to the Catholic Study Class of Saint Mary's Cathedral, in San Francisco, in February, 1942, outlined the circumstances of the physician's death. He "insisted on walking on his knees, from his bed to the front door of the house, supported by two members of the family—and on his knees holding a blessed candle accompanied Our Lord to his room where he received Him for the last time. He died that night and was buried with military honors."

Manuel Quixano served his faith, his nation and his profession well. He deserves to be remembered among the pioneers of California.

JAMES RYDER RANDALL (1839–1908)

The prominent prose writer and essayist, James Ryder Randall, was born at Baltimore in 1839. After completing his education at Georgetown, he journeyed to Latin America and the West Indies, where he worked briefly in the printing trade.

In 1859, Randall moved to New Orleans and there accepted the Chair of English Literature at Poydras College, then a flourishing Creole Institution. His writings soon won for him a wide reputation in the world of letters. Unable to fight for his beloved Confederacy because of ill health, he became a journalist and, in 1861, wrote the famous war song of the Confederacy, "Maryland, My Maryland."

After the war, Randall continued to work as a newspaperman as the Washington correspondent for a number of southern newspapers. He subsequently became editor of the *Constitutionalist* at Augusta, where he made his home for some years.

In 1905, Randall came to the West Coast for the national conclave of the Knights of Columbus, which was held at Los Angeles. The nationally–known writer was hailed by the local press for his many patriotic, romantic and religious writings. Joseph Scott offered to give Randall everything but the climate.

Randall was described by *The Monitor* as "a youthful old man in vigorous health" which the newspaper credited to his "strong, natural constitution and correct living." Randall was astounded "with the developments and phenomena of the Pacific Coast, especially along the great Southern Pacific Railway." Also greatly impressed with "the beautiful and sublime scenery," Randall stated that even the City of Rio de Janeiro "is not at all as attractive as Los Angeles or San Francisco."

During his western sojourn, Randall wrote a number of elaborate letters for publication in three eastern newspapers, *The Chronicle* (Augusta), *The Columbian* (Columbus) and *The Morning Star* (New Orleans). In one of the vignettes, he said that "when I crossed the Colorado desert and got a glimpse of the irrigated Eden, I felt as the Jews of old did when they beheld the Promised Land, or as the traveller from Jerusalem does when, on the mountain top, he beholds Damascus, the emerald jewel in the wilderness." Randall promised that upon his return to the east, he would "endeavor to persuade many persons in other sections to come this way," insisting that those who have not visited the area were only half educated.

James Randall returned to Augusta where he continued his work. Much of his work in those final years breathed a deeply religious tone. The man often referred to as the "Poet of the Lost Cause" (for his support of the Confederacy) died on January 14, 1908.

FREDERICK L. REARDON (1879–1906)

A. SOUTHLAND LITTERATEUR

The first of the Catholic directories issued in California's southland, now a rare and prized collector's item, was conceived and produced by a man worth remembering as one of the area's literary forebears. Frederick L. Reardon (1879–1906) the son of a well–known officer in the Union Army, was born in Peoria, Illinois. His parents brought their family of five youngsters to Los Angeles "when Fred was a little lad in knickerbockers."

He was always a dominant personality in his many endeavors. A friend recalled that even as a student at Saint Vibiana's School, Fred "led us all, and on the tree–shaded playground, as well as in our holiday ram-

bles over the hills, he was our leader. We realized his ability and accorded him recognition, looking up to him and following in his footsteps."

Reardon's intellectual acumen was equally outstanding. He achieved a splendid record at Saint Vincent's College, winning "practically every medal or other scholastic honor offered in those days." The Vincentian faculty looked upon Reardon "as one of the brightest young men ever enrolled at the college." After obtaining a master's degree at The Catholic University of America in Washington, Reardon returned to California with plans for a Catholic directory to serve the far–flung Diocese of Monterey–Los Angeles. The energetic and youthful writer was well trained for such an ambitious undertaking.

At Saint Vincent's he had "organized a monthly paper and launched it upon the seas of college journalism." His interest in writing continued and, upon his arrival back in Los Angeles, he proudly displayed his most treasured possession, a volume of Maurice Francis Egan's poems which bore on the fly–leaf the writer's prediction that his young friend would become the laureate of the Pacific.

With the exception of two years at Hastings College of Law in San Francisco, Reardon lived out his few remaining years in Los Angeles, lecturing on English, Latin and Medieval History at Saint Vincent's College. He served with Charles C. Conroy as co–editor of *The Tidings* for several months in 1905–1906. The originality of thought and neatness of phraseology evidenced in his prose and verse give every indication that had Frederick L. Reardon lived beyond his twenty–seventh year, he might well have won that laureate foretold by Maurice Francis Egan.

FREDERICK L. REARDON (1879–1906)

B. CATHOLIC TREASURE TROVE

One of the most remarkable books associated with early California is the *Catholic Directory and Census of Los Angeles City and Parish Gazetteer of the Diocese of Monterey–Los Angeles*. Edited and published by Frederick L. Reardon, the 377 page book was envisioned as "a means of making Catholics known to each other and so foster the many good things that would necessarily result from a more perfect union between our co–religionists."

In the Preface, Reardon said the book was intended "to be a factor in bringing about a better state of affairs among the Catholics" of Southern California. It was a noble objective and one he certainly accomplished. Printed by L. R. Jones, whose firm was then located at 235 West First Street, Los Angeles, the book contained several hundred advertisements, mostly from the various religious institutions then serving the area.

A Catholic census of the City of Los Angeles was taken in preparation for the directory. A total of 18,857 Catholics are represented (those fifteen years of age or older), plus another 418 "inmates" of Religious Houses. Another ninety–three living outside the city limits were added for various reasons.

Each person listed in the directory is identified with his or her parish. The 19,275 Catholics residing in Los Angeles, in September, 1899, were divided into the six parishes of Saint Vibiana, Our Lady of the Angels, Saint Vincent, Saint Joseph, Sacred Heart and Saint Mary.

Of the six parishes then canonically functioning, only Saint Joseph lacked specific boundaries. It was established for the accommodation of the German–speaking Catholics of the whole city. According to the directory, there were ninety priests serving in the 75,984 square mile diocese. There were twenty–three seminarians (eight studying for the diocese and fifteen for religious orders), forty–six churches with resident priests, forty–two mission churches, twenty– nine station churches and two chapels.

Educationally, there were 2,497 enrollees in twenty–two academies and twenty–four parochial schools. 1,198 orphans were cared for in eight orphanages, as well as 400 children in three Indian schools.

At that time, the jurisdiction was bounded by Arizona, the Pacific Ocean, Peninsular California and the 37th degree, 5th minute northern latitude. It embraced the portions of Merced, Santa Clara and Santa Cruz counties lying south of that line. It was pointed out that the Church owed much of its strength in the area "to the efforts of the old *padres* who lived and died for the Faith of our Fathers more than a century ago."

A careful study of this book would make for a splendid sociological survey of the Catholic Church in Southern California. It really is a monumental tome for which the people of this and future generations should ever be greatful.

OLIVER REARDON (1904–1992)

During the late summer of 1978, I noticed an elderly gentleman showing three youthful, smartly–dressed, naval cadets through the historic church at San Buenaventura Mission. It didn't take much imagination to identify him as the "legendary" Oliver Reardon (1904–1992). We became instant friends.

After the proper introductions, I asked Oliver when he had last played the organ at the Old Mission. "I think it was Bastille Day in 1938," he responded. "Father Patrick Grogan put me on suspension for playing the French National Anthem after High Mass."

Though he had been away from San Buenaventura for thirty years, during which time he had a most successful career with the United States Navy Band, Oliver was widely–revered as the senior member of the famous Reardon family whose mortuary had served the area since 1911.

Then embarking upon a well–deserved retirement, Oliver readily agreed to resume his service at the Old Mission and, for most of the next decade, he played at the 10:30 Hispanic Liturgy every Sunday.

Oliver's first concert had been given at the Armory Hall which was built in San Buenaventura to accommodate the bands of Sousa and Gilmore. His initial public appearance, as a boy soprano, was staged at the Lagomarsino Opera House for a Saint Patrick's Day gala.

In 1919 and 1920, Oliver began playing at the local Isis Theatre. Known as "The Liberty," the theatre was more popularly referred to as the "Flea Palace." It was outfitted with an automated piano–organ whose removable rolls allowed Oliver to operate it manually.

Later, he played the accompaniment at "The Apollo," which was located near the intersection of Chestnut and Main streets. He provided the music for silent films and comedies and, occasionally, for vaudeville shows. In 1936, when the parish choir sank to unprecedented depths, Oliver was enlisted to rescue the angelic voices. The years that followed were classic ones for the old Mission because Oliver insisted on observing all the directives of Pope Pius X about using Ambrosian and Gregorian chant.

In the years after Oliver's return to the keyboard of the Old Mission's historic organ, the two of us spent at least an hour each week reminiscing about the lore of San Buenaventura. Oliver began where the history books left off.

Born July 30, 1904, Oliver grew up in the building just to the west of the mission's garden. Later used as a hotel and now housing the parochial offices and a Gift Shop, the building served as a mortuary in Oliver's early years. Though he never mentioned it, I learned that Oliver had studied at the Fountainbleu Paris Conservatory, the University of Southern California and Emerson University, where he obtained his doctorate.

If my funeral homilies were relevant during those years, it was because Oliver had coached me about the decedent's life span. What he didn't remember didn't need telling. In whatever he did, whether teaching music at Villanova, counseling cadets in the military or serving as armchair historian for the Old Mission, Oliver Reardon epitomized the role of exemplary Catholic layman.

He couldn't recall a person's faults, only his virtues. When faced with an embarrassing or compromising query, he would invoke Saint Paul's suggestion that "certain things are better left unsaid."

Everyone probably remembers that game played as

youngsters, where one person would suggest a word, and another would respond with a synonym, Whenever someone mentions San Buenaventura Mission, the name of Oliver Reardon automatically flashes on my memory screen.

AGNES REPPLIER (1885–1950)

Agnes Repplier was one of the first Catholics to receive a gold medal from the American Academy of Arts and Letters. And she did it in 1911, when few women were recognized for their talents in the literary world. Encouraged by such prominent people as Father Isaac Hecker and Thomas Bailey Aldrich, Agnes contributed stories and essays to the *Catholic World* and the *Atlantic Monthly*.

Even in contemporary times Miss Repplier is regarded by discriminating readers as one of the nation's most delightful essayists. Scholarly but not pedagogical, she charmed thousands with volume after volume of delicately written, thoughtfully composed stories.

No Philadelphian missed her vignettes of that city; no cat lover overlooked her reflections on felines and no tea drinker denied her literary interpretations of that popular beverage. It was (and is) understood that a collection of English essays would be incomplete without at least one of Agnes Repplier's contributions.

The great writer was also a biographer of considerable note. Her two fine books on "Pere Marquette" and "Mere Marie of the Ursulines" are regarded among the most beautiful and distinguished works of American biography.

Early in her career, Miss Repplier professed a great admiration for Fray Junípero Serra and his missionary work along *El Camino Real*. She promised one day to write his life. In the early 1930s, Agnes was able to fulfill that desire. New York's Doubleday and Company suggested she complete her trilogy with a volume about the Mallorcan friar and his work on the Pacific Slope.

She finished her work in 1932. The "Dean of American Essayists" produced a book which Theodore Maynard said was "written with great literary skill and with a special Catholic insight." Miss Repplier built her reconstruction of the great Franciscan pioneer's troubled and triumphant life on all the right sources—Francisco Palou, Herbert E. Bolton and George Wharton James. The volume was applauded as a vivid history of colonization and a portrait of an outstanding pioneer.

Though Agnes laid no claim to profound historical scholarship about the early history of California, she understood the period and its problems better than many self–proclaimed authorities. She found in Serra "purity of intention, which is one thing; fidelity of execution,

which is another; and farsighted wisdom, which is a third, and which insured the success of everything he undertook."

To Miss Repplier, "Spain's gift to America was one of disinterested benevolence, and Fray Junípero Serra was her almoner." She looked upon the friar as "seraphic in spirit, simple in faith and pure of heart."

Subsequent and more scientific studies have confirmed those observations. All told, Miss Repplier came quite close to portraying Fray Junípero Serra as he really was. One acquainted with her other writings would not find this surprising.

JOSEPH WARREN REVERE (1812–1880)

Joseph Warren Revere (1812–1880) grandson of the famous hero of revolutionary times, made a number of outstanding contributions to the post mission era of California history. Born in Boston, May 17, 1812, Joseph entered the navy as a midshipman and, in 1828, sailed on his first visit to California. His ship, the *USS Portsmouth*, under the command of Captain John Montgomery, arrived at Monterey in April 1846, "to watch over the rapid developments immediately preceding the war with Mexico."

In the absence of army personnel, Revere personally lowered the Bear Flag and unfurled the American standard at Sonoma, on July 9, 1846. He remained for about six months, establishing the usual routine of patrols and scouts. Revere was also able to make numerous excursions, during which he visited all the parts of the district subject to his jurisdiction.

In October, 1846, Lieutenant Revere acquired the estate of San Geronimo, about five miles from San Rafael. Shortly thereafter, he was transferred to San Diego. He participated in hoisting the stars and stripes at La Paz, thus having the honor of raising the American flag at the most northerly and southerly points of the Californias. After the war, Revere returned by ship to Boston, but was ordered back to California as agent for the protection of live oak and other Naval timber lands.

In 1850, Revere resigned from the Navy and entered business as a merchant seaman. He purchased part interest in a clipper ship in partnership with Sandy McGregor. Revere served briefly as an instructor in artillery for the Mexican Government. He returned to the United States, in 1853, and in later years functioned as a military consultant to various European governments. He associated himself with the United States Army in 1861, where he eventually rose to the rank of Brigadier General.

Revere was an educated and practicing Catholic throughout his life. While serving in California, he wrote a fascinating letter to Archbishop Samuel Eccleston of Baltimore, advising the American prelate of the problems facing the nascent Church along the Pacific Slope. That eleven–page letter, written from New York, on October 29, 1848, now reposes in the Baltimore Cathedral Archives.

Revere's firm belief in the future of California and the duty of Catholics is amply illustrated on the last page of *A Tour of Duty in California* (New York, 1849), in which he said:

> Perhaps a hundred years hence some curious book–worm . . . will be tempted to find out what was said and predicted of California at the eventful period of her annexation to the United States. . . . The poor Indians will then have passed away; the *rancheros* will be remembered only as the ancient proprietors of broad lands . . . the Grizzly Bear will live only in books and tradition . . . and California . . . will she have become populous and enlightened, the seat of arts and learning, the generous rival of her elder sisters in all that is lively and of good report among men ? Will not her arts of peace flourish beyond example and the majestic tread of man still press onwards towards a yet more glorious destiny?

WILLIAM ANTONIO RICHARDSON (1795–1856)

William Antonio Richardson (1795–1856), "a handsome man, above medium height, with an attractive face and a musical voice," arrived in San Francisco aboard the British whaler *Orion*, on August 2, 1822. The London–born Richardson sought out Fray Thomas Esténaga and asked the friar for employment at Mission San Francisco as a bricklayer and carpenter. In addition to his chores at San Francisco, Richardson was engaged, at various times, to vaccinate the Indian neophytes at several other of the nearby California missionary foundations.

In October 1822, Richardson petitioned Governor Pablo Vicente de Sola for permission to become a permanent resident of the province. The governor acquiesced, "being aware that the petitioner, besides being a navigator, is conversant with and engaged in the occupation of a carpenter." Richardson's association with the friars proved spiritually rewarding. He was baptized at Mission San Francisco, on June 10, 1823, at which time Fray Jose Altimira bestowed upon him the name "Antonio."

Two years later, Richardson married Maria Martinez, the daughter of the *comandante* at the Presidio of San Francisco. Their marriage was ultimately blessed by three youngsters, Mariana, Francisco and Estevan. A skillful sailor and an energetic man of business, Richardson built a launch and a small vessel with which he collected, traded and sold the produce of the neighboring missions. He was renowned as an experienced pilot and navigator and, on numerous occasions, was employed to "bring in" foreign ships to San Francisco Bay.

In 1829, Richardson journeyed to the *Pueblo de Nuestra Señora de los Angeles* on a trading expedition and, two years later, went to Peru for a similar purpose, during which time his family remained as guests at Mission San Gabriel. Early in the 1830s, Mr. Richardson approached Governor Jose Figueroa with a request for authorization to establish a commercial town at Yerba Buena, on the San Francisco Bay. Official approval was given by Governor José Castro, on October 20, 1835. Richardson erected the first dwelling in the new settlement, a shanty of boards with a sail–cloth roofing. He subsequently replaced it with an adobe structure on a piece of land that is now the northwest corner of Clay Street and Grant Avenue.

In 1841, the Richardsons moved to San Diego, where William became the grantee of the Sausalito Rancho. It was there that the "founder" of Yerba Buena, present–day San Francisco, died on April 20, 1856. The name of William Antonio Richardson is written in capital letters in the annals of California.

PHILIP AUGUSTINE ROACH (1820–1889)

Peter Thomas Conmy has observed that "the California pioneers were a varied lot. A number came as part of a supply of cheap labor. Some gave mechanical leadership and others offered commercial craftsmanship. Among them were educators, capitalists, poets, artists and ministers of religion. A few of them may be classed as advocates of truth and the cause of the people. To this latter type belonged Philip Augustine Roach."

Roach, a native of the Emerald Isle, was born at Cork in November 1820. He was brought to the United States two years later and grew up to become one of the outstanding men of his time. His early years were crowded with activities. He became a newspaper editor in 1844 and shortly thereafter entered the United States Foreign Service where, because of his linguistic abilities, he occupied several consular positions around the world before bowing to the "gold fever" of 1849. Once in the west, Roach entered public life and was elected *alcalde* or mayor of Monterey where he was characterized by "determination and bravery." The "silver tongued orator" served until his entry into the state legislature in 1852. From the very beginning of his law making career, "he emerged as one of the dynamic members of the senate." After some years as United States Appraiser for San Francisco, Roach entered private business in the

Bay City. It was during these years that he became a moving force behind the Roman Catholic Orphan Asylum of San Francisco. Always a man of intense activity, in 1865 Roach and two friends inaugurated the *Daily Examiner* and saw the publication eventually "become the leading democratic journal of California."

Roach was a popular figure in the community. In 1876, he was spoken of as one who had "attained local celebrity by reason of his rollicking good humor and innocent pleasantries, which are perhaps intensified by the venerable appearance his premature white locks fix upon him." In 1873 Roach was again nominated for the state Senate and later that year returned to the legislative chambers where he had served so illustriously two decades earlier. He was a leading candidate for governor in 1875, and seven years later was elected Public Administrator for San Francisco.

When Archbishop Patrick W. Riordan announced plans for a new cathedral in 1887, Roach was asked to deliver the central address for the opening festivities at the Mechanic's Pavillion. In his traditional style, the renowned lawmaker urged the people of the Bay Area to cooperate with the archbishop in erecting one of the grandest cathedrals of our country. Roach characterized the structure as one that, fifty years hence, would be a monument to the piety and zeal of the Catholics of the present time. The years had taken their toll on the noted pioneer and on April 27, 1889, he succumbed to complications resulting from a fall at his home. It is a fortunate man whose eulogy is written while he is still alive to read it. Such was the case with Philip Augustine Roach, for in 1878, Hugh Quigley wrote that,

> Senator Roach is a man of character—a natural born leader of men, and would have made his mark in any community. Of fine personal appearance and gentlemanly instincts, he displays marked public spirit and a thoroughly upright and honest heart. His character is agreeably impressive, and he never fails to command respectful attention when he has anything to say. He is like Cato of old, a man of action as well as an elegant orator, and it is in action that his large and generous resources find fitting expression.

HERMAN J. RODMAN (c. 1851–1907)

Herman J. Rodman was posthumously characterized by a longtime friend, as the classic example of "the eagle caged by circumstance." The son of a wealthy Saint Louis merchant, Herman was able to attend the United States Naval Academy by virtue of a presidential appointment. He had achieved an enviable academic record at Annapolis by the time of his graduation in 1873. The prospects of a career in the navy of those days was not encouraging and the young cadet decided to join his father in mercantile pursuits, something that ultimately proved wholly uncongenial.

Shortly after the turn of the century, a Japanese naval officer who had known Rodman at Annapolis offered him a commission in the Imperial Navy. Rodman had just lost his only daughter in death and his wife was nearing the end of a final illness. Reluctantly, he was forced to decline the position When Mr. Rodman's mercantilistic endeavors proved unsuccessful, he turned to journalism and there it was that his innate creative talents reached their fullest potential.

According to an article in the *Graphic*, Rodman "was an active newspaper man whose specialites—real estate and commercial work—brought him into close personal relations with men of affairs" in all walks of life. He worked for several Eastern newspaper chains before coming to Southern California as city editor for the Los Angeles *Express*. During his years with that newspaper, Rodman "read and prayed" his way into the Catholic faith.

On August 31, 1906, Bishop Thomas J. Conaty, President of The Tidings Publishing Company, approached Rodman with a proposal that he join the staff of the diocesan newspaper as editor–in–chief. Rodman brought to *The Tidings* "the experience of a life–time spent as a newspaper man." From the very onset, he infused new life and vigor into the weekly publication, from his editorial offices in the W. H. Hellman Buildng. Gradually the paper was enlarged to a twenty–four page spread. In December, 1907, Rodman published the first annual edition of eighty–six pages with a format that was to perdure until 1936.

The editorship of *The Tidings* was anything but a lucrative position. Yet like many converts to the faith, Rodman was filled with enthusiasm for the spread of Catholic principles and he felt that in no sphere could he be of greater assistance than as editor of the southland's only Catholic publication. Throughout his relatively few years as a Catholic, Rodman gave "manly service' in the cause of the Church. He was ranked among the "most prominent and involved" members in the local Knights of Columbus.

Unfortunately, Mr. Rodman's association with *The Tidings* lasted less than a year. The veteran journalist died suddenly and unexpectedly on July 26, 1907. Short though his tenure was, the name of Herman J. Rodman will be long cherished in California annals for "the goodness of his life, the sincerity of his purpose, the earnestness of his life work, his unflagging duty to religion, his love of the Church and his country, his apostolic spirit in the interest of Catholic truth as expressed in the Catholic newspaper."

JOSE DE LA ROSA (1790–1892)

Though the claim that Jose de la Rosa was California's first printer is disputed, it is known that his was the first printing of English in the area, a distinction he achieved while working for Thomas Oliver Larkin, the United States Consul at Monterey.

Born at *Puebla de los Angeles*, to Jose Florencio and Maria Antonia de la Rosa, the youngster was raised in a family long respected for its skills in the printing trade. Jose served in the War for Mexican Independence and during that time held a prominent position in the government's printing office at Mexico City.

In 1833, General Antonio Lopez de Santa Ana dispatched de la Rosa to Monterey with a printing press. There are nine extant publications bearing de la Rosa's imprint, all of them dating from 1844–1845. Jose moved to Sonoma in the early 1840s, where he became a protege of General Mariano Guadalupe Vallejo, the military *comandante* for San Francisco Bay.

After the Bear Flag Revolt, de la Rosa remained a close personal friend of Vallejo, whose family referred to him as "Don Pepe." He was named *alcalde* of Sonoma, in 1845, and became the grantee of the nearby *Ulpinos Rancho*. About 1880, Jose moved to San Buenaventura, where he took up residence with Harold L. Kamp and his family. He worked in a host of trades. He was a skilled tailor, expert watchmaker and talented musician.

During his last dozen years, the never–married de la Rosa became a familiar character in the community of San Buenaventura. He was known by his contemporaries as a cheerful man, a "quiet, polite and intelligent gentleman."

A statewide celebration was held in San Buenaventura's Union Hall to mark his 100th birthday. Jose spoke on that occasion and then played his guitar for the guests. One news account remarked that "his accuracy of touch and the agility of the movements of his hands and fingers was wonderful."

Mary M. Bowman noted that shortly before Jose's death, "time had dealt gently with him. His hair was quite abundant and not entirely gray. The upper teeth were firm and even, the eyesight dim, but his hearing good and memory clear." Jose de la Rosa died at 101 years of age on December 28, 1891. His funeral was held at the Old Mission, where he was eulogized as a fine Christian gentleman of high moral standards and strict religious observance. The local newspaper editorialized that "it was a fitting send–off for one who had been such a respected formulator of the area's objectives."

WILLIAM STARK ROSECRANS (1819–1898)

An impartial study of this nation's Civil War will indicate the pivotal role exercised by William Stark Rosecrans (1819–1898) in military strategy. This "last survivor of the generals who commanded an army, on the Union side," is a pioneer of whom California is justly proud.

Rosecrans graduated from West Point in 1842, the fifth in a class of fifty–six. He was then assigned to the engineer corps as a second lieutenant and during the half century that followed, he achieved an outstanding reputation as soldier, politician, educator and diplomat. It was while teaching philosophy at West Point that the young soldier was first attracted to Catholicism. He was fond of recalling how it happened: One day while out walking with a fellow–officer, George Deshon, the two came across a poor man trudging along the road with a basket on his arm The future general asked the man what he had to sell. To this he replied, "Catholic books." Rosecrans was not favorably inclined to the Church and was amazed that the peddler was so unashamed of his occupation. The oil–cloth covering of the basket was removed, revealing an excellent selection of Catholic literature—from which Rosecrans purchased *The Catholic Christian Instructed*, by Richard Challoner. He also bought a copy for his companion (who later became a priest and Superior General of the Paulist Fathers) and through that volume "read his way into the Church."

After his own conversion, Rosecrans was ever anxious to share his good fortune with others. In 1846, he interested his brother, Sylvester, in Catholic teaching. Sylvester went on to be the first Bishop of Columbus, Ohio. Rosecrans was equally successful with other members of his family, including his wife, who embraced the Faith some years after their marriage. In 1861, after a brief interval as president of the Coal River Navigation Company, William Rosecrans returned to the Army where he subsequently, "was one of the ablest strategists among the Union generals," serving as commander of the forces of the Cumberland in 1862 and 1863. It is recorded that "on the morning of every important engagement, or perilous undertaking, it was his invariable custom to attend Mass and commit himself and his army to the keeping of the God of battles."

Though known as a lifelong Democrat, the general was offered a place on the Republican ticket with Abraham Lincoln in 1864. Had it not been for a mix–up of telegraph messages, Rosecrans, and not Andrew Johnson, would have succeeded to the presidency in 1865. The following year, General Rosecrans refused the Union nomination for the governorship of Ohio. Two years later, he retired from the Army and journeyed to California.

Public service did not end for the eminent military

man with his arrival on the West Coast. He served a number of years as Ambassador to Mexico, and between 1881 and 1885, he was a member of the California delegation in the United States House of Representatives. In 1885, he was named Registrar of the Treasury.

The man for whom the old Spanish Fort of Guijarros in San Diego was named "exhibited a familiarity with controversial theology that made him a formidable antagonist to the best read." He was no less accomplished in the field of patrology, where the vehemence of his intellect was frequently heard in the Church. At the general's funeral, held in Saint Vibiana's Cathedral, Bishop George T. Montgomery noted that William Stark Rosecrans needed no eulogy—"He has written his own panegyric upon the hearts not alone of the American people, but upon that of the race."

JAN HENRYK DE ROSEN (1891–1982)

Jan Henryk de Rosen, a "Renaissance man in the 20th century," was described in early 1979 as "the pre–eminent religious artist in the world." It was a title he richly deserved. His murals and mosaics adorn churches around the globe, including the private chapel of Pope John Paul II at the summer papal palace, Castel Gandolfo. In 1939, de Rosen decorated the Polish Pavilion at New York's World Fair. His largest mosaic (believed to be the most massive in the world) was done for the 13,000 square foot dome of the Cathedral at Saint Louis.

Anaheim is among the half dozen California places where de Rosen's work is represented. The famed artist was commissioned by the Dominican Sisters to paint the "Descent of Truth" mural for the chapel of Saint Catherine's Military School. That mural represents a span of 1900 years during which Christ's truth has been preached by word and example to all nations, by men and women of every generation and under all guises— philosophy, theology, literature and the arts and sciences.

Christ the Teacher dominates and gives meaning to the ninety foot mural as He stands, arms outstretched, transmitting His eternal truths to all ages, through men at His left and women at His right. Christ's flowing robe is joined by a clasp upon which are portrayed the four evangelists, the immediate bearers of His truth. Overhead is the image of Christ crucified and to one side is the ancient Greek symbol for resurrection.

To the Lord's left are nineteen men, apostles, fathers and doctors of the Church, theologians and mystics, courageous Christians who entered into the problems of their age with learning and sanctity. Saint John the Evangelist stands next to Christ. He holds in his hand the chalice of wine from which a snake emerges, recalling

the occasion when his enemies attempted to poison him.

Saint Peter bears in his hands the keys to the kingdom. Inscribed in his halo is the Greek work, *Cephas*. In the background, the obelisk of Saint Peter's square in Rome marks the place of the vicar's martyrdom. Saint Paul, author of fourteen masterly epistles, stands before the Athenian altar to the unknown god from which he preached on the Holy Spirit. In his hands he holds a sword, the instrument of his earthly demise.

The other figures in the mural are equally symbolic in their portrayal, concluding with Cardinal Mercier and Pope Leo XIII who bears in his hand the encyclical which made scholastic philosophy obligatory for all divinity students. To the right of the majestic Savior are seven women who have played a part in history as bearers of truth saints Elizabeth, Monica, Gertrude, Catherine, Jane d'Aza, Teresa and Joan of Arc.

And so Jan Henryk de Rosen, a poet in Paris, a soldier in Poland and a diplomat in New York lives on at Anaheim in the greatest of his roles—an artist for God.

M. DE ROUISSILLON (1772–1803)

The initial Polish imprint on Alta California can be traced to May 1, 1805, when Captain William Shaler's 175 ton *Lelia Byrd* put into a bay on Santa Catalina Island for repairs. Because the bay which served the weary seamen as an hospitable haven had not yet been designated with a name, Shaler, the proto navigator to visit and survey the area, "took the liberty of naming it after my much respected friend, M. de Rouissillon." The conferral of his Polish companion's name was the first such appellation applied in California by an American.

John, the Count of Rouissillon (1772–1803), was a Polish nobleman of considerable prominence in his native land. An accomplished scholar in the fields of astronomy, mathematics and music, the count was conversant with almost every European language and dialect. Rouissillon had fought for the liberty of his country as an aide–de–camp to Tadeusz Kosciuszko — when that famed Polish general led a force of 4,000 peasants, armed only with crude scythes and other farming implements, against the Russians at Raclawice.

Subsequently exiled in Hamburg to avoid reprisals from his nation's enemies, Rouissillon met William Shaler and Richard Cleveland when the two New England merchant–adventurers arrived to purchase a vessel on which to visit the western shores of America. Reared on the continent, Rouissillon had never been to sea. Yet such a challenge fascinated him and he readily accepted the offer to join Shaler and Cleveland on their epochal journey.

The *Lelia Byrd* sailed from Cuxhaven on November

8, 1801. After a brief stop at the Canary Islands, the ship reached Rio de Janeiro early the next year. Rounding Cape Horn, Shaler, Cleveland, Rouissillon and their eight crewman sailed into the harbor of Valparaiso on February 24th. There the entire crew was briefly imprisoned for infringing on the Spanish trade monopoly.

The *Lelia Byrd* encountered further difficulties at San Blas, Mexico, where officials raised new objections to their docking. After personally appealing to the local governor and then to the viceroy himself, Rouissillon finally secured permission to dispose of their wares and reprovision the ship. Then it was on to Alta California.

Though he remained behind in Mexico to acquaint himself with the seat of an ancient and vibrant culture, Rouissillon fully intended to rejoin his friends in the United States, where he hoped to live out his years in an atmosphere of liberty. Those expectations were unfortunately thwarted by his premature death in 1803.

Richard Cleveland described the count as a strong "advocate of liberty" who "could not brook the subjugation of his country." He was likewise an outstanding Catholic, whose knowledge of theology and practice of virtue further endowed his valiant personality.

Though Port Rouissillon does not survive in the Golden States geographic nomenclature, present–day Avalon remains the scene of the first link in what has become a formidable Polish presence in California.

WILBUR RUBOTTOM (1914–1993)

The "mark of excellence" is a term associated with the works of the late Wilbur Rubottom, the Ventura craftsman who fashioned a lasting gift to his city, in the person of Fray Junípero Serra. Born in 1914, Rubottom was a man of many talents. He launched his career at Fremont High School in Los Angeles in 1930, with a cabinet–making course that included four shop periods a day.

While mechanization and mass production have, over the decades, greatly reduced opportunities in the trades, there will always be work for true craftsmen who take pride in their accomplishments. In 1946, he moved to the scenic and historic seaside city of San Buenaventura and there began his company, W.L. Rubottom Cabinet Makers. For the next thirty–six years, he provided as many as 130 jobs to local carpenters.

Through a long and productive life, Rubottorn urged that others be given the opportunity to develop their talents. As a man who made the most of his own skills, he wanted others to share those blessings. Mr. Rubottom designed and personally crafted an ancient–looking vestment case for the sacristy which had all the qualities of a modern cabinet.

A noted Jesuit historian visited the mission a few years later and commented "how well the vestment case had withstood the years since 1784. It was the supreme compliment for its maker."

Perhaps the greatest and surely the most visible Rubottom legacy is his work on the statue of Fray Junípero Serra that stands serenely atop California Street in front of the San Buenaventura City Hall. That statue is a copy of the original concrete likeness by Juan Palo Kangus in 1936. The story of the replica's creation is one that needs to be recorded.

In the mid–1980s, the concrete statue began deteriorating, to the extent that a drive was launched for replacing it with a bronze figure. Wilbur Rubottom stepped forward and offered his skills for the project.

The master carver began what was a tedious and year–long process of carving a wooden replica of the nine foot statue. The end result, warmer and more beautiful than either the original or the finished product, is displayed in the City Hall atrium. When Rubottom and his crew had finished, their wooden replica was used as a mold for the bronze statue that was unveiled on its California Street pedestal in 1989.

For his devotion to this project, the Chamber of Commerce for San Buenaventura bestowed upon Mr. Rubottom the " Citizen of the Year" award. His was probably the most popular choice ever made. Rubottom lived on another five years and often could be seen waving at Fray Junípero Serra as he drove along Poli Street. After all, they were good and close friends.

Rubottom's work on the statue is his most valued legacy to the city. The Ventura *Star Free Press*, in an editorial published at the time of his demise in 1993, said that San Buenaventura "is blessed to be able to share some of his pride in the statue that graces the city's magnificent City Hall. It is there—and will be there forever—because Mr. Rubottom and his colleagues lovingly shared their talents with their community.

PAUL SALAMUNOVICH (b. 1927)

Those who read the documents of Vatican Council II will eventually stumble across the passage which affirms that "the musical tradition of the Universal Church is a treasure of immeasurable value, greater even than that of any other art." Such a statement comes as no revelation to Catholics in California where music has always played a paramount role in the development of the Church. From the earliest mission times, choral music has occupied a unique place in the religious and social life of God's people.

On the local scene, Paul Salamunovich has played a vital role in sustaining that heritage. He has aptly been referred to as "California's High Priest of Choral Music." His friends recently observed Paul's fiftieth anniversary as music director at Saint Charles Boromeo Parish in North Hollywood.

Born in Redondo Beach, on June 7, 1927, the youngest of five sons Paul was reared in a loving and caring environment which emphasized strong familial ties. He first became interested in music at the age of ten when he joined a boys choir founded by Father Louis Buechner in Redondo Beach. The years he spent there instilled a true feeling for the authenticity of Gregorian Chant as unfolded on the pages of the *Liber Usualis.*

Early on, Paul became enamored with the choral renditions of Roger Wagner and later he profited from lessons which helped to produce that fullbodied sound attained through proper voice support and placement. In 1940, the Salamunovich family moved to Hollywood and there Paul became affiliated with the liturgical outreach of Richard Keys Biggs at Blessed Sacrament Church. During those Hollywood years Paul also regularly attended and carefully observed Roger Wagner's rehearsals.

He entered the armed forces in 1945 and served as part of the United States Navy in Pearl Harbor. After his discharge, in 1946, he signed up for courses at Los Angeles City College. In 1948, he received his associate degree in music. During that time he also sang with Biggs and Wagner who alternated as coordinators of youth choruses from the Los Angeles City Bureau of Music.

A charter member of the Los Angeles Concert Youth Chorus, which later became the Roger Wagner Chorale, Paul became music director of Saint Charles Borromeo in 1949. In June of 1961, he was awarded his graduate degree from Mount Saint Mary's College and from 1957 to 1976 he was choral director for that college. In May of 1950 he married Dorothy Hilton. His four sons and one daughter inherited his love for music and his expertise in choral arrangements.

In July of 1969, Paul was named music director for Saint Basil's Church in the Wilshire district and, in 1973, he began teaching full time at Loyola–Marymount University. Also, in the years 1957 through 1972 Paul taught at UCLA as a substitute for the frequently–touring Roger Wagner.

Paul Salamunovich believes that choral music is not a substitute but an adjunct to community singing. Anyone who wants to hear that objective set to music should plan to attend Sunday Mass in North Hollywood.

JOSE DE LOS SANTOS (1815–1921)

A faded, unidentified newspaper clipping in one of the John Steven McGroarty scrapbooks tells about the funeral of Jose de los Santos who was buried with grand solemnity from San Gabriel Mission on February 21, 1921. According to the account, "he was the last of the 16,000 of his race won from savagery to Christianity through the efforts of the Mission fathers and the last who could tell from personal experiences the story of the California missions when they were in their glory."

"Juncio," as he was known to his friends, had reached the venerable age of 106! Born in 1815, he had "passed his entire life within the sight of the same mountains and within a radius of twenty miles of his birth." Father Rafael Serrano, the Claretian priest who officiated at the funeral, related that Juncio had been born six years following the birth of Abraham Lincoln. A convert to the faith, he was confirmed at San Gabriel Mission about a decade prior to the outbreak of the American Civil War.

Many of the details in McGroarty's "Mission Play" had been inspired by Juncio's tales of his childhood. In his homily, the priest described the deceased as one "whose life was a tribute to the good and lasting work done by the Mission play." The newspaper account of the funeral liturgy is interesting. The Mission Church was filled to overflowing and another crowd of mourners gathered outside while the ceremony was in progress.

Many of the scores of Indians assembled to pay tribute to "the most venerable citizen of Southern California," were outfitted in their native costumes, a feature that added a touch of colorful picturesqueness to the event. The newspaper description noted that the crowd mingling at the threshold was refreshingly unique. The drama, music and art critic of a prominent *Pacific Coast Magazine,* a dusty African, an Indian laborer and scores of children came to say goodbye.

The coffin containing his remains was carried down the narrow aisle of the historic old church and into the street by six young Indians, lineal descendants of the men who, like Juncio, had been born within the confines of the mission. "The scene was fraught with revealing impressions." As the cortege moved out of the church, Chief Youngturtle of the Chickasaw tribe acted as coordinator for the guard of honor. The six young braves who acted as pallbearers were followed closely by Chief Manitou of the Pueblos Indians.

One hundred singers from the cast of the Mission Play followed the Indian escort and chanted the ancient hymn of the *Alabado* which Juncio learned in his first years as a member of San Gabriel's Christian family. At the grave, after the ceremony, the Indians invoked an old custom and threw a handful of dirt into the open grave. Each then brought forth a single flower which was reverently arranged in the form of the cross which Juncio had embraced so many decades earlier.

"If old Santos knows the honor that is being paid him today, I'm sure he's very happy," said a wrinkled faced old woman who had followed the coffin to the grave. It was a tribute well befitting the last of a remnant race. As the newspaper account concluded "his passing marked the severing of the last living tie between the romantic past and the present."

JUAN DE DIOS SANTOS (ff. 1850s)

Juan de Dios Santos was one of California's legendary *bandidos* who flourished in the 1850s. Christened in early childhood by devout parents, he later earned the name of *El Lobo* (the wolf) because of his uncanny ability of avoiding capture for his unsavory lifestyle.

Like many stories handed down from the past without solid documentation, Juan's life has several variations. This one was told by Angus MacLean in *Legends of the California Bandidos* which was released by Pioneer Publishing in 1977. There are no dates for Juan. He was among that band of rebellious *revolucionaries* who never recognized or acknowledged Mexico's relinquishment of California to the United States.

One day, while resting in an unguarded camp in the Cuyama Valley, Juan and several of his companions were ambushed by a posse. The others were shot immediately, but Juan, though wounded, managed to escape on horseback.

With great determination, Juan de Dios Santos urged his weary mare to great effort—though he knew it would be his last ride. It was as though death on an invisible black charger rode by the side of the wounded bandit. At the first opportunity to pause and rest, Juan tightly bandaged the wound where the bullet had shattered a rib as it tore into his body. The bullet was lodged deep inside, so deep that there was no possibility of removing it. Bleeding was profuse.

Finally Juan de Dios Santos arrived at a remote canyon in the rugged Sierra Madre, a place where many caves offered the solitude he needed for a peaceful death. Taking his bedroll and saddlebags with him, *El Lobo* sought out one of the caves for his last moments. His instinct told him that his own death should not be witnessed by the unsympathetic eyes of the curious.

With reverent hands the man who had been christened with such a pious name took from his saddlebag a small, exquisitely–carved figure of the Madonna which he had salvaged (or purloined) from the ruins of *Nuestra Señora de la Soledad* Mission some years earlier. He carefully placed the holy image from the Mission days in a niche on the rock wall of the cave where, in his dying hours, it facilitated a review of his life and sorrow

for his lawlessness. Recalling the prayers of his youth, *El Lobo* made his peace with the Lord.

It was another thirty years before a group of youngsters on a hiking expedition came upon the bones of Juan de Dios Santos in the cave. Little was left of his clothing and saddle bags. His hunting knife with its staghorn handle, a handful of scattered cartridges, some mother–of–pearl buttons and a silver belt buckle were all that remained.

The small Madonna was still enthroned in its niche among the rocks and it was that remnant from *Nuestra Señora de la Soledad* Mission that identified Juan de Dios Santos, an outlaw who had disappeared into the mountains after being wounded in a skirmish with lawmen. The story or legend of Juan de Dios Santos is worthy of remembrance mostly because it recalls a *bandido* whose lifelong devotion to the Blessed Mother provided a solace in his final hours. Has it not always been thus with clients of the Blessed Lady?

VIRGILIO SCATTOLINI

Father Robert Graham, a native of San Francisco who became an outstanding Jesuit scholar, is credited with unraveling one of the most dramatic historical hoaxes of modern times. For many years, Graham had been working on a book about the activities of Pope Pius XII and other Vatican officials during World War II. During his studies, Graham stumbled across the shadowy figure of Virgilio Scattolini.

In 1979, Graham finally tracked down the file on Scattolini which he then pried loose from the Central Intelligence Agency with a Freedom of Information Act request. Therein Graham's suspicions were finally confirmed.

In mid 1944, Scattolini approached the United States Office of Strategic Services, wartime precursor of today's CIA, with the offer of intelligence reports from the Vatican. Scattolini's subsequent reports became so valuable and prolific that the OSS kept a man in Italy occupied full time translating and forwarding them on to Washington officialdom.

Those reports included verbatim dialogues between Pope Pius XII and Church leaders throughout Europe. Transcriptions of secret audiences with the German and Japanese ambassadors were rushed to the White House for review by the president.

Grace Tully, FDR's private secretary, told the OSS in January, 1945, to keep the reports coming. "The President finds this material most interesting and reads every one carefully." Scattolini was the intelligence source for the first peace feelers from Japan and the first signs of civilian unrest in war–torn Germany. He informed the Americans of what the Russians were telling the Japanese about their intentions in the Pacific.

And he flashed the news that Japan was thinking of breaking its links with Germany and that Japan's industrialists were gaining influence over their nation's militarists. Father Graham discovered that there was one major problem with the Scattolini intelligence reports—they were entirely manufactured. It was a classic scam, apparently concocted because Scattolini needed the $500 monthly payment from the OSS.

When the OSS finally figured out the hoax, two of its top officers quickly buried the 1,700 cables and documents on a farm in Maryland. They were unearthed and returned to the CIA in 1960. The San Francisco priest whose research brought the Scattolini episode to the the surface said that "it was a farce to think that President Roosevelt, the State Department and the joint Chiefs of Staff were fed these complete fabrications—it's incredible."

No one at the OSS ever met Scattolini. His reports were passed through an intermediary. Scattolini *claimed* to have been in contact with Msgr. Giovanni Battista Montini, the Vatican's pro–Secretary of State (who later became Pope Paul VI).

Montini supposedly kept the archives where Scattolini said the minutes of the Pope's secret audiences were kept. Scattolini hinted that he had access to those archives. Graham became suspicious when he found that there were no records anywhere in the Vatican of the audiences which Pope Pius held with diplomats, church leaders or anyone else.

And Washington would have kept its secret, had it not been for a San Francisco–born Jesuit!

ERNESTINE SCHUMANN–HEINK (1861–1936)

From the front window of his grocery store across the street, from San Buenaventura Mission, Nick Peirano watched the famous, infamous and unfamous make their way in and out of the Old Mission for over half a century. Near the top of his list of renowned visitors was Madame Ernestine Schumann–Heink (1861–1936) who never traveled the coast route without making a visit to her "favorite mission."

Though she admitted to "wandering from the embrace of Mother Church," the world's greatest contralto never forgot the lessons she learned as a youngster at the Ursuline Convent at Prague. Born at Lieben, the daughter of an Austrian army officer and an Italian housewife, Ernestine studied under Marietta von Leclair. After making her debut in 1878, she went on to become the most famous member of the Berlin Opera.

In 1898, Ernestine came to the United States, where she eventually was associated with the Metropolitan Opera. Seven years later, she proudly took the pledge of allegiance as an American citizen. Though her operatic

repertoire numbered over 150 roles, Ernestine never stopped learning and polishing. (When she moved into Grossmont, people living in the El Cajon Valley five miles away said that often they could hear her singing as she worked!)

Schumann–Heink's success was due not alone to her majestic voice. Her audiences adored her as a person. They loved her naturalness, her motherliness, her wit and humor and her kindness. Critics used adjectives to describe her performances they hadn't utilized for years.

After retiring from the Metropolitan, Madame Schumann–Heink devoted most of her time to concert work giving as many as 100 recitals annually. Year after year her popularity grew, to the extent that she became a legendary figure in her own lifetime. In 1912, Ernestine moved to San Diego, where she quickly became that city's most famous citizen. She loved being a Westerner and in Southern California this "greatest box office draw in the United States" enjoyed her family, her pets, her career and her fellow artists.

Her heart was broken during World War I when she had sons fighting in both the American and German armies. Yet she toured the nation selling Liberty Bonds with record–breaking success. She had the honor of being the first woman Honorary Colonel in history. The San Francisco *Chronicle* noted editorially that "America will not soon forget Schumann–Heink's war–time service. Schumann–Heink is genuine and she is safe in America's heart."

When "the Heink" died in 1936, a large crowd gathered in San Diego to hear Verdi's Solemn Requiem Mass sung for the beloved songstress by Saint Joseph's Cathedral Choir. Msgr. John M. Hegarty, Vicar General for the Diocese of San Diego, spoke eloquently and touchingly about the great diva, who gained not only the plaudits of the entire world, but also its universal affection.

And, at San Buenaventura Mission, Father Patrick Grogan also prayed for Madame Ernestine Schumann–Heink, "Gold Star Mother, a Star of the World."

JOSEPH SCOTT (1866–1958)

A. Biographical Sketch

Joseph Scott was not a politician; he was "the great elder statesman of the west, and one of our most beloved citizens." It would be difficult to say whether the growth of the city whose name he bore paralleled the life of Joseph Scott or *vice versa*. Born in Penrith, England, Joe Scott was educated at Ushaw College, Durham, where he had the privilege of studying under Rafael Merry del Val, later the papal Secretary of State under Pius X. After his graduation from London University, Scott came to the United States in 1889, and was admitted to the bar five years later.

The Los Angeles of 1893 had seemingly little to offer; but in the City of Our Lady of Angels Joseph Scott found his wife, his career and his fame. Of the eleven children born to Joe and Bertha Roth, two became priests, one a judge, and all became respected members of a society that owed a large debt of gratitude to their loving father.

Scott never held public office except for a short tenure as President of the Los Angeles Chamber of Commerce and the City Board of Education some years after the turn of the century. Rather, he devoted his energies to social and cultural betterment which he felt was easier and less conflicting for a private citizen. A patriot, nationally famous for his sterling leadership in public affairs, Joseph Scott preferred to sit on the sidelines; nevertheless, he was a powerful force in the Republican Party as is evidenced by the privilege accorded him in 1928, of nominating Herbert Hoover for the presidency. A tribute printed in the *Congressional Record* to commemorate his 90th birthday spoke of Scott's "driving ambition and his boundless energy that wrote an American success story for him." One member of Congress noted that "if any man has lived a more full and vigorous and useful ninety years than Joseph Scott, I have yet to hear of him."

The fame which Scott acquired for his achievements as a patriot and civic leader never clouded his brilliance as an outstanding and respected member of the legal profession. The list of his favorable court decisions over more than fifty years is exceedingly impressive. Eulogized by the press as "Mr. Los Angeles," Joseph Scott was, in the words of James Francis Cardinal McIntyre, "a gentleman of God, a noble citizen, a soldier of truth and justice."

Los Angeles has its long list of benefactors, but as Herbert Hoover once observed, "I will suggest to you that one of the men, perhaps the greatest of the men of this city who have kept the democracy functioning with its tolerance, with its willingness to action taken with its constant devotion to public service is Joe Scott."

He was not just a statesman who was a Catholic, he was a "Catholic statesman." His name was at the head of every group of laymen and no one has yet had the time to tabulate the number of organizations to which he belonged or the ones which he helped to finance. Perhaps no other Catholic layman in all of "California's Catholic Heritage" was a more articulate and zealous proponent of the Church. Certainly no one maintained that position so long or so consistently. He used his stature as a statesman to further Catholic ideals, not a common virtue in America's Catholic annals.

Of all the many characters who have gone forth from Ireland to inspire and stimulate the finer qualities of human nature, there is none who transcended in nobility of character the man known and respected as "Mr. Los Angeles," Joseph Scott!

JOSEPH SCOTT (1866–1958)

B. MR. LOS ANGELES

Early in 1902 the Los Angeles *Daily Herald* published an informative article on Joseph Scott, already one of the city's leading attorneys and one whose services to California's southland would span yet another fifty–six years.

> To arrive friendless in a strange land, to fail in finding newspaper employment, to reach one's last $2 bill and take a job of hod carrying, and to resign the position as deputy hodman to accept a position as professor of English and rhetoric in a college—sounds romantic, doesn't it?
>
> Sounds as if it were fiction rather than real life. But it isn't, and the man who had this career, full of pluck, perseverance and pathos, lives in Los Angeles today. You probably know him. He is a successful lawyer, and he is called Joe Scott.
>
> No matter how many years ago, he landed at New York. He was a stocky, sturdy, athletic chap, 21 years old, a graduate of Ushaw College in the north of England, and modestly bearing the honor of having matriculated with a gold medal in London University. He had been a leader in athletic sports in his college, had specialized in history and literature, and had left with the idea that he would come to this country and be a great journalist.

The interesting sketch goes on to relate Scott's experiences in the newspaper world, his brief sojourn as a laborer and his three and a half year teaching career at Saint Bonaventure College, Allegheny, New York. By 1893, after completing his legal training, he had established himself in Los Angeles as an attorney. The *Daily Herald's* "snapshot" article continued:

> Those who know Joe Scott today know him as primarily a rarely good friend and thoroughly sound man, serving his clients and his friends with an energy that is as indefatigable as it is intense; secondarily, as the secretary of the Newman Club, the association of prominent Catholic gentlemen with which his strong personality has become identified; as the secretary of the Stephen Mallory White monument fund; as a robust basso in St. Vibiana's choir; as president of the Hibernians; as a fine cricketer, evolving now into a baseball fan; as a natural orator and champion organizer of banquets.

"Such versatility," the article concluded, "may be traceable not only to a dash of Irish in his blood but to the varied experiences of his youth." That a local newspaper would so dwell upon the accomplishments of a Catholic personage in 1902 indicates the esteem Scott enjoyed among his non–Catholic brethren even at that early time. Indeed, Charles F. Lummis noted that when Scott spoke "to an audience of Catholics, Methodists, Baptists, Presbyterians, Episcopalians, Christian Scientists, Adventists and Agnostics, he seemed to fuse them all to a common feeling."

Those characteristics which so charmed his contemporaries became more pronounced in the decades that followed. When Joseph Scott died, in 1958, it was justifiably said that he had been "a simple citizen who won more battles than the generals, who upheld more laws than the judges, who built more structures than the engineers and whose influence remains with us as a more potent force than any political power."

JOSEPH SCOTT (1866–1958)

C. FOREFATHER OF AMERICAN CIVILIZATION

Joseph Scott (1866–1958) spoke often and he spoke well. Whenever the legendary "Mr. Los Angeles" was scheduled to deliver an address, the local press was on hand to record his observations. The following excerpted discourse, given by Mr. Scott early in 1904, was reproduced in *The Columbiad*. It later appeared in most of the nation's Catholic newspapers.

It may appear as an act of exceeding temerity for anyone to brush up against the traditions of the so–called Simon–pure Americans by raising a doubt as to who were the genuine forefathers of American civilization.

The Westerner who invades the domain of cultured Boston is liable to be greeted with a reception as chilly as a New England winter if he raises a doubt as to the claim of the Pilgrim Fathers to this glorious prerogative, and this contention is somewhat sturdily supported occasionally by men of Catholic faith.

A few historical facts may be found not unworthy of attention and to this end it may be well to consider the civilization as organized and developed by the followers of Columbus and the Mission Fathers in the Southwest; a land civilized and developed by the Spanish *padres*, and yet to many of our own faith a country distant and unknown as the land of Tibet.

Plymouth rock was first struck in 1620. In 1534, nearly a century earlier, Fray Pedro de Gante founded a school for Indians in the city of Mexico. Two years later, the first Bishop of Mexico brought from Spain the first printing press. In the year 1539, a Bible was printed in the Aztec language for the Indians.

The first English Bible that ever saw the light of day was printed just one year previously, so that the forefathers of the Pilgrim type of civilization were but one year ahead of the Indians of the Southwest.

It has been said, rather irreverently, of these same Pilgrim Fathers that when they reached the Atlantic seaboard, they first fell on their knees and then fell on the Indians, as they wished the brutes to learn English.

If they had been a little less strenuous in their exercise and allowed the Western Catholic missionary to travel eastward, he might ultimately have reached the Yankee Indian with an Indian Bible, and the ceremony of making him English or dispatching him might possibly, to a large extent, have been dispensed with.

There are no Yankee Indians, there are no Puritan Indians; and Charles F. Lummis, Puritan for five generations, a native of Massachusetts and a graduate of Harvard, now known to the entire continent as a recognized authority on the Indian says: "I have known a great many Indians of a great many tribes and countries; I have never known a Protestant Indian."

Father Juan Padilla, the first martyr of the United States, and his companions were the pioneers—not the argonaut of California, who came looking for gold, not the modern tourist and camera fiend who gets out of his palatial Pullman after three days of incarceration therein, but the priest who lifted the Cross of Christ, and preached Him crucified.

And this preaching went on until the Southwest was covered with churches and schools, and the Indians were educated and trained so that modern American architecture can produce nothing better, nor more substantial, nor more artistic than the cathedrals and mission churches built by Indian artisans, with Catholic missionaries as architects and superintendents.

While the east was in the throes of the revolution of the colonists, California was in the thick of the fight for spiritual emancipation under Fray Junípero Serra, which culminated in the establishment of the missions from San Diego to San Francisco.

JOSEPH SCOTT (1866–1958)

D. DEFENDER OF THE JEWS

Throughout his long and productive life, the late Joseph Scott (1866–1958) was a tireless campaigner for civil rights and personal justice. Known to several generations as "Mr. Los Angeles," the Irish–born patriot spoke out on numerous occasions about breaches in the fabric of human dignity. The following letter, made available through the kindness of Rabbi Edgar G. Magnin, illustrates the nobility of Scott's concern for injustice. It was written to a Mr. Jack Stewart, proprietor of a motel in Phoenix Arizona, on December 15, 1942:

This will acknowledge receipt of your literature about the Camelback Inn, which attracted my attention and satisfaction until I came to the end of your pamphlet, when I noticed this phrase: "Clientele is rigidly restricted to 125 Gentiles."

It is difficult for me to restrain my feelings to put into respectable language my views upon this amazing exhibition of racial and religious intolerance. I don't know what has been your experience with Jews; perhaps, you have unfortunately met with one or two annoying examples of that race, for every group has its "black sheep."

But for you, a hotel man, catering to the public as you must have done, to have set a prohibitive restriction of that kind upon the personnel of your guests, seems utterly incredible if it were not in black type in your own literature.

That you should have undertaken to advertise this matter in these perilous critical days for our beloved country, when men of every race and every religion and every national stock are facing death to save you and me from the abomination of Hitlerism, make it particularly exasperating and offensive.

I have been living in this section of California for about fifty years. The Jew was here before me, spreading the kindliness and benevolence of his race far beyond the confines of his own group, and from that day to this our social welfare, benevolent and philanthropic activities have been largely led and upheld by the people of the Jewish race, although they are numerically an extremely small percentage of our population.

With many of these Jewish leaders I have been on terms of social intimacy for more than two generations. They are sympathetic, kindly, congenial folks, thoroughly anxious and concerned for the future of this country with wholesome patro–amenities which make life worth living; but altogether outside of my own personal views and experiences, I am shocked and dismayed to think that you should have the amazing effrontery to publicize your views in this crude and cruel fashion.

As to my identity, I beg to advise you I have been President of the Los Angeles Chamber of Commerce, President of the Los Angeles City Board of Education, President of the Los Angeles' Community Chest and now (am) Chairman of the Citizens Committee for the Army and Navy, Inc.

I came from a persecuted race myself. My father and mother were married in Wexford, Ireland. Time was when the Irish could see in the advertising columns of the daily press in New England: "No Irish need apply." Therefore, it is ingrained in me to resent persecution, discrimination and superiority complexes in anybody.

The more I see of snobbishness and caddishness, if I were an embittered man, I would recall Lord Byron's lines: "The more I see of men, the more I love dogs." For a piece of literature I recommend you to read Dickens' *Christmas Carol*. It may warm your soul with the Christmas spirit of kindliness, friendliness and tolerance. God help you.

JOSEPH SCOTT (1866–1958)

E. A LOYOLA TRADITION

In 1952 the regents of Loyola Law School instituted the Scott Moot Court Honors competition whose purpose was "to stimulate excellence in brief writing and oral advocacy." Fittingly, the man the students sought to emulate was the late Joseph Scott (1866–1958), who had served as second dean of the law school, a man whose name came to be identified with legal profession in California.

Born in England, Scott attended Ushaw College and London University before emigrating to New York City in 1890 at the age of twenty–two. A short while later, he was hired as professor of rhetoric and literature at Saint Bonaventure College in Allegheny, New York.

When Joseph Scott arrived in California in 1833, it was still possible to practice law without a formal degree. He became a student clerk in the office of Judge J. S. Anderson and, in 1884, was admitted to the State Bar of California. Throughout his long and distinguished public career, Scott was extremely generous with his time and talents. He was involved in drafting the City Charter for Los Angeles, spent fifteen years on the Board of Education and eleven years as a member of the Chamber of Commerce.

Scott became Dean of Loyola Law School in 1924 and remained in that position long enough to influence a whole generation of youthful legal aspirants. Being one of his proteges was a distinction of honor.

Known for his dramatic and effective courtroom presence, Scott's greatest fame came as a trial lawyer. Among his more fascinating clients were such nationally–known figures as Aimee Semple McPherson, Joan Berry (who sued Charles Chaplin in a paternity suit that gained world–wide attention) and the Finn Twins (who were prosecuted for stealing a C–47 airplane).

On his ninetieth birthday, politicians, educators, jurists, attorneys and friends met to honor Scott for his many contributions to the commonweal. Among those signing a special birthday scroll (which is on exhibit at the Archival Center, Archdiocese of Los Angeles), were then President Dwight Eisenhower, former President Harry S. Truman, Senator John F. Kennedy, Chief Justice Earl Warren, Eleanor Roosevelt and a host of other outstanding Americans.

The naming of the Moot Court at Loyola Law School for Scott was indeed a fitting memorial. It was meant to be and has become a continuation of Loyola's commitment to excellence in appellate advocacy. In the three decades of its existence, the competition has produced an elite group of talented advocates, most of whom had their first real taste of courtroom life as apprentice competitors.

Chosen to act as moderators for the yearly events are prominent jurists. At the finals in 1955, for example, were Justice Maurice T. Dooling (First Appellate District), Associate Justice John W. Shenk (California Supreme Court) and Justice Thomas P. White (Second Appellate District).

The Scott Moot Court is a student–run program that focuses on the development of individual appellate advocacy skills. It is one of the most prestigious activities at a university known for its long list of contributions to the public arena of Southern California.

JOSEPH SCOTT (1866–1958)

F. FATHER OF CALIFORNIA COLUMBANISM

The Knights of Columbus, a fraternal and beneficent society of Catholic men, was founded on February 2, 1882, by the Reverend Michael J. McGivney, Assistant Pastor of Saint Mary's Church in New Haven, Connecticut. The purpose of the society was to develop a practical Catholicity among its members, to promote Catholic education and charity and through its insurance department, to furnish at least temporary financial assistance to the families of deceased members.

Genesis of the Order's activities in California dates back to 1901 when Edward L. Hearn, Supreme Knight sent James J. Gorman to California for interviews with Archbishop Patrick W. Riordan of San Francisco and Bishop George T. Montgomery of Monterey–Los Angeles. Originally, it was suggested that there be only two Councils, one in San Francisco and the other in Los Angeles. From these two units, the organization would develop at its own rate and eventually spread throughout the state.

An inspection of the California foundation was made in the summer of 1902 by the Supreme Knight, Edward L. Hearn.

Upon his departure, the late Joseph Scott was named Territorial Deputy for the incipient Pacific Coast organization. Almost immediately, Scott inaugurated a third Council at Oxnard, in order to qualify for establishment of a State Council. The actual establishment took place in May of 1903, "in a bedroom of the Hotel Angelus in Los Angeles." Other Councils were subsequently set up by Scott at such places as Oakland, Fresno, Vallejo, Pomona and San Jose.

By a clever parliamentary move, Scott won approval of the national board to hold the annual convention of 1905 in Los Angeles. Several special trains brought members from all over the nation to Southern California where a gigantic welcome was staged by civic and religious dignitaries.

Under Scott's direction, the K. of C. grew so rapidly that when the devastating earthquake and fire of 1906 struck San Francisco, it was among the first agencies on the scene distributing food and clothing. One hundred thousand dollars was appropriated for the purchase and dispersal of the primary necessities of life to the Bay City's homeless residents. Commenting on an article Scott wrote about the Knights in 1936, one commentator noted, "if criticism might be directed, then let it be said that personal modesty forbade Mr. Scott to mention his own life of devotion to Columbanism through these many years."

Raymond J. Rath, Past Grand Knight, went on to say that "the Catholic men of California, as in fact the entire citizenry of California, can well be proud of the record of achievement of Joseph Scott. A relentless and stub-

Joseph Scott

born warrior in those matters that affect the right of man to worship according to the dictates of his conscience; a champion in the cause of protecting the youth of our land against those perverted minds that would ruin their moral structure; a tireless and fearless worker in support of those ideals that make for true Americanism; the name of Joseph Scott remains dear to the hearts of both young and old."

When the State Council met at Oxnard in 1905, overtures were made to give Scott a third term as State Deputy. He declined the honor, telling the delegates that "George Washington's philosophy was good enough for me." Though he held no office in the K. of C. for the next fifty years, the "Father of Columbanism in California" continued to be an active force in all the activities of the Knights of Columbus.

The debt of the California K. of C. to Joseph Scott was expressed in writing over thirty years ago:

> To us he has not only been a great leader but a kind, gentle and devoted counsellor, to whose wisdom and judgment, always freely given, we owe the solution of many trials and tribulations that have beset us during the years. In the hours of trouble and adversity he has been ever with us, and strengthened by his presence when we heard him say, "Courage Brothers, Courage!"

FIDEL VICENTE SEPULVEDA (1880–1942)

Fidel Sepulveda's earliest memories revolve around the happy years he spent at the orphan asylum of the Immaculate Heart of Mary in Pajaro Valley. He admitted to being spoiled by the friars who had operated the historic institution since 1869.

Born at San Juan Capistrano Mission, on April 24, 1880 the son of Jose Vicente and Maria Delfina Sepulveda, he was entrusted to the care of the Franciscans when only five years of age. Young, energetic and intellectually talented, Fidel became proficient in both English and Spanish and was fluent also in several of the local Indian dialects. He was often called upon to act as interpreter for legal cases.

After a long courtship, Fidel married Lugarda Dominguez Jimenez in 1903, during ceremonies conducted at San Juan Capistrano Mission. It was a gala affair which brought together some of the state's most celebrated historic personages.

The Sepulvedas built a modest home on property belonging to the Dominguez family on Ramon Street. Fidel became a cowhand on *Rancho Santa Margarita* where he supervised personnel, rode horses and herded cattle. With the birth of his daughter, Delfina Juanita, Fidel gave up his earlier work and organized the first post office for the village of San Juan Capistrano. He became a notary and served as the town's unofficial linguist.

Later, Fidel supervised the installation of a PBX switchboard for San Juan Capistrano and, in 1912, he became the agent for a regular telephone exchange. The first installation was a crank manual, three position device connected to Riverside.

In his role as "operator" for the Home Telephone Company, Fidel became an appendage to every family in the area. He was especially popular for ascertaining the results of races and bull–fights. Fidel was "central" to the town and its outlying inhabitants. During World War I, when troop trains stopped at San Juan Capistrano for wood and water, the telephone lines added to Fidel's stature. Those were busy and sad times, especially when War Department communiques came in notifying parents and friends of deaths on the battlefields.

Throughout his long and busy life, Fidel remained close to the Old Mission. He organized pageants and fiestas for adults and school children and nothing was official until it bore the endorsement of Fidel Vicente Sepulveda. In 1927, when Pacific Telephone took over the Home Telephone Company, Fidel retired from his position and returned to Rancho Santa Margarita where, once again, he engaged in cowpunching.

Father Arthur J. Hutchinson, the pastor of San Juan Capistrano Mission, was one of Fidel's close friends. He was once quoted as saying that Fidel was "a living chapter from the history of California. He and his family personify what the early missionaries had in mind for this portion of the Lord's vineyard."

Fidel's death, in 1942, signalled an end to an era. Yet, in many ways, it was not an end at all. The name of Sepulveda will always be prominent in the story of California.

FRANCISCO XAVIER SEPULVEDA (1742–1788)

While the names of saints adorn more cities, towns and villages in Alta California than any other comparably sized area of the world, the names of prominent Catholic pioneers are also deeply imbedded on the Golden State's cartography. The Sepulvedas were among a whole litany of family names that continue to dot the California landscape. Catholics all, the Sepulvedas were outstanding pioneers who moved with great dignity along *El Camino Real*.

The patriarch of the Sepulveda family was Francisco Xavier (1742–1788). A native of a small town in northwest Mexico called Villa de Sinaloa, he came to California in 1780 as part of an expedition to reinforce the influence of the *presidios*.

Sepulveda was accompanied by his wife Candelaria (Redondo) and their seven children. One of his offspring, Francisco *segundo* served as a soldier at San Diego before marrying Francisca Avila and moving to Los Angeles in 1815. Humble man that he was, the elder Francisco Sepulveda would find himself very much at home in the modern metropolis where his name continues to perplex easterners unfamiliar with the Spanish language. He was the first adult Hispanic interred at San Gabriel Mission.

The younger Francisco (1775–1853) served as a city councilman for the *Ayuntamiento de los Angeles*. He later became *alcalde* or mayor, a position he occupied from 1836 to 1837.

The Sepulveda family played a significant role in ranching and local government in the early days of Los Angeles. Francisco *segundo* was the first of his family to settle in the San Fernando Valley. His family name was given to what was once the longest road in the country, stretching from the mountains to the sea. Prominent along Sepulveda Boulevard is a Junior High school name for Francisco in 1960.

In 1827, the *Rancho Los Palos Verdes* was given to the family and that grant, covering an area of 31,62.9 acres, was ratified in 1846. At Sepulveda's Landing (Timm's Point) a port subsequently developed. Almost the entire area of what is now San Pedro was carved out of *Rancho Los Palos Verdes*. Francisco *segundo* was also entrusted with the *San Vicente y Santa Monica* land grant in 1839. An energetic man of great personal warmth, Francisco was later deputized as commissioner for the secularized San Juan Capistrano Mission.

By the time of Francisco's death, several branches of the family were scattered around California. The census books indicate that he had at least fourteen children of his own. Among the many Sepulvedas whose names appear in the history books is Jose Dolores who was killed during an uprising of Indians at La Purisima Concepcion Mission in 1824

The Sepulveda House, located in *El Pueblo de los*

Angeles State Historic Park, was built in 1857 as a combination residence, hotel and boarding house. It was named for its owner, Eloisa Martinez de Sepulveda. One of the few such structures surviving in the city, the house is a remarkable example of Victorian architecture. It is located in the forty–acre park on Olvera (Wine) Street.

The "Sepulveda" name was applied to the train station east of the present town bearing the family name when the railroad was extended from Los Angeles to San Fernando Valley in 1873. The city of Sepulveda is likely named for Fernando Sepulveda whose adobe was near the base of the Verdugo mountains. On and on we could go. Surely the Sepulveda heritage is very much alive in the 1990s.

HECTOR (ETTORE) SERBAROLI (1881–1951)

Because of their accuracy of detail, the paintings of Hector (Ettore) Serbaroli (1881–1951) are today regarded equally as "historical landmarks" as pieces of art. His legacy of religious masterpieces is of even greater importance to the Church in California. Born in Rome, Hector Serbaroli's early life fell under the tutorial influence of Alessandro Ceccarini, a painter known throughout Italy for his ecclesial embellishments.

Later Hector was apprenticed to the famous Cesare Maccari. It was that Sienese muralist who took Serbaroli to Loretto where he played an important role in completing the interior of the city's great basilica. After several extensive courses at the *Academia di San Lucca* in Rome, Hector left for Mexico City, where he was assured of work in several of the public buildings then under construction or being repaired.

It was in the *Distrito Federal* that Serbaroli met the renowned soprano, Luisa Tetrazzini. She had an opera company performing in Mexico and needed a talented artist to design and paint the scenery for her productions. Serbaroli was also employed to help decorate the new Senate building, as well as the *Teatro de Bellas Artes.* Several commissions for churches provided further income for the struggling artist.

Among the mansions he was asked to decorate was one in Chihuahua that belonged to Josefina Sini. It was a providential task for he subsequently married Josefina in 1912, shortly after completing a contract at the local governor's palace.

The political unrest in Mexico motivated Hector and his bride to emigrate to the United States. They resided for a while in El Paso and then moved on to San Rafael. There the artist found several lucrative commissions for the California Building at the Panama Pacific International Exposition.

Probably Serbaroli's most celebrated painting there was the huge (4 1/2 x 20 feet) panorama of Mount Tamalpais and its upland meadows. That painting was later moved to the San Francisco Ferry Building and then to the Mill Valley Bank where it hung from 1928 to 1947.

Serbaroli opened a studio in San Rafael, taught at Tamalpais Military Academy and did contract work for Congressman William Kent. His painting of Mac Neer Point, commissioned by the congressman, hangs in the national capitol in Washington.

In 1922, Serbaroli met William Randolph Hearst who asked the artist to do restorative work on some ceiling murals recently imported from Europe. Serbaroli, his wife and their four children lived at San Simeon for several years while he worked at the castle.

Through the auspices of Adela Rogers St. John, Serbaroli moved to Hollywood, where he worked for some years designing sets at the First National Studios (now Warner Brothers). His paintings of Tyrone Power, Darryl Zanuck, Bette Davis and H.B. Warner, to mention but a few, are classical renditions of Hollywood's greatest personalities.

A decade later, Serbaroli determined to spend the rest of his life at his real love, religious art. His murals adorn Holy Family Church (South Pasadena), the Rosary Chapel of Immaculate Conception Church (Los Angeles), Saint Ignatius (Highland Park) and Saint Monica's (Santa Monica). There were many others too.

Serbaroli's greatest religious works are probably those done for the sacristy catacombs at Saint John's Seminary, Camarillo. The one over the central altar portrays the Sacred Heart of Jesus, surrounded by the various saints connected with the propagation of that devotion, including Pope Leo XIII.

JUDY SERBAROLI (1914–1979)

Though often unrecognized and more often undercompensated those gifted people whose lives are spent designing and furnishing houses–of–worship surely warrant our attention and demand our gratitude. They are the ones who bring the empty shell of a church alive with color and atmosphere.

What is true of most male artists is especially the case with a woman, the more so when she works with churches. Fifty years ago, there were few enough ecclesial artists and even fewer who were women. One such person who rose above the narrowness of her times to a pinnacle of prestige was Judy Serbaroli.

During the years she spent beautifying the churches of the Archdiocese of Los Angeles, Judy Serbaroli (1914–1979) became known to laity and clergy alike as "Miss Gold Leaf." It was a term of the utmost respect and endearment.

A native of Mexico City, Judy came to the United States with her family in the early 1920s. She attended Immaculate Heart High School and then took graduate studies in art at several local ateliers. She studied drawing and oil painting with the highly–acclaimed Joseph Mason Reeves II, the son of the Rear Admiral of the United States Navy. Her encyclopedic knowledge of art history proved exceedingly useful for portraying the rich symbols of Catholic tradition.

During much of her adult life, Judy worked with her internationally–recognized father at various churches along the Pacific Slope. In the Southern California area, she assisted in painting at Cathedral Chapel, the Rosary Chapel of Immaculate Conception, Saint Ignatius (Highland Park), Holy Family (South Pasadena) and Saint Andrews (Pasadena.)

In 1954, Judy was commissioned to oversee the installation of the famed Escaray Altar furnishings in the Chapel of Queen of Angels Seminary, San Fernando. After deciding how the 16th century Baroque woodwork could be fitted into the available space, Judy began the delicate task of applying layers of gold leaf to the reconstructed reredos.

Christened "Miss Gold Leaf" by Father William H. Ready, Judy thereafter used that terminology in printed descriptions of her artistic accomplishments. One newspaper columnist suggested that "gold was likely the substance of her soul as well." A decade later, Miss Serbaroli was also influential in suggesting the ornamentation and color scheme for Saint James Chapel at the seminary college in Camarillo. Her sketches of the reredos and altar were brought to completion by an artist in Valencia, Spain.

Probably Judy's "culminating masterpiece" was her work at Saint Charles Church in North Hollywood. There she designed the church and painted the life–size Stations of the Cross in tones of sepia. Her artistic genius is especially obvious in the Fourth Station which portrays the meeting of Christ with His Blessed Mother. In 1967, at the suggestion of James Francis Cardinal McIntyre, Pope Paul VI publicly recognized Miss Serbaroli, awarding her the *Pro Pontifice et Ecclesia* medal as a token of the Church's gratitude.

In her final years, Judy lived quietly and modestly in an apartment in North Hollywood. Though never in robust health, she attended daily Mass and remained available for artistic consultation and advice.

Judy died at Saint Joseph's Medical Center in Burbank on July 10 1979. In his homily at the Mass, Timo-thy Cardinal Manning described her as "an inspiration and a guide in the development of ecclesiastical art in the Archdiocese of Los Angeles."

JOSEPH WILLIAM SHARP (1879–1915)

Joseph William Sharp was proud of recalling that he was born on the Feast of Our Lady's Assumption. It was in 1879 that Robert and Catherine Sharp welcomed their second son, a year remembered locally for the diptheria epidemic. Reared in a family of boys, Joseph learned the skills of competition and cooperation. He was among the first students enrolled at Sacred Heart Parish School which opened its doors in 1890.

According to the early records of the school, Joseph was chosen to read a poem honoring Saint Patrick and then to present a "garland of flowers and wishes" when Father Patrick Harnett visited the youngsters on March 17th.

After his graduation from Saint Vincent's College, Joseph entered his father's furniture business. He went on to become one of the city's pioneer funeral directors. In those days, morticians built their own caskets or, as they were then known, coffins. The early directories for the City of Los Angeles record that in 1898, Joseph was the Vice President of Robert Sharp & Son Co., Undertakers. From all indications, he was highly regarded by the community which he served with great dedication.

In the *McFaul Caulfield Newsletter* for December, 1991, there is a notation that "young Joe was generously endowed with with the talents requisite for success in his chosen field: sympathetic understanding toward his clients; loyalty and geniality to family and associates; and integrity and a competitive spirit in business matters."

When the Right Reverend Thomas J. Conaty arrived in the southland as Bishop of Monterey–Los Angeles, he and Joseph became close friends. The Sharp limousine, one of the first in the area, was placed at the prelate's disposal. There are photographs in the archives of Conaty being driven on confirmation tours.

Not only was Joe Sharp among the earliest benefactors of Sacred Heart parish, he forged a close bond with the local clergy. Bishop Conaty later recalled that Joseph "was one who was loved by all who knew him and he was held in particular esteem by the clergy of the diocese."

In 1908, Joseph and his father built a handsome brick mortuary at 1218 South Flower Street. By then he was being called upon to expand his business into the suburbs. Later that year, on September 17th, Joseph married the lovely Florence Ganahl, daughter of Franz Joseph and Louise (Lebrun) Ganahl, who were prominent in the lumber business. Their marriage was blessed by two children.

In May of 1915, Joseph was stricken with cerebro–spinal meningitis, a serious and painful illness which eventually proved fatal. He died at the youthful age of thirty–six on May 20th at the family home on Dalton Avenue. The funeral Mass was held at Saint Agnes Church. A large concourse of friends and admirers gathered to pay their respect to a man universally loved and esteemed. Bishop Conaty presided at the funeral obsequies. In his homily, the prelate said that "the true value of life is in the knowledge and love of God, and the perfection of life is to die in God's holy love. This was our dear friend's faith, that was his hope, and in that hope he died, and has gone to his eternal home."

The memory of Joseph Sharp is writ largely in the annals of Los Angeles. He left his family "a legacy of loyalty, business integrity and love for God and the Church."

REGIS DAVID SHEPHARD (1859–1948)

Regis David Shephard, known theatrically as R. 0. MacLean, was born at New Orleans on March 7, 1859. Today he is most remembered as the man who portrayed Fray Junípero Serra in *The Mission Play*.

Shephard studied at the University of Virginia and later at Washington and Lee University, where he became a member of the Delta Psi Fraternity. He majored in modern languages, history and chemistry.

It was at the University of Virginia that R. D. developed his fondness for Shakespeare. He made his stage debut in an amateur performance as Brutus in *Julius Caesar*. During the years that followed, R. D. appeared in various Shakespearean roles, including the title role in *Othello* and Spartacus in *The Gladiator*. He was hailed by the New York *Mirror* as "a man of superb physique and handsome features. His voice is deep and powerful and his entire personality bears the stamp of inborn dramatic talent."

During the 1902–1903 season, R. D. and his wife played stock in San Francisco and it was there that he developed his abiding love for California and its people. He was to make his most dramatic performances in the west.

Throughout his long career on the stage, critics acknowledged that R. D. was "widely–known throughout the country for his King John, Macbeth, Malvolio, Petruchio, Jacques, Orlando, Charles Surface, the Prince of the Senate in *Adrea* and his role in *The Heart of Maryland*. In later years, however, as interest in Shakespearean productions lessened, the number of stock companies began diminishing and R. D. found work hard to find. It was then that he joined the cross–over to vaudeville.

In 1920, R. D. took permanent residence in California

and there pursued a career in the movies. Unfortunately, his film career was filled with more hope than success and his performances were anything but memorable.

In 1914, at the age of sixty–five, R. D. assumed the leading role of Fray Junípero in *The Mission Play*, the outdoor production written by California's poet laureate, John Steven McGroarty. A copy of an undated "Program of the Mission Play" has a full page copy of the actor's portrait and under it "R. D. MacLean, In the Crowning Role of His Great Career as Father Serra in the Mission Play." MacLean played over 1,500 performances of the play through 1941.

So well did R. D. portray Serra that the University of Southern California bestowed upon the veteran actor an honorary doctorate "in recognition of generous public service and achievements in the field of Letters."

A notice in the *Hollywood Reporter* said that on June 28, 1948, R. D. MacLean died of heart aliment after several months of illness. He was buried in Hollywood Cemetery. The death notice in MacLean's hometown newspaper hailed the actor for "his fame as being the personification of Serra," placing that role ahead of his earlier–won laurels as a Shakespearean actor.

R. D. MacLean found great satisfaction in finishing his long and successful career with the mantle of a Franciscan mendicant. He once told a reporter that "Serra was a totally authentic man who came by his love for the natives supernaturally." To R. D. and the many who applauded his portrayal of the friar, the world was Serra's stage and his performance was other–worldly.

ALBERT SHUMATE (1904–1998)

On May 21, 1975 Mayor Joseph Alioto honored Dr. Albert Shumate for his "enduring contributions to the preservation of San Francisco's history." The citation went on to say that the recipient, "more than any other single person, has helped to keep alive and meaningful those great traditions which have made San Francisco numbered among the great cities of the world, and which have made it a viable one for all its residents."

The California pedigree of Albert Shumate can be traced to 1852, when his maternal grandfather, John Ortman, reached San Francisco. Born on August 11, 1904, he was the third generation of his family to occupy the historic and splendid century old Victorian residence at Scott and Pine Streets.

At Lowell High School, Albert was a classmate of Governor Edmund G. (Pat) Brown. He went on to the University of San Francisco, where he was a member of the Class of 1927. Four years later, Albert was awarded a doctorate at Omaha's Creighton Medical School. His specialty was in the field of dermatology.

Dr. Shumate has contributed mightily in time and energy to organizations and campaigns concerned with preserving the state's heritage. For more than half a century he was acknowledged throughout California as the Catholic Church's most prominent "guardian" of local history. A consistent advocate of a "balance between progress and preservation," Dr. Shumate worked tirelessly to develop the Cable Car Museum and rehabilitate the old United States Mint. He was the first president and continued to be an active member of the San Francisco Landmarks Preservation Board. Dr. Shumate was also Chairman of the History Committee for San Francisco's Twin Bicentennial.

A devoted public servant, the quiet, mild–mannered physician occupied the presidency of the Good Shepherd Advisory Board, the California Genealogical Society, the Roxburghe Club, Saint Mary's Hospital Staff, the California Historical Society and the Book Club of California. He was one of the two honorary members of the Society of California Pioneers. (The other was Richard M. Nixon).

A trustee and regent for the College of Notre Dame, Shumate also served on the Board of Trustees for Saint Patrick's Seminary. He was a Knight in the Order of the Holy Sepulchre and a Knight Commander of Isabella, the Catholic.

Over the years, Dr. Shumate amassed an outstanding collection of Californiana books, pamphlets and broadsides. Among his outstanding titles were numerous examples of fine and exceptional printing by western pressmen. Devotion to art, books and learning was reflected in Dr. Shumate's service with the San Francisco Art Commission, the Gleeson Library Associates and the Friends of the Bancroft Library.

The Shumate name adorns a host of book reviews in learned journals, several articles in the *California Historical Quarterly* and the *Pacific Historian* and at least two books, including the life of George Henry Goddard. He completed a biography of the *ranchero* Francisco Perez Pacheco.

Dr. Albert Shumate was not alone a recorder of the past, but a prophet for the future. He falls into that exclusive category of California pioneers described by Rockwell Hunt:

These build the fabric of our State
  And rear the temple of her fame;
These are the great, the truly great,
  Whose deeds the ages shall proclaim.

MARY HIGGINS SINCLAIR (c.1890–1971)

During September of 1968, the Archdiocese of Los Angeles paid a well–earned debt of gratitude to an outstanding woman who rounded out her fiftieth consecutive year of service to the People of God in Southern California. The pace of life had quickened considerably since the daughter of James and Mary (Higgins) Sinclair began her work in the Chancery Office at Los Angeles, as secretary to the late Bishop John J. Cantwell, in 1918. Only a handful of the 177 priests then serving the 190,000 faithful in the old Diocese of Monterey–Los Angeles were still at their posts. The Catholic population had increased over 900%, while the area served by the present jurisdiction had been reduced to one–eighth its earlier size.

Four popes, nine presidents and six mayors had come and gone during the half century that Mary E. Sinclair labored on behalf of an ecclesiastical area even then among the largest and most influential in the nation. Oddly enough, Mary served only two ordinaries during her long tenure, one for twenty–nine years, the other for twenty–one.

Shortly after graduating from Polytechnic High School, Mary inaugurated her professional career as legal secretary to Willis I. Morrison, an attorney for the Guaranty Mortgage Company. In September of 1918, following Willis' appointment to the bench, Miss Sinclair joined the staff of the recently–installed Bishop of Monterey–Los Angeles, then housed on the eighth floor of the old Higgins Building at Second and Main Streets. The manifold friends Mary won over the years, especially among the clergy, were not all concentrated in the City dedicated to Our Lady of the Angels. Visitors to the chanceries at San Francisco, San Antonio, Fresno, Sacramento and Dallas routinely returned with greetings to the gracious lady whose cheerful disposition had become a familiar trademark to bishops, priests, religious and laymen alike. Those having business at 1531 West Ninth Street were welcomed, as their parents and grandparents before them, with the kindly smile and courteous demeanor characteristic of one personally interested in whatever brings them to their Chief Shepherd.

In addition to her professional duties, Miss Sinclair was active in most of the major organizations, clubs and societies functioning in the archdiocese over the preceding five decades. Among her favorites were the Young Ladies Institute, the Catholic Daughters and the Ladies of Charity. Mary had also been a long–time enrollee of the Perpetual Adoration Society at the Plaza Church of *Nuestra Señora de los Angeles*. Her tireless attention to charitable works brought a special decoration from the Vatican, in April of 1943, when Pope Pius XII bestowed the *Pro Ecclesia Pontifice* medal on Mary to commemorate her silver anniversary in the service of the Church.

Miss Sinclair's long association with the manifold Catholic functions of Southern California gave her a rich background in the Church's historical lore. On the innumerable occasions this writer turned to Mary as a source–of–last–resort, she rarely failed to supply what the written record lacks; her vivid memory a veritable storehouse for even the most insignificant items of the area's ecclesiastical story. Those busy about the works of God and His people generally take little time to think about their own place in the overall montage of Church history.

It would not be presumptuous to suggest that one as intricately involved as Mary Sinclair in the pageantry of California's Catholic heritage, unquestionably merited the words reserved by the Book of Proverbs for the most faithful of servants: "Many are the women of proven worth, but she has exceeded them all."

JAMES FRANCIS SMITH (1859–1928)

James Francis Smith was born at San Francisco, on January 28, 1859. His parents, Patrick and Ann Smith, had immigrated from Ireland to Sonoma County about 1840. Following his graduation from Santa Clara College in 1878, James took up the study of jurisprudence at Hastings Law School. He was admitted to the bar in 1881.

For a few years he practiced law in partnership with Frank J. Murphy, a locally prominent jurist who later became a judge of the Superior Court. On August 13, 1885, James married Lillian A. Dunnigan. Active in ecclesial affairs, James was a founder of the Young Mens Institute. He was also active as an officer of the League of the Cross, a Catholic abstinence society.

Inasmuch as military affairs interested the youthful lawyer, James affiliated himself with the First California Infantry. In April, 1898, when hostilities between the United States and Spain broke out, he was made a colonel of the regiment. The contingency sailed from San Francisco to the Philippines on May 23rd, aboard the *U.S.S. Charleston*. Under Colonel Smith's leadership, the First California regiment achieved a fine military record in the Philippines, including the capture of Manila, on August 13th.

Smith served as President of the Military Commission and later was deputized to confer with Emilio Aguinaldo's commissioners in January of 1899. He was commended for "gallantry in action" in recognition of his activities during February and March of that year. On April 24th, he was made Brigadier General of Volunteers and assigned to command the Department of Visayas.

The Chief of the American Army of Occupation, General Elwell Otis, regarded Smith as one of the most capable leaders in his command and entrusted him with the delicate and difficult task of pacifying and administering Negros Island as Military Governor. During his tenure as governor, the records indicate that Smith "accomplished as much . . . by tact and diplomacy as could be effected by a whole army."

When the First California regiment returned to San Francisco, Smith stayed behind to devote himself to constructive projects such as road building, civil administration and education of the native population. He served as Collector of Customs in Manila and then, in mid 1901, President William McKinley appointed Smith Associate Justice of the Philippine Supreme Court. Two years later, he became Commissioner of Public Instruction.

In 1906, President Theodore Roosevelt named Smith Governor General of the Philippines, a position he held for four years. Upon his retirement, he was credited with rendering "more different kinds of distinguished public service than any American who had ever been in the Philippine Islands from the time Dewey's guns first thundered out over Manila Bay." After his return to San Francisco, Smith was selected to serve on the newly–created Customs Court of Appeals by President William Howard Taft and he remained at that post until his death, on June 29, 1928.

San Francisco's lawyer–soldier–diplomat was buried with military honors at Holy Cross Cemetery in Colma.

FRANK HAMILTON SPEARMAN (1859–1937)

Lee Shippey once wrote that "some men are admirable without being likeable, and vice versa. There is a quiet friendliness about Frank Spearman which makes him lovable and a quiet strength which makes him admirable." Known throughout the English–speaking world as the creator of *Whispering Smith*, Frank Hamilton Spearman was born in Buffalo, New York, in 1859, and grew to adulthood in Wisconsin. He was fond of recalling how his own father had been among those who greeted Lafayette on his visit to Philadelphia in the late 1830s.

Frank studied at Lawrence College and there "read his way into the Church" through *Faith of Our Fathers* which was written by Archbishop (later Cardinal) James Gibbons. The two later became close friends.

Spearman began life as a business man in Chicago. For health reasons, he decided to move west, to the rugged frontier town of McCook, Nebraska. There he started a small bank at a railroad division mark.

Railroad pioneering was as exciting in those days as interplanetary travel is today. Spearman met many interesting characters and he decided to write about them. First he composed articles, then short stories and finally a novel for the *Saturday Evening Post*. From that time onwards, Spearman became a regular contributor to *Harper's Weekly* and other monthly magazines.

Early in his storyhood days, Spearman met a "Mr. Porter" who was enthralled with his work. When he later discovered that the man was O. Henry, Frank decided it was the Lord's way of telling him to devote the rest of his life to writing.

He moved to Cheyenne and it was there, in 1906, that Spearman invented "Whispering Smith" for some short stories in *McClures*. He modelled that famous character on O.E. Le Fors. One of the greatest American critics declared that in Whispering Smith Spearman "had created the rarest thing in literature, a distinctly new character." Within a short period, dozens of imitation personages appeared.

Spearman and his wife, the former Eugenie Lonergan, then came to Los Angeles, where they established their permanent home. One of Frank's sons became a distinguished Jesuit priest and another owned and operated a religious goods store on Flower Street.

Whispering Smith achieved the ultimate success in 1915, when it was made into a film. Many of Spearman's other novels also found their way into the Hollywood scene. *Nan of Music Mountain* was probably among Spearman's most popular motion pictures. Spearman's books quickly found their way onto the shelves of America's libraries. *The Marriage Verdict, Selwood of Sleepy Cat, Spanish Lover* and *Carmen of the Rancho* were among his historical tales. One of his novels, *Robert Kimberly* was praised by the critics as being an impressive defense of the sanctity of marriage.

Spearman was nationally recognized when, in 1935, he received the *Laetare Medal*. He also was awarded honorary degrees from Notre Dame, Santa Clara and Loyola. Within the Hollywood circle, Spearman's name was held in high esteem.

In a statement released to the press at the time of Spearman's demise, Archbishop John J. Cantwell of Los Angeles praised the writer, noting that his career had been "as versatile as it was distinguished."

VERONA SPELLMIRE (1889–1975)

For well over half a century, a cheerful little lady had criss–crossed the whole of California's southland giving Christian witness to her religious convictions. For Verona Spellmire, it had been "a great privilege to be His instrument in helping lead little children to a knowledge and love of God and His Church." Verona, one of eight children, was born in Kansas City, Missouri, on May 8, 1889, the daughter of Anthony Henry and Theresa Eleanor (Marshall) Spellmire. At a tender age she was brought to Flagstaff, Arizona, where the family

stayed only a few years before moving on to California and more abundant educational opportunities.

Upon completion of her studies at local schools, Verona entered the University of California at Berkeley, in 1909. Eager from her earliest years to involve herself in the field of social work, she subsequently took special courses along those lines at Santa Barbara Normal School. Miss Spellmire taught Home Economics at several southland institutions, mostly in the poorer sections of the city. In addition to her classroom schedule, she found time for home visitations, parental counselling and a myriad of other activities related to her Sunday–school apostolate at the Brownson House. She began her catechetical work informally, during the summer of 1920, when she and a group of other teachers instituted weekly classes in Christian doctrine at Simon's Brickyard, a Mexican–American colony near Montebello. It was Verona's use of a forced period of convalescence that later facilitated her work among peoples of various nationalities.

Aware of the work so successfully being performed among the immigrants by the Missionary Confraternity of Pittsburgh, Verona was anxious to see a similar program inaugurated in the Diocese of Monterey–Los Angeles. She was greatly encouraged by a teaching stint at the Catholic school in Monterey, where she learned some exceedingly useful teaching techniques from Father Ramon Mestres, who had been actively associated with the highly effective work of the Barcelona Confraternity. Early in 1922, Verona approached Father Robert Emmet Lucey, director of Catholic Charities, with plans for organizing, promoting and uniting a corps of volunteers for teaching Christian doctrine to youngsters otherwise out–of–touch with Catholic agencies. The energetic priest passed the proposal along to Bishop John J. Cantwell and the Irish–born prelate immediately seized upon the apostolate as a unique means of furthering his own plans for Christianizing California's southland.

On June 17, 1923, following the appointment of Father William Mullane as diocesan director, the work of the Confraternity of Christian Doctrine was "solemnly and forever" consecrated to the Sacred Heart of Jesus. A subsequent appeal from Bishop Cantwell enlisted an additional 300 volunteers in the first of the major steps towards training youngsters.

Except for an eight month postulancy with the Holy Family Sisters, Miss Spellmire continued her pioneering work during the Confraternity's earliest years. She conducted a series of surveys to determine places where the Confraternity apostolate was most direly needed and, afterwards, devoted full time to organizing and implementing various teacher training programs. Together with Father Leroy Callahan, she was instrumental in inaugurating the summer school program, in 1928, with six pilot ventures which, the following year, were extended throughout the diocese. In the fall of 1941, when her earliest supporter, now an archbishop, was transferred to San Antonio, Miss Spellmire went to Texas, where she spent eight fruitful years coordinating the C.C.D. program for the Most Reverend Robert Emmet Lucey in the far corners of his 33,025 square mile archdiocese.

After her return to California's southland, Verona worked for a while in Saint Elizabeth's Parish, Altadena, under Father William Mullane. After 1954, she helped in the more intensive organization of C.C.D. activities in Pasadena. Known to the late Archbishop John J. Cantwell as the "Confraternity's Number One Bushwacker," Verona Spellmire still pursued her lifelong commitment to those poor families and individuals not as yet touched by the saving message of Jesus Christ. May her tribe increase!

ROBERT STEERE (1833–1910)

Robert Steere "was one of the pioneers of California who labored to develop this great state along the material lines which have given glory to it, while at the same time he contributed to it the influence of his magnificent moral character." The son of Rufus Steere and Eliza Brown was born in Laurens, Oswego County, New York, on December 27, 1833. He was "reared in his native county, receiving a primary education in the schools in the vicinity of his home."

While growing to manhood, young Steere assisted his father in the business. Later he learned the trade of tinsmith, working at various times in Saint Paul, Sioux City and Omaha. It was from the latter city that Robert Steere fitted out an ox team expedition for crossing the plains to California. After arriving on the west coast, Steere settled for a while at Placerville. He later moved to El Dorado, where he purchased and successfully managed a hardware business.

During his years at El Dorado, Steere served as postmaster and Internal Revenue collector. He was soon known as an upright citizen, "always ready to do his duty in the defense of good government and civic betterment, to which cause he liberally contributed much of his time and money." Four years after his marriage to Anna Higgins, Robert became ill and he was forced to sell his business holdings. He subsequently returned with his wife and two children to Illinois, where he lived a quiet and unpretentious life for a number of years.

The Steere family came back to California in 1875, and shortly thereafter settled in Los Angeles. In the southland Robert operated a furniture business and, in

1882, was elected to the City Council. "Wealth and honor were to him only stepping stones toward a better service of God," and in the 1880s, he joined his wife and family in the Catholic Church. He subsequently became a charter member of the Los Angeles Catholic Beneficial Society. One commentator noted, "as a friend of the poor his charity knew no bounds."

Steere was an intense Californian, particularly enthusiastic about the development of Los Angeles, which he saw grow from a *pueblo* to a large city. From the back porch of his home, Steere saw the daily transformation from village to city. One of his hopes was to see the Owens River water brought to Los Angeles and its power harnessed for the development of electric light and power.

As a merchant, Robert Steere was connected for many years with the commercial interests of this city and while acquiring a competence won a place of importance among business men and representative citizens. At the time of Steere's demise, on April 29, 1910, the Bishop of Monterey–Los Angeles, Thomas J. Conaty, said of him: "Death has summoned to his reward one of the elders of the congregation. A man of venerable years and honorable life. A man of intense loyalty to all the interests of religion and of the community in which he lived!"

ALICE STEVENS (1860–1947)

The Catholic newspaper for the Diocese of Monterey–Los Angeles has long been "an equal opportunity employer," as evidenced by the enlightened tenure of a lady editor from July 15, 1908 to October 15, 1913. Born a Methodist, in Sutter County, Alice J. Stevens (1860–1947) began her journalistic career with the Los Angeles *Times*, where she worked for several years as a real estate editor. She was first associated with *The Tidings*, shortly after her conversion to the Catholic faith, as a contributor to the "Womens" page.

In 1906, at the encouragement of Bishop Thomas J. Conaty, Alice inaugurated the "Young Peoples' Column" which ultimately became one of the weekly newspaper's most popular features. Father John J. Clifford, who served briefly as editor *pro–tem* of *The Tidings*, following the death of Herman J. Rodman, nominated Miss Stevens as his successor, a candidacy subsequently confirmed by the paper's Board of Directors.

Reared in a literary family, Alice found no difficulty in expressing her personal viewpoint. It was she who started the editorial column, *El Rodeo*, which was to become (and is) a hallmark of *The Tidings*. A profoundly "human" approach characterized Miss Stevens' editorship. She personally interviewed and wrote feature stories on such leading contemporary personalities as

Mother Francis Xavier Cabrini, John Cardinal Farley and Father Bernard Vaughan.

In addition to her journalistic expertise on behalf of the Catholic press, Miss Stevens was an accomplished administrator who insisted that *The Tidings* he operated as a sound business venture. Among her many notable contributions was that of moving the editorial quarters to the Higgins Building, at Second and Main Streets, in 1912. Miss Stevens felt that it was expedient and proper to have the newspaper's offices adjacent to those of the diocesan curia, where day–to–day Catholic events could be more easily monitored.

In 1911, Miss Stevens attended the charter gathering of the Catholic Press Association, which she helped to establish as an organization "to promote the educational, literary, news and business interests of the papers concerned and to establish a closer fraternity among Catholic editors of the United States." At that formative meeting, Alice was unanimously chosen as a member and secretary of the directorate.

In the fall of 1913, Alice resigned the editorship to accept what she said was "a woman's higher place in life" as the wife of William Tipton, a leading legal expert on the question of Spanish land titles. Following her husband's death, Alice moved to Pacoima, where she lived until her own demise, in 1947.

Innovator though she was, Alice J. Stevens was basically a very humble lady. She was the first member of her sex to address the Knights of Columbus and the Newman Club and that she did in the masculine–oriented era prior to World War I. At the same time, popular as she was in her role as spokeswoman for the Church, Alice adamantly refused to allow her name to be carried on the newspaper's masthead.

Her five years as the only woman editor of *The Tidings* are remembered as a time of unparalleled gentility in both expression and tone. Or, as one writer noted, "Alice J. Stevens brought a lot of class to Southern California's Catholic newspaper and she did it in a time when class came at a premium."

GEORGE C. ST. LOUIS (b. 1848)

George C. St. Louis, a pioneer Fresno Catholic, was born on January 6, 1848. In the 1930 Annual Review edition of the *Central California Register,* George related some of the incidents that occurred during the six month journey by covered wagon that brought his family from Missouri to Sacramento in 1852.

In his account, excerpted from an address to the Native Sons of the Golden West, George said that the caravan of twenty–two wagons followed a guide book which told where "the feed was good and where water could be had for the whole train." At night the wagons were arranged in a circle, the tongue of the second wagon was pushed under the first wagon and so on until a complete circle had been formed. The cattle were kept within the circle to keep Indians from stampeding them.

"The whole train was managed in a sort of military style, as my uncle Charles had served under General (John) Fremont and used military tactics when practical." Those precedures must have worked well because the caravan "had very good luck all the way from St. Joseph in good old Missouri until we reached Sacramento."

George went on to say that "it was not many more days when we came to where elk and deer were plentiful and different men were sent out to supply the train with meat. What was not used for dinners was cut into strips and boiled in salt water and hung out to dry and was called jerky. The hides were tanned and were used to make pants and coats for the men." "Just before Pikes Peak, a heavy dark cloud arose and in no time a thunder storm was upon us and the men had barely time to unyoke the cattle when it began to rain, not in drops but in sheets.

"After a little it began to hail and some of the hail stones were as big as pigeon's eggs and with the double–forked lightning and the noise of the thunder reverberating over the hills and the utter darkness and the men hollering, the cattle and horses nearly all stampeded, before the corral could be formed."

One day the caravan was held up by about two hundred Indians. "Maybe you will think that we were scared. Well, I will say we were scared some and then a great deal more. The women and children were all crying, the men all excited and did not know what to do, except Uncle Charles who seemed cool and ready for all emergencies.

"He spoke French to them and asked what they wanted and it happened that a few of them knew him as they had seen him with General Fremont a few years before and they understood French and they told him that one of our sharpshooters had shot and killed one of their tribe and that unless the murderer was delivered to them they would send 500 more of their tribe and burn the wagons.

"Uncle Charles told them there must be some mistake as his sharpshooters were all French and he knew they would not shoot an Indian unless in self defense. They then asked where we had camped last night. Uncle Charles told them; they said it must have been someone in the train ahead of ours.

"Sure enough they found their man and when the I Indians returned with him, he pleaded with Uncle Charles to save him. But nothing could be done for him and what the Indians did with him we never heard."

There are several other interesting sidelights to the narrative. Hopefully, at some future time, the whole account will be reprinted for wider distribution. In any event, after arriving in California, George's family bought a farm in Yolo County and there he later became successful raising wheat. He later moved to Woodland and learned the confectioner's trade.

He concluded by noting that "now I am expecting to go on another journey, sometime within the next few years. It will not be in a covered wagon, but it will be empty–handed and alone to meet my God in that place called heaven. I hope to see you one and all in due time."

CHARLES STODDARD (1843–1909)

When Charles Warren Stoddard (1843–1909) passed away at Monterey, he was eulogized by George Wharton James as "one of the sweetest, kindliest and truest of men." Indeed, the death of the noted writer, poet, scholar and educator left a void in the literary ranks of the Pacific Coast that was keenly felt at every level of local and national society.

"Uncle Charlie" Stoddard had a warm, emotional and sensuous nature. For him, the rolling peals of the solemn organ, the mysteries of the Faith, the odor of incense and the elaborate ceremonials of the Church had profound meaning and influence. Eventually, Stoddard became a Roman Catholic and ever after the Church provided him full scope for the genius of his writings. Fittingly, he chose for his patron and model Saint Anthony of Padua.

In 1884, Stoddard was invited to teach at the College of Notre Dame in Indiana. Two years later, according to Joaquin Miller, the Holy Father "put out his hand over the heads of the hundred thousand learned men of Europe who would have been proud of the place, and chose Stoddard professor of English literature for The Catholic University of America in Washington, D.C."

For thirteen years, Stoddard lectured to students and the great outside world. Then he retired to private life and, characteristically, he burned the whole of his lectures lest he be tempted to use them again. Stoddard regarded the past as a stairwell to the future.

If it is true that people are measured by the quality of their friends, Stoddard rated highly. He was a confidant of such people as Robert Louis Stevenson, Rudyard Kipling, Bert Harte and Thomas Starr King.

Stoddard was a long–time friend of Mark Twain too. In fact he lived with him for several years in England. He once said that "I've heard nearly all the great speakers, orators, actors and preachers of modern times. Either in Washington or in Europe I had the best opportunities. I've heard bishops and archbishops and all the great notables of the Church read, but never in my life

did I hear anything as rich and sweet and impressive and beautiful as was Mark's reading of the Book of Ruth."

The famed writer was in San Francisco when the earthquake and subsequent fire struck the city. For him it was a traumatic experience and one from which he never fully recovered. He later took ill and succumbed on April 24, 1909.

Never did Stoddard's muse rise in such power and strength as in his "Bells of San Gabriel" which appeared in *Sunset Magazine*.

Therein the vivid picturing of the missions in their golden days bring before the listener the sad refrain which tolled the end of one era and the beginning of another. According to one critic, had Stoddard written no other than that poem, his name would occupy a unique status in the list of the poets along the Pacific Coast and the nation itself.

Stoddard's mortal remains are buried in the cemetery of San Carlos Borromeo Cathedral in the old Monterey he loved so well. Nearby stands the building founded by Fray Junípero Serra, the pioneer whose work aroused in Stoddard's heart an enthusiasm and exuberance that invariably led to tears of deep emotion.

THOMAS STORKE (1876–1971)

During most of his long and eventful life, Thomas Storke (1876–1971) was Santa Barbara's most influential private citizen. An outstanding Catholic layman, with a personal life beyond reproach, Thomas numbered among his ancestors such local luminaries as Jose Francisco de Ortega and Daniel A. Hill.

Following his graduation from Stanford University, Thomas worked briefly on his uncle's sheep ranch on Santa Rosa Island. Later he became a cub reporter for the *Morning Press*.

After a tour of America's more prominent cities, Thomas Storke returned to Santa Barbara to become night editor for the *Press*. Later he purchased the ailing *Daily Independent* and on the first day of the twentieth century, he formally launched his career as editor and publisher.

Storke subsequently bought the *Daily News* and for twenty or more years published the two papers under the masthead *Daily News and Independent*. During that time, very little that happened in those environs escaped Storke's always provocative editorials.

In 1904, Thomas married Elsie Smith. Their three children (and a later son born to his second wife, Marion Day) became pillars of Santa Barbara's social and religious atmosphere. Always active in Democratic politics, Mr. Storke was appointed postmaster for Santa Barbara in 1914. A close friend of Senator William Gibbs McAdoo, Storke was several times a member of the California delegation to the Democratic National Convention. Storke used his friendship with President Franklin D. Roosevelt to bring several Federal programs to Santa Barbara.

In 1937, Storke merged his newspaper with the *Morning Press* and from that time onward published the Santa Barbara *News–Press* During that era Storke was, as reported by *Time* magazine, Santa Barbara's "benevolent dictator."

Journalism buildings were erected at both Stanford University and the University of California at Santa Barbara. Storke Tower was built at UCSB as a tribute from "Mr. Santa Barbara's" fellow regents. Governor Frank Merriam appointed Storke to serve out the unexpired term of Senator McAdoo. One local commentator noted that Storke went back to Washington and "accomplished more in six weeks than most senators accomplish in six years."

A series of editorial articles written by Storke about the controversial John Birch Society in the early 1960s won the *News–Press* a Pulitzer Prize, together with other awards from universities, colleges and businesses. From all quarters, Storke was hailed as a man brave enough to speak out on the crucial questions and challenges of his time.

After more than six decades in journalism, Storke sold the *News–Press* in 1964. Thereafter, he presided as elder statesman of Santa Barbara, finally dying on October 12, 1971, just a few days short of his ninety–fifth birthday.

The eulogy for Storke's funeral was delivered by his long–time friend and admirer, Chief Justice Earl Warren. The former California governor accurately hailed Thomas Storke as "the most powerful citizen of the century" in Santa Barbara.

In his foreword to Storke's autobiography, published in 1962, Adlai Stevenson said that Storke had been "a courageous spokesman for what is good and true and just, and in the forefront of the never–ending battle against exploitation, corruption, graft and crime." Warren and Stevenson, political rivals, surely agreed in their assessment of Thomas M. Storke.

WILLIAM P. SULLIVAN (d. 1901)

Massachusetts–born William P. Sullivan came to California as a teenager. He studied at the Lincoln Grammar School and subsequently spent three years in what would be equivalent to present–day secondary school. William chose a business career and shortly after completing his educational courses entered the dry goods house of Mosgrove and Company, where he mastered all the details of the firm from salesman to bookkeeper.

When a financially more lucrative opportunity beckoned, he became affiliated with the prestigious firm of Keane & Company as accountant, a position he held until that organization terminated its services. Sullivan's next venture was that of forming his own business. With two partners, he established the firm of Sullivan, Burtis and Dewey, a dry goods store on Market Street, the first such attempt in that area of San Francisco.

William Sullivan was probably best known in commercial circles through his association with the nationally–known Pacific Rolling Mills. There he worked for many years as secretary and chief accountant. His innovative methods did much to increase the earning power of that company. For sixteen years he was an active member of the California National Guard. He enlisted as a private in the First Regiment and worked himself up, rank by rank, to that of colonel. He was a tactician by nature, a characteristic that never left him.

Mr. Sullivan first appeared in the political arena during the campaign of 1894, when he was elected as a delegate from the Thirty–Seventh Assembly District to the Democratic County Convention. Two years later, Sullivan became chairman of a reorganizing committee for local government. James Phelan was nominated for and then elected Mayor of San Francisco and Sullivan became his senior deputy. He held that influential position until February 14, 1900, when he was named Chief of Police for San Francisco.

Throughout his life, Sullivan was a devoted Catholic. A member of Saint Agnes Parish, he took an active part in all the local parochial activities. He rarely missed ushering at Sunday Mass and was a monthly participant at the Communion breakfasts. He was a charter member and ardent supporter of the Young Mens' Catholic Union. And when Archbishop Patrick W. Riordan organized the League of the Cross Cadets, Sullivan was chosen as colonel of the regiment.

A family man in every way, William spent all his available moments with his wife and three children. A reporter once noted that at home Sullivan was kind and gentle, but fair and resolute. His whole existence was family–oriented. The funeral of Chief Sullivan, in mid–November, 1901, was described by one local newspaper as "one of the most impressive ever held in this city." And rightly so, for William P. Sullivan's religious and civic lifestyle epitomized the Catholic contribution to San Francisco at the turn–of–the–century.

ALFRED SULLY (1820—1879)

Alfred Sully (1820–1879), one of the two sons of the noted American artist Thomas Sully, was a skillful draftsman and painter in his own right. A number of his works survive, mostly watercolor sketches which he composed during his various tours of duty in the military.

Choosing to follow a career in the army, Sully obtained an appointment to West Point in 1837, where formal training in topography and perspective sharpened the informal lessons his father had supplied. Graduating in 1841, he fought in the Seminole War and along the southern frontier.

In 1847 he landed with the forces of Scott at Vera Cruz, and campaigned all the way to Mexico City. After a brief return to New York, Sully sailed for California in November of 1848. Here he lived for the next four years, marrying the daughter of a rancher and taking part in the development of the new state. After his duty in California, Sully spent most of the 1850s Indian fighting on the plains. He served with the Army of the Potomac, and is best known in western history for his campaigns against the Sioux in 1864–1865.

Following the Civil War, worn out by the campaigns and embittered by being passed over for promotions, Sully spent what remained of his life in frontier posts until his death in 1879. While Alfred was clearly not the artist his father was, he still inherited considerable ability from Thomas. His early watercolor of the parade ground at West Point, presumably done during his student days, illustrates his command of topographical technique.

Sully's watercolors represent very early original pictorial records of California, done as they were by an American who was there at the time. They are charming and important views that add much to the historical scene.

The artist's sketch of the "Church at Monterey, California, July, 1849" is a masterful rendition. After having returned to New York, Alfred was assigned to Monterey, the capital of California. Since almost all the soldiers had deserted for gold, his first trip to the area was anything but boring.

It was there that Sully met the grand daughter of Jose de la Guerra, Manuela. She was destined to become Sully's wife. This was to be the happiest and then the saddest part of the artist's life. The sketch of the church is a delightful, skillfully rendered view of a Spanish house-of-worship. It has exquisite detail, down to the friar and peon tipping hats to each other.

In 1850, Alfred and Manuela, much to her parents consternation, eloped. At first her family was enraged but gradually they became reconciled, especially when Manuela gave birth to a baby boy. Unhappily, in April of 1851, Manuela died violently after eating an orange, perhaps sent by an ex-suitor. Three weeks later, Sully's son also succumbed. Within a few short weeks, Sully's whole life was changed. He decided to leave California.

He then went to Santa Barbara to say farewell to the patriarch of the family, Jose de la Guerra. It was at that time that Sully made his first drawing of Santa Barbara. He later spoke of that sketch as of "the mission a mile back in the hill overlooking the town . . . a noble old building made of sandstone."

That particular sketch is a wonderful, yet poignant view of the village and mission. As Sully noted, it was "pure California in all its habits." A nice added touch are the pencil-sketched mountains in the background.

Another sketch of the mission appears in Sully's book *No Tears for the General*. There he described the church where his late wife was confirmed as a splendid old building . . . which would put to blush many churches in Philadelphia.

ROGER BROOKE TANEY (1777–1865)

It was through the kindness of Dr. Doyce B. Nunis, Professor of History at the University of Southern California, that the Chancery Archives acquired the signature of Roger Brooke Taney (1777–1865), the first Catholic Chief justice of the United States.

The Maryland-born jurist was one of the most prominent of the nation's great pioneers. A graduate of Dickinson College, Taney entered political life, in 1799, as a member of the Maryland General Assembly. He was elected to the state's Senate in 1816, where he served with distinction until 1821. Six years later, he became Attorney General of Maryland and, in 1831, Taney was appointed Attorney General of the United States, the proto-Catholic ever to serve in a presidential cabinet.

President Andrew Jackson named Taney to be Secretary of the Treasury, in 1833, but his nomination failed to win confirmation by the United States Senate. In 1835, Jackson appointed Taney Associate Justice of the Supreme Court. Later that year, following the death of John Marshall, the President recalled his earlier nomination, and submitted Taney's name for the vacant post of Chief Justice.

During his twenty-eight years as the country's highest judicial officer, Chief Justice Taney swore into office eight Presidents of the United States, from Martin Van Buren to Abraham Lincoln. Historians place Taney second only to John Marshall in the history of the Supreme Court. He was especially noted for reversal of earlier theories that property rights were more sacred than human rights.

In 1852, Bishop Joseph Sadoc Alemany journeyed to Washington, where he sought the advice of the nation's fifth Chief justice about Catholic claims to the Pious Fund of the Californias. The Bishop of Monterey was graciously received but, as Alemany's biographer stated, "Taney could be of little help with regard to the Bishop's perplexities regarding the Pious Fund because, in this case, the Mexican government was directly at odds with the Church" and not with officials at Washington.

Taney was a deeply religious man. When his wife and daughter died, during the epidemic of 1855, he wrote: "Most thankful I am that the reading, reflection, studies and experiences of a long life have strengthened and confirmed my faith in the Catholic Church, which has never ceased to teach her children how they should live and how they should die." Attorney General Edward Bates wrote in his famous diary that Taney "was a man of great and varied talents. He cannot be forgotten, for his life is interwoven with the history of his country."

The signature acquired by the Chancery Archives is attached to a receipt for payment of $15,000 to the Treasury Department. The note, dated January 17, 1834, is especially rare inasmuch as it bears Taney's title, "Secretary of the Treasury," a position from which he was subsequently forced to resign for lack of Senate confirmation.

TIBURCIO TAPIA (1789–1845)

The story of Tiburcio Tapia's lost treasure chest is one of California's most repeated (and believed) legends. It was most recently featured in an issue of the *Tombstone Epitaph*. Tiburcio Tapia (1789–1845) was a respected and successful Los Angeles merchant. By the time he was thirty–nine, he had been *presidente* of the local *ayuntamiento* and *alcalde de constitucional*. In 1840, he was named judge of the district embracing all of the southland.

When fears of war with the United States began to circulate through California, Tapia reportedly moved an iron–bound chest of coins from Los Angeles to his home at Rancho Cucamonga for safe keeping. The chest contained most of his own fortune, together with funds collected to build a chapel in Cucamonga.

One version of the legend contends that after the war, Tapia decided to move his family to Mexico, before the California countryside was ruined by *gringos*. During the long trek to Sonora, he and his family were attacked by Cahuilla Indians, near present–day Banning. Critically wounded, Tapia lay beside the road for several days before being found by a roving priest. Though delirious from his wounds, Tapia was able to tell the priest about the money chest which he had hidden at Cucamonga.

Tapia claimed to have given a map containing directions for finding the treasure to one of his *vaqueros* before the Indian attack, but he didn't know whether the *vaquero* had survived the raid. Then Tiburcio Tapia died. The priest had promised the dying man that he would look for the treasure. Eventually, the *padre* found his way to Cucamonga and, after a lengthy search, he concluded that the whole story had been the figment of Tapia's fevered imagination.

Soon after the priest's visit to the ranch, treasure seekers began flocking to Cucamonga. Several hundred acres were dug up, all in vain. Finally, the story was passed off as a colorful yarn. Several years later, an elderly *vaquero* arrived at Cucamonga. He refused the hospitality of the house, bought some provisions and camped along the road. Next morning, he was gone. But close to the Tapia house, near the base of a giant oak tree, were six deep holes.

During the depression, numerous groups journeyed to the adjoining Red Hill Country Club on weekends. They would camp out and spend a few pleasant days digging up the golf course. They removed so much dirt from beneath two large oak trees standing near the fifth and ninth tees that both trees died. Another favorite digging site was on the bank near the east side of the sixteenth hole. Tunnels resembling mine shafts were burrowed there. A giant cactus patch was devastated by the fortune hunters. All, apparently, to no avail.

The warm desert winds still blow each autumn over the clay bluffs of Red Hill in Rancho Cucamonga. The winds rustle the thin leaves of the eucalyptus trees surrounding the new condominia perched on the hill. The homes standing on or near that hill were once the site of the Tapia *rancho*. Where the trees shade the sidewalk was once a grand adobe home, massive as a fortress. And somewhere, near the red bluffs, is rumored to be a treasure—buried California gold hidden there in 1845.

ALEXANDER TAYLOR (1817–1876)

Alexander Taylor was one of the few emigrants in the 1840s not drawn to California by the "gold fever" then sweeping the nation. Though he arrived "in that earliest motley and variegated band of adventurers," he was a pioneer of another type, "predestined to become the first bibliographer of California."

For some years Taylor was clerk of the United States District Court at Monterey, but later moved to Santa Barbara where he married the socially prominent daughter of Daniel Hill. Not a Catholic at the time of his marriage, Taylor later became a convert and was buried on July 28, 1876, amidst great solemnity from the old Mission at Santa Barbara. His entire life, to quote one commentator, proved him to be a "most indefatigable historical worker in the days when such work was not appreciated."

It was while living in Monterey that Taylor began amassing Spanish documents relating to California's history between 1770 and 1846. There were over 6,000 items in his collection, of which forty or fifty were letters written by Fray Junípero Serra. In 1854 Taylor offered his "documents and papers of public character consisting of letters from the authorities, religious and civil to the Library of Congress. It has long been a painful memory to Washington officials that the generous bibliographer's offer was not accepted.

Taylor waited some years and in 1860 presented 2,560 of the documents to Saint Mary's Library Association. This group had the letters bound into eight volumes and provided funds for an index to their contents. The collection then passed to the Archives of the Archdiocese of San Francisco where it remains today. Three sets of five volumes of transcripts were later made, one for the Santa Barbara Mission Archives, another for the Academy of American Franciscan History in Washington, and a final one for the Huntington Library at San Marino. The numerous references to "Archbishop's Archives" found in California source books refer to the Alexander Taylor Collection.

Another facet of Taylor's collection was the 400 specimen newspapers of early California between 1846 and 1854. This assortment, presented to the Mercantile Library of San Francisco was destroyed in the 1906 fire, Taylor was also a prodigious author. Four scrapbooks of his writings were donated to the Santa Barbara Mission Archives, most of them dealing with Indianology of California. Several other miscellaneous volumes contain data on the development of journalism in the state.

There is much to commend in the works of Alexander J. Taylor. Unfortunately, far removed from the centers of culture and learning, he was, like other and greater men, "too big for the company in which he was obliged to live." Hubert Howe Bancroft had the last word on Taylor when he noted that it is well to judge a man not alone by what he has accomplished, but "also by what he has conscientiously tried to perform." In that vein, we would join in saying, all honor to such men as Taylor, who have "toiled under more or less unfavorable auspices to save from destruction the data of our history."

THOMAS WORKMAN TEMPLE (1905–1972)

Thomas Workman Temple III, a sixth generation Californian and one of the West's most knowledgeable genealogists, was a dedicated scholar who doggedly preferred accuracy to popularity. Though he held a legal degree from Harvard, Tom never actually practiced law. In 1930, he was encouraged by San Francisco's Archbishop Edward J. Hanna, to pursue his genealogical interests as a lifetime vocation. Since then, he earned a modest livelihood by fulfilling commissions from families, foundations and historical agencies.

For over forty years, Temple patiently transcribed entries from the old Baptismal, Confirmation, Marriage and Burial Registers of mission times. In 1965, the Chancery Archives of the Archdiocese of Los Angeles acquired the Thomas Workman Temple Collection of Historical Transcripts, part of an extensive survey made of California's missions, *padres* and people. The 2,000 typed pages also include data on the *gente de razón* from sixteen of the state's twenty–one missions, as well as several foundations in Peninsular California.

Oldest of four children, Tom was born January 4, 1905, at Mission Vieja, on the Rancho La Merced, near present–day Montebello. His father, Walter Pablo Librado Workman Temple, once owned the 800–acre spread east of San Gabriel which ultimately developed into Temple City. The family name was also perpetuated in Los Angeles, where a major traffic artery was designated, in 1858, to honor Jonathan Temple, one of the southland's first merchants. Tom's mother, Lorenza Librado González Alvitre y Alvarado de Bermudez Lugo, was descended from Manuel Ygnacio de Lugo, one of the seventeen soldiers who escorted the *pobladores*, or founders, to *El Pueblo de Nuestra Señora de los Angeles*, in 1781.

When he was nine years old, Tom made an interesting discovery while gathering wild flowers and onions on a hillside near the family home, Rancho La Merced. He saw a tiny pool of rain–water, bastioned in the rocks, its surface bubbling fumes of gas. Further investigation disclosed a jet of natural gas. Tom's mother returned to the area frequently, to amuse friends by frying eggs over the natural jet. The obvious indication of oil beneath the surface attracted the interest of the Standard Oil Company and, in 1917, drilling commenced on what eventually became one of the nation's richest fields.

As a youngster, he attended, appropriately enough, Temple Grammar School, near the location of the original Mission San Gabriel, on the bank of the Rio Hondo. Later he studied at Santa Clara and, in 1926, went to Harvard Law School, in New England, "for a little polish."

In 1938, Tom married Gabriela Quiroz, whose ancestors can be traced back to the Spanish *conquistadores* who came to Mexico with Hernando Cortés. Their small, five–room house on Euclid Avenue became the focal point for much of the southland's historical lore. For many years, at Fiesta time, Tom edited the *Bulletin of the Old Mission Parish*, at San Gabriel, where he functioned as historian and consultant. He wrote and translated over a dozen articles for different western journals and engaged in extensive research on Antonio Jose Francisco Yorba, grantee of the Santiago de Santa Ana Rancho. His "Sources for Tracing Spanish–American Pedigrees in the Southwestern United States," a talk given at Salt Lake City, explains, in considerable detail, his overall approach to genealogy. That address was reproduced and distributed by the Genealogical Society of the Church of Jesus Christ of Latter–Day Saints.

While doing research in Spain, during 1968–1969, Tom was instrumental in having a bronze commemorative medallion struck, at Barcelona, to honor Fray Junípero Serra, on the occasion of California's bicentennial. Already that exquisitely–cast medallion has become a collector's item. No living authority was better versed than Workman Temple III about the familiar relationships of California's Provincial era as recorded in the old mission registers, *presidio* muster rolls and early census reports.

PATRICK J. THOMAS (1830–1901)

Patrick J. Thomas was born in Ireland's County Galway in 1830, where his family had lived in relative affluence for centuries. He grew up "with printer's ink in his veins" and during "his early years acquired considerable knowledge in the field of journalism, under the tutelage of the (Tuam) *Herald*." When his apprenticeship expired, Thomas "ran away to sea, was shipwrecked and returned to Galway. Later he sailed for New York and was there employed in a newspaper office." At the age of twenty–five, Thomas arrived in San Francisco, where he found work on the *Cosmopolitan*, a weekly controlled by an erratic genius, Hugh McDermott.

Such was the industry of the Bay City's first printer and publisher that he managed to work his way through Santa Clara College while doing part–time editorial research for the *Daily Evening Bulletin*. He even found time to serve as the first secretary of the San Francisco branch of the Saint Vincent de Paul Society.

In 1858, Thomas was one of the three founders of the San Francisco *Monitor*, which the trio envisioned as "a Catholic journal, free from the rancor of polemics and devoted to the cultivation of Catholic literature." Though the paper was welcomed by the community, ecclesiastical journalism was not a lucrative occupation in those days and within a year, Thomas found it financially expedient to relinquish his interests in *The Monitor* to Bartholomew Dowling, the well–known Irish poet.

In subsequent years Thomas was associated with several other Bay area newspapers. He was on the staff of Charles H. Webb's *Californian* during the era when that journal boasted such luminaries as Samuel Clemens, Bret Harte and Charles Warren Stoddard. He was also one of the original founders of the *Evening Post*. Already a prolific writer himself, Thomas purchased an interest in a job printing firm in 1870, a business he soon developed into one of the city's most successful enterprises. It was from this press that he issued his now rare *Our Centennial Memoir* to commemorate the first century of Catholicism in San Francisco. In many ways this book symbolized Thomas, who had long dedicated himself to depicting "in truthful colors the aims and objects of the devoted men who raised the banner of Christianity and of civilization where one of the greatest cities of the world is now established."

Even in his times Thomas realized that "the documents remain in the libraries of the few—too few—who feel an interest in the story of the vicissitudes of the Golden City of the Pacific," and he was anxious to put before his contemporaries evidence "to vindicate the character of the zealous missionaries to whose earnestness in the cause of the Gospel San Francisco owes its origin." When the veteran printer and publisher died on February 27, 1901, the following excerpt from Archbishop Patrick W. Riordan's eulogy appeared in *The Tidings*

> The life of the deceased was that of a true Christian, and although his demise was sudden and unexpected, death found him well prepared. His sterling qualities, his honesty and integrity of life, his charity for the poor, made him generally respected and beloved.

ALICE S. TIPTON (1860–1947)

During five of its many years as the official Catholic newspaper for Southern California, *The Tidings* was edited by Alice Stevens, one–time real estate reporter for the Los Angeles *Times*. Alice was a native of Sutter County, where she was born, in 1860 A sister of Carrie Stevens Walters, a poet and contemporary of Joaquin Miller, "Aunt Alice" came from a Methodist family, long steeped in literary traditions.

Miss Stevens was first associated with *The Tidings* as a regular contributor to the Women's Page and Young People's Department. Her name was submitted as a candidate for the editorship by Father John J. Clifford, from whom Alice had taken instructions and been received into the Church a few years earlier. The late C. C. Desmond, Chairman of the Board of Directors for *The Tidings*, had reservations about entrusting the editorship to a woman, until Father Clifford convinced him that "Aunt Alice" possessed all the qualities needed for operating a Catholic newspaper.

On July 15 1908, Miss Stevens became the editor, a post she occupied with distinction until the fall of 1913. An unassuming person, Alice never permitted her name to be carried on the newspaper's masthead. Yet with her literary background, she found no difficulty in expressing herself during the years of her association with *The*

Tidings. "Aunt Alice" carried on an intellectual enlightenment campaign in which she "exposed" the evils of radical socialism. And through that and other journalistic forays, *The Tidings* retained dignified and aloof from the more controversial and debatable issues of the day.

Miss Stevens interviewed a host of famous personalities, including Mother Frances Cabrini, Cardinal John Farley and Father Bernard Vaughan, the famous English Jesuit. She was the only woman present when the nation's Catholic editors met in Columbus, Ohio, in 1911 to form the Catholic Press Association, a group geared to promoting "the educational, literary, news and business interests of the papers concerned and to establish a closer fraternity among Catholic editors of the United States." "Aunt Alice" was unanimously elected as a member and secretary of the directorate. During that journey, the editor of *The Tidings* was invited to Worcester by Father Bernard Conaty, the brother of the Bishop of Monterey–Los Angeles, where she was introduced to that area's leading journalists.

In the fall of 1913, Alice resigned her position to "accept a woman's high place in life" as the wife of William Tipton, a legal expert on Spanish land grants. During the later years of her life, "Aunt Alice" lived in a modest little cottage at 12527 Bromwich Street, in Pacoima. In an editorial, Charles C. Conroy, her successor as editor of *The Tidings*, said that during her years, Alice "had done most excellent work and had been recognized as one of the leading Catholics editors in the United States."

It is indeed unfortunate that the feminist movement began with women claiming men's rights instead of equal rights or specific rights as women. Alice Stevens carved her niche in journalistic history as a first class woman, not a second class man!

ROBERT J. TOBIN (1828–1906)

Robert J. Tobin, the last of those who were founders of the Hibernia Bank, died at San Francisco, on September 19, 1906. It marked the end of an era for Northern California. In the local newspaper accounts of his demise, Judge Tobin was acknowledged as "a prominent figure among the men of affairs and in the financial and commercial world of the metropolis of the Pacific.

"He was a pioneer and an argonaut, and from the days of the first rush of gold–seekers in which were laid the foundations of the city's material and social greatness, his name was identified with the expansion and development of San Francisco's civic and commercial activities."

Born at Waterford, Ireland, in 1828, Robert was taken early in life to Australia. Four years later, the family moved on to Chile, where they remained until 1847.

In the latter year, the nineteen year old Tobin emigrated to the Island of Tahiti. When news reached him about the discovery of gold in California, Robert set out for the United States. He reached San Francisco the following fall and was among the first to engage in mining along the Gold Dust Trails.

Tobin was later the driving force behind the establishment of the Irish Benevolent Society. When that fraternal organization was transformed into the Hibernia Savings and Loan Society, Robert and his brothers became actively associated with its business affairs. Under the careful and sagacious administration of Tobin, the Hibernia Savings and Loan Association grew into one of the six largest such institutions in the nation.

During the earlier years of his varied career, Tobin served for a time as Justice of the Peace. He occupied that position when it was one demanding exceptional qualities of determination and courage. He was also a Police Commissioner under several succeeding municipal administrations covering almost a quarter century. In that office too, he served the community fearlessly and well.

The judge was an energetic and sympathetic worker in religious, social and benevolent enterprises. Devoted to his Catholic faith, Tobin enjoyed the confidence and respect of both the clergy and laity of San Francisco. Tobin was always interested in the cause of his native Ireland and he never missed an opportunity to promote its welfare by voice or purse. He was traditionally a fixture in the annual Saint Patrick's Day parades.

At his funeral obsequies, Archbishop George T. Montgomery praised the jurist–banker, noting that he was an outstanding public figure in the social and civic life of the Bay Area. The prelate paid special tribute to the character and charitable record of the departed pioneer. Judge Tobin succumbed after a long illness which he bore with enviable Christian strength and resignation. He related to one priest how easy it was to die after a life of honest endeavors.

PATRICK CHARLES TONNER (1841–1900)

As one of the southland's outstanding pioneers, Patrick Charles Tonner (1841–1900) was also a prophetic versifier of no mean ability. Thus it was that he wrote of "The Flocks of Palomares:"

> I see a thousand vineyards,
> All o'er that lovely plain,
> I see the fair haired Saxon
> Where dwelt the sons of Spain.

The Irish–born educator came to the United States as a youngster of sixteen. He studied with the Jesuits in Philadelphia, and in 1863, joined his two brothers in the mining fields of the Mother Lode Country. For a while Patrick taught classics at Saint Mary's College near San Francisco and later held similar positions in Marysville and Monterey. He moved to Los Angeles in 1869, where he became associated with the legal firm of Howard and Kewen. Even after taking a post as teacher in the Palomares School District near Pomona in 1872, young Tonner maintained his interest in the legal profession. His private collection of tomes of jurisprudence eventually became one of the most extensive in the West.

In his many civic activities, Tonner contributed to upgrading the western image around the nation. *Harper's Weekly* reported to its readers in 1912, "There are coming out of that great nursery great children, whose thoughts and discoveries and deeds will do for human life, wherever it exists, greater far greater, services than any prophet dare predict." The pioneers who were responsible for that "suspicion abroad in the East that 'the West' was a good place to raise men" are indeed worthy of gratitude for their descendants.

George Wharton James observed that these men forsook all luxury and comfort, all ease and self–indulgence, and bravely, boldly, resolutely and daringly threw themselves into the wilds, resolving to master them or die in the attempt. The same writer went on to say of those pathfinders, among whom Patrick Charles Tonner must be included:

> It was the pioneers who blazed the trail, cut out the pathway, hewed the wood. It was their deeds that called across the mountains to the halting ones, the waiting, the hesitant, the fearful.
>
> It was their bravery and courage that heartened the tens of thousands who followed. It was their spirit that has entered so largely into the making of the new land they won so hardly, they loved with so fierce and intense a love that men of lesser natures and poorer, less lovable lands, wondered at them, or laughed and scoffed.
>
> It was their rugged strength, their simple–heartedness, their direct frankness, their robust honesty, their uncorrupted sincerity that laid the foundations so secure for this last, greatest, and most needed civilization of the Western World.
>
> It was their spirit that has leavened and is leavening the lump of civilization,—civilization that has always— so far in the world's history—sunk into dissolute luxury and faded away to nothingness, poisoned by the evil of its own sensuousness, lulled to sleep by the lotus flowers of its growing, when it should have been alert, awake, in battle–array.

J. F. REGIS TOOMEY (1898–1991)

While out–of–town a few years ago, I read in a local newspaper about the death of J. F. Regis Toomey, one of Hollywood's most durable and widely–known actors. According to the wire reports, Toomey's most notable and memorable accomplishment was "taking part in what was billed as the longest on–screen kiss in Hollywood history."

Perhaps that 158 second encounter with Jane Wyman, in "You're in the Army Now," is reason enough for a headline. But I have more authentic memories of Toomey than that. I knew him thirty years ago when I was a youthful curate at Saint Victor's Parish in West Hollywood. To me, he was all the things one could associate with a Catholic layman, an actor who epitomized the very best in the Motion Picture Industry.

I once introduced Regis to the members of the Altar and Rosary Society as "an actor who is a Catholic." He didn't like that description and pointed out that he preferred being a "Catholic who is an actor." Being Catholic came first in Toomey's priorities. And his wasn't just a nominal affiliation with the Church. He attended daily Mass and took an active part in all our parochial functions.

He lived with his wife in a modest little home at 1257 Sunset Plaza Drive. Jobs were hard to find in the industry—even for a man of his stature. We always knew when Regis was working because he tithed on every pay–check he ever received.

Regis was a native of Pittsburgh. Born on August 13, 1898, he did graduate work in drama at the Carnegie Institute of Technology. Initially he wanted to be a lawyer and he looked the part of a jurist in his always neatly–tailored suits. But he signed on temporarily with a vaudeville act and later decided to make the stage his career.

He toured England in George M. Cohan's "Little Nelly Kelly" and, in 1928, he appeared with Chester Morris in "Alibi," the first all–talking melodrama. Three years later he played opposite Clara Bow in "Kick In." Once he let me page through his scrapbook, where there were playbills of his starring roles in "Spellbound," "The Bishop's Wife," "Show Boat" and "Voyage to the Bottom of the Sea."

In television, Regis often played a priest or a policeman. He appeared in several series, including "Dante's Inferno," "Hey, Mulligan" and "Petticoat Junction." He often played the victim of screen violence. "I die well," he once said. He was "killed" so often that he wondered if he qualified as the "mortician's 'Man of the Year'."

Cecil B. De Mille once asked Regis to play a part in "Union Pacific" where he would be terminated by Anthony Quinn. He said it wasn't all that bad because he died in Barbara Stanwyck's arms. "If you gotta go, that's as good a way as any."

Regis had reached the grand age of ninety–three

when he died peacefully at the Motion Picture Hospital in Woodland Hills. He played his screen and stage roles well, but he really excelled in his private life. For what you saw was what he was—a role model for contemporary Catholics.

FRANZ TREVORS (1907–1980)

Memorial services were conducted on April 3, 1980, at San Buenaventura Mission, for Franz Trevors, an internationally–acclaimed "conservator" of fine paintings. A long–time local resident, Mr. Trevors succumbed after a lengthy illness brought on by a reaction to the toxic chemicals of the restorative profession.

Trevors was a man who must be accorded a place of artistic prominence in the annals of the Golden State. Born at Philadelphia, in 1907, he grew up in San Francisco. His father was a muralist and restorer and the younger Trevors often recalled how his first paintings were landscapes executed in the backyard of his Bay Area home. His apprenticeship under such talented craftsmen as Harold Thompson and Walter Ufer brought alive a series of unique talents hidden by God in the very recesses of Trevors' soul.

Franz was a painter of numerous Western subjects and between 1945 and 1951 he completed no fewer than 140 murals which can still be seen in the gambling casinos of Nevada. He and his beloved Grace traveled extensively. But Franz always regarded Southern California as his first and last homestead. He came to be, among other things, a recognized authority on such Western America giants as Ed Borein.

In addition to being an artist in his own right, Trevors achieved considerable acclaim as an art historian and "detective." He traced down the dubious authenticity of numerous paintings purporting to be old masters, including fake works of Rembrandt, Renoir and Raphael.

Known internationally as a true master of scientific restoration he was called in as consultant by the Italian Government, in 1966, when the Arno River flooded Florence. For many months, Franz worked in the basement of the Uffizi Palace repairing and restoring some of the world's greatest artistic treasures. Franz also had entree into the major museums and galleries in Western America. Few there were who didn't occasionally send him a damaged or dimmed painting for restoration.

Trevors was well known to the various directors of the California missions. His restoration of two historic paintings at Santa Barbara Mission was widely heralded in the columns of the *New–Press*. In 1971, Trevors restored the famous Leonardo Barbieri portrait of Fray José Maria de Jesus González Rúbio which was originally painted in the 1850s. Franz removed the overlay of an earlier restoration and then treated the fragile canvas with a preservative synthetic resin to protect it from further deterioration.

He also worked at a half dozen other missions. Trevors' most lasting contribution was made at San Buenaventura where he restored the famed *Via Crucis* in the mid 1960s. In an essay written for *Westways*, Robert S. Bryan described how Trevors spent thousands of hours removing layers of mildew, fungus, candle smoke and calcium deposits from the fourteen canvases. Those historic works of art were and are the "crowning glory" of the Old Mission's restoration program.

Though he once described himself as a "happy heathen," Franz Trevors was a man of deep faith and abiding principles. San Buenaventura Mission was indeed an appropriate place for his obsequies and the homilist aptly noted, in words originally applied to Christopher Wren, "If you are looking for his monument, just look around you."

BENJAMIN CUMMINGS TRUMAN (1835–1916)

Benjamin Cummings Truman (1835–1916) was a pioneer journalist who portrayed the California missionary enterprise as representing "an energy as forceful, a courage as unfaltering, a devotion as true as that manifested by the Puritan fathers upon the bleak and inhospitable shores of New England." Between 1867 and 1872, Truman made a tour of the missions. Many of the observations he recorded during that trek appeared in Southern California's first newspaper, the Los Angeles *Star*, which Truman edited between 1873 and 1877

Truman's comments about San Fernando, the seventeenth of California's historic frontier establishments, reveal his viewpoint that those foundations were "monuments of energy, of courage, of religious fervor, and of advancing civilization that should not be left to perish."

This mission . . . is situated near the centre of a vast plain about twenty–four miles northerly from Los Angeles, and may be seen from the Southern Pacific Company's roads running to Santa Barbara and San Francisco.

The Indian name of the locality was Achois Comihabit; the ceremonies of consecration took place on the 8th of September, 1797, and were performed by Padre (Fermín) Francisco Lasuén.

The first marriage took place on the 8th of October, 1797, and Laureano and Marcelia were joined in the holy bonds of wedlock according to the custom of the Roman Catholic Church; and, curiously enough, the first legitimate birth was a male child to the parents of the first wedlock, and occurred on the 29th of July, 1798, and was an episode of pleasant and unrestrained commotion.

I visited this mission in company with Don Señor Eulogio de Celis, Jr., in March, 1872, and stayed three days as guest of the occupant, Gen. Andrés Pico, who fought a victorious battle with the United States troops near Los Angeles during the Mexican war. Gen. Pico gave me a great deal of information and told me that at one time there were once a mile and a half of buildings, including residences, schools, workshops, and storehouses, nearly all of which are now in ruins.

There is, however, one noble structure left standing, which was the residence of the General. This structure was erected as an adobe for the *padres* and their servants, and is the most substantial of any of its kind from the Mission Dolores to San Diego. It is now in a rare state of preservation. It is 300 feet long and 80 feet wide between its walls.

The building is two stories high, and the walls, which are perfect specimens of solid masonry, support a roof of tile which weighs more than two hundred tons. The beams and rafters were cut in the mountains, many miles off, and hauled down in such a way that they were "planed" on all sides by the process of transportation.

The great attraction of the structure is its corridor, 300 feet in length, with columns and arches of superb masonry, and tile roof and floor. The penitentiary–looking windows are all barred with heavy English twisted rod iron, and the massive doors are made to swing with a shivering creak, like the turning of ponderous gates on rusty castle hinges.

The interior constitutes a collection of apartments unlike any other private residence in America. There is a reception room 35 by 40 feet, where the old missionaries used to sit and toast their shins and play upon their violins and drink their native wines and chat of their boyhood days in Madrid and Seville and Barcelona.

This apartment looks as massive at night as if it had been carved out of solid rock, and the same may be said of the *salle à manger*, adjoining, 35 by 70 feet; then there is the kitchen, in which could have been produced a *déjeuner* for the standing army of California when it attacked the American eagle on its perch at San Pasqual;

And there are great square 24 by 24 feet chambers like unto the sleeping apartments of the house of Pindarus; and there is a library 25 by 40 feet, where have been hoarded hundreds of thousands of Spanish doubloons. Near by is the store–room, 20 by 80 feet, and a wine cellar underneath of the same dimensions.

Gen. Pico took me down into this cellar, and locked up in a huge Spanish chest, were many of the ancient trinkets and implements and "bric–a–brac" of this old landmark, some of which were of solid silver, including censors, *naveta*, incense vessels, a box of sacred forms, and pieces of a solid silver and gold cross. There were portions of two of the tallow candles used at the first Mass, nearly seventy–five years before, in commemoration of the Holy Virgin; also the original cattle brands, old flint–lock guns, spears, half a dozen small cannon, and an old pair of copper scales, made in 1795; and— this is strictly private—in one corner, or, more properly,

at one end of the cellar (which marked the hospitable Pico as one of Epicurus's sons) were promiscuous elevations of empty vessels upon which were such hieroglyphics as "Château Laurose," "Château Yquem," "East India Pale Ale," "Krug Private Cuvée," and such, which made my mouth water, notwithstanding the cobwebby emptiness of the vessels aforesaid.

The old church near by, which presents that sameness for which all these ancient structures are noted, looked hoary with time and decay. Its exterior seemed a sign of "no admittance on account of my shaky condition," but of which I took no heed. I had borrowed the key of an old lady who occupied an adobe on the crest of a neighboring hill, and who had watched the movements of the constellations long before Padre Lasuén placed into position the cornerstone of the tottering edifice nearly seventy years before.

This building was 150 feet in length by 50 feet in width. To my surprise the interior was far from harmonizing with the uninviting picture of neglect and dilapidation of its outside. The altar was tastefully decorated and close by was all the glittering paraphernalia of Catholic ceremony, which was performed once a month by a priest from Los Angeles.

There were evidences of rude attempts at fresco work and here and there a painting. I call freshly to mind that the interior was as silent as a grave. Not a sound broke the solemn stillness, except the flapping of a monster owl that winged its way awkwardly across that sacred chamber, and took its perch upon the altar.

There were two gardens attached to this mission, each containing 32 acres, and respectively owned by Gen. Pico and Don Señor De Celis, Jr. The Pico garden had 300 olive trees, 12,000 grapevines, and a large number of peach, apple, pear, orange, lemon, fig, walnut, almond and pomegranate trees. The De Celis garden had 7,000 grapevines, 320 olive trees, and all of the other fruits mentioned above and which had been planted by the missionary fathers in 1800.

The ranch upon which San Fernando is situated contains 121,542 acres, and was sold by Gov. Pio Pico (brother of Andrés) to Don Eulogio De Celis for $14,000, which money was used in 1846 to resist the Americans.

Fifteen years ago, 59,550 acres were sold for $115,000. 1 have seen since then one sweep of 40,000 acres of wheat growing on this piece of property. It is largely divided up now, and the 121,542 acres that the elder De Celis paid $14,000 for in 1846 is now taxed for nearly $2,000,000. Gen. Andrés Pico died about twelve years ago, but his brother, Pio Pico, the last Mexican Governor, is still living and is hale and hearty and fine looking, and is over ninety years of age.

There are more than a thousand homes at present in what is termed the San Fernando Valley and upon the foothills which amost entirely encircle it, while the scream from the locomotive and from the factory may be heard at all times of the day. Yet it is not so many years since Padre Dumetz stood within the corridor of the venerable structure I have described and, directing his gaze toward the west and taking a vast expanse of mountain, valley and plain and "cattle upon a thousand hills," soliloquized with Selkirk:

"I am monarch of all I survey."

JOHN W. TRUXAW (1883–1952)

Early in 1952, Orange County's last country doctor in Anaheim retired. Dr. John W. Truxaw (1883–1952) had served without interruption for over forty years. His retirement marked the end of a medical era for a south-land community.

Born in Saint Mary's Parish, Wymore, Nebraska, John was brought by his parents to Riverside in 1903, and there he spent the remainder of his childhood. After various jobs in Fresno and San Francisco, he entered the old medical school conducted by the University of Southern California in 1907.

He served his internship at the Los Angeles Country General Hospital and while there he met his future bride, Louise Wallberg, who was then nursing at the hospital. They were married in Long Beach in 1913. Eight children were to grace their lives.

Having completed his education and internship, Dr. Truxaw hung out his shingle on the street entrance of Anaheim's old Nagel Building. He joined the staff of Saint Joseph's Hospital at Orange in 1928. At the same time he found time to treat a goodly number of the emergency cases that were brought in to the Anaheim Hospital. He also functioned for some years as official health officer for the city.

The lives of the Truxaw family closely paralleled the ecclesial history of Southern California. For example, the oldest of John's sons was born the day after Bishop Thomas J. Conaty died in 1915. Another son became a journalist and devoted his life to *The Tidings*, the official diocesan newspaper. And John's brother, Joseph, became a priest of the Archdiocese of Los Angeles, occupying a host of important positions, including that of pastor of Immaculate Conception Church in Los Angeles.

"Doc," as he was known through the years, was a fixture of the Anaheim community. A journalist writing in the *Bulletin* said that "he was more than a doctor of medicine. He was advisor and counselor and served often as a 'father–confessor.' He knew his people, their health and their problems."

Many of the 3,500 babies he delivered were born on the once–proud *haciendas* of Santa Ana Canyon. He had hurried there in the early days by horse and buggy to deliver the babies of the Yorba, Dominguez and Peralta families. Written into the memories of many in Anaheim are pictures of Dr. Truxaw hurrying about on his calls in his small white Buick coupe, the car an identification for those who needed to find him fast, day or night.

Though his office hours read from 11 to "something," they actually never ended. Breakfast hour for him was around 4 a.m., but he did try to "cat–nap" during the morning or between operations. A charter member of the Rotary Club, a veteran in the Knights of Columbus and a pillar of the local Elks Club, "Doc" was identified with all the activities in Saint Boniface Parish.

Though ill health forced his retirement some months before his demise, Dr. Truxaw continued to see patients at his family home on Los Angeles Street. It proved very difficult to erase "Doc's" image from the scene of a lifetime of service.

A measure of the esteem held for Dr. Truxaw can be seen in the first page coverage given to his death, on October 22, 1952. The *Bulletin* news story suggested that "flags in Anaheim should be lowered to half mast Saturday morning in deep memory of a 'soldier' at home who served through two World Wars." He was indeed that and much more.

YSABEL VARELA DEL VALLE (1837–1905)

The final chapter in the long and noble history of Camulos, "the most notable of Southern California's *ranchos*," was written on March 31, 1905, with the disposition in Calvary Cemetery of the earthly remains of Ysabel Varela del Valle (1837–1905). According to newspaper accounts, "no more touching tribute could have been offered in memory of the gentle mistress of Camulos than that of the orphaned little ones" assembled at the roadside in front of the Orphan Asylum in Boyle Heights to pay a last honor to her who "in life had deemed it a pleasure to listen to the tale of the homeless and friendless."

Ysabel, the daughter of Cerval Varela and Ascensión Avila, was a familiar figure in Southern California's annals. Her marriage to Ygnacio del Valle, on December 14, 1851, in the Plaza Church of *Nuestra Señora de los Angeles*, united descendants of two outstanding provincial families. The *señora* of Camulos, a model of Christian womanhood, was "an exemplar among a people where the reign of honor and hospitality seemed to reach no bounds." For the whole southern district, the ranch house at Camulos served as a center of religious life for all who came in contact with it. Probably at no other place in the state were the traditions and customs of the past so faithfully kept.

During the days when great herds grazed the hills and valleys of the famous *rancho*, Señora del Valle attended personally to the details of the home life. From the break of dawn, when the chapel bell beckoned worshippers to morning devotions, she watched over her family and the servants of the household with a firmness and gentleness that won a love and respect which time never altered. At sunset every evening, the old bells from the San Fernando mission, then hanging in a frame south of the wide veranda, summoned the family and employees to the chapel in the garden, for the rosary.

One newspaper account reported that "a cardinal doctrine in her piety was a practical charity which reached out to such an extent that those most intimately connected with the life of the *Señora* did not even realize its lengths." Recorded instances of Señora del Valle's charity are innumerable. Race or creed never entered her thoughts when she was called upon to care for the poor or distressed.

Señora del Valle's deep–seated love for the Church was manifested in many ways. Each year, for example, the first gift of her olive harvest was used for the oil at Saint Vibiana's Cathedral for the Holy Thursday ceremonies. At the time of her demise, Bishop Thomas J. Conaty characterized the "Last Mistress of Camulos" as that "type of womanhood, the glory of the Church, as well as the community in which it is found." She was, the prelate noted, "a woman whose life was dominated by the spirit of absolute and simple faith which led her through a long life to untold deeds of kindness and charity. Her faith was something more than profession, it expressed itself in the everyday act of religion and charity. Her home was the center of her affections and the love of husband and children caught its glow from the love of God which characterized her entire life."

Ysabel Varela del Valle's life testified to the beauty of a home where the service of God is the source and the spirit of God its inspiration. Such women have been and are the bulwarks of California's civilization and the pride of humanity everywhere.

MARIANO GUADALUPE VALLEJO (1808–1890)

The year 1846 was a significant one for California. Governor Pio Pico and other prominent leaders were urging secession from Mexico and annexation either to England or France. Opposing that notion, but recognizing California's intolerable relationship with Mexico, was Mariano Guadalupe Vallejo. He favored annexation to the United States.

Born in California of Mexican parents, Vallejo was known for his integrity, judgment and ability. A nominal Catholic, he was one of the area's most respected figures. In March of 1846, less than three months before the Bear Flag Revolt, Vallejo delivered an impassioned speech which was recorded by Joseph Warren Revere, a lieutenant in the United States Navy. The following is excerpted from that address.

We possess a noble country, every way calculated,

from position and resources, to become great and powerful. For that reason I would not have her a mere dependency upon a foreign monarchy, naturally alien, or at least indifferent, to our interests and our welfare.

What possible sympathy could exist between us and a nation separated from us by two vast oceans? But waiving this insuperable objection, how could we endure to come under the dominion of a monarchy? For although others speak lightly of a form of government, as a freeman, I cannot do so.

I come prepared to propose instant and effective action to extricate our country from her present forlorn condition. My opinion is made up that we must persevere in throwing off the galling yoke of Mexico, and proclaim our independence of her forever.

Our position is so remote, either by land or sea, that we are in no danger from a Mexican invasion. Why, then, should we hesitate still to assert our independence? We have indeed taken the first step, by electing our own governor, but another remains to be taken. I will mention it plainly and distinctly: it is annexation to the United States.

In contemplating this consummation of our destiny, I feel nothing but pleasure, and I ask you to share it. Discard old prejudices, disregard old customs, and prepare for the glorious change which awaits our country.

Why should we shrink from incorporating ourselves with the happiest and freest nation in the world, destined soon to be the most wealthy, and powerful? Why should we go abroad for protection when this great nation is our adjoining neighbor?

When we join our fortunes to hers, we shall not become subjects, but fellow–citizens, possessing all the rights of the people of the United States, and choosing our own federal and local rulers. We shall have a stable government and just laws.

California will grow strong and flourish, and her people will be prosperous, happy and free. Look not, therefore, with jealousy upon the hardy pioneers who scale our mountains and cultivate our unoccupied plains; but rather welcome them as brothers, who come to share with us a common destiny.

JOSE MARIA VERDUGO (1751–1831)

Jose Maria Verdugo was born in 1751, at Loreto, the son of Juan Diego and Maria Ignacia de la Concepcion Carillo Verdugo. He is first mentioned by name on July 13, 1772, at San Carlos de Monterey, where he acted as *patrino* at the baptism of a converted Indian.

The youthful *soldado de cuerca* or leatherjacket was assigned to the presidial guard at San Diego in 1775 and, two years later, was sent to San Gabriel Mission. There he continued to serve in the guard provided for the safety of the foundation by the Spanish government.

On November 7, 1779, Jose married Maria de la Incarnacion Lopez in a colorful ceremony at the presidial chapel of San Diego. Fray Antonio Cruzado witnessed the exchange of their vows. The couple then took up residence at San Gabriel. Jose's popularity with the natives is attested by the many times he and his wife were called upon to act as sponsors at baptisms.

An ambitious person, Jose gradually acquired cattle of his own which he grazed in the fertile plains and valleys surrounding the mission. His family prospered and, early in 1782, Jose was promoted to corporal and put in command of the mission guard. Life at San Gabriel in those days, routine for the *gente de razon*, was enlivened by exploring and hunting parties, by bull and bear fights and by visiting soldiers and settlers who occasionally stopped at San Gabriel enroute to or returning from Monterey.

The chief social events were those held in conjunction with the numerous holydays and conferral of the sacraments. Often the soldiers, bored by their comparatively calm existence, organized hunting parties which brought back deer, antelope and bear. On Sundays and feastdays, Jose and his family attended Holy Mass. Throughout his long life, he was known and recognized as a fervent practitioner of the Catholic faith.

Jose petitioned Governor Pedro Fages for permission to use a tract of land called the Arroyo Seco for grazing his ever–increasing herds. The governor granted his request in 1784. It was an area abounding in long grassy plains, well–watered by streams. There were heavily wooded hills, rich in oak, alder, willow and evergreen. Deer, antelope, bear and fox also contributed to the desirability of the location.

Early in 1788, Verdugo was given authorization to use his own brand. With that distinction came confirmation of his large cattle holdings and the consequent need for pasturage. In 1797, Jose submitted his request for retirement, noting that he was no longer capable of fulfilling the duties attached to military service. He erected some adobe houses on his San Rafael *rancho* where he planned to spend his less strenuous final years.

Jose continued to expand his flocks, often times at the expense of both San Gabriel and San Fernando Missions. Though physically debilitated, he never lost his mental agility in his many financial dealings. He lived on until April 12, 1831, when, surrounded by his family he gave back his soul to Almighty God. The following day he was buried in the cemetery at San Gabriel Mission by Fray Geronimo Boscana.

ALICE VIGNOS (1872–1940)

It was in the 1930s that New York's Cardinal Patrick Hayes singled out Alice Vignos as the most persuasive and effective catechetical apostle in the United States. Born in Canton, Ohio, September 21, 1872, the daughter of Augustus and Phoebe (Devinny) Vignos, Alice came to California shortly after the turn of the century. In her adopted home, she dedicated herself to a lifetime of imparting Christian ideals and objectives to the young.

Alice pioneered what was known as the Hewitt Street Center, in Saint Vibiana's Parish, in 1925. Later, as superintendent of Our Lady of Talpa Center for nine years, she saw it grow from a handful of youngsters to an enrollment of well over 500. The catechetical program developed under her direction included a vacation school, week–day after–school classes for elementary and high school students and a discussion club for young men and women. Alice even persuaded civic officials to make available a nearby playground for club work, Christmas pageants and social functions.

Miss Vignos also elicited the cooperation of the local public school principal and teachers. A fishers' club composed of the children supplemented the work of regular home visitors assigned to each section of her district. The center was soon so crowded for Sunday Liturgy that it had to be enlarged. Not content with three groups of First Communion classes each year, Alice worked out a plan whereby each child was accompanied by one or more parents to the communion rail.

Through individual follow–up work done prior to First Communion day, she was instrumental in having a number of marriages validated by the Church. "Wherever there was a little child to be reached, no sacrifice was too great for her," as her pastor later noted. He added that "thousands of young men and women who are practical Catholics today owe it to her influence."

By making speeches, demonstrating new methods of teaching catechism and urging corporate action for the Church on the part of the laity, Alice focused attention upon the Archdiocese of Los Angeles as a pioneer and leader in Confraternity work. And yet, there was nothing parochial or provincial about the methodology of Alice Vignos. She believed that a successful religious instruction program of one area should be made available to others. She was ever mindful of the Church's missionary goal of bringing all peoples everywhere to Christ.

It was an outgrowth of her expansionary temperament that inspired Alice to write a series of religious project booklets which were eventually adopted in the vacation schools throughout the United States. Her practical work on behalf of Mexican–Americans was another noteworthy aspect of Miss Vignos' educational achievements.

The zeal and enthusiasm of that little lady were paramount features in the decision to hold the 1940 National Catechetical Congress in Los Angeles. Though her participation at that conclave was negated by a fatal cerebral hemorrhage, on August 18, the spirit of Alice Vignos was evident in all the sessions of that national gathering. At a memorial liturgy for Alice held during the Congress, Bishop Edwin V. O'Hara of Kansas City, Chairman of the Episcopal Committee for the Confraternity of Christian Doctrine, spoke eloquently of the affection and esteem shared for Alice Vignos by all those engaged in confraternity apostolate.

The prelate noted that Alice saw "the image of Christ in every child, in every man and woman." He concluded by praying that such a spirit might live on in all those committed to furthering the ideals of the CCD.

EDWARD VISCHER (1809–1879)

"Many of the most important illustrations of California scenes and incidents are preserved to us only through the painstaking sketches of early travelers or pioneer residents." Edward Vischer (1809–1879) was one whose artistic talents resulted in many valuable contemporary treasures. "He more than any other, loved the Old Missions, the work of a generation anterior to his. . . ."

Edward Vischer saw the world through the eyes of an educated man familiar with the highest cultural accomplishments of Europe. His paintings portrayed the California missions "with the sense of an author and an artist." Born at Regensburg, Bavaria, Vischer went to Mexico in 1827, and established himself as a commercial agent with the firm of Kayser Hahn and Company of Mazatlan and Acapulco. Although he was the first to start regular commercial relations between Mexico and California, and was said to be pre–eminently the greatest artist in the early history of our state, the name of Edward Vischer is almost unknown to the present generation.

Vischer first journeyed to California in 1842, at which time he toured the missions and enjoyed the hospitality and friendship of the Franciscan friars. In 1849, he took up permanent residence at San Francisco. Though the majority of his time was devoted to commercial activities, Vischer's talent for drawing, and an appreciative eye for the picturesque, led him to make sketches of scenes and objects wherever he went.

In the years after 1842, Vischer produced sixty or seventy views of the missions. His works, drawn with photographic details, are frequently the "only source of pictorial data on the condition of the mission establishments before the hand of neglect had crushed their roofs and left their walls to the mercy of winter rains." The missions had entered their period of decline by the time Vischer came to California, and one writer remarks that "he was especially attracted by the ruins of the Spanish missions and his drawings of them form a valuable record of their appearance at that time."

"Young California's foremost artist" set himself to the task of trying to preserve faithfully in picture form that peaceful patriarchal life of the missions as he first knew them. In 1870, fifteen drawings of the missions were published in *Vischers' Pictorial of California*. A description of these now–rare volumes notes that the drawings were made before these famous institutions were greatly overtaken by the earlier period of decay or the later process of restoration. Vischer was especially attracted to the Golden State's southland and once remarked that "the southernmost part of California contains many monuments of the mission period and is for this wonderland what Italy is for Europe."

ROGER WAGNER (1914–1993)

Martin Bernheimer, music critic for the Los Angeles *Times*, said that Roger Wagner (1914–1993) was something of a genius on the podium, and a splendidly feisty old walrus off it. He knew how to blend vocal sounds with uncanny flexibility, sensuality, color and point. He was a showman par excellence and, luckily, his generous ego was matched by his talent.

Born at Le Puy, France, Wagner orginally wanted to be a priest. At the age of seventeen, however, he decided to pursue a career in music. He spent five years studying organ and researching Gregorian chant. Coming to Los Angeles, Wagner sang in the MGM Studio chorus in the mid–1930s, where he worked with Jeanette MacDonald and Nelson Eddy in the film "Naughty Marietta."

Later he served as organist and music director for Saint Joseph's Church, a post he occupied for over thirty years. Annual choral concerts attracted music lovers to downtown Los Angeles and led to Wagner's selection as supervisor of youth choruses for the Los Angeles Bureau of Music.

He established the Los Angeles Youth Concert which evolved into the Roger Wagner Chorale in 1948. The chorale toured Europe and Latin America, sang for movies and even performed at rock concerts. Wagner served as guest conductor with choruses around the world and was often accompanied by his wife Janice and their three children.

An authority on medieval and Renaissance music, Wagner wrote scholarly essays and engaged in teaching for several decades on the UCLA faculty. He was noted for identifying such talented opera stars as Marilyn Horne and Marni Nixon.

Praised by critics as a conductor who drew rich sounds from his singers, Wagner possessed the flair and energy of a showman. He was passionate about music and demanding of those who worked with him. Possessed with a quick, frequently wicked wit, Wagner's considerable charm was easily matched by his acerbic tongue. More often than not, his sarcasm was benign, such as when he greeted a sing–along audience with this admonition "I hope you're in better voice than you were last year."

After a 1957 appearance at New York's Town Hall, music critic Howard Taubman called Wagner's group "a highly disciplined ensemble which can cope with anything." Leopold Stokowski observed that "there are supremely great choruses in England and Italy, but yours is second to none in the world."

In 1964, Wagner co–founded the Master Chorale, an aggregation of more than a hundred professional and amateur singers. That group functioned as a Los Angeles–based group, while the separate Roger Wagner Chorale, with fewer singers, concentrated on touring.

Upon his retirement in 1986, Roger Wagner was given the title "music director laureate." In later years, Wagner continued working as his health permitted. By the time he died in Dijon, France, on September 17, 1992, Wagner had become a nationally acclaimed music figure whose career spanned nearly five decades.

Referred to by one writer as a "mercurial conductor," Roger Wagner was a dominant figure in American choral music. There was a "priestly" ingredient in his work which gave the talented musician a unique status in the world's entertainment capital.

BERNHARDT WALL (1872–1956)

At the midpoint of the 20th century, Bernhardt Wall was described by a columnist for the Los Angeles *Times* as "the only man in the United States to make a career of etching whole books." With his engraving needle and acid, Wall traced onto copperplates a host of superbly executed portraits and inscriptions, demonstrating a phenomenal, exquisite and unique craftsmanship.

Born to Bernhard and Friedricka (Holtz) Wall, on December 30, 1872, the talented artist educated and amused himself as a youngster by copying pictures and scenes from newspapers and magazines. He served in Cuba during the Spanish–American War, with the 202nd New York Volunteer Infantry Regiment. It was mainly through his subsequent efforts that Congressional legislation was enacted to raise the famous battleship *Maine* from its watery grave in Havana Harbor.

Wall began his career as a lithograph artist in 1889. He later worked commercially and, between 1902 and 1913, taught various phases of art at several New England institutions. His work for Schlesinger Brothers, as the designer of over 5,000 comic "greeters" won for Wall the title of "Postcard King" for the nation in 1911. Shortly after his marriage to Jennie Hunter on December 25, 1899, the Buffalo–born engraver originated the pop-

ular series of Sunbonnet postcards, many of which became collector's items.

During World War I, Mr. Wall decided upon the medium of etching for his life's vocation. His method was very rare in bookmaking; instead of the usual letter-press, each page was printed by hand from an etched plate, including the text as well as illustrations. Wall's earliest work, *World War Etchings*, was a collection of portraits depicting that conflict's foremost statesmen and combatants.

In January, 1921, the artist completed the initial number of *Wall's Etched Monthly*, the first all–etched periodical in the history of graphic arts. Issued at New York, the innovative publication received instant acclaim from book lovers, librarians and collectors. The proto volume, which sold for $50, contained twelve numbers, averaging five picture plates and seven of engraved text.

The 125 copies of the magazine, printed by hand from copperplates on Japan paper, were signed, numbered and forwarded to subscribers as first class mail. Though envisioned for only one year, several series of the journal appeared over the decades, including *The Etcht Miniature Monthly Magazine*, produced at Sierra Madre, in 1948. The stories of famous people and historical incidents became the focal point of Wall's remaining years. He compiled and issued pictorial biographies for such famous personages as Thomas Jefferson, Marquis de Lafayette, Sam Houston, Franklin D. Roosevelt, Stephen F. Austin, Andrew Jackson, Edwin Markham and James McNeill Whistler. Among his miniature books were such titles as *Abraham Lincoln's Chronology, Lincoln's Gettysburg Speech* and *Walliana*.

Wall's magnum opus was the eighty–five volume *Following Abraham Lincoln*, which was privately issued at Lime Rock, Connecticut, between 1931 and 1942. Only thirty–six sets of the numbered and signed work were completed, each with 1,035 hand–printed pages, 445 of which were finely–executed etchings. The masterful set, for which the Lincoln Memorial University awarded Wall a doctorate of Humane Letters, was indexed by the noted Civil War scholar, Harry E. Pratt. A splendid dual color reproduction of the original etchings was released in a single volume of 415 pages by Wise–Parslow Company of New York.

In 1943, Wall published his widely–heralded *Following Fra Junípero Serra and Others*. That book, with its twenty–seven plate etchings, was limited to 200 copies. The handsome edition is only surpassed, in rarity, by Wall's subsequent miniature portrayal of *The California Missions*, in 24 plates, measuring 1 3/4 by 1 1/2 inches.

Known throughout his long career as the nation's foremost etcher, Bernhardt Wall maintained studios at New York City, Lime Rock, Connecticut, Houston,

Texas and Sierra Madre, California. After the death of his first wife, in 1938, and his later marriage to Doris Turbet, Wall settled at Pasadena, where he lived for the final years of his life. Bernhardt Wall's death, in 1956, concluded a unique contribution to the field of graphic arts. His work remains as the prize of the *cognoscenti*, the delight of collectors and the pride of librarians.

THOMAS WALL (1845–1910)

Judge Thomas Wall (1845–1910) "was subject always to the demands of the needy. Nobody ever called on him in vain . . . though his charity was forever concealed and knowledge of his kindness to the poor came to light only in the most unexpected ways."

A native of Stourbridge, Worcestershire, England, Thomas was one of a family of twenty–two children born to John Wall and Ellen Corbett. He received private tutoring in his early days and only later was enrolled in the school of his native town. At the age of sixteen, young Wall passed the preliminary law examination, after which he was admitted to the formal study of jurisprudence. In 1867, he was licensed as a solicitor. The following year, he opened a legal office at Stourbridge, where he practiced for the next decade. In 1879, he was appointed to a vacancy in the office of Clerk to the Board of Guardians, a position he held for twenty–two years. During this time, he was, according to one journalist, "imperturbable and courteous to a degree, he was exceedingly painstaking and his service was always listened to, and commanded respect. The accounts published in the English papers at the time of his departure for the United States mention, with considerable pride, the victories which Wall won for the people in matters of municipal interest.

Thomas had embraced the Catholic Faith at the age of twelve and afterwards dedicated much of his time to the Church's manifold charitable activities. He married Emily Perks in 1874. Of their dozen children, two subsequently became priests in England.

After his retirement, Judge Wall brought his wife to California to join several of his sons who had journeyed to the west coast some years earlier. For a short while Wall operated a ranch on Signal Hill near Long Beach. During his nine years in the latter city, Wall took little part in public affairs owing to his poor health and natural reserve but he was always ready to help in his quiet way and financially any plan for local improvement.

The judge, however, maintained his concern for ecclesiastical affairs. His "great interest centered in the Church; first in the church which he and his family attended some miles away at Wilmington, and later in the church which he helped to found, and generously

support at Long Beach." In his final years, the versatile jurist even acted as choirmaster at Saint Anthony's. Although the greater part of his life "was passed in quietude, his studious nature, and his association during a long life with people in every walk of life combined to give him a thorough knowledge of human nature with all its virtues and its weaknesses." Thomas Wall died on May 23, 1910, after a life spent in kindness and good works.

FREDERICK BARKHAM WARDE (1851–1935)

Remembered as one of the last of the great tragedians, Frederick Barkham Warde (1851–1935) is forever immortalized for his role as Fray Junípero Serra in John Steven McGroarty's "The "Mission Play." Born in the village of Deddington, Oxfordshire, the son of Thomas and Anne (Barkham) Warde, Frederick studied law and attached himself to a prestigious firm of attorneys in London.

Never really interested in the legal profession, young Warde defied his parents and joined a small provincial acting company, making his first appearance on stage at Sunderland, September 4, 1867. Later he received valuable thespian training and experience at Glasgow, Leeds and Manchester. He was a natural actor with a fine resonant voice. In 1874, he journeyed to New York, where he became a leading man at Booth's Theatre.

For over thirty years, Warde toured the United States continually in Shakespearean roles. Soon known as "America's foremost dramatic actor," he was probably among the greatest exponents of the classics. In 1871, Warde married Anne Edmondson, an English actress. She obligingly left the stage to play the role of mother of their four children, remaining at his side for over half a century.

Warde became almost as noted as a professor as an actor. Every year, for example, he lectured three times at the University of Southern California and at the Los Angeles campus of the University of California. A collection of his lectures was published in 1913 under the title *The Fools of Shakespeare*.

Once, when speaking to students at Loyola College, Warde recalled that the name of God or Christ occurred 850 times in the thirty–seven plays of Shakespeare. He always felt that was significant in the great writer's philosophy.

John Steven McGroarty used to say that he wrote "The Mission Play" with Warde in mind for the role of Fray Junípero Serra. When the actor first portrayed the friar, in 1919, the reviewers were enthralled. One said that "to hear and see the old Franciscan Father reincarnated is to again live and feel the spirit of the missions."

Another critic wrote that "Mr. Warde's interpretation is sympathetic, powerful and impressive. His natural poise, superb enunciation and fine dramatic judgment make Fray Junípero a character to be long remembered."

Shortly after his first season with "The Mission Play," Frederick Warde wrote his autobiography, *Fifty Years of Make–Believe*, wherein he painted with deft strokes a picture of life behind the footlights. It was a simple, unaffected story of a great and good man in a field of public endeavor.

As a direct result of his sterling performance of Fray Junípero Serra, Warde was given an "open contract" in the Motion Picture Industry. Among his films were *King Lear, Richard III, Silas Marner* and *The Vicar of Wakefield*. He also became in demand on radio. Near the end of his active life, Frederick Warde said that "in my almost sixty years on the stage, no role was more satisfying than that of Fray Junípero Serra. It was the only time I ever portrayed a saint."

EARL WARREN (1891–1974)

During ceremonies at Petra marking the 250th anniversary of Fray Junípero Serra's birth, the United States was represented by Chief Justice Earl Warren, whose observations about the Mallorcan friar are a worthy addition to the public record. Noting that it was "always good to recall the deeds of a great man who has influenced the lives of generations," Justice Warren spoke "chiefly as a Californian, whose State has been especially enriched thanks to the fact that Fr. Serra passed through it and because the lives of my wife and my children have, like my own, been especially benefited by this."

The one–time California governor pointed out that while Serra belonged equally to Spain and the United States, "it was in California where his deeds bore fruit after a long life of dedication, sacrifice, courage and achievements." The missions inaugurated by Serra and his companions "are not great cathedrals, nor even impressive churches. They are simple houses of prayer. They were built despite great difficulties and sacrifices exceptional in those times. It has been said that when they were raised, they were as humble as the place where Jesus Christ was born. All their characteristics are typical of the modest origin of our nation."

The "Apostle of California" planted "the cross in San Diego in 1769, and over the next fifteen years he created a chain of missions from there to San Francisco, along the entire length of the *Camino Real*. He faced and overcame all the obstacles of jungle and desert. Though he was not in good health, he came and went, and pressed ever onwards teaching European civilization and Spanish culture at the same time as the Christian religion."

The eminent jurist went on to state that "Fr. Serra was a man of great gifts. His major passion, it goes without saying, was his religion, but he also thought it a part of his obligation to bring civilization to that new world. This was the case in all the missions he raised. He taught the Indians to read and write, to sing lovely Spanish songs to the sound of the guitar. He taught them to work, to build houses, the trades of carpenter and bricklayer. He showed them the mysteries of agriculture, sowing, planting fruit trees, looking after cattle; to tan, to spin. And more important, to live in peace and happiness in a community. He instilled a feeling for the law without which no orderly society can exist. He contributed to all this, as well as preaching the Gospel with apostolic zeal."

In the opinion of the Chief Justice, "the era of the California missions came to be the most charming and marked in the dawn of American history. It was full of romance. The beautiful Spanish songs, the fiestas, the hospitality to kin and stranger, the hundreds of names of Spanish saints with which just so many places were named have left a mark on California which still survives. We still greet the stranger as in those days, and it's for that reason that millions from all over the world flock there, some to visit us, others to stay and share what we have, as was the practice in the times of Fr. Serra."

Concluding his remarks, Justice Warren noted that "it has been said, and rightly, that the history of the world is the history of great men. This thought moves us to revere the memory of Fray Junípero Serra, so that it may persist in the minds and the hearts of our peoples; (that is) why we lavish his effigy in churches, parks and public buildings throughout California, and why his statue figures in the Hall of Fame in the capital of our Nation, in Washington, so that whoever passes by there shall see it and understand."

G.M. WASEURTZ AF SANDELS (d. 1852)

One of the most curious of the early reflections on the California Missions were those of G. M. Waseurtz af Sandels, who visited San Carlos, San Francisco, Sonoma, Santa Clara, Santa Barbara, San Fernando, San Buenaventura, San Gabriel, San Luis Obispo, San Rafael and Santa Ines in 1842–43.

By his own admission a physician, mining expert and naturalist, Waseurtz spent a number of years in Brazil.

After losing a fortune in Mexican mining operations, he journeyed from Acapulco to Monterey with Captain John B. R. Cooper aboard the *California*. Concise though they are, Waseurtz's descriptions are at once fascinating and accurate. In recording his impressions about the seventeenth of the California missionary outposts, the Swedish scientist noted:

> The nearer one approaches to San Fernando, the more bold becomes the scenery. The hilly, steep ridges which separated the gold plains from those of San Fernando were really romantic. Steep broken rocks, green flower clothed hills tufted with mountain oak, and brooks lined with salix gave a softness to the landscape which was enchanting. The river at the gold places was very shallow, and not always plentifully supplied with water, though encouragement was held out for the gold–washer to obtain it out of the sand of the gulches of the river by turning the river, as they called it. That means leading off the stream to another channel. The willow and oaks were plentiful in this neighborhood and first rate for turning.

Following Waseurtz's departure aboard the *Diamond* for Honolulu, in September, 1843, he eventually found his way to New Orleans, where he died sometime between 1850 and 1852. The manuscript of his observations seems to have surfaced before 1848, when it came into the possession of Colonel Thomas Bangs Thorpe, an amateur naturalist and able journalist, who was known to the literary world as "Tom Owen the Bee Hunter."

Thirty years later, when the elusive manuscript re–appeared at a meeting of the Associated Pioneers of the Territorial Days of California, the Society determined to publish part of it in the San Jose *Pioneer and Historical Review*. Another portion was incorporated by Samuel C. Upham, in his volume of *Notes on a Voyage to California*, which was published at Philadelphia, in the same year.

The sketch of "The Sea Town and Port Yerbabuena in San Francisco Bay," along with part of the manuscript, was published in the *Quarterly of the Society of California Pioneers*, in 1926. A more complete version was edited for the Grabhorn Press by Helen Putnam Van Sicklen and issued in 1945, as *A Sojourn in California by the King's Orphan–The Travels and Sketches of G. M. Waseurtz, a Swedish Gentleman who visited California in 1841–1843*.

The noted Jesuit historian, Father Arthur D. Spearman, claimed that Waseurtz's sketch of Mission Santa Clara made "on the spot" is very accurate. One of the few portrayals of the fourth church at Santa Clara, the sketch is excellent in both detail and perspective. The Waseurtz treatise is not especially new or novel. The strong element of fiction found in certain parts of the text was probably intended to enliven the narrative, rather than deceive the reader. Conflicting as are the stories about the author, all who mention G. M. Waseurtz af Sandels refer to him as a kindly and gentle person who was sincerely interested in the scenic grandeur and prospective development of California.

GEORGE WASHINGTON (1732–1799)

The handsomely–fashioned bronze likeness of Fray Junípero Serra, located in the Statuary Hall of the nation's capitol, appropriately faces the one depicting George Washington. Surely there was something more than coincidence in the proximity of the two great pioneers, one the "Father of his Country," the other a "Father" of his Church. George Washington (1732–1799) and Junípero Serra (1713–1784) were contemporaries in ideals as well as in time. They worked for a common cause, each in his own sphere.

In 1776, the year associated with the Declaration of Independence, Fray Junípero Serra established the Mission of San Francisco beside the Golden Gate. By the time of his death, less than a decade later, a new nation had been born.

While George Washington and his patriots fought for independence, Fray Junípero introduced Christian civilization into an area that would eventually join forces as the thirty–first member of the American commonwealth. At the time there was little more than a vast wilderness and a few French colonies between the Atlantic and Pacific oceans. Chances are that Washington gave very little thought to California.

When Spain entered the war with the English, the "perfidious heretics," Serra's sentiments identified immediately with those of Washington. He asked his fellow missionaries, in 1780, to be "most attentive in begging God to grant success to this public cause which is so favorable to our holy Catholic and Roman Church."

Personality–wise, Washington and Serra were resourceful innovators, stern disciplinarians and exemplary pacesetters, the one dedicated to his people in the civil realm, the other to serving them in the religious sphere. Both men fit into the category of "charismatic" leaders. Washington and Serra fulfilled their particular commissions, not alone by mandate, but rather by virtue of dynamic personalities which instilled an incredible loyalty and devotion among their respective peoples.

Though George Washington and Junípero Serra differed considerably in their religious convictions, secular vocations and human endowments, the qualities they shared are exceedingly more impressive than the ones they differed in. "Great places make great men," Oliver Wendell Holmes once observed. Washington and Serra, each in his own way, proved the enduring wisdom of Holmes' aphorism.

As widely divergent as were their concepts about God, George Washington and Junípero Serra would surely have identified their sentiments in that beautiful–prayer subsequently composed by John Henry Newman:

> God created me to do Him some definite service; He has committed some work to me which He has not committed to another. I have my mission—I may never know it in this life, but I shall be told it in the next. I am a link in a chain, a bond of connection between persons. He has not created me for naught. I shall do good; I shall do His work. I shall be an angel of peace, a preacher of truth in my own place, while not intending it—if I do but keep His Commandments. Therefore will I trust Him. Whatever, wherever I am, I can never be thrown away. If I am in sickness, my sickness may serve Him: in perplexity, my perplexity may serve Him; in sorrow, my sorrow may serve Him. He does nothing in vain. He knows what He is about. He may take away my friends; He may throw me among strangers. He may make me feel desolate, make my spirits sink, hide my future from me—still He knows what He is about.

DOUGLAS SLOAN WATSON (d. 1948)

Douglas Sloan Watson (d. 1948) was the author of several books in the field of Californiana. His *Santa Fe Trail to California (1849–1852)*, published in 1911, contained some excellent drawings on the missions, together with pertinent textual materials.

And, in 1934, Watson edited *The Expedition into California of the Venerable Fray Junípero Serra*, the first book issued under the imprint of the Nueva California Press. A second edition of that book was released as *The Founding of the First California Missions . . .* In addition to the writings issued under his own name, Watson worked with the Grabhorns in the publishing of their famous "Americana" series. Numerous of his learned essays also appeared in the *California Historical Society Quarterly*.

Though he occupies a respected place in the historical bibliography of the west, Watson is best remembered for a charming narrative about a small boy, his wagon and his devotion. That story became one of the most popular programs presented by Jack Webb in his television series "Dragnet" which aired in the 1950s.

The episode's origin is a story entitled "Tony's Christmas" first printed by the Grabhorn Press in a limited press run of 100 copies in 1932. Thirty years later, another edition was printed by Lederer, Street & Zeus at Berkeley as a Christmas greeting for select friends of the Watson family. The second edition was illustrated by Tom Lubbock.

The story itself is based on an incident that occurred at the Church of Notre Dame de Victoires on Bush Street in San Francisco. (Another tradition places the event at the Church of Sts. Peter and Paul in North Beach.)

The plot revolves around the creche or crib set that had been set up by parishioners in the local church as part of the seasonal decorations. The day after Christmas the figure of the Infant Jesus mysteriously disappeared from its place in the manger.

Police officals were notified and a frantic search of the neighborhood was initiated. Eventually a small boy, one Georgie Potter, was observed pulling a little red wagon down the sidewalk. Inside was the missing Infant Jesus carefully wrapped in a brightly colored afghan. When asked what he was doing, the youngster innocently replied: "I asked Jesus for a red wagon. I promised that if He bought me one, I'd give him a ride in it. He did and I am keeping my promise."

Though Webb was the first to make use of the story for television, he was not the first to broadcast it. That distinction goes to Mel Venter, the KFRC storyteller, who related it on his "Pictorial" program in December of 1946. The script for that broadcast was written by a former newspaperwoman named Betty Turner Friendlich. She, in turn, recalls first encountering the story as a journalism student at Columbia University in 1934.

The late Alexander Woollcott, famous critic and raconteur, appeared as a guest lecturer at Columbia one December day and he rated "The Little Red Wagon" among the finest examples of modern Christmas stories. Only a few people know the background of this narrative. In any event, "The Little Red Wagon," now a Christmas classic, is aired worldwide each year. It now has a permanent place in the fabric of the nation's Yuletide celebrations.

JAMES JOSEPH WATSON (1840–1910)

One rarely reads about the Civil War within the context of California history. Because of its distance from the point of conflict, the Golden State had no quota of soldiers assigned to it by the Lincoln administration. Nonetheless, it is interesting to note that about 16,000 men in California enlisted in the Union Army. Mostly they were trained and kept in the west in the event of a Confederate invasion.

California, although a consistently loyal state, probably due to the influence of Governor Leland Stanford, had a strong minority of southern sympathizers. And then there was a third faction which favored joining California and Oregon into an independent Pacific Republic.

One of the most outstanding California personages involved in the Civil War was James Joseph Watson

(1840–1910), who later boasted that he was the only Native Son combat veteran of the Civil War. Born in Monterey to parents who had come to California from England, six year old James witnessed the raising of the American flag over his native city by Commodore John D. Sloat on July 7, 1846.

James grew to maturity in Bolinas. Shortly after the beginning of the Civil War, he went to San Francisco and there enlisted as a combat troop in the California One Hundred. He was officially inducted on December 10, 1862. Following a period of training at Redville, the California One Hundred, part of the Second Massachusetts Cavalry, was sent to Fort Monroe, Virginia, and for a number of weeks underwent further training and picket duty.

James was severely injured in the Battle of the Wilderness, when his horse was shot out from under him. Despite a dislocated leg, he returned to combat and, on November 1, 1864, was promoted to Corporal. Five months later, the war ended when General Robert E. Lee surrendered at Appomattox Court House in Virginia. The California One Hundred was disbanded on July 20, 1865, just two days after Watson had been advanced to sergeant.

After the war, Watson returned to Bolinas and when the Grand Army of the Republic was organized, he became a member of Lincoln Post #1 of San Francisco. A member of the Society of California Pioneers, James was active in other civic groups. He engaged in the restaurant business and later was licensed to operate a tavern.

On February 16, 1876, James married Mary O'Connor, a native of Ireland. The Watsons had four sons and a daughter. James later served as Constable of San Rafael. Following incorporation there he was elected Marshal and later tax collector. James Watson was always proud of his birth in Mexican California. He is reported to have driven an ox team in several Admission Day parades, thus portraying his ancestry.

When Watson died on June 2, 1910, he was buried from Saint Raphael's Church, located on the actual site of the mission established by the Franciscans in 1817. He was among that small group of patriots who served the stars and stripes in both war and peace. Watson's greatest boast was that he was the only native of California and the only member of the Native Sons of the Golden West to have engaged in combat on the bloody battlefields of the Civil War.

CHARLES M. WEBER (1813–1881)

Charles Maria Weber (1813–1881), dreamer, adventurer, pioneer, argonaut and entrepreneur, was born in Steinwenden, Bavaria, a city west of the Rhine River, where people were still inspired by the spirit of the French Revolution. In 1836, Charles left his native Germany and journeyed to New Orleans. Later he went to Texas and became affiliated with Sam Houston's forces in the War with Mexico, an event that considerably influenced his later life.

In May of 1841, Weber joined the Bidwell–Bartleson Party which was subsequently hailed as "the first serious intrusion into California by Americans." Enroute he met Father Pierre Jean De Smet, the Belgian missionary–explorer. De Smet gave him a rosary which he used for the rest of his life.

After working briefly with John Sutter in Sacramento, Weber experimented with the first plantings of tobacco in California. In 1842, he moved to San Jose where he opened the first shoe factory in the area. Soon he began acquiring thousands of head of cattle for market beef and shoe leather. He also made soap, operated a bakery and ran a blacksmith shop. In February of 1844, "Carlos" became a naturalized citizen of Mexico and, the following year, he purchased the *Rancho El Campo de los Franceses*. From that time onward, Weber had a firm economical footing.

During the Bear Flag Revolt, in 1846, Weber accepted a commission as Captain in the United States Cavalry from John B. Montgomery. By then, he was an American in spirit, caught up in the westering movement that drove so many emigrants to the west.

In the summer of 1847, Captain Weber selected the area later named for Commodore Robert F. Stockton. Initially, the city was known at Tuleberg. Shortly thereafter, he organized the first mining company in California. In July of 1850, Stockton became the county seat for San Joaquin. In that same year, Charles married Ellen Murphy, daughter of Martin Murphy, Sr. There were three Weber children.

The captain held many important positions, including that of President for the State Agricultural Society. He and his family lived for over thirty years at Weber Point, in the shadow of Mount Diablo.

Throughout his life, Weber donated property sites for all the churches of Stockton, regardless of creed. They included the Methodists, Presbyterians and all the other congregations organized at that time. He made substantial contributions to the Catholic Church and underwrote the bringing of the Dominican Sisters of San Rafael to Stockton. Weber also built Saint Agnes convent.

An innovative farmer who reportedly gave away over 14,000 acres of land, Weber was fiercely pro–Union during the Civil War. He proudly flew the American flag atop a 120 foot staff in front of his home.

The captain died from pneumonia at the age of sixty–eight while on a trip to Virginia City. He was buried in the Weber family mausoleum in San Joaquin Catholic Cemetery, Stockton, California.

At his funeral, Archbishop Joseph Sadoc Alemany of San Francisco said that Weber "was a noble–hearted man" who fulfilled his role "as a good citizen and Christian." The *Evening Mail* reported that the Dominican prelate spoke "very feelingly of Weber's charitable bequests to the Church and to the poor."

ELLEN MURPHY WEBER (1822–1895)

From today's popular version of Western American history, it could easily be concluded that the feminine force of California's pioneer ancestors was made up exclusively of dance hall matrons and drab, bitter wives. Dorothy Tye points out that "facts, however de–glamor-ize the dance–hall girls and properly credit the adulation they received to a lack of feminine competition in that rough, bathless, masculine world. The typical frontier woman had something more substantial to offer than bare shoulders and alcoholic companionship. By the manner with which she accepted hardships and heartaches, yet clung to her aspirations and dreams, she inspired in her men the strength and confidence that won the West."

Ellen Murphy Weber (1822–1895), the daughter of Martin and Mary (Foley) Murphy, was among California's first ladies who challenged the loneliness of a harsh new world with the fortitude and courage charac-teristic of her Hibernian forebears. Ellen's maternal descendants achieved considerable importance in the ecclesiastical annals of the United States. The Foley name was associated with archbishoprics at Baltimore, Chicago and Detroit.

The Murphys came to the United States, in 1840, and settled in the prosperous community of Irish Grove, in Holt County, Missouri. Disappointed with that region's religious advantages and educational facilities, Martin Murphy and his family decided, in 1844, to emigrate to California. Ellen's father and brothers joined the first overland party of pioneers to venture westwards from Missouri. The twenty–six ox–drawn wagons headed into the unknown wilderness for 2,000 miles on a journey that lasted nine full months.

The hardships and dangers of their journey, complete with "hostile Indians, threats of starvation, separation, and loss of cattle and supplies," led over the identical summit which the Donner Party crossed two years later. On one scouting expedition, Ellen Murphy was among the first white people to enjoy the beauty of Lake Tahoe.

Shortly after arriving in California, Martin Murphy purchased a 40,000 acre ranch at San Jose. In 1851, Ellen married Charles Weber, the original proprietor of Stockton, a marital union subsequently blessed by three children. Following her husband's death, in 1881, Ellen graciously filled the position of a lady of wealth and cul-ture for fourteen years, until her own demise at the age of seventy–three. Her biographer notes that "Ellen Mur-phy Weber's life couldn't have been easy in any way— even during the settled years of her marriage. She had to face with her husband the enmities and resentments he incurred in developing his city in the way he wanted, which turned him into a dour, mistrustful, withdrawn man."

Like others of her sex, Ellen traded security for dan-ger and leisure for constant watchfulness and hard labor. And with them, she shared spirit—a quality fast losing importance under the softening influence of today's mechanized living. One can only regret the absence of documentation about other courageous women who helped to tame the Golden State!

LAWRENCE WELK (1903—1992)

Raised in a sod farmhouse in North Dakota, Lawrence Welk (1903–1992) was described by *Newsweek* maga-zine as one who "always thought his heartland values could survive, undistorted, in electronic images on mil-lions of American TV screens." And they did.

The son of German immigrants, Welk didn't speak English until he was twenty–one. He began his musical career playing the accordion at weddings and barn dances.

His "champagne music," a sedate blend of wood-winds, strings and muted brass, tripped through familiar melodies above ripples of accordian and organ. His lis-teners said that his music was "bubbly like champagne."

Of all the superb musicians in his band, Welk was the most inadvertently telegenic of them all, reading the cue cards in his Alsatian accent and dancing with ladies in the audience.

Welk epitomized the best qualities of the entertain-ment industry. A survey once showed that 85 percent of his viewers found him "believable." The rest admitted to tuning in week–after–week because they just couldn't believe him. His ratings went off the charts.

This foursquare defender of the family caused more than his share of Saturday night squabbles as youngsters clamored for "Have Gun Will Travel," while their par-ents preferred Welk and such popular entertainers as the Lennon Sisters. His television show, which ran from 1955 to 1982, was the longest–lived in television his-tory. When ABC finally dropped the show in 1977, Welk began a syndication on other networks and took with him 95 percent of his viewers, setting a trend later followed by other shows.

Welk's popularity was easily explained. He played

what people knew and understood. Though a jazz enthusiast and a Dixieland player at heart, Welk accommodated his own preferences to those of his audiences. And it worked. Reportedly Welk got richer than any of his contemporaries in the entertainment business. But he shared his wealth, as is plainly evident in the correspondence at the Archival Center, Archdiocese of Los Angeles.

Lawrence Welk, the "champagne music maker," was a longtime member of Glendale Council 1920 Knights of Columbus. In 1966, he was honored by the Knights for his great proficiency as a band leader, for his leadership in promoting international understanding among people of all nations, creeds and colors, for his contribution to moral entertainment for the entire family and for his outstanding services to the community, state and nation in the charitable field.

At a gathering in the Hollywood Palladium, letters of congratulations were read from President Lyndon Johnson, General Chiang Kai–shek, Queen Elizabeth II and the heads of state from Israel, Mexico, Canada, Germany, Ireland, Spain, Japan and Italy.

Welk's philosophy of life was expressed in an address given to students at his hometown of Strasburg, North Dakota and reported in the Congressional Record for September 16, 1968. Among other items worth recalling is the following:

> I know that with God's blessings on our labors, we can accomplish miracles in the field of human relationships and in our fight for a better America and a better world.

JEAN DAYTON WEST (b. 1894)

The colorful oil painting of Father Maynard Geiger (1901–1977) that hangs in the library of the Santa Barbara Mission Archives is one of the major artistic works of Jean Dayton West, a talented portraitist of considerable renown.

Father Maynard was anything but a willing subject for the artist. That he agreed to sit for the painting is due to the persistent encouragement of the board members for the archives. The artist was herself a fascinating person. Born in 1894 at Iowa City, she became interested in art through her father, an attorney who was also a watercolorist. She often tagged along on his outings to sketch and paint.

Her natural facility at drawing prompted Jean to take classes in high school and later to earn a bachelor's degree in art at college. Even her earliest sketches show definite signs of natural talent. West and her husband, an Air Force surgeon, were married in 1918. The couple moved to New Brunswick, Canada and subsequently to Des Moines, Iowa, where they raised their children.

Though she suffered from polio, Jean continued her work, winning an assortment of medals at the Iowa State Fair and other statewide competitive contests. Practically all of her entries were awarded ribbons. During the years when her husband was stationed in China, Jean and her three children stayed behind. It was during that period that she completed her work for a master's degree in contemporary art.

During World War II, Mrs. West and her husband were able to visit the major European museums, including the Louvre (Paris), the Del Prado (Madrid) and the British Museum (London). At each of those places, her portfolio grew.

After her husband's demise in 1964, Jean devoted most of her time to painting. She served for a while as President of the Palos Verdes Community Art Association. It was in 1972, at the suggestion of Dr. and Mrs. Charles Heiskell, that Mrs. West was commissioned to paint an oil portrait of Father Maynard Geiger, longtime archivist at Santa Barbara Mission and prominent Western American scholar.

Though an affable man, Father Geiger resisted the suggestion for some months. He finally agreed to the proposal only after some gentle nudging by his superiors and friends. Mrs. West was brought to Santa Barbara Mission several times by the Heiksells and there she completed a preliminary pencil and charcoal sketch. The actual painting was completed at the Canterbury, a retirement facility in Rancho Palos Verdes where the award–winning artist then resided.

The painting of the friar is unquestionably among the finest in the long litany of Jean Dayton West's masterpieces. It occupies a prominent place at the Santa Barbara Mission Archives.

At the time of its dedication, a local newspaper reporter had this to say about the painting: "Father Maynard Geiger now shares with another Franciscan, Jose Maria Gonzales Rubio, the distinction of being rendered in oil for the edification of future generations. It is a well–deserved honor for both artist and subject."

RICHARD EDWARD WHITE (1843–1918)

California's mission lore has always attracted poets. One of the first to call attention to this rich and long–neglected theme was Richard Edward White (1843–1918), whose "Midnight Mass," written in 1875, at Mission San Carlos Borromeo, is one of the state's best known poems. It tells the story of the ghostly return of the *padres* to Carmel on the eve of Saint Charles' feastday.

In 1884, White published a thirty–two page opus on *Padre Junípero Serra and the Mission Church of San*

Carlos del Carmelo as part of the commemoration marking the centenary of the friar's death. That rare work, circulated by P. E. Dougherty and Company of San Francisco, is now among the most elusive of Californiana items. Among Richard White's more celebrated contributions to the *Overland Monthly* was his versification of a quaint tradition which he excerpted from Francisco Palóu's *Relación Histórica*:

Bright angels, guarding o'er the land,
Were looking down from heaven afar;
Each held a lantern in his hand,
The light of which men call a star.

And o'er the plain, as night came on,
Two weary pilgrims held their way;
They came from Mission of San Juan,
And sought the Mission Monterey.

Spoke Junípero: "Brother, here
Must we one night at least remain
So gratefully and without fear
Let us repose upon the plain."

As on the ground knelt down the two,
A light amid the darkness shone:
And suddenly upon their view
A house appeared, some distance on.

Said Palóu: "Surely food and rest
The Devil brings us now to tempt;
My flesh is weak, and from such test
I'd rather wish to be exempt."

But vanished soon all fear away,
For by the door an old man stood,
Who welcomed them and bade them stay
And share his humble roof and food.

They entered; everything was neat,
A lady fair and lovely boy
Received them; 'twas a home complete,
Where all was love, and peace, and joy.

That night the pilgrims rested there,
And soon as came the dawn of day,
Thanking their hosts for rest and fare,
They went rejoicing on their way.

Soon met they with a muleteer,
Who said: "So far from men's abode,
I wonder much to meet ye here;
How fare ye on this desert road?"

"Some two miles hence last night we stayed."
Then wondered more the muleteer;
"Good *padre*, some mistake you've made
No house for sixty miles is near.

"So if two miles from this last night
You stayed and met with kindly fare,
And slept in peace till morning's light,
'Twas God who entertained you there."

"I'll show you where the house doth lie,"
The *padre* said; but lo 'twas gone;
And as they turned, in azure sky
The morning star in beauty shone.

Spoke, after pause, the *padre* thus:
" Slowly the truth has come to me,
Bright angels ministered to us,
And very blessed were the three.

"By spirit hands was built that house,
And the old man whom we saw there
Was Joseph, the good Virgin's spouse,
And Mary was the lady fair.

"And well I know the youth was he
The meek and lowly Nazarene,
Who died for us on Calvary
The thief and penitent between."

STEPHEN MALLORY WHITE (1853–1901)

According to a columnist for *The Monitor*, the Catholic newspaper for the Archdiocese of San Francisco, Stephen Mallory White (1853–1901) was "a steadfast adherent to the Catholic faith, a man of strict integrity and lovable qualities, a true, loyal friend, generous to a fault."

Raised on a farm in Santa Cruz county, Stephen received his early schooling in the local public system. He then went to Saint Ignatius College in San Francisco and finally to Santa Clara College where he studied law. Following his admission to the California state bar, young White became one of the highest ornaments in legal circles. He settled in Los Angeles, where he was soon recognized as being among the most successful of juridical practitioners.

In 1875, White ran for the post of District Attorney of Los Angeles. Though he lost that bid by a handful of votes, he went on to win that office in 1882. Three years after his marriage to Hortense Sacriste, White was elected to the state senate, where he served as President *pro tempore* and Lieutenant Governor from 1886 to 1890.

A respected member of his own party, Stephen White attended the Democratic National Convention at Chicago in 1892. There it was his privilege to nominate Adlai E. Stevenson for Vice President.

White was elected to the United States senate in 1893. It was in that legislative body that the young Californian was the backbone of the historic fight for a harbor at San Pedro, pitting his strength against those who were using their mighty resources to have the harbor developed on their own property at Santa Monica Canyon. He served a full term in the senate before returning to Los Angeles and becoming an active member of the local southland community.

White reportedly once told the President of the United States that he "would rather be a lawyer whose word was as good as the rich man's bond, and whose opinion upon intricate questions of judicial science were valued . . . than to hold in his hands all the honors that were ever won by appeals to the passions and prejudices of men."

White's premature death did not find him unprepared. The last rites of the Church were administered by the Right Reverend Frederick Horstmann of Cleveland, a long time friend of the family who was visiting in Los Angeles at the time. White's funeral services were conducted by Bishop George T. Montgomery at Saint Vibiana's Cathedral. Horstmann preached what a local newspaper reporter described as "an eloquent and touching tribute" over the distinguished jurist.

Noting that the press of the state was "unanimous in its judgment" about the former senator's character and ability in public life, the bishop dwelt on the fact that White "commanded the respect and admiration not only of his own party, but also of his adversaries. As a citizen he was always ready to cooperate in every good work for the welfare of his city, state and country. In public life, he looked on office as a trust, to be ministered for the benefit of the whole people."

"A born leader and a broad–minded statesman," Stephen Mallory White's "faith was his dearest treasure. He lived ever a Catholic life." The monument to White in downtown Los Angeles attests to the respect in which this outstanding Catholic layman was held by his contemporaries.

THOMAS P. WHITE (1888–1968)

In speaking of the Honorable Thomas P. White, one

editorial writer noted that "justice for all has been the keystone of his long life of service. That has applied to his decisions on the side of both law enforcement and of the accused."

Thomas Patrick White, the son of Peter White and Catherine Clark, was born in Los Angeles on September 27, 1858. His early education was acquired at Sacred Heart and old Saint Vincent's College. After leaving school in 1905, White took a business–college course in shorthand and typing, at the conclusion of which he entered the employ of Santa Fe.

When he left the railroad in 1908, to begin the study of law, he was assistant to the trainmaster at Needles. Following a distinguished three–year stint at the University of Southern California, during which time he represented the institution on its intercollegiate debating team and acted as student body president, White graduated in 1911, with a legal degree.

For several years, the young attorney practiced his profession with the firms of Randall, Bartlett and White and, later, with Irwin, White and Rosecrans. In 1913, when Henry H. Rose became Mayor of Los Angeles, the Board of Supervisors named Thomas P. White to the former's unexpired term on the Police Court as Justice of the Peace. The following year, he was elected to a full term. Though, at the age of twenty–five, White was the youngest jurist in the United States, his years on the Police Court brought about the innovation of the famed woman's court, first of its kind in the nation. Judge White also inaugurated a probation department for the inferior courts in 1915, and two years later the first work–farm for rehabilitation of inebriates.

Between 1919 and 1931, White engaged in private practice and soon gained a reputation as one of the city's most outstanding trial attorneys. He returned to the bench in 1931, when Governor James Rolph named him to the Superior Court. While serving in the latter position, Justice White was assigned by the Judicial Council as a *pro–tempore* member of the District Court of Appeals. In 1937, Governor Frank Merriam named the well–known jurist Associate Justice of the District Court, to which position he was elected and re–elected by the people. He was advanced to the presiding Judgeship by Governor Earl Warren in 1949.

White's appointment to the California Supreme Court in 1959, "capped one of the grandest judicial careers on record," and gave the judge the unique record of having served on the bench at every level of the state's judicial system. Upon naming the life–long Republican to the Supreme court, Governor Edmund G. Brown noted that "Justice White has been a great jurist in California for more than thirty years. This appointment comes late in his career, but it carries with it a recognition of the gratitude and confidence of the people of California."

Throughout his long and useful years, Justice White was an outspoken and respected member of California's Catholic community. He served as State Deputy and Supreme Director of the Knights of Columbus, Grand President of the Young Men's Institute and the Los Angeles Archdiocesan branch of the Holy Name Union, and for sixteen years as president of the southland's Saint Vincent de Paul Society. He was also a founding member of the Perpetual Adoration Society at the old Plaza Church. Equally active in civic affairs, the justice served on the Executive Board of the Boy Scouts of America and on the Board of Directors of the Community Chest (now United Crusade), and on the faculty of Loyola College of Law.

Even after his official retirement, Judge White sat occasionally with the Supreme Court on assignment by the chairman of the Judicial Council. In the philosophy of Thomas P. White, "it is the duty of a judge to look beyond the form of law to find the facts and substance of Justice." This he consistently did by practicing those virtues which he once said should adorn every man sitting on the bench: "heart, conscience and common sense.

FELIX PAUL WIERZBICKI (1815–1860)

Felix Paul Wierzbicki (1815–1860), "the most famous Polish pioneer of California," was born at Czerniawka, a village in the Province of Volhynia. He fled to the United States, in 1834, on the heels of an unsuccessful insurrection in his native Poland. Shortly after arriving in New England, the youthful enthusiast had the good fortune of meeting an American family who financed his education through medical school.

Wierzbicki functioned as a physician briefly in Providence, Rhode Island, before enlisting as a volunteer with Colonel Jonathan D. Stevenson's regiment during the hostilities with Mexico. Believing as he did of California, that "there is no country, probably where the soil is so grateful to the hand that cultivates it," Wierzbicki subsequently determined to make his home in the Golden State. At the conclusion of the war , he resumed his medical career in San Francisco where he soon achieved a reputation for his surgical abilities. He took a lively part in the public life of the Bay City and soon became known as "a one–man Chamber of Commerce and California booster."

The Polish–born physician is best remembered for his writings. In 1841, he published a philosophical treatise on *The Ideal Man* and, in 1846, a series of articles on the history of Poland in *The American Whig Review*. His "Essay on the History of Medicine" was among the first articles on the subject written in the state.

The most esteemed of Wierzbicki's works, *California As It Is, And As It May Be, Or, A Guide To The Golden Region*, was written after an intensive four–month tour of the El Dorado on foot and horse, in 1849. The sixty–page work, published at San Francisco by Washington Bartlett, was "the first book of an original nature printed in California, in English." Described as "a bibliographical rarity, valued at more than its weight in gold," Wierzbicki's was the first book about the gold rush "to separate fact from fancy, to sift information through the sieve of common sense, and to give

really sound and practical advice to those proposing to seek their fortunes in the Western El Dorado."

Wierzbicki is immortalized in a mural depicting the history of medicine in California by Bernard Zakheim and Phyllis Wrightson in Toland Hall at San Francisco's University of California Hospital.

Felix Paul Wierzbicki was among that select group of Poles who compiled a noble record in the annals of California. It has been said of those exiles that "were it not for the Pacific Ocean, which closed the shores of America, they would still go further west in order to be as far as possible from the home of slavery into which their country was changed by oppressors." Happily in California, they found friends and a measure of prosperity. They repaid the young commonwealth with the best that was in them."

JOHN T. WILSON (1857–1947)

In the early years of this century, the tall and erect John T. Wilson was a familiar figure as he moved in and about the vast and mostly undeveloped areas of San Fernando Valley. He first trod the dust of San Fernando as a barefoot boy. He was a colorful pioneer who, like others of his historic era, overcame all manner of human and natural obstacles in order to transform the valley into one of the world's garden spots.

Wilson first came to the southland in 1871 with his father, C.N. Wilson. His early manhood was spent on the old Wilson Canyon Ranch, where the Olive View Sanitarium was later erected. During those years, he drove the team which hauled the last rail into place that completed the Southern Pacific Railroad line between Los Angeles and San Francisco.

It was as a small boy that Wilson first saw the landmark with which his name was to be so closely linked in subsequent years—the San Fernando Mission. He used to recall that he had once been the luncheon guest there of the infamous Pio Pico. Wilson had the good fortune to choose as his bride the lovely Grace Lopez, daughter of Francisco Lopez, the first person to discover gold in California when he found a nugget under the oak of golden dreams in Placerita Canyon, five miles from Newhall, on March 9, 1842.

Wilson was an innovative man, always anxious to improve his own life and the fortunes of those with whom he lived and worked. He was the first to bring electricity to San Fernando. Through an arrangement with what residents called the "highline," he purchased electricity and redistributed it to dwellers of the area under the name of the San Fernando Light and Power Company. That company was later purchased by Southern California Edison. Prior to that, Wilson served for many years as manager of the Porter Land and Water Company. He was also supervisor for the San Fernando Mission Land Company.

Always active in the country's political and civic life, the pioneer resident made one campaign for supervisor and he also ran, again unsuccessfully, for the office of sheriff. There were few people in the area unacquainted with John T. Wilson. After first seeing the San Fernando Mission as a grand, historic structure, Wilson watched its decline through the years, until it was finally used as a stable for farm animals. Then, with his son, Wilson did much toward restoring the mission to its original form and purpose.

Death finally came to the ninety year old Wilson on April 16, 1947, at his rambling home, 317 Mission Road. There, for decades, scores of California's leading figures had attended gala *fiestas* as guests of the amiable patriarch.

Fittingly, his funeral Mass was offered at San Fernando Mission, in the place that awed him as a youngster seventy–six years earlier. Like other pioneers, he lived beyond his time. It was a wholly new San Fernando Valley in 1947—but that very "newness" would have been impossible without the dreams and ambitions of people like John T. Wilson.

HANNAH VICTORIA WINSLOW (1828–1905)

Hannah Winslow was a lady of great refinement and deep learning. Possessed of a lovable disposition, she is remembered chiefly for the high ideals she had of the duties and responsibilities of parents to educate their children in the Catholic lifestyle. She expected her youngsters to be loyal children of the Church, good citizens of the country and praiseworthy members of society.

Born in Wilmington, Delaware, on April 7, 1828, Hannah Victoria Sherry had all the natural and supernatural ingredients needed for achieving a permanent niche in the annals of womankind. During the early years after her marriage to Michael Winslow, on June 15, 1847, Hannah worked diligently at fulfilling all the Scriptural exhortations associated with home–making. Her two sons, Edward and James, had the good fortune of being raised in a familial atmosphere firmly attached to Catholic principles.

Shortly after hearing about California from those who had gone west in pursuit of gold, the Winslows decided to make their home along the Pacific Slope. They joined one of the western caravans and arrived in San Francisco during December, 1851. From their earliest days in the Bay Area, the Winslows were close friends and confidants of the Most Reverend Joseph Sadoc Alemany, Archbishop of San Francisco. He was a frequent guest in their home.

In 1868, the family moved to Contra Costa County, where they purchased the large and beautiful acreage known as Sunny Side Farm. There Hannah and her loved ones remained for twenty years, entertaining hosts of friends who came from all parts of the state to spend their summers at her country home. Twenty years later, Hannah gave the farm to her son James and built a smaller residence in the City of Martinez for herself and devoted husband. There she lived for the final seventeen years of her life.

Hannah passed into the Lord's presence from the family home at Martinez, on June 27, 1905. Her remains, among the first to be embalmed in California, were kept until July 1st, when the funeral took place. The funeral cortege, the largest ever witnessed in Contra Costa County, passed from the home to Saint Catherine's Church, where a solemn Requiem Mass was sung by the Dominican pastor. The church was crowded with mourners, relatives and friends who came to pay their last tribute of love and respect to one who had proven herself a faithful friend to them in life.

Generous, charitable and kind, Hannah Victoria Winslow was wise in counsel and helpful in need to those who came to her doorstep. She left in her wake a half century's accomplishments in California, little cornerstones that meant much to the future women pioneers for whom she was a model and exemplar.

SAMUEL D. WOODS

It was in the mid 1850s that Samuel D. Woods, the son of a Protestant minister, first visited Los Angeles. His memories of that journey, published a half century later in his *Life on the Pacific Coast* is a fascinating and informative part of California's Catholic Heritage.

Drawn to Southern California by the area's "salubrious and healing climate," Woods set out for Los Angeles by sea, taking passage on the *Senator*, a famed vessel that operated for many years between San Francisco and San Pedro. Upon arrival in the southland, Woods traveled by "a rude stage" through a treeless plain to Los Angeles. In the *pueblo*, he encountered a "mixed population of Spaniard, Mexican, American and Indian (which) did not exceed twelve hundred."

He remembered that "the old cathedral (actually the Plaza Church of *Nuestra Señora de los Angeles*), facing its ancient plaza, was the center from which radiated the streets, along which were grouped the houses in more or less compact clusters." For Woods, the Los Angeles vineyards and orchards resembled the atmosphere of the Orient. The charm of these first days in Los Angeles fascinated him and he could not "forget the little *pueblo*, where adobe *casas*, one story in height, were sufficient for the simple homes of those who here lived, satisfied with the blue skies, the bloom and the romance."

Woods was impressed that "Spanish was the common tongue. Both Mexican and Indian spoke it, with no more violation of its idiom or accent than the uneducated American in his speech violates the English tongue. The habits of the people were faithful copies of Spanish customs." As a Protestant, Woods marveled that "the little *pueblo* was under the dominion of the Catholic Church" and how the Church influenced both the home and school. "Other faiths," he said, "struggled for a foothold, but made no inroads upon this dominion of the Mother Church."

"The priest was in authority, and held his flock with firm hand." Woods felt that "at no place in all of California was the authority of the Roman Catholic Church more obeyed and revered. Its services were crowded with devotees, to whom its decrees were inviolable." Woods was amazed how Catholics "made no question, but in absolute faith knelt at its altars and worshipped, according to the form and in the phrases of the Holy Church."

The cathedral had daily services; "its doors were never closed. In and out of its portals, during the hours of the day and night, a steady stream of old and young, rich and poor, devout and sinful, poured, seeking consolation. The Church's "calendar was crowded with Saints' Days, and it was a most frequent sight to see from the doors of the cathedral issue a procession of priests and acolytes, marching in solemn order with the Exalted Host and banners, around the plaza, while multitudes knelt in reverent attitudes." Woods admitted that "this manifestation of reverence impressed me greatly, and many a time, as I passed before it, I instinctively uncovered my head, for somehow the spell of the old church was irresistible."

Such glimpses into the past are the "stuffing" of local history. Recollections of people like Woods are vitally important for arriving at a balanced history of any city, certainly Los Angeles.

MARIA JULIA WORKMAN (1871–1964)

Mary Julia Workman (1871–1964) was a woman of outstanding stature during the many years she helped to pioneer the religious and social betterment of her native Los Angeles. "Miss Mary," as she was known to her friends, was the daughter of one–time Mayor William Henry Workman. Much of her early life was spent in educational circles. After graduating from Oakland's College of the Holy Names and the State Normal School, Mary taught for twenty–one years in the Los Angeles school system. Between 1926 and 1928, she served as president of the Civil Service Commission.

Never one to avoid public responsibility, Miss Workman was active in the foundation of Brownson House in 1901. Subsequently she campaigned for child labor and Indian welfare legislation. She was the first president of the Los Angeles Council of Catholic Women and the initial recipient in Southern California of the "*Pro Ecclesia*" decoration from Pope Pius XI. Many other projects which she inspired were forerunners of the essential neighborhood services which developed all over the city, and in time were united in the Community Chest after its founding in 1924.

Proponents of a more intense involvement of the Catholic laity in social issues would do well to take a leaf from Mary Julia Workman's book. One outstanding example of her noble concern is mirrored in a public letter on "The Hopelessly Defective," which she wrote in the 1924 *Bulletin* of the Municipal League of Los Angeles. Arguing against euthanasia, Miss Mary noted:

> The principal objection is that God alone has the supreme dominion over human life. No committee of social workers or physicians or legislators may presume to trespass upon the right of the Creator. God is the author of life and it is for him to decide when the service of His creatures is to terminate. Any law authorizing a committee of physicians to do away with the lives of the hopelessly defective would be invalid, first of all, because it contravenes the higher law of God. The second reason is that such a practice would bring mental anguish and fear to the minds of the sick and suffering, who would be in continual fear of death, in addition to their other afflictions. The case of those who would not realize the impending fate or who would desire it, would not change the fact that an avenue would be opened for all forms of injustice toward the helpless.

Miss Mary reiterated that "no physician or social worker has any moral right over life. Their function is to prolong life, to lessen human suffering and to promote the general welfare of the community. The only safe social doctrine is that no one under any conditions may take the life of an innocent person. Every human being, no matter how afflicted, has an inherent dignity which must be respected; each one has an immortal soul capable of union with God and each one has certain inalienable rights among which is the right to life."

To Mary Workman, man was bound to "consider the law of God, the rights of the individual, the social effects" of all moral actions. For that reason, "we may never do wrong that good may come. Because good may result in some specific case from a wrong policy, the policy is not vindicated."

Throughout her ninety–three years, Mary Julia Workman was a tireless worker for a social justice based squarely on the message of the Gospel. Shortly before her death, Miss Mary received the following letter from Archbishop Robert Emmet Lucey:

God has been good to you and has given you a long life which you have spent for His honor in the service of mankind. Your interests have transcended the limitations of your city and country, going out to the poor, the needy and the exploited in all parts of the world.

YELLOW SKY (b. 1789)

In the fall of 1919, Bishop John J. Cantwell conferred the Sacrament of Confirmation upon Yellow Sky, a venerable Indian of an unknown tribe and the last of the California "heathens." The account of the historically–significant ceremony was related for readers of *The Catholic Herald* (1919–Annual), Catholic newspaper for the Diocese of Sacramento.

Clad only in an overcoat and carrying in his hand the only hat he ever owned, Yellow Sky, believed to be more than 130 years old, knelt at the altar of a century–old mission and was confirmed by Bishop Cantwell of Los Angeles.

As far as is known, Yellow Sky was the last heathen in the diocese which now constitutes the territory of the old missions. Two years ago he was baptized and then it was found that he had never worn clothes and spoke a tongue lost even to the Indians of the Southwest.

A mission Indian was assigned to the duty of learning the language of Yellow Sky. A year of study brought mastery of the tongue and then came a year in which Yellow Sky was taught the story of the lowly Nazarene and the lessons of Christianity.

Word was sent to Bishop Cantwell that Yellow Sky desired to be Confirmed. The bishop, accompanied by John McGroarty, Los Angeles writer and authority on Indian and mission lore, started off across the mountains following the trails which Fray Junípero and the other leaders of the golden days of the California missions first trod.

Word of the coming of the bishop was sent throughout the Southwest. The scenes of the old mission days were re–enacted as Indians started to El Cajon. Camp fires burned and by night signal lights flashed from the mountain peaks. Finally the day came, and with the direct descendants of those who had received their first communion from Fray Junípero Yellow Sky was confirmed.

After the service McGroarty presented Yellow Sky with his first corn cob pipe and a can of tobacco, and the Indians gave him the money for his first suit of clothes.

JOSE ANTONIO YORBA (1746–1825)

José Antonio Yorba (1746–1825), "a devout Christian who walked humbly before God," was the first of the state's land barons with holdings that amounted to a principality. Born in the town of San Sadurni de Noya,

near his ancestral village in the district of Barcelona, Jose Antonio early in life enlisted in the Spanish Army and, as a member of the Royal Catalan Volunteers, came to New Spain, in 1767.

Two years later, he was among the twenty–five Catalans chosen to accompany the California expedition. His contingency aboard the flagship, *San Carlos*, arrived at San Diego after an exhausting 110 day voyage from La Paz. Yorba was further honored by being among Gaspár de Portolá's exploratory party which left for Monterey on July 14, 1769, and arrived back at San Diego, following a harrowing journey, on January 24, 1770.

José Antonio Yorba remained in California, serving at various *presidios* and missions. On May 17, 1782, he married Maria Joséfa Grijalva at San Francisco. Their thirteen children, nine of whom lived past infancy, are represented by descendants numbering in the thousands.

In 1789, José Antonio was attached to San Diego Presidio where he served until his retirement as sergeant, in 1797. While there, he applied to Governor José Arrillaga for a land grant subsequently known as the *Rancho Santiago de Santa Ana*. The acquiescence of his petition, together with that of his nephew, Juan Pablo Peralta, placed Yorba among the few holders of grants authorized during the Spanish regime. (The present cities of Santa Ana, Orange, Tustin, Olive, El Modena, Costa Mesa and a portion of Newport Beach have grown out of that *rancho*.) José Antonio lived there until his death in 1825, cultivating a large orchard and vineyard, as well as herds of cattle, sheep and oxen.

José Antonio Yorba's spiritual testament testifies to the noble character of one who participated most intimately in the initial and very important phase of California's occupancy and settlement by Spain:

I commend my soul to God who created it and by the merits of the precious blood of our Lord Jesus Christ, who redeemed it—I beg and ask a general pardon of the offenses that I have committed against Him, in order that when it leaves this miserable body it may go to praise Him with the blessed in Heaven; and it is my will that my body be given up to the earth from which it came, remaining in deposit for the day of judgment, and that it should be shrouded in the holy habit of the sacred religion of the Seraphic Patriarch Saint Francis.

LORETTA YOUNG (1912–2000)

Loretta Young, "a woman born to cause excitement," is still one of Hollywood's most dynamic, tireless and dedicated "big–name" personalities. Today she retains every bit of the beauty, charm and glamour that characterized the busiest years of her dramatic career. "Gretchen" was brought to California from her Salt Lake City birthplace, in 1916. Her artistic talents were recognized almost from the moment of arrival in the Golden State. She became a child extra, at four; a juvenile bit–player, at eleven; a studio contractee, at twelve and a star in adult roles, at fourteen.

Her schooling was necessarily sporadic. Though she briefly attended sessions at Saint Brendan, Saint Thomas, Ramona Convent and Conaty High School, her classroom was mostly the corner of whatever studio stage she happened to be working.

The "most awarded actress in Hollywood" has never kept a diary or a scrapbook and can give no statistical account of her performance record. A little research revealed that she had completed 252 productions; eighty–seven major pictures and 165 teleplays of "The Loretta Young Show."

In 1947, Loretta won the coveted Oscar from the Motion Picture Academy for her performance in RKO's "The Farmer's Daughter." She was nominated for a similar honor after portrayal in 20th Century Fox's "Come to the Stable."

Through her NBC television series, Loretta Young became a cherished weekly visitor in millions of homes throughout the United States, Canada, Australia and Latin America. That show, aired in the years after 1952, won the distinction of being TVs most awarded anthology program.

Married, in 1940, to Thomas H. A. Lewis, Loretta has always given a priority to familial obligations. Even today, her three children and two grandchildren receive "top billing" in a life crowded with a host of varied public commitments. "Woman's greatest asset is her motherhood, all else is secondary and accidental." It is a rare week that Loretta doesn't dart out from her home for several hours of volunteer work at neighboring hospitals. Though she doesn't sing, dance or tell jokes, the Loretta Young charism is as evident as ever as she gracefully moves from bed to bed.

A part of Loretta's life was written, in 1961, by her long–time friend and public relations representative, Helen Ferguson. Released by the Bobbs Merrill Company, as *Things I Had to Learn*, the volume did much to focus world attention on Miss Young's Christocentric behaviorial pattern.

For over half a century, Loretta Young has echoed the theme that" a life without religion is, truly, an impoverished existence." That stance, maintained in the face of numerous personal and public confrontations, has caused her considerable anxiety. Her adamant refusal, for example, to glamorize immorality in any of its manifestations, is the basic reason for her premature "retirement." Loretta harbors no regrets. She considers her career artistically fulfilled, inasmuch as she was able, in her television series, to perform every role she dreamed about, without compromising her philosophy that permissiveness cannot be the norm in the interpretative art of acting.

Possible no single "trademark" of Loretta's life–style is more demonstrative, among her professional peers, than the "Swear Box," which she invented to counteract the maze of blasphemous language so common to production sets. "The four letter words were free," she recalls, "but any irreverence to the Lord's name cost a quarter, while 'hell' and 'damn' brought a dime." At first, as much as $100 was collected weekly and dispatched to some local charity. Gradually the air cleared, but for the practice Loretta was dubbed by the industry's pseudo–sophisticates as "Miss Goody–Two–Shoes." "I was just a little proud of that," she admits in retrospect.

Loretta Young's successful life is a most difficult and competitive industry bespeaks a generous portion of that Christian orientation, disciplined professionalism and ethical deportment one necessarily looks for in persons of great and lasting accomplishments.

III. Clergymen
In General and Individual Clergymen

CALIFORNIA'S PRIESTLY MARTYROLOGY (1734–1812)

According to one historian, "the hope of martyrdom had lured not a few friars from Spain to California, and some of them were gratified." That the early friars considered martyrdom a very real possibility of their missionary endeavor is obvious from the remark made by Junípero Serra when he was informed of the cruel death of Fray Luis Jayme at San Diego. "Thanks be to God; now that the terrain has been watered by blood the conversion of the San Diego Indians will take place."

By definition, "martyrdom" is the testimony a person renders to Christian teachings by voluntarily undergoing death inflicted out of a hatred toward Christ and His religion. If, one day, a special martyrology is written for California, the following format could well be followed:

October 1, (1734), Father *Lorenzo Carranco*, Mexican–born member of the Society of Jesus, killed during an uprising at Mission Santiago de las Coras in Peninsular California;

October 3, (1734), Father *Nicolás Tamaral*, attacked and brutally slain by the Uchintíes Indians at his mission post of San José del Cabo in Baja California;

April 12, (1738), birthday of Fray *Francisco Garcés*, the missionary hero of Yuma, who suffered martyrdom at the Colorado River foundation of Purísima Concepción on July 17, 1781;

November 4, (1775), at San Diego, the anniversary of Fray *Luis Jayme*, proto–martyr of Upper California, who was given the crown of glory by the San Diegan Indians;

July 17, (1781), Fray *José Matias Moreno*, who came to the California missions out of a "desire of winning souls and the longing for martyrdom," won his aurora at Mission San Pedro y San Pablo del Vado de Bicuñer;

July 17, (1781), at present–day Fort Yuma, the youthful friar, *Juan Antonio Barreneche*, was slain under orders of the dissident chief of the Yuma Indians;

July 17, (1781), at Mission San Pedro y San Pablo del Vado de Bicuñer, the Queretaran friar, *Juan Diaz*, suffered a painful death inflicted by the Yuma Indians;

July 8, (1782), commemoration of the birth of Father *Jose Ygnacio Argüello*, first native–born priest of California, son and brother of early governors, who assumed the crown of martyrdom in Torin, Sonora, at the hands of the Yaqui natives;

October 12, (1812), anniversary of the cruel death at Santa Cruz inflicted by the ungrateful Indians on Fray *Andres Quintana* who "strained all his faculties as far as zeal and industry carried him in order to improve and advance them."

AND ELSEWHERE MANY OTHER HOLY MARTYRS, CONFESSORS AND HOLY VIRGINS. THANKS BE TO GOD.

The desire for martyrdom is usually something an individual keeps between himself and God. But one friar, writing to his sister, notes that "the opportunity of spreading the Faith of Christ and of suffering martyrdom is always at hand . . . . It is true that there is much hardship in enduring hunger, thirst, intolerable heat, and making painful journeys, but what is this in comparison with the price paid by Christ for these souls which would almost infallibly fall into the net of Satan, if no one had the courage to undertake their conversion?"

Junípero Serra left the Balearic Isles in 1749, never to return. The next thirty–five years of his life belonged to California. But Mallorca has not forgotten. All of Spain and all of California can thank Almighty God for the early Iberian missionaries who brought the Gospel to an unknown land!

PRONOTARIES APOSTOLIC IN LOS ANGELES

Pope John Paul's designation of Msgr. Arthur Lirette as a Protonotary Apostolic called to mind the relative rarity of that distinction in California's southland. The pastor–emeritus of Holy Family Parish in Glendale was only the ninth priest of the Los Angeles jurisdiction ever to bear that title.

The office of notary has a long and distinguished history in ecclesial annals. Already by the 5th century those entrusted with that title formed a separate college, the head of which was known as the Protonotary. During the Middle Ages, the protonotaries were high papal officials who were often raised directly from that position to the cardinalate. In the late 16th century, the office gradually declined in importance until, at the time of the French Revolution, it had almost disappeared.

In 1838, Pope Gregory XVI re–established the college of Protonotaries Apostolic and fixed their number at seven. The pontiff also provided for a limited membership of honorary appointees who were to enjoy many of the same prerogatives conferred upon the real members of the college.

The office of Protonotary Apostolic, as it now exists, can be traced to February 9, 1853, and the issuance, by Pope Pius IX, of a papal brief outlining the faculties and privileges of the college. Several minor alterations were made by Pius X (1905) and Pius XI (1934).

The first American named a Protonotary Apostolic was Msgr. Robert J. Seton (1839–1927), a priest of the Newark diocese, who was given the distinction by Pius IX, on August 17, 1867. The honor was bestowed a second time, December 13, 1881, on Msgr. Thomas S. Preston (1824–1891) and again, July 5, 1889, on Msgr. George F. Doane (1830–1905). Interestingly enough, the initial three appointees all eventually became bishops.

The initial Californian to become a Protonotary Apostolic was Msgr. Patrick Harnett (1858–1924), Vicar General for the Diocese of Monterey–Los Angeles. The title was bestowed by Pope Pius X, in 1909, four years after the longtime Rector of Saint Vibiana's Cathedral had been invested as the Golden State's initial monsignor. The appointment was conferred on Harnett's successor, Msgr. John J. Cawley (1882–1953) in 1925. That distinguished prelate bore the honor for twenty–eight years until his death in Geneva, enroute home from the papal consistory of 1953.

It was almost another quarter century before the title of Protonotary Apostolic was again conferred, this time on Msgr. John M. McCarthy (1864–1951), the Pastor–Emeritus of Saint Andrew's Parish in Pasadena. The former "horse and buggy missionary" received the distinction in 1950, on the occasion of his sixtieth anniversary in the priesthood.

In 1959, another veteran cleric was added to the College of Protonotaries Apostolic in the person of Msgr. Michael Galvin (1888–1974), Pastor of Holy Family Parish in Glendale for almost a half century. Msgr. Galvin served as *officialis* or Chief Justice for the Archdiocese of Los Angeles from 1937 until his death.

Though the office of Protonotary Apostolic, as it exists outside the City of Rome, is strictly honorary, its very rarity bespeaks the pre–eminence and esteem associated with the persons so designated for that honor.

REMEMBER THE PRIESTS

Some of the most fascinating entries in the Priestly Hall of Fame belong to clerics who walked along California's *El Camino Real*. A fairly significant number have been memorialized for the edification of future generations.

Rank has its privileges and that explains how the names of so many of the area's early bishops are attached to educational institutions. There are high schools named for Bishop Francisco Garcia Diego (Santa Barbara), Joseph Sadoc Alemany (Mission Hills), Thaddeus Amat (La Puente), Francis Mora (Los Angeles), George T. Montgomery (Torrance), Thomas J. Conaty (Los Angeles) and John J. Cantwell (Montebello).

Probably the highest human tribute that can be bestowed is that of having a youngster named in someone's memory. During Bishop George T. Montgomery's episcopate (1896–1903), dozens of children were christened "George Thomas." The last vestige of that era was a priest in Orange County, Father George Thomas Breslin, whose father was named for the southland's fifth bishop.

But there are others memorialized too, at the local level. The parish hall at Saint Clare of Assisi in Canyon County honors the work of Father Henry Banks (1910–1976). While at Newhall, Banks built the church, school, hall, library and rectory and it was he who "reached out" to open a Sunday Mass center at Canyon Country High School.

On April 17, 1982, as a monument to Msgr. Ramon D. Garcia, the Los Angeles Department of Parks and Recreation attached his name to the Fresno Playground, a park located in a triangle of land formed by the junction of westbound Santa Ana and Pomona freeways. The first priest ordained from Saint John's Seminary in Camarillo, Msgr. Garcia (1913–1972) was a leading promoter for the new Santa Marta Hospital and the Bilingual Community Adult School at Salesian High.

There is a council of the Knights of Columbus in Sherman Oaks, at Saint Francis de Sales parish, named for Father James O'Mahony (1890–1960), pastor at Sherman Oaks from 1940 to 1960. Prior to his arrival there, Father O'Mahony had served as pastor of seven southland parishes.

In Burbank, an auditorium was erected in the mid 1980s as a memorial for Msgr. Martin Cody Keating (1883–1971) who was pastor of Saint Robert Bellarmine parish between 1930 to 1968. The colorful Keating, a chaplain in World War I, sought to dramatize America's dedication to freedom and human rights by modelling the parish church on Thomas Jefferson's home at Monticello and the high school on Independence Hall in Philadelphia.

At Saint Jane Frances de Chantal parish in North Hollywood is Lahart Hall, so designated to memorialize Father Thomas Lahart (1905–1982). The building had served as the parish church during Lahart's pastorate. The "Vincents" were a group of teenagers organized by the late Father Vincent Haggin (1919–1990) during his years as associate pastor of Epiphany parish in El Monte. Father Haggin served most of his ministry in the United States Army Chaplain Corps where he rose to the rank of Colonel.

The parochial hall at Saint Catherine parish is named for Msgr. John Hackett (1905–1983) who served the Reseda area as pastor for thirty–two years. The monsignor was eulogized as a priest "always present to his people." And there is Buechner Hall which commemorates the dedicated efforts of Father Louis Buechner (1900–1986) who labored as pastor of Saint John of God parish between 1950 and 1972.

SACERDOTAL MEMORIALS

The late Archbishop John J. Cantwell was fond of saying that "there's nothing so dead as a dead priest, except perhaps a dead bishop." Cantwell presumably escaped the usual obscurity associated with defunct clergy by having a high school named for him. Few priests have been so fortunate. Here are some other notable exceptions.

There are two streets in West Hollywood named for the "Padre of the Films," Msgr. John J. Devlin (1898–1977). The co–founder of the Legion of Decency is remembered by Devlin Drive and Devlin Place in the hills above Sunset Boulevard.

The parish hall at Saint Bruno's parish in Whittier was so designated as a memorial to the founding pastor, Father John McCormick (1910–1973). In San Buenaventura, the parochial hall at Assumption parish is named for Msgr. Daniel Hurley (1894–1982), founder of the parish and emeritus–pastor of the Old Mission.

Lynch Hall at Saint Matthew's in Long Beach recalls the longtime and beloved pastor, Msgr. James Lynch (1897–1986). And there's Jinks Hall at Saint Paul of the Cross in La Mirada, so designated in memory of Father Owen Jinks (1911–1983).

Rarely is the name of a living person bestowed upon a street. Coffield Avenue in El Monte, listed now for several decades in the gazeteer, honors the still very much alive Msgr. John Coffield (b. 1914) of Capistrano Beach.

In Northridge is Stroup Hall, named as a memorial for Msgr. Paul E. Stroup (1917–1983) who established Our Lady of Lourdes Parish in that area of San Fernando Valley in 1958. Gratian Street in East Los Angeles was so designated many years ago to honor Father Gratian Ardans, O.S.B., the long–time Benedictine pastor of the other archdiocesan parish named for Our Lady of Lourdes.

Martinez Hall in Granada Hills is named for Father Frederick Martinez, C.M. (1904–1967), who helped on weekends at Saint John Baptist de la Salle for many years. Father Martinez boasted of being born near what is now first base in Dodgers Stadium.

Molloy Hall at Saint Maria Goretti Parish in Long Beach was named for Father Vincent Molloy (1913–1970). And Conlin Hall at Saint Mary Magdalen Parish in Los Angeles recalls the legendary Father John Conlin (1899–1960), who was pastor there from 1931 to 1955.

Dublin Street in Leimert Park was originally slated to be Buckley Drive. But Father (later Msgr.) James Buckley (1894–1965), pastor of Transfiguration Parish, asked that the name of his native city be used instead of his own. And city planners went along with the priest's wishes. Hunt Avenue in San Gabriel is named for Father Michael Hunt (1915–1984) the gentle Irish–born pastor of Epiphany parish in South El Monte. Father Hunt died while administering the Sacrament of Reconciliation.

Finally, there is Hawkes Residence, a housing unit for women at the Good Shepherd Center, which was opened at Queen of Angels Hospital to honor the memory of Msgr. Benjamin G. Hawkes (1919–1985).

But given the thousands of priests who have served long and well in this area of the Lord's vineyard, the old dictum of Archbishop Cantwell remains the rule: "There's nothing so dead as a dead priest. . . ."

PRIESTLY NECROLOGY

Some interesting observations can be made about the 547 secular priests included in the 1965 edition of the *Sacerdotal Necrology* for the Archdiocese of Los Angeles and those California areas making up the state's original ecclesiastical jurisdiction. The first native Californian raised to the priesthood was Jose Ygnacio Arguello (1782–1808), son of the well–known Captain Dario Arguello. This proto–priest was killed in an uprising of the Yaqui Indians in present–day Sonora.

Father Clement Molony (1874–1949) headed the long list of residents in the old Diocese of Monterey–Los Angeles ordained for service in the southland. He was advanced to the priesthood by Bishop George Thomas Montgomery in Saint Vibiana's Cathedral on April 19, 1897. The first ordination on California soil was performed at Santa Barbara on June 29, 1842, with the conferral of Holy Orders on Miguel Gomez. Shortly after returning to Guadalajara, Father Gomez died on December 4, 1856.

The initial death among the secular clergy in the Golden State was that of Father José de los Santos Avila on March 25, 1846. Only thirty–six years later, the Right Reverend Francisco Garcia Diego y Moreno (1785–1846), Bishop of the parent Diocese of "Ambas California," succumbed at Santa Barbara.

Longevity of the southland's clergy has followed irregular patterns. The priestly, life–span averages out to 60.3 years, although forty priests lived beyond their 80th birthday; seven of these well into their 90s The oldest was Father Francis Taton (b. 1861) who died November 29, 1956, at the age of 95 years and 68 days.

The average years in the ministry after ordination was only 33.7, though the 547 deceased secular priests of Southern California amassed an impressive overall total of 18,434 years in the apostolate. The longest tour of duty was that of Father Ananias Bouret (1873–1963), who lived 69 years after his ordination.

The shortest span was the 84 days of Father José de los Santos Avila. Among the archdiocesan clergy alive in 1965, half of whom had been ordained since 1948, were eleven priests who had functioned for over half a century. The eldest received the Sacrament of Holy Orders 67 years earlier.

As far as nationality is concerned, 42 percent of the priests dying before the beginning of 1966, were Irish–born, while 49.6 percent were American–born, California accounting for 24.6 percent. The percentage of Irish clergy is gradually diminishing for presently the Emerald Isle lays claim to only 39 percent of the priests in the Archdiocese of Los Angeles.

In former times, honorary papal titles were quite a rarity. The first Californian made a monsignor was Father Patrick Harnett (1858–1924), who was created a domestic prelate by Pope Pius X early in 1905. Father Francis Mora (1827–1905) enjoyed a canonically equivalent status during his years as the first diocesan vicar general.

While statistics may well be the "dry bones" of history, they do have certain valid applications. In the case of the diocesan priests serving Southern California 1840–1965, these figures are not only impressive—they are a standing tribute to decades of sacrifice rarely paralleled in United States Catholic annals.

CHAPLAINS IN WORLD WAR II

The story of the priest–chaplains in the United States Armed Forces can be traced to 1775, when the Continental Congress authorized that chaplains be inducted into the Army with captain's rank. First among the Catholic priests to serve as a naval officer was Father Adam Marshall, a Jesuit who served aboard the *North Carolina* from 1824 until his death the following year. During the Mexican–American War, President Polk was anxious to commission Catholic priests as Army chaplains to avoid criticism of the war as an "anti–Catholic crusade."

Fathers John McElroy and Anthony Rey were released by Bishop Hughes of New York to serve with General Zachary Taylor's troops. Father Rey was killed in Mexico, and Father McElroy served a year before returning east to found Boston College.

At the outbreak of the Civil War, there were an estimated three million Catholics in the United States, primarily German, Irish and other European immigrants, in a total population of about 30 million. Volunteer units from various states were often accompanied into active duty by their local priests. Some forty Catholic clergymen served as chaplains with the Union Army. Out of 600 chaplains serving the Confederacy, twenty–eight were known to have been Catholic.

It was in 1888 that the United States Navy commissioned its first priest, Father Charles Henry Parks of New York, as a chaplain. By the turn of the century, three more priests had joined him and during the Spanish–American War, twelve priests held commissions in the Army and Navy.

It was also in 1888 that the Archbishop of New York was granted special faculties by Rome to appoint chaplains. In 1917, the pope appointed Bishop Patrick Hayes of New York to serve as the military bishop for the United States. Hayes established the military diocesan headquarters in New York with five regional vicariates. That diocese was known as the Military Vicariate and its offices became the Military Ordinariate.

In 1939, Pope Pius XII designated Archbishop Francis J. Spellman as Military Vicar for the United States. Between Pearl Harbor and V–J Day, 2,453 priests served as Army chaplains and 817 as Navy chaplains. Of that number, seventy–six died in service. And those figures do not include another 2,000 civilian auxiliary chaplains who also came under the vicariate's jurisdiction.

It was during World War II, for the first time in history, that chaplains in large numbers became prisoners of war, thereby giving invaluable service to fellow prisoners in the most primitive conditions.

Records at the Archival Center indicate that thirty priests from the Archdiocese of Los Angeles served as military chaplains during World War II. They were:

Bell, Alden J.
Bramble, William Keith
Collins, John J.
Cook, Ozias B.
Deady, John P.
Diamond, James P.
Dougery, Edward F.
Eyraud, Joseph L.
Flannery, Patrick J.
Gannon, Robert J.
Gunn, Francis G.
Hiss, Martin C.
Kass, Frederick
Kielty, Daniel
Lundy, William
McArdle, Joseph K.
McGoldrick, Patrick
O'Connor, Michael J.
O'Gorman, James A.
O'Malley, Thomas J.
O'Reilly, Aubrey J.
Osborne, Francis J.
Pick, Louis V.
Quatannens, John C.
Sharpe, Joseph F.
Sherwood, Gervase G.
Spotter, Otto E.
Strange, Donald J.
Treboal, Herve M.
Trower, William J.

In describing these men, John Cardinal O'Connor said that "no priest can ever watch blood pouring from the wounds of the dying . . . without anguish and a sense of desperate frustration and futility."

INDIVIDUAL CLERGYMEN

JOACHIM ADAM (1837–1907)

In the historical annals of Southern California, Father Joachim Adam was known as "simple, approachable as a little child, with a saintly humility and a true Christian charity." It was on October 12, 1837 that Jose Joachim Adam was born at Barcelona. After completing his studies at Rome's Urban College of Propaganda Fide, Adam was ordained on December 2, 1863.

Upon his arrival in the Diocese of Monterey–Los Angeles, Father Adam was appointed curate at Visalia. He served subsequently at Watsonville and Santa Barbara prior to being named to the pastorate of Santa Cruz in October of 1868. On February 28, 1883, Bishop Francis Mora named Father Adam Vicar General of the diocese, and rector of Saint Vibiana's Cathedral, both of which positions he occupied until ill health forced his retirement, in 1899.

A prolific author, Father Adam wrote many articles, most of them historical in nature. One of his more outstanding contributions was a two–part treatise on the development of devotion to Our Lady of Guadalupe, which appeared in the April, 1889, issues of *Ave Maria*. Father Adam's most ambitious literary endeavor was a truncated translation, the first in English, of Francisco *Palóu's Relación Histórica de la Vida y Apóstolicas Tareas del Venerable Padre Fray Junípero Serra*, which was published at San Francisco, in 1884, by P.E. Dougherty and Company. The 156–page book, issued as the *Life of Ven. Padre Junípero Serra*, was occasioned, according to an early advertisement, by the finding of the friar's remains, on July 3, 1882, during the restoration of San Carlos del Carmelo Church. Father Adam's central purpose was, in his own words, "to perpetuate the memory of a poor Franciscan, who left honors, relatives and friends to spend his life in laboring for the conversion of the aborigines of Alta California."

The Vicar General was a long–time member of the Historical Society of Southern California and a frequent contributor to that organization's annual publications. At the time of Adam's death, the society reprinted a letter from the Los Angeles *Evening Express* wherein Henry Dwight Barrows stated that "the reverend—truly revered—cleric, had long been a resident of our city, and his good deeds and gentle, courtly ways had endeared him to many of our people outside of his own communion."

In 1888, when discussions were first held between Archbishop Patrick W. Riordan of San Francisco and Bishop Francis Mora of Monterey–Los Angeles, about creation of a new diocese in the southland or the appointment of a coadjutor, Mora submitted the name of

Joachim Adam

his Vicar General as a worthy candidate for the episcopate. While admitting in a subsequent letter to Rome that the priests of Southern California "would overwhelmingly prefer Adam," Archbishop Riordan counseled the appointment of a younger man, and, if possible, one born in the United States. No action was taken either way for almost a decade. Adam's own disposition seems rather obvious from his refusal, in 1890, of the Vicariate Apostolic of Brownsville. In March of 1906, Bishop Thomas J. Conaty announced that Father Adam, by then retired and living in Spain, had been named a private chamberlain by Pope Pius X.

Father Adam died in London on July 30, 1907. At a memorial Mass subsequently offered at Los Angeles, Bishop Conaty characterized the one–time Vicar General as a man who possessed "a nobility of resignation, a priestly patience, a splendid manifestation of faith in God and reliance upon His infinite mercy to bear him safely through all the difficulties of life."

VALENTINE AGUILERA (1872–1907)

Father Valentine Aguilera worked for the salvation of souls in California when duty laid upon priestly shoulders a heavy burden of toil. It is part of the historical record that he met that challenge with distinction.

Aguilera was born at Barcelona on February 29, 1872. After completing his primary education, he enrolled in the Jesuit College at Manresa, just north of the famous shrine dedicated to Our Lady of Montserrat. After some years of study with the Society of Jesus, the youthful Catalan expressed a desire to prepare for the priesthood. He was eventually accepted as a clerical candidate for the Diocese of Vich.

In 1869, Aguilera met Bishop Thaddeus Amat, who had stopped at the seminary enroute to Vatican Council 1. After listening to the prelate's appeal for priests to work along California's *El Camino Real*, Aguilera volunteered for service in the Diocese of Monterey–Los Angeles.

Amat sent the cleric to All Hallows College, Dublin, where he remained for some months learning English and completing his priestly studies. Aguilera then set out for the New World, arriving in Los Angeles in September of 1871. He was ordained to the priesthood on June 28th of the following year.

Father Aguilera was first assigned to Castroville and then to Visalia. In 1876, he was advanced to the pastorate in the latter city. That gigantic parish encompassed over 32,000 square miles in what is now Fresno, Tulare, Kern and Inyo counties.

A local newspaper reported that "too much praise cannot be given Father Aguilera for the noble work he has performed in his chosen calling, when it is considered that in this parish at that time" there was such an extensive field of endeavor. The account went on to say that "aside from his many other duties of visiting the sick, attending baptisms and funerals, in out of the way sections, we must give him credit of building the rectory in Visalia."

Aguilera also erected Saint John's Church, Fresno, which was the largest brick and stone church in the county at the time. Other houses–of–worship were built at Medeira, Borden, Hanford and Tahone.

After 1882, Father Aguilera gave his time exclusively to Fresno, where he continued furnishing the churches in his charge with everything necessary for divine services. He also dedicated a beautiful new cemetery near Fresno. In 1891, Bishop Francis Mora transferred Aguilera to San Luis Obispo Mission and there he labored faithfully for many years. While at the Old Mission, he built additional churches at Santa Margarita, Cayucas and Cambria Pines.

There was no diminution in Aguilera's pace during the final years of his priestly life. He made many improvements at San Luis Obispo and did everything within his power to keep that historic foundation a vital link in the chain of parishes then comprising the Diocese of Monterey–Los Angeles.

In 1907, Bishop Thomas J. Conaty suggested that Father Aguilera take a prolonged European vacation in order to regain his failing health. But the priest died of pneumonia at Claremont, a suburb of Barcelona, on February 24th of the next year.

In the obituary notice published by *The Tidings* for March 27, 1908, the editor noted that Father Aguilera was always "ahead of civilization . . . long before the railroads entered any of the parishes he so zealously labored in, he was making his daily calls, going on horseback or driving in all kinds of weather . . . often travelling all day without seeing a human being, carrying his own provisions and water, often going without sleep and food to make a hurried call of 300 miles."

MAXIMIANO AGURTO (1815–1870)

According to the prescriptions of Canon Law, every priest must "belong" somewhere. Either he is incardinated in a diocese or is a member of a religious order or community. The code specifically forbids a priest to be a "*vagus*" or wanderer.

Yet, over the years since 1769, numerous clergymen have "wandered" in and out of the shadows to exercise their ministry in California, many of them leaving little or no record beyond a few entries in sacramental registers. Among those wanderers who appeared in Provincial California was Father Maximiano Agurto (1815–1870), a native of Cauquenes, Chile, the son of Bartolome and Doña Maria (Castillo) Agurto. Maximiano was ordained for the Diocese of Concepcion and during the earliest years of his priestly ministry, he served in Santiago and Rancagua.

Precisely why Agurto came to California is unknown. He arrived in the company of gold seekers who departed from the Port of Valparaiso in 1849–1850, possibly as their chaplain. Archbishop Joseph Sadoc Alemany, who was desperate for priests, welcomed Agurto with open arms, giving him faculties for the Archdiocese of San Francisco and appointing him to look after Catholics living on Contra Costa, across the bay.

Agurto appears to have been a tireless worker, serving both Indians and Hispanic settlers alike. *The Metropolitan Catholic Almanac* lists Agurto as the only priest in Contra Costa county in 1853. Happily, the priest kept two register books, one for baptisms and confirmations, the other for burials.

During his years in the area, the priest lived at the home of Vicente Peralta of Temescal, on one of the four parcels of land comprising the original *Rancho San Antonio*. There was a small chapel on the *rancho* which had been built sometime before 1842.

Between September, 1850 and November, 1853,

Agurto made 130 entries in the register for baptisms and confirmations, fifty–six for native Americans and the rest for settlers. The priest always followed his name by the initials " S.L." which may have been an inversion for *locum sigillum* or the seal of the place. There were fifteen entries of the burial register, ending with that of Carmen Peralta who died of cholera. She was buried on a knoll in a private cemetery overlooking Pinole.

Sometime after November of 1853, Father Agurto disappeared from the California scene. A note by Alemany in the *Libro de Gobierno* says only that "permission is given to Rev. Maximiano Agurto to return to Chile." After arriving back in his homeland, Father Agurto had an illustrious career, serving the last years of his life as a parish priest and diocesan missionary, much beloved by those to whom he ministered.

Agurto published a long letter in the newspaper *El Nuble* for November 14, 1857 in which he complained "about the increasing number of *ceranderos* (quack doctors) ruining the health of those placed in their care."

In 1862, Agurto became chaplain and director of the House of San Francisco Javier in Concepcion and there he wrote a 396 page book entitled *Directorio Pronutario de los Ejercicios Espirituales del Gran Padre San Ignacio de Loyola* which was published at Santiago by *El Independiente Press*.

Maximiano Agurto died on October 14, 1870 and was buried the next day from the parish church of Concepcion in the "cemetery of this city." His passing was prominently noted in the local secular press. Father Maximiano Agurto was but one of those unheralded priests who served the pioneer Church in California. Catholics of that time were greatly indebted to the ministries of these good men.

DOROTEO AMBRIS (d. 1883)

Doroteo Ambris was an ecclesiastical student who responded to the invitation of serving the People of God in the newly–established Diocese of Both Californias. He was one of the trio of seminarians who arrived with Bishop Francisco Garcia Diego y Moreno in December, 1841.

Young Ambris continued his studies under the personal direction of the prelate, first at Santa Barbara, and later at the seminary founded at Santa Ines. The youthful native of Mexico was ordained to the priesthood, at Mission Santa Barbara, on January 1, 1846, by Bishop Garcia Diego.

His first appointment was to San Carlos Borromeo, at Monterey, from which he occasionally visited San Antonio and Soledad. After the arrival, in early 1851, of Bishop Joseph Sadoc Alemany, Father Ambris was transferred to Mission San Antonio as its resident pastor, where he resided until his death on February 5, 1883.

The last resident priest at San Antonio, Father Ambris shared the hardships and privations of his parishioners and although the bishop offered him other appointments where he could be more at ease, the dedicated cleric elected to remain with those who needed him most. His remains were interred in the sanctuary of Mission San Antonio, where, according to Zephyrin Engelhardt, the "Franciscan Fathers (are) awaiting with him the call to rise on the Last Day."

Father Joachim Adam related, for the readers of *Ave Maria*, his visit to San Antonio, in 1867, and his reflections on its legendary pastor:

I was very anxious to make his acquaintance. He was the only Mexican secular priest in the diocese, had the early history of the country treasured up in his memory, and was eye–witness to many facts connected with the secularization of the missions and the surrender of the country to the United States. Father Ambris came to California when quite young, as a seminarist to the first Bishop of California, the Right Rev. Garcia Diego, and was it seems the Benjamin of his Grace. Whether saying Mass, at table, or traveling, young Ambris was always at the bishop's side. Many are the amusing anecdotes I have heard from the lips of this good father, and many the pleasant hours I spent in his company, amused at their recital. Among others was one in which the good father himself was a leading character—one which marks the almost patriarchal simplicity of the persons concerned. It was the 3rd of October, eve of the Feast of St. Francis of Assisi; the bishop, calling Ambris, told him to go to the tower and ring the bells, as customary on the eve of great festivals, in honor of the Seraphic Founder of the Franciscan Order. The young man did as he was told; but while in the tower, an old friar being much annoyed by the sound of the bells at this unusual time, and not understanding the reason of their ringing, called one of the lay brothers and asked who was making such a noise. Being told that it was young Ambris, he ordered the door of the belfry to be locked. The seminarian having finished his commission, came down only to find himself locked in, and although he made all the noise he possibly could there was no one around to hear him. So he had to stay where he was, and bide his chances. Dinner–time came; but when the dinner–bell rang, poor Ambris had to make up his mind to keep fast in honor of St. Francis, whether he willed it or not. The aged bishop, going to the table as usual, asked for his seminarian; being told that Father had him locked up in the bell–tower, he felt displeased, and without saying a word he retired to his room without touching the dinner. The poor old friar did the same. Meantime, Ambris being still a prisoner for his apparent misconduct in the eyes of an ancient dignitary of the house, the bishop finally gave orders for his liberation. As soon as he came out, the old father spoke to him in a complaining manner for having gone to ring the bells on his own hook—but what was his dismay— and consternation when told that it was done by the order of his superior, the bishop, and that his grace was grieved and displeased with the good friar for having locked him in. The latter at once went to the bishop's room and humbly apologized for his conduct and the grief it had caused him, stating that if he had known his grace had ordered the bells to be rung he would not have interfered. The two aged men shed tears, embraced each other, and they concluded that as Ambris was now at liberty to join them they would go to dinner, which they accordingly did.

Twice afterwards I had the pleasure of visiting San Antonio, and each time found Father Ambris at home. This good priest wishes only to live and die amid the ruins of San Antonio. He was the first, and so far the last parish priest, *propria dictus*, appointed in California at the time that Canon Law was in full force this country then belonging to Mexico.

JOSE IGNACIO MAXIMO ARGUELLO (1781–c. 1815)

San Gabriel Mission was the scene of an event in the early fall of 1809, which brought much joy and satisfaction to the missionaries, neophytes and settlers. Father José Ignacio Maximo Argüello, the son of Captain José Dario Arguello of Santa Barbara, returned to his birthplace and there offered his first Solemn Mass for the residents of San Gabriel. It was indeed a happy occurrence for Father Argüello was the first native Californian raised to the priesthood.

Jose's father, later to become the most prominent, influential and respected man in California, had been in the company of soldiers who, in July of 1781, escorted forty families of recruits by the way of the Colorado River to San Gabriel. The group lingered at the mission until March of 1782, before moving on to establish the *Presidio* at Santa Barbara.

The wife of the youthful ensign, Ignacia, was about to give birth and remained behind at the mission. On June 8th, the infant son was born and that same day was baptized by Fray Miguel Sanchez in the mission church. The oldest of nine children born to the Argüellos, José grew to manhood at Santa Barbara. He was the first person to be confirmed in the original chapel of the *presidio* by Fray Junípero Serra in 1783.

When he later manifested a desire to study for the priesthood, José's father sent him to Mexico, where he pursued the necessary philosophical and theological studies. Ordained for the diocesan ministry at Sonora, Father Argüello sought permission for a visit to his family and friends in Santa Barbara. It was enroute that California's proto–priest paused at San Gabriel.

As soon as Fray José Maria de Zalvidea heard about the impending visit, he began preparations for the solemn festivities. The mission choir was rehearsed and all was put in readiness. The Old Mission church was decorated as never before, with every imaginable color of flowers. Zalvidea preached an eloquent sermon on the priesthood, noting that young Argüello was only the first in what would be a long line of native responses to the call of the Gospel.

The event was duly recorded in the margins of the *Registro de Bautismos*, where opposite Argüello's baptismal entry it was written: "He was a priest, and on passing by way of this mission, he sang a High Mass."

The new priest journeyed north and was present for the dedication of the new church at San Buenaventura Mission on September 6, 1809. He offered the first Mass in that historic church on the following Sunday. Argüello visited with his parents and then returned to his diocese in Mexico. Nothing more is recorded about the priest except the notation by Hubert Howe Bancroft that he "later became curate of Torin, on the Yaqui River, in Sonora."

Father Argüello was subsequently killed in an uprising of the Yaquis and thus won another distinction, that of having a place on the roll of California's martyrology.

JOSE DE LOS SANTOS AVILA (1819–1846)

James Cardinal Gibbons once observed that "the life of a missionary priest is never written nor can it be. He has no Boswell. His biographer may recount the churches he erected, the schools he founded, the works of religion and charity he inaugurated and fostered, the sermons he preached, the children he catechized, the converts he received into the fold; and this is already a great deal, but it only touches upon the surface of that devoted life. There is no memoir of his private daily life of usefulness and of his sacred and confidential relations with his flock—all this is hidden with Christ in God, and is registered only by the recording angel."

One such man was José de los Santos Avila, whose privilege it was to be the first vocation to the secular priesthood for California. The son of Guadalupe Avila and María Antonia Linares was born at Monterey, on January 22, 1819. According to the register book of San Carlos Borromeo, José de los Santos Avila was baptized the following day by Fray Juan Amorós.

The youngster's education was acquired mostly from the various friars attached to the mission. In his earliest years, José was recognized as a highly intelligent and industrious individual. He served as secretary at Branciforte and then went to Mexico for his clerical training. Returning with Bishop Francisco García Diego y Moreno, in 1841, he continued his studies at the seminary operated by the prelate at Santa Barbara and later at Inés. José was among those present, on May 4, 1844, when the first ecclesiastical seminary in the Californias was established under the patronage of *Nuestra Señora de Guadalupe*. The twenty–seven year old native of Monterey was ordained priest at Santa Barbara on January 1, 1846, by Bishop García Diego and, early the following month, was placed in charge of Santa Clara and San Jose Missions.

Avila's was the shortest span of ministerial service in the Golden State's annals. He succumbed unexpectedly after only eighty–four days of priestly work, on March 25th, at Santa Clara. The initial priest to die among the secular clergy in California was interred beneath the Epistle side of the altar in the old mission church. A simple clay plaque recounted his services to God's People.

The ever–so–short ministry of José de los Santos Avila recalls the description of priestly dedication penned by the Jesuit theologian, Karl Rahner:

> The priest is not an angel sent from heaven. He is a man chosen from among men, a member of the Church, a Christian.
>
> Remaining man and Christian, he begins to speak to others about the Word of God.
>
> That Word is not his own. No, he comes to serve only because God has told him to proclaim His Word.
>
> Perhaps he has not entirely understood it himself. Perhaps he adulterates it, but he believes it and despite his fears he knows that he must communicate God's Word to his people.
>
> For must not some one of us say something about God, about eternal life, about the majesty of grace in our sanctified being. Must not some one of us speak of sin, the judgement and the mercy of God?
>
> So dear friends, pray for him. Carry him so that he might be able to sustain others by bringing to them the mystery of God's love revealed in Christ Jesus.

JOAQUIN BOT Y CUSANT (1836–1903)

At the time of his demise, Father Joaquin Bot y Cusant was eulogized by a local southland newspaper as "one of our oldest and best priests." He certainly was that—and considerably more. Born in 1836, at Mataro, in the environs of Barcelona, the young Joaquin was recruited for the Diocese of Monterey–Los Angeles, by Bishop Thaddeus Amat, a close friend of the Bot family.

We are told by a contemporary essay in *The Tidings* that Joaquin "early evinced a predilection for a religious life which his pious mother fostered." After making preliminary clerical studies in Spain, the youthful Bot came to the United States and completed his training at Saint Vincent's Seminary in Cape Girardeau, Missouri.

Ordained December 12, 1862, Father Bot was assigned to Our Lady of Sorrows in Santa Barbara. He afterwards served at Santa Ines Mission and later at San Gabriel and San Luis Obispo Missions. He was pastor at San Gabriel for many years. Bot's delicate health was further complicated by a fall from a horse. In 1887, he returned to his homeland "in the hope that his native air would assist in restoring him to moderate health."

An article in a recent issue of *Antiques and Fine Art* tells that during that visit to Spain, Father Bot "acquired a substantial number of paintings which he brought back to California." In his essay, Norman Neuerburg suggests that the priest purchased the entire stock of an art dealer thinking that "there might be a market for religious paintings" in Southern California. It appears to have been a poor investment, however, because of the financial "bust" that befell the southland in the late 1880s.

In any event, Bot returned with as many as eighty–seven paintings, twenty–one of which are still at the Southwest Museum and thirty at San Gabriel Mission. The key to identifying the paintings lies in a numbering system which the priest wrote in pencil or black ink on the back of the stretchers and frames.

With few exceptions, the Bot collection was religious in nature, with several Old Testament subjects. About a third are mid–19th century paintings and there is even one chromolithograph after Carlo Dolci. Others of the paintings are copies of Raphael and Murillo. There is one landscape, possibly mid–European and three genre paintings of Spanish scenes, two by Grensner and one by Pinals dated 1854.

According to Neuerburg, one of the religious paintings, *Madonna of the Ring*, is attributed to Antonio Palomino with a date of 1690. A mid–19th century painting of *Salome with the Head of John the Baptist* is a copy of one still at San Gabriel Mission.

The year after Bot's death, Charles F. Lummis was instrumental in raising funds for purchasing the unsold paintings and books accumulated by the priest. Most of the books went to the Los Angeles Public Library, while the paintings were consigned to the Southwest Society of the Archaeological Institute of America, the predecessor of the Southwest Museum.

Father Bot succumbed on July 14, 1903 at Los Angeles. He was buried from old Saint Vincent's Church at ceremonies attended by friends, parishioners and admirers of many years. In his homily for the funeral Mass, Bishop Thomas J. Conaty aptly referred to the beloved priest as "the last of those fine Catalan clergymen who brought the refinement and culture of Spanish society to America."

ROBERT E. BRENNAN (1908–1986)

The late Msgr. Robert E. Brennan (1908–1986) was a long–time priest attached to the Archdiocese of Los Angeles. Ordained in 1932, he served for many years as head of the Music and Liturgy Commission. He was also pastor of several parishes, including Our Lady of the

Holy Rosary (Sun Valley), Saint Elizabeth (Altadena) and Saint Gregory (Los Angeles).

The monsignor was deeply interested in liturgical art and, over the years, gathered a rather formidable collection of treasures from earlier times. Twenty–nine of those items recently found their way to San Fernando Mission and the Archival Center where they will be permanently enshrined.

The four Russian items in the collection include a 19th century Christ Pantocrater with enamel and silver reza, an icon of the Blessed Virgin, and enamel decorated bronze icon of Saint John Chrysostom and a twenty–three inch hanging vigil light.

The copper reliquary fashioned by William Van Erp of San Francisco is especially imposing. Its peaked case has a pair of doors which open to reveal twelve relics. The flared rectangular base has raised lettering which reads PRETIOSA.

Another reliquary, this one attributed to Egidius Weinert of Cologne, is designed in the form of a cross with ornamented rock crystal, colored stones and neillo. A final Spanish colonial gilt–wood reliquary, dating from the 18th century, encases a splinter of the true cross. Its frame, in the scrolling foliate form, served as an anchor for the tiny silver case.

Oldest of the items are two ceramic tiles from the 12th or 13th century, reportedly removed from Forde Abbey, near Salisbury. Another memento from those times is a carved and polychromed wooden figure of a seated bishop holding an empty reliquary.

A bronze statue of Saint Paul stands out prominently in the collection. Signed by J. Lambert Rucki, the stylized seventeen inch figure is resting his hands on a downturned sword.

There are four enamel plaques, all attributed to Gertrude Stohr of Vienna. One is a two–sided Austrian Crucifixion scene, another represents Saint Elizabeth and five monks, a third portrays the Blessed Mother and Child and a final one shows the Last Supper in the shape of a cross inset with twelve small tiger's eye stones. A twenty–three inch bronze figure of Saint Joseph is also attributed to Egidius Weinert of Cologne. It is contrasted by a companion cast–iron relief plaque of Saint Michael, the archangel.

Surely the most attractive item in the collection is a 13 x 12 inch mother–of–pearl creche set which can be illuminated by a hidden light. This beautiful Nativity scene is displayed in the convento building of San Fernando Mission each year at Christmas time.

The Blessed Mother is featured in three other items: a Yugoslavian icon on a wooden panel, a carved wood figural group of Virgin and Child from the German Tyrol and a carved rosewood and ivory portrayal signed by Heuvelmans on a stepped onyx base. There are also carved bone figures of the Blessed Mother and two kneeling figures, along with a Mexican polychrome wooden figure representing God holding a sceptre in his right hand.

This fine collection of artifacts will be intermingled with the other historical treasures on exhibit at San Fernando Mission and the Archival Center. Msgr. Brennan will long be remembered for these artistic gems.

JEAN–BAPTISTE–ABRAHAM BROUILLET (1813–1884)

Father Jean–Baptiste–Abraham Brouillet was a priest who wandered in and out of California's Catholic heritage on several occasions. He merits being remembered among the Golden State's ecclesial pioneers.

Born December 11, 1813 in the Province of Quebec, the son of Jean–Baptiste and Charlotte (Drogue–Lajoie) Brouillet was educated at the minor seminary of Saint Hyacinthe, 1826–1833. After taking his theological studies at the local major seminary, the young Brouillet was ordained priest on August 27, 1837 by Ignace Bourget, Bishop of Montreal in the old St. Jacques Cathedral.

Father Brouillet taught philosophy at the College of Chambly in Quebec from 1837 until 1844, during which time he also served as associate priest at the local parish of St. Joseph. In 1841–1842, he was editor of *Melanges Religieux*, the diocesan newspaper for Montreal. He also functioned as pastor at Saint George in Henryville (1842–1846) and Saint Marguerite in L'Acadie (1846–1847).

In 1847 Brouillet received permission to work with Augustin–Magliore Blanchet, the legendary Bishop of Walla Walla in the Territory of Oregon (which is now the state of Washington). Father Brouillet became the first canonical pastor of San Francisco in December of 1848. Zephyrin Engelhardt recorded that finding "neither the town nor the mission a suitable place to stay," he resided temporarily at Santa Clara.

The administrator of the vacant Diocese of Both Californias, Fray Jose Maria Gonzalez Rubio, asked Brouillet to erect a church at San Francisco. Brouillet began by arranging an oratory in a room of the house belonging to Major James A. Hardie, military commander of the United States troops at the port of San Francisco. It was there that Holy Mass was offered for the first time at the former Yerba Buena, on the third Sunday after Pentecost, 1849.

A journal kept by Father Anthony Langlois states that "Religion now began to be practiced a little in spite of the natural obstacles thrown in its way by the pursuit of gold; gold, of which all had come in search from every part of the globe; in spite, moreover, of the drawbacks of uncertain employment, of various inconveniences, of the inter-minglings of people, strangers to one another, and this in tents for a considerable number; in spite of the temptations of barrooms and saloons on every hand for the multitudes that frequented them, to amuse themselves, drink and spend their time; in spite of the smallness of what was at once church and residence, and the poorness of its exterior; all taken in conjunction with the shortcomings of its curate [Father Langlois himself] who was called upon to speak English, Spanish and French in the same sermon, that he might be understood by all; as well as the lack of time needed to go and invite Catholic households to church and let them know that it was possible for a person to save his soul in San Francisco."

During his brief time in California, Brouillet organized the parish of Saint Francis, built the first church and invited the Jesuits to San Francisco, all noble and important contributions to the story of California Catholicism.

Unhappily for California, Father Brouillet was recalled to Walla Walla by his bishop. In 1872–1874, he was sent to Washington, D.C. where he and General Charles Ewing organized what became the Bureau of Catholic Indian Affairs. He remained there for the following decade as the official agent for the American hierarchy.

Death claimed the veteran missionary on February 5, 1884 at Providence Hospital in the District of Columbia. His funeral was conducted by Father Louis–Placide Chapelle, later Archbishop of Santa Fe and New Orleans. Brouillet was buried at Mount Olivet Cemetery where there is a monument to his memory.

ANTHONY BROUWERS (1912–1964)

Monsignor Anthony Brouwers (1912–1964) was recognized internationally as an "Apostle of the Missions." His memory is very much alive today, even a quarter century after his premature demise.

Born in Los Angeles, young "Tony" Brouwers attended Sacred Heart Parochial School, Cathedral High and Los Angeles College. He was ordained a priest in Rome on December 8, 1938. A few years later, he was appointed to the archdiocesan matrimonial curia. In 1947, he became secretary to the then Bishop Timothy Manning and the following year, he was named director for the Propagation of the Faith.

Always a popular speaker, the energetic young priest was a favorite of young and old alike. In 1950, he established the Saint Vibiana's Guild to encourage and train aspiring artists. Five years later the far–sighted priest "began one of the most advanced and visionary developments in the Church" with his establishment of the Lay Mission Helpers, a group of people who volunteered to serve a minimum of three years in the missionary outreach of the Church.

The next year, he founded the Mission Doctors for the same purpose. Since the first departure ceremony on July 4, 1956, over 800 people have been sent to the missions, all because a dynamic priest had the courage to pursue a dream. Shortly thereafter, Father Brouwers began establishing a network of Mission Circles whose function it was and is to offer their prayers and financial support for the missionary program. Over 200 of the circles were ultimately erected.

Carpenters, teachers, nurses, pilots, administrators, doctors and journalists were only a few of the professional and non–professional people recruited for the missions. Before long they were running hospitals, operating schools and editing newspapers throughout Africa, Latin America, New Guinea and parts of the American southwest.

Brouwers was honored by two pontiffs when he was made a papal chamberlain by Pope Pius XII in 1950 and a domestic prelate by Pope John XXIII in 1959. The Papal Volunteer program inaugurated by the Holy See was modeled in great part on the program developed in Los Angeles. The monsignor was active in a host of other projects too. And somehow he found time to administer the busy, inner–city parish of Saint Paul between 1959 and 1964.

Monsignor Brouwers made four extended tours of the African continent to determine the needs of the missions there and to visit the Lay Mission Helpers already at work in that huge area. He authored a weekly column, "Mission Chats" for *The Tidings* wherein he kept alive the spiritual and physical challenges of the missions.

His final missionary labor was on the frontier of suffering Though stricken with spinal cancer in his last years, he never slackened his pace or lessened his enthusiasm. As mentioned in an editorial by Alphonse Antzcak in *The Tidings*, "it should not be forgotten that there was a holy man here named Anthony Brouwers. *Que en paz desance.* "

ALEXANDER BUCCI (1875–1959)

Surely one of the most colorful and memorable clerics ever to function in California's southland was Father Alexander Bucci (1875–1959). He bears the distinction of being the only priest in California's religious annals to have been publicly reprimanded on the pages of the local Catholic newspaper.

Ordained on May 14, 1899 for service in the Italian Diocese of Larino, Bucci came to the United States in 1905. He served briefly at Saint Patrick's Cathedral in New York City and then journeyed west to Salt Lake City.

Coming to the Diocese of Monterey–Los Angeles in March of 1906, he was assigned to serve the local Italian community at Saint Peter's Parish in downtown Los Angeles. He officiated there for the following twelve years. In 1918, Father Bucci was transferred to Cayucas. Later that year, he was appointed to Tres Piños, a community in Central California. It was there that Bucci's actions began getting him into trouble.

A resourceful man, he raised funds for his poverty–stricken parish by installing a distillery in the sacristy of the church. Those were prohibition times and because of the eighteenth amendment, manufacture of alcohol was a Federal crime. Though permission was obtainable for the production and use of altar wine, Bucci's activities went considerably beyond acceptable practices. On several occasions, he was warned by Chancery officials.

In the summer of 1922, Bucci was formally arrested for violation of the Volsted Act. Officials agreed not to prosecute if the Bishop of Monterey–Los Angeles would administer an appropriate penalty.

Since there was some question about Bucci's canonical status, Bishop John J. Cantwell directed the priest to return to his native diocese. By then an American citizen, Bucci adamantly refused on the grounds that the bishop had no right to punish a priest for violation of a public law.

It was then that Cantwell, invoking Canon 985, suspended the priest and had the following notice placed in *The Tidings*: "It is officially announced that a certain priest, by name Alexander Bucci, for many months past and at the present time, has not and does not enjoy the faculties of the Diocese of Los Angeles–San Diego."

Bucci never acknowledged or abided by the canonical decree or the revocation of his faculties. He took up residence in Burbank, performing baptisms, marriages and funerals, often from a makeshift chapel in his sister's home. In December of 1933, Father Bucci asked the bishop for reinstatement. "There's nothing to reinstate," he was told. "Return to your diocese in Italy!" A letter from the Apostolic Delegate re–affirmed Cantwell's earlier decision.

It was then that Bucci "went public." He began performing funerals and weddings at Forest Lawn Cemetery, something that especially annoyed Cantwell who expressly forbade all his priests to officiate there. Bucci went a step further. On at least one documented occa-

sion, he celebrated Mass in the funeral parlor of Godeau and Martinoni.

In May of 1935, Father Bucci gained national notoriety by offering Holy Mass in the "Wee Kirk o' the Heather" chapel at Forest Lawn for Trent Durkin, a popular teenage film star who had been killed in an auto crash. The Los Angeles *Examiner* featured a photograph of "Father A. Bucci, retired Catholic priest of Burbank" leading a procession of mourners to the grave.

Then, two months later, Bucci once again hit the headlines when the Los Angeles *Times* reported that he officiated at Forest Lawn for the funeral of Leland Deveraigne, known in Chicago's underworld as "two Gun Louis" Alterie. "Two Gun Louis" was killed when enemies fired twelve shotgun slugs into his body after he allegedly turned government informant on a bond case. Another story in the *Examiner* said that "Bucci, now resigned from an active pastorate, was a friend of Alterie."

Father Bucci had some rather shady relatives too. He was a brother–in–law of Nicola Pietrantonio who was assassinated in a raid by Federal agents looking for alcohol. Reports of that incident stated that "the Pietrantonio home served also as a private chapel for Father Alexander Bucci."

Bucci continued his unorthodox ministry until his own health began to fail. In his later years he lived quietly in Burbank with a younger sister. He remained on close terms with Msgr. Martin Cody Keating and was reconciled to the Church prior to his death. He was the first priest interred in the "new" San Fernando Mission Cemetery in 1959.

ALEXANDER BUCKLER (1883–1930)

Father Alexander Buckler (1883–1930) came to Southern California in mid 1903, after serving the earliest years of his ministry in Oakdale, Minnesota. Bishop Thomas J. Conaty appointed the German–born priest to Santa Ines in July of 1904. There he remained for over twenty years caring for the spiritual needs of his people and restoring what was earlier the nineteenth of the Franciscan missionary outposts along *El Camino Real*.

The physical pace of those days was staggering. One Sunday a month, Father Buckler conducted the Liturgy at Santa Ines, one at Los Alamos, another at Sisquoc and whenever there was a fifth Sunday, he journeyed to the village schoolhouse of Las Cruces for Holy Mass. Buckler's indomitable spirit and tenacity of purpose served him well in his great desire to restore the Old Mission and at no time would he allow himself to be discouraged or swayed from that purpose.

Though he was a man of aristocratic birth, reared in

culture and refinement, Father Buckler's affable, genial and sympathetic disposition endeared him to old and young alike. The welcome mat was always out and many "knights of the road" enjoyed hospitality at Santa Ines Mission.

When Father Buckler died, on March 7, 1930, John Steven McGroarty made the long journey to Santa Barbara for his funeral. Three weeks later, California's poet laureate had this to say in his Sunday column for the Los Angeles *Times*:

> A while back, we made a sad journey to Santa Barbara. It was to attend the funeral of an old friend who has been our friend these long and many years, and who also was a friend to many who had few friends in this world.

> We started out on the high road before the break of day in order to be in time for the funeral at the Old Mission Church of Santa Barbara. It was a thrilling experience to speed upon the King's Highway and along the shores of the sunset sea as dawn was breaking.

> But our heart was heavy as lead within us notwithstanding all the splendor that Nature was showering upon us. We could not help but know our friend would never behold again the dawn of a new day upon this good earth.

> It is about Alexander Buckler that we are talking. For long years he had been the *Padre* at the Old Franciscan Mission of Santa Ines which stands still, altho in ruins, upon a sunlit mesa between Santa Barbara and San Luis Obispo.

> When *Padre* Alexander was first sent to the Mission Santa Ines the roof had fallen and the floor was littered with the debris that the vandals had flung upon it. With him was a devoted niece who kept his house. Together they cleaned away the litter of the years and rescued from dust and decay sacred old vestments of priceless value, and many another relic that museums might well quarrel over today.

> They cleared the place and made it clean and holy again. They lighted candles on the old altars where the earlier ones had burned away. They struck again the listening ear of the morning and of the evening music of the *Angelus* from the rusted Mission bell. The house that was fallen was reared anew.

> This was a great thing that *Padre* Alexander had done with the help of his devoted kinswoman. What he did was to fully restore that traditional hospitality of the missions in the days of their glory when their doors were never closed against the stranger.

> Perhaps some day there will be a monument builded in memory of this wonderful man, but it will not matter whether a monument be builded or not. He builded his own monument in the remembering heart of God, Who knows and sees all things, even to the sparrow's fall.

> The life of a man so generous, so charitable, so forgiving and so good constitutes a monument greater than any that can be builded of bronze or hewn of stone.

> In the Old Mission Church of Santa Barbara he was given, as he lay silent in his coffin, the greatest honors that his church is able to bestow upon any man. Had he been a cardinal in scarlet robes he could not have been more honored.

JUAN CABALLERIA (1861–1932)

A. LEARNED SCHOLAR

Father Juan Caballeria (1861–1932) was known throughout California as "a gentleman of great energy and versatility. Early in his priestly life he decided to follow the example of a distant cousin, Archbishop Joseph Sadoc Alemany, by pursuing his apostolic activities in California. Prior to coming to the Diocese of Monterey–Los Angeles, the Barcelona–born priest had achieved prominence in his native land as a journalist and a literary man of distinction.

Father Caballeria's initial assignments in Southern California were at Riverside and San Bernardino. He was given the pastorate of the old plaza church of *Nuestra Señora de los Angeles*, on July 14, 1903.

During his years in Los Angeles, Father Caballeria's lingual abilities enabled him to serve the cosmopolitan needs of his English, French, Basque, Italian and Spanish–speaking parishioners. Father Caballeria was a great organizer and in his time at the plaza groups such as the Saint Cecilia Choral Society, the Sons of Montezuma, the League of the Sacred Heart and the Christian Doctrine Society functioned as integral participants of parochial life.

The poverty of his people and disrepair of their church prompted Father Caballeria to dispose of his personal collection of thirty–four paintings which he had amassed over the years. Purchased by the Southwest Society of the Archeological Institute of America, the valuable works of art are presently displayed at the *Casa de Adobe*.

"A gentleman of ripe scholarship," Father Caballeria was "known to all over the coast for his literary ability." He had taught in Barcelona's *Academia Taquigrafia* and the *Colegio Josefino* before coming to the United States. In his adopted land, Father Caballeria wrote a textbook on phonetic stenography and, in 1892, published his *History of the City of Santa Barbara California From Its Discovery to Our Own Days*. That volume, now quite rare, was reissued in a limited edition of one hundred copies, in 1928, by the Schauer Printing Studio of Santa Barbara. Shortly after the turn of the century, the Times–Index Press published Father Caballeria's 130–page *History of the San Bernardino Valley From the Padres to the Pioneers, 1810–1851*.

It was during his tenure at San Bernardino that Father Caballeria founded *La Actualidad*, an eight–page weekly "devoted to the instruction in Catholic truth and doctrine" of the Spanish people in Southern California. That paper flourished between 1895 and 1902.

Though forced by ill health to spend the last of his years in retirement, Father Caballeria kept abreast with happenings in Southern California, hoping always that one day he would be able to resume the active apostolate. When death claimed Father Juan Caballeria, on January 5, 1932, California and Spain lost a good priest, one amply endowed with a love for ancient historical lore, and the spirit that impels men to search for knowledge.

JUAN CABALLERIA (1861–1932)

B. CABALLERIA COLLECTION

In the fall of 1904, the Southwest Society of the Archaeological Institute of America announced that it had acquired the Caballeria Collection of thirty–four paintings which hung in the old Franciscan missions prior to secularization. The Spanish–born originator of the collection, Father Juan Caballeria (d. 1932), had amassed the paintings during the early years of his ministry, in California. Caballeria was well acquainted with the area's Catholic heritage. He had published a history of the city of Santa Barbara in 1892, and a decade later an illustrated tome on the development of the Church in the San Bernardino Valley between 1810 and 1851. The indefatigable priest even found time to publish *La Actualidad* from 1895 to 1902, a newspaper "devoted to the instruction in Catholic truth and doctrine" of the Spanish–speaking people in Southern California.

It was shortly after his arrival at the Church of *Nuestra Señora de los Angeles* that this last secular priest to serve the old Plaza found it necessary to sell his paintings to finance long–needed repairs on the dilapidated edifice. While many of the paintings were executed in Spain, several were obviously done in Mexico by artists who came to the New World soon after the conquest. One observer noted that the canvases "even in their crudity have high associations and value, not only for the artist but for the historian." Sixteen of the works predated 1700. The oldest is a depiction of Saint Anthony dating from the early 1600s. It had been purchased many years earlier from Father Doroteo Ambris at Mission San Antonio de Padua.

The painting of Our Lady of Sorrows had been brought from Mexico by the sea–expedition of 1769. By the texture of its canvas, the pattern of its stretcher, and the technique of its workmanship, the painting can easily be judged as belonging to the pre–1700 era. This artistic and historic masterpiece was pillaged from Mission San Gabriel about 1834, and purchased later by Father Joachim Bot. It has, perhaps, more intimate historical association with California than any other picture in the collection. Pre–eminent among the works is the "Madonna of the Ring." This excellently preserved canvas, with the empiric wreath of flowers, is unquestionably of Spanish origin. Aside from the floral garland, the workmanship is inevitably suggestive of Murillo. One writer noted that "it would be no artistic impiety to attribute it to him."

Although the Caballeria Collection was purchased for the relatively low price of $1,000 the paintings represented a collection of venerable works all intimately connected with the southland's ecclesiastical history for nearly 150 years. They are "all of a romantic association and record whose fame is world–wide."

Shortly after its acquisition by the Southwest Society of the Archaeological Institute of America, the Caballeria Collection was displayed in the Los Angeles Chamber of Commerce building. It was later moved to the Southwest Museum and is now at the Casa de Adobe. Few persons suspect how much old art, serious as well as ancient, there was in the Golden State before the coming of the Americans. The Caballeria Collection is but one example. There were others.

LEROY CALLAHAN (1900–1940)

Father Leroy Callahan (1900–1940) was "a Christ–like priest" ever anxious to extend "a kindly hand to those in need." His relatively short life was crammed with able achievements, any one of which would have assured him a prominent place in the southland's historical annals.

The Illinois–born Callahan studied at several schools in Nebraska, Kansas and Los Angeles prior to entering, in 1918, Saint Patrick's Seminary, Menlo Park, as a clerical aspirant for the Diocese of Monterey–Los Angeles. His theological training was pursued at Rome's North American College and Fribourg University. He was ordained to the priesthood by Bishop John J. Cantwell, on December 20, 1924.

After a short stint as curate at Saint Vibiana's Cathedral, Father Callahan returned to Fribourg where he completed his doctoral studies and a dissertation on the "Early Life of Serra."' His thorough and extensive research on California's pioneering missionary, though never published in monograph form, did appear in the Franciscan *Provincial Annals* between 1942 and 1944.

In 1926, Father Callahan was named director of the Confraternity of Christian Doctrine for the Diocese of Los Angeles–San Diego. Quickly and efficiently he "built up the model organization now adopted by practically every diocese throughout the country." New centers and chapels were erected, and, in 1928, Father Callahan inaugurated the first religious vacation school in the southland. He drafted and published a manual which found its way into almost every vacation school classroom in the United States.

Father Callahan was especially sensitive to the Church's obligation for the southland's Mexican–American community. He felt that among those people, most of them forcibly exiled from their native land, was as truly missionary in scope "as the evangelization of the heathen, with the sole difference that we are laboring amongst those who are Catholic by tradition."

Among the organizations he established to further that ideal were the Mexican Young Mens' Association, the Mexican Young Womens' Association and the *Damas Católicas*. Another of his foundations was the Santa Teresita Sanitorium for Mexican girls which was placed in charge of the Carmelite Sisters. For his tireless efforts on behalf of the Mexican–Americans, Father Callahan was honored, in 1929, by being named an honorary canon, or "blue monsignor," of the metropolitan chapter attached to *Guadalajara's Catedral de la Asunción de María Santisima*.

Father Callahan stated his concept of the lay apostolate thusly: "Not piety for piety's sake; rather personal piety as a preparation for God's work. Not study for its own sake; rather knowledge to better break the Bread of Life to others; Not action for activity sake; rather action which is directed to bring about the Peace of Christ in the Reign of Christ."

Through the years Father Callahan held numerous other posts. He cared for deaf mutes for many years and participated in most of the local activities of the Conference of Catholic Charities, as well as the broader–based Catholic Rural Life Program. He was successively administrator of San Antonio de Padua and pastor of Sacred Heart and Saint Bernard's Parishes in Los Angeles. Though the greater quantity of his work involved the various facets of the active apostolate, Father Callahan retained his scholarly interest. It was, in fact, his encyclopedic knowledge of the life and work of Fray Junípero Serra that inspired him to carry the work of California's first apostle to yet another generation.

ANGELO DELFINO CASANOVA (1833–1893)

Father Angelo Delfino Casanova (1833–1893), a native of Switzerland, began his studies for the ministry at *Il Colegio Brignole Sale Negroni* in Geneva. He was ordained priest May 26, 1860. Having been incardinated in the Diocese of Monterey–Los Angeles, at the suggestion of the prefect of Rome's Sacred Congregation of Propaganda Fide, Father Casanova journeyed to California, where he was welcomed on December 3rd by Bishop Thaddeus Amat, C.M.

After spending several months perfecting his English, Father Casanova was sent, in September of 1861, to San Juan Bautista. Two months later, he was placed in charge of the parish of the Immaculate Heart of Mary in the Pajaro valley.

Casanova was subsequently transferred to Santa Cruz and there he remained until October 28, 1868. He was then named Vicar Forane for the northern part of the diocese and entrusted with the pastorate of San Carlos Borromeo at Monterey. At Monterey, Father Casanova built a rectory and a schoolhouse. He also looked after the abandoned mission at Carmel, where Fray Junípero had been buried in 1784.

Casanova became a close friend of Mrs. Leland Stanford and it was he who suggested that she commemorate the arrival of Serra at Monterey with an appropriate monument. In the late 1880s he gave Mrs. Stanford his extensive collection of California music which later came into the possession of Stanford University.

Though Father Casanova was the recipient of many benefactions from Mrs. Stanford, he never retained them for any other than ecclesial needs. His account book indicates that he was exceedingly generous. In October of 1892 , for example, he made a sizable personal contribution toward the erection of a new church at Watsonville. According to an entry in the *Libro de Difuntos* for the Old Mission at Carmel, Father Casanova opened the grave of Fray Junípero Serra on July 3, 1882, in order "to satisfy the desires of many to behold the tombs of the reverend Fathers buried in the sanctuary." He removed the still–preserved violet stoles and distributed them as mementos to local residents. The tombs were then closed and remained unopened until Harry Downie's work in 1943.

Late in 1891, Edward J. Nolan visited San Carlos Mission and, in a subsequent address to the Catholic Club of Philadelphia, he recalled that Father Casanova customarily came to Carmel every year to offer Mass in the abandoned church: He "read the service in a melodious voice wearing, as he afterwards told us, one of the chasubles originally belonging to Father Junípero."

> The sermon was on the parable of the tribute money. It was in Spanish and although we were unable to follow the discourse with precision, it was certainly voluble and doubtless eloquent.
>
> After Mass we called on Father Casanova and were delightfully entertained by him with an account of the Mission, notes of his experiences and anecdotes of Fr. Junípero Serra.

Casanova's health was never robust and during the winter of 1892–1893 he suffered from the effects of cancer. On March 11, 1893, after a life of hard work and privation, he passed to his eternal reward at Monterey. In one of his articles, the late James Culleton praised Father Angelo Delfino Casanova, noting that "he deserves a lasting shrine in the hearts of all Californians. He, and he alone, saved the most famous of all missions from ruin."

JOHN CASSIN (1847–1932)

John Cassin (1847–1932), a native of New York City, was brought by his parents to San Francisco in 1856. After expressing his wishes of becoming a priest, he was sent by Archbishop Joseph Sadoc Alemany to All Hallows College in Ireland for his theological studies.

Ordained in 1874, he was assigned to Marin County. Later he served for a while at Mission Dolores in San Francisco and, in 1878, he was appointed to Bodie, where he organized a parish for that distant mining town.

In her book, *The Story of Bodie*, Ella M. Cain told about Father Cassin's pastorate in the "rip roaring, hell–bent mining camps of Bodie and Lundy." The narrative was written in the casual language used by miners.

> It was about '78 that a young priest came to these parts. His name John B. Cassin. Think of the Archbishop sendin' a young, inexperienced missionary up to a hell roarin' camp like Bodie. Well, he proved equal to the task, an afore he left he'd received a liberal education on human nature in the rough.
>
> Comin' in on the stage coach he was sittin opposite a sportin' woman an' a gambler. It was a cold day in winter an' the father had a big muffler wrapped around his church collar, but when the talk went to the point where it offended him, he pulled off his muffler an' asserted himself. Not another word was spoken until the stage pulled into Bodie.
>
> When the news was spread around that a real sky pilot had invaded the camp, some rejoiced, some sneered. He had been commissioned to build a Catholic church, so he set out to do it, and later on he found the people were more generous than pious.
>
> The funds were quickly subscribed, an' a site for the church was given by the minin' company. It was on a rocky hillside on the eastern slope of town; but from there on Father Cassin's difficulties increased. He seemed to be left to his own resources as to plannin', architecture, etc.
>
> He could be seen pacin' up and down over the rocky hillside, where the church was to be built, in a befuddled sort of way, and if some kind hearted carpenters hadn't taken pity on him he would probably be walkin' around there yet.
>
> Well, after a time, the church stood completed, a very plain sort of buildin' with a steep, slantin' roof an' lots of windows, an' a heap larger than was needed for th' people who attended.

> It was generally so cold in winter durin' services that the congregation did ample penance for their sins. The archbishop had told the father to honor the man who had done the most towards its construction, so he called it St. John's, after hisself.
>
> Father Cassin was called on many a time to go to the dyin', those who died in bed, an' those who died with their boots on. At one time he was called after a shootin' fracas. The feller with a bullet in him was lyin' on the saloon floor in a pool of blood. When the priest bent over him, he thought it was his adversary comin' at him, again he pulled the trigger of his gun, an' the bullet went just over the priest's head.
>
> Many a time a dispute that would have ordinarily ended in gun play was left to him to settle; yes–siree, Father Cassin was known to be fair an' unprejudiced.

Father Cassin spent five years at Bodie. He was a zealous, patient and self–sacrificing man whose deeds of kindness were long remembered in that mining community by peoples of all religious and other persuasions.

By the time of his demise as pastor of Santa Rosa, Father Cassin had reportedly "been in Holy Orders longer than any other priest in California." Interestingly, what was left of the mines and mills of Bodie were destroyed by fire on the very day of Cassin's death.

JOHN J. CAWLEY (1882–1953)

The late Monsignor John J. Cawley "had no other model than the great High Priest. His sublime faith, childlike in its simplicity, was the key to his character, even as it was the inspiration and motivation of all his work." He was born March 31, 1882, "of goodly Sligo stock, which, long strengthened by discipline of the spirit, could gladly sacrifice the vain pleasures of life for the enduring rewards of religion."

Sensing the world's greatest needs at an early age, he decided to dedicate himself to the noblest service on earth, that of ministering to men in the things that pertain to God. John studied for the priesthood at Maynooth College, where he acquired a broad culture and a deep grasp of the sacred sciences, so much so that in the halls of his *alma mater* he is remembered as one of her finest students. He was raised to the priesthood, June 17, 1906. Following ordination, Father Cawley did graduate work in the Dunboyne establishment and taught classics at Saint Mary's College, the Achonry diocesan seminary.

The Irish–born priest came to Los Angeles, in 1909, at the invitation of Bishop Thomas J. Conaty. He served as curate at Holy Cross Church and Saint Vibiana's Cathedral and later at Saint Patrick's in Watsonville. In December of 1917, Father Cawley was named chancellor of the Diocese of Monterey–Los Angeles and secretary to the newly installed Bishop John J. Cantwell.

Three years later he was made a papal chamberlain. In 1924, Monsignor Cawley was entrusted with the pastorate of the cathedral and appointed Vicar General of the Diocese of Los Angeles–San Diego. The following year, Pope Pius XI honored him with the rank of prothonotary apostolic.

During the twenty–nine years Monsignor Cawley served the People of God at Saint Vibiana's, he built and maintained La Immaculada and Holy Rosary Mission stations, supervised the erection of the new rectory and a modern five–story school and convent complex. He was also instrumental in establishing Our Lady's Chapel and the Catholic Information Center for the inner–city area. Upon the installation, in 1948, of Archbishop J. Francis A. McIntyre, Monsignor Cawley was re–appointed Vicar General for the Archdiocese of Los Angeles, a position he shared, in his final years, with Auxiliary Bishop Joseph T. McGucken.

The last act of public worship he attended was presided over by the Vicar of Christ in the magnificent Basilica of Saint Peter in Rome where Monsignor Cawley had gone to see his archbishop elevated to the cardinalate. "As the Holy Father and his Cardinal Archbishop looked down upon that great assemblage, their eyes could not rest upon anyone who rivalled him in love for the successor of St. Peter, or reverence and respect for, and obedience to his Princely Ordinary."

In seeing the Red Hat bestowed on the people he loved, Monsignor Cawley's most lofty ambitions for the Church in Southern California had been realized. The long–time Vicar General, known to his sacerdotal confreres as a man "kindly in thought, wise in counsel, prudent in action," had finished his course.

VALENTINE CLOSA (1841–1916)

Among the clerical pioneers of the Diocese of Monterey–Los Angeles, none surpasses in virtue or accomplishments those of Father Valentine Closa (1841–1916), a native of Vich, Spain. Born to humble parents, Valentine was educated at the local diocesan seminary. Adopted for service in California by Bishop Thaddeus Amat, he was ordained to priesthood on June 19, 1872.

After a few months of service at the Plaza Church of *Nuestra Señora de los Angeles,* Father Closa was assigned to San Juan Bautista Mission as associate to the legendary Father Cyprian Rubio. He eventually succeeded Rubio and spent the rest of his earthly sojourn among the small community attached to the Old Mission.

Like most priests then and now, there was nothing dramatic in Closa's life. He was content with performing his ministry away from the limelights of center stage. One commentator wrote that "Closa never allowed the boredom of daily routine to distract him from his primary goal of administering the sacraments and looking after the needy. He was one of that legion of clergymen who serve out their lives in happy anonymity. But he was no less a hero to his people."

A rare glimpse into Closa's life occurred in 1874, when a young man wrote about his visit to San Juan Bautista Mission for the San Jose *Herald.* He noted that after dining, he "walked out to the old Catholic Mission and wondered at its ancient tumbledown adobe walls, and from its peculiar surroundings became anxious to know something of its history." The door was locked so he "knocked at the door of the Father's study, and upon his answering the bell, made acquaintance with the object of our visit. He is a gentlemanly, modest, unassuming, mild–mannered man, and without inquiring, we saw upon the door, 'Rev. V. Closa.'"

"He took us to the entrance and unlocked the swinging gates and we walked into the ancient cathedral that has stood there for nearly one hundred years. There is

John J. Cawley

something supernatural about this place of worship; everything was as still as death, nothing being heard but our footfall on the bare thick floor."

The writer said that Closa told him that the paintings hanging in the church "were painted many years ago, in Mexico." He described the baptismal font at which seven thousand people were baptized. As they passed through the church, Closa "reverently pointed to a slab near the altar, saying that directly under it, Father Estevan Tapis was buried" seventy years earlier. Closa showed his visitor some clothing that belonged to Tapis. He had seen the remains of Tapis and told how "the hair and beard of the priest looked as natural as ever."

The Old Mission was severely damaged in the earthquake of April, 1906. Father Closa asked Fremont Older, editor of the San Francisco *Bulletin*, to help inaugurate a movement for restoration. Older organized a fiesta which raised enough funds to stabilize the building and keep it from collapsing.

Closa suffered most of his life from chronic bronchitis and, on March 8, 1916, he died quietly in his quarters at San Juan Bautista. In its issue of March 13, *The Tidings* told its readers that "the Angel of Death last Thursday morning called to his eternal home one of the oldest priests of the diocese." The account said that Father Closa "had been ill for some years, and almost blind, having suffered several strokes of paralysis."

The funeral was described in great detail. We are told that "all San Juan Bautista and the surrounding country mourned when, on Monday last, the remains of the beloved priest were laid away at the foot of the Cross in the cemetery overlooking the mission and the beautiful San Juan Valley."

HAROLD E. COLLINS (1899–1980)

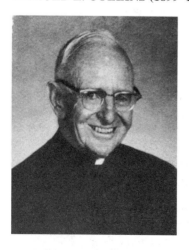

Every priest who studied in an American seminary prior to Vatican Council II knew and cherished a 192 page book entitled *The Church Edifice and Its Appointments*. It was "the" handbook of the time—and a good one at that.

The author of that book was a member of the San Francisco presbytery, Msgr. Harold E. Collins (1899–1980). Longtime pastor of Saint Cecilia's Church, Msgr. Collins was one of California's most beloved churchman.

A native of San Francisco, he grew up in the mission district. A protegé of the famed Msgr. Charles A. Ramm, he studied for the priesthood at Menlo Park and was ordained by Archbishop Edward Hanna on June 20, 1925. During the first decade of his ministry, Father Collins worked in Richmond. He taught for many years at Sacred Heart and Saint Ignatius High schools and later at Lone Mountain College. Always interested in liturgy and rubrics, he earned a doctorate from the University of Santa Clara in 1935

It was while studying for his degree that Father Collins began gathering materials for his landmark study. He defined the book's purpose as that of bringing into "a handy volume a summary of the laws governing the building, the dedication and the furnishing of a Catholic church."

In his foreword to the book, Archbishop John J. Mitty said that "the bishop, the pastor, the architect and the contractor, even the firms that supply church furnishings, all will find the work a valuable addition to the shelves of their libraries." Mitty's observations were quickly endorsed by the enthusiastic reviewers and the volume went through numerous editions.

Father Collins touched other bases too during those busy times. He became, for example, the first chaplain for the Serra Club of San Francisco, a position he held with distinction for thirty–three years. He was named secretary to the archbishop in 1939 and shortly thereafter was designated a papal chamberlain.

In 1946, Msgr. Collins was entrusted with the parochial family of Saint Cecilia and there he remained for three activity–packed decades of dedicated service. Probably no parish anywhere was as well organized. Thoughtful to the last degree, the pastor saw that every couple married there received a special blessing from the Holy Father. The church became the center of Collins' life. Like that great exponent of poverty, the Cure of Ars, Msgr. Collins rightly believed that anything used for divine worship should be beautiful, inspiring and uplifting.

And he also loved the beauty of God's house in the human heart. He loved his parishioners and, above all, he loved the children. He spoke to them about God and taught them, in turn, to love the beauty of God's house.

In a letter to this writer, Archbishop John R. Quinn said that "Monsignor accepted the changes in the liturgy more easily than many because of his desire to follow 'the mind of the Church' in all matters great and small. This gave him, I believe, that equanimity and peace of mind which so many find elusive today." Msgr. Collins returned his magnificent soul to the Lord at San Rafael's Nazareth House on December 16, 1980. He who had been the model of priestly hospitality to his peers was finally at home in his Father's house.

JUAN COMAPLA (1824–1878)

The provenance of the six volume set of *La Santa Biblia* given to the Archival Center by Miss Rosario Curletti of Santa Barbara is most interesting. Written onto the title page of each book is the simple phrase: "*Ad usum* Rev. Juan Comapla."

Juan Comapla, the son of Juan and Francisca (Senna) Comapla, was born at Batet, Spain, on May 10, 1824. He entered the seminary as a clerical candidate for the Diocese of Gerona, in 1845. Shortly before completing his theological training, John affiliated himself with Bishop Joseph Sadoc Alemany and was incardinated into the Diocese of Monterey. He came to the United States in 1853.

If one were to accept the evidence available in the annals, John was ordained to the priesthood no less than three times! Records in the San Francisco Chancery Archives indicate that he was advanced to holy orders on January 10, 1853, while the Catholic Directory for 1878, gives the date as January 1, 1854. A third authority suggests March 13, 1854.

In any event, Father Comapla was appointed to Santa Ines on April 25, 1854. While in that position, he also served as Vice Rector and later Rector of the diocesan seminary. The Catalan priest subsequently ministered at San Luis Obispo.

In 1861, Comapla was appointed Pastor of San Buenaventura Mission. A local historian wrote that the priest eventually became "the best loved, and in some ways perhaps the most remarkable of the long line of priests" at the Old Mission. Sol N. Sheridan goes on to state that Comapla's "rule, gentle, benign, always seeking for the best of his people, lasted until 1876. No man in all the sleepy old village of San Buenaventura was more highly regarded than this good priest." The parish at that time embraced everything between Rincon Creek and San Fernando and never did Comapla "hesitate to go upon a call, however long nor however he might be fatigued by his labors."

The priest "drove an old surrey, and might be seen at any time, night or day, on the rough roads of that time going about his parochial duties." Benjamin Cummings Truman, a pioneer California journalist, visited San Buenaventura in the late 1860s and he referred to Father Comapla as "a very pious, but an altogether delightful man and a person of brilliant attainments."

According to Truman, "Father Comapla had a very good library . . . and he pointed with marked respect to three engravings which adorned the walls of his study— George Washington, Stonewall Jackson and Robert E. Lee—whom he looked upon, so he informed me, as great soldiers and good men."

The initial steps toward restoring the old church at San Buenaventura occurred during Father Comapla's pastorate. In addition to covering over the exposed roof beams with a false ceiling, he had a wooden encasement placed atop the disintegrating floor tiles.

The popular and energetic pastor died unexpectedly at Los Angeles, on January 11, 1878. His name remains enshrined at San Buenaventura and it was he for whom Padre Juan Canyon, eight miles up the beach toward Rincon, was named.

The books in question were likely used by Comapla in his seminary studies. Published by *Libreria Religiosa* and printed by Pablo Riera at his shop on Barcelona's *Nueva Calle de San Francisco*, the scholarly tomes were translated from the Latin Vulgate and edited for publication by Felipe Scio de San Miguel. It was probably after the priest's demise that his books were either sold or given to friends. Miss Curletti recalled that the books had belonged to her mother as long as she could remember.

CHARLES E. COUGHLIN (1891–1979)

Father Charles E. Coughlin, the pastor of Royal Oak, Michigan, rose to national prominence in the early 1930s as a radio preacher. Ever–so–gradually, his talks on the social encyclicals drifted into political tirades. Though at first favorable to the New Deal, Coughlin turned against Franklin D. Roosevelt and launched a series of derogatory remarks about the president during the 1936 campaign to re–elect.

With the depression as a backdrop, Coughlin preached a message of "want in the midst of plenty." Anti–capitalist as well as anti–communist, the priest was heard by millions of people and his name became a household word. So popular did he become that he received more mail than the president. At one time he needed an army of a hundred secretaries just to handle correspondence. Football games stopped so that players and fans could listen to his Sunday afternoon sermons.

People walking down the street remember hearing out of every window the voice of Father Coughlin blaring from the radio. A person could walk for blocks in the big cities and never miss a word.

Early on Father Coughlin became an embarrassment to his fellow priests and the members of the American hierarchy. Though he had the backing of his own bishop, his name evoked sharp controversies at annual meetings of the National Catholic Welfare Conference.

In Los Angeles, Father Coughlin's shenanigans were carefully monitored by Archbishop John J. Cantwell. On September 16,1936, Cantwell asked the editor of *The Tidings* "to treat Father Coughlin's advent as he would treat the advent of any politician." The archbishop did not want to interfere personally, noting that "a priest has a right, according to our present customs, to come into any diocese as a priest . . . to make speeches."

Cantwell went on to say that "the only time we can control a priest is when he comes in to talk on religion." He didn't expect Coughlin to call on him and he felt reluctant "to deny him the privilege of saying Mass if he bears a celebret from his bishop." Though he didn't favor Coughlin's viewpoint in many areas, Cantwell didn't think there was any precedent for denying the priest permission to speak in Los Angeles. The archbishop observed that Coughlin had spoken in several cardinalatial sees without local episcopal interference.

The Archbishop of Los Angeles thought that Coughlin might win some votes for Alfred Landon, but he had "no doubt that Roosevelt will be elected in California." And such was the case.

Cantwell concluded his observations by saying that "as Father Coughlin appears as the champion of the oppressed and is certainly against capital, it would be very invidious for the Church to take sides."

The patience exhibited by Cantwell was not shared by the Archbishop of San Francisco. In response to an earlier letter, John J. Mitty, a man of few words, said that Coughlin "is harming the Church and I hope that after the election he will at least tone down."

Following the 1936 campaign, Coughlin began a weekly newspaper, *Social Justice*, in which he escalated his attacks against communism. Unhappily, he also branched out to attack Jewry and that tactic eventually proved to be his downfall. When Archbishop Edward Mooney eventually forced Coughlin off the air for technical reasons, the famed radio priest remained faithful to the Church and obeyed his superiors. He died in 1979, a fallen, but not forgotten hero.

JOHN P. COYLE (1856–1908)

The public manifestation of sorrow at the demise of Father John P. Coyle was without precedent in the annals of early California. One of San Francisco's best loved priests returned his soul to the Heavenly Father on March 3, 1908.

Born on November 4, 1856, John received his elementary education in public schools. He later studied under the Christian Brothers at Saint Mary's College, where he graduated with a master of arts degree. The youthful Coyle was greatly esteemed by his classmates in college. Strong and vigorous, he was the star athlete of the school. His name appeared in the line–up of every game and event.

John's preparation for the priesthood was made at the *Grand Seminaire* in Montreal, where he enrolled as a candidate for the Archdiocese of San Francisco. There he was guided in his philosophical and theological studies by the Sulpician Fathers.

Coyle was one of the four Johns (others were Cottle, McGinty and Sullivan) ordained by Archbishop Charles Fabre on December 18, 1880. It was an historic occasion for John Coyle was the first native son of San Francisco raised to the priesthood. Father Coyle's first priestly assignment was to the pastorate of Saint Patrick's Church. There he labored with great success for about a year, until his health began to fail.

The archbishop then suggested that Coyle might find the climate of Oakland more conducive. In later years he served at Saint Joseph's and Holy Cross. In 1894, he was made Pastor at Star of the Sea Parish in Richmond. According to contemporary accounts, Father Coyle was "one of the hardest working priests we have ever known. He was a zealous pastor, who never tired of his chosen work, but rather, overtaxed his strength in laboring for his people."

The report went on to say that Father Coyle's "sincere modesty only served to increase his ardor, for he was eager to accomplish, but never sought publicity or reward. Display he avoided, and was content with work alone."

Star of the Sea Church was a living floral piece for Father Coyle's funeral obsequies. Newspaper reports say that "the edifice was thronged to the utmost, to say nothing of the crowds who could not gain an entrance. Archbishop Patrick W. Riordan joined almost a hundred clergymen in paying tribute to San Francisco's proto priest.

Margaret G. Barrett, Secretary of Holy Rosary Sodality, noted that "by Father Coyle's death the Church has lost one of its greatest advocates, his dear mother a devoted son, and California one of its brightest minds and kind hearts."

JOHN P. CREMINS (1916–1994)

Maureen Johnson, a graduate music major at Oxford University, devoted a year "travelling and listening" in all but four of these United States. She spent three whole months in the Archdiocese of Los Angeles, visiting different parishes and interviewing cantors, choirmasters and organists.

After returning home, she wrote with this question: "Can you explain the historical reasons why your archdiocese appears to be: (1) far ahead of other areas in its congregational singing, (2) considered considerably further along in grass roots appreciation of liturgical singing and (3) more advanced in the basics of cantor training?"

The response to all three queries is the same: Msgr. John P. Cremins. Though long retired, he was the one who launched a program in 1948 to train seminarians, novices and college students in the then novel notion of liturgical music. Fourteen years before the conciliar fathers of Vatican II called for giving chant "the pride of place in liturgical services," Father Cremins was preparing for that eventuality.

It was an uphill struggle. After convincing Archbishop J. Francis A. McIntyre that he needed specialized training, he journeyed to Rome for courses at the Pontifical School of Music. Upon completion of those studies, he went to the Benedictine monastery at Solesmes for a lengthy apprenticeship in choral and liturgical chant.

Back in Los Angeles, he fell into a grueling routine that included teaching at Los Angeles College, Immaculate Heart College, Mount Saint Mary's College, Saint John's Seminary and half dozen novitiates. Like all good teachers, Father Cremins instinctively knew that any major innovation had to begin among young people. By concentrating on seminaries and novitiates, he would vicariously reach thousands of people down the road.

Father Cremins subsequently became Director of Music for the archdiocese and, in that position, he practically lived out of his car. Msgr. Thomas F. Fogarty was once overheard responding to a telephone call: "God knows all things, except where Father Cremins is at any given time."

Over the years, Cremins organized myriads of music festivals for the archdiocesan school system. He served as facilitator for concerts at the Shrine Auditorium and directed a thousand voice choir which performed throughout the state. He was everywhere, sometimes almost in defiance of the law of bilocation.

Father Cremins pestered James Francis Cardinal McIntyre until he received permission for what was then known as a *missa recitata* (recited Mass), wherein the entire community responded to all the prayers formerly reserved to the server. He had that practice adapted at the major seminary.

He was the first to conduct *tenebrae* services at Saint Vibiana's Cathedral during Holy Week. And, on one occasion, he was given a unique permission by Rome allowing Terce to be chanted in English. That was back in the 1950s!

In 1952, Father Cremins established the National Catholic Music Institute and through his work at the national level was able to export from Los Angeles his methodology for appreciation of liturgical music at the parochial level.

If the Archdiocese of Los Angeles slipped so effortlessly into the conciliar mode of "community singing," it was because every priest ordained from Saint John's Seminary in the 1950s and 1960s bore the gentle but lasting imprint of John P. Cremins.

Deacons at Camarillo were asked to compile a list of the five or so priests who had most influenced their spiritual formation by example or deed. The name of Father Cremins appeared on every list and was invariably in top place. In 1961, Father Cremins was entrusted with a parish in Torrance where he was able to implement personally the principles he had so persuasively imparted to his students.

In later years, others took up his baton and continued his work. When ill health forced his retirement from parochial duties, Father Cremins returned to the classroom. In short order he became a respected and loved figure at Bishop Amat High School.

When Cardinal Manning announced that Father Cremins had been made a monsignor in 1983, His Eminence said that it was the first time in the history of this archdiocese that a priest had achieved distinction by "popular acclaim."

THOMAS CRINNIAN (1823–1867)

In one of the few extant references to Father Thomas Crinnian, a newspaper article dated March 2, 1867, it was noted that the "spirit of self–denial ever characterized his life. Even when, during the last years of his life, he had to attend to an extensive mission in California, his flock will remember with what cheerfulness he cared for the wants of his own district."

Born in Drogheda, Ireland, in 1823, Thomas Crinnian studied for the priesthood at Armagh. So proficient was the young man that he was chosen to complete his studies at the Irish College, in Paris. He was ordained in that city in 1848. Upon his return to Eire, Father Crinnian was appointed to missionary work, principally in Armagh, Belfast and Drogheda, during the period when cholera and famine swept over the land.

One newspaper reported that "in those trying days nothing could equal his zeal in the discharge of his several duties. His disposition was most amiable, and never failed to relieve distress whether he patiently watched over the victim of a ravaging fever or bravely stood by the departing soul of one dying in the agonies of cholera."

Father Crinnian answered the appeal for priestly assistance in far–away California and, in mid–1861, he was assigned to Yreka where, despite a host of physical maladies, the determined cleric labored to advance the Gospel message. It was on a trip to attend dying man, in the winter of 1862, that he became affected with rheumatism, which was caused by exposure in a snow storm, as he was crossing the mountains between Yreka and Weaverville. From that time onwards, his lot was one of patient suffering. His health deteriorated and, in October 1863, he was transferred to Eureka, where it was hoped that the stimulating ocean air might prove to be beneficial.

As the first resident priest in Humboldt County, Father Crinnian's duties extended to the distant parish of Crescent City, in Del Norte County. Unfortunately, the unsettled coastal climate, with the frequent fogs that prevail in that region, only aggravated the priest's health and, in November, 1865, Bishop Eugene O'Connell sent Father Crinnian to the warmer and dryer climate of Oroville, in the Sacramento Valley. Death claimed the Irish–born cleric, on January 2, 1867, after "a short but fruitful and very edifying missionary career in a stubborn corner of the vineyard."

At the time of his demise, *The Monitor*, Catholic newspaper for the Archdiocese of San Francisco, reported that "by word and example, even when painful suffering was depicted in his pale features, did he show himself a devoted follower of Him who came not to do His own will, but that of his Heavenly Father. Now this devoted priest has entered the house of eternity. What a consolation it must be to his friends to look back and count the perils of his life, which his angel guardian gathered up and placed to eternal glory."

JAMES CROKE (1827–1889)

Father James Croke (1827–1889) is known in the annals as one of the noblest and most heroic souls that trod the footsteps of Padre Junípero Serra on the Pacific Slope. Born at Charleville, County Cork, Croke came from "a race of staunch defenders of the Church and loyal patriots." His eldest brother, Thomas, became Archbishop of Cashel and one of Ireland's most celebrated and outspoken loyalists.

Upon completion of his priestly studies in the Irish College, at Paris, the young cleric volunteered to spend his ministry with Archbishop Francis Norbert Blanchet of Oregon City. Croke arrived in San Francisco during the 1851 plague, where he spent three months administering the sacraments to the area's fever–stricken victims.

Father Croke's subsequent years were passed in the Northwest among the sparsely–scattered Irish farmers, French Canadians and Indian tribes of Oregon, Montana and Idaho. There he spared no pains and incurred all manner of risks in caring for the spiritual needs of his people. His church was a small frame building, in the

sacristy of which he slept and cooked his meagre meals. During the winter months he attended those living within a radius of thirty miles of the church. As soon as spring arrived, he mounted his horse and traveled in all directions "fearing neither floods, nor rains, nor lurking wild beasts, where there was a soul to be saved."

Father Croke's always precarious health eventually forced him to transfer his apostolate to San Francisco, where his zeal, devotedness and large–hearted charity in the plague had already endeared him to the people. His vigorous frame recuperated and soon he found himself able to resume his missionary efforts in a more conducive climate. Under Archbishop Joseph Sadoc Alemany, Father Croke served as Vicar General and Rector of Saint Mary's cathedral. A universal favorite with all classes and creeds, he was Alemany's first choice when discussions were held, in 1859, about creating the Vicariate Apostolic of Marysville. Father Croke was administrator of the Archdiocese of San Francisco during Alemany's attendance at the First Vatican Council.

The noble–hearted charity and unselfish spirit which attracted Father Croke to all segments of society accounts for his success in raising funds for the erection of Saint Mary's College, which he envisioned as an instrument to equip young people to uphold their religion and account for their faith.

Croke's final priestly years were spent as chaplain for Saint Vincent's Home, at San Rafael. "Whatever he touched prospered under God's blessing" and the Irish–born priest was able to renovate and enlarge the central building, erect a new chapel and build churches for several neighboring mission stations. Whether it was among the wilds of the Northwest or in the more refined atmosphere around San Francisco Bay, Father Croke sacrificed as much as could any man brought up in competence, independence and refinement.

The sentiments expressed in a memorial book, published shortly after Father Croke's demise, are worthy of recalling.

> . . . through all apparel shone the genial priest, and the scholarly gentleman. He shunned notoriety, was rather shy with strangers, and generally reserved in his manners; but with his friends he was always pleasant company, rich in dry, quiet humor, and full of anecdote. His was a noble soul, generous to a fault, large–hearted and kind and charitable. He was a warm friend, and steadfast as he was warm, and never wanting in the hour of need.

DENIS O. CROWLEY (1852–1928)

A. EARLY YOUTH WORKER

"A man whose deeds live after him in very truth is

one Reverend D. O. Crowley (1852–1928) whose benign life was filled to overflowing with works of zeal for the welfare of his fellowmen." The Irish–born priest spent much of his youth around Boston. In 1875, he came to California by way of Panama and sought his fortune in the gold and silver mines of Nevada. His experiences on the contract lode brought him sufficient money to realize a long cherished purpose for the priesthood.

After taking preparatory courses at Saint Vincent's College in Los Angeles, young Denis Crowley entered Saint Mary's Seminary at Baltimore. He was ordained for service in the Archdiocese of San Francisco on December 22, 1883. Early in 1887, Archbishop Patrick W. Riordan placed Father Crowley in charge of the Youth's Directory, an organization begun some years earlier to care for abandoned boys in San Francisco.

Shortly after assuming his new position, the talented priest launched, on March 26, 1887, *St. Joseph's Union*, a periodical that subsequently provided most of the revenues needed by Father Crowley in his educational and welfare work. In 1902, Father Crowley established an agricultural school in Napa County which he was able to staff with Xaverian Brothers. There homeless and destitute boys lived under proper discipline while being taught at the same time the theory and practice of scientific agriculture.

The school at Napa "embodied an extremely advanced idea of education, because an increasing number of people were awakening to the realization that the real wealth in California was not in its gold but in its rich soil." Father Crowley was active in practically all the Bay's Area's charitable activities. During the 1906 fire, he and his co–workers supplied 72,000 persons with provisions daily until the rehabilitation committee could take over their work. In subsequent years, the tireless priest also served as vice president of Associated Charities, chairman of the Commission on Parks and Playgrounds and a vociferous member of the Protective Committee of the Juvenile Court.

Concerning his longtime work as Playground Commissioner, it is recorded in the annals, "probably no other city in the world has more to show in practical results for the work of its playground commission, and for these results the resourcefulness and ever ready counsel and assistance of Father Crowley have been the chief factors." Though the active apostolate occupied most of his time, Father Crowley found time to use his literary talents. In the preface to a collection of his writings, Maurice Francis Egan, United States Ambassador to Denmark, noted that, ". . . poets like Father Crowley . . . are all the more legitimately exercising their vocations when they express the emotions of religion, the passing shales of sentiment which result from those deep convictions which spring from the sources of spiritual life. . . ."

Had not Crowley been assigned to youth work, his genuine literary ability would have obtained far wider recognition. In a book review of Father Crowley's verses, A.J. Waterhouse of Berkeley wrote: "Splendid American that he is; beloved by young and old, by Catholic and Protestant, Jew and Gentile, Christian and pagan; beloved by these because of good deeds that have known no creed distinctions."

Four decades after Crowley had been charged with building a home for destitute boys at Howard and 17th Streets, three institutions had been built and 20,000 youngsters cared for in both their moral and physical well–being all without a penny of public aid. Well could Rockwell Hunt remark that Father Crowley's residence in California has been distinguished by many and notable services to his fellow men, well deserving the titles of priest, poet and philanthropist.

DENIS O. CROWLEY (1852–1928)

B. IRISH POETS AND NOVELISTS

The library at the Archival Center acquired a most interesting (and quite rare) volume from Dr. Albert Shumate of San Francisco, the distinguished Western Americana collector.

Compiled by Father D. O. Crowley (1852–1928), the book is entitled *Irish Poets and Novelists*. Profusely illustrated, it embraces "complete biographical sketches of those who at home and abroad have sustained the reputation of Ireland as the land of song and story." In his preface, Father Crowley tells how he gathered the sketches and poems from the *Celtic Magazine*. Confessing that many of Ireland's best poetical writers had been omitted, Crowley said that he sought not so much "to measure the fame of well–known poets as to popularize those comparatively unknown, but whose works, nevertheless, entitle them to our gratitude and admiration."

In a review for the October, 1892 issue of *St. Joseph's Union*, an anonymous writer characterized the book as "not only interesting and edifying but . . . valuable as a work of reference." A score of standard authors, whose works have been in demand for years, are pictured both in pen and portrait. Sketches of Irish Poets, R. D. Williams and James J. Callanan, for example, appear in print for the first time.

The reviewer went on to say that "the Rev. editor shows research and labor in procuring and publishing hidden treasures. To him also is due credit of first bringing to light the life, history and character of Bartholemew Dowling." Father Abram J. Ryan, the "poet priest of the south," is featured prominently in the book. Crowley's memoir about that famed cleric contains considerable biographical information not previously known.

Another reviewer of Crowley's book, writing for *The Monitor*, said "the lover of Irish literature can fully appreciate this work only by careful study of its pages. The book is well printed, and handsomely bound in cloth, with marble edges. Its table of contents is nicely arranged, and the size is commendable." He concluded by saying that "this work may have some faults; but taking it all in all, the biographical sketches are well, we may say, brilliantly written, and the selections are such as can be made only by one who has a keen appreciation of the beautiful, and a broad and thorough knowledge of literature."

In his introduction to the book, Thomas R. Bannerman noted that the pen of the compiler "could not have been more fittingly employed than in spreading the fame of those who, without the exception of material reward, devoted their genius and talents to a poor and helpless motherland in order that she might perpetuate the existence of her ancient nationhood."

Published at San Francisco, in 1892, the 423 page book was electrotyped and printed by P. J. Thomas in his shop at 505 Clay Street. Unfortunately, most of the copies of this fine book were destroyed in the earthquake and fire that ravaged the city a decade later. This book was only one of the many literary accomplishments of Father Crowley.

JOHN J. CROWLEY (1891–1940)

The solitary cross rising from a neat, whitewashed circle of rocks amid the majesty of the desert has a special meaning for motorists speeding along U. S. Highway No. 6 near Freeman Junction, for that rough–hewn monument recalls to memory the beloved "desert *padre*," John J. Crowley. Civilian Conservation Corps boys erected the cross, simply inscribed with the priest's name, "as a reminder of the love that came to him from the frontiersmen and prospectors, laborers and desert rats of his parish. It stands off the highway a little, framed in the vast cloudless blue of the desert sky against the changing hues of the Mojave Mountains. Only the twisted Joshua trees rise with the cross in wilderness memorial to the spirit of Father Crowley."

John J. Crowley was born in Killarney on December 8, 1891, the son of Michael F. Crowley and Nora M. Layne. He was brought by his parents to Worcester in 1903, where he was enrolled in the public schools and later Holy Cross and Clark Colleges. After completing his studies for the priesthood at Saint Mary's Seminary in Baltimore, John was ordained on May 18, 1918, at Fall River, Massachusetts, for service in the old Diocese of Monterey–Los Angeles.

The young priest was curate briefly at Saint Agnes Church in Los Angeles before being entrusted, in 1919, with the pastorate of a cluster of mining settlements in Inyo and San Bernardino counties. It was an exhausting apostolate. He was forced to travel day and night in rough stagecoaches to every part of his 20,000 square mile parish without sleep or food or the simple refinements of life in a Herculean effort to satisfy the spiritual needs of his parishioners.

Shortly after the installation of Bishop John B. MacGinley in the Diocese of Monterey–Fresno, Father Crowley was named chancellor. In 1925, he was designated a papal chamberlain by Pope Pius XI, and five years later, he became pastor of Saint John's Cathedral. As chancellor, Monsignor Crowley helped to build, at an amazing rate of speed, churches, hospitals and schools until illness forced his retirement from the hectic pace of curial activity.

At his own request, the ailing monsignor was restored to his earlier pastorate in Owens Valley, where he hoped to spend the final years of his life in the towering shadows of the 14,500 foot Mount Whitney. Ever so gradually, however, his health returned as the monsignor threw all his energies into the battle of providing badly–needed water for the valley's parched earth. About his activities, one writer commented: "Father Crowley was not only a devout churchman, but a tireless worker for the material prosperity of his people. He knew what every missionary knows; that it is easier to save a man's soul when he is prosperous and happy than when he is worried by adversity and embittered against the world and against God."

In the years that followed, Father Crowley devoted himself earnestly to the welfare of the area and largely because of his work, Owens Valley is today a peaceful and increasingly prosperous region. The weeks, month and years stretched into a decade. Death finally came to the busy desert *padre* on March 17, 1940, but not before he had guided to completion the details of erecting a massive dam to reclaim the Owens Valley for his people. On October 19, 1941, Crowley Lake in Mono County was named to honor its chief benefactor.

One writer recorded the impact this indefatigable "dying" priest had in the final years of his life by observing that he had never "known a man more loved and honored and leaned upon by any people." Perhaps the reason for this phenomenon was correctly described in an article for the *Saturday Evening Post*, where monsignor was epitomized as primarily "a man of the cloth" whose "first efforts belonged to the Church."

JAMES HILLIS CULLETON (1898–1978)

James Hillis Culleton, the first native of Fresno

ordained to the priesthood, was born on December 11, 1898, to Patrick and Mary (McCrory) Culleton. His early education was acquired at Saint John's School. In 1916, James was accepted as a clerical aspirant for the old Diocese of Monterey–Los Angeles. After completing his initial preparation for the ministry at Saint Patrick's Seminary, Menlo Park, he was sent to Rome's North American College. There he studied at the Urban College of Propaganda Fide.

Following his ordination at Saint John Lateran Basilica, on December 19, 1925, Father Culleton pursued his doctoral studies, earning degrees in both theology and canon law. He returned to the recently–created Diocese of Monterey–Fresno, in 1928.

Bishop John B. MacGinley appointed Father Culleton Chancellor in 1933, a position he held for thirty–four years. He did much to stabilize the shaky financial status of the diocese in the hectic depression years. In 1939, Pope Pius XII named Culleton a Domestic Prelate. With the division of the jurisdiction, in 1967, Msgr. Culleton became Vicar General for the Diocese for Fresno. He was made a Protonotary Apostolic in 1968.

Always interested in history and the preservation of early records, Msgr. Culleton established, in 1944, the "Church History and Art Research Institute of California." He asked each of the state's residential ordinaries to name delegates for a meeting at Fresno. Unhappily, that noble endeavor was blocked when the representative from San Francisco withdrew over a dispute about financing.

The Academy of California Church History was inaugurated some years later. Its publication, *Academy Scrapbook*, appeared in 1950 and continued through five volumes, the last being issued in 1959. Over the years Msgr. Culleton compiled a number of most interesting essays for the *Academy Scrapbook*, including treatises on "Father Casanova's Account Book," "Father Serra's Grave," "Monterey Church Property" and "California's First Library."

In 1950, Culleton published his superb work on the *Indians and Pioneers of Old Monterey*, a volume described by one reviewer as "a very precisely constructed enumeration of historical facts" for the years 1542–1819. The Academy Library Guild, which succeeded the earlier historical organization, continued Culleton's objective of providing spiritual literature for the Catholics of predominantly agricultural Central California.

In 1955, the Monsignor encouraged foundation of the apostolate of Fatima and actively participated in that group's publication, *Divine Love*, which began in 1957.

A remarkably versatile priest, Msgr. Culleton wrote several other books, including one on guardian angels.

His works on "How to Enjoy the Races" and "Pari–Mutuel Betting" have become classics and are still avidly circulated among racing enthusiasts.

At the time of his death, in 1978, Msgr. Culleton was praised for his many accomplishments in various fields, literary, historical, biblical and theological. More than that, he was first, foremost and always a priest—one who placed his ministry above all other considerations.

THOMAS DALTON (1826–1891)

Throughout the many years he labored along California's Gold Dust Trails, Father Thomas Dalton (1826–1891) was a friend of the sinner and the unfortunate. He was a priest " known and loved by everyone in return." Born in Colierstown, County Wesmeath, he studied briefly at Mullinger, before entering all Hallows College as a clerical aspirant for the Diocese of Nesqually, Oregon. During his student days, young Dalton distinguished himself as a scholar in theology and canon law. Following his ordination, on July 3, 1853, Father Dalton worked for a short time in Brooklyn.

The "young ecclesiastic of brilliant talents" came to San Francisco, in early 1855, and on May 7 was appointed Pastor of Nevada City and Grass Valley. He took up residence at the latter place, where many quartz mills were operating at full capacity. From the very beginning, the populace took to Father Dalton, Catholic and non–Catholic alike, men and women of every nationality. In 1857–1858, he constructed a handsome new church, dedicated to Saint Patrick, for which "he received generous donations from the citizens of every race and color and creed."

Edmund E. Kinyan, editor of the *Morning Union*, is the authority for the story that "Father Dalton caused gold to be put in a bell made for the local parish church. When the bell was consecrated he uttered a prophecy that gold would always be found in the mines within hearing distance of the bell's peal."

Father Dalton brought the Sisters of Mercy to Grass Valley, in 1863, where they opened a day school and, later, an orphanage. It is doubtful "if there was anyone who covered a greater extent of territory than Father Dalton did on his missionary journeys during the many years he spent in the foothills of the Sierras." In the course of time he erected houses of worship at Iowa Hill, Forest Hill, Auburn, Moore's Flat and Washington.

A man of considerable influence, the Irish–born priest was known to have changed the course of many a stubborn or bigoted indivdual by the force of his good example. The indefatigable cleric was a spiritually–orientated man. It was said that "neither press of business, nor weariness or sickness could prevent him from the faithful recitation of his beads." One chronicler noted that Father Dalton's heart was as "tender and affectionate as a woman's and his moistened eye and sympathetic voice naturally responded to every appeal of stricken humanity."

In 1868, with the creation of the Diocese of Grass Valley, replacing the Vicariate Apostolic of Marysville, Father Dalton, "a man of soldier–like bearing, possessing a massive frame, crowned in later years by a snow–white leonine head," became Vicar General of the newly–formed ecclesiastical jurisdiction. After thirty–six years of unselfish service to the People of God, Father Dalton succumbed, on December 27, 1891. One of his clerical associates left the following tribute to his priestly confrere:

> Long years o'er mountain ways he trod
> With messages of faith and God,
> Bearing with love, like faithful friend,
> The Master's burden to the end.

JOHN J. DEVLIN (1898–1977)

A. *PADRE* OF THE FILMS

The sacerdotal career of Msgr. John J. Devlin bridged the deaththroes of one era and the birthpangs of another. Though he considered himself "old–fashioned," his parishioners looked upon their priestly shepherd as the most relevant of his peers.

He said his prayers after Mass, recited the breviary in Latin, poured over the beads and made his daily visits to the Blessed Sacrament long after such practices went out–of–vogue. Somewhat hesitant in implementing liturgical directives, perhaps overly touchy about pastoral prerogatives and definitely close–minded on the question of clerical discipline, he enjoyed pointing out that his initial plans for a new church were rejected as "too modern."

Well into the "post–Marian" age, he insisted on a May procession in honor of the Blessed Mother. For more than four decades he conducted and preached at weekly devotions to Our Lady of the Miraculous Medal. Solemn Novenas continued to be an annual occurrence.

Though asking little from priestly associates, he did demand that liturgical services begin promptly, that the housekeeper be notified about visitors and that someone be always on hand for emergency calls. He was formal in speech, casual in conversation and bashful in demeanor. His curate was always "Father."

He delegated broadly, except in spiritual areas. He reserved to himself the instructing and questioning of youngsters for first Holy Communion and no occasion occupied a greater portion of his time or prayers than the day scheduled for that annual event.

Abreast of all activities in the school, he was always on hand to distribute the report cards. Rare was the youngster whose name he didn't know. He frequently startled old–timers with his ability at almost total recall.

His attitude about finances was pre–Keynesian. He had a built–in aversion to incurring debts, paying top prices or writing checks. At the same time, he adamantly refused to badger the people about pecuniary shortages. His many depression years without a salary precluded any thought of a personal "fortune."

Steeped in the traditions of the archbishop whom he once served as secretary, he expected meals to be served at 12:15 and 6:15. The food was ample in supply and ordinary in quality. Clerical attire was the presumed dress for meals.

Though bent by, age, impaired in health and unstable of gait, he mounted the pulpit every week to share his knowledge of Christ with others. His clear, resonant voice, trained in youth for music, retained the tonal qualities of a much younger man. During the years of his pastorate, he built first a convent, then a rectory, afterwards a school and finally a church.

He may have been, as he often claimed, an "old–fashioned" relic from an earlier era. If that be so, it would behoove modern–day Catholics to pray Almighty God for more priests like John J. Devlin "God's man" at Saint Victor's Church, in West Hollywood, for almost fifty years.

JOHN J. DEVLIN. (1898–1977)

B. GET "FATHER DEVLIN"

From the very outset of the Legion of Decency, the Right Reverend John J. Cantwell insisted that all Catholic film advising fall under his mantle as Bishop of Los Angeles–San Diego, and, later, as Archbishop of Los Angeles. He chose Father John J. Devlin to be the official liason with the Motion Picture Industry.

A whole chapter in Frank Walsh's book *Sin and Censorship* is devoted to Devlin's work on behalf of the Legion of Decency. "Get Father Devlin" became the watchword for any studio considering the production of a film touching on the Catholic Church. For the next four decades, Devlin regularly reviewed between forty and fifty scripts annually from big budget films like *Going My Way* to Red Ryder's potboilers at Republic.

Occasional articles on "the movie priest" in the Catholic and secular press made Devlin a household name for people across the country. His mail, much of it on file at the Archival Center for the Archdiocese of Los Angeles, includes letters from Hollywood moguls to aspiring starlets, all of it painstakingly answered. Devlin claimed in one interview that all his job required was a thorough knowledge of the moral code given by God to Moses on Mount Sinai, plus the ability "to relate that knowledge to modern trends and changing conditions."

While patience was paramount among his virtues, Devlin could be awfully blunt at times. After reading one MGM script for a story about a woman with a split personality, he advised the producer to "consign the script to an incinerator where it would certainly make a good fire."

While many producers feared Devlin, others welcomed and even sought his advice. He helped them to avoid such mistakes as putting a Gideon Bible in the home of an Irish–Catholic family, and making sure that priests were properly attired for whatever function they were performing.

Much of Devlin's time was devoted to correcting the minor mistakes that crept into films dealing with Catholic priests. He once allowed a bullet to shatter a holy picture, provided it did not touch Christ's head or heart.

The use of the confessional was especially sensitive. He demanded that Jack Warner delete a scene from *Angels with Dirty Faces* in which a gangster is shown confessing to his boyhood friend, a priest. Alfred Hitchcock's *I Confess* presented even more difficulty. On learning that Devlin had serious reservations with the initial script, the New York Bankers' Trust insisted that Hitchcock satisfy the priest before it would provide financing.

Aware that "Hollywood never let the historical record get in the way of a good movie," Father Devlin spent a great deal of his time defending the Church's image and he was ever careful that films should "carefully and sympathetically convey a Catholic viewpoint." Devlin's influence forced Arthur Schlesinger to complain that "the movies were being filmed according to ground rules set by a minority religious faith."

Devlin followed productions from beginning to end, observing some of the filming and reviewing the daily rushes. He was never arbitrary but followed the code religiously. Only when a producer endeavored to "stretch" the rules did the priest get upset.

Probably his biggest success was *Going My Way* where Devlin did his best to interject some spiritual values into the film while trying to tone down what he considered the "undignified conduct" of "Father" O'Malley. That film swept the 1944 Academy Awards and prompted one cardinal to say that "it did more for the Catholic Church than a dozen others could have accomplished in a year."

JOHN DUNNE (1903–1995)

For eleven years *The Tidings*, official newspaper for the Diocese of Los Angeles–San Diego and later the Archdiocese of Los Angeles, was guided by a remarkable man, Father John Dunne.

Things were a lot different in 1931 when young Father Dunne, fresh from a three year course in Moral Theology at The Catholic University of America, walked into the cramped offices of *The Tidings* for the first time. The paper was then located on the second floor of a building at 130 East Second Street.

There were only 2½ people on the editorial staff–Patrick Henry, George Andre and Charles Conroy. Old "Doc" Conroy, himself a former editor, "only counted for half because he was also a professor at Loyola College in Westchester."

There was no ticker tape machine in those days. International and national news was delivered from NCWC by post, except for those non–infrequent days when the mailman "fell in" with friends at the local pub. There were two ancient typewriters in the office and they could be heard clanking away from early morning until late evening. Occasionally a friend from *The Times* would drop by to share a juicy ecclesial morsel for local Catholic consumption.

Dunne saved his pennies and was eventually able to purchase a linotype machine along with the other equipment needed for printing the newspaper. From there on the weekly was produced at its own plant, a factor which saved money and improved efficiency.

Things were vastly different for the Church in those days. The old Diocese of Los Angeles–San Diego stretched from Santa Maria to the Mexican border. There were 284 parishes serving a Catholic population of 292,000.

Interestingly enough, though there are now eleven times as many Catholics in about a fourth of the area, the circulation of *The Tidings* is not greatly larger than it was seventy–five years ago. And that doesn't speak very well for the reading habits of contemporary people.

Though the curial offices were just a block away, Bishop John J. Cantwell rarely came to *The Tidings* office, and even less frequently did he use the telephone. "He left us alone," said Dunne, "except when he sent Barney (Msgr. Dolan) over with some official notices."

Dunne recalls only once being called on the episcopal carpet. He had hinted editorially that President Hoover favored certain actions of the Ku Klux Klan. "His Grace was displeased, to say the least." It was a brief scolding which began in this fashion: "Father Dunne, a gentlemanly priest would not have accused the President of the United States of being anti–Catholic. Your little Irish mother would not approve."

Then, just as curtly, the bishop stood up and said:

"You may go, Father." As he passed through the office, he heard one of the secretaries whisper: "Go, and sin no more Father!"

When asked whether he "liked" Bishop Cantwell, Dunne replied: "We came from the same part of Ireland. The Cantwells had been prominent churchmen for generations—it ran in their blood. Though he lacked the commoner's touch, he was the right man for this rinky–dink diocese at the time."

The Tidings was more magazine than newspaper in the 1930s. There were upwards of a dozen regular columnists and weekly features that came by mail or messenger each week. "First we put the ads in place, then the regular fare and, finally, the news." And "when there was space left, we flipped a coin as to who would write the fillers."

There were concerned Catholics around the diocese in the 1930s who acted as unpaid stringers, mailing or bringing in local items. Photographs were mostly amateurish but quite usable. There was no sports section, but there was a great enthusiasm for such literary items as book reviews. Father John Devlin, for example, attended the Philharmonic every week and would often mail in the program along with his observations on a performance.

Pastors and others were good about keeping *The Tidings* informed about activities at the parochial level. Mary Sinclair and Ethel Bosert cranked out whatever official items there were. "We were much more a family in those days," said the monsignor.

While there may have been less journalistic sophistication during the Dunne years, the paper was attractively printed and highly informative. There was no television and little radio, so Catholics appreciated the role of *The Tidings* as the official newspaper for the sprawling diocese.

The energetic Father Dunne served as diocesan spokesman for eleven years until October of 1942, when he received his "Dear John" letter thanking him for his years of editorship. Then it was on to the pastorate at Saint Teresa's.

One stands in utter amazement at the marvelous things people like Msgr. Dunne were able to accomplish in those years. What fun it was to talk with this living testament of an earlier age. People in the 1990s need to know what the pioneers of earlier times did to make the Church in Los Angeles what it is today.

MICHAEL DURAN (1830–1889)

Some people are remembered because of the deeds (or misdeeds) of a famous relative or namesake. Such was the case with Father Michael Duran, a distant cousin of Fray Narciso Duran (1776–1846). That famed Franciscan was eulogized by Hubert Howe Bancroft as "a most earnest and successful missionary" who served as first Vicar General for the Diocese of Both Californias.

About the only extant reference to Michael Duran's priestly service along California's *El Camino Real* is a short notice in New York's *Catholic News* for November 17, 1889, wherein editor John Gilmary Shea recorded that Father Duran had died the previous October 29th "at San Juan Capistrano, California, where he was the rector for some time."

The clergy book for the Diocese of Monterey–Los Angeles indicates that Duran was born on November 3, 1830 at Arbuelas, Province of Gerona, Spain. His earliest education was in a school attached to the local Catholic church. Duran became acquainted with the legendary Father Cajetano Sorrentini who suggested that Duran enter the seminary of Brignole–Sale as a clerical candidate for the California jurisdiction then presided over by another Catalan, Bishop Thaddeus Amat.

After ordination at Brignole–Sale on December 21, 1859 by Allesandro Cardinal Barnabo, Father Duran set out for the New World, arriving in Los Angeles early the following year.

The youthful priest spent several months as associate at the Plaza Church of *Nuestra Señora de los Angeles*, during which time he studied English and learned the customs and practices in what were then the borderlands.

Michael Duran

In 1863, following a severe smallpox epidemic, Bishop Amat sent Duran to look after the spiritual needs of the native Americans living on the west side of the Colorado River. Three years later, Duran was appointed pastor of San Juan Capistrano which was described by Adeline Stearns Wing as a "quaint little village, with everywhere old adobe ruins." There wasn't much left of the one–time "jewel" of the California missions. Writing in the May 16, 1886 issue of *Ave Maria*, a visitor said that only a segment "of the devout and heroic work of the eighteenth century remains."

Duran was also delegated to care for San Luis Rey Mission and the still–active Indian community clustered around San Antonio de Pala, a grueling assignment that lasted until 1866. Though hampered by illness, Father Duran assisted when he could. He looked after the Plaza Church in the absence of Father Francis Mora in 1877, returning to San Juan Capistrano in 1881.

In mid–1881, Father Duran, always in precarious health, suffered a "shock of apoplexy" which left him partially paralyzed. He never fully recovered and thereafter was unable to accept any full–time assignments.

After his demise in 1889, Duran's remains were brought to Los Angeles for obsequies which took place in Saint Vibiana's Cathedral. He was buried in old Calvary Cemetery. Though his works for the Lord went mostly unrecorded in the early annals, Father Michael Duran is eminently worthy of being remembered by those who walk in his footsteps.

JOHN T. DWYER (1916–1987)

Though Msgr. John T. Dwyer (1916–1987) was an historian, author, archivist and lecturer, he was foremost a priest and it was in that role that he will be best remembered along *El Camino Real*. A clergyman of the Diocese of San Jose, John Dwyer was ordained for San Francisco on June 13, 1942. His earliest years in the ministry were spent in and around "the City." For a long time he was pastor at Gilroy and while there he wrote a most interesting monograph on the historical development of Saint Mary's parish.

With dismemberment of the San Jose diocese from its parent jurisdiction, Msgr. Dwyer became one of that area's more prominent pastors. He served as a consultor to Bishop Pierre Dumaine, dean of his district and chair of the Pastoral Resources Committee.

In 1955, Dwyer compiled his first major work, *One Hundred Years an Orphan*, which was a superbly–written history of Saint Vincent's Home for Boys at San Rafael. That 159 page monograph was published by the Academy Library Guild of Fresno. Later he wrote several essays in the *Academy Scrapbook* which was edited by Msgr.

James Culleton, the long–time Chancellor for the Diocese of Monterey–Fresno. Among the more important of those articles was one dealing with the Reverend John Shanahan, the "pioneer priest in Nevada County."

Surely the most outstanding of his many works was *Condemned to the Mines*, the biography of Eugene O'Connell (1815–1891), the proto Bishop of Northern California and Nevada. That 301 page treatise told the story of an Irish professor–turned–missionary bishop who blazed a religious trail across the mining country of America's western territory and laid the foundation for continued growth of the Catholic Church in that region today.

Msgr. Dwyer supervised and wrote much of the text for *Catholics in the Gold Country* in collaboration with parishioners in Auburn. He also compiled a chronicle of the Sisters of Mercy in Grass Valley. His last historical work was related to the centennial celebrations for the Diocese of Sacramento, where he served as chairman of the History and Art Committee. Several of the newspaper columns that appeared in the *Catholic Herald* bore his name and reflected his scholarship.

Msgr. Dwyer had retired early and was planning to spend his final years pursuing his interest in the Catholic history of Northern California. For a long time he had been gathering information for a book about the pioneering Irish priests along the Gold Dust Trails. He died on September 2, 1987.

In the final chapter of Dwyer's book about Bishop Eugene O'Connell, he remarked that "perhaps the Church in Northern California and Nevada owes more to this man than meets the eye. It is about time that his remarkable accomplishment for the Church should become known, recognized and appreciated and his memory and his virtues be resurrected for our own inspiration and edification."

It would not be far off course to apply those same words to the man who wrote them. Msgr. John Dwyer wrote much and he wrote it well. This man who once described himself as "an educator, social worker, hospital chaplain, cemeterian, psychologist and pastor" will be long remembered along California's Gold Dust trails.

HENRY EUMMELEN (1862–1933)

Father Henry Eummelen (1862–1933) was "a very modest and unassuming man" who "endeared himself to all by his unselfishness, his devotion to duty, his generosity, and his genial nature." Born to John Mathias and Mary Elizabeth Eummelen, in the City of Lutterdale, Province of Lombardy, on December 8, 1862, he studied at the Jesuit College, Sittaert, before coming to the United States in 1878.

Young Henry pursued his education at the Franciscan

College, Teutopolis, Illinois and Mount Angel Seminary. His theological training was interrupted for a few years, during which he taught linguistics at Saint Vincent's College, Los Angeles. On February 28, 1890, Eummelen was ordained a priest for the Diocese of Leavenworth, Kansas. He subsequently served as curate at the cathedral and a small parish in a predominantly black neighborhood.

Ill health induced Father Eummelen to transfer his priestly ministry to Vancouver, where he worked for nine years. It was in 1896, during his apostolate in the Pacific Northwest, that he was named a papal chamberlain by Pope Leo XIII, an honor that Monsignor Eummelen bore only until the pontiff's death, in 1903.

Father Eummelen's labors, begun on the Plains of the Middle West, continued on the Northern Shores of the Pacific, were extended to the Diocese of Monterey–Los Angeles, shortly after the turn of the century.

He served in Imperial Valley at Brawley, El Centro, Calexico, Holtville and Otay, where he erected four churches amid the hardships of pioneer country. After three years, Bishop Thomas J. Conaty assigned Eummelen to National City and, later, to Saint Joseph's Church, in Santa Ana.

Among the priest's many accomplishments at Santa Ana, were the enlarging of the church and parochial residence, purchase of educational facilities and inauguration of a parish school. Long interested in the logistics of formulating Catholic model communities, Father Eummelen actively circulated statistical and agricultural prospects to those wishing to relocate in California or any other locality in the western part of the nation. Over the years, a well–integrated program gradually evolved and, in 1910, he formally established the Catholic Homeseekers Information Bureau and Catholic Colonization Society.

The words spoken at Father Eummelen's silver jubilee flavored the atmosphere of the modest El Modena dwelling to which deteriorating health confined him during the final years of his life.

> Well may he pause to look back with satisfaction and thanksgiving to Almighty God, for his work has extended over a wide field, east, north and south, and last of all, to Southern California. He has held the plow in God's field and has watched the seed which grows up into life everlasting. He has done many good works, eased aching hearts, consoled the sorrowing, saved souls and brought a good crop into God's barns and in doing so, in the intensity of the cultivation, his indomitable energy and burning zeal has caused his health to break down and even brought him to the brink of the grave.
>
> He has ministered to many nationalities, mastered their languages and customs, and, as St. Paul said: "I have become all things to all men in order that I might gain all for Christ." He is the friend of children, adults, sick and dying, but his activities have not been confined solely to those lines; he is a successful builder of churches and schools, many times at a great expense to himself, an organizer of parishes and a colonizer, assisting people to find homes suitable to their mode of life and religious convictions.

LAWRENCE H. FARRELL (1907–1983)

The Reverend Lawrence H. Farrell was often called Monterey's "public priest." His beard, cape and lusty laugh were known throughout the Monterey Peninsula. He was once described as "the only man of the cloth whose prayers are frequently greeted by a round of spontaneous applause."

Farrell was born in Monterey on September 17, 1907, in his family's home on Larkin Street. He was baptized by the legendary Father Ramon Mestres at San Carlos Church. After two years at Monterey High School, Farrell attended Saint Joseph's College in Mountain View and then moved on to the University of Fribourg in Switzerland. He finished his education at Oscott College in Birmingham, England.

After ordination to the priesthood in 1937, at Saint Austin's Church at Stafford, he returned to Monterey to offer a Mass at San Carlos Church. He then reported for his first parochial assignment in Royal Leamington Spa, England. Later he was sent to Saint Patrick's Church in Birmingham. The latter parish, Father Farrell once told an interviewer, was a downtown enclave complete with "a prison, a looney bin and a workhouse and a huge hospital . . . we really worked there in those days."

When World War II began, Farrell joined the British Army and served as chaplain to the 59th Newfoundland Heavy Regiment Royal Artillery. The vestments he wore during the war years hang in a shrine in the city hall of Saint Johns, Newfoundland, which honored the priest with the title "Free Man."

Father Farrell returned to the United States after the war and spent four years as Catholic chaplain at the California Correctional Facility for Women at Tehachapi. After several years as chaplain at the Carmelite monastery at Point Lobos, Farrell began his more than twenty years serving in the same capacity at Soledad Prison.

Following his retirement from the prison post, Father Farrell remained available for counseling and "fill in" posts at a wide range of parishes on the Central Coast. Everywhere he went, he continued enriching his already formidable knowledge of history.

During ceremonies in which be was named "Citizen of the Year" in 1972, Farrell was introduced as "he of the golden voice, the cape, the flowing beard, a great humanitarian, the last of the Irish *paisanos*." The fortieth anniversary of his ordination was marked in 1977 by a heavily attended picnic in Monterey's Memory Garden. There he received a papal blessing from the Holy Father and numerous plaques from civic officials.

A brilliant conversationalist and speaker, linguist and poet, Father Farrell was always in demand at public functions. His witty, provocative and memorable invocations and benedictions were the high points of many otherwise stuffy events.

The "dean" of Monterey's clergy died on July 30, 1983. His funeral at Carmel Mission Basilica was attended by over 700 persons, all of them friends and admirers of a truly outstanding cleric. Farrell was eulogized by Bishop Thaddeus Shubsda as "a priest beyond compare, a priest without peer." He was a man "determined to help, inspire, encourage, enlighten and create joy, one who cared deeply about the individuals with whom he came in contact."

His long–time friend, Harry Downie, once said of Father Farrell: "They don't make priests like that anymore. He was a cut above all the others. He was a throwback to apostolic times."

PATRICK J. FISHER (1850–1918)

Patrick J. Fisher was born, on February 24, 1850, the son of James J. Fisher and Catherine M. Brady. He studied for the priesthood at All Hallows College and was ordained in that Dublin Seminary, on June 24, 1880. The freshly anointed priest arrived in Los Angeles a few months later,where Bishop Francis Mora gave him an assignment as curate at Saint Vibiana's Cathedral. A few years afterwards, he was transferred to Saint Joseph's Church in San Diego.

It is recorded in the annals that Father Fisher's "characteristics as a priest were no less striking than his powers of endurance physically. From early youth he has been fond of exercising his powers as an athlete. . . One afternoon, while in San Diego, he swam across the bay of San Diego and back again, this being the first time such a feat had ever been attempted."

In April of 1886, shortly after the creation of Saint Joseph's Church in Pomona as a distinct parochial unit Father Fisher was entrusted with the newly formed jurisdiction. The tireless pastor built a frame church and rectory at Pomona and, in 1899, was instrumental in plans to open the Academy of the Holy Names. In addition to his other duties, Father Fisher cared for missions at Ontario, Chino and Azusa. One writer noted that "working for the religious progress of the people and their spiritual development, he has been a contributor to the moral development of the state."

In 1902, Father Fisher went to Santa Cruz as successor to Father Hugh McNamee, just when that pretty seaside city was beginning its period of growth. At his new post, Father Fisher continued his feverish activities, redecorating the church, building a rectory and refurbishing the educational facilities. In 1907, he was named a diocesan consultor and the following year Vicar Forane for the Santa Cruz deanery. On June 15, 1909, Father Fisher was designated a papal chamberlain, at that time an unusual and rare distinction for priests living outside the confines of the Eternal City. The appointment was reconfirmed, in October, 1918, by Pope Benedict XV.

Fisher's reputation was not confined to Santa Cruz. The diocesan newspaper noted on April 25, 1903, for example, that "there is a rumor in circulation that the archbishopric of Manila has been offered to and refused by the Rev. pastor of Santa Cruz." The southland paper went on to observe that "so far as worldly comfort and enjoyment of life are concerned, we are certain that the position of rector of Santa Cruz is much more desirable than that of Manila." Mention was made of the monsignor's name a dozen years later for the vacant Diocese of Monterey–Los Angeles. Unfortunately, the prelate's age ruled out the practicality of such an appointment by that time.

When Monsignor Fisher succumbed at Santa Cruz, on December 3, 1918, the editor of the local newspaper wrote:

> If any man loved his fellow men with heart big enough to take in all the pure and the sinning, the young and the old, the laborer on the streets as well as the man who had won prominence in commercial or professional life, Father Fisher was such a man.

ROBERT FITZGERALD (1835–1912)

One of the most elusive and mysterious books ever to appear on the California scene was written by the Very Reverend Robert Fitzgerald, a Canon of the Cathedral Chapter, Diocese of Kilkee, County Clare, Ireland. Entitled *The 'Frisco Debacle*, the sixty–eight page book appears to have been written to describe the terrible earthquake and subsequent fire which ravaged San Francisco in April of 1906.

According to the author, the *raison d'etre* of the volume was "the strong bond of sympathy and kinship which connects the Catholic people of the Old Land with the Catholics of "The Queen of the West." He went on to say that "we have grown accustomed to talk of and to rely upon the 'Greater Ireland of the States,' and nowhere has the greater Ireland been stronger, more generous and more true to the Faith of our fathers than in the fallen city of San Francisco."

Although the author does not indicate whether he was in San Francisco during the disaster, he describes in great detail how "suddenly in the bowels of the earth a thunderous roaring like the rush of a mighty sea, the earth, whose stability seems a law of nature, rocking and heaving like the deck of a ship on a raging ocean."

Canon Fitzgerald goes on to tell how "the City of the Golden Gate, which lay at dawn a thing of peace and beauty above the placid sea, was through that awful day a veritable inferno, where the seismic destruction and slaughter was small compared with the ruin wrought by the flames."

The author continues to chronicle, with great detail, the events that transpired over the following days. He tells, for example, how "hundreds who escaped the shocks were roasted to death in the flames. People rushed wildly about, apparently without aim, by a mad impulse, sometimes into the very jaws of death." All told it was a vivid though probably imagined portrayal.

Fiztgerald's book was published at Dublin, by James Duffy, that same year, possibly in early August. The only known copy to have reached California is possessed by Dr. Albert Shumate of San Francisco.

Subsequent research has unearthed very little about the Canon. He was born in 1835, at Kilfinane, County Limerick, and studied for the priesthood at Maynooth College. Ordained in 1858, for service in the Diocese of Limerick, his earliest priestly years were spent at Ruan, Tulla and Ennis. He was parish priest at Ballyna for fourteen years.

An engaging speaker, the young priest was active in a host of benevolent activities. After becoming pastor at Kilkee, he did herculean work to have that place recognized as a tourist resort. With his demise on March 26, 1912, local civic officials publicly acknowledged the Canon for his "kindly disposition, genial nature and many other qualities."

It is interesting to speculate why Canon Fitzgerald's book was never circulated in the United States. One can suspect that local ecclesial officials frowned upon its obvious exaggerations and prevailed upon Fitzgerald to restrict his readership to Ireland. But that is only a speculation.

Whatever the reason, *The 'Frisco Debacle* deserves a place in the bibliography of San Francisco. What other book identified the "City" as "the Queen of the West" in 1906?

THOMAS F. FOGARTY (1902–1966)

For the longtime pastor of Saint Brendan's Church, the "whole world was, as it ever should be for the pastor, his parish and people." This alone accounts for the spon-

taneous expression of grief manifested by the overflow crowds of faithful parishioners flocking to the four public obsequies for their departed shepherd.

Though born in Brooklyn, on August 27, 1902, Thomas Francis Fogarty, was raised and educated in Ireland. He studied for the priesthood at Saint Patrick's Seminary and was ordained in the Thurles' Cathedral for service in the Diocese of Los Angeles–San Diego on June 12, 1927. During his first thirteen years in

Thomas Fogarty

the southland, Father Fogarty served as curate at Saint Monica's Church (Santa Monica), Saint John's and Sacred Heart Churches (Los Angeles), Holy Rosary (San Bernardino) and Saint Anthony's Church (Long Beach). In 1938, he was named pastor of Saint Francis of Rome Parish in Azusa. Two years later, following a brief period as administrator at Saint Kevin's, Father Fogarty was entrusted with the pastorate of Saint Brendan's.

In the physical order he found indebtedness when he came to his flock and the early years there were occupied in retiring that obligation. For the Sisters, he renovated and later rebuilt completely the convent. The school was first modernized and then replaced altogether. He brought to completion the shell of the parish's landmark Gothic church and subsequently saw it consecrated. For his fellow priests there was the dream of a new home and that too eventually became a reality.

Possessed of a keen Irish wit, a scholarly mind and a deep human sympathy, Father Fogarty became a part of each family in his square–mile parish, ever acknowledging the dignity of the laity and their prominence in the overall mission of the Church. It has been remarked that "with jealousy for his flock's welfare, he sought always the best, the perfect—and even when it was man's best, he felt the lack of Divine perfection and went on and on, still searching . . .

Thomas Francis Fogarty entered personally into every activity affecting the spiritual and material welfare of his parishioners, thus anticipating by several decades the role of the contemporary priest as outlined by Vatican Council II. Long ago this zealous shepherd realized that the clergy "cannot be of service to men if they remain strangers to the life and conditions of men."

To the pastor of Saint Brendan's as to the prelates of the recent ecumenical council, the priestly office was not confined to the care of the faithful as individuals, but also properly to the formation of a genuine Christian community. This concept of public service explains why Father Fogarty was no less accessible to his people after being elevated to the domestic prelacy in 1957.

Ever a man in a hurry, the last of the monsignor's many projects was finished only weeks before his death. At last he could and did repeat those lovely words of the evangelist: "I have brought you honor upon earth, I have completed the task which you gave me to do."

Rarely has such genuine grief been recorded at the loss of a pastor as when news of Monsignor Thomas F. Fogarty's sudden and unexpected demise spread among his people. But this good shepherd left something more enduring than mere human sadness. Those who knew him best would have no hesitation in re–echoing those sentiments formulated into eulogistic terms by a former curate:

> We rejoice that a good soul, afflicted with the rest-lessness of Augustine here on earth, has crossed through the portals of death to find the eternal rest that awaits the just . . . and, while, in the words of the Canticle "he is now standing on the other side of this very wall—gazing through the windows, peering through the lattices" of his memorable works among us, each, in our turn, will call to him for help as we continue on the same road going home.

RAPHAEL FUHR (1860–1935)

Throughout the long years of his priestly career, Father Raphael Fuhr was "the good shepherd, the kind judge, the devoted teacher, the loving pastor and the loyal associate." Born January 4, 1860, at Elberfeld, near Cologne, Raphael was brought to the United States, in 1875. He entered the Order of Friars Minor at Teutopolis, Illinois, on June 29, 1876, and was ordained to the priesthood as a Franciscan, on May 12, 1883, at Saint Louis, Missouri.

Between 1884 and 1898, Father Fuhr was a professor at Saint Francis Seminary, in Quincy, Illinois and during those years he also looked after the small parish of Saint Joseph, at nearby Columbus. Besides being "a constant and prolific contributor of articles, especially on church music and the liturgy, to a number of periodicals, both in the United States and foreign countries," Father Fuhr also compiled several editions of Wapelhorst's *Compendium on the Sacred Liturgy.*

In vacation periods from school work, "Father Raphael's favorite work was to give retreats to the various sisterhoods and this made him hundreds of friends among the priests and sisters of the Middle West." It was also in those years that the indefatigable friar served several terms as head of the German Catholic State Federation. In 1898, Father Fuhr was named to the pastorate of Saint Anthony's Church, in San Francisco. Upon his completion of service in the Bay Area, Father Fuhr came to Los Angeles as Pastor of Saint Joseph's Church, a position he filled with his traditional zeal. It was during his tenure that the handsome schoolhouse was erected.

At the invitation of Bishop Thomas J. Conaty, Father Fuhr affiliated himself with the Diocese of Monterey–Los Angeles, in 1909. During the five subsequent years, the priest engaged in missionary work in Inyo County, a 27,000 square mile desert apostolate encompassing portions of the Sacramento and Salt Lake dioceses. He returned to the Southern California community of Gardena–Torrance, in 1914, as pastor of Saint Anthony's Church. On February 20, 1918, Father Fuhr took over the pastorate of Saint Michael's Church, Los Angeles, which he retained until his death. The splendid school which he built at 87th Street and Vermont was dedicated, on October 17, 1926, by Archbishop Edward J. Hanna of San Francisco. The next year he began a new rectory and convent for the Dominican Sisters. "Crowning a long life and priestly duties including arduous parish and missionary work, a life of scholarly attainments and always unfailing zeal in the vineyard of the Lord," Father Fuhr was named a Papal Chamberlain, in April of 1930, by Pope Pius XI. At the monsignor's death, it was said that "where he was there was no rest and as the years of his long life went by he might be said to have grown young like the eagle in the service of God."

HUGH GALLAGHER (1815–1882)

Father Hugh Gallagher is described by the biographer of Archbishop Joseph Sadoc Alemany as "one of the most important helpers" of San Francisco's pioneer prelate. Born in Killygordon, County Donegal, on March 26, 1815, Hugh Gallagher completed his clerical studies at Saint Charles Seminary, Philadelphia, where he was ordained to the priesthood in 1840.

Father Gallagher's earliest years in the ministry were spent in various parts of Pennsylvania. There he built churches, established schools and won considerable acclaim for his defense of the Catholic faith against the Native Americanists. He later served as rector of the diocesan seminary and founding editor of the Pittsburg *Catholic.* Gallagher was also influential in launching another publication known as the *Crusader.*

It was while serving as a theologian at the First Plenary Council of Baltimore that Gallagher met the Right Reverend Joseph Sadoc Alemany. The Dominican Bishop of Monterey encouraged the Irish–born cleric to transfer his apostolic endeavors to California. In the fall of 1832, Father Gallagher came to Benicia, where he secured ground and collected funds for the erection of a church. His next task involved supervising the building of Saint Mary's Cathedral in San Francisco. Daily he solicited money for that purpose along the streets, wharves and alleys and out in the sand hills of the scattered city.

Gallagher utilized his journalistic experience too by establishing the first Catholic weekly newspaper on the Pacific Coast. The earliest issues of the *Catholic Standard* were published on May 6, 1854. Father Gallagher is also credited with the establishment of the parochial school system for the Archdiocese of San Francisco. He served as steward of the working classes when the Adams' Express and Banking Company failed in 1855. Millions of dollars passed through his hands during the time he watched over and protected the meager savings entrusted to his care.

As the years progressed, the tireless priest founded parishes and erected churches in Oakland, Sacramento, Carson City, Virginia City and Yreka. He was also the driving force behind the opening of the Magdalen Asylum in 1865. Four years later, Father Gallagher convinced the State Legislature to embark upon a program for improving Golden Gate Park, a project which gave employment to thousands of willing workers.

Throughout his ministry, Father Gallagher was a loyal and dedicated friend and confidant of Archbishop Alemany. He it was who brought back the pallium for the prelate. And on that same journey to Europe, he recruited the Presentation Sisters and the Mercy Sisters for service in the Archdiocese of San Francisco.

The " extremely talented and competent priest" died as Pastor of Saint Joseph's Church on March 10, 1882. His passing marked the ending of an era in the northern part of the state.

ANDREW GARRIGA (1843–1915)

Although Father Andrew Garriga was not one of California's earliest missionaries, he personally knew many who were. He was a learned man with a keen eye for details. Born at Vich, in the Catalonia region of Spain, on December 19, 1843, his preparation for the ministry was initiated in his homeland and concluded at All Hallows College in Dublin. It was there that he was raised to the priesthood on June 24, 1868, for service in the Archdiocese of San Francisco.

The newly–ordained cleric was named curate of Saint Francis Church in the Bay City on December 5, 1868, and remained in that capacity until 1875, when Archbishop Joseph Sadoc Alemany entrusted his fellow Catalan with the recently established national parish of Our Lady of Guadalupe, formed within the parochial confines of Saint Francis. With the permission of Archbishop Patrick W. Riordan, Father Garriga was released for service to the Diocese of Monterey–Los Angeles in 1890, as pastor of Saint John's Church in Fresno. There he opened a parish school in 1893 and "accomplished great and lasting good, for which his name should ever be held blessed."

In October of 1896, Garriga was appointed to the pastorate at Bakersfield, an assignment he was soon forced to relinquish because of ill health. Between 1900 and 1905, he served the combined parishes of Saint Theodore (Gonzales) and Saint John (King City). In that position he also cared for the spiritual needs of those few Catholics attached to San Antonio Mission.

From 1907 onwards, the Vich–born priest served at San Luis Obispo. At the time of his death, on March 27, 1915, Father Garriga was eulogized by Bishop Thomas J. Conaty as "a man beloved by all who knew him because of his devotion to his priestly office."

Garriga was the author of several books and pamphlets, among them *Counsels for All Colors and Truths of All Flavors* and *Advice to Good Catholics on the Practice of Their Religion*. A Spanish edition of the former work, *Consejos de Todos Colores y Verdades de Todos Sabores* was published at Chihuahua in 1899.

During his years of service at Gonzales, King City and the environs of San Antonio Mission, Father Garriga composed a manuscript on herbs which he based on his own research and that done earlier by Father Doroteo Ambris. Sometime between 1907 and 1915, during a visit to San Luis Obispo, Father Zephyrin Engelhardt transcribed Garriga's manuscript. The Franciscan chronicler subsequently included fifty–eight of the "Medicinal Herbs of Early Days in Use and Collected in the San Antonio Mission District" in his book on *Mission San Antonio de Padua*.

At the time of Garriga's demise, the original manuscript on herbs was given to the mother of P. J. Lojo. According to Lojo, family tradition confirmed that the priest "had collected these while covering the then extensive territories of Mission San Antonio, Soledad, Jolon from King City." In 1978, this writer published *Andrew Garriga's Compilation of Herbs & Remedies Used by the Indians & Spanish Californians Together with Some Remedies of His Own Experience*.

JOSEPH M. GLEASON (1869–1942)

The story of an epoch is the story of the men who made it. Among the more prominent of such personages was Monsignor Joseph M. Gleason (1869–1942), a name still remembered in the Bay Area for his outstanding priestly virtues. The San Francisco–born cleric attended Sacred Heart School and Saint Ignatius College prior to taking post–graduate work at the University of California. His studies for the priesthood were made at Saint Mary's Seminary in Baltimore, where he received holy orders at the hands of James Cardinal Gibbons, in 1892.

Following additional scholarly work in Rome and Paris, Father Gleason served as an army chaplain in the Spanish American War. He subsequently accompanied the troops during the China relief expedition at the time of the Boxer Rebellion. From 1909 to 1928, Father Gleason was pastor of Saint Thomas Aquinas Church in Palo Alto. In the latter year, he was transferred to Oakland and the pastorate of Saint Francis de Sales where he finished out his priestly years.

In his various apostolic endeavors, Gleason's feet were not chained to the sanctuary. Rather, he went forth "even as Christ, Himself, among the scattered children of the Redemption." Throughout his life, Gleason exhibited a sustained interest in the history of California and of his native San Francisco. He was, in the view of Zephyrin Engelhardt, "a competent judge of historical matters" and during his years at Palo Alto, Father Gleason lectured frequently on that subject, at nearby Stanford University.

To Gleason, "California was first the missionary field, hitherto untilled, of the Franciscan friars; afterwards, or even contemporaneously with this, the broad, unbounded range of the lavish and independent Spanish and Mexican cattle kings; later the fighting ground of the frontiersman and the American desperado; become by the discovery of Marshall on Sutter Creek one vast mining camp, to which flocked the ambitious adventurers of the world, whose only thought was to amass wealth and leave as soon as possible; finally appreciated for its unrivalled fertility and excellent commercial position, and in consequence settled by the families, who, with their children, make the population of the State today."

Over the decades Monsignor Gleason carefully gathered a fine collection of books dealing with California history and related matters. That library, later the property of the San Francisco College for Women, was once described as the "greatest gift to Catholic education in the history of the State."

Perhaps Gleason's most noteworthy contribution to the written record was his valuable series of essays on "Fifty Years of Catholic California" which appeared on January 23, 1904, as a special golden jubilee edition of *The Monitor*, official newspaper for the Archdiocese of San Francisco. Therein, Father Gleason pursued his theme that "more than any other part of the United States, more perhaps than any other country in the world, the story of California has been the story of the Catholic Church . . ."

In his busy schedule, Gleason found time to help establish the Academy of Pacific Coast History, at the Berkeley campus of the University of California. Twice he served as president of the Pacific Coast branch of the American Historical Association. He was a founder of the San Francisco College for Women and head of that institution's history department. Joseph M. Gleason once observed that "the biography of a priest ordinarily lacks the melodramatic matter found in the histories of those of more eventful lives." If that be true, then Monsignor Gleason was no "ordinary" priest.

WILLIAM GLEESON (1829–1903)

"As a preacher, lecturer and conversationalist; a priest and patriot; patron of Catholic education; exemplar of piety, faith and priestly zeal, the life of Father William Gleeson is one that the Catholic youth may well study with much profit." The man about whom this was said was born in the northern part of County Tipperary in 1829. He entered All Hallows College at Dublin in 1848, and was ordained for the Diocese of Agra in India two years later.

A decade of feverish missionary activity among the Hindus undermined the young priest's health and forced his withdrawal from those enervating conditions in late 1860. When a throat infection further curtailed his actions, Gleeson became chaplain of the English soldiers in the mutiny of the Sepoys. Later he went to Smyrna where he acquired a speaking knowledge of the Syrian and Arabic tongues. After a short tenure in Chicago, Father Gleeson came to California at the invitation of a former professor, Bishop Eugene O'Connell of Grass Valley, a prelate who described the Gold Dust Trails to Gleeson as "an Elysium on earth."

In September of 1868, O'Connell wrote to a friend that he had given the parish in Carson City, Nevada, to the Irish priest, a city "where the Legislature sits and Father Gleeson prays." Leaving Grass Valley, Gleeson joined the faculty of Saint Marys College where he became a highly respected professor of history. It was while teaching there for the Christian Brothers that Father Gleeson published a series of his lectures under the title of *History and the Catholic Church in California*, a two volume treatise released in 1872. The volumes suffered from the customary defect of a contemporary approach and have never been of great use as source materials; however, they remain valuable, especially to book collectors, since most of the edition was destroyed by the San Francisco fire.

In 1871 Gleeson was made pastor of the newly created Saint Anthony Parish, a jurisdiction containing only thirty persons and extending over half of Oakland and all of the town of Alameda. The "Athens of the Pacific," as Oakland was known in those days, had little pretension to the beauty and culture it later attained. Nonetheless, in 1877 the pastor of Oakland managed to open Our Lady of Lourdes Academy under the direction of the Sisters of Mercy.

The San Francisco *Call* described the dedication ceremonies of the lovely new Gothic Church of Saint Anthony in late February of 1886. It was an historic event, presided over by Archbishop Patrick W. Riordan. The church continued to serve its people for over seven decades until 1957.

> Father William Gleeson, bearded, venerable, learned zealous, holy, first pastor of Saint Anthony's Parish, died after an illness of a few days on January 29, 1903. Though the parish has had a most illustrious list of pastors, including the justly famous Father Peter C. Yorke, it seems that it would not be unfair in the least to say that its first pastor knew no peer among his great successors. One reads with awe the tale of his labours for God and souls in the proud second oldest parish of the beautiful City of Oakland.

MIGUEL GOMEZ (d. 1856)

Miguel Gomez entered religious life as a Franciscan *donado* or lay brother of the Third Order Regular, at the Apostolic College of Zapopan, in Guadalajara. In those surroundings, he was known by his confreres for the industry and zeal with which he performed the duties of his office.

Early in 1841, the newly–ordained Bishop of Both Californias, Francisco Garcia Diego y Moreno, visited Zapopan, appealing for clerical recruits for his faraway diocese. Miguel was one of the few who responded affirmatively. Arrangements were made for Gomez to receive minor orders and the subdeaconate, with the understanding that he would complete his clerical studies in California. The ceremony took place at Guadalajara, on July 25, 1841

Several months later, Gomez journeyed to San Blas, where he joined the bishop's party en route to Alta California. The small group sailed aboard the *Rosalind*, arriving at San Diego on December 10, 1841. The surroundings there militated against making that town the permanent episcopal seat, and Bishop Garcia Diego, with his companions, decided to relocate at Santa Barbara early the following year.

Formal classes were instituted for the handful of seminarians, in the rear apartments of Mission Santa Barbara. Gomez completed his preparatory courses at that embryonic institution within a few months and was advanced to priestly orders on June 29, 1842. In November, Father Gomez, the first priest ordained in and for the Diocese of Both Californias, was appointed pastor at the former Missions San Luis Obispo and San Miguel, which, at that moment, became the first regular parishes in Alta California.

The bishop transferred Father Gomez to La Purísima on February 28, 1844, and from that post the priest also looked after the spiritualities of Santa Ines. By the time of his appointment at La Purísima, there were only about 200 souls attached to that old mission. Father Gomez worked diligently at his various assignments under the episcopate of Bishop Garcia Diego and his two successors, Bishops Joseph Sadoc Alemany and Thaddeus Amat. He left California, on June 27, 1856, for Guadalajara, for a long–cherished reunion with his family, and friends. There, quite suddenly, he succumbed on December 4th.

Father Gomez was a unassuming cleric whose apostolate in California received little mention in the state's early annals. The prayer of California's proto–priest might well have been that of Ralph S. Cushman:

> I do not ask
> That crowds may throng the temple,
>   That standing room be priced:
> I only ask that as I voice the message
>   They may see Christ!
>
> I do not ask
> For churchly pomp or pageant
>   Or music such as wealth alone can buy:
> I only ask that as I voice the message
>   He may be nigh!
>
> I do not ask
> That men may sound my praises,
>   Or headlines spread my name abroad:
> I only pray that as I voice the message
>   Hearts may find God!
>
> I do not ask
> For earthly place or laurel,
>   Or of this world's distinctions any part:
> I only ask when I have voiced the message
>   My Savior's heard!

GUSTAVO GONZALES (1913–1942)

Though "torn away by a tragic death from the land of the living in the flower of his youth—a youth already laden with the rich and well founded hopes of a long and brilliant future," Father Gustavo Gonzalez (1913–1942) was a priest whose virtues, zeal and activities "earned for him the esteem and confidence of his hierarchical superiors, the respect and admiration of his brother priests and the gratitude and veneration of all the faithful."

Born in San Benito, Texas, the young clerical aspirant studied for the ministry at Lugo, Spain, and Menlo Park, California. He was ordained at Saint Vibiana's Cathedral, on March 28, 1936, for service in the Archdiocese of Los Angeles. During the earliest years of his priestly work, Father Gonzalez served as chaplain at the Los Angeles County General Hospital. There his ceaseless, methodical and persevering attention to thousands of patients won an unforgettable place in the hearts of all those with and for whom he labored. In 1940, he was transferred to the Cathedral, where his chief pastoral duties centered around the mission chapel of Holy Rosary.

The tragic chain of events leading to his untimely demise revolved about a nurse whom he had instructed in the Faith while at the county hospital. Subsequently dismissed for stealing and using narcotics, the distraught woman nurtured her acquaintance with the priest by periodically expressing a wish to reconcile herself to the Catholic Faith, from which she had wandered many years previously. Though frequently warned about the "wayward, unruly, inconsistent and Machiavelic" wiles of the chronic psychopath, Father Gonzalez expressed the hope of eventually alleviating her manifold spiritual distresses.

On the afternoon of November 16, 1942, the lady telephoned the cathedral rectory with an urgent, almost hysterical plea for the priest's immediate assistance. Assuming that she had met with some sort of accident, Father Gonzalez grabbed the holy oils and sped to the indicated address. Arriving at the residence, he found the atmosphere calm and serene, so much so that he consented to a cup of coffee before returning to the rectory. "All the venom of her poisonous heart" was contained in that cup, along with a lethal dose of cyanide.

Once he had realized the situation, the moribund priest managed to get ahold of the phone to call the cathedral, and then slumped into a chair. His demented hostess, after summoning a nearby nurse to ascertain that the priest was actually dead, then took cyanide herself and died soon thereafter. In his touching homily, preached before the largest congregation of clergy and laity ever assembled in Saint Vibiana's Cathedral, Father Manuel Canseco pointed out that even the tragic circumstances of his premature death were powerless to dim the brilliancy of Father Gonzalez life "a life short indeed, but fruitful in good works, a life in which we discover a continuous 'crescendo' of apostolic activity and zeal."

JOSEF GORAJEK (b. 1908)

Father Josef Gorajek was enthusiastically welcomed at San Fernando Mission on April 10th, 1988. He had journeyed to the United States, as the guest of the Valley Beth Shalom Temple, to participate in ceremonies recalling the six million Jews killed in World War II.

Eugene Winnik had arranged for the visit of the eighty year old priest to California, explaining in the courtyard of the Old Mission how Gorajek, a short man with a beak nose and alert eyes, had become a hero among the Jewish community at the Simon Wiesenthal Center in West Los Angeles.

It was in 1941 that Winnik and his mother fled Nazi–occupied Warsaw by train, leaving behind his father, an affluent dentist (whom he never saw again). When they arrived in Wawolnica, they and others were greeted by Father Gorajek who offered to pretend that Winnik and his mother were Catholic villagers.

The priest arranged for the young boy to care for the village's herd of cattle. Eugene dug up potatoes and cooked them over small fires he made from dried cow dung. When Nazis came through town, he hid in wheat silos. He did not attend school until after the war. At night, when he returned from the forest, Father Gorajek taught him catechism. But the priest never tried to convert him, telling the youngster that someday he would be free to live as a Jew.

After the war, Winnik and his mother emigrated to Argentina and then to the United States. Eventually he came to Sherman Oaks, where he became and still is a successful furrier.

Winnik never forgot the Roman Catholic priest who risked his life to help him and his mother by providing them with false papers and shelter, insisting all the while that local villagers keep their heritage a secret.

In the summer of 1987, after coming across the communion certificate signed by the priest among his mother's effects, Winnick and his wife decided to make a return visit to Poland. They found that little had changed in the rural area, a 2½ hour drive from Warsaw. The village had few cars, minimal electricity and no plumbing. When the Winnicks pulled up to Gorajek's church, a young priest bounded out the front door to greet them. When they showed him the certificate, he disappeared inside and returned with Gorajek.

Early in 1988, plans were made for Father Gorajek to be honored on the occasion of ground–breaking ceremonies for a Holocaust monument at Pan Pacific Park in Los Angeles. Rabbi Harold M. Schulweis noted that "to hide a Jew, to give him a meal or to help transport him in those days was to be exposed to the threat of death. The Holocaust left a legacy of despair, hopelessness and cynicism. We need to search out the good as much as we have correctly hunted down the evil."

Father Gorajek admitted to being only one of many priests in Poland who harbored or in other ways sheltered Jews from detection by the Nazis. "It was an awful chapter in our history," he said, "and one which must never occur again." That sentiment, spoken through an interpreter, was echoed by the people of San Fernando Mission as they applauded for the aged and heroic priest following the morning Gospel homily.

THOMAS KIELY GORMAN (1892–1980)

According to local clerical folklore, the first priest in the southland to own his own car was Father Thomas Kiely Gorman (1892–1980) longtime editor of T*he Tidings* and, later, the first Bishop of Reno.

Gorman was anything but an armchair journalist. He travelled widely through the sprawling Diocese of Los Angeles–San Diego looking for feature stories and augmenting the advertising revenue for the area's Catholic newspaper.

Gorman once confided to this writer that Bishop John J. Cantwell was not pleased with Gorman's "showy" car, a gift of his parents on the occasion of his completing doctoral studies at the University of Louvain. During the ensuing years, other priests purchased automobiles, to the annoyance of Bishop Cantwell who never drove a car himself. The bishop felt that parishioners were better served by a less mobile clergy.

One day, Fathers John Conlon, Patrick Coleman and James Leheny were involved in a "spectacular" car accident enroute to the Santa Anita racetrack. Though no one was injured, the incident received coverage far wider than its importance. Shortly after reading about the crash in the morning edition of the Los Angeles *Times*, Bishop Cantwell directed Father Martin McNicholas to draft a canonical ordinance curtailing the possession of cars by diocesan priests.

There had already been, since 1927, a prohibition in the statutes against buying or procuring "luxury" cars by the local clergy. In those days, Buicks and Packards fell into that category and a few of them were still parked in rectory garages.

The new regulation, which was promulgated by the chancellor on October 26, 1934, was annexed to #38 of the existing diocesan statutes. The expanded regulation forbade "any curate from either directly or indirectly buying or possessing his own car." Any violation of the prohibition incurred an automatic suspension removable only by the bishop.

In his letter to the priests, Father Bernard Dolan cautioned that "the Most Reverend Bishop requires its strict observance." He went on to say that "any request for exception to this law must be made to the bishop personally."

Pastors were exempted from the ruling, though relatively few of them actually owned their own cars, preferring instead the use of an auto bought and paid for by the parish.

There was considerable negative reaction to Cantwell's directive. Probably the most outspoken cleric was the colorful Father William Mullane who felt that the new ordinance was a violation of the natural law. While not agreeing with that objection, the bishop did concede that each parish would thereafter provide and maintain a car for the use of curates—at no expense to them. Even Mullane had to conclude that it was a fair exchange.

In 1942, when the first synod was held in what became the Archdiocese of Los Angeles, the prohibition about automobiles was confirmed and it remained in effect until the synod held under James Francis Cardinal McIntyre in 1959. Though no longer regulated by statue, the practice of curates or associate pastors not owning cars still perdures in the archdiocese. And, given the cost of purchasing and maintaining cars in the later years, most priests are grateful for Bishop Cantwell's letter of 1934.

PATRICK "PATSY" GROGAN (1860–1939)

The jovial "Patsy" Grogan (1860–1939) was the patriarch and pastor of San Buenaventura Mission for well over forty years. He was one of the legendary "characters" of the Catholic Church in Southern California.

Born October 13, 1860, the son of John and Helen (Cahill) Grogan in Ballintober, County Roscommon, Ireland, young Patrick received his elementary education at the local national schools. He entered Saint Patrick's College at Castelrea in 1878 and, four years later, enrolled at All Hallows College from which he was ordained priest on June 19, 1887 for service in the Diocese of Monterey–Los Angeles.

Arriving in the southland, Father Grogan served in many assignments, including Hollister, the old Plaza Church and Saint Joseph's in San Diego. His first pastorate was at Saint Joseph's in Santa Ana.

In 1891, Grogan was named pastor of Saint Andrew's Parish in Pasadena. Subsequently, he served for two years in Whittier before being appointed to Santa Paula on July 20, 1897. At that time, the farflung parish of Santa Paula included Camulos, Lancaster, Mojave, Tehachapi, Lone Pine and San Buenaventura. Though never officially posted at the Old Mission, Father Grogan took up residence there and soon became the acknowledged "dean" of the county and city named for Saint Bonaventure.

Those were busy years. Father Grogan built a rectory, a schoolhouse (which he enlarged twice) and a convent for the Holy Cross Sisters whom he brought from Notre Dame, Indiana. Mindful of the historical heritage of his parish, Father Grogan carefully preserved the few remaining relics of earlier times by opening a museum, first in the bell tower and later in a building he erected in the garden area adjoining the old Washington Hotel.

"Patsy" Grogan figured prominently in both the history and the folklore of Ventura County and it is often difficult to separate the man from his legend. His was the happy duty of welcoming President William McKinley to the Old Mission on May 10, 1901. If one were compiling a list of the truly significant pioneer priests who have served the Church in California's southland, preference would necessarily be given to Patrick Grogan, the veteran pastor of San Buenaventura Mission.

Among Grogan's many distinctions was that of attending the fourth (1887) and fifth (1927) diocesan synods, thus becoming the only priest to survive that enormous span of time. The mayor of San Buenaventura once referred to Grogan as our "living history book." By the time of his demise, on the Feast of Saint Patrick in 1939, Father Grogan had exceeded all other archdiocesan priests in length of service. He was the last link with the Spanish *padres*.

Just a year after Los Angeles was created as an archdiocese, Father Grogan celebrated his golden sacerdotal jubilee. Archbishop John J. Cantwell and over a hundred priests gathered at San Buenaventura Mission for that gala occasion.

Upon his demise, the Ventura *Star Free Press* referred to Father Grogan as "one of Ventura's most famous and most beloved characters," a man who "had a kindly smile and a greeting for everyone, Catholic or Protestant. He was a great favorite with the children, for whom he always had a smile and a cheerful word."

B. FLORIAN HAHN (1850–1916)

German–born Father B. Florian Hahn (1850–1916) was once described by the head of the Bureau of Catholic Indian Missions as "a good, pious, zealous and prudent priest who got the good will and confidence of all who knew him." Young Hahn came early in life to the United States, where he spent some years as a printer before entering the Congregation of the Precious Blood. He was ordained at Castagena, Ohio, on June 8, 1882.

After serving at a number of parishes in the midwest, Father Hahn was appointed pastor of Assumption Church in Reed, Ohio. There he reorganized the parish and became a local celebrity. He was later transferred to the Indian school at Rennselaer, Indiana, and it was while ministering at that institution that he decided to devote the remainder of his life to caring for the spiritual needs of native Americans.

Bishop Francis Mora heard about Father Hahn's work with the Indians and, in 1890, invited him to take charge of Saint Boniface Industrial School at Banning, in the Diocese of Monterey–Los Angeles. For almost a quarter century, Father Hahn rode on horseback, by wagon and in automobile across the desert areas of the diocese preaching to the (mostly Indian) inhabitants from San Gorgonio Pass to the Mexican border and as far east as Indio.

By the time of his death, Hahn left a legacy of eleven mission churches and two parishes, one in Banning and the other in Beaumont. It was indeed an impressive record and one for which Hahn was given the papal title,"missionary apostolic."

During his years at Banning, Father Hahn utilized his skill at printing by writing and publishing T*he Mission Indian*, a monthly periodical which assisted substantially to support the Indian school. He also published several books during those years, including Archbishop J.B. Salpointe's *Soldiers of the Cross*, a collection of notes on the ecclesial history of New Mexico, Arizona and Colorado.

Father Hahn's twenty piece band became famous throughout the diocese. The talented priest, an expert on Gregorian chant, reportedly could himself play every instrument in the band. Though his native language was German, Father Hahn developed a fluency in English surpassed by few priests on the west coast. Bishop Thomas J. Conaty, a gifted orator in his own right, once said that he "preferred Father Hahn over all the preachers he had ever heard."

Despite the fact that he was plagued by ill health in his final years, Father Hahn never slackened in his pace. He was a perpetual motion machine for Christ. He died at Oxnard, on August 3, 1916. Father Hahn was among the most admired priests in California. In the homily preached at Hahn's funeral obsequies, Msgr. Thomas J. Fitzgerald attributed Hahn's intellectual and missionary success "to a unique and observable spiritual depth."

"Those who have heard him at the altar recite the Holy Sacrifice of the Mass could not but be struck with the intelligent, natural devotion that seemed to have possession of the man in the articulation of every syllable; in parts he seemed to go outside of himself and be, as it were, carried off in ecstasy."

PATRICK HARNETT (1858–1924)

Patrick Harnett "came of a goodly Limerick stock, which, long strengthened by discipline of the spirit, could gladly sacrifice the vain pleasures of life for the enduring rewards of religion." The young son, born in November, 1858, to Patrick Harnett and Johanna Relihan studied for the priesthood at Saint Patrick's College,

Carlow. He was ordained in his native Ireland, on June 3, 1882.

Shortly after his arrival in the Diocese of Monterey–Los Angeles, Father Harnett was assigned as curate to the Cathedral of Saint Vibiana. In 1886, he was appointed secretary to Bishop Francis Mora, a post he held for two years. For a brief time in 1887–1888, he was *pro–tempore* rector of the Cathedral. In August of 1888, Father Harnett was named the founding pastor of a new parish placed under the patronage of the Sacred Heart. Enclosed within the confines of the parochial unit was most of the area between Los Angeles and San Gabriel. There Father Harnett built a church and a school.

Harnett's fluency in Spanish and his keen Irish wit, scholarly mind and human sympathy made him the logical choice to succeed Father Joachim Adam, when the rectorship of Saint Vibiana's Cathedral fell vacant in 1899. At the same time, Bishop George T. Montgomery named Harnett Vicar General. Upon Montgomery's promotion to the coadjutorship of San Francisco, Father Harnett was the unanimous candidate of the diocesan consultors to succeed as Ordinary of the Diocese of Monterey–Los Angeles. His candidacy was given additional impetus from retired Bishop Francis Mora, who wrote from Spain to Rome on Harnett's behalf.

A petition favoring Harnett's appointment signed by the priests of the diocese, was also dispatched to the Holy See expressing the "conscientious belief in his eminent fitness for the position of Bishop of this diocese." When the nod ultimately fell to the former Rector of The Catholic University of America, Bishop Thomas J. Conaty, the new prelate asked Father Harnett to remain as Vicar General and not long thereafter, the Irish–born vicar received the distinction, unusual for those times, of being formally elevated to the domestic prelacy. The investiture of the state's first monsignor took place on July 31, 1905. An eyewitness later recalled that "the ceremony which preceded the Mass was the first one of its kind in California, and was singularly impressive in view of the high place Msgr. Harnett occupies among the people of Los Angeles." Four years later, Harnett was advanced to the rank of Protonotary Apostolic.

During the latter years of his episcopate, Bishop Conaty proposed his Vicar General's name as a candidate for the auxiliaryship of the far–flung Southern California jurisdiction. Conaty's recommendations was warmly endorsed by the diocesan consultors who, on April 14, 1915, "moved and seconded and unanimously carried the suggestion regarding the appointment of an auxiliary in the person of Rt. Rev. Mons. Harnett." Had the Vicar General been younger, such an appointment would very probably have materialized.

Monsignor Patrick Harnett "came to California when the Spanish clergy were about to pass on the lamp of faith which they kindled on our Pacific Slope. That flame he faithfully guarded throughout the years!"

PATRICK HAWE (1847–1923)

Father Patrick Hawe (1847–1923) was once described as a "simple, unassuming, meek and gentle" man, who was an "inspiration to his brother priests and a model to the laity." Patrick was one of the seven children born to John and Bridget (Freehan) Hawe. A brother, John, also studied for the ministry and served the People of God for many years in the Diocese of Dubuque.

At sixteen, Patrick entered the Classical Academy of the Carmelites and, three years later, began his formal preparation for the priesthood, at All Hallows College, Dublin. He was ordained in the college chapel on June 24, 1872, by Bishop John F. Whalen, for the Diocese of Monterey–Los Angeles. The newly–anointed priest then journeyed to California, where he received his first assignment the following fall.

In subsequent years, Father Hawe occupied curacies at San Bernardino, San Buenaventura, San Luis Obispo, Santa Cruz and Santa Barbara. After a few months caring for the vacant pastorate at San Bernardino, the Irish–born cleric was named to Saint Boniface Parish, in Anaheim, in 1885. During his two years there, Hawe built the first priests' residence and added a tower to the small church.

In May, 1886, Bishop Francis Mora entrusted Father Hawe with the challenge of organizing the Catholic populace of the Bay District into the Parish of Santa Monica. Under his able administration, that parochial family became one of the foremost in the diocese. In addition to his extensive building program at Santa Monica, the venerable and beloved priest built chapels at the Palms (Saint Augustine), the Soldiers' Home (Holy Trinity), East Santa Monica (Saint Anne) and Ocean Park (Saint Clement).

During his thirty–seven year pastorate, Father Hawe personally baptized 2,600 souls and united in wedlock 700 couples—at Santa Monica alone! The esteem and regard in which his people held him is illustrated by a touching incident related by a confrere. One afternoon, at the Soldiers' Home in Sawtelle, where Father Hawe was chaplain, he was waiting for the priest when an elderly patient approached and sat down beside him. After a few moment's conversation, Father Hawe came along and seeing him, the old soldier remarked: "Here comes the most perfect model of the meek and gentle Jesus."

In a tribute to his brother priest, Msgr. Thomas J. Fitzgerald said that "from Santa Cruz to San Diego, from San Bernardino to the sea was the field of (his) labors. Sick calls of many days' duration; missionary travels for distances of hundreds of miles on horseback and afoot, days without food and shelter, sleeping under trees on the King's Highway, was the lot that this young priest drew so that the blessings of Holy Mother Church could be given to the sick and dying."

His hospitality, friendship and virtue endeared Father Hawe to clergy and laity alike. Truly could it be said, at his death on August 30, 1923, that a marked figure in the annals of the southland had gone home to God.

BENJAMIN G. HAWKES (1919–1985)

In an interview, James Francis Cardinal McIntyre casually referred to Msgr. Benjamin G. Hawkes as the archdiocesan "concert–master." His explanation of that term and his response was very meaningful:

"The concert–master selects the programs, rehearses the orchestra and then steps aside for the conductor. The musicians often bristle at the concert–master's methods, but they all respect his ability to blend their individual efforts into soothing music."

Monsignor Hawkes, the "concert–master" for Los Angeles' two cardinals, fell asleep in the Lord on September 22, 1985 at Queen of Angels Hospital, but not before handing over to the newly–installed archbishop a performance–ready archdiocese.

Born in Lakeport, New York, on August 18, 1919, Benjamin George Hawkes acquired his earliest religious training at Saint Vincent's School in Buffalo. Later, his parents and older brother, William, moved to Los Angeles and Benjamin completed his primary education at Immaculate Heart of Mary in Hollywood.

In 1932, he enrolled at Los Angeles College, the preparatory seminary for the Diocese of Los Angeles–San Diego. Upon graduating, he entered Loyola University, where he majored in economics.

In 1940, he joined the staff of Lockheed Aircraft Company and there he rapidly advanced in the accounting department to the position of steward. At the end of World War II, Benjamin sought out the advice of Fathers Vincent Lloyd–Russell and Charles Casassa and then decided to complete his theological studies at Saint John's Seminary as a clerical candidate for the Archdiocese of Los Angeles. He was ordained priest on April 26, 1950

After two years as a curate at Saint Michael's Parish in central Los Angeles, Father Hawkes was named secretary to Archbishop J. Francis A. McIntyre. Early the following year, he accompanied the archbishop to Rome for his formal investiture as the first American cardinal of the far west.

During the following thirty–three years, Msgr. Hawkes served the curial offices of the archdiocese as secretary (1952–1962), Chancellor (1962–1967) and Vicar General (1967–1985). He was also active in other areas as a board member for the Dan Murphy Foundation, a trustee for The Catholic University of America and Vicar Delegate for the Military Ordinariate.

In 1965, Msgr. Hawkes began his long association with Saint Basil's Parish, first as consultant for the new church and, in 1969, as canonical pastor. The completed Saint Basil's was aptly described by the Mayor of Los Angeles as "one of the most significant examples of contemporary church architecture in the world."

Msgr. Hawkes' distinguished service to the Church of Los Angeles was recognized by Pope Paul VI on November 15, 1975, when the Holy Father conferred upon him the title of Protonotary Apostolic, a distinction given only seven times in the history of the jurisdiction.

During the years of Timothy Cardinal Manning's tenure, Msgr. Hawkes was publicly recognized by such publications as *Los Angeles Magazine* as "one of the most powerful men in the city." He was the subject of several in–depth studies by the mass media over the years. The Los Angeles *Times* referred to him as "a legend—a priest who for years has wielded immense power for two cardinals."

Interestingly enough, the reporters generally overlooked the fact that this same priest was a dedicated pastor of souls who offered a scheduled Mass every day, counselled people in the evenings, took his turn in the confessional and in the pulpit and performed all the other duties associated with the priestly ministry.

Though plagued throughout his life with miserable health, he rarely missed a full day in the chancery or on the road looking after the material needs of churches, schools and other institutions. His no–nonsense demeanor and abrupt style belied a man who quietly channeled a lion's share of the Church's assets into projects benefiting the inner city's poor and downtrodden.

Just a week before his death, he emerged ever–so–briefly from the background to serve as archpriest for Pope John Paul II in the ceremony that saw his long–time friend, Msgr. Justin Rigali, advanced to the archbishopric. He remarked to friends that the occasion was the capstone of his priestly life.

Much more might be said, but one feels that Msgr. Hawkes would prefer to slip away unnoticed. Perhaps it's enough to record that he cared only for the Church, the archdiocese and his parish.

Cardinal McIntyre concluded the above–mentioned interview with these words: "No man can lead the orchestra unless he returns his back to the crowd."

JOHN M. HEGARTY (1884–1954)

It used to be said, in clerical circles, that the only canonical "right" a priest had was to Christian burial. Certain pastors, however, enjoyed another right that closely paralleled the "tenure" held in academic circles, that of being "irremovable."

A celebrated example of pastoral irremovability concerned Msgr. John M. Hegarty (1884–1954), a priest who had served as Vicar General in the Diocese of San Diego for five years. Born in Ireland, Hegarty studied for the Diocese of Monterey–Los Angeles. He was ordained on June 17, 1910 and served at posts in Riverside, Long Beach and San Diego.

Hegarty was highly regarded by everyone. Upon his departure from Long Beach, in 1928, B.F. Tucker was quoted in the local newspaper as saying that "through his personality and determination," Hegarty was one of those responsible for "changing the entire community thinking." At the time of his silver priestly ordination, when Hegarty was serving as Vicar Forane for San Diego and Imperial counties, Bishop John J. Cantwell personally journeyed to San Diego to honor the area's "foremost priest."

Hegarty had a rare gift with words. His essay on "The Franciscan Path to the Stars" was featured in the September, 1931 issue of the *San Diego Magazine*. Therein he stated that "the glory of the Franciscans is not that they did so much, but that they did anything at all."

In 1940, Bishop Charles Francis Buddy asked Hegarty, then in charge of Saint Joseph's Cathedral, to assume the pastoral care of Our Lady of Angels with the title of "irremovable pastor." In his letter, Buddy commended Hegarty for being distinguished in "learning, piety, culture and a vigorous defender of the faith."

For reasons unknown, (his file in the San Diego chancery archives has been "purged" of the details), Hegarty was asked to resign in August of 1943. The bishop even threatened to remove his name from the list of Domestic Prelates which, of course, could only be done by the Holy Father.

Hegarty complained to Cantwell, by then the Metropolitan Archbishop of the Province of Los Angeles, that Buddy had compiled a twenty–three page list of grievances, including charges of perjury, threat of civil suit

and delinquency of paying his debts. The embattled priest engaged a canon lawyer, Father James W. Richardson, C.M. (a renowned canonist who later became Superior General for the Congregation of the Mission) to defend him against being removed.

When the bishop, known for his irascible outbursts, threatened to have the pastor evicted by the local sheriff "as an unwanted tenant," Hegarty took refuge outside the diocese. Happily, Richardson eventually won the case in canonical court and the bishop was instructed to re–instate Msgr. Hegarty. Buddy refused and Archbishop Cantwell had to intervene. Cantwell told the Apostolic Delegate that "the good Bishop of San Diego is very autocratic in his dealings" and that he had conspired to manufacture false or at least unsubstantiated evidence in the legal proceedings.

Several months later, Cantwell told the Apostolic Delegate that Buddy had agreed to restore Hegarty to the diocese, in another pastorate, at Ontario. Though Cantwell felt that such a decision was considerably short of being fair or just, he advised Hegarty to accept.

The monsignor was left alone by the bishop for the final years of his life. He died peacefully as pastor of Saint George in Ontario on March 30, 1954. The then Auxiliary Bishop Timothy Manning told this writer that "Hegarty should be remembered as a martyr for that he truly was."

THOMAS F. HUDSON (1829–1907)

To those whose privilege it was to know him, Father Thomas J.F. Hudson (1829–1907) exhibited that rugged, old–fashioned piety which made his life a constant prayer. Shortly after completing his studies at Dublin's All Hallows College, on June 26, 1864 the young son of James and Ann Hudson was ordained to the priesthood in the chapel of his alma mater for service in the Diocese of Monterey–Los Angeles.

When the newly–anointed priest arrived in California's southland later that summer, Bishop Thaddeus Amat gave him his one and only appointment in the northernmost parish of the far–flung jurisdication. Father Hudson proceeded at once to take up his work in the Chapel of San Martin, in the Santa Clara Valley, midway between Santa Clara Mission and San Juan Bautista. In the words of one chronicler, "what happened in the life of the Catholic Church in this community between November 4, 1864, the date of his appointment as Pastor of the Church of St. Martin, and his death on June 10, 1907, was all due to one man."

In 1865, the Irish–born pastor received permission to relocate his parish on a fifteen–acre site in the newly developing community of Gilroy (Hot Springs). There he erected a wooden frame church which he placed under the patronage of the Blessed Mother. Not long afterwards, a rectory was built and property acquired for a cemetery. In late 1870, Father Hudson began raising funds for a Catholic school. A two–story edifice was built housing classrooms on the ground level and quarters for the sisters above. The institution began operation, in September of 1871, under the direction of the Sisters of the Immaculate Heart of Mary.

Father Hudson insisted on participation in the various parochial enterprises. Among the more active of the organizations he initiated were the Altar Society, the League of the Sacred Heart, the Young Mens' Institute and the Catholic Ladies Aid Society. Only once in the forty–three years of his pastorate was Father Hudson known to have been absent from his parish. During his long tenure at Gilroy, he baptized 1,655 persons, witnessed 272 marriages and made 1,000 burial entries, in the parish registers.

On November 25, 1905, Father Hudson received the rare honor from the Holy Father of being named a papal chamberlain. Though he thus became entitled to the title of "monsignor," the name "Father" Hudson was so ingrained in the vocabulary of the community that he was effectively denied the honor given by Pope Pius X.

Father Hudson served many years as the Vicar Forane in the northern part of the diocese and in that capacity proved of valuable assistance to the bishop. It was as the "most beloved of all our associates" that he was eulogized by Bishop Thomas J. Conaty at the time of his death, in 1907. The long–time pastor at Gilroy was memorialized, in 1962, when Archbishop Joseph T. McGucken purchased a site for a future Catholic High School which he designated as "Hudson Memorial High."

WILLIAM McDERMOTT HUGHES (1880–1939)

Though he was a priest of the Diocese of Monterey–Los Angeles, Father William McDermott Hughes (1880–1939), first native of Sacramento raised to the priesthood, spent most of his ministry working among or for the nation's Catholic Indian population. Just two years after his ordination, Bishop J. Conaty sent the Dunwoodie–trained priest to San Jacinto, a small mountain town close to the northern end of the Sierra Nevadas as missionary to the Soboba, Cahuilla, and Coyote Indians.

Though he endured many hardships in the lonely 5,000 square miles area making up his parish, Father Hughes reckoned it of little importance compared to what hundreds of priests in early California days had undergone. He commented that the "inconveniences of the far–flung apostolate gave him an encouraging feeling of kinship with those truly heroic men on whom first fell the trials and to whom is now accorded the glory of the grandest work of religion in the United States, the Indian missions of early California." Among his earliest achievements among the natives was the construction of a beautiful old mission–style chapel on the Soboba Reservation.

The talents and skill of the California missionary soon attracted the attention of the national hierarchy, and in 1910, Hughes was named to the staff of the Bureau of Catholic Indian Missions. At the time of his appointment one newspaper described the indefatigable priest as "a clear–eyed, clean–skinned, bright–brained priest . . . who is the type that any church . . . should be glad to have carrying its banner."

On April 17, 1912, two years after his arrival in Washington, Father Hughes became assistant director of the Bureau under the supervision of the Reverend William H. Ketchum. During World War I, Father Hughes served in France as chaplain for the 335th Field Artillery, of the 87th division. After the hostilities he returned to Los Angeles as Pastor of Saint Basil's Church, where he erected the frame building later moved to Wilshire Boulevard. On December 1, 1921, Cardinal Dougherty nominated Hughes to the directorship of the Bureau of Catholic Indian Missions at Washington.

Upon his return to the national capital, Hughes immediately launched a campaign for promoting more friendly relations and cooperation between the Catholic missionaries and the United States Government. "His genuine interest in Indians, his understanding of their problems, his personal uprightness and singleness of purpose, his friendliness, his sense of justice, and his good judgment won him the abiding confidence and respect of Congressmen and officials in the Indian Service." So successful was the Los Angeles priest in his endeavors that he was soon recognized throughout the country as the mainstay of the Indian missions. His own years of hardship as a missionary not only gave Father Hughes an understanding and sympathy with those engaged in the Indian apostolate, but it also led him to emulate them in the simplicity of his own personal life.

The director was able to report in 1931, "The Catholic Church today ministers to Indians in thirty–three dioceses in twenty–one states and to Indians and Eskimos in the Territory and Vicariate of Alaska. There are nearly 400 mission chapels attended by 200 priests." The Bureau was then also maintaining seventy Catholic Indian day and boarding schools and other missionary activities on eighty–one reservations in the United States and Alaska.

Upon his retirement from the Washington post in

1935, Monsignor Hughes, a domestic prelate since 1924, came back to the west as pastor of Avalon on Santa Catalina Island, off the Southern California coastline. His last pastorate was that of Saint Catherine in Laguna Beach. Even in his final years, the monsignor continued to live as a missionary. "His intense love of the poor and the unfortunate, his zeal for the Church, and his love of Christ called forth that tireless energy with which be devoted himself to the Indian missions" for a quarter century.

ARTHUR J. HUTCHINSON (1876–1951)

It was during the pastoral tenure of Father Arthur J. Hutchinson that San Juan Capistrano Mission came to be known as the "jewel of the California missions." "Hutch," as he was known to contemporaries, was born at Brooklyn, New York on November 14, 1876, the son of Arthur and Honora (Carey) Hutchinson. From his earliest years, Hutch wanted to be a priest. And few doubted that he would achieve that goal.

After attending Saint Francis College, Hutch entered Saint Bernard's Seminary in Rochester as a clerical aspirant for the Diocese of Buffalo. He was ordained by Archbishop John Farley in St Patrick's Cathedral on June 10, 1911. During World I, Hutchinson was among the first of the Army chaplains to serve in the overseas Air Corps. It was while stationed abroad that he fell victim to gas inhalation by the enemy.

Because of the precarious health that resulted, Father Hutch came to California after the hostilities and was given several assignments in the old Diocese of Monterey–Los Angeles. He served at Our Lady of the Sacred Heart in San Diego and, in 1921, established Our Lady of the Valley Parish in Canoga Park.

In 1933, Father Hutchinson was sent to San Juan Capistrano where, according to one chronicler, "he reached for and grabbed ahold of the stars." It was the perfect position for a man of his temperament. The November 22, 1936 issue of the Los Angeles *Times Sunday Magazine* carried an extensive article on the excavations made at the old Mission by Father Hutch.

In a period of eighteen months, the priest and his co–workers "uncovered the workshops and storehouses of former mission days. . . . This spurred the diggers onward and, near the stoves, layers of earth were taken from two large vats. These undoubtedly were used as tallow vats," said Father Hutchinson. Conical in shape, they were nearly ten feet deep. Beneath each is a small furnace. These and other discoveries clearly indicated to Hutch that "tallow making was one of the most important industries in the old mission days."

He went on to say that "the Indians of the early mis-

sion days were highly skilled in the tanning and curing of hides. San Juan Capistrano was especially famous in this craft.

It was at San Juan Capistrano that Richard Henry Dana, in his book, *Two Years Before the Mast*, described taking on a boatload of hides. The stiff pelts were carried to the sea cliffs three miles away by ox–cart. Here they were unloaded and thrown down the 300 foot slope to waiting boats below.

As he reflected on what the early missionaries accomplished with their bare hands and iron wills, Father Hutchinson said that the priest then "was not only a saver of souls. He was also of necessity an explorer, an architect, a builder, a trader and an executive. Converting the Indians to Christianity was his mission in the New World—but teaching them to raise their own food, make their own clothes and live in a civilized society" was vitally important to their overall objectives.

In an essay published in 1976, Carmen Oyharzabal said that Father Hutchinson "was a man of deep faith, love and gratitude. Gratitude for the pleasant happenings as well as the not so pleasant, he believed that they were both stepping stones to heaven."

ANTHONY JACOBS (1894–1964)

The Homiletic and Pastoral Review is a journal published for Catholic clergymen since 1900. In recent years it has carried a monthly column on "My Favorite Priest." The issue for June, 1989, featured a reflection on "The Bishop of Oxnard," Msgr. Anthony Jacobs, by Catherine Mervyn.

A native of Ooltgensplaat, the Netherlands, Anthony J. Jacobs was born on December 16, 1894. After completing his theological Studies at the University of Fribourg, he was ordained on July 25, 1920 for service in what was then the Diocese of Los Angeles–San Diego.

One of the more interesting monographs in the Archival Center, Archdiocese of Los Angeles, is a thirty–two page *Feestgids* that was issued as a tribute to the newly–ordained priest at Brussels in 1920. It was an elaborate program commemorating the conferral of his theological degree.

His first assignment along the Pacific Slope was Santa Clara in Oxnard, as associate pastor. Afterwards, he served as pastor at three parishes in various parts of California's southland. In 1934, Father Jacobs returned to Oxnard, this time as pastor. In subsequent years he erected Santa Clara High School, Saint Anthony's Elementary School and Christ the King Church. Pope Pius XII named Jacobs a papal chamberlain in 1940 and, ten years later, he was advanced to the domestic prelacy.

Though the monsignor performed many other functions within the local Church, he is most remembered for his long tenure as a chairman of the archdiocesan Building Committee. There, according to a local newspaper he advocated "a blending of the significantly religious elements and simple, modern lines in church architecture."

Jacobs was a voracious reader and a discerning bibliophile. Most of his extensive collection of architectural and art books eventually found their way to the library at Queen of Angels, the archdiocesan preparatory seminary at Mission Hills.

In 1959, parishioners at Santa Clara honored the monsignor's silver jubilee as pastor with a handsome monograph outlining, in pictorial fashion, his major contributions to the city and environs of Oxnard. In March of 1964, "Oxnard's Dutch Monsignor" was featured in a special issue of P/C, the weekly magazine of Ventura County. Bob Horner gave Jacobs the ultimate accolade by referring to him as "a contemporary priest" in every area touching his people.

The monsignor's death, on June 16, 1964, occasioned a remarkable show of affection throughout Ventura County. He was interred alongside his predecessors in the stately mausoleum of the parochial cemetery.

In her article for the HPR, Mrs. Mervyn noted that Msgr. Jacobs left "an indelible imprint on the life of his parishioners." He was "brilliant, compassionate, erudite, stern. There was an aura of dignity about him that commanded respect. He practiced the apostleship of presence zealously and made the sacraments readily available to his parishioners."

In his years as Pastor at Oxnard he "emerged as a powerful ruler on behalf of the Church's affairs, and a benevolent, considerate, kindly human being in his dealings with the people he shepherded."

ANTONIO JIMENEZ DEL RECIO (f. 1815–1853)

A suburban third grader who was being exposed to a history course for the first time voiced a complaint about the subject to her parents, noting that "nobody lives more than two pages!" Using that little lady's yardstick, the role played by Father Antonio Jiménez del Recio in the Catholic pageant of California would rate only a few letters of a single line.

The Franciscan chronicler reported that Jiménez del Recio's "antecedants are not known." The young clerical aspirant came to California from Mexico with Bishop Francisco Garcia Diego y Moreno, in December, 1841. Prior to his ordination to the priesthood, Antonio served as the bishop's pro–secretary. In that capacity, he assisted the Franciscan prelate in drafting the first *Pastoral Letter* issued on California soil. Published at Santa Barbara, on February 4, 1842, the pastoral outlined the various programs which Bishop Garcia Diego hoped to inaugurate for the People of God in the newly–created Diocese of Both Californias.

Antonio was received into the clerical state at San Diego, on December 19, 1841. He was advanced to the deaconate on the following June 29th. His ordination to the priesthood was conferred in the old Mission at Santa Barbara, on October 8, 1843. It is recorded that Jiménez del Recio joined Bishop Garcia Diego and several other priests in taking the oath of allegiance to the new Mexican Government.

Throughout the short years of his sacerdotal ministry, Father Antonio Jiménez del Recio was sickly and infirm. The precise nature of his illness cannot be ascertained. Hubert Howe Bancroft stated only that he was chronicly enfeebled. On December 5, 1843, Father Jiménez del Recio was named curate to Fray Tomas Esténaga at Mission San Gabriel. One of the historians of that foundation later wrote that the priest served as "chaplain on one of the San Blas transports."

During his short tenure at San Gabriel, the priest cared for the *Asistencia de Nuestra Señora de los Angeles*. He was apparently highly esteemed by the populace of the *pueblo*, who petitioned that he be named permanent pastor. Unfortunately, there were not funds enough available to support an autonomous ministry at Los Angeles.

The national Catholic Directory for 1854 states that Father Jiménez del Recio died at Los Angeles, on April 23, 1853. Though attached to Mission San Gabriel and assigned to *Nuestra Señora de los Angeles*, there are indications that the priest succumbed at Mission San Fernando. A reporter for the Los Angeles *Times* reported, in 1905, that the bones of the "bygone priest" were among those disinterred by Father Alexander LeBellegay.

Very little else is known or recorded about the priest. Father Zephyrin Engelhardt wrote that "having been rapidly promoted to the priesthood on account of the dearth of priests, his studies could not have been brilliant." Possibly that was true, though there is no way of determining how far advanced the clerical aspirant was in his ecclesiastical courses at the time of his arrival in California.

Quite possibly, future historians will discover more about Father Antonio Jiménez del Recio. One prominent commentator on the American scene, Father Peter K. Guilday, once observed that

> History never stays written. Every epoch and every generation since the beginning of the modern research school of historians has witnessed the revelation of new documents, new archaeological sources, new discoveries of all kinds.

JOHN PATRICK LANGUILLE (1925–1985)

John Patrick Languille, a priest whose lifeline was c–h–a–r–i–t–y, returned to his native Seattle—there to surrender his gentle soul to the Lord. A few years after his birth, Victor Languille and his infant son moved to Long Beach, California, where "Pat" entered Saint Matthew's school. It was under the watchful tutleage of Msgr. Bernard J. Dolan that "Pat" enrolled at Los Angeles College, preparatory seminary for the newly–created Archdiocese of Los Angeles.

Ordained to the priesthood on May 7, 1949, Father Languille was assigned to Saint Andrew's parish in Pasadena, which at that time was shepherded by Bishop Joseph T. McGucken. From that relationship evolved a life–long friendship.

Early in 1950, Father Languille began his long association with the charitable works of the archdiocese. His first appointment was assistant director of the Catholic Welfare Bureau and then, the following year, his apostolate was broadened to include the Catholic Youth Organization.

During the ensuing decades, Father Languille found himself engaged in a host of activities related to the Church's outreach programs. These included the Neighborhood Youth Corps, several refugee projects, the commission on aging and, finally, Las Torres Corporation for seniors.

The Languille imprint was felt even more widely when he became director of the CYO (1958), the Catholic Welfare Bureau (1973) and the Saint Vincent de Paul Society (1974). One of the friends from USC noted amusingly that "Pat got more mileage from his ACSW degree than all his classmates combined." In his "spare time," Msgr. Languille was director of Mary's Hour, Moderator of the Catholic Alumni Club and Coordinator for the Cardinal's Christmas Parties, to mention but a few his "sideline" involvements.

He was fiercely proud of the Church's front–line identification with the poor. If he ever bragged, it was only to point out that he presided over the largest family service agency west of the Mississippi River!

Twice honored by the Holy See, Msgr. Languille remained a "street priest" in every sense. Besides keeping a firm hand on the pulse of the Los Angeles *barrios*, he was a respected member of the local French community. His command of Spanish and French was the envy of his priestly collaborators.

Since 1967, Msgr. Languille had been pastor of Our Lady of Loretto parish in downtown Los Angeles. Though several times offered other pastoral assignments, he opted to remain in the inner city "with the people I love the most."

"Pat" Languille was not alone a first class administrator of Catholic charities. He went several steps beyond and dedicated his life to eradicating the causes of poverty and need. His name was probably on every city administrator's Rolodex.

His sixty year "war on poverty" terminated in the city of his birth on September 23, 1985. The Catholics in California's southland can join in saying: "Thank you Seattle for a fine priest, a loving pastor and a great exemplar!" Msgr. Languille lived close to death, having lost all his relatives at an early age. On his desk was a laminated copy of Alan Seeger's poem "I have a Rendezvous with Death:"

> I have a rendezvous with Death
>   At some disputed barricade
> When Spring comes round with rustling shade
>   And apple blossoms fill the air.
> I have a rendezvous with Death
>   When Spring brings back blue days and fair.
>
> It may be He shall take my hand
>   And lead me into His dark land
> And close my eyes and quench my breath;
>   It may be I shall pass Him still.
> I have a rendezvous with Death
>   On some scarred slope of battered hill,
>
> When Spring comes round again this year
>   And the first meadow flowers appear.
> God knows 'twere better to be deep
>   Pillowed in silk and scented down,
> Where love throbs out in blissful sleep,
>   Pulse nigh to pulse and breath to breath
>
> Where hushed awakenings are dear .
>   But I've a rendezvous with Death
> At midnight in some flaming town
>   When Spring trips north again this year,
> And I to my pledged word am true,
>   I shall not fail that rendezvous.

EDMOND E. LAPOINTE (1882–1932)

Father Edmond E. Lapointe (1882–1932) was famed, according to the Los Angeles *Times*, "as a virtual reincarnation of the early mission *padres* of Southern California." Ordained priest at twenty–one, by papal dispensation, the Canadian–born cleric came to California, in 1903, at the request of Bishop George T. Montgomery "to walk for twenty–nine years the warm and tangled back country hills of San Diego County."

Father Lapointe plunged immediately into his work with the descendants of the old mission Indians. During his three decade apostolate, he established outposts at Descanso, Campo, Sequan, Mesa Grande and Jamul. The chapel he built at Palm City was destroyed by the floods of 1916. Envisioning the old site of Santa Ysabel as a mother church to the neighboring group of missionary stations, Father Lapointe rebuilt the church there and then had it re–dedicated, with colorful pageantry, in 1924. An auditorium, rectory and grotto were subsequently added at the site.

In earlier years he made the rounds on foot, accepting the humble hospitality of back–country settlers along the road. Later he was presented with a horse which he rode constantly until failing health made it necessary that he travel by car. Upon the demise of his parents, Father Lapointe inherited a personal fortune of $60,000. The indefatigable missionary "held good to the tenets of his life and gave every cent of it to the Indians of his flock." He was aided in his later works by the philanthropic interest of Ellen Browning Scripps.

Over the years, Father Lapointe "revived or kept alive there many of the old customs and ceremonies celebrated by the ancestors of the present–day Indians." The observance of the harvest festival annually attracted 500 Indians and a thousand whites. "All the afternoon of the first day barbecued beef and Indian–cooked foods were served to residents and visitors alike. In the evening a procession, led by three men each carrying a large cross made of sheaves of grain, was formed at the *fiesta* grounds from whence it proceeded to the chapel where a Mass of thanksgiving was sung. After the Mass came the bonfires and games so loved by the Indians. On the second day the religious ceremonies were repeated and then came another barbecue. followed by the games of *peon*, *pelota*, *gome* and *monte* played by the older men, for the younger ones have taken to baseball."

Prematurely worn out by his arduous missionary tasks, Father Lapointe died at Mercy Hospital, in San Diego, on November 19, 1932. At the request of his beloved Indian flock, the latter–day missionary was interred at Santa Ysabel, there to rest among the people for whom he had labored so unceasingly. Perhaps more than any of his contemporaries, Father Lapointe typified the Church's missionary apostolate by readily adapting to the strange customs and changing circumstances of a backward people. His sympathetic mind and responsive heart endeared the dedicated priest in the hearts of his flock as few have been—before or after.

ALEXANDER LeBELLEGAY (1855–1941)

Father Alexander LeBellegay (1855–1941) was "a Frenchman of venerable appearance and gentle manners, well loved by the Mexican families of the valley and revered by the few remaining Indians" of the area. A native of France, Father LeBellegay came to the Diocese of Monterey–Los Angeles after serving as a missionary in Guatemala. He was assigned to the parish at San Fernando between November, 1903 and November, 1906.

The priest resided in a couple of bare rooms within the little church in San Fernando, living a life almost as simple and devoid of worldly comforts as did his early predecessors. Father LeBellegay was an "eccentric priest" according to a long feature article which appeared in the Los Angeles *Times* for March 4, 1905. The essay complained that the one–time missionary had unroofed certain parts of the mission buildings and carried off the timbers and tiles to San Fernando, where he was erecting a summer pavilion outside the parochial church.

It was disinterment of his sacerdotal predecessors that most irritated the reporter's sensitivities. The account is fascinating for the background it contains about conditions as they existed at San Fernando just after the turn of the century: "In vaults beneath the floor of the cloister, brick–lined, brick–floored, brick–ceiled, reposed the crumbled forms of several of the old fathers. There they had slept for sixty years and more, even their names forgotten though their works still stood."

An ancient Indian lady, Catalina Lopez, told Father LeBellegay "the names of the dead men who lay in the narrow vaults beneath the cloister floors, and in what relative position they slept." "Then behold," the reporter continued, "the queer priest standing, paper in hand on which the old squaw had traced in trembling outlines a plot of the vaults; he is directing several workmen who with picks and spades are digging up the ground of the cloister floor.

"When the horizontal wall of flat adobe bricks was reached which formed the ceiling of the vaults, Father LeBellegay ordered them to break it through, and they obeyed. After a little more toiling they hoisted up to him, there in the sacred shadows of the Mission roof, some armfuls of human bones and punky wood, which were the remains of the bodies and the caskets of Pedro Cabot and Thomas Stenaga (sic), the last of the Franciscans, and Antonio Jiménez, a bygone priest. Assembling their gruesome relies in a heap, Father LeBellegay went through the ceremony of blessing them.

"A few days later, he placed the exhumed remains of the three fathers in two ordinary lemon–picking boxes, and lowered them into the vaults. This done, he caused earth and stones to be tumbled into the yawning cavities, and planted a rude cross in the careless mound. On this headboard he pasted a sheet of note paper on which he had written in ink an epitaph identifying the remains." The *Times* reporter noted that "during the interval between the exhuming and the reburying of the bones the sacred relics reposed in picking boxes, free to the curious fingering of a number of tourists who paused in passing that way."

The story quite naturally came to the attention of chancery officials and Bishop Thomas J. Conaty wrote to the priest, saying: "The Los Angeles *Times* of this morning has a very exciting report in which you appear as destroying portions of the Old Mission. I am anxious to know what explanation you have for it." Unfortunately, if Father LeBellegay answered by letter, the correspondence has disappeared. In any event, *The Tidings*, in its issue for March 10, 1905, stated that reports about the "alleged exposure of the desecration of the old San Fernando Mission . . . were not based upon adequate foundation."

The official Catholic newspaper for the Diocese of Monterey–Los Angeles went on to say that "both Father LeBellegay and those of his parishioners who know the upshot of his work in connection with the old mission affirm that, instead of destroying any portion of it, Father LeBellegay's efforts have been directed towards preserving it from the destructive work of vandals seeking treasure on the old site."

The report in *The Tidings* maintained that the bones had been unearthed several years earlier by "persons in search of the buried gold that was supposed to have been hidden away at the time of the secularization movement." To prevent further desecration, Father LeBellegay had simply gathered the bones together and reburied them. He then erected a cross on the spot that was believed by tradition to have been the burial place of the venerable Father Pedro Cabot.

Unfortunately, the explanation by *The Tidings* received scanty attention in comparison to the untrue "expose" by the *Times*' reporter. The account, with all its inaccuracies, found its way into the historical annals and even today occasionally comes to the surface—much to the annoyance of seekers after the truth.

EUGENE McNAMARA (f. 1840s)

Father Eugene McNamara, "native of Ireland, Catholic priest and Missionary Apostolic," arrived at Monterey aboard the British vessel, *Juno*, in mid June, 1846. He was to inaugurate a movement still shrouded in secrecy as to its full motivations.

The previous year, Father McNamara petitioned the President of Mexico for permission to settle a large group of Irish colonizers in California. The Irish cleric claimed to have a threefold reason for his plan: to advance the cause of the Catholic faith, to contribute to the happiness of his countrymen and to thwart any further "usurpation on the part of an irreligious and anti–Catholic nation (United States!)."

Initially, thousands of colonists were to settle on the Bay of San Francisco. Later, McNamara planned to establish colonies near Monterey and Santa Barbara. With these three establishments, he felt "the entire coast would be completely secured against invasion and pillage of foreigners."

The priest wanted 4,428 acres given free to each family. And their offspring would later receive half that much land as a "national gift." The colonists would also be freed of taxation for a given number of years. McNamara told the President that his plan had the "fullest approbation of the Archbishop of Mexico City, the venerable head of the Church" in the Republic.

The Irish cleric claimed that if his plans were not speedily adopted, "the Californians will form a part of the American Nation." And should that happen, he went on to predict that "Catholic institutions will become the prey of the Methodist wolves, and the whole country will be inundated with the cruel invaders." A reply to the request was issued by the Minister of Foreign Affairs, Government and Policy, Joaquin Castillo, on January 19, 1846. It was an ambiguous statement which referred the whole matter to local officials in California.

Father McNamara then went to Monterey and there presented his proposal directly to Governor Pio Pico. This time he increased the number of colonists to 10,000. They would, he said, "be bound by and subject to the established laws" and would "lend their services to the legitimate government in defense of California against all enemies who might invade her."

McNamara asked for a specific area, namely the land "between the River San Joaquin, from its source to its mouth, and the Sierra Nevada. The limits being the River Consumne on the north, and on the south, the extremity of the Tulares, in the neighborhood of San Gabriel." It was obvious that the priest knew little about local geography. The governor was favorable to the proposal and sent it on to the California Assembly. A grant was issued, but being dated a few days after the United States had taken possession of Monterey, it was never recognized or even promulgated.

But there is a footnote to this scheme which causes observers to question the integrity of the Irish Priest. Researchers have discovered evidence to indicate that Father McNamara was a British agent who worked in conjunction with James Forbes, the British Vice Consul. The whole plan was hatched under the auspices of the British Legation. McNamara himself, though seemingly a priest in good standing and one duly authorized to function in California by ecclesial officials, was a full–fledged member of the British government. In any event, with the arrival of United States troops, Father McNamara hastily left California on the English flagship, *Collinwood*, for the Sandwich Islands and thereafter disappeared completely from the searching glance of historians.

JOAQUIN MASMITJA (1808–1886)

Bishop Thaddeus Amat had every right to be a "name dropper." The Vincentian prelate was a personal friend of three saints—Anthony Claret, Catherine Laboure and John Neumann. The candidacy for beatification of another of his acquaintances, Canon Joaquin Masmitja y de Puig, has recently been initiated. And that venerable cleric has other claims to renown in California for he was the founder of a religious community that grew to maturity in the Golden State.

Joaquin Masmitja was born at Olot (Gerona, Catalonia) to a respected family known for its piety and social position, on December 29, 1808. It was an eventful time for Spain which was then being invaded by the armies of Napoleon.

Upon completion of his studies in the humanities, Joaquin entered the seminary in 1825 as a clerical aspirant for the Diocese of Gerona. In 1829, he enrolled at the University of Cervera and there excelled in philosophy and theology. He was awarded a licentiate in jurisprudence on June 17, 1834. Ordained to the priesthood on February 22, 1834, Masmitja was offered a coveted teaching position at the University of Barcelona. Preferring the parochial ministry, he asked the local bishop for permission to remain at La Bisbal and Olot.

After serving in several parochial positions, Father Masmitja was appointed Pastor of the diocesan cathedral in 1848. Five years later, he was made a canon and then in 1975, archpriest of Gerona. A forward–looking and

Joaquin Masmitja

apostolic priest, Canon Masmitja instituted a perpetual adoration society, organized the Court of Mary and established the Confraternity of Our Lady of Victory.

It was at the urging of Librada Ferrarons that Masmitja founded the Congregation of the Sisters of the Immaculate Heart of Mary, on July 1, 1848. Envisioning the community as a means for catechizing young girls, he personally wrote the original constitution and way–of–life.

The initial group numbered seven women, as a tribute to the dolors of Our Lady. Approved in April of 1850 by Queen Isabella II, the congregation had grown to forty sisters and fourteen novices serving in six houses by 1860. Though he was long a prominent priestly figure in the Diocese of Gerona, once even serving as Vicar Capitular, Canon Joaquin Masmitja y de Puig is best remembered for his work as founder of the Immaculate Heart Sisters.

The venerable canon succumbed on August 26, 1886. His earthly remains were re–interred in the chapel of the Motherhouse for the Immaculate Heart Sisters at Olot in 1965. He is a candidate for beatification.

FRANCIS FLORENCE McCARTHY (1884–1948)

It is often fascinating to know the background of how a book came to be written and published. A case at hand is the work of Francis Florence McCarthy (1884–1948)) which occupies a prominent place in the bibliography of the California missions.

The McCarthys came from Bardstown, Kentucky to California, where Francis was born at Napa. A few years later, the family moved to San Francisco and it was there that the youthful boy came to know Archbishop Patrick W. Riordan.

Educated in California, McCarthy was enamored by history, much of which he learned from his mother's tales of Irish America and early California. Several of his articles were published in the years after McCarthy was ordained a priest for the Archdiocese of San Francisco.

He served as assistant and later as pastor of several parishes and, in each of those assignments, he studied about the local area and wrote parochial histories. It was while pursuing a planned reading program established by his mother that Francis McCarthy discovered that San Jose Mission was the only one of the historic foundations along *El Camino Real* that lacked its own history.

To remedy that lacuna, McCarthy devoted his spare time during the final decade of a very busy life. Shortly before his demise, the pastor of Sacred Heart parish in Oakland finished his manuscript.

Compiled from data unearthed in the Santa Barbara Mission Archives, the archives for the Archdiocese of San Francisco and materials in the Bancroft Library at Berkeley, the completed work filled a long–felt need in the field of Californiana especially for those interested in Alameda county's earliest beginnings.

McCarthy knew Professor Herbert Eugene Bolton and he sent the manuscript of his book to the esteemed historian and scholar for review. So impressed was Bolton that he offered to write a preface for the book. Though Bolton himself died before he could complete that commitment, he had earlier noted that the manuscript "should be published because it contains precious data which has not yet found its way into print." Sister M. Serena, a member of the community staffing the Dominican College of San Rafael, contacted Msgr. James Culleton who agreed to publish the work under the imprint of the Academy Library Guild. Issued as *The History of Mission San Jose California 1797–1835,* the book was prepared for publication by Dr. Raymund F. Wood who wrote an epilogue covering the 1835–1855 period at the mission. The previous year, Dr. Wood had published his own *A Brief History of Mission San Jose* which he acknowledged was "based largely upon the more complete" manuscript written by McCarthy.

McCarthy's 285 page book was described by J. Thomas Owen of the Los Angeles Public Library as "a factual account presented with freshness which would deny the original ink on those recordings dried more than a century ago." An article in the San Francisco *Sunday Tribune* for November 23, 1958 stated that McCarthy's book "brings us a score of stories that have been heretofore unknown or known by only a very few."

As is the case for many writers, McCarthy's book was his only major publication. But it alone won for its author a cherished place on the bookshelves of Californiana.

JOHN M. McCARTHY (1864–1951)

One of the last "transitional" priests was Msgr. John M. McCarthy, whose six decades of service to the Church in California's southland made him Dean of the Clergy, in fact as well as in esteem. John Michael McCarthy was born on April 10, 1864, in New York City, the son of Silvester McCarthy and Bridget O'Brien. Though there were other children in the family, only John lived to manhood. As a youngster, one of his most vivid memories was that of attending the opening of Saint Patrick's Cathedral in 1878.

After studying at New York's Saint Francis College, John was selected for a scholarship at the Urban College of Propaganda Fide in Rome, a privilege he won at the intervention of his pastor, Father Joseph O'Connell, uncle of the titular archbishop of Marianne. For reasons of health, the young seminarian subsequently transferred to All Hallows College at Dublin where he was adopted by Bishop Francis Mora for the Diocese of Monterey–Los Angeles. He was ordained on June 24, 1890.

Arriving in Southern California in the fall, the newly ordained priest was assigned to the *Iglesia de Nuestra Señora de los Angeles.* The *"adobe padre,"* as he was known at the Plaza Church, was placed in charge of Saint Vincent's Hospital and the nearby orphanage of the Daughters of Charity. After a few rapid instructions in Spanish, Father McCarthy achieved considerable proficiency in the language. While in the downtown parish, he organized the Sacred Heart League and introduced the practice of the Holy Hour and congregational singing in Los Angeles.

In the fall of 1893, Bishop Mora sent Father McCarthy to Riverside as that area's first resident pastor. During his years as the "horse and buggy missionary," he led a successful fight against the American Protective Association to gain recognition of Catholic principles. By the time of his departure five years later, the young priest had built a rectory at Riverside and a church at Corona, then known as South Riverside. In 1898, McCarthy was sent to Central California as Dean of the vast northern territory which later became the Diocese of Monterey–Fresno. There he opened up a new and vital era in the Catholic growth of the Fresno vicinity. Among his first acts at Saint John's was that of building a new Romanesque–Gothic church on property he acquired near the parochial school. Services in the completed edifice, destined to become a cathedral in 1922, were first held on Easter Sunday of 1903.

Soon after becoming a diocesan consultor in 1906, Father McCarthy became one of the state's first monsignors, the rank of papal chamberlain. He was advanced to the domestic prelacy in 1909, just after finishing the newly located parish school in Fresno.

On October 15, 1918, as he was completing his sixteenth year in the San Joaquin Valley, Msgr. McCarthy was recalled to the southland and entrusted with the pastorate of Saint Andrew's Church in Pasadena. Two years after assuming his duties in the Crown City, the church was condemned when a decision was made to widen Walnut Street. The monsignor purchased property at Chestnut and Raymond, and began construction on a new church modeled after Rome's 5th century Santa Sabina. Over half of Msgr. McCarthy's priestly life was spent in Pasadena. By the time of his semi–retirement in 1944, he had completed a church, high school, grammar school, rectory and convent.

On the occasion of his sixtieth sacerdotal jubilee in 1950, the pastor emeritus of Saint Andrew's was made a protonotary apostolic. The insignia of his new office was displayed for the first and last time after his death on July 28, 1951. In his eulogy for the man who had served the diocese longer than any other priest in its 111 year history, Bishop Joseph T. McGucken, the monsignor's successor in Pasadena, noted:

> To the educated, he was a gracious and cultured prelate. To the irreligious he was instantly fearless in defense of Christ and His Church. To his brother priests he was a kindly father, always ready with wise counsel and encouragement.

THOMAS McCARTHY (1911–1978)

Father Thomas McCarthy (1911–1978) was a remarkably endowed priest who never really reached his ultimate potential. In 1942, shortly after receiving a doctorate in psychology at The Catholic University of America, McCarthy was named editor of *The Tidings* by Archbishop John J. Cantwell. His facile mind quickly mastered the intricacies of journalism and, before long, the paper was achieving added local distinction and merited national acclaim.

McCarthy opened the pages of *The Tidings* to new columnists and fresh features that appealed to all levels of Catholic readership. He was once quoted as saying that "the essence of journalism is sensation on the wing." A scholar himself, McCarthy enlarged the paper's library and outlined procedures whereby staff members could study as they prepared their stories for publication.

Each employee was encouraged to read a book every month. McCarthy's system worked too and, in 1945, a writer in the Los Angeles *Herald Express* said that "in its own specialized field, *The Tidings* has become one of the leading Catholic papers in the nation."

Editorially, the paper kept abreast of the times. Archbishop J. Francis A. McIntyre was enamored of McCarthy and often noted that he was "the finest jewel I inherited when my predecessor went home to God." A man with a high sense of morality, McCarthy was easily outraged. He fearlessly waged personal feuds with such luminaries as Drew Pearson ("vicious slander and irresponsible smearing") and Louella Parsons ("cheap, meretricious twaddle") and with any other careless columnist who treaded on the truth.

McCarthy's successor at *The Tidings* said that it was always his aim to give the paper proper proportion lest it merit Mencken's sophomoric jibe of a "dismal diocesan rag." And so, *The Tidings* became everybody's newspaper, with features for every member of every household, not alone an archdiocesan chronicle, but concerned as well with the momentous issues at home and abroad, in the turbulent years that have now passed.

Msgr. William North went on to observe that McCarthy's pen "surveyed the contemporary scene with courage and conviction. It was slow to wrath except when Christian principles were openly affronted. Hedging was foreign to his resolute and independent mind and integrity belonged to the essence of his character."

McCarthy early on entrusted the managerial aspect of the newspaper to Robert S. Labonge, a seasoned journalist who looked after the editorial department, and Robert F. Nichols who became business manager. By the time of his retirement from the editorship, one writer said McCarthy had been "our most forceful spokesman" in every arena of public affairs. "And he had been to all a zealous, kindly priest; and to many, a fast and faithful friend."

The Worcester–born priest remained at the helm until 1949, when, in the words of *Time* magazine, "the editor of the hard–hitting Los Angeles Catholic weekly, *The Tidings*, and a leader among the younger, liberal element in the Church," was appointed director for the Bureau of Information attached to the National Catholic Welfare Conference in Washington.

McCarthy excelled in whatever pursuit came his way. He was a zealous pastor, an entertaining speaker, an informative homilist and an effective author. He was, as one contemporary put it, "one classy cleric." During his years in the nation's capital with the Catholic Press Association, McCarthy spoke frequently on the Catholic Hour, a weekly program broadcast by NBC in cooperation with the National Council of Catholic Men.

His addresses for the five Sundays, October 28 to November 25, 1945, were later issued in monograph format and widely circulated around the country. In those presentations, McCarthy delved into the spiritual fibre of John Henry Cardinal Newman, Saint Augustine, Saint Thomas Aquinas, Saint Thomas More and Matt Talbot.

A measure of McCarthy's facility with words is revealed in his remarks about Thomas More: "Very few of us will be called upon to die on a scaffold in a public place and very few of us will ever be forced to spend long months in prison for our principles. Every one of us, however, does have the obligation of testifying always to what is right. If fear of what others might say would deter us from giving that testimony, let us remember that serene and merry man of England, Thomas More, who now in eternity enjoys a rich reward for his singular devotion to principle. May his example be to us a source of sustenance and renewed courage."

WILLIAM DANIEL McKINNON (1858–1902)

Father William Daniel McKinnon (1858–1902) "was a man of sterling qualities, an honor to his country, a fountain of Christian influence . . . His walk through life, though shorter than most, has been rewarded with results that few attain. The son of Alexander McKinnon and Mary Morrison was "raised in a strict Catholic upbringing" according to his biographer. He studied at Santa Clara College, where he was cited upon graduation as "first in morals, obedience, and general application."

After taking preliminary courses at Ottawa College, McKinnon entered Saint Thomas Seminary, in 1884, as a clerical candidate for the Archdiocese of San Francisco. He completed his seminary training at Baltimore and was ordained in the premier city by James Cardinal Gibbons on June 11, 1887. The young priest spent his first months as curate at Saint Bridget's Church, in San Francisco. He then served briefly as personal secretary to Archbishop Patrick W. Riordan.

In June, 1888, Father McKinnon was named Superintendant of Saint Vincent's Boys Orphanage at San Rafael. In his five years there, he "eliminated the grievances lodged against the previous administration, introduced competent teachers, and advanced the institution's status in the eyes of public officials. During the time immediately following, Father McKinnon held pastorates successively at San Pablo, Rio Vista and Suisun.

At the outbreak of the Spanish–American War, in May, 1898, Father McKinnon enlisted as chaplain of the First Regiment, California Volunteer Infantry. Commissioned as captain, he sailed for the Philippines, where he shared the dangers of the preliminary fighting leading up to the battle of Manila. During his tenure as chaplain, Father McKinnon "was the friend of hundreds of soldiers, famed throughout the nation and esteemed by his contemporaries in ecclesiastical, civil, and military life."

The San Francisco priest was the initial American to enter Manila at the siege of that town, having braved the fire of the Spanish sharpshooters to confer with the archbishop for a capitulation. After participating in the "unglorified chore of winning the peace," McKinnon served as superintendant of schools and cemeteries as well as chaplain at the San Lorenzo Hospital for lepers. When he was mustered out of the services, in 1899, Father McKinnon re–enlisted in the regular army. Among his other positions was that of advisor to the McKinley administration on the delicate and highly controversial question of Catholic monastic orders in the Philippines.

Father McKinnon's last years were spent in the Near East and it was while attending the stricken in the plague hospitals that he himself acquired a fatal case of cholera, in the epidemic of 1902.

In speaking of his many accomplishments, the San Francisco *Chronicle* accounted Father McKinnon's work in the Philippines as far more reaching than that of any other American. A touching editorial in the Solano County *Republican* noted that "many a noble life has been given under the American flag in the Philippines, that the cause of human happiness might be advanced and maintained but none was a greater sacrifice and none was given more willingly than that of a simple priest, beloved by his people at home, honored and esteemed by the greatest men in the greatest nation the world knows . . . the priest whose patriotism was second only to his love of God."

HUGH McNAMEE (1840–1902)

A few weeks before the untimely death of Father Hugh McNamee, an editorial in *The Monitor* had this to say: "To such men the Catholic Church owes its success, its triumphs and achievements." This doesn't appear to be an overstatement.

Hugh McNamee was born in the historic county of Armagh on February 73, 1840. After taking his preliminary courses in classics at the Catholic University of Dublin, he entered the famed missionary college of All Hallows as a priestly candidate for the Diocese of Monterey–Los Angeles. Ordained on June 24, 1873, he set out for what was still considered "the rim of Christendom." In subsequent years, Father McNamee served at Watsonville, San Diego and San Gabriel. He always revelled in the distinction of having been the first assistant pastor of Saint Vibiana's Cathedral.

Father McNamee was named Pastor of Sacred Heart in Hollister and there, according to newspaper accounts, he found "a nice little church but no parochial residence." In characteristic form, he hastily set about to remedy the lack of those facilities. After completing an extensive building project at Hollister, McNamee was called back to Los Angeles as pastor and rector of Saint Vibiana's Cathedral, a position he held under Bishop Francis Mora from 1880 to 1883.

Because of failing health, Father McNamee resigned the cathedral rectorship and, after a short convalescence, accepted the pastorate of Holy Cross in Santa Cruz. At that post he was called upon to build a church for the sprawling parochial family scattered over a huge area.

In the 1899 issue of the *Catholic Directory and Census of Los Angeles City and Parish Gazetteer*, the parish at Santa Cruz was described as a community "in the central part of Santa Cruz County" which "extends northerly to the boundary of the San Francisco Archdiocese and southerly to the Watsonville parish."

Following close on the erection of the church came

the centennial of Santa Cruz Mission. According to an early account in the Archival Center, "It seemed well to Father McNamee to commemorate the event by something to perpetuate the memory of the missionary fathers. At his suggestion the citizens decided to erect a triple arch, surmounted by a cross. It was placed in front of the new church and conforms to it in architecture. The following inscription was engraved over the central arch:

"Erected by the citizens of Santa Cruz, September 25, 1891, to commemorate the establishments of the Santa Cruz Mission by the Franciscans."

The next project was erection of a school for boys to complement the existing institution operated by the Daughters of Charity for girls. While raising money for that project, Father McNamee toured Europe and secured for his people the personal blessing of Pope Leo XIII. McNamee entered into negotiations with the Christian Brothers to staff his new school. He was especially pleased when the Brothers of Saint John Baptist de la Salle decided to enlarge their apostolate in the Diocese of Monterey–Los Angeles.

Finally, "the last and crowning act of his life" was the purchase of an old Methodist Church as a hall for his parishioners. It was named to honor the local ordinary, "Montgomery Hall." McNamee was highly sought after as a speaker. His address on the "Virtue of Charity" was quoted extensively in the very first edition of *The Tidings*, which appeared on June 29, 1895.

Father McNamee's poor health finally caught up with him and he died in the parochial home on October 3, 1902. Bishop George Montgomery journeyed to Santa Cruz for the funeral and interment. Father John F. Nugent preached the homily for the occasion.

RAMON MESTRES (1865–1930)

A. *PADRE* OF THE RESTORATION

The name of Ramon M. Mestres, long–time pastor of Monterey–Carmel, must be numbered among the more memorable clerical giants of early Californiana. Known as the "*Padre* of the Restoration," Mestres is remembered for his attempts to preserve the historic edifices at Monterey and Carmel. His dedication to restorative mission projects won formal recognition from the Spanish Government, in 1915, when he was awarded membership in the Royal Order of Isabella, by King Alfonso XIII. Ten years later, in 1925, Mestres was made a domestic prelate by Pope Pius XI.

Born at Barcelona, on October 19, 1865, the son of a distinguished Catalan family, Mestres began his studies for the priesthood under the auspices of the Society of Jesus. He subsequently enlisted for service in the Diocese of Monterey–Los Angeles. Bishop Francis Mora sent the young seminarian to Ireland, where he rounded out his clerical training in surroundings more attuned to the California apostolate. Mestres was ordained to the priesthood, in Saint Vibiana's Cathedral, on October 14, 1888. His first years in the ministry were spent at Los Angeles, San Diego and Santa Cruz. On April 7, 1893, upon completion of special studies at The Catholic University of America, Father Mestres was entrusted with the pastorate of Monterey–Carmel.

The energetic Catalan priest at once began a program of improvement which resulted in repair and restoration of both the *presidio* chapel at Monterey and the Mission of San Carlos Borromeo at Carmel. He erected a school in 1898, for which he secured the Saint Joseph Sisters; built a rectory; remodeled the tower of the mission and contracted for the handsome sarcophagus near the tomb of Fray Junípero Serra.

The monsignor was a charming man with unusual oratorical abilities. His erudite demeanor gave the colorful cleric entry in social and political circles as well as among the poorest families of his flock. His acquaintance with Miss Lou Henry, a school teacher, has special significance. Mestres and the Henry family became close friends after the local school–house burned down. The priest graciously put the parochial facilities on half–day schedule so as not to deprive the public youngsters of their educational opportunities. For some time San Carlos School served both church and state.

Father Mestres achieved national prominence during the presidential campaign of 1928, when it became known that he had officiated at Lou Henry's marriage to Herbert Hoover on February 10, 1899. Both Hoover and Miss Henry were members of the Society of Friends. There was no Quaker meeting house in the vicinity of Monterey and Lou Henry's father, a prominent banker, asked Father Mestres, if he would witness the ceremony in the capacity of a civil magistrate. Mestres sought and received permission from Bishop George T. Montgomery and the marriage ceremony was held before a small assemblage in the front yard of San Carlos Church. Thus it was that Herbert Hoover later claimed the distinction of being the first President of the United States married by a Catholic priest!

The monsignor died at the Garden City Sanitarium in

San Jose, after a brief illness, on August 5, 1930. The Mestres name is perpetuated in the annals of Monterey and Carmel, where his accomplishments are indelibly engraved for the edification of future generations.

RAMON MESTRES (1865–1930)

B. CATHEDRAL GHOST

Catholic theology says nothing against the possibility of "ghosts," in the sense of an apparition of one dead. It surely is within God's providence to permit departed souls to appear on earth to fulfill some purpose or other.

In any event, one of the most popular of California's ghosts is that which has frequented the old Royal Presidio chapel and rectory at Monterey for over half a century. Most of the commentators who have written or spoken about Monterey's "ghost" associate it with Father Ramon Mestres (1865–1930), the longtime pastor at San Carlos.

The priest's hand–worn breviary would be found at various places in the church or rectory, always opened to the office of the day. Memorial cards of his deceased friends would appear in the sacristy *ordo*, neatly fitted into place to mark their anniversaries. Though the ghost of the venerable priest moved from church to rectory with great alacrity, it seems to have spent more time in the latter place than what is now the Cathedral for the Diocese of Monterey.

Heavy footsteps are the chief instrument which the ghost uses to manifest his presence. He also likes to move around furniture, books and papers. Most of these activities occur in the deep of night. Randall A. Reinstedt recalls that "one of the most mystifying events to take place at the rectory happened only a few short years ago. On a typically foggy Monterey evening, a local security officer—accompanied by his police trained German Shepherd and a greatly respected peninsula citizen—were about to enter the building only to discover that the dog had suddenly become "spooked." His hair bristled and he began to whimper and whine—all to the amazement of his owner who had never seem him react in such a way.

"With a great deal of coaxing the dog obediently followed his master into the building. But as they approached the main staircase, it suddenly broke and dashed for the stairs, snarling and snapping as it went. Nearing the top of the stairs, it gave a mighty leap and viciously bit at something in the air. The two men stood dumbfounded. Whatever the dog had so furiously attacked remained invisible to them."

Another story about the ghost of the Spanish–born cleric tells about a visiting priest who stopped at the rectory enroute to a hunting expedition. About midnight, the others in the house heard a gunshot. Rushing to the guest room, they were told how a "shadowy image" had approached their visitor. He, in turn, had grabbed for his gun and fired at the would–be robber. The next morning, upon careful investigation, nothing was found to be disturbed and there were no signs of forced entry. Obviously, the Mestres ghost had appeared again, much to the panic of the rectory visitor.

Other stories abound about falling books, banging doors and blinking lights, all apparent manifestations of the restless ghost of Father Ramon Mestres.

Though the sacerdotal ghost has not been so active in recent years, old–timers at Monterey still recall how he often lit the candies and rang the hand bell at Holy Mass.

RAMON MESTRES (1865–1930)

C. LOST GOLD MINE

Father Ramon Mestres (1865–1930) served at Monterey for almost forty years. Among the many stories attributed to the popular priest is one related by Antoinette Gay who, in turn, claimed to have heard it from one of his confidantes.

It seems as if, during his early years at Monterey, Father Mestres was told about a "lost" gold mine not far from the old Presidio Chapel where the Indians "picked free gold out of black dirt." Wishing to expand the Catholic facilities then at Monterey, the priest was anxious to locate the mine and exploit its treasures for his worthy programs.

Eventually, he managed to find an elderly Indian woman in Salinas who knew the whereabouts of the mine and, after much persuasion, she agreed to accompany him to the site. The first trek was aborted when an owl startled the woman. The second attempt two months later was considerably more successful. Mestres and his guide first prayed at the tomb of Fray Junípero Serra and then went to a peaked, almost inaccessible overpass at Point Lobos.

The squaw unrolled a heavy coil of rope and, tying one end to a gnarled cypress whose roots dug deeply into the rocky soil, she slowly let herself down over the cliff. She disappeared under the overhanging ledge and a few minutes later shouted to Mestres that he should follow her. The priest complied and, on the rocky surface, found a precarious foothold, lapped by angry waves.

The Indian guide laid her wrinkled bronze hand on a faded cobalt cross, painted prominently on a rock a little above and to the left of a subterranean cave entrance. But the tide was too high and they could proceed no further. Apparently Indians of earlier times had entered the cave by boats, and then gone down a dark passageway that widened into a series of cavelets.

In the crevices of the walls was a sticky black "dirt" from which free gold shone. The Indians would scratch or pluck the gold as they paddled around with burning torches. Father Mestres subsequently studied the tides and determined that only in one month each year were they low enough to accommodate entry into the cave. Deciding that the risk was too great, he made no further attempt to visit the area in his quest for gold.

Later, Mestres heard that Indians had also found gold in a thirty–five foot well in the field between the old Martin ranch and the mission, directly in line with the vein which was said to run under Point Lobos. Father Mestres left instructions about finding the cave, with the condition that half of any treasure discovered be given to the church at Monterey. Here are his instructions:

> Stand outside the SE corner of the Carmel Mission, with your hand on the door opening to the altar. As you face SE in the direction of Point Lobos you will see across the corner of the mission the approximate location of the mine.

But, don't forget, the Church at Monterey gets half!

RAMON MESTRES (1865–1930)

D. MONSIGNOR RETURNS TO CARMEL

When the long–time Pastor of Monterey died, on August 5, 1930, a local newspaper reporter wrote that "as long, as the Church exists in California, Msgr. Mestres will be remembered." That statement surely has proven prophetic.

Few other priests made a deeper impression along the Pacific Slope than the Spanish–born, Irish–educated and American–ordained clergyman who took up the presbyteral mantle on October 14, 1888. The youthful Father Mestres was the first Californian to study at The Catholic University of America. While ostensibly studying theology, he specialized in catechetical methodology, a field in which he became a recognized national authority.

On April 7, 1893, Father Mestres was named to the pastorate of San Carlos Borromeo in Monterey. There he used to claim as his rightful title "unworthy successor to Fray Junípero Serra." He was that, in thought, word and deed.

In addition to his restorative work in Monterey and Carmel, Mestres established San Carlos School, erected a rectory, founded the Mission Restoration League and launched numerous parochial organizations and support groups. Decorated by Spain's King Alfonso XIII, honored by Pope Pius XI and loved by his parishioners, Monsignor Mestres remained at his post for almost forty years, until ill health brought about his forced retirement.

During the early days of his illness, Mestres lived with the Munras family. Later, he was confined to the Garden City Sanitarium in San Jose. His death elicited a statement from President Herbert Hoover (whom the priest had married to Lou Henry in 1899), that "a cedar of Lebanon has fallen in California."

When Mestres' successor at San Carlos suggested that he be given the honor of being the first priest interred in the new Calvary Mausoluem at Los Angeles, Bishop John J. Cantwell readily acquiesced. Apparently no heed was given to the monsignor's oft–expressed wish to "lie among my people."

On November 25th, 1930, the solid copper casket bearing Mestres' remains was removed from the Field Vault at Monterey, and sent in the funeral coach of George L. Grunnagle to Los Angeles. At Santa Ines Mission, the body lay in state before the high altar and news reports stated that Father Vincent Kerwick brought out a wealth of rare old ornaments preserved from the founding of the mission in preparing the church for the event.

At dawn the following day, the Old Mission bells tolled softly and Requiem Mass was offered by Father J. B. Roure. Leaving Santa Ines, the solemn procession wended its way through mountain passes and across the valleys, reaching Calvary Mausoleum shortly after noon. Prayers were said by the priests of the diocese and the casket was placed in a couch crypt near the altar.

The late Harry Downie had long desired to fulfill Msgr. Mestres' wish of being interred at Monterey. Finally, in early 1984, Bishop Thaddeus Shubsda agreed with the notion. Because the vault at San Carlos Cathedral had been sealed several years earlier, it was decided to inter Mestres in the cemetery at San Carlos Borromeo Mission.

On March 19th, we removed the copper casket from its vault at Calvary Mausoleum and drove it overland to Carmel. The next morning, Bishop Shubsda, a dozen priests from the Diocese of Monterey and a number of people who had known or been baptized by Msgr. Mestres gathered for the Mass of the Resurrection. Finally, after fifty–four years, the wishes of Msgr. Mestres had been realized!

CLEMENT MOLONY (1874–1949)

Father Clement Molony, the first native priest ordained from the City of Los Angeles, was born on April 12, 1874, the son of Richard and Ellen (Murphy) Molony. Baptized at the old Plaza Church of *Nuestra Señora de los Angeles*, Clement was raised in the traditions of the Spanish aristocracy that pervaded the Cathedral Parish during the years when Father Joachim Adam was pastor of Saint

Vibiana's and Bishop Francis Mora was Ordinary for the Diocese of Monterey–Los Angeles.

After completing his studies at Saint Vincent's College, Clement decided to prepare for the priesthood. At the age of eighteen, he traveled across the nation by train to Allegheny, New York, where he enrolled at Saint Bonaventure's Seminary. With the opening of Kenrick Seminary, in 1894, he transferred to Saint Louis for the completion of his clerical courses.

Clement was too young for ordination and had to wait until the spring of 1897 before reaching the canonical age. He was raised to the priesthood on April 19 by Bishop George T. Montgomery. Shortly thereafter, the young cleric was appointed secretary to the bishop, a post he held also under Montgomery's successor, Bishop Thomas J. Conaty. During his years in the curial office, Father Molony occupied several positions, including that as director of cemeteries. It was he who laid out and opened present–day Calvary Cemetery.

In 1903, Father Molony was made pastor of the newly–created Saint Agnes. His parochial boundaries extended to Redondo Beach on the south and Santa Monica on the west. In the forty–six years he served God's People at Saint Agnes, Father Molony built a temporary, then permanent church, a rectory, a convent, a school and, finally, the first parochial (and co–educational) secondary school in the diocese.

Most impressive of his many building projects was the graystone, twin–spired Gothic church which was dedicated in 1907. The handsome edifice, a miniature of Saint Patrick's Cathedral in New York, was consecrated by Auxiliary Bishop Timothy Manning, on October 15, 1953.

The organizational methodology of Father Molony was innovative in many respects. He originated, for example, the envelope practice of church maintenance in Los Angeles. Yearly fairs were staged for both societal and support purposes. A careful parochial census accounted for every soul living within the parish boundaries. So impressed was Bishop John J. Cantwell with Molony's administrative abilities, that he made him an irremovable pastor, the only such distinction ever conferred in the Los Angeles jurisdiction.

Auxiliary Bishop Joseph T. McGucken, whom Father "Clem" had baptized at the Cathedral, referred to the colorful priest as "always a man of strong views and fair principles." Though he suffered from a host of physical maladies during the final years of his life, Father Molony never wavered from his demand that the liturgy at Saint Agnes be performed with meticulous care and perfection. On the occasion of his death in 1949, Archbishop J. Francis A. McIntyre described Father Clement Molony as "a man of strong character, deep faith, diligent in the preservation and maintenance of the House of God, and of great administrative capacity.

HENRY NOEL MORGAN (1839–1888)

There were several attempts to establish "Catholic colonies" in California. One such project took form in 1885, when promoters sought to enlist the interests of Europeans. The matter received publicity in London and elsewhere but, unfortunately, the plan failed because of the dishonesty of organizers.

In any event, the services of a priest, Father Henry Noel Morgan, scion of a Welsh Catholic family, were enlisted as chaplain of the expedition and that, in itself, provides a link in California's Catholic heritage. Morgan, born on July 18, 1839, had originally been ordained as a Redemptorist on October 13, 1865, under the tutelage of Father Edmund Vaughan. According to notes discovered recently, Charles Conroy reported that Morgan "passed through an interesting and varied career." He enlisted as a chaplain for the 23rd Regiment of the British army, the so–called and famous Welsh Regiment.

Later, he served in the Franco–Prussian War of 1870–1871. Imprisoned by the Germans, he later was released and journeyed to Rome where he became the private tutor of the Italian crown prince, later King Victor Emmanuel III. Subsequently, Father Morgan returned to England and, after a visit to Australia, he resumed his ministry as a preacher of parochial missions, a position in which he gained wide acclaim.

It was during that time of his life that Father Morgan was approached about offering his services for a group of Catholics who wanted to emigrate to the United States, hopefully California. When that project failed, Morgan decided to continue on to the west coast, where he was welcomed into the Diocese of Monterey–Los Angeles by Bishop Francis Mora. At the time, Mora was desperately looking for clergymen who could minister to the growing English–speaking Catholic community.

Morgan was assigned to Wilmington, where a church or chapel had been erected twenty years earlier but which never had enjoyed the services of a resident priest. Morgan was ideally suited to that position. The still youthful priest directed his energies toward upbuilding the community which, at the time, covered the entire southern coastline of the present Los Angeles county, as well as many miles into the interior. Father Morgan found himself being almost a "circuit" rider as he moved among his scattered people.

After paying off the parochial debt and enlarging the church, Father Morgan engaged in a host of other spiritual endeavors for his parish, not the least was advising local civic officials on the needs of the Church. The priest's reputation as a preacher brought invitations to speak at numerous other local parishes and soon Morgan's zeal outdistanced his delicate health. In the fall of 1888, Bishop Mora recalled the priest to Los Angeles and a post at Saint Vibiana's Cathedral.

Shortly thereafter, Father Morgan became critically ill and, on December 19, 1888, he succumbed. In accordance with his previously expressed wishes, he was buried in the Catholic section of the cemetery at Wilmington.

Father Ramon Mestres offered his funeral obsequies and Father Aloysius Meyer, the pastor of Saint Vincent's parish, preached the homily. Morgan was eulogized as a priest whose dedication to the ministry of souls was "the all consuming concern of his life." He was likened to the "Moses of old who led his people to the brink of the promised land."

MICHAEL J. MULLINS (1891–1976)

The Irish–born founder of the Catholic Motion Picture Guild of American came to the Diocese of Monterey–Los Angeles, in 1920, after a distinguished career as a military chaplain of Europe's western front. His had been the privilege of administering the last rites to Lieutenant William Fitzsimons, "the first American officer killed in action in World War I," on September 3, 1917. Though he was initially assigned to California's southland on a "temporary basis" from the Irish Diocese of Achronry, Father Michael J. Mullins observed the golden jubilee of his service to the People of God in the Golden State.

In 1923, Father Mullins was entrusted with carrying out Bishop John J. Cantwell's goal of providing a strong Catholic organization among the ladies and gentleman engaged in the moving picture industry. At the first meeting of the subsequently established Catholic Motion Picture Guild, held in June of 1923, at the old Blessed Sacrament Hall, the Guild was charged with the formidable challenge of advancing the "spiritual, charitable and material welfare of all Catholics in the motion picture industry." In addition to cooperating with other agencies within the industry, the Guild served the further function of "unofficial spokesman for the church on various happenings in the entertainment world." Chosen to serve as the Guild's first president was the well–known and popular Thomas Meehan. As Bishop Cantwell later noted, "the task set to Father Mullins was a difficult one," especially in view of the wide–spread bigotry then directed against the Church from many quarters of the Hollywood community.

When the initial headquarters at Sunset Boulevard and Western Avenue proved inadequate, space was acquired in Hollywood's Taft Building. Monthly social and business meetings were held for members at the Knights of Columbus Hall. The Guild's manifold activities were financially sponsored by a modest dues paid by members as well as by annual vaudeville show staged by such theatrical luminaries as Jack Coogan, Sr., John

W. Consedine, Irene Dunne, James Gleason, Tommy Gray, Neal Hamilton, Johnny Hines, May McAvoy, James Ryan, Winfield R. Sheehan and Ben Turpin.

The Catholic Motion Picture Guild News, a monthly journal launched in December, 1923, under the editorship of Bert Ennis, was founded "to acquaint Catholics of the world as to the identity of those of their Faith who are carrying on actively in the motion picture profession, both on the screen and in executive positions."

At the conclusion of a week's retreat scheduled generally for March, it was the duty of members "to give evidence of their faith" by being present at and participating in the Annual Communion of the Guild. Following the Mass, a breakfast was served at the Beverly Hills Hotel attended by Bishop John J. Cantwell. The yearly celebration afforded the prelate an opportunity of meeting Catholics in the entertainment world and offering them a few words of fraternal counsel and advice.

Father Mullins served as the "sparkplug" of the Guild for almost a decade, during which time he also found time to erect a church, rectory and school for Good Shepherd Parish, in Beverly Hills, which he established, in 1923, with a nucleus of a hundred families. The activities of the Guild were gradually phased out with the establishment, in the years after 1934, of the Episcopal Committee on Motion Pictures and its agency, the Legion of Decency.

The challenge courageously undertaken and admirably fulfilled by the Catholic Motion Picture Guild has yet to be fully appraised. That the Guild, with its 2,400 members "exercised a salutary influence in Hollywood" during its decade of service goes without dispute. For that contribution, historians of California's Catholic heritage doff their hats to Father Michael J. Mullins, who lived on as pastor–emeritus of Holy Spirit Church in Los Angeles until 1976.

DANIEL W. J. MURPHY (1876–1913)

Often times, those who live the shortest lives have the greatest impact in historical annals. Surely that was true of Father Daniel W.J. Murphy (1876–1913), the founder of the Church in Hollywood. Daniel Webster John Murphy was born in County Cork, Ireland, on January 12, 1876. Two days later he was baptized in Conchford, one of the many natives of that area destined to leave deep imprints in the New World.

Five years later, John and Nora Murphy emigrated to the United States, where they settled in Cambridge, Massachusetts. An early newspaper account states that the elder Murphy became "the faithful servant of a good New England family."

Daniel attended Washington Grammar School until graduation in 1891. In that year, the Murphys moved again, this time to the west coast. Daniel enrolled in Redlands High School. When Sacred Heart parish was established in that area a few years later, Daniel became the first altar server, a distinction he cherished the rest of his life.

It was the Reverend John T. Fitzgerald who suggested that Murphy consider the priestly vocation. After finishing secondary studies, Daniel was accepted by Bishop George T. Montgomery as a clerical candidate for the Diocese of Monterey–Los Angeles. Daniel was sent to the Sulpician Seminary in Baltimore for his philosophical and theological studies. There he was befriended by the kindly James Cardinal Gibbons who would often ask that Daniel accompany him on his daily walks. His Eminence ordained Murphy in the nation's premier cathedral on June 19, 1900.

Father Murphy's first and only assignment as curate was at Saint Vibiana's Cathedral. Among the youthful priest's tasks was that of looking after the spiritual needs of Catholics then residing over the ridge of Fort Hill in a place known as Hollywood.

In 1903, plans were made for establishing a parish in that area and, on the following January 15th, Father Murphy was named proto–pastor of the newly–designated Blessed Sacrament. He was then only twenty–eight years old. That such a heavy responsibility was placed on one so young was a testimonial to his ability as an organizer

Bishop Thomas J. Conaty's trust was not misplaced. The youthful pastor worked with dispatch, purchasing property at the corner of what is now Hollywood Boulevard and Cherokee Street. There he had a church ready for occupancy by the late fall. That temporary structure served the growing community until 1923.

Father Murphy seemingly moved on all fronts at the same pace. He established a council for the Knights of Columbus in Hollywood. In that fraternal role, as in his work in the cathedral parish, he was very successful and won the esteem of his brother Knights. The Knights later sponsored installation of a stained glass window directly over the main altar. The theme was Columbian, depicting Queen Isabella handing her crown jewels to the explorer.

During the following years, Father Murphy also supervised the building of two auxiliary chapels at Sherman and East Hollywood, both of which subsequently became centers of thriving Catholic parishes. After a bout with illness, in the spring of 1913, Father Murphy took a vacation in Illinois. While at Joliet, he died on June 9th. His remains were returned to California for interment in old Calvary Cemetery.

An editorial in the diocesan newspaper for June 13th noted that Father Murphy's demise "removed from the ranks of the clergy one of the best known and most popular members."

JOSE MUT Y ROSE (c. 1835–1889)

Jose Mut y Rose (c. 1835–1889) was among the clerical candidates recruited for the Diocese of Monterey–Los Angeles during one of Bishop Thaddeus Amat's visits to his native Catalonia. After completing his theological studies with the Vincentian Fathers at Cape Girardeau, Missouri, Mut came to Southern California where he was ordained on December 12, 1862. His first assignment was at the Plaza Church of Our Lady of the Angels.

In 1866, Father Mut was appointed pastor of San Juan Mission. In that position, he was also entrusted with the care of Catholics at San Luis Rey Mission and the *Asistencia* of San Antonio de Pala.

At Capistrano, Mut took up residence in a "mere hole in the mission building" and for the next two decades the dedicated cleric tended his scattered flock. A visitor to the Old Mission in the 1880s described Mut's living quarters, noting that "by no possibility could any chamber be more gloomy, unfurnished, generally dilapidated and desolate."

"A battered old pine table stood in the middle of the floor and, beside it, a mended chair. Another, with a rawhide bottom, stood beside the door. There was no glass in the one window. An old and worn black priest's coat hung against the wall and the cheapest variety of cotton umbrella leaned beside it. The only sign of creature comfort, the one human weakness of the place, was a little bag of cheap tobacco and a wooden pipe that lay beside the spectacles."

Zephryin Engelhardt told how "on one of his trips to the various Indian mission stations, Father Mut had occasion to bless the grave of a man whose name figured somewhat prominently in the early days." The man was Jose Antonio Pico, the elder brother of the notorious Pio Pico.

Benjamin Cummings Truman visited San Juan Capistrano and published his views about Father Mut. One fascinating story revolved around an old record kept by Fray Gregorio Amurrio dated May 7, 1778, in which were recorded these words: "We prayed fervently last evening for the success of the colonists under one George Washington, because we believe their cause is just and that the Great Redeemer is on their side."

Early in May of 1888, Father Mut was transferred to the north and made pastor of San Miguel Mission. It is recorded that "to his energy it is due that the row of buildings comprising the ancient *convento* was preserved. Many of the rafters were decayed and others broken, so that the roof with its heavy tiles threatened to collapse at any time . . ." With $3,000 collected from local inhabitants, "the energetic priest replaced the rotten timbers and broken tiles with new material and, thus, rendered the rooms habitable and safe."

Charles F. Wilcox attended Mass at San Miguel in

1889 and, in a subsequent essay for *Ave Maria* magazine, he noted that "the Spanish priest, Father Mut, was the celebrant, and preached, in a quaint but pleasant manner, a practical sermon on the gospel of the day. The English tongue, spoken by a Spaniard, takes on a certain dignity and softness, decidedly foreign but delightful to the ear." Wilcox was much impressed by Mut who, he said, was "cheerfully giving his life to the obscure and arduous care of this post and three or four more outlying chapels of this parish."

Worn out by his missionary labors along California's *El Camino Real*, Father Joseph Mut died on October 15 1889. His remains were interred in the cemetery at San Miguel, where a modest stone marker recalls the memory of the Catalan priest.

WILLIAM BERNARD O'CONNOR (1814–1911)

During his forty–three years in the priestly ministry, Father William Bernard O'Connor (1814–1911) personified "the catholicity of a gospel that was meant for every man." From his earliest days in Ireland, the son of John and Mary (Rea) O'Connor was regarded by friends and acquaintances as the embodiment of common sense, broad–mindedness and religious fervor.

Young William's initial education was obtained from private tutors on the family farm, in the parish of Ballyhea, Charleville, County Cork. He subsequently entered Mount Melleray and for several years studied with the Trappists. In 1863, he enrolled at All Hallows College, in Dublin, as a clerical student for the Archdiocese of San Francisco.

Father O'Connor came to the Bay City a few months after his ordination, in 1868. He served as curate at Saint Patrick's and Saint Joseph's before his unusual ability, piety and zeal induced Archbishop Joseph Sadoc Alemany to entrust him with pastoral responsibilities at Stockton. With his arrival at Saint Mary's, Father O'Connor entered his new labors with that vim and ardor and quiet determination which characterized his whole life.

A builder and organizer par excellence, Father O'Connor's first major accomplishment, at Stockton, was the erection of Saint Agnes Academy in 1876, and its staffing with the Sisters of Saint Dominic. Shortly thereafter, he built Saint Joseph's School to serve Catholics in the city's northeastern area. In 1884, Father O'Connor induced the Brothers of Mary to open educational facilities for boys in a temporary frame building at the southwestern corner of San Joaquin and Washington Streets. Whether it was redecorating the church, raising funds to house the elderly, replacing a dilapidated rectory, securing property for a new cemetery or spearheading local temperance movements, Father O'Connor

"shunned public notice and self–advertisement, and taught the lessons of humility by the daily routine of his life."

At the time of his death, the editor of Stockton's *Daily Evening Record* published a tribute to the memory of the local pastor. Couched in eloquent terms were the sentiments of the priest's many friends, admirers and parishioners:

> Father O'Connor was no ordinary man. It is not taking license with words to say he was a great man. One test of true greatness is the performance of good and noble deeds out of the sight of men—the dislike for praise for praiseworthy acts—a repugnance for the flattering unction which soothes so many willing ears. That was Father O'Connor's way; it is the way of the truly great. He labored quietly, unostentatiously, through the days and through the years for the betterment of his fellows, and screened his good works behind a modesty, real, inherent, simple and true.
>
> He was an exemplar of all the virtues of the priesthood, compelling the respect of men of all creeds and the admiration of his brother priests. As a pulpit orator he was logical, forceful and convincing. Bombast was not in his vocabulary, but he was rich in words and spoke fluently; his diction was faultless and his delivery natural, easy and graceful.
>
> The community respected him and paid him deferences because he adhered strictly to the things within the purview of his holy calling, and never offensively interfered or intruded in matters worldly and secular in character.

THOMAS J. O'DWYER (1896–1966)

Monsignor Thomas J. O'Dwyer will long be remembered as a priest of strong simple faith, rare prudence, exceptional administrative ability, with a spirit that expended itself in self–sacrificing zeal. Born on March 31, 1896, at Cashel, County Tipperary, Ireland, Thomas O'Dwyer studied at the Christian Brothers School and Saint Patrick's College at Thurles before beginning his seminary course at Wexford. In the last year of his teens, the son of Edmund and Nora (Storman) O'Dwyer came to the United States where, on June 10, 1922, after completing his clerical training at Saint Bernard's Seminary in Rochester, he was ordained a priest for the old Diocese of Los Angeles–San Diego.

Upon finishing graduate studies at The Catholic University of America, Father O'Dwyer was named assistant director of the Catholic Welfare Bureau. In 1926, Bishop John J. Cantwell advanced the young priest to the directorship of the Bureau. The ensuing four decades were filled with tireless dedication to the social needs of Southern California's growing Catholic populace. In the years before such campaigns were popular,

Thomas J. O'Dwyer

Father O'Dwyer asserted the essential rights each person enjoys in the overall societal structure.

A workingman's claim for those things necessary for his wellbeing was a theme often repeated by Father O'Dwyer. At the Catholic Conference on Industrial Problems in 1930, the highly respected priest pointed out "It is our duty to sponsor and support in every way possible legislation that will secure for the workman his fundamental right to a living wage, adequate protection against industrial hazards and an income that will provide properly for old age."

As for the workingman's health needs, Father O'Dwyer observed that "ordinary wages are entirely inadequate to meet the expenses of medical care. The cost of sickness appears to be a necessary part of the cost of production. The burden should be placed on industry. Churches, community chest and tax supported relief agencies are at present assuming an obligation that seems to belong to industry."

Three years after receiving papal recognition for his accomplishments in the social realm, Monsignor O'Dwyer reminded the National Conference of Catholic Charities of their obligation "to submit proposed social remedies to the touchstone of Christian principle." In his presidential address, he further noted that the Church has "never accepted, and can never accept a status quo, and

will be found protesting, as ever, against social and individual injustice, knowing that any wrong done the lowliest creature is a wrong done Christ Himself. And while we bind up, as best we may, the wounds of the victims of modern greed and confusion, we do not accept the conditions of social life today as final or unchangeable. We strive for a more Christian social order. Our cry is Catholic Action."

Though Monsignor O'Dwyer was a nationally known authority on social and welfare work, hospitals, public housing and labor relations he found time in his busy schedule for pastoral duties at Saint Mary's (1937–1960) and Saint Thomas (1960–1966), both busy inner city parishes. Whether as chairman of the California State Housing Commission, archdiocesan consultor, or board member (and one of the founders) of Blue Cross of Southern California, Senior Citizens Committee, Los Angeles Community Welfare Federation or the Urban Renewal Advisory Committee, the monsignor could always be expected to put forth solid Christian proposals.

Few were the state legislators and city councilmen who did not seek out Monsignor O'Dwyer's advice on social problems over the forty years he directed charitable activities in the southland. As any of his friends would have expected, the monsignor was on a charitable mission at the time of his death at San Diego on June 7, 1966. Space allows only a mentioning of the highlights of this good priest's contribution to Catholic life. Suffice to say that few men in the history of Southern California sacrificed more for others or accomplished more for suffering humanity than Thomas J. O'Dwyer.

HUGH O'FLAHERTY (1898–1963)

"The Scarlet and the Black" is a movie that appears occasionally on late night television. Featuring Gregory Peck, it relates the fascinating and true story of Msgr. Hugh O'Flaherty, the "Scarlet Pimpernel of the Vatican."

In subsequent years, Msgr. O'Flaherty (1898–1963) came to the Archdiocese of Los Angeles, where he served for a while as chaplain at Saint Catherine's Military School in Anaheim. His life was featured in a full length book by J.P. Gallagher in 1968.

Born at Killarney, County Kerry, the oldest child of James and Margaret O'Flaherty, Hugh won a King's scholarship at Waterford College where he fell under the tutelage of the Brothers of Saint John Baptist de la Salle. At fifteen, he secured a junior academic post at the local monastery, where he taught for three years. He then went to Mungret College, a missionary seminary at Limerick operated by the Jesuits.

Late in 1921, Hugh was accepted as a clerical candidate for the Vicariate Apostolic of Cape Town in South

Africa. Sent to Rome for theological studies, he was ordained priest on December 20, 1925.

Almost immediately after ordination, Father O'Flaherty was appointed Vice Rector of the Urban College of Propaganda Fide. In the following years he earned the triple doctorate in Divinity, Canon Law and Philosophy. After becoming associated with the Vatican's diplomatic service, he became *Charge d'Affairs* at the apostolic legation in Egypt. In 1935, he was sent by Cardinal Eugenio Pacelli to the adjacent republics of Haiti and San Domingo.

But it was in the Eternal City that O'Flaherty became famous. Even today, the very mention of his name among Romans is enough to start a flood of reminiscences. To the thousands of people he saved, O'Flaherty remains one of the great heroes of World War II.

During the months of 1943–1944, for example, O'Flaherty made arrangements for hundreds of escaped war prisoners, from privates to generals, to be hidden away in the homes of anti–Facist Romans and in convents and monasteries.

Each night would find him standing alone on the shadowy steps of Saint Peter's Basilica, waiting for those in trouble to sneak across the boundaries of the Vatican. His rescue network even functioned for a while inside Rome's German College.

Most of the incidents related in the movie actually happened. The genial, gentle and guileless priest was ever ready with a helping hand. He became the most wanted man in Rome, the scourge of the Nazis and the rescuer of more Allied lives than probably any other single person during World War II.

To quote his biographer, O'Flaherty "was unlucky enough to become a legend in his own lifetime and this, in itself, combined with the traditional chauvinism of Vatican officialdom, clouded his last years." Some of his colleagues stood beside him, while others were bitterly and publicly jealous of his notoriety. There were those who called him a saint because they couldn't think of any other term to explain his character. And yet nothing is more damaging in ecclesial circles than being canonized while still alive.

After leaving Southern California, O'Flaherty went back to his native Ireland, where he died on October 30, 1963. The obituary notice that appeared in the Mungret College *Journal* was as accurate as any:

> Hugh O'Flaherty was above all a generous honest–to–God Irishman without guile. His big heart was open to any and every distress and he was lavish in his efforts to assuage suffering in any form . . . His life was always ordered to using his powers in fair weather or foul for the glory of God. Can any of us hope to achieve more?

EUGENE O'GROWNEY (1863–1899)

The name of Eugene O'Growney "stands for the great Ireland of the past reborn in the great Ireland of the future." A native of Ballyfallon, near Athboy in County Meath, Eugene resolved early in life to restore Ireland's national language to its rightful place of prominence. In January of 1879, he became a clerical candidate at Saint Finian's, the diocesan seminary of Meath, near Navan. O'Growney avidly studied the Irish lessons of the famous Gaelic scholar, John Fleming. His holidays were spent in Irish–speaking districts, notably in the Aran Islands near Galway Bay, where he was all but idolized by the local country–folk.

After completing his theological training in June of 1889, at Maynooth's Saint Patrick College, Eugene O'Growney was ordained and appointed curate at Ballinacargy, County Westmeath. Already widely known as an Irish scholar, the young priest was made editor of the *Gaelic Journal*. An article Father O'Growney wrote in the *Irish Ecclesiastical Record* on "The National Language" brought about restoration of the Irish Chair at Maynooth, a position to which O'Growney was thereafter appointed.

In 1893, Father O'Growney began his great work, "Simple Lessons in Irish." The series first appeared in the *Weekly Freeman* and, the following year, in book form. O'Growney felt that if the Gaelic language were to be once again a universally spoken tongue in Ireland, the movement in its favor had to come from and through the common people. With this in mind, he traveled around the country, stirring up enthusiasm for the language through the newly formed Gaelic League.

His delicate health collapsed under the manifold duties. When he contracted tuberculosis, physicians advised the stricken priest to seek a cure in the warmer climates of the Western United States. At the time of his departure, the Archbishop of Dublin wrote: "I am sure you do not need any letter of introduction to any bishop, priest or layman of our Irish race at home or abroad."

Father O'Growney journeyed to San Francisco, where he assisted Archbishop Patrick W. Riordan until March of 1895 when he sought the drier atmosphere of Arizona. Though separated from adequate library facilities, the famous Irish–language scholar continued writing. Hardly an issue of the *Gaelic Journal* appeared without a contribution from his learned pen.

A fair amount of his final months was spent in Los Angeles and it was in the City of Our Lady of the Angels that he died on October 18, 1899 just as the sound of the *Angelus* was coming softly up the hill on the breeze of the evening. After a brief but active life of only thirty–six years, "beloved and lamented within the four seas of Erin and known in every land where an Irishman finds a home, as an ideal patriot, a saintly priest and a learned scholar, he died a happy death."

In September of 1903, the remains of the priest were removed from Old Calvary and sent back to Ireland for interment in the cemetery adjacent to Maynooth College, where he had inaugurated his brilliant career as Professor of Gaelic Language and Literature. Though his reputation in the field of letters was firmly secured, Laurence T. Brannick felt that O'Growney's real greatness consisted "not in his great learning, nor in the fame which came to him unsought but in the humility of his life and in the humilty of his heart."

MICHAEL O'HALLORAN (1890–1970)

Michael O'Halloran was born near Ardfert, County Kerry, Ireland, on August 26, 1890, the son of Patrick and Mary (Horgan) O'Halloran. He studied at Kilmoyley National School and Saint Brendan's College from 1895 to 1908. His preparation for the ministry was made at Dublin's All Hallows College, where he was ordained for the Diocese of Monterey–Los Angeles, on June 21, 1914.

In his initial priestly assignment, at Saint Thomas Church, Father O'Halloran made parish visits and sick calls by jitney bus or streetcar. Later, in Watsonville, his only transportation was horse and buggy. In 1920, the industrious young cleric was given his first pastorate, at Taft. The following year, Father O'Halloran was asked by Bishop John J. Cantwell to assume the spiritual direction of Saint Augustine's Church, in Culver City. During those pioneering days there were only three movie studios clustered along Washington Boulevard.

The year 1923, a record one in the growth annals of Los Angeles, saw the erection of ten new parochial jurisdictions in the far–flung southland diocese. In July, Father O'Halloran was entrusted with establishing the parish of the Precious Blood, in the Wilshire District of Los Angeles. During his early months there, he celebrated Holy Mass at 686 South Carondelet Street, in the home of Mr. and Mrs. Charles Murray. As soon as possible, he erected a temporary frame church at Third and Coronado Streets for his sparse flock which, at that time, was "made up mostly of elderly people residing in large homes interspersed with vacant lots."

The generous response of the People of God in the Wilshire District made it possible to purchase a triangular site at Occidental and Hoover, upon which was built a beautiful reinforced concrete structure of Italian Romanesque design. Opened on October 31, 1925, the church was formally dedicated, November 25, 1926, by Bishop Cantwell. It was also in that year that the residence at 525 South Occidental was occupied.

In the initial years, when there were few youngsters in the parish, Father O'Halloran and a group of women journeyed regularly across town to teach catechism to the children at Our Lady of Talpa Center. In 1950, a parochial school was opened at Precious Blood under the direction of the Daughters of Mary and Joseph. The next year, Father O'Halloran supervised erection of new auditorium facilities.

O'Halloran's support for the work of the Legion of Mary stemmed from his conviction that it was "the single most effective in the whole spectre of parish organizations." He was named archdiocesan spiritual director of the Legion, in 1938, a post he occupied throughout the remaining years of his priesthood.

The Wilshire District pastor, honored by the Holy Father, in 1937, and again, in 1965, served Precious Blood for forty–seven years, until his death, on February 19, 1970, a priestly career that spanned the decades from the horse and buggy to the interplanetary era. Michael O'Halloran typified the "recipe for holiness" enunciated by Pope Saint Pius X:

> The priest who is moved by the spirit of zeal for the glory of God and the salvation of souls is not afraid of weariness, is not fearful of danger, does not consider sacrifices, does not indulge himself in comforts, knows no rest, does not trouble about repose. Though contradicted and persecuted he does not lose heart, because he knows that the heritage of the Church Militant is the hatred of the gloomy, and the greater obstacles he encounters the more there increases in him a burning desire to show himself a true Minister of God in everything.

PATRICK O'KANE (1841–1926)

One of the most colorful of the Irish–born pioneer–priests along California's Gold Dust Trails was Father Patrick O'Kane (1841–1926), a native of the Emerald Isle's County Kerry. Patrick entered All Hallows College, at Dublin, in 1860, as a student for the Vicariate Apostolic of Marysville. Upon completion of his studies, he journeyed to San Francisco and, in 1866, was ordained by Bishop Eugene O'Connell.

The "big strapping cleric" subsequently filled appointments at Weaverville, Nevada City, Gold Hill, Shasta, Trinity, Butte and Colusa, to mention but a few. He "bears the distinction of having served on more missions of Northern California than any of the priests" in the Diocese of Grass Valley.

Being one of thirteen children, Father O'Kane early accustomed himself to regard the practice of poverty as much an economic necessity as an evangelical virtue. Throughout sixty years of ministry, his clothes, fare and lodgings "were those of traditional apostolic simplicity." To this nephew of Bishop Patrick Keane, life was one long, sweet summer's day, and neither hurry nor worry nor the opinions and the arguments of his fellow men could cause him to deviate one bit from the even tenor of his way.

One of Father O'Kane's more noteworthy attributes, whether a virtue or a vice, was his utter disregard for schedules. That time was a negligible quantity in Father O'Kane's scheme of existence is obvious from a sign posted on his church door to the effect that "Mass at Coloma at 8 o'clock. Mass at Georgetown, generally speaking, at 10 o'clock."

Numerous anecdotes are associated with Father O'Kane's pastorate at Georgetown during the years between 1901 and 1923. One of his parishioners related this tale of a Sunday occurrence:

> By ten o'clock one Sunday morning we were all assembled for the Mass in goodly number. I generally waited outside until I saw the father nearing the church before I went in. On this particular occasion, ten–thirty rolled around and still no Father O'Kane. About twenty minutes to eleven, he drove up in his buggy, having said Mass over at Coloma. While helping him to tie up his horse, he engaged me in conversation, and it was eleven o'clock before he made any movement to enter the sacristy. By eleven–fifteen he appeared in the sanctuary with his server.
>
> Whilst he was arranging the Missal, he seemed to be disturbed a bit and calling the altar boy, whispered to him to get the window pole out of the sacristy. Bidding the boy to go ahead of him, he strode solemnly down the aisle, wielding the pole in his right hand, much after the manner of a Bishop. The reason for this maneuver was the presence of a woodpecker, which had chosen that particular time to pick a hole in the corner of the church.
>
> Having successfully accomplished his mission, without saying a word, and assuming an episcopal air again, the priest proceeded slowly up to the altar, put away his crozier and at last commenced the service.
>
> But Father O'Kane was not satisfied to begin the Mass according to the Latin rite. There were some preparatory prayers in English which it was the custom to recite in the old parish church in Killarney, where he came from, and these must first be said. Finally the Mass was safely on its way, and after a half–hour's sermon on the Gospel of the Day, the Mass was eventually brought to its conclusion about half–past twelve.

The Irish *padre* of Trinity County was one of those rare actors on the stage of life whose every word and movement was flavored with the spice of the dramatic. He represented the best in that generation of pioneers whose influence still pervades the folklore of California's Catholic heritage.

JAMES J. O'KELLY (1884–1938)

James J. O'Kelly was born in Ireland on December 23, 1884. Ordained at Wexford, in 1909, the young priest spent his earliest years in the ministry working among the slums of London. He later became a military chaplain to the British Expeditionary Forces and was serving in that capacity when World War II began. In subsequent years he earned several medals for valor and devotion to duty.

In 1922, Father O'Kelly came to the Archdiocese of San Francisco, where he served as curate at Saint Monica, Saint Francis and Saint Patrick Parishes. He also spent a short while as curate at Saint Gertrude in Stockton. Knowing O'Kelly's background as chaplain, Archbishop Edward J. Hanna asked him to him to take up the cause of merchant seamen in the Bay Area. The tireless Irish priest founded the Apostleship of the Sea and then served as arbitrator during the difficult years of unemployment that followed the waterfront strike.

During the depression years, when many ships were tied up, Father O'Kelly furnished more than 200,000 meals to needy seamen in one twelve month period. He also provided hospitalization for sick seamen, as well as clothing and tobacco. Known throughout the waterfront area as the "rightest guy on the Embarcadero," Father O'Kelly labored until November 12, 1938, when he was stricken with a heart attack as he stepped from a Berkeley streetcar.

Early in 1943, it was announced that a liberty vessel would be named after the dedicated priest. The keel of the ship, built by the Permanente Metals Corporation, was laid on August 26th. Archbishop John J. Mitty delivered the invocation on September 19, 1943, when *The James J. O'Kelly* was officially launched at the Richmond Shipyards.

Among the dignitaries attending the ceremonies were labor leaders, ship crews, steamship executives and civic, fraternal and religious representatives. Delegations were present from the Knights of Columbus, Hibernians and Catholic Daughters.

The vessel was christened by Mrs. John Curran, president of the Women's Auxiliary for the Apostleship of the Sea. Father Edward Lenane pulled the trigger releasing the ship. The launching of *The James J. O'Kelly* was a dramatic event, one filled with color, excitement and suspense. Few modern rites, apart from those of a purely religious origin, have a background that harkens back 4,000 years in recorded history.

And it was an historic day too, especially for Catholics—one of the few times in American annals that such a distinction was accorded to a priest.

LUIS AMEZCUA OROZCO (c. 1890–1930)

In the early months of 1930, the superintendent at Calvary Cemetery informed Bishop John J. Cantwell that hundreds of people were coming each day to pray for a miracle at the tomb of Father Luis Amezcua Orozco. An undated clipping from the Los Angeles *Times* substantiated the report by noting that "the silence of the congregation of the dead at Calvary Cemetery again was broken yesterday. A procession of the sorrowful and maimed streamed to the grave of *Padre* Orozco all day, where beside the flower–strewn mound of earth they sought a miracle to heal and comfort them."

Father Luis Amezcua Orozco, a cleric belonging to the Diocese of Zamora, spent many of his early priestly years as director of the *Asociacion de Juventud Catolica Femenina* in the Archdiocese of Guadalajara. Coming to Los Angeles in 1927, during the religious persecution in his homeland, Orozco was assigned to the parish of Our Lady of Talpa. With the encouragement of Bishop Cantwell, Father Orozco organized twenty–five branches of his *Asociacion* in the southland. Its purpose continued to be the "application of Christian principles to modern social problems."

Father Orozco was killed in an automobile accident enroute to a retreat in El Paso. His funeral was conducted on February 15, 1930, at Saint Vibiana's Cathedral. Bishop Jose Manriquez of Huejutla offered the final obsequies and presided at the internment in the priest's plot of Calvary Cemetery.

Several weeks later, "a rumor of a miraculous cure at the grave of this humble Mexican priest" spread through the local Hispanic community. "Fathers and mothers with tears streaming from their eyes laid the little forms of sick children on the grass beside the grave. They sprinkled its earth on the little bodies while their lips moved in prayer." Mixed in among the crowd of sincere Catholics "were curiosity seekers who peered over the heads of the kneeling throngs at the flowers, already wilting in the sun."

Cars lined the narrow cemetery roadways "with Illinois, Ohio and Alabama licenses. Cameras clicked and a few occupants joined the devout and dropped to their knees on the grass."

Father Orozco's grave was located near the midway point of the *Via Crucis*. Throngs stood on the pedestal of the Seventh Station of the Cross overshadowing the grave. "They tramped over the graves of scores of priests and Sisters of Mercy whose bodies are mingling with the dust at this quiet, beautiful spot; and always new bands of the devout came bearing flowers to the heaped–up mound."

Another clipping from the Los Angeles *Examiner* is preserved at the Archival Center in Mission Hills. It relates that from the time "the gate of the city of the dead was opened until it was closed last night, the living came in reverence to kneel on the soft grass and petition for health and happiness." Thousands of flowers were brought to the grave and handfuls of dirt were removed as relics. The clipping told how, two weeks earlier, "it was rumored that several Mexicans who had come to pray at the grave of the *Padre* had been cured of disease."

All day long "the procession ebbed and flowed. At one time in the afternoon, there was no one near the grave. Within five minutes, there were thirty or more present. The crowd is never large, attendants say, seldom more than two score at a time."

But now, many years later, the grave of Father Luis Amezcua Orozco is just one of the many hundreds resting unattended in the priests' plot at Calvary Cemetery. John J. Cantwell used to say that "no one is deader than a dead priest except, perhaps, a dead bishop!"

ST. JOHN O'SULLIVAN (1874–1933)

When Msgr. St. John O'Sullivan died on July 22, 1933, he was eulogized by his one–time professor, Archbishop Edward J. Hanna, as "a holy priest, a great man, a high–minded citizen and a gentleman of the old school".

Born on the Feast of Saint Joseph in 1874 at Louisville, Kentucky, St. John was the son of Michael and Anne (O'Dwyer) O'Sullivan. He studied at Notre Dame University before entering Saint Bernard's Seminary in Rochester.

He was ordained for the Diocese of Louisville on June 12, 1904. Shortly thereafter, he fell seriously ill and was sent on sick leave to San Antonio, Texas. He was told by physicians that he had only a short time to live, so he came to Los Angeles to reside with a brother in May of 1909.

When his health improved, Bishop John J. Cantwell suggested that the priest go to San Juan Capistrano Mission where there had been no resident priest since 1886. It was a providential appointment. Upon his arrival, Father St. John O'Sullivan lived in a tent, surrounded by the ghostly remnants of "the lordliest of the California missions." From the outset, he began to advertise the mission. Curious visitors began appearing and paying an admission fee of 25¢, thus creating the revenues necessary for the work of restoration.

The mission was in almost total ruin. The priest worked with his hands in putting the historic foundation back into place. He devoted numerous hours to recovering the furnishings and other items carried away by peoples of earlier times. Father O'Sullivan took justifiable pride in his restoration of the Serra Church. It was and remains the oldest building in California and the only one still standing which Fray Junípero Serra personally knew. When the work on the church was completed in 1920, Bishop Cantwell gave the cedar high altar and reredos which had been carved four centuries earlier in Spain.

Characterized by the Los Angeles *Times* as a "kindly, zealous, sincere" priest, Father St. John O'Sullivan infused new life into a community of worshippers who had been without a spiritual leader for over a generation. His name was given to countless youngsters born and baptized during those years.

From 1912, when he had rehabilitated the old Mission living quarters until 1929, when the north wing containing school, rectory and convent was dedicated, the work of restoration continued without interruption.

Archbishop Hanna recalled how "out of ruin, Father O'Sullivan made a garden of delight. His rebuilding of the mission was worthy of the heroic *padres* who founded it on the wastelands." Indeed, O'Sullivan was "singularly touched by the life and the mystery of Christ. He was simple and spoke as you might expect Christ to speak. In the humility of Christ, he found his peace and rest."

Just a month before his demise at Saint Joseph's Hospital in Orange, Father O'Sullivan was made a domestic prelate by Pope Pius XI. It was a fitting recognition for a man who came to California to die and lived to re–establish one of the most famous landmarks along *El Camino Real*.

With as much ingenuity as that associated with the work of his priestly forebears, Msgr. St. John O'Sullivan brought back to center stage the foundation which Blessed Junípero Serra lovingly referred to as the "Jewel of the California Missions."

LUCIANO OSUÑA (ff. 1870s)

Luciano Osuña was a colorful young man who came from his native Guadalajara to San Francisco in 1862 at the request of Archbishop Joseph Sadoc Alemany. He was, in the view of one commentator, "the finest acquisition" during those pioneering years. Having already completed his clerical training, Osuña was ordained a priest on January 11, 1863.

Shortly thereafter, the energetic clergyman was sent to what was then the Vicariate Apostolic of Marysville, later the Diocese of Sacramento. As he spoke both English and Spanish fluently, his ministry was to all the Catholics then residing in the far–flung vicariate.

From the outset, Father Osuña was especially preoccupied about the spiritual welfare of the Pomo Indians in Mendocino and Lake counties, most of whom were conversant in Spanish as a result of their contact with earlier missionaries and settlers. Osuña's concern for the Indians is reflected in a letter written to Bishop Eugene O'Connell on August 29, 1872:

> I have been with the Indians most of the time, they are sick and hungry and so I am hungry with them. We have no place to live.
>
> The Indians are starving in both respects, in the body and in the soul. We must do something, otherwise our charity will not reach them. As winter is nigh, we must take hold of every chance, lest by neglect some of these little ones may perish, obliged to pass the winter with the rain upon their heads and with empty stomachs; and what is worse without the shelter of religion.

Father Osuña's casual and independent attitude antagonized the local Indian agent, Reverend J.L. Buchard, the Methodist minister in charge of the government's Round Valley Reservation in Mendocino. Buchard seemed to have been especially irritated at Osuña's strange, ragged, soiled, habit–like robe and open sandals. He was also annoyed that the priest usually arrived at the reservation unannounced and without the customary authorization.

One day, in November of 1873, a nasty confrontation ensued. Tempers flared, words flew and the exasperated agent struck the priest with his cane and then had him unceremoniously escorted off the reservation. Undaunted, Osuña kept returning until Buchard finally had him arrested and charged with insanity by the local justice of the peace. Though the charge was dismissed, Bishop O'Connell advised Osuña to discontinue his visits to the Catholics on the reservation.

Several years later, Osuña borrowed funds to purchase acreage near the reservation, where he established a worship community dedicated to Saint Turibius. Buildings were erected (including housing for the Indians), crops planted and livestock acquired. At last the indomitable priest was free to conduct his ministry unhampered by hostile government agents.

The Mexican–born priest continued his work and ecclesial records show that between 1870 and 1879, he baptized 567 persons, most of whom were native–Americans. In 1879, Father Osuña returned to Mexico where, presumably, he served out the remaining years of his ministry.

According to Father Zephyrin Engelhardt, Osuña was a tireless man and a pious priest. What few deficiencies he had were in the area of patience. In the *Catholic Directory* for 1866, Father Osuña reported that there were over a hundred Indians in his mission, all of them active Catholics.

Osuña was an activist for Indian rights long before it was fashionable. For all his years in California, Father

Luciano Osuña campaigned to have his people treated with justice and kindness. He deserves to be remembered.

JOSEPH PHELAN (1839–1903)

The life of Father Joseph Phelan (1839–1903) was a precious reminder of the very human side of those heroic men who served the Church in her beginnings in the Far West. Born at Knockahaw in one–time Queen's County, Ireland, young Joseph left his native home early in life for the adventure and excitement of California's gold dust trails. He spent almost a decade working in the mines before entering Mount Melleray Seminary as a clerical student for the Diocese of Grass Valley. He was ordained in 1874, after completing studies for the priesthood at All Hallows College, in Dublin.

Father Phelan subsequently served as pastor at Austin for eighteen years before ill health forced his premature retirement in 1894. He then became resident chaplain for the Sisters of Mercy at their motherhouse in San Francisco, a position he occupied until his death. Among Father Phelan's many talents was that of versifier. As the "poet laureate" of the Diocese of Grass Valley, he reeled off a raft of memorial pieces and lamentations for the sorrows and indignities of the "Ould Sod" with uniform infelicity.

Tradition has undoubtedly credited Father Phelan with considerably more than he actually composed. Spurious, for example, is the verse: "Of all the Bishops now in vogue, the greatest of all is Pat Manogue." The authentic version of that particular verse is: "Times and people shall always change, and fresh men come into vogue, but few will have the heart and range of the lamented Bishop Manogue."

Shortly before his death, Father Phelan completed arrangements to immortalize his versifications in book form. The sumptuous volume was released at San Francisco, in 1902, by the Commercial Publishing Company, as *The Poetical Works and Biographical Remarks of Rev. Joseph Phelan, with Album Scraps and Catholic Poems.*

It is recorded that a copy of the book found its way into the hands of the Archbishop, Patrick W. Riordan, who immediately interdicted the publication, much to the dismay and pecuniary loss of the author. Admittedly, the book contained "some of the most appalling doggerel ever committed to writing and set in type. Pious priest though he was and zealous missionary, Father Phelan was grievously in error in mistaking a facility for rhyming for the genuine gift of poesy."

There is considerable doubt that the sacerdotal bard's book would have caused any serious scandal or disgrace had it been circulated. Because of the numerical poverty of extant copies, what the author envisioned "to win souls to God through his poetic inspiration" has become, instead, a rare and widely sought after gem of Western Americana. Perhaps in the Mother Lode country, where Father Joseph Phelan's name is still invoked, a verse he wrote on the occasion of Bishop Eugene O'Connell's death might be applied to himself:

In religious matters he was most exact;
For business matters he had no tact;
Theological points he could decide;
The Church lost an aegis when he died.

JOHN J. PRENDERGAST (1834–1914)

John J. Prendergast, described by one writer as "a Christlike comforter of troubled hearts," was born in 1834. He studied for the Archdiocese of San Francisco at Ireland's Mount Melleray and later at All Hallows, where he was raised to the priesthood on June 26, 1859. Though offered a position on the seminary faculty at Dublin, the newly ordained priest refused the honor "and repaired to his destination to take up his labors in a distant country, known, at that time, chiefly to the gold-hunter, the adventurer and the speculator."

Soon after arriving in the Bay City, Father Prendergast was appointed to Stockton. A short while later he was moved to Mission Dolores as assistant to Father Richard Carroll. In May of 1860, Father Prendergast was named rector of Saint Thomas Seminary at Mission Dolores as well as pastor of the parish which then covered two–thirds of the area of San Francisco. After the seminary was closed, Prendergast remained on at the mission as pastor.

During the1860s, Father Prendergast preached missions in many areas of Northern California where his zeal and priestly dignity was often recalled by miners in later years. The Irish–born priest was widely in demand as a speaker for he had the " grand manner" of the great pulpit orators and he knew how to fit sonorous words and rhythmic periods to the high themes of religion.

It was during his years at the mission that Father Prendergast founded the Holy Family Sisters, whom he envisioned as the "gleaners" of those souls he could not personally reach. "In this Order, and in the noble work of the good women who daily carry out the instructions of their revered Founder, a monument has been raised" which "shall proclaim aloud to all generations the glory of the saintly priest whose generous and unswerving zeal gave it life and inspiration."

Father Prendergast was also instrumental in persuading the Sisters of Notre Dame to establish a school for girls in his parish, an institution which has since gained fame as the College of Notre Dame. Another project launched with the approval of Archbishop Joseph Sadoc Alemany was the Youth's Directory, which Prendergast organized for the protection and education of neglected boys.

On August 23, 1874, the archbishop appointed Father Prendergast Vicar General of the Archdiocese of San Francisco and pastor of the cathedral parish, then located on California Street, both of which positions he occupied for the next four decades. Advancements only increased Prendergast's working capacity. When the malign spirit of bigotry manifested itself during the 1870s, Prendergast calmly exposed the false statements and gave a manly definition of Catholic doctrine.

Although he was an energetic and effective campaigner for the Church, the Vicar General's reputation among non–Catholics never waned. As a correspondent for one paper noted: "There is not a more retiring, a more modest priest on the entire Pacific coast than Monsignor Prendergast, nor one who has done half as much for the spread of religion and the diffusion of knowledge."

Archbishop Alemany proposed his Vicar General for the coadjutorship of San Francisco in 1874, only to discover that Father Prendergast had already declined the mitre in Grass Valley. Even a petition signed by the majority of the Bay City's clergy left Prendergast unmoved, a gesture which one observer felt was "a rare instance of humility in this selfish age."

When Monsignor Prendergast, a domestic prelate since 1909, died on January 19, 1914, the words spoken at his golden jubilee five years earlier seemed all the more appropriate: "He has been all the time the consistent, dignified scholar, the perfect gentleman, the real Christian priest."

HUGH QUIGLEY (1819–1883)

Hugh Quigley was born within two Irish miles of Tulla, in the County of Clare, in December of 1819. He was dedicated by his pious father to the services of the Church, when about four years of age, at a "blessed well" named Tubber VicShane, where religious services used to be performed by outlawed priests during the penal times of Saxon Persecution. After completing his early education, Quigley went to Dublin, "where he joined the numerous bands of young men employed in the trigonometrical survey of Ireland.

Soon afterwards, Hugh entered Maynooth College to prepare for the priesthood. Because he refused to take the oath of allegiance to the British government, the young seminarian was forced to flee to Rome, where he continued his ecclesiastical studies at the Sapienza.

Upon completion of his work in the Eternal City, the newly ordained priest was given the exclusive title of *juvenus doctissimus* by the seminary authorities. The young priest returned to Eire and was made a curate in his native parish of Tulla. Later he went to Killahoe, where he labored under the direction of the well known Father (later Bishop) Daniel Vaughan. Father Quigley was pressured to leave his curacy at Killahoe when government officials discovered that the zealous cleric had advised his people that "it was no sin to feed their starving children and wives, even if compelled to take it from the rich neighbor's property." The exiled priest spent some years on the English and Scotch missions during the great Irish famine during which time he learned to admire the candor, independence, and sincerity of the English Catholics, both clergy and laity.

In 1848, Father Quigley was invited to New York, where his reputation as a writer and lecturer had preceded him. He worked in the Diocese of Albany for the following decade. While at Troy in 1849, he wrote the now celebrated story from real life, *The Cross and the Shamrock*, a handbook on the means of defending one's faith. That work, together with the book on *The Prophet of the Ruined Abbey*, circulated over a quarter million copies.

Quigley lectured widely in New York City and in Sheffield and Bradford, where his appearances were well reported in the daily press. During his pastorate at Lansingburgh, Father Quigley got himself involved in an expensive and widely heralded lawsuit over the use of the Bible in public schools. He was subsequently appointed rector of Saint Mary's in Chicago but resigned after a few years to become a missionary among the Chippewa Indians about Lake Superior.

Father Quigley came to California with the intention of working among the miners along the Gold Dust Trails. It was while in the west that the learned priest made his most lasting contribution to the literary world, *The Irish Race in California, and on the Pacific Coast*, published at San Francisco in 1878 by Anton Roman. The book is especially valuable for the biographical data it gives on the many Irish–born pioneers of the far west. After a few years in California, Father Quigley returned to New York and spent his last days at Troy, where he died at his residence, 196 Third Street, in May of 1883.

The esteem in which the Irish–born priest and scholar was held is obvious from an address given at the time of Father Quigley's departure from Eureka:

> You have proved yourself an honest man by your candor and love of truth, a scholar by your learned and moving discourses, a defender of the faith by your vigorous writings and lectures, a patriot by your love of country and advocacy of the independence of your native land; but above all these noble qualities for which we honor you, we place the highest estimate on your

piety as a priest of God, in your solemn ministrations at the altar, your attention to the instruction of our children, and your exact regularity in the discharge of all your sacred duties.

CHARLES A. RAMM (1863–1951)

A. BIOGRAPHICAL SKETCH

Charles A. Ramm (1863–1951) was born on a large ranch near the little town of Camptonville, in California's Yuba county, on August 4, 1863. His parents were immigrants from Hanover, Germany and he was reared in the Lutheran Church.

Although undoubtedly attracted to California by the discovery of gold, Ramm's father was more interested in raising grain, vegetables and cattle than in dredging the Yuba River for gold. Young Ramm entered the University of California in 1879 and, four years later, graduated with highest honors. He then did three years of graduate work in mathematics and physics at Johns Hopkins University before entering Saint Mary's Seminary at Baltimore as a clerical candidate for the Archdiocese of San Francisco. He was ordained priest on September 24, 1892.

Father Ramm's ministry was legendary. His early parochial work took him to many of the parishes in the archdiocese. With his degrees, Ramm was uniquely qualified for teaching and other academic posts. His talents were widely recognized and he enjoyed the unusual distinction of serving for thirty–two years as a regent for the University of California.

He often recalled the devastating day of April 18, 1906 when he stood on the steps of Saint Mary's Cathedral watching the Richelieu Hotel burning across the street. A little boy tugged at his cassock and said, "Look Father, the church is burning." Smoke was fanning from the tower below the cross. Firemen shrugged, knowing they couldn't get a hose high enough to extinguish the flames.

Somehow Ramm managed to climb the tower below the cross and directed firemen in putting out the blaze. "I was drenched to the skin," he recalled, "but we saved the cathedral."

Ramm is probably best remembered for a book published the year after his death under the title *Invocations and Other Prayers*. That sixty–eight page tome, edited for publication by Sister Catherine Marie Lilly, O.P., contained many of his priestly utterances between May, 1935 and December, 1944.

Probably the most memorable selection was his "Address before a Marriage Ceremony" which became part of Catholic marriage ceremonies throughout the English–speaking world. It has yet to be matched in con-

tent or expression and Catholics married prior to the 1960s will readily recall those beautiful words, part of which we here reprint:

My Dear Friends: You are about to enter into a union which is most sacred and most serious; sacred because ordained by God Himself, and serious because it will bind you together for life in a relationship so close and intimate that your whole future will be profoundly influenced by it.

And yet, what the nature of that future will be you do not know. You know neither its length of days nor its vicissitudes. Its hopes and disappointments, its successes and its failures, its pleasures and its pains, its joys and its sorrows, are all hidden from your eyes. You only know that these elements in varying proportions are mingled in every life, and are, therefore, to be expected in your own. And so, not knowing what is before you, you take each other for better or for worse, for richer or for poorer, in sickness and in health, until death.

Truly these are serious words, fraught with an almost fearful meaning. It is a beautiful tribute to your unclouded faith in each other, and to the splendid courage and generosity of our human nature, that recognizing their grave import, you are nevertheless so willing and ready to pronounce them.

And because they involve such solemn obligations, it is most fitting that you should, by these words, rest the security of your wedded life upon the great principle which lies at the base of everything that is holiest and best in human achievement. That principle is sacrifice.

Inasmuch as you are free, you can take each other only when you have first given each other. And so you begin your married life by the voluntary and complete surrender of your individual lives in the interests of that deeper and wider life which you are to have in common. Henceforth, you will belong wholly to each other; you will be one in mind, one in heart and one in affection. And whatever sacrifices you may hereafter be required to make for the preservation of this common life, will already have been included in that perfect and unreserved sacrifice with which you are about to begin it.

CHARLES A . RAMM (1863–1951)

B. GOLDEN TONGUED ORATOR

Charles Adolph Ramm, a man endowed by God with exceptional qualities of mind and soul, was born into a Lutheran family of eight children near Camptonville on August 4, 1863. Young Ramm entered the University of California upon graduation from the Berkeley Gymnasium in 1880. He studied in the College of Engineering, and on May 28, 1884, was awarded his degree along with designation of being the most distinguished graduate of the year. Soon after completing his studies, Ramm entered the Church. He later authored a pamphlet on

"Why I Became a Catholic," in which he attributed the grace of his conversion to the eloquent sermons of Father James Bouchard, the famed Indian priest.

Ramm stayed on at Berkeley as Recorder of the University until 1888, when he applied for admission to Saint Mary's Seminary in Baltimore, as a clerical aspirant for the Archdiocese of San Francisco. He was ordained in the premier see by James Cardinal Gibbons on September 24, 1892. At the suggestion of Archbishop Patrick W. Riordan, Father Ramm remained at Baltimore an additional two years as a graduate student of John Hopkins University. He returned to San Francisco in 1895, to become a curate at Saint Mary's Cathedral.

Ramm's knowledge of history, his literary ability and deep spirituality were virtues not easily concealed. Already by 1902, his famous "Address Before a Marriage Ceremony" (My dear friends—you are about to enter. . .) had an established place in Catholic marriage rituals throughout the English–speaking world.

Father Ramm accompanied Archbishop Riordan to the Hague in 1902, when the International Arbitral Court heard the plea of California's hierarchy for a settlement to the long–pending Pious Fund Case. Two years later, Riordan named Ramm his secretary, a position he occupied until 1914, when he went back as pastor to the same cathedral he personally helped save during the devastating post–earthquake fire of 1906.

The widely known and highly respected priest held a number of positions in the ensuing decades. He served as a Regent for the University of California from 1912 to 1944, and for many years was a member of the State Department of Social Welfare.

Created a Domestic Prelate by Pope Benedict XV in 1919, Monsignor Ramm was traditionally expected to speak at all the Bay City's important civic and religious functions. He gave the dedicatory address for both the Golden Gate Bridge and the San Francisco–Oakland span. A collection of his *Invocations and Other Addresses* was published shortly after his death on December 23, 1951.

Msgr. Charles A. Ramm approached death as an inspiration and example to his fellow priests. On the occasion of his golden jubilee, the articulate advocate of truth noted that,

> When one is on the threshold of the scriptural fourscore span of life, he knows he is descending the western slopes towards the sea. That need not be a lonely descent under a burden of gloom. The setting sun, too, has its glory, as well as the midday splendor. So one may go on slowly, not in fear, but in peace, carrying in his heart the treasured experiences of God's unfailing mercies through the years. Unworthy though he knows himself to be, yet he trusts that his gracious Master will guide and protect him to the last.

JAMES ARTHUR MORROW RICHEY
(1871–1934)

It is important that the paradigmatic stories of the "converts" from earlier days not be lost among the present generation of Roman Catholics. James Arthur Morrow Richey was one such convert who transferred his spiritual allegiance from the Protestant Episcopal Church in America to Rome.

Born on February 21, 1871, at Georgetown, Prince Edward Island, James was the son of a prominent minister in the Canadian Anglican Church. In 1889, after a short tenure at Racine College, James entered the preparatory department of Nashotah House, a "High Church" seminary in Wisconsin. He graduated in 1893, and was ordained deacon at Hobarth Church on the Oneida Indian Reservation. The Reverend James Richey was elevated to the Anglican priesthood by Bishop Lee Nicholson of Milwaukee. Not long afterwards, he married Mary Bryant.

James parented four children and pastored two parishes between 1895 and 1905, when the family moved to San Diego. In the latter city, Richey served as Rector of the local Anglican "High Church." He also published *The Crusader* which later became *The American Catholic*. The avowed aim of *The American Catholic* was to "help drive Protestantism out of the Episcopal Church." This he endeavored to do by convincing Episcopalians that they were truly Catholics and by demanding recognition by the Roman Catholic Church.

Shortly after his wife's death, in 1908, Richey returned to Chicago where he became Rector of Saint George's Church. A while later he moved to Quincy and there became a close friend of Father Michael J. Foley, editor of the *Western Catholic*.

Richey eventually became a Roman Catholic, receiving conditional baptism on December 8, 1910, at the hands of Archbishop John J. Glennon of Saint Louis. His children were also received into the Church at that time. James then decided to prepare himself for the Catholic priesthood. He entered Kenrick Seminary briefly for theological studies. He didn't stay too long, thinking it better to look after the raising of his children.

He worked at various journalistic pursuits and then went to Graymoor as associate editor of *The Lamp* and *The Antidote*. Several of the hymns he composed in those years were widely circulated, including "That All May Be One." His book on *The Sciences Dependent* (Boston, 1931) was applauded for its success in drawing out the relationship between science, philosophy and religion.

In 1931, James returned to Kenrick Seminary. After a year of further study, he was ordained a priest for the Diocese of Los Angeles–San Diego. The sixty–one year old cleric plunged into the busy round of pastoral activity as curate at Precious Blood Church in Los Angeles.

Father Richey's health declined and, on January 4, 1934, he died at Queen of Angels Hospital. In an editorial appearing in *The Lamp*, it was noted that "Richey forcefully reminded his own time that *phileia* and *agape* are basic to the Christian life, just as his life story reminds us that no genuine ecumenism is possible without authentic human friendship and active Christian love."

A lengthy biographical sketch of Richey's life in *Mid–America*, summarizing his career in the Protestant Episcopal and Roman Catholic Churches, related his contributions as pastor, journalist and apologist during a period of widespread ecclesial and social change

PATRICK ROCHE (1912–1982)

In 1957, the pastor of Holy Name parish in central Los Angeles, Msgr. Patrick Roche (1912–1982) was named editor of *The Tidings*, the sixth priest to occupy that position since 1895. Born in Lynn, Massachusetts, Patrick graduated from Holy Cross College before entering Saint Mary's Seminary in Baltimore as a clerical candidate for the old Diocese of Los Angeles–San Diego. He was ordained in 1938.

During the earliest years of his ministry, Father Roche worked mostly in educational assignments, both as assistant principal and associate superintendent for Catholic Schools. Like his two sacerdotal predecessors, Roche held a doctorate from The Catholic University of America and that training served him well for the sixteen years he shepherded the grand old lady of the Catholic press. Admittedly succeeding to the editorship of *The Tidings* was a tremendous challenge. There was still a steady flow of local news stories about the continued growth of parishes and schools, development of the seminary system, expansion of the Confraternity of Christian Doctrine and the activities of such organizations as the Lay Mission–Helpers who were sending people from Los Angeles to missionary areas around the world.

Roche consistently encouraged his staff members. He told one writer, just a few days before he died, that "Catholics walk taller when they learn about their roots. The honest writing of history is an apostolate that influences the mainspring of the commonwealth." He frequently quoted and endorsed John Steven McGroarty's definition of a friend which states that "a friend is one who writes the faults of his brothers and sisters in the sand for the winds to obscure and obliterate and who engraves their virtues on the tablets of love and memory."

Those who read Roche's *El Rodeo* columns between 1957 and 1973 were as impressed by his style as they were by his content. To the very last, the monsignor was a master of phraseology. The record needs to show that Roche departed significantly from his predecessors insofar as he was exceedingly conservative, almost reactionary in many of his views. During his editorship, *The Tidings* lost much of its credibility among those imbued with the so–called "spirit" of Vatican Council II.

Yet, when he retired, he was praised by Timothy Cardinal Manning for his "sensitive and capable management of the paper. *The Tidings* has reflected a true image of the Church and the archdiocese under your loyal priestly mind and heart."

His Eminence went on to express the hope that "we can all call upon your experience regularly for the continued guidance of the official newspaper of the Archdiocese." And that he did for the following decade.

JOHN ROHDE (1933–1995)

Someone once observed that the virtues of priests must be those not merely of men on a pilgrimage, but of the advance guides, scouts, who are at the head of the pilgrimage plunging into the wilderness, exploring the unknown and leading the way into the future.

In 1947, Msgr. John Rohde (1933–1995) and I were freshmen at the old Los Angeles College on Detroit Street. And for all those years, I have looked up to him as the ideal priest. There was nothing dysfunctional about John Rohde. What you saw was what he was—a 100% priest who had no other interests in all the world but his service to the Lord.

John was blessed with two lovely parents who worked long and hard to raise a family in the days before welfare checks and social legislation. It is no disservice to recall that he was born dirt poor and, by choice, he remained that way throughout his life, turning necessity into virtue. He didn't leave a will because he had nothing left of this world's treasures beyond a few trinkets in his apartment. Life was never easy for John. The oldest of a large family, he bore much of the burden in rearing his brothers and sisters while his mother was ailing and his father was working two full time jobs.

His vocation to the priesthood, recognized early, was planted firmly in concrete. He never looked back. He knew what he wanted to be and he defied all odds in attaining that goal. For six long years, he daily journeyed forty–five miles to and from the minor seminary and those were pre–freeway miles in a car that was barely roadworthy. By the time he had finished helping his father at night, there wasn't much time left for study and yet, somehow, he squeaked through the seminary, something he always attributed to that wonderful Vincentian, Bernard J. McCoy.

John was a good priest because he was a good seminarian. Deprivation and suffering came almost naturally to him, both before and after ordination. On a holy card given out at the time he became a priest, in 1959, was a quotation from Saint John Chrysostom which said that "according to the mind of Christ, a good shepherd may be compared to many martyrs. A martyr dies but once for Christ; the shepherd dies a thousand times for his flock."

Throughout the years of ministerial life, John Rohde was a peoples' priest whose demeanor was appreciated and recognized by laity and clergy alike. He genuinely liked people—all kinds of them—the rich and the poor, the learned and the ignorant, the simple and the mighty, the orphan and the needy, the homeless and the forgotten. He was most at home in what we used to call the "box" where people flocked to tell him their sins, listen to his advice and receive absolution.

Sertillanges once observed that "One has no faith in the jewel merchant who sells pearls and never wears them." Msgr. Rohde lived what he preached and people instinctively knew that. He wore the pearls of priestly service where everyone could see them.

John Rohde was the ideal role model for the American priest. He worked hard, laughed often, recreated sparsely, listened much, counseled wisely and prayed a lot. He had some difficult assignments, but he never complained. He was the good and faithful servant spoken about in Holy Scripture. He was a company man— and his company was the Lord.

Through it all, John was always happy. His joy didn't rest on a better definition of the priesthood or even on the experience of its effectiveness. Rather it rested on the total trust which he placed in the Lord who called him out of weakness to participate in His ministry.

The observations of an old Cheyenne Indian Chief who lived in the last century fit the context of this reflection most appropriately:

> There is a mountain in this vicinity known by every Cheyenne. The mountain is high and strong and many years old. Our forefathers knew it as well as we do. When children, we went out hunting and cared little whether we knew the way or not. When men, we went out to meet our foes no matter where they came from. Though the way ran high up and down low, our hearts trembled not; because that mountain was ever a safe guide and it never failed us. When far away, on seeing it our hearts leaped for joy because the mountain was the beacon which told us that we were approaching home. In summer, the thunder shook it from head to foot and fire bored holes in its sides. But the noise soon passed away and the mountain stood there majestically. In winter, storms rushed around to take it out of our sight and cover it with layer upon layer of snow. Only with difficulty could we distinguish it from the others. Only its height told us it was our mountain. But during the spring all the snow disappeared and the mountain, clothed with green grass, stood before us and the trees upon it stood firmer. This mountain is the priest of God . . . We know he has but one word and that his heart is as firm as a rock. He comes to instruct us, and what the mountain is in our journeys, that is his word. The priest is the mountain that leads us to God.

For many people, John Rohde was that mountain. When storms blew and rains fell, he was always there with words of comfort and assurances of hope. But now it is winter time and we must wait till spring to see him again. Like the Cheyenne's mountain, John's life is changed, not ended. The mountain never goes away.

TOBIAS ROMERO (1913–1996)

The first Hispanic American to receive a papal knighthood is also the first to have been given all the Church's sacraments, including that of Holy Orders. It could only happen in Los Angeles!

Tobias Romero was born into a family that had lived in New Mexico for nearly three centuries. In 1934, while working as a clerk for J.C. Penney, he married Maria Claudia who was a schoolteacher in Taos County.

The youthful couple was eventually blessed with three sons, Tobias Jr., Gilbert and Juan. Those early years were depression times and it wasn't easy for Tobias to support his family on a wage of $1 a day. Shortly after the outbreak of World War II, the Romeros emigrated to Los Angeles, where Tobias found employment in the machine, accounting and systemizing areas.

In subsequent years he was employed by Lockheed Aircraft Corporation, the Richfield Oil Company, Carte Blanche and CBS Television. Happily, the three Romero boys entered Los Angeles College, the preparatory seminary for the Archdiocese of Los Angeles. Gilbert and Juan were ultimately ordained priests. Tobias Jr. provided his father with two granddaughters.

Tobias took an active part in the Holy Name apostolate and was appointed archdiocesan president in 1964. Three years later, he was made a Knight Commander of Saint Gregory by Pope Paul VI, upon the recommendation of James Francis Cardinal McIntyre.

When Maria Claudia died in 1969, Tobias thought

about becoming a priest. He was discouraged initially by the Passionists because of his advanced age. Fortunately, the Claretians did not feel that age was a liability, and Tobias was accepted as a candidate. He was able to complete his seminary training in four years.

Ordained by Timothy Cardinal Manning on May 17, 1975, the sixty–one year old Father Tobias Romero was appointed to the staff of *Nuestra Señora de los Angeles*, the Old Plaza Church in downtown Los Angeles.

It proved to be a busy assignment. Over 15,000 people crowd into the small church for Mass every weekend. There are over two hundred baptisms every single week. During his years there, Father Tobias Romero also served as chaplain for the Nocturnal Adoration Society. He later was named archdiocesan director of the Hispanic Branch of the society.

Though he admits to having enjoyed "the best of both worlds," Father Romero does not recommend a married clergy. "If you are married, your first duty is to your wife and family, and that is a full–time commitment.

"If you are a priest, your first duty is to your flock. You can't do justice to both commitments. One or the other will suffer if you try to combine the two. I'm sure a celibate clergy is more effective." At priestly gatherings in and around Los Angeles, people often confuse Fathers Tobias and Juan as brothers. In reality, they are more than that for Father Tobias is a two–fold "father", to his three sons and to his parishioners at Our Lady of Solitude.

It is the only time in United States Catholic annals where father and sons have served together in the priesthood.

JOSE MARIA ROSALES Y PACHECO

José Maria Rosales y Pacheco was the first person advanced to the clerical state in California. He received tonsure and the minor orders at San Diego, on December 19, 1841. The youthful cleric accompanied Bishop Francisco Garcia Diego to Santa Barbara early the following year, and there continued his theological courses under the personal guidance of the bishop.

Rosales was ordained on October 8, 1843, at Mission Santa Barbara and, on the following November 9th, was placed in charge of the spiritualities at San Buenaventura. With his arrival, that mission became one of the first canonically–erected parishes in the Diocese of Both Californias.

The Zacatecan–born priest served at San Buenaventura until August 20, 1848, when the Administrator of the vacant bishopric, Father José Maria de Jesús González Rubio, abruptly terminated his pastorate. There are several interpretations as to what provoked

Rosales' removal from office, none of which satisfactorily answers the question. One suggests that the priest was guilty of doctrinal irregularities, another that he had an altercation with an American official and the third that he was insubordinate.

The Franciscan chronicler reported that González Rubio had informed Governor Richard B. Mason that "he had been insulted by the Presbyter Don José Maria." That statement cannot be verified or elaborated upon. That the administrator subsequently entrusted another pastorate to Father Rosales indicates that his offense certainly was not of a serious or incriminatory nature.

In any event, Father Rosales was given permission for a trip to Guadalajara. He returned to California and, early in 1850, "on seeing the people without spiritual guidance and comfort" at San Juan Capistrano, he volunteered for that vacancy. Rosales served there for some months as a curate and, on August 28th, was confirmed in the position and formally appointed pastor. He was a popular and enthusiastic clergyman and the Franciscan chronicler noted that the older people at San Juan Capistrano remembered him as a forceful speaker. As the first secular priest to minister at Capistrano, Father Rosales began a whole new tradition of apostolic ministry among the white inhabitants and the few remaining Indians.

Rosales was proud of the historical role he played in the ecclesial affairs of the new diocese and once wrote, in the register book at Capistrano, that he had been in "the company of the first Bishop of California, who died in the year 1846. I was the first ecclesiastic in this new diocese." (By this he obviously referred to his being tonsured. Father Miguel Gómez was the proto–priest ordained for California on June 29, 1842.)

Father Rosales remained at Capistrano until November 22, 1853. With the authorization of Bishop Joseph Sadoc Alemany, he then returned to Guadalajara "as he had intended to do when the pitiable condition of San Juan Capistrano detained him." Beyond a renewal of his permission to remain in Mexico in 1856, there is no further record of the priest extant in the annals. Quite likely he served out the remaining years of his parochial ministry somewhere in his native homeland.

LUIGI ROSSI (1817–1871)

Though hardly a prototype Catholic missionary, Father Louis Rossi wrote an exceedingly colorful account of life along the west coast of America in the 1880s. Born Abramo De Rossi, on June 14, 1817, the son of Graziado and Anna (Finzi) De Rossi, the young native of Ferrara was a convert from Judaism at the age of twenty–one. It was then that he adopted the name Luigi Angelo Maria Rossi.

In January of 1838, Rossi entered the Passionist Order at Paliano. Though later expelled for being "choleric and impetuous," Rossi was eventually allowed to re–enter the Order at Monte Argentario. He made his final religious profession on October 29, 1839 under the name of Pelligrino del Cour di Gesu. After further theological studies, Rossi was ordained priest in April, 1843.

Rossi spent his early priestly years teaching rhetoric, philosophy and theology at various Passionist houses in the Italian province and, during his stay in Rome, he wrote a biography of Saint John of the Cross. In 1853, he was instrumental in establishing a Passionist foundation at Bordeaux, France.

Rossi came to the United States in 1856, and spent the following six years along the west coast. Those were times of expansion and excitement and Rossi was confronted with great loneliness and isolation in the relatively unpopulated vastness of Western Washington and Northern California.

Upon his return to Europe in 1863, Rossi cared for the parish of Saint Joseph in Paris. The rest of his life was spent in parochial assignments at Maisons, Alfort and Ile–Saint–Denis. During those years, Rossi also worked at writing his memoir which was published at Paris and Brussels in 1863, *as Six ans en Amerique Californie et Oregon.*

It is a remarkable book which offers interesting insights to what was occurring in a considerable area of the west coast. He knew San Francisco, for example, as a burgeoning, post gold–rush city.

An Italian with a solid overlay of French influence and discernible anglophobic tendencies, his admiration for the then infant American system is refreshingly devoid of the patronizing attitudes often present in European visitors of the time.

Throughout the narrative, Rossi communicates an immediate feeling for the natural grandeur of a region in the very early stages of exploitation by white men. He also conveys the sense of excitement that must have been present in all those who were seeing the richness and appreciating the potential of a vast, raw territory.

Very little is known about Rossi's personal life after his return to Europe. He had left the Passionists in 1855, and possibly became affiliated with Bishop A.M.A. Blanchet of Nesqually. He died on September 9, 1871.

The 1863 edition of Rossi's book was re–issued the following year, under a slightly different title. W. Victor Wortley has prepared an English translation which has been published by the University of Utah Press.

GEORGE M.A. SCHOENER (1864–1941)

Santa Barbara's "*Padre* of the Roses," George M.A. Schoener, was born in Steinbach Baden, Germany, on March 21, 1864. His early studies included courses in botany at universities in Germany and Switzerland. In 1886, Schoener was adopted as a clerical candidate for the Diocese of Pittsburgh. Coming to the United States, he completed his classes in theology at Saint Vincent's Seminary, Latrobe, Pennsylvania, where he was ordained on April 2, 1892.

In the following two decades, Father Schoener served at various parishes in the Pittsburgh area, including Saint Mary's (Altoona), Saint Peter's (Pittsburgh) and Saint Leo's (Allegheny). One source indicates that he designed and directed the building of Saint Cecilia's Cathedral. The young priest subsequently went to Oregon for his health and, in 1910, was appointed Pastor of Assumption Parish, in Brooks. There, as he walked through the hills and woods, he was enthralled with the variety of wild roses climbing over granite boulders and up into the branches of oak and fir trees.

Father Schoener decided to refresh himself on the study of botany and before long began his hybridization work with roses, a pursuit in which he rapidly gained a national reputation. From the outset of his work, the priest endeavored to produce new strains of roses that would have all the beauty of household plants. He soon began growing roses in the neglected soil of his little churchyard at Brooks.

In 1914, Father Schoener exhibited sixty of his hybrid plants at the Portland Rose Festival and had the extreme pleasure of seeing one of his creations christened by the Rose Festival Queen. The next year he displayed roses at the Panama Pacific Exhibition in San Francisco.

On October 8, 1915, the church, rectory and rose garden at Brooks were destroyed by fire. Following the conflagration, the priest moved to Portland, where be established the Schoener Gardens on the peninsula at McKenna Park. There he continued his work among the plants and flowers.

The final twenty years of his life were spent at Santa Barbara, where he assisted the resident priest at Our Lady of Guadalupe Parish. Through the kindness of the Royal Botany Gardens and others, he obtained seedlings to develop still more roses. His garden contained a "rose avenue" 225 feet long and lined with giant rose trees.

The title of "*El Padre de las Rosas*" was conferred upon the priest by the *Salem Journal* in 1936. According to an article in the *American Magazine*, Father Schoener developed his 236th new rose that same year. It was a "little coal–black rose" of considerable beauty. The priest named it for Chief Justice Oliver Wendell Holmes who helped collect funds to assist Schoener in his work at Santa Barbara.

At the time of his demise, on February 10, 1941, Father Schoener had some 5,000 bushes, including a giant rose eight inches in diameter and rose trees towering twenty–five feet high. He was busy at work striving to produce a pure blue rose, a dream of rose fanciers. At his own request, the internationally recognized botanist was buried from Santa Barbara Mission. And that was surely fitting for like the early friars before him, Father George M. A. Schoener was truly a pioneer in the development of the far west.

MARTIN FRANCIS SCHWENNINGER (1809–1866)

Martin Francis Schwenninger, referred to along the Gold Dust Trails as the "Padre of Paradise Flat," was born at Innsbruck, the capital of the Tyrol Province in Austria, on July 30, 1809. In the early years after his ordination in 1832, Father Florian, as he was known by his Benedictine confreres, was Professor of Sacred Scripture and Oriental languages at Feicht.

After coming to the United States in 1844, Father Florian worked for some time among the German immigrants around Utica, New York, and later in the northern part of New Jersey. He was editor of a Catholic periodical called the New York *Sion* before accepting the invitation of Bishop Joseph Sadoc Alemany to journey westward in 1852.

In his first year in California, Father Florian was attached to Saint Francis Church in San Francisco where, among other duties, he had charge of the Bay City's German–speaking Catholics. In 1853, he was sent to Shasta and enroute became the first priest ever to penetrate the northernmost districts of California. Not long after arriving in Old Shasta Town, Father Florian started work on a little frame church at present–day Cemetery Hill.

Florian's ministrations were not restricted to Shasta. He visited all the neighboring regions, journeying on foot as far as Red Bluff in Tehama County, Dog Creek, up the Sacramento River Canyon, and Fort Redding and Pit River on the east. He built churches at Horsetown and Weaverville and soon earned a reputation for being the most "traveled" priest along the gold belt.

In August of 1858, Father Florian took up residence at Sawyer's Bar, located on the North Fork of the Salmon River. It was there that he became known to prospectors, Catholic and non–Catholic alike, as the "Padre of Paradise Flat." There he erected Saint Joseph's Church, which became the central point of his missionary activities in subsequent years. A contemporary newspaper clipping described the priest as "a remarkable man, a German Benedictine monk, most thoroughly instructed in ancient and modern languages, music and other accomplishments of the German schools. He is also a music composer of great excellence and, above all, he is a good, kind–hearted, faithful man

of God, who is content to live in waste places for the advancement of what he believes to be the Holy Church." The account went on to speak about the church he was building at Paradise Flat, noting that "every timber shaped by his feeble hands in the solitude of the mountains is a work as worthy of consecration as a cornerstone in the church of St. Peter."

The tireless missionary lived another decade and though illness plagued his final years, there was little evidence of its effects on his many activities. He died with Bishop Eugene O'Connell at his side in the foothills of the Sierras on July 28, 1866. Some years after his death, the following epitaph on "The Padre's Grave" was penned by Myron C. X. Shuey:

> He needs no costly tomb, no mark of stone
> To tell the passing world of warfare's strife;
> For lives redeemed give homage to the soul
> That led the way to higher, nobler life.
> Within the hearts of millions yet unborn,
> His deeds will burn, a glorious beacon bright
> To lead them to the shrine that Faith makes real;
> A shrine resplendent with God's holy light.

LUIGI SCIOCCHETTI (1878–1962)

The ceilings, walls and dome of the recently refurbished Saint Joseph's Cathedral in San Jose are elaborately adorned with murals and paintings designed and executed by Father Luigi Sciocchetti (1878–1962).

Luigi was born in Ripastransome, Italy. His earlier education embraced his two great loves—the priesthood and the palette. He seems to have integrated these interests in a most admirable way. When Archbishop Edward J. Hanna met Father Sciocchetti in Assisi, during 1922, he urged the young priest to affiliate himself with the Archdiocese of San Francisco which was then preparing to celebrate the golden jubilee of Saint Joseph's Church in San Jose.

Two years later, after being formally entrusted with redecorating the church in anticipation of its jubilee, Father Sciocchetti brought two compatriots, Professor Armando Marchigiani and Ruggero Faggioni to assist in the project. Marchigiani was an expert in color coordination and Faggioni in the fabrication of paper mache and other design elements.

Nephews and nieces of the priest acted as models for the various figures in the murals. Guido Sciocchetti, his brother, was himself an artisan and he was charged with providing and erecting the scaffolding for the project.

Father Sciocchetti spent about five months in his San Francisco studios working on the drawings. The most difficult part of the designs was executing the original sketches. They had to be drawn on paper, then divided into small squares and, finally, transferred to canvases.

The canvases were painted in the empty school building in back of Saint Joseph's church. Once the murals were finished, the artist spent another five months gluing them to the walls, ceiling and domes.

Newspapers of the time carefully recorded the artistic program and packages of clippings from the San Francisco *Chronicle* explain in great detail how the work advanced over a three year period. In the *Chronicle's* rotogravure pictorial section for August 27, 1933, Father Sciocchetti is also featured and applauded for his work in the Salesian Church of Saint Joseph in Oakland.

The only extant photograph of the priest is one showing him at work in his studio in San Francisco. On his easel is a portrait of Padre Giovanni, a boyhood friend who died in 1905. According to the clippings, Giovanni was then being considered for canonization and Father Sciocchetti had been asked by Roman officials to produce a likeness of the Passionist priest.

Sciocchetti's mural of Don Bosco as a peasant shepherd is one of his finest works. His murals can still be viewed at Immaculate Conception and at Saint Paul of the Shipwreck. Father Sciocchetti remained active in a host of pastoral activities over the years he spent in the Bay Area. He was a confessor of wide renown and his Sunday homilies were noted for their simplicity and sincerity.

The highly respected priest celebrated his fiftieth and sixtieth sacerdotal anniversaries in residence at Precious Blood parish in San Jose. He fell asleep in the Lord in 1962, a legendary figure in both his native land and his adopted country.

JOHN SHANAHAN (1792–1870)

Known as the "Pioneer Priest of Nevada County," Father John Shanahan was among the first resident Catholic clergymen along California's Gold Dust Trails. Ordained at Baltimore on September 19, 1823, for the Diocese of New York, the Irish–born cleric spent the early part of his ministry as one of the half dozen priests in the entire State of New York and the greater part of New Jersey.

Concerning his days as pastor at Troy, one commentator speaks of the "virtuous, hardworking Father Shanahan, of whom the tantalizing scanty glimpses we got of his history make us hungry for more. Church histories tell naught of him but in praise of his zeal and industry during his long missionary life in these regions."

In 1849, after a siege of the ill health which plagued him throughout his life, Shanahan "contracted the habit of traveling" and set out for the gold regions of California, then a part of the Archdiocese of San Francisco. Two years later, at the request of Archbishop Joseph Sadoc Alemany, the fifty–nine year old priest accepted the pastorate of Nevada City. His parish was one of the largest in the archdiocese, reaching over to Downieville in Sierra County on the north, and as far as Michigan City in Placer County on the south. To travel from one boundary to another took the missionary three weeks of continuous journeying, on mule or horseback through one of the most rugged sections of the Sierra foothills.

"In Father Shanahan's time great freight wagons drawn by ten or twelve oxen were arriving daily from Sacramento; there were at least 3,000 miners in town continually, the majority drinking gambling, and carousing. . . . The newly arrived missionary, although he came from the gay city of New York, had to avow that never in all his experience had he ever witnessed anything like Nevada City in the pioneer days."

The exceedingly wet and stormy winter of 1852 cut off communications with Monterey and Sacramento for almost two weeks and "Father Shanahan then witnessed a unique condition of affairs, the saloons ran out of liquor, and he found himself in a mining town that actually went dry!" Though his sojourn in Nevada City was relatively short, Shanahan built several churches for his people and achieved a far–flung reputation as "an apostle on horseback, bringing the same Faith and the same sacraments to the men who dug, the Erie Canal and the men who dug deep into the earth in search of gold."

Failing eyesight forced Father Shanahan's retirement from California in 1853, and during the final fifteen years of his life, the "Pioneer Priest of Nevada County" served at New York City's Saint Peter's Church on Barclay Street. "With pleasant memories of old California, and with a final prayer for his beloved children of the rugged mining camps in the hills he loved so well, Father Shanahan passed away on the eighth day of August, 1870."

Though his years as a California missionary were short, Father Shanahan came as a witness to his Faith, mindful perhaps what an earlier priest in the area had said: "One cannot enkindle fire in others who permits it to be extinguished in himself!"

DANIEL SLATTERY (c. 1827–1860)

There were three Slatterys who served the People of God along California's Gold Dust Trails, in the early days of the 1800s, *viz.*, Maurice, William and Daniel. Father Daniel was a favorite with the miners of the area. One of thirty–six children of an Irish family from Kerry, Daniel studied for the ministry at Maynooth College before his arrival in San Francisco in 1854

He lived only six years in the priesthood before succumbing to pneumonia, on October 9, 1860. But in that short time, the priest became something of a legend among his people. Though very little biographical data is available on Father Daniel Slattery, there is much of his personality portrayed in a letter that Mrs. Elizabeth Sanborn wrote to Thomas Colin of Columbia, in 1923:

> One of the happiest days of my life was when we were told that the Bishop of San Francisco was coming to Sonora to confirm us. Well, we all hurried, getting ready to receive confirmation. Even babies in arms were confirmed, and we were told beforehand that the Bishop would confirm us by making the sign of the Cross on our forehead, and give us a slap on our face, of which we were afraid. We did not know much about church, so everything was new to us at the time. As I remember it, we all went to the church on that famous Sunday and everything seemed changed, because Bishop Alemany was there; and I need not tell you anything about him, because anyone who ever knew him can realize the kind of man he was—a pure Castilian Spaniard and Father Slattery beside him. I still think, as I did at that time, that two better or kinder men were never before in this big beautiful world. We marched up and knelt before the Bishop and were confirmed, and the wonderful man, Father Slattery, wiped the oil from our foreheads. He was so gentle and kind to us that we all thought he was related to God, and I have always thought so ever since. I honestly think he was made in the image and likeness of God. At that time he made his home in the house of Mrs. Holden, on a wide street opposite the church, and I shall never forget how badly Father Slattery and all of us felt when, shortly after this, our dear Mrs. Holden was taken from us. She was burned to death. She fell over a candle in some kind of fit when she was helping her dear old father. The next day she sent for me and said: "Lizzie, come and kiss me goodbye. I will be your guardian angel;" and I really believe she always has been.

> We had wonderful people and wonderful friends there in those days. Mrs. Holden and Mrs. Harmon were two perfect women. I hope some day to meet them again. And our two wonderful pastors, the Bishop from Spain and dear, good, kind Father Slattery from Ireland. Those two countries had wonderful representatives right here, working under great difficulties, but they won the love and the good wishes of every soul in the land of gold and sunshine.

> Father Slattery loved the children especially, and gave his time to us, and what he did for us could not be done today by any living person. He was always arranging picnics for us. I remember one picnic in particular which was held at Madame Lacassis' Garden, out of town on the road to Soulsbyville, on the 15th of August, the Feast of Our Blessed Lady. This wonderful garden was made to represent a fairyland, the children were all dressed in dainty attire and healthy and happy, the most wonderful man, Father Slattery, looking out for their comfort. We started on this never–to–be–forgotten picnic, first by going to Mass in Sonora Church, where there was wonderful music and singing. Then we went to the schoolroom and Father came in smiling, and as he came by every little girl he would say: "Well, my child, how much money have you to spend for ice cream?" And if she said: "None," he would say, "I was afraid of that," and drop 25 cents in her lap. He brought the boys outside and threw dollars and dimes around for them to scramble for. You would think he had eyes in the back of his head, he was such a keen observer and so good to all.

CAJETAN SORRENTINI (1815–1893)

Though Father Cajetan Sorrentini was undeniably one of the most controversial of California's post–mission clerics. his fifty–four years in the ministry constitute an intriguing chapter in ecclesial annals. Born in Italy on August 7, 1815, the son of Giuseppe and Anna Maria Sorrentini, Cajetan studied at the Eternal City's prestigious *Colegio Romano*. He was ordained on September 19, 1839

An "Apostolic Missionary" attached to the Sacred Congregation of Propaganda Fide, Father Sorrentini was assigned to the Chair of Theology at the diocesan seminary in Amalfi, Naples, a post he occupied for several years. Early in the 1840s, Sorrentini was sent to Jerusalem as a special "visitor." His delicate assignment was that of investigating charges of Franciscan affiliation with the Masons. During his three years in the Holy Land, Sorrentini was also influential in building Saint John's Hospital. He was eventually recalled to Rome because of ill health.

Sorrentini was present in the private oratory of the Urban College of Propaganda Fide for the episcopal ordination of the Right Reverend Thaddeus Amat. In November, 1854, Sorrentini arrived in California with Bishop Amat and shortly thereafter was entrusted with the pastorate at Monterey.

A few years later, Father Sorrentini was transferred to Santa Barbara as Pastor of Our Lady of Sorrows. He figured prominently in the dispute that Bishop Amat had with the Franciscans. In 1857, he was sent to Rome with a detailed account of the controversy. Unfortunately for all concerned, Sorrentini had previously run afoul of Father Bernardino de Montefranco, the Franciscan Master General, in the Holy Land. Sorrentini was not one who could easily disguise his hostile attitude to the friars.

Upon his return from Europe, Sorrentini was released from the jurisdiction of Bishop Amat for service in what is now the Diocese of Alexandria, Louisiana. In 1861, he was made Pastor of Saint Mary Magdalen dei Pizzi, in

Philadelphia. Between 1864 and 1871, Sorrentini occupied a similar position in New Castle. After four years at Pottstown, Pennsylvania, Father Sorrentini was appointed Pastor of Saint James, in Wilmington, Delaware. He also served as chaplain for the Italian work crews brought into that area for railroad construction.

Sorrentini then got into a dispute with the local bishop, an encounter which motivated his return west. Back in California, the priest was assigned to Sacred Heart Parish, Salinas. There he remained for sixteen years, building a new church, parochial residence, schoolhouse and cemetery. Father Sorrentini observed the golden jubilee of his priestly ordination in 1889, an event attended by hundreds of his friends from all over the country. He lived on until June 30, 1893.

A profound scholar, accomplished linguist and talented musician, Father Sorrentini was a colorful priest whose contributions are still evident in the landscape of California's Catholic heritage.

POLYDORE JUSTIN STOCKMAN (1843–1924)

One of the outstanding priestly pioneers of the Church in Southern California was Msgr. Polydore Justin Stockman (1843–1924). Among his many distinctions was that of serving as the proto–chancellor for the huge Diocese of Monterey–Los Angeles.

Born in Ghent, Belgium, Stockman came to the United States in December of 1873, after completing his theological studies in Europe. He was ordained by Bishop Thaddeus Amat on March 25, 1874. Following a six month stint of pastoral work in San Diego, Father Stockman was assigned to San Bernardino, then a frontier community composed mostly of non–Catholics and peoples of no religious persuasion.

"*Padre* Agostin," as he became known to the native Americans, set out to establish a Catholic presence in San Bernardino county. Within the next two decades, the imprint of the tireless priest was indelibly etched onto the map of the area. Among his brick and mortar accomplishments were ten or more churches and chapels, plus the first parochial school in what has become the Inland Empire. To his clerical friends, Father Stockman was a "pastoral cyclone" who somehow managed to extend his influence even to faraway Needles and Yuma.

In October, 1895, Father Stockman was transferred to the pastorate of Our Lady of Sorrows in Santa Barbara. There he once again demonstrated his solicitude for spreading the Gospel to all who would listen.

In mid 1906, Father Stockman was able to obtain seven Sisters of Notre Dame to take charge of his parish school. And, two years later, again at Stockman's behest, Franciscan Sisters of the Third Order agreed to establish Saint Francis Hospital in Santa Barbara. Between 1898 and 1914, Father Stockman fulfilled the duties of chancellor for the Diocese of Monterey–Los Angeles. In January of 1906, he was named a consultor and spokesman for the bishop in Santa Barbara county.

Failing health compelled Stockman to resign his pastoral duties in 1908. Shortly thereafter, he took up residence in Los Angeles, where he served as chaplain for the Sisters of the Immaculate Heart in Pico Heights.

In 1909, Father Stockman was made a private chamberlain to Pope Pius X, one of the first priests so honored in California. He was renewed in that office by Popes Benedict XV and Pius XI. During his years as chaplain at Immaculate Heart, Msgr. Stockman turned his energies and attention toward compiling a catechism for teenagers, as well as his classic *Manual of Christian Doctrine* which was published in 1921.

In a letter to Stockman, Father John J. Cawley said that Bishop John J. Cantwell found the manual "in every way an excellent book for the purpose for which it was written. It was," said the prelate, "an indispensable manual for those who are aspiring after perfection." Cantwell felt that a copy "should be on the priedieu of every religious" and, with that in mind, he ordered fifty copies "to place in the various religious houses" of the diocese.

The venerable cleric lived on for another three years, until his demise on December 1, 1924. After a moving eulogy by Msgr. Thomas J. Fitzgerald of Redlands, Stockman was interred in the priests' plot at Calvary Cemetery.

GIUSEPPE TONELLO (1851–1933)

The origin of our national anthem, "America," vociferously disputed in the 1930s, was a controversy that received wide coverage in the southland's secular press. The basic melody was used in a dozen or so countries. Adapted from "God Save the King," it was claimed by the Irish, Germans, English and others.

In Los Angeles, Father Giuseppe Tonello (1851–1933), a "valiant defender of the rights of Italy," told a reporter for the *Examiner* that "the tune is Italian and originated with Giambattista Lulli," a Florentine who was often thought to be a Frenchman. Tonello, an acknowledged authority, was regarded as "one of the leading figures in the American music world." He had written a number of compositions which were played by the Los Angeles Philharmonic Orchestra.

The newspaper account referred to the priest as a "scholar" whose "investigations on the subject of

'America' carry weight." While admitting that the names of Handel, Carey, Anson and others were associated with "America," Tonello insisted that the sole credit belonged to Lulli.

Tonello recalled that during a visit to Saint–Cyr, King Louis XIV "was deeply moved as the burst of bright, fresh, young faces sent up in the anthem which was a household sound for more than 100 years." He also related that the Dames of St. Louis (Saint Cyr) attributed the melody to Lulli. Finally Tonello quoted L'Abbe Nisard who declared that the anthem was composed by Lulli and sung at Saint–Cyr when, on the holy days, Louis XIV would enter the chapel. Handel was the means of making the hymn known in England.

Tonello was himself a colorful person. He was a member of the Order of Charity (Rosemenians). Ordained on September 8, 1878, he was later sent to the United States to establish a college in Illinois. Tonello subsequently served as pastor in Galesburg, an area that was then predominantly Italian. In 1912, Father Tonello came to Los Angeles for health reasons. For many years the Italian–born priest administered to Catholics at Our Lady of Lourdes parish in Tujunga.

A story in the Los Angeles *Examiner* for January 30, 1973, told how the gentle priest had been awarded a Knight Chaplaincy in the Sacred Military Order of St. George, "one of the rarest and highest honors given by the Vatican." Described in a newspaper account as "an intimate friend of Caruso and known affectionately by Pope Pius X," Father Tonello wrote a number of musical compositions, including the popular ballad "Souvenirs of Italy."

In order to further document his contention that Giambattista Lulli was responsible for "America," Father Tonello provided a biographical sketch of the composer for the local press. He concluded his interview by saying that "plainly, historical facts prove that Lulli was an Italian and that he composed the original tune, *Grand Lieu Suave le Roi*" which became "America."

When word reached Los Angeles that Father Tonello had died at Turin, the conductor of the Los Angeles Philharmonic Orchestra announced that Chopin's Funeral March would be played in Tonello's memory during the following week's performances.

FRANCISCO TORRENS Y NICOLAU (1856–1924)

Foremost among the literary memorials which the gifted pens of writers dedicated, in prose and verse, to Fray Junípero Serra on the two hundredth anniversary of his birth was the *Bosquejo Histórico del Insigne Franciscano VP.F. Junípero Serra, Fundador y Apóstol de la California Septentrional*. The 227–page work, published at Petra by B. Reus, was one of the many schol-

arly productions of Father Francisco Torrens y Nicolau (1856–1924), a well–known ecclesiastical notary in the archpresbyterate of Manacor.

During the years following his ordination, on December 2 1, 1834, Father Torrens engaged in parochial activities. He quickly began to excel as a leader and organizer and, within a relatively short time, had achieved an enviable reputation as orator throughout the Balearic Isles. In addition to his manifold duties, Father Torrens broadened his education by acting for several years as a chaplain in the service of the Spanish Transatlantic Company. He also functioned for almost a decade as spiritual advisor to the influential Alejandro Maria Pons of Barcelona.

Torrens was an accomplished historian. He wrote a documented narrative about Petra and the popular *Apuntes Históricas de Santuario de Nuestra Señora de Bonamy*. In 1904, he participated in two literary contests, one at San Andrés de Palomar in Barcelona, the other at Zaragosa. The first prize was awarded to Torrens in both. For the latter, Torrens submitted an exquisite theological dissertation on "*La Concepción Inmaculada de Varlay el Pecado Original.*"

Torrens' interest in Junípero Serra stems from a copy of Francisco Palóu's biographical account which he providentially stumbled across in an idle moment. Through that seemingly casual event, he became a fervent and enthusiastic admirer of his countryman. From the very outset, Torrens used his influence to popularize Fray Junípero and the work of the California missionaries among his kinsmen. In 1892, at his request, the old *Plaza de la Constitución* was renamed *Plaza del VP. Junípero Serra, R.F.*

Two decades later, Father Torrens published his own work which was welcomed as a "wonderfully brief, yet complete resume" of Serra's accomplishments. The classically written account was regarded as "the last and most reliable work on whatever appertains to the intimate life of the founder of the California Missions, especially in reference to the first period of his life in Spain." The Torrens tome was divided into two parts, the first embracing the life of the pioneering missionary, the second outlining what California and Spain had done to honor his memory, since 1784

The writer's own inventive nature is amply displayed in his assessment of the various printed works, poems, plays and monuments to the great hero of *El Camino Real*. As an appendix, Torrens included an interesting collection of unpublished letters and documents relating to the California missionary enterprise. Though subsequent research has rendered the Torrens narrative obsolete, one can readily appreciate the ingenuity and resourcefulness which made such a publication possible in an era when Fray Junípero Serra was practically an unknown quantity in his homeland.

EGISTO TOZZI (1882–1961)

Even in these days of inflated monetary values, there are relatively few millionaires. The statistical charts indicate that in the 1990s only a small percentage of people can be classified in that distinctive category.

California once had a millionaire priest. In addition to his financial holdings, Monsignor Egisto Tozzi was among the more colorful of San Francisco's early clerics. All the while he wore his fortune well.

Born to Nicola Tozzi and Maria Guglielmi on April 28, 1882, Egisto was baptized in the parish church of Civitella d'Agliano, a suburb of the Eternal City. Tozzi was fond of recalling that his pastor predicted on the day of his baptism that he would one day be a priest.

The Tozzi family had close ties to Rome's so–called "Black Nobility." And when the youthful Egisto expressed a desire to study for the ministry, he was enrolled at *Bagnoregio Seminario*, Vescovia. Ordained for the Diocese of Bagnoregio, on June 18, 1905, by Bishop Eutizo Parsi, Father Tozzi spent the earliest years of his priestly life devising methods of uplifting the disadvantaged peoples of his poverty–ridden parish.

Shortly after his ordination, Father Tozzi was befriended by one of Italy's leading bankers, A.P. Giannini. While still in his twenties, Tozzi was advised to invest his family inheritance in shares of Giannini's Bank of Italy. It was probably the best advice of his life.

The investment proved a shrewd one and the habit of playing the stock market stayed with Father Tozzi over the next half century. In time, the Bank of Italy became the wealthy Bank of America and Father Tozzi's original investment was multiplied many times.

Father Tozzi came to San Francisco in late 1908 and from that time onwards served in many capacities for Archbishops Patrick W. Riordan, Edward J. Hanna and John J. Mitty. Incardinated in 1921, Father Tozzi was named Pastor of Saint Peter's parish in Cloverdale. Later be served in pastorates at Saint Anthony's (Manteca), Saint Paul's (San Pablo) and All Souls (South San Francisco). In all of those places, Father Tozzi was known for his charitable benefactions and his willingness to share his financial expertise.

In 1939, Father Tozzi was named a papal chamberlain and, eight years later, a domestic prelate. He lived on until October 11, 1961, when he was killed in an automobile accident. When an inventory of his assets was filed in San Mateo county superior court, Redwood City, it showed that the priest had left an estate of $1,123,139. The inventory disclosed that Monsignor Tozzi owned shares of forty–four blue chip stocks.

Monsignor Tozzi left small bequests to friends, his former parish church in Rome and All Souls Church in South San Francisco, where he had been pastor. But the bulk of his estate, more than $1,000,000 went to the Colegio Egisto Tozzi, a boy's high school and junior college in Rome named after the priest. The college, which required no tuition from the sons of poor families, was founded by a nephew in 1952. It had been the major source for the monsignor's benefactions in the later days of his life.

GEORGE M. TRUNCK (1870–1973)

The oldest person ever to contribute a regular newspaper column to an American publication was a Catholic priest who lived in retirement at the Church of the Nativity, in San Francisco. Father George M. Trunck (1870–1973) began writing for Cleveland's *Amerikanski Slovence* in 1924. On July 21, 1971, he addressed his 2571st column in a bold, firm flourishing script. And it was not his last.

George Trunck was born in the small village of Bace. He was ordained priest in the now–defunct nation of Corinthia, in 1895. As a young clergyman, he actively supported the social encyclicals of Pope Leo XIII.

Also vociferous in politics, Father Trunck was named delegate from Corinthia to Versailles Treaty Conference following World War I. There he met the world leaders, including president Woodrow Wilson of the United States. Before a special election to determine whether Corinthia should join Austria or Yugoslavia, Father Trunck campaigned vigorously for union with Yugoslavia. When the majority vote favored Austria, Father Trunck was jailed for a time. He was accused of Slovenian nationalism, a charge to which he readily agreed.

Trunck put aside political involvement in 1921 and left his native country, never to return. He came to the United States and for the next four years served the German Catholic parochial community of Berwick, North Dakota. Subsequently, he was offered the pastorate of the "highest church" in the country, Saint Joseph's Slovenian Church, in fabled Leadville, Colorado. There he remained for twenty–two years, 10,190 feet above sea level.

While there, Father Trunck covered the walls and ceiling of the church with brilliant paintings from the New Testament. The edifice has since been declared a National Slovenian monument because of the paintings which are considered a fine example of primitive art.

When he retired in 1946, Father Trunck came to San Francisco, where Archbishop John J. Mitty assigned him to the Church of the Nativity. There the genial priest quickly endeared himself to the local populace. Four years later, Father Trunck completed his final book, *Spomine*, which contained his memoirs. Earlier he had written books in English, German and Yugoslavian.

His small room was a little library, containing all the latest publications on theology, scripture and history. In a feature story for a San Francisco newspaper, Marilyn McNulty reported that his rectory quarters "might not look like heaven to some people but to Father Trunck whose spirit is as bright as the red geraniums in the attic window boxes, it's his heaven."

The writer went on to describe how "the walls were covered with murals of his native Corinthia, once a small country between Yugoslavia and Austria. The murals depict scenes from his childhood surroundings."

During the final phase of his long and eventful ministry, Father George M. Trunck also became the oldest Catholic priest in the United States—maybe even the world—to remain active in offering Holy Mass. Before he was finished, he logged seventy–eight years at the altar.

ANTHONY UBACH (1835–1907)

Father Anthony Ubach was among those early California pioneer–priests born at Barcelona in the first decades of the 19th century, one whose zeal and devotion to the cause of Catholicism in California will always be remembered. Shortly after his ordination at San Francisco in 1860, Father Ubach was sent to Mission San Juan Bautista where, the following year, he opened an orphanage and day school staffed by the Daughters of Charity.

In 1866 Ubach began his long tenure of duty at San Diego in the adobe church on Conde Street. He soon became the intimate and trusted friend, not only of the whites but also of the many migratory Indians in the region. So great was his influence with the natives that Ubach is credited with preventing a bloody reprisal from the Temecula Indians when they were forcibly ejected from their homes by unprincipled Anglo settlers. Always a defender of the Indians, Ubach once wrote to Bishop Thaddeus Amat that "sad, indeed and very gloomy is their future, unless the Government takes very stringent measures against those whites who rightly or wrongly settle on their lands, without consulting them about it or even inquiring of the poor Indians. . ."

From the missionary's pen came the testimony that the natives were basically a good people. Those under his care were "very well disposed, friendly and peaceable when unmolested, sober, industrious and of a naturally quiet disposition. . . ."

In July of 1865, Bishop Amat laid the cornerstone at Ubach's new Church of the Immaculate Conception in Old Town. Four years later, after much of the area had been destroyed by fire, Ubach moved his congregation southward and in 1875, "on the mesa west of town" saw a new church dedicated, this time to Saint Joseph, by Bishop Francis Mora. The tireless Spanish–born priest

was almost ubiquitous and records of his services can be found at Santa Ysabel, Banner City, Julian, Agua Caliente and El Capitan Grande.

It was at Ubach's suggestion and encouragement that the Sisters of Saint Joseph of Carondelet came to San Diego in 1882 to open Our Lady of Peace Academy and, five years later, Saint Anthony's Indian School near the old mission. San Diego's pastor also arranged for the erection of Saint Joseph's Hospital (now Mercy Hospital) when, in 1890, he brought the Sisters of Mercy to Southern California. Always concerned about affairs of civic importance, Father Ubach campaigned to bring the Texas and Pacific Railroad to the west and gave public support to the candidacy of Zachariah Montgomery for District Attorney.

Though he died in Saint Joseph's Hospital on March 27, 1907, Ubach has lived on as the fictionalized "Father Gaspara" in Helen Hunt Jackson's novel, *Ramona*. Those who knew him best testify that this humble missionary has a right to be remembered in his own name, for he personifies the greatness of that litany of dedicated Spanish churchmen who came to California for the sole purpose of spreading the Gospel.

CYRIL VAN DER DONCKT (1865–1939)

Father Cyril Van der Donckt (1865–1939) was a native of Quaremont, Belgium. He was ordained in Louvain on June 24, 1887 for service in the Vicariate Apostolic of Idaho. Within three months, the youthful cleric had arrived and was busy at work in that far–flung post.

According to his own testimony, Father Van der Donckt was the first priest ordained for the vicariate. During his earliest years in Idaho, he attended to the spiritual needs of native Americans scattered around the fourteen counties comprising the vicariate. He served as pastor of a parish in Pocatello in the late 1890s.

For reasons of health, Father Van der Donckt came to the Diocese of Monterey–Los Angeles in 1921 and for the next decade was chaplain at the Los Angeles County Hospital. A letter in his file indicates that "he acquitted himself well and was devoted to his work."

Father Van der Donckt wrote several books over the years, including *Eucharistic Miracles*, *Christian Science and Spiritism Tested* and *Christian Motherhood and Education*. A writer in *Ave Maria* characterized the latter book as being "full of good advice for parents and educators."

The priest was a prolific versifier. He kept a quasi–diary into which he recorded his reflections in verse form. Father David McAstocker, a prominent Jesuit writer, encouraged Van der Donckt to have a selection of his verses published. In 1934, Father Van der Donckt issued a limited edition of *Metrical Memories*, a 382 page book bearing the *imprimatur* of Bishop Edward J. Kelly of Boise.

Three years later, a second, expanded edition appeared, along with an index to the larger text. Reviewers liked the book. R.H. Thompson said it was a "fine contribution to poetic literature."

Though Van der Donckt doesn't appear to have been one of John J. Cantwell's favorites, the priest dedicated his collection of *Metrical Memories* to the Bishop of Los Angeles–San Diego.

Included among his verses are two tributes to Cantwell, both composed to honor the prelate's silver anniversary of priestly ordination in 1914.

J oy gratitude and lawful pride
O' erflow your followers' hearts to–day,
H igh Priest dear, long with us abide!
N e'er poured God powers in nobler clay.

C hampion o' the Spirit's sword and spear,
A ngels nigh envy your career:
N o monuments, reared by human hands
T ow'r higher than those your toil hath raised,
W hile loos'ning sins' and sorrows' bands
E ternally God hence be praised!
L ook down on you the Queen of priests,
L ure she us all to Heaven's feasts!

J oin, priests, nuns, women, maidens, boys
O n this day, to acclaim our grand
H igh priest: his thanks to share and joys.
N one's more revered throughout the land;

J ust, true, his words and deeds e'er urge

C harity to all: hence efforts surge
A ll men to teach, for Christ to win.
N eath his enlightened, prudent lead,
T o war 'gainst error, vive and sin;
W hilst giving host the Apostoles' creed,
E nlarging bounds of higher freedom.
L oud sing we hence: "Through Christendom
L oved, praised be Christ "*in aeternum*"!

PETER VERDAGUER (1835–1911)

The 1880s were difficult times for the struggling Diocese of Monterey–Los Angeles. So depleted were the diocesan finances that on two occasions their administration was removed from the control of Bishop Francis Mora.

Early in 1887, Isaias W. Heilman, one of Mora's closest friends and advisors, devised a plan whereby the property on which the Old Plaza Church of *Nuestra Señora de Los Angeles* was located would be sold to commercial developers. It was indeed an attractive offer which Father Joaquin Adam, the Vicar General, and others felt would greatly benefit the diocese. Though no public announcement appears to have been made, news of the sale was leaked to the press. By the time Bishop Mora took the pastor of the Old Plaza Church, Father Peter Verdaguer, into his confidence on the matter, the whole city was astir over the impending loss of the historic church.

Father Verdaguer thought about and prayed over the proposal for several days. Finally, on October 4th, he wrote a lengthy letter to the bishop, outlining his opposition to the transaction. Excerpts of that letter, one of the most important in the Archival Center, are repeated here:

> As a priest and, particularly one well known in Los Angeles, I probably have more than the average opportunity of knowing the opinions, feelings and sentiments of the community on this subject than the bishop. Understandably, people express their sentiments more freely to a priest than to a bishop. There is generally a certain reverence that impedes them from being frank and open to their bishop.
>
> Since the people are not afraid of priests, they open their hearts and speak plainly and freely on any subject. And, on the matter of selling the property of the old church, I assure you they have spoken out to the extent that, should Your Excellency consult all the citizens of Los Angeles who have been here for the last fifteen

Peter Verdaguer

years, I have no doubt that, with the exception of a few real estate and business men, all would advise you not to sell the old Church. Sell part of the property, if you must, but keep the Church where it has been for many years; it is the only remnant left of the old city of Our Lady of the Angels.

Do not destroy it. That would be the general response from the old and the young Catholics, as well as from the majority of non–Catholics. And, if I were to judge from what I have heard from many priests, they would give the same answer: "Do not destroy the old Church." They look at the Church as a monument worthy of being preserved, for most of the older inhabitants of the city and its environs were baptized and married there and many of their ancestors were buried from it. It was the first place they went to hear the Word of God and the place where they received their religious instruction.

No wonder they feel so strongly about its being removed. You and I would feel the same way had we been baptized, made our First Communion, been ordained and gone to Mass there since infancy.

There are those people of good judgment, learning and experience who say that religion will suffer in Los Angeles if the church is removed. And such is also my personal opinion.

How many there are who would never go to Mass were it not that the presence of the church reminds them of their duty? How many there are each day who are moved to enter and pray there! People arriving from the east see the church as the first edifice in the city. They know at once where to attend Mass. And how many who stop at the different hotels will not go to Mass, if they have to look for a church. Yes, I have said it and I repeat it: considering everything I have written, should the church be moved to some other place, religion will suffer and there will be great talk and scandal.

Finally, may I repeat that as an old parish priest attached to an even older church, I am convinced that sentiment and good sense militate against moving the church away and building it anew in another place. I feel that in conscience I had to send this letter. If I have unintentionally offended Your Excellency in the process of expressing myself, please hold me excused.

Father Verdaguer's letter must have tilted the scale against selling the property for the bishop did not pursue the matter and there is no extant evidence of any further negotiations about the sale. Had it not been for Father Verdaguer's intervention, the Old Plaza Church would likely be remembered today by a bronze plaque atop a marble standard somewhere along Sunset Boulevard.

Nor did Verdaguer's outspoken opposition lessen the esteem held for the priest by Bishop Mora. Verdaguer went on to become Vicar Apostolic of Brownsville and titular Bishop of Aulon.

FRANCIS WAJDA (1908–1972)

Father Francis Wajda, a valiant Polish priest who endured imprisonment in four Nazi death camps during World War II, allowed the story of his confinement to be dramatized on the Heritage TV program . There he told, without bitterness, of the human degradation, the revolting brutality of the camp overseers; the inhumanity of the apostles of totalitarianism.

Like so many other priests imprisoned then and later by the Communists, especially in China and Korea, Father Wajda maintained his faith and remained essentially beyond reach of the crushing forces brought to bear on him. During the final decades of his ministry, Father Wajda served the Archdiocese of San Francisco at Mary's Help Hospital in Daly City. When he died on April 18, 1972, he left behind a letter to the "dear Sisters and all Mary's Helpers." It was a beautiful letter, one well worth sharing with priests and laity of another generation.

> I am now approaching the point where my joyful hope is becoming a vivid, joyful reality. So many times did I assist the dying in my twenty–one years plus years of service at Mary's Help. Every time I stayed with the dying I thought of my own death as surely and inevitably coming to me. I thought of it in terms of our Faith.

> I am now about to join those who 'have gone before us marked with the sign of faith,' and along with them I will be waiting for all of you, to visit you again one–by–one. Please do not be less realistic about this than I am.

> With all my crowded thoughts in mind I would like to express my gratitude—to the archbishop and the priests and my Polish fellow priests for their gift of friendship;

> to all the Sisters, Daughters of Charity—for giving me an opportunity to share in their zeal and dedication to the service of the sick;

> to my personal doctors, to all medical and nursing staff members and to all Mary's Help employees—who have shown me their personal love and deep understanding of my priestly work for the sick;

> to all relatives and friends of Mary's Help patients, to all our patients for their appreciation and generosity to me for years;

> to all people I came in contact with, to all Polish people in the area—who helped me to take care of their religious needs in the years past.

> I ask all and each one of you to forgive many of my shortcomings, and I particularly beg for forgiveness if I ignored, neglected, hurt or scandalized anyone of you.

> Thank you, thank you and *au revoir*, until I see you again. In the name of the Father, and of the Son, and of the Holy Spirit. Amen.

The small religious family at Mary's Help Hospital gathered at Mission Dolores Basilica the day after

Father Wajda's letter was read for the final obsequies. Archbishop Joseph T. McGucken and a handful of priests offered the joyful Mass of the Resurrection for the happy repose of a truly beloved priest.

"Hospitality is a state of soul, a kindness which some people possess," observed the homilist. "Father Wajda learned in the school of suffering—on his body before you, he has the number of a prison camp."

GEORGE WILLARD (1836–1890)

How many priests and religious there have been in California whose years of faithful service go unmarked and unheralded by later generations. And yet, where would the Church of the 1990s be, were its peoples not standing on the shoulders of the pioneers?

Father George Willard (1836–1890) was one of those early trailblazers. He was a latter day "Indian Missionary" whose name is reverenced today only by a handful of native Americans served by the Bureau of Catholic Indian Missions and its affiliates. Born in New York, the son of a Protestant minister, young Willard was converted to the Catholic faith early in life. He was ordained on June 29, 1863, for the Diocese of Milwaukee. During his first years in the ministry, he taught in the seminary conducted by Bishop John Henni.

He was subsequently pastor of several parishes, including one at Fond du Lac, where he served from 1870 to 1879. It was said that the church there was just across the street from the one formerly cared for by Willard's father, an Episcopalian priest.

Father Willard had always wanted to work with the Indians and, in 1888, he was asked to supervise the erection of Saint Joseph's Indian School in Rennselaer, Indiana. He remained on for a while as director of that institution. In the late 1880s, Father Willard was "loaned" to the Bureau of Catholic Indian Missions as associate to the famed Msgr. J.A. Stephan. Early the following year, he came west as director of Saint Boniface Indian School, in Banning, California His first task there was completion of the central building.

Willard's work at Banning was cut short when be contracted the dreaded typhoid fever. After a brief illness, he succumbed to that illness. His remains were interred in the cemetery at the northeastern edge of the property and there they remain in an unmarked grave.

A little girl, Mary Slater, wrote a letter on July 17, 1896, to the editor of The Mission Indian in which she asked about Father Willard. Here is part of that twelve year old's letter:

> He was the pastor of Fond du Lac for many years. The people loved him very much. He left here and went to Dakota, then he went to California to build an Indian

school. He died while there. My mother says every one in Fond du Lac thinks that Father Willard is a saint in Heaven. He was so good.

Father B. Florian Hahn answered her query in The Mission Indian, noting that "Father Willard's last place of rest has yet no monument. All his relations being Protestant, even the church vestments, chalice, etc., had to be given to them, besides the property he possessed in the East. A warning for everybody. Do the good whilst you live and when yet enjoying health, lay up treasures and provide for your own spiritual welfare. When you are dead your relatives will pocket all you possess and you will be forgotten forever."

The rest of Father Hahn's letter was not so severe. He told about Willard's ministry and how he became interested in the welfare of the Indians and why he had come to California to look after Saint Boniface Indian School. During his earlier priestly years, Father Willard had been editor of The Catholic Citizen, the diocesan newspaper for Milwaukee. It is indeed fitting that this rare glimpse into his personal life also emanated from a Catholic newspaper, this one edited at Banning, California.

PETER C. YORKE (1864–1925)

A. Consecrated Thunderbolt

Father Peter C. Yorke (1864–1925) was aptly eulogized by Archbishop Edward J. Hanna as "a man of distinction among his fellows, a constant, loyal friend, a faithful earnest priest, a mighty teacher." Born in Ireland's small seaport city of Galway, Peter prepared for the ministry at Saint Patrick's College (Maynooth) and Saint Mary's Seminary (Baltimore). He was ordained for the Archdiocese of San Francisco, on December 17, 1887, by James Cardinal Gibbons.

At the suggestion of Archbishop Patrick W. Riordan, the young cleric took graduate studies at The Catholic University of America, where he was among the first recipients of that institution's licentiate in theology. Although the faculty wanted Father Yorke to remain in Washington, as Professor of Semitic languages, Archbishop Riordan needed the brilliant young levite on the west coast. Shortly after arriving in San Francisco, Yorke was appointed chancellor and editor of The Monitor. In the years that followed, the colorful cleric defended the Catholic Church against bigotry, championed the rights of labor and advocated Irish nationalism.

Father Yorke had all the earmarks of "episcopal timber" and his biographer notes that "had he been willing to sit and not rock the boat, there is little doubt that he would have gotten a bishopric." But Yorke was anything but a careerist. He didn't care enough about clerical advancement to engage in even the most innocent kind of politics. When his name did appear on the first of several *ternas*, for the Diocese of Nesqually, a local San Francisco Jesuit did a "hatchet job" on Yorke that rather effectively blocked any further suggestions along episcopal lines.

Yorke's relationship with Archbishop Riordan began deteriorating in the years after 1898, and never again did the popular Irish priest regain the confidence of his Ordinary. Yet, in spite of Riordan's exasperation over some of Yorke's flamboyant antics and the priest's consequent resentment of the archbishop, there seems to have been a mutual respect, even affection, among the two churchmen. San Francisco was just too small for two such forceful personalities.

Yorke sorely missed the public exposure that terminated with his removal as editor of *The Monitor* and, in January, 1902, he launched his own newspaper, *The Leader*, which served thereafter as his journalistic platform and mouthpiece.

Throughout his thirty–eight priestly years, Yorke was a man of extraordinary energy and in no sphere was his tireless zeal more obvious than at the parochial level. In 1903, he was entrusted with the parish of Saint Anthony's, in Oakland. A decade later, Riordan recalled Yorke to "the City" as pastor of Saint Peter's. By that time, Father Yorke's catechisms on Christian doctrine were being used in much of the nation's Catholic school system.

Yorke's contributions to Christian education were as rewarding as his genius was promising. He was a founder of the National Catholic Educational Association and he served for many years as a regent for the University of California. Some of Yorke's more prominent pedagogical pronouncements were published, in 1933, as *Educational Lectures*.

The tall and handsome priest was a commanding and dynamic speaker. His engaging speeches, lectures and sermons were written and delivered in a clear, vigorous and idiomatic tone. In 1913, Yorke published *Altar and Priest*, a collection of fifteen addresses delivered at various anniversaries, dedications and funerals in the Bay area. Two additional volumes of *Sermons by Rev. P. C. Yorke, D.D.* were issued under the editorship of Father Ralph Hunt, in 1931.

Father Yorke's consuming passion for justice was used to further the interests of fellow Catholics, oppressed workers and persecuted politicians, to say nothing of downtrodden Irishmen. His penchant for pushing principles to extremes often involved him in political hassles, some of which were as embarrassing as they were unfortunate. Observers of the Western Americana scene would agree with the editorial appearing in *The Call*, at the time of the priest's death, that the history

of San Francisco could not be written "without bringing in the name of Father Peter C. Yorke again and again." He was indeed, in the words of John J. Barrett, a "consecrated thunderbolt."

PETER C. YORKE (1864–1925)

B. CHAMPION OF CATHOLICISM

If ever there lived a man who typified the best in the land of his birth and one who was part of his adopted land's greatest deeds for God, that man was Peter C. Yorke. Born in Galway, Ireland, on August 15, 1864, Yorke left his six brothers and sisters early in life and after some years at Eire's famous Maynooth College came to the United States. He entered Saint Mary's seminary at Cardinal Gibbons for the Archdiocese ordained priest by James of San Francisco.

After refusing the Chair of Semitic languages at The Catholic University of America, young Father Yorke came to the Bay City where he spent the first years of his priesthood as assistant in the cathedral parish. Archbishop Patrick W. Riordan soon recognized Yorke's outstanding abilities and named him chancellor of the Archdiocese and a short while later editor of the San Francisco *Monitor*. With the emergence of the anti–Catholic *Argonaut* and *Jolly Giant* publications, Yorke took up his pen in defense of the Church and made *The Monitor* "the best known and most widely read Catholic weekly in America." Father Yorke's brilliant declaration of Catholic principals not only struck the death–blow to the American Protective Association in San Francisco, but it also revealed the genius and powerful talents of one of California's truly gifted clerics. As one author has stated it, "Peter C. Yorke made many a man proud to be a Catholic."

His "second" career began early in the 1900s when Father Yorke took up the cause of the Catholic worker, thus becoming one of the first to challenge the masters of industry with the teachings of Leo XIII's *Rerum Novarum*. The question to Yorke was whether "men for whom Christ died to teach them that they were free, men with free rights, shall be crushed beneath the foot of the least bright of all the angels that fell from heaven, Mammon, the spirit of Greed." So successful was the energetic cleric in his defense of the workingman's dignity that upon his death, the San Francisco Labor Council stated that it would ever cherish and respect his name as being among those we recognize and number as founders and leaders of the San Francisco labor movement."

In addition to establishing the Catholic Truth Society and inaugurating the *Leader*, a newspaper dedicated to the cause of Irish independence, Yorke wrote a number of books and served on the board of the National Catholic Educational Association. His contributions to this latter field were recognized by state officials who named him a regent of the University of California. In the midst of his campaigns for labor in March of 1903, Father Yorke was given the pastorate of Saint Anthony's Church, a parish on the mainland side of San Francisco Bay. Ten years later he was transferred to Saint Peter's Church where he remained until his death on Palm Sunday of 1925.

PETER C. YORKE (1864–1925)

C. PIONEER LABOR LEADER

If the bishopric could be "deserved," then Father Peter C. Yorke (1864–1925) should have been a bishop. No one would have enhanced that office more strikingly, certainly no one would have been so eloquent.

But Peter was ahead of his time and those in authority resented and feared him. He was already a threat to the establishment as a priest, as a bishop he would have proven unbearable—as have been many great ecclesial personages.

Among his many other qualities, Father Yorke was an advocate of the labor principles enunciated by Pope Leo XIII in his encyclical, *Rerum Novarum*. The cleric became an active union spokesman and leader in a strike that proved to be one of the longest, bloodiest and most important in California's history.

In August, 1901, strike leaders in San Francisco approached Father Yorke for assistance against the Employers Association which had locked out union teamsters. Yorke addressed a rally of 15,000 strikers on August 8th, telling them that the effort to break the Teamsters Union was a violation of the Holy Father's encyclical.

Yorke denounced a local court ruling against picketing because it was based on philosophy that labor was a "commodity" on the market. He quoted *Rerum Novarum* to the effect that "if through necessity of fear of a worse evil the workman accepted harder conditions because an employer will afford him no better, then he is the victim of injustice." Yorke contended that the "worker had a right to a livelihood and that it was a gross injustice to leave him to the mercy of the so–called laws of supply and demand."

Father Yorke spoke often during the strike. On one occasion, he told strikers that "they could not afford to accept peace at any price, but only peace with honor." He said that there were two irreconcilable principles at stake; the Employers Association held that unionism must be destroyed, while strikers believed that unionism must be preserved.

Declaring that he could be no friend of those who concealed the issues, Yorke realized the potential danger of a showdown battle. But he told listeners that they were "fighting for a principle that makes life worth living, that gives dignity to everything people do."

The rectory at Saint Peter's Church served as a gathering place for strike leaders. In addition to composing all strike publicity, Yorke helped organize a soup kitchen and moved about the city raising funds for the campaign. He even denounced the mayor for "prostituting the police force to the service of the capitalists." He called the police chief a "lackey" of the Employers Association.

Then Yorke took the campaign to the city's newspapers with full page advertisements claiming that Pope Leo XIII "comes out plump and square for unions." He quoted the pontiff as saying that unions were the "most important means" by which workers could better their conditions.

When the governor was asked to send in the militia, he consulted with Father Yorke who advised him to close down the affected businesses and bring all parties to the negotiating table. That ploy worked and within an hour, the strike was settled. So great was the morale and solidarity engendered by the strike that unionism swept all before it. Unionists formed their own party and elected the President of the Musicians Union, Eugene Schmitz, mayor of San Francisco.

While militant action was criticized by some, it brought honor and respect to the working man. Today, Father Yorke's portrait still hangs in the Teamsters Union Hall in San Francisco.

PETER C. YORKE (1864–1925)

D. DEPARTURE OF A GIANT

The panegyric delivered by Archbishop Edward J. Hanna at the funeral of Father Peter C. Yorke has long been regarded as a classical tribute to a most deserving cleric. We here recall some excerpts from that sermon preached at Saint Peter's Church, on April 8, 1925.

> A man of marked distinction among his fellows, a constant, loyal friend, a faithful earnest priest, a mighty teacher, Christ's champion on the ramparts of Israel, has passed from life to his reward.
>
> We, who loved him, have come into the shadow of the Tabernacle where Christ dwells to pay our poor simple tribute to his memory and to lay at his feet our testimony of sorrow, our hymn of praise.
>
> For a moment I thought silence might be more eloquent than any poor words I might speak—for there is a silence more eloquent than speech; but no, someone must speak, someone must tell the story of his life, someone must make known the power by which he

wrought, a power so often hidden from the gaze of men.

There is, in every noble life, a compelling vision. What did Father Yorke see that compelled his great soul, which drove him, as the years ran on, to toil, to labor, to ceaseless activity?

His great faith made him see in Christ the healing of the nations; in Christ the only hope of salvation. When he reached his prime, for more than a hundred years the princes of the earth, the men of wealth and of station, had risen up against God and against His Christ; they had promised a new era of brotherhood, of freedom, of peace.

They spoke of Christ as a step in the world's evolution, but for them Christ's day had gone, and a new era had dawned for the world. The Reformaton had come to its logical conclusion, and they who began by rejecting the Church, in the end rejected Christ—yea, and God. Europe was an armed camp, and even in our prosperity here there was unrest.

He saw clearly that the struggle must come and for it he must be ready. And as the vision deepened, he saw Christ on the summit of the ages; he saw the Church as the world's hope; he saw the battle was in behalf of the poor and the downtrodden; he saw Christian education as the supreme work of the Church, especially in America.

He is gone from us, and the world of great men is poorer because of his going. He has left us a memory that will last unto coming generations, and he has imposed on us a task that we must follow even unto the end.

Like him we must battle for the rights of Catholic men in this land to which we have consecrated our energy; like him we must stand for the poor and the downtrodden; like him we must uphold the banner of Christian education, for in it , and in it alone is our hope of salvation.

I need not tell you that Father Yorke's life was a constant battle, and as he spared not himself, so was he not spared. Should he have erred through human frailty, should stain still mar his great soul, our prayers, our sacrifices, especially the Mass he loved so well and said so faithfully, will aid him.

In Father Yorke the poor have always had a friend; and as he stands today before his Master in judgement his advocacy of the weak of the world will, perhaps, be his great title to praise and to mercy.

The archbishop concluded with a prophecy that the name of Father Yorke will be written in letters of gold on what possibly will be the proudest page in our history.

III. Friars
In General and Individual Friars

APOSTOLIC COLLEGES IN NEW SPAIN

The missionary system, as it evolved in Upper California, formed part of a general plan carried under Franciscan auspices to the frontiers of New Spain. Those missionaries who accompanied the first Spanish *conquistadores* to America soon achieved for their work of conversion a recognized place in the over–all Spanish system of colonization.

By virtue of faculties given to the Franciscans in 1521 by Pope Leo X, the friars were empowered to preach, administer the sacraments, absolve from reserved sins and to settle practically every type of marriage case without recourse to the local bishop. Before 1683, the Franciscans in Mexico were organized along the same lines as in other parts of the world, into provinces over which provincials ruled. Late in the seventeenth century a new concept of missionary endeavor grew up, that of missionary or apostolic colleges. Their purpose was to gather, educate and orientate friars toward a more ascetical life than that common in the provinces. Their chief apostolate was to be converting the Indian tribes on the frontier and conducting missions among the faithful in the homeland.

The first such college inaugurated in the New World was Santa Cruz in Querétaro founded by Antonio de Llinaz, a Mallorcan. It was this college, together with *Nuestra Señora de Guadalupe* at Zacatecas (1707) and San Fernando in Mexico City (1734), which provided missionaries for California; San Fernando predominated in length of years, in personnel and in achievement. All of the apostolic colleges were subject directly to the Commissary General of the Indies. Each was autonomous and operated in its own designated area. This methodical organization merited for the friars an unparalleled place in early colonial foundations.

Official Spanish policy toward the native had a three-fold objective: to convert him, to civilize him and to exploit his services. But it was only in those frontier areas where the friars had charge of the social, economic and spiritual guidance of the culturally inferior natives that this principle received its proper focus for only there did the Indian's spiritual life achieve greater importance than his material usefulness. The friars, entrusted with the temporal as well as the spiritual welfare of the Indians, became not only preachers of the word, but doers also, in the literal sense, priest, teacher, disciplinarian were all combined in the Franciscan.

Two predominant traits of this system, independence from episcopal jurisdiction and combining of the spiritual with the material, played important roles in the events leading up to the establishment of a hierarchy in California. When it became obvious that the original system could no longer operate effectively, the friars suggested an entirely new structure of ecclesiastical organization, that of the episcopal curia. Had the Apostolic Colleges been allowed to function in California without governmental interference, the system would have developed of its own accord to the diocesan phase as indeed it has done and is doing in other mission lands throughout the world.

California was unprepared and ill–suited for the bishopric in 1840 and only in the gold–rush decade that followed was the Church able to constructively initiate that phase under the leadership of Joseph Sadoc Alemany, O.P. In any event, the work of the Apostolic Colleges in California between 1769 and 1840 was phenomenal and as one *Comisario–Prefecto* stated:

> I have before me a document which assures me that the number of souls baptized to the year 1832 reached 87,739 Such a multitude rescued from barbarism, instructed in Religion according to their capacity, cannot but excite sweet satisfaction

APOSTOLIC COLLEGE OF SAN FERNANDO

The seven apostolic colleges founded in New Spain between 1683 and 1814 were subject directly to the Commissary General of the Indies. Each was autonomous and operated only in those districts designated and approved by the commissariate. The basic purpose for establishing a college was that of gathering and training an elite corps of friars known for their exalted spiritual ideals, strict ascetic life and austere living for the apostolate of the Indian missions and the regeneration of Christians in civilized areas

The Apostolic College of San Fernando, the "Motherhouse of the California Missions," was established by a royal decree, October 15, 1733, as an extension of the existing College of Santa Cruz de Querétaro. During the years of its existence, San Fernando's friars, recruited mostly from the many provinces and colleges of Spain, were active in missionary endeavors throughout the Sierra Gorda region of Mexico and in both Baja and Alta California.

The college was responsible for the great development between 1769 and 1833 in the entire area of present–day California. Of the 142 friars from three such foundations, 127 were missionaries from San Fernando. Fifty–eight of those zealous men died during their tenure in the area, two of them (Frs. Luis Jayme and Andrés Quintana) at the hands of the natives.

After a relatively brief, but illustrious career, San Fernando was abolished as a college, in 1908, and was incorporated as a religious house in Mexico City's Province of the Holy Gospel. The old college no longer exists, having been demolished to make room for modern buildings and new streets. The church of San Fernando, recently restored, continues in service as it has since 1755

Over the years, the personnel of the Apostolic College of San Fernando, an independent, specialized institution within the framework of the Franciscan Order, had its saints, mediocrities and a few sinners. And yet "the sons of San Fernando, as well as those of other colleges, who excelled in observing their high ideals were not easily forgotten in literature, in painting or in the memory of their confreres."

GREY AND BROWN–ROBED FRIARS

Visitors to the California Room of the Los Angeles County Museum can see displayed there an authentic grey habit worn by the Franciscan missionaries of provincial times. Many may wonder why it is that the garb used by Junípero Serra and the other colonial *padres* differs from the brown worn by the friars of our time.

A glance back into history reveals that while Saint Francis himself wore a grey habit, he did not indicate any preference along those lines for his followers, provided they "disassociate themselves from the silk and satin trappings of the rich and the gaudy frills of the frivolous." Many of the early friars wore grey in imitation of Francis, but such a custom never became universal and in various parts of Europe, black, white, or blue habits were common. One chronicler aptly noted that "the first brethren of Rivo Torto and Portiuncula certainly were not remarkable for the exaggerated uniformity of their garb."

A measure of "uniformity" did come during the generalship of Saint Bonaventure, when the Constitutions of Narbonne (1260) directed all Franciscans to don grey in deference to the color used by their founder. The regulations went unenforced during the 16th and following centuries until the late 1800s, when it was stipulated officially that the "Franciscans could wear black, brown, and blue habits according to the approved customs of the Provinces."

Pope Pius IX suggested that it would be fitting for the friars of the Colleges in America to wear the grey habit without dye, since that color "had been worn by the brethren in all Central America from ancient times." With the exception of the Province of Jalisco (where blue was used) and the convent of San Diego in Mexico City (which clung to the brown), the color of the habit of all the Apostolic Colleges in Mexico was grey, woven from white and black wool. The customs of using the grey in California lasted until 1885, when the Golden State's friars were annexed to the American Province of the Sacred Heart whose members wore the brown habit.

Franciscan Priest, California, late 18th century

On October 4, 1897, Pope Leo XIII issued his famous letter, *Felicitate Quadam*, to the newly reorganized Order of Friars Minor with an international directive that "the artificial color of the outer garments shall resemble the color of wool naturally blackish or dark brown which is called *Marrone* in Italian and and in French *marron*." Hence it is that, since the turn of the century, all members of the Order of Friars Minor have worn the brown robes, most of them accepting the transition as a matter of obedience and uniformity rather than a strict observance of tradition. The last of California's "grey friars," Guadalupe del Rio, was buried on May 21, 1939, in the "brown habit" now universally symbolic of followers of Francis of Assisi. Today, while it is no longer associated with the Order of Friars Minor, "the traditional Franciscan grey survives throughout the world in bishops who were once Franciscans." But there is a note of irony, for prelatial clothing is made of silk, never wool!

A FRANCISCAN CENTENNIAL

A vibrant part of the Franciscan family celebrated its hundredth year in California during 1994. The Secular Franciscans, or the Third Order, was established in Los Angeles during the "Gay 90s."

Actually, the Secular Franciscans first emerged about 1212, when Francis of Assisi was preaching in the countryside of Tuscany and Umbria. It was in that year that Francis motivated the whole village of Cannata to adopt his way of following Christ.

By 1221 Francis and Cardinal Ugolino, protector of the emerging order had written a Rule for the Order of Penance, as members were first called. In that official rule, one reads that "the Franciscans, as one among many spiritual families raised up by the Holy Spirit in the Church, unites all members of the People of God . . . who recognize that they are called to follow Christ in the footsteps of Francis of Assisi."

In the mid–1890s, Bishop Francis Mora, wanting to provide for the spiritual needs of the many German–speaking people in the southland, erected a German parish at Los Angeles under the patronage of Saint Joseph. The Franciscans were invited to take charge in September, 1893. On the following January 21, Father Victor Aertker began a branch of the Third Order Secular at Saint Joseph's by receiving forty–two applicants. That number was doubled just a week later.

During the initial twenty years, German was the predominant language. However, with the outbreak of World War I, English became the accepted language for the parish and its secular Franciscans.

Although the order was identified with Saint Joseph's for most of the next century, there were numerous outreaches into other parishes throughout Southern California, where members were involved in all kinds of social and spiritual activities. In the mid–1940s, Saint Joseph's Fraternity was instrumental in founding the Hour of Saint Francis, a radio program that developed into what is now known as Franciscan Communications.

By the early years of the following decade, the Fraternity had grown to 1,160 members. To create a greater familiarity among members, branches were begun in Santa Monica, Gardena, West Los Angeles, Lake Arrowhead and Long Beach.

During the 1960s, the Fraternity provided for young married people by a group called the Troubadors. They, like other segments of the Fraternity, were active in performing acts of mercy. In 1970, Father Hugh Noonan encouraged the Fraternity to open Saint Francis Center to minister to the needs of the poor and downtrodden in central Los Angeles.

The activities of the Secular Franciscans were not restricted to the Archdiocese of Los Angeles. When the Lay Mission Helpers were founded, Saint Joseph's Fraternity began assisting the Papago Indian Reservation in Ajo, Arizona. Similar programs evolved in later years.

The Tertiary, founded in September of 1925, later became the *Third Order Bulletin*. As the official newsletter for the Secular Franciscans, its function was capsulized in this way: "If life is not a journey heavenward, then it is but a pilgrimage to death and nothingness. If you succeed, let your deeds speak, if you fail, say nothing."

The whole thrust of the Third Order is summed up in its rule: "Let the Secular Franciscans seek a proper spirit of detachment from temporal goods by simplifying their own material needs. Let them be mindful that according to the Gospel, they are merely stewards of the goods received for the benefit of God's children."

TRIBUTE TO FRANCISCANS

The late Willa Cather spoke, in eloquent terms, about the missionary zeal of the friars in her classic essay on "Father Junípero's Holy Family" which was first published, in 1926.

Those early missionaries threw themselves naked upon the hard heart of a country that was calculated to try the endurance of giants. They thirsted in its deserts, starved among its rocks, climbed up and down its terrible canyons on stone–bruised feet, broke long fasts by unclean and repugnant food. Surely these endured hunger, thirst, cold, nakedness of a kind beyond any conception St. Paul and his brethren could have had suffered.

Whatever the early Christians suffered, it all happened in that safe little Mediterranean world, amid the old manners, the old landmarks. If they endured martyrdom, they died among their brethren, their relics were piously preserved, their names lived in the mouths of holy men. Such was not the case in California.

A similar portrayal was made by the eminent non–Catholic Professor of Western Americana, Herbert Eugene Bolton, in an address delivered in the winter of 1912, and reported thusly in *The Monitor*, official newspaper for the Archdiocese of San Francisco:

"In the whole history of the United States there is no more inspiring chapter than the work of the Missionary Fathers in the Southwest," said Professor Bolton of the State University, speaking at Newman Hall recently. "They came to America inspired by the highest ideals. Many were college men of the old world, learned in the arts and sciences; many were of noble blood; all of them might have had brilliant careers in Europe. Instead they came to the new world where they endured toil, exile, extreme suffering and even death at the hands of the natives they were trying to save. The list of missionaries who were martyrs to the Indians in the Southwest is over two hundred."

Prof. Bolton went on to explain that, contrary to the popular idea, the mission did not consist of a church alone, but was a definitely planned and carefully executed religious, educational and industrial plant. While always the salvation of souls was the supreme aim of the Fathers, yet their greatest labor was along educational lines. The Indians were taught to settle in the mission *pueblo*, where instruction was given them in the secrets of agriculture; they were taught to sew, spin, weave and card; the men learned mechanical arts, their carving, metal work and masonry enduring to the present day. Nor did the education stop here. The training in the practical science of government afforded the Indians is yet visible in the more civilized tribes of New Mexico and Arizona. "Records show," said Prof. Bolton, "that the mission *pueblo* was almost entirely governed and policed by the Indians themselves. The Mission *pueblo* of San Gabriel in Los Angeles at one time consisted of three thousand Indians, self–governing and self–supporting, guided only by half a dozen *Padres* and guardsmen."

As outposts of civilization the missions were most valuable; thus it was that they received the support of the Spanish Government. The marvelous foresight of the Superiors at the Mission Headquarters of San Ilfonso, Mexico, is shown in the efficient distribution of these centers of Christianity. From eastern Texas, throughout New Mexico, Arizona and along the *camino real* of California were scattered a chain of missions, all contributing to the spiritual and educational uplift of the native Indians.

Prof. Bolton paid glowing tribute to the efficiency of the educational work of the *Padres* and showed the disastrous results both from the viewpoint of the government and Indian of the secularization of the missionary plants.

THE "LEGEND" OF PADRE VICENTIO

The literature about gold in California is extensive. In 1949, for example, the late Carl Irving Wheat enumerated no fewer than 239 "significant" books dealing with various phases of the "placer days."

There are numerous theories about the "first" discovery of gold along *El Camino Real*. The precious substance was supposedly unearthed in 1839 by W.F. Thompson in Sierra County. Other authorities suggest even earlier dates.

No one pushed the discovery further back in the annals than Bret Harte (1829–1902), the great Catholic literary giant who testified by his writings that "to live in California is to breathe, to see, to feel poetry at every turn." In one of Harte's most charming essays, "The Adventure of *Padre* Vicentio," Harte tells about a friar attached to Mission Dolores who was brought by a "mysterious stranger" to the scene of a sinking ship and there asked to assist a dying man.

Opening his feeble eyes, the sufferer addressed the friar, pleading that his "only hope of absolution" lay in imparting "a secret which is of vast importance to the Church, and (one which) affects greatly her power, wealth and dominion on these shores." The friar asked about the secret, but was told that it could be disclosed only after the Sacrament of Penance had been imparted. The two argued briefly whether the disclosure of the secret or the giving of absolution would come first.

Suddenly the vessel, upon which the scene took place, fell to pieces amidst the surging waters which at once involved the dying man, the priest and the mysterious stranger. Here's how Harte concluded the story:

"The *Padre* did not recover his consciousness until high noon the next day, when he found himself lying in a little hollow between the Mission Hills and his faithful mule a few paces from him, cropping the sparse herbage. The *Padre* made the best of his way home, but wisely abstained from narrating the facts mentioned above until after the discovery of gold, when the whole of this veracious incident was related, with the assertion of the *Padre* that the secret which was thus mysteriously snatched from his possession was nothing more than the discovery of gold, years since, by the runaway sailors from the expedition of Sir Francis Drake."

Harte likely used Fray Vicente Pascual Oliva (1780–1848) as the central personage for his story. Oliva, who served at San Francisco between 1815 and 1818, was described by one observer as one who labored "with zealous intrepidity" for his people.

In 1939 Hans Weilder and Ellen Bentley issued a beautifully printed and illustrated edition of *The Adventure of Padre Vicentio: A Legend of San Francisco* in a press run of 450 copies. That volume, now almost as elusive as the gold it describes, is considered among the most "collectible" of California volumes.

Francis Drake came to Alta California in 1579. Was the story only a "legend?" Could it have been that gold was really discovered as early as that? Could Harte's love for romance and legendary lore of California have gotten in the way of truth? When he referred to the whole event as a "veracious incident," what did he mean?

FRANCISCANS AS RECORD–KEEPERS

It is eminently appropriate that the Franciscans, who figured so prominently in colonizing this frontier outpost on the Spanish borderlands, should also be the trailblazers for collecting, preserving and utilizing the records of the gigantic undertaking, Surely, no greater misfortune could possibly befall a people than to lack a historian to properly set down their annals; one who with faithful zeal will guard, treasure and perpetuate those human events which if left to the memory of man and to the mercy of the passing years, would be sacrificed upon the altars of time.

A host of historically–orientated and socially–concerned friars must be accorded a portion of today's acclaim. Among those worthy of mention are such names as Owen Da Silva, Francis Guest, Finbar Kenneally, Eric O'Brien, Charles Piette, Alban Schwartze, Francis Borgia Steck, Joseph Thompson and Antonine Tibesar. Three personages, however, deserve special recognition for their practice of the beatitude which states that "he who records the good deeds of others is himself a doer of good deeds."

The "Palou" of post–mission times was Father Theodore Arentz. Besides an innate love for the past and a natural ability for recording it, Arentz was a first–hand witness to much of what transpired at the important junctures of his order's history. In his various positions as pastor, missionary, provincial visitor, novice master, orphanage director and guardian, he methodically collected and saved all the newspapers, magazines, photographs and letters in any way related to Franciscan activities along the Pacific Slope.

Throughout his seventy–four years, Father Arentz was a lover of books, a promoter of studies and a hard–working chronicler. He had the foresight and took the time to preserve the accomplishments of the pioneers. He was a careful scribe. With tireless energy and a minute eye for detail, Father Arentz recorded, in a clear and legible hand, several thousand pages of history about the apostolic college, the commissariate and the province which otherwise would have eluded succeeding generations.

It was Zephyrin Engelhardt, the second person of Santa Barbara's historical trinity, who effectively utilized the musty old archival materials locked away at the mission. After giving an organizational structure to the valuable holdings, to which he added several thousand pages of his own transcripts, Father Engelhardt breathed life into the Santa Barbara mission archives by allowing the documents to speak for themselves on the printed page.

With that inordinate passion for truth and accuracy characteristic of the German–born, Zephyrin Engelhardt composed a veritable library of historically–relevant volumes, each one painstakingly researched and thoroughly documented. What niceties he lacked in methodology, Engelhardt compensated for by his carefully exact style. Ever the crusader, the venerable friar was anything but a colorless compiler of records. His zeal in spreading the account of Franciscan accomplishments in the Far West was slowed by neither illness nor advanced age. He had printers' ink in his veins.

Father Zephyrin Engelhardt was not, nor did he ever claim to be, a professional historian. He envisioned, as his successor, a scholar more artistically–inclined and educationally–qualified than he. To that man would belong the duty of couching the story of the California missions in a style as readable as it was accurate. The mantle fell to Maynard Geiger, whose familiar figure had graced Santa Barbara since 1919.

Soon after returning to the mission with a doctorate in history, Father Geiger was entrusted with the office of archivist. Over the ensuing thirty–three years, a steady stream of books, brochures and learned articles bore the Geiger imprint.

Subscribing to the adage that "there is no substitute for documents," Father Geiger continued the Engelhardt tradition which acknowledged that chroniclers, documents and history form one indispensable link in the flow of knowledge from one generation to another. His contributions as archivist and historian speak eloquently for themselves and, in defense of Father Maynard Geiger, there is no need to wave flags, explode fire works or blaze forth with bands.

EARLY FRIARS AT SACRAMENTO

Probably the most succinct account of the early Franciscans in the region of Sacramento is that written by Father Zephyrin Engelhardt (under his pen name, "*Esperanza*") in *The Monitor* for February 17, 1912. The essay was entitled "An Important Document: Who Named the Sacramento?"

"Captain Pedro Fages and Fray Juan Crespi, in 1772, went up the eastern shore of San Francisco Bay, passed the sites of Oakland and Berkeley, followed the southern bank of Carquinez Strait, and finally reached the vicinity of the present Antioch, where they discovered the two rivers which united and formed what Father Crespi christened the *Rio San Francisco*.

"Later, various expeditions went over the same ground, but no name seems to have been applied which would cling to either stream until the year 1806. In September of that year, Ensign Gabriel Moraga, accompanied by Fray Pedro Munoz, set out from Mission San Juan Bautista for the northeast. Moraga on this trip named the southern branch of the *Rio San Francisco* for his father, Joaquin Moraga, *Rio San Joaquin*. As such it has been known ever since.

"In October, 1811, Fray Ramon Abella and Fray Buenaventura Fortuny accompanied by Sergeant Jose Antonio Sanchez made an extensive examination by water to the San Joaquin, which they renamed San Juan Capistrano, and thence along the Two Mile Slough to the northern river, which on that occasion they concluded was the main branch of the *Rio San Francisco*, and therefore applied the same name—San Francisco.

"It is most probable that other expeditions visited the

two rivers during the next five years, but thus far no record of them has been discovered in the religious or secular archives.

"Lately (1911) Dr. Frederick J. Teggart, Curator of the Academy of Pacific Coast History, Berkeley, has unearthed the journal of an expedition to the river hitherto spoken of as the *Rio de San Francisco*."

The diary is in the handwriting of Fray Narciso Duran, of Mission San Jose, and also bears his signature. Father Duran and Father Ramon Abella of Mission San Francisco, accompanied by guards of the garrison of San Francisco, set out from the beach below the *presidio* on May 13, 1817. They crossed the bay, moved up the strait and *Rio San Francisco* until they reached the junction of the two rivers at nightfall the next day.

"One river comes from the north and northeast," reports Father Duran, "and it is called the Sacramento, and the other from the east and southeast, and is called the San Joaquin, and the two, united at their mouth, appear to be the river which the maps have put down under a single name, *Rio de San Francisco*."

Here, for the first time in history, we meet with the appellation "Sacramento" as applied to the stream in question, but who first gave it that name? Father Duran uses the present tense . . . we therefore believe that the beautiful and significant name must have been given to the stream on some previous occasion, and that it was not one of the friars who merits honor.

"One reason is that otherwise there would be some record of the incident in the various archives. Yet the document bearing testimony to the fact may be discovered some day. An earlier expedition may have found itself on the shores of the river about the Feast of *Corpus Christi* or on Holy Thursday. That would account for the name. But the question of who led the expedition and who applied the name is still an unresolved issue."

TRIBUTE TO THE OLD FRIARS

William Heath Davis (1822–1909) came to California in 1831 and for sixty years was in a position to observe its change from the latter mission period almost to the dawn of the twentieth century. The result of his observations was a splendid book entitled *Sixty Years in California.*

He frequently visited the Old Missions on his many business tours and came in contact with a number of the old *padres*. He was thoroughly acquainted with the commercial, maritime, agricultural, military and social side of early California. Of special interest is his resume of the missionaries:

> The priests at the various missions were usually men of very pure character, particularly the Spanish priests. The first priests who established the missions were directly from Spain. They were superior men in point of talent, education, morals and executive ability, as the success of the missions under their establishment and administration showed.
>
> They seemed to be entirely disinterested, their aim and ambition being to develop the country, and civilize and Christianize the Indians, for which purpose the missions were established.
>
> They worked zealously and untiringly on this behalf, and to them must be given the credit for what advancement in civilization, intelligence, industry, good habits and good morals pertained to the country at that day, when they laid the foundation of the present advanced civilization and development of the country.
>
> After the independence of Mexico, and its separation from Spain, the missions of California passed under the control of Mexican priests, who were also men of culture and attainments, generally of excellent character."
>
> They were always hospitable to strangers, all visitors were kindly received and entertained with the best they could offer, and the table was well supplied. The wine which they made at the missions was of a superior quality and equal to any that I have drank elsewhere.
>
> In trading through the country and traveling from point to point it was customary for travelers to stop at the missions as frequently and as long as they desired. This was expected as a matter of course by the priests, and had the traveler neglected to avail himself of the privilege, it would have been regarded as an offense by the good Fathers.
>
> On approaching the mission, the traveler would be met at the door or at the wide *veranda* by the *Padre*, who would greet him warmly, embrace him and invite him in, and he was furnished with the best rooms to sleep in, attended by servants, and everything possible was done to make him at home and comfortable during his stay.
>
> On leaving he was furnished with a fresh horse, and a good *vaquero* was appointed to attend him to the next mission, where he was received and entertained with the same hospitality, and so on as far as the journey extended.

Davis was especially enamored with Fray Jose Maria Gonzalez Rubio. "He was a noble man, a true Christian, very much respected and beloved by all his people, and by all who knew him." He was, in the opinion of Davis, "the Saint on Earth."

While admitting that there were some exceptions among the priests, "as there are everywhere," Davis thought that "as a class they were a fine body of men of superior character who accomplished a vast deal of good. The priests were much respected by the people, who looked to them for advice and guidance."

FRANCISCANS IN HISPANIC CALIFORNIA

With the financial assistance of the James Irvine Foundation, The Huntington Library of San Marino published Maynard J. Geiger's study of that "corps of soldiers of the cross who, two hundred years ago, effected the first triumphs of religion and civilization in what is now the golden state of California." Issued under the title, *Franciscan Missionaries in Hispanic California, 1769–1848*, the 304–page text gathers in one handy volume, the hitherto scattered and often inaccessible data on the Seraphic Foreign Legion. In addition to sketches of nine friars who merely visited the area during the period, the scholarly study represents a collection of succinct biographies of the 142 Franciscan missionaries who evangelized California in the initial seventy–nine years after its permanent colonization.

The treatise is monumental in its scope. Material was gleaned for over a quarter century from annual reports, register books, official governmental documents, secular and religious historians, memoirs of visitors, etc. These widely scattered sources were diligently sought out in Seville's *Archivo de Indias*; Mexico's *Archivo General de la Nación, Biblioteca Nacional* and *Biblioteca del Museo Nacional*; the archival centers of the various Franciscan provinces, apostolic colleges and bishoprics of Spain and Mexico; the Roman Archives of the Sacred Congregation of Propaganda Fide and the Santa Barbara Mission Archives. The work was complicated inasmuch as many of the friars who left California after their missionary service were forced, through secularization, revolution or war to live outside their religious communities.

The mountain of information gathered is arranged into unified essays outlining the chronology of each missionary's life, "the areas of his activity, the principal contributions resulting from his labors, the physical, spiritual, intellectual and social description and appraisal of his person, all in a relatively balanced manner." The 142 friars from the three Apostolic Colleges of San Fernando (Mexico City), Our Lady of Guadalupe (Zacatecas) and Santa Cruz (Querétaro) invested 2,269 man years, or an average of sixteen years on the California frontier "to bring into the Christian fold and into the Hispanic civilization nearly one hundred thousand aborigines, while they also attended to the spiritual needs of the conquering Spaniards and Mexicans in *presidios, pueblos*, and ranches."

This latest study from the industrious and meticulously accurate Maynard J. Geiger continues the tradition of impartial objectivity evident in his earlier works. While assigning their just praise to the good and saintly, the Franciscan historian makes no effort to minimize the shortcomings of those early friars who were unequal to their arduous calling. The composite picture of Franciscan activity reveals the friars to have been generally men of talent, ability and eminent virtue who accomplished great things against overwhelming odds. The appearance of this book recalls the words of Ecclesiastes:

Now, let us call the roll of famous men that were our

fathers long ago. . . . Here were men that had power and bore rule, men that excelled in strength or in the wisdom that dowered them. . . . Here were men that had skill to devise melodies, to make songs and set them down in writing. . . . Here were men of noble aim, that dwelt peacefully in their homes. They were the glories of their race, the ornament of their times. . . . These were men of tender conscience; their deeds of charity will never be forgotten. . . . Their bodies rest in peace; their name lasts on, age after age. Their wisdom is yet a legend among the people; wherever faithful men assemble, their story is told.

FRANCISCAN HERITAGE

The issuance of a 20¢ commemorative stamp by the United States Postal Service honoring Francis of Assisi, in October of 1982, calls to mind the debt that Californians and all Americans have for the seraphic saint. The imprint of Francis has penetrated deeply into the fibre of the nation. Franciscan priests first entered what is now the United States in the early 1500s, when they accompanied exploratory treks along the coast from Florida to Texas.

Fray Juan Padilla accompanied Coronado in 1542, when the great explorer journeyed into the central plains. Padilla, later killed by Indians in present–day Kansas, is generally identified as the nation's proto martyr. There were friars associated with the Christian beginnings in Florida, Nebraska, Texas, Lousiana, Michigan and Minnesota. Subsequently they were also active in southwestern Illinois.

Possibly the greatest accomplishment associated with the followers of Francis of Assisi was the establishment and development of the California missions in the years after Fray Junípero Serra founded San Diego de Alcala. Between that time and 1823, twenty–one missions were planted along that trail that became known as *El Camino Real*. It was a venture that represented incalculable effort and sacrifice.

The friars gathered the natives, taught them the rudiments of the Christian faith, instructed them in the arts and crafts of civilization and inducted them into the mainstream of contemporary life. The literature about the Franciscan work along the Pacific Slope forms an inspiring chapter in the story of North America. These seraphic men of God braved the perils of the wilderness, blazing trails, living on native foods, and overcoming unsanitary conditions. But it all came as second nature to the Franciscans because they were soldiers of Christ.

During the years after secularization, the friars gradually left the missions, most of them returning to other tasks in Mexico or Spain. The small group that remained was eventually affiliated with Holy Name Province of Saint Louis.

In the 1880s, Bishop Francis Mora asked the friars to take charge of an orphanage in the Pajaro Valley. Two years later, Archbishop Patrick W. Riordan entrusted them with a German parish in San Francisco. In 1892, he commissioned them to found a German parish in Oakland. Bishop Manogue asked the Franciscans to take charge of a new parish in Sacramento, near Sutter's Fort.

Vocations to the Order flourished and, in 1901, a seminary was inaugurated at San Luis Rey Mission. In November of 1915, the Province of Santa Barbara was established, encompassing California, Arizona, Oregon and Washington. Since then, the Franciscan family in California has been enhanced by the arrival of two other branches, the Capuchins and the Conventuals.

The stamp issued to honor Saint Francis extends his influence to 1982, a clear indication that the little man from Assisi reached far beyond his death in 1226. The Franciscan spirit brought to San Diego 231 years ago continues to grow as an important element of the overall Christian apostolate.

If the past be any gauge for measuring the future, the Franciscans in California will confront the new challenges of the post conciliar age if only they keep a clear eye on the *poverello* whose seraphic message is forever relevant.

INDIVIDUAL FRIARS

FRAY JUAN AMOROS (1773–1832)

Henry W. Henshaw observed, in 1890, that "it is doubtful if a purer and more devoted set of men ever labored for the good of the heathen than the early missionaries of California." One such friar was surely Juan Amoros.

In remarks delivered for the centennial of Mission San Francisco de Asis, General Mariano Vallejo recalled that "Friar Juan Amoros was sanctity itself." He was "a model of virtue, charity, humility, and of Christian meekness—a man without blemish, of a candid heart, and of most exemplary life; he was the admiration of his contemporaries and the astonishment of the tribes of the aborigines."

Amoros was born at Porrera, in the Catalan region of Spain, on October 10, 1773. He entered the Franciscans at Gerona, in 1791, and six years later was ordained priest at Solsana. Animated by his great zeal for the conversion of the gentiles, the tall, thin, pockmarked black–haired friar came to New Spain, in 1803, and the following year arrived in California. He labored on behalf of the Indians at Mission San Carlos Borromeo for the next fifteen years of his priestly ministry.

Amoros had a practical knowledge of at least two of the seven Indian dialects in the Monterey region. A broadminded, candid man of vision, his penetrating reply to the request of the Spanish Government concerning the native culture of the Indians at San Carlos, was published by Father Zephyrin Engelhardt in 1934. It was re–issued, with annotations, by Father Maynard Geiger in *The Americas*, sixteen years later. In 1819, Amoros was transferred to San Rafael, where he "worked with astonishing perseverance until his death." Serving at that mission for thirteen of its seventeen years, the Catalan friar put in granaries, corrals and workshops. Baptisms outnumbered deaths two–to–one and the overall neophyte population nearly doubled, even though many natives were moved to San Francisco Solano. In 1828, the mission inhabitants reached the all–time high of 1,140 persons.

Though known as the "Diplomat of the Frontier," Amoros refused adamantly to take the oath of loyalty to the Mexican Constitution of 1824. He also protested, though much less successfully, against attempts to collect export duties on mission goods. Throughout the twenty–eight years he spent in California, Amoros was known for his religious zeal, characteristic industry and keen ability in conducting the temporal and mechanical activities of the mission.

According to a report submitted by Father Mariano Payeras, Amoros' merit was outstanding, his aptitude for the apostolic ministry in both spiritual and temporal matters above the average. He was, according to his superior, "fit for some official position in the Order." Amoros died on July 14, 1832, at San Rafael. In his entry in the *Registro de Difuntos*, Fray Buenaventura Fortuny stated that Amoros had labored for the neophytes with enviable constancy. He went on to add: "I have known this priest since 1792 and have always considered him to be a saint."

FRAY FELIPE ARROYO DE LA CUESTA 1780–1840)

To Felipe Arroyo de la Cuesta "belongs the honor of rescuing from oblivion the only literary monument of its kind in California." His *Vocabulary or Phrase Book of the Mutsun Language of Alta California* is neither a dictionary nor a grammar but consists of 2,884 phrases of the Indian dialect spoken at Mission San Juan Bautista. The small book was published in 1862, by John Gilmary Shea under the auspices of the Smithsonian Institution as Volume VIII of the *Library of American Linguistice*.

The more common prayers, some music and several routine formulas, all in the Mutsun tongue with their Spanish equivalents, can be found at the end of the vocabulary. The treatise was reproduced from a forty–seven page manuscript purchased by Hubert Howe Bancroft from Alexander S. Taylor.

Explanations and footnotes are given in exquisite Latin. In his Introduction, de la Cuesta writes,

> Here begins our effort on this Collection of Indian sentences in the sounds or words of the inhabitants of this Mission of San Juan Bautista. It comprises everything written by me heretofore. Some remarks must precede, however. They are as follows:
>
> Firstly, I have not found any word written in the language of said Indians. Secondly, scarcely a syllable or suitable letters can be devised for expressing what is spoken. Thirdly, in this idiom some letters of the alphabet are lacking such as B, D, F, and Z and others, besides the definite and indefinite articles.
>
> Fourthly, in order to pronounce correctly, the tongue, bearing, mouth and nose must be exercised so that the Indian word may come out agreeably, in accord with the manner of the Indian lest he be moved to ridicule. Fifthly, one must practice beforehand with children and old people who, being ignorant of Spanish sounds, will easily and perfectly pronounce the words without foreign sounds. Sixthly, although I have read this many times, nay thousands of times, and find this

idiom ineloquent and inelegant, it is in reality not so. It is very copious, oblong, abundant and eloquent, as experience has taught me.

Father Felipe de la Cuesta was a remarkable man. A native of the Villa de Cubo in Old Castille, he first came to San Juan Bautista in 1808, and spent almost a quarter–century at the mission, retiring only when the Zacateano friars arrived to staff the northern foundations in 1833. Despite paralytic rheumatic pains, the old missionary continued at his work even when it became necessary that he be carried to administer the sacraments.

De la Cuesta had great facility with languages. Father Vicente de Sarria notes in his *Sketches* that the priest "applied himself most assiduously to the learning of the respective languages with such success that I doubt that there is another who has reached the same proficiency in understanding and describing its interesting syntax." Concerning his book, Sarria goes on to say, that "He even reduced to some sort of rules the confusing formations of its verbs, adverbs and the rest of the parts of speech. . . . I have animated him to compose a work on the subject. He has labored . . . with good success."

The phrase book was many years in preparation but the veteran missionary was hard at work early. In a *interrogatio* filled out for the Spanish Government in 1812, de la Cuesta remarks that "the Indians of this Mission and of this region speak the language of the district in which they were born, and, although apparently of distinct idioms their languages are only accidently different."

FRAY ANTONIO DE LA ASCENSION (ff. 1600s)

A modern sociologist asserts that "the priest must be a man of intellectual curiosity, a man who is never satisfied with the answers he has, the techniques he uses, the advice he gives." Such a person was Fray Antonio de la Ascención, who came to California in 1602, as a cosmographer with the expedition of Sebastian Vizcaíno. Born in Salamanca, about 1573, Antonio studied for the priesthood and was ordained for service with the Order of Discalced Carmelites, sometime in the 1590s. He was assigned to graduate studies in cosmography at San Telmo School, in Seville. In 1597, Fray Antonio de la Ascención volunteered for missionary work in New Spain.

The young priest was initially attached to the Convento de San Sebastian in the Carmelite Province of San Alberto. There, for his first years, Fray Antonio taught clerical aspirants. On February 20, 1602, the friar was assigned to accompany Fray Andrés de la Asumpción and Fray Tomás de Aquino on the expedition to California in search of a safe port for the Manila galleons. In addition to his religious duties, he was also to serve as assistant cosmographer to the legendary Sebastian Vizcaíno. The expedition sailed from Acapulco on May 5, 1602, and charted the California coastline from Cabo San Lucas, in Peninsular California, to Cape Mendocino in the far north. Upon completion of the epoch–making voyage, Fray Antonio assisted Vizcaíno in drawing up the final report which was submitted to Viceroy Gaspar de Zúñiga y Acevado.

Fray Antonio's minutely–drafted charts contained a

host of invaluable sailing directives. With the utmost precision, he described landmarks, noted depths, catalogued wind–directions and recorded latitude and anchorage. In the years that followed Fray Antonio wrote several additional accounts of the voyage and compiled a number of memoranda relating to his findings for the king and various other governmental officials. His description of Alta California as a land of great potential wealth has been borne out by the development of the past century.

There can be little doubt about the friar's enthusiasm for colonizing the area. For well over thirty years after the famous voyage, Fray Antonio continued to praise California and promote its settlement. His account of the Vizcaíno expedition, published in 1757, by Father Miguel Venégas, was used by other historians of the 18th century as their source of information about California.

Though Fray Antonio de la Ascención died about 1636, the impact of his "propaganda" continued to influence the scene for centuries. The prominent Western America historian, W. Michael Mathes, ranks the Carmelite friar as "not only California's first, but one of its most dedicated and effective propagandists."

FRAY JOSE BARONA (1764–1831)

Fray José Barona was born near Burgon, at Villanueva del Conde, on August 5, 1764. He received the Franciscan habit at Villa de Velardo on July 18, 1783. Along with twenty–eight other missionaries, Barona set out for the New World in 1795 aboard the Santiago de España. His passport described him as of regular build, with lemon–colored skin, hazel or dark brown eyes and hair, a thick beard and a scar on his forehead.

Upon his arrival in Alta California, Barona was assigned by Fray Fermin Francisco de Lasuen to San Diego Mission. There he labored faithfully until 1811. That Barona was beloved at his post is indicated by the invitation extended to him in 1813 to dedicate the new and final mission church. His return there occasioned great bursts of jubilation from the neophytes.

The last two decades of Barona's life were spent at San Juan Capistrano Mission. There was much to do and over the years he built a hospital containing bedrooms and corresponding reception areas for the sick and elderly. He also erected a small chapel adjacent to the hospital.

Barona endured the terrifying earthquake of December 8, 1812, during which some fifty Indians attending Holy Mass were killed. It was a traumatic experience which he recalled many times in future years. On January 23, 1823, the friar was the victim of what one writer has called "the most scandalous case which has been witnessed in California." It seems as if two soldiers,

Juan Alipas and Hilario Garcia, tried to forcibly detain the friar from travelling to San Luis Rey, where he had been summoned by Fray Antonio Peyri.

The soldiers, comprising the military guard at San Juan Capistrano, felt that it was unsafe for the friar to travel alone. A scuffle ensued when one of the soldiers kicked Barona's horse. The frightened animal fell to one side atop the friar, causing him considerable physical pain and compelling him to cancel his journey. A sensational affair, it was duly reported to the *Presidente* of the California Missions, Fray José Señán, as well as to Governor Luis Antonio Argüello.

It would appear that the sixty–year old Barona never fully recovered from the indignity and shock suffered at the time. The last entry he made in the Baptismal Register at San Juan Capistrano was in a trembling hand, on October 14, 1830. Shortly thereafter he became wholly incapacitated.

The friar died at San Juan Capistrano Mission on the night of August 4, 1831. Though known throughout his life as a man with a "weak constitution," he was always known as a zealous and hardworking friar, a fact that is substantiated by a glance at the register books which reveal almost 1,200 Baptisms during his tenure.

Like many of the early missionaries, Barona's apostolate in Alta California has gone mostly unheralded. But such a fate is welcomed by those who work only for a spiritual reward.

FRAY GERONIMO BOSCANA (1775–1831)

The Franciscans from the Apostolic College of San Fernando represented a cross section of practically all the Spanish provinces. Sixteen of the friars, or eight percent of the total missionary personnel working in California, originated on the Balearic Isles. Together these tireless monks logged 341 years of service to the Pacific Slope. Mallorcan influence in California was a lasting one for there was constantly one or more of these missionaries on the scene between 1769 and 1823. Truly, "the isle of calm and beauty was and remains California's spiritual godmother."

Among the twelve Mallorcan friars who died at their posts was Geronimo Boscana (1775–1831). Born in the Villa of Lluchmayor, he was invested with the seraphic habit at Palma on August 4, 1792, and eleven years later came to New Spain as a missionary of the Apostolic College of San Fernando in Mexico City. Father Boscana's quarter–century of service to the Church in California was spent at Missions Purisima Concepcion (1806–1811), San Luis Rey (1811–1814), San Juan Capistrano (1814–1826) and San Gabriel (1826–1831). While at his last position, the friar served intermittently as chaplain to the *Asistencia de Nuestra Señora de los Angeles*.

That the Mallorcan friar had earned a place of respect among his confreres is attested to by Father Mariano Payeras, who noted of Boscana: "I consider his merit above the medium and his aptitude the same for the ministry among the faithful and the unbelievers as also for some kind of office or commission."

The indefatigable Franciscan is well known to students of California ethnology. During his tenure at San Juan Capistrano, Father Boscana took great pains to ascertain and record the beliefs, notions, traditions and habits of the Juaneño Indians. These observations were discovered among the papers of Jose de la Guerra and published by the Wiley and Putnam Company at New York in 1846, under the title *Chinigchinich*. The introduction to the tome, penned by Alfred Robinson, is known to readers as *Life in California*. The Boscana narrative has been referred to as "the one penetrating piece on aboriginal ethnology written by a California missionary." A. L. Kroeber described it as "easily the most intensive and best written account of the customs and religion of any group of California Indians in the mission days."

Geronimo Boscana was among that pioneering group of Catholic missionaries who brought the Christian message to an uncharted land. He was one of those responsible for that system which elicited praise from the pen of Thomas Jefferson Farnham:

> I could not forbear a degree of veneration for those ancient closets of devotion; those resting–places of the wayfarer from the desert, those temples of hospitality and prayer, erected by that band of excellent and daring men, who founded the California missions and engraved on the heart of that remote wilderness, the features of civilization and the name of God.

FRAY JUAN CABOT (1781–c. 1856)
FRAY PEDRO CABOT (1777-1836)

The quest for sources relating to California's Catholic Heritage has led in many directions and truly it can be said that "the pleasure of a search, like that of a hunt, lies in the searching and ends at the point at which the pleasure of certitude begins." Recently, for example, the following account of two early California *padres* was unearthed in an issue of the San Francisco *Bulletin* for April 22, 1864. It is here reproduced exactly as published.

> We are kindly favored by Bishop Amat with the annexed original notice of the death of Friar Pedro Cabot, a celebrity in this country forty years ago, from the entry at No. 2,115 of the *Book of Obituaries* of the Mission San Fernando, in Los Angeles County, which we insert as a curiosity in California chronicles.

Father Cabot, at the time of his death, was about sixty years of age, and had served in the Missions of California for over thirty years, having arrived in this country from Mexico about the year 1806. He was born on the Isle of Mallorca, and had a brother, Juan Cabot, who served also many years at San Miguel Mission, thirty miles below San Antonio, at which place his brother Pedro served from 1808 to 1830. Being so near each other, and the only two brothers among the old missionaries, their habits and characters were much noted by the natives and old foreigners.

Pedro was a fine, portly, gentlemanly, educated man of courteous, dignified manners, well up in the theological lore of the Catholic Church, and universally beloved and esteemed in the country for eminent piety and devotion to his duties as a priest—the very pattern of a Christian gentleman after the Spanish model. On the other hand, Juan was a burly, rough sailor like man, of plain schooling and knotted thoughts; full of snaps and turns; generous and hospitable to a fault; and immensely popular among the *ranchero* people.

He left California about the year 1831, and returned to the island of Mallorca at the time of the Carlist wars of 1835, where, as we are informed, he was heard from by Bishop Amat, when in Spain, in 1856. Shortly after that date the old California friar ended his mortal career, being a great celebrity in those Spanish parts as a *returned Californian*, of which country, after the news of the gold discoveries of 1848, he was never tired of talking, and people were never tired of listening—for the Mallorcans all loved California gold better than the friar's sermons.

While serving in the Missions, the country people nicknamed Pedro, *El Caballero*, and Juan, *El Marinero*; and these two names stuck to them to the last. The brothers are often mentioned in the works on California, published between 1830 and 1846. The sailor–*padre* was the only one of the California fraternity left between 1846 and 1856, except Altimira, the *padre* of San Rafael and Sonoma about 1824, who was said to be living, at the Canary Islands in 1860; and we understand that this "last reminder" of the ancient Baron priests of California has come to the mortal finality since.

The following is the obituary notice referred to: On the 12th day of October, 1836, in the cemetery of this Mission of San Fernando, I gave ecclesiastical burial to the body of the Rev. Father Pedro Cabot , minister of the same, having on the day before made confession and received Extreme Unction. For the truth of which I hereby affirm and sign . . . . Friar Franco Gonzales de Ibar.

FRAY MAGIN CATALA (1761–1830)

A. HOLY MAN OF SANTA CLARA

The "Holy Man of Santa Clara," Fray Magín Catalá, was one of twins born at Montblanch, Province of Tarragona, Spain, on January 29, 1761. He entered the Franciscans at Barcelona and was raised to the priesthood sometime in 1785.

Soon after ordination, Catalá volunteered for the American missions and was assigned to the Apostolic College of San Fernando in Mexico City where he labored until coming to California in 1794. Catalá's tenure at Mission Santa Clara lasted without interruption for the next thirty–six years until his death in 1830. One can glean very little from extant records about Magín's personal life for he wrote few letters and spent most of his time instructing the Indians and watching over their moral conduct.

A careful investigation of the old registers at Santa Clara reveals that the indefatigable missionary personally baptized 3,067 persons, buried an equal number, and performed 1,905 marriages—a phenomenal record for even thirty–six years. His rigorous adherence to abstinences and penitential practices eventually brought about chronic inflammatory rheumatism which plagued him throughout the last years of his life. In fact, Catalá was so disabled by infirmities during those years that he could neither stand nor walk; nonetheless, he had himself propped up in the sanctuary where he daily taught Christian doctrine to the Indians. The natives were understandably grieved when the tolling mission bells announced the friar's death on Monday, the 22nd of November, 1830. An immense crowd of people filed into the church to pay their final respects to the venerable missionary who had been their father and friend for almost four decades.

In 1882, fifty–two years after his death, inquiries were made at Santa Clara about the formalities for possible process of beatification. The Jesuit Fathers petitioned Archbishop Joseph Sadoc Alemany of San Francisco to institute a canonical investigation pointing out that "inasmuch as more than fifty years have already passed since his blessed death, it is to be feared that the memory of his virtues and labors may be lost and his fame decline, unless everything relating to the servant of God be at once diligently collected from those that still survive and may remember him. . . ." Father Benedict Picardo, S.J., the notary, set out to gather evidence from the few remaining eyewitnesses. The archbishop became deeply interested in the cause and was tireless in his efforts to trace down the details of Catalá's early life in Spain. Unfortunately, little was done on the cause after Alemany's retirement in 1884, and it was another two decades before Catalá's biography was published by Father Zephyrin Engelhardt. In 1907 the missionary's body was moved to a new location in the church, and in the next year the Sacred Congregation of Rites ordered the process *de non cultu*.

Nothing of any real importance has been done on the cause in recent years, and in view of the complications usually involved in such cases, the possibility of beatifying the humble Franciscan friar is not promising. But beatified or not, Fray Magín Catalá, from his place in heaven, still watches over the destinies of the California missions!

FRAY MAGIN CATALA (1761–1830)

B. COFFIN REMNANT

One of the more precious and treasured items in the Historical Museum of the Chancery Archives is a 3 1/2 inch fragment from the redwood coffin of Fray Magin Catalá. Known in the annals as the "Holy Man of Santa Clara," Fray Magin (1761–1830) came to Alta California in 1793. The next year he arrived at Santa Clara Mission, where he ministered to the Indians for the next thirty–six years.

During Catalá's last decade, he was plagued with many physical afflictions. When he could no longer ascend the pulpit or stand up to preach, he addressed the neophytes seated in a chair. As early as 1799, the friar was referred to as "Blessed Father Magin."

Zephyrin Engelhardt wrote of Catalá that "despite his infirmities he observed the Franciscan rule strictly, used the discipline and penitential girdle, tasted nothing till noon, and then and in the evening would eat only a gruel of corn and milk . . . The venerable missionary was famed . . . for his miracles and prophecies, as well as for his virtues." The Catalan missionary died at 7 o'clock in the morning, on November 22, 1830. According to the *Libro de Difuncto*s, he was buried the next day near the presbytery, on the Gospel side of the altar.

Fray Magin Catalá

On April 2, 1860, the tomb was opened before a large gathering of Spanish, Mexican and Indian people. Juan Crisostomo Galindo, the *majordomo* at Santa Clara mission, identified the remains, noting that only the skeleton and parts of the Franciscan habit were in evidence. The tomb was subsequently closed and sealed.

In 1882, the process for Catalá's beatification was inaugurated. Persons were interviewed who had known him and could testify to his reputation for heroic sanctity. Archbishop Joseph Sadoc Alemany took the findings to Rome. When the tomb was next opened, in 1907, Catalá's remains or *restos* were removed to the foot of the altar of the Crucifixion. This time the old coffin was found to be mostly disintegrated, with only a few bones, some hair and pieces of habit remaining.

The *restos* were placed in a large tin box, the lid of which was fastened down hermetically. It was lowered into a new sepulchre. Over the new casket was placed a marble slab containing biographical data, the Franciscan coat–of–arms and the scriptural inscription: "His memory is held in benediction."

In 1908, the Sacred Congregation of Rites advanced Catalá's cause and Father Zephyrin Englehardt was named Vice Postulator. The documents gathered were again forwarded to Rome. No further action has been taken on the cause. Henry L. Walsh, the Jesuit historian, wrote that Catalá's remains were exhumed after the fire of 1926 and, after due authentication, were re–interred in their present location.

The piece of Catalá's coffin displayed in the Historical Museum was removed in 1860. It was presented to the Historical Museum of the Archival center by the late Father Arthur D. Spearman, long–time achivist for the University of Santa Clara.

FRAY MAGIN CATALA (1761–1830)

C. *EL PROFETA*

The life of Magin Catalá (1761–1830) was described by one of his contemporaries as "exemplary, industrious, and edifying." Many fascinating incidents are associated with Catala's thirty–seven year missionary sojourn at Santa Clara. Perhaps none is more interesting than the Franciscan's reputation for prophecy, a fact widely confirmed among the people of Central California.

In an article in *The Century Illustrated Monthly Magazine*, Mariano Vallejo recorded that on more than one occasion before his sermon, the friar would ask the congregation to join him in prayers for the soul of one about to die, naming the hour. In every case this was fulfilled to the very letter, and that in cases "where the one who died could not have known of the father's words."

Another early witness testified that "all that this sainted priest foretold came to pass." One Sunday, for example, as Magin Catalá was about to celebrate Mass, he called an attendant and directed him to tell two men who were stealing flour from the storeroom to come to holy Mass, lest they commit two sins at one and the same time. The two culprits, all besprinkled with flour, really appeared in the church. The stifled amusement of the worshippers may be imagined.

In 1908, Mrs. John M. Burnett, daughter–in–law of the first governor of California, recalled after the late San Francisco disaster by shock and flame that many old Spaniards had told her that Fray Magin Catala had predicted the rise of a great city on San Francisco bay. The *padre* had further foretold that the builders would be a new race of people, and that the city in time would be punished for its sins and vanity by a visitation of earthquake and fire.

Merced Ortega Castro related, "When her nephew one day made himself ready to catch a horse with a lasso, his mother said to him. 'Don't go out. Fr. Magin announced today that a man and his horse would be killed.' The wilful youth nevertheless went out with his brother and cousin. In throwing the lasso both horse and rider were tangled up, and both fell so unfortunately as to break their necks on a rock." This incident was later confirmed by Mrs. Maria Teresa Hartnell. Additional evidence was offered by Petra Pacheco, who noted that Fray Magin predicted that a cholera epidemic would visit San Jose, and that the dead would be hauled out by the carloads. This was verified about 1850.

One of Catala's most interesting predictions concerned the discovery of gold. The southland's Catholic paper noted, "It is not improbable that Father Magin Catala knew about the existence of gold in California a half century before its discovery by James Marshall, for it is recorded that while the *padre* was journeying in the mountains with some Indians, one of the latter found a stone which aroused the wonder of the natives. When the *Padre* saw it he exclaimed, throw it away, or California is lost. Nor could it be found afterward by the Indian. It is thought that the stone was rich gold quartz, which, indeed became the ruin of the natives wherever it was discovered." In his last sermon be thus addressed the Indians at Santa Clara:

> We are situated upon a great treasure which will be discovered, chiefly toward the north. This treasure will be the occasion of many crimes and murders. There will be discord in families; parents will stand up against their children, children against their parents, brothers against brothers, and all on account of their greed. From all parts of the globe will come people whose language you do not understand, and who will take your homes, your lands, your cattle, and leave you nothing.

The prophetic utterances of the friar were only one aspect of his many–sided personality. Even a most cursory glance at the activities of *Padre* Magin Catala compels the reader to agree with the evaluation of Beryl Hoskin: "The beauty of his character was such that it left a lasting impression on Santa Clara Mission."

FRAY JUAN CRESPI (1721–1782)

A. ILLUSTRIOUS SON

The notion of "hero" is very much alive in the Catalan culture of modern times. An example would be Fray Juan Crespi (1721–1782) who, on December 31st, 1993, 211 years after his earthly demise, was enrolled as an "Illustrious Son" of Palma de Mallorca.

Crespi studied under Fray Junípero Serra at the Convento de San Francisco, and there made his profession as a friar on January 9, 1739. A decade later, he left for the New World, where he spent his first years as a missionary in the Sierra Gorda.

In 1767, Crespi was one of the friars chosen to replace the expelled Jesuits in the missions of peninsular California. He later joined Serra and others who were to spend the rest of their lives working in the two Californias.

Serra named Crespi chaplain and chronicler for the expedition to Alta California in 1769. He subsequently wrote seven diaries of the explorations, performed one of the first baptisms in the area and was among the first Europeans to see the Bay of San Francisco.

It was Crespi who bestowed the name of *Nuestra Señora de los Angeles* on the little river on the eve of the feast of the Portiuncula. That appellation passed on to the *pueblo* which evolved into the present megapolis of Los Angeles.

With the exception of a few months in San Diego, Crespi was posted at San Carlos Borromeo most of his time in Alta California. During these years, he served as diarist for several important expeditions.

Following a short illness, Crespi died on New Year's day in 1782. He was buried by Serra in the sanctuary of the church. His remains were later moved to the present edifice where they were exhumed and identified in 1856.

Crespi was highly esteemed by his contemporaries, one of whom recalled him as a man of "blameless life and exemplary virtues." Professor Herbert Eugene Bolton summed up his estimate of Crespi in these words:

> Among all the great diarists who recorded explorations in the New World, Juan Crespi occupied a conspicuous place. Gentle character, devout Christian, zealous missionary, faithful companion, his peculiar fame will be that of diarist. Of all the men of this

half–decade, so prolific in frontier extension, Crespi alone participated in all the major path–breaking expeditions. In distance, he out–traveled Coronado.

Today, Crespi is memorialized by a hall at Carmel. His name has also been given to numerous streets and roadways in many cities, including his birthplace, Palma de Mallorca.

December 31, the principal holiday in Palma, recalls the defeat of the Arabs of King Jaime I of Aragon in 1229. In 1993, at ceremonies in the city's cathedral, Bishop Theodoro Ubeda offered Holy Mass attended by all the major officials of the Autonomous Community of the Balearic Isles and the municipal government of Palma. Juan Fageda Aubert, the mayor of Palma, proclaimed Crespi as one of the city's "illustrious sons." Henceforth, Fray Juan Crespi's portrait will hang next to that of Serra in the city hall.

Crespi's city of origin now recognizes him as "a pioneer explorer, chronicler and civilizer," terms long ago conferred on Crespi by his friends and admirers along California's *El Camino Real*.

FRAY JUAN CRESPI (1721–1782)

B. PORTRAYAL OF A FRIAR

There are tens of thousands of books about California, many of them classic portrayals of the area's history since 1769 and the arrival of white men from the "old" world. Among the score or so of best written volumes, at least from the aspect of basic prose, is the rather elusive tome by Charles Francis Saunders on *The Wild Gardens of Old California*. Published at Santa Barbara by William Hebberd in 1927, the book is "a presentation of Padre Juan Crespi and how he went on a journey."

Saunders was a botanist who came to California shortly after the turn of the century. It has been said of him "that the subtle atmosphere and charm that literature creates for a country he has helped to weave about California and by writings occupying a field distinctively their own."

The author begins by doubting if even the most enthusiastic naturalists would want to be transported to the California of the 1770s, where they could accompany Fray Juan Crespi in his long journeys between San Diego to Carmel. Saunders felt, and probably rightly so, that the opportunity of seeing California in the beauty of its unspoiled nature would be more than offset by the monumental inconveniences of primitive life.

The author's portrayal of Crespi was as accurate as it was sympathetic. Loving God, Fray Juan Crespi "naturally enough loved all His works, both great and small, and in the records he has left us, his lively enjoyment of the scenes that met his eyes in that early California, which was still a virgin land—scenes no white man had before looked upon—finds hearty expression."

To the Indians, Crespi "was little less than a saint—nay, something more than a saint, so quickly responsive was he to their needs and so understanding of their weakness." It is part of the public record that Crespi was "so sunny natured, so humble and warm of heart, so altogether *simpatico*, that he was affectionately known among his companions as *el beato*—the blessed one."

Crespi had accompanied Gaspar de Portola on his famous marches up and down the California coast between San Diego and the north, seeking the Port of Monterey. He had a unique vantage point from which to record his impressions. Crespi is correctly characterized as a friar better versed in theology than in the natural sciences. But even though his observations are at times incomplete and obscure, they capture the features of the landscape in a remarkably accurate fashion.

The beauties of flowers and birds, the glories of valleys and mountains did not escape Crespi's reverent eye. He spoke about the bright–hued flowers which, in the springtime, lent a fleeting glory to the hills and valleys.

Crespi was extraordinarily observant, one who had a keen eye for all growing things. A botanist he was not, but that makes precious little difference because nearly every plant in the California of 1769 was as innocent of name as Adam found the flowers of Eden.

Charles Francis Saunders wrote more than a dozen books about California. None is more enjoyable than his slim volume on T*he Wild Gardens of Old California* and his portrayal of Fray Juan Crespi.

FRAY JUAN CRESPI (1721–1782)

C. FRIAR REVISITED

Ironically, those who keep the diaries, write the chronicles and compile the records of the past are often the least written about of all the pioneers. Surely that was true on the California scene.

Fray Juan Crespi (1721–1782), the most vivid of the missionary diarists, is a perfect example of one who carefully recorded the accomplishments of others while himself remaining in the shadows. Happily, Bartolome Font Obrador has published a monograph under the title *Juan Crespi, Explorador i Cronista Francisca a l'Alta California* which provides a new dimension on the Mallorcan friar.

Issued as Volume XIX in the *Biografies de Mallorquins* series published by the *Ayuntament de Palma*, the extremely well–documented and copiously illustrated, eighty–two page book is written in Crespi's native language, a version of Catalan.

Crespi studied philosophy under Fray Junípero Serra at the Convento de San Francisco in Palma. Ordained in 1746, he volunteered for services in the Indies where he arrived in 1750. The friar ministered in several of the missions in the Sierra Gorda district of Mexico between 1752 and 1767. He joined Serra two years later in Peninsular California, where plans were afoot to move northward.

Crespi was asked by Serra to serve as diarist for the first arm of the military expedition bound for San Diego under Fernando Rivera y Moncada. On June 22, 1769, Crespi wrote the first letter by a Franciscan in Alta California.

Crespi and Fray Francisco Gomez had the distinction of administering the first baptisms in Alta California when they came across two dying Indian girls north of San Clemente on July 22, 1769. It was Crespi who recorded the first earthquakes experienced by Europeans in California.

The diaries written by Crespi, both in Baja and Alta California, were meticulous and detailed. He gave Christian names to the villages, rivers and sites encountered along the way. Interestingly, of all the names he bestowed, only two remain—Los Angeles and Santa Cruz. Los Angeles was named on August 1st in memory of the Portiuncula Indulgence attached to the Franciscan Chapel of Our Lady of the Angels at Assisi.

Professor Herbert Eugene Bolton said of the friar that "among all the great diarists who recorded explorations in the New World, Juan Crespi occupies a conspicuous place." He was a gentle man, a devout Christian, zealous missionary and faithful companion whose fame will be that of diarist. Of all those prolific in frontier extension, Crespi alone participated in every major path–breaking expedition.

The Mallorcan friar worked mostly at San Carlos Borromeo Mission during his years in California and it was there that he died and was buried in 1782. He was interred on the Gospel side of the sanctuary near the main altar in the existing church. His remains were later moved to the present edifice, next to those of Fray Junípero Serra.

Font's new treatise testifies how the archives of California, Mexico and Spain are enriched by Crespi's correspondence with officials and friends. In his "precious diaries, the human tolls, adventures, thrills, hopes and fears of three historic journeys are forever enshrined."

FRAY JUAN CRESPI (1721–1782)

D. CALIFORNIA XENOPHON

Often the most eloquent and convincing testimony about churchmen comes from those who do not share the Catholic faith. An example would be Herbert Eugene

Bolton's esteem for Fray Juan Crespi (1721–1782).

In the July, 1927 issue of *Touring Topics*, the distinguished Professor of History at the University of California, Berkeley, wrote that "without the diaries of Crespi, this age would be apprised of but little of the history of the conquest of California." Certainly among all the great diarists who recorded explorations in the New World, Juan Crespi occupied a conspicuous place. For more than three decades, he pioneered the wilds of North America.

Like Francisco Palou, he was a pupil of Fray Junípero Serra and for many years his close companion. Like them he was a Mallorcan and he accompanied them to the New World in 1749. Beside them he went as missionary to the Sierra Gorda and with them he was sent to Peninsular California when the Jesuits were expelled in 1767. For a while, he was in charge of Mission Purisima Concepcion.

Two years later, he was one of the friars selected by Serra to join the Gaspar de Portolá expedition to Alta California. Crespi was among those who planted the cross of Christ and the banner of Spain at San Diego. Since Crespi was the only friar who made the whole march from Vellicatá to San Francisco and back, he was commissioned to prepare the composite diary of that epochal journey.

Carmel was Crespi's home in Alta California and there he spent twelve years as Fray Junípero Serra's faithful companion. During that time he was often in poor health, suffering from burning fevers.

In all his various treks as diarist, Crespi also served as chaplain. "With fingers benumbed by cold, with inflamed eyes, in drenching rain, under burning desert suns, or in his berth on a pitching ship, he faithfully chronicled the happenings of those historic journeys." He kept superb records that have come down to us through two centuries. Bolton characterized Crespi as "missionary, globe trotter and journalist." He suggested that "breviary, pack mule, caravel and quill might appropriately decorate his coat of arms or his book plate."

In the Sierra Gorda, on the Baja California peninsula and at Carmel, the baptisms, marriages and burials are recorded in Crespi's distinguished script. The archives of California, Mexico and Spain are enriched by his correspondence with officials and friends.

He died a relatively young man of sixty–one. His years were few, but his deeds were many and memorable. As Fray Junípero Serra made ready for death in 1784, he made only one request—that his human remains be placed next to those of his faithful and devoted Juan Crespi.

FRAY NARCISO DURAN (1776–1846)

A. Zealous Mssionary

Narciso Duran (1776–1846) was described by one outstanding historian as a person who "retained the esteem of most adversaries and was always beloved by people of all classes, being popular and influential in Santa. Barbara."

Born in Catalonia Duran came to New Spain as a young priest in 1803. His passport portrayed him as medium in height, somewhat stout, with fair complexion and blue eyes. He arrived at Monterey, in 1806, and was first assigned to San Jose Mission. The twenty–seven years Duran spent at his first post were times of great challenge and accomplishment.

Duran's musical talents were developed at San Jose. When Alfred Robinson visited the Old Mission, in 1831, he wrote that "the music was well executed, for it had been practiced daily for more than two months under the particular supervision of Father Narciso Duran." Without doubt, Duran was the *padre* musician *par excellence*.

Captain Frederick Beechey visited San Jose, in 1826, and reported that the mission "was all neatness, cleanliness and comfort." He also praised the choir, hospitality and character of the resident missionaries. Another prominent visitor, Alfred Robinson, recorded that Duran was "universally beloved, and the neighboring village bore testimony to his charitable heart, while many a transient traveler blessed him, and thanked God that such a man existed among them."

Duran declined to take the oath of allegiance to Mexico, in 1826, and for that failure, suffered greatly at the hand of the various public officials. His superior had nothing but praise for Duran. Fray Mariano Payeras said that "his merit is distinguished and his aptitude is for a complete apostolic man in both fields (spiritual and temporal) and for such offices and prelacies which may be deemed best to bestow upon him."

In 1824, Duran was named *Presidente* of the California missions. Six years later, he was again elected to that office. He was also named Vicar Forane and thus became the chief ecclesial figure in California. For the final years of his life, Duran was stationed at Santa Barbara. Even after the creation of a diocese for *Ambas Californias*, Duran continued to function as *comisario prefecto* for the Fernandino friars.

Duran lived at Santa Barbara until his demise in 1846. He had the distinction of being the first *Presidente* to administer the full twenty–one missions. During his forty years in California, Duran had been in touch with all the important persons of his time and area.

The great chronicler of the missions, Father Zephyrin Engelhardt, said of Duran that during the troublous times of the secularization and sale of the missions, it was Father Duran who fought the pillagers step by step, though in vain, and fearlessly unmasked the real aims of the despoilers. For virtue, learning and missionary zeal he ranks with the most brilliant of his predecessors.

FRAY NARCISO DURAN (1776–1846)

B. *PROLOGO*

The most valuable extant document bearing on the Church's music of the California missions is the *prólogo* compiled by Fray Narciso Duran at San Jose Mission in 1813. Unique among documents of its kind, the *prólogo* emphasizes the place that ecclesial music holds in the expression of Christian life and worship. It exemplifies the practical problems that confronted the early friars in teaching the Indians how to sing and otherwise participate in the Church's liturgy.

Father Owen Da Silva, the great Franciscan authority on the subject, contends that beyond providing a marvelous insight into Duran's pedagogical abilities, the *prólogo* serves as "the musical charter of Indian California." After dedicating his work to Saint Joseph, Fray Narciso Duran describes the *prólogo* as a guide to the principal feasts and celebration of the liturgical year. Noting that sacred chant is "more ancient in its origin than the Church herself," Duran explains how "the Church adapted the chant as a principal part of her liturgy from the time of the apostles."

He then briefly outlines the place that sacred chant occupies in the writings of the Church's early fathers, recalling how Saint Paul exhorted the Ephesians to fill themselves with the Holy Spirit by "singing hymns, psalms and spiritual canticles." Throughout the *prólogo*, Duran strove mightily to conform the beat of the chant upon the ear to that of the word upon the heart.

Though not a trained musician, Duran was gifted with a hearing sufficiently delicate to discern the basic tones of hymnology. This he did while admitting to never having been able to understand the theoretical rules of chant.

The friar trained the boys at San Jose Mission according to a set of rules or principles adapted to local needs and capabilities. He carefully avoided taxing their limited retentive faculties with undue memorization. After several months of tedious practice, Duran had brought the singers to the point where they could read and sing whatever notes were plainly written or graphed. Occasionally, the friar would color the notes for easier recognition.

Duran's system called for instrumental accompaniment whenever possible. This allowed the singers to more easily sustain their voices and to observe uniform intervals in their chants. He insisted that the instruments be kept at an unchangeable pitch, tuned to wind instruments like the flute. Eventually Duran developed a formula for transposing all the traditional chants for use by the Indian singers. By thus simplifying the system, Duran achieved a rather professional choir at San Jose within a relatively short span of time.

Once trained for choral work, the Indians continued to utilize their musical expertise throughout their lives. Duran was careful to see that their subsequent employment at the mission enabled them to be available whenever there was need for singing or playing. The complete text of Duran's *prólogo* can be found in *Mission Music of California*, a book published by Warren F. Lewis in 1941.

FRAY NARCISO DURAN (1776–1846)

C. GREATEST MISSION MUSICIAN

Among the most precious relics of colonial days is the Choir Book of Fray Narciso Duran (1776–1846). This "musical charter of Indian California" forms part of the Hubert Howe Bancroft Library at the Berkeley campus of the University of California. It is a large, heavy tome, executed on parchment and bound in calf–skin. "The most valuable document extant on the church music of the California Missions" is encased between half–inch–thick board–covers overlaid with tanned leather. The volume is knitted together with twine and five strips of cowhide. Two pairs of iron clasps serve as fasteners for the cover.

The first six of the 156 pages contain the famous *Prologo ad Lectorem*, wherein Father Duran emphasized the place church music holds in the expression of Christian life and worship by unfolding problems with which the friar musician was confronted, and the methods he employed in resolving the difficulties at hand. In the musical portion of the tome, the square notes are imprinted in large size on the folios of the manuscript—easily readable at some distance. Notes are written on single staffs of five lines in four different colors. White notes outlined in red indicate the part for the first voice or instrument; white notes outlined in black, for the contralto; solid red notes, for the tenor; and solid black notes, for the bass. In his system of teaching music to the neophytes, Duran explained that he did away with a diversity of clefs and used solely the clef of F flat, a method enabling the Indians to read notes and sing by themselves whatever is plainly written.

It is known from other sources that Duran had a secret system for calling attention to false notes occurring during the *Gloria* or *Credo* at Mass. The Indians were told "to watch his hands resting on his knees as he sat in the sanctuary during those two portions of the

Mass, and that if they saw him raise his forefinger, it was to be a signal to them that some musician had blundered on a note."

That Duran's music was effective is testified to by Alfred Robinson, who recorded that at Mission San Jose "the music was well executed, for it had been practiced daily for more than two months under the supervision of Father Narciso Duran. The number of musicians was about thirty; the instruments performed upon were violins, flutes, trumpets, and drums." Though in the *Prologo* he admits having no special musical training, Father Duran was naturally gifted with a highly acute appreciation for tone variance. The genial choirmaster could detect a discordant note instantly–much to the amusement of his well–trained singers.

While other of the early missionaries may have been better informed about musical theory, no friar labored more indefatigably with choirs and orchestras than this outstanding friar from Catalonia, and no one achieved better results. Narciso Duran's carefully prepared parchment, compiled at San Jose in 1813, remains the most complete collection of mission music, and his *Prologo* to the book is without question the most valuable musical testament from Spanish days.

FRAY TOMAS ELEUTERIO ESTÉNAGA (1790–1847)

No history of Los Angeles would be complete without a biographical sketch of Fray Tomas Eleuterio Estenaga (1790–1847) who administered the sacraments to the earliest residents of *El Pueblo de Nuestra Señora de los Angeles.*

Born at Anzuola, Vizcaya, Spain, Tomas entered the Order of Friars Minor in the Province of Cantabria. He came to the New World in 1810 and was ordained at San Fernando College in Mexico City. Estenaga journeyed to Alta California in 1820, where he was described by Mariano Payeras as "manifesting a spirit of religion and prudence, sufficiently apt for the ministry, but in poor health."

After laboring a few months at San Carlos Borromeo, he went to San Miguel and then on to Mission Dolores. Records indicate that Fray Tomas looked after San Rafael Mission in the early 1830s.

When the British Navy's Captain Frederick W. Beechey visited San Francisco in 1826, he noted that he had been hospitably welcomed by Estenaga who supplied him with horses for his men free of charge. He found the friar to be a man of genuine humor and an affable friend. Later, Auguste Duhaut–Cilly met Estenaga who received him "with great demonstrations of friendship." He related that the friar was glad to hear

news from Spain, to which Californians no longer owed allegiance.

In 1833, Estenaga was assigned to San Gabriel Mission, where he was to serve for the final fourteen years of his life. By that time, secularization had begun and Fray Tomas found it difficult dealing with the problems unleashed by those who treated him like an ill–paid state servant.

During his years at San Gabriel, Estenaga also cared for the native Americans in and around San Bernardino *Estancia*, as well as the *Asistencia de Nuestra Señora de los Angeles*. During the years 1837 to 1843, the friar was the only priest in what would become the metropolis of Los Angeles.

In his many journeys to San Bernardino, Estenaga customarily travelled in a horse–drawn buggy, something that few other missionaries in California had done. It was part of the Franciscan rule that friars walk wherever possible. Estenaga's poor health was a factor, however, and he took advantage of his superior's wishes that he conserve what little strength he had.

From time–to–time, Estenaga officiated at San Fernando and San Juan Capistrano missions. On November 4, 1841 he blessed a cemetery at Los Angeles which had been acquired through subscriptions from local residents.

Estenaga died at San Fernando Mission in 1847 and was buried in the sanctuary of the church near the pulpit. According to Eulalia Perez, an old–time resident at San Gabriel, Estenaga was somewhat tall, thin, quite light in complexion and "very intelligent in the management of what little remained at the mission." She testified that he always treated everyone with much amiability.

There was much tragedy in Estenaga's life. General Mariano Vallejo recalled that Estenaga, who had been in charge of the choir at San Francisco Mission for the centennial celebrations of 1830, was "a young man of medium height, the personification of activity, of jovial disposition, select and varied in his conversation, an excellent and very sincere priest. He had seen a great deal of the war of the Revolution in Spain and was there during the French invasion, when Napoleon I and his brother Joseph tried to appropriate to themselves that privileged land."

FRAY FRANCESCO ANTONIO A FARNESIO (c. 1746)

The *Real Patronato de las Indias* was a concession granted by the popes, whereby Spanish monarchs provided for the temporal maintenance of religious activities in the New World. It was based on a succession of papal bulls, the most important of which was *Universalis Ecclesiae* of 1508.

Among the many royal prerogatives associated with the *Patronato Real* was that of nominating to ecclesiastical offices and benefices. Through the method of "presentation," the king could and did directly name all such personages, from archbishops to sacristans. Philip II, for example, sent to the Indies 2,682 religious and 376 clerics during his reign. Yet it can readily be seen how the Church, in many areas, was virtually absorbed in and became a part of governmental machinery.

One example of this "enslavement" of the Church centers about Fray Francesco Antonio a Farnesio, an Italian friar who arrived at Monterey, on the *Concepcion*, enroute from China via the Philippines, in the later part of December, 1804. The fifty–eight year old Farnesio had labored for a number of years as a missionary in the Far East, until he was forced, for reasons of health, to seek a milder climate. From Monterey, Farnesio proceeded to Mission La Purisima Concepcion, where he

was cordially welcomed and given permission to offer Holy Mass and perform limited other ecclesial functions.

Evidently Farnesio was unaware of the provisions of the *Patronato Real* which controlled the sending of missionaries to Spanish overseas possessions. In any event, he liked California and shortly after his arrival at La Purisima, he wrote to Fray Estévan Tápis, the *Presidente* of the Missions, for authorization to remain in the jurisdiction on a permanent basis.

On January 7, 1805, Fray Tápis wrote his Italian confrere that he would gladly grant him the customary facilities, if the matter were his to decide. However, the *Presidente* pointed out that only priests sent to California by "our Catholic Spanish King" could be approved for the priestly ministry. Nonetheless, Tápis obligingly forwarded the request to the Guardian of the Apostolic College of San Fernando, in Mexico City. The latter, in turn, presented the matter to the viceroy for formal consideration. The decision of the viceroy, acting in the name of the king, was negative, and on June 10, 1805, he notified Tápis that Farnesio should continue on to Italy.

The Franciscan *Presidente* informed Farnesio of the ruling, noting that his earlier appointment from the Sacred Congregation of Propagana Fide, as a missionary to China, could not be interpreted as a license to pursue the ministry in California. Shortly after receiving the *Presidente's* reply, along with provisions from the Franciscan procurator in Mexico, Farnesio made arrangements to leave for Europe. He departed from San Diego, on the *Princesa*, November 6, 1 1805.

Francesco Antonio a Farnesio was only one of the missionaries lost to the Church in California through the *Patronato Real*. With due allowance for the benefits of royal patronage, it was always a grave source of potential and real danger to the freedom of religion for God's people in early California.

FRAY PEDRO FONT (1738–1781)

The diary kept of the expedition led by Juan Bautista de Anza from the little village of Horcasitas in Sonora to the Great Bay of San Francisco and back again, is one of the most fascinating accounts in Western American annals. Certainly the 3,000 mile journey was an important one for it opened the overland route from Sonora to Monterey and it resulted in the eventual founding of San Francisco.

The original manuscript of the diary is one of the treasures in the John Carter Brown Library at Brown University. It was first published by Herbert E. Bolton in 1930. The author of the diary was Fray Pedro Font (1738–1781) who had been appointed cartographer and diarist of the expedition because of his extensive background in mathematics.

Dr. Bolton said that "few episodes in Western Hemisphere history left a richer legacy of records than the Anza expeditions." And of the various accounts of the expeditions, he awarded the palm to Font. "Of all the chronicles," he wrote, "Father Font was the master . . . he wrote a superb diary, one of the best in all western history."

Readers of the diary must agree with Bolton that Font was both a remarkable narrator and an outstanding man. In character, he was typical of the best of his Order who shared in the making of California—consecrated, self–sacrificing, sincere, militant in the cause of righteousness, humble before God, but insistent that people should respect his office as a priest.

He walked unafraid among dangers, living always in the presence of the unseen, consumed by passionate devotion and loyalty to the faith which he preached and professed.

Because of his mathematical training, Font was able to calculate latitudes with reasonable accuracy. These accomplishments, coupled with unusual powers of observation and a rare capacity for description, make his diary a valuable guide–book even for the present day. As Bolton remarked in his preface, "Father Font's observations were keen. He had a sharp eye for landmarks, and a canny knack of telling what he saw. His record of distances and directions is so accurate and his description of natural features is so graphic that nothing surprises the explorer of his trail."

He missed nothing and set down everything. He gives the details of the small company of less than 200 persons who began that perilous journey, the number of pack and riding animals, even the contents of the saddle bags. There are anecdotes of meals eaten, conversations spoken, services offered, Indians encountered, games played and marches made. Font was a fastidious man whose personal health was poor. Though he didn't understand the Indians, he wrote well about them and his diary gives some of the clearest accounts of their customs and practices.

The importance of Fray Pedro Font's diary to Californians and others is obvious. You cannot know the story of the Anza expedition unless you've read it. Aside from its importance historically, the volume is worth reading for its sheer narrative interest. Put aside the novels, the truth is far more fascinating.

John Steven McGroarty once concluded an address by saying: "Give me a jug of water, a Franciscan crown rosary and a copy of Pedro Font's diary and leave me alone on a deserted island for a week. I'll return a far better man, physically, spiritually and intellectually."

FRAY FRANCISCO GARCES (1738–1781)

A. PIONEER FRIAR

On May 7, 1939, a statue of Fray Francisco Garces (1738–1781) was unveiled, blessed and dedicated to the memory of the illustrious *padre* of the deserts of California and Arizona. On the same date, in 1776, the friar became the first white person to visit the area now known as Bakersfield.

With voluntary contributions and the aid of funds allocated by the Federal Art project, the statue was erected to commemorate the many accomplishments of Kern County's great pioneer. The statue was carved from Indiana limestone. Standing fifteen feet high, it was erected on a base of carnelian granite, situated in the traffic circle just north of the city of Bakersfield. It was sculpted by John Palo–Kangas.

The figure of Garces, dressed in the grey robes which the friars of that period wore, is considered to be an excellent likeness because it represents him as a man of faith, courage and simplicity. If the youthful appearance of the friar is surprising, it should be remembered that when Garces visited the site of Bakersfield, he was only thirty eight years old. Always an out–of–doorsman, possessed of an excellent physique, he would still have been in the vigor of manhood.

Perhaps the most unique feature of the heroic statue, for it is larger than lifesize and smaller than colossal, is that it represents Garces with the friar's hat which the Franciscans of that era customarily wore. This flat brimmed, fairly large crowned chapeau was similar to the headpiece of the contemporary Spanish dons. Though commonly worn by the friars, whose work took them out and into the heat of the western sun, it is one of the few examples of that headgear in any of the memorials. The staff carried by the missionaries is also shown in the depiction.

At the dedicatory services, Dr. Herbert E. Bolton, Professor of History at the University of California, Berkeley, gave an address in which he eulogized the life and work of Garces. He paid the friar high tribute as a missionary and explorer, unexcelled perhaps in the roll of greats who came from Spain to work among the native American peoples.

And surely Fray Francisco Garces was a notable figure. He was the first recorded white person to see the Kern River, the first priest in the San Joaquin Valley, the trailblazer of the route later used by the Sante Fe railroad between Needles and Los Angeles, the first Spaniard to see the Grand Canyon and the first to open a trail from California to New Mexico.

Besides all these distinctions, he travelled more miles, visited more Indian tribes and made more explorations than any missionary of his period. And he travelled over five thousand miles without military escort, accompanied most of the time by his faithful Indian friend, Sebastian.

Inscribed on the base of his statue in Bakersfield is the following tribute to the valiant friar:

> Francisco Garces (1738–1781). Spanish Franciscan. Padre Garces, seeking a new route between Sonora, Mexico, and Monterey, California, crossed Rio de San Felipe (Kern River, May 7, 1776) at Ranchería San Miguel, now Bakersfield. He brought Christianity to the Indians and on Rio Colorado, his brave life was crowned with martyrdom.

FRAY FRANCISCO GARCES (1738–1781)

B. HERO OF YUMA

Padre Francisco Garcés was born at Morata del Conde, Avagon, on the 12th of April in 1738. From infancy he felt called to the service of God and his fellowmen. He entered the Franciscan Order at the age of fifteen and was ordained priest ten years later. Attached to the Apostolic College of Santa Cruz at Querétaro in Mexico, Garcés asked to be sent to the Indian missions and eventually was assigned to Mission San Xavier del Bac in Arizona.

His first visit to the Yumas was in September of 1771. The tribe impressed Garcés and he wrote that one could learn true humanity, politeness and attention from those gentle people. The Yuma Indians wanted Garcés to set up a mission in their midst similar to the ones in California. The government promised Palma, the Yuma chief, that his request would be answered and two missions were established in October of 1780, under the titles of *Purísima Concepción* and *San Pedro y San Pablo de Bicuñer*.

Unfortunately the foundations were not modeled on their California counterparts since the government's plan provided only a chapel for the settlers where the neophytes were expected to congregate on Sundays and feast days. Although the *padres* protested this arrangement and predicted disaster, the commanding general could not be dissuaded. Hoping for an eventual remedy to the situation, Father Garcés promised the natives that the system would be altered at the earliest opportunity The settlers agitated the already–strained relations by appropriating the best available lands and allowing their horses to graze on the crops of the natives.

On Tuesday, July 18, 1781, an uprising burst out. The women and children in church and the men in the fields were set upon and nearly all killed. Chief Palma seems to have taken no part in the bloody raid, and afterwards gave orders that a search be made for Father Garcés and the "good and innocent" man brought back uninjured. Among the Indians sent out to seek the venerable friar was a renegade from the Nefora tribe. Upon finding Garcés, the traitor incited his followers to murder the priest along with the three other missionaries, Fathers Juan Diaz, Matías Moreno and Juan Barrenecbe.

Such was the "criminal blunder" as Bancroft styles it of Commander General Teodoro De Croix's new way of converting the Indians to the Christian Faith! An official expedition was sent out to punish the guilty natives but it only increased their hostility.

In 1884 Fort Yuma was transferred to the Department of the Interior. Several unsuccessful attempts were made to win over the Indians until finally the Sisters of Saint Joseph took up the work. From that time on conditions improved and a school was soon flourishing. Chief Palma himself ultimately embraced the Faith. At the request of Bishop John J. Cantwell, the Franciscan Fathers resumed their work of looking after the spiritual welfare of the Yuma Indians in 1919, and their efforts in succeeding years have been crowned with success.

A large statue of Padre Francisco Garcés stands in front of Saint Thomas Mission on the Yuma Reservation, and annually thousands of tourists traveling along the transcontinental highway stop to hear the story of Yuma's hero and to pay their tribute of respect to one of the world's great benefactors.

FRAY FRANCISCO GARCES (1738–1791)

C. GARCES MEMORIAL

Over sixty years ago, Father Tiburtius Wand, a German–born Franciscan, conceived the notion of honoring Fray Francisco Garces (1718–1781) with a statue erected at Saint Thomas Indian Mission, Yuma, Arizona. Wand entrusted the sculpting of the statue to Joseph Fleck, a noted artist whose renditions even then were represented on the five continents of the world. The prominent philanthropist, Charles D. Baker, provided the major part of the necessary funding.

An elaborate base fashioned from petrified wood was erected and when the statue was completed, it was shipped from Germany by sea via the Panama Canal to San Pedro and thence by rail to Yuma. A newspaper reporter reflected that Garces' statue came more easily to the New World than the missionary did. With the assistance of heavy hoisting machinery lent by the U.S. Bureau of Reclamation, the statue was moved from the rail car, carried up Mission Hill, and firmly mounted on the prepared base. The formal dedication was scheduled for October 21, 1928.

A crowd of over 3,000 attended the inaugural ceremonies presided over by the Right Reverend John J. Cantwell, Bishop of Los Angeles–San Diego. Among those in attendance were Apache Indians and representatives from the Pima and the Papago tribes. Dr. Frank C. Lockwood of the University of Arizona opened the program with an interesting historical dissertation on the exploring expeditions and missionary activities of Garces and his Franciscan collaborators.

Bishop Juan Navarette of Sonora portrayed Garces as the ideal of missionaries and exhorted his hearers to appreciate and practice the religion of the cross preached by the heroic friar. In his address, Bishop Cantwell contrasted the supernatural motives of faith and charity which actuated the labors of Father Garces with the selfish and material motives so often found in the lives of worldly–minded people. The Yuma Indian Band interspersed the program with such music as the "Star Spangled Banner."

Occupying the highest point on Indian Hill and having Saint Thomas Church and mission tower as a background, the imposing white stone group of the Garces Memorial dominates the entire Yuma Valley and fully merits the admiration it arouses. The seven foot statue of Garces holding aloft a cross is flanked on the one side by a kneeling Indian and on the other by a small angel who lifts up to him the palm of victory. The statue is illumined by flood lights.

The inscription on the bronze plaque affixed to the base of the statue reads as follows:

Born April 12, 1738
Died July 19, 1781
Fray
Hermenegildo Francisco
Garces
Daring Explorer, Zealous
Missionary and Unfailing
Friend of the Yuma Indians
Padre Garces Founded the
Yuma Indian Mission and
Nearby Gave his Life
for their Souls
His Faith was Unshakable
His Hope was Tranquil, His Charity Joyous
His Zeal Triumphant

FRAY FRANCISCO GARCIA DIEGO Y MORENO (1785–1846)

In the summer of 1832, Fray Francisco Garcia Diego, the Commissary–Prefect for the Apostolic College of *Nuestra Señora de Guadalupe*, in Zacatecas, together with nine of his Franciscan confreres, set out for Alta California to replace a portion of the depleted and aged Fernandiño friars.

When the crew of the ship on which they were travel-ling mutinied, at Cape San Lúcas the overly–anxious missionaries rashly decided to proceed northward on foot through the arid Peninsula of Baja California. Fray Garcia Diego hastily realized the "utter ignorance" in the decision of travelling in the desolate wasteland. So discouraged did the *Comisario–Prefecto* become, that he seriously doubted whether he and his companions would "ever get to the missions." Fortunately Governor José Figueroa eventually regained control of the ship, and the friars were able to resume their sea voyage, without further complications, to Monterey.

Some years later, Garcia Diego reflected upon the "providential misfortune" of the Baja California escapade in a long letter to the Metropolitan Chapter of Mexico City. During that time the friar had "dealt with many of its inhabitants, preached to them, heard their confessions" and acquainted himself "with their miseries."

He described the territory as extending for more than four hundred leagues, from the Cape of San Lúcas to Mission San Miguel. In 1832, the entire area was served "by only five Dominicans, stationed at such distances from each other that made it impossible to properly care for the souls of their charges." For that reason, the *Comisario–Prefecto* said that "most of the populace could not hear Mass nor comply with their other spiritual obligations." He reported that "many died without spiritual assistance and never, or at most rarely, did they hear the Word of God."

"Understandably," the friar noted, "they did not comprehend their religious faith and their lives were hardly distinguishable from those of barbarians or savages." There were no schools in the peninsula, except for the one at La Paz, and "its poorly–trained teacher, more harmful than useful, passed along serious errors to his unfortunate pupils." In such a state of affairs, the natives found it "difficult to resist the seductions of dissident and perverse people who live or visit there."

The climate was "quite balmy, even in October, and the temperature reached ninety–eight degrees on most days." Suffering "hunger, lack of food and an insufferable plague of mosquitos," most of the friars fell ill, "some from the fever and others from recurring discomforts which attacked their urinary system."

The friar never returned to the peninsula, even after his episcopal ordination as the proto–Bishop of Both Californias. To provide for the spiritual care of that vast territory, the prelate conferred upon the Dominican *Presidente* the title and prerogatives of Vicar Forane. One need only read about the misfortunes that plagued Fray Garcia Diego and his companions, in 1832, to understand his reluctance to re–enact that "providential misfortune."

FRAY JOSE GASOL (ff. 1800s)

A. THE *PATENTE*

Among the register books associated with the California missions was the *Libro de Patentes* in which communications from church or civil officials were recorded. It was an important book which functioned as a local archive.

Among the items transcribed into the *Libro de Patentes* were directives from royal ministers and viceroys, copies of apostolic briefs, letters from bishops and religious superiors and other materials of a similar nature.

The *Libro de Patentes* also served occasionally as a book of inventories, listing the material possessions of a particular mission. In the volume for Santa Barbara Mission are annual reports covering the years 1787 to 1835. Spiritualities were also enumerated, including the number of baptisms, marriages and deaths for each year, along with such mundanities as the quantity of buildings, livestock and harvest.

The only complete *Libro de Patentes* are those for Missions Santa Barbara and San Luis Rey. Those for other missions are either missing or incomplete. In the Santa Barbara Mission Archives are partial books from San Carlos Borromeo, San Juan Bautista, San Antonio, San Luis Obispo and Nuestra Señora de la Soledad.

In a recent issue of *The Americas*, Father Francis Guest reproduced an annotated copy of a letter sent by Fray Jose Gasol, the Franciscan guardian, to the missionaries of Alta California on October 1, 1806. The text of that directive is important because it exemplifies the type of document that constituted the typical *Libro de Patentes*. Among the many items treated by Gasol about mission government are suggestions about the conduct expected from the friars, directives for liturgical ceremonies and the importance of catechetical training.

Other things mentioned are the administration of the sacraments, work schedules for neophytes, punishment of the Indians, observance of religious poverty, business dealings with smugglers and journeys from one mission to another. Fray Jose Gasol also carefully instructed the missionaries about expenses incurred in travelling, annual spiritual exercises for the friars, transferal from one post to another and the use of firearms.

At the end of the lengthy letter, Gasol directed that "the original text be circulated throughout all the missions. And, in each one, after the contents have been read, let the substance of it be entered into the Book of official communications (*Libro de Patentes*) and after this letter has reached the last of the ministers, let him certify that it has been read and copied. It will then be returned by the last of the ministers to the Reverend Father President. And he will notify me that all have been informed of it."

The final two pages of the manuscript confirm that, at each mission, the official letter of the guardian to the friars was indeed dutifully read and transcribed. That the administration of the California missions followed a carefully prescribed format is evident from even a cursory glance at any copy of the *Libro de Patentes*.

FRAY JOSE GASOL (ff. 1800s)

B. SMUGGLERS

Reading letters and other documentary sources of yesteryears can be a fascinating and challenging experience and one which often involves considerable insight and interpretation. An example would be the *patente* or official communication sent to the missionaries of Alta California by Fray Jose Gasol, Guardian of the Apostolic College of San Fernando, on October 1, 1806.

In paragraph #10 of that lengthy *patente*, Gasol remonstrates with the friars for their failures in observing the vow of poverty. In particular, he was upset with "the use of silver watches" which he felt were not in keeping with the rule of Saint Francis of Assissi.

He directed that "those who have silver watches or other expensive articles for personal use" immediately send them to the *Presidente* who would have their value applied to the respective missions. What is more intriguing than the possession and use of the watches is how those *relojes de plata* got to California in the first place. Certainly, the friars did not bring them from the Apostolic College of San Fernando in Mexico City.

The strongest clue is a subsequent paragraph of the *patente* wherein Gasol reminds the friars that "no one, neither of himself nor through the interposition of another, is to have any dealing with smugglers!" Though stopping short of making any direct accusations, Gasol obviously knew or suspected that the Alta Californians were engaging in business dealings with American, English or French ship captains along the coast.

It was a violation of Spanish law for subjects of the king, even in remote areas like California, to trade with foreign vessels. But Gasol also realized that the arrival of regular supply ships from San Blas had been infrequent and would ultimately cease altogether. The friars knew that laws of their very nature are designed to promote the common good, but in that distant outpost of the empire, much of the mercantilistic code was impractical or even unjust.

Father Francis Guest, the distinguished Franciscan historian, has noted that "the Spanish civil code made provisions for legislation that was no longer applicable by allowing the subject to observe the principle which stated: "I obey but I do not execute."

In circumstances when supplies were unobtainable

from any other source, "natural rights took precedence over civil legislation" and hence the friars, because of physical necessity, could justifiably trade with foreign vessels. Theologians have always taught that there are some laws which the lawgiver did not intend to be binding in conscience but which are regarded as obligatory insofar as the sanction is concerned. Those are called "penal" laws.

So, if Gasol considered smuggling by the missionaries only a penal law, why did he forbid them to engage in such practices? He answered the question himself: "In order to avoid the reprimand that the college would have to suffer from the Most Excellent Lord Viceroy," should he find out.

FRAY JOSE GODIOL (1829–1902)

Fray José Godiol (also spelled Godayol) was born at Vich, in the Province of Catalonia, on January 16, 1829. Early in his life he met and was befriended by a young Dominican, Joseph Sadoc Alemany, who later became Archbishop of San Francisco. It was at the behest of Alemany, that Godiol decided to do missionary work in Alta California. After completing the classical and philosophical studies in his native town, José and two other clerical candidates left for the New World.

On July 23, 1854, it became Godiol's distinction to be the first novice to receive the Franciscan habit in California, with his installation as a lay brother in the Order of Friars Minor. And with that ceremony, the College of Our Lady of Sorrows was declared solemnly and canonically established "amid the joy and edification of those assembled, the ringing of bells, the discharge of cannon and muskets, followed by other festive demonstrations." Six years later, on August 15, 1860, Fray José Godiol was ordained to the priesthood by Archbishop Alemany. He was subsequently affiliated with the Sacred Heart Province when the west coast friars joined their counterparts in the eastern United States.

The first thirty–five years of his ministry were spent as professor and procurator at the *Colegio Franciscano*, Santa Barbara. There he helped in the training of many young men whose names later became prominent in the historical annals.

In an interview with the editor of *The Monitor*, in 1901, Godiol noted that at the time of his arrival at Santa Barbara, the surrounding country was all pasture land, under the control of the mission, as far as the eye could reach. "Near the mission was a village of 400 Indians, living in adobe houses, arranged on streets with considerable regularity. This was the only congregation. Farther down were the Spanish dons, to whom Santa Barbara points with proud historic finger—the Ortegas,

De la Guerras and Carrillos, and others of like wealth and distinction."

During his years at the mission, Padre José, as he was widely known, laid out and opened the street through the property owned by the friars. Water from the mountains was brought through the ancient stone aqueducts for five miles and into the big reservoirs. The fountain in front of the mission was always running and there was water enough for everyone,

One chronicler notes that Fray José Godiol did not restrict himself to Santa Barbara Mission in those years. He was responsible for building the little church at Montecito, where he frequently journeyed for Mass. After his departure from Santa Barbara, Father Godiol spent a dozen or so years at Saint Francis Orphanage near Watsonville. There too he spent much of his time in outlying villages administering the sacraments.

"The last of the Spanish friars" died at Santa Barbara Mission on October 30, 1902. He was buried in the vault of the Old Mission cemetery along with the remains of Fray José Maria de Jesús González Rúbio, and the other Franciscan giants of the early Provincial era.

FRAY FRANCISCO GONZALEZ DE IBARRA (1804–1875)

In an article appearing in *The Popular Science Monthly*, for August of 1890, Henry W. Henshaw doubted "if a purer and more devoted set of men ever labored for the good of the heathen than the early missionaries of California." One of those early friars was Francisco González de Ibarra (1804–1875), who spent twenty–two years of his priestly life ministering to the neophytes of Missions San Fernando, San Luis Rey and Santa Barbara.

Born at Viana, in the Spanish Province of Navarre, González de Ibarra journeyed to Mexico, in 1819, arriving the following year in California. During the subsequent decade and a half he served the Indian population at Mission San Fernando. He was an efficient and dedicated friar and throughout his tenure at the seventeenth of California's missions, Father González de Ibarra managed to bring a measure of prosperity to that extended district.

It is recorded in the annals how the friar's activities on behalf of the neophytes won for him the nickname of "*Padre* Napoleon" for his tendency to boast and insist on the superiority of everything at San Fernando. Another source states that the outspoken missionary, though not an unpopular man even among those whom he derided, was known "for the independent style in which he criticized the acts of the authorities in secularizing the mission and disposing of its lands." The intolerable conditions imposed on San Fernando eventually frustrated Father González de Ibarra and, in 1835, he returned to Mexico in utter disgust.

Upon his return to California four years later, Father González de Ibarra was assigned to Mission San Luis Rey. There, Eugene Duflot de Mofras recorded, the friar was "compelled to sit at the table of the administrator and to endure the rudeness of cowboys and *mayordomos*, who a few years before esteemed themselves happy if they could enter the service of the friars as common servants."

Francisco González de Ibarra was a "witty and merry" man whose concern for the material necessities of the neophytes was hardly less obvious than that he exhibited for their spiritual welfare. Alfred Robinson described the business–like *padre* as a short, thick, ugly–looking old man, whose looks did not belie his character. The reputation of the friar among those for whom he labored speaks for itself. Hubert Howe Bancroft declared that "he was well liked by the Indians for his sunny disposition and plain, unassuming manners, which latter trait won for him the affectionate title of *Tequedeuma*."

Father González de Ibarra was a typical friar in many ways. What has been said about his Franciscan confreres by such openly hostile writers as Frances Fuller Victor can be predicated of him:

> The spectacle of a small number of men, some of whom certainly were men of ability and scholarship, exiling themselves from their kind, to spend their lives in contact with a race whom it was impossible in a life–time to bring anywhere near their level, excites our sympathy and commendation.

FRAY JOSE MARIA DE JESUS GONZALEZ RUBIO (1804–1875)

A. Refusal of Bishopric

Though the peninsula of Baja California remained within the geographical confines of the Diocese of Monterey, the government of General Mariano Arista, which came to power in early 1851, categorically refused to recognize Bishop Joseph Sadoc Alemany's episcopal jurisdiction there. When an appeal was made to Rome for a separate ecclesial district, officials at the Sacred Congregation of Propaganda Fide replied that such a move would depend on Mexican assurances of financial support previously promised, but never given, to the larger Diocese of Both Californias.

Meanwhile Bishop Joseph Sadoc Alemany made the conciliatory gesture of offering faculties to any priest designated for work in the peninsula by the Archbishop of Mexico City. The prelate went a step further, and, in December, 1852, demanded and obtained from the Holy See guarantees that the area would be severed from his diocese. Shortly thereafter, the bishop approached Father José Maria de Jesús González Rubio with a direct offer of the Baja California apostolate.

González Rubio (1804–1875) a Franciscan attached to the Apostolic College of *Nuestra Señora de Guadalupe*, had labored in California since 1833. He had served as Administrator for the Diocese of Both Californias in the years after Bishop Francisco Garcia Diego's death and was described as "an enlightened, zealous and educated man" and one whom "all the clergy are fond of."

The Metropolitan Chapter at Mexico City also wanted the friar to assume spiritual leadership in Baja California and put his name forward as their official candidate to Rome. Fray González Rubio was "advised that his name had been sent to Rome as vicar apostolic of Lower California *cum ordine episcopabili*." Not long afterwards, a journalist for the *New York Freeman's Journal and Catholic Register* reported to readers that it had been "stated in one of the papers that the Very Rev. *Padre* González had been appointed Bishop of Lower California."

Meanwhile, on December 4, 1852, the Archbishop of Mexico City advised González Rubio that he had been chosen vicar–apostolic of Lower California. Twice he declined the promotion. In reply, the Franciscan friar expressed "great surprise that he who was without merit or aptitude should be chosen for that difficult assignment especially since there were so many worthy and capable men, both secular and religious, in Mexico, who could fill the position." Neither his physical strength nor his moral powers measured up to the assignment, he wrote. He thanked the archbishop for the honor, but declined, asking that another pastor be assigned "to lead Lower California to everlasting life." On March 11, 1853, a second letter arrived from Mexico City urging him to reconsider the appointment to Baja California. He repeated that he was "not the one destined by God for this office."

The delicate matter was finally resolved, on April 17, 1853, when Bishop Joseph Sadoc Alemany received notification from Rome that Peninsula California had been removed from its attachment to Monterey and entrusted to the Metropolitan District of Mexico City, Whatever may have motivated the gentle González Rubio to decline the episcopal appointment, the fact remains that he was an outstanding priest and an exemplary religious. Archbishop Alemany, in a letter to Rome, declared that he had not "seen a man so observant and so venerated in all California for his knowledge, prudence and virtue" as Fray José Maria de Jesús González Rubio.

FRAY JOSE MARIA DE JESUS GONZALEZ RUBIO (1804–1875)

B. KIDNAPPING OF VICAR GENERAL

In the words of one California historian Fray González Rúbio, the last survivor of the California missionaries, was "a man respected and beloved by all from the beginning to the end of his career; one of the few Zacatecanos who in ability, missionary zeal, and purity of life was equal to the Spanish Fernandinos."

González Rúbio arrived in California in 1833, with Fray Francisco Garcia Diego y Moreno, O.F.M., and for the next forty–two years lived a remarkable life of obedience and sacrifice. Chosen as Garcia Diego's secretary when the latter became bishop, Rúbio subsequently became administrator of the vacant diocese and served under two succeeding bishops as Vicar General. Recommended by the Mexican Government for the post of Vicar Apostolic of Baja California, first in 1851 and again in 1853, the humble friar vehemently opposed the appointment. "I humbly supplicate that you will accept my refusal and, at the same time, have pity on Lower California, by giving it a pastor who may lead it to ever-lasting life and thus exonerate me of the fatal risk of being oppressed by such a heavy weight."

For about a decade of his life in California, González Rúbio was pastor at Santa Barbara. It was during his long tenure in that city that his "kidnapping" took place, an event that ranks unique in the state's ecclesiastical annals. On May 6, 1855, Rúbio had been elected Guardian of his college or motherhouse at Zacatecas in Mexico. He immediately notified the college authorities that his removal from Santa Barbara would leave the struggling Diocese of Monterey without a Vicar General and would add considerably to the problems of the local bishop who was desperately short of priests.

The appeal went unheard and so, good religious that he was, González Rúbio made ready to depart for Mexico by steamer. Delegations of every class called at the parish trying to dissuade him from leaving, but "neither pleading, reasoning nor circumstantial remarks, succeeded in altering his insistence on obeying his superiors, lest he give bad example by violating the obedience he so frequently made the subject of his sermons." It was then that the people, seeing that every other method of persuasion had failed, resolutely determined to prevent his departure. When the smoke of the steamer was seen at ten o'clock on the morning of January 22, a large concourse of people was on hand at the beach where a small boat had been sent in for the passengers. Almost a thousand "men and women of every nationality and creed, all moved by instinct and a common desire to detain the respectable gentleman, formed a single body surrounding his carriage."

Just then Don Francisco de la Guerra came up and announced to the startled missionary that the "towns-people were determined to prevent his leaving by every means and it was therefore impossible for him to move another step closer to the ocean." An order was given to the carriage driver and the venerable *padre* was taken back to his parish, "where I discovered that my small traveling equipment had already been returned."

Through the subsequent intervention of Archbishop Joseph Sadoc Alemany of San Francisco, the "kidnapped Vicar General' was allowed by his superiors to remain at Santa Barbara where he happily lived until his death on November 2, 1875. González Rubio was a great churchman, one of the bright lights in "California's Catholic Heritage." One non–Catholic visitor to Santa Barbara had this to say about its pastor: "He was a noble man, a true Christian, very much respected and beloved by his people, and by all who knew him."

FRAY JOSE MARIA DE JESUS GONZALEZ RUBIO (1804–1875)

C. BARBIERI PORTRAIT

Sir George Simpson described Father José Maria de Jesús González Rúbio (1804–1875) as a "truly worthy representative of the early missionaries." Indeed, the humble Franciscan was a man widely known for his piety and learning. For well over a century, a painted depiction of Father González Rúbio, "Santa Barbara's most beloved friar," has hung in the visitor's foyer of California's tenth missionary foundation.

The painting portrays the Guadalajara–born priest as a vigorous man in the prime of life seated at a desk, pausing from writing in a large book. In the lower right corner is lettered the inscription:

> The Most Illustrious Father José María de Jesús González Rúbio of the Franciscan Order, Administrator for the Diocese of Both Californias, which the people of Santa Barbara had painted in testimony of their warm affection and public appreciation and which is to be preserved as a precious memorial of his eminent virtues and as a grateful memory of his unquenchable charity towards the poor and his love for everyone.

The painting was executed by the famous Leonardo Barbieri, who opened a portrait studio at Santa Barbara in 1850. It was paid for by the local citizenry who raised $391.20 in public subscriptions.

In 1906, while being cleaned, the painting was severely damaged and torn. It was subsequently repaired and restored by another Santa Barbara–based artist, Robert Wagner. The tears were patched and an overlay of paint was applied, changing the color of the friar's from a dark gray to the coffee brown shade worn by the Franciscans since 1885. The table and chair in the background also received an overlay of paint.

In recent years the canvas, on public display in the mission foyer, had become dimmed with accumulated grime. Through the intervention of Father Maynard Geiger, the painting was sent to Ventura, in 1971, to be cleaned by F.A. Trevors, a restoration expert, who received his experience in the Uffizzi Galleries of Florence, Italy. Trevors, in restoring the painting to its original brilliance, was able to remove the 1906 overlay and treat the fragile canvas with a preservative synthetic resin to protect it from further deterioration. During the process, he rectified the changes caused by Wagner, more than half a century earlier, and once again Fray José Maria de Jesús González Rúbio became a "grayfriar."

The historic Barbieri painting was then replaced in its place of prominence at the mission where it reminds the countless visitors to Santa Barbara of Father González Rúbio, a friar for whom religion was a golden cord, which ran through every action of his life, endearing him to all, whether Protestant or Catholic.

FRAY JOSE MARIA DE JESUS GONZALEZ RUBIO (1804–1875)

D. SEARCH FOR A BIOGRAPHER

Fray José Maria de Jesús González Rúbio was "a noble man, a true Christian, very much respected and beloved by his people, and by all who knew him." Born in 1804, to José Maria González Rúbio and Manuela Gutiérrez, José spent the earliest years of his life in Guadalajara. He entered the Franciscan College of Zapopan where he was ordained to the priesthood on December 22, 1827. In later years, he transferred to the jurisdiction of the *Colegio de Nuestra Señora de Guadalupe* at Zacatecas.

The young priest came to California in 1833. He was assigned to Mission San Jose where he toiled for the following decade. While there he occupied a host of positions, including those of *Presidente* and *ComisaroPrefecto* of the Zacatecan Missions. George Simpson visited San Jose during Fray González Rúbio's tenure and recorded that the mission there was "in a more perfect state of preservation than almost any similar establishment in the country." From 1842 onwards, this worthy representative of the early missionaries served at Santa Barbara as secretary to Bishop Francisco Garcia Diego, diocesan vicar general, pastor, guardian and professor.

With the death of the bishop, in 1846, Fray González Rúbio became administrator of the vacant Diocese of Both Californias, a post he occupied until 1850. Those were strenuous years. Priests were scarce, the missions had been secularized and thousands of people were pouring into the area in search of fortune. The several pastoral letters he issued indicated his concern for the spiritual welfare of those in the vast diocese.

González Rúbio was vicar general under the two subsequent prelates. During Bishop Alemany's time, the gentle friar declined episcopal appointment at least twice when overtures were made for erection of a separate vicariate apostolic for Baja California. In 1855, González Rúbio was elected guardian of his apostolic college at Zacatecas, a position he avoided only through the strenuous intervention of his long–time friend and supporter, Alemany, by then the Archbishop of San Francisco.

José Maria de Jesús González Rúbio was, according to Hubert Howe Bancroft, "one of the few Zacatecanos who in ability, missionary zeal, and purity of life were equals to the Span. Fernandinos." The selfless Franciscan lived on at Santa Barbara until November 2, 1875, when he slept away, replete "with the fame of uncommon virtues, especially with that of prudence and exquisite tact in governing."

It is stated, in a *History of Santa Barbara County*, published in 1883, that "none knew him but to love the man. Whether in his church or among those of different religions, his face wore the same benevolent, cheerful feeling."

Unquestionably, Fray González Rúbio deserved a biographer. Michael Neri of Seattle has responded to the challenge with an excellent book on the friar whom Father Maynard Geiger says "is the most consistently described by a plethora of witnesses without benefit of collusion, and this throughout his entire public career."

FRAY LUIS JAYME (1740–1775)

One of the brightest chapters in the history of humankind is that which relates the spiritual accomplishments of North America's Franciscan pioneers. And perhaps the most glorious and long–lasting of the many contributions associated with the disciples of Saint Francis is the distinction of having provided the proto–martyrs for Mexico, Canada and the United States. In North America alone, no fewer than 115 friars willingly underwent the supreme sacrifice in a saga of dauntless courage, inspiring heroism and wholehearted devotion unparalleled in ecclesial annals.

The Franciscans were especially lavish in bestowing their blood and virtue on the Church in California. Prominently etched onto the Golden State's martyrology are the names of six outstanding friars whose testimony for Christ is forever a monument to Christian endurance and bravery.

On the eve of the nation's bicentennial, the People of

God gathered at San Diego to honor the memory of Fray Luis Jayme, a cherished member of that Seraphic contingency who affected the initial triumph of religion and civilization in what was to become the thirty–first commonwealth of these United States. It was just two hundred years earlier that the soil of the Pacific Slope was reddened by the blood of that youthful friar.

Sixteen of the Franciscans who carried the banner of Christ along *El Camino Real* hailed from Mallorca, the largest of the Balearic islands, off the Spanish coast. Luis Jayme was one of those who bore in his temperament and exemplified in his demeanor the charm of that picturesque isle which writers have long referred to as the "spiritual god–mother" of California.

Melchor Jayme was born in the tranquil farming village of San Juan, about six miles west of Petra, on October 18, 1740. His earliest schooling was acquired from the local parish priest. When their son reached his fifteenth birthday, the elder Jayme brought him to Petra, the capital city of Mallorca, and enrolled him at the convent school of San Bernardino, where the famed Fray Junípero Serra had earlier studied.

On September 27, 1760, Melchor Jayme was invested with the Franciscan habit, in the *Convento de Santa Maria de los Angeles de Jesús*. Following a year of strict seclusion and rigorous discipline, Jayme solemnly promised to observe the rule of the Friars Minor for the rest of his earthly lifespan. From then onwards, he was known as Fray Luis. The friar made his theological studies at the *Convento de San Francisco*, which then served as the motherhouse for the Franciscan Province of Mallorca. He was ordained to the priesthood on December 22, 1764. Upon completion of his courses, Fray Luis was appointed Lector of Philosophy, a position he occupied at San Francisco from 1765 to 1770.

It was during the year of Spanish penetration into Alta California that Luis Jayme determined to spend his remaining years as a missionary in the New World. He wrote for permission to the Commissary General of the Indies and was assigned to Mexico City's Apostolic College of San Fernando.

After a farewell visit to his native village of San Juan, Fray Luis left Palma early in 1770, for Cádiz. There an official for the Board of Trade provided the only extant description of the friar, recording that he was a "person with well proportioned physique, somewhat thin, and of a darkish complexion." Jayme arrived in New Spain after a long and arduous trans–Atlantic voyage. There he began the special training course wherein soldiers of the Cross were conditioned to the privation, fatigue, mortification and penance encountered on the missionary frontier. Finally, in October, Fray Luis and nine other priests set out for California, where they had volunteered to spend a minimum of ten years in winning over the hearts and souls of the primitive, marginal peoples then inhabiting the outer rim of the Spanish realm.

Jayme was happy when Fray Junípero Serra, the *Presidente* of the California Missions, appointed him to what would be his first and last assignment, San Diego de Alcala. That foundation had special significance for Fray Luis, since that was where it had all begun for Christ in Alta California.

The Yuman Indians at San Diego were the most treacherous and uncooperative of all the tribes in the coastal areas. Generally described with such words as thievish, egocentric and untrustworthy, they consistently provided a formidable challenge to the evangelization endeavors of the Spanish missionaries. A clever and talented friar, Jayme's earliest efforts at San Diego were devoted to mastering the complexities of the local native language. Once he had gained a facility with its vocabulary, he was able to compile a polyglot Christian catechism.

The extreme scarcity of water, combined with the proximity of the military personnel, induced Fray Luis to ask for and receive permission to move the mission from its original site, atop Presidio Hill, to the valley where it is presently situated. The new location proved eminently more practical. Almost immediately there was a notable upsurge in the number of conversions which, by 1775, numbered 431. Such success obviously infuriated the devil who seems to have held the natives in bondage during aboriginal times. In any event, a plan was hatched by a handful of pagan sorcerers and others to rid the area of all traces of Hispanic influence,

At about 1:30, on the brilliantly–lit night of November 4, 1775, 600 or more warriors from some forty *rancherías* silently crept into the mission compound. After quietly plundering the chapel, they set fire to the other buildings. The crackling of flames soon awakened the two missionaries, the guards and the Christian neophytes. Instead of running for shelter to the stockhold, Fray Luis Jayme resolutely walked toward the howling band of natives, uttering the traditional Franciscan greeting: "*Amar a Dios, hijos!*" In a frenzied orgy of cruelty, the Indians seized him, stripped off his garments, shot eighteen arrows into his body and then pulverized his face with clubs and stones.

The attack on the mission was only terminated when a well–aimed shot from a musket unnerved the Indians and caused them to flee in panic. Early the next morning, the body of the thirty–five year old missionary was recovered in the dry bed of a nearby creek. His face was so disfigured that he could only be recognized by the whiteness of his flesh under a thick crust of congealed blood.

The friar's mangled body was initially buried in the *presidio* chapel. When the new church at the mission was completed, it was re–interred in the sanctuary. There it rested until November 12, 1813, when it was transferred to the third and final church. Today the remains of Fray Luis Jayme repose in a common vault between the main and side altar.

The reaction of the Franciscan *Presidente* to the news of his confrere's death speaks volumes about the attitude of the early friars. Far from being saddened or disappointed, Fray Junípero Serra said: "Thanks be to God; now that the terrain has been watered by blood, the conversion of the San Diego Indians will take place." That proved to be a prophetic statement too, for by 1834, the number of Baptisms at the mission reached 6,638.

Little else can be said about Fray Luis Jayme. There is a trinity of physical reminders of the Mallorcan friar: a concrete cross beside the *arroyo* where he died, a stone monument above the city hall of the village where he was born and a painting in the sacristy of the church where he was baptized.

It was only the mortal body of Fray Luis that was consumed in that November massacre two hundred years ago. His spirit and influence were born into eternity on that winter's night. Fray Luis Jayme lives on in the affections of latter–day Californians as a noble pioneer who mortgaged his lifeblood to implant the principles of Christianity into California's landscape.

Through the centuries, martyrs have been regarded as objects of veneration, models of perfection and friends of God. Martyrdom was and is a praiseworthy ideal of dedicated followers of the Nazarene for it is the ultimate proof of love and dedication to the Christian lifestyle.

Yet, two hundred years after the death of California's proto–martyr, those who trek along *El Camino Real* are reminded that death by the shedding of blood is far from being the only way whereby a Christian is transformed into the likeness of the Savior.

FRAY FERMIN FRANCISCO DE LASUEN (1736–1803)

On April 16,1979, Fray Fermin Francisco de Lasuén (1736–1803) returned to San Buenaventura Mission to take up permanent residence, after an absence of 185 years. San Buenaventura was in its infancy when Lasuén assumed direction of the California Missions in 1785, following the death of Fray Junípero Serra. For the next eighteen years, Lasuén's shadow hovered prominently over the spiritual destinies of the "Mission by the Sea."

The Spanish–born friar made his first official visitation as *Presidente* to San Buenaventura in January of 1791, when, on the Feast of the Epiphany, he conferred the Sacrament of Confirmation on 380 persons, nearly all of whom were Indians. He returned the following

June 5th and confirmed another thirty–five candidates. Two years later, in November, Lasuén's name appears once again in the register books. He also came in February, September and November of 1794. His faculty for administering that sacrament, granted by Pope Pius VI, expired the following year.

A kindly and gracious man, Lasuén was considerably more popular than his Mallorcan predecessor. George Vancouver, whom Lasuén met in 1792, at San Carlos Borromeo, was greatly impressed by the *Presidente's* gentle manner, noting that he was fitted "in an eminent degree for presiding over so benevolent an institution" as the California Missions. It was that English seaman who immortalized Lasuén in California nomenclature by bestowing his name on two points in the Bay of San Pedro, Point Fermin and Point Lasuén

Fray Fermin occupied the presidency of the missions for eighteen long and arduous years, during which time he established nine additional frontier outposts along *El Camino Real*. The missions as they are known today date from Lasuén's time. The older buildings were expanded and sturdier ones were erected.

His writings were published in two volumes by the Academy of American Franciscan History in 1965 and, eight years later, Father Francis Guest completed his definitive biography of Fray Fermin Francisco de Lasuén.

The larger–than–life size statue of the friar, which vivifies his memory at San Buenaventura, was fabricated early in 1960 as an adornment for the central administration building of Fermin Lasuen High School, situated on a promontory about two miles from Point Fermin. Fashioned from a monochromatic fibreglass substance, the twelve foot statue was a familiar landmark in Palos Verdes for almost two decades, even after the closing of the seventeen acre campus at the conclusion of the 1971 academic year.

Early in 1979, Timothy Cardinal Manning suggested to the Little Sisters of the Poor, whose new Home for the Aged is located at Palos Verdes, that the statue of Lasuén be given to San Buenaventura Mission. The venerable *Presidente* arrived back in the Poinsettia City late in March. Now firmly affixed to the facade of the old Washington Hotel, *Padre* Lasuen peers down from his anchorage upon visitors to the Old Mission, just as his Franciscan predecessor does barely two blocks away.

FRAY JULIAN DE LESCANSO (ff. 1530s)

Juan Rodriguez Cabrillo became one of the richest landholders and most intrepid adventurers in the New World. Author, slaveholder, shipbuilder and professional soldier, he was also a family man, perhaps even a

religious one. The account of the voyage made to Alta California by Cabrillo in 1542 and 1543, constitutes the written record of human activity along the west coast of the present United States.

When the Spanish viceroy dispatched the armada of three ships from the harbor at Navidad, at high noon on Tuesday, June 27, 1542, the main purpose was "to discover the coast of New Spain." The question of whether there was a priest aboard the flagship, the *San Salvador*, has long been a matter of conjecture among historians. Royal directives normally required a chaplain but, in the absence of the usual log, verification has been impossible until quite recently.

In his recent book on Juan Rodriguez Cabrillo, published by the Huntington Library at San Marino, Dr. Harry Kelsey, an official at the Los Angeles Natural History Museum, reports that an Augustinian monk, Fray Julian de Lescanso, testified in 1547 that he had gone to California with Cabrillo's armada.

A notary of the royal audience of Mexico, Juan León is credited with compiling a narrative of the voyage from interviews with survivors of the armada. His "annoyingly brief" account has been the source for most of what has been written about the trip to Alta Califor-

nia. A synopsis of the Leon report, some of it possibly composed by Fray Julian de Lescanso, is presently in the *Archivo General de Indias*.

From research there and other places in Spain, Dr. Kelsey has found that Fray Julian de Lescanso came to the New World in 1535, arriving at the Port of San Juan de Ulloa a couple of months after Viceroy Antonio Mendoza. His parents, Licenciado Lescanso and Teresa Alvarez Gil, seemingly did not come with him, so the presumption is that the friar was attached to the household of the viceroy or some other official, possibly as chaplain.

The friar claimed to be a native of the *villa de voles tierra del reyno de Toledo ques en los reynos de Castilla*. However, his emigration permit says that his parents came from Socuellamos. Julian de Lescanso was an Augustinian "Mass friar" (*frayle profeso de la orden de Señor san Agustin de esta ciudad de Mexico frayle profeso de rnysa*). In other words, he had been ordained not to preach or otherwise evangelize, but strictly for the purpose of providing the Eucharist for the monks, a practice not uncommon in those times.

On September 28 the Cabrillo sea expedition discovered "a sheltered port . . . to which they gave the name of Saint Michael." This was the first landfall by outsiders in the area that would become Alta California. There is every reason to presume that the chaplain aboard the *San Salvador* would have offered Mass shortly after going ashore. Hence, based on the latest evidence, Fray Julian de Lescanso was the first priest to offer Holy Mass in what is now the State of California, an event that took place on September 18, 1542.

FRAY RAMON LULL (1235–1314)

In his pre–American years, Fray Junípero Serra was Scotistic Professor of Theology at the "Pontifical, Imperial, Royal and Literary University of Mallorca," or more succinctly, the Lullian University. The man for whom that institution was named has never ceased to captivate the minds of Mallorcans.

Born in Palma de Mallorca in 1235, Ramon Lull was the son of one of the island's conquerors. In his youth, he followed the path of a worldly cavalier and became an artist and a musician. His misspent early years were followed by a sudden conversion after which Lull, talented, zealous and energetic, devoted himself to the perfection of his moral life and the spread of Christianity.

To facilitate the conversion of the Moslems, he founded a school for the study of Arabic. He became a writer on a variety of subjects including mathematics, mysticism, navigation, law, warfare and horsemanship. It is conceivable that if it had not been for Blessed Ramon Lull, and the Franciscan vision which he had and typified, there would have been no America as we have come to know it.

After he was almost eighty years old and had spent three score years in toil, Blessed Ramon Lull was stoned, all but to death, at Bougie on the Algerian Coast, where the natives are still stoning missionaries. He was left on the beach half dead. Two merchants from Genoa, who had a ship in port, found him dying and offered to take him by sea to Genoa. Those two Italians had heard about Ramon Lull and recognized him when they found his body on the beach.

They wanted to have his remains in Genoa so, before he had a chance to die, they picked him up and put him aboard their boat. The idea was that he would succumb in Genoa and be interred there. The capricious winds of the Mediterranean drove them instead to Mallorca. During his death agony on the deck of the Genoese ship, the Franciscan missionary asked his two rescuers to lift him up so he could fix his eyes on the horizon.

With his last strength, he pointed out beyond the rail of the ship and said: "Beyond the curve of the sea which washes England, France and Spain, opposite this continent which we see and know and love, there's another contintent which we have never seen, which we don't know. It is a world which is ignorant of Jesus Christ. Send men there." One of the Genoese merchants never forgot those words and he told the story time and time again to his family. His name was Stephen Columbus, the grandfather of Christopher Columbus!

In Serra's time, the relics of Blessed Ramon Lull were enshrined in one of the twenty–three chapels in the church attached to the Monastery of San Francisco, in Palma. Serra had great great devotion to Lull, whose relic he wore about his neck in life and death. Scholarly man that he was, Serra undoubtedly knew about that other "continent" mentioned by Lull. Could it have been in response to Lull's directive to "send men there" that Serra decided to inaugurate his own missionary conquest? And, if so, does that not bind Ramon Lull closely to California's religious heritage?

FRAY ANTONIO PERELLO MORAGUES (1673–1749)

Among the friars who occupied a "vicarious" role in evangelizing Alta California, none is more celebrated or worthy of recalling than Fray Antonio Perello Moragues (1673–1749), a native of Petra.

Perello was a close friend of Fray Junípero Serra and, in fact, clothed Serra in the Franciscan habit in 1730 in his role as Provincial. The funeral oration preached at Perello's funeral was later published with Serra's approbation as canonical and theological censor.

In 1995, a copy of that homily, which had previously belonged to Buenaventura Serra y Ferragut, was acquired by the Santa Barbara Mission Archives. A translation of the now rare treatise appears in Antonine Tibesar's *Writings of Junípero Serra.*

Perello entered the Franciscan Order and went on to become one of the most outstanding members of the Mallorcan province. He obtained doctorates in both philosophy and theology and taught both subjects. He was regent of studies for his province and held the Chair of Scotistic Theology. In addition, he filled various administrative positions in the Order, serving twice as Guardian of San Francisco in Palma and three times as Provincial of the Mallorcan area.

At his death, Perello had spent sixty years in the Franciscans. And he had served as Definitor General for all of Spain, a position in which he exercised influence over all the friars in that country. In his book on Serra, Francisco Torrens quoted extensively the account by Francisco Bordio Tallades about Perello. The following is taken from a translation by Norman Neuerburg.

Perello was "a truly great, generous, wise and holy man without leaving his regular state." He was, "among the sons of this Province (of Mallorca), the one upon whom the most honors were bestowed."

The friar was a very renowned preacher and a consummate theologian in all sorts of dogmatic and moral matters. His manifold talents, "accompanied by a fervent zeal for the greater good of souls, gained for him a great reputation as a wise and holy man of the cloth." Perello had such an attractive manner and such a vivacity and sweetness in his speech that everyone felt great affection for him since the splendor of his manner and conversation had a singular modesty. Not only in Mallorca but in many parts of Spain, Perello was known "for his wisdom and his graciousness" and considered "to be exceptionally highly–qualified" for his role of service to both community and the public.

For all these qualities, Perello "was greatly beloved by all the religious, who admired in him a great mind and a singular inspiration as an administrator. Many monuments testify to Perello's zeal in adorning the House of the Lord and serve to perpetuate his memory, especially in the Friary in Palma.

"Finally, as for all, the end came and, in his last illness, he demonstrated his love for God and the Most Holy Virgin." He asked that he be dressed in his habit to receive the last sacraments.

The account concluded by observing that in his funeral homily, Fray Bartolome Rivera "demonstrated, with singular erudition, the virtues and heroic actions of the deceased." It is that homily that is now preserved in the Santa Barbara Mission Archives.

FRAY FRANCISCO PALOU (1723–1789)

Franciso Palóu was born at Palma de Mallorca on January 22, 1723, the son of Sebastian and Miquela (Amengual) Palóu. He entered the Franciscans in 1739, at the *Convento de Santa Maria de los Angeles.* After studying philosophy and theology under Fray Junípero Serra at San Francisco in Petra, Francisco was ordained to the priesthood in 1743. Six years later, he responded favorably to an invitation by Serra to join the missionary apostolate in New Spain.

At the time of his departure, Palóu's passport indicated that he was "a person of medium height, swarthy in complexion, with dark eyes and hair." It is the only physical description on record. Upon arriving at the Apostolic College of San Fernando, in Mexico City, Palóu volunteered for the missions of the Sierra Gorda and there he worked alongside Serra at *Misión Santiago* for eight years.

He served briefly as *Presidente* of the Sierra Gorda missions and, in 1767, was allowed to join the friars who were going to Peninsular California as replacements for the banished Jesuits. Palóu was assigned to San Francisco Xavier, about twenty–two miles southwest of Loreto. Following Serra's departure for Alta California, Francisco Palóu became *Presidente* of the friars remaining in the peninsula, a position he occupied until 1773,

He later journeyed north and, in Alta California, served as diarist on two expeditions to San Francisco under Captain Fernando Rivera y Moncada. It was Palóu who laid the cornerstone for the present Mission Dolores on April 25, 1782.

Palóu was with Serra when the famed friar died, August 28, 1784. Though he had already been given permission to retire, he remained on as acting *Presidente* until the formal appointment of Fermin Francisco de Lasuén. After Serra's death, Palóu began writing a biography of the "Gray Ox." That volume, published in 1787, enjoys "the double distinction of being the earliest California biography and the best biography of California's most renowned character.'

In 1785, Palóu returned to Mexico City where, contrary to his personal wishes, he was elected Guardian of San Fernando. He died in that office on April 6,1789 and is buried at *Santa Cruz de Querétaro.*

An able missionary and excellent administrator, Palóu is best remembered as California's first historian and biographer. His *Noticias de la Nueva California* was the first general history ever written of Alta California.

Professor Herbert Eugene Bolton once said that had the University of California bestowed a degree upon Francisco Palóu it would have read:

> Fray Francisco Palóu, diligent student, devout Christian, loyal disciple, tireless traveller, zealous missionary, firm defender of the faith, resourceful pioneer, successful mission builder, able administrator and fair–minded historian of California.

FRAY PABLO JOSE DE MUGARTEGUI (1736–1804)

Through the course of seventy–nine years, 142 friars spent 2,269 man years to bring into the Christian fold and the ambient of Hispanic civilization nearly 100,000 aborigines. They also looked after the spiritual needs of the Spaniards and Mexicans attached to or living in the *presidios, pueblos* and *ranchos* of Alta California.

In 1959, Ignacio Omaechevarnia published a biography of one of those distinguished friars. Entitled *Fray Pablo Jose de Mugartegui en su Marco Social y Misionero,* the 333 page book was issued by *Selecciones Graficas* of Madrid.

The son of Pedro and Maria (de Ormoza) Mugartegui was born at Marquina, Spain, in October of 1736. He became a Franciscan at Bilbao in 1757 and several years later a professor of theology. A member of the Franciscan Province of Cantabria, Pablo came to the New World in 1769. At that time it was recorded that he had "a good physique, a large face and dark brown hair." He was one of thirty–nine friars who arrived at San Fernando Apostolic College during the tenure of Fray Rafael Verger.

Mugartegui was assigned to accompany Fray Junípero Serra back to Alta California following the *Presidente's* visit to Mexico City in 1773. He travelled with Serra in a coach to Guadalajara and then aboard the *Nueva Galicia* for the rest of the journey. Enroute the youthful priest became seriously ill and had to stay behind in San Diego.

Fray Pablo Mugartegui was assigned to Missions San Antonio, San Luis Obispo and San Juan Capistrano. In the latter post he acted as co–founder with Fray Gregorio Amurrio. Mugartegui served at San Juan Capistrano Mission until his retirement to Mexico in 1789

When Fray Fermin Francisco de Lasuen was named *Presidente* of the missions, Mugartegui was appointed second–in–charge of the southern missions from Santa Barbara to San Diego, a jurisdictional innovation. At the same time he was designated to assume the presidency in the event of Lasuen's death.

After his return to Mexico City, Mugartegui was elected Guardian of San Fernando Apostolic College, a position he occupied for the traditional three years. Later he became professor of philosophy and theology for seminarians then living at the college. He was made Visitor–General of his own college in 1795, a rare and unusual distinction. Three years later, he asked for and was given permission to return to his homeland, where he became *custos* for the Province of the Holy Gospel.

On July 17, 1802, the friar petitioned for re–affiliation with San Fernando Apostolic College. He returned there and lived quietly until his demise on October 21, 1804. Because of his early association with Serra and his experience as a missionary at three of the outposts along *El Camino Real*, Fray Pablo Mugartegui was uniquely qualified for the administrative positions he subsequently occupied in Mexico City and elsewhere.

When Mugartegui served in Alta California, it was considered by soldier and missionary alike as "the last corner of the earth." Never would the area be as primitive or rugged as it was in the 1770s. It was a distinct advantage to have Mugartegui at the helm in Mexico City during many of those pioneering days.

For a host of reasons, few of the accomplishments of the early friars were ever recorded. It is indeed fortunate that Fray Pablo de Mugartegui's labors along *El Camino Real* have been chronicled for the edification of later generations.

FRAY MARIANO PAYERAS (1769–1823)

A. *PRESIDENTE* OF MISSIONS

California and Mariano Payeras (1769–1823) entered the recorded annals the same year that brought Spain to the bold step of extending its Pacific Coast holdings hundreds of miles to the north. Born at Inca, on the isle of Mallorca, Payeras's life spanned the history of the region from its founding to just beyond its final curtain as effected by proclamation of the new Mexican republic.

After arriving in the province in 1796, Payeras spent some years at Carmel, Soledad and San Antonio. In the fall of 1804, he was transferred to *La Purisima Concepcion* where, except for a short while in 1819, he remained for the rest of his life. Payeras was serving at Purisima when the mission was virtually destroyed by the major earthquake of 1812. The church collapsed, the other buildings fell down and most of their contents were ruined. With the consent of all involved, the friar sought and gained permission to relocate the foundation to a more suitable place three and a half miles away.

Named fifth *Presidente* in 1814, Mariano Payeras was initially charged with looking after the purely internal affairs of the missions. Later, he also was made *Comisario Prefecto* as well as vicar forane for the Bishop of Sonora which gave him full ecclesial authority in the area. He proved to be a superb administrator both spiritually and temporally

Though the native population at the missions did not decline markedly during the decades of his service in Alta California, it was clear to Payeras that the census could only be sustained by importing Indians from elsewhere. With that in mind, he suggested and championed the notion of extending the missions into the internal regions, especially Central California. Payeras established *vistas* and *asistencias* at Pala and San Bernardino but, because of a dearth of clergy, his expansionary plans were never fully implemented.

Payeras deserves to be remembered by Angelenos for it was he who coordinated a building program for the parochial church on *Nuestra Señora de los Angeles*. In addition to raising the funds necessary for erecting the area's proto–house of worship, the friar arranged to have Indian laborers from several of the missions work for builder Jose Antonio Ramirez until the edifice was completed. Payeras thus became the "patron of the pioneer church" in what was to become the west's largest city.

With the recent publication of his writings, Payeras joins three of his predecessor *Presidentes*, Junípero Serra, Fermin Francisco de Lasuen and Jose Señan whose writings are accessible to researchers. Hopefully, the making available of such resources will eventually assuage the antagonistic and erroneous views of those whose interpretation of mission times is based more on sentiment and bias than on documentation and fact.

The magnificent collection of letters, carefully translated and expertly annotated by the emeritus professor of Southwest History at the University of New Mexico, has been published by Bellerophon Books for the Academy of American Franciscan History. The writings reveal the Mallorcan as a hard–working and conscientious friar. Though neither a scholarly nor deeply theological thinker, Payeras was a pragmatic leader whose writings indicate a conscientious concern for the rights, privileges and responsibilities of both his Franciscan collaborators and the natives under their tutelage. No less an authority than Hubert Howe Bancroft is on record saying that "there was no friar of better and more evenly balanced ability in the province" than Mariano Payeras. Surely this collection of writings substantiates Bancroft's observation.

FRAY MARIANO PAYERAS (1769–1823)

B. TOMB

A number of the more astute visitors to Missions La Purísima Concepción and Santa Barbara have long wondered about the seeming "bi–location" of Fray Mariano Payeras (1769–1823) who appears, from tombstone markers, to have been buried at both institutions. The Mallorcan–born friar, a popular man on account of his affable manners, kindness of heart and unselfish devotion to the welfare of others, died on April 28, 1823. Entry No. 2197 in the Purísima register book states that he was given ecclesiastical burial in the mission church, after having died "with religious and exemplary edification to the Fathers as well as for the *gente de razón* and the neophytes."

For many years it was presumed that the one–time *Presidente* of the California missions had succumbed at Purísima and, for one reason or another, was later moved to Santa Barbara. That viewpoint was sustained by a careful study of the Franciscan chronicles which revealed that the Payeras vault, at Santa Barbara, had been opened, in August, 1911. On top of a small wooden box containing some bones and a bottle was the incription: "*De ossibus Rev. Patris Mariani Payeras, O.F.M.*" An entry in the *Libro de Difuntos* states that Father Payeras "*restos* were transferred to this Mission of Santa Barbara by Rev. Father Francisco Sánchez."

During the excavation and reconstruction of Mission La Purísima Concepción by engineers of the United States Government, the workers came upon a skeleton in the sanctuary. They contacted Church officials for permission to open the vault and identify the remains. On July 27, 1936, the tomb, located at right angles to the communion railing, was unearthed and the bones identified as belonging to a non–Indian male, with precisely the pathological and anatomical conditions predicated of Fray Mariano Payeras.

According to testimony of the scholarly Maynard Geiger:

> One of our first impressions on seeing the skeleton was that it was surely a friar. The arm bones were crossed, just in the manner in which a friar is buried, his arms in his habit sleeves. It was pointed out in the course of the ensuing conversation that only one of higher standing or of unusual rank would be given the honor of burial in the sanctuary. So the skeleton was that either of a friar or of some official. But the position of the arms, as well as the total absence of any metal remains, buttons, etc., again seemed to exclude any official, soldier or officer, and again pointed to a friar.

Pathological study and other convincing evidence confirmed Geiger's impressions and indicated that the unearthed remains at Purísima were, in fact, those of Mariano Payeras.

Once the place of interment had been determined, however, the question of Payeras' purported entombment at Santa Barbara had to be resolved. Most likely, only a portion of the remains were moved to the Channel City by Fray Francisco Sánchez. Undoubtedly, the term *restos* can be understood as "relics" or partial remains. Just what may have motivated Sánchez to move the *restos* is not clear, though it may have been out of deference to Payeras' position as *Presidente* or his widely known reputation as a man of virtues, good qualities, talent and energy.

The apparent contradiction between the burial register of Purísima and the tombstone at Santa Barbara presents an interesting, if baffling side–light to the story of California's missionary foundations. Whatever be the precise explanation for the friar's post–mortal peregrinations, he would surely endorse the plea of Saint Thomas More: "Pray for me, as I will for thee, that we may merrily meet in heaven."

FRAY TOMAS DE LA PEÑA SARAVIA (1743–1806)

Tomas de la Peña Saravia (1743–1806) a native of Burgos, Spain, became a Franciscan in 1762. He volunteered for missionary work and left for the New World in 1769, the year that Fray Junípero Serra arrived in San Diego.

After working in the peninsula, Peña came to Alta California in 1772. He served as chaplain aboard the *Santiago*, during which time he kept a log of that ship's voyages.

Accusations of impropriety against the clergy are not peculiar to the 1990s. In 1786, Fray Tomas, then stationed at Santa Clara, was formally charged with having struck and killed two Indians attached to the mission. The confused manner in which the case was resolved reflects its unusual nature.

Governor Pedro Fages appointed a military officer to investigate the matter and to take the necessary testimony. In a departure from the normal procedures, the governor himself conducted an additional inquiry of several witnesses.

The two hearings were held in April and May. The friar had not been incarcerated and the governor neglected to inform Fray Fermin Francisco de Lasuen about the charges. It was several weeks before word of the matter reached the *Presidente* of the missions.

Lasuen immediately delegated an ecclesial court to look into the charges. In his final report, Lasuen not only declared the innocence of Peña, but strongly criticized the governor for conducting proceedings outside a canonical forum, a clear violation of the *Recopilacion de leyes de Indias*. Both the governor and the *Presidente* communicated the results of their investigation to the *comandante general* of the Internal Provinces and there matters remained for about four years.

The evidence was contradictory and ultimately the *comandante* determined that although Peña was innocent, it would be prudent to remove him from California, a recommendation passed along to the viceroy.

For his part, the viceroy ordered a fourth hearing and appointed two neutral parties to hear the evidence. One was the commander of the *presidio* at San Diego and the other a Dominican missionary from peninsular California.

At this fourth hearing, held at Santa Clara Mission in July of 1793, Peña was completely exonerated. In 1795, nine years after the original accusation, the viceroy declared the friar innocent. It had been a long, drawn–out affair, unusual both for its nature and for the procedures used to deal with the accusation.

Subsequent discoveries indicate that the charges originated with a local official whom Peña had reprimanded for misbehavior. On January 2, Fages wrote that Peña "comes out innocent of the calumny, with his credit and reputation clear." A soldier attached to the mission, Joaquin de Castro, frequently accompanied the friar on his journeys and he declared that "he had noticed nothing but a love for them (Indians) that was too trustful, an extreme good humor, and a degree of patience and courtesy that was unusual."

Even Hubert Howe Bancroft, no lover of the friars, defended Peña. Though he described him as "hot tempered and occasionally harsh," he said he was "innocent of the charges to which the Indian witnesses had falsely testified."

Fray Tomas later interceded with authorities to mitigate the punishment of his accuser, who was released after issuing a public apology. The friar subsequently left California, arriving back at San Fernando College in Mexico City where he served as counselor and, for a period, was procurator for the California missions.

FRAY MIGUEL DE PETRA (1741–1903)

Fray Miguel de Petra is classified by historians as "among the most famous men that Petra de Mallorca gave to the world." He had the added distinction of being the nephew of Fray Junípero Serra. The son of Juana Maria, Serra's only sister (husband of Miguel Robot), he was born on January 11, 1741. Miguel was only a small boy when his distinguished uncle sailed for the New World in 1749.

Miguel made his primary studies at the Franciscan Convent of San Bernardino in Petra and then took his course in rhetoric under the Jesuit scholar, Juan Reines. Wishing to become a priest and religious, he sought the religious habit from the Minims at the convent of San Francisco de Paula, but was refused because of his extraordinarily small stature.

In this he resembled his famous uncle who also was judged as too short when he applied for entry into the Franciscans. Miguel then applied to the Capuchins and was given the habit on October 15, 1757, at the age of sixteen. After studying philosophy, Miguel devoted himself to mathematics and drawing. So proficient did he become in those two disciplines that he was named a member of the *Sociedad Economica Mallorquina*. He

was the first in his convent to teach experimental philosophy after the plan of Raymond Lull.

Versed in the complexities of architecture, Miguel drew the plans and then directed the construction for the convent of the Capuchins at Palma, arranging therein a museum of antiquities and natural history. He also is remembered for enriching the contents of the convent's library.

Miguel was ordained to the priesthood on March 2, 1765. Shortly thereafter, he travelled to Madrid where he was able to obtain grants from King Charles III. He was also given the royal title of "*gran matematico.*"

Fray Miguel de Petra must have been a man of varied talents and interests, if one is to judge by the type of writings he left behind. They comprise books and learned articles on history, philosophy, mathematics, theology, homiletics, geography, drawing, architecture and even sundials. In him too were the instincts of the historian, archivist and librarian. He gathered and saved what valuable things had been written by or concerning his uncle and, in 1790, these were placed in the archives of the Capuchin monastery at Palma. They were discovered by Fray Francisco Torrens y Nicolau, great grandnephew of Serra, in the 19th and early 20th century.

Two of the most touching letters retained by Fray Miguel were written by Junípero Serra from the Apostolic College of San Fernando In Mexico City. One is dated September 29, 1758 and the other August 4, 1773.

Torrens published these materials in his *Bosquejo Historico del Insigne Franciscano V.P.F. Junípero Serra Fundador y Apostol de la California Septentrional* in 1913, the bicentenary of Serra's birth. Father Eugene Sugranes, C.M.F., then stationed at the Plaza Church of *Nuestra Señora de los Angeles*, translated much of the *Bosquejo* into masterful English for readers of *The Tidings*.

Fray Miguel de Petra died on February 11, 1803. His portrait is prominently displayed in the Sala de Sesiones in Palma de Mallorca.

The Capuchin friar is still influencing the cause of history and, when his famed uncle is canonized he will have aided the cause considerably by his own writings and research.

FRAY ANTONIO PEYRI (1769–1832)

In the very year of California's penetration by white men, there was born, in faraway Catalonia, one who was destined to play an important role in the area's growth and development. Antonio Peyri aligned himself with the Franciscan Order at Reus, on October 21, 1787. He was sent to study at Escornalbu and, later, at Gerona, where he was ordained priest on March 16, 1793

Two years later, Antonio was one of the twenty friars who sailed from Cadiz for missionary work in New Spain. He paused briefly at the Apostolic College of San Fernando, in Mexico City, and then journeyed on to San Francisco, arriving there on June 18, 1796.

Fray Antonio served for a short time at San Luis Obispo. He was afterwards designated by the Franciscan *Presidente*, Fermín Francisco de Lasuén, to found the eighteenth of the California missions, under the patronage of San Luis, Rey de Francia. For the rest of his years in California, Peyrí was associated with that missionary outpost. In addition to caring for the mission itself, he also looked after the *ranchos* of San Juan, Santa Margarita, San Jacinto and Las Flores. He was closely identified with the *Asistencia de San Antonio de Pala*.

In a report for 1820, Fray Mariano Payeras noted that Peyrí's "merit is distinguished as founder and builder of a beautiful mission in the spiritual and temporal matters which it enjoys." Described by Eulalia Pérez as "very amiable and endearing," Fray Antonio is credited as having erected and successfully managed the largest and most populous Indian mission in both Americas.

During his tenure at San Luis, Rey de Francia, Fray Antonio Peyrí hosted such historically prominent personages as Alfred Robinson and James Ohio Pattie. Auguste Duhaut–Cilly recorded that on his visit to the mission, in 1827, he was greeted with "affability and politeness" by the friar. Failing health induced the friar to leave California, in 1832. He took with him two prospective seminarians to Rome and then sought vainly to find a medical respite for his deteriorating physical condition.

The Franciscan chronicler, Father Zephyrin Engelhardt, regarded Peyrí as a zealous friar and the "most practical of the missionaries." Indeed, the fact that he was able to build up the mission from a brush hut to the largest establishment in California tends to support that assertion. At the time of Peyrí's departure, 2,189 Christianized natives were attached to the mission. Since 1798, 5,295 Indians had received the Sacrament of Baptism. The temporal growth was even more phenomenal. By the end of 1831, there were 26,000 head of cattle and 25,000 head of sheep!

The friar was unable to return, as he had hoped, but his mark had already been indelibly placed on the California scene. Alexander Forbes quite accurately prophetized that "this worthy man . . . will live long in the memory of the inhabitants of California."

FRAY ANDRES QUINTANA (1777–1812)

Father Andrés Quintana (1777–1812) was described by Governor Pablo Vicente de Sola as "a very pious missionary" whose compliance with the duties of his ministry brought about his premature death. The circumstances of the Spanish–born friar's demise were discovered only some years afterwards. On the evening of October 12, 1812, Father Quintana was roused from his sleep at Mission Santa Cruz by a feigned sick call. Showing the "innate kindness credited to him," the missionary, not wishing to disturb the guard, went alone to the reportedly–ill victim.

When he was a distance from the Mission, the Indians attacked him and "dispatched him in a most revolting and diabolical manner." After his death, the remains were secretly returned to his quarters, where it was made to appear that he died of natural causes. The following morning, he was found dead in his cell, with the holy oils and the Blessed Sacrament clasped to his breast. A contemporary account of how Father Andrés met his death was recorded by Nasario Galindo, in a manuscript later published by the California Historical Society:

> The Indians led the priest to the orchard, where they suddenly seized him and hung him. So that no one would know the manner of his death, they took the body to his room, they put him in his bed, covering him with a blanket, and locked the door of his room.

Two years later, an old Indian neophyte of the mission confided on his deathbed that "the good *Padre*, having been summoned in the dead of night to a dying Indian, had been treacherously murdered under a tree." The remains of Father Andrés were disinterred and Dr. Manuel Quixano conducted the first recorded autopsy ever performed in California. The surgeon discovered that the missionary had been so revoltingly murdered that the details were kept from public disclosure.

Fray Narciso Durán later spoke of "the horrible assassination" to a Franciscan confrere. Noting that Quintana had been murdered in a torturous manner Durán doubted "if such cruelty has ever been resorted to in the most barbarous nations." Eight Indians were arrested and questioned. They acknowledged their guilt, alleging as their motive that Father Andrés had treated them cruelly by punishing them with the lash.

Governor Sola looked into the methods of punishment at Santa Cruz and ascertained "that this good Father went to excess, not in punishing his Indians but in the love with which he regarded them." The governor further stated that Quintana "strained all his faculties as far as zeal and industry carried him in order to improve and advance them. He distinguished himself among many for the solicitude and tenderness of his paternal care to relieve his neophytes of whatever savored of troublesome vexation."

In 1885, when excavations were being made for a new church at Santa Cruz, the remains of the slain priest were unearthed and reburied in a stone vault. The name of Father Andrés Quintana is perpetually enshrined there as one of the missionary heroes of Santa Cruz and all of California.

FRAY FRANCISCO SANCHEZ (1813–1884)

The accomplishments of Francisco Sánchez in provincial California were immortalized by Helen Hunt Jackson, who portrayed the friar as Father Salvadierra in her famous novel, *Ramona*. The personage of the humble priest was no less edifying in real life. Born in August, 1813, at León in the State of Guanajuato, Mexico, Francisco had originally studied for the diocesan ministry at Morelia.

In February, 1837, he applied for admission to and was accepted in the Franciscan College of *Nuestra Señora de Guadalupe*, Zacatecas. He completed his theological studies and was ordained to the priesthood in 1838, by Bishop Diego Aranda y Carpintero of Guadalajara.

During the earliest years of his ministry, Sánchez was assigned to the teaching staff at Zacatecas. A popular and forceful speaker, he also gave numerous parochial missions in the territories then served by the Apostolic College.

Sánchez was one of the few who answered the call of Bishop Francisco Garcia Diego y Moreno for clerical recruits to serve in the newly–created Diocese of Both Californias. He journeyed with the prelate to the area, where he was named to the faculty of the nascent diocesan seminary. He lived at Santa Barbara with Bishop Garcia Diego until 1844, when separate quarters for the seminary were provided at Santa Inés. Sánchez served as Vice Rector of the institution and professor of Philosophy and Latin.

On April 20, 1854, Sánchez was called as a witness before the United States Land Commission concerning the ownership of mission properties. His testimony before that forum figured prominently in the ultimate decision confirming the claims of Bishop Joseph Sadoc Alemany for the Diocese of Monterey. In subsequent years, Sanchez traversed all of California preaching missions to the Indians, Mexicans and *paisanos*. Though he never learned to speak English fluently, he was a favorite of the Americans who began flocking into the area during and after the gold rush days.

The Franciscan chronicler relates how the zealous and indefatigable friar hunted out the "lost sheep" in the mountains and *ranchos*, inducing them to make their peace with God. "He possessed a special gift for making the men confess their sins wherever he found them. If he met one on the road (he always traveled in his habit, barefoot and alone), Fray Sánchez would insist that the poor fellow make his confession right there and then."

Many years after his death, other priests could experience the influence of good Sánchez's ministrations; for the penitents, on being asked when they had last received the Sacraments, would answer, "when Fr. Sánchez was here." The Zacatecano friar served briefly at Missions San Buenaventura, San Gabriel and Santa Barbara. In later years, with the establishment of Our Lady of Sorrows College, he was novice master and professor. A deeply–pious and mortified friar, Sánchez communicated his own spirit to the novices and all others with whom he came in contact.

In 1874 and 1875, Sánchez was attached to Saint Francis Orphanage and the Parish of the Immaculate Heart, in the Pajaro Valley. The exemplary *padre* succumbed at Mission Santa Barbara, on April 17, 1884. Two days later, the *Daily Independent* stated editorially that

> His virtues as a priest, religious and missionary, are well known throughout the State, especially his ardent Christian piety and zeal for the good of souls for whom he never spared either labor or fatigue.

FRAY JUAN SANCHO (1772–1830)

Only one of the recent histories of music in America mentions the music of the Spanish colonists in Alta California. "Is it possible." asks William John Summers, Associate Professor of Music at Dartmouth College, that "these recent publications share an unvoiced racial, political or perhaps even an anti–Roman Catholic bias?"

Even if this disregard for such a large part of American history is unintentional, one can hardly ignore the obvious indifference that typifies the euro–centrism found in accounts of "American" music written prior to 1945. In a paper delivered at Madrid in April of 1992, Summers took a preliminary step toward reversing this pattern of silence and neglect.

Of particular interest to Summers was a collection of music manuscripts, prepared by and brought to Alta California from Mallorca in 1804 by Fray Juan Bautista Sancho (1772–1830) which long ago disappeared from the Stanford University Library. Only a few transcribed excerpts and a small number of photographic plates of selected leaves from Sancho's manuscripts survived at the Santa Barbara Mission Archives.

Providentially Summers discovered photostatic copies of Sancho's original manuscripts in the California Folk Music Archives of the Works' Progress Administration which are housed in the Music Library at the University of California, Berkeley.

Made sometime prior to 1942, the copies had gone unnoticed for many years. While the polyphony in Sancho's manuscripts cannot be considered folk music, the inclusion of his manuscripts in the original WPA filming project proved to be a most pleasant development.

All but four of the fifty–two polyphonic compositions in the collection have never been described or discussed in scholarly literature. The materials consists of approximately 145 pages with varying measurements. Assembled by Sancho while he was a choir director in the *Convento de San Francisco* in Palma de Mallorca, they are variously dated from 1795 to 1797.

Sancho arrived in Alta California in August of 1804 and spent his entire missionary career at San Antonio de Padua, where he died at the age of fifty eight. His music served as the foundation of that mission's musical programs from 1804 to 1846.

The Sancho manuscripts are truly significant. They constitute the largest single body of polyphony that can be associated with a particular individual and a single mission church. It was the very first collection of its kind brought to California.

Sancho's music was a personal, working collection. None of the pages appears to have been sewn together in book form. Their size and shapes suggest that they were intended to be portable. Without question, the friar was a musician of considerable competence who had been systematically trained in music. He carefully and methodically recorded a great deal of polyphonic music which he believed would be useful in his priestly ministry.

The Sancho materials alone confirm that the Spanish musical heritage in the United States must be recognized as a vibrant and integral part of the artistic legacy of North America, a musical patrimony that can be embraced with pride by scholars on both sides of the Atlantic Ocean.

FRAY VICENTE DE SANTA MARIA (1742–1806)

Fray Vicente de Santa Maria (1742–1806) one of California's more outstanding missionary personages, was warmhearted and impetuous, two qualities that often occur together and sometimes make for difficulties with prescriptive authority. The Spanish–born Franciscan journeyed to the New World, in 1769, where he became attached to the Apostolic College of San Fernando in Mexico City. He served briefly in Peninsular California, at Loreto and San Xavier prior to the replacement of the friars by the Order of Preachers.

In 1774, Santa Maria was appointed chaplain for the *San Carlos*, which sailed to California under the command of Juan Bautista de Ayala and won the distinction of being the first Spanish ship to pass through the Golden Gate. The party remained anchored in the bay for forty days before returning to Monterey. At the request of Junípero Serra, *Presidente* of the Missions,

Fray Vicente de Santa Maria remained in California, where he served at San Diego, San Francisco, San Antonio and San Buenaventura.

The friar's friendly and generous nature deeply impressed Captain George Vancouver who regretted "the short time I was to be indulged with the society of a gentleman whose observations through life and general knowledge of mankind rendered him a most pleasing and instructive companion." On November 24, 1793, the British seaman named one of the points at the extremity of San Pedro Bay for Padre Vicente. The designation appeared for the first time on Eugene Duflot de Mofras' map of 1844.

The friar's most enduring literary contribution was the journal or "catalogue of trials" which he carefully kept while chaplain aboard the *San Carlos*. Long the object of search by historians, the elusive manuscript was recently discovered and published by John Galvin. The 130–page treatise, an enthralling record of discoveries, "exhibits the talent, industry and pertinacity of a careful observer."

Fray Vicente wrote solidly, with a glint of humor, about the Indians whose antics greatly amused him, His telling of how a native mimicked his manner of praying is a "rarity in the soberness" of Hispanic colonial literature. An earnest reporter of what he observed, Fray Vicente's reflections belie his friendly and generous nature. His journal is crammed with human interest rather than descriptions of the shapes and colors of a new land or the earthly pleasures of fresh adventure.

He was evidently captivated by the natives, welcoming them aboard the ship and returning with them to their dwellings. His examples of Indian languages, descriptions about their clothing and commentaries on their way of life, adornment and behavior provide valuable insights into native culture. The recent publication of Vicente de Santa María's journal enshrines at least one facet of the multi–talented friar. He has left such an enduring presence to later generations that a wanderer on the quiet shores of Angel Island can almost hear, from round some rocky corner, an echo of his voice in the *Alabado* "to an accompaniment of Indian rattles.

FRAY JOSE FRANCISCO SEÑAN (1760–1823)

A. MODEL MISSIONARY

José Francisco Señan was born at Barcelona in the Province of Catalonia on March 31, 1760. He was admitted to the Franciscan novitiate early in 1774, and ordained ten years later. Almost immediately after his ordination, Father Señan arrived at Mexico City and three years later came to Mission San Carlos Borromeo at Carmel to begin his California apostolate.

Señan's early years were routine enough and by the middle of the 1790s the missionary was given a sabbatical in the Mexican capital. After a brief respite from his labors, Señan returned to where he spent the next quarter century. In 1812 he was elected *Presidente* of the California Missions, a position he held intermittently until his death. Most of Señan's life centered around the gentle and civilized Chumash Indians, probably the most advanced people on the entire California coastline. They were exceptionally responsive to his labors and were, for the most part, excellent Catholics.

The Letters of Jose Señan recently translated and published by Leslie Byrd Simpson, reveal "the endless and appalling amount of housekeeping a missionary had to do" in colonial days: planting, harvesting, cultivating of the crops; breeding and slaughtering the cattle, sheep and hogs; handing out tallow and lard and packing it in skins; making soap; shearing the sheep; carding and bailing hemp and wool; weaving blankets, dressing hides and otter pelts; marketing the mission produce; keeping the account books and overlooking the general welfare of the entire community were routine duties. All of these things were above and beyond the heavy spiritual cares of the missionaries which included teaching the neophytes; baptizing, marrying and burying, them; nursing the sick and chastising the poorly behaved; staging festivals; preaching sermons and celebrating Holy Mass.

While admittedly a humble and scholarly friar, Señan never excelled as an administrator; however, though he intensely disliked exercising the authority of his office, his terms as *Presidente* were tolerably well–managed. A great enemy of apathy, Señan had little time for those who would neglect the California missions. His sharp words to the stay–at–homes were more than obvious. "Fortunate are they who can sit apart in some little corner, telling their fat beads and calmly saying their prayers, while in fact this sad world produces nothing but hardship and bitterness!"

The Commissary General of the Indies directed Señan to write a history of the California missions in 1818, but, even though the aging *Presidente* believed that "the suggestions of one's superiors should be looked upon as commands and accepted as such in all the humility befitting one's station," he was unable to comply with the request because of the other duties of his office. Señan went home to God on August 24, 1823, the last of the pre–1790 friars to die. Bancroft comments that "he was a model missionary . . . always ready to respond to the frequent calls of his confreres for advice."

FRAY JOSE FRANCISCO SEÑAN (1760–1823)

B. HISTORIAN

In his provocative essay on "The California Background," John D. Hicks defines history as the "record of human experience. Its purpose is to explain the present, and to enable us to make intelligent judgments on the shaping of the future." Of all the California missionaries, Fray José Francisco de Paula Señan (1760–1823) fulfilled most perfectly the portrait of a historian sketched by Lord Bryce, who maintained that the highest kind of research demanded "unwearied diligence in investigation, a penetrating judgment which can fasten on the more essential points, an imagination which can vivify the past and that power over language which we call style."

Recognizing that "only a few are capable of the concentration and endless labor implied in successful research," Father Buenaventura Bestard, Commissary General of the Indies, directed Señan, in 1818, "to write a history of the California missions." The Franciscan chronicler, Zephyrin Engelhardt, later remarked that it was not known what progress he made, if any, on that task.

That Señan's historical abilities were recognized is evident from other sources. On December 31, 1820, Fray Mariano Payeras reported his view that the friar was "very capable of compiling a historical narrative of these missions, at which he is already working by direction of the Most Rev. Commissary General."

Fray Vicente Francisco de Sarría also considered Señan especially qualified "to write the history of the California missions and urged him to do so." It would seem that he declined on the grounds that such a commission would seriously interfere with his spiritual and temporal work at San Buenaventura.

The Barcelona–born friar did compile a thirty–seven page handbook of questions and answers concerning the commandments and precepts for use with his Chumash natives. Representing the oldest extant text for any California language, it illustrates the social and material culture of a group of Mission Indians about whom little is known and less has been published. In 1967, that work was translated and edited by Madison E. Beeler and published by the University of California Press as *The Ventureño Confesionario of José Señan, O.F.M.*

A scholarly man with a remarkably retentive memory, the fourth *Presidente* of the California Missions wrote a detailed account of the customs and habits of the Ventureño Chumash in response to an 1815 questionnaire from the Spanish Government. Though similar reports were made by other missionaries, Señan's account is longer and more detailed than any of the others.

The letters written by the humble and self–effacing

priest were gathered, edited and published, in 1962, by the distinguished Western Americana historian, Lesley Byrd Simpson. The neatly–written letters, translated by Paul D. Nathan, are an astonishingly vivid portrayal of missionary activities in California.

José Señán was one who recognized the folly of becoming a prisoner of contemporary pressures. He would have fully endorsed the sentiment so forcefully spelled out in the 1968 Statement by the National Conference of Catholic Bishops to the effect that "our continuity with Christ and the apostolic age survives all the changing patterns of the past and yet presupposes a continuing relationship with the perennial elements of our religious past." One can only lament that Fray José Señán did not write that history of the missions for which he was so eminently qualified by talent, experience and disposition.

PRAY JUNÍPERO SERRA (1713–1784)

A. *IN VINO VERITAS*

There is an old Latin dictum in ascetical theology that says "*bonum est diffusivum sui*", or goodness spreads itself all over. It is always interesting to trace the effects of goodness, especially in a secularistic society. An outstanding example of this principle is the influence of Blessed Junípero Serra, a friar who probably touches the lives of more people in the 1990s than he did when he first walked along California's *Camino Real*.

Pick up the telephone directory for any of California's large cities. Serra's name will be seen adorning a pharmacy, a shopping mall, numerous schools, a myriad of highways, streets, roads and alleys, a laundry, a "liberty" ship, a printing shop and a stamp store.

Statistically, it is easier to become a canonized saint in the Roman Catholic Church than to appear on a stamp issued by the U.S. Postal Service. Yet, within a few months in 1985, Fray Junípero Serra achieved the harder of those goals and made notable progress on the other.

Most recently, the grey–robed friar has taken to the bottle! On July 24, 1984, while in the only bar in the tiny village of Petra de Mallorca, Serra's birthplace, I spotted a wine bottle on a back shelf with a very artistic label bearing the name "Fray Junípero."

A closer examination revealed that it was a "*vino de mesa*" (table wine) bottled locally by Miguel Oliver Juan. Measuring 13% in alcoholic content, it had been released to the market under governmental permit R.E. 3025–PM.

Portrayed on the label is the artistic tower of the *Convento de San Bernardino,* a Franciscan monastery located just a few hundred yards from Serra's birthplace. There the youthful Serra learned Gregorian chant in

what is regarded as the "pearl of all the churches of the province." Some months later, someone sent a label from another wine, this one distilled in Mexico by Vinos Pedro Domecq. It also bore the name "Fray Junípero," though there appears to be no connection between the two products.

The Mexican version, a *vino blanco* or white wine, comes from the *Valle de Calafia* in Peninsular California. With an alcohol content of 10% it is distributed under license number 125631 "B". At the top of the label, Serra is portrayed wearing his Franciscan *sombrero*, holding a bunch of grapes in his right and a farmer's hoe in the left. To the rear of the scene is the massive facade of a church, somewhat reminiscent of the one at Santa Barbara Mission in Alta California.

On the verso side of the bottle is a 3 X 2 1/4 inch secondary label which reads in Spanish: "This pleasant white wine recalls Baja California where the Franciscans, guided by Fray Junípero Serra (1713–1784) founded various missions. Produced in an area where the making of wine has reached great importance. This wine was made especially for you by La Casa Domecq".

Though this writer is anything but an expert on viniculture, he suspects that Blessed Junípero Serra is one of the few ecclesial figures in history for whom two brands of wine were named. Featuring Blessed Junípero Serra on wine labels of two separate continents, 216 years after his demise, says a lot about the friar's enduring influence and popularity among peoples of all races and creeds. All of which confirms the ancient dictum that *bonus est diffusivum sui!*

FRAY JUNÍPERO SERRA (1713–1784)

B. SERRA IN MALLORCA

Fr Junípero Serra, Mallorca–Mexico–Sierra Gorda–

Californias is the title of a magnificently–printed and tastefully–bound book issued by the Cultural Commission for the Isle of Mallorca, to commemorate the quint-centenary of European presence in the New World. This collection of eighteen essays about Fray Junípero Serra (1713–1784) is profusely illustrated by eighty–two color and twenty–seven black and white photographs, many of them never before published and all of them of superb quality.

Authored by Bartolome Font Obrador and translated from Spanish and Catalan by Norman Neuerburg, the 190 page book is a product of the prestigious Mallorcan firm of Graficas Miramar. In his Foreward to the book, Commission President Pilar Ferrer points out that, as one of the outstanding Mallorcans in the New World, Fray Junípero Serra has left the indelible imprint "of his name and his work on every river and stream, every mountain and pathway along the Pacific Coast." Beyond that, the friar imported a "new accent and a new style to the direction of colonization . . . one saturated by the evangelical spirit identified with the hearts of Mallorca's country people."

Following an introductory enumeration of dates in Serra's life, along with an outline of the major events occurring during those years, the author selects fourteen topics around which to build his narrative. Though there are no factual surprises or additions to the existing record, the presentations are attractively presented and carefully documented.

Two chapters are of special interest. One about Our Lady of Guadalupe, the "Empress of the Americas," and the other on "The Missionary's Doctrine." Serra's long devotion to the "Dark Virgin," which dated from his youth on his native isle, is dramatized by his visit to the famous shrine at Tepeyac on December 31, 1749, the very afternoon of his arrival in the capital of New Spain–after travelling 500 kilometers on foot from the Port of Vera Cruz. Serra was especially anxious to celebrate the first Mass of the New Year at the altar of Guadalupe because, as he wrote in his diary, "I am the only one among the clergy who was not seasick and while the others were almost dead, I never really noticed I was at sea."

The chapter on "The Missionary's Doctrine" would be more accurately entitled "The Missionary's Manual" for it explains the relevance of the *Itinerario para Parrochos de la India*, the handbook or manual written by *Alonso de la Peña Montenegro*, on which Serra and his collaborators based their missionary work among the native Americans of Central Mexico and the Californias.

Happily, several long translated excerpts from the *Itinerario* are reproduced in this book, including those dealing with forced baptisms (which were considered null and void) and punishment of the Indians (which was restricted to the secular realm). This truly attractive and informative tome belongs in every serious collection of Western Americana.

FRAY JUNÍPERO SERRA (1713–1784)

C. SERRA IN MISSION HILLS

Surely no person in California's historical annals has been more portrayed in statuary, paintings, windows or even postage stamps than Fray Junípero Serra, the humble Mallorcan friar who brought Christianity to the Pacific Slope. The most recent depiction of Serra is the one blessed on November 8th 1992, on the grounds of San Fernando Mission by Father Noel Francis Moholy, the Vice Postulator of the Serra Cause.

Commissioned by William H. Hannon in memory of his mother, the striking statue at Mission Hills was designed and sculpted in bronze by the talented Sacramento artist, Dale Smith. George Wharton James, a Methodist and the author of many superb books on California, considered Serra among the outstanding pioneers of all time. He dedicated a chapter to the friar in his book on the *Heroes of California*. His sentiments were hauntingly present to this writer as he watched the blessing of Serra's statue:

While admitting that "there are some things about this great and good man that do not appeal to me as they do to those of his own faith," James "extolled the spirit of *Padre* Serra" saying that "in many respects I bow my soul in reverence before him." James affirmed that he had written "honestly and truthfully what I feel in regard to his self–abnegation, his self–discipline (and) his historic pioneering."

In these days of material progress, and with our whole nation regarding the acquisition of riches as the clearest proof of success, it seems to me that it is well for our youth to look closely into the lives of those men who constructed the foundations upon which our State is built.

Serra was a very simple–hearted man, yet in three special realms he claims the reverent attention of the youth of the State of which he was the first and greatest of a large army of pioneers.

Serra dared to do the thing that appealed to the very highest in his nature. He dared to fling himself in absolute and perfect trust upon God. He had but one aim—to serve God in blessing the savages to whom he asked to be sent. He dared to be free!

It is hard for us of today to realize what it meant for Serra to come to California. He left congenial work, devoted associates, loving friends, honor, applause, fame and advancement in the eyes of men, to bury himself in the unexplored wilds of a new country.

In his own land, he had been one of the most popular and appreciated preachers, honored and beloved. Here, the best that can be said is that he received the half ador-ing reverence of a part of the ignorant, though rudely affectionate, aborigines to whom he came to minister, while the remainder bore him open hostility and bitter hatred.

Even those who gave him their allegiance did not have the faintest comprehension of what he was endeav-oring to do for them, and he had to humor their whims and caprices, their prejudices and superstitions, as a mother humors her petulant and self–willed child.

Here was a pioneer, indeed, in that he had no home to come to. His home had to be in his own soul. In one sense, he had not where to lay his head, for there were no homes—in the way in which we use the word—in the land to which he came.

There were only the rude, open, wicker–work or tule shacks of the aborigines, full of filth and vermin, and foul with the accumulated odors of the uncleanness of many seasons. The hard but hospitable bosom of Mother Earth became his pallet; like Jacob, he used a stone for a pillow; the open air was his coverlet, and the ineffable blue of the sky, pictured with moon, planets, stars and Milky Way, his ceiling; the howling of coy-otes, the wild shriek of the panther, the growl of the grizzly, the hoot of the owl, the soft cooing of the morn-ing dove and all the queer, soothing, startling, conflict-ing night sounds of trees, shrubs, insects, birds and beasts became the varied orchestra that sang him to sleep, or quickened his waking hours,

FRAY JUNÍPERO SERRA (1713–1784)

D. SERRA ON WILSHIRE BOULEVARD

One of the most artistic and beautiful houses–of–worship in Los Angeles is an Italian Gothic church located on Wilshire Boulevard at Plymouth. It is one of the most photographed ecclesial structures in the United States.

Forming a sort of frieze along three sides of the church, high up on the walls below the ceiling is a long list of names considered famous by the builder and selected to represent those who have best served their confreres in religion, learning and service.

Among that select number is Saint Francis. There is also a window dedicated to the seraphic saint, whom the official book of the church describes as "a saint revered in all branches of the Christian Church. Certain it is that no follower of the Christ has ever shown greater devo-tion to God and humankind than the gentle founder of the Franciscan Friars." And Dante, Michelangelo, Columbus, Magellan, Copernicus, Gutenberg, Galileo and Pasteur are also there, Catholics all, some of them tertiaries of one or the other Franciscan Orders.

An examination of the church's architecture reveals further Franciscan themes. The facade is inspired by the Church of Saint Francis in Brescia, Italy; the pulpit is a replica from the church of Saint Francis at Viterbo and the altar closely resembles the one dedicated to Saint Clare in the basilica at Assisi.

While all these bring Franciscanism to a focial point within and without the church, the anomaly is that this beautiful building is NOT Franciscan, not even Catholic. It belongs to the Wilshire United Methodist Church.

The late Father Maynard J. Geiger was deeply impressed when he visited the church in 1945. Here was his reaction: "Built to seat 1400 persons, the church could be used for Catholic services on short notice. All it needs is a tabernacle on the altar." The Franciscan histo-rian, reflecting the mood of those pre–ecumenical times, suggested that "the secular and heretical personages commemorated, of course, would have to be removed, and a few statues erected."

Today's resourceful visitor could discover something even more fascinating. This magnificent church is the only non–Catholic edifice in Los Angeles having a win-dow dedicated to Fray Junípero Serra! The Methodists anticipated Serra's beatification by half a century.

The window is situated to the left near the chancel. It is fabricated of colored or stained glass with a Gothic point. It is beside two others bearing likenesses of Shakespeare and one of the voyagers on the *Mayflower*. Serra is attired in a brown (instead of gray) habit. He is standing, blessing an Indian who kneels at his feet, rem-iniscent of a scene from the *Mission Play*. Above are inscribed the words: "The memory of him will never depart away," a sentiment applied to Serra by Fray Fran-cisco Palou in his *Vida*. Below are the words: "To John Steven McGroarty who enkindled our devotion to Junípero Serra."

Next time you are driving out Wilshire Boulevard, stop at Plymouth and check the historic chunk of rock after which the street is named. It reads: "In memory of noble men and women having received from Pilgrim Fathers the faith in religion and learning." Then take a tour of the beautiful church. Before the window of Fray Junípero Serra, say a prayer that the Mallorcan friar might use his influence to restore unity to the Christian family.

FRAY JUNÍPERO SERRA (1713–1784)

E. MOUNT JUNÍPERO SERRA

In his monumental and classic life of Fray Junípero Serra, the late Maynard Geiger said that "in a sense Serra attained a certain immortality in memory. His fame has grown since his death, particularly since 1849. Monuments to him line his *Camino Real* from Petra to San Francisco."

Truly this humble Mallorcan friar who was so vital in life has projected his influence from the grave. His name has been bestowed upon buildings, ships, museums, highways, license plates and on and on. There is even a mountain that bears his mark.

Early in 1907, Lilly Reichling Dyer, founder of the Native Daughters of the Golden West, launched a campaign throughout the State to have one of California's mountains named for Junípero Serra. Chosen for that distinction was the highest peak, of the Santa Lucia mountains, a majestic eminence within view of the picturesque San Antonio de Padua Mission.

Mrs. Dyer introduced a resolution before the Grand Parlor to acknowledge "the life work and extraordinary achievements of Fray Junípero Serra in the exploration of the unknown territory which afterwards became the State of California." The proposal was enthusiastically endorsed and forwarded on to the United States Department of Commerce and Labor in Washington, D.C., Mrs. Dyer saw to it that others also were informed of her campaign. Letters of support were acquired from prominent people in every strata of anxiety throughout the nation, including President Theodore Roosevelt and members of his cabinet.

The well–known scientist, George Davidson, wrote a most favorable recommendation: "In that remarkable range over–hanging the Pacific for fifty miles, are peaks which are landfalls of our navigators and they were familiar to the early fathers. The name of Junípero Serra upon one of these coast peaks that barred the expeditions of 1769 and 1770 will be a living designation, appealed to every day by the mariner and traveler."

Harry Gannett, chairman of the United States Board on Geographic Names wrote from Washington:

> The Santa Lucia peak is the highest summit in the Santa Lucia Range, forty miles southeast of Monterey, in the midst of the scenes of the Father's labors. It is probably the highest peak in the coast ranges south of San Francisco and has an altitude of very nearly 6,000 feet. How appropriate to have it named for Serra.

The Secretary of the Geographic Board, C. S. Sloane, subsequently informed Mrs. Dyer and other members of the Native Daughters that "at the last meeting of the United States Geographic Board, the name of Junípero Serra was established for the name of the peak in the Santa Lucia Range formerly known as Santa Lucia."

The designation of the peak as "Mount Junípero Serra" was officially announced by Sloane to the press at Washington, D.C., in mid–summer of 1907. The news was released to Californians by *The Monitor* in its issue for August 17th.

FRAY JUNÍPERO SERRA (1713–1784)

F. UNIVERSAL APPEAL

Despite a plethora of printed evidence to the contrary, many Americans still unconsciously cling to the notion that nothing of any great significance has yet occurred west of the Mississippi River. With the possible exception of a few major movie stars and several recent presidents, the country's religious and secular heroes are still pretty much associated with the so–called "eastern establishment."

It is always fascinating to watch audience reaction when one points out that California is not alone the most populous state in the Union (since 1963!), but has more inhabitants than 111 nations. Its economy ranks sixth among the world powers, its gross product is exceeded only by that of the United States, the Soviet Union, West Germany, the United Kingdom and France.

On and on the statistics could go, but perhaps most importantly California has the historical distinction of being the only territory in the Western World where modern civilization was founded by the cross and not by the sword. The same month and year that the Liberty Bell, on the Atlantic seaboard, rang out the birth of a nation at war for freedom, mission bells at San Francisco, on the Pacific Slope, chimed forth the arrival of messengers for the Prince of Peace!

Prior to the 1960s, California's ecclesial history was also largely neglected (or even ignored) by national scholars and writers who somehow concluded that the Hispanic flavor of Western America just didn't fit neatly into the tidy flow of pre–Gold Rush narratives.

Since, for the most part, the printed histories of California have been locally published and not widely circulated in the east, it is easy to understand why Americans generally have been unfamiliar with such personages as Fray Junípero Serra, the religious founder of California. Unaware that George Washington and Junípero Serra were contemporaries in ideals as well as time, visitors to Statuary Hall in the nation's capitol have been heard to ask who the friar was, when did he live, why is he included with this country's pioneers.

What is true at the national level, has certainly not been the case within the Golden State, where Fray Junípero Serra is among the most written–about persons in California annals.

That anyone would remember, much less write about and extol someone dead for two centuries is remarkable, the more so when the individual in question was a mendicant friar who worked among an aboriginal people on the very outskirts of civilization. Yet, amazingly enough, the tradition of Serra's fame has been spontaneously handed down by verbal tradition and written memoir from the very moment of his demise to the present day. He just won't stay dead! Most recently, Pope

John Paul II, in his homily at Fray Junípero Serra's beatification, has extended the friar's influence to the entire world. What Serra has meant for Californians is now extended to all peoples everywhere.

The late Father Maynard Geiger put it very well thirty years ago when he said: "In a sense Serra [has] attained a certain immortality in memory. Monuments to him line his *Camino Real* from Petra to San Francisco. His missions have been restored–about a million people from all parts of the globe visit them annually. His name is a household word in California!" Indeed, Blessed Junípero Serra, the man who was so vital in this life, has projected that vitality even from the grave!

FRAY JUNÍPERO SERRA (1713–1784)

G. SERRA AND THE CALIFORNIA MISSIONS

What appears as a lack of sincerity in certain recent newspaper portrayals about Fray Junípero Serra and his companions may well be a lack of understanding as to what the mission program was and how it functioned in California.

To begin with, the time sequence is vitally important. The dreadful violation of Indian rights in California came after and not during the mission era. And those who suffered most from the encroachments of the gold rush days were descendants of the Indians never attached to the missions. (Demographers estimate that not more than 40% of the total Indian population was affiliated with the missions at any one time)

Put another way, the friars can be held accountable only for what transpired during their incumbency, and that would be 1769 to the 1830s. They warned that secularization was premature in California and subsequent events more than confirmed that viewpoint.

Contrary to the practice in the English and French settlements of colonial America, the relationship of native Americans to Hispanic explorers and settlers along the Pacific Slope was carefully regulated by a series of royal statutes. This *Recopilación de las Leyes de los Reinos de Indias*, first published in 1552, was revised and updated several times in subsequent centuries. To the early missionaries in California, the *Recopilación* was as familiar as their breviary. Copies of this multi–volumed handbook or manual were available in every mission library.

As agents for the crown, as well as missionaries for the Church, the friars patterned their activity on the directives contained in the *Recopilación* There is no evidence that any of the missionaries in Alta or Baja California had any serious reservations about carrying out the royal mandate.

Concern for the spiritual and temporal welfare of the native peoples was a recurrent theme in the decrees codified in the *Recopilación* An example of the king's concern can be seen in an edict issued in 1526, whereby Charles exhorted "priests and religious who might participate in discoveries and in making peace (with the native tribes) . . . to try, with very great care and diligence, to bring it about that the Indians are well treated, looked upon and favored as neighbors."

Missionaries were instructed not to allow "the Indians to be forced, robbed, injured or badly treated." The emperor went on to say that "if the contrary is done by any person, regardless of his position or condition, the justices are to proceed against him according to law; and in those cases where it is proper for us to be advised, let it be done as soon as the opportunity is available . . . in order that we may be able to give orders for justice to be provided and that such excesses be punished with all rigor."

Philip II issued further directives on December 24, 1580, charging the viceroys, presidents and *audiencas* with the duty of protecting the Indians and of issuing corresponding orders so that they may be protected, favored and alleviated. He went on to say that "we desire that the injuries they suffer be remedied and that they may be without molestation or vexation, this viewpoint being now in force and keeping in mind the other laws of the *Recopilación*, the Indians are to be favored, protected and defended from whatsoever harm, and these laws are made to be observed very exactly. Transgressors are to be punished."

The king concluded by charging ecclesial prelates "to obtain this end as their true spiritual fathers of this new Christianity and to conserve for them their privilges and prerogatives." These were the laws of the land. There is no indication that Fray Junípero Serra and his companions did any other than observe them to the fullest.

FRAY JUNÍPERO SERRA (1713–1784)

H. RECIPE FOR OLIVES

In the United States, the olive culture has become established only in California, where it was introduced by the Hispanic missionaries in the years after 1769. There were many uses for olive oil in the old Missions. It was burned in lamps, used in cooking, prescribed as a medicine and utilized for the lubrication of machinery. There are two species of olives trees; the low gnarled type with willow–like leaves (like those at San Fernando Mission) and the tall and slender poplar–shaped type.

The olive tree is at least ten years old before it begins to produce the precious fruit. From that time onwards it continues to bear for generations. The black ripe olive is used for eating, whereas the green species is the one from which olive oil is extracted. Generally the crop is harvested about the middle of November. Nutritionists advise that olive oil is the most easily digested fat found in foods.

There are many recipes for preparing olives. One thinks immediately of those in Bess Cleveland's book, *California Mission Recipes*, released in 1965 by the Charles E. Tuttle Company. Therein are several pages of instructions for preparing olives.

Probably the most popular recipe for curing mission olives can be traced to Fray Junípero Serra. It was most recently adapted by "Uncle Ben Dixon" of San Diego for Ethel Reed's *Pioneer Kitchen. A Frontier Cookbook*, published in 1971 by Frontier Heritage Press. Dixon is known in bibliographical annals for his editorship of *Diario—The Journal of Padre Serra*, a 116 page correlation of the three known texts of the diary written by the Mallorcan friar as he journeyed from Loreto to San Diego.

> Gather about 4 gallons of olives; wash and clean thoroughly; place in an oak or crockery container—a vinegar barrel or 8 to 10 gallon stone jar is excellent. Cover with sufficient water so they can be stirred or agitated with a wooden paddle. Pour 1 gallon of concentrated lye in the container and macerate for 48 hours, more or less, depending on the state of maturity of olives. Stir several times daily to permit lye to work evenly. Test several times by slitting fruit with knife to determine the action of the lye.
>
> Very ripe olives must be processed carefully to prevent crushing, or breaking the skins. Very green olives can be cured, but will need a stronger solution, or a longer time for maceration, to soften and loosen from the seeds.
>
> After curing, wash olives in fresh water 2 or 3 days or longer to eliminate lye. Change water occasionally, until it tastes fresh, or is neutral to litmus.
>
> *To start brine*: Dump in 1 pound of salt. Add salt daily until suitable brine is formed. This is not stable, and should be renewed occasionally. Olives will keep much longer in a very heavy brine. *WARNING: Do Not Seal!*
>
> These olives should be kept in an open container. Like all unpasteurized fruits and vegetables, if sealed they may develop the anaerobic *Botulisni bacillus*, which is a dangerous organism. An open container will obviate this deadly risk.

FRAY JUNÍPERO SERRA (1713–1784)

I. FRIAR'S WELL–TRAVELLED SERMONS

The rediscovery in Petra de Mallorca of four sermons preached by Fray Junípero Serra to the Poor Clares of Palma in 1744, gives occasion to recall the interesting history and peregrinations of those now famous discourses. Serra was only thirty–one years old and recently named to teach Scotistic theology at the University of Mallorca when he was asked to prepare and deliver a retreat for the nuns. He spent several months writing the twenty–seven pages in his forceful script.

One writer observed that "from the said sermons we gather that Father Junípero was very much given to the study of the Sacred Scriptures which he used with great frequency to buttress the beautiful concepts and Christian sentiments that came forth from his learned lips." When Serra left for the New World, five years later, he took the sermons with him. Later, when he departed for the missions of Baja and Alta California, he left them behind at the Apostolic College of San Fernando in Mexico City.

Likely they were used by other friars engaged in giving conferences and retreats to nuns. Eventually they came into the possession of Fray Juan Bestard, another Mallorcan missionary, who later returned to his homeland where he became Commissary General of the Indies.

Bestard brought Serra's sermons with him when he came back to Mallorca, sometime prior to 1815. They were later entrusted to Fray Raimundo Strauch who penned the following notation on the last page:

> There are the original sermons of the Venerable Father Junípero Serra who took them with him to America, and afterwards Fray Juan Bestard, founder of the College of Orizaba, gave them to me. . . .

(An interesting sidelight might be that Strauch is also a candidate for beatification)

When Father Maynard Geiger was in Mallorca looking for original Serra documents, the sermons had been missing for some years. Fortunately, Francisco Torrens y Nicolau had made copies of them and photographic reproductions were made for the Santa Barbara Mission Archives.

In 1949, the elusive sermons were found by Miguel Ramis Moragues. They were exhibited during celebrations marking the bicentennial of Fray Junípero Serra's departure for the New World. Geiger wrote to Ramis, asking for copies of the originals which would be needed for the Serra Cause. Imagine his surprise when, on July 6th, 1949, a large envelope arrived at the Old Mission containing the documents themselves!

The next morning, the documents had been photostated and were enroute back to Petra de Mallorca. Those sermons, in the course of their history, had crossed the ocean four times! Father Maynard guestimated that the total mileage of the once–missing Serra sermons has so far exceeded 24,000 or enough to circumnavigate the globe. They have travelled slightly more than Serra himself!

And that's quite a journey for sermons written for a convent of Poor Clares whose members are committed to life–long stability.

FRAY JUNÍPERO SERRA (1713–1784)

J. ALONG THE *PRESIDENTE'S* TRAIL

Though the bishopric in Alta California can be historically documented only since 1840, the Golden State's poet laureate (who was also an accomplished historian) suggested an earlier derivation that lends itself readily to the present context. In 1910, John Steven McGroarty said that he had always thought of Fray Junípero Serra as the first bishop of the Diocese of Monterey–Los Angeles. He was never consecrated a bishop, but he exercised some of the faculties of the high and holy office. For a time he was empowered to administer the Sacrament of Confirmation, and many thousands of Indians together with a large number of white persons were confirmed by him."

McGroarty went on to say that "in addition to this, he was the first President of the California Missions, in which capacity he directed the work of the Church here and exercised authority over priests and people." He concluded by saying that "Father Junípero was, therefore, in effect a bishop, although not one in fact."

The consecration of three new bishops to serve God's people along *El Camino Real* in 1987 was indeed an appropriate way to inaugurate an exciting year, one in which Pope John Paul II visited the tomb of Fray Junípero Serra at the Mission Basilica of San Carlos Borromeo.

And though today's world may be a vastly different one than Serra knew, the basic apostolate of the Church is the same in the 1990s as it was in the 1760s when Serra arrived in this rim of Christendom. The skins of those whom Serra served was red, while today's are white and brown and black and yellow. But the differences are only cosmetic, because then and now God's people come in all colors.

This ceremony puts in place the first phase of the curial reorganization begun in September, 1985, with the installation of the Most Reverend Roger M. Mahony as the fourth Archbishop of Los Angeles Each of the newly–created vicarial districts is now governed by an auxiliary bishop who will exercise all the duties envisioned for that position by the new Code of Canon Law.

The senior of the prelates fittingly chose for his episcopal seal the familiar motto of Fray Junípero Serra, "*siempre adelante.*" G. Patrick Ziemann (b.1941) is the second oldest of the seven children born to Judge J. Howard and Helen (Scott) Ziemann, longtime residents of Pasadena. A grandson of Joseph Scott, the bishop has many of the oratorical skills of his legendary forebear. After attending Mayfield, Sacred Heart and Saint Andrew schools, Patrick entered Queen of Angels Seminary in 1955. A dozen years later he was ordained to the priesthood by James Francis Cardinal McIntyre in Saint Vibiana's Cathedral.

During the early years of his ministry, Father Ziemann served in Huntington Park under the tutelage of Msgr. Patrick Shear. He began his teaching apostolate in 1967, at Saint Matthias Girls High School, later transferring to Mater Dei in Santa Ana. In 1974, Father Ziemann was attached to the faculty of the minor seminary at Mission Hills, serving at various times as Spiritual Director, Dean of Studies and Vice Rector. He has two masters degrees and a secondary life credential in education. Armando Ochoa (b.1943), a native of Oxnard, California, studied in that city's primary and secondary Catholic schools. After a year at Ventura College, he entered Saint John's Seminary College in 1962, as a clerical aspirant for the Archdiocese of Los Angeles. Ordained in 1970 by Timothy Cardinal Manning, Father Ochoa filled parochial positions at Saint Alphonsus, Saint John the Baptist and Saint Teresa of Avila. In 1984, he was named Administrator (and later Pastor) of Sacred Heart Parish, one of the oldest and most active of the parochial units in the historic city of *Nuestra Señora de los Angeles*.

Since 1975, Bishop Ochoa was active in the diaconate training program for the archdiocese. He was named Episcopal Vicar for the San Fernando Region, as well as Titular Bishop of Sitifi. He later became Bishop of El Paso, Texas.

Carl Fisher (1945–1993) was born at Pascagoula, Mississippi, where he attended Saint Peter the Apostle parochial school. Attracted by the ideals of the Saint Joseph Society of the Sacred Heart, which since 1871 has been working among the black peoples of the United States, Fisher enrolled at Epiphany College High School in Newburgh, New York. Later he entered Mary Immaculate Novitiate, completing his priestly studies at Saint Joseph's Seminary in Washington, D.C. He was ordained in his home parish on June 2, 1973.

Following graduate work at the American University in Washington, D.C., Father Fisher served in several parochial positions, including Saint Veronica's in Baltimore. For many years he was national vocation director for the Josephite Fathers, and during that time he became a prime spokesman for the ideals of racial equality.

For five years, Father Fisher was pastor of Saint Francis Xavier, America's oldest black parish in the premier See of Baltimore. There his priority was the evangelization through the charism of preaching and the participation of the laity, a program that quadrupled parochial membership. Bishop Fisher was named to the titular See of Tlos by Pope John Paul II. In the Archdiocese of Los Angeles, he became Episcopal Vicar of the San Pedro region.

Those who have studied the growth of the scriptural seed planted along the Pacific Slope would surely agree with Aimee Semple McPherson's observation that in California one can find "God's great blueprint for man's abode on the earth."

In imitation of the Mallorcan friar who began it all, Californians of modern times have been characteristically more willing than others to experiment and break with tradition. It was their willingness to try difficult things, to look at sagebrush and mesquite and see farms and cities, to gaze at missions and envision cathedrals, which has pushed California to its present position of spiritual and national prominence.

Looked upon in its historical context, the ordination of this trio of bishops became another chapter in the long and challenging pageant of God's people along *El Camino Real*. The story of California bequeathed by Fray Junípero Serra to succeeding generations is surely among the most remarkable in all of recorded history. And how would Serra react at seeing his vineyard as America's number one center of religious, political, economical and social power? Likely he would simply smile and repeat once again: "In California is my life and there, God willing, I hope to die."

CARMEL, Calif.

Fr Junípero Serra

BAPTISMAL FONT

BIRTH PLACE

FRAY JUNÍPERO SERRA (1713–1784)

K. MUSICAL TRIBUTES

If it's true that "he who sings prays twice," then Fray Junípero Serra has doubly blessed California since that day in 1784 when he fell asleep in the Lord at San Carlos Borromeo Mission. Among the many melodious tributes composed to honor Serra, we have singled out here some of the more prominent published pieces as worthy of being preserved in the public record.

The historian Theodore E. Treutlein recently recalled that "one of the most pleasant traditions" associated with his *alma mater*, the San Diego State Normal School, was a musical tribute to Serra originated by Professor Irving Outcalt. Treutlein noted that in 1921, Outcalt composed the verses of "The Junípero Serra Song" for use by the college's Men's and Women's Glee Clubs. The music department tried to find a tune which fitted the words and ultimately came up with the music for 'Lord Jeffrey Amherst'

Though there were subsequent problems about copyright infringements, students at the school continued to use the tune for many years as their semi–official college song. L. Deborah Smith provided a musical nota-

tion for 'The Junípero Song' which ultimately appeared in an issue of the *San Diego Historical Quarterly*.

Arthur Michael Bienhar wrote a "Mass in Honor of *Padre* Junípero Serra, Apostle of California" which was performed under the direction of the composer at San Carlos Borromeo Mission on August 28, 1934. It was later edited by Father Owen de Silva and published by the Franciscan Fathers of California. The twenty–three page monograph was distributed by the Delkas Music Printing Company of Los Angeles.

Richard Keys Biggs composed a 'Mass dedicated to Fray Junípero Serra, O.F.M. Pioneer of the Faith and Builder of Civilization in California', which was copyrighted in 1937, by J. Fisher and Brothers. It was printed in a twenty–eight page monograph at New York under the "Fisher Edition" label.

One of the most meaningful melodic tributes to California's Gray Ox was Wells Hively's opera, 'Junípero Serra' which the famed pianist played throughout the United States Europe in the mid 1950s.

In the April, 1982, issue of *Apostol y Civilizador*, Fray Salustiano Vicedo gathered and printed ten hymns and ballads, written to commemorate various facets of Serra's life. Among the more noteworthy of those is "*Goigs a llaor del Venerable Fra juniper Serra*," written by Rubi Darden, with music by Juan Rubi. This piece, composed in Serra's native tongue in 1980, was widely used through the Isle of Mallorca.

Another popular ballad in that collection is "Fray Junípero Serra" written at Mexico City in 1974, by Salvador lbarra Padilla. The same musician composed '*En la Sierra Gorda. Cancion del Recuerdo*' five years later.

During the year marking the 200th anniversary of Serra's demise, several musical renditions about California's religious pioneer were popularized. Probably the most appealing, the '*Cancion de Fray Junípero Serra*,' with words and music by Justin Kramer, was adopted as the official hymn of the Serra Bicentennial Commission.

FRAY JUNÍPERO SERRA (1713–1784)

L. Some Symbols of the *Presidente*

In October of 1957, Father Maynard Geiger was asked to recommend a series of symbols that would epitomize the apostolate of Fray Junípero Serra. The following were among his suggestions.

The *saw* and *hammer* indicate his parents' name. *Sierra* is the Spanish word for saw, as is the Mallorcan word of *Serra*. That name is equivalent to the English "carpenter." The hammer of the blacksmith would indicate his mother's name *Ferrer* which in English would be "Smith." It's an appropriate combination for, like most priests, Serra was born of the working class and those tools commemorate the fact that in his missions he carefully provided that the Indians were taught self–sufficiency by a variety of trades.

Serra's own attitude toward manual work was shown by his strenuous helping of the unskilled laborers in the Sierra Gorda region of Mexico. Only a few days before he died, the friar was busy cutting up bolts of cloth at Carmel Mission to make clothing for the Indians.

Another symbol would be the *book* for it reminds us that Fray Junípero Serra was a bookman as student, professor and librarian in his monastery on the isle of Mallorca. His writings showed a familiarity with such classics as Virgil, Seneca and Terence. He brought to Alta California books on theology and morals, on ecclesial and civil law, as well as tomes on farming, building and medicine. In each of his missions there was a library.

And, of course, the symbol would refer primarily to "the" book, the Holy Bible, which Serra seemed to know by heart. Through all his letters from 1749 to 1784 there runs the thread of Scripture which he wove into his thoughts and exhortations.

And then there is the symbol of the *cross*. It was the first thing that Serra set in place at the establishment of a mission. In front of the cross the friar said his daily prayers. Overlooking the different missions a large cross was raised upon a hill as a holy landmark.

Serra was careful to see that each of his churches had the Stations of the Cross. When he once asked for a crucifix to be sent from Mexico, he called it "the chief object of our preaching." And when he was found dead on his bed of boards, he was holding in his arms the cross he had received as a missionary in 1750.

Finally, one might associate the *halo* with Serra. It brings to mind that he had a great devotion to the saints. He knew the stories of their lives and used that knowledge not only in his sermons and devotions, but also in his conversation.

He was especially devoted to Saint Joseph, not only because his own baptismal name was Miguel *Jose*, but also because Saint Joseph had been named the official patron of the conquest of California when the area was in danger of Russian occupation. When California was about to be abandoned, in 1770, the friar led his countrymen in a novena to Saint Joseph for the safe arrival of the supply ship. The long overdue ship was sighted offshore on the last day of the novena, Saint Joseph's feast-day, March 19th. From that moment onwards, on the 19th of every month, Fray Junípero Serra sang a high Mass in thanksgiving to the saint, a practice that he continued to the last month of his life.

The saw and hammer, the book, the cross and the halo are but a few of the symbols which call to mind the apostolate of Fray Junípero Serra.

FRAY JUNÍPERO SERRA (1713–1784)

M. in the Santa Clara Valley

The fact that portrayals of Fray Junípero Serra (1713–1784) are proliferating throughout California and around the world is another graphic indication of the Mallorcan friar's popularity within and without the Christian faith. An example would be the "Junipero Serra Mosaic" which was unveiled on the evening of July 30, 1970, on the Bank of America building in the Serra Shopping Center, Milpitas, California.

After dedicating and blessing the colorful mosaic, Bishop Floyd L. Begin of Oakland noted that "Serra has now come to the crossroads of our society—a fitting culmination to a busy and effective apostolate." Nearly two centuries earlier, Serra first arrived in the Santa Clara Valley and there he put in place the cornerstone of the adobe church at Santa Clara Mission.

The site of the exterior mosaic was the third structure of what was then the world's largest financial institution. On May 1, 1936, Bank of America purchased the Bank of Milpitas which had served the local community since January 2, 1912. The impressive mosaic was commissioned by the Donovan family, developers of the Serra Shopping Center. Standing six feet wide and 10 1/2 feet high, the mosaic was designed and executed by Magda Chambers, who was assisted in the intricate work by Sister Joachim O'Connor. Recalling the period of California's history, 1769–1840, the mosaic incorporates native flora, such as Sand Hill dandelions, mission bells, California poppies and Indian paint brushes.

The small scene in the upper left portion of the mosaic depicts two friars, one absolving the other. A spot along the creek was chosen by the friars as a convenient meeting place because it was equidistant between San Jose and Santa Clara missions. The creek accordingly became known as *La Penitencia* which is Spanish for penitence.

In the lower right panel is the facade of the present Basilica of *San Carlos Borromeo del Rio Carmelo*. Within the sanctuary lies the remains of California's pioneering missionary and it was there that Pope John Paul II prayed during his visit to Carmel. Finally, in the lower right panel is a representation of the statue of *Nuestra Señora de Belen*, Our Lady of Bethlehem, which was brought to California by Serra and is now enshrined in a special chapel of the mission–basilica.

The hundreds of tiny pieces called *tesserae* used in creating the mosaic are made of stone, colored glass and gold leaf smelted on glass cubes and glazed ceramic tile. They have a variety of textures. By their nature they suggest a unique quality of simplicity and strength. Combined into an artistic work, such as the Serra mosaic, they add brilliance and luminosity to the overall field. The gifted mosaicists, Magda Chambers and Sister Joachim, completed the monumental panel of Fray Junípero Serra during the summer of 1969 at the Dominican College of San Rafael.

In the official description of the mosaic, it is noted that "during the 18th century, Spain's expanding colonial empire engaged the energy of its people. From his first days as a Franciscan novice, Fray Junípero was attracted to the responsibilities of the vocation of Apostolic Missionary and he volunteered for service in the New World in 1749."

FRAY JUNÍPERO SERRA (1713–1784)

N. EXHUMATION OF FRAY JUNÍPERO

As the cause for the beatification of Fray Junípero Serra moved toward its final resolution, there remained the task of disinterring and identifying the friar's remains. This "canonical recognition" took place at Carmel Mission Basilica on November 13, 1987.

California's religious pioneer died at San Carlos Borromeo on August 28, 1784. He was buried the following day in what was then the fifth church at Carmel. The present edifice, built some years after his demise, was erected over Serra's grave.

The 1987 proceedings actually marked the fourth time that Serra's vault had been opened. He was first identified in 1856, by Father Cajetano Sorrentini, later seen by Father Angelo Casanova in 1882, and finally removed and reinterred by Harry Downie in 1943.

The vault was opened during the afternoon and evening hours of November 12, 1987, under the careful supervision of Richard Menn, curator of the Old Mission. Serra's remains, enclosed in a gray copper casket, were brought to the surface and placed on a catafalque. The church was then locked for the night.

Shortly after 9 o'clock the next morning, Bishop Thaddeus Shubsda and about a dozen official witnesses entered the church to begin the canonical process. A short prayer was recited and the oaths were administered to several of the participants, among whom was Joseph Hinojos, the only survivor present who had been at the 1943 exhumation.

Hinojos testified that the open vault was indeed the one in which Fray Junípero Serra's remains were placed forty–four years earlier. He recounted briefly the circumstances surrounding the 1943 identification. Then Mrs. Virginia Klepech, notary for the event, read aloud an abridged description of the 1943 proceedings from an account written four decades previously by Father Eric O'Brien, who was then Vice Postulator for the Serra Cause.

Afterwards, the notary read an historical resume prepared by Harry Downie whose association with San Carlos Borromeo Mission dated back to 1913. Therein he carefully explained how the bones of Serra had been removed from the vault, identified and then replaced in the metallic casket. The documentation for that occurrence has been published and is available to researchers. Parts of the report prepared by Dr. Theodore McCown were also read. An anthropologist from the University of California at Berkeley, McCown had conclusively identified Serra's remains by physical evidence totally apart from oral tradition.

For those who had not been present the previous day, Richard Menn described the details of opening and removing the casket from the vault. Then, after ascertaining that the seal of the casket was still intact, Bishop Shubsda severed the brass wire and opened the airtight glass lid of the casket. Dr. Osmund Hull, a local pathologist, and Dr. David Huelsbeck, an anthropologist at

Santa Clara University, then carefully removed the ninety–three pieces of remaining bone fragment from the casket. Each was identified and checked off the 1943 inventory.

Father Noel Moholy, Vice Postulator for the Serra Cause, then gathered a small quantity of bone for transferral to Rome. The remaining *restos* were then replaced in the casket. A scroll attesting to the proceedings was added to the earlier one and a new piece of wire was put in place, after which the seal was attached with the diocesan coat–of–arms. The canonical examination was finished at 2:30 p.m., at which time the bishop concluded the recognition ceremonies with a prayer for Serra's beatification.

FRAY JUNÍPERO SERRA (1713–1784)

O. SERRA NAMED SECONDARY PATRON

The Archdiocese of Los Angeles now has a "secondary patron" in the person of Blessed Junípero Serra. A commemoration of this new patronage was observed for the first time on August 26th 1989.

In a liturgical sense, a patron is a saint or blessed who is celebrated as "an advocate before God." The practice of designating ecclesial patrons dates from the early Church. By the 4th century, Christians were already being named after apostles and martyrs. Patrons found their greatest popularity in the Middle Ages. Towns, for example, were named after saints and nearly every circumstance of daily life was assigned its heavenly protestor.

The rescript naming Blessed Junípero Serra secondary patron for the Archdiocese of Los Angeles, dated May 12, 1989, was accompanied by a letter from Archbishop Vergilius Noe, the secretary of the Congregation for Divine Worship. Therein, Archbishop Noe said that he agreed with the petitioner that such a declaration would "prove a source of spiritual richness" to the archdiocese "which already had a very special bond with Blessed Junípero Serra."

Following is the writer's translation from the Latin of Prot. N.CD. 1008/88:

> In view of the fact that Blessed Junípero Serra, a religious of the Order of Friars Minor, preached the Gospel in California, ignited the flame of Christian charity in the area and devoted his whole life to the spread of the faith, the clergy and faithful of that region now and for over two centuries have honored him with a special and constant veneration.
>
> For these reasons, His Excellency, Roger M. Mahony, Archbishop of Los Angeles in California, echoing the sentiments of his people, has recommended the naming of Blessed Junípero Serra as secondary patron before God of his archdiocese.

In a letter dated April 26, 1989, the archbishop earnestly and forcibly outlined the reasons why this proposal should be approved and confirmed. This he did in accordance with the accepted norms governing the naming of patrons as outlined in the Instruction for the Revision of Particular Calendars and Propers for the Divine Office and Holy Mass.

Since the request followed the norms of canonical law regarding these matters, this Congregation for Divine Worship and the Discipline of the Sacraments, in virtue of the faculties entrusted to it by the Supreme Pontiff, John Paul II, all things set forth and having been considered, hereby grants the request and thereby confirms Blessed Junípero Serra as secondary patron before God for the Archdiocese of Los Angeles in California, with all the corresponding rights and privileges allowed by the rubrics of liturgy.

What all this means is that the ministry begun by Serra in Alta California in 1769, has been prolonged and renewed. He is once again a primary and duly designated spokesman for God's people in this portion of his earlier apostolate. What was an apostolate to thousands has been enlarged to encompass 3.39 million Catholics in the largest See in the United States.

In his new and expanded ministry, Fray Junípero Serra no longer intercedes for his flock from a humble cell at San Carlos Borromeo Mission. From now on, Blessed Junípero Serra watches over us from a heavenly vantage point.

FRAY JUNÍPERO SERRA (1713–1784)

P. PICTORIAL BIOGRAPHY OF SERRA

Fray Junípero Serra is one of those rare historical personages who won't stay dead. Though he died 216 years ago, his name is still a household word along California's Pacific Slope. The most recent in the long litany of books about the Mallorcan friar is among the most informative. Martin Morgado's treatise, *Junípero Serra. A Pictorial Biography*, is a colorfully illustrated, 137 page book published by Siempre Adelante of Monterey.

The author's fascination with Serra led him "to identify and document Serra's possessions and physical environment that are still in existence today." In this volume, he carefully describes those items within a biographical framework based largely on Serra's own writings.

Since the friar had taken the solemn vow of poverty, "possessions" used in this context refer only to what Serra touched, used and valued as tools of his missionary life. It was no easy task to separate and distinguish legend from fact in the author's quest for authenticity. There are many traditions, some of them probably true, that this or that vestment, statue, cross, chalice or book belonged to or was used by Serra. The only items enumerated are those for which there is solid documentation.

In several cases, the author also demonstrates how documentation can disprove a claim. An example would be the "Serra chalice" at San Carlos Borromeo Mission that was thought to be a companion to the monstrance given by Bucareli to the *Presidente* in 1778. Careful research proved that the chalice in question did not arrive at Carmel until twenty years after Serra's death.

Also included in the scope of this book is every item Serra ordered for a California mission or that was present in his day and survives. The 144 entries are listed chronologically as they touched upon Serra's life. To each description is added the present location.

Among the most interesting items featured is the San Antonio *regalito* given by Serra to Jose Francisco Ortega in 1774. The wooden figure of the saint holds the infant Jesus and a loaf of bread. The statue's provenance can be traced through six generations of Ortegas.

Serra's Indian reliquary, probably made for him by a neophyte craftsman, had an attached description which a handwriting expert identified as having been written by the Mallorcan friar. And there is the Biblical concordance with its note "for the simple use of Fray Junípero Serra, Observant Order of Friars Minor." This volume, given to Pope John Paul II at San Fernando Mission in 1987, is now kept among the "Precious Books" at the Vatican Library.

Of the multitude of Serra tributes mentioned in this book, from statues and medals to comic books, and even a World War II Liberty ship, only those commemorating an important site or event in Serra's life are featured, as well as those with national or international significance.

By examining what Serra surrounded himself with in life, one can gain further insight into the nature of the man himself. Prophetic indeed the utterance about Serra when he died: "Unfading will be his memory". (Sirach, 39, 9)

FRAY JUNÍPERO SERRA (1713–784)

Q. SERRA'S "HOLY FAMILY"

Willa Cather's essay on "Father Junípero's Holy Family," an excerpt from her classical treatise, *Death Comes for the Archbishop* was printed, in monograph form, by Carolyn Reading Hammer at The Anvil Press, in 1956. There it is told how Fray Junípero Serra and a companion arrived on foot without provisions. The friars welcomed their two confreres in astonishment, believing it impossible that they could have crossed so great an expanse of desert in such a fashion.

But Father Junípero replied that they had fared well and had been most agreeably entertained by a poor Mexican family on the way. At this a muleteer, who was bringing in wood for the Brothers, began to laugh, and said there was no house for twelve leagues, nor anyone at all living in the sandy waste through which they had come; and the Brothers confirmed him in this.

Then Father Junípero and his companion related fully their adventure. They had set out with bread and water for one day. But on the second day they had been traveling since dawn across a cactus desert and had begun to lose heart when, near sunset, they espied in the distance three great cottonwood trees, very tall in the declining light. Toward these they hastened. As they approached the trees, which were large and green and were shedding cotton freely, they observed an ass tied to a dead trunk which stuck up out of the sand.

Looking about for the owner of the ass, they came upon a little Mexican house with an oven by the door and strings of red peppers hanging on the wall. When they called aloud, a venerable Mexican, clad in sheepskins, came out and greeted them kindly, asking them to stay the night.

Going with him, they observed that all was neat and comely, and the wife, a young woman of beautiful countenance, was stirring porridge by the fire. Her child, scarcely more than an infant and with no garment but his little shirt, was on the floor beside her, playing with a pet lamb.

They found these people gentle, pious, and well–spoken. The husband said they were shepherds. The priests sat at their table and shared their supper, and afterwards read the evening prayers. They had wished to question the host about the country, and about his mode of life and where he found pasture for his flock, but they were overcome by a great and sweet weariness, and taking each a sheepskin provided him, they lay down upon the floor and sank into deep sleep.

When they awoke in the morning they found all as before, and food set upon the table, but the family were absent, even to the pet lamb, having gone, the Fathers supposed, to care for their flock.

When the Brothers at the monastery heard this account they were amazed, declaring that there were indeed three cottonwood trees growing together in the desert, a well–known landmark; but that if a settler had come, he must have come very lately.

So Father Junípero and Father Andrea, his companion, with some of the Brothers and the scoffing muleteer, went back into the wilderness to prove the matter. The three tall trees they found, shedding their cotton, and the dead trunk to which the ass had been tied. But the ass was not there, nor any house, nor the oven by the door. Then the two Fathers sank down upon their knees in that blessed spot and kissed the earth, for they perceived what Family it was that had entertained them there.

Willa Cather's appraisal of the story is also worth recalling, for she thought there was "always something charming in the idea of greatness returning to simplicity

. . . but how much more enduring was the belief that they, after so many centuries of history and glory, should return to play their first parts, in the persons of a humble Mexican family, the lowliest of the lowly, the poorest of the poor, in a wilderness at the end of the world, where the angels could scarcely find them!"

FRAY JUNÍPERO SERRA (1713–784)

R. THE *PRESIDENTE* IN LOS ANGELES

The handsomely–sculptured statue of Fray Junípero Serra, the spiritual Father of Alta California, moved in 1955 to historic ground in the old Plaza of Los Angeles, embodies one of the nation's most meaningful tributes to a religious pioneer. In *pueblo* days, the area of Serra's statue provided a site for the adobe townhouse of Ignacio del Valle of Rancho San Francisco. Don Ignacio's presence lent social prestige to the Plaza and within the thick–walled enclosure of his home were held many of the political meetings of the early American period.

Don Ignacio's neighbors were other *rancheros* bearing such well–known names as Lugo, Olvera, Pico, Carrillo, Sanchez and Sepulveda. In the 1850s, their town houses almost ringed the plaza which was dominated, then as now, by the church of *Nuestra Señora de los Angeles*. There was the setting for the significant, the colorful, the prosaic events of the Spanish, Mexican and early American phases of Los Angeles history. In modern times, that area was formed into a state historical monument or park in order to preserve the atmosphere of earlier days.

The bronze statue of Serra, a replica of the one in Statuary Hall at the nation's capital, was the work of Italian– born Ettore Cadorin of Santa Barbara. It was paid for by public subscription, a gift to the City of Los Angeles by the Southern California Chapter, Knights of Columbus. The statue was not erected without bigotry raising its ugly head. Because of numerous complaints, the Los Angeles Board of Public Works was obliged to convene a meeting to hear arguments for and against the statue. It was an eloquent plea by Joseph Scott that won the case for Fray Junípero.

Artistically designed, the statue portrays Serra in his religious habit, holding aloft in his right hand a cross at which he is gazing with intense fervor. In his left hand is a miniature California mission. inscribed on the plaque are the words: "Fray Junípero. Serra, *Padre* of the California Missions, 1713–1784. Presented to the City of Los Angeles by Southern California Chapter, Knights of Columbus, August 26, 1934."

The statue was unveiled and dedicated during the sesquicentennial year of Serra's death, at ceremonies attended by 6,000 spectators. It was accepted on behalf of the Los Angeles populace by Mayor Frank Shaw, with "a sense of humility and reverence." Father Louis Schoen, O.F.M., delivered an address on "Serra, California's Apostle and Pioneer," while John Steven McGroarty read his famous poem, "Dreamers of God." Though the Franciscan *Presidente* founded no mission in Los Angeles and was, in fact, opposed to the establishment of the *pueblo* itself, "nowhere else does Serra have so conspicuous a location today."

FRAY JUNÍPERO SERRA (1713–1784)

S. A SAN DIEGO MONUMENT

On July 16, 1913, a group of San Diegans, city officials, business and professional men, history buffs and ordinary citizens, armed with pick and shovel, gathered on Presidio Hill to begin the work of reclaiming the precious bits of tile which were once part of the original little chapel built upon that spot by Fray Junípero Serra and his sturdy band of Franciscan confreres. Those tiny fragments of tile, the result of the first manual labors of the friars on the soil of California, were to be transformed into a giant cross in memory of the Franciscan *Presidente*.

The use of those old worn and broken tiles, so intimately associated with the past and which had lain for nearly a century and a half buried and forgotten in the dirt and debris of the hillside, lent the crowning touch of genius and sentiment to the occasion. The project had been proposed by David Charles Collier, a man who devoted most of his means and the best years of his life to upbuilding and developing San Diego.

Collier suggested the plan to the Order of Panama, whose membership quickly–endorsed and generously–financed the project. The land for the envisioned monument was acquired by George W. Marson and then signed over to the Order of Panama. Throughout the summer of 1913, the building of the cross proceeded without interruption and with the most wonderful spirit of cooperation on the part of all who had the opportunity of participating in the work.

It was decided to have the solemn dedicatory services on September 28th. A large crowd gathered for the occasion to honor the "memory of Fray Junípero Serra, that saintly priest who, on July 16, 1769, on that same sacred spot raised the first Christian Cross in California." The Spanish Ambassador to the United States presided at the event, as did an official legation from President Woodrow Wilson. Bishop Thomas J. Conaty represented the Catholic populace of the state.

Charles Fletcher Lummis composed the inscription for the monument, which visitors today can read, in English and Spanish, at the base of the cross:

In this ancient Indian village of Cosoy, discovered and named San Miguel by Cabrillo in 1542, visited and christened San Diego de Alcala by Vizcaino in 1602

Here the First Citizen
FRA JUNÍPERO SERRA
Planted Civilization in California
Here he first raised the Cross
Here began the first Mission
Here founded the first town–San Diego
July 16, 1769

In memory of him and his works
The Order of Panama, 1913.

There, atop Presidio Hill, a little back from the river and the bay, one can see today all that remains of the one–time Mission San Diego de Alcalá which served the Indian *ranchería* of the Diegueños. But then again, in human annals, does anything outlast the cross?

FRAY JUNÍPERO SERRA (1713–1784)

T. RELIGIOUS FIBRE OF THE *PRESIDENTE*

Martyrs are a shining example of that genuine faith which will have nothing to do with ambiguity or false compromise in whatever is held as sacred. Theirs is a faith that is never afraid to declare its convictions. The martyrs are not just dim figures in the shadowy past, but definitive individuals. Some were squat and dumpy, others lean and bald, a few wealthy but most poor, and so forth. But they were all alike in their fierce love for Christ. Almost universally, those brave People of God strike a note of joy, urbanity, humanism, hope, unconquerable determination and unconquering love.

Though he never achieved the goal of personal martyrdom, Fray Junípero Serra embodied its ideals. Prior to his coming to California, he made an agreement with José de Gálvez that in the case the natives might take his life, they were not to be punished. When, in 1775, the Indians rose up in rebellion at San Diego, and killed Fray Luis Jayme, Serra recalled his earlier pact with Gálvez and pleaded for lenience and mercy.

If the Indians kill a missionary, what good are we going to obtain by waging a military campaign against them? Allow the murderers to live so that they can be saved. This is the purpose of our coming here and which justifies our presence here. . . . Thus we shall fulfill our (Christian) law which commands us to forgive injuries and not to seek the sinner's death but his eternal salvation.

In this and in others of his many letters, one can see how the record of Fray Junípero's spiritual orientation was so integral a part of California's heritage, inextricably interwoven with the history of the commonwealth.

In 1927, the great American essayist, Elbert Hubbard, published his now famous *Note Book*. Contained therein is his appreciation of the noble Franciscan pioneer:

Among the world's great workers—and in the front rank there have been only a scant half–dozen—stands Fra Junípero Serra. This is the man who made the California Missions possible. In artistic genius, as a teacher of handicrafts, and as an industrial leader, he performed a feat unprecedented, and which probably will never again be equalled. In a few short years he caused a great burst of beauty to bloom and blossom, where before was only a desert waste.

The personality of a man who could not only convert to Christianity three thousand Indians, but who could set them to work, must surely be sublimely great. Not only did they labor, but they produced art of a high order. These missions which lined the Coast from San Francisco to San Diego, every forty miles, were Manual Training Schools, founded on a religious concept.

Junípero taught that, unless you backed up your prayer with work God would never answer your petitions. And the wonderful transformations which this man worked in characters turned on the fact that he made them acceptable and beautiful. Here is a lesson for us! He ranks with Saint Benedict, who rescued classic art from the dust of time and gave it to the world. Junípero is one with Albrecht Durer, Lorenzo the Magnificent, Michelangelo, Leonardo da Vinci, Friedrich Froebel, John Ruskin and William Morris. These men all taught the Gospel of Work, and the sacredness of Beauty and Use.

Junípero was without question the greatest teacher of Manual Training which this continent has so far seen. Without tools, apparatus or books, save as he created them, he evolved an architecture and an art, utilizing the services of savages, and transforming these savages in the process, for the time at least, into men of taste, industry and economy.

FRAY JUNÍPERO SERRA (1713–1784)

U. SERRA ON POSTAGE STAMP

Over the years, there have been several attempts to have a postage stamp bearing the likeness of Fray Junípero Serra issued by the United States Postal Service, so far to no avail. In 1962, Mayor Samuel Yorty of Los Angeles asked Postmaster General J. Edward Day to authorize such a stamp pointing out that the famed missionary was "historically acknowledged as the Apostle of California."

Yorty told the postmaster that he felt "the issuance of such a stamp would be singularly appropriate and well received, particularly by those of us in California who honor the role played by Father Serra in California's early development long before statehood."

Always go forward and never turn back.
SERRA

Fray Junípero Serra was a complex and highly intelligent man whose spiritual and practical vision guided him to the successful settlement of California. Born on the Spanish island of Mallorca, Serra traveled to Mexico with a group of Franciscan friars. Later he accompanied the explorer, Gaspar de Portola, along the California coast and on July 16, 1769, founded a mission at what is now San Diego. The Spanish settlers eventually established 21 missions and for 65 years made great strides in developing farming and industry in the area.
Aristocrat Cachets

Fr. Junípero Serra
1713-1784

First Day of Issue

Some months later, Representative James C. Corman introduced Bill No. 13062 to provide for issuance of a stamp commemorating the 250th anniversary of the Mallorcan friar's birth. Corman's bill was endorsed by numerous prominent individuals organizations and public officials. The proposal passed but was shelved by the Post Office Department. They explained that the selection of themes was governed by a Citizens Advisory Committee consisting of stamp collectors, artists, historians and experts on designing and printing who meet four times a year.

To narrow the list of proposed themes, the committee routinely eliminates anyone (except presidents) not dead for ten years (with exceptions made in the past for Walt Disney and Winston Churchill). Stamps must honor significant anniversaries and have "widespread national appeal and significance," but no commercial impact.

Two other criteria prohibit stamps honoring fraternal, political or religious organizations, and stamps for charitable organizations "whose funds are supplied in whole or in part by voluntary contributions." Fray Junípero Serra was proposed not as a religious personage, but as an historical pioneer.

In 1969, when the Postal Service agreed to issue a special stamp for California's bicentennial, it was suggested again that the stamp feature Fray Junípero Serra. It was pointed out that six commemorative stamps bearing Serra's portrait would be released by the governments of Spain, Mexico and Portugal, in 1969, all of them in observance of the 200th anniversary of European penetration into Alta California.

In 1985, the United States Postal Service finally issued a stamp for Serra in its "Pathfinder Series." A year earlier, the Spanish Government issued a commemorative stamp for California's Grey Ox.

FRAY JUNÍPERO SERRA (1713–1784)

V. STUNNING MEMOIR OF SERRA

Aside from Father Maynard Geiger's two volume biographical study on T*he Life and Times of Fray Junípero Serra, O.F.M.*, one of the most ambitious and fascinating books about the famed founder of the California Missions will surely prove to be the treatise on *Junípero Serra in His Native Isle (1713–1749)*.

Prepared by the longtime, American–born "ambassador" to Mallorca, Dina Moore Bowden, this copiously–illustrated tome provides, with text and photographs, a wholly fresh insight into the traditions and culture of that islandic cradle where much of California's heritage originated.

From a lifetime of on–the–scene studying and researching into every aspect of Serra's life, Mrs. Bowden deftly blends already–known facts with a new found ambiance that flowers forth in these pages with rare fragrance and beauty. Concentrating on the period 1713 to 1749, the years prior to Fray Junípero Serra's departure for the New World, the book captures the religious and cultural atmosphere which the *Presidente* and other Mallorcan friars brought to the California story.

Mrs. Bowden's understanding of Serra's character, the ideals which inspired him and the faith and fortitude with which he carried them out, results in her portraying him as a living reality, as well as a protagonist of history. Apart from its treatment of Serra, the book provides a framework for evaluating and appreciating the contributions of the other fifteen Mallorcan friars who invested 341 man–years in spreading the Christian message along the Pacific Slope.

Mallorca, that majestic isle of calm and beauty, has long been regarded by historians as the "spiritual god–mother" of Alta California. The genius of this graphic presentation is its capturing in print of that historical link which Serra and others forged between their Mediterranean homeland and the Pacific shoreline. This significant and offbeat approach has produced a book that easily qualifies as an "absolute must" for any Western–Americana collector or enthusiast. And its attractively–written style and value–laden contents assure the volume a place of prominence for even the casual reader of the California experience.

The 170 page tome, with its fifty–two stark and stunning photographs by Stefan Laszlo, is further enhanced by a number of outstanding pen–sketched drawings. Artistically bound in blue cloth, the volume was printed by Graficas Miramar at Palma de Mallorca.

Bartolome Font Obrador, the President of Palma's *Sección Junípero del Circulo de Bellas Artes*, has said that the reading of this book is "balm to the spirit."

FRAY JUNÍPERO SERRA (1713–1784)

W. MARKER PLACED AT MONTEREY

Fray Junípero Serra and his companions landed in Monterey during 1770. There, on the Feast of Pentecost, under an old oak tree, he offered Holy Mass on an improvised altar dominated by a statue of the Virgin Mary.

The Franciscan *Presidente* reported to his Guardian that "everyone arrived singing, while the bells hung from the old tree were ringing at full peal. . . . A large cross had been laid out on the ground; we lifted it together and planted it upright in the earth. . . . Then we buried, at the foot of the cross, a cabin boy who had died aboard the San Antonio."

For many years, that holy spot was marked by a wooden cross. It was replaced several times, due to the ravages of time and weather. In late 1907, James A. Murray decided to erect a permanent monument to commemorate and perpetuate "the most important event in the history" of Monterey. He enlisted the assistance of Douglas Tilden, a talented San Francisco sculptor, who had earlier designed the statue of Fray Junípero Serra in Golden Gate Park.

After carefully considering a number of sketches, the final draft for the proposed monument was approved by Murray. Then he contacted officials at the United States War Department for permission to have the monument placed at the entranceway to the *Presidio* Reservation.

The actual execution of the finished monument was entrusted to the M.T. Carroll and Sons Company of Colma. A fifteen ton piece of granite was brought by railroad from Westerly, Rhode Island. It was necessary to lay a foundation thirty–six feet deep in order to support the massive five feet square and sixteen feet long stone.

On the face of the granite is carved a raised Celtic cross, its outlines extending around the sides. In the center portion of the cross is the partly–hooded head of Fray Junípero Serra, his eyes uplifted and his hands clasped in prayer. Above, on either side and below are panels of Celtic interlaced carving, executed in high relief and made to form a cross on the center of each. The inscription is very simple, the words appearing on the stone being "Junípero Serra."

Next follows another panel of Celtic carving, that too being endless interlaced work. Lastly is San Carlos Borromeo Mission, with its every graceful lines carved in perfect proportion. The workmanship is remarkably well–executed, the fine lines and moldings of which were finished by pneumatic tools designed especially for the intricate chiseling.

The picturesque monument to Fray Junípero Serra was dedicated with impressive ceremonies in April, 1908. As noted in one newspaper account, the graceful granite tribute forms a striking and forceful unity "telling in two simple pictures and words that Junípero Serra the saintly priest, was the founder of the Missions of California."

FRAY JUNÍPERO SERRA (1713–1784)

X. SPIRITUAL FATHER OF ALTA CALIFORNIA

With prophetic insight, John F. Davis wrote, in 1913, that the pathetic ruin at Carmel is a shattered monument above a grave that will become a world's shrine of pilgrimage in honor of one of humanity's heroes." He went on to say of Fray Junípero Serra that "the memory of the brave heart that was here consumed with love for mankind will live through the ages. And, in a sense, the work of these missions is not dead—their very ruins still preach the lesson of service and of sacrifice."

The dedicated missionary who is regarded by all peoples as the spiritual Father of Alta California was a man of outstanding personal qualities. The testimony of his contemporaries and subsequent commentators are unanimous in their praise of the Mallorcan friar.

Serra's apostolic philosophy was stated in a letter he wrote to his superior, shortly after arriving at San Diego. "It will be necessary in the beginning to suffer many real privations. However, to a lover all things are sweet." Serra expected no Utopia. He presupposed hardships and even embraced them. He took setbacks and disappointments in stride.

The friar was made of tough spiritual fibre. For years be was accustomed to four or five hours of sleep only. He spent long hours in prayer. In the matter of food, he was most abstemious and seemed to care little about its quality. He had prepared himself well for the rigorous apostolate of a cheerless frontier.

A measure of the esteem generally held for Fray Junípero Serra by his contemporaries is evident from a confrere who wrote to a friend, on August 26, 1773: "Because of the austerity of his life, his humility, charity and other virtues, he is worthy to be counted among the imitators of the apostles."

Like all truly spiritual people, Serra spoke rarely and with great reservations about his own interior life. The friar did pull aside the curtain long enough to observe that "the only quality that I can feel pretty sure I have, by the kindness and grace of God is my good intentions, As to anything else, what means have I of knowing whether I am right or wrong? May God direct us in the way of truth!"

Isidore Dockweiler said that "this man whose memory is indissolubly one with the epic of California, was great in humility. He triumphed by his courage, when everything would have appeared bound to discourage him and beat him down. He is one who is worthy of first place among the immortal heroes who created our nation. So his memory will never die, and his name will be blessed from generation to generation."

Over half a century ago, Hiram Johnson, California's outstanding senator and governor, made bold to say:

> To the memory of Junípero Serra, California owes an everlasting tribute. He brought civilization to our land, and in deed and character, he deserves a foremost place in the history of our state.

And surely that he has attained!

FRAY JUNÍPERO SERRA (1713–1784)

Y. MONTEREY RECALLS THE *PRESIDENTE*

The first public symbol of an appreciative posterity to Fray Junípero Serra was dedicated at Monterey in 1891. Interestingly enough, the donor of this monument was Jane Leland Stanford, a non–Catholic. Located on the military reservation, it was unveiled on June 3, 1891, in the presence of over 5,000 people from every part of the west coast, many of whom arrived in specially chartered railroad cars.

Monterey was elaborately decorated for the occasion. All along the principal streets pine and cypress boughs were interplaced and there was a goodly show of bunting. At the ceremonies, Father Clementine Deymann gave a brief history of Serra's life, followed by a sketch of the friar's far–reaching influence on the history of California by Judge W.H. Webb.

The site commands a grand view of Monterey Bay, the city and the exquisite countryside around. It is picturesquely located and is sufficiently close to the identical spot to insure its historical relevance. Standing about fifty feet above the high water mark, in a conspicuous place, the statue is about 100 yards from the actual ravine where the Carmelites first offered Holy Mass in 1602 and where Serra himself repeated the Liturgy in 1770.

The figure and pedestal are fashioned entirely of granite and the front faces almost due northeast. On a polished surface of the pedestal an inscription notes that "here, June 3, 1770, landed Very Rev. Father Junípero Serra, O.S.F. . . ."

Beneath that inscription, a dedicatory sentence attests that "this monument erected by Jane L. Stanford, in the year 1891. In Memory of Father Junípero Serra, a Philanthropist seeking the Welfare of the Humblest, a Hero Ready and Daring to sacrifice himself for the Good of his Fellow Beings, a Faithful Servant of his Master."

The notion of commemorating the landing of Serra originated with Father Angelo Cassanova who discovered the friar's body in 1882 and began restoring San Carlos Borromeo Mission in 1884. The contract for the statue was entrusted to the Western Granite & Marble Company of San Jose. A block of sixty tons of Crystal Lake granite was cut from the quarry at Emigrant Gap.

At the time of its dedication, the Monterey *Cypress* noted that "the press throughout the coast had been exceedingly liberal in its mention of this great gift, and the people all along the line between San Diego and San Francisco evinced an ardent desire to see the monument erected to the memory of a man whose life had been devoted to the work of Christianization in this then wild and uncivilized sphere."

FRAY JUNÍPERO SERRA (1713–1784)

Z. RARE FIND AT ZACATECAS

During a journey to Mexico, in 1954, Harry Downie discovered a faithful copy of what may have been the only painting Fray Junípero Serra ever posed for. In an interview for the Monterey *Peninsula News*, the renowned restorer of San Carlos Borromeo Mission

noted that "it is the only one I have ever seen showing Father Serra in a sick, weakened condition. And historical documents say he was ordered to sit for a painting during his illness just before he died."

A prominent local artist in Monterey, Abel G. Warshawsky, confirmed Downie's assertion that "it could be a true sketch of the original painting, which has been missing ever since a revolution in 1912." An inscription on the painting testifies that it was "a sketch by Pedro Pablo Miquez, Convent of the (Holy) Cross, Province of the Holy Gospel, Querétaro." It is known that the original painting hung at Santa Cruz de Querétaro about 1773.

Warshawsky said the brush marks indicated that it was probably a true copy because they are delicate and deliberate. And the general features are the same as those in other Serra paintings. He said the canvas was the type used about 1780 and the artist probably went to the convent and copied the original at the request of someone. "Most other pictures," said Harry Downie, " show Father Serra with a face that has been used to luxurious living, but this shows him rather gaunt and hard worked. And remember, he was dying when the original was made."

How the painting came to be discovered is fascinating. The Downie family was visiting places in Mexico associated with the famed Franciscan *Presidente*. North of the capital, Harry met a man who told him to seek out a particular second–hand store along the main highway leading into Zacatecas. And there it was that he came upon the painting. The proprietor of the store wasn't overly anxious to part with the painting, but Downie was

finally able to purchase the treasure for about sixteen American dollars—indeed the bargain of the century!

The sketch of Serra depicts the friar's cowled head and shoulders. His face, with its marked Spanish lineaments, reflects sadness, suffering and patience.

Visitors to San Carlos Borromeo Mission can see the painting upon request, as well as an elaboration of the Zacatecas version painted by Mr. Warshausky. Harry Downie had the portrayal copyrighted by the United States Government. And that was fitting too, for Fray Junípero Serra belongs to San Carlos Borromeo in a very special way—for there his remains are solemnly entombed.

FRAY JUNÍPERO SERRA (1713–1784)

AA. CHURCH AT JALPAN

Jalpan is situated in a narrow valley through which the Rio de Jalpan lazily flows, flanked by huge shady sabino trees. The only flat portion in the town is the area in which the church and the town *plaza* are located. From the plaza the narrow streets of cobblestone and dirt or ledges of rock run downhill.

The church in Jalpan is the one remaining piece of evidence of Fray Junípero Serra's building program during his missionary career. (The mission buildings of California built during his years, with the exception of the adobe chapel at San Juan Capistrano, have given way to more sturdy structures) In a letter written on March 28, 1758, Fray Pedro Perez de Mezquia said that Serra built the church of "rough stone and mortar and with vaults without any further help than that of God."

Likely, however, Serra utilized the talent of a master mason from Mexico City, Querétaro or San Luis Potosi. Known as Santiago, the church has, at the left of the facade, an imposing tower about ninety feet in height, surmounted by a five foot ornamental iron cross.

Measuring about forty feet in width and about seventy–five feet in height, the tower has a profusion of detail in low and high relief, with statues and symbols. The style is a mixture of churrigueresque and baroque. The church is cruciform with an octagonal cupola. It is built entirely of stone, with three groined vaults forming the nave. The choir loft, supported by a rather flat arch, occupies half of the first third of the nave. Midway up the nave, on the Gospel side, a high arched doorway leads to the octagonal side chapel, similar to but larger than the one at San Luis Rey Mission.

The outside stones of this chapel look fresher than the rest of the church and within there are unmistakable signs that they were added later. The sacristy opens directly from the end of the right transept. It has a vaulted stone roof, not groined, but of barrel design.

The pulpit is fixed to the wall at the corner of the nave and the transept and is reached by a stairway through a wall, as in many of the California missions. It is located on the Epistle side. The four windows on each side of the high walls are splayed Arabic design, similar to those at Santa Barbara Mission.

The colors within the church are subdued pinks, blues and greens. They are tints and, in this respect, similar to Santa Ines and San Miguel Missions. In the general aspect of the interior, with its cross piece and octagonal dome and its modern altars in classic design, Jalpan is more like the interior of San Luis Rey Mission. Several statues are all that remain of the original interior furnishings. Especially interesting is the one depicting Our Lady of Solitude which stands in a side chapel near the Cristo del Santo Entierro, the image of the dead Christ lying in a glass–walled coffin.

Adjoining the church to the right, is a quadrangular one–story building formerly used as a monastery. Quite plain and simple in its lines and structure, the monastery is in full accord with the ideals of Franciscan poverty.

Santiago is surely the one architectural gem of Jalpan. The lacelike finery of saints and vines and scallops and shell designs on the graceful tower and exquisite facade radiate the magical effect of golden yellow under the light of the full moon.

FRAY JUNÍPERO SERRA (1713–1784)

BB. SHRINE FOR CALIFORNIANS AT PETRA

The welcome mat is always out for Californians at the little dwelling at No. 6 Calle Barracar, on the southeastern edge of the small town of Petra de Mallorca. There, on November 24, 1713, Miguel Jose Serra was born. That insignificant home of Antonio Serra and Margarita Ferrer has become famous because it once cradled a Christian hero who added a realm to the Church and a continent to the empire.

Built of stone, with a frontage of twenty–eight feet, the two–story dwelling is a typical farmer's house of the early 18th century. An ample doorway, with a round arch, served as the entrance for the mule, as well as the family.

A corridor leads from the parlor, arranged with period furnishings, to a long narrow garden in the rear. That passageway divides the mule's corral on the right from the small kitchen and bedroom on the left. The second story, reached by a staircase from the parlor, contains another bedroom and an area for storage. Two small windows admit light and air. The bake oven and woodshed are in the rear garden.

Today there is a plaque on the facade of the home indicating its role in the life of its famous son, Fray Junípero Serra. Town officials at Petra guard the building as a museum. During the early years of this century, the historic structure was unoccupied and used as a corral for livestock. Its entrance door was unhinged, its stone walls both in front and rear were flaking and moldering. Refuse and debris of more than a century were everywhere.

In 1930, Jaime Oliver Febrer and Miguel Ramis authenticated the home as Serra's birthplace. This they did through records found in the archives of the local parish church. Shortly afterwards, the ancient stone dwelling and adjacent garden were purchased and the interior of the house was restored by a group of historically–minded Mallorcans.

The Rotary Club of Mallorca acquired title to the Serra birthplace on December 2, 1931 and, after making some minor repairs, the house was offered to the City of San Francisco. The Bay Area's Board of Supervisors were elated at the proposal and commissioned Juan Cervera Cebrian to take formal possession of the deed. Governor James Rolph then proclaimed May 12, 1932, as Junípero Serra Day in recognition of the gift.

In 1958, the Society of California Pioneers took responsibility for maintaining and administering the Serra House as a shrine/museum. Expenses were defrayed from a subsidy levied by the San Francisco hotel tax authority.

Following the passage of Proposition 13, San Francisco's Chief Administrative Officer decided that the annual operational costs of the Serra House were excessive and should be discontinued.

Kevin Starr, a popular local columnist, deplored the decision and said that "the withdrawal of this paltry subsidy is just one more nail in the coffin of San Francisco." He did admit, however that the public support of Serra's birthplace must seem like "a naive provincial oddity" in an "era when tens of thousands of taxpayer's dollars are used to underwrite a parade for the gay community."

In any event, the return of the title to Petra in no way reflects upon or diminishes the love and affection Californians still harbor for their beloved religious founder.

FRAY JUNÍPERO SERRA (1713–1784)

CC. EVER OLD AND ALWAYS NEW

Definitive is a characteristic rarely associated with oral or written history. The wise and dedicated researcher is ever alert to the need for revising the public record in light of freshly unearthed evidence. An interesting example of this principle is the "Schumacher Crayon" likeness of Fray Junípero Serra which, prior to the turn of the century, was generally accepted in California as an authentic depiction of the Mallorcan friar.

The first prominence given to the work came in May of 1860, when a woodcut of this "Portrait of Father Junípero Serra" appeared in *Hutchings' California Magazine*. Serra, arrayed in the traditional Franciscan habit, is shown with his leftward–looking face slightly elevated in a spirit of reverent adoration. Over his shoulders rests a stole ornamented with a pattern of oak leaves. The original crayon version, commissioned by Antonio F. Coronel and executed by the San Francisco artist, Arthur Nahl, was based on an excerpted bust from a scene in which Serra was kneeling before the altar of San Carlos Borromeo Mission the day before his death. The crayon was fashioned at the Los Angeles studio of Frank G. Schumacher, 107 North Spring Street, in August of 1884.

For some years the framed depiction hung at Los Angeles Orphanage. Shortly after the turn of the century, it came into the possession of Mission Santa Barbara. When Charles C. Pierce inquired about its location, in 1904, he was informed "that it had been sent some time before to a local loan exhibition with other mission relics and rarities. When these were returned to the mission the crayon was missing." Fortunately, Mr. Schumacher had photographed the crayon and that portrait of the Venerable *Presidente* appeared in a number of publications as the authentic likeness of Junípero Serra.

There are two theories about the model used for the crayon. George Watson Cole was of the opinion that the Nahl depiction was copied from an old painting, which as near as Schumacher could remember, was executed on parchment. He recalled that it had been borrowed expressly for the purpose of making the crayon copy. If such a model ever existed, it has long since disappeared. The eminent Franciscan historian, Father Maynard Geiger, on the other band, suspects that the Nahl version was based on a photographic reproduction made by William Rich, in 1853. In any event, since both the purported models were copies of Mariano Guerrero's 1785 painting of Serra's reception of the last sacraments, the authenticity of Nahl's crayon is obviously related to the faithfulness of the earlier work.

The Guerrero painting, now hanging in Chapultepec Castle's Hall of the Spiritual Conquest, was examined, in 1904, by Father Zephyrin Engelhardt. After a careful investigation, the Franciscan chronicler concluded that the *Verdadero Retrato del Apostólico Padre Predicador Fr. Junípero Serra* was nothing more than "a fanciful production of an artist in Mexico [done] after the death of the venerable mission founder." Engelhardt studiously documented his view denying that the Guerrero work was really "a true likeness." There was a factor, however, which he did not consider: In the Antonio Coronel Collection are several fragments of Serra's clothing, among which is a piece of the friar's stole, with oak leaves woven in gold thread. The design is practically identical with that in the Guerrero painting and the

Schumacher crayon. Whether this is a mere coincidence, or indicative of the original artist's familiarity with his subject is still an open question.

Should further evidence come to light, it might well happen that the Schumacher crayon, once accepted as a faithful likeness of Serra and later categorized as "a fanciful production," may swing full circle. Presently, there is no "definitive" answer. One can only repeat an opinion stated in 1910: "The whole question concerning portraits of Serra is involved in considerable obscurity."

FRAY JUNÍPERO SERRA (1713–1784)

DD. LETTERS OF THE *PRESIDENTE*

Students of California happily welcomed the long–promised fourth volume of the *Writings of Junípero Serra*. That the tome actually did appear, even ten years late, is a story of dogged determinism by the Academy of American Franciscan History. Part of the type was lost when the printing office was taken over by the government, and the matter was further confused when the manuscript itself was misplaced while the Academy was moving to its new quarters.

It was activity incident to the contemplated beatification process that originally sparked attempts to gather a complete set of the extant letters, reports, memorandum, etc., of Fray Junípero Serra into one central location. In 1937, Father Maynard J. Geiger was entrusted with locating and integrating all the Serra materials into the Santa Barbara Mission Archives.

The feasibility of publishing this data was first suggested by the late Maximin Piette, O.F.M. It was rightly thought that Serra's writings would be an effective measuring rod for interpreting the life and character of the founder of California's mission chain. During the last years of his life, Piette carefully arranged to have the Spanish text and English translations of the various "Serrana" set in type.

With Piette's premature demise in 1948, the overall program was orientated along more restrictive norms. The documents were painstakenly edited and arranged into a uniform style of spelling, punctuation, accentuation and capitalization. It was decided that explanatory notes should be minimized in view of the already published scholarly tomes of Maynard J. Geiger. Each of the letters was identified as to designee and place and date of origin with a brief prefatory digest. Other materials were prefaced with descriptive headings and date and place of origin.

The first of the four contemplated volumes of the *Writings of Junípero Serra* was published by the Academy in 1955, under the capable editorship of Antonine Tibesar, O.F.M. Two subsequent volumes appeared the following year. The final tome is perhaps the most important in the series, providing as it does, in addition to the normal text, an indispensible thirty–nine page index to the entire series.

Volume Four brings to 231 the number of extant Serra writings available for the public record. That the total document count falls considerably short of the stated estimate is due to the omission of items which proved little more than extracts from longer originals. Most critical readers agree that documents differing only in date and/or addressee should appear only under one heading. Complete as these four volumes are, however, they surely do not exhaust the correspondence of the gentle friar who once complained that he had spent half of his life writing letters.

If the text of this final volume lacks the polish of the earlier tomes, readers must remember that these are the letters of an old man, worn out by labors, encompassed by difficulties and confronted by frustration from every direction. The issuance of this book calls to mind a remark made by Hiram W. Johnson on November 24, 1913, at the bi–centennial celebration's of Serra's birth: "To the memory of Junípero Serra, California owes an everlasting tribute. He brought civilization to our land, and in deed and character be deserves a foremost place in the history of our state."

FRAY JUNIPERO SERRA (1713–1784)

EE. A CALIFORNIA SAINT?

Canonization, or the formal declaration by the Catholic Church of a particular individual's personal salvation, has been described as "the most complicated legal process in the world." Such a proclamation usually marks the end of centuries of research, discussion and purposeful delay.

In 1909, Charles Fletcher Lummis, the prominent historian and non–Catholic founder of the Southwest Museum, noted, "Without authority, I have started a campaign to find out why Junípero Serra has not been canonized." Though Lummis never published the results of his searching, the answer to the original query was given years later by Serra's biographer. "The principal unfavorable factors against the opening of a cause of sainthood in favor of Serra in colonial California were distance, the absence of a bishop, a lack of personnel, great expense, and the changing political situation not too long after Serra's death." The question became so compelling that in 1934, the name of Fray Junípero was formally proposed for the honors of the altar by the Very Reverend Novatus Benzing, Provincial of the Franciscan Province of Santa Barbara.

An historical commission was established by the Bishop of Monterey–Fresno on December 17, 1943. Three well–known scholars, one of them a non–Catholic, were instructed to collect all existing writings of Serra and all data concerning his life, character and reputation. The work of finding, gathering and assembling the necessary materials from over 125 libraries and archives around the world took five years of dedicated effort on the part of Father Maynard J. Geiger, O.F.M.

People of Mexican, Spanish, Indian and early American ancestry were interviewed on what they knew of Junípero Serra from family tradition. Out of this testimony, the vice–postulator drew up a series of statements to be proven in an ecclesiastical forum.

Formal court proceedings began on December 12, 1948, at Fresno, presided over by Bishop Aloysius J. Willinger. Oaths of fidelity and secrecy were taken by all attached to the cause. Specially chosen judges were empowered to interrogate witnesses with questions submitted by the Promotor of the Faith, or the "Devil's Advocate." At this hearing the 2420 documents (7500 pages) of Serra's writings were carefully examined for doctrinal content. All sessions were held behind locked doors to prevent any possible collusion. The vice–postulator, after an initial appearance, took no part in the investigative process, "the only court in the world in which the man who is pleading the case is not allowed to be present!"

After four days at Fresno, the court reconvened at Carmel, the burial place of Junípero Serra. There another process was inaugurated to ascertain whether any unauthorized veneration had taken place. The judges, seated in the sanctuary, questioned a number of early pioneers as to the nature of the pilgrimages and devotions in honor of Serra after his death in 1784. Subsequently, testimony was given by members of the Diocesan Historical Commission concerning the 5000 pages of materials written about Serra by kings, viceroys, clergymen, military people, civilians and confreres. At the conclusion of these and later court sessions, reports of the meetings were packed in boxes, stamped with the episcopal seal, and shipped to Rome's Sacred Congregation of Rites for further examination.

FRAY JUNÍPERO SERRA (1713–1784)

FF. RELICS OF FRAY JUNÍPERO SERRA

The veneration of Christian relics is a practice that can be traced back to the middle of the 2nd century. Even today, the Catholic Church permits and even encourages the veneration of relics as a way of honoring those temples of the Holy Spirit raised to eternal glory.

There are several categories of relics. For example, "first class" relics are parts of the human remains of a holy person; "second class" relics are items associated with the person during his or her earthly sojurn and "third class" relics are anything having been remotely connected with the person in question.

Over the years, a number of people have written to ask about the possibility of obtaining relics of Fray Junípero Serra.

The practice of venerating relics has been minutely regulated since the time of the Council of Trent. Among the many stipulations is one that forbids the issuance of new relics without episcopal authorization. When Fray Junípero Serra's remains were officially identified in 1943, the Bishop of Monterey–Fresno made it clear that he did not wish anything to be removed, especially for public veneration.

Very likely the bishop had in mind the observation of Fray Francisco Palou who cautioned those who had items belonging to Serra that the term "relic" could only be associated with those whom the Church had officially proclaimed "blessed" or "sainted." Palou's advice was good theology.

Given that caveat, relics of Fray Junípero Serra cannot be venerated until the Holy See formally beatifies the friar. Those who might have such items should be careful to treat them primarily as historical treasures and nothing more. That there are some of those "relics" around is amply evident. Following Serra's interment, Palou blessed scapulars which had been made from Serra's extra tunic. Some of those may well have survived.

There is a piece of the *Presidente's* bone in the Historical Museum attached to the Archival Center, Archdiocese of Los Angeles. It is encased in a mosaic–filled cross bearing depictions of the four Roman basilicas. Several pieces of Serra's original coffin are also preserved in the Historical Museum, along with a piece of a nail which was found when the remains were exhumed and identified at Carmel. The latter was presented by Marie Harrington in 1982.

Serra's chalice, monstrance and many of his books can still be seen at San Carlos Borromeo Mission. His extant writings have been carefully preserved and his autograph turns simple paper into currency among Western Americana collectors.

Another interesting "relic" is a fragment removed from the heart of the tree beneath which Fray Junípero Serra celebrated Holy Mass for the first time at Monterey, June 3, 1770. It was authenticated by J.K. Oliver on August 28, 1905.

One final Serra "relic" is a copy of the *Relación Histórico*, a small book which belonged to and was used by Serra during his years as *Presidente* of the California missions.

FRAY JUNÍPERO SERRA (1713–1784)

GG. OUTFITTING THE *PRESIDENTE*

In the never–ending task of untangling California's history, no aspect has proven more fascinating and enlightening than ascertaining the costumery of those living in the earliest years of European penetration.

In their book on *Early California Costumes, 1769–1847*, Margaret Gilbert Mackey and Louise Pinkney Sooy devote a whole section to the vesture of "the Father President of All the Missions," Fray Junípero Serra.

HAT: Broad, stiff, round brim; low, rounded crown; gray to match robe. Sometimes the cowl was used.

HAIR: Hair clipped short around ears; small tonsure on crown of head. Face clean–shaven.

ROBE: Of gray "sackcloth," woven like a woolen twill or heavy, coarse serge; made like a tunic; full–skirted and full–sleeved; capuche or cowl made separately and left to hang between shoulders behind. Franciscans in California did not change the color of their robes to russet–brown until the latter part of the nineteenth century.

CORD: Double; white, heavy, twisted ropes; passed around waist and drawn through knotted loop on right hip; ends extended to bottom of robe, where each was finished in a knot; the forward rope of the two, as it hung from the waist to the hem of the robe, was knotted in three places, the knots being five or six inches apart.

ROSARY: String of wooden beads on a small chain, consisting of fifteen sets of small beads (*Ave Marias*), ten beads in each set, separated by a length of chain and a larger bead (*Paternoster*). The Rosary was fastened together at the bottom by a medal carrying the image of the Virgin or of some saint. From this medal hung a larger bead (*Paternoster*) separated by a length of chain from three more small beads (*Ave Marias*) followed by a second bead (*Paternoster*) and finished at the end with a wooden cross carrying the image of Christ. The rosary was looped through the cord about the waist and hung on the left side.

SANDALS: Of brown, heavy leather; thick sole; single strap, about an inch broad, crossing base of toes; a leather strip protecting the heel; fastened by leather thongs around ankle. Otherwise, the feet were bare.

The description of life inside the mission's "monastery" was also interesting. Life was simple and comfortless. Floors were earthen or tiled; there were few fireplaces, and the windows were glassless. The furnishings consisted of plain, straight oak chairs with rawhide seats and backs, or straight, hard benches, hand–hewn and without paint or decoration.

The refectory or dining room tables were long, heavy and plain. Tallow candles at night gave forth the only light in the small rooms. Beds were of rawhides stretched on wooden frames and covered with coarse blankets, while the monastery dishes and implements were of simple earthenware, iron or copper.

A library containing a few volumes of saints' lives and sermons offered the chief mental recreation for the friars. When a stranger arrived for the night, the friars not only extended their generous hospitality but enjoyed an evening of interesting conversation.

In pastoral California, there were no hostelries. Travelers had to depend on the missions for a night's lodging. Knowing this, the friars posted an Indian at the door day and night to look after the needs of visitors.

A whole section in the book is devoted to the vestments worn by priests at Holy Mass and another for the special vesture used on such feastdays as *Corpus Christi* and Pentecost. The friars endeavored to have the finest vestments for the celebration of the holy mysteries.

As far as they were from the bustling centers of contemporary life, the California missions were remarkably well adapted to meet the needs of frontier life.

FRAY JUNÍPERO SERRA (1713–1784)

HH. SERRA IN NATION'S CAPITAL

In 1864, the Honorable Justin Smith Morrill, senior senator from the State of Vermont, authored legislation in Congress to set aside as Statuary Hall that portion of the national capitol building formerly used by the House of Representatives. Each state of the union was asked to submit two marble or bronze statues, of its most distinguished citizens "illustrious for their services to their fellow men."

There were several attempts in succeeding years to have California represented at Washington but differences of opinion delayed action until 1927, when a committee of the Legislature officially proposed Junípero Serra and Thomas Starr King for the honors.

The acceptance and unveiling ceremonies took place in Statuary Hall on March 1, 1931, in the presence of a host of the nation's civil and religious leaders. In his invocation, Bishop Thomas J. Shahan, Rector–emeritus of The Catholic University of America, recalled that the hard trails Serra's "weary feet traversed are to–day a royal road along which are strung great cities, on which nature exhibits all her riches, and human progress, its every latest attainment." The magnificent statue, fashioned by the Venetian–born Ettore Cadorin, was seen by one observer as "a silent figure in bronze, holding the cross aloft, a tribute to his noble life and an inspiration to future generations."

President Herbert Hoover was represented at the ceremonies by Ray Lyman Wilbur, Secretary of the Interior, who eulogized Junípero Serra as the west's torchbearer of civilization who "bravely, zealously, lovingly, and indefatigably remained steadfast" in gaining the devotion and respect of the California Indians. The official representative of California referred to Serra in his remarks as a man "devoted to the inculcation of the principles of Christianity and modern civilization in a new land and among a primitive people." Senator Hiram

Johnson noted that the humble Mallorcan friar had identified himself with California "in order to educate, train, and help the Indians dwelling in that region" once a savage land, now a wondrous empire.

Isidore B. Dockweiler, a well–known Los Angeles businessman, delivered the principal address. He portrayed Serra as the 'legitimate precursor of the later–day civil authorities established by the American Government upon the shores of the Pacific." Dockweiler, himself an outstanding western pioneer, concluded his remarks by quoting from California's poet laureate to the effect that "it is perhaps quite safe to say that there is not in all the history of civilization one other single man whose individual labors for God and humanity bore such a bountiful harvest. The name of Junípero Serra is to–day the best–loved name in California, without distinction of class or creed. His memory is honored and revered by all the people."

FRAY JUNÍPERO SERRA (1713–1784)

II. MEXICO CITY RECALLS SERRA

The Mexico City that Fray Junípero Serra left forever in 1773 has changed so much that he would have difficulty recognizing the metropolis which is fast moving toward being the largest in the world. Though the college no longer exists, the Church of San Fernando (largest in the city except for the cathedral) is still very much in evidence. It is still staffed by the Order of Friars Minor.

There is abundant evidence that Serra has not been forgotten in Mexico City or, as it is now called, the Distrito Federal. Visitors entering the Church of San Fernando from Guerrero Street, for example, pass through a modern portal appropriately called *La Puerta de Fray Junípero Serra*, named to honor the Mallorcan friar who started it all along *El Camino Real*.

Within the vestibule of *La Puerta*, half hidden in the darkness, stands a large statue of Serra chiseled from gray *canteria*, a substance common in many Mexican churches, public buildings and private homes. In Serra's hand is a replica of San Carlos Borromeo Mission. In the sacristy of the church, atop one of the vestment cases, is a possibly contemporary oil painting of Serra which authorities are unable to date or otherwise verify.

Father Zephyrin Engelhardt suggested that Serra may have sat for a painting by Joseph Paez when he visited Mexico City in 1773. It was a custom of religious institutes to have portrayals done of their more famous members. The portrait of Serra seated in a chair and leaning a little forward, which Engelhardt used in several of his historical volumes, and which, according to Dr. Nicolas Leon, formerly hung at San Fernando, has long since disappeared.

In the park before the church stands a monument of the statesman and soldier, Guerrero. The trend in Mexican monuments for many years has been toward portraying Indian chiefs and military policiticans–not missionaries. Perhaps one day soon the pendulum will swing the other way and the statue of Serra now in La *Puerta* will be moved outside among the green trees of the *plaza*.

In the Museum of History at the Castle of Chapultepec, near the far end of the *Paseo de Reforma*, there is a painting of Fray Junípero Serra in a prominent room dedicated to the spiritual conquest of New Spain. The painting was done posthumously (1785) and depicts Serra receiving Holy Viaticum from the hands of his friend, Fray Francisco Palou, in the mission church of San Carlos Borromeo. Bishop Rafael Verger, once Serra's guardian at San Fernando College and later a bishop, paid for the painting which was executed by Mariano Guerrero.

One can still see the building which once housed the printing shop of Don Felipe de Zuñiga y Ontiveros on Mexico City's *Calle de Espiritu Santo*. There, sometime between March and December, 1787, the *Relación Historica de la Vida y Apostolicas Tareas del Venerable Padre Fray Junípero Serra* was published.

That book enjoys the distinction of being the earliest California biography and the best account of the area's most renowned character. Copies today fetch a handsome price among Western Americana enthusiasts.

Who from California can visit the Shrine of Our Lady of Guadalupe, the religious heart of Mexico, without recalling the evening of December 31, 1749, when Fray Junípero Serra first knelt before Our Lady's depiction with a prayer for guidance over his new apostolate in America?

FRAY JUNÍPERO SERRA (1713–1784)

JJ. *PRESIDENTE* AND MUSICIAN

As in other things, so also in music Fray Junípero Serra was an example to his brethren. The first *Presidente* of the California missions not only fostered music by verbal approval, but taught it as well. Many a service he enhanced by his singing for he was endowed with a sonorous voice which he used for the glory of God.

During his youthful days in Petra de Mallorca, he attracted attention by his singing and it was on this account that he was admitted into the choir of the local Franciscan monastery. Before little Miguel Serra was tall enough to reach the choir rack, he was skilled in plainsong.

When Serra came to Mexico in 1749, he edified all at the great College of San Fernando by his faithful attendance at choir. He made his time spent at the College a second novitiate. Later, in the Sierra Gorda at his first missions, he converted his Indians by song, as well as by preaching and good example.

He celebrated Holy Mass whenever possible with chant. The services of Holy Week were a special delight to him. On Sunday afternoons he made it a practice to gather together his neophytes for songs in honor of Our Lady of Mercy.

Another more impressive custom he inaugurated was a procession every Saturday evening in honor of the Blessed Mother during which all would chant the rosary. This inspiring devotion always ended with the beautiful chant *Tota Pulchra es Maria* which Serra translated into Spanish and which the Indians learned by heart and chanted with great solemnity.

In the missions of both Baja and Alta California, Fray Junípero Serra continued with those same devotions. He fondly recalled Saint Benedict's advice that "to sing is to pray twice." At San Carlos Mission, Serra took personal charge of the choir, teaching his singers not only the necessary Masses and reponses, but also his favorite hymns. We are told by his biographer that whenever the natives sang the rosary, Serra would shed tears of tenderness and devotion. The same thing would happen when he celebrated the services of the Passion and the Divine Mysteries of Holy Week.

Serra died singing. Toward the very end of his life, when he was most feeble, he insisted on praying and singing with the neophytes. On hearing him one afternoon conclude Vespers with the hymn composed by Fray Antonio Margil in honor of Our Lady's Assumption, Palou remarked to a soldier that the *Presidente* did not seem to be very ill. The soldier replied: "We must not be too confident; he is sick, but this saintly priest, when it comes to praying and singing, is always well; but he is almost finished."

On the day following this incident, because it was the nineteenth of the month, Serra asked that Mass be celebrated in honor of Saint Joseph. Weak as he was, Serra sang along with the Indian choristers. That afternoon he recited the usual prayers and sang the regular hymns to the Blessed Mother.

Next day he joined with the faithful in the devotion of the *Via Crucis*. Some days later, while the Angel of Death hovered over his weakened body, the beloved Apostle of California startled those kneeling about him in church, when immediately before receiving Holy Viaticum, he sang the *Tantum Ergo Sacramentum* in a loud voice.

Like his holy Father, Saint Francis, psalms of praise were on his lips until the very last. His Requiem, however, the neophyte choristers did not render flawlessly; they could not sing with ease, for tears and weeping choked their voices within them.

FRAY JUNÍPERO SERRA (1713–1784)

KK. CALIFORNIA'S EDUCATOR

By training and years of service, Fray Junípero Serra was a university professor—and a good one at that. He put it all aside, journeyed to the New World, and then spent the remaining years of his life teaching aboriginal peoples the rudiments of the Catholic Faith.

Serra's "second career" was surely more challenging than his first. Many of Christianity's abstract teachings could not be expressed in the native California languages and dialects. The simple minds of his listeners had great difficulty in grasping philosophical concepts.

Hence it came about that the friars adopted the system their predecessors found useful in other areas of the New World, the *Doctrina*. The missionaries would have the Indians recite, until they knew it by heart, the Sign of the Cross, Our Father, Hail Mary, Creed; Acts of Faith, Hope and Charity; the *Confiteor*, Ten Commandments, Six Precepts, Seven Sacraments, the Necessary Points of Faith and the Four Last Things. Known throughout Latin America as the *Doctrina Cristiana*, this summary of the Deposit of Faith was required of the Indians before they were allowed to be baptized.

The *Doctrina* was recited each day before Holy Mass and again in the evening before retiring. With a minimum of effort, even the dullest natives would gradually absorb the basic groundwork of the Faith in a relatively short time.

Spanish was used in the learning process since it was a uniform language and could be taught throughout California, an area filled with a multitude of local dialects. Not only did the natives quickly pick up the basic foundations of the new language but they profited from the unifying effect it had on the separate tribes.

Sunday sermons centered about the *Doctrina*, usually isolating and explaining some aspect of the teaching. In the early years, sermons were translated into the local dialect by an interpreter. Later the missionaries mastered the Indian tongues and were able to converse in their own languages. As the *Doctrina* was intended primarily for adults, a special type of catechetical instructions was used for the youngsters. In the morning as soon as the grown people began their daily chores the friars gave instructions to the boys and girls who were five years old and over.

In order to demonstrate more graphically the truths of the *Doctrina*, depictions and statues were often placed in the corridors, living quarters and around the mission compound of Our Lord, the Blessed Mother, the saints and various mysteries of the Faith.

Another supplement used in religious instruction of the natives was a series of religious dramas based on the liturgical cycle. The Christmas season was especially appealing in this regard and the story of Our Lord's Nativity was portrayed as vividly as possible, with the natives themselves acting out the various parts.

This daily schedule of religion, work and play arranged by the missionaries was designed to keep the neophytes occupied from dawn to dusk. While it was the most important part of their daily duties, religious instruction was only one aspect of that mission culture upon which men of a later day reared the structure of history, the cornerstone of California art, literature and sentiment.

Experts who have studied the pedagogical system used by Fray Junípero Serra and his Franciscan collaborators tell us that their methods were surprisingly progressive, efficient and well-integrated. Representing as they do the Hispanic American system in the culminating stage of its development, the educational methods introduced in California by Serra help to explain the transformation of much of aboriginal Latin America in the Colonial era.

FRAY JUNÍPERO SERRA (1713–1784)

LL. SERRA AND THE CALIFORNIA INDIANS

What appears as a lack of sincerity in certain recent newspaper portrayals about Fray Junípero Serra and his companions may well be a lack of understanding as to what the mission program was and how it functioned in California.

To begin with, the time sequence is vitally important. The dreadful violation of Indian rights in California came after and not during the mission era. And those who suffered most from the encroachments of the gold rush days were descendants of the Indians never attached to the missions. (Demographers estimate that not more than 40% of the total Indian population was affiliated with the missions at any one time). Put another way, the friars can be held accountable only for what transpired during their incumbency, and that would be 1769 to the 1830s. They warned that secularization was premature in California and subsequent events more than confirmed that viewpoint.

Contrary to the practice in the English and French settlements of colonial America, the relationship of native Americans to Hispanic explorers and settlers along the Pacific Slope was carefully regulated by a series of royal statutes. This *Recopilación de las Leyes de los Reinos de Indias*, first published in 1552, was revised and updated several times in subsequent centuries. To the early missionaries in California, the *Recopilación* was as familiar as their breviary. Copies of this multi-volumed handbook or manual were available in every mission library.

As agents for the crown, as well as missionaries for

the Church, the friars patterned their activity on the directives contained in the *Recopilación* There is no evidence that any of the missionaries in Alta or Baja California had any serious reservations about carrying out the royal mandate.

Concern for the spiritual and temporal welfare of the native peoples was a recurrent theme in the decrees codified in the *Recopilación*. An example of the king's concern can be seen in an edict issued in 1526, whereby King Charles exhorted "priests and religious who might participate in discoveries and in making peace (with the native tribes) . . . to try, with very great care and diligence, to bring it about that the Indians are well treated, looked upon and favored as neighbors."

Missionaries were instructed not to allow "the Indians to be forced, robbed, injured or badly treated." The king went on to say that "if the contrary is done by any person, regardless of his position or condition, the justices are to proceed against him according to law; and in those cases where it is proper for us to be advised, let it be done as soon as the opportunity is available . . . in order that we may be able to give orders for justice to be provided and that such excesses be punished with all rigor."

Philip II issued further directives on December 24, 1580, charging the viceroys, presidents and *audiencas* with the duty of protecting the Indians and of issuing corresponding orders so that they may be protected, favored and alleviated. He went on to say that "we desire that the injuries they suffer be remedied and that they may be without molestation or vexation, this viewpoint being now in force and keeping in mind the other laws of the *Recopilación*, the Indians are to be favored, protected and defended from whatsoever harm, and these laws are made to be observed very exactly. Transgressors are to be punished."

The king concluded by charging ecclesial prelates "to obtain this end as their true spiritual fathers of this new Christianity and to conserve for them their privileges and prerogatives." These were the laws of the land. There is no indication that Fray Junípero Serra and his companions did any other than observe them to the fullest.

FRAY JUNÍPERO SERRA (1713–784)

MM. EDITOR WRITES ABOUT *PRESIDENTE*

Michael Williams (1877–1950) was among the most prominent Catholic writers of the early twentieth century. A native of Halifax, Nova Scotia, Williams worked for many years as a journalist for papers on the east coast. Just the day before the earthquake, Williams became editor for the San Francisco *Examiner*, where he worked assiduously to record the drama of that catastrophic occurrence. He subsequently returned to New York and, in 1924, founded the weekly journal *Commonweal*.

A lifelong devotee of Fray Junípero Serra, Williams wanted to write the definitive biography of California's Gray Ox. One of his essays on Serra, published by the New York *Catholic News*, July 29, 1922, reveals his esteem for the Franciscan *Presidente*. To Williams, Serra "exemplified the mystic paradox of the grain of mustard seed of his Master's parable, that was cast into the earth, and died, so that from it might spring a mighty tree."

William's interest in Serra was partly an outgrowth of his belief that "it would be well for Catholics to enhance their private and public interest in history, and in particular become better acquainted with those Catholic heroes of history whose lives are in themselves a living protest against the materialistic conception of human origin and human destiny." He felt that "the ideals and truths of the Catholic faith were exemplified and made visible realities" in such personages as Serra.

After carefully pouring over the extant evidence, Williams concluded that "Serra in his youth and early manhood was even more distinguished intellectually than he was spiritually, although his religious fervor was notable. There had been born in that passionate, fervent lad of the remote isle of the Balearic group a forceful, mighty brain, as well as a powerful and devoted soul. For such a one the highest paths of power in the Church were open and easy of ascent. Even in his early twenties the fame of his preaching and of his teaching, and of his exceptionally magnetic personality, was rife in Spain." Williams noted that "thoughtful ecclesiastics" found in Serra "the stuff of greatness, the material from which leaders are fashioned. Eminently fitted by nature and by culture to hold his own in the highest ranks of European affairs of Church and State, Serra seemed predestined to achieve splendid success in the eyes of the world."

But he had other ideas. "Without regret or sorrow, but with joy and thanksgiving he gave up all thought of fame and position in Europe and passed from the plain of pomp and power—a silent, gray–robed, bare–footed friar, disappearing from the eyes of men into the wilderness—into the far–away and incredible depths of pagan and almost mythical California."

In appraising the resurgence of interest in Fray Junípero Serra, Williams thought it was significant that the friar's fame "owes its great and constantly growing proportions less to the appreciation of his fellow religionists, as such, than to the broad development of California patriotism, quite outside the limits of class or creed."

"To Catholics, Serra is first of all the saintly apostle,

but he is the special admiration, beyond all, of those who admire the pioneers, which is only as it should be, for Serra as a civilizer appeals to universal human qualities."

Though the book once envisioned by Williams never materialized, the renowned editor did record for posterity his view that Fray Junípero Serra was the "quint essential type of the Man of the West—a cornerstone of its civilization and its material progress as well as of the missions with which he adorned and sanctified the wilderness he came to transform."

FRAY JUNÍPERO SERRA (1713–1784)

NN. WHERE ARE SIGNATURES?

Since the turn of the century, a considerable percentage of the extant letters and signatures of Fray Junípero Serra has disappeared from various archival holdings, only to re–appear in dealers' catalogues or in private collections. One such document, a whole page ripped from a register book at San Francisco de Asís, recently surfaced. Happily it was returned to its rightful place at Mission Dolores through the diligent work of Rosario Curletti.

The "when," "how" and "why" of these disappearances have long been a major puzzlement. There is seemingly no consistent pattern and none of the theories batted around within historical circles completely answers the question.

It has long been a logical assumption that the missing materials were purloined at various times for monetary reasons. In fact, a number of recovered items can be rather accurately traced from the very day of their "departure." The whole question of the missing Serra letters has been further complicated by a chance discovery made by James Abajian, Archivist for the Archdiocese of San Francisco.

Abajian came across a letter written by George Cardinal Mundelein, on June 26 , 1922, to Msgr. James Cantwell, Chancellor for the Archdiocese of San Francisco. Therein the Archbishop of Chicago, known even then as an avid autograph collector, thanked Cantwell for "the two splendid letters of Fr. Junípero Serra and of Archbishop Alemaney (sic.)." The cardinal went on to say, "I assure you that I prize these autographs most highly, especially that of such a historic character as Fr. Junípero."

Though the correspondence pre–dating this exchange could not be located, it is known that His Eminence actively sought out letters and signatures for his collection from friends in the American hierarchy. Obviously officials at San Francisco had responded affirmatively.

Since the Archbishop of San Francisco and his duly–appointed Chancellor were canonically and legally entitled to alienate property, the gift of the letters was a perfectly legitimate gift. Knowing that much of Mundelein's collection is still intact, at Saint Mary's Seminary, Abajian wrote the librarian there, hoping to ascertain the date of the missing letter. Unfortunately, it seems to have wandered off in still another direction!

Lacking the date of the Serra letter sent to Cardinal Mundelein, one must conclude that there is now a shadow over all the other fugitive Serra letters, since any one of them could be the one given to His Eminence of Chicago. Hence, the long–accepted notion that all Serra letters appearing on the open market are purloined must now be discarded. (Of course, how the missing Mundelein letter came to be removed from the cardinal's collection is yet another matter) .

To serious collectors, this is more than an academic question. Letters written by Fray Junípero Serra are worth upwards of $7,000 on today's market. Even his signature sells for no less than $750. All of which speaks highly for Serra whose letters are worth considerably more than those of George Washington and Abraham Lincoln.

FRAY JUNÍPERO SERRA (1713–1784)

OO. MISSION RATIONALE

The renown that has come to Fray Junípero Serra is based almost entirely upon his apostolicity, that is, the zeal with which he announced Christ to the Indian tribes of California by word and example. In fulfilling that missionary apostolate, the humble Mallorcan friar experienced every vicissitude, disappointment and type of opposition which life is capable of presenting.

Throughout the whole of his years among the natives of Mexico and California, Serra exhibited an undaunted determinism that made him a "prince among missionaries." That attitude he expressed in a letter to his Capuchin nephew in 1774:

> When I left that beloved land of mine, I made up my mind to leave it not only in body . . . but if I was to retain forever in memory what I had left behind, what would have been the purpose of leaving it in the first place?

The ardent, optimistic and eager missionary stated his apostolic philosophy in simple, but meaningful terms, noting that for those who work among aboriginal peoples, "it will be necessary in the beginning to suffer many real privations. However, to a lover all things are sweet. But these, my poor creatures (the Indians) have cost incomparably more to my Lord Jesus Christ."

Known to historians as "the man who never turned back," Junípero Serra allowed no obstacle to deter his apostolic endeavors, observing only that "great undertakings have always been accompanied by great difficulties." He was a man "who never knew the meaning of rest or who could understand the reason for delay." Serra's missionary philosophy, as rephrased by his biographer, can be summed up as follows:

> First of all, give up everything and this completely, not only externally but internally so that your apostolate may be an all–out dedication. Do not let physical impediments, such as illness, hardships in travel and living conditions, climate, food, isolation bother you. Allow no difficulty to impede or discourage you from whatever source, diabolical or human, it may come.
>
> Face every issue head–on. Dodge none. You are fighting for God and souls. Be kind and gentle, if possible. If you must show a holy anger and enter a principled controversy or fight, do not hesitate to do so. Be a man and not a mouse. A missionary must practice the militant virtues.
>
> Work in harmony with all men insofar as it is possible, but not on the principle of "peace at any price." Where injury and opposition is sustained, be forgiving as is your Heavenly Father. Never allow your zeal to abate. Try to do all that you can, but if your superiors do not see eye to eye with you, present your case, but whatever the answer, obey. Obedience, first, last and always.
>
> Once you embark upon your work, you are God's servant in behalf of souls. Never turn back. Love your flock with the tenderness of a mother and help them with the providence of a father. Presuppose the pattern of hardships, contradiction, opposition and misunderstanding.
>
> You are in a vale of tears. Heaven is earned by such coin. Heaven awaits you as a reward. Be a man, but above all be God's man. The Church will increase and heaven will flower in souls.

The missionary *credo* of Junípero Serra, the Apostle of California, is indeed impressive. This man had the stuff of which saints are made!

FRAY JUNÍPERO SERRA (1713–1784)

PP. CALIFORNIA'S GREATEST CHARACTER

In an essay for *The Kingdom of the Sun*, John Steven McGroarty reflected that "in the fascinating history of California, Serra, the gray–robed Franciscan, stands out clear–cut and ennobled as its greatest character. He is, indeed, one of the greatest characters of all history, a true priest, an ideal soldier, an evangelist, an empire–builder, a dreamer with a poet's soul.

"Travel, if you will," writes California's poet laureate, "the seven hundred miles of *El Camino Real*—the 'King's Highway'–from San Diego to Sonoma, with its chain of twenty–one Mission buildings; think of the labor of all that, the surpassing genius of construction

and the marvel of its endless and intricate detail; recall the savage snatched from degraded barbarism to the uses of husbandry and the nobility of toil, his soul uplifted to the Crucified Christ, ear and lip trained to music, his eye taught to art; scan the fields, the hillsides and valleys found waste and desolate but made to blossom as the rose and to feed numberless flocks and herds; try to grasp all this and you will sit with the soul of Junípero Serra in the empire he created.

> Old Conquistadores, O gray priests and all,
> Give us your ghosts for company as night begins to fall;
> There's many a road to travel, but it's this road today,
> With the breath of God about us on the King's Highway.

McGroarty, accomplished as he was in the knowledge of history, noted that "from the first moment (Serra) saw California he loved it, and as his eyes swept backward over the Bay of San Diego shining blue against the sea, and in through the laughing valleys and tumbling hills of the off–shore, he claimed them all for the God whom he adored with the wild passion of his soul."

Happy the day when Junípero Serra came to San Diego–happy for the Place of First Things and the Harbor of the Sun, and happy for him who was to be its glory. "'Tis a goodly land," he wrote, "the wild vines are loaded with grapes, and the roses are like the roses of Castile."

Fifteen days after his arrival Father Serra sang the Mass from top of the hill where the Spaniards had erected a fort, the historic spot now known as Presidio Hill. "The bonnie banner of Castile and Leon was unfurled to the winds, the guns fired a salute and a new city was born on the western shores of the western world. They called it San Diego, as men call it still and will call it yet when the pennants of every nation beneath the swinging sun shall crowd its glowing harbor, havened and buttressed safe against the booming thunders of the Sunset Sea."

As to what the arrival of Serra in California meant to other generations, John Steven McGroarty stated that "it means that, had it never been, the wonderful Franciscan Missions of California had never risen, standing as they do today [1915], most of them in ruin, but still the most priceless heritage of the Commonwealth. Came never that day on Presidio Hill with Junípero Serra on his knees, there would have been no Mission San Diego de Alcala in the Mission Valley, no Pala in the mountain valleys, no San Luis Rey, no San Gabriel or Santa Barbara's towers watching above the sea, no San Luis Obispo or Dolores or any of the twenty–one marvelous structures that dot the Royal Road between the Harbor of the Sun and the Golden Gate, and which to see, untold thousands of travelers make the pilgrimage to California every year."

Noting that Mission San Diego was then a "pathetic ruin," McGroarty predicted that "some day, the slow but sure step of the restorer will come. It cannot crumble to dust. Its strong facade, its brave old archway through which the neophytes thronged in happier times, the ancient bell that still mounts the crumbled tower, are not yet gone. Some day some great, strong step shall find the place–holy with blood of martyrs and the tears of penitents–some great, strong hand will reach out lovingly, and morning suns and mellow moons will look again on the shrine rebuilt in the Place of First Things where California began."

FRAY JUNIPERO SERRA (1713–1784)

QQ. SERRA AND COLUMBUS

Here's a *Jeopardy* question: What did Fray Junípero Serra and Christopher Columbus have in common?" If you answered "Blessed Ramon Lull," go to the head of the class!

In his youth, Ramon Lull (1135–1314), the son of one of Mallorca's conquerors, followed the path of a worldly cavalier. An artist and musician, he misspent his early years until his conversion to the Catholic faith. Thereafter, the talented, zealous and energetic young man devoted himself to the perfection of his moral life and the spread of Christianity. Among his many accomplishments was the foundation of a school for the study of Arabic.

Ramon Lull became a prolific writer on a variety of subjects, including mathematics, navigation, law, warfare and horsemanship. When a university was established at Palma de Mallorca in the late 15th century, it was named for Lull. From 1692 onwards, the Franciscan held the chairs of Scotistic philosophy and theology at what was then officially known as the Pontifical, Imperial, Royal and Literary University of Mallorca.

On October 16, 1743, Fray Junípero Serra was unanimously selected to occupy the chair of Scotistic theology, then one of the most prestigious academic positions in all of Spain. Ramon Lull has never ceased to captivate the attention of Mallorcans and Serra was no exception. When Serra's remains were exhumed at Carmel, a reliquary was found in which a relic of "B. Raydi. M" (Blessed Ramon Lull of Mallorca) was enclosed.

The Columbus connection to Blessed Ramon Lull, which is even more fascinating, centers around the martyrdom of Lull at Bugia. After forty five years of strenuous activity, Lull journeyed to North Africa where he devoted himself to bringing the Moslems into the Church.

It was a severely hostile environment. At the age of almost eighty, Lull was attacked and beaten for his beliefs and left for dead on the seashore. Two Italian merchants rescued him and took the Mallorcan aboard their ship which was bound for Genoa. As Lull lay dying on the deck, he sat up one final time and, fixing his eyes on the horizon, said: "Beyond the curve of the sea which washes England, France and Spain, opposite this continent which we see and know and love, there is another continent which we have never seen and which we do not know. It is a world ignorant of Jesus Christ. Send men there."

One of the merchants told the story many times to his family and friends, some of whom recorded it for posterity. That man's name was Stefano Columbus, grandfather of Christopher Columbus!

Whether Fray Junípero Serra knew about the prophecy is unclear. But the fact remains that both Christopher Columbus and Junípero Serra fell under the influence of Blessed Ramon Lull who surely deserves a place of prominence in the annals of our nation as a whole, and California in particular.

History is chock full of such fascinating relationships, many of them as yet unravelled. Only on the final day will the last word be known about such personages as Christopher Columbus and Junípero Serra. And that's the way it was meant to be for us who stand alongside *El Camino Real*.

FRAY JUNÍPERO SERRA (1713–1784)

RR. MISSIONARY IN SIERRA GORDA

In the early days of the Church, saints were proclaimed by the people and priests of certain locales. The first solemn canonization was that of Saint Ulrich by Pope John XV in 993. If that old system were still in effect, Fray Junípero Serra would long ago have been canonized by the people of the Sierra Gorda region for nowhere is his reputation for holiness and heroic virtue greater.

The fame of Serra transcends his supporters as evident in Central Mexico where he labored before coming to Alta California and where very little had been written about him until contemporary times. The Franciscans were active in the Sierra Gorda for roughly a quarter century. There the friars succeeded in fulfilling their dual goals of converting the natives to Christianity and turning them into productive citizens of the Spanish empire. That Serra and the other Franciscans were successful in the Sierra Gorda is all the more impressive in light of earlier futile attempts at bringing the peoples there into the Catholic faith.

Serra's work in Central Mexico and that of his collaborators was crucial to their later activities in Alta California because the area was a training ground for many of the friars who subsequently worked along *El Camino Real*. Today, Serra is the most remembered of all the early missionaries working in that portion of the Lord's vineyard. He was assigned to the Santiago de Jalpan in 1750 and remained there for eight years.

Serra's success in his earliest missionary endeavors can be attributed to the polices upon which he based his ministry: teaching his marginally agricultural people new techniques of farming and caring for livestock.

The perfecting of their agricultural pursuits allowed the neophytes to improve their standard of living, thus giving them parity with other citizens of the empire. Unlike his predecessors who relied on translators, Serra actually learned the Pame language and was able to teach and converse in that tongue. Serra's missionary policies were not so easily realized in Alta California even though the lands were more fertile and easily irrigated. The natives also were still at the "hunting and gathering" stage and, until 1769, had no contact with outsiders. They had no traditions of farming or husbandry.

There was no common Indian language in Alta California. Within that outpost of the empire were no less than sixty–four (perhaps as many as eighty) mutually unintelligible languages, along with numerous dialects. The linguistic perplexities forced Serra and the other friars to encourage the Indians to learn Spanish.

Despite the more challenging problems in Alta California, Fray Junípero Serra was able to establish nine missions along the coast of California. And there, as earlier, Serra was loved and venerated by those brought into the embrace of the Catholic faith.

The missionary outposts in the Sierra Gorda are very much in place today. Visitors to that remote area can still see the churches built and cared for by Serra and his companions two and a half centuries ago. What is more fascinating are the verbal traditions about Serra and the good work he and others did in that region. The people there long ago "canonized" Serra and, today, he continues to walk tall in the Sierra Gorda.

FRAY JUNÍPERO SERRA (1713–1784)

ss. Serra–Jefferson Correspondence

As part of the planning for America's bicentennial celebration in 1976, Frances Ring, editor of *Westways*, asked Dave Dutton and Larry Meyer to create a Correspondence between Fray Junípero Serra and Thomas Jefferson that would inform East about West.

Meyer volunteered to speak for Thomas Jefferson and Dutton for Junípero Serra. They composed an exchange so realistic in style that many readers believed the letters to be authentic. The essay was subsequently reproduced in *A Western Harvest*.

According to the perpetrators of the hoax, a small bundle of letters was discovered on April 1, 1976, at a Pico Rivera garage sale. The correspondence pointed to an early contact between the founder of the California Missions and the illustrious American statesman.

In one of his letters, Serra explained how the California Indians made possible the founding of what became the California freeway system. It seems that a delegation from Santa Barbara approached the friar one day with an astonishing revelation. They had found an innovative use for the black tarry substance that oozed from the fissures and faults along the coast.

"By mixing this substance with crushed gravel, they have devised a material which can be applied to the ground as a sort of pavement upon which men, animals and vehicles can travel." Serra went on to tell how they had "petitioned me for a contract to apply the substance to sections of *El Camino Real*." Serra gave the scheme his whole–hearted blessing and the results were highly encouraging.

Serra was fascinated by the notion. "Think of it, Jefferson, a broad, smooth band of ooze fault stretching from San Diego to San Francisco, and beyond—the speed, the ease, the economy of travel on such a road!"

Such a roadway "would have neither tollgates nor impediments and would therefore be, as Brother Desideratus jestingly remarked after vespers the other evening, a free–way. I rather like the sound of the word."

After trial applications in Monterey, "we shall begin immediately to lay ooze–fault all along the route. The work shall be paid for by the imposition of a grass tax levied on all horses and mules which travel the road."

The governor "suggested that we also impose a tax on shoe leather, since many pedestrians will use and benefit from this oozefault free–way, but my colleague Fray Crespi (an ardent walker and arch–conservative in matters fiscal) remonstrated thusly: 'But Governor, would you tax men's soles?' De Neve relented, but he has power and is not one whose toes should be carelessly stepped on."

Jefferson was fascinated by the idea of a new highway. "I would suppose this substance to be akin to what we sometimes call pitchtar, and believe that were we to have it here we could well apply it to our own roads." On and on the correspondence goes, all of it one gigantic hoax. But what if the exchange had really taken place? The letters today would be a prized possession of an archives, rather than a nondescript bundle unearthed in a garage sale.

FRAY JUNÍPERO SERRA (1713–1784)

tt. Serra's Oak Tree

In the yard of San Carlos Cathedral, a stone marker in front of a gnarled old stump attests to a once–majestic tree which sheltered Fray Junípero Serra as he offered

the Liturgy inaugurating present–day Monterey. That almost–forgotten relic from an earlier age is, in reality one of the oldest and most important historical mementos in the Western United States.

Though now scarred and sadly–neglected, this bit of wood remnant, held together with chicken wire and concrete, has been associated with the area since the first white explorers entered Monterey Bay. Originally standing near the edge of the harbor, the majestic oak tree has witnessed over three centuries of historical events. Records of its existence date to 1602 and notations by Sebatián Vizcaíno and his chaplain, Fray Antonio de la Ascension.

It was in that year that the famed Basque navigator unfurled the Spanish flag prior to Holy Mass being offered by Ascension under the spreading limbs of the stately tree. It was another century and a half before the great oak and picturesque harbor were visited again by colonizers. In 1770, Gaspár de Portolá and Fray Junípero Serra arrived in Monterey. Serra too offered the Eucharistic Liturgy under the limbs of the aged tree.

That Mass marked the beginning of the *presidio* at Monterey and San Carlos Borromeo Mission.

As the years rolled on, the tree withstood weather, wars and a growing influx of people. Progress took its toll in 1903, when a road construction crew exposed the tree's roots to sea–water. The salt proved lethal and before long the beautiful tree died. Two years later the "Junípero Oak" was removed by overly–ambitious workers and pitched into the sea.

Through the efforts of Father Ramon Mestres, the tree was rescued. Its remaining branches were fondly installed on the grounds of the Royal Presidio Chapel. Its broken stump was placed upright directly behind the church. Today, the "Junípero Oak" is still visible to sight–seers. Unfortunately, its cracked, cement–filled form does not present the image of the revered landmark it truly is.

(There is a piece of the tree in the Historical Museum of the Chancery Archives. It was presented to J.K. Oliver on August 24, 1905, by the Corporal of the Guard in charge of laying the foundation for the permanent memorial).

According to a widely–accepted legend, Hattie Sargent Gragg planted an acorn from the "Junípero Oak" in the front yard of the Stokes adobe, on Hartnell Street, at the turn of the century. That tree still exists and flourishes—the last living remembrance of the original 1602 tree.

FRAY JUNÍPERO SERRA (1713–1784)

UU. SERRA AND SAN FRANCISCO

The picturesque statue of Fray Junípero Serra in San Francisco's Golden Gate Park depicts the Franciscan *Presidente* as the virile and vibrant personage he most assuredly was. The history of that portrayal can be traced to the early days of the 20th century.

On December 10, 1903, Archbishop Patrick W. Riordan submitted a petition to the City's Park Commissioners, in which he said the Honorable James D. Phelan had "most generously offered to place in Golden Gate Park a statue of Father Junípero Serra, the founder of the Franciscan Missions, provided the Park Commissioners will give the required permission." The archbishop said he would be "deeply grateful" if the commissioners acted favorably, noting that "such a measure will meet with the hearty approval of all who love this State."

Commissioner Frank Sullivan's motion that the generous offer be accepted was incorporated into the following resolution:

> Whereas, the Most Reverend Archbishop Riordan has this day requested the Board of Park Commissioners to receive a statue of the illustrious Junípero Serra, founder of the Franciscan Missions of California, to be donated by Hon. James D. Phelan, and, if the design is

satisfactory, to select a site for the same in Golden Gate Park; and

Whereas, it appears just and proper that this Board of Park Commissioners should show its appreciation of the pioneer of pioneers of California, whose devoted spiritual children as early as 1769 crossed this very ground of Golden Gate Park on their way from Laguna de la Merced in their mission of civilization; and

Whereas, the history of California of the past is the record of progressive steps from Paganism to Christianity, evidenced by the missions erected through the labors of Father Junípero Serra; and

Whereas, the bay and Mission and Presidio of San Francisco owe their names to Father Junípero Serra, and to him alone; therefore be it; and

Resolved, That this Board of Park Commissioners feels honored by the fact that it has been made one of the means of commemorating the name and memory of the illustrious Franciscan; and

Resolved, That the chairman of the board select a committee to confer with the Most Reverend Archbishop Riordan in reference to the site and design for said statue.

In introducing the matter, Mr. Sullivan said he felt "great pleasure in proposing the preamble and resolutions in reference to the acceptance of the statue of the earliest pioneer of California, Father Junípero Serra." He noted how "it was fitting that the initiator of the memorial should be the distinguished Prelate who presides over the Catholic Church in California. In him the brilliancy of Bossuet is united to the gentleness of Fenelon." After speaking at length on the accomplishments of Fray Junípero Serra, Sullivan concluded his remarks by asking the commissioners to "unite in the patriotic duty of selecting a fine position for the monument of him who did so much for our State."

The President of the Commissioners appointed a committee to select the precise site for the monument. A local artist was entrusted with the work and the completed statue was unveiled in 1907.

It was indeed fitting that San Francisco, the "ultima thule" of Serra's travels, honor the Franciscan *Presidente* with an appropriate monument.

FRAY JUNÍPERO SERRA (1713–1784)

VV. PURPORTED *NOVENA*

Historians of California have long regarded the writings of Fray Junípero Serra "as indispensable for an understanding of men and events" in the Hispanic era. Known for the tireless attention given to the mechanics of his office, Serra once complained that "half my life is passed at a writing desk."

In the years between 1955 and 1966, four volumes of Serra's writings were translated into English and pub-

lished, under the editorship of Antonine Tibesar, O.F.M., by the Academy of American Franciscan History. The 231 writings of the friar include a whole array of letters, reports, memoranda, register entries and the like.

One treatise, attributed to Serra by bibliographic scholars, is the *Novena de Alabanzas en Honrra de la Purissima Concepcion de Maria Ssma. Con el Titulo de Prelada*. The small book is a collection of prayers to Our Lady under her title of the Immaculate Conception. In March, 1942, the Reverend Demetrio Garcia, a Spanish–born priest who had long labored in Mexico, presented an incomplete copy of the Novena to Father Maynard Geiger, O.F.M., for inclusion in the Santa Barbara Mission Archives.

The thirty–three page *Novena* had been printed at Mexico City by D. Xavier Sanchez, in 1765. According to data on the title page, the work was attributed to "*la balbuciente Lengua de un menor subdito de la Sra. del Colegio Apostólico de S. Fernando la ofrece á sus devolos*," an indication that the author was a Franciscan attached to the Apostolic College of San Fernando in Mexico City. Apart from the donor's claim that the *Novena* was authored by Fray Junípero Serra, the testimony of Mexico's two most prominent bibliographers sustain that contention.

José Mariano Beristáin y Souza, a prominent scholar, credits Fray Junípero Serra with a work which he described as *La Prelada de S. Fernando: Novena á la Concepción Inmaculada de María, distribuida por las nueve Letras de Ave Pulchra*, which was printed at Mexico City in 1765. Beristáin (1756–1817) was a knowlegeable bibliographer who, as a contemporary of Serra, would have had access to first–hand evidence about the novena's authorship. His monumental *Biblioteca Hispano Americana Setentrional* was first published in 1796. Another outstanding bibliographer, José Toribio Medina, in his *La Imprenta de Mexico* (1539–1821), published at Santiago de Chile in 1907, also attributes the *Novena* to Junípero Serra.

A second edition of the Novena was published, in 1770, by Phelipe de Zuñifa y Ontiveros, at Mexico City. A copy of the latter edition, comprising forty–eight pages and measuring 21 by 31 inches, was offered for sale several years ago by a prominent Western Americana bookdealer.

Fortuitously or not, the 1770 edition was printed at the same press as Francisco Palóu's subsequent *Relación Histórica de la Vida y Apostólicas Tarreas del Venerable Padre Fray Junípero Serra*.

Medina records only two extant copies of the 1770 edition, his own and one belonging to Vicente de P. Andrada, a discriminating collector and bibliographer in his own right. Medina noted that his personal copy had an engraved portrait of the Virgin Mary which is lacking in the other copy.

If the *Novena* was indeed authored by Fray Junípero Serra, and its stylistic composition lends credence to that supposition, then it has the distinction of being the only one of the friar's writings published during his lifetime.

FRAY JUNÍPERO SERRA (1713–1784)

WW. SERRA VIEWS BISHOPRIC

It has long been the practice of the Holy See to bestow broad faculties on priests laboring in missionary areas for the administration of the sacraments. One such prerogative, generally delegated to local superiors, concerns the conferral of Confirmation, a faculty customarily reserved in most parts of the Christian world for those enjoying episcopal ordination.

Such an apostolic concession was exercised in California by Fray Junípero Serra. The venerable Franciscan *Presidente* sought and received the authorization "so that he could visit the missions and confirm the neophytes, lest they be deprived of the great spiritual good to be had from the effects of this holy sacrament." Judging from remarks of his biographer, there were those apparently who viewed such action on Serra's part as indicative of episcopal aspirations. Not so, according to Francisco Palóu: Junípero Serra "was so far removed from seeking this dignity or even desiring it, that he rather devised means to flee it, because of his profound humility and his fervent desire to labor in the vineyard of the Lord."

Palóu further mentions that after the establishment of Mission San Carlos, "His Reverence learned that a courier at Madrid had written to the Reverend Father Guardian of our college . . . that a great honor was waiting the Reverend Father Junípero." When word reached Monterey of the "great honor," so fearful was Serra that he would "lose before God the merit of his labors in these spiritual conquests through receiving in this world the reward that was foretold in that letter," immediately resolved to refuse the distinction or any other which would forestall his being able to live "as an apostolic missionary among the infidels and to shed his blood for their conversion." Palóu confided that Serra may not have made a vow to that effect, "though I am inclined to believe he did, for he did not explain the matter to me in full detail."

The possibility of such an appointment was not so remote as might initially appear. A diocese was established at Sonora, in 1779, for example, while that vast area was almost entirely missionary territory. One outstanding Franciscan historian states categorically that "Spain should have asked for a bishop for the Califor-

nias, considering the huge territory, even though churches were few and the income nothing."

So disturbed was the *Presidente* at the thought of becoming a bishop that he took the extreme precaution of writing an influential acquaintance at the royal court asking him to "serve rather as his censor than as his agent" if the issue of bestowing regal favors on his person ever came up for discussion.

At a meeting of the Newman Club, held at Los Angeles on May 26, 1910, John Steven McGroarty had this to say about the Franciscan *Presidente* and the bishopric:

> I always think of Father Junípero Serra as the first bishop of the Diocese of Monterey–Los Angeles. He was never consecrated as a bishop, but he exercised some of the faculties of that high and holy office. For a time he was empowered to administer the Sacrament of Confirmation, and many thousands of Indians, together with a large number of white persons, were confirmed by him.
>
> In addition to this, he was the president of the California Missions, in which capacity he directed the work of the Church here and exercised authority over priests and people. Father Junípero was, therefore, in effect a bishop, although not one in fact.

FRAY JUNÍPERO SERRA (1713–1784)

XX. DEPARTURE OF A MISSIONARY

Why does a man become a missionary, leave home, oftentimes never to return? This abridged letter of Padre Junípero Serra may offer a clue. It was published to commemorate the 250th anniversary of Serra's birth at Petra.

> I am writing this letter in farewell. The day fixed upon is unknown to me, but the trunks containing our baggage are locked and strapped and they say that after two, three, or possibly four days, the ship will sail.
>
> I want to ask you again to do me the favor of consoling my parents, who, I know, are going through a great sorrow.
>
> I wish I could give them some of the happiness that is mine; and I feel that they would urge me to go ahead and never turn back.
>
> Tell them that the dignity of an apostolic preacher, especially when united with the active ministry, is the highest vocation they could have wished me to follow.
>
> After all, considering their advanced age, their life is mostly spent. Their remaining days are obviously short and if they compare those days with eternity, they will see that it is no more than an instant. This being the case, it is very important, and according to God's Will, that they do not depend on what little help I might be to them were I to remain behind. By so doing they will merit greatly from Almighty God. And if we are not to see each other again in this world, they may rest assured that we will all

be united forever in eternal glory. Tell them how badly I feel at not being able to stay longer and make them happy by my presence. And yet, they know full well that first things come first; and our first duty is to do the will of God. Nothing else but that love has led me to leave them. And, if, for the love of God and with the help of His grace, I can muster the courage to leave, might I not suggest that they also, for the love of God, can be content to forego the happiness of my presence.

Let them listen attentively to the advice of their confessor; and they will see that God has truly entered their home. By practicing holy patience and resignation to the Divine Will, they will possess and attain eternal life.

They should hold no one but Our Lord God and Him alone responsible for the separation. They will find out how sweet His yoke can be, that what they now consider and endure as a great sorrow will be turned into a lasting joy. As a matter of fact, nothing in life should cause us sorrow. Our clear duty is to conform ourselves to His Will and thus prepare well for death. Beyond this, nothing else matters.

Happy are they who have a son a priest—however bad and sinful—who, every day in the Holy Sacrifice of the Mass prays for them as best he can and very often offers exclusively for them his Mass so that the Lord will send them help and the necessities of life; that He may grant them grace of patience in their trials, and finally, at the proper time, a happy death in God's holy grace.

If I succeed in being a good priest and missionary these prayers of mine will be all the more useful and my parents will be the first to profit by them. And the same is to be said regarding the rest of my family.

I well remember that, while assisting my father when he had taken severely ill, sometime back, he said to me: "Son, what I am most anxious about is that you be a good religious." Well, father, rest assured that I keep your words always before me, just as if I hear them from your mouth at this very moment. But bear in mind that it is to become a good religious that I have undertaken this voyage. You must not feel badly that I am doing your will, which is, at this time, the will of God. As for my mother, I know full well that she has never missed offering up her prayers for me to God for that same purpose, that I be a good priest. No wonder then that God, hearing your prayers, has directed me in this way. Rest assured then with the way in which God has allowed things to work out.

Let us bless God who loves and cares for us all. May the Lord bring us all together in eternal glory and keep us all for many years.

FRAY JUNÍPERO SERRA (1713–1784)

YY. THE "GREY OX"

Elaborate preparations were made in 1963 on the small Balearic Isle of Mallorca to commemorate the 250th anniversary of the birth of its famous son, Fray Junípero Serra. Festivities began with an official reception at Palma on May 29th. The *Asociacion Amigos de Fray Junípero Serra* scheduled civic and religious functions for June 4th at Petra, birthplace of the founder of the California missions.

Petra has shown great regard for its renowned missionary. The house on Calle Barracar where Antonio Serra and Margarita Ferrer brought up their son is now a national monument. In 1930 its authenticity was established by Miguel Ramis Moragues, a scholar whose entire life has been devoted to furthering interest in the Serra cause. The ancient stone dwelling and its adjacent garden, restored by a group of townspeople, was presented to the City of San Francisco on May 12, 1932, by the Rotary Club of Mallorca. In 1958 the Society of California Pioneers assumed responsibility for maintenance of the house. A museum, library and conference hall were set up in 1959 to honor and perpetuate the memory of Petra's famous pioneer. Designed by one of Spain's leading architects, the center represents the many features of traditional Mallorcan 18th century architecture.

It was in the parish church of San Pedro that the infant Serra was baptized as Miguel José on November 24, 1713. The font used for the ceremony was removed from the church in 1858 and made over into an ornamental flower vase in the rectory garden. It was restored in modern times with a plaque indicating its connection with Serra. California visitors can see the baptismal record in the sacristy along with other objects pertaining to the Grey Ox. Serra received the name "Junipero" in 1730, upon making his religious vows in the Franciscans.

The youthful Serra was educated at San Bernardino Convento, the "Pearl of all the churches of the province." Founded in 1607, the present church houses many baroque side–chapels whose patronal names later became associated with the California mission chain. A beautiful depiction of Our Lady of the Angels dominates statues and paintings of Santa Clara, San Antonio de Padua, San Francisco Solano, San Juan Bautista, and the Virgin Purísima. Serra's parents are interred in the church's crypt.

The church and monastery of San Francisco at nearby Palma was the home of Fray Junípero for eighteen years and is now staffed by the Third Order Regular Franciscans. "Mallorca's prized ecclesiastical structure" is situated close to the heart of the ancient city and contains the remains of Blessed Ramon Lull. It has housed a boys' college since 1951.

The *Plaza de Junípero Serra* with its handsome monument is located in the center of Petra. Dedicated in 1892, the *plaza* received its sculptured statue of Serra on September 29, 1913, when more than ten thousand pilgrims gathered to honor his memory. An oil painting of Fray Junípero Serra and one of his nephews, Miguel de Petra, hang in the Town Hall. Miguel was a well–known architect and cartographer. In 1949 the Municipality of Petra erected a cross on the slope of the Sanctuary of *Bon–Any* to commemorate Serra's departure from Mallorca. This famous shrine was one of Fray Junípero's favorite memories and he often referred to *Bon–Any*, the "title by which Most Holy Mary is known in my beloved homeland."

Mallorcans are proud of their native son and have done much to perpetuate his memory.

FRAY BENITO DE LA SIERRA (1729–1778)

Fray Benito de la Sierra (1729–1778) arrived at Loreto on April 22, 1769, where he was assigned to the peninsular Mission of Santa Rosalía de Mulegé. The Spanish–born Franciscan labored among the neophytes of that region for four years, until being replaced by the Dominicans, in 1773. He then returned to Mexico City and was appointed librarian at the Apostolic College of San Fernando.

On November 18, 1774, Father Sierra was assigned to the "disagreeable position" of co–chaplain for the *Santiago*, which sailed from San Blas the following March 16th. The vessel journeyed to the waters of Northern California where, at the *Puerto de la Santísima Trinidad*, a cross was planted on June 11th. Captain Bruno de Hazeta took possession of the area for the Spanish crown as Frays Miguel de la Campa and Benito de la Sierra conducted the customary liturgical services. In his homily, Sierra exhorted the crew to courageously continue their exploratory expedition until the desired objective had been accomplished. The friar visited a nearby Indian *ranchería* and explained, as best he could, that he or others would one day return and take up permanent residence among them.

The expedition proceeded further north before reversing direction. Enroute back, the mouth of the Columbia River was named *La Asunción de Nuestra Señora*. The *Santiago* or *Nueva Galicia* as it was occasionally called, arrived at Monterey on August 29th. Fray Benito de la Sierra kept a journal of the historic sea venture which he apparently confided to his superiors at the apostolic college upon his return. Most of that institution's documents and books subsequently passed into the hands of private individuals.

The friar's journal was acquired by José Maria Agreda, a collector of books and historical materials. Sometime after his death, in the 1920s, the Sierra memoir was purchased by G. R. C. Conway. It was translated into English by A. J. Baker and published in 1930, with an introduction and notes by Henry Raup Wagner, for the California Historical Society.

The Hazeta expedition was an important and historic voyage for it greatly increased Spanish knowledge of coasts, harbors and anchorages north of Monterey. Considerably more important was the added perspective it afforded of the native inhabitants—their appearance, clothing, weapons, habitations, diet and temperaments. The expedition also relieved Viceroy Antonio Bucareli of anxieties about possible Russian encroachments.

The friar's journal, published under the title *Fray Benito de la Sierra's Account of the Hazeta Expedition to the Northwest Coast in 1775*, takes on further significance inasmuch as it chronicles the activities of the first European to set foot on that area of the continent. Its story of human endeavors and endurance of hardships, on sea and shore, is a vital part of the larger pageant that brought about the development of Western North America in the 19th century.

Little more is known about the person of Fray Benito de la Sierra. He acted as chaplain for two later expeditions to Monterey and died, unexpectedly, at the Port of San Blas, in 1778.

FRAY BUENAVENTURA SITJAR (1739–1808)

A. *DICCIONARIO*

A writer for the San Francisco *Bulletin* noted, in the edition for September 7, 1864, that "in turning over the records" he had discovered that Fray Buenaventura Sitjar "had compiled a very lengthy dictionary of words and sentences in the Indian language" of San Antonio Mission. Observing that the dictionary "was drawn up in a little old parchment–covered volume, difficult to decipher," the writer said "it was a very curious and laborious affair, and of value to scientific linguists, whom he knew nothing about."

The account of Sitjar's dictionary concluded with the comment that "it effectually enabled him . . . to instruct his Indians in the *doctrina* and to work up little manuscript catechisms in their language." The compilation of such a work must have involved considerable effort. Fray Pedro Font noted in his diary that the Salinan linguistic group (and that included San Miguel and *Nuestra Señora de la Soledad* missions) was "very rough and most difficult to pronounce because it has so many crackling sounds."

Font further testified that the language has been learned by Fray Buenaventura Sitjar through continual application and hard labor, and he has written the catechism in their language but since there are no letters to express such barbarous and ridiculous cracklings and whistling and guttural sounds, he had made use of the K and of various accents and figures, whereby the catechism is as difficult to read as to pronounce."

In the late 1850s, Alexander Taylor acquired Sitjar's manuscript. He later agreed to loan the precious treasure to the Smithsonian Institution, on the provision that it eventually be published. Arrangements were subsequently made to include Sitjar's dictionary as Volume VII in John Gilmary Shea's Library of American Linguistics, a series that also numbered Fray Felipe Arroyo de is Cuesta's grammar of the Mutsun language.

Finding the 442 page manuscript difficult to edit, Shea slightly rearranged the contents. He then consigned the burdensome task of printing to the talented J. Munsell at the Cramoisy Press in New York. The *Vocabulario de la Lengua de los Naturales de la Misíon de San Antonio* appeared in print during 1861 as a *Vocabulary of the Language of San Antonio Mission, California.*

In print, the dictionary covers forty–three pages of double columns. Preceding the *diccionario*, on ten pages, the editor endeavored to construct a sort of grammar from the sample sentences furnished in the original manuscript. The talented Fray Buenaventura Sitjar (1739–1808) proved to be an able linguist of Mutsun, not an easy task for one familiar only with European languages.

FRAY BUENAVENTURA SITJAR (1739–1808)

B. SAN ANTONIO MISSION

The "moving spirit" of Mission San Antonio de Padua was Fray Buenaventura Sitjar (1739–1808). The Mallorcan–born friar was indeed the chief founder and civilizer of Christianity in the area and one whose name is worthy of honorable mention in the literary as well as the religious and historical annals of California.

Father Sitjar died at San Antonio, on September 3, 1808. The entry by his successor, Fray Pedro Cabot, in the *Registro de Difuntos*, translated and published in the San Francisco *Bulletin* for September 10, 1864, is a most revealing and informative document:

> He [Sitjar] was strong and robust of body and in spirit equally as patient to sustain the heavy and arduous labors of those times of peril and privation, trying as much to the soul as to the body, but in all of which his zeal never tired or flagged, nor the charity and love which had drawn to him, from first to last, all and each of the people of this Mission.
>
> The condescension, zeal and entire confidence with which he lived in the midst of the natives, shed a cheerful pleasure and peace on his labors and greatly assisted him in acquiring a thorough knowledge of their language, by which he was effectually enabled to instruct these poor gentiles for the reception of the holy rites of baptism, and to administer to them the Sacraments of

> our Holy Church, and thus in their idiom to impart to these simple converts the sanctifying bread of the ever-lasting Word of God.
>
> In his 58th year he was directed by the Father Presidente Fermin de Lasuén—whom God preserve—to lay the foundation of the Mission of San Miguel. After the accomplishment of this, in 1797, he returned to this, the scene of his old labors, on 29th August, and celebrated the office of the Holy Mass for the happy results of the same.
>
> He was still able at this advanced age to accompany his Indians in their works and labors, and to instruct them in things necessary for their spiritual and temporal benefit. In nothing did he seem either afraid or terrified or fatigued; and neither the frosts of winter, nor the heats of summer, nor the painful complaint under which he so long suffered, which caused the compassion and sympathy of those friends who witnessed the painful affliction and distress of his infirmity, was sufficient to quench his devoted zeal and diligent labors in the arduous services of his Mission.
>
> I, who assisted him in his last moments, in company with the Rev. Father Juan Bautista Sancho, my much loved brother co–minister, commended his soul to the mercy of Almighty God in humble prayer; . . .
>
> On the following day, the 4th of September, after the chanting of the Mass, we interred his body in this church of San Antonio, on the Gospel side of the Presbytery, between the High Altar and the wall, next to that of the Fray Francisco Pujol, preceeded by solemn and pompous funeral ceremonies after the manner of the most devout convents.
>
> In these offices we were assisted by the Reverend Ministers from La Soledad and San Miguel, the friars Antonio Jayme and Juan Martin, and accompanied by the soldiers of the troop, all of whom desired that he might be buried in this place for the edification of the faithful and the ministers of the church who might succeed him in the sacred offices of the ministry.
>
> And of the truth of all of which is herein written, and for all time, I hereto sign my name in this Mission of San Antonio de Padua, on the 9th of September, 1808.

FRAY ESTEVAN TAPIS (C. 1756–1825)

Fray Estevan Tapis (c. 1756–1825) was "a truly evangelical priest and a fervent preacher" whose personality was characterized by Franciscan sweetness and gentility. A native of Colona de Farnes, Catalonia, Tapis entered the Order of Friars at Gerona, in 1778. At the time of his departure for the New World, in 1786, he was described as a man of "regular stature, thin, with dark eyes and hair."

Shortly after arriving at Monterey, in 1790, Fray Tapis was assigned to San Luis Obispo Mission. He served there for three years prior to being transferred to

Santa Barbara. During his years at the latter foundation, Tapis was responsible for many physical improvements, including the third church. He also built the chapel of San Miguel, at Cieneguitas, an *estancia* between Santa Barbara and Goleta.

Held in high esteem for his learning and piety, Tapis composed music as a means of eliciting devotion, worship and veneration among the Indians at their liturgical festivities and celebrations. In 1800, Tapis prepared a detailed description of the methods and practices used in the missionary system of California, a report generally considered the finest and most comprehensive written during the period.

During his many years of pastoral work, Tapis became familiar with several Indian languages. He was noted for his habit of studying the individual peculiarities of the neophytes. Appointed Coadjutor *Presidente* of the California Missions in 1798, Tapis, succeeded to that post in 1804. Throughout the eight years of his tenure, the friar performed his duties ably, and was popular with both missionaries and military officials."

Tapis was *Presidente* during the so–called "Golden Age" of the missions, a time in which more natives were converted to the Catholic faith than in any other period of similar length. The *Presidente* fostered several expe-

ditions into the interior country to explore sites for possible future missionary foundations. The number of missions increased to nineteen in 1804, with the establishment of Santa Ines. Tapis had completed preparations for that establishment in 1798, but the actual order was delayed for some years by the governor.

In September, 1810, Fray Tapis asked to be relieved of his post as *Presidente*, to which he had been re–elected three times. A chapter meeting held at Mexico City's Apostolic College of San Fernando, on July 11, 1812, appointed Fray José Señán to succeed Tapis. The Catalan missionary happily returned to ordinary pastoral work and during his final years served at Missions La Purísima Concepción, San Carlos Borromeo, Santa Ines and San Juan Bautista.

Tapis died at San Juan Bautista, on November 3, 1825. He was described by Hubert Howe Bancroft as having "left less of his individuality in the records than any other of the friars who filled the presidency."

FRAY JOSE VIADER (b. 1765)

Fray Jose Viader (b. 1765) spent thirty–seven of his priestly years ministering to the natives of Santa Clara Mission. Known as the "*Padre de Gallinas*," Viader was described by Auguste Duhaut–Cilly as "a modest and truthful man."

Among the documents gathered and left behind by Viader at Santa Clara is one dated May 19, 1798, wherein Pablo Soler, a brilliant physician and surgeon, explains the crude but effective method of inoculating against the dreaded small–pox. It's an important document because it proves that a method of immunization was practiced in California prior to the one developed by Dr. Edward Jenner.

The document appears to have been copied from a circular letter sent by Soler to all the missions from San Carlos Borromeo. It was translated by the late Father Arthur D. Spearman.

> Method of practical inoculation with smallpox, by the simple use of which innumerable deaths can be avoided, that experience at all times has shown, and most recently in New Spain, according to general reports.
>
> The point of the lancet or similar instrument, is moistened by inserting it in a ripe, white pustule of smallpox, preferably from a case arising from previous inoculations. The point thus loaded is introduced by the large finger and the index finger so lightly that the blood barely flows.
>
> Then on withdrawing the instrument, apply one's finger over the wound so that the serum will be kept in. No bandage is to be applied and the blood dries of itself.
>
> The diet should be of a light kind, and cooling, such

as atole or mush of barley, corn meal, etc., and for beverages the same, juice from lettuce, maidenhair fern, or whey.

The use of medicines or other more perfect means of treatment are not suggested on account of the circumstances of the country. The inoculation can be practiced upon all ages, even though they be suffering from eczema, or of other similar sickness, enjoining, above all, cleanliness, ventilation, cheerfulness, and other points that have been suggested in the case of chickenpox.

I do not doubt that the reverend missionaries will procure this benefit for the Indians in view of the ravages which they have experienced, both Christian Indians and heathens, in Baja California, in the year 1781, when the Missions San Fernando (de Velicatá) and San Jorja survived on account of not catching the contagion, while the mission of San Ignacio conquered it by the inoculation practiced, on his own initiative by the Rev. Father Crisostomo, Gomez, with the accustomed success.

It is to be desired that all the poor heathens partake of this benefit through the medium of their relatives for the directions here given are intended for the good of humanity.

Pablo Soler was indeed a benefactor of the Indians. In one of the record books at Carmel, he was described as "a great physician and surgeon. Had not his humanity prompted him to give his profession to the services of the California colony, he would have been renowned in Spain, but he gave the best years of his life for the welfare of the people, traveling many miles to minister to officers and soldiers . . . to all with equal kindness."

FRAY JOSE MARIA DE ZALVIDEA (1780–1846)

José Maria de Zalvidea (1780–1846) was considered by his Franciscan superiors to be one of the best and most zealous of California's friars—as priest, teacher and manager of temporalities. Born at Bilbao, Vizcaya, Spain, the youthful Zalvidea entered the Franciscans on December 13, 1798. He left for the New World in 1804, arriving in San Francisco the following year.

The friar was stationed briefly at San Fernando and then, from 1806 until 1827, he was the resident missionary at the fourth of California's missionary outposts, San Gabriel. Zalvidea found the chief field of his labors at San Gabriel and there he toiled incessantly for over two decades building up the temporalities of the mission and caring for the spiritual needs of the neophytes.

A man of many talents, Zalvidea was able to master the Indian dialects with relative ease. Such an accomplishment was a feat in itself, as the Gabrielino tongue was one of the most complicated.

Zalvidea was the first to introduce viniculture on a wide scale at San Gabriel. And it was he who built the old grist mill (*El Molino Viejo*), the first of its kind along the Pacific Slope.

Robert Glass Cleland, a longtime researcher of things historic at San Gabriel Mission, refers to Zalvidea as a "forceful, intelligent, practical leader, the exalted religious devotee, who helped to bestow upon San Gabriel the sobriquet of the "richest of the missions."

Though he was a firm, hard–driving administrator, Zalvidea was respected and loved by his people. The non–Catholic Cleland went on to say that "he was doubtless in those days a model missionary, and then and later was regarded by the common people as a saint."

Michael C. White, who knew the friar personally, described how he planted fruit trees in the ravines for the benefit of the Indians. It was White who suggested that Zalvidea was something of a Franciscan Johnny Appleseed. A tall, stout man with light complexion and fine presence, Zalvidea was known as a courteous friar with a smile and kind word for everyone. Contemporaries are unanimous in crediting the friar with unusual intelligence.

Throughout his years in California, Zalvidea suffered greatly from asthma. It was for that reason that the friar was transferred to San Juan Capistrano in 1826. He labored there until 1842, when he went to his final assignment at San Luis Rey.

The friar succumbed at San Luis Rey early in 1846. He was buried in the mission church, to the left of the altar. Thus passed from the scene a man who was a great figure in the annals of early California.

Even this short biographical sketch helps to confirm a report submitted in 1817, by Fray Vicente Francisco de Sarria, which states that, in his judgement, Zalvidea was "one of the best missionaries in this land. . . ."

III. Religious
In General and Individuals

RELIGIOUS: IN GENERAL

CABRINI SISTERS

A. LOS ANGELES

In early 1892, long before she had began her foundations in Chicago, Denver and Seattle, Mother Frances Cabrini (1850–1917) was thinking about an establishment on the Pacific Coast. She predicted that "One day we shall have to go to California, where we will do something for the glory of God."

Bishop Thomas J. Conaty wrote to her later, asking for Missionary Sisters of the Sacred Heart in his Diocese of Monterey–Los Angeles: "I feel that a great deal of good could be done by them in this city in our work among the Italians."

Mother Cabrini shared the bishop's views. She sent Mother Umilia and Sister Angelica to California as the vanguard. They rented a room in a small house at 817 Alpine Street in the Italian quarter. Cabrini herself arrived in Los Angeles on July 23, 1905. A few weeks later she confided to the Apostolic Delegate, Archbishop Diomede Falconio, that "coming here I have found a great opportunity for doing good, because I perceive our Italians are in much need."

In the community annals is a vivid description of the challenges faced by the Sisters: "For more than thirty years our poor Italians of Los Angeles have been without a priest who speaks their language. . . . Many have become Protestants." A later entry complains that "The Protestant sects here grow like mushrooms . . . Mother [Cabrini] thinks it will be much easier to do good for the souls of our immigrants when their material needs have been provided for, so she will do everything possible to establish a school, orphanage, nursery, etc."

During August of 1905, Mother Cabrini went around California's southland looking for an appropriate place for the new mission. In a letter to one of her Missionary Sisters she related: "The city of Los Angeles is widespread and seems to grow recklessly. Property is very expensive. . . . The climate is excellent so I recuperate while I am working."

Winding up her initial work, Cabrini happily related in November: "Here in Los Angeles we have a stupendous house on top of a hill which dominates the city, and at its base are all the Italians we take care of." The "stupendous house," built in 1887 as the home of J.W. Robinson, a pioneer merchant of Los Angeles, was situated at Sunset Boulevard and Hill Street.

The establishment was important to Mother Cabrini, who was not satisfied with her earlier projects of teaching at Saint Peter's parochial school and Holy Angels kindergarten which had been confided to the Sisters by Bishop Conaty. The new house, which she called Regina Coeli Orphanage, served as a center for the Italians, a place where they could come to tell their troubles and seek whatever assistance they might need.

On a return trip to Los Angeles the following year, Mother Cabrini bought 120 acres of land dotted with olive trees and grape vines in Burbank. The small structure on the property served as a summer house for the orphans for many years and was used for small groups of children whose physical health was poor.

Cabrini viewed 1905 as a turning point for her institute. It was the twenty–fifth anniversary of the original foundation in Codogno, Italy. Bishop Conaty surprised her with a gala anniversary celebration. Public excitement in Catholic circles ran high, because it was the first time that a foundress of a religious order was present in Los Angeles on such an auspicious occasion.

The nation's first citizen–saint wrote to a friend In Rome: "We were always hidden until now now everyone is interested in us." From 1905 on, Cabrini's name was featured in the religious and secular press whenever she arrived or inaugurated new charitable work.

Mother Cabrini came to Los Angeles several more times in her busy life. Even as she approached the twilight of her loving service, she never wavered in her activities. She came a final time to the west coast late in 1916 for a last visit with her sisters, orphans and youngsters

CABRINI SISTERS

B. MARIAN SHRINE IN SAN FERNANDO

One of the most picturesque Marian shrines in the United States was that dedicated to Our Lady, Help of Christians. Erected high atop Mount Raphael, overlooking the San Fernando Valley, the little white chapel was a familiar landmark to travelers along the Golden State freeway. In 1916, two women looked out over a desolate San Fernando vista. One saw "nothing but sand and snakes." The other, Mother Frances Cabrini (1850–1917), envisioned lush vineyards and orchards and small children regaining their shattered health in the compassionate sunshine.

Mother Cabrini's dream materialized and her Missionary Sisters of the Sacred Heart built first an orphanage and preventorium, then a boarding and day school for girls on the site, nestled against the Verdugo Hills, near Burbank. The tiny chapel was completed in 1917, the year Mother Cabrini died in Chicago. It was supposedly one of the last buildings erected under the personal supervision of America's first citizen–saint. Situated on the 475 acres that eventually became Villa Cabrini Academy, the hilltop chapel has an interesting history. Several times it narrowly escaped destruction.

Recalling the brush fire that encompassed the Verdugo Hills, one of the Sisters noted that the conflagration of 1949 was "a terrible one in which over 200 local homes were destroyed. We were all watching the fire reach the hill where the chapel is. Flames went all the way up the side, burning everything. Finally, the smoke and fire died down—and the chapel was still there. Some reporters here at the time wanted to know what we thought, a fire destroying everything but our little chapel," she smiled. "Of course, you can't intimate that it was a miracle or anything like that, but I know some of us were praying hard to both Our Lady and Saint Frances."

Six years later, in November, 1955, the disastrous La Tuna Canyon fire completely surrounded the shrine, but did no damage to it or to the trees immediately surrounding it. During World War II, the chapel was painted a luminous white to guide pilots over the foothills, down to Lockheed Air Terminal, just a mile away.

The one room chapel has been reconstructed several times, most recently in 1952, by the Knights of Columbus. Late in 1973, the historic Marian Shrine was moved to the grounds of nearby Saint Francis Xavier Parish.

Mother Frances Cabrini epitomized the role that women religious play in contemporary society. A measure of her warmth and kindness remains today atop the mountain she frequently climbed to pray and meditate. Standing there, in those peaceful surroundings, one would have to agree that Saint Frances Cabrini was for California, as indeed for all the world, a "deaconess of salvation."

THE CAPUCHINS

The Franciscan heritage can be stated succinctly: living the gospel life in this world honestly, simply and joyfully. The Capuchins are a living fulfillment of that dedication in California. Father Luke Sheehan was the first of the "Irish" Capuchins sent to the United States. He came to Oregon, in 1910, at the invitation of Bishop Charles O'Reilly.

Origins of the Irish Capuchins in California can be traced to 1920, when they were called upon to replace their English counterparts in Mendocino County who had been recalled to India. Two years later, Bishop John J. Cantwell invited the Irish Capuchins to the Diocese of Monterey–Los Angeles, with the suggestion that they take charge of Saint Lawrence Brindisi parish in Watts.

Shortly thereafter, the friars were given a similar charge at Burlingame, for the Archdiocese of San Francisco.

The parishioners at Santa Ines Mission look upon Thursday, November 20, 1924, as their "brown–letter day" for it was then that a group of Capuchins arrived to look after the spiritualities of Solvang. They were welcomed with a peal of mission bells from the nineteenth of the frontier outposts along *El Camino Real*. The Capuchins enlarged their apostolate that same year when they agreed to assume responsibility for the parish of Saint Francis of Assisi in Los Angeles.

The years between 1910 and 1927 were momentous ones for the Capuchins. Twenty–three centers of apostolic work were either founded or taken over—almost one and a half institutions every year! In 1946, the friars opened Saint Francis High School in La Canada. Built aside a hill overlooking Pasadena, the institution quickly became a highly respected college prep school.

Seventeen years later, another dream was fulfilled with the establishment of a novitiate in the beautiful Santa Ynez Valley, a few miles from the Old Mission. San Lorenzo is already the *alma mater* for a number of young Capuchin priests.

In the early 1970s, the California Custody became a Vice Province, thus giving it greater autonomy and flexibility. At the same time, the student friars studying in the east were transferred to San Francisco's Buenaventura Center, located in a converted apartment building. That facility subsequently was moved to Oakland. The student training program for the Capuchins has always been both innovative and sound, involving active participation in the apostolic life of the friars. Opportunities include summer day camps, parish census, parochial life, chaplaincy training and summer school teaching.

A formal petition was drafted in 1977, asking the Minister General of the Capuchin Franciscans for an independent province. The request was formally approved on April 18, 1979. The Irish Capuchins in Our Lady of the Angels Western American Province personify those beautiful words of Francis of Assisi: "The world is our cloister."

CARMELITE SISTERS

A. DIOCESE OF MONTEREY–FRESNO

The first Carmelite nuns arrived in the United States in 1790. According to tradition, the Order had its origin with the ancient hermits of Mount Carmel and the prophet Elijah or Saint Elias who is considered the founder.

In 1925, the year Therese was canonized, Bishop John B. MacGinley invited the Carmelites to establish a monastery in Carmel. According to Father Ramon Mestres, the nuns were attracted "by the natural grandeur and beauty of the valley, its mountains, the river and the bay of Carmel." The area had been named in honor of Our Lady of Mount Carmel by the Carmelite friars who accompanied the Vizcaino expedition to California in 1602.

The nuns acquired a parcel of land that commanded an unobstructed view of the ocean. A two story, sixteen room wooden building was erected with a capacity for ten nuns. On October 23rd, the first contingency of nuns drove to their new home. After a few days, the closure was sealed and the quiet routine of monastery life began.

In November of 1931, Carmel of Our Lady and Saint Therese emerged from its chrysalis and moved the short distance to permanent quarters provided by Francis J. Sullivan on San Jose Creek. The Boston firm of Maginnis and Walsh designed the Monastery of Our Lady and Saint Therese. A newspaper reporter wrote that "seldom does one see such solid harmony between a building and its natural surroundings as exists here, where one seems only to enhance the beauty of the other."

The modified Romanesque architecture of the monastery conveys a feeling of stability and strength. The bell tower suggests something of the lofty serenity of life within the monastery. Decoration is used only sparingly. The monastery stands three stories high and contains some ninety rooms. Its exterior is constructed of reinforced concrete. Cut stone and terra cotta are used in many parts.

Forming the core of the monastery is the chapel and connected to it are wings that reach out to both the north and south. In the north wing are the extern's quarters, the parlors and the area where the nuns meet visitors. As is the case in all such monasteries, the extern sister manages the temporalities, does the shopping and serves as general agent for the cloistered community.

Since the nuns are a mendicant order, they are largely dependent on alms, most of which come from their numerous friends and collaborators. The monastery is totally self–supporting and the nuns perform many duties for which they receive a modest stipend.

The Carmelites are cloistered which means that their contact with outsiders is carried on with the parties invisible to one another, except when a nun greets members of her own family. Cells for the twenty–one nuns (the community may not exceed that number) are located above the first floor. The chapter room, library, archives, recreation areas and several work rooms make up the total of ninety.

One writer observed some years ago that the Carmelite nuns are enclosed, but not vacuum packed. Like painters and writers, they feel they must have seclusion in order to do their best work . . . Their vow of poverty assures them of a freedom which few in the outside world will ever know.

CARMELITE SISTERS

B. SAN FRANCISCO MONASTERY

There are several versions of the story (or legend) of how Rita Marie Shomo (1870–1954) became interested in the Carmelite Sisters and their work in San Francisco. One fanciful version, which the Carmelites themselves consider mostly apocryphal, tells how one day a lady rang the bell at the Jesuit faculty house attached to the University of San Francisco. She asked the porter if the superior might be available.

Presuming that the superior was busy about many more important things, the porter brazenly asked what she wanted. The unpretentious lady said she wished to make a contribution to the Society of Jesus. The porter, in a gesture of impatience, suggested that she go down the street and make her donation to the Carmelite Sisters.

After thanking him, she walked to the ramshackled convent at 2246 Fulton Street, where she gave the cloistered nuns a million dollars!

Or so the story goes. Other versions are even more embellished. The Carmelites question the above account. The present prioress wrote to say that the story "has always seemed to us very strange, and we are almost sure that it refers to somebody else." In any event, the beautiful monastery that presently stands at 721 Parker Avenue was given in its entirety by the Scottish–born Rita Marie Shomo.

An essay that appeared in the *Monthly Bulletin* for Saint Ignatius Church makes the very likely suggestion that Rita Maria was "a Carmelite in spirit all her life, for the secrecy shrouding her is even more complete than that of a cloistered nun." Among Mrs. Shomo's effects at the time of her death was a card bearing this message: "Saturday, July 13, 1929, my first meeting with my Carmelite family."

Rebecca Harkness was born in 1870. Her formative years were probably spent in the British Isles and France. She was received into the Church during January of 1894 and, thereafter, she was known by her Confirmation name, Rita Marie. She was a personal friend of Rafael Cardinal Merry del Val and through his kindness she met Pope Pius X on several occasions. She married Jean Andre Shomo in Tacoma, Washington on June 7, 1913.

Quietly and mostly unknown to the Carmelites, Rita had been a benefactor from the time of their arrival in San Francisco. Father D.J. Kavanagh, S.J., whom the nuns consider their California founder, asked Mrs. Shomo to assist them on several occasions. Mrs. Shomo's plans for their new monastery were delayed by the outbreak of World War II and later by her protracted illness.

Shortly after her death on September 7, 1954, it was announced that Rita Marie Shomo's entire fortune had been dedicated to the erection of a new monastery in honor of Christo Rey.

In August of 1958, Archbishop Jose Garibi Rivera, who later became Mexico's first cardinal, journeyed to the Bay Area to dedicate the chapel. The remains of Rita Marie were subsequently entombed beneath the Shrine of Our Lady of Guadalupe in the chapel which she provided to enhance the spiritual skyline of San Francisco.

CHRISTIAN BROTHERS

In what the Los Angeles *Times* described as a "really sad day for the Napa Valley," The Christian Brothers sold their winery in 1989 to the Hueblein division of Grand Metropolitan PLC of Great Britain.

Surely the largest winery sale in the nation's history, the transaction brought another of the great legacies of California's wine–making traditions to a halt after 107 years of successful operation.

It had all begun in 1879, on twelve acres of property purchased by the Brothers of the Christian Schools for a novitiate. Recognizing the possibility of augmenting their meager income, the Brothers planted additional vineyards, while improving those already under cultivation.

Brother Victorick McDonald subsequently conducted a "little experiment" which he intended only for the Brothers' table. He dumped the year's crop into a large watering trough, pounded it with a huge club, drew off the grape juice, and then set it aside for fermenting. Such was the humble beginning of the large, modern Christian Brothers Winery of present time.

Brother Victorick's modest attempt at winemaking was a delightful success, so a small crusher was purchased in 1883 to replace the "huge club" earlier used. Soon the Brothers began selling their products to pastors for use as sacramental wine.

As the business expanded, the Brothers began purchasing grapes from farmers around Martinez. By 1887, the winery had become a real commercial enterprise, doing business under the title of De La Salle Institute.

Shortly after starting the winery, Brother Victorick was given other duties at Villa De La Salle and Brother Azarie Vignon was appointed in his place. He managed the operation until 1897. The winery continued to expand and, in the early years of this century, the Brothers wisely decided to hire an expert vintner to taste and blend the wine.

In 1904, a new three story building was constructed to house the expanded operations at Martinez. The advent of Prohibition in 1919 did not materially affect the winery because the Brothers produced at that time mostly sacramental wine for liturgical use. They were also permitted by the government to make some wine for "medicinal purposes," to be sold at drugstores with a physician's prescription.

When the Brothers moved to Mont La Salle in 1932, they brought their winery equipment and inventories with them. The city of Martinez helped out by providing free ferry service to Benicia.

Shortly after the move to Mont La Salle, an event occurred which radically altered the Brothers' wine making business. That was the repeal of Prohibition in 1933, an action which greatly endeared President Franklin D. Roosevelt to the Brothers.

Only so much wine could be sold for altar use or to the general public in Washington and California, where the Brothers' main markets were then located. The prospect of enlarging their market presented itself in 1937 when Alfred Fromm of Picker–Linz Importers in New York City approached the Brothers with an offer to merchandise their wines.

Brother David Brennan, president of the Christian Brothers, said that "the decision to sell . . . was a difficult one, but this action allows the Brothers to give the highest priority to their educational work."

The Brothers teach in 1,600 schools in eighty countries and, until 1989, that work had been largely supported by the sale of wines and brandy. Cathedral High School in Los Angeles was among those profiting from the activities of the winery.

DAUGHTERS OF CHARITY

A. SOUTHLAND FOUNDATION

In his chapter on "Soldiers of Christ, Angels of Mercy," the Jesuit author of *Frontier Faiths* (Albuquerque, 1992), provides the best survey yet about the works of the Daughters of Charity in Southern California.

The initial band of Sisters left Emmitsburg, Maryland, during October of 1855 in the company of Bishop Thaddeus Amat and a group of clergymen newly–recruited for the Diocese of Monterey. They finally arrived at the *Pueblo de Nuestra Señora de los Angeles* on the Feast of Our Lord's Epiphany. Like other religious women on the frontier, often referred to in the annals at "gentle tamers," the Daughters of Charity were destined to contribute mightily to the ongoing Americanization of the Catholic Church.

In his careful research, Father Michael Engh tells how this blue–robed band became the most flexible and adaptive Roman Catholic presence in the *pueblo*, proving that members of the Catholic Church could grapple creatively with the exigencies of pioneer life from a *pueblo* convent. Invited to establish a school and an orphanage, the sisters involved themselves in hospital nursing, disaster relief, job placement, fund raising for charitable causes and care of smallpox victims.

Because of their greater numbers, range of ministries and broader contacts with the community, they often contended more directly and effectively than the clergy with local pastoral problems. Through their manifold involvement at all levels of society, the Daughters of Charity in Los Angeles repeatedly demonstrated their facility of moving with the changing complexities of life in this farwestern community of diverse peoples. They demonstrated quite forcibly by their prayer and life style the Church's willingness to engage in flexible responses to contemporary demands.

The Daughters of Charity also provided role models for women engaged in a variety of educational, charitable and welfare activities, often doing work deemed inappropriate for women. Theirs was a simple philosophy, "if it needs doing, do it."

There was an undercurrent of hostility to the Daughters of Charity by those who questioned Catholics about the nature of their allegiance to the pope. After all, he was at that time, a temporal king, as well as a spiritual leader. Many Protestants sincerely believed that Catholicism was a religion incompatible with a democratic society. The Sisters effectively proved that contention false.

In Southern California and elsewhere in the United States, the Daughters of Charity were at the forefront of those pioneer sisters who played crucial roles in the difficult adjustments that Old World Catholics faced in nineteenth century America. The notion of pluralism was a worrisome challenge to many Catholic immigrants.

When Bishop Amat attended Vatican Council I, he bragged to his fellow ecclesiastics about the relationship between the Daughters of Charity and peoples of diverse faiths and cultures. "They do not deprive us, we enrich them." Had the council not been prematurely concluded, the Vincentian Bishop of Monterey–Los Angeles might have proposed the Daughters of Charity as exemplars for that ecumenism which, unfortunately, had to wait for yet another council to find its expression.

DAUGHTERS OF CHARITY

B. MIRACLE DRUG

The Daughters of Charity, long associated with the care of the sick and elderly in Southern California, are credited with introducing a remarkable new "curative medicine" into the area at the turn of the century. Their "curative medicine" is still effective and is probably the safest and most widely used drug in the world today— though doctors still don't fully understand why it works.

Despite the fact that its roots can be traced to ancient times, present–day researchers are finding new ways to use what has been referred to as the original "wonder drug." Probably the cheapest medication presently available, this incredible drug is nothing more than plain aspirin or, as chemists classify it, acetylsalicylic acid.

More than 2,300 years ago, Hippocrates, the Greek "Father of Medicine," prescribed willow leaves to treat women at childbirth. Those leaves contained salicin, a natural compound related to aspirin. In 1826, two Italian researchers isolated the magic ingredient and, twenty seven years later, a French chemist produced acetylsalicylic acid in his laboratory. Chemists employed by the Bayer Company in Germany continued experiments with aspirin in the 1890s. They discovered its value as a pain reliever and fever reducer.

Aspirin was first marketed by the Bayer Company in 1899 and the new medication was hailed as a wonder drug in medical circles. It has been relieving aches, pains, swelling and fever ever since.

The first of the little white pills were brought to Los Angeles from the Paris motherhouse of the Daughters of Charity in 1901. Since that time, aspirin has become a household curative throughout the United States. Over twenty billion aspirins are sold every year in this nation alone—and that averages out roughly to ninety–one pills for every man, woman and child.

It is not only the world's safest drug, but the most widely used. Marketed worldwide under scores of labels, aspirin is also still sold under the label of its originator, the Bayer Company. In more recent times, researchers have discovered that aspirin also has anti–blood clotting properties that can be used to treat cardio–vascular diseases. After all these centuries, medical science continues to be puzzled by this deceptively simple drug. Its anti–fever effect is a mystery—for it lowers bodily temperature only when there is a fever.

And, to their eternal credit, the Daughters of Charity can be thanked for introducing this "curative medicine" to the western part of the United States a century ago.

DAUGHTERS OF CHARITY

C. 125TH ANNIVERSARY

The recent 125th anniversary observed by the Daughters of Charity brings alive a host of thoughts and reflections on and about these good people and their role in the spiritual development of Southern California since their arrival in 1856. Perhaps the secular historian would describe the Daughters of Charity as the first multi–national conglomerate to settle in these parts. Their holding company, located in Paris, had branches in many of the world's great population centers.

This multi–national conglomerate marketed charity. And like all efficient organizations, it had subsidiaries which packaged the product for local consumption under a variety of labels. This area of the Lord's vineyard, being mostly undeveloped, materially and spiritually, provided a ready outlet for almost all the services traditionally associated with the Daughters of Charity. And so, in the years since 1856, the heavily–starched coronet became a familiar feature to patients, orphans, the elderly, student nurses and the underprivileged in Southern California.

There's a moving letter in the Archives of the Daughters of Charity Motherhouse, on Rue de Bac. It was written by Bishop Thaddeus Amat and it pleaded for a foundation of the Sisters in Los Angeles.

Amat's letters were all persuasive, but this one especially stands out. It said: "You give me five Daughters of Charity and the six of us will make California into a new Rome." By God's grace, they said "yes" and he did it!

The 125th anniversary of the Daughters of Charity in California could easily cause people to wonder if those early pioneers had some secret ingredient that made them so effective in the society of their time.

Sociologists could likely dream up a host of theories, some of them credible, others silly. But very likely, the answer is quite simple and rudimentary. The Daughters of Charity were practitioners of virtue. Though neither trained nor commissioned as preachers of the Word, their lives were spent in the pulpit of good example. They didn't have to tell people about charity, it flowed from their very finger–tips.

That term "Daughters of Charity" really epitomized what those good ladies were about. They spent their long days catechizing, nursing, teaching and watching out for the less fortunate. Their white linen coronets quite naturally came to be identified with that queenly virtue which today many so–called Christians are content just to talk about.

When historians begin seriously searching out the activities of the Daughters of Charity in Southern California, they will find more charity than history, more deeds than words. It will be a glorious chapter for it will reflect all the ideals that Jesus intended for the spiritual well–being of His people.

Indeed, the Daughters have helped to make Los Angeles the "new Rome."

DOMINICAN FRIARS

A. ORDER OF PREACHERS

Dominican activity on the west coast of North America dates from 1772 when the missions of peninsular California were transferred to the Order of Preachers by the Franciscans of San Fernando College. After secularization a few Dominicans remained in the area; others came northward to Alta California. One of those pioneers, Father Ignacio Ramirez de Arellano, was widely known and respected in provincial days.

The first American–born Dominican to serve in California was Father Peter Augustine Anderson. He worked at Sacramento and erected in that city its first church, dedicated to Saint Rose. His apostolate was prematurely terminated by death on November 17, 1850, during the cholera epidemic.

Reactivation of the Order in modern times is usually reckoned from the appointment of Joseph Sadoc Alemany to the Bishopric of Monterey on May 31, 1850. The former provincial of Saint Joseph brought with him to California Father Francis Vilarrasa whom he authorized to establish the Order of Preachers in the west. Permission for the foundation of the Province of the Holy Name of Jesus was given by Father Jerome Gigli, Dominican Vicar General, on July 3, 1850. Formal inauguration took place on February 4, 1852, when six young novices from Spain arrived at Monterey, the first male novitiate in the Golden State. From its earliest days, Saint Dominic's Monastery was conducted according to the strict observance as is evident from one of Vilarrasa's letters:

> In our convent we do not know the taste of meat; but we have good fish and eggs. Every morning at three we say Matins. . . . This climate agrees with all the religious.

The community moved to Benicia in March of 1854 because of that town's promising position on the Carquinez Straits of the Sacramento River. A Novitiate and House of Studies were erected. Alemany, by then the Archbishop of San Francisco, entrusted to the Dominicans Vallejo along with the area from the meridian of Mount Diablo to San Pablo.

Noting that "it is of the greatest importance to our Order to have a convent in San Francisco, which is one of the most important and richest cities in the whole of America and even of the world," Vilarrasa established Queen of the Most Holy Rosary Convent in the Bay City in 1863 and on adjoining property built a parochial church under the patronage of Saint Brigid. This parish and the one of Saint Francis reverted to the archdiocese soon after Saint Dominic's Church was erected in the western part of the city.

In his *Chronicle*, written at the end of 1873, Father Francis Vilarrasa noted that

> the Order has progressed slowly up to now, but if it be recalled that only one Father was sent here in the beginning that he was for a long time the only priest of his Order here, that the Order was completely destitute of any temporal help, and furthermore, that the Order

received little or rather no incentive from the Archdiocese, then it will seem wonderful that there are now found in California two houses of the Brethren with seventeen priests, six students, and six lay brothers!

DOMINICAN FRIARS

B. DOMINICANS IN PENINSULAR CALIFORNIA

Since their foundation in 1215, by Domingo de Guzmán, the Order of Preachers has worked diligently to make the world their cell and the ocean their cloister. Coming to the New World in 1510, the Dominicans settled on Española, a small island in the Caribbean Sea. There they opened a campaign on behalf of native peoples unparalleled in the annals of humanitarian endeavor. The names of Pedro de Córdova, Antonio de Montesinos, Bartolomé de Las Casas and Luis Cáncer are only a few of those who threw themselves wholeheartedly into the task of advancing the spiritual and material welfare of the Indian population.

In practically every corner of the two American continents penetrated by Spain, the Order of Preachers labored with distinction. As early as 1526, they moved on from the Caribbean Islands to new fields of conquest. Dominican missionaries were the first to preach the Gospel within the present borders of the continental United States, possibly with Ponce de León, in 1513, and assuredly with Lucas Vázquez de Allyón, in 1526.

While never so influential in New Spain as the Franciscans, the Order of Preachers worked with singular success. Their missionary foundations in Oaxaca, for example, were considered outstanding models of evangelic accomplishment. The Dominicans were the first to gain a successful foothold in the Sierra Gorda region where, by the close of the seventeenth century, they were operating six flourishing missions.

On April 7, 1772, the Dominicans were officially entrusted with all the Jesuit foundations in Peninsular California, as well as the recently-founded frontier establishment of San Fernando de Velicatá. The actual transferral of authority took place in mid 1773, when the last of the Franciscans departed for their new apostolate in Alta California. The territory was of immense proportions and included what one writer aptly called "the decadent area south of Velicatá and the virgin territory north."

The Dominican presence in Baja California lasted for over eighty years, during which time the friars established eight new missions. Between 1772 and 1854, fourteen Dominicans occupied the office of *Presidente*. The fortunes of missionary work in the area were irrevocably altered in the years after 1804, when the peninsula was politically severed from Alta California. Initially, the region's isolation had the beneficial effect of insulating it from many of the vexations confronting the mainland, but eventually time caught up with Baja California and placed insurmountable obstacles in the path of the friars.

Complications totally beyond their control rendered Dominican missionary efforts in Peninsular California considerably less productive and surely less dramatic than their exploits in other areas of the New World. Yet the emerging records, scant though they still are, show that the self-sacrificing friars "labored as effectually for the Indians, and accomplished as much good for religion, as either the Jesuits or the Franciscans. And these fruitful labors the friars of St. Dominic continued until they were deprived of all means of subsistence, and were forced to leave the country by the destructive secularization measures of the past century."

FRANCISCAN SISTERS OF THE SACRED HEART

It was on August 20, 1908, that four Sisters from Joliet, Illinois came to establish a hospital in Santa Barbara. The institution was named after the patron of the Franciscan Sisters of the Sacred Heart. The desire at the time was to locate a hospital in Southern California which would supplement the work already begun by the Sisters at Saint Joseph's in San Francisco.

The Sisters purchased the Quiesesana hospital which had been erected several years previously on East Arrellaga Street. The earlier foundation had been launched by a trinity of physicians who were delighted to step aside for the Franciscan Sisters.

In 1910, a new fireproof addition to Saint Francis Hospital was built. It had space for a modern surgical department, operating room, sterilization and anaesthetical equipment and supply rooms. Five years later the surgical unit was further strengthened by the installation of a powerful X-ray plant and an up-to-date kitchen facility. By that time, Saint Francis Hospital was looked upon as one of the state's finest.

Ever-so-gradually, the Franciscan Sisters carried the hospital through the trying days of its foundation, each year making it more complete and functional. Their interest and devoted zeal attracted many patients, so many, in fact, that soon there was need for additional space.

It was eventually decided to expand and erect a new building. A site of more than three acres was available on East Micheltorena Street and plans were announced for a new structure. A four story building was designed, constructed of steel, concrete and brick. There was even a roof garden for patients needing prolonged periods of convalescence. The campaign to raise funds began on

December 7, 1921. The entire community responded and on January 6, 1924, Bishop John J. Cantwell journeyed north from Los Angeles for the dedication. Unhappily, less than two years later, the new building was shaken to the ground by an earthquake, a mass of crumbled mortar and twisted steel.

The work of seventeen years lay in ruins. Whole sections of the main walls had fallen outward to the ground; stairways were torn from their anchors; tiles were ripped from the partitions. No one was injured in the earthquake, but the building itself was a total loss.

With their hospital wrecked, with no place to put their patients, and even without rooms in which they themselves could sleep, the Sisters were tempted to leave the area. But, as Sister Rosina said, "we are at least no worse than when we came to Santa Barbara. We will start anew." The old Quiesesana building was pressed back into temporary service and the Sisters stayed at their posts, determined to overcome the tremendous handicaps placed in their path.

The courage shown by the Sisters aroused the interest and support not only of the people of Santa Barbara, but other areas of the state. On May 6, 1927, the cornerstone of a new building was put in place. The day on which the Sisters and nurses transferred their patients to the new hospital marked the end of two decades of struggle.

Those years were only a prelude to the decades of service to follow. Today, the Franciscans Sisters continue their work of bringing solace and love to the hurting people of Santa Barbara.

HOLY CROSS BROTHERS

The news about the discovery of gold in California travelled rapidly around the world. In the midwest it became a favorite topic of conversation among the faculty and students at Notre Dame University.

Given the university's severe shortage of operational funds, the temptation to join the gold seekers was overpowering. On September 28, 1849, the Local Council for the Holy Cross Brothers "unanimously resolved" to send three of its members "to dig gold in California." The council admitted that its actions would "appear strange and extraordinary to some," though they were "in no way unjust and unlawful." Father Edward Sorin, the superior, said that the decision was "justified before God to two powerful motives" namely that of repairing the damage of a recent fire and that of paying arrears of indebtedness.

The Brothers who eventually became part of the expedition were Lawrence Menage, Justin Gautier, Placidus Allard and Gatien Monsimer. They were accompanied by three other "prospectors" who formed what became the St. Joseph Company.

Father Sorin devised a set of twenty–three regulations by which the company was to be guided. The "regular observance" of religious exercises and other pious practices were of paramount importance.

The group departed on February 28, 1850 for a journey that would take about four and a half months of arduous travel over nearly 3,000 miles. On a good day, when road conditions, grass supply and weather permitted, they could hope to travel twenty–five to thirty miles at most.

The correspondence from the Brothers enroute is fascinating. Brother Gatien reported that "the number of emigrants to California is immense. People say we are very early & still there are 200 teams ahead of us: yesterday we saw 9 teams within one mile."

There wasn't adequate time for the Brothers to pray as they moved westward and they had to travel on Sundays which made Mass attendance difficult. To dramatize their lack of opportunity for prayer in common, Gatien told how once, "when the horses broke loose without a driver, Brother Lawrence promised a thousands *Aves*. We do not have the time to say them. Would you have them said for us? It is a small miracle that the horses with our large wagon galloped 3 miles alone without any accident."

Another letter described their camping arrangements. "Every evening, we have pitched our tent, scattered over the damp or frozen ground a little hay or straw, when we could procure it; and when we could not, we would, for a substitute, rake a few leaves with our fingers or mow a little prairie grass with our knives."

It must have been a challenging journey. "We see on the road young and old, rich and poor, men and women, children and babies—some with baggage; some with carts or wagons; others packing or walking." A full account of the journey has been published by the Indiana Province Archives Center of Holy Cross from a transcript edited by Brother Francis Cullen.

The "company" arrived at Placerville on July 31. There they were surrounded by "infidels" who even worked on Sunday in their drive to find gold! "Like everyone we have neither tent nor house. Our neighbors are six feet from us . . . We often say our prayers in bed so as to avoid scandal."

Brother Placidus died early in November and another member of the "company" succumbed early in 1851. The remaining members returned to Notre Dame about mid year—without the hoped–for riches of the gold mines. For many years there was criticism of the trek to California. Yet one suspects that the venture would have been widely acclaimed had the Brothers returned with sacks of gold dust.

While the 1850 expedition to California was an ill–conceived attempt to resolve the financial problems then beseiging the community, the temporary foundations in Northern California were serious efforts to engage the human resources of Holy Cross in the evangelization of the west, efforts that would pay rich spiritual dividends in a later age.

HOLY CROSS SISTERS

The Congregation of the Sisters of the Holy Cross recently observed the 150th anniversary of its establishment by Father Basil Anthony Moreau. Originating at Le Mans, France, the first missionary contingent came to the United States in 1843.

Early in 1914, Father Clement Molony invited the Holy Cross Sisters to teach in the elementary school which he had erected to serve the Catholics of Saint Agnes Parish in downtown Los Angeles. Eight years later, a parochial school was erected at San Buenaventura Mission by Father Patrick Grogan and once again the Sisters of the Holy Cross were asked to staff the institution. At the formal dedication on August 20, 1922, Bishop John J. Cantwell warmly greeted the Sisters and prophesied that they would become an integral part of the local community.

Such indeed was the case and, a few years later, the sisters opened Saint Catherine–by–the–Sea, a private academy for young girls which served the people of San Buenaventura for many years. Since 1968, that facility has functioned as a retirement center for the sisters.

Other grade schools in the southland were staffed by the community over the years, including Saint Paul's in Los Angeles (1922–1979), Good Shepherd in Beverly Hills (1930–1976), Saint Barnabas in Long Beach (1946 onwards) and Saint Philip Neri in Lynwood (1954–1986).

The sisters have also been active at the secondary level, teaching at Bishop Conaty High School (Los Angeles), Saint Pius X (Downey), Notre Dame (Sherman Oaks), Paraclete (Lancaster), Mater Dei (Santa Ana) and Santa Margarita (El Toro). In addition to their service in the local Catholic educational system, the Sisters of the Holy Cross have been leaders in the field of health care, a ministry dating from the Civil War years when more than eighty sisters answered the call for nurses.

Historically, the sisters served the old west as nurses and teachers in the mining towns, responding to the needs of prospectors and miners in and around the Salt Lake area. Bishop Thomas K. Gorman once observed that "the sisters planted the Holy Cross deeply in the soil of Utah."

Holy Cross Medical Center first opened its doors at Mission Hills in the 1950s as a Catholic response to the health care needs of the San Fernando Valley. When the facility was destroyed in the 1970 Sylmar earthquake, a new, larger building was erected with a capacity of 316 beds.

Designated as a level II Trauma Center, Holy Cross Medical Center offered a broad range of innovative services with its staff of highly–skilled physicians, nurses, technicians and support staff. Today, the Holy Cross Health System operates eight major health care corporations in seven states from Maryland to California. These foundations include a dozen acute care hospitals, eight extended care facilities, four residential centers for the handicapped and elderly, numerous ambulatory care and surgery centers, several clinics for the poor, a college of nursing and three preferred provider organizations.

HOLY FAMILY SISTERS

Elizabeth Armer was born at Sydney, Australia, on April 30th, 1851, and soon after was brought to California to be raised by a foster mother, Mrs. Richard Tobin of San Francisco. Attracted early in life to the religious state, Elizabeth consulted Archbishop Joseph Sadoc Alemany about her vocation and was told by the San Francisco prelate, "There are little ones to be cared for while their mothers are off to work. And who is to instruct the children of our big city in the ways of faith, hope and love? They must be prepared for the Sacraments; they must be brought to the knowledge, love and service of God. There are the poor to be visited in their homes. There are hearts to heal and souls to save in our busy city streets. This is the work God wants you to do, Elizabeth!"

Responding to the archbishop's request, Elizabeth moved into a rented apartment on San Francisco's Pine Street in November of 1872, to begin what later became Holy Family Institute. The spiritual director of the enterprise, Father John J. Prendergast, outlined a rule of life for Elizabeth and her few companions encompassing the earlier directives of Archbishop Alemany. The first years were dark ones, for vocations were slow in coming. Almost two years passed before the second recruit made her appearance, but soon other generous girls volunteered for the work and the number began to grow.

In order to give the foundation canonical status, Alemany sent one of the young ladies to the Dominican convent at Benicia, and in 1878, she pronounced her vows as Sister Teresa of Jesus. In 1880 the entire group repeated the ceremony and California had its first native religious institute. At the suggestion of the archbishop, the Sisters opened a series of day homes for youngsters whose mothers were obliged to work. When San Francisco's *presidio* became the center for sick and wounded soldiers during the Spanish–American War, the nuns acted as nurses. Despite the danger of contamination with typhoid fever, the Sisters never hesitated to perform their tasks with optimistic generosity.

In the devastating fire and earthquake of 1906, the Sisters converted their motherhouse into a temporary shelter for the insane and, in addition, took in many of the homeless religious of San Francisco. Mother Dolores, the Elizabeth Armer of earlier days, continued to guide and direct the activities of the community until her death on August 2, 1905. Since then the work has continued to meet the challenges of a growing city and an ever expanding state.

By 1951 the Sisters were instructing 79,000 public school children throughout 225 parishes in an apostolate stretching into three archdioceses and six dioceses. 2,000 children of all races and creeds were being cared for in the day homes operated by the Community. Growth has not altered the original aims of the institute. Even in 2000, one can still read in the constitutions the central idea of the Holy Family Sisters, "to instruct and educate children in the doctrine and practice of the Catholic faith . . ."

IMMACULATE HEART SISTERS

Catalonia's small town of Olot witnessed the foundation of the Institute of the Daughters of the Immaculate Heart of Mary on July 2, 1848, by Canon Joaquin Masmitja. Three years after its establishment, the new congregation received permission from the Royal Council of the Republic to engage in catechetical instruction. Formal approbation of their rules and constitutions came when the Bishop of Gerona endorsed their work on April 18, 1861.

The Right Reverend Thaddeus Amat, C.M., himself a native of Catalonia, was familiar with the community and anxiously hoped to introduce the sisters into the Diocese of Monterey–Los Angeles. Enroute to the First Vatican Council, in November of 1896, Amat approached Canon Masmitja for the necessry authorization. Acting upon the recommendation of Archbisbop Anthony Claret, Masmitja acquiesced and soon ten nuns were busy preparing for the long journey to California. The Franco–Prussian War of 1870 delayed their departure for over a year during which time the sisters learned to speak the English language.

In July of 1871, Father Francis Mora, Vicar General of the Diocese of Monterey–Los Angeles, went to Spain to escort Mother Raimunda and her nine companions to California. Leaving Gerona on the Feast Of Our Lady of the Angels, Mora found that by the time his group arrived in Liverpool, the boat on which they were to sail had already departed. The inconvenience and hardships of arranging for subsequent passage on another ship were compensated for, when word arrived that the earlier vessel had been lost at sea, never to be seen again!

The ten sisters docked at San Francisco on August 31, 1871, where they were met by Bishop Amat and Archbishop Joseph Sadoc Alemany. Five of the sisters were sent to Gilroy and the others to the orphanage at San Juan Bautista. The arrival of the nuns at their new homes occasioned a warm public reception by the local populace. Their convent in Gilroy was about a mile from the city on land adjacent to Saint Mary's Church, whose pastor, Father Thomas Hudson, was overjoyed at their coming.

An academy and a private day school were soon in operation with an enrollment of thirty–five pupils. Boarding accommodations were ready within a month, and the number of students steadily grew despite the distance from town. Amat authorized the establishment of a novitiate, and in October the first English–speaking postulant, Miss Ann Garvey of San Francisco (Sister Mary Conception), applied for admission. The extent of the sisters' activities broadened in 1874 with the erection of a parochial boys' school.

A block of land in San Luis Obispo had been given to the diocese in 1857 by Don Dolores Herrera for a convent. After clearing the title to the land in 1872, the bishop heeded pleas of the town's inhabitants and arranged for a school to be opened there. Several years passed, and on August 2, 1876, the foundation was taken over by the Sisters under the name of the Immaculate Heart Academy.

There were countless hardships in the early years. The convent at Gilroy, for instance, stood in the middle of an uncultivated, treeless, fifteen–acre oasis. Crammed within the two story frame structure were two classrooms, two music rooms, several poorly-lighted dormitories, a kitchen, and a dining room. But from these humble beginnings the Sisters prospered and expanded until they found themselves scattered over the entire Pacific Coast. The Sisters of the Immaculate Heart of Mary, later an independent community, are a credit to their Spanish "founder," a tribute to their California "adapter," and a monument to the value of prayer and sacrifice.

THE JESUITS

A. SUPPRESSION OF SOCIETY

On the eve of its 450th anniversary, the Society of Jesus was described as "the most prestigious missionary order in the Catholic Church." Their general is aptly known the world over as the "black" Pope. Talleyrand once said that "whether or not one agrees with them, one always finds in the Jesuits that precious note of reason; they are reasonably severe, reasonably focused on what is possible, reasonably moral, reasonable enemies, reasonable even in their devotion to the papacy. Always, that note of reason."

But there have been dissenters to Talleyrand's view. Webster's Third International Dictionary, for example, defines a Jesuit as "one who is given to intrigue or subterfuge; an astute person." What concerns us here is the banishment of the Society of Jesus from Baja California in 1767, an event that triggered the coming to the area of Fray Junípero Serra and his Franciscan collaborators. One of the most frequently asked questions from readers of this column is: "Why were the Jesuits expelled?"

Unfortunately there is no simple answer, partly because many of the documents in the historical archives of the Society have not been made public out of deference to the wishes of the Holy See. One factor figured into the decision above all others and it was the political climate of Europe.

Proponents of the Enlightenment wanted to establish another religion, one based on pure reason called deism—belief in a distant god who doesn't concern himself too much with humankind . . . hence a rather non–demanding god. But the Jesuits got in the way of that movement. At that time they held almost a monopoly in the education of the laity throughout most of the Europe's Catholic countries. Only by removing the Society of Jesus could the deists be assured that people would no longer be reared and trained according to the Gospel.

The Jesuits were also active in another ministry that thwarted deism–that of giving parochial missions and retreats in both the rural and urban areas of Europe. Their catechetical network worked well, perhaps too well!

While easily the most brilliant, influential and effective arm of the papacy, the Jesuits were easily the most detested. And, interestingly enough, they were suppressed not by the revolutionaries but by the "Catholic" kings who themselves would eventually be guillotined and/or overthrown.

The "enlightened" philosophers had their way. The Society was abolished in Portugal and its territories in America and Asia (1759), in France (1764), in Spain and its colonies (1767) and finally by the Pope himself (1773). Only in Russia did the Tsarina refuse to publish the papal decree.

Pope Clement XIV allowed himself to be convinced that "it is absolutely impossible to maintain a true and lasting peace within the Church as long as that order exists." His successors long regretted that statement and eventually repudiated it. That Pope Clement XIV wasn't as "astute" as the Jesuits he banished is amply clear from

subsequent history. The Society was eventually re–established and regained its place of prominence within the Church.

And what about today? As late as February of 1989, the "black" Pope (Father Peter–Hans Kolvenbach) reiterated the sentiments of Ignatius Loyola that "the sole true reason for the existence of the Society is the service of the Church in dependence on the Roman Pontiff; to remove ourselves from that purpose would be to sign our death warrant."

THE JESUITS

B. RETURN OF THE JESUITS

Jesuit missionary activity in Baja California, "remote as was the land and small as was the nation," has brought the comment that "there are few chapters in the history of the World on which the mind can turn with so sincere an admiration."

With their expulsion from the Spanish realm in 1768, the Society of Jesus closed the book on seventy years of apostolic activity in the peninsula and turned over to their Franciscan successors the foundations and traditions that later bloomed forth along *El Camino Real* in Alta California. Although the Society was briefly reinstated in Mexico between 1816 and 1820, the Spanish ministry irritated Mexican sentiments by ordering the Jesuits again expelled without any reasons given or offered.

Bishop Francisco Garcia Diego y Moreno petitioned the Mexican Government on July 16, 1841, to use "its full power to have the Jesuits established in Upper California and thus cheer up the territory . . . so needy in every respect." The prelate's request was approved by President Anastasio Bustamente but was revoked when General Santa Ana seized control of governmental machinery later in the year. The general subsequently relented but no action was taken because of the paucity of means available to transport the priests from Europe.

Shortage of clerical personnel in California became desperately acute in the years after Bishop Garcia Diego's death. The Administrator of the Diocese, Father González Rubio, hopefully turned to Archbishop Francis Norbert Blanchet of Oregon City for assistance. The prelate's response was effectively sympathetic:

> I have received your most welcome letter . . . but its reading filled my soul with grief. . . . In the midst of so many and such great causes of affliction you ask me for help when we ourselves need help. . . . The news of the discovery of gold in California is fascinating the mind of everybody, and is unsettling and attracting the minds of various persons in our diocese. Determined to provide for their spiritual need, I had already thought of

sending after them the Very Reverend Brouillet, Vicar General of Walla Walla.

It was to be Brouillet's work to care for the spiritual needs of that massive number of his countrymen (estimated at two–thirds of the able Oregonians) settling in California. Brouillet arrived late in 1848 and was soon joined by Father Anthony Langlois who was on his way back to Canada to enter the Jesuit Novitiate. Langlois's superior, Father Michael Accolti, advised him to remain for a while in California to work out the details necessary for eventually bringing the Society of Jesus back to the Golden State.

After a year of negotiations, Accolti himself and several companions started out for California and landed on the "longed–for shores of what goes under the name of San Francisco, but which, whether it should be called madhouse of Babylon, I am at a loss to determine; so great in those days was the disorder, the brawling, the open immorality, the reign of crime, which, brazen–faced, triumphed on a soil not yet brought under the sway of human laws." The arrival of the Jesuits was a great boost to Catholicism in California, and Fray González Rubio immediately presented the Society with the first in a long series of difficult challenges.

The words of Michael Accolti still echo down through the decades—"Once our Society shall, like a vine, have been lawfully planted in California and shall have taken root, it will be easy for it afterwards to spread its branches."

THE JESUITS

C. Recruitment of *Californios*

Though Spanish–speaking students comprised at least a fourth of California's school–aged youngsters in the 1850s, they did not have immediate or equal access to public instruction. In a superb essay on "Hispanic Californians and Catholic Higher Education," Father Gerald McKevitt recently pointed out that the state was slow to establish schools and even slower to provide for the area's Mexicans or *californios*.

The Catholic bishops and educators, on the other hand, with acculturation as their ultimate objective, established schools and colleges that attempted to meet the needs of the post–conquest *californios*. An outstanding example would be Santa Clara College. Founded by immigrant Italian Jesuits in 1851, the all male school enjoyed a wide Hispanic patronage.

The value that Catholics placed upon religious instruction reinforced Santa Clara's attractiveness. James Alexander Forbes called the college "the best there is in California," because its faculty is "concerned about the religious education of the students without which there can be no true instruction."

In his enlightening article for *California History*, McKevitt used Jesus Maria Estudillo (born 1844) as an example of a student struggling with the challenge of adapting to a new political, economical, cultural and ethnic order as the state moved from an Hispanic to an Anglo orientation. For Estudillo and others, the Jesuit college served as a mediating influence between the old and new cultures while, at the same time, providing continuity with the Hispanic past of the *californios*.

Jesuit pedagogy placed a high priority on *eloquentia perfecta*, or the cultivation of style. The professors rightly felt that the ability to speak and write well correctly reflected a disciplined and educated mind.

Other features made the Santa Clara milieu even more inviting. The mixed student body provided opportunities for forging friendships with both Anglo and Hispanic classmates in a closely–knit familial atmosphere. Religion forged the strongest bond with *californio* culture. Sermons in Spanish were still preached in the old mission church, public processions were common and Marian devotions were encouraged.

Estudillo's diary illustrates how the Church often served as the "first line of defense" behind which ethnic groups, threatened with loss of identification, organized to preserve their group singularity. Religion for Estudillo and others remained a valued last vestige of an old order that was quickly passing, but which provided continuity and help in coping with the new.

The apparent ease with which Estudillo moved in both worlds mirrored his ever–increasing Americanization. After attending a Fourth of July parade in 1862, he wrote in his diary that "though not a free born American, I feel a little of that spirit which raises and makes every American's heart leap with gladness at the very name of Liberty."

McKevitt concluded his essay by portraying Santa Clara College as "a bridge between change and continuity . . . a safe haven in which young *californios* could make the difficult transition from pre– to post–conquest culture."

THE JESUITS

D. Ignatian Year

Probably the question most asked of a diocesan priest is something like this: "Are you a Jesuit?" In the early days of my ministry, that question irritated me; later I found it amusing and now, in my final years, I rather like being identified with the Society of Jesus.

So why this attraction to the Jesuits? Perhaps it had its origin in a decree addressed to Ferdinand and Isabella, on May 4, 1493, by Pope Alexander VI. Therein the Holy Father said:

"We order you in virtue of holy obedience that you

dispatch to the designated mainlands and islands virtuous and God–fearing men endowed with training, experience and skill, to instruct the natives and inhabitants before mentioned and to imbue them with the same Christian faith and sound morals, using all speed in the premises." With this and subsequent papal mandates, the Spanish monarchs inaugurated the Christianization and colonization of the New World.

That portion of the vast apostolate assigned to the Jesuits demanded great heroism. One historian attributes to it the superlative praise of being a task unparalleled in the history of the Western Hemisphere in its demands for courage and the significance of its fruits.

An agreement between Pedro Menendez de Aviles and Saint Francis Borgia introduced the Society of Jesus to the Atlantic seaboard of North America in 1566. Already by September 28th of that year, Father Pedro Martinez had won the privilege of shedding the first Jesuit blood on the Isle of Tacatacuru (Cumberland), near the mouth of the San Juan River.

Even the history of Virginia opens, not with the founding of Jamestown, but with the martyrdom there of eight Black Robes in February 1571. It was a saddened General of the Society of Jesus who complained some months later that his priests "have seen little or no fruit of their labors, which is the greatest suffering of all for those who seek only the good of souls for the greater glory of God."

The Florida enterprise, which had proven to be about as disastrous a failure as the Society was to experience in colonial America, was terminated when the survivors of the Carolina revolt and the Virginia massacre were transferred in 1572 to Mexico and a new apostolate which would endure, without interruption, for the next two centuries.

The decades following the coming of the Jesuits to Mexico are possibly the most glorious of the Society of Jesus. In 1591, the spiritual *conquistadores* began moving northward from Mexico City along the west coast of the mainland, establishing a series of missions against the rugged Sierra Occidental, and to spread east and north over the plains into present–day Chihuahua. Directly opposite and parallel to these coastal foundations was Peninsular California which, along with modern Nayarit, Durango, Sinaloa, Sonora, and most of Chihuahua and part of Arizona, comprised the northwest province of the Society of Jesus.

It is now four centuries since the Jesuits began reaching out to areas that would eventually include California. The year of 1991 was an "Ignatian Year" during which the world observed the 450th anniversary of the Society of Jesus and the 500th anniversary of the birth of Ignatius of Loyola.

These celebrations provided an ideal opportunity for remembering Ignatius, Francis Xavier, their early companions, the missionaries and martyrs, the scientists and teachers, the preachers and pastors and the confessors and retreat masters of the New World who have labored so faithfully in the shadow of the cross.

MERCY SISTERS

The Sisters of Mercy arrived in San Francisco in 1854, on the very day that Pope Pius IX promulgated the dogma of Our Lady's Immaculate Conception. How much good they have wrought since then is known to God alone.

During the cholera epidemic of 1855, the Sisters were asked to take charge of the suffering population. They accepted, refusing any payment for their services and asking only that the bills of the hospital be met. And the proposition was applauded by the general populace.

Political and religious antipathy, however, found vent in the daily publication of calumnious attacks on the Sisters in the columns of the San Francisco *Bulletin*. Mother Mary Baptist Russell, after some months of this, invited the Grand Jury to investigate. By its official report the public was, to its surprise, made aware that for seven months the Sisters had received not one cent in cash from the city to meet demands, and were actually forced to borrow money to do the city's work.

Nevertheless, the Sisters continued their gratuitous services until April 1, 1857, when by previous notice to the Board of Supervisors they cancelled their contract because of the city's refusal to pay its bills. Shortly thereafter, Archbishop Joseph Sadoc Alemany began a drive for funds with which the Sisters were able to purchase the hospital from the city and rename it Saint Mary. A series of fairs was held in the area to clear the mortgage and make extensive repairs.

A new location was eventually decided on, at the summit of Rincon Hill, then in the heart of the fashionable district of San Francisco. On the afternoon of September 3, 1860, their new building was ready to receive its first patient.

In the summer of 1868, there was a terrible outbreak of smallpox. The Sisters of Mercy offered to take charge of the patients in the smallpox hospital, and the offer was eagerly accepted. One of the Protestant newspapers at that time paid the following tribute to the Sisters:

> It was almost with a feeling of shame for Protestantism that we saw, the other day, when the continual complaints of mal–administration and neglect of patients at the Variola Hospital in this city seemed to be without remedy, none of our religious denominations save the Catholic Church had any organization which could furnish intelligent help—competent, kind, female nurses to enter that home of misery and take charge of its ministrations to the crowd of suffering humanity it contains.

Those devoted Sisters of Mercy willingly presented themselves and entered on a mission of charity from which all others shrink in dismay and affright. That their presence there will have a beneficial effect none can doubt.

Already the good results of their presence are apparent. Their fearless, self–sacrificing love is an honor to their Church and to their Order be blessed for their work by God who sees everything.

One of the patients during those gloomy days later wrote a letter to the San Francisco *Morning Call* in which she too praised the Sisters. It is here presented in summary form:

Oh, what work they did for their suffering fellow–creatures! I shall begin with the youngest, a noble specimen of God's work. There she might be seen from 6 A.M. till a late hour at night, going through the wards, carrying a tray with medicine, beef–tea, wine, egg–nog, always with the kind look and benevolent smile that did more good to our hearts than anything the doctor could do for our health.

After enumerating several other such devoted Sisters, the correspondent noted that "these works were done for God, not for the praise of any one. May God protect them all–they are real Sisters of Mercy and mothers of the afflicted."

ORANGE SISTERS

The Australian Island of Bougainville is probably best known as the place where the late John F. Kennedy and his crew of sailors were stranded in 1943. But a whole year before that, another chapter of interesting history unfolded on that Solomon isle and it figures prominently in California's Catholic heritage.

It was in 1940 that the Sisters of Saint Joseph of Orange answered the plea of Bishop Thomas Wade for two teachers and two nurses to engage in missionary work in his Vicariate Apostolic of the Northern Solomons. The four volunteers from Orange were appointed to assist the Marist priests and Sisters at their dispensary station on the small island of Buka. There they worked with the people in almost every capacity, but not without contracting malaria, pneumonia and dysentery.

Soon after the outbreak of World War II, Bishop Wade felt that the contingency would be safer on the large island of Bougainville. For a year, the group of religious lived and camped in the hills, always avoiding the high mountains where cannibals were known to exist. When the Japanese landed on the east coast, in the late months of 1942, Bishop Wade instructed Father Albert Libel to have the Australian coast watchers contact the United States Navy for advice on evacuation.

The message eventually sent to Admiral William F. "Bull" Halsey read: "Urgently request the evacuation of American women from Bougainville. Fear repetition of crimes committed at Guadalcanal. Tinputz and Teop harbors convenient and safe."

The admiral reacted quickly. He dispatched the U.S.S. *Nautilus* to the scene and ordered a temporary cessation of bombing until the evacuation was completed. Six days later, the Nautilus reached Kessa point off the harbor. Meanwhile, the twenty–nine people to be evacuated (two elderly priests, ten Marist Sisters, four Orange Sisters and a group of local people attached to the mission) had journeyed through the crocodile–infested waters of several rivers and over a jungle path opened for them by the natives.

It was during the darkened hours of New Year's Eve that the small group of evacuees was rowed halfway to the submarine in canoes. They changed, midway, into a motor launch for the rest of the five mile journey to the *Nautilus*. After a four day under–water voyage, they were transferred to a sub–chaser for the last part of the journey to Guadalcanal. There they boarded the *Hunter Liggett* for New Zealand.

Upon their eventual arrival in San Francisco, the four Orange Sisters pushed the doorbell of their convent at Our Lady of Victory Parish. It was the first anyone had heard about the fate of the "four lost Sisters." They had been presumed dead. The rescue was later woven into a plot for a segment in the television presentation, the "Silent Service." Network officials report that the "Nautilus and the Nuns" was one of the most popular stories in the series.

Following the war, two of the original Orange contingency returned to Bougainville for resumption of their missionary work. It marked the end of a long but fascinating trek for the California Sisters.

PICPUS FATHERS

The first association of the Picpus Fathers, the Congregation of the Sacred Hearts, with California occurred in 1832, when Fathers Alexis J. A. Bachelot and Patrick Short arrived at San Pedro after being banished from their missionary stations in Hawaii. By 1848, the Picpus Fathers could see that California was going to be an important country. "Everybody is going thither. Soon there will be over a million inhabitants. There is gold everywhere: in the rivers, in the plains, and in the mountains."

One of the Picpus Fathers, Louis Desirée Maigret, the Vicar Apostolic of Hawaii, suggested to Archbishop Pierre Dominique Marcellin Raphael Bonamie, Superior General of the Picpus Fathers, that their community offer its services to California on the condition that one of their number be named bishop of the area. Maigret's interest in affairs there was based on his concern for the large number of Hawaiians who were then migrating to the Pacific Coast. There is no evidence that the Vicar Apostolic informed the Administrator of the Diocese of Both Californias, Father José Maria de Jesus González Rúbio, about the extent of his "intervention" with Roman officials.

Bonamie endorsed Maigret's proposal and from his headquarters at Paris, the archbishop wrote the Cardinal Prefect of the Sacred Congregation of Religious that his community would assume spiritual direction of the shepherdless Diocese of Both Californias, if a member of the Congregation of the Sacred Hearts be named to the vacant bishopric. Allesandro Cardinal Barnabo favored Bonamie's suggestion and recommended it formally to Pope Pius IX. On June 21, 1849, Cardinal Giacomo Fransoni notified Bonamie of the pontiff's sympathetic viewpoint.

The archbishop's candidate for the vacancy was Father Bernard Tignac, a priest of outstanding piety and exemplary character, whose previous twelve years in the ministry had been spent in Valparaiso. The Holy Father was living at Gaeta, near Naples, a factor which disrupted the normal channels of communications between the various agencies and congregations through which episcopal nominations were processed.

Meanwhile, the question of California's orphaned Church came before the American prelates as they gathered at Baltimore for the Seventh Provincial Council. They recommended to Pius IX that the candidate for the California episcopate should be an American citizen. The name of their nominee, Father Charles Pius Montgomery, was forwarded to the cardinals comprising the governing board of the Sacred Congregation of Propaganda Fide.

The congregation voted to support the proposal of the American hierarchy in preference to the one by Archbishop Bonamie. In effect then, what began as a grandiose plan to evangelize California under a Picpus bishop was modified by the decisions of the Baltimore Council and Pope Pius IX. In his letter explaining the turn of events, Cardinal Fransoni suggested to Archbishop Bonamie that the Picpus Fathers might be satisfied with taking charge of Peninsular California.

The proposal for a Picpus vicariate in California appears to have been an ambitious and well-motivated attempt to provide for an area otherwise neglected by church authorities. In retrospect, however, it is doubtful whether the appointment of any other than an American citizen would have adequately served contemporary ecclesial demands.

SACRED HEART SISTERS

In 1990, the Society devoted to the Sacred Heart celebrated the fiftieth anniversary of its foundation and, in what is probably a unique record for any religious society, none of its members died in that first half century! It was in 1940 that a young Hungarian woman made her lifetime profession of poverty, chastity and obedience. Sister Ida Peterfy was then and remained throughout her long life a woman of singular dedication and unparalled commitment.

Things weren't very favorable to the Church in Hungary during the early years. World War II, followed by the Communist occupation, created untold challenges for any and all religious communities.

Following the arrest of Josef Cardinal Mindszenty, the Sisters of the Sacred Heart were advised to leave the country and this they did on February 14, 1949. They went first to Austria, then to Canada and, finally, to the United States. In 1956, the Sisters responded to the invitation of James Francis Cardinal McIntyre and began an establishment in Los Angeles. Soon young women from all parts of the country found themselves drawn to the vibrant joy and dedication of the Sacred Heart Sisters.

In their motherhouse, then located on property intended for a new archdiocesan cathedral, the Sisters installed a printing press and one of their first publications in 1961was the monograph on *Francisco Garcia Diego y Moreno, First Bishop of the Californias*.

With the encouragement of Msgr. John J. Clarke, the Sisters became an important arm of the Confraternity of Christian Doctrine and, especially, of the Borromeo Guild. A host of brochures and monographs published by the Guild in the 1960s were printed at the Sisters' press on Hudson Avenue.

In that decade, the Sisters became actively involved in youth retreats and, later, in the Cursillo movement. They also played an important role in summer camps for children. Family Retreat Camps were established to nourish and sustain the basic familial unit.

Later, Sister Ida pioneered in the field of communications. The Sisters produced twenty–seven childrens' religious educational programs for KABC–TV. Their celebrated video catechesis, "Sacred Heart Kids' Club," began in the 1980s. They were also busy in the spiritual formation programs for the Permanent Diaconate and in that area they concentrated on training the candidates' children, a concept then unique in the country.

In their First General Chapter, in 1976, the Sisters formally adopted constitutions which were later approved by Timothy Cardinal Manning. In 1985, Roman approbation was given and the Sisters of the Sacred Heart took their place as a fully recognized religious community. Outreach became a familiar pattern for the society, first at Sacred Heart Camp in Big Bear and, later, with the establishment of Heart of Jesus Center in Orange County.

In 1985, the Sacred Heart Sisters established a mission in Taiwan. At home they have continued their interest in any and all sorts of religious educational programs, from catechesis to ethnic ministries. May they long endure!

THE VINCENTIANS

The oldest community established in Southern California's post mission times, in 1965 observed the centennial of its work in the Golden State. Founded at Paris in 1625, the Congregation of the Mission received papal approval eight years later as a community of priests and brothers dedicated to the dual purpose of evangelizing the poor and educating the secular clergy. So rapid was the early success, that during Vincent de Paul's life, the work spread to lands as far away as Poland, England, Ireland, Scotland, Italy and even Algiers, Tunis, and Madagascar.

The community's influence expanded to the New World in the early years of the 19th century. The Lazarist Fathers, as they were known in France, arrived in the United States in 1816, and a separate province was erected at Perryville, Missouri on September 2, 1835. One of the community's outstanding Spanish–born pioneers, Father Thaddeus Amat, was sent to California as Bishop of Monterey on July 2, 1853. The young prelate attempted to enlist Vincentian interest in his infant diocese from the very beginning, but it was a dozen years before his confreres were able to make a west coast foundation. On May 9, 1865, the Congregation of the Mission entered the educational field in California's southland.

Two months later, on August 17, 1865, in the rented rooms of the Lugo House, the Fathers opened "St. Vincent's Select School for Boys" in the Los Angeles Plaza district. By the time they were able to move to more permanent quarters the next year, a local newspaper noted that "the gentlemen who are in charge of the College of Saint Vincent are well known to us and we assert that no more accomplished scholars and gentlemen can be found in any institution in or out of the State of California."

The cornerstone for a parochial church was set in place during July of 1866, but a fire gutted the building before its completion and another two decades passed before a parish could be organized under the patronage of Saint Vincent in Los Angeles. During the intervening years, the chapel of the college was occasionally pressed into service for quasi–parochial functions.

On January 25, 1887, the Very Reverend Aloysius J. Meyer celebrated the first Holy Mass in the newly–completed Saint Vincent's Church, then located at Grand Avenue and Washington. Father Meyer served as both president of the college and pastor of the newly–erected parish. Vincentian activity in California centered around this parish church, especially in the years after 1911, when the Congregation of the Mission withdrew from the administration of the college.

In 1926, after an absence of fifteen years, the Vincentians once again returned to the academic scene to staff Los Angeles College, the new diocesan minor seminary. The community expanded its operations again in 1939, when Archbishop John J. Cantwell opened Saint John's Major Seminary at Camarillo. Parochial commitments were widened too, first in 1950, when Our Lady of the Miraculous Medal was opened in Montebello under Vincentian auspices and again five years later when the community accepted charge of Sacred Heart Church in Paterson and Saint Charles Borromeo in San Francisco.

Continued expansion necessitated more priestly personnel and in the early 1950s plans were formulated for a preparatory seminary on a fourteen acre ranch given to the Vincentians by the Andrew Pansini family. A multi–unit plant, partially financed by the late Carrie Estelle Doheny, was dedicated on July 19,1958, by His Eminence, James Francis Cardinal McIntyre. It was in the same year that a separate filial province was established for California encompassing all the territory west of the continental divide.

With the dedication of Saint Mary's Novitiate at Santa Barbara, the Vincentian Fathers rounded out their first century of service in and to California. The Congregation of the Mission, grateful for its past blessings, looks to the future and even greater conquests in the spiritual sphere.

RELIGIOUS: INDIVIDUALS

MARIA DE JESUS DE AGREDA, C.O.
(1602–1665)

Throughout the southwest, the name of Maria de Agreda jumps out at the historian. Who she was, what she reportedly did, the credence of it all, has been the subject of widespread speculation.

Alonso de Benavides was instructed by the Minister General of the Franciscans to visit the town of Agreda and interview Madre Maria in 1631. There he was told by the mystic of her miraculous visits to America. Benavides discovered that the woman's family name was Coronel though she was commonly known to her contemporaries as Maria de Agreda. A native of a small town in the Province of Storia, about fifty miles from Saragossa, she was born on April 2, 1602. When her family home was converted into a nunnery in 1619, she entered the Conceptionist Order and adopted a habit somewhat similar to that worn by the Franciscans. At the age of twenty–three Maria was elected abbess of her community, an office she held almost continuously until her death in 1655.

From her earliest years, Maria claimed to have experienced supernatural revelations concerning the life of the Blessed Virgin. Her own account of these visions appeared in print around 1670. The work was translated into English and published in four volumes in 1914. Scholars have accepted her writings with some skepticism and the books have been on and off the Index several times. Few critics, however, have questioned Maria's reputation for holiness. During the preliminary proceedings for her beatification, it was shown beyond reasonable doubt that she truly did possess extraordinary sanctity.

Sor Maria de Agreda is mentioned several times in Fray Junípero Serra's diary, for the story of this Spanish nun was a recognized phenomenon in the southwest. "The Blue Lady of the Plains, as she has come to be known in the literature of the West, was a factor in the thinking and activity of the Franciscan missionaries in the American borderlands, and therefore the story is of importance for its effect in California."

Palou mentions the narrative of the "miraculous" instructions given to the Indians at San Antonio in pre–mission days. It was commonly accepted that Sister Maria de Agreda had made repeated journeys to various places in New Mexico and California. One elderly native asking for baptism was interrogated as to why she was embracing the Faith. She responded that, "when she was young, she heard her parents tell of a man coming to their lands who was dressed in the same habit the mis-

sionaries wore. He did not walk through the land but flew. He told them the same things the missionaries were now preaching. Remembering this, she had determined to become a Christian."

Palou goes on to state that, "When I heard this news from the Fathers, I immediately recalled the letter which the Venerable Mother, Sister Mary of Jesus of Agreda, wrote in the year 1631 to the missionaries engaged in the spiritual conquests of New Mexico. In it, among other things, she tells them that Our Father Saint Francis sent to these nations of the north two friars of our Order to preach the faith of Jesus Christ, who, after having effected many conversions, suffered martyrdom. Having compared the time, I judged it could have been one of these friars of whom Agreda spoke."

The old *padres* at the Apostolic College of San Fernando in Mexico City accepted the Agreda tradition and eventually passed it on to Spain in one of their memorials to the king. Congratulating their monarch on proclaiming the Immaculate Conception as Patroness of Spain, one report noted it had been the pious wish of the "most faithful and venerable woman of Spain, the honor of the nation, Sor Maria de Jesus de Agreda."

Whatever the Church's eventual decision of Maria de Jesus, it is an undeniable fact that she influenced California's Catholic Heritage for Serra, Palou, Crespi and even the King of Spain piously believed that their missionary efforts were aided in a supernatural manner through the instrumentality of Sor Maria de Jesus de Agreda, known in American literature of the southwest as 'The Blue Lady of the Plains.'"

PETER AUGUSTINE ANDERSON, O.P.
(1812–1850)

The history of the Catholic Church began in Northern California. with the advent of a priest of the Dominican order. Peter Augustine Anderson (1812–1850) was a native of Elizabeth, New Jersey. Shortly after his conversion to the Catholic Faith, Anderson became a candidate for the priesthood at Saint Rose's Priory.

He was ordained on April 5, 1840, and spent the early years of his ministry in Kentucky and Ohio. After working briefly on the missions in Canada, the young Dominican turned up in California where, according to his superior, he had journeyed for the purpose of bringing "spiritual assistance to those of our American Catholics who have already started from our congregation here or elsewhere to that country."

In August of 1850, Father Anthony Langlois notified

the Catholics of Sacramento that he was sending Anderson there "to commence a religious establishment in your midst and so to have more opportunity to worship our God, to promote the good of holy principles and, particularly, for you to profit in spiritual and moral ways and, by so doing, to procure future salvation."

Father Anderson bore "the distinction of being the first priest of the San Francisco Diocese to set out for the mining regions." He celebrated the initial public or parochial Mass at Sacramento on August 11th. The young friar, soon recognized as a very zealous and exemplary cleric, came highly recommended. One authority noted that there were few young priests who labored harder on the missions of this country than Father Anderson.

No missionary ever entered upon his work under such adverse and discouraging conditions. Father Anderson managed, however, to obtain temporary quarters for a church and soon had a permanent edifice under construction at the corner of K and 7th streets. The new place of worship was placed under the patronage of Saint Rose.

The *Sacramento Illustrated* noted, "During the memorable season of cholera, Father Anderson labored unceasingly. He visited the Cholera Hospital several times daily, sought out the poor and afflicted in their uncomfortable tents, administered all the consolation and relief within his power and procured medical aid for such as had no one to care for them. Overcome and exhausted by excessive labors, he contracted typhoid fever and fell victim to his self–sacrificing charity and zeal." He died on November 27, 1850. Catholics and non–Catholics alike mourned the loss of this real martyr of charity who had given his life in the service of the plague–stricken.

Four years after Anderson's death, Archbishop Joseph Sadoc Alemany had his confrere moved to the Dominican monastery in Benicia and buried beneath the altar of the old church. In 1859, the remains were transferred to the nearby cemetery.

Peter Augustine Anderson was the first martyr of charity among the priests who came to minister to the inhabitants of Gold Rush California. "As such, he walks in history's pages in the distinguished company of Fray Junípero Serra and a host of others who should not be forgotten."

and took the time to lay the groundwork for recording the history of his time.

The German–born friar, one of seven children, entered the Franciscans in 1871, and was invested with the habit on the following March 2nd. He made his studies for the priesthood in the United States and was ordained on June 4, 1876, by Bishop Patrick J. Ryan of Saint Louis. During his early years in the ministry, Father Arentz filled a number of missionary and parochial appointments in Illinois, Missouri, Nebraska and Ohio. From the pastorate of Saint Joseph's Church in Cleveland, Arentz was called to the provincialate of Sacred Heart Province in 1897.

Upon completion of his term, Father Arentz occupied a host of other positions including that of Commissariat of the Holy Land. After the turn of the century, Arentz came to California, first as novice master at Santa Barbara and later as director of Saint Francis Orphanage and Pastor of Immaculate Heart Church near Watsonville. In 1904, he was transferred to Saint Elizabeth's Church in Fruitvale.

One of the friar's most interesting and effective extra–parochial accomplishments was his official visitation to the Franciscan Provinces in Mexico which he made, in 1905, with Father Zephyrin Engelhardt. The results of that trip were so successful that he received another such commission in 1906, to the American Province of Saint John the Baptist. In June of 1908, Father Arentz returned to Santa Barbara where he was to spend the rest of his life as guardian, custos and definitor.

Throughout his multi–phased activities in the west, Father Arentz collected and saved all the newspapers, magazines, photographs and letters in any way connected with Franciscan pursuits in California. He was especially interested in the post–mission years between 1853 and 1922. Arentz was a careful chronicler. With his tireless energy and gift for detail, be wrote in his clear and legible hand several thousand pages of history for the Apostolic College (1853–1885), the Commissariat (1885–1915) and the province (1919–1922).

The astonishing range of his interests, the industry of his pen, the care and precision of his statements, his ability at correlation and his foresight as to the value of his work assure Father Theodore Arentz's reputation as "the Palóu of modern times among the Franciscans on the West Coast."

THEODORE ARENTZ, O.F.M. (1849–1923)

His Franciscan confreres remember Father Theodore Arentz (1849–1923) as a lover of books, a promoter of studies and a hardworking chronicler. He was among the few of California's great pioneers who had the foresight

CONCEPCION ARGUELLO, O.P. (1792–1857)

In September of 1805, Nicolai Petrovich Rezanof, Russian Ambassador Extraordinary to Japan, journeyed to Sitka on the mainland of Alaska to inspect his nation's northeastern frontier. Finding the colonies on the verge of starvation, Rezanof determined to visit California for supplies. Obviously a man of exceptional humanity, Rezanof's decision to establish trade contacts with California was a risky one in view of the Spanish government's strict laws forbidding any dealings with foreigners.

Upon arriving at San Francisco in April, Rezanof contacted Don José Arguello, Captain of the *Presidio*. Rezanof noted in his report that, "among the lovely sisters of the *comandante*, Doña Concepcion has the name of being the beauty of California." The subsequent relationship of the Russian chamberlain and Doña Concepción has become the subject of prose, verse and song and has given rise to one of California's most romantic sagas. And while it is true that "truth speaks louder than fiction," the veracity of many accounts is wholly unreliable.

Rezanof was a forty–two year old widower "of fine appearance with a remarkably attractive face." The dashing courtier certainly fascinated the sixteen year old daughter of the future governor. On the other hand, it is probably true that "the bright eyes of Doña Concepción had made a deep impression upon his heart," and the ambassador found himself personally and diplomatically attracted to the youthful maiden. The historian, Hubert Howe Bancroft, remarked that the courtship "had a very solid substratum or superstructure of ambition and diplomacy." Rezanof hardly disguised his intentions and, in his own words, "seeing that my situation was not improving, expecting every day that some misunderstanding would arise . . . I resolved to change my politeness for a serious tone.

Rezanof might have foreseen that asking for Doña Concepción's hand would bring up a delicate question of disparity of cult (Rezanof was Russian Orthodox). In any event, the local friars agreed to petition for the necessary dispensations and "Baron Nicolai Petrovich de Rezanof and Senorita Doña Maria de la Concepción Marcella Argüello were formally betrothed." It was here "that rather unpleasantly merges the lover into the diplomat" for as a *de jure* member of the family, Rezanof admitted that he managed this part of his Catholic Majesty as my interests required." Soon thereafter the ambassador was able to complete his negotiations and set out for Alaska.

Rezanof's health had been seriously impaired by his travelings. On the return trip he died at Krasnoyarsk, a small town in western Siberia, and thus "the fates with a voice more powerful than that of emperors and kings forbade the banns." Doña Concepción remained loyal to her fiancé, waiting for his return with the necessary dispensations. She lived with her parents in Baja California and later returned to Santa Barbara where she dwelt with the De la Guerra family. Just when she learned the fate

of her lover or the circumstances of his death is not known, although Sir George Simpson noted that "she knew not, until we mentioned it to her, the immediate cause of the chancellor's death."

A long–time member of the Third Order of Saint Francis Doña Concepción asked to be accepted as a novice when Bishop Joseph Sadoc Alemany opened a convent for the Domincan Sisters at Monterey in 1851. She was formally received on April 11th under the religious name, Maria Dominica. As the first nun professed in California, she lived on at Benicia until December of 1857, when she died at the age of sixty–five.

Whatever may have been Reznof's intentions about returning to California, those of Doña Concepción cannot be denied. When she realized that her fiancé would not come back, she spent the weeks, months, and years of her life in the service of others. Entering the convent at an advanced age only formalized a life of dedication most of which was spent before the luxury of religious life came to California.

HENRY AYRINHAC, S. S. (1867–1930)

One of the most respected leaders in the American seminary movement was that of Father Henry Ayrinhac, a Sulpician priest long associated with Saint Patrick's Seminary, at Menlo Park. Born on March 21, 1867, at Aveyron, France, the youthful Ayrinhac studied at Rodez prior to completing his theological preparations in Rome. As was the custom in those times, he earned doctorates both in theology and Canon Law.

Ordained in the Eternal City on March 28, 1891, Father Ayrinhac's earliest years were spent in the classrooms of Saint Mary's Seminary, Baltimore. There he became a close friend and advisor of James Cardinal Gibbons. It was Gibbons who suggested his name to the Archbishop of San Francisco.

In 1904, Ayrinhac was assigned to Saint Patrick's Seminary and he remained at Menlo Park until his death, in 1930. A versatile professor, he was equally at home teaching Moral or Pastoral Theology, Canon Law or Church History. In the years after 1924, Ayrinhac discontinued teaching and devoted himself energetically to the compiling of a series of commentaries on the new Code of Canon Law.

Archbishop Edward J. Hanna said that Ayrinhac's "was a nature endowed with mental gifts of a high order, an intelligence quick and profound, a memory retentive and responsive, a faculty of analysis and coordination that no problem could confuse. When one followed laboriously the processes which seemed to outline themselves so naturally and spontaneously in his thoughts, one realized what powers had contributed to his decision."

The archbishop went on to say that Father Ayrinhac's "intelligence was thoroughly illumined by Faith; the judicial function ever took the tempering of Charity. Father and Reason cooperated in harmony, with the higher command; the jurist became the priest."

The fame of the Sulpician priest probably became more widespread after his death. His books were read and studied throughout the nation and in many areas of the English–speaking world. Even today, there are few priests who don't have one of Ayrinhac's books in their library.

Charles J. Murphy, a student and friend, wrote that "Father Ayrinhac belongs to the ages. He was a builder, a man of vigorous action, relentless with himself in the realization of a constant ideal, and that ideal expressed itself in the formation of young men for the priesthood." Many of the older priests in California and the west still speak about the indelible impression Father Henry Ayrinhac made on their lives a generation ago. To them, "he was a man of God declaring the Law."

When the famed Sulpician went home to God, Archbishop Hanna expressed the mind of those who mourned when he said: "We bow our heads to God's decree in taking from us a great man who for many years guided the souls of our students in the tradition and piety of the Seminary. He is gone. May his soul be in peace. May he, from his high place, look down upon us and bless us."

JOHANN JACOB BAEGERT, S.J. (1717–1772)

"The only comprehensive account written by an actual participant" of experiences among the aboriginal inhabitants of the rugged, sterile and uninspirational peninsula of Baja California is the *Nachrichten von der Amerikanischen Halbinsel Californien*, compiled from notes made by Johann Jacob Baegert (1717–1772) during his seventeen years at San Luis Gonzaga.

Baegert's encyclopedic observations were published, according to one authority, to counteract "the illusory information that was currently widespread" regarding peninsular affairs that had appeared in such works as Miguel Venegas' three volume *Noticia de la California y de su conquista temporal, y espiritual, hasta el Tiempo Presente* (Madrid, 1757). Obviously, Father Baegert considered the more unattractive aspects of the California apostolate as "the best weapon of defense in the controversy between the Jesuits and their sovereign."

Though not generally esteemed as an impressive record of missionary accomplishments among the natives, the *Nachrichten* contains "a good account of their culture, languages, and distribution." Indeed, the naively objective compilation represents an abundant fund of anthropological information as well as on–the–scene geographic and descriptive observations of considerable value to subsequent generations.

Baegert communicated "the feeling of the time, place, and people of which he wrote." A sense of humor pervades the factual, literal, mathematical and realistic narrative as do occasional shafts of sarcasm. The author's descriptions of the area's geography, botany and zoology, while well done, reflect his personal distaste for Baja California and the hardships endured there by himself and his confreres. Bitter at seeing the Society of Jesus banished from New Spain, Baegert's scathing account of the treatment meted out to the Jesuits graphically reveals the "shocking conditions existing among the natives of Lower California, whom he considered but one step above the wild beasts that surrounded them." He concluded his eyewitness journal on the note "that California is without exception the most miserable country under the sun, or, if an equally miserable or worse one was ever discovered by the Argonauts, then California was used by the Almighty Creator as a model for making it."

The vigorous and amusing account was completed by Father Baegert shortly after his return to Europe, in 1769. The 358–page work was published anonymously, in 1772, by the Electoral Court and Academy at Mannheim as *Nachrichten von der Amerikanischen Halbinsel Californien: mit einem zweyfachen Anhang falscher Nachrichten*. A folding map bearing the description "*California per P. Ferdinandum Consak S.I. et alios*" facilitates the location of the Jesuit missionary foundations, showing as it does the routes along the west coast of Mexico over which Father Baegert travelled in 1751 and 1768. A second edition of the *Nachrichten* was issued the following year, containing only minor alterations with the same map and plates as the earlier imprint. An abstract of the work appeared, in 1777, in the *Berlin'sche Litterarishe Wochenblatt*.

In its annual report for 1863, the Smithsonian Institution published an English rendition by Charles Rau (1826–1887) of the initial four chapters of the *Nachrichten*, dealing with the life and customs of Baja California's native population, under the title, *An Account of the Aboriginal Inhabitants of the California Peninsula as given by Jacob Baegert, a German Jesuit Missionary, who lived there Seventeen Years during the Second Half of the Last Century*. The remaining four chapters were issued by the Smithsonian Institution the following year.

Rau's translation was reprinted as a monograph from the electrotyped plates of the annual Smithsonian reports and, in 1882, was included in an anthology of *Articles on Anthropological Subjects, Contributed to the Annual Reports of the Smithsonian Institution from 1863 to 1877* (Washington, 1882).

In 1942, Pedro R. Hendrich's 262–page Spanish translation of the entire *Nachrichten* was published at Mexico City by the *Antigua Libreria Robredo de José Porrua y Hijos* as *Noticias de la Peninsula Americana de California por el Rev. Padre Juan Jacobo Baegert*. Included in that edition was the brilliant thirty–page ethnographic study of Indian mores in the area by Paul Kirchhoff.

A wholly new annotated translation, based on the original German, was prepared by M. M. Brandenburg and Carl L. Baumann and published in 1952, by the University of California Press. Issued as *Observations in Lower California by Johann Jacob Baegert, S.J.*, the 218–page treatise, with its nine illustrations and analytical index, faithfully rendered the author's stylistic peculiarities into readable and accurate English.

Johann Jacob Baegert has not fared well among the chroniclers, characterized as he has been as "arrogant" by one writer, and a "career ecclesiastic" by another. Plainly, the stalwart Jesuit missionary lacked much of the ardor, optimistic zeal and human sympathies of his predecessors in the peninsula. Nevertheless, even the critic can discern that Baegert recognized the disabilities of the natives as cultural, not inherent qualities. His overall observations confirm that "his heart was with his poor children of the wild among whom he had labored, for whom he had sacrificed, and toward whom he tried to be an instrument of eternal salvation."

WILLIAM P. BARR, C.M. (1881–1964)

The late Father William P. Barr was eulogized by Archbishop Timothy Manning as "the greatest master of the spiritual life we have known." Indeed, the Vincentian educator combined, in his priestly role, the offices of father, advisor, legislator and disciplinarian without diminishing or compromising the paternal atmosphere within which he trained two generations of clerical aspirants.

Born in New Orleans, on January 7, 1881, William Patrick Barr's pre–seminary education was acquired from the Christian Brothers. He entered the Apostolic College of the Vincentian Fathers, at Perryville, Missouri, in 1893, and pronounced his vows as a member of the Congregation of the Mission, on January 8, 1899. Subsequently sent to Rome's Apollinaris Seminary for completion of studies in philosophy and theology, both of which disciplines awarded him doctorates, he was ordained on December 19, 1903, by Archbishop Joseph Ceppetelli, the Patriarch of Constantinople.

Father Barr returned to the United States, in 1905, to become director of students and novices at Saint Mary's of the Barrens, in Perryville. For the following decade he also taught dogmatic theology at the Vincentian motherhouse. In 1923, Father Barr was appointed rector at Perryville, a position he occupied until 1924, when he was sent to Denver to manage the erection of that city's new theological seminary. In 1926, he was named Provincial of the Western Province and it was during his tenure that the Vincentian Fathers assumed direction of the newly constructed preparatory seminary at Los Angeles.

Upon completion of two terms as provincial, Father Barr became rector of Kenrick Seminary, Webster Groves, Missouri. In that more relaxed atmosphere, he became a well–known figure as speaker and educator in the Saint Louis area and a popular retreat master for clerical groups throughout the nation.

Father Barr began another term as provincial in 1938, but was forced to resign a year later because of ill health. With the opening, at Camarillo, of Saint John's Seminary, Father Barr heeded Archbishop John J. Cantwell's plea to assume the rectorship "on a temporary basis" until the institution was firmly established. During his ten years there a host of the southland's future levites were inflamed with the desire to emulate Father Barr's sublime ideal of priestly perfection, of which his life was so striking an example. In the years after 1949, Father Barr served as rector of Saint Mary's Seminary, in the Galveston–Houston Diocese. It was there that the renowned educator quietly observed the golden jubilee of his priestly ordination.

That his "communicability" with young people never faltered explains how Father Barr could return to the teenage level, during the latter part of his life, as a popular professor of religion at Queen of Angels Seminary, San Fernando. His active apostolate was terminated by a paralytic stroke which forced him to spend the remaining years confined to Saint Vincent's Hospital, in Los Angeles, where he died on June 20, 1964.

Throughout his sixty–one years in the priesthood, Father William P. Barr exhibited all the desirable traits and none of the negative qualities associated with leadership. To his loyalty for the Church, love for learning, impatience with mediocrity and insistence on theological precision he added a very understanding attitude towards the frailties of human nature. He was among the last of a long line of outstanding Vincentian seminary professors whose very presence commanded respect and emulation.

MATHIAS BARRETT, B.G.S. (1900–1990)

Brother Mathias Barrett (1900–1990) , founder of the Little Brothers of the Good Shepherd, was once described by an Irish newspaper as "a legend in his own lifetime." He was that and more. The diminutive Irishman was born in Waterford City on March 15th, in the first year of this century. At the age of sixteen, he entered the Brothers of Saint John of God and for the rest of his life worked in convalescent homes and care facilities for the ill, elderly and homeless.

In 1927, Brother Mathias went to Montreal and there founded seven institutions for the poor. He then came to Los Angeles where, in the 1940s he became a close friend and confidant of Archbishop John J. Cantwell. Through collaboration with a cousin, John Barrett, he rented a house on skid row where he welcomed, fed and re-trained transients. Later he was able to move to another house which cost $45 a month to rent.

Feeding his patrons day-old bread and whatever else he could scrounge from local merchants, Brother Mathias managed to sustain his ministry. Then, with the help of the archbishop, he rented a still larger facility which he used as a novitiate for his religious community. He also found time to inaugurate a Catholic maritime club.

In later years, Brother Mathias looked back upon his early days in Los Angeles: "The bishop gave me his blessing, but no money. I think he was testing me, so I would go to the Saint Vincent de Paul Society and they gave me ten dollars. I really never knew where the next meal or rent payment would originate, but God always provided."

Brother Mathias subsequently went to Boston and there looked after both aged and ill priests. Archbishop Richard Cushing became his great mentor and personally underwrote and otherwise sponsored many of Brother's outreach programs for the poor.

In 1949, Brother Mathias joined Father Gerald Fitzgerald who had founded a center for sacerdotal rehabilitation at Jemez Springs, New Mexico. It was a providential venture for it was there that he befriended Archbishop Edwin Byrne of Santa Fe. Several years later, at the urging of Byrne, Brother Mathias founded the Little Brothers of the Good Shepherd in Albuquerque, a community that has since become a worldwide religious force for helping the homeless and needy of God's children.

Brother retired in 1976 from the leadership of his community. In 1983 he was awarded the *Lumen Christi* Award by the Catholic Church Extension Society. Three years later, the city fathers of Waterford named the street on which he was born "Barrett Place."

Brother Mathias was frequently referred to as the "Mother Teresa of America." A co-worker testified that "this man was truly an innovator. As many people saw him, he was probably the closet thing to a saint on earth. When it came to the homeless and the impoverished, he did not know what the word 'no' meant."

The thousand friends and admirers who attended Brother Mathias's funeral at Albuquerque's Church of the Immaculate Conception heard about his many wonderful accomplishments from bishops, priests and laity. Sir Daniel Donohue perhaps put it best in his eulogy by observing "that Brother Mathias was a practitioner of virtues most of us only hear or read about. His sanctity and influence radiated outwards towards all people, but especially those in most need."

Brother Mathias left behind a legacy that few will or can emulate. His was a living endeavor that brightens the busy existence of the more fortunate by showing so eloquently what one man can do with the work and example of a well spent ministry

ANDRE BASSETTE, C.S.C. (1845–1937)

Champlain's Mont Royal dominates the skyline of Montreal. Near its summit shines a tremendous egg-shaped dome crowned with a tall lantern. It is the Oratory Shrine of Saint Joseph, a splendid monument to a man and his faith.

That man, Brother Andre Bassette (1845–1937), a member of the Congregation of the Holy Cross, was solemnly beatified by Pope John Paul II on May 23, 1982. Born in a village near Montreal, Brother Andre was orphaned at an early age. He had no formal education and was chronically ill. As a young man, he emigrated to New England, where he found work in textile mills. He returned to Canada in 1867, and three years later joined the brotherhood.

For the first forty years of his religious life, Brother Andre served as porter at Notre Dame College in Montreal. He would take time after his duties to visit the sick, urging them to pray to Saint Joseph. Many were cured instantly and the number of visitors seeking the Brother's intercession grew daily.

His faint laugh and merry ways gave no clue to his long fasts and penances or to the austerity of his life. The slight, unassuming lay brother had healing in his hands. Each time Brother Andre went to answer the door, he looked up to the summit of Mount Royal. In his mind a dream slowly took shape—a dream of a great shrine to Saint Joseph, who had been the patron of Canada since 1624.

In 1904, Brother Andre obtained permission to build a tiny oratory dedicated to Saint Joseph in a wooded area across the street from the school. From this structure evolved the towering Oratory of Saint Joseph, one of the largest church edifices on the continent.

The crypt church was ready for use in 1917, but the great basilica was not completed until 1966. To this place come many thousands of pilgrims every year seeking cures or spiritual assistance. Today the shrine is one of the most prominent centers of the Christian world. On feastdays, pilgrims make their way to the massive church. And there, Brother Andre lives on in the glory of his patron, Saint Joseph.

In November of 1921, the "Miracle Man of Montreal" visited the Diocese of Los Angeles–San Diego as a guest of John Doran, a wealthy businessman from Ontario. Brother Andre was then seventy–six years old. While the trip to California was planned as a vacation, the local pastor arranged a reception for the famed lay brother. About 500 persons came and his biographer recorded that there were seven cures, one of a blind man and another of a deaf person.

Brother Andre returned to Montreal and lived on until 1937, when he died at the age of ninety–one. During the seven days before his entombment, an estimated one million persons passed by the bier of the humble man.

Since his death, the shrine instituted by Brother Andre has become a powerful place of prayer for innumerable pilgrims. The recent declaration by Pope John Paul II came as no surprise to Canadians.

ALBERT BIBBY, O.F.M. CAP. (1878–1925)

In a reference to Father Albert Bibby, O.F.M. Cap., the Catholic *Bulletin* for April, 1925, declared: "To pass through life without meeting one who conveys the impression that he is cast in the mold of the Redeemer is to miss meeting an influence for the permanent uplifting of the soul. Those who had the joy of Father Albert's friendship can well look forward to meeting him in Heaven."

Thomas Francis Bibby was born at Muinebheag (Bagenalstown), County Carlow, on October 20, 1878. The youngster grew up in Kilkenny, within the shadow of the Capuchin Abbey, and, on July 7, 1894, joined the Franciscans at Rochestown. Fray "Albert" was ordained priest on February 23, 1902. Always a brilliant student, the young cleric took graduate courses at the Royal University. After completing his studies there, he was appointed Professor of Philosophy and Theology at Saint Kieran's College.

Father Albert spent many years at Church Street, where he served as provincial secretary from 1913 to 1919. It was while working in that capacity that he became one of the pioneers of the Gaelic League. During his years in Dublin, Father Albert was known for his marked piety. His saintly selflessness endeared him to all walks of life. His confessional was one of the most sought–after in all of Ireland. Always a frail and delicate man, Father Albert was buoyant in spirit. His cheerfulness in adversity was possibly the most attractive aspect of his many–faceted personality.

In the uprising of 1916, Father Albert served the spiritual needs of the Volunteers in the North Dublin Union area. From that time on, he was prominently identified with the movement for national independence. Father Albert's views eventually incurred the displeasure of British authorities and he was exiled from the country in mid–1924.

The Irish friars were entrusted with the old mission at Santa Ines in that year and on November 20th, Father Albert was named pastor of the historic California missionary foundation. Although his enforced exile was a mighty burden, Father Albert welcomed the opportunity of serving under the patronage of Saint Agnes, for whom he had long been a devotee.

The famous Irish patriot–cleric died on February 14, 1925, far from the land he loved so dearly and the people he served so faithfully. The first of the Irish friars to succumb in Western America, Father Albert was buried at Santa Ines. In 1958, his remains were returned to Ireland, where they were interred at the friars' cemetery at Rochestown, County Cork. At the time of his death, the Catholic press in Eire proclaimed that "the Catholic Church has lost a gifted scholar and a saintly priest; Ireland a loyal and devoted patriot."

ALFRED BOEDDEKER, O.F.M. (1903–1994)

From his cluttered office at Saint Boniface Church, in San Francisco, Father Alfred Boeddeker launched a worldwide movement to mark the 2000th birthday of Jesus Christ. It mattered not to the eighty year old friar that he likely wouldn't be around to join in those festivities.

In an interview shortly after announcing his plans, Father Boeddeker said "after all, we mark our calendars from His birthdate. Yet not enough people know Him. I mean know Him personally. . . .

Boeddeker drafted four five–year plans for popularizing Christ and ushering Him into the 21st century with worldwide celebrations. The bishops with whom he had spoken endorsed his notion enthusiastically.

Father Boeddeker was best known in San Francisco for his charitable work among that city's poor. Since 1949, his name became synonymous with efforts to feed and house the less fortunate in "the Tenderloin." Shortly after arriving at his San Francisco pastorate, Boeddeker established Saint Anthony's Dining Room in an unused machine shop next door to the parish church. Over 1,400 dinners are served there daily.

The stout, smiling friar estimated that over 15 million meals have been dished up at the Dining Room in the past thirty–three years. He used the term "dining room" because, as he said, "soup kitchen was too insulting. Our diners are guests."

Boeddeker did it all without any assistance from the state, church or parish. Everything comes from voluntary contributions. And somehow the friar managed to pay the bills and to feed all comers. He attributed this modern–day miracle to Saint Anthony.

The ingenious priest operated a 900 acre farm in Petaluma where much of the food originates. And he liked to observe that over 1,200 men who have labored there have returned to the active work force. He attributed their "healing" to the experience of helping others. Father Boeddeker also ran an employment service, a shelter for homeless men, a Thrift Shop and a clinic. His last project was a retirement home for elderly women.

The cherubic friar is remembered for his charitable activities in other parts of the world. Following World War II, he established a center for European refugees in West Germany, dining rooms for the needy in Naples and Bologna and housing for the poor in the Dominican Republic.

He also founded a community of Franciscan Sisters to work with the poor in Tijuana. These Missionary Sisters of Our Lady Queen of Peace operate orphanages, dispensaries, dining facilities and a leper clinic.

Father Boeddeker's many activities are a logical outgrowth of love which he considered "the most important thing in the world." He once said that it would be "a sad thing to stand before God on judgement day knowing you hadn't really loved anybody. You'd get a cool reception."

Given his track record, one didn't doubt that Father Boeddeker's plans to honor the 2,000th birthday of Christ would materialize.

JAMES BOUCHARD, S.J. (1823–1889)

A. ELOQUENT INDIAN

According to his autobiography, James Bouchard (1823–1889) was born at the Village of the Muskagola in the Delaware River, a portion of the Indian Territory," on a reserve located southeast of the modern city of Leavenworth, Kansas. "Watomika" (the swift–footed one) spent his early years as a typical Indian brave. Introduced to Christianity by the followers of John Calvin, Bouchard became a convert to Catholicism in May of 1847, and was baptized in Saint Francis Xavier Church in Saint Louis by the Jesuit, Father Arnold Damien.

Within a year after embracing the Faith, Bouchard entered the novitiate of the Society of Jesus. Concerning his character, the annals record that "he is posesed of good talents, devoted, has good health, good judgment and . . . the necessary indifference. . . ." With his ordination by Bishop James Van De Velde of Natchez on

August 15, 1855, James Bouchard (or Beshor as it is sometimes spelled) earned the distinction of becoming the first American Indian ordained to the priesthood in the United States of America.

Coming to San Francisco in 1861, the zealous missionary quickly earned the respect and love of westerners. It is recorded that ". . . the west had never heard such soul–stirring, feeling eloquence . . ." as came from the mouth of James Bouchard, S.J.

The name "Chrysostom" given to Bouchard at the time of his confirmation could hardly have been more appropriate, for the "Indian Priest" wasted no time in becoming one of the most distinguished Catholic orators of his time. Richard Gleeson recalled that Bouchard's first sermon in the Bay City won him a place in the hearts of the people. The "listeners were charmed by the sound of his silvery voice, by the power of his nervous eloquence, and by the pleasantness of his address, by the lucidity of his explanations and by the vigor of his stringent logic."

Archbishop Joseph Sadoc Alemany had little appreciation for Bouchard's long, flowing beard even though the editor of the San Francisco *Monitor* thought it added "a peculiar dignity and even majesty to his figure." When it was hinted that removal might be in order, Bouchard addressed a petition to the Holy See and received what may well be the only "bearded indult" ever granted a Californian.

Always a controversial figure even among his Jesuit confreres, Bouchard had his share of critics; but as one contemporary states, "He was possessed of such urbanity and modesty that he never lost his self–control . . . rather, he was accustomed to speak highly of those who criticized him." That his popularity among the people was never questioned is obvious from various sources. One Jesuit historian noted that "Probably no other Catholic clergyman in that section of the country was ever more effective in the ministry of the pulpit. . . ."

Bouchard suffered from what his biographer calls "a restless and overly sensitive personality," a failing common to men of great stature. On the pastoral level, "his lively faith, for which he was remarkable, made him unspeakably earnest and effective. He went straight to the hearts of poor sinners and made them return to God, and many Protestants placed themselves under instruction and were baptized."

Of James Bouchard, California's "Eloquent Indian," Archbishop Patrick W. Riordan had this to say:

> To no man in all the West is the Church of God more beholden than to Father James Bouchard. . . . He kept the faith in the mining districts; he sustained the dignity of God's Holy Church in the midst of ignorance and misunderstanding and everywhere championed her rights.

JAMES BOUCHARD, S.J. (1823–1889)

B. BEARDED INDULT

Known as "one of the most celebrated missionaries of the Pacific Coast," Father James Bouchard (1823–1889) has the dubious distinction of being the first priest in California's ecclesiastical annals to win papal reversal of a decision rendered by a residential ordinary: The differences between the Jesuit cleric and Archbishop Joseph Sadoc Alemany arose over the Dominican prelate's attempt to implement legislation adopted by the Second Plenary Council of Baltimore forbidding the wearing of beards by priests in the United States.

Viewed apart from its historical context, the conciliar action seemingly contradicts the Mosaic prohibition against shaving which isolated the chosen race from their idolatrous neighbors. Canonists explain, however, that this divine precept, as well as the other ceremonial observations of the old law, expired with the death of Christ. The Romans of apostolic times were clean–shaven and had been since the days of Scipio the African. This practice was adopted by that city's clergy in much the same way as the toga evolved into the soutanne. Although the Roman custom was effectively ended by the influx of the "barbari," it was retained by civil and religious leaders and was canonized in succeeding codifications of ecclesiastical law.

In 1865, the Bishop of Freising asked for procedural directions regarding certain priests in his diocese who had inaugurated the habit of wearing beards. The prelate was informed by Archbishop Matthew Eustachius, Apostolic Nuncio to Bavaria, that the Holy See preferred the clergy of that entire country to conform to the discipline of Rome where the wearing of beards had not been in vogue for centuries.

When the hierarchy of the United States met at Baltimore in 1866, they voted to censure any undue care of the hair and beard, appealing to the recent directive issued under the auspices of Pope Pius IX to Bavaria and directed that the custom then observed at Rome be adopted as the official policy throughout the nation.

There is no evidence as to precisely when Father James Bouchard first began wearing his beard, though his decision surely pre–dated the Second Plenary Council. A correspondent from Austin, Nevada, reported in 1868, that "it has been seven years since we have seen Father Bouchard. His appearance is much changed since then but, to our mind, for the better. The venerable beard which he has permitted to grow till it sweeps down his breast adds a peculiar dignity and even majesty to his figure.

The reason for the Jesuit Indian–priest's actions was revealed in another newspaper account which spoke approvingly of the "venerable appearance" afforded by Bouchard's long white beard, which served the utilitarian purpose of protecting the famed orator's throat and vocal chords which had become weakened by constant lecturing. Early in 1869, Archbishop Alemany notified the Jesuit provincial about the Plenary Council's decree and his personal wishes that Father Bouchard fall in line with the accepted discipline then observed throughout the country. The Bay City prelate stated he would prefer that Bouchard "cut the hair short with scissors, as practiced by St. Alphonsus, and have the neck protected with something warm" which, he felt confident, would bring about the desired effect. There is no recorded evidence about Father Bouchard's reaction to the archbishop's entreaty. In any event, the widely–known missionary apparently made no effort to heed the prelate's directive.

Though empowered in individual cases and for a just cause to dispense from decrees of the plenary council, the misopogonic archbishop exhibited no inclination to exercise that prerogative. Hence, "after due consultation, a petition was addressed to the Holy See by the Jesuit superior," asking that Alemany's ruling be set aside. The appeal undoubtedly pointed out to Roman authorities that beards had never been forbidden to clerics by any general law of the Church; what prohibitions there were referred to the "fastidious care" of the beard and not to its existence as such.

No response to Bouchard's appeal has yet been unearthed but the fact that the Jesuit was allowed to continue his missionary travels throughout the west, including the Archdiocese of San Francisco, is assurance enough that he was indeed successful in obtaining some kind of "bearded indult" exempting him from the restrictions imposed on the American clergy by the Second Plenary Council of Baltimore.

FRANCES CABRINI, M.S.C. (1850–1917)

Mother Frances Cabrini (1850–1917), the first citizen–saint of the United States, came to California in 1905, at the behest of Bishop Thomas J. Conaty to establish a foundation of her Missionary Sisters of the Sacred Heart. As was her custom, Mother Cabrini kept a careful log of her journey. Even today, her account of the trip west at the turn of the century is enjoyable reading.

As she approached the Golden State by rail, the Italian–born nun observed, "The train was running amidst clusters of orange groves, hedges of eucalyptus, and the most beautiful green meadows of flowers," all of which emphasized that, at last, "we were in California. With good reason," she observed, "this State is often compared with Italy and especially with our so–called Riviera, and those who say it should be compared with the land of promise flowing with milk and honey are not mistaken." To the never–tiring social worker, educator and friend of all humanity, every valley was "a natural sanatorium, where, by just remaining in the open air night and day one is cured of some special disease. . . ."

With the encouragement and cooperation of Bishop Conaty, Mother Cabrini carefully searched out a location for her foundation, noting that there was not a hill or valley which she did not visit, and always with an increasing admiration of God's goodness, which was so clearly seen in this privileged country.

While exploring the foothills of San Fernando, Mother Cabrini recorded, "The fruit has a special fragrance and flavour. Here, near Los Angeles, lives the celebrated naturalist, Burbank, who, adding new wonders to the wonders of Nature by his ingenious experiments and graftings, has produced new kinds of fruit and flowers, apricots and prunes without stones and grapes without seeds."

With the nuns located in their new Regina Coeli Orphanage at 610 North Hill Street, Mother Cabrini wrote, "Already our Sisters are well settled, and have begun their work, not only in behalf of the Italians, but also for the poor Mexicans who are numerous here and in great need of help." That Saint Frances Cabrini was a remarkable personage is evidenced by her establishment, in only thirty–seven years, of sixty–seven houses and institutions throughout the nation, all with practically no financial resources among peoples where she herself was a stranger.

She lived in an era marked by the bustle of ceaseless activity, of speed, of quick decision, and restless tempo. Mother Cabrini "walked, or rather ran, in step with this spirit, so active, so energetic, so tireless, that her life has well been described as a quiet whirlwind." Mother Frances Cabrini returned to Chicago in 1905, shortly after attending a Solemn Mass at Saint Vibiana's Cathedral marking the silver jubilee of her community's foundation. In the Windy City she carried on her charitable work for another dozen years, rejoicing when the work "began with a Cross, which is the seal of all good enterprises."

ROSA CASTRO, O.P. (1815–1878)

Remembered in the annals as "Don Joaquin's saintly daughter," Maria Antonia Jacinta Castro was born near Santa Cruz Mission on January 21, 1815, the daughter of Jose Joaquin and Maria Antonia (Amador) Castro. Maria Antonia lived quietly with her four siblings, Guadalupe, Jose Ygnacio, Joaquin and Maria de los Angeles at the Villa Branciforte which was located on the east side of the San Lorenzo River.

The youngest of the Castros spent most of her childhood at Santa Cruz Mission, where her father served as majordomo. In 1818, the pirate Hippolyte Bouchard entered Monterey Bay and sacked the city, causing great anxiety and excitement.

Maria Antonia later became the owner of the 12,147 acre *Rancho Refugio* which stretched six miles along the northern coast of Santa Cruz. Records indicate that in 1840, Governor Juan Alvarado also granted her a portion of property near the mission.

In another reference, Maria Antonia was listed as a seamstress. Later, she did washing and ironing for Pierre Richard, a French trader. That the young lady was a well–to–do woman in her own right is well–documented. Maria Antonia's biographer, Marion Dale Pokriots, said that according to oral family tradition, Maria Antonia had intended to marry a wealthy Spanish merchant. However, on an outing, the young man broke a leg and later died in Spain.

Shortly after the arrival in California of the Right Reverend Joseph Sadoc Alemany, the new Bishop of Monterey announced plans for opening a convent in the city of Monterey. On the Feast of Saint Rose of Lima, in August of 1851, Maria Antonia decided to abandon her worldly possessions and to dedicate herself to the Lord in California's first convent. She was invested with the white veil of a novice and took the name of Sister Rosa.

On August 31, 1852, Sister Rosa made her final vows. On that day she exchanged the white veil of a novice for the black one of a professed nun. In keeping with her new vocation, Sister Rosa had deeds of conveyance drawn up whereby her properties were distributed. Each of the documents was signed in a bold, strong hand that differed from the penmanship in the rest of the documents.

The convent was later moved to Benicia. Before leaving Monterey, in 1854, Sister Rosa Castro made her last will and testament. She gave and devised to her community all her rights, titles and interest in the house that had been occupied by the Sisters of Saint Dominic in Monterey. Sister Rosa served as a member of the General Council of the Dominican community from 1863 to 1876. She passed away at her convent on June 22, 1878, at the age of sixty–three. She is buried on a wind–swept hill overlooking Suisun Bay in the historic Dominican cemetery.

The pioneering nun is remembered in the annals of her community for her "great sanctity and her love of flowers." There is a tradition which says that she carried plants from the convent garden in Monterey to Benecia. Don Joaquin's pious little girl who had assisted the friars at Santa Cruz Mission in her youth helped to found one of the state's foremost educational institutions. Saint Catherine's Academy continued to operate for eighty–eight years after Sister Rosa's death. Its doors were permanently closed in 1966.

Unquestionably, the story of the religious women who served the Church in its pioneering days in California has not been adequately told. When it is, the name of Maria Antonia Jacinta Castro, Sister Rosa, will surely occupy a prominent place.

MARY JOSEPH JOHN TERESA COMERFORD, P.B.V.M. (1821–1881)

In a recently published monograph, it is noted that "Mother Teresa was a wonderful personality, a woman of great prudence, sound judgment and common sense, gifted by nature and grace for the work for which God intended her." Bridget Comerford was born on February 19, 1821, at Coolgrancy, Gowran, County Kilkenny. After completing her education at the Brigidine convent, Tullow, she entered the novitiate of the Presentation Sisters in Kilkenny.

Given the name Sister Mary Joseph John Teresa, Bridget made her solemn vows on January 17, 1844. From that time onward she was dedicated to the charitable instruction of poor female children within an enclosure. Sister Teresa was familiar with California through correspondence with one of her brothers who had journeyed there in 1849. She asked the local bishop for permission to join a group of Presentation Sisters who had volunteered to serve in the Archdiocese of San Francisco.

Leaving Dublin on September 20, 1854, Sister Teresa and her travelling companions arrived in faraway California two months later. Archbishop Joseph Sadoc Alemany provided the Sisters with a house in Saint Francis parish and almost immediately, they began their work of evangelization. Several years later, the archbishop named Sister Teresa superior and the small group continued their work, financed almost exclusively by Patrick Fenton and other prominent Irish residents of the Bay Area. Ever–so–gradually, Mother Teresa and her companions expanded their activities. In 1857, she opened a school for Black and Indian girls, the first such institution in the state.

The Jesuits encouraged Mother Teresa to establish a convent in the newer section of the city, near Saint Ignatius College. In 1867, she returned to Ireland, where she recruited additional sisters for her San Francisco apostolate.

By 1874, there were sixty sisters at the two foundations in San Francisco, despite the fact that the small community had sustained a dozen deaths due to tuberculosis. In addition to teaching 1,700 children, the Sisters were busily catechizing adult Catholics and potential converts. Mother Teresa established the Apostleship of Prayer and the Children of Mary Sodality as aids to the evangelization work of the Sisters.

In 1878, she established a school in Berkeley. Later that year, she revealed plans to begin a novitiate in Ireland for girls wishing to work in California. This she wished to do so that "our mission here, and elsewhere, may be maintained and extended for the greater glory of God and the benefit of the poor little ones of Christ."

Mother Teresa died on August 2, 1881. She was buried at Berkeley. In the Kilcock Annals one reads "no doubt she did much for religion in California as it was at a low ebb in those early days. She insisted that the Sisters were to devote their free time in the evening to instruct converts, to encourage negligent Catholics to return to their duties, to prepare adults and children for the reception of the Sacraments."

The fact that many of Mother Teresa's objectives were realized only after her death speaks highly for her foresight. Her memory lives on in the persons of the Presentation Sisters.

MARY OF THE INCARNATION CROWE, R.G.S. (1850–1906)

The extension to California, in June of 1904, of the educational and vocational program used so effectively with wayward and unruly young ladies in eastern cities was largely due to Mother Mary of the Incarnation (1850–1906) So effective was her foundation of the Good Shepherd Sisters that within a few months after the Irish–born nun had introduced their work in California, city and state officials took official cognizance of a new force for good in the community.

Mother Mary of the Incarnation, whose family name was Crowe, arrived in the United States in 1866. She entered the convent at Saint Louis eight years later and, shortly thereafter, was named prioress in Detroit. Mother Mary subsequently occupied a similar position in Minneapolis, after which she served a term as assistant provincial.

In mid–1904, at the invitation of Bishop Thomas J. Conaty, Mother Mary journeyed to the Diocese of Monterey–Los Angeles to inaugurate the spiritual, social and educational rehabilitation program for girls, most of whom, ranging in age from twelve to twenty–one, were referred by the juvenile court. The bishop provided temporary accommodations for the nuns at 1918 South Grand Avenue until the larger, permanent quarters, later located on Arlington Avenue, could be completed. There the nuns took up their apostolate among the outcast, the despised and the neglected of young womankind.

Mother Mary was not long in winning the respect of the southland's leaders in her attempts to reform the girls and women who, for some reason or another, had fallen into ways of evil. The local Catholic press attributed the early success of the Good Shepherd Home "to her splendid executive ability, her masterful tactfulness, and above all, to her excellent traits of sympathy with all causes of misfortune." Indeed it was recognized that "her sense of keen hospitality and broad–minded charity have gathered around her hosts of friends who have stood loyally by her in the upbuilding of an institution which is alike an honor to the Church to which she belongs and a pride to the city in which she has made her home."

There were no lines of nationality, creed or color in the Good Shepherd Home and Mother Mary's policy of admitting anyone desirous of correction or reformation earned the admiration and good will of judges, humane officers and welfare workers. Though she was only active for twenty–two months in California's southland, Mother Mary "laid the foundations of a great work in this community" which has continued over succeeding decades in ever– growing proportions

At the time of her premature death, Mother Mary of the Incarnation was eulogized as the "perfect" religious. "She had the sweetness that comes from great virtue. She had the kindness that won for her the love of all who met her. She had the hospitality of a good Mother, the devotedness of the Good Shepherd. Her life was the sweetest of influences, her tact, unselfishness and sympathy made her success. She was a woman of great business ability, splendid executive power, clear–headed and direct. She was grateful to God and to the friends who rallied to her aid and her heart filled with deep affection for all the kindness which she received."

WILLIAM H. CULLIGAN, S.J. (1869–1940)

When one remains faithful to the service of God for over half a century, laboring constantly and without other remuneration than the consciousness of helping others, there is evident proof that seeds of piety sown in early youth, at home and at college, have borne abundant fruit for one's own sanctification and that of others. One such servant was Father William H. Culligan (1869–1940), an energetic Jesuit whose life personified the virtues that Ignatius of Loyola envisioned in his spiritual sons.

San Francisco–born Culligan received his early education at Saint Ignatius College. After entering the Society of Jesus, in 1877, he studied at Santa Clara and later taught undergraduates at his *alma mater*. He pursued his theological training at Woodstock, Maryland, and was ordained by James Cardinal Gibbons, June 29, 1893.

Father Culligan's subsequent assignments at Santa Clara, Saint Ignatius College and Sacred Heart Novitiate revealed innate organizational abilities possessed by few of his contemporaries. The older parishioners at Santa Clara used to recall with pleasure Father Culligan's pastoral zeal during his years there. His work at the old mission church, his labors for the young men, the building of the Sodality Club and his kindly offices as minister and treasurer of the college still linger in the annals of that community.

In 1909, he went to San Jose as curate and, later, pastor, of Saint Joseph's Church. There he was a zealous and untiring laborer in advancing the Kingdom of Christ along spiritual and temporal lines. He erected Saint Leo's Church and school, Newman Hall, a convent and Santa Maria Hall for brothers. All that could tend to the greater glory of God met with his wholehearted and self–sacrificing approval, and the sorrow–stricken and distressed always found in him a ready and sympathetic advisor and friend.

The spiritual zest and assiduity with which Father Culligan ministered his flock was again demonstrated in the years after 1918, when he served as pastor of Seattle's Church of the Immaculate Conception. It was there that he established the "Dollar Standard" envelope system for weekly contributions which has since become a national practice.

In his many assignments and roles over the sixty–three years he served in the Society of Jesus, Father Culligan worked "with no fixed home, no choice of personally preferred labors, no hope of advancement except with God's graces." His God, his Order and the greater good of all were the dominant notes in a life of constant and hidden sacrifice. The name of Father William H. Culligan immediately comes to mind when reading David Thoreau's words:

> It is something to be able to paint a picture, or to carve a statue, and so to make a few objects beautiful. But it is far more glorious to carve and paint the atmosphere in which we work, to effect the quality of the day. This is the highest of the arts.

MARY MICHAEL CUMMINGS, S. M. (1853–1922)

Mother Mary Michael Cummings was known to her contemporaries as "one of those whose heart and whose charity are as broad as the circle of suffering humanity." The youngest of seven children, Rose Anna Cummings was born on July 8, 1853, at Madisonville, Illinois. In 1870, she entered the convent as a novice for the Sisters of Mercy at Saint Louis, and was given the white veil and her religious name on November 14, 1871, by the Right Reverend Patrick John Ryan.

After a few years at the motherhouse the young nun

was sent to Colorado, and in 1888, she became superior of the hospital at Ouray. She worked briefly in Salinas prior to answering the plea of Father Anthony Ubach to establish a hospital in San Diego. Bishop Francis Mora welcomed Sister Mary Michael and her companions in June of 1890 expressing the hope that God would prosper and multiply their work in Southern California. Quarters were rented in the upper stories of the Reed Building at Sixth and H Streets, and after the first bursts of intolerance and misapprehension had passed away, the Sisters won a respected position in the growing community.

The nuns subsequently acquired a new site north of the city on University Avenue for a permanent foundation. The central building of the new complex was located on an eminence near the area where the road begins its descent into historic Mission Valley. Expansion continued. Mother Mary Michael brought about completion of the hospital in 1904, along with a lovely new chapel. A two–story convent had been added in 1900, and a school of nursing in 1904

Though "humiliation was the community's badge, poverty its watchword, the cross its refuge and final victory," Mother Mary Michael guided her Sisters through even further growth, establishing a branch hospital at El Centro in 1910, and another at Oxnard in 1915. Just a year and a half before her death in 1922, one of Mother Mary Michael's great desires was fulfilled when the Mercy Sisters of Arizona, San Francisco and San Diego voted to amalgamate their personnel and resources into a single religious community.

On the occasion of Mother Mary Michael Cumming's Golden Jubilee, Bishop John J. Cantwell of Monterey–Los Angeles said of this pioneering nun:

> Until Mother Michael's arrival in San Diego, this city was without a hospital; through her untiring and wholehearted efforts, Saint Joseph's Hospital was built. The jubilee of a nun is not altogether a personal affair; it brings before us in a concrete way the ideas of self–sacrifice, of self–denial, of humility, justice and patience. . . . The recording angel alone can tell how many souls have been rescued from the pit of darkness, how many times a heart has turned to God when before his dying eyes the figure of Jesus crucified was lifted up. . . .
>
> We trust that when the sun sinks down to rest in crimson, purple and gold in the western sky, that it will be to her a promise of a better land, the promise of the good things that Almighty God has for those who serve, the promise of an eternal life which passeth not away.

OWEN DA SILVA, O.F.M. (1906–1967)

The involvement of religious personages in popular musical renditions is not an exclusively post–Vatican development. In the mid 1930s, the late Father Owen da Silva, a talented Franciscan composer–priest, organized a group of his fellow friars, at Mission Santa Barbara, into the *Padre Choristers*.

In 1938, the *Padre Choristers* inaugurated a series of music programs over Radio Station KTMS which was transmitted nationwide by the National Broadcasting Company over its Blue Network. The fortnightly concerts quickly made the tone of Santa Barbara's Mission bells familiar throughout the United States. One observer noted that "the peace and beauty which has been Santa Barbara's compelling attraction since the valley on the channel was first sighted by Spanish explorers" was available for all the country to hear and enjoy. Reaction to the program was favorable at the local level too, as is evident from a Channel City newspaper report that "within Santa Barbara no community endeavor has ever met with such prompt and unanimous approval and appreciation."

The major portion of credit for the success of the *Padre Choristers* was due to the affable Father da Silva (1906–1967), whose musical compositions have been sung by numerous choirs and choruses throughout the country. Best known of his works are a "Mass of Our Lady" and the "Peace Prayer of Saint Francis" which was later recorded by Bing Crosby.

A native Californian, Father da Silva was baptized, ordained and, ultimately, buried from the Church of Mission Santa Barbara. Though involved in a host of positions during his priestly years, the tireless friar will be remembered longest for his contributions to the field of religious music.

Father da Silva's monumental treatise on the *Mission Music of California*, published by Warren F. Lewis in 1941, is a source book of distinctive merit in which he reproduced, without omission or addition, the manuscript music used by the friars at the California missionary foundations. The first complete and authentic collection of early provincial music ever published, the 132–page volume, with its chirography by Arthur M. Bienbar and pen sketches by Paul Moore, has been described as that "type of book that only a person of musical talent as well as ability in historical research could produce."

One of the most popular of his many recordings, *Songs of the Missions* released in 1951, consisted of two ten–inch records (four sides, 78 r.p.m.). Embodying a cross section of the Golden State's musical heritage, it was produced by RCA Victor. Music critics were lavish in their praise of the records, acknowledging them to be a noteworthy contribution to the art and culture of Franciscan California. A reviewer for the *Catholic Educator*, commenting on the handsomely packaged album said that "those who are interested in the nostalgic saga of missionary achievements in California will find their reveries enhanced greatly by the sound of the *padres'* songs in this album. "

Though he did not personally participate in the deliberations of Vatican Council II, Father da Silva's philosophy of music parallels that contained in the conciliar *Constitution on the Sacred Liturgy*:

> The musical tradition of the universal Church is a treasure of immeasurable value, greater even than that of any other art. The main reason for this pre–eminence is that, as sacred melody united to words, it forms a necessary or integral part of the solemn liturgy.

BLESSED JOSEPH DE VEUSTER, SS. CC. (DAMIEN OF MOLOKAI) (1840–1889)

In 1864, John Stoddard went to the 'Hawaiian Islands to recover his health and there he met Father Joseph De Vuester, known to the world as Damien of Molokai. Three years later, Stoddard became a Catholic and later wrote his famous book about *The Lepers of Molokai*,

It is a sympathetic and tender account of the lives of those "despairing but unresisting souls, swallowed up in the transfiguration of the sunset, snatched from the breast of sympathy and from the arms of love, doomed to the hopeless degradation of everlasting banishment, and borne in the night to that dim island whose melancholy shores are the sole refuge of these hostages to death." Stoddard's tender and gentle sympathy manifests itself throughout the pages of this beautiful little book. He is especially impressed by the good people who were sacrificing their own lives for those from whom the world turns in disgust.

He gives a moving portrayal of Father Damien: "The chapel door stood ajar; in a moment it was thrown open, and a young priest paused upon the threshold to give us a welcome. His cassock was worn and faded, his hands stained and hardened by toil; but the glow of health was in his face, the buoyancy of his youth in his manner, while his ringing laugh, his ready sympathy, and his inspiring magnetism told of one who in any sphere might do a noble work, and who has chosen to do the noblest of all works. This was Father Damien, the self–exiled priest, the one clean man in the midst of his flock of lepers."

Stoddard tells how "we were urged to dine with him. Good soul! He was conscious of asking us to the humblest of tables, but we were a thousand times welcome to the best he had." Awhile later, the priest "brought from his cottage into the churchyard a handful of corn, and, scattering a little of it upon the ground, he gave a peculiar cry. In a moment fowls flocked from all quarters; they seemed to descend out of the air in clouds; they lit

upon his arms, and fed out of his hands; they fought for footing upon his shoulders and even upon his head; they covered him with caresses and with feathers. He stood knee–deep among as fine a flock of fowls as any fancier would care to see; they were his pride, his playthings."

In the epilogue of his book, which was written after Father Damien had himself contracted leprosy, Stoddard quotes the letter apprising him that "I am now the only priest on Molokai, and am supposed to be myself afflicted with this terrible disease . . . Those microbes have finally settled themselves on my left leg and my ear, and one eyebrow begins to fall. Having no doubt myself of the true character of my disease, I feel calm, resigned and happier among my people. Almighty God knows what is best for my own santification and with that conviction I say *fiat voluntas tua.*"

Stoddard concludes by prophesying for Damien the universal honor that the world accorded the priest when he was gone. Out "of this corruptible body springs heavenward the invisible blossom of the soul."

After resting nearly half a century in the little leper colony cemetery at Kalawao, the remains of Father Joseph De Veuster (1840–1889), known more familiarly as Damien of Molokai, were being returned to Louvain. At the personal request of the King of the Belgians, the famous Picpus missionary was to be permanently entombed near his birthplace of Tremeloo.

Enroute to his native land, Father Damien's remains passed through San Francisco where they were received at Fort Mason Army Transport Docks, on February 11, 1936. The body was conveyed to Saint Mary's Cathedral and, for five days, tens of thousands paid their respects at the bier in one of the most impressive and historic events in the city's history.

The image of Father Damien had captured the hearts and souls of his fellow Christians the world over and, as Father James McHugh noted in his sermon for one of the several Requiem Masses:

> No story of sacrifice and love thrills the heart of men more than the story of Damien, the Samaritan of Molokai.
>
> The history of Damien's work and success is known to all. It tells how completely he sacrificed himself, becoming all things to all men for the love of Christ. No difficulty was too great, no obstacle stayed him. As a result the lepers called on him in all their needs, physical as well as spiritual.
>
> Damien instructed their children, washed their sores, amputated when necessary. He built their cabins, painted their houses. Yes; he made their coffins and dug their graves. His tenacity of purpose, his dogged perseverance, secured government aid, focused the attention of the world on this small island and brought honor to his country and church.
>
> After a few years on the island—some historians place the date as early as 1876—Damien could refer to

the inhabitants as "we lepers," for he had contracted the dreadful disease. As soon as his misfortune became known the whole world became concerned.

Money, gifts, medicine arrived on every boat. The heart of mankind grieved for Damien, as it had for none other. Millions of prayers were offered for his cure. Under this frightful handicap he carried on till 1889 when, on April 15th, his soul appeared before God. Damien had read the law aright and eternal life was his.

In explaining the enthusiastic welcome afforded the remains of Father Damien in the Bay Area, Archbishop John J. Mitty noted that the people of San Francisco represented all America in paying tribute to a man who, in seeing beneath the festering sores of his fellow sufferers, had "come to grasp with the realities of life, that in retreat, in meditation with God he realized the one thing that counts, the salvation of immortal souls."

The People of God in California still cherish the privilege that was theirs of paying personal homage at the bier of a missionary whom Robert Louis Stevenson ranked as "one of the world's heroes and exemplars."

DOHENY, WILLIAM, C.S.C. (1898–1982)

Among the correspondence of Carrie Estelle Doheny on file at the Archival Center, Archdiocese of Los Angeles, are 189 letters to and from Msgr. William J. Doheny, presiding judge of the Sacred Roman Rota. Because most of the Doheny correspondence prior to the 1940s was destroyed, it is unclear precisely how Msgr. Doheny was related to the California branch of the family. He appeared to be a second cousin to Edward L. Doheny and in her letters, Carrie Estelle consistently referred to the monsignor as "Cousin Billy."

In any event, Msgr. Doheny's claim to a place in historical annals is based on his own accomplishments, quite apart from whatever his relationship was to the California branch of his family.

William Joseph Doheny was born on May 30, 1898, at Merrill, Wisconsin, the son of William and Bridget (O'Connor) Doheny. His earliest education was acquired at the parochial school of Saint Francis Xavier. He entered the Congregation of the Holy Cross at Notre Dame, Indiana, in 1919, and was solemnly professed on October 15, 1923. Ordained June 27, 1924, by Bishop Francis W. Howard, Father Doheny was sent to The Catholic University of America where he was awarded the J. U. D. degree in 1927.

Doheny taught Canon Law at Holy Cross College, Washington, D.C., from 1924 until 1929. He was then made superior of Holy Cross International College, a position he occupied for five years. He was named first American advocate and Procurator of the Tribunal of the Signatura of the Sacred Roman Rota in 1932.

From 1941 to 1945, Father Doheny was assistant Superior General of the Congregation of the Holy Cross. After returning to the United States, he taught Legal Ethics at the University of Notre Dame. At different times, he held other positions, including that of charter member of the Riccobono Seminar in Washington (1927), first President of the Canon Law Society of America (1938) and General Supervisor of Studies for the Congregation of the Holy Cross.

During most of his years in Rome, Doheny was among the few Americans holding significant positions at the Vatican. By virtue of his rank as a judge of the Roman Rota, Doheny was given the title monsignor in 1948, a rare distinction indeed for a member of a religious order.

In the field of Canon Law, Msgr. Doheny was an internationally known scholar and writer. Besides his series of books on *Canonical Procedures*, he published volumes on the legal aspects of ecclesial property and practical problems connected with church financing.

During his frequent visits to the United States, Msgr. Doheny gave numerous retreats to priests and religious. He edited several ascetical books, including a *Life of Christ* that went through numerous editions. He also wrote for such professional journals as the *American Ecclesiastical Review* and *The Jurist*.

Msgr. Doheny performed many services for American prelates. At the request of the Archbishop of Los Angeles, Doheny wrote a sixty–two page book on Cardinal McIntyre's titular Church in Rome which appeared in 1956. Entitled *Saint Anastasia. The Saint and Her Basilica in Rome*, it was an imprint of Angelo Belardetti.

After his retirement in 1967, Msgr. Doheny spent much of his time editing an extensive series of spiritual classics. When the eighty–three year old priest died on May 1, 1982, in Salvator Mundi Hospital, he was interred in the Vault of the Holy Cross Fathers in Rome's Campo Verano.

GERARD DONOVAN, M.M. (1904–1937)

The mortal remains of Father Gerard Donovan, the first Maryknoll priest to meet death on the mission field, were returned to the United States aboard the S. S. *Chichibumaru*, early in 1938. At the behest of Archbishop John J. Mitty, a formal liturgical reception was held at San Francisco, on April 27th. The archbishop personally met the ship and escorted the funeral cortege to Saint Mary's Cathedral.

In his brief address, the archbishop directed his remarks principally to the young people present, holding up to them the ideal "spirit of sacrifice which is in every boy and girl and which flowered in the heart of the smiling boy, Gerard Donovan, when he offered himself to the service of God and who finally surrendered his very life a captive, slowly starving to death—all alone, with nothing to cling to save Christ."

Gerard Donovan, the youngest of three brothers who became Maryknoll priests, was born at Pittsburgh, on October 14, 1904. A bright and talented youngster, Gerard made his early studies at Saint Peter's School in McKeesport and it was from there that he entered Maryknoll College, at Clark's Summit, Pennsylvania.

Those who taught him recall his pranks, his boisterousness and his wholesome joyousness. Following his theological courses, Gerard was ordained to the priesthood on June 17, 1928. He was sent to The Catholic University of America for graduate work and later taught for three years at Maryknoll College.

Father Donovan was able to fulfill his missionary ambitions in 1931, when he was assigned to Hsin Pin in Manchukuo. A while later, he moved on to the isolated village of Linkiang, the most remote of Maryknoll's stations. Father Donovan was totally engulfed in his apostolic activities. He wrote once about a Christmas celebration, noting that he would not trade "the hushed, expectant Christians" in Linkiang for "the most gorgeous cathedral in Christendom."

In September, 1937, the priest was moved again, this time to the center of the Prefecture of Fushun, and it was there, in a suburb called Hopei, that the final stage of his life unfolded. The tragic ordeal that culminated his seven years of missionary work began while he was kneeling at prayer. On October 5, 1937, a group of bandits kidnapped Father Donovan and held him for ransom.

Authorities failed to acquiesce to their demands and the captors murdered their hostage on the Feast of Our Lady of Lourdes. They left his mortal remains alongside a highway, near Huaijen, not far from T'ung Hua.

The three days that Father Gerard Donovan's body remained in San Francisco was a time of great spiritual blessing for the local Catholic community. Archbishop Mitty expressed that sentiment well when he noted that "while we dare not bespeak the Holy See, we feel that he has already gone to God. Nevertheless, we offer our prayers for him, hoping he will bring choicest blessings on our city and archdiocese."

Today Father Donovan's tomb can be visited at Ossining, New York, the motherhouse for the Maryknoll Fathers.

ROSE PHILIPPINE DUCHESNE, R.S.H.M. (1769–1852)

Rose Philippine Duchesne (1769–1852) is known in America's ecclesial annals as the "pioneer missionary of the New World." She has been declared a saint by Pope John Paul II. She who was to be the foundress of the Religious of the Sacred Heart in the United States was born at Grenoble, France, in the year that Fray Junípero Serra brought the Catholic faith to Alta California.

Though early attracted to religious life, Philippine was discouraged by her father who felt that she could "find a better way to achieve happiness." His attempts in that direction were eventually frustrated. During the French Revolution, Duchesne risked her life to bring food, medicine and news to cholera victims in prison and to dress the dead for burial. Her willingness to help others knew no earthly bounds. Shortly after the revolution, Philippine became acquainted with St. Madeleine Sophie Barat, founder of the Society of the Sacred Heart at Amiens. She affiliated herself with that community and subsequently served as treasurer, secretary, infirmarian and teacher.

In 1817, Sister Philippine was given permission to answer Bishop Louis William Dubourg's plea for missionaries in the United States. She and four companions left for America on March 21, 1818. Later that year, she opened the first free school west of the Mississippi River with twenty–one pupils of all ages. Sister Philippine was never proficient at languages and later wrote a friend that "God has not bestowed on us the gift of tongues. Perhaps He wants His missionary nuns to sanctify themselves by failure."

Sister Philippine then set about to open a novitiate and thereby the Society of the Sacred Heart became a potent factor in the religious and educational life of the Mississippi Valley. The rest of her active life was devoted to opening schools and training younger Sisters for educational pursuits. Certainly Philippine Duchesne can be credited as one of the pioneers of what became the nation's parochial school system.

At the age of seventy–two, she was sent to work among the Indians at Sugar Creek, Kansas. There she was deeply impressed by the solid piety of the native Americans and their responsiveness to her ministry. Philippine Duchesne died at Saint Charles, Missouri, on November 18, 1852. Her thirty–four years in America had merited for her a unique place on the pages of America's Catholic heritage. Mother Rose Philippine Duchesne was beatified by Pope Pius XII on May 12, 1940

Mother Duchesne's connection to California began in October of 1951, when one of the Sisters at the San Francisco College for Women, Lone Mountain, began praying to Duchesne for the cure of a throat cancer which was diagnosed as terminal. Without any further medical treatment, the cancer was cured. Sr. Mary Henry, a registered nurse who cared for the afflicted Sister and who served later at the infirmary of the religious in Menlo Park, testified to the cure at the formal deposition held in September, 1961.

This then is the story of a frontier missionary. Like other pioneer women of equal intrepiditon, she took in her stride hardships whose mere enumeration makes a softer age recoil. "Some names must not wither," says the bronze table bearing the Pioneer Roll of Fame in the Jefferson Memorial in Saint Louis. Duchesne surely heads that list of women!

NEWMAN EBERHARDT, C.M. (1912–1995)

Newman Charles Eberhardt (1912–1995) spent almost his entire priesthood, well over half a century, walking along California's *El Camino Real*. He endowed the priestly image with all the virtues the world associates or should associate with priesthood.

Born in Chicago on July 10, 1912, Newman Eberhardt attended local Catholic schools before his affiliation with the Congregation of the Mission. Professed in 1932, he was ordained to the priesthood in 1939, just prior to World War II. The youthful Vincentian was then sent to Rome where he acquired a licentiate's degree in Sacred Theology at the Athenaeum Angelicum. Some years later, he received his advanced degree in history from Saint Louis University.

Assigned to Saint John's Seminary at Camarillo in 1941, Father Eberhardt spent his early professional years teaching philosophy, patrology and history. During the summers, he taught at De Paul University in Chicago. Eberhardt's reputation was firmly established on the national level with his publication, in 1961–1962, of *A Summary of Catholic History*. That two volume compendium was described by one reviewer as "an accurate, readable and comprehensive" treatise.

Another scholar writing for the *Catholic Historical Review* was "impressed by the generous bulk of material succinctly compressed into its 900 pages; by the prevailing tone of objectivity; by the refusal to slur over awkward facts; by the adroit summaries of major issues, [and] by the great attention given to the secular background."

The name "Eberhardt" thereafter became a recognized tradition in seminaries throughout the nation. One prominent authority explained that phenomenon by observing that "Father Eberhardt's style is simple, uncomplicated, historical rather than apologetic, with an occasional touch of humor."

In 1964, Eberhardt's supplementary study, *A Survey of American Church History*, appeared on the book-

stalls. It too was greeted with wide acclaim. The late Hugh H. Nolan described the 308–page book as "a truly valuable work for seminaries, novices, college students, and the general Catholic reader." It is a sound, attractively written and carefully documented study.

In 1972, without slowing his pace at Camarillo, Father Eberhardt embarked on a third career, a teaching apostolate for the Permanent Deacon Program in the Archdiocese of Los Angeles. Two nights a week, after a full schedule with the seminarians, he drove fifty–five miles to Los Angeles, where he functioned as academic coordinator and teacher in the training classes. Eberhardt's national reputation was confirmed in 1981, when fellow members of the American Catholic Historical Association elected him second vice–president.

In his lectures and books, Father Eberhardt always treated the Church with deference, respect and love. Perhaps more than others, he knew the Church's human imperfections and shortcomings, but he always chose to dwell on what was good and uplifting.

Vicariously, as spiritual director and academic professor, Father Eberhardt touched the lives of hundreds of thousands of Catholics in the Metropolitan Province of Los Angeles. He epitomized what is best in the evolving traditions of the Church—probably because he always abided by his own dictum: "An historian ought to give testimony, not prophecy."

Eberhardt died suddenly in his room after returning from his customary morning walk on May 26, 1995. He had turned in his grades for the semester and was working on a homily for the Feast of the Ascension. Placed next to his casket at Saint Vincent's Church in Los Angeles was the *Pro Ecclesia et Pontifice* medal which he had been awarded by Pope John Paul II in 1989. Roger Cardinal Mahony, seven bishops and over 300 priests concelebrated the Mass of the Resurrection.

Eulogizing Newman Eberhardt would be redundant. Everyone has his or her memories of "Ebbie" as they knew him. He was one who performed well all the priestly tasks: He recited his breviary, he read Holy Scripture, he made his meditation, he said the rosary, he did his spiritual reading and he practiced the virtues. Truly Ebbie did all things well. And he did them in an unobtrusive, almost hidden way. In a busy world, he found time for the Lord, for students and for everyone who knocked on his door. Seeing his light on was a sign that all was right with God and man. And that light was like a vigil lamp in the sanctuary, it never seemed to go out.

"SISTER ELSIE"

Over the years, this writer has received numerous requests for information about "Sister Elsie Peak," located at the foot of the northern slope of the Verdugo Hills.

Who was Sister Elsie, when did she live and how did she come to have her name attached to a large piece of California's real estate? It's a valid enough question and surely there must be an answer.

Investigation of the historical record indicates that Phil Begue bought land in the area about 1882. Using the original survey made by Frank Lacovreur, in 1871, Begue seemingly originated the interesting story of Sister Elsie Well and Sister Elsie Peak. His account was subsequently put into print by Grace J. Oberbeck in her *History of La Crescenta–La Canada Valleys*, a ninety–three page book published at Montrose by The Ledger, in 1938.

According to this account, a group of Sisters operated an orphanage on *El Rancho de las Hermanas*. They maintained there a herd of cows which were looked after by several elderly Indians.

Reportedly, Sister Elsie was the much beloved nun who worked with the herd and the Indians. Gradually her name came to be associated with the well where water for the herd was acquired. Almost directly north of the well towers a high peak of the Sierra Madre range. Out of respect and love for their favorite nun, the Indians also bestowed her name to the 5,020 foot peak.

On this mountain was situated for many years the forestry department lookout known as "Lukens" where, during the fire hazard months, rangers were stationed. In 1937 the tower was abandoned. *El Rancho de las Hermanas* was subsequently incorporated into the holdings of the Begue family. The well was made a motif of a hotel, built in 1932. Two years earlier, "Sister Elsie Well" was dedicated by the Native Sons and Daughters of Glendale Parlors and a bronze plaque was hung over the well.

Just behind Sister Elsie Peak is Mount Josephine, named for Mr. Begue's daughter when she was just a tiny girl. Although it is 500 feet higher than Sister Elsie Peak, it cannot be seen in the background.

That's where the story stops. So far, this writer has been unable to further identify Sister Elsie or her Community. The Daughters of Charity apparently did own property in the area at one time, but there is no Sister Elsie listed on their necrology.

The Dominican Sisters have been an integral part of La Crescenta since 1930. But, in a search of their archives, Sister Mary Paul reports "there is nothing in our records to substantiate . . . any Sister named Elsie." Whether Sister Elsie ever lived is questionable. Surely there was no Catholic orphanage in the area during the time of Phil Begue. Maybe the good Sister was kidnapped by Martians!

ZEPHYRIN ENGELHARDT, O.F.M. (1851–1934)

Although libraries abound with books on the Califor-

nia missions, there are few that add substantially to the studies of Father Zephyrin Engelhardt, O.F.M., the first Catholic historian to wade through the maze of source materials scattered around the state.

Born at Bilshausen, Hanover, Germany, on November 13, 1851, young Charles Anthony Engelhardt was brought to America in 1852, where he spent the remainder of his eighty–two years. He was ordained in 1878, and shortly thereafter was sent to do missionary work among the Menominee Indians of Wisconsin. Serving in various capacities during the next decade, he was well–prepared for the appointment to the Indian Boarding School at Harbor Springs in 1894. There he installed a printing press and published a monograph on the saintly Indian maiden, Katherine Tekakwitha, in the Indian language of the Ottawans.

In 1900 Father Zephyrin came to Banning's Indian School and remained there until his transfer to Mission Santa Barbara. Already the author of several small volumes, he directed his whole attention to the now famous historical collection known as the Santa Barbara Mission Archives. His notes from the United States General Land Grants Office in San Francisco include many of the 2,000 original letters, reports and orders written by missionaries, governors, and viceroys which were subsequently destroyed by fire.

Among the first works published by Engelhardt at Harbor Springs was his *Franciscans in California* which appeared in 1897. This slender volume served in later years as the ground–plan for his series on *The Missions and Missionaries of California*. The four books were issued between 1908 and 1915, and rated from one reviewer the comment that "from many points of view . . . Father Engelhardt is the most indispensable of all the historians of California."

In the years after 1920, the well–known German friar began issuing small monographs on the local history of individual missions. Sixteen volumes ultimately appeared in the highly useful series and, in most cases, these books remain the principal sources on their subjects. The "Dean of California Historians" did not restrict his endeavors to books alone. He was a frequent contributor to periodical journals, both under his own name and under his two pen–names, "*Der Bergman*" and "*Esperanza.*"

Ever the crusader, Engelhardt was anything but a retiring, colorless compiler of records. He wrote with a view to historical accuracy of fact rather than to attractiveness of style and method. His works represent an exhaustive study of the work of the Franciscans on the mission frontier. Charles Chapman observed that it was as "a great chronological sourcebook of mission history, as a kind of Franciscan Bancroft that Father Engelhardt's work is primarily important."

The passage of time, discovery of new sources and

development of a more scientific approach suggests that Engelhardt's tomes should be revised and updated. But until that is done, it can be said that his writings are the principal thesaurus of historical lore regarding a glorious chapter in this nation's ecclesiastical annals.

ANNA RAPHAEL FITZGERALD, S.N.D. (1842–1915)

Sister Anna Raphael possessed that rare combination of wide knowledge and personal enthusiasm which characterizes "great" teachers. The memory of her kindliest deeds, selfless devotedness and gentlest counsels still pervades the religious community which she served for just five months short of half a century.

Born into one of California's best known pioneer families, on October 23, 1842, Anna A. Fitzgerald entered the Sisters of Notre Dame in 1865. She was professed on January 1, 1868.

The simplicity of her noble character revealed itself in the gently insinuated remarks, in the apt allusion and in the spontaneous outpouring of sentiments which permeated her whole being with loving reverence for the things of God. Throughout the many years of her classroom apostolate, Sister Anna Raphael's scientific and literary work brought her considerable prominence, especially in the Santa Clara Valley, where she was aptly regarded as the Poet Laureate.

At the time of her demise, in 1915, one of the nun's many students wrote most descriptively that

> Her noblest poem was a life that bore
>   On every page the seal of sanctity.
> The sweet–voiced singer may forgotten be;
>   The scientist, who, versed in Nature's lore,
> Made it her dearest pleasure to explore
>   Of seed and shell and star the mystery,
> And seemed to hold of Nature's heart the key,
>   May be remembered by us here no more.
>
> But memory of the kindly gracious word,
>   The daily selfless giving of her best,
> The life of prayerful calm beneath God's Eye, –
>   This is to Notre Dame her rich bequest,
> By this to nobler impulse hearts are stirred,
>   And leaving this, she left what cannot die.

Her serenity of spirit along with kindness in word and deed, made Sister Anna Raphael's classes at Notre Dame as enjoyable as they were instructive. Simple and unobtrusive in her relations with others, Sister Anna Raphael never spoke hastily or judged unkindly. It was her mission to inspire others with high ideals and thereby to lead them to thoughts about God.

Auxiliary Bishop Edward J. Hanna said of Sister Anna Raphael that she was about the work of salvation "from the beginning; nothing daunted her spirit, and in spite of danger and difficulty, she simply pressed on, knowing to Whom she had given her trust and to Whom she had plighted her troth."

> She had a great mind. Not only was there a great mind, there was also a great spirit of sacrifice to give all to God. And the fifty years that have passed in this work are indications, not only of greatness of mind, but the spirit of sacrifice.
>
> She crowned this gift of sacrifice, this gift of consecration, with a magnificent intelligence, with a love for things that are beautiful, with a love that brings men out of themselves and makes them see God in all that is beautiful and glorious and great.

MARY BRIGID FITZPATRICK, C.S.J. (b. 1921)

Those who complain that the Catholic Church is male dominated don't really know much about its inner workings. No other institution on planet earth has a longer history of utilizing the talent and leadership qualities of women!

One obvious example would be the Catholic school system. The largest private educational institution in the United States (or anywhere else) was grounded, supported and administered by female religious. In our own archdiocese, religious and lay women can be found at every level of ecclesial leadership.

Among the many outstanding women who occupy significant positions of leadership in the Archdiocese of Los Angeles is Sister Mary Brigid Fitzpatrick, who served as administrative assistant to Roger Cardinal Mahony. Born December 17, 1921 at Cisco, Texas, the eldest of seven children of James and Mabel (Keough) Fitzpatrick, Mary Catherine was brought to Los Angeles in 1923 when the family relocated in Saint Anselm's parish.

After completing her schooling at Saint Brigid's, Mary Catherine enrolled at Saint Mary's Academy, where she remained until graduation. She then became a postulant for the Sisters of Saint Joseph of Carondelet. Taking the name of Mary Brigid, she was professed on the community's feastday in 1942.

After a brief stint at historic Saint Boniface Indian School in Banning, Sister Mary Brigid was posted at Saint Cecilia's and Saint Mary's Academy. She made her final vows in 1945.

Most of her academic work in later years centered around Mount Saint Mary's College, where she taught classes in social welfare and sociology. For two years she was a classmate of Terence Cooke (who later became Cardinal Archbishop of New York) at The Catholic University of America and it was from there that she received her master's degree. She finished her doctoral studies at Notre Dame University in 1962.

In addition to her professorial duties at the Mount, Sister Mary Brigid served as dean of both the faculty and the graduate school. She lived at the downtown campus and, during the years 1962 through 1965, the daughter of an immigrant oil driller served as superior and mistress of the home once owned by the legendary oil tycoon, Edward L. Doheny.

Following her tenure as regional superior (1968–1974), Sister Mary Brigid returned in 1979 to the Mount as associate director of the Academic Advancement Center. She remained there until joining the administrative team organized by Archbishop Mahony in 1985.

The history of the institutional Church in any given area must be recorded and told within the context of those who make it work. Sister Mary Brigid typifies that corps of dedicated people, mostly women, who labor unobtrusively behind the facade of every episcopal curia.

In a talk about the dignity of womanhood which aired on television in the 1950s, the late Bishop Fulton J. Sheen observed that, " God created man, then He paused and said: 'I can do better than that,' and He created woman."

MARIE THERESE GAGNON, C.S.J. (1900–1992)

It is written in the Talmud that "God did not create woman from man's head that he should command her, nor from his feet that she should be his slave, but rather from his side that she should be near his heart." Sister Marie Therese Gagnon perfectly exemplified that truism.

Born to Onesime and Adele Gagnon on September 23, 1900, at Lyslet County in Quebec, Marie Rose was the thirteenth in a family of eight boys and six girls. When she was eight years old, her family moved to Biddeford, Maine.

About the time Marie Rose was completing grammar school, Mother Frances Lirette was touring Maine, looking for young women interested in joining the Sisters of Saint Joseph in California. Though only fourteen, Marie Rose answered the call and journeyed to distant Eureka.

On July 10, 1915, Marie Rose formally joined the Congregation and thereafter was known as Sister Marie Therese. She took final vows on July 2, 1917. When it was discovered many years later that her vows were invalid because of her youthful age, Sister happily repeated them a second time.

Throughout a religious life that spanned seventy–seven years, Sister Marie Therese served the Congregation of Saint Joseph of Orange in a host of assignments, five of them involving service as "supe-

rior." Though remembered in many areas, Sister was especially wedded to West Hollywood where she served as principal of Saint Victor's grammar school on three separate occasions: 1933–1939; 1944–1950 and 1961–1967.

During the 1970s, she returned for a fourth time to West Hollywood as a "parish nun" and, in that capacity, became a beloved and revered fixture in the life of the local community. In an issue of the parochial bulletin for West Hollywood, dated August, 1972, it is noted that Sister Marie Therese belongs to West Hollywood and it is here that her heart will continue to reside. Her life among us has been, as the Vatican Council directed, 'one of total dedication to the profession of the evangelical counsels.'

> Consecrated as her years have been to the interior life, Sister Marie Therese has always looked upon her religious vocation as having a necessary role to play in the circumstances of the present age.

Another tribute to her, appearing in a local newspaper at the time of her "retirement," quoted Pope Paul VI: "The Church loves you, for what you are and for what you do on behalf of the People of God; for what you say and for what you give; for your prayer, for your renunciation, for the gift of yourself."

A natural leader, Sister Marie Therese accepted and met the challenges of daily life in a calm and cheerful way. Her pastor once recalled that during depression days, when school tuition was a dollar a month, parishioners often complained that they couldn't afford it. That was okay with Sister. She charged a quarter a week— and collected it!

Though she always spoke with a gentle French accent, Sister Marie Therese was thoroughly American in her demeanor and prayer style. She loved nothing more than telling youngsters about God and His Church. She never grew old because she always thought as a child.

By the time of her demise at Orange, on August 7, 1992, Sister Marie Therese was the longest professed and the oldest living pioneer in her community. And that was indeed fitting because, as Longfellow once observed, "there is no death. What seems so is transition."

MAYNARD J. GEIGER, O.F.M. (1901–1977)

A. Golden Jubilee

On May 23, 1972, Father Maynard J. Geiger, long–time archivist and historian at Mission Santa Barbara, quietly observed his golden jubilee in the Order of Friars Minor. Characterized by the late W. W. Robinson

Maynard J. Geiger, O.F.M.

as one who "writes as he talks, with clarity, ease and frankness," Geiger's "carefully researched publications have won him the respect and admiration of the profession by reason of the thoroughness of his research, his unceasing labor and the high integrity with which he has told the story of his religious family."

Born in Lancaster, Pennsylvania, August 24, 1901, the son of Joseph and Catherine (Kray) Geiger, young Joseph came to Los Angeles a dozen years later. There he was enrolled in Holy Cross School and, later, Loyola High School. In 1919, he entered Saint Anthony's Preparatory Seminary, in Santa Barbara, as a clerical candidate for the Order of Friars Minor. At the time of his investiture with the Franciscan habit, July 15, 1923, young Geiger was given the name "Maynard," which has since become a familiar entry in the library card catalogues around the literary world.

Upon completion of his philosophical studies at Saint Elizabeth's, in Oakland, he was ordained to the priesthood by Bishop John J. Cantwell, on June 9, 1929, at Mission Santa Barbara. Between 1933 and 1937, Geiger took advanced courses in history at The Catholic University of America and it was during those years in the nation's capital that his proto–publications appeared, dealing not with California, but Florida. The friar's doctoral thesis, published in 1937, prompted the observation that "the work of Dr. Maynard Geiger on the *Franciscan Conquest of Florida* probably represents the best single specialized volume on Spanish Florida."

After finishing his graduate work in Washington, Father Geiger's interest turned westward. His imprint, however, remained indelibly impressed on Florida's annals and authorities in that field conceded that the meticulous Franciscan had "accomplished an undertaking of great importance for historical scholars interested in Spanish Florida." His work was formally recognized, ten years later, with bestowal of the Cervantes Medal Award by the Hispanic Institute.

Soon after returning to Santa Barbara, Father Geiger was appointed mission archivist, in which position he organized and augmented the vast quantities of original manuscripts and documents that Father Zephyrin Engelhardt and others had accumulated over the decades. The first tangible result was a *Calendar of Documents in the Santa Barbara Mission Archives*, which historians and other scholars greeted as "an outstanding contribution to the study of California mission history."

After 1947, Father Geiger's energetic efforts to update the archival relevancy have tripled its quantity of holdings. The initial collection has been enriched with an additional 8,000 pages of transcripts relating to the Serra Cause alone.

Inasmuch as a well–written life is almost as rare as a well–spent one, special attention must be given to Geiger's monumental biography of Fray Junípero Serra. Between 1941 and 1958, he traveled 100,000 miles through Europe and the United States locating, photostating and collecting materials in 150 public and private libraries and archives for the beatification process. His personal involvement in the subject never compromised the friar's impartiality and he unswervingly treated Serra with less sentiment and more objectivity.

In Geiger's opinion, the role of chronicler was one of utmost importance for it is he who makes available the basic sources. "There is no substitute for documents: no documents, no history, and I might add, no chroniclers, no documents." The works of Maynard J. Geiger are now and will long remain among the truly significant contributions to the field of American ecclesiastical history. The subtitle of his Serra biography, "The Man Who Never Turned Back," also characterizes the energetic friar who spent the long hours of seven days a week, for almost forty years, in a bare–walled Santa Barbara cell, slowly but ever so accurately grinding out the story of the Franciscan spiritual conquest along the New World's Pacific Slope.

Like the Master whom he has served so faithfully in this life, Father Maynard Geiger was a prophet in his own land: yet generations after the peace marchers, draft protestors and social dissidents are relegated to the annals, the scholarly works of this humble friar will be remembered and utilized as achievements of lasting merit.

MAYNARD J. GEIGER, O. F. M. (1901–1977)

B. PASSING OF ARCHIVIST

The Vatican Council reminds us that "when we look at the lives of those who have faithfully followed Christ, we are inspired with a new reason for seeking the city which is to come." Surely that was so as his earthly friends bade farewell to an esteemed colleague and fellow levite, Father Maynard Geiger. This good and gentle friar met his final challenge without fear for he anticipated death as one of the last functions of the priesthood. It was his last Mass!

One does not dare to write nor think as a judge. That's a prerogative happily left to God. Yet we do know that a person's life can be at least partially evaluated by the range of its interests, the skill of its performance and the measure of its fulfillment.

Though he was first, last and always a priest, and a good one at that, Maynard Geiger was other things too. By obedience, he was an archivist; by training, he was an historian and by acclaim he was a scholar. His priestly specialty was that of breathing life into the dry old bones of earlier ages. Most of his attention since June 9, 1929, the day of his ordination, was given to studying, preparing and writing several shelves full of the finest historical works yet published in the field of Western Americana. His name is known to every competent librarian in the United States.

The patience for details, accuracy of expression and passion for truth that characterized his works needs no further elaboration. The publication of his bibliography, in 1971, is tribute enough to what a single priest accomplished in response to the scholarly mandate.

Like the great Fray Junípero Serra, whose biographer he was and in whose footsteps he walked, Father Maynard Geiger was a tireless worker. With Edna Saint Vincent Millay he could say: "My candle burns at both ends; it will not last the night; But, oh, my foes, and oh, my friends, it gives a lovely light."

This humble friar accepted the Pauline exhortation about being all things to all people:

To clerical students, he was a fascinating and engaging professor;

To researchers, he was a helpful and accommodating archivist;

To scholars, he was a distinguished and recognized historian;

To attentive audiences, he was a sought–after and provocative lecturer;

To hostile protagonists, he was an ever–patient and polite apologist;

To thousands of visitors, he was the genial and cheerful host;

To those in the pews, he was an effective and moving preacher;

And to his religious confreres, he was an affable and generous companion.

Great men need no eulogies. May we only say that spiritually, intellectually and every other way, the earthly sojourn of Maynard Geiger measures up most perfectly to Robert Louis Stevenson's definition of one who has achieved the maturity of manhood:

That man is a success
who has lived well, laughed often and loved much;
who has gained the respect of intelligent men and the love of children;
who has filled his niche and accomplished his task;
who leaves the world better than he found it whether by an improved poppy, a perfect poem or a rescued soul;
who never lacked appreciation of earth's beauty or failed to express it;
who looked for the best in others and gave the best he had.

Something of the Franciscan Order was interred with Maynard Geiger. It is hoped that the example of his priestly zeal may become the seed that springs up anew for still other generations of service along *El Camino Real* for the Order of Friars Minor.

MARY OF THE CROSS GOEMAERE, O.P. (1809–1891)

Catherine Adelaide Goemaere, the daughter of Ignace Joseph and Euphemie (Demailly) Goemaere, was born at Warneton, Belgium, on March 20, 1809. She entered the Dominican Convent of the Cross, at Paris, in her fortieth year.

Soeur Marie Goemaere had just completed her novitiate when Bishop Joseph Sadoc Alemany visited Paris in search of volunteers for the Diocese of Monterey, in far–away California. With two companions, Sister Mary joined the Dominican prelate "with the intention of founding a monastery of the Third Order for the education of girls." The small band of religious pioneers crossed the Atlantic to New York, where the two younger nuns disembarked and journeyed on to the Dominican Convent at Somerset, Ohio, for further training. Alemany, Father Francis Vilarrasa and Sister Mary Goemaere took another ship to Aspinwall. Crossing the Isthmus of Panama, they continued on to San Francisco, arriving, on December 6, 1850, just as "the echoes of the last gunshot that celebrated the admission of the free and Sovereign State of California died away."

Sister Mary opened a convent and school "in a land of sand and thorns" at Monterey where, in April, 1851, she received the first California applicant for religious life, Concepción Arguello. The gray adobe building which housed the "first religious community of women in the state" had previously belonged to the prominent William E.P. Hartnell. With the canonical erection of the

Convent of Santa Catalina, on July 18, 1851, Sister Mary became prioress and was thereafter known as Mother Mary of the Cross Goemaere.

Mother Mary's two years in convent life at Paris "had sufficed to form her in the contemplative way, to enkindle more strongly the fire of love that had burned in her heart since childhood." One writer observed that "the striking resemblance of her features to those of Savonarola was a reflection of strong traits of character within, qualities most needed in the work of organization." While the years at Monterey were filled with hardships and poverty, Mother Mary insisted that the Sisters follow the strict Dominican conventual observances.

At the suggestion of Archbishop Alemany, Mother Mary transferred the convent and school to land donated by Judge S. C. Hastings at Benicia, in 1854, where their foundation was henceforth known as Saint Catherine. The new facilities were completed there and formally inaugurated in 1860. Though ill health brought about Mother Mary's resignation as Prioress in 1862, the tireless Dominican remained faithful to her religious commitments until claimed by death, on October 4, 1891.

The modest tomb bearing her remains, in Benicia's cemetery of Saint Dominic, recalls a great religious whose "engrossing solicitude for God's service was directed preeminently to the spiritual advancement of her sisters." Soeur Marie Goemaere, who presided over the first foundation of Dominican Sisters on the Pacific Coast, was a religious pioneer filled with the spirit of her founder and deeply imbued with the traditions of the past.

ROBERT GRAHAM, S.J. (1912–1997)

One of the Church's leading experts on the war years, 1939 to 1945, and a staunch defender of Pope Pius XII against accusations that the pontiff turned a deaf ear to atrocities committed by the Nazis is Father Robert Graham.

Born March 11, 1912, at Sacramento, Graham was ordained a Jesuit priest in 1941 as a member of the California province. Two years later he joined the staff of *America*, the society's New York–based magazine. Father Graham remained with *America* until 1966, except for a sabbatical during which he earned his advanced degree at the University of Geneva.

Next, Graham became affiliated with *La Civilta Cattolica*, the influential Jesuit journal published in Rome. There he contributed numerous learned articles on a myriad of historical and kindred subjects. In 1968, Graham began a series of monthly essays for *Columbia* magazine, which is published by the Knights of Columbus. He remained as a columnist for a quarter century, writing over 300 articles, all of them penetrating insights into the workings of the Church.

Long at work on a book about Vatican diplomacy, Father Graham spent many decades rummaging through the Vatican's secret wartime documents. During those busy years, he somehow found time to edit a twelve volume series of World War II documents.

According to Catholic News Service, Graham has collected abundant evidence of false reports for his "hoaxes, howlers and humbug file." False reports in spy terminology, are called disinformation. To Graham, such reports and disinformation are what ordinary people call "just plain lies." Graham notes that historians have given a lot of attention to the great revolutions of the past two centuries, the French of 1789 and the Bolshevik of 1917. Both left their scars on the 19th and 20th century, respectively.

Those revolutions were openly antagonistic to religion and both pronounced the death sentence for Christianity and the Catholic Church. While things looked bad for a while, today those once–powerful and dangerous movements are so many wrecks strewn along the highway of history.

The Jesuit scholar suspected that future confrontations will take place not at the level of politics (the state), but at the cultural level. The state seems to be out of the running as the war of ideas is heating up. The media has taken over from the state, as far as the destiny of Christianity is concerned: "Is it too much to suppose that the massive outpourings of the media, incessantly marked by anti–Christian and anti–human tenets, will not in the end be revealed as the new incarnation of the foe with which the Church has had to cope in the centuries of revolution?"

Graham was optimistic for the future. He claimed that the Vatican Council came too late for Europe, too soon for the Third World, but providentially just at the right time for U.S. Catholics: "One shudders to think what disastrous confusion would have been felt in the United States, from top to bottom, without the renewal program sanctioned beforehand, in calmer months, by the council."

Those who read *Columbia* will miss the monthly columns by Father Graham because the California Jesuit always put a positive spin on world events, pointing out that "the rite of passage is also a purifying process."

JAMES HART, O.M.I. (1874–1959)

One of the legendary "fixtures" at San Fernando Mission was Brother James Hart who looked after visitors and conducted tours during the years before, during and after World War II. Born in Lowell, Massachusetts, on June 15, 1874, James Hart entered the Novitiate of the Missionary Oblates of Mary Immaculate of Tewksbury at the age of twenty. He wore the habit for sixty–five years!

In 1895, Brother James pronounced his first vows and during the following year was assigned to a community house in Brownsville, Texas. There he taught and looked after the community's temporalities.

He was transferred to Saint Anthony's Seminary at San Antonio, Texas, as athletic coach in 1906. While there he also taught English and Mathematics as well as coordinating the various outreach programs sponsored by the Oblates. When asked to join the staff at San Fernando Mission in 1934, Brother James agreed to take the position temporarily. That pro–tem appointment lasted almost twenty years.

Though not a trained historian or an accomplished speaker, Brother James spoke eloquently about the development of San Fernando. It was almost as if he had witnessed the mission's foundation in 1797 by Fray Fermin de Lasuen. His memory of dates and happenings was as phenomenally long as it was factually accurate.

During the long and tedious years of restoration, Brother James played an active role in the work. He was at once a tour–guide, a carpenter and a brick mason. Father Augustine O'Dea, who supervised much of the rebuilding, said that "Brother James was far more useful than a dozen historians or architects. He seems to sense what belongs where, how and why."

When tourists returned to San Fernando Mission, a generation later, they invariably asked for "the little brother with the floppy black hat." He often made a deeper impression that the ruins he explained so well.

With the opening of Queen of Angels Seminary, adjacent to San Fernando Mission, Brother James was transferred to his community's southern province and, for the final years of his life, he served as sacristan at Saint Mary's Italian Church in New Orleans.

The file on Brother James at the provincial headquarters in San Antonio contains only three items, one of which is a newspaper clipping from the Los Angeles *Examiner* for November 11, 1951. Inset into the photo is this description: "Brother James Hart of San Fernando Mission finds the park across the street from the mission a delightful spot for rest and meditation. Seen from this bower of natural beauty, the edifice, founded in 1797, seems doubly impressive." Following Brother James Hart's demise on June 8, 1959, a chronicler attached the following observation to his death notice: "Brother Hart was deeply devoted to the Holy Eucharist and assisted at several Masses each day. He died suddenly at San Antonio, Texas, where he had gone to make his annual retreat."

MARGARITA HERNANDEZ, O.C.D. (1903–1989)

Maria de la Concepcion Hernandez was born in the City of Ameca, Jalisco, Mexico, on February 25, 1903, the first of four children of Nestor and Maria (Gonzales) Hernandez. Growing up in a simple but pious environment, Maria studied with the Franciscan Sisters and the Sisters of the Incarnate Word. At the age of seventeen, she received her credentials as a teacher.

After giving classes in typing, shorthand and bookkeeping to the in Carmelite Sisters in Guadalajara, Maria herself entered the convent in 1913, taking the religious name Margarita Maria of the Sacred Heart. In 1927, she came to California with Mother Luisita, where the community was seeking refuge from the religious persecutions and the Cristeros uprisings then rampant in Mexico. Three years later, Sister Margarita took charge of the newly opened Sanatorium for tubercular girls in Duarte.

In addition to Santa Teresita Sanatorium, which later became a 283 bed medical facility, Mother Margarita established a Retreat House, Little Flower Missionary House and *la Casa de la Virgen Nazarena*, together with several outreach programs, all of them related to the medical needs of the local populace.

In 1981, Mother Margarita was instrumental in adding a five story medical office building with thirty–two suites to Santa Teresita. And the chapel she erected there is one of the southland's architectural gems. Mother remained at Santa Teresita for fifty–seven years, until she retired in 1986. She stayed for a few more years longer working on physical contracts and directing fund raising. Recognition of the valuable contributions Mother Margarita made to the community came in 1961, when she became a Life Fellow of the American College of Hospital Administrators.

From her earliest years in California, Mother Margarita established a close working relationship with Bishop John J. Cantwell and his successors. Her charm was such that even James Francis Cardinal McIntyre endorsed her many projects, many of them poorly underfinanced. During those years, *The Duaretian* newspaper referred to her as the "Queen of the Valley."

In 1973, Timothy Cardinal Manning preached at Mother Margarita's Golden Jubilee. He acknowledged that Mother Margarita "was that unique combination of Martha and Mary; a women who was busy about many things—caring for her household and caring for all the temporalities that involve the service of the Lord. Yet, all the while she had that reservation of the inner–self for the presence of the Lord." The cardinal foretold that one day people will say " that she is the embodiment of the woman who graces that last chapter of the Book of Proverbs. She is like the ideal woman who rises in the night, who weaves clothes for her family and feeds them."

Mother Margarita returned her noble soul to the Lord on September 21, 1988, at which time a fourth archbishop of Los Angeles, Roger Mahony, gave tribute to her "great faith, vision and courage as she helped lay the foundations for a marvelous Carmelite community which now has so many wonderful apostolates through the archdiocese."

The diminutive Carmelite sister probably said it best when she advised her community "to think that each hospital room is like another chapel, each bed is an altar, each patient another Christ."

BERNARD R. HUBBARD, S.J. (1888–1962)

One of California's most renowned priests was Father Bernard R. Hubbard (1888–1962). The famous Jesuit's career as an explorer began as a youth, when he climbed the Santa Cruz mountains with camera, gun and dog. Because of his interest in geology, young Hubbard enrolled at Saint Ignatius College and later Santa Clara. At the age of twenty, he was received into the Society of Jesus.

While studying theology at Innsbruck, Hubbard devoted much of his time to probing and photographing the alpine peaks and glaciers of the Tyrol. It was then that he became known as the "Glacier Priest." During the summer of 1927, Father Hubbard made his first major expedition to Alaska, where he explored the Mendenhall and Taku glaciers. That journey, over country never before traversed, brought nation wide attention to the Jesuit priest.

The following year, Hubbard became "the first human ever to reach the rugged and almost inaccessible interior of Kodiak Island" and there he found mountains six thousand feet high of which "no one had previously known the existence." He was later employed by the United States Coast and Geodetic Survey as a guide for a party interested in erecting triangulation stations in that wilderness area.

In 1929, Father Hubbard trekked to the rarely–visited and spectacular Valley of Ten Thousand Smokes towards the summit of the towering volcano Mount Katmai. The Santa Clara professor was often accompanied by campus athletes chosen, as one newspaper put it, "to stand hardship." On one trek, however, in 1931, he travelled with only thirteen dogs from the interior of Alaska to the Bering Sea, a distance of 1,600 miles.

After 1930, Hubbard was released from his classroom responsibilities for full–time lecturing, writing and exploring of the Alaskan wilderness. It was also in that year that he first visited Aniakchak, the largest active volcano in the world. In 1931, he was on hand to photograph the spectacular display of fire and molten rock erupting from that volcano. That accomplishment merited Hubbard a place in the pages of the *National Geographic*.

In 1934, the National Geographic Society partici-

pated in his expedition to explore and map both the Alaskan Peninsula and the adjacent Aleutian Islands, whose topography had been greatly altered by the recent volcanic upheavals.

The adventures of this unusual Jesuit priest were featured in a series of articles appearing in *The Saturday Evening Post* during 1932. From that time onward, the "Glacier Priest" was a household name throughout the United States. Hubbard wrote several accounts of his many travels. His first book, *Mush You Malemutes*, appeared in 1932 and three years later came the famous *Cradle of the Storms*.

While football teams were capturing headlines for the University of Santa Clara across America, the "Glacier Priest" was making the university's name known in lecture halls from Los Angeles to New York. In one eight month period, Hubbard delivered no fewer than 275 talks, probably a world record, at least according to the *Literary Digest*.

The thousands of feet of motion–picture and still film with which Hubbard illustrated his lectures provide a valuable visible record about many aspects of Alaskan geography and the life of its people that have long since disappeared.

EUSEBIO KINO, S.J. (1644–1711)

A. CATTLE KING

The Jesuit missionaries who came to Baja California in 1683 are remembered in the annals as the first to establish a permanent foothold on the peninsula. Among their number on that historic trek was Father Eusebio Kino (1644–1711), who later brought the Gospel to the great southwest region of what is now the United States.

The non–Catholic historian, Herbert Eugene Bolton, wrote a monumental biography of Kino which was published in 1936 under the title, *Rim of Christendom*, a book that is still recognized as the last word about the "Pacific Coast pioneer." The words of Bolton speak more eloquently than any testimony by this writer. Here are some of his observations about the "Apostle to the Pimas of Arizona" in his role as " Cattle King."

> The problem of the biographer of Father Kino is to tell much in little, so many and varied were his activities. Great as missionary, church builder and explorer, he was no less great as a pioneer of secular civilization.
>
> The work which Father Kino did as a ranchman or stockman would, alone, stamp him as an unusual business genius. He was easily the cattle king of his day and region.
>
> From the small outfit supplied him from the older missions, within fifteen years he established the beginnings of ranching in the valleys of the Magdalena, the Santa Cruz, the San Pedro and the Sonoita rivers. The stock raising industry of no less than twenty places on

the modern map owes its beginnings on a considerable scale to this indefatigable man.

And it must not be supposed that he did this for private gain, for he did not own a single animal. It was to furnish a good supply for the Indians of the missions and to give these missions a basis of independence.

Characteristic of Kino's economic efforts are those reflected in a letter thanking him for 150 head of cattle and as many sheep for the beginnings of a ranch at Caborca.

In 1699, Kino established a ranch at Sonoita for the triple purpose of supplying the little mission there, furnishing food for the missionaries of Baja California and establishing a base of supplies for the explorations which Kino hoped to undertake to the Yumas and Cocimaricopas. The next year, when the mission of San Xavier del Bac was founded, Kino rounded up 1400 cattle from his ranch at *Nuestra Señora de Dolores Mission*, divided them into two equal droves and sent them off to San Xavier.

Not only his own missions but those of sterile California must be supplied; and in the year 1700 Kino took from his own ranch several hundred cattle and sent them to Father Juan Maria Salvatierra across the Gulf at Loreto, a transaction which was several times repeated. And it must not be forgotten that Kino conducted this cattle industry with Indian labor, almost without the aid of a single white man. An illustration is the fact that the important ranch at Tumacacori, Arizona, was founded with cattle and sheep driven, at Kino's order, more than 100 miles across the country from Caborca by the very Indians who had earlier murdered a priest.

There was always a danger that the mission Indians would revolt and run off the stock, as they had done in 1695. And there was the added peril that the hostile Apaches, Janos and Jocomes would attack. But Kino knew his people and trusted them.

Father Kino indeed deserves remembrance as founder of the stock industry of Arizona. On one hand, he carried the Bible; in the other the branding iron. Where his churches arose, famine fled. He transformed his neophytes from nomads to a people of a settled life and they loved him for it all.

EUSEBIO KINO, S.J. (1644–1711)

B. LETTERS TO DUCHESS

According to no less an authority than John Gilmary Shea, "Father Eusebio Francisco Kino (1644–1711) stands . . . as the greatest missionary who laboured in North America." It was in 1683 that the Jesuit missionary journeyed to Baja California. On April 1st, he and others reached the palm–fringed Bay of *Nuestra Señora*

de la Paz. The following day they went ashore, fashioned a "great cross, and set it up on a height and, raising the Standard of Faith, they took possession of all this land in the name of the King of Heaven, and of Spain."

During the ensuing thirty months, over 400 Indians were instructed in the rudiments of Christianity. Unfortunately, the inclemency of the weather and the scarcity of drinking water eventually brought about abandonment of the enterprise. With heavy heart, Kino reluctantly returned to the mainland in May of 1685, promising, before his departure, that the program of conversion would be continued.

Leaving the peninsula was especially hard for Father Kino for as Hubert Howe Bancroft said, "as the heart of the conqueror is elated at the prospect of a new kingdom to vanquish, so the heart of the Ingoldstadt votary glowed with pious rapture as he contemplated the spiritual conquest of this virgin field of paganism in the far northwest." Kino never relinquished the hope of one day returning.

Only the barest outlines of Kino's activities in Baja California were known prior to 1922. In that year, a collection of letters written by the Jesuit to his patroness, the Duchess d'Aveiro d'Arcos, came into the possession of Maggs Brothers, dealers in fine and rare books, prints and autographs.

From their bookstore on New Bond Street in London, Maggs compiled a catalogue of the letters which they entitled *Bibliotheca Americana* (432). Copies of that catalogue were sent to the leading libraries and collectors of Western Americana.

Herbert Eugene Bolton, the most distinguished historian in the field, approached officials at the Huntington Library in San Marino, with the suggestion that they purchase the entire collection. The thirty–three documents proved to be a treasure–trove of information about Kino and his missionary apostolate in Baja California. In one case, for example, the missionary told how "the natives were highly impressed by the attitude of the Spaniards and of what we have come to teach."

In another letter, Kino relates the history and discovery of Baja California. He noted that the area around *Nuestra Señora de los Dolores* is "a most fertile country which can, and does, easily yield such abundant harvests of wheat and maize that we could easily supply other missions or new converted communities poorer or shorter of supplies than ourselves."

Probably the most important of the letters was that written from San Bruno on December 15, 1685. It is an extraordinary account wherein Kino mentioned that "we found many Indians who are very meek, friendly, affable and docile, who come to see us every day, in all friendship, and give us the greatest hope of being able to convert them quickly."

In the 1960s, Father Ernest J. Burrus gathered together the Kino letters at the Huntington and those from other sources into his monumental treatise, *Kino Writes to the Duchess* which was published by Rome's Jesuit Historical Institute. That book confirms Shea's reference to Kino as "the greatest missionary who laboured in North America."

ARTHUR LIEBRENZ, O.F.M.

Everyone knows about the twenty–one missions along California's *El Camino Real*. This is the story of another "mission" founded by a friar and sometimes referred to in the annals as "California's 22nd Mission."

In the 1950s Father Arthur Liebrenz pursued a new path along U.S. Highway 99 through the passes of the Sierras and up the back roads leading to the ranches and farms of San Joaquin Valley. The mission's parishioners, like the neophytes of Fray Junípero Serra's time, were also nomadic people of the soil, migratory farm workers, who inhabited the flatlands and foothills of the San Joaquin and whose contact with the teachings of Christ and His Church were as fleeting as their mode of life.

The Franciscan mobile church, a twenty–seven foot trailer with a miniature sanctuary, opened out to the very fields where the people of another generation lived, worked and often died. Next to the trailer chapel was the friar's monastery, a 1947 one–and–a–half ton Dodge truck which was Father Arthur's cell–on–wheels. It was once described as the "only mobile monastery in the world."

Father Liebrenz's associate, a youthful friar attached to Santa Barbara Mission, had a small bunk aft in the trailer which was as compactly outfitted as those in contemporary submarines. The name of the chapel, conferred by a journalist who interviewed the priests, was San Francisco–on–Wheels. It could travel further in a few days than Fray Junípero Serra traversed in his whole lifetime.

The two friars preached upwards of forty missions, novenas and retreats annually at the valley's migrant camps where many of the inhabitants had not seen a priest or received the sacraments in many years. Father Arthur reported that "they take each other for better or worse without benefit of clergy" and children often remained unbaptized into adolescence.

During the early years of the Franciscan Mobile Mission, Father Arthur, known among his people as *Padre Arturo*, rectified 600 marriages and performed some 300 baptisms of youngsters aged six days to sixteen years. In the first two years, he arranged for the First Communion of hundreds of adults whose average age was twenty. He heard thousands of confessions and aided many in making their "reconciliation" to the Church. About 70% of the camps' inhabitants were Mexican nationals and the rest mostly Oklahoman.

Padre Arturo brought to his work a long experience of pastoral activity at Saint Turibius parish located at 16th and Essex streets in Los Angeles. He spoke Spanish fluently and moved easily among his transitory parishioners.

Congregations during an average mission or novena usually numbered from 300 to 400 people. "They kneel on the cold ground and often built fires out of scrap–wood and old tires just to keep warm." The people asked for medals or crosses and the friars spent a good deal of their time seeking those precious items from friends and supporters back home. The local populace anticipated the arrival of the missionaries with great enthusiasm. It wasn't infrequently that whole families of Oklahomans, previously non–Catholic, came into the Church.

At each stop, Padre Arturo said he "left behind a bit of his very self." Like their great mentor, Fray Junípero Serra, the two friars followed a harvest of souls, a rewarding apostolate in so many ways.

MARY SCHOLASTICA LOGSDON, D.C. (1814–1902)

In the words of Henry T. Hazard, Mayor of Los Angeles, Sister Mary Scholastica Logsdon (1814–1902) was a "kindhearted, generous, true and devoted" member of the Daughters of Charity. The following address was given by the City Treasurer, William H. Workman, at Caledonia Hall on October 7, 1902, just a month after the eighty–eight year old nun passed to her eternal reward.

> The life of Sister Scholastica was a retired one; but her days and and nights were filled with a noble devotion to the cause of humanity. Her name did not appear in public periodicals, her deeds were unrecorded, she cared not for worldly fame, but the good work she accomplished so quietly and unostentatiously, is manifest today in the lives of countless women of Southern California, and radiating from their lives to the lives of their children and their children's children. It is but just and meet that some one that knew her should speak of her now that she has gone from our midst, for the lives of noble men and women have a mighty influence on the lives of all. In our age of selfishness, it is refreshing to dwell on the life of one who labored always for others; who, without material recompense, or even a desire for such remuneration, gave freely and lovingly of her best efforts for the cause of the orphan and the helpless, and for the education of the young.

Sr. Scholastica was born in Maryland in March of 1814. In her girlhood she was associated with the family of our late honored pioneer, J. De Barth Shorb. In August of 1839, she became a member of the well–known Order of Sisters of Charity, that, in every part of the civilized and uncivilized world carry on the work of devotedness in behalf of the helpless—this being the peculiar characteristic of their Company.

Nobly did Sr. Scholastica exemplify in her life the true spirit of her Order. She labored first in Mississippi, was called thence to important offices of trust in the Motherhouse of the Sisters of Charity at Emmitsburg, Maryland, and in 1855 was named leader of a band of six Sisters appointed to exercise their gentle ministry in the far distant and newly–inhabited region of California.

It required a brave and faithful spirit to undertake this work, and Sr. Scholastica and her associates were well chosen. Every pioneer knows how far away California seemed in those days when no railway stretched its connecting band of steel across the American continent; when vague and strange reports were circulated regarding the primitive life of the Far West; when prairie schooners led travelers through the terrors of Indian attack. Across the plains, or a long voyage by steamer, via the Isthmus of Panama was a tiresome journey. It required indeed a staunch heart to venture into this unknown world; and above all, it demanded a courage inspired by such faith as Sr. Scholastica possessed for women to undertake this journey that they might minister to those in need. All honor to the noble pioneers of California!

Sister Scholastica and her companions reached San Francisco on the steamer *Sea Bird*, in January, 1856. By the sixth of the same month they had arrived at San Pedro. General Banning's celebrated stage conveyed them to Los Angeles, the scene of their future lifework.

Ignacio del Valle, with characteristic hospitality, gave the Sisters shelter until a home was secured to them at the corner of Alameda and Macy Streets. Here the Sisters lived for many years; the property, on which was a small frame house, was purchased from Mr. B.D. Wilson. The house, familiar to all, had been brought in sections from New York, via Cape Horn. The sections were marked to facilitate reconstruction.

Ere long the Sisters gathered around them the orphans, who have always been their special care. In connection with their Asylum they had a school for children and young ladies, and in this school many of the prominent and worthy mothers and grandmothers of Southern California received their education. The people of Los Angeles regardless of religious differences, gladly welcomed the Sisters and gave them generous assistance. To need their help was the only ticket of admission to their sympathy; color, race, or creed, did not enter into the consideration.

In the year 1889, on the fiftieth anniversary of the life of Sr. Scholastica as a Sister of Charity, her friends gave her a substantial proof of their love and esteem in the gift of a purse of $3,000 which the good Sister at once devoted to the building fund for the erection of a new and more commodious home for the rapidly increasing number of orphans. On February 9, 1890, the corner–stone of the magnificent Orphanage now over-looking the city was laid.

When the home was completed, the Sisters took possession of it and here, surrounded by a family of nearly four hundred orphans, Sr. Scholastica whose life was all gentleness and peace, even in the midst of trials, folded her willing hands in the last long sleep.

JOHN BERNARD MCGLOIN, S.J. (1912–1988)

A. CALIFORNIA RESEARCHER

If it is true, as New York's Archbishop John J. Hughes

once observed, that "he who records the good deeds of others was himself a doer of good deeds," then Father John Bernard McGloin surely qualifies as a man of singular virtue.

The long–time Professor of History at the University of San Francisco was himself a native of "the city." Born to Daniel Joseph and Mary Loreta (Kelly) McGloin, on March 8, 1912, John received his earliest education in the local public schools. He later attended Saint Ignatius High School and Saint Louis University.

He entered the Society of Jesus on August 2, 1929 and, after the usual theological training, was ordained to the priesthood by Archbishop John J. Mitty on June 7, 1941. Most of his subsequent professorial duties were associated with the University of San Francisco.

Long interested in California's ecclesial history, Father McGloin wrote numerous scholarly and popular articles for various journals, including the *British Columbia Historical Quarterly, California Historical Society Quarterly, American Ecclesiastical Review, Southern California Quarterly, Utah Historical Quarterly, Nevada Historical Society Quarterly, Pacific Historian, Historical Bulletin* and *America*.

McGloin's historical work can be divided into four major areas; the first describes the state of the Church in California between 1846 and 1850, the second is concerned with the arrival and early efforts of the Jesuits in Alta California, the third treats of Bishop Joseph Sadoc Alemany and the subsequent growth and development of Catholicism and the final covers the secular and religious history of San Francisco.

Though much of Father McGloin's works have dealt

with Alemany, the Spanish–born prelate who became San Francisco's first archbishop, he has written about other outstanding religious personages too, such as Michael Accolti, Charles Etienne Brasseur de Bourbourg, Thomas Cain, Anthony Langlois, Patrick Manogue, John Nobili, Gregory Phelan and Joseph Phelan.

McGloin's first major publication was *Eloquent Indian. The Life of James Bouchard, California Jesuit.* Published by the Stanford University Press in 1950, that 380 page study was described by Bishop Thomas K. Gorman as "a really worthwhile piece of research in a little explored field."

Next came his biographical study on *California's First Archbishop. The Life of Joseph Sadoc Alemany, O.P.*, a volume in the "Makers of American Catholicism" series. It told the story of a beloved Dominican—whose human and spiritual talents were spent in the service of the church in California. The Alemany treatise was subsequently translated into Spanish by Alberto Collell Costa and appeared in 1974 as *El Primer Arzobispo de California.*

Jesuits by the Golden Gate. The Society Of Jesus in San Francisco was the "first attempt at a complete telling of the 120 years of Jesuit history" in the area. It was intended as a complement to Joseph W. Riordan's monumental opus which was completed in 1905.

McGloin's most outstanding book, *San Francisco. The Story of a City*, was published by Presidio Press at San Rafael, in 1979. That 443 page tome was described by one reviewer as a "most useful as well as enjoyable" tool "in helping to provide a clearer perspective" of San Francisco's history.

For more than forty years, Father John B. McGloin's historical endeavors served to confirm the ageless dictum that "he who cannot see very far backward cannot see very far forward."

During the summers, Father McGloin would select a small California town, along the Gold Dust trails, and volunteer to serve there while the local parish priest took a vacation. Then he would invite his students to join him for what surely must have been the highest form of educational seminar.

McGloin was a stickler for accuracy. He delighted in debunking myths and deflating errors. He once observed that "there is more romance in the truth of history than in a thousand untrue legends."

Though never unduly impressed by the many accolades he received over the years, McGloin was fond of recalling how once, after delivering an address in the presence of Archbishop John J. Mitty, the grumpy old prelate came about as close as he ever did to a compliment by noting: "Your version will do until something better comes along!"

Forced into retirement by illness in 1981, Father McGloin retained his interest in things historical. Just several weeks before his death, he wrote to say that "the Church will have a better future when it learns to pay closer attention to the past."

McGloin was an early campaigner for the cause of Fray Junípero Serra. He frequently visited San Carlos Borromeo Mission and there offered Mass at the friar's tomb. Unfortunately he died prior to Serra's beatification.

JOHN BERNARD MCGLOIN, S.J. (1912–1988)

B. HISTORIAN'S LEGACY

In mid–1986, Father John Bernard McGloin, Professor Emeritus of History at the University of San Francisco, authorized a limited reprinting of twenty– five articles, homilies and newspaper essays he had written between 1948 and 1978. Entitled "Some Events and Persons in the San Francisco and California Catholic Story," the 139 page booklet, limited to a press run of fifty copies, will surely become a rarity among Western Americana enthusiasts.

Subject matter for the essays varies widely, beginning with a history of the 5,284 pound "St. Ignatius Church Bell" (largest steel bell ever produced in England) to "Benediction at the Bellarmino" (which houses the largest Jesuit community in the world.)

"Fortress for Christ" tells about the fifth Saint Ignatius Church in San Francisco, a magnificent edifice whose erection in 1910–1914 elicited the unfulfilled prophecy that it "would hold back the work of education and the progress of the then St. Ignatius College" (later the University of San Francisco). "Where California's Catholicism Began" is a charming essay about *Nuestra Señora de Loreto Mission* in peninsular California, referred to by historians as the "*Cabeza y Madre de las Misiones de Baia y Alta California.*" Written after a journey to the area in 1960 the survey traces the historic foundation from October, 1697. The centennial homily delivered for the Sisters of Notre Dame at Mission Dolores, in 1966, traces the saga of religious commitment along *El Camino Real* from the time of Joseph Sadoc Alemany to that of Joseph T. McGucken.

Personalities dominate this collection of essays. An example would be Peter Malloy, the first Jesuit novice in California, who entered the small novitiate attached to Santa Clara College in 1857. Unfortunately, the Irish–born Malloy succumbed only a few months later at San Francisco.

A particularly interesting chapter of San Francisco's history is explored in the essay "Why St. Ignatius Church is not a Parish." Therein McGloin carefully traces the relationship between the archbishops of San Francisco and the Society of Jesus and how the parochial autonomy that existed between 1855 and 1863 was terminated. The treatise on "Our Lady's Chapel,

Presidio of San Francisco" is as interesting as it is informative. The restored chapel, dedicated on September 14, 1952, can still be seen, not far from the former parade ground and general headquarters for the military presence in the Bay Area.

In his "Requiem for a Cathedral," the Jesuit historian recalls the history of Saint Mary's Cathedral and its destruction by fire on September 7, 1962. Of special interest is the account of the most impressive of all the processions that took place in the cathedral, the one in which the archbishop removed the Blessed Sacrament from the smoldering edifice. Probably the most historic event recorded in these pages is the return to San Francisco of Archbishop Joseph Sadoc Alemany's *restos* in February of 1965. Father McGloin preached an inspiring homily on that occasion at old Saint Mary's in China Town.

The 100th anniversary of the proto Mass in Sacramento is described in an address given in April of 1950. McGloin deftly sketches the setting in which Father Peter Augustine Anderson first offered the Eucharistic Liturgy in the area named for the Blessed Sacrament. The only negative factor about this booklet is the paucity of copies. Perhaps one day this superb collection of historical occurrences will be republished in book form. Surely it deserves that status.

MARY PIUS MARBAISE, O.P. (1883–1974)

Eugenie Marbaise was "a woman who walked in faith and in the clear uncluttered light of truth." Born in Hoboken, New Jersey, to Otto and Eugenie (Deveaux) Marbaise, on May 6, 1883, she grew to adulthood in an atmosphere of culture and refinement. Taken to Europe early in life, the young lady lived for many years in and around Cologne. There she attended Saint Leonard's School and, later, the Teachers' Training College. Upon completion of her studies, Eugenie received a certificate allowing her to teach at any school in the Empire.

But the young Miss Marbaise had other ideas. In 1903, she entered the Dominican Novitiate, at Moresent–Neutre, where she had been drawn by the Order's strong liturgical orientation. Owing to her facility with English, the new novice was almost immediately sent to San Francisco. There she was assigned to teach at both Saint Anthony's and Saint Boniface Schools.

In June, 1904, Miss Marbaise received the Dominican habit. In deference to her maternal relationship with the family of Pope Pius VI she asked for and was given the religious name of Pius. In the years that followed, Sister Mary Pius taught in various schools in the Bay Area. When she was named Mistress of Novices, in 1912, she reorganized the whole training program to allow time for studying Liturgy, Church history and the spiritual life.

During the years 1922–1936 Sister Mary Pius worked in revolution–ridden Mexico. Her handwritten memoirs of those dark days of religious persecution reads like an adventure story. For long periods her very life was seriously in jeopardy. Ironically, the President of Mexico during those years, Plutarco Calles, later brought his two sons to Saint Catherine's, where Sister Mary Pius was Prioress. Nothing was said, but the tradition of Mexican youngsters studying at Anaheim began a practice that still perdures.

Following her forced departure from Mexico, Sister Mary Pius served as superior or prioress at Dominican houses in Anaheim, San Francisco and Mission San Jose. In all her duties, she was openly recognized as "a woman of integrity whose life was shaped by the totality of her dedication."

At the General Chapter, in 1949, Sister Mary Pius was chosen fourth Prioress General for the Dominican Sisters of Mission San Jose. The twelve years of her tenure was a time of rapid expansion, characterized by large numbers of vocations and wholly new educational ventures. It was also during that post–war era that a beautiful new chapel and commodious infirmary were erected at the motherhouse.

Mother Mary Pius died on January 31, 1974. At the time of her demise, she was aptly eulogized as a religious of staunch principles "whose intense prayer life fed the fires of charity that burned so steadily in her great soul."

LEO (FRANCIS MEEHAN), F. S. C. (1881–1966)

In the 1920s, Brother Leo (Dr. Francis Meehan), the distinguished Professor of Literature at Saint Mary's College, Oakland and Moraga, was acknowledged to be "the shining star among the new constellation of Christian Brother intellectuals." Born on October 8, 1881, the son of James Meehan and Mary Ellen Gallagher, Leo graduated from Saint Peter's School in San Francisco and, in 1897, entered De La Salle Institute at Martinez. A mostly self–educated man, Brother Leo served as instructor in English at Sacred Heart College between 1903 and 1908.

He then went to Saint Mary's College, where he became a full professor. In the following decade, he was sent to The Catholic University of America and there earned a doctorate in humane letters. During subsequent years, Brother Leo became the most famous Christian Brother in the United States. He lectured to more than two thousand different audiences in the 1920s and 1930s, often in the opera house at San Francisco.

He participated in lecture series which featured such figures as Winston Churchill and Sherman Anderson. It was an exciting time for Brother Leo who also offered courses at the College of the Pacific (Stockton) the University of California (Berkeley) and U.C.L.A. Speaking on education and literary topics Brother Leo was also a regular commentator over the then massive radio network of the National Broadcasting Company.

In 1930, Brother Leo was named Chancellor at Saint Mary's College, a position in which he functioned as college president and academic dean. In that role he determined to enhance the intellectual atmosphere at the college by making Moraga a cultural center for the whole bay area. He launched a rather ambitious extra–curricular program of public academies, faculty lectures, dramatic productions, symphonic recitals, operatic presentations, civic awards and learned publications.

Throughout his academic career, Brother Leo represented the viewpoint that exalted humanistic and literary studies at the expense of vocational and technical education. Within a relatively short time, Saint Mary's became a center for liturgical music in the western United States. And during that time, Brother Leo was also instrumental in launching *The Moraga Quarterly*, a journal that became a leading literary publication. Though he claimed that his resignation, in 1932, was prompted by a desire to devote more time for outside academic interests, it was widely known that Brother Leo was opposed to Saint Mary's becoming a "football factory."

Critics conclude that Brother Leo's publications were neither profound nor distinguished, but he had few peers in the country. Often writing under such pen names as "Will Scarlet" and "Leslie Stanton," he authored hundreds of articles, four plays, a few novels and several literary critiques. His college textbook on English literature was used throughout the nation.

In August of 1941, after forty–two years in religious life, Brother Leo received a dispensation from his vows and returned to lay life. Writing his famous *Living Upstairs* a year later, Leo said that "I feel that I have done my work, such as it is, it is now time to retire." He married DeNaze Brown, a convert to the Catholic Church, in 1946 and lived out the final years of his life at Casa Della Madonna in Southern California's Lake Sherwood area.

When he died, in 1966 at the age of eighty–five, he was still referred to, even in obituaries, as "Brother Leo."

ALOYSIUS MEYER, C.M. (1839–1898)

Father Aloysius Meyer was a true man, a gentleman, a man of profound erudition, a good educator, and a true priest of Christ. He was a man of strength, determination and indomitable energy. Aloysius Joseph Meyer was born on December 19, 1839, at Baden, Germany. He came to the United States in 1856, and lived for a while with relatives near Quincy, Illinois.

Aloysius Meyer, C.M.

Though he first considered entering the Society of Jesus, the young clerical aspirant was led, it would seem by the special Providence of God, to the house of the Lazarists or Vincentian Fathers. After his ordination in 1863, by Archbishop Peter Richard Kenrick, Father Meyer began his priestly career by filling teaching assignments at Perryville and Cape Girardeau. He later performed parochial duties in Saint Louis and Baltimore.

In 1877, Father Meyer was named President of Saint John the Baptist College in Brooklyn, as well as pastor of the adjoining parish. "Here, as elsewhere, he toiled unceasingly and such was his success, not only as a pastor of souls, but as an able educator, that he soon won the love and esteem of all who had the pleasure of his acquaintance." With the resignation of Claude Mary Dubuis, Bishop of Galveston, in 1881, Archbishop James Gibbons of Baltimore proposed Father Meyer for the vacant jurisdiction. Upon learning that papal bulls had been issued, Father Meyer was successful in asking Pope Pius IX to withdraw the nomination.

In 1884, Meyer came to Los Angeles and the presidency of Saint Vincent's College. Under his wise and prudent management the college entered upon an era of unprecedented prosperity and began to take on new life and vigor. Two years after his arrival in Southern California, Father Meyer moved the college to new and larger quarters at the corner of Grand and Washington. During those years, the indefatigable Vincentian also served as founding pastor of Saint Vincent's Church.

Throughout the southland, Father Meyer was known as "a man of firm character and strong personality, of fine physique and commanding presence, modest and unassuming though of noble and dignified bearing." In 1893, his superiors named Father Meyer rector of the newly organized Kenrick Theological Seminary in Saint Louis. The following year he returned to Los Angeles and began with even greater energy and zeal than before to forward the interests and the temporal as well as the spiritual welfare of both college and parish.

That Father Meyer was highly regarded by his parishioners is evidenced by the formal "resolution of affection" adopted at the time of his death on February 12, 1898:

> He was not alone the beloved pastor, the finished educator, the man of affairs, whose consummate genius stands portrayed on every page of the history of this parish, he was a lover of mankind, and fully typified the words: "He loved his fellows and their love was sweet." No line of creed did he know in his friendship and among those who mourn today are many attached to other forms of religion. He was an example in his every transaction, whether as a priest, teacher, man of business or citizen. His impress was always as plain and simple as it was touching and well formed. To live such a life was to elevate mankind, to leave such a chapter was to add materially to the great book wherein man's noblest deeds are told.

CHARLES PIUS MONTGOMERY, O.P. (1806–1860)

The long vacancy in the See of Both Californias was a cause of great concern to the members of the American hierarchy when they met at Baltimore for their Seventh Provincial Council, in May of 1849. Three names were recommended to the Holy See with a plea for immediate action to remedy the sad plight of the orphaned California diocese.

On November 20, 1849, Pope Pius IX nominated the former Provincial of the American Dominicans, Father Charles Pius Montgomery, to the See of Monterey. Having received no prior notice of his selection, Montgomery refused the mitre on the grounds that " . . . my health is such . . . as to render me totally unable to discharge the duties attached to it."

The humble and retiring pastor of Saint Thomas Church in Zanesville, Ohio then faded from the California scene as quickly as he had appeared on it. He remained at Zanesville until his death, on April 8, 1860.

The appointment itself, issued at Naples by Pope Pius IX, on November 20, 1849, is here reproduced in its entirety:

> The duty of apostolic ministry divinely entrusted to us demands that we should look to the salvation of souls with every care and zeal, and take thought for the provision and control of churches that are vacant. Consequently since our venerable Brother, the Archbishop of Baltimore, and other Bishops, his suffragans, at the Sacred Council recently held, concerned for the welfare of California missions, are of the opinion that there should be an immediate election of a new Bishop to the vacant See of Monterey; and since further, beloved son, they have earnestly recommended you to Us for this purpose, We, with the advice of Our venerable brothers, the cardinals of the Holy Roman Church in charge of the Congregation for Promoting the Faith, have decided that We should accede to their wishes with all possible cordiality.

> Wherefore beloved, son, wishing especially to honor you, distinguished as you are for the moral uprightness, prudence, religious sentiment, piety and proven learning, as well as for your foresight in spiritual matters and your caution in temporal; and for this purpose solely absolving you from any censures of excommunication, suspension or interdict, in whatever way or for whatever cause imposed, if you have happened to incur any, and regarding you as in future absolved; by Our Apostolic authority and by means of this letter we choose to announce and constitute you bishop and pastor for the vacant episcopal Church of Monterey. And we make provision of this church by means of your person, acceptable to Us because of the qualities of your merits; and we fully entrust to you the care, control and administration of the same church in spirituals and temporals.

> We trust in Him Who gives and bestows gifts, that He will direct to advantage and success the measures you take under the Lord's guidance by the exercise of your diligence and caution in the said church of Monterey and that the Catholic religion will gain increase in the spiritual and temporal domains. Accordingly, embracing with prompt devotion of spirit the yoke of the Lord upon your shoulders, the aforementioned care and administration do you so consider.

JOSEPH M. NERI, S . J. (1836–1919)

Students of California's Catholic Heritage are fond of recalling that it was Father Joseph M. Neri (1836–1919), who first introduced electricity to the State of California. As far back as 1869, the Jesuit professor at Saint Ignatius College in San Francisco was quietly examining the newly discovered force and its possible uses.

Neri perfected an electrical system for lighting in one of the college's lecture halls using carbon electric lights. In 1874, he installed a massive searchlight in the tower with rays so powerful they could be seen in many nearby cities. Three of Neri's arc lights were strung across Market Street to illuminate the opening parade of San Francisco's Centennial Exposition in 1876—the first time such a system had ever been used in the Bay City or anywhere else in the nation. Lectures given by the renowned Jesuit at the Exposition attracted crowds so large that many had to be turned away from the Mechanic's Pavilion.

In May of 1873, Neri instituted the Loyola Scientific Academy whose object was "the cultivation and promotion of the study of the natural sciences." Neri thought the spread of new discoveries was an excellent form of missionary work, since it removed prejudices from the minds of non–Catholics and strengthened the Faith of the ill–instructed. Starting out with large batteries and later converting over to magnetic machines, Father Neri was a pioneer in mastering the use of dynamos. The first magnetic electric machine in California was a product of this ingenious son of Saint Ignatius.

Neri was dedicated to the principle that there was no true advance of science that the Church could not bless and foster, since there could be no conflict between true science and true religion. Officially, Neri was professor of physics, analytical chemistry, geology and mineralogy, but his restless mind wandered into other fields and merited numerous citations and commendations from scientific academies and learned societies all over the world. His relentless schedule eventually resulted in partial blindness casting a shadow of darkness over the last sixteen years of his life. This affliction, however, only served to increase his interest about "the wonderful works of God," and his final years were anything but inactive.

Thought to be the first Jesuit ordained in California, Father Neri lived until November 17, 1919, when he slept quietly away at Santa Clara where he had labored since 1877.

> Father Neri was an enthusiast in his love for the natural sciences and though always in delicate health, and able to take such a small quantity of food that even living seemed marvelous, he was nevertheless able to work long and laboriously day after day, ever keeping pace with the newest discoveries of the hour and seeming to tire only when exhausted nature could bear no more.

JEREMIAH J. O'KEEFE, O.F.M. (1843–1915)

Father Jeremiah Joseph O'Keefe (1843–1915), an eminently social being with a smile and sense of humor, is remembered as one of the most colorful and best–known characters among the California Franciscans between the Old Mission days and modern times. The Irish–born lad was brought to the United States by his parents, Dennis O'Keefe and Margaret Smith, in

Jeremiah O'Keefe, O.F.M.

1852. Eight years later, after a short stint as a clerical student for the Archdiocese of San Francisco, he joined the Franciscans at Santa Barbara. He was ordained to the priesthood by Bishop Thaddeus Amat, on September 19, 1868.

As his initial assignment, Father O'Keefe was appointed to the faculty of the college operated by the friars in the Channel City. There he taught Latin, Greek and Mathematics prior to becoming president of the institution in 1870. Throughout his association with the college, Father O'Keefe was regarded as a kind and fatherly priest by the students, some of whose memoirs are still available. Upon completion of his term, Father O'Keefe became vicar of the old mission, a post which he held with distinction until 1885.

It was during his tenure at Santa Barbara, which lasted until 1891, that Father O'Keefe wrote the first of a long series of handbooks, chock full of scientific data and useful information on the history of the famed edifice. The forty–page "handbook of authentic information" was based on the registers, reports and other documents in the mission archives. It was published, in 1886, by Santa Barbara's Independent Job Printing House.

In 1891, Father O'Keefe was sent to San Luis Rey

where he acted as architect and builder in repairing the church, erecting a two–story monastery and restoring the beautiful arches on the south side of the mission.

"The best known Franciscan in the United States," so described by one newspaper, celebrated his golden jubilee in 1909. On that occasion, the Santa Barbara *Daily–News* portrayed Father O'Keefe, "the kindly man some 20–odd years ago, when he was in charge of that venerable old pile that the world knows as the 'Old Mission Santa Barbara' the object which, alone, has probably attracted a million visitors to pass more or less time in this city. We recall this man and his very few brothers who were the custodians of that old religious institution; how few the brothers were; how poor they were and the good works they were doing continually–even to this day–in the walks among the poor, particularly among the poorer classes of Californians and Mexicans."

In his final years Father O'Keefe worked at the diocesan orphanage in Watsonville. When death finally claimed the "widely loved, and faithful missionary, whose deeds are inseparably interwoven with California's history," the last link with the Golden State's pioneering Franciscans was forever severed.

MARTIN J. O'MALLEY, C.M. (1889–1943) AND NICHOLAS CONNEALLY (1879–1949)

For over fifty years, the two films *Going My Way* and its sequel, *The Bells of Saint Mary's*, have been classics for moviegoers of all faiths. Much of what people know or think about the Catholic Church derives from those two productions.

In *Going My Way*, Father O'Malley (Bing Crosby) sells a song to pay off the parochial mortgage—but then the church burns down so the priest and his pastor, Father Fitzgibbons (Barry Fitzgerald), set out to rebuild it. The film's director, Leo McCarey, based the role of the two stars, Bing Crosby and Barry Fitzgerald, on two prominent priests that long served in the Archdiocese of Los Angeles, both of whom deserve a posthumous Academy Award.

In an interview, McCarey said that the idea for the story came to him in a conversation with an elderly Irish priest with "a brogue as thick as a peat bog" who had erected a church near McCarey's home in Santa Monica. The cleric had approached McCarey for a contribution for a new loudspeaker. During the course of their conversation, McCarey asked the priest how he got along with his younger counterparts. "They're nice fellows," he replied, "who are figuring out how they can change things around here when I die."

The priest was Father Nicholas Conneally (1879–1949) who served as pastor at Santa Monica

parish from 1923 to his demise a quarter century later. Nicholas, one of three Conneallys who became priests, immigrated to the United States and completed his clerical studies at Saint Mary's Seminary in Baltimore.

Ordained July 11, 1907, Conneally subsequently became pastor of several Southern California parishes, where he gained a reputation for building projects. At Saint Monica's he built a beautiful church, an elementary school and a high school. Father Nick was often abrupt in his dealing with people, but always gracious and humorous. He loved children and he was often seen on the school playground, where he knew all the kids and parents by their first names.

The role immortalized by Bing Crosby was based on Father Martin J. O'Malley (1889–1943), the Lazarist pastor of Saint Vincent's parish in downtown Los Angeles. O'Malley had earlier taught at Kenrick Seminary where, according to the St. Louis *Register*, he gained renown as a pulpit orator, being ranked by many as "the foremost speaker in the country."

McCarey used to attend Mass at Saint Vincent's church and there he became enamored with O'Malley's sermons. It was the fine choir at the "Doheny church" that gave McCarey the idea for introducing music into the plot of his films.

Going My Way garnered no fewer than seven Academy Awards, including best picture, best director (Leo McCarey), best actor (Bing Crosby) and best supporting actor (Barry Fitzgerald). It was also cited for being the best original screen story, the best screenplay and the best composition for the song *Swinging on a Star*.

Though sequels are rarely as memorable as their models, *The Bells of St. Mary's* was equally as charming as its predecessor. In that film, McCarey based the role of Sister Benedict upon his own aunt, a role played to perfection by Ingrid Bergman.

There are critics who complain that Leo McCarey's two classic films delineated priests as unrealistic and out of touch with contemporary society. Maybe yes, probably no. Leo portrayed priests as he knew them, not as icons out of a book about saints. What McCarey depicted came from his heart and that's what movies were all about in those days.

FRANCOIS GERMAINE PETITHOMME, SS. CC. (1796–1860)

The late Archbishop John J. Cantwell was fond of reminding clergymen at their annual retreat, that "there is nothing quite so dead as a dead priest, except perhaps a dead bishop." There is abundant evidence to sustain Cantwell's observation. A case at hand is Father Amable Petithomme, a priest who did much spiritual good for people on three continents and who rates only scant mention in the chronicles.

Francois Germaine Petithomme was born in the municipality of Pre–en–ail on December 20, 1796, or to use the terminology of the period, on the 26th of Mercedor in the Fourth Year of the French Republic. Those were chaotic times in France which was then under the rule of the infamous Robespierre and the Directory.

When the youthful Petithomme entered religious life as a member of the Congregation of the Sacred Hearts, on September 16, 1826, he took the name "Amable" and that is how he is remembered. Since no record of Petithomme's ordination has yet been unearthed, the presumption is that he was already a priest by the time he became affiliated with the "Picpus" Fathers.

In July of 1833, Petithomme was sent to the United States, where he received an assignment in the Diocese of Boston. His apostolate was that of spreading the Gospel message among the Indians of northern Maine and, later, in Nova Scotia.

In 1840, Father Petithomme was appointed to Latin America. He worked for a while in Valparaiso, Chile and later in Santiago. From there he was transferred to the Spanish Marquesas Islands in the South Pacific. Father Petithomme established a mission on the Island of Tahuata. He labored among the local inhabitants, hoping to baptize the aged king. Though his efforts were not immediately successful, the area subsequently became predominantly Catholic. He had planted the seed well.

Petithomme returned to Chile, where he taught at the newly–established College of Coplapo. Subsequently, the priest–missionary assumed the duties of pastor of the church in Chanaral.

In 1851, "Padre Amable" was sent to California, where he was entrusted with inaugurating a school in Los Angeles. He arrived at San Pedro in May and shortly thereafter was busy looking after Catholic youngsters in *El Pueblo de Nuestra Señora de los Angeles*. The records about Petithomme's activities in the southland are sketchy at best. In November, he signed the register book at Santa Ines Mission where he was functioning as Vice Rector of the Diocesan seminary under the direction of Father Eugene O'Connell.

Petithomme affixed his signature to the Baptismal book at San Fernando Mission on September 3, 1852. Very likely he was then functioning as a "circuit priest" among the *ranchos* and *pueblos* scattered around the area. It was about that time that Father Petithomme first encountered the community of Agua Mansa in the San Bernardino Valley. The local inhabitants wanted him to remain as their resident priest and, while there, he erected *la Capilla de San Salvador*.

It was while at Agua Mansa that the Picpus priest was stricken with a partial paralysis. For health reasons, in the fall of 1855, Petithomme sailed for the Sandwich Isles and there spent the final years of his life.

On April 23, 1860, "Padre Amable," as he is remembered in the annals, died in Valparaiso after a long illness. He was buried in the cemetery of the Fathers of the Sacred Hearts in Chile. And that's all that is recorded about this good man's earthly accomplishments.

PATRICK PEYTON, C. S.C. (1909–1992)

For almost half a century, Hollywood tour buses have paused in front of 7201 Sunset Boulevard, the world headquarters for Father Patrick Peyton's "Family Theatre of the Air." It is a recognized "monument" to prayer.

Pat Peyton (1909–1992) was the Holy Cross priest who coined the household truism that "the family that prays together stays together." And how fitting it was that he first uttered those words in the media capital of the world. The Irish–born cleric, one of the nine children from a rural family in County Mayo, began his Family Rosary program at Vincentian Institute High School in Albany, New York, shortly after ordination on June 15, 1941. His goal was to have ten million American people reciting the rosary every day.

Early in life, Peyton had promised the Blessed Mother that if he were cured of tuberculosis, he would spend the rest of his ministry promoting devotion to the Mother of the Savior. She did and so did he. Long before television, Peyton spread Marian devotion throughout the world by radio and the movies.

His weekly series of radio programs was aired without interruption for twenty–two years. For three consecutive seasons, while critics shook their heads in utter amazement, it was proclaimed "America's Favorite Dramatic Radio Program." For his radio and television presentations, as well as his international tours and crusades, Peyton enlisted a formidable legion of famous personalities, including Bing Crosby, Rosalind Russell, Ronald Reagan, Loretta Young, Grace Kelly and Mother Teresa.

Peyton's campaigns rapidly exceeded even his own ambitious projections. He conducted rosary crusades in over fifty countries, including the former Soviet Empire where the "Rosaries for Russia" program was personally endorsed by Boris Yeltsin.

While Father Peyton and the rosary slipped from the front pages after Vatican Council II, they never lost their effectiveness. Peyton often recalled that Our Lady promised at Fatima that if enough people recited the rosary, Russia would return to the faith. "After all," he said, "the rosary always bounces back in times of great crisis."

J. Peter Grace credited Father Peyton with invoking "miracles," including the overthrow of Brazil's leftist President Joao Goulart in 1964. Brazil was "going communist when a Family Rosary Crusade enlisted dozens of movie teams and outdoor movie screens to reach millions of people in the South American nation! Family Rosary billboards proclaimed try prayer to a nation with low morale. Women marched in the streets, praying. Goulart scorned their 'silly beads,' but eighteen hours later, his army rebelled and seized control of the government. Women with their rosaries brought down Goulart."

In a letter to Father Peyton, Pope John Paul II said that "from the beginning, you understood the dynamic role of the mass media of social communications. You motivated the artists of stage, screen, radio and television to extend the crusade's messages to people of all faiths and creeds. Many of these artists gave their name and ability to glorify the Rosary, dramatize its mysteries, pray its prayers, sing its songs, and present it to the world in all its beauty, as the joyful, sorrowful, and glorious history of our salvation through the Son of God, who became incarnate through the Virgin Mary."

Few other priests in all of history have touched so many millions of people with the simple message of prayer. Death will not still either the voice or the work of the handsome Irish priest who made a promise to Mary and kept it.

BLESSED MIGUEL PRO JUAREZ, S.J. (1891–1927)

One of the four people beatified along with Fray Junípero Serra, on September 25th, 1988, was the famed Jesuit martyr, Father Miguel Pro Juarez, who was executed by the Mexican government during the celebrated "Cristero" rebellion.

Most of the priests who lost their lives during the 1927–1929 uprising died in obscurity, "speechless witnesses of the refusal of the Mexican priesthood to obey a governmental order to abandon their sacerdotal duties." The fact that Father Pro escaped that anonymity and became an internationally known figure can be attributed to the pictures that were taken of his execution. Copies of those photographs were distributed to news agencies who spread them all over the world. It was a public relations scheme that backfired and brought outcries from major leaders everywhere.

Miguel Agustin Pro Juarez (1891–1927) was born at Guadalajara, Mexico, of a socially prominent family. He entered the Society of Jesus novitiate in El Llano during August of 1911. Because of the religious unrest in Mexico, he was sent to Los Gatos, California, where he lived, studied and prayed in 1914 and 1915. After further stud-

ies in Spain and Nicaragua, the youthful Pro went to Belgium, where he was ordained in 1925. When he returned to Mexico, the following year, public worship had been suspended under the persecution of Plutarco Elias Calles.

The Pro family were members of a militantly Catholic opposition group, the National League for the Defense of Religious Liberty. There is no evidence anywhere indicating that Father Pro engaged in anything but peaceful efforts to bring about a cessation of hostilities.

During those frantic months, Father Pro busily spent himself in his "bicycle ministry," bringing Holy Communion to thousands upon thousands of the faithful. "*Viva Cristo Rey*" became his motto as he moved among the eucharistic stations established by the Church.

Pro and his brother were seized by police during the early winter of 1927 and falsely charged of being involved in a car–bombing attempt on the life of former President Alvaro Obregon. Pro and his brother, Humberto, along with two others, were killed by a firing squad on November 23, 1927. The actual account of his death is told by Father Wilfred Parsons, S.J.

> Father Pro was the first to die. When he went to the wall in the prison yard, he knelt a moment, and held his eyes on the Crucifix he had received when he took his vows of religion. He pardoned his enemies, and refused to be blindfolded. He held his arms out in the form of a cross, and at the very moment of the command to fire he cried: "*Viva Cristo Rey*, Long Live Christ the King!" and fell riddled with bullets. A sergeant gave him the *coup de grace* in the temple.

The cause for Father Pro's beatification was begun in January of 1952. When the Vatican announced plans for the actual ceremony, November 10, 1986, it was noted in the official announcement that the Mexican priest was "killed in hatred of the faith."

The grave of Plutarco Elias Calles in Mexico City is marked by a large and cold slab of stone. There are never any flowers beside it and hardly ever does anyone stop to look or say a prayer. But not far away, the small and humble grave of Miguel Pro Juarez is always surrounded by colorful floral decorations. People approach it day and night on their knees. Dictators come and dictators go, but Blessed Miguel Pro, the Jesuit martyr, will never be forgotten by the grateful people of Mexico.

BLAS RAHO, C.M. (1806–1862)

One of the most beloved priests ever to serve in the Diocese of Monterey–Los Angeles, was the Reverend Blas Raho (1806–1862), a pious and zealous, if sometimes implusive and irrascible Vincentian who accompanied Bishop Thaddeus Amat to California, in 1835.

Blas Raho, C.M.

Born in Naples, Raho came to the United States, in 1835, and occupied a host of missionary assignments in Illinois, Missouri, Mississippi and Louisiana. He served as pastor at La Fourche, Louisiana, and succeeded Thaddeus Amat as rector of the Saint Louis diocesan seminary, in 1844. During that period, Father Raho supervised the erection of the new Saint Vincent de Paul Church, which was dedicated on July 8, 1844. Possessed of "so lively a imagination" that his provincial was called upon to remove him from at least two administrative positions, Father Raho's character is attested by proposals made, in 1843, that he be named to bishoprics in Chicago and Milwaukee.

During Raho's earliest years in California, he was superior of the "*petit*" seminary attached to Bishop Amat's residence in Santa Barbara. The "genial, broad–minded" Italian also served briefly as pastor of the Channel City's Church of Our Lady of Sorrows. On August 10, 1856, Raho reopened, in a rented adobe building, the school formerly operated by the Picpus Fathers in Los Angeles, as Saint Vincent's College. The earlier institution had benefited by a code passed on July 9, 1851, whereby the City Council provided a sum of money toward "the support of any educational institution in the city, provided that all the rudiments of the English and Spanish languages" be taught. There are no extant records of the school and no indication as to how

long it survived. The curtailment of public assistance by statewide legislation in 1856, greatly hampered its activities and it is believed that the small school had a very short existence.

It was also in 1856 that Father Raho was named pastor of *Nuestra Señora de los Angeles*. He began at once to redecorate the church. One commentator noted that "the historic edifice, so long unchanged, was practically rebuilt. The front adobe wall, which had become damaged by rains, was taken down and reconstructed of brick; some alterations were made in the tower; and the interesting old tiled roof was replaced—to the intense regret of later and more appreciative generations—with modern, less durable shingles."

In 1858, Bishop Amat appointed Father Raho Vicar General and in that capacity he governed the sprawling Diocese of Monterey during the prelate's lengthy absence in Europe. While serving in various diocesan administrative positions, Father Raho compiled a set of twenty–three regulations and directives which Bishop Amat had published at San Francisco, in 1870, as *Reglas para Las Señoras de la Sociedad del Altar*.

Though the years of his active ministry were relatively short, Father Raho achieved an enviable reputation as an outstanding ecclesial pioneer. Santa Barbara's Charles E. Huse put it well when he recorded that the Vincentian priest was a "very intelligent, liberal, devout, lovable" shepherd of the flock.

WILLIAM H. READY, C.M. (1913–1992)

Father William Ready, C.M., (1913–1992) was a familiar and beloved figure in the Church of Los Angeles for well over a half century. The Archdiocese of Los Angeles, the Congregation of the Mission and the Catholic populace of Southern California are much diminished by his passage to a better life.

Ordained for the Vincentians in 1939, Father Ready was sent to Los Angeles College which was then the preparatory seminary for the archdiocese. He remained on the faculty until long after the institution was moved to Mission Hills under the patronage of Our Lady, Queen of the Angels. His only other appointment during the long years of his ministry were the two stints he was posted at Montebello's Saint Vincent's Seminary and its successor, De Paul Center.

During his earliest years at old L.A.C., Father Bill served as procurator and, in that capacity, he had to provide meals for the boarding students. One day he would cook, another he would do the dishes and yet another scour the local area for reasonably–priced food staples. He did all that while teaching a full course load and supplying for daily Mass at one of the neighboring parishes.

He spent what little time was left overseeing the student bookstore.

For many of his years at L.A.C. and Queen of Angels, Father Ready served as Vice Rector. That he wasn't impressed by that position is evident from his observation that his "chief responsibility centered about walking the rector's cocker spaniel." In later times, Father Bill served as the seminary librarian. Those were the days before accreditation and only meager funds were available for books, and even less for accessioning new additions. Saturdays would invariably find Father Bill at the main branch of the Los Angeles Public Library carefully transcribing index cards. Most people presumed that he worked there and he was the only outsider with a key to the staff bathroom.

When the college seminary gained its autonomy and moved to a separate campus, w. h. r (as he was known far and wide) chose to stay behind where, he rightly observed, "the youngsters need me." Had there been equitable role recognition during his academic career, Father Ready would have been a full professor of English Literature at U.C.L.A.. He had memorized more Shakespeare, read more poetry, produced more plays and parsed more sentences than a dozen classicists.

A careful record keeper, Bill kept abreast of the numerous priests he had taught over the years. He was especially proud of having taught an archbishop and a dozen bishops. He possessed autographed annuals for every class, along with lengthy annotations as to where priests were assigned, when they were made pastor, etc. He never forgot a name and often the whole of his paltry allowance was spent on cards, notes and well wishes. He answered his voluminous correspondence the day each letter arrived.

The final years were physically painful ones. He once confided to a friend that he had "more physical maladies than Job and far less patience." Actually his considerable patience was only outdistanced by his many other virtues. Father Bill loved to talk and unlike others with that tendency, he was never boring. Bill had thousands of stories, hundreds of recollections and dozens of tales. And his conversation never bordered on the uncharitable.

Always the priest and ever the Vincentian, Father Bill Ready was a unique person in many ways. A friend and confidant, he will long live vicariously in the students he taught, the people he evangelized and the persons he influenced.

JEROME S. RICARD, S.J. (1850–1930)

In the words of Archbishop Edward J. Hanna, the Reverend Jerome S. Ricard, S.J., was "a high–minded, noble man, a great citizen of his adopted country, a holy priest, a faithful Jesuit." Jerome Sixtus Ricard was born on January 21, 1850, at Plaissans, Drome, France. In addition to a fine training in the classical studies, the youngster travelled widely with his parents in Africa, Italy and France.

After a year at the Apostolic School in Avignon, Jerome transferred to Turin and in 1872 entered the Jesuit Novitiate at Monaco. The next year he came to the United States where he taught at Santa Clara and Saint Ignatius prior to his ordination at Baltimore in 1886. Ricard returned to Santa Clara in 1891, as Professor of Physics and Higher Mathematics. Some years later he became interested in astronomy and made further studies on the subject at Creighton University.

In 1895 an eight–inch refracting telescope was acquired by Santa Clara and " with this as his one scientific instrument," the Jesuit founded a little observatory on the colorful grounds of California's eighth mission. Father Ricard startled the world by his discovery in 1907, that sunspots influence weather conditions, tidal waves, earthquakes and tornadoes. Though a recognized member of the American Association for the Advancement of Science, Ricard's theory was not well received by his contemporaries.

The undaunted Jesuit, already known as the "Padre of the Rains" for his weather predictions, continued "his research while his opponents had their say." In March of 1925, Ricard was vindicated when Dr. Charles C. Abbott of the Smithsonian Institution revealed that extensive study actually confirmed the relationship between sunspots and climate conditions. Ricard's seasonal weather forecasts were widely circulated and his monthly journal the *Sunspot* was used by farmers, industrialists, movie producers, etc. Several almanacs reproduced Ricard's weather charts annually. Shortly after his golden jubilee in 1921, the Knights of Columbus erected at Santa Clara The Ricard Memorial Observatory as a permanent monument to the famed Jesuit's discoveries. To Father Jerome Sixtus Ricard, the study of the universe was only another insight to the Maker of such beauty. This sentiment he once expressed in a preface to a high–school yearbook:

Astronomy is the noblest of the natural sciences. None so elevates the soul, so satisfies its yearnings, as this which brings us into the ante–chamber of the Creator. In other sciences we touch, we measure, we weigh, we handle, we test in the laboratory their activities and receptivity.

Our sight can hardly claim to reach the heavenly bodies. From our instruments we have but data. What we learn of distances and volumes, of numbers the limits of which are not yet reached, of temperatures and compositions of mutual influences, of orbits and velocity, all is the result of pure intellect. Wonderful it is in its variety; yet but a faint foreshadowing of what is to be revealed when passing from the antechamber we enter into the Creator's presence.

MARY BAPTIST RUSSELL, S.M. (1829–1898)

When Mother Mary Baptist Russell died on August 6, 1898, one newspaper reporter referred to her as the "best–known charitable worker on the Pacific Coast." It was a distinction earned by a lifetime of good works for others.

The cholera epidemic was one outstanding example. When that disaster hit San Francisco, on September 5, 1855, it didn't daunt the young Irish–born nun. Though only twenty–six years old at the time, she had been through it all before in her native land. She quietly instructed her seven Sister companions on how best to care for the stricken. It was a terrible epidemic. Five out of every ten of the afflicted people actually died from the plague. The city fathers were perplexed as how to handle the problem for the local populace was on the verge of panic.

As the scourge gradually spread, Sister Mary Baptist Russell and her companions headed toward the places of greatest need. Much of their care was directed to the Marine State Hospital at Stockton and Vallejo. The filthy buildings there were staffed by people too ignorant to earn a living in any other way, even in a Gold Rush boom town. Their idea of care was often to render the indigent patients senseless.

For six weeks the nuns ministered to the sick and comforted the dying. There was no time for rest. Somehow the nuns restored calm to a city that had been filled with fear. The legislature had directed each county to care for its own indigent sick. Hence the San Francisco Board of Supervisors asked the Sisters of Mercy to organize and operate a local hospital.

The supervisors weren't as generous in their funding as they were in awarding obligations. That didn't slow Mother Mary Baptist Russell whose tenderness for the ill was matched by her tenacity for finding financial support. She sought out lucky gold miners and buttonholed business leaders.

Though the supervisors ignored the hospital bills for two straight years, the nuns managed to keep the hospital operational. Finally, in 1857, Mother Russell ended the management contract. Ten days later, she launched Saint Mary's Hospital and, despite the chronic shortage of funds, that institution became the flagship for the state's medical progress.

Mother Russell further expanded her outreach after the epidemic. Risking the wrath of the vice lords, she opened a shelter for teenage girls who escaped from Barbary Coast dens. She and her companions began regular visits to San Quentin and local jails. No one was beyond her care and interest. During the rare moments between her many projects, Mother Russell found time to visit the poor and ill in their homes, bringing along medicines, clothing and hot foods.

In 1861, Saint Mary's Hospital moved into bigger quarters at First and Bryant. Mother Russell was then able to focus on other concerns by opening schools in San Francisco and Sacramento. She also organized night classes for the illiterate and immigrant population.

Homes for the aged were built to care for the elderly who flocked to the hospital. The nuns were known for never turning anyone away who appeared at their doors, be they Catholics, Protestants or Jews. There was always room for one more.

To quote one observer, Mother Mary Baptist Russell was a "mixer of mercy and moxie." Another publication included her as the only woman among the fifty "Makers of California." Others remember her as the "Mother of San Francisco."

BLESSED DUNS SCOTUS, O.S.F. (1270–1308)

Once in my early schooling, the teacher proclaimed me a "dunce" and set me on a stool with a conical cap on my head. After confiding that humiliating experience to a priest, I gained a wholly different perspective on dunces.

The term derives from the followers of John Duns Scotus (1270–1308) the greatest British philosopher and theologian of the Middle Ages. Two centuries after his death, the "Duns–men" or dunces were falsely accused of resisting the new learning discovered in the early Greek and Roman classics.

The experiences of earlier times came alive again when I entered Saint John's Seminary in 1953. The most spectacular and colorful window in the theologate chapel is dedicated to John Duns Scotus. I immediately felt at home, dunce cap and all.

On March 20, 1993, Pope John Paul II confirmed an ancient custom by proclaiming Scotus "blessed" and giving him as a feast day, November 8th, the day he died. The gentle friar had waited almost seven centuries for that well– deserved distinction.

Born in the little town of Duns, in the southwest corner of Scotland, John entered the Franciscan Order at the age of fifteen. He was ordained priest on Saint Patrick's day in 1297, at Northampton.

After receiving the highest credentials in theology from the chancellor of the University of Oxford, the "subtle doctor" went on to stand beside such medieval giants as Thomas Aquinas and Bonaventure.

Though he didn't live long enough to write his own *Summa*, Scotus was indeed a remarkable theologian, a true giant in his field. It was he who championed (against many others) the doctrine of the Immaculate Conception of the Virgin Mary. He put it this way: "God could do it, it was fitting that he do so, so therefore he did (preserve from all sin)."

When Pope Pius IX solemnly declared that the Virgin Mary was "from the first moment of her conception, by a singular privilege and grace, preserved exempt from all stain of Original Sin," the presence of John Duns Scotus could be felt in the alcove of Saint Peter's Basilica.

Scotus applied his "God is Love" to philosophy because he believed and taught that "love is more important than knowledge, the free will more than the mind and the practical more than the theoretical." He held that "the happiness of heaven is love."

Pope John Paul observed that though he died at only forty–two years of age, John Duns Scotus presented "himself not only with his sharp mind and extraordinary ability to penetrate the mystery of God, but also with the persuasive power of his holiness of life, which for the Church and the whole of humanity makes him a teacher of thought and of life." Thomas Merton was a modern disciple of Scotus. He once proclaimed after reading a treatise by Scotus, that "your book, O Scotus, burns me like a branding iron."

Oh yes, one final consideration. In 1743, Fray Junípero Serra was entrusted with the Scotistic Chair of Theology, a position held by the friars at the Lullian University at Palma since 1692. So, if ever you are called upon to don the dunce's cap, wear it with pride.

ELIZABETH SETON, D.C. (1774–1821)

The canonization of Mother Elizabeth Seton has special significance to the story of California's Catholic heritage. The Golden State has profited from the spiritual legacy of that noble lady since November 14, 1855, when the first contingency of her Daughters of Charity arrived in San Francisco on the Pacific Mail Company's steamship, John C. Stephens.

Described by Pope John XXIII as "the first officially recognized flower of sanctity which the United States offers to the world," Elizabeth Ann Bayley was born in New York City, two years before the Declaration of American Independence. Though not reared as a Catholic, Elizabeth was concerned about spiritualities from her earliest days. She drew up for herself, from the pages of Sacred Scripture, a plan of perfection. Using that as her guide, she examined her conscience, usually in writing, every evening and then reproached herself for her faults and negligences.

The years after Elizabeth's marriage to William Seton were happy ones. They were blessed with five healthy children, three girls and two boys. Following William's death in 1803, at the age of thirty–five, the family was left with practically no funds or sources of livelihood. For a while Elizabeth was forced to live by the charity of her friends. During those times, Elizabeth was "reaching out" for the Church, even though she realized that her conversion to Catholicism would further impede her position in New York society.

Finally, on February 27, 1805, she walked up to Saint Peter's Church, on Barclay Street, and asked to be received into the faith. As she did so, she looked up at the cross on the steeple and exclaimed: "Here I am my God, I give you my heart and my soul from this day forward." As news of Mrs. Seton's conversion spread among her friends and relatives, it was a signal for them to desert her. Many of those whom she dearly loved completely disowned her.

Elizabeth Seton must surely have known that there was a special mission reserved for her by God. Yet she had no apparitions and heard no voices. Rather, she prayed, pondered and consulted. Then she waited for God's manifestation. It came in short order. Not long afterwards, the friendly and vivacious Elizabeth was able to open a boarding school for girls on Paca Street, in Baltimore. There she gathered a group of ladies together who were interested in the teaching apostolate.

On March 25, 1809, Elizabeth Seton pronounced vows of poverty, chastity and obedience—binding for one year—in the presence of Archbishop John Carroll. It was the Baltimore prelate who conferred upon Elizabeth her title of "Mother Seton." She and her Sisters adopted a formal religious habit, patterned after the standard widow's weeds worn in Italy, a style of dress Mother Seton had worn since her husband's death. Mother Seton's desire to affiliate her nascent community with Saint Vincent's Daughters of Charity was thwarted during her own life by the Napoleonic Wars. Yet she modeled the rule for her Sisters after the Paris foundation, subject only to a few minor modifications suggested by Archbishop Carroll.

On February 22, 1810, Mother Seton opened the first free Catholic parochial school in America, at Saint Joseph's Valley, Emmitsburg. That foundation was the primary cell of the modern Catholic educational system. It was with Mother Seton's successors at Emmitsburg that Bishop Thaddeus Amat arranged for the Daughters of Charity to extend their numbers to California in 1855. Since then, the gentle shadow of Elizabeth Seton has cast its radiance over the People of God in the Golden State.

XAVIER SHAUER, D.C. (1838–1912)

Archbishop Fulton J. Sheen tells how Almighty God, after He had created Adam, looked around and said to Himself: "I can do better than that! Then He created woman."

Sister Xavier Shauer was born in Munich, in 1838. She was brought to the United States ten years later, where she subsequently entered the Daughters of Charity, at Emmitsburg. She made her religious vows in 1857.

Shortly after her profession, Sister Shauer was among a group of six nuns who volunteered to serve the People of God along California's *El Camino Real*. Her tiny band sailed from New York, on November 22, 1855, arriving at San Pedro early the following January. The final miles of their journey to Los Angeles were traversed on a stage provided by Phineas Banning.

On May 29, 1858, the Sisters opened the first medical dispensary, in the house of Cristobal Aguilar, a small adobe building at Barth and Alameda Streets, near the Plaza. Sister Xavier was among the historic pioneers who moved on to larger quarters, in a two–story edifice, on Chavez Lane in the early 1860s. Though the new infirmary was bigger, it had no water and all the linen had to be carried to the river for washing.

Gifted with a rich, sweet voice, Sister Xavier organized the choir and led the youthful chanters in singing the praises of God. She taught herself Spanish and was soon able to communicate with her students in their native tongue. In 1859, Sister Xavier was transferred to San Juan Bautista. Although privations there were many, her "light heart and sunny disposition cheered all and the Sisters recalled with pleasure the happy days she spent" with them. She went from San Juan to Virginia City as one of the pioneers for a foundation to assist orphans and after a few years of faithful work there, was recalled to Los Angeles.

The German–born nun proved to be a heroine during the smallpox epidemics that ravaged California's southland. For three months in 1877, she courageously fought the dreaded scourge at the isolated "pest house" in Chavez Ravine. She was also on hand to assist victims of the virulent disease when it re–occurred in 1885. In whatever duties she was employed, Sister Xavier always displayed tact and devotedness. During her long religious life "only the good Master knows how many souls, blinded by error or passion, were by her brought back to the service and love of God." In her final years, frequent attacks of illness gradually weakened her robust consitution. She died at Los Angeles, on November 26, 1912.

The accomplishments of women such as Sister Xavier Shauer recall Pope Pius XII's statement that "Christianity pure and simple, grasping the essential values in womanhood, has discovered and cultivated in woman missions and offices which are the true foundation of her dignity and the reason for a more genuine exaltation of her sex." This brief glance at the life of Sister Xavier gives a deeper understanding of a hymn used in the *Roman Breviary* for the Feast of Holy Women:

> High let us all our voices raise
> In that heroic woman's praise
> Whose name, with saintly glory bright,
> Shines in the starry realms of light.

THOMAS EWING SHERMAN, S.J. (1856–1933)

Father Thomas Ewing Sherman, eldest son of the famous Civil War General, is a largely forgotten cleric whose contributions have yet to be fully recognized by ecclesiastical historians. Born in San Francisco, on October 12, 18S6, to William Tecumseh and Ellen (Ewing) Sherman, Thomas received much of his earliest education at Georgetown University. He entered Yale, in 1876, and subsequently studied law at Saint Louis.

Against his father's advice, Tom entered the Society of Jesus at Roehampton, England, on June 14, 1878. He took his philosophy at Woodstock College, Maryland, and, as a scholastic, taught physics and classics at Saint Louis University and the University of Detroit. After his ordination to the priesthood, on July 7, 1889 by Archbishop Patrick Ryan of Philadelphia, Father Sherman returned to Saint Louis University, where he acquired a reputation as pulpit orator and Catholic spokesman.

In the years after 1895, he concentrated almost exclusively on missionary preaching. His subsequent career was described by one writer as "one of brilliant promise and tragic failure." He was a powerful and persuasive speaker and during the years 1892 to 1907, "he was easily America's foremost Catholic voice" on a host of controversial topics.

Father Sherman idealized his father. He served briefly as Chaplain with the Fourth Missouri Regiment and later as resident priest for American troops stationed in San Juan, Puerto Rico. He returned to the missionary apostolate in 1899, and became a proponent for the advanced education of women. Two years later, he founded the Catholic Truth Society of Chicago.

In 1911, the controversial priest suffered a nervous breakdown. Upon his recovery, he took up residence at Santa Barbara. Archbishop Robert Dwyer notes that "one of the saddest features of his illness was his illusion of persecution at the hands of his Jesuit brethren. This finally assumed the proportions of mania, and he spent his last decades away from the order, living in a cottage in Santa Barbara, California, offering Mass daily, but haunted by nameless fears and terrors." Father Maynard Geiger remembers seeing Sherman on his daily walks through the Channel City. The Franciscan historian recalls that the Jesuit priest "lived quietly in retirement. He had a stentorian voice and was an able preacher." In 1931, Sherman suffered another nervous disorder and was hospitalized at De Paul Sanitarium, in New Orleans, where he succumbed on April 29, 1933

The elder Sherman, who was baptized on his deathbed, never countenanced the concept of Thomas studying for the priesthood. He once referred to his son as "some sort of Catholic divine" who should have taken an active "part in the great future of America."

In fact, the priest did just that. His stormy career as an apologist demonstrated that he was indeed his father's son and when the story of Catholic involvement in social questions and ecumenical relations is ultimately chronicled, the name of the renegade Jesuit will occupy a prominent place.

ALOYSIUS STERN, S.J. (1875–1966)

Long before the convocation of Vatican Council II, Father Aloysius Stern (1875–1966), the "only living landmark in San Francisco," embodied the notion that religious life "is intended above all else to lead those who embrace it to an imitation of Christ and to union with God through the profession of the evangelical counsels."

The seventh child of William and Elizabeth (Kurz) Stern was born at Gassersweiler, Bavaria, on June 21, 1875. He was educated by the Redemptorists prior to entering the Josephinum Seminary as a clerical aspirant for the Diocese of Vancouver Island, British Columbia. Young Stern was ordained priest on June 14, 1902. Thereafter, he received an appointment as chaplain at Saint Joseph's Hospital and curate at Victoria's cathedral.

In 1904 Father Stern was named resident priest for Nootka island. There he diligently set about learning the local Indian dialects and customs. His efforts for the natives were described by one Canadian government inspector as those of "a gentleman of untiring energy and zeal." A measure of the affection for Father Stern was evident in a letter sent by a delegation of Indian youngsters to Pope Pius X, on February 26, 1908, thanking the pontiff "for sending us a priest here, who is doing very good for our souls." The Holy Father was so impressed that he sent a personally written note to the Indians which is still preserved at Nootka:

> To our beloved sons, the chiefs and their children of Nootka, B.C., with the wish that the Lord may reward them for their attachment to the Holy Catholic Church, We, from the bottom of Our heart, bestow upon you Our Apostolic Blessing.

Father Stern's pastoral activities were described by Arthur D. Spearman, S.J., in an essay on the "Padre of Nootka Island," which initially appeared in the June, 1954, issue of *Saint Ignatius Church Bulletin*. During his years at Nootka, Father Stern championed the beatification cause of Fray Magín Catalá, the renowned Franciscan missionary of Santa Clara, who had visited the island briefly, in the winter of 1793, as chaplain of the ship *Aranzazu*. In subsequent years, Father Stern was influential in having an article by Archbishop Amleto Cicognani on "The Holy Man of Santa Clara" published in monograph form and circulated widely throughout the nation.

After Father Stern's entry into the Society of Jesus, he performed parochial duties at Lewiston, Yakima, Pendleton and San Jose. He also taught for a brief while at Gonzaga and Seattle Colleges. In 1925, he was appointed chaplain of San Francisco City and County Hospital. The twenty–two years he lived and worked at the hospital abounded in spiritual accomplishments. In one year (1940), he baptized 215 persons, anointed 1,459, heard 3,288 confessions and brought Holy Communion to 4,370 patients!

After 1947, when he took up residency at Saint Ignatius Rectory, Father Stern became one of the Bay City's favorite confessors and spiritual directors, sought out by clergy and laity alike. The popularity of the German–born priest among students at the University of San Francisco was a natural result of the rare gift he had of "explaining things very simply and pointing out the correct solution of a problem without telling the person what to do." The life of Father Aloysius Stern gives proof to the declaration by Vatican Council II that "a life consecrated by a profession of the counsels is of surpassing value. Such a life has a necessary role to play in the circumstances of the present age."

ARTHUR DUNNING SPEARMAN, S.J. (1899–1977)

Arthur Dunning Spearman was born at Wheaton, Illinois, on August 26, 1899, the youngest son of Frank Hamilton Spearman and Eugenia (Lonergan). A prominent novelist, Frank (1859–1937) brought his family to Hollywood and in later years achieved national notoriety with his numerous railroad stories and movie scripts.

The youthful Arthur studied with the Jesuits in Los Angeles and Santa Clara and, in July of 1918, entered the Society of Jesus. Ordained to the priesthood in 1931, he subsequently received degrees in history and theology from Gonzaga and Saint Louis Universities.

From 1935 to 1947, Father Spearman served as Director of the Library at Loyola University in Los Angeles. For most of those years he also functioned as coordinator for the Apostleship of Prayer in the Archdiocese of Los Angeles. An engaging preacher, Father Spearman was active in the retreat movement between 1947 and 1959. He was also widely known for his ministry among Hispanic parishes throughout Southern California.

His *Spanish–English Confessors Guide* was (and still is) the most widely–used book of its kind ever published for priests in the west and southwest areas of the country. Always adept at writing, Spearman authored short stories and articles on Indian lore in the great northwest between 1922 and 1932. His *Out of the Northland*, first published in 1930, went through several printings.

In 1956, the tireless Jesuit was assigned to Santa Clara University as Director of Manuscript Collections and Exhibits. He later served as Archivist in the Orradre Library and in that position assisted young scholars in their preparation of many learned studies.

After a number of years studying about the missionary activity of Fray Francisco Garcia Diego y Moreno at Santa Clara, Father Spearman published a thirty–nine page brochure on *Our Lady, Patroness of the Californias* in which he traced the development of Marian devotion under the title, Refuge of Sinners.

Father Spearman's masterful treatise on *The Five Franciscan Churches of Mission Santa Clara, 1777–1825* was published by The National Press in 1963. That 164 page book was the first complete record of the great social, cultural, religious and educational adventures associated with the eighth of the missionary foundations along *El Camino Real*.

In 1967, Spearman's book on *John Joseph Montgomery. Father of Basic Flight* was published by the University of Santa Clara. The profusely–documented and interestingly–written biography of the first man to fly successfully a heavier–than–air glider re–enkindled interest in the great aviation pioneer for whom a freeway, school and airfield had been named. His work on Montgomery had other ramifications too for it spurred the Lockheed Missiles and Space Company to reconstruct the original Montgomery plane from remnants. A second edition of the book was issued shortly before Father Spearman's demise. Full of earthly honors, Father Spearman returned his soul to the Lord at Santa Clara on April 9, 1977. He left behind a noble array of historical achievements as his contribution to California's Catholic heritage.

EUGENE SUGRANES, C.M.F. (1878–1942)

The story of San Gabriel Mission could not be told without reference to Father Eugene Sugranes (1878–1942) who came to the "pride" of the California missions early in this century. Born at Castellvell, Spain, the youthful Sugranes entered the seminary at Tarragone where he was known by his classmates for a "spirit of piety and love of books."

Entering the Missionary Sons of the Immaculate Heart of Mary (Claretians) in 1902, he completed his theological training at *Santo Domingo de la Calzada*. Ordained priest on July 5, 1903, he left shortly thereafter for Mexico. He came to the United States and, in 1905, was assigned to San Marcos, Texas.

At the invitation of Bishop Thomas J. Conaty, the Claretians took charge of San Gabriel Mission in 1908. Father Sugranes was among the first members of his community to serve in California, working at Yuma and the Old Plaza church of *Nuestra Señora de los Angeles*.

Sugranes became acquainted with the legendary Father Zephyrin Engelhardt and through him developed an interest in the history of the missions. He wrote numerous articles for the *Southern Messenger, The Tidings* and *Our Sunday Visitor*. Though he spoke English with a pronounced accent, he was able to write the language with an impeccable accuracy.

He published a life of Anthony Claret, as well as a manual of prayers, the *Florilegium*, which was for many years the official manual in Claretian houses throughout the United States. In 1927, he wrote a history of the Claretians in California.

In 1909. Sugranes published *The Old San Gabriel Mission* which he based on "historical notes taken from old manuscripts and records." The book was basically a compilation of articles written earlier for *The Tidings*.

John Steven McGroarty issued a "commendation" for the volume which he characterized as constituting "the most elaborate and complete history of the Mission San Gabriel that has yet appeared in print." He emphasized that the book had been compiled "from the mission records handed down by the Franciscans who built it and held possession of it until secularization and after." In McGroarty's view, Father Sugranes was "eminently fitted by education, training and experience to be the historian of San Gabriel. Moreover, his whole nature and his sacred profession of the missionary priesthood and his nationality makes him a sure interpreter of mission history and tradition."

In an ad which Charles Fletcher Lummis wrote for the *Out West Magazine*, in August of 1910, the book was described as "a critical study of art, antiquity and architecture of this best–preserved landmark by one who has for years been in touch with mission customs and traditions."

That the book was well–received is attested by a revised version which appeared in 1917 under the title *Glory of San Gabriel*. Four years later, another edition was issued to commemorate the 150th anniversary of the mission's foundation.

After his service in California, Father Sugranes established a house of studies for the Claretians in Washington, D.C. During his final years, he served in Chicago and it was there that he died on April 15, 1942.

Father Sugranes left behind an enviable reputation for learning and piety. Especially he is remembered in the bibliographical annals of California for his writings about San Gabriel Mission where even today his indelible imprint is plainly visible.

ALOYSIUS VARSI, S.J. (1830–1900)

Aloysius Varsi (1830–1900), a deep philosopher, a

profound theologian, a fervent religious, a talented administrator and a natural leader was among that galaxy of learned and holy Jesuits given by Italy to the California apostolate. Young Aloysius entered the Society of Jesus just three years prior to the devastating revolution of 1848. After his novitiate, he and several companions fled to Belgium where they took refuge with the Brother Hospitallers of Saint John of God,

Owing to his extraordinary ability as a mathematician and scientist, Varsi was sent to Paris, where he attended the lectures of the most distinguished scholars of the day. That training was to prepare him for duty at China's Imperial Observatory. After his ordination, in the Convent of the Madames of the Sacred Heart, in Laval, France, Father Varsi completed his theological training with considerable acclaim. Gifted with a brilliant mind, he gave himself with ardor to his studies and distinguished himself in Jesuit Houses of Studies in Belgium and France.

In 1862, Father Varsi journeyed to the United States, where he served briefly as a chaplain in the Civil War. He subsequently taught physics and chemistry at Georgetown and Boston Colleges. During those years, Varsi was a sought–after speaker. One of his Boston lectures, on the question of electricity, was the first of its kind ever given in the nation.

Between 1868 and 1876, Father Varsi occupied the presidency of Santa Clara and during his incumbency he devoted all his energies to improving the college and building a new dormitory and theater. From 1877 onwards, Varsi was associated with Saint Ignatius College, in San Francisco. His tall and commanding presence admirably suited the large mind and larger heart of the Cagliari–born Jesuit. The very simplicity of his manners brought out, in striking relief, the real greatness with which nature and grace had gifted him.

Widely recognized for his theological expertise, Father Varsi served as the official theologian or *peritus* for Bishop Patrick Manogue at the Third Plenary Council of Baltimore. As a director of souls, Varsi ranked with the ablest of his contemporaries in wisdom, prudence and charity. Throughout California, the name of Aloysius Varsi was known as a true orator with a far–reaching eloquence.

His rare prudence made him a favorite counselor with his friends and one never felt embarrassed in his presence, his patient forbearance hiding any hint that his time was urgently needed by pressing business. He preferred to restrict the hours of his sleep rather than inconvenience those that confided in him. His trust in Saint Joseph and in Divine Providence was deep and child-like; and though severely tested by the long years of crushing debt, he came forth from the trial purified and intact.

EDMOND VENISSE SS. CC. (1823–c.1856)

Edmond Venisse was born at Folligny (Manche) on September 29, 1823. He joined the Congregation of the Sacred Hearts of Jesus and Mary (Picpus Fathers) on August 15, 1846. In July, 1849, while still a seminarian, young Venisse was sent to Chile. There he continued his theological studies and, on March 15, 1851, was ordained to the subdiaconate.

Later that same month, Venisse was assigned to the *Pueblo de Nuestra Señora de los Angeles*, in Alta California, where he was to teach in the recently–opened school which Bishop Joseph Sadoc Alemany had entrusted to the Picpus Fathers. Recalling his work in that pioneering educational institution, Venisse noted that he had become a "real schoolmaster, teaching a little of everything to some poor children."

The priestly–candidate was also attached to the Church of *Nuestra Señora de los Angeles*, as an associate to Father Anaclet Lestrade. There he organized a choir for the great feasts composed of Indians, the "survivors of those happy times when the talented Franciscan Fathers taught the arts with so much success." Venisse said that while he served in Los Angeles, he felt that he was "among the angels."

In the spring of 1853, Venisse petitioned his superiors at Paris for advancement to the priesthood. The permission was granted and the usual dimissorial letters were dispatched to California. Alemany, the newly–designated Archbishop of San Francisco, bestowed the priestly imprint on Venisse on November 20th.

Enroute back to Los Angeles, Father Venisse stopped at Santa Barbara Mission, where Fray José Maria de Jesus Gonzáles Rubio insisted on having a grand ceremony honoring the recently–ordained priest. He was lodged in the episcopal quarters once occupied by Bishop Francisco Garcia Diego y Moreno and, on the Feast of Santa Barbara, offered his first Solemn High Mass. Following the liturgy, everyone in the congregation came forward to greet the celebrant personally.

Father Venisse spent some further days at Santa Ines Mission and then journeyed on to San Fernando Mission, which had been without a resident priest for some years. The school operated by the Picpus Fathers at Los Angeles lasted until mid 1853, when Father Felix Migorel left the diocese. In the following months, Venisse toured California, assisting at various places in the administration of the Sacraments.

In the summer of 1855, Venisse made a trip to Hawaii for his health. But when he found the climate there no more conducive, he returned to California, arriving in time to witness the initial visit of Bishop Thaddeus Amat to the southland.

The youthful priest, anxious to pursue his teaching apostolate, asked his superiors for an assignment more in keeping with his considerable talents. Sometime later, he noted that since "the principal aim of our Congregation in this country has been the establishment of a college, and the time marked by Providence did not seem to have come, it was decided that I was to leave for Chile."

Venisse departed early in 1856, arriving at Valparaiso on May 22nd. He was then sent to Copiapo, where the Picpus Fathers operated the thriving College of Our Lady of Mercy. He is last heard of on June 20, 1856, when he wrote a letter to his homeland, recalling his service to the Church in California. The date and place of his death are not presently known.

HENRY VETTER, C.P. (1911–1977)

In 1984, Godfrey Poage wrote a book about Father Henry Vetter in which he recalled the life of *The Magic Padre*, with special emphasis on his apostolate in Mexico. A reading of that book explains why the Passionist missionary burned deep scars of gratitude in the memories of those to whom he ministered.

Born December 17, 1911, Henry Vetter lived his earliest years within the shadow of Saint Michael's Passionist Monastery in South Pittsburgh. He and his twin brother entered the seminary in 1924. Later Henry was sent to Sacred Heart Monastery in Louisville, then to Holy Cross in Detroit and finally to Immaculate Conception in Chicago. He took final vows in 1930 and, on June 11, 1938, Vetter was ordained to the priesthood.

Father Vetter's first appointment was in Birmingham, Alabama. There, with his older brother Arnold, he established a mission for blacks in an area called Tuxedo Junction. A clinic, school, church and hospital were ultimately erected there as part of the parochial foundation.

The next years were spent preaching retreats and missions in the midwest parts of the nation. In 1950, Father Henry was sent to Citrus Heights, a suburb of Sacramento. It was there that he began studying Spanish and learning about the Hispanic heritage along the Pacific Slope.

As he moved among the little towns of Northern California and Nevada, Vetter gradually perfected his linguistic abilities, eventually becoming totally conversant in Spanish. Following a hasty visit to Tijuana, he began to realize that his future work would be in Mexico.

In June of 1953, Vetter was transferred to Mater Dolorosa Monastery in Sierra Madre. From there he began weekend forays to Tijuana, where he commenced a series of missions and reach–out programs. Vetter was concerned for the needy people of the area, many of whom lived in cardboard shacks along the dry river beds. He also became interested in the hundreds of orphan children who roamed the streets of the border towns.

Youngsters liked Father Vetter. They were initially attracted to him by his magic tricks and sleights–of–hand. He was a talented prestidigitator and an accredited member of Hollywood's legendary Magic Castle. Ever–so–gradually, Vetter expanded his apostolate into Mexico, especially the peninsula of Baja California. He visited villages that had gone for generations without priestly ministrations. The Bishop of Tijuana empowered Father Vetter with faculties for the entire peninsula.

In 1963, Father Vetter organized a group known as Aid for Baja California (A.B.C.), a non–profit charitable program that eventually made possible the establishment and support of several orphanages and schools. Each week, Vetter's truck could be seen making its way south from Sierra Madre to Rancho Nazareth orphanage, Tecate. It would be loaded with lumber and other supplies for building homes, churches and structures for the needy.

It was on one of his many errands of mercy that Father Vetter and his ancient truck were involved in the fatal crash that took his life.

On May 24, 1977, the gentle priest returned his noble soul to the Lord. An issue of *The Tidings*, published a few weeks after the priest's death, showed a picture of the boys at Rancho Nazareth standing around his grave. The inscription read: "They are bidding farewell to the man who had been their father in everything save blood. He fed and clothed them, provided an education and disciplined them. He listened to their woes and always was available."

BUCHARD VILLIGER, S.J. (1819–1902)

Though his priestly ministry in California lasted only five years, Father Buchard Villiger (1819–1902) is remembered as one of the most talented Jesuits ever to serve on the west coast. Born on May 14, 1819, in Switzerland, the youthful Buchard early in life exchanged the wealth and comfort of his parents' home for the persecution and annoyance to which the sons of Saint Ignatius were then the victims.

Scarcely had he commenced his studies for the priesthood, when an edict was issued by the government expelling the Jesuits from every canton in Switzerland. His disguised flight into Savoy and his subsequent romantic escapes in the midst of hostile soldiery constitute a page of the most fascinating interest to those concerned about the very core of human rights.

The opposition to the Jesuits in his own native country and in other parts of Europe inspired Villiger to select the United States for his haven. He became affiliated with the Maryland Province of the Society. Early in his priestly ministry, Father Villiger became Provincial and in that capacity did much to spread the Catholic faith along the eastern seaboard of the country.

In 1861, following completion of his term in office, Villiger was appointed Superior of the Jesuits in California and rector of Santa Clara College. His journey to the new post was a story in itself for he boarded the last train out of Baltimore for New York prior to the rails being torn up as a military precaution for the Civil War.

After travelling via Aspinwall and Panama, Father Villiger arrived in San Francisco early in May, there to be welcomed personally by Archbishop Joseph Sadoc Alemany. During the four years that Villiger spent at Santa Clara, he diligently labored to inculcate the students with the lessons of practical charity and patriotism which later became a hallmark of the alumni.

He enlarged the intellectual scope of the college, added several new buildings, liquidated a substantial debt and brought Santa Clara up to the standards maintained by the older Jesuit institutions in the east. One of his last acts there was to sponsor a drama, on February 22, 1865, for the benefit of soldiers wounded in the Civil War.

The following spring, Villiger was transferred to San Francisco, where he became President of Saint Ignatius College and superior of the local Jesuit community. After only a year in the Bay Area, Villiger was recalled to the Maryland Province. He later became Pastor of the Gesu parish in Philadelphia, a post he held for twenty years. In 1868, he began work on a new church at 17th and Stiles streets. When finally completed, the magnificent new Church of the Gesu was a monument to Villiger's years of anxious labor, patient striving and genius for work. Good administrator that he was, Villiger served in numerous other capacities over the years, including that of Rector for Sacred Heart College at Woodstock.

In the midst of his many temporal cares, Father Villiger never lost sight of the things of the mind or of the spiritual interests. He was, at all times, the profound student and thinker. He found relaxation in the study of Scripture. He was a preacher of marked attainment and was always most diligent in his preparations. Though a foreigner by birth, his letters and writings were done in the most faultless and engaging English.

WILLIAM G. WARD, C M. (1891–1958)

Near the end of his long and eventful life, it was said of Father William G. Ward that "he is a soft–spoken, devout man; a quiet person who almost gently declares his position on a matter, but the position inside the gentle declaration is surprisingly hard, like a rock in a snowball."

Born September 11, 1891, William Goodman Ward fondly recalled the hazards of walking through his Polish neighborhood to his father's stoneyard. Then and throughout his life, Ward was a person whose convictions were set in stone.

Upon graduation from Chicago's De Paul Academy in 1912, young "Willie" Ward entered the Congregation of the Mission. He was ordained priest by Archbishop John J. Glennon on June 13, 1918. The young priest's first appointment was a professorship at Dallas University High School. From 1920 to 1922 he served as prefect for Saint Vincent's Seminary in Cape Girardeau, Missouri. Then he went to De Paul Academy where he spent four years as principal.

In 1926, he was named treasurer for Saint Thomas Seminary in Denver. After a brief stint at Kenrick Seminary in Saint Louis, Father Ward worked in the offices of the Miraculous Medal in Perryville. And, in 1931, he came to California as an associate pastor of Saint Vincent's Church.

In Los Angeles, Father Ward became a close friend and spiritual advisor to Mr. and Mrs. Edward L. Doheny. After Mr. Doheny's death in 1935, Ward helped his widow organize and administer her philanthropic outreach. Mrs. Doheny had the "right of presentation" for the pastorate of Saint Vincent's parish and for the rest of her life, Father Ward occupied that post—for a total of twentytwo years.

Stories abound about Father Ward's strictness at Saint Vincent. Funerals and weddings began precisely at the strike of the hour, confessions were heard before and after every Mass and priests were on duty at all hours to care for the needs of parishioners. The other priests found it hard to complain, however, because their pastor took an equal turn at every duty. They were less forgiving about the padlocks he attached to the rectory refrigerator!

After Mrs. Doheny developed glaucoma, an illness that darkened the final years of her life, she established the Estelle Doheny Eye Foundation at Saint Vincent's Hospital. Following her death in 1958, Father Ward saw to it that her wishes for that foundation were scrupulously fulfilled.

In addition to his chairmanship of the Carrie Estelle Doheny Foundation, Father Ward monitored endowment trusts set up to provide for Saint Vincent's Church in Los Angeles, the Edward Laurence Doheny Memorial Library at Camarillo and the Vincentian Fathers House of Studies in Washington, D.C. He also administered funds and acted in an advisory capacity in building the chapel and two buildings at the Los Angeles Orphanage (Maryvale), a chapel and three buildings at Saint Vincent's Center in Montebello and Saint Mary's Seminary in Santa Barbara.

Father Ward was active in many ancillary positions too, including the chaplaincy of the Ladies of Charity. Though his final years were spent at Saint Vincent Hospital, Father Ward continued his work without interruption well into his mid nineties. An essay written for *Update*, a publication of the Estelle Doheny Eye Foundation, stated that "his has been an unusual ministry and his has been a very special stewardship. He has resisted pressures from various sources that would have bent other men, but stone does not bend; he has outlasted all of his family and most of his generation—stone is durable; but he has shown a compassion and concern for his fellow man that tells us there was no hardness in his valiant heart."

VII. Ecclesial Institutions
1. Churches & Chapels

CALIFORNIA AND ITS CATHEDRALS

The religious life of a diocese centers around its cathedral, the chief church of the bishop. Even in the 21st century, with its concentration on the parochial level of Catholic life, the cathedral continues to serve as the "Mother Church" of the faithful within a given ecclesiastical jurisdiction.

Greatest among the New World's "Mother Churches" is Mexico City's Metropolitan Cathedral, now the oldest religious edifice on the continent. Interestingly enough, the facade of its adjoining *sagrario*, begun in 1750, is reproduced at Camarillo, California, over the entrance of the Edward Laurence Doheny Memorial Library.

In the papal bull erecting the Diocese of Both Californias in 1840, Pope Gregory XVI directed that "the principal church in the said territory of San Diego be raised and elevated to the honor and dignity of a cathedral church." The honor then, of being the state's oldest cathedral belongs technically to Mission San Diego although there is no evidence that it ever functioned in that capacity.

Bishop Francisco Garcia Diego y Moreno fixed his headquarters at Santa Barbara, making the old Mission there the first real pro–Cathedral in California. With the changing of the title of the diocese in 1849, the episcopal residence was officially transferred to Monterey and the Royal Presidio Chapel became Bishop Joseph Sadoc Alemany's cathedral. With his removal to San Francisco in 1853, Alemany used old Saint Francis Church temporarily as his pro–cathedral. Within a year after becoming the Metropolitan of the new Province of San Francisco, Alemany dedicated the Cathedral of "Saint Mary, Ever Virgin and Conceived Without Sin," the first in the world to be placed under the patronage of the Immaculate Conception. The Bay City received its second cathedral dedicated to Mary in 1891, when Archbishop Patrick W. Riordan erected Saint Mary of the Assumption. When the latter church was destroyed by fire in 1962, it was replaced by a modern structure which has become a fixture on the Bay City's skyline.

In the southern jurisdiction, Bishop Thaddeus Amat of Monterey–Los Angeles used the *Asistencia de Nuestra Señora de los Angeles* for his cathedral until 1876, when Saint Vibiana's was opened in Los Angeles. Modeled after Barcelona's *Puerto de San Miguel*, Saint Vibiana's was the most imposing building in the city at the time of its consecration.

It was a half century after Garcia Diego's arrival in San Diego before work was begun on the Gothic brick church later to be known as Saint Joseph's Cathedral. The handsome edifice was dedicated by Bishop Francis Mora in 1894, and elevated to cathedral dignity in 1936.

Sacramento's Italian Renaissance Cathedral of the Blessed Sacrament owes its origin to Bishop Patrick Manogue, who had the seat of his diocese changed to that city in 1886. When the cornerstone was laid on June 12, 1887, one local newspaper declared that "there is nothing that so beautifies a city as a handsome temple of God and the Catholics have shown a magnificent example."

Saint John's in Fresno has served the city as a parish since 1882. The present church was dedicated on June 7, 1903, by the Most Reverend George T. Montgomery, Coadjutor Archbishop of San Francisco. When the Diocese of Monterey–Fresno was erected in 1922 Saint John's became the "Cathedral in the Valley."

Among the state's other cathedrals is Saint Eugene's in the Diocese of Santa Rosa. Built in 1950, it achieved its status by designation in 1962, when the diocese was erected. Stockton's Saint Mary of the Annunciation antedates Saint Eugene's by twenty years, while the Cathedral of Saint Francis de Sales in Oakland traces its origin back to 1886. It was later destroyed by earthquake.

Other cathedrals in California are Holy Family (Orange), the Basilica of Saint Joseph (San Jose) and Our Lady of the Holy Rosary (San Bernardino). A magnificent new cathedral is under construction in Los Angeles which will be dedicated to Our Lady of the Angels.

CARDINAL DELVES INTO THE PAST

The Archival Center had a distinction unmatched by any other such facility in all the world—it enjoyed the status of having a "cardinal on staff." Each Friday, Cardinal Timothy Manning drove out to Mission Hills, where he worked among the hundreds of thousands of documents and memorabilia related to the development of the Catholic Church in California.

One of the cardinal's projects, and one about which he was uniquely qualified, was that of recording how the parishes of the archdiocese got their saintly names. Though this was originally intended as an "in–house" project, we felt that readers might like to share a sampling of the results.

The parish of Saint Elizabeth in Altadena, for example, was shepherded in its earliest years by Father (later Msgr) Victor Follen (1885–1953). His mother's name was Elizabeth.

The parish dedicated to Saint Frances Cabrini was given to the care of the Holy Cross Fathers because of Cardinal McIntyre's longtime and close relationship with the President of Notre Dame University, Father John O'Hara (later Archbishop of Philadelphia). It was named for Mother Cabrini who had purchased the property in that area for what became Villa Cabrini Academy.

There was always some confusion as to whether Santa Catalina parish in Avalon was named for Catherine of Alexandria or Catherine of Siena. The question was put to rest in 1949, when a parish was dedicated to Saint Catherine of Siena in Reseda.

Saint Robert Bellarmine was established at Burbank, in 1909, under the title of Holy Trinity. Because of Msgr. Martin Cody Keating's (1883–1971) great devotion to Robert Bellarmine. Archbishop Cantwell agreed to change the parochial patronage.

Finbar was the first bishop and later patron for the Diocese of Cork, Ireland. His monastery was at Goughan Barra, the native homestead of Cardinal Manning.

Saint Joseph the Worker parish in Canoga Park was established in 1956. Its title derives from the new feast-day honoring the foster–father of Jesus which was proclaimed by Pope Pius XII in 1955.

Our Lady of Perpetual Help in Downey was originally dedicated to the patronage of Saint Anthony. After the Redemptorist Fathers took over administration of the parish, they had the title changed.

The parish in Hawaiian Gardens, established in 1986, was named for Saint Peter Chanel, the only canonized saint and martyr of the Pacific Islands. Feastdays play an important part too in the naming of parishes. An example would be the parish established at Lakewood, in 1953. Its erection took place on or near the feast of Saint Pancratius.

Holy Innocents in Long Beach was initially intended to fall under the patronage of Saint Luke. However, local officials of the Episcopal Church objected because of their own parish by that name. The nearby parish of Our Lady of Refuge was so named, in 1948, to honor the original patroness of the Church in the old Diocese of Both Californias.

Our Lady of Lourdes in Northridge received its patronage in honor of the hundredth anniversary of the apparitions to Saint Bernadette Subirous in 1858. The Assumption of the Blessed Virgin Mary was commemorated, in 1950, the year that doctrine was infallibly defined, by a parish bearing that name in Pasadena.

Cardinal Timothy Manning was a priest for over fifty–five years. When the retired Archbishop of Los Angeles came to this area, in 1934, he made the acquaintance of many senior clerics, thus extending his purview of the Church in Southern California back another half century.

His Eminence committed to paper some of his reflections of the near and distant past at the Archival Center. Here are some more of his reflections as to how various parishes received their patronage.

In the late 1930s, Archbishop John J. Cantwell got the notion of naming parishes for saints enumerated in the Roman Canon (now Eucharistic Prayer #1). Thus it was that San Marino received its patronage of SS. Felicitas and Perpetua.

The parish of the Epiphany in South El Monte was named to complement the neighboring enclave of Nativity from which it was separated in 1956, thus keeping the two great mysteries of Our Lord side–by–side.

James Francis Cardinal McIntyre paid tribute to Msgr. Anthony Jacobs (1894–1964), long–time pastor of Santa Clara parish in Oxnard, by placing the daughter parish of that city under the spiritual tutelage of Saint Anthony.

Another parish named for its pastor was that of Saint Andrew's in Pasadena. Established in 1886, it remains today a reminder the work of Father Andrew Cullen (1845–1890).

National parishes have never been fashionable in Southern California. At a dinner in the Polish House at Rome, Karol Cardinal Wojtyla asked the Archbishop of Los Angeles if he would grant territorial recognition to Our Lady of Bright Mount. Manning noted, in parenthesis: "Fortunately, I did it, before he became pope. "

Nellie Cantwell, the sister of the archbishop, was a fixture in Southern California for many years. She was honored in 1931, by having a parish in South Gate named after her patron saint, Helen (Nellie).

Sister Genevieve McArdle was a Daughter of Charity who worked for many years at Saint Vincent's Hospital. Her name was bestowed upon the parish in Panorama City because of her special concern for ill priests of the archdiocese. Saint Anastasia, created shortly after Archbishop J. Francis A. McIntyre was elevated to the Sacred College of Cardinals in 1953 was named for the titular church in Rome assigned to the care of Los Angeles.

Saint Eugene was selected for the parish established on South Van Ness Avenue, in 1942, as a way of honoring Pope Pius XII, whose given named was Eugenio Pacelli. Saint Ignatius Parish in Echo Park was originally staffed by the Society of Jesus (before they moved to Blessed Sacrament in Hollywood). It was logically named for the founder of the Jesuits, Ignatius Loyola.

In 1943, the parish of Saint Paul the Apostle was divided. The new enclave was envisioned to occupy a site then on Manning Avenue (later moved). Archbishop Cantwell thought it would be appropriate to name the parish after his secretary's patron saint, Timothy.

Saint Philomena Parish in Carson was named for the favorite saint of the Cure of Ars, to whom he attributed his miracles. When a question arose about her historicity, Cardinal Cushing was heard to say: "If she is not for real, then somebody up there is answering her mail." Chancery officials wanted the patronage gradually changed to Saint Jude. It never materialized—which probably says more about Philomena than is recorded in the annals.

THE STREET OF CATHEDRALS

"The only street in the world that has had three cathedrals" is the proud claim of California Street in San Francisco. Such was the contention of a feature article that appeared in the San Francisco *Chronicle* during the Century of Commerce celebrations in 1935.

Old Saint Mary's at California Street and Grand Avenue, is now surrounded by a thriving Chinatown whose people cherish the one–time cathedral as a vital part of their local heritage.

There is also Grace Cathedral on California, between Taylor and Jones Streets. Few people are aware that there was an earlier Grace Cathedral whose cornerstone was put in place by Canon William Kip in May of 1860. It stood majestically as the Mother Church for the Episcopalian community at California and Stockton Streets.

The foundation for old Saint Mary's was laid on June 17, 1853, by Joseph Sadoc Alemany, the Spanish–born Dominican who became the first Archbishop of San Francisco that very year. Though it has suffered extensively from fires and other maladies associated with the passage of time, old Saint Mary's remains among the most historical structures extant in early downtown San Francisco.

The article in the *Chronicle* suggests that the one–time cathedral vied with its neighbors, the John Parrot block which was built of stone brought back from China and the Montgomery block where James King of William died in 1856.

The first Mass was offered in Old Saint Mary's in Christmas Eve of 1854. That venerable house–of–worship served as Cathedral for the Archdiocese of San Francisco until 1891. Bricks for its walls came from the Atlantic coast by sailing ships around the Horn. Stone for its foundation was imported from China and lumber for its superstructure was purchased in San Francisco at the price of $324 per thousand feet.

During the 1906 fire, the roof, altars, pews and most of the interior were destroyed. Even the massive bell came crashing down from its moorings in a half molten mass. Happily, the foundation withstood the devastation and the sturdy brick walls proved impregnable enough for rebuilding.

Atop California Street, "Nob Hill" was first christened when the area was selected as the site of many residences by the bonanza, commercial and financial leaders of the time. There were located the mansions of Flood, Hopkins, Fair, Huntington, Colton and Stanford. The handsome Victorian home of the Crockers also adorned the hill on the present site of Grace Cathedral.

The foot of California Street in earlier times formed a study in contrasts, with its beach and water lots, its mud flats and low tide. One observer said "it was possible to close one's eyes and imagine oneself in heaven or hell—all at one time."

During the celebration for the Century of Commerce, elaborate re–enactments of earlier times were staged. For a brief time, the area's fabled characters and famous landmarks lived again. Even "Emperor" Napoleon came strolling down California Street, waving at bystanders along the "pathway of Cathedrals." It was a vivid portrayal of what was, and maybe still is the most famous of all the Golden State's historic streets.

SOUTHLAND'S "PRO CATHEDRAL"

It wouldn't be hyperbole to describe the Los Angeles Memorial Coliseum as the "pro–Cathedral" for the Archdiocese of Los Angeles and perhaps for all of Southern California. Like the ancient Coliseum at Rome and the Parthenon at Athens, the Los Angeles Memorial Coliseum has been associated intimately with the Church since its earliest days, and that relationship will likely continue for many years to come.

William M. Bohen, known in local annals as the "Father of Exposition Park," spearheaded the movement to have the title of the area vested in the people of California. In 1910, the City of Los Angeles leased the premises which would eventually embrace the contemplated coliseum.

The actual location was once a gravel pit from which hundreds of tons of sand and crushed stone had been carted away over the years. That removal, leaving a wide and deep hole, made it a logical place for a large structure. Work on the coliseum was finished in June of 1923. Bishop John J. Cantwell delivered the invocation at the dedication and was present for the first major sporting event which featured a memorable football game between the Trojans and Golden Bears.

Throughout the rest of his long episcopate, Cantwell was a frequent visitor at the Coliseum. The religious establishment of *El Pueblo de Nuestra Señora de los Angeles* was commemorated at the Coliseum on September 6, 1931, with a solemn Pontifical Mass at which 105,000 Catholics gathered to offer gratitude to Almighty God.

That celebration, attended by the Apostolic Delegate and eighteen members of the American hierarchy, was referred to by a local newspaper as "the most magnificent public demonstration of Catholic faith ever witnessed on the shores of the Pacific."

A decade later, on October 13, 1940, the centenary of the establishment of the bishopric in California was observed with another gigantic gathering of Catholics. This time, forty–nine prelates, 750 priests and over 100,000 came to hear Msgr. Fulton J. Sheen reflect on the "Peace of Christ in the Golden State."

The "Catholic" association with the Memorial Coliseum has been renewed biannually in recent times by the USC– Notre Dame football tradition. In 1947, that game resulted in the largest gross gate for any single event, with 105,236 spectators passing through the turnstiles.

In 1949, Mary's Hour became a yearly tradition, drawing Catholics from all over Southern California to honor the Mother of God. That event, continued for twenty years, is publicly memorialized by a large bronze plaque portraying a bust of James Francis Cardinal McIntyre.

And then, of course, there was the visit of Pope John Paul II on September 15, 1987. The Coliseum was filled to capacity for the pontiff's liturgy in honor of Our Lady of Sorrows. It was the high point of the Holy Father's second pastoral visitation to the United States.

Like the city whose name it bears, the Memorial Coliseum is walled in by mountain ranges whose highest peaks are whitened by December snows. Having grown from an experiment to an institution, it represents different things to different peoples. But, to Catholics, it is our largest church where no less a personage than the Vicar of Christ has offered Holy Mass.

ALL SOULS CHAPEL — CALVARY CEMETERY

The recent sanctuary refurbishment in the historic All Souls' Chapel at Calvary Cemetery, calls to mind the influence Zachariah Montgomery exerted on ecclesial affairs in Southern California. The genesis of the ornate Gothic chapel can be traced to the turn of the century and the inauguration of "new" Calvary, just a half mile beyond Odd Fellow's Cemetery.

Though the cemetery had been one of the greatest of Bishop Francis Mora's many achievements in the Diocese of Monterey–Los Angeles, it was his successor, George T. Montgomery, who actually opened and developed the burial grounds. From the outset, Bishop Montgomery was anxious to erect a chapel in the cemetery. By virtue of several sizable benefactions from a number of prominent Catholic families, Montgomery was able to initiate plans early in 1902.

It was the bishop's uncle, Zachariah Montgomery, who suggested reproducing a facsimile of the parochial church in Eaton's rural district of Stoke Poges, Buckinghamshire. Montgomery had visited the southeast areas of England near the end of his life and was deeply impressed by the scene which motivated Thomas Gray (1716–1771) to write his famous "Elegy in a Country Churchyard." (Composed about 1742, the "Elegy" is considered the most popular piece of prose in the English language)

A fairly accurate reproduction of the quaint old–world edifice, with its gabled–tower and heaven–pointing spire, was erected on a slightly elevated tract of land overlooking the entire cemetery. On All Souls Day, 1902, Bishop Montgomery offered a Solemn Pontifical Mass on a temporary altar at the site and, afterwards, presided at the setting in place of the cornerstone. His homily on that occasion was fittingly devoted to "Victory over Death."

Interestingly enough, shortly after World War I, Dr. Hubert Eaton, founder and developer of Forest Lawn, received permission from Bishop John J. Cantwell to use the plans for All Souls' Chapel to erect the "Little Church of the Flowers." Though altered in some respects from All Souls,' that church is probably the most authentic of the many edifices built by Eaton.

During the thirty–four years after 1902, All Souls' Chapel became one of the most visited houses–of–worship in Southern California. Thousands of people journeyed there to pray for their loved ones.

With the completion of the new chapel in the Mausoleum, in 1936, the older edifice gradually lost much of its usefulness. In recent years, it has been associated with the local clergy, hundreds of whom are buried in its adjoining ground.

And now, like its mentor in faraway Stoke Poges, All Souls' Chapel has evolved into a shrine of love and sacred memories, forming a beautiful link with Old World traditions.

CALVARY'S DOHENY CHAPEL

Everything has a history. Unhappily, only a small percentage of human events are properly and/or accurately recorded. Reconstructing the past can involve an enormous investment of time and effort and, even then, the results are often inconclusive.

Some time ago, a visitor to Calvary Mausoleum wrote to ask about the background of the Doheny Chapel. More specifically, she wanted to know "how it is that a priest is buried there."

A valid query deserves an accurate response. So, off we went to the files. Already we knew that the priest in question was Father William Ward, C.M.(1891–1985), long–time private chaplain to Carrie Estelle Doherty (1875–1958).

At the time that Edward Laurence Doheny died, on September 8, 1935, work was nearing completion on the new chapel in Calvary Mausoleum. Surrounding the sanctuary were several unfinished private crypt rooms. One of those areas, which is to the east side of the main sanctuary, was "designated on the records of said cemetery as Room # 356—the Doheny Chapel."

According to the late Archbishop Joseph T.

McGucken, an arrangement was made with Carrie Estelle whereby she would pay for installing the altar and furnishings in the first crypt and, in return, Bishop John Cantwell would allow her husband and other members of the family to be buried there.

Cantwell issued a memorandum stating that "The Roman Catholic Bishop of Los Angeles–San Diego" promises that Mass would be celebrated in the chapel "on every Wednesday morning, when the rubrics permit, for a period of fifty years . . . for the repose of the souls of those who lie buried therein."

After entrusting the cemetery's chaplain with this duty, "inherent in his office," the prelate said that if, in any week, it is impossible to fulfill the obligation, "the aforesaid Mass must be celebrated on the next most convenient day." In a document signed in December of 1956, Thomas F. Bower, the superintendent at Calvary, confirmed the earlier memorandum.

The following January, Mrs. Doheny wrote to Archbishop J. Francis A. McIntyre with suggestions as to what would happen to the Doheny chapel after her own demise. In particular, she made several requests, provided only that they are in accordance with "the laws, regulations and discipline of the Holy Roman Catholic Church as determined by the Ordinary of the Archdiocese of Los Angeles."

After designating her own crypt, the one above her husband, she asked that, at the proper time, the remains of Father William G. Ward, "may be entombed in any other crypt which at the time of his death may be vacant." She also provided a place for her faithful housekeeper, Miss Rose Kelley, which was never used.

Mrs. Doheny also requested that any other descendants of Edward L. Doheny be placed there, should they have embraced the Catholic faith before or at the time of their death. Any crypt not used by twenty–five years after her own death, would "be placed at the disposal of the Ordinary of the Archdiocese of Los Angeles for such use as he may deem fit and appropriate."

In February of 1957, Msgr. Edward V. Wade, Director of Catholic Cemeteries, notified Mrs. Doheny that her wishes were perfectly acceptable with the discipline of the local Church.

CHAPEL OF MEMORIES — MISSION INN

During a tour of California in the early 1930s, Dorothy Cottrell recorded her memories of Frank Miller's legendary Mission Inn at Riverside. She was especially fascinated with the charming little chapel dedicated by Msgr. John M. McCarthy on December 15, 1932.

According to her account, the great doors of Mexican mahogany typified the spirit of the chapel. Within their tall and stately form was a smaller entranceway which could be opened independently by visitors and others who came to pray.

The chapel was known as the "International Shrine of Birdsmen." An artistic panel invoked "St. Francis, Patron of the Birds" asking his protection for "the men who fly." To the little chapel came hundreds of the early aviators from all nations who knelt in prayer for their absent and deceased comrades. It was a place "where memories of loss and grief became memories of tenderness and hope."

Among the other sentiments associated with the chapel were those of "simplicity and valor of the Old West with its Indian nations, heroic priests and mighty trappers." To the left of the doorway was an old copper font with its elaborately carved pedestal from the Church of Taos, New Mexico. Reportedly, Kit Carson's children were baptized at it, as were other descendants of the great scouts who forged trails across the Rockies.

The chapel was bare of furnishings, with plain grey walls, beamed ceiling and dark floor. The carved heads atop the choir stalls, age darkened and worn smooth, were acquired from a centuries–old Belgian convent.

The sanctuary of the chapel was filled by a magnificent altar, once the property of the Rayas family and shipped from Guanajuato, Mexico. "Both coloring and carving of the altar are most intricate, saint rising above saint to the quaint and crowning presentation of the Trinity."

The altar shines in the soft light of the little chapel with a glitter and gleam so deep and warm that it suggests the beauty of massed chrysanthemums or golden lilies. Ms. Cottrell felt that there was something childishly appealing in the painted faces of the saints. "The little figure of the Infant Jesus is as delightful as a plump, brown–complexioned doll; He is so tenderly fashioned, so living and so lovable."

Both the altar and its saints were carved of cedar, heavily overlaid with gold leaf, as brilliant as when it was first hammered into place by cunning craftsmen hundreds of years earlier. The windows of the chapel were thought to rank with its altar in loveliness. Designed by Stanford White and crafted by Louis Tiffany, they were originally intended for a Presbyterian Church in New York City.

The windows were thought to be "the most artistically lovely ever produced in America and in them the little city of Riverside shelters great treasures that will be increasingly loved with the passing of years." The jewelling of the details, with delicate thickness and seemingly–hewn texture, bespoke a rugged and simple splendor resembling the treasures of the earth more than the work of a great glass maker.

Dorothy Cottrell was not alone in her appreciation of the chapel. Bishop John J. Cantwell was equally impressed and once observed to an eastern prelate that "nowhere, not even in Assisi, is the memory of Saint Francis more beautifully and tastefully captured and portayed."

CHRIST THE KING IN HOLLYWOOD

The first church in the United States named for Christ the King stands in its majestic Byzantine architecture on a triangle of land between Rossmore and Arden, just south of Hollywood's Melrose Avenue. Established in the mid 1920s as part of Bishop John J. Cantwell's formula for "square mile parishes," a concept pioneered in Chicago by George Cardinal Mundelein, the parochial enclave was placed under the invocation of Christ the King.

Timothy Cardinal Manning later observed that "there were inspired reasons for the creation of the parish of Christ the King. Hollywood was a byword across the globe. Its life style and values were exalted for the emulation of lesser mortals."

Cantwell had decided on that patronage after reading one of Pope Pius XI's masterful encyclical letters which alluded to "Christ the King of all Nations." In 1925, the Holy Father proclaimed a feastday under that title. Father Peter Corcoran, superintendent of Catholic schools for the Diocese of Los Angeles–San Diego and principal of Bishop Conaty High School, was named pastor. It all came together, fittingly enough, on the Feast of Christ the King in 1926.

The artistic church was erected the following year by the Joseph A. McNeil Company from designs executed by T. Franklin Power, a local architect of considerable renown who had earlier participated in designing Blessed Sacrament Church.

The church has been referred to as "a little jewel box nestled within sight of the Hollywood Hills." It was further described by H. M. Kurtzworth as fulfilling "the high traditions established by Fray Junípero Serra when he built the first of the twenty–one mission churches at San Diego."

With its attractive Byzantine tower, the church's interior combines a tasteful use of stained glass, mural paintings and sculpture which illustrates the life and spiritual emotions of Christ and His followers.

Joseph Tierney, the New York artist who had done the stained glass windows for the chapel of Saint John's Seminary in Camarillo, designed the colorful windows along a theme depicting the kingship of Christ. Between the windows are a series of mural paintings executed by L. G. Marrissael in 1946, each portraying a scene in the life of the Lord. One visitor felt that "the murals give substance to the Biblical narrative."

There are many exquisite pieces of sculpture in the church, including the fourteen Stations of the Cross or *Via Crucis*, together with eight statues recessed into the walls. When the interior art work was completed, as part of the parish's silver jubilee celebration, the secular press echoed praise for the beauty of the stately church. *The Mirror* recorded in superlatives that "the beauty of Christ the King Church is regarded as a prime example of the improvement of art in the service of the people."

Outside the church, facing the world's film capital, is a twelve foot tall Carrara marble statue of Christ the King standing on a huge base representing the world. Inscribed around the globe are the words: "King of Kings, and Lord of Lords" from I Timothy, 6, 15–16. Designed by A.J. Arany and carved in Italy by Biaigny, the statue was solemnly dedicated by Bishop Timothy Manning on the Feast of the Epiphany in 1951.

Among the church edifices in Los Angeles, Christ the King stands as a distinctive, artistic and meaningful expression of religious piety. It is one of a dozen or so churches that visitors to the city will surely want to see.

BENJAMIN WILLIAM FOXEN MEMORIAL CHAPEL

The "Foxen Memorial Chapel," so designated by the Santa Maria Parlor of the Native Daughters of the Golden West, in 1950, became the first official historical landmark of Santa Barbara County, on April 30, 1967. Silhouetted against the sky and commandingly situated on the mesa at the head of a canyon, the chapel and the nearby Benjamin William Foxen (d. 1874) grave and monument stand as sentinels over a region redolent with romantic and historic interest.

The property on which the chapel and its adjacent cemetery are located was purchased from the United States government, in 1872. It is about two miles southeast of the Frederick Wickenden adobe and the 8,874–acre Rancho Tinaquaic, a land grant authorized by Governor Juan B. Alvarado, on April 29, 1842. Two years after Benjamin Foxen's death, Father John B. McNally of Mission Santa Ines approached Ramona Foxen Wickenden for assistance in erecting a chapel at Sisquoc for the sixty–five Catholic families residing in that area. The completed chapel, placed under the spiritual patronage of San Ramon by Bishop Francis Mora, was dedicated in 1879. Identical frame buildings, "suggesting in miniature the lines of Santa Barbara Mission," were erected at Lompoc and Guadalupe with lumber transported from San Luis Obispo, where it had been brought through old Fort Hartford. The isolation of the Sisquoc chapel enhances its quaint charm and invests it with a solemnity which is altogether just for a memorial to Benjamin Foxen.

Benjamin Foxen Memorial Chapel

In succeeding decades, services were held monthly in the little white, twin–steepled chapel. After the area became a station of the Santa Maria parish in 1907, the chapel was utilized only for funerals. Between 1908 and 1933, San Ramon was abandoned to the elements. On July 29 of the latter year, however, the chapel was restored as a public landmark to Benjamin William Foxen. At the time of its rededication, one newspaper reported that "the markers in the long–abandoned cemetery, now overgrown with weeds, bear the names of families famous as founders of California." Representing the broken mast of a ship, the marble monument to Benjamin Foxen aptly symbolizes the colorful life of the courageous "Don Julian," as he was known to his contemporaries.

Colorful is the chronicle of the old chapel, and many the services held within its shelter. The steep driveway ascending to it has been worn deeply by the feet of mourners and solemn processions into the cemetery. There lie many descendants of the soldiers who accompanied Fray Junípero Serra on the expedition to California, among them the wife and sister–in–law of Benjamin Foxen. "To trace their stories is to read intimately into the early history of Spanish–Californian settlement."

CHAPEL OF THE HOLY CROSS —
SANTA CRUZ ISLAND

It is known that the Islands of San Lucas in the Santa Barbara Channel were populated by native tribes from the earliest times. Three of the Islands—San Miguel, Santa Cruz, and Santa Rosa—were discovered by Juan Rodriguez Cabrillo in October of 1542.

For one reason or another the islands have figured only accidentally in California's Catholic Heritage. Fray Estévan Tápis seemed to have been anxious to found a mission for the natives in the channel areas, but nothing came of his plans because the requisites for such an establishment were lacking. Of all the islands, Santa Cruz probably has the most interesting history. The island is known by several names. It was called *Limu* by the Indians. Ferrer in 1543 named it San Sebastian. Vizcaino called it *Isla de Gente Barbuda* in 1602, because of the bearded natives living there. Santa Cruz as a title dates from the landing of the ship *San Antonio* in 1769.

There was a penal colony on Santa Cruz in the 1830s. About thirty men were sent out with a supply of cattle and fish hooks and left there to live as best they could. Most of them managed to escape within a few years.

In the latter part of the 1800s Justinian Caire took his

772 ENCYCLOPEDIA OF CALIFORNIA'S CATHOLIC HERITAGE

family to the island where he built a home and lived for some decades. The hilly landscape reminded Caire of his native French Alps and the area around Liguria, Italy, where he had spent his childhood. Caire petitioned Bishop Francis Mora for permission to erect a chapel on his property for the use of his family and employees. Through the intervention of a friend, Father Michael King of Oakland, the request was eventually granted by the Bishop of Monterey–Los Angeles.

Practically all the building materials were produced on the island itself. Bricks were baked from local clay; stone was quarried by an Italian stone–mason and even the lime was prepared in a home–built kiln. The wrought iron railing separating the sanctuary from the nave was the work of an imported Sicilian blacksmith. The little rectangular–shaped chapel was finished in red brick. Carved stone quoins decorated the corners and even a small belfry peeked out through the shingled roof. Symbolically enough, the chapel was located in the very midst of a lovely vineyard. Colored glass windows broke the lines of the white plastered walls and its gently vaulted blue ceiling. A simple wooden altar was placed beneath a large ebony–hued crucifix.

When the tiny chapel was completed in 1891, Bishop Mora delegated the Jesuit, Father Caspar Genna, to bless the new edifice and give a mission to the island's several dozen inhabitants. At the conclusion of the services, a solemn blessing was imparted to the adjoining orchards and fields.

It would appear that the Caire family spent only part of each year on the island after the death of Justinian in 1897; hence, no regular chaplain was appointed to care for the few Catholics there. Through the years however various priests have ventured out to Santa Cruz, more as sight–seers than missionaries. In 1929 Father Thomas Sherman, son of the famous Civil War general, celebrated Holy Mass there at Christmas time.

Today the Hacienda Chapel of the Holy Cross on Santa Cruz Island stands out as a relic of the past, a reminder of another century. But it has its attractions, especially to those interested in California's Catholic heritage!

A CHURCH FOR SAN DIEGO

San Diego's second Catholic church was erected by the Reverend John Chrysostom Holbein, a Picpus Father from the Sandwich Islands. There is no record of any name being applied to the adobe edifice in its early days, although it was later given the patronage of the Immaculate Conception by Bishop Thaddeus Amat.

The October 9, 1851 issue of the San Diego *Herald* carried the following story for the laying of the cornerstone from the pen of its editor, I. Judson Ames:

The ceremony of laying the cornerstone for a new Catholic Church at San Diego, Old Town, was per-

formed on the afternoon of the 29th, with all the gorgeous rites of that most poetic faith. The mild and tranquil beauty of the day was in fit harmony with the occasion, whilst the deep and measured tones of the church bells gave additional solemnity to a scene already sufficiently imposing.

At 4 o'clock, precisely, the folding doors of a large apartment in the house of Don José Antonio Estudillo, used for private worship, were thrown open, and a procession composed of the esteemed and cherished members of the Church Universal, with the learned and devout "*Padre*," in full canonicals at their head, preceded by the interesting youths dressed in snow white frocks, and bearing in their hands silver vases and gold and silver candlesticks of great length, issued into the Plaza, and was increased every moment by the addition of citizens, male and female, Catholic and Protestant, until it reached the sacred spot.

In the center of the area already marked out in the form of a large parallelogram, was placed a table richly ornamented with solemn ecclesiastical devices, and covered with cloths of the richest fabric. The never–failing emblem of the sins of men and the atonement by the crucifixion of our Divine Saviour, occupied a conspicuous place, towards which the procession slowly wended its way with solemn chants.

A circle being formed, the chief Priest and his assistant officials commenced the prescribed services. The deep responses of the males, and those more gently breathed by the dark–eyed daughters of Castile, attested the sincerity of their interest in the scene, and of their devotion to the religion of their fathers. Many saints, with the most poetic names, and in whose gentler influence over the holy edifice about to be erected, and over all who might enter therein, the fair devotees seemed to have the fullest faith, were invoked to bless this effort, and those who contributed to its success.

The prayers being over, the priest consecrated with holy water the foundations of the building; after which a scroll containing a memorandum of the date and place —the class of persons from whom the contributions were received (of which we were glad to see many Protestants) together with the names of several who formed part of the procession, was securely sealed in a vessel of indestructible nature, and placed under the cornerstone about to be laid.

The procession over, we returned to our humble domicil [*sic*] deeply impressed with the solemnity of the scene, and more convinced than ever that there are no influences over the mind of man like those of religion and women. The one exalts and ennobles, the other regulates and purifies.

IMMACULATE CONCEPTION ANNIVERSARY — LOS ANGELES

The Church of the Immaculate Conception, located atop an elevated area on the north side of Ninth Street between Green and Whittier, is surely one of the more architecturally attractive buildings built in Los Angeles during the 1920s. The property had been acquired in 1903 as a site for the Cathedral of Our Lady of Guadalupe which Bishop Thomas J. Conaty enthusiastically envisioned for the then Diocese of Monterey–Los Angeles.

A considerable amount of national attention was given to the southland's proposed cathedral. The very first issue of *Christian Art*, for example, gave the prominence of its front page, along with some details of the building's design together with strong words of praise for the architects.

Approval of the plans was not at all universal, however. Archbishop Patrick W. Riordan of San Francisco, a strong dissenter, told his suffragan that he would "find that the contemplated building will be very expensive and entirely too large." The metropolitan suggested delaying the whole project for some while, since he believed that the envisioned church was at least a quarter of a century ahead of its time.

As an alternative, Riordan advocated erecting "a temporary church on the site," which could be used while construction on the cathedral was in progress. Admittedly, the building project would stretch over many years. Planning went ahead and in March of 1906, *The Tidings* told its readers that "the new cathedral, when completed, will perhaps typify better than any other public building, the progress of the southland."

The unforeseen financial depression of 1907, however, brought to a grinding halt the entire cathedral project. Even this disappointment did not daunt Bishop Conaty. But realizing that the project might be delayed for some years, the prelate decided to follow Archbishop Riordan's advice and erect a chapel on the projected site.

On June 27, 1909, the Vicar General of the diocese, Msgr. Patrick Harnett, blessed the new chapel–of–ease, placing it under the patronage of Our Lady of Guadalupe. "It was intended," he said, "for their accommodation until such a time as the new cathedral shall be completed." Generally referred to as the "Cathedral Chapel," it was envisioned to serve the needs of Catholics living in the Westlake district.

In 1910, a prominent Los Angeles newspaper spoke in great detail about "Bishop Conaty's determination to proceed with the erection of the $1,000,000 cathedral in this city, the plans of which have just been approved and accepted." Though he never totally abandoned the notion of erecting a new cathedral for the diocese, Bishop Conaty was never able to get the project off the drawing and planning boards. Even some years after his death, there was speculation about possibly building "Conaty's Cathedral," and, in 1923, sketches of the proposed edifice appeared in at least one national architectural publication.

The title of the chapel was changed to Immaculate Conception in October of 1925 and the following year Conaty's nephew, Reverend Francis J. Conaty, began construction of the present church.

Brought to completion with the installation of artistic Marian windows by Msgr. Joseph J. Truxaw, the church was solemnly consecrated by James Francis Cardinal McIntyre on October 11, 1954.

KING'S COLLEGE CHAPEL — CAMBRIDGE

During his visit to England in 1850, the newly–consecrated Bishop of Monterey, Joseph Sadoc Alemany, made a journey to Cambridge, where he toured what he felt was the "most gorgeous church in all of Christendom," King's College Chapel.

Several years ago, while in Cambridge gathering material for an essay on the American National Cemetery, I too visited the Anglican chapel whose foundation stone was set in place by King Henry IV on Saint James Day in 1446.

The stonework was completed for the building in 1515. The glass and woodwork followed and, with the erection of the original high altar in 1544, the chapel was completed. Stonework of the final period can be distinguished by the Tudor emblems which it bears: crowned roses, portcullises, fleurs–de–lis, dragoons, greyhounds and King Henry VII's royal arms.

The proportions of the chapel's interior are truly spectacular. An example would be the Great Vault, one of the finest surviving examples of fan vaulting, a form of roof peculiar to England and arguably the most beautiful ever devised.

Filled with stained and painted glass, the Great Windows were put up between 1511 and 1531. They contain the world's most elaborate series of pictures in glass on a large scale. They were made in England by glaziers from the continents, many of them designed in Antwerp by Barnard Flower. Galyon Hope is also thought to have had a part in these magnificent productions.

The series begins with the youth of the Virgin Mary and the birth of Jesus. The ministry, passion and resurrection of Christ surround the choir; other scenes feature the Acts of the Apostles and the last years of Mary.

Possibly "the finest piece of woodwork on this side of the Alps" is the screen which dates from 1533, when Ann Boleyn was queen. It is the work of Philip Carver, a foreigner of unknown nationality, who carved the queen's initials into the larger panels. The choir stalls, also Carver's handiwork, are executed in the Renaissance manner. The detailed ornamental work is without parallel.

The Stone Armorials in the antechapel were completed early in the 1500s by Thomas Stockton. They show the arms of Henry VII, supported by a dragon and collared greyhound.

Eighteen side chapels were arranged into the spaces between the buttresses. They too have fine stone vaults, some decorated with woodwork and ancient glass. The first chapel is set aside for private meditation and, in the second chapel on the south is the tomb of a son of the Duke of Marlborough who died while a student at King's College.

Built by Renatus Harris in 1688, the Organ Case bears ornaments from the late 1600s. It incorporates parts of earlier cases built by Thomas Thamar, Lancelot Pease and Thomas Dallam.

The lower parts of the north and south stalls were fashioned by the same craftsman who built the Screen. The carved panelling behind shows the arms of Eton and King's, Oxford and Cambridge, as well as the sovereigns from Henry VI to Charles I. The canopies date from 1678.

Ruben's "Adoration of the Magi" was painted in 1634 as an altarpiece for the Convent of the White Nuns at Louvain. It was given to the College in 1961.

King's College Chapel, predating as it does Henry VIII, recalls an era when England was still Mary's dowry. Perhaps it was meant to witness the eventual return of that dowry to Rome!

LOS ANGELES ORPHANAGE

Bishop Thaddeus Amat's proposal to open an orphanage in Los Angeles met with immediate approval on the part of the city's civic leaders, and, in December of 1855, a committee was formed to work out the necessary details for such an undertaking. Great jubilation was evident in most quarters when the six nuns arrived at San Pedro the next month even though it was recorded that as they rode into Los Angeles on the old Banning coach, "the few Indians and Spaniards on the street eyed the newcomers with curiosity."

Civil officials saw in the advent of the sisters the beginning of a new era in education and community service and, as one historian remarked, ". . . immediately they formed an important adjunct to the Church in matters pertaining to religion, charity and education." The Daughters opened their school and home for orphans with seven youngsters, a small number but one destined to grow as the years moved on. By June 7th, 1856, there were 120 children in attendance, Catholic, Protestant and Jew.

Conditions were far from ideal for "it was a primitive town . . . primitive in society, business and government. Its three thousand inhabitants had among them many restless and reckless characters, disgruntled Mexicans and depraved Indians whose number was augmented by criminals driven from the north by the vigilantes."

Annual Orphan Fairs were inaugurated by the nuns, the first of which was held in October of 1857. One chronicler notes that "socially, for many years, the biggest events were the fairs that were given for the support of the Sisters of Charity and their good work. The date of the fairs was always set for steamer day, which meant the day the boat came in from San Francisco."

A foundation was made at Santa Barbara late in 1856, where neglected and orphaned Indian youngsters were gathered from the area on oxcarts, wagons, donkeys, ponies, and on foot to attend the first English–speaking school in the city, Saint Vincent's Institution. A third contingent of the Daughters of Charity opened the southland's first "county hospital" in 1858, in a small adobe building at Bath and Alameda streets near the plaza. Eleven years later an announcement in the local paper recorded that the "Sisters of Charity would respectfully announce to the suffering members of the community, that, having completed a large, commodious, well–ventilated building for the use of the County Patients, they can now accommodate a number of both male and female Patients with Private Rooms, where they shall receive the care and attentive solicitude of the devoted Sisters."

In 1861 the nuns opened an orphanage and school at San Juan Bautista and in subsequent years enrolled as many as 120 day pupils and thirty–five orphans in the old mission. The year 1862 saw the inauguration of an orphanage and school at Santa Cruz in the old adobe Eagle Hotel. In May of 1861, a novitiate was launched at Los Angeles Orphanage to train young girls from the west wishing to enter the Daughters, but it lasted only until October of 1870, when it was closed for lack of financial means and a dearth of vocations.

It required staunch hearts to venture from the comfortable surroundings of Emmitsburg to California a hundred years ago but such courage the Daughters of Charity exhibited, and glancing back over a century of devoted service to the Church in California—those of another generation gratefully salute their zeal and sacrifice!

MANRESA OF THE WEST — AZUSA

The spirit of Saint Ignatius Loyola is very much alive in the 1980s, especially at the retreat house operated by the Jesuits in Southern California for the past three and a half decades. "Manresa of the West," located between Azusa and Glendora, stands on land originally inhabited by Shoshonean Indians, many of whom were later christianized by the friars attached to San Gabriel Mission. Following secularization, the area was included in the Rancho Azusa, which was granted to Luis Arenas, a Mexican trader, on April 26, 1842. Arenas was the first to utilize the fertile terrain for crops.

Several years later, Arenas sold his ranch to the adventurous Englishman, Henry Dalton. Around 1880, most of Dalton's holdings were purchased by Jonathan Sayre Slauson, one of the founders of modern–day Azusa. Slauson's daughter, Louise MacNeil, eventually inherited that part of the property known as the *Rancho de los Cacomites* (ranch of the Wild Hyacinth—so called because of the small white wild flowers that grew so abundantly over the hillsides)

In 1932, after four years of intensive planning, Louise MacNeil built the lovely southern French chateau which had been designed by the talented and renowned architect, Robert D. Farquahr. (Farquahr later designed the Pentagon for the United States Department of War).

The chateau was occupied only rarely during its earliest years. In 1947, it and seven surrounding acres were sold to the Society of Jesus for use as a retreat house. It was formally blessed for its new spiritual purposes by the Most Reverend Joseph T. McGucken, Auxiliary Bishop of Los Angeles, on July 13, 1947.

The Azusa site had long been associated with Catholic endeavors. For many years it served as the meeting place of the old Sunset Club of Los Angeles, whose members included such outstanding personages as Bishops George T. Montgomery and Thomas J. Conaty. Five "hermitages" were constructed in 1949 for retreatants. They were scattered on the hillside olive grove around the old home. One newspaper reporter noted that the hermitages qualified Manresa for the title of being "America's most unusual retreat quarters for laymen."

Upon the death of Louise MacNeil, in 1950, the earlier family residence was purchased, along with additional acreage of landscaped gardens and lawns. The twelve room wooden structure was aptly known as the "White House." A strikingly beautiful French–Norman style chapel was erected in mid 1953. Constructed of brick, granite and driftwood, it is one of the most distinctive houses–of–worship along the Pacific Slope.

Those pilgrims fortunate enough to have visited the original Manresa, a small town in Northeast Spain, will agree that the Hispanic atmosphere of solitude and prayer have been successfully transplanted in Southern California by the spiritual descendants of Ignatius Loyola.

MARE DE DEU BON ANY — MALLORCA

The hilltop Shrine of *Nuestra Señora de Bon Any* is among the most precious of religious centers in the Balearic Isles. Located southwest of the tiny village of Petra, birthplace of Fray Junípero Serra, its church and monastery tower 500 feet above the surrounding plain (or 1289 feet above sea level).

From the lofty eminence of Bon Any, one can experience a breathtaking view of the valley, mountain and sea. Three–fourths of the isle of Mallorca can be seen with glimpses of the Mediterranean, north, east and south. Over twenty towns and cities are easily discernible from the shrine. And the most picturesque of all is Petra, standing out like a jewel in the center of the valley.

The Shrine of *Nuestra Señora de Bon Any* is as alive in consciousness of the Petrenses today as it was in the time of Serra and long before. The Mallorcans speak of the shrine in terms of pride, tenderness and devotion. Indeed the shrine has a long history which is intimately connected with the islanders' concern for good crops. Dependent as is the plain area on rain, there have been many severe droughts over the centuries.

It was a drought in the 16th century that inspired the people to build a shrine on the hill in honor of Our Lady. Following construction of the original chapel in 1609, the Mallorcans made their pilgrimages and the rains fell. It was a "good year" and the people named the shrine "*bon any.*" Hence the title for Our Lady of the Good Year, or *Nuestra Señora de Bon Any*.

Even in the 1970s, the Petrenses visit the shrine singly and in groups, with petitions, in thanksgiving, at great moments of their lives as well as on minor occasions. Those about to leave on a journey always pay a courtesy call to *Bon Any*. Expectant mothers traditionally visit the shrine, where candles are lit and prayers recited for safe delivery. On the Tuesday after Easter, housewives bring their *empanadas* or meat pies to *Bon Any*.

The seated statue of Mary, with the Christ Child on her lap, dates from the 16th century and portrays Our Lady of the Rosary. A fanciful legend has it that the statue was found accidentally by a Mallorcan shepherd after the Spanish conquest of the Moor–dominated land.

Fray Junípero Serra went to the shrine in the drought year of 1749, and there led the people in prayer. Afterwards he preached to them about Mary's concern for God's people. Today when the Petrenses sing their hymn, "*Joix de Bon Any*," they include a verse in which they recall the visit of Serra to the shrine shortly before his departure for the Indies:

> From that hill *Padre* Serra left for the New World, there one day to spread the faith, even in its most distant place. Give us a good day and a good year. Give us a good year, O Lady, for you are the key to it all.

Though Serra never returned to *Bon Any*, the hilltop shrine was etched deeply into his loving memory. That holy place was part of his life and many memories would remain with him as persistently as his heartbeats and the ceaseless pounding of the surf at Carmel Bay.

MONASTERY OF THE ANGELS — HOLLYWOOD

People growing up in Hollywood during the 1940s developed wholly different perspective into "Tinseltown" than that portrayed on the marquees of the nation's moviehouses. There was (and is) a spiritual dimension to the area that one rarely reads about in the newspapers, hears on radio, sees on television and watches in the theatres.

The Monastery of the Angels has been a vital part of the Hollywood scene since the 1930s. There many of the local celebrities could be seen at daily Mass.

The cloistered Dominican nuns are an ancient and valued fixture in the Church. They were founded by Saint Dominic Guzman at Prouille, near Fanjeaux, France in 1208. According to tradition, the first group was made up of converts from Albigensianism. In subsequent years, numerous filial foundations were made from Prouille until the time of the French Revolution, when the original monastery was mostly destroyed and its inhabitants scattered.

In 1880, the monastery was re-opened and staffed by Dominican nuns from Nay. The Hollywood foundation traces its roots to Prouille and thence to Ouillin, where a French lady of nobility established a convent whose principal devotion centered around Perpetual Adoration of the Blessed Sacrament.

Eventually, Julia Crooks, a niece of Newark's Archbishop Michael Corrigan entered the cloister at Ouillin with the intention of later bringing the Dominicans to the United States. In 1880, Saint Dominic's Monastery was formally inaugurated at Newark.

In 1924, Bishop John J. Cantwell invited a contingency of the Sisters to the Diocese of Los Angeles–San Diego. The nuns, under the superiorship of Mother Mary of the Eucharist, initially resided in a convent at 728 West 28th Street.

On November 18, 1934, quarters for their new Monastery of the Angels at 1977 Carmen Place was blessed by Msgr. John J. Cawley. The diocesan Vicar General enthusiastically welcomed the nuns to Hollywood where, he said, "they would impart a badly-needed tradition of spirituality to the area."

The twenty-six nuns comprising the cloistered Dominican community in Hollywood continue the practice of Perpetual Adoration of the Blessed Sacrament. They also chant the Divine Office and pray the Rosary of the Blessed Mother around the clock as their predecessors have done for centuries.

Totally self-supporting, the nuns not only pray together, but do much of their work in common. There is no more peaceful and joyful place in Southern California than their lovely chapel which is open to the public during the daylight hours.

The Monastery of the Angels is still very much among us and perhaps most of what is good in Hollywood owes its origins to the cloistered nuns who spend their lifetime at prayer so the rest of us can live and rest in peace. If ever the Academy of Motion Pictures were to give an award for the "best prayers said in Hollywood," the perennial front-runner will be the Dominican Sisters at the Monastery of the Angels.

SAINT MARY'S CATHEDRAL — SAN FRANCISCO

Bishops Thomas J. Conaty and John J. Cantwell both designed and planned new Cathedrals on the west coast. But it was another Angelino, Joseph T. McGucken, who brought their dreams to completion. And it was just a few years ago that the magnificent new Saint Mary's Cathedral in San Francisco was opened to worshippers.

Archbishop Joseph T. McGucken rose above the odds makers and confounded his critics by building what will probably be the last, and surely the most striking cathedral erected in North America in the 20th century.

San Francisco, alone among the great cities of the nation, is made for monuments. The setting of the hills and ocean, as well as the rhythm of the bridges that span its Bay, demands an architecture to match its natural endowments.

Built around the cornerstone of its seventy-one year old predecessor, the "People's Cathedral" was erected by eleven thousand contributors of all races and creeds who shared in providing an eight million dollar replacement for the historic Saint Mary's destroyed by fire on September 6, 1962.

Situated atop a picturesque incline, at Geary Boulevard and Gough Street, on a rise that dominates the Civic Center and much of the downtown area, the cathedral is located axially on O'Farrell Street. Its two square block site provides a generous plaza on the north and a dramatic vista toward Market Street on the east. The overall complex, which includes a high school, faculty residence and rectory, also houses an archdiocesan convention center, a parish hall, kitchen facilities, functional sacristy, historical museum and covered parking.

A daring architectural departure from tradition, much of the design is credited to Italian engineer Pier Luigi Nervi and Boston architect Pietro Belluschi, who served as consultants to local architects Angus McSweeney, Paul A. Ryan and John Michael Lee.

Professor Neri, one of Europe's most renowned structural engineers, outlined the chief theme of the building as based upon "the great concept of four monumental sculptured pylons, symmetrical geometrically, supporting the great dome." He described the overall plan as "a modern but simple idiom of unobstructed lines." Neri said that "it is not a church to be built for a single group of intellectuals, or avant–garde artists; our idea was to build a cathedral for all people, which all can understand and appreciate. It is the 20th century, not a century of the past or indeed of the future."

As different from traditional cathedrals as an abstract painting is from a Flemish masterpiece, the decisive structure engendered civic rejoicing for its bold originality. Already one of San Francisco's major attractions, it ranks as one of the nation's great ecclesial structures.

The whole edifice is designed on the geometric principle of the hyperbolic paraboloid, where a cube curves upward in graceful lines from all four corners, while retaining its squareness. From the giant monolithic pylons supporting the superstructure spring concrete vaulting, spanning 140 feet in each direction, rising to a square perimeter opening fifty feet above the floor.

Curved, yet composed of straight lines, the geometric shapes blend harmoniously with the reinforced concrete structure. One thousand, six hundred and eighty pre–cast, triangular–shaped concrete pan forms constitute the inner surface of the cupola shell. The exterior of the beams, sprayed with gunnite, gives the bonding shell of concrete.

The beams formed by the coffered pans create a face–like pattern of concrete ribs which soar upward following the curved contours of the hyperbolic shapes. The building's stone form softened into the antiglare of solar bronze glass at its corners, creates a truly prodigious achievement in mystic, graceful design.

Much of the cathedral is faced with Italian travertine marble. The acoustically–treated, ivory–smooth wall surfaces are patterned into delicately–shaped segments. The church is 189 feet high, the equivalent of an eighteen story building.

Its inner perimeter provides 40,000 square feet of floor area; the pews, situated in a fan–shaped pattern, accommodate 2,400 persons in such a way that no one is more than seventy–five feet from the predella. The handsome baldachin over the symmetrically–placed altar, with its thousands of anodized aluminum shimmering rods, symbolizes a living bond of grace between God and His People.

Designed by Hungarian–born Gyorgy Kepes of Massachusetts Institute of Technology and executed by the Willet Stained Glass Studios of Philadelphia, the window patterns portray the four elements: the blue of the north window, water; the lighter colored south windows, air; the red–stained west window, fire and the green east window, the earth.

As the colors modulate upward, their tint moves from blues, reds and others into a unified sparkle of gold that crosses the ceiling like two arches at right angles to one another. The six feet wide windows extend from 1,139 feet up the edge of four wall–like roof sections, forming a multi–colored cross at the top, symbolic of the Resurrection.

The eighty–nine rank, seventy top electro–pneumatic organ, executed in Padua, Italy by Antonio Ruffati, is a grand, comprehensive and multi–dimensional ensemble of almost pure tonality.

What is surely California's most distinctive church is easily its most controversial. A group of stoics protested that it should never have been built; a cluster of radicals complained that funds for its construction would better have served the poor and a handful of Puritans threatened to burn it down. Probably to those who believe that man exists on bread alone, Saint Mary's will always be a sin and a scandal. Yet the cost of religion is clearly legitimate.

A nation that expends hundreds of thousands on pets, millions on cosmetics and cigarettes and billions for filling stations and supermarkets surely has room in its economy for noble houses of worship.

The building of churches and the helping of the poor have never been mutually exclusive projects and surely no society in all recorded history so desperately needs points of repose and rest, places of silence and peace or centers of worship and community than that of the 1990s.

Opened on October 15, 1970, and formally dedicated the following May 5, the "People's Cathedral" of San Francisco is a landmark structure. Bishop Mark Hurley predicts that future generations "will say that when Vatican Council II was enjoying a new liturgy and a new renewal to 'serve the dignity of worship with beautiful signs and symbols of heavenly realities,' a courageous archbishop and his people on the phoenix–ashes of the old cathedral began the Cathedral Church of 1965. It was not a replica of medieval gothic, or 19th century byzantine nor even a projection of the 21st Century.

It was and is a church of Vatican Council II, today's church in a revolutionary era."

CATHEDRAL THAT NEVER WAS — LOS ANGELES

Shortly after the turn of the century, the Catholic Church in the United States passed through a cathedral–building era. So widespread was the movement that by 1907, cathedral churches had been completed or were under construction in twenty of the nation's ecclesiastical jurisdictions.

That Southern California was not immune from this national trend is obvious from action taken by the Ordinary of Monterey–Los Angeles, the Right Reverend Thomas J. Conaty. On January 26, 1904, the bishop and his consultors voted to relocate Saint Vibiana's Cathedral about two miles southwest of its existing site. A formal petition was drafted and sent to the Sacred Congregation of Propaganda Fide asking permission to "demolish the present Cathedral" in order to erect a larger church in a more suitable area of the town. As soon as a favorable decision had been handed down by Roman officials, Bishop Conaty engaged the Boston firm of Maginnis, Walsh and Sullivan to draw up plans for a magnificent new cathedral for the City of Our Lady of the Angels.

Approval of Conaty's plans was not at all universal. Archbishop Patrick W. Riordan of San Francisco, for instance, told his suffragan that "you will find the contemplated building to be very expensive and entirely too large." Such discouraging remarks did not visibly affect the tireless southland prelate for he recalled that similar observations had been made to Bishop Thaddeus Amat in the 1870s when he built the city's first cathedral. Conaty reminded his metropolitan that "I am in no great hurry and do not intend to do anything until I know all the details."

Originally, cornerstone–laying ceremonies were scheduled for June 23, 1905 but delays in acquiring the property and the absence of Archbishop Riordan caused postponement of the event until after Conaty's proposed trip to Rome the following year. Planning continued and in March of 1906, *The Tidings* told its readers that "the new cathedral, when completed, will perhaps, typify better than any other public or semi–public building the progress of the southland."

The unforeseen financial depression of late 1907, however, brought the project to a grinding halt. Even this disappointment did not deter the bishop, for he felt that suspension of cathedral planning gave him an opportunity to develop charity work. Realizing that his cathedral would be delayed for some years, Bishop Conaty decided to erect a chapel in honor of Our Lady of Guadalupe on the projected site and on July 27, 1909, the Vicar General of the Diocese, Monsignor Patrick Harnett, blessed the new edifice. (In later years the title was changed to the Immaculate Conception, and in 1926, the present church was erected.)

Even with all the problems he encountered, Conaty did not entirely abandon the idea of one day having a new cathedral. It is known, for example, that as late as 1912, he made a bid on property at Vermont and Wilshire as a possible future site.

OUR LADY OF MOUNT CARMEL — MONTECITO

Among the most distinctive houses–of–worship in Southern California is the remarkable edifice erected in

1936 at Montecito under the patronage of Our Lady of Mount Carmel. The features of that beautiful church were explained in a brochure prepared by the Schauer Printing Studio in the 1950s.

Consecrated by Archbishop John J. Cantwell on October 1, 1938, the church was the gift of three sisters who were local parishioners. Its status among the handful of consecrated churches is attested by the twelve crosses with candles affixed to the interior walls.

The building was designed by Ross Montgomery to resemble the missionary chapels erected for the Pueblo Indians in the Franciscan Province of *Santo Evangelio de Mexico*. With the limited facilities then available, the friars developed an architectural style that combined characteristics of aboriginal design with Spanish Colonial concepts.

Visitors to the great southwest can see those chapels of earlier times, many of them still intact. The design of Our Lady of Mount Carmel is a good cross section of those old custodial buildings, not Californian but entirely Catholic and altogether American.

Among the distinctive features of the New Mexican chapels recognizable at Montecito are the walled–in forecourt, the plastering (which is primitive but very serviceable), the flat roof, the logs (*vigas*) on the ceiling and their adjacent eucalyptus saplings (*savinos*), the raised sanctuary roof, the windows above the nave, the uneven walls, the organ loft, the altars, the flagstone floors and the massive hand–made doors.

While the art and spirit of earlier times remain intact, the church of Our Lady of Mount Carmel incorporates a host of modern features that make it functional for local parishioners. Examples would be its reinforced concrete (instead of crumbling stone and adobe), a waterproof roof (instead of parched clay), glass windows (instead of oiled sheepskin or selenite slabs), gas heating equipment (instead of crude stoves), electric lights (instead of candles or oil lamps), electronic organ (rather than clarions, bassoons and trumpets) and pews.

The tin lighting fixtures and frames for the Stations of the Cross were fashioned in Santa Fe by native American craftsmen. Tin has long been utilized for those ornaments and the architect carefully used traditional artistry in his series of patterns.

The tabernacle and sanctuary lamp are made of repoussé copper and bronze covered with silver plating. The silver–plated altar crucifix and candle–sticks were designed to follow the spirit and design of 17th century artisans.

The original landscaping, some of which has been altered in recent years, embraced the New Mexican character of the church. The plants in the forecourt were reminiscent of those brought to California and cultivated by the early friars. Among their number were jasmine, oleander, rosemary, lemon verbena, lavender, potato vine, pomegranate, penny royal, mint, mother of thyme, angel's trumpet and balm. Of special interest was the celebrated "Crucifixion Thorn."

Probably no other church in the Archdiocese of Los Angeles is more historically relevant or architecturally fascinating than the one at Montecito. It is eminently worthy of a visit by those travelling along the California coastline.

OUR LADY OF ASSUMPTION CATHEDRAL — PALMA DE MALLORCA

The historic Cathedral of Our Lady's Assumption, at Palma de Mallorca, played an important, if vicarious, role in the spiritual formation of Alta California. There Francisco Palou was baptized in 1723 and Juan Crespi in 1721. Commenced shortly after the Spanish conquest of the island, in 1229, the medium–sized Gothic edifice is uniquely sturdy, somber and imposing.

Dedicated to Our Lady's Assumption, centuries before that doctrine was infallibly defined, the cathedral is the crowning architectural glory of Mallorca. Many were the great architects, master–builders and artists over the centuries who contributed to its construction and adornment. Even today, the handsome cathedral stands out prominently, just above the sea wall and ancient foundations of Palma, its flank to the Mediterranean and its façade to the west.

Santiago Rusiñol gave perhaps the most discerning description of the edifice when he noted that "few cathedrals give the impression that this one does, of having been erected with one single blow of the hammer, in one single moment of creation, and of one solid block." He goes on to say that "it does not look as if it had been built; you would say, rather, that it is a huge block of stone that has been chiselled by a sculptor, carving frameworks, windows and buttresses. as one molds a statue; and that he left it just so high, that the sun could kiss it at all hours of the day, covering it with a reddish glow and kindling it like a flame every afternoon in the agony of sunset And that, not satisfied with building one only, he placed it on the seashore so that it could reflect another; solid and massive the one, unsteady and vibrating the other."

Rusiñol concluded his observations by saying that the cathedral "is a great flower in the garden of humanity. Rarely has man so spiritualized the material of his work. Such are the world's happy moments, moments in which mysticism embodies itself in a work of art; where thought can find a refuge and the soul takes shape. The cathedral of Palma is an island in the heart of an island."

Fray Junípero Serra preached in the cathedral on three occasions, the first being in January, 1742, when he recalled and expanded upon the story of *El Nino Perdido*, the loss of Jesus in the Temple. He also preached there on the Feast of *Corpus Christi*, in 1743, and, on that occasion, the great doors of the central entranceway overlooking the sea were flung open.

It was a singular honor to occupy the pulpit on *Corpus Christi* for that feast was and is the most memorable on the liturgical calendar of Palma. Only the area's best preachers rate such a distinction. A number of the other sixteen Mallorcan priests were closely associated with the cathedral in their earlier years, especially those born in Palma, Francisco Dumetz, Antonio Jayme, Miguel Pieras and Antonio Ripoll.

Their recollections of the magnificent Cathedral are evident enough to its reputation as "the heart of religious life in Mallorca.

PENDLETON'S RANCH HOUSE CHAPEL

The picturesque chapel overlooking the Valley of Santa Margarita is the oldest structure at Camp Joseph H. Pendleton. Erected possibly as early as 1810, a portion of this historic edifice served as the temporary quarters for the Pico family when they moved their ranch house from Ysidro Flats to its present location in 1828.

With completion of the new home, the older structure reverted to its prior use as a winery. It was later utilized as a tool shed. Under the ownership of Richard O'Neill, it was made over into the living quarters for the blacksmith.

In March of 1942, the old Santa Margarita Ranch became one of the largest military camps in the world, as the west coast base for combat training of the United State's Marine Corps. When President Franklin D. Roosevelt dedicated Camp Pendleton, he suggested that the historic heritage of the *rancho* be preserved wherever possible. The ranch house and the adjoining buildings were restored to illustrate Spanish colonial architecture.

Among the structures selected for restoration was the old winery. Initially, it was proposed that it be a museum, but as work progressed, it was decided to make it into a house–of–worship. It was a wise choice for by locating a chapel at the historic center of the base, recognition was given to the influential part played by the early missionaries in developing the area.

The Santa Margarita Ranch House Chapel continues to serve as the focal point of devotional life at the marine installation. Military personnel of all denominations find the spiritual strength to carry on the work of their choice. There are many historical treasures associated with the restored chapel. The stone doorstep embedded in the entraceway to the courtyard is from the old *capilla* at nearby Las Flores. The bell came from the railroad station at Capistrano, where it hung for many years after being taken there by Juan Forster from Las Flores.

Tradition has it that the large crucifix, used at the ranch house for many years, was taken from San Juan Capistrano Mission after the 1812 earthquake. The old

Spanish chair is a replica of the one used by King Carlos III. The vestments, given by a private family, likely belonged in previous times to San Luis Rey Mission. The altar is a copy of one in Istanbul. Its gilded cross of wood, about two feet high, was at one time used by the friars in Peru. The large wooden candle–sticks came from a little chapel outside Cordova. Also from the Spanish chapel is the silver sanctuary lamp and the altar canopy. The four bracket candelabra, two in the sanctuary and two in the chancel, also came from a chapel in Spain while the red brocade on the wall in the main body of the edifice probably originated from Florence.

The Santa Margarita Rancho House Chapel is the strongest link between Camp Pendleton and the glorious history of Southern California Whereas the old Franciscan foundations were on the front lines as the friars ministered to the primitive peoples, today the little chapel helps to train men and women for front line service where they will do their duty for God and country throughout the world.

RANCHO CAMULOS CHAPEL

Probably no spot in Ventura County, aside from its historic mission, has the interest and glamour of *Rancho Camulos*, whose adobe is among the most famous in California Originally part of the larger *Rancho San Francisco*, Camulos was a grant to Antonio del Valle in 1839. The *rancho*, encompassing the towns of Saugus, Newhall and Castaic, remained in the Del Valle family until the mid 1920s.

Ygnacio del Valle served as treasurer of the civil government in California in 1846. Later he was *alcalde* of *El Pueblo de Nuestra Señora de los Angeles* (1850) and an elected member of the City Council and State Legislature. He resided in Los Angeles until his retirement to Camulos, where he died in 1880.

The oldest part of the adobe at Camulos, built in 1853, contains four rooms. A granary and kitchen, independent of the house, were later joined to the structure, thus creating a quadrangle surrounding a patio. Ysabel Varela del Valle had a separate wooden building erected, apart from the family adobe, for exclusive use as a chapel. Mass was offered regularly there for the family, employees and Indians living in the vicinity.

The quaint little chapel was immortalized by Helen Hunt Jackson in her best selling book, *Ramona*. While seeking atmosphere for her novel, Mrs. Jackson visited Camulos and was fascinated by the pressing of olives in the old *morteros* and the making of wine which was stored in a huge cellar beneath the house.

The chapel remains today much the same as it was when priests from San Buenaventura Mission came to offer Mass. One can still see the Roman vestments given to Ysabel Varela del Valle by Bishop Francis Mora. In March of 1928, floodwaters from the break of the Saint Francis Dam cut through the garden and missed the chapel by only a few feet.

Among the few references in the annals about the chapel at Camulos is one written by Charles Francis Saunders and included in his book *Under the Sky of California,* which was first published by the Robert M. McBride Company of 1913. That short account is significant because it was written by a recognized historian at a fairly early date (early 1900s). The writer was escorted to the chapel by Frasquita, "a bright–faced young girl, whose black hair, olive skin and vivacious eyes proclaimed her Spanish blood."

> We were let into the little rustic chapel within the garden's shade, and saw an altar cloth as white and fresh as though just from Ramona's hands. And Frasquita told us all the news about the chapel, how they had to keep it locked now for the American visitors have carried away every thing for—what you call?—keepsake.

> And once they did—Mother of God, the heretics!—steal a holy crucifix that had been the family's for a hundred years—two hundred years yes,—two hundred years maybe; and now they still hold services in the chapel once a month, and Father John comes up from Ventura, and there is Mass, and everybody attends from the *rancho,* and sometimes some of the neighbors too. O yes, a gift for the chapel? Many, many thanks; and *adios,* Señora . . .

"Father John" was Juan Comapla who served at San Buenaventura Mission between 1861 and 1877. He was especially fond of Camulos (an Indian word meaning "My Fruit") and its pioneering family, the del Valles.

RESURRECTION PARISH — FIFTIETH ANNIVERSARY

Throughout their fifty years as a distinct parochial family, the People of God in Southern Boyle Heights have exhibited a consistent attachment to and love for their parish Church of the Resurrection. In many ways, they prefigured the sentiment verbalized in the *Ordo Missae,* which reminds the faithful that their local church is a sign of "the spiritual Church which their Christian vocation commissions them to build and expand."

Catholic presence in the eastern section of Los Angeles is generally reckoned from 1896, and the establishment of Saint Mary's Parish, in Boyle Heights. In the quarter century that followed, the thinly–populated area expanded considerably and, by the early 1920s, the whole tableland of vineyard days was covered with comfortable homes.

It was just seventy years ago, on December 12, 1923, that the Board of Consultors for the Diocese of Monterey–Los Angeles conferred parochial autonomy on that geographical area bounded by Whittier Boulevard, Euclid Street, Pasadena Avenue and Eastern Avenue. Acting upon the recommendation of his advisers, Bishop John J. Cantwell entrusted the pastoral care of the newly–created Resurrection Parish to Father William J. O'Regan (1882–1950).

After carefully canvassing the Southern Boyle Heights district of Los Angeles and speaking at length with the Catholics living there, the Irish–born cleric rented a frame residence at 3571 Atlantic Street, which he converted into a temporary church–rectory–hall complex. Within a few weeks, there were people enough to justify the scheduling of two Sunday Masses.

Early in 1924, after acquiring property on Lorena Street, Father O'Regan contracted with Emmet C. Martin for a modest church. As soon as the escrow proceedings were completed, the youthful pastor moved into a residence adjoining the church site, at 1124 South Lorena. A new church was ready for occupancy by mid–summer and, on August 10th, it was solemnly dedicated by Bishop Cantwell.

It was Father Daniel Sweeney's initiative that brought about the erection, in the fall of 1944, of Our Lady of Victory Chapel, at Union Pacific and Herbert Streets. That edifice was envisioned to serve the spiritual needs of those living in the eastern portion of the parish, many of whom were land–locked for lack of surface transportation.

On February 24, 1949, in what was surely among the first demonstrations of its kind, the youngsters of the parish "picketed" their elders after the Sunday Masses, with placards calling for the erection of their own Catholic school. Shortly thereafter, property for that purpose was acquired at Eighth and Lorena. Groundbreaking for the projected schoolhouse took place on February 21, 1950. Actively participating in that long–awaited event were the Franciscan Sisters of Mary Immaculate, whom the new pastor, Father Henry Alker, had engaged to staff the institution. The completed edifice, one of the initial links in the chain of facilities made possible by the Youth Education Fund, opened its doors the following September with 211 enrollees in the lower four grades.

Father Ramon D. Garcia (1913–1972) became pastor in March, 1953. He added substantially to the "physical plant" of the parish, but, more importantly, he gave identity to the mostly Mexican–American community which, by that time, had replaced the pioneering Italian, Irish, Hungarian and Polish populace. Three years later, a single–story, three classroom addition was made to the schoolhouse. With that expansion, one thousand public school youngsters were able to utilize one or another of the various programs offered by the Confraternity of Christian Doctrine, over and above the 435 full–time enrollees.

The long–envisioned church became a reality when plans drafted by E. J. Samaniego won approval. Ground was broken for the modern concrete masonry building on May 24, 1964, following ceremonies at which Father Garcia was invested with the title and office of papal chamberlain. It was a gala occasion for it reminded the whole community of the Holy Father's concern for his peoples everywhere. The monsignor's health began deteriorating in 1969, and on June 11, he suffered a near–fatal stroke. A second seizure affected his eyesight and the following spring, Msgr. Donald Montrose, archdiocesan superintendant of secondary schools, was named parochial administrator. Shortly after the pastor's demise, in 1972, Montrose was designated as his successor by Timothy Cardinal Manning.

In their constitution, *de Ecclesia*, the conciliar Fathers stated that the Church of Christ "is truly present in all legitimate local congregations of the faithful which, united with their pastors, are themselves called churches in the New Testament." Elsewhere in that same constitution, it is noted that "within the Church particular churches hold a rightful place" and "retain their own traditions without in any way lessening the primacy of the Chair of Peter." Thus it was in 1923, and ever shall be at Resurrection Parish!

SAINT ANASTASIA'S CHURCH — ROME

In addition to their other duties, members of the College of Cardinals also serve as pastors of churches in Rome, thus preserving the ancient practice of having the pontiff elected by the clergy of Rome.

The first church in the Eternal City assigned to a California "pastor" was Saint Anastasia, entrusted to the care of Archbishop J. Francis A. McIntyre at the time of his cardinalatial investiture. According to a dispatch written for the Chicago *Daily News* by George Weller on January 6, 1953, "Rome's saddest, coldest and most deserted church had a happy Italian Christmas when Pope Pius XII turned over the 1,800 year old Saint Anastasia to the new American cardinal."

The account went on to tell how "icy rainwater lay in pools on the church's marble floor. Blackened wooden panels covered the chapel windows. Thick green moss covered the gigantic arches of the church which perches upon the stables of chariot horses."

McIntyre had never "seen the tottering but surpassingly beautiful church which fell under his care. The cardinal, who passed from the Archdiocese of New York to the gigantic congregation of California, found himself pastor of a church without a single worshipper." At that time, Saint Anastasia Church was used only a few times each year. Teresa Celsi, wife of an unemployed carpenter, looked after the church and rang the rusty old bell to tell the hours.

Though the church was rarely used, it enjoyed a long and noble heritage. The earliest popes used to come on horseback to say the *aurora* or dawn Mass on Christmas. The church was mentioned in every copy of the *Missale Romanum* as the "station" church for the Nativity. Weller reported that "the Romans find it wholly appropriate that this somewhat sad gift should be given to an American cardinal on a day (January 6th) when Italians do their giving and piazzas are piled high with gifts, even for the police."

By 1953, there was nothing near Saint Anastasia but the Roman ruins and the last tenements which were being evacuated as the city moved outward. Anastasia's patrician life was as bound to those few acres beside the muddy Tiber as was Teresa Celsi's. In the garden beside the circus, a patrician lady had buried Anastasia's ashes after the lovely matron refused to renounce Christianity and was burned at the stake.

McIntyre was the latest of a long list of cardinals to look after Saint Anastasia. Two Germans and two Italian protectors rest under a single wooden cross. One of Spain's last grand inquisitors, Portuguese Nono Cardinal Acunha, lies beneath the marbled flagstone. The most recent "pastor" had been Michael Cardinal von Faulhaber of Bavaria who was too busy struggling with Hitler to realize that both his coat–of–arms and the pope's were blazoned on twin metal shields flanking the main doors.

The Catholics of Los Angeles responded generously to Cardinal McIntyre's pleas to restore the 4th century shrine. Over a million dollars was raised and used to bring the historic church into the modern world.

Today, only McIntyre's shield recalls the church's association with Los Angeles. Like his many predecessors, McIntyre's name is only a memory at Saint Anastasia.

SHRINE OF SAINT ANNE — BEAUPRE OF THE WEST

Although the Shrine of Saint Anne is among the least ornate centers of worship in the Christian world, thousands of pilgrims flock to the "Beaupre of the West" for the annual devotions honoring the mother of the Virgin Mary. If in more recent times the greatest number of participants in the religious festivities at the shrine have been outsiders, the origin of the devotions has a distinctively parochial tone.

The first chapel for the area, erected with volunteer help, early in 1908, by Father Patrick Hawe (1847–1923), was envisioned as a mission station for the Mexican–Americans then living in that section of the mother parish known as "East Santa Monica." Bishop Thomas J. Conaty dedicated the small frame church, located at 21st Street and Colorado Avenue, on April 12, 1908, placing it under the spiritual protection of Saint Anne, the mother of the Blessed Virgin.

From the very outset, a strong loyalty to their patronal saint characterized the inhabitants of the area. In 1912, Father Hawe gave the already–existing public devotions a permanent form with provisions for a special annual observance between July 19 and 27. Father Henry Weber, a Redemptorist, inaugurated the yearly devotions which have continued, without interruption, since 1912. The following year, a relic was secured from Saint Anne de Beaupre. Canada. It was venerated at the shrine for the first time on March 6.

Attendance at the annual novena increased to such proportions that, by 1916, additional facilities were required. An outdoor shrine was erected to accommodate a statuary depiction of Saint Anne and Child Mary, presented by Mr. and Mrs. William Doleshall. The enlarged shrine was solemnly dedicated on December 16, 1916. In 1935, an outdoor altar enclosure of wood and stucco was installed at the pilgrimage site. Further enlargements to the shrine came in 1955, four years after Saint Anne's had achieved parochial autonomy, when a new marble altar of the crucifixion was placed beneath an artistic twenty–four foot baldacchino supported by Gothic arches of laminated wood.

Devotion to the Mother of the Virgin Mary has continued to be a vital part of Catholic life in Southern California. Today, the Shrine of Saint Anne, located in a less affluent section of Santa Monica, retains its unusual distinction as a pilgrimage center of national prominence.

SAINT ANNE'S CHURCH — MOTHER LODE

There's an old house–of–worship in Columbia that parishioners and friends wouldn't allow to die. Though twice abandoned, Saint Anne's Catholic Church dates back to 1856, when it was erected by gold miners in California's historic Mother Lode.

The small but stately church and its handsome bell tower stands on a hill overlooking the onetime gold camp at Columbia. Locals claim that it is the oldest brick church in the state.

After a half century of distinguished service, the church was first closed in 1910, when the city's population dwindled to a handful of diehards. Sorely neglected and in considerable disrepair, the edifice was boarded up and abandoned. Such furnishings as statues, the baptismal font, Stations of the Cross, pews, prayer and song books were removed and stored with the few Catholic families remaining in the area.

Weather and vandals accounted for the front and back doors being ripped off. Knights of the road and wild animals used the church for shelter in times of rain and hail storms. Several of the tombstones in the graveyard remained intact, one of them engraved with the names of fifty parishioners of Saint Anne's dating back to the 1850s. Walking through the cemetery was like taking a stroll through an old history book.

When chancery officials announced plans to sell the building and move the graves and markers to nearby Sonora, some of the old–time families decided to raise funds to revivify Saint Anne's as the spiritual center of the community. With assistance from the Sons and Daughters of the Golden West, the red brick church was carefully, lovingly and artistically restored. Most of the valuable artifacts were returned.

Then, in 1974, Saint Anne's was condemned by public officials as being structurally unable to pass earthquake standards. Services were discontinued and once again the furnishings were moved to private homes for safekeeping.

Five years later, Saint Anne's went on the auction block. A "Save Old Saint Anne's" committee was formed by grandchildren of earlier parishioners. "We're going to raise enough money to make Saint Anne's structurally safe and restore her to her original beauty" said one of the local inhabitants.

Over the next decade, $90,000 was raised for earthquake proofing and bringing the church back to its original specifications. A new roof was put on, steel beams were implanted for stability and walls and ceilings were strengthened.

A new electrical system was installed and the original altar paintings, reputedly the work of James Fallon, were restored and remounted. The window jams were reset and the pews anchored in place.

The old bell at Saint Anne's, cast in New York and shipped around the Horn to San Francisco in 1857, was hoisted into place. Soon it began ringing out the call to Sunday liturgy. Once a month, a priest comes from Sonora for Mass and visiting priests are always welcomed.

Today the venerable church continues its earlier role as a vibrant part of Columbia's spiritual life—a lasting tribute to the prospectors and their descendants along California's Gold Dust Trails.

SAINT AUGUSTINE PARISH — CULVER CITY

Saint Augustine Parish in Culver City, recently observing the eightieth anniversary of its parochial autonomy, once encompassed the major part of the extensive valley formed by La Ballona Creek as it flowed toward Playa del Rey. The area was populated by permission of Commander José De la Guerra, as early as 1819, when settlers reported occupying, with their grazing stock, the place called "Pass of the Carretas," forerunner of present–day Washington Boulevard.

Rancho La Ballona was subdivided in 1886, and from that time onwards, was known as "The Palms." Catholic activities pre–date the subdivision by two years during which time priests from Saint Vibiana's Cathedral ministered to the Spanish–speaking people in the area. The initial church, placed under the patronage of Saint Augustine, as a tribute to the local pioneer, Augustine Machado, was built by Father Patrick Hawe (1847–1923) shortly after Victor Ponet purchased a 150–acre parcel of land adjoining The Palms, in 1886.

Spiritual needs of those attached to the mission church were cared for in subsequent decades by priests from Santa Monica, Redondo Beach and Saint Agnes. In the years after 1917, when a city was inaugurated at "Ivy Park" bearing the name of Harry H. Culver, "the fields became transformed and in their stead homes began to sprout and groups of industries and marts were springing up where barley leaves waved gently in the breeze."

On November 26, 1919, Bishop John J. Cantwell entrusted the newest pastorate in the Diocese of Monterey–Los Angeles to Father Thomas N. O'Toole ((1884–1960). During his short tenure the Irish–born pastor built a rectory and formulated plans for future parochial development. Shortly after Father John O'Donnell's arrival as pastor, in 1923, the plans for expanding the small frame church were implemented to provide for the growing number of new Catholic arrivals in the area. The educational needs of the parish, by then the "Heart of Screenland," were considered and it was decided to erect a new rectory on Jasmine Street and convert the earlier house into a convent. A school building program was inaugurated and, in the fall of 1926, the Daughters of Mary and Joseph initiated their work in California's southland by welcoming 123 pupils to their four classrooms in the converted parish hall.

It had been recorded in the local press as early as 1906, that "a grand church in the near future for The Palms was the leading topic of conversation" whenever a group of that area's Catholics assembled. Finally, late in 1936, construction began on a Gothic–type church with a capacity of 650 worshippers. The completed edifice, dedicated on May 2, 1937, created national interest as a prototype of reinforced steel construction whereby a network of pre–fabricated parts was welded into a single unit.

A permanent thirteen–room school was brought to completion during Father Leo Murphy's pastorate on property between Clarington and Jasmine Avenues. That building, along with a new convent, was ready for occupancy, late in 1948. Most recent addition to the vibrant Christian community at Culver City is the magnificent concrete church built in 1957–1958, by Monsignor James F. McLaughlin (1893–1968). By that time the creaking of ox–drawn carts along the Pass of the Carretas was only a hazy memory to the oldest of the city's residents.

A characteristic of parochial sketches is the tendency to eulogize the visible accomplishments of those specifically entrusted with the growth and development of a particular parish. Certainly that forms part of the picture, but the real and integrated history of the People of God, in any given area, is the record of the unnumbered souls who were its inhabitants, the saints and the sinners, the gay and the morose, the rich and the poor (with a fair sprinkling of those who were neither), the devout and the indifferent, the generous and the penurious. Though the names of those good people may escape the chroniclers, their place in the overall pageantry of God's plan is a feat worthy of continued emulation.

SAINT BRENDAN PARISH — VOCATIONAL PROFILE

If it's fair to use labels, one might designate the years 1940 through 1966 as the "golden vocational age" for Saint Brendan Parish in mid–town Los Angeles. During those often tumultuous years, one man monopolized the spiritual life of that square mile enclave. His name was Father Thomas F. Fogarty (1902–1966) and his shadow still hovers over the Catholic families populating that area of the Lord's vineyard.

The school was the apple of his pastoral eye. He refurbished it several times, ultimately relocating it and building it anew. His "kids" ran away with all the sports trophies and literary awards offered in the Wilshire District. He knew every youngster by first and last name.

Each September, he and the principal of the school began measuring up candidates for the priesthood and sisterhood. Rarely did a graduation pass that didn't find him proudly announcing that one or another youngster was entering the seminary or convent.

Though no records were kept, one can pretty accurately reconstruct the vocational profile during those years. The first two priests were Fathers Martin Hiss (ord. 1938) and Joseph Schneiders (ord. 1941). Though pre–Fogartarian they were the models he held up for emulation.

The first ordination was that of William Steffan (ord. 1946). Bill had studied for the archdiocese, then went off to serve in the military during World War II. When he returned, he was accepted as a clerical candidate for the Diocese of El Paso.

About the same time, there was John Fader (ord. 1947), who spent most of his active ministry as a chaplain in the armed forces. He retired with a senior commission and lived on in Clearwater, Florida. It was also in 1947 that Louis F. McKean was ordained for the Diocese of Reno. He later became a monk at New Melleray Abbey in Dubuque.

Maine–born Harold L. Ford, later pastor of All Souls Parish in Alhambra, was ordained on May 7, 1949. Harry was an accomplished carpenter in his seminary days. Probably the most intriguing seminarian associated with Saint Brendan's in those times was Harry Morgan, a former Episcopalian priest who became a Catholic in 1948. Harry lived at the rectory during his student days and was ordained for the Diocese of Gallup in 1954.

The year 1946 stands out prominently because three youngsters of the parish went off to Los Angeles College, the prep seminary for Los Angeles. Thirteen years later, Father John A. Mihan, later archdiocesan superintendent for secondary schools and Father Francis J. Weber celebrated their first Solemn Masses at Saint Brendan's, with a very proud Msgr. Thomas F. Fogarty serving as archpriest and delivering a stirring panegyric on the priesthood.

Fogarty once confided the "fall–back" approach he used with a promising youngster who was a little reluctant about entering the seminary after grammar school: "I send them to Loyola High and let the Jesuits snag them down the road." It was a highly successful tactic, judging from the statistics.

The list of Jesuits ordained from Saint Brendans is indeed impressive. There were Edward (ord. 1958) and John (ord. 1959) Callanan of the prominent mortuary family. And there was Francis Buckley (ord. 1958), professor of theology at the University of San Francisco; Anthony Sauer (ord. 1971), President of Saint Ignatius College Prep and Paul Pollock (ord. 1973), a missionary in Chiang Mai, Thailand.

Finally there were Jack Boyle (ord. 1960), a professor at the Jesuit School of Theology at Berkeley and his nephew, Gregory (ord. 1984), who is now assigned to Mission Dolores Parish in Los Angeles.

The Mitchell Boy Choir was a very active part of the parochial scene in the Fogarty years. Two youngsters from that group later grew into the priesthood— Michael Driscoll (ord. 1965), now Bishop for the Diocese of Boise and Dave Windsor, C.M. (ord.1974), rector of the American College in Louvain.

Though he came along three pastorates after the "golden vocational age" of the parish, John Woolway (ord. 1980) only served to confirm the adage that "one man sows, another reaps." Possibly the same could be said for Michael Scully (ord. 1986).

Recruitment was only the first part of the Fogartarian formula. Once a candidate was firmly ensconced into the seminary saddle, the genial pastor supported him in moments of turmoil, helped pay his bills, entrusted him with responsibility, gave him a key to the rectory, listened to and often acted on his suggestions and made sure that he had a part in every parochial ceremony and celebration.

In one of his sermons, all of which are carefully filed away at the Archival Center, Msgr. Fogarty waxed eloquently on the pastoral dimensions of the ministry. He concluded by reminding his listeners that "priests are fishers of men, not keepers of the aquarium."

The Archdiocese of Los Angeles does not need more vocations. It needs more priests like Thomas F. Fogarty to ferret out the vocations already implanted by the Lord!

SAINT BRIGID PARISH — LOS ANGELES

The origins of Saint Brigid's parish, in Los Angeles, can be traced to December 6, 1920, when Bishop John J. Cantwell asked Father John J. Egan to look after the People of God in that area of Los Angeles known as "the Mary of the Gael." Father Egan (1880–1964) was no stranger to the district, inasmuch as he had served previously as curate in the parent–parish of Saint Cecilia. At the time of its establishment as an autonomous parochial unit in the Diocese of Monterey–Los Angeles, three quarters of the territory comprising the parish was one gigantic corn field.

The pastor rented a small bungalow at 51st Street and Gramercy Place, where he offered Mass, for the first time on Christmas Day, 1920. Shortly thereafter, property was acquired for a church on nearby Western Avenue, then a narrow, rutted dirt road bounded on both sides by wide–open expanses. A frame building, occupied on the first Sunday of Lent, was dedicated by Bishop John Cantwell, on May 22, 1921. The small house adjoining the church, at 5214 Western Avenue, was subsequently acquired for a rectory.

Early in 1923, the Irish–born pastor announced plans for new facilities designed to serve the dual purpose of church and school. At the same time he notified the parishioners that the Sisters of Saint Joseph of Carondelet had agreed to staff the school. The formal dedication ceremonies took place on the last Sunday of October, 1923, when Monsignor John J. Cawley blessed the completed parochial plant. The Vicar General congratulated the faithful for the "magnificent new building" which he described as "an asset to the diocese, a pride to the city" and one "of which all can be justly proud."

Parochial life progressed in the subsequent decades in a most Christ–like atmosphere. In 1940, Archbishop Cantwell, feeling that a permanent church would befit the people of Saint Brigid, asked Father Egan to have plans drafted. The work was delayed by World War II and the actual ground–breaking ceremonies only took place on August 30, 1953. The handsome church, described as "a profession of faith spoken in steel and stone to challenge the materialism of our age," was dedicated by James Francis Cardinal McIntyre on May 22, 1955.

Built under the supervision of Father James Nash, the church won national honors for its striking architectural design. An imposing statute of Saint Brigid, the parish's fifth century patroness, graces the ceramic tile facade of the church. The 124–foot tower, surmounted by an eighteen–foot metal cross, contains four specially–designed bronze bells, fashioned by the Vanduzen Bell Foundry of Cincinnati. An electrically–programmed ringing device simulates the rhythm of swinging bells, while eliminating the tremendous strains of ponderous weight.

The initial schoolhouse was replaced a few years later by the present U–shaped re–inforced concrete block–building, with facilities for eight classrooms and an assembly hall. Bishop Alden J. Bell dedicated the new school on February 12, 1961. Parochial history, wherever it transpires recalls the comment of Pope John XXIII.

> Oh, what a gift of the Lord the parish is in the life of the Church, The parish, the parish . . . what an oasis of grace, of delight, and of blessings for all who belong to it, of all ages, of all social classes, in every sad and joyful event in life.

SAINT CATHERINE PARISH — AVALON

In one of his many historical monographs, W. W. Robinson tells how "Cabrillo discovered Santa Catalina Island for white men. Vizcaíno named it. The ships of nations and generations visited it, Before the American period it became a *rancho*, and remains one. It has been lived on by hunters, pirates, smugglers, stock raisers, miners, millionaires, fishermen and young people on vacations. Its setting is deep, clear waters, with undersea gardens at its base, a fertile sea life in its currents and fascination on its shores."

The history of the island is adorned with some of California's highest adventures—involving Spanish exploration, Indian life, sea–otter hunting, mining and real–estate booms, military action, fishing, stage–coaching, swimming and yachting. The twenty–one mile long island, varying in width from half a mile at the isthmus to eight miles at its widest part, also boasts the distinction of having "the most picturesque parish in the United States." From the 2,100 foot–high Mount Orizaba to the schools of flying fish that cavort in the warm off–shore waters, Saint Catherine's parish is a panoply of colorful quirks and contrasts serving the residents of the picturesque island.

White men first visited Catalina in 1542, but there is no available record as to when Mass was initially celebrated on the island. A decree from the Sacred Congregation of Propaganda Fide, February 12, 1871, specifically states that all the coastal islands belonged to the closest mainland jurisdiction for ecclesiastical purposes. When Father Alphonse Miller was appointed the first resident chaplain, late in 1903, the diocesan newspaper reported that "about two years ago they built a little church where Mass was said occasionally." Provisions were made for more serviceable quarters in 1912, and on April 28, Bishop Thomas J. Conaty dedicated the newly constructed church to Saint Catherine of Alexandria, for whom the island had been named. A fire completely destroyed both the church and rectory on the following December 23.

Work was begun anew and, on April 27, 1913, the bishop returned to Catalina for the dedication of the island's third Catholic Church, this one "perched high above the town and the semicircular Bay of Avalon." Living quarters for the pastor were located in the sacristy of the church. A reinforced concrete structure was erected to accommodate the growing number of tourists in 1950. The new church, built in the California mission style, and located in Avalon Valley at the entrance to Canyon Terrace, was blessed on August 27, 1950, by Archbishop J. Francis A. McIntyre. In 1963, ground was broken for a hall to serve the social needs of the parish.

Though present–day facilities provided at Saint Catherine's have all the modern conveniences, one is still inclined to agree with a statement in the southland's Catholic newspaper in 1905: "Robinson Crusoe could not have found a more elusive spot" for a parish than the seventy–six square mile parochial enclave on Santa Catalina Island!

SAINT JOSEPH CATHEDRAL — SAN DIEGO

The Cathedral of Saint Joseph figures prominently into the historical montage of California's Catholic heritage. Though divine worship has been offered at the present location for a mere hundred years, the parochial family of Saint Joseph legitimately claims lineal descent from that proto–missionary foundation on nearby Presidio Hill.

On September 29, 1851, Father John C. Holbein laid the cornerstone for an adobe church in Old Town to suc-

ceed the disintegrating mission and *presidio*. Several years later, that never–completed edifice was abandoned in favor of a small chapel in the home of Mr. John Brown. Those facilities, dedicated to Our Lady's Immaculate Conception, on November 21, 1858, served the spiritual needs of the local populace until the era of Father Anthony Ubach, the second "founder" of Catholicism in San Diego.

When that renowned cleric came to the area, in 1866, he had only two parochial boundaries: "The Pacific Ocean and the Colorado River." From the very outset of his ministry in San Diego, Father Ubach determined to restore at least a portion of the dignity conferred on the city, in 1840, by a pope and withdrawn, in 1842, by a bishop. If he could not make San Diego a diocese, he could build for the city a cathedral. And that he set out to do.

The first of his long–term plans was a magnificent celebration to commemorate the centennial of Mission San Diego, on July 18, 1769. Ubach invited Bishop Thaddeus Amat to preach on that occasion and the Spanish–born prelate happily complied. At the conclusion of the festivities, Bishop Amat set in place the cornerstone for the first church of Saint Joseph, in Old Town. Father Ubach's decision to invoke the patronage of that saint had considerable historical precedent, for it was through Saint Joseph's intercession that the abandonment of the whole San Diego enterprise was miraculously averted in 1770.

Work on the new church had not progressed very far, however, when the disastrous fire of April 20, 1872, totally destroyed the edifice. The conflagration was a sign to Father Ubach. He prayed and pondered and then decided to relocate the parish atop a mesa west of town, on a parcel of property at Third and Beech, donated to the Church by Alonzo Erastus Horton. A frame church, the second dedicated to Saint Joseph, was erected, in late 1874, and dedicated by Coadjutor Bishop Francis Mora on the following January 31st.

The growth and development of the parish and the city in the next decade and a half made possible the fulfillment of Father Ubach's dream for a "cathedral–like" church for San Diego. By 1894, the walls of a handsome Gothic church were firmly etched onto the San Diego skyline. The brick structure was erected adjacent to the older frame building, which continued its service under the appropriate title of Junípero Serra Hall. When Mora returned to San Diego for the solemn dedication of the new Saint Joseph's Church the bishop told a local reporter that "Father Ubach has not erected a church, but a cathedral."

That judgment was confirmed by the Catholic newspaper, which stated that Saint Joseph's "has no equal in church architecture in San Diego, and apart from the cathedral [of Saint Vibiana in Los Angeles], is said to be the most beautiful church in the diocese."

Father Ubach had indeed reared a "cathedral" for San Diego, though it would be another forty–two years before that title was officially bestowed. Yet, despite the fact that he had built a cathedral, Father Ubach would not be buried as a bishop. At his own insistence, the fabled priest laid in state in the old Junípero Serra Hall.

The fascinating story of this cathedral has yet to be fully told. Suffice to say that in 1936, San Diego received what was promised almost a century earlier, a residential bishopric. Restating the decree of his predecessor, five times removed, Pope Pius XI raised and eleveated San Diego "to the honor and dignity of a cathedral city."

SAINT PATRICK — WATSONVILLE

Late in 1863, Father Apollinarius Roussel (1823–1891) began planning for a church in Watsonville. After seeking the advice and support of the area's prominent Catholic lay people, Roussel asked James Waters to draw up the necessary plans.

The Hibernian Bank of San Francisco agreed to advance the funds, on a three year note, and the building program was inaugurated. On Sunday, July 3, 1864, Bishop Thaddeus Amat journeyed to Watsonville, where he put in place the cornerstone. The completed edifice was occupied in early fall. It was a spacious church by the standards of the time. The *Pajaronian* once referred to it as "the largest building of its kind in Santa Cruz County." The newspaper went on to describe how trees and flowers planted around the church further enhanced the beauty of the area.

The church was given parochial status in the Diocese of Monterey–Los Angeles in 1869. Following that distinction, sacraments other than Holy Mass and Confession were dispensed within its walls. The first Baptism was conferred on October 11, 1869, when Timothy Craig was initiated into the Catholic faith. That same day, Maria Vibiana Noriega was buried from the church. Patrick Kelley and Elizabeth Curran were the initial couple to exchange their marital vows in the historic edifice. Two years later, Bishop Amat bestowed the Sacrament of Confirmation on twenty–nine candidates.

With retirement of the parochial indebtedness in 1874 it was decided to complete the interior furnishings of the church. Bishop Francis Mora came from Los Angeles to offer the Sacred Liturgy in the handsomely outfitted church. By the turn of the century, the church had become too small for the needs of the ever–expanding congregation and plans were set in motion for its replacement with a commodious English Gothic building.

On September 6, 1901, the cornerstone of the edifice was excavated. Under the stone was a piece of hermetically sealed gas pipe. It contained several scrolls written by Father Roussel. One read:

> This church erected to the greater glory of God. Its cornerstone, put in place in honor of Saint Patrick, was blessed on July 3, 1864, during the reign of Pope Pius IX as Roman Pontiff; Abraham Lincoln as American President; Frederick Lowe as Governor of the State of California and Bishop Thaddeus Amat as Bishop for the Diocese of Monterey–Los Angeles.

According to an account in *The Monitor*, of those who had witnessed the putting in place of the cornerstone, "a large majority have laid down the burden of life and passed to eternity, and those who are still in the land of the living are nearing their journey's end and are waiting for Death's final summons."

Though it existed for a relatively short thirty–seven years, the initial Saint Patrick's church beautifully symbolized an early phase of early California's religious history when primacy was given to providing the very best of temporal surroundings for the "presence of God among His people."

SAINT PETER BASILICA IN LOS ANGELES

Among the most fascinating exhibits in the Treasury of Saint Peter's Basilica in Rome is a model of that historic church whittled by hand from more than 400,000 tiny pieces of wood. Attilio Savola and his son, Lucio, two famous Italian architects, carved the scale model from three kinds of wood. The miniature is exactly 300 times smaller than the real church.

As exhibited, the model is fifteen feet long, nine feet wide and eight feet in height from floor to top of the main dome. Seven massive crates are needed to contain the model when it is moved. To call it "little" is perhaps the wrong description because this woodcarving weighs nearly three tons!

In addition to the more than 140 statues of saints in the exhibits, the model reproduces the 284 columns in front of the basilica. A miniature lighting plant inside shines through the stained glass windows which are only three inches tall.

Attilio and Lucio created their masterpiece in 1:100 scale, using beech, birch and cirmolo (a soft white wood) to depict the stone and marble portions of the church. They copied the basilica even to the identical colorings.

Built underneath the model is a complete water system, so carefully crafted that the tiny fountains in the square actually spout with water. A sound tape makes the bells of the basilica ring, replicating the actual sounds so familiar in the Eternal City.

The entire display is such an exquisite work of art that Pope Pius XII became interested in it and asked to have the miniature set up inside the Vatican for his personal inspection. After blessing the model, the Holy Father expressed the hope that it could be taken on a world–wide tour so that millions of people could view and enjoy it.

The masterpiece was brought to Southern California in October of 1953, where it was exhibited on the sixth floor of the Broadway department store in the downtown area of Los Angeles. Leaders of local religious communities were invited to see the model. In addition to thousands of school children, James Francis Cardinal McIntyre, Bishops Joseph T. McGucken and Timothy Manning and Mayor Norris Poulson came to view this unique replication.

A handsome brochure, made available for visitors, featured the history of the basilica and how the model came to be crafted for the Holy Year of 1950. Accompanying the model were the Savola family members who made themselves available to answer questions about their work.

Ever–so–patiently, they explained how the Basilica of Saint Peter in Rome was "among the most exacting examples of devotion to an inspired idea ever recorded by great people from all walks of life." They told how, from 1453 onwards, "eleven renowned architects and thousands of collaborators and artisans lent their great talents, their magnificent artistry and their diligence to construct, through the reign of twenty–two popes, one of the best known and most famous buildings in all the world."

SAINT PETER DIAMOND JUBILEE — LOS ANGELES

Shortly after the turn of the century, the burgeoning Italian population of Los Angeles was creating something of a "little Italy," though it never became a virtually homogenous, characteristically Italian settlement, as in many other American cities. Saint Peter's Church was established in the spring of 1904 by Bishop Thomas J. Conaty to accomodate the growing number of Italians concentrated in central Los Angeles. By 1905, the predominantly Italian church was functioning in a temporary frame structure on North Spring Street under the pastoral care of Father Tito Piacenti.

On July 4, 1915, Saint Peter's was moved to its present site on North Broadway, in the heart of the Italian community, when the red sandstone memorial chapel, built in 1890 for old Calvary Cemetery, was entrusted to the Italians. The religious, cultural and social life of the Italian people quickly came to center around Saint Peter's and its modest hall. From throughout the community people came to the Italian church for their baptisms, weddings and funerals.

Under the auspices of Saint Peter's, they gathered to celebrate their various feastdays. There were even religious carnivals held four times annually, on the feasts of San Trifone, San Vittoriano, Madonna della Stella and Madonna di Costantinopoli.

In the years just prior to World War II the Italian families living in the vicinity of Saint Peter's began moving out to the suburbs and surrounding hills. And, with their departure, the area became mostly Chinese. The so–called " golden years" of the Italian community had come and gone. Italian shops closed their doors and popular Italian restaurants shut down. Other Italian firms relocated in different sections of the city.

Meanwhile, on June 13, 1944, a disastrous fire destroyed the church. A new edifice was built and dedicated on April 13, 1947. In the mid 1950s, canonical parochial status was given to Saint Peter's. Though the Italians had spread across the giant megalopolis, blending into the great sieve of peoples and cultures, they did not forget their common bond. They maintained their contacts, upheld their loyalties and clung to their ethnic roots. In the 1960s, the impetus for coordinating community activities and events passed back to old Saint Peter's—and rightly so. The historic foundation had always been an umbrella embodying the religious and cultural roots cherished by every Italian. Many began returning to Saint Peter's for their sacramental needs.

The Italians in Los Angeles have pulled themselves up by their bootstraps and joined the mainstream growth and development of a dynamic section of God's vineyard. From very meager beginnings, at the foot of the Elysian Hills, they continue their objectives of enriching American life with Italian culture.

Work on the envisioned Casa Italiana began in 1967, a project finally brought to completion in 1972. Fittingly enough, one of the central art objects in the Casa is a bust of Bishop John Baptist Scalabrini, named by Pope Leo XIII, "Apostle of the Emigrants."

SAINT TERESA — A HUNDRED YEAR LEGACY

What Saint Teresa's Parish on San Francisco's Potrero Hill observed during October of 1980 was the centennial of its establishment or a time of celebration for much of the city's older generation.

The *"potrero"* (new pasture) was the land grant bestowed by Spain to the *alcalde* Francisco de Haro for whom one of the nearby streets is named. It is a term familiar in the local nomenclature. After the Spanish came the Irish who worked in the Union Iron Works and Shipyards. Over the succeeding years, the Irish were joined by peoples of every race and color.

In the early days, spiritual guidance originated from

the priests who celebrated Mass on Sundays in the Breslan Hotel's dining room, at 22nd and George Streets. About 1878, Archbishop Joseph Sadoc Alemany designated the area as a "mission" of Saint Peter's. And, in 1880, the Dominican prelate advanced the "mission" to full parish status and appointed Father John Kemmey the first resident pastor. During the next hundred years, eight pastors and a host of assistants served the spiritual needs of Saint Teresa's Parish.

Erected originally at 19th and Tennessee streets, the church was a charming old Victorian building. It underwent a major structural renovation in 1974, in order to comply with the design of its original architect. New plaster and paint, modern terrazzo stairs and freshly–poured sidewalks gave the historic edifice a wholly refurbished appearance.

Even more important than the building was the renewed outlook imparted to the parochial community. Adult education courses were inaugurated, leadership training sessions were begun and programs for seniors were established. Emphasis on liturgical awareness created a new atmosphere for worship.

Prior to the 1970s, Saint Teresa School was regarded as a model institution and student teachers came from other areas of the city to observe its operation. However, urban renewal brought about a reduction in enrollment and, in 1974, the decision was made to close down that phase of the parish commitment. It was a time of real anguish for the whole parish.

Although the surrounding parishes could easily accommodate all the children from Saint Teresa, the loss of an institution that had been so vital a part of parish life for sixty–two years was a painful one. A key factor in the accomplishments of the parish has been the Presentation Sisters who first came in 1912. After the closing of the school, they remained at Saint Teresa's, serving the community in an expanded ministry as parochial associates. Their efforts cover a wide spectrum, planning Liturgies, helping with the seniors, directing social programs, educating children for First Communion and counseling the troubled.

The priests and people of Saint Teresa can look back upon an eventful past as they grapple with the challenges of the new millennium. They are confidant that the new century will find them as relevant as they've always been.

SAINTS PETER AND PAUL "ITALIAN CATHEDRAL" — SAN FRANCISCO

For well over a hundred years, San Francisco's Church of Saints Peter and Paul has served the Catholics of the North Beach area with respect and admiration. It was and is the church which symbolizes the "American Dream" to thousands of Italian immigrants.

Serving the first national Italian parish in California, the historic edifice stands as a monument to the dedication of immigrant clergy and laity alike who worked long and hard to build a church reflecting the artistic and historical heritage of Italy in the New World. The church's twin spires and Romanesque facade lend grace and beauty to North Beach which was one of the first "little Italys" in the United States. For the immigrants and their children, the church has always represented a typical Italian cathedral.

Saints Peter and Paul was more, however, than a church providing the sacraments for an ethnic people. Priests attached to the parish have offered communicants a place to learn and to play, and to celebrate the simple joys and major triumphs of daily life. The history of the church reflects the pioneer spirit of the Italians who first came to California during Gold Rush days and remained to participate in the building of the west.

From the church's Americanization classes emerged citizens who have contributed greatly to the country. One merely has to look at what has been accomplished in agriculture, education, science, law, politics, banking, architecture, opera, theatre, music, dance and all other aspects of the American experience to discover evidence of their offerings.

When there was poverty and despair, it was their "cathedral" which offered hope and assured human dignity. And, when there was fear from such events as the earthquake and fire, the Great Depression and five wars, it was their "cathedral" which sheltered them.

As new generations came into being, it was the "cathedral" which established a school to educate their children. And it was the "cathedral" which founded a boys' club and a girls' club to combat delinquency by harnessing their energies through athletic endeavors, showcasing their talents and stimulating their minds with culture.

Through Saints Peter and Paul, equality was given great significance, integration was emphasized and discrimination was prohibited. Today the parish has entered into its second century and there still persists a zealous commitment to serve its parishioners with respect and affection. And while it will never lose its pride of *Italianita*, it stands ready to serve a new wave of immigrants, this time the Chinese.

In 1984, the head of the Salesian Order wrote a letter paying tribute to the presence of Saints Peter and Paul in San Francisco. Therein he said:

> Your parish, which was the first Salesian foundation in the United States, was established to serve San Francisco's immigrants at a time when they were confronted with the problems connected with a new place and a strange language and with the rampant religious indifference and anti–clerical spirit of the age. Our immigrants were in dire need of priests who could understand

Saint Timothy Church

them, and who would take a personal interest in their families and especially their children.

It was a challenge met with zealous enthusiasm. The story of this magnificent parish is told in a book recently published under the title *Saints Peter & Paul Church, The Chronicles of the Italian Cathedral of the West 1884–1984.*

SAINT TIMOTHY CHURCH — LOS ANGELES

Unlike many cities in the east and even San Francisco on the Pacific coast, Los Angeles has only a half dozen architecturally significant Catholic churches.

Among the outstanding exceptions is Saint Timothy on West Pico Boulevard at Beverly Glen. The founding pastor, Father William T. O'Shea (1902–1963), spent six years planning and bringing to completion a church that ranks among the truly precious jewels in the Archdiocese of Los Angeles. Designed by Harold Gimeno and built by Robert B. Hedberg, the shell of the church was erected by a crew that was mostly Mormon—men who simultaneously built the Mormon Temple in Westwood.

The church is unusually rich in its decorative features. Its altarpiece was fabricated in Spain at some

undisclosed date. Early in the 1900s, it was sent to Yucatan, where it was confiscated by the Mexican government. Subsequently acquired by an art dealer in New York, the altarpiece was brought to New York City and purchased by a benefactor who intended to have it installed in Saint John Episcopal church at Adams and Figueroa.

In the mid 1940s, the altarpiece was once again put on the market. Officials at 20th Century Fox Studios alerted Father O'Shea who was able to acquire it at auction. Also included with the central altarpiece were a number of frames and panels.

The tabernacle was designed by craftsmen in the special effects department of Metro Goldwyn Mayer under the direction of Thomas McCorry. It is made up of figured brass castings, gold–plated with silver figures of the twelve apostles.

Another distinctive feature of the church is the ornate pulpit which is composed of two separate pieces. The base, consisting of three carved eagles, came from the William Randolph Hearst collection.

Even the pews have an interesting background. During a strike at 20th Century Fox, the woodshop stood idle and studio moguls allowed carpenters to build the pews with lumber donated by Arthur J. Harff.

The *Via Crucis* or Stations of the Cross, acquired from the Vatican Mosaic Studios, were donated by a

Jewish man in the Motion Picture Industry in gratitude for the technical advice given by Father O'Shea on one of his films. There are no fewer than sixty–seven stained glass windows in the church, nearly all of them crafted in Ireland. The one over the main entrance portrays winged symbols of the four evangelists—the ox for Luke, the eagle for John, the lion for Mark and the seraph for Matthew.

The church is replete with artistic paintings, including one of the Presentation of the Child Jesus in the Temple which is thought to be a work of the school of Bartolome Esteban Murillo (1617–1692), one of the great names in artistic annals.

Saint Timothy, under whose patronage the church was erected, is represented four times in the church, once in a window, once in a painting and twice in statues. He and other saints are often depicted with emblems by which they can be identified.

The late Donald Kennedy, a journalist with a life–long interest in architecture and arts, is the author of a monograph on *The Altar and Decorative Features of Saint Timothy's Church* which examines in great detail this truly beautiful house–of–worship.

There is nothing incongruous or unliturgical about designing a church that is also devotional and artistic. Until fairly recently, plain and drab churches were intended to serve only until resources allowed for more ornate monuments to the Lord.

God is praised in artistic expression. It is a profound misreading of Vatican Council II documents that attempts to justify the uninspirational Catholic churches that are beginning to dot the country's landscape.

SAINT VIBIANA CATHEDRAL

As early as 1869, Bishop Thaddeus Amat announced plans for a Cathedral to serve the Diocese of Monterey–Los Angeles. Upon his return from Rome after Vatican Council I, a site was selected further north yet considerably south of the plaza. Amat had acquired property in that area in August of 1858 from Amiel Cavallier. It was an attractive piece of land with a small stream flowing through the middle. The bishop petitioned the city for a deed of quitclaim and received assurance that such a request would be granted. In May, 1871, Amat gave his formal approval and the work of clearing the ground began.

The enterprise, like all others of the time, was closely linked to the ups and downs of agricultural and sheep raising interests. The winters of 1868–1870 were exceptionally dry and, therefore, economically unfavorable. Hence, in order to adjust the original plans along more modest lines, a smaller church was designed by the local

architect, E.F. Kyser, who in later days was assisted by W.J. Mathews with whom he formed a partnership. The general plan of the structure was suggested by that of the *Iglesia de Puerto de San Miguel* in Barcelona and provided for a building eighty feet wide and 160 feet deep.

Beyond the clearing of the property, little work was done in 1871. The outer walls took form in 1872 and 1873 in a seemingly endless succession of delays. Bishop Amat went to Europe for his health in 1874 and during his absence his coadjutor, Bishop Francis Mora, renewed efforts to complete the structure before Amat's return. Louis Mesmer took charge of the construction program in the winter of 1874–1875 and "inaugurated a renewal of the work by bringing to it an energy which never flagged until the structure was ready for divine services. "

By the end of June, 1875, the building had been roofed. The giant bell of Mission San Juan Capistrano, cast in Massachussetts in 1828, was blessed on July 4 and on the following day a festival was held to raise funds for the continuance of the work. A group of ladies sponsored the gala affair within the bare brick walls and it was estimated " that at least three thousand visitors were present during the day and partook of the elegant bounty." On Sunday afternoon, January 2, 1876, the foundation stone of the high altar was blessed and set in place. Later additions were no less newsworthy:

> The cupola of the new Church is, without exception, the most graceful specimen of architecture in California. It is a marvel of symmetrical beauty and comely shapeliness. The eye just naturally lingers on it, and never tires of admiring its elegance and handsome proportions. That beautiful tower will yet be sung in verse and commemorated in lasting prose.

In the first months of 1876, the work of decorating the interior and exterior of the church was undertaken by Joaquin Amat, the bishop's nephew. The artistic stonework for the railing in front of the building was manufactured in blocks in East Los Angeles at the artificial stone factory of Messrs. Bashard and Hamilton. Railings, fabricated from iron, products of Page and Gravel, formed a beautiful and suitable enclosure which lasted for many years. The two niches flanking the rose window received statues of SS. Peter and Paul, and on the upper front wall of the transepts images of the four evangelists were attached. Statues of SS. Patrick and Emigdius were placed at either side of the main altar.

At last, on Palm Sunday April 9, the first services were held within the cathedral walls. The palms were blessed at ten o'clock after which a solemn pontifical Mass was celebrated in the presence of the city's leading dignitaries. The spacious new church easily accommodated the immense throng gathered for the joyous occasion. Immediately after the Mass, Bishop Amat imparted a special apostolic blessing and offered a few words of gratitude to his flock.

The colorful ceremonies of consecration were scheduled for the second Sunday after Easter, April 30. Archbishop Joseph Alemany of San Francisco officiated and celebrated the Mass. The renowned Indian Jesuit priest, Father James Bouchard, gave an historical description of the symbolic ceremonies of which the only extant report says the

> . . . eloquent divine gave a graphic description of the ceremonies of consecration, and illustrated in a lucid manner all the symbols and mysteries of the magnificent spectacle. He spoke of the building of the Temple of Solomon, and compared the work of erecting a modern Tabernacle of God; he made a fervent appeal on behalf of religion and religious works, and adjured his hearers to turn from the sinful ways of the world and consecrate their souls to God.

At the conclusion of the consecration rite, Bishop Amat was host to the archbishop and various civic officials at a banquet in the episcopal residence. Alemany delivered an interesting address outlining the historical background of the California apostolate, recalling the somewhat–forgotten trials and tribulations that plagued the early missionaries. To these pioneers, Alemany gave the credit for planting the seed that blossomed forth into Saint Vibiana Cathedral.

SAINT VICTOR CHURCH — WEST HOLLYWOOD

Among the more obvious disadvantages arising from the Golden State's constantly growing influx of people is the gradual disappearance of the "little country churches" that once dotted the skyline of California. Growing parishes have been forced to replace these quaint landmarks with larger and more efficient buildings.

One of the last of these churches to be dismantled in the southland was Saint Victor's in West Hollywood. Erected in 1906 by Victor Ponet and given the name of his patron saint, the tiny church served the area for over fifty years and came to be known throughout the country as a truly "period church." On the day of its dedication, one commentator noted that "in all California there is no more romantic Church, its gilded cross on the hill, a beacon to the western sea; its sweet–toned bell calling to prayer the lovely valley before it. Saint Victor stands the last link in the chain from Mount San Bernardino to the Pacific."

The Church served the old Diocese of Monterey–Los Angeles as a mission until 1925, when it was given autonomy and a resident pastor. From those years onward there were recorded in its parochial registers the names of many men and women who became later prominent in Church and civic affairs of California. Most of the people in West Hollywood (or Sherman as it was known in the early days) worked in the nearby Doheny Oil Wells or at the large railway repair yard that M.H. Sherman had built adjacent to the roadbed at the foot of the hills.

Continuing for several decades as the only church under the patronage of the fourteenth pope, Saint Victor had its share of distinctions in its fifty–three years. The Legion of Decency, for instance, was born, nurtured, and propagated from the sanctuary of this humble church in the 1930s Spread over the pages of several national magazines, the rustic frame church found its way into most of the country's homes. On dozens of occasions, the large and rambling camera vans from the nearby Hollywood studios were driven to its doorsteps for the shooting of scenes for a major film. At one time or another, most of the movie industry's great names attended weddings or funerals there or perhaps enrolled their names as parishioners. It was not uncommon at all to kneel beside Loretta Young, Jimmy Durante, Jane Wyatt or Steve McNally at Holy Mass.

Truly a mother to its people, the church grew into a fully–developed "parochial plant." During the long pastorate of Msgr. John J. Devlin, a school, convent, and rectory were added, until gradually the little white church stood as a dwarf among its offspring. When

Saint Victor Church

progress and the march of time finally caught up with this last of the city's little country churches, a reluctant pastor and flock put aside personal attachments to lay plans for a more commodious church to serve another generation.

It was a sad July 29, 1959, when the wreckers arrived to begin their work. One loyal parishioner was heard to say, "Ours was a church that smiled and beckoned and called and contributed its fragrance and beauty as only cultivated places can. A church where the old, the ailing and the feeble found a helping hand. A church where the young could gather, listen and understand. It was a church, Father, born a church!"

Now there stands a lovely new Saint Victor's, modern in every way, artistic and serviceable. Only the "sweet–toned bell" remains as a reminder of the past. Not infrequently there is heard, be it just a whisper, a longing sigh for its noble predecessor. While the passing of the "little country churches" may be a sign of Catholic maturity, it is hardly a welcome event in the lives of those who grew up in California and remember it as a truly "Golden State."

Saint Vincent Church

SAINT VINCENT DE PAUL — LOS ANGELES

The history of Southern California's most beautiful parochial church is almost as fascinating as the artistic embellishments that make it a distinctive landmark along the Pacific Slope. The cornerstone of the first church dedicated to Saint Vincent de Paul was set in place during July of 1866. Unfortunately, a fire gutted the building before its completion and another two decades passed before a church could be erected under the saint's patronage. During the intervening years, the chapel of old Saint Vincent College was pressed into service for quasi–parochial functions.

On January 15, 1887, the Very Reverend Aloysius J. Meyer celebrated the first Mass in the newly–completed Saint Vincent Church then located at Grand Avenue and Washington Boulevard. Attached to the parish were Catholics from the city's downtown area as well as those scattered west to Santa Monica and south to San Pedro. Father Meyer served as both president of the college and pastor of the parish.

In 1907, a location for a second church was acquired at the corner of Adams Boulevard and Figueroa Street. A local newspaper stated that the number of parishioners had made St. Vincent the largest parochial enclave in the diocese. Plans for the new church were delayed during World War I. A fund drive was inaugurated in the early 1920s and ultimately, at the request of Bishop John J. Cantwell, Edward Laurence and Carrie Estelle Doheny agreed to finance the new edifice. Earlier the Dohenys

had contributed substantially to the erection of Saint John Episcopal Church to the east of Figueroa.

The Boston architect, Ralph Adams Cram, known in those days as "America's greatest designer of churches," was asked to draft plans for a Spanish Renaissance building that would incorporate the major features of Santa Prisca in Taxco, Mexico. Mr. Doheny placed few restrictions on the architect. He did insist, however, that, with the exception of the mosaics and marbles, all the furnishings and decorations for the church should be made in the United States.

The first Mass was offered in the new Saint Vincent Church on April 5, 1925. A scroll presented to the bishop read thusly: "We, humble members of St. Vincent Parish, and spiritual children of Your Lordship, deeply sensible of the God–given privilege of building the new St. Vincent Church, beg to tender to Your Lordship, as the Roman Catholic Bishop of Los Angeles–San Diego, this new temple to God; and we pray Your Lordship to accept it for the greater honor and glory of God, for the good of souls, and as an expression of our Catholic faith and thanksgiving to Our Blessed Savior." Several years later, an endowment fund was established by the Dohenys whereby the maintenance of the church would be provided for in ensuing years. Mr. Doheny was a shrewd observer of demographics.

In October of 1930, Bishop J. Cantwell consecrated

the church, assisted by Bishops Francis Clement Kelley (Oklahoma), Henry Tihen (Denver) and John J. Mitty (Salt Lake City). On the 24th, Patrick Cardinal Hayes of New York offered the first Solemn High Mass in the church.

Each of the artistic features of the church has historical significance and none more than the reredos of the main altar wherein are portrayed the twelve apostles, together with Saint Edward which closely resembles Mr. Doheny. One of the early architectural handbooks for Los Angeles tell its readers that "no one has seen Los Angeles until he or she has visited and prayed in Saint Vincent Church."

That's still true.

SAN JACINTO CHAPEL

According to R. Bruce Harley, Fray Antonio Peyri is credited with erecting and successfully managing the largest and most populous mission in both Americas during Spanish and Mexican times. Among the outposts of San Luis, Rey de Francia, which Peyri inaugurated in 1797, were San Antonio de Pala Asistencia and four *estancias* or cattle ranches, all of which were notable additions to California's skyline.

The *estancia* of San Jacinto was located a few miles west of the present-day city of that name, along what is now the Ramona Expressway. It was begun in or around 1819, on the feast of Saint Hyacinth, August 16th. Included in the complex of buildings forming the central patio were a granary for wheat and barley, an adobe house and a "pretty chapel," where Holy Mass was periodically offered.

There is a record that Fray Mariano Payeras and Fray Jose Sanchez visited San Jacinto in September of 1821. Then the most distant *rancho* of San Luis Rey Mission, San Jacinto had a fair number of cattle. Here is how they described the *rancho*: "On the whole stretch, there are no trees. On reaching San Jacinto, the land, although used for pasture, proved to be of little value on account of the alkali."

In 1822, Fray Antonio Peyri enumerated the holdings of San Luis Rey, pointing out that the land in that area was "to a great extent sterile, much of it entirely so. For that reason, the livestock needs it all; indeed, in years where there is little rain, the stock dies for want of pasture."

Five years later, Auguste Bernard Duhaut–Cilly told how "every Sunday the *majordomos* or overseers come to the mission to give an account to the Father regarding the work of the past week and the state of the *ranchos.*" When the properties of San Luis Rey Mission were secularized, on August 22, 1835, San Jacinto Rancho was appraised as being worth $10,258, which was a considerable chunk of money in those days.

The original *rancho* encompassed 130,000 acres, extending from a point near the foot of Mount San Jacinto to today's city of Corona. It included all of the valley except canyon mouths, such as the later Soboba Indian Reservation.

In the years after Mexican independence, the original grant was divided into several parcels and sold for paltry sums to various persons. In 1842, Governor *pro tem* Manuel Jimeno signed over the eastern portion of the 35,000 acre *rancho*, where the original buildings were located, to Jose Antonio Estudillo.

When Eugene Duflot de Mofras visited the site, he found the main compound to be still intact and in fairly good shape, but described the San Jacinto ranch buildings as being "nearly all in ruins." Estudillo portrayed the ranch headquarters as being "a dilapidated earthen-roofed" building. Estudillo erected a house near the old chapel and his widow lived there for several decades after his death. His son built a two–story brick house in 1880 about two miles from the chapel.

In 1900, Francisco Pico erected an addition to the original chapel, converting the whole building into an L–shaped dwelling for his family. The chapel–turned–ranch house was destroyed by fire in 1969, thus terminating the last tangible physical connection with the colonial period, 150 years after its construction.

NUESTRA SEÑORA DE SAN JUAN DE LAGOS

Shortly after the Spanish conquest, a small statue of Our Lady's Immaculate Conception was brought to the New World by missionaries and placed in the parish church of San Juan de Lagos, not far from Guadalajara.

In 1623, a professional acrobat travelling with his wife and two daughters stopped at San Juan de Lagos, to give some performances.

While practicing their act, one of the daughters lost her balance, fell from the swing–bars and was killed.

As her parents were preparing the young acrobat for burial, an old Indian lady reportedly touched her with the statue of Our Lady and she was restored to life. News of the incident spread rapidly, thus giving rise to widespread devotion to *La Virgen de San Juan de Lagos*.

Although Fray Francisco Garcia Diego y Moreno, the proto–Bishop of Both Californias, was a frequent visitor to the Marian Shrine at San Juan de Lagos, devotion to *Nuestra Virgencita* in the southland can only be traced back some fifty years. According to local legend, one day in 1925, Mary Silva was suddenly stricken with an excruciating pain in her back and carried upstairs by her husband. She began to choke and by the time a physician arrived, she gave every indication of being dead.

The family refused to accept the medical verdict about Mary's demise. Following a series of invocations to Our Lady of San Juan de Lagos, Mrs. Silva's vital signs returned and eventually she recovered her health completely. She then vowed to build a shrine to Mary in thanksgiving. Two years later, Mary arranged with an elderly sculptor at the Plaza Church, in Los Angeles, to have an image of Our Lady carved in wood. The likeness was to follow the general features of the statue at San Juan de Lagos.

The statue was subsequently enthroned in a converted wash–house, at the rear of the Silva home, near the intersection of Foothill Boulevard and Woodward Avenue. In subsequent years, devout pilgrims, mostly Americans of Hispanic descent, travelled from as far away as Mexico and Texas, to the nondescript shrine for private devotions to *Nuestra Señora de San Juan de Lagos.*

The daughters of the Silvas, Carmen Jones and Dolores McDole, dutifully maintained the shrine. Each day they opened the make–shift chapel to the fifty or sixty pilgrims who came for prayers to "*Nuestra Virgencita.*"

Nuestra Señora de los Lagos

A few years ago, following arrangements to sell the Silva property, plans were made to move the statue of Our Lady to a specially constructed grotto–shrine at Santa Rosa Church, in San Fernando. And there, on February 27, 1975, Bishop Sinforiano Lucas, the Vicar Apostolic of Pilcomayo, presided at impressive enthronement ceremonies for Our Lady of San Juan de Lagos.

SAN MIGUEL DEL PUERTO — BARCELONA

Snuggled away at the head of *Calle de la Alegria,* just one street behind Barcelona's *Paseo Nacional* is the stately *Iglesia de San Miguel del Puerto,* a church that played an important part in the historical annals for the Archdiocese of Los Angeles. It was the Baroque Spanish style of that parochial church which Bishop Thaddeus Amat used as the model when he had plans drawn for Saint Vibiana's Cathedral in the 1870s.

The Barcelona "model" has its own distinctive history, quite apart from the role it occupied in the far–away Diocese of Monterey—Los Angeles a century ago. Once a majestic structure, it was built in a period when the "Queen City" assimilated the cultures of East and West with such proficiency as to achieve a flourishing municipal life and a wide and vigorous political, military and commercial expansion. Many features of that era are reflected in the architecture of San Miguel del Puerto. Erected in the early months of 1775 and dedicated with great solemnity on October 3rd of that year, the church was a monument of gratitude for the return of Bishop Benito de Sala and 300 of the Barcelona clergy from exile.

That the church was long among the city's more celebrated houses–of–worship is testified to by two valuable printed treatises issued at the time, one the *Sermon en la Dedicación del Templo de San Miguel del Mar* and the other *Sermon que en el tercero dia de las Fiestas, que se hicieron en el Nuevo Templo.* The church was severely damaged by an earthquake toward the end of the last century, a fact which necessitated a great deal of renovation and alteration in the original design. The passage of time has taken its toll also. Today there are notable discrepancies in the stateliness of the exterior from the magnificent proportions of the interior. And it must be noted that Saint Vibiana's Cathedral "suffered" several major modifications too over the years—all of which lessen the obvious similarity between mother and daughter.

It is not surprising that Bishop Thaddeus Amat used the design of San Miguel del Puerto as the basis for his cathedral in Los Angeles. He had grown up in the port district of Barcelona and often participated as a server in the liturgical ceremonies of that church. But there was more than that. The historic edifice stood on the spot occupied by a former church erected through the munificence of an ancient ancestor, Pedro Amat.

Pedro was a Commissioner for Barcelona and a private chamberlain to King Martin I of Aragon. A great patron of the church, Pedro had given the property and a partial endowment for the earlier building. (It was, by the way, from Pedro's line of the Amat family that Luigi Cardinal Amat (1796–1828) was descended). How fitting that something so prominent as an archdiocesan cathedral serve as an embodiment of an architectural excellence from the once proud capital of the Catalan–Aragonese monarchy.

SAN SALVADOR'S BELL

The original parish *capilla* erected at San Salvador collapsed before it was completed, probably because its foundation rested on quicksand. Another more sturdy edifice was built at Agua Mansa in 1851–1852. It was used until 1893. Nothing remains today of Agua Mansa, except the little burial ground on the hill above the river, near which once stood the chapel. It is the oldest cemetery in the area and many early pioneers are interred there.

One of the most treasured items publicly displayed in the fore court of Riverside's Mission Inn is the bell of the one–time church of El Salvador at Agua Mansa. The historic artifact has the unusual distinction of being made in the area. It was carefully fashioned in a manner that incorporated all the best features of California's noble traditions.

The bell was cast in 1866, by means of a furnace and mold specially made in front of the adobe home of Cornelius Jensen, adjacent to the Agua Mansa church. (The present Jensen home on Riverview Drive was erected four years later.)

The church had no bell during its early years. But, when Father Peter Verdaguer came to the area as pastor, he set his heart on a bell with which to announce the calls to worship. Parishioners joined forces to complete that priestly dream.

Several local residents, among them Cornelius Jensen, offered to help mold a bell. It was a rather heroic effort and one unparalleled in that part of the state. Father Verdaguer later recalled that the total cost was two horses and twelve dollars.

People from nearby environs brought in their jewelry and silverware to be melted down. Even the poorest neighbors tossed some small mementos into the pot. Remnants of an earlier bell were also utilized. A throng of interested persons gathered to witness the bell being taken from its mold. Unfortunately, to the regret of all the bystanders, there were two small holes near the top of the bell.

Though the imperfections marred the purity of the tone, the bell did make a joyful and welcome noise, one which resounded throughout the Santa Ana river lowlands. It was dedicated to *Nuestra Señora de Guadalupe*. The bell survived the disappearance of San Salvador church. For some years it hung from a tree on the site of the old Agua Mansa Church, the last vestige of a once–active parochial family.

Later, the bell was removed to the Church of the Holy Rosary which was built in nearby Colton. There it hung until a fire destroyed that church. The bell was found among the ashes, still intact.

Frank Miller ultimately purchased the bell from the Catholic community of Colton, much to the distress of the history–minded. Today, the bell can still be seen at the Mission Inn, Riverside, crammed full of historic associations and nostalgic memories.

SAN SECONDO D'ASTI CHURCH

Although there are few raisin or table grapes produced in Southern California, over a hundred tons of wine grapes are grown annually in the western part of San Bernardino County. Today some of the finest quality–wines in all of California, along with champagnes, vermouths, and brandies originate in that "oldest wine–producing district" in the state.

It was the recognition that viniculture dates from provincial times that prompted Secondo Guasti to erect a modest little church in the midst of his vast vineyards as a memorial to "the many and glorious missions of California." The scenic edifice, with its thick walls and enchanting bells, is located at the foot of the Cucamonga Mountains, forty–three miles east of Los Angeles, in the center of 5,000 vine–covered acres of the Italian Vineyard Company.

Secondo Guasti, for many years "one of the leading viticulturists in the states," built the attractive little edifice in 1924. He personally supervised the smallest parts of its construction and furnishing, including such objects as the five wrought–iron chandeliers that hang from the big wooden beams of the ceiling.

Built originally to provide for the spiritual needs of those employed in "the world's largest vineyard," the white–washed adobe church retains all the simplicity associated with an earlier generation in California. In design, the church was patterned after the one in Guasti's native Italian village dedicated to his patron saint, the protector of the Piedmontese, San Secondo d'Asti. The large circular stained–glass window above the white marble altar depicts San Secondo arrayed in a purple mantle. In his right hand he holds the reins of a horse, while grasping a picture of the city of Asti to his heart with his left hand.

On Palm Sunday, in 1926, Secondo Guasti donated the church to the Diocese of Los Angeles–San Diego and, on the following October 3, Bishop John J. Cantwell asked Father John Cotta to look after the Catholics inhabiting the cluster of villages located on and around the three nearby wineries. Through subsequent decades, the Church of San Secondo d'Asti has continued to serve the area. Each year the pastor blesses the grape crop from the portico in front of the church.

Some years after his death, the residents of Guasti made provisions for a bronze bust of Secondo Guasti, founder of their community, on a pedestal in the courtyard of the church he generously provided for their convenience. Visitors to the wineries invariably pause in the small church of San Secondo d'Asti, there to ponder the historical heritage and traditions of a community, an industry and a legend—all the dream of Secondo Guasti.

The late Archbishop John J. Cantwell included Guasti in that select list of Italian–born pioneers who "brought to us not only a love for the finer things of life, for music and the arts, but also a bright intelligence, a business acumen and a tireless industry."

STANFORD MEMORIAL CHURCH

The Memorial Church on the campus of Stanford University, known widely for its artistic stained glass windows and masterful mosaics, impressed one visitor as "being Catholic in every way except name." Certainly it embodies all the Christian traditions of earlier centuries.

From the outset, Senator Leland Stanford and his wife, Jane, envisioned that the educational institution named for their son should include a house–of–worship. Today the church stands as the central building of the main quadrangle.

Several years after the university was opened, Mrs. Stanford decided to complete the original plans by building the church as a memorial to her recently deceased husband. Dedicated on January 25, 1903, the church was severely damaged in the 1906 earthquake and had to be restored, stone–by–stone.

Charles Allerton Coolidge, the architect, decided to adopt, for educational purposes, the style of the California missions, which was an outgrowth of Moorish and Romanesque architecture. That style is distinguished by long, low buildings, connected by wide colonnades and separated by open courts. The basic plan of Stanford is a quadrangle arrangement, with low buildings grouped symmetrically about a central court.

The altar, font and chancel steps are all fashioned from marble. The pulpit is made of intricately carved stone, while the three double doors at the main entrance are of solid bronze. The twelve apostles that once occupied the niches of the chancel were damaged beyond repair by the 1906 earthquake.

Probably the most striking feature of the church is the vast expanses of mosaic. They are all of Venetian origin, based on 15th century models. The reproduction of Cosimo Rosselli's "Last Supper" is the most spectacular of the many mosaic masterpieces. Largest of the mosaics, featuring "the Sermon on the Mount," adorns the facade of the church. No fewer than forty–seven persons are depicted in that colorful scene which has become a hallmark of Stanford University.

The windows, American in design and construction, are the work of Frederick S. Lamb of New York. Their theme is taken from the New Testament. Most colorful of the windows are the three in the chancel representing the birth, crucifixion and ascension of Christ. One newspaper account said that "the whole life of the Savior is mirrored" in those windows.

On significant occasions in the life of the university, the church has played an important part by providing the setting for the ceremonial. It is indeed more than a building famed for its architecture and mosaics; it is a place specially hallowed by devotion and memories of the Stanford family and community. Mrs. Stanford retained her interest in the church. She once remarked to Dr. John C. Brannet, then President Emeritus, that "while my whole heart is in the university, my soul is in that church."

Today the memorial church remains an integral part of the university life. Baptisms, weddings and occasionally funerals are held there. It is committed to reflect the highest Christian traditions and in its work and services (it) seeks to unite the insights of faith with achievements of knowledge. Among the many inscriptions carved into the church's sandstone walls is one which is especially meaningful: "God is all in all; and if we cannot appreciate and worship Him in all things, we worship only part of God."

WORLD'S LITTLEST CHURCH

The designation of 1983–1984 as a Holy Year had special significance to the Catholic residents of Grimes, California. For them it was already a special jubilee occasion—a hundred years since the erection there of the "world's littlest church."

The brick shrine, located a mile and a half south of Sycamore, on the Colusa–Grimes highway, commemorates the first Roman Catholic service in Colusa county, celebrated on May 1, 1856 by Father Peter Magagnotto, C.P., of Marysville. During subsequent years, whenever a priest came to the area, he offered Mass in the home of Jacob Meyers, on the Sacramento River, an area then known as Grand Island.

In 1864, Father P.G. Laufhuber preached a mission to the people of Grand Island. Later that year, Ann Myers promised the Lord that if He would send rain to save her barley crop, she would "do something for You." The prayer was answered and shortly thereafter Ann donated a parcel of land for the purpose of one day erecting a church. She and others then set out to raise a twenty–seven foot wooden cross as the first stage of dedicating the property to the Lord.

The actual genesis of the shrine dates from the arrival at nearby Our Lady of Lourdes Parish of Father Michael Walrath (1841–1917) a Prussian–born priest destined to spend thirty–five years in Colusa county. Father Walrath was a remarkable person, one of California's great sacerdotal pioneers. A chronicler noted that "in the whole history of the missions of Northern California there was perhaps no more interesting character in the priesthood." His efforts in building up the Church in Colusa would form a volume in itself.

In 1883, Father Walrath began building a miniature church on the site earlier given by Ann Myers using bricks he personally fired in an open kiln. It took him about a year to complete the little edifice. His work was recorded too and the historian for the area noted that "a brick shrine with an altar was built at Grand Island under the title of Our Lady of Sorrows, to which a pilgrimage was made every year."

Holy Mass was offered on certain designated feast-days during the subsequent years of Father Walrath's tenure. Rosary devotions and other services were conducted and the old wooden cross was eventually replaced by one of concrete.

The centennial of the "world's littlest church" was observed in 1983 when Father Robert Coffey offered the Eucharistic Liturgy at the tiny shrine for several hundred people. The church, with two doors and twin steeples, has barely enough room for altar, priest and a couple of worshippers. Robert Ripley in his "Believe It Or Not" newspaper column referred to the structure as the "World's Littlest Church" nearly fifty years ago and that designation endures.

(Despite the earlier recognition by Ripley, the Guinness Book of World Records gives the nod for the smallest house–of–worship to Union Church in Wicasset, Maine)

Bishop George Montgomery was especially enamored with the tiny shrine and often bragged that California had both the largest area and the tiniest church in America. He once wrote a relative in Kentucky: "Come west and I'll show you a church where the two of us will make a crowd."

VII. Ecclesial Institutions
2. Schools & Universities

MISSIONS AND SEMINARIES

Much has been written about the "romance and beauty of the missions, but rarely, if ever, has their role as seminaries been dwelt upon. And yet, surprisingly enough, nine of the twenty–one missions have served in that capacity at one point or another in the drama of California's Catholic heritage.

California's first seminary was opened by Bishop Francisco Garcia Diego y Moreno in March of 1842 at Mission Santa Barbara. Located in the rear apartments off the corridor facing the patio, this embryonic institution functioned for two years until more commodious quarters could be built.

On May 4, 1844, Bishop Garcia Diego opened a new seminary on grounds adjacent to Mission Santa Ines under the patronage of Our Lady of Guadalupe. Unhappily, the early years were bleak ones and the bishop himself was forced to admit that "the seminary which with wretched means I have started, offers no hope of prosperity." The *Catholic Directory* for 1853 notes that Father Eugene O'Connell is pastor of Mission San Francisco (Dolores) and "superior of the seminary." Established by Archbishop Joseph Sadoc Alemany and known as Saint Thomas, the seminary limped along until 1863, when the archbishop was forced to close it for lack of candidates. Some twenty years later, a second seminary dedicated to Saint Thomas was opened at Mission San Jose under the care of the Marist Fathers. Archbishop Patrick W. Riordan ended its short existence in 1884, sending off what few students there were to Saint Mary's in Baltimore.

The first Jesuit seminary, established about the year 1854, was located at Santa Clara College and, unlike its California predecessors, enjoyed continuing success. It was transferred to Los Gatos in 1888. True to the tradition of their Franciscan pioneers, the Friars Minor have utilized the old missions as educational institutions. The old Mission at San Miguel now houses the Novitiate for their province while the House of Philosophy is part of San Luis Rey Mission near San Diego. An apostolic college for exiled Zacatecan friars was opened at Mission San Luis Rey as early as 1892 under the protection of Our Lady of Guadalupe. By 1897 the Catholic Almanac notes that there were already a "Novitiate and apostolic college of the Franciscan Monastery" at San Luis Rey.

The establishment of Queen of Angels Seminary by His Eminence, James Francis Cardinal McIntyre, in 1954 was as rich in historical precedent as it was significant for the future growth of the Church in the most populous state of our nation. A minor seminary functioned for the Claretians at San Gabriel for a while.

Hence, in a very concrete and obvious way, it can be said that the work of Christian education, inaugurated by Junípero Serra at San Diego in 1769, influences even our present Catholic life in California. Priests have been and still are being trained at those centers which saw the introduction of Christianity into the state.

CHURCH AND STATE IN EDUCATION

There was very little of an educational nature going on in California when the state came into the Union in 1850. In the subsequent five years, the exploding population caused the allotting of public funds to all schools, denominational and otherwise. Between 1850 and 1855, all education in the state, except that in San Francisco, was under church direction; however, as the ideas of Horace Mann gained ascendancy, the attitude of the California legislature towards private schools quickly changed.

Sincere advocates of a state monopoly in educational affairs gradually found themselves allied with those critics of the Church who characterized Catholic schools as propaganda mills of "popish plots." One such "progressive thinker" was D.R. Ashley, who led his fight to deny funds to non–public schools into the state legislature. The acceptance of Ashley's proposals in 1855 was due, in great measure, to Know Nothingism, then strong in the state. The Ashley Bill withheld all public money from schools where sectarian or religious subjects were taught. Proponents of the bill argued that its passage would promote erection of schools in areas where population counts were low, an aspect of the legislation never fully realized.

An attempt was made in 1861 by Zachariah Montgomery, uncle of the future Coadjutor Archbishop of San Francisco, to secure public funds for religious schools on a *pro rata* basis. Pitted against such outspoken and influential opponents as John Swett and John Conness, Montgomery's efforts were eventually frustrated.

The Constitutional Convention of 1849 made practically no provision for education, stating only that the common elementary schools "were to be supported by the sale of land granted to the State by the United States Government." Article II, Section XIII, provided that "taxation shall be equal and uniform throughout the State. All property in this State shall be taxed in proportion to its value, to be ascertained by law." Subsequent court decisions ruled that the drafters meant to exclude non–public schools, although the phraseology was admittedly misleading. In any event between 1849 and 1868, non–public schools did not pay taxes. With the revision of the state's consitution in 1879, there was included a stipulation that public money was to be denied to any school "not under the exclusive control of the officers of the public schools." In addition, it was stated that "all property in the State, except in this Constitution provided, not exempt under the laws of the United States, shall be taxed in proportion to its value." The revised constitution squeaked through to a narrow victory on May 7, 1879 and the Church–affiliated schools found themselves not only denied public funds but taxed for their very existence!

The exemption from the tax rolls of Stanford University in 1900 marked the first break in the "iron–clad" Constitution of 1879 for subsequent attempts were based on that precedent. An effort was made in 1926 to remove the tax burden from nonpublic schools, but this attempt, together with a similar one in 1933, failed to win sufficient public support and revealed that "the savage antagonisms of the Eastern Seaboard were transplanted in California" even if on a reduced scale.

In 1951 Laughlin Waters proposed legislation to exempt non–public schools from taxation pointing out that California, alone of all the states, imposed this "penalty" for private education. The bill passed with little objection and was signed into law by Governor Earl Warren on May 3rd. Opposition to the legislation came only after its passage when the matter was put to a referendum vote in November of 1952. The movement by the California Taxpayers Alliance was soundly defeated by the state's electorate. The opponents then resorted to the courts but in this endeavor they were no more successful.

In 1957 the "Californians for Public Schools" obtained enough signatures to call for an initiative to repeal the 1952 law. This measure, brought to a vote in November of 1958, was once again rejected by the people of California and the Catholics of the Golden State were assured that their education system could remain without taxation. Their sentiments echoed those precious words of California's constitutional preamble, "We, the people of the State of California, grateful to Almighty God for our freedom. . . ."

FIRST CATHOLIC SCHOOL IN LOS ANGELES

Throughout the annals of history, the Catholic Church has been the patroness and promoter of education. Hers were the great universities of Faith, and hers too, the hedge schools in which knowledge of things human and divine was imparted in penal times. So it was along the Pacific Slope. Even before much thought could be given to plans for revamping the obsolete system of mission times, churchmen were looking for new means of providing religious instruction for God's people.

Plans were afoot to inaugurate a Catholic school for the growing *Pueblo de Nuestra Señora de los Angeles* as early as 1849. On June 9th of that year, Father Sebastiano Bongioranni submitted a petition for an allotment of land to the *Ayuntamiento*. The council reacted favorably and granted, from the unappropriated property belonging to the *pueblo*, a parcel some distance north of the *plaza*. For one reason or another it became impossible to fulfill the purposes of that land grant and the property reverted to public domain. The next year, at the instigation of Fray José Maria de Jesús González Rubio,

Administrator of the vacant Bishopric of Both Californias, a second petition was submitted by Fray Antonio Jiménez, this time for property adjoining the old plaza church. Again, no action was taken.

The Right Reverend Joseph Sadoc Alemany visited Los Angeles in December of 1850. Anxious to pursue the earlier plans, the newly–appointed Bishop of Monterey renewed the initial request to the council, promising to begin immediately the erection of suitable educational facilities. The Dominican prelate noted in his diary that the institution was opened on May 8, 1851, with twenty–six "scholars." Direction of the area's first Catholic school was entrusted to three Picpus Fathers.

It is impossible to identify the exact location of the school, "but there is good reason to think that it was "not far from the French Hospital on College Street, whose name itself probably refers to the Picpus" foundation. The school was assisted by public funds. On July 9, 1851, the Los Angeles City Council had stipulated that a sum not exceeding $50 a month could be granted toward "the support of any educational institution in the city, providing that all the rudiments of the English and Spanish languages be taught therein." Practically nothing further is known about the institution. The national Catholic directory for 1852 and 1853 state only that there was a "Boarding and Day school at Los Angeles under the direction of the Fathers of the Sacred Hearts."

One commentator conjectured that "the Picpus Fathers undoubtedly introduced some higher subjects in the school, but the curriculum must have been predominantly elementary." The school was in full operation on January 17, 1853, when two members of a city committee for education made an inspection and reported the attendance at twenty students. The school continued for another six months. Its disappearance coincided with the departure of Father Felix Migorel, who volunteered for service in the missions of Baja California, and left the diocese in the autumn of 1853.

Three years later, Father Blas Raho reopened the school for the expanding city in a rented adobe building. The institution, placed under the patronage of Saint Vincent de Paul, must have "enjoyed some prosperity, for in 1859, there were eighty boys enrolled."

The curtailment of public assistance by statewide legislation greatly hampered the school's activities and is believed to have shortened the "second life" of the city's proto–Catholic school. Short and interrupted though its existence was, the institution was a healthy seed whose blossoming forth would come in later times.

SAN FRANCISCO'S FIRST CATHOLIC COLLEGE

The Congregation of the Sacred Hearts, or Picpus Fathers, first served in California in 1832, when several of their number arrived as exiles from the missions on the Sandwich Isles. When conditions improved, a few years later, the priests returned to Hawaii.

In 1848, it was recognized that "California is going to be an important country. Everybody is going thither. Soon there will be over a million inhabitants. There is gold everywhere; in the rivers, in the plains, and in the mountains." With this in mind, two Picpus Fathers were sent to the area hoping to find "some resources for our Sandwich Mission and to see there someday a house of our institute." Soon after arriving in California Father Stanislaus LeBret, serving at San Francisco, wrote to his superior general for permission to inaugurate a college in the Bay City. In August of 1849, the Titular Archbishop of Chalcedon notified Fray González Rubio, Administrator of the Diocese of Both Californias, that he authorized "a party of some religious who can open a school or college in the vast establishment" of the west.

While Rubio apparently had no objections to a college, he politely reminded the archbishop that in his capacity of administrator, he was unable to make a firm commitment "without consulting the Holy See and without its authorization." Archbishop Bonamie then contacted officials of the Roman Curia and early in 1850 told Rubio that it was "agreeable to the Congregation of the Propaganda if a college for the education of youth he opened at San Francisco by priests of our congregation."

The news alarmed certain members of the Society of Jesus who had plans of their own for a college in the Bay area. Father Michael Accolti suggested to the diocesan administrator that "the southern part of the vast territory should be assigned to the Picpus Fathers." Rubio quickly agreed and invited the Congregation of the Sacred Hearts "to establish themselves at different points in the old missions situated in Southern California." There matters stood until the arrival of Father Flavian Fontaine at Mission Dolores late in 1850. Not an easy man to dissuade, Father Fontaine consulted with the newly appointed Bishop, Joseph Sadoc Alemany, and then took positive steps toward setting up a college. Early in 1852 "the enterprising missionary was teaching in a building to the north of Mission Dolores."

The three–room school, with an equal number of teachers and about twenty pupils, was located "in an adobe building to the north of the Mission Church, and separated from it by a line of houses." In 1853, Father Fontaine acquired eight additional acres and announced plans for a brick building to accommodate day–students as well as boarders. Unfortunately, the expansion program overextended the meager assets and creditors forced the priest's hand by demanding immediate payment. Father Michael Nobili of nearby Santa Clara College agreed to guarantee the bonds but in so doing laid claim to the property and all other holdings. The institution was reopened under Jesuit auspices early in 1854 but lasted only until the following October.

Thus it was that the school which Father Flavian Fontaine opened "with the expectation that it would be built up into an institution of higher learning" achieved a fate far less noble than its founder envisioned. One authority attributed the failure of the Picpus Fathers "to the interference of the Jesuits who were seeking a monopoly on education in Northern California." While there may be some justification to that charge, "the suggestion that the Fathers of the Sacred Hearts concentrate their activities in Southern California had some merit," for it was not in their interest to be dispersed over an immense territory where already they staffed several churches.

In any event, when the Picpus Fathers realized that their plans were not being well received, "they preferred to leave California and to dedicate themselves to their flourishing projects in Chile."

ALL HALLOWS COLLEGE — DUBLIN

The annual celebration of Halloween, vigil–day of All Hallows (All Saints), brings to mind that great missionary college in Dublin which has supplied priests for California since 1858 when Fathers Patrick Cotter, James Largan, Edward Morris, and Patrick O'Reilly arrived to begin their apostolate in San Francisco.

All Hallows College traces its origins back to its titular feastday in 1842, when an old manor house in a northern suburb of Dublin near Drumcondra was set aside to train priests for the English–speaking missions. Founder of the college was Father John Hand, a priest of the Diocese of Meath, whose bishop encouraged his work by personally appealing for material support to the Irish hierarchy. In his initial report to the Sacred Congregation of Propaganda Fide, Father Hand could state that "it is cheering to see so many candidates presenting themselves. This fact shows what an abundant supply of zealous priests the faith and piety of Ireland could yield for the foreign missions . . . ."

It was the founder's aim and it remained the objective of his successors "to form missionaries of a practical type, men who would throw themselves with zeal into the advancing civilization of the New World." All Hallows was and is a "spiritual, scholastic, enthusiastic and patriotic" institution. Even today a most remarkable spirit of camaraderie bubbles forth from the college. Visitors (especially graduates) are treated in kingly style with one of the most contagious types of cordiality known to man.

Since 1891 All Hallows has been staffed by the priests of the Congregation of the Mission (Vincentian Fathers) but its original purposes have gone unchanged. Serving directly under Propaganda Fide, the college faculty is practically autonomous. Appointment to the All Hallows ends only with death. The strong bond linking the college with its graduates helps to explain how the institution manages to support itself solely on the financial assistance of its priestly alumni. Noble traditions abound at All Hallows. For example, graduates around the world are accustomed to write each year to the President of the College telling of their work. Much of this correspondence has found its way into the *All Hallows Annual*, which is sent out each year to the priest–graduates.

The Diocese of Sacramento, whose first and third bishops came from All Hallows, has gratefully accepted priests from the college since its erection as the Vicariate Apostolic of Marysville in 1860.

From All Hallows have gone forth more than 3,000 priests, including seven archbishops, about thirty bishops and one cardinal. Alumni can be found in all the pioneer areas where the Faith is preached in the English language. There is something in the Irish character that makes him an excellent missioner, or as one writer has put it, "His restless spirit will never be content on the bog and the fen with the fogs and winds of his native land. The Celt must wander, his youthful foot itches, and the mind and body are keen to follow."

MOUNT SAINT MARY'S COLLEGE — LOS ANGELES

The need for a Catholic college to augment the work of Saint Mary's Academy was voiced by Bishop John J. Cantwell soon after his installation as the Ordinary of the old Diocese of Monterey–Los Angeles. When Mount Saint Mary's finally opened its doors in September of 1925, Cantwell noted that the Sisters of Saint Joseph of Carondelet were placing a "capital stone upon the many educational structures that they so efficiently preside over in this diocese."

Located in the early years at Slauson Avenue and Mesa Drive in Los Angeles, the college acquired a thirty–six acre tract of land in the Santa Monica mountains and in the spring of 1931, the sisters moved into their lovely new home overlooking the Pacific Ocean.

Building expansion over the next decades was slow but constant. The picturesque Spanish–Gothic chapel, erected in 1940, was used for the first time on Christmas Eve when Archbishop John J. Cantwell presided at a colorful solemn midnight Mass. A faculty residence hall was put up the next year, and by 1947, the Charles Willard Coe Memorial Library was ready for occupancy. The Marian Hall of Fine Arts was dedicated in 1956, followed after two more years by Carondelet Hall. The five–story Humanities building was opened in the spring of 1965.

From the earliest days, Mount Saint Mary's ranked high in academic circles. The college was affiliated with The Catholic University of America in 1930, and was recognized by the Association of American Colleges and the Western College Association. In August of 1953, Mount Saint Mary's joined with ten other small accredited educational institutions to form the Independent Colleges of California, and two years later the Mount was empowered to offer its first graduate program for higher studies. Through the munificence of His Eminence, James Francis Cardinal McIntyre, a downtown campus was opened in 1959, on the estate of the late Carrie Estelle Doheny in Chester Place. By 1962 a full–time program was in operation "at the southland's newest college campus, the first of its type type among Catholic colleges on the West Coast."

The Mount has had its dark days too. A devastating conflagration swept the college on November 6, 1961, but it was was an ordeal out of which emerged a lesson of complete dedication on the part of the college itself. The sisters refused to surrender the work of three decades, and although two buildings were completely destroyed and a third severely damaged, within two days classes were resumed amid the char and dust of a burnt campus. This dogged determination can perhaps be best explained when one recalls that the work of education brooks no delay. It is a work to which the Sisters of Saint Joseph have dedicated their lives. It is a task that has survived many previous trials, obstacles, heartaches, loneliness, poverty and pain. In their efforts to form the characters of young women in the pattern of the great women of our time and in the image of her who was the most valiant of them all, these educators have traditionally employed the arts and skill of their profession in a most exemplary manner. One observer believes "that is why in their future lives, the students of Mount Saint Mary's College will be distinguished for their fortitude, their sense of responsibility and their devotion to duty."

CALIFORNIA'S PROTO SEMINARY — OUR LADY OF GUADALUPE

In view of the paucity of funds and personnel available, it was a courageous decision on the part of Bishop Francisco Garcia Diego y Moreno to establish a diocesan seminary for the Diocese of Both Californias in the 1840s. Indeed, that institution can be looked upon as the prelate's "greatest contribution to the Church of California."

Shortly after taking up his episcopal residence at Mission Santa Barbara in 1842, the bishop inaugurated formal classes for his handful of seminarians in the rear apartments off the corridor facing the patio. The embryonic institution functioned for almost two years until the number of students and lack of facilities necessitated more commodious quarters.

Early in 1844, Bishop Garcia Diego asked friars Jose Jimeno, Juan Moreno and Francisco Sánchez to petition Governor Manuel Micheltorena for a grant of land adjacent to Mission Santa Ines, on which a permanent building could be erected to house a conciliar seminary. The governor responded on March 16, by allotting to the Diocese of Both Californias the four *cañadas* of Sotonocomu, Alisguey, Calabaza and Aquichurruno, an area of six square leagues. That original grant was augmented, the following September 26, by an additional two square leagues on the northern and western sides of the initial area.

It was a generous gesture and the bishop hastened to thank the governor for the parcel of land, which eventually amounted to 35,499 acres, as well as for $500 which he personally pledged as an annual subsidy to offset the cost of caring for youngsters unable to pay the modest tuition.

Shortly thereafter, construction began at Santa Ines under the supervision of Fray Jimeno. The top floor of the two–story adobe edifice, devoted to dormitory quarters, had a porch or balcony facing the front wing of the mission. On the first floor were classrooms and apartments for the professors. The handsome structure, with its roof of red tiles, was an altogether imposing and comfortable building, suited to the educational needs of the times. The extensive *Bibliotheca Montereyensi–Angelorum Dioeceseos*, already numbering several hundred tomes, was located in a room near the central part of the old mission.

For reasons not exactly clear, the first educational institution in what is now the State of California was erected, not on the governor's vast land grant, but within the confines of Mission Santa Ines quadrangle itself. The day of May 4, 1844, was set aside for the formal dedication ceremonies of California's proto–seminary, placed under the protection of Our Lady of Guadalupe. Though Bishop Garcia Diego inaugurated the enterprise with practically no financial assistance, he was confident of the institution's eventual success. He looked upon the seminary as the seed from which zealous and charitable priests would sustain divine worship and, through their teachings and example, maintain the good customs of the country.

The bishop personally composed the rules and operational procedures, or constitution, whereby the seminary was to function. A monastic–like horarium was adopted much like that followed at the Apostolic College of *Nuestra Señora de Guadalupe*, at Zacatecas. Students were to study the standard theological authors then used in the seminaries of Mexico and then present their observations and problems to the various faculty members for further elucidation.

The seminary was never really successful, at least by present–day standards. And yet, while only about ten of its graduates became priests, the institution is representative of that period between the glorious days of old when saintly and industrious frairs reaped a harvest of souls and the modern far–flung province that developed to take its place.

OUR LADY OF LORETTO — CONATY HIGH SCHOOL

The origins of Our Lady of Loretto–Bishop Conaty High School can be traced to the early days of this century, when the parochial school of Saint Vibiana's Cathedral was expanded to include secondary classes for girls. Bishop Thomas J. Conaty, a veteran educator and former Rector of The Catholic University of America, had long wanted to provide such opportunities for the then Diocese of Monterey–Los Angeles and it was he who encouraged the initial steps along those lines.

With the cessation of World War I, Conaty's successor, Bishop John J. Cantwell, approached the Sisters of the Immaculate Heart of Mary with a proposal to purchase the grounds on which their former academy was located as a site for a new diocesan school. The Sisters had already transferred most of their own educational facilities to Hollywood and the earlier site on Pico Boulevard was thought to be an ideal place for inaugurating a secondary school for girls.

In 1922, Cantwell formally announced plans to adopt a modified form of the "central high school idea" used by Bishop Philip McDevett in Philadelphia. The idea was to accept young ladies from all over the city on a competitive basis.

Cantwell's announcement of plans to erect a new facility in Pico Heights was well received by the local Catholic populace. The old building was razed and in November, 1922 the cornerstone was set in place for the new Los Angeles Catholic Girls High School.

In his address for the occasion, Joseph Scott explained the purpose of the establishment and how it was envisioned as the focal point of a whole new educational thrust for the Church in Southern California. Father Peter C. Yorke, the highly respected "labor" priest from San Francisco, then delivered an eloquent panegyric on the necessity of a Catholic education, pointing out that "the first American schools and colleges were religious and we are following the best American traditions when we build schools like this to give fair play to our children. . . ."

The Tudor Gothic structure was hailed by local newspapers as one of the "finest buildings of its kind in all the west." And indeed it became the showpiece of Cantwell's tenure, visited by politicians, celebrities and such churchmen as Patrick Cardinal Hayes and Arbp. Diomede Fumasoni–Biondi. It was Cantwell who suggested that the school be named for Bishop Thomas J. Conaty. A beautiful statue of the prelate, carved from a solid piece of white carrara marble, was placed in a niche over the main entrance.

On the first day of classes, September 4, 1923, the school roster numbered upwards of 500 students. On that day, Father Peter Corcoran, the principal, formally inaugurated the first unit of what became the largest and most successful system of private high schools in the nation.

Five years later, a similar institution was provided for boys at the new Cathedral High School. On that occasion, Cantwell said that he wanted "every high school boy and girl in our diocese to feel that school is a place not for the rich, not for the poor nor for any other class in particular, rather it is a place for all Catholic boys and girls to be educated."

Though demographics have called for changes of focus in the overall educational apostolate, Bishop Conaty High School has retained its position as the flagship of the Catholic educational system in Southern California. It is joined with Our Lady of Loretto High School, established in the 1950s as the first outreach of the Youth Education Fund by Archbishop J. Francis A. McIntyre.

SANTA CLARA UNIVERSITY

On July 30, 1910, the Very Reverend Joseph S. Glass announced to Bishop Thomas J. Conaty that the Lazarist Fathers had decided to withdraw from Saint Vincent's College in Los Angeles. As abrupt as it was inexplicable, the decision to close the southland's leading educational institution has been traditionally interpreted as a desire on the part of the community to concentrate attention on its recently opened University of Dallas.

Recent discoveries, however, reveal that there may have been other factors at work. On the day after Father Glass' disclosure, Father James P. Morrissey became president of Santa Clara College and it may well have been more than coincidence that Morrissey had openly advocated moving the Jesuit campus either to Mountain View or Southern California. The move would have been a logical one for a disastrous fire had swept Santa Clara in December of 1909, destroying the faculty building and severely damaging several other structures. In addition, it was well known that the two other Catholic men's colleges in the Bay area were more than adequate to care for that region's needs.

The Jesuit–trained Bishop of Monterey–Los Angeles and Father Herman J. Goller, local provincial of the Society of Jesus, toured a site in Los Angeles earlier selected by the Vincentians for an expanded campus and quickly approved Morrissey's proposal to move Santa Clara to the area in September of 1910. Only the unexpected and premature death of the youthful Goller stalled the actual transfer to the eighty–nine acre tract of land known as Rancho La Cienega.

As a true friend of Los Angeles youth with their best interest at heart, Father Glass agreed to keep the Grand Avenue campus of Saint Vincent's open for the year 1910–1911, or until the Jesuits could establish themselves in the region. Meanwhile at Santa Clara, housing accommodations had become desperate and with no official authorization to move, Father Morrissey felt obliged to go ahead with a building project on the mission campus. As one chronicler has pointed out,

> A person desirous of catching Father Morrissey's vision of Saint Vincent's on its Angelus Mesa campus can go to Santa Clara today fifty years afterwards, where the buildings he wished to grace View Park still flank Father [Cornelius] McCoy's New Mission Church.

The Society of Jesus did fulfill its commitment in the south, however, and in the spring of 1911, Father Richard Gleeson secured property in Garvanza where, on the following September 11, he opened a boys high school to absorb the students of old Saint Vincent's. After a suspension of three years, college classes were renewed at the old site in 1914, and Los Angeles College and its successors, Loyola College and University, carried on the tradition planted by the Vincentians in 1865.

Without Santa Clara's resources of a thirty–man faculty and Father Morrissey's buildings, the southland's new educational project had a severe struggle in the early years. Nonetheless, when Father Joseph S. Glass, later the Bishop of Salt Lake, gave his commencement address in 1914, his words were strangely prophetic:

> Rest assured that when the present faculty shall have passed away, other loyal sons will continue the work through countless years to come.

SAINT BONIFACE INDIAN SCHOOL

In 1888, Bishop Francis Mora announced plans to erect an Indian School in a beautiful valley between the foothills of the Grayback and San Jacinto Mountains, about a mile north of the small desert community of Banning. The object of the institution was "to build up religion in the hearts of those children of presumably Catholic people, the Mission Indians.

The school, to be built by the Bureau of Catholic Indian Missions with funds provided by Mother Katharine M. Drexel, "was to be under the care of Benedictine monks from Beatty, Pennsylvania, who would in time, by, the establishment of a monastery, further extend their influence with an abbey school and by missionary endeavor to the surrounding territory." Three monks arrived early in 1890 to inaugurate the foundation. Unfortunately, a change in governmental policy towards contract schools brought about the withdrawal of the Benedictines a few months later.

Father George L. Willard, an official in the Bureau of Catholic Indian Missions, replaced the monks for a time but the elderly priest succumbed within a few months from the ravages of typhoid fever. With the death of Willard, Father B. Florian Hahn, a missionary from Rensselaer, Indiana, was named superintendent. At the same time, in response to a request from Archbishop

Patrick J. Ryan of Philadelphia, the Sisters of Saint Joseph of Carondelet sent six nuns to Banning under the superiority of Sister Celestine O'Reilly. The school was opened on September 1, 1890, with an enrollment of 120 youngsters.

The three–story brick structure, placed under the spiritual patronage of Saint Boniface, was formally dedicated on January 6, 1891. Several months later the children were honored by a personal visit of President Benjamin Harrison who took time from his busy schedule to greet each of the Indian students individually. In its early years, the institution received limited Federal assistance for one hundred of its children, but even that meager sum was later terminated. Thereafter, most of the operating funds came from the Bureau of Catholic Indian Missions, diocesan collections and the free–will offerings of generous benefactors.

The youngsters helped in the support too. Almonds, pears, peaches, nectarines, plums, apricots, apples, quinces, figs, olives and oranges were cultivated in the thirty–five acre orchard. Children would study half a day and work at designated tasks the other half. In the overall educational program, vocational instruction paralleled the elementary branches, and thus it was that horticulture became the speciality of the boys while the accomplishments of the girls included excellent bead work and proficiency in the making of Cluny and Torehon laces.

The art of printing was introduced with the publication of *The Mission Indian*, a bi–monthly periodical which told of the school, gave useful instruction, and provided no little amusement to the children themselves. Father Hahn, the superintendent, was also a musician of note, as well as a painter by trade. The band which he established and trained at the mission was a prominent feature of the school.

Facilities were enlarged at Banning, in 1894, with the erection of a two–story building for class and recreation rooms and dormitories for the boys. When the building was destroyed by fire in 1911, it was replaced by Bishop Thomas J. Conaty and the generous people of the Diocese of Monterey–Los Angeles. A visitor to Saint Boniface in 1921, just after the Franciscans had taken charge, noted that travelers and motorists anxious "to get away from strife and commercialism" would enjoy "a trip to a haven of peace, where unselfish sacrifice and enduring of unwarranted hardship for the good of fellowmen obtain in the fullest sense."

SAINT CATHERINE MILITARY SCHOOL — ANAHEIM

The history of Orange County's oldest Catholic educational establishment can be traced to 1886, and the dauntless enthusiasm of Father Peter Stoeters, Pastor of Saint Boniface Parish. On July 2nd of that year, the priest wrote to the Dominican Sisters of the Third Order, at Mission San Jose, asking about the possibility of staffing the school he was planning for Anaheim.

The proposal was favorably received and forwarded on to the community's motherhouse, which was then located in Brooklyn. After considerable discussion, Mother Seraphina Staimer formally authorized the envisioned project, on May 8, 1887. Early the following September, Mother Pia Backes journeyed to Southern California for further consultation with the Right Reverend Francis Mora, Bishop of Monterey–Los Angeles.

Father Stoeters welcomed Mother Pia to Orange County for a personally–guided tour of what was then the largest grape growing district in the state. The Dominican superior was fascinated with "the little city of Anaheim," which she described in her diary as "a delightful place with about 1,300 inhabitants."

Inasmuch as Mother Pia and her consultors preferred to make their own foundation, rather than merely staff a parochial school, she purchased a three acre tract of land in Anaheim, on Palm Street. She contracted for erection of a three story brick edifice, consisting of two classrooms and providing accommodations for the Sisters and a few boarding students. The building operations proceeded rather quickly and, by early March 1889, the new structures were ready for occupancy.

Mother Pia and the faculty of three returned to the southland for the formal dedication, which was scheduled for the Feast of Saint Joseph. After placing the first foundation by the Dominicans in the area under the patronage of Saint Catherine, Bishop Mora celebrated Mass in the small chapel. Father Joachim Adam, the Vicar General, preached an eloquent sermon in English and then in Spanish.

The foundation was generously supported by the people of Anaheim from the very outset. There were nineteen day scholars at the formal opening of the school, on March 25th and that number had swollen to forty by the fall, with an additional fifteen boarders.

Early in 1894, due to a decrease in pupils, the Sisters decided to phase out the boarding school, in favor of an orphanage. In June, the enrollment was restricted to boys and the institution became a school for homeless youngsters. In its new role, Saint Catherine's began to grow. Additional land was purchased and the institution eventually expanded to twenty–six acres. By 1903, there were 200 orphan and half–orphan boys from two to fourteen years of age.

In subsequent years, however, the state inaugurated a new policy of placing homeless boys with private families and the Sisters found it expedient, once again, to take in day students. Saint Catherine's School for Boys was officially proclaimed a military academy, in 1925.

Today, the famed landmark of Anaheim, one of the

largest Catholic institutions of its kind in the west, continues the basic pedagogical traditions inaugurated over ninety years ago by a pioneering pastor and a courageous religious community.

SAINT JOHN SEMINARY — CAMARILLO

A. BACKGROUND

Over sixty years have passed since that day in March of 1939, when the cornerstone was laid at Saint John's Seminary at Camarillo. It was an historic event, one worthy of recalling. Even though seminaries had existed in California since 1842, it was only in the years after World War I that the southland was able to take permanent steps toward establishing its own institutions for training priests.

Early in 1926, plans were unveiled for a minor seminary in the old Diocese of Los Angeles–San Diego. By September of that year a temporary building was in operation on 21st Street, west of Grand Avenue. The completed Los Angeles College at 241 South Detroit Street opened its doors in March of 1927, with fifty–five students. Graduates from the preparatory seminary continued their studies at various institutions throughout the nation, including Saint Patrick (Menlo Park), Saint Thomas (Denver), Saint Mary (Baltimore), Mount Saint Mary (Emmitsburg), Saint John (Collegeville), the *Seminaire de Sant Sulpice* (Paris), and numerous other major seminaries.

Although it has only recently celebrated its diamond jubilee, Saint John's Seminary traces its origins back to March 3, 1927, when the late Juan A. Camarillo offered the diocese a hundred acres of land near the town bearing his family name for a senior seminary. The institution, dedicated to the donor's patron, was to occupy a knoll dividing the two historic *ranchos* of Calleguas and Las Posas. Depression years delayed further action and it was December 27, 1937, before Archbishop John J. Cantwell formally announced plans for opening the major seminary in a special pastoral letter. The subsequent campaign for funds was the most effective hitherto done to consolidate the apostolic endeavors of more than a century and a half of Catholic crusading in the southland.

Ground was broken on May 10, 1938, by the Right Reverend John J. Cawley, and just a year later, on March 19th, Archbishop Cantwell presided at the laying of the cornerstone. Classes began the following September 12th when sixty–seven students took their places for the initial roll call. The completed seminary was dedicated on October 4, 1940, by the Most Reverend Amleto Giovanni Cicognani, Apostolic Delegate to the United States. Mexico City's Archbishop Luis Maria Martinez celebrated Solemn Mass in the company of some fifty members of the American hierarchy.

Capacity of the seminary was boosted to 178 in 1955–1956 when a new residence wing and utility building were erected east of the existing facilities. Adoption of a three unit system of seminary training in 1962 by James Francis Cardinal McIntyre brought about further expansion at Camarillo when Saint John's College was separated from the two existing archdiocesan seminaries and formed a self–contained institution on property adjacent to Saint John's. The new complexus of buildings was dedicated on June 25th, 1966, by Francis Cardinal Spellman.

In the first twenty–seven years of its service to Southern California, Saint John's Seminary with its Vincentian and archdiocesan faculty sent forth 424 priests (including a bishop and a mitred abbot) to seven different ecclesiastical jurisdictions. Through the munificence of its benefactors, the seminary looks forward to even greater strides in the new century.

SAINT JOHN SEMINARY — CAMARILLO

B. ST. JAMES CHAPEL

One of the most beautifully and colorfully furnished houses–of–worship in the Archdiocese of Los Angeles is Saint James Chapel, at the seminary–college in Camarillo. Of special interest are the thirty–one stained glass windows executed by the Paul L. Phillips Studio of Altadena.

The windows portray symbolically the relationship of God with His people. As one enters the chapel, the first window on the right depicts Adam and Eve, hearing the welcome news of a Redeemer, a prophecy fulfilled in the opposite window where Christ is shown with His Mother and foster father.

Next on the right is Moses, the great legislator and mediator of the Old Covenant, promising a land flowing with milk and honey in return for observing the decalogue of Mount Sinai. Opposite is Christ assuring the Beatific Vision to those obeying the New Covenant.

Then the prophet Jeremiah conveys Yahweh's assurance of providing spiritual leaders for his people. This is extended to the whole world by Christ who passes along the mandate of leadership to the apostles and their successors. The fourth panel on the right portrays Noah holding in his arms the Ark, a notion expanded in the New Covenant by the presentation of the keys to Peter, keeper of the ark.

In the following panel, Melchizedek offers a thanksgiving sacrifice for Abraham's military victory. On the Gospel side, Christ offers his own body and blood for the life of the world. The sixth window portrays Cain slaying his brother Abel, a scene echoed in the New Covenant when Christ pours out his blood on the cross.

Saint John's Seminary

Jonas is shown in the seventh window as being spewed up by the sea monster while, in the opposite panel, the Lord is rising triumphantly from his earthly tomb, as a sign of victory over death. The final window in the series shows Yahweh as he appeared to Moses in the burning bush. On the Gospel side, the Holy Spirit descends on the apostles in the form of tongues of fire on Pentecost.

Then a new series of windows on the Gospel side depicts the various minor and major orders leading to priestly ordination. First is the Tonsure ceremony during which the bishop cuts the candidate's hair as a sign of worldly abandonment.

The next four windows graphically portray the orders of Porter, Lector Exorcist and Acolyte, followed by the major orders of Subdeaconate and Deaconate. The priesthood and episcopate are omitted since they are symbolized by the altar and episcopal chair. The ninth window on the Epistle side depicts Aaron who was chosen for the priestly role by the miraculous blooming of his staff. The next six windows designate the sacraments, except for the Holy Eucharist which is reserved in the tabernacle.

Like all art forms, the windows must be interpreted within the timeset of their fabrication. The Tonsure, for example, has been superseded in the post–Vatican Church by a candidacy ceremony. The minor orders are reduced in number, there are no longer subdeacons and the humeral veil has been banished to museums.

James Francis Cardinal McIntyre was a man of a single book—the Bible. How fitting it is that his love for the Scriptures is embodied in the windows of the chapel bearing the name of his saintly patron.

SAINT MARY COLLEGE — MORAGA

Saint Mary's College grew out of the stubborn determination of San Francisco's Archbishop Joseph Sadoc Alemany to establish a college which would serve as a kind of preparatory seminary. Alemany laid the cornerstone of the college in 1862 on a sixty acre site located some four miles from the center of town, along the Old Mission Road to San Jose.

Placed under the patronage of Our Lady, the institution was described as possessing "all the advantages of a salubrious situation, commanding an extensive view of the Bay and surrounding scenery."

The single academic building which housed the college was set in the middle of a seven acre campus; the remaining fifty–three acres of the property consisted of cultivated farmland which supplied the school with all the milk, vegetables, potatoes and hay it needed.

The archbishop personally supervised the construction of the college building, an imposing Gothic edifice with recessed arches, a rose window, buttresses and a lantern tower. Wishing to "protect the virtue of its students," Alemany did not want the young students at the college to succumb to the delights of the Barbary Coast district, where gambling and prostitution flourished during those years.

Saint Mary's was formally dedicated on July 9, 1863. Alemany entrusted the administration of the college to the archdiocesan clergy who, unfortunately, were not academically qualified for that task. By 1868, the college was in desperate straits, due mostly to the inefficient management of its faculty. It was evident to the archbishop that only a qualified religious community could keep the doors open.

When overtures to the Paris headquarters of the Brothers of the Christian Schools proved unsuccessful, Alemany asked the newly designated Vicar Apostolic of Marysville to bring a small group of Christian Brothers from Ireland. That request also fell on deaf ears. Then the archbishop decided to ask Pope Pius IX personally for assistance. Armed with the Pontiff's endorsement, Alemany visited the Brothers of the Christian Schools to plead his cause. This time he was successful.

Chosen to inaugurate the California foundation was Brother Justin McMahon and eight confreres, most of them of Irish birth or extraction. The small contingency left New York City aboard the *Ocean Queen* on July 16, 1868. At Aspinwall, the brothers crossed Panama by train and wagon and then boarded the *Montana* for the final leg of their journey to San Francisco. They arrived on August 10th.

The early years in California were not without their problems. One contemporary document notes that only "the spirit of self–sacrifice forgets present hardships and hope for better times." The brothers began immediately to revitalize Saint Mary's College. Alemany aided their efforts by issuing a pastoral letter urging his flock to support the work of the Institute in the archdiocese.

By 1875, the thirty students had grown to 240 and soon the college would become the largest institution of higher learning in the whole state, even outstripping the University of California at Berkeley.

SAINT PATRICK SEMINARY — MENLO PARK

A. HISTORICAL SKETCH

In the words of Bishop George T. Montgomery, the opening of Saint Patrick's Seminary at Menlo Park, in August of 1898, was "the realization of the hopes of every Bishop that is or has been on the Pacific Coast, and marks an epoch in the history of the Church west of the Rocky Mountains." Though it was not the first institution of its kind to function in California, Saint Patrick's achieved a success denied to earlier diocesan seminaries at Santa Ines, San Francisco and San Jose.

Archbishop Patrick W. Riordan realized that the Bay City archdiocese was the only jurisdiction on the coast which could hope at that time to undertake the burden of building and maintaining a seminary. With such an institution, the prelate was able to provide an adequate and steady supply of good and well–trained priests for the Church in the far west.

After considerable consultation it was decided to locate the seminary on an eighty–six acre tract of land, in Santa Clara Valley's Menlo Park, given to the archdiocese by Mrs. Kathryn Johnson. The plant was designed by the noted architect Charles I. Devlin. Construction was begun in 1894, and four years later the administration building, one wing and several smaller units were ready for occupancy. The Romanesque structure was formally opened on September 20, 1898, with thirty–four students enrolling in the classical department.

The Sulpician Fathers came to California from Baltimore to staff the new institution, which the archbishop had dedicated to Saint Patrick, "the patron saint of a great Catholic race to which the vast majority of our own people belong." It was the prelate's hope that the saint's "apostolic spirit may be given in large measure to the teachers and their students, so that their studies and their lives may be unto the increase of Divine faith and the salvation of many souls."

In the first year of its operation, Father John B. Vuibert, S.S., the Seminary rector, divided the student body into three classes of high school. Each subsequent year, there was to be an additional year until the full quota of twenty–four semesters was attained. In 1904, the "Grand Seminaire" was fully inaugurated with the addition of a theology department.

Extensive damage was sustained by the seminary in the earthquake of 1906. The upper story front wall of the college pavilion was rattled loose and huge sandstone blocks from the tower crashed through corridor walls, while others tumbled down on the granite steps at the main entrance. "With that courage and tenacity of purpose" so characteristic of Patrick W. Riordan, the archbishop set out at once to repair the damages and complete the remainder of the building. In 1918, the beautiful central chapel was dedicated by Riordan's successor, Archbishop Edward J. Hanna.

From the very outset, Saint Patrick's was envisioned as an institution that would serve the whole Pacific coast. Prior to 1939, it functioned more or less as a provincial institution and most of the native–born priests were trained for the ministry at Menlo Park. In 1924, the younger students were moved from Saint Patricks to a new minor seminary at Mountain View. Two years later, the college wing was remodeled for use by philosophy students.

Further improvements were brought about in 1937, when Archbishop John J. Mitty had the entire institution refurnished and modernized. The archbishop spent much of his time at Saint Patrick's and took personal interest in the seminary's day–to–day activities. With the destruction of San Francisco's cathedral in 1962, Saint Patrick's Seminary remains the last of the "brick and mortar" monuments to Patrick W. Riordan, a prelate who wisely "regarded vocations to the clerical state as an infallible sign of the spiritual life of a people."

SAINT PATRICK SEMINARY — MENLO PARK

B. ARCHBISHOP RIORDAN'S CONCERN

The interesting collection of artistic masterpieces, many of which still adorn the walls of Saint Patrick's Seminary, have fascinated numerous visitors who have toured the historic buildings at Menlo Park over the years. Early in 1940, Archbishop John J. Mitty suggested that an investigation be made as to the origin of the splendid collection. A partial result of that inquiry was published in the April, 1946, issue of *The Patrician*.

It was discovered that the notion of gathering a representative collection of paintings, prints and pictures originated with Archbishop Patrick W. Riordan. The report noted that "he never went anywhere without being on the watch for some additions."

Indeed he was remembered to have left more than one home with a new prize tucked away under his arm and his friends wondering what to put in its place. When in Europe, he secured personally whatever he could, and when not there he left orders with friends to forward their finds from wherever they happened to be.

Scholarly man that he was, Riordan took great pleasure in acquiring the collection for the seminary. And he had a definite purpose in mind—wishing to put within the reach of all his students the wealth of art in the possession of the Church.

Eventually he acquired some five hundred paintings, prints and pictures. His own travels and especially his library showed that he had studied art. He knew its great value and power, and his desire was to place it where, viewed day after day, it would make lasting impressions.

For Riordan, Christian art was a silent but eloquent preacher. Its purpose was to lead people from earth to the things above the earth, to teach virtue, to make people more holy, to dispense the religion that inspired it. The towering of its Gothic steeples would turn heart and mind to the Lord; the Madonna would leave an impression of chastity; the Crucified Master would sanctify His people and so on.

For this reason, the archbishop wished to give his seminarians the art of the Church, and to give it to them in abundance so that along with their other spiritual exercises, it might become an added means of making them more Christ–like. The archbishop also felt that a cultural and educational development would follow upon the acquaintance with these fine specimens of Christian art. The first was most in line with the dignity of the priesthood, the second most beneficial when one's ministry might require the erection or decoration of another House of God.

Riordan realized that the crowded seminary curriculum did not permit lengthy courses in such subjects, but he considered them so valuable that he arranged that all would have a six year visual course in them. In his art collection, he placed a lecture on every wall.

Oil paintings, etchings, mezzo–tints, pen drawings, engravings and photographs at Menlo Park remain among the priceless gifts left to the modern era by a far–sighted archbishop whose chief purpose was to see his priests given a well–rounded education.

SAINT VINCENT COLLEGE — LOS ANGELES

The story of Saint Vincent's College has yet to be fully related, for much research remains to be done on this pioneering educational institution in California's southland. In April of 1865, Bishop Thaddeus Amat, C.M., called together a group of Los Angeles' civic leaders to discuss the feasibility of beginning and supporting a college in Southern California. Soon thereafter, a local newspaper observed that

> The citizens of this place have been awakened to the necessity as well as the benefits that will flow from the founding of a college in the southern part of California. Meetings have been held . . . to cooperate with the bishop . . . in securing the aid necessary to carry out the idea.

The college opened its doors in September of 1865, in the rented adobe house of Don Vicente Lugo with Father John Asmuth acting as president. The early years were precarious ones, for the institution was soon jeopardized by lack of funds and by the death of several members of the faculty. Anxious to see the educational work continue, the city then offered to donate a tract of land to the college. However "the place was anything but healthfully or conveniently situated, and hence the proposal was rejected." A short while later, Mr. Ozro W. Childs deeded the Fathers enough property to enable them to erect a suitable structure. "Amid a large concourse of citizens," the cornerstone of the new building, located on a nine acre tract of land on Broadway between Sixth and Seventh streets, was put in place by the bishop in 1866.

The handsome brick building was begun with "contributions from the county and city and from prominent citizens." Finished the following March, the city's tallest edifice served the college for the next nineteen years. A newspaper account of the dedication ceremonies concluded by stating:

> . . . We feel no hesitation in saying that nowhere on the Pacific coast will parents or guardians find a more desirable institution in every requisite for the education of those under their charge than the one to which we refer.

On August 15, 1869, the college became one of two such institutions of higher learning in the State of California to qualify for a charter. At the same time, Governor Henry H. Haight empowered Saint Vincents to confer a series of graduate degrees on deserving students. A third floor was added to the building in 1884, along with a distinctively designed tower. The structure itself lasted as a Los Angeles landmark until 1913, when it was razed to make way for the Hollingsworth Building.

During a visit to Los Angeles in 1876, the Archduke Ludwig Salvador spoke about "The College of Saint Vincents, situated in the west end of town in a pleasant garden." He went on to say that

It is a large ugly building, with seven windows and a gable, in front surmounted by a cross and ball. Through the building runs a central corridor. On the second floor are the dormitories. The College also contains a library and a small chapel. From the terrace, an excellent view may be had over the city of Los Angeles. Out in the garden is a vine covered pergola where the boys gather. In front of the house stands a small fountain. This institution has three classes with the enrollment last year of some seventy students.

Relocated on the northwest corner of Washington and Grand in 1887, the magnificent edifice erected there became as much a part of the Los Angeles skyline as the Plaza Church or Saint Vibiana Cathedral. Although the perplexing economical atmosphere in California's southland continued to thwart increased enrollment Saint Vincent was able to educate the area's leading young people with considerable success well into the 20th century. Shortly after a devastating fire destroyed the Jesuit college at Mission Santa Clara in 1909, it was suggested in certain quarters that the Society of Jesus might prefer to relocate in Southern California. The proposal was endorsed by Bishop Thomas J. Conaty, and on July 30, 1910, Father Joseph S. Glass, C.M., President of Saint Vincent's, offered to withdraw in favor of the Jesuits, a move that actually materialized two years later. The closing of the college marked the end of an era, for from that day onward no Catholic educational institution in Southern California has been so closely associated with a given area.

Saint Vincent College

Certainly "if Los Angeles is a religious city today it is due as much to Saint Vincent College's intellectual superstructure built on Los Angeles' Franciscan foundations, as to the great heritage received from Junípero Serra and his missionary companions of the 18th and 19th centuries."

SAINT VINCENT SCHOOL — SANTA BARBARA

Among the oldest Catholic schools in the Archdiocese of Los Angeles is that opened at Santa Barbara by the Daughters of Charity under the patronage of Saint Vincent de Paul. The blue–robed Sisters arrived in Santa Barbara during Christmas week, wading ashore on December 28, 1856, where they were enthusiastically greeted by the local populace after a grueling journey through the Isthmus of Panama.

Early the next month, the Sisters selected a three acre site of government land in an area known as *Las Cieneguitas*, about four miles north of the town of Santa Barbara. Work was soon underway on a three room adobe schoolhouse. The Sisters took up temporary residence in the *Casa de Aguirre* on East Carrillo Street. The daily commute to school and back was a major undertaking.

The initial students were orphaned native Americans from the various tribes scattered around the mountains and villages of the area. Eventually, day school students began coming from the town and neighboring ranches.

In 1883, the Sisters moved into Santa Barbara to property at De la Vina and Carrillo Streets, where they built a two–story brick schoolhouse from materials brought from San Francisco. When fire destroyed the building a few months later, it was rebuilt through public subscription.

There were many outstanding women associated with Saint Vincent over the years, among them Sister Mary Polycarp O'Driscoll, described by one writer as "a woman of great presence and learning who exerted a fine influence upon the youngsters under her care." There were also many prominent lay persons affiliated with the Sisters in those early days. One was Dr. James L. Ord who served as volunteer physician, counselor and friend of the institution for many years.

A complete register of all the pupils attending Saint Vincent between 1858 and 1879 was published by Wilberta M. Finley in an article for *Noticias*, the publication of the Santa Barbara Historical Society, in 1959.

In 1924, the school was moved back to its original location on *Las Cieneguitas* ranch, where the students could enjoy the wholesome and happy blessings of the country. The character of the school has changed over the years. It is no longer an orphanage, but is devoted to a training program for children with learning disabili-

ties. The educational program follows specialized techniques for training and is geared to the capacities of its students. The school is rated as one of the best of its kind west of the Mississippi River. The Daughters of Charity send their finest teachers to Santa Barbara and the city has long accorded this fine school a special place in its esteem.

When the downtown structure was sold to the Knights of Columbus in the spring of 1924, the old orphanage cornerstone was opened. Its contents were exceedingly interesting, reflecting as they did the needs and demands of an earlier age. Along with names of the early Sisters, local clergy, diocesan administrators, public officials and others, was this observation: "Teaching God's children will always remain the noblest of vocations."

SAINT VINCENT SEMINARY — MONTEBELLO

The decision to close Saint Vincent Seminary in Montebello rang down the curtain on sixty years of training teenage aspirants for the priesthood in Southern California by the Congregation of the Mission.

Vincentian activity along the Pacific Slope began with the arrival of the Right Reverend Thaddeus Amat, Bishop of Monterey, in 1854. In addition to bringing members of his own community to the area, Amat was largely instrumental in establishing Saint Vincent College in 1865.

The opportunity for opening their own preparatory seminary in the Archdiocese of Los Angeles came when the Vincentians were offered property for that purpose by Mr. and Mrs. Andrew Pansini. The historic site, which the Pansinis had owned since 1918, was part of the old Rancho San Antonio, once the property of Francisco Salvador Lugo, who had been present for the founding of *El Pueblo de Nuestra Señora de los Angeles* in 1781.

The architectural firm of Barker and Ott was entrusted with drawing up plans for buildings which would accommodate eighty boarding students. The modified California–style plan was brought to completion by the J. A. McNeil Construction Company, at a cost of $700,000. Ground–breaking ceremonies were scheduled for July 8, 1954. James Francis Cardinal McIntyre was assisted on that occasion by a host of well–wishers, including two Vincentian prelates, Archbishop Francis Beckman of Panama City and Bishop Charles Quinn of Yukiang, China.

Located on a twenty–six acre site at Bluff Road, south of Washington Boulevard, on a height overlooking the Rio Hondo, the attractive brick structures were targeted for at least partial completion the following fall. Opening the new high school facilities at Montebello made it possible to transfer back to the west coast those Vincentian students from the eight Western states then taking their classes at Cape Girardeau, Missouri. Chosen to supervise the spiritual and material needs of the new foundation was Father John O'Malley Sharpe, a native of Los Angeles, whose brother was principal of Saint Pius X High School in Hollydale.

Classes opened at the campus on September 15th with twelve students initially taking their studies outdoors and in the old Pansini home. Each successive year brought about an additional class until the full high school program was operational. By the time the seminary was formally dedicated, on July 19, 1958, there were 120 students enrolled at Saint Vincent.

Though all the buildings are architecturally–appealing and educationally–functional, the most exquisite of them all is the chapel which was erected through the generosity of Carrie Estelle Doheny. A tall belltower flanks the facade of the brick edifice, with a glass mosaic tile forming a grid pattern on plaster. The altar is a table of dark green marble supported by tapered legs of the same material. Behind is a reredos of glass mosaic that terminates at a wood–framed skylight, which bathes the sanctuary in natural light.

In 1933, Andrew Pansini and his family planted an oak sapling near the ancestral home, on the bluffs overlooking the Rio Hondo. The oak grew full–limbed and thick–trunked, a living calendar of family events: anniversaries, birthdays, marriages and a son's entry into the seminary. That tree still grows at Saint Vincent.

UNIVERSITY OF SAN FRANCISCO

The University of San Francisco observed the 125th anniversary of its establishment during October of 1980. A review of its history is a capsulized glance at the "City" itself from 1855 onwards.

It was in 1854 that Archbishop Joseph Sadoc Alemany addressed a plea to Baltimore, asking about the possibility of acquiring some priests interested in opening "a good college for the education of male youth." Providentially, there were, at that time, three Italian Jesuits, Anthony Maraschi, Charles Messea and Aloysius Masnata, who very much wanted to extend their apostolate to the Pacific Slope.

Father Maraschi (1820–1897) had arrived in the United States in 1849 and, for several years, he taught at Jesuit colleges on the east coast. He was the first to respond to Alemany's appeal.

The three "Black Robes" began the long and treacherous sea voyage to California, entering the Golden Gate aboard the *Sonora* on November 1, 1854. Maraschi was greeted by the archbishop and assigned to Saint Francis Church. Alemany agreed that the Jesuits could locate their school on the site of the present–day Emporium Department Store. The area was among sand dunes, in a small valley.

The optimistic Maraschi replied to critics of the site that "someday this will be the center of a great city." A worthy prophet he proved to be too. One need only look at San Francisco's street guide to confirm Maraschi's enthusiasm.

In July of 1856, Archbishop Alemany blessed a one–room structure which was known as Saint Ignatius Church. He named Maraschi its first pastor. The building program continued and, on October 15th, Saint Ignatius Academy was formally opened. On the following April 30th, the State of California granted a charter to the academy whereby the institution was empowered to grant degrees. In 1862, Saint Ignatius College erected a brick structure adjacent to the earlier buildings. By the late 1870s, the area was becoming too congested and the Jesuit community decided to move the college to property at Hayes Street and Van Ness Avenue.

Father John B. McGloin, in his history of the University of San Francisco, labels the years 1880–1906 as the "Golden Age" of the institution. That era was abruptly ended by the devastating earthquake of April, 1906, during which the college was almost completely destroyed.

Once again relocated and rebuilt, the college entered its "Iron Age." Classes continued and another generation of San Francisco's young people advanced in wisdom, age and grace before God and man. The present church was erected in 1914 and, thirteen years later, building began on Campion Hall. This development inaugurated the present "Ignatius Heights" phase of the historic educational facility.

Re–christened the University of San Francisco in 1950, the campus now numbers a whole litany of imposing structures. Then, in 1978, the Lone Mountain campus was incorporated into the university and the Jesuit educational apostolate entered its present age of service to San Francisco.

VII. Ecclesial Institutions
3. Archival Center

Library of Archival Center
Mission Hills, California

HISTORICAL SKETCH — ARCHIVAL CENTER

The dedication of the new Archival Center for the Archdiocese of Los Angeles in 1981 was the latest phase of a program inaugurated over two decades earlier by the late James Francis Cardinal McIntyre.

Though an archivist had been named for the old Diocese of Los Angeles–San Diego, as early as 1927, Msgr. Peter Hanrahan never functioned in any other but a titular role. He later described the collection of those early days as "a mass of unarranged materials in a walk–in vault with a combination lock at the old cathedral rectory."

Charles C. Conroy served the ecclesial community of Southern California for many years as unofficial historiographer. A retired University professor, Dr. Conroy utilized the archives for his monumental treatise on *The Centennial 1840–1940*, but he never made any headway at organizing the holdings.

In the final months of 1962, Cardinal McIntyre had a new wing added to the northeastern end of the Chancery Office which was located at 1531 West Ninth Street in Los Angeles. An archivist was formally appointed and, on the following July 8th the Chancery Archives were formally blessed and designated as an archdiocesan department.

A reporter was present for that ceremony and he later ventured the opinion in the Los Angeles *Times* that the Chancery Archives would "eventually constitute the largest collection of ecclesiastical documents in the Western United States." Indeed there was a prophetic ring to those words.

During the ensuing nineteen years, efforts were made to augment and catalogue the widely diversified assortment of documents, brochures, books and other historical mementos associated with the development of the Catholic Church in California's southland. The initial holdings were quadrupled within the first decade and it became increasingly clear that the quarters on Ninth Street would not be able to adequately serve the ever–growing needs of the archdiocese.

On a number of occasions, the necessity for larger quarters was discussed with Timothy Cardinal Manning and Msgr. Benjamin G. Hawkes. Several possible solutions were presented, all of which were carefully studied by His Eminence and the Vicar General.

Early in 1980, Msgr. Hawkes, a member of the Board of Directors for the Dan Murphy Foundation, presented a letter from the cardinal requesting a grant with which to build a wholly separate structure for the archives on property adjacent to San Fernando Mission. With the endorsement and encouragement of Sir Daniel Donohue, the foundation generously agreed to erect a building which would serve as the major participation by the Catholic Church in the bicentennial celebrations for *El Pueblo de Nuestra Señora de los Angeles.*

Ground was broken on the Feast of Saint Pius Vth, April 30th. On the following February 5th, the first of twenty– three truckloads of historical materials arrived from the Chancery Office, thus launching the Archival Center on its tenure of service. It was especially fitting that this first independent archival facility erected under diocesan auspices in the United States be located within the shadow of a California mission—for it was among those venerable foundations that it all began for Christ along *El Camino Real.*

The Chancery Archives exists to preserve and make available documents and other pertinent historical materials essential to the effective administration of the Archdiocese of Los Angeles. As the final repository for the permanent records of the Church in Southern California, the collection is a treasure–trove for historians, economists, political scientists and many others.

NEW ARCHIVAL CENTER

Located adjacent to the old *convento* at San Fernando Mission, the Archival Center for the Archdiocese of Los Angeles incorporates all the traditional aspects of provincial architecture. Its nine distinctive arches, framed in wood and finished in adobe stucco, reflect the most outstanding features of Hispanic influence.

Though barely distinguishable as a contemporary building, the two–story edifice is an extremely functional facility, equipped with all the modern devices associated with efficient record management. Designed by Harold L. Cass for maximum utilization of existing space, the eleven room building, with its 5,198 square footage, accommodates the massive quantity of archival materials accumulated since 1962 and previously housed in the archdiocesan Chancery Office.

The first floor, with its commodious offices for the archivist and secretary, together with ample restroom area, also houses the Historical Museum and Library sections. In addition to the several thousand reference volumes available for researchers, the attractive room has sixteen panelled display cases wherein are exhibited hundreds of interesting and often unique mementos related to the ecclesial development of California and the West. Provisions have also been made for four revolving displays which are changed bi–monthly.

The general public is invited to tour the Historical Museum on Mondays and Thursdays, between 1 and 3 o'clock, at which time members of *Las Damas Archivistas* conduct lectures and answer questions about the holdings. Researchers are welcome by appointment.

In the upstairs area of the Archival Center, which is not open to visitors, there are housed several hundred thousand documents that comprise the core collection of the Chancery Archives for the Archdiocese of Los Angeles.

Erected with a grant from a private foundation, the Archival Center has been engineered to withstand the normal onslaught of earthquake and fire. Its floors on both levels are concrete, faced with vinylized asbestos tile. The bottom floor is carpeted with a patterned, commercial covering. Fire resistency is rated at one hour for most of the building.

Heated in the winter by a Lennox forced air gas unit and refrigerated at other times by an expansion valve air–conditioning system, the Archival Center is also serviced by a humidifier which assures consistent moisture readings for the more fragile and aging documents.

Though the exterior is finished in a stucco substance, the building's surface closely resembles the adobe used throughout California during provincial times. The roof is covered with replica mission tiles fashioned by the San Valle Company. In order to secure ultimate security, wrought–iron bars have been installed on all windows, along with lock templates and a sensitized alarm system. A fire panel provides further assurances of safety.

Other novel features in the new edifice are restrooms equipped for the handicapped, a hydro–electric elevator activated by braille switches and doors outfitted with panic bars for quick egress. The building is furnished throughout with cabinets specially fabricated from domestic birch by the Wilson Company. In several areas, formica counters are also installed to more effectively utilize space.

Erected under the supervision of Dick Adams for the M.T. Patrick Construction Company, the Archival Center for the Archdiocese of Los Angeles encompasses the best of the past for the service of the future.

INAUGURAL OF ARCHIVAL CENTER

The dedication or setting aside of a building or area for God's work has always been intimately interwoven with the Church's rich liturgy. Hence it is highly appropriate that the Chief Shepherd of Los Angeles inaugurate the new Archival Center for the archdiocese within the framework of the Eucharist.

It has long been part of the public record that a dozen years prior to the directive from the National Conference of Catholic Bishops encouraging local ordinaries to open their archives to researchers, the leadership of the Church in Southern California had dedicated itself to the ideal of making available the heroic, varied, productive and inspiring deeds of our forebears.

The very discernible and sincere concern exhibited in this portion of the vineyard for keeping an accurate record of God's dealings with His people will be looked back on as an outstanding precedent and an enviable watershed in the story of the American Church.

This is not alone the observation of a biased spectator. The Dean of American Catholic historians, Msgr. John Tracy Ellis, visited on June 27th and he later wrote a glowing letter saying how much he was impressed by this "splendid archival achievement."

Those who are the benefactors of this foresight pledge to keep its objective alive for future generations. And this they do, at least partially, by carefully acknowledging how it came to fruition.

There was a trinity of persons who translated this dream into reality; the instigator, the provider and the catalyst. Like its divine model, this trinity of persons was interdependent in all its works.

The instigator, of course, was Timothy Cardinal Manning. It was he who got this ambitious undertaking off the ground. Even during the days before he was archbishop, he encouraged with his presence and interest any and all efforts towards accurately perpetuating the Church's spiritual and human pageantry.

Next there is Sir Daniel Donohue (and the Dan Murphy Foundation), the generous provider of the material components comprising the building itself. Throughout the months of its erection, he took a most active role in seeing the building brought to completion.

Finally, Msgr. Benjamin G. Hawkes was the catalyst whereby skeletal and ethereal plans evolved into an exceedingly practical and modern building all within the architectural simplicity of the mission era.

To this trinity of persons must be added dozens of others, each of whom in his or her own way, can take great consolation in knowing that the Lord always blesses those who have the courage to break fresh ground and forge new pathways. It is a special blessing that this new facility should be attached to one of California's historic missionary foundation—for it was along *El Camino Real* that it all began for Christ and it is in that context that the story should be told.

The first building of its kind ever erected by the Catholic Church in the United States, the archival center will, prayerfully, become the flagship for a whole new fleet of sister–foundations dedicated to recording the accomplishments of the past for the enrichment of the future.

"YEAR OF THE ARCHIVES"

For Catholics in California's southland, the year 1981 was not alone the bicentennial anniversary for *El Pueblo de Nuestra Señora de los Angeles*, it is also, for the Archdiocese of Los Angeles, the "Year of the Archives." It has long been recognized that responsible preservation of documents is absolutely essential for authentic history. For it to be above evasion or dispute, history must be grounded on documents, not on opinion or hearsay.

Forty–five years ago, this nation's first Catholic President journeyed to the National Archives to participate in ceremonies opening the John Adams papers to researchers. On that occasion, he pointedly observed that "there is little that is more important for an American citizen to know than the history and traditions" of the past.

He went on to say that "without such knowledge," a person "stands uncertain and defenseless before the world, knowing neither where he has come from, nor where he is going." Surely those observations apply in a very special way to the story of salvation. No less an historical skeptic than George Bancroft studied the roots of the human saga and he was forced to acknowledge that he found "the name of Jesus Christ written on the top of every page of modern history."

The Archival Center erected by the Archdiocese of Los Angeles at San Fernando Mission is a measured response to the Church's obligations to collect and preserve those documents and other records associated with the human activities comprising California's Catholic heritage.

The need for such a repository is clearly demonstrated in contemporary times when the quantity of knowledge is increasing so rapidly. It has been estimated, for example, that in the last century, the sum total of human knowledge doubled every fifty years. By the beginning of this century, the time it took to double that knowledge was down to twenty–five years. By mid–twentieth century, the doubling was occurring every fifteen years.

At present, the storehouse of knowledge is doubling in less than ten years. Put another way, enough scholarly papers are being published every day to fill seven sets of a twenty–five volume encyclopedia! The Archival Center is envisioned as occupying a vital role in the on–going challenge of keeping the local Church abreast with modern demands and needs, some of which are not only new, but totally unprecedented in ecclesial annals.

The tragedy of Caiaphas and his associates resulted from their clinging to the past, their unwillingness to lay aside their privileged positions and to welcome a new day. They were blind to the signs of the times. That same tragedy, in painful though less significant ways, has been repeated at every period of transition in the history of religion. And it is being repeated today by those who fail to provide for the future by ignoring the past.

While there is much wrong with modern times, there is more that could be right if people would only take time to look at the record, make creative interpretations and then arrive at reasoned conclusions. This they can do only by going to the documents.

A GUTENBERG FRAGMENT

An essay about displaying leaves from the Gutenberg Bible at the three archdiocesan seminaries and the Archival Center occasioned a minor avalanche of queries, most of which could be paraphrased in this way: "How could you countenance removing pages from the Gutenberg Bible at Camarillo for the purpose of exhibit?" One reader put it a little more bluntly: "I regard tearing out pages of a Bible as only slightly less revolting than vivisection."

Well, we didn't and wouldn't do such a thing. The pages in question were removed from a damaged and incomplete copy of the Bible over half a century ago. And while this is surely not a case of bibliasection, perhaps an historical explanation is in order.

From the very outset of her collecting days, Carrie Estelle Doheny was enamored with the work of Johannes Gutenberg. During the years she patiently waited for the opportunity of purchasing an entire edition of his famous Bible, Mrs. Doheny acquired fragments whenever they became available.

Most of those pages had been tipped into a limited edition of "leaf books" published by Gabriel Wells of New York, in 1921, for A. Edward Newton (1863–1940). Here we will discuss one of those books, identified as Item #2899 in the Estelle Doheny Collection.

The bookplate affixed to that volume indicates that it was purchased by Melvin S. Wood, a collector of some prominence. Shortly after acquiring this cherished page as the cornerstone of his library, Wood sent it to D.F. Howe of Hermosa Beach, California, a nationally recognized scriptural scholar for analysis.

Howe identified the leaf as the "latter part of the 7th and the first part of the 8th chapter of II Esdras of the Apocryphas." Howe goes on to comment that "the Apocrypha consists of 14 books. They were not admitted to the Hebrew Canon of the Scriptures. But they were admitted as genuine to the Septuagint version." He then goes on to speak about the canon of scripture in such a way as to indicate that he was a Protestant scripture scholar.

Though he digressed from his original purpose, Howe admitted to Wood that "you surely have a treasure in this leaf." Annexed to his handwritten reply, Howe translates the last fifty–three verses of Chapter 7 and the first twelve verses of Chapter 8. Mrs. Doheny acquired this page sometime between 1946 and 1955. It is tipped into a full black morocco binding fabricated by Stikeman and Company of New York and blind stamped with geometrical cover designs.

In the bibliographical essay written for this copy of A *Noble Fragment. Being a Leaf of the Gutenberg Bible, 7450–1455*, A. Edward Newton traced the history of the famed "Mazarin" Bible, so named for the French cardinal in whose library the first copy was discovered. After carefully explaining how the leaf was printed in Gothic type, in double columns of forty–two lines, Newton notes that "the Bible from which this fragment was extracted was itself imperfect, chiefly in that it lacked a number of pages.

Newton's sensitivity to possible criticism of his use of the leaves probably accounts for his remark that had the dismantled "book been perfect, or even had it lacked a few pages which could be supplied in facsimile, as is usually done in books of great value, it would have been an act of vandalism to remove the leaves. . . ."

What one can say about Item #2899 can be applied to the other fragments or leaves that have been retained for public viewing. The Dyson–Perrins–Doheny Gutenberg remains unscathed by the archivist!

CALENDAR OF DOCUMENTS

December 23, 1990 was a banner day at San Fernando Mission. Early in the morning a gigantic wooden crate arrived from Hong Kong containing copies of Volume One of the long–awaited *Calendar of Documents and Related Historical Materials in the Archival Center*. The genesis of this book and the other volumes in the series goes back almost thirty years, to November of 1962, when James Francis Cardinal McIntyre inaugurated the ecclesial archives for the Archdiocese of Los Angeles.

Father Maynard Geiger, the long–time director for the Santa Barbara Mission Archives, was the inspiring force behind the notion of publishing a finding device for materials in the archdiocesan repository. His own calendar of the historic treasures at Santa Barbara, an exemplary tool for researchers, was later used as a model for the twelve volume series cataloguing the United States Documents in the Propaganda Fide Archives, that began appearing in 1966 under the editorship of another southland cleric, Father Finbar Kenneally, O.F.M., a member of the Academy of American Franciscan History.

In 1983, Sister Miriam Ann Cunningham (1916–1987), a member of the Congregation of the Holy Cross, became affiliated with the Archival Center. She was entrusted with the monumental chore of cataloguing the holdings between 1903 thru 1917, an era encompassing the episcopate of the Right Reverend Thomas J. Conaty. Prior to that time, the Conaty documents had been arranged, but uncatalogued.

Each document was assigned a code number and described as to correspondents, date, language, pagination and place of origin. A digest was made of contents and, finally, the information was typed onto stencils for index cards. By the time she was finished, Sister Miriam Ann had become the most informed person alive on Conaty's activities as Bishop of Monterey–Los Angeles.

Since an archival collection remains sterile and useless until scholars know of its existence and the scope of its contents, plans were formulated for publishing the calendar. In addition to chronologically enumerating 3,427 individual letters, the calendar lists 292 homilies, addresses and lectures which Conaty wrote and delivered during the years of his incumbency.

A twelve page biographical index enumerates the persons mentioned in the correspondence, along with a guide to the letters in which their names appeared. The book also contains a lengthy biographical sketch of Thomas J. Conaty excerpted from the editor's *Century of Fulfillment*, a history of the Roman Catholic Church in California's Southland.

The initial volume in an open–ended series, the *Calendar of Documents and Related Historical Materials* in the Archival Center is the first guide of its kind ever issued for an ecclesial jurisdiction in the United States. Its appearance makes it possible for researchers the world over to know what materials are available at Mission Hills.

Lord John Acton is credited with saying that "history to be above evasion must stand on documents, not on opinion." That has been the philosophy motivating the preparation of this and succeeding calendars.

THE OAK AUTOGRAPH ALBUM

One of the truly great treasures at the Archival Center, Archdiocese of Los Angeles, is an album entitled "Autographs of California Pioneers." Measuring 17" tall, 14" wide and 5" thick, the book contains more than 1,650 autographs (1,150 individuals) of Californians and visitors to the area prior to 1849. The material is skillfully mounted on thin sheets inlaid atop the original leaves of the album. Appended to most of the entries are printed biographical sketches which the compiler excised from newspaper accounts or other early printed sources.

The people represented were all pioneers in the life of the Golden State, men and women who came by ship around the Horn, by weary journeys on foot or horseback across uncharted deserts or by dangerous and tiresome trails in the oxcarts and wagons of the pre–Gold Rush days. Friar and scout, captain and sailor, author and adventurer, trapper and *alcalde*, lawyer and merchant are all part of a collection unique in western annals.

For many years, the fascinating scrapbook belonged to Ora Oak, a one–time employee of the A.L. Bancroft

& Company of San Francisco. She sold the album to Ernest Dawson about 1927. Charles Yale, then an employee of Dawson's Book Shop, was asked to write a comprehensive description of the album to enhance its saleability. In so doing, he leaned heavily on the biographical insertions for the essay which he and his assistant, Eleanor Reed, prepared for publication in Catalogue #53 which was issued by the book shop in January of 1928. A copy of that now–rare catalogue was given to this writer by Glen Dawson, along with permission to quote liberally from its contents.

Yale concluded the lengthy description of the album by noting that, since duplication of such a work would be an impossibility, it was being "moderately–priced" at $6,000. Though there was no dearth of interested and prospective buyers, the cost was considered prohibitive, even in those pre–depression times. Finally, a year later, "father" Dawson reduced his price and Carrie Estelle Doheny purchased the album as the centerpiece of her Western Americana collection.

In 1940, the album became part of the Estelle Doheny Collection of Books, Manuscripts and Works of Art and, as such, was presented to Saint John's Seminary in Camarillo. There it remained, a cherished historical jewel, until 1987, when it was moved to the Archival Center, at Mission Hills, as part of the newly–constituted Estelle Doheny Collection of Californiana.

The compiler of the album was Henry Lebbeus Oak (1844–1905), a native of Maine who came to California in 1866. He was an avid autograph collector. During a tour of the California missions in 1874, for example, he interviewed people such as Benjamin Hayes, Cornelius Coe, Alfred Robinson, Andres Pico, B.D. Wilson and J.J. Warner. And, in every case, he sought and was given either an autograph, a document or a letter for his personal files. Later, whenever an important individual came to the library, he left behind something for the Oak collection. It can easily be seen how a man of such diligence came to acquire such a varied and exquisite collection. Everything about this volume indicates the methodology of its compiler. The contents are neatly mounted, carefully cross–indexed and minutely researched. The sketches, mounted next to the autographs, subsequently became the basis for the pioneer register and index which began appearing under the name of Hubert Howe Bancroft in 1885.

The missionaries occupy a prominent section in the album. *Primer inter pares* would be Fray Junípero Serra (1713–1784), founder and *Presidente* of the California missions. Actually there are two Serra autographs, one clearly dated at San Carlos de Monte–Rey, July 17, 1774. Others included in this section are Fermin Francisco de Lasuen, Estevan Tapis, Jose Señan, Vicente de Sarria, Mariano Payeras, Jose Sanchez and Francisco

Garcia Diego y Moreno who became the first Bishop for the Diocese of Both Californias.

They are all here—those valiant men and women who came from all parts of America and from many foreign countries to lift California high upon the crest of world–wide acclaim.

DOYLE–ALEMANY POWER OF ATTORNEY

Among the several hundred thousand documents housed at the Archival Center, Archdiocese of Los Angeles, is one of particular interest to legal historians. It is the original power–of–attorney given to John Thomas Doyle by Archbishop Joseph Sadoc Alemany whereby Doyle is empowered to represent the archdiocese in its legal battle with the United States over the ownership of lands.

The document itself, issued by George L. Kenny, agent at the Old Stand, Naglee's Building, was sealed and delivered in the presence of David Bixler and F.J. Thibault. The text of the handwritten power–of–attorney reads as follows: "Joseph S. Alemany, Roman Catholic Archbishop of San Francisco, State of California, have made, constituted and appointed John T. Doyle my true and lawful attorney to oppose and protest against the issuing by the United States of any and all patents for lands in the state of California, claimed by the Roman Catholic Church and confirmed to me as 'Bishop of Monterey,' to any other person or persons than to me."

It goes on to say that "in case it should be deemed advisable by my said attorney, for me and in my name to compromise and settle all such conflicting claims to said lands as he may deem proper and on such terms and in such manner as to him may seem best." The text concludes by Alemany's "giving and granting to my said attorney full power and authority to do and perform all and every act and thing whatsoever requisite and necessary to be done in and about the premises . . . as I might or could do if personally present. . . ."

It was signed by Archbishop Alemany on May 7, 1858. There is a small yellow seal next to the archbishop's signature and a large pink notary slip on the verso. There is some minor soiling to the last page, but otherwise the historic document is in superb condition. Measuring 12 1/2 x 7 3/4 inches, the text covers 1 1/2 pages on a single folded sheet. The docket on the last page reads: "Power of Attorney. Jos. S. Alemany, Archbp, S.F. to Jno. T. Doyle."

John Thomas Doyle, among the most outstanding of the state's early lawyers, is probably most remembered for his work on the Pious Fund of the Californinas. He was also founding president of the California Historical Society.

It would be interesting to know how this document wandered into the public domain. The external markings are similar to those made on documents in the Chancery Archives, Archdiocese of San Francisco. However, it is possible that this important document was retained by John T. Doyle himself. In any event, it was either lost, stolen, given away or sold from one of those two sources.

About twenty years ago, it was purchased by Kenneth M. Johnson, a prominent author, historian, lawyer and lecturer. Johnson was a prolific writer who compiled several volumes in the "Famous California Trials" series published by Dawsons Book Shop. After Kenneth Johnson died in 1983, his books were sold by the California Book Auction Galleries, Inc. The document in question was listed as Entry #433.

DOCUMENTS ACQUIRED BY ARCHIVAL CENTER

Through the kind offices of Glen Dawson, a prominent Los Angeles bookseller, the Archival Center acquired a valuable collection of documents and transcripts relating to the ranches, orchards and vineyards once comprising San Fernando Mission. The packet of materials contains surveys and related items used as evidence in the numerous legal suits filed at various levels about land holdings at or near the Old Mission. A number of petitions and affidavits contain statements by such historical personages as Andres Pico, John Wilson and James McKinley.

Among the materials are eight boundary surveys of what is known in the annals as "Ex Mission San Fernando" between 1852 and 1878. The 116 pages in that deposition encompass field reports made by Henry Washington, Ralph W. Norris, Henry Hancock, John Goldsworthy, W.P. Reynolds and others.

Several "Transcripts of Record" are among the acquisitions. One of the more noteworthy deals with the United States versus Eulogio de Celis, filed on December 6, 1855, about "a place named San Fernando." (Eulogio is memorialized in the City of San Fernando by a street named for him and his son) There is also the entire transcript of the Southern District Land Case 173, the United States of America versus Manuel Garcias, including the "Opinion of the Land Commissioner," issued by George Fisher on December 19, 1854.

A handwritten copy of the "Contract of Lease of Mission San Fernando" was probably transcribed from the original copy which was burned in the conflagration following the disastrous San Francisco earthquake. There are also some agreements and deeds drawn to the Lankershim Ranch Land & Water Company

(1887–1891), along with a forty–eight page " Extract of Field Notes of the ReSurvey of the Exterior Boundaries of the Rancho Ex–Mission San Fernando by Surveyors C.A. Ensign and E.T Wright." It bears the confirmation date of 1892.

Possibly the most intriguing item is a holographic will of Ygnacio Coronel (father of the famed Antonio), in which he proudly declares himself "a citizen of the Mexican Republic and a resident of the City and County of Los Angeles, in the State of California." Dated December 6, 1862, it is witnessed by Ignacio Sepulveda and Juan Hoogstrater.

Most valuable of these treasures is a "rubbing" of the three page document whereby Pio Pico sold the mission and all its lands to his crony, Eulogio de Celis, for the paltry sum of $14,000, a sale later invalidated by President Abraham Lincoln. The document, with its rare seal bearing the words "*Gobierno del Dept. California*," was signed by Pico and witnessed by Jose Matias Moreno. It bears the historically significant date June 17, 1846.

The approximately 200 square miles of land that once belonged to San Fernando Mission is now populated by people living in nineteen Los Angeles communities and two incorporated cities. It has evolved into the eighth largest of the nation's urban markets, accounting for a population of upwards of 1.3 million. Demographers contend that if the San Fernando Valley were itself a city, it would rank sixth in the United States of America. More people reside there than inhabit Detroit, Dallas, Baltimore and San Diego!

How the ownership of that land has developed since mission times can only be traced through such documents as those which are now available to researchers at the Archival Center.

THE CANTWELL CHALICE

The chalice is the most important of the "sacred vessels" used for the celebration of Holy Mass. The earliest chalices, even the cup used by Our Lord at the Last Supper were large and had two handles to accommodate the laity who communicated under both species until the 14th century.

Through the kindness of the Marymount Sisters, the chalice that belonged to the late Archbishop John J. Cantwell (1874–1947) was recently entrusted to the Historical Museum of the Archival Center at Mission Hills. Measuring 9 3/4 inches tall, the heavily filigreed chalice is elaborately decorated around the cup with six amethysts interlaced by an equal number of tiny emeralds.

Linked to Cantwell's birthplace by a single, circular piece of jade, the 5 inch cup is set among four silver–

plated angels. Inlaid in the node or centerpiece of the chalice are four miniature rubies. There are four cloisonne scenes on the base of the chalice: The Blessed Mother and Saint John the Evangelist at either side of the crucified Christ, Saint John the Divine, Mary and the Christ Child and Saint Joseph with the Infant. Between the colorful cloisonne portrayals are four larger rubies and eight opals.

On the bottom of the base are these words in Latin: "From Patrick W. Riordan, Archbishop of San Francisco, to Father John J. Cantwell as a sign of cherished friendship. 1910." The name of the goldsmith is also visible, along with the coat–of–arms used by purveyors to the Holy See.

The chalice is housed in a handsomely fabricated wooden case covered with black leather. Its accompanying paten fits snuggly into a hidden drawer at the bottom of the case, while an intinction spoon hangs in a felt stirrup.

The background of this chalice is long and historically interesting. The youthful Father Cantwell was appointed to the curia in San Francisco in 1904 as personal secretary to Archbishop Patrick W. Riordan. Writing to a friend, Riordan said that he had selected Cantwell for many reasons. "Since he came to the diocese he has been a most priestly character in every sense of the word and a man of great refinement and gentlemanly character, and while he has had no business experience, he is a man of intelligence and gradually will pick up the information necessary for this office."

On the occasion of Cantwell's first journey back to Ireland in 1908, the archbishop presented him with a cash gift "as a slight token of my great friendship for you and also as a mark of my gratitude for your service to me in the Archdiocese of San Francisco." Father Cantwell decided to use Riordan's gift to purchase a chalice. While in Europe, he journeyed to Fulda in Prussia and there placed an order with William Rauscher, an internationally–known goldsmith.

When the completed chalice finally arrived in San Francisco, Cantwell showed it to Riordan who consecrated it and used it himself several times. It was the archbishop who suggested the wording that was eventually engraved on the chalice.

Cantwell used the chalice for thirty–seven years in San Francisco and then in Los Angeles. In the southland, it was kept first at his episcopal residence on Burlington Avenue and then at 100 Fremont Place. It was used by Eugenio Cardinal Pacelli when the future Pope Pius XII offered Mass in the chapel at Fremont Place on October 29, 1936. Shortly after Cantwell's death, his sister, Nellie, gave the chalice to the Sisters at Marymount where she had volunteered for many years as a member of the Marymount Tabernacle Society.

THIRTY PIECES OF SILVER

Through the generosity of a prominent local numismatist, the Historical Museum of the Archival Center acquired an ancient "shekel" of Tyre which is identical to and contemporary with the "thirty pieces of silver" paid to Judas Iscariot for his betrayal of Christ.

Mentioned for the first time in Ezra 2, 69, coins figure often in the passages of Holy Scripture. Our Lord Himself frequently used them as a teaching device for the telling of His parables.

The silver Shekel of Tyre is represented by at least three biblical references: (a) it is the only coin accepted as payment for the annual Jewish temple tax, according to the Talmud; (b) it was therefore the coin found in the mouth of a fish, since that coin was used to defray the temple tax for Jesus and Peter and (c) most notorious of all, it was surely the coinage paid to Judas Iscariot for his betrayal of the Lord.

None of the evangelists gives a character study of Judas and, whenever the apostles are enumerated in the pages of Holy Scripture, Judas is always placed at the end of the list. It seems likely that the major crisis for Judas was the same as that faced by the other apostles, the revelation of a suffering Messiah. Scripture scholars conclude that Judas' courage and faith must have been unequal to such a profound challenge.

The seeming waste of perfume at the Bethany anointing disturbed a number of the apostles, but Judas is singled out as being particularly offended by It. We are told that shortly thereafter "Judas Iscariot, one of the twelve, went to the chief priests to betray Him."

Saint Matthew recalls how Judas later rid himself of the "blood money" by hurling it into the Temple. The precise enumeration of "thirty pieces" may have been symbolical. Thirty shekels was the prescribed fine imposed on the owner of an ox that killed a slave.

There are different accounts of Judas' death in the early Christian writings. According to Saint Matthew, he hanged himself but, in the Acts of the Apostles, Peter is quoted as saying that Judas "fell forward and burst open." Probably both accounts are meant to be symbolic. Of all the biblical references to coins, the thirty pieces of silver associated with Judas is perhaps the best known. Over the centuries, there has been a persistent curiosity about those historic coins that recall the greatest betrayal in recorded annals.

The obverse of the silver shekel is idolatrously adorned with the laureated head of Melqarth, a Phoenician god, while the reverse exhibits a proud eagle sitting on a ship's prow. A palm branch appears behind the eagle with the legend in Greek reading: "Tyre Sacred and Inviolable Sanctuary."

The coin is marked with a Phoenician date and was struck in the first century before the birth of Christ. It is interesting to note that even with the shekel's high grade of silver, its monetary value was, to the best of present–day reckonings, only a little over $30 in American money.

SCRIMSHAW AT MISSION HILLS

The making of scrimshaws was the folk art of American whalers. A superb example of that delicate and attractive art can be seen in the Historical Museum of the Archival Center at Mission Hills.

Scrimshaw was a form of art practiced during what is termed the golden era of whaling, from 1825 to 1865. It was prevalent earlier and later but that forty year period marked its peak.

No one knows the origin of the art. Some link it with the ancient practice of Oriental landsmens' ivory carving. Others associate it with Eskimos working on ivory or bone, and still others identify it with the Indians of the Caribbean, South America and Pacific Islands working in shells and wood. The word itself is said to have been derived from skrimshander. Being of Dutch origin, the term eventually came to be identified exclusively with the folk art of the American Whalers.

The men aboard whale ships used these materials readily at hand which had little commercial value in their raw state. These were the teeth of the sperm whale. A good sized sperm had approximately fifty teeth from four to ten inches long, all in the lower jaw.

There was an unwritten understanding that the lower jaw of a sperm whale, with its teeth, belonged to the crew. The teeth were doled out by the second or third mate. When removed from the jawbone, the teeth are rough and rigid, but soft. They harden with age.

After removal of the teeth, the first step was to smooth the surface with a file, grindstone or sharkskin. Final polishing was with pumice or ashes, rubbed gently with the palm of the hand to produce the proper sheen. Sometimes the teeth were placed in brine or hot water to soften before being worked upon.

The seamen had special tools to carry out their projects. These would be sail needles with wood or bone handles, gimlets fashioned from nails, a sharp jack knife, files for turning and making lace–like filigree, saw blades and other cutting or scraping instruments.

The subjects of scenes placed on the scrimshaw were varied. Closest to the men would be their daily activities and they often depicted, to the best of their ability, the various phases of whaling industry. Thoughts of home inspired romantic subjects. Many copied scenes from magazines or newspapers of the day. Naval heroes and scenes were popular.

The designs were carefully scratched and pricked on

the tooth, because a slip of the hand might ruin the entire project. With the design successfully etched on the surface, the next step was to add color. India ink, paint, soot, tar or dyes were worked into the incised lines. Excess color was wiped off leaving the picture sharp and defined.

The scrimshaw in the Historical Museum at the Archival Center has a scene of two wives standing atop a roofed platform, looking out over the city of Nantucket for their returning husbands. Like most scrimshaws, it is undated. The scene is quite accurate, according to contemporary portrayals of the city.

According to an oral tradition passed down through the family of its donor, the scrimshaw at Mission Hills dates from the 1820s and was given to Archbishop Joseph Sadoc Alemany just prior to his departure for Vatican Council I. It may have been intended as a gift for Pope Pius IX.

THE RAILROAD COLLECTION

Among the interesting materials on exhibit in the Historical Museum of the Archival Center in Mission Hills is a collection of handcrafted models of the "World's Greatest Locomotives" fashioned from solid pewter. It was presented to the museum in 1988 by Don Hildreth. Railroad buffs and others are fascinated by these models which represent trains that rolled out of the yards at Altoona, Cheyenne, Bath and Chicago, mechanical giants on tracks of steel.

From iron works across Europe and the Orient, they signaled a world–wide revolution in travel and commerce. From the early wood burners to the new streamlined expresses, they were objects of awe and symbols of adventure. Sponsored by the Railway and Locomotive Historical Society, the collection at Mission Hills is the first ever to capture the drama of railroading as it unfolded in the west and around the world.

The twenty–five authentically detailed models in the collection portray the most important locomotives of all time. Selected by leading railroad experts, each sculptured miniature is individually cast in solid pewter and entirely finished by hand.

Beginning with the legendary John Bull of the 1830s, the collection includes such important American locomotives as: Engine 999 of the Empire State Express, which claimed a world speed record of 122 miles per hour in 1893; the Pennsylvania Railroad's K–4, a pioneer on runs like the Detroit Arrow and the sleek West coast Daylight–type of 1941.

From the other great railroading nations of the world are reproductions of England's "Flying Scotsman," Japan's "Asia Express" and Germany's S/36, the pride of the Rheingold Express. The superbly–crafted miniatures show such fine details as handrails, suspension, fittings and cab layout in hand–rubbed pewter. The casting molds were refined by hand to ensure accuracy.

Displayed in a specially–built wooden shelf, the tiny locomotives are exhibited on five tiers, each outfitted with miniature tracks which hold the engines securely in place. All of the locomotives are described by interesting commentaries written by A. William Johnston and other experts in railroad history and mechanical design. The commentaries are housed in an attractive box.

Bishop Thaddeus Amat (1811–1878) traveled extensively by railroad during his years of service in the Diocese of Monterey–Los Angeles. In one of his letters, he told about his ride on old *Jupiter* #60, a standard type 4–4–0 locomotive that hauled passengers to Nevada's White Pine mining country.

Jupiter became famous for its key role in the ceremonies linking the east and west portions of the transcontinental railroad on May 10, 1869, at Promontory, Utah. *Jupiter* pulled the two cars bearing Governor Leland Stanford to the ceremonies.

Early in 1991, a visitor to the Historical Museum wrote in the Guest Book: "An amazing place—there's something for everyone here. A fascinating place to visit."

A COLUMBUS MEMENTO

Among the items currently displayed at the Historical Museum of the Archival Center at Mission Hills is one which highlights and recalls the 500th anniversary of European penetration into the New World. It is a hundred year old copy of Francesco Tarducci's *The Life of Christopher Columbus*.

Tarducci (1841–1906), a distinguished Italian historian, based his extensive study on previously unknown documents. His story of Columbus' life and discoveries, written in a graceful and natural style, was the finest account written to that time. Samuel Eliot Morrison considered the Tarducci account a classic.

The two volumes, boxed and bound together in artistic hand–tooled leather, were translated from the Italian by Henry F. Brownson (1835–1913), the lawyer–son of Orestes A. Brownson, and issued under the Brownson imprint at Detroit in 1891. On the front cover is a three–colored, finely–fashioned cloisonne seal bearing the insignia of the Knights of Columbus.

Inside the book is the elaborately etched bookplate of Archbishop John J. Cantwell (1874–1947). For many years the book was housed in the library of the episcopal residence at 100 Fremont Place in Los Angeles. It was among the many volumes consigned to Saint John's Seminary by this writer when James Francis Cardinal McIntyre moved his residence to Saint Basil's Rectory.

What truly distinguishes the book and gives it historical significance is the calligraphed inscription which reads:

> San Francisco Council No. 615 of the Knights of Columbus beg Right Reverend Bishop Conary to accept this volume as a slight expression of their gratitude for the learned and eloquent words, in which he set before them the life and virtues of their great Patron, on the occasion of their Annual Celebration, October 16, 1904.

The Knights of Columbus, a fraternal and beneficent society of Catholic men, was founded on February 2, 1882, by Father Michael J. McGivney. Its purpose was that of developing a practical Catholicity among its members, to promote Catholic education and charity and, through its insurance department, to furnish at least temporary financial assistance to the families of deceased members.

Genesis of the Order's activities in California dates back to 1901, when Edward L. Hearn, Supreme Knight, sent James J. Gorman to California for interviews with Archbishop Patrick W. Riordan of San Francisco and Bishop George T. Montgomery of Monterey–Los Angeles. Originally, it was suggested that there be only two Councils, one in San Francisco and the other in Los Angeles. From these two units, the organization would develop at its own rate and eventually spread throughout the state.

An inspection of the California foundation was made in the summer of 1902 by Hearn. Upon his departure, the late Joseph Scott was named Territorial Deputy for the incipient Pacific Coast organization. Almost immediately, Scott inaugurated a third branch at Oxnard, in order to qualify for establishment of a State Council. Other Councils were subsequently set up by Scott at such places as Oakland, Fresno, Vallejo, Pomona and San Jose.

Bishop Conaty had been an enthusiastic supporter of the Knights of Columbus and his eloquent speech at their annual gathering in 1904 was a masterful treatise on Christopher Columbus and his role in the discovery of the New World. The book presented to Conaty on that occasion has itself become a cherished memento of the great "Admiral of the Ocean Sea."

SAINT PATRICK CATHEDRAL — NEW YORK

One of the nation's most celebrated houses–of–worship celebrated the centenary of its formal opening on May 25th, 1979. It was just a hundred years earlier that John Cardinal McCloskey solemnly opened the doors of Saint Patrick's Cathedral to the people of New York.

A memento of that historic event is prominently displayed in the Historical Museum attached to the Archival Center, Archdiocese of Los Angeles. It is a 31 x 6 inch ticket to "Grand Pontifical Vespers," ornately printed by the firm of Schumacher & Ettlinger. The handsomely–engraved memento was given to Archbishop J. Francis A. McIntyre shortly after his arrival in Los Angeles by Msgr. John M. McCarthy, Pastor of Saint Andrew's Church in Pasadena. A native of New York City, one of McCarthy's earliest recollections was that of being taken, as a fifteen year old youngster, to the opening of Saint Patrick's Cathedral, on May 25, 1879.

Put into service three years after its Los Angeles counterpart, Saint Patrick's Cathedral has become a national landmark for peoples of all faiths. A visit to the Empire State is incomplete without a tour of the familiar Gothic edifice facing Rockefeller Center, between 50th and 51st streets. The historic church was a quarter century in the building,

Archbishop John Hughes initiated the project in 1853, when he entrusted James Renwick with the task of erecting a monument that would be "worthy of God, worthy of the Catholic religion and an honor to this great city."

The cornerstone was laid on August 15, 1858. Work was discontinued during the years of the Civil War, but taken up again in subsequent decades. Renwick erected the church in granite arid marble, using a Gothic revival common in Europe during the 13th, 14th and 15th centuries. The floor plan for the huge edifice, based on the Latin cross, allows for a seating capacity of 2,500 people.

Atop the huge bronze doors are depictions of the apostles, Mary and John the Baptist. The six statues decorating the massive doors are Saints Patrick, Joseph, Isaac Jaques and Kateri Tekakwitha, together with Frances Cabrini and Elizabeth Seton, both of whom worshiped there. The colorful stained glass windows portray the principal mysteries of the Catholic Faith and warm the monotony of the stone groining and pillars. Hanging from the ceiling are the cardinalatial hats of John McCloskey, John Farley, Patrick Hayes and Francis Spellman, vestiges of the leadership given to the Church along the Atlantic seaboard.

That Saint Patrick's is woven into the joys and sorrows of American life is attested by a proclamation issued to commemorate the centenary by the Mayor of New York City:

> The Cathedral has provided a welcoming presence for travelers and immigrants from all over the world. ... It has been an inspiration for millions and a place where Catholics and people of all faiths find quiet and peace and an opportunity for reflection and meditation.

IVORY FIGURINES IN MUSEUM

Ivory is a type of dentine found only in the tusks of elephants. Its use as a material pecularly adapted for sculpture and decoration has been universal in the history of civilization.

The Historical Museum attached to the Archival center has two mounted ivory tusks, both of them rich in religious and historical significance The more outstanding of these works–of–art was given to the late James Francis Cardinal McIntyre by Oba Adeniji Adele II, the tribal king of Lagos during the All Nigerian Marian Congress of 1954.

Cardinal McIntyre had gone to the west coast of Africa as the papal legate of Pope Pius XII who had fallen ill and was unable to personally participate in the Marian Congress. During the final ceremonies of the Congress, Oba Adeniji Adele presented the Archibishop of Los Angeles with the full–sized tusk as a gesture of gratitude on behalf of Nigeria's 700,000 Catholic inhabitants.

Because of its density, whiteness and ability to take a polish, African ivory has always been highly valued in commerce. In most recent years, the exporting of the substance from Africa's Ivory Coast has been almost totally curtailed.

The finely–polished memento presented to McIntyre was delicately engraved by hand with his cardinalatial coat–of–arms. Measuring thirty–nine inches and weighing forty–two pounds, it is anchored to a cleverly balanced wooden base.

The other smaller tusk is mounted horizontally. It is also expertly carved, with scenes of tribal life in the South Pacific. It was presented to Timothy Cardinal Manning by the Poor Clare Missionary Sisters in 1972. While Asiatic ivory is a coarser grain and doesn't possess the transverse ridges and grooves characteristic of the African form, it has always been regarded among the finest media for artistic expression.

Another exquisite figurine in the Historical Museum is a hand–executed statue of Saint George and the Dragon which Carrie Estelle Doheny had fashioned from a single piece of African ivory. The 9 1/4" high work–of–art, anchored to a mahogany base, was given to Archbishop John J. Cantwell in 1936 as a memento of the creation of the Metropolitan District of Los Angeles, an event that gave California the distinction of being the only state in the union with two ecclesial provinces.

A related item, inasmuch as it belonged to Countess Doheny, is a seven inch ivory totem pole carved in the form of stylized bird–like figures. This is one of a series that belonged to the Estelle Doheny Collection housed at Saint John's Seminary, Camarillo, California.

A final ivory masterpiece is a small bust of Saint Pius X, affixed to a teakwood base. Carved and mounted at the Britannia Fine Arts & Ivory Works, Port Trivandrum, it was presented by Msgr. Lawrence O'Leary. The use of ivory has long been of special significance for religious expression. In its whiteness and firm texture, the substance itself symbolizes moral incorruptibility and strength.

The Historical Museum is abundantly blessed with its ivory figurines.

REMINDERS OF THE PAST

Within the past few years, a considerable number of historical objects connected with California's Catholic Heritage have found their way into the Chancery Archives of the Archdiocese of Los Angeles. These items permanently displayed in several large glass showcases, have provoked considerable comment from scholars and research students visiting the archives. In order to make these fascinating mementoes more accessible to the general public, arrangements are made from time–to–time to exhibit the collection at various educational centers throughout the southland.

Among the more notable objects is Bishop Francis Mora's silver napkin ring, discovered at Sarria, in 1962, after an absence from California of over half a century. Worn by years of constant use, the napkin ring was manufactured at Watsonville where Mora was pastor, in 1856.

The *Libro de Difuntos de la Mision del Señor S. Fernando* is the famous "wandering register book" of Mission San Fernando. It was alienated from the church for five or six decades until its discovery and return by the late Henry Huntington, in the 1920s.

An especially prized item is the beautifully decorated wine cask presented by Monsignor John J. Ward to James Francis Cardinal McIntyre at the former's consecration as Titular Bishop of Bria in Saint Vibiana's Cathedral, on December 12, 1963. The episcopal ring of Bishop Thaddeus Amat, removed from his finger in 1962, reflects the simplicity of the Vincentian prelate in its plain gold band topped with a single semi–precious jewel.

Archbishop Joseph Sadoc Alemany's precious mitre was presented to the author by Antonio Alamany at Barcelona, in 1962. Family tradition associates this mitre with the Dominican bishop's consecration at Rome's Church of San Carlo al Corso in 1850. The slippers of Archbishop John J. Mitty of San Francisco, used at the consecration of Thomas Connolly, Duane Hunt, James Sweeney, Hugh Donohoe, James O'Dowd, Merlin Guilfoyle, Robert Dwyer and John Scanlon, were given to the Chancery Archives by the Right Reverend Thomas Bowe, former Chancellor for the Archdiocese of San Francisco.

Another rare item is one of the four known copies of the *Ilustrísimo y Reverendisimo Fray José Sadoc Alemany Conill, O. P.*, a collection of the archbishop's letters published by his nephew, in 1925. Most of the volumes were burned during the Communist take–over in Barcelona in 1936. The freshly polished crozier of Bishop Thaddeus Amat was displayed for many years at San Fernando Mission. Experts believe the four–part staff was "rolled" in Spain in the 1850s. Threads now connecting the joints of the crozier were added in later years, as was the thin silver coating.

NORMAN ROCKWELL'S "KENNEDY" IN ARCHIVES

The "Rembrandt Of Punkin Crick" is generally acknowledged as this century's most beloved American artist. And the genius of Norman Rockwell (1894–1978) enhanced the image that most people have of this nation's thirty–fifth president. Rockwell's classic oil painting of John F. Kennedy is surely the best known and most popular portrayal of the first Roman Catholic ever to reside at 1600 Pennsylvania Avenue.

Commissioned by the *Saturday Evening Post* when Kennedy was forty–three years old, it was painted in the summer of 1960 during the hectic presidential campaign waged between Kennedy and Richard M. Nixon. The painting originally appeared on the cover of the *Saturday Evening Post* for its issue of October 29th. Used again on December 13, 1963, it became the only Norman Rockwell painting ever used three times when the new *Post* reproduced it in September of 1975. A very straightforward portrait, the Rockwell painting conveys the look of John F. Kennedy's boyish determination that so captivated the electorate in 1960.

During his long career, Norman Rockwell did 317 covers for the *Saturday Evening Post*. A tremendously versatile painter, his work also appeared in more than twenty–five other magazines. Over the years, he illustrated advertisements for everything from cough syrup to airlines, varnish to socks and bicycles to soft drinks. Rockwell had the unique distinction of seeing his work reproduced more often than all of Michelangelo's, Rembrandt's and Picasso's work put together!

(Oh yes, Rockwell did another, less–heralded portrayal of John F. Kennedy which appeared on the cover of the *Saturday Evening Post* for April 6, 1963. Quite different from the earlier work, it presented the Chief Executive in a pensive mood to illustrate a lead story on "A Worried President.")

From February, 1972 to April, 1973, the original oil paintings of JFK were included in a travelling exhibition entitled: "Norman Rockwell, a Sixty Year Retrospective." People in nine American cities and Japan flocked by the thousands to see it and other works by the nation's most popular artist in more than half a century.

The painting was purchased by Robert A. Drew in late 1975 and three years later it was sold to the Stockbridge Museum for the unprecedented sum of $90,000. Measuring 16" by 12", the painting was able to be reproduced "life size" on the original cover of the *Saturday Evening Post*. It has all the traditional warmth, humor, character and tenderness associated with Norman Rockwell.

Among the treasures in the Historical Museum of the Chancery Archives is a framed postage stamp reproduction of Rockwell's portrayal of Kennedy, issued by Sharjal & Dependencies in 1972, to commemorate the tenth anniversary of the President's assassination. Rockwell signed the mounting in his customary square–letter style, at his home in Stockbridge on October 6, 1976.

REMBRANDT AT MISSION HILLS

One of Europe's greatest artists, Rembrandt Hermenszoon Van Rijn (1606–1669) is represented in the Historical Museum of the Archival Center with an etching of "Christ Crucified between Two Thieves." The son of a miller, Rembrandt was born near the Rhine at Leiden. His background was Dutch Calvinist of middle–class society—prosperous, democratic and proud of its recent independence from Spain.

Spanning the classic period of that society, Rembrandt's life ranged from the noisy realism of Frans Hals's generation to the quiet refinement of Vermeer's. Unfortunately, many scholars believe that Rembrandt outlived his time. The one towering genius in Holland's golden age of little masters, Rembrandt died in poverty and isolation, a fate not uncommon to great people.

A prodigious artist, Rembrandt produced about 600 paintings and 1600 drawings. He is known to have executed about 300 etchings. Among his diverse works are landscapes, portraits, mythologies and Biblical scenes.

Described as one of the little masters who were in fact portrait and genre specialists, Rembrandt was also a universalist who engaged all the themes of his life. He excelled in religious portrayals, in spite of the limited demand and total prohibition of their display in Calvinist churches. Rembrandt interpreted Biblical content in familiar, humanizing terms, concentrating on individual reaction to the divine.

The unsigned print in the Historical Museum is on a rectangular sheet with oval dimensions. The ink is a deep rich tone approximating the color artists know as burnt umber. The lower portion of the print is quite deep in tone and the upper portion, particularly between the

two thieves is relatively light. The chiaroscuro effect of the print is thus very striking in its resemblance to Rembrandt's paintings.

It was purchased from the San Francisco firm of S. and G. Gump and Company about 1929 by James P. Barry of Los Angeles and for many years hung in his private collection. In April of 1981, it was given to the Archival Center by Mrs. Marianne Peterson, through the kind intervention of Mr. Jeff Weber, an associate of Zeitlin and Ver Brugge.

A similar print sold by the English firm of Craddock & Barnard, in 1974, brought 1750 pounds at auction. It was listed as item No. 199 in their catalogue No. 140. The description read: "Extremely fine and rich impression . . . showing the plate–mark almost all round."

Rembrandt's etchings have always excited enthusiasm among the great collectors and today some of them are almost as sought after as his paintings. The rendition of "Christ Crucified between Two Thieves" is considered among Rembrandt's finest etchings.

THE PICZEK TABLEAUS

One of the most interesting (and surely the most artistic) features of the Archival Center at San Fernando Mission is the series of six mosaic tableaus adorning the eastern wall of the building. Designed by the talented Isabel and Edith Piczek from a theme suggested by Timothy Cardinal Manning, the 48" by 32" panels portray the geographical history of the Church of Los Angeles since its inception, in 1840, as the Diocese of *Ambas Californias*.

The making of these mosaics followed a complicated procedure which dates back to pre–Roman times. The initial sketches were made, revised several times and then a final color plan was drawn to scale. Finally, the six scenes were rendered to full size in a black and white cartoon. The Piczek Sisters then dispatched the cartoon to the Italian fabricator, where a reverse photocopy was made.

The mosaics were fashioned in one of the many studios at Pietra Santa. This ancient, sister–city of Carrara has been the world's mosaic center for uncounted centuries.

There are over a hundred different colors and shades of Byzantine tile in the completed mosaic renditions. The only non–ceramic pieces are the gold ones which are glass overlaid with 14 carat gold leaf. The mosaicists glued the thousands of tiny pieces of tile into place on the photocopy. When completed, match marks were drawn on the reverse of the paper in blue crayon.

The completed mosaics were then sealed into zinc containers (to protect them from dampness), crated and shipped to San Pedro aboard the *Zini Genova*. They arrived early in March.

Installation is a crucial part of the overall project and requires the careful craftsmanship of a master tilemason. Ralph McIntosh, who was the recipient of numerous national awards, was chosen for the task.

The methodology for installing mosaics is as old as the art form itself, little changed from Roman times. After anchoring galvanized metal lath firmly to the structure, the installer mixed a non–organic solution of lime, sand and cement as the base into which the mosaic tiles were imbedded. Each tiny piece was fitted securely into place, following carefully the numerical master plan drawn up by the fabricator. Using a water solution, the paper was peeled off. The entire surface was then grouted and cleaned with a mild chemical solution.

The erection of these stunning mosaic tableaus is not alone a feat of artistic excellence, but an historical panorama of California's Catholic heritage. How fitting its use for the new Archival Center.

ALBRECHT DURER IN GLASS

The two circular windows in the Archival Center at San Fernando Mission are outstanding for both their artistic qualities and their historical provenance. They were acquired through the good offices of Msgr. Clement Connolly.

Robert H. Schafhausen, the donor of the windows, provided the interesting background for the dual panels. He estimates that about a hundred years ago, they were acquired by Father Johannes Ritten, a parish priest in the town of Dollendorf. The priest likely had them installed in the parochial house which he shared with his two sisters overlooking the Rhine River. Upon Ritten's death, the windows were inherited by his nephew, Casper Schafhausen, a member of the German diplomatic corps. Prior to World War II, Schafhausen was the German Consul General in Ottawa.

With the outbreak of hostilities, Schafhausen's possessions were impounded by the Canadian government. Schaufhausen's son, Robert, was allowed to purchase his family's treasures at public auction, thus re–affirming his family's ownership of the two windows.

Forty years later, when Robert Schafhausen disposed of his home in Encino, he decided to donate the windows to the Archdiocese of Los Angeles. It was subsequently determined that they be used in the new archival facility at San Fernando Mission.

Isabel Piczek was called in for consultation. After careful examination and testing of the monochrome, graphic treatment, she ascertained that the designs of the two panels were copies patterned after the woodcuts of the German renaissance mastercraftsman, Albrecht Durer (1471–1528).

Durer's connection with stained glass is well founded in art history. The two windows at Mission Hills were likely fashioned at Cologne, where artisans were especially captivated by Durer's style. The exact years the windows were made is unclear. Quite likely, they date from the "era of stained glass revival." They are correct to the finest details, with no attempts made to improve on Durer's designs.

The panels are very well preserved. Though severely warped or bent, due to the insufficient temperature control of a wooden kiln, the circular panels are otherwise in excellent condition.

Miss Piczek was entrusted with the delicate task of designing an appropriate frame for the panels. She ultimately decided on a diamond background, incorporating red borders to enhance the contrast of the interior.

The upper panel, depicting the Coronation of the Blessed Mother as Queen of Heaven, exhibits a later style of Durer, probably dating from about 1511. A departure from his earlier renaissance style, the scene shows indications of the German baroque. The lower panel is a copy of Durer's renowned Virgin and Infant receiving the homage of Saints Joseph, John the Baptist, Anthony, Jerome, Paul and Catherine. Executed between 1497 and 1500, it exhibits a keen sense of artistic detail.

PRESIDENT OF THE UNITED STATES

The destiny of American democracy has been in the hand of thirty–eight men since 1789. Swearing "to preserve, protect and defend the Constitution of the United States," the Presidents have guided the nation through times of turmoil and eras of tranquility, seasons of change and decades of stability. Each president has brought his hopes, strengths, beliefs and ideals to the nation's highest office and each, in his own way, has pledged himself to George Washington's first precept: "the preservation of our sacred fire of liberty."

One of the treasures of the Historical Museum attached to the Archival Center for the Archdiocese of Los Angeles is a pewter sculpture collection of "the Presidents of the United States." Each of the 2 1/2 inch high sculptures is authentic in every detail.

Fashioned by David LaRocca, one of America's most gifted sculptors, each of the tiny figures is individually hand–polished to bring out the full luster of the metal. A number of steps were required to create each original clay model and the entire process took weeks to complete. First, extensive research was done to insure that each sculpture was historically accurate. Then a skeleton was built to mold the clay around. Next the clay figurine was modeled and then clothing was added in several layers. Lastly, the minute finishing details were added.

Each president is depicted exactly as he looked during the time he held the nation's highest office. Every article of clothing, every pose and facial expression is portrayed in accurate and intricate detail.

Featuring the presidency from George Washington to Jimmy Carter, the thirty–eight figures are both true to history and true to life. Each sculpture is hand–cast in fine American pewter.

Pewter is an especially appropriate art form in which to portray the United States' presidents because pewter has been popular in this country since colonial days. The warm finish of the fine pewter highlights to the utmost the delicate detail of the originals.

The presidents mirror American history. For example, Theodore Roosevelt hunted buffalo in the Dakotas, shot lions in Africa, led cavalry charges in Cuba and took the country into the twentieth century. He dug the Panama Canal, set aside 150 million acres of timberland for public use, fought for a national pure food law and, gave America her role as peacekeeper among nations.

And then there was Thomas Jefferson. He was a man of many interests, but freedom concerned him most of all. Author of the Declaration of Independence and our third president, Jefferson showed how practical a man of vision could be when he purchased from Napoleon the great empire of Louisiana, more than doubling the size of the United States.

The collection of presidents is displayed in a custom–crafted, free–standing cabinet whose soft, rich glowing tone of hardwood complements the warm finish of the pewter sculpture. This really attractive collection of the presidents at Mission Hills are not alone exceptional works of art but they honor the achievements and aspirations of the nation as reflected in its leadership.

VATICAN STAMP COLLECTION

One of the most popular of the many exhibits at the Historical Museum of the Archival Center is the one featuring the postage stamps issued by the Vatican since 1929. It is among the few complete collections in existence.

The several hundred stamps, each carefully mounted in White–Ace dual purpose binders, are exhibited chronologically as originally issued. The collection was presented in November, 1984, by Mrs. Christie Bourdet, a member of the Executive Board, Friends of the Archival Center.

Stamps have always been regarded as miniature documents of human history. They are a means by which people give sensible expression to their hopes and needs, beliefs and ideals. In the case of the Vatican collection, the stamps mirror the past and presage the future; they delineate cultural attainments, industrial works, domestic, civil and social life. The late Francis Cardinal Spellman once observed that stamps are "vignettes that give a vivid picture of the world, its occupants and their multifarious endeavors."

It was by virtue of the Lateran Treaty, signed with Italy on February 11, 1929, that Vatican City was empowered to establish its own postal services. The first stamps of the newly–created city–state were released on August 1, 1929. That issue was composed of fifteen values, seven of the thirteen regular stamps depicting the papal tiara and crossed keys of Saint Peter, and the higher orders portraying Pope Pius XI.

Each of the attractive stamps in this collection has its own distinctive relationship to ecclesial history. The most valuable items are probably the set of six supercharged stamps issued on June 16, 1934. They had orig-

Vatican Stamp Collection

inally been released in 1929 and then re–evaluated for later use.

Another highly esteemed set is that issued to honor the International Congress of the Catholic Press which met at the Vatican in 1936. Portrayed on those eight stamps are Saints Francis de Sales and John Bosco, both of whom were active in disseminating truth.

The highly–coveted 500 Lire airmail stamp honoring the younger Tobias, his heavenly guide and a dog is also included in the collection. The design is taken from a little known painting of Alessandro Botticelli.

A colorful and unique item is the Roman States centenary sheet released to commemorate the hundredth anniversary of postage stamps in 1952. Its design shows a mail coach coming out of the historical Pontemollo Bridge in Rome. In addition to the core collection, there are numerous other first day covers, lettersheets and related postal materials in the exhibit, some of them issued by other nations to coincide with one or another event chronicled by a Vatican stamp.

Brilliant in color, exquisite in design, the Vatican stamps in this collection are the work of outstanding contemporary designers and are among the most beautiful ever issued by any state. Most postage stamps display proud national symbols; parliaments, flags, inventions and statesmen. The tiny posters at Mission Hills carry forth a message of universality: Out of the enduring and creative faith of God's people have arisen treasures and traditions precious to all mankind.

BISHOP ALEMANY'S LOST DIARY

Recording the ecclesiastical activity in the Diocese of Monterey between 1850 and 1854 has always presented something of a problem because of the almost total lack of documentation for the period. Nor do the various "blotter" books of the bishops shed much light devoted as they are mostly to official duties.

It was known that Bishop (later Archbishop) Joseph Sadoc Alemany was a better–than–average bookkeeper and that he kept a diary of his activities during his tenure in California. The Archives of the Archdiocese of San Francisco contain much of the post 1854 data, but the 1850–1854 years were not to be found.

The missing portions of his diary were apparently among the effects Alemany took back to Spain when he returned in 1885. Some of these objects were given to the Alamany family (they spell their name with an "a" instead of "e") after his death at Valencia. His glasses, two mitres (one of which is now in the Los Angeles Chancery Archives), his chalice and other items have long been handed down as treasured mementoes in the Alamany family.

Over the years, the Archbishop's grand nephew, Antonio, gathered together the letters of his distinguished relative, and in 1925, he had them published in a limited edition under the title *Biografia del Ilmo. y Rmo. Fray Jose Sadoc Alamany Conill, O.P.* This was a fortunate move, for barely a decade later when the communists took over Barcelona, most of the original letters were seized by the Communists and burned.

What few belongings of the archbishop did survive were hidden in a hollow spot beneath the floor of the family residence at Avila 72. Several times during the Red occupation, the home was searched by officials and on each occasion great numbers of books and other items were burned. Anything of a religious nature was destroyed immediately. It was presumed by Antonio that the archbishop's diary was among those documents burned, since it could not be located after the war. Antonio had, in fact, not the slightest hope of ever seeing the precious document.

When this historian visited the Alamany family in 1962, the subject of the diary was brought up and, more out of accommodation than anything else, a thorough search of the two Alamany houses in Barcelona was made—in vain. The archbishop's great grand nephew, Jose, then drove the author to Vich, where Antonio spent his summers in the home where Archbishop Alemany was born in 1814. But here again no trace of the elusive diary could he found.

Some weeks later it was decided to have the family apartments in Barcelona painted and refurnished. During the restoration process it was necessary to remove parts of the antique panelling in the library and it was there that a workman discovered a wad of folded old notes on blue and white paper hidden behind a loose board—the long lost diary of Joseph Sadoc Alemany!

It was easy to recognize Alemany's script, sometimes in English, often in Italian, but mostly in Spanish. It was immediately obvious that these pages were the missing link in the life of the one–time Bishop of Monterey. The Alamany family graciously entrusted the diary to the Chancery Archives of the Archdiocese of Los Angeles. It has been published by the California Historical Society and is now an important adjunct to California's Catholic Heritage.

THE CARDINALATIAL VESTURE

Several times during the tenure of James Francis Cardinal McIntyre, the vesture prescribed for members of the Sacred College was altered and simplified by the Holy See. Some of the cardinalatial and/or episcopal garments were totally put aside, including the train, gremial, buskins, sandals, *cappa magna* and other insignia formally associated with ecclesial rank or position.

In order to graphically illustrate the vesture in use during the McIntyre years, a mannikin is on display in the Historical Museum of the Archival Center, attired in the various pieces of clothing used by Cardinal McIntyre. The color–scheme of the vesture is uniformly scarlet–red. Until fairly recent times, watered–silk or moire was used for their clothing, except for that worn at funerals and during the penitential seasons of Lent and Advent.

The choir–cassock or soutane is a long, close garment covering the entire body. It is known in the older manuals as the *vestis talaris* reaching as it does to the heels. It is held in place by a sash with two tassels. Over the cassock is a linen surplice which replaces the earlier rochet. A loose white garment with wide sleeves, it is the choral and processional dress of the secular clergy worn while administering the sacraments.

The stole, which cardinals may wear at all times as a sign of the jurisdiction they share with the Roman Pontiff, symbolizes hierarchal order. This particular one is fashioned from cloth–of–gold and bears the colorfully embroidered coat–of–arms used by Cardinal McIntyre.

Worn atop the surplice and stole is a scarlet red mozetta or short cape. It covers the shoulders, is buttoned over the breast and has a small hood attached. By long tradition, cardinals may wear the mozetta even outside their own jurisdiction. The pectoral cross, suspended at the neck with a gold chain, is hollow to allow for enclosure of relics. By regulation, it portrays the Latin form of the cross, that is, the upper part and the arms are of equal length.

This particular cross, Celtic in design, was given to Cardinal McIntyre on the occasion of his episcopal ordination as Auxiliary Bishop of New York, January 8, 1941. It was presented by the "Maren Fellowes."

The zucchetto or calotte is a skull cap which was used initially to cover the tonsure. It is worn under the scarlet–red biretta with its three "horns" or projections at the top. (The zucchetto given to Timothy Cardinal Manning at the time of his elevation to the Sacred College is on display in another area of the Historical Museum.) The scarlet–red stockings and leather shoes are prescribed for liturgical functions in place of the earlier sandals. They are to be used whenever the cassock is worn.

It is in accordance with ancient customs that cardinals and other ministers in the Catholic Church wear distinguishing dress while performing their sacred functions and otherwise exercising their office. Though greatly simplified in recent times, the vesture of the Roman clergy continues to reflect the rich background of liturgical awareness that has always characterized divine worship.

CARDINAL MINDSZENTY VISITS

Of all the prominent people to have visited the Chancery Archives, none surpasses in historical stature the person of Josef Cardinal Mindszenty, who toured the facilities on June 13, 1974.

Born Josef Pehm in the village of Csehimindszenty, on March 29, 1892 (he subsequently adopted the village name as his own in defiance of the Nazis), Mindszenty initially attracted governmental disdain in 1919, for opposing the first Communist revolution in Hungary. The patriot–priest was named Bishop of Veszprem, in 1944, just as the German armies were beginning their occupation of his nativeland. Within a year, Mindszenty was arrested and imprisoned for harboring Jewish refugees.

Late in 1945, Mindszenty was advanced to the Archbishopric of Esztergom and named Primate of Hungary. The following February, he was flown to Rome in a United States aircraft for investiture in the Sacred College of Cardinals. It was at that conclave that Pope Pius XI foretold that one of the newly–created princes would become a "confessor to the faith."

The primate was arrested by the Communists on December 26, 1948, and submitted to trial in a people's court on charges of espionage, treason and currency manipulation. He was convicted and sentenced to life imprisonment. Cardinal Mindszenty spent eight years in jail prior to the Hungarian Revolt of 1956. At the time, he was liberated from prison, but subsequently forced to take asylum in the United States Legation, when Soviet forces invaded Budapest.

During the following decade and a half, the cardinal remained under the "protective custody" of the American flag, supported by funds provided from the United States hierarchy. At the behest of Pope Paul VI, His Eminence left Hungary for the last of his "exiles," in 1971.

The famed Prince of the Church devoted the final years of his life ministering to the spiritual needs of Hungarians scattered throughout the world. It was during a tour of the United States, that Cardinal Mindszenty toured the Chancery Archives.

There he personally investigated an exhibit of newspaper and documentary accounts of his trial, imprisonment and subsequent exile. He was clearly surprised to see the extensive coverage given to his person by the secular and religious press of the United States. Still a gracious and thoughtful man, the eighty–two year old cardinal left behind his zucchetto or skullcap, which is now permanently displayed beside a silver medallion bearing the likeness of the longtime Primate of Hungary.

Msgr. Tibor Meszaros, the cardinal's secretary, himself a prisoner of Communist oppression for eight years in Siberia, later sent from Vienna the worn and faded zucchetto which Mindszenty wore during his residency at the United States Legation in Budapest. In an article for the Los Angeles *Times*, Arpad Kadarkay wrote that "history knows many dark times when, despite persecution amid public silence, a man stands up and speaks in defense of human dignity, love and truth. One such man is Joseph Cardinal Mindszenty!"

TWO SERRA ITEMS ON DISPLAY

The exhibit of materials relating to Fray Junípero Serra, first displayed to commemorate the bicentennial of the friar's demise in 1984, continues to be a popular feature at the Historical Museum of the Archival Center, in Mission Hills. Two items seem to attract special attention.

The sandblasting of glass is a challenging task. The work must be done in reverse of how one traditionally paints or sketches. Rather than adding shadow (or color), the artist must rely solely on highlighting; the fainter the surface, the more intense the process. The 16 1/2 by 10 inch deep–cut glass etching of Fray Junípero Serra was sculpted at the Hooper Studios in Atascadero by Mark Hiteshew, a talented painter, sculptor and artist. It is an outstanding tribute to California's religious founder.

The glass rendition was fashioned by forcing abrasive sand through the nozzle of a "gun" with compressed air. Ever–so–gradually, the artist sculpted the glass into three–dimensional relief. Tape and other marking materials protected those areas not affected. At various stages in the painstaking process, Hiteshew patiently removed tiny slivers of masking materials from the glass and then proceeded on to another portion of the surface.

Faintly at first and then more clearly, the personage of Fray Junípero Serra began to emerge. When the work had been completed, bathed and dried, the friar could be seen in surplice, stole and humeral veil imparting the Eucharistic blessing with a raised monstrance.

The prayerful scene received its final touch when the glass panel was fitted into a wooden base, thereby imparting a proper balance to the truly meaningful portrayal. This fascinating rendering was presented to the Archival Center by the Serra Bicentennial Commission in 1985.

Another feature of the exhibit is a keepsake prepared by David Magee for the Roxburghe–Zamorano gathering which took place at San Francisco during the month of September, 1958. Magee was able to obtain a damaged, incomplete copy of Fray Francisco Palou's *Relación Historica de la Vida y Apostólicas Tareas del Venerable Padre Fray Junípero Serra*, the first literary work ever undertaken in San Francisco.

The book was dismantled and its usable pages were tipped into 177 copies of another book entitled *An Original Leaf from Francisco Palou's Life of the Venerable Father Junípero Serra 1787*.

The Magee book, printed at the famed Grabhorn Press with an explanatory essay by the compiler, is now itself a collector's item which only rarely appears on the bookstalls. The page tipped into the copy on exhibit at the Archival Center is 19–20. It is one of the few examples of a page that has adorned two books, one printed in 1787, the other 171 years later.

In his essay, Magee notes how to Californians, and San Franciscans in particular, "Father Palou's life of his good friend and mentor, Junípero Serra, must have special significance, for it is more than the record of a zealous and saintly man; it is the very bones from which our history is fashioned."

That Fray Junípero Serra's fame is growing on the national and international level is plainly evident from the interest demonstrated for the Mallorcan friar by visitors from all over the universe. Rare is the visitor to the Archival Center, Catholic or non–Catholic, who doesn't ask about and want to see the Serra exhibit.

JOURNEY OF A BOOK

When a mission in California was established it was given a set of six blank folio books by the Apostolic College of San Fernando in Mexico City. Into these registers went records of baptisms, marriages, deaths, confirmations, patents and padrones. With the secularization of the mission system in 1834, some of these books were destroyed, a few disappeared and still others withstood the hectic times to become treasures of another generation.

The old registers were usually uniform in size and binding, the pages measuring 11 3/4 by 8 1/2 inches of excellent quality paper. The bindings were mostly made of a flexible brown leather material with the back side long enough to fold over the edge and top with two leather loops and two thongs with crossbars to serve as clasps. A special type of carbon ink was used, and for the most part the script remains quite legible. Only occasional areas of faded and indecipherable writing appear in the majority of the books.

Of all the twenty–seven extant burial registers, perhaps none has experienced a more varied existence than the *Libro de Difuntas de la Mision del Señor S. Fernando*. Very little is known about the whereabouts of the book after 1852, when the last entry was recorded in its pages. Bancroft states that he had examined the mission–books of San Fernando at the mission in 1874. Apparently even at that time the burial register was missing since he omits it in his enumeration. Eulogio Celis purchased San Fernando Mission from Pio Pico on June 17, 1846, six years before the last notation was made. How the volume subsequently, found its way into the Andres Pico Collection is not clear; although Andres had rented the mission prior to its sale to Celis. In any event, the *Libro* was known to have been in the Andres Collection in 1904, for in that year Father Zephyrin Engelhardt examined the volume and copied several large extracts from it.

When the collection was deeded to the Southwest Museum in the next decade, the register was apparently taken out and sold to a private party. It passed through several hands before coming into the possession of Henry E. Huntington of San Marino, Knowing nothing of its improper alienation, Mr. Huntington purchased the manuscript in good faith. As soon as he was informed of its illegal removal from the mission, Huntington gra-ciously restored the register to the Chancery Archives of the Diocese of Los Angeles–San Diego, legal heir to San Fernando Mission property.

First entry in the register "*en la iglesia de esta Mision*" was the Indian neophyte, Jose Antonio. Fray Francisco Dumetz signed the notation April 7, 1798, seven months after the mission's foundation. Roque Cota was the first non–Indian entered in the register on September 30, 1798.

The *Libro* is little more than half filled and closes with the entry of a child of Mexican parents on July 10, 1852, the 2,425th notice placed in the venerable old book. With the return of the *Libro de Difuntos de la Mision del Señor S. Fernando* to the Church by the generous Henry Huntington in 1925, the register ended its long peregrination and became once again a source of edification for those interested in the zeal of Christianity in mission times.

VIII. Memoirs

MARIA ANA MONTIELO (1785) — THE YUMA MASSACRE

In December, 1785, Fray Francisco Antonio Barbastro asked Maria Ana Montielo, an eyewitness of the Yuma massacre and widow of Ensign Santiago Islas, to describe the uprising. The account provides historians with important details of that disastrous occurrence along the Colorado River in July of 1781.

Father Juan Barreneche celebrated the first Mass that morning, which I myself attended. Father Francisco Garces had the second Mass. His server was my deceased husband. As my husband was moving the missal from one side of the altar to the other, for the Gospel of the Mass, the war whoops of the Indians began.

Corporal Pascual Baylon was the first to fall into their hands. As they were putting him to death with their war clubs, Father Barreneche rushed out just in time to force his way through the yelling Indians and witness the corporal's last act of life.

Realizing that the whole Yuma nation had risen up against us, I gathered the women together and we fled for our lives back to the church. There we found more refugee Spaniards arguing with Father Garces about who should be blamed for the uprising. 'Let's forget now whose fault it is,' Father Garces replied, 'and simply consider it God's punishment for our sins.' His voice was compassionate though his face was an ashen grey.

That night the Yumas began to burn our houses and belongings and kill as many of our people as they could. That was the night my heart was broken, when my beloved husband was clubbed to death before my very eyes.

As day dawned on July 18th, Father Barreneche encouraged those of us who were still alive with the words: "Let us sing a hymn to Mary, most holy, that she favor us with her help, and let us praise God for sending us these trials." All during that night, Father Garces had moved stealthily about the village, administering the sacraments to the wounded and dying.

Father Barreneche offered Mass for all of us, as we awaited death at any moment. After Mass, he occupied himself by pulling out arrows and spears from the walls of the church.

About three o'clock in the afternoon, when the Indians had finished killing Captain Rivera and his party, on the other side of the river, Father Barreneche arrived from ministering to the last of the dying and told us that each of us should try to escape as best we could.

He picked up his breviary and crucifix and, together with Father Garces, the women and rest of the people, started out of the settlement, leaving behind forever the new mission of La Purisima Concepción

Father Garces warned us: 'Stay together, do not resist capture, and the Yumas will not harm you.' This was the last we saw of the two fathers as we sat huddled together waiting death at any moment.

Through another Spanish woman captive, who was not with my group, I later learned that Fathers Garces and Barreneche were not killed until three days later (July 21st). After leaving the lagoon, the fathers were discovered by a friendly Yuma whose wife was a fervent Christian. He hurried the fathers to his own *rancheria*.

The enemy fell upon them as they sat in the Yuma's dwelling, drinking chocolate. The rebel leader shouted: 'Stop drinking that and come out side. We're going to kill you.'

The Indians tell the story that at the first attack of the executioners, Father Garces disappeared from their sight, and they were left clubbing the air. Word had spread among the Yuma nation that he was more powerful than their own witch–doctors.

Time and again I heard that many of the Yumas did not want to see the fathers killed. Nevertheless, their blood was spilled, and the woman who told me this was close enough to hear their pitiful moans as they lay dying. The husband of the pious woman recovered their lifeless bodies and buried them.

WILLIAM HEATH DAVIS (1831) — MEMOIRS OF SIXTY YEARS

Life in California before the advent of the gold seekers was truly idyllic. Never were people happier or more contented. Poverty was virtually unknown, for at the hospitable home of every *ranchero*, be ever so high in caste or rich in cattle, was a welcome for the stranger until he decided to continue on his journey.

Travellers wandered from San Diego to Sonoma, stopping leisurely along one mission to another, or at some *rancho*, where he was received with warmest greeting, and at the end of his stay he was supplied with a fresh horse. Hospitality could go no farther than that extended to the traveler while a guest at the *hacienda*.

"I look back almost two generations ago," says William Heath Davis, the author of *Sixty Years in California*, "to those merry days with pride and joy at the kindnesses which I received and the manliness and simplicity of the welcome of the fathers of the families, and the womanly deportment of their wives and daughters, and their innocent amusements, and think that these native Californians of Spanish extraction were as sincere people as ever lived under the canopy of heaven."

The houses of the *rancheros*, he says, were usually built entirely upon open ground, overlooking a wide stretch of the country round, in order that they might look out to a distance on all sides—they having always in view security against the Indians. The buildings were erected on the general plan of the missions, one story in height and built of adobe, with broad piazza, and a large court yard.

Among the Californians, there was more or less caste. They were naturally, whether rich or poor, of a proud nature, and though always exceedingly polite and courteous and friendly, they were possessed of a native dignity which was apparent in their bearing, walk and general demeanor. They were descended from the best families of Spain and never seemed to forget their origin.

Notions of propriety and morality were so strict among the people that young lovers engaged to be married were permitted little association by themselves. They were scarcely allowed to see each other or converse together except in the presence of their parents.

The carnival festival, which is celebrated with merriment and revelry in Catholic countries during the week preceding Lent, was observed by the Californians. One of the amusements they brought with them from Spain and Mexico was the custom during the carnival season of breaking upon the heads of the opposite sex egg shells filled with fine scraps of pretty colored silver or gold paper, or with cologne water, or some harmless and agreeable substance.

There was more strenuous entertainment for the men than music and dancing. They found their recreation, as they did their occupation, chiefly on horseback. On feast days, which were general holidays, the *vaqueros* were relieved from duty, wore their best clothes, were allowed to mount the best horses and had their sport. These races were usually from two to four hundred yards.

Contests for deciding questions of superiority with the *riata* were also familiar. This amusement was especially popular at the killing time. When cattle were slaughtered, bears came to the place at night to feast on the meat that was left after the hides and tallow were taken. The bears coming, the *rancheros* with *vaqueros* would go there for the purpose of lassoing them. This sport was highly exciting and dangerous. Except at horse races, when bets of cattle and horses were sometimes made, there was little gambling. People were cattle rich and money poor.

Mr. Davis concludes his account by noting that he had never known of a case of dishonesty among the early Californians. "They were faithful in their promises and engagements of every kind. The Californians were too proud to do anything mean or disgraceful."

FRAY JOSE DE MARIA DE JESUS GONZALEZ RUBIO (1833) — REPORT ON THE MISSIONS

Probably one of the most comprehensive assessments of the Golden State's provincial era was that penned by Fray José Maria de Jesús González Rubio (1804–1875),

who recorded the status of the California missions, at the time of his arrival, in January, 1833. Following are the highlights of his report.

On my landing in this country, there were in existence from San Diego up to San Francisco Solano 21 Missions, which provided for 14,000 to 15,000 Indians. Even the poorest Missions, those of San Rafael and Soledad, provided everything for divine worship, and the maintenance of the Indians.

The care of the neophytes was left to the Missionary, who, not only as pastor, instructed them in their religion and administered the sacraments to them, but as a householder, provided for them, governed and instructed them in their social life, procuring for them peace and happiness.

Every Mission, rather than a town, was a large community, in which the Missionary was President, distributing equally burdens and benefits. No one worked for himself, and the products of the harvest, cattle and industry in which they were employed was guarded, administered and distributed by the Missionary. He was the Procurator and Defender of his neophytes and, at the same time, their Chief and Justice of Peace, to settle all their quarrels, since the Mission Indians were not subject to the public authorities, except in grievous and criminal cases.

This system, though criticized by some politicians, is the very one that made the Missions so flourishing. The richest in population was that of San Luis Rey; in temporal things, that of San Gabriel. Mine was that of San Jose, and although I was promised, as it was on the gentile frontier, it would not be secularized, it too, succumbed in 1836.

In the inventory made in January, 1837, the result showed that said Mission numbered 1,300 neophytes, a great piece of land, well tilled; the store–houses filled with seeds; two orchards, one with 1,600 fruit trees; two vineyards—one with 6,039 vines, the other with 5,000; tools for husbandry in abundance; shops for carpenters, blacksmiths, shoemakers, and even tanneries, and all the implements for their work.

The fields were covered with live stock; horned cattle, 20,000 head; sheep, 500; horses, 459. For the saddle 600 colts of two years, 1,630 mares, 149 yoke of oxen, 30 mules, 18 jackasses and 77 hogs.

As long as the Missions were in the hands of the missionaries, everything was abundant; but as soon as they passed into the hands of laymen everything went wrong, till eventually complete ruin succeeded, and all was gone.

We have to acknowledge that a manifest punishment from God was the cause of the destruction of the Missions, since theft alone could not accomplish it and the subsidy given to the Government would not affect them.

On the contrary, left to the priests, the Missions would have prospered and other establishments still more opulent would have been erected in the Tulares, even without any protection from the Government.

If the revolution of Spain in the year 1808 and that of

Mexico in 1810 had not put an end to the prosperity of the missionaries . . . if zealous missionaries had been left amongst the savage tribes roaming through this vast territory, from the Sierra Nevada to the Coast Mountains . . . would have been converted to Christianity.

As I was not only a witness but a victim of the sad events which caused their destruction, I have tried rather to shut my eyes that I might not see the evil, and close my ears to prevent hearing the innumerable wrong, which these establishments had suffered.

Fray González Rubio concluded his letter, written to Joachim Adam, in September, 1864, with these words: "My poor neophytes did their part, in their own way, to try and diminish my sorrow and anguish."

✠FRAY FRANCISCO GARCIA DIEGO (1836) — REFLECTIONS ON THE MISSIONS

The author of California's first "letter to the editor" signed himself only as "a lover of truth and of the missions of Alta California." Clearly in the hand of Fray Francisco Garcia Diego, the lengthy intervention to the editor of *Diario del Gobierno* also gives internal evidence of being composed by the then *Comisario–Prefecto* for the Zacatecan friars.

Written in 1836, at Mexico City (where Fray Garcia Diego had gone to plead with governmental officials on behalf of the missions), the letter takes exception to remarks made by Colonel Mariano Chico, on May 27, 1836, which tended "to blacken the conduct of the missionaries."

Especially irritating to the writer were charges that "the missionaries effected the most frightful slaughter of cattle, destroyed valuable vineyards and in fine abandoned every kind of resources which would have enriched California." Pointing out that "only the half–wild and unbranded cattle" were killed, the correspondent charged that "this was one of the calumnies by means of which the enemies endeavored to blacken the missionary religious from the time the innovations began, in order to have a pretext for driving the missionaries from the management of the property of the Indians."

As for the alleged destruction of the vineyards, the writer observed that only at San Luis Obispo had there been any such action. And, in that case, the vines had been found unproductive and the soil unfavorable for grapes. He went on to regret the slanderous accusations against the friars "whose conduct has always been irreprehensible, and whose aims had no other object than the welfare and happiness of the Indians as well as of the white people."

The writer then observed that the Franciscans "have abandoned their country, their parents, their brothers and sisters, their friends and relatives, solely for the sake of the missions. They have embraced a life full of privations and almost without society among a people by whom they are hardly understood and appreciated."

They have endeavored to extricate these poor Indians from barbarism, and they have given them secular as well as religious instruction. They have supplied them with suitable teachers who give instructions in the arts that are beneficial to the whole territory. Indeed, those missionaries have made slaves of themselves.

They have been the consolation of the afflicted who obliged through misfortune arrived at their doors. They have been the refuge and relief of the travellers whom they sheltered, tenderly refreshed and conducted to the next mission to be there received in the same way, and enjoy the like services of Christian charity.

They cared for the Indians as a father cares for his beloved children. They defended them against the insults, injury and ill–treatment which it was the fashion of the white people to inflict upon Indians.

They looked after the property interests of their Indians as though they were their own. They fed them, clothed them and attended them in their sickness. They took great pains to keep the neophytes from intercourse with vicious white people in order to preserve them from corruption.

The lengthy intervention concluded by noting that "these are the crimes which the missionaries of Alta California have committed."

Then addressing himself to the friars, the writer said: "If you see yourselves slandered in a distant land, know for your consolation that there are many who esteem your merit and who will rise in defense of you, as I have done, and with better weapons than mine."

THE MONITOR (1850s) — REMINISCENCES OF CATHOLIC CALIFORNIA

In mid 1904, the editor of *The Monitor* asked several early pioneers to submit their "Reminiscences of Catholic California" in the 1850s for a series of articles in the San Francisco Catholic newspaper. The following are extracted from the resultant compilation.

Previous to 1835, there was not a house on the present site of San Francisco, if we except the venerable Mission Dolores church and the group of adobe and sun–dried brick houses around it. During that year, Captain Richardson erected the first wooden building. In 1847, the town commenced to fill up and in June of that year, the population was about five hundred.

It was also in 1847 that Washington Bartlett, first *alcalde* of Yerba Buena—a naval officer of the Pacific squadron who subsequently emigrated to New York— issued an ordinance doing away with that name and ordering the place to be thereafter known as San Francisco.

During this and succeeding years, foundations were laid for large fortunes. Fifty *vara* lots sold then for $6, which could now be bought for a quarter of a million. In 1848, the population increased to eight hundred and fifty souls, and the town had about two hundred dwellings, principally improvised cabins. During the great exodus of '49, it was impossible to obtain sufficient lumber with which to build houses and canvas tents were freely used for domiciles.

On approaching the city from the sea, a truly magnificent sight could be beheld. It seemed a moving panorama of natural scenery, lofty hills, fine valleys and level stretches of sandy beach studded with glittering and beautiful shells, and its general lines very much resembled Lisbon or Constantinople.

Up to 1849, there was but one Catholic church in the young city, and in July of that year, Father Anthony Langlois, a pious French priest, erected the first Saint Francis church. Becoming too small, it was torn down and a larger, barn–like structure was hauled to the site and made into a church. It was lined on the inside with cotton muslin, which fluttered and shook omniously whenever strong gusts of wind whistled through the cracks between the wall timbers. The church was reached by scrambling over uneven, rough hills and large congregations of worshippers attended every Sunday. Of course, they were thoroughly cosmopolitan in caste. There were the dreamy Spaniard with high *sombrero* and gorgeous serape, the phlegmatic Indian, some Portuguese, Frenchmen, Americans and many Irish—faithful old race, were they not?

At the very time when solemn services were being celebrated, only a stone's throw away, around Washington and Clay streets, gambling saloons would be thronged with the desperate devotees to the goddess of Luck. Their curses, high words and blasphemy contrasted strangely with the humble supplication of the adoring priest.

The nightly scenes at these dens of vice and degradation were wild, fascinating and incongruous. The gambling room was brilliantly lit with lamps and candles, and frequently at the back of the hall, or in front of it, a band of music played with the idea of attracting the ubiquitous miner to the place, much after the way of the Caprean siren who wiled her victims with a lute.

Gambling at that time was indulged in by all classes and kinds of people, and was the principal amusement of the reckless and extravagant. Still the Catholic element of the population was very devotional and attended Mass regularly.

The two churches, Saint Francis and Mission Dolores, used to be more than crowded on the Feasts of Good Friday, Easter and Christmas. On these great festivals, the ceremonies and services were very magnificent and impressive, and always attracted the entire population, irrespective of creed or nationality. Uninviting as were conditions in 1849, God's religion prospered, the city grew out of its nothingness into a great commercial and industrial center and we are happy to add, a great Catholic center as well.

CHARLES ENOCH HUSE (1850s) — SANTA BARBARA AT MID CENTURY

One prominent California historian has stated that life everywhere in the southland during the 1850s "was still rude and violent, crime remained a normal feature of society; schools and churches found foothold only in the largest communities; culture and refinement, like exotic plants, blossomed with difficulty in the harsh environment."

That it was indeed a confusing time is obvious from a glance at affairs in Santa Barbara during the mid–century. The emerging city suffered a severe jolt that affected its social, economic, political, religious and institutional life. Robberies, assassinations, infanticide and other nefarious crimes succeeded one another with impunity. Justice was mocked because of perjury, hung trials, payoffs, promises and threats.

The former patriarchial simplicity of the *rancheros* quickly faded from the scene. When wealth came to the Barbareños, as a result of the Gold Rush, immigration and the rising cattle prices, they splurged in dress, furnishings and entertainment. Enthusiasm for horses, gambling, cock fights and festivals reigned over every other sentiment. Out of fifty business licenses issued for Santa Barbara during the early part of the decade, thirty two were for liquor establishments!

Judge Charles Enoch Huse, a prominent Harvard Congregationalist wrote in his diary that he had "never known such meanness as exists here in this settlement . . . the greater part of the people are indolent; do not work; do not pay their debts; do not keep their word.

Two diocesan priests of the time, Fathers Jayme Vila and Cipriano Rubio, agreed that corruption existed in a higher degree among persons holding the highest positions either because of their office or of their wealth. And the two clerics noted that "this immorality was aped by people of the rank and file." Father Rubio went on to describe the Barbareños as "indolent, with a low standard of conduct and an ignorance in religious matters that at times borders on superstition."

In a memorial sent to Pope Pius IX, Bishop Thaddeus Amat declared that "there are no townspeople . . . even in California, according to the judgment of various families who have lived in Santa Barbara for some time, who are so vicious and corrupt as those of that city."

Another commentator of the period, Ramón de la Cuesta, viewed Santa Barbara as "a corrupt and hypocritical town," while Francis Maguire considered the people there "lazy, inclined to lying, totally uneducated, grossly ignorant in religious matters stressing external observances."

Father Maynard Geiger, the prominent Franciscan historian, wrote that "aside from personal viewpoints and interpretations the many unfavorable testimonies of this dolorous decade are sufficient evidence that Santa Barbara was anything but a desirable place in which to live. . . . Religiously, morally, socially and culturally, much was lacking to make the town even respectable."

Fortunately, with the passage of time, a cleansing process began fashioning a better people through purer religion, decent citizenship and cleaner living, all of which brought new opportunities for educational and economical betterment. But the fact remains that many Barbareños of the 1850s reflected the more unsavory characteristics of the post–missionary era in California.

GREGORY PHELAN (1850s) — REFLECTIONS OF MANHATTAN

During most of the 1850s, Dr. Gregory Phelan (1822–1902) acted as California correspondent for several Catholic newspapers in the eastern states. His columns, appearing most often in the New York *Freeman's Journal*, were signed with his favorite pen name, "Philos."

A native of New York, Phelan was one of Sacramento's pioneer physicians from 1849 onwards. The doctor also occupied several political positions, including a seat on the Board of Aldermen. He was the first Commissioner of Common Schools for Sacramento.

Phelan journeyed to the east in 1855, where he married Cecilia Blancher on June 19th of that year. Upon his return to California, the doctor was elected President of the Board of Education. His remaining years were filled with a litany of civic and religiously oriented public services.

Probably Phelan's greatest, or at least his most enduring accomplishment, centered around the literary contributions he made to the sparse literature concerning Catholicism along the Pacific Slope. The first among his many essays dealt with the cholera epidemic. He recorded the arrival and subsequent activities of Bishop Joseph Sadoc Alemany, as well as other items of historic significance. The writings of "Philos" ceased after 1858 with the establishment of *The Monitor*, the "Irish and Catholic newspaper" of California.

Early in 1876, Dr. Phelan returned from Europe where he had visited religious shrines–and other places of historic interest. He had earlier been asked by Richard O'Sullivan, editor of *The Monitor and Guardian*, to provide some observations about his recent journey. The ever agreeable physician consented and wrote a series of essays, among which are five concerning his travels through California enroute to Sacramento. Instead of resurrecting "Philos," Dr. Phelan this time used the pen name "Manhattan," probably in deference to his birthplace.

In his letter of September 30, 1876, Dr. Phelan had the following to say about his meeting with the Bishop of Grass Valley:

While traveling across the mountains, of which I made mention in my last, it was the pleasure of your correspondent to have the company of his Grace Bishop (Eugene) O'Connell. The good Bishop is now on his periodical visits to all parts of his distant diocese, which covers a vast area of territory. Notwithstanding all the labor of traveling which his Grace undergoes, and which would affect a much younger man, the Most Rev. gentleman looks hearty and did not show the least sign of fatigue.

Having reached Reno, it was with some regret I parted with the good Bishop. Here I was obliged to wait several hours before taking the train on the Truckee and Virginia Railroad for Virginia City—the center of the mining interests of Nevada. The road from Reno to Nevada is, I suppose, one of the greatest pieces of engineering in the world.

The curves on the road above Carson are so numerous and so sharp that they are obliged to drop the sleeping car at Carson. Reaching Virginia, if the traveler has formed any pleasant ideas of beautiful walks, drives, etc., they are instantly dispelled as soon as he alights from the cars and commences the ascent of the mountain–street leading from the depot to the main street. He naturally stops mid–way in the block to breathe, and wonders what inticed (sic) him to Virginia.

To give your readers an idea of the hilly proportions of the town I might say that in one of my visits I entered a house at the first floor on one street, went to the third floor and came out on the level street in the rear! Strangers do not linger long here, I assure you.

Virginia is proverbial for its liquor saloons and its gambling propensities; the former are numerous and must form an immense source of revenue to the State. I do not suppose that in any town in the Union you will see more men on the street. I averaged the number of men to a block, and I found there were about ten men to every front of about twenty feet.

Dr. Gregory Phelan continues his fascinating account of a journey through California and Nevada. He is now at Virginia City, the center of mining interest in the area:

The fire of last year was a severe blow to Virginia,

but, owing to the pluck of its citizens and the immense amount of capital represented here, they are clearing away all vestige of the fire, and the city is being fast rebuilt. Among the buildings consumed was the Catholic church, which was quite a handsome brick edifice.

This was a terrible misfortune, not only to the Catholics, but also to the pastor, Rev. Father (Patrick) Manogue, who had only a short time previous to the fire erected a splendid building for hospital purposes. Nothing daunted by reverses, however, the Rev. Father, aided by the proverbial liberality of the mining class, is fast pushing towards completion a new edifice, which the good people of Virginia expect to worship in by next Christmas.

While here I visited Gold Hill, about a mile distant from Virginia, and resembling the latter in every respect. Rev. Father (William) Clarke is the pastor here, and I found him a genial and sociable gentleman. He is building quite a large parochial residence, and as it is situated on a prominence, it will, when finished, enhance the appearance of Gold Hill. Here, as in nearly all the parishes, you find good educational institutions under the charge of Sisters.

Leaving here, tired and foot sore from clambering mountains, after an hour's ride I arrived at Carson, a very prettily–situated town half way between Virginia and Reno.

Rev. Father (Luke) Tormy, who invariably displays a most genuine hospitality, is the pastor here. The Catholics have really a handsome little church, and through the working of the reverend gentleman the Sisters of Charity have purchased the ground known as the old race track, which contains a number of acres, with several buildings thereon.

A few days later, Phelan left Carson and soon arrived at Reno. "Here you can see the nucleus of a large town. Reno has everything to give it promise of being the largest town on the Central Pacific. The Catholics here are as yet few; but, notwithstanding their small number, through the exertions of Rev. Father (Andrew) O'Donnell they have quite a large church, and during the past year have added a number of improvements to the edifice."

The reverend gentleman has a large extent of territory included in his parish, and no doubt it will surprise some of your readers when I state that his parish is larger than the whole of Ireland! The trials and perils of the pastors of this diocese, in attending to the wants of their scattered flocks, are very severe.

I soon left Reno. Before reaching Palisade the first place of interest on the line is Humboldt, an oasis in the desert. This is no doubt a very beautiful spot, and the sparkling fountains of clear water are certainly a relief to the monotony of a ride of hours through an alkali desert.

After breakfasting here you again board the cars, and

in five hours reach Palisade, where you find the cars of the Eureka and Palisade Railroad awaiting to convey you to Eureka.

Rev. Father (James) Hynes is pastor of Eureka, and, by dint of hard work and the liberality of his parishioners, has built a large church. He is holding a fair to make more extensive improvements to the church, and, owing to the unbounded generosity of his people on former occasions, is assured of this being a success. Like other clergymen in this diocese, he has quite an extensive parish—reaching to near Salt Lake, a distance of nearly 400 miles

Leaving the smoky precincts of Eureka I took the stage for Austin. This is a ride of eighty miles through an almost trackless desert. You see nothing but an immense tract of country before you, with not the slightest thing imaginable to relieve the monotony. After riding fourteen hours you finally reach Austin, choking with dust and very tired.

What a change! Here you see almost an Eden as compared with Eureka. Austin is very prettily situated, and is one of the oldest mining camps in the State. It has long ago got over the boisterous excitement that you usually find in younger camps, and has settled itself down to the even tenor of old towns.

On last Sunday Right Rev. Bishop O'Connell visited this place, and gave the good Austins the pleasure of hearing a discourse from his Grace. The Bishop spoke in the highest terms of the people of Austin to your correspondent, as I had the pleasure of meeting him after returning from here. The church of Austin is one of the finest finished edifices outside of San Francisco and speaks highly for the good taste of the Austins.

✟JOSEPH SADOC ALEMANY, O.P. (1851) — REBUKE TO SPAIN

In his early years at Monterey, Bishop Joseph Sadoc Alemany leaned heavily on the support provided by the Paris office of the *Propagation de la Foi*. Established some years previously to further missionary activities, the society depended entirely on free will offerings sent in from all parts of the world.

Alemany's native Spain had been suffering for a number of years from internal strife, much of it directed toward the Church, its clergy and religious. It came then as no surprise when the Duke of Victory, General Baldomero Espartero, announced a complete withdrawal of his nation from the works of *Propagation de la Foi* in 1840. In mid–1851, some months after the Spanish Government had signed a new concordat with Rome, the authorities of *Propagation de la Foi* asked the recently consecrated Bishop of Monterey to pen a gentle exhortation to his fatherland about its missionary responsibilities. This Alemany did on July 19th. Whether the plea ever reached Madrid or not is uncertain. In any event, the appeal, produced here in an abbreviated form, was put on record at Paris. It reads as follows:

On Catholic Spain, how glorious for thee was the day on which thou didst send forth from thy most eastern shores to this land of America such apostolic men as Fathers Junípero Serra, Magin Cátala, José Viader, and many others! How deserved didst thou wear the name Catholic, when thou didst foster the spirit of those holy, religious and apostolic men, whose missionary field of labor was the world and who did not dread to cross two oceans to go and live both among the bears and savages of California. There they hoped that God would deliver them from the terrors of the former, and that the divine spirit of the Catholic Church would convert the ferocity of the latter into the mildness of the lambs of the children of Christ!

Oh Catholic Spain! Missionaries from thy shores effected a perfect change on the face of California! Thy arts, traders, music, language, hospitality, honesty, piety and Catholic Faith were engrafted and nurtured with success in this vast region of the farthest west. Thou didst stud these shores with a variety of monuments, whose picture alone makes the Anglo–Saxon pause and admire the greatness of the enterprise.

Oh Catholic Kingdom! How truly Catholic thou wert when thou didst promote those rich memorials of faith, those apostolic institutions, those missionary colleges and religious orders from whose bosom walked out so many apostles to evangelize the most distant regions of the east, and the barbarous unexplored confines of the west!

But, Oh how uncatholic thou wert, when in a raving fit of impiety thou didst exclaustrate those holy cloisters! How uncatholic that hour in which thou didst refuse admission into thy dominions of the noble catholic work of the Propagation of the Faith for the foreign missions, for fear that thy own poor should suffer from it!

Blot out, my country, those black stains from thy history! Efface them from the pages of history for they give lie to thy name of Catholic. Let the world know that thou art no longer ashamed to admit into thy precincts men who practice the catholic apostolic precepts of poverty, chastity and obedience.

Let the Head of the Catholic World know that thou art one of those Christian nations which charitably sends alms for the glorious work of propagating our Holy Faith!

GREGORY PHELAN (1851) — A BISHOP COMES TO SACRAMENTO

The following item, written at Sacramento on February 27, 1851, appeared in the New York *Freeman's Journal and Catholic Register* for April 19, 1851. It gives an interesting insight into the thinking of Catholics during the Gold Rush Days.

In the Council of Baltimore, held in May, 1849, the See of Monterey was created and Dr. Alemany, Provincial of the Dominicans in the United States, was selected first Bishop. This Diocese extends over the State of (Upper) California, but for the present the Bishop has jurisdiction over Lower California also, where I understand there are only about half a dozen priests.

Some years since San Diego was erected into an Episcopal See and a Bishop appointed, but finding it almost impossible to live there at that time, the Bishop removed to Santa Barbara, where he died.

The state of religion in California is assuming a different and more encouraging appearance than that which it presented a few years or even a few months ago. Then I believe no institutions, charitable or literary existed, except that of San Ignace. A very small number of Priests were located in the southern portion of the territory; but that vast northern region, including the valleys of the San Joaquin and Sacramento, was rarely visited by our missionaries; nor did there exist a spire, surmounted by a cross, to gladden the eye of the weary traveller and point to the Temple of the true God.

Mexican oppression and California spoliation impeded the progress of religion and civilization. But now, in almost every portion of the State, churches are being erected, charitable and literary institutions are being founded, and with the blessing of God, we hope, in a short time, that California will shine forth a bright spot on the map of the Catholic Church. Yes, we hope soon to have colleges and schools, churches and convents, asylums and hospitals; with a numerous body of devoted clergy, and those good Sisters of Charity, who have ever devoted themselves to the care of the orphan, and the relief of the sick and distressed.

On Sunday morning, 23d inst., Bishop Alemany, accompanied by Very Rev. A. Langlois, and Rev. Mr. Llebaria, arrived in our city for the first time. They proceeded immediately to the residence of the pastor, Rev. J. Ingoldsby, and made the necessary preparations for the ceremonies to be performed. The Bishop commenced the dedication of the church at 10 A.M., and was assisted by the clergymen above named. An immense concourse of persons were present, and many went away, unable to gain an entrance. After the dedication the Bishop celebrated High Mass, and at the conclusion of the reading of the Gospel, preached an excellent and eloquent sermon, taking his text from that portion of Scripture relating to the dedication of Solomon's Temple. The audience was very attentive and appeared much pleased. At the close of the sermon, Rev. Mr. Llebaria read the Bishop's Pastoral in Spanish, and preached in the same language; at the conclusion of which he preached again in French. Father L. is an able and fluent preacher and a zealous missionary. He was in this city during a portion of the cholera season and has since been in Marysville, where he has commenced the erection of a church. The Bishop has changed the field of his labors to Santa Cruz, where his knowledge of the

Spanish and French languages will afford him a wider sphere for the exercise of his talents and acquirements, probably, than Marysville.

At Vespers the Bishop preached again on the Catholic Church, proving that it was the same to–day as it was eighteen hundred years ago, and that it was unchanged and unchangeable, having the pledge of the Omnipotent to sustain it. He pointed to the writings of the Fathers to show that similar ceremonies to those performed here now were performed a thousand years ago; that St. Augustine prayed for the departed soul of his mother, and in fact that all the doctrines now taught by the Church were taught by the Fathers of the earliest period of Christianity. And, said he, it is in a measure owing to the investigation of the writings of the early Fathers, that so many learned and distinguished divines of the English Church have been led into the true fold of the One Shepherd.

In the evening, Murray Morrison, Esq., in the name of the Catholics and citizens of Sacramento, delivered a beautiful and appropriate address to the Bishop, who replied in a very happy manner.

EUGENE O'CONNELL (1815–1891)

The following letter is one of priceless gems of California's Catholic Heritage. It was written by Father Eugene O'Connell in 1853, describing to his confreres at All Hallows College in Dublin the San Francisco of Gold Rush days.

Your welcome letter, after an unsuccessful search about the solitude of Santa Inez, reached me a few days ago in this noisy city. How then can I express to you my gratitude for your kind invitation to All Hallows after my wanderings in the Far West? I only await the arrival of one of the six missionaries whom Dr. Alemany expects from All Hallows previous to my departure. You would really pity the poor bishop were you to see the fluctuating soldiers he has to fight his battle; like Dr. Whelan of Virginia, he was obliged to make the two seminarians he has swear to remain with him. Therefore, under these circumstances, I presume on your leave to remain. . . .

You must, I'm sure, have received letters from Dr. Alemany since March 5th which show you the urgent need he has of Irish clergymen and the provisions he is making to secure a constant supply from All Hallows now, in order to keep up an unbroken succession in this diocese of All Hallows missionaries. For the present, he can do no more for the institution than he has done, in consequence of being engaged in building St. Mary's Cathedral, which it is calculated will cost $100,000—a work he is bound to get through with, for many reasons, but principally to secure a fire–proof church in the neighborhood, that he himself and his clergymen may be without the daily and nightly apprehension of being burnt out.

Owing to the scarcity of stone in this country and dearness of brick buildings, most of the houses here are constructed of wood and the six or seven fires that have already occurred haven't taught many to make an effort to build brick houses. Since the Bishop transferred me from Santa Inez to this city about three or four months ago, there has been a fire almost every month and the value of thousands of dollars consumed. . . .

The temporal burnings of which I am speaking naturally remind me of the everlasting one which they presage to thousands of the citizens of San Francisco, unless they stop their career of iniquity. The rage of duelling, the passion for gambling and barefaced depravity prevail to a frightful degree. . . . Venus has numerous temples erected to herself in this city, but thank God, the Catholic church is not deserted all the while.

The two Catholic churches are crowded every Sunday and, notwithstanding the enlargement of one of them by Architect O'Connor, it is full to overflowing. William Hamill, formerly of Maynooth, is the teacher of the Bishop's English school. Doctor Barry was translated to the Dolores seminary with a salary of $50 a month. Mr. Hamill's salary is $60 a month in consideration of his acting as Sexton to the Church—in fact $50 a month is the salary even of cooks in this country.

I don't know whether you are aware of some of our California liberties which beat the Gallican ones hallow. Take, for example, that of eating meat . . . on every Friday except the Fridays in Lent—and don't infer from this that the finest salmon in the world don't abound on our shores! There is again the universal custom of smoking cigars save at Mass or at meals. The only scandal to my knowledge given by a smoking clergyman was owing to his having repeatedly put the ignited end into his mouth instead of the opposite extreme. Hence you perceive it is neither the simple fact of smoking per se, nor of drinking per se, but the unlucky combination of both by a clergyman which makes him confound both ends of a lighted cigar. Then, and not till then, do the ladies and gentlemen receive a slight shock!

Oh, my dear Father and brothers, please all pray for me and my speedy return to Alma Mater, where I hope to find rest for my soul.

Adieu, dear Father until then.

GREGORY PHELAN (1855) — CATHOLICITY IN CALIFORNIA

For many years the New York *Freeman's Journal and Catholic Register* carried sporadic columns sent from California and signed only with the name "Philos." Reliable evidence identifies "Philos" with Gregory Phelan, the city physician for Sacramento from 1849 onwards. A highly educated man, Phelan was associated with Sacramento for over forty years and was always a great champion of the Church. The following report on

Catholicism was sent in by "Philos" to the *Freeman's Journal* in 1855 and printed on December 22nd.

This State is Catholic at heart; its history and traditions and reminiscences are inseparably connected with the Church and her ministers. And shall we not hope that its future will be Catholic;—that its enterprising population will profess the true faith, and that commissioned teachers may everywhere be found comforting the afflicted, instructing the ignorant, and enlightening those in error or in doubt.

Time, and the grasping hand of Mexican officials, followed by American utilitarian progress and improvement, and but too often by acts of vandalism on the part of our enlightened countrymen, have not yet effaced the evidences of the labor and zeal of the Franciscan missionaries who first planted Christianity and civilization upon these shores.

Let the work go on. The field has widened and become vastly more important. A few years ago, the Missionary labored to implant the great truths of Christianity in the untutored mind of the poor savage, and at the same time sought to draw him forth from his miserable habitation to teach him the arts and duties of civilized life. Large churches, comfortable dwellings, commodious workshops, were part of the fruits of their labors. I need not speak of the spiritual blessings showered upon them. But a change, sad in many respects, came o'er the scene. Since the Golden Era of California, a majority of those who came in search of the precious metal, were not Catholics. The vast immigration was composed of the bold, enterprising youth of every race and creed and country.

It is true that there was a mixture of the vicious and the good. Convicts, desperadoes, and others, who deserted from vessels and got here by various means, have, by their lawless acts, cast a foul stain upon our young State that will require years to wipe away.

There are good and bad in every community, and this is no exception. Still I believe our character abroad is below what justice requires. I will venture to assert that in proportion to her population, California possesses the most active, bold, energetic and educated people in the world. There are some illiterate persons from the Western states and other places; but nearly all who come from the Eastern states, and they number thousands, have received a common school education, and not a few from other portions of the Union, have received literary instructions, to a greater or less extent. Many are graduates, and some are distinguished in the learned professions.

There are Catholics scattered in every town and village—upon every mountain and valley. Many have grown careless and indifferent—some are in districts rarely visited by a Priest, having but few opportunities to perform their religious duties, and many obstacles are in their path.

Such is the field of our Missionaries—a people whose conversion would be a great triumph to the Church, as well as an inestimable blessing to the recipient of graces and consolations following their conversion.

A great deal has been done by our devoted and self-sacrificing Prelate and his zealous assistants, and, no doubt, in a short time the wants of the people will be supplied, and the harvest will yield a hundred fold.

SAMUEL WOOD (1856) — SANTA BARBARA

It was 1856 and an eight year old boy stood on the deck of the *Senator*, as the old and proud veteran of the waterways between San Francisco and San Pedro made its way south. The little boy's memories of that voyage would later become a permanent part of the Pacific Slope's literary heritage. Up and down, sideways and crisscross, the *Senator* rolled and tossed and bounded, her throbbing engines driving her steadily past the headlands and the Farallones, into the open roadway of the sea.

Though at first hectic, the waters calmed and Samuel Woods recalled that "with the dawn came peace, and as we lifted our eyes across the waters to the shoreline, we saw in the perfect beauty of a typical California morning the Bay of Monterey with its historic town, where first floated our Flag, symbol then and now of dominion; of freedom and justice."

Woods sensed that "we were in an atmosphere of history and romance," the ship halted long enough only to send off the mail and passengers," and then headed on to the south, to Santa Barbara, "then a sleepy Mission town, which in the radiant sunshine sloped from the shore toward the hills." Santa Barbara was a "typical town of that Church which in the past century had possessed the most favored spots of the State, lifted the Cross, and under the roofs and in the cloisters of cathedrals, now world–famed, gathered together the native tribes that they might be taught the old, old story, and become familiar with the arts of civilization."

Woods lamented that "many of these old cathedrals (he is referring to the missions) with their outlying buildings, the home for long years of priest and devotee, are falling into decay. And while the lovers of the historic and romantic are making some effort now to save them from the teeth of time, the State itself has, for fifty years, practically done nothing to preserve these historic places from ruin . . .

In what proved to be a prophetic statement, Woods said that "future generations of those who love romance and beauty will regard as most worthy of preservation these historic Missions. As a State, we have been unmindful of our rarest treasure and we have sat idly by while priceless things have been perishing."

Woods went on the say that "we have never, in a public way, gathered together any traditions or lore to fill the storehouses from which some future Prescott shall be able to gather marvelous data, and write of real things, more brillant and fascinating than all the dreams of imagination." Oh, "some great names like Junípero Serra are immortal, and the story of their heroism is the world's permanent possession, but no record has been kept of many simple, patient, lonely lives devoted to work and prayer among the natives."

"The *Angelus* floated out from the old Mission tower" as the *Senator* weighed anchor in the calm of a summer evening and made its way past the hills of the Coast Range and on to San Pedro. This was the scene of the Channel City and its mission that Samuel L. Woods would recall fifty–five years later when Funk & Wagnalls published his reflections about life on the Pacific Coast.

✚JOSEPH SADOC ALEMANY, O.P. (1859) — PURPOSE OF NORTH AMERICAN COLLEGE

The North American College was established by the bishops of the United States in 1859, as a residence and house of formation for seminarians and graduate priests in Rome. Students appointed to the college took their theological courses in the various seminaries of the Eternal City, principally the Pontifical Gregorian University. In a pastoral letter to the people of San Francisco, on January 31, 1859, Archbishop Joseph Sadoc Alemany explained the purpose and need for the college.

The Prelates of the United States, deeply impressed with the many advantages which the Church in this country would derive from instituting, in the capital of the Christian world, an Ecclesiastical Seminary for the education of young aspirants to the American ministry, have repeatedly expressed their wishes to the Holy Father on the subject, and earnestly solicited his approval.

By letters dated the 12th of February, 1856, and addressed to the Bishops of the United States, the common Father of the faithful, to whom, in the person of St. Peter, the Lord committed the care of "feeding his lambs and sheep," not only cordially approved of so important an undertaking, but was even graciously pleased to cooperate most efficiently in the work, by the magnificent donation of a large and spacious building.

Leaving it to the zeal and prudence of the several Bishops of the States to adopt whatever means they may deem most efficient to further so desirable an object, the Holy Father urgently exhorts them to fit out this Seminary as speedily as possible, and prepare it for the reception of American students; and for that purpose, to appeal to the generosity and acknowledged liberality of the faithful committed to their pastoral charge.

The rapid progress of the faith, and the daily increasing demand of the Catholics throughout the Union for

pastors to break the bread of life to the little ones of Jesus, render it an imperative duty on the Chief Pastors to labor with energy to supply their wants, by procuring zealous and efficient cooperators.

Ecclesiastical Seminaries, it is true, have been established in the various Dioceses of the States, for the purpose of supplying our most urgent wants; and they have furnished, and will continue to furnish, with God's blessing, a large number of efficient missionaries; but as a sufficient number of priests cannot be spared from the active exercise of the Ministry to conduct these Seminaries, many of them cannot afford those advantages which the student of Divinity would possess in a higher and more fully organized establishment, such as it is the wish of the Bishops of the United States, with the aid and sanction of the Holy Father, to render the American College in Rome.

Where can the young student be more thoroughly educated in the various and intricate duties of the holy ministry, or imbibe the full spirit of the priesthood and the fervor of a missionary, than in Rome, the cradle of Christianity, and the faithful mother of so many Apostles?

Instructed by Professors who have made Divinity the study of their lives, and at the feet of the successor of St. Peter—walking amidst the graves of the countless martyrs, and surrounded by so many glorious evidences of the past struggles and splendor of the Spouces of Christ—he possesses advantages for study in every branch of ecclesiastical learning, of which he would necessarily be deprived in a Diocesan Seminary.

Other nations have their colleges at Rome, where young men for every clime and country are educated and ordained. The English and the Irish colleges have stood there for centuries, under the protection of successive Pontiffs, and during the dark ages of the Penal code, have sent forth many a pious and learned priest to console his countrymen, and many a martyr to shed his blood for the ancient faith.

The day has come, we hope, when America too shall have her college in the Mother City, and thus, if possible, be more closely linked to that great centre of Catholic unity.

In our (arch)Diocese of San Francisco, where "the harvest is so great and the laborers so few," Catholics must feel more than an ordinary interest in the establishment of this seminary.

It is, therefore, with full confidence that we appeal (for) aid in carrying out an undertaking so dear to the heart of the Holy Father, and so well calculated to promote the glory of God and the salvation of souls.

ANONYMOUS (1875) — SILVER JUBILEE OF ARCHBISHOP JOSEPH SADOC ALEMANY

On July 29, 1875, the Catholic populace in Northern California feted the twenty–fifth anniversary of the Most Reverend Joseph Sadoc Alemany as Archbishop of San

Francisco. The tributes given to the Dominican prelate on that occasion were indeed moving. One speaker, for example, noted how the archbishop had found himself "on these remote shores in the midst of an heterogeneous people, made up of portions of all the races on this globe, differing from each other in national, political, social, religious and moral traits." He went on to say that "the field of your labors was not old Christendom, but a new domain, unsettled and unformed–a field, *sui generis,* in which many of the old rules of old countries were worse than useless.

> Old lessons in diocesan policy had often to be unlearned and new plans to be devised and adopted. Great courage, zeal and wisdom were demanded in Your Grace's isolation from brother prelates, whose advice might have been of much service, had distance not precluded it.
>
> But like Peter, Your Grace bravely weathered the storm, skillfully piloted our bark clear of the shoals, and landed us safe in a goodly land watered by the dews of heaven and abounding in the bread of life.

The speaker continued: "Under Your Grace's administration, the Church has fairly distanced all her competitors in this new field of religious rivalry. With scarcely equal advantages, and without earthly favor, the State in general and this metropolis in particular, have become more and more Catholic with the advance of years."

> So numerous are the monuments of Your Grace's wisdom, charity and zeal, that the emblem of salvation surmounting them meets every eye. Hospitals supply a couch to the diseased and feeble. Asylums furnish a home to the orphans and a refuge of reform to the victims of vice.
>
> Schools unfold their treasures of Christian wisdom and love. Convents afford to sensitive and fervent souls a sanctuary from the blighting blasts of worldliness. Churches everywhere open wide their doors to the suppliant.
>
> Spacious sanctuaries are spread with the banquet of divine love. Altars have been erected wherever the prophecy of Malachi has at length been literally and completely fulfilled, for "in every place there is a sacrifice, and there is offered to my name a clean oblation."
>
> We regard the success of Your Grace's career and the consequent blessings; we, your spiritual children enjoy, as due, under God, to the assiduous cultivation and practice of Apostolic zeal, such as infuses into man's efforts far more continuous and untiring energy than any earthly interests could inspire—evidence that the sacrifices made under its influence are prompted by higher than material or ephemeral considerations of prudence—so necessary to moderate that zeal and to restrain the soul fired by it from blind and impetuous attempts to attain ends without the possession and use of proportionate means.

The speaker concluded his tribute to the archbishop by publicly acknowledging the "simplicity, personal disinterestness, self–privation and poverty and kindred virtues, with which God has been pleased to adorn the chief pastor of this (arch)diocese."

✝JOSEPH SADOC ALEMANY, O. P. (1876) — AMERICAN CENTENNIAL

The centennial of American Independence was solemnly observed by the Catholics of California at San Francisco, on October 8, 1876. Fortunately for the historical record, the details of the celebration were incorporated by Patrick J. Thomas into a now–rare book entitled *Our Centennial Memoir.*

That 192 page opuscula endeavored to enshrine for posterity the story of "the Christian fortitude, the heroic perseverance of those Catholic Friars and pioneers who devoted life, energies, everything they possessed to the service of their Divine Master."

Archbishop Joseph Sadoc Alemany of San Francisco sounded the theme for the Catholic observance of the nation's hundredth birthday in a Pastoral Letter issued on June 26, 1876. Parts of that letter are worth recalling, even in the 1970s.

> This is the Centennial year of our proud independence as a nation. A hundred years since our country was a wilderness, her lands untilled, her resources undeveloped, her population sparse, and war being waged against the thirteen poor colonies by one of the most powerful Governments of modern times.
>
> But thanks to the noble patriots of the Revolution, who, yielding to none—not even to the historic Spartans—in their devotion to liberty, honor and chivalric arms, we came through the ordeal a glorious and free people.
>
> They left us their Declaration of Independence as a model of sublimity for the admiration of mankind. They framed for us a Constitution whose provisions secure for every soul that dwells beneath it—together with ample protection for 'life, liberty and the pursuit of happiness' as much genuine freedom as is the happiness of man to enjoy, if not the fullest enjoyed in any portion of the civilized world.
>
> Under the benign influence of the Republic our disenthralled country has experienced a hundred years of wonderful success, and has made gigantic strides towards prosperity and refinement.
>
> Our citizens are enlightened, our laws respected; our fields teem with luxuriant crops, our orchards are laden with choice and delicious fruits; we produce three–fourths of all the precious metals dug from the earth and we look with pride at our national prosperity unsurpassed.
>
> Our intelligence, industry and valor are known, rec-

ognized and respected throughout the world, and we stand today one of the first and grandest nations of the earth.

Are these not reasons for congratulation and thanksgiving? Whence all this prosperity? True, our fathers labored well and wisely for it, for which we respectfully tender them our sincerest filial gratitude; but we must not forget that though Paul sow and Apollo reap, it is God that giveth the increase.

We ought, therefore, to thank God from our hearts for mercifully bestowing upon us such choice favors and with such a lavish hand. As Catholics, too, we have special reasons for thanksgiving. We cannot forget that our land was discovered by a Catholic, that the spirit of religious toleration—which happily echoed in the letter of our Constitution—was breathed over the land and given to the world by the noble Catholic colony of Maryland, and that our noble Catholic sires fought and bled alongside their fellow patriots of other creeds, with whom they have always shown how dear to their hearts are the Stars and Stripes, the inheritance of the fathers of the Republic.

It was under that equitable and wise provision of the Constitution, which guarantees to every man the right to 'worship God according to the dictates of own conscience,' our Church has flourished and increased from the little seed of a century ago into the stately and towering oak of today, beneath whose branches millions of faithful souls find shelter and repose.

In thanksgiving for these and so many other signal blessings from on high, we ought to celebrate in a becoming manner the Centennial day of our country. To this end we proclaim a Mass of Thanksgiving, as solemn as circumstances will admit, with an appropriate oration to be celebrated in every church in this archdiocese at such hours on the morning of July 4th as will not be likely to conflict with the local civic celebrations.

✢RAMON MARIA DE SAN JOSE MORENO (1876) — ECCLESIAL AFFAIRS IN BAJA CALIFORNIA

The Right Reverend Ramón Maria de San José-Moreno (1839–1890) arrived at La Paz on March 17, 1875, as the newly–designated Vicar Apostolic of Baja California. From the very outset of his episcopate, the Carmelite bishop was beset by troubles with civil officials. Colonel Francisco Miranda, the Governor of the peninsula, finally incarcerated and then deported the bishop. Moreno came to Los Angeles, where he gave an interview to the press on November 16, 1876, explaining the problems he had encountered. The following excerpt was published a month later by the New York *Freeman's Journal and Catholic Register*:

In 1875 a system of religious persecution against the Catholic Church was commenced in Lower California,

instigated, I think, by some unknown secret organization. The first demonstration against me was made in June, 1875, when a Captain of the militia, named Palacio, attempted to take my life in my own house. The assassin fired a revolver at me, but I was saved from death by a friend who sprang forward and raised the hand of the murderer on the instant, thus directing the weapon from me. Palacio was placed under arrest and sent to Mazatlán, but he was never punished for the offense.

The next attempt was made in San José a town on the lower coast where I was presented with a dish of dessert sent in through one of the servants of the house at which I was stopping. Before I had partaken of the dish, I was warned by a conscience–stricken accomplice in the scheme that it contained a deadly poison. I thus escaped death a second time from the secret outlaws.

In the same place, shortly afterwards, when I was entering the church, a man named Pedrino sprang forward from the crowd and raised his arm to strike me with a poignard, but for a second time a friendly hand interfered and arrested the weapon before it fell. Pedrino escaped without punishment, although the populace were so incensed that they would have killed him had it not been for my interference on his behalf.

After that, insults of the grossest character were heaped upon me, and the dignities of my office, as head of the Church in that diocese. I have with me copies of these assaults, made through the public press, but they are too indecent to be reproduced. Some of the calumnies which were even too gross in character for the press of La Paz, were sent to Mazatlán, where they were printed and scattered far and wide over Lower California.

Francisco Mirando, who assumed the Governorship of the State of Lower California last Spring, it seems, was pledged to further the ends of the secret organization to which I have referred. On making my accustomed pastoral visit to the town of San Antonio, the people received me with the ringing of bells and the explosion of fireworks, for which demonstration they had previously obtained permission from the local authorities. Notwithstanding this warrant for the proceedings on this occasion, five or six days afterward I was arrested on a charge of disturbing the peace, and taken, under a guard of soldiers, like a criminal, to a town named *El Triunfo*, some six miles distant, and there cast into a calaboose or military guard–house.

The squad of soldiers who made the arrest–some forty in all–were under the command of a captain named Contreras, and I have no right to think otherwise than that he received his instructions from the Governor. I remained in the calaboose twenty–four hours, and was there insulted by three men sent in for that purpose.

Then I was removed to the criminal prison, where I was retained five days and received no attention whatever from the authorities. I subsisted on contributions from charitable and religious people about the place, who came to me with food and the necessities of life.

Finally a guard of forty men escorted me to La Paz,

where I was in turn incarcerated in the station–house for several days. Here I received most considerate treatment from the captain in charge of the station–house, named Gutiérrez, but at the same time was supported by provisions brought from my own house.

Overtures were made to me at this place to the effect that I would be released on condition of leaving off my religious habit while walking the street. I tacitly accepted the terms, intending to wear a large cloak while on the street, so that my manner of dress might not be visible. In passing to the church, I was arrested a second time, by a squad of soldiers, on a warrant from the Governor. They conducted me at the point of the bayonet to the station–house where I had been previously confined.

With the forced exile of the Vicar Apostolic, there was no leadership whatsoever for the Church in Baja California. Finally, when it became obvious to the Holy See that the prelate would not be allowed to return, Pope Leo XIII transferred Bishop Moreno to the See of Chiapas, and temporarily placed the vacant jurisdiction under the care of Guadalajara's Archbishop Pedro Loza.

✝THADDEUS AMAT, C.M. (1877) — REFLECTIONS ON LENT

As long as there are attics, closets and garages, historians will be discovering new insights into the past. An example is a hitherto unknown pastoral letter which Frederick Dockweiler recently found among his father's papers.

Written by Bishop Thaddeus Amat on February 5, 1877, the letter contains directions that it be read aloud to the Catholic People in the Diocese of Monterey–Los Angeles on "the first Sunday after its reception." Intended as a pastoral exhortation for the approaching season of Lent, the letter reiterates many of the traditional practices common in the Church during the later decades of the 19th century.

Amat himself came from an area where Lent was a time for prolonged prayer, bodily discipline and generous alms–giving. Those memories are evident as he writes to the peoples of his far–flung jurisdiction.

The bishop begins by recalling the Church's concern for the spiritual welfare of her people, pointing out that "by the wholesome practice (of Lent), we may satisfy divine justice for our sins and excesses." He stresses the notion of reconciliation that comes through the worthy practice of penance.

Amat encourages his people to begin the holy season "with an earnest desire of profiting by it," quoting Saint Paul to the effect that this is "the acceptable time and the day of salvation." Observing that all people have offended God in one way or another, the prelate suggests that, especially during Lent, they abstain from "those worldly amusements which are opposed to the spirit," remembering that "he who jokes with the devil will be excluded from the enjoyment of Christ."

"By the faithful observance of Lent," Catholics "draw down upon themselves heavenly blessings and, with them, the grace of sincere conversion of heart." Amat proposed that "we unite our fasting and our humble and fervent prayer" because such actions will penetrate "the clouds of heaven and attract upon the soul the salutary dew of God's grace."

Then, to put a positive spin on his exhortation, Amat suggests that his people remember the needs of the orphans and widows, the ill and the poor, thus making them partakers of the temporal blessings which God's providence will dispense. And, in that vein, he announces that there will be a collection for that purpose on the Sunday after Easter. He knows that Catholics "will generously contribute" to this annual appeal for the less fortunate.

Finally, and probably most importantly, Amat asks that his people "fast from sin and from satisfying their rebel inclinations." After all, he observes, fasting and abstaining would hardly profit a people given to sin.

Noting that it was "the principal object of the Church, during the season of Lent, to prepare her children to celebrate with pure conscience the great mysteries of the passion, death and resurrection of our loving Redeemer," he points out that Catholics are expected to confess their sins and receive the Holy Eucharist during the Easter season. He allows the local clergy to have solemn Benediction on Easter or during its octave and to that, he attaches a forty day indulgence.

There is a very human aspect to the pastoral letter. Bishop Amat had been ill for some time and he asked the people to pray that Almighty God "grant us health if it be His divine will." He then concludes his remarks with his paternal blessings, given at Los Angeles on the feast of Saint Agatha.

It was the bishop's last pastoral letter

THE MONITOR (1878) — NATIVE AMERICANS

Through the centuries, the Church has consistently championed the cause of minorities—especially those deprived of their human and/or natural rights. The native peoples of California are a case in point. In 1878, the State Legislature passed a joint resolution asking the United States Congress to provide for the dessandts of the original mission Indians.

The House Committee on Indian Affairs recommended the purchasing of reservations, but their pleas went unheeded by politicians who argued that they had more pressing problems to solve. So the Catholic hierarchy of California (all three of them) mounted a campaign to force some action in Congress. A series of articles was prepared for *The Monitor*, explaining the needs and desires of the Indians. The following excerpt from those essays provides some idea of how poorly the natives were faring.

The Missions Indians of California are a peculiar people. They are among the most docile and tractable of the native races within the United States. They are so by nature and by circumstances.

All observers agree that the red men of the south are less savage than those of the north; that the Indians of the lower Mississippi lack the fierceness of the Sioux and other northern tribes, and that the red men of Mexico, at the time of its conquest, were much milder in disposition than those encountered by the English in Virginia and New England or the Iroquois who determinedly withstood the French occupation of the country north of the St. Lawrence and the Great Lakes.

Our Indians are akin to those of Mexico, and partake of their nature. Circumstances have done much to confirm the natural characteristics of the race. The first encounter with the white race was peaceful, and for a considerable period their treatment was not cruel.

Franciscan missions were established along this coast with the intention of converting and civilizing the natives. For a long time the immigration of Europeans in any numbers was not encouraged. The whole attention of the missionairies was directed toward the Indians who, at San Diego, San Luis Rey, San Bernardino, Santa Barbara and San Francisco, were gathered into the fold of the Church and taught the agricultural and mechanical arts.

Hence the Mission Indians gained their name. Since the withdrawal of the Franciscans friars and the sequestration of their missions, the Indians have doubtless degenerated, but for many years after they suffered little from the encroachments of the whites.

The country, under the rule of Mexico, was too sparsely settled and considered of too little value to make the dispossession of the Indians a temptation. But since the rapid settlement of the state as a member of the Federal Union, the fate of the Mission Indians has been a sad one and is shameful to contemplate.

Had they been a fierce people, or had their first contact with whites been such as to arouse their resistance, it would have been better for them. They would have been better cared for by the Government and supplied with food, clothing and arms. But they are unwarlike, patient, submissive, uncomplaining and the result has been that they have been deprived of assistance and protection, and at the mercy of aggression, the extent of which if understood, would arouse a profound feeling of indignation.

As they now exist, the Mission Indians are chiefly located in San Bernardino and San Diego counties. They dwell in communities of from fifty to one hundred, and although they share some of the vices of their race and of all downtrodden people, are better behaved and more disposed to industry than their treatment would seem to warrant.

As has been stated, the very virtues of the Mission Indians, natural or acquired, are turned against them to their harm. It would seem that their uncomplaining and peaceable disposition has been crushed into an acquiescence. But if they cannot speak, and appear incapable of acting for themselves, the honor of the Government and the interest of humanity dictate that their situation should be ameliorated.

They ask for no supplies, but that when they work they shall be paid in coin and not be robbed of half their earnings. They are willing to maintain themselves, but experience has taught them that the Government should guarantee them a small portion of that domain which once was theirs, and which they relinquished without opposition, believing in the justice of the whites who first came to them in the garb of religious teachers and in the role of material benefactors.

Nor are their demands unreasonable. They are extremely moderate.

ZACAHARIAH MONTGOMERY (1883) — LOS ANGELES

The name of Zachariah Montgomery (1825–1900) was prominently identified with educational progress in California for many years. One of the state's ablest jurists, Montgomery's "journalistic campaign against the defects in our public schools" endeared his name to all who appreciated the grandeur of religious morality in the arena of daily life.

An editorial in *The Tidings* for June 16, 1900, characterized Montgomery as one who believed that a true Catholic "would rather abide in chains with truth, justice and an upright heart, than with a guilty conscience to rule the world from an imperial throne built upon the ruins of justice and the wreck of human liberty." Montgomery took his campaign for a "free education" to Los Angeles, during the summer of 1883. In a subsequent issue of *The Family's Defender*, he described "that charming city of the angels" and the "wonderful growth and increase of business" which had recently come to the Southern California community.

From a modest little town of three or four thousand inhabitants, Los Angeles has within the last two or three years grown to be a thriving city of considerably over twenty thousand, and is still advancing.

A few years back when we first saw Los Angeles it was confined to the narrow limits of a small valley, where, like a smooth gentle stream it pursued the even tenor of its way without any apparent hope or prospect of materially extending its limits.

But, as a rising river swollen by the mountain torrents, as they came pouring down from the melting snow of the Sierras, overflows its banks and spreads its waters far and wide over all the adjoining country, so does the rising city of Los Angeles, swollen by the inpouring tide of immigration, rise above the adjacent hills, and sends its beautiful streets and splendid blocks of buildings for miles beyond the ancient limits of the town.

We have neither the time nor the space to enter into a minute description of Los Angeles, the queenly city and thriving metropolis of Southern California. But had we both the time and the space, still we should despair of our ability to do justice to the subject.

Imagine a busy, active, commercial young city, covering some four miles square or about sixteen square miles, with splendid churches, and schools, beautiful residences and blocks of business houses, interspersed with gardens, apple and peach orchards, vineyards and groves of figs, oranges, lemons and pomegranates, all watered by ever–living streams of clear water.

Listen to the noise and bustle and ceaseless clatter of commerce, as it mingles with the cheerful songs of ten thousand wild birds, sporting amidst the dark foliage and sweet blossoms of the lemon, the orange, and multitudes of other ever green and ever blooming trees of tropical lineage;

Picture to yourself a spot which nature and art, city and county, mountain and valley, earth, air, and water, spring, summer, and autumn, have all combined to enrich, adorn and beautify, and you will have a more perfect likeness of Los Angeles than any which we can paint with our pen.

✛JOSEPH SADOC ALEMANY (1885) — THE ARCHBISHOP BIDS *ADIEU*

The departure of Archbishop Joseph Sadoc Alemany from San Francisco was "sorrowful in the extreme." After thirty–five years, the Dominican prelate had retired, "full of years and honors," and set out for his native Spain "to round off a glorious and self–sacrificing life." The following account of that farewell, here shortened and edited, appeared in the New York *Freeman's Journal and Catholic Register*, June 20, 1885.

Besides the immense material progress that he had witnessed and left behind, he took leave of friendships that had become the very fiber of his life. There certainly was never a day in his life that was more crowded with affecting scenes, and feelings of joy and sorrow.

On Saturday evening he sat in the confessional in the Cathedral hearing, till a late hour, the confessions of people whom he has guided in religion for years. At 7:30 o'clock Sunday morning he stood at the altar in Saint Mary's Cathedral and faced an audience that packed every seat, aisle and nook of the edifice.

He celebrated Mass, and then for the last time administered the Communion. He was unassisted in this work, preferring to do this last office with his own hand, bestowing his benediction on the kneeling communicants. It seemed that every one in the Cathedral pressed forth to receive the last Communion from the Archbishop, and it was late when he finished the ceremony.

After a short rest he entered the Cathedral again, and assisted at the celebration of High Mass by Archbishop Riordan. As the choir finished Mozart's "Twelfth Mass," the aged Archbishop rose and walked to the center of the altar and began a Confirmation address to several hundred children, who gathered about the altar. His voice quivered with emotion and tears filled his eyes.

As the Archbishop concluded his eloquent address he was overcome with emotion. Tears were in the eyes of those with him on the altar, and the audience was moved deeply by the words, which seemed to them as authoritative as though they had fallen from the lips of a prophet of old. The congregation left the church sadly, and the Archbishop repaired to his rooms for a brief rest before undertaking the final ordeal of parting finally from his friends.

At 2 o'clock the vestibule and hall of the residence of the clergy were filled with people, and a crowd waited on the sidewalk to catch a last glimpse of the face of the Archbishop. A carriage stood before the door ready to take him to the ferry. The door leading into the hall opened, and Archbishop Riordan and Vicar General Prendergast, followed by Archbishop Alemany, tried to move to the door.

As soon as the throng caught sight of the aged Archbishop they all, men, women and children, fell upon their knees. The women sobbed and cried bitterly. The Archbishop blessed the kneeling company, but they did not rise.

As he passed among them to go to the door they took his hand and pressed it to their lips, many hot tears falling upon it. He spoke a consoling word to each, which, instead of allaying the sorrow, seemed to give it voice, and a wail followed him as he pressed his way to the door and through the crowd to the street. As he entered the carriage the crowd rushed to the open door and clung to the Archbishop's hand, pressing kisses upon it.

The carriage door was at last closed, and the Archbishop, with Archbishop Riordan, Vicar General Prendergast and D. J. Oliver, were driven to the ferry, where they took the 2:30 boat and crossed to the Oakland mole. A car had been chartered to take the clergy and a few laymen to Port Costa, to say a last farewell.

About eighty persons took the 3 o'clock boat and crossed the bay, where Archbishop Alemany was found in the last seat in the chartered car. The scene at St. Mary's was repeated on the Oakland mole. The clergy and laity that intended to go to Port Costa found seats in the car, but a large number of people stood at the window to catch a last glimpse of the Archbishop.

Men and women came into the car to shake his hands

and wish him a happy journey. The train soon drew out of the depot, and the Archbishop sat down by the side of one of the aged priests.

As the train approached Port Costa the Archbishop rose to take final leave of the men who have been laboring with him for years. With one accord the clergy and laity knelt in the aisle and received the Archbishop's final blessing. As the old man passed through the cars to a Pullman at the head of the train, he was received with respect by every one. As the train ran on board of the ferryboat, the Archbishop stood on the platform and waved farewell to his friends, who bade him God speed with full hearts.

LOUIS COOK (1885) — PARISH MISSIONS

During the summer months of 1884, Bishop Francis Mora wrote to the Redemptorists in New Orleans, asking that four priests be sent to the Diocese of Monterey–Los Angeles for the purpose of conducting a series of parochial missions. The priests (Father Louis Cook, James McLoughlin, Timothy Enright and J. O'Shea) arrived in Los Angeles on December 28th and for the next seven months busily moved around the diocese fulfilling their spiritual tasks. Father Cook's diary is the source of the following reflections.

We began in the cathedral on January 4th with a good attendance which increased daily until standing room was scarce. We continued the mission and heard 1,572 confessions. Then they moved on to San Bernardino. This place was described as the most God–forsaken of the diocese. In fact, it was doubtful whether it was worth our trouble to go there at all. But God blessed our labors. . . . The people did nobly. They afforded us the greatest consolation by the large and earnest attendance and by their perseverance after the mission.

On February 5th, Father Cook "started on his long journey through the Mojave desert to the Calico mines, a distance of ninety–seven miles and a ride of forty–eight hours in a wagon. The place was a forlorn mining camp of 1,500 people." The missionaries found at Hanford "a God–forsaken people but not their fault. This station should have been attended from another mission but was neglected and hence the number of apostates was great. However, the Bishop promised publicly to send them a priest, and in one hour, the grateful people subscribed $2,500 for a priest's house."

It was at Watsonville that "we first experienced the novelty of an earthquake. The house began to sway to and fro as if moving on waves. The sensation is peculiar and terrifying. You seem to lose all courage in an instant and feel an inclination to hurry into the open air that you may avoid being buried in the ruins of the building."

Later, at Santa Cruz "we experienced our third earthquake. The church was packed to suffocation and the sanctuary was filled with boys and girls in gala dress. As Father Cook was saying the beads in the pulpit, three tremendous knocks were suddenly heard. The rumbling of the earth was so marked that we feared the chandeliers and the statue on the temporary altar would be tumbled."

Father Cook described San Gabriel Mission as being located in "a little town nine miles distant from Los Angeles." Its setting "is the most beautiful in the state. There used to be a large convent attached to the solid old adobe church. Most of the other buildings have gone to ruin for want of care. The church was most neglected and had become a home for owls and bats. During the sermons, these filthy birds would hold their meetings of indignation at our intrusion upon their quiet. It was seldom indeed that their place had been disturbed by a loud word. The sanctuary floor was but a mass of rotten carpets and bird dung. A foul air pervaded everything in and around the church."

Bishop Mora must have been extremely pleased with the Redemptorists because Father Cook noted that "the good bishop has kindly offered us this venerable adobe pile and its surroundings for a foundation." He felt its "possibilities are great."

Others were pleased with the parochial missions. The Vicar General of San Francisco declared that "we had carried the state of California by storm." Cook thought that was the supreme compliment "when it is remembered that the Jesuits, Dominicans, Franciscans, Paulists and Sanguinists had all tried their missions there and failed."

✚JOSEPH SADOC ALEMANY, O.P. (1885) — REFLECTIONS FROM ROME

Shortly after his retirement as Archbishop of San Francisco, the Most Reverend Joseph Sadoc Alemany returned to his native Spain, where he became active in a movement to re–establish the Order of Preachers in Valencia. Enroute, the Dominican prelate visited Pope Leo XIII in Rome. On August 22, 1885, he wrote a newsy letter to *The Monitor*, outlining his reflections on the Eternal City.

It is truly a great treat to every Catholic, who has the opportunity, to visit the Eternal City. He feels he is no stranger in it, he finds himself at home; and at home he is while remaining in it. His Father is here; his brethren in faith are here, the trophies of his immortal ancestors are also here; and, from street to street, from church to church, he is carried back through countless generations of noble heroes, who had the same faith, received the same sacraments, were all of the same holy communion under the same visible head, the successor of St. Peter, and who left to future generations the most brilliant examples of Christian virtue.

It is particularly in Rome that a Catholic feels proud of his faith and of his kindred in the faith, the countless illustrious children of the same mother who, for well nigh nineteen hundred years, have shone brilliantly in every land and climate—glorious men, rich in virtue, who left behind them those who would worthily sing their praises.

A Catholic here feels a holy satisfaction in going around and paying his visit to the shrines of these glorious men. He goes to Piazza Navona, and there he visits St. Agnes in the beautiful church erected to perpetuate the praises of the youthful virgin, whose purity and divine love were stronger than the fire and sword of her pagan executioners.

He travels to the Basilica of St. Lawrence and there again his heart exults with Christian joy, finding himself brought back to the days of Pope St. Sixtus II, whom the holy deacon used to serve at the Altar of God.

The archbishop goes on to describe the numerous other shrines of Rome in considerable detail. In speaking of Saint Paul's Basilica, he wished that he might "take to this magnificent church every Protestant in California and even of the whole world, and present to them the two hundred and sixty–three Popes, who stand there in double line, around the grand Basilica, in exquisite mosaic, commencing with St. Peter and ending with the gloriously reigning Pontiff Pope Leo XIII, a most worthy heir of the Apostolic keys."

Alemany had special fascination with Saint Peter's Basilica, "the most magnificent church in earth." He noted that "it stands as the wonder of the world, the admiration of man, the most beautiful, most precious and largest church in the world. The heart of the Catholic visitor expands with joy on gazing upon this marvellous work of human hands, and is directed to contemplate the heavenly Jerusalem, built by the hand of the Omnipotent, infinitely surpassing all the works of man."

The archbishop observed that a visitor "at the Vatican is constantly enraptured in contemplating the exquisite works of art, the monuments, the statues, the marvellous mosaics and the thousand beauties, which give the beholder some idea of the triumphant church in heaven."

Alemany concluded by saying that he knew "that many Catholics in and out of California are familiar with Rome and its precious monuments; but some may not be. Hence it may not be amiss to have given a short though imperfect account of some of them."

✛JOSEPH SADOC ALEMANY, O.P. (c. 1885) — VIGILANTE DAYS

Shortly after his retirement as Archbishop of San Francisco, the Reverend Joseph Sadoc Alemany was requested to relate a portion of his reminiscences during those stormy days when the Vigilantes ruled with a rod of iron. Though at first reluctant to speak, for publication, the Dominican prelate finally consented to the interview, though he protested that his recollections were likely of little value to the permanent record.

The Catholic Church did not have to face the prejudice in this state which it encountered in the other parts of the country. In the early days of Tennessee, the bishop and the Church were subjected to a great deal of annoyance, and even to open insult.

The people there did not comprehend the mission of the Catholic religion, and consequently did not welcome it as one of the elements of the civilization that was growing up there, and which would mold the destinies of its people.

But the bishop calmly, quietly, politely and conscientiously performed his duties, and silently and gradually won the respect of the people, and sailed smoother seas. I was fortunate in not being compelled to face any such opposition.

The elements which combined to form the civilization of the Pacific Coast made respect and tolerance of all doctrines and beliefs necessary. People came here from all quarters of the globe, and each with a different opinion and belief. In such a variety of ideas, mutual tolerance and respect for the views of each other were demanded and conceded without debate.

Arbp. Joseph Sadoc Alemany

That made the missionary life here—for this was a missionary station—very easy. In addition to that I have found the people here are more generous and open–hearted than in any other country in the world. They have treated me very kindly, very considerately. Yes, the people here are noble–hearted, warm–hearted and they have been very kind to me.

The prelate was then asked whether, in the early days, he had anticipated so great a future for the state and Church in California and the nation as a whole.

Yes, I think all we early Californians looked forward to great things for this State. Gold was found in such large quantities, and people thronged to this country in such great numbers, that it took no gift of prophecy to foretell that a great State would rise on the furthest shore of America. Our Church must grow and spread in proportion to the population.

When I first came here in 1850, all of California, both the upper and lower portions—that is the old and new California were included in my diocese. I was here but a short time when I had to leave to attend the Council at Baltimore, which was held in 1852.

Then old California was placed under the ecclesiastical authorities in Mexico, and the diocese of Monterey was divided into two, one being made a Metropolitan See for the northern portion of the State, the title being Archdiocese of San Francisco, to which I was transferred, for the whole State was too much for a small man.

In 1860, I again asked that the diocese be divided, and all that portion of my territory north of the 39th degree to the 42nd degree of latitude was set aside and a bishop appointed over it, who was first stationed at Marysville and afterwards was removed to Grass Valley.

Our Church in this city, I feel sure, embraces half the population. The best way to determine that is to compare the burials of our Church and those of other churches. There are as many burials in a twelve month by our Church as by all the other churches and people combined.

The archbishop was then asked whether he foresaw the day when a conflict would exist between the Church and the state.

That can never be. That is an old prejudice that is gradually and surely dying out. People are beginning to look on the Catholic Church in a different way than they used to. Formerly it was said that all the ignorant and riotous and vicious were embraced in the Church, but as people have observed learned men in all professions, judges, lawyers, physicians and teachers join the Catholic Church, non–Catholics have formed a higher and more rational opinion of the Church.

There is nothing in our religion antagonistic to the form of government of the United States. When President [Andrew] Jackson wanted to appoint a Chief Justice of the United States, a friend of his told him to select a practical Catholic, and then the rich man and the poor man would receive justice alike. Jackson appointed [Roger Brooke] Taney, and he fulfilled all that was expected of an upright and honest judge.

REGINALDO F. DEL VALLE (1899) — MISSION INDIANS

In an address before the Newman Club of Los Angeles, late in 1899, the Honorable Reginaldo F. Del Valle spoke about "The Mission Indians" and the efforts of the Franciscan friars towards their conversion.

Upon the constant efforts and patient endeavors of the Christian teachers developed the duty of demonstrating that man in a barbarous state, living on the traditions that had been handed down through the generations for centuries, unrestrained in his natural inclinations, except by imperfect tribal laws, could be molded to the ways of civilization and reclaimed from the almost brutal state to which he would sink if left in his then condition.

The evidence of history is sufficient to convince us that two hundred years before the Mission fathers arrived in California the peoples who inhabited the regions to which these good men gave their attention were a superior people. The savages found here afterwards by Fray Junípero and his followers were stubborn in their paganism, and only by persistent work was success achieved.

What was accomplished in the limited time that the missionaries held full sway over the Missions, is sufficient to prove that the entire disappearance of these races was not due to natural causes and the infallible destiny of all weaker peoples, but rather to the lack of effort in reclaiming them.

A little more than a generation had passed from the time that the cross was planted on the shores of San Diego, and the mission of Christianizing had commenced, when the missionaries were divested of the properties that they had created, and the work of secularization of the Missions had begun.

The great estates upon which the labor of the neophytes had been bestowed were parcelled out among settlers and the power of the missionaries passed away, and as rapidly disappeared the wards whom these good men had led into greater light.

The ruins of the old churches still give evidence of the character of training that the Indians had received. They were the artisans who built the many monuments of stone and brick from Sonoma to San Diego, silent witnesses to the energy of brave men and symbolizing religion on the Western shore. They were the artists who borrowed from mother nature the colors which they used to ornament the paintings still extant on the walls of the houses of God.

At the height of the power and influence of the missionaries, there were fifteen thousand neophytes living, and connected with the various Missions of California. This had been the work accomplished by the friars during a very short period.

The principal motive that induced these good men to abandon the comparative comforts of life to face danger from privations in an uninviting territory known to be peopled by unfriendly savages was partially attained.

The evolution had been perfect. They had followers counted by the thousands who had shattered their idols to follow the teachings of the true religion. They were happy and content in their beliefs and it is a fact replete with the salutary lessons of sincerity that the Indians who were attached to the Missions died professing the Catholic religion, and all their descendants have lived in it.

There was a great contrast between the Mission Indians and those belonging to the same or neighboring tribes and who preferred to remain in their original state. One acquired the advantages which followed from the contact and teachings of superior men, the other was lost in the monotony of barbarism.

The end, came, however, and today the California Indian, the master of this mighty empire a little more than a century ago, is almost an extinct race. Disease, the vices taught him by civilized man, the abandonment to his own resources and the encroachment on his possessions have been the primary causes of his destruction. There seems to be no room on this fertile and productive land for the native plant and it has been uprooted and new seed sown in its place.

A GIANT AMONG THE GIANTS

California never numbered among her sons a nobler character, a more imposing pioneer or a more splendid figure than Zachariah Montgomery (1825–1900). Massive, physically and intellectually, he was a giant among the race of giants to whom is owed the foundations of the California commonwealth. Fearless and unswerving in his loyalty to principle, he stood forth conspicuously as the champion of right, whenever right was assailed, and always with an absolute disregard of the cost to his own personal interests.

Like others of the rugged pioneers, whose names are associated with the material and social upbuilding of the state, Mr. Montgomery's gifts and qualifications found many opportunities leading to position and wealth, but in his case, these were spurned and cast aside, without a moment's hesitation, in the pursuit of higher and grander aims, looking to the community's betterment and permanent advancement along every line of real human progress. Had it not been for his rare devotion to the public good and the cause of better things, the venerable publicist and philanthropist might easily have been

numbered among the opulent "great" men of the coast.

He had a philosopher's contempt for riches merely as a means of self–gratification, his ideals were antagonistic to those which inspire the sordid neo–pagan dollar worship of modern society. Zach Montgomery was a type of broad, sound, robust American manhood which, unfortunately, is less commonly found that it might be. Strong without coarseness, cultured without pedantry, religious without cant or pretense, his life affords a splendid illustration of the fruits of a potent, living, active Christian faith consistently carried out to the minutest detail of everyday conduct.

Captain James Connolly, one of the founders of *The Tidings*, spoke about Zachariah Montgomery at the time of his death. A life–long friend, he was thoroughly competent to estimate the worth of Montgomery's contribution to the California scene.

I knew him well in the trying times of political strife, social change and religious intolerance, and saw him stand up intrepid through it all in defense of original American principles and of God's eternal laws. At times he seemed to stand apart and almost alone as the exponent and advocate of the parental against the State right and duty of educating the children.

The home and fireside he believed to be the most sacred and productive nursery of the best American man and womanhood. This belief was an inheritance which he cherished with a religious fortitude rarely equaled. Mr. Montgomery's Christian spirit pervaded every act and endeavor of his life. Nowhere was its influence more helpfully felt, and its usefulness more conspicuously seen, than in his long and successful practice of law. I have known him to spend weeks in defense of the rights of poor widows and orphans from whom he could hope no pecuniary fee. Few men had more cultured or refined literary tastes, and it was in speaking of things literary that you got at the inmost heart of the man.

Socially he was as entertaining a host and pleasant a guest as one ever met. For hours together he could lead one delightedly through the interminable charms of natural beauty or the pleasing labyrinth of art.

The world of mankind is poorer for his loss, and his friends must take heart from the hope of meeting him where sorrow is no more.

JAMES McCLATCHY (1901) — CALIFORNIA AT MID CENTURY

James McClatchy came to the United States as a land reformer and, in New York, found employment with Horace Greely on the *Tribune*. He served as President of the Homestead Club and later became known for his campaign against land monopoly in California.

In San Francisco, McClatchy met Henry George and gave him a position on the editorial staff of the *Times* which he edited. One prominent writer felt that George's book, *Progress and Poverty*, was "largely due to this land reforming Catholic Irishman."

In July, 1876, McClatchy went to Santa Clara College to attend a theatrical reproduction of the debate on the Declaration of Independence in the Continental Congress in which his son had a role. While there, McClatchy befriended a man identified only as "An Old–Timer," to whom he related several accounts of his early days in California. A quarter century later, in November, 1901, that chance aquaintance recalled his meeting with McClatchy in an article for Buffalo's *Catholic Union and Times*.

> Coming to California in 1849, I travelled with a party overland by way of Mexico. At Mazatlan we hired a vessel that was not seaworthy and was wrecked off the coast of Lower California. Everything we brought with us was lost and we were destitute of clothing and boots.

> The Mexicans were the only people in the country then and their ranches were few and far between. Besides, there was no very great welcome for Americans in the country.

> Of course our destination was the mining region which was situated in the northern portion of the State and far away. We were forced to all kinds of straits. We ate anything we could find that was not absolutely poisonous, not excepting rattlesnakes.

> We were compelled to walk through fields of cacti and wild briars, through gulches and boulders and all kinds of country, including swamps and lagoons. It was slow progress.

> The nights were cold and the days hot. When night came we had no shelter only such as heaven's canopy offered. When we reached a Mexican ranch we had no welcome and were driven to appropriate whatever we could lay our hands on such as poultry and turkeys.

> We had no shotguns to pursue wild game. We were sometimes arrested and hauled before the *alcaldes* for our transgressions, but we were such pitiful sights, they were glad to get rid of us and let us go.

> A number soon grew so weak and faint that they could not proceed. They would turn aside to a ravine or clump of shrubbery, lie down and die. I was one of those who was able to hold out. But my clothes were in tatters and my feet were enjoying the freedom of earth and air.

> I was soiled and unshaven and no tramp ever presented a more forlorn aspect. I was thin and wasted and bruised and blistered, and my own mother would not have known me. My eyes did not have their own look, my voice was changed and my walk was altered.

> When I struck this Alameda, I felt as if I had reached the promised land, but not till then. When I reached San Jose I was alright. Here were many of my own countrymen in good circumstances—the Murphys, Reads, Welches, Falons, Dallys and others were here long before the gold discoveries and were well off and glad to befriend a fellow–countryman.

It was an interesting story of a pioneer who later became a respected journalist and business merchant in Northern California.

T. P. McLOUGHLIN (1901) — SAN MIGUEL MISSION

Father T. P. McLoughlin visited San Miguel Mission in 1901, and later recorded his impressions of that frontier outpost for the press. The following excerpt is taken from his sketch.

> He that has not seen California in the spring time has not seen the land of flowers at its best. And oh! how romantic is the old mission, standing in the heart of the Salinas Valley with the swift flowing river at its feet, and the landscape for miles as far as the eye could reach covered with tapestries of golden poppies, and baby blue eyes, and all kinds of purple, yellow and pink wild flowers, that delight the senses, and make one involuntarily say: 'Isn't that perfectly beautiful'?

> We found ourselves one fine spring morning in February, ready to investigate the ruins and relics of the old San Miguel Mission. When we approached the cloisters we saw the *padre* seated on a wicker rocking chair saying his office, and he reminded us of the gentle Francis of Assisi, for at his feet crouched two very fine dogs, one an immense greyhound, the other an Irish setter.

> Back of him stood his pet mare, who seemed to be intent on the Breviary which the priest was reading, while in front of him, only six feet away, was his favorite cow, chewing her cud. It was a picture for an artist, this self–sacrificing priest, away thousands of miles from his native land, living alone in this bleak, ghostly monastery, having no society but that of these lowly animals of the field, no exchange of intellectual, refining thoughts, save with his books.

> The dogs rose of their own accord at our near approach, the horse and cow remaining in their fixed positions, while the Father on seeing us stood and 'shooed' the hen and her little ones out of the way.

> He led us first to the old Mission chapel with its sweet sounding bell, and to our great amusement, the horse, the cow and the two dogs followed us to the great door of the chapel. The *padre* turned around and bade them begone and the dogs obeyed, but the horse and cow simply moved away about ten feet and stood there looking after us as we entered the ancient portals.

> We saw the fine vestments and sacred vessels and pictures, and were examining some antiquated statues over the high altar when we were shocked at hearing the *padre* shout: 'Shoo! get out of there!' We turned, and, heavens preserve us! there was that blessed cow in the church, and horror or horrors! she was actually drinking the holy water out of the font.

> I regret to confess that we laughed outright in church. His reverence, however, did not see the comical side of it as we did, but indignantly said: 'That is the

boldest cow I ever saw, she would enter the sanctuary if I permitted, and last evening she ate the cover off my Bible.'

The visiting priest concluded his observations about the ravenous cow by noting that "I have laughed many times over the incident, for it always reminds me of the funny saying of the vaudeville actor anent the chasing of the cow out of the hammock."

THE MONITOR (1902) — CHRISTMAS IN EARLY CALIFORNIA

In the Christmas issue of *The Monitor* for 1902, an unidentified writer recorded the details of "A Christmas with the Early Californians." It is a classical description well worth repeating, in abbreviated form, to another generation.

Navidad! *Pasquas*! *Noche Buena*! Christmas! What memories of good old times gone, never to return, must the above words being back to the minds of old Californians. *Noche Buena* meant to us merriment in the full sense of the word, but with of course religious thoughts as well. With all the uproarious *fiestas* and racket, the thought that to the world was born a Savior, was not forgotten, and the great event was kept in the minds of the people by the continuous and merry ringing of the bells.

Among the quaint and pretty customs in celebrating Christmas none was prettier than the observance of the Holy Night. Nine days before Christmas a novena was commenced in every home in honor of the Christ–child and a ceremony called a *posada* was inaugurated. Literally, the word signifies an inn, and in this was commemorated our Blessed Mother and St. Joseph, seeking for shelter in the inns of Bethlehem.

Beginning on the evening of the sixteenth of December and continuing every night until the twenty–fifth, the family and servants in every household assembled and with lighted tapers they sang the Litany and formed a procession down in the patio or courtyard. Four men were chosen to carry the *nacimiento* or crib, wherein to lay the Holy Child. They walked in the center and halted before each door in the house as the procession moved on.

In exquisite Spanish verses were then begged the *posada* for the Blessed Virgin and St. Joseph, but from the closed door angry voices called out that there was no room for the travelers. The Litany was again resumed until a halt was made at several other doors and the *posada* again asked for and was refused.

The last door was finally reached, the *posada* was entreated and sweet voices from within bade the travelers welcome. The door was thrown open, the procession filed into a room beautifully illuminated.

The *nacimiento* was placed upon a temporary altar, and after a hymn of thanksgiving and the recitation of the Rosary, the sacred part of the *posada* was terminated and the social programme begun. When the last *posada* had taken place all repaired to the churches to assist at Mass at daybreak. The altars and statues were all magnificently dressed to welcome the new born King.

And the lowly Indian and opulent Californian, kneeling side by side, vied with each other in offering their devotion to the Holy Child. All kneeling with arms outstretched in the form of a cross holding lighted tapers, so emblematic of their ardent faith, and at the *Venite Adoremus* every head was bowed to the ground.

At every Mass on Christmas Day a procession took place in the churches. The crib was reverently carried about, and the people follow with lighted tapers singing the Litany. With the Benediction of the Blessed Sacrament which was given after the last Mass, ended the religious celebration of the feast of Christmas.

ELEANOR C. DONNELLY (1902) — MEMORY OF THE MISSIONS

Writing in *Mosher's Magazine*, in 1902, Eleanor C. Donnelly paid tribute to the memory of the California Missions. Her words are all the more significant, insofar as they come from the pen of a non-Catholic.

Enemies of the friars . . . seem to have ignored the fact that those good religious were the founders and rightful owners of the missions . . . the first fathers of the land; that they did whatever was done for it, and for the people who originally inhabited it.

It is indisputable that they were the first explorers, the first tillers of the soil, the first cattle raisers, the first educators of the natives in all branches of secular as well as religious knowledge.

From the time officious outsiders began to interfere in the affairs of the friars, the prosperity of their people began to diminish—faith and morals to languish and decay.

The Mexican soldiers and colonists were alone responsible for the deadly disorders introduced, more than a half–century ago, among the Catholic Indians of California.

The Franciscans of California were deprived of their missions . . . about the year 1826; and, after a year's disastrous experience without their guiding care, were implored to take charge again of their helpless flock abandoned to the wolves of circumstance, like sheep who had lost their shepherd.

Let the foes of the friars do what they may, or what hell and its myrmidons may prompt them to do, to expel the missionaries from their sacred abodes, and dispossess them of their lawful rights–they are powerless to erase the recollection of those apostles, often martyrs, of

Christ from the spots they consecrated for ages by their self–sacrifcing toil and prayer; from the soil they have enriched by their sweat, their tears and their blood.

Sacrilegious hands may level the convent belfry to the dust, and pluck out the metal tongue that has long and lovingly invited the favored aborigines to the true worship of his God, yet the music of the ancient mission–bell will ever continue to echo through the corridors of romantic history, bearing melodious witness against the vandals who conspired to rob a happy people of that angel summoner to the blessed realms of prayer and peace.

Ruthless bigots of crafty diplomats may succeed in demolishing or purloining the antique mission–houses and schools; but the picturesque phantoms of the old–time *padres* and their gentle neophytes will never cease to flit through their primitive haunts, whispering constantly to all godless intruders the names of the patrons of their shadowy shrines—titles as immortal as are the holy ones who bore them, and whose memory is held in benediction by angels and men.

Full tenderly and loyally then may each one of us unite in conclusion with the gifted author who has been privileged to wander and muse in the footsteps of the *padres*, when he thus apostrophizes the genius of the departed mission–bell:

> Ring gentle *Angelus*! ring in my dream,
> But wake me not, for I would rather seem
> To live the life they lived who've slumbered long
> Beneath their fallen altars, than to waken
> And find their sanctuaries thus forsaken;
> God grant their memory may survive in song.

THE MONITOR (1902) — SAINT MATTHEW'S CHURCH

The ceremony for consecrating a church, "one of the most beautiful and symbolic which finds place in the ritual," was performed for the first time in the Archdiocese of San Francisco, on July 2, 1902. A description of that colorful event, at Saint Matthew's Church, San Mateo, appeared in the pages of *The Monitor* later that week.

The preparatory rites were observed on Monday evening, the day being one of fasting for some of those to participate in the offices, and the relics of the saints which now have place within the miniature sepulchre carved out of the block on which the altar stone rests, were temporarily set in a convenient place without the church.

The consecration ceremony proper began with the closing of the church, no one remaining within in excepting the deacon. . . . The Archbishop, wearing his alb, cope and mitre, and carrying his crozier . . . made the circuit of the church three times, blessed the walls on the outside in the formula prescribed, sprinkling with

water which had been previously blessed with the special prayers of the church.

The blessings were given to the upper walls, the foundations and the intermediate spaces. After each circuit the Archbishop ascended the front entrance steps of granite, and standing before the closed doors knocked with the lower end of his crozier and asked admittance, the deacon responding from within.

At the third demand the doors were opened, and the Archbishop scaling the threshold stone with the sign of the cross made with his crozier, entered.

The consecration services then continued within the church. Three times the procession circled within, blessing the walls as had been done without. The twelve brass crosses set in the walls, three on each side and corresponding in number to the twelve apostles were then anointed with chrism and blessed.

They are to remain perpetually encrusted on the walls in testimonial of the ceremony having been performed. They will also hold as a proof of the fact in case all documents of attestation are lost.

The door posts were also touched with the holy chrism and sealed within with the sign of the cross. The crosses set in the walls are mounted with sconces holding wax tapers which were lighted at the word of command from the Archbishop during the services.

One of the characteristic symbolic features of the ceremony was the spreading of ashes to the breadth of a palm transversly along the central aisle from the sanctuary to the entrance, one path of ashes being from right to left and it was crossed at the center with another path running from left to right.

Along one of the paths was inscribed by the Archbishop with his crozier the letters of the Greek alphabet; along the other he set the Latin alphabet. This suggested instruction and the catechizing of the newly baptized in the elements of faith and piety. The crossing of the lines in the center betokened the cross and Christ crucified as the central point in the teachings of the Church.

Further the figure and the letters stand for the universality of the Church stretching out to bring all nations within the arms of the cross. Salt indicating the strength and wholesome virtues, and recalling the words of Christ to his Apostles, 'You are the salt of the earth,' wine suggesting the hallowed plenty of heaven; water, a fountain of blessing, and ashes recalling mortality, were all used in the ceremony, together with chrism, oil of the catechumens and incense.

A church to be consecrated must be of brick or stone, perishable materials are not allowed, and further the church must be out of debt. Never while it remains a structure can it be used for other purposes than a church. It can not be rented, leased, mortgaged or encumbered in any particular. It is a gift whole and complete offered to God and must remain such.

J.S. THOMPSON (1903) — SOUTHLAND CATHOLICISM

The Reverend J.S. Thompson, Pastor of the Independent Church of Christ, in Los Angeles, preached a remarkable sermon on April 6, 1903. Therein he stated unequivocally that "the Catholic Church is the grandest organization in the world." Dr. Thompson's sermon, part of a series on "the providential purpose of the various denominations", is here excerpted from the San Francisco *Monitor*.

> The Catholic Church is the grandest organization in the world. It has a place of consecrated duty for all types or groups of mind.
>
> It is an imperialistic church. The Pope is a real monarch on a powerful throne, holding in his hands a sceptre of wondrous influence over the souls and destinies of men. The present Pope glorifies the papal crown; for he is a scholar, a thinker, a poet, a genuine philanthropist, a true friend to every wise measure for the benefit of the race, a skillful and practical manager of vast and complicated affairs, a member of a noble family, a gentleman and a saint; and yet the Catholic Church is thoroughly democratic in its aims, policies and efforts.
>
> The poor, the common and the rich people meet together in that Church, as children of the common Father. The poor hard working man and woman are found in that Church.
>
> It is an ancient Church. It was an ancient Church before the birth of Protestantism. It has cohesion and unity and continuity. The very fact of its great age is a proof of its providential purpose. It traces its descent to the founder of our common Christianity.
>
> The gates of hades have not been able to destroy it. It stands today against the opposition of centuries. It is the strongest religious force in Christendom.
>
> Many reasons might be given for the success and power of this wonderful organization. That Church believes sincerely and profoundly in the necessity for the salvation and happiness of men and women in this world and the next.
>
> It preaches this necessity and it acts accordingly. It does not neglect the religious education of its children, expecting them to grow up some way or other to be religious members of society.
>
> The keys of knowledge which that Church possesses are wisely used to admit the worthy into the kingdom of heaven, and to prepare them to seek that kingdom with consecrated hearts.
>
> Religious knowledge frees and strengthens the soul; but a religion that cannot command loyalty and consecration is worthless.
>
> In the dark ages it was the monks who kept the fires burning upon the altar of literature. Our divine and glorious Bible was guarded and saved by the Catholic Church for us.
>
> In England and in many other places, the priest made

> the dying slave owner emancipate his slaves. Its priests are consecrated workers. They sacrifice many things to minister at the altar.
>
> The Catholic Church has always favored education. Before the Reformation that Church had established colleges and other institutions of learning. Was not Luther educated in a Catholic college? The Catholic Church is the mother of all Protestant denominations.

The Los Angeles minister concluded his sermon by asking this question: "Why should not these children give gratitude, respect and honor to that mother, who has done and is doing so much good for the world ? It will not hurt our Protestantism to be grateful."

THE MONITOR (1903) — SPANISH LANDOWNERS IN CALIFORNIA

Even by the turn of the century, much had been written about the picturesque life among California's Spanish landowners during the days their herds roamed the vast expanses of the Golden State. The "Idyllic Life in California before the Gringo Came" was portrayed in a feature story for *The Monitor*, official Catholic newspaper for the Archdiocese of San Francisco, on March 21, 1903. Some excerpts of that essay are worth recalling.

> The golden era of Spanish occupancy in California dates from 1830 to 1835. It was the time when Richard Henry Dana visited the coast and the life that he told about in his *Two Years Before the Mast*. The Spanish owned nearly two–thirds of the whole State.
>
> The Spanish, with their herds and enormous stretches of fertile soil, were the most independent people alive. Each family lived in a sort of pastoral barony, dreaming in a soft climate, under cerulean skies, and amid more than plenty, practically cut off from the rest of the busy, ambitious world .
>
> Charles Dudley Warner has said that the days of the herds and Spanish life in California were the most picturesque in American history. In those days the rollicking steer was a mighty factor in affairs, for his was about the only visible means of support of his ease–loving, generous and dreamy Spanish owner. Several generations of the Spanish and their descendants failed to take advantage of the agricultural resources of the new El Dorado, except in a very limited and listless way.
>
> The history of the California 'beef critter' is an interesting one. He came in with the Franciscan missionaries in the latter part of the eighteenth century, and with the waxing of his numbers grew wild and long of horn.
>
> He it was that made possible the idyllic life so charmingly told about in pre–American times in California, when few worked, because it was really unnecessary, but put in most of their time taking life easily and unconsciously making a historical background for future efforts in fiction. He it was who laid the founda-

tion of colossal fortunes. Now the herds have gone, and so, too, have most of the Spanish fortunes built out of beef, hide and hoof.

From the days that the Franciscan monks brought to California a few cattle away around Cape Horn from their homes in Spain, and taught the native Indians how to become Christian herdsmen, to 1855. The increase in herds of the beasts was marvelous, notwithstanding the tens of thousands that were slaughtered every year.

In the Spanish days, when a man's herd increased so that it was too much bother to keep it together and provide grazing land, the owner allowed the stock to run wild, with the result that the animals lost all trace of domesticity and were extremely hard to round up.

There was probably never anywhere in the whole world such hospitality as the homes of the Spanish offered previous to the early sixties. There are hundreds of early pioneers now in California who tell of having visited at a Spanish *rancho* for weeks at a time when they were 'broke' and when they could not speak a word of Spanish or hold any conversation with the numerous hosts and hostesses.

But all this—the picturesqueness of the halcyon cattle days—passed away over thirty years ago. Money–making propositions took its place, and the *ranchos* of the proud, hospitable, non–commercial Spanish were absorbed by Americans and English.

Now the days of the big herds of cattle under the American regime are fast passing. The agriculturist has demonstrated the marvelous capabilities of the soil of California, and has taken many thousands acres formerly used for cattle purposes.

The railroads have cut through the immense valleys where King Steer roamed at will twenty years ago, and cities and towns have sprung up in the very heart of the best grazing land in the State.

SEÑORA CASTRO (1903) — EARLY CALIFORNIA

Upon completion of his duties as commandant of the Mexican forces at San Francisco *Presidio*, in 1824, Ignacio Martinez acquired a large grant of land once belonging to the *Rancho del Pinole*, near the present town bearing the family name.

Shortly after the turn of the century, a reporter from the local newspaper in Martinez, interviewed the only surviving member of the family, at her home on Escobar Street, in San Francisco. The eighty year old woman had a keen memory and provided some valuable glimpses into early California pastoral life. Several of the more interesting reflections of Señora Castro, excerpted from *The Monitor* in its issue of April 9, 1903, are here presented in edited form.

Long before the treaty was made with Mexico, California was occupied by a civilization which, though dif-

ferent from our own, was possibly preferable to it in some essential particulars. You are familiar with the history of the missions, in which the disciples of Junípero Serra labored for the conversion and civilization of the Indians.

The mode of living in California was exceedingly primitive up to 1820, the inhabitants being mostly half–caste natives who occupied the land instead of legally owning it. There were no roads. There was no means of saving timber, that used for building purposes being hewn from logs with axes by the Indians. There were no fireplaces or stoves, nor were any in use until introduced by American settlers in 1846.

Before the Gringo came there was not a great deal of bustling enterprise in this live, eager, restless young land of today, but there was more of comfort, plenty and genuine contentment than it will probably again enjoy. The lords of the great *ranchos* dwelt in houses of adobe, deep–walled, deep–galleried, warm in winter, delightfully cool in summer, which suited the exigencies of the climate perfectly.

These homes were the scene of a liberal hospitality. The wealth of the landowners was largely in their cattle, which ranged in great herds over the hills and through valleys now planted with rich vineyards and orchards. These animals commanded a good price and the cost of raising them was nominal.

Money came easily and was spent generously. The traveler was warmly welcomed to those early *haciendas;* he was entertained with a hospitality almost Arabian; if his horse was tired and worn out he was given a fresh steed, usually much more valuable than his own mount, and was sent on his way rejoicing.

It seems strange to consider the half–patriarchal social system under which the Californians lived during the Mexican regime. The system was semi–socialistic, and semi–feudal at the same time. If the rancher had more than enough for his needs and his neighbor had less than enough, the neighbor was welcome to help himself from the rancher's store and nobody thought of calling it stealing.

When my grandfather first came to this country the family went to the Santa Clara mission, the nearest church. Mind the distance? Ah, the country was a paradise in those days! A ride of sixty or seventy miles was a pleasure. When the old church, which still stands in Martinez, was first bought and made into a place of worship, the Spanish for miles around gathered there for Mass on Sundays. They rested in the afternoons and the younger people enjoyed a horse race and dance sometimes before going home.

Concluding her remarks, Señora Castro noted that "we have developed California's resources and opened wide the Golden Gate to the world's commerce. But are her sons and daughters the better for being ours? Have the lessons we have taught them been of good or evil import? If not, on us the burden lies and from us shall be exacted a full account of our stewardship."

JOHN GALLAGHER (1904) — REFLECTIONS ON SAN FRANCISCO

The Right Reverend John Gallagher, Bishop of the Australian See of Goulburn (now Canberra), had words of singular praise for San Francisco. His remarks, given to a reporter at Sydney, on February 5, 1904, were carried in newspapers during the early days of the following month.

The prelate, just returned from a twelve months' tour of the world, was asked what country made the greatest impression upon him during his travels. Swiftly and unhesitatingly came the answer, "America." Bishop Gallagher referred to the thousands of stories of material progress which he said were no exaggeration.

But has not this material progress, this commercial spirit, this hurry–scurry after dollars, this rapidly expanding greatness submerged her spiritual tendencies?

As far as the Catholic Church is concerned, I can say no—emphatically no, replied His Lordship. "I think the Catholic Church in America despite many difficulties and some leakage, is making more progress than in any other country.

And I am glad to add that this progress does not consist in the mere erection of churches; the greatest evidence of this progress is to be found, perhaps, in the system of intermediate education which the Church has established, especially, for girls, in academies and high schools. These educational establishments reach a level of excellence higher than that to be found attained by the Church in any other country.

Their parochial primary schools' education is also receiving a very large measure of development. In fact, over a million children are being educated under that system alone. And, just as we are accustomed in Australia to see the Press notifying the success of pupils from our parochial schools when brought into fair competition with the pupils of the richly endowed schools of the State, so in America the Church can claim similar educational triumphs.

There, as here, they are not subsidized in any way by the State, but do their work through the devotedness of the people.

The reporter asked Bishop Gallagher if the Americans were as bitterly opposed to the principle of subsidizing private schools as a section of the Austrialian people are.

I must admit that the prejudice which operates against us here is still strong among certain sections in the United States. But a strong sympathy for the Catholic body is steadily growing among the public of America. Some of the best educators and broad minded legislators are in full sympathy with a grant of some kind to Catholic schools, for the exceeding merit of their work is a matter of constant comment.

I happened to be in San Francisco during Holy Week, and I can assure you that I was edified by what I saw. As you know Dr. Higgins, Dean Slattery and I were together, and the remark that passed between us in friendly conversation was that we had never in Australia nor, as far as our memory went, in Dublin, or any part of Ireland, seen greater evidence of practical Catholicity than those that fell under our observation in the city of San Francisco.

As an example, I need only refer to the number going to Communion on Holy Thursday and Easter Sunday. During the whole of those days, at every Catholic church in the city, there were perpetual streams of people pouring in and out of the doors.

B. FLORIAN HAHN (1904) — CHAMPION OF THE INDIANS

Father B. Florian Hahn was a champion and defender of Indians in the years before such apostolic activity was popular. The following descriptive account of conditions among the Indians at Saint Boniface Indian School, in Banning, is excerpted from a letter Father Hahn sent to *The Monitor*, in 1904.

The real truth is that there is much suffering and destitution among the Indians in Southern California. This fact has been repeatedly reported to the Government officials, albeit very little has been done by them.

The Government has barrels of money for its non–sectarian schools. Just now one hundred thousand dollars is being expended at the Riverside school (Sherman Institute); the new sewage system there will cost another one hundred thousand dollars. And if the money spent on football, baseball, railroad and electric car trips, ice cream parties, dances, etc, were wisely distributed there would not be any hungry relative of the Government schools' pupils.

Why does not the Government give one hundred and sixty acres of land to each Indian family? White citizens are given that much by way of homestead. The officials are forever quarreling with the Indians on the land question and lately the Agent threatened the desert Indians, saying if they did not accept twenty acres in severality the Government would compel them to accept any amount the authorities saw fit.

Then let us consider the Government's failure to suppress or control vice. The Indians here have a well defined moral sense; they well know the difference between right and wrong, and they recognize the difference between precept and example.

Were they managed firmly and charitably, much could be done for their moral well being. Instead, the Agent employs as chief of police a man living in an adulterous union; another policeman is an *emancipado*.

The whole Indian service is wanting, to say the least. Pala has not been a success, and never will be under the present system, still the Government is doing more for the Pala Indians than it has done for any other tribe in the vicinity. There is a good Agent on the place and a large school.

Work has been given to the Indians. But it is questionable whether a model reservation will be built up. The fifty houses on the place were bought in the East and hauled on freight car to California! It was stated that the price for each house was three hundred dollars; one hundred dollars for the house and two hundred dollars freight on each edifice!

The Indian land is one, two or three miles from the village—how are they to care for their crops at so great a distance from their dwellings? The Government undoubtedly tried to do its best for the Pala Indians but the ways of the Indian Department are surely beyond comprehension.

There are some Indian villages in San Diego county where dire poverty exists. Formerly these unfortunates were given medical and other assistance from the Government, but no physician has visited them for five years. They may blame their present neglect largely to a preacher in Southern California who reported that the Mission Indians were well–to–do and thriving. From henceforth the Government stopped issuing proper rations to the needy.

As you know, I have had many year's experience among the Indians of California and I would respectfully suggest the following to the officials concerned:

Give to each Indian family, and to each single man, one hundred and sixty acres of land; give to each indigent person unable to support himself, two rations a month (three dollars worth of provisions is a ration here); encourage the young strong man to stay at home and help support his hungry kinsfolk; appoint a decent force of policemen—men who will prevent the sale of liquor and not sell it themselves; send the strong young women and men above the age of twenty, who are at the Government schools, home to help their people.

Were these measures taken and enforced with justice and common sense the Indian problem in Southern California would cease to vex.

AN "ENGLISH PRIEST" (1904) — THE OLD MISSIONS

An interesting European glance of the missionary foundations along *El Camino Real* was published in *The Monitor* for April 30, 1904. The unidentified author, referred to only as an "English Priest," wrote his observations from Liverpool.

Arriving in San Francisco, the capital [*sic*] of California, the traveler finds much to see. This is a cosmopolitan city, a seaport that fronts on Asia and takes its tribute from the regions north and south as well—from Puget Sound, from treasure–laden Alaska, from Hawaii, from Mexico, from Central America, and the thriving nations of the West Coast of South America.

However it is not San Francisco I am to write about, but a more congenial subject—the Old Missions of California. From San Francisco to San Diego, a distance of nearly six hundred miles, the traveler rides on the Coast line of the Southern Pacific Railway through an atmosphere of religious romance.

The whole road was traversed more than a century and a quarter ago by sandaled Spanish priests, and it is now overhung by memories of a strange and romantic past.

The Franciscans who came from the sunny land of Spain called the trail they made on foot through the wilderness *El Camino Real*—the Royal Road, or less literally, the King's Highway, and along it, a day's walking journey apart, they planted the Old Missions, the last monuments of their heroic faith and laborious work.

Along that highway now run the gleaming rails of steel, and the traveler of today rides by these monuments of the past in as many hours as the good monks of old took days to cover the same distance.

The quaint structures which they built are many of them now unoccupied. The first mission was established by Father Junípero Serra, the pioneer missionary at San Diego, in 1769, in the extreme southern part of New Spain, which is now California, having been annexed by the United States in 1846.

The last mission was founded by the Franciscans, north of San Francisco, at Sonoma, in 1823. It is the mission of San Francisco Solano—the twenty–first and last link of a glorious chain. God alone, Who knows all things, knows what good was done by the sons of St. Francis among the Indians in the long–gone past.

The Franciscans who founded those missions and raised the buildings with the aid of convert Indians were men of courage, of indomitable energy, and were under the necessity of inventing a building material called adobe, which is like the material of the mud wall cabins of Ireland, but made in slabs, and built up like bricks. With this they built the massive walls, the graceful towers, and the long lines of arched cloisters and colonnades.

The immensity of this work is still apparent even in its ruins, and the difficulties under which the founders toiled are seen today in the rawhide thongs which did duty in place of nails, binding braid and rafter to beam, the beams being smoothed by being dragged by ropes down the mountain side, where they were roughly hewn.

The above buildings are all that is ancient in California: 'a remnant of the wealth and prime, with the halcyon grace around them, of the dreamy Spanish time.'

They amply repay study, and with their old–time beauty, their quaint surroundings, and legendary lore draw thousands of visitors to California.

✛THOMAS J. CONATY (1905) — INDIAN AFFAIRS IN SOUTHERN CALIFORNIA

Early in 1905, Bishop Thomas J. Conaty released a statement containing his views about the remaining Mission Indians in the Diocese of Monterey–Los Angeles. The following excerpt is taken from *The Monitor* for February 11th:

In Southern California, "there are four thousand Catholic Indians distributed in several reservations. There are two Indian schools maintained by the Catholic Church; one, the industrial at Banning, with one hundred and fifteen children, and one at San Diego, Old Mission, with sixty children."

These schools are presided over by clergymen and taught by the Sisters of St. Joseph. The Indian Bureau, (Bureau of Catholic Indian Missions) through general annual contributions in our churches, and contributions from Mother Katherine Drexel, maintain these schools which cost $30,000 per year.

The missions among the Indians reaching to all the reservations in the diocese, as well as the schools, are cared for by seven priests, whose maintenance and support come from diocesan funds.

The Government policy for the past year of having the Catholic children of the Indian schools cared for in their spiritual development by the Catholic Church has necessitated considerable expense, and the creation of a church and parsonage outside the Sherman Institute has been provided for from our diocesan treasury. Father [Cornelius] O'Brien, the priest in charge, has at present two hundred and forty–eight Catholic Indian children whose religious instruction is cared for by him and such is the case in all the different reservations in Southern California.

I make this statement in order that the public may see how strenuously we have striven to do our duty to our Indian people and their children and we are doing it at considerable expense, while not one cent of Government money reaches the Catholic Church for the benefit of the Catholic Indian Missions of Southern California, and the same is true of Northern California.

The study of conditions among our California Indians is most important as well as interesting. Visiting the different reservations, as I have, hearing the reports from those in charge of them, I feel keenly the small results that come from the labor done.

Much is being done to remedy many of the existing abuses and I feel satisfied that it needs the cooperation of all good people to work out a solution of these Indian problems, and to bring to these people some measure of improvement and contentment.

Many of them are noble souls who appreciate very

Bishop Thomas J. Conaty

keenly the kindness done, but in the breasts of many there rankles a very bitter feeling of the wrongs committed against them.

We are, on our part, striving to do our duty to those who are bound to us by their Catholic faith and in no way do we interfere with those who differ from us in religious principles. We are striving to do our duty to our own and we are glad to see others do their duty to their own.

As Catholics we ask no favors from the Government as such, but we also ask that there be no discrimination against us because we are Catholics. Those who know us best have always recognized our ability and willingness to do the duty of loyal citizens in all the affairs of Government.

The Bishop of Monterey–Los Angeles concluded his observations by noting that "it seems to any fair–minded man that Indians who are Catholics ought to be guaranteed their conscience rights just as well as any other people in the land." Bishop Conaty was thus championing "human rights" decades before the current popularity and awareness of such campaigns.

WILLIAM McDERMOTT HUGHES (1910) — MISSION INDIANS

There hovers about the old missions of California a halo of romance and heroism. The ancient adobe churches were artistic to a wonderful degree even though they were built by unskilled Indian workmen under the direction of priests scarcely more fit by training for such a task than their red-skinned neophytes. The thousands of savages converted to ways of peace and progress, the long journeys afoot or on horseback into the mountains to win new converts are among the features of California life which will always appeal to man's sense of romance, beauty and heroic faith.

The question occasionally arises about the final disposition of those people who once inhabited the area's earliest foundations. According to an account of a missionary, written in 1910, "the graves where lie their fathers are scarcely more silent than the footfall of their Indian children in the missions which their fathers built." Father William Hughes (1880–1939) reported that the natives, whose numbers had dwindled in Southern California to 3,000, were robbed by the early governors, dispossessed by secularization and denied protection by the American government. Ultimately they had been "driven to the mountains or forced out on the desert, where the coyote's howl is more welcome than the white man's voice."

Recognizing the plight of the Indians, the Church, with the solicitude which the mission *padres* learned at her knee, continued to send forth missionaries to the burning desert and the cold mountain–top to seek out the scattered sheep lest they perish without a shepherd. The Sacramento–born priest described the circuit of missionary posts under his charge, pointing out the necessity of riding about 200 miles on horseback. This journey had to be completed between Sundays, lest one or more of the six towns in the valley be deprived of its monthly Mass.

Great as were the problems he encountered in crossing the mountains, fording the rivers and traversing the desert, Father Hughes regarded it as "nothing compared to what hundreds of priests in early California days underwent." The indefatigable missionary to the Sobobas, Cahuillas and Cayotes recorded the vicissitudes of one day's encounters after leaving San Jacinto.

> The first mission is five hours by horse over the shortest trail. At the summit, where the trail divides, the two demons, Darkness and Fog, overtook me, covering my eyes (as the Indians would say) from both the little traveled trail and the mountain peaks, which serve as landmarks.
>
> Fully realizing that I had hopelessly lost my way, I calmly cast about in the fast–falling darkness and fog, to find a spot on which to rest my weary body. The poor pony was supperless. So was I. He might be hobbled, but the grass was short, even here in the mesa, at the head of the trail, which furnishes Cahuilla all of the pasturage for its cattle.
>
> A likely place was found for a camp. A fire was soon kindled with *manzanita* wood torn by hand from the river bank. The sandy bed of the river—it was an *arroyo seco*—was as dry as the desert. Here a hole, long and wide enough for a bed, and six inches deep, was made, and a fire built in it. When the wood was reduced to coals, it was covered with a layer of sand deep enough to retain the heat and yet not to burn. The device is a familiar one among the Indians. Reclining upon this improvised bed, I placed over me the saddle blankets, now thoroughly dried by the fire.
>
> With the saddle as a pillow, a good night's rest was enjoyed. In the morning it was not hard to get one's bearings and to reach Cahuilla in time to say Mass for the waiting Indians.

While admitting that the apostolate among the Indians was "frought with considerable personal discomfort to the missionary," Father Hughes looked upon such hardships as giving "an encouraging feeling of kinship with those truly heroic men on whom first fell the trials and to whom is now accorded the glory of the greatest work of religion in the United States, the Indian missions of early California."

ROCKWELL D. HUNT (1911) — TRIBUTE TO FRAY JUNÍPERO SERRA

Fray Junípero Serra's place in the annals of history does not rely solely or even predominately on the writings of Catholics. Secular historians such as Rockwell D. Hunt (1868–1966) also recognized the Mallorcan friar as a man of singular destiny.

A native Californian, Dr. Hunt served for many years as Professor of History at the University of Southern California. He authored many works on the state's history, including a biography of John Bidwell.

Professor Hunt's portrayal of Serra is here taken from *New California the Golden* (Sacramento, 1937), an updated version of the 1911 edition which was published by the California State Department of Education.

> Through all time Fray Junípero Serra will be remembered as California's 'Knight of the Cross.' He stands supreme among those pioneer Christian missionairies from Spain whose high courage and sublime faith made possible the occupation of Alta California.
>
> With Junípero, friendship was a master passion. The affectionate attachment which he early formed for Francisco Palou and other friends was never permitted to wane in later life. His loving devotion to the Indian converts in the California mission was as constant as the north star, as fervent as the southern sun.
>
> After his student days in the Majorca convent, Serra earned the title of doctor and became a professor of theology. But never for a moment was his ardor for mission work dampened despite the strict routine of the monastery and the years of delay. His soul was on fire with unquenchable zeal—New Spain was ever before him as a goal.
>
> In 1749 Serra and his companions were granted per-

mission to join a company of missionaries about to embark for Vera Cruz. This opportunity meant the turning point in his life work.

The difficult voyage to Mexico occupied ninety–nine days. Serra proceeded at once to the City of Mexico, eager for his work in the New World. Then followed nineteen years of unflagging labors in founding missions and preaching in Mexico. But what he deemed the great work of his life lay still before him.

Serra was fifty–six years of age when his supreme opportunity came. Not until after the suppression of the Jesuits in 1767 was the way fully opened. We can imagine something of the holy joy that flooded his soul when he received his appointment as Father–President and his commission, giving him control of the religious forces which were to occupy Alta Calfornia. All his life he had been preparing for such an opportunity and now he embraced it with sacred rapture and yet with humble gratitude, unable for a time to speak for his tears.

The years of the first Father–President of the Franciscan Missions of California were years of ceaseless toil and struggle and of unbelievable sacrifice, all endured with surpassing fortitude and crowned with heroic achievement. There seemed no limit to his endurance, no bound to his desires, nothing daunted his courage or chilled his faith.

His soul was ever serene, apparently superior to the physical suffering that was constantly his. To baptize the simple natives into the Christian faith was his consuming passion; to feel that he had saved a soul from death filled him with unutterable joy. To him religion was everything; his outstanding traits were humble sincerity, godly zeal and utter consecration.

At seventy years of age, lame, weary, scarcely belonging to this world, he made for the last time the loving pilgrimage on foot along the trails that we know as *El Camino Real*, from San Diego to his dear Monterey, not failing to turn aside into the Indian *rancherias* to bestow comfort upon his many loving disciples.

It was his last long journey—his labors had come to an end. On the afternoon of August 28, 1784, the tolling of the mission bell at Carmelo announced his death to the grief–stricken poeple. Of all the tributes paid to him none was more touching than the tears of his adoring Indian converts.

ALICE J. STEVENS (1911) — THE OLD MISSION

Among the early apologists for the Franciscan missionary conquest was Alice J. Stevens (1860–1947), one–time editor of *The Tidings*. On March 28, 1911, Alice Stevens addressed the Knights of Columbus in their new club rooms at 107 North Spring Street, on "The California Missions in Literature." Miss Stevens said, in part:

While the lofty mountains and fertile valleys of our Golden State have been a source of inspiration to some of the really great writers of the west, whose work will live so long as men love the handiwork of God; and while the mining days, with their attendant hardships have been portrayed in song and story by virile pens, no theme in the entire west replete with romantic interest, has so gripped the heartstrings and fired the souls of all classes of writers, good, bad and indifferent, as have the old, historic missions of California. Their spirit breathes in our literature and their influence is impressed upon our western art.

To the commercial citizen they appeal as a stock in trade to promote business enterprises, as he exploits them as a drawing card for the tourists. He never spoils what he considers a good story for the sake of the truth, but by deviating from the truth he invariably spoils a better story than the best that a distorted fancy possibly could picture.

Our book stores are filled with literary junk dealing with the subject of the missions, purporting to depict life and scenes incident to the days of their greatest glory, written by authors whose sole aim seems to have been to weave a cobweb of fiction around a sacred subject whose character they were utterly incapable of comprehending, in order that they themselves might pose as western writers with the stamp of the dollar mark to measure the merits of their work.

Others have even stooped to lower depths of degradation in this line, and utilized the pictures of the old missions for trade marks. What a sacrilege! A law should be enacted prohibiting such desecration.

There is another kind of writer who, unintentionally, does quite as much harm, and that is the undependable and indefensible enthusiast, who skims along the surface of things, weaves a tale from the fabric of dreams, clothes it in beautiful flowers of rhetoric and sends it out into the world with a message wholly at variance with actual conditions and yet founded upon just enough fact to give it the semblance of truth. The pens of such writers must be muzzled. They are too superficial to delve deeply into the subject, and they impose upon the lack of authentic information of their readers.

To artists the old missions appeal in diverse ways. To some they are a "study," to others they have a higher meaning, but at least it is a matter for commendation that the average artist possesses sufficient of the artistic temperament to adhere to the lines of the subject.

In architectural art, the missions have afforded an abundant source of inspiration for purely typical California buildings, although what is generally accepted as the mission style often bears but slight resemblance to the original.

But there is a spirit pervading these missions which eludes commercialism and defies materialism, and unless that spirit rests, upon the pen of those who tell the story or depict the glory of the old missions of California, they will labor in vain, and that is the same spirit which prompted their building, a deeply religious spirit which seeks but the glory of God and the salvation of souls, the spirit of the Catholic Church and its Divine Founder abiding with it.

In conclusion, Miss Stevens said that "as long as time and the elements shall spare these missions, they will ever stand as the concrete embodiment of a living faith, and those that would seek to incorporate into an enduring literature the spirit of the missions must be inspired by the same faith that prompted their buildings. These old missions, even those whose ruins are the abode of bats and birds, are yet the most priceless possessions that California can claim as her own."

CHARLES PHILLIPS (1912) — THUMBNAIL SKETCHES OF CALIFORNIA

During the fall of 1912, Charles Phillips, editor of *The Monitor*, asked some of the foremost Catholic journalists and diplomats in the United States and Europe to submit "thumbnail" sketches about California for the Christmas issue of his newspaper. Here are some of their replies:

Humphrey J. Desmond, editor and publisher of the *Catholic Citizen*, the *New Century* and the *Catholic Journal of the South* said: "We must look to the West for the ideas and tendencies which will best enable us to forecast the future of this country. Not in the oligarchy–ridden south, not in the factory feudalism of New England, are nation–wide social and political movements cradled. But in the West—out on the Pacific Slope. Free men, sun–crowned, will come to us from the soil that still nurtures the Big Trees."

Archibald McLean of the Buffalo *Catholic Union and Times* replied by saying that friends and travellers return "with such glowing stories of the wonders of your city (San Francisco) and your state that we are filled with envy."

Father William P. Cantwell, editor of the Trenton, New Jersey *Monitor* gave this as his resume of the west: "Physically—vastness and variety—beauty in streaks; politically–fadsome, but earnest and honest; in business—wide awake and energetic; socially—honestly and rather effusively hospitable to strangers . . . vastly more interesting than their cousins of the East, strait–jacketed with society's customs and absurd monkey imitations of foreign snobbery; religiously—the Catholic Church alone answers fully the mighty summons of an eager, honest–hearted people for a religion worthy of the name."

The editor of the *Western Watchman* responded that "the front door of the greater United States will open out on the Pacific. The sovereignty of the East is doomed. San Francisco is destined to be the port of entry of the New World." He concluded by noting that Thomas Benton had said, a half century earlier, when pointing to the sun, "There lies the West."

Mr. Phillips also asked several American diplomats for their comments. Writing from Denmark, Maurice Francis Egan said that the people there look upon California as "a garden of wonders, and they scan the records closely to see how much butter and cheese she produces." They think of Californians "as a people of almost superhuman energy and capacity."

T. St. John Gaffney observed that "no part of America is better known in Europe or more highly as well as curiously regarded, than California; and no American city attracts more attention abroad, or excites more interest than San Francisco." He went on to say that "California has for some magic reason appealed at all times to Europeans as if it were quite another America, distinct from the America of Boston, New York and Chicago."

Writing from Switzerland, Dominic I. Murphy, speaking of those Europeans who are "travelled" said that those "who were fortunate enough to have visited the Pacific Coast, were enthusiastic over California. There they found a most genial atmosphere, delightful climate, charming landscapes and glimpses of orange groves and vineyards."

WILLIAM McDERMOTT HUGHES (1913) — TRIBUTE TO BISHOP THOMAS CONATY

Bishop Thomas J. Conaty (1847–1915) was a great champion for the descendants of the Golden State's original inhabitants. In a report submitted to the Bureau of Catholic Indian Missions in 1913, Father William McDermott Hughes referred to the Bishop of Monterey–Los Angeles as the "Apostle of the California Indians." In part, his report reads as follows:

When the monument to the memory of Padre Junípero Serra was dedicated recently in San Diego, generous reference was made to Bishop Conaty as the successor of the great *Presidente*. But I wonder how many who heard him applauded, really understood how truly the militant Bishop is the successor to the missionary *Padre*.

How many there present knew that the Bishop has raised more than ten monuments dearer to the heart of that priest and truer symbols of his faith, than the cross itself which marks the site of the first mission in San Diego.'

Truer than the cross is the cross–crowned church where the sacrifice of the cross is enacted daily. Dearer than the cross are the Indian souls redeemed by the cross, the souls which gather from the desert sands and the mountain rocks to worship in the chapels which Bishop Conaty has provided for the Indians in his diocese.

Ask the Indians themselves who is their living *Padre Junípero*. Ask the Sisters that are laboring unobserved at Banning with one hundred and twenty Indian children who it is adds to their supernatural motive the strongest human sympathy.

Or, ask the priests who ride the lonesome trail to the Indian camps, who lightens their labors and sweetens their burdens by understanding their hardships and attempting to provide both means and words of encouragement. They will answer: "Bishop Conaty."

Humanly speaking the figure that towers above the living missions in California is the bishop. Humanly speaking, I say, because it is the spirit of Christ he breathes and inspires and it is the person of Christ he reflects and represents.

The inspired writer has sung the praise of the beauty of them that bring the gospel of peace. Just praise of the messenger does not diminish but rather enhances the glory of the message.

The contentment of the priests on Indian missions is the striking fruit of the California field. They feel that Indian missions are held in honor here as they should be everywhere; that it is not alone in the glorious but dead past but also to the living and present that honor is paid.

It is not of themselves they think so much as of the souls to be saved. They are jealous of these souls. They wish that these shall be held in the same priceless value with the souls of white men.

Well, what if missionaries are a bit jealous of the bishop's appreciation They are very human. Their life, the primitive people and the silent wilderness make them more human, more sensitive to sympathy and encouragement. They feel the greater need, too, of a stronger brother's aid to hold up their weary arms while the battle wages.

There is a marked personal devotion to the bishop, a fealty, in the service of the priests of this diocese. But nowhere are the proofs of it stronger than among the Indian missionaries.

ROGER BAUDIER (1914)—YOSEMITE

Of all the country's national parks, Yosemite is easily the most popular. Each year, visitors throng to the area in record numbers. The quantity of literature about Yosemite is extensive enough to fill two large bibliographies.

One of the early reflections about Yosemite was written by Roger Baudier, a teacher at Watsonville's Saint Francis Orphan Asylum, after his visit in 1914. It is here excerpted from a neatly–written, four page journal in the archives for the Archdiocese of New Orleans.

On July 7th, Baudier, a seminarian from Santa Barbara, and a forty–two year old Frenchman set out for their trek. The trio were accompanied by an aging horse that Baudier purchased in Santa Cruz and renamed Han-nibal. The trip was a rugged, outdoor adventure for the two young men and their older companion. They traveled just over 500 miles in thirty–one days, mostly on foot. They camped out under mulberry trees, along rivers and in abandoned houses.

The travelers passed through several scattered small towns on the way to and from Yosemite. Merced was "a fine little town with tree–shaded, paved streets, a fine courthouse, park and busy business quarters" as well as a railroad depot.

Coulterville, on the other hand, was a "dying town" that had suffered three fires which helped reduce the population from 3,000 to 250. San Felipe consisted of one barroom, one barn and two houses, while Los Banos was "a thriving, ambitious little center."

Baudier jotted down his impressions of the rugged scenery: the "dry, parched, brown hills" around Mountain House; the "miserable, flat, swampy country" at the San Joaquin River; the "fine mountain scenery" and abandoned gold mine on the approach to Coulterville; the "rough, steep, zigzagging trail" to the summit of Yosemite Falls; and the "splendid panorama" from Glacier Point.

He noted that the old road from Hazel Green to Bower's Cove was the same one that Indians and oxen had used in the 1850s. Baudier's box camera captured some of the rugged beauty described in the journal.

The trio met a few travelers on the way to and from Yosemite; a hostile Dane at San Luis Ranch who "growled because our horse was hitched in front of his domicile," two strangers at Hazel Green who shared a pan of fried potatoes and Father Jerome Enright who preached a good "simple sermon" to the small tourist community at Yosemite Village.

The return trip from Yosemite to Watsonville was agonizing for the three adventurers. Baudier and Castell both came down with malaria and had to allow Hannibal to pull them in the rickety wagon. On July 31, Baudier wrote: "so tired and out of spirit that Edward Poetzl and I ate out of the same bowl to avoid washing dishes and work." They tried to avoid the intense heat by walking through the San Joaquin Valley at night.

When the exhausted pilgrims reached Los Banos the following day, they made a "bee–line" for the nearest saloon "and feebly asked for something to drink." The weary travelers finally marched into Watsonville on the afternoon of August 6. Baudier and Castell both needed a doctor while Hannibal was so worn out that he had to be shot.

Each night during the trip, Baudier sat by candlelight and recorded the day's main events and his own impressions: the number of miles traveled; impressions of towns people and mountain scenery; personal weariness, discomfort and delight; and the newspaper accounts of the ominous outbreak of war in Europe. He even noted his dream of tarantulas after one "spooked" the trio by crossing their outdoor table.

✢EDWARD J. HANNA (1916) — ARCHBISHOP LOOKS AHEAD

Among the more notable of the many sermons delivered by the erudite Archbishop Edward J. Hanna of San Francisco is the one he gave for the silver jubilee ceremonies of Saint Mary's Cathedral, on Van Ness Avenue, in 1916. Always a fascinating orator, Hanna drew, in masterly strokes, the picture of a greater city and a more magnificent cathedral in the future. The following excerpts indicate the versatile genius of an outstanding American churchman.

We belong to a young, a vigorous race, and we feel that the Church of today is little when compared to the glory of the Church that is to come, and the vision of the future holds us as we gather here to tell the story of the past. Ours, indeed, has been a glorious past, the glory of the Missions that brought unto this land religion and civilization; the glory of the Argonauts, who blazed the trail that we have followed; the glory of our fathers whose bigness and whose generosity have passed into proverb; the glory of the city with its romance, its spell, its charms.

But, oh, how little will all this appear to him who unrolls the mightier vision of the future! Ours is a chosen land, a blessed land. Our mountains contain treasures that would enrich a whole world; our valleys, teeming with fertility, can sustain hundreds and hundreds of millions.

We are in the seat of an empire, and we reign over land and sea. Around the ocean that washes our shores dwell almost three–fourths of the human race, and in this vast empire we have a dominant place; the men of the Orient are just stirring into life, and of their awakening, and of their power, who can tell?

In our magnificent harbor the navies of the earth can ride at anchor, and freighted with the riches of our vast country, the ships of the world must come and go. And all we need are men, men of intelligence, men of firmness, men of faith, men of strong moral fibre, men loyal unto truth.

If we are true to our American traditions of simple life, traditions of high–minded dealing, traditions of self– sacrifice, traditions of courage and bravery, if we are, above all things, faithful to the teachings of Holy Mother Church and her higher moralities, true to the Church to which this land of God owes so much, then here must arise an Empire by the Pacific wave of which no man can tell the greatness.

In this new kingdom, at the world's edge, the great Church to which we belong will ever have a mighty influence, for it teaches those things unto men which make for a vigorous manhood, which make for the possession of what is best in life, which must ever make for greatness, yea, and for stability, and while it teaches it also gives strength for realization,

And when our dream of Empire is realized, then unto Jesus the King, will arise from the heights of the City of St. Francis a cathedral worthy of His name, worthy of Serra and his noble band, worthy of the men of the past, the mighty men of pioneer days, worthy of the best traditions of art and of architecture of the great old Church, worthy of our place among the cities of the world, worthy of the grandeur and the glory of San Francisco, that in splendor and magnificence will reign as Queen over the Empire around the Western Sea.

✢LAWRENCE SCANLAN (1916) — CATHOLIC CHURCHMAN IN UTAH

Shortly after Bishop Lawrence Scanlan's demise on May 10, 1915, the following article, here digested, appeared in *All Hallows Annual*, the publication of Ireland's famous Vincentian missionary seminary.

Forty–six years ago, on June 24th, 1868, Lawrence Scanlan was ordained a priest in this College. From every point of view, he promised to be a splendid missionary. In physical fitness, intellectual vigor, and moral strength of character, none of his contemporaries surpassed him. He was tall, athletic, and powerfully built— a leader in all the games, and a keen pedestrian. He possessed an acute, logical mind that loved discussion, a wonderful facility in mastering languages, and such a capacity for acquiring and assimilating knowledge that, as years advanced, he seemed to be well–informed on every subject, no matter how remote from his professional studies.

Such was the young Tipperary priest who, soon after his arrival in America, was appointed to the wild mining settlements of Pioche, in the year 1869. Pioche was situated about four hundred miles from the nearest railroad. Its population consisted of adventurers. The toughest characters in the West had congregated there. Each man was a law unto himself. Father Scanlan's efforts to lessen the depravity of the place soon got him into trouble. But he kept up the fight and won. One afternoon big Dan O'Leary approached him and said: "Father, you have conquered us. We all admire your pluck. We'll all be with you next Sunday."

When he left the camp in 1874 he was loved by every man, woman and child in Pioche, and every one of them signed so strong a protest against his removal that the Archbishop of San Francisco postponed his departure.

About the middle of 1874, Archbishop Alemany was called upon to supply a priest for the mission of Salt Lake, Utah. It was a parish of 85,000 square miles in extent. One church only graced that immense territory, the old brick church on Second East Street. Only a man possessed of extraordinary physical health and strength and zeal could hope to cope with the difficulties of the situation. In looking over the list of his priests, one figure stood out among all the rest—the young giant of Pioche fame. Scanlan gladly acquiesced, and Utah won the services of one of the most exemplary missionary priests in the annuals of the Church in America.

From that day in July, 1873, until late in the nineties Bishop Scanlan's life was one long and ceaseless effort to organize Catholicity in Utah. Even today the diocese is territorially the roughest and the most difficult to govern wisely of all the dioceses in the United States.

Between Salt Lake City and Ogden there were, perhaps, ninety Catholics, while the entire census for Utah, with its 85,000 square miles, scarcely numbered 800. Father Scanlan's labours in those early years were truly herculean. He was constantly on horseback, travelling hundreds and even thousands of miles, from one mining settlement to another, entering into the thoughts and lives of the humblest folk, founding missions, and erecting churches and schools and various charitable institutions.

His energy and zeal, his perseverance and prudence, were rewarded with success. The Catholics increased in numbers and influence; and in 1887 the Holy Father appointed him Bishop over the vast territory of Utah and a portion of Nevada.

For almost thirty years he ruled the Diocese of Salt Lake City, with results which today astonish the visitor from the Eastern States. "Words," said Cardinal Farley, "fail to convey the impressions I carried away with me on leaving Salt Lake City. The fine spirit of the Catholic population, their cordial relations with their non–Catholic brethren, the imposing edifice which rivals any of the cathedrals of the land, the institutions of charity and mercy reared under a wise and active administration—all these filled me with a sense of admiration and have been a source of inspiration to me."

His death was as edifying as his life was blameless. His whole life was a preparation for the final dissolution. He retained his faculties to the end. Whilst the last prayers for his parting soul were being said, he held up his hand for the ring to be placed on his finger, and in less than three minutes, without any struggle, he peaceably passed away.

JOHN STEVEN McGROARTY (1915) — HARBOR OF THE SUN

One of the most beautifully phrased essays ever published about San Diego was written in 1915 by John Steven McGroarty, for the illustrated quarterly, *The Kingdom of the Sun*. It is here reproduced in digest form, for the edification of a new generation of Californians.

The place of San Diego de Alcalá, the Harbor of the Sun, is the Place of First Things, where California began. It was the first American harbor—as the United States is now constituted—to hail a white man's sail, as it was the first port on the Pacific to greet and welcome the ships of the mighty armada that sailed from Hampton Roads, under command of the Fighting Admiral on that epoch–making day of December 16, 1908. Here was reared on Americas western shores the first cross: here the first church was built, and the first town. It was here too, that sprang from primeval wastes the first cultivated field, the first palm, the first vine and the first olive tree to blossom into fruitage beneath a wooing sun from the life–giving waters of the first irrigation ditch.

And here, also, was flung to the winds of conquest in the West, the first American flag. The Harbor of the Sun will still be first, through the centuries to come, to greet the ships that sail from India or cleave the continents in twain with eager prows through Panama.

San Diego is very old in history, yet very young in destiny. She looks back on a past that stretches nearly four hundred years into the now dim and misty pathways of civilization. She knew the white man's wandering ships before Columbus was much more than cold in his grave. Her tiled rooftrees and her Christian shrines sang to the crooning tides before the Declaration of Independence was signed and before Betsy Ross wove from summer rainbows and wintry stars the miracle of Old Glory.

Yet upon the ruins of a past hallowed and sacred and great with the memories of strong men, San Diego thrills today with youth as lusty as the youth of Hercules. Where once rocked the galleons of the Spanish explorers now anchor the mighty leviathan burden–bearers of all the seas. In the canyons of the giant hills from which crept the uncertain streams that watered Junípero Serra's first Mission fields are now stored reservoirs of water that would care for San Diego though she were twice her present size, and though never a drop of rain were to fall for a thousand nights and a thousand days.

We do not wonder that San Diego lures the wanderer and the traveler from every land, as well by the charm of her wondrous beauty and her gateways to opportunity as by the glamor and fascination of a past rich in romance as a lover's dream. For it was upon the glinting waters of San Diego's Harbor of the Sun, and upon her shining hills, that our California of today drew its first breath of life and ventured its first uncertain footstep on the long road to power and fame and greatness.

It would be impossible to tell how many tourists have visited California since the traffic was commenced, but the fact is well established that it was to San Diego that the first tourists came. It was very long ago—nearly three and three quarter centuries have passed since then, in fact. They remained six days, had a most delightful time, according to their own accounts, and were doubtless afterward sorry as all tourists always are that they did not stay longer.

This was the voyage from Mexico—the "New Spain" of those days—of Juan Rodriguez Cabrillo, "brave old Cabrillo of the ships." It marked the first successful attempt to carry out the exploration of the fabled land to the north which red–handed Cortez and his successors believed to be India, not knowing it was richer and more beautiful country. So, on a golden morning of September, 1542, Cabrillo and his swart sailormen steered their two brave little wind–jammers, the *San Salvador* and the *Victoria*, into San Diego's Harbor of the Sun. Never before had the eyes of Caucasian man looked upon it; wherefore the name of Juan Rodriguez Cabrillo became immortal. Never shall time blot out his name, or the memory of his name, until God shall call back the sea and the last chanty is sung. Yonder, northward on the Golden Coast, somewhere on an island that hears the Mission bells of Santa Barbara, in the hush and quiet of Sabbath mornings, he sleeps the last, long sleep, heedless of passing sail and singing tide. And so God rest him, the immortal Portuguese who was first to "put San Diego on the map."

In all the world there is no more beautiful estuary than the Bay of San Diego. It was in the gladness of His dreams God made it when he fashioned our beautiful earth and flung it from the hollow of His hand through myriad meteors and the shimmering tracery of the stars. You have but to look at your map of the globe to grasp instantly the fact that San Diego Bay was intended by nature to be one of the most magnificent of harbors. On all the wide–flung pathways of the seas, since the Phoenician ventured them, never has prow sought a safer haven from the wind and storm.

Lying land–locked under the bluest of ever faithful skies, the navies of all the world might anchor within the twenty–two square miles of the harbor and still have room. Let commerce crowd its sunny gateway as it will, tomorrow and throughout all the tomorrows that are to be, there will still be place and more, within the gate, for all that come. When the argosies of the great ocean and all the oceans, and the masts of the seven seas, hastening through Panama, shall signal San Diego, as they must, she will beckon them to enter, no matter how many they may be, that they may find waiting the spoils of desert and plain and hill and valley to carry back with them to Europe and Africa the limitless Orient and far Cathay.

All this for him who dreams of conquest, of rearing wheels and smoking funnels, caravans and the trading marts. But they, nor those who would whip the seas with commerce and crowd the land with trade, can rob him who is but a dreamer of dreams, of San Diego. Still will break above the dear and lovely morning hills the glory of the dawn. Still will sunset's purple wrap in its royal robes the crooning waters, headland and cape and the long shores.

Peace will be there—peace and rest and infinite content breathed like balm on the waters and the circled clasp of bright lomas in the Harbor of the Sun. Men shall come to dream—each with what dream he loves the best—and if they go it shall be but to come again. In the heart of man there are two times of longing—the time of youth that longs for wealth and power, and time of retrospect when the soul grows wiser. And for these times and all times, the Harbor of the Sun waits with both a solace and a reward.

In the days to come—and they are coming thick and fast—San Diego will rank among the great cities of the world; no doubt of that. God made much land and still more sea, but He did not make many harbors that man can use handily. And when the engineer draws his calipers upon the maps, it is seen that what harbors there are have been placed where they ought to be.

And now as time advances the work of man to meet his needs, the Bay of San Diego comes to its own. Behind it lie the fertile hills, the great plains and the limitless desert made opulent by the irrigation ditch and canal. From these, even now, come teeming the wealth of farm and orchard and forest to find outlet and the waiting barter on the shores of the great ocean. Where rail and sail meet is the gateway of San Diego. The day when she depended on men to make her great is past, and the day has come when men depend on her to make them great.

The San Diego of tomorrow will be a place of crowding domes that will stretch upon the wide–flung uplands everywhere that eye can see. Ships shall come and go ceaselessly into her wondrous harbor, and she shall match the glory of Carthage and of Tyre that was of old.

Then, as now, men will journey far across many lands and many waters to look upon her beauty. Then as now men will come to her for peace or gain, each as his need may be. Nor shall her beauty fade or her glory vanish. What she has wrought and what she has won shall still be hers through all the centuries to be—the place where Padre Serra knelt; the Place of First Things that guards the Harbor of the Sun.

CHARLES FLETCHER LUMMIS (1918) — PRESERVING THE OLD MISSIONS

Charles Fletcher Lummis (1859–1928) was once described by *The Tidings* as "a fearless upholder of religious toleration, the staunch defender of the downtrodden and oppressed of every clime." As Americanist, conservationist, archaeologist and founder of the California Landmarks Club, Lummis gave much of his time, talent and inspiration to many worthwhile causes.

Following is an example of his forceful, direct writing when urging Californians to preserve their heritage. Written in pencil in his own hand about 1918, it was found among his papers by Dudley Gordon:

We have many calls upon our Patriotism. It is always bringing new duties—but never absolves us from the old. Like charity, it may cover the ends of the earth—but it begins at home.

We cannot point the finger at any soldiers who bombed a noble cathedral used as a fort by their enemies, if we in peace and fatness allow our own historic temples and monuments to be destroyed by the elements. Our vandalism is far less excusable than that of war—ours isn't 'military necessity' it's just laziness and stupidity.

The Old Missions of California are just as valuable to this state and this country as the cathedral at Rheims. They are more important to California than any monument in Europe. They are the largest material asset of the Golden State, as our foremost men of affairs admit. Artists and historians acknowledge they are the chiefest monuments of architecture, heroism and romance that the United States possesses.

No hostile armies are blowing them up—or we'd get out and fight. But the California rains are eating them down—and have been for half a century—and we sit around, vandals of carelessness and lavish our time, money and knitting on every other country but our own.

The Landmarks Club of California began 23 years ago. It has saved all that is left at the Missions San Diego, San Juan Capistrano, Pala and San Fernando; besides helping seriously, by money and influence, in saving many other landmarks.

It has just finished another $7,500 work of repair on the venerable (1797) church of San Fernando. The preservation of those great walls is the most remarkable feat of engineering ever done on a historic landmark in the United States.

It needs $1,500 more to tile the roof of San Fernando and finish the interior. We have our own kiln ready on the spot to burn the tiles for roof and floor, from the ancient claypit.

All the work of the Landmarks Club has been done by voluntary subscription.

These remarks are typical of Lummis, for to him "the old Missions are worth more money, are a greater asset to Southern California than our oil, our oranges, even our climate." And such words from a non–Catholic, in 1918, were forceful indeed!

✝JOSEPH S. GLASS, C.M. (1924)
TRIBUTE TO THE CHURCH

One of the most moving discourses ever heard in Saint Vibiana's Cathedral was that delivered on February 3, 1924, by the Right Reverend Joseph Sarsfield Glass (1874–1926). In that memorable panegyric, the Vincentian Bishop of Salt Lake described the Church as it rose from the catacombs, "a glorious Church without spot or wrinkle." In that atmosphere, "men were taught the value of human dignity and the splendor of their supernatural destiny, the family was reconstructed upon divine lines, and the state was made to know that its proper purpose and its greatest glory are the welfare and happiness of its people.

Forests were cleared, fields were planted, and the lovers of poverty, chastity and obedience, saving the literature and treasures of the past, worked magnificently to place society on its upward march toward culture, progress, learning and true civilization.

Everywhere throughout Europe the Church preached the message Peter brought to Rome. In all places and among all people the missionaries of Christ taught His doctrine, and gave evidence in their own saintly lives of its sublime, spiritual power. The Church grew and waxed strong, and there sprang up, as if by magic, churches and temples, and schools and monasteries.

With the Church and her divine influence came consciousness of the rights of man and the dignity of women; the weak were protected and the strong restrained; there was order and respect for authority; men learned to know liberty and to love justice, to grant mercy and to seek things spiritual.

Her elementary and cathedral schools and universities became the pride of nations, and her superb churches and cathedrals are the glory of the ages. She gave culture and refinement, she taught the arts and

Bishop Joseph S. Glass, C.M.

crafts, she encouraged painting and sculpture, she urged to greater endeavor the seekers after knowledge and the lovers of science; and many of the greatest and the most important scientific truths were imparted to the world by her children.

She saved the Bible and translated it before Luther's time into the languages of the people; she established the Truce of God, the right of asylum, and gave the world its age of chivalry.

Strong with the strength of Christ abiding in her, the Church resisted the onslaught of error and heresy, and stood imperishable amid the wreck and ruin of the so–called Reformation.

Unchanged and unchangeable in her divine constitution, she kept the deposit of faith untouched; and neither emperors nor kings, nor powers or principalities, nor the loss of nations could make her faithless to her divine commission.

Rationalism and materialism and the basest passions of mankind sought to destroy her; but after nineteen centuries, she stands supreme, the divinely–commissioned teacher in spiritual things, the Church as Christ founded her, preaching the same doctrines and administering the same sacraments as in the days of Peter.

In the words of Gladstone, she has marched for fifteen hundred years at the head of civilization and has harnessed to her chariot, as the horses of a triumphal car, the chief intellectual and material forces of the world.

Her greatness, glory, grandeur and majesty have been almost all that in these respects the world has had to boast of. Her children are more numerous than all the members of the sects combined; she is every day enlarging the boundaries of her vast empire.

Her altars are raised in every clime and her missionaries are to be found wherever there are men to be taught the evangel of immorality and there are souls to be saved.

And this wondrous Church, which is as old as Christianity and as universal as mankind is today . . . as fresh and as vigorous and as fruitful as on the day when the Pentecostal fires were showered upon the earth.

✠JOHN J. CANTWELL (1924) — BISHOP RECALLS THE RECORD

In April of 1922, the Bishop of Monterey–Los Angeles authorized a complete renovation of Saint Vibiana's Cathedral. After almost a half century of service, the historic church was badly in need of modernization and expansion. Besides renovating the cathedral proper, a gallery was erected over the main entance, in the area provided by the new facade. Marble steps and railings were added to the considerably enlarged sanctuary. The walls were replastered and richly finished in liturgical ornamentation

A new pulpit of white carrara, offset by colored marble columns and inlaid panels was installed opposite the episcopal cathedral or chair. The renovation process lasted almost two years, though it never interfered with the normally–scheduled divine services.

On February 3, 1924, the Apostolic Delegate to the United States, Archbishop Pietro Fumasoni–Biondi journeyed to the Pacific Coast for the formal opening of the newly–refurbished cathedral. In one of the addresses given on that occasion, Bishop John J. Cantwell provided the Apostolic Delegate with a capsulized view of Catholicism on the West coast:

> You will permit me to remind Your Excellency that the old *pueblo* known as *Nuestra Señora de los Angeles*, was ministered to in a spiritual way by the Franciscan Fathers from the Mission of San Gabriel.
>
> The Station Church, or as it was called, "The *Asistencia*," still exists in this city. It links us with the past and perpetuates the intelligent and heroic work of the Sons of Saint Francis, who in early days conquered California for Christ, and tenderly cared for their flocks in a chain of Missions extending from San Diego to the Valley of the Seven Moons in the North.
>
> It is sadly true, Your Excellency, that the Old Missions are in ruins; but the light of faith which burned in these sanctuaries has never gone out.
>
> The old land consecrated by the labors of the *Padres* has been preserved for a new people. Where once a small church in a Mexican *pueblo* ministered to a few hundred souls, now in a hundred churches and chapels the Bread of Life is being daily broken, and the Word of God caught up from the lips of the Saints is proclaimed in all its majestic simplicity to younger generations.
>
> Where once a few priests shepherded a little flock, now an ever growing army of diocesan clergy and the spiritual sons of the Saints, stand as sentinels in the City of Sion.
>
> In a special way do we realize today that we on the Pacific Coast are the objects of his (Pope Pius XI's) paternal care. Your Excellency may take back from us to the Holy Father the most profound expression of our homage, obedience and love.
>
> You may say to him also, that while California has been blessed beyond measure by the generosity of nature in the fertility of her soil, in the riotous beauty of her landscape, in the golden and purple hues of sea and sky, we are not unmindful of Him from whom all blessings flow.
>
> Here the splendors of the past shall live again, and a new and more glorious temple shall rise under the providence of God to the Majesty of His Holy Name.

J. WISEMAN MACDONALD (1934) — CATHOLIC ACTION

During Catholic Action Week, held at Los Angeles between April 29, and May 3, 1934, the Society of Saint Vincent de Paul sponsored a symposium presided over by the Archbishop Amleto Giovanni Cicognani, the Apostolic Delegate. Most prominent of the speakers addressing the conclave, J. Wiseman Macdonald, placed the whole question of Catholic Action within the context of California's evangelic history.

The term "Catholic Action" as a name–unit, is of very recent Origin—that is to say, it is only within the past few years that the words "Catholic" and "Action" have been fixed together in juxtaposition so as to form a special name or appellative.

The very day that our California was founded was the day that Catholic Action commenced here—and, mark this well—*it was Catholic Action itself that founded the State*—nothing more, and nothing less.

In the year 1769, the saintly Father Junípero Serra and some of his brother Franciscan monks, left the College of San Fernando in Mexico City, and, in two parties, passed overland, going by way of the most northerly of the missions of Lower California, bent on their work of evangelizing Upper California.

From the Missions of Lower California the good Fathers brought with them, for immediate use and future sustenance, and to aid in founding the new territory, hundreds of heads of horned cattle, horses, hogs, sheep and domestic animals of other kinds. They carried provisions, medicines, clothing, and abundant necessaries of life. They brought farm and, agricultural implements, and experienced craftsmen to use them and thereby to cajole into productiveness the faces of Mother Earth.

In their *carretas*, or old–fashioned, springless wooden carts, they carried building and industrial implements of many kinds to aid in developing the new territory. Grape vines, slips of olive and other fruit trees, and quantities of grain seed, were in their train, and, later, all were planted and grew profusely in the fecund soil of our own California.

It is well for us to know that *every single grape and olive, and every blade of barley and grain*, originally grown in this great State, *was here produced directly through Catholic Action*, for Catholic money paid for all of them, and Catholic hands planted everything.

Every animal which the good fathers brought to California in 1769 and, later, for food and for labor, and every industrial and agricultural instrument, every plow and harrow which they carried with them, distinctly represented Catholic Action. *Catholic money paid for it all, and Catholic hands did the work.*

Every penny that was spent by the good Missionary fathers in animals, implements, fruits and grains, was money obtained from "*El Fondo Piadoso de las Californias*"—"The Pious Fund of the Californias" a great charitable trust fund of between a million and a million and a half dollars, *contributed by Catholics in Spain and Mexico*, and assembled by the Jesuit Fathers in those countries in the first half of the Eighteenth Century for the specific purpose of evangelizing both Californias—Alta and Baja—Upper and Lower—then, of course, Spanish colonies.

A notable reflection in this connection is that *even the wages of the few soldiers who accompanied the fathers for protection against Indians, came from Catholic Action. Those wages were paid from the same Pious Fund.*

Catholic Action indeed began very early in California. Seventy years before 1769, it had incepted in Lower California, when the Jesuits commenced the foundation of their thirteen Missions in that territory.

Great, spreading arrays those pioneers of our State and their animals presented, as they marched slowly and resolutely to commence the building of California—to open up its great destiny; and I say, and declare to you *that, when the first man of those historic marchers stepped across the imaginary line then stretching between Lower and Upper California, and placed his evangelizing foot on the soil of Upper California, our own California of today—at that very instant Catholic Action commenced in this State*, and, ever since that moment, it has continued efficiently, progressively, gloriously, and with ever–widening range, until the present moment.

The twenty–one great Mission buildings in this State subsequently erected by the *padres*, running from San Diego, northerly, six hundred miles to the Mission of San Francisco Solano, forty miles north of San Francisco, *were built through Catholic Action*, and those Mission buildings, today the pride and joy of all Californians; irrespective of creed—some of them in disintegrations of sad but beautiful and romantic ruins; others restored to stately strength and grandeur and still performing their sacred functions—all remain as glorious monuments attesting the zeal, the fervor, and the charity of a bygone and unforgettable century, and they stand as wonderful tributes to Catholic Action, dating back to the very first day of the State's existence.

Surely, more the 87,000 benighted souls brought from paganism into the light of the Gospel constitute the brightest jewel placed in the crown of Catholic Action, or any other action, in this State, at that time, or at any time.

ETHEL MURTHA HUXLEY (1939) — SAN FRANCISCO

"There's one thing about San Francisco. 'Tis hard to leave,'" said Rudyard Kipling, famous English writer. Mark Twain and Robert Louis Stevenson, two other literary gentlemen who delighted the world with their magical mating of words, both found a haven in San Francisco and agreed with Mr. Kipling that the city had charm. James M. Barrie, the Scotch novelist and playwright, said that "charm is the bloom on a woman. Charm too, is the bloom on a city."

The City by the Golden Gate has long been a center for Catholics of German extraction. In the summer of 1939, the "city" was eulogized by Ethel Murtha Huxley, in an article on "Glamorous San Francisco," lead feature for the handsome souvenir booklet issued for the 84th annual convention of the *Catholic Central Verein of America*.

Miss Huxley pointed out that "San Francisco's charm, like that of many a lovely lady, is variable,— old–world at the same time that it is ultra–modern . . . dinky cable cars mounting the straight, steep inclines that are San Francisco's streets, up, up and up go the tiny cars, chauffered by a corps of witty gripmen who take life and the hills in their stride, all the while merrily clanging their car bells . . . the flower stands at every street corner, a glorious clamor of color and fragrance."

> San Francisco's foreign air,—Chinatown, its pagodas, carved temples, gilded doors, scarlet and indigo roofs and Oriental bazaars forming the largest Chinese city outside of the Orient.
>
> Fisherman's Wharf, with its cluster of pale–blue boats riding at anchor while swarthy–skinned fishermen sit calmly mending their great brown nets preliminary to an early morning haul, and the little shops that line the wharf prepare for the day's business, steaming crabs and other sea food in great sidewalk cauldrons for visitors who await the tasty dishes.
>
> San Francisco's pride in her romantic and colorful past . . . Sutro's old–fashioned gardens of the eighties overlooking the ocean, replete with quaint statuary in close communion with strange tropical trees, shrubbery and flowers.
>
> San Francisco's surprising vistas—her fascinating little alleys housing shops,—the fountains, flower gardens and tree–bordered walks of Civic Center with hundreds of pigeons and sea gulls bathing in the fountains and greedily pushing each other out of reach of the proffered peanuts of admiring visitors.
>
> San Francisco's matchless views of shimmering waters of the bay and the oft–time turbulent Pacific, ships from the Seven Seas slipping by and out to the Orient or dropping anchor at the Embarcadero to unload passengers and cargoes from other countries.
>
> San Francisco's skyline hides its vast areas of pure vacation–land from the eyes of the visitor. Nowhere in the world can the sportsman or sportswoman enjoy as many of his or her favorite sports as in San Francisco.
>
> You can fish, you can play tennis. You can ride horseback, or hike, or mountain climb. You can golf, You can go bicycling. You can swim. You can sail, You can cruise. You can bowl on the green. You can go to the races. And, you can enjoy any and all of these vacation sports throughout the year, due to San Francisco's equable climate.

Miss Huxley concludes her essay with the observation that "no city in the United States can boast of such a gay, romantic custom as can San Francisco with its downtown flower stands. No story of San Francisco's flower stands should be told without speaking about the gallantry of the flower stand salesmen, nearly all Italians, who own their own stands, and are gentlemen, one and all.

"With a dash, a verve, a manner all their own, they pin on the bouquets on any fair lady's shoulder with an intent and artistry that is something else to remember of the City by the Golden Gate."

✚TIMOTHY MANNING (1948) — REFLECTIONS ON THE *PUEBLO DE NUESTRA SEÑORA DE LOS ANGELES*

The city dedicated to *Nuestra Señora de los Angeles* is a metropolis of legendary limits. It was within the context of the archdiocese that sprung from this *pueblo* that the Most Reverent Timothy Manning made the following observations, on March 19, 1948: This wonder–city "is yet the progeny of the new age, still seeking to find its ultimate strength, awkward in its growth, yet inching its way upward to tower above its contemporaries in the American family of towns."

> Over the hills and into the adjacent valleys it spills like something poured out, waiting to assume its permanent form, to congeal and settle. It knows only the restless Pacific and the rock–rimmed desert for its boundaries.
>
> Much of its fame is founded on intangible things: the green and gold of its citrus orchards, outlined against the snow of its hills; the languid climate slowing the pace of mind and body, and enriching our language with the lovely word *mañana*; the latent wealth of the black and liquid gold in the earth below us; the dubious brilliance of our stellar system over the holy wood; the spurious sowings of a thousand creeds in a wheat field, waiting for the harvester; the unpredictable instability of the earth beneath, reminding us that we have not a lasting city; the ceaseless ebb and flow of the great heart of humanity that is contained within our streets.
>
> Our roots are altogether Catholic. We are Catholic by conquest and the blood of the *conquistadores* flows in our veins. The little Plaza Church is hidden under the shadows of the great municipal buildings, but hidden only as a pearl of great price.
>
> Its origin is coeval with the *Pueblo*, they bear a common name, they share a common patronage. It was a place of worship (1781) five years before the first Catholic structure was erected in the City or State of New York.

✚JOHN J. MITTY (1952) — OAKLAND CENTENNIAL

On May 18, 1952, the religious and civil leaders of Oakland gathered in Saint Francis de Sales Church to publicly thank Almighty God for a hundred years of His "countless blessings and favors" on their City of the Oaks. The Archbishop of San Francisco, Most Reverend John J. Mitty, summarized the importance of the occasion with a most fitting address.

The life of a great city is inseparable from the lives of the men and women who gave it birth, sustained its youth and guided its maturity. From its citizens it receives its personality and character, the vigor of its youth and the honor of its age. So it has been with the great city of Oakland.

Born under the shadow of the American flag just one century ago, Oakland's history has been written in the lives and achievements of its citizenry.

It was a small group of seventy–two who secured the charter and called the new city "The Land of the Oaks," a title suggested by the sturdy trees that dotted the hills and shoreline of the Eastbay.

They stood as symbols and a pledge of the strength, stability and endurance with which God would endow this city during its years.

Throughout its history the city of Oakland has been in the vanguard of cities pioneering the colossal expansion of the Golden West. In all walks of life, as leaders in industry, business and transportation; in the government and the military; in art and culture; and in the things of the spirit, its citizens have served well the great State of California and our beloved country.

In 1906 the citizens of Oakland demonstrated that greatness was something of the soul and spirit. After the great earthquake had wreaked havoc over Northern California, in spite of its own wounds, this city opened its hearths to some hundred thousand neighbors fleeing disaster.

This fraternal charity which graciously crossed the San Francisco bay joined the hands of two great cities in everlasting friendship, a union symbolized today in the linking steel of a world famous bridge.

The Church, too, has been part and parcel of this century of progress. Even more than a century ago, *padres* walked "The Land of the Oaks" and christened the water of its estuary "San Antonio."

Within a very few months after the foundation, priests from Mission San Jose established a mission in the nascent city. The intervening years have seen the success of parish churches, elementary and secondary schools, institutions of higher learning, hospitals, homes for the aged and infirm and countless educational and welfare services that have become incorporated into the warp and woof of Oakland, and part of the everyday life and blood of its sons and daughters.

But while we salute the men and women of the past who have built a great city, while we honor the present citizens who sustain that greatness and express our confidence in future heirs of this heritage, we humbly acknowledge that it is God who has given the increase and who will insure the future.

May I, as your Archbishop, in the name of all the Catholics of the archdiocese, humbly salute you, citizens of the city of Oakland, and pray that God will bless each one of you and will remain with you forever.

RICHARD M. NIXON (1959) — CATHOLIC EDUCATION

The place of parochial schools within the nation's overall educational system was spelled out clearly and forcibly by (the then) Vice President of the United States, Richard M. Nixon, on June 15, 1959. Lauding the "tremendous possibilities" of the University of San Diego, Mr. Nixon said that "here in the United States we have deficiencies in the educational system, which we understand and endeavor to eradicate. We saw this too clearly when the Sputniks were put up by the Soviet Union."

But nevertheless, here in this country, then and now, more students receive a better education than in any country in the world today. It still isn't as good as we should like it and we are always working to make it better.

There is a place here for the great public educational system at the grade, high school and college level, and there is also a place for the private schools as well.

And rather than have any warfare between the two we realize the need for both and recognize that about 20% of the funds spent on education in the United States come from private sources and 80% come from public funds.

On the other hand we also realize that it is important and desirable to leaven our public education with private education. We never want uniformity or conformity in education.

Once we put all the burden of education on government, we will have government domination of education.

As long as we have institutions supported as this institution is, we are assured that new ideas will alter education.

The Vice President's remarks were delivered during commencement exercises at the University of San Diego. Mr. Nixon had journeyed to the Alcala Park campus for dedication of the Hall of Science, last major unit of the newly established Catholic school of higher learning.

Bishop Charles F. Buddy also used the occasion to confer the university's first doctorate of laws on Mr. Nixon for his "eminent achievement . . . in statesmanship, splendid scholarship and constructive measures in Congress." A handsome bronze plaque commemorating the festive gathering was hung in the Hall of Science. It was a historic day for San Diego.

ALBINO CARDINAL LUCIANI (1974) — REFLECTIONS OF SAN BUENAVENTURA

Pope John Paul I

Saint Bonaventure of Bagorea (1221–1274), for whom the ninth and last of Fray Junípero Serra's missions was named, is known in historical annals as a teacher of theology, general of the Franciscan Order, cardinal of the Catholic Church and much appreciated orator at the Council of Lyons. In 1974, Albino Cardinal Luciani, the Patriarch of Venice (later to be Pope John Paul I), wrote the following 'letter" to San Buenaventura, on the occasion of the seventh centenary of his death:

Most gentle Saint Bonaventure! Your contemporaries who had the good fortune to hear you, were intoxicated by your words. They wrote: 'He spoke with angelic tongue.' I wish you would still speak like an angel: especially to parents, to educators, to politicians, to all those who, today, are responsible for the young.

And I wish you would say: 'Do not fear any effort, any just reform, any expense, any dialogue, if it will help these sons of ours. It is for their good, but also for your own good. In fact, those who fear effort and expense today may have to pay dearly tomorrow.'

Tolstoy would be prepared to underline these last words of yours with a parable.

In the little Principality of Monaco, many years ago, the judge sentenced a rogue to the guillotine, but then they realized that, to carry out the sentence, they had neither a guillotine nor an executioner. The Principality of Monaco was so tiny!

They asked to borrow both things from their neighbor France, but when they heard what the charge would be, they took flight: 'Too expensive!' They made a similar inquiry at the court of the king of Sardinia. Again the price was too high.

So they left the rogue in prison: but the jailer, the cook, the prisoner's food also cost money. 'We'll open the jail door,' the judges decided, 'and let him go off on his way.'

Seeing the door open, the prisoner went out for a stroll along the seafront. But at noon he went to the prince's kitchen to claim his meal. He did this the first day, the second, the third, and for many days thereafter.

The matter was becoming a serious threat to the budget of the principality. The authorities decided to send for the man. 'Haven't you realized yet that you must go away?'

And he answered: 'All right, I'll go, but first you must pay me.'

They had to pay him. And thus, with the excuse that it was too expensive, and with constant postponements, another criminal was set loose in the world to continue his misdeeds.

So you must not keep saying, 'It costs too much !' if you want to stop the criminal, furious, revolutionary protest from traveling about the world.

Solutions of problems, expenditures, dialogue must not be put off. Let us speak with these people, and let us try to help them with new assistance and new methods, suited to the times, but with the same impassioned love with which you, dear saint, helped them, in your own times.

IX. Topical

THE *AD ALTARE DEI* CROSS

The scouting movement, begun in England by Sir Robert Baden Powell, was formally established in the United States on February 8, 1910, by William D. Boyce. The first troop formed in California under Catholic auspices can be traced to 1917, when Bishop John J. Cantwell endorsed and encouraged scouting for the Diocese of Monterey–Los Angeles.

Catholic interest in the movement is evident from many sources, none of which is more demonstrative than the origination of the now famous *Ad Altare Dei* cross. That award has been conferred upon young scouts in Southern California for meritorious religious service for almost half a century. It has proven to be a most effective way of encouraging and recognizing the contribution made by these young people to the liturgical life of the community.

It was in the 1920s that the Diocese of Los Angeles–San Diego became the first to publicly acknowledge the loyalty and fidelity of scouts in such a fashion. Father James E. Dolan is credited with the idea of bestowing the *Ad Altare Dei* cross, a distinction reserved for those scouts outstanding in "the spiritual phase of scouting."

From the very outset, the award proved to be immensely popular and within a relatively short period of time, many other dioceses throughout the nation followed the example of scout leaders in Los Angeles.

By formal action of the Scout Chaplains' Conference, at Savannah, Georgia, in 1939, a request was made to the Bishops Committee on Scouting to adapt the *Ad Altare Dei* cross on a national scale. And then, two years later, the cross was formally approved as an official award by the Boy Scouts of America National Council. That action, of course, gave the award a more profound meaning and significance.

The requirements for obtaining the *Ad Altare Dei* cross are stiff. To qualify, a scout must have attained the rank of First Class, know all the responses to the prayers at Mass and have served at the altar for no less than 250 hours. His pastor must certify that the candidate is worthy of receiving the cross, by reason of punctuality, fitness, decorum and devotion at the altar.

The award itself is a bronze cross suspended from a ribbon in the papal and national colors. Under the bar pin is a plate bearing the inscription *Ad Altare Dei*. It is attached to the scout's uniform on the left breast, just above the pocket.

Bestowal of the awards on the "soldiers of peace" has traditionally been associated with colorful liturgical ceremonies. In Los Angeles, the crosses are given at Saint Vibiana's Cathedral, during the month of February, often by the archbishop himself.

The establishment of the *Ad Altare Dei* cross is one further example of the innovative genius possessed by the religious and lay leaders of the Church in Southern California.

ADOBE

People who visit the California missions often recall their adobe construction as if that element were an element from the distant past, something foreign to the building practices of the 1980s. Nothing could be further from the truth. It is estimated that at least one third of the world's current population lives in some sort of earthen housing, most of it adobe. The practical appeal of adobe construction lies in that material's worldwide availability and in the fact that its use requires a minimum of technology.

Contemporary builders and architects on the local scene speak about adobe in terms of quaint and primitive techniques. Actually, a growing number of experts believe that adobe construction is not only an interesting way of building, but one that offers special advantages which are vitally important to an energy–conscious world.

Like many Spanish terms, "adobe" is derived from Arabic. It refers to mud bricks and/or the clay soil from which they are fashioned. It has a long and fascinating background that stretches into prehistory.

Adobe was used quite commonly in the early civilizations of the Middle East and Mediterranean. The Roman architect, Vitruvius, devoted a section of his classic treatise on architecture to the making of adobe bricks which were utilized for a variety of purposes.

The esthetic appeal of adobe is somewhat difficult to describe. The gentle visual delights of thick walls, softened edges and the not–quite–plumb construction are reflected in many very attractive adobe buildings, especially in the rural areas of New Mexico.

Adobe itself is a mixture of clay and other materials, usually sand and silt. Its properties vary with the way it is mixed and used. The standard size of adobe bricks used in early California was 4 X 4 X 16 or 8 X 4 X 16. The early adobe buildings along the Pacific Slope usually had roofs covered with a layer of earth about twelve inches thick.

According to the National Bureau of Standards, the ideal adobe brick is composed of 19% coarse sand, 42% fine sand, 22% silt and 17% clay. Vitruvius recommended allowing bricks to dry for two years before use. Straw is frequently mixed into an adobe of high clay content to prevent it from cracking. Adobe bricks with a high clay content generally resist weathering better than more sandy combinations which absorb water through capillary action. Natural adobe will last for centuries if properly maintained. Much of Taos Pueblo in New Mexico has been standing for at least four hundred years and some parts might date back to the thirteenth century.

In addition to the historical interest of adobe construction and the beauty of various building traditions, adobe has a relevance to the energy crunch. Its combination of heat storage capacity and rate of heat conductance makes it usable for thermal storage mass in passive solar applications. An adobe building, properly built with bricks of the right components, can store enough heat to carry it through a cold night or sufficient coolness to see it through a hot day.

Augustus Caesar boasted of finding Rome a city of brick (mud) and leaving it a city of marble. Contemporary planners might consider the advisability of reversing that procedure in the future.

ADOBES — HISTORIC

The oldest and largest adobe building in Southern California is the Convento at San Fernando Mission. But there are other historic adobes dotting the southland skyline. Among those surviving the 1994 Northridge earthquake are the following.

The *Michael White Adobe* in San Marino, built in 1845 on a parcel of land known as *Rancho Ysidro*, stands in the middle of the campus of San Marino High School. *El Molino Viejo*, originally attached to San Gabriel Mission, became the home of James S. Waite, editor of the first English language newspaper, the *Star*.

Also in San Gabriel is the *Ortega–Vigare Adobe*, built by Juan Vigare sometime between 1792 and 1805. Vigare's family lived there until the 1930s. Today it is a private residence and not open to the public.

In Pomona is *La Casa Primera*, built in 1837 by Ignacio Palomares, a cattle rancher. This five room adobe, now the home of the Pomona Historical Society, is located close to *El Adobe de Palomares*.

There are two adobes on the *Rancho La Puente* in the City of Industry, the first built in 1842 by William Workman. In 1920, Walter Temple built a more modern adobe nearby. The Homestead Museum offers free tours of both adobes.

The *Sanchez Adobe Museum* in Montebello was built by Casilda Soto de Lobo in 1845 to fulfill a condition of ownership of the 1,363 acre *Rancho la Merced*. Juan Matias Sanchez took over the property in later years.

Rancho Los Alamitos in Long Beach was originally built in the early 1800s by retired soldier Juan Jose Nieto. It was renovated in 1842 by Abel Stearns for his bride, Arcadia Bandini.

The adobe on the *Rancho Los Cerritos* in Long Beach was built by Jonathan Temple in 1843 on a bluff overlooking the Los Angeles River. Nearly a dozen cities were carved out of *Rancho San Pedro*, the 76,000 acre grant given to Juan Jose Dominguez in 1784 by the Spanish Crown. Manuel Dominguez inherited the ranch and began building the U–shaped, one–story *Dominguez Adobe* in 1824. His wife, Maria Engracia, who lived there for fifty–five years, raised ten children, six of whom inherited more than 40,000 acres.

The *Vicente Lugo Adobe* in Bell Gardens was at the heart of the vast 29,413 acre *Rancho San Antonio*, home of Antonio Maria Lugo, a Spanish Cavalier and his heir, Vicente Lugo. In later times Henry T. Gage, a former California governor, got title to the home as part of his wife's dowry.

The *Gilmore Adobe* is shrouded by vegetation in the middle of the famous Farmers Market in Los Angeles. Built in 1828, the adobe was the residence of Antonio Jose Rocha on the *Rancho La Brea*. In the 1870s , Arthur F. Gilmore bought the property and it was his son, Earl, who founded the Farmers Market in 1934. Unfortunately, this adobe is only rarely open for special events.

Finally, there is the *Avila Adobe* on Olvera Street. Built in 1818 by Francisco Avila, once a mayor of Los Angeles, this 179 year old adobe, the oldest in the central area of the city, was occupied in the 1930s by the indomitable Christine Sterling, the "Mother of Olvera Street."

There are other adobes in the area, including the *Lopez Adobe* (San Fernando), the *La Casa de la Centinela Adobe* (Inglewood), the *Pio Pico Mansion* (Whittier), the *Casa Adobe de San Rafael* (Glendale), the *Leonis Adobe* (Calabasas) and the *Andres Pico Adobe* (Mission Hills).

"ADORATION OF THE MAGI"

Those interested in the Catholic heritage of California's southland will be pleased to know that the 1988 Stained Glass Christmas plate, sponsored by the United States Historical Society, was based on the renowned Nativity window of Saint Vibiana's Cathedral.

Reviewers have acclaimed this "Adoration of the Magi" as the height of the platemaking art. A distinguished art critic described the 1988 plate as an embodiment of "one of the finest Nativity windows in the world."

Artisans applied seventeen separate transparent colors to each piece of the genuine cathedral glass. The colors became fused permanently into place when fired to temperatures in excess of 1100 degrees Fahrenheit. The Jefferson Pewter Company, whose craftsmen produce museum pieces for the United States Department of State and the Boston Museum of Fine Art, fashioned rims for the plates using highly–polished, lead–free pewter.

As were the other windows in the Cathedral, the "Adoration of the Magi" was designed by the grand master of stained glass art, John Mayer of Munich. His work can be seen in other California churches, including Saint Paul's in San Francisco.

Father William Cantwell had journeyed to Europe in early 1922 and personally visited the Mayer Studios. He highly endorsed their work in a letter to the Bishop of Monterey–Los Angeles, noting that the Mayers "have a reputation that they are living up to and not living on." It was a recommendation enough and the contract was signed.

Into this particular window, the elderly Mayer poured all he had learned from a lifetime of perfecting the unique beauty of stained glass art. Critics believe it ranks among his finest works. His colors are today extraordinarily deep and rich, with stunningly intense blues, reds and golds, together with a host of other colors, ranging from subtle pastels to rich variations of the primary spectre. The skin tones are amazingly realistic.

Modern–day artisans are overwhelmed by Mayer's skill as were those of a half century ago. The "Adoration of the Magi" was a milestone achievement, and its influence on stained glass art makes it one of the more important windows on the Pacific Slope. Working with his three sons, John Mayer based his depiction on Saint Matthew's Gospel which graphically records how shepherds and village people gathered at the manger to adore the newborn King of the Jews.

One distinguished art critic, comparing the 1988 facsimile to the original, notes that when the light strikes this plate, it becomes alive with fiery colors. Its polished pewter 'rim' creates a halo effect uncommon in works of this kind. Collectors will want to know that the stained glass Christmas plate comes in an elegant upholstered box. A lucite display stand is included and each plate is registered and numbered. Special "Art Glow" lights are also available to illuminate the plate.

THE *AGNUS DEI*

The *Agnus Dei*, a small flat piece of wax impressed with the figure of a lamb and a cross or banner, is an ovalar cake about six inches in diameter. The reverse side of the disc bears an impression of a papal coat–of–arms. Enclosed in a small leather case with a glass overlay, the *Agnus Dei* in the Historical Museum attached to the Chancery Archives, was blessed by Pope Pius XII and conveyed, at his personal behest, to the late Archbishop John J. Cantwell.

The historical origin of the *Agnus Dei* is clouded in considerable obscurity. Very likely the practice was initially devised as a counterreaction to the pagan beliefs in charms and amulets. If so, it is a good example of how the Church "baptized" a custom which, though misguided, did demonstrate an instinctive reliance on higher powers.

An *Agnus Dei* was found in the tomb of Maria Augusta, the wife of Emperor Honorius, which dates it to the fourth century. Their use was common in the 800s, when they were sent by popes to sovereigns and other distinguished personages. During penal times in England, the *Agnus Dei* was specifically forbidden as a "popish trumpery" and its possession was regarded as a felony.

In former years, it was the practice of the Holy Father to bless the *Agnus Dei* during the first year of his pontificate and every seventh year thereafter. On Wednesday of Holy Week, the discs were brought to the Vatican. The pope dipped them into a vessel of water mixed with chrism and balsam, while reciting various consecratory prayers.

The blessing used for the *Agnus Dei* makes special mention of the perils of storm and pestilence, fire and flood and the dangers associated with childbirth. Distribution would then take place with solemnity on Easter Saturday, when the pontiff, after the *Agnus Dei* of the Mass, placed packets of the discs into the inverted mitres of each cardinal or bishop coming to receive them.

The solemnity with which this sacramental was blessed and distributed by the Holy Father, the graces which were besought in the consecratory prayers and the symbolical meaning which it possessed indicate that the *Agnus Dei* was an efficacious means of grace and a powerful protection against the evils threatening body and soul.

Just as the blood of the paschal lamb protected each household from the destroying angel, so the purpose of those consecrated medallions was that of protecting those who used them from all malign influences. The wax of the *Agnus Dei* symbolized the virgin birth of Christ, while the cross associated with the lamb suggests the idea of a victim offered in sacrifice.

Though it was an important sacramental, there were no indulgences attached to the *Agnus Dei*. Its efficacy derived from its symbolism of Christ and the lamblike virtues of innocence, meekness and indifference to the world. All of which is to say that there's much of the Church's rich historical heritage attached to the *Agnus Dei* exhibited in the Chancery Archives.

ALTAR WINE IN EARLY CALIFORNIA

In the years immediately following the mission era, the making of altar wine in California became a serious concern for Church officials. It was and is a difficult task to satisfy the stringent regulations of Canon Law.

The processing of sacramental wine is not exactly the same as that for ordinary wines. The code prescribes that "the wine must be the natural and uncorrupted juice of the grape."

"Natural" wine is that which has no added water or other chemical substances. Nor may it contain matters which should have settled out during aging, which are sometimes called yeast or excess cream of tartar. If conditions require, a small quantity of spirits (grape brandy or alcohol) may be added to guard against spoiling during transportation. Such "spirits" must meet certain conditions. They must have been distilled from grape, they must not exceed eighteen per cent of the whole and they must be made during the process of fermentation.

Hence altar wine cannot be extracted and prepared from other fruits. Also restricted are the so–called artificial wines, even if their chemical constitution is identical with the genuine juice of the grape. Although the wine may be white or red, weak or strong, sweet or dry, it must be produced from the mature grape, that is, grapes that have begun to ripen. The fermentation process must be long enough to change the grape into wine. And care must be taken so that fermentation stops short of producing vinegar.

From these specifications, it can be seen that the production of altar wines measuring up to the requirements of Canon Law demanded the constant care and vigilance of Archbishop Joseph S. Alemany and other churchmen.

The archbishop came from a family well versed in the chemistry of wines and other spirits. (Until the early 1970s, the family produced some of Spain's finest brandies.) Early in the 1880s, Alemany pointed out to an old friend, Joseph Concannon, the difficulties in obtaining altar wine. At the prelate's behest, Concannon purchased forty–seven acres of land in the heart of a gravel strata in the south end of the Livermore Valley.

The archbishop had observed that growing conditions in that area were comparable to those of the famous wine producing grape district of Bordeaux. Joseph journeyed to France and returned with choice cuttings and oak casks in which to age the wine.

Thus was established a firm that has made wine history in California for almost a century, Today, in addition to altar wines, a large variety of table, dessert and sparkling wines bear the Concannon label.

A plaque placed on the property testifies that "here in 1883 James Concannon founded the Concannon Vineyard. The quality it achieved in sacramental and commercial wines helped establish Livermore Valley as one of America's select wine growing districts."

Some years ago, Vivienne L. George wrote that "even if there were no medals, ribbons or landmarks, this family knows that in every section of the United States and even in thirty foreign countries, Concannon wine is daily used in the Holy Sacrifice of the Mass; it is daily being transformed into the Body and Blood of Christ."

And it came about at the suggestion and encouragement of Archbishop Joseph Sadoc Alemany of San Francisco.

THE AMERICAN BIBLE

The Word of God at the Archival Center for the Archdiocese of Los Angeles has been enhanced by a gift of the four volume *American Bible* from the Ernest and Helen Chacon Trust. This landmark publication presents, for the first time, the dramatic history of the Bible in America through a display of thirty–eight original leaves from the most precious and significant editions printed in the geographical area of what is now the United States.

The pages, spanning a period of over two hundred years (1663–1878), are from the collection of the noted bibliophile, Michael Zinman, who selected them and provided an introduction for each page. The leaves have been carefully removed from incomplete Bibles by skilled conservators and are archivally mounted. It is important to emphasize that no complete, intact Bible has been used, only partial or damaged copies.

The entire collection provides a striking exhibition of educational, aesthetic and religious import. The informative introductory essays, bibliographical descriptions and commentaries are printed on individual sheets and can be detached for display purposes.

The leaves are divided into four groups: (1) Bibles in the languages of the native peoples of America, (2) and (3) Bibles in English from the 18th and 19th centuries and (4) Bibles in other languages. Each group of mounted leaves and explanatory material is housed in a custom–made portfolio box. The edition is limited to one hundred sets.

Nowhere in the world did the Bible have a greater impact than on the virgin continents of the New World as they were exposed to European civilization. And especially was that true in the United States. The discovery of large Indian nations led to a period of missionary activity unparalleled since the earliest days of Christianity. Explorers, missionaries and settlers joined forces to spread the Gospel to unbelievers.

By the time of the exploration of the North American continent, the invention of movable type had made the Bible accessible to large numbers of people and even those of modest means could afford the luxury of a Bible. Possessing a Bible on the American frontier was considered a necessity of home life and family Bibles became heirlooms for their descendants. Bible production increased to supply the needs of the growing colonial populations.

Prior to the Revolutionary War, the Bible could not be printed in English in America because that right was legally reserved to English printers. While no restriction was placed on Bibles in other languages, there wasn't a Spanish Bible printed in the New World until 1824.

The earliest Bibles printed in America were in Indian tongues. Often this required an Indian language to be crafted into written form for the first time and, in some editions, special phonetic characters were cast in type for the first time.

In Philadelphia, Mathew Carey, an immigrant from Ireland, printed the Douay Bible in 1790. It was the first English Catholic Bible published in America and today is the rarest of the early Bibles. A page from this "vulgate" edition is now at the Archival Center.

AMERICAN PROTECTIVE ASSOCIATION IN SAN FRANCISCO

"The man who would introduce religious dissension into this community is a moral monster, an ogre, a traitor to the flag." This sentiment of the Reverend Peter C. Yorke was unhappily not shared by many persons in San Francisco at the turn of the century.

Throughout American history, organizations have risen up against the Catholic Church, most of them basing their appeal on nativism and hostility to things Catholic. While the Know–Nothings and the Klu Klux Klan are outstanding examples, they are only two among the "thirteen orders which sought to rally Protestant America against the threat of the foreigner and papist." Of special interest to Californians was the American Protective Association, founded on March 13, 1887, in Clinton, Iowa, by Henry F. Bowers. This secret organization was imported to California several years later, and, in 1893, the first chapter of the A.P.A. was opened in San Francisco.

The Bay City was fertile territory for the A.P.A. That area's large number of foreign born (many of them Irish) gave the Church a strength that frightened many non–Catholics. This, coupled with the growing stature and importance of Catholicism on the national level, agitated certain peoples. It must be mentioned that not a small amount of anti–Catholic sentiment was caused by the faithful themselves. The indiscreet flying of the green flag over City Hall on Saint Patrick's day is one outstanding example!

The igniting spark came with the adoption of Meyer's *Medieval and Modern History* textbook by the city's public schools. Archbishop Patrick W. Riordan personally presented a list of objections about the anti–Catholic book to the Board of Education, thus setting off a whole series of claims and counter claims. That the A.P.A.'s tactics were violent needs little emphasis. Members were required to take an oath denouncing "Roman Catholicism . . . the pope sitting at Rome or elsewhere . . . his priests and emissaries, and the diabolical work of the Roman Catholic Church." In addition, members were obliged to swear that they would labor for the exclusion of Catholics from public office, boycott Catholic merchants, and refuse to employ Catholic workingmen.

The A.P.A. had effective means to disseminate these charges. Weekly patriotic meetings, a private newspaper and hundreds of posters and pamphlets flooded the Bay Area. Forgeries were common too—and even a bit humorous. An encyclical originating in Oakland and attributed to Pope Leo XIII called upon Catholics to rise up in a bloody revolution on the feast of Saint Ignatius of Loyola in 1894, and hand over the country to the pope!

The Catholic position was defended by Father Peter C. Yorke, who became editor of *The Monitor* in 1894. Yorke's public controversy with the Unitarian minister, Charles W. Wendte, effectively demonstrated the A.P.A.'s charges against the Church as garbled quotations and outright forgeries. The American Protective Association faded swiftly from the scene in the years after 1896, due to the persistence of Yorke's tactics. Of course the decline had other reasons too. On the national scene the organization, failing materially to influence the political conventions of 1896, lost much of its nation–wide image. Locally, Yorke uncovered several major internal scandals which rocked the Association's foundations apart. In retrospect, the effects of the A.P.A. were lasting for, among other things, it "helped to insure San Francisco from any renaissance of organized anti–Catholicism." Its defeat "must also be recognized as an important step forward in the growth of the Catholic Church in California,"

ANCIENT ORDER OF HIBERNIANS IN SOUTHLAND

Historians trace the origin of the Ancient Order of Hibernians to the Emerald Isle's County of Kildare in the Province of Leinster. There in 1565, Rory O'Moore and his "Defenders" rallied the Irish people to a defense of their religion and country against the English invaders.

During the stormy penal days, members accompanied the priests in their midnight missions of mercy. They were entrusted as sentinels to guard the heights and defend the priest and his flock from surprise attack.

The annals relate how, sometimes, in spite of their vigilance, "they were surrounded and the kneeling congregation was slaughtered and the venerable white–haired priest at the rude altar was slain and his lifeblood flowed near the Adorable Body and Blood of the Redeemer he was offering up for the living and the dead."

Through the following centuries the A.O.H. has continued to be the great defender of its native land and the chosen rulers of the Irish people. In the stirring days of the "Land League" the mighty moral and financial support of the society was largely responsible for the nation's eventual emancipation.

The Ancient Order of Hibernians was formally established in the United States in May of 1836, when that bigotry and prejudice which assailed Irish Catholics in their homeland was transplanted with added virulence to the New World. In the constitution adopted by the A.O.H. in 1908, the intent and purpose of the fraternal society was geared to promoting friendship, unity, and Christian charity.

Loyalty to Catholic principles has been a trademark of the Ancient Order of Hibernians. Each county chaplain was instructed by the constitution to see that nothing is done or countenanced within his jurisdiction which is contrary to the laws of the Catholic Church, the decrees of the Plenary Councils of Baltimore and the Synodical Constitutions of the Diocese.

To this oldest Catholic fraternal society in existence "belongs the honor and distinction of being the first American society to raise $50,000 for the support of The Catholic University at Washington, as an endowment of a chair for the preservation of the language, literature, history and antiquities of Ireland." The initial division of the A.O.H. in Los Angeles was instituted on September 17, 1875, and "for a good many years the shock troops of Catholic Action in the diocese were the members of that order which insists upon the qualification of Irish birth or descent through either parent."

By the turn of the century the Ancient Order of Hibernians had the largest membership and the strongest financial standing of any Catholic organization in Southern California. When disaster struck the Golden State in 1906, earthquake and fire victims of San Francisco received substantial assistance from the A.O.H., which promptly raised $40,000 for the Bay City's homeless refugees. The Ancient Order of Hibernians in California has faithfully carried on the good work intended by its founders. Its activities have extended to all the corporal and spiritual works of mercy. Whether it was caring for the needy, visiting the sick, burying the dead, comforting the sorrowful or praying for the living, the A.O.H. has set an enviable record of Christian accomplishment.

ANGELS FLIGHT

In a letter to his priest–brother, Bishop Thomas J. Conaty observed that "Los Angeles has everything, including the shortest railroad in the world." He was referring, of course, to the Angels Flight Railway Company.

The prelate must have ridden Angels Flight often. In one of his breviaries, now in the Historical Museum of the Archival Center, was found a partial book of tickets (#953) for Angels Flight—"good for one ride if presented with book."

Christened by fruit punch on December 31, 1901, Angels Flight, the miniature funicular, was financed and built by Colonel J. W. Eddy as a practical means of providing access to Olive Heights and Bunker Hill. A poster advertisement issued in the early days of its operation referred to Angels Flight as "the most unique, interesting and useful inclined railway in the world." It went on to state that "it is in the heart of the city–Hill and Third Streets. The ride is inspiring and perfectly safe."

Angels Flight

Oldtimers will attest that Angels Flight truly was the city's most efficient form of public transportation. It was rarely more than a few minutes late and there were never any interruptions along its lines. Crowded, the cars could accommodate a maximum of fifty persons.

The two squealing funicular cars, *Sinai* and *Olivet* hauled an estimated 100 million commuters and tourists up and down Bunker Hill between 1901 and 1969. It was the only "movable" landmark in Los Angeles. The cost of riding Angels Flight never varied—a nickel. Traversing the 365 feet took only about forty–five seconds. Interestingly enough, the city classified Angels Flight as an elevator, rather than a railway.

Bishop Conaty came to the editorial defense of Angels Flight in 1913, when the cable controls failed and the *Sinai* careened into the *Olivet*, causing a spectacular and "'horrendous accident." (Fortunately, no one was seriously injured in the mishap). Conaty pointed out that Angels Flight was still the safest mode of transportation in the city.

Dismissed in 1935 as "outmoded," the "Old Lady of Bunker Hill" outlasted most of its detractors, making 400 trips each day, seven days a week, from 6 o'clock in the morning until midnight. On a marker erected by the Native Daughters of the Golden West, it was estimated that Angels Flight carried more passengers per mile than any other railway in the world during the first fifty years of its operation.

In his Introduction to Walt Wheelock's book on *Angels Flight*, the late W. W. Robinson said that the story of the "inclined railway that carries people to the heavily populated summit of Bunker Hill, is part of the story of local transportation." It is an account that began with horses and mules, continued with ox–drawn carretas, carriages, wagons, stages, railroads, horse–cars, cable–cars and electric lines.

THE *ANGELUS* AT THE MISSIONS

One of the early commentators on the western scene recalled, in 1913, that "every Californian as he turns the pages of the early history of his state feels at times that he can hear the echo of the *Angelus* bell of the missions that are dead and gone." Indeed, the tri–daily recitation of the *Angelus*, a pivotal part of the daily routine for the neophytes attached to the Golden State's missionary foundations, was a practice deeply rooted in the Christian life–style.

The *Angelus*, named for the first word of the appellation of the Archangel Gabriel, commemorates the mystery of the Incarnation through recitation of certain versicles, three Hail Marys and a special prayer, at 6 a.m., 12 noon and 6 p.m. It is a prayer formula that developed gradually over the centuries. Though it can be traced to the 900s, the *Angelus* was given papal sanction only in 1308, when it was approved and promulgated by Pope John XXII.

The ringing of a bell at each of the versicles was a device used in monastery villages to remind inhabitants of their obligation to thank Almighty God for His most stupendous message to mankind .

Annie Wynne's memorable poem, *The Angelus Bell*, recalls the pious practice as it was heard in mission days.

> HAIL holy bell! angelic lips
>> First breathed thy wondrous numbers,
> At fresh'ning dawn thy mellow voice
>> Awakes the world from slumbers;
> My heart exults each morn with thee,
>> That one more day I'm given
> To sever earthly shackles free
>> And strive for God and heaven.
>
> Aweary of life's endless toil
>> When mid day thou art chiming,
> The jangling and discordant strains
>> Blend sweetly to thy rhyming;
> One moment from the noisy world
>> Thou bidst each soul to sever,
> And read the hopeful lesson o'er
>> That God is with us ever.
>
> When day is waning to a close
>> And beauteous glow of even'
> Has merged its sapphire, gold and rose,
>> The valley, hill and heaven;
> How softly sounds the Angelus
>> To tired mortals bending
> With contrite, meek and grateful hearts
>> Their orisons ascending.
>
> 0 blessed bell! Sweet bell of peace,
>> We hail each holy pealing,
> At morning, noon and even' close
>> Redemption's price revealing;
> E'en as the ages roll along
>> To man thy peace pledge giving
> The mystic burden of thy song,
>> That makes our day worth living.

ANTIPHONALE — AN EARLY EDITION

An *antiphonale* or antiphonary is a liturgical book intended for use in the choral praise of the Lord. Originally it included the antiphonal chants sung by cantor, congregation and choir at Mass and the canonical hours. Later its use was restricted to the Divine Office.

The *antiphonale* was normally placed on a movable podium or lectern and rotated so that monks, friars and canons could read the music as they alternated in singing the verses of the psalter. By design it was an oversize book with plainly visible markings.

The beautifully hand–illuminated *antiphonale* on exhibit at San Fernando Mission can be traced to Palencia, Spain, where it was used for choral rendition of daily Vespers.

A heavy and large folio, the handsomely–executed volume dates from the late 16th or early 17th century. It is written in Latin on 180 leaves of heavy, durable parchment measuring 18.5 by 13.5 inches. The text is inscribed in very large Gothic letters, with music provided in square notes on five line staves. There are numerous calligraphic capitals and initials in red and blue with elaborate penwork of the opposite color.

Headings, antiphons and rubrics are colored in red. The opening initial "S" (*Salve crux pretiosa . . .*) measures 5.5 by 5.5 inches and is artistically painted in red and blue with two–color penwork. The lower margin of the same page is also filled with a decorative border which is partly cropped away.

Like other manuscripts dating from the same period and now displayed in leading libraries and museums, the *antiphonale* has three sections, each of different but more–or–less contemporary origin: There is the Proper of the Saints (*Sanctorale*) which consists of 125 leaves from Saint Andrew (November 30th) through Saint Clement (November 23rd). The Feast of Saint Lawrence is uncommonly long, perhaps because of a special relationship to the local church.

Then comes the Common of Saints which stretches over thirty–seven leaves, ending with the propers for the dedication of a church. Finally, there are some local feasts like Joachim and Anne, Antoninus (patron of Palencia), the Visitation of Mary and Mary Magdalen. Bibliophiles feel that this last section may have been added to the book late in the 17th century. The *antiphonale* can easily be identified with Palencia, a village 120 miles NNW of Madrid because of liturgical and stylistic considerations. There is also an explicit inscription which reads, "*quibus utitur Ecclesia Pallantina.*"

Bound in full leather over wooden boards, the covers of the manuscript are decorated in blind–tooling, with the name Miguel Piña de Campos on the front cover. The cover is further enhanced with four large corner pieces, plus a rather elaborate brass boss in the center.

Though the *antiphonale* lacks distinctive artistic quality, its lettering and music are obviously the work of skilled scribes. The rubrication and decoration of initials is simple but clear and precise. It is evident that this manuscript was used for many years. There are numerous hand stains and somewhat clumsy repairs. The margins and corners have obviously been thumbed for a long, long time.

It is not known precisely how the manuscript got to California. It was purchased by William Wreden from the estate of one of the California Crockers in 1945. He later sold it to a collector who, in turn, passed it along to Bernard M. Rosenthal, a bookdealer in Berkeley, California.

ARCHCONFRATERNITY OF BLESSED JUNI-PERO SERRA

The origins of the Archconfraternity of Blessed Junípero Serra can be traced to July of 1988, when Archbishop Roger M. Mahony authorized the inauguration of such a pious association "to coincide with the friar's beatification" which was scheduled to take place in Rome on September 25th of that year. The motivating objective was to launch "a prayer crusade" that would eventually culminate in Serra's canonization.

On July 26, 1988, the archbishop enthusiastically endorsed the proposal. After agreeing to become the canonical "protector" of the new archconfraternity, he directed that the program proceed "as you suggest."

The formal establishment of the archconfraternity took place on October 1st, at a con–celebrated Mass in the chapel of the Convento de San Bernardino, just a few steps from the house where Junípero Serra was raised in the tiny village of Petra de Mallorca in the Baleric Isles.

Assisting this writer at that Liturgy were Fathers Salustiano Vicedo, Vice Postulator for the Serra Cause in Spain and Father Thom Davis, a priest attached to the Archdiocese of Los Angeles. Among the forty charter members enrolled at Petra were two non–Catholics: Marly Daily of Santa Barbara and Mervin Eide of Granada Hills, California.

Canonically the archconfraternity is an ecclesial association having the three–fold purpose of advancing the canonization for Fray Junípero Serra, promoting vocations to the priesthood, religious life and lay ministry and intensifying the spiritual lives of members. By virtue of its authority of aggregating to itself confraternities erected for the same objectives in other localities, the association was referred to as an "archconfraternity." Members in the Archconfraternity of Blessed Junípero Serra, along with other confraternities established elsewhere, share in all the spiritual blessings, indulgences and works of virtue performed by associates throughout the world.

In addition to several newspaper accounts of its establishment, the first official recognition of the archconfraternity occurred in the 1989 issue of the *Los Angeles Catholic Directory* where it was described as a "non–profit organization dedicated to the canonization of Fray Junípero Serra."

In notices circulated to prospective members, it was stated that the names of enrolled and/or affiliated members would be recorded in the central headquarters. Membership is perpetual and requires only a daily prayer incorporating the objectives of the archconfraternity.

On November 9, 1988, this writer suggested to Bishop Thaddeus Shubsda that he consider establishing a branch of the association in the Diocese of Monterey. The bishop was initially hesitant only because he didn't have a priest available to direct the project. When it was explained that sacerdotal leadership was not necessary, the bishop reconsidered and, in mid 1989, he asked the late Martin Morgado to begin the Confraternity of Blessed Junípero Serra in the Diocese of Monterey.

The origins of the newsletter, later issued under the title *Siempre Adelante*, go back to 1983 and the first issue of the *Serra Bicentennial Commission Newsletter*. The eleven newsletters published between April of 1983 and September of 1985 were devoted to outlining the proceedings of the ten meetings held by the Serra Bicentennial Commission in various parts of the State.

There were several subsequent editions issued under the watchful eyes of Miriam Downie and Elizabeth Hilleary. In January of 1990, the newsletter became the official organ for the Monterey branch of the Confraternity of Blessed Junípero Serra. Its title was changed to *Siempre Adelanta* by its new editor, Martin Morgado.

ARCHIVES OF THE INDIES

As long ago as 1917, the eminent California historian, Charles E. Chapman, observed that "the history of Spanish America, so far as the documents are concerned, is preserved almost completely in Spain. . . . The most essential parts of those documents are contained in the *Archivo General de Indias* of Seville."

That famed collection, with which this writer had the privilege of working on two occasions, was set up at the behest of King Charles III in 1785, with the aim of bringing together all the records about America which until then were scattered in Simancas, Cadiz and other places.

The project was instigated by Jose de Galvez and put into practice by the historian and academic, Juan Bautista Muñoz, the renowned *Cosmografo Mayor de Indias*. The archives were brought together in a splendid building called the *Casa Lonja*, which had been constructed during the rein of Philip II. That edifice continues to house the Archives of the Indies to this day. The materials filed there are of exceptional interest for the historical study of Spain's activities in Latin America, concerned as they are with the vast area from the south of the United States to *Tierra de Fuego*, as well as the Philippines.

The documents were mostly issued by the various administrative organizations involved in the Spanish presence in Latin America and they include the *Virreinatos, Audiencias, gobernadores, capitanes generales, corregimientos*, etc.

Divided into fifteen sections, according to the origin of the documents, the Archives of the Indies also contain maps and drawings sent by the earliest colonizers to illustrate and explain their reports. Materials are grouped in bundles, around 43,000 in all, averaging a thousand sheets in each, most of them crammed with information on both sides of the page. The drawings and maps comprise about 7,000 items and there are an estimated nine kilometers of shelving in the Archives of the Indies.

The contents of the bundles are indexed in a variety of guides, inventories and catalogues, none of them complete and many inadequate. There are several alphabetical indices (of names, topographical materials and subjects) available to researchers. But those finding devices, prepared as they were over many decades by a host of different people, reflect a remarkably different depth and range of information. The most successful researchers are those who learn the mindset of earlier cataloguers.

Even with all its complexities, the Archives of the Indies is a fascinating and challenging treasure trove which scholars approach with excited anticipation. Each year, researchers from all over the world scramble to occupy the seventy available seats in the reading room and there are rarely any empty chairs.

In 1987, to cite one set of statistics, 72,368 requests were processed by the staff. Almost 5,000 of those inquiries were concerned with maps and drawings and an equal number for books in the auxiliary library. In that year, 874 researchers visited the Archives of the Indies, 62% of them were Spanish, 29% American and 8% European.

Until a scholar in the field of Western American has worked at Seville's Archives of the Indies, he remains an historical neophyte. And once there, that same scholar is humbled and edified by the recorded accomplishments in Latin America.

ART AND THE PAPACY

During the final months of 1983, California hosted the first–ever traveling show of art treasures from the Vatican's ten museums. The event was described as the "greatest art coup of all."

Described by *Newsweek* as the artistic "blockbuster

of the decade," the two hundred and seventeen works were on public display at San Francisco's M.H. de Young Memorial Museum.

In 1979, Philippe de Montebello, the director of New York's Metropolitan Museum of Art, asked Terence Cardinal Cooke to propose the idea to Pope John Paul II during the pontiff's visit to the United States.

A number of gifts from corporate and other sources, notably Philip Morris, Inc., made possible the financing needed for transportation and insurance. The collection was insured for $91,410,000. The selection of art and artifacts was chosen not alone for their intrinsic quality, but also as didactic illustrations of the papal collections from the fourth century to the present.

Emphasis was placed principally on what the works reveal about the papacy and only secondarily on the artists themselves. Bernini's bronze bust of Urban VIII was included, not for its beauty, but because it was Pope Urban who consecrated the new Saint Peter's Basilica in 1626.

The exhibit was divided into five sections which were intended to give some notion of the innumerable artistic holdings in the Vatican museums. Included were sculptures from the Egyptian Musuem and works from the Collection of Modern Religious Art.

The history of the papacy has been closely intertwined with that of art. Constantine's earlier basilica was crammed with artistic embellishments by the time of Pope Julius in 1503. Three years later, the Holy Father laid the foundation stone for the present Saint Peter's Basilica wherein the greatest of the Renaissance art works were incorporated.

Though Michelangelo's *Pieta* was not in the exhibit, the *Belvedere Torso* was brought to San Francisco. Two sets of small predella panels by Raphael likewise were on display.

The artistically–superb Vatican collections have an evangelical function. They also have a rare historical value inasmuch as they are the only pieces of art which, from Renaissance times, have the same owners and have been on the same site. The Renaissance popes—who hoped the art they fostered would convey the Christian vision could surely not have imagined that it would be seen as far away as California.

The exhibition proved extremely beneficial to the collection itself. Funds generated by various groups have enabled the Vatican to complete several major restorations previously delayed for lack of means.

Teeming with art that portrays miraculous interventions in the human pageant, the exhibition was probably the only chance many Californians ever had to see how the Vatican helped to shape the course of Western art.

ART CAPTURES HISTORIC MOMENT

September 15 is an important day in these environs for it recalls the beginnings of Mexico's revolution in 1810 from Spain. On the evening of that day, Ignacio Perez informed Juan de Aldama, Ignacio Allende and Father Miguel Hidalgo that the government had discovered their plans for independence.

The following morning, church bells called hundreds of peasants to the town square where they heard the leader of the conspiracy cry out for independence (*El Grito*). A large peasant army quickly mobilized and the movement spread to other regions of the country.

In March of 1811, Hidalgo, Aldama and Allende were defeated near Guadalajara and captured. They were executed a few months later, but their revolution continued until independence finally came in 1821.

These events were important for the far–away town of *Nuestra Señora de los Angeles* because at the conclusion of the revolution, Spanish control of Los Angeles ended. For the ensuing twenty–six years, the Mexican flag flew over the city.

In recognition of its historical and cultural ties with Los Angeles, the Mexican government, in 1968, donated to the one time *pueblo* a replica of the Bell of Dolores which Hidalgo rang on that fateful morning of September 16, 1810.

Dedicated by President Jimmy Carter in 1979, the *Placita de Dolores* was developed to display that gift. As part of the project, a competition was held in 1977 for a mural to serve as a backdrop for the bell. The design, which was won by Eduardo Carrillo, portrays the key people at the beginning of the revolution. On the viewer's left, Josefa Dominguez stands in front of her daughter and a group of school children.

To their left, a peasant hangs a poster proclaiming "Down with Bad Government" and "Foreigners Who Have Stolen Our Land" which Father Hidalgo courageously proclaimed on that September day. Dominguez's messenger, Ignacio Perez, rides a brown horse. Next to him, Captain Ignacio Allende is portrayed astride a blue stallion. A soldier bearing the revolutionary flag, with its depicting of a skeleton, stands next to Jose Maria Morelos, the leader of the revolt in southern Mexico.

At the center of the mural, Juan de Aldama, who was captured and betrayed Hidalgo, points an accusing finger at the priest who holds a paper with the sign of the *olin*, the Aztec symbol for movement and earthquakes. A peasant carrying the standard of the revolution, with its rendition of Our Lady of Guadalupe, stands slightly ahead of another revolutionary leader, Maria Estrada, who is displaying the scales of justice.

Three musicians signify the importance of music in Hidalgo's life, while stalks of corn in the background and peasants preparing food fix the beginning of the movement at the end of harvest season. Organized around a single point perspective, reinforced by the stonework pattern in front of the mural, the church at Dolores and its adjacent buildings focus action on a stage outlined by the sign of *olin*.

The mural is constructed of 300 handmade ceramic tiles, each one inch square. The artist prepared a full sized cartoon to help impose the composition onto the individual sections of fresh clay. Before he dried and fired the squares, Carrillo applied glazes over colored oxides.

Eduardo Carrillo's mural captures an historic moment. The 8 by 44 foot portrayal incorporates both the event and its artist into the long and colorful history of *El Pueblo de Nuestra Señora de los Angeles*.

BAJA CALIFORNIA — ALEMANY SPEAKS OUT

Early in December, 1876, Bishop Ramon María de San José Moreno y Castañeda (1839–1890), the Vicar Apostolic of Baja California, arrived in San Francisco. The Carmelite prelate had long been at odds with Governor Francisco Miranda over the enforcement of certain aspects of the Mexican Constitution in Peninsular California. After being seized and incarcerated, Bishop Moreno was expelled from the vicariate.

The exiled bishop gave an interview to the press on November 6th. Therein he briefly outlined the problems the Church faced in what easily amounted to an open persecution in Baja California. On December 10th, Archbishop Joseph Sadoc Alemany and the priests comprising the Archdiocese of San Francisco entertained Bishop Moreno in the basement of Saint Mary's Cathedral.

It was a noteworthy event. Not alone did it draw the largest assemblage of clergy in memory, but it provided the usually tranquil and gentle Archbishop Alemany with an ideal opportunity for publicly censuring the Mexican Government.

> Your visit to San Francisco is a singular event indeed, and speaks plainly of the rapid strides Mexico is making in its march to 'progress.' When I was in Mexico in 1852 knowing that the Government intended to imprison me should I personally exercise my official duties in Lower California, which then formed part of my diocese, I tried to persuade them that in a spirit of justice and in the name of liberty they would allow me, a Catholic bishop, to minister to my Catholic flock placed by the Sovereign Pontiff under my jurisdiction; but they obstinately refused, because I was not Mexican.
>
> Now you, Monsignor, a Mexican, have just been ignominiously imprisoned and sent into exile for doing your duty to your Mexican flock!

The archbishop noted that when he was last in Mexico, there was still regard in high places for the Sisters of Charity and for the local hierarchy. But now, "in a few years they have made such progress in their enlightenment and view of liberty as to banish from the capital its saintly and most learned Archbishop [Lazaro de] Garza, who, crushed with grief, died in a foreign land.

> They have proscribed and exiled a thousand Sisters of Charity, whose only crime was charity; they are constantly enacting anti–Christian laws which would disgrace even a Caligua or a Nero.
>
> And were I asked a proof of my assertions, your very presence among us furnishes it most abundantly. For under the quibble that your episcopal dress should be, not as the episcopal ceremonial points out, but as lay officials may fashion; without an alleged crime, without the least semblance of trial, you were imprisoned and banished from your country and from your flock.
>
> All this is truly progress, only in the wrong direction. When the Roman leaders emerged from the thick darkness of paganism, and they exiled the bishops and popes, they acted as pagans deprived of the light of Christian civilization. What can exculpate a handful of officials, electing themselves into high places over a truly Catholic people, and who, in the name of liberty and civilization, trample on the most sacred rights, plunder the nation's goods, keep the country in a constant state of agitation, sedition and anarchy, paralyze the energies of the people, and render one of the finest countries on earth a wreck to society and civilization.
>
> It is not my hatred, it is my love for Mexico, which makes me utter such expressions; for Mexico should at present rank among the highest nations of the world, for it is blessed with an excellent climate; it has safe harbors on the Gulf and on the Pacific; its soil is most productive; its mineral resources exceedingly rich and inexhaustible; the people are sprightly, intelligent and humane, and the nation, as a whole, is sincerely devoted to the interests of their faith.
>
> Americans are a noble people and in their keen sense of right they truly sympathize with such as, like you, suffer persecution for justice sake. This is the sentiment which animates us all here now, in coming together before you on this occasion, to tender you, Right Reverend Sir, our highest regard and veneration.

BAJA CALIFORNIA — HISTORICAL OUTLINE

One of the most fascinating and surely the most elusive publications to appear in the mid–nineteenth century was the anonymously–edited *Historical Outline of Lower California*. The seventy–nine page pamphlet, translated from the Spanish by "M.E.R.," was printed at the office of *La Voz de Méjico* and published in San Francisco, probably early in 1863, by Henry Payot.

Envisioned as a promotional effort for emigrants, "as well as those intending to become such," the stated purpose of the publication was "solely to contribute . . . some additional light upon a few subjects likely to give information about the state of that country from its discovery to the present time." The treatise was known to J. Ross Browne, who travelled through the peninsula in 1866. He refers to and quotes the work in which "detailed statistics are given of the names, locations, ownerships and products" of the various mines.

The fact laden pamphlet touches a wide variety of bases. It contains tracts from the posthumous work of Francisco Javier Clavijero (1789), an essay on mineralogy and commerce (1856), a decree on colonization (1857), portions of the memorial of Ulises Urbano Lassepas (1859), a census of inhabitants (1861), a descriptive list of operational mines and several miscellaneous decrees.

Certainly the most interesting item in the pamphlet is a report on the peninsular missions written by Sebastian Viosca. Early in 1861, Baja California's Governor, Teodoro Riveroll, commissioned Viosca, a local official, to visit all the missionary outposts of the Territory, as far as that of San Borja, and to "take therefrom all the manuscripts, pictures and antiquities deemed useful for the Museum and History of Mexico."

Viosca began his tour through the labyrinth of steep and tortuous hills, narrow ravines, steep descents, mountain valleys and low inclines on February 14th. A recognized authority on the mining districts, Viosca was "a gentleman qualified by his official position to furnish authentic data." He attributed most of the problems encountered by the area's missionaries to the continuous political dissensions which had destroyed the vitality of the unhappy Republic since its independence.

Obviously a man of considerable education and experience, Viosca spoke affectionately about "those habitations of stone, brick, mud and palm trees" where the "few vestiges of art, taste and luxury" indicated "man's aspirations to a better state."

He recalled how the missionaries had engineered irrigation canals to refresh "the earth with their fertilizing waters," how they had planted the "trees bending under the weight of branches loaded with figs, oranges, lemons, olives, pomegranates and peaches," how they had built roads along "the sides of steep and rugged mountains" and on the border of immense precipices, how they had laid out fields "covered with grape vines, corn and sugar cane," and how they had introduced cattle and sheep on the hills of the peninsula.

In his report, which was submitted to the "Citizen Governor of the Territory," on April 14, 1862, Viosca spoke longingly about the missions "whose ruins are admired by the intelligent traveller."

The Viosca memorial is valuable for the historic record. There the observant reader can easily see that "each and everything pertaining to the three Kingdoms of Lower California is the result of the long and patient work of an enterprize initiated one hundred and sixty five years earlier."

BAJA CALIFORNIA — MISSIONS ON THE *FRONTERA*

The Order of Preachers engaged in missionary, parochial and educational work in the new world from the earliest days of the conquest. With their many convents and schools, the Dominicans enjoyed a long and spiritually profitable existence in New Spain.

In 1767, the Society of Jesus was suppressed and the Jesuit Missions in the New Spain were entrusted to other religious orders. Those in Baja California were turned over to the Franciscans who, a few years later, transferred them to the Dominicans.

Upon their arrival, in 1773, the Dominicans were commissioned by the king to establish five coastal missions in the *frontera* or northernpart of Baja California, as a means of connecting the existing foundations with those already established or projected for Alta California. The purpose for the coastal missions was basically strategic and military. They were to become a part of that Hispanic defense system whose missions and *presidios* brought Christianity and civilization to numberless aboriginals and, at a minimum cost to the Crown, effectively prevented encroachments by the English, French and Russians.

The Dominicans founded the coastal missions in 1774 (Rosario), 1775 (Santo Domingo), 1780 (San Vicente), 1787 (San Miguel) and 1791 (Santo Tomas). Then they established two additional outposts in the mountain area, namely San Pedro Martir (1794) and Santa Catalina (1797). San Pedro was founded for purely spiritual objectives, while Santa Catalina was established because of its ability to support the natives of a fairly densely populated area. The latter foundation was also envisioned as a necessary communicational link between the *frontera* and Sonora.

The period of growth for the Dominican missions on the *frontera* occurred between 1774 and 1804, when the peninsula was separated politically from Alta California. During those three decades seventy–nine Dominicans labored in the area.

In the fifty years after 1805, only fifteen additional friars came to the peninsula. The sharp reduction in their number can be attributed to a number of causes. To begin with, after the political separation of the Californias, the peninsula no longer enjoyed any strategic value and Spain shifted its interest to Alta California. Secondly, the Mexican Revolution, in 1810, severely complicated the processing of new recruits for missionary endeavors.

Thirdly, the "reforms" of the Mexican Empire, introduced in 1821, practically dealt a death blow to mission life. Though the Indians remained under the general supervision of the friars, they were freed from any constraints of work and residence. Fourthly, the secularization movements of 1825, 1830, and 1833 gradually dispensed the Indians from all remaining forms of accountability to the friars.

The Dominicans were asked to remain at their posts, which many did until 1855. But the Indians were not ready for the unrestrained liberty which they abused with great abandon. Gradually they drifted away from the missions, looking for food and clothing, while epidemics and diseases greatly reduced their numbers. Smallpox ravaged the peninsula several times in the late 1700s, killing hundreds of Indians in its wake.

In 1834 the ninth and last Dominican mission was founded, some miles east of San Miguel and placed under the patronage of *Nuestra Señora de Guadalupe*. It was established with the vain hope of salvaging what little was left of the old mission system.

After 1822, there were no resident ministers at Rosario, Santo Domingo and San Miguel and, after 1825, San Vicente was without a priest. In 1839, *Nuestra Señora de Guadalupe* was sacked by the Indians and, the following year, Santa Catalina was burned. The last Dominican missionary on the *frontera* was Fray Tomas Mansilla, who resided at Santo Tomas. He was in charge of the whole mission system from 1840 to 1850. The various ruins were illegally sold between 1849 and 1859. From the spiritual viewpoint, the harvest of souls was great, considering the Indians' hostile tendencies, the paucity of their number and their wide dispersion in the mountains, caves and *arroyos*.

Socially, the primitive peoples were brought together into organized villages and community life. They were fed, clothed and taught some of the amenities of civilization. They enjoyed security and learned a healthy respect for law, peace and order.

Educationally, the *frontera* missions were also giant industrial schools. The women taught cooking, sewing, spinning and weaving, while the men were instructed in masonry and carpentry, as is clearly evident from the buildings, dams, reservoirs, canals, corrals, tanning pits and kilns.

The natives also learned how to plant, cultivate and harvest crops, such as wheat, barley, corn, beans, vegetables and grapes. Likewise they were taught to care for and breed cattle, sheep, horses, mules and hogs. This practical industrial education had the obvious result of making the natives somewhat self–supporting and providing the discipline necessary for the rudiments of what we know as civilized life.

BANK OF AMERICA

When the cornerstone was set in place for the new San Francisco headquarters of the Bank of America, on May 6, 1941, the trowel used by A. P. Giannini symbolized the building blocks of California.

The handle of the trowel was fabricated from tiny pieces of wood gathered from each of the state's fifty–eight counties. Most of the fragments were associated with historic events which marked California's beginnings. Others were identified with literary figures who found fame portraying the romance of the area, while still others were reminders of California's scenic beauty which has captured the admiration of peoples everywhere.

Featured prominently among the tiny wooden fragments were the California's historic missions which Fray Junípero Serra and his Franciscan collaborators erected along what became known in historic annals as *El Camino Real*.

Marin County is represented by a piece of pear wood from one of the original trees planted in 1819 at San Rafael Mission. Founded in 1817, the mission was later abandoned and, by 1941, only the pear trees remained to recall the once–proud frontier establishment.

A chunk of redwood recalls San Juan Capistrano Mission which was established in 1776. This particular piece of wood was taken from the storeroom where the friars kept food and dried meats.

It is believed that the first use of redwood in the southern part of the state occurred at San Juan Capistrano. Historians conjecture that the timbers used at that mission were brought from small groves in the San Simeon area.

The wood chosen to represent San Diego Mission, the first of the frontier outposts in Alta California, was incense cedar. Timbers for that mission were hauled from the Cuyamaca mountains, some fifty miles east of San Diego. Plans were underway, in 1941, for restoring the church to parochial use.

San Luis Obispo is portrayed by a fragment of pine from the mission founded in 1772 in honor of Saint Louis, the Bishop of Toulouse. It was at San Luis Obispo Mission that an inventive friar perfected the manufacture of tile, which was used for the erection of the adobe church.

The wood from Santa Barbara County, also pine, was extracted from a door of the Old Mission. Though the site for the "Queen of the Missions" was selected by

Fray Junípero Serra in 1784, two more years passed before Fray Fermin Francisco de Lasuen actually inaugurated the mission.

Finally, another variety of pine was used to recall Ventura County, whose mission of San Buenaventura was founded on Easter Sunday in 1782, the last of the nine established by Fray Junípero Serra. By 1800, this mission was raising more cattle and grain than any other in California and was famous for its large olive groves and vineyards. In 1873, part of the grounds were used for a new court house.

The other pieces of wood are enumerated and described in a pamphlet issued by the Bank of America in 1941 under the title *Cornerstones of California*. In that sixty–four page publication, the author writes that "upon these foundations, California, with the vision and spirit of its founders, has continued ever building for the future."

BARBAREÑO CATHECHISM (1798)

The oldest extensive text yet discovered in an Alta California Indian tongue has long been among the manuscripts and rare books, in Mexico City's *Biblioteca Nacional*. Compiled by Fray Juan Lope Cortés (b. 1772), the thirty–two page booklet is entitled *Oraciones de la Doctrina Christiana, Methodo de Confesar, y algunas otras cosas . . .* It was sewn together in December, 1798, for use at Santa Barbara Mission.

The compiler was a friar from Toledo, Spain who had worked in California since 1796. He served at Santa Barbara between 1798 and 1805, at which time he returned to the Apostolic College of San Fernando. From 1821 to 1828, he was procurator of the California missions.

Cortés intended that his manuscript would contain the basic "elements of Christian doctrine" along with an easy formula for interrogating those neophytes wishing to avail themselves of the Sacrament of Penance. He wrote the text in the Indian dialect most frequently used at Santa Barbara, with an accompanying Spanish translation. As a reflection of Indian culture, the manuscript is a truly significant document.

The priest compiler modeled his little handbook on those developed earlier in the missions of New Spain. The basic format dates to when the bishops drafted the statutes of the Third Mexican Provincial Council.

Cortés work includes the Act of Contrition, Lord's Prayer, *Ave Maria*, the Creed, a version of the *Salve Regina*, Ten Commandments, Precepts of the Church, Seven Sacraments, a catechism, guide for confession and a brief exhortation to be read to those about to receive Baptism, Penance, Matrimony and Extreme Unction.

The catechetical part of Cortés manuscript is a direct translation of Bartolomé Castaño's *Catecismo Breve*. Cortés later wrote that the Castaño version was recited twice daily at Santa Barbara, once in Spanish and once in the native dialect. The use of both languages was an attempt to find a middle road between a royal decree that only Castilian be used and the experience which showed that many neophytes simply could not learn the new language. The Cortés manuscript was apparently one of those books intended to be read aloud to the penitent in the confessional or to a group of penitents just before confession to help them recall their offenses.

The original manuscript is soiled from hard use. The lower outside edges of the pages containing the prayers and catechism are heavily smudged from oil and perspiration. Apparently the author unconsciously rubbed the inked page between his thumb and forefinger while reciting these texts day after day with his Indian neophytes. One of the few contemporary records of religious education in the California missions, the manuscript is the only known text in Barbareño Chumash.

Harry Kelsey, Chief Curator at the Natural History Museum in Los Angeles, has translated the fascinating manuscript which is now available in a 124 page book, *The Doctrina and Confesionario of Juan Cortés*.

BELL MARKERS AT THE MISSIONS

Shortly after the turn of the century, a group of Californians became conscious of their history, and, out of this awareness, came the desire to honor their state's traditions and to establish some visible historical monuments. At the suggestion of Mrs. A. S. C. Forbes, it was decided that erection of replica mission bells along the 700 mile route of *El Camino Real* would be a "distinctive, emblematic and appropriate guidepost" to remind residents of the Golden State about their noble historical heritage

The first bell, erected outside the *Asistencia de Nuestra Señora de los Angeles*, was dedicated on August 15, 1906, in connection with the festival held each year to mark the patronage of the old Plaza church. Each of the 100 pound cast–iron bells was suspended on an iron pipe resembling in shape the shepherd's crook. The guidepost was of a plain, severe design to represent the simple austere life led by the early missionaries. A marker was attached to each standard giving explicit directions to the traveler and information regarding the missions as stations along the way.

Initial interest in the project of marking the meandering road connecting the missions was widespread and numerous organizations cooperated in raising funds to erect the bell standards. By 1913, there were 450 markers stretching along *El Camino Real* from the Mexican border to Sonoma. Unfortunately, there were no funds available to sustain or replace the bells in the years prior to 1921. At that time, however, the Automobile Club assumed the task of maintaining the markers throughout the state.

In the years after 1933, the work of caring for the bells was supervised by the California Division of Highways. Gradually the bells began disappearing. Some were lost when state roads were widened or relocated. Vandals and souvenir hunters despoiled others, and by 1959, there were only seventeen bells remaining in Los Angeles County. In 1959, the California State Legislature approved a proposal authorizing the Division of Highways to re–erect the bells. More than thirty were recovered from various private parties. In addition, a Los Angeles firm agreed to produce a facsimile bell for the original price of $25.

Today, the mission bells once again mark California's *El Camino Real* and in 1963, Chief Justice Earl Warren and a delegation of other notable figures personally delivered a bell to Fray Junípero Serra's birthplace on Mallorca to commemorate the 250th anniversary of the Franciscan's birth.

Travelers driving through the state today might find it historically relevant to recall those words written in 1903, by the originator of the bell markers:

> They are the voice of the past,
> Of an age that is fading fast,
> Of a power austere and grand,
> When the flag of Spain unfurled
> Its fold o'er the Western world
> And the priest was lord of the land.

BELLS — FOR WHOM THEY TOLL

Though the origin of bells is obscure, history reveals their dual and somewhat strange function. They convey a signal, a message or a warning in a code understood by the people concerned. Besides this useful duty, bells perform a ritual function as a component of solemn ceremony and worship.

The liturgical use of bells reaches far back into antiquity. Chinese chronicles dating from 2262 B.C. mention bells. The ancient Egyptians and Indians used them. The canopy of the hearse bearing the remains of Alexander the Great (324 B.C.) was adorned with bells calling the populace to join the funeral procession.

There is no mention of bells in the Old Testament, and the first centuries of Christianity are devoid of bells. The liturgical use of the bell among Christians originated in Ireland. Irish monks brought their bells to the continent, where the use of the Roman bell had apparently been forgotten or discarded.

The bell of Saint Gall, a monastery in Switzerland founded by Irish monks, served as a model for a type of bell used widely in western and central Europe. That design has been transmitted to contemporary times without much alteration. They can still be found on the green slopes of the Alps—and the pastures of Wisconsin–tinkling joyfully on the necks of the placid cattle.

In earlier times, bells were dedicated to their spiritual and practical vocation by a long and magnificent liturgical ceremony. The rite was established during the sixth century and was performed by a bishop. A lesson from the Book of Numbers recalled the command of Moses, to make two silver trumpets. Christian bells are to the new law what trumpets were to the old. The celebrant asked the god–parents to name the bell. They answered: "Under the invocation of Saint ———, we commend this bell." This custom of naming the bells comes from remote Christian antiquity. For example, the largest bell at Notre Dame in Paris is called "John."

Throughout the Middle Ages, bells were used in the defense of cities. A special bell with a high–pitched tone was rung during great disasters, civil wars, riots, looting and murder. First it was rung at long intervals, then in quick succession, which echoed the call of a person in distress. When destruction threatened a city through fire, all the bells were rung simultaneously, their rapid peals simulating a cry for help.

The bell also served to call the people to prayer. At the founding of San Antonio Mission, it is recorded that Fray Junípero Serra took "the bells brought along" and had them suspended from the branches of an oak tree. He rang them in a lively manner, shouting: "Hear, Oh Gentiles, Oh come to the holy Church of God."

Pope Gregory IX introduced midday prayer. The association of the *Angelus* with these prayers, asking the bell to summon Gabriel of the Annunciation, dates from the fourteenth century. In 1456, Pope Callistus III established the *Angelus* as a universal custom in commemortaion of the miraculous liberation of Belgrade from the Turks during that year.

Yet another duty of the bell is the "tolling of the knell." This toll for the dying—three peals for a man and two for a woman—is of great antiquity. In Rheims, the bell used at the death of a Canon of the Cathedral was called "the bark of death." During the Italian wars in the Middle Ages, the bell was carried into the battlefields on a chariot in the shape of a belfry pulled by oxen and protected by a special guard. Some of the chariots served as chapels where, before the battle, Mass was celebrated.

BENEDICT'S CASTLE

In the early 1950s, the Order of Servants of Mary, also

known as Servites, was looking for a site to open a seminary for the Western United States. Through a providential series of circumstances, they selected a "castle" in Riverside. Located near the present intersection of Central and Chicago Avenues, the castle has a history which closely resembles that of Scotty's Castle in Death Valley.

Charles W. Benedict was a native of Riverside who had left his native surroundings to find his fortune. He returned to Southern California in 1919, and began plans for his Spanish–style home. Shortly thereafter, Charles met and then married a talented young woman musician and together they started the actual construction of their dream castle in 1922.

We are told that disagreements over the details of the building added to the Benedict's marital problems and, in 1925, their marriage was legally terminated. Understandably, for a few years, progress on the construction faltered. In 1931, upon completion of the castle, Mr. Benedict named the building "*Castillo Isabella*" for his mother. The ninety foot tower was christened "*Torre Luisa*" to honor Benedict's new wife, Louise. Despite those formal titles, local inhabitants still refer to it as "Benedict's Castle."

During the subsequent seven years, the Benedicts staged numerous glorious parties and banquets at their castle. Charles died in 1938, but Louise continued to live there until 1949, when she finallly allowed the castle and its expensive furnishings to be sold.

The new owners rented out the castle for various events and during the years between 1949 and 1952, the castle figured prominently in the social calendar of the Riverside–San Bernardino area. With the arrival of the Servites in 1952, the castle's interior was altered to allow for dormitories and classrooms, together with a large cooking and dining area. The central parlor was made over into a chapel, and windows were painted to resemble stained glass.

A swimming pool and tennis courts were added for the seminarians, but the Servites carefully avoided making major alterations to the historic structure. The castle became a favorite also for television and movie production. In the 1960s, the Servites opened the castle's doors to the public for such events as art festivals, musical programs, social gatherings and fundraising activities.

A change of focus within the Servites brought on the decision, in 1970, to abandon the seminary program. Several proposals were made for use of the property, but eventually it was decided to sell the castle and its adjoining property. Benedict's Castle was purchased by Teen Challenge of Southern California. Today that ministry institute, affiliated with Oral Roberts University, operates a 28,000 square foot facility consisting of twenty–three acres and five main buildings capable of accommodating seventy live–in residents.

Benedict's Castle is now a Riverside landmark. Visitors are impressed to see many of the religious symbols placed there by the Servites still being preserved. There is a bronze plaque with the name "Our Lady of Riverside Seminary–*Ordo Servorum B.M.V.*" and around the patio are the Stations of the Cross.

BIBLE — GOD'S WORD IN THE SOUTHLAND

In addition to being the inspired Word of God and thus the cornerstone of the Catholic faith, the Bible has been and remains the greatest document of Western culture. Its history is synonymous with that of the people edified and guided by its message.

The importance of the Bible is without parallel. In the Middle Ages, for example, its influence can be found in virtually every facet of medieval life and culture. In the long centuries before printing, manuscripts preserved the text of Holy Writ for future generations.

Printing by movable type was invented by Johann Gutenberg and, fittingly, his first book was the Bible which he completed around 1454–1455. Over the past 500 years, the Bible has been printed in more versions, editions and translations than any other book.

There is a long and rich history of Bible collecting in California's southland. The earliest significant collection was amassed by Henry E. Huntington in the years after 1911, when he bought Robert Hoe's copy of the Gutenberg Bible on vellum. In subsequent years, Mr. Huntington gathered a remarkable variety of manuscripts and printed editions of the Sacred Scriptures.

Another early southland collector was Carrie Estelle Doheny who has been described as "without doubt Los Angeles's greatest woman collector and its most zealous collector of Bibles." At one time, Mrs. Doheny owned more than a dozen Bibles printed before 1501, including two elegant editions printed by Nicolas Jenson, the first in Dutch and an illustrated edition in German.

Ultimately, she was able to purchase her own copy of the Gutenberg, the Dyson–Perrins copy. While only a single volume, it was gloriously illustrated by a Mainz artist and sturdily bound by a contemporary craftsman.

Mrs. Doheny has also been acknowledged as having "the honor of being one of the most generous donors to the cultural institutions of Los Angeles." She built libraries at USC and Camarillo and gave away several sets of the Complutensian Polyglot Bible, as well as copies of the *Book of Kells* in facsimile.

The vast majority of the rare books at the J. Paul Getty Museum, including its Bibles, came to that institution in 1983, when officials there acquired the famed Peter Ludwig Collection from Germany. A few of the more choice Doheny materials were acquired by UCLA's Department of Special Collections for the Ahmanson–Murphy Collection of Italian Printing, including the Nicolas Jenson Latin Bible of 1476. The collections of Holy Writ at the Getty and at UCLA display the rich character and diversity of both illuminated manuscripts and printed copies over the course of a thousand years of human history.

Since the arrival of Spanish missionaries in Alta California in 1769, the Bible has been a source of consolation, instruction and inspiration to the peoples living along the Pacific Slope. Today, the Huntington Library, the Getty Museum and the Special Collections Department at UCLA preserve a rich array of Bibles to be studied as texts, historical artifacts and works of art.

The historical thread that stretches back to the ancient kingdom of Israel and Judah is amply represented in Southern California.

BIBLE — PLANTS AND FLOWERS

"More than skies or clouds, more than valleys or hills, more than sentient creatures of high or low degree, the trees, shrubs and flowers of a land give character to its scenery, impressing the mind by their grandeur, or charming it by their beauty." So says William Groser in a delightful book published at London in 1888.

In the west and southwest areas of the United States halfway around the world from Palestine, in the same latitude and under climatic conditions governed by a similar relation of mountains to valleys and desert to sea, many of the plants first mentioned in Holy Scripture can be seen in great abundance.

During the May of 1935, Paul J. Howard exhibited a collection of those plants at the Second Annual San Fernando Valley Flower Show in North Hollywood. The following parts of that exhibit were among those catalogued by Mary van Barneveld.

BARLEY (John 6,9). "There is a lad here with five barley loaves." The Hebrew name for barley means "long–haired" grain as contrasted with wheat. It grows wild in Syria and Palestine.

FIG (Luke 2,29). "Behold the fig tree . . . ." Biblical references to this tree begin with the Garden of Eden and end with the Apocalypse, illustrating the frequency of its occurrence and the value of its shade.

GRAPE (Genesis 9,20). "Noah began to be a husbandman and planted a vineyard." The predominance of vineyards was a prominent feature in the scenery of ancient Palestine as well as an important element in the sustenance of its people.

CEDAR (I Kings, 5,8). "My servant shall bring trees from Lebanon." The grandest of all the trees known to the Hebrews were the Cedars of Lebanon. And they were used in the construction of Solomon's Temple.

LENTILS (Genesis 25,30). "Jacob gave Esau a pottage of lentils." Barzillai and his companions brought lentils for David and his soldiers. On the border of Egypt stood Phakussa, "the lentil town."

LILIES (Luke 12,27). "Consider the lilies of the field." Many scripture scholars believe that the biblical lilies were not white, but red and purple. This is confirmed by the implied comparison with royal robes.

MUSTARD (Mark 4, 30). "It is like a grain of mustard seed." A traveler has been quoted as saying that "I have seen this plant on the rich plains of Akka (Phoenicia) as tall as the horse and his rider."

OLIVE (Hosea 14,6). "His beauty shall be as the olive tree." These trees grow on Mount Olivet. Solomon's groves were probably near the coastal plain or in the low hills between the central highlands.

PALM (Deuteronomy 34,1). "The valley of Jericho, the city of palm trees." The art of cultivating the date–palm was first practiced in the plain bordering the Lower Euphrates and Tigris.

POMEGRANATE (Samuel, 14,2). Saul tarried under a pomegranate tree." Throughout the Orient, the palm tree is looked on as a symbol of luxuriant fertility and life. It was known to be a favorite fruit in Egypt before the Exodus.

WHEAT and TARES (Matthew 13,30). "Gather the wheat into my barn". Wheat is mentioned in some of the earliest pages of holy scripture. There are sundry varieties. The tares is usually identified as darnel or wild rice, which belongs to the grass family.

Authors in many lands, writing about Palestine, have been touched by the imagery furnished by the trees and plants in the Bible, many of which can be seen flourishing in Southern California.

BIBLIOTHECA MONTEREYENSIS–ANGELORUM DIOECESEOS

A. HISTORICAL SKETCH

In early 1968 the old *Bibliotheca Montereyensis –Angelorum Dioeceseos* was removed from storage and transferred to Queen of Angels Seminary, where it was catalogued and categorized. The historic library was eventually placed on permanent display in a newly restored room of the adjacent Mission San Fernando. The provenance of the *Bibliotheca* is fascinating. Though most of the books had long been in California, it was only in the years after 1842 that they found their way into the theological library formed by Bishop Francisco Garcia Diego y Moreno for the area's initial seminary.

What books had been gathered from the missions and private donors were moved from Santa Barbara, in 1844, to quarters provided at nearby Santa Ines for the newly autonomous Seminary of Our Lady of Refuge. During its four decades at Santa Ines, the collection occupied a large room in the central part of the the old mission building, not far from the two–story adobe housing the seminary proper.

When the seminary's prospectus was broadened to include nonclerical aspirants, the college, later placed under the patronage of Our Lady of Guadalupe, was moved to another site about a mile and a half from the mission, on the vast 36,000 acre ranch. While students continued to have access to the *Bibliotheca*, the seminary library was never transferred to the new location.

No specific check list of titles for any given period has been discovered, though an inventory drawn up, in 1853, mentions 744 volumes as belonging to the library. In 1874, Hubert Howe Bancroft visited Santa Ines and recorded seeing about 600 tomes in the *Bibliotheca*. Sometime between November, 1882 and the spring of 1884, Bishop Francis Mora had the library moved to his residence in Los Angeles, adjacent to Saint Vibiana's Cathedral. When a new three–story edifice was erected, in 1888–1889, the books were placed in specially designed quarters off a tunnelway connecting the rectory with the tower of the church.

The *Bibliotheca Montereyensis–Angelorum Dioeceseos* remained at the cathedral until 1933, when an earthquake so damaged the building that it had to be completely replaced. At that time the collection was taken to the diocesan preparatory seminary, located in Hancock Park. Accommodations were made for storing the library in the basement area, immediately beneath the central foyer. From that time onwards, the *Bibliotheca* ceased to be utilized as a learning tool. Shortly after the opening, at Saint John's Seminary, of the Edward Laurence Doheny Memorial Library, on September 22, 1940, the *Biblio-theca Montereyensis–Angelorum Dioeceseos* was again crated and transported the sixty–five miles to Camarillo. There it was placed in two caged rooms on the bottom level of the reference stacks. Sporadic attempts were made to acquisition the collection and a number of obviously valuable tomes were indeed assimilated into the active seminary library. Several of the more attractively bound book sets were used to fill out the shelves left vacant in the seminary's parlor by the removal of a large collection of rock specimens.

On February 7, 1968, authorization was obtained from chancery officials of the Archdiocese of Los Angeles to reactivate the *Bibliotheca Montereyensis–Angelorum Dioeceseos* as an historical collection. The books were carefully cleaned, repaired and arranged into the ten–category system used at the Apostolic College of San Fernando in Mexico City. Post–mission accession marks were removed and mutilated or faded bookplates replaced. In the later months of 1964, the *Bibliotheca Montereyensis–Angelorum Dioeceseos*, once the largest and most complete of the mission libraries, emerged from the shadows of another era.

BIBLIOTHECA MONTEREYENSIS–ANGELO-RUM DIOECESEOS

B. *OBITER DICTA*

Booksellers and librarians testify that people tend to put things in books to protect them (rose petals from a casket spray), to safeguard them (money or love letters) and to preserve them (ticket stubs from a Notre Dame–USC football game).

Bibliotheca Montereyenis-Angelorum Dioceseos

During 1968, when the 1760 volumes comprising the *Biblioteca Montereyensis–Angelorum Dioeceseos*, were being organized and accessioned a number of interesting and fascinating items from earlier times were discovered in the books.

Probably the most intriguing single item was a small "confession ticket" which was dated October 31, 1804. It read: "*Se confeso en cumplimiento del precepto anual de Ntra Madre la Sta Iglesia anno de mil ochocientos quarto.*" (The holder made his confession in accordance with the annual precept of our Holy Mother Church in 1804).

Such "tickets" were handed to converts, soldiers and others in provincial times on the occasion of their yearly reception of the Sacrament of Penance. Presumably, it was the practice that Catholics had to provide evidence of compliance with ecclesial law.

Another item was a printed notice inviting friends to a funeral. Dated at Los Angeles, December 8, 1867, it read: *Mañana, a las nueve de la mañana, tendre lugar en la Iglesia Catolica, en entierro del finado Dn. Jose Maria Davlos (Q.E.P.D.). Su esposa, familia y amigos, esperan les honre con su asistancia.*"

There was even a "holy ticket" testifying that Armando Contreras had visited Rome in 1768 and there received a special indulgence by "attending the Mass of the Holy Father." (Pope Clement XIII). Another ticket gives evidence that Jose Maria Jimeno participated in a solemn portrayal of the Stations of the Cross at the church of San Felipe de Jesus "*En el dia 15 de Enero de Ano de 1843* " (January 15, 1843).

A rose–colored "holy" card indicates that its owner was a "religious client" of Saint Eulalia. That would refer to the cathedral in Barcelona where many of California's pioneer priests and soldiers were earlier associated.

There were *ex libris* labels attached to some of the books. The first bookplate designed and printed in California was made for General Mariano Guadalupe Vallejo, commander of the northern frontier. His library contained more than 12,000 books, some of which are still displayed at his Sonoma home and in the Bancroft Library at Berkeley.

Jose de la Rosa, one of the first printers in California and an employee of Vallejo, undoubtedly printed the general's bookplates. There are at least two of his bookplates in the *biblioteca* which is now on exhibit at San Fernando Mission.

Bishop Francis Mora had bookplates made for the books in the *biblioteca*. There were four words: "*Biblioteca Montereyenis–Angelorum Diocececos*, along with a blank space for the shelf number. There were also a number of "holy cards" found in the books, including several with depictions of Our Lady of Guadalupe and one with a reference to Our Lady of Montserrat.

THE *BIBLIOTHECA SANCTI FRANCISCI ARCHDIOECESEOS*

One of the most intriguing and historically relevant book collections in California, long housed at Saint Patrick's Seminary in Menlo Park, has been catalogued and made available to competent researchers. Though not associated with the mission period of California's history, many of the tomes predate that era by well over two centuries.

In a description of the *Bibliotheca Sancti Francisci Archdioeceseos*, made in 1878, Flora Haines Apponyi noted that "in the library of J. S. Alemany, Archbishop of California, at San Francisco, there are two thousand, seven hundred and fifty volumes, consisting principally of various versions and editions of the holy bible, commentaries on the same, the writings of the fathers and doctors of the church, bullarisms, canon law, theology, history, liturgy and classics."

There are presently 1,612 tomes in the *Bibliotheca*, under 621 separate titles. In addition to an undisclosed number of volumes accessioned into the active seminary library, a fair proportion of the books obviously have been lost, borrowed or otherwise alienated in the ninety four years since the appearance of the Apponyi treatise.

The origin of the library can be traced to August 8, 1850, when Bishop Joseph Sadoc Alemany, newly appointed to the See of Monterey, recorded in his diary that he had shipped a large parcel of his personal books from Marseilles to California. Indications are that the prelate kept the volumes at his residence in Monterey, until 1853, when he moved to San Francisco as the area's first metropolitan archbishop.

Whether the tomes were placed at Mission Dolores, where the archbishop opened Saint Thomas Seminary, is only a conjecture. In any case, clerical aspirants surely had access to the valuable library during their years of training in the Bay City.

There is no evidence to substantiate the theory that the collection was once part of the older *Bibliotheca Montereyensis–Angelorum Dioeceseos* which was located for so many years at Mission Santa Ines for students attending the southland's nearby college.

Sometime after January 15, 1883, the *Bibliotheca Sancti Francisi Archdioeceseos* was moved to the seminary inaugurated at Mission San Jose. There it remained until the opening, in Menlo Park, of Saint Patrick's shortly before the turn of the century. A brochure, issued in 1898, notes that "the shelves of our library already contained a few thousand volumes—the greater number purchased; the remainder coming from the Old Seminary at Mission San José, or donated by His Grace, the Most Reverend Archbishop."

While some of the more basic volumes were integrated into the general students' library, the *Bibliotheca* remained a seldom–used autonomous collection. With the passage of the decades, it gradually became more of an historical oddity than a useful source of information. Most recently, upon the opening of the McKeon Memorial Library at Saint Patrick's, the *Bibliotheca* was placed in its present location, in two caged compartments on the upper level of the stack area.

With the assistance of Mr. Paul Kelly, this writer catalogued the old library, many of whose volumes bear the inscription, "Joseph Sadoc Alemany, O.P." or "*Dioecesis Sancti Francisci*" in the archbishop's own hand. Books were classified into a series of ten categories based on subject–matter. Each volume was assigned a code number, based respectively on tier, shelf and location. The system allowed researchers to avoid the necessity of defacing the spines with unbecoming call–letters.

History, theology and humane letters, in that order are the greatest number of titles. Well over a third of the books were printed in Latin, with French, Italian, English and Spanish following in descending order. The oldest book in the *Bibliotheca* is *Sacratissima*, printed at Venice in 1514. 187 of the 621 titles bear publication dates in the 1800s, 296 in the 1700s, ninety–four in the 1600s, and twenty–five in the 1500s. The year of publication cannot be determined in nineteen instances. About a third of the collection is bound in faded, but well–preserved vellum.

By making the *Bibliotheca Sancti Francisci Archdioeceseos* once again accessible to scholars, the seminary authorities affirm John Henry Newman's dictum that "it is our duty to live among books."

BICENTENNIAL REFLECTIONS

Historical commentators are quick to observe that almost everything in Southern California has been imported—plants, flowers, shrubs, trees, water and even religion! More than three decades ago, the late Carey McWilliams pointed to the unprecedented influx of people–a factor that today accounts for the multi–ethnic nature of the onetime *Pueblo de Nuestra Señora de los Angeles*.

The Indians were the first to inhabit the area. And though they are mostly gone now, they left an indelible mark behind in such names as Cahuenga, Malibu, Mugu and Pacoima.

Then came the Catholic *pobladores* from Sonora who laid out the original *plaza* on a bluff above the river named by Fray Juan Crespi to honor Our Lady of the Angels. For a while after the war with Mexico and the discovery of gold, Los Angeles remained a small and insignificant town. But that was soon to change.

Statehood came, in 1850, and then, following the Civil War, the railroads reached out to touch Los Angeles, bringing newcomers from the south and midwest, many of them lured westward by the well–publicized sunshine.

(The roots of the King James edition of the Bible were solidly transplanted by the great midwestern migration. Los Angeles remains predominantly Protestant, though the importance of the Catholic faith was first attested, in 1953, when the Archbishop of Los Angeles became the first cardinal in the western United States. Though the city is famous for its revivalists and cultists, they have probably drawn attention out of all proportion to their numbers. Studies indicate that the great majority of churchgoers belong to the traditional faiths.)

The Chinese and Japanese arrived; French, Poles and German Jews also came and many of the beach areas became popular resort meccas for English tourists. Early in this century, the Mexican population began rising again, this time forming the bulk of the migratory work force. The Blacks, who presently constitute 12.5% of the population, began their treks in 1900.

And the waves of immigration roll on. In recent decades Vietnamese and Koreans, with their distinctive contributions, have flooded into Los Angeles to join dozens of other Asiatic groups, like the Samoans, more of whom live in Los Angeles than reside on the Island of American Samoa itself. The people thronging to the area have generally been an adventurous and inventive lot. In Hollywood, for example, creative minds have entertained and informed the whole world, reflecting both America's manifold problems and its unique promise.

A major port city, the aircraft and electronics industries expanded to meet the challenges of World War II and then spun around to handle contemporary transportation and communication needs.

As it celebrated its 200th anniversary, this largest of the world's cities dedicated to Our Lady provided a haven for its perpetual transplants. It amazes, amuses and eventually absorbs. New arrivals are confronted with culture shock—the climate, the freeways, the lifestyles and the ethnic mix.

But one can rest assured that new blood will keep Los Angeles alive, vigorous and growing as it inches towards its tricentennial.

BIGOTRY

A. IN GENERAL

By the grace of God, Californians are now living in an age of ecumenism. Such was not always the case. Much of the ill–feeling toward the Catholic Church in the Golden State can be traced to the anti–clerical attitudes of the historian, Hubert Howe Bancroft. Noted chronicler that he was, Bancroft had little use for priests and on more than one occasion spoke of "friars being squeezed for their desire to hold on to the temporalities," as if to imply that this concern for the material welfare of the natives somehow violated the Franciscan vow of poverty.

Bancroft's views are reflected in many quarters where genuine hostility can easily be detected. It was charged by one author, for example, that neophytes were kept in a state of chronic undernourishment in order to retard the tendency to fugitivism. Though it is true that ignorance and prejudice are not interchangable terms, the results are often the same. Even a fair number of the casual writers were imbued with this spirit. One said of the friars:

> The day of their supremacy and influence in California has gone by never to return. This they had the sagacity to foresee; and thus only can we account for the rigid silence as to the existence of gold in the country, maintained for more than a century. That these priests were cognizant of the abundance of the precious metal at that period is now well known; but they were members of the extraordinary society of the Jesuits, which jealous of its all–pervading influence, and dreading the effect of a large Protestant emigration to the western, as well as to the eastern shores of America, applied its powerful injunctions of secrecy to the members of the Order; and their faithful obedience during so long a period, is another proof of the strength and the danger of their organization.

On another occasion, when a priest advised his people against joining the Free Masons, a certain J. Judson Ames retaliated in the San Diego *Herald* by calling "the Romish Church . . . the most corrupt and wicked institution ever organized since the creation of the world!" The attitude of a hostile press can be seen in other areas too. The Santa Barbara *Gazette* derided the arrival of Saint Vibiana's relics in 1855, by sarcastically observing that the relies might "possess a miraculous influence, in which case that town will become a resort. . . ."

Anti–Catholic publications were not uncommon. One such journal, established at San Francisco in 1874, as the *American Citizen*, was devoted to essays, lectures, speeches and remarks on the relations between church and state, most of them directed against the Catholic Church. Probably the greatest abuse suffered by the Church in California has been in the field of education where, it was noted in 1861, "American Protestants will never consent to see their educational system destroyed by the interference of Romish priests." The Public Schools Welfare League of California at San Francisco circulated a petition in 1922, supporting the K.K.K. campaign aimed at compelling children of school age to attend only schools maintained by the state of California.

This constant barrage against the very existence of Catholic educational institutions forestalled any tax relief for private schools until recent times and for many years gave California the unenviable position of being the only state in the union to tax parochial schools. Though opposition in this field has abated, some apparently still believe "that Catholics want to either destroy the public schools or else introduce sectarianism into them." The savage antagonisms of the eastern seaboard were transplanted to California, though on a reduced scale. For example, the American Protective Association was brought to the west in 1893, and soon became militantly anti–Catholic. Their brutal campaigns were slowed when an editorial in the San Francisco *Monitor*, revealing the lodge oath and other secrets of the A.P.A., undermined the unity of the organization.

An associated press dispatch from Los Angeles in September of 1894, related: "J. K. Gosper, a local politician and an A.P.A. man, was invited to address the Unity Club. In the course of his remarks, he charged that under the Catholic cathedral in this city were 500 stands of arms. D. F. Dongan, a contractor, arose in the audience, and, displaying a $1,000 certificate, declared that the statement was a lie, and that he would give the money to the A.P.A. if it were true!" As more and more people are educated in the history of the Golden State, the incidence of anti–Catholic bigotry subsided, for it is hard to propagate antipathy toward the Church that introduced civilization to the western shores almost four centuries ago!

BIGOTRY

B. RUSTON EXAMPLE

The ugly spectre of bigotry against the People of God has not been lacking in the annals of California's Catholic heritage. There were, of course, various reasons behind the Church's persecution. The conflict between Catholic and non–Catholic ideologies has not been simply a disagreement of creeds, but one reaching out to the social and political implications inherent in Catholicism.

A classic example of bigotry is couched in George Augustus Frederick Ruxton's 1849 depiction of the "presiding *padre*" at Mission San Fernando as a man of "great paunch, vain and addicted with little occupation but eating, drinking and sleeping away his time, addicted to the *cigarito* and *aguadiente*, a man around whom gathers half–breed Mexican women and sundry beef–fed urchins of whitey–brown complexion . . . exhibiting a curious resemblance to the strongly marked features of that worthy *padre*."

Happily, there were counteracting forces to such denigrating and unfounded narratives, one of which was the proclamation, by Governor Hiram Johnson, in 1913, calling for public demonstrations to mark the bi–centenary of Fray Junípero Serra. The editor of the *Notre Dame Quarterly* felt that the governor's action indicated that "the Age of Bigotry" was passing. He went on to say that a time would soon come when, freed from trammels of the lies of centuries, men no longer connect the Catholic Church with superstition, tyranny, ignorance and the chaining of the human intellect, but acknowledge the world's debt; the long, slow debt of civilization to her, the Mother of Arts, the Nurse of Industries, the Patroness of Science, the Civilizer of Nations."

The same writer went on to point out:

> What Serra did for the California Indians, the Church has done for humanity. Serra could not have been what he was, had he not been a Catholic. The Catholic Religion alone can inspire sacrifice, devotedness, zeal, self abnegation such as was his. So, to the Catholic Church, California owes the debt she would pay this day, in part to this loyal son of St. Francis of Assisi. All that Serra did, Religion inspired; Religion was the animus of his being. To Religion then, to the Catholic Religion, then, our California owes the germs of her splendid achievement; we say nothing of the after debt.
>
> There is a personal element , too, in this celebration. Not only do we honor a Founder and a Builder; a Laborer and a Teacher; but we honor a MAN. There is something sweetly attractive in the personality of *Padre* Serra. It is said, "All the world loves a Lover." And when this Lover is a Lover of God, how much the more is he lovable! *Padre* Serra loved God with all the intensity of his intense nature. He loved Christ, the Man God, with something of that ardent flame which consumed the Seraph of Assisi, he whom the sweet legend pictures as being embraced by the Beloved Crucified; he who went singing over the hills of Italy calling the Sun and Moon and the Stars to praise the Lord. *Padre* Serra had a poet–soul, as had his gentle Father Francis, a soul keen to Nature's beauty, and to human sympathy and love; for the Saints are not steel–hearted, they love intensely and humanly, but the human is so interfused with the Divine, that nothing selfish or sordid is mingled there. *Padre* Serra loved Nature, and so he loved the fair new vineyard given him to toil for; he loved the brown mountains' and the blue sea; the rosy sundowns and the purple dusks; he loved the golden mornings, and the languid noons, and the white star–glory of the lonely nights; he loved the giant trees with their glittering foliage, and the sweet blossoms swaying at their feet, the golden poppies that sheeted the fields with flame, and the pale silken harebells, or the fragrant briar rose. It was doubtless he who had brought the first fair Castilian roses from sunny Mexico, those beauteous compacts of a thousand odors, sweeter than orient urns. He had an artist's spirit and he aimed at the highest and best in the decoration of God's house, as truthful Time attests. He was a man of keen and lofty intellect and he bent that mind of his to the simple and lowly things of life."

BLACK ENRICHMENT OF LOS ANGELES

When Pope Paul VI visited the martyrs shrine in Uganda, he reflected on the theme of how Black peoples had enriched "the Church with their unique and treasured gifts of negritude." Indeed that gift was present in the New World from almost the beginning of European penetration. The first blacks came with the Spanish Explorers like Cabeza de Vaca and there was reportedly a Black priest with Coronado's expedition in the 1500s.

When the City of *Nuestra Señora de Los Angeles* was established in 1781, its founders were Hispanic peoples of mostly Black and Indian ancestry. One of the area's earliest landowners was Maria Rita Valdez de Villa, a Mexican lady whose grandparents were black.

Shortly after the turn of this century, Black Catholics are recorded in parochial register books throughout the southland, many of them having migrated from Louisiana. One writer observed in 1918 that "negros are to be found in almost all the Christian denominations in Los Angeles. There are a large number of Roman Catholics, most of whom are members of the cathedral parish and their numbers are constantly increasing."

One of the more prominent civic figures in those years was Noah Thompson, a Black writer, journalist and politician. His wife, Eloise Bibb Thompson, a devout Catholic, was a poet and writer who often had her work published in *The Tidings*.

Bishop Thomas J. Conaty was highly esteemed by the area's Black Catholics. When he died in 1915, *The California Eagle* noted that "The (Black) race indeed loses one of its staunch friends." In an earlier issue, the editor said that "Bishop Conaty in line with Archbishop Ireland, Cardinal Gibbons and others of this great Church have been in the last decade a mighty force in scales of justice for the Negro."

Conaty's successor was also an outspoken champion of Blacks. On November 28, 1921, Bishop John T. Cantwell delivered a benchmark address to the N.A.A.C.P. in which he put on record his strong feelings toward the race issue as it effected the local scene. At the same time, Cantwell foresaw new opportunities for missionary work among the Blacks in the United States. His goal was to give those living in Los Angeles "one of the best organized social centers in the country."

When Saint Victor's Center was launched in 1922, Cantwell noted that there would be further openings for Black Catholics as they became aware "of their hopes and aspirations and a fuller development of the fine qualities that characterize their race, a deep religious instinct, love of family life and a devotion to their Church."

In 1927, a large church and a two–story rectory were inaugurated at 53rd Street and Hooper Avenue under the patronage of Saint Odilia. It was not a center for Blacks alone, as indicated by the census rolls which abounded in Irish and Italian names.

It was also in 1927 that a chapter of the Knights of Saint Peter Claver, a Catholic fraternal society, was established in Saint Patrick's Parish. The first chapter established in the west coast, it became a vibrant organization for Catholic activities in the southland. Though he had provided a fraternal organization for the Blacks, Cantwell was never pleased about their being excluded from other groups. He wrote to Joseph Scott, a prominent Catholic layman, complaining that "there should be a place in the Knights of Columbus for our Negro Catholics." He eventually won his point.

The manifold contributions made by Black Catholics to California is nowhere more evident than in the Hollywood film industry, together with television, night clubs and theaters, all of which attracted Catholic actors and actresses, performers, musicians and other entertainers from other parts of the nation and the world.

As early as 1917, jazz pianist Jelly Roll Mortin arrived on the southland scene. Others came in later years, notably film actor–comedian Steppin Fetchitt (converted to the Catholic Church in the 1930s), actress–singer Ethel Waters, actress Fredi Washington and singer–actress Lena Horne.

Jazz singer Billie Holiday came to Los Angeles in the early 1940s and took an active part in the establishment of the Capitol Records Company in Hollywood. Later she was a popular performer on the night club circuit.

Another group who contributed mightily to the arts were the Rene Brothers. Initially, Otis worked as a bricklayer and Leon as a pharmacist. They later started an orchestra and wrote numerous hit songs, including "When the Swallows Come Back to Capistrano."

Other Black Catholics native to Los Angeles were band–singer Ivie Anderson, writer–musician Elizabeth Laura Adams, dancer Carmen de la Vallada and *prima ballerina* (with the Metropolitan Opera) Janet Collins. Another singer–actress who identified herself with the Catholic Church throughout her life was singer–actress Dorothy Dandridge.

In the mid 1940s, the Catholic Interracial Council was established "to oppose all forms of discrimination directed at minority groups of all races and colors and to make known the Catholic point of view on both legal and extra legal practices of segregation on account of race or color."

Chairman Daniel Marshall spoke to a gathering of the council in February of 1945, assuring his listeners that the superintendent of Catholic Schools for the Archdiocese of Los Angeles "would not permit discrimination in the parochial schools on account of race and color." In 1948, the Catholic Interracial Council was involved in what became a major civil rights victory. Father Joseph

della Torre, a priest attached to Saint Patrick's parish in Los Angeles, appealed to the council for assistance in having the state's anti–miscegenation law nullified.

A legal case was instituted and tried in the courts. On October 2nd, the California State Supreme Court ruled the law unconstitutional, thus allowing Sylvester Davis, a black, and Andrea Perez, a white, the legal right to marry in a Catholic ceremony. By 1986, California had become one of the states with the largest number of Black Catholics (102,895). On December 29th of that year, Pope John Paul II announced the appointment of a black auxiliary bishop for the Archdiocese of Los Angeles. Father Carl A. Fisher, a Josephite priest, was consecrated auxiliary bishop.

Though their numbers are relatively small in relationship to California's overall population, Black Catholics have made their presence felt in the artistic, social, civic, and political sphere of influence. Researchers like John LeFlore are gradually unearthing historical evidence and statistics that confirm the tremendous contributions made by Black Catholics to the Golden State.

BLESSED VIRGIN MARY — GOLDEN ROSE OF TEPEYAC

Each year on the 12th of December, at Mexico City's Basilica of Our Lady of Guadalupe, roses are solemnly blessed after High Mass to commemorate the Blessed Mother's appearance to the Indian peasant, Juan Diego. At the same time, a rose of pure gold is awarded to some person who has distinguished himself in a special way for the cause of Christ and His Church. This ancient custom dates back to the times of King Ferdinand VI of Spain.

Recipients of the golden rose were formerly made members of the Royal Congregation of Our Lady of Guadalupe. After 1821, Agustin de Iturbide instituted the Order of Knights of Guadalupe and handed over its administration to national officials. Through the centuries many great personalities have received the honor, among whom are Maria Barbara of Portugal, Isabel Farsenio of Spain, Philip V, Maria Teresa, and numerous churchmen.

No roses were distributed in the fifteen years prior to 1931, because of the religious persecution in Mexico. In that year the presentation was made to the Right Reverend John J. Cantwell, Bishop of Los Angeles–San Diego, as a solemn gesture of gratitude for that prelate's great hospitality and charity toward exiled Mexican priests during the years of persecution. Archbishop Pascual Diaz of Mexico City and the canons of the Basilica of Our Lady of Guadalupe unanimously selected Southern California's bishop for the distinction of receiving

La Rosa del Tepeyac. In 1929 the bishop had been cited by the Holy See for similar reasons and made an Assistant at the Papal Throne.

The Golden Rose was brought from the Mexican Capital by Señor Juan Laine, Grand Knight of the Council of Guadalupe, who presented the award at an informal gathering of Los Angeles' Mexican community. Symbolically, *La Rosa del Tepeyac* recalls the beautiful roses which miraculously grew in the desert soil at Tepeyac when the Blessed Mother made her appearance to Juan Diego in 1531. It will be remembered that a number of these roses were carried to the first Bishop of Mexico City, Don Juan Zumarraga, by the Indian who had gathered them in his cloak—that same garment upon which the miraculous image of Our Lady of Guadalupe is venerated today at the famous Mexican shrine.

Awarding of the Golden Rose to Bishop Cantwell was all the more symbolic because of the association of California's first bishop with the national shrine. Fray Francisco Garcia Diego y Moreno was consecrated within those hallowed walls on October 4, 1840, and from there he carried the message of Guadalupe to all of California. Mindful of this Marian tradition, Garcia Diego placed his seminary at Santa Ines under the heavenly protection of Our Lady of Guadalupe. Today the State of California boasts no less than twenty–nine churches dedicated to the Mother of God under that august title.

BLESSED VIRGIN MARY — *LA CONQUISTADORA*

Probably the "oldest shrine of Our Lady on the West Coast of America" is located at Mission San Carlos Borromeo del Rio Carmelo. *Nuestra Señora de Belén* was a favorite of Fray Junípero Serra and even today forms an integral link in California's Catholic Heritage. Devotion to "*La Conquistadora*" has its roots deep in history, for her image was venerated by Prince Henry the Navigator at Rastelo near Lisbon as early as the 15th century.

An Iberian tradition states that in July 1497, Vasco de Gama, accompanied by King Manuel I and his court made a solemn pilgrimage to the shrine invoking Our Lady's intercession on behalf of his impending expedition to India around the Cape of Good Hope. In thanksgiving for their successful journey, the king changed the name of Rastelo to Belén (Bethlehem) and erected that magnificent church to Our Lady now used as a national mausoleum for Portugal's celebrated dead. Through the years, "*La Conquistadora*" gained in prominence and became the patroness of sea adventurers. The devotion spread to Spain in the years of the dual monarchy. Mis-

sionaries brought the devotion to the New World, and, by the late 1700's, the Blessed Mother was widely known under that title.

When plans were made to take possession of Alta California, Archbishop Francisco de Lorenzana of Mexico City presented a replica of Our Lady of Bethlehem to José de Gálvez. The statue was brought on the *San Antonio* to San Diego where it arrived in April of 1769. In the summer of the next year, the image was taken to Monterey and enshrined upon the altar before which Junípero Serra sang the solemn *Te Deum* on Pentecost Sunday.

Pilgrimages to Our Lady of Bethlehem date to 1775, when the crew of the ship *Sonora* lost its way at sea and made a vow to visit her shrine if they made port safely. Despite a heavy incidence of scurvy and the fierceness of the waters, not a single life was lost and every member of the crew marched over the hills to Carmel Valley in thanksgiving. Our Lady was venerated at Carmel until the 1840s, when the mission was secularized and its people scattered. The statue was moved to the private home of Doña Ignacia Nocha, a devoted woman of Spanish–Mexican ancestry. Doña Ignacia stipulated that after her death the statue was to be given to Gertrude Ambrosia, a descendent of a soldier on Serra's original expedition.

La Conquistadora

In the process of restoring the mission, overtures were made by Harry Downie for the return of *"La Conquistadora"* and on Christmas night of 1944, Our Lady of Bethlehem was restored to her shrine where the pilgrimages began anew. Today the lovely statue of the Madonna stands on the Gospel side of the high altar, "clad in regal robes, complete with ear–rings, pearl necklace and silver crown, surmounted by a cross."

BLESSED VIRGIN MARY — *LA VIRGEN DE LA CARIDAD DE COBRE*

The Cuban community that inhabits Southern California has great devotion to the Blessed Mother under her title "Our Lady of Charity of *El Cobre*." The Shrine of *La Virgen de la Caridad del Cobre* is located about ten miles from Santiago, Cuba's second largest city, in Oriente Province, near the United States Naval Base, at Guantanamo.

Devotion to *La Virgen de la Caridad* can be traced to the early 1600s, to an area on the slopes of the Sierra Maestra Mountains, where Indian and African slaves mined copper for the Spanish government. Juan and Rodrigo de Hoyos, together with a ten year old black youngster, Juan Moreno, discovered an image of Our Lady mounted on a piece of wood bearing the words: "I am the Virgin of Charity." The three carried the statue to their master who fashioned a makeshift chapel for the sacred image. Devotion spread quickly and, as early as 1688, the Archdiocese of Santiago looked into the story of *La Virgencita*.

The first shrine to Our Lady under that title was erected in the 1730s. It was later replaced with a more sturdy edifice that lasted well into the present century. In 1927, the Basilica of brick, mortar and stone was erected. Located on a tiny hill, the handsome edifice is graced by eternal spring breezes. Daily thousands of pilgrims stream into the Basilica.

To the rear of the Basilica is the "altar of miracles," where the figure of *La Virgen* is prominently displayed. From a balcony to the left can be seen five other magnificent wooden altars each fashioned from a different kind of Cuban stalk.

The image of Our Lady measures about fifteen inches in height and stands on a board above the altar. Atop her head is a golden crown, made to resemble the sun's rays, with which she was proclaimed "Patroness of the Island of Cuba." In her right hand, the statue holds a cross of gold and in the other the Infant Jesus bearing a sphere representing the world. At the base are the traditional words: "I am the Virgin of Charity."

In 1915, the Cuban volunteers of the Spanish–American War petitioned the Holy See to proclaim the Virgin of Charity patroness of their nation. This Pope Benedict XV did on May 10, 1916, selecting September 8th as the day of her official feast. In 1940, Thomas Merton made a pilgrimage to the Shrine. He later publicly thanked the "little black Virgin" in his book *Seven Story Mountain* for assisting him to make the decision about entering the monastery.

The medal of the *Virgencita* graces the chests of practically every Cuban man, woman and child, wherever they live. *La Virgen de la Caridad* has become and will always remain the Mother of Cubans and their hope for eventual religious freedom.

BLESSED VIRGIN MARY — MADONNA OF HOLLYWOOD

The devastating fire which gutted the historic Hollywood branch of the Los Angeles Public Library on April 13, 1982, destroyed upwards of 70,000 books, along with an extremely valuable collection of theatre arts. Miraculously spared in the conflagration was the tiled Madonna, "The Lady of Silence," which had been anchored to the entrance wall at 1623 North Ivar Avenue, after gracing the garden fountain of the previous library site for many years.

According to a 1924 article in *Holly Leaves*, the architect suggested the notion of embellishing the library garden with "an interesting historic tile" which he discovered while touring Mexico. E.A. Sage, a man devoted to "the art interests of the community," influenced James Warrington to purchase the tile and got Mr. Edwards of the Simpson Construction Company to set it in a charming design drawn by the architect.

Even in 1924, the eighty tiles were thought to be over a hundred years old. Measuring three by three feet, the Madonna was described as "a link of association with California's early history."

Tile–making had been developed in Mexico by the Dominican friars who were trained at Talavera. After coming to Puebla, they combined the virile art of Spain with the refining influence of Italian and Oriental traditions.

The exquisitely–produced Madonna at the Hollywood Library is very likely a version of Our Lady of Covadogna, one of the great symbols of the Spanish nation. As such, she is very much at home in Tinsel Town.

From ancient times, the cave at Covadogna was regarded as a sanctuary of Our Lady. Her image in the dark hills and mountains of Asturia had been venerated since pre–Visigothic times.

In 718, the Moors sent an army into Asturia with orders to destroy the final vestiges of Don Pelayo and his soldiers. After praying to Our Lady of Covadogna, the small Christian army was victorious.

Though the area remained for several more centuries under Moorish domination, the victory had great significance for the future of the peninsula. Don Pelayo became King of Asturia and united the remaining Visigoths and the Hispano–Roman tribes. With this unification began the creation of historic Spain. And ever since, the Virgin of Covadogna has been identified with the Spanish nation. The Spanish national sanctuary has been featured on postage stamps, described in travel books and portrayed in mosaic.

Traditionally, this particular image of Our Lady has been the most beautiful. One writer said that Asturians claim "that even if a painter were to come down from Heaven, he would be unable to reproduce the beauty of this lovely statue." And yet many have tried. Today one can see images of *Nuestra Señora de Covadogna* throughout Spain and Latin America, each one a beauty unto itself. To portray this Madonna was considered the ultimate accomplishment of every true artist.

When the Hollywood Library was rebuilt, the "Lady of Silence" was refurbished and incorporated into the new building. One could hardly think of one without the other.

BLESSED VIRGIN MARY — THE MARIAN YEAR

The Holy Father's declaration of 1987–1988 as a Marian Year recalls the similar action of Pope Pius XII in 1954. The earlier designation was commemorated in the Archdiocese of Los Angeles by the dedication of the preparatory seminary under the patronage of Our Lady, Queen of the Angels.

California's early *padres* were clients of Mary and were responsible for introducing her devotion to the area, so much so that the Vice Postulator of Father Serra's cause has said that "If Mother Church should raise the Apostle of California to the honor of the altars, we know whose hand will weave for him the garland of sainthood."

Nuestra Señora de Belen, christened *La Conquistadora by Galvez*, had been shipped to Monterey and was used in taking possession of the land there for Spain. The statue was later returned to Mexico, but found its way back to Mission San Carlos in subsequent years. Special veneration to Mary during the colonial period is attributed to that statue and today it is considered California's oldest and most historic replica of the Mother of God.

Two missions in Alta California, *La Purisima Concepción* and *Nuestra Señora de la Soledad* were dedicated to Our Lady as were seven of the twenty–five establishments in peninsular California. The first Bishop of Both Californias, Francisco Garcia Diego y Moreno, was consecrated in the magnificent Marian Shrine of Our Lady of Guadalupe near Mexico City where the Virgin is venerated as the "Empress of the Americas." On January 4, 1843, Bishop Garcia Diego declared Our Lady, Refuge of Sinners, the Patroness of Californias. This patronage has never been revoked and the feast is still observed with great solemnity.

Old Saint Mary's Cathedral in San Francisco was dedicated to Our Lady in 1854, under her title "Saint Mary, Ever Virgin and Conceived Without Sin." This century–old edifice was the first cathedral in the entire world named in honor of the Immaculate Conception after that doctrine was defined.

A second cathedral in the Bay City was also a Marian Shrine. Dedicated in 1891 to Mary's Assumption, it was in constant use until the fall of 1982 when it was reduced to ashes by a ravaging fire. Stockton's Saint Mary of the Ascension Cathedral also claimed the protection of the Blessed Virgin.

California's largest city was named in honor of *Nuestra Señora de los Angeles del Rio de Porciuncula*, where Portola's expedition camped enroute to Monterey in 1769. The virgin's name was given to numerous other towns and villages. The seminary erected by Bishop Garcia Diego at Mission Santa Ines, in 1844, was dedicated to Our Lady of Guadalupe and served the diocese for several decades, first as a training center for prospective priests and later as a boarding school.

Personal devotion to the Mother of God has always characterized California's Catholic heritage. For example, on May 7, 1873 Father Joachim Adam wrote from Santa Cruz, "The image of Our Lady has been venerated in this place for more than fifty years, first in the Old Mission Church, now in ruins, and since July 4, 1858, in the new frame church on the main altar. In 1870 I built a nice side chapel in one of the towers of the Church and the image was taken in solemn procession from the main altar to the new chapel, March 25, 1870, where it has been venerated since, with great devotion, by peoples of every condition in life."

California's devotion to Mary forms a chapter all its own and we have space here only to mention in briefest outline the more prominent manifestations of this allegiance. But from these few words, it can be seen that the Mother of God deserves a lion's share of the credit for California spiritual and material attainments.

BLESSED VIRGIN MARY — OUR LADY OF ANGELS EXHIBIT

Those who were charmed and fascinated by the Los Angeles bicentennial presentation staged by Tony Duquette at the County Museum of Science and Industry were anxious to see his display of antique madonnas and miniature shrines exhibited at San Fernando Mission in 1984 and 1985. The noted Catholic playwright and stateswoman, Clare Booth Luce, once said that "there has not been in the history of art, nor is there today in the art world, a designer of spectacles and environments with more imagination than Tony Duquette."

That observation was certainly confirmed by the colorful and magnificient *objets de art* at San Fernando. Many of the madonnas were acquired by Mr. Duquette during his frequent trips to Europe and Latin America.

Handsomely carved shrines from Venice, Sicilia, Florence, Austria and Mexico were accommodated to house the madonnas. One had *faux lapis lazuli* columns, another portrayed a garden scene, while yet a third supported a wrought iron baldachino.

The depictions of Our Lady were uniformly tasteful and appealing. Mostly dating from the 18th century, one dressed in period robes and a silver crown, another in gold embroidered muslin robes with a butterfly wing halo. One of the Spanish madonnas had an amethyst trimmed gown and a silver filagree crown. The Bolivian colonial madonna was especially charming. Dressed in her original Chinese robes and European brocade cape, she was acquired years ago in the Philippines.

A Peruvian colonial madonna, with human hair and turquoise earings, was attired in an embroidered red robe and silver crown. A consensus of viewers rated this as the "favorite" in the collection. Much of the artistic statuary at San Fernando, which remained in place for almost two years, was destined to be re–incorporated into the Angels Exhibit when it was scheduled to open again at Exposition Park.

In her preface to the official booklet for "A Bicentennial Celebrational Environment," Mrs Luce also said that if Tony Duquette "had lived in the days of the great monarchs and art–loving princes of Europe, they would have vied furiously with one another to engage his creative services for their balls, fetes, pageants, processions, stage and opera sets, ceremonials and spectacles."

The Madonna Exhibit at San Fernando, beautiful and attractive as it was, was finally put aside for an even more magnificient (and permanent) tribute to Our Lady of the Angels.

BLESSED VIRGIN MARY — OUR LADY OF THE ARCHIVES

Marian iconography is an element of Christian art that has been of great importance in Orthodox and Catholic countries from the third century to the present day. With deep roots in early Christian thought, together with a continuous history through subsequent ages, it embraces single representations and liturgical Marian

Our Lady of the Archives

art; narrative cycles of her life, dormition and glorification; portrayals of her miracles and apparitions and other symbolic Marian themes. It has been an ancient tradition in Western iconography to link the crowned Madonna with particular places or groups such as sanctuaries, shrines and associations.

Because of the Church's ancient role as "preserver of culture," it was thought that Our Lady's patronage for this vital function should be dramatized by depicting her as "Our Lady of the Archives." And how fitting it is that the first depiction of the Blessed Mother under this title should be affixed to the building housing the Archival Center for the Archdiocese of Los Angeles.

The 6 x 11 foot ceramic tile portrayal was designed by Isabel Piczek. After several trial sketches, the final cartoon was executed in charcoal and then taken to Franciscan Ceramics for final execution. The original cartoon was laid out atop a large piece of tracing paper and then transferred to the sixty–six pieces of Terra Floor bisque tile. Finally the colors were added.

The tiles were then carefully inserted into a gigantic kiln and fired for about an hour at temperatures ranging up to 1500 degrees Fahrenheit. It was important that each of the individual tiles receive exactly the same heat application.

After a lengthy cooling process, the tiles were disassembled and packed for shipment to San Fernando. The installation was entrusted to Ralph McIntosh, an award winning tilemaster who most recently laid the mosaic flooring for the restored state capitol building at Sacramento.

A brass frame was attached to the north end of the building and McIntosh gently began placing the tiles into a bed of modified cement–based emolument. It was an exciting installation insofar as the slightest mishap would have necessitated a wholly fresh fabrication. On the second day, November 9th, with all the tiles finally in place, the craftsmen applied the grouting which renders the completed depiction waterproof. Several bystanders spent the whole day watching and photographing the installation.

Interestingly enough, Our Lady of the Archives will long be known for reasons over and above its artistic excellence. It is the final creation of Franciscan Ceramics, a California tradition since 1875, when Gladding McBean began producing clay products. Since 1923, the firm has been manufacturing floor tile and decorative pottery at their factory on Los Feliz. Financial considerations caused the parent company, Wedgwood Ltd., to discontinue operation.

The portrayal is the latest of the artistic masterpieces adorning the churches of this country that bear the name of Isabel and Edith Piczek. The distinctive style of their work bestows a modern relevancy on the Archival Center known primarily as a bastion of the past.

BLESSED VIRGIN MARY — OUR LADY OF GUADALUPE

Devotion to Our Lady of Guadalupe is the oldest Marian observance in the Californias. All the earliest missionaries from Spain had visited the massive sanctuary built at Tepeyac near Mexico City.

According to historical tradition, it was during December of 1531 that Juan Diego beheld a "beautiful lady" as he crossed the hill of Tepeyac en route to Holy Mass. Identifying herself as the Virgin Mary, she told him to ask Bishop Juan de Zumarraga to build a church on the site.

Dismissed at first as a religious eccentric, Juan Diego (beatified in 1990) had two subsequent encounters with Our Lady. Finally he returned to the episcopal residence, this time bringing out–of–season roses he found at the scene of the apparitions. As he was speaking with the bishop, Juan opened his cloak or *tilma* and, on the rough cloth, there was an image of the Virgin as she had appeared to Juan Diego.

Called Our Lady of Guadalupe to avoid confusion with the Medieval apparition of the Virgin at Guadalupe in Spain, the occurrences of 1831 had a greater impact upon the Western Hemisphere than any other single event during the past five centuries.

In 1556, a hermitage was established on Tepeyac hill to house the *tilma*. Due to extensive flooding between 1629 and 1634, the *tilma* was displayed in the Metropolitan Cathedral in Mexico City. Devotion to our Lady of Guadalupe was formalized in 1737, when she was named Patroness of Mexico City. A college was founded at the sanctuary and, in 1910, Pope Pius X declared her Patroness of all Latin America. It was Pope Pius XII who proclaimed Our Lady of Guadalupe as Empress of the Americas.

During the years 1695 to 1709, a large baroque church was erected at Tepeyac. In 1895, it was raised to the status of a minor basilica by Pope Leo XIII who also authorized the coronation of Our Lady's image.

In 1976, the *tilma* was moved to a newly–erected modern basilica adjacent to the 18th century building and it was there that Pope John Paul II said Holy Mass on January 27, 1979.

In every one of the California missions, a painting of Our Lady of Guadalupe was accorded a place of special prominence. The friars were fond of reminding the neophytes that Mary's first appearance in the New World was to one of their own native Americans.

The shrine of Our Lady of Guadalupe has taken on even greater significance for the Californias since 1840, when Fray Francisco Garcia Diego y Moreno was consecrated there as the proto bishop of the Diocese of *Ambas Californias*. As the patroness of the insurgents under Father Miguel Hidalgo, the image of Our Lady of Guadalupe appeared on the banner of the independence movement. And, with the establishment of the empire and republic of 1821 and 1824, she became the official "protector" of the nation.

Today more than 20 million pilgrims annually visit the basilica which is the largest Marian shrine in the world. An estimated 300 million faithful, representing every continent, make Our Lady of Guadalupe the largest single devotion in the Catholic world.

BLESSED VIRGIN MARY — OUR LADY OF LIGHT

In a recent article in *The Journal of San Diego History*, the painting of *La Madre Santisima de la Luz* is described as "one of the most interesting works in the California missions."

The central part of the canvas replicates a painting executed in Palermo, Sicily, in the early 18th century, and now venerated in the Cathedral of Leon in the State of Guanajuato, Mexico. The painting, now cleaned and restored, is on display in the Serra Museum at San Diego. Expertly restored by Elizabeth Court of the Balboa Art Conservation Center, the painting of Most Holy Mother of Light is probably brighter and more attractive than it was when it arrived in San Diego sometime prior to 1776.

The oil rendition appears to be one of two paintings that survived the 1775 destruction of the fledgling mission. First mentioned in the report of 1776, it also appears in an inventory for 1777 and another in 1783. A second, smaller painting has since disappeared.

It is known that the portrayal of Our Lady of Light was in the adobe chapel of the Immaculate Conception where it was probably brought when that chapel was dedicated in 1858. The chapel remained in use until 1916, when the new parochial house–of–worship was built. The Franciscans were in charge there until 1945. When the church was turned over to the secular clergy, the art works were removed to San Luis Rey.

In a long essay about the painting, Dr. Norman Neuerburg told about the background of the original painting, the details for which were provided by a "devout lady" who purportedly had frequent visitations from the Virgin Mary. Devotion to Mary under this title was brought to Mexico in 1732 where it became popular. It was first spread by the Jesuits and later by the Franciscans throughout the missionary area of Latin America.

Images of *La Madre Santisima de la Luz* are known in Ecuador and Venezuela, perhaps as the result of Jesuit missionaries who had earlier worked in Mexico. Besides reproductions of the painting on canvas in all sizes, there were engravings and sculptures, both in relief and in the round, and medals.

A sermon on *La Madre Santisima de la Luz*, preached at Merida in 1749, merited publication in the Holy Year of 1750. Confraternities in her honor were organized throughout Mexico and gained widespread popularity in the 1750s and early 1760s.

The portrayal of our Lady of Light at San Diego was probably executed in the 1760s. It was painted by Luis de Mena, journeyman artist of some renown in 18th century Mexico.

Included in the "busy" painting are, at the top, Saint Joseph and a redeemed soul to his left, two persons of the Holy Trinity in the center and Saint Francis with a redeemed soul to the right. Indian chieftains can be seen in the lower corners, with Our Lady as the central figure about to be crowned as queen by two angels.

There are some departures from the original portrayal, especially the inclusion of native Americans. Exactly how and why these changes came about is yet to be ascertained.

BLESSED VIRGIN MARY — OUR LADY OF MONTSERRAT

Devotion in California to Our Lady of Montserrat, first brought to the area by the Franciscan missionaries, received a whole new emphasis with the arrival of the earliest diocesan priests, most of whom were born and raised in the shadows of the famed shrine bearing her same name. Situated almost at the center of Catalonia, some sixty miles northwest of Barcelona, the Marian monastery has figured prominently in the annals of history for almost a thousand years.

An ancient legend testifies that in pagan times there was a temple erected at Montserrat dedicated to Venus. It was supposedly destroyed by the intervention of the Archangel Michael. The presence of a hermitage at the site can be traced to the 8th century. Early in the 11th century, the Bishop–Abbot Oliba, a figure of considerable importance in the formation of medieval Christendom in Catalonia founded a little monastery beside the hermitage of Saint Mary.

The foundation at Montserrat grew in fame and influence during the subsequent centuries—mostly because of the devotion engendered there to the Blessed Mother as portrayed in an image known as *La Moreneta*.

The Christ Child, with hand raised in blessing, is seated in the lap of Our Lady. Over the centuries the facial and flesh areas of the Romanesque statue have taken on a dark color. The "Black Virgin" is esteemed not only as a religious treasure, but as a work of artistic excellence.

Devotion to Our Lady of Montserrat spread eastward with the Mediterranean conquests of the Catalan–Argonese monarchy. Throughout the Italian territories, there were over 150 churches and chapels dedicated to the Madonna of Montserrat.

The imperial dynasty of Spain carried the fame of Our Lady of Montserrat westward with the discovery of the New World. The Benedictine monk, Bernard Boyl, a one–time monk at Montserrat, accompanied Christopher Columbus on his second voyage in 1493. He it was who brought that Marian devotion to the new continent.

Many of the earliest churches in Mexico, Peru and Chile were dedicated to the Madonna of Montserrat. Her patronage was also bestowed upon an island and different mountains, to say nothing of numerous towns and villages. The Madonna of Montserrat became the first of the names of Our Lady to be known on a really world–wide scale.

Though the hallowed sanctuary at Montserrat suffered almost total destruction during the Napoleonic invasion and in later civil wars, it underwent a rebirth in the 19th century, with the return of Our Lady's statue from its place of hiding. The Blessed Mother, under her title Madonna of Montserrat, was declared the Patroness of the dioceses in Catalonia by Pope Leo XIII. Some forty years later, the entire Spanish nation was placed under the spiritual mantle of the Madonna.

In more recent times, the monks attached to the famed Marian shrine have returned to practices of the 16th century, with their cultivation of history, classical literature, natural sciences, painting and music. A pilgrimage to the shrine of Our Lady of Montserrat still remains among the most thrilling of religious experiences. It is a journey into the best of California's past.

BLESSED VIRGIN MARY — OUR LADY OF PEACE

The parish of Our Lady of Peace, Santa Clara, can rightfully claim the distinction of having the largest depiction of the Blessed Mother in the United States, possibly even in the world. It all began in 1975, when Father John Sweeny and a group of his parishioners decided to acquire a statue of Mary for the many persons who gathered on the first Saturday of each month for devotions in honor of Our Lady of Fatima.

The noted sculptor, Charles Parks, was commissioned to build a 90 foot statue which would tower over the Bayshore Freeway and be visible to travelers arriving and leaving the San Jose Municipal Airport. Initially, Parks built a 10 foot statue, and then the present 32 foot model, preliminary to the 90 foot version. It was decided, however, for reasons of maintenance, to concentrate on the middle size madonna.

The $340,000 cost of the gigantic statue was met entirely from voluntary donations mailed in by 3,700 persons throughout the world. It took five years and 12,000 hours of work to complete the statue.

Moving the 7,200 pound stainless steel statue from Delaware to Philadelphia to Chicago and then across the nation was a feat in itself. Onlookers stood in awe as the huge rendition of Our Lady of Peace inched its way along the highways. The driver of the pilot car who escorted the flat–bed truck and its precious cargo from Reno to Santa Clara said "I'm not a Catholic, but I am a Catholic–Protestant now."

Thirty–five bay area businesses donated time, supplies and labor to the construction of the 14 foot high foundation of the shrine. Interestingly enough, much of the freely–given materials came from non–Catholics.

Dedication of the statue was scheduled for the Feast of Our Lady of the Rosary, October 7th 1983. Bishop Pierre DuMaine gathered for the event with upwards of 3,000 faithful on the six acre grounds of Our Lady of Peace parish in Santa Clara.

Fittingly, the ceremonies at the shrine marked the first diocesan observances of the jubilee Year of Redemption which Pope John Paul II proclaimed for the Christian world. Bishop DuMaine designated Our Lady of Peace a pilgrimage site for the rest of the holy year.

In his dedicatory remarks, the bishop said that modern peoples are strengthened by God's promise to be among believers when they pray. "We ask Christ to fill the world with His peace and we call on Mary, the Queen of Peace, to intercede for us that we may walk in the ways of peace." Members of the Knights of Columbus Color Guard, Saint Victor's Choir and more than fifty priests from the Diocese of San Jose recited the rosary during a post–vespers procession from the church to the shrine.

Historically speaking, the shrines to Our Lady are very much a part of the world's story—of crusade and conquest, martyrdom and sainthood—as the works of writers, archeologists and scientists show. And the role of Marian shrines is not a static one, belonging merely to the past. Quite the contrary. At this very instant, the cumulative effect of a dynamic faith through the centuries quickens new generations to prayer.

BLESSED VIRGIN MARY — OUR LADY'S SHRINE AT SAN DIEGO

The following article appeared in the *Ave Maria* in 1894. It is reproduced here as an indication of Marian devotion at the turn of the century.

The proposed shrine of Our Lady near the Indian school at San Diego, California, is now an accomplished fact; the nucleus, at least, of what we hope may some day be an offering more worthy of her in whose honor it has been erected. Perhaps it would be well, in connection with the announcement, to give a short account of its first inception; as there are, no doubt, among the readers of our Lady's magazine some who have forgotten, and others who have never heard, how the shrine had its origin.

In the winter of 1890–91 Southern California was visited by a sharp shock of earthquake, the worst it had experienced in many years; and, although no damage whatever was done, many persons were thoroughly alarmed. Among these were the Indian children at St. Anthony's School, which is situated within a very easy stone's–throw of the ruins of the old San Diego Mission building, founded by the saintly Fray Junípero Serra more than 125 years ago; the first of the numerous missions which gave name to the various coast towns and settlements from which the foot of the Spaniard has long since departed.

These children fell upon their knees, and promised the Blessed Virgin they would build, with their own hands, a shrine in her honor, if she would be their intercessor for protection from the danger of the earthquake. They intended to build it of adobe, and at once began to work by carrying stones for the foundation from the valley to the summit of the hill, where they proposed erecting the shrine.

Their intention having been given publicity through a short account of the circumstances in these pages, several persons expressed a desire to contribute. One lady generously offered to pay for a statue, another an altar; and various small sums of money were given through other channels.

The cornerstone was laid on July 16, 1892, the Feast of Our Lady of Mount Carmel and the 127th anniversary of the foundation of the mission. Afterward a departure from the original plan was decided upon; and instead of being constructed of adobe, the shrine has been built of wood and plate–glass, after the pattern of that at Auriesville, New York. It was also decided to dedicate it to Our Lady of Sorrows; and on the Feast of the Seven Dolors, last September, the ceremonies were performed with great solemnity.

The shrine is very tastefully built, open to view on all sides; and in the rainy weather, which occurs here but seldom, the interior will be amply protected by the plate–glass which forms its outer sides.

A beautiful statue of Our Lady of Sorrows (*la Pieta*) surmounts the altar, which is white, "'picked in" with gold. Here daily come the Indian children with flowers to adorn the shrine; here they assemble with their little petitions and prayers. Here are novenas constantly being offered for their benefactors, as well as for many who ask prayers for special intentions.

From the top of what is now called Our Lady's Mount may be seen the crumbling ruins of the Mission, with the famous olive groves from which have originated the finest California olive orchards. They are still flourishing and fruitful, after more than a century of existence, All around breathes peace and contentment; it is a favorable spot for meditation and seclusion. Blessed by the labors of the early missionaries, baptized in the blood of the martyred Father Jayme, whose body was found not far distant and consecrated anew by the erection of this shrine to Our Lady of Sorrows, surely this privileged land will find favor in the eyes of Her Divine Son.

It seems appropriate, too, that near the spot where the brave pioneer priests built a mission house for the evangelization of the Indians, the descendants of those Indians should now, when old San Diego is crumbling into dust, rear a new shrine in honor of that Faith, which has made the annals of California rich in examples of heroism and devotion. May the fruit sown in love be gathered in abundance!

BLESSED VIRGIN MARY — PATRONESS OF THE CALIFORNIAS

For over 120 years the Blessed Mother has been the Patroness of the Californias under her title, Our Lady, Refuge of Sinners. So declared on January 4, 1843, by Bishop Francisco Garcia Diego y Moreno, O.F.M., the proclamation has never been repealed, although the individual dioceses have since adopted their own local patrons. The Diocese of San Diego retains an annual feastday in honor of Our Lady, Refuge of Sinners, Patroness of the Californias, celebrated each year on the 4th of July.

The text of the proclamation can be found in the *Libro de Patentes* of Mission Santa Clara. After quoting the early Church fathers on the practice and spiritual benefits of naming patron saints, the bishop declared:

> We make known to you that we hereby name the great Mother of God in her most precious title *Del Refugio* the principal patroness of our diocese . . . . With so great a patroness and protectoress, what can we not promise ourselves? What can be wanting and whom do

Our Lady, Refuge of Sinners

we need to fear? If through the centuries this most worthy Mother of God has shown goodness and compassion to all peoples and nations . . . will She not do likewise for those peoples who bind themselves to her as their Refuge and special Patroness?

The bishop continued with almost prophetic faith,

We have said that the greater part of her benefactions are invisible, for in the dark night of this miserable century we can see only those blessings that are visible to our bodily senses. But that glorious day will certainly come when each of us will be astonished and will exclaim with overflowing joy and gratitude the words of the Book of Wisdom.

One of the mission reports described the local proclamation of The Virgin's patronage in colorful language:

After the people had been informed and invited a month before, the bells were rung at different times after Vespers of April 15, 1843. In the Church which had been adorned as well as possible, to the right and left of the tabernacle were placed the images of Our Lady of Refuge.

Next day, after the bells had been rung repeatedly, High Mass was offered before the Blessed Sacrament exposed. After the Gospel a brief exhortation was made, followed by the Oath of Allegiance. At the conclusion of the Holy Sacrifice the *Te Deum* was sung, and this closed the ceremony.

A painting of the newly proclaimed patroness was borne in solemn procession after which a detailed explanation of the history of the devotion and its fittingness was given. Most of the missions have a depiction of the Virgin under title, Refuge of Sinners. From an artistic standpoint, they are very much alike. The Virgin is shown with the child Jesus. Usually the mantle of the Blessed Mother carries the monograms JHR and IMR, a set of alternate stars and a fringed border. The child has a tunic of transparent gauze adorned with lace work. That part of the Virgin's mantle falling across the child is bordered with red and fringes of gold. A collar of painted pearls is visible in most cases.

The heads of both figures lean together with no background between them. Mary's eyes are turned toward the observer while the gaze of the child seems to be a bit to the left. With few exceptions, the pictures of Our Lady of Refuge of Sinners are uniform in design and execution.

On January 15, 1982, Archbishop Giuseppe Casoria, Pro–Prefect of the Sacred Congregation for the Sacraments and Divine Worship, acting upon a request from the California Conference of Catholic Bishops, signed a decree authorizing the Feast of Our Lady, Refuge of Sinners, to be celebrated in California on July 5th.

BLESSED VIRGIN MARY — THE SOUTHLAND AND KNOCK

The visit by Pope John Paul II to Knock recalls the pilgrimage to that famous Marian Shrine in Ireland made by James Francis Cardinal McIntyre in the fall of 1954. During his sojourn, the Archbishop of Los Angeles made arrangements for a beautiful stained glass window to be placed in the right transept of the parish church. Designed and executed by the Henry Clarke Studios of Dublin, the window was dedicated to Our Lady of the Angels in gratitude for the many priestly vocations provided by Ireland to Southern California.

It was the evening of August 21st, in the rainy, famine–struck summer of 1879, that Father Bartholomew A. Cavanaugh, pastor of the County Mayo village of Knock, first heard voices and shouting from the direction of the parish church. About fifteen persons had witnessed an apparition of Mary, the Mother of the Savior clothed in a white silken mantle, with a crown of glittering gems on her head,

Saint Joseph stood alongside, his head bowed. On her other side was Saint John the Evangelist, vested in the ceremonial robes of the Eastern Church, one arm raised, the other holding a copy of the Roman Missal. Behind the three figures stood a white marble altar containing a small lamb and a cross. One writer conjectures that the altar, cross and lamb "were to remind us that we must make every sacrifice to be faithful to the Mass, the sacraments and rosary."

The apparition lasted for almost two hours and though witnesses stood in heavy rain, the grass beneath the gable on which the figures appeared remained dry. Word of the apparition spread rapidly through the village. And though there were skeptics, they were confounded with additional appearances on the following January 6th, February 10th and 12th.

A series of "hearings" about the authenticity of the event were held by the Archbishop of Tuam. Composed of prominent clergy from surrounding districts, the commission questioned witnesses and later confirmed the apparitions. After the Church made its official pronouncement regarding the authenticity of the shrine at Knock, thousands of people began bringing the sick and afflicted to the site.

During the Marian year of 1954, Pope Pius XII blessed and decorated the banner of Knock in Saint Peter's Basilica. And, twenty years later, Pope Paul VI blessed the foundation stone for a new church which was to be built at Knock in honor of Our Lady. Over a million persons annually visit the shrine. The local pastor has noted that "Knock is a place for returning, for finding lost faith and greater devotion; the conversion of hearts, minds and souls are top priority here."

During August of 1979 Timothy Cardinal Manning

visited Knock and renewed there the relationship established a quarter century earlier between the people of Ireland and those of the Archdiocese of Los Angeles.

BLESSED VIRGIN MARY — SUTRO MARIAN REPOSITORY

One of the truly important Marian repositories in the United States is the Sutro Library at San Francisco which was established by Adolph Sutro (1830–1898) in the 1880s. Among the treasures at the Sutro is a certified copy (the original is lost) of the hearings of the first miracle attributed to Our Lady of Guadalupe which was filed in the archives of the Cathedral at *Puebla de Los Angeles* on October 28, 1864.

Comprising 186 leaves and written in a calligraphic hand by Secretary Jose Maria Catalani, the manuscript is finely bound in leather. The original copy was dated December 9, 1755 and was prepared at the convent of *Santa Catarina de Sena*.

According to the account, Mother Jacinta Maria de San Jose became increasingly ill and began vomiting blood. During the following days, her condition rapidly declined. Medication had no effect and, on December 12th, she was thought to be on the verge of death. The sacrament of Extreme Unction was administered.

In a weakened state, Mother Jacinta uttered a prayer to Our Lady of Guadalupe, asking for a miracle to glorify her name. Immediately she began to recover and shortly thereafter was able to eat the first solid food in days. Within a few more days her health was completely restored. She lived on until May 20, 1792.

As a result of this rapid recovery, hearings were heard in 1755 and 1756 before Gaspar Antonio Mendez de Cisñeros, the treasurer of the Metropolitan Cathedral and commissary of the Holy Office of the Inquisition, to determine the legitimacy of the events.

Eleven questions relating to the seriousness of the illness, the immediacy of the recovery and whether it appeared miraculous were put to fifteen witnesses comprising nuns, novices, physicians and theologians. The depositions were then submitted to a panel of three judges. Positive opinions were eventually rendered and, on June 11, 1759, the recovery of Mother Jacinta Maria de San Jose was canonically determined to be a true miracle.

In addition to this most extraordinary documentation at the Sutro are other items pertaining to Our Lady of Guadalupe, including copies of the earliest printed likeness of Our Lady (a copper engraving by Samuel Stradanus) and a devotionary with nine separate images produced in Mexico for the opening of the sanctuary in 1622.

And there is a copy of *Regla y Ordenaciones de las Refigiosas* by Archbishop Francisco Manso (1635) which contains a woodcut of Our Lady repeated in several works during the 17th century. Another great treasure is the first published account in Nahuatl, taken from the Nican Mopohua of Antonio Valeriano which was printed at Mexico City by Juan Ruiz in 1649. More than a hundred prints of Our Lady of Guadalupe published prior to Mexican independence also form part of the vast holding in the Sutro's Mexican Collection.

Later, major imprints in the Sutro Library include the prayer to Our Lady of Guadalupe composed by Archbishop Francisco Antonio Lorenzana which appeared from the press of Jose Antonio de Hogal in 1770; the *Manifiesto Satisfactorio* of Jose Ignacio Bartolache which discusses the scientific composition of the *tilma* and the *Pensil Americano* of 1790 and 1797.

BLESSING OF ANIMALS

From the earliest times, the Church has had official prayers imploring Almighty God's protection upon the animal kingdom. These invocations, in addition to showing the strong agrarian sympathies of the Church, remind the faithful in rural areas of the materialistic spirit often discernible in an ever–growing industrial civilization.

The custom of blessing animals goes back 1,600 years to the days of Saint Anthony, a fourth century hermit of the Egyptian desert, who first called attention to the service rendered man by these creatures of Providence. In 356, the holy abbot composed an invocative prayer which is still used in the liturgical benediction:

> Almighty Father, we bless these animals for all they have done for us in supplying our food, in carrying our burdens, providing us with clothing and companionship and rendering a service to the human race since the world began.

The *Golden Legend* associated with the memory of Saint Anthony tells "wonderful stories of how the crows brought him food, how the beasts of the forest used to show him his way, how two lions came out of the desert to help him dig a grave in the sand for his brother hermit, Paul." We are further told that the wild animals never harmed him, but, on the contrary, helped him in many ways, and he certainly loved these four–footed, furry companions of his solitude. His great heart had room for all, God, man, and beast. He was a champion of animals and as their faithful friend after so many centuries, he still wants to obtain a blessing for them on his feast day.

The annual *Benedicto equorum aliorumve animalium* was originally held in Rome on Saint Anthony's feast day, the 17th of January. It is related how in the square before a church located near the city's biggest market place, the four–footed congregation was dutifully assembled:

"Hunting dogs, German police dogs, wire haired terriers, white woolie dogs, black curley ones, a little Roman *lupetto*, all made up a right noisey and restive congregation. There were canaries in cages and other birds, and even an elephant from a passing circus." Shepherds from the country areas brought their flocks, to which were added cows, horses, donkeys and goats, their presence secured by the promise of a generous meal right after the blessing. One commentator remarked that the whole assembly might have walked out of Noah's Ark onto the piazza.

Even such elusive creatures as chickens, too independent to be gathered with the others, were blessed for "they too must serve well their master, man, to whom God gave all the goods of the earth."

The annals further describe how "at ten o'clock, while inside the church a solemn High Mass was being celebrated in honor of the saint [Anthony] a priest and acolyte in white surplices came out on the steps; there was a hush in the congregation and some attempt made at order." A short Latin prayer from the ritual was read asking the blessing of God on the animals. The intercession of St. Anthony was invoked in order that they might be preserved from all bodily harm. A generous sprinkling of holy water concluded the brief ceremony.

In subsequent centuries, the blessing of animals gradually became associated with Holy Saturday morning, as is still the custom in many Spanish–speaking countries. One competent writer, commenting on the various festivals observed by the Catholic Church between Christmas and Easter, notes that little or nothing has been written about their celebration in mission days. The same authority goes on to relate, however, that "within recent years there has been revived among the Mexican people of Olvera Street and the old Plaza Church, the ceremony of *La Bendicion de los Animales*. There, on the appointed day, domestic animals and pets—horses, cows, cats, dogs, birds, squirrels, chickens, ducks and even goldfish are brought in procession from the picturesque little Mexican street to the courtyard of the old *pueblo* church where each in turn is blessed by the smiling officiating *Padre* for its health and fertility.

Surely there was a similar custom followed in mission times, especially in those years when it was so vitally necessary that the flocks and herds increase as rapidly as possible. Moreover, it is not reasonable to suppose that the *padres* would bless the newly–planted fields, the crops, the water as it was turned into new ditches, and not bless the livestock.

The ceremony, as observed in contemporary times, includes all pets, from a turtle to an ox. An observer, in 1965, described the event: "On the day before Easter, dogs, cats, rabbits, roosters, turtles, parrots, horses, and their owners throng the narrow street and the Plaza of Los Angeles. Some pets are ridden, driven or led; others are carried in arms, cages, paper bags, or bowls. Many of the people are in Mexican costume; many of the animals sport garlands of flowers or ribbons. In Plaza Park, a *padre* and his altar boys stand on a flower–bedecked platform, and bless each of the animals as it goes by."

The recent Vatican Council strongly recommended and encouraged those practices of piety commended by long usage in the Church. Surely the annual blessing of animals at the Plaza on Holy Saturday fits eminently into the conciliar exhortation.

BOOK OF KELLS

Scholars have long agreed that the combined skill of eye and hand exhibited in the *Book of Kells* ranks it among the most wonderful examples of human workmanship. The original is on public display in the Trinity College Library, Dublin. It is known as the "*Book of Kells*" because it was used for many years at liturgical services in the Abbey of Kells, in County Meath.

During a raid by the Vikings, the book was stolen by vandals who ripped off its gold–embossed, jewel–studded cover. It was later buried for several months, during which time considerable damage was inflicted. After the volume was recovered, a new binding was fashioned, but the missing pages were never replaced. In 1539, when the Abbey was surrendered to King Henry VIII, the *Book of Kells* came into the possession of Gerald Plunkett. During the Cromwellian years, it was given to Dublin's Trinity College, where it has remained since 1661.

Produced between 1100 and 1200 years ago, the *Book of Kells* was likely the work of four different persons. It contains the four Gospels written in Latin, together with prefaces, summaries, tables of references, part of a glossary and blank pages (on which have been inserted historic land grants).

The handwriting is bold, well–rounded and print–like. The ink is brownish–black for the most part, some is red, some is bluish–black and purple. Sentences range from sixteen to eighteen words per line. Thirty–one pages are fully illustrated. The designs include geometric, trumpet–like spirals, animal shapes and leaf patterns. Nearly every creature of earth is represented, like the interlacing of water snakes with earth and sky birds. The key pattern is fire.

The variety and beauty of the opening pages is especially striking. Reference figures and lists of parallel passages are set out in the framework of Byzantine architecture with pillars, capitals, bases and tympana finely decorated. The oft–recurring theme of the Evangelists is presented with ingenuity and beauty.

There are 340 leaves still remaining, measuring thirteen by nine and a half inches. They are all made of thick–glazed vellum or parchment. Authorities generally agree that the "Monogram" page, with its outstanding Greek symbol for Christ, is the culminating splendor of the entire manuscript.

The late Archbishop John J. Cantwell was long an admirer of the *Book of Kells*. In 1940, he acquired a facsimile page which had been printed for the Irish Government by Eyre and Spottiswoode of London. Cantwell gave the page to Carrie Estelle Doheny and from that time onward, the countess was avidly interested in the *Book of Kells*.

In 1950, when the firm of Urs Graf announced plans to reproduce the entire volume, Mrs. Doheny became a charter subscriber. When the three volume edition was completed, in 1951, the Doheny copy was numbered 17. Using the latest methods of scientific color photography and reproduction technique, the printers fashioned one of the most gorgeous and beautiful works of the century.

When Mrs. Doheny died in 1958, her copy of the *Book of Kells* was given to James Francis Cardinal McIntyre. Entrusted to the Archival Center a decade later, it can be seen by special appointment.

BOOKPLATE — CATHOLIC

A bookplate is a detachable label, usually adorned with artistic scenes or witty sayings which indicates the ownership or use of books. The world's oldest bookplates date back to the 18th dynasty of Egypt, when Amenhotep III ruled Thebes.

In the literary world, bookplates are often referred to as "*ex libris*," a Latin phrase meaning "from the books of . . ." For the early California missionaries and others bound by the vow of poverty, the term "*ad usum*" ("for the use of. . . .) was common. Bookplates have been executed in many media over the years—including woodcuts, engravings, lithographs, etchings and line drawings. Here we will dwell on some of the more prominent Catholic "*ex libris*" on the local scene.

The missions are frequently featured in bookplates. Santa Barbara for example, occupies center place in the fanciful *ex libris* of the California Bookplates Society. That historic foundation was also on the cover of the first edition of *California Bookplates*, November 1906.

The plate of Thomas Wayne Morris depicts San Carlos Borromeo Mission in the days before its restoration. A cloud of swallows nest in the eaves of historic San Juan Capistrano Mission in the bookplate of Harry Bennett Abdy. In the *ex libris* of Herbert Eugene Bolton, distinguished scholar and head of the department of History at the University of California, Berkeley, is featured the signature of Father Eusebio Kino, the famed Jesuit "Cattle King of Arizona," along with three other prominent early pioneers.

The bookplate of Chaffey Library suggests the tranquillity of scholastic learning. An early friar is shown reciting his breviary, with San Antonio mountain in the background. Patrick William Croake, one–time editor of the *The Tidings*, is portrayed at a table lined with books, including John Steven McGroarty's famous *Mission Play*. Appropriately, the artist, Bernhardt Wall, included an issue of *The Tidings* in the frontal area of the table.

The bookplate of Msgr. Francis J. Conaty is especially ornate and meaningful. His musical and literary interests are indicated in the design of the artist, Mary Eleanor Curran, who also sketches the exterior and interior of the Cathedral Chapel of Our Lady of Guadalupe. The prelate's written signature completes the design. A genial Dominican portrayed in Monsignor Joseph M. Gleason's bookplate is vested in a cowl, habit and merry look bespeaking the mellow San Francisco priest. Seated at a book laden desk, the abbe is transcribing into a blotter book.

The *ex libris* of Carrie Estelle Doheny was designed by Riviere & Sons of London. Experts consider it to be "one of the supremely beautiful leather" bookplates in several continents. The plate is an adaptation from a binding designed by Clovis Eve and found on a book *Las Ordonnances de la Ville de Paris en 1587.*

Collecting bookplates or *ex libris* is a superb way of pursuing one's interest in the pioneers of earlier days. A useful guide in this field is Clare Ryan Talbot's treatise *Historic California in Bookplates* which was published by the Graphic Press in 1936. There is also a *Newsletter of the American Society of Bookplate Collectors and Designers* which is issued under the editorship of Audrey Spencer Arellanes. Interestingly enough, Catholic themes on bookplates give evidence of widespread use.

BORROMEO GUILD

According to an early promotional brochure, the Borromeo Guild was established for the purpose of "furthering Catholic knowledge and information" through a wider dissemination of doctrinally sound books, pamphlets and other printed materials. The brainchild of Msgr. John K. Clarke, for thirty–three years director of the Confraternity of Christian Doctrine for the Archdiocese of Los Angeles, the Guild became a separate and autonomous organization in April of 1943. In its earliest months, it shared quarters with the Catholic Welfare Bureau at Second and Hill streets.

Clarke envisioned the Borromeo Guild as the publishing arm of the Confraternity of Christian Doctrine and in that role the Guild provided religious textbooks and teaching devices for Confraternity classes at various grade levels. With its removal to No. 2 Chester Place in 1944, the Guild, named for Saint Charles Borromeo, expanded its stock of available books, concentrating on those titles then in demand by the Catholic reading public. Pastors and principals were encouraged to establish parochial libraries and to enlarge classroom resources. By 1968, there were 136 parish libraries functioning in the archdiocese, all of them under the direction or encouragement of the Borromeo Guild.

In an effort to better serve the Catholic populace of the four county archdiocese, the Borromeo Guild moved in 1955 to quarters especially designed in the new building erected for *The Tidings*, across the street from the Chancery Office. The handsome reinforced concrete and brick structure allowed for further expansion of the Guild's activities. Within a year, the modern facilities at 1530 West Ninth Street housed the largest selection of Catholic books on the west coast.

In the post Vatican years, when religious texts began appearing from a host of national publishing houses, the Borromeo Guild withdrew from most of its involvement in that area and concentrated on other phases of the Catholic apostolate. Later, the Borromeo Guild provided services in a diversity of fields including visual aids, catechetical materials, religious records and cassettes, greeting cards, childrens' books and reading devices.

The inventory of 55,000 books includes Bibles, encyclicals, missals, prayerbooks, lives of saints, devotional works, popular novels and a veritable litany of theological, moral, scriptural and liturgical commentaries and essays.

And the Guild continued to serve the needs of religious education classes, parochial seminars, renewal programs and other areas of catechetical outreach in an archdiocese serving 2,561,602 Catholics. What was begun as a way of satisfying the need for upgraded religious textbooks evolved into a multifaceted operation for the entire Catholic booktrade, all in accord with the founder's dictum that "the Borromeo Guild is more a service than a bookstore."

Since mid 1987, the Borromeo Guild has functioned as a unit of Cotter Church Supplies, its staff still committed to providing the widest possible spectrum of Catholic teachings at the least possible cost.

BROWNSON HOUSE

The need for a Catholic Settlement House in California's southland was realized in 1901, when Bishop George T. Montgomery endorsed plans drawn up by Fathers M. S. Liebana and John J. Clifford. As stated in its constitution, "the object of this association shall be to maintain a Catholic Social Settlement which shall be a center for personal service and mutual helpfulness, for civic, social and religious betterment where conditions of living are difficult, and where Catholics of poor circumstances and foreign birth abound. . . .

Inspired by the indefatigable zeal of Orestes Brownson, the new settlement was given the name of that noted American Catholic author of the last century. In 1904 Bishop Thomas J. Conaty purchased property at 711 Jackson Street, and erected a house which was ready for occupancy early the next year. The field of work for Brownson House was the poor and foreign people, most of whom were Mexican Catholics; however, the activity of the House extended to other peoples of every race and creed. Constructive social work and promotion of civic, social and religious betterment through personal service and mutual contact achieved amazing results in a city previously so little concerned with that problem. To carry out these ideals, a staff of experienced workers was brought together, each of them specially trained in his respective fields. As early as 1915, there were 160 people active in the movement, many of them volunteer workers.

The Settlement carried its apostolate to the homes of the less fortunate through field workers. Another beneficiary of their attention was the county's General Hospital. Sewing clubs were organized and many needed garments prepared for worthy families. Brownson House officials cooperated with public agencies and other social organizations to solve specific problems. Indiscriminate giving was discouraged in favor of a self–help plan through friendly cooperation.

Realizing that any work of solid construction is necessarily slow, skilled personnel were constantly available in a never ending attempt to solve the complex problems of poverty and need. A truly remarkable unanimity and devotion of its workers was always the hallmark of Brownson House and demonstrated once again that only a high, true, religious motive can effectively and permanently inspire unselfishness and genuine, lasting self–sacrificing devotion to any cause.

In the years after the First World War, when Southern California started its phenomenal growth, Bishop John J. Cantwell organized a Bureau of Catholic Charities (now the Catholic Charities) to extend the work of Brownson House to a diocesan level. Gradually certain functions of the earlier organization were handed over to the larger agency until today the establishment known as Brownson House operates solely as a youth center under the C.Y.O. In these times we are accustomed to large–scale charitable foundations, both public and private; but at the turn of the century such was not the case and Catholics are forced to tip their hat to those great pioneers who made Brownson House a high mark in California's Catholic Heritage!

BUBONIC PLAGUE OF 1924

In today's medically secure years, it is hard for contemporary peoples to realize that just a generation ago, here in Southern California, there was an outbreak of the bubonic plague. It all began during a hot summery day in 1924, in a bustling Hispanic neighborhood east of downtown Los Angeles. Jesus Lajun was recounting a humorous tale of how he had come across a dead rat beneath his house.

Less than a month later, the gossip around the area had stopped. Lajun began to nurse a bloody cough and a painfully swollen gland. He was mourning the death of a daughter who had been declared a victim of "double pneumonia" by the coroner. A neighbor, Lucena Samarano, had also died recently. By the end of October, Lajun was dead too. So were three other boarders in his house. Within days, there had been a dozen unexpected deaths in the immediate neighborhood.

Once properly diagnosed as the plague, according to medical records of the period housed at the University of Southern California, the community between Alameda Street and the Los Angeles River and from Macy Street to Alhambra Avenue was placed under strict quarantine.

Rope barricades were set up and armed guards were brought in. Food was rationed, a temporary medical facility established and undertakers throughout the city were instructed not to embalm any bodies until health inspectors had been called in. Priests were cautioned by Bishop John J. Cantwell about the outbreak and told to report any unexpected deaths or extraordinary illnesses. Funerals of known victims were to be conducted privately, with only family members in attendance.

Due mostly to the careful enforcement of strict health measures, the Los Angeles epidemic was quickly over, although before its end forty people were known to have been infected, and all but three of them had died. Medical historians now believe that the plague that infected Los Angeles came from San Francisco. It had apparently came aboard a ship that had entered San Francisco Bay from the Orient.

After lying dormant for most of the previous 200 years worldwide, the plague resurfaced in March, 1900, striking a Bay City wood seller who was staying in a hotel in San Francisco's Chinatown. At least this is the theory of a 1955 essay in the *Stanford Medical Bulletin*.

Although the city board of health placed a quarantine on Chinatown, the action was widely opposed by the cit-izens of San Francisco. Nob Hill matrons were miffed that they were being deprived of their household help. Downtown businessmen feared that publicity about the quarantine might devastate trade. In headline after headline, the city's newspapers lampooned the alarm as a result of the "figment of medical imaginations." Even the Chinese opposed the quarantine, claiming that it was a form of discrimination.

As a result of the opposition, the quarantine was generally ignored in San Francisco. It was not until the epidemic had spread across the state and Mexico had closed its ports to California shipping that San Francisco took the plague seriously—almost four years and 119 victims later!

People of earlier times lived with the realization that plagues and epidemics were an accepted (and dreaded) part of the human cycle. With the advent of the so-called "wonder drugs," these great killers of the past have been controlled and/or eliminated. Such was not the case, even in California, a generation ago.

BULL–FIGHTING IN SOUTHERN CALIFORNIA

Catholic authorities have condemned bull–fighting on a number of occasions. Pope Saint Pius V imposed a universal prohibition on the "sport" and even threatened local princes who allowed it with ecclesiastical penalties. The restriction of the Dominican pontiff was moderated for Spain (and its territories) by his successor in the papacy, Gregory XIII. The ban was further relaxed so as to include only Sundays and holydays.

A limited amount of bull–fightings took place in Southern California in provincial times. Auguste Bernard Duhaut–Cilly described one such celebration at Mission San Luis Rey thusly:

> This exercise offered nothing very remarkable: it took place in the inner court. Each rider proceeded to tease the bull, which rushed with lowered head, now upon one, now upon another; but such is the agility of men and horses that they are almost never overtaken, though the bull's horn appears to touch them every instant. . . . The bull was not killed as in Spain. After it had been provoked, tired, teased for a half–hour, a small gate leading onto the plain was opened; no sooner had the animal seen this way of escape, than it made for it with all speed; the horsemen flew like arrows in its pursuit; the swiftest, upon reaching it, seized it by the tail; and, at the same instant, giving spurs to his horse, he overthrew the bull, sending it rolling in the dust; only after this humiliating outrage was it permitted to gain the pasture in freedom.

Another version of the "sport" common to Alta California was the bull–bear fight. Theodor Cordua noted in his memoirs, in 1841, that he had "an opportunity to witness the cruel entertainment," which is rather popular in California, of a fight between a large grizzly bear of about six hundred pounds and a spirited steer of about twice the size. In a circular enclosure a fore–leg of one animal was tied to that of the other by a rope 20 yards long.

> As soon as the steer saw the bear and felt that the latter was hindering it from moving about freely, it rushed toward the poor grizzly and ran his horns into the bear's ribs. After many such violent thrusts, the bear finally clutched its great paws around the neck of the steer and embraced it so tightly that the bull could not move and showed its fear by frantic bellows.
>
> Frequently the bull is strangled in this manner while the bear clings to its neck with its entrails dangling. The two animals participating in the fight we observed, were still alive after a struggle of two hours, although they were mortally wounded. The butcher gave them the death–blow with his knife.

Horse–racing, cock–sparring and bull–fighting were still fairly common in the *Pueblo de Nuestra Señora de los Angeles*, in the 1850s, though "an element for the preservation of cruelty was constantly being increased by an influx of Americans of the better class, and especially the American women." (The old bull–fighting arena in the *pueblo* occupied the site of the present French Hospital, in old "Sonora Town.")

In his *Annals of Los Angeles*, J. Gregg Layne states that "during the year 1860 occurred the last bull–fight to be staged in Los Angeles, the death of a little child at one of these encounters causing them to be done away with as a form of public entertainment."

BYZANTINE DIOCESE OF VAN NUYS

The Catholic Church has unity of faith in all things divinely inspired or revealed, but it does not have uniformity in worship, in matters of spiritual life or areas of ecclesial discipline. In apostolic times, the Church grew into prominence in the cities of Antioch (in Syria) and Alexandria (in Egypt). Saint Peter, who established the Church at Antioch, later travelled to Rome where he was martyred.

While Rome became the center of Christianity in the West, it is from Antioch and Alexandria—as well as from the Church in Jerusalem—that the Eastern rites evolved. The Byzantine rite originated with the Church at Constantinople during the 4th and 5th centuries. When the rite spread into the Slavic countries, it took on a spirit of reverence related to the Christian life and worship of those areas. Ruthenian Catholics have come to be known for their simple devotion and "spiritual songs" which have been handed down through the centuries.

With almost 5.7 million members worldwide, the Byzantine Rite is by far the largest of the five Eastern Rites. The others are Alexandrian (Coptic and Ethiopian Rites), and Antiochean (Pure Syrian, Maronite and Syro–Malankarese), Armenian and East Syrian (Chaldean and Syro–Caldeo–Malabarese). In the United States, about 73% of the one million Eastern Rite Catholics are members of the Byzantine Rite.

Most of the communicants in the four Byzantine–Ruthenian dioceses of Pittsburgh (Pa.), Parma (Ohio), Passaic (New Jersey) and Van Nuys (Calif.) trace their ancestry to Czechoslovakia, Hungary, Rumania and other eastern European countries. Many have been persecuted peoples.

Interestingly, while Christianity along the Pacific Slope was taking root, Russian missionaries and traders, acting under the protection of the Russian Imperial Government, made a serious attempt to introduce Eastern Orthodoxy into the area. They built Fort Ross, about thirty miles north of Bodega Bay, near the mouth of a small stream, named by them Slawianski River. Russian Orthodox priests remained there until about 1841. In 1900, there were about 8,000 Ruthenian Catholics in the Western States, with parishes in Seattle, Portland, Denver, Pueblo and Stockett. There was also a monastery in Calhan County, Montana.

The Eastern Rites were brought permanently to California in 1926, when Saint Anne Melchite parish was established in Los Angeles. Ten years later, Saint Andrews Parish was founded for Russian Catholics by the Jesuit Fathers. The first Byzantine–Ruthenian parish of Saint Mary's traces its origins to 1956, and the arrival of Father Eugene Chromoga.

During the next quarter century, the parish of Saint Mary was administered by the Byzantine Bishop of Parma. Gradually, additional parochial foundations were made at San Diego, Fontana, Anaheim, Sacramento and San Mateo. On December 15, 1981, Pope John Paul II established the Diocese of Van Nuys, as a suffragan to the Byzantine–Ruthenian Metropolitan Province of Pittsburgh. Chosen to head the new diocese was Bishop Thomas Dolinay, formerly Auxiliary for the Byzantine Diocese of Passaic and episcopal vicar for the anthracite region of Pennsylvania. Dolinay was the son of a priest and both his maternal and paternal grandfathers were priests. The first Ruthenian bishop, appointed in 1924, was his great uncle.

The new diocese encompassed the eleven western states, Alaska and Hawaii. At its inception, the Diocese of Van Nuys included some 10,000 Catholics in fifteen parishes, five missions and approximately ten communities. The parishes in Van Nuys are relatively small in numbers of families, averaging perhaps 150. Ethnically, the core group of each parish may be Carpatho–Rusyn,

Slovak, Hungarian and Croatian ancestry. The parishes in Anaheim, San Diego and Sacramento often use Spanish in their liturgy.

The prime thrust of the Byzantine diocese today is among the unchurched and fallen away. The Metropolitan Province as a whole is striving towards an "American" Byzantine Church, with emphasis on retaining what is best of each group's natural heritage.

CALENDAR SURGERY

The year 1752 was a peaceful time for the Hispanic world. In Jalpan, Fray Junípero Serra began construction of the beautiful church of Santiago, the one remaining evidence of the friar's building program initiated in the New World. But that same year was one of turmoil for the American colonies. It was a year of only 271 days, when George Washington slept from September 2nd to the 14th. It was a year with no January or February and only six days in March.

Although painful complications followed, the operation of 1752 was necessary to correct an error that had begun in 46 B.C., when Julius Caesar ordered a new calendar put into use. It was the length of the solar year that created the problem. It takes the earth almost 365 1/2 days to complete a revolution around the sun—a period of time that cannot be evenly divided into either days or months. Since it is difficult to put one–fourth of a day on the calendar, Caesar added a day every four years.

However, his arithmetic was too much by an average of eleven minutes and fourteen seconds annually, or a day every 128 years. By the time sixteen centuries had passed, there was a noticeable discrepancy between the calendar year and the solar year. The calendar was no longer synchronized with the seasons.

Pope Gregory XIII was concerned because the Feast of Easter, whose date is determined by the spring equinox, was arriving too early. And he realized that the discrepancy would only worsen with the passage of time. To synchronize the calendar with the seasons required drastic action, so the Holy Father directed that in October, 1582, the 4th would be followed by the 15th, making a month of only twenty–one days and an abbreviated year.

This new Gregorian calendar also established January 1st as the beginning of the year because until then the date had been optional, (Many countries had begun the year on March 25; others had used Christmas or Easter).

The new calendar was immediately adopted by the Roman Catholic countries of Europe—Spain, Portugal, Italy, France and Poland. But the Protestant nations balked. The turmoil, therefore, did not end in 1582. England, undaunted by the prospect of becoming a "time island," did not make the change for nearly 200 more years. By the time the new calendar was adopted in the British Isles and in the American colonies, the Julian calendar had accumulated another day. This time eleven days had to be omitted.

Thus it was that "surgery" for the calendar in the colonies was scheduled for Wednesday, September 2, 1752. The next day was Thursday, September 14th. Benjamin Franklin found it the great delight of sleeping for twelve days. It's interesting to note that the whole operation had to be repeated in Alaska, when the United States purchased that area in 1867. Russia was still using the old Julian calendar. The treaty bears two dates: March 18th and March 30th.

Had Fray Junípero Serra known what confusion was transpiring in the American colonies in 1752, he would have smiled. It had taken Protestant England almost two centuries to catch up with Catholic Spain.

"CALIFORNIA ARCHIVE"

Though most scholars doing research in the field of Western Americana are familiar with the historical materials on file in the Santa Barbara Mission Archives, few are aware of the nearby Karpeles Manuscript Library whose "California Archive" is without peer among private holdings in the United States and abroad.

Founded in 1978 by David Karpeles, the archive is part of a larger collection which now has branches in New York, Tacoma and Jacksonville. According to a printed finding–device, there are fifty–five manuscript pages of Jose de Galvez and twenty–one of Fray Junípero Serra in the "California Archive."

Serra and his biographer, Fray Francisco Palou, are well represented with no fewer than 130 manuscript pages. The Palou diary is generally regarded as one of the greatest treasures from the provincial period. The letters of Galvez to Serra and Palou spell out the plans, locations, base camps, personnel, supplies and schedules of that momentous undertaking of 1769–1770.

Perhaps the most poignant of these documents is the "Christening of California," a letter from the Visitator General to Serra wherein the contemplated missions are named for the first time. The proto chapter in the history of Alta California's colonization closes with the drawing of the priceless "Founding Map of California," an appropriate commemoration to the success of the expedition.

Another treasure is a silver–encased illuminated manuscript awarded by King Charles III to Galvez, presenting the Visitator General with the title of "*Marques de Sonora*" for his success of the Sacred Expedition. It was given to Galvez shortly after his return to Spain in 1771.

Among the materials of local interest are descriptions of establishments at Santa Barbara, Los Angeles and Santa Ines as related by the founding father of each of the establishments. The destruction by Indians of the first mission at San Diego in November of 1775, a tragic setback to the achievements of the first years, is related in one of the documents. And there are founding maps of Northern California and Alaska which were made on the expeditions to complete the uncharted coasts of the New World.

The first years of the Mission Period are documented by reports and letters of Fray Junípero Serra and succeeding *presidentes*. Included therein are materials from Palou (130 manuscript pages), Fermin Lasuen (43), Estevan Tapis (9), Mariano Payeras (27), Narciso Duran (1 13) and Jose Bernardo Sanchez (3), as well as administrative letters from Teodoro de Croix, Antonio Bucareli, Juan Vicente, Revilla–Gigedo, and Miguel Branciforte.

The more important topics mentioned in these and other documents include the founding and construction of San Francisco Mission, the announcement of the successful opening of the overland trail to California by Juan Bautista de Anza, the planning and naming of each new mission, as well as reports on the "Council for the Development of California".

The "California Archives" at the Karpeles Manuscript Library is indeed among the richest storehouses of Western Americana.

CALIFORNIA ARROW

The history of the dirigible in California dates back to 1849, when Rufus Porter of New York first suggested flying argonauts to the gold fields of California in a giant "aerial locomotive." Not long thereafter, ingenious and intrepid San Francisans, capitalizing on the area's superior weather conditions, experimented with a variety of schemes to link California and the east coast by air.

Many of California's pioneering "aeronauts" experimented with the notion of affixing an engine and rudder to an elongated gas–filled balloon. This resulted in the invention of the dirigible which basically is a balloon that can be steered.

A number of San Francisco inventors operating in obscurity achieved many important firsts. In the same year, for example, that land–lovers completed the transcontinental railroad (1869), a balloon–glider made America's first powered flight near San Francisco. And, in 1904, a former tight–rope walker flew the country's first dirigible over a baseball field in Oakland. His cigar–shaped gas balloon was christened the *California Arrow*. A newspaper reporter watching the events observed that "California has the brightest sunshine, the thickest fogs and the most gigantic frauds of any state in the Union."

The subsequent successes of the Wright Brothers and the biplanes of Glenn Curtiss signaled a new era in aeronautics and, by 1910, the airship had been upstaged as too expensive, slow and unreliable. In the 1920 and 1930s blimps and zeppelins made a comeback in the American skies. They were used effectively during World War II, when the United States Navy had 168 of them hovering over convoys in submarine–infested waters.

The first Mass ever celebrated aboard an airship was that offered by Father Paul Schulte on May 7, 1936. It was offered in the social hall of the *Hindenburg* during that ship's maiden voyage.

The first Goodyear airship based in Los Angeles was the *Pony Express*. It came in 1919 when the company's factory was under construction at Central and Florence Avenues. It plied the skies of Southern California until 1923. According to the late Msgr. John J. Devlin, Bishop John J. Cantwell was the first prelate in the United States to fly in a Goodyear Blimp. Though the event is unrecorded in Cantwell's desk book, the flight took place sometime early in 1923.

On February 19, 1964, Msgr. Devlin was once again a passenger on a Goodyear blimp, this time aboard *Columbia II*. The story of that flight is the subject of a recently–issued miniature book on *The Goodyear Blimp*.

The present Goodyear airship, Columbia III, is perhaps the most recognizable corporate symbol in the nation, if not in the world. It and its predecessors have carried over one million persons aloft without a single injury! Wherever the massive silver and black airship travels, heads turn and wide–eyed children point and gasp. The 192 foot long airship looms above like an enormous thundercloud.

CALIFORNIA CATHOLIC CONFERENCE

The *Decree on the Bishops' Pastoral Office in the Church* considered it "supremely opportune everywhere" that bishops belonging to the same nation or region form an association which meets together at fixed times. Such had long been the practice in the United States. In the years immediately following the council, the nation's bishops reorganized the existing National Catholic Welfare Conference into the United States Catholic Conference.

Incorporated on January 1, 1967, under the laws for the District of Columbia, the Conference assists the American bishops by uniting the People of God where voluntary collective action on a broad interdiocesan range is needed. The USCC provides an organizational structure and the resources needed to insure coordination, cooperation and assistance in the public, educational and social concerns of the Church at the national or interdiocesan level.

California is one of the twenty–eight states which has adapted many parts of the USCC structure to the local Church. There are variances, of course, but the California Catholic Conference has generally the same objectives and goals as the larger organization, except that it deals exclusively with the fifty–eight counties of California.

The California Catholic Conference was formally established by the Golden State's hierarchy in February, 1971. It was an outgrowth of the California Conference of Catholic Health Facilities and the Catholic Schools of California, organized two years earlier. The functions of the Conference fall into three general categories: (a) providing liaison with state departments and with the legislature, (b) disseminating information to Catholic associations and organizations, to other state conferences and to the USCC and (c) coordinating interdiocesan activities in the areas of education, welfare and related items.

An informational newsletter is published monthly and a large amount of correspondence is maintained with the archbishops and bishops attached to the twelve ecclesial jurisdictions of California. Organized as a direct result of Vatican Council II and the 1971 Synod of Bishops, the California Catholic Conference is actively involved in a myriad of public affairs integral to the preaching of the Gospel and the betterment of justice, peace and general welfare.

The California bishops are a policy making body. An executive director coordinates the day–to–day activities of the Conference, assisted by office personnel who serve as staff to the bishops. Associated with the CCC are the diocesan directors of welfare and social service agencies, the superintendents of schools and coordinators of religious education, campus ministries and Catholic cemeteries.

Among the arms of the California Catholic Conference are Divisions of Education, Hispanic Affairs and Social Welfare. Another satellite group closely affiliated with the California Catholic Conference is the California Association of Catholic Hospitals.

The existence of the CCC confirms the conciliar belief and ideal that "when the insights of prudence and experience have been shared and views exchanged, there will emerge a holy union of energies in the service of the common good of the churches."

CALIFORNIA CATHOLIC FIRSTS

Some years ago, a list of "California Catholic Firsts" was published. Since then, people have responded with a host of notes on other outstanding first events, individuals and things. Here is a sampling.

The first baptism to be administered in Alta California took place at "*Los Christianos*" or "*La Cañada de los Bautismos*" on the initial expedition of Gaspár de Portolá to Monterey. Maria Magdalena was the name given to the infant christened on July 22, 1769 by Fray Francisco Gomez. First annulment in California was granted to Casilda Sepulveda who had been married to Antonio Teodoro Trujillo against her wishes. It was signed by Bishop Francisco Garcia Diego y Moreno at Santa Barbara in January, 1842.

First use of the name "redwood" for the famous California native tree now universally known by that name can be traced to Fray Juan Crespi's diary where, in an entry dated October 10, 1769, he says, "as we knew not the names of the trees, we gave them that of the color of the wood, *palo colorado*."

The initial excommunication was handed down by Fray Juan Fuster at San Diego Mission. In 1775, Fernando Rivera y Moncada, military *comandante* in Alta California, demanded custody of an Indian neophyte who had sought sanctuary in an improvised chapel after being accused of killing Fray Luis Jayme. When the friars refused to surrender the Indian, Rivera forcibly entered the area and removed the suspect. The first California boundary line was established some fifteen miles below the present international boundary with Mexico on August 19, 1773, when Fray Francisco Palou raised a cross to mark the line of jurisdiction between the two Californias.

The proto elopement in the area was that of Josefa Carrillo and Henry Delano Fitch. The couple left San Diego on the *Vulture*, in 1828, and were married at Valparaiso, Chile. Their action caused a tremendous sensation, resulting in a canonical trial at San Gabriel Mission. First vaccinations made in California were done by James Ohio Pattie, an American trapper and "sometimes surgeon extraordinary to His Excellency, the Governor of California." He made the exaggerated claim of innoculating 22,000 persons. Probably the first irrigation project in Alta California was undertaken and completed by the friars at San Diego Mission. It consisted of a stone dam 254 feet long, twelve feet thick and fourteen feet high and a dozen miles of stone and tile flume from the site of the dam to the mission lands. It was completed in 1781. The initial marriage witnessed on this "rim of Christendom" occurred at San Antonio Mission on May 16, 1773. The couple was Juan Maria Ruiz and Margarita de Cortona, an Indian neophyte.

First foreigner to settle permanently in California was John Gilroy (aka John Cameron) who landed at Monterey from the *Isaac Todd*, an English vessel in 1814. He was baptized as Juan Antonio Maria on September 29,

1814, by Fray Vicente de Sarria. He later married into the Ortega family and left a number of children.

The first roofing tiles made in California were manufactured at San Luis Obispo Mission about 1790. Once adopted at the Old Mission, their use spread rapidly to the other foundations along *El Camino Real*. First land grant, consisting of a parcel of land in the Carmel Valley, near San Carlos Borromeo Mission, was made by Fernando Rivera y Moncada to Manuel Butron on November 22, 1775.

The prominence of the Catholic Church in California can be traced to the very day when it all began for Christianity along the Pacific Slope. Here are some more of the "firsts" associated with the People of God in this choice portion of His vineyard.

The first permanent settlement in Alta California was begun when soldiers and sailors of the "holy expedition" of 1769, under the command of Vicente Vila, Fernando Rivera and Pedro Fages, on May 17, 1769, were moved from a temporary camp on San Diego Bay to what is now known as Old Town, at the foot of Presidio Hill. First earthquake recorded in California by Spaniards was experienced by Gaspár de Portolá on his initial journey from San Diego in search of Monterey. It occurred at a camp site on the present Santa Ana River, July 28, 1769, and he named the river, in consequence, Rio de Jesús de los Temblores (River of Jesus of the earthquake).

Apart from the speculations that there was a priest with the Cabrillo expedition, the first recorded Christian religious services consisted of Holy Mass conducted on November 12, 1602, on the San Diego Bay by Fathers Andrés de la Asumpcion, Antonio de la Ascension and Tomas de Aquino. These priests were Carmelites attached to the exploratory expedition of Sebastian Vizcaino.

The first martyr for the Catholic faith in California was Fray Luis Jayme, who was slain by natives at San Diego Mission on November 4, 1775, during the course of an attack and the burning of the foundation by non–Christianized Indians. First navigation of the Sacramento River was accomplished by an expedition headed by Fray Ramon Abella of San Francsico Mission and Buenaventura Fortuni of San Jose Mission. The explorers ascended the San Joaquin River, crossed through Two–mile Slough and descended the Sacramento, October 15 thru 30th, 1811.

First American to arrive in California was John Groehem (or Graham), the son of John and Catherine Groehem of Boston. He came with the Spanish exploring expedition of Alejandro Malaspina in the royal corvettes *Descubierta* and *Artevida*, arriving at Monterey on September 113, 1791. Groehem seems to have died on the day of his arrival and was buried at San Carlos Mission.

The initial contact between the white man and the notorious California flea was recorded by Fray Juan Crespi who was diarist for the Portola Expedition seeking the Port of Monterey. The fleas were encountered on October 17, 1769, at an Indian village near Half Moon Bay. A creek in the vicinity for many years bore the name *Las Pulgas* to commemorate the event. First murder mystery occurring in Alta California was that of Fray Andrés Quintana who died mysteriously at Santa Cruz on October 12, 1812. Thought originally to have died of natural causes, an investigation two years later revealed that the friar had been murdered by five Indians.

The first *pueblo* or city in California was organized and recognized as such by the Spaniards as San Jose de Guadalupe. It was founded November 29, 1777 by Lieutenant Jose Joaquin Moraga with five settlers who had come from Sonora with the expedition of Juan Bautista de Anza in 1776. On and on the list could go. Perhaps some enterprising person will one day compile a full–length book of Catholic "firsts" in California.

CALIFORNIA — THE GOLDEN STATE

No less a personage than Fray Junípero Serra once said that "in California is my life and there, God willing, I hope to die." Most of us can identify with those sentiments, even two hundred years after they were expressed.

Pocahontas is portrayed three times in the Capitol rotunda, California is shown only once, in a single panel of a frieze near the top of the dome depicting the Gold Rush. Yet California has been setting the trend for the nation for decades—in movies, in style, in business and, most recently, in politics. The state with the single star on its flag easily has the rest of the country outnumbered in just about everything that really matters.

By the 1990s, California had become indisputably *numero uno*. It is the trend–setting, politically dominating, racially diverse, cultural capital of the country, much to the dismay of outsiders.

Among its sister commonwealths, California ranks first in manufacturing, agriculture, foreign trade, entertainment, high tech, aerospace, biotechnology, enviro–technology, church attendance and political contributions.

The good and the bad co–exist in California. The state has more rich people and more unemployed workers, more terror bombings and more professional sports teams, more legal immigrants and more illegal ones, more colleges and universities, and more prisoners than any other state.

California leads the country, if not the world, in racial

and cultural diversity. By the year 2002, the non–Latino population will dip below 50% and the state will be inhabited entirely by minority groups. Even now, its public schools teach in more than forty languages, including Puniabo, Mixteco, Serbian, Lao, Hmong, Armenian, Farsi, Hindi, Portuguese, Tongan, Gujarati, Urdui, Khmu, Mien and Pashto.

And the rapid growth keeps moving ahead. Since World War II, California has been producing a bumper crop of freeways, water projects, research institutes, military bases and defense–related businesses. Its population is now over thirty–two million.

With fifty–four electoral votes, 20% of those needed to elect a President, California is the biggest prize in national elections. Only twice since 1916 has a President won an election without capturing California. California has sparked social movements that have spread nationwide. The rise of environmentalism, the tax revolt, term limits for elected officials, victims' rights and tougher prison sentences began in California.

Kevin Starr, the state librarian, says that every other state can see something of itself in California. Early settlers brought with them such place names as Manhattan Beach and Bosnia in Southern California; Yankee Hill, Chicago Park, Iowa Hill and Michigan Bluff in Gold Country; the Dixie Elementary School District and the town of Alamo in the Bay Area.

Even in the make believe world, California excels. There are more movies and television programs set in California and about Californians than any other state in the country.

"CALIFORNIA HOTEL"

The "California Hotel" was an historic adobe associated for many years with Santa Clara Mission. It was erected by the Indian neophytes under the supervision of the friars, about thirty years before John Marshall found the glittering treasure that maddened half the world. It was solidly built with standard adobe bricks, each earthen cube being two feet long, one foot wide and three inches thick. The thickness of the walls was between three and four feet.

When the adobe was erected, in 1818, Santa Clara Mission had already seen its halcyon days. A few years later came Mexican Independence which was followed by a period of political greed and avarice. Once the dwelling place of the mission *majordomo*, the adobe was seized by sheer physical force and converted into a wayside inn. In the late 1840s, the edifice was styled the "California Hotel."

It is likely that many of the pioneers of the golden era were lodged there—that the Gwins and Fremonts, the Sutters and Kearneys, the Larkins and Rileys and Danas made it a halting place in their journeys up and down *El Camino Real*. Father John Nobili, the founder and proto president of Santa Clara College, in order to avoid friction with the claimants of the hotel, paid their price for it in 1854. With acquisition of the adobe by the college, students were given an on–campus residence hall.

Like all the original mission buildings at Santa Clara, the "California Hotel" was only one story in height. Father Nobili added a second floor built of a peculiar light–colored, fire–baked brick substance. From that time onwards, the upper floor was used as a dormitory. while the ground level served as classrooms. The title "California Hotel" remained intact, at least among the students.

When, in 1871, Father Aloysius Varsi constructed the Exhibition Hall, the dormitory for the elder students was removed from the "California Hotel" to the first floor of the new building. The lower story of the adobe continued to be used for classes, while the upper floor was converted into apartments for the secular employees of the college.

In 1876, the building was given over to the college debating societies. In subsequent times, the first American Literary Congress was organized at Santa Clara and given the "California Hotel" as its headquarters. Time took its natural toll and early in 1906, the historic adobe was razed to make room for more modern structures. It was at that time that Charles D. South wrote a charming tribute in the San Jose *Mercury* about the historic "California Hotel:"

> The old adobe, with its roof of tile, its rude exterior, and its long, low-ceiled halls; with its ten thousand treasured memories and associations and a history extending far back into an age before the Gringo came—the old adobe has gone the way of all structures material.

> It served many a turn, it answered many a purpose; it furnished the educators of the country with an immeasurably valuable, original American idea; and, when its time came, it went down all of a sudden, and buried itself in its own congenial mold.

> Yet, even there—its dust commingled with its mother dust—the old adobe will be eloquent still; for, when the winds of winter blow, and moisture clouds the air, and the soil of the valley drinks its annual libation to prosperity—then will there be a re-awakening of the life that was imprisoned in the adobe's massive walls, and the scattered remains of the building will be robed in springtime verdure.

CALIFORNIA AND CATALONIA

California Catholicism owes a great debt of gratitude to its Spanish forebears from the ecclesiastical Province of Tarragona in the Principality of Catalonia for no other area in all the world has given so freely of its leaders than this 12,464 square mile gem of the Iberian Peninsula.

Three of Calforina's bishops were natives of Catalonia. Joseph Sadoc Alemany, O.P., first Archbishop of San Francisco was born at Vich on July 13, 1814. Retiring in 1884 from this thirty–four year episcopate, Archbishop Alemany returned to his native Spain where he died on April 14, 1888. Thaddeus Amat, C.M., longtime Bishop of Monterey–Los Angeles came from Barcelona. Born on December 31, 1811, he arrived in the United States in 1838 and for the next four decades devoted his energies to American Catholicism. Coming to California in 1854, Amat wore the mitre for a quarter century during which time his jurisdiction acquired all the characteristics of a modern diocesan unit.

Amat's successor, Bishop Francis Mora, was also a Catalan. He was born on November 24, 1827, in the small moutain village of Gurb, a few miles north of Vich. A serious carriage accident resulted in his resignation in 1896 and the latter years of his life were spent in the relatively obscure little town of Sarria near Barcelona. Distant relatives of both Alemany and Mora still live in Catalonia. Through the kindness of the archbishop's grand-nephew, who attended his funeral in 1888, this writer was taken to Vich for luncheon during 1962 in the very house where Alemany was born.

Grandchildren of Bishop Francis Mora's brother reside in Sarria. It was their cooperation that made it possible to return the bishop's remains to California.

Among the mementoes now in the Chancery Archives of the Archdiocese of Los Angeles are Alemany's mitre (the one used at his consecration in 1850!), Amat's episcopal ring and a precious copy of Archbishop Alemany's life written in 1925 by his grand-nephew, Antonia. Mora's silver napkin ring, taken with him to Spain in 1896, is also among the mementos. A valuable painting of Bishop Thaddeus Amat, executed at Barcelona in 1873, was presented to James Francis Cardinal McIntyre by the bishop's great grandniece, Mrs. Carmelita Burton of Santa Barbara. The painting, still in remarkable condition, now hangs in Saint John's Seminary at Camarillo.

There are other connections between California and Catalonia. The *Iglesia de San Miguel de Puerto* in Barcelona's waterfront area served as the model for Saint Vibiana's Cathedral in Los Angeles. Now in a state of poor repair, it was obviously an artistic church in an earlier era. Some sixty miles north of Vich in the City of Olot is the motherhouse of the Sisters of the Immaculate Heart of Mary. Brought to California in 1871 by Bishop Francis Mora, the sisters became one of the largest religious communities in the west.

Countless missionaries of the earlier periods of our heritage owed their origins to Catalonia. Even the diocesan era boasts such names as Anthony Ubach, Joachim Adam and Cyprian Rubio. Nor would it be out of place to mention that the tiny Island of Mallorca, birthplace of Junípero Serra, lies but twenty miles due south of Barcelona.

The door of history closed off Catalonia from California on August 3, 1905, when Francisco Mora y Borrell slept away quietly at Sarria. True enough that event marked the passing of an era. But it was a long and happy association, one of which both Spain and California are justly proud!

CALIFORNIA'S FIRST MARRIAGE CASE

Early in 1842, Casilda Sepulveda informed Fray Tomas Estenega that she had been "forced" by her father to marry Antonio Teodoro Trujillo. She wondered if she had grounds for an annulment.

When Estenega failed to take any immediate action, Casilda approached the civil authorities with the same question. Formal proceedings were initiated and Estenega was asked to submit his views. After assuming jurisdiction over the case, a judge cited the parties, examined witnesses and then handed down a sentence granting Casilda an annulment from Trujillo.

Upon hearing of the action, Bishop Francisco Garcia Diego y Moreno immediately filed a complaint with Santiago Arguello, charging that the judge had acted in violation of competent ecclesial authority. The Bishop of Both Californias pointed out that the Church alone had jurisdiction in the case and that he had neither deputized that tribunal nor any other to undertake even the preliminary investigation required in such a case.

He said that "although marriage is founded upon a contract arising from the natural law and confirmed by civil statute, Jesus Christ elevated it to the dignity of a sacrament and, at that moment, it took on a holiness over which the Church remains the sole guardian." Bishop Garcia Diego noted further that "judging the validity or nullity of a marriage, investigating the motives whereby one may opt for a permanent or temporary separation is absolutely reserved to the ecclesiastical domain."

The prelate concluded by invalidating the civil decree and suggesting that the case be re–introduced before the diocesan tribunal. Fray Tomas Estenega was instructed to formally look into Casilda's claims and to grant her a temporary separation if one seemed justified.

Fray Tomas gathered all the evidence, interrogated the witnesses and submitted his findings or *expediente* to the bishop. On August 20, 1842, Bishop Garcia Diego ruled in favor of matrimonial nullity. An addenda to the decree stipulated that "in the unforeseen circumstance that Casilda is not properly treated by her father and step–mother, try to have her housed in an honorable home, with provision that her food and subsistence be paid for by her father or the civil arm."

Fray Tomas Estenega was then instructed to publish and explain the decree to his parishioners at *Nuestra Señora de los Angeles*, stressing "the grave sin and danger of excommunication for all those who knowingly do violence to one another by forced marriages."

In his *History of California*, Theodore Hittell noted that "the novel character of the complaint and the prominence in social life of the parties rendered the case one of extraordinary interest to the Californians of those times." And beyond that, it was the first "marriage case" recorded in California's Catholic annals.

According to an article by Winifred Davidson in the Los Angeles *Times Sunday Magazine* for September 6, 1931, "Don Enrique Sepulveda, once more with a daughter on his hands, returned to Los Angeles; and thereafter, in spite of the benign bishop's parting injunctions, neither by look nor word could the relations between these two be considered even remotely actuated by loving kindness."

CALIFORNIA — ANOTHER DISTINCTION

The world of the 1490s was troubled, anxious and introverted. Long established ecclesial, academic and political institutions were pulling apart at the seams from scandals, betrayals and compromises.

For Christians especially, there were many symptoms of impending doom in those days of Pope Alexander VI. The Church was confronted with such manifestations as witchcraft, black magic, aberrational lifestyles and underground liturgies.

The *Nuremberg Chronicle*, in a folio dated July 12, 1492, even predicted the imminent end of the world by a combination of flood and fire. Many intelligent Christians took refuge in studying the classics, while others directed their attention to astrology, contestation and dissent.

That enormous flight from reality proved to be a blessing in disguise, for it triggered the Renaissance. Interest in past accomplishments brought on a fresh enthusiasm for art, architecture and poetry. Gradually, a whole new cultural influence came to be felt at all levels of society. At the same time, geographical findings in The New World re–enkindled hope and thereby dispersed much of the gloom and despair plaguing the very heart strings of humankind.

The Renaissance, coupled with the discovery of a new continent, changed the whole complexion of life.

The English produced fewer witches and gave the world a series of gifted writers, headed by Shakespeare; the French grew weary of sorcery and turned their energies to art, poetry and theatre; and the Spanish de–escalated their military commitments in favor of expanding the frontiers of European influence. Missionaries planted new foundations for Christianity, conquistadors expanded the influence of civil rulers and humanitarians shared the benefits of civilized life with less fortunate peoples.

There was a discernible parallel between the world of the 1490s and that of the 1990s in religion, politics and culture.

The very tenets of Christian belief were being questioned and disregarded; the governmental components of modern society were crumbling from dry rot, while the moral tone of contemporary life wallowed in the gutters of nudity, profanity and disdain for spiritual values.

Yet Christians, optimistic as they must always be, can see a promise of better things. They suspect that the accomplishments of the astronauts hold out even greater challenges than the explorers offered the world of the 1490s. Though its impact may be temporarily delayed, the movement into outer space is God's way of renewing His covenant with a troublesome people.

Christians also sense a Renaissance engendered by recent happenings. They recognize a new love for Scripture, a fresh concern for theology and a reborn appreciation for liturgy.

Saint Paul remarks that "in everything, God works for good within those who love Him." That's the underlying motive Christians have for placing these disturbed times in their historical perspective. That's why God's people have the courage to call for a strengthening of FAITH, a heightening of HOPE and a maturing of LOVE.

CALIFORNIA — TEN YEARS OF GROWTH

Catholicism in the State of California during the past decade shows one of the most phenomenal growth patterns of the Church in modern times and the following figures reflect, if only confusedly, the major results of this development.

Based on the latest national figures, there are 8,907,905 Catholics in the state's ecclesiastical jurisdictions. A cardinal, an archbishop and twenty-eight bishops direct the activities of 2,150 diocesan and 1,552 religious priests caring for 1,069 parishes, and 196 missions.

4,966 sisters and 489 brothers staff 113 diocesan and private high schools, 580 elementary schools and nine protective institutions. Enrollment is fixed at 70,833 in Catholic high schools and 180,083 in parochial grammar schools. Thirteen colleges and universities serve 41,197 students. There are five diocesan seminaries with 236 aspirants coupled with seventeen religious seminaries or scholasticates serving 178 seminarians.

Under the release–time program on the secondary level 84,850 public school students receive Catholic instruction each week while 435,430 youngsters participate in the program on the elementary level.

A large percentage of California's clergy teach in the Church's educational system: 205 are exclusively engaged in this work with another 88 brothers and 845 sisters devoting the major part of their time to the classroom; 13,596 lay teachers augment the program on a full–time basis.

Forty–nine general hospitals serve California's Catholic population. This past year 5,159,338 people were treated in Catholic hospitals. The Church operates nine orphanages with 849 resident children and last year supervised the placing of 1,488 youngsters in foster homes.

193,433 infant Baptisms were recorded in parochial registers, while 9,138 adult converts were received into the Faith. 31,429 couples were united in holy matrimony, and 39,210 were listed in the burial records.

Within the state, Catholicity has grown at a proportionately slower rate than it has in the nation at large. In the California Catholics make up 27% of the population as contrasted with 20.9% a decade ago.

CALIFORNIA — FIRST RECORDED MASS

In the closing months of 1931, a bronze plaque attached to a three ton boulder near the present site of the Fort Guijarros Monument was solemnly dedicated by the Very Reverend John Hegarty who represented Bishop John J. Cantwell. On the plaque were these words: "This boulder erected November 1, 1931 by Court San Diego De Alcalá, No. 1099 of the Catholic Daughters of America, to commemorate the first Holy Mass celebrated in California, November 11, 1602 upon the arrival on this site of Sebastian Vizcaino who named the port San Diego in honor of the feast of Sénor San Diego de Alcalá and who was accompanied by three Carmelite friars Fray Andrés de la Asumpción, Fray Antonio de la Ascención and Fray Tomás de Aquino."

The story of the three priests with the Vizcaino expedition can be traced to November 24, 1601, when the Viceroy of New Spain asked Carmelite officials to appoint chaplains for the contemplated voyage up the California coast. They were to have two major tasks— administering the sacraments to those aboard the expeditionary ships and instructing and converting "all heathen Indians" in the area.

The trinity of ships left Acapulco on May 5, 1602. The voyage up the coast of peninsular California proved to be extremely treacherous. After a journey of more than six months, the ships finally arrived off the Southern California coast.

On November 10, Vizcaino had his ships anchor in a bay off what later became known as Ballast Point. Two days later, on the Feast of San Diego de Alcalá, Vizcaino, his officers and chaplains went ashore.

According to the captain's diary, once on shore "a hut was built and Mass was said in celebration of the feast of San Diego." Since there were three priests, one can presume that it was a Solemn High Mass. Con–celebration was not then allowed, so it is unclear which of the friars was the actual celebrant of the Mass on that historic day in California's history.

It was another three hundred years before there was any commemoration of that important event. It came about in July of 1911 in conjunction with the groundbreaking of the Panama–California Exposition buildings. The military sponsored a Mass on the shores of San Diego Bay at the exact location of the 1602 celebration. Bishop Thomas J. Conaty came to represent the Diocese of Los Angeles–San Diego.

It wasn't until 1932 that plans were finalized for dedicating a plaque to commemorate the first Mass in California. Speaker for that event was Father Martin Cody Keating who paid tribute to the adventurous Spaniards who carried the cross of Christianity and the banner of their king to what was then the rim of Christendom.

Unfortunately, because of military restrictions, the area in which the marker was placed proved to be almost totally inaccessible to the general public. In 1963, the United States Navy moved the plaque to its present location in front of the submarine base chapel.

CALIFORNIA — LAND OF PROMISE

California has experienced everything in recent years–riots, floods, droughts, fires, earthquakes and, now, killer bees. Yet, the Golden State is still the garden spot of old planet earth. One often recalls and affirms what Fray Junípero Serra said: "In California is my life and there, God willing, I hope to die."

California is truly a state of superlatives. Twelve percent of the nation's residents live in California, an area that boasts of 64,500 millionaires, 57% of them women! Well over 56% of the state's population own their own homes, and 90% have at least one car.

Despite the rape, mayhem, robbery and murder, California is still *El Dorado* to refugees from boredom, poverty, stagnation and despotism. A favored statistic, quoted for the benefit of easterners, is that Blue Canyon, California, is the snowiest town in the country with a mean average of 243.2 inches.

However decadent it may appear to outsiders—weakened by unemployment and inflation, demoralized by crime, deluded by cultists, corrupted by pornographers, debased by junk bond dealers, decimated by psychopaths and pillaged by rioters—California remains a never–never land of riches, fame and freedom to millions around the world. Despite pockets of poverty, Californians are fabulously wealthy in other ways.

In a booster pamphlet issued in 1886 by the Illinois Association, one reads that "in this grand country, we have the tallest mountains, the biggest trees, the crookedest railroads, the dryest rivers, the loveliest flowers, the smoothest ocean, the finest fruits, the mildest lives, the softest breezes, the brightest skies and the most genial sunshine to be found anywhere else in North America." The pamphlet goes on to say that "we welcome those sojourning in a 'City of Angels' where their hearts will be irrigated by living waters from the perennial fountains of health, happiness and longevity."

Angelenos are used to being misunderstood. The November 22, 1943 issue of *Life* carried a feature story about California's southland which stated that "Los Angeles is the damnedest place in all the world," a comment typical of eastern cynics.

Realistically, Los Angeles is the most interesting metropolis in all the world. In altitude, it ranges from 5,049 feet in Tujunga (which is higher than all but a few mountains east of the Mississippi) to below sea level at Terminal Island. Los Angeles is divided by both a river and a mountain range. It is the only major city in the country large enough to have forest fires within its limits! It boasts of snow–clad mountains and sunshine beaches at the same time, with a 40 degree difference in temperature in a single day. Los Angeles completely surrounds full–fledged municipalities and unincorporated county areas.

There has always been a strange loyalty to the rhythmic flow of life in Southern California. Perhaps that was best expressed by a youngster who, when asked where she came from, answered, "I was born in Los Angeles at the age of six."

CALIFORNIA — A FOUR YEAR INTERREGNUM

Some years before he died, California's first Bishop, Francisco Garcia Diego y Moreno, warned the Mexican Government that failure to meet its financial obligations to the Church would certainly militate against the imme-

diate appointment of his successor. The prophecy was peculiarly accurate. When the bishop's death came on April 30, 1846, his secretary, Fray Gonzalez Rubio became the custodian of the orphaned diocese and functioned in that capacity for the next four years. The gentle friar fought bravely against the most trying odds, but was not able to offset the decline inherited from mission days. Contemporary accounts of those years reveal, "This state is Catholic at heart . . . there are Catholics scattered in every town and village, up every mountain and valley" but "many have grown careless and indifferent . . . such is the field of our missionaries, a people whose conversion would be a great triumph to the Church, as well as an inestimable blessing to the recipient of the graces and consolations following their conversion. Archbishop Francis Norbert Blanchet of Oregon City noted in one of his letters to Rubio that his soul was filled with grief for the utter desolation in the diocese and the descriptions of the evils, anxieties and perils oppressing Rubio's soul. The sad state of ecclesiastical affairs was also known in the Premier See of Baltimore where letters came to Archbishop Samuel Eccleston representing the condition of affairs written by intelligent Americans, Catholic and Protestant. News of California's plight reached New York too, and, late in 1848, Archbishop John Hughes contacted Don Jose De la Guerra of Santa Barbara and asked the prominent Catholic layman to submit a report on the status of Catholicity in the area.

De la Guerra informed the archbishop that there were about twenty–five or thirty thousand Catholics in the state before the discovery of gold. He estimated the number of Christian Indians at between ten and fifteen thousand. To serve that vast number of souls, there were only four secular, four extern and eight religious priests. The closing pages of the De la Guerra report echoed a plea for a Spanish prelate to guide the Church in California: "I judge that to be fitting, because the Catholics of this country are almost all Spanish–American, with whom the Spaniards are in sympathy."

Relief did not come immediately and the deplorable status of the Church during the period can be read into Gonzalez Rubio's appeal to Europe in 1849, "From that day on which Divine Providence in its inscrutable decrees disposed that we should bear the heavy and delicate burden of the administration of this diocese, we have ever kept before our eyes the chief and most important duty of providing evangelical laborers." Everywhere there was the need for priests—but nowhere could they be found.

It must have been a happy May 13, 1850, when Archbishop J. D. Bonamie's letter came with its news that a Bishop for the Diocese of California had been chosen. The subsequent arrival of Joseph Sadoc Alemany was a great satisfaction to the state's Catholic population. The Spanish–born Dominican prelate was joyfully greeted and the populace expressed its feelings on the occasion. John A. McGlynn welcomed Alemany with these words:

> We dwell with pleasure on the contemplation, that for you and your fellow laborers, it may be in the Providence of God reserved, to complete the good work so zealously commenced by diffusing, not only among the aboriginal inhabitants, but the unconverted also, who have come hither of late years from the various nations of the world, a knowledge of that Faith by which alone their temporal and eternal happiness can be truly rescued.

CALIFORNIA — DIVIDING THE STATE

Because of the question of diverting the waters of the delta of the Sacramento and San Joaquin Rivers to the arid areas of Southern California one hears talk (mostly from the north) about dividing California into two sovereign commonwealths. Such proposals are not new.

During the Spanish and Mexican eras, California was envisioned as extending from the Pacific Ocean to the Colorado River, thus including present–day Nevada and part of Utah. When the Constitution of 1849 was drafted, the state's official boundaries coincided with what is presently considered California. There were valid reasons for such a determination.

First of all, the framers wanted to exclude the Mormons and their inferred practice of polygamy in the state. Secondly, Nevada was looked upon as a worthless area which would be unproductive and hard to manage.

Interestingly enough, many of the framers personally wanted a separate state in the southern section of California. Though that movement had some powerful adherents, it never mustered sufficient support to pass.

Two years after California was admitted to the Federal Union, new demands were raised in the legislature for dividing the state. This time the rationale was that the north was inhabited by peoples from divergent backgrounds who engaged in multiple occupations, while the southern population, considerably smaller in numbers, was primarily agricultural and Hispanic.

The 1852 proposal was revised seven years later when Andres Pico introduced a bill envisioning a state comprised of San Diego, Imperial, Riverside, San Bernardino, Orange, Los Angeles, Ventura, Santa Barbara, San Luis Obispo and parts of Kern and Inyo, together with the Territory of Colorado.

The Pico bill passed both houses and was signed by Governor Milton Latham. It allowed resident voters of those areas to be detached if they could win a two–thirds vote, which they did. The Civil War thwarted congressional approval, mostly because of the touchy issue of "slave versus free" status.

Governor James G. Downey later brought up the matter again, claiming that the Pico bill was still effective inasmuch as Congress had never voted on it. Downey wanted the southern counties of Arizona added to the package.

In 1907, the movement for division came alive again, this time because the State Board of Equalization increased the assessed valuation in the southland at a higher rate than in the north. Various groups, including the Native Daughters of the Golden West, opposed division.

Over the years, other proposals have been made including one in 1941 (and again in 1976) to combine the counties of Lassen, Siskiyou, Trinity and Del Norte with Curry and Josephine (in Oregon) to form the State of Jefferson. Most recently, the sixteenth effort to divide California was introduced, in 1965, and would have brought the counties of Ventura, Los Angeles, Orange, San Bernardino, Riverside, Imperial and San Diego into the State of Southern California.

Because California is so large, so greatly diversified and so heavily populated, the matter of dividing the state will probably continue to be discussed. Possibly, at some future date, the proposal will carry.

CALIFORNIA CATHOLICISM

It is usually more fun and always more rewarding to recommend books in a given field. Occasionally, however, one needs to "warn" potential readers about a volume that is really off the wall. Unhappily, *California Catholicism* by Kay Alexander is one such tome.

This book is the first in a projected series of nine volumes on "The Religious Contours of California," a project sponsored jointly by the Center for the Study of Religion, University of California, Santa Barbara and the California Historical Society. Compiled by a specialist in the histories of "Christian Origins and Religions in America," this study begins with an introduction to the Catholic faith as brought to Alta California in 1769.

Both informative and misinformative, this study endeavors to cover too much territory in only ninety–seven pages of text. And, to make matters worse, the author devotes over a third of those pages to a fanciful interpretation of Vatican Council II and what it did and didn't do for the Church. Especially aggravating is Chapter 5 on "The Mythic Boundaries" which ranges from folk–Catholicism in Mexico to Liberation Theology in Latin America, neither of which she seems to understand.

The text suffers from an exorbitant number of factual inaccuracies. Examples would be—San Carlos Borromeo Mission was *not* named to honor Charles III, Saint Joseph is *not* the patron saint of California and San Gabriel was *not* established "in the vicinity of Los Angeles" which it predated by eleven years. While perhaps unimportant in themselves, the enormous quantity of such errors tends to compromise what is good about this treatise.

Though the author has included a long and impressive "bibliographical essay," she appears to have used her sources poorly, with little or no attention to their objective accuracy or the competency of the writer. Among the many examples would be her repetition and presumed endorsement of the totally unfounded remarks by Mike Davis that Cardinal McIntyre "sent undercover priests and monsignors with hidden tape recorders into the homes of underground Catholics. Scores of dissident priests and nuns were removed and some exiled to McIntyre's favorite Siberia—Orange County." That scenario never occurred. Those on the curial staff in those days can testify that such happenings are little more than someone's idle imagination. To see such foolishness like this repeated in what is purported to be a serious attempt to understand the "spiritual tradition in California" is disconcerting.

There were other occurrences reported inaccurately or incompletely, like the 1969 Christmas Eve fracas at Saint Basil's in the mid–Wilshire district of Los Angeles. The author failed to report, if she knew, that the protesters were arrested because they broke into the already–filled church and attempted to disrupt the services. She could easily have checked this by looking at the police blotter for that event.

There is really little to recommend in this book because bad history is worse than no history. If this book were a hotel, it would barely rate a single star. Hopefully, the rest of the volumes in this series, edited by Phillip E. Hammond and Ninian Smart, will be in better focus.

CALIFORNIA'S BICENTENNIAL

To Californians, 1969 was a most historically significant year, marking as it did the bi–centennial anniversary of Hispanic penetration into an area previously known only from crudely drawn nautical charts and maps. Official recognition of this important milestone was manifested in many concrete ways. The United States Post Office, for example, issued a special stamp to commemorate the occasion, in July. The highest representatives of the Spanish government journeyed to the Pacific Slope for public observances. Books and learned articles were published, symposia conducted and pilgrimages organized—all to honor an unparalleled feat in New World expansion.

Relevant history must be defined in terms of men, their origin, life and destiny. In this regard, one man, above all others, epitomizes the spirit which motivated California's colonizers to their noble accomplishments. He was, of course, Junípero Serra, the gray–robed friar to whom, according to Hiram Johnson, "California owes an everlasting tribute." From the silver strand of San Diego to the Golden Gate on San Francisco Bay, this "torch bearer of civilization" inaugurated a movement whereby the natives of the forest and plains were able to turn their faces toward the celestial light of Christianity and immortality.

The heroism associated with *El Camino Real* were unknown quantities to Junípero Serra who forged the initial links of that tortuous highway through unknown terrain where tragedy and despair plagued every forward step. As to the permanency of Serra's contributions and those of his pioneering collaborators, the distinguished non–Catholic historian, Robert Glass Cleland, had this to say:

Consider the Missions of California. How shall we view them. As interesting examples of architectural adaptation. As monuments to the members of an adventurous, heroic Order. As outposts of Christianity and civilization upon a barbarous frontier. They are all of these, surely, and something more. Break off a piece from one of their century–old adobe walls. Crumble it to dust between your thoughtless fingers. Then place this dust in the open palm of your hand and hold it so that the wind from the sea will blow it away forever. Only from the dust of a crumbling adobe brick from a crumbling Mission wall, you say with an idle shrug. Yes, but a trifle more. The dust you held so carelessly in your open hand was the dust of an empire, if you had only understood the glory of an ancient, heroic race. And the wind which blew it so utterly away. Ah, that was the wind which men call time.

The esteem for Junípero Serra's name, now a household word in California, has grown progressively since his demise. The tide of mental enlightenment and spiritual uplift that followed in his wake has nowhere been more aptly stated than in an address delivered, a lifetime ago, by Dr. Warren D. More, pastor of Santa Barbara's First Presbyterian Church:

Other states may point to a great event or a great name, or even to a succession of great names and events, but the name of Fr. Junípero Serra brings before us an epoch, stirring and eventful, a civilization unique, different, a bit of the oldest world mingling fascinatingly with the newest world, a faith, self–sacrificing, heroic, unconquerable before difficulties, yet ultimately yielding to the inevitable changing order of things, a man with the faith and zeal of the saints, with the courage and fortitude of the soldier, with the vision and dreams of the prophet, with the sacrifice and gladness of the martyr, and yet all—epoch, civilization, faith, man, losing themselves as in the dissolving picture, and in their stead there appears the radiant, glorious, enduring name—California.

CALIFORNIA'S CENTENNIAL

For a brief moment, on September 18, 1949, the Los Angeles Memorial Coliseum became an "open air cathedral" as Catholics in the Archdiocese of Los Angeles gathered to celebrate the centenary of California's statehood under the title "*El Camino Real de la Cruz.*" The devotional drama about the California missions unfolded on a Sunday evening in the presence of over 35,000 people in response to an invitation from Archbishop J. Francis A. McIntyre.

Presented on three giant stages on the Coliseum green, the event consisted of an historic prologue depicting the founding of the City of *Nuestra Señora de los Angeles*, a living tableaux of the Stations of the Cross and Benediction of the Blessed Sacrament. The story of California's Catholic background and the heroic saga of the Franciscan friars were intertwined with events in the Passion of Christ written for the occasion by Father Michael Sheahan, pastor of Santa Isabel parish in downtown Los Angeles.

Nearly a dozen stars of screen and radio took part in the narration and in leading the prayers of the Stations of the Cross. They included J. F. Regis Toomey, George Murphy, Stephen McNally, Gene Lockhart, Pedro de Cordoba, MacDonald Carey, J. Carrol Naish and Rod O'Connor. Choreographer Hermes Pan directed the overall pageant. Setting the early California mood was the band of Our Lady of Talpa parish, a 100 strong group of boys who played a serenade beginning at 7:20 P.M., forty minutes before the pageant began. Choral music for the evening was provided by the Roger Wagner Chorale.

Prior to the prologue, which began at precisely 8:00 p.m., the archbishop and a long procession of priests, religious and ministers entered the coliseum in procession.

During the prologue, on the first stage, the audience saw friars and Indians together with Mexican settlers, on the trek from San Gabriel where they raised the cross on the site of the present church of *Nuestra Señora de los Angeles*. This they did as part of a ceremony of thanksgiving for having been brought safely from their homes in what is now Mexico.

Each of the stations was portrayed in living tableaux

on the second stage in the center of the Coliseum. At the close of the *via crucis*, Benediction of the Blessed Sacrament turned the arena into a huge church. All lights in the stadium were turned out and thousands of candles were held by participants.

The monstrance used for Benediction was the same one used in mission days by Fray Junípero Serra at San Carlos Borromeo del Carmelo. It was brought to Los Angeles for the event by Harry Downie. Donated long ago by Antonio Bucareli, Viceroy of New Spain, the monstrance was and is among the great historic treasures of California. Following Benediction, the event was brought to a close with the singing of the Star Spangled Banner and the hymn, Holy God, We Praise Thy Name.

Members of the Catholic Youth Federation ushered the event. A small booklet was issued containing the prayers used for the celebration. Each person was also provided with a candle.

The whole event was patterned after one which Saint Leonard of Port Maurice performed in the Coliseum at Rome on December 27, 1750, to mark the jubilee inaugurated that year by the Holy Father. A local newspaper account described the event in great detail, concluding with the observation "What an example these early missionaries have left for us. Truly they were prophets in their own right."

CANDIDUS — SHRINE

According to Alban Butler, Candidus was a member of the Theban Legion, a group of Christian soldiers recruited by Maximian Herculius in Upper Egypt for the purpose of putting down a recalcitrant tribe of the Gauls called Bagaudae. When Maximian ordered all his soldiers to join in offering sacrifice to the pagan gods for the success of their expedition, the members of the Theban Legion refused to take part in the rites.

Candidus, known as the *senator militum*, was among the leaders of the Theban Legion who led the opposition to Maximian, noting that "we are your soldiers, but we are also servants of the true God. We cannot renounce Him who is our Creator and Master, and also yours even though you reject Him."

Maximian, seeing no hope of overcoming their constancy, ordered that the entire legion be put to death. This all occurred near Agaunum (c. 287 A.D.) and September 22nd is the day that Candidus and his companions are commemorated in the Roman Martyrology.

Saint Eucherius, the Bishop of Lyons during the first half of the 5th century, is the source for the story about Candidus. Though certain aspects of the account are ambiguous, it seems clear that the martyrdom is an historical fact. For many centuries, the principal relics of

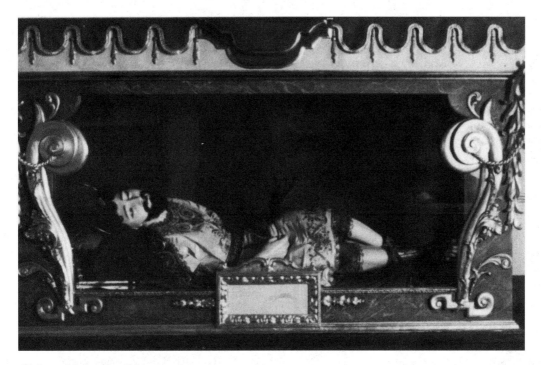

Shrine of Saint Candidus

Candidus and his companions of the Theban Legion were preserved in a 6th century reliquary at the Abbey founded by Saint Theodore of Octodurum.

Prior to the 3rd century, Candidus was a name without Christian significance and one probably derived from pagan ancestors. That Candidus was fairly well–known by the 9th century is attested to by at least two prominent clerics who took his name, Candidus of Fulda (d. 845) and Candidus, the Anglo–Saxon disciple and confidant of Alcuin.

Very little is known about the peregrination of the relics of Saint Candidus which were enshrined in the Serra Chapel at San Fernando Mission in the latter weeks of 1992. The presumption is that shortly after they were encased within a waxen portrayal of the Saint, the relics were brought from Rome by Bishop Thaddeus Amat, probably in January of 1868.

In any event, upon his return from the Eternal City, Bishop Amat entrusted the relics to the care of the Lazarist Fathers who then conducted Saint Vincent's College in Los Angeles. It was probably at that time that the bishop removed a portion of a bone from the reliquary. Since the 1860s, over 90% of the altar stones used in Southern California contain relics of Saint Candidus.

Shortly after the new church of Saint Vincent de Paul was dedicated by Bishop Francis Mora, on February 20, 1887, the relics were moved from the college chapel to the new edifice at the northeast corner of Grand Avenue and Washington Boulevard.

In 1892, new altars were installed in the church and the relics of Saint Candidus were placed beneath the shrine of the Sacred Heart, at the far end of the Gospel side of the Sanctuary. The relics remained in place for the next thirty–eight years, until 1925, when the present Saint Vincent's Church was opened at West Adams Boulevard and Figueroa Street.

Father Terence O'Donnell, C.M. a former pastor of Saint Vincent's Parish, explained that when the relics were moved from the old to the new Saint Vincent's Church in 1925, the documentation (along with one of the parochial Baptismal registers) were stored in a wastepaper basket. An overly zealous custodian threw the basket and its contents into the trash.

For some unknown reason, there were no provisions made in the Spanish Renaissance Church for Saint Candidus, although portions of his relics were placed in the altars of the Miraculous Medal and Saint Joseph for their consecration in 1930. The wooden sarcophagus was placed atop the vesting cabinets of the easternmost sacristy and there they remained until the mid 1980s when they were consigned to a storage area in the church's cavernous basement.

In September of 1991, the massive sarcophagus and its contents were moved to San Fernando Mission. The waxen figure of Candidus was sent to the South Coast Fine Arts Preservation Center for cleaning and the wooden case to Carmel where it became the model of a wholly new altar–shrine built by Richard Merin.

CANOVA MEDAL

On June 17, 1985, the *Monumenti Musei e Gallerie Pontificie* notified Timothy Cardinal Manning that he had been awarded the prized Canova Medal in recognition of his exceptional services on behalf of the Vatican Museums. On one side of the large medal is the portrait of Antonio Canova (1757–1822.), sculptor, and director of the Vatican Museums from 1802 until his death two decades later.

Born at Possagno, in the Venice region of present–day Italy, Canova lived in Rome during most of his life, a city that still bears his unmistakable artistic imprint. He returned to Venice only to die. His contemporaries considered Canova a second Phidias, that is, an artist who evoked in his sculpture the perfection and beauty of ancient art which he had studied, loved and admired.

Canova's works were extremely well received during his lifetime and were coveted by collectors both in Italy and abroad. Presently, three of his works are exhibited at the Metropolitan Museum. Canova was the creator of three papal monuments, numerous works portraying outstanding personalities of his day, both sacred and profane. A deeply religious man, he was very faithful to the papacy which earned him many honors and commissions.

From 1802 onwards, he was Superintendent of Fine Arts for the Vatican. He was President of the Rome Archeological Academy, "lifetime Prince" of the San Luca Academy where the finest artists of the day met. In 1815, Pope Pius VII put Canova in charge of retrieving the works of art purloined from the Papal States by Napoleon in 1797. He diligently accomplished that arduous task even to the satisfaction of France.

On his return to the Eternal City, Canova was made Marquiz of Ischia by the Pope, a position which provided him with a sizable yearly income. Those funds he gave to the young artists and to the academies over which he presided. During a period in which restoration of ancient sculpture meant complete reintegration, he understood with an avantgarde sensitivity the intangible beauty of the Parthenon marbles. He supported the view that they should be left unrestored.

Thus Canova was not only a great artist, but a symbol of moral integrity, love towards his fellows, loyalty to the Holy See, generosity and sensitivity. It was surely appropriate that the image of the artist, so closely associated with the history of the Church's museum, was chosen for the front of the medal bestowed on Cardinal Manning.

The original medal was cast in 1816. It has been faithfully reproduced from a design by a pupil of Canova, Salvatore Passamonti, a sculptor highly esteemed in Rome. The reproduction of the Apollo Belvedere which appeared on the back of the original medal has been deleted in favor of the following inscription:

H. E. Timothy Cardinal Manning
GRATI ANIMI SIGNUM
PRO LIBERALITATE TUA
MUSEIS VATICANIS COLLATA
MCMLXXXV

CAPITAL PUNISHMENT ALONG THE PACIFIC SLOPE

That "the morality of the Californians was somewhat closely looked after by authorities" in provincial times, is evident in the case of José Antonio Rosas, the first recorded victim of the death penalty along the Pacific Slope. Born at Los Angeles, the youthful Rosas was one of the fifty–nine soldiers attached to the Santa Barbara Presidio. In June, 1800, while looking after the animals at La Mesa, the eighteen year old soldier was observed by two Indian girls committing a *crimen nefando* which was considered, in those times, the most grievous of all violations of chastity.

By order of Captain Felipe de Goycoechia, criminal proceedings were immediately initiated. Indicted by a military court, the accused culprit confessed that he had been overcome by *El Demonio*. The brief trial ended in a guilty verdict. Acting on the recommendation of the prosecuting attorney, *Alfrérez* Pablo Cota, the soldier was condemned to death. The court proceedings were then referred to Governor José Arrillaga who sent them to vice–regal officials at Mexico City for a final review.

Fray Estevan Tápis, the future *Presidente* of the California missions, made a fervent plea for clemency to authorities. A similar appeal was voiced, for less lofty reasons, by Felipe de Goycoechia, who stated that a prevailing illness among the presidial force at Santa Barbara would make it extremely difficult to spare Rosas. Despite the two interventions and the eloquent plea by Rosas' attorney, José Maria Ortega, the sentence was confirmed, in September, and directives were issued to the governor that the convicted soldier be hanged and his earthly remains burned, together with those of the mule *"en quien cometieó tan horible delito. "*

There being no hangman in California at the time, Rosas was shot, on February 1801. The rest of the sentence was then carried out on a burning heap of wood. It was recorded, on the certificate of execution, that "the charred remains of the victim, fitted by the purification of flame for rest in consecrated ground," were buried in the *presidio* cemetery.

If José Antonio Rosas cannot be remembered for his virtue, then surely his name has a legitimate claim to prominence in the long story of capital punishment in California.

CARDINAL MANNING HOUSE OF PRAYER

When ground was broken for the new Cardinal Manning House of Prayer, the memory of Earle C. Anthony cast a long and memorable shadow over the proceedings.

The property on which the new facility is located, more recently known as the Villa San Giuseppe, was developed by one of California's most innovative and fascinating characters. Earle C. Anthony was a radio executive (KFI), a composer ("What Hawaii Means to Me"), a bridge–builder (San Francisco Bay Bridge) and a television pioneer—all in one lifetime!

But above all those accomplishments, Earle C. Anthony is credited, as early as 1927, with making Los Angeles "a completely motorized civilization." Anthony sold Packard automobiles to Los Angeles as a total way–of–life.

Kevin Starr tells how he did it: When a person purchased a Packard from Anthony, he bought into a club as well as a franchised service system. Anthony established a chain of gasoline stations, which he lighted with neon lights (a concept he imported from Europe), so that his clients might gas up or have their Packards serviced in uniformly identifiable surroundings.

"Like Helena Rubenstein or Ralph Lauren in the years to come, Anthony understood that in conditions of emergent taste, a brand, a label, a neighborhood, a specific make of car anchored identity. Nowhere was this anchoring more necessary than in Los Angeles of the 1920s and nothing could do it more dramatically than an automobile, especially a shiny new black Packard."

Anyway, in 1923, Anthony acquired eight and a half acres in the Los Feliz area overlooking Los Angeles, Hollywood, Burbank and Glendale. There he decided to build his dream home. Earle dreamed big. He and his wife traveled throughout Europe gathering thousands of photographs of castles and other historic buildings. He entrusted the plan for the building to renowned architect, Bernard Maybeck, who had earlier designed such landmarks as San Francisco's Court of Honor.

Maybeck, a proponent of mixing styles, eventually settled on a medieval, Gothic–styled mansion unlike any other ever erected in the west. Stone was imported from France, tile from Spain and wood from Italy. The completed specifications called for a classical Mediterranean estate, patterned after the early Renaissance.

Beginning in 1927, the building of the mansion stretched over three years. When completed, it covered over 23,000 square feet and became the largest house under one roof on the west coast, with twenty–eight rooms and sixteen bathrooms.

The Earle C. Anthony estate was purchased in the 1950s by Sir Daniel and Countess Bernardine Donohue. It was then christened Villa San Guiseppe in honor of Saint Joseph. The Donohues landscaped the gardens and added European art treasures throughout the mansion. The property was deeded to the Sisters of the Immaculate Heart of Mary in 1971 and has since become the community's motherhouse. Donohue Manor, now used as a convent, was added in 1983.

Earle C. Anthony's wife died within the embrace of the Catholic Church. Surely she and her husband would rejoice at seeing how their estate at 3431 Waverly Drive is being used seventy-seven years after its birth in the Los Feliz Hills.

CARDINALATIAL HAT

The *galerum rubrum* has been in California's ecclesiastical nomenclature only since January 15, 1953, when Pope Pius XII formally bestowed the "red hat" upon the Archbishop of Los Angeles, as the first and most distinctive feature of the princely role entrusted to the Most Reverend J. Francis A. McIntyre.

Next to the Roman Pontiff, there is no dignity in the Catholic Church higher than that of the cardinalate. Since the early 11th century, the College of Cardinals has functioned as the Pope's principal advisory agency in the administration of Church affairs. This vital role was emphasized by Pope Eugene IV who stated that just "as the door of a house turns on its hinges, so on the cardinalate does the Apostolic See, the door of the whole Church, rest and find support."

As a recompense for their numerous responsible duties, both tradition and canon law have long accorded cardinals privileges more ample and extensive than those enjoyed by any other ecclesiastics. One of the oldest, and surely the most singular adornments of the cardinalatial office is the *galerum rubrum* which has been a special insignia of the electors and candidates of the papacy since its initial bestowal by Pope Innocent IV, in 1245. In earlier centuries, the *galerum rubrum* served a functional use as a form of head–wear. The cardinals rode on horseback directly behind the Pope in processions, their red or scarlet hats held in place by golden cords tied under the chins.

Use of the colorful appendage was discontinued after the loss of the Papal States, in the 1870s. As a sign of "mourning," cardinals were directed to express their displeasure about the lack of civil autonomy given to the Church by refusing to wear the *galerum rubrum*.

Directives stated that after its acceptance, the *galerum rubrum* was to be stored in a safe place in the cardinal's permanent residence. At his death it was to be placed at the foot of the catafalque, after which it was to be suspended from the ceiling of his cathedral as evidence of the spiritual authority once exercised by a prince of the Church. There it hangs until crumbling to dust! The design of the unique hat, reproduced in each cardinal's personal coat–of–arms, is as simple as it is singular. Its crown is small and shallow; the brim flat, rigid and very broad. Attached to the crown are two crimson–colored cords, each of which terminates with fifteen tassels arranged triangle–wise.

Prior to 1953, the *galerum rubrum* had been conferred on only eleven American bishops. The prayer used for its bestowal recalls both the princedom and martyrdom symbolized in its bright cardinal–red or scarlet color.

> In praise of Almighty God and as an ornament of the Holy See, receive the Red Hat, the particular sign of the dignity of the Cardinalate, by which is signified that you must show yourself to be steadfast even to death and the shedding of your blood for the exaltation of the Holy Faith, for peace and tranquility among all Christian people, and for the welfare of the Holy Roman Church, in the name of the Father, and of the Son and of the Holy Spirit.

CARMEL MEMORY

Robert Louis Stevenson visited Carmel in 1879. Roaming over the wooded hills and along the shores of bay and ocean, he absorbed and then verbalized the natural beauties of the Monterey Peninsula. Stevenson's description of the area, first published in *The Old Pacific Capitol*, remains today a masterpiece of American literature. Here is how he portrayed the scene at San Carlos Borromeo del Rio Carmelo:

> In comparison between what was and what is in California, the praisers of times past will fix upon the Indians of Carmel. The valley drained by the river so named is a true Californian valley, bare, dotted with chaparral, overlooked by quaint, unfinished hills.
>
> The Carmel runs by many pleasant farms, a clear and shallow river, loved by wading kine; and, at last, as it is falling towards a quicksand and the great Pacific, passes a ruined mission on a hill.
>
> From the mission church the eye embraces a great field of ocean, and the ear is filled with a continuous sound of distant breakers on the shore. But the day of the [Franciscan] has gone by, the day of the Yankee has succeeded, and there is no one left to care for the converted savage.
>
> The church is roofless and ruinous, sea breezes and sea–fogs, and the alternation of the rain and sunshine, daily widening the breaches and casting the crockets from the wall.
>
> As an antiquity in this new land, a quaint specimen of missionary architecture, and a memorial of good deeds, it had a triple claim to preservation from all thinking people; but neglect and abuse have been its portion.

> There is no sign of American interference, save where a headboard has been torn from a grave to be a mark for pistol bullets. So it is with the Indians for whom it was erected.
>
> Their lands, I was told, are being yearly encroached upon by neighboring American proprietors, and with that exception no man troubles his head for the Indians of Carmel.
>
> Only one day in the year, the day before our Guy Fawkes, the *padre* drives over the hill from Monterey; the little sacristy, which is the only covered portion of the church, is filled with seats and decorated for the service.
>
> The Indians troop together, their bright dresses contrasting with their dark and melancholy faces; and there, among a crowd of somewhat unsympathetic holiday–makers, you may hear God served with perhaps more touching circumstances than in any other temple under heaven.
>
> An Indian, stoneblind and about eighty years of age, conducts the singing; other Indians compose the choir; yet they have the Gregorian music at their finger ends, and pronounce the Latin so correctly that I could follow the meaning as they sang.
>
> It was to them not only the worship of God, nor an act by which they recalled and commemorated better days, but was besides an exercise of culture, where all they knew of art and letters was united and expressed.
>
> And it made a man's heart sorry for the good fathers of yore who had taught them to dig and to reap, to read and to sing, who had given them European Mass–books which they still preserve and study in their cottages, and who had now passed away from all authority and influence in that land—to be succeeded by greedy land thieves and sacrilegious pistol–shots."

CASA ADOBE DE SAN RAFAEL

Tomas A. Sanchez (1826–1882), a popular figure known throughout Southern California for his chivalry and bravery, was born at San Gabriel Mission. He served as Sheriff for Los Angeles County from 1859 until 1867. Following Sanchez's retirement from law enforcement, he moved his family toward the mountains, locating on a 100 acre tract of land on the old *Rancho San Rafael*.

At first, the Sanchez family lived in a small wooden house. Sometime between 1870 and 1872, Tomas began erecting an artistic, *hacienda* type adobe home. It was a costly and time–consuming project that occupied several years.

The new Sanchez adobe was typical of the California *rancho* homes of that time, its overall design restricted only by the limitations of site and money. The rather long rooms were limited in width by ceiling and roof spans. The *sala* or living room was designed to accommodate the family's nineteen sons and two daughters.

Adjoining the *sala* was a smaller, less formal family room known as an *antesala* or *salita*. The other two main rooms in the Sanchez adobe were used primarily as bedrooms or *recamaras*. At the east end of the rambling adobe was a large, enclosed area, devoted mainly to cooking and related activities. This was known as the *cocina*.

On the south, west and a portion of the north side was a covered porch or *veranda*. Structurally, that corridor area protected the adobe from rains and erosion.

As is typical for adobe buildings, the walls of the main structure were nineteen inches thick, built of blocks. The floors and ceiling areas were finished in wood, while the roof was covered with shingles. (This latter feature was a Yankee invention).

Surrounding the home were informal gardens, with trees affording both fruit and shade. There was also an herb garden close to the kitchen area. Eucalyptus trees were planted as windbreaks.

With the death of Tomas Sanchez, on June 24, 1882, the adobe passed to Andrew Glasswell. Numerous owners held title in subsequent years and, by 1895, the property had dwindled to 1.2 acres.

In 1930, the old *rancho* with its historic adobe was purchased by the California Medicinal Wine Company.

Casa de Adobe

Two years later, the deed was acquired by the City of Glendale. Plans were then formulated for restoring the Sanchez adobe. The restoration was entrusted to J. Marshall Miller who had earlier been engaged at San Diego Mission. Work was completed in January, 1935, and shortly thereafter, the Sanchez Adobe was formally christened "*Casa Adobe de San Rafael.*"

The State Historical Resources Commission officially designated the *Casa Adobe de San Rafael* as Historical Landmark No. 235. For those wishing to visit this relic of an earlier age, the present address is 1330 Dorothy Drive, in the northwest section of Glendale.

CASA DE ADOBE CHAPEL

Located along the *Arroyo Seco*, the *Casa de Adobe* is a replica of a Spanish–Colonial *hacienda* or ranch house in Old California, one built about 1800 and occupied for fifty years. In 1915, officials at the Hispanic Society of California decided to erect a facsimile ranch house and to furnish it with period items. It was completed and presented to the Southwest Museum in 1925.

Jesus Velasquez was the unassuming Mexican–American who masterminded the construction of the adobes. The bricks were fashioned on site by a crew who carefully followed the procedures used in the area a century and a half earlier

The floor tiles are reminiscent of the pattern in the original flooring of San Juan Capistrano. In the *capilla* or chapel, the tiles form darts pointing to the altar. The corridors and other rooms are floored with historic tilings typical and suitable for the purpose.

The "priest's room" in the *Casa de Adobe* is reminiscent of the one set aside for visiting friars who occasionally would come to offer Holy Mass, preside at marriages and perform baptisms for the family and its retainers. Known as the *cuarto de capellan*, the room has a four poster bed, an old fashioned table, a small wash stand and mirror, a writing desk and a Latin and Spanish dictionary. Its starkness and simplicity is surely in keeping with Franciscan poverty.

The *capilla* adjoins the *cuarto de capellan* and is the focal point of the house. Its decorations and artistic embellishments are all reminiscent of provincial days. The doors of the chapel and the main entrance have both historic and artistic merit. There are no nails in their construction. one door resembles the chapel entrance of San Carlos Borromeo and the other is much like the Palo Verde *haciendas*.

Through the kindness of Bishop John J. Cantwell, who was a trustee of the Southwest Museum for several decades, many of the statues, including the small crucifix and other religious articles were donated by Santa

Ines Mission. On the lectern is a Latin *Missale Romanum* printed at Madrid in the latter part of the 18th century.

The Spanish colonial benches were made by Indians and brought from New Mexico by Charles Fletcher Lummis. His distinctive stamp is evident in many other areas of the *casa*.

According to a booklet about the *Casa de Adobe*, "the capsheaf of the chapel's furnishings is the massive cavern throne–like armchair which Dr. Lummis secured from San Juan Capistrano." He contended it had been used by Fray Junípero Serra when the venerable *presidente* officiated at that mission. There are others who say that the style of the chair indicates a later period. In any event, it is a fine memento, similar to those associated with Santa Barbara Mission at a later time.

In the mid 1980s, Dr. Norman Neuerburg restored and expanded much of the design work painted on the walls at the time of the building's dedication. And it was he who made arrangements for several additional furnishings to be borrowed from San Fernando Mission.

CASA DE BANDINI

When the Right Reverend Francisco Garcia Diego y Moreno, first Bishop of Both Californias, arrived at San Diego, on December 10, 1841, he was given lodgings in the magnificent *Casa de Bandini* which thereby gained the distinction of being the first episcopal residence in Alta California. The *Casa de Bandini* is still very much in evidence today as a restaurant in San Diego's Old Town. An outstanding relic of California's colorful heritage, the structure was built in 1829 by Juan Bandini who had arrived from Peru a decade earlier.

The *Casa* was erected on a parcel of land granted to Juan in 1827 by Governor Jose Maria de Echeandia. In its early years, the *Casa de Bandini* served both as a headquarters and a home for Commodore Robert Stockton. During the mid 1800s, the gracious home figured prominently in the social life of San Diego. In its grand ballroom, dignitaries danced the waltz for the first time in California. Its U–shaped construction, along with its outbuildings and walls, prepared it to fend off possible attacks by the Diegueño Indians in the early years.

Juan Bandini was an active participant in both the Mexican and early American periods of California's history. In his home, he devised many of his political sentiments, including disputes with various factions ruling the area prior to 1846.

An opponent of Governors Manuel Victorio and Juan Alvarado, Bandini took a leading role in revolts against both leaders. He served as secretary for Pio Pico and later furnished supplies for the American cause.

Between 1830 and 1865, there was a dramatic and rapid transformation of life in California. The Spanish Dons endeavored to secularize the vast lands, converting them to prodigious *ranchos* where tremendous herds of cattle became the mainstay of business. Those years were characterized by Indian conflicts and revolutions, conquest and defeat, rugged frontier conditions that rivaled those of the later Wild West. The lavish days of the Spanish Dons came to an unhappy end with the great drought of the 1860s that destroyed enormous herds of cattle.

Following the Mexican War, financial reverses forced Juan Bandini to dispose of his *Casa*. It was purchased by a Frenchman named Adolph Savin for $600. A portion of the house was then converted into a dry goods store and later the dwelling also served as an olive factory. In the watery deluge of 1862, downpours washed away the adobe walls of the corrals, outbuildings and the entire east wing of the *Casa de Bandini*. It was a sad time for a once–proud structure.

After the Civil War, the *Casa de Bandini* was purchased by Albert Seeley. He operated a postal service and stagecoach line between San Diego and points north. He added a second story to the *Casa* and renamed it the Cosmopolitan Hotel.

In July of 1928, the *Casa de Bandini* was sold back to the Bandini family in the person of Cave J. Couts, Jr., Bandini's grandson. He had the house restored and then leased it to a number of tenants for use as a hotel and restaurant known as the Miramar Hotel An abundance of trellises were added to the facade and the gardens were heavily vegetated around a lovely fountain.

The architect Richard Requa was called in to modify the structure in 1945. It was subsequently operated as a motel by Nora Cardwell. Finally it was acquired by the State of California and declared a State Historic Site. Today it functions as a period restaurant.

The *Casa de Bandini*, with its lavish furnishings, is a delightful reminder of the San Diego that greeted Bishop Garcia Diego in 1841.

"CASTLE" ON FIGUEROA STREET

Over the years, many readers have asked about the "castle" located at 2421 South Figueroa Street near Adams Boulevard, in downtown Los Angeles. In an article for a recent issue of the *Branding Iron*, official publication of the Los Angeles Corral of Westerners, Ray Zeman, a retired journalist at the old Los Angeles *Mirror*, answers all those queries quite fully.

The red sandstone structure, with its impressive tower, does indeed conjure up the notion of a medieval castle. But the one on Figueroa Street, built in 1891 and

"Castle" on Figueroa Street

now owned by Mount Saint Mary's College, has no connection with royalty, its grandeur notwithstanding. Its builder was neither king nor nobleman, but an affluent Seattle lumberman. Thomas Douglas Stimson left an indelible imprint on Los Angeles by erecting a stunning, four story mansion, each of whose rooms is panelled in a different kind of wood, much of it imported to the United States from abroad.

From the octagonal tower, with its crenelated battlements, to the picturesque rathskeller, the builder spared no expense. The architect, Carroll Brown, described the design as Richardson Romanesque. Others, probably more accurately, termed it Queen Anne. Wrought iron gates and massive doors provided protection as well as access. Stained glass windows overlooking the porte–cochere added a distinctive beauty. The hand–carved balustrades and the enormous fireplace were and remain as impressive as they were functional.

The castle's huge refrigerator has marble walls. And eighteen massive marble pillars line the tiled porch. The game room on the lower floor of the adjacent carriage house reflects the recreational interests of the Stimson family. Even today, the carefully manicured lawns, trees and shrubs are reminiscent of those adorning castles of Europe.

The Stimsons took up resident in their mansion in 1891 and lived there the rest of their lives. Later, Eddie Maier, a mogul for one of the nation's largest brewing companies, purchased the castle and used it for the gala parties he had for notable visitors to California's southland.

The Pi Kappa Alpha fraternity at the University of Southern California acquired the castle in the late 1920s. Carrie Estelle Doheny bought it in 1947 and, thereafter, it became an appendage to the vast property holdings of the Dohenys. Its charming chapel was inaugurated and outfitted in 1947 when the castle was first used as an extension of the convent for nearby Saint Vincent's parochial school.

In more recent times, the building has been used as a residence facility for the Doheny Campus of Mount Saint Mary's College. Though technically not a part of Chester Place, the castle enjoys what might be called "extra territorial privileges." Today, the "castle" on Figueroa Street remains a picturesque reminder of an earlier age in Los Angeles. Though it has no moat, torture chamber or chopping block, the Stimson mansion abounds in fanciful legends.

CATALINA IN 1905

The visit to Santa Catalina Island, in 1905, of Mother Frances Cabrini (1850–1917), was described by the nation's "first citizen saint" in a diary which was published some years after her death.

Mr. Banning, the proprietor of a well–known island in the Pacific, gave me a pleasure trip, favouring me with passes on his steamer. I had heard so much about the Island of Saint Catherine, that I was anxious not to leave California without being able to tell you something about it. I went there one day when the sky was of a cobalt colour and the sea justified its name.

In the contemplation of the immense ocean, as we could see nothing but water, the hours in crossing passed very quickly. When we arrived at the principal bay of the island, which serves as a little port, a transparent fog extended like a veil before the immense mass of rock, thirty miles long, which forms the island, so that we could only see its outline.

As we drew near the island this great curtain of fog raised itself, and there before our vision was as it were, the scenery of a theatre, but prepared by Nature. I can assure you I thought I was in a dream. I thought I had been transported into a terrestrial paradise. The background was a whole blaze of saffron colour, under which lay the imposing mountains. In the midst of these graceful rocks were small houses with a dark background of pines and palms.

The air was so clear that one could not measure the distance, and one's power of vision seemed to increase. The sea was of such a transparent blue, that myriads of fish could be seen deep down, whilst flying fish darted into the air like arrows and then sank into the waves. Cod fish imported from Newfoundland where it is found in abundance has become a source of great trade with the English. The boat moved slowly in the water without frightening the fish, which seem accustomed to the company of human beings. They even appear to have lost all fear of man, so harmonious is Nature here. Less still is there any fear among the aquatic birds which continually hover about the fisheries.

Thousands of these birds live on the shore of the beautiful bay of Avalon, in the waters of which they take their morning bath, and at other times float or rock on the waves. We also saw them resting on the nets of the fishermen's boats, on the edges of the steamers and on the rocks. In fact, there is no prominence standing out of the water which they do not adorn by their elegant form and pure whiteness.

But the most wonderful sight is that which one enjoys in gazing at some of the boats which have glass fitted into their keels. I had been told of the aquatic gardens of the Island of Saint Catherine, and had imagined it was some ingenious arrangement of lenses designed to produce the illusion of a garden in the waters of the sea. Of course, I should not have gone had I not been invited to make a trip. On one of these boats I can assure you I did not regret going, for I found everything beyond my expectations and imagination.

In the bottom of the boat there is an opening with a glass window through which you can see everything in the sea. We had hardly left land when the sea which appeared smooth and sandy at the bottom, gradually became full of rocks and then of green mountains. Between these were plains and valleys, all covered with green sea plants which in some places reached a height of one hundred feet, waving to and fro with the movement of the sea.

There is a never–ending variety of aquatic plants, some of which bore bunches of violets, different kinds of fruit of delicate tints, fresh like the blossoms of spring, and they were continually moved by the waters, as by a breeze. If the view of the land park is beautiful, I can assure you that a marine park is much more so, especially when you behold it inhabited by every kind of fish, including the goldfish, and its rocks adorned by hills of the most brilliant colours. After two hours of these wonderful sights we landed on the beach of moonstones. These are of a reddish colour, and when cut and polished they are made up into various kinds of ornaments. The chalcedony of which these are formed must have fallen from some high mountain. Who knows how far away? It is beaten by the waves on the beach.

CATECHISMO Y EXPOSICION BREVE

Treasures are where one finds them. An example would be the copy of Geronimo de Ripalda's *Catechismo y Exposicion Breve de la Doctrina Christiana* which surfaced in Los Angeles during the XXIII California International Antiquarian Book Fair.

Held at the Airport Hilton Hotel, the Book Fair featured 134 dealers from Europe and the United States, each specializing in one or another of the 198 categories enumerated in the official guide prepared by the Southern California Chapter of the Antiquarian Booksellers Association of America.

The catechism was discovered among the materials offered for sale by Roy Bleiweiss Fine Books and Autographs of Berkeley. Given the book's age (188 years), it is in extremely good condition.

Though printed in large press runs, the book is quite scarce today, probably because most copies were long ago worn out and thrown away. Catechisms are basically textbooks and, as such, they generally have a short lifespan.

This edition of Ripalda's catechism was printed at *Puebla de los Angeles* (the one in Mexico!) in 1802 on presses operated by Pedro de la Rosa, possibly a relative of the early California printer, Jose de la Rosa. In an introductory note, the editor explains that the publisher had been authorized to reproduce a faithful copy of the catechism originally approved for distribution at Mexico City on July 16, 1783.

The format of the vellum–bound catechism was that established as normative in 1585, when the bishops of Mexico met in solemn session to promulgate and implement the decrees enacted by the Council of Trent. According to a commentary on the bishop's gathering by Mariano Galvan Rivera, "all those charged with the care of souls, both secular and regular clergy, must have a text containing the basics of Christian Doctrine; namely, the Lord's Prayer, the Angelic Salutation, the Apostles' Creed, the antiphon *Salva Regina*, the Twelve Articles of Faith, the Ten Commandments of the law of God, the Five Precepts of the Church, the Seven Sacraments and the Seven Capital Sins."

Another decree of the same episcopal synod directed that Indians had to be taught in their native language with the aid of catechisms approved by the Church's magisterium. Ripalda was a Jesuit whose catechetical methodology was extremely popular throughout Mexico. His textbook gained official endorsement from the Mexican Synod of bishops. It was probably used more widely than any other in the New World.

The Ripalda version of the *Doctrina* was especially identified with Baja and Alta California where it was the basic doctrinal text for the first generations of Christians in the missions and *pueblos*. It was simple in language and followed a regular question–and–answer format.

As suggested earlier, the Ripalda catechisms were printed in the thousands for the Californias and then used until they fell apart. For that reason, readable copies are exceedingly rare today.

The one acquired at the XXIII California International Antiquarian Book Fair is now on public exhibit at San Fernando Mission. Those who want to see how peoples of earlier times learned about God are invited to view the historical tome.

CATHOLIC CALIFORNIA

California is a remarkable place, by almost any measuring rod. With only 10 to 15% of its 158,693 square miles regarded as comfortably habitable, the state has been the most populous in the Union for over a decade. With 3/4th of its surface consisting of rolling hills or mountains, the Golden State still accounts for more inhabitants than 111 nations!

For whatever value they serve, statistics indicate that California deserves "empire" status. With an economy ranking sixth among the world powers, its gross product is exceeded only by the United States, the Soviet Union, West Germany, the United Kingdom and France. Californians are more prosperous, longer–lived and more mobile than their counterparts in other states. Per capita income exceeds that of any country, including the United States. Presently California is edging out Japan for fifth place in Free World Manufacturing. Its overall export–import trade outranks a hundred nations.

California wineries produce four of every five bottles consumed in the United States and over 200 farm products are grown on the 8,000,000 acres of land in 400 varieties of soil composition. Residents of California have more telephones than any country, except the United States. At last count, the vehicular registration placed the state fourth in the community of nations. Variety is the spice of life too. California has the driest and wettest climatic zones in the nation. It snows more in the mountains of California than it does at the North Pole!

These are but a few of the reasons why California, as late as 1848 the most distant place on earth from major population centers, affords such fascination to onlookers. Religiously and historically, it is doubtful whether any section of the American continent offers a more absorbing montage of projects, events and personages. In his welcoming address to Bishop Joseph Sadoc Alemany, John A. McGlynn stated that "no portion of this great continent" presented a more interesting field for the missionary than California. Every bay and river, every mountain and valley, throughout the length and breadth of this beautiful land is, in the name it bears, a silent but unimpeachable witness of the efforts . . . in extending the Kingdom of Christ.

Another pioneer struck a similar vein, pointing out that the saga of California's discovery and development, is the story of its religion. "The sweetly suggestive Catholic nomenclature of the mountains and valleys, coast–line and interior plains of our State, are the legacy of the Apostles of the land." Nowhere in the world has the calendar of saints and the sacred objects of Catholic devotion been drawn upon as in California to designate even the most insignificant places.

As it did a half century ago, the Golden State shines with renewed luster to the world as the home and haunt of beauty—"a region where abides the creative spirit of art, and where there remains for the American world to cherish and make use of one of the most precious possessions any people may have, namely, visible symbols and links of tradition, joining the recent with the past and supplying a glorious perspective for the future. And these symbols are the missions." The late Michael Williams said that "every crumb of adobe in their walls is precious. Every scrap of history or legend concerning them is more valuable than fine gold from the Californian hills. There inspiration for the millions of people who have gazed upon them, or who will so gaze, the influence they exert upon thought and so upon life itself, and the gracious history of the period from which they spring, these things are what put California in a place by herself—and make her a state *sui generis*."

CATHOLIC CEMETERIES

Historians can frequently fit together the variant pieces of an historical puzzle more easily by walking through a cemetery than pouring over a shelf of books. The entire cast of earlier generations can be reassembled by computerizing interment records.

One day, while looking for the grave of a local pioneer, I happened over the tombstone of the legendary journalist and propagandist, Benjamin Cummings Truman (1835–1916). I had written a book about Truman and never had determined where he was interred.

The obvious often evades the casual observer. It is fascinating that the producers of the television series about "the rich and famous" have not done at least one sequence in a cemetery where everyone eventually gathers to await the final resurrection.

In the Archdiocese of Los Angeles, there are eleven Catholic cemeteries and mausolea, all of which have their litany of prominent interees. Most of our early bishops, for example, are entombed in the episcopal vault at Calvary Mausoleum in east Los Angeles. Among the many other early and influential Catholics represented in the mausoleum are such family names as Doheny, Hancock, Wilcox, Dominguez and Barrymore.

At San Fernando Mission Cemetery in Mission Hills are graves of pioneer rock 'n roller Ritchie Valens, television star Chuck Connors, comedy actor Walter Brennan and character performers William Bendix and Rosalind Russell.

Those with gravesites at Holy Cross Cemetery in Culver City are actors Ray Bolger, Jackie Coogan, Kevin "Chuck" Connors ("The Rifleman"), Bela Lugosi ("Dracula") and Jack Haley; comedians Jimmy Durante and James and Marian Jordan ("Fibber McGee and Molly"); sports figure Walter O'Malley; musicians Lawrence Welk and Lindley "Spike" Jones; singers Mario Lanza and Dennis Day; and producers John Ford and Mark Sennett. Interred near the lovely Grotto of Our Lady of Lourdes at Holy Cross are several well–known southland Catholics, including Harry Lillis "Bing" Crosby and Rita Hayworth.

There used to be an agency in Hollywood known as the "Grave Line" which conducted bus tours of local cemeteries, where tombs of prominent figures were identified or pointed out. Many cemeteries will provide lists of notable gravesites upon request.

Sometimes the inscriptions on a tombstone provide a clue to the descendant's personal life. At Evergreen Cemetery, for example, is a marker which proclaims that "Peter, Peter, pumpkin eater, had a wife but couldn't keep her." Whether he was a widower, divorced or alienated is not mentioned and a check of the cemetery office files adds nothing more to the equation.

Inscriptions are not always infallible. I know of a very prominent southland lady who directed her executor (under threat of disinheritance) to have her birthdate post–dated by ten years. The old time chiselers couldn't always spell or read too well. A marker at one cemetery reads: "May she rest in pieces."

Genealogists armed with hand computers have drawn up some fascinating profiles of local inhabitants by tracing and identifying familial interments. Sometimes more problems emerge than facts. For example, when infant death rates were higher, parents would often bestow the name of a deceased child on the next baby.

The democracy about death is reinforced by the simple plaques laid flat on the ground, a provision made in fairly recent times for safety and maintenance reasons.

CATHOLIC CHURCH EXTENSION SOCIETY (1905)

The imprint of Father Francis Clement Kelley (1870–1948), firmly engraved on the ecclesial fibre of the United States, was especially visible in the Diocese of Monterey–Los Angeles. Though the Canadian–born priest was ordained for the ministry of Detroit, he engaged in an apostolate which led him to almost every jurisdiction in the nation.

Very likely, Kelley's most durable contribution was that of establishing the Catholic Church Extension Society to assist America's destitute missionaries in their efforts to spread the Gospel message. It was on October 18, 1905, that Kelley delivered his moving appeal to a Chicago meeting of bishops, priests and laymen about the physical and spiritual challenges confronting the Church's work in the backward areas of the country.

Shortly thereafter, he and a group of nineteen men founded the Catholic Church Extension Society as a "means of assisting those priests across America who were daily struggling to introduce and preserve the faith in the isolated, thinly–populated and poverty–ridden parts of the nation." The headquarters for the Society were located at Chicago in 1906, and there Father Kelley was selected to preside over the Society, a position that he held for the next nineteen years. Among the principal fund–raising efforts, none was more successful than the *Extension Magazine* which Kelley launched over seventy years ago.

During the intervening years, the Catholic Church Extension Society has helped to build, remodel and furnish thousands of chapels, catechetical centers, rectories and parochial utility buildings. Of special concern to the Society were those areas where the work of the Church was (and is) seriously handicapped by lack of personnel, organization and finances. The work touched many bases: home mission priests were subsidized, needy seminarians educated, teaching sisters supported, children instructed and the poor of every color and language had Christ brought into their lives.

Over the years, the Society has erected no fewer than 7,000 small churches or chapels. By mid–1924, the Society had contributed substantially to the then improverished Diocese of Monterey–Los Angeles. Houses–of–worship were built at Bishop (Our Lady of Victory), Catalina Island (Saint Catherine), Chino (Our Lady of Guadalupe), Colton (San Salvador), Corona (Saint Edward), El Cajon (Saint Mary), La Verne (Our Lady of Guadalupe), Oro Grande (Saint Cecilia), Owensmouth (Our Lady of the Valley), Palmdale (Saint Mary) and Seal Beach (Our Lady of the Rosary).

In addition, assistance from the Extension Society was granted to Saint Boniface Indian School (Banning), the Old Mission (San Juan Capistrano) and the Japanese apostolate (Los Angeles). In 1924, Father Kelley was named Bishop of Oklahoma City–Tulsa, where he served with distinction for the remainder of his priestly life.

Bishop Kelley continued his association with South-

ern California even after his departure from the Catholic Church Extension Society. He was especially forceful in his defense of the Mexican hierarchy and clergy exiled from their homeland by hostile and anti–Catholic governmental leaders.

CATHOLIC INFORMATION CENTER

Throughout his long life, Archbishop J. Francis A. McIntyre identified with the spiritual needs of working people. One of his favorite apostolates in New York City had been the establishment of Our Lady of Victory Chapel in downtown Manhattan.

Shortly after coming to Southern California, the archbishop began planning for a similar chapel in Los Angeles. He acquired an old hat factory and warehouse on South Flower Street and, at that strategic location in the city's business district, he established what would become Our Lady's Chapel.

In addition to remodelling and transforming the building into an attractive house–of–worship, McIntyre also made provisions for an Information Center and a Catholic bookstore. Space was made available on the second floor for a library, counselling room and accommodations for resident priests.

Father Paul Stroup, the senior priest at Saint Vibiana

Catholic Information Center

Cathedral was placed in charge of Our Lady's Chapel which was erected specifically "for the service of the people engaged in business and commerce" in the area. From that moment, God became "a neighbor all day long" in downtown Los Angeles.

Besides the five daily Masses offered at the chapel, novenas, missions and retreats were scheduled at regular intervals. Confessions were heard at specified times and the Blessed Sacrament was exposed daily. The rosary and other devotions conducted throughout the day were often broadcast by radio.

After the formal opening of the chapel, on December 8, 1948, men and women began organizing groups from among the Catholics in their respective business firms to sponsor and attend Mass on given days of the week. From those groups came the eventual development of the Catholic Center Men's Club and *Las Ayudantas de Nuestra Señora*. The latter group did volunteer work at the center and maintained its 4,000 volume library.

In time a choir was formed under the leadership of John Ruivenkamp, a distinguished musician from Holland. The Bob Mitchell Choir also provided music for the chapel on many occasions.

Attached to Our Lady's Chapel was the Catholic Information Center which was envisioned to represent the Church in its youngest mood "its missionary personality reaching out to all peoples everywhere." Father John V. Sheridan, so many years a fixture at the Center, said that "this is the Church on the Street in the tradition of Christ among the multitudes. Here is the truth at the mind's fingertips for those who seek it. This is a proof of God's Providence and goodness. To hundreds, Flower Street is one of the labyrinthine ways."

In an effort to publicize the Church and its teachings, the Catholic Information Center used every appropriate method of modern pedagogy, communications and business practice. Its primary purpose was that of conveying knowledge about the Church quickly, effectively and authoritatively. Such services as a round–the–clock telephone service, the largest pamphlet rack in the city and a staff of nine people all helped advance the Center's scriptural motto: "Be ready always with an answer to everyone that asks a reason for the hope that is in you."

For well over forty years, Our Lady's Chapel and the Catholic Information Center have fulfilled the ancient prayer of the people of God: "that every material expansion of the Church may be accompanied by even greater spiritual progress."

CATHOLIC LABOR INSTITUTE

On February 12, 1947, a group of Catholic laymen and priests began discussing plans for establishing a Labor Institute in Los Angeles. Father Thomas Coogan, who acted as temporary chairman, suggested an organization modelled after the encyclical letters of Popes Leo XIII and Pius XI.

Working closely with Joseph E. Doherty and other locally prominent labor and management officials, Father Coogan convened the first official meeting on March 10th at Immaculate Conception Parish Hall. Those in attendance agreed that the primary focus of the Institute would be educational. Labor schools, public forums and days of recollection would be their means of operation.

Father Coogan proposed that the Los Angeles foundation be patterned after the already functional labor groups in Hartford, Chicago and New Orleans. The local institute would meet twice monthly at various areas in the four county archdiocese.

The establishment of labor "schools" was an early objective of the Catholic Labor Institute. Their purpose was to promote a better understanding of the mutual problems of labor and management and to provide a basis in Christian principles for their solution. In addition to the two schools organized in those early months, the Institute sponsored a management panel for local industrialists and a seminar for priests and religious.

After Father Coogan's untimely and premature death, later in 1947, the spiritual leadership of the Catholic Labor Institute was entrusted to Father Joseph Kearney and it was he who secured the endorsement and encouragement of the new Archbishop of Los Angeles, J. Francis A. McIntyre.

At ceremonies marking the Catholic Labor Institute's first anniversary, Auxiliary Bishop Timothy Manning noted that the Institute was already doing "much to bring people closer to a knowledge of their faith and of its application to their daily lives." By the end of 1948, there were five schools operational, with over 300 members enrolled in the sixteen week sessions. Courses were offered in public speaking, industrial ethics, parliamentary procedure, debating, propaganda analysis, grievances and arbitration, profit sharing and collective bargaining.

The teaching staff was selected from the area's outstanding leaders in labor and management. It included Arthur Roemero, Martin Work, C. C. Stoddard, Felix de la Torre, Jim Carbray and Vincent Lawler, to mention but a few.

In October of 1953, the Catholic Labor Institute opened Padre Serra Labor School at Our Lady of Talpa Parish, in the heart of the largest Hispanic settlement in the United States. The classes there were geared to the special needs of East Side workers.

Other projects suggested by Archbishop McIntyre were added, including a program whereby resident Hispanic aliens over fifty years of age could qualify for citizenship under provisions of the McCarran Act. During the following dozen years, more than 2,700 persons, mostly Mexican Americans, completed the training courses and became American citizens.

Since the 1950s, the Catholic Labor Institute has given annual awards to companies, unions and individuals for their contributions to industrial peace and social justice. A Labor Day Mass is sponsored to honor the working people of America.

Much has been *written* and more has been *said* about Catholic teachings on social problems. But, in Los Angeles, something has been *done* about the papal encyclicals.

CATHOLIC MOTION PICTURE ACTOR'S GUILD

In March of 1923, Bishop John J. Cantwell entrusted Father Michael Mullins ((1892–1976) with the task of organizing a Catholic presence within the Motion Picture Industry.

The resultant Catholic Motion Picture Actor's Guild was given the formidable challenge of advancing the spiritual, charitable and material welfare of all Catholics in the industry. In addition, the Guild was to function as the "unofficial spokesman for the Church on various happenings in the entertainment world."

Thomas J. Gray, one of the organizers of the Guild, eloquently explained the benefits that would accrue to those joining the new organization and, by the time of the initial meeting, on June 14th, over 200 people had become affiliated with the Guild. Bishop Cantwell was proud of the Catholic involvement in Hollywood and said that "there is no reason why the moving picture actors should not appear before our people as men and women of high integrity, of character, of reverence and obedience of law."

One of the most effective outreaches of the Guild was *The Catholic Motion Picture Guild News* which was launched in December of 1923 "to acquaint Catholics of the world as to the identity of those of their Faith who are carrying on actively in the motion picture profession."

By the end of 1924, there were more than a thousand names on the Guild's roster. A constitution was drafted and officers were chosen. People like Thomas Meighan, Jack Coogan and Mary O'Connor were installed in leadership positions.

Father Mullins, known as the *"padre* of the stars," eventually devoted his full energies to the Guild. Headquarters were opened at 5507 Santa Monica Boulevard and later in the Taft Building on Hollywood Boulevard.

Membership fees were set at $2 per year. Guild members were anxious that Catholic subjects in the films be treated with accuracy and decorum. Any item touching upon the Catholic belief or practice was considered worthy of attention and the Guild offered its consultation services gratis.

The industry generally welcomed the work of the Guild and the contents of its monthly publication. Each year, the Guild sponsored a public Mass and Communion breakfast to which all Catholics working in the industry were invited. The event took place at Blessed Sacrament Church in Hollywood and outstanding Catholic homilists from all over the nation occupied the pulpit.

Bishop Cantwell traditionally attended the annual gatherings and such Catholic luminaries as John Steven McGroarty, J. Wiseman Macdonald and James Mahoney were engaged to speak at the breakfast. The Guild was affiliated with Catholic theatrical organizations throughout the world. A branch office was opened in New York City to deal with the corporate heads of the various production companies.

After 1934, with the establishment of the Episcopal Committee of Motion Pictures, the activities of the Guild were gradually phased out or transferred to the newly formed Legion of Decency.

CATHOLIC TRUTH SOCIETY

Late in 1891 Archbishop Patrick W. Riordan of San Francisco established the Catholic Truth Society in the Bay City "to make known the doctrines of the Catholic religion, such as they are taught by the Church; to give reasons upon which the doctrines of the Church rest; to refute the errors and misrepresentations that are not uncommon in the minds of so many outside the pale of its organization."

As envisioned by the archbishop, the Catholic Truth Society would publish tracts and pamphlets, scatter leaflets and give courses of lectures in public halls. The organization was established independently of exisitng parochial endeavors and placed under the capable direction of Father Peter C. Yorke. The San Francisco group was modelled on the one set up in England during 1884 by James Britton as "an organization of members of the Catholic faith, clerical and lay, men and women, founded to promulgate the truths of the Catholic Religion by means of the written word."

Because of the pressing responsibilities incumbent on pastors towards their flocks, Riordan saw the need of a group dedicated to "the special work which the parish organizations cannot do, or at least cannot do well, nor can be expected to do." The Bay City's prelate recognized that "in carrying out the command of our Blessed Lord our first duty as Catholics is to our own." And, in this regard, Riordan felt that the "laity must be educated in a strong, robust masculine enthusiasm," for he knew that "the more enlightened her children are the more will they be inclined to love her and to serve her."

The Catholic Truth Society attempted to equip Catholics with a philosophical concept of their religion geared to accommodate the various speculations and tendencies of the age. Controversies raised in San Francisco in those years made it expedient for the faithful to know and be able to define the Church's relations with contemporary society. The archbishop had several specific aims for the Catholic Truth Society which were outlined in an article for the *Angelus Monthly* early in 1898. These included providing literature for the sick in hospitals, prisoners in jails, and seamen entering the San Francisco Port. Riordan was especially solicitous about the infirm people of the city and noted that "if ever there was a city in the world that should be ashamed of the care it gives its indigent sick, it is this rich City of San Francisco."

As a student of history, Riordan realized that the English tongue of his time was essentially anti–Catholic, coming into its beauty as it did at the time of the English Reformation. "It was taken hold of by the great classical writers 300 years ago, and it was moulded so as not to carry Catholic expressions or Catholic truth." Though the Bay City's Catholic Truth Society anti–dated by three years that organization's formal establishment in the United States, 1898 was, indeed, an appropriate time to call attention to the people of this country to the claims of the Catholic Church, its marvelous history, its undying life, its services to humanity. . . ."

Archbishop Riordan was no stranger to bigotry and he knew that Catholics are much closer to the Church during times of stress. The prelate jokingly admitted, "a slight grudge against my dear friend, Father Yorke for having opposed so strongly the society of the A.P.A." for had he 'let them alone for two or three years more I should have been able to pay for my new seminary and endow it".

California's second metropolitan was ever on the move. "We do not want to keep things as they are," he said, "we want things to grow. We want to stir up activity and continued efforts to advance the cause of truth, and charity, and civilization." The archbishop realized that "Catholics must go forward, or cease to be a factor in the social, the intellectual, or even the religious life of the country." Riordan's establishment of the Catholic Truth Society was one of his programs for "moving forward" and a further proof of a statement the prelate made on his arrival in San Francisco:

There may be among you men older than I, and there may be men wiser and who have had more experience than I, but in one thing I yield to no man among you— in my love for the Church of God.

CATHOLIC WOMAN'S CLUB

During the early winter months of 1916, a group of Catholic ladies decided to form an organization that would give them a greater voice in the activities of the Church in Southern California. The "Catholic Woman's Club" held its first official meeting at 2123 Estrella Avenue, Los Angeles, on December 20th and, at that time, the sixteen founders agreed that the organization would work for the advancement and promotion of literary and educational interests. They also committed themselves to aiding the poor, irrespective of creed or nationality.

The ladies also agreed "to carry on such benevolent work of any character that may from time–to–time be possible and expedient." They decided to lease or purchase any real estate necessary to carry out their benevolent purposes.

In order to facilitate their operations, the ladies voted to have, take and receive gifts, endowments and personal property. And, finally, they pledged to do "all acts and things which may be necessary, proper, useful or advantageous to the full carrying out of the benevolent purposes" of their organization.

Helen M. Higgins was elected first President of the Catholic Woman's Club and it was also she who spearheaded the club's incorporation by Secretary of State Frank C. Jordan on January 23, 1917. Later that year, Mrs. Higgins asked the newly–named bishop for the Diocese of Monterey–Los Angeles, the Right Reverend John J. Cantwell, to formally endorse the work of the club. In one of his first public pronouncements, Cantwell "gladly accepted the invitation to give the Catholic Woman's Club" his approval. He noted that the club "is to the Catholic public what some great engine is to a factory; it is the motive power of a surprisingly large number of social, civic, religious and patriotic activities."

Years later, the bishop observed that the club had fulfilled an obvious need in supplying the desires of cultured women for an opportunity to acquire a knowledge and a fuller appreciation of the great contribution that the Church has made to the world in the schools of Science, of Art, of Literature and of Music. He went on to say that the club "in supplying such needs has made for the greater usefulness and for a fuller development of these fine characteristics of womanhood which contribute so much to the stabilization of the home and family life."

Bishop Cantwell was "particularly pleased with the

positive and unhesitating stand which the Catholic Woman's Club had taken upon social questions and upon pernicious theories which if adopted would go far to undermine the very principles upon which Christian civilization and the Christian home rests."

The club acquired an old mansion at the corner of San Marino Street and Menlo Avenue for its headquarters. In 1937, the building was extensively renovated and enlarged to accommodate the many activities of the Catholic Woman's Club. Elaborate annual reports were published in which the various programs of the club were outlined in considerable detail. A collection of eight of those now–rare volumes recently was acquired by the Archival Center and is available to researchers.

There were at various times thirty departments or outreaches operated by the club, including drama, literature, gardening, public speaking, landmarks and California history. Regular meetings were held on the first and third Wednesdays, generally followed by luncheons at which civic leaders were featured.

Loss of membership and change of focus eventually curtailed the activities of the club and, in 1970, the officers decided to shut down the club's programs. Two years later, the few remaining assets were transferred to the Archbishop's Fund for Charity.

During its heyday, the Catholic Woman's Club was a pioneering force for good within the Church of Southern California. Its many accomplishments confirm the dictum that each new generation stands on the shoulders of those who have gone before!

CATS TO THE RESCUE

The delicate balance of nature was severely compromised with the introduction of rats into California. Unknown before the arrival of European ships those dangerous and destructive stowaways became a real problem both to natives and settlers. Seriousness of this new challenge is confirmed by medical historians who estimate that more people have died from diseases transmitted by rats than from all the wars in history!

The early missionaries, knowing the basic principles of ecology, sought to counteract this threat by importing felines to the area. Fray Pedro Font (1738–1781), the chaplain and diarist to the Anza Expedition of 1775–1776, noted that when they were returning to Mexico City, they were asked by the resident priest at San Carlos to deliver "cats, two for San Gabriel and two for San Diego at the request of the friars who urgently asked for them." Reminders of their existence at the missions are found today in the cat holes cut in some of the original doors at San Gabriel, San Fernando, San Juan Bautista and Santa Ines.

About the same time, another missionary, Father Thomas Eixarch, working among the Yuma Indians, living miserably in a brush hut overrun by rats, noted tersely in his diary for the benefit of his successors: "Bring cats." John C. Luttig also confirms the value of felines on the American frontier in his journal of 1812–1813:

> This morning we left old she Cat at Camp, at breakfast I missed her, and Mrs Manuel sent a man for the Cat. He returned in the Evening with the Cat, to our great satisfaction. This Remark may seem ridiculous, but an Animal of this kind is more valuable in this Country than a fine Horse. Mice ate in great Abundance and the Company have lost for want of Cats several Thousand Dollars in Merchandize. . . . There was not a night passed since I got that Cat , that she has not caught from four to ten Mice and brought them to her Kittens.

Following the discovery of gold, the shortage of cats prompted numerous appeals. Thomas J. Bidwell wrote his brother, in January,1851, "the mice here are actually worse than the rats ever were at Sacramento City! Nothing is safe from them—not even our noses at night. Let this touch your heart, my dear brother, and induce you to bring home one cat at least, pregnant if possible."

In his *Reminiscences of a Ranger*, Horace Bell described how entrepreneurs took advantage of the cat shortage:

> In 1849 San Francisco was over–supplied with rats, without a corresponding supply of cats.. The supply of cats in Los Angeles was overabundant while of rats there were few. It was therefore left to the fertile brain of a distinguished Virginian to equalize this seeming inequality in the nature of things. Consequently he went to work and gathered up all the cats he could get, either by hook or crook, caged them up and shipped them to San Francisco. . . . Pete was supreme dictator as to prices and sold his cats, several hundred in number, at prices ranging at from #16 to $100 each.

Reginald Bretnor, writing in a recent issue of T*he American West*, observed that "it is very difficult to access the part cats played in helping settlers defeat the wilderness." While admitting that "without cats, the American West would have been settled," he admitted that "we owe those frontier cats a debt of gratitude."

CENTRAL CALIFORNIA — NEW DIOCESES

Plans for a separate ecclesiastical jurisdiction for that district of the old Diocese of Monterey–Los Angeles comprising Central California were considered as long ago as 1866. In a letter to a friend, Bishop Thaddeus Amat predicted that "within a few years another bishop will certainly be established and form a new diocese."

No official action was taken at that time but early in 1889, Giovanni Cardinal Simeoni told Bishop Francis Mora that Roman officials found it difficult "to see how one person, however industrious, can effectively provide for the demands and necessities of the Church" in so extensive an area.

The matter was given serious attention and, in September of that year, Archbishop Patrick W. Riordan of San Francisco suggested to officials of the Sacred Congregation of Propaganda Fide the feasibility of a separate diocese at Monterey encompassing the six counties of San Luis Obispo, Monterey, San Benito, Tulare, Fresno, Inyo and those parts of Merced, Santa Cruz and Santa Clara not already attached to the Archdiocese of San Francisco.

Bishop Mora exhibited little enthusiasm for the proposal believing as he did that smaller units would not be financially viable. On February 24, 1890, the Archbishop of San Francisco reported that those he had consulted in the matter "were of the opinion that the line should be drawn north of Santa Barbara County and south of Kern County and south from San Bernardino." Several additional reports were submitted to Rome later that year and circulated among the members of the congregation. In 1894, the cardinals endorsed Bishop Mora's views and voted to put aside the question of dividing the diocese in favor of appointing a coadjutor for California's southland.

Rumors of a division were revived after Bishop Thomas J. Conaty's death in 1915, and the long delay that ensued before the appointment of a successor. The territorial integrity of the Diocese of Monterey–Los Angeles remained intact, however, until 1922, when Bishop John J. Cantwell, acting on the advice of Gaetano Cardinal De Lai, petitioned Pope Pius XI to divide the unwieldy jurisdiction into more manageable units. Favorable response to the request came in June of 1922, with the announcement that the Holy Father had approved plans for removing the twelve northernmost counties from the Diocese of Monterey–Los Angeles and forming them into the separate ecclesiastical jurisdiction of Monterey–Fresno.

An estimated Catholic population of 50,000 souls was included in the new diocese whose geographical confines encompassed 43,714 square miles in the counties of Fresno, King, Tulare, San Luis Obispo, Kern, Inyo, Stanislaus, Merced, Santa Cruz, Madera, San Benito and Monterey. The boundary line between the new Diocese of Monterey—Fresno and the Archdiocese of San Francisco was adjusted to allow all of Santa Clara County to revert to the metropolitan see and all of Merced County to the newly erected diocese.

Archbishop Edward J. Hanna of San Francisco presided at the formal canonical erection ceremonies which were held in Fresno's newly designated Cathedral of Saint John the Baptist, on December 3, 1922. Appointed by the Holy See as interim Apostolic Administrator of the diocese was Bishop John J. Cantwell who continued as Ordinary of the southern counties, now known as the Diocese of Los Angeles–San Diego. On March 27, 1924, Bishop John B. MacGinley of Nueva Caceres in the Philippines was chosen by Pope Pius XI as the first Ordinary of the Diocese of Monterey–Fresno. He was installed on July 31, 1924, by Dennis Cardinal Dougherty.

In the first statistical survey made of the area, it was reported that there were fifty–three priests maintaining forty–two parishes and twenty–one mission stations to accommodate 51,265 faithful. The educational system was composed of four academies and seven elementary schools to care for the upbringing of 2,061 youngsters. A long series of financial reverses, coupled with chronic illness, brought about the retirement of Bishop MacGinley on September 26, 1932. Designated as second Ordinary of Monterey–Fresno was the diocesan general, Father Philip G. Scher, who was elevated to the episcopate, on June 29, 1933.

The great population shifts during and after World War II are reflected in the figures for 1950, which revealed 204 priests, eighty–one parishes, eight high schools, thirty–one elementary schools and seven hospitals to fill the needs of Central California's Catholic community which had grown, in a quarter century, to 214,615 souls.

For a period of four months in 1946–1947, the senior Auxiliary of Los Angeles, Bishop Joseph T. McGucken administered the Diocese of Monterey–Fresno with an apostolic indult. Late in 1946, the Holy See announced that Bishop Aloysius J. Willinger of Ponce had been transferred to the titular see of Bida and would function as coadjutor in the Monterey–Fresno jurisdiction. With Bishop Scher's death on January 3, 1953, after a long illness, his coadjutor automatically succeeded. Four years later, the diocese was given an Auxiliary in the person of Father Harry A. Clinch. He was consecrated at Fresno as titular of Badiae, on February 27, 1957.

Diocesan statistics, adjusted to 1966, indicated a Catholic population of 442,588 out of a total count of 1,653,900. The twelve counties were being served by 114 parishes, twelve high schools, fifty elementary schools and seven general hospitals. A diocesan minor seminary enrolled eighty–seven students preparing to join the 290 priests already active in the apostolate.

Another adjustment of ecclesiastical boundaries affecting Central California's twelve counties resulted in separate episcopal seats being established at Fresno and Monterey. With the acceptance of eighty–one year old Bishop Aloysius Willinger's resignation and his assignment to the titular See of Triguala, Pope Paul VI named the Auxiliary of the Metropolitan See of Los

Angeles, Bishop Timothy Manning, to the Diocese of Fresno. Included in that jurisdiction are Fresno, Kern, Tulare, Merced, Madera, King, Inyo and Mariposa counties wherein reside 315,000 Catholics. The former Auxiliary of the parent jurisdiction, Bishop Harry A. Clinch, was chosen as Ordinary of the Diocese of Monterey. Embracing an area of 8,475 square miles in the four counties of Santa Cruz, San Benito, Monterey and San Luis Obispo, the latter bishopric accounts for 133,000 Catholics in a population of 450,000.

CHANCELLOR OR MODERATOR OF CURIA

The new Code of Canon Law, promulgated in early 1983, states that the "principal office" of Chancellor or Moderator of the Curia is "to ensure that the acts of the curia are drawn up and dispatched" and see that they are kept safe in the archives of the curia."

Ordinarily, the Chancellor delegates the latter function of watching over the archives to someone else, which explains my own humble position. "Chancellors" in the American Church have traditionally been entrusted with administrative duties which more than occupy their time.

It is interesting to trace the office of Chancellor here in Southern California. Father Polydore Stockman (1843– 1924), known to his contemporaries as *Padre Agostin,*" came from Belgium in 1873. He served as proto–Chancellor for the Diocese of Monterey–Los Angeles between1898 and 1914. In 1909, he was among the first priests in California named a Private Chamberlain by Pope Plus X. Later in life, Stockman compiled a *Manual of Christian Doctrine* which Bishop John J. Cantwell said "should be on the priedieu" of every priest and religious.

> 1898–1914 Very Reverend Polydore Stockman
> 1915–1918 Reverend Francis J. Conaty
> 1918–1924 Very Reverend John J. Cawley
> 1924–1938 Right Reverend Bernard J. Dolan
> 1938–1948 Most Reverend Joseph T. McGucken
> 1948–1956 Most Reverend Timothy Manning
> 1956–1962 Most Reverend Alden J. Bell
> 1962–1970 Right Reverend Benjamin G. Hawkes
> 1971–1986 Msgr. John A. Rawden
> 1986–1994 Bishop Stephen E. Blaire
> 1994–1997 Msgr. Terrance Fleming
> 1997 onwards Sister Cecilia Louise, C.S.J

In 1915, shortly before the death of his episcopal uncle, the Reverend Francis J. Conaty (1880–1950) was named Chancellor, a post he held until the arrival of Bishop Cantwell who came from San Francisco in 1917.

It was once said of Msgr. John J. Cawley (1882– 1953) that "he had no other model than the great High Priest."

Cawley served the diocese and archdiocese for thirty–five years as Chancellor (1918–1924) and Vicar General. A graduate of Ireland's Maynooth College, he is thought to have turned down several offers of the bishopric.

In 1924, Father Bernard Dolan (1890–1968) succeeded to the Chancellorship, a position he occupied for fourteen years. In the later three decades of his life, "Berny" Dolan was pastor of Saint Anthony's Parish in Long Beach.

The fifth person to serve as Chancellor was Msgr. Joseph T. McGucken (1901–1983) who functioned in that capacity between 1938 and 1948. McGucken subsequently became Bishop of Sacramento and, later Archbishop of San Francisco.

Auxiliary Bishop Timothy Manning (1909–1989) was entrusted with the title of Chancellor in 1948. Upon his accession to the office of Vicar General, he relinquished the post to Msgr. Alden J. Bell (1904–1983), who also served as Rector of Saint Vibiana's Cathedral. Bell rounded out his priestly ministry as Bishop of Sacramento.

Msgr. Benjamin G. Hawkes (1919–1985), the most visible of the Chancellors for the Archdiocese of Los Angeles, occupied the position from 1962 until 1970, when he became Vicar General. Hawkes served in leadership roles for three archbishops and during many of those years he also acted as Pastor of Saint Basil's Parish in the mid–Wilshire district.

Serving in the role of Chancellor during the Manning years was Msgr. John A. Rawden. For much of those fifteen years, he was also administrator and then pastor of Immaculate Conception Parish, just across the street from the Chancery Office.

Among the first appointments made by Archbishop Roger M. Mahony was that of Father Stephen E. Blaire who became Chancellor and Moderator of the Curia in 1986. Eight years later, Blaire, by then Auxiliary Bishop, became Episcopal Vicar for the Region of Our Lady of the Angels.

CHANCERY OFFICE — LOS ANGELES

The Chancery (curial or pastoral) Office of a (arch) diocese is the administrative headquarters for the spiritual and temporal affairs of the local (arch) bishop and his clerical and lay assistants. The first curial offices in California were established at Santa Barbara Mission in January of 1842, when the Right Reverend Francisco Garcia Diego y Moreno arrived to assume his position as Bishop of Both Californias.

During the tenure of Bishop Joseph Sadoc Alemany, the administrative function of the diocese was moved to Monterey, where it was located adjacent to the old Presidio Chapel of San Carlos.

Bishop Thaddeus Amat lived in Santa Barbara for the early years of his episcopal tenure. And during those mid years of the 1850s, the *mitra* was also associated with the Channel City. In 1859, the Vincentian prelate had the residence and offices of the diocese moved to Our Lady of the Angels in Los Angeles. Since that time, the curial offices (or chancery) have been situated in California's southland.

In 1879, a new episcopal residence was erected just north of Saint Vibiana's Cathedral on Main Street. The administrative offices of Bishop Francis Mora and his staff were located in that building. A decade later, a new house was built on East Second Street, around the corner from Main, and provisions were made therein for the business matters associated with the curia.

The house on Second Street was used as a chancery office by Bishops George Montgomery and Thomas Conaty. It wasn't until the arrival of Bishop John J. Cantwell, in 1917, that the need for larger quarters became imperative.

Accommodations were then acquired in the Higgins Building at 108 West Second Street, across the street from the cathedral. The offices remained there until the spring of 1932, when the growing Diocese of Los Angeles–San Diego once again necessitated larger quarters. At that time, Mr. Edward L. Doheny offered accommodations for the Chancery Office on the 7th floor of the new Petroleum Securities Building on West Olympic Boulevard at Figueroa.

Early in 1951, Archbishop J. Francis A. McIntyre announced plans for new two–story chancery facilities on the northwest corner of Ninth and Green streets, across from Immaculate Conception Church.

The building was to cover a frontage of 180 feet along Ninth Street. It was to be 147 feet wide, built of re–inforced concrete and brick. The new building was opened near the end of August, 1951 . Immediately north of it on the neighboring lot was to be the new Immaculate Conception Parish building which consists of an auditorium, meeting rooms and a library.

With the exception of two later additions, one to house the Chancery Archives, the office remained virtually the same. Several satellite buildings were erected nearby to house education, welfare and literary apostolates for the ever–expanding Archdiocese of Los Angeles. The archbishop's office was still located at 1531 West Ninth Street.

In 1997, the curial offices were moved to a twelve story building at 3424 Wilshire Boulevard, the former headquarters of the Thrifty–Payless Drug Company.

CHICANO CATHOLIC CHURCH

According to the Bureau of Census, the largest group of Hispanic persons in the United States today are those Americans of Mexican origin, with upwards of 6.5 million members. Whatever the census takers call them, the increasing number of Mexican–Americans proudly refer to themselves as *Chicanos*, a word derived from the ending of the word "Mexicano," which Aztecs pronounced "Meschicano."

The "sh" sound doesn't exist in the Spanish language, so the conquistadors simply put an "X" wherever unfamiliar sounds occurred. The word "Mexicano," shortened to "Xicano" (pronounced "shicano") finally became "Chicano." At the *La Raza Unida* Conference, in El Paso in 1967, young Mexican–American youth leaders called themselves "Chicanos," and the word took hold as a symbol of pride among many Mexican–Ameriacans.

The Chicanos have much reason to be proud. Centuries before Christopher Columbus was born, their predecessors, Mayas and Aztecs, had founded a sophisticated civilization in the hemisphere. And, by the time the Pilgrim Fathers struggled ashore along our eastern seaboard, the Chicanos' forebears already had at least twenty–five missions and some ninety communities well established in what is now Texas, New Mexico, Utah, Colorado, Kansas and Nebraska.

As often happens when people join a nation through war and conquest, the Mexican–Americans became victims of prejudice. The Treaty of Guadalupe–Hidalgo promised them full citizenship and property rights, but that pledge was not fully honored. Many of the new Americans lost their lands and even their language was taken from them. Testifying in court in Spanish became illegal.

As recently as World War II, some states permitted discrimination against Mexican–Americans at lunch counters, bars and hotels. In many places, separate times were set up for Mexican–Americans to use department stores and recreational areas.

In spite of this, Mexican–Americans served with extraordinary distinction during World War II. Infantrymen of the all–Chicano Company E, 141st Regiment of the 36th Division became one of the nation's most decorated groups. Seventeen Mexican–American servicemen won Congressional Medals of Honor. And that tradition continued in Vietnam. Although Hispanic Americans made up less than 8% of the national population, they represented 21% of our casualties in Vietnam.

Since World War II, however, Mexican–Americans have developed new unity and determination to win their fair share of rights and opportunities as citizens. Discrimination has been fading in response to efforts by Chicano groups and leadership of people like Cesar Chavez, Reies Tijerina and Rodolfo Gonzales. As a group, Chicanos are using the vote to get things done. A growing cluster of Chicano representatives is in Congress, the state legislatures and governorships. They are working at the grass–roots level to change things the democratic way.

The Catholic Church has been at the forefront of efforts to share the American dream with peoples of Hispanic origin. Pope Gregory XVI named Mexican–born Fray Francisco Garcia Diego y Moreno the first Bishop for the Diocese of Both Californias in 1840. From that time to the present, the Church in California has marched under the banner of Our Lady of Guadalupe—before whose shrine in Mexico City the proto bishop was given the insignia of his office.

All of which means that the Catholic Church in California was "Chicano" 167 years before the term was coined!

CHIEF CAHUENGA

Most dictionaries define legend as a narrative based chiefly, or even partly on tradition, hence of dubious veracity. One of California's more fanciful legends deals with "Cahuenga," allegedly an Indian chief for a tribe that inhabited the area now known as Hollywood.

The name itself probably came from a Gabrielino Shoshonean word. Used for three Mexican land grants, it is found repeatedly, with variant spellings, in documents issued since the 1840s. The name "Cahuenga" gained historical significance when Andres Pico surrendered to Captain John Fremont at *Campo de Cahuenga* on January 13, 1847. There was at one time an Indian *rancheria* called Cahuenga.

The "legend" of Cahuenga is generally attributed to Seward Cole who wrote about it in an old newspaper printed in the boom days of Hollywood. Then, in mid 1931, when attempts were being made to change the name of Cahuenga Pass and Lankershim Boulevard to Highland Avenue, Seymour Millikan updated the legend for the Los Angeles *Times Sunday Magazine*.

Early in 1771, according to Millikan's version of the legend, a large band of Indians swooped down from the region north of Tehachapi and fell upon Chief Cahuenga's people. After a desperate battle in which many were killed, the northern invaders withdrew, taking with them nearly a hundred captive women and children and leaving behind a number of their own warriors in the hands of Cahuenga's people.

Fray Junípero Serra who was then at San Gabriel Mission, heard about it and arranged to have a field hospital established to care for the wounded warriors of both sides. After a day or so, the friar learned that Cahuenga and his people were planning to roast alive their twenty–seven captives. Appalled, he went at once to the chief and pleaded for mercy.

"But that obdurate old heathen only chuckled with glee at the prospect of seeing his enemies writhing amid the flames, and the good father soon found that nothing could be done to divert him from his purpose."

When his efforts were rejected, Serra "with his utmost earnestness and well–known tact," proposed an exchange of prisoners, a totally foreign but attractive idea to the chief. The friar offered to personally arrange the exchange if Cahuenga would postpone the holocaust.

After a perilous journey of eight days, Serra reached the blue–wooded Tehachapi mountains surrounding a great lake of calm and beauty. After some diplomatic wire–pulling, the chieftains agreed to the proposal and released their captives to Serra's care. When they returned to the south, Cahuenga complied with the agreement and set his prisoners free.

The success of Serra's intervention, so novel in its purpose, added greatly to the friar's prestige among the Indians. In succeeding months, many of the tribe, including the chief, become neophytes at nearby San Gabriel Mission.

Is there any truth to the legend? Maybe yes, maybe no. It is not mentioned in Palou's life of Fray Junípero Serra, nor does the late Father Maynard J. Geiger record the story. But knowing Serra and his love for the Indians, it surely could have happened. And in the words of John Steven McGroarty, "there is ample room in the California story for legend. In imitation of the Bible, the Golden State surely deserves its apocrypha."

CHINESE CALENDAR OF ANIMALS

In an address given to a delegation from China, in 1906, Bishop Thomas J. Conaty thanked his visitors for inviting "the local Catholic bishop to greet you in this year of the Horse." Alluding to the place that the horse occupied in the development of the western United States, the bishop commended those born in that year, noting that "they would be popular, independent, cheerful and wise."

The Bishop of Monterey–Los Angeles had been a pastor, an educator and a university rector. Having dealt with people from all over the world, he was attuned to the cultural and religious sensitivities and diversities of Orientals as few others in the Los Angeles of 1906.

This essay is written in response to Conaty's observation that "we are all richer for knowing and studying about the traditions and practices of others." And, "where," asked the bishop, "but in Los Angeles could we have the opportunity of greeting such distinguished visitors in our own homes."

Chinese folklore relates how an early emperor once invited all the animals in his kingdom to share in a New Year's celebration. Twelve animals turned out to pay homage to the emperor and, in return, he named a year for each one. The proto day of the Chinese New Year falls on the first day of the new moon after the sun enters Aquarius. (On the Christian Gregorian calendar, used in the western world, it would fall somewhere between January 21st and February 20th.)

Unlike the western zodiac, which is divided into twelve months, the Chinese counterpart is a twelve year cycle. The animal which represents the year of a person's birth becomes his or her animal sign.

For centuries, the Chinese have believed that a person's animal sign helps to determine much of his or her character and human destiny. Very often decisions about such important issues as marriage, friendship and business are made according to the guildeline of one's animal sign. The twelve animals whose names are attached to the dozen year cycle are the Dragon, the Rat, the Ox, the Tiger, the Rabbit, the Snake, the Horse, the Sheep, the Monkey, the Rooster, the Dog and the Boar.

In order to calculate the cycle, and which year belongs to each animal, one can begin with the rat (in 1900). The years since then bearing that designation would be 1912, 1924, 1936, 1948, 1960, 1972, 1984, and 1996.

Here are some of the characteristics associated with the various years. The Dragon (1904, 1916, 1928, 1940, 1952, 1964, 1976 and 1988) would include people known for their honesty, brilliance, sensitivity and bravery. They can also be stubborn, short-tempered, excitable and fastidious.

Those born in the year of the Snake are generally wise, determined, passionate, beautiful and emphatic. Yet they can also be vain, obstinate, volatile and doubtful. The so–called "Dog" people (1910, 1922, 1934, 1946, 1958, 1970, 1982, and 1994) are loyal, trustworthy, patient, protective and honest. Many also tend to be exceedingly eccentric.

Bishop Conaty himself was born in the year of the Sheep (for shepherd?). He would have been (and truly was) elegant, artistic, gentle and wise. Those falling under the sign of the Sheep are also known for their leadership abilities.

While there had been Chinese in California since 1847 (the year Conaty was born), there isn't much indication that loyal leaders paid any serious attention to their cultural background. It all changed with Bishop Thomas J. Conaty.

CHRIST ON THE CROSS

The centerpiece of the Los Angeles County Museum of Art's 15th century gallery is a recently acquired altarpiece, "Christ on the Cross," thought to have been destroyed during World War II. It is plainly worth a trip to see.

Known more formally as "Christ on the Cross with Saints Mark, John the Baptist, Vincent Ferrer and Blessed Antonius," it was painted by an artist known only as the "Master of the Fiesole Epiphany." The richly–colored portrayal of a bejeweled Christ is surrounded by four holy men and a host of angels.

Now displayed in a new tabernacle frame carved by a Florentine craftsman to match the original, the altarpiece is a fine example of late 15th century art which, according to Curator Philip Conisbee, is a "beautiful and moving image."

The artist, probably a student of Domenico of Ghirlandaio, had earlier achieved fame for his majestic and unparalleled rendition of the Adoration of the Magi which was executed for a church near Florence. The "Christ on the Cross" was painted between 1485 and 1490 for the Chapel of the Holy Cross in the Dominican Church of San Marco in Florence, the place made famous because of its frescoes by Fra Angelico.

It was known chiefly by photographs until fairly recently. Removed in the 16th century while the chapel was being remodeled, the altarpiece disappeared until 1830, when it surfaced in England.

It was purchased by a collector in 1935 and hung as the collection centerpiece in Italy. When the home burned to the ground during the allied bombing raids, it was presumed that "Christ on the Cross" had also been destroyed.

Happily and unknown to the art world, the painting had been crated and moved to a nearby warehouse for storage. Though terribly dirty, the artistic masterpiece remained substantially intact, waiting only for the loving hand of a restorative artist. When the many layers of grime and varnish were removed, the painting was once again a stunning rendition of the *Christus*, with a startling range of vivid colors and distinctive patterns.

In an article for the Los Angeles *Times*, Suzanne Muchnic described how the painting depicts the Crucifixion, with Christ's body corresponding to the shape of a cross. "He is also a resurrected Christ who hovers above a chalice and displays the stigmata on his hand."

The Renaissance painting was purchased for the Los Angeles County Museum of Art with funds provided by the Ahmanson Foundation. The roughly 6 feet square altarpiece was placed on public exhibit in mid 1992. With the acquisition of "Christ on the Cross," LACMA filled a void in its holdings. The museum already had 16th and 17th century altarpieces, but lacked anything comparable for the 15th century.

And while there was no chance of getting a major work by Botticelli, Lippi or Ghirlandaio, "Christ on the Cross" is far more than an attractive substitute. It is unique in many ways, as viewers will readily agree.

"Christ on the Cross" is larger and more important

than the artist's other works in Fiesole, according to Conisbee. Indeed, the Curator feels that the painter rightly deserves a new moniker: "the Master of the Los Angeles Christ on the Cross."

THE CHRISTINES

Founded in December, 1949, the Christines was a Los Angeles woman's group that attempted to counteract the communist threat to world peace "through an activation of the social encyclicals and the Sermon on the Mount." The group came about through the efforts of Anne Sullivan Reber, a Los Angeles housewife who lived in Westwood. Anne's idea was to form a lay organization which could speak for Catholics in the southland.

She enlisted eleven other Catholic ladies in Saint Paul the Apostle parish as the "twelve nuclear apostles." Encouraged by the Paulist Fathers, the Christines expanded into eleven parishes where members regularly attended monthly meetings.

The pattern of their meetings was considerably more than a mere club gathering and something less than a full day spiritual retreat. Adapted to a busy mothers' routine, the meetings began at eleven o'clock with prayer, spiritual reading and the rosary led by a priest.

After lunch, which the ladies brought in brown bags, they engaged in intensive study and discussion periods which lasted far into the afternoon. These centered mainly upon papal encyclicals and the doctrinal and catechetical basis for the social apostolate.

The Christines quickly grew to a membership of 900. A threefold program of study, prayer and action involved them in discussions of Catholic social theory, industrial relations, interracial challenges, marriage problems and even the controversy then raging over the programs of the U.N. and UNESCO.

In a description of the work of the Christines, Jesuit Father Albert S. Foley wrote an essay in *Integrity* magazine in which he said that "in their obedience to the call of the Holy Father and in their quest for peace, these courageous ladies moved out into the arena of public life. Eventually, however, they were caught in the crossfire between the extreme rightists and the leftist," a factor which eventually thinned their ranks, crippled their organization and forced them to withdraw from many facets of their work.

In promoting Pope Pius XII's Fourteen Point Peace Plan, the Christines encountered resistance within the Los Angeles community from another allegedly Catholic group known as the American Public Relations Forum. The Forum initiated a campaign of intimidation against the Christines. Pressure was exerted on a local Catholic college to cancel its invitation to a Christine–sponsored program. That, in turn, caused a number of clergymen to rethink their association with the Christines.

After a while, following a barrage of doorbell ringing, phone calls and letters, even the parish that had given birth to the Christines hesitated to allow them to meet in its hall. In the Spring of 1953, the Christines got an interview with James Francis Cardinal McIntyre and presented him with a list of nineteen problems they had encountered. McIntyre assured Anne and the others that lay Catholics were free to follow the dictates of their own consciences in political affairs. Though the cardinal would not endorse the views expressed by the Christines, he never made any attempt to thwart their work.

In later years, the Christines withdrew from the arena of public affairs and reshaped their program along the patterns of a pious association, quietly pursuing the study of the Sacraments and eschewing all controversial topics.

CHRISTMAS IN 1849

(The following article is abridged from Santa Barbara's *Daily Press*, December 29, 1885)

"Our early California Christmases were passed very much as other days, quietly by the people in their houses, and there was no feasting or outward sign that the day was not like any other. The people were, in fact, preparing themselves for the coming celebration, for busy were the good parishioners with the church, decking it with evergreen for the performance of the *pastorela*. A few hours before midnight, the town was astir, and as my happiest recollections are with Monterey, let us speak of that city, which you know was the capital of California prior to the American occupation.

"About ten o'clock the townspeople began to dress for church, and long before the mystic hour of 12 struck they were assembled before the sacred edifice. It was indeed a decorous and solemn assemblage, for you know in those days there were no dissenting creeds; all were Catholics, and on Christmas Day all were good Catholics.

"Punctually at midnight, the church doors were thrown open, and what a sight greeted the congregation! The church was a mass of green, the altar was a dense mass of foliage, and at the foot of it was the grotto, where, in figures, sat the Holy Virgin with the infant Jesus. Right by it were the feeding oxen—in truth it was a perfect representation of the birth of Our Lord.

"When the congregation had filed into the church, the *pastorela* commenced. Then could be seen the six or eight shepherds who sang the holy hymn and who reverently brought and laid before the Babe their offerings.

And pretty offerings they were too, consisting of honey and sweet incense and other donations, to resemble the biblical story. Then, in the distance, came a body of holy men who had come to pay reverence, and among them were the three magi, or wise men. The devil himself was impersonated, with all his terrible equipment of horns, hoofs, and tail; and he went about the assemblage whispering to them and attempting to prevent the good men from carrying out their intentions. Then came one who would seem to be a priest and between him and the devil there would take place a long discussion, the devil of course sneering and mocking at their devotion, and the priest attempting vainly to convince his satanic majesty of the error of his ways. The Star of Bethlehem would also appear, and in truth everything was done to give a realistic appearance to the performance.

"I would have you bear in mind that there was no burlesque about this. It was intended and played as a holy performance, a play which would more vividly call to remembrance this great event in Christianity.

"The *pastorela* occupied about one hour and a half, and when it was over, all withdrew to their several homes. Everyone was welcome. No man was made to feel that he was a stranger in a foreign land, for Christmas Day was really a day which brought peace to men of good will. The supper that followed was a grand one, and the principal feature of it was the abundance of fish cooked in as many different ways as the ingenuity of its preparer prompted. This feast was called the *aguinaldo* or in other words keepsake. No person left the home without being presented with some little token of the happy day. Generally the presents would be made by the young ladies of the household, and consisted of some pretty little hand–worked ornament or a handkerchief or scarf. After the *aguinaldo* was finished, at which were also given some specially prepared sweetmeats, those who were not too tired, paid a call upon the governor and serenaded him. With this, terminated the festivities of Christmas Day, for mind you, when the parties broke up, the day of December 26th had well advanced."

Thus were spent Christmas days in Monterey, Santa Barbara, San Diego, San Jose and San Francisco, in the days when California was under Mexican rule.

CHRISTMAS IN EARLY CALIFORNIA

A. MISSION ERA

The earliest known descriptions of Christmas in Alta California were written by Fray Juan Crespi and can be found in the diary which he kept while accompanying Governor Gaspar de Portolá on his trek to Monterey in 1769.

In the entry for December 24th, the friar recorded that "on this day before Christmas . . . we set out on the same road by which we came. . . . The march covered three leagues and we halted on the identical spot as on the 10th of September, which was in the valley of *El Osito de San Buenaventura*. It was God's will that we should celebrate the Nativity joyfully, which was done in this way:

> More than two hundred unbaptized natives of both sexes came to visit us, bringing us Christmas gifts, for many of them came with good baskets of *pinole* and some fish, with which everybody supplied himself, so that we had something with which to celebrate Christmas Day. Blessed be the Providence of God, who gives us more than we deserve.

The entry for the following day was not so joyful. "On this day of the Nativity, we could not celebrate in any other means than by offering Holy Mass. . . . The cold is so biting that it gives us good reason to meditate upon what the Infant Jesus, who was born on this day in Bethlehem, suffered for us."

The friar went on to write that "we made three leagues and a half today, and went to stop a little further to the south of the estuary of Santa Serafina, close to a small village of Indian fishermen, from whom a great deal of fish was obtained, in exchange for beads."

It was there "that we celebrated Christmas with this dainty, which tasted better to everyone than capons and chickens had tasted in other places, because of the good sauce of San Bernardo hunger which we all had in abundance."

In the winter of 1775–1776, Captain Juan Bautista de Anza led 240 persons, including thirty soldiers, twenty–nine soldiers' wives, four families of colonists, 115 children, 355 head of cattle and 450 saddle horses and pack mules overland from Sonora to Monterey. At the Christmas season, the de Anza caravan camped in Coyote Canyon, in present–day Riverside County. It was a cold and foggy time. Three children had been born between the *presidio* of Tubac in southern Arizona and Coyote Canyon, and one woman had died.

On December 24th, the soldiers drank brandy given to them by their commander. That afternoon, Fray Pedro Font heard the confession of Gertruda Linares, a soldier's wife, who had been in labor since the day before. Gertuda was afraid she was going to die, so the priest consoled her and then returned to his tent. At half past eleven at night, she gave birth to a son. Font noted in his diary that "because a little before midnight on this Holy Night of the Nativity, the wife of a soldier happily gave birth to a son, and because the day was raw and foggy, it was decided we should remain here and I solemnly baptized the boy, naming him Salvador Ygnacio."

Later on, when the missions had been established and life had become normalized in California, the friars taught the Indians to play the flute, violin, bass viol, trumpet and metal triangle and to sing a plain chant or Gregorian Christ's Mass (Christmas) in Latin and *villancicos* or carols in Spanish. For those attached to the missions, the Feast of the Nativity was the most festive day of the year.

Gloria a Dios en las alturas y paz al hombre en la tierra!

CHRISTMAS IN EARLY CALIFORNIA

B. LATER TIMES

During the earliest centuries of the Christian era, the Feast of Our Lord's Nativity was celebrated on different dates. At various places the occasion was commemorated on January 6th, February 2nd, March 25th, April 19th, May 20th and November 17th.

The variation was probably compounded by the five different systems for reckoning times that were used in differing geographical areas of the world during those years. Saint John Chrysostom related that in the fourth century, Pope Julius I sought advice on the matter from knowledgeable historical and scriptural authorities. Concluding that December 25th was the most likely date, he decreed, in 353, that henceforth Christmas be observed on that day.

Thus it came about that *Kerst–Misse* in Holland, Noel in France, *Weihnachten* in Germany, *El Natal* in Spain and *Christes Mass* or Christmas in the United States is observed on December 25th. Whether this is the true and authentic day for observing the Lord's birth or not (and many scholars contend that it is NOT), it has since become a hallowed feast for peoples of many religious persuasions.

In 1909, the San Francisco *Call* published the reminiscences of Joseph J. McCloskey and Hermann J. Sharmann, two sturdy goldrushers who recalled their hardships on Christmas day a half century earlier, in 1849. McCloskey recalled that he once was wandering through the goldfields with two companions, Steve and Mat, after the trio had lost nearly all their provisions and tools in a flash flood. While fixing breakfast one morning, Mat looked up and exclaimed:

"Good Lord, boys!" he says. "Do you know that this is Christmas?" Well, it was pretty tough, coming that way. I felt as if some one had pulled a prop away from under me with a jerk. We stared at each other a minute and then we all looked away again. It was Christmas. The land was green and pleasant, but it had lost its charm for us. . . . It was the first time I had ever been away from my mother at that time of the year.

I'm not ashamed to say that I stepped away from my companions, went around to the other side of the bushes and sat down and cried. I was pretty young. Through that solitude, in the untrodden wilderness, 100 miles from any living soul, there came the musical chant of voices. Sweet and true the melody filtered down to us through the trees "*Adeste, Fideles*," the hymn of all hymns for Christmas!

We looked up, baring our heads mechanically. I don't think we would have been surprised after the first strain to see a troop of angels among the branches. . . . Steve let out a whoop and dashed on up the hill. We followed him to the top and in a little open space we found our angels. There were four of them, young men from Boston.

It appeared that they had belonged to a church choir and traveled to California together. They were in the hills prospecting and were making the most of their Christmas.

They were well supplied with provisions, flour and sugar and bacon, and they welcomed us joyfully. You may be sure we were grateful to the Lord.

CHRISTMAS CARD IN CALIFORNIA

For Californians, whose state's economy ranks sixth among the family of nations, the exchange of Christmas cards has become an unavoidable, yet curiously revelatory means of communication. Denounced as illogical, frivolous and unnecessary, Christmas cards have become, nonetheless, an institutionalized part of American life, representing handsome profits for two hundred manufacturers and thousands of retailers scattered throughout the United States.

The colorful harbinger of holiday cheer has an historic background, rich in originality, romance and inspiration. The practice of sending and receiving yuletide cards, a rekindling of the ancient tradition whereby small tokens of affection were bestowed upon loved ones, can be traced to the early years of England's Victorian Era.

Sir Henry Cole, an art dealer and publisher, is credited with dispatching the first printed Christmas greeting, in 1843. His initial card, designed by a well–established artist, John Calcott Horsley, was printed from a lithographic stone on a single stiff cardboard, measuring 51 by 31 inches, with dark sepia ink.

About a thousand of those "proto–Christmas cards," produced by Jobbins of Warwick Court, Holborn, were circulated by Felix Summerly's Home Treasury Office, located at 12 Old Bond Street, London. A rotund English gentleman and his family are portrayed around the wassail bowl toasting their friends. The side panels contain elaborately–executed scenes of feeding the hungry and clothing the naked.

The first Nativity greeting in the United States was a

lithograph produced in the early 1850s, by Richard H. Pease, an engraver and merchandiser from Albany, New York. Subsequent development of the trade, however, is generally associated with Louis Pranz, who strides through the annals as the "Father of the American Christmas Card." Today, the purveyors of Pranz's brain-child preside over a multi–million dollar operation, employing thousands of people and producing more than 2.5 billion cards annually.

The deplorable absence of a Christian theme on mod-ern–day cards prolongs a custom evident from the earli-est times. Studies of Victorian collections indicate little fluctuation in the percentage of "religious cards" circu-lated in the last century, even for those areas of predom-inantly Christian persuasion. Apparently, from its beginning, the greeting card was more closely identified with the season's social aspect than with its religious origins.

Since World War II, the trend has ever–so–gradually shifted to a greater emphasis on the central theme of Christmas. Hopefully, in the years ahead, the spiritual significance of the Nativity, portrayed artistically more than any other single episode in history, will also be reflected more substantially in Christmas greeting cards.

Perhaps, by putting Christ into Christmas cards the universal practice of exchanging seasonal wishes, fre-quently followed from mere conventionality, will become a means for "ending strifes, cementing broken friendships and strengthening family and neighbor ties in all conditions of life."

CHRISTMAS TREE

High in the Sierra Nevada Mountains of Central Cal-ifornia, in the Kings Canyon National Park, stands an ancient and majestic *Sequoia gigantea*. The General Grant Tree is known to the world as the nation's Christ-mas Tree. Each year since 1925, on a Sunday in Decem-ber, people of all faiths make a fifty–four mile pilgrimage from Sanger, California, to hold a religious ceremony at the tree.

A Christmas wreath is placed at the foot of the tree by the Superintendent of Kings Canyon and Sequoia National Parks. Hymns are sung by choirs and guests of all denominations. Scripture readings, prayers, invoca-tions, a homily and other religious services are con-ducted by the clergy of different faiths.

This Sierra redwood, thought to be from 3,000 to 4,000 years old, is one of the oldest living things on earth. It was 500 years old when King David composed his beautiful psalter, 1,500 years old when the Christ Child was born and more than 3,000 years old on July 4, 1776, when United States independence was pro-

claimed. Standing 267 feet high, with a 107–foot cir-cumference and a forty foot diameter, it would take more than twenty men, women and children, holding hands to form a chain around its base.

People come to see the ancient Sequoia from all parts of the United States. In 1925, Charles E. Lee, a local res-ident, thought the General Grant Tree deserved the honor of being designated as the nation's Christmas Tree. The following year he registered the request with the Department of the Interior. That same year, the first annual religious ceremonials were held at Christmas time.

On April 28, 1926, the tree was formally dedicated as the nation's Christmas Tree. Thirty years later, on March 29, 1956, by an act of Congress, it became a national shrine. Fleet Admiral Chester Nimitz, repre-senting President Dwight D. Eisenhower, dedicated the tree as a "living memorial to those men and women of the armed forces who since the beginning of our country have made the supreme sacrifice."

An old Indian legend tells about the grove of giant trees—sugar pines, ponderosa, silver fir and the grandest of them all, the *Sequoia gigantea*. The legend contends that the Great Spirit created the tree when he was in one of his happiest moods. The tree was first seen by white men in 1858. The news of the giant tree drew visitors from far and near. It was named for the eighteenth Pres-ident of the United States, by Lucretia Parker, in 1867. The Chief Executive later wrote to Mrs. Parker and thanked her for the honor of having his name attached to what was believed to be the largest of the big trees. A living symbol of immortality, the General Grant Tree is scarred and beaten by time and the elements. It is dedi-cated to the theme of "Peace on earth to men of good will."

How fitting it is that this ancient Sequoia, which was growing in the Sierra Nevada Mountains on the night the Infant Jesus was born, should be known in the annals as the official Christmas Tree for the United States of America!

CHRISTOPHER MOVEMENT

For over forty years, the Christopher Movement has been emphasizing God's claim over His people, encour-aging individuals to use their talents well for God by responding to the movement of the Spirit. The founder of this remarkable movement which now reaches people in 125 nations, was a native of Oakland. James Keller was born on June 27, 1900. He entered Saint Patrick's Seminary in 1914. Later he left to work in his family's business, but returned the following year.

We know from his autobiography that while pursuing

his theological studies at Menlo Park, "a small party of missionary priests led by Father James Anthony Walsh visited St. Patrick's on their way to China." They were part of a new organization called Maryknoll. Keller was "deeply impressed by the forthright manner of these frontier–breaking men of God, and the missionary side of the Church took on a new and deeper meaning" to him.

In 1920, Keller asked for and was given permission by Archbishop Edward J. Hanna to join this new group. Five years later he was ordained a priest in his home parish of Saint Francis de Sales in Oakland. To his great disappointment, however, he was not sent overseas but was chosen to do promotional work at home.

The youthful Father Keller went from city–to–city gaining friends and supporters for Maryknoll. He preached a message of hope: God calls each one to some specific task; the individual is important; one person can make a difference.

In 1945, Father Keller founded The Christophers out of the conviction that, with God's help, a single person can do something to change the world for the better. The name "Christopher" is taken from the Greek and means "Christ–bearer." Tirelessly, Keller proclaimed the Christopher ideal by stimulating millions to show personal responsibility and individual initiative in raising the standards of all phases of human endeavor.

His famous book, *You Can Change the World*, was published in 1948 and was an instant best seller. Later Keller launched *Christopher News Notes* which were sent to nearly a million people seven times a year. Weekly radio and television programs, inspirational commercials and a daily newspaper column brought the Christopher message to a world starving for spiritual nourishment.

To accentuate the positive, Keller adopted as the Christopher motto the Chinese proverb, "Better to light one candle than to curse the darkness." The Prayer of Saint Francis became the daily supplication of millions.

Keller, a man of prayer, great hope and magnificent vision, was consumed with the idea of reaching as many people as he could in his lifetime with the love and truth of Christ. Though ill health forced his retirement in 1969, Father Keller continued to assist the Christopher Movement until his death in New York City on February 7, 1977

His autobiography, *To Light a Candle*, embodied Keller's message that "Our Lord and Savior, Jesus Christ, had given mankind the divine formula nearly two thousand years ago. All the Christopher Movement is trying to do is to encourage people to apply it to modern times. The idea is far from new or original—it is as old as the hills of Galilee."

COLLEGE OF THE CARDINALS IN CALIFORNIA

A faint thread of purple moire or watered–silk in California's Catholic Heritage can be traced to September 17, 1875. In a letter to his cousin, Luigi Cardinal Amat, the Right Reverend Thaddeus Amat, Bishop of Monterey–Los Angeles, expressed his happiness about Pius IX's elevation of New York's Archbishop John McCloskey to the cardinalate, noting that "someday, possibly within a century. that honor will come to Los Angeles." The Vincentian prelate went on to say that "when I asked the Holy Father to move [my] episcopal *sedes*, it was from a contention that Los Angeles would one day rank among the great cities of the republic and even the world." Bishop Amat concluded by observing that he was planning "a cathedral fit for an eminent Cardinal!"

The Golden State was honored, in the latter part of 1887, with a visit by James Cardinal Gibbons, the ranking dignitary of the Catholic Church in the United States. After a brief stop in San Francisco, the prelate proceeded to the southland. The first cardinalatial visitation to the City of Our Lady of the Angels began with a liturgical ceremony at Saint Vibiana's Cathedral and an official greeting by the Right Reverend Francis Mora, Bishop of Monterey–Los Angeles.

In responding, His Eminence of Baltimore observed that the growth and progress of the Pacific Coast far exceeded his "wildest expectations." The prelate went on to say that "the glory of your State after all lies not so much in your climate and soil, but your prosperity consists in your manhood, intelligence and the zeal and earnestness which the American people bring to every enterprise they undertake." The cardinal's biographer later wrote that the presence of Gibbons in the far west "aroused a great deal of interest and enthusiasm among the Catholic people of those regions. It was their first glimpse of a prince of the Church, and their pride in playing host to a member of the College of Cardinals was heightened when they observed the generally friendly manner in which their non–Catholic friends and neighbors greeted the visitor."

On October 15, 1902, a half century before the distinction actually came to California, a world–wide news agency reported that the favorable decision handed down by the International Court of Arbitration concerning the Pious Fund of the Californias was a sweeping victory for San Francisco's Archbishop Patrick W. Riordan. It would make him, according to the story, "a prominent figure when the question of the next cardinal for the United States comes up."

The cardinalatial dignity ultimately came to the Golden State, in 1953, with Pope Pius XII's bestowal of the red hat on James Francis McIntyre, Archbishop of

Los Angeles. The nation's twelfth cardinal was welcomed by the Catholic populace of the southland, in Amat's "cathedral fit for an eminent Cardinal," on January 21, 1953

The distinction was renewed, two popes and twenty years later by Pope Paul VI's elevation of Archbishop Timothy Manning, as America's twenty–eighth member of the Sacred College.

Los Angeles, one of the nine cities in the continental United States honored with the cardinalate over a span of ninety–eight years, enjoyed the further distinction of being one of the four ecclesial jurisdictions in all the world possessing two living cardinals at one time.

Cardinals are commonly referred to as "brothers of the Pope," a terminology especially apt for the shepherd of God's People in Southern California. There is much that binds the City of *Nuestra Señora de los Angeles* to the See of Peter.

One writer conjectured, at the turn of the century, that Los Angeles was destined to become "to the world in its day what Roman civilization at its purest was to its." Such it has become.

Father Henry L. Walsh, the eminent Jesuit historian, once commented that there was an "air of nobility in the bishops" chosen by the Vicar of Christ to watch over the spiritual destinies of California. Each of them measured up to the Pauline requirements of apostolic zeal, extraordinary charity and unswerving faithfulness to the People of God.

Timothy Cardinal Manning embodied that tradition in a more "eminent" manner, giving substance to James Gibbon's observation that "it is not the cardinal who ennobles the man, but the man who ennobles the cardinal."

COLMA — CALIFORNIA'S NECROPOLIS

There's no priest shortage in Colma, California. Guestimates place the number of Catholic clergymen there at upwards of 1,500, probably the largest concentration in any incorporated city outside of Rome.

Unhappily, the sacerdotal population of the town are all dead. Colma is a necropolis whose 1.5 million residents are all tucked away in one or another of the sixteen cemeteries that line the quiet streets.

In a recent interview, Ted Kirschner, the mayor of Colma, said that "you could call us the Death capital of the United States." More burial permits are issued there daily than in any other American jurisdiction.

Kirschner claims to "have more corpses packed into our two–square mile town than any other comparable area in the country." He said that's why folks "have nicknamed our town "Coma.""

The name Colma first appears in the Wells Fargo & Company's Express Directory for 1872. Possibly the name derives from Walter T. Coleman, the "Lion of the Vigilantes," who lived in the area during the 1870s. There is also an Alsace a Colmar in Switzerland.

There are no grocery stores, hospitals, schools, libraries, post offices or churches in the small suburb of San Francisco in San Mateo county. What it does have are graves—lots of them.

The president of the local historical society notes that "we have governors, congressmen and a bevy of San Francisco mayors at rest here. We have the famed gunslinger Wyatt Earp, who died in 1929—forty years after his legendary gunfight at the O.K. Corral in Tombstone, Arizona." Another resident is the original "Citizen Kane," newspaper magnate William Randolph Hearst. There are also lesser known people buried in Colma, including circus clowns, Alcatraz inmates, a former emperor and a Hell's Angel named "Harry the Horse" who was buried with his Harley Davidson.

Scores of skilled artisans work in the town, from gravestone makers to mausoleum builders. The cemeteries are designed to fit every taste and need, from fancy mausoleums to frill–free tombstones.

There are cemeteries for Catholics, Protestants, Jews, Japanese, Chinese, Serbians, Italians and Greeks. There is even a pet cemetery, where rock star Tina Turner's pooch is interred wrapped in a fur coat.

Since the inauguration of Holy Cross Cemetery at Colma, on June 7, 1887, well over 95% of the local Catholic clergymen have been buried there. All of San Francisco's archbishops are interred in Holy Cross Mausoleum which was opened in 1921. Even the remains of California's first archbishop, Joseph Sadoc Alemany (1814–1888) are now at Colma, moved there in 1965 from their original resting place in Vich, Spain.

Unlike other cities in California and throughout the United States, Colma is financially sound. Though business is "dead," the city's coffers are overflowing, with a typical annual surplus of $500,000.

Julie Kirschner enjoyed growing up in the necropolis. She was instrumental in designing the bumper stickers passed out at the Town Hall which carry the words: "It's Great to be Alive in Colma."

CONFRATERNITY OF CHRISTIAN DOCTRINE

The origins of the Confraternity of Christian Doctrine can be traced to Milan and the establishment there of the first "Schools of Christian Doctrine" by Father Castellino de Castello, in 1536. The movement was re–vitalized by Pope Pius X in his encyclical letter, *Acerbo Nimis*, of 1905.

The practicality of founding a branch of the CCD in the Diocese of Monterey–Los Angeles was initially broached by Verona Spellmire, a public school teacher long active in catechetical work among the ever–growing community of Mexican–Americans. Father Robert Emmet Lucey, Director of Catholic Charities, was responsive to the idea and arranged for a series of exploratory discussions during which the need for a local unit of the Confraternity was thoroughly studied.

Episcopal endorsement came on March 11, 1922, with Bishop John J. Cantwell's call for an organizational meeting at which he gave his unqualified approval of the CCD. Father William J. Mullane was named director of the new unit which closely followed the pattern of the Pittsburgh Missionary Confraternity in its activities among the immigrants scattered through the rural districts of southwestern Pennsylvania.

While the work of the CCD in Los Angeles was not restricted to Hispanic immigrants, it was among that segment of the Catholic population that its earliest and most far–reaching accomplishments were realized. The first foundation, on the parochial level, was made at Saint Mary's Church in East Los Angeles. On April 16, 1923, a formal constitution was approved, and, shortly thereafter, the initial catechetical center was opened under the patronage of Santa Maria at Belvedere Park.

The apostolate was warmly supported by Bishop Cantwell who expressed grave concern for the "thousands of children in and around our city, especially among our immigrants, who are in danger of being lost to the faith" through lack of proper catechetical instruction. Of those heeding the prelate's invitation for personal involvement in the CCD objectives, more than 300 completed the training course and qualified for assignment in one or another of the twelve centers in key locations of the diocese.

Further expansion came, on March 5, 1924, when the bishop lent his support to the parish unit system of organization which he endorsed for adoption in all of Southern California. With the establishment of a Diocesan Union of Confraternities, minutely structured programs were inaugurated for teacher–training, home visitation, transportation of students and relief to the poor and needy. What began as a missionary movement on behalf of children living in the immigrant districts had blossomed into a well–knit bond of parochial confraternities.

A new phase of involvement came in the years after 1926, with the appointment of Father Leroy Callahan to the directorship. Among the first of his innovations was the affiliation of the Los Angeles branch with the Archconfraternity of Christian Doctrine in Rome. Father Callahan, a recognized scholar, initiated a series of model catechetical lessons which was widely utilized as a pioneering handbook for CCD teachers, Within a few years,

some thirty–five comparable publications were circulating around the country bearing the Los Angeles imprint.

In 1928, the CCD ambit was further enlarged to encompass courses for religious vacation schools. *The Handbook of Suggestions for the Daily Vacation School*, first compilation of its kind ever produced, was subsequently adopted by over fifty centers in the eastern and southern parts of the United States.

The planning, vitality and spirit of CCD activities in the Diocese of Los Angeles–San Diego prompted similar undertakings in other areas. Father Callahan's hope of seeing the Confraternity established nationally was championed, in the early 1930s, by Father Edwin V. O'Hara of the Catholic Rural Life Conference who recognized the program's merits and its relevance to the Church on the national scene.

To O'Hara, the Los Angeles plan provided a partial answer to the perplexing challenge posed by the tremendous numbers of children unable to participate directly in the already functioning Catholic school system.

There were other epoch–making proposals emanating from California's southland such as the formation, within the CCD framework, of teacher institutes and study groups to better equip members for their particular apostolate. By 1936, the Confraternity of Christian Doctrine in Los Angeles was a vital organization with an effective catechetical program reaching the largest number of public school children in the country.

The manifold accomplishments of the Confraternity of Christian Doctrine in its earliest years helped to create interest, encourage programs and upgrade instruction in CCD activities in practically every area of the nation. Eventually, a goodly portion of the country's affiliated branches had adopted the basic guidelines used so effectively in Southern California.

COPA DE ORO

There have been several books published with recipes of old Spanish California dishes. Here are some typical items served in the Monterey home of Maria Antonia Field on feastdays and holy days. . . .

Albóndigas—meat balls, mixed with bread, eggs and lard, seasoned with mint, thyme, crushed garlic and saffron, boiled in water, or soup stock, also seasoned with onion, thyme and mint.

Conserva de calabaza—pumpkin preserves made by cutting pumpkin into pieces about two inches in length, cutting off the rind, soaking in lime over night, boiling several hours with plenty of sugar and water, seasoning with sections of orange, lemon and cloves. Pumpkin becomes almost candied. It is delicious. The syrup is excellent for *buñuelos*.

Empanadas—These delicious "turnovers" were made of dough rolled thin and filled with apple sauce or any berry or fruit preserves. Also, they may be filled with purée of pumpkin, sweetened, or they may be filled with meat hash, containing raisins and chopped hard boiled egg. There are also *empanadas de frijol*—for which the filling is made of cooked beans, seasoned with onion, and fried in their natural gravy. Then the *empanada* is pierced with a fork and fried lightly in deep fat. The bean *empanada*, properly made, is substantial, but not nearly as rich or heavy as may be imagined.

Guizado—(stew) may be made of potatoes and hard boiled eggs, cut in pieces, and stewed in water seasoned with tomato and minced onion. Or a good *guizado* may be made of meat and potatoes seasoned the same way. Soup stock may be used instead of water for stewing, or half water and half soup stock.

Aroz guizado—put rice, minced onion and garlic into a skillet of well heated lard, stir until golden brown, then pour water, in proportion of two cups of water to one cup of rice, pepper and salt to taste, then simmer until rice is tender, but do not stir, once you have put water in skillet. If the rice gets too dry, add a little more water as needed. It must be moist, but not mushy. If desired, small pieces of sweet pimento, prawns or Spanish sausage may be added to rice, about five minutes before taking off the stove.

Chiles rellenos—(stuffed peppers) select green peppers, clean and skin them, by putting them in the oven long enough to loosen the skins—stuff with minced cheese and onion, or with meat hash with raisins and minced hard boiled egg and roll in egg batter, fry lightly, then cover with water or soup stock seasoned with tomato and let simmer about forty minutes.

Carne adobáda—put beef, pork or venison roast into porcelain bowl, cover with half water, half vinegar, seasoned with rosemary, thyme and crushed cloves of garlic. Allow to stand for three days, then roast, using some of the vinegar and seasonings for basting.

Salsa de chile verde y tomate—may be made easily with canned pepper and tomato. Mince equal parts of green pepper and tomato. If fresh tomatoes and peppers are used, they must be skinned, and peppers freed from seed. Add minced onion, salt, oil and vinegar to taste. Enough vinegar is needed to impart tartness. Makes excellent sauce to serve with meat, especially with roast or broiled steak.

Buñuelos—lightly fried tortillas, made of egg batter, rolled very thin, fried until just golden. When cold, break into large pieces, and heat well in syrup just before serving.

These are some of the tasty dishes served in the California of an earlier era. And all these goodies came before today's fast food shortcuts.

CORNERSTONES

Many significant ecclesial buildings and most churches erected in this area of the Lord's vineyard have a cornerstone which was put into place with appropriate ceremonial fanfare. With a stage–setting of dust and dirt, fallen mortar, broken bricks, unfinished concrete and scattered scaffolding, this impressive ceremony is usually performed by a local religious or civic dignitary.

As soon as the foundations are laid and the walls are ready to receive the cornerstone, the Church invokes the blessing of God on this stone and on the foundations which it supports. The liturgical setting is designed to manifest that all the work must begin with the help of God and must be built on the rock, which is Christ. Therefore, the directives call for the singing or chanting of Psalm 128 which begins: "Except the Lord build the house, they toil in vain who erect it.

In a very strict sense, it appears that the cornerstone should be a real foundation stone; the first, as it were, to be laid. The stone is to have a real as well as a figurative role in the finished building.

Precisely when this practice of blessing cornerstones began is not easily determined. A twelfth century English liturgist notes that "when the foundations have been dug, it is necessary that the bishop sprinkle the place with holy water, and that he or some other priest lay the first stone of the foundation."

In a wider sense, however, the cornerstone may be understood as a block of stone placed in a prominent part of the foundation on which the superstructure of the church or other building is to be erected. This stone is to unite the walls into a single unit.

The Old Testament mentions cornerstones many times, often appling the term symbolically to the future redeemer: "Behold, I will lay a stone in the foundation of Sion, a tried stone, a cornerstone, a precious stone, located in the foundation." (Isaias 20, 26) In the Psalms it was foretold of Christ: "The stone which the builders rejected, has become the cornerstone; by the Lord has this been done, and it is wonderful in our eyes."

In his letter to the Ephesians, Saint Paul tells us: Jesus Christ, Himself, being the Chief cornerstone, in Whom all the building being framed together, grows into a holy temple of the Lord." Thus Christ is to be the cornerstone of every church and Church–related building, binding together the foundations and the joints of the walls in fulfillment of Holy Scripture.

In form, the cornerstone ordinarily is a hewn block of stone in which there is a cavity. Not only has the laying of the cornerstone a deeply religious meaning, but it also has a definite historical significance.

Into this cavity in the cornerstone there is customarily placed a small metal box, containing a written record of all pertinent matters of the day. Perhaps a local newspaper, parish bulletin or other records of the events can be added. Various coins of the realm and other suitable memorabilia are often included.

Usually an inscription of some kind is chiseled on the outside of the stone to convey briefly what is contained inside. With the inscription are the dates and other useful information.

CORONATION OF THE VIRGIN

The colorful stained glass window in the church at San Fernando Mission depicts the "Coronation of the Virgin." It is surely among the finest such portrayals in California's southland. The window was probably executed by one of the Meyer studios in Germany during the mid 1920s. It was one of several windows installed in the Chapel of the Miraculous Medal, Saint Vincent's Hospital, Los Angeles, in 1927.

Blessed early in 1928, the window remained in place for the following forty–seven years in the lovely chapel erected by the widow of John Fillmore Francis. Of all the artistic expressions in the "oldest hospital in the metropolitan area of Los Angeles," none surpassed the "Coronation of the Virgin." When the chapel was dismantled in 1975, the window was removed, crated and placed in storage by Isabel and Edith Piczek. In 1985, the window was reframed and installed in the balcony of the church at San Fernando Mission in memory of Joseph L. Szajko.

The German style of the window is shown in the delicacy of the flesh and fine detailing in the garments and background. There is also a careful use of silver stain to produce the delicate, yet bright, yellow golds. Soft flesh and gray enamels are used in the hair and flesh as subtle shading and highlights. Stick lighting in the half toning is also very typical of this style.

Walter W. Judson, a local designer and craftsman of stained glass, graciously journeyed to the Old Mission to look at the "Coronation of the Virgin." His fascinating report of the window is the basis for these reflections.

Central is the Blessed Virgin kneeling with her arms folded across her breast, her eyes cast slightly down and head tilted a little to the side, all signs of humility and acceptance. This pose is similar to the one in which she would be shown at the Annunciation saying: "Be it done to me according to Your word." She is robed in blue for heavenly strength and white and gold for purity. White represents purity as an abstract concept and gold, like the metal, represents purity in concrete terms. The Blessed Mother's nimbus is golden with stars to remind viewers of Revelation XII, and upon her hand a crown of twelve stars."

God the Father is shown as the regal Old One with gray hair and full robes. He holds the orb representing His creation and above the orb is a cross meaning that creation will be fulfilled with the rule of Christ. The Father is in purple, the color of royalty. His nimbus is triangular depicting Him as the Father. God the Son is robed in ruby, green–white and white. His nimbus is of white with gold in a treform, reserved to the Trinity. He holds a scepter or staff representing His authority and as a symbol of the Second Coming.

God the Holy Spirit is shown as the descending dove with graceful rays emanating from His being etched onto the crown held by the Father and the Son. Finally, the setting is depicted as heaven shown by the clouds and stars and by the edges of the open gates of heaven between the outer border and the figures of the Father and Son.

While purists will point out that stained glass was not used in mission times, they will admit that the reason was because of its inaccessibility. The contemporary churches in Europe abounded in that artistic medium. Had stained glass been available in the 1700s, the California missions would certainly have been adorned with it. So perhaps it is only right that at least one window in the rosary of missions be endowed with stained glass.

CORPORATION SOLE IN CALIFORNIA

Corporation Sole is a term applied to a person, some of whose rights and liabilities are permitted by law to pass to his successors in a particular office, rather than to his heirs, executors or administrators. Such corporations are chiefly designed to insure the proper devolution of property pertaining to ecclesiastical establishments upon legitimate successors.

The process is one not common to the entire United States but regulated by individual state legislatures, some of whom "have leaned against it, believing that the church was asking for an undue privilege."

In other states no such legislation has been sought and bishops have hence been held not to possess corporate rights. In still other states, legal decisions have gone as far as creating quasi corporations sole without any express legislative authority.

The first American provision for Corporation Sole, passed by the Maryland Legislature on March 23, 1833, decreed,

> That it shall and may be lawful to, and for the trustees of any Roman Catholic Church, in whom the title to any lot or lots of ground, whereon any Roman Catholic Church is now erected, or which is used as a graveyard attached to any such church, to convey the same deed to be executed, acknowledged and recorded in the usual manner, to the Most Reverend James Whitfield, the present Archbishop of Baltimore, and his suc-

cessors in the Archiepiscopal See of Baltimore, according to the discipline and government of the Roman Catholic Church, forever; and it shall and may be lawful to and for any person or persons or body corporate, to convey unto the Roman Catholic Archbishop of Baltimore, for the time being, and his successors as aforesaid, forever, by deed as aforesaid, any lot piece or parcel of ground. . .

Legal opinion, however, was not universally favorable to this arrangement and contentions were made in some quarters that Corporation Sole is "somewhat of a contradiction in terms, and a useless feature of law." Hence, attempts to imitate the Maryland provisions in other areas of the nation were often strenuously opposed, especially by proponents of Nativism.

In 1844, the Bishop of Chicago, William Quarter, succeeded in obtaining a charter from the Legislature of Illinois empowering him and his successors to hold property in trust for the diocese. A subsequent act provided that "gifts, grants, deeds, etc., heretofore made to any bishop shall be construed as conveying the property to such person as the Catholic Bishop of Chicago, and that title shall vest in this corporation sole."

Prior to 1850, the California legislation stipulated that real estate held by a religious body could not exceed two whole lots in a town, or twenty acres in the country. However, on May 12, 1853, the state removed the restriction and adopted into its statutes that "curious thing which we meet with in English law called a Corporation Sole." The new law read, in part:

> Whenever the rules, regulations and discipline of any religious denomination, society or church require for the administration of the temporalities thereof, and the management of the estate and property thereof, it shall be lawful for the bishop, chief priest or presiding elder of such religious denomination, society or church to become a sole corporation. . .

The measure went on to state that " . . . all property held by such bishop, chief priest or presiding elder, shall be in trust for the use, purpose and behalf of his religious denomination, society or church."

The State Legislature restored the restrictive clause regarding property on May 13, 1854 and it was twenty–four years before the limitation was taken away for the final time by a measure which gave Corporation Sole "the power to buy, sell, lease or mortgage property and in every way deal in real and personal property in the same manner that a natural person may." In essence, the present law reads:

> A corporation sole may be formed hereunder by the bishop, chief priest, presiding elder or for the purpose of administering and managing the affairs and property of such religious organization. . . .

The Civil Code modified certain aspects of Corporation Sole common to English law. For example, the California legislation erects the ecclesiastical office itself into a Corporation Sole, thus making it possible for the incumbent to create an attorney of fact to survive his death and administer the Corporation Sole until a new appointee is named.

Determination of the rightful incumbent is safeguarded by the law which directs that a vacancy in the office must "be filled by the rules, regulations or constitutions of the denomination, society or church" in question. The Corporation Sole has considerable power. It can sue and be sued; borrow money; make contracts; buy, sell or mortgage property; receive bequests; and appoint attorneys of fact. Although every Corporation Sole has perpetual existence, it may be dissolved and its affairs concluded voluntarily by filing with the state a declaration of dissolution signed and verified by the chief officer of the corporation.

CORPUS CHRISTI IN CALIFORNIA

The Feast of *Corpus Christi*, inaugurated to solemnly commemorate the institution of the Holy Eucharist, dates to the year 1246, when it was introduced at Liege in Belgium. It was extended to the universal church calendar in 1264, and fixed as an annual feast for the Thursday following Trinity Sunday. In California, the first observance of *Corpus Christi* was held in 1602, according to an account by Juan de Torquemada, O.F.M. The Franciscan historian learned of the event from one of the priests accompanying the three ships of Sebastian Vizcaino, which anchored in a bay east of Cape San Lucas on the southern extremity of Lower California on June 11th:

> On landing, the general (Vizcaino) commanded a great awning to be spread, in order that an altar might be set up there, where the Religious (the three Carmelite Fathers, Andres de la Asumpcion, Antonio de la Ascension and Tomas de Aquino), might say Mass on the days the fleet should be detained there, as they always did. On the last day of the Octave of *Corpus Christi* the Religious there celebrated the feast. There was a grand procession with the Most Blessed Sacrament, and with a statue of Our Lady of Mount Carmel, which the Religious brought with them for the consolation of all. On that day, too, all the members of the expedition made their confession and received Holy Communion, and there was a High Mass with a sermon which was a great consolation to all.

More proximately, however, the Feast of *Corpus Christi* was first observed in Alta California 170 years later with the arrival at Monterey of the land and sea expeditions of 1770.

Soon after establishing himself, Fray Junipero Serra started preparations to celebrate the approaching feast. At first the Mallorcan friar thought it would be a difficult and almost impossible enterprise, since the small group lacked the wherewithal to carry it out. Nevertheless, Serra was adamant, for he was anxious to celebrate the feast and hold the procession of *Corpus Christi*, even though it be done in a poor fashion, in order "to drive away whatever little devils there may be in this land."

Once he had resolved that the ceremony could not be dispensed with, Serra set in motion the formal planning for the observance which, that year, was scheduled for June 14th. Lanterns were borrowed from the ship *San Antonio* to augment the six silver candlesticks brought from Loreto. Tallow candles were lent by Captain Juan Perez. The circle or square around which the procession was to march was swept clean and adorned with green branches so as to form aisles. Men from the ship fashioned a temporary church under the roof of the half–completed warehouse by arranging the flags of the various nations in the form of a canopy.

According to Serra, bells were rung, guns were fired, hymns and sacred songs were sung—everything went off in a fine fashion and could not have been improved upon. The statue which had been lent to the expedition by Jose de Galves, the Visitador General, occupied a place behind the monstrance.

After the procession, the Sacred Host was broken into particles and distributed as Holy Communion. The ceremony was closed with a hymn. In the opinion of Fray Juan Crespi, the liturgical service "was for all a source of rejoicing and extraordinary delight, as every Roman Catholic Christian will understand."

In a letter subsequently sent to the *Visitador General*, Serra said that the first Feast of *Corpus Christi* in Alta California had been celebrated with such splendor that it could have been witnessed with pleasure had it taken place in Mexico!

CREOLE AND CAJUN CATHOLICS

Of all the peoples who reside under California's umbrella of color, none is more historic and interesting than the Creoles and Cajuns known for their Catholic faith, French language and large families.

The Cajuns living in Los Angeles emigrated to the west from southern Louisiana. They were immortalized by Henry Wadsworth Longfellow in an epic poem telling about their expulsion from New Brunswick and Nova Scotia (Acadia) by British troops in 1755, when they refused allegiance to the British crown. By 1790, about 4,000 of those Acadians had settled in the fertile bayou swamps along the Gulf of Mexico.

Linguists reckon that the name "Cajun" is a corruption of "Acadians." Their speech patterns combine bits of ancient French with words taken from English, Spanish, German, native American languages and Afro American. Their distinctive music, played by fiddles, distonic accordians and triangles, often has a haunting quality of sadness.

Creoles have a different background. They are a people who originated in one of the New World's possessions of France, Spain or Portugal. "Creole" is a French word which came from the Spanish "*criollo*" which, in turn, was adapted from the Portuguese "*crioulo*." According to Webster's dictionary, it means "a slave born in the master's household."

The Creoles came to New Orleans prior to migrating north through rural Louisiana where some remained. Their dialect is a soft, idiom–rich jargon grounded in French.

Zydeco, the Creole counterpart of Cajun music, incorporates blues and jazz. Its unique Afro–Caribbean sound comes from a percussion instrument known as the *frottoir*, a corrugated metal vest which the instrumentalist plays with spoons.

Louis H. Metoyer, editor of *Bayou Talk*, a monthly newspaper circulated to Creoles in twenty–five states, says that most of the 20,000 families in Los Angeles came from Louisiana in two major migrations. The first occurred after World War II when they journeyed west to find employment and good schools for their youngsters. They settled in what is now known as South Central Los Angeles.

Metoyer points out that "When we left Louisiana, we didn't leave our values there. We packed them and brought them with us. And they are interwoven within the Catholic faith." He goes on to note that "one of the distinct things about the Creoles, as well as the Cajuns, is that they have large families. Extended family is just as important as immediate family."

The second migration took place in the 1960s and it was then that Metoyer and others came to the Pacific rim. The archdiocesan Creole Cultural Heritage Liturgy was inaugurated at that time.

In Los Angeles, the Cajuns and Creoles have preserved what is best in their traditions. Over 5,000 gathered in June of 1993 at Long Beach for the seventh annual Southern California Cajun and Zydeco Festival. There, actor John Delafise and the Eunice Playboys exhorted the people to reach out and touch a hand.

One Anglo observer at that event wrote that "the music is part of the pie. The rest of it is these wonderful people who are very family oriented. They're real Catholics, and I feel at home here. They get together, and they celebrate life and community. And that's their gift to the Church."

CROWN OF THE ANDES

The Crown of the Andes is sculptured from a solid piece of pure Incan gold. It is encrusted with what is said to be the largest collection of fine emeralds in the world. The history of the Crown began in the 16th century in the Spanish territories which Pizarro captured from the Incas of Peru.

A devastating epidemic had spared the city of Popayan, high in the Andes, in its sweep across the west coast of South America. The people of the city, attributing this miracle to their devotion to the Blessed Mother, determined to make the most beautiful crown in the world as an act of thanksgiving.

Into the Crown they poured the gold and emeralds captured from the Incas. Expert lapidaries were brought in from Spain to shape and polish the gems. And after six years of work by twenty–four expert goldsmiths, the masterpiece was finally completed.

There are 453 genuine emeralds in the Crown, with a total combined weight of 1,521 carats. The seventeen pear–shaped emeralds which hang as pendants inside the Crown are solid stones weighing from twelve to twenty–four carats each. The jeweled cross contains ten jewels.

The Crown was carved by hand from a huge block of pure Incan gold weighing over one hundred pounds. No portion was cast or soldered. It was literally sculptured out of a solid block of gold, exactly as a modern sculptor carves a statue out of marble The Crown was made in six sections, joined together with bolts and nuts of pure gold, so that it could be taken apart and buried in six different places in times of danger.

On December 8, 1599, in the great Cathedral at Popayan, amidst Spanish pomp and pageantry, the Crown was placed atop the statue of the Madonna, whom local people called Our Lady of the Andes.

Then, in 1650, the Crown was stolen by pirates. It was quickly recovered and retained by the Spaniards until the revolution of 1812. During succeeding uprisings the Crown was buried for safe–keeping and exhibited in the Cathedral only on great feastdays.

The Vatican gave special permission, in 1909, to sell the Crown to obtain funds for hospitals and orphanages. Czar Nicholas II of Russian wanted to buy the Crown but he and his family perished in the Russian Revolution before the sale could be consummated.

In 1936, the Crown was finally sold to an American for an undisclosed sum. (Its value had been placed at between four and five million dollars by connoisseurs of antiquity). The Crown was later brought to Southern California and, for several weeks, was displayed at Pasadena by the J. Herbert Ball Jewelry Company.

CROSS OF CARAVACA

Over the centuries, the most widespread and venerated symbol of the Christian religion has been the cross because it was upon a wooden cross that Our Lord died to redeem the world. There is a Feast of the Holy Cross observed each year in the Roman liturgical calendar. There are many varieties of crosses. The *Cruz de Caravaca*, a development of the traditional patriarchal cross, has two cross bars, forming part of the heraldic arms of a patriarch and carried before him in religious processions.

Among the treasured museum artifacts at San Fernando Mission is a larger than usual *Cruz de Caravaca* which was presented by Richard Joseph Menn, longtime curator of San Carlos Borromeo Mission at Carmel. Though about two inches taller than the one worn by and interred with Fray Junípero Serra, it is the same vintage and design and was likely brought from the Isle of Mallorca by one of Serra's collaborators in the late 1700s.

An ancient legend associates the *Cruz de Caravaca* with a battle during which the Moors were defeated and then converted to the Catholic faith. The incident reportedly followed a supernatural vision in 1132 wherein the distinctive design was revealed to Gines Perez de Hita (c. 1544–1619), a priest imprisoned in the southern town of Caravaca during the Moslem occupation of Spain. The *Cruz de Caravaca* was also a favorite of Saint Teresa of Avila (1515–1582). Since the time of Philip III, Teresa has been the secondary patron of Spain, ranking next to Santiago (Saint James).

There are five indentations in the bronze cross, each of which very likely housed a relic of one of the saints. In Serra's cross, which was discovered during the excavation of his tomb at Carmel Mission Basilica in 1943, there was still visible a part of the authentic testifying to the presence of a relic of Blessed Raymond Lull, a 13th century Mallorcan who was stoned to death by the Moslems in 1315 at Bugia in Africa.

Ministering angels at either side of the cross are artistically portrayed as supporting the central shaft of the two–tiered crucifix. Firmly anchored into place, they are probably part of the original cast. The verso side of the cross portrays two additional angels, a chalice and uplifted host together with a praying rendition of Saint Francis of Assisi. Several undecipherable symbols are also embedded into the cross.

The design and workmanship of the *Cruz de Caravaca* clearly confirms that it was the product of European craftsman, probably Italian or Spaniard. Similar crosses in museums throughout Spain are of comparable design and composition. Still an attractive work-of-art, the cross–reliquary measures 6 3/4" tall (6" with eyelet) by 3 1/8" (lower arm) or 2 1/2" (upper arm). Though hinged above the *titulus*, the cross is frozen or crystallized into a closed position. There are no longer any indications of relics.

It was the practice in those days for the Mallorcan friars to wear a *Cruz de Caravaca* under their religious habit, much the same as Catholics of the 20th century wear a Miraculous Medal. The one at San Fernando Mission gives evidence of long usage and is covered with the residue of verdigris and lime.

CRUCIFIXION AT FOREST LAWN

The painting which no one wanted to own has become the painting which everyone wants to see. Jan Styka's portrayal of "The Crucifixion" at Forest Lawn is rightly considered the world's most tremendous dramatic religious rendition. It was Ignace Paderewski, the famed Polish musician and statesman who, in 1894, first conceived the notion of capturing on canvas an oil depiction of Christ's sacrifice on the cross.

Paderewski confided his dream to a fellow countryman, Jan Styka, who immediately took up the idea and made its realization the culminating artistic experience of his life. In preparation for the project, Styka made a pilgrimage to the Holy Land. In Jerusalem he personally experienced the spiritual drama of that tragic day when the Son of God bought back the human race from its bondage to sin.

On his return from the Holy Land, Styka paused briefly in the Eternal City and there knelt before Pope Leo XIII who blessed the palette on which he would mix his colors. Provisions were made to acquire from Belgium a gigantic canvas measuring 195 feet long by 45 feet high. It was sent to Poland where Paderewski had it suspended from the vaulted ceiling of a large public building. There, atop a wooden scaffolding, Styka began the years-long project.

When finally it was ready for unveiling, "The Crucifixion" was hailed throughout Europe as the greatest artistic protrayal of the century. Its viewers were enthralled by the staggering realism of the scene.

Unlike conventional renditions, Styka chose to portray that moment of suspense before Christ was placed upon the cross on Mount Calvary. A vast concourse of people stands in awe of what was about to occur.

In 1900, Styka brought the huge painting to the United States where, unfortunately, there was no building available large enough to accommodate its exhibition. After several futile attempts to publicly display the painting, the artist reluctantly rolled it up and placed it in storage. And, to make matters worse, the financially embarrassed Styka was eventually forced to sell his masterpiece and to return home without it.

It was in the 1940s that Hubert Eaton heard about the discarded, unwanted painting. Realizing its spiritual potential, he convinced the Council of Regents at Forest Lawn to adopt provisions for enshrining it permanently in Glendale, California.

During part of the time while the giant Hall of the Crucifixion was being constructed, the painting was displayed at the Shrine Auditorium in Los Angeles. Finally, when the cathedral-like edifice, with its huge stained glass windows, soaring black marble columns and massive vaulted ceilings was completed, the Styka masterpiece was brought to Forest Lawn.

People from all over the world daily stream through the Hall of the Crucifixion to view Jan Styka's great painting, surely one of the largest in the world. They come away with the conviction that, in the history of religious art, "The Crucifixion" will always stand unique.

When Karol Cardinal Wojtyla visited Los Angeles, in August of 1976, the then Archbishop of Krakow asked to be shown Jan Styka's painting. While at Forest Lawn, the future Pope John Paul II scribbled a note that is still on display to the effect that Styka's work was among the greatest contributions made to the world by his native Poland.

CURSILLO MOVEMENT

The contribution of the Isle of Mallorca to Provincial California was outstanding, varied and continuous. Sixteen of the early missionaries invested 341 man-years in spreading the Christian message to the Indians along the Pacific Slope.

Father Maynard Geiger, the Franciscan historian, has stated that "the state of California owes much to persevering and determined men from a small island in the Mediterranean. Mallorca, especially in the beginning, provided many of California's early conquering heroes. For this reason, the isle of calm and beauty was and remains California's spiritual god-mother."

Nor did that contribution stop in 1856, with the death of Fray Juan Cabot, the last of the Mallorcan friars. Indeed, there is much of that same missionary enthusiasm evident almost two centuries after the passing of those early pioneers. In 1944, Eduardo Bonnin, a convert from Judaism, invited about thirty priests and laymen to join him in counteracting the personal immorality and religious indifference then creeping into Spanish society. His aim was to transform the small group into militant Catholics whose lifestyles would revolve about the sacraments. Shortly thereafter, Bonnin approached the Right Reverend Juan Hervás y Benet, and asked the Bishop of Mallorca for guidance and approval of the movement. Bishop Hervás heartily endorsed the proposals and personally assumed direction of what would later be known as the *Cursillos de Cristianidad*. From the very outset, the prelate insisted that the retreat–like movement be carefully structured.

The Cursillo, as envisioned by Hervás, was to be "a short, intensive course, in which priest and lay leaders, in close collaboration, develop a particular method, the aim of which is the Christian renewal of the *Cursillistas* and their apostolic projection into society, so that they will extend the Kingdom of Christ." The prelate's apostolic zeal is further revealed in an article written for *The Americas*, in January of 1950, in which he called for a re–kindling, in a new generation, of "that same peace and good–will of the Gospel which Fray Junípero (Serra) succeeded in planting in the New World."

After completing a carefully–prepared course of instruction, a squad of teachers conducted the first Cursillo on January 7, 1949, in Palma's *Convento de San Honorato*, under the personal supervision of the bishop. Teams were subsequently sent to Barcelona and from there to the other major population centers of Spain. Within a few years, the "spiritual revolution" had spread through much of Latin America as well.

In May, 1957, two flyers from the Spanish airforce, Agustin Palomino and Bernardo Vadell, while on a training program in Waco, Texas, joined with Father Gabriel Fernández, to launch the Cursillo program in the United States.

The initial Cursillo was held in Los Angeles under the direction of the Claretian Fathers, in 1962. Cardinal James Francis McIntyre welcomed the movement and, within four years, thirty–three Cursillos had been conducted in the archdiocese.

Bishop Hervás, later the Prefect Apostolic of Ciudad Real, described the Cursillo as "an instrument of Christian renewal in which the most modern pedagogic, religious, social and psychological methods are brought into harmonious fusion with the traditional doctrine of the Church." Today, the intensive apostolic collaboration of priest–laymen teams are busily bringing to modern generations of believers what Fray Junípero Serra and his companions brought to the pagans of earlier times: "faith, tenacity and self–sacrifice." And Mallorca once again lights a candle in the New World!

DAYLIGHT SAVINGS TIME

Most people don't mind Daylight Savings Time as much as they do adjusting their clocks. At San Fernando Mission, there is an automated carillon, three chime clocks, numerous desk clocks and a host of other time pieces all of which need special attention when DST begins and ends.

Benjamin Franklin is credited with devising the concept of DST. According to the *Encyclopedia Americana*, he suggested that some method be devised to save candles and provide longer daylight for evenings.

The early missionaries in California used the concept of DST, without the actual practice of advancing their clocks. Lighting the interior of the mission buildings was costly, impractical and inefficient. The daily schedule was adjusted for maximum use of daylight. An example would be daily Mass which was "movable" insofar as it began shortly after the "rising" of the sun.

Daylight Savings Time as we know it dates back to World War I when both England and Germany adopted the practice as a means of conserving fuel and power. It wasn't popular in the United States and was suspended when farmers voiced their opposition. It was reinstated year–round during World War II.

Late in 1929, in order to place DST on the ballot, the California Daylight Savings League was established by Dr. Rufus B. Von Kleinsmid, President of the University of Southern California and other southland leaders, including Bishop John J. Cantwell.

In a colorful brochure distributed throughout the state, proponents told how "Daylight Savings would give residents an added hour of playtime in California's Golden Sunshine." Among other features mentioned in the brochure, were three weeks of extra vacation (154 additional hours of sunshine), substantial savings on electric bills, the opportunity of enjoying out–of–doors recreation every day, additional time for swimming, fishing, golfing and motoring.

Further, if the ballot measure were to be approved, there would be extra time for home gardening, private business and personal affairs, together with closer companionship with family, healthier and stronger children, added prosperity and better radio programs. Though the arguments were somewhat overstated, proponents of DST were convinced that passage of the initiative would bring about "greater efficiency and more time for pleasure and relaxation."

There was considerable opposition to the measure which was submitted to the electorate in November of 1930. "California's Alright" was established as "a league against the Daylight Saving Menace." In a letter mailed out to voters, Jeff Lazarus pointed out that "Daylight Saving was in operation throughout the entire country as a National war measure, in 122,186 communities. Because of confusion, inconvenience and financial damage, it was abolished in most places. Only 263 communities now use it! Experience condemns it; no doubt about that!"

Many newspapers campaigned against the DST measure, including the influential *Sacramento Bee*. One prominent religious leader observed that it was "preposterous for us to try to improve on the way God created the universe." The measure didn't carry.

At the national level, Congress passed the Uniform Time Act in 1966 whereby DST was standardized from the last Sunday in April to the last Sunday in October. Twenty years later, an additional three weeks was added by moving the opening date back to the first Sunday of April.

The controversy continues. For the moment, proponents of DST have the edge with their convincing argument that it conserves precious fuel. The early California missionaries achieved the same result by rising and retiring an hour earlier during the winter months.

DIOCESE OF BOTH CALIFORNIAS

The historical framework surrounding the formation of curial government for the Church in the Californias can be traced to 1681, when spiritual jurisdiction over the Peninsula . . . was in dispute between Juan Garabito, Bishop of Guadalajara and Fray Bartolomew de Escanuela, Bishop of Durango. The latter, contending that Baja California belonged to Nueva Vizcaya, customarily delegated faculties to California–bound missionaries, until he was gently told not to meddle in peninsular affairs.

The feasibility of advancing the internal provinces of northwestern New Spain to diocesan status was formally suggested as early as 1760. Renewed impetus for the plan came eight years later with the proposal to form Sonora, Sinaloa and Lower California into a separate ecclesiastical jurisdiction.

In 1775, Bishop Antonio Marcarulla informed Fray Junípero Serra that his Diocese of Durango exercised authority over future Spanish settlements in California by virtue of the canonical prerogative assigning all undesignated territories to the nearest established jurisdiction. That claim was flatly rejected by Fray Junípero Serra, as was the less convincing assertion of the Bishop of Guadalajara who argued that Alta California belonged to his diocese as "a logical extension of the peninsula over which he did have legitimate authority."

On May 7, 1779, acting upon a recommendation from Spanish officials at Madrid, Pope Pius VI created the Diocese of Sonora, comprising the provinces of Sonora, Sinaloa and Both Californias. For the first time, Alta California, hitherto a totally independent field of missionary endeavors, fell within defined canonical boundaries. The newly created Diocese of Sonora, entrusted to Fray Antonio de Jos Reyes, was almost entirely a missionary territory, Communications between Sonora and the Californias by land was impossible and the Franciscan prelate, finding himself isolated from the furthest confines of his diocese, satisfied his episcopal obligations by delegating the Franciscan *Presidentes* as Vicars Forane for Sonora.

At least one prominent historian felt that "Spain should have asked for a bishop for the Californias, considering the huge territory, even though churches were few and the income nothing." Indeed, the thought of a mitre for Fray Junípero Serra possibly did cross the minds of Spanish officialdom. The *Presidente's* biographer recalls that after the establishment of Mission San Carlos, "His Reverence learned that a courier at Madrid had written to the Reverend Father Guardian of our college . . . that a great honor was waiting the Reverend Father Junípero." As soon as news of the "great honor" reached Monterey, Serra decided against any distinction that would forestall his work as an apostolic missionary among the infidels. He even took the extreme precaution of writing an influential acquaintance at the royal court, asking that he veto any further consideration of regal favors, should such ever come up for discussion.

The faculty of administering the Sacrament of Confirmation, bestowed by succeeding popes on the *Presidentes* in California, was not renewed, in 1803. That factor greatly disturbed Fray Narciso Durán. In a letter to the Mexican chief of state, written on September 22, 1830, Durán was the first to suggest that it was time to petition for the erection of a diocese and the appointment of a bishop. The frightful chaos that befell the Church in the post–secularization period strengthened Durán's views that a canonically established curial government would be an effective and practical alternative to the existing status.

At a meeting in Santa Barbara, on May 27, 1835, Frays Narciso Durán and Francisco Garcia Diego drafted a formal memorial to the government suggesting that creation of a bishopric was the only means of providing adequately for the ecclesial needs of Alta California. That proposal was widely discussed and carefully studied by both Church and civil authorities at the Mexican capital and, on September 12, 1836, a formal request to that effect was approved and submitted to the Holy See. On April 27, 1840, Pope Gregory XVI approved the petition and issued the customary papal bulls inaugurating a diocesan system of government for the Californias.

The modern era of the Church had then begun.

DIVINA PASTORA

Through the kindness of Sir Harry Downie, famed restorer and curator of Mission San Carlos Borromeo, the Chancery Archives for the Archdiocese of Los Angeles acquired an exceedingly rare imprint bearing the name of Fray Francisco Garcia Diego (1785–1846) proto–Bishop of Both Californias. The twenty–two page the memory of D. Ygriacio Villaseñor, is an 1830 edition of the *Novena á la Smâ. Virgen Maria en la advocación de la Divina Pastora*, printed by Alexo Infante.

The background of the novena itself is interesting and can be traced to Fray Isidro, who lived in an old Capuchin monastery at Seville. One night after the others had retired, the friar remained in chapel praying for an end to the growing corruption then prevalent among the local citizenry.

Suddenly, the Blessed Virgin appeared, in the guise of a shepherdess, with the Infant in her arms and a flock of lambs frolicking about her. Fray Isidro was instructed to inaugurate a devotion to the *Divina Pastora* as a means of winning sinners back to the service of Christ.

Bartolomé Estéban Murillo had lived at that monastery and one of his pupils, Bernardo Germán de Llorente, painted the apparition as it was described by Fray Isidro. From that time onward, veneration of the Divine Shepherdess began spreading throughout the Spanish empire.

Devotion to Our Lady under her title *Divina Pastora* was common among the missionaries of Latin America. The home missions conducted by the Franciscans from the Apostolic College of San Fernando, for example, were given under the patronage of the Divine Shepherdess.

The *Novena* acquired by the Chancery Archives was compiled and prepared for publication by Fray Francisco Garcia Diego, in 1830, while the young priest was serving as Commissary Prefect of the missions attached to the Apostolic College of *Nuestra Señora de Guadalupe*, Zacatecas. The exquisitely–drawn portrayal of the popular *Nuestra Señora de la Divina Pastora* enhancing the otherwise unadorned publication is obviously adapted from a celebrated painting of *La Divina Pastora* by the Mexican artist, José de Páez.

Our Lady sits under a large tree, surrounded by, seven sheep whose eyes resemble those of humans. Mary holds the crozier or pastoral staff in her right hand and the Infant Jesus in her left. The face of the virgin has an afflicted, somewhat Victorian charm. There are paintings of the *Divina Pastora* at Missions San Juan Capistrano, Santa Ines and Santa Barbara.

Following the general format of other novenas used in 19th century Latin America, the simply–structured collection of prayers honoring the Divine Shepherdess is arranged for recitation on nine consecutive days.

The novena begins with an Act of Contrition, followed by an opening and closing prayer which remains unchanged. Particular orations are then provided for each day. The devotion concludes with a *trisagion* and hymn, which very likely were chanted by the community.

The translated *Novena* was included in a volume of Fray Francisco Garcia Diego's writings in 1976, as part of the Catholic participation in the nation's bicentennial observance.

Received in exchange for a fugitive volume from the historic mission library at Carmel, the only known extant copy of Fray Garcia Diego's *Novena* has been placed on permanent display in the historical museum attached to the Chancery Archives, along with a host of other memorabilia associated with California's Catholic heritage.

DOHENY LIBRARY AT U.S.C.

An article in the September 13, 1932 issue of the Los Angeles *Times* reported how, on the preceding day, "A key of gold turned smoothly in its lock and the massive bronze doors, portals to knowledge and culture, of the new Edward L. Doheny, Jr., Memorial Library swung wide for the first time."

The genesis of the library at the University of Southern California can be traced to the middle months of 1929, when Mr. & Mrs. Edward L. Doheny began looking for a suitable manner of perpetuating the memory of their lately deceased son. It was Dr. Rufus B. Von KleinSmid, the President of U.S.C., who suggested that a library would be an ideal memorial to "Ned" Doheny (1893–1929) who had served on the University's Board of Trustees since 1919.

A masterpiece of perfection to the minutest detail, the building took over a year and a half to erect. Located in the center of a city block, facing the university's administration facility, the library cost over $1,000,000. It was designed in the shape of the letter H in order to allow a maximum of light and air to filter through its hallways and reading rooms.

The exterior was done in marble, brick and stone, while the interior was constructed from finely textured and exquisitely carved European marble and rich–appearing oak, walnut and other woods. In accordance with Carrie Estelle Doheny's wishes, preference was given to American materials whenever possible.

Entrance to the library is gained through a pair of two ton bronze doors, the largest ever cast on the Pacific coast. In the tall marble delivery room, light is shed from a multipiece chandelier, hanging from a cathedral–like ceiling three stories above. In the nearby stained glass windows are depicted various university shields.

Nine murals adorn the Treasure Room which was designed to contain the rare and ancient books of the university. It was Dr. Von KleinSmid's hope that one–day the Estelle Doheny Collection of Rare Books, Manuscripts and Works of Art would be housed in that room.

Other points of interest in the building are Roger Haywards' mosaics, statues of Shakespeare and Dante and a sculptured panel above the archway, the cloister and patio with its tiled pool, trees, shrubs and flowers and Edward L. Doheny, Jr.'s portrait bust.

During the summer months of 1932, more than 147,000 books, periodicals and related materials were moved into the spacious new building. For the first time, the University of Southern California had a library worthy of its academic standing among America's educational institutions.

The dedicatory services, broadcast over Radio Station KFAC, then the official broadcasting unit for the *Evening Herald and Express*, marked the first time a Trojan program was sent out over the air waves. The invocation for the event was given by Father Thomas C. Powers, C.M., Pastor of Saint Vincent's Church.

For the dedication, Mrs. Doheny arranged for a collection of her rare books to be exhibited in the Treasure Room. According to the catalogue issued for that occasion, the exhibit featured "the history of the book during the last ten centuries . . . starting with the earliest relics of the Middle Ages."

A host of dignitaries attended the dedication, including Governor James Rolph who hailed the library as "an ornate and artistic structure of which any university of the world would be proud."

DOMINGUEZ *RANCHO* ADOBE

Among the more devotional and celebrated chapels in Southern California is the one at *Rancho San Pedro*, known more commonly as the Dominguez Rancho Adobe in Compton. The adobe was the original building erected on the *rancho* in 1826 by Manuel Dominguez, a nephew of Juan Jose Dominguez, a member of the 1769 Portola expedition. Located on a slight rise at the northeast side of a sloping hill, the house was typical of the pattern used by the *rancheros* of the time.

In 1784, as a reward for his service to the king, Juan Jose received the first Spanish land grant in California from Carlos III. At the time, *Rancho San Pedro* extended from the south boundary of the *pueblo de Nuestra Señora de los Angeles* to the marshy Bay of San Pedro, an area of 75,000 acres, and west from the Los Angeles river to what is now Redondo Beach. Its original territory now encompasses eleven cities and the Port of Los Angeles.

When constructed, the house was a rectangular one–story building, with covered porches on three sides. It consisted of five rooms, with sheds, and other out–buildings for use by ranch–hands. Eventually the edifice was expanded by adding wings on the north and south sides, eventually becoming a wide U–shaped building with ten rooms.

Don Manuel and his wife, Maria Engracia, lived there for over a half century and, after their passing, the building was occupied by their children for another forty years. In 1922, the home was deeded to the Claretian Missionary Fathers.

The room selected for the chapel had been a family parlor. An altar and pews were installed and it was here that Bishop Thaddeus Amat and others came to offer Holy Mass on special occasions. Behind the altar, on the east side, is an elegant imported stained glass window inscribed with the Dominguez name. The year "1826" is still visible. The family acquired a beautiful crucifix from Mexico which hangs above the altar. A statue of the Immaculate Conception was brought from Barcelona and vestments were acquired in Mexico. From Italy came an oil painting of Saint Peter, patron saint of the *rancho*.

Registered as a California State Landmark in 1945 and a National Historic Landmark in 1976, the *rancho* and its chapel have probably been "plaquerized" more extensively than any other place in the Golden State.

In 1964, the Dominguez Adobe achieved the ultimate distinction by being featured on a 13 cent postal card issued by the United States Postal Service. The card commemorated "the contributions made by the *ranchos* to the rich heritage of Southern California." It also marked the two hundredth anniversary of *Rancho San Pedro* which witnessed the birth and growth of agriculture, cattle raising, industry and family life in California. The multicolor postal card was designed by Earl Thollander of Calistoga, who earlier had executed the Alta California stamp released in 1977. The romantic adobe, with its historical chapel, is graced with curved–arch porticos and a sloping, tile–gabled roof, recalling a colorful heritage under flags of three nations: Spain, Mexico and the United States.

While visiting the adobe and its chapel, be sure to see the painting of Manuel Dominguez in the family room. It was done by Solomon Nunes Carvalho and is thought to be the first oil on canvas portrait executed in California.

EARTHQUAKE OF 1994

Who says that history doesn't repeat itself? On January 17th, just two weeks short of twenty–three years after the Sylmar earthquake, another major temblor devastated the San Fernando Valley.

In 1971, the Old Mission was seven miles from the epicenter. This time it was less than three miles away. Perhaps that proximity explains why this more recent experience seemed so much more severe.

There were ominous similarities to the earlier quake for this writer. Once again I was sitting at my desk and once again I was writing my weekly column for *The Tidings*. (This time it was about William Ide, California's only President).

My day starts early at 2:00 a.m. Following some prayers in the Serra Chapel, I had arrived at my office in the Archival Center about 4:10. After feeding the pooch and winding the clocks (a regular Monday ritual), I had turned on my ancient IBM electric typewriter as a prelude for grinding out the first draft of my essay.

At precisely 4:32, there was a penetrating noise and the entire room began swaying. Something crashed down and gashed my head as I slid under my desk, the same desk that saved my life in the 1971 earthquake.

After what appeared like an eternity (it was more like thirty seconds), there was utter silence. It was pitch black as I began to crawl out of the building. It took about twenty minutes to get around, over and between the several thousand books that had rained down from the shelves.

I hurried back to my apartment, secured the dog and then went over to the seminary where I found, happily, that the students were still on holiday (in honor of Martin Luther King).

Aftershocks are commonplace following major earthquakes, but they are terribly unnerving. Newspapers reported a number of 5.6 "rollers" throughout the next few days.

While the complete contents of the Archival Center were strewn everywhere, the archdiocesan "memory bank" was basically safe and intact. It would easily take six months to re–shelve our 20,000 books and to sort out the contents of 1,500 storage boxes. Fortunately, the file cabinets remained upright. The only item still in place was a porcelain statue of the Blessed Mother that Msgr. Benjamin Hawkes gave us in 1981. The cases and their contents in the Historical Museum sustained considerable damage and much breakage.

It would have been easy to feel sorry for ourselves. Thirty–two years of collecting, sorting, arranging and cataloguing had been poured out on the floor. But, after hearing of the loss of life (fifty–one killed, including one of our seminarians), there wasn't any room left for self–pity.

It took most of Monday just to become operational. Happily, our telephones were up by mid–afternoon and a few hours later, DWP had power for most of our buildings. Much of our area remained without power for several more days.

As soon as communications were restored, I called Cardinal Mahony's residence and was told that he was enroute to the San Fernando Valley. He arrived here at about 5 o'clock, after personally visiting the damaged area from one end of the valley to the other

His Eminence is always at his best in times of crisis. His presence among our ruins was a badly–needed and much–appreciated dose of encouragement. He repeated Job's observation that "The Lord gives, the Lord takes away, blessed be the name of the Lord." We all needed that reminder.

The first priority was to get the Valley's Mother Church ready for the three funerals scheduled for Tuesday. We had a crew busily at work by 6 a.m. the next morning and the church, rebuilt after the 1971 earthquake, was totally functional in a few hours. The other mission buildings hadn't fared as well. But everyone pitched in to clean up the debris and, with only a few days out for clean–up, San Fernando Mission was open for visitors on January 24th

There's a lesson in everything that God allows to happen. Often we have to pray hard to understand and accept His will. More often than not, we must wait until the afterlife for a full explanation. But, it's God's world. He sets the rules and if we want to play the game, we have to follow His gameplan.

EARTHQUAKE SAINTS

Every time there is a major temblor in California, reporters first call Caltech for a reading of intensity and then the Archival Center for a list of saints invoked against earthquakes. According to Butler's *Lives of the Saints*, there are three names which have long been associated with earthquakes, all of whom come with impressive credentials in the field.

Saint Francis Borgia (1510–1572) was proclaimed patron of earthquakes by Pope Benedict XIV in 1756, a few months after a quake killed upwards of 50,000 people in Lisbon, Portugal. Francis had an interesting pedigree, descended as he was from illegitimate heirs of Pope Alexander VI and King Ferdinand of Aragon. After a happy marriage, the widowed duke joined the newly founded Society of Jesus and there excelled in evangelization and administration. His labors in Portugal were widely heralded and he became the unofficial patron of that country, with a feast day celebrated on October 10th.

Then, there is Saint Gregory, known as the "wonder–worker," who died in 268. Gregory was a convert to the faith at age fourteen, when he abandoned the practice of law to study philosophy and theology at Caesarea. After a few years, Gregory became Bishop of Neocaesarea, a city then having only seventeen Christians. Because of Gregory's zeal, learning and charity, it is said that by the time of his death, only seventeen pagans were left in his diocese. He is known to have administered to his flock through the persecutions of Decius and a Gothic invasion.

Gregory was much admired by the Cappadocian Fathers and they recorded a series of dramatic miracles that gave Gregory his nickname. Those included phenomena associated with earthquakes, such as altering the flow of a river. Gregory's relics were later translated to Calabria in southern Italy, where he is still invoked against earthquakes and flooding. His feastday is observed on November 17th.

Finally and most importantly, there is Saint Emygdius, long a favorite in California. Even in mission times there is evidence that the friars invoked his intercession against temblors. Bishop Thaddeus Amat was aware of the devotion to Saint Emygdius as it existed throughout much of Europe. He felt that such an intercessor would have special relevance for the Diocese of Monterey.

Emygdius, Bishop of Ascoli Piceno, devoted his life to caring for the spiritual needs of his people. With three companions, Emygdius was beheaded during the persecution unleashed by Diocletian, on August 5, 303. His earthly remains were discovered towards the end of the 10th century. In subsequent years, the cult of Emygdius spread through Italy, where he was and is considered an effective protector against earthquakes.

Following the disastrous temblors at Fort Tejon, on January 9, 1857, Bishop Amat petitioned the Holy See for the faculty of observing the feast of Saint Emygdius (August 9th) in the Diocese of Monterey. The prelate also asked for permission to grant a special indulgence on that day to those who received Holy Communion and prayed to Saint Emygdius for his assistance against earthquakes. Just a year later, on January 9, 1858, Amat was informed that the Pope Pius IX had acceded to his request.

In the Synod for May, 1862, the priests attached to the jurisdiction of Monterey–Los Angeles petitioned Rome to name Emygdius a principal patron for the diocese. On February 1, 1863, the Holy Father complied with that request and also authorized recitation of special readings for the local editions of the Roman Breviary.

And, thereafter, the Feast of Saint Emygdius, on August 9th, was observed in Southern California with special emphasis as a "Day of Devotion."

EARTHQUAKE — SAN FRANCISCO

Early in the morning of April 18, 1906, a massive earthquake shook the ground along the San Andreas Fault from Salinas in the south to Cape Mendocino in the north. The epicenter of the temblor was near San Francisco and, although California had experienced greater quakes, none was so devastating in its effects on the Golden State's populace.

Broken electric wires turned the City of San Francisco into one blazing holocaust and swept through block after block of apartments and residences until 28,199 buildings had been levelled to the ground. A general breakdown in the water system delayed for precious hours any effective rescue attempts. For three days and two nights the fires raged through 500 blocks leaving Nob Hill, Chinatown, and almost the entire northeastern part of the city in complete ruins.

Coadjutor Archbishop George T. Montgomery reported that "twelve churches were burnt and the parishes absolutely wiped out of existence. In the burnt district we lost, along with the churches, every institution with it—the parish schools, colleges, academies, hospitals, homes for the aged and abandoned children. . . ."

Aid to the 300,000 left homeless by the tragedy came from all over the world. Even the traditional enmity between California's north and south (characterized by a report in the San Francisco *Examiner* consoling its readers that "a great tidal wave had buried most of Southern California.") melted away and Bishop Thomas J. Conaty of Monterey–Los Angeles, whose own losses at Salinas and nearby areas were serious, set up relief stations throughout the southland and within hours had food and clothing dispatched to San Francisco by rail and ship.

The Bay City's new Cathedral of Saint Mary was badly damaged, so much so that the following Sunday, Archbishop Montgomery was forced to celebrate Holy Mass on the outside steps "overlooking the blackened waste" of a once beautiful city. Saint Patrick's Seminary at Menlo Park was also severerly damaged. The upper story front wall of the college pavilion was torn away and "huge standstone blocks from the tower crashed to the granite steps at the main entrance." The chapel walls were crumbled to the ground.

Archbishop Patrick W. Riordan was in the east at the time and his coadjutor was immediately looked to as a symbol of hope among a despondent people. At one church it was related that " as the priest finishes Mass at the improvised altar, an automobile drives up. It is the bishop, who is going the rounds of the city this morning with a message of courage and hope to the people. They kneel in the street for his blessing, and as they rise you may read many things in their faces but never, never despair."

With destruction staring in every direction, it was amazing how "the thorough and surprising vitality of the Catholic Church in San Francisco was splendidly exemplified in the promptness with which the work of reconstruction was taken up after the great fire." An article appearing in the *Overland Monthly* for November of 1907 took note of the progress and reported that " today, all the destroyed churches are again open to worshippers." Peace and calm had returned to the City by the Bay.

EARTHQUAKE — SANTA BARBARA

The earthquake which jolted Santa Barbara, in mid–1925, caused the worst damage in The Channel City's history and resulted in the loss of eleven lives. Father Augustine Hobrecht, superior at the mission, subsequently published his recollections of that fateful day in *Noticias*, a quarterly bulletin of the Santa Barbara Historical Society. That account, here abridged, is a most interesting part of California's Catholic heritage.

The earthquake occurred at exactly 6:40 in the morning of June 29th, 1925. Besides the student friars and the lay brothers, there were only two elderly priests with me at home. At 6 o'clock that morning I had gone to the organ loft of the Old Mission church to join the student choir in singing for the solemn high Mass for the feast of Sts. Peter and Paul.

And then it happened. . . . While I was standing close to the console of the organ, suddenly I felt a violent jolt that seemed to come from the very depths; then the Old Mission church began to sway with a crunching sound. Soon after, several large statues were catapulted from their pedestals; one of the statues was headed directly toward Father Raphael Vander Haar, who had celebrated the Mass and was now running from the sanctuary.

At that very moment Brother Michael Lamm, who served for many years as tourist guide at the Old Mission, saw in a flash the statue was on the way down and quickly drew Father Raphael aside, while the large wooden statue landed on the floor of the sanctury. The large silver crown from the head of the figure of Our Blessed Mother Mary rolled away unharmed.

After a brief interval the quake increased in violence, more things began to fall and the noise became deafening. . . . When the quake had subsided, I said to Father Cornelius:

"Now let's go." The door to the choir loft would not budge; it was jammed. Only after both of us had charged several times on the run did the heavy door yield suddenly. How fortunate we were not to have run immediately we discovered when, after emerging into the upstairs corridor we found our passage blocked by large stones that had fallen from the tower above, and the air filled with dust so thick, we could see only a few feet ahead.

Both of us quickly returned to the two aged brothers that were with us in the organ loft, took hold of them and half carried, half dragged them with us over the rubble of rock that covered the stairs down to the second story level of the corridor into the living quarters of the Old Mission.

We halted for a moment to decide what direction to follow now. Father Cornelius suggested entering one of the rooms on the west side, and then quickly kicked upon the light door leading to the room of Father Zephyrin Engelhardt, the well–known historian of the California Missions.

As I took a few steps forward, I found myself plunging downward in what appeared to be just a black hole. . . . When I landed below and began groping about, I found that Brother Firmus had fallen ahead of me. . . . In a flash, I had the good old brother in my arms; half dragged and half carried him to the outdoors. As we passed under the bell tower, half of which had already fallen, I could see one of the bells hanging from one of the beams that was still clinging to one side of the tower opening, and at that moment the earth trembled again, enough to toll the bell, as if in mourning..

I made a quick survey of all the buildings . . . and after gathering the entire community around me, gave orders to stay out of all the front wing and the church. The front wall along the venerable old corridor was already leaning heavily outward and, as I thought, could easily have fallen with additional shocks. Later we brought out beds from enough rooms to house the community. And from then on for several weeks, we slept out under the trees in the lower garden away from the buildings.

The facilities were gradually rebuilt and, on December 3, 1927, Bishop John J. Cantwell and the entire California hierarchy gathered at Santa Barbara for the dedication of the restored buildings and consecration of the mission church.

ECUMENISM IN SOUTHLAND

It is satisfying to discover that the leaders of God's People in California have promoted ecumenism, the quest for unity among Christians, from the earliest times. In the Golden State, bishops and priests have insisted that no one animated by the charity of Christ can look upon his separated brethren as strangers or enemies. In his first pastoral letter as Bishop of Monterey, for example, issued early in 1851, Joseph Sadoc Alemany noted that "we should never indulge the least uncharitable feeling towards those who do not possess the gift of faith; on the contrary, we should earnestly pray for all who unfortunately are deprived of it."

The Vincentian Bishop of Monterey–Los Angeles, Thaddeus Amat. held similar views and stated that there was no place in the Catholic Church for the "religious bigot" who "trades on the sensitivities of God and man to satisfy his own interior religious unrest." Bishop Francis Mora, who suffered personal abuse because of his foreign birth, appealed for Christian unity on many occasions. He was especially anxious that Catholics edify their neighbors for, as he said. though they may have different religious beliefs, "yet they are your brethren. Our Creator is theirs. The sunshine and day fall alike on the field of Catholic and non–Catholic." The prelate went on to say that "God wishes the salvation of all. Be kind and considerate to your non–Catholic acquaintances, and let no animosity ever exist between you; have confidence in them."

Mora's successor as Bishop of Monterey–Los Angeles, George Montgomery, was always a popular speaker before non–Catholic audiences, mostly because of his broad–minded approach to daily problems. One local newspaper commented that "no public function is now considered complete without the presence and active cooperation of the Catholic bishop." It was largely Montgomery's ecumenical demeanor that brought about the freedom of the Catholic Church in San Francisco, "from religious factiousness, and polemical strife, and the existence of a happy and cordial *entente* between Protestant and Catholic."

When Thomas J. Conaty, former Rector of The Catholic University of America, came to Los Angeles as bishop, he brought with him the ideal that an American was "a broad–minded and just man, demanding liberty for himself, and desirous that it should be enjoyed by others." On the occasion of his installation in the Bishopric of Monterey–Los Angeles, John J. Cantwell noted that it would be "his constant aim to lend our feeble assistance to every movement that makes for the salvation, the betterment and happiness of ALL the people irrespective of creed or other consideration. Our door and our heart shall ever be open to all our fellow citizens."

What religious strife there has been in California cannot be attributed to Catholic leaders, for they have been exceedingly watchful to avoid that disunity which contradicts the will of Christ, scandalizes the world and endangers the effectiveness of the Gospel message. The annals show that ecumenism, one of the principal concerns of Vatican Council II, has long been a characteristic of God's People along the Pacific Slope. Though believing that "it is only through Christ's Catholic Church" that mankind "can benefit fully from the means of salvation," they long ago endorsed the conciliar viewpoint that non–Catholic churches, "deficient in some respects," have not been deprived of significance and importance in the mystery of salvation.

EIN FESTE BURG

Some years ago, following Holy Mass at San Buenaventura Mission, the choir sung *Ein Feste Burg* during the incensation of the gifts. It was a glorious rendition which fit beautifully into the theme of the day's liturgy. After Mass, a distraught, youngish–looking man stormed into the sacristy and launched into a ten minute diatribe on the inappropriateness of the hymn which he attributed to Martin Luther.

A check with the choir director confirmed that "A Mighty Fortress" was indeed written by the one–time Augustinian monk, though she felt that the sentiments of the hymn more than compensated for the questionable status of its author. Further research revealed that Luther was alone among the Protestant reformers of the 16th century in commending the use of music for the nourishment of Christian life and worship.

He insisted that Gregorian chant and classical polyphony be taught to the youngsters, never discarding his own medieval musical heritage, but adapting it for the use by the whole community of believers. Hence it came about that many of his hymns were revisions of earlier materials.

There are several reputable historians, including the eminent Wilhelm Baumker, who contend that "A Mighty Fortress" was derived from Gregorian music in the *Missa de Angelis*. But while many of his hymns have uncertain origins, *Ein Feste Burg* is among those most convincingly credited to Luther.

Probably composed in 1529, *Ein Feste Burg* is based on the 46th psalm and its melody closely resembles an old *Credo* chant. It received its English translation at the hands of Frederick Henry Hedge in 1852.

Beyond all that, there was a precedent for using *Ein Feste Burg* in the foundations along California's *El Camino Real*. It is verified in an account of a visit to Santa Barbara Mission in 1841 by Sir George Simpson (1792–1860) of the Hudson Bay Company.

In his *Narrative of a Journey round the World* (London, 1847), Simpson concludes his description of the church in these words:

> In the music gallery there was a small but well–tuned organ, on which a native convert was executing several pieces of sacred music with considerable taste, and amongst them, to our great surprise, Martin Luther's hymn *Ein Feste Burg*. This man was almost entirely self–taught, possessing, like most of his race, a fine ear and great aptitude; and his countenance was rather a singular one for an organist on active service, consisting of a handkerchief that confined his black locks, and a shirt of rather scanty longitude belted around his waist.

I gathered all these facts into a letter which was mailed to the Salinas home of our complainant. He scribbled the word "hogwash" on the letter and returned it—postage due!

The whole experience recalled an inscription on a face stone of the National Shrine of the Blessed Mother in Washington, D.C.: "Bigotry, prejudice and bias, all perversions of truth, have one thing in common—they die hard."

EL HOGAR FELIZ

The society of *El Hogar Feliz* was founded on May 5, 1897, under the patronage of Bishop George T. Montgomery, to care for the neglected Catholic children of Los Angeles. It was the initial institution of its kind in Southern California. Principle aim of the organization was to teach the abandoned little ones that by leading virtuous lives they could become useful members of society and a credit to their Church and community.

Through a system of planning and supervising the temporal enjoyment of the youngsters, the staff of *El Hogar Feliz* was able to win their gratitude and confidence in a way that made possible the moulding of their young minds. Bishop Montgomery personally paid the rent for the school building during the first four years and this, coupled with periodic musicals and other entertainments, helped provide the revenue to support the daily activities.

Night classes were conducted for the benefit of working boys and girls not able to attend the normal sessions. Professional men of the city arranged several series of lectures for the evening classes. In the first year of its existence, sixty–five youngsters enrolled under the organization's banner, and the number increased so rapidly that within fifteen months larger quarters had to be sought. These were generously provided by G. Allan Hancock.

Donations of chairs, benches, tables, pictures, and other necessary furnishings were secured from the Catholic populace of Los Angeles, and gradually the nucleus of a small library was put together. Games, dress material and kindergarten supplies were collected as the labor of reclaiming the neglected urchins progressed. A three room home with a large playground was secured at 647 Buena Vista Street, and the name "Happy Home" given to the place. Children from six to fourteen years of age were taken in from all parts of the southland.

The early years of *El Hogar Feliz* were exceedingly productive and the organization was enthusiastically supported by succeeding generations of clergy and laity. On February 22, 1920, Bishop John J. Cantwell blessed the group's beautiful new headquarters and a short while later placed it under the spiritual patronage of Saint Rita. The settlement house was located in a neighborhood where 88% of the families were of Mexican origin. Other national groups served by the Santa Rita Settlement included Austrians, Poles, Spaniards, Armenians, Irish, French, Germans, and natives of Finland, Cuba and Arabia.

During Bishop Cantwell's time, facilities were greatly expanded. A clinic was established to care for sick and needy people from all over town who took advantage of the medical services offered to all applicants, regardless of race or creed. Within a short time, over 300 patients were being treated weekly at the clinic by its volunteer staff of thirty–four doctors. In later years the settlement was attended as a mission from the old Plaza Church and Mass was celebrated there on feast-days and Sundays.

El Hogar Feliz and its successors, Santa Rita Settlement and Clinic, exhibited to the people of Los Angeles that the Catholic Church had an interest in their physical as well as spiritual development. It was among the first of this nation's effective "Catholic Action" groups.

EL MOLINO VIEJO

San Marino's *El Molino Viejo* is a colorful symbol of the enduring legacy left by the friars of earlier times to the Californians of today, This first water–powered grist mill in California was erected by Fray José Zalvidea. Its construction is described in the register books of San Gabriel Mission for December 31, 1816.

Prior to the erection of the Old Mill, all grain at San Gabriel had been ground by hand in stone *metates*, a slow and laborious process. That crude method soon proved an inadequate means of supplying food for the rapidly–growing population. Fray Zalvidea figured that the new mill would not only supply all the necessary grain, but would also make it possible to free a large number of Indian women for other works.

The grist mill was built where the shallow but rugged *arroyas* (Los Robles and Mill Canon) came close together, at the foot of the Pasadena tableland. It was a two–story building with roof of red hand–molded tiles. The walls were of masonry and adobe brick nearly five feet at the base and approximately three feet wide at the top. They were strengthened further by massive buttresses on the eastern corners.

The lower story contained three large rooms known as the wheel chamber. Water, channeled through ditches, was stored in a twelve foot cistern at the southwest end of the mill. From there it was forced through a horizontal spout–flume into the brick–arched wheel chambers.

The wheels were horizontal affairs with a vertical shaft extending upward into the second story, where the grain was ground. On the upper level were heavy millstones fashioned from slabs of volcanic tufa. The friars ingeniously dammed up the lower end of the pond and utilized the flow of water to furnish power for a sawmill, tannery and wool works further down the slope.

The Old Mill served for about seven years until Joseph Chapman was able to erect a new mill just opposite the mission compound. From that time onwards, it was abandoned by the missionaries. Its subsequent history has been catalogued with great detail by Robert Glass Cleland in his superb treatise *El Molino Viejo* (Los Angeles, 1950).

Located as it was in the midst of a very wild and isolated land, the Old Mill was a highly important factor in the life and expansion of the remarkably self–contained agricultural, industrial, educational and ecclesial community at San Gabriel. Though long abandoned, the building stubbornly survived the oblivion that quickly overtook the other buildings at San Gabriel Mission. Since October, 1965, *El Molino Viejo* has housed offices for the California Historical Society.

ENREQUITA MINE

Alexander Edouardt (f. 1858–1892) was among the pioneer artists of California who bequeathed a rich visual heritage to historian and art lover alike. Not alone a skillful man with his brush, Edouardt was a printer and photographer as well. His works in all three of those media, amply described in brochures and books, can be found on the walls of numerous art galleries and museums.

One of Edouardt's most historically significant paintings, depicting the "Blessing of the Enrequita Mine," can be seen hanging in the San Francisco gallery of the Society of California Pioneers. The handsomely–framed painting delineates the colorful ceremony of blessing a quicksilver mine at New Almaden, an event associated with Hispanic miners about to launch their work in a new shaft.

There were a number of such mines in the valley of the Guadalupe Creek, about a dozen miles from San Jose. Mostly dating from Hispanic times, those mines were for many years the largest producers of quicksilver in the country. The name, New Almaden, was derived from their counterparts in Spain.

When the Enrequita mine was opened in 1859, Father Anthony Goetz (1812–1870), the Jesuit Pastor of Saint Joseph's Church in nearby San Jose, was invited to offer Holy Mass at the site. Alexander Edouardt, who was present for that occasion, decided to preserve the ceremony in glowing colors that retain their freshness even after a century.

The picture of the priest offering the Eucharistic Liturgy in a brush–shelter chapel is full of vigor and movement. In the foreground a small plateau is portrayed, perched like a stage above the canyon. The entranceway to the mine appears to be in the hillside behind the altar. Kneeling before the altar are a group of miners with bare heads. Dominating the center foreground are the mine superintendent and his wife.

They are followed by a demure maiden, partially obscured by a parasol. She is very likely their daughter, Enrequita Laurencel, for whom the mine was named. A dog peers intently at some of the men who are preparing a mound of firecrackers that would be exploded at the conclusion of the Mass. No fire–arms are visible. To the right, some latecomers are making their way up the steep hillside on burros. At the extreme right is a plume of steam arising from the smelting furnaces below.

The dominating shades of the canvas are the warm brown of the summer–touched hills and the green of California live oak. The gently rolling hills serve as an excellent backdrop for the stage upon which the whole scene is enacted. Edouardt's portrayal, bathed in sunshine, conveys a feeling of activity, warmth and gaiety. It is California visual history at its very best.

EPISCOPAL HERALDRY

History is replete with instances where coats–of–arms on gravestones, bookplates and documents have proven to be the only means available for identifying personages or offices. The science of heraldry can be traced to the dawn of recorded history. Primitive peoples painted or tattooed tribal badges on their bodies; the ancient Hebrews, Egyptians, Chinese and Japanese used symbols comparable with the insignia of heraldry; the Aztecs of Mexico carried shields and banners bearing personal or tribal devices and the heroes of ancient Greece and Rome inscribed hereditary ensigns on their shields. Centuries later, the Norman invaders of England bore shields emblazoned with crudely–devised insignia.

True heraldry, in the sense of a systematized science containing hereditary armorial bearings, dates from the early twelfth century. There is no record of the use of such bearings during the First Crusade (1096) and they were extremely rare during the Second Crusade (1147). But, by 1189, a number of the shields borne in the Third Crusade were emblazoned; and the great seal of Richard the Lion–Hearted shows his shield charged with a lion rampant.

Several factors contributed to the rise of heraldry: first, the natural desire to enhance personal appearance, which found expression in the ornamentation of military equipment; secondly, the need, among warriors who covered their heads and bodies with armor, for identifying marks easily recognizable in the press of battle and thirdly, the need, in an age when few could write and personal seals served instead of signatures on official or private papers, for seals of clearly identifiable design.

Heraldry was the answer for those times and, with remarkable swiftness, it came into general use. From the beginning of the thirteenth century, princes, nobles, knights and gentry displayed their arms in architectural and household decorations, in jewelry and in embroidery as well as on the paraphernalia of war. The practice of putting the family device on the surcoat, worn over the coat of mail, is credited with giving rise to the coat–of–arms.

In the earliest days of heraldry, arms were chosen indiscriminately by the bearer. Crosses in many forms were adopted, in some instances perhaps to commemorate service in the Crusades, but more often merely as the symbol of Christianity. Broad horizontal, vertical, or slanting stripes of vivid colors across the shield were chosen as being simple to emblazon and easily recognizable. Beasts, dragons, birds, fishes, heavenly bodies, trees, fruit, plants and objects familiar to everyday life of the Middle Ages were adopted as charges. Lions, eagles and foxes representing the virtues which the medieval mind attributed to these creatures, were frequently employed.

The complete composition of a coat–of–arms includes the shield of arms, the helmet, the crest, the wreath, the mantling and the motto. The shield, on which is displayed the armorial device, is the most important part of the composition. It represents the old knightly shield and may vary in shape according to the taste of the artist. The helmet, derived from the defensive armor, is placed above the shield and may be used even though the coat–of–arms includes no crest. The crest, principal accessory of the shield of arms, surmounts the helmet. Like the shield and helmet, it has its origin in the accoutrement of the knight who wore on his helmet, as a special mark of distinction, an ornament of painted wood, metal or leather. The motto, which is inscribed on a scroll either above or below the shield, is not an essential part of the composition, is not necessarily hereditary and may be changed at will. Many of the oldest coats–of–arms do not include mottoes.

The Roman pontiffs and lesser prelates began using personal coats–of–arms in the mid–twelfth century. This they did because they were landowners who needed official identification or documentation pertaining to their ecclesiastical property. For the most part, ecclesial coats–of–arms follow the general rules of heraldry. One distinctive feature is the use of tassels whose color and number indicate whether the bearer is a cardinal, archbishop, bishop, monsignor or simple priest.

Today, practically all official Church documents carry the printed or impressed coat–of–arms of the residential bishop or the diocese over which he presides. Many of the documents pertaining to the California phase of the nation's Catholic heritage can be identified by the personal coat–of–arms emblazoned upon the page. Devised in remote days of chivalry, borne by armed knights in tournaments and on ancient battlefields, cherished by illustrious forebearers of ages past, and handed down from generation to generation as a sacred emblem of family honor, the coat–of–arms is an object of pride and distinction for its bearer today and an heirloom which generations will treasure.

THE "ESTELLE"

The first home of Edward L. and Carrie Estelle Doheny was a railroad car. And it was aboard that "mansion on wheels" that they exchanged their marital vows on August 22, 1900.

The "Estelle"

In the listing of marriages in the local Albuquerque newspaper was this entry: "Oil magnate Edward Doheny was married yesterday to Carrie Betzold aboard their private railroad car, parked on a siding near the main transcontinental line."

Doheny's private railroad car played an important role in his busy life. For over three decades, the "mobile mansion" rolled back and forth across the United States and Mexico with great regularity.

According to railroad historian, Lucius Beebe, the "Katharyne" was distinguished for its "classic purity of line and refinement of decorative treatment." In his book, Beebe reproduces a picture of the car resting on the transfer table at Pullman, Illinois, with the company's venerable clock tower in the background.

Manufactured by George Mortimer Pullman's Palace Car Company the "Katharyne" was listed on the company's records as Private Car Number 2093. Delivered on November 30, 1894, it was constructed according to Plans Number 1115–A.

The car was luxuriously outfitted with carpeted floors, upholstered chairs and artistic chandeliers. The black walnut panelling was embellished with bevel edged French mirrors. The car even boasted an ice activated air conditioning unit.

Built to the specifications of Richard C. Kerens as his personal property, the car was assigned to its home carrier, the West Virginia Central & Pittsburgh Railway, a company in which Kerens was a director.

Though not a railroad operative in the professional sense, Kerens was a heavy investor in such firms as the St. Louis, Iron Mountain & Southern, and the St. Louis–Southwestern. In addition, Kerens was associated with Montana's Senator William Andrews Clark in the incorporation of the San Pedro, Los Angeles & Salt Lake Railroad which later evolved into the Union Pacific.

The deluxe private railroad car "Katharyne" transported Kerens in comfort and safety, sometimes pausing at the four towns named for its owner in Texas, Arkansas, West Virginia and California. The "Katharyne," named for Kerens' oldest daughter, was acquired by Edward Laurence Doheny just prior to the turn of the century. On the day of his wedding, Mr. Doheny rechristened the car "Estelle" for his new bride.

The "Estelle" had begun its career during the golden years of steam railroading. Private railroad cars were a familiar scene from the high passes of the Rockies to the fashionable resorts of California. Yet, almost without exception, private cars remain aloof, serene and impervious to popular availability. To own and operate a private car was a rare distinction.

Since many of the files at the Pullman company were destroyed and others remain "classified," it is presently impossible to determine what eventually happened to the "Estelle" after Mr. Doheny sold it in the early 1930s. Several family friends conjecture that it was given to the President of Mexico.

EZCARAY ALTAR PIECES

In 1934, Bishop John J. Cantwell was approached with a plan for acquiring the complete interior of the famous Chapel of Ezcaray. Built in 1608, and removed to the United States in 1926, the collection comprised several altars, a pulpit, organ, confessionals, statues, paintings and bells.

Though the Bishop originally demurred, for financial reasons, the historic furnishings were ultimately purchased by Raymond Gould of Pasadena. After the new owner's death, a consortium chaired by Edward T. Foley acquired the collection for use in the cathedral that Archbishop John J. Cantwell was planning for Los Angeles on Wilshire Boulevard.

At the suggestion of Mark Harrington, who supervised most of the restoration work at San Fernando Mission, the pieces of the "Spanish chapel" were stored in several rooms at the Old Mission. A few years earlier, when Harrington drafted plans for the sanctuary area of the mission chapel, his design for the altar and reredos were based on his "accommodated sense" of what was there originally He had no photographs, oral tradition, or sketches on which to base his designs.

In a letter to Harry Downie, written shortly after the Ezcaray altar pieces arrived at San Fernando, Harrington said that he "had discussed the possibility of using the altar pieces in the chapel of the Old Mission" with Auxiliary Bishop Joseph T. McGucken.

Apparently McGucken sensed that there might never be a new cathedral in Los Angeles, for he assured Harrington that "if the Ezcaray pieces aren't used for the cathedral, you can have them for San Fernando Mission." Harrington was "delighted" and, in his letter to Downie, said that "if ever we install the Ezcaray pieces in the chapel of the Old Mission, ours will be the finest and most attractive of all those along *Camino Real*."

On June, 18, 1941, the "Ezcaray Chapel Exhibit" was opened to viewing by the public at San Fernando. According to the brochure issued for that occasion, James A. Tierney, the artist who supervised the installation in several rooms of the convento, said that the Ezcaray items had "found a becoming, if not a permanent home." Harrington had, in fact, placed several of the pieces in the chapel, *viz.*, the hand–carved pulpit, the sound chamber above the pulpit, several statues and a group of paintings. Visitors said that "they looked as if they had always been there."

In 1953, it was decided that a large portion of the

Ezcaray collection would be assembled and used as a reredos for the newly–erected student chapel at the adjoining Queen of Angels Seminary. Miss Judy Seraboli, a well–known California artist, was asked to oversee the installation. Many observers complained that in its reconstructed form, the reredos lacked much of its original embellishment. In the place of the central statue of Saint Philip Neri, for example, an ornate crucifix was mounted onto the middle panel.

EX LIBRIS IN CALIFORNIA

Detachable bookplates or *ex libris* labels, some of them pre–dating the age of printing, are an outgrowth of the armorial symbols found in medieval manuscripts. Their *raison d'étre* has always been, that of putting the owner's name to the plate's most conspicuous outpost. The artistic embellishments or tiny scenes illustrating the actual name, possessing as they do an uniquely revelatory quality, are historical remnants of art and society whose style reflects the customs and practices characteristic of a particular era.

In the days before invention of movable type, bookplates formed part of the book itself and were put in place as a matter of course by the scribe who copied the manuscript. Though designed primarily as declarations of ownership, bookplates served also to express the owner's preferences and character. Such was the case in Germany, where the use of plates can be traced from the 15th century.

In early California, the most ingenious, legible, and accurate method of indicating ownership was the *marca de fuego*, or brand, which was burned onto the top edges of the leaves or on the vellum or sheepskin binding. It was irremovable and thus served well the missions whose supply of books was always scanty.

Probably the oldest bookplate in California annals is the typographical imprint of Mariano Guadalupe Vallejo, a copy of which is preserved in San Marino's Henry E. Huntington Library. It was most likely printed at Sonoma, between 1837 and 1839, by Jose de la Rosa, on the press of Agustin Zamorano. The earliest dated bookplate made in California belonged to William B. Olds who arrived in the Bay Area about 1849. His plate was attached to the legal tomes that subsequently formed the nucleus of the San Francisco Law Library.

The Golden State's earliest ecclesiastical bookplate was commissioned by Bishop Francis Mora for the books comprising the *Bibliotheca Montereyensis–Angelorum Dioeceseos*, that outstanding collection of theological, biblical, historical and scientific tomes which was housed in Los Angeles, at Saint Vibiana's Cathedral, in the years after 1884. The distinctive plate, measuring 3 1/4" by 2 3/4," was printed on a dull coated rag paper, by a commercial firm in Los Angeles. While there is no way of judging the quantity of those bookplates printed, certainly over a thousand would have been needed to provide each of the books with a plate.

Even today, bookplates lend character and individuality to books. For enthusiasts of Californiana, the historic imprint associated with the *Bibliotheca Montereyensis–Angelorum Dioeceseos* is a highly prized addition to their private collections. The art of the bookplate or *ex libris*, ever the harbinger of the book, is the *avant courier* of progress. Beauty in plates is not confined to a few specimens of the past. It is a living ideal reflected in many contemporary examples of the bookplate.

FAMILY ROSARY CRUSADE

Newly ordained and burning with determination to spend his life in the service of the Blessed Mother, Father Patrick Peyton set out to proclaim the value and necessity of family prayer. The ingenious Holy Cross priest hit upon the idea of popularizing the rosary as the most logical and effective device for proving his theory that "the family that prays together stays together."

The Family Rosary Crusade was launched in 1942, as a world–embracing movement offering peoples of every race and creed the option for life and love and unity within the family circle. Though the crusade was universal in its appeal, the movement has very special associations with Los Angeles. Southern California won the distinction of being Father Peyton's quasi–domicile early in the 1940s, when the indefatigable priest began his radio apostolate.

Father Peyton chose London, Ontario, as the locale for the first formal convocation. From there, the crusade spread like wildfire throughout the globe. Between 1942 and 1977, some 375 crusades took place on all six continents, with rally attendance ranging from hundreds to hundreds of thousands. Newspapers reported more than 500,000 attended the rally at San Francisco's Stadium. In excess of a million were counted at the crusades in Manila, Madrid, Rio de Janeiro and Sao Paolo.

The whole operation reflected precision planning. Forty tons of projectors, films and parts were moved by vans into the crusade area. Armies of local parishioners were recruited to act as projectionists and catechists. Peyton and his co–workers utilized every modern means of communications–advertising, salesmanship, radio, the press, motion pictures, television and personal visitations. No rosary bead was left unfingered by Peyton in the efforts to further devotion to Our Lady. Nor was the follow–up neglected. After the rally at Sao Paolo, hundreds of thousands of lay volunteers went from door–to–door soliciting pledges for the daily Family Rosary.

Throughout most of the United States, the crusades have taken the form of a family–oriented parish renewal program called "Families for Prayer." Like the earlier format, they stress the importance and values of family life.

From the very outset, Father Peyton's crusade received approbation and encouragement from Rome. Pope Pius XII sent a letter on the occasion of the crusade at Wembley Stadium, London, which read:

> There is no surer means of calling down God's blessings upon the family . . . than the daily recitation of the Rosary . . . in which parents and children join together in supplicating the Eternal Father, through the intercession of their most loving Mother.

More recently, Pope Paul VI sent a special message to Father Peyton in which he said:

> You, beloved son, mindful of this ancient devotion to the Blessed Mother, and with great confidence in her powerful protection, founded the Family Rosary Crusade in 1942. Those were the days when the world was particularly afflicted not only by extreme material dangers, but by moral evils as well. You strove to alleviate the sufferings of families, as you likewise do today, by making known to them the necessity, the power and the ease of prayer, especially that of the Rosary.

Like the Church, the crusade is now in a state of flux. It may well take different forms in the future. Whatever route it goes, one can rest assured that the rosary and family prayer will have the place of prominence.

FAMILY THEATRE OF THE AIR

The apostolate of Father Patrick Peyton on behalf of family prayer has no parallel in United States Catholic annals. From January, 1942, the tireless Holy Cross priest devoted himself to strengthening the family unit through daily corporate prayer, especially the Rosary.

A vital part of Peyton's campaign involved utilization of radio as a means for furthering the notion that "the family that prays together stays together."

After meeting with the leaders of network radio in Hollywood, Father Peyton decided on a format for the "Family Theatre of the Air" patterned after that used by professional shows: a "drama" to gain the audience, followed by a "commercial" to sell the product. The drama would be presented in a family setting, so as to prepare the listeners for the message of daily corporate prayer, which Peyton termed the "lost notion of our age."

The first office of the Family Theatre in Hollywood was a room at the old Immaculate Heart Convent. That and "sundry telephone booths" served as headquarters until permanent facilities were acquired at 7201 Sunset Boulevard. The initial program was aired over the Mutual network on February 13, 1947. It was a play entitled "Flight from Home" and starred Loretta Young, James Stewart and Don Ameche.

The reaction of the general public was overwhelmingly favorable. Eventually 700 stations throughout the United States subscribed to the program. The Armed Forces Radio network beamed them to troops overseas and independent stations in other countries also picked up the series. Even certain areas behind the Iron Curtain heard the program by shortwave.

The tremendous impact of the program in favor of family prayer was sustained. Four hundred and eighty–two separate presentations were carried by the Mutual Broadcasting System every Thursday evening at 7 o'clock, for almost ten years.

The "Family Theatre of the Air" was also well–received in professional circles. It won the Thomas Edison Award, as well as the American Legion award. *Time* magazine called the series "outstanding" and *Radio Daily* selected it as the Mutual network's best of the year.

The program continued into the mid 1950s, until the radio media began losing much of its audience to television. Even a decade later, however, reruns of earlier shows were reaching 150 stations, as well as millions of listeners in Latin America, Spain, Australia and the Philippines.

Though Father Peyton's radio productions were only one of his many–faceted endeavors on behalf of daily family prayer, they were perhaps his most important. His identification with those programs provided an exposure which eventually enabled Father Peyton to project his Rosary and prayer crusades to diocesan, national and international audiences.

Father Peyton's pioneering radio apostolate anticipated by fifteen years Vatican Council II's decree advocating "Catholic broadcasting" as an ideal means for bringing listeners "into communication with the life of the Church."

FAZZINI IN LOS ANGELES

Visitors to the Paul VI Hall of Audiences in the Vatican are fascinated with Pericle Fazzini's monumental sculpture of the "Resurrection." The breath–taking rendition has been the source of countless articles and newspaper accounts. The artist has Christ rising from a grove of olive trees swept by the wind. The trees recall the Mount of Olives, Christ's passion and the blind violence of war.

This sculpture is symbolic of a continuous rejuvenation of the world, and this rejuvenation is not progress but a conservation of youth, freshness and novelty. In Christ, Fazzini has imprinted his deep–seated conviction that life is not progress towards a far–away, unidentified goal, but a submergence in the eternity of that act.

Those who have seen Fazzini's "Resurrection" sense that there is something of an invasion of the world by God in the sculpture, the reality of God coming to earth and transforming it. All boundaries between time and eternity, between heaven and earth, are blown away in the resurrection.

At the Historical Museum of the Archival Center is another of Fazzini's masterful works of art, this one fashioned in the same spirit as the "Resurrection" in the Paul VI Hall of Audiences. The "Redeemer" is a bas–relief completed by the artist on the occasion of the Extraordinary Redemption jubilee in 1983–1984. Christ is depicted with an intense expression, a dramatic pause in Pilate's consulate.

Behind a close–up portrayal of Our Lord's face is the consulate paved with stones. Two Roman soldiers can be seen, waiting their turn to torture Him. It is a picture of suffering, violence and betrayal from another era, yet one all too recurrent in contemporary times.

In his own description of this work–of–art, Fazzini said he wanted to bring back to life the face of Christ in front of Pontius Pilate. "He is demonstrating compassion and mercy to the arrogant people of those times and ours for the conceit and presumption that necessitated His passion."

The Fazzini sculpture at San Fernando is #18 of a series commissioned by the Knights of Columbus. It was presented to Timothy Cardinal Manning by Supreme Knight Virgil C. Dechant in June of 1984. For more than twenty years, Fazzini's name has won worldwide recognition. Important art critics in all the major countries study his work and methods. During his simple and solitary life, Fazzini cultivated rare friendships, including that of the late Pope Paul VI who gave him the commission for the immense Resurrection scene that dominates the Hall of Audiences.

Fazzini's portraits, bronzes, engravings and graphic arts have been praised by critics the world over. No less an authority than F. Bellonzi said that the figures fashioned by Fazzini for a chapel in Rome's Saint Eugene's Church render that edifice "the most beautiful complex of sacred art effected in the Eternal City since the early 1800s." Like all the other items entrusted to the Historical Museum of the Archival Center, Fazzini's "Redeemer" is available for public viewing on Mondays and Thursdays from 1 until 3 o'clock and at other times by appointment.

"FELICITA "

One of the most significant events in southland history was the Battle of San Pasqual, which occurred in December, 1846. Though the greatly outnumbered American troops were defeated, the Mexican Government realized thereafter what was entailed by "manifest destiny," or the inevitability of United States expansion to the Pacific coast.

For many years in the 1930s, that dramatic encounter of United States dragoons and Mexican lancers was recreated in an outdoor pageant staged about four miles from the scene where the forces of Stephen W. Kearny faced those of Andrés Pico. Written by the talented Benjamin F. Sherman, director of the Escondido Community Arts Club, "Felicita" opened with Indians gathered for a *fiesta* in the San Pasqual Indian village.

One of the features of that *fiesta* was a "marriage race" to determine which of several contenders would win the hand of a highly–coveted tribal maiden. In this particular case, three Indian braves and a Spanish–Indian, Caspár, who was the villain, vied for the honor of marrying Felicita, the daughter of Chief Pontho.

Shortly after the racers started their long course, a friar from San Luis Rey Mission arrived to administer the sacraments to the sick and to baptize children and catechumens. Among the baptismal candidates was Felicita. Caspár cheated in the race, won and claimed the hand of Felicita. She refused, however, to go with him, saying that, as a Christian, she was no longer obliged to follow heathen customs.

Just as the villain was about to take the pretty Indian maiden by force, a messenger arrived with news that white men were approaching the Indian village. Caspár immediately departed to inform Captain Pico. Then came the renactment of the San Pasqual Battle. Some fifty, horsemen, representing the Californians of 1846, charged up the hill where the outdoor play took place. Guns were fired and a mock battle ensued. The Americans were shown huddled and making plans to send for outside assistance.

The principal male character of the play, Richard, a private under Kearny, took the scene. He was seriously wounded and at the point of death after a short sword duel with Caspár. Felicita came across him and nursed Richard back to health.

Apart from the authentically–recreated battle scene, there is a ring of historicity about the central plot. Indian legend has it that one of Kearny's wounded soldiers was found by a San Pasqual Indian girl and cared for. Legend also is clear that her name was Felicita. Shortly after the turn of the century, an Indian by that name was found residing at San Pasqual. She claimed to be more than one hundred years old and, in talks with pioneers of the area, told of the Battle of San Pasqual and her rescue of an American soldier.

The pageantry of "Felicita," woven as it was about the principal struggle in winning California to the United States, was long a vital and visible chapter in the story of the Golden State.

FEMALE PRIESTHOOD — ALEMANY'S VIEWS

While acknowledging the directive from Vatican Council II about the importance of having women participate more widely in the various fields of the Church's apostolate, most theologians see no justification for altering the traditional practice of excluding them from the sacrament of holy orders.

From apostolic times the tradition of the Church has denied women the privilege of becoming ordained ministers, a custom also evident in the Old Testament priesthood. Though very important roles were given to such women as Esther and Judith, they were never permitted to perform services at the altar. The continuing practice of the Church has been based on Saint Paul's teaching in I Corinthians 14, 34 and I Timothy 2, 11 which absolutely opposes the ministry of women in the Church. Several of the early Fathers, among them Irenaeus, Epiphanius, Ambrose and Augustine, felt it would be heretical to admit women to the office and dignity of the priesthood.

Archbishop Joseph Sadoc Alemany of San Francisco also had some very definite ideas about the question of a female priesthood. The Dominican prelate expressed himself "with devastating thoroughness" in a letter of May 26, 1883, which appeared four days later in T*he Monitor,* the Bay Area's Catholic newspaper,

> St. Paul was not much in favor of women's preaching, for he says: "Let women keep silence . . . for it is a shame for a woman to speak in the church. Let women learn in silence . . . I permit not a woman to teach, nor use authority over a man; but to be silent.
>
> This agrees perfectly with the designs of the Son of God who, although He loved His Blessed Mother more than He did, or ever will, love any other of His creatures, yet He did not commission her to preach or to exercise any of the functions of the sacred ministry; but He conferred those offices upon men, who were to be ordained with due powers by the Sacrament of Holy Orders.
>
> Upon which the learned Epiphanius observes (Heresy 59) "that from the beginning of the world, among the followers of the true religion, never has a woman performed the offices of the priesthood, neither Eve or any of her daughters."
>
> And this is true in the New as well as in the Old Testament. "For if the function of the priesthood," says the same holy Doctor, "had been confided to women, to no one should the priestly offices have been entrusted with greater reason than to Mary, upon whom so great an honor was conferred that she was chosen to conceive in her chaste womb the Lord of all things the God of Heaven, the Son of God."

Concluding his observations, the archbishop said that women would be well advised to heed the apostolic mandate about doing what was not confided even to the Mother of God. Archbishop Alemany expressed himself on this overall question as an appendage to another, more-pressing issue. Had he dwelt on the topic at any length, very likely he would have leaned more heavily on the positive element of womanhood as contained in The Talmud:

> God did not create woman from man's head, that he should command her, nor from his feet, that she should be his slave, but rather from his side, that she should be near his heart.

FESTA DE SERRETA

A study of the religious festivals common to various nationalities reveals much about a peoples' ideals, beliefs and culture. Over the centuries, the Catholic Church "has used in her preaching the discoveries of different cultures to spread and explain the message of Christ to all nations, to probe it and more deeply understand it, and to give it better expression in liturgical celebrations and in the life of the diversified community of the faithful."

The Azorean Portuguese colonies traditionally engage in a host of religious celebrations during the summer months, most of them centering around the *Divino Espirito Santo* and *Rainha Santa Isabel.* One of the most popular and unique of the religious festivals in California is that of *Nossa Senhora des Milagres.* Known popularly as the "*Festa da Serreta,* " the festival is observed annually at Gustine.

Historically, the observance can be traced to and associated with the beautiful devotion to Our Lady of the Miracles, in Terceira, Azores. There, in a rude chapel, in the sixteenth century, a statue of *Nossa Senhora* became the focal point of numerous cures and miracles. In later years the shrine was enlarged to accommodate the growing crowds and then formally dedicated with great solemnity, in 1842.

The initial purpose of introducing the festival along the Pacific Slope was that of uniting all the Portuguese people of California into a more cohesive community. The mechanics of the festival were organized by John Mattos, who worked with and directed the program from 1932 to 1947. Overall management of the religious pageantry was later entrusted to a group of men known as the *Irmandade do Nossa Senhora dos Milagres.*

Focal centers of the festival are the Catholic Church (the *Igreja do Divina Espirito Santo*), the city park and the nearby fraternal hall. Before the beginning of the annual novena, the young Portuguese girls learn a series of melodies to Our Lady. The images of sixteen saints are decorated with satins, flowers and laces. The novena itself begins on September 8, and lasts until the 15th. Upon completion of the religious services, the statues are taken in procession through the town on *andores* or litters. Thousands of people participate in the various liturgical and para–liturgical events.

The incorporation into the festival of *cantorias ao desafio* (song contests), the *bodo de leite* (milk banquet) and *bolos doces* (sweet dough) exemplify what the conciliar fathers of Vatican Council II meant when they said that "there is hardly any proper use of material things which cannot be directed toward the sanctification of men and the praise of God."

In a detailed study of the religious festivals associated with the Portuguese, financed by a John Simon Guggenheim Memorial Fellowship, one researcher classified the "*Festa da Serreta*," at Gustine, as one of the most elaborate and popular festivals of the "exiled" Portuguese. Certainly, one would agree with that same observer who stated that the festival was guaranteed to kill nostalgia.

FIRE HOUSE #1

The Old Plaza Engine House, at the corner of Plaza and Los Angeles streets, was erected in 1885. It has the distinction of being the first station in the city named for *Nuestra Señora de los Angeles.*

The adobe residence of Pio Pico stood just west of the firehouse, with the famed Pico House Hotel on the same side of the Plaza, across Sanchez street. On the west side stands the restored *Asistencia de Nuestra Señora de los Angeles.*

Mrs. Bigelow, the owner of the two story brick building first leased it to the Los Angeles Fire Department's Chemical Company Number One for $50 a month. That was a bargain even in those days. It was occupied by the "Thirty–Eights Engine Company No. 1," a volunteer company named in memory of the thirty–eight volunteers who provided the initial fire protection for local inhabitants.

There was a meeting room, with living quarters for the fire fighters in the rear of the second floor. The street level was occupied by the horses and fire equipment. When the alarm sounded, the fire fighters came down a brass sliding pole. In 1872, the Thirty Eights acquired a 2nd size Amoskeag. With that purchase, Los Angeles emerged directly from the bucket brigade to the era of the steam engine. Fire fighting took on new dimensions.

Fifteen years later, the city purchased an Ahrens 2nd size steam engine which was proudly christened the "Walter S. Moore" in honor of their chief. Thereby began Engine Company No. 4. And shortly thereafter, the station house was connected to the new Richmond alarm system, one of the first street box–alarms introduced to the west coast.

In 1891, Engine Company 4 was moved and Chemical Company No. 1 took possession of the station–house. The priests at the Old Plaza Church referred to this group as the "shock troops" of the Fire Department. Their duty was to get water on the fire immediately, while the steamers were taking time (four to six minutes) to build up sufficient steam to operate—a minimum of eighty pounds of pressure. The chemical engine was operable simply upon being rotated 180 degrees.

The four horse stalls were located near the back of the lower floor. From there the horses moved forward and under the harnesses attached to the engine. There was a turntable which made it unnecessary to back into the station.

After the fire station was relocated, the building was used as a hotel, restaurant and saloon. Today, restored with great care, authenticity and precision by the State Division of Architecture, it is a major feature of the *Pueblo de los Angeles* Historic Park.

The Old Plaza Engine House has been declared a state historical landmark. Within is displayed fire fighting equipment from the 1880s, including an original pumper and chemical wagon.

FIRSTS IN CALIFORNIA

The subjects of "firsts" has received much local, national and international attention in recent years, especially since 1933, when the first edition of Joseph Nathan Kane's Famous First Facts was issued. A few of these "first" relating to Catholic development in California are gathered for those interested in such statistics.

The initial christening administered in California has been the subject of some dispute. According to one authority, "The first Indian Baptism in California was on July 22, 1769, when Fray Juan Crespi on the Portola expedition in search of Monterey Bay baptized a dying Indian girl whom he named Margarita, in the northwest corner of the present San Diego County." Apparently unmindful of this happening, Fray Junipero Serra noted in the record books at Monterey that on December 26, 1770, "Bernardino de Jesus Fages (became) the first Christian among the natives of Upper California." The first white child baptized within the confines of California was Juan Jose Garcia, born on November 11, 1774, at San Luis Obispo.

Father Francisco Palou's *Relacion Historica de la Vida y Apostolicas Tareas del Venerable Padre Fray Junipero Serra* (Mexico, 1787) was the first book written in California to find its way into print. The first writing of a literary nature produced by a native in California was written about 1854, by Pablo Tac (1822–1841), an Indian seminarian from Mission San Luis Rey.

The first bishop actually to touch California soil was Fray Francisco Garcia Diego y Moreno who took up his episcopal residence at San Diego, on December 10, 1841. The first officially proclaimed Thanksgiving Day was observed with the active cooperation and support of Fray Gonzalez Rubio and the Catholic clergy of California on November 29, 1849.

The initial convent opened was that of Santa Catalina, commenced at Monterey in early 1851, by Sister Mary Goemere, O.P. Father Jose Ygnacio Arguello, the proto–priest of California, was ordained in 1808. The first novice to join a religious order of women was Arguello's sister, Maria Concepcion, who received the Dominican habit on April 11, 1851. To Juan Bautista Mugazabal, S.J., belongs the distinction of being the first man to pronounce the vows of poverty, chastity and obedience in California.

In 1893, an alumnus of Santa Clara College, California's first Catholic college founded exclusively for laymen, Stephen M. White (1853–1901) became the first native son of California to serve in the United States Senate. Father Michael King (1829–1904), pastor of Saint Mary's Church in Oakland, was the first priest to celebrate a golden jubilee of service to the Church in California. This was on July 12, 1903.

These items are but a sampling of a long litany of events recorded in the annals of the Golden State—a commonwealth whose privilege it was to be discovered, explored, colonized and civilized by men professing the Catholic Faith.

GOLDEN STATE'S FLAGS

Since Egyptian times flags have been regarded as real, though sometime vicarious reminders of sovereignty. The bright colors and striking designs of a nation's pennant symbolize the land, government and ideals associated with a particular segment of the world's populace. Such was surely the case in California.

Though claiming nominal suzerainty over the area from 1542 onwards, the Spanish government actually flew its colors in California only during the fifty–three years between April 29, 1769, and April 11, 1822. Prior to the adoption of a distinctive national flag, in 1785, the colorful standard of Charles V, its shield bearing the quartered arms of Castile and Leon, denoted Iberian dominance in California.

Between 1785 and 1822, the national ensign replaced the royal standard as the symbol of Spanish authority. It consisted of a wide yellow band bordered at top and bottom by a red stripe, with an escutcheon bearing a crown and displaying the arms of Castile and Leon. With the official sanctioning of independence by a *junta* at Monterey, the standard of the Mexican Empire was substituted for the Spanish national banner. The green, white and red flag stood for the Catholic religion, national autonomy and monarchial government. Superimposed on the white field of the tri–colored banner was a design derived from an old Aztec legend foretelling the location of Mexico City. Replacement of the short–lived empire by a republic, in 1824, brought about a slight alteration in the design and proportions of the eagle and wreath.

The California Republic was proclaimed on June 14, 1846, by hoisting the flag bearing a five–pointed red star in the upper corner facing the figure of a grizzly. A red stripe edged the broad, white band. Barely four weeks later, the red, white and blue national flag of the United States was raised by John D. Sloat over Monterey. At that time, there were twenty–eight stars in four rows on a blue field of thirteen stripes.

Other flags have been associated with California during its history, though none was ever more than a gesture of minor importance. Most outstanding of these were the pennants of England (Drake, 1579) and Russia (Kuskof, 1812–1842). The personal streamers of such individuals as Hippolyte Bouchard (1818) and John C. Fremont (1843–1846) also deserve inclusion. The present state flag, following the basic design of the one used by the California Republic, was officially adopted on February 3, 1911.

Owning a flag and displaying it properly bespeaks patriotism and respect for the people whose sovereignty it represents. Those reflecting on the history of their government's official standard can easily appreciate the message of its symbolism.

FLIGHT INTO EGYPT

Aficionados of Los Angeles will want to know that the United States Historical Society honored Saint Vibiana's Cathedral by designating the famed "Flight into Egypt" window for its 1982 Christmas plate. Reviewers and critics alike have already acclaimed this colorful item as the height of the platemaking art. Robert Ramsay has described it as a "masterful artistic achievement."

Artisans applied fifteen separate transparent colors to each piece of the genuine cathedral glass. The colors became fused permanently into place when fired to temperatures in excess of 1100 fahrenheit.

The Jefferson Pewter Company, whose craftsmen produce museum pieces for the United States Department of State and the Boston Museum of Fine Arts, fashioned rims for the plates, using highly–polished, lead–free pewter. As were the other windows in the Cathedral, the "Flight into Egypt" was designed by the grand master of stained glass art, John Mayer of Munich. His work can be seen in many California churches, including Saint Paul's, San Francisco.

Father William Cantwell had journeyed to Europe in early 1922 and personally visited the Mayer studios. He highly endorsed their work in a letter to the Bishop of Monterey–Los Angeles, noting that the Mayers "have a reputation that they are living up to and not living on." It was recommendation enough and the contract was signed.

Into this particular window, the elderly Mayer poured all he had learned from a lifetime of perfecting the unique beauty of stained glass art. Critics believe it may have been his finest work.

His colors are today extraordinarily deep and rich, with stunningly intense blues, reds and golds, together with a host of other colors, ranging from subtle pastels to rich variations of the primary colors. The skin tones are amazingly realistic.

Contemporary artisans are overwhelmed by Mayer's skill as were those of a half century ago. The "Flight into Egypt" was a milestone achievement, and its influence on stained glass art makes it one of the most important works of all time—as well as one of the most beautiful.

Working with his three sons, John Mayer based his depiction on the second chapter of Saint Matthew's Gospel, where an angel of the Lord appeared to Joseph in a dream and said, "Rise, take the child and his mother, and flee to Egypt." The distinguished art critic, Robert Ramsay, compared the 1982 facsimile to the original and noted that "when the light strikes this plate, it becomes alive with fiery colors. The polished pewter 'rim' seems to focus the light—a halo–effect never before seen in a collector's plate."

Collectors will want to know that "the only annual genuine stained glass cathedral Christmas plate in the world" comes in an elegant upholstered box. A lucite display stand is included and each plate is registered and numbered.

FORE–EDGE PAINTINGS AT CAMARILLO

Probably the most curious and fascinating of the graphic arts is that of fore–edge painting. Tiny scenes, mostly done in watercolor, are applied to the front edges of a book while its leaves are secured in a fanned position. The world's richest and most varied assemblage of these interesting book decorations was in the Estelle Doheny Collection of Rare Books, Manuscripts and Works of Art, located on the grounds of Saint John's Seminary. In the Camarillo collection were 614 fore–edge books, including about fifty "double" fore–edge paintings.

A rudimentary kind of "edge–decoration" can be traced to the tenth century on the European continent. The edges of large and heavy volumes, most of them shelved horizontally rather than vertically, offered librarians a natural and obvious convenience. Often the inscribing of a book's title on the fore–edge saved the labor of lifting a weighty volume from its place to determine the nature of its contents.

With the invention of the printing press, smaller books became more common and the fore–edge was relieved of its duty as titlebearer. In subsequent years mottoes, royal monograms and fine adornments were occasionally applied to select books as a means of enhancing the tome's overall worth. Just when the "fanning" method of decorating the fore–edge came into vogue is not precisely known. The process involves spreading the leaves and, while holding them in that position, applying an elaborate design or scene. When the leaves spring back to their normal position, the inscription becomes indiscernible.

When a painting has been put on the leaves fanned in one way, it disappears entirely when the direction of the leaves is reversed. This fact attracted the attention of resourceful artists and suggested the possibility of painting the edge in both directions. One scene appears when the leaves of these "double" fore–edge paintings are fanned to the right; and another when they are fanned to the left and neither is obvious when the leaves are in their usual position. Estimates place at seven percent the number of "double" paintings among the total extant fore–edge scenes. "Double" fore–edge paintings truly represent a "lost art." Even the most talented craftsman found it difficult to paint two scenes without allowing one to mar the color sequence of the other.

Unfortunately, but necessarily, fore–edge paintings commonly result in the segregation, if not the concealment of the volumes they decorate. Their quantity is most generally limited to books published in England between 1775 and 1850. A most interesting study on the subject, written largely around the Estelle Doheny Collection, is Carl J. Weber's A Thousand and One Fore–Edge Paintings (Waterville, Maine, 1949) which chronologically locates a representative assortment of books in the United States with decorated edges.

Those who refer to fore–edge paintings as "pretty but petty" are seemingly oblivious to that basic principle for determining artistic quality which clearly states that size is no gauge for grandeur.

FORT YUMA BICENTENNIAL

There were two missionary establishments in Alta California staffed by friars from the Apostolic College of *Santa Cruz de Querétaro*. They were not patterned after the plan used so successfully in the coastal foundations.

The arrangement proved to be an unfortunate blunder, in the opinion of one chronicler. Another authority characterized the plan as calling for neither a *presidio*, a mission nor a *pueblo*, each of which was intelligible to a Spaniard. The first of these two "mongrel" missions, dedicated to *La Purísima Concepción de Maria Santisima*, was established on December 8, 1 1780, the feast of Our Lady's Immaculate Conception.

For a host of reasons, the foundation didn't function well and, on July 18, 1781, an uprising broke out among a small dissident group of natives. The mission was totally destroyed. The founder, Fray Francisco Garces and three other friars were martyred.

The mission was never rebuilt. Hubert Howe Bancroft observed that the Yumas were not subdued, peace was not made and the rebel chiefs were not captured. The nation remained independent of all Spanish control and was always more or less hostile. The Yumas occupied the area until 1846, when United States troops, under the command of Stephan Watts Kearny crossed into California and took possession of the territory.

Union soldiers were stationed at Fort Yuma during the Civil War and the Butterfield Stage Line passed through the area enroute from Saint Louis to San Francisco. The first residential priest in modern times was Father Patrick Birmingham, who arrived in 1866. Twenty years later, the Sisters of Saint Joseph of Carondelet came from Saint Louis to teach the Indian children.

The United States government withdrew its support from the school in 1895, and the Sisters were soon forced to leave. It wasn't until 1923, after twenty years of negotiations, that the Catholic Church was once more able to reclaim the site and build a new and permanent mission.

In the late 1930s, jurisdiction of Fort Yuma was transferred to the newly created Diocese of San Diego. From that time onwards, diocesan priests have served the area. Built and dedicated in 1923, the present church is located at the strategic Yuma crossing, an area which once controlled the land route from Mexico in California.

On November 23, 1980, the Indian Mission at Fort Yuma observed the bicentennial of La Purisima and its latter–day successor, Saint Thomas. Two bishops, a host of priests and hundreds of local inhabitants joined in the gala commemorative event.

Saint Thomas Indian Mission remains today as a visible monument to early missionary work among the Yumas. And, fittingly, a statue of Fray Francisco Garces greets visitors to this desert outpost of Christianity.

FRENCH IN CALIFORNIA

The French played a prominent role in the interesting drama of California's heritage. Handicapped though they were by internal revolutions and faltering governments, the French were just as eager as others for a place in the Pacific sun. Not being powerful enough for unilateral action to acquire the area outright, France played a discreet role, striving to cultivate the good will of the Californians. Her agents were enthusiastically received and her subjects were treated as natives rather than foreigners.

The first effective contact dates from 1786, and the arrival, at Monterey Bay, of the first foreign contingency to visit California after Spanish occupation. Jean Francois de Galaup, Comte de La Pérouse, had been commissioned by King Louis XVI to expand geographical knowledge by searching out such areas as the Northwest Passage. The Comte de La Pérouse was equally intent on appraising the commercial and political potentialities of the whole Pacific Slope.

That seaman's attractive and colorful personality is reflected in his personal observations about the California missions, where "the monks, by their answers to our questions, left us in ignorance of things concerning the regime of this kind of religious community."

Wright Howes maintains that "of all modern exploring voyages to the Pacific those of Cook, La Pérouse and Vancouver were the most important."

In 1817, Camille de Roquefeuil dropped anchor in San Francisco Bay. His ship was the first one flying the French flag to enter that port. A lieutenant in the merchant navy, Roquefeuil's objective was to demonstrate the possibility of trade with China which was then almost at a standstill.

A decade later, Auguste Bernard Duhaut–Cilly sailed along the Pacific Slope and became the initial "outlander" to be intimately acquainted with Hispanic California. That French navigator's published observations constitute the most extensive contemporary account of California's missions and settlements for the period.

Abel Aubert Du Petit–Thouars came in 1837. A keen observer and a man of considerable intelligence, he kept a careful diary of his voyage which he envisioned as helpful for French foreign commerce, especially the whaling industry.

The colorful flag of Orleanist France was brought to California, in 1839 by Cyrille Pierre Theodore Laplace, who was concerned about the possibility for French colonial establishments in the Pacific.

Eugene Duflot de Mofras, a young attaché at the French embassy in Mexico City, ploughed the California waters, in 1841, examining and reporting on the area's institutions, resources, history and prospects. An advance scout of King Louis Philippe, Duflot de Mofras industriously sent back his findings and later published a two volume illustrated account of his trek.

An observer of later generations, Frank Monaghan, wrote that "it was enthusiasm rather than bitterness that prejudiced the minds of French travellers to America during the eighteenth century." On the California scene, "the English and French travellers were the most prominent, and their results were the most far–reaching; but of those voyages visiting and writing of Mexico and California, the French easily surpass the English."

Even this most cursory glance at early French influence in and concern for California indicates that before the admission of California to the Union, there were not a few who hoped to acquire the area for France.

FRONTIER FAITHS IN SOUTHLAND

A book by Father Michael Engh, a local Jesuit scholar, tells about *Frontier Faiths, Church, Temple and Synagogue* inLos Angeles between 1846 and 1888. It is published by by the University of New Mexico Press at Albuquerque. This penetrating study about the role of religion in a frontier community offers a fresh insight into the complex beginnings of social and ethnic diversity in Los Angeles.

Religious life in the one–time *Pueblo de Nuestra Señora de los Angeles* differed significantly from that in other frontier regions of the nation because of the area's geographic isolation, local demographics and ministerial diversity. As a frontier, Los Angeles stood as an exception to the pattern of religious pioneering in the United States. The area was "discovered" and colonized by Catholics and, as one Baptist preacher noted in 1851, the population was still attached to the "ridiculous observances of the Roman Church." In his opinion, "no place needed the Gospel more than Los Angeles."

However, adherents to non–Catholic creeds faced new and unfamiliar challenges in the area, not the least of which was the language. No Protestant minister could speak Spanish until the arrival of Reverend William Mosher in 1871. Such Hispanic customs as Sunday bullfights, gambling, horse racing and cock fighting appalled the Protestant divine.

Dr. James Woods, a Presbyterian clergyman who established the first Protestant religious body in Los Angeles, confided to his diary that the city's Hispanic aristocracy were a dark complexioned set with darker minds and morals."

With the gradual improvement of transportation, more immigrants streamed to Los Angeles. For religious sects, this meant increased membership, construction of churches, formation of ecclesial jurisdictions and a proliferation of denominations.

No group felt the impact of this influx more than the descendants of the city's founders. Spanish–speaking Roman Catholics comprised the earliest pioneers and their congregations constituted the oldest of the creeds, not only in Los Angeles but throughout California and the Southwest. Because of their numbers and influence, Catholics remained the most prominent of the city's institutional religions well into the 1880s.

In his meticulously–researched and carefully–annotated study, Father Engh demonstrates how, in spite of considerable religious prejudice and racial violence, Protestants, Catholics and Jews developed an unparalleled religious cooperation based on civic boosterism and the desire to attract newcomers to the city and its churches.

Without any question, the best of the nine chapters in this book is the one dealing with the "Soldiers of Christ, Angels of Mercy" which tells about the Daughters of Charity in Southern California and their work among peoples of diverse faiths and cultures. Those good ladies demonstrated how members of the Roman Catholic community could also grapple creatively with the exigencies of pioneer life from their *pueblo* convents.

Jesuit Engh is a better historian than a sociologist. His treatment of Bishop Thaddeus Amat's attempts to implement the directives of the Baltimore Councils, for example, needs considerably more "seasoning." The giants of yesteryears, religious and otherwise, cannot be properly understood or appreciated in a context outside the era in which they lived.

Hopefully, this truly fascinating study is only the first in a series about religious diversity in what is now the largest city in the world dedicated to the Mother of God.

GALERO

The *galerum rubrum* has been in California's ecclesiastical nomenclature only since January 15, 1953, when Pope Pius XII formally bestowed the "red hat" upon the Archbishop of Los Angeles, as the first and most distinctive feature of the princely role entrusted to James Francis McIntyre.

Next to the Roman Pontiff, there is no office in the Catholic Church higher than that of the cardinalate. Since the early 11th century, the College of Cardinals has functioned as the Pope's principal advisory agency in the administration of ecclesial affairs.

This vital role was emphasized by Pope Eugene IV who stated that just "as the door of a house turns on its hinges, so on the cardinalate does the Apostolic See, the door of the whole Church, rest and find support."

As a recompense for their numerous responsible duties, both tradition and canon law have long accorded cardinals privileges more ample and extensive than those enjoyed by any other ecclesiastics. (A 485 page book *De Cardinalis Dignitate el Officio*, published at Rome in 1836, is given to those enrolled in the Sacred College).

The actual wearing of the colorful appendage was discontinued after the loss of the Papal States, in the 1870s. As a sign of "mourning," cardinals were directed to express their displeasure about the loss of the Church's civil autonomy by refusing to wear the *galerum rubrum*.

Traditional norms stated that after its acceptance, the *galerum rubrum* was to be stored in a safe place in the cardinal's residence. At his death, it was to be placed at the foot of his *catafalque*, after which it was to be suspended from the ceiling of the cathedral or church to which he was attached as evidence of the spiritual authority exercised by princes of the Church. There it was to hang until crumbling to dust!

The design of the unique hat, reproduced in each cardinal's personal coat–of–arms, is as simple as it is singular. Its crown is small and shallow; the brim flat, rigid and very broad. Attached to the crown are two crimson–colored cords, each of which terminates with fifteen tassels arranged triangle–wise. (The hats were fabricated by the Roman firm of Tanfani & Bertarelli, on Via S. Chiara.)

Prior to 1953, the *galerum rubrum* had been conferred on only eleven American bishops. The prayer used for its bestowal recalled both the princedom and the martyrdom symbolized in its bright cardinal–red or scarlet color.

> In praise of Almighty God and as an ornament of the Holy See, receive the Red Hat, the particular sign of the cardinalatial office, by which is signified that you must show yourself to be steadfast even to death and the shedding of your blood for the exaltation of the Holy Faith, for peace and tranquility among all Christian people, and for the welfare of the Holy Roman Church, in the name of the Father, and of the Son and of the Holy Spirit.

The conferral of the *galerum rubrum* was discontinued following the investiture of 1967, when the ceremonial for installation was simplified. Hence the red hat entrusted to James Francis Cardinal McIntyre was both the first and last presented to a Californian. Because Cardinal McIntyre was retired at the time of his demise (and therefore, no longer canonically attached to his former cathedral), the *galerum rubrum* was hung at Saint Basil's Church where His Eminence resided during his final years.

GHIRARDELLI CHOCOLATE

Centuries before the advent of Europeans, the natives living around the Gulf of Mexico made use of the beans of chocolate plants that grew abundantly in that area. There were no fewer than a dozen species of cacao growing along the shoreline from Mexico south to the mouth of the Amazon River, some of the plants reaching heights of twenty–five feet.

The purplish–yellow pods are eight or nine inches long and have a diameter of three or four inches. The seeds or beans within the pods are in five rows, with five to twelve beans in each rows. The Aztecs referred to the plants as "choclath." So highly esteemed were the beans that often they were used as a means of exchange. Several early writers were so enhanced with the taste that they called it "God's food." When Hernando Cortes and his adventurers arrived at Vera Cruz, in 1518, they found Montezuma and his Aztec followers drinking huge quantities of chocolate. One creditable historian recorded that Montezuma had as many as fifty jars or pitchers of chocolate prepared daily for his personal use and another 2,000 jars for his immediate family and court.

Knowing something about the background of chocolate helps one to understand how it came to be introduced into Alta California by the early missionaries. Alfred Robinson substantiated its use in his account of a visit to San Juan Bautista Mission, where he was served the drink at breakfast by Fray Felipe Arroyo de la Cuestra. George Ruxton, telling about spending a few days with a Mexican family at El Gallo, recorded how, at daybreak, "the females of the family rise and prepare the chocolate or *atole*, which is eaten first thing in the morning. "

Similar references to the use of chocolate are found in a number of other contemporary accounts dealing with California and the west. Fray Francisco Palou, the biographer of Junípero Serra, wrote about the importance of chocolate in the diet of the early missionaries. Speaking about the extreme shortage of water aboard their ship, enroute to the New World, he noted that "it was impossible even to make chocolate."

Some years later, Juan Bautista de Anza told the *Presidente* about the privations suffered at Monterey when his people "did not have even a single bar of chocolate" for breakfast. That remark is said to have brought tears to Serra's eyes. The Spaniards carried the cocoa beans back to Spain. From there they were introduced to France, England and other countries of Europe. Chocolate was a very fashionable drink in 18th century Spain–but not before it had become a favorite in far–away California.

All of which proves that the still–thriving business introduced to California by Domingo Ghirardelli, in 1856, had roots that stretched back well over a century to the earliest mission times.

Glass Paperweights

GLASS PAPERWEIGHTS

The production of antique paperweights fuses the genius of glassmaker and artist in such a way as to allow emerald, amethyst, ruby, sapphire, mossy agate, gold and silver to sparkle forth in a rich myriad of attractive designs.

One of the world's most colorful and extensive concentrations of these "manmade jewels" was on permanent display among the treasures of the Estelle Doheny Collection of Rare Books, Manuscripts and Works of Art, on the campus of Saint John's Seminary, at Camarillo. The 228 superb specimens in the fascinating, yet little known collection of glass paperweights were displayed on lucite mounts in four specially constructed walnut cases in the oval foyer of the Edward Laurence Doheny Memorial Library. Most of the weights are individually lighted through a special condenser control system which enhances their widely divergent color schemes. While no catalogue of its holdings in this area was ever issued, the Camarillo collection was remarkable for its artistic originality which incorporates French, British and American examples from almost every period during which the art flourished.

Glass, with its components of two–parts lead or lime and five parts pure sand, is an excellent medium for preserving artistic expression. It loses none of its original substance and weight when heat is applied and its versatility allows for utilizing designs of great diversity and beauty. Venetian glass makers produced the first paperweights in the early 1800s, but by mid–century, they were rapidly outstripped by French artisans at Saint Louis, Clichy and Baccarat. The exceptional quality, workmanship and beauty evident to the superlative French specimens represent the ultimate expression of the art.

In the actual production of paperweights, the first step was to take a thick piece of crystal or colored glass and decorate it as desired. The component elements were then heated uniformly to avoid cracking on the inside of the weight around the pattern. As soon as the glass became pliable, thongs, shears, spatula and blow pipe were used to apply different shades to the existing depressions and erections. At this point, the artist would seat himself in a cradle with its set of metal arms across which rested the pontil rod. The craftsman manipulated the rod quickly back and forth with his left hand, while a spatula, held in his right hand, shaped the molten mass into its proper size and form.

Though it was virtually impossible to exactly duplicate a design, glassmakers generally avoided even related productions. Each was a masterpiece in itself, with a unique decorative singularity incorporating such chromatic subjects as flowers, fruits, snakes and lizards.

Glass weights were never made for commercial purposes, a fact which partially accounts for their present–day paucity. In addition, relatively few artisans possessed the skill and technical knowledge essential to the fabrication of fine paperweights.

A rather sizeable number of variations could be found in the Doheny Collection, some fashioned into bases for vases, pen holders and bottles, others molded into decorative mantel ornaments. Over a dozen miniature weights were included, one of which is attributed to the Sandwich Glass Works. The exquisite glass door-knobs were probably fashioned by Apsley Pellatt. The fascinating collection of glass paperweights assembled by the late Carrie Estelle Doheny, outstanding for their lustrous softness and excellent craftsmanship, was highly regarded for the fine artistic sense clearly evident in the diverse nature of its carefully selected specimens. Truly they are *mille fiore* poems in glass!

GOLDEN GATE — OPENING

Juan Manuel de Ayala was born on December 28, 1745 at Osuna, Spain. He entered the royal navy on September 19, 1760, where he served in various capacities until his retirement with the rank of captain in 1785. In the fall of 1774, Ayala was sent to New Spain.

Two months later he was appointed commander of the *Felicidad* or *Sonora*. He set out for San Blas, where he was to take over his ship.

While at San Blas, Ayala's orders were changed and he was placed in charge of the small packet boat, *San Carlos,* with orders to proceed north to Monterey with supplies for the mission and garrison. Viceroy Antonio Bucareli also instructed Ayala to continue to the Bay of San Francisco. There he was to make a detailed survey and then report back to Naval Department Headquarters at San Blas.

The San Carlos reached Monterey near the end of June, 1775. Ayala was warmly welcomed by Fray Junípero Serra. It was arranged for him to act as sponsor for the infant Juan Francisco Belano upon whom the *Presidente* conferred the Sacrament of Baptism. Serra was most cordial to Ayala and his crew. Fresh vegetables, meat and milk were supplied for the *San Carlos.* Such delicacies were welcome to men who had eaten jerked beef and the tack for so long at sea.

Following a month's layover, Ayala sailed for San Francisco, where he arrived in early August. With only the light of a nine day old moon rising to the east, Ayala edged his ship through the Golden Gate. For forty–four days, Ayala remained in San Francisco Bay, exploring every arm and inlet. He and his men went as far north as the mouth of the San Joaquin River. Most of the time, the San Carlos was anchored in the sheltered cove at Angel Island (*Isla de los Angeles*), where there was abundant wood and fresh water.

The survey ordered by Bucareli was completed by the intrepid pilot, José Cañizares. He used a dugout which Ayala had ordered his carpenters to make from a large redwood tree found on the Rio Carmelo.

Fray Vicente de Santa Maria, a Franciscan from the Apostolic College of San Fernando, acted as chaplain for the voyage and he became the first priest to set foot on the northern shore, where a *rancheria* of friendly Indians welcomed him.

With the completion of his mission, Ayala returned to San Blas, via Monterey, arriving on November 6th. It was one of the most successful naval voyages in Pacific annals. The City of San Francisco observed "Ayala Day" on August 5, 1975, as part of the bicentennial celebrations. And it was fitting too for the development of community, commerce and industry at one of the world's great ports can be traced to Ayalas' entry into San Francisco Bay in 1775.

GOLDEN GATE — CAR SPANGLED SPANNER

There probably isn't any single icon more identified with a city than the Golden Gate Bridge is with San Francisco. Like the Eiffel Tower and the Statue of Liberty, the bridge acts as a sort of pictorial shorthand for its setting, announcing to all who cross it that they have arrived in the promised land.

With all its other distinctions, the Golden Gate Bridge is the nation's most visited tourist attraction. And, unhappily, it is also the world's number one suicide spot—920 at latest count.

The famous gateway was considered both the most obvious and the most impossible place for erection of a suspended roadway. Most people scoffed at the whole idea when it was proposed by Charles Crocker in 1872. The frequent gale–force winds, persistent fog and unpredictable tides made the whole notion "unbridgeable."

Ground was broken for the famous gateway on January 5, 1933. Built at the height of the Depression, the Golden Gate Bridge was financed entirely from local sources in a program that employed over 13,000 people for most of four years.

The project was costly in many ways. It was rumored that about one life was lost for each million dollars spent on the bridge. Actually, only eleven people died during the $ 37 million undertaking, mostly because workers were required to wear hard hats, tie–on lines and filter glasses. The most innovative safety feature was an ingenious net strung below the unusual mid–air construction site.

Though many persons were involved in its construction, the bridge owes its existence to the vision and persistence of civil engineer Joseph Strauss, who became involved with the project in 1919 and saw it through to completion. Among the most important trivia associated with the bridge is the distance which it is designed to sway—an astonishing twenty–seven feet from side–to–side, the largest of any bridge built before or after.

The span is painted "International orange" rather than gold. That distinctive hue has become the virtual embodiment of the Golden Gate itself. The orange is a subdued terra cotta that resembles the rich earth tones of the Grand Canyon, contrasted against the green Marin hills, the blue sky and the bay.

The "Car Spangled Spanner," a nickname bestowed on the bridge by newspaper columnist, Herb Caen, opened on May 27, 1937 when over 200,000 people walked across the span between 6 a.m. and 6 p.m. Today, the bridge is traversed annually by more than forty million cars.

On May 29th, Msgr. Charles Ramm (1863–1951) gave the invocation for the formal opening of the Golden Gate Bridge, a prayer that has been reprinted many times over subsequent years:

> Almighty and Everlasting God, we bow down before Thee, and we offer unto Thee this finished work with humble hearts of joy and gladness. Let its garlands of grace and beauty, hanging between Heaven and earth, sing unto Thee the perpetual song of praise and thanksgiving of a happy, grateful people.
>
> As the ceaseless lines of traffic, coming and going, North and South, and East and West, on the surface of this bridge and of the waters beneath it, will make the sacred sign of the Cross, may that saving symbol, constantly traced by the streams of living men and women at this gateway of the West, be an abiding pledge of Thy Fatherly love and protection, and of our healing and redemption.

GOLDEN LEGEND VERIFIED

If a contestant on "Jeopardy" were asked to identify the first discovery of gold in California, the answer would likely be: "John Marshall—the tailrace of Sutter's Mills, 1848." Alex Trebek would then push the "no" button and, if the other contestants also failed to respond correctly, he would say: "Wrong. Francisco Lopez–Placerita Canyon, 1842."

Actually, tales of gold in Alta California can be traced back to Sir Francis Drake who, in 1579, reported a "reasonable quantity of gold and silver" around San Francisco Bay. Like the story of his "Plate of Brass," Drake's contention about gold has proven elusive.

Explorers along the Colorado River supposedly picked up some nuggets of gold in the 17th century. And there were scattered references to mining activities in the Frazier Park area about 1775.

In 1824, Jedediah Smith found "free flowing gold" in the Owens Valley and there were reports of similar phenomena at San Isidro a short time afterwards. The annals testify that Antonio Mendoza, a veteran miner from Sonora, was working in the Santa Clara River in 1833. And the de Celis family is on record for staking a claim in the San Francisquito Canyon five years later.

In 1834, Richard Henry Dana wrote in his classic *Two Years Before the Mast* that "we also carried a small quantity of gold dust, which Mexicans or Indians brought down to us from the interior . . . I heard rumors of gold discoveries, but they attracted little or no attention and were not followed up."

Despite these and other unsubstantiated claims, it was Francisco Lopez (b. 1802) who made the first authentic gold discovery in the Placerita Canyon, an area long associated with San Fernando Mission. Francisco was anything but an "illiterate peon who didn't know what he was doing." A graduate of the Mexico City University, he had studied mining at the *Colegio de Mineria*.

The actual discovery was made on Francisco's fortieth birthday, March 9, 1842. He was looking for herbs and spices for his wife, Maria Antonia Feliz, when he found gold while digging onions under a grove of sycamore trees. When the gold he discovered was later tested, it weighed 18.34 ounces, with a fineness of twenty–two carats, worth about $344.75 in those days when gold sold for $19 an ounce.

While it is difficult to ascertain how much gold was subsequently mined in the area, production possibly averaged 260 pounds per year between 1842 and 1847. That would amount to $70 million by today's calculations. It was surely more than a casual strike.

For historians of the missions, there is something significant in the fact that the San Fernando Mission District bears the distinction of having supplied California's first substantiated gold, six years prior to John W. Marshall's discovery in the north. Of those tumultuous times, nothing remains today except a gnarled old oak tree in a county park. But a valid discovery it truly was. Of the many "golden legends" associated with California missions, this one stands undisputed.

GOLDEN ROSE

There was a long and historical precedent for the bestowal of the Golden Rose of Tepeyac upon Timothy Cardinal Manning by the Metropolitan Chapter of the National Shrine of Our Lady of Guadalupe. In the early centuries of the Church, it was the custom for the Pope to give a golden rose that he had blessed at Eastertime to one or another of the prominent monarchs or nobles of Europe.

The rose's stem, leaves, buds and blossoms were fashioned of pure gold, sometimes set with rubies and sapphires, and anointed with balsam and musk. It was a symbolic message from heaven. Originally the golden rose was an annual gift from the popes to the city prefects of Rome. Its bestowal entailed an elaborate series of ceremonies lasting the better part of a day.

On the fourth Sunday of Lent, known then and now as "Rose Sunday," the Holy Father carried a crimson–dyed golden rose in solemn procession from the Lateran Palace to Santa Croce in Gerusalemine. There he would celebrate Mass and deliver a homily on the rose as a symbol of the spiritual joys attached to the approaching Feast of Easter. The rose's fragrance, he would note, foretold the splendor of the Resurrection.

As the pope returned to the Lateran, he was met by the city's prefect who would accept the golden rose and then carry it inside the church, accompanied by a solemn procession of religious and civil officials. What began as a purely Roman custom of cementing the relationship between the city of Rome and its clergy gradually spread to other locales. After 1309, when Pope Clement V took the papacy to Avignon, the golden rose was awarded to French and Tuscan personages.

During ensuing centuries, the golden rose evolved from a pastoral Easter greeting into a conscious instrument of international diplomacy. In 1490, Isabelle of Castile received a rose in recognition of her accomplishments against the Moors. In 1521, a rose was sent to King Henry VIII of England, along with a letter bestowing upon him the title "Defender of the Faith." The last male monarch to receive a rose was the Austrian Archduke, Ferdinand, in 1780.

Occasionally, the golden rose is still awarded to female sovereigns—the Grand Duchess of Luxembourg received one in 1956. And recent Popes have begun the practice of bestowing golden roses upon notable shrines, such as those of Our Lady of Fatima (1965) and the Virgin of Luyan (1982).

No one who has ever seen *Der Rosenkavalier* will forget that magical moment when the youthful Octavian enters the palace bearing the perfumed symbol of betrothal, the silver rose. To Sophie, for whom it was intended, the rose seemed "like heavenly, not earthly roses; roses from the highest paradise . . . like a message from heaven."

The opera's "Presentation of the Roses" alludes to a custom much older than Richard Strauss and Hugo von Hofmannsthal. And one suspects that the long and engrossing history of this most sumptuous and symbolic of Easter presents, the Golden Rose, is far from finished.

GREGORY XVI CREATES A DIOCESE

One of the most historically significant documents of the Archival Center for the Archdiocese of Los Angeles is the papal bull appointing Fray Francisco Garcia Diego y Moreno the proto bishop for the Diocese of Both Californias. The remarkably well–preserved document has rightly been described as the "corner–stone" of California Catholicism.

Bearing the date April 27, 1840, the bull was issued in the name of Pope Gregory XVI. The manuscript is executed on vellum, 28 x 21 inches, with ties and lead seal attached. It was acquired by J. Francis Cardinal McIntyre in 1961 from John F. Fleming.

The historic bull was one of four issued in response to a petition filed on the part of the Mexican Government requesting the erection of a diocesan seat or curia to serve the area of Baja and Alta California. After a careful investigation of the plea, Pope Gregory XVI approved the recommendation and ordered the appropriate bulls to be issued. (A copy of the Consistorial Process conducted by the Holy See on that occasion is also at the Archival Center)

Documents of this nature are customarily issued in triplicate. In this case, one copy was sent to Bishop–elect Garcia Diego, another was dispatched to the Metropolitan Province of Mexico City and a third was filed in the central archives of the Ministry of Religion. Bishop Garcia Diego's copy remained in his possession until his death in 1846 and then disappeared for several decades. It was found and presented to the Santa Barbara Mission Archives by Dr. Ernest Forbes and Mr. Frank C. Drew on August 24, 1920.

The bull at the Archival Center is probably the one from the Ministry of Religion whose papers and documents were scattered during the persecutions in Mexico. Many of those items found their way into the hands of private collectors.

In the bull, the Holy Father explained how the lack of priestly personnel for the Church in California had motivated him to establish a canonical diocese for the purpose of more adequately providing for the temporal and spiritual administration of the area. Fray Francisco Garcia Diego was instructed to receive episcopal consecration from any Catholic bishop in good standing with the Holy See. Included in the bull is a suggested formula for the oath of allegiance required then and now before conferral of the episcopal office. Therein was included a promise (unfortunately never fulfilled) of visiting the tomb of Peter every six years.

A complete translation of this interesting document has been made and is on deposit at the Archival Center. The first draft of that English rendition was made several decades ago by the late Father Maynard J. Geiger, long–time Archivist at the Santa Barbara Mission Archives.

The bull was placed on deposit in the Estelle Doheny Collection at Camarillo after its acquisition in 1961. It was later removed to the Archival Center where it is on permanent exhibition. The diocese for Both Californias established in 1840 has blossomed forth (just in the Golden State) into two metropolitan provinces with twelve separate ecclesial units. Pope Gregory XVI read the signs of those early times exceedingly well.

GREYSTONE MANSION

Greystone Mansion has been aptly described as " the most impressive home ever built in Beverly Hills," a distinction it retains to this day. It was built by Edward Laurence Doheny on a twenty–five acre parcel of property that originally belonged to the larger, 415 acre Doheny Ranch, now Trousdale Estates.

Completed in 1917, at an estimated cost of four million dollars, the fifty–five room mansion is as massive and solid as an ancient castle. Its walls of reinforced concrete are three feet thick. The Greystone name derives from the outer coating of Indiana limestone which blends with the pale roof of slate imported from Wales as an adornment.

The rooms are castle large, from the former grand dining room, complete with a balcony for an orchestra, to the restaurant–sized kitchen and pantry. The upstairs trophy room features lighted gun–cabinets and an adjoining sun porch with louvered roof and glass windbreaks.

The grand stairway is enhanced by handcarved banisters and balustrades, descending to a black and white marble floored main hallway as large as an entire suburban home. Graceful arches lead to the terraced–edged game room. The quarters for the staff, which accommodate upwards of thirty people, lend a hotel atmosphere to that wing of the house. This largest mansion in Beverly Hills encompasses 46,000 square feet.

There is a regulation sized gymnasium and, down a circular stairway, a family entertainment center that includes a motion picture theatre, a bowling alley and a billiard room with a concealed bar.

Greystone even had its own fire station, riding stables, tennis courts, swimming pools, badminton courts and dog kennels. The formal sixteen acres of gardens consisted of wooded areas, orchards, manicured lawns and picturesque walks. Over a hundred species of plants from all over the world have been identified and recorded among the reflection pools, waterfalls and lakes.

Edward L. Doheny, Jr., and his family moved into Greystone Mansion in 1928. The thirty–six year old "Ned" Doheny was tragically killed there in February of the following year by a deranged secretary, Theodore Hugh Plunkett. Doheny's widow eventually remarried and continued her residence at Greystone and later at a smaller home on the property, until the mid 1950s.

The City of Beverly Hills purchased the property in the 1960s for its much–needed reservoir which was built beneath the parking lot. In September of 1971, "Greystone Park" was formally dedicated and five years later the mansion was declared a landmark and placed on the National Registry of Historic Places.

The Doheny name is still firmly imprinted on the street map of Beverly Hills. Greystone Mansion is surrounded on two sides by Doheny Road and on another by Doheny Drive. And the influence the Doheny family had on the area will probably last as long as the city it enhances.

Visitors to the legendary Greystone Mansion will agree with one writer who wrote that touring the magnificent estate was something like walking through the pages of a Gothic novel.

GUAJOME RANCHO

About thirty miles north of San Diego, amid a landscape of gently rolling hills, stands the spacious adobe of *Rancho Guajome*, a beautiful and representative example of Spanish *hacienda* architecture. The *Rancho Guajome* was presented to Cave Johnson Couts (1821–1874) and his bride Ysidora Bandini in 1851 by the legendary Abel Stearns. The original patent described the *rancho* as consisting of 2,219 acres.

Located just five miles from San Luis Rey Mission, the *rancho* was well supplied with ponds, lakes and frogs. Its farming lands were exceptionally fertile and productive.

Couts began construction of the adobe residence at Guajome following his resignation of a commission in the United States Army. Development of the *rancho* thereafter became the driving force of his life. Couts planted extensive orchards, started a vineyard and set up the earliest irrigation system in the county by enlarging the existing ponds into a network of basins and streams of running water.

His laborers built barns, stables, sheds and corrals for the growing herds of cattle and horses. It was primarily through the sale of these animals that Couts was able to finance his operations. It was Couts' ambition to make the *Guajome Rancho* into the grandest, if not the most successful of all the Southern California *ranchos* and there is abundant evidence that he achieved that objective.

Couts' lofty objectives were probably best expressed in his stately ranch house which was several years in the building. An elegant dwelling, it harmoniously combined methods of architectural construction employed in both low, rambling Mexican adobes and the more elevated styles of American woodframes.

The thousands of adobe bricks used in its building were made by Indian laborers. The majority of the roof tiles came from San Luis Rey Mission. Finding the mission abandoned and in partial ruin, Couts obtained permission from Bishop Thaddeus Amat to utilize the tiles.

A graduate of West Point Military Academy, Couts never forgot his obligations to God and country. After completing work on the central building, he decided to erect a private chapel for which he even obtained the unusual permission of reserving the Blessed Sacrament from Pope Pius IX.

According to a log at the Archival Center, Archdiocese of Los Angeles, Bishop Amat journeyed to the *Guajome Rancho* on December 24, 1869, and there blessed the "Chapel of St. John the Evangelist . . . the gift of Colonel Cave J. Couts." In the years that followed, the chapel was widely used, especially by the eight children of Cave and Ysidora. Catechism lessons were taught there, Mass was offered when a priest was in the area and marriages performed for neighboring families.

Probably the most notable event that took place in the chapel was the marriage of Elizabeth B. Clemens to Cave Couts Jr. on January 14, 1887. "Lily Bell," as she was more popularly known, was a niece of writer Samuel Langhorne Clemens, better remembered as Mark Twain. The *Guajome Rancho* was acquired by the County of San Diego in recent times and is now being preserved as a living landmark of California's colorful *rancho* period.

Of special interest to visitors is the chapel where such personages as General Ulysses S. Grant, Lew Wallace and Helen Hunt Jackson worshiped the Lord over a century ago.

GUTENBERG BIBLE — DOHENY COPY

Among the most treasured items in the Estelle Doheny Collection of rare books, manuscripts and works of art housed at Saint John's Seminary, Camarillo, was a copy of the *Biblia Latina* printed at Mainz in the 1450s. Johann Gutenberg (c. 1394–1468) used the recension of the Latin Vulgate text to print a book comparable in quality to the finest products of the highly developed art of hand–lettering. The craftsman's perfection of movable types resulted in an edition of the Scriptures still regarded as the masterpiece of all printed books.

For three centuries after his death, Gutenberg's *Biblia* remained unheralded. In 1763, Francois Guillaume de Bure discovered and identified a copy in the library of Jules Cardinal Mazarin, in Paris. Gradually scholars searched out other copies until today's total of forty–seven was reached. Based on the assumption that Gutenberg printed about 185 copies, probably 150 were executed on handmade ragpaper and thirty–five on vellum or parchment. Each complete copy of the forty–two line Bible necessitated 340 folio sheets of four pages.

Although there had been as many as eight consecutive Gutenberg leaves in her collection for some time, it had long been Carrie Estelle Doheny's cherished dream to add a copy of the *Biblia Latina* to her already impressive assortment of scriptural editions. The opportunity first presented itself, in 1947, when the copy of C. W. Dyson Perrins, its leaves still encased in their contemporary leather binding, was sold at Sotheby's Auction, in England. At that time, however, the book was acquired by Ernest Maggs, a London bookseller, for Sir Philip Frere. Mrs. Doheny's disappointment was alleviated three years later when the Gosford–Amherst–Perrins copy again became available. It was purchased and, in turn, donated to the Edward Laurence Doheny Memorial Library at Camarillo.

Once the property of the Earl of Gosford, the tome was originally bought by a London agent, sometime prior to 1800. It found its way into Lord Amherst of Hackney's library about 1885. When the Amherst collection was dismantled, in 1908, Bernard Quartish, Europe's leading bookseller, acquired it for C. W. Dyson Perrins who retained the tome until 1947.

The page headings on the Doheny Bible are in Lombardy capitals with the letters alternately in red and blue. Chapter numerals follow a similar pattern. Artistically executed initials, many intertwined in vine and leaf work, begin the individual prologues and books of the *vetus testamentum*. The braided leather button attached to the edge of some leaves, intended as a placemarker, is a forerunner of the modern thumb–index system. The 15th century dark–brown binding, with its five metal bosses on each cover, is attributed to a Mainz bookbinder.

With the acquisition of the Gutenberg Bible, Mrs. Doheny put in place the cornerstone of her outstanding library. Since its founder's death in 1958, the prominence of the Estelle Doheny Collection continued to expand in learned circles. Johann Gutenberg's masterpiece contributed immeasurably towards making Camarillo a respected center of scholarship and learning.

HALF HOLY DAYS

The recent discussion by the National Conference of Catholic Bishops about the number of holy days for the United States brings to mind an earlier California practice of observing the half–holy days. Ecclesiastical feasts or holy days commemorate the sacred mysteries and events recorded in the history of redemption. Special liturgical services are traditionally held on those days and Catholics are expected to rest from work.

Every religion has its feasts, but none has such a rich and judiciously constructed system of festive seasons and days as the Catholic Church. The succession of these events form what is known as the liturgical year. The feasts of Our Lord form the framework and those of the Virgin Mary and the saints the ornamental tracery. Prototypes for this system are the Jewish solemnities of Easter and Pentecost. Together with the weekly Lord's Day, they remained the only universal Christian feasts down to the third century.

Two feasts of Our Lord (Epiphany and Christmas) were added in the fourth century, then came the feasts of the apostles and martyrs in particular provinces. Later on, those of certain confessors were added. In the sixth and seventh centuries, feasts of the Blessed Mother were brought into the calendar.

After the triumph of Christianity, sessions of civil courts were prohibited on all feasts, as well as games in the circus and theatrical performances. This provided adequate time for Christians to hear Mass.

In the course of time, the ecclesial calendar expanded considerably. Each bishop had the right to establish local feasts. It was only later that a reduction of feasts took place, partly because of revolutions in state and Church.

The Decree of Gratian (about 1150) mentions forty–one feasts besides local patronal celebrations. The Decretals of Gregory IX (about 1235) enumerate forty–five public feasts and holy days. That would mean a total of eighty–five days when no work could be done and ninety–five days when no court sessions could be heard.

From the thirteenth century to the eighteenth, there were dioceses in which the holy days and Sundays amounted to over one hundred, excluding the feasts of certain monasteries and churches. The long–needed reduction of feast days was begun by Pope Urban VIII in 1642. In his provisions, there remained thirty–six feasts or eighty–five days free from labor. And the pope went a step further and limited the right of local bishops to establish new holy days.

A reduction for Spain (and its colonies) was inaugurated by Pope Benedict XIII in 1727. Only seventeen feasts were left unchanged and on the nineteen abrogated holy days, only the hearing of Mass was obligatory. This arrangement gave rise to the term "half–holy day."

There were additional changes over the following years. In 1779, word reached Fray Junípero Serra in Alta California that Pope Benedict XIV had further reduced a significant number of full holy days to "half" ones.

Always meticulous observers of the rubrics as outlined in the *ordos* or directories, the friars noted the latest alterations and announced the feasts when they occurred, noting that on the half–holy days "work was permitted after Mass had been heard."

HALLEY'S 1986 VISITATION

Comets are enormous "snowballs" of frozen gases (mostly carbon dioxide, methane and water vapor). In 1986, one of the world's most famous comets once again approached perihelion or the point of its closest orbit to the sun. For the first time since 1910, Californians caught a glimpse of Halley's comet.

Named for Sir Edmund Halley (1656–1742), the comet's earliest recorded encounter with earth occurred in 240 B.C. Since that time, it has frightened, inspired and puzzled millions of the world's inhabitants.

A number of early Scripture scholars, including Joseph Lagrange, identified Halley's comet with the star that shone over the manger of Jesus. Modern exegetes have generally discarded that theory, mostly because the "star" was seen only by astronomers and astrologers, not by the people of Jerusalem. A bright comet would have caught everybody's attention.

The historian Josephus reported that in 64 A.D. a comet resembling a sword foretold the destruction of Jerusalem. Later calculations identify it with the large, bright comet seen during the Norman Conquest of England (1066) and portrayed in the Bayeaux Tapestry of that time.

Peoples of the Middle Ages were especially perplexed by the appearance of comets. To them such astronomical phenomena portended all manner of problems, spiritual and otherwise.

On June 29, 1456, when the celebrated comet could be prominently seen in the sky at night, there were many who feared it would bring on a plague, famine or some other disaster. Pope Callistus III called upon Christendom to pray that the comet, a symbol of "God's vengeance" would be fended off.

In 1704, Dr. Halley carefully measured the orbit of the comet and found that earlier comets in 1531, 1607 and 1682 moved through an identical orbit. He correctly concluded that the appearances were roughly seventy–six years apart. When the comet appeared on schedule, in 1758, it was appropriately christened "Halley's comet."

William Shakespeare said that "when beggars die, there are no comets seen; but the heavens themselves blaze forth the death of princes." Edward VII's biographer noted that when that monarch succumbed, on May 6, 1910, Halley's comet was at its brightest point.

Mark Twain was fond of telling how he was born

during the comet's 1835 visit. He was heard to say that he would be disappointed if he didn't depart when it came again. He died right on time, April 21, 1910 just before the comet's tail brushed the earth.

There was considerable profiteering attached to the 1910 visitation. Merchants found a ready market for such items as anti–comet pills to counteract illnesses induced by the "gases" released from the tail of the highly–visible visitor.

That dirty old snowball from the freezer of twilight space returned as expected for another peek at planet earth. There are those who predict that the 1986 visitation of Halley's comet would be its last.

HIERAPOLIS

In a recent travel magazine there was an advertisement sponsored by Turkish Airlines for "touring in history." It extolled the advantages of a trip to "ancient Hierapolis, the holy city near Panukkale bequeathed to Rome in 133 B.C. by the last King of Pergamum." The ad goes on to say that "today you can still sit at the ancient theatre and imagine Romans acting a play by Seneca. Or take a plunge in the Magic Pool of History nearby. Thermal waters that nature keeps a warm 35 degrees will give you a crystal clear look at the Holy City. And a sun tan."

So, what is the connection of Hierapolis to California? Just this—the Right Reverend Francis Mora served as titular Bishop of Hierapolis from 1896 until his death in 1905. It was and is the practice of Rome to assign auxiliary, coadjutor and retired bishops to titular sees, usually areas where there was once a flourishing Christian community but which, in later times, reverted to other or no religious persuasions.

This writer was never able to unearth many details about Hierapolis. Its vernacular name is *Tambuk–kalesi* which is probably the Panukkale mentioned in the advertisement for Turkish Airlines. Various references indicate that Hierapolis indeed was a "holy city" of one kind or another. There is some confusion in the sources about the exact spelling of the name, with some listing it as Hierapolis and others as Hieropolis.

Readers will recall that Bishop Mora had been severely injured in a carriage accident in the early summer of 1882. He had interrupted a pastoral visitation to confirm a bedridden Indian woman in the backwoods near San Bernardino. On his return trip, the insecurely-fastened seat on the spring wagon jolted loose and spilled the prelate backwards off the carriage. So severely was his spine wrenched that Mora lay unconscious for some hours until a passerby came on the scene. Even then, as his successor later related, the

injured prelate "lay in an Indian hut without receiving any care" for a number of days.

Mora's recovery was slow and incomplete. Though he was able to resume many of the burdensome duties of his office, it soon became evident that he would never fully recover from the effects of the accident. In any event, Bishop Mora began what was then the unusual procedure of retiring from his position as Bishop of Monterey–Los Angeles. Finally, in May of 1896, he was informed by Miecislas Cardinal Ledochowski that Pope Leo XIII had agreed to his request. In a subsequent letter, Cajetan Cardinal De Ruggieno notified Mora that he had been transferred to the titular See of Hierapolis.

When notified about his new title, Mora told a friend that he "wouldn't need a miter or crozier in that spiritual oasis. Nor will I need my winter overcoat." There is no evidence that Mora ever visited the "holy City" of Hierapolis. Yet when he died, the only identification on his bronze marker were the words: Episcopus Hierapolis.

In 1962, Mora's tomb was located in the little Barcelona suburb of Sarria. When the prelate's grand nieces were contacted, they knew nothing about Mora's work in California—only that he had been Bishop of Hierapolis.

HIGGINS BUILDING

Referred to by Steve Harvey in the Los Angeles Times as a "derelict landmark," the old Higgins Building at 108 West Second Street was once a showplace of architecture in the City of Los Angeles. Located across the street from Saint Vibiana's Cathedral, the nine story building served as the Chancery Office for the Diocese of Monterey–Los Angeles for seventeen years.

Prior to 1917, Bishops George T. Montgomery and Thomas J. Conaty conducted business matters in a house on Second Street, next door to the cathedral. With the arrival of Bishop John J. Cantwell, the curial offices were moved to the 7th floor of the Higgins Building.

It was considered a spacious structure in those days. Opened for occupancy on May 15, 1910, the building was erected under the direction of A. L. Haley, architect and Albert J. Martin, engineer. In a brochure on file at the Archival Center, the building was advertised as being "convenient to the leading hotels, clubs and cafes" and within "two blocks of every trolley line in Los Angeles."

Located in the heart of the business district, within three blocks of the Court House, City Hall and Federal Building, the building had a full–length basement, fourteen storerooms and 238 offices. Built of "absolutely fireproof and reinforced monolithic concrete, it was earthquake–proof throughout."

The building's exterior was modeled after the Renaissance style of architecture "with concrete grouted to a smooth sandstone finish." The large entrance hall was faced entirely in marble, with a beautiful stairway leading to the second floor and basement. The floors of mosaic tile were the first of their kind in the city. The hallways and lavatories were surfaced with white tile and marble wainscoting.

In a letter to his brother, Bishop Cantwell bragged that "all the water in the building is thoroughly purified by passing through large filters to storage tanks and thence to each room." There were three passenger elevators "of the hydraulic type, each having a speed of 400 feet per minute—the safest type" then known. The large cabs were lavishly fitted and equipped with the latest signalling and stopping devices.

In addition to the Chancery office, the building was also occupied by prominent lawyers and businessmen. Probably the most famous occupant was trial lawyer Clarence Darrow who took a ninth floor office in 1911, when he came west to defend the McNamara brothers, the defendants in the Los Angeles *Times* bombing case.

The offices of Llano del Rio Company were head-quartered in the Higgins Building, as were those of Job Harriman. Charles F. Horan operated a Religious Goods Store opening onto Second Street. Known in local annals as the County Engineers Building, the Edwardian skyscraper is now characterized as "a derelict, long abandoned, with rusting iron barricades blocking its once stately entrance."

The late Mary Sinclair and Ethel Bossert who, between them, spent nearly 120 years working at the curial offices, were fond of recalling their association with the old Higgins Building which once served as the hub of Catholic activities in California's southland.

HISPANIC HERITAGE

Hispanics in the United States rightly point out that their ancestors were here long before the Pilgrims. The image of the nation as a land settled exclusively by immigrants from northern Europe is a pious myth which, historically, has anti–Catholic roots.

Especially is that true in California where the Spanish–speaking population has grown enormously in recent years. Los Angeles has become one of the world's largest Hispanic metropolises and the growth pattern gives no indication of diminishing. Recent demographical studies indicate that Hispanics in Los Angeles comprise well over a third of the population, thus forming the largest single ethnic market in the United States.

While such Catholic prelates as Archbishops John J. Cantwell and J. Francis A. McIntyre foresaw the trends, even they would have been astounded that nearly one–fifth of the entire Hispanic population in the United States and 54% of the state's Hispanics now reside in Los Angeles.

Figures such as these explain what motivated Pope John Paul II, during his 1987 pastoral visit, to say that "This land is a crossroads . . . experiencing both the enrichment and the complications which arise from this phenomenon." He noted that this massive influx is "a symbol and a kind of laboratory, testing America's commitment to her founding moral principles and human values."

Of the millions of persons of Hispanic background in the United States today, an estimated 85% identify themselves to census takers as Catholics. Yet there is precious little room for complacency because the loss of Spanish–speaking Catholics to proselytism is disturbingly high.

In an address to the National Conference of Catholic Bishops, the papal Pro–Nuncio observed that "much of the challenge to the Church . . . lies precisely in stemming this outflow of our brothers and sisters from our faith. And this will happen by providing them the same supportive ecclesial environment that nurtured the faith of earlier generations of Catholics of other ethnic and cultural origins—Irish, German, Italian, Polish and the rest."

The Church in California has even closer ties to its Mexican–origin Hispanics than other areas in the southwest. Its proto bishop, a native of Lagos de Moreno, was consecrated for the newly–created Diocese of Both Californias in Mexico's National Shrine of Our Lady of Guadalupe. The inaugural of a Spanish language Catholic newspaper in Los Angeles, *Vida Nueva*, is the most recent recognition by the Church of the importance attached to Hispanic culture and its survival along the Pacific Slope.

A few years ago, voters in California joined sixteen other states in approving a controversial measure designating English as the state's "official language." Those Catholics who favored that initiative were probably unaware that the state's earliest missionaries couldn't speak English, that its first bishop was Mexican–born, that three of his successors were Hispanics, and that the area's first pastoral letters, homilies and catechetics were written and communicated in Spanish.

HISPANIC INFLUENCE IN CALIFORNIA

The heritage of Catholic Spain and the nations which emerged under her umbrella is clearly evident in the western part of the United States, especially in such states as California where the very nomenclature is saturated with Hispanic overtones.

There are other areas too, on the national level, where the influence of the *conquistadores* is deeply imbedded.

One writer suggests that George Washington may have thrown a silver *piastre* across the Potomac River, instead of the traditional "dollar" for, interestingly enough, Mexican coinage was legal tender in the United States until 1857.

Shortly after Hernando Cortez captured the Aztec capital Tenochtitlan (Mexico City) on August 13, 1521, King Charles I issued an edict establishing a mint at Mexico City. Nearly seventy million gold dollars and over two billion silver coins were produced there between 1537 and 1821.

The earliest coins were made with comparatively crude methods. A sheet of metal was rolled to the proper thickness and planchets for the individual coin were cut off with heavy shears. Later, the mint began issuing the so–called "cob" money which was made by chiseling off sections from roughly rolled bars and then hammering those crude planchets between a pair of dies.

In the course of time, the Spanish milled dollars of eight *reales*, better known as "pieces of eight" and these became the most widely circulated coins in the 18th century. With its extensive circulation, the famous pieces of eight (the Spanish silver *piastre*) played a significant, even epochal role in the coinage of many other countries, not the least of which was the United States.

Thomas Jefferson was named to a committee charged with making recommendations for a coinage system suitable for the emerging nation. He it was who suggested that the United States pattern its coinage on the milled dollar struck at Mexico City, a measure formally approved by the Congress in 1784. And so it came to be that the man who wrote the final draft of the Declaration of Independence was also responsible for the adoption of Hispanic coinage system in the United States.

All of this is said to illustrate how the origin of the two bits, four bits and six bits terminology found its way into American usage. It was a custom at Mexico City to divide the eight *reale* piece into four parts for change purposes. Hence "two bits" denoted a quarter dollar, "four bits" a half dollar and so on.

In California, the "bit" was an imaginary coin valued at 12 1/2 cents. Its use grew out of the necessity of having some medium of exchange understood by both the native Californians and the newly–arrived Americanos. The Mexican *reale* and the American "bit" had the same value, 12 1/2 ¢. The American coin approximating nearest the "bit" was the dime. Those who purchased articles priced at a "bit" gave the dealer a dime, which was 2 1/2¢ short. Generally speaking then, either the dealer or the purchaser was "short" in those early transactions.

In any any event, one can see how customs and figures of speech originate. In California, the diversity is due, to a large extent, to the influence of Catholic Spain.

HISTORIC SPOTS IN CALIFORNIA

One of the most useful and comprehensive works about the Pacific Slope is *Historic Spots in California*, a 642 page book published by the Stanford University Press. A Catholic priest was responsible for the 1966 edition.

Father William N. Abeloe (1933–1982) was a widely–known and highly–respected priest–historian attached to the Diocese of Oakland.

He served in a number of parishes during his ministry and wrote histories of most of them. Among others of his writings are parochial sketches of Saint Leander's Parish (San Leandro), Saint Anthony's (Oakland) and Saint Joseph's (Mission San Jose). His *Parish Directory for Mission San Jose* is one of the most thorough such works ever published in California. Though he denied that it was a "comprehensive" sketch, the well–articulated text would surely indicate otherwise.

Born in Oakland, "Bill" Abeloe was raised in the Santa Clara Valley. He became a convert to the Catholic Church in 1952 and shortly afterwards began his studies for the priesthood. His ministry was open–ended in the sense that it often extended beyond the confines of the Oakland diocese. He was Vicar for Eastern Rite Catholics and was probably as well or better informed on the eastern Church than most of its adherents.

Described by one newspaper account as "a man with an abiding faith in God, and a deep interest in California history," Father Abeloe had a dream about one day restoring the old mission church at San Jose. In the year after his appointment to the pastorate of Saint Joseph's in Fremont, he began directing his considerable talents towards that project. Unfortunately he did not live to see the fulfillment of his dream in 1984.

In 1962, the Stanford University Press engaged Father Abeloe to revise, update and expand *Historic Spots in California*, a work initially issued in three volumes in 1932, 1933 and 1937 by Mildred Brooke Hoover, Hero Eugene Rensch and Ethel Grace Rensch.

The purpose of the already famed text was "to stimulate the interest of Californians in the rich history of their native or adopted state; to guide travelers to places where this history was made, to call attention to the need for immediate action and to preserve the rapidly disappearing landmarks of California's heritage."

The lucid introduction to the earlier editions by Robert Glass Cleland was retained in the 1966 edition. Over 200 photographs were added in an effort to identify lesser–known or unmarked historic buildings and places. Abeloe's edition was the first to enumerate all registered State and National Historic Landmarks in California. Also included were exact measurements of the Old Spanish and Mexican land grants.

Father Abeloe died unexpectedly on October 9, 1982,

while in Reno, Nevada attending a convention of Serra International. He was buried in Gate of Heaven Cemetery in Los Altos. Though he wrote much and well, Father Abeloe will be remembered foremost for his scholarly and meticulous work in revamping one of the great classics in western annals, *Historic Spots in California.*

HOLLYWOOD OR HOLY WOOD

Whence came the term Hollywood? Is it true that the word is a hyphenated form of "Holy Wood," a reference to the Cross of Christ, which Catholics formerly commemorated each year on the 3rd of May?

There is a legend to that effect and it can be traced to Father Daniel W. J. Murphy, who was named the first Pastor of Blessed Sacrament Church on January 12, 1904. Murphy is quoted as saying that "I am informed that Mrs. Beveridge so named the settlement—Hollywood comes from the Old English Holly, our word Holy —and wood with it, makes the Holy Wood of Calvary." Thinking as he did that "the day on which Father Serra first held divine services in this city," was May 3rd, it comes as no surprise that Father Murphy scheduled the ground–breaking ceremonies for Blessed Sacrament Church on the Feast of the Exaltation of the Holy Cross, May 3, 1904.

Since there was no documentation available to substantiate the legend, several writers set out to invent some. A souvenir brochure published by the Jesuit Fathers in 1923 put these words into Crespi's diary:

> Out by sea, his day's journey ended, in the uncertain light of the moon Father Junípero Serra wrote: May 3, 1769, Feast of the Finding of the Cross. Said Holy Mass this morning under some oak trees near an Indian village.

The sea voyage alluded to actually took place in 1770, not in 1769. On May 3, 1769, Serra had not yet arrived at Velicatá. Only on the 14th of that month was the mission founded there under the title of San Fernando, the only one of the missionary establishments in Baja California founded by the Franciscans.

But the legend persisted. Travelers to Hollywood in the 1920s gazed up at the mounted mission bell in front of the old Blessed Sacrament Church and read there, on a small tablet under the bell, that "near this spot on May 3, 1769, Father Junípero Serra read the Mass of the Holy Wood of the Cross." While in recent years the plaque has been removed from its post (it was last seen in the basement of Blessed Sacrament Church), the story of Serra's visit to the area persists, the facts notwithstanding.

A more logical (and factual) explanation of how Hollywood came by its name, while perhaps less edifying, does not in any way detract from the romantic background of the City of the Stars. Historically, the term "Hollywood" seems to have been associated with the ranch Harvey H. Wilcox acquired in the area in 1886. During later years, after the 120 acre tract had been subdivided, the name gradually became identified with the budding village earlier known as Cahuenga Valley. The name was a common one throughout the nation in the 1880s. There were "Hollywoods" in Arkansas, Georgia, Maryland and North Carolina.

Holly is not native to California, except perhaps Toyon and even that species is hardly impressive enough to justify having its name applied to a city. One can only speculate that the term was "transferred" to the southland probably by those familiar with the imported holly plants grown in the private greenhouses of the Wilcox family.

In 1903, when its 700 citizens elevated their community to the status of a city, the term Hollywood was formally adopted to designate the area. By the time the Motion Picture Industry brought prominence to the region, however, Hollywood had lost its identity and was merely one of the many suburbs of the rapidly expanding Los Angeles City. Today the origin of Hollywood's name may seem an academic point to many of its inhabitants. "After all," they might say, "Hollywood is neither a city nor a town, it is a state of mind!"

HOLY DAYS IN CALIFORNIA

Holy days are special feasts on which the People of God are seriously obliged to participate in the Eucharistic Liturgy. Current discipline binds Catholics in the United States to satisfy that obligation on all the Sundays of the year, as well as on six other specified feast-days. In California, as in Texas, New Mexico and Arizona, the calendar of feast and fast days was based on the one promulgated by the Third Council of Mexico. It was formidable too. Besides the Sundays of the year, there were forty–seven additional feasts on which attendance at Mass was mandatory.

The modification of the list by Pope Benedict XIV, in 1750, meant that the Catholic pioneers of California were expected to take part in Holy Mass on Sundays and the Feasts of the Circumcision (January 1), Epiphany (January 6), Candlemas (February 2), Easter Monday, Annunciation (March 25), Whit–Monday, *Corpus Christi,* Ascension, Saint John the Baptist (June 24), Sts. Peter and Paul (June 29), Saint James (July 25), Assumption of Mary (August 15), Nativity of Mary (September 8), All Saints (November 1), Immaculate Conception (December 8), Christmas (December 25), Saint Stephen (December 26) and the local patron.

There were special provisions for the Indians

attached to the California Missions. By virtue of a decree from Pope Paul III, in 1537, a distinction was made between the spiritual obligations of whites and Indians. Since the neophytes lived a "most precarious existence," they were only bound to attend the Eucharistic Liturgy on Sundays and ten designated feastdays. That exemption in favor of the natives was universally recognized in Spanish America.

The number of non–Dominical holydays remained at eighteen until September 19, 1850, when California became the thirty–first of the United States. Then, by virtue of a dispensation given to all the North American dioceses by Pope Gregory XVI, in 1837, the obligation for Mass attendance on Easter Monday and Whit–Monday was removed from Catholics in California.

Bishop Joseph Sadoc Alemany further reduced the number of precept–days by eliminating the feasts of Saint James and Saint Stephen. His published listing for the Diocese of Monterey was:

The Circumcision	Saint John the Baptist
The Epiphany	Sts. Peter and Paul
The Purification	The Assumption
Saint Joseph	The Nativity of Mary
The Annunciation	All Saints
The Ascension	The Immaculate Conception
Corpus Christi	The Nativity of Christ

In addition, Alemany named three "days of devotion," on which participation at Holy Mass was strongly recommended, namely, the Feasts of Our Lady, Refuge of Sinners (July 4), Saint Emidius (August 9) and Our Lady of Guadalupe (December 12).

On December 31, 1885, Pope Leo XIII, at the request of the American hierarchy, allowed the Feast of *Corpus Christi* to be solemnized on the following Sunday. Since the decision by the prelates attending the Third Plenary Council of Baltimore, to follow a uniform discipline throughout the United States, Catholics in California have been enjoined to hear Mass only on Sundays and the Feasts of Circumcision, Ascension, Assumption, All Saints, Immaculate Conception and Nativity.

HOLY NAME SOCIETY

The inauguration of the Holy Name Society as an organized effort to promote that reverence enjoined by the Second Commandment can be traced to the thirteenth century and the violent attacks then being made on the Divinity of Christ and His supernatural character. The society itself, founded in 1274, was an outgrowth of attempts by the Council of Lyons to foster special devotions in reparation for the excesses of the Albigenses and other blasphemers.

In succeeding centuries, crusades honoring the Holy Name were led by the illustrious personages of the time. When the ravages of a violent plague ceased in Portugal, during the 1430s, a series of lectures advocating devotion to the Holy Name was credited as divine approval of the devotion. A grateful nation responded with a gigantic public procession.

The movement received its societal orientation at Burgos, Spain, in 1450. Objective of the society as then stated "was the suppression of blasphemy, perjury and the profanation of the Sacred Name in conversation." On April 13, 1564, Pope Pius IV elevated the society to the status of an ecclesiastical confraternity. At that time the primary purpose was stated as "the honor and glory of God and the personal sanctification of its members by acts of love and devotion to the Holy Name." In addition, affiliates were exhorted, "to suppress blasphemy, perjury, oaths of any character that are forbidden, profanity, unlawful swearing, improper language, and, as far as possible, to prevent those vices in others."

On the second Sunday of Lent, in 1809, Father Charles Nerincks established the first Holy Name Society in America at Saint Charles Church, Hardin's Creek, Marion County, Kentucky. To Bishop Thomas J. Conaty must be given credit for initiating the Holy Name Society in Southern California. In 1910, his campaign to check profanity and indecent language resulted in the foundation, by Father Thomas F. Fahey, of a branch of the society in Holy Cross Parish under the presidency of M.H. Kearney. A new impetus was given to the movement, in November of 1920, when Bishop John J. Cantwell named Father Frederick A. Wekenman as diocesan director. The Illinois–born priest inaugurated a campaign for increased membership in the course of which he "proved the adaptability of the Holy Name Union as a vehicle for organizing lay effort."

On January 15, 1922, the scattered units of the Holy Name Society, the only lay confraternity then existing in the Church with a purely spiritual objective, were organized into a diocesan union. The growth of the Holy Name movement has continued into present times. Current membership of the 230 parochial units in the Archdiocese of Los Angeles exceeds 100,000 affiliates.

During these post–conciliar years, the Holy Name Society, in addition to fulfilling its original historical purpose of spreading and increasing love for the Sacred Name of Jesus through word and example, exhorts its members to "'witness Christ" in all their personal and social actions through a carefully planned program of information, which covers relationships in the family, the parish, the Church, the world of work, the community and society at large.

HOLY YEAR OF 1750

Over the centuries since 1300, when Pope Boniface VIII announced the first of the Christian jubilees, the Holy Year celebrations have given rise to a number of historical curiosities. One interesting facet of the jubilee observances has been the assortment of medallic illustrations that have become prominent since the pontificate of Sixtus IV and the Holy Year of 1475.

In December, 1973, Dr. Gloria Ricci Lothrop, Assistant Professor of History at California State Polytechnic College in Pomona, presented to the Chancery Archives, a collection of twenty–six papal coins, several of which date back to the early 1700s.

The most fascinating specimen in the collection and certainly the most relevant in the current Holy Year, is the one issued to commemorate the jubilee of 1750. The eighteenth of the Holy Years was announced and inaugurated by Benedict XIV, "the greatest scholar among the popes." During the months of that celebration, the pontiff called especially for a renewed interest in the Gospel message.

The jubilee of 1750 was announced and popularized throughout Christendom. The Confraternity of the Holy Trinity alone provided accommodations for 194,382 pilgrims to the Eternal City. One is startled at reading, in an Italian account about the opening of the Holy Door, in that year, that "there assisted at the ceremony, in a special loge or grand–stand magnificently decorated, His Majesty of Great Britain."

The medal recently acquired by the Historical Museum of the Chancery Archives, a memento of the 1750 jubilee, is an outstanding "relic" of bygone times. On the front side are portrayed the apostles Peter and Paul, with the letters "*SS. Pet Pa AP Roma.*" On the reverse side, Pope Benedict XIV is depicted, wearing his tiara, as he strikes the *Porta Santa* in Saint Peter's Basilica with a silver hammer. Surrounding the pontiff are two cardinal deacons, the Grand Penitentiary, the apostolic subdeacon and a papal master of ceremonies.

Contemporary accounts of that event describe how the Holy Father then intoned the *Te Deum*, knelt briefly in prayer and finally passed through the Holy Door bareheaded. A papal medal will also be struck during the current Holy Year, the twenty–seventh such Christian jubilee. Very likely, it will bear a depiction of John Paul II standing before that same threshold, proclaiming to the Christian world "a year of prayer, penance, pilgrimages and all the other ritualistic exercises common to the jubilee festivities."

The story of the Holy Year medals forms an interesting commentary on the devotional thoughts to which the opening of the *Porta Santa* has given rise through the centuries.

HOLY YEAR IN LOS ANGELES

For the seventh and last time in the 20th century, a Holy Year, was proclaimed for Roman Catholics by Pope John Paul II. The theme for the 1983–1984 jubilee was "reconciliation." The Holy Father noted in his announcement that this "special" jubilee year (the 1,950th anniversary of Christ's death) pointed the way to the "Great Holy Year of 2,000.

In the Archdiocese of Los Angeles, Timothy Cardinal Manning formally inaugurated the Holy Year with a Pontifical Mass at Saint Vibiana's Cathedral on the Feast of Our Lord's Resurrection.

In former times, the local observance of the Holy Year took place throughout the Christian world during the twelve months following the celebration at Rome. That process has been modified in recent times as a means of honoring "the local churches, active members as they are of the one and universal Church of Christ."

The 1983–1984 observance was rich in historical precedents. The Christian "jubilee" derives from the ancient Jewish practice of a "sabbath" every seven years, during which there was to be neither sowing nor harvesting.

When seven times seven years had passed, a trumpet or "jobel" was sounded to usher in the fiftieth or golden year. That year was made sacred "by proclaiming liberty in the land for all its inhabitants." (Leviticus 25, 10) The Jewish practice was adopted by the Savior Himself, who announced, in the synagogue at Nazareth, "a year of favor from the Lord." (Luke 4, 19)

The first of the recorded Christian "Holy Years" was proclaimed by Pope Boniface VIII, on February 22, 1300. Those who journeyed to the Eternal City within the appointed time were promised "great remissions and indulgences for their sins."

So successful was the proto–jubilee, according to Dante Alighieri's *Inferno*, that a strong barrier had to be constructed along the bridge of the Holy Angels, in order to keep the crowds flocking to Saint Peter's from mingling with and obstructing those coming in the opposite direction.

It had been the intention of Boniface to have a Christian jubilee at the beginning of each century. However, Saint Brigid of Sweden and other influential personages appealed to Pope Clement VI for a shortening of the ninety–nine year interim since, as they argued, the average lifespan would not allow everyone to partake of the spiritual privileges attached to the jubilee.

Clement VI acquiesced and, in 1343, decreed that a Holy Year be proclaimed every fifty years, beginning in 1350. The number of pilgrims visiting the Roman shrines during that jubilee reportedly reached a million.

During the pontificate of Boniface IX, two jubilees were celebrated, the first in 1390, and another ten years later. Pope Martin V announced the fifth Holy Year for 1423, apparently in deference to a decree of 1390, calling for such a celebration every thirty–three years thereafter, to correspond with the human lifespan of Jesus Christ.

Fortunately, for mathematicians, the fifty year practice was restored by Pope Nicholas V, who designated 1450 as a year of thanksgiving for the end of the schism caused by the anti–popes. That jubilee is remembered for the catastrophe that occurred when a panic on the bridge leading to Castel Sant Angelo resulted in twenty–two pilgrims being trampled to death.

On April 19, 1470, Pope Paul III, "having regard for the shortness of human life," further reduced the interim between celebrations of the Holy Years. From 1475, it became customary to observe a Holy Year four times each century.

The Holy Year of 1525, called by Pope Clement VII, was notable for the sharp criticisms of Martin Luther on the "bull of induction." The one–time Augustinian monk's ties with the Church had been decisively severed on January 3, 1521.

It was part of an earnest attempt to bring about a reform in the Church that motivated Pope Julius III to announce a Holy Year for 1550. There were discernible spiritual results too, not the least of which was a temporary restoration of the Catholic faith in Queen Mary's England.

The innovative Pope Gregory XIII proclaimed the Holy Year for 1575. Pilgrims returning from Rome told about the revision of the Julian Calendar, which the pontiff introduced into most Catholic countries three years later. The jubilee of 1600 bore witness to the papacy, renewed and updated by the Florentine Pope, Clement VIII. Over three million visitors crammed into the Eternal City for that year of grace.

So much in evidence was the "counter–reformation" during the *Anno Santo* of 1625, that Pope Urban VIII found it necessary, on several occasions, to caution extremists against inciting pilgrims with their inflammatory orations. It was shortly after the conclusion of that jubilee that Urban solemnly dedicated the new Basilica of Saint Peter.

Though physically weak and frail, the elderly Pope Innocent X insisted on proclaiming and presiding over the ceremonies for the Holy Year of 1650. Whenever possible, the pontiff personally greeted the pilgrims who jammed the confines of Rome.

The convocation of a jubilee year for 1675 was the most notable accomplishment of Emilio Altieri, who was already an octogenarian by the time of his election to the papacy as Clement X. Pope Innocent XII died during the Holy Year of 1700 and was succeeded in the Chair of Peter by Clement XI. The newly–elected Vicar

of Christ concluded the jubilee with the customary walling–up of the *Porta Santa* in the Vatican Basilica.

During the jubilee of 1725, Pope Benedict XIII discharged personally the duties of Grand Penitentiary and is said to have seriously considered (and happily rejected) the notice of reviving public penances for certain grave offenses. The eighteenth of the Holy Years was announced and inaugurated by Benedict XIV, the greatest scholar among the popes, in 1750. During the months of the celebration, the pontiff called for a renewed interest in and observance of the Gospel message.

Six years after the Christian penetration of Alta California, pilgrims began gathering at Rome for the jubilee of 1775. They were greeted by Pope Pius VI who reminded them that personal holiness was to be the hallmark of those publicly demonstrating their commitment to Christ.

Owing to the Napoleonic Wars and the presence of a French army within the very shadows of the Vatican, the next jubilee was delayed until 1825, when Pope Leo XII designated the twentieth of the Holy Years.

The omission of the observances for 1850 and 1875 was again due mostly to political disturbances. Gioacchino Pecci, a young seminarian of fifteen during the Holy Year of 1825, took an active part in the solemn celebrations at Rome. Then, seventy–five years later, in the evening of his own pontificate, Pecci, now Leo XIII christened the 20th century by announcing a jubilee for 1900.

Pope Leo's proclamation was universally interpreted as the harbinger of better days for the Church. Though still a "prisoner of the Vatican," the venerable pontiff personally visited Saint Peter's and dispatched cardinalatial legates to the other three of Rome's major basilicas to open the Holy Doors.

In 1913, Pope Pius X called for an "extraordinary" Holy Year of thanksgiving to commemorate the sixteenth centenary of the Edict of Milan, in which Constantine recognized the rights of Christians to worship in accordance with their consciences. The twenty–third *Anno Santo* was inaugurated by Pope Pius XI, in 1925, On that occasion, the Holy Father also announced his desire to resume the sessions of Vatican Council I with the "greatest international Christian congress . . . since the foundation of Christianity nearly two thousand years ago." Eight years later, the same *Pontifex Maximus* called for another Holy Year, this one to "honor with unusual solemnity the nineteenth centenary of the Passion and Death of our Divine Lord."

Pope Pius XII designated the Holy Year of 1950, on June 2, 1948, as a period devoted to "the sanctification of souls through prayer and penance." The twenty–fifth of the Christian jubilees brought unprecedented throngs of the faithful to the Eternal City.

On May 27, 1949, Msgr. Giovanni Battista Montini explained that the celebration for 1950 was to be looked upon as a "contribution to peace and fraternity." That same prelate lived on to convoke the next jubilee in his own name, as Pope Paul VI.

CHRISTIAN HOLY YEARS

1. 1300 – Boniface VIII	14. 1650 – Innocent X
2. 1350 – Clement VI	15. 1675 – Clement X
3. 1390 – Boniface IX	16. 1700 – Innocent XII
4. 1400 – Boniface IX	17. 1725 – Benedict XIII
5. 1423 – Martin V	18. 1750 – Benedict XIV
6. 1450 – Nicholas V	19. 1775 – Pius VI
7. 14 75 –Sixtus II7	20. 1825 – Leo XII
8. 1500 – Alexander VI	21. 1900 – Leo XIII
9. 1525 – Clement VII	22. 1913 – Pius X
10. 1550 –Julius II1	23. 1925 – Pius XI
11. 1575 – Gregory XIII	24. 1933 – Pius XI
12. 1600 – Clement VIII	25. 1950 – Pius XII
13. 1625 – Urban VIII	26. 1975 – Paul VI

HORSERACING — SPORT OF KINGS

Arabian horses were brought to the New World by Hernando Cortés, in 1517. Their colors and markings were variously described as chestnut, sorrel and gray. Descendants from those horses were gathered by Fernando Rivera for the expedition to California, in 1769. They were small, fast animals of remarkable endurance.

Horses subsequently became indispensable in the care of the cattle herds. During the *rancho* period, they could be purchased for about three dollars, less than the cost of a saddle and bridle. Capable of great speed, the horses, mostly mustangs, acquired a skill in rounding up and branding cattle hardly less extraordinary than that of their riders. In the mission era, horses were never used for work in the fields or for hauling. Such labor was performed by oxen. Mules were utilized as pack animals. A comparatively small number of burros were also found in the mission droves.

Large numbers of *vaqueros* or cowboys were needed because of the absence of fences in the territory. Free–running stock became so wild and fierce that it was unsafe to go among such herds on foot or unarmed. The horses in California multiplied at such a rate that they often ran wild. Chroniclers report that some met their death by being driven over precipices into the sea or rivers to drown.

The "sport of kings" or horseracing was among the most popular pastimes for early residents of San Gabriel. Thomas Workman Temple II traced the sport to 1839, and a race between José Avila and Andrés Duarte, *mayordomo* for the mission. Stakes for the event were a barrel of San Gabriel *aguardiente* or brandy, two gentle horses and five pesos in silver. The race course was south of the mission over an area of 600 *varas*, or approximately 600 yards, all to be fenced with no blocking allowed.

Duarte's jockey broke the rules by giving Avila's horse a blow on the head and blocking the way. Avila complained to *Alcalde* Manuel Dominguez, at the *Pueblo de Nuestra Señora de los Angeles*, and appeared with witnesses to demand the prizes, although Duarte's horse came in ahead by half a length.

Avila, however, failed to prove his contention. The *alcalde*, after hearing the testimony, decided that as the course had not been properly fenced, in conformity with the governor's regulations, the parties should pay a fine of $10 each and that the race should be repeated within twenty days, in the presence of a *regidor*, or councilman.

Temple reported that there was no record about the eventual outcome of that race, but that the barrel of mission brandy could hardly have lasted very long in the festivities which probably followed the race. Under the lash of an ill– defined puritanism and nativism, the California legislature passed a law, in 1855, prohibiting the sport on Sunday. Thus, for a while, horse races, described by one Protestant clergyman as one of the "fruits of Popery," were banned from the scene.

Fortunately, or perhaps not so, depending on one's viewpoints, the "sport of kings" was temporarily interdicted in the Golden State.

HOTEL DE CORONADO

Having no divinity degree, Bishop Thomas J. Conaty (1847–1915) was often given to speaking in terms more descriptive than theological. An example would be an observation made in a letter to his brother in 1906: "My concept of heaven is Coronado Island off the shoreline of San Diego. Whenever I am in the area, I stay on the island. I think of the grounds of the Coronado Hotel in terms of the Garden of Eden."

Conaty was not alone in his appreciation of the Hotel del Coronado. One early promotional booklet about the hostelry said that "guests may well fancy themselves in a veritable terrestrial paradise." Legend had it that a rabbit hunt actually occasioned the hotel. In 1884, Elisha S. Babcock and H. L. Story had gone to the island to shoot rabbits. Babcock was impressed with the setting and reportedly said, "what a splendid site for a great resort hotel."

Babcock's enthusiasm was infectious and Story soon became infatuated with the dream of a magnificent hotel on what had previously been an ignored and brush–covered island. The two men purchased 4,185 acres on the island in 1885 and within a year they had organized and

Hotel Coronado

incorporated the Coronado Beach Company. In order to finance their venture, they began a nationwide campaign to auction off part of the property to private developers.

Tracks were laid and shortly thereafter the tiny Coronado Railway began hauling construction material across the island from the docks. Pipe lines were installed under San Diego Bay to bring water to Coronado from wells near Old Town. The potential impasse of obtaining sufficient lumber was avoided when exclusive rights to that commodity were entrusted to the Dolbeer and Carson Lumber Company, one of the largest suppliers on the west coast.

In March of 1887, the first shovel of earth for the hotel's foundation was turned. Most of the several hundred workers were unskilled and received vocational training on the job. The whole operation was skillfully orchestrated. The Hotel del Coronado was among the first of its kind to have electric lights from the beginning. All the wiring was channeled through piping designed to supply gas for lighting. And that was only one of the many innovative and distinctive features of the hotel.

The spacious building was ready for occupancy on February 19, 1888. In the pages of the San Diego *Union* was this description of the grand dining room: "The vast and elegant room, with its wealth of appointment, is a rare sight, especially under the brilliant incandescent lights that illuminate it. The polished floors, over which an army of trained servants noiselessly glide, the high inlaid ceilings, the snowy linen and the glitter of the silver and glassware combined to make a most charming picture. The room may have its equal, but it certainly is not surpassed anywhere."

Indeed, the completed hotel was fittingly regarded by contemporaries as "one of the wonders of this wonderful age, and a great credit to our glorious Republic." Bishop Conaty, one of the earliest admirers of the Hotel del Coronado, died within the shadow of his "concept of heaven," on September 18, 1915.

IMMACULATE CONCEPTION

The day on which the Christian world honors Our Lady's preservation from all stain of original sin, from the very first moment of her conception, is pre–eminent among the Marian feasts in New Spain's annals.

The flagship on which Christopher Columbus journeyed to the New World was named "*Santa Maria de la Inmaculada Concepción.*" While he fittingly christened the first of the islands he discovered in the name of *San Salvador* (Holy Savior), the "Admiral of the Ocean Sea" conferred the title of Mary's Immaculate Conception on the second.

Just a century later, on December 8, 1603, Sebastian Vizcaíno gave the appellation *Limpia Concepción* to that area near Santa Barbara, where the California coastline turns from east–west to north. To this very day Point

Conception recalls that great navigator's devotion to the Mother of the Savior.

In 1620, the fifth of the missionary establishments founded by the Society of Jesus in Peninsular California was placed under the Patronage of *Purísima Concepción*. Founded by Father Nicolas Tamaral, that frontier outpost served the spiritual needs of the natives from Cadegomo for over a century.

On November 8, 1760, the Blessed Mother, under her title of the Immaculate Conception, was declared the principal patroness of all the possessions attached to the Spanish Crown, including those in America. Eighty–six years later, at the Sixth Provincial Council of Baltimore, the Bishops of the United States voted to proclaim Our Lady of the Immaculate Conception the nation's official protectoress.

Fray Juan Crespi, official diarist for the expeditionary penetration into California, named a small Indian village in the western portion of present–day Santa Barbara County, *Concepción de Maria Santísima* in August, 1769. One of the two quasi–missions established, in October, 1780, at the *Puerto de Concepción*, by friars from the Apostolic College of *Santa Cruz de Querétaro*, was entrusted to Mary's patronage of *Purísima Concepcion*.

Seven years later, the eleventh missionary outpost along California's *El Camino Real* was established, near present–day Lompoc, as *Mision de la Purísima Concepción de la Santísima Virgen Maria*.

The Cathedral erected in San Francisco by Archbishop Joseph Sadoc Alemany, dedicated to "Saint Mary, Ever–Virgin and Conceived Without Sin," was the first in the world named for the Immaculate Conception following that doctrine's formal definition on December 8, 1854, by Pope Pius IX.

The dedication of the United States to Our Lady, by the Sixth Provincial Council of Baltimore, repeated in later gatherings of the American hierarchy, was given visible expression, on September 23, 1920, when the cornerstone was put in place for the National Shrine of the Immaculate Conception, in Washington, D.C. That magnificent church, the seventh largest religious edifice in the world, is but one of the 515 churches (including fourteen cathedrals) in the United States bearing the appellation of Our Lady's freedom from original sin.

The image of the Virgin Mary's Immaculate Conception is at the heart of Western Society, a presence so familiar that it would be impossible to measure. So many names of days in the calendar, places, customs, landscape, language and literature bear her sign.

Daniel–Rops has pointed out that Our Lady's witnesses are the great cathedrals at Amiens, Chartres, Rheims, Florence and Cologne, as well as the crowds that throng on pilgrimage to Lourdes and Fatima. The most tender of Christian traditions is this love for the humble young maiden who was the instrument of the will of the Most High. By it each one of us seeks to find our way back, through the most intense of our sufferings, to that secret unattainable but never abandoned desire, the pure heart of our childhood."

The message addressed to the Catholics of the United States by nation's hierarchy, in 1849, bears repeating in this new century:

> We exhort you, brethren, to continue to cherish a tender devotion to the Mother of Our Lord, since the honor given to her (Immaculate Conception) is founded on the relation which she bears to Him.

THE IMMIGRATION MOVEMENT

During the 1990s, more than four million immigrants found their way to the United States legally and several million others entered the country illegally. Many of those who come from Asia and most from Hispanic America are professedly Roman Catholic.

California presently accounts for 3.5 million (out of 14 million) of America's foreign–born population. With one in four of these people residing in the Golden State, California has become the nation's melting pot.

About one in every four residents in the metropolitan Los Angeles area (and almost one in six in greater San Francisco) is foreign–born. If the Statue of Liberty were built today, it would probably be perched near the ocean approach of the Los Angeles airport or on an incline at the international border near San Diego.

The Koreans on the assembly line in Silicon Valley, the Vietnamese fishermen in Monterey Bay, the Hmong tribesman learning new skills in San Diego, the Hispanic Americans working in construction are evidence that California is showing America its future. For more than a century, magnetic California has pulled the tide of migration westward. It has been the last stop of the great westward movement that has underscored the history of European civilization since the Middle Ages.

Immigration is a painful process because the newcomers invariably bring along strange languages and cultures. Their differing etiquette, diet, religion and hygiene can be irritating and threatening to the established order.

Historically, each new wave of immigrants has been met with a measure of open hostility. Yet it is important to recall that hybrid vigor is a phenomenon as vital to societies as genetics. With immigrants comes a strengthening of the collective gene pool.

Naturally, the current immigration, be it legal or otherwise, poses some problems. But it is an enduring myth that immigrants consume vast amounts of the public dole, while contributing paltry sums to the public treasury.

In fact, studies show that about three quarters of them (even illegals) pay social security and income taxes and only a minuscule number (perhaps as few as 3%) accept any form of public assistance. The vast majority of immigrants come to California for one reason only, to work.

Upon their arrival, immigrants face obstacles at least as serious as those encountered by disadvantaged Americans—they have few skills, little education, no knowledge of the area and, in most cases, little if any command of the language. Yet they are finding and creating jobs. The bottom rung of the ladder is a step up for most of them. And because they expect less in the beginning, they are on their way to gaining more in the end.

The immigrants who came across the border in the 1920s and 1930s transformed California life. Their customs, heritage , language and energies merged into the mainstream of our culture, enriching it and changing it forever.

IRISH SETTLERS IN GOLDEN STATE

The names of the first Irish settlers in Alta California will probably always remain in oblivion, with their deeds unrecorded, unhonored and unsung, like those of their forefathers whose memories have so often perished from the annals of history.

There were a number of American whaling ships which made voyages to the Pacific Coast in the years after the Revolution. Many of the crewmen on those vessels were Irish and not a few of them were driven to desertion by the intolerable treatment they received because of their religion and nationality.

A possibly apocryphal tradition notes that a man named "Logue", in 1800, a seaman on a whaler, became involved in a quarrel with the mate because the latter pushed a piece of pork to his mouth on Good Friday. He stabbed him in the heart and then leaped overboard, escaping to the mainland and later taking up residence in the neighborhood of Mendocino.

The first extant record of an Irishman coming overland to California was Captain J. Smith, who reached the coast with a party of immigrants or trappists in 1826. Smith's presence alarmed the Spanish inhabitants and they sent a messenger to inquire about his intentions. Smith, a native of King's County, Ireland, stated that his object was trapping. He signed his reply as "your stranger but real friend and Christian brother, J. Smith."

The Smith party, numbering about forty, were mostly murdered by Indians. Among the few who escaped were two natives of Galway who settled in Northern Califor-

nia. Smith himself somehow avoided the massacre and afterwards obtained a lucrative position as chief trader for the American Fur Company on the Green River.

There were several Irish officers on the sailing vessels which visited the coasts of California and some of them established residences in the area. Mostly they married Spanish or Mexican wives and learned to speak the Hispanic language, transmitting nothing Irish to their descendants save their names.

One very remarkable Irishman who came at an early date was John J. Read, who was among the first to settle permanently. He was born in Dublin, in 1805, and left Ireland fifteen years later. Eventually he located in Marin County, where he lived until his demise in 1843

Timoteo Murphy, who came by sea from South America early in 1828, was born in Wexford. Daniel Hill, another native of the Emerald Isle, arrived in California during Hispanic times. Dr. Nicholas Den, a son–in–law of Hill, made California his home well before the proclamation of the Bear Flag Republic.

Martin Murphy and James Miller undertook the hazardous journey to the Pacific as early as 1844. There were sixty members of their party. Three years afterwards, the Donner party attempted what the Miller–Murphy people had done before them, and fell into all sorts of unfortunate tragedies. Several members of the Donner party were also Irishmen, including the Breens, Dolans and Hallorins.

The "revolt" of 1836 was headed by the two Irishmen, Coppinger and Graham. It is estimated that fully a fourth of Captain John Fremont's sharp shooters were natives of Ireland. General Stephen Kearny, the first military governor of California, often boasted of his Irish birth.

IRISH TEAM AT SANTA INES

The colorful inaugural of the XXIII Olympiad year at Los Angeles calls to mind an event that occurred during the 1932 games, when the Olympics were first held along the Pacific Slope. Simultaneously with the impressive ceremonies that brought the Xth Olympiad to a close, the team from Ireland motored 150 miles north to Santa Ines, where they paid tribute to the memory of a famed Irish patriot.

The team gathered in the graveyard of the Old Mission to place a huge wreath representing the tri–color Irish flag over the grave of Father Albert Bibby (1878–1925). Their heads bowed in silent homage, the team listened intently to a tribute honoring the renowned Irish Capuchin.

A columnist for *The Monitor* noted that Father Albert was one of those persons remembered for his goodness, his sweetness, his meekness and his charity. Father Albert—of whom poets and writers with their feeble words have tried to render' homage. Father Albert—at whose passing, the bells of Erin and old Santa Ines united, their muffled peals ringing out a dirge of mournful sadness.

"In death as in life, this true follower of the saint of Assisi has a place in the affections of our hearts. He who was a true priest, soldier and patriot is held in loving memory on our shores of the Pacific, as well as in his own homeland."

Rocky Dana, a writer for the Santa Maria *Valley Vidette*, asked one of the athletes if he had known Father Albert personally. He replied that "all Ireland knew him."

Father Albert Bibby was among the pioneers of the Gaelic League. Although a frail and delicate man, he was buoyant in spirit. His cheerfulness in adversity was possibly the most attractive aspect of his many–faceted personality.

In the uprising of 1916, Father Albert served the spiritual needs of the Volunteers in the North Dublin Union area. From that time on, he was prominently identified with the movement for national independence. Father Albert's views eventually incurred the displeasure of British authorities and he was exiled from the country, in mid–1924

The Irish friars were entrusted with the Old Mission at Santa Ines in that year and, on November 20th, Father Albert was named pastor of the historic California missionary foundation. Although his enforced exile was a heavy burden, Father Albert welcomed the opportunity of serving under the patronage of Saint Agnes, for whom he had long been a devotee.

Father Albert died at Santa Ines, far from the land he loved so dearly and the people he served so faithfully. At the time of his demise, the Catholic press in Eire proclaimed that "the Catholic Church has lost a gifted scholar and a saintly priest; Ireland a loyal and devoted patriot."

The tributes cabled into Santa Ines were numerous and effusive. The Catholic *Bulletin* declared that "those who had the joy of Father Albert's friendship can well look forward to meeting him in heaven." But one suspects that Father Albert would have treasured above all the others the posthumous honor bestowed when the Irish team visited his grave at the close of the Xth Olympiad Year.

IRISH IN CALIFORNIA

At the turn of the 19th century, some fifty years before the disastrous Irish famine, legend has it that a saintly old monk living near a tiny Christian enclave in the confines of Old Tunisia, had a prophetic vision wherein he beheld a great exodus from an island he knew only as Hibernia. A million bedraggled natives were seen leaving their thatched cabins on the fens and the moors, dragging their emaciated forms westward. From there, tall–masted ships bore them over the wide bosom of the ocean to the great veldts on the flats of Southern Africa. After a brief time mining diamonds, the exiles travelled on to the colonies of the South Seas. Still further they sailed, some choosing the ports of New England as their haven.

On the western coast of North America, where "nature smiles the whole year through," the monk could see a glorious empire magically springing into existence, where golden treasure abounded on every hill. The valleys promised wealth to those who would nourish and harvest them and the inhabitants were blessed with freedom, contentment, and brotherly love, Here it was that the homeless children of Erin settled—and Almighty God, remembering their love for Him and His Church, kept their Faith ever flourishing by sending along to them a new generation inspired by the Holy Ghost and consecrated to His service, to break for them the Bread of Life and direct their souls in the paths of righteousness and Christian piety.

Be this prophetic legend, fact or myth, such a migration really did take place during California's Gold Rush Days. Great as it was numerically, however, the great surge of *Esos Irlandeses* post–dated by almost a century, Irish influence in California. Indeed, the initial movement toward possession and settlement of the area was prompted by Irish–Spaniards and directed by a native of Dublin, the Conde Alejandro O'Reilly. It was an order of this Generalissimo of the Spanish Armies that eventually culminated in the coming of Fray Junípero Serra and Gaspar de Portola in 1769. But Irish influence did not end there. It was due largely to the aid and direction of Thomas Fitzpatrick, a veteran trapper and guide, that the overland trail to California was opened, and that the Carson, or Tahoe Pass, was discovered. When this route was menaced during the Civil War by possible action of the Southern Army and by Indian insurrection, the roadway was kept open and contact with the east maintained by Major Patrick E. Conner. California, then, was saved for Mexico and subsequently for the United States; a trail was opened for the argonauts; and vital communications between east and west assured, all through the efforts of three Irishmen!

Save for the Spaniards themselves, the only men appearing in the record of achievement to extend the frontiers of New Spain into the wilderness of *Las Californias* were Irish–Spaniards. Certainly it was altogether fitting, that those two great nations, Ireland and Spain, which had shared the Faith since penal days, should have cooperated so harmoniously in Christianizing California.

That the Golden State is a beneficiary of the Irish spirit hardly needs emphasis. Here, the sons of Erin have added much to the composite American, made up as he is from various European, Asiatic and African stocks. The spiritual disciples of Saint Patrick, the co–patron of the Archdiocese of Los Angeles, have softened California wit, added to its tenderness, increased the spirit of good fellowship, augmented our social graces and increased our poetical imagination.

The Irish priesthood has a long and noble heritage in the Golden State, though, in all fairness, it should be noted that even before her ministers came, the Faith carried over from Ireland was securely locked away in the hearts of a people who never forgot their religion, despite being deprived for many years of its priestly services. There is something in the Irish character which readily takes up the call of the missions. As a playwright put it, the restless spirit of an Irishman "will never be content . . . with the fogs and the winds of his native land. The Celt must wander. His youthful foot itches, and the mind and body are keen to follow!"

One historian of California, speaking of the Irish missionairies who followed Eugene O'Connell to Grass Valley, described the stream of the Emerald Isle's clergy who have so faithfully served this far–western apostolate:

From the Apostolic colleges of Ireland, they came; from St. Kieran's in Kilkenny, from St. Patrick's in Carlow, from St. John's in Waterford, from St. Patricks in Tipperary and from All Hallows in Dublin. Nor were these messengers of peace all silver–haired divines who had borne the heat and burden of the day, but bright young clerics, just fresh from the anointing at the hands of the bishop, fortified with the continence of the Virgin, the burning zeal of the Apostle, and the spirit and welfare of their fellowmen till death would meet them at the end of the trail.

That long list of Irish missioners perdures to the present day. In Southern California alone, 42 percent of the deceased secular priests and 39 percent of those presently serving in the Archdiocese of Los Angeles proudly claim the Emerald Isle as their place of birth. California takes justifiable pride in the accomplishments of those who have been with her through the years since her infancy, those who have helped to make her name glorious in the eyes of the world. California is grateful to those trail–blazers who assisted in pushing back the forces of ignorance and barbarism. She is mindful of those who, in the not–so-easy pioneering days, struggled, sometimes at the sacrifice of their own lives, to see that justice prevailed within her borders; of those who

freely gave of their time, talent and resource that a stable government might be universally established. California is thankful for those children who have brought her honor and glory in the field of literature, arts and science. The Golden State, if she is highly respected today as a benevolent and godly commonwealth, a peaceful and desirable place to live, recognizes her great Irish builders as humble men of God, who by teaching and good example, added their share of knowledge, culture, courage and faith to the state's development.

Pope Pius XI once said of the Irish: They are "everywhere, like the grace of God." Truly, the monuments of Ireland are erected "everywhere," not monuments of cold marble or chilled stone but monuments of living nations whose Faith she had founded, fostered or revived and whose manners she has purified, refined and gilded with superb Christian wisdom.

It would indeed be difficult to define the limits of the spiritual service of the Irish race in this or any other area, and that, perhaps, is why the Holy Father said they are "everywhere, like the grace of God." Everywhere," they are found the champions of morals, the apostles of liberty and the emancipators of peoples, and races. "Everywhere," like God's sunshine giving warmth and glow to a cold and neo–pagan civilization. Truly the Irish pioneers of California were great men and the reward of great men is that, long after they have died, one is not quite sure they are dead!

ITALIAN CATHOLIC FEDERATION

California is the story of a heritage fulfilled, resources developed and beauty cultivated. Catholicism in the Golden State is likewise the narrative of saint–named cities and mission–marked heroism brought to the twentieth century with vitality and promise.

The influence of Italians in the mosaic of California Christian life can be traced to the dawn of another century when the Florentine navigator, Alesandro Malaspina first anchored in the warm waters along the Pacific Slope. Since that time, Italians have participated in agriculture, fishing, mining, constructing, manufacturing, wholesaling, retailing, farming, law, politics and almost every other field of human endeavor.

In the early 1920s, a survey indicated that a vast majority of the Italians and Italo–Americans in California had become alienated from the traditions of their Catholic religion. Mainly responsible for that sad condition were such factors as anti–clericalism, lack of Italian–speaking priests, poor education and, above all, the mentality that economic and social betterment would be accelerated by breaking all ties with their background, foremost of which was the Catholic faith.

In an attempt to reverse that trend, Father A!bert Bandini and Mr. Luigi Providenza decided to establish an organization whose primary and ultimate aim would be the reactivation of the spiritual seed which was dormant in so many Italian hearts and souls. The first meeting of the Italian Catholic Federation took place on June 15, 1924, in San Francisco's Church of the Immaculate Conception. Archbishop Edward J. Hanna approved the structure and statutes and, on December 7, the initial branch of the I.C.F. was inaugurated with 300 members.

It was the founders' intention that the I.C.F. should be the instrument for anchoring the Italian descendants to a family apostolate, uniting husband, wife, children and relatives in sacred enthusiasm. That ideal was further implemented through establishment of the *Bollettino*, which has been published monthly since 1925.

From the very outset, the Italian Catholic Federation sponsored missions, retreats and radio programs by Jesuits, Salesians, Josephites, Franciscans and Dominicans to awaken "a more intense Christian life among the Italian population of California." The I.C.F. was introduced to California's southland in 1931, with foundation of the San Roque branch at Santa Barbara, on November 22. Presently, the Archdiocese of Los Angeles is the largest field of work for the I.C.F., with fifty–eight branches in the three county area.

Though envisioned as primarily a parochial society upon which the local pastor could rely for his work the I.C.F. was destined by God's grace to encompass a spirit and vitality that has grown to 225 active branches and 25,000 persons. The Italian Catholic Federation observed the golden jubilee of its establishment in 1974, with publication of a 112 page book on *The First Fifty Years*. Therein, the "reason" for the I.C.F. was nobly stated by Msgr. Robert Brennan: "to bring back people to the Body of Christ."

The long–time archdiocesan director of the I.C.F. for Los Angeles went on to describe the organization as "an idealogical, beautiful expression of Catholic Action."

JAPANESE APOSTOLATE

The origin of the Japanese mission on the west coast was related by *The Monitor* of San Francisco in 1913. A certain Leo Hatakeyama of Los Angeles wanted a priest to hear his confession. Speaking no English, he wrote to his native land offering "to send his confession in a registered letter" and asking that a priest "return the penance and absolution by mail."

Apparently the case was referred to the Bishop of Monterey–Los Angeles, the Right Reverend Thomas J. Conaty. The prelate immediately contacted the Maryknoll Fathers in Massachusetts who, in turn, forwarded the request to the Paris Foreign Mission Society. One of their priests, Father Albert Breton, was sent to Los Angeles and told to organize facilities for the Japanese Catholics in the Golden State. Father Breton arrived in Los Angeles on October 12, 1912, where he found a Japanese colony of 10,000. Although a relatively small number was Catholic, those who did profess the Faith were found immensely anxious to have their needs cared for by a fellow countryman.

It was noted in one journal that "the work of locating the Japanese Catholics in California is being done by Fr. A. Breton, a member of the Society of Foreign Missions in Paris. Long residence in Japan had given Father Breton the advantage of a thorough knowledge of the language and literature of the country. His present residence is Los Angeles, and he has succeeded in gathering together the Japanese members of the Church in that city and neighborhood." In the foundation at Los Angeles, "there were about fifty Japanese members of this first Catholic Mission dedicated to the Japanese in America," originally located at 707 West Second Street.

Education of the children was the first perplexing problem. Of the 60,000 Japanese in California, 8,000 were going without a Catholic education. At Father Breton's request, four Catechist–Lovers of the Cross (later known as the Japanese Sisters of the Visitation) from Nagasaki came to Los Angeles to open Saint Francis Xavier Mission School. "With the aid of the Franciscans, Daughters of Charity and the Helpers of the Holy Souls, the education and evangelization of the emigrated Japanese advanced rapidly and was greatly encouraged. Many works sprang up . . . Kindergartens, orphanages, sanatoriums, grammar schools, language schools, music schools, night schools and Sunday Schools."

Breton's influence was felt throughout the state. In San Francisco Archbishop Patrick W. Riordan set up a home and club room at 2158 Pine Street, for classes on "religious and secular instruction." The priests of Saint Mary's Cathedral looked after the foundation during Father Breton's absences in the southland. One contemporary journal told its Catholic readers that "it is needless to speak of the merits of the work, or to suggest the propriety of cooperation. The success of Saint Francis Xavier's mission, and the zeal and self sacrifice of his converts shows us what grace can do among these wonderful people; and the labors of the modern Catholic missionaries in Japan should inspire us to supplement their work on the Pacific Coast."

After World War I, Father Breton was recalled to Japan where, ten years later, he became the Bishop of Fukuoka. In San Francisco the Jesuits took over the work and the Society continued its activities among the Japanese until 1925, when the Divine Word missionaries assumed the charge. Sacramento's apostolate was assumed by the Franciscan Sisters of Niagara, while in Los Angeles and Seattle the Fathers and Sisters of Maryknoll took up the task.

The Japanese apostolate came to a thundering halt on Pearl Harbor day, and overnight the streets of the Japanese communities were abandoned. When the hostilities ended, the people returned to their homes "taller in stature, with the pride of men and women who had proven their faith and loyalty to the land of their adoption by the sacrifice of their sons in that nation's defense."

SAINT JOSEPH IN CALIFORNIA

The Feast of Saint Joseph was observed with great solemnity in provincial times. Visitador General José de Galvez had asked the Franciscans to celebrate a monthly High Mass in honor of the Holy Patriarch "in order to obtain the most complete success for the California enterprise." This Fray Junípero Serra did throughout his years as *Presidente*. Alfred Robinson wrote about the festivities attached to the observance at Mission San Jose. His eye witness account contains many facets of a practice common throughout the missionary system.

> The music was well–executed, for it had been practiced daily for more than two months under the particular supervision of Fray Narciso Duran. The number of the musicians was about thirty; the instruments performed upon were violins, flutes, trumpets and drums; and so acute was the ear of the priest that he would detect a wrong note on the part of either instantly, and chide the erring performer. I have often seen the old gentleman, bareheaded, in the large square of the Mission beating time against one of the pillars of the corridor, whilst his music was in rehearsal.

> After Mass was concluded we passed out of the church to the priest's apartment through a shower of rockets, which were fired off incessantly in every direction. Dinner was served early to give us time to witness the performances of the Indians, and as there are many strangers at the Mission, a very lengthy table had been prepared, so as to accommodate all.

> An abundance of good things appeared and disappeared, till at length the cloth was removed; cigars were smoked, and the good old friars retired to enjoy their "*siesta*," whilst we repaired to the front of the corridor to behold the fun.

> At a signal from their "Capitan," or chief, several hundred Indians presented themselves at the corner of one of the streets of the "*Rancheria*" and gradually approached towards us. They were dressed with feathers, and painted with red and black paint: looking like so many demons.

> There were several women amongst them. Soon they formed a circle, and commenced what they called dancing, which was one of the most ludicrous specimens of grotesque performance I had ever seen. It did not appear to me that they had any change of figure whatever; but fixed to one spot, they beat time with their feet to the singing of half a dozen persons who were seated upon the ground.

> When these had performed their part, they retired to an encampment beyond the building and another party appeared, painted and adorned rather differently from the former, whose mode of dancing also, was quite dissimilar. They retired after a while, and arrangements were made for a bear fight.

> Whilst these amusements were going on, the *Padres* had risen, and we were called to chocolate; but the enthusiasm of the Indians hardly gave us time to finish, when we heard them crying "*Aqui traen el oso!*" He was soon ready, though almost dead from confinement, and the bull made a few plunges, ere he laid him stiff upon the ground.

> This part of the amusement concluded, (Ferdinand) Deppe and I walked to the encampment, where the Indians were dancing in groups, as we had seen them at the Mission. Around the large space which they occupied were little booths, displaying a variety of ornaments, seeds, and fruits. All was hilarity and good feeling; for the prudence of Father Narciso had forbidden the sale of liquor.

> At sundown the bells were rung—rockets were let off—guns were fired; and long after supper, at a late hour of the night, we could hear from our beds the continued shouts of the multitude.

JOURNALISM IN CALIFORNIA

The Catholic press has consistently been an active force in California Catholic life. As early as 1850, the New York *Freemans Journal and Catholic Register* carried a regular column from a California correspondent signing himself only as "Philos" but thought to be Gregory Phelan of Sacramento.

Between, 1854 and 1855, the *Catholic Standard* was published at San Francisco but was eventually discontinued for lack of patronage. *The Monitor* was founded in March of 1858, by James Marks, Patrick J. Thomas, and James Hamill. It was published constantly since except for two months in 1865, when its offices were wrecked after the assassination of Abraham Lincoln. Its title has varied slightly. From 1875 to 1877, it was the *Monitor and Guardian* and between 1920 and 1926, it came out as the *Monitor and Intermountain Catholic*. In 1877 *The Monitor* became the official organ of the Archdiocese of San Francisco.

The Universe replaced *The Monitor* between April 14 and June 10, of 1865. The *Catholic Guardian*, first published in 1872 under the editorship of Dillon Francis Eagon, was merged with *The Monitor* three years later. Los Angeles was the headquarters of the *California Catholic* in 1888. Written in English by a group of laymen and issued weekly, the newspaper only lasted one year.

O Amigos dos Catolicos was begun at Irvington in 1888. The Portuguese publication was inaugurated by Father Manuel Francisco Fernandez and José Francisco Tavares. After some years the paper passed under lay control and moved to Pleasanton. From 1892 to 1896 it was printed in Hayward. The name changed in 1896 to *O Arauto*. It was purchased in 1917 by Pedro L. C. Silveira who merged it with *O Jornal de Noticias*.

Published weekly and devoted to "the interests of the Catholic Church in America," the *Cause* was launched on October 4, 1890, by Edward Robertson, Isidore Dockweiler, and Joseph Mesmer. It was succeeded by the *Voice* sponsored by W. D. S. Harrington. Unfortunately, the advertisers refused to support the publication because of pressures from the American Protective Association and the paper soon died from fiscal malnutrition.

The Catholic Tidings appeared on June 29, 1895, and became the official newspaper for the Diocese of Monterey–Los Angeles on October 7, 1904. Its title had been shortened to *The Tidings* in 1897. The *Southern Cross* also began as an independent newspaper in 1912, and became the authorized publication of the Diocese of San Diego on August 18, 1937.

In 1897 Constantino C. Soares originated *O Reporter* in Oakland. From 1910 to 1914, the weekly was owned and issued by the Reverend José Silva. *La Actualidad* was printed for several years from 1895 at San Bernardino under the direction of Father John Caballeria. Its primary concern was the "interest of the Spanish–speaking people of Southern California."

The *Catholic Herald* began in 1908 at Sacramento under the editorship of Thomas A. Connelly. It ceased publication on December 28, 1929, and the next month was replaced by the *Register* as the official paper of the Diocese of Sacramento. In 1945 its name was changed to the *Superior California Register* and in 1949 to the *Superior California Catholic Herald*. Since 1958, the paper has reverted to its original title, the *Catholic Herald*.

Monterey–Fresno's official–diocesan organ is the *Central California Register*. It was established in 1929 as part of the *Denver Register* system and became independent in 1955.

La Luz began in 1949 as the Spanish language paper of the Diocese of Monterey–Fresno. Its name was changed to *Excelsior* in 1950. Since 1961, it has been combined with the *Central California Register*.

Other California newspapers known to have been published by Catholics or in Catholic interests include *La Cronica* (1872–1892), *Las dos Republicas*, successor of *La Cronica*, and *O Uniao Portuguese* which was printed at San Francisco between 1889 and 1942 at irregular intervals.

CATHOLIC JOURNALISM IN CALIFORNIA

NAME	YEARS	PLACE
Catholic Standard	1854–1855	San Francisco
Monitor	1858 onwards	San Francisco
Universe	1865	San Francisco
Catholic Guardian	1872–1875	San Francisco
La Cronica	1872–1892	Los Angeles
California Catholic	1888–1889	Los Angeles
O Amigos dos Catolicos	1888–1896	Irvington
Cause	1890–1892	Los Angeles
Voice	1892–1893	Los Angeles
La Actualidad	1895–1902	San Bernardino
Catholic Tidings	1895 onwards	Los Angeles
O Arauto	1896–1917	Hayward
O Reporter	1897–1914	Oakland
Catholic Herold	1903 onwards	Sacramento
Southern Cross	1912 onwards	San Diego
O Journal de Noticias	1917–1932	San Francisco
Central California Register	1929 onwards	Fresno
La Luz (Excelsior)	1949–1961	Fresno

JOURNALISM — CATHOLIC PRESS

Among all the important auxiliaries of the Church, according to John Steven McGroarty (1862–1944), the Catholic press ranks "first in importance and usefulness." California's poet laureate applied the term "Catholic press" to that weekly newspaper or magazine, countenanced, approved and endorsed by the proper authorities, whose sole aim and purpose is "to labor in the Church's behalf."

The one–time Congressman decried the fact that many Catholic journals of his time sought "to ape the methods of the secular press" giving all too little attention to purely Catholic literature. Such an approach was paradoxical, in McGroarty's view, since Catholic editors had at hand the most priceless treasures to spread before their readers, if only they would use them. McGroarty said that were an editor "to print his journal twice every day for a hundred years he could not exhaust his vast supply of golden treasure."

McGroarty also felt that "acrimonious controversies with our non–Catholic brethren not only fail to accomplish any good end, but that, on the contrary, they do untold harm." He noted that the only worse thing was "the scandalous manner in which Catholic editors quarrel with one another." His conception of the "ideal Catholic journal" was the weekly or monthly paper or magazine so conducted, edited and managed "that it can enter the Protestant home with the same assurance of polite and friendly welcome that a Catholic gentleman or gentlewoman would receive in that same home."

Despite his fierce loyalty to the religious press, McGroarty was not overly favorable to the widely discussed plan for inaugurating a Catholic daily on the national level. Such a venture, he believed, was not necessary inasmuch as Catholics generally had no reason to complain about the treatment they received at the hands of the secular press: "It would be misdirected effort and energy on our part to invade the field of daily journalism, where there is no necessity for us to go, and where we would but create distrust and invite attack."

His long experience as a journalist with the Los Angeles *Times* convinced McGroarty that journalism should be of such quality as to dispense altogether with the need for apology, excuse or explanation. He said that "the Catholic press must be dignified, it must be pure and true, it must be sweet and kindly, and above all, charitable. The Catholic journal must seek the highest planes, it must live where it can catch the breath of God from the mountain tops of the earth."

As for the Catholic journalist, McGroarty counseled him to regard his publication as a father regards his child so that when he sends it forth to walk among the haunts of men, he sends it with his prayers, the loving touch of his hand upon its shoulders and the light of his own soul in its eyes.

JUAN CARLOS VISITS LOS ANGELES

The welcome extended to King Juan Carlos and Queen Sofia by the hybrid population of *El Pueblo de Nuestra Señora de los Angeles* marked the first time a Spanish monarch had ever visited the city chartered by King Carlos III in 1781. During ceremonies dedicating a statue to his distinguished ancestor, the king extolled Los Angeles as a "center of economy and culture worldwide," the most prosperous gem in the Hispanic galaxy of nations and cities.

Carlos was "the king of Spain and Mexico and California," said Carmelita Lorenzano Flores. "How can you argue with history?" Juan Carlos didn't. Dedicating the statue was a "moment of deep emotion," and a "symbol of brotherhood that unites all people, the people of Los Angeles and the people of Spain."

As he stood in the Old Plaza before 150 descendants of the city's original *pobladores*, the king expressed his gratitude at finally being able to visit what was once known as the "rim of Christendom."

When given the key to the city of Los Angeles, King Juan Carlos expressed his hope that having that symbolic memento would "help to keep the doors open for all future activities between the United States and Spain." Though fluent in five languages, including English, Juan Carlos spoke in Spanish as a mark of affection for California's colonizers.

Later that afternoon (September 30, 1987), the descendant of Ferdinand and Isabella, Louis XIV (of France) and Victoria (of England) journeyed across town to the Century Plaza Hotel, where he was scheduled to meet with still another group of well–wishers.

It was there that I was able to greet the royal couple, thanks to a gracious invitation by the local consul general, Pedro Temboury. (The king and queen had intended to visit Mission Hills and the venerable 1797 Spanish outpost named for *San Fernando, Rey de España*. Unfortunately, that part of their journey was cancelled for lack of time.)

There were in excess of a thousand people gathered in the vast Los Angeles Ball Room of the Century Plaza Hotel to meet the king and his lovely queen. He entered at precisely 6:15 p.m. and spoke for about ten minutes, recalling the colonizing accomplishments of such outstanding people as Gaspar de Portolá, Pedro de Fages and others.

Fray Junípero Serra was given considerable mention, as were the other friars who helped to plant the seed of Christianity along the Pacific Slope in the last years of the 18th century. After his brief speech, the royal couple greeted a number of those present. Queen Sofia was given the little miniature book written about Fray Junípero Serra in 1984. She appeared pleased with the presentation and paged through it briefly before placing it in her purse.

Indeed the royal family is quite knowledgable about Serra and his place in Western American annals. In October of 1984, the king and his entire family visited Petra de Mallorca, the birthplace of Serra, for celebrations honoring the California pioneer on the 200th anniversary of his demise.

The visit of King Juan Carlos and Queen Sofia to Southern California was considerably more than an exercise in diplomacy. Our European roots in California are Hispanic and contemporary peoples honor their forebears by extending cordiality to their monarchy.

"JUST CALIFORNIA"

(The following is a paraphrase of John Steven McGroarty's classic tribute to California—a land apart from all others—like no other and distinctively itself.)

To find romance in America, it is to California that you must go. In romance was California born, and in it nurtured, and steeped in it she still is, down to this very day. Came the gray–robed, sandaled Brothers of St.

Francis, to build the missions and to set the glow of their candles on high altars in poppy–strewn valleys and upon green hill tops, and to ring the bells of the *Angelus* from one cross–crowned tower to another, all the way from San Diego's harbor of the sun to Sonoma in the valley of the seven moons.

The ruins of the old Franciscan missions constitute the only historical landmarks of consequence within the territory of the United States. And, in a way, they may be said to be as ancient as things can be, for the reason that they tell a story that is forever closed. Whoever travels by the overland route of the Santa Fe to California is landed at the outset of his arrival into the very heart of the dreams of this old Franciscan adventure.

He will be brought down through the mountain passes of the San Bernardinos, passing near San Gabriel into Los Angeles, and then on by San Juan Capistrano to San Luis Rey and San Diego. On the shores of the Bay of San Diego one will behold the spot where the first habitation of white men was reared on the western shores of our America.

Then up and yonder from San Diego, league upon league, the wander trail beckons to us. It is a road that the *padres* and their Indian neophytes built in the long ago, to be a chain for their missions, each hospice a bead in their rosary of faith and achievement.

They called it "*El Camino Real*," the King's Highway. Today it is paved with concrete for the flying wheels of the automobile, as broad and smooth as the Appian Way, and a thousand miles from end to end.

The pathway of the missions it is—that old King's Highway; and as you trudge it you shall live in the glamour of the past. You shall sit by the sunny fountain at San Fernando, pass the ancient tower of San Luis Obispo and see the candles glowing on the altar of Santa Barbara— which is the one gray fortress of the faith that never surrendered. And still onward you will wander from one ruined fane to another, beyond Carmelo and Monterey, even, and "Dolores" in the city of Saint Francis, to the Moon Valley of Sonoma.

The charm of California is not a fitful one. She has never known a faithless lover. Whoever has fallen under the spell of her beauty seeks no other mistress. Son and daughter that she has borne worship at her very name. The expatriate from other lands clings to her with a deep affection that ends only with death.

There is no other land so lovely, so constant, so generous. It lies between the desert and the sea—God's two great sanatoriums for weary body and weary mind.

KU KLUX KLAN

Founded atop Stone Mountain near Atlanta, Georgia, on Thanksgiving Day, 1915, the Ku Klux Klan began its activities in the Southern California town of Anaheim seven years later.

Although William Joseph Simmons stated repeatedly that the K.K.K. was merely "a secret fraternal and patriotic order drawing romantic inspiration from, the Civil War," the Klan's founder and his cohorts speedily saw the sales value of old hates and prejudices, especially those directed against Catholics and Jews. There were open Klan meetings in Anaheim throughout 1923 and 1924, in parks, squares and schoolhouses. Most of the speakers were imported from Oklahoma and Texas where K.K.K. activities were on the decline. An ex–minister, Leon Myers, was the "Exalted Cyclops" of the Anaheim Klavern and, as such, the moving force behind the organization's machinations in that area. (He is the same Leon Myers who in 1913 entered into a conspiracy with J. E. Hosmer in Silverton, Oregon, where they planted a woman in Mount Angel Convent under subterfuge. This woman later became the subject of Hosmer's book entitled *The Last Stand for Despotism or The Escaped Nun from Mt. Angel Convent*.)

Klan activities in Anaheim were implemented by the *Plain Dealer*, a daily newspaper which later became the official organ of the K.K.K. for Orange County. Catholic merchants were boycotted, citizens intimidated, public officials attacked, and airplanes, fiery crosses, and parades used to create interest. At one meeting in the Anaheim City Park, the speaker advocated burning down and wrecking Catholic churches, convents, and monasteries. Klansmen actually managed to win public office early in 1924 and during their brief tenure Catholic employees were discharged from office and a generalized "police state" harassed the Church's activities. The District Attorney for Orange County, A. P. Nelson, himself a non–Catholic, vigorously opposed Leon Myers and threatened to jail him if rioting occurred as the results of Klan meetings. Though Nelson was continually intimidated and insulted, he managed to thwart much of the strife planned by K.K.K. officials.

Late in 1924 the Knight of Columbus organized the U.S.A. Club to spearhead efforts to remove Klansmen from office. A list of Klan members was secured and made public and with that the "reign of terror" gradually began to subside. A recall election was scheduled for February 3, 1925, and with the support of leading Protestant ministers, the Anaheim *Bulletin*, the Chamber of Commerce, and the Elks, Lions, Rotary, and Kiwanis Clubs the bigots were turned out of office. The K.K.K. lost effectiveness after its defeat at the polls. A new set of Trustees reorganized the police force and other city departments and returned to Anaheim a type of government more acceptable to the ideals of its founders.

KNIGHTS OF COLUMBUS

In mid 1904, Joseph Scott was asked to write an article for *The Monitor* outlining the rationale for the Knights of Columbus. He was ideally suited for that task, inasmuch as he was then serving as State Deputy.

The Knights of Columbus were founded by Father Michael McGivney, a priest serving in New Haven, Connecticut. He was a far–sighted man with a keen knowledge of human nature. New Haven, the home of Yale University, was for years honeycombed by influences diametrically opposed to the welfare of the Catholic Church and this in spite of the educational enlightenment of Yale's educational center. The bigotry and prejudice to all things Catholic was phenomenal.

Father McGivney felt that his little band of devoted Catholic men needed the strength of organization to keep them together for mutual protection and support. Accordingly, he assembled a few of the leading spirits among his congregation and established in a very quiet, unpretentious way, the society of the Knights of Columbus.

Originally, the Knights were envisioned as simply a fraternal insurance organization, with the usual beneficial advantages that accompany such associations. Gradually the unselfish and devoted efforts of Father McGivney and his followers attracted attention throughout Connecticut and the Order spread until its ramifications were in every quarter of the "Nutmeg State."

It was hardly anticipated by its most sanguine members that the Order would ever branch outside of its native jurisdiction. Yet it crossed into Rhode Island with some trepidation and, in 1893, it landed in Boston. Its total membership at the time was 3,500. From its entry into Massachusetts until 1904, the development of the Order was most rapid and wonderful. In fact, at times, the growth alarmed its more conservative element. Shortly after the turn of the century, there were 125,000 members in almost every state of the Union.

Mr. Scott assigned several reasons to the rapid growth. At the outset, a solid Catholic faith was impregnated into its very vitals by the respected Father McGivney. And those lessons continued to impress younger people. Further, those elected to national office were men of unquestioned integrity. Their obviously sincere faith and devotion to the Catholic Church was unyielding.

The various state jurisdictions have generally been well operated. In the west, though the membership was initially smaller, men of sound judgement and unspoiled character were called to leadership. There never was any class distinction in the Knights, socially, financially, racially or politically. Candidates need only be men of sterling Catholic character and reasonable intelligence.

Mr. Scott then outlined the various charitable activities engaged in by the Knights, noting that they had just recently endowed a Chair in History at The Catholic University of America, in Washington, D.C. The work resulting from the endowment of that Chair would demonstrate that the Catholic Church had converted thousands of Indians into devout adherents "long before the Pilgrim Fathers landed on Plymouth Rock."

He concluded by noting that the work of the Knights will be carried on "with charity to all and with fear of none and with the firm hope and belief that there is enough disposition of fairness in the average American to do adequate, if tardy, justice to the facts of Catholic history."

KNIGHTS AND LADIES OF THE HOLY SEPULCHRE

The Equestrian Order of the Holy Sepulchre of Jerusalem has the distinction of being the oldest and certainly the most celebrated of the Pontifical Military Orders in the long history of the Catholic Church. The Order traces its lineage back to 1099, when it was established by Sir Godfrey de Bouillon, the Duke of Brabant. Godfrey bestowed his own insignia, the red cross of the Five Wounds of Christ, on the Order.

Today the insignia (consisting of a large central cross surrounded by five smaller ones) can be seen at all the sacred shrines cared for by the Franciscans in the Holy Land. This "Crusader's Cross" is also mounted atop each of the stations along the *Via Dolorosa*.

Following the crusades, the Knights of the Holy Sepulchre returned to their countries of origin. During the ensuing centuries, the Order maintained its identity in most areas of Europe. In the 13th century, the Order was placed under the leadership of the Franciscan Custos of the Holy Land and members were entrusted with the maintenance of churches, abbeys, convents, shrines, hospitals and schools within Palestine.

In 1847, when the Holy See restored the Latin Patriarchate in Jerusalem, Pope Pius IX placed the Order under the jurisdiction of the new patriarch. Forty years later, Pope Leo XIII approved formation of the Ladies of the Holy Sepulchre and thereafter women were admitted to full membership, in all degrees of rank.

The present apostolate of the Knights and Ladies of the Holy Sepulchre remains essentially that enunciated by Pope Pius IX, namely the support of the living Church, the poor Christian community attached to the Patriarchate of Jerusalem. Though the Order has been formally constituted in the United States for only fifty years, there are already four Lieutenancies and one Magistral Delegation. The Western Lieutenancy, which includes California, was divided in the 1990s.

According to the 1977 statutes, the Knights and Ladies of the Holy Sepulchre are chosen "from among persons of a deep and practical Catholic Faith and of unblemished moral reputation who have acquired particular merits on behalf of the Works and the Catholic Institutions of the Holy Land and the Order." While membership in the Order is considered a great honor, it carries with it the serious responsibilities in keeping with its original character, requiring its members to serve the Church with their prayers, alms and activities.

Since its inception, the Western Lieutenancy has held annual meetings in San Diego, San Francisco, Tucson, Anchorage, Los Angeles and Honolulu. In 1975, members had the opportunity of visiting Jerusalem, where they received the Pilgrim Shell, the ancient badge of pilgrims, from Patriarch James J. Beltritti.

Ancient as it is, the Order still represents something alive, functional and excellent in the modern Church. Their well–defined charitable objectives and duties confirm the Knights and Ladies of the Holy Sepulchre as a valid and vibrant force in a troubled world.

KNIGHTS OF PETER CLAVER

In November of 1909, four Josephite priests and three black Catholic laymen joined forces to establish the Knights of Peter Claver at Mobile, Alabama. The purpose of the fraternal order was "to give financial help to the members and their beneficiaries, solace to the sick and disabled and to provide social and intellectual fellowship for members."

Another objective envisioned by the founders was that of encouraging members in their practice and propagation of the Catholic faith. Bishop Edward Allen of Mobile suggested the name "Knights of Peter Claver" be given to the nascent order.

The patronage of Saint Peter Claver (1602–1654) had special significance. That famed Jesuit missionary spent his whole life ministering to the spiritual and material needs of the sick and wretched at Cartagena. During the forty years Claver spent as a "Slave of the Negroes," he baptized more than 300,000 persons. The Catalan priest was a familiar figure at the chief slave market of the West Indies.

From the very outset, membership in the Knights was intended to embrace the whole family. Thus the junior Knights (1917), the Women's Auxiliary (1922) and the junior Daughters (1930) were inaugurated in succeeding decades. The first council of the Knights of Peter Claver established in California was Queen of Angels–87. Chartered on April 20, 1941, this proto council was headquartered in Los Angeles. It was the first branch west of San Antonio, Texas.

One of the largest and oldest of the Catholic fraternal orders, the Knights of Peter Claver are mostly black, though membership is open to Catholics of all races and colors. James Francis Cardinal McIntyre once remarked that the Knights were "always a source of comfort, consolation and edification." He had worked closely with them while serving in the Archdiocese of New York. After his transfer to Los Angeles, McIntyre became even more outspoken in his regard for the Knights.

Timothy Cardinal Manning was no less supportive of the Knights of Peter Claver, whom he once described as the "stand–ins for Christ." In 1977, he became personally involved in a drive to recruit members and, at that time, he defined the aims and goals of the order as that of supporting the local clergy, participating in parochial and archdiocesan activities, promoting civic improvement, creating brotherhood and furthering a love of Church and community.

Members have their own insurance and medical programs, together with the nationally funded Don Bosco Credit Union, a Federal Credit Union affiliate. Any member of the Order and others in his family may participate. Regular meetings of all councils and courts are held monthly and a special effort is made to be of some service to the Church and to practice charity while leading a good Catholic life.

The Knights of Peter Claver are in the forefront of the contemporary Catholic struggle to reverse disruption of society, family life and community. Their record in this noble objective has been especially outstanding.

KNIGHTS OF MALTA

The Hospitallers of Saint John of Jerusalem were founded in the middle of the 11th century. Their earliest work was that of financing and staffing a hospital in the Holy City for pilgrims. During the Crusades, the hospital was enlarged and the Knights endowed it with their properties.

With the advent of the Moslems, the Knights retired to Acre and later to Cyprus. They participated in the conquest of the Isle of Rhodes which they fortified as a Mediterranean military stronghold.

The Order enjoyed sovereign rights and, following the victory at Rhodes, became an autonomous state, with its own laws, army and naval forces. Knights fortified its rocky coast and established a fleet to patrol the Mediterranean and cleanse it of Turkish pirates. The Order of Malta ultimately became one of the foremost naval powers in Europe.

The "Knights of Malta" occupied the island for almost three centuries, until Napoleon forced their surrender in 1798. Four years later Admiral Horatio Nelson captured the island. With their departure from Malta, the Knights ceased to be a military or political body. They wandered from place to place until Pope Leo XIII invited them to locate their headquarters at Rome.

In all their peregrinations, the Knights made establishment of hospitals for the poor and needy their first priority. That apostolate was subsequently enlarged to include all the works of charity.

So well recognized has been its charitable and hospital work that under the Geneva Convention the Cross of Malta became entitled to the same recognition by belligerents in war as is accorded the Red Cross.

Although long deprived of its territorial autonomy, the Order retains its sovereign character. It issues its own passports and entertains diplomatic missions and legations in several countries. In 1927, the American Chapter of the Knights of Malta was established by Pope Pius XI at the special request of Alfred E. Smith. There are about a thousand members currently in the states.

In California's southland, the Knights of Malta have an enviable tradition of charitable works. They maintain a free clinic in Los Angeles, provide transportation for the elderly and occasionally arrange for terminally ill patients to visit Lourdes.

The Maltese Cross, with its four equal arms expanding outwardly in width, is the badge of the Order. The four arms of the cross represent the virtues of temperance, prudence, justice and fortitude. The white in the arms of the cross symbolizes the purity of deeds, and the eight points of the cross are in honor of the eight beatitudes as proclaimed by Christ in His Sermon on the Mount.

The Grand Master, elected for life, enjoys the rank of prince. He is referred to as the "Custodian of Christ's Poor." The Grand Prior is generally a member of the Sacred College of Cardinals. The constitution and by–laws of the Association of Master Knights of the Sovereign Military Order of Malta in the United States were promulgated on November 7, 1932 and amended on April 30, 1977.

Establishment of the Knights of Malta along the Pacific Slope links the Catholic life of California with the history, traditions and glories of the Church's medieval peoples.

KNIGHTS OF SAINT GREGORY

Peoples of the Pacific Slope have long held the memory of Pope Gregory XVI in high esteem. He was the pontiff who created the Diocese of Both Californias, on April 30, 1840, and appointed the first bishop in the person of Fray Francisco Garcia Diego y Moreno.

Gregory XVI (1765–1846) was the first of the "mod-

ern" popes. Formerly a Camaldolese monk, he had occupied many positions in the curia prior to his election to the Chair of Peter, including that of Prefect for the Sacred Congregation of Propaganda Fide. His fifteen year pontificate marked an important milestone in the effective exercise of papal authority.

The great revival of missionary activity, for example, dates from Gregory XVI who created seventy dioceses and vicariates apostolic, including ten in the United States. The former Bartolomeo Cappellari was both an accomplished theologian and a skillful diplomat.

Among the Holy Father's many innovations was the establishment of the Order of Saint Gregory the Great in 1831, as a way of honoring people of unblemished character who had "promoted the interests of society, the Church and the Holy See." Because of his great admiration for Saint Gregory the Great (540–604), the pontiff named the new order for his illustrious predecessor and namesake.

There were no knights appointed for the United States in those earliest years after 1831, mostly because of the commonly held belief that it was improper (and possibly unconstitutional) for Catholics in this country to receive titles from the head of a sovereign government. Recall that prior to the suppression of the Papal States, the popes were also temporal kings. (That, by the way, explains why there were no cardinals in the United States until 1875.)

Shortly after re–organizing the Order and making it more responsive to the needs of contemporary society, Pope Pius X issued a decree on February 7, 1905, extending to local bishops the prerogative of nominating candidates for the papal knighthood.

It was in 1919 that Bishop John J. Cantwell first responded to the Holy Father's invitation by proposing Joseph Scott as a Knight Commander of the Order of Saint Gregory. Cantwell bestowed the honor at a pontifical Mass offered at Saint Vibiana's Cathedral on Pentecost Sunday, May 15, 1921. The Bishop of Monterey–Los Angeles praised the recipient for "having interested himself during his entire career in all questions affecting the welfare of the people."

Three years later, the Order was again conferred on an outstanding Catholic layman, Isidore B. Dockweiler. At that investiture ceremony, on June 5, 1924, a writer for *The Tidings* said Dockweiler's "talents have ever been at the command of the Church."

Others cited in subsequent years were W. I. Moore (1935), P. H. O'Neil (1937) and Harry E. Johansing (1944). Though the record keeping has been less than perfect, it would appear that ninety–nine men have been honored with the Order of Saint Gregory the Great since 1921.

KOLPING SOCIETY IN SOUTHLAND

In the view of Father Adolph Kolping (1813–1865), "active charity heals all wounds." Well over a century ago, this German born "Apostle of the Workingman" noted that if the life of the people is again to become more according to the spirit of the Church, then the Church must again become popular.

Even before the first of the Vatican Councils, Father Kolping recognized that the priest "must concern himself with the social, the civil, the community life of the people; that he ought to stoop down to the ground to lift up any one or every one who stretches forth his hand imploring help." Imbued with the motivation that working people should recognize God better and love Him more deeply, Father Kolping organized the Catholic Journeymen Society at Cologne, on May 6, 1849. Interestingly enough, just two blocks away, on that very night, Karl Marx was urging workers of the world to unite against God and country.

Envisioned as a spiritual family to substitute or supplement a young person's home conditions, the society was to encourage Catholic men, young and old, to be good Christians in the Kingdom of God, industrious workers in their respective trades and professions, solicitous fathers in their families and loyal citizens in the community of their people. Fittingly, the work of the society was placed under the patronage of Saint Joseph. In an effort "to bring back the active charity of Christ among the people as a healing power for the social evils of the time," Kolping asked teachers, mastercraftsmen and artists to give lectures on the means of rising above the educational level of ordinary workers.

Father Kolping's basic formula to help young workingmen is shown in his writings: "Give these men a moral background, extend a helping hand, let them have a decent meeting place, sound instruction, social entertainment, corporal religious practices and so forth, and such means will give the journeymen joy in God and cheer in labor."

The Catholic Kolping Society, as it later became known, was brought to the United States, in 1863, in order to provide opportunities for social life in suitable Catholic surroundings. A branch was inaugurated by Anton B. Voss, in Los Angeles, around a group of German immigrants who gathered in Saint Joseph's parish hall, on February 23, 1928. Four years later, plans were formulated for a Kolping House on South New Hampshire Street. Although the scope of the society was broadened to meet the needs and customs of the Los Angeles area, its character, aims and traditions retained intact.

On November 18, 1945, Archbishop John J. Cantwell officiated at the dedication of the refurbished Gillett Mansion, 1101 South Westmoreland Avenue, as the 323rd residence of its kind in the world. Subsequently another site was begun on South Union Avenue.

Aside from regular monthly payments made by members to cover room and board, the society depends mostly on its social activities for support and maintenance. The Kolping Society's claim as "the first union of a genuine social character in the entire world" is one of which its members are justly proud. Surely the wide success of the movement is due to its founder's realization that the happiness has its foundations in personal achievements, in religious and civil virtues; the future of the people rests in a well–skilled youth.

KOREANS IN LOS ANGELES

The most significant celebration during the 25th anniversary of the Korean Catholic Apostolate in North America was the blessing of the Shrine of Saint Andrew Kim Tae–gon at Holy Cross Cemetery, Los Angeles, on November 7, 1993.

Saint Andrew Kim, the first Korean priest, spear headed efforts that brought the Catholic faith into his native land two hundred years ago. Only twenty–three years old when he died, Kim's martyrdom symbolized the peace and harmony that the Catholic message offers to a local society.

When the final pages of the history of the Catholic Church in Southern California are written, the chapter on Korean Catholics will figure prominently. The City of Los Angeles presently boasts of having the largest Korean Catholic population outside the Orient.

The faith came to Korea in a most unusual way, through diplomatic envoys who journeyed to China each year to pay taxes at the Imperial Court in Beijing. There, they encountered Jesuit priests who gave them Catholic books and religious articles. And so, with the help of neither true missionaries nor priests, a group of Korean scholars began to study Catholic doctrine. They are recognized among the founders of the Church in Korea.

The Catholic community in Korea was formally established by Yi Sung Hun. The nascent grouping, calling one another "believing friends," abolished class distinctions, stopped offering sacrifices to their ancestors and spread the faith through books written in the Korean alphabet.

In 1785, the first in a long series of persecutions broke out. The growth of the Korean Catholic Church, up to 1883, was one of tremendous sacrifice. In 1869, alone, some 10,000 Catholics were sent to their death.

Father Andrew Kim (b.1821) began his ministry in 1843. He was arrested and beheaded just a year later. A number of French priests made other incursions, most of them members of the Paris Foreign Mission Society. In

1886, the Korean–French Treaty ended the persecutions and, thereafter, native seminarians were trained in Seoul.

Pope John Paul II travelled to Korea in 1984 and there canonized 103 of the Korean martyrs, including ninety–four lay people from nearly every walk of life. Also canonized was Saint Andrew Kim in the first such ceremony performed outside of Rome since the 13th century.

The first Koreans moved to Los Angeles in 1905, settling along Jefferson Boulevard. Koreatown now stretches between Hoover Street on the east, Crenshaw Boulevard on the west, Jefferson Boulevard on the south and Beverly Boulevard on the north.

The strongest element in Korean society is the Church and it is there that the major portion of their social interaction takes place. About 75 % of Koreans attend weekly Mass, a remarkably high number in these days.

In his greeting on an earlier anniversary, Roger Cardinal Mahony acknowledged "the vitality of the Korean Catholic communities within the Archdiocese of Los Angeles" as "a marvelous blessing and we thank God for the energy and strength of your Catholic commitment. "Today," he said, "in the Church at Los Angeles, Christ is Anglo and Hispanic, Christ is Chinese and Black, Christ is Vietnamese and Irish, Christ is Korean and Italian, Christ is Japanese and Filipino, Christ is Native American, Croatian, Samoan and many other ethnic groups."

THE *LAETARE* MEDAL

In the year 1883, Pope Leo XIII was in the Vatican and Charles A. Arthur occupied the White House. Karl Marx died and Benito Mussolini was born. The Metropolitan Opera and the Brooklyn Bridge both opened. The Orient Express carried its first passengers and the United States adopted four separate time zones. And it was that year, 1883, that the University of Notre Dame first issued its *Laetare* Medal.

At that time, neither Notre Dame nor Catholics generally loomed very large on the national horizon. There were less than two hundred students enrolled at Notre Dame and American Catholics, for the most part, were far removed from the mainstream of national life.

That was the context in which Professor James F. Edwards proposed that the university honor each year a man or woman "whose genius has ennobled the arts and sciences, illustrated the ideals of the Church and enriched the heritage of humanity." The first honoree in 1883 was the historian John Gilmary Shea, the man called "the Father of American Catholic history." His

massive *History of the Catholic Church in the United States* later brought further fame and recognition to this humble layman.

Until 1973, the *Laetare* Medal was restricted to laymen, but since then priests and religious have also been eligible. Through the years, the medal has been conferred on statesmen and soldiers, artists and industrialists, diplomats and philanthropists, educators and scientists.

The *Laetare* Medal is the American counterpart of the "Golden Rose," a papal honor antedating the eleventh century. It is so named because the recipient is announced on Laetare Sunday, an occasion of joy in the liturgy of the Church.

The medal is considered the most prestigious award available to Catholics. More importantly, it celebrates the lives of men and women and their contributions to their professions, the nation and the Church. While it is not looked upon as a prelude to beatification, the *Laetare* Medal does signal a Catholic of uncommon distinction.

In 1918, the *Laetare* Medal was awarded for the first time to a Californian, Joseph Scott (1867–1958). The English–born recipient had come to the Golden State in 1893, and a dozen years later became the first Catholic to serve as President of the Los Angeles Board of Education.

Thirty years later, the award was bestowed on Irene Dunne, "the first lady of the Talkies." A five–time nominee for an Academy Award, she chaired the Field Army of the American Cancer Society, the American Heart Association and the American Red Cross. There were others who had associations with California, including General William Starke Rosecrans (1819–1898), who prospected in California after turning down the Democratic Party's nomination for the governorship of Ohio.

In recent years, there was serious discussion as to whether Notre Dame should continue making the annual award. Catholics are hardly an immigrant minority anymore, with twenty–one members of the United Senate avowed members of the Church.

But it is still salutary to recognize persons of excellence and faith who exemplify best what it means to be both American and Catholic. Likely there will continue to be a *Laetare* Medal as long as there is a Notre Dame.

LANDMARKS CLUB

Known as a "missionary enterprise of a peculiar character," the Landmarks Club, founded and maintained by Protestants, had for its object "primarily and principally the preservation of the old Missions." So successful was the Club that its founder, Charles F.

Lummis, "forced the armchair historians to rewrite the pioneer period of American history, and particularly those chapters which bear upon the lives and deeds of the early Spanish explorers."

To Charles F. Lummis, himself not a Catholic, the mission system employed in California was "the most just, humane and equitable system ever devised for the treatment of an aboriginal people." It was this tireless man who helped to relegate Prescott and his New England school of historians to the "literary scrap–pile" they so richly deserved.

According to Lummis's own account, "among the last days of 1895 a number of Californians, restive under our general American carelessness of history and its legacies, incorporated the Landmarks Club to conserve the missions and other historic sites in Southern California." He further observed that "the old Franciscan Missions were inevitably the first point of attack for the Landmarks Club, and will continue to be its chief concern, though not its only one." Lummis felt that the missions as a group were "by far the most imposing, the most important, and the most romantic landmarks in the United States, architecturally and historically."

Relatively few people, then as now, had even a remote appreciation of those missions built for the Indians of California, some of them even before this nation's Declaration of Independence was signed. There was never anything but cooperation between the Landmarks Club and California's hierarchy for Lummis and his fellow members believed the title of the missions should remain with the Church—"an ideal status." He recognized that "if there be any institution which is permanent and invariable, it is the Catholic Church." Ownership was not the primary consideration, for the founder of the Southwest Museum remarked in his journal, the *Land of Sunshine*, that "the fact is that whoever owns these monuments, they are yours and mine, and every other one's who cares for beauty and romance."

The restorative work done by the Club cannot be adequately gauged for if the members and their friends had not concerned themselves, at least three of the foundations, San Juan Capistrano, San Diego and San Antonio de Pala would have returned to the dust from whence they came. Careful management by unsalaried volunteers enabled the Landmarks Club to get at least 30% more work for its money than market ratings, an important consideration in those days when money was not so plentiful.

As probably the first incorporated body in the nation to undertake such a work on a grand scale, the Landmarks Club received no public funds but operated solely with resources contributed by private parties from all over the world. An editorial in a publication of the Southwest Museum did not overstate the case when it observed that "the Landmarks Club . . . has saved these

noble monuments of architecture and faith for generations to come. He [Charles F. Lummis] supervised the reconstruction of more than an acre of roofs and one half mile of walls!"

LAS POSADAS

The custom of celebrating *Las Posadas* is especially appropriate to Southern California with its large Hispanic population. It resembles the English custom of caroling; and it cuts through much commercialism and sophistication to the essential Christmas message.

Las Posadas or The Lodgings, re–enacts Mary and Joseph's search for a birth–place for the Christ Child. It's a custom which goes back to an open air *Misa de Aguinaldo* (Mass of the Gifts) which was authorized by Pope Sixtus V and observed, beginning in 1586, from December 16th until Christmas Eve, at the Monastery of San Agustin in Acolman, Mexico.

As part of the Mass, priests and Indians, while making their way around the monastery's courtyard, stopped at *posas* (small chapels) for songs and prayers. Aztec priests had held ceremonies during the winter solstice in pre– Cortesian times in which they carried an image of their war–god Huitzilopochtli, who was born in December. Hence it was fitting for Augustinian priests and their communities to carry images of Mary and Joseph at the head of a procession. Gifts, probably inexpensive baubles, were concealed in clay *ollas* or *piñatas* which were broken at the end of the liturgical services. *Las Posadas* changed from a sixteenth century liturgical ceremony conducted by priests to a eighteenth century Christmas pageant staged by friends and neighbors.

From December 16th to Christmas Eve, celebrants in Mexico and early California held candles and walked in procession headed by bearers carrying images of Mary and Joseph and an angel. The creche or *nacimiento* was usually not borne in *Las Posadas*.

Participants paused at different homes to ask in song for a place to rest. As the procession was admitted to only one home each evening, the owners of the area took turns so all of them would have an opportunity to entertain the group.

At the last stop, the travelers asked in song for shelter. The man of the house denied them entrance; then, upon learning their Biblical identities, he threw open the door and the guests entered rejoicing.

After much additional singing and dancing, a *piñata*, or figure of a bird, animal, flower or star, made of paper around a clay *olla* or wooden frame, was lowered from the ceiling. Children who were blindfolded, tried to break open the *piñata* with sticks as it swung to and fro in order to release the sweets within.

The custom of breaking *piñata* began during the Italian Renaissance. In Spain, people used to break *piñata* on the Sunday after Ash Wednesday. Many of the moralists interpret the *piñata* as a moral symbol. Andrade Labastida, for example, wrote how "the *olla*, beautifully disguised, represents Satan or the spirit of evil which tempts the human race. The candles and food inside are the unknown pleasures which he holds out to attract people to his kingdom. The blindfolded person represents Christian faith which must be blind and is charged with destroying the malign spirit."

The moral is that man, supported by faith, must struggle to destroy evil passions. In California, the ceremony was originally performed for the benefit of Indians and became in time a popular *mestizo* custom.

LAS SEÑORAS DE LA SOCIEDAD DE ALTAR

Modern–day altar societies can be traced to the establishment of the Sodality of Saint John Berchmans by Father John Basile, a Jesuit missionary who worked among the Slavonic peoples. The objective of the sodality was to recruit members who would care for vestments, sacred vessels and other items used in liturgical services. Although not a confraternity properly so–called, the sodality was approved by Pope Pius IX on September 21, 1865

Las Señora de la Sociedad del Altar was established at Los Angeles in August of 1860. It predated by almost a decade its Jewish counterpart, the Hebrew Ladies Benevolent Society and thus has the distinction of being the oldest womens' organization on the west coast.

The founder of *Las Señoras de la Sociedad del Altar* was Father Blas Raho (1806–1862), one of the most beloved priests ever to serve in the Diocese of Monterey–Los Angeles. A Vincentian, he had accompanied Bishop Thaddeus Amat to California in 1855.

In 1856, Father Raho was named pastor of the Old Plaza Church of *Nuestra Señora de los Angeles*. Two years later, Raho became Vicar General for the sprawling diocese. It was during his earliest months at the Old Plaza Church that Raho founded *Las Señoras*. In 1870, the printing firm of Mahon, Rapp, Thomas & Company, then located at 505 Clay Street in San Francisco, published the *Reglas para Las Señoras de la Sociedad del Altar*.

In his Introduction to that twelve page pamphlet, now one of the rarest of the early Los Angeles imprints, Raho noted that the primary object of the society was to provide whatever means were necessary to properly adorn the House of God.

He also pointed out that the society had been established to promote the spiritual growth of its members. Since external works can do little more than reflect internal disposition, he said it was always necessary to advance personally in wisdom, age and grace before God.

One of the spiritual practices of the society was the offering of a Solemn Mass for each deceased member at the earliest opportunity following death. A Mass was also offered monthly for all deceased members. There were twenty–three basic *reglas* or rules for members, beginning with the requirement that each applicant had to be known as a person of good reputation and conduct.

There was an initiation fee and monthly dues. Each member was provided with a set of the regulations which had been drawn up in accordance with the practices of the Catholic Church. The society encouraged frequent reception of the sacraments, especially on *Corpus Christi*, the Assumption, Resurrection and Christmas. Members were expected to fulfill their Easter duties.

Meetings were held on the first Monday of each month and members were exhorted to attend as many of the gatherings as reasonably possible. There were also periodic elections for officers. There are no extant records as to the size of the society. However, in the 1870 imprint, it is noted that seven members constituted a quorum, an indication that total enrollment was at least fifteen, and likely twice that number.

In the *Catholic Directory and Census of Los Angeles City* for 1899, *Las Señoras* was among the parochial societies listed as still in operation. Members met "in the priests' house in the afternoon of the second Sunday of each month."

LAY MISSION HELPERS

The Lay Mission–Helpers Association was born into a world in which one–third of humanity had never heard the name of God. Founded by Monsignor Anthony J. Brouwers to help correct this universal tragedy, the organization was canonically erected as a Pious Association under the patronage of His Eminence, James Francis Cardinal McIntyre, Archbishop of Los Angeles.

A constitution was drafted outlining the specific duties and obligations of the Mission–Helpers. Members receive no salary, but are given an allowance of twenty dollars per month for food and clothing, enabling them to have the same standard of housing, board and medical care as do the local clergy. Their transportation is paid and it is understood they will remain at their posts for a minimum of three years.

A contract is signed with the local bishop stipulating the particular functions of each Mission–Helper. Men and women between twenty–five and thirty–five years of age are eligible and, beyond normal health, applicants are required to take the Minnesota Multiphasic Personality Inventory. Once accepted they take no Religious vows and wear no distinctive garb.

By September of 1956 there were eight workers in Africa, where it was soon discovered that lay missionaries are frequently able to enter into the life of a community more completely than priests or nuns. So quickly did the organization develop that within a year after its establishment, a similar group was set up by Bishop James A. McNulty of Paterson under the title of the Association for International Development.

A carefully–trained staff conducts an intensive training program lasting an entire year and including such courses as ascetics, theology, Scripture, first aid and history of the area of assignment. Reports from members already in the field are carefully examined and scrutinized in seminar sessions.

While college–trained applicants are preferable, others have been accepted. Teachers, doctors, mechanics, carpenters, electrical and metal workers, pressmen, journalists, social workers, pilots, radiomen and farmers are but a few of the skills and trades represented over the years. The training period emphasizes the spirit of personal mortification. Prospective members are acquainted with the climatic discomforts, transportation inconveniences, strange foods and pesty insects they may encounter.

The Lay Mission–Helpers and its sister organization, the Mission Doctors Association, are geared to provide skilled lay men and women to assume tasks that will advance the cause of Christianity on the mission frontiers. Members undertake no regular form of community life but they follow a well–organized plan of spiritual practices. Daily Mass, regular prayers, reading of Scripture, obedience to authority, monthly reports and annual Retreats are their chief spiritual weapons.

Monsignor Brouwers' Lay Mission–Helpers antedated the papal volunteer program by several years and served as a "pilot system" for that world–wide organization set up by the late Pope John XXIII. Another proof of its effectiveness is seen by the fact that by 1960 there were seven separate diocesan groups on the national level paralleling the Los Angeles foundation and functioning in Brooklyn, Evanston, Paterson, Chicago, Washington, D.C., and Weston, Massachusetts.

As could be expected of any agency in the jurisdiction of James Francis Cardinal McIntyre, the Lay Mission–Helpers was and is an economically healthy organization. Compared to the cost for a three–year period of the Peace Corps, a Mission–Helper can be transported to and from his post and maintained for his tour of duty for approximately 1/8th what it costs the Peace Corps.

Embedded in the minds of these dedicated soldiers of Christ was Pope Benedict XV's reminder that "missionary work surpasses all other works of charity."

LEAGUE OF THE CROSS

From his earliest days in San Francisco, Archbishop Patrick W. Riordan endeavored to foster the principle of temperance among Catholic young people. Part of his program included the practice of administering the pledge to youngsters on the occasion of their receiving the Sacrament of Confirmation.

The archbishop decided to establish the League of the Cross in San Francisco, patterned after the organization founded at Liverpool, in 1872, to combat the wave of intemperance then sweeping England.

According to an article in the San Francisco *Examiner* in 1886, the League of the Cross was inaugurated in the Bay Area at Saint John's Church. Father George T. Montgomery was the chief pioneer in the movement and, on April 1, 1887, he expanded the League to Saint Peter's Parish.

San Francisco's participation in the League was formalized in early 1891, with the installation of Thomas H. Fallon as director. Fallon was an indefatigable worker with splendid executive ability. The first meeting of the League took place at Archbishop Riordan's home on Eddy Street. There it was decided to provide branches of the League in every parish of the archdiocese.

The "pledge" adopted for members read as follows: "I promise you Father and the League of the Cross, that with God's help I will abstain from all intoxicating drink, and from visiting places where liquors are sold until twenty–one years of age; and that I will discourage, as far as in me lies, the habit of drinking in saloons."

In December, 1893, Father Montgomery noted that "the purpose of the League of the Cross is to promote temperance and total abstinence and it owes its existence to a custom introduced about two and one half years ago by the Most Reverend Archbishp on the occasion of administering the Sacrament of Confirmation."

Upon Montgomery's elevation to the bishopric, in 1894, Father Peter C. Yorke became Spiritual Director of the League. He was already deeply interested in the work and his enthusiasm made the organization an outstanding feature of Catholic life in California.

In the fall of 1894, the first issue of *The Sentry*, a periodical devoted to the interest of the League of the Cross Cadets, appeared. It was an eight page monthly which, according to one source, "presents a very neat and attractive appearance in addition to a journalistic merit which speaks well for the efforts" of its editor. The title of the journal was later changed to the *League of the Cross Bulletin*.

The League was further structured on April 29, 1896, when a constitution and by–laws were adopted. Three years later, it was incorporated under the laws of California. Among the activities of the League was an annual essay contest in which all the members were invited to submit entries. A gigantic meeting would include the contest at the Mechanics Pavilion, presided over by the archbishop.

In 1899, the League was described as an "organization embracing both religious and military features yet waging their chief warfare against the most insidious and fatal foe of young manhood, the drink habit." In an address to the League of the Cross Cadet in 1901, President William McKinley congratulated the "great body of young men . . . associated together for the purpose of self–restraint, determined to lead sober lives."

By 1904, the League had become the largest and most active society of boys in the nation. With the passage of another decade, more than 20,000 young men had passed through the ranks of the League. Within the realm of contemporary social problems, the excessive use of alcohol was outstanding, especially among younger people. And it was characteristic of ecclesial leaders in San Francisco that something effective be done to counteract that degrading practice.

LEGAL SYSTEM IN CALIFORNIA

During the half century after 1769, Alta California was essentially a military frontier and was governed as such. The missions, together with the *presidios* and *pueblos*, represented the triad of Spanish frontier governance.

The legal system used in the area was as rudimentary as its colonization. The abundant laws in force were codified in the *Recopilacion de leyes de los Reynos de las Indias* of 1680. While formal Spanish law was used in the resolution of disputes, the California population had little need of the procedural law and the specialized tribunals detailed in the *Recopilacion*.

In addition to formal Spanish law, there was a great deal of provincial law in California, almost all of it public law. For example, on December 2, 1817, the governor forbade card games on Catholic feast days. Then there was a plethora of regulatory laws. Hubert Howe Bancroft once lamented that "if the three great principals underlying ethics, namely law, government and religion, are proper criteria of progress, the Hispano–Californians were the most civilized of peoples." He complained that people "were made to eat, sleep by law, to work, dress, play and pray by law, to live and die by law."

Public laws were enacted by the *cabildo* or, more commonly, by the *ayuntamiento*, the locally elected town council, a body presided over by the *alcalde* who also played a role in criminal litigation. The *alcalde's* or mayor's judicial role was paternalistic and benevolently dictatorial. He could resolve local conflicts as he saw fit,

constrained only by the cultural and religious practices of the village over which he presided.

In 1781, the Spanish king approved provisions whereby the *alcalde* could function in a judicial and executive capacity. Two *regidores* would act with the *alcalde* in forming the town council or *ayuntamiento*. The governor would appoint these three officials for the first two years, after which the inhabitants could elect their own *alcaldes* and *regidores*, subject to the governor's confirmation.

Because so many of the candidates for the office of *alcalde* were illiterate, the process of electing qualified people was often delayed. Los Angeles was not permitted to have an *alcalde* until 1788. Punishment for petty offenses was summary. The corporal of a mission guard could punish insubordination, for example, by flogging or placement in the stocks for such minor offenses as public drunkenness.

The friars at the missions asserted a paternal power over their Indian charges, including the responsibility of discipline. There was nearly constant friction between the governors and missionaries as to how far the latter's power of punishment extended. The friars disliked immensely being in charge of punishment and, wherever possible, they delegated that role to others.

Sampling the evidence recorded by Bancroft and others, it appears that the majority of infractions in Spanish California were offenses against morals. Most of the Spanish crimes committed against the natives were sex offenses. The missionaries constantly complained of this conduct which explains why they endeavored to obtain married men with families to serve as mission guards.

To some, the legal procedures of early California may seem crude and primitive. But any legal system must be judged by the society it serves and the region was a thinly populated area which required less law and legal mechanisms than other places.

LEGION OF DECENCY

The first organization of Catholics in the movie industry was launched by Bishop John J. Cantwell in June of 1923, under the title of Catholic Motion Picture Actor's Guild of America. While the Guild served a useful purpose, it was never recognized as anything more than a social agency and was unable to wield any lasting influence in bettering motion pictures.

Bishop Cantwell's concern for the blatantly irreverent attitude exhibited in certain of Hollywood's productions convinced him that some sort of officially sponsored organization was needed to inform Catholics about the dangers inherent in such entertainment.

At the 1933 annual assembly of the American hierarchy in Washington, the Bishop of Los Angeles–San Diego read a detailed status–report on Hollywood's productions in which he confirmed what many of the prelates had long suspected about the movies and their producers. Cantwell noted that, in many cases, the films had taken "to preaching a philosophy of life" and were overly concerned with such delicate social problems as "morals, divorce, free love, race suicide, unborn children" with no obvious restraint.

At the first meeting of the newly established Episcopal Committee on Motion Pictures, in June of 1934, the prelates established the Legion of Decency to act as a clearing house for their subsequent activities. Sole purpose of the Legion was "to arouse millions of Americans to a consciousness of the dangers of salacious and immoral pictures and to take action against them." Catholics throughout the nation were urged to enroll in the Legion of Decency and subscribe to its pledge of avoiding "indecent and immoral motion pictures" and those that "glorify crime and criminals."

In the Diocese of Los Angeles–San Diego, Bishop Cantwell's campaign was tremendously successful. Talks were given throughout the southland to various Catholic and non–Catholic groups, and much of the Legion's support came from sources outside the Church.

Results of the nationwide campaign were soon obvious. By the end of 1934 the Committee announced that many theatres were reporting a curtailment of patronage directly traceable to Catholic boycotting of objectionable films. The columnist, Raymond Moley, was to say two decades later that "the Catholic Church has had a vital part in the 35 years' revolution which transformed a rowdy and tasteless film world into an orderly, self–regulated industry."

Bishop Cantwell, as a prime mover behind the Legion of Decency, had no illusions about the problems still facing the group, realizing as he did that "the task before the Church in striving to improve the productions of Hollywood is a difficult one." But with all the obstacles connected with such an undertaking, the Bishop of Los Angeles–San Diego never faltered in his determination to elevate the moral tone of the movies. His contribution to this first national attempt by the Church to discipline, according to Catholic morals, an industry dealing with all Americans, an industry at once the richest, most influential, and most tightly coordinated of all pressure groups in the United States, was a major factor in the ultimate effectiveness of the Legion of Decency.

LIBRO GOBIERNO

Until recently, Father Zephyrin Engelhardt's treatise was the only reliable source of ecclesial activities in Peninsular California for the years since 1840. Using as the basis for his study the *Libro Gobierno del Vicariato de la Baja California*, the Franciscan chronicler credited Father John Rossi (1869–1939) with possessing the volume, as late as 1929.

Further investigation disclosed that Rossi, a priest from the *Seminario dei Ss. Apostoli Pietro e Paolo di Roma per le Missioni Estere*, had served as "Superior of the Missions of Baja California" between 1905 year, he and his companions were forcibly exiled by the hostile Mexican Government. Rossi subsequently journeyed northward to the Diocese of Monterey–Los Angeles, where Bishop John J. Cantwell entrusted him with the parish of Our Lady of Guadalupe in San Bernardino. Apparently, the deposed superior brought with him to California the *Libro Gobierno* and a few other of the more precious curial documents to save them from confiscation by the government.

The whereabouts of the *Libro* after Father Rossi's death at Los Angeles, on March 28, 1939, remains a mystery. His books were eventually acquired by Camarillo's Edward Laurence Doheny Memorial Library, but there is no accession record there of any tome resembling the missing register. Quite probably the volume was returned to Baja California late in 1939, when the Holy See assigned the Holy Ghost missionaries to look after the peninsula's spiritual needs.

The narrative might end there, were it not for a fortuitous discovery made some years ago in the archdiocesan Chancery Office at Los Angeles. This writer was cleaning out a closet when he came across a rather unpretentious cardboard box containing two certified typewritten copies of the *Libro Gobierno del Vicariato de la Baja California.* Exactly how and when these transcripts originated is uncertain. It can be conjectured, however, that they were made as part of the program Archbishop John J. Cantwell initiated, in the 1930s, to accommodate the many refugee priests seeking religious asylum in Southern California during the Mexican persecutions.

The initial entry in the journal, dated December 3, 1840, announces the death, on the preceding July 11, of Father Felix Caballero, O.P., Vicar Forane of the Missions in Baja California. The entries of Caballero's successor, Father Gabriel González, a methodical record–keeper, are a valuable record of his first years in the presidency. Though González made notations in the journal rather consistently, there are none for the nine years after October 16 (or 18), 1845, despite the fact that the Dominican undoubtedly remained at his post until 1854.

Father Juan Francisco Escalante (1792–1872) revived the *Libro* after his arrival, in 1854, and during his years on the peninsula numerous entries were made.

Succeeding prelates and administrators were considerably less solicitous about keeping their records, as is evident from the sporadic notations made at widely different times. The volume concludes with this note: "La Paz, December 27, 1895. By order of the Most Reverend and Excellent Bishop, I delivered this book to the Reverend Luis Pettinelli, vicar *pro tempore* of this territory."

One of the most interesting entries in the *Libro Gobierno* is Bishop Buenaventura Portillo's account of the pastoral journey he made through parts of the peninsula in the spring of 1881. The narrative is important, insofar as the prelate's subsequent report to Rome, based on this journey, brought about the division of the State of Sonora into two ecclesiastical jurisdictions, one of which, with Portillo as Ordinary, assumed charge of the Church's affairs in Baja California. The Portillo memorandum was reproduced as a supplement to Volume XI of Glen Dawson's *Baja California Travel Series*. It gives an extremely revealing insight which those interested in peninsular California affairs happily welcomed to their ever–expanding reading lists.

LINCOLN MOVES TO ORANGE

On July 30, 1979, Timothy Cardinal Manning authorized transferral to the Diocese of Orange of a treasured document entrusted to the Bishopric of Monterey–Los Angeles over a century ago. It was on February 19, 1853, Bishop Joseph Sadoc Alemany instituted a lawsuit for recovery of that part of the original mission holdings at San Juan Capistrano consisting of the church, clergy residence, cemetery, orchard and vineyard.

The complicated legal proceedings were eventually decided in the prelate's favor and, on March 18, 1865, President Abraham Lincoln signed a proclamation returning to the Church those tracts of land embraced and described in the petition. Attached to the Lincoln document are six pages containing the patents, land survey and tracts, together with a Plat of the forty–four acres of land surveyed by Henry Hancock for the United States Surveyor General in February of 1860.

Beautifully executed by hand on a fine quality of parchment, the pages measure seventeen by thirteen and a half inches. Written onto the title page is a note by J. W. Gillette, Recorder for Los Angeles County, to the effect that the deed was officially registered by Bishop Thaddeus Amat, on December 15, 1875.

The surveyor's report indicates that there were five tracts of land received by the claimant: the first comprised the mission buildings and vineyard (about ten acres), the second an area north of the rear cemetery wall (about one and a half acres), the third a "new cemetery" (two thirds of an acre), the fourth an orchard (two and one fifth acres) and the fifth another vineyard and orchard (about thirty acres).

The actual text of the Lincoln document now part of the Chancery Archives, Diocese of Orange, reads as follows:

Now Know Ye,

That the United States of America, in consideration of the premises and pursuant to the provisions of the Act of Congress aforesaid of 3rd of March 1851. Have given and granted, and by these presents do give and grant, unto the said Joseph S. Alemany, Bishop of Monterey and to his successors, "in trust for the religious purposes and uses to which the same have been respectively appropriated," the tracts of land embraced and described in the foregoing survey, but with the stipulation that in virtue of the 15th section of the said Act, the confirmation of this said claim and this patent shall not affect the interests of third persons."

To have and To Hold the said tracts of lands with the appurtenances, and with the stipulation aforesaid unto the said Joseph S. Alemany, Bishop of Monterey, and to his successors, in trust for the uses and purposes as aforesaid.

In testimony where I, Abraham Lincoln, President of the United States, have caused these letters to be made patent, and the Seal of the General Land Office to be hereunto affixed.

Given under my hand at the City of Washington, this eighteenth day of March, in the year of our Lord One Thousand Eight Hundred and Sixty Five, and of the Independence of the United States the Eighty Ninth.

Lincoln's is the "most sought–after signature" according to Charles Hamilton, the world's acknowledged authority on signatures. This particular document is all the more valuable insofar as the nation's sixteenth Chief Executive wrote out his full name, rather than the more commonly used "A. Lincoln."

LOPEZ ADOBE

Though massive signs proclaim that San Fernando is "The Mission City," the title is a complete misnomer. Years ago, short–sighted planners gerry mandered the city's boundaries so as to avoid providing the historic institution and its surroundings with public utilities.

But San Fernando is not completely lacking in historic sites. The Lopez adobe, better known as *La Casa de Geronimo Lopez*, stands at the northwest corner of Maclay Avenue and Pico Street. That edifice cradles a long and picturesque history of early California. The adobe is not the first built in San Fernando, but it is likely the oldest remaining edifice, adobe or otherwise, that has managed to circumvent the modernizers.

The two–story adobe was erected in 1882–1883 by Valentino Lopez for his cousin, Geronimo and his wife, Catalina. Geronimo, the first postmaster in the San Fernando Valley, operated a stagehouse which was later demolished when the Van Norman Reservoir was built in 1913.

One writer has noted that "the Lopez home was the local focus of activities when the pastoral life of Southern California still retained its Spanish–Mexican flavor, and gracious living was deemed more important than promoting land development." The Lopez family and their descendants resided at or owned the adobe until 1967. In that year, Louise M. Penney of Long Beach disposed of the property. (Her mother, Catherine Millen, resided there from 1935 to 1961)

It was a sturdily–built adobe, constructed with two foot thick walls. The original shake roof was replaced, about 1928, with tiles in an attempt to relate the building to the early mission period. The Lopez adobe was severely damaged on the 9th of February, 1971, when an earthquake rocked that part of the San Fernando Valley. A year later, the city acquired the house and grounds and began to repair the edifice.

In an effort to rehabilitate the adobe and enhance its authenticity, the city replaced a large portion of the roof tiles and plastered the inside and outside walls with a new type of reinforced cement adhesive. The wooden floors and stairs were repaired and all the wood surfaces refinished. Light fixtures from Mexico were installed and the patio area was re–tiled with a colorful theme. The exterior was painted with traditional "Spanish brown."

On March 8, 1975, the Lopez adobe was formally re–dedicated as a city–owned museum. The event was all the more significant inasmuch as it coincided with San Fernando's centennial as a city.

The Lopez adobe, *La Casa de Geronimo Lopez*, remains an outstanding example of that early California architecture which characterized the colorful transitional period between the decline of the missions and the expansive development of the America era.

LOS ANGELES — *PUEBLO* OF OUR LADY OF ANGELS

The *Pueblo de Nuestra Señora de los Angeles* was established on September 14, 1781, within the parochial confines of San Gabriel Mission, with a contingency of eleven families, or forty–four people. Four square leagues of land, good for planting all kinds of grains and seeds, about three–fourths of a mile west of the river, on a ledge rising above the present Alameda Street, were set aside for the furthest extension in the presidial district of *San Diego de Alcala*.

Fray Junípero Serra first visited the *pueblo* on March 18, 1782, seven months after its foundation, en route to San Gabriel. He referred to the town endearingly as *La Porciuncula*, though he did not describe it. His biographer relates how the inhabitants of those days worked in the fields, ate tortillas, beans and tamales and, for recreation, played cards.

Though Serra and his confreres harbored serious reservations about the expediency of establishing the *Pueblo de Nuestra Señora de los Angeles*, the foundation, like its sister metropolis to the north, San Francisco, bears that distinctively Seraphic imprint that can only be predicated of the earliest penetrators into this far–away Province of California.

Franciscan influence in Los Angeles reflects, at the local level, what the friars accomplished along the whole expanse of the Pacific Slope. Even Governor Pedro Fages, whose relationship with Serra was anything but cordial, admitted, in 1789, "that the rapid, pleasing, and interesting progress both in spiritual and temporal matters . . . are the glorious effect of the apostolic zeal, activity, and indefatigable labors of these missionaries."

That viewpoint has been generally sustained, even by the most hostile of observers. The openly antagonistic Frances Fuller Victor, for example, once remarked that "the spectacle of a small number of men, some of whom certainly were men of ability and scholarship, exiling themselves from their kind, to spend their lives in contact with a race whom it was impossible in a lifetime to bring anywhere near their level, excites our sympathy and commendation." The early Franciscan heritage has perdured into the 2000s. Indeed, Fray Junípero Serra's biographer stated that "nowhere else does Serra have so conspicuous a location today" as he does in contemporary Los Angeles.

The handsomely sculptured bronze statue of the *Presidente*, now prominently enshrined in the Old Plaza area of the city, embodies one of the nation's most meaningful tributes to a religious founder. Fray Junípero is also remembered in the names of numerous streets, schools, plaques, buildings and institutions.

The Franciscan influence has been manifested rather consistently since the earliest days. One creditable author acknowledges that up to 1854, the only organization in Los Angeles upholding any standard of morality whatever was the Roman Catholic Church. "It erected houses of worship, hospitals and schools; it was the pioneer in all good works."

Little wonder that there is a renewed interest in the work that Serra and his band of Franciscan collaborators accomplished in California the more so when one recalls that Los Angeles today is second only to Mexico City in the number of inhabitants who carry the blood and speak the beautiful tongue of the old vice–royalty of New Spain.

LOS ANGELES — LARGEST ARCHDIOCESE

Since 1983, the Archdiocese of Los Angeles has been the largest ecclesial district in the United States. Interestingly enough, the runner–up to Los Angeles in California is the Diocese of Orange, which was only severed from its parent jurisdiction in 1976. The figures are based on those reported by the nation's thirty–five Latin and Eastern Rite archdioceses and 150 Latin and Eastern Rite dioceses as enumerated in the *Official Catholic Directory*.

Naturally, the Church's growth reflects the civil structure. The metropolitan area of Los Angeles continues to grow at a phenomenal rate. Its 34,000 square miles encompass an area larger in population (13.4 million) than all the states except California, New York and Texas.

By 1986, it had the largest Hispanic market, with 27% of the population of Hispanic heritage or origin, as well as the largest Asian/Pacific islander market, with 8.2% of the population of Asian heritage or origin.

There were 157 separate incorporated cities in the district, ranging in size from Los Angeles (3.3 million) to Vernon (ninety) people. It was first in manufacturing shipments, with 75.7 billion in 1986 as compared with 71.5 billion for second–place Chicago. (The Archdiocese of Chicago was formerly the largest in the nation.) Upwards of 77 million tourists came every year, many of them to shop in an area which was fourth in production of apparel after New York, California and Pennsylvania.

Ranking third in the manufacture of furniture, to cite another example, Los Angeles and its metropolitan area was a major market for imported cars. And the area was not all highway either, but ranked just behind Washington and Oklahoma in the quantity of land devoted to agriculture.

Financially, the area had a firm base. It was the savings and loan capital of the United States, having eleven of the fifty largest such institutions headquartered here. Savings deposits totaled 104.4 billion, nearly twice that of second– ranked Chicago. For those who distrusted American banks, there were 120 foreign banks located here.

In terms of gross national product, the metropolitan area of Los Angeles ranked tenth among the nations of the world. In 1986, the GNP was 275 billion, putting it ahead of Brazil, India, Mexico, Australia, Spain, the Netherlands and Switzerland.

In 1968, James Francis Cardinal McIntyre said that "Los Angeles would become a world center with an orientation to the Pacific." His Eminence may not have been a prophet in the scriptural sense, but he was exceedingly shrewd at reading the signs of the times. His successor was no less astute. Timothy Cardinal Manning likened Los Angeles to Ellis Island (in New York), a multi–cultural archdiocese, destined to take its rightful place as the flagship of the American Church.

When Pope John Paul II came to the archdiocese, in September of 1987, he found the Church experiencing what Archbishop Roger Mahony described as "a New Pentecost, a vigorous growth in faith and in diversity of peoples, a renewal of spirit and joy in our Lord Jesus Christ and in the tradition of Fray Junípero Serra."

LOS ANGELES — POLYGLOT ARCHDIOCESE

The Archdiocese of Los Angeles probably has the most diverse Catholic population of any jurisdiction in North America and perhaps in the whole world. One writer has suggested that this diversity explains why the area is "so precious in the sight of the Lord."

According to the latest figures, there are ninety–nine ethnic groups represented in the Archdiocese of Los Angeles. Holy Mass is offered regularly in thirty–seven languages and occasionally in twelve additional languages.

Ethnic groups are served in California's southland by fifty–five priests who have come from all over the world to serve peoples of their nations of origin. Clergy gatherings resemble the General Assembly of the United Nations.

The largest number of foreign–born priests hail from Ireland (105), while twenty–eight are natives of Mexico and twenty–seven come from the Philippines. The next largest groups are from Spain (14), Vietnam (14), Korea (8), India (6) and Italy (6).

The diversity of peoples in this area of the Lord's vineyard is hardly a recent development. On April 27, 1927, Bishop John J. Cantwell wrote to the Apostolic Delegate in Mexico telling him that "we have here a large number of refugees, lay and cleric, and I think that this diocese in the past few years, has become the largest Mexican diocese outside of Mexico.

Fourteen years later, Cantwell, by then the Archbishop of Los Angeles, addressed a letter to the clergy in which he observed that "California, and our own City of Los Angeles, have been joined by many bonds to the great country of Mexico." He went on to say that "the large number of Mexicans who have come to California, and indeed to the Southwest," have brought "the finest traditions of their own land in music, in art, in sculpture and in painting."

Cantwell, preparing for a trip to Mexico's Shrine of Our Lady of Guadalupe, invited those interested in accompanying him to participate in this tribute to the "Empress of the Americas." He said that "a visit by our people to the City of Mexico would be a gracious compliment to the hierarchy and Catholics of a country that has sent so many of its children to California."

In more recent times, in addition to the continuing influx of Hispanics, other nationalities have flocked to the area, including large numbers from European countries that had fallen behind the Iron Curtain. The Asian–American population in Southern California has shifted from a predominantly U.S. born, Japanese–American to a predominantly foreign–born population representing many ethnic groups and Asian cultures. This began occurring after relaxation of the quota system in 1965.

A breakdown of the Asian–American population living in the southland would be Chinese (25%), Filipino (23%), Korean (15%), Japanese (13%), together with Thai, Cambodian and Vietnamese. According to statistics released by the Los Angeles *Times*, there are 954,485 Asian–Americans in Southern California, an increase of 767,162 in only twenty years. A remarkable phenomenon.

The Archdiocese of Los Angeles is a primary beneficiary of these wonderful migrations of people.

LOS ANGELES ARCHDIOCESE

The geographical derivation of the 8762 square miles presently comprising the Archdiocese of Los Angeles can be traced to April 27, 1840, when Pope Gregory XVI created the parent jurisdiction from the already–established See of Sonora. Boundaries for the gigantic Diocese of Both Californias were the Colorado River in the east, the 42nd degree of north latitude (Oregon line), the Pacific Ocean in the west and all of Baja California. The title was officially changed to Monterey in 1849.

The subsequent transfer of sovereignty in California made a further delineation of boundaries imperative. On April 17, 1853, Bishop Joseph Sadoc Alemany received word that the Sacred Congregation of Propaganda Fide had removed Peninsular California from its attachment to the Diocese of Monterey.

Several months later, on July 29th, Pope Pius IX created a Metropolitan District at San Francisco. The southern parallel of the parish at San Jose was fixed as the demarcation between the new Archdiocese of San Francisco and the larger but suffragan Diocese of Monterey.

The Monterey jurisdiction, which encompassed all of Southern California, remained territorially intact for the next seven decades. On July 8, 1859, Bishop Thaddeus Amat was authorized to move his episcopal seat to Los Angeles. At that time he was also permitted to add that city's name to the diocesan title.

During the subsequent years, there were a number of proposals for dividing the large and unwieldy Diocese of Monterey–Los Angeles. As early as 1866, Bishop Amat confided to a friend that he expected, "within a few years," to see another bishopric formed in the southland.

While no official action was taken by Amat, his successor, Bishop Francis Mora, petitioned the Holy See several times for a reduction of his jurisdiction. The proposal was shelved temporarily, in 1894, when Mora was given a coadjutor. Rumors of a division were revived after Bishop Thomas J. Conaty's death, in 1915, and were sustained by the long inter–regnum that ensued before the appointment of John J. Cantwell.

Early in 1922, Bishop Cantwell asked that the 90,000 square mile Diocese of Monterey–Los Angeles be dismembered, with twelve counties formed into a separate jurisdiction. Pope Pius XI acquiesced and, in June, created the new Diocese of Monterey–Fresno. The larger area, known as the Diocese of Los Angeles–San Diego, embraced the remaining southland counties stretching to the Mexican border.

The final major alteration in the southland occurred on July 11, 1936, with the erection of a second Metropolitan District in California, at Los Angeles. Simultaneously, the four southernmost counties were fashioned into the Diocese of San Diego. Included in the newly–formed Province of Los Angeles were the suffragan Sees of Monterey– Fresno, San Diego and Tucson.

In January of 1948, the Apostolic Delegate informed officials at Los Angeles that in order to avoid confusion with the older Archdiocese of Puebla, in Mexico, the southland's jurisdiction would henceforth be known officially as the Archdiocese of Los Angeles in California.

The archdiocese retained its geographical integrity from 1936 until June 18, 1976, when Pope Paul VI created a new diocese for Orange County. Remaining in the parent See were the counties of Los Angeles, Ventura and Santa Barbara.

LOS ANGELES — SOME CATHOLIC TRIVIA

A local quiz show asked for a number of Catholic trivia questions about Los Angeles. The following were part of the response:

(1) *What Catholic Bishop went un–entombed after his death*? Bishop Thomas J. Conaty died at Coronado on September 18, 1915. His remains were temporarily stored in a receiving vault where they remained until July 18, 1936, when they were placed in the newly–opened Episcopal Vault at Calvary Mausoleum.

(2.) *Is it true that The Garden of Paradise was located in California*? Yes, opened at Los Angeles in 1858, the German–style beer garden and amusement park on Main Street was operated by George Lehman until its closure in 1879.

(3) *What city in the United States has the greatest diversity of religious persuasions?* According to historian Christopher Reed, "there are probably more religions in Los Angeles than in the whole previous history of mankind."

(4) *Who was the first native–born person in Los Angeles to become a priest?* Father Clement Molony (1874–1949) was fond of claiming that distinction. Baptized at the Old Plaza Church, he was ordained for the Diocese of Monterey–Los Angeles in 1897.

(5) *What is the official flower of Los Angeles and how did it get to the area?* "Birds of Paradise" were introduced in California's southland by the Spanish friars from Mallorca.

(6) *Why is Saint Patrick's Day held in such high esteem by the priests of the Archdiocese of Los Angeles?* Since 1903, March 17th has been a "holiday" for the pastors. It predated by several decades the practice of giving a weekly day–off to the clergy.

(7) *What is the "largest Mexican diocese outside of Mexico"?* That distinction has belonged to the Diocese of Monterey–Los Angeles and its successors since 1927, according to a letter sent to the Apostolic Delegate in Cuba by Bishop John J. Cantwell.

(8) *What is the authentic name of Los Angeles and where did it originate?* It was Fray Juan Crespi who introduced the Feast of the *Portiuncula, Nuestra Señora de los Angeles*, into California's vocabulary.

(9) *Who were the first Catholics to visit Los Angeles?* Actually the Catholic "presence" pre–dates the city of *Nuestra Señora de los Angeles* by a full dozen years. The mostly–Catholic expeditionary force came through the area in 1769, the city was established in 1781.

(10) *Was there ever an "established" religion in Los Angeles?* Don't tell anyone but, on January 17, 1837, just a year after Los Angeles had been raised to city status, the *ayuntamiento* passed, without a dissenting voice, a resolution declaring that "The Roman Catholic apostolic religion shall prevail throughout this jurisdiction." It was a short–lived, but unique distinction in Western American annals.

(11) *Who was the first occupant of the papal throne to visit Los Angeles?* Eugenio Cardinal Pacelli (who became Pope Plus XII) toured Los Angeles in 1936.

LOS ANGELES — PAPAL VISIT TO LITTLE TOKYO

The Commission on Ecumenism and Interreligious Affairs in the Archdiocese of Los Angeles enjoys premier status among the juridic units of the Catholic Church in the United States. Hence, during the planning stages for the Holy Father's visit to North America, it was early on decided that the customary meeting with Jewish, Islamic, Hindu and Buddhist religious personages should occur at the "gateway to the Pacific."

During his three day sojourn in Los Angeles, Pope John Paul II fulfilled that commitment by a visit to the Japanese American Cultural and Community Center in Little Tokyo for a brief interreligious observance of the celebrated *Nostra Aetate*.

The perspective of twenty–two years confirmed the generally held view that Vatican Council II's "Declaration on the Relation of the Church to Non–Christian Religions" ranks among the most outstanding utterances that emerged from the Church's twenty–first ecumenical gathering. Though the shortest of all the conciliar documents, *Nostra Aetate* has exerted a lasting and profound impression throughout the world, and especially in the United States where religious diversity is a way–of–life.

The emphasis of *Nostra Aetate* is on the Christian relationship with those who do not share the Christian tradition. The motive and ultimate aim of dialogue at that level is the fostering of a deeper understanding and respect for the richness and integrity of other faiths.

There are other aims too, such as increased awareness of the basic life principles which each of the world's greatest religions has in common. The term "pluralism" must have been especially coined to describe the diversity of peoples and faith traditions in the one–time *Pueblo de Nuestra Señora de los Angeles*. Here, as perhaps nowhere else, it is imperative for Catholics and all believers to develop a sensitivity about the special relation of Abrahamic faith to the history of salvation based on the uniqueness of God's revelation through the Law, the Prophets and His Son.

In the Archdiocese of Los Angeles, the commitment to interreligious activities has been strongly expressed through involvement by the Commission on Ecumenical and Interreligious Affairs in dialogues with both the Jewish and the Islamic communities, as well as programs with other World Religions.

After being welcomed by the Japanese American Cultural and Community Center by a Japanese Buddhist, the Holy Father listened to a short presentation by selected Jewish, Islamic, Hindu and Buddhist speakers. The papal response underscored the ultimate aim of such dialogue, namely, the fostering of a greater grasp of and appreciation for all faiths and traditions.

LOS ANGELES CITY HALL

Reflections of the Catholic influence can be seen in practically all aspects of the Golden State's growth and development. An example is the present City Hall for what was originally *El Pueblo de Nuestra Señora de los Angeles*.

When the builders erected the twenty–seven story

building in 1925–1926, they used sand from every California county and water from each of the state's twenty–one missions. Even the landscaping reinforced local pride, containing a rich sprinkling of the city's official flower, the bird of paradise, brought to the area by missionaries.

Today the most recognizable landmark in Los Angeles, the City Hall was the Daily *Planet* in the old "Superman" television series; it was destroyed by Martian invaders in the movie "War of the Worlds" and it survived to portray the United States Capitol and the Vatican in other productions. In real life, it has been the scene of bombings, riots, suicides, marriages and shouting matches. It has also played host to kings, queens, presidents and the homeless.

With its Byzantine–style pyramidal tower, the City Hall was the tallest building in Southern California until the late 1950s when the municipal height limit was repealed. The building replaced a two–story brick edifice on Broadway. It was built across the street from what was the earliest adobe seat of government from 1853 to 1884, a structure familiar to Bishops Joseph Sadoc Alemany, Thaddeus Amat and Francis Mora.

According to *A Guide to Architecture in Los Angeles*, the form of the building was influenced by Bertram Goodhue's design for the Nebraska State Capitol. The top of the tower appears to be an interpretation of what the Mausoleum of Halicarnassus might have looked like. Concerned that the structure would be too tall in earthquake–prone Los Angeles, the architects provided the tower with compressible joints at each floor, something like a human spine, so that it could safely ride out the waves of a temblor.

The City Hall's dedication, on April 26, 1928, was billed in local newspapers as the largest civic gathering west of Chicago. President Calvin Coolidge pressed a telegraphic key in the White House to activate the tower's beacon.

The Spring Street entrance is a portrayal of local history. Its two large bronze doors feature panels commemorating such events as the arrival of the Portola expedition in 1769 and the opening of the Los Angeles Aqueduct in 1913. In the tradition of Europe's great cathedrals, the floor of the rotunda consists of many kinds, colors and forms of marble laid in geometric designs, producing intricately–shaped circular patterns, interlaced bands and checkered fields.

Along the marble–faced corridor, the wooden doors recall the four governments that have served the area: the lion and castle (Spain), the eagle and serpent (Mexico), the grizzly bear (California Republic) and the Stars and Stripes (United States). Inside the cathedral–like council chamber, with its barrel–vaulted ceiling, are marble columns decorated with the seals of the forty–eight commonwealths that comprised the United States when the building was erected.

In the early 1950s, a carillon was installed on the twenty–fourth floor, along with amplifiers that allowed carols to be heard during the Christmas season. Also at that time, before the courts ruled such actions as unconstitutional, the lights of the City Hall were left on at night to form a huge cross.

LOS ANGELES—CITY OF OUR LADY

The City of Our Lady of the Angels has always taken cognizance of its Catholic beginnings. One obvious example of that historical awareness is the official seal prominently displayed at all civic functions.

According to one explanation, the seven–decade rosary surrounding the sixty year old seal "suggests the part played by the Mission *Padres* in founding the City." At the time of the seal's adoption, there was considerable anti–Catholic feeling in Los Angeles, most of it spawned by the American Protective Association. It was through the efforts of the Native Sons of the Golden West, who insisted that the missionaries be remembered, that the rosary was included. The original seal, formally adopted on March 27, 1905, contained ten decades. In the interest of correct heraldry, some slight modifications were made in 1949, and now the traditional seven decade Franciscan crown rosary encompasses the four–part pictorial emblem.

Herbert L. Goudge, one–time deputy city attorney and designer of the seal, felt that the crown rosary was the most characteristic reminder of the grey–robed pioneers of California, both because of its traditional association with the friars and because of the actual name bestowed on the area in 1781.

The rosary itself has an interesting history. It was introduced in the early 1400s by a young Franciscan novice to commemorate the Seven Joys of the Blessed Mother. It later became customary to add two additional beads to coincide with the seventy–two years Mary was thought to have lived on earth. Sprays of olive, orange, and grape just outside the field suggest the fertile location of Los Angeles in a semi–tropical land of picturesque scenery. The shield within the circlet of beads contains four significant emblems. The lion of Leon and Castile recalls Spanish dominance over the tiny *pueblo* from 1781 to 1822. An eagle holding a snake in its mouth represents the Republic of Mexico whose sovereignty over the City of Our Lady of the Angels lasted from 1822 to 1846.

That era prior to the Golden State's entry into the union is represented by the old Bear Flag of the California Republic. The emblem of the stars and stripes shows

Our Lady of the Angels

that Los Angeles has been under democratic forms of government, both Federal and State, from its incorporation in 1850 to the present time. Certainly it is fitting that the nation's largest city dedicated to the Blessed Mother should publicly recognize that fact in its official seal.

LOS ANGELES AIR RAID

Many years ago, an elderly priest of the archdiocese recalled an interesting story which he charitably classified among the apocrypha. It dealt with a mysterious phone call made during the early morning hours of February 25, 1942. Msgr. Nicholas Conneally, the pastor of Saint Monica's Church in Santa Monica, reportedly telephoned Archbishop John J. Cantwell with the startling news than an enemy air attack on Los Angeles was imminent.

According to the story, the archbishop was singularly unimpressed and politely informed the distraught monsignor that he "would have his secretary look into the matter next day *during office hours.*"

In a recent essay on "The Air Raid that Never Was," Eric Shuman examines military records about the beginning months of World War II. Therein he discloses information that makes the Conneally phone call a very plausible occurrence. It seems that on the day in question, air defense radar picked up a mysterious blip approximately a hundred miles offshore. The presumption was that unidentified aircraft, presumably hostile, were inbound and closing fast.

Air raid sirens sounded. Interceptor planes scrambled. Troops rushed to their posts and a great city of two million people was awakened by the steady, terrifying wail of warning devices. During the predawn hours, Los Angeles distinguished itself by becoming the first (and only) city in the continental United States ever to undergo a real enemy air attack or, what was thought to be one.

As a blackout was imposed upon the metropolitan Los Angeles area, traffic was halted and white helmeted civil defense wardens took to the streets. Giant army searchlights began probing the darkness. The sky glowed with shell bursts as ack–ack gunners shot some 1,500 rounds of high explosive ammunition into the air. Amid the din, fear and rumor ran rampant.

By the time of sunrise, the smoke had cleared and the whole incident was soon dismissed as nothing but a grandiose false alarm. While California politicians and the Navy chortled, the Army conceded jittery gunners might have been carried away by the sight of shadowy weather balloons, clouds or whatever.

After the war, historians discovered that the Japanese submarine operating offshore at the time, the I–17, carried a collapsible, catapult–launched float plane. And some years later, a reporter learned that the Army in 1942 had hushed up a key fact; existence of a coastal radar station at Santa Monica that had confirmed an inbound blip on the evening of February 25, 1942.

It is still not known how Msgr. Conneally heard about the danger some hours before the general alert. Possibly someone at the coastal radar station informed him, or asked him to call the Archbishop of Los Angeles. In any event, what was once thought to be a harmless, but interesting tidbit of clerical gossip now has to be upgraded from apocrypha to believable, all of which makes the initial story all the more fascinating.

LOS ANGELES INTERNATIONAL AIRPORT

With the landing of TWA's Shepherd I at Los Angeles International Airport, on September 15, 1987, the one–time *Rancho Sausal Redondo* received its most distinguished visitor ever. A local newspaper described the event this way: "Pope John Paul II has arrived in the promised land."

The site itself was part of a large Mexican land grant that took its name from a clump of willow trees stretching along the coast from present–day Playa del Rey to Redondo and then inland to Inglewood.

A hundred and fifty years before the papal visit, Governor Juan Alvarado approved a land grant for *Rancho Sausal Redondo* to Antonio Ygnacio Avila. In 1868, the heirs of Avila sold the ranch to Robert Burnett, a Scottish Lord. Burnett also acquired adjoining property and re–designated his holdings as *Rancho Centinela*.

In 1873, with Burnett's return to Scotland, Daniel Freeman leased (and later purchased) the major portion of the ranch. Originally a sheepherder, Freeman subsequently turned to dry farming and, by 1880, was producing a million bushels of barley each year. Andrew Bennett began purchasing parcels of the ranch in 1894 and, by 1922, he was growing wheat, barley and lima beans in the portion now occupied by the Los Angeles International Airport.

It was during the 1920s that a makeshift landing strip first emerged. In 1927, a group of local citizens began a campaign to start a formal airport on the old Bennett homestead. William W. Mines, a real estate developer, sold 640 acres of the ranch to the City of Los Angeles and, on July 25, 1928, Mines Field was proclaimed the city's official airport.

In September of that year, the National Air Races were staged there and, in 1929, the Graf Zeppelin landed at Mines Field after its historic trans–Pacific flight from Japan. Over the following decades, the airstrip was enlarged and improved and, in December of 1946, commercial airline service was formally established. As terminal facilities and runway space were added, the airport replaced Burbank as the principal hub for all five of the major airlines of the time.

In mid 1961, new accomodations inaugurated jet–age travel. The completion of the Tom Bradley International unit, in 1984, marked the opening of the largest terminal of its kind in the United States. Today, Los Angeles International Airport, known around the world by its call letters LAX, is situated on a 3,500 acre complex to the south and west of the population center it serves. With 579,081 landings/takeoffs and 41,417,867 passengers in 1986, LAX ranks as the third busiest air travel station in the world, as well as the third among the world's airports in volume of air cargo.

It funds more than 40,000 jobs in addition to the employment provided by cargo and tourism in the related businesses near the airport. LAX has become the prime gathering, shipping and communications network for the metropolitan area of Los Angeles.

Pope John Paul II may have landed at older airports, but certainly he has never arrived at one more closely linked to the lives and destinies of local inhabitants than LAX.

LOS ANGELES — CHRISTMAS SEASON IN 1850S

In the latter part of the 1850s, Christmas Eve and the Feast of *Los Pastores* (Epiphany) was celebrated with a tableau presenting the Nativity and the pilgrimage of the adoring shepherds. The characters for *Los Pastores* were taken from the Bible: *La Madre de Dios* (Mary), *San Jose* (Joseph), *El Angel* (Gabriel), *La Hila*, (Elizabeth), *El Ermitano* (Hermit), *Bartolo* (Bartholomew), *Caifas* (Satan), *El Diabola Cojo* (Lame Devil) and *Los Rejes* (Three Kings), all of whom took part in portraying the pageant of the Savior's birth.

The ladies were dressed in their rustling silk grosgrains, with filmy–webbed *mantillas*, while the men sported their best suits. The shepherds carried staffs decorated with rainbow–colored feathers, flowers and trailing ribbons.

For weeks the twelve *Pastores* rehearsed their lines and songs at *La Casa de los Feliz*, in what is now Griffith Park. A much–traveled trail was worn by *caballeros* on trotting and prancing horses, bustling in preparation for the fiesta to and from the *rancho*.

The Plaza area of *El Pueblo de Nuestra Señora de los Angeles* formed the nucleus for the portrayal. There the procession of actors stopped at the *casa*s of the old Spanish–Californian families. Their presentation was repeated in the homes of the Aviles, Olveras, del Valles, Carrillos and Alvarados, all of whom warmly welcomed the *pastores* with large assemblies of guests.

Gradually, the *Pastores* made their way along what is known as Main Street, to the *casa* or home of Maximo Alaniz; then down San Pedro Street to Seventh and Central, where the rambling adobe of Antonio Coronel stood. Special music was provided for that venerable pioneer from the tinkling guitars and lamenting violins, while the chorus sang the greetings of the season. Filing indoors, the *Pastores* were applauded by the guests, who settled back to be entertained in the spacious *sala* of the Coronel home.

The basic portrayal adored *El Nino* in song and poetry. *La Hila* detached herself from the group for a special musical piece. Then *El Ermitano* stepped forward to introduce the Ox, whose warm breath shielded the Infant from the cold wintery breezes.

The masked and horned *El Diablo* jeeringly cast slurs at *El Nino*. Then, with fluttering wings, *El Angel* dropped beside *El Diablo* and struck him with a sword.

As the devil slumped to the ground, the angel triumphantly placed his foot atop *El Diablo*'s neck and exclaimed: "I have conquered you, O lame Devil."

Following each performance there was dancing and feasting. Tables were adorned with lavish food and drink. Attractively–dressed señoritas mingled among the guests, serving *bunuelos* and *puchas* dripping with sugar and anise syrup. The portrayals generally started from the Los Feliz *rancho*, in Griffith Park, and continued through *El Pueblo de Nuestra Señora de los Angeles,* out to *ranchos* in La Cienega (now Culver City) and La Ballona (now Venice), until winding up at the home of Francisco Higuera.

LOS ANGELES — ARCHDIOCESAN CONSECRATED CHURCHES

One of the most ancient Catholic ceremonials is the solemn and impressive consecration (as opposed to dedication) of a church. Only fourteen times has the colorful rite been performed in the Archdiocese of Los Angeles. To qualify for consecration, churches may not be built of wood, iron or other metallic substances. The walls must be of stone, or at least of brick or reinforced concrete. Twelve places on the inside walls and two on the posts of the main entrance are marked with an engraved, painted or fashioned cross.

Fittingly, the first church consecrated in the southland was Saint Vibiana Cathedral. Archbishop Joseph Sadoc Alemany of San Francisco officiated at the ceremonies on April 30, 1876, just ninety–two years after the inauguration of the nearby *Asistencia de Nuestra Señora de los Angeles.*

It was another four decades before the rite was repeated. On May 5, 1918, another Archbishop of San Francisco, the Most Reverend Edward J. Hanna, consecrated Oxnard's Church of Santa Clara, a handsome edifice patterned after a Gothic design of the fourteenth century.

The Right Reverend John J. Maiztegui–Besoitaiturria C.M.F., Vicar Apostolic of Darien, exercised his newly–conferred episcopal prerogatives on October 22, 1926, by consecrating the Carmelite Convent Chapel in Alhambra. Built as a memorial to Mr. and Mrs. Victor Ponet, the artistic house–of–worship was described by local newspapers as "a gem in the crown of the diocese."

The consecration of the rebuilt Church at Mission Santa Barbara was performed on December 3, 1927, by Bishop John J. Cantwell. The entire California hierarchy gathered in the Channel City for ceremonies marking restoration of the earthquake–devastated building.

Bishop Cantwell consecrated Saint Vincent Church, in Los Angeles, on October 23, 1930. Erected through the munificence of Mr. and Mrs. Edward L. Doheny, the modified Spanish Renaissance building was copied from the historic Santa Prisca, in Taxco. The first church consecrated after the creation of a Metropolitan Province at Los Angeles was that dedicated to Our Lady of Mount Carmel. Archbishop Cantwell officiated at the ceremonies in Montecito, on October 1, 1938. A gift of Mrs. William N. Nelson and her sisters, the structure reflects the architectural style developed by California's early missionaries.

The artistic Byzantine chapel at Saint John's Seminary, Camarillo, was solemnly consecrated by Archbishop Cantwell on October 8, 1940, just a few days prior to the formal dedication of the entire institution by the Apostolic Delegate and fifty members of the American hierarchy.

Auxiliary Bishop Joseph T. McGucken pontificated at the next consecration, in Los Angeles, on May 1, 1943. The attractive church bearing the patronage of Saint Cecilia, is reared in the Lombard Romanesque style.

Four years later, on June 16, 1947, Auxiliary Bishop Timothy Manning consecrated the parochial Church of Santa Monica. Erected during 1924, the Indiana limestone house–of–worship is thought to be among the finest examples of Romanesque in the state.

Bishop Manning repeated the three hour ritual on October 15, 1953, for the graystone, twin–spired Gothic Church of Saint Agnes. The impressive edifice, a miniature of Saint Patrick's Cathedral in New York City, is the only one of the southland's fourteen consecrated churches to have been subsequently torn down.

The following year, on October 11, 1954, Bishop Manning attached the twelve crosses to the walls of Immaculate Conception Church, located on the site of a once–envisioned new cathedral. The steel and masonry edifice has long been regarded as one of the finest Marian shrines in the west.

Thirty years after its opening, Bishop Timothy Manning traced with his crozier the Greek and Latin alphabet in ashes on the floor of Saint Brendan's Church, in Los Angeles. The steel–reinforced stone building, echoing the best forms of the classic Gothic tradition, had just been outfitted with new altars and other sanctuary furnishings.

The indelible mark of consecration was imprinted by Auxiliary Bishop Alden J. Bell on Saint Alphonsus Church, in east Los Angeles, on February 14, 1961. A brick and concrete edifice, the attractive building conforms to the modern Romanesque style. Bishop Bell officiated at the services which climaxed fifty– seven years of history for Saint Michael's Church, in southwest Los Angeles, on November 18, 1961. Erected in 1938, the church combines modern design with tradi-

ARCHDIOCESAN CONSECRATED CHURCHES

(1) Saint Vibiana's Cathedral	Los Angeles	April 30, 1876
(2) Santa Clara Church	Oxnard	May 5, 1918
(3) Carmelite Convent Chapel	Alhambra	October 22, 1926
(4) Santa Barbara Mission Church	Santa Barbara	December 3, 1927
(5) Saint Vincent's Church	Los Angeles	October 23, 1930
(6) Our Lady, of Mount Carmel Church	Montecito	October 1, 1938
(7) Saint John's Seminary Chapel	Camarillo	October 8, 1940
(8) Saint Cecilia's Church	Los Angeles	May 1, 1943
(9) Saint Monica's Church	Santa Monica	June 16, 1947
(10) Saint Agnes Church	Los Angeles	October 15, 1953
(11) Immaculate Conception Church	Los Angeles	October 11, 1954
(12) Saint Brendan's Church	Los Angeles	May 16, 1957
(13) Saint Alphonsus Church	East Los Angeles	February 14, 1961
(14) Saint Michael's Church	Los Angeles	November 18 , 1961
(15) San Buenaventura Mission	San Buenaventura	December 19, 1976
(16) Carmelite Chapel	Duarte	June 25, 1977

tional accents of Norman Gothic.

The historic church at San Buenaventura Mission, erected in 1809 and presently the second oldest house–of–worship in the Archdiocese of Los Angeles, was solemnly consecrated by Timothy Cardinal Manning on December 19, 1976. It was the first such edifice in the United States at which the revised liturgical formula was used.

Most recently consecrated was the Carmelite Chapel at Santa Teresita Hospital, in Duarte, a ceremony performed by Cardinal Manning on June 25, 1977.

Catholic concern for their houses–of–worship, as manifested in the ceremonial for consecration, is nothing more than recognition that for centuries churches have served humankind as places of prayer, galleries of art and incentives to devotion.

LOS ANGELES — "ROME OF THE WESTERN SLOPE"

Oscar Wilde's description of Los Angeles, in 1882, as "a sort of Naples," confirmed the feeling of many local residents who looked upon Southern California as the Mediterranean of America. They envisioned the sub–tropical environment as bringing forth in the New World, as it had in the Old, a series of great classical civilizations,

Writing from the Eternal City on "What We Can Learn from Rome," Grace Ellery Channing pushed the comparison even further, noting "those subtler potentialities which made a City of Rome of our City of the Angels." After establishing the physical relationship, Miss Channing reflected on other areas of cultural similarity:

> Here we touch the core of the matter. Can all this alikeness be for nothing? Is it possible for two cities to be born so much alike by nature, and the destiny of one bear no natural proportion or relation to the other? Is its geography, climate, scenery, vegetation,to go for naught; exercise no similar influence upon the race in   constant contact with them? . . . Caesars and Colosseums and an Hierarchial Church we do not look to produce on our free Western shores; but a civilization which shall be to the world in its day what the Roman civilization at its purest was to its—a city which shall be to that new civilization what Rome was to the old—is that unreasonable?

In the book on *California of the South*, the authors noted that the favorable combination of climate and terrain provided the ingredients of an exceptional future for the area:

> If there is any truth in the law of improvement of race by selection and elimination and in that other law of the power of climatic surroundings to influence race development, history shows that the fruitage may be. It was in the analogue of this climate, as found about the east shores of the Mediterranean, that, two thousand years ago, grew up the Graeco–Latin civilization which for centuries swayed the destinies of the world, and to–day, after all the ages, still stamps itself upon the mental life of the races.

Even such an eminent scientist as David Starr Jordan contended that because California demanded a more varied background of her pioneers than did other parts of the nation, "the processes of natural selection have favored the survival of the ingenious, and the quality of adequacy has become hereditary."

Franklin Walker, in his appraisal of the literary history of Southern California, observed that the enthusiastic embracing of all things Spanish that overtook the area in the last quarter of the nineteenth century was the result "of this strong desire to establish cultural traditions in as short a time as possible. Although an Italiano–Roman or even a neo–Greek civilization had at first greater appeal for the hundred thousand Anglo–Saxon settlers who came by emigrant excursion coach and Pullman Parlor car in the boom days, the Spanish tradition—stemming, as it did, from the Mediterranean—had many advantages, even though acceptance of it by the preponderately Protestant society involved tribute to an alien Catholicism."

It's easy enough to ridicule the inhabitants of Southern California who thus turned to Old Worldish traditions, but to do so is hardly just. Franklin Walker points out that they were merely following a tendency, common throughout the United States "to emphasize the romantic elements of this historic past, even though the material they had to work with was fairly thin and sometimes had to be much altered to meet their needs. The construction of a synthetic Spanish California past was neither more reprehensible nor unnatural than the manufacturing of legends about the Pilgrim Fathers or the building of a tradition of an ideal Southern chivalry. In Southern California, however, the process of creating a past was perhaps more rapidly achieved and can be more clearly traced than elsewhere."

LOS ANGELES — THE UNRELIGIOUS FOUNDERS

Though it seems particularly fitting that the birth of a city, like that of a nation, should be historically arrayed within a colorful framework of dramatic circumstances, such was not the case for the inauguration of the largest metropolis in Western America.

The circumstances surrounding the foundation of the *Pueblo de Nuestra Señora de los Angeles* are almost as obscure as the legendary beginnings of Venus, who, the myths recount with a sad lack of detail, sprang full–blown from the sea. However disconcerting they might be, the basic facts are that the founding, on September 4, 1781, even among a ceremony–loving people, did not involve processions, speeches, fanfare or music. Mostly it consisted of tired, dusty and sweaty people unpacking their mules and getting temporarily settled.

Unfortunately, the absence of eye–witness accounts to the event has been no deterrent to the many descriptions of it. One commentator, observing the high incidence of pure fantasy and romance surrounding the event in the imaginative writings of many early chroniclers, wryly concluded, "No respectable author passes through our *pueblo* and touches his pen to its history without describing that scene."

The legendary "pomp and circumstance" that has grown up over the years can be traced to Helen Hunt Jackson who, in 1883, described how the friars from San Gabriel Mission, Indian neophytes, the military governor and his showy guard of soldiers ceremoniously erected the cross, hoisted the Spanish flag and unfurled the banner of Our Lady of the Angels over the envisioned town. The Jackson legend, rapidly assuming a tone of factuality, was embalmed in many of the popular accounts of later decades. Most ornate of all the descriptive narratives was that of Harrie Rebecca Forbes who portrayed the "picturesque caravan" with all " the pomp and ceremony possible for the leaders to provide" (and authors to invent!).

Certainly the governor *could have* accompanied the colonists, but there is no evidence to support his presence. As for the priests, they may have been on hand, but the lack of documentation raises serious doubts about that too. The Franciscans, after all, were opposed in principle to the founding of Los Angeles. Fray Junípero Serra felt that the establishment of Spanish towns was still premature, fearing as he did that they would be prejudicial to Indian and mission rights.

It should also be borne in mind that of itself the founding of a California *pueblo* did not demand processions, speeches or music. It did not even call for the presence of governor, priests or pageantry. Henry Raup Wagner based his doubts about any formality involved on the fact that "the other *pueblo*, San Jose, which was authorized at the same time as Los Angeles, seems to have come into existence without any of the accustomed ceremonies."

Fanciful though the statement may appear, there is absolutely no corroborative evidence yet available to substantiate the contention "that the explanation for the city's present unmistakably Christian character, its prosperity and all–around greatness, should be sought in its auspicious beginning." One local writer put it well by noting that " some ruthless historian always comes along to kick the romance out of all the best stories !"

LOS ANGELES IN 1905

Already in 1905, the City of *Nuestra Señora de los Angeles* was showing traces of the growth patterns that would eventually transform it into the nation's most vibrant metropolis. The following recollections are excerpted from the diary of Mother Frances Cabrini, who visited the area just after the turn of the century.

Los Angeles in 1880 had only eleven thousand inhabitants, now it counts one hundred and fifty thousand, and in the winter this number is increased by tourists who come to spend the winter there. Whilst I was there, thirty thousand more were added to the population.

It is only about sixteen miles from the sea, which is easily reached by an incomparable system of electric trains. The most elegant palaces, not to be found in other States, adorn the streets, while villas and parks extend from the brow of the hills to the plains. There is no house, however small, that has not a flower garden and palms give the city an elegant aspect.

It was precisely on one of these hills that I found a place adapted to our work, and I can really say it was prepared for us by the Sacred Heart, for the palm trees in front of the house hide it so nicely that it seems like a real Convent. At the same time we are but a short distance from the town, and at the foot of the hill where our house is situated the Italian families live so that the Sisters find themselves in a few minutes right on the field of work and are able to quickly reach the school that Bishop Conaty is erecting for us.

The perfect scheme of electric trains which connects Los Angeles with its suburbs, affords foreign visitors the opportunity of a beautiful pleasure trip, which I was able to avail myself of through the kindness of friends.

In less than four hours after leaving the shores of the Pacific, we reached the top of Mount Lowe, six thousand feet high. Leaving the beach, we ran through vineyards and fields which reveal the fruitfulness of the soil. There you have only to sow the seed and leave it to the care of the sun and rain, and in the Autumn you get an abundant crop.

In less than half–an–hour, Los Angeles appeared like a majestic queen with her beautiful white palaces that peep through the perennial green of the hills that crown here. Then between new hills, we reached the aristocratic city of Pasadena, where the millionaires of the United States pass the winter. In the midst of green carpets dotted with flowers and amidst the perfume of orange trees, we reached the foot of Sierra Madre. To the inhabitants of California, the word "foothill" suggests all that one can imagine as good, beautiful and healthy. There, orange and lemon flower and ripen without danger of frost, and there one gathers even in winter the most delicate vegetables. There also the sick recover lost health.

From Altadena, which is at the foot of the mountain, you can ascend in a "funicular" to a height of five thousand feet. At this height begins the most attractive part of the sight, because when once there you immediately enjoy the splendid panorama of the open valleys and plains.

An electric railway, constructed by the characteristic boldness of the Americans, spreads its lines from peak to peak, suspended over dizzy abysses below, and then climbs the rocks of granite, which seem inaccessible , to such a height of six thousand feet. And so one enjoys the whole beauty of the mountains without being Alpinists

I spent several hours contemplating the splendid sight that one enjoys up there, and stretched my vision as far as the ocean, which one can see on clear days.

LOS ANGELES BURIES ITS DEAD

William Gladstone once said, "Show me the manner in which a nation or community cares for its dead and I will measure with mathematical exactness the tender sympathies of its peoples, their respect for the laws of the land, and their loyalty to high ideals."

Before 1822, those dying in the *Pueblo de Nuestra Señora de los Angeles* were buried in the cemetery of Mission San Gabriel. The first burial plot in the city, located on the northern side of the old Plaza Church, was opened in the 1820s and served the area for about twenty years. A formal petition was presented to the Los Angeles *Ayuntamiento* on August 16, 1839 to the effect that "the old cemetery was totally inadequate to the present needs and endangering the health of the community."

The request was referred to committee and no action was taken until 1844, when the area had become so unhealthy that a grave cannot be dug without offense being given the neighbors. On October 28, 1844, a new cemetery site was set aside by the "Illustrious Council of Los Angeles" on Buena Vista Street (now North Broadway) at the southwest corner of Bishop's Road. Plans for removing the bodies from the Plaza were drawn up and Bishop Francisco Garcia Diego y Moreno authorized the local priest to bless the twelve acre site "as soon as it is properly fenced in."

A few days later the *alcalde* of Los Angeles was asked to have a large cross, "the height of a man, erected in the cemetery" along with a "small stake with three slates of wood at equal distances driven into the ground for the purpose of holding three candles." The new burial ground was blessed on November 4, 1844, by Fray Thomas Esténaga. It was formally consecrated twenty–two years later by Bishop Thaddeus Amat, C.M., under the title of Calvary Cemetery. (With the removal of the bodies from the Plaza, the northern part of the old cemetery area adjacent to the church was made over into a lovely flower garden. That area to the south became an orchard and, in later years, a parking lot.)

There were a number of expensive ground vaults erected in the new cemetery over the years, many of them containing Mass chapels. The vaults faced the main avenue leading from the entrance on Buena Vista Street and extending to a circular hillside mound on which was placed a handsome and artistic crucifix. Old Calvary Cemetery served the City of the Angels for the next six decades until expansion called for a second relocation.

After the land boom of the 1880s a fifty–two acre tract of property was purchased by the diocese on the eastern edge of Los Angeles. On September 28, 1895, Bishop Francis Mora reported to the City Council that "I have determined to close as early as possible the old cemetery grounds situated on Buena Vista Street and to open for cemetery purposes a piece of ground belonging to the diocese, situated on the extreme eastern border of the city. . . ." The Board of Health approved the prelate's plans but because of pressures from the powerful American Protective Association, the Colgrove property was exchanged for acreage further out of town "on Stephenson Avenue, only a half a mile beyond the Odd Fellows' Cemetery, on a direct line to Whittier."

Burials in the old cemetery were suspended in 1910 by order of the Los Angeles City Council, though few interments had been made since 1896. On June 9, 1925, the council passed an ordinance directing that all the bodies on Buena Vista Street were to be moved to New Calvary by January 1, 1928. Although over a thousand interments had been made in the old cemetery between 1844 and 1910, few of the relatives could be located. According to the *Catholic Tidings*, "the site for New Calvary was chosen by Bishop Mora, as one of the last of the many monuments which attest his untiring zeal in a long and laborious episcopate." With the opening of the new burial plots, Los Angeles could be said to measure up to the criterion set forth by Gladstone for judging the city's "respect for the laws of the land" and "its loyalty to high ideals."

LOS ANGELES — DREAM ON

Though already launched toward its tricentennial, there is still something fresh and exciting about the one-time *Pueblo de Nuestra Señora de los Angeles*. The story of its progress, from Hispanic colonial foundation to international center for learning, art and commerce is as much a work of imagination as it is of history.

Historians and others maintain that more than any other major city, Los Angeles has achieved its unique place in human annals because a handful of pioneers— from the Kings of Spain to the barons of land, rail and industry—dreamt and decreed that it would be so, and because thousands of others, working people from Sonora and Indiana, Shanghai and Odessa, bought and built accordingly.

Los Angeles is not perched aside the confluence of major waterways or along a vital commercial route; it is not blessed with a great natural harbor or outstanding physical location; neither was it built atop some ancient center of human habitation or upon a pre-existing religious cult. About all the city ever had and continues to have is an unequalled place in human imagination. But, alas, that's what really counts when all the chips are down.

If New York is identified on bumper stickers as the "big apple," and Chicago as "gangsters gulch," then Los Angeles must surely be the city of the giant dream, the grand illusion and the hard reality.

Unimpressed by its own past and certainly not intimidated by that of its sister-cities, *El Pueblo de Nuestra Señora de los Angeles* is a place where everyone is entitled to a second, even a third chance.

Angelenos have never measured the cost nor considered the contradictions of their accomplishments. Their quest for water, to cite an outstanding example, is a monumental feat of human ingenuity and skill.

Or, again, when pressing demands of new immigrants and the financial interest of aggressive developers converged in postwar Los Angeles, the San Fernando and San Gabriel valleys blossomed forth with suburban housing tracts that defied demographers around the globe.

Probably no community in all of recorded history managed to house so many of its working-class and middle-income people so well, while continuing to provide them with amenities usually associated only with the wealthy. For the thousands who continue to pour into the area annually, Los Angeles is the community that invented itself. It remains the city of exceptions and exceptional "dreamers."

And why not? After all, was it not the "Dreamers of God" who began it all for *El Pueblo de Nuestra Señora de los Angeles*?

LOS ANGELES REACHES 200

Celebrations for the bicentennial of *El Pueblo de Nuestra Señora de los Angeles* began early and continued until September 4th, 1981, It was a time for recalling the "Catholic roots" of Los Angeles.

Even those outside her fold must accord the Catholic Church a special "historical pre-eminence" in discussions about the city's earliest days. Especially is that true as this largest of the world's Marian cities prepared to observe its 200th birthday.

The "Catholic presence" in the area now comprising the City of Los Angeles actually pre-dates the city by a dozen years. The very name derives from the diary of Fray Juan Crespi, who introduced the Feast of the *Portiuncula* into California's vocabulary.

And it was a group of Catholics, most of them predominantly Negro in racial strain, who effected the actual foundation of *El Pueblo de Nuestra Señora de los Angeles*, in the fall of 1781.

Fray Junípero Serra, the *Presidente* of the California Missions, first walked the dusty pathways of the *pueblo* the following year. Interestingly enough, he and his Franciscan companions initially objected to the establishment, feeling that premature Spanish towns would infringe upon the Indian and mission prerogatives. And they did!

In any event, despite the reservations of the friars, the

pueblo has borne, from the very outset, the unmistakable seraphic imprint of those dedicated pioneers who came to share their religion and civilization with an aboriginal people.

Los Angeles continued for some years to be a "Catholic" enclave, with most of its inhabitants worshipping, at least sporadically, at the Old Plaza Church. Oh, that's not to say that the *pueblo* was, by any means, a virtuous city. Unfortunately, the Catholic Church has always been blessed (or cursed) with more than its share of renegades.

On January 17, 1837, just a year and a half after Los Angeles had been raised to the status of a city, the *Ayuntamiento* or council passed, without a dissenting voice, a resolution declaring that "the Roman Catholic apostolic religion shall prevail throughout this jurisdiction." While there is no evidence that this expressed but never enforced "establishment of religion" benefitted Catholics, it did provide adherents with a unique distinction in Western Americana's historical annals.

Plans were unveiled to begin a Catholic school in the city in 1849 and two years later the institution opened its doors with twenty–six "scholars." Bishop Joseph Sadoc Alemany entrusted the administration of the school to the Picpus Fathers.

As late as 1853, Harris Newmark said that "nearly all the population was Catholic." Another creditable authority noted that "up to 1854, the only organization in Los Angeles upholding any standard of morality whatever was the Roman Catholic Church. It erected houses of worship, hospitals and schools, it was the pioneer of all good works." And while it all changed following the onrush of the gold seekers, Los Angeles continued through the decades to be a unique haven for religious–minded peoples of all creeds.

In a survey of local history published in 1967, Christopher Rand observed that "there are probably more religions in Los Angeles than in the whole previous history of mankind." And it all started with the Catholic Church, in 1781.

LOS ANGELES — OFFICIAL TREE

Of all the flowering trees adorning the city dedicated to *Nuestra Señora de los Angeles*, none is more spectacular than the erythrina or coral tree. Fittingly, in an Arbor Day ceremony on March 7, 1966, Mayor Sam Yorty issued a proclamation designating the erythrina as the city's "official tree." Los Angeles is one of the few areas in the United States where conditions are favorable for the tree's growth.

Erythrina trees have been ornamentals in Mexico since Aztec times. Members of the Pea Family, their flowers are modified pea–shaped blossoms in various forms. Fifteen or more species of the coral tree are presently grown in California's southland and each year their adaptability to the local microclimate is improving.

Some coral trees do better in the mild coastal areas, while others grow well inland. Some are shrubby and others develop into large shade trees of forty or more feet.

Erythrina is the Greek word for red. The actual flowers vary from pink through crimson, scarlet and burnt orange. The blooming period lasts from four to six weeks or longer and different species bloom in various seasons.

Coral trees can be propagated by cuttings taken from mature wood, and all grow from seeds after filing and soaking. Cuttings from trees of flowering age bloom one or two years after planting.

They are vigorous and able to tolerate smog and other traffic fumes. Relatively pest free, they are susceptible to oak root fungus if soil builds up around their base.

The Franciscan missionaries brought the first coral trees (probably erythrina coralloides) to California. A dozen or more kinds are currently under cultivation. (There are nineteen at the county arboretum in Arcadia).

The coralloides or naked coral is one of the hardier trees. Its blossoms stand upright like crimson candles, in clusters on the ends of branches. They bloom for about six weeks between March and May when the tree is without leaves.

The naked coral seldom exceeds twenty feet and the branches bend down, requiring judicious pruning. A "Flame Tree Forest" of over 1,000 of this species was planted by the Camp Fire Girls in Harbor Park to commemorate their 50th anniversary in 1962. The earliest friars were men of culture, accustomed to the natural beauty of their Hispanic homeland. That they wanted to share those treasures with California comes as no surprise to anyone appreciative of flora and fauna.

And how appropriate that present–day Los Angeles recognized and permanized one of the prettiest of all New Spain's flowering trees, the erythrina or coral tree.

LOS ANGELES — CHRISTMAS

The oldest devotional reproduction of the Nativity scene is the marble group carved by Arnolfo di Cambio when he remodeled the Oratory of the Crib in Rome's Basilica of Saint Mary Major. But it was Saint Francis of Assisi who really launched the crib devotion with his *presepio* at Greccio in 1223. The home crib became popular in Catholic Europe after 1600, owing to the efforts of the Capuchins.

For centuries, five small boards of Levantine

sycamore preserved in Rome have been venerated as part of the original crib of the Infant Jesus. Evidence indicates their presence in the Eternal city since the 7th century.

One of the most beautiful and colorful portrayals of the Nativity on the west coast is the one erected each Christmas season in the Marian Chapel of Immaculate Conception Church in downtown Los Angeles. For almost half a century it has attracted worshippers from all over the southland.

Artistic talent of the Old World combine with that of the New to produce the lifelike splendor of the Nativity scene. The entire sanctuary is transformed into the stable of Bethlehem. Twenty–one nearly life–size figures, representing the Christ Child, the Blessed Virgin, Saint Joseph, the three Magi, shepherds and animals of the manger, are featured in the tableau.

The statues were made by Brother Joseph Schmalzl, member of a family which for 300 years has been famous for wood carvings in Italy. The background shows the city of Bethlehem and the hills of Judea and was painted by Joseph Dupont, a Pasadena artist.

Msgr. Joseph Truxaw was fond of recalling that each of the figures was carved from a solid block of wood. The entire display represents more than a year's work by the famous wood carver and his family who still live near Italy's famed De Prato Church. In its original setting, the background scenery was installed and lighted for display by Richard W. Jung, Pacific Coast Vice President of the Oidtmana Studios of New York.

For almost fifty years, people have come from near and far to view and pray before the elaborate Christmas display. In many families, a visit to Immaculate Conception Church during the last week of the year has become an annual tradition, a holy pilgrimage.

In a feature story appearing in the Los Angeles *Times* for December 26, 1939, a writer noted that as the worshippers approached the scene they were overcome by its graphic reality, kneeling in prayer before the Biblical figures. Mothers explained to their children the glory and humility of the old, old story of the Nativity and of the Three Wise Men who came bearing gifts to the newborn Jesus.

An earlier story in *The Times* described the scene as "the most elaborate presentation of its kind in the nation." Another reporter was equally impressed, saying that "the religious display is regarded as the most realistic ever presented in a Catholic Church."

While minor changes have been made in the scene in recent times, the portrayal of the Nativity remains essentially the same. A visit to the church comes highly recommended at Christmas time.

LOS BANOS DE PADRE ARROYO

Etymologists estimate that there are as many as 150,000 place names in California. Descriptive titles probably outnumber all others in geographical nomenclature, although a diversification has been brought about by names arising from incidents, superstitions, beliefs, the forming of landed estates and the desire to honor persons.

The latter case, that of perpetuating historical personages, accounts for the now apocopated title of *Los Baños*. Oldtimers in that area of Central California are wont to recall how the appellation came to be associated with the third largest community in Merced County. Now the center of industry, including the production of fruit and dairy items, the city traces its origin to "the baths," a cluster of deep, clear pools near the source of that body of water known as Los Baños Creek. The pools were initially referred to as *Los Baños de Padre Arroyo*. There, in the years between 1808 and 1833, Father Felipe Arroyo de la Cuesta, the missionary at San Juan Bautista, often journeyed for relief of his chronic rheumatic pains.

Fray Arroyo de la Cuesta (1780–1840) was "one of the most celebrated of the religious founders of the State of California, and a man who has left his mark on her history and the literature of her aboriginal languages." The Spanish–born friar, a good–natured, hospitable, cheerful and amusing conversationalist, labored in California for thirty–two years. Unfortunately, the priest suffered throughout his ministry with a host of debilitating illnesses. Fray Mariano Payeras reported, in 1820, that his confrere was afflicted with "grave infirmities which are already chronic and which for years have made him think at least of death."

Governor José Echeandía noted, ten years later, that the friar was so crippled and incapacitated, that he often had to be carried on a stretcher to answer sick calls. Fray Arroyo de la Cuesta sought relief from his illness in the refreshing pools of the San Joaquin Valley whenever possible. He was especially fond of those near the source of the creek which later bore his name.

Despite his paralytic condition, Arroyo de la Cuesta was a man of numerous accomplishments. He invented a perpetual calendar, wrote a vocabulary and phrase book for the local natives, composed musical pieces and engaged in all sorts of mechanical hobbies. The annals indicate that "to the end he showed himself a man of active and penetrating mind and of elevated affection and esteem." The Franciscan historian later wrote that "nothing short of the word heroic can be applied to him when one considers that he accomplished so much amid physical pain."

The populace of Los Baños are fortunate indeed to have, as their ancestral patron, the gentle Spanish friar who combined so well his interesting personality with his religious zeal.

LOURDES OF THE WEST

It is certainly appropriate that a shrine honoring Our Lady's appearance to Saint Bernadette should be located in America, the only large nation possessing the Immaculate Conception for its national patroness. Indeed, James Cardinal Gibbons once said that Bernadette Soubirous "might be declared in a peculiar sense the American saint. . . . Chosen out of all the earth to proclaim the Immaculate Conception, she is doubly linked to the United States throughout all ages."

"Lourdes of the West" was conceived by Monsignor William E. Corr (1882–1940) as a means of sharing the spiritual benefits of the world–famous Shrine of Our Lady in France with the people of California. Located in the shadows of the Sierra Madre Mountains in Altadena, the shrine fills one end of a spacious garden area on property of Saint Elizabeth's Church. The artistic replica, constructed to resemble the riverside grotto of a most cherished place of Catholic devotion, is the work of the nationally known craftsman, Ryozo Fuso Kado.

The twenty–five foot high shrine is fashioned in 135 tons of rusty–red volcanic rock and ninety tons of cement. Graceful pine, spruce and deodar trees form a pleasant background for the carrara marble statues of the Blessed Mother and Saint Bernadette, shepherdess of the apparitions. Bits of moss are interspersed among the volcanic rocks, and sprigs of sedum grow out of the lava crevices. A hidden lighting system illuminates the grotto for evening devotions. Half way up the shrine and to the right is seen the figure of Our Lady, poised with a firm but ethereal grace upon a jutting ledge that half extends over the cool waters of a pool below.

The grotto has a genuinely natural appearance. The two overhanging cantilever arches, built on an angle to each other and joined at the top, avoid completely any concept of artificiality One newspaper reporter observed at the time of the shrine's dedication in 1939, "No Canyon torrent ever hollowed out its grotto more unobtrusively than has the careful hand of the rock artist, R. F. Kado."

Throughout the early years of the shrine's existence in Altadena, a constant flow of devout Marian clients gave evidence of the enthusiastic response with which they accepted the opportunity of honoring the Mother of the Savior. Within the first twelve months after its opening, nearly half a million people, onlookers as well as pilgrims, visited the shrine. While the number of organized pilgrimages gradually diminished in the years after the Second World War, the grotto continues to attract individuals from all over Southern California. Such prominent churchmen as the Bishop of Tarbes–Lourdes have journeyed to the Marian Shrine patterned after its European counterpart.

Devotion to the Blessed Mother has taken many forms in California. "Lourdes of the West" has served its purpose "in giving the people of our land a place of refuge in time of trial and trouble, a place where they may come at any time of the day or night to call upon Our Lady of Lourdes to help them to combat the battles of life in this vale of tears."

MAIN STREET OF AMERICA

When Archbishop J. Francis A. McIntyre was appointed to Los Angeles in late 1947, the priests of the Archdiocese of New York presented him with a new Dodge automobile, the first and only car he ever owned.

Early in 1948, McIntyre arranged to have the car driven to California. Following the advice of the Automobile Club of Southern California, the archbishop suggested that the driver first journey to Chicago and then go west on Route 66, America's most famous highway.

The route which the little Dodge followed west was indeed a famous one, over which most of the Catholic immigrants traversed when coming west after World War II. If the "black box" of that little car could ever be located, it would be possible to recreate its journey to California.

Route 66 was an asphalt ribbon that enjoyed the sobriquet "the Main Street of America." Opened in 1925 (and named in the following year), it was later christened the "Will Rogers Highway." It stretched 2,200 miles from Chicago to the pier at Santa Monica. And for those who travelled its entire length, it presented an unparalleled lesson in geography.

The highway was made even more famous through songs, books (especially *The Grapes of Wrath*), films and even a television series. During the early 1960s, the names of Tod and Buz and their Corvette were synonymous with a carefree lifestyle along Route 66.

For those travelling west, the trip involved a long, forbidding, monotonous stretch of highway from Needles to the Pacific Coast. Drivers faced a brutal desert and every effort was made to avoid the road during the searing midday heat. In the era before antifreeze, prudent drivers carried extra water and kept a close watch on the heat gauge.

Windows were rolled down and the water–cooled air conditioners attached to the outside of the vehicle often failed. All too frequently, the heat and rolling hills overcame every precaution.

Towns with names like Barstow, Ludlow, Bagdad and Needles offered succor to the bleary–eyed driver and a chance for the car to cool off. Because of radiator problems, roadside business sprang up, not unlike those of the previous century. Many of those towns were dominated by a gas station, diner, motel and auto camp. A unique architecture developed, designed to attract the motorist.

With the opening of Interstate 40 in 1984, Route 66 was eclipsed as the national artery. But, because of the highway's historical role, admirers of American culture set out to record the once lively past of Route 66. Attempts were made to preserve portions of its buildings and landmarks.

The memory of Route 66 is kept alive today in many ways. A collection of postcards, brochures, maps and related memorabilia, put together by Adrian Verburg of Santa Monica, was donated in 1993 to the California State Library at Sacramento.

That collection and at least three major books pictorially document the highway from Los Angeles to the Change of Rocks Bridge at Saint Louis, where it crossed the Mississippi River into Illinois.

MALIBU — HOLY FATHER VISITS

Pope Clement VII (1592–1605) is alive and well in Malibu, or at least that's the contention of officials at the J. Paul Getty Museum, where visitors are ushered into the presence of the Holy Father.

Early in 1992, Sebastiano del Piombo's commanding oil portrait of the pope, measuring 41 1/2 x 34 1/2 inches, was unveiled for viewing in the museum's Renaissance Gallery. It had been purchased for $11 million.

Clement VII, once described as "beloved, beleaguered, spiritually exalted (and) worldly wise," survived the sack of Rome in 1527 to become one of the great art patrons of the Renaissance. "This painting would be a welcome addition to any collection," museum director John Walsh recently declared. "It is very hard to buy High Renaissance paintings of any kind, let alone a great masterpiece of papal portraiture by an artist who was the greatest painter in Rome."

Curator George Goldner said that "this is a terribly important picture for our collection," noting that the Sebastiano is one of only three significant High Renaissance paintings in Los Angeles. "The Sebastiano is interesting in terms of the subject, whom the artist knew very well, and in terms of the experimental technique." The first to use slate for portraits, Sebastiano liked the permanence and the tonalities that result from painting on the dark stone surface.

Michelangelo testified that Clement VII commis-

sioned the Getty portrait as a more permanent form of a painting done earlier on canvas. The artist painted the three–quarter length portrait with the figure seated diagonally to the picture plane, a form that later became the norm for depicting pontiffs.

Very little is known about the history of the painting after its completion. An English collector appears to have taken it out of Italy in the 17th century. Its whereabouts were unknown until 1987, when it surfaced at one of Sotheby's auctions.

Filthy and nearly unrecognizable, it was identified by Michael Hirst of London's Courtauld Institute. Later that year it sold for $752,000 at Christie's.

Julian Agnew eventually acquired the painting and had it thoroughly cleaned. After emerging from centuries of grime, the papal portrait was acclaimed as one of the great masterpieces of its time. According to Getty conservator, Elisabeth Mention, the painting is now in wonderful condition. Its only notable losses are tiny flecks of pigment in the red garments.

Mention acknowledged that the painting's obscurity might have protected it from the rough cleaning and restoration that other works endured. "Some restoration was done in the 17th century, but it is essentially untouched. That's quite amazing for a painting of this importance and age."

Sebastian (1485–1547) had journeyed to Rome in 1511 to paint frescoes in the Villa Farnese. He became a close friend of Clement VII who appointed him "Keeper of the Papal Seals" and, thereafter, he was known as "Piombo" which refers to the lead from which seals were made.

The papal portrait at the Getty Museum is the only one by Sebastiano del Piombo on the west coast. Visitors are invited to a papal audience with the Holy Father at Malibu.

MALTESE "VICTORY DAY"

Among California's more historic "festival days is that observed in San Francisco on September 8th. "Victory Day and the Nativity of the Blessed Virgin" is a Maltese observance which celebrates the lifting of the Great Siege of Malta in 1565

The Phoenician population of Malta was converted early to Christianity, 58 A.D. Conquered and governed successively by the Romans, Arabs, Normans and Spaniards, the little island was a defenseless prey to raiding Turks and Saracens until, in 1530, it became the property and stronghold of the Knights Hospitalers.

The Order of the Knights Hospitalers of Saint John of Jerusalem was organized during the first crusade, in the 11th century, to nurse the sick and wounded and to aid the pilgrims to the Holy Sepulchre. When that city fell, the Knights moved their Order to Acre, then to Cyprus and Rhodes, thus acquiring the status of a sovereign power in Europe.

The continual loss of their strongholds to the infidels developed the military spirit of the Order and its property and wealth acquired through connection with all the great houses of Christian Europe gave it prestige and power. Rhodes fell to the Turks and, in 1530, the Order received a grant of Malta, Gozo, Conino and Tripoli from Emperor Charles V. Malta was then a barren place, with little water or vegetation. There were twelve thousand impoverished inhabitants living there. Under the energetic Knights, its resources were developed and it was fortified against the inevitable Turkish attack.

Malta was a stepping stone for the Turkish advance on Europe, and, on May 18, 1565, the great armada of the Sultan Ottoman I attacked the island. During the four month siege, thousands died, including a large number of children. On September 7th, what was left of the Turkish fleet withdrew from the island, their defeat hastened by a vision of the Virgin Mary with Saint John and an angel holding the shield and buckler of the Knights Hospitalers.

The following day, the Nativity of the Blessed Virgin Mary, was proclaimed a day of thanksgiving by the victorious Grand Master de la Vallette. It was thereafter celebrated annually with great religious and civil pomp by the Knights until they lost the island to Napoleon's forces.

There is still a plaque commemorating the event, near a schoolhouse in St. Elmo. It is dedicated "to the glorious memory of the children who, during the battle of 1565, sacrificed their lives fighting by the side of their elders for faith and country."

In San Francisco, the Maltese observe Victory Day and the Nativity of the Virgin with a two day celebration on the Saturday and Sunday following the 8th of September. In former times, a parade, headed by the Maltese Band, and made up of members of the Maltese Club and children in Knights of Malta costumes, floats depicting "Victorious Malta" and "The Hero of La Vallette" marched to the Maltese Church of Saint Paul of the Shipwreck, where thanksgiving services were held with great pageantry.

Then the Maltese Club takes over the day's festivities, with programs of patriotic speeches, historical sketches, musical numbers and dioramas, followed by a grand ball. Thus is observed but one of the customs and ceremonials, religious rituals and folk festivals associated with a cosmopolitan area where many peoples live amicably side–by–side, enjoying the freedom of thought and expression that is so characteristic of America.

MANUELO'S NARRATIVE

Sometime prior to 1847, a musty and mutilated old manuscript relating to Alta California was discovered at a monastery in the City of Evora, in the Portuguese province of Alemteji. It was written in a mixture of Spanish, Portuguese and Italian.

The manuscript was reportedly found in a secret closet, carefully wrapped in an envelope of untanned skin and covered with the accumulated dust of many ages. No one could recall exactly where the manuscript originated or precisely how it came to Evora. The wrapping about the bundle indicated that its origin may have been a frontier town in America and a single expression on one of its pages pointed toward Acapulco as the place where it could have been written.

There was a tradition at the monastery that an old member of the Dominican Order, Justino by name, had returned from Mexico with the manuscript. "Father Justino's one aim in life had doubtless been to instruct the rude natives of the New World in the sublime doctrines of the Christian religion."

The writing may have been intended as the basis of a missionary movement in the direction of Alta California and, for that reason, the character of its people, their habits of life, their capacity for civilization, and their fitness for conversion to Christianity, were largely dwelt upon.

It was only in subsequent years, when California became celebrated throughout the world as the depository of nature's choicest mineral treasures that the manuscript gained notoriety.

The manuscript opened up to the world a chapter in the remote history of that part of America, which antedates them all by many years and which is far more instructive than anything as yet disclosed concerning that region which had been until then a *terra incognita*.

Eventually the manuscript was brought to California where it was translated and then published at San Francisco in 1888 by the Samuel Carlson and Company under the title *California Three Hundred and Fifty Years Ago*. The book's subtitle, "Manuelo's Narrative," referred to the original author who is identified only as "the first white man whose feet ever pressed the sacred soil of California."

The knowledgeable Robert E. Cowan had little regard for the book and noted in his monumental bibliography that the 333 page volume was "a singular book ascribed to Cornelius C. Cole (1822–1924). Being apparently a weird fiction, to ascertain its purport would be as difficult as to find the individual who has read it."

Cowan went on to observe that pages 141 thru 186 "are occupied by a remarkable poem in superlative doggerel, relating chiefly to San Francisco, from the arrival of the San Carlos to the advent of Denis Kearney and the spring valley water ring, which is only one of the numerous incongruities found in the narrative."

If indeed the distinguished Senator Cole was the author and/or translator, he managed to produce a most fascinating tome. Though dismissed in *An Annotated Bibliography of California Fiction* as "an imaginative tale of early exploration" the book surely deserves further examination.

To have produced an imaginative or unfactual book seems totally out–of–character for Senator Cole. Nor does there appear to be any "reasonable cause" for such an action, especially at a time when such a spurious volume would have served no useful purpose.

MARY'S HOUR

In one of his masterful editorials for *The Tidings*, Msgr. Patrick Roche recalled how "here in Los Angeles a beautiful tradition has grown. Each year we pluck one hour and vest it with a lasting glory and loveliness. We sign and seal it in solemn testament. We give it to Mary."

He went on to say that "we do this publicly, to share her with the city and the world. For she is, first of all, Christ's mother and by that role she encompasses the world in her love, even where neither He nor she may be known and recognized.

Roche was referring to Mary's Hour which had begun in 1948 in response to Father James Keller's program calling people to "light a candle in the darkness." A group of Catholic college students in Los Angeles, with the enthusiastic approval and endorsement of Archbishop J. Francis A. McIntyre, organized a public rally called Mary's Hour.

The first Mary's Hour was held on May 2, 1948, in the Hollywood Bowl. It was a remarkable assemblage sponsored by "the Catholic people of the Archdiocese of Los Angeles" for the intention of "peace in America and in the world." The program featured sacred music by Roger Wagner, a sermon by Msgr. Edward Wade, hymns directed by Msgr. Robert Brennan and the mysteries of the Holy Rosary recited by Herbert Ybarra, Marian Mooney, Louis E. Euler, Mrs. A. J. Bender and James I. Prince. Benediction was given by Archbishop McIntyre.

Because the Hollywood Bowl was barely able to accommodate the huge crowd, it was decided to stage the 1949 Mary's Hour at the Los Angeles Memorial Coliseum and, once again, the arena was filled to capacity. Each succeeding year, growing throngs of people journeyed to the coliseum from the four counties of the Archdiocese. Especially impressive were the busloads of Catholics who motored from the northern areas of Santa Maria and Santa Barbara to participate in the "Living Rosary."

In 1959, the event was described by a reporter for the Los Angeles *Mirror News* as "one of the most impressive events held in the nation."

Surely it was the largest Marian gathering on record. In that same year, a headline of the Los Angeles *Examiner* proclaimed: "Rite Turns Coliseum into a Gigantic Cathedral." A photograph depicted the "vast throng . . . filling the coliseum to its brims, its collective heart and mind equally brimful with man's solemn desire for peace."

Fittingly Mary's Hour is memorialized at the Los Angeles Memorial Coliseum with a huge bronze plaque portraying the bust of James Francis Cardinal McIntyre who never missed the annual observance.

During the 1960s, attendance began to dwindle. In 1969, Mary's Hour was moved to Dodgers Stadium. About 27,000 persons took part in the twenty–second and last Mary's Hour.

The rationale for Mary's Hour was spelled out in an essay for *Our Lady's Digest* in 1962: "Mary belongs to our city and Archdiocese under her title, Our Lady of the Angels. She was here when the city was founded and by its dedication, she became forever associated with its fortunes and its people. The years between have served to show her love for us."

MARYMOUNT TABERNACLE SOCIETY

In a talk to the Marymount Tabernacle Society, Bishop Fulton J. Sheen observed that "some of the strongest links between members of the Church Universal are forged with needle and thread." The genesis of the Marymount Tabernacle Society can be traced to early 1926, when Bishop John J. Cantwell asked the Religious of the Sacred Heart of Mary to inaugurate the Society in Los Angeles. He suggested that the west coast branch might be modelled after those already established in Baltimore and New York.

Cantwell envisioned that the Society's weekly meetings would enable "members under capable direction to engage in making vestments for poor parishes" so that the Church's liturgy "might be conducted in a becoming and decent manner." The bishop noted that "for several years the priests of this diocese, especially those engaged in the large Mexican settlements, were obliged in their poverty to apply to New York, St. Louis and San Francisco for vestments. He felt strongly that the women of the Los Angeles–San Diego area would respond to local needs if given the opportunity. And, indeed they did.

During the first year of its existence, forty–one mission areas were supplied with 150 vestments, twenty copes, 1,500 altar linens, fifteen albs, fifty cinctures and numerous other altar appurtenances. Spiritualities were cared for too. Members were expected to make a monthly holy hour as part of their commitment to the Society. The annual dues of $10 was to be set aside for purchase of vestment materials.

Within a few months after the establishment of the Marymount Tabernacle Society, Bishop Cantwell was able to have the group affiliated with the Central Tabernacle Society in Rome, thus allowing members to participate in the rich indulgences granted to those who labor for poor churches.

The bishop asked his sister, Nellie Cantwell (1889–1978) to assist in the work of the Society. Early on she took an active role, serving for almost half a century as secretary–treasurer. Quietly and without fanfare, the Marymount Tabernacle Society functioned as one of the area's most useful and effective groups. In the early years, the bishop would frequently accompany Nellie to the meetings and then assist at Benediction of the Blessed Sacrament for the ladies.

Prominent local and national churchmen and civic leaders were invited to the Society's annual exhibits which were generally held in February. Those who addressed the Society generally echoed Cantwell's theme that "tawdry and worn out vestments are not worthy of a congregation that is well dressed itself."

During the war years, the ladies made special light weight Gothic vestments for army and navy chaplains throughout the world. A priest from the Pacific front wrote that "the Marymount Tabernacle Society brought beauty and dignity to our Masses offered amid the horror of war and death." The extant figures indicate that by 1966, the Society had supplied 3,960 vestments and 37,943 altar linens to needy rural and poor Christian communities in Africa, South America, Europe, the Fiji Islands, India, Korea, Mexico, the Philippines, Puerto Rico and Taiwan.

Faced with the myriad of new vestment designs that followed in the wake of Vatican Council II, the aging members of the Marymount Tabernacle Society decided in 1972 that their organization had fulfilled its goals and should be disbanded. In a final gesture of charity, the Society turned over its few remaining assets to Marymount High School.

MARYSVILLE AND GRASS VALLEY

The Vicariate Apostolic of Marysville, established in 1860, by Pope Pius IX, was not, as many have falsely conjectured, named to honor the Mother of God. When Theodor Cordua located a ranch at the site in the fall of 1842, he gave to modern Marysville the name of New Mecklenburg, after his native home in Germany, hoping thereby to share it with many of his own countrymen.

The present city was laid out by Auguste Le Plongeon, a French surveyor, who acquired the Cordua property early in 1850. At that time the area was known as Jubaville, probably after nearby Yuba City. When asked how the city of 6,000 souls, one–third of whom were then Catholic, acquired its Marian appellation, Bishop Eugene O'Connell, the newly–appointed Vicar Apostolic of Marysville, explained that the seventeen counties of his new jurisdiction were named for Mary Murphy Covillaud, a survivor of the ill–fated Donner party. The Irish born prelate pointed out on another occasion that "the names of several places in the Diocese are not vey euphonious" since most of the new settlers had not bestowed "as expressive and appropriate names as the Spaniards."

When the vicariate was advanced to diocesan status on March 22, 1868, the episcopal seat was moved to the more centrally located city of Grass Valley in Nevada County. The title of that ecclesiastical jurisdiction was even more perplexing to Bishop O'Connell than its earlier one. The prelate recorded that Grass Valley is a misnomer "for in truth there is no grass upon it any more than on the Hill of Howth in Dublin Bay."

In the bishop's opinion, "Aspramonte" (rocky mount) would have been a far more appropriate and expressive name for the diocese "because it is situated only five miles from Rough and Ready, and besides it is rough enough itself and rocky too." Though he felt that neither of the titles used for the immense area embracing the territory between the 39th and 42nd parallel of latitude was really appealing, the bishop apparently preferred the earlier appellation of Marysville for he never abided by the "fiction of law" which directed him to take up his residence in Grass Valley.

In Bishop O'Connell's eyes the matter of a more descriptive title for the episcopal jurisdiction confided to his care was of considerable importance. The prelate retired in 1884, but he had the pleasure of living to see the most exalted title of all bestowed on his former diocese—that of Sacramento.

MASS IN CALIFORNIA

It is of no little significance that "the first white men to settle on these western shores were Spaniards and Roman Catholics, representatives of a powerful nation that was the citadel of united faith." There are several opinions as to when these Christian pioneers made possible the first celebration of Holy Mass in the New World. It has long been a legend in the Franciscan Order that Juan Perez, the Prior of *La Rabida*, came with Columbus on his maiden voyage in 1492. No evidence to substantiate the view, however, can be found either in the ship's journal or in any of the accounts written by contemporaries.

A similar tradition among the Mercedarians relates how one of their number, a certain Juan de Solorzano de Aguilar, accompanied the "admiral of the ocean sea" on his initial voyage. But here again, a search of Spanish archives fails to corroborate the opinion. A third priest, Pedro de Arenas, is thought by one prominent Jesuit historian, to have been with the first Columbus expedition. According to a manuscript discovered in the National Library at Madrid in 1891, Arenas remained in the New World after the admiral's return to Europe. Most present–day scholars are inclined to agree with Samuel Eliot Morison, who dismisses the subject by noting that "certain pious souls, worried by the absence of a priest, have tried to invent one."

The Benedictine, Bernard Buil, and several clerical assistants accompanied Columbus on his second trip and offered the first eucharistic sacrifice on the Island of Hispañola, January 6, 1494 The initial Mass on the mainland of the North American continent may have been celebrated by Father Alonso Gonzalez, chaplain of the ill–fated Fernando Hernandez de Cordova expedition which was blown against the west coast of Florida in 1517. The landing of secular and religious priests with Juan Ponce de Leon in the spring of 1521,is the first positively authenticated instance of the presence of Catholic priests in the mainland of the present United States."

Catholic penetration of the west coast took place only twenty–one years later with the explorations of Juan Rodriquez Cabrillo. The question of dating the first Mass offered in California is still a matter of controversy. An affidavit made eighteen years after the Cabrillo voyage states that there was a priest with the 1542 expedition though neither in the document nor elsewhere is anything further said about his identity. On October 18, 1587, two Franciscans, one of whom was Father Martin Ignacio Loyola, nephew of the sainted founder of the Society of Jesus, went ashore in the vicinity of San Luis Obispo. These chaplains of Pedro de Unamuno most probably celebrated Holy Mass during their brief visit.

There is every reason to presume that the holy sacrifice was offered in November of 1595, by Father Francisco de la Concepcion, Franciscan chaplain of the *San Agustin*, which put into San Francisco or Rodriquez Carmeno Bay above the Golden Gate on the way back from Manila to Acapulco. In any event, the first recorded or substantiated celebration of the Eucharistic Banquet took place in 1602. The annals state: "On the 12th of said month (November), which was the day of the glorious San Diego, the general, admiral, religious, captains, ensigns, and almost all the men, went ashore. A hut was erected, and Holy Mass was said to celebrate the feast of Señor San Diego."

In California, as well as in all the other parts of the New World, the Catholic sea and trail–blazers literally carried out the mandate of spreading the faith to all the corners of the globe. Thus can it be said that in California, "the altar is older than the hearth."

MEDALLIC HISTORY OF CALIFORNIA

Among the medallic holdings in the Historical Museum of the Archival Center at Mission Hills, is a complete collection of "California Commemorative Medals" issued in 1970 to mark the 200th anniversary of European penetration along the Pacific Slope. There are sixty events portrayed in this "medallic history of California," each of them selected by R. Coke Wood for its importance in the 425 year pageant of the state.

The medals at the Archival Center belong to what is known as the "Collector's Edition." They were struck at the Franklin Mint in sterling silver, each one individually numbered. Probably the most important of the sixty medals is #13, the "Old Custom House" at Monterey. The word "California" is misspelled on the verso of the medal. Replacements were offered for this medal, but the one at Mission Hills was never exchanged, a factor that increases its value.

Starting point of the medallic series features the landing of Juan Rodriquez Cabrillo in San Diego Harbor in 1542. His entrance into the bay formally marked the discovery of what became the thirty–first state in the Federal Union.

Fray Junípero Serra is portrayed on Medal #4. The "Apostle of California" is shown blessing the site of San Diego Mission on July 16, 1769. The next medal features the actual mission itself, the first of the twenty–one establishments along *El Camino Real*.

The first Christian baptism in California is also commemorated. Two dying infants, Maria Magdelena and Margarita were welcomed into the Catholic faith by Fray Juan Crespi and Fray Francisco Gomes near present–day San Onofre.

A friar walking a burro by San Juan Capistrano Mission is shown on another of the earlier medals. This "Mission of the Swallows" was wrecked by a ferocious earthquake in 1812. Today an enlarged replica of that church is located nearby.

The only other mission in the series is that dedicated to San Francisco Solano. That final link in the frontier establishments was founded in 1823 at Sonoma by Fray Jose Altimira.

The 1932 Olympic Games were featured along with the Panama Pacific Exposition (1915), the First Transcontinental Air Flight (1911) and the erection of the Golden Gate Bridge (1937). The Pony Express (1860), the Butterfield Stage Line (1858), the First Public School (1850) and the California Gold Rush (1849) are also commemorated in what is a very good choice of topical events.

Artistically, the medals are of top quality. Though unmarked as to engraver, each of the medals exhibits the workmanship associated with a master craftsman. In a newspaper review of the series, Orcutt Jamieson wrote that "the California Commemorative Medals represent the best of our profession. They can only appreciate in value. "

The panorama of subjects, the quality of the casting and the artistic embellishments of the engraver rank this remarkable collection among the most coveted items in the Californiana collection of the Archival Center.

MEDICAL STORY IN CALIFORNIA

When his book on *California's Medical Story* appeared in 1932, Charles Singer said that "California presents quite exceptional advantages. The geographical isolation of its population makes a true local study more valid than would be the case in most states." He went on to note that "the earliest records have been better and more lovingly preserved in California than in any other civilization that has developed so recently and so rapidly."

Five years later, the Federal Art Project was offered an excellent opportunity to portray the state's medical history in mural decoration for Toland Hall, the medical amphitheater at the University of California Medical School in San Francisco. The work was begun in 1937 by Bernard Zakhelm and Phyllis Wrightson and completed the following year. It forms one of the most impressive art efforts associated with medicine in the country.

The story told by the colorful murals begins with the domestic life and hygiene of the California Indians. A young native reaches out in a greeting to the sun as he dries himself after a sweat bath and a plunge into the river. Three Indians illustrate native California healing methods.

To the left of this central scene, Sir Francis Drake grimly supervises an autopsy which the ship's surgeon is performing upon his younger brother. To the right, four sailors are burying comrades who have perished from disease while their chaplain offers a prayer.

Completing the panel, three Indians present to Fray Junípero Serra the three most important herbs con-tributed by California to modern medicine: *Yerba santa*, *cascara sagrada* and *grindelia robusta*. Behind them is a group of Spanish soldiers who connect this scene with the adjoining panel. The latter is a symbolic portrayal of the invasion of California by a strange people, a new religion and unknown diseases.

Leading the band of soldiers is Juan Bautista de Anza. The central figure of the main group is a native Californian standing between a friar who baptizes him and a soldier who offers him something to drink. In one of the other panels, this one dealing with medicine in Southern California, the first group shows a Spanish soldier watching several mission Indians clustered around a shrine.

The central and largest portion of this scene is devoted to a representation of the first hospital in California, the crude shelter erected at San Diego de Alcala Mission in 1769 for the members of the Portola expedition who were suffering from scurvy. A table in the background provides a place for medical supplies and an altar, beside which two friars are waiting to assist the patients.

The remaining third of this panel deals with the American trapper James Ohio Pattie who is shown negotiating his freedom from jail by offering to vaccinate the Indians against smallpox. These and other panels at Toland Hall constitute an artistic masterpiece of high excellence and remarkable intellectual value. Carefully planned and brilliantly executed, the frecoes reveal an exciting chapter in California's history. Without question, the murals tell their story artistically, graphically and ethically.

METHUSALAH TREE

The omnipotence of God is manifested among His people in many and diverse ways. One doesn't have to look far before seeing the divine imprint on things human. The world's oldest living testimony to Divine Providence happens to be in California. It was already 2,622 years old when the Christ Child was born at Bethlehem, almost twenty centuries ago!

Located high in the White Mountains of California, the bristlecone pine known as "Methusalah" is a stunted, gnomish–looking tree that belies its incredible age. Yet it represents an awesome antiquity that predates recorded history. Methusalah is not alone. There are approximately twenty bristlecones that have lived for more than 4,000 years. They are twisted, misshapen and battered forms of life that cling precariously to the spare soil that somehow sustains them.

Imagine! Methusalah was hundreds of years old when the Egyptians built the pyramids; it had lived over a millenium when Moses led the Israelites out of Egypt and it had survived over 3,000 mountain–top winters when Charlemagne was proclaimed Holy Roman Emperor!

Bristlecone pines grow in arid, hostile environments where growth can literally be microscopic. Their annual rings of growth are often only a few thousandths of an inch.

Dendrochronologists (scientists who measure time by counting growth rings) have discovered that tree chronologies extending back thousands of years are very useful in historical and archaeological studies. For example when an archaeologist finds a wooden beam used in an ancient building, he can often date the edifice by matching the pattern of tree rings.

Climatic fluctuations and weather conditions over the past several thousands years can also be determined by examining the tree–ring patterns of bristlecone pines— those most durable of God's living things. Through discovery of logs and stumps, bristlecone chronology has been extended back over 8,000 years. One might ask how this accords with the widely–held belief that God created the earth and all living things about 6,000 years ago?

Several scriptural scholars maintain that God created trees with the appearance of age—complete with all their characteristics, including rings. Others claim that the Bible allows for a world before Adam and a universe that may be billions of years old. As for the flood of Noah, did the trees survive the deluge? Probably yes, for the flood described in Genesis killed primarily animal life. (Remember, the dove returned with a palm leaf!)

Outliving even California's giant sequoias by nearly 2,000 years, the bristlecone pine is proving to be a treasure trove of intriguing and useful information.

METODO DE MISIONAR

It is not commonly known, even among ecclesiastical historians, that Fray Francisco Garcia Diego y Moreno (1785–1846) was an accomplished and widely known preacher throughout Central Mexico in the early days of his priestly ministry. The Lagos–born friar's initial clerical appointment was that of assisting the home–mission program then flourishing, on an annual basis, in many of the established parishes of his native land. During those days, Fray Francisco Garcia Diego developed a format for that worthwhile apostolate not unlike the one popularized, in later years, by the Cursillo movement.

The clear and succinct ten–chapter *Metodo de Misionar* speaks eloquently of the early years of Francisco Garcia Diego. It also reveals much about the means employed so successfully by the Franciscans as

they traveled through the countryside enkindling and intensifying the faith of the local populace.

Shortly after his episcopal ordination as *Obispo de Ambas Californias*, Garcia Diego was persuaded by the Franciscan Guardian of the Apostolic College of *Nuestra Señora de Guadalupe*, Fray José Maria Guzmán, to issue the *Metodo* in printed form as a legacy to the younger friars who had succeeded him at Zacatecas. This the prelate did for, as he said, "experience has taught that this method brings much benefit to souls." The bishop devoted some months to carefully revising the text in such a way as to accommodate the exigencies personally encountered during the many years of his own activity among the faithful.

Copies of the initial edition, printed at Zacatecas, on March 11, 1841, are exceedingly rare. The text was subsequently incorporated into Jose Francisco Sotomayor's 1874 edition of the *Historia del Apostólico Colegio de Nuestra Señora de Guadalupe de Zacatecas*.

A more modern, but less well–edited text was released, in 1931 under the patronage of Archbishop Francisco Orozco y Jimenez as *Metodo de Misionar Fieles, que ha Usado Siempre el Colegio Apostólico de Ntra. Sra. de Guadalupe de Zacatecas*. That fourteen–page monograph was published at Guadalajara by *Talleres Graficos "Radio."* it was also reproduced in the *Boletin Eclesiástico de la Arquidiocesis de Guadalajara y de la Baja California*, for January, 1932. The *Metodo* was translated into English by Maynard J. Geiger, O.F.M. and appeared in *Provincial Annals*, for October, 1944. A new rendition, based on the 1841 text, was published recently by the American Catholic Historical Society.

Measured by the standards of the time, the *Metodo* was a radical departure from traditional religious presentations. Each mission, conducted by a team of friars, and lasting from nine to forty days was placed under the spiritual patronage of Our Lady, Refuge of Sinners.

Historical personages are frequently so identified with the era of their greatest prominence that earlier accomplishments go unheralded. So it has been with Francisco Garcia Diego's *Metodo de Misionar*, a noble work that deserves to be remembered for its own intrinsic merit.

MEXICO'S BICENTENNIAL STAMP

The colorful airmail stamp issued by the Republic of Mexico, on July 12, 1969, to commemorate California's bicentennial, has become a collector's item for reasons best known and appreciated by historians. As indicated by the inscription directly above the central field, the stamp was envisioned as a tribute to Fray Junípero Serra,

Colonizador de las Californias. Ironically, however, the personage actually portrayed is not that of Serra, but another friar, usually identified as Francisco Palóu.

The bust on the eighty centavo stamp was reproduced from a prominent painting encompassing no less than fifteen portraits. That the engraver should confuse the identity of the two central characters is an error of considerable historical proportions

The background of the painting itself is an interesting, if not pivotal sidelight to this philatelic miscarriage. A copy of the letter in which Fray Francisco Palóu initially proposed the painting, dated September 13, 1784, is in the Santa Barbara Mission Archives. Therein Serra's biographer suggested that "the most edifying scene would be to have him wearing his stole and kneeling before the altar of Our Lady, with the Child in her arms, and a priest vested with a cape before the altar, with a small host for giving him viaticum. . . ."

When Palóu's proposal was conveyed to Rafael Verger, the Bishop of Nuevo Leon, a long–time friend and admirer of Serra, the prelate endorsed the idea and offered to defray whatever expenses might be involved. Mariano Guerrero was commissioned to execute the painting which, according to an inscription on the canvas, was completed in 1785. Though described as a "true likeness," there is no available documentary evidence that Serra ever sat for a portrait nor is there any way of determining what pattern or sketch the artist used to base his interpretation of Fray Junípero's features.

The dominant color schemes of the five–by–five feet painting are red, blue, gray and walnut brown. Its greatest defect is the artificiality of the poses, according to the eminent historian, Maynard J. Geiger, O.F.M. He points out that "Palóu had a very vivid recollection of the moving scene in which he participated but in suggesting the scene for canvas he gave the painter a difficult task to perform realistically. Again all the facial features are wax–like and stereotyped. Serra's features do not portray a man of seventy years nor the face of a person in pain and approaching death."

The Guerrero painting undoubtedly hung at the Apostolic College of San Fernando in Mexico City for the first seventy years after its completion. Certainly it was there, in 1853, the year it was partially photographed by William Rich, a member of the United States legation. This print was subsequently reproduced (in reverse!) along with Rich's statement certifying the daguerreotype to be a copy from a painting in the convent of San Fernando.

Sometime during the turbulent years of the Benito Juarez regime, the Guerrero painting was appropriated by the government and moved to *El Museo Nacional*, where it was seen, in 1904, by Father Zephyrin Engelhardt. It was later stored for a number of years before being transferred to its present place in the Hall of the Spiritual Conquest of New Spain, at the Historical Museum in the Castle of Chapultepec.

Historical purists may bemoan Mexico's release of the wrong stamp for the right reason, but collectors and Californiana enthusiasts will look upon this commemorative issue as a *felix culpa*, inasmuch as it automatically increases by one the membership in that select category of "philatelic oddities" whose immortality is assured.

MIDNIGHT MASS IN SAN FRANCISCO

Shortly after Pope Pius IX's infallible definition of the Immaculate Conception, on December 8, 1854, California won the privilege of having the first church dedicated to Our Lady under that patronage. Archbishop Joseph Sadoc Alemany scheduled the formal inauguration of Saint Mary's Cathedral for Christmas eve of that year. Still devoid of all ornamentation, the unfinished edifice was readied for the ceremonies by scores of carpenters and masons.

In addition to the local Catholic populace, a considerable number of representatives from other religious persuasions were anxious to participate in the dedication of the new cathedral. A half century later, one of those fortunate enough to be on hand for that historic event recorded her observations for the November 5, 1904 issue of *The Monitor.*

> At eight o'clock on the evening of the Vigil of Christmas day, 1854, the carpenter work was sufficiently advanced to justify the celebration of midnight Mass in the half–finished edifice.
>
> As the mechanics marched out of the building the motley congregation commenced to pour in, so as to procure good positions for seeing and hearing religious services which a large majority of the attendants had never witnessed before.
>
> The girders of the building were not enclosed and the floor joists of the galleries were in the same condition, so with that happy–go–lucky disposition so characteristic of the miners of California, a large number of the gold–seeking fraternity climbed up the sides of the building.
>
> They seated themselves on the girders of the ceiling and the rafters of the galleries, their rough and rubber boots dangling down over the heads of the congregation on the main floor, where some unpainted pews and rough benches had been improvised for the accommodation of those who did not care to roost like crows in the upper portion of the unfinished building.
>
> On that memorable Christmas eve of 1854 the dedicatory Mass was celebrated by Archbishop (Joseph) Alemany. The sermon to the cosmopolitan congregation was preached by Rev. Hugh P. Gallagher. The orchestra for the festival, which was comprised of bass and

stringed instruments, was placed on the Gospel side of the altar, the choir under the leadership of George Loder, rendering Haydn's Third Mass.

It was nearly two o'clock Christmas morning before the services were concluded, and it took nearly another hour before the last of the miners had descended from his high perch and commenced his homeward march through the sand dunes that then environed the city south of California street.

Indeed, it was a momentous occasion for the Catholics of California. Two days after the event, Archbishop Alemany wrote to his mother, describing the great crowd that came to the dedication:

> The Cathedral of which I sent you the plan is large, not so large as that of Vich, and all were surprised to see it as full as an egg. One hour before the ceremony the people were hurrying to the bell tower and to the galleries which at present have nothing but the beams. . . . I do not remember having seen a church more crowded and they told me that more than a thousand people had to turn back not being able to enter.

As the first Archbishop of San Francisco watched his flock file out of the new cathedral that Christmas morning, he might well have thought: "Surely, now Christ is born in this house raised for His glory—the most magnificent structure among all the pursuits of men in this city of San Francisco."

MINIATURE BOOKS — CATHOLIC THEMES

Miniature books, representing as they do an ultimate accomplishment in printing, illustrating and binding, exemplify the craftsman's technical and manual dexterity for cutting, casting and setting midgetized letters. In many cases, the initial purpose served by miniature books, some as old as movable type, has given way to the more mundane pursuit of satisfying mini–bibliophiliacs, those "Lilliputians with whale–sized appetites for literary plankton."

Eight of those "typographical curiosities" are devoted to Californiana Catholic themes, including Francis F. Guest's work on *The Symbolism of Santa Barbara Presidio,* an interestingly–written treatise portraying the final link in the mighty chain of conquest forged by Iberian soldiers to symbolize the culture and civilization associated with Spain's expansionary activities in the New World. The forty–page book, printed by Grant Dahlstrom, has a red and black frontispiece and is bound in hand–tooled green crushed morocco.

The little volume by Frank J. Thomas on *Mission Cattle Brands,* issued by the Tenfingers Press and bound in vellum over boards, contains twenty–four designs cut in linoleum and printed in various colors on textured kozo paper. *Hollywood's "Padre of the Films,"* pub-

lished by Dawson's Book Shop, is a thirty–page biographical sketch about the Right Reverend John J. Devlin's work with the Motion Picture Industry. It was issued to commemorate the monsignor's golden anniversary of priestly ordination.

The eye–witness report of the extensive damage inflicted on the San Fernando Valley by the tremblor of February 9, 1971, *An Earthquke Memoir,* was printed by Cathay Press Limited of Hong Kong in a press run of 400 copies. Rarest of all the miniatures based on a California Catholic theme is Bernhardt Wall's *The California Missions,* a pictorial portrayal in twenty–four plates printed by the author in Sierra Madre in 1947.

Christmas in Pastoral California is an account of the *Pastorela* truncated from a description appearing in the Santa Barbara *Daily Press,* December 29, 1885. The twenty–five page book was handset, printed and bound by Bela Blau in both red and green morocco, Two hundred copies of Emily and Norman Whytock's fifty–one page opus on the *Franciscan Missions of California* were printed by William M. Cheney to coincide with California's bicentennial, in 1969.

The smallest book ever devoted to the philatelic theme is the twenty–nine page *What Ever Happened to Junípero Serra?* That 1 $1/4$" by 1 $7/8$" treatise, printed from handset type and bound in gilt–tooled, dark green morocco, contains a mint edition of the colorful eighty centavo airmail stamp issued by the Republic of Mexico to commemorate the 200th anniversary of California's colonization.

"MIRACULOUS" STAIRWAY

In one of his homilies, Bishop Thaddeus Amat told about a "miraculous" staircase he had either seen or heard about in Santa Fe, New Mexico. He noted that there were thirty–three steps, one for each year of Our Lord's earthly sojourn.

Indeed there was (and is) such a stairwell. It is located at what was formerly the chapel of Our Lady of Light, attached to the onetime convent school operated by the Sisters of Loretto, in Santa Fe. The story behind the stairwell is most fascinating. Projectus Mouly, a prominent European architect, had drafted plans for a chapel for the nuns, patterned after the famed *Sainte Chapelle* in Paris. He was, however, an absent minded man and it seemed that his design for the choirloft failed to provide for an access.

The Sisters were indeed perplexed about what to do. They called in a half dozen local artisans for advice and not one of them was able to figure out an answer to the problem of where to put the supports necessary for a stairwell. Then one cool morning in early December, a bearded man appeared at the convent door. He was a strongly–built, tall and handsome fellow who said he was a carpenter and could quite easily remedy the architectural mistake. And, he would do it for nothing!

Each day thereafter, the man with the windburned face appeared, his small gray burro weighed down with lumber and delicacies for the Sisters. He worked quietly, asking only that no one enter the chapel until he was finished. He labored on for a little over a week. Late on Christmas Eve, the carpenter rang the convent bell and informed the portress that he had completed his chore and would be leaving shortly. Then, suddenly, he vanished.

When the nuns proceeded to the chapel for midnight Mass, there it was! Like a curl of smoke the staircase rose majestically before them. Its base was on the chapel floor; its top rested against the choirloft. Nothing else supported it—it almost appeared to float on air. There were no banisters. Two complete spirals were in evidence. The polished wood gleamed softly in the candlelight. All present for that first glimpse felt that something very special had occurred.

The mother superior moved forward and almost trance–like, she slowly put her foot on the first step, then the second and the third. There was no tremor. She looked down bewildered, unable to explain how the work could have been done at all, and how it could have been finished so rapidly.

That stairwell mentioned by Bishop Amat a century ago stands today as it did when the chapel was dedicated in 1878. Only a banister has been added to allow the older sisters to walk more securely up its steps. The thirty–three steps make two complete turns without central support. There are no nails in the stairwell, only wooden pegs. Authorities brought in to look at the workmanship marvel at its craftsmanship.

The curved stringers are put together with exquisite precision, spliced in seven places on the inside and nine on the outside. The wood itself is said to be a hard–fir variety, not found in New Mexico. The full story of the miraculous staircase is told by Arthur Gordon in a book published in 1974 under the title *A Touch of Wonder*.

MISERERE HOUSE

Among Cardinal McIntyre's priorities when he came to Los Angeles was his desire to provide a place "out of the free–eating and free–lodging house category" for needy men. He knew from his experiences in New York that the need existed.

A 15,000 square foot, two–story building was acquired at 231 Winston Street, in the heart of the city's skidrow district, in 1954. It was remodelled at a cost of $100,000 and opened on February 21, 1955 as Miserere House.

Maintained and operated by the Saint Vincent de Paul Society, the steel and concrete building included a chapel with a seating capacity for 200 people, counseling offices, reading quarters, letter writing and smoking rooms, space for showers, television and games. It was unlike any other similar facility in the area.

A survey among the early users of Miserere House revealed that most of them were seasonal workers, living in neighborhood hotels or halfway houses. Others saw Miserere House as a wholesome environment for transients between jobs and residents of the poorer neighborhoods, many of whom were living on small pensions or holding odd jobs.

In the beautiful and peaceful second floor chapel Mass was celebrated daily at 12:07 p.m. by one of the priest counselors who was also available for confessions and other types of spiritual services. Assisting the priests in their work were several professionally–trained workers who rendered advice or provided social rehabilitation to clients and users of the facility.

Miserere House was open from eight in the morning until eight at night. An estimated seventy–five men used the shower facilities every day and 150 the shaving provisions. On opening day alone, more than 600 men dropped in and within two weeks that number reached 10,000. The first year, 350,000 names were listed on the rolls. The house was not only a haven for migratory workers, but "a visible sign of an earnest effort to restore temporarily disadvantaged men to their rightful place of human dignity."

Miserere House was advertised as "something clean and fresh in a drab area." Its programs gave a promise of hope and a pledge of the "good life" to many who had fallen on bad times. Supported wholly by donations and through proceeds from the Saint Vincent de Paul Society, Miserere House provided a base of operation for men in the course of their rehabilitation. In addition, it gave users a healthy place to pass their leisure time.

There were all kinds of services available. For example, through employment services provided by Matt Campion, the House was able to find employment for 3,260 men during the first ten months of its existence. In an early mission statement for Miserere House, it was recorded that its main purpose was to provide "for the mental and spiritual upbuilding of homeless and transient men" in whatever way possible.

Miserere House was Cardinal McIntyre's own special project for needy men. A local newspaper article about the facility stated that McIntyre "saw the clients of Miserere House not as bums, but as souls in need of salvation."

MISNOMERS — SOME OUTSTANDING ONES

California is especially fortunate in having a rich and diversified nomenclature for its many cities and towns. As could be expected, there are some interesting misnomers among the 150,000 place names in the Golden State and we here point out some of the more obvious ones.

The word CALIFORNIA itself is of mysterious origin. Older textbooks perpetuated the theory that the designation grew out of the words *callida fornax* (hot furnace). Most modern scholars, however, believe the term originated in Garcia Ordonez de Montalvo's *Las Sergas de Esplandian* (c.1500), a story about an earthly paradise, CALIFORNIA, where beautiful women, gold and pearls abounded.

The Puerto de MONTEREY was so designated by Sebastian Vizcaino, in 1602, to honor the memory of Gaspar de Zuniga y Acevedo, the *Conde de Monterrey*, viceroy of Mexico. How the title of the bay (and later the city) came to be misspelled is puzzling, for the older city of Monterrey in Mexico has always been written with a double r. It was this inaccuracy which accounts for the term *Dioecesis Montis Regis*, used in several early papal bulls.

LOS ANGELES is a shortened version of *El Pueblo de Nuestra Señora de los Angeles*, the City of Our Lady of the Angels. Though the term La Reina (the Queen) frequently appears in the city's title, it is a spurious insertion, not etymologically justified.

In 1868, when the seat of the Vicariate Apostolic of Marysville was moved to the old City of Centerville in present–day Nevada, a diocese was established under the title GRASS VALLEY. Bishop Eugene O'Connell protested the use of the term, pointing out that "in truth there is no grass upon it any more than on the Hill of Howth in Dublin Bay." GRASS VALLEY'S first ordinary suggested that the area might be called Aspramonte (rocky mount) "because it is situated only five miles from Rough and Ready, and besides it is rough enough itself and rocky too."

Originally designated *La Asuncion de Nuestra Señora* by Father Juan Crespi, the present City of VENTURA derives its name from the mission founded there in 1782. Though dedicated to Saint Bonaventure (San Buenaventura), the city that subsequently developed was tabbed VENTURA when it received county–status in 1872.

The little town of SAN ARDO has the distinction of being the only point in California bearing the name of a saint canonized by the United States Post Office. Originally known as San Bernardo, the city's name was later changed by postal officials to distinguish it from San Bernardino.

New Mecklenburg, now the city of MARYSVILLE, thought by many to be named after the Blessed Mother, actually got its title in 1850, from Mary Murphy Covillaud, a survivor of the Donner Party. Despite the fact that it advertises itself as "SAN FERNANDO, the Mission City," the town really has no claim to such a distinction, since it arbitrarily adjusted property lines to exclude the mission in the 1930s. Mission San Fernando, now in the City of Los Angeles, proudly boasts the second oldest church in the City of Our Lady of the Angels.

These misnomers demonstate that California is indeed a land of abundant diversification!

MISSION BRAND

Fresh oranges were a delicacy in the mid west and eastern parts of the country. To find one or two oranges in a Christmas stocking was the answer to a child's prayer.

But fresh oranges played another very important role, coming as they did individually wrapped in a light tissue paper emblazoned with a picture of a California mission. They provided my first exposure to those wonderful historical outposts established by the Franciscans along *El Camino Real*.

Upon each of the wooden orange crates was a large label portraying three friars leaning against a table inside a colonnade, sampling oranges. In the background was a mission splendidly arrayed in a vast orchard of trees. The mission resembled the one founded at San Gabriel in 1771.

At the lower left of the colorful label was a printed attestation that "this fruit is scientifically grown and ripened on the trees. (It is of) superior quality and uniform in grade." At the other side of the label were the words: "Grown and packed by Charles Chapman, Fullerton, Orange County, California."

Long after their content had been scattered to the four corners of Indiana's Marion County, the sturdy wooden crates, with their colorful labels intact, were used for all sorts of purposes. It was only fifty or so years later that the origin of those rare delicacies was unravelled. The story is told in the autobiography of Charles C. Chapman (1853–1944), the man for whom Chapman College was named.

Mr. Chapman, a pioneer in the citrus industry since 1895, was responsible for perfecting what was known as "Valencia" oranges. From the outset, he felt his product should have a distinctive name or brand. Though at first discouraged by others in the field, Chapman persevered. He recalled being "greatly interested in the old missions" some of which he had visited. "We thought a mission building with palm trees and orange orchards would make a beautiful picture."

He commissioned an artist to capture those sentiments artistically. Along with the original design were the words: "Chapman's Old Mission Brand." That label was attached to all his products, even walnuts.

According to one source, "The Old Mission Brand" soon became favorably recognized on the larger markets of the east. Not only did his brand become the best known of California oranges, it represented the best in quality.

The *Fruit Trade Journal* of New York proclaimed that "the fame of Old Mission is world–wide and justly so. Its claim to fame begins in California with its grower and shipper, Mr. Chapman of Fullerton, who produces fine fruit and allows only the best to come to market."

Chapman soon became known as the "Orange King of America" and his brand of oranges was the most famous and sought after in the world. "Old time buyers never opened a box for inspection because they knew every one was always the same quality."

For well over thirty years, "Chapman's Old Mission Brand" brought the highest price ever received for California oranges. The brand became the envy of shippers as well as consumers. And beyond all that, Charles Chapman introduced me and countless others to the California Missions, where the orange industry began in North America."

MISSION DAYS — A REINCARNATION

The history of California's internationally–famous "Mission Inn" can be traced to 1902, when Frank A. Miller erected the first part of the concrete and brick structure at Glenwood. Modeled after the old missionary foundations along *El Camino Real* and containing rare art from all over the world, the Cloister, built in 1911, with its Music Room and Cathedral Organ; the Spanish Art Gallery, built in 1915, with the Patio of the Fountains, and the Garden of Bells, with 650 bells of many shapes and sizes; the Rotunda with its Galeria, Saint Francis Wedding Chapel, and Oriental Court, built in 1931—are only a few of the beautiful treasures of the Mission Inn.

More enthusiastic lines have been written by famous authors spontaneously and unsolicited—and more praises have been spoken by world–travelers and globe-trotters about the Glenwood Mission Inn at Riverside, California, than have been written or said about any other hotel on earth. In 1912, John Steven McGroarty wrote about the renowned Riverside establishment for *Touring Topics*. Extracts from the essay are worth recalling, even six decades later.

No man or woman has ever visited this beautiful institution—for that's really what it is, an institution—without searching not only their minds, but their hearts also, for words with which to describe its quite indescribable charm.

It is true that the Glenwood Mission Inn is located in one of the most beautiful places known to travelers, but there are many other hotels of which the world at large seldom or never hears that are located in beautiful places. The Glenwood Mission Inn, located in any other spot would fascinate the guest as truly. Or, to put the matter another way, if Frank Miller, the Master of the Inn, had built and conducted a hotel anywhere else, it would be an inn that would not fail to acquire the same fame that the Glenwood at Riverside enjoys.

When the good Quaker parents of the Master of the Inn decided to give him the name Francis, they were doubtless not aware that they were doing something psychological. It is not at all likely they dreamed that they were to give California one who was destined to rear in the curve of the old King's Highway, a reincarnation of the lost glory of the Franciscan Missions that are now in ruin, but which once stood along the golden stretches of *El Camino Real*, each a day's journey on foot from the other, between San Diego's Harbor of the Sun and Sonoma in the Valley of the Seven Moons. For that is exactly what the Mission Inn is–a reincarnation of California's Mission days . . . a hospice on the King's Highway, although in a newer day.

No one has put the matter in a more enlightening manner than Dr. David Starr Jordan when he said: "It has been left for you, Frank Miller, a genuine Californian, to dream of the hotel that ought to be, to turn your ideal into plaster and stone, and to give us in mountain–belted Riverside the one hotel which a Californian can recognize as his own."

The Mission Inn was a hotel in a class by itself long ago, but the dream was not completed until the past few years when the addition known as "The Cloister" was built. As the establishment now stands, it is one of the largest hotels in America. Yet, large as it is, it is filled with guests during the season. There are very many people who come from the East and other far distances to spend the winter in the Glenwood as regularly as they spend the summers in their own homes.

The architecture of this great building includes so many faithfully reproduced features of so large a number of the old Franciscan Missions of California that it may be said to be a composite of them all. The campanile of San Gabriel, the towers of Carmel, the arches of San Juan Capistrano, the cloisters of San Luis Rey— this feature and that of one mission after another—they are all there to make mellow the dreams of the romantic and hallowed past.

Doors of massive oak, hewed as are the rafters above them, and hundreds of patiently wrought details down to the very keys and latches of the rooms, work their spell on the happy guest. The one deep word that describes it all is "peace." It rests the tired heart; it soothes the very soul.

The saints stand in the niches and on the crochets of the walls bestowing their benedictions upon you. At noontide the Mission bells call you to the waiting meal and at evening they ring out the twilight music of the *Angelus* in soft, sweet chimes.

MOBILE CHAPEL CAR

American entrance into World War II brought about startling changes in Los Angeles with respect to population, industry and agriculture. The ideal climate, for example, encouraged the erection of numerous factories which beckoned workers from all areas of the nation. Almost overnight, Los Angeles became one of the country's most important cities.

The Catholic Church in Los Angeles kept apace with all the new demands for its services. Hence it comes as no surprise that "the first maritime service chapel on wheels" was "launched" under the auspices of the Catholic Maritime Club.

Early in 1944, Father James Nevin approached Mrs. Charles Von der Ahe with a request that she provide funds for purchasing a mobile unit that could be outfitted as a chapel. With her gracious financial backing and the endorsement of Archbishop John J. Cantwell, Father Nevin acquired a trailer and had it thoroughly rebuilt along the lines used by the Catholic Church Extension Society for its railroad chapels.

When completed, the twenty–two foot unit accommodated an altar, confessional and office for counseling. There were ten chairs inside the trailer and, on the rear, an overhang apparatus for protection against inclement weather.

On May 23, 1944, Father Nevin had the truck towed to the schoolyard of Cathedral Chapel Parish, just west of Hancock Park, where Archbishop Cantwell and a small group of clergymen blessed it. The prelate concluded his benediction with this acclamation: "May she sail true and strong and come into port well loaded with souls."

Newspaper coverage of the "launching" was wide-

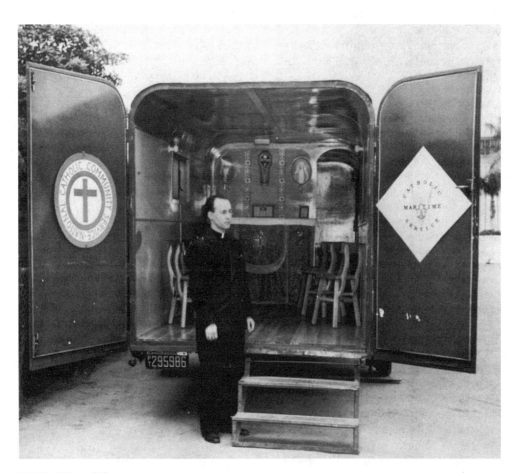

Mobile Chapel Car

spread. For example, the new mobile facility was described by the Los Angeles *Herald–Express* as "a trailer chapel equipped with an altar, at which Catholic members of the armed forces may receive the administrations of the Church on the Los Angeles docks before embarking for combat."

Another local newspaper, the Los Angeles *Examiner*, reported to its readers that the mobile chapel would "sail among the docks and wharves of the Harbor area, bringing spiritual comfort" to service people. Following its dedication, the mobile chapel "was indeed used extensively by Father Nevin, its "skipper." As the director for the Catholic Maritime Services in the Los Angeles Harbor, it was Father Nevin's duty to look after the spiritual needs of the thousands of sailors who daily moved in and out of the busy area.

The mobile chapel was of special assistance in caring for those Catholic military personnel whose naval units were too small for regular chaplain services. An elaborate scheduling system was devised which allowed the chapel to move about with great adaptability.

Fortunately, the war lasted only another year. With cessation of the hostilities, the mobile chapel lost its primary function. It was "de–commissioned" in 1946, and sold to one of the major trucking lines. One occasionally hears a veteran of World War II speak findly of "Old PT 295" which rolled into place just in time for daily or Sunday Mass. It was just one more example of the local Church reaching out to meet the needs of the time.

THE MONITOR

The San Francisco *Monitor* was founded in March of 1858, by James Marks, Patrick J. Thomas and James Hamill as an eight–page weekly newspaper under the masthead, "Unity in essentials, freedom in things debatable, charity always." In the March 6, 1858 issue of the *Daily Evening Bulletin* it was noted that "the first number of *The Monitor* appeared today. This is a weekly Roman Catholic journal, of 8 pages, published in this city by Marks, Thomas and Company. It is finely printed and contains a great variety of reading matter. Two columns are devoted to items in the Spanish language."

Throughout the early years, James Hamill dedicated the journal to publishing "all domestic and foreign newsworthy events of interest to the Catholics of California." In addition to wide coverage of Irish news, Hamill assured his readers that "no pains will be spared to make our mining, agricultural and commercial intelligence ample, interesting and reliable."

According to the San Francisco *Herald*, *The Monitor*'s early editorials exhibited talent "far above the standard which generally obtains in California" and merited the support of "our Roman Catholic population, who, in point of intelligence, worth and numbers, require a representative through the press of their sentiments."

Though the paper's founders avoided political discussions as matters "outside the scope of a religious journal," that policy was abandoned by Thomas A. Brady who purchased *The Monitor* from Bartholomew Dowling in 1860. A former law reporter from the *Herald*, Brady had decidedly pro–Southern leanings during the Civil War. In his first years as editor, *The Monitor* reflected those views to such an extent that Hubert Howe Bancroft spoke of the paper as a "disloyal, Catholic journal." So embroiled did the publication become that Archbishop Joseph Sadoc Alemany publicly disavowed responsibility "for articles and statements" issued without his approbation. The prelate further stated that certain "Periodicals and journals . . . are not always faithful exponents of the doctrines and wishes of the Catholic Church which in this diocese has no official organ."

The rebuke cooled the atmosphere and Brady subsequently endorsed the Democratic platform calling for "a speedy and honorable peace." Nonetheless, when Abraham Lincoln was assassinated, a mob led by Warren C. Butler wrecked *The Monitor* office and everything "went into the street in a splintered heap." Between April 14 and June 10, 1865, *The Universe* replaced *The Monitor*, but within a month Brady had restored his paper's earlier title, noting that "we have the satisfaction of resuming today the publication of *The Monitor*."

Through the decades, the newspaper's title has varied slightly. From 1875 to 1877, it was the *Monitor and Guardian,* and between 1920 and 1926, it was published as the *Monitor and Intermountain Catholic*.

Archbishop Alemany and several of his priests purchased a half interest in the paper on December 27, 1876, and the issue of April 7,1877 carried the following letter signed by the Archbishop of San Francisco:

> Right Rev. Bishop Amat, of Monterey–Los Angeles, Right Rev. Bishop O'Connell, of Marysville, and myself take pleasure in declaring to our respective flocks that we beg to avail ourselves of your useful and ably edited *Monitor* as our official organ.

Four years later, the Monitor Publishing Company was created as a partnership consisting of Bishop Eugene O'Connell, Fathers James Croke (acting for Alemany), Patrick Manogue, Peter Grey, Andrew Cullen and Mr. Frank L. McCormick. In February of 1892, the proprietorship of *The Monitor* was formed into a joint stock company and incorporated by the State of California as an agency of the Archdiocese of San Francisco.

The Monitor has been an active force in the Bay City's public life since its very foundation. During the editorship of Father Peter C. Yorke the paper was "the best known and most widely read Catholic weekly in America." At the formative meeting of the United Nations in San Francisco, the United States Department of State impounded *The Monitor*'s equipment and personnel and "With linotype operators, copy readers, etc., flown directly from the Soviet Union, and with striped–pants diplomats rubbing shoulders with *The Monitor*'s own employees, the original charter of the United Nations was set in type in the Russian language."

THE MONITOR AND THE UNITED NATIONS

The United Nations was born of a resolve by World War II leaders to prevent future battlefield conflicts. It was a noble endeavor and one to which all peoples of good will were dedicated. Associated originally with the pursuit of unconditional victory, the resolve was manifested progressively in the 1941 Atlantic Charter (stating the peace aim of England and the United States), the 1942 Declaration of the United Nations (in which twenty–six allies accepted the ideals of peace), the 1943 Moscow Declaration (in which China, Russia, England and the United States pledged their continuous international cooperation) and the 1944 Dumbarton Oaks Conference.

On February 12, 1945, John C. Grew, Acting Secretary of State, informed Mayor Roger Lapham that "San Francisco had been selected as the site of the United Nations Conference—for the purpose of preparing a charter . . . for the maintenance of international peace and security."

The proceedings began on April 25 and lasted until June 26th, when the Charter was signed by the fifty member nations. On the following October 24th, with the requisite ratification by the five permanent members of the Security Council, the Charter went into operation.

Though it is not generally known, the official Catholic newspaper for the Archdiocese of San Francisco, *The Monitor*, played an integral and unique role in the dramatic events of those days. Governmental officials were desperately looking for a print shop which could set in type the United Nations Charter in the Russian language, one of the agreed–upon languages of the Preparatory Conference. To everyone's surprise, The Monitor was the only shop on the Pacific Coast that could do that job. As a result, the United States Department of State impounded *The Monitor*'s equipment and personnel.

Linotype operators, proofreaders and other technicians were flown directly from the Soviet Union to assist in the composition of the Russian version. Striped–panted diplomats and security agents rubbed shoulders with *The Monitor*'s employees as the original Charter was set into type. It was truly an historical few days.

The Monitor continued to be printed in its own composing room until mid 1977, when the editor signed a termination agreement with the International Typographical Union. Afterwards, the paper was produced at the Industrial City Publishing Company.

The United Nations Charter was a product not alone of the statesmen assessing contemporary political realities, but also of the determination by religious authorities, scholars and groups of citizens that the lessons of history should be written in terms of moral principles for the guidance of the future. How appropriate that a Catholic newspaper play such a prominent role in inaugurating and achieving such lofty ideals.

MONTEREY JACK CHEESE

Since 1955, the soft country cheese introduced to California by the missionaries, made by the pioneer settlers and produced by early dairies, has been officially designated by the United States government as "Monterey Jack." Today, "Monterey Jack" cheese is no longer made in Monterey County, but comes from Sonoma, Pleasanton and Crescent City. On a larger scale it is manufactured in such states as Wisconsin and Oregon.

The California Milk Advisory Board refers to "Monterey Jack" as the only one truly native to California. In the 1770s, a cheese known simply as *queso blanco* (white cheese) or *queso del pais* (country cheese) was processed at the missions. The Franciscan friars had imported the formula from their native Mallorca. They taught the Indians to make cheese as a practical way of utilizing the excess milk produced by the mission herds.

Mission cheese was a descendant of that semi–soft dairy product originating from the Roman Empire. It had been brought into Spain by Roman legions when colonization of that area began in 200 B.C. Gradually it became commonly–made household cheese.

Cheese quickly became a popular product of early settlers. Some families brought their own cheese–making recipes from such diverse places as the Azores or the Italian Swiss Alps. Milk surplus was common where families had a dairy and it was commonplace for them to turn the excess into either butter or cheese. Such products could be easily marketed in surrounding towns or sold to neighbors. There were upwards of 150 dairies between Big Sur and Marina. In those times, three cows constituted a dairy and many were family–owned and operated.

There were also numerous dairies in the Salinas Valley. Countywide dairy farming dates to 1865, when

Carlisle Abbot began selling dairy products from his acreage near Spreckels. The Swiss immigrants in that area also produced commercial dairy products—first butter, then cheese.

Large–scale commercial marketing of the locally processed cheese began in 1882. David Jacks, who owned acreage in various parts of Monterey, began to ship the product by rail to San Francisco and Sacramento. Some of his cheese came from dairymen leasing his properties and others he purchased from private family–run dairies.

While there had been an outside demand for the Monterey County cheese before Jacks, earlier attempts at marketing were largely unsuccessful. Prior to railroads, cheese had to be crated and sent up the coast by ship. The resulting delays, temperature changes and water intrusion often led to spoilage.

When Jacks began to market his product, Anglos found it difficult to pronounce *queso del pais*, so it became known as "Jack's Monterey Cheese." Later the "s" was dropped and the name reversed to "Monterey Jack Cheese." Today's "Monterey Jack Cheese" has been compared in consistency to other native American cheeses, such as Muenster, Wisconsin Brick and Colby.

But whatever its consistency and however it acquired its name, the dairy product that is today a staple throughout the United States, had its origins in the California missions.

MOST BEAUTIFUL DIOCESE IN AMERICA

The following description of the Diocese of Monterey–Los Angeles is taken from an address delivered, on May 26, 1910, by John Steven McGroarty before the Newman Club. It was published under the caption: "The Most Beautiful Diocese in America."

There are times when the use of the superlative is justified by the facts and when it is alone by its use that the truth can be construed. Wherefore, when we speak of our Diocese of Monterey–Los Angeles, stretching half way down the golden length of the Land of Heart's Desire, in the glow of the snow–crowned Sierras and by the white, sweep of the shores of the Sunset Sea, as "The Most Beautiful Diocese in America," we have the facts to justify us and the truth to make us strong. We can make the assertion in a two–fold sense, because our diocese is not only pre–eminent in its physical beauty but in its spiritual beauty as well.

Human government divides the earth into nations; the divine government of the Church divides it into dioceses, each diocese is a spiritual principality with a prince of the Church in the person of a successor of the apostles to rule over it. America is a young land, as nations go, so young that until a few months ago it was still regarded as a missionary country by the Church.

Now in America, there are many of these diocesan principalities older in point of existence than the nation itself, and some as young as yesterday. The Diocese of Monterey–Los Angeles is neither the oldest nor the youngest American diocese, but that it is the most beautiful I do contend.

It has in it the soul of eternal summer, the heart of undying June. It lies between the shining waters of the Bay of Monterey and San Diego's Harbor of the Sun–between the spot where the first recorded Mass was celebrated on the Pacific Coast and the spot where the first church was built with its altar of sacrifice on the western rim of our America; between the grave of Junípero Serra and the grave of Father Jayme the first martyr in California to the faith of Christ. Down upon it look Mt. Whitney, Mt. San Antonio, Mt. San Bernardino and Mt. San Jacinto, glorious and peerless among the mountains of the world; its shores are flecked with the magic isles of Santa Barbara, Santa Catalina and the Coronados. It was first hailed by a Catholic sailor and its hills and valleys were first trod by a Catholic soldier. It was once a wholly Catholic province from end to end and from sea to mountains; and it still holds within its possession the ruins of the Franciscan mission buildings which are the oldest and most priceless relics of the Church and the nation inside the present borders of the United States.

When you think, therefore, of the beauty of the Diocese of Monterey–Los Angeles, we must think always of that combination of physical and spiritual beauty which make it pre–eminent among the dioceses of America. For, a country or a province or a diocese may be like a human being who possesses both spiritual and physical beauty, or just the one and not the other. There might well be and there doubtless are dioceses in the Arctic or in the blazing deserts, most repellant in their physical desolation yet divine in their spiritual beauty and the conditions exactly turned about elsewhere. Here in our Diocese of Monterey–Los Angeles there has come down to us from the splendor of the past a heritage of religion so sweet, so gentle, so unselfish and so glorified that I know of none other to compare with it; while the heritage of nature that God has bestowed upon it is today the wonder of the world. It is a thing to be inexpressibly grateful for, a heritage to be proud of, and yet withal something that puts upon us the responsibility of striving as best we may to bring back the spiritual beauty that has been lost to keep company with the natural beauty that God in His goodness has not taken from us.

It is a diocese filled with great achievements of great men of the Church, clerical as well as lay; it has always had a great bishop in authority as it has today; it has always had true priests as it has today. The splendor of the self–sacrifice of grey– robed friars of St. Francis has been nowhere more eloquent than was made here. Its mountain peaks, its hills, its valleys, its cities and towns, its rivers and lakes and harbors bear to this day the holy names of the saints of Christ's Church. Its episcopal see bears the name of Our Lady of the Angels. It has had more than one saint of its own who but wait the authority of the Church that they may be so revered; it has the record of miracles that also but await the seal of authority upon them. The blood of martyrs is upon it, it has known bitter persecution and suffering, it has felt the thrill of glory and the sting of shame, but it never lost the faith; and today it lifts its head from the dust of the past to greet new altar lights that crown the old King's highway like stars in the night of a summer sky.

Within this marvelous principality of the Church, set in the golden heart of California, a man might spend his whole life yet never satiate his soul with its beauty. Let him set foot from the sea at San Diego as did Cabrillo, the great Portuguese Catholic navigator . . . and begin his journey to Monterey where Father Junípero sleeps in his quiet and hallowed grave. Before him will stretch *El Camino Real*, the old King's Highway that the grey–robed priests built for the flocks of the fold in the long ago when the world was young. Before him will lie the long road over which Father Serra and his brethren made innumerable journeys and which they consecrated with their blood and with the waters of life poured in baptism on the heathen gentiles' heads.

MUSIC — SPANISH SONGS OF OLD CALIFORNIA

The name of Charles Fletcher Lummis (1859–1928) is known to every Californian. His journalistic accomplishments, historical books and native American concerns are without parallel in the annals of this and the last century.

Not so widely known was Lummis' interest in music. He amassed a large collection of more than 450 unrecorded folksongs of the Southwest from the years 1884 onwards.

In November of 1923, Lummis published fourteen "Spanish Songs of Old California" which he envisioned as the first in a series destined "to preserve a fair showing of the quaint, heartfelt and heartreaching Folksong which flowered in the California That Was." Now itself a rare and collectible item, the book is valued for many reasons, not the least of which is its preface entitled "Flowers of Our Lost Romance" wherein the compiler reminisced about "old California before the gringo came—the California of the Franciscan missions."

Lummis felt that "we who inherit California are under a filial obligation to save whatever we may of the incomparable Romance which has made the name California a word to conjure with for 400 years." He said that "we cannot decently dodge a certain trusteeship to save the Old Missions from ruin and the Old Songs from oblivion." Lummis was "convinced that from a purely selfish standpoint, our musical repertory is in crying need of enrichment—more by heartfelt musicians than by tailor–made ones, more from folksong than from pot–boilers."

A collector of old songs for thirty–eight years, long before the phonograph, Lummis said that "it was a sin and a folly to let such songs perish. We need them now! They are of the kindred of our own undying favorites. My versions are authentic, both in music and in text. Frankly, I do not know when such a muster of such songs has ever before knocked at our door in a body."

In California of earlier days, "there was no Grand Opera and no folk songs. There were Songs of the Soil, and songs of poets and of troubadours, in this far, lone, beautiful, happy land; and songs that came over from Mother Spain and up from Step–mother Mexico. But everybody sang; and a great many made their own songs, or verses to other songs. Not being musical critics, they felt music, and arrived at it; and the Folksong of Spanish America is a treasure of inexhaustible beauty and extent."

Noting that the songs of every soil have beauty of their own, Lummis felt that the "Folksong of the Spanish blood—whether in the Old peninsula, or in the New World that Spain gave to the Old—has a particular fascination, a naiveté, and yet a vividness and life, a richness of melody, with a certain resilience and wilfulness—that give it a preeminent appeal. It has more Music in it–more Rhythm, more Grace."

"It is more *simpatica*. It not only jogs my hearing and tickles in my pulses, but cuddles in my heart more happily than the songs of any of the score of other nationalities to which I have given friendly ear. Song then was born of emotion, and never of the commercial itch. It came from the heart—and it reached the heart."

Lummis recalled that "in the California days of my young manhood it seemed there was always somebody singing at work or play Carmen or Nena or Pichona or Ysabel—and nightly, by dusk or moonlight, twenty or thirty of us would sit in the long corridor, forgetting the hours as we sung our hearts out in these very songs and a hundred others—maybe with *Padre* Pedro marching up and down, conducting; a choirmaster with a voice as the Bulls of Bashan.

One cannot help but love the songs in his book—the homely quaintness of some, the sheer beauty of others and the charm of them all. Like many noble projects, however, this "first book" on the subject was the last, a shame indeed and a great loss for lovers of yesteryears.

NATIONAL ASSOCIATION FOR THE ADVANCEMENT OF COLORED PEOPLE

On November 28, 1921, at a time in this nation's history when indifference to the physical and spiritual welfare of the black man was nothing short of scandalous, the Bishop of Monterey–Los Angeles accepted, "with much pleasure and delight," an invitation to address a convocation of the National Association for the Advancement of Colored People. The very appearance of Bishop John J. Cantwell, to say nothing about the tone of his remarks, was courageous for he enunciated principles not at all popular in the country at large. To the prelate, however, there was "no place where a Catholic bishop or priest should be more at home than among the children of the colored race."

The bishop expressed a kinship with his audience by remarking that neither they nor their fathers, nor the people he represented, were strangers to intolerance: "You and I know too well, to our sorrow be it said, what comes from an intolerant bigotry, from an unchristian appreciation of human character." Cantwell acknowledged that it had been hard for the members of his church to battle against the forces of that public opinion which "tolerates" the colored people and makes no effort to develop a black clergy within the ecclesial structure.

Past injustices not withstanding, the bishop called for a strong alliance wherein black and white could stand shoulder–to–shoulder against the world, the flesh and the devil. Without such an accommodation, he foresaw the whole human family sinking "into an ocean of degradation and corruption." "Religion teaches us," the prelate noted, "to see in every man, no matter what may be the color of his skin, a human soul upon which is stamped the image of God. That image was defaced by original sin and cleansed again in the Blood of Christ, so that a human soul has been redeemed and purchased in the Life Blood of the Son of God. If men realize the dignity of the human soul, apart altogether from external appearance, they will be forced to recognize the equality of all men in the sight of God."

The Bishop of Monterey–Los Angeles attributed the ills heaped upon the colored race to "the absence of the spirit of charity, and ignoring of religious principles." In obvious contrast to the commonly accepted view, Cantwell regarded the vast majority of the black race as "exemplars and models" after which white people would do well to conform their manners. He decried the calumnies levelled by organizations, the subsidized press and propaganda, noting, that such lies account for the fact that "a bigoted section of our fellow citizens has been able from time to time to usurp even the majesty of our courts." While unable to speak for the nation as a whole, Bishop Cantwell did express the hope that Catholics in the Diocese of Monterey–Los Angeles "will henceforth be your friends and, be entirely without prejudice." He assured his listeners "that the colored people of this city, whether they are of my church, or of another church, or of no church at all, will never be denied by me or my priests."

NATIVITY STORY

The Christmas season is a very special time at Fig Tree Spring, Coyote Canyon in present–day Anza Borrego State Park. There the Child Monument recalls an event that occurred on Christmas Eve, 1775.

It all began with the Juan Baptiste de Anza expedition of colonists who came from Mexico, up through Southern California, and then on to found the City of San Francisco. The story itself is reconstructed from the diaries of Fray Pedro Font.

The diarist records that 1775 was a terrible winter. Driving rain and bitter cold had slowed progress to a few miles each day. Cattle and horses were dying daily and at night the colonists huddled around fires, many of them ill with the flu. It was still sleeting at daylight on December 23rd. When the downpour stopped briefly, scouts could see snow ahead on the Sierra ridges up the canyon. But on they went.

Friendly Indians approached the beleaguered colonists with presents of food and firewood. Next morning De Anza and his people moved another nine miles up the canyon to camp at what later became Fig Tree Spring. During that night, Gertruda Rivas Linares, the wife of a soldier, began experiencing birth pains. About half an hour before midnight, Fray Font reported to bystanders that a baby boy had been born.

The Christmas Eve child was baptized with great solemnity next morning immediately after Font's third Mass. Appropriately, the youngster was christened with the name "Salvador." Afterwards, Salvador and his parents continued with the other colonists up the California coast to become one of the founding families of San Francisco. But the little fellow's only recorded place in history is in the lonely canyon of his birth.

The Child Monument, constructed by the "Roads to Romance" of stones washed down the mountain above it, bears a plaque telling of Salvador's birth. It was put in place on May 7, 1950, by the California Centennial Committee.

Whether little Salvador was truly the first immigrant child born in California is open to some conjecture. Other women from Mexico had already joined their husbands along El Camino Real. But certainly no baby could have entered the world in California under more dramatic circumstances. Even today those who hike into the area from Borrego are exposed to one of the most picturesque nature preserves in the United States.

The passage of more than two centuries has all but buried the story in its wilderness setting, Relatively few Californians have heard of the Child Monument and fewer still have journeyed to see it.

NEWMAN CLUB

The Newman Club was established, on May 25, 1899 by John Filmore Francis and several other Catholic laymen of California's southland with the avowed purpose of promoting religious toleration in accordance with the Constitution of the United States, and considering and discussing subjects germane to Catholic thought and history and giving expression, on proper occasions, to the sentiments of members about matters of Catholic concern.

According to John Alton, "the idea of such a club had its inception in the mind of that American Churchman whose memory we all revere and cherish, the late Most Reverend George Montgomery," during his years as Bishop of Monterey–Los Angeles. An early journalist noted that "the formation of the Newman Club came at a most opportune time, and its object was mainly to have a body of laymen whose tact and firmness would be a great assistance to the Catholic people in general." Such an observation is understandable when one considers that the Newman Club was launched in an era when many citizens believed that a Catholic American was not a fit person to be a citizen.

Though it was essentially a literary organization, one of the Club's principal purposes was the defense of those few Catholics in public positions whose religious convictions subjected them to injustice or oppression. That the Newman Club achieved its purpose is obvious from remarks recorded just a few years after its establishment: "Whilst maintaining the strictest Catholicity, the club has done a noble work. . .in giving to the Church in this community a standing among the non–Catholic body that it never had before." It has done "a generous service in breaking down unhappy prejudices that have too long made enemies of those who should be friends."

These outstanding effects on the educational life of Los Angeles were recognized by Bishop Montgomery, who reckoned that the Newman Club was "one of the promising features of Catholic life in the city and for the diocese."

Men of prominence in the professional and business life of the community have always considered membership in the Newman Club a distinct privilege. Even in 1903, it was noted that the organization "is made up of some of our best men in almost every walk and profession of life. They are men who enjoy the respect and confidence of their fellow citizens, irrespective of party or denomination."

At the same time, social status has never been a criterion for membership. The Newman Club is open to Catholics in all walks of life, provided only that they have " a liberal education and sufficiently cultivated literary taste . . . to appreciate and discuss the activities, which under the purview of the constitution, may be brought up in the papers which each in turn will be required to present."

The passage of time has not altered the Club's original format. Since May of 1899, when Madame Modjeska read her paper before the group on "Christianity and the Stage," members have met monthly to hear and discuss the major problems encountered by the Church in an ever–growing community. Over sixty years ago, the Newman Club was referred to as "probably the only society of its kind in the United States," a distinction that would very likely go unchallenged even today.

It would be hard indeed to improve on the observations of the poet, publicist and author, James R. Randall, who wrote, in 1905, that "The Newman Club of Los Angeles is a splendid representative body of Catholic men. It is an admirable combination of religious and literary motives and purposes."

NEWMAN CLUB MOVEMENT

Students at the University of California at Berkeley were among the first in the nation to set up a means for supplementing their secular education along Catholic lines. After several unsuccessful attempts to establish a permanent organization, a "Newman Club" was founded in 1899, to honor the great English cardinal by that name. The object of the Club was "not alone the spiritual but also the social and intellectual improvement of its members."

Berkeley's Newman Club received the sanction of Archbishop Patrick W. Riordan in 1901, and was given as its spiritual director the assistant pastor of nearby Saint Joseph's Church, the Reverend John J. Cantwell. The future Archbishop of Los Angeles guided the students with such initiative and perseverance that within a few years the Club had grown large enough to warrant more permanent quarters than the Golden Sheaf Bakery. In 1907 Archbishop Riordan purchased a twelve–room residence in a choice section of Berkeley only 200 feet from the northeastern entrance to the university and for the next three years this building served their purposes until Newman Hall with its chapel, lecture room, and chaplain's residence could be erected. The new edifice was financed with the $40,000 presented to Riordan on the occasion of his silver jubilee. Upon completion, the building was placed under the protection of Thomas Aquinas, patron of Catholic education.

Riordan's sponsorhip of the Newman Club movement was in complete harmony with the sentiments of Pope Leo XIII and his dealings with the long–disputed problems of Catholic students attending Oxford and Cambridge in England. The archbishop recalled that students of John Henry Newman's life can easily observe the cardinal's sentiments favoring the attendance of Catholics at great secular universities, provided their schooling could be given a Catholic orientation. Father Thomas Verner Moore of the Congregation of Saint Paul took charge of the work at Berkeley in mid–1907, and initiated the traditional association with the Paulist Fathers.

The introduction to an early edition of the Club's constitution notes that "once organized, the Club more than realized the sanguine hopes of its founders," and this fact remains true even after the passage of another six decades. Over the years Newman Hall has expanded its usefulness by helping students secure suitable lodgings, serving as an employment agency and arranging social events for its members. One alumnus noted years ago "the Newman Club has never considered a successful social event foreign to the great cardinal's idea of a University."

Fully appreciative of the generous assistance of clergy and laity, the Newman Club at Berkeley quickly took a prominent place in university life and lent its active support to programs elevating the intellectual and moral tone of the institution. Today the Newman Club at the University of California at Berkeley has the distinction of having served as the "Pilot plan" for a whole network of allied groups spread over the major secular colleges and universities of the State of California.

NOCTURNAL PERPETUAL ADORATION SOCIETY

In the first sermon preached by a Roman Catholic since the Reformation, in Oxford's Church of Saint Mary the Virgin, Gordon Wheeler said:

> The call to holiness is specially underlined by Vatican II. And it would be a terrible impoverishment of the Church's life if mere activism took its place. . . . What we are and what we do interact on one another. Personal renewal is the key to the right kind of reform. And this postulates prayer.

Surely it is appropriate, while experimenting with new methods of popularizing Catholic devotional life, that perpetual adoration of the Blessed Sacrament would continue as a climactic part of that intricate pattern of prayer woven around the Mass and the Church's other liturgical and paraliturgical practices.

For over thirty years, the members of the Nocturnal Perpetual Adoration Society have spent thousands man–hours annually kneeling "in the subdued light of an alcove chapel, where most of the radiance comes from flickering tapers guarding a sacramental presence." The old Plaza Church of *Nuestra Señora de los Angeles* has been the scene of special eucharistic devotion since

April 1, 1921, when a group of ladies organized the *Vela Perpetua,* to keep a guard of honor before the tabernacle through the daylight hours.

The *noche feliz*, or nocturnal adoration, inaugurated on the third Saturday of each month, was subsequently launched by a dedicated corps of Mexican American parishioners in the downtown area. On May 13, 1932, the Pious Sodality was recognized as an autonomous affiliate of Rome's Convent of the Perpetual Adoration. On October 27, 1938, the late Joseph Scott gathered a group of men at the Plaza Church to discuss the possibility of extending the practice of daytime adoration around the clock. Preparations were made for appointment of thirty–one captains, each responsible one evening each month for seeing that every hour is supplied with a sufficient number of adorers.

The inauguration of nocturnal adoration took place in 1939, following a colorful procession through the streets of Los Angeles. Saint Basil's Holy Name Society had the privilege of keeping the first night watches, with two men on duty hourly from 10 o'clock until 5 in the morning. Timidly begun by a few simple but faithful people, the practice prospered under the spiritual tutelage of Father Victor Marin, C.M.F. The adoration has continued, uninterrupted, in succeeding years. Even during the period of church reconstruction, the watch was maintained at temporary quarters, 755 North Hill Street.

Joseph Scott, the founder and first president of the Nocturnal Adoration Society, considered that work "one of the most consoling of my humble activities," noting how edifying it was to see the variety of ages, races, occupations, and social strata united faithfully in devoting an hour each month in adoring Our Blessed Lord. Indeed, the membership represents a cross section of the southland's manhood. Doctors, lawyers, merchants, mechanics, laborers and priests bring to the little chapel every sort of local community, each "united in one objective, to stimulate devotion to our Eucharistic Lord in the Sacrament of His love."

Members of the Nocturnal Adoration Society still gather at the historic *Iglesia de Nuestra Señora de los Angeles*, one of California's truly cherished religious shrines, to recite the appointed prayers with uplifted voices. There, secluded before the Blessed Sacrament, they perpetuate a public cult that stretches back to the 13th century. That spiritual work, performed during the dark and lonely hours of the night, is a Catholic "first" along the Pacific Slope. Perpetual Adoration, the first and highest privilege of the angelic choirs, certainly carries with it a special assurance of heavenly favor in Los Angeles, where it thrives under the patronage of Our Lady of the Angels.

NOMENCLATURE IN CATHOLIC CALIFORNIA

William Hazlitt, the English critic and essayist, once likened "a name fast anchored in the deep abyss of time" to "a star twinkling in the firmament, cold, silent, distant, but eternal and sublime." The preservation of the place—names from the days of early Spanish occupation has always been a matter of state pride to Californians.

The joy of the tourists "in the stately names which distinguish California from the Smithville States" was a human and laudable reaction, according to Charles F. Lummis, and one that should be shielded against the "simple carelessness" of those unaware of what those appellations signify. That the Golden State's rich and diversified nomenclature perdures is no accident of history. As early as 1905, the legislature directed that "as far as possible, the old Spanish names, where given to cities, towns and villages in this state, should be preserved in their original forms." Around many of the early California names hovers "an atmosphere of consecration, the aroma of ancient and romantic associations, the poetry of a pastoral age such as no other state in the union and no other country of the world ever had."

That nomenclature is especially cherished by Catholics diffusing as it does "a delightful aroma of piety" over the vast expanses of the noble California commonwealth. A journalist once suggested that the constant recurrence of this sacerdotal terminology "gives California an air of belonging to the patrimony of St. Peter." He further observes that "Holy Mother Church stands well in this notable land of gold and the vine. It was Catholics—the noble and ingenious Franciscan monks—who taught Californians what was in their soil, and created the conditions which render life so delicious here today. It is a land worth striving for to a verity."

Even with the passage of two centuries, dictionaries abound in the richly significant place–names which the missionaries scattered with a zealous prodigality over the area. One authority boldly asserts that there are "more saint names—more 'Sans' and 'Santas'—on the map of California than on the map of any similar–sized area of the world." Those names, harkening back to the beginnings of unique movement in history, allow something of the charm, challenge and sacrifice of the pastoral age to linger in the smog–cluttered atmosphere of modern times.

The reverence which an area should bear for its place–names was spelled out by Robert Louis Stevenson:

> None can care for literature in itself who does not take a special pleasure in the sound of names; and there is no part of the world where nomenclature is so rich, poetical, humorous and picturesque as the United States of America. There are few poems with a nobler music for the ear, a songful, tuneful land; and if the new Homer shall arise from the Western continent, his verse will be enriched, his pages sung spontaneously, with the names of states and cities that would strike the fancy in the business circular.

NORMANBY HOARD

One of the more unusual historical attractions on exhibit in the Historical Museum of the Archival Center is a set of five coins dating from the last days of the Roman empire. They were part of a long–hidden treasure unearthed in December of 1985 in the farmland of Normanby, twelve miles north of Lincoln, by Thomas Cook, who was sweeping the area with a metal detector.

Cook discovered the "Normanby Hoard" buried not more than three feet beneath the surface in a huge earthenware jar. A Roman pot of ancient design, it is still in perfect condition, protected and strengthened through the years by layers of soil. The ancient Roman coins were untouched and intact. When brought to the surface, they were exposed to light for the first time in seventeen hundred years!

Historians conjecture that the Hoard was buried around the year 293 A.D., a time when Rome was in great turmoil. The provinces were under seige, and the empire struggling with breakaway rebels. Normandy was especially vulnerable to attack by the Saxons. The coins were probably hidden underground from the invading forces in a spot where they would be undisturbed for centuries.

Shortly after its discovery, the Hoard was shipped to the British Museum in London for authentication. In a long and arduous process that stretched over many months, each coin was carefully inspected, cleaned and catalogued.

Close examination confirmed the significance of the coins from not only an historical point of view, but a numismatic one as well. The Hoard contained pieces previously unrecorded. The coins also revealed important information about Roman mintage and the sequence of minting in ancient times. The British Museum was so intrigued with the contents of the Hoard that they retained many specimens for their own collection. A book was subsequently published on *The Normanby Hoard and other Roman Coin Hoards*.

The five coins at the Historical Museum are different denominations, each dating from 260 A.D., to 274 A.D. and each bearing a portait of the emperor in power at the time of mintage. There is Gallienus (260–268 A.D.), an emperor to whom historians have ascribed every imaginable vice; Claudius II (268–270 A.D.), a valiant warrior who died tragically at the height of his power; Victorinus (269–271 A.D.), whose reign was marked by great victories on the battlefield; Tetricus I (274–277 A.D.), a simple, good and honest man of peace who abdicated and died peacefully at a very advanced age and Tetricus II (271–274 A.D.), a handsome, popular and intellectual leader who became a respected senator in his later years.

Each of the emperors led his life in a different and exciting way. One waged war, another wanted peace; one sought knowledge, another revelled in pleasure; one died on the battlefield and another succumbed in bed.

Each of the coins is incapsulated for protection. The set is attractively boxed in an attractive cherry–wood case. They carry with them a document of authentication signed by an official of the British Museum.

NOVUM PSALTERIUM PII XII

Prior to entering religious life as a lay brother at Oakland's Dominican House of Studies, William Everson enjoyed an enviable reputation for his writings, especially those he personally set in print at The Equinox Press. In 1951, shortly after his profession in the Order of Preachers, Brother Antoninus, as he was subsequently known, embarked on the ambitious task of providing the first fundamental printing of the newly translated Roman psalter promulgated by Pope Pius XII.

Though the initial phases of the contemplated six–year project at Saint Albert's Press progressed rapidly enough, serious complications were not long in arising. Extreme temperature variations in his working quarters, difficulties in dampening the paper and lack of uniformity between the meagre quantities of paper he was able to purchase at any one time eventually forced Brother Antoninus to conclude that his "vision of a great book" was an impractical task for "an obscure hand-pressman in a new monastery on the periphery of Christendom." When he reluctantly discontinued work in 1954, at the conclusion of Psalm 53, thirty–six of the envisioned 300 leaves had been completed.

Inasmuch as a number of advance subscriptions had been accepted, Brother Antoninus inquired about the possibility of releasing the unfinished work under the imprint of Dawson's Book Shop. Glen and Muir Dawson purchased the leaves, but shortly thereafter acceded to an offer from Carrie Estelle Doheny who wanted to personally sponsor completion of the fragment and its distribution to select collectors and centers of learning.

Composition of a title page, introduction and colophon was entrusted to Saul and Lillian Marks who agreed to print the necessary additional pages on hand–made English Tovil paper identical to that used in the earlier runs. A Foreword by Robert 0. Schad and "A Note on the Psalter of Pope Pius XII" by Brother Antoninus along with other preliminary matter was set in matching eighteen point Frederic Goudy Newstyle and printed at the Plantin Press in Los Angeles.

The books were bound by the Chicago firm of R. R. Donnelly & Sons in full blue morocco with five raised bands. On the front cover was embossed a large Latin cross above the words: *Novum Psalterium PII XII*: Inside the cover was placed the oval bookplate of Estelle Doheny. Each of the books was fitted with a felt–lined, light–blue slipcase.

Nineteen of the forty–eight copies of the stately and handsome edition were numbered and inscribed with the name of the recipient. The remaining volumes were distributed to various educational institutions after Mrs. Doheny's death, in 1958.

From the quantity of extra and rejected leaves subsequently given to Muir Dawson, an additional twenty copies of the *Novum Psalterium PII XII* were assembled, each containing twelve pages of the psalter. Together with the introduction, printed on machine–made paper, this unfinished folio edition was bound at London by Sangorski and Sutcliffe in full buckram over beveled boards. There are five other sets of overruns and strays, each with a different number of non–consecutive leaves, which were gathered and enclosed in slip cases from unused portions in the possession of Saul and Lillian Marks.

The *Novum Psalterium PII XII*, a classic example of beauty, devotion and craftsmanship, is an outstanding achievement in the history of Western printing which surely "will long stand in the foremost ranks of California press books."

NUESTRA SENORA DE GUADALUPE

Seven peninsular missions and three in Alta California were dedicated to the Blessed Virgin under one or another of the various titles of her heavenly patronage. Paramount among Marian devotions in Mexico, since 1531, has been that honoring Our Lady of Guadalupe, the unofficially–proclaimed "patroness" since the days of Cortés.

Devotion to *Nuestra Señora de Guadalupe* has long been a hall mark of Catholicism along the Pacific Slope. Indeed, the first church in all of California was dedicated to her, in 1683. Father Eusebio Kino stated in his diary:

> On Monday we began to build a small church and a little fort or *Real de Nuestra Señora de Guadalupe*, and from this day we began to sleep and live on the land. (April 5, 1683).

One of the most cherished depictions of Our Lady of

Guadalupe is that prominently displayed in the parish church of Guadalupe, small town in the northwestern corner of Santa Barbara County. The colorful painting was commissioned by a relative of Bishop Francisco Garcia Diego, shortly after the friar's episcopal ordination, in the National Basilica of *Nuestra Señora de Guadalupe*, in Mexico City. It bears the inscription:

> A devoción de Doña Maria Antonia Moreno, para el Obispado California. Lagos, Año 1841, Mariano Borja fecit. .

Upon the arrival of California's proto–bishop in his newly created diocese, the handsomely framed portrayal of *La Virgen* was entrusted to the Church at Mission Santa Ines.

In the fall of 1875, when Father John B. McNally erected a frame church under the patronage of Our Lady, on the one–time *Rancho Guadalupe*, in Santa Maria Valley, the historic depiction of the virgin was enshrined above the main altar. The painting hung there for over eighty years, until the erection, in 1959, of the present stucco church. During 1940, the centennial year for the establishment of the hierarchy in California, the painting was publicly displayed at Saint John's Seminary, for ceremonies sponsored by the Holy Name Society.

Today, in the small community bearing her name, the cherished depiction of Our Lady of Guadalupe is still venerated by Marian clients. It presently occupies the place of prominence in a special shrine of the parochial church. The painting, executed by Mariano Borja, represents the virgin standing with the right foot on a crescent moon, supported by a cherub with outstretched wings, and hands clasped upon her breast. A rose–colored tunic, richly embroidered with gold covers her form, and a girdle of velvet surrounds her waist. The mantle, decorated with stars, partially covers the head, on which rests a ten–pointed crown.

Devotion to Our Lady of Guadalupe in California, especially in the picturesque "Valley of the Gardens," recalls or perhaps foreshadows the statement of Vatican Council II that true devotion to Mary consists neither "in sterile or transitory affection, nor in a certain credulity, but proceeds from true faith, which teaches the excellence of the Mother of God, and by which we are moved to a filial love toward our mother and to the imitation of her virtues."

OCEAN MAIL SERVICE

One of the major problems facing the Church in California during the early years of the 1850s was the slow and often undependable mail service between the "states" and the Pacific Coast. The Pacific Mail S.S. Company had the government mail contract and operated a shuttle line of mail steamers between San Francisco and Panama. As a general rule, all correspondence sent through San Francisco went by the regular steamers via Panama over that line. A similar line of shuttle mail steamers operated on the Atlantic from New York to Aspinwall, connecting with the mail brought east across the Isthmus.

For a short period of time, the postmaster at San Francisco, in order to accommodate the public more efficiently, authorized the sending of mail by the "Laws Opposition Line of Steamers," a line connecting with the Pacific Mail. Letters sent in that manner simply had to be marked with the name of Laws Steamers. This irregular practice was stopped by order of the Postmaster General and correspondence by Laws is now quite rare among collectors.

The Ocean Mail service was practically the only link the gold miners and other pioneers had with relatives and friends in the "states." The arrival and departure of the mail steamers was always a time of prime importance. Most business activity was regulated in accordance with "Steamer Day." The arrival of the mail steamers was also important for local residents anxious for news contained in the eastern newspapers.

There were complaints, of course, about the infrequency of service. Initially, the sailings were monthly on the 15th—then bimonthly and finally trimonthly. And many people strongly disliked the notion that the mail was a gigantic monopoly.

The Post Office Department experimented with other contract routes. One of the earliest was from New Orleans to Vera Cruz, then to Acapulco, there to connect with the Pacific Mail Steamers for San Francisco. That service boosted delivery at San Francisco to four times a month. Another interesting contract route was established over the Isthmus of Tehuantepec in Mexico. It was a convenient route but the lack of popular support eventually brought about its abandonment.

The mail steamers were the sole means by which the argonauts could maintain their communicational link with the "states." For this service they gladly paid handsomely in gold and services.

Correspondence between the "premier" episcopal seat of Baltimore and the bishopric at Monterey was almost non– existent in the 1850s, at least if one were to judge by surviving letters. During the earliest years of his tenure, Bishop Joseph Sadoc Alemany managed his vast jurisdiction with little if any assistance from the "states."

Yet what scanty communications there might have been with the American hierarchy most assuredly had to come by the Ocean Mail Service.

OLIVAS ADOBE

In May of 1841, Raimundo Olivas and Felipe Lorenzana applied to the Mexican Government for a grant of land near the mouth of the Santa Clara River, in present–day Ventura County. Because of their faithful service in the army, the petition was favorably granted and the two received a parcel of land "one and one half square leagues" which they named in honor of San Miguel.

Raimundo (1809–1879), a native of *El Pueblo de Nuestra Señora de los Angeles,* had married Teodora Lopez in 1832. During the forty–seven years of their marriage, twenty–two children were born. Lorenzana married Maria de la Navidad Ruiz at San Fernando Mission in 1821.

A condition of the grant was the proviso that a house be erected on the *rancho.* Olivas had already built a small one room adobe there in 1837. Later incorporated into the larger complex, the original adobe still stands.

Olivas was able to satisfy the other requirements of planting grain, fruit trees and grapevines by acquiring seeds from the friars and administrators of nearby San Buenaventura Mission. A diligent worker, Olivas prospered from the sale of tanned hides and tallow rendered from the fat of cattle. During the gold rush, he drove herds north to meet the needs of the miners.

In 1847, the two story adobe was begun to accommodate the growing Olivas family. It was patterned after the Monterey–style adobes popular in the northern areas of Alta California.

According to an article in the Los Angeles *Star* for May 9, 1859, there was a spectacular robbery at the Olivas adobe during which a group of *banditos* took upwards of $30,000 in gold. The man believed to be the culprit was captured and hanged by a posse of vigilantes.

The title of *El Rancho de San Miguel* was confirmed by the United States Land Commission in 1853. By that time the *rancho* had been divided, with Olivas taking the area on which the adobe was located. Another newspaper reported that in 1879, the *rancho* encompassed 2,500 acres, with about half of it under cultivation. The rest was used for grazing horses, sheep and cattle.

The Olivas family set aside the largest room in their adobe as a chapel and fairly often a priest from San Buenaventura Mission would come to offer Holy Mass. At other times, Don Raimundo would gather his family in the chapel for private devotions.

A visitor to the adobe in the 1870s later wrote that there were forty–three members of the Olivas family residing there. The practice of having a so–called "extended family" living together was a common practice in Provincial California. Raimundo's youngest daughter was the last family member to own *El Rancho de San Miguel.* After the turn of the century, Julius Alford made some major alterations in the adobe.

In 1927, Max Fleishmann bought the adobe and during his years of ownership used the house in conjunction with a duck reserve where he and his friends hunted until the 1950s

The City of San Buenaventura acquired the adobe in 1963 and, with funds from the Fleishmann Foundation, restored the building and acquired period furnishings, some of them originally associated with the Olivas family.

Today, the Olivas Adobe, surrounded by colorful gardens and plants, is among the state's more attractive and authentic early adobe buildings. Open to the public, it is maintained and operated by the Recreation Department, City of San Buenaventura.

ORANGE — THE DIOCESE

The Origins of the Diocese of Orange, the tenth ecclesial district formed for the State of California, can be traced to March 11, 1889, when the presently–designated county was established from the loosely–knit cluster of *ranchos* then comprising the southeastern part of Los Angeles County. Though it is generally assumed that the county's name was chosen to accentuate the citrus industry, there is a greater likelihood that the appellation was imported by Andrew Glasswell, a native of a Virginia county named to honor the son–in–law of George II.

The area is rich in Indian–Spanish traditions. There are 160,168 people in the county with Hispanic surnames and 108,167 of them, or roughly 13% of the total population, speak Spanish as their mother tongue. Probably no other of the nation's 3,049 counties can match the temperate climate, geographical attractions and scope of religious, educational and recreational facilities adorning the 782 square mile area known as Orange County. It is bounded geographically by the counties of Los Angeles, San Bernardino, Riverside, San Diego and forty–two miles of Pacific coastline.

The county seat is located at Santa Ana, which is thirty–one road miles southeast of Los Angeles. Of the twenty–six incorporated cities in the county, Anaheim has the largest population (185,105), followed by Santa Ana (168,205). The figures for 1976 place the count for the City of Orange at 82,795.

Orange County has been one of the nation's most spectacular growth areas. During the 1960s, its advance in population exceeded that recorded in forty–one of the United States. There were 1,605,700 recorded inhabitants in the county.

Orange has evolved from an abundantly–rich agricultural region into a progressive, industrially–oriented metropolitan area. Inasmuch as three–fourths of the county's 500,480 acres are subject to urbanization, there is every reason to believe that Orange is destined to be an even more dominant force in the industrial and financial life of California. Indeed, its average rainfall (15 inches), rate of sunshine (from 60 to 80% of the year) and mean temperature (from 48 to 76 degrees) all portend a future of unlimited proportions, to say nothing of the recreational facilities and potentials.

Catholic penetration, on a permanent basis, can be traced to All Saints Day, in the year of American Independence, when Fray Junípero Serra founded the seventh of California's missions at San Juan Capistrano.

In 1860, Bernardo Yorba built the chapel of *San Antonio de Santa Ana* on his extensive lands. Priests from San Gabriel attended the distant outpost in the years immediately following. When Saint Boniface Parish was created at Anaheim in 1889, its boundaries were co–extensive with those of the newly–formed county.

Regular mission stations were cared for at Santa Ana (Saint Joseph's) and Yorba (San Antonio). That year also saw the inauguration of Catholic education, with the establishment of Saint Catherine's Academy at Anaheim.

The Church's facilites in the county have been considerably expanded in recent years. In 1975 there were forty–three parishes and eight mission stations serving a Catholic population of 333,860.

Six high schools and thirty–five elementary schools enrolled 17,768 youngsters. The People of God in the Diocese of Orange were served by 108 diocesan priests, fifty–seven religious and 484 Sisters, with sixty–six candidates studying for the ministry.

ORDEN DE ISABELLA CATOLICA

During one of the oral interviews conducted with the late James Francis Cardinal–McIntyre in 1970, the then retired Archbishop of Los Angeles was asked, "which of his many honors stood out as the most significant?" After acknowledging that such distinctions matter little in eternal life, the cardinal responded: "I have always appreciated the Grand Cross of Isabella the Catholic because it symbolizes my love for peoples of Hispanic heritage."

The Order of Isabella the Catholic was established by Ferdinand VII, King of Spain, to honor the memory of the Queen of Castile and wife of Ferdinand of Aragon whose financial support made it possible for Christopher Columbus to launch the voyage leading to the discovery of America.

Ferdinand's decree of March 24, 1815 was enthusiastically endorsed by Pope Pius VII the following year.

Initially awarded for services rendered on behalf of the Spanish–American colonies, it is now granted for distinguished diplomatic, civil and military merit.

Having its own fascinating history, the Order has undergone various reforms. Abolished in 1873 by the first Spanish Republic, it was reestablished upon the restoration of the monarchy. After failing into desuetude again, it was returned to its primitive splendor in 1938, when Caudillo Francisco Franco made it into Spain's highest ranking Order of Merit.

Queen Isabella (1451–1504), for whom the Order was named, was a native of Madrigal. Devoted to the religious and political unity of Spain, she ushered in the "modern phase" of her nation's history. Isabella became Queen of Castille after the death of her brother, Henry IV. And it was she who united Castille with Aragon with her marriage to Ferdinand in 1469.

Together, the *reyes Catolicos* suppressed civil war and banditry, reformed the judiciary, encouraged sheep-breeding and trade, organized a regular army, re–conquered Granada and strengthened the Church through the nomination of worthy bishops. Oh yes, she also established the Inquisition which, unhappily, betrayed her trust in later years.

Her Majesty was also active in founding universities and reviving the traditions of learning. A pious woman of proven virtue, her cause for beatification was introduced at the behest of the Spanish hierarchy.

The first recipients of the Order of Isabella the Catholic in the New World were Viceroy Francisco Javier Venegas and General Nemesio Salcedo, both of whom pledged "to live and die in our sacred, apostolic and Roman religion and to defend the mystery of the Immaculate Conception of the Virgin Mary."

In modern times, the Grand Cross of the Order of Isabella the Catholic was conferred on Charles Fletcher Lummis by Alfonso XIII. The king also bestowed the honor on California's Poet Laureate, John Steven McGroarty, in 1930. The insignia of the Order, a gold medal bearing an engraved portrayal of the ship *Santa Maria*, was presented by Dr. Gregorio del Amo. At that time, according to an article in the Los Angeles *Times*, "the highest of the five decorations conferred by the Spanish monarchy is said to be possessed by only six men in the world." Among the other distinguished Californians honored with this award in subsequent years were Herbert Eugene Bolton, Maynard Geiger, Harry Kelsey and James Francis Cardinal McIntyre.

McIntyre's Grand Cross, bestowed in 1968 by the Spanish Ambassador Marquis Merry del Val (nephew of the famous Rafael Cardinal Merry del Val), was given "in recognition of his humanitarian and religious service" to Hispanic peoples in the New World.

THE *ORIZABA*

On practically all his many visitations to California's southland, San Francisco's Archbishop Joseph Sadoc Alemany travelled on the historic coastwise vessel, the *Orizaba*. The ship was originally built for service between New York and Vera Cruz. Launched in 1854, it was brought to California two years later and for the rest of its service plowed the waters of the blue Pacific.

Between 1856 and 1864, the *Orizaba* operated between San Francisco and Nicaragua and Panama as the flagship of the Pacific Mail Steamship Company. Its list of passengers on those trips is impressive indeed.

The *Orizaba* was a steamer of 1,334 tons. Measuring 246 feet in length, it could accommodate seventy–five cabin and 200 steerage passengers, as well as 600 tons of cargo. It was one of the larger vessels in the coastwise trade prior to 1880. In 1867, Holladay & Brenham purchased the ship and five years later it was sold back to the Pacific Mail Steamship Company. In 1875, it was acquired by Goodall, Nelson & Perkins, a firm later known as the Steamship Company.

The *Orizaba* sailed under the Maltese Cross house flag until her retirement from service in 1886. By then, the thirty–two year old ship was the last of the side wheelers in coastwise service. At that time, the *Orizaba* was far outclassed by such iron, propeller–driven steamers as the *Queen of the Pacific* and the *Santa Rosa*. In 1881, the historic old vessel was sent to a shipbreaker.

During the years that Archbishop Alemany sailed aboard the *Orizaba*, there were fifteen steamers and two sailing vessels in operation by the Goodall, Nelson & Perkins firm. Together with her sister–ships, the *Ancon* and the *Senator*, the *Orizaba* maintained an express service from San Francisco to Port Harford (now San Luis Obispo), Santa Barbara, San Buenaventura, Santa Monica, San Pedro, Anaheim Landing and San Diego.

Though the company published a schedule stating days and hours of arrival and departure there was always the annexed warning that "hours of sailing are not entirely reliable; steamers liable to be later, not earlier." Coastal traffic was fairly commonplace. In 1875, for example, nearly 12,000 passengers landed at San Pedro and over 8,000 departed. Some 85,000 tons of cargo was unloaded there in that year. The coastwise carriers had no real competition prior to 1876, when the Southern Pacific opened its line to Los Angeles via Tehachapi. And it was only in 1904 that the railroad's Coast Line was completed.

An oil painting of the *Orizaba* was executed by Joseph Lee of San Francisco. It was destroyed in the fire of 1906, but a photographic copy is still on file at the San Francisco Marine Museum.

OUR LADY OF GUADALUPE

Traditionally, paintings of Our Lady have been the most treasured depictions in the Christian world. The Madonnas of the Renaissance, those of Raphael, Michelangelo and Murillo, are internationally famous for their beauty and artistic style. Yet there is one likeness of Mary that surpasses them all, for it was presented by the Mother of God herself to a humble Indian neophyte, on an insignificant little hill, near far–away Mexico City, over 400 years ago. The story of Our Lady of Guadalupe, proclaimed the "Empress of the Americas" by Pope Pius XII, is most fascinating and inspiring.

On Sunday, December 9, 1531, Juan Diego, a fifty–five year old Indian, was rushing down Tepeyac Hill to Mass when suddenly there burst forth a beautiful song, as if thousands of birds were singing. For an instant it ceased and the mountains echoed a response. Looking up to the crest of the hill, he saw a white shining cloud from which a multi–colored rainbow projected rays of dazzling light. Then it was very quiet and Juan Diego heard a woman's voice coming from the cloud saying,

> Know, my son, my little one, that I am the ever Virgin, Holy Mary, Mother of the true God, who is the Author of Life, the Creator of all things, the Lord of heaven and earth, present everywhere. It is my wish that a church be erected to me in this place. Here I will show myself as a loving Mother to you and to all those born in these lands, and to all those who love me and trust me, for I am your loving Mother. Go to the palace of the Bishop and tell him what you have heard and seen.

Bishop Zumarraga was understandably incredulous. He questioned the Indian extensively and then told him to ask for a sign that it really was the Blessed Mother whom he had seen. On December 12, Our Lady appeared again and Juan Diego asked for the sign. She directed him to climb up the hill and gather an armful of roses. In spite of the winter weather and the barrenness of the soil, he found, at the summit, fragrant Castilian roses covered with dew. He brought them to Our Lady who arranged them in his *tilma* or cloak.

Then she instructed him to return to the bishop as her ambassador and to tell him again that she wanted a church erected there. Juan related what Our Lady had told him and then, unfolding his *tilma*, the roses spilled out. The bishop's eyes were fixed on the *tilma*, whereon was now imprinted a life–size image of Holy Mary of Guadalupe. The picture was venerated and guarded in the bishop's chapel and soon thereafter was taken back to Tepeyac and given a place of honor in the temple erected to honor Our Lady of Guadalupe.

The coarsely–woven material bearing the picture is as thin and open as poor sacking. It is made of vegetable fibre and consists of two strips, about seventy inches long and eighteen wide, held together by weak stitching.

The miraculous depiction of Our Lady can presently be seen, encased in a golden glass–covered frame, atop the main altar in Mexico City's National Basilica of Our Lady of Guadalupe. That ancient shrine, begun in 1709, is a pilgrimage center for all of Mexico and much of Central and South America. Before that precious image, the first Bishop of Both Californias, Fray Francisco Garcia Diego y Moreno, was ordained to the episcopacy, on October 4, 1840.

In a radio message beamed to the Western Hemisphere in 1945 Pope Pius XII said:

> On the *tilma* of poor Juan Diego was painted with brushes not of this world a most sweet Picture, which the corrosive work of centuries was most wondrously to respect. The amiable Maiden asked for a Sign from which she might show and give all her love and compassion, help and protection . . . to all the inhabitants of that land and to all others who would invoke her and trust her. Since that historical moment, the total evangelization has been accomplished. Furthermore, a banner was hoisted and a fortress erected against which the fury of all the storms would break. One of the fundamental pillars of the Faith in Mexico and in all America was thus firmly established.

The residents of the Californias, whose privilege it was to have their first church placed under the protection of *Nuestra Señora de Guadalupe*, in 1683, pay homage to Our Lady on her annual feastday, December 12th.

OVERLAND MONTHLY

Foremost among the bibilophilic treasures in the library of the Archival Center at Mission Hills is a complete set of the *Overland Monthly*, one of the few extant sets bound in the original publisher's cloth. The magazine was founded in July of 1868 by Bret Harte, the most famous short story writer of the early west, and Anton Roman, then the leading publisher on the Pacific Slope.

Associated in the editorial work of the magazine in the early years were such notable writers as Charles Warren Stoddard, Ina Coolbrith, Joaquin Miller, Jack London and Samuel Clemens (Mark Twain).

During the following quarter century, the *Overland Monthly* mirrored the thrilling romance of the west. It was the first publication to reflect the area's distinct literary culture. Most critics agree that with the founding of the *Overland Monthly* coincided the beginning of the artistic and literary life of Western America.

Publication of the *Overland Monthly* created a sensation throughout the world. Its monthly installments were anticipated with feverish anxiety in the east, where people yearned to learn about the picturesque romance of the new frontier. Mark Twain's monthly contributions to the *Overland Monthly* revealed an understanding of human nature that brought him recognition as the century's greatest humorist and its gentlest, kindliest and noblest delineator of character.

Today the *Overland Monthly* is regarded as much a part of the west as the lofty snow–capped Sierras. Behind the *Overland Monthly* lies the tradition and the spirit of California magic. The journal encompassed in its pages the romance of the past, the prosperity of the present and the amazing promise of the future—all portrayed in fact and fiction.

The provenance of the forty–three volumes at Mission Hills can be traced back to June of 1931, when Ernest Dawson offered the set to Carrie Estelle Doheny. It was, to the best of his recollection, "the first entirely complete run" which he had ever handled. In a note tipped into the initial volume, Dawson traced the history of the journal, noting that the "first series" was issued between 1868 and 1875, under the editorship of Bret Hart. From 1880 to 1881, it appeared as *The Californian*.

Then, in 1883, its name reverted to the *Overland Monthly*. Appearing for another twenty–two volumes until 1893, the journal reached "the highest point of literary excellence." Dawson noted that the many poems, articles and stories appeared in the *Overland Monthly* "for the first time in print."

The Los Angeles bookseller told Mrs. Doheny that it was safe "to say that no magazine was ever published in the west containing so much of real literary excellence as was contained in this set. To locate it all complete and in the original publisher's cloth, and in fine condition, will always be difficult.

According to a small, rectangular bookplate in certain of the volumes, the set of the *Overland Monthly* now at the Archival Center belonged to Ira P. Rankin prior to its purchase by Dawson. Dawson's cost of the set was $300. Guesstimates of its present value soar into the thousands.

The *Overland Monthly* was the premier magazine in its time and one of the few that made any valid pretensions to literary merit. It was rightly advertised as "the grandest magazine in its field in the world."

PALACE OF LIVING ART

It is no longer necessary for California residents to visit the great museums of Europe in order to appreciate the fine masterpieces of religious and secular history. Orange County's "Palace of Living Art" recreates, in third dimension, many of the world's most famous artistic creations. Visitors can virtually look over the shoulders of artists, to see the models who posed for the original works.

Located adjacent to the Movieland Wax Museum, in Buena Park, the "palace" is the realization of a dream by Allen Parkinson whereby people can vicariously experience the thrill of seeing truly outstanding art. Among the more notable of the religious works exhibited at the Palace of Living Art is a startling realistic wax reproduction of "The Crucifixion." A taped commentary of the words of Jesus further dramatizes this supreme moment in the history of humankind.

The sculpture work in the half acre of displays is magnificent. Michelangelo's "David" is carved from a single piece of marble, as was the original. Towering eighteen feet high and weighing ten tons, it took two years to complete. And Michelangelo's "Captive" is also reproduced from the original at the Louvre. It was one of the figures initially intended to adorn the tomb of Pope Julius II.

A copy in marble of the same artist's "Moses" is on display. Finished in 1545, it was also commissioned by Pope Julius for his tomb in Saint Peter's Basilica. Probably the most outstanding replica is, "The Pieta," which was copied to the greatest detail from the one in Rome. Exact in all proportions, it too was carved from white Carrara marble and weighs nearly eight tons.

El Greco's masterful portrayal of Cardinal de Guevera is especially captivating. The aged prelate's fingers, distorted by an advanced case of arthritis, are expertly reproduced. Philippe de Champaigne's famous figure of Cardinal Richelieu also occupies a place of honor in the gallery.

The ceiling of the Foyer is graced by a copy of a mural painted in Rome's famous Gesu Church by Andrew Pozzo. Designed to be viewed from a point in the center of the nave, the mural creates the illusion of a palace opening onto a sky filled with angelic figures hovering in imaginary space. Leonardo de Vinci's "The Last Supper" is reproduced on an entire wall. The slanting lines formed by the pattern of the ceiling and walls draw the viewer's eyes toward the figure of Christ, which is silhouetted by the light from a window in the background.

Among the dozens of other statues, busts and bas reliefs depicting great religious painting and sculpture are a tablet of "Saint George Fighting the Dragon," a seven foot Carrara statue of the Sacred Heart of Jesus, a copy of Heinrich Hoffman's "Christ in the Garden" and a replica of Guido Reni's "Salome Receiving the Head of John the Baptist."

PAPAL CHALICE

The chalice used by the Holy Father during the Eucharistic Liturgy at Dodgers Stadium has a long and historical association with the Church in Southern California. Fashioned by one of Europe's most outstanding silversmiths, it was presented to Archbishop John J. Cantwell by Pope Pius XII in 1940, to commemorate the hundredth anniversary of the establishment of the hierarchy in California.

The artistic cup and its paten were brought to Los Angeles by the Apostolic Delegate to the Church in the United States, Archbishop Amleto Giovanni Cicognani. It was used for the first time locally at the Memorial Coliseum on Sunday, October 13, 1940, for a Mass attended by over a 100,000 people, including remaining members of the family of the Right Reverend Francisco Garcia Diego y Moreno, the Mexican–born first Bishop of Both Californias.

The inscription emblazoned on the chalice is in Latin:

Saeculo I Exeunte ab Eccla Hierarchia in California regione constituta Pius XII Pont. Max. Excmo. Viro Johanni J. Cantwell Angelorum Archiepiscopus benevolentis animi pignus D. D. V Kal. Maj. A MCMXXXX.

Translated into English, it reads:

On the occasion of the completion of the first hundred years of the ecclesial hierarchy in the State of California, Pope Pius XII, Supreme Pontiff, presents this chalice to the Most Distinguished John J. Cantwell, Archbishop of Los Angeles, as a loving tribute of a well–wishing soul, on this, the 27th of April, 1940.

Each of the eight scenes engraved on the cup and base of the chalice relate different phases in the life of Christ. Surrounding each of the portrayals are the following inscriptions:

Missus est angelus Gabriel a Deo
The angel Gabriel was sent from God
Venit Jesus cum illis in villam Gethsemani
Jesus came with them into the garden of Gethsemani
Natus est nobis hodie Salvator
There is born to us today a Savior
Baptizatus est a Johanne
He was baptized by John
Crucifixerunt eum
They crucified Him
Acceperunt ergo corpus Jesu
They then received the body of Jesus
Posuit illo in monumento suo
He placed him in his tomb
Cognoverunt Eum
They knew Him

Around the base of the chalice are inscribed the words: *Calicem salutaris accipiam et nomen Domini invocabo*: I will take the chalice of salvation and call upon the name of the Lord. Finally, surrounding the cup is the formula of consecration: *Haec est calix sanguinis mei*. This is the cup of my blood.

After the chalice was used at dedication ceremonies

for Saint John's Seminary, Camarillo, it was consigned to the care of that institution. In subsequent years, it has become something of a fixture, being used for numerous important and commemorative liturgical functions.

PATRON SAINTS OF CALIFORNIA

In the last several years, Raymond Wood and Norman Neuerburg have published superb studies about the patron saints of the California missions. Few people remember that, over a half century earlier, another writer has also become fascinated with that theme. And though her small booklets are now rare collectors' items, the works of Phebe Estelle Spalding are certainly worth being mentioned.

Born in 1859, Phebe's early life was spent teaching grammar school in New Hampshire and Vermont. In 1880, she accompanied her father, a Methodist clergyman, to the northern Dakota territory. Later, Phebe returned to the east, where she finished her education at Carleton College, a Congregationalist institution in Northfield, Minnesota. With her degree in Literature, Miss Spalding headed west.

In 1889, Phebe Estelle Spalding arrived at Claremont Hall in Pomona. There she taught and tutored, while working on her doctoral dissertation about William Shakespeare's histories. It was in those pioneering years at Pomona College that Phebe began work on her series about the Spanish name–saints of California. According to one authority, those studies were "essentially searches for the meaning of their claims to sanctity."

Phebe wrote that "California's saints are a more distinctive asset than her matchless climate with its flowers and fruits, her mines of gold and silver, or even her heroic and far–famed history. For her saints, by the mere mention of their names, connect us in art and literature and religion with centuries of old–world legend, and give that poetic glow to our prosaic present which is the soul of beauty and the spirit of life itself."

There appear to have been two series of the "Patron Saints of California." The Franciscan series includes essays about San Francisco, San Antonio de Padua and San Diego and Santiago. Another was entitled "The Virgin Series" and featured Santa Barbara and Santa Catalina. Both series, finally issued in print in 1934–1935, were published by the Saunders Studio Press at Claremont, California.

Phebe was not so much a chronicler or commentator as an interpreter. She also wrote a number of short stories. Those and other of her works indicate that Spalding was a proponent of equal education for the sexes, something quite revolutionary in those times.

We are told by a college historian that Phebe Estelle Spalding "was the guardian angel of the college's meager collection of books, whose nucleus, a gift apparently from Carleton College, she had brought with her to Claremont." Spalding acquired most of her knowledge of art through reading and European travel. Her early interest in religious paintings and architecture broadened to include a wide range of European and American art.

She was one of the founders of the Rembrandt Club in 1905 and remained a leader in that club's activities throughout her lifetime. Phebe lectured on art and invited others to address students and friends. Retiring from the classroom in 1927, Phebe Estelle Spalding died a decade later. Her writings on "Patron Saints of California" remain her chief literary contribution to Western American bookshelves.

PATRONAGE — RELIGIOUS IN CALIFORNIA

The earliest ecclesiastical patronage in California dates from January 4, 1843, when the first bishop, Francisco Garcia Diego y Moreno, placed his jurisdiction under the spiritual protection of Our Lady, Refuge of Sinners. When the diocese was divided in 1853, the metropolitan at San Francisco adopted another heavenly intercessor while the southland retained its earlier allegiance. On September 1, 1856, Pope Pius IX gave the Diocese of Monterey as its patroness Vibiana, a saint unearthed in the Roman catacombs a few years earlier. The term "Los Angeles" had been a part of the episcopal title since 1859, but that appellation , a shortened form of *Nuestra Señora de los Angeles*, has never figured in the religious patronage of Southern California.

It has been suggested that a transfer of patronage to Our Lady of the Angels would be highly appropriate for the Archdiocese of Los Angeles. Possibly the late Archbishop John J. Cantwell had that in mind when plans were drafted for a proposed cathedral by that name in the 1940s. That the present title has no connection with the archdiocesan patronage, however, is not without precedent in the United States where only four of the twenty–eight archdioceses identify title and patron.

Fray Juan Crespi recorded in his diary that late in the afternoon of July 31, 1769, the expeditionary force of Gaspar de Portola crossed an *arroyo* of muddy water and stopped a little further on in a wide clearing. He stated that the following day was set aside to celebrate the jubilee of Our Lady of the Angels *de Porciuncula*. The next morning on the vigil of the feast, the party continued its journey and came through a pass between two hills into a broad valley abounding in poplar and alden trees. A beautiful brook crossed the valley and later turned around a hill to the south. After traveling another twenty miles, the Spaniards camped along a river which they fittingly named in honor of *Nuestra Señora de los Angeles de Porciuncula*, title derived from the day's liturgical calendar.

According to Canon Law, the patron of a place is the saint honored as the special protector of that locale. In the case of Los Angeles, this distinction was accorded to Our Lady of the Angels when the name given to the *Rio Porciuncula* was extended in its alternate form to the *pueblo* founded in the fall of 1781.

Since the feast of Our Lady of the Angels of the Porciuncula was not observed in the universal liturgical schema, the patronage of Mary under that title could not be applied to the *pueblo* as a formal ecclesiastical patron except by privilege and even then only after consultation with the clergy and laity of the place. In this, as in other similar cases it has been the practice of the Holy See to bestow as the titular feastday, that of Mary's Assumption into heaven. Hence as early as 1814, Fray Luis Gil of San Gabriel spoke of laying the cornerstone of the church at Los Angeles on the 15th of August on which it, the *pueblo*, celebrates its titular feast.

Although canonical legislation pertaining to patrons of places applies less strictly to churches (the patron or title of a church is the person or mystery to which the edifice has been dedicated), it is also an established custom that churches dedicated to the Blessed Virgin Mary, without the addition of one of her liturgical titles should celebrate their patronal feast on the 15th of August. Thus it is that the city's oldest church, located on the *plaza*, also observes Assumption Day, not August 2nd, as its annual feast day.

To rephrase more succinctly what has been said, religious patronage in the Archdiocese of Los Angeles has no connection with that of the City of Our Lady of the Angels, which proudly salutes its patroness each year on the 15th of August under her original title, *Nuestra Señora de los Angeles.*

POLISH PRESENCE IN CALIFORNIA

The initial Polish imprint on Alta California can be traced to May 1, 1805, when Captain William Shaler's 175 ton *Lelia Byrd* put into a bay on Santa Catalina Island for repairs. Because the bay which served the weary seamen as an hospitable haven had not yet been designated with a name, Shaler, the proto navigator to visit and survey the area "took the liberty of naming it after my much respected friend, M. de Roussillon." The conferral of his Polish companion's name was the first such appellation applied in California by an American.

John, the Count of Roussillon (1772–1803), was a Polish nobleman of considerable prominence in his native land. An accomplished scholar in the fields of astronomy, mathematics and music, the count was conversant with almost every European language and dialect. Rouissillon had fought for the liberty of his country as an aide–de–camp to Tadeusz Kosciuszko

when that famed Polish general led a force of 4,000 peasants armed with only crude scythes and other farming implements, against the Russians at Raclawice.

Subsequently exiled in Hamburg to avoid reprisals from his nation's enemies, Roussillon met William Shaler and Richard Cleveland when the two New England merchant–adventurers arrived to purchase a vessel on which to visit the western shores of America. Reared on the continent, Roussillon had never been to sea. Yet such a challenge fascinated him and he readily accepted the offer to join Shaler and Cleveland on their epochal journey.

The *Lelia Byrd* sailed from Cuxhaven on November 8, 1801. After a brief stop at the Canary Islands, the ship reached Rio de Janerio early the next year. Rounding Cape Horn, Shaler, Cleveland, Rouissillon and their eight crewmen sailed into the harbor of Valparaiso on February 24th. There the entire crew was briefly imprisoned for infringing on the Spanish trade monopoly. The *Lelia Byrd* encountered further difficulties at San Blas, Mexico, where officials raised new objections to their docking. After personally appealing to the local governor and then to the viceroy himself, Roussillon finally secured permission to dispose of their wares and reprovision the ship. Then it was on to Alta California.

Though he remained behind in Mexico to acquaint himself with the seat of an ancient and vibrant culture, Roussillon fully intended to rejoin his friends in the United States, where he hoped to live out his years in an atmosphere of liberty. Those expectations were unfortunately thwarted by a premature death in 1803.

Richard Cleveland described the count as a strong "advocate of liberty" who "could not brook the subjugation of his country." He was likewise an outstanding Catholic whose knowledge of theology and practice of virtue further endowed his valiant personality. Although Port Roussillon does not survive in the Golden State's geographic nomenclature, present–day Avalon remains the scene of the first link in what has become a formidable Polish presence in California.

Though their numbers have never been large, the Poles have left a noble record in western American annals. One writer says that "here in the sunny land they found freedom and new homes, they found friends and a measure of prosperity. They repaid the young commonwealth with the best that was in them." This they surely did and today their numbers even include a member of the California hierarchy, the Most Reverend Thaddeus Shubsda, who served as Bishop of Monterey.

POPES AND CALIFORNIA

The influence of Peter's successors in California has been evident in many ways over the years since Christianity was first proclaimed in this area. The first of the popes to make his mark in California was Clement XIV (1769–1774). It was he who issued a special indult, on July 10, 1774, whereby Fray Junípero Serra was authorized to confer the Sacrament of Confirmation in the missionary foundations along *El Camino Real*.

The documentary evidence concerning episcopal jurisdiction in Alta California can be traced to Pope Pius VI (1775–1779) who created the Diocese of Sonora on May 7, 1779. Although the popes who governed the Church between 1800 and 1830 (Pius VII, Leo XII and Pius VIII) are not known to have personally dealt with the inhabitants of California, there is recorded evidence that their presence in Peter's Chair was known and acknowledged.

Pope Gregory XVI (1831–1846) created the Diocese of Both Californias on April 27, 1840 and appointed Fray Francisco Garcia Diego y Moreno to be the area's new bishop. On July 29, 1853, Pope Pius IX (1846–1878) created a Metropolitan Province for California, advancing the Right Reverend Joseph Sadoc Alemany to the Archbishopric of San Francisco and the Reverend Thaddeus Amat to the Bishopric of Monterey. Three years later, he named Vibiana patroness for the Church in Southern California.

Pope Leo XIII (1878–1903) further provided for God's people along the Pacific Slope by creating the Vicariate Apostolic of Marysville (1860), Diocese of Grass Valley (1868), Diocese of Sacramento (1886) and the Diocese of Salt Lake City (1891).

It was during the pontificate of Pius X (1903–1914) that Patrick Harnett, Rector of Saint Vibiana's Cathedral and Vicar General for the Diocese of Monterey–Los Angeles was created California's first monsignor. The first pontiff to send a special message to the inhabitants of California was Pope Benedict XV (1914–1922), who conveyed his greetings through Archbishop Edward J. Hanna.

Lay people were honored by Pope Pius XI (1922–1939) who bestowed the *Pro Ecclesia* medal on Mary Julia Workman and a papal knighthood on J. Wiseman Macdonald in 1924. He created the Diocese of Reno in 1931 and the Metropolitan Province of Los Angeles in 1936.

Cardinal Eugenio Pacelli, who became Pope Pius XII (1939–1958) was the first pontiff to have visited California. He blessed the San Francisco–Oakland Bay Bridge on October 28, 1936. In 1939, he conferred the first title of papal nobility in the area upon Carrie Estelle Doheny and, in 1952, he named the Archbishop of Los Angeles to the Sacred College of Cardinals.

The papal consistory at which Pope John XXIII (1958–1963) was elected to the Chair of Peter was the first in which a Californian, James Francis Cardinal McIntyre participated. In 1962, the Holy Father created dioceses at Oakland, Santa Rosa and Stockton. Pope Paul VI (1963–1978) also provided for growth development in the Golden State by creating dioceses at Fresno, Monterey and San Bernardino–Riverside.

POPE JOHN PAUL II

Karol Joseph Wojtyla, who visited Los Angeles as Pope John Paul II, was born on May 18, 1920, in the town of Wadowice, not far from Cracow, near the Czech border. His father was a junior officer in the Polish army and his mother a schoolteacher. The youngster was raised in an atmosphere of religious piety and strict discipline.

Karol's mother died giving birth to her third child. Three years later, his older brother succumbed to scarlet fever. The boy and his father moved to Cracow, so that the young man could study philosophy at the celebrated Jagellonian University. On September 1, 1939, while he was serving as an altar boy at Mass, German bombs began failing on Cracow. Although the Nazis closed the university, young Wojtyla and a few others secretly continued their studies. Karol worked full time in a stone quarry and later at a chemical company to support himself.

During hospitalization following a streetcar accident, Karol began to think for the first time about becoming a

Pope John Paul II

priest. A few months later, he narrowly escaped death when he was crushed by a truck. That same year, he was suddenly orphaned when his father died of a heart attack.

In 1942, Karol began secret preparatory studies for the priesthood, while continuing to be active in the banned Rhapsodic Theatre and UNIA, a Christian democratic underground organization. He helped save the lives of many Jews and others during the Nazi occupation.

Karol Wojtyla was ordained priest on November 1, 1946. Later he became a recognized scholar and expert in many languages, earning doctorates in philosophy and theology. He was professor and then chairman of the Philosophy Department at the Catholic University of Lublin. In the 1950s, Father Wojtyla emerged as a prolific writer of moral and philosophical works, and even poetry.

In 1958, Wojtyla was made Auxiliary Bishop of Cracow and, six years later, residential archbishop. Always conscious of pastoral responsibilities, he established adult religious study groups in parishes, a Family Institute and a ministry for the sick and disabled.

Archbishop Wojtyla attended all the sessions of Vatican Council II. In the discussion about the Constitution on the Church, he spoke from personal experience about the denial of freedom of conscience which he had experienced under both the Nazis and the Communists. He was also vociferous about the Declaration on Religious Freedom and the Decree on the Instruments of Social Communications. Wojtyla often mentioned how the council had significantly broadened his perspectives beyond those of the Polish Church.

Pope Paul VI recognized the cardinal's special talents by using him as a theological consultant and asking him to conduct his personal lenten retreat in 1976, the meditations from which have been published as *Signs of Contradiction*. In 1969 and 1976, Cardinal Wojtyla toured Canada, the United States and Latin America, visiting Polish communities. The latter visit centered on the Eucharistic Congress in Philadelphia, where he delivered a moving homily on the human hunger for religious freedom.

On October 16, 1978, Pope John Paul II, 264th successor of Saint Peter, stepped forward on the balcony of the Basilica to bless the crowd and to begin a dramatic new chapter in the history of the Catholic Church.

PORTIUNCULA CHAPEL

Though there is no evidence that Fray Junípero Serra or any of his Franciscan collaborators along *El Camino Real* ever personally visited the picturesque village of Assisi, perhaps no town anywhere had a greater influence on the landscape and nomenclature of the Pacific Slope than the one associated with Saints Francis and Clare.

Even two hundred years ago, visitors to the various Franciscan churches and shrines in and around Assisi must have felt, as did Pope John XXIII in 1962, that truly "The gates of heaven are hinged to the Umbrian Hills." Among the numerous monuments at Assisi, none is more historically relevant to modern times than the Basilica of *Santa Maria degli Angeli* situated in the village at the base of the mountain, a short distance from the railroad station.

Of particular interest to residents of California's southland is the Portiuncula chapel located within the basilica for it was that tiny chapel that gave its name to the Pueblo of Our Lady of the Angels (Los Angeles) in 1781. A simple, rustic oratory, fashioned from Subasio stone, it was one of the spots loved most by Saint Francis and it was there that he passed to everlasting life on October 3, 1226. Founded by four pilgrims on their return from the Holy Land, it was supposedly erected to house a fragment of the Virgin Mother's tomb.

The later name "Portiuncula" derives from the "smallness" of the chapel. It was known as Our Lady of the Angels because of an ancient tradition that angels were often heard in the area chanting praises to the Lord.

Looked after by the Benedictines from the 6th century onwards, the chapel was entrusted to Francis in 1211 in exchange for an annual bowl of fish from the Tescio River, a practice that continues to this day. Francis personally restored the crumbling walls of the chapel and it was there that he welcomed Saint Clare on March 19, 1212, after she fled her family in search of a life of sacrifice and poverty.

In 1216, Francis inaugurated the *Festa del Perdono* which was celebrated thereafter on August 2nd. All who went to confession and received Holy Communion could visit the chapel and there receive a special indulgence. The Portiuncula Indulgence is still given each year in most Franciscan churches throughout the world. The facade of the chapel is decorated below by geometrical ornaments and above by a frescoe painted by J. F. Overbek of Lucech (1829) portraying the Institution of the Feast of Pardon.

On the right wall of the tiny chapel are 15th century frescoes with a Sienese flavor. Several other frescoes depict various Marian themes, with special emphasis on the Annunciation. The mosaic atop the entrance to the Old Plaza church, in downtown Los Angeles, was reproduced by Isabel Piczek from an original in this revered chapel.

Pilgrims accompanying Roger Cardinal Mahony to Rome for his investiture in the College of Cardinals, in

1991, journeyed to the Basilica of *Santa Maria degli Angeli* where they joined the Archbishop of Los Angeles in reaffirming the historic linkage of Los Angeles to its Franciscan roots.

POSTAL HISTORY

People have been writing letters since the advent of civilization. Saint Paul's letters to local churches and friends have long been enshrined in sacred literature. The subsequent spread of Christianity is mirrored in the letters of the early Church Fathers.

Postal history then is a vital part of the Christian heritage and nowhere is that more obvious than in California. In the western part of the nation, postal history is a saga of tragedy and romance, often poignant and occasionally comic.

In his book, *Letters of Gold*, Jesse L. Colburn tells of hopes denied and dreams fulfilled as he illustrates the postal history of California. In its totality and with homely detail, the postal history of the far west records the decay of the Hispanic empire and the expansion of a vigorous new nation as it spread across a continent from the Atlantic to the Pacific shores.

The story tells of people venturing into the unknown, yet eager to keep in touch with their roots. Happily, today we know the intimate details of their adventures because people wrote letters to their friends, relatives and acquaintances.

Historians and archivists value a letter for its content, for the information it gives about its times, culture, civilization and the personalities of the writer. The postal historian not only respects the content of the letter, but he studies the postage stamps and postal markings, the cancellations and other factors related to the passage of the letter from writer to addressee.

Collectors of postal materials, and there are many in today's society, place an additional value upon letters, namely the monetary cost of such items in the contemporary marketplace. The value of a cover is determined by its rarity, condition and the demand of collectors. Physical condition of an envelope (cover) or the address–portion of a folded letter is secondary to its scarcity.

Many covers were damaged as they were carried in the rough pockets of the senders or were carelessly opened by the receivers. And many were carried under extremely adverse conditions. For those reasons, rarity must outweigh aesthetic appeal.

The postal history of California began when an inhabitant first sent a letter to someone else. Among the earliest such letters written in and to California were those originating with Fray Junípero Serra and many of them are still very much in existence at various archival repositories.

Prior to 1849, there was no government mail service in the far west. A letter writer made individual arrangements with a ship's officer to carry his letters. In the case of eastbound letters, the ship's officer was required to deliver these letters to the post office at his eastern port–of–entry, at which place the letters received their first postal markings. For this service, the ship's officer was paid a fee of two cents, provided the ship was American owned. There was no way to prepay the postage, so all mail was sent collect.

On westbound mail, postage to the port–of–departure was prepaid, and a ship's officer usually delivered a letter to a west coast custom's officer to await pickup by the addressee.

The period between 1849 and 1869 is of special interest because it encompassed the fumbling attempts of the United States Post Office to solve problems which it did not seem to understand. In 1869, the transcontinental railroad was completed and that climactic event largely ended the postal role of other transportation agencies in California. By then the government Post Office had surmounted most of the problems which had vexed its western users, problems that had created the unique postal history of the period.

POSTCARD — HISTORY

Among the many unique distinctions enjoyed by California is that of being the postcard capital of the world. Experts in the field claim that postcards portraying the fire falls at Yosemite National Park have been the "very best sellers all through the years." Even many of the runnersup are California–based, such as scenes of Hollywood and Vine, the Queen Mary, the Franciscan Missions, Disneyland, Dodger Stadium, Hollywood Bowl and a host of others.

California's postcard vision has always been pastoral, wholesome and a bit crazy, and the movie industry did little or nothing to alter that view. Early postcards showing the inside of a studio could be a block in any modest suburb. The white frame houses are there, the beds of daisies and marigolds, along with the intensely ambitious Cecil Brunner roses.

Later cards portray stars' homes amidst banks of flowers trailing across lawns and over towers and terraces. Hollywood may appear exotic to the rest of the world but, somehow, to America, California's promised land still flows with nothing stronger than milk and honey.

If postcards provide a clue to the hopes and dreams of common people, it's only natural that Southern California would offer a thriving market and an amazing opportunity for glitter and boast. The movie industry aside, California always had what the rest of the country lacked, reasonably good weather and scenic splendor.

Years before the first movie, people were flocking to California. Postcards featured trains steaming through orange groves and over mountains, announcing smugly: "Throw snowballs at me, and I will throw oranges at you."

The earliest California scenes on postcards were lithographed on stone. Probably the best work was done by the Detroit and Leighton companies and the first printing was executed in Europe. Early California postcards can be dated fairly easily. The "undivideds" came first in this century (before 1906). Thereon, only the recipient's name and address were allowed on the blank side of the card. By the 1920s, hand–tinted postcards became popular and, for a while, California's orange trees, snow–covered mountains and desert wild flowers predominated the field.

Several categories of postcards are represented at the Archival Center for the Archdiocese of Los Angeles, including a large mint collection purchased and preserved in their original wrappers by Carrie Estelle Doheny during her tour of Europe early in this century.

The collection of mission postcards is especially significant. Seven large scrapbooks contain numerous scenes from all of the twenty–one missionary outposts along *El Camino Real*, together with numerous portrayals of *asistencias*, *ranchos*, friars and related subjects.

Several dozen of California's Catholic churches are featured on postcards, along with schools, and other institutions associated with the ministerial outreach of the Church in California. A person can learn a lot of history by studying and maybe even collecting old postcards. Aside from the paper shows, postcards can still be found at reasonable prices in thrift shops, book stores and rummage sales.

Postcards sum up all that's memorable about the places, times, events and people of earlier times. No period in human annals has been devoid of a medium to express its own particular beauty and fascination. When seen in their proper historical perspective, postcards certainly express the tone of California's provincial atmosphere more effectively than many other of the less ephemeral survivors of the era.

POZOS DE SAN JUAN DE DIOS

During the year of American independence, while on a journey from Arizona's San Xavier del Bac Mission to San Gabriel, Fray Francisco Garces (1738–1781) paused to spend the night at a group of waterholes in the Mojave desert. Following the custom of Hispanic missionaries, Garces named the area in honor of Saint John of God, whose feastday it was. Since March 8, 1776, *Pozos de San Juan de Dios* has been the only place in the United States immortalized by the name of the hospitaller saint.

The marker that has identified the area since October 28, 1972 has its own story. It began when Brother Benignus Callan arrived in Apple Valley in 1969. Local residents told how Fray Francisco Garces, discoverer of the Mojave River (which he called the River of the Martyrs), had also charted the springs named for Saint John of God.

Brother Callan made several trips to the area, about 130 miles southwest of Apple Valley. Eventually, he acquired a copy of the Garces diary which had been edited and then published by Elliott Coues in 1900. It proved to be a fascinating account of travels through Sonora, Arizona and California.

Callan found that the 1776 journey was Garces' longest exploration. He traveled along the Colorado River to a point near the present location of Needles. Turning westward, he crossed the desert into Southern California, ultimately reaching San Gabriel Mission.

The entry in Garces' diary for March 8, 1776, read thusly: "I went six leagues westsouthwest, in part through the *cañada* and in part through the *medano*. I arrived at some very abundant wells which I named *Pozos de San Juan de Dios*, and there is sufficient grass there." The diary indicates that Garces returned to the exact spot on May 22nd, shortly prior to departing for the Colorado River. While there he noted a group of Indians (Beneme) who lived mainly on herbs and roots.

Further investigation by Brother Callan indicated that the *Pozos de San Juan de Dios* were redisovered in the 1860s, when horse–soldier forts were set up across the Mojave desert to protect early immigrants. A small stockade was erected at Marl Springs and ruins of the early settlement can still be seen at the foot of Kelso Peak.

Callan convinced his religious community to pursue the possibility of marking the area. A special Mass was offered at the remote setting on January 29, 1972. Afterwards, a bronze plaque affixed to a brick platform was unveiled. It read:

"On March 8, 1776, Fr. Francis Garces, O.F.M., on his most famous journey of over 2,000 miles from Mission San Xavier del Bac, Tucson, Arizona, to Mission San Gabriel, California, rested here and named these waterholes 'St. John of God Springs.' (Marl Springs)." Present–day visitors can locate the site and its plaque midway in the vast triangle created by highways 66 and 99, about ten miles due north of the small hamlet of Kelso.

The story of *Pozos de San Juan de Dios* would be

incomplete were it not mentioned that barely five years after discovering the springs, Fray Francisco Garces, the intrepid pathfinder, became a martyr to the Faith—just fifty miles away!

PRESIDENTIAL MEDALS IN MISSION HILLS

Attached to the wall leading into the Historical Museum at the Archival Center in Mission Hills is a large wooden, three doored, glass case exhibiting forty–one presidential medals from George Washington to Bill Clinton. A gift of Msgr. James Hourihan, long-time pastor Saint Andrews parish in Pasadena, the massive case was fabricated from oak in the early years of this century.

Presidential medals date back to the earliest days of the republic. Medals bearing a likeness of the president on one side and symbols of peace and friendship on the other were presented to Indian chiefs and warriors at treaty signings and other events.

On their expedition to the Pacific coast in 1804–1806, Lewis and Clark carried a supply of "Indian Peace Medals" bearing the portrait of President Thomas Jefferson for presentation to important personages. The tradition of giving peace medals continued until the latter part of the 19th century.

After the term of President Andrew Johnson, these medals became the official souvenirs of presidential inaugurations, with individual reverse designs featuring inaugural dates, terms of office, official symbols, seals and even excerpts from speeches.

Traditionally, the pursuit of numismatics has been devoted primarily to coinage. While several million Americans would describe themselves as serious coin collectors, comparatively few would identify themselves as medalists.

Medals have a totally different appeal. They do not serve as a medium of exchange, but as commemoratives of individuals or moments in time. Although prepared in precious metals, they have no prescribed face value and the significance of a specimen is found in the delicacy and boldness of the craftsman who produced it.

Since medals are generally larger than coins, there is more room for detail. And, because they do not circulate as a medium of exchange, there is no need to protect their image with a high rim.

The official inaugural medal occupies a unique position in the nation's medallic heritage. While other issues are struck at one time over a brief period, the inaugural medal spans decades and represents the skill of artists and medalists from many backgrounds.

A new inaugural medal appears for every new President. Silver and gold editions are limited in advance of sale. Production of the bronze specimens ceases when the inaugural committee disbands or curtails its authorization. (The ones at the Archival Center are all executed in bronze.)

Over the years, a fairly large number of medals have appeared to commemorate presidential administrations. But only the inaugural committee or the President himself can authorize an official issue.

The entire American presidency is recorded in the medallic collection exhibited at the Archival Center. There are relatively few complete sets and even fewer that are so handsomely displayed as the one at Mission Hills. The latest addition to the series is an artistic medal celebrating the inauguration of William Jefferson Clinton, as the forty–second Chief Executive of the United States.

PRINCESA — VOYAGE

Pilots were highly–skilled professional seamen who enjoyed a lofty status among the peoples of Hispanic times. There may have been as many as a dozen pilots along the Pacific Slope in the 1780s.

In addition to their other tasks, pilots were charged with mapping the ports and coasts they visited. Their ships supplied Alta California's military outposts, missions and pioneers.

Juan Pantoja y Arriaga was one of their number. Based at San Blas, on the west coast of Mexico, he was among that select group described as "the most colorful of the major officials in the Spanish Naval Department." Juan Pantoja was specially gifted in cartography. His map of San Diego was referred to in the Treaty of Guadalupe–Hidalgo, in 1848. That treaty defines the location of the international boundary line between Mexico and the United States as "one marine league due south of the southernmost point of the Port of San Diego according to the plan of said port made in the year 1782 by Don Juan Pantoja."

After matriculating from the *Seminario de San Telmo* in Seville, Pantoja was assigned to the Naval Department of Colloa de Lima, where he served with distinction for six years. He received the title of *pilotin* in 1777. Following his appointment to San Blas, Pantoja served as navigator and cartographer on various supply vessels to Alta California. In 1779, he was pilot aboard the flagship *Princesa* on an expedition to Alaska.

In May of 1781, Pantoja was entrusted with the command of the *Aranzazu*. Later he took an active part in exploring and mapping voyages to the lower coasts of Nicaragua.

Pantoja's visit to Alta California aboard *Nuestra Señora del Rosario* or the *Princesa* in 1782 is important because of the log which he meticulously kept of that voyage. As others had before him, Pantoja found that the California coast was particularly tricky, mostly because of its prolonged calms and persistent fogs which make every landfall count. His sketch maps make it possible to visualize the Southern California coastline as it was known two hundred years ago.

Pantoja had a careful eye. He recorded every incident relating to the ship's progress—wind direction and force, fog banks, storms, showers, currents, waves, ship's speed and direction, use of various sails, accidents, sightings, arrivals, departures and whatever else might have an influence on the voyage.

The *Princesa* anchored at Santa Barbara from August 2nd to the 16th. Pantoja missed Fray Junípero Serra for the ailing *Presidente* had left a few months earlier for Carmel. He did meet Serra the following year, when he acted as sponsor for two Baptisms performed by the friar at San Carlos Borromeo. Little is known about Pantoja in subsequent years. Though Spanish voyages to the northwest coast ceased in 1797, Pantoja is known to have been stationed at San Blas as late as 1803. He likely retired then and returned to Spain.

Pioneers such as Pantoja brought back priceless pilotage information. Spanish authorities carefully guarded his and other charts and a few expert navigators like Jean Francois de Galaup, Comte de la Perouse and George Vancouver made use of their knowledge.

PRIVATE REVELATION IN CALIFORNIA

An article on "Watsonville's Miracle Tree Phenomenon" tells how, on a quiet summer morning in June, Anita Contreras Mendoza knelt to pray beside a tree . . . and came face-to-face with the Virgin Mary." That experience held the power to change lives, both for her and for countless others—men and women, young and old, able bodied and infirmed—who would follow in her footsteps.

Catholic theologians have consistently taught that formal divine revelation ceased with the demise of John the Evangelist, the last of the apostles to die, about 90 A.D. There have been, however, numerous claims of "private" revelations during succeeding centuries. Among the more spectacular examples would be the appearances of the Blessed Mother at Tepeyac, Lourdes and Fatima.

"Private" revelations only bind the persons to whom they are made. And, traditionally, the Catholic Church has been exceedingly reticent about approving or publicizing such reported revelations.

Over the past century, several dozen private revelations have reputedly been made in the United States, none of which has been given formal recognition by the Church. California has had its share of these phenomena, including the locutions at the Hill of Hope in Orange County during the 1960s.

The most recent claimant to this category reportedly occurred during June of 1992 at Pinto Lake Country Park in Watsonville, where the Virgin Mary supposedly appeared to Anita Contreras Mendoza. Mrs. Mendoza, a fifty-three year old cannery worker, told friends that the vision of Our Lady of Guadalupe "spoke with her at length, giving her three messages" which she refused to publicly disclose.

At a place about twenty feet high on a tree, just below the fork of a limb, Anita saw what she described as distinct markings that she believed to be miraculous, irrefutable evidence of the Virgin's appearance. A reporter for the *Alta Vista Magazine* noted that during the subsequent months people poured into the park in a steady steam to look at the "supernatural image of the Holy Mother herself, carved into the tree by the very hand of God."

"Whether real, imagined or a complete fabrication," the visions of Anita Contreras Mendoza created unprecedented problems for park officials "whose training in emergency preparedness failed to cover religious phenomena."

Since the initial "visions," the oak tree itself has taken on what Sharon Randell described as the appearance of a Christmas tree "decorated by gypsies, colorful and exotic but lovely nonetheless, adorned with bits and pieces of countless broken hearts."

Everything else happens in California—why not private revelations? Years ago, a message reportedly intended for Timothy Cardinal Manning was brought to the archbishop's attention. His response, not meant in jest, was both logical and amusing: "The Lord knows where I make my daily holy hour. If He wants me to do something, He can tell me personally. I will then happily comply."

PROPAGANDA FIDE

Students of American Catholic history are acutely aware of the vital importance attached to the Roman Archives of the Sacred Congregation of Propaganda Fide. This is especially true of those areas in the west where original documentation is nowhere to be found on the local scene.

An understanding of the basic purpose and structure of Propaganda Fide is necessary for a proper appreciation of the pivotal significance of that congregation's archival holdings. Organized in 1622, to oversee the expansion of the Catholic apostolate in underdeveloped areas, the Sacred Congregation of Propaganda Fide controls the faculties, or delegated powers, of all missionaries within its carefully defined sphere of influence. Even today a considerable number of residential bishops and practically all prelates in territories not yet elevated to diocesan status are subject to the congregation. The cardinal prefect, referred to in clerical circles as the "red pope," and his advisors have plenary power over spiritual affairs in mission lands.

Perhaps in no other country was the congregation of Propaganda Fide more successful in fulfilling its purpose than in the United States between the time of American Independence and 1908. For that reason, the correspondence between this nation's prelates and officials of Propaganda makes that congregation's archives more important for historians of the American Church than all other record depositories taken together.

Since 1955, the Academy of American Franciscan History has been preparing a systematic calendar of Propaganda Fide's documents with the patient collaboration of a leading European researcher, Mr. Anton Debevec. In addition to paying a tribute to the memory of the many Franciscan missionaries who had labored in the Americas under the guidance of Propaganda, the calendar was envisioned "as a service to the church historians of our beloved country."

The initial volume of Series One, covering the years between 1673 and 1844, was released under the capable editorship of Father Finbar Kenneally, the highly respected compiler of the Fermin Lasuen letters. Without question, this calendar of *United States Documents in the Propaganda Fide Archives* is the singularly indispensable reference tool issued in the last quarter century for historians of American Catholicism. The format of the 2278 entries is extremely useful. Each document is identified with its own call number and then located by its designation in the Propaganda Fide archives. It is further described by names of correspondents and the date and place of origin. Following a brief digest of each entry is a note about the language employed. A useful bit of information, usually lacking in such works, is an enumeration in each entry of "persons mentioned" in the text of the original document. Publication of this book is another in a litany of reasons calling for the gratitude of American Catholics to the intellectual contributions of the Academy of American Franciscan History.

PROTESTANT "REQUIEM MASS"

An interesting news story appeared in *The Monitor*, official Catholic newspaper for the Archdiocese of San Francisco, on March 14, 1908, to the effect that the first Protestant "Requiem Mass" had been offered in California.

It noted that "down in Los Angeles the Episcopalians—some of them, at any rate—are getting very 'high church.' Last week they 'celebrated a requiem Mass for the repose of the soul of the late Rev. Father Braun.'"

The short, two column report observed that "this was the first time a 'Requiem Mass' was ever celebrated in the Episcopal Church in this State." (Attempts to corroborate this "first" with the Diocese of Los Angeles have been unsuccessful. Mr. Edward White, historiographer for the Episcopal Church in Southern California, thinks that Christ Church in Ontario may have been liturgically orientated as early as the mid 1890s).

In any event, the account goes on to say that the "Catholic Club" of the Episcopal Diocese "has lately introduced in several churches of California ritualistic services which very much resemble, in fact, are almost exact copies of the services of the Catholic Church."

Those affiliated with "Catholic Club" professed a belief in the Real Presence in the Blessed Sacrament. For this reason the members kneel on entering and leaving, and each time in passing before the altar, a custom that is not usually observed in the Episcopal Church except in those designated as "high."

The Monitor account mentions the little chapel of Saint Matthias in Los Angeles as "a good exemplification of the ritualistic services now being introduced. (Saint Matthias was long located on Washington Boulevard, just west of Rosedale Cemetery. Founded as a mission in 1905, it was advanced to parochial status in 1907. Its present–day congregation gathers weekly in the chapel of the old Villa Cabrini in Burbank).

According to the 1908 news release, Saint Matthias "resembles any Episcopalian church in its furnishings, with the exception that high above the altar is a crucifix, with the figure of Christ in ivory. Just before this is an altar lamp, a tiny light in a red glass vessel constantly burning."

"In the altar itself there is a slight change, the tabernacle being introduced as in Catholic Churches. On either side of this, for the 'Requiem Mass,' were three lighted candles, while below and at each end were single lighted tapers. The altar cloth, usually plain, was ornamented with very beautiful lace. Above the tabernacle was the usual metal cross."

Apparently, "the vestments used differ greatly from those commonly seen in Episcopal churches. The celebrant's white surplice has been lengthened into an alb, with long, tight–fitting sleeves in the place of flowing ones. This alb is held at the waist by a cincture. The chasuble and maniple of the Catholic Church are also used. The stole is worn by all the Episcopal clergy and in addition, birettas have been introduced into the vestments of the officiating clergy. Incense also is used. The Mass was sung in English."

Since the appearance of *The Monitor* article, in 1908, the "Anglo–Catholic" movement within the Protestant Episcopal Church has grown considerably in California.

PUEBLO DE NUESTRA SEÑORA DE LOS ANGELES

Authorities are in general agreement that the name of the town established adjacent to the *Río Porciúncula*, in the fall of 1781, was taken from the title of the nearby river. Fray Francisco Palóu, a contemporary observer, related that "work was begun with a few families in founding the projected town of *Nuestra Señora de los Angeles* on the banks of the river named *Porciúncula*." When Felipe de Neve decided to set up the town, he incorporated the religious title of the river and the popular appellation of Assisi's chapel in the name, and the result was *El Pueblo de Nuestra Señora de los Angeles de Porciúncula*.

The origin of the spurious appellation *la reina* (the queen) presents an interesting study in heuristics. Earliest mention of the term in connection with the *pueblo* seems to be December 27, 1779, when plans were drawn up for a foundation "*con el titulo de Nuestra Señora la Reyna de los Angeles, sobre el Rio de la Porciúncula*." The term was used again two years later, on September 13, 1781, in a statement of Antonio Villavicénsio, who referred to the "*Pueblo de la Reina de los Angeles*."

It would seem logical that the valid use of *la reina* depends on the literal meaning and etymological significance of Porciúncula along with the intention the original writers wished to convey in employing the word. Fray Juan Crespi's familiarity with the term Porciúncula grew out of the *toties quoties* indulgence gained at Franciscan churches, on August 1st and 2nd, as well as the devotion to Our Lady of the Angels prevalent in the Convento of San Bernardino at Petra.

The Marian patronage in that Franciscan church can easily be traced to the small village at the base of the steep mountainous town of Assisi in Italy. There the small community of *Santa Maria degli Angeli* (near present–day Perugia) developed around the monastery where Francis Bernardone is said to have received his vocation to the ministry on February 24, 1208. The humble friar lived there on a tiny plot of land alongside a chapel supposedly erected by hermits from the Valley of Josephat. There is no evidence linking *la reina* with the shrine and, that being the case, the term must be regarded as an unwarranted interpolation based on an erroneous understanding of the etymological derivation of *Porciúncula*.

Evidence notwithstanding, *la reina* appears in a number of contemporary chronicles, though it must be noted in defense of the term's wide usage, that many of the early commentators were unaware of the word's true significance. Such an intellectual lacuna is hardly surprising in such men as Hubert Howe Bancroft, Theodore H. Hittell and Zoeth Eldredge, none of whom belonged either to the Church which canonized the term or the country which popularized it. Since formal sources are breeding places of factual errors, most of the major California historians of subsequent generations have innocently perpetuated the practice of including *la reina* with the title of the *Pueblo de Nuestra Señora de los Angeles*.

As could be expected, those most familiar with the term *Porciúncula*, the friars, are uniformly on record as favoring the term itself or its equivalent, *Nuestra Señora de los Angeles,* for the *pueblo* which grew from forty–four *pobladores* into the world's largest city dedicated to the Virgin Mary.

Although any association between *la reina* and the *Porciúncula* is historically unwarranted, it is one thing to underscore a popular misconception and quite another to evaluate the reasons giving rise to the initial error. The explanation of how this etymological stillbirth came about is a very simple one. *La Reina* is an epithet applied to the Virgin Mary from ancient times, beginning as far back as the fourth century with Saint Ephraem. It is repeated no less than a dozen times in the Litany of Loreto, a familiar and popular prayer among the Spanish and Mexican people. *La Reina de los Angeles* has special prominence in the litany because of its position as first of the queenly titles. The phrase is also traditionally appended to the rosary in Latin countries where both devotions, designedly "dialogue prayers," are committed to memory for daily use as part of one's spiritual vocabulary.

The precise distinction between *Nuestra Señora de los Angeles* and *Nuestra Señora La Reina de los Angeles* is not immediately obvious or, for that matter important, to those unschooled in the finery of ecclesiastical verbiage. It came about that references to the Feast of the *Porciuncula* could, and very often did, trigger the concept of queenship where none ever existed. The hyperbolic expression found its way into print where it was stereotyped by writers more interested in historical development than in etymological evolution.

PURITAS DISTILLED WATER

Historians may write glowingly about the past, but few would care to live in those bygone days. One reason would be the lack of conveniences and pleasantries that people of modern times take for granted. Most of these 21st century "perks" didn't exist even a hundred years ago.

An example would be the bottled water that people buy at the market or have delivered to their homes. What is a luxury in most areas of the world seems to have become a dire necessity for a great majority of Americans. In 1910, Bishop Thomas J. Conaty observed to a friend in Worcester, Massachusetts, that the "mountain water of Southern California is surely among the most attractive features of this far western portion of the Lord's vineyard."

The bottled water industry was then in its infancy. It began with the Ice and Cold Storage Company of Los Angeles. Residents of Southern California got their first taste of bottled drinking water in 1894.

Puritas Distilled Water was produced from municipal water supplies in much the same fashion as it is today and sold in five gallon bottles from horse–drawn wagons. The first plant for this purpose was located on the *arroyo* near Eagle Rock and later was moved to more updated quarters at Seventh Street and Santa Fe Avenue. In mid 1928, the company was sold to California Consumers, a firm then selling ice cream and cold storage units.

Puritas Distilled Water was unrivaled until 1905, when the Arrowhead Springs Corporation began selling spring water in Los Angeles. The water came from the San Bernardino Mountains, its name taken from the great natural arrowhead design on the mountain–side above Arrowhead Springs, a health spa known for its mineral–rich hot springs. The first bottling was done in the basement of the hotel, where the water was packaged in pints, quarts and gallons. As its popularity increased, the water was bottled in five gallon units and shipped to customers via Pacific Electric Railway.

In 1917, the company constructed a bottling plant in Los Angeles, and in the September 23rd issue of the *Los Angeles Times*, the following announcement appeared: "One of the most important of the recent industrial acquisitions of Los Angeles is the new and modern bottling plant of the Arrowhead Springs Company at the corner of Washington Street and Compton Avenue. . ... it is the largest establishment of its kind in the West."

A pipeline had been constructed at the springs, and water was transported to a reservoir above the hotel and brought to the new plant in glass–lined railroad tank cars. In 1929, the three major water companies operating in Los Angeles merged into the California Consolidated Water Company and opened new facilities on a 162,000 square foot acreage. The company was easily the largest bottled water concern in the world, with a business estimated about five times as great as that of any other company in Los Angeles.

Quantities of both Arrowhead Spring Water and Puritas Distilled Water were available for shipment east. One journal of the time noted that "the Fred Harvey system has Arrowhead Spring Water on sale throughout all of its dining rooms." The product was also being shipped to Shanghai–Hong Kong.

QUEEN'S DAUGHTERS

There exists in California's southland a small army of faithful women whose unsparing response to the needs of orphans and the poor has been a vital part of the local scene for well over half a century. Once each week, the Queen's Daughters gather at their new headquarters, on West Twenty–Third Street, behind the Stella Maris House, to sew for the needy. Over fifty layettes (twelve diapers, two blankets, two night gowns, two shirts, two bibs, a kimona and a pair of socks) are produced monthly for distribution by the Catholic Welfare Bureau.

Long an important feature in the philanthropic activities of Saint Louis, Missouri, the Queen's Daughters was inaugurated in the Diocese of Monterey–Los Angeles on October 8, 1914, as a benevolent association of Catholic Women interested in works of charity. A group of thirteen resourceful ladies, gathered at the old Los Angeles Orphan Asylum, decided to formalize their already extensive involvements in Catholic charities by affiliating with a proven and effective organization dedicated to the needs of underprivileged girls.

Though primarily concerned with helping the "orphan and the needy," the Queen's Daughters diffused their activities in many related fields. They taught Sunday school, engaged in welfare duties during World War I and established a loan fund for scholarships and apprentice programs. Their many charities were financed through sewing circles on the parochial level.

In June, 1915, the Queen's Daughters opened the Stella Maris Club in a rented house on Sunset Boulevard. Accommodations were provided there for young women in the lower income brackets unable to acquire adequate housing elsewhere. Larger quarters were later utilized on Grand Avenue. Still further expansion of their apostolic works came in 1924, when a handsome building was erected on Witmer Street. The activities continued, over subsequent decades, culminating in the founding of Saint Vibiana's Club on South Union Avenue.

The Queen's Daughters were incorporated in 1917. Four years later the organization was structurally revamped by Father Robert Emmet Lucey, Director of the Bureau of Catholic Charities. It was through Lucey's efforts that the Queen's Daughters qualified for and were accepted in the Community Chest Program, inaugurated in 1924.

This work continues. Members still gather at regular meetings and thousands of useful and beautiful garments are sewn each year for underprivileged youngsters. For over fifty years this dedicated organization has been a faithful witness to the Catholic involvement in Southern California's remarkable growth. The Queen's Daughters prefigured that movement known as "public commitment," perhaps by realizing the advice uttered many years ago by Henry Ward Beecher:

> Do not keep the alabaster boxes of your love and tenderness sealed up until your friends are dead. Fill their lives with sweetness. Speak approving, cheering words while their ears can hear them and their hearts can be thrilled by them.

RAMONA THE HEROINE

The story of *Ramona*, the nation's first novel staged in Southern California, was intended as a kind of *Uncle Tom's Cabin* to arouse concern about the abuses heaped upon the area's native peoples. It all began on March 24, 1883, when an Indian woman watched in horror as a white man emptied the rounds of his double–barreled shotgun into the body of her defenseless husband. The woman's name was Ramona.

The account of that cold–blooded murder was first related by Helen Hunt Jackson in her official *Report on the Condition and Needs of the Mission Indians of California* which she submitted to the Bureau of Indian Affairs in July of 1883. She repeated the narrative a few month's later in a New York *Independent* article entitled "Justifiable Homicide in Southern California." But it was the fictionalized version of the event that eventually won nationwide attention.

In 1884, Helen Hunt Jackson published *Ramona* in which she recast and embellished the story in great detail. Therein she graphically told how the orphaned Ramona had met and married Alessandro, her star–crossed Indian lover.

The novel became an instantaneous best–seller. One reviewer called it "unquestionably the best novel yet produced by an American woman." The Jackson book became intertwined into the history of California's southland.

Aside from being a compelling love story, what eastern readers found most appealing in *Ramona* was its beautiful new vision of Southern California's landscape and its fresh romantic image of the area's pre–American past. Life on the Mexican *ranchos* was portrayed as full of courtesy, generosity, piety and gaiety.

And so the "myth" of Ramona was launched as a strange mixture of fact and fancy that generations of readers would accept as history. The trappings of Ms. Jackson's story far outweighed the storyline.

Probably the greatest contributor to the mythology was Edward Roberts who came to Los Angeles in 1886. He is credited with associating the Camulos ranch with Ramona. Thereafter, the Santa Clara Valley ranch was identified as the "real" home of Ramona and the de Valles, who inhabited the ranch, were delighted with their new found popularity.

Ramona landmarks burst forth all over Southern California, An adobe near San Gabriel Mission was hailed as her "birthplace." San Diegans advertised the Estudillo adobe as "Ramona's marriage place." In her fictionalized role, Ramona became the most travelled and idolized of all California's Indians.

In 1905, the first theatrical presentation of *Ramona* was staged at the Mason Opera House in downtown Los Angeles. Five years later, D. W. Griffith filmed what would be the first of four feature films bearing the name *Ramona*. It became a story that never grew old.

Ramona the Heroine

On April 13, 1923, the Ramona Pageant was performed for the first time at Hemet and that pageant has become a major tourist attraction every succeeding spring. Getting a ticket to a performance was a recognized and cherished status symbol.

It has now been well over a century since Helen Hunt Jackson wrote her best seller and there is every reason to believe it is now as popular as the day it first appeared. Ramona lives on with ever greater affection as California's best loved heroine.

REAGAN LIBRARY — THE DEDICATION

For the first time in history, five chief executives of the United States gathered on November 4, 1991 for the dedication of the new Ronald Reagan Presidential Library, located just miles west of San Fernando Mission in the Simi Valley.

The presidents, along with their wives, Lady Bird Johnson and a host of dignitaries and Hollywood stars, joined with 4,100 invited guests to witness the turning over to the Federal Government of the 53,000 square–foot complex.

Thanks to an unexpected and welcome phone call from former American Ambassador to the Vatican, William A. Wilson, this old country priest was able to be present for the historic event that brought together the largest assemblage of its kind in the history of Southern California.

It was indeed a gala occasion and one which very much impacted on nearby San Fernando Mission, whose cattle roamed those very hills in the early years of the 1800s. There is much about the Ronald Reagan Presidential Library that bespeaks the California missions. The outdoor lamps, for example, are replicas of the mission bells that line *El Camino Real*. And through the generosity of Justice William P. Clark, a large bronze likeness of Fray Junípero Serra will eventually be placed at the site.

The mission style archives and museum buildings, located atop a windswept hill overlooking suburban Simi Valley, is the largest and most expensive ($56.8 million) repository for documents ever built. Erected with private donations, on twenty–four acres of land that once served as a backdrop for Hollywood westerns, the facility will contain a collection of over 55 million documents—an archivist's delight!

According to stipulations in the 1978 Presidential Records Act, all files maintained in the White House between 1981 and 1989 became public property when Mr. Reagan left the office. Most of the historic treasures are hidden away in the cavernous basements, including the 75,000 gifts presented to the Reagans during the eight years they resided at 1600 Pennsylvania Avenue. A mammoth piece of the Berlin Wall graphically reminds visitors of the dramatic changes that have transformed the world since 1981.

The Reagan Library, the tenth of the presidential libraries, will be the last of its kind, due to a congressional edict sharply curtailing the size of any future documentary collections. The research center will be open to anyone wishing to utilize materials at the facility. In addition to the documents for scholars, a chief attraction for visitors in the 22,000 square foot museum is a replica of the Oval Office and exhibits tracing Reagan's life as actor, governor and president.

Everyone has different memories of the man whose name has adorned the world's marquees for the past sixty years. The Ronald Reagan Presidential Library will allow scholars and others to sort it all out. Much of what Ronald Reagan accomplished in his long and eventful life was undoubtedly an outgrowth of his love and esteem for the one he once identified as "the most admired man" in his life—"the Galilean fisherman."

THE "RED" MASS

In a growing number of areas throughout the United States, the inauguration of the fall court term is marked by the celebration of a "Red" Mass during which the blessings of Almighty God are implored for the equitable administration of justice during the coming year. The custom of such yearly observances can be traced to 1245, and the inauguration of King Louis IX, a new era in the lives and practical affairs of his people. The monarch established a high court of justice consisting of nobles, clergy and lawyers to which he entrusted the enforcement of a uniform legal code throughout the nation.

The jurists composing that court were annually invited to *La Sainte Chapelle* at Paris, the private chapel of the French royalty, to join in a *Messe Rouge* asking God's blessings and guidance on their juridical activities. Rapidly the custom spread throughout Catholic Europe. In England, the practice was popularized under the auspices of Edward I, who began a whole new concept of juridical reforms based on the *Magna Carta*.

As in France and Italy, the Bench and Bar had but one purpose in joining the ordinary and traditional celebration of Mass to the traditions and processes of the Courts and the Law. In essence, the Red Mass was meant to call upon God the Holy Ghost, the Third Person of the Holy Trinity, to grant light and inspiration to the lawyers in pleading and to the judge in adjudicating during the coming term of the court.

Inauguration of the centuries–old custom in the

United States is credited to Monsignor William E. Cashin who celebrated a "Red" Mass, on October 6, 1928, at Saint Andrew's Church, for jurists living in the New York area. The practice was introduced on the west coast, in 1942, at San Francisco. On August 24, 1958, the first "Red" Mass was celebrated in Los Angeles as a prelude to the opening of the 81st annual meeting of the American Bar Association.

Traditionally, in Los Angeles and throughout the United States, Protestant and Jewish, as well as Catholic members of the judiciary and legal profession attend the annual event. The Mass is offered to honor the Holy Spirit, source of wisdom, understanding, counsel and fortitude, gifts which must shine forth preeminently in the lives of those dispensing justice.

The term "Red" Mass may have derived from the color of the priestly vestments though, more probably, it was a descriptive appellation of the vivid hue given to the occasion by the scarlet robes of the attendant judges. Possibly the color scheme has even a deeper significance. One writer noted that "from the beginning this Mass was celebrated exclusively as an invocation of the Holy Spirit. The red robes and the red vestments of the celebrant were the red of Christian significance. So close in the life of the lawyer is the truth inspired by the Holy Spirit and the willingness to defend that truth at the cost of blood that it takes little effort for the Christian lawyer to join the two together as he stands at the beginning of the term of the court. He implores the help of God on his work and asks the Holy Spirit to keep him true to the truth of justice even to the shedding of the blood."

RELACION HISTORICA

During the bi–centennial year of Christian penetration into California, considerable attention was focused on the printed sources from which the story of the area's pioneers is gleaned. First and foremost among the materials pertaining to Fray Junípero Serra must be given to the written account of his long–time companion and biographer, Francisco Palóu. Certainly no one was better qualified, by opportunities and ability, for such a task. Most of the early literature about Serra was based totally or in part on Palóu's *Relación Histórica de la Vida y Apostólicas Tareas del Venerable Padre Fray Junípero Serra.*

Palóu's monumental opus exhibits a host of positive qualities. It has, for example, the dual distinction of being the earliest California biography and the best account of California's most renowned figure. Even today, Palóu's work is the chief source "into which essayists, preachers, orators, poets and playwrights have dipped their pens for their materials, and in this manner

it enjoys an influence beyond the wildest dreams of its author."

Though primarily intended "as a treatise for edification," the *Relación Histórica*, published in 1787, at the printing shop of Felipe de Zuñiga y Ontiveros, on Mexico City's *Calle del Espiritu Santo*, proved to be the "most vitally important work on the early years of the Spanish occupation of California." The sixty chapters, with their almost 100,000 words, occupy 344 pages of text. Apparently the cost of publishing that "first book written in California to find its way into print," was borne jointly by the College of San Fernando and certain of its benefactors. Some copies read "*a expensas de Don Miguel González Calderon síndico de dicho apostólico colegio*" while others merely have "*a expensas de varios bienhechos.*" A few typographical discrepancies indicate at least two impressions, if not separate editions.

Though circulated widely, Palóu's original work has never been in plentiful supply. In a preface to the first English edition, published in 1884, Bishop Francis Mora of Monterey–Los Angeles observed that even then, "Fr. Serra's life by Palóu is so scarce in the mother tongue that the few copies extant are estimated at the highest value." The fortunate discovery, just after the turn of the century, by W. W. Blake, a bookseller in Mexico City, of fifty copies at the Apostolic College of Santa Cruz de Querétaro, has greatly alleviated the demand of Western Americana enthusiasts, many of whom regard the treatise as the cornerstone of their collection.

The *Relación Histórica* was republished at Mexico City, in 1852, as a supplement to Juan R. Navarro's edition of the *Historia de la Antigua o Baja California Obra Póstuma del Padre Francisco Javier Clavijero.* Four years later, an edited version appeared serially in San Francisco's *El Estandarte Católico* and, the following year, in *La Estrella of Los Angeles.* In 1856, Roa Barcena published a lengthy three–part digest of the work under the caption "*Estudios Biograficas, El Padre Franciscano Serra*" in *La Cruz.*

A truncated edition, the first in English, was translated in 1884 by Father Joachim Adam and issued from the San Francisco publishing house of P. E. Dougherty as the *Life of Ven. Padre Junípero Serra.* The late Henry Raup Wagner considered copies of this 156 page work as "even scarcer than the original." George Wharton James published a complete English version of the *Relación Histórica*, at Pasadena, in 1913. Unfortunately, a considerable number of inaccuracies in the textural rendition of *Francisco Palóu's Life and Apostolic Labors of the Venerable Father Junípero Serra* found their way into that 338–page translation by G. Scott Williams. In 1944, another reproduction of the work, this one in Spanish, was published as *Evangelista del*

Mar Pacífico, at Madrid, under the editorship of M. Aguilar. The 317-page treatise, with its lengthy prologue by Lorenzo Riber, was regrettably marred by numerous typographical errors.

The "only truly scholarly edition in any language of the *Relación Histórica*" was published, in 1955, by the Academy of American Franciscan History, under the title *Palóu's Life of Fray Junípero Serra*. Translated in a smooth and accurate style by the eminent Father Maynard Geiger, O.F.M., the extremely valuable and pertinent editorial notations of the 547-page narrative correct some of Palóu's misstatements and clarify a number of hitherto obscure points. *An Original Leaf from Francisco Palóu's Life of the Venerable Father Junípero Serra, 1787*, assembled from a dismantled copy of the first edition, was tipped into each of the 177 copies of a bibliographical commentary on the *Relación Histórica* which David Magee published at San Francisco, in 1958, for members of the Roxburghe and Zamorano Clubs.

Even those literary critics unwilling to rank the *Relación Histórica* as a serious historical opus, by today's standards, agree that "Palóu's work will remain for just what it is, the most valuable account ever published on early California history, though covering only a portion of that field."

RELIGION IN THE AMERICAN WEST

Among the more positive elements in the field of Western Americana is the renewed interest in religion and how the spiritual values of colonizers and settlers figured into the overall pageantry of history. An example of that concern is reflected in a book of essays recently published by the University Press of America entitled *Religion and Society in the American West*. The 491 page book is edited by Carl Guarneri and David Alvarez.

While there have always been divergent definitions and views of the west, the saga of gold rush immigrants and other pioneers, of gamblers, ranchers, cowboys and Indians has tended to dominate the historical treatment of the west. In his Introduction to this collection of essays, Professor Guarneri points out that popular magazines, movies and television have tended to prolong that rather stilted and stereotyped portrayal of the west.

And though professional historians and amateur buffs generally paint a more comprehensive and realistic picture of western history, they also have focused much of their attention on the frontier themes of conflict, settlement and development. Happily, in recent years, a small cadre of local, regional and denominational historians has begun incorporating the growth and impact of religious institutions, business enterprise and family values into the written accounts. This collection of twenty essays clearly reveals the pivotal role religion had in shaping the character of the colorful and distinctive region known as the American West.

The group of distinguished scholars here represented explore areas where religion either influenced local life or shaped public policy. Some of these articles offer thematic or topical overviews of religion, while others dwell on particular facets of religious development. One could hardly read and study these presentations without concluding that the west has indeed been the scene of religious events and movements which have profoundly influenced millions in the area and in the nation as a whole.

This reviewer's nomination for the best of the essays would go to that of Eldon G. Ernst, whose treatise on "American Religious History from a Pacific Coast Perspective" provides a marvelous window to the era through the plateau of bibliography.

Apart from its rich contents, there is great value in a book of this nature. It brings together a wide spectrum of informative essays that otherwise might be lost or go unrecorded in the literary shuffle. Of course, like all anthologies, the treatment of the various topics is uneven and somewhat unrelated. But having these essays in a central sourcebook is a plus factor that far outweighs any negative considerations.

Of special interest to Catholics are chapters 3, 11, 13, 15, and 18. The essay on "Peter C. Yorke: Advocate of the Irish from the Pulpit to the Podium" tells about one of San Francisco's most popular priests and his influence on life in the Bay Area.

RENO — THE GENESIS OF A DIOCESE

According to the historian for the Diocese of Reno, that territory within the Great Basin between the Rocky Mountains and the Sierra Nevada, "uninhabited by white men and possessed of no missions," had no historical relevance prior to American occupation. When the Diocese of Both Californias was erected, on April 30, 1840, the 110,829 square miles forming the present jurisdiction comprised part of the northernmost area of the vast ecclesiastical unit. With the exception of an alteration in title, the initial diocese remained geographically intact until the formation, on July 29, 1853, of a metropolitan district incorporating the Archdiocese of San Francisco and the Diocese of Monterey.

The population influx into Western Nevada during the 1850s necessitated a further division of responsibilities and, in September of 1860, the area between the Pacific Ocean and the western line of the 39° of latitude was formed into the Vicariate Apostolic of Marysville and, later, the Diocese of Grass Valley. That portion of Nevada south of the division–line remained attached to the Archdiocese of San Francisco.

In May of 1866, borderlines of the Diocese of Grass Valley were extended to include Sacramento and that city became the residential seat of the local bishopric. Those six counties of Southern Nevada remaining in the Archdiocese of San Francisco, along with the State of Utah, were erected into a vicariate apostolic on January 23, 1887. The area was advanced to diocesan status four years later.

The possibility of an independent diocese at Reno was discussed shortly after the turn of the century. A notice in *The Tidings* for November 10, 1905, stated that the "Rt. Rev. Bishop Grace of Sacramento was received in audience with the Pope a few days ago, and when the question of dividing the immense territory, comprising his diocese, came up for discussion, Bishop Grace pointed out that the diocese is entirely too big, and too widely separated to be properly attended to by one man, who has to make a yearly visit to every portion thereof—for it includes nearly all of Upper California and all of Nevada."

Not long afterwards, the same paper commented that "it is probable that as a result of the visit of Bishop Grace of Sacramento to Rome his extensive diocese, embracing something like 100,000 square miles will be divided and the seat of the new Episcopal See will be at Reno, Nevada. The division is another evidence of the progress of the Western world. Bishop Grace will preside over the diocese of Sacramento covering Northern California."

No action was taken, however, until March 27, 1931, when the Holy See detached all the territory of the State of Nevada from the existing ecclesiastical jurisdictions at Sacramento and Salt Lake to erect the Diocese of Reno. Appointed to the new bishopric was Father Thomas K. Gorman, the editor of the Catholic newspaper for the Diocese of Los Angeles–San Diego.

In subsequent years, Bishop Gorman was fond of relating how Nevada, the last of the forty–eight states elevated to diocesan rank, came to be given that honor. "Cardinal Mundelein of Chicago was riding through on the train one day and asked his secretary who was the bishop of Nevada. When he found out there was none, being very patriotic and politically minded, the cardinal felt it was not right for one of the sovereign states of the United States to be without a bishop so he persuaded the Holy Father to erect a new diocese."

The new ecclesiastical unit, with a Catholic population of 8,000, began its operation as an autonomous diocese on August 19, 1931, with the installation of the new bishop in Reno's Cathedral of Saint Thomas Aquinas.

RERUM NOVARUM IN SAN FRANCISCO

In a superb article for the summer, 1990 issue of *U.S. Catholic Historian*, Father Richard Gribble explained how Pope Leo XIII's encyclical *Rerum Novarum* affected the labor movement in San Francisco.

The progressive nature of the encyclical, with its statements on workers' rights and the importance of ecclesial intervention on the part of labor, melded well into the San Francisco labor scene of 1891. Among other things, it provided workers with a greater insight into their own worth and merit.

The standard bearer for implementing the teachings of Leo XIII in San Francisco was Father Peter C. Yorke who had come to the area shortly after his ordination at Baltimore in 1888. From 1891 onward, Yorke called for applying the precepts of the encyclical in his advocacy of labor versus capital. He became the "champion of labor, the oriflamme which served to rally the hard pressed ranks of labor in the city."

Peter Yorke was truly a force to be reckoned with. His style, whether as a speaker or a writer, compelled attention. His mind could strip questions to their essentials and he clothed his logic in language that was often picturesque and always vigorous.

As an orator, Father Yorke was in great demand. Archbishop Patrick W. Riordan chose him to head the campaign against the American Protective Association and so successful was he that Riordan eventually named Yorke chancellor and editor of *The Monitor*.

Early on, the priest found the general attitude among local employers inconsistent with the precepts of *Rerum Novarum*. Many industrial leaders, opposed to the right of workers to organize, fought against the pressure of collective action.

Yorke was the principal labor advocate in several major work disputes during the years 1900–1910. In the teamsters and waterfront strike of 1901, for example, Yorke successfully worked for the achievement of additional rights and more equitable wages.

He began his own newspaper, *The Leader*, and it became a forceful mouthpiece for workers' rights as outlined in *Rerum Novarum*. Yorke was especially outspoken in the Planing Mill strike of 1900 and the steel strike of 1916.

Giving official Catholic sanction to workers' associations, *Rerum Novarum* unleashed the polemic of Peter Yorke against the oppression of labor by capitalism. In 1901, he supported the rights of teamsters and waterfront workers to unionize. The high percentage of Irish and German Catholics in those organizations gave added incentive to the involvement by Yorke for workers to organize,

Although the Church supported the right of workers to organize, many employers in San Francisco were at best tolerant of such organizations. The Law and Order Committee, founded in 1916 to combat the city dock strike, exemplified attempts by employers to destroy unions and eliminate rights obtained earlier.

Roman Catholics and organized labor in San Francisco can be characterized as mutually supportive. Yorke came to personify the call by Pope Leo to unite the workers, while seeking to alleviate the plight of the poor and oppressed in society.

Yorke's brash tactics and unorthodox methods were remarkably successful in bringing positive results for the working classes in San Francisco. While not always supported by his archbishop, Yorke lived to see most of his policies vindicated. Today, he is enshrined as a pioneer in the Church's struggles on behalf of workers.

THE RESURRECTION

In the preface to a booklet about the magnificent trilogy of paintings adorning the walls of the mausoleum at Holy Cross Cemetery, Roger Cardinal Mahony has observed that the murals capture "the totality of our belief and understanding of the Resurrection of Jesus Christ."

The artist, in a remarkable fashion, "has allowed that wonderful theology of the Church to come to new and vibrant life through these pictorial renderings. She has brought together in one place all of the themes surrounding the unfathomable mystery of the Lord's Resurrection." Truly, in an unprecedented manner, she provided "a glimpse into aspects of that total mystery heretofore never seen."

Painted by the internationally–acclaimed Isabel Piczek, the mural is of special interest during the Paschal season of the year. It occupies a surface of 1,300 square feet. Executing the sketches was a monumental task that took the artist twenty–eight months. In order to accommodate the acrylic resin paintings, the walls were pre-coated with a lime and plaster base.

The entire eastern wall is dominated by the gigantic portrayal of the Risen Christ, four times life–size. The figure attired only in light and flames, victoriously embraces all things, filling them with his glory.

Christ is shown emerging from the superenergetic tomb in which the new life of cosmic creation is born. The tomb is represented by a deep violet color contoured by an outburst of light in a circular form.

The two smaller Christ figures representing the descent into Sheol (the gates of hell) and the ascent to heaven were intended as secondary features akin to a revelation. There is only one Risen Christ and the secondary depictions are merely expressions of redemptive actions.

The two arrows piercing the Risen Christ emphasize the direction of the descent and ascent. A dark arrow explains the descent from heaven into the lives of God's people. A blueish arrow starts out of Sheol on the left bottom and widens toward the right, embracing the ascending Christ.

The two figures emerging from a rainbow and the waters are Noah and his son Shem. Noah holds a cluster of grapes which symbolize the Eucharistic wine. The hands of Shem are submerged in the waters of the deluge, a sign of the universal waters of Baptism or initiation into Christ.

Noah's other hand is lifted toward the universal gate of Faith, reminiscent of Abraham and Isaac. Abraham looks upward towards a ladder made of light and enveloped by the body of Jacob.

Also standing in the gate and emerging from a harp and crown is David. As the hand of Christ opens the gates of Sheol, a man on the far left steps out from two stone tablets. This is Moses through whom comes the decalogue. Above Moses stands Ruth holding the wheat, which is the other Eucharistic symbol.

Taken as a unit, the central mural portrays Christ as the Savior of universal creation. The gates of Sheol were thrown open for all people who, at some point in history, encounter Christ.

The portrayal of the Risen Christ at Holy Cross is a meditation that unfolds gradually and fully into the beautiful theology of Easter, a wonderful source of reflection during that holy season.

RETABLOS: MASTERPIECES IN OIL OR TIN

Saints and other holy personages played an important role in the daily lives of the people in colonial Mexico and their descendants in the American west and southwest.

A collection of a hundred 19th century Mexican paintings (or retablos) in oil or tin was exhibited by Joseph P. Peters at the Philadelphia Art Alliance in the fall of 1989. This remarkable collection, one of the largest of its kind ever assembled, constituted a visual history of early Catholic devotional practice in areas like California.

In the printed program for the exhibition, Mr. Peters explained how the intimacy and preoccupation of Mexicans with the divine was a result of the unique forces that shaped the history of Latin America during preconquest and colonial times. People of those times felt themselves completely in accord with the religious sentiments and rites of the Catholic Church to such an extent that there was a complete fusion between the symbology of the Gospels and the people's capacity to express in personal and artistic terms what the Gospel narrative meant to them.

The Gospels and the traditions of the Catholic Church permeated to the marrow of their bones. When wedded to indigenous preconquest beliefs and rituals, the result was a unique form of religious expression that puzzled many 18th and 19th century Anglo–Saxon visitors to Mexico.

It almost seems to be a national characteristic of the Mexican people, as with most Ibero–Americans, that they are on intimate terms with God and His saints. It is not surprising, then, that artists were asked to supply paintings and statues of favorite saints for private veneration. The more affluent could afford paintings on canvas, but the poor had to be content with smaller paintings on wood panels or other less costly materials.

Late in the 18th century, the metallurgic process of applying a thin coat of tin to a leaf of iron was developed. Tin sheets were inexpensively produced and were used by self–taught artists as a ground for oil paintings (*retablos*).

These paintings were either specially commissioned or purchased from peddlers who hawked them door–to–door or sold them in stands set up around churches after Sunday Masses. In time, *retablos* were produced throughout central Mexico, mainly in the states of San Luis Potosi, Zacatecas, Guanajuato, Queretaro, Jalisco and Michoacan. They were also painted in other parts of Latin America, especially in Ecuador and Guatemala.

Although there are great differences in style and quality of the *retablos*, many of which found their way into California, their technique and production are quite similar. Most of the still extant *retablos* are permeated with devotion, intensity and folk stylization, often with charming simplicity. They range from crude and primitive depictions to very skillful representations which reflect the higher standards of more sophisticated guild artists.

With the development of cheaper printing methods in the 19th century, the production of tin *retablos* began to decline. Yet the lovingly–handcrafted *retablos* of yesteryears say much about the depth of faith as it unfolded in Hispanic America.

ROMAN VIEWS

A fascinating exhibition of drawings and watercolors from the collections of the *Biblioteca Apostolica Vaticana* was opened to the public at the Santa Barbara Museum of Art on November 11th, 1989. "Views of Rome" is a representative gathering of eighty–one items from the collection assembled by Thomas Ashby

(1874–1931), director of the British School at Rome, a vibrant center of studies in archaeology and topography.

Ashby began collecting his treasures in 1899, with the purchase of six albums of unpublished sketches by Carlo Labruzzi. By the time of his death, he had put together, generally through purchases in London, an estimable collection of about 6,000 prints and perhaps 1,000 drawings, together with a host of maps bearing directly or indirectly on the Roman countryside.

Several years after Ashby's death, the collection was acquired from his widow by the then Msgr. Eugene Tisserant, Pro–Prefect of the Vatican Library. Though carefully catalogued at the time, the collection remained virtually unknown until 1975. While not presenting a historic survey of European drawings of the Eternal City, "Views of Rome" exemplifies the richness and importance of the Vatican Library collection, as well as presenting a reflection on the development of public and private taste.

The exhibition at Santa Barbara provided visitors with a unique opportunity to observe European draftsmanship of the highest order from the Renaissance to the age of Romanticism. Dr. Donald McClelland of the Smithsonian Institution Traveling Exhibition Service personally arranged and supervised the exhibit at the Santa Barbara Museum of Art. A specially–prepared 304 page catalogue was prepared by Raymond Keaveney, an official at the National Gallery of Ireland. (copies are available from either the museum or Scala Publications of London.)

The gala opening of "Views of Rome" at Santa Barbara, sponsored by Daniel J. Donohue, featured an address by Archbishop Justin Rigali, President of the Pontifical Ecclesiastical Academy, who came from Rome to attend the event. Archbishop Roger Mahony expressed his pleasure that Santa Barbarans, who hosted the first bishop of the Californians just 150 years earlier, were now being honored again, this time as the hosts for one of the world's truly spectacular artistic collections.

Among the eighty–one renditions of Roman monuments and sites, none is more symbolic than Ferdinand Becker's "South Flank of St. Peter's Basilica," a pen and gray ink sketch. Another brush and gray ink 18th century rendition portrays the Palatine Hill with the Church of San Buenaventura. There is no visible trace or sign of the Palatine's former glory, only the ruins of a church built thereon by Pope Calixtus.

From its foundation, the Vatican Library has been regarded as unique among the great European libraries. This exhibition at Santa Barbara, which remained in place until the end of the year, serves to confirm the predominate role which the Vatican Library still serves for bibliophiles, collectors and researchers.

THE ROSE PARADE

For five or six hours each year, Pasadena, California, the Emerald City, becomes the capital of the world. On New Year's Day, Colorado Boulevard takes center stage as the most famous roadway in the world, surpassing Pennsylvania Avenue, the Champs Elysees and Picadilly Circus.

The Rose Parade began as a celebration of California's mild climate. Its founders, Francis Rowland and Charles Holder, patterned their floral festival after the annual "Battle of Flowers" in Nice, France. From its inception in 1889, the parade consisted of a modest procession of flower–covered carriages converging on a dusty park for a day of picnicking and sports.

It was Charles Holder who first referred to the parade as a "Tournament of Roses" and the name struck the general fancy. Today that name is prominently listed in gazetteers, almanacs and encyclopedias. In its description of the inaugural parade in 1889, the Pasadena *Evening Star* called the event "the greatest festival of a similar nature ever held in the country." If it wasn't then, it surely has become so today.

Dr. Francis F. Rowland served as the first Grand Marshal of the parade, a position he held seven times between 1890 until 1916. Since then, some of the world's most distinguished individuals have served in that capacity including actors, astronauts, writers, artists, athletes and political figures.

During the early years, members of the Valley Hunt Club would gather to decorate their carriages with elegant and exotic flowers. They would then ride down Colorado Street in what one writer called the "cavalcade of color."

Shortly after the turn of the century, the management of the event was entrusted to a group of public–minded citizens, the Pasadena Tournament of Roses Association. Today, that group of men and women still give up their evenings, weekends and holidays to ensure the success of the animated floral floats, high–stepping equestrian units and precision marching bands.

Initially there was more emphasis on events than on the parade. There were polo games, *vaquero* feats, hurdle races, a tourney at rings, bicycle races and tugs of war. In 1902, the organizers added a football game in which Michigan routed Stanford, 49–0. The next year, there was a chariot race instead. Football was re–instated as the afternoon attraction in 1916 and today that game is one of the most popular college events of the year.

By 1907, 30,000 people witnessed the floral parade which stretched for two miles. The chief feature that year was a prairie schooner, covered with blossoms and drawn by four mules, with a pioneer who had crossed the plains in 1845 sitting alongside his wife on the wagon.

In 1923, Tournament of Roses members financed the construction of a new stadium which was appropriately called the Rose Bowl. A Rose Queen has presided over the annual celebration since 1930. Her Royal Highness is selected from hundreds of local student contestants between the ages of 17 and 21. In 1995, through the medium of television and radio, 450 million people watched and heard what one television commentator called the "only mobile wonder of the world" in ninety countries, more than any event in history.

The theme of the Rose Parade for 1995 was "Sports–Quest for Excellence." Rose Queen was Aliya Haque, the Grand Marshal was Juan "Chi Chi" Rodriguez and Oregon and Penn State played in the Rose Bowl.

RUBRICAS

"Rubric" is a term applied to portions of old manuscripts and books which, for typographical embellishment, were printed in red. In Hispanic countries, the *rubricas* take on the added significance of denoting those post–signatorial flourishes which are frequently the most conspicuous features of a page.

A study of the Spanish documents in the Chancery Archives of the Archdiocese of Los Angeles covers a wide spectrum of peculiar and interesting *rubricas* used by the friars who labored in the California missions during provincial times. The intricate variety of loops, circles and zigzag lines reveals a wide variety of "lattice work," some of it quite artistic. In fact, the *rubricas* were wonderfully constructed calligraphic devices used principally as a precaution against forgery in subscribing, signing or sealing letters and statements.

Each of the friars developed his own rubric which he practiced until memorizing fully its curves, figures and scroll work. The device was so essential an ingredient of the signature that its absence called the validity of a document into question. The rubric was the only recognized manner by which a friar could "certify" or guarantee the authenticity of his signature on official documents. Its intricate design effectively defied even the most practiced forgerers. While there have been several rather prominent and fascinating forgeries uncovered within the context of California's Catholic heritage, their paucity confirms the difficulty experienced by those schooled in the art of spurious documentation.

The "paraph," a particular type of flourish, served as valid identification even when it stood alone, as was often the case with royal personages. In effect, paraph took precedence over the writer's signature.

The artistically constructed *rubricas* incorporate a myriad of designs, some resembling the interior of a maze, others the shape of a coiled snake about to strike and still others a mattress for the name to rest upon. Described by one writer as "autographical monstrosities," the *rubricas* often reflected the writer's temperament, advancing age, debility or illness. Generally, the rubrical eccentricities are remarkably accurate interpretations of character. Odd zigzag lattice work, for example, often betrays the writer as either a very nervous person or one well advanced in years.

Whether the linear markings are rapid, slow, vertical, sloped, large, small, compressed, expansive, simple, ornate, careful, slipshod, consistent or varied can also shed light on a wide range of character and personality factors. A careful study of rubrical graphology, a deductive as well as an inductive science, is still a largely unexplored means of determining and/or confirming the dominant personalities responsible for California's ecclesial foundations.

SACRAMENTAL CALIFORNIA, 1769–1846

The purpose of the Sacraments is "to sanctify men, build up the Body of Christ and give worship to Almighty God." Those divine channels of grace not only pre–suppose faith, but by words and objects they also strengthen and express it. It was a "sacramental mission" that brought the early missionaries to California. The record of their work among the native population attests to the success of their apostolate.

The 156 extant mission registers indicate that between 1769 and 1846, there were 98,055 Baptisms, 28,040 Marriages and 75,340 funerals performed by the 142 friars who staffed California's twenty–one missionary foundations.

The earliest administration of the Sacrament of Baptism was performed at *Los Cristianos*, July 22, 1769, when Frays Juan Crespi and Francisco Gómez christened two dying Indian girls Maria Magdalena and Margarita. Unknowingly, Fray Junípero Serra subsequently claimed that privilege for himself, noting in the parochial register at Monterey, that on December 26, 1770, Bernardino de Jesús Fages (became) the first Christian among the natives of California. The first white child born in California, Juan José Garcia, was baptized shortly after his birth, November 11, 1774, at Mission San Luis Obispo.

The initial conferral of Confirmation took place on June 29, 1778, at Mission San Carlos Borromeo, where Junípero Serra anointed ninety–one children. The proto–*confirmatus* was Junípero Bucareli, son of Tatlun, chief of the Carmeliño Indians. Though the Eucharistic liturgy was very likely offered along the Pacific Slope as early as 1542, the first *recorded* instance dates from November 12, 1602, when the Holy Sacrifice was celebrated at San Diego, by Carmelite priests attached to the Sebastián Vizcaíno expedition.

The first whites married in California were José Lorenzo de Esparza and Maria Josefa Davila, who exchanged matrimonial promises before Fray Junípero Serra at San Gabriel, on April 19, 1774. The Golden State's proto– priest, Father José Ygnacio Argüello, was ordained in 1808. A son of Captain Dario Argüello, the youthful priest died during an Indian insurrection at Sonora, soon after receiving holy orders.

Miguel Gómez, a native of Guadalajara, was the first cleric ordained to the priesthood in California. He received the imposition of hands from Bishop Francisco Garcia Diego y Moreno, at Mission Santa Barbara, on June 29, 1842. The first bestowal of Extreme Unction occurred on August 15, 1769, when Junípero Serra anointed José Maria Vergerano. The youthful native of Magdalena, near Guadalajara, was killed in an Indian rebellion at San Diego.

The sacraments are not merely vehicles of grace for the individual, but vital actions whereby the Church, Christ and His Spirit live and grow and become ever more truly a holy people of God. The early California missionaries understood, perhaps better than subsequent generations, how vital were the sacraments to the fabric of human society.

SACRAMENTO — DIOCESE

History must be defined in terms of people, their origin, life and destiny. For that reason, one might profitably think about the the Diocese of Sacramento in the context of the leaders chosen to shepherd its people. Bishop Patrick Manogue (1831–1895), the most typically Californian of all the state's prelates, was a gold–prospector turned cleric. His benign and kindly influence spread itself into the mansions of the mighty and the modest dwellings of the poor.

Succeeding to the bishopric of Grass Valley in 1884, Manogue soon realized the growth patterns within the diocese and asked Rome to transfer his episcopal seat to Sacramento, the state capital. The prelate's biographer said that "the thriving Diocese of Sacramento is a living testimony to the foreseeing wisdom of Bishop Manogue."

Thomas Grace (1841–1921) was an intrepid Irishman who became "a universal favorite among his people" because, as one contemporary noted, he had "not the slightest leaven of selfishness in his nature." He became administrator of the diocese in 1895 and a year later was made Bishop of Sacramento by Pope Leo XIII.

In his new position, the dauntless prelate exhibited

the energy and capacity for hard work that characterized him as a humble missionary along the gold dust trails. With his death, the great romance of California's golden days came to an end.

Bishop Patrick J. Keane (1872–1928) was among the principal heirs and benefactors of the noble heritage left behind by his priestly predecessors. Named Auxiliary of Sacramento in 1920, he succeeded two years later. Keane's most notable contribution, besides his spiritual leadership, was the extension of the school system. By the time of his demise, it could be said of Keane that he had planted deep in the hearts of the western youth the vigorous roots of eternal truth. Few there were who didn't love and respect him.

If it be true that only the humble deserve to rule, then Robert J. Armstrong (1884–1957), by his simplicity and humility of heart, was admirably fitted for the bishopric of Sacramento, a position he occupied for over a quarter century.

Consecrated March 12, 1929, Armstrong built more churches, schools and other religious edifices than had been erected in the entire previous history of the Sacramento jurisdiction. An unusually lovable and colorful character, Robert Armstrong is remembered for his human qualities of charity, patience and humility.

Joseph T. McGucken (1902–1983) became Bishop of Sacramento early in 1957, a position he occupied for five years before moving on to the metropolitan seat at San Francisco. During his short tenure, McGucken completed the seminary and expanded the religious education programs.

Alden J. Bell (1904–1982) spent most of his early ministerial years in various positions with the Catholic Welfare Bureau. After serving as Auxiliary of Los Angeles, Bell was transferred to Sacramento in 1962. His years there were busy ones, establishing parishes. opening schools and updating other facets of the apostolate.

Bishop Francis A. Quinn (b. 1921) brought an educational, journalistic and pastoral background to Sacramento. He was well prepared for shepherding the ninety–three parishes comprising the 42,597 square mile Diocese of Sacramento.

SACRED TOMB OF THE REDEEMER

For half a century, Nathaniel Currier and James Merritt Ives served as "printmakers to the American people." Today they retain that distinction in the 7,500 extant prints that bear their names, a whole heritage of artistic tradition.

Nathaniel Currier, born in 1813 in Roxbury Massachusetts, was apprenticed at an early age to William S.

and John Pendleton, the first to use lithography in the United States. In 1834, Currier left their employ to start a business for himself in New York. James Ives came into the firm in 1852, as a bookkeeper. He became a partner and general manager five years later. Their store in those early days was located on Nassau Street.

Currier and Ives were businessmen and craftsmen. Ives had some claims as an artist, but primarily the two men are mirrors of the national taste, weathervanes of popular opinion, reflectors of American attitudes from 1835 to 1907. In their prints can be found the whole florid panorama of our national life in the mid–nineteenth century, from the baroque elegance of urban *mores* to the idyllic simplicities of country life. Their prints featured fashionable turnouts in Central Park, Thanksgiving celebrations in New England and the perils of crossing the plains.

Harry T. Peters has noted that in their prints can be found that wholesome national flavor which makes their work the finest representation of the habits and customs, life and tastes, history and achievement of the exciting era which witnessed the building of a great republic.

Probably most of the "Home Sweet Home" pictures seen in American households during the 1890s can be traced directly to Currier and Ives. In perfect tune with the public taste of the times, they turned out many prints on courtship, marriage and family life. There was even a large number of lithographs on the subject of temperance.

The political prints produced by Currier and Ives are marked by a shrewdly–acid quality which makes them an invaluable commentary on the personalities and issues of contemporary political life. Drawn by highly competent artists, colored by hand in what may have been the earliest experiment of mass production, the prints are an important American art form. From their five story factory at 33 Spruce Street, in New York City, prints were distributed continually between 1866 and 1907.

That the two partners were not devoid of humor is evidenced by the fairly large quantity of social and political satires, together with many cartoons. Most of the social satire doesn't deviate far from the slapstick pattern. Another prominent category of their work is that of the sporting print. Those concerned themselves with many facets, but racing scenes were probably the best. They were especially good at featuring trotting horses.

Religion was an exceptionally potent factor in those days and a large number of Currier and Ives religious prints were made to order, while others were copied from European paintings. The Archival Center has one lithograph from the Estelle Doheny Collection. Numbered 69 it is entitled "The Sacred Tomb of the Redeemer." Hand–colored and printed on woven paper with margins, it is considerably timestained, yet is still a precious remnant from the "printmakers to the American people."

SAINT BRIDGET'S CATHOLIC CHINESE CENTER

There was a strong affinity for the Chinese among Western missionaries who lived and worked in China for generations and were forced to leave after the outbreak of war with Japan. While the Chinese had their roots deep in California history, their numbers in the southland did not grow rapidly until after the turn of the century and what few there were did not profess the Christian faith. However, by the time of World War II, there were enough in Los Angeles to launch what became Saint Bridget's Catholic Chinese Center.

As noted by Sister Noemi Crews in "A Pictorial History of the Catholic Chinese Center in Los Angeles Chinatown, 1940–1990", the center was launched with several unique challenges: First, the central part of Los Angeles already included three other major ethnic Catholic churches, as well as two established Catholic schools. Secondly, the center's location, between Cathedral High School and the Pasadena Freeway, precluded any appreciable growth and, finally, the garb and culture of Anglo priests and religious provided a major obstacle to the initial reception of the Church in the residential and commercial sections of Old Chinatown.

It was in 1939 that Father John Cowhig, a missionary from China who had returned to the United States for health reasons, first began to organize a Catholic presence among the southland's Chinese community. Archbishop John J. Cantwell was highly sensitive to the need expressed so eloquently by Cowhig and other members of the Columban Fathers. Cowhig took up residence temporarily at Cathedral High School as he began reaching out to the local Chinese community.

After making a thorough demographic study of the area, Father Cowhig chose the present site at the north end of Chinatown for his foundation. The edifice on Cottage Home Street was opened on Christmas day in 1940.

A language school was also begun and that endeavor proved to be enormously successful. Young people were anxious to learn more about their roots and, soon thereafter, a club was organized for sporting activities. The Sisters of the Immaculate Heart of Mary were asked to assist in the project and formal classes were offered at Queen of Angels Grammar School, a program that lasted until 1951. The Catholic Chinese Academy that flourished in Chinatown was highly esteemed by all the local inhabitants, most of whom had relatives or friends evangelized by Catholic missionaries in their homeland.

The archbishop was an avid supporter of the center as evidenced by a letter to a benefactor in New York: "You will be happy to hear that our Chinese Mission is filled to capacity and overflowing." The donor had paid for the original building and it was he who asked that it be called "Saint Bridget's Catholic Chinese Center". He also stipulated that Holy Mass be offered there weekly.

Except for the nursery and kindergarten, the center's school was closed in 1951, at which time the youngsters were sent to a Catholic school a few blocks away. In the mid–1960s, new waves of Chinese immigrants called for enlarging and modernizing the center. Expanded facilities were also made for liturgical activities. Today, Saint Bridget's Catholic Chinese Center is recognized as a permanent and cherished part of the Los Angeles Chinatown community.

SAINT ELIZABETH'S DAY NURSERY

Saint Elizabeth's Day Nursery has the distinction of being the oldest institution of its kind in the City of Los Angeles.

The nursery was founded in 1906 as an extension of the old Brownson House. It opened in September of that year "to care for children whose mothers were forced to work away from home." In 1910 Saint Elizabeth's was given autonomy and its own staff.

An average of eighty to a hundred children were cared for and fed during a six day week that began each morning at 6:30 a.m. Childrens' ages ranged between three months and ten years.

In 1907, Bishop Thomas J. Conaty invited a group of the leading Catholic women in the Diocese of Monterey–Los Angeles to inaugurate an auxiliary or guild whose purpose it would be to assist and finance the nursery's activities. Membership in that exclusive group included Mrs Lucian N. Brunswig, Mrs Louise M. Cole, Mrs Joseph Farrell, Mrs Daniel Grant, Mrs Richard J. Hanna, Mrs Maurice S. Hellman, Mrs Elsie Kerckhoff, Mrs Oscar Lawler, Mrs Susan E. Lynch, Mrs Ambrose McNally, Mrs Marie Rose Mullen, Mrs Daniel Murphy, Mrs. Margaret E. Nelson, Mrs Thomas W. Phillips, Mrs Arthur W. Redman, Mrs William R. Rowland, Mrs Louis C. Scheller, Mrs Eunice Ward, Mrs. Shirley Ward and Mrs William H. Workman.

Located in a two story bungalow at 135 North Anderson Street (later Mission Road), Saint Elizabeth's Day Nursery existed in the early years mostly from funds raised from a citywide pencil drive. One reporter said that "this entire city is pencilled by the good ladies from Saint Elizabeth's." The surrounding neighborhood in those days was a congested residential district of working people, many of whom were aliens or first generation Americans.

An article in *The Tidings* for April 17, 1914 solicited readers who "would journey to the home of the nursery, and spend a morning amidst the pleasant and homelike surroundings provided for the children whilst their mothers are elsewhere earning their daily bread."

The following year, the nursery was incorporated by Bishop Thomas J. Conaty in one of the last of his actions prior to his premature death. During those years, Mrs. Nellie Peyton served as director. In 1926, Saint Elizabeth's Day Nursery joined the Community Chest Agency and from that time onwards the institution became a model for similar nurseries established up and down the west coast.

An annex to the original building was erected in 1949, providing a dormitory, dining room, kitchen and laundry. Then, in 1951, a modern and functional building was constructed. Further extentions were made in 1963.

SAINT PATRICK'S PURGATORY

In the document on "Reconciliation and Penance in the Mission of the Church," the Bishops of the Sixth General Synod lamented that "at times we have lost or at least weakened the sense of penitential prayer, fasting, almsgiving, works of mercy and ascetical practices." One place where that loss has gone unfelt is Saint Patrick's Purgatory, located on a tiny islet in a lake of Donegal called Lough Derg, the Sanctuary of Station Island.

The Lough Derg devotion provides a glimpse from the twenty-first century into the fifth. Every emerging pilgrim is a sort of Rip Van Winkle who returns with experimental knowledge of Celtic Christianity. We mention this place of pilgrimage, located in the north of Ireland, because it was a favorite of the late Timothy Cardinal Manning. Customarily he visited Lough Derg every time he returned to his native land.

There are records of pilgrimages to Lough Derg from France, England, Hungary, Portugal and other places that date from the 12th century and the extent and severity of the penitential exercises were even more exacting in earlier times. That Patrick was the founder of Lough Derg is one of the oldest and most tenacious of Irish traditions. Even when persecution destroyed all the buildings on the tiny island, the pilgrimages never ceased. Since 1613, nothing has changed.

About the size of a city block, Lough Derg is an unattractive, craggy knoll less than an acre in extent. It is set in a grey, quiet lake, enfolded by a chain of low, rolling, barren, gray mountains. On the island is an imposing basilica which accommodates 1,200 people. There is a hostel for men with three stories of facilities for bunk beds, and a similar but larger building for women. A smaller church is used for confessions and nearby is a residence for the priests that staff the island.

Because of the severe weather limitations, pilgrimages to Saint Patrick's Purgatory are conducted only from May to mid–August. About 25,000 people journey to Lough Derg every year. The pilgrimages last for seventy–two hours and consist of prayer, penance and fasting. There is a light repast of dry bread and black tea or coffee each day. On arrival, pilgrims remove their shoes and stockings and go barefooted for the length of their stay. Sleep is replaced by prayer vigils on the first night.

The prayers are simple, but long. The posture of kneeling and standing at prayer near the water's edge makes an indelible impression on a person's consciousness. Holy Mass is offered in the morning and evening, with Stations of the Cross recited in the afternoons.

Pilgrims leave the island hungry, tired and sore–footed. It is a unique experience in the Church and one that Cardinal Manning made no less than twenty-six times in his eighty years. He once observed that while he dreaded nothing more than going to Saint Pattrick's Purgatory, it was a spiritual experience that he cherished above all others. It was his first priority upon arriving in Ireland.

SAINT PATRICK BATTALION

On the wall of an 18th century stone house, next to San Jacinto Church on Mexico City's historic San Angel Plaza, is a large plaque commemorating members of Saint Patrick's Battalion who were executed for having defected during the American–Mexican War. California is well represented among the names engraved on the stone memorial. The inscription reads:

> In memory of the Irish soldiers of the heroic Battalion of Saint Patrick, martyrs who gave their lives for the cause of Mexico during the unjust North American invasion of 1847.

At the top of the large plaque is Mexico's national emblem, an eagle with a snake in its mouth, along with the Irish Celtic cross. Beneath the inscription are the names of seventy–one deserters revered as Mexican heroes.

The battalion was captured by American forces during the battle of Churubusco and was tried for treason. Some were executed on the gallows erected in San Angel Plaza on September 12, 1848 and others were strung up the same day on a scaffold near Chapultepec Castle.

The background of how these one–time Irish–Americans became deserters is worth recalling. In the context of history and the social implications of that time, it is understandable why the defections occurred. About half the American forces were composed of foreign–born soldiers and probably half that number were Irish immigrants who had come to the United States during the great famine. The vast majority remained loyal to their new country during the war.

Mexico's President, Antonio Lopez de Santa Ana, publicly appealed to foreign–born soldiers in the American army "not to fight against the Catholic country from which you receive no harm." He promised every American soldier who defected 320 acres of land in a nation "without religious or ethnic prejudices."

The conflict with Mexico was never a popular one in the United States and officials place the number of deserters at 9,207 in what is generally regarded by historians as an unpopular and poorly–managed war. While most of the deserters simply left the United States, at least 300 are known to have crossed the border and signed up with the Mexican army. Of that number, about half, nearly all Irish immigrants, formed the San Patricio Battalion which fought under a green banner featuring a shamrock, a harp, a cross and a likeness of Saint Patrick.

While some deserters may indeed have defected for the promise of land and wealth, probably the majority were disgusted and appalled by the wholesale disregard and wanton destruction of the Catholic Church in Mexico by the invading American army. Irked by the pillaging of the Church and the murder of priests, sisters and even the faithful attending Mass, many Irishmen felt a sense of duty to fight for their Catholic faith.

Time has a way of eroding prejudices and today the revisionist historians are re–appraising the role of the Irish–Americans in the Mexican–American war. New questions are being asked. For example, if the lure of wealth and land were the primary reason, then why did not more of the non–Catholic deserters fight for the Mexicans?

SAINT VINCENT HOSPITAL — ROMAN INTERVENTION

Saint Vincent's Hospital is one of the most historic institutions in all of Los Angeles. Under various titles and at several locations, it embodies that unbroken chain of charity first brought to the Pacific Coast in 1855. For 145 years, the good Sisters have continued their spiritual ministrations in the name of and under the banner of the great apostle of charity, Saint Vincent de Paul. The opening of the cornerstone, at old Saint Vincent's Hospital, in 1974, was only the most recent in a long litany of historical events associated with the Daughters of Charity and their services for God's People in the United States and California.

Why has Saint Vincent de Paul favored this nation by allowing the Daughters of Charity to work so feverishly on its behalf? Perhaps part of his intercessory favor is a response to an incident that occurred many years ago— one about which the history books are strangely silent.

It all began on the second Sunday after Easter, 1830, when the relics of Saint Vincent were carried in solemn procession from the residence of the Parisian archbishop to the church at 95 *rue de Sèvres*, adjoining the Maison–Mère. It was the greatest religious celebration held in Paris since the Reign of Terror. At the conclusion of the ceremonies, the relics, encased in a beautiful silver reliquary, were hoisted to a specially–designed shrine atop the high altar of the church. But peace was not to last for long. When the dark days of the Commune descended upon Paris, the Catholic city where he wrought his marvels of charity, the relics of Saint Vincent were threatened with despoliation.

The American Consul General in Paris at the time was Andre Bienvenu Roman (1795–1866), a prominent Catholic and a former two–term Governor of Louisiana. One of his five children was a Daughter of Charity and another, then a young lady, lived in the consulate with her parents. She was quick to realize the imminent danger that one of the mobs would violate or steal the silver reliquary with its precious contents. And so, with her father's permission, the young Miss Roman had the reliquary wrapped in the American flag and secretly brought to the consulate for protection. There she kept a lamp burning constantly before the relics and spent much of her time praying that God, through the intercession of Saint Vincent de Paul, would restore peace to the agitated French capital. With the ultimate restoration of order, the reliquary was returned to its shrine on the *rue de Sèvres*—saved from destruction by the American flag that today flies over Saint Vincent's hospital.

And there is a sequel to the story. After both her parents had died, the young lady in question asked for reception as a Daughter of Charity. Her request was granted and she joined her sister in the motherhouse, on the *rue de Bac*.

The Californians of another generation hope and pray that the gratitude Saint Vincent de Paul surely has for this nation, its flag and the governor's daughter who became a Daughter of Charity will continue to manifest itself by blessing the good Sisters in their ministry to those in need,

SAINT VINCENT DE PAUL SOCIETY

The story of the Saint Vincent de Paul Society in the United States can be traced to November 20, 1845, when it was launched in Saint Louis, Missouri, by Bryan Mullanphy. Just a dozen years earlier, a young Frenchman,

Frederic Ozanam, with a group of seven or eight men, inaugurated the society in the offices of a Catholic newspaper in Paris.

Ozanam, an apologist, writer, historian, lawyer and professor, had in mind an organization that would counteract attacks against the Catholic Church by the unbelievers, deists, and rationalists of his time. After the very first meeting, Ozanam carried a supply of wood to a poor family and those symbolic logs ignited a tremendous conflagration of charity that spread throughout the world.

The first parochial conference of the Saint Vincent de Paul Society was established at Los Angeles in 1904 in Saint Vibiana's Cathedral parish. From there it rapidly spread to scores of parishes reaching a high of ninety parochial conferences with more than 750 active members.

When Bishop John J. Cantwell founded the Bureau of Catholic Charities in the Diocese of Monterey–Los Angeles in 1919, the Saint Vincent de Paul Society was made part of the Family Welfare section. Five years later, with the establishment of the Catholic Welfare Bureau, the Saint Vincent de Paul Society was restored to its original autonomy. At that time, the field of the society's work was defined as including all parochial welfare and relief cases, supplemental relief to families, society welfare problems for the homeless and spiritual and temporal works of mercy.

By 1945, in the words of Archbishop Cantwell, the society organized when "we were yet a little more than an outpost of the Catholic world," was "strong and healthy with that vigor which emanates from the charity of Christ." By then it was made up of a network of parochial conferences that served the entire Catholic population in the four county archdiocese. All of the funds from poor boxes in the parish churches were turned over to the Society to enable it to carry on its work among the needy. Thousands of worthy recipients received assistance each year.

The objective of the conferences was to sustain its adherents "by mutual example, in the practice of a Christian life." Members visited the poor, brought them needed assistance and afforded them religious consolation. Arrangements were also made for Catholic instruction for the imprisoned, through the distribution of moral and religious books. No work of charity was considered foreign to members of the Society.

In 1945, the central headquarters for the Society in Los Angeles was located downtown at 254 South Broadway, Room 228. That office was headed by the secretary and three assistants who were on duty eight hours daily. Legal and medical aid were provided by members of the Lawyers and Doctors Guild which had been established in 1927.

Beyond the poor boxes, one of the chief sources of support for the Society was the salvage operation begun in 1917. By 1945, there were four stores and a central warehouse with trucks traveling the streets of the city and county.

Archbishop Cantwell believed that "of all organizations of the laity," the Saint Vincent de Paul Society came "closest to the heart of Christ, for His heart was love personified. It sees Christ in the person of every human individual, but especially in those who are needy, for with them Christ has specifically identified Himself."

Founded in the days when charity still resided in the churches and other local organizations, the Saint Vincent de Paul Society was the fore–runner of today's social welfare programs. Especially was that true in Los Angeles.

SAN BERNARDINO — DIOCESE

The creation of a new ecclesial district encompassing the two counties of San Bernardino and Riverside was announced by Archbishop Jean Jadot from the Apostolic Delegation on July 18, 1978. Appointed chief shepherd of the new Diocese of San Bernardino was Father Philip Straling, Pastor of Holy Rosary Church (now the Cathedral), a forty–five year old native of the area.

Carved from the massive 36,000 square mile parent jurisdiction of San Diego, the new diocese was the eleventh established within the State of California. It was one of the last authorized by Pope Paul VI. Embracing approximately 235,665 Catholics (out of a total population of 1,250,000), the new diocese comprised a geographical area of 27,047 square miles.

The five deaneries of Ontario, Palm Springs, Riverside, San Bernardino and Victorville were being served by 128 diocesan and forty–three religious priests, together with 280 religious women. An impressive eighty–five parishes were in operation in the two counties. Catholics comprised 29% of the total population in San Bernardino County and 17% in Riverside.

Almost 10,000 youngsters were enrolled in twenty–nine elementary schools, two secondary schools and three seminaries (two in Riverside and another in Victorville). There were also two hospitals in the diocese, as well as retreat centers at Cherry Valley, Newberry Springs and Redlands. Newman chaplaincies had been established at eleven colleges and universities. The bulk of the diocesan combined populace was centered in what economists dubbed the Riverside–San Bernardino–Ontario metropolitan area.

Borders of the Golden State's newest jurisdiction extend from the 11,000 foot high Telescope Peak to the floor of Death Valley, some 2,280 feet below sea level in San Bernardino County and from the 10,830 foot high

San Jacinto Peak to the Salton Sea, 230 feet below sea level in Riverside County.

The physical boundaries of the two counties are larger than four New England states. The area abounds in such geographic and geological features as twisted rocks and fossil beds, all of which indicate that the Pacific Ocean once extended into what is now desert land.

Within the diocese, desert comprises some 90% of the area. About 15 to 20% of the total population resides in that thermal area. Both counties have districts of varied economic scale, ranging from Palm Springs and Lake Arrowhead to the *barrios* of the inner cities where large families struggle with direct poverty.

The entire diocese boasts of rich agricultural lands, with farming, milk and egg production high on the list of economic mainstays. (Almost all the dates sold in the United States come from the Coachella Valley). There are seventeen incorporated cities in Riverside County and fifteen in San Bernardino. Among the incorporated areas, the City of Riverside is the most populous, with 154,000 residents. There are 104,000 in the City of San Bernardino.

SAN BUENAVENTURA — CITY

If the origin and correct usage for the picturesque name bestowed upon California's "Poinsettia City" is unknown to the majority of the area's inhabitants, perhaps this brief reflection might be useful.

It all began at Bagnarea, in 1221, with the birth of a youngster christened John Fidanza. As a child of four years, he became seriously ill and hovered dangerously near death. His mother hastened to Saint Francis of Assisi, who was preaching in the vicinity, begging him to come and intercede with the Lord on behalf of the youth. The saint acceded to her request, prayed over the child, and immediately there was a cure.

Francis was then heard to utter the prophetic words: "*0 buono ventura*," "0 blessed things to come!" From that day onwards, the child was called Bonaventure, a name he retained even in religious life. Bonaventure later became a Franciscan and, in 1257, was elected Minister General of the Order. A gifted theologian, Bonaventure governed the friars for eighteen years, later becoming Bishop of Albano and a cardinal. It was he who inaugurated the practice of reciting the *Angelus*.

Fray Junípero Serra brought to fulfillment a desire first envisioned by Jose de Galvez when, on Easter Sunday of 1782, he founded the ninth and last of his missions along *El Camino Real*, placing it under the patronage of San Buenaventura. An attempt to formally inaugurate a town near the mission in 1848 was not suc-

cessful, but a Post Office was established and named after the mission in 1861. A county was created from part of Santa Barbara County in 1872, and given the abbreviated name "Ventura."

In 1891, because they found the name too long to write and too difficult to pronounce, postal officials began using the shortened form "Ventura" for the city and a decade later the Southern Pacific started referring to its station as simply "Ventura" in the timetables.

Zoeth Eldredge, in his campaign to restore Hispanic names, wrote the following obituary to the old name in the April 10, 1905 issue of the San Francisco *Chronicle*:

> And now comes the Post Office Department which is the most potent destroyer of all. I have spoken before of the injury done the people of San Buenaventura. They cling to that name and use it among themselves. But they are doomed. Mapmakers of a pocket guide following the lead of the post office, call the place Ventura, and the historic name will be lost.

Legally, the city is still "San Buenaventura" and that name proudly adorns the Fire Department's hook and ladder truck, as well as the city's official stationery. One can also observe a gradual resurgence of the title on certain street signs and other markers. It is heartening that a few purists continue to utilize the traditional nomenclature. And why not? The name San Buenaventura reflects the area's history and differentiates the city from the county.

There is little enough of the spiritual left in contemporary society. How appropriate it is that there's still a place along the Pacific Slope whose official name recalls a miraculous intervention that occurred at Bagnarea, in 1221.

SAN BUENAVENTURA — MASS ON THE PIER

Among the many centennial celebrations held at San Buenaventura during 1882 was the offering of Holy Mass by Father Cyprian Rubio (1827–1905) on a makeshift altar at the far end of the old Ventura pier. Though there is no known account of the liturgical event, it must have been a festive occasion. Presumably it occurred on or around March 31st or possibly even on Easter Sunday.

The Ventura pier is still very much in evidence. It juts out from its bluff below the freeway like a giant hockey stick. Inasmuch as the coast faces south at that point, the 1,700 foot pier, except for its broad outer end, also faces in that direction. The present pier, last rebuilt in 1928 and repaired a number of times since, is ideally situated to withstand the storm waves running down the ferocious Santa Barbara Channel, an area described as the "naval graveyard of the Pacific."

The earliest photographs of the Ventura wharf portray railroad tracks along its length. They were probably placed there by the Southern Pacific Railroad which extended its lines to San Buenaventura in 1882. The first wharf, dating from 1872, was built by Captain Robert Moody, an English mariner, who had settled in San Buenaventura after a lifetime at sea. Originally the wharf was 1200 feet long and easily accommodated large ocean–going vessels.

The pier flourished in its early days. Unfortunately, its redwood pilings were dislodged in the terrific winter storms of December 1878, probably because the pitch of the pier was wrongly slanted. The pier was eventually rebuilt and served the small town of San Buenaventura very effectively. During a storm, in December of 1914, the steamship *Coos Bay*, which was tied alongside, broke loose and drove itself completely through the pier, destroying the ship and severely damaging its moorings.

In 1917, the pier was once again fixed and this time extended about 500 feet out into the Pacific. Nine years later, it was destroyed by a powerful electric storm. Inasmuch as the pier was essential for the lumbering and petroleum trades, it was rebuilt and served until 1935, when it was ravaged by fire. In its next reconstruction, a four foot gauge–railway was placed atop the pier.

Though damaged in the swells of 1983, the Ventura Pier is still in place. It is now used mostly by fishermen who compete with the seagulls for mastery over the once commercial thoroughfare

SAN DIEGO CATHOLICITY

Among the Christian communities of this great nation, few if any have a greater claim to antiquity than the city and people bearing the hallowed and revered patronage of Saint Didacus. Discovered by Rodriquez Cabrillo in 1542, named by Sebastián Vizcaíno in 1602 and inaugurated by Junípero Serra in 1769, San Diego bears the added distinction of being the seat of the first bishopric for the Californias.

Indeed, this is where it all began for Christ along the Pacific Slope. Here, on America's western shores, was reared the first cross, built the first church and established the first modern city. Here too sprang the first cultivated field, the first palm, the first vine and the first olive tree to blossom into fruitage. And most important of all, here the blood of the first martyr was poured out upon the ground as the seedling for Christianity. From this missionary outpost, at the very edge of the known world, the gray–robed sons of Saint Francis pushed the Spanish frontier north to Sonoma, carving out of the wilderness that path later popularized in literature as the King's Highway.

Along that *Camino Real* went emissaries of the Spanish realm to claim and possess the land, to develop and harness its natural resources and to acquaint its inhabitants with the duties and privileges of citizenship. Down that same roadway traveled the missionaries of Christ to proclaim and extend the Kingdom of Heaven, to evangelize and civilize its diverse peoples and to win a whole new race to the Christian way–of–life.

In this newest of the world's empires, Christ was King and the friars were His soldiers. They claimed this golden land in His name and possessed it for His glory— by living and practicing those Christ–like virtues of poverty, chastity and obedience. Through the ministry of Fray Junípero Serra and his confreres, the Mission of San Diego de Alcalá became the first tabernacle of God in Alta California. From this far–Western cradle of Christianity, the Gospel message was brought first to the Indians and then to their multiracial successors as God's People.

San Diego, though it be very old in years, is yet quite young in its destiny. With all their rich historical background, San Diegans do well to honor the past, but they would do poorly to worship it. A backward glance into the dim and shadowy passage of 458 years serves contemporary Christians well only if it motivates them to renew their dedication to Him whose banner was first unfurled here, just thirty–six years after the earthly remains of Christopher Columbus were laid in the tomb.

SAN FRANCISCO — HEAVENLY CITY

The city named for Saint Francis is nearly surrounded by the ocean and the Bay. First sighted by Jose Ortega in 1769 and entered by Juan Ayala and Jose Cañizares in 1776, it lies on the northern tip of its peninsula and covers just 46.38 square miles. Settled in the year of American independence, the city built on forty–three hills is unlike any other in all the world. And, in that sense, it resembles the saint of Assisi whose patronage and image it bears.

"San Francisco was zero in 1848, a Mexican village," says columnist Kevin Starr. "And in 1870 it was the tenth–largest city in the United States." The author of *Americans and the California Dream* goes on to say that ne'er–do–wells found themselves making fortunes on minerals or dry goods. Young Yankees rode into town by the thousands, looking for adventure and gold. "It was never your average American City . . . San Francisco, right from the very start, was second chance, a new beginning."

From its earliest days, San Francisco stretched out the welcome mat to immigrants from China, Italy and Ireland, all of them anxious for a better life through hard work. And, following the devastating earthquake, there were abundant challenges. The city's two world–famous bridges and half of its presently–standing buildings were erected between 1906 and the onset of World War II.

Like America itself, but more urban and less buttoned down, San Francisco's mild but foggy climate tends to nurture eccentrics. When the local loony Norton I, self–proclaimed Emperor of North America and Protector of Mexico, died in 1880, 30,000 people flocked to his funeral. No wonder that Rudyard Kipling characterized San Francisco as "a mad city—inhabited for the most part by perfectly insane people."

San Francisco's size, one tenth that of Los Angeles, gives it many economic advantages over the sprawling metropolis to the south. The land supply is so small and the demand so great that residential real estate value surpasses that of any other place in the nation. The exotic centerpiece of downtown's rising skyline is Archbishop Joseph T. McGucken's magnificent Saint Mary's Cathedral. That award–winning house–of–worship has set a whole new architectural trend. Between 1982 and 1984, *Time* magazine reported that a new skyscraper was topped off every five weeks!

The Census Bureau places the San Francisco's Asian population at a conservative 22%, just about equal to that of blacks and Hispanics combined. The city has no fewer that eight Chinese daily newspapers! San Francisco has a charisma that defies description. It has always been so and probably always will be. The city was gay when that term meant merry and blithe, when its 49ers were gold prospectors, rather than football players.

Chances are that Francis of Assisi would feel right at home in the city that bears his name. It is a beautiful, vivacious, dramatic city, one that is funky but clean, elegant but spunky, modern but provincial. It is probably the closest thing America has to a heavenly city!

SAN FRANCISCO'S "STATUE OF LIBERTY"

Herb Caen, the popular columnist for the San Francisco *Chronicle*, once described Beniamino Bufano (c.1898–1970) as a "beatnik before the term was coined, an ancient hippie" who somehow managed to become "a legendary figure before his death." Bufano liked to work big because, as he was fond of saying, he didn't want to create small elegant objects of art for the cloisters of the rich, but works for all the world to see and enjoy, preferably in the open.

One of Bufano's most revolutionary ideas was an 180 foot statue of Saint Francis of Assisi, which the artist envisioned atop Twin Peaks, overlooking the city bearing his name. Executed in stainless steel, the statue would be even taller than the State of Liberty.

The proposal was rejected in the first skirmish with the San Francisco Art Commission. Members did agree, however, on one thing—that Bufano was one of the few American artists with either the background or the ability to produce a statue of such gigantic proportions.

The issue soon became a *cause celebre* bringing forth scornful as well as enthusiastic letters to local newspapers. Dozens of news stories in the *Chronicle* reported the pros and cons of the statue.

Archbishop John J. Mitty wrote to the Commission expressing approval and saying that "it will be a tremendous asset to the city and it will become one of the most distinctive, outstanding monuments throughout the world."

Others expressed contrary viewpoints, including several members of the California Federation of Women's Clubs who called it "a dressmaker's dummy," "a wooden thing," " grotesque" and other equally unflattering things. Maynard Dixon, a noted realistic painter, signed a petition in favor of the statue, but drew sly cartoons of a Saint Francis accompanied by a goose, from which he had evidently extracted an egg.

The nationally–syndicated columnist, Westbrook Pegler, made hilarious capital of the proposed monument. In one of his diatribes, Pegler called it "a tombstone cutter's nightmare," declaring that he himself could do a better job of design.

Pegler posed in a smock and beret for newspapers, which picked up the story eagerly. A reporter in the Bay Area wrote, when seeing the Pegler photograph, that the statue "may one day frighten off a Japanese armada," but that "civilization were better served should some dear foe sail close enough to blow it down."

On February 3, 1937, the Art Commission authorized the statue and on the following May 8th, Mayor Angelo Rossi inspected and approved a revised model of Saint Francis. By this time, however, Bufano had become totally disillusioned by the opposition to his masterpiece.

The proposed statue was never completed or, for that matter, ever started. Bufano made seven or so different models, but none was ever dignified by enlargement. As noted by Bufano's biographer, "the whole project fizzled and faded." Bufano lived on for many years and today his artistic accomplishments are coveted by museums and private collectors. As is the case with many persons of great talent, Bufano's spirit was simply ahead of his time.

And so San Francisco never got its Statue of Liberty.

SAN FRANCISCO CHANCERY ARCHIVES

The prominence of the San Francisco Chancery Archives has long been recognized by historians, many of whose footnotes bear the familiar code, *Archb. Arch.* The pivotal importance of this archival depository is a natural outgrowth of the ecclesiastical and jurisdictional development in the state. Prior to 1936, San Francisco was the metropolitan seat for all of California and very little escaped the attention of the residential ordinaries entrusted with governing the archdiocese, in the years after 1853. Its gradual reduction in size and influence did not diminish appreciably the archdiocese's valuable historical documentation, much of which remains even now virtually unexplored.

A fairly well–organized curia has functioned in the Bay City since 1878, when Archbishop Joseph Sadoc Alemany instituted the office of chancellor in the person of Father Peter J. Grey. A progression of exceptionally qualified and able chancellors in succeeding decades established a tradition of efficiency in record preservation unequalled in any other part of the state.

Much of the system presently discernible in the archives, housed on the fourth floor of the Chancery Office, at 441 Church Street in San Francisco, can be credited to the late Monsignor Charles F. Ramm, who catalogued the collection's more outstanding materials shortly after the turn of the century.

The most historically treasured holding in the San Francisco Chancery Archives is the Alexander S. Taylor Collection, a group of papers ranging from 1770 to 1846, amassed during the years Taylor functioned as Clerk of the United States District Court at Monterey. In 1854, Taylor offered his documents, consisting of letters from the civil and religious authorities of both Baja and Alta California, to the Library of Congress. It has long been a painful memory to Washington officials that the generous bibliographer's offer was not accepted. Some years later he presented 2,560 of the documents to Saint Mary's Library Association. There the letters were bound into eight volumes and chronologically indexed by John Ruard. The collection subsequently passed to the Chancery Archives where it has remained ever since.

In the 1940s, the papers were microfilmed and prints placed on deposit at the Academy of American Franciscan History in Washington, D.C. and at the Santa Barbara Mission Archives. In 1966, Archbishop Joseph T. McGucken graciously allowed the Taylor Papers to be xeroxed for inclusion in the Chancery Archives of the Archdiocese of Los Angeles.

Typical of the quality of other materials in the San Francisco Chancery Archives are three volumes of documents relating to the Pious Fund of the Californias which were presented to the archdiocese by the heirs of the famous legal adviser, John Thomas Doyle. The bulk of holdings pertain to the diocesan period, that is, the years after 1840. Included therein are files of the various archbishops and bishops, parochial correspondence, clergy personnel records, letters to religious communities and the usual run of categories associated with ecclesiastical affairs.

While their primary function is not that of serving the general public, the San Francisco Chancery Archives are generally available to qualified scholars having a legitimate interest in their contents. Anyone wishing to consult this unique archival depository may address a written request to the archdiocesan chancellor, outlining the petitioner's purpose and competence, along with the dates and times he wishes to visit the archives.

SAN FRANCISCO'S HISTORIC *CATHEDRA*

The throne or *cathedra* is the chair from which a bishop comments on the scriptural readings. Initially a piece of furniture in the Roman Emperor's palace, it became a chair of distinction for orators and judges and finally a symbol of their office.

Gradually adopted into Christian worship services, the *cathedra* was placed in the vertex of the apse, raised above the priests' seats which adjoined it on both sides. Originally constructed of wood, it was later fashioned out of stone and, in the Byzantine period, was made to resemble the throne of civil officials. The church where it was placed came to be known as the "cathedral" or bishop's church.

The historic *cathedra* used by California's first metropolitan archbishop, Joseph Sadoc Alemany, is one of the Golden State's most historic relics. It has been removed from storage and placed on public view in the chapel of Holy Cross Mausoleum, at Colma.

Though the exact age of San Francisco's *cathedra* or archiepiscopal "throne" has not been determined, it was likely constructed for Old Saint Mary's Cathedral at California and Dupont (now Grant Avenue) in the late 1870s. The original cathedral served the Archdiocese of San Francisco from 1854 to 1885, when circumstances forced the newly–installed Archbishop, Patrick W. Riordan, to move its functions (and its *cathedra*) to temporary facilities on Eddy Street,

With the formal dedication of the Romanesque edifice on Van Ness Avenue, in January of 1891 the *cathedra* was once again moved, this time to a cathedral named for Our Lady's Assumption. From its place of prominence in the new Saint Mary's Cathedral, the historic seat witnessed a long series of liturgical functions presided over by Archbishops Patrick W. Riordan, Edward J. Hanna and John J. Mitty.

Though there was some cracking and breaking in various parts of the edifice, the cathedral suffered no serious damage during the earthquake and subsequent fire of 1906. The story of Father Charles A. Ramm's successful efforts to save the cathedral form an exciting chapter of California's Catholic heritage.

When Archbishop Mitty had the sanctuary of the cathedral renovated, he commissioned Miss Charleton Fortune of Carmel to design a new *cathedra* with a tester, dossal etc. With the installation of the new seat, the Alemany *cathedra* was relegated to a storage area in the basement of Saint Mary's. Because it was placed on a slight elevation, it escaped water damage when the cathedral was destroyed by fire on September 7, 1962. A few days after the conflagration, the *cathedra* was moved to the sacristy of San Francisco de Asis (Mission Dolores), where it remained until the summer of 1979.

The throne, with its wooden canopy, stands about 10' 3" in height. It is executed in oak, with a good deal of excellent carving. Above the Ordinary's seat is the carved and gilded coat–of–arms associated with metropolitan archbishops.

SAN FRANCISCO — OAKLAND BRIDGE

Probably no bridge in all of United States history was inaugurated with such ecclesial fanfare as was that which spanned the central part of the bay between San Francisco and Oakland. It was indeed a notable accomplishment. Erected at a cost of $77,000,000, the eighty mile double–tiered bridge was the largest ever built, a distinction it retained for another decade.

When plans were announced that Eugenio Cardinal Pacelli, the Papal Secretary of State, would visit San Francisco in late October, 1936, Mayor Angelo Rossi suggested that the bridge be blessed on that occasion by the man whom the San Francisco *News* nominated as "the most probable successor to Pope Pius XI."

Cardinal Pacelli and his three travelling companions, Bishop Francis J. Spellman of Boston, Count Enrico Galeazzi of Vatican City and Raymond Riesgo arrived on the evening of October 27th, aboard a special United Air Lines plane chartered by Mrs. Genevieve Brady of Long Island.

The next day, following a Pontifical Mass at Saint Mary's Cathedral, Cardinal Pacelli and Archbishop John J. Mitty were driven to the Oakland side of the bridge over the upper tier and then back to San Francisco on the lower level. The actual blessing took place at West Tower 1. Following the brief ceremony, "the highest ranking dignitary of the Catholic Church ever to visit the United States" said he "very much marveled" at the gigantic bridge and had "greatly enjoyed" his trip by car over the span.

It was easy enough to understand why the cardinal was so impressed by the "beauty and charm" of the bridge. The glistening Transbay bridge includes (in the west crossing) two suspension bridges of 2,210 feet sharing a joint center anchorage in deep water and a cantilever bridge of 1,400 feet, together with approach truss and girder spans of various lengths. One of the pier foundations is carried down to a record–breaking depth of 240 feet.

The giant structure of steel and concrete is approached at its western end by ramps that lead over certain downtown streets in San Francisco to the first span over the water near Pier 26, at the Embarcadero. A land link of the bridge is constructed on Yuerba Buena Island, midway between the two cities and just within the boundary of San Francisco City and County.

Prior to the City opening of the bridge, on November 12th, Monsignor Charles A. Ramm delivered a formal invocation, asking God's blessings on "this wondrous creation, upon its designers and its builders, and upon us all for whose use and joy it is this day dedicated and opened."

The monsignor continued in what must be the most beautifully–phrased invocation yet recorded in California's Catholic heritage:

> As it binds together our separate shores by the strong strands of steel that reach into the very hearts of two great communities so, we pray Thee, let it also be a symbol of those invisible bonds that will bind these communities together in friendship, in common interests and in abiding peace.
>
> Lifted high above the restless waters, let this Royal Highway, laden with its freight of human life, and with the products of busy industry, be a safe channel of traffic for the ceaseless stream of travelers who will speed over it on their lawful quests of business and pleasure. Guard them against dangers, and save them from accidents.
>
> And as by shortening time and space, it will bring us outwardly closer to one another, so let it also help to bring us inwardly nearer together in those social and spiritual relationships which are Thy precious gifts to the common family life of all Thy children.

SAN JOSE — PUEBLO BICENTENNIAL

On November 29, 1977, *El Pueblo de San Jose de Guadalupe*, the oldest civil settlement in Alta California, observed the bicentennial of its establishment. The founding of the *pueblo* was occasioned by the difficulty the Spanish government encountered in supplying provisions for the existing *presidios*. Governor Felipe de Neve felt that *pueblos* would be the most efficient means of utilizing the fertile California lands for agricultural production.

Acting on instructions from the governor, Jose Joaquin Moraga led an expedition of sixty–eight persons including nine soldiers from Monterey and San Francisco, five colonists, their families (and one servant) to an area two and a half miles from Santa Clara Mission, along the eastern shoreline, near the source of the *Rio Guadalupe*.

The traditional foundation site is marked on the grounds of Jefferson School, at 73 Hobson Street, San Jose, adjoining the property on which formerly stood the Vendome Hotel.

As provided in the *Laws of the Indies*, the *pueblo* was laid out around a central plaza or square. Homesites were measured off, and each family received a plot on which to erect a dwelling.

There were also agricultural plots and they too were carefully measured out, a separate parcel for each settler. These latter plots could not be subdivided and they also were "inalienable forever." Timber and water rights were retained by the Crown.

Half of the *pueblo* was retained by the town government. It was rented out and the accruing income applied to expenses of the Crown. There was also a common land surrounding the *pueblo*, equal in area to the size of the town. There the inhabitants recreated and grazed their herds. The first *pueblo* houses were erected in the area where modern Taylor Street abuts the Guadalupe River.

Fray Junípero Serra and the friars at Santa Clara opposed the location of *El Pueblo de San Jose de Guadalupe* on the grounds that its closeness to the mission specifically violated the *Laws of the Indies* and thus was prejudicial to the rights of the natives. In any event, the *pueblo* continued its existence, though not without a long series of unfortunate incidents that did indeed compromise the best interests of the Indians.

The first specifically religious function associated with the *pueblo* occurred two years after the town's inauguration, on November 6, 1779, when Fray Junípero Serra confirmed a group of the colonists at Santa Clara Mission.

In 1803, the friars from Santa Clara built a small adobe *capilla* or "chapel of ease" on the plaza of the *pueblo*. Nine years later, the local residents sought and obtained permission from the *Presidente* of the California Missions to have Holy Mass said in their chapel on those rare occasions when it was necessary to provide Viaticum for the dying. From this it can be inferred that the Liturgy was offered only sporadically at San Jose in those early years.

Though weakened by an earthquake the year after its erection, the chapel lasted until 1835, when it was considerably enlarged. It was thoroughly renovated by Fray Jose Maria Mercado in anticipation of the first episcopal visitation of Bishop Francisco Garcia Diego y Moreno which took place on July 13, 1844. After the chapel was destroyed by fire, in 1859, it was replaced, on the same site, by the present stone church which was dedicated to

Saint Joseph just a century after the establishment of *El Pueblo de San José de Guadalupe*.

The United States Postal Service officially recognized and solemnized the bicentennial of the first civil settlement in Alta California with a special 13 cent commemorative stamp, issued at San Jose, on September 9, 1977.

SAN SIMEON

San Simeon is probably the most spectacular private residence ever built in the United States. The magnificent *La Casa Grande* and its guest houses were located atop "Enchanted Hill" on the 265 acre ranch belonging to William Randolph Hearst (1863–1951).

The "castle" with its 146 rooms was begun in 1919 and took twenty–eight years to complete. It houses Hearst's vast collection of paintings, sculpture, tapestries, antique silver, furniture and books. Shortly after Mr. Hearst's death, San Simeon became a California State Historic Monument and was opened to the public for the first time. It is among the most popular tourist attractions on the west coast.

Of special interest to Catholics are the numerous religious items that Mr. Hearst gathered from European churches, dealers and palaces. In 1946, this writer was given a tour of the warehouse on the wharf at San Simeon and even then it was packed with choir stalls, stained glass and statuary destined for *La Casa Grande*.

The main entrance to the castle is fashioned like a Gothic cathedral, with limestone portrayals of Sts. Peter and Paul guarding the door. The virgin and Child, enshrined in a niche above, were acquired from a defunct Spanish convent.

A favorite of visitors is the impressive bedroom furnished with the bed of the French Prime Minister, Jean Cardinal Richelieu. It is described as "carved and gilded walnut; Lombardic, late sixteen century." The bedboard, carved to simulate a copy of fringed drapery, embodies the cardinal's coat–of–arms. On each side of the Florentine lectern in the vestibule are tiny elaborately carved sanctuary chairs.

Of all the rooms in *La Casa Grande*, the refectory was Mr. Hearst's favorite. The Gothic choir stalls and other artifacts give the room a distinct dignity. Covering the walls between the banners are Flemish tapestries portraying scenes from the life of the prophet Daniel and his encounters with King Nebuchadnezzar of Babylon.

The Della Robbia suite is dominated by works of art from the family for which it is named. Over the French Louis XII fireplace is a bas–relief of Saint Joseph and Child, flanked by a pair of angelic candlesticks. On the right wall, above an ornate table is a painting of the

Immaculate Conception attributed to Bartolome Murillo.

In almost every room are delicately carved statues of St. Anthony, Saint Catherine of Siena, Saint Francis and others. When once asked why there was no chapel, Mr. Hearst responded: "Every room is a chapel. Nowhere in this home does one feel isolated from God or His saints."

Hearst was a highly–educated man well versed in the scriptures. At one time he possessed one of the finest collections of Bibles in the world. The kind of art that pleased him most was religious. His love and respect for the Blessed Mother is evident from the many depictions of Mary in tapestries, needlework, marble, terra cotta and glass.

Nominally an Episcopalian, Mr. Hearst exhibited respect and tolerance for all forms of worship. Through the years he presented substantial gifts to Notre Dame University and the California missions. He reserved for his own suite an early 14th century Madonna by Segna, a masterpiece of Renaissance art and probably the single most valuable item in the collection.

SANTA ANA WIND

Myths die hard, especially those which appeal to the imagination. One such local myth revolves around the hot, dry wind that blows over the central plain of California's southland in fall and winter. That "east wind" has been labelled in various ways over the years. One rather charming story claims that the wind was named after the Mexican general, Antonio Lopez de Santa Anna, whose horsemen stirred up clouds of dust in their forays through Southern California. But that contention can be dismissed for two very good reasons: The general never entered the area and he spelled his name with two "n's."

Another theory maintains that the true name is "Santana," derived from Indian usage. Hating the wind, they referred to it, in their own language as, "the Wind of Evil Spirits." The mission friars supposedly preferred "Satan's Wind," a term gradually corrupted into "Santana." The most logical explanation is that "Santana" is merely an Anglo version of Santa Ana.

In 1847, Commodore Robert Stockton encountered a Santa Ana while camping at the mouth of Santa Ana Canyon, in present–day Orange county. He recorded that the "wind blew a hurricane and the atmosphere was filled with particles of fine dust so that we could not see and but with difficulty breathe . . ."

The wind was thereafter called "Santa Ana" because it appeared to originate in Santa Ana Canyon. Actually it begins in the high pressure air masses beyond the moun-tains and, seeking the lower pressure of the coast, is heated by compression as it pours down the slopes.

Historically, the term "Santa Ana" was first used in an article on "The Philosophy of Sandstorms" which appeared in the Los Angeles *Evening Express* on November 15, 1880. That essay began: "In parts of the Los Angeles Valley, the Santa Anas pour their blasts of desert sand, making the house the only comfortable retreat."

In December of 1901, a Western Union dispatcher filed a story about a "Santa Ana" wind that had allegedly toppled trees, blew off roofs, piled up sand and other-wise wrought havoc on his city. There was objection to the report from local officials who were competing with other Southern California cities for their share of eastern immigrants. Outraged by the bad publicity, the Chamber of Commerce formed a committee to discourage news-papers from using the term "Santa Ana" to describe the wind. Undaunted, the United States Weather Bureau, in its 1903 publication of "Climatology of California," spoke about a wind known in the area as the "Santa Ana."

Thirty years later, Father St. John O'Sullivan of San Juan Capistrano Mission told a reporter from the Los Angeles *Times* that an old friend, Magdalena Murillo, who was born on the Las Bolsas ranch in 1848, always spoke about the wind as a "Santa Ana" because it came down from the Santa Ana canyon.

In his short story "Red Wind," Raymond Chandler used the correct terminology when he told how "there was a desert wind blowing that night. It was one of those hot, dry Santa Anas that come down through mountain passes and curl your hair and make your nerves jump and your skin itch." Call it what you will, but the east wind that continues to blow over Southern California will be forever associated with Santa Ana, the name it bears.

SANTA BARBARA MISSION ARCHIVES

The inauguration of new and modern facilities for the Santa Barbara Mission Archives was widely applauded, especially in scholarly circles, where that research cen-ter has long been recognized as one of the most impor-tant depositories in the United States for manuscript material pertaining to the Hispanic era.

Mission Santa Barbara has housed the central archives of the Franciscans since 1833. Researchers first utilized the rich collection as early as 1877, when agents of Hubert Howe Bancroft examined the holdings and transcribed twelve folio volumes of about five hundred pages each. Since that time, serious and accredited scholars have produced a whole library of books,

Santa Barbara Mission Archives

brochures and pamphlets based on materials in the Santa Barbara Mission Archives.

Among the carefully catalogued documentary data are annual and biennial reports of the missions, register books, inventories correspondence of missionaries and civil officials and personal diaries dating from the period of Franciscan penetration into Baja California, in 1767.

There were no fewer than 2,842 entries enumerated in a calendar of the archives, published in 1947, exclusive of reports, statistics, tables, lists and a considerable number of documents not belonging to the Californiana collection. Since that time, the quantity of holdings has been tripled. The archives have been enriched, for example, with an additional 8,000 pages of transcripts relating to the Serra Cause; 2,300 from the Alexander Taylor Collection and about 1,000 from Rome and the Archives of the Archdiocese of Los Angeles. The nearly 2,000 original documents from the De la Guerra Papers are the most recent acquisitions.

In addition to primary sources, the Santa Barbara Mission Archives has a unique collection of printed materials dealing with almost every aspect of the multi–phased California missionary enterprise. The extensive assortment of newspapers, magazines, directories and other related historical ephemera is also extremely useful to researchers.

The growing interest in the archives in recent years, evidenced by the increasing flow of authors, historians, geographers and ethnologists, etc., rendered provision of more adequate quarters a matter of utmost urgency. The massive collection, formerly housed in the small cell and adjoining veranda once inhabited by Father Zephyrin Engelhardt, has been relocated on the ground floor of the recently completed western wing of the central mission corridor. Provisions have also been made for a small, but highly select and relevant library to accommodate the immediate needs of researchers.

Erection of the new facilities, fully equipped with temperature control for better preservation of the documents, provides permanent quarters for the extensive materials pertaining to missionary activity on the west coast. Not envisioned as a competitive agency to existing historical institutions, the Santa Barbara Mission Archives, with its unique treasures, will continue its accustomed role as a center for diffusing knowledge about the Church's place in Hispanic America. The purpose of the archives will continue to be, according to Father Maynard Geiger, "to preserve and serve the public."

SANTA BARBARA — THE ROMANCE

The effects of the eloquent plea addressed by Charles Fletcher Lummis to the people of Santa Barbara, in 1923, are plainly evident in the Channel City. First published in the Santa Barbara *Morning Press*, the exhortation became the cornerstone for the subsequent activities of the Plans and Planting Committee of the Community Arts Association.

Don't let them skin Santa Barbara of its romance! And they are sure to do it, unless you watch and stand fast! This is essentially the Vandal Age—and a thousand times as much damage has been done in the world by the vandalism of ignorance and carelessness and greed as was ever done by the Huns.

Lummis felt that Santa Barbara was among the few towns that had not exchanged her birthright for a "mess of Potash and Perl–mutter." He wondered whether she would follow others in casting the rich pearls of her dowry before the swine of blundering materialism or stand erect, queenly and alone in her purple beauty of romance.

Do you dream that anybody will ever build in Santa Barbara another building that will mean so much to Santa Barbara and to the world as the grey Old Mission? No one ever will. Does that mean anything?

There will never be another Pantheon, another Sphinx, another Coliseum—another Santa Barbara Mission. Our Today will sometime be Antiquity—but it will be a machine–made, standardized antiquity, without mystery, atmosphere or Romance. We must lay hold upon the noble Old Romance that is left us, and hold fast to it—for we shall never get anything to take its place.

What I would like to see—what the world would like to see—what everybody would like, but cannot see yet—is a Santa Barbara that shall be not just another yard off a tiresome bolt of machine–pattern, stencilled, unimaginative, and rather tawdry American Calico— but Santa Barbara, the one and only.

I know of no law of God or man that would forbid an American community to dwell in a town as beautiful, as artistic, as well worth crossing the world to see, as are any of five hundred towns along the Mediterranean. There is no reason to suppose that we would sicken and die if set in an environment that was not an insult to the God of Beauty right here in California.

Santa Barbara should have an Architecture of its own . . . Obviously it should be based on the Spanish. The Spaniard—whether from Andalusia or Aragon or Castille—was too intelligent an architect, when he came to the New World, to build here precisely as he had built for a thousand years Back Yonder. He adapted his homes and his public buildings to the new environment, the new climate, material, conditions and the Spanish–American architecture is a class by itself.

Now, I would like to see Santa Barbara set its mark to be the most Beautiful, the most Artistic, the most Distinguished and Famous little city on the Pacific Coast. It can be, if it will—for it has "the makings." And those makings are not its landscapes but its Romance, its Past, to build on.

There are enough clear–seeing, right–thinking people in Santa Barbara to bring this about here, even as such a civic atmosphere was brought about in Santa Fe. Here centered the cream of the old Spanish aristocracy of the beautiful days of the California That Was . . . The old spirit, the old pride, are still here, as nowhere else in the Golden State.

The worst curse that could fall on Santa Barbara would be the craze to get big. . . . Get a City Planning Commission of architects, artists and scholars. Get together for a town that shall be a dream of beauty. Save every landmark.

I am no Visionary, but a hard-headed, hard-fisted graduate of the Frontier. . . . As explorer, historian, student of architecture, of migrations, of peoples, for forty years, I have become convinced of certain infallible and inflexible laws. Beauty and sane Sentiment are Good Business, as well as good ethics. Carelessness, Ugliness, blind Materialism are Bad Business. The Ideal lasts longer than anything you can buy or sell or build. And Romance is the Greatest Riches of Any People.

The Honor of Santa Barbara is in your hands. . . . And more than that, the responsiblity for all California is pretty much dropped down on your Barbareno shoulders. You hold the Last Trench of that California which has shone for centuries in song and story, which has fascinated the world and put a new sentiment and beauty in American life. So it is up to you, both to save Santa Barbara Romantic, and save California's romance in Santa Barbara.

SANTA CLARA UNIVERSITY ARCHIVES

The origin of the archives at the University of Santa Clara can be traced to 1777 and the inauguration of the eighth of Fray Junípero Serra's missionary foundations along *El Camino Real*. The basic collection of manuscripts and printed books presently forming the core of the archival collection has been carefully stored at the campus since 1851, when the remaining Franciscan friars turned over Santa Clara Mission to the Society of Jesus. In subsequent years, a Jesuit university has developed on the site and the materials were moved several times.

With the passage of the years, other related books and historical materials have increased the overall holdings and transformed the collection into one of California's more valuable primary repositories. Included among the documents are several hundred tomes dating from mission times, some of them obviously a part of the state's oldest library which is now housed at San Carlos Borromeo Mission.

The 220 titles collected by the Franciscans between

1777 and 1851 are in excellent condition considering their age. Many of them bear evidence of having originated at the Apostolic College of San Fernando in Mexico City.

Father John Nobili, the first President of Santa Clara College, wrote to Alexander S. Taylor in 1853, noting that "Santa Clara and San Jose Missions had in their archives numerous manuscripts, but the late Fr. Jose Maria Real took the whole of them with him to Lower California, saying that they contained private accounts and memorandums belonging to his Franciscan order." The letter further states that the collection remaining behind at Santa Clara still contained some pastoral letters of Bishop Francisco Garcia Diego and a copy of the *Apostolicas Alfanes de la Compania de Jesus*.

While there is no evidence to indicate any organization of the holdings of the archives at Santa Clara prior to 1961 it is known that Father Henry L. Walsh did a good deal to collect and preserve what records he could find. In 1956, the late Father Arthur D. Spearman (1899–1977) was named Archivist and Director of Manuscript Collections and Exhibits and during the years of his tenure, the treasures housed at Santa Clara were catalogued and made available to researchers.

The current archivist reports that there are presently 950 linear feet of manuscripts, publications and records, together with 25,000 photographs documenting the history of Santa Clara. Archival holdings include baptismal, marriage and burial records from 1777 to 1900, along with a raft of contemporary correspondence and documents relating to life at the California missions. Among the later acquisitions are the papers, photographs and films of astronomer and meteorologist Jerome Sixtus Ricard, gold rush pioneer Bernard J. Reid and famed "glacier priest" Bernard R. Hubbard.

The archives also contain the papers of the presidents and administrative officers of the university, account books, scrapbooks, student collections and the records of Jesuit community consultations from 1851 to the present. Since 1964 the archives have been housed in the Orradre Library building on the campus of the University of Santa Clara, a building named in honor of famed California rancher and university regent, Michel Orradre.

SANTA PRISCA AND LOS ANGELES

Edward L. Doheny visited the city of Taxco many times during the years he was exploring and developing the oil fields of Mexico. He and his wife, Carrie Estelle, were especially impressed by the beautiful church of Santa Prisca.

In the early 1920s, Mr. Doheny was asked by Bishop John J. Cantwell to assume the burdens of financing the new Saint Vincent's Church on property adjacent to his home in Chester Place. Doheny agreed to do so, on the condition that the basic design of the envisioned church be based on Santa Prisca.

Interestingly enough, Santa Prisca had also been designed and funded by a single patron, Jose de la Borda, one of the most illustrious personalities of Mexico's colonial period. His fortune had come from the ground. He was a silver miner. Construction was begun on Santa Prisca in 1748 and finished a decade later.

The magnificent new church was formally dedicated on May 11, 1759, by Manuel Antonio Rojo de Rio Lubian. The exterior of Santa Prisca is baroque, with hints of churriguera style. Its towers resemble carved wood and were probably meant to resemble Chinese carvings (there was, at the time, a flourishing trade with the Orient through Acapulco) In the Los Angeles counterpart of Santa Prisca, Mr. Doheny refined and enhanced many of the artistic features of the earlier church, but always in a manner that retained the basic designs.

So careful was Mr. Doheny to emulate Jose de la Borda that he allowed a statue of his patron saint, at the far left in the base of the reredos, to bear a striking resemblance of himself. A small enough indulgence for the gift of a church!

Architectural historians could prepare a thick manuscript of similarites between Saint Vincent's in Los Angeles and Santa Prisca in Taxco. The reredos of the main altar, for example, is a magnificent example of the powerful churriguera style.

The facade and tower of the church, which are an overture to the theme of the interior, are truly remarkable. One writer ventured the opinion that Santa Prisca's facade "is probably the most sophisticated work in Mexico," reflecting as it does the trends of mid–century Andalusia. Again like Santa Prisca, the side altars and shrines at Saint Vincent's are of the same structural distribution as the main altar. The Marian theme is everywhere evident, for in Spain and its colonies, there was a strong devotion to Mary.

The setting of Saint Vincent's is unique in that the axis of the building is at a 45–degree angle with both Adams Boulevard and Figueroa Street. This feature is due alone to the foresight of the donors who wished to so place the building that there would be no danger of adjacent commercial structures detracting from the beauty of the church.

The exterior of the church is of plaster with Indiana limestone trim, ornament and statues, ornamental tile covering the dome and Spanish tile on the roof. Actual construction of the church is of very substantial reinforced concrete designed to withstand wind and earthquake. Floors and roofs are of reinforced concrete.

SANTA ROSA ISLAND

In Cabrillo's time, there were several thousand Chumash Indians residing on Santa Rosa Island. Today only about a dozen or so people live there and they are mostly *vaqueros* or cowboys. An account of Cabrillo's voyage notes that the Indians were "very poor. They are fishermen, they eat nothing but fish; they sleep on the ground; their sole business and employment is to fish. They say that in each dwelling are fifty souls." With the removal of the last Indians to the mainland in the early years of the 19th century, the island gradually reverted to its natural habitat and until recently was operated as a cattle ranch.

Named for Saint Rose of Lima, the island is fifteen miles long and ten miles wide. Like the other three northern channel islands, the eighty–four square mile Santa Rosa visually represents a seaward extension to the west of the Santa Monica Mountains.

Santa Rosa has a mild climate, with dry and occasionally foggy summers and cool rainy winters. The almost constantly prevailing winds come from the northwest. There is abundant fresh water from springs and streams. The island is blanketed predominantly with gentle, rolling hills and grasslands. I was driven to the southwestern section of the island where the marine terrains are deep and rugged. The coastline is variable, with broad sandy beaches on the north, east and west.

The modern history of the island dates from 1843, when Governor Manuel Micheltorena issued a grant for Santa Rosa to Jose Antonio and Carlos Carrillo. In the following year, John Jones and Alpheus Thompson moved cattle onto the island. By mid–century, there were 8,000 head of cattle and 2,000 head of sheep on Santa Rosa.

The earliest structures were erected in the late 1840s. During the tenure of T. Wallace More (1858–1902), Santa Rosa Island was primarily a sheep ranch. Walter Vail and J. V. Vickers purchased the island in 1902 and gradually the sheep ranch evolved into a cattle ranch.

Since 1987, the island has been owned by the United States government. There are temporary National Park Service facilities on the island and plans are afoot to eventually utilize an abandoned Air Force complex for permanent quarters. In 1877, Thomas Savage said that Santa Rosa Island provided "a unique and colorful window to California's past." That remark was made 123 years ago! Or was it last week?

SANTA TERESITA CHAPEL CAR

Late in 1928 Bishop John B. MacGinley announced plans to have a mobile chapel outfitted for "the benefit of souls and the advancement of Catholicity" in the Diocese of Monterey–Fresno. The new "Catholic Chapel Car" was envisioned as a means of giving Catholics in communities where there was no church the opportunity of attending Mass and receiving the sacraments.

The chapel car was also intended to present a partial solution to the spiritual needs of those transient Mexican–Americans who came to Central California for the purpose of harvesting crops. Always a large element of the Catholic population, many of those people were fugitives from the religious persecution then raging in their homeland.

Having studied plans for other chapel cars in neighboring dioceses, MacGinley adapted their best features and, wherever possible, improved upon them. That the mobile chapel was both designed and built entirely in Fresno was a great source of satisfaction to those who cooperated in the project.

The foundation of the chapel car was the chassis of a reinforced Ford truck, outfitted with a powerful, four cylinder engine. Its gearing system was revamped to allow for the mountain highways crisscrossing the diocese.

The altar was situated in the rear of the car, enclosed by two large doors which were thrown open during the services. It was beautifully finished in Philippine mahogany, the upper portion of which was ornamented with graceful spirals. On either side of the altar were small stained glass windows.

Altar linens, vestments and other articles used in the liturgical services were donated by various religious communities of women. The school children of the diocese provided the chalices and ciboria. There were modest living quarters for the priest in the space between the enclosure of the altar and the driver's cab. It was a tiny area, but totally adequate. In the actual "living area" were two tables and a long seat or lounge that formed into one of the beds. A folding upper berth was available for a second priest. In the kitchenette were a two–burner stove, a small water heater and a diminutive refrigerator. Opposite was a sink attached to a small work table and a cabinet.

There was even a shower and a tiny dressing room, with hot and cold running water. Four different storage places were provided for luggage and other items necessary for daily living. Panelled in the same wood as the altar, the living quarters were as attractive as they were compact, complete and comfortable. Electric power for the needs of the car and hydrogen gas for cooking and heating were generated in tanks located in the driver's cab.

Christened the "*Santa Teresita*" in honor of the diocesan patroness, the chapel car was formally blessed by Bishop MacGinley on Washington's birthday, in 1929. Father Leo Kulleck, a Redemptorist priest, was placed in charge of the new "outreach" program for the Diocese of Monterey–Fresno.

In the years that followed, the *"Santa Teresita"* visited all portions of the vast diocese. The mobile chapel became a "veritable cathedral" for thousands of Catholics who eagerly awaited its annual appearance.

SANTIAGO DE COMPOSTELA

During his youth, Bishop Thaddeus Amat and members of his family travelled from Barcelona to Santiago de Compostela, the city dedicated to Saint James the Apostle. It was an experience he recalled with fondness throughout his life.

Santiago has long been the religious and cultural center of Galicia. Since the Middle Ages, it has been visited by pilgrims from all over the world. Every good Spaniard considers it a pious obligation to go there at least once in his or her lifetime. From earliest times, Saint James has been associated with Christianity in the Iberian peninsula. Around forty–four, he travelled to Jerusalem for a last meeting of the apostolic family and there was decapitated by the grandson of Herod the Great.

Athanasius and Theodore retrieved his body and brought it back to the mountain called *Liberius donum*, the site of present–day Santiago de Compostela, located between the rivers Sar and Sarela. In the 9th century, during the reign of King Alfonso II, the tombs of Saint James and numerous other early martyrs were discovered in the area where the cathedral is now located. A city was born and dedicated to the "Son of Thunder."

The main altar of the romanesque cathedral has great significance for peoples of the New World. Its altar appears to be covered with silver, a gift from an early Archbishop of Mexico City. It was executed by 17th century silversmiths. The two chandeliers, made in Rome, are also of silver.

On the upper part of the canopy is portrayed Saint James on horseback. Above the altar of the Apostle are represented all kinds of people, religious authorities and kings, magnates, famous noblemen and thousands and thousands of pilgrims kneeling in prayer. Pilgrims go up the stairway to give the traditional embrace to Saint James.

Though it is not known in what year Amat visited Compostela, it was probably during one of the local holy years. At those times, a special "holy door" is opened and pilgrims passing through that entryway gain special indulgences.

In one of his letters, Amat also remembered seeing the fine equestrian statue of Saint James, carved in wood by the 18th century Gumbino. It is the one carried through the streets of the city every year on July 25th.

From the tenor of another letter, Amat appears to have visited Compostela on the actual feastday of Saint James. He was present for the ceremony of the *Botafumeiro*, the swinging of the censer, an event that still occurs on July 25th.

Hanging from the crucifer of the cathedral ceiling is a long cord attached to a special pulley which allows the gigantic censer to be activated. Victor Hugo christened the 118 pound *Botafumeiro* the "King of the Censers." Eight men, known as *tiraboleiros*, specially trained for their work, use a swinging motion, like the pendulum of a clock, making the censer rise until it almost scrapes the dome. During that event, the *chirlmias* provide a musical accompanyment.

The incense of the *Botafumeiro* not only purifies the stagnant air of the vaulted cathedral, but perfumes the great naves of the building and the tribunes where the pilgrims gather to watch and pray. An old tradition states that once during the reign of Catherine of Aragon, the *Botafumeiro* suddenly broke loose from its moorings, and crashed through a window, injuring several onlookers.

SAVAGES AND SAINTS

Aside from its unfortunate title, *Savages and Saints* is a tolerably good historical novel based on the early days of European presence in what is known as Alta California. In great detail and with considerable enthusiasm, Mrs. Fremont Older describes the heroic achievements of Padre Pedro, a handsome, aristocratic, young, charming and erudite friar in a strange land.

His early fall from grace into the arms of a European enchantress (the details of which are discreetly vague), his return to the fold; his penitential assignment to the remote and haunted Santa Lucia Mission; his subsequent adventures in shepherding a highly heterogeneous flock and his ultimate triumph over hate, avarice and pride crown with success his years of work among a fascinating people.

Padre Pedro's flock included two murderers, a virago, a Belgian countess and a Serbian princess, a decayed gentleman doctor from Vermont with two wives and a number of illegitimate children, an assortment of mongrel dogs and a cat. The life of Padre Pedro was truly an exciting one. Yet he was never too weary to mount his horse for an invigorating fifty mile journey to the coast or the Sierra to comfort a lost soul. Nor did he ever appear to have the wrong answer to a problem, whether the advice was sought on the quality of a tamale or the entanglement of a thorny dilemma.

If the friar had any failing, it was that of being overdrawn. He is almost too perfect, a hero from the enthusiastic brain of a great optimist. Yet that was an accurate reflection of many of the early Mallorcans who came to this area of the Lord's vineyard.

Mrs. Older was probably better equipped as an historian than a novelist. Her tale reads like one long lyric of praise and admiration. Moreover, she tends to overwork certain devices like coincidence and accident so that everything fits perfectly into place. And life isn't really like that.

Any novel which indulges in a long series of pleasant surprises suffers from artificiality. It is really unfortunate that such an interesting plot was not treated more realistically—with less adjectives and fewer superlatives. The overall plot makes for an absorbing tale and, in a sense, a thrilling one. But it loses much of its thrust in being over embroidered in too flowery a style.

With those reservations stated, it must be said that no one interested even remotely in the theme will be bored. And once the reader decides not to be annoyed unduly by the style, he or she will spend a very pleasant afternoon in old California. And, after all, is that not why people read novels?

Cora Miranda Older was a close friend of the late Herbert Eugene Bolton. He wrote the foreword for her book on the *California Missions and Their Romances* when it was published by Coward McCann, Inc. of New York in 1938. He pointed out that hers was an interesting book, one written in the popular vein with a considerable amount of factual information. Dr. Bolton resisted the temptation of saying that Mrs. Older was more adept at writing history than she was at penning novels.

LOS SEISES

Shortly after the turn of the century, Father E. L. Taunton visited the Cathedral at Seville. There he witnessed the "quaint but altogether beautiful and reverential dance of *Los Seises*," a moving event which he described for *Rosary Magazine*. His observations were reprinted in the November 8, 1902, edition of *The Monitor*.

It was the Feast of La Purisima and an enormous altar had been moved into place to support a huge silver monstrance. "The effect against the red velvet drapery . . . is very grand, and gives the idea that no expense is spared by the [Cathedral] Chapter in celebrating the feast."

At 5:30 p.m. the Canons had concluded the final verses of *Lauds* which, in those days were anticipated. "The beautiful silvery blue of the incense is still clinging round the altar . . . curling upwards round the throne, bearing to Him the prayers of His faithful."

Los Seises (ten vested choirboys) enter and take their places, five on either side of the altar. "Their dress is very becoming. It dates from the time of Phillip III. The tunic, of blue silk, shaded with gold, has long streamers from either shoulder; knee breeches of white satin, white stockings and shoes with blue and gold bows."

"In their hands they carry three cornered hats of blue and gold trimmed with white ostrich feathers and they hold in their hands small Spanish castanets. They stand waiting. Meanwhile a small orchestra takes up its place just behind them on the Gospel side of the sanctuary."

The archbishop and his ministers arrive and go to their places while *Los Seises* chant a processional hymn. When everyone is in position, *Los Seises* genuflect and put on their hats.

"Then, singing the praises of the Lord, who has made Mary Immaculate, the boys advance one row towards the other, keeping time with the music, one step to each bar. Then one row crosses the other; they form squares, stars, circles and various figures, all the while singing.

"Towards the end of each verse, they so manage their steps that, one by one, they return to their original positions by the benches and at the last note they mark the conclusion by a rapid twirl on one foot.

"Then, as the band plays the interlude, they advance again, row towards row, not singing now but playing their castanets while they dance. First a faint click which swells with the music and dies away to the merest sound. After the interlude the boys sing another verse and dance in the same way."

The whole ceremony lasted for about twenty–five minutes. Father Taunton said "the scene is very beautiful in the darkening church, for now all the light comes streaming from the silver altar and lights up the happy bright faces of the boys, and the deep, earnest look of the Spanish congregation who gaze on much moved at the touching spectacle."

He goes on to describe how, "when the dance is over, the Archbishop ascends the altar and kneels there while a motette is sung. . . . The great bells of the cathedral ring out joyously, the organ crashes, and the instruments play while the concluding verse of the *Tantum Ergo* are sung. "Then, after some prayers, the Blessed Sacrament is veiled from sight and the prelate gives his final benediction and all depart down the long drawn and vast aisles which are lit only by great waxen torches fixed in sockets onto the vast columns."

SERRA RETREAT

It was the dream of Frederick Hastings Rindge (1857–1905) to find and acquire "a farm near the ocean, and under the lee of the mountains; with a trout brook, wild trees, a lake, good soil and excellent climate, one not too hot in the summer." In 1892, he purchased the 13,000 acre Rancho Malibu and there built a large Victorian ranch house. Rindge was a pious man who referred to the site as "*Laudamus* Hill," a term that portended the area's future spiritual dimensions.

Rindges great "castle" overlooking the sea was eventually built by his widow in consultation with the internationally famous architectural firm of Morgan, Walls and Clements. The fifty room mansion was to be an authentic Mediterranean edifice. Among the features in the castle–like structure was a lavish use of marble, hand–carved mahogany and exquisite tile.

The "castle" never reached completion and the great structure stood on its hilltop as an unfulfilled dream. When Rhoda May Rindge died in 1941, the administration of her estate passed into the hands of the Marblehead Land Company

In 1942, the unfinished "castle" and its contents, together with twenty–six acres of land, was acquired by the Order of Friars Minor. The Franciscans initially hoped to utilize the buildings and grounds for a seminary. Several Franciscan brothers, together with local volunteers, undertook the task of completing the "castle" along the original plans. From supplies of tile and other unused materials still in storage, they were able to bring the Rindge dream to completion.

The Friars eventually concluded that the foundation would serve a better purpose as a retreat house. Thus it was that "Serra Retreat," named for the founder and *Presidente* of the California missions, was inaugurated in October of 1943 under the directions of Fathers Augustine Hobrecht and Owen de Silva.

The beautifully–illustrated and carefully–written book on the *Ceramic Art of Malibu Properties*, published by the Malibu Lagoon Museum in 1988, tells how "the gardens, by careful planning, had achieved an atmosphere of peace and quiet rare in this busy world.

> Softly the *Angelus* bells summoned retreatants to prayer and holy song led by brown–robed, sandal–clad Franciscans. Week after week, Catholic laymen and their friends of all denominations and creeds, in quest of spiritual renewal come to meditate, to pray, and to hear God's voice in the quiet sanctuary of the Malibu hills,

Unfortunately, on September 25, 1970, the colorful "castle of *Laudamus* Hill" was mostly destroyed in a brush fire that also consumed many other homes and buildings in the Malibu area. In subsequent years, a new cluster of buildings was erected on the site. Many of the original Malibu tiles were salvaged and utilized in fireplaces, walkways and garden areas of the rebuilt complex. The salvaged tile in the Serra Retreat evokes both in the casual observer and the knowledgeable ceramist, an appreciation of the incredible artistic skills of the fabricators who designed and fashioned the tile.

Today, Serra Retreat quietly and effectively pursues its role as a spiritual refuge amidst a busy and pre–occupied world. And this it does from its pinnacle overlooking the "American Riviera" on a site first charted by Frederick Rindge.

SIERRA GORDA

It is not widely known in Alta California that the name of Fray Junípero Serra is also venerated widely in the Sierra Gorda region of Central Mexico. Indeed, that area is one of the bright chapters in the evangelization of New Spain.

The Franciscans were active in the Sierra Gorda for roughly a quarter century. In that area the friars succeeded in fulfilling their dual goals of converting the natives to Christianity and turning them into productive citizens of the Spanish empire. That Serra and the other Franciscans were successful in the Sierra Gorda is all the more impressive in light of earlier futile attempts at bringing the peoples there into the Catholic faith.

Serra's work in Central Mexico and that of his collaborators was crucial to the later activities in Alta California because it was a training ground for many of the friars who subsequently worked along *El Camino Real*.

Today, Serra is the most remembered of all the early friars working in that area of the Lord's vineyard. He was assigned to the mission at Santiago de Jalpan in 1750 and he remained there for eight years. Happily, the activities of Serra at Jalpan were carefully recorded by his biographer who was with him most of the time.

Serra's success in his earliest missionary endeavors can be attributed to the two policies upon which he based his ministry: teaching this marginally agricultural people new techniques of farming and caring for livestock, as well as learning and teaching in their native language.

The perfecting of their agricultural pursuits allowed the neophytes to improve their standard of living, thus giving them parity with other citizens of the empire. And, unlike his predecessors who relied on translators, Serra actually learned the Pame language and was able to teach in that tongue. Serra's two missionary policies were not so easily realized in Alta California even though the lands were more fertile and easily irrigated. The natives were still at the "hunting and gathering" stage and, until 1769, had no contact with outsiders. They had no traditions of farming or husbandry.

There was no common Indian language in Alta California. Within that area were no less than sixty–four (perhaps as many as eighty) mutually unintelligible languages, along with numerous dialects. The lingual perplexities forced Serra and the other friars to insist that the Indians learn Spanish.

Despite the more challenging problems in Alta California, Fray Junípero Serra was able to establish nine missions along the Pacific Rim. And there, as earlier, Serra was loved and venerated by those brought into the embrace of the Catholic faith.

The missionary outposts in the Sierra Gorda are still very much in place. Visitors to that remote area can still see the churches built and cared for by Serra and his companions two centuries ago. And what is more fascinating are the verbal traditions about Serra and the good work he and others did in that region. The people there long ago "canonized" Serra and, today, he continues to walk tall in the Sierra Gorda.

"SIGNERS" OF THE DECLARATION

The Declaration of Independence has been regarded, and rightly so, as this nation's great charter of freedom. The original document is enshrined in the Exhibition Hall of the National Archives. Sealed in a bronze and glass case filled with helium, it is screened from harmful light rays by special filters and can be lowered, at a moment's notice into a large fire and shockproof safe.

Drafted by Thomas Jefferson, in conjunction with a committee comprising John Adams, Benjamin Franklin, Roger Sherman and Robert Livingston, the Declaration was adopted on July 4, 1776, though most of the fifty-six signatures were affixed on August 2nd. The lawyers, physicians, merchants and plantation owners who signed the important document had been chosen by their respective communities. While a few of the "signers" lived through the subsequent struggle for independence to become judges, legislators and governors, most of them suffered greatly from their act of public bravery.

Understandably, the signatures of many of those who ascribed their names to the Declaration of Independence are exceedingly scarce. As of 1926, there were only twenty-seven complete sets of autographs by the "signers," eighteen owned by institutions and nine by individuals. One of the rare sets of the "signers" was housed in the Estelle Doheny Collection, at Saint John's Seminary, in Camarillo. The priceless autographs were gathered by the late Carrie Estelle Doheny over the twenty years after 1929, and her acquisition of a letter by Elbridge Gerry.

Included in the Doheny collection was "the only letter written by a signer on the very day of the Declaration of Independence." Mailed by Caesar Rodney, at Philadelphia, on July 4, 1776, the rare document was originally a part of the extensive collection of Colonel James H. Manning. Another fascinating signature is that of Richard Henry Lee, who introduced in Congress the Declaration of Independence. Penned on June 2, 1776,

the three-page missive called for "a proper confederation by which internal peace and union may be secured. The letter of Thomas Lynch, written from Charles Town, August 22, 1775, is exceedingly "dear" inasmuch as the South Carolina freedom fighter's signature is generally considered the rarest of all the "signers."

The Doheny collection of "signers" was completed, in 1948 with the purchase of a letter from the Marine Committee of the Continental Congress, dated July 12, 1776, containing the signatures of Button Gwinnett, John Hancock, Francis Lewis, Arthur Middleton, Robert Morris and George Read. Button Gwinnett's signature, another of the more elusive ones, rounded out Mrs. Doheny's holdings. That letter enjoys the additional distinction of containing more of the original "signers" than any other document, except the Declaration of Independence itself!

The priceless run of "signers" at Camarillo, one of the more remarkable components of the Estelle Doheny Collection, helped to rank the overall holdings among the most elite in the nation.

SKID ROW — CATHOLIC PRESENCE

Like all the great cities of the world, Los Angeles has its Skid Row district, an area where homeless and destitute people, mostly men, gather to count away the hours, days, months and years. According to the author of a prominent history of Los Angeles, "Skid Row" encompasses the area bounded by Los Angeles Street, Central Avenue, Third and Seventh Streets. The populace, though including a traditional body of transient Anglo males, is varied in gender, ethnicity and permanence.

The "modern era" for Skid Row can be dated from the early 1930s, when unemployment in Southern California hit an all-time high. Many of those out of work, having turned in desperation to alcohol, drifted into the area and remained there for the remainder of their lives. For them the depression never ended.

From the outset of his administration in Los Angeles, James Francis Cardinal McIntyre was anxious to establish a Catholic presence on Skid Row. In 1954, with money borrowed from local banks by the Saint Vincent de Paul Society, he purchased an old creamery building located at 231 Winston Street.

After having the two-story edifice thoroughly refurbished and brought up to code, the Cardinal opened the new facility on February 21, 1955. It was known as Miserere House, named for the motto emblazoned on McIntyre's episcopal coat-of-arms. The 25,000 square foot building had accommodations for a chapel, counseling offices, reading and letter writing, game rooms and bathing. It was, for many years, the only facility of its kind operating on Skid Row without any governmental subsidy.

Chosen by McIntyre to supervise Miserere House was Matt Campion, a recovered alcoholic, whose whole life had been dedicated to the social apostolate of the Church. Campion remained in charge for thirteen years. It was McIntyre's expressed thought that "by restoring man bodily and re–establishing his spiritual status, the hope prevails that many troubled and unfortunate persons may return to useful and gainful pursuits."

Over the subsequent years, Miserere House continued its outreach to the alcoholics, transients, pensioners and emotionally distraught on Skid Row, dispensing meal and bed tickets, clothing and job referrals. The doors were open for rest and recreation, showers, shaves, companionship and counseling. Miserere House had no soup kitchen, no beds, no hymn singing. Nothing was asked and nothing expected. There were no strings attached to the Catholic presence on Skid Row.

During a typical year, 1967, disbursements at Miserere House included 3,710 meal and 1,130 bed tickets, 2,100 articles of clothing, 625 job placements and uncounted thousands of referrals to allied agencies. Over 550,000 people moved in and out of Miserere House that year, a phenomenal statistic! In October of 1972, after extensive remodeling, Miserere House's name was changed to Saint Vincent's Center, the better to reflect the charitable spirit associated with the worldwide ministrations of the sponsoring agency, the Saint Vincent de Paul Society.

A host of persons have been associated over the years with Saint Vincent's Center. Tom Cassidy, Bill Carroll, Raymond Healy, Fathers Dominic Pontolillo, Roderick Potstada and Don Kribs, Mother Teresa's Brothers of Charity—all practitioners of Christ's charity to the forgotten people of Skid Row.

smallPAXweber

smallPAXweber (1974–1990) was among that small but select cadre of Shetland sheep dogs that have watched over the California missions since 1769. According to such early commentators as Richard Henry Dana, smallPAXweber's ancestors were imported to the Pacific Slope by the Spaniards and traders.

Canines served a very important role in early California. Especially was that true of sheep dogs because there were no fences and few natural barriers to segregate the domestic cattle on the vast terrain of the mission ranches. Originating in Scotland, Shetland sheep dogs were well suited for the task of keeping the herds in their assigned pastures. Few of the missions were without their "toy collies."

Mentioned frequently in the annals, "shelties," as they are popularly known in canine circles, are an even–tempered breed. There appears to be a telepathy–like and unbreakable bond between the dogs and their masters.

Born in 1974, smallPAXweber came to San Fernando Mission seven years later and thereafter served as senior guard dog and favored mascot for all the other members of the animal kingdom attached to California's seventeenth mission.

He became something of an international celebrity. His name appeared numerous times in local newspaper columns, his face was familiar to television viewers around the nation and his likeness was captured and preserved in several major artistic renditions. One TV commentator, speaking about the visit of Pope John Paul II to San Fernando Mission in 1988, went so far as to say that smallPAXweber had become one of "the most photographed and talked–about dogs since Fala."

When asked about the dog's unorthodox moniker, a reporter for the Los Angeles *Times* explained to readers that smallPAXweber was "named not for the disease, but for his mother, PAX (Latin for peace), who was born on the day the Vietnam peace treaty was signed."

One reason for his renown was the dog's popularity as a model. He is featured at the feet of Fray Junípero Serra by Isabel Piczek in her tile memorial for the papal visit. And he was sketched in pen and ink by the famed artist, Leo Politi, a likeness later reproduced in a book about the artist. For these and kindred reasons, smallPAXweber brought fame and honor to his breed.

Like others of his kin, smallPAXweber was innately bashful. When someone touring the Old Mission recognized him, he generally scampered off to hide with the cats behind the boxwood. Some years ago, one of the little dog's fans from Spain had a specially–made tile set in place on the mission grounds. It portrayed the bust of smallPAXweber above the words *"Cuidado con El Perro."* The pooch rightly felt that warning was a bit of overkill.

His position at the mission was that of monitoring and overseeing the twenty or so cats, the seven roosters, twenty–three peacocks, uncounted squirrels, numberless raccoons and an ancient desert tortoise. Though he was the "last of the mission shelties," smallPAXweber provided for his succession by allowing his breed and his name to be franchised for future generations.

Likely there will always be a PAX at San Fernando Mission and probably at many other missions as well. The vast herds of cattle are gone now, but there will ever be a need for the distinctive love, friendship and loyalty imprinted on the California landscape by Shetland sheep dogs, the most famous of whom was smallPAXweber.

SNUFF IN THE CALIFORNIA MISSIONS

Among the historical artifacts in the museum attached to the Chancery Archives for the Archdiocese of Los Angeles is a snuff–container, hand–fashioned from the antler of an elk, bearing the date, 1782. Engraved with the name of James Welch Baker, it was given to Fray Jose Senan (1760–1823) by Captain George Vancouver on the occasion of the British seaman's visit to Mission San Carlos Borromeo, December 2, 1792.

The outstanding Franciscan historian, Father Maynard J. Geiger, states that "it was almost a universal custom in former times for the friars to use snuff." Even Fray Junípero Serra "was a snuffer, at least, later on in California, though he did not smoke." Serra complained, in a letter of June 21, 1771, about a shipment of snuff which the friars felt was little more than "pure dirt" and unusable. Fortunately, after removing the top layers, they found the rest of the consignment more compressed and of better quality.

Snuff, a powder manufactured from tobacco, can be either chewed or inhaled through the nose. Only the choicest portions of fine leaf tobacco are used for the finer grades of snuff, while for the ordinary commercial brands, the thick, stemmy portions, the midrib and scrap tobacco are employed. The tobacco is subjected to two forms of fermentation, whereby strength and aroma are acquired and nicotine and organic acids removed. The leaves and stalks, moistened with salt water to prevent putrefaction, are pressed into cakes, sliced and then left in open chambers for about six months to ferment and develop aroma.

Afterwards the tobacco is ground in mills out of contact with the air and the resulting powder is dampened and placed in wooden chambers for a second ten–month fermentation period. Finally, the snuff is gathered from the fermenting rooms into one large chamber where it matures for another month. It is ready then for stamping into casks.

Certain of the dry snuffs are slightly adulterated with quicklime which imparts a biting desiccating effect. Snuffs are scented with musk, essences of bergamot, lavender, attar of roses, tonka beans, cloves, orange flowers, jasmine and other scents. Austrians, Germans, Italians and Spaniards were notorious snuff consumers and, with them, it was nothing short of a national custom, Europeans claimed that snuff was beneficial for the eyes. It was often used as a cure for catarrh and head colds, a common malady among the friars. The damp cells aggravated sinus conditions and made the use of snuff more a matter of practicality than of pleasure.

When snuff taking was one of the habits of society, pocket snuff boxes for holding small quantities of the powder came into use—and many of those artistic containers became museum pieces. All of which helps to explain the snuff–container in the Chancery Archives for the Archdiocese of Los Angeles and its historical relation to the provincial period of California's Catholic heritage.

SOTTERRANEO IN CALIFORNIA

One of California's great artistic treasures is the reproduction of Michelangelo's *Sotterraneo* which is housed in a specially constructed, tunnel–like area in the museum at Glendale's Forest Lawn Memorial Park. The original sketches are in the basement of the Medici Chapel in Florence, a tiny room in which the artist hid for ninety–two days under the threat of death by influential members of the curial family.

According to Irving Stone, the distinguished author of *The Agony and the Ecstasy*, the life of Michelangelo, the reproductions at Glendale are faithful and unique in the art world.

It all began in August of 1530, when the Medici family laid siege to Florence from which they had been ejected by the local citizenry. Having been innocently involved in the fracas, as overseer of the city's fortifications, the artist had been placed under a sentence of death.

Michelangelo was, at the time, working in the Medici Chapel on his great allegorical statues "Twilight and Dawn" and "Day and Night." Local church officials hid the artist in a secret basement area directly beneath the chapel and during his three months in that tiny area, the fifty–five year old artist executed some of the most exciting charcoal sketches ever made. The sketches included such designs as Saint Peter's Basilica, with its majestic dome.

As he passed the long days and longer nights, Michelangelo, with only the light of a candle, drew on the walls fifty–six sketches, ranging from reflected memories to plans for future projects. With so little space he crowded the drawings and intermingled them. On and on he worked, aware that the alternative was certain death. From August to November, the artist worked feverishly and then, after his release, the walls of the Sotterraneo were covered over with whitewash for the next 445 Years.

In 1975, the director of the Medici Chapel came upon a trapdoor in a sacristy storeroom, with a staircase leading down to a long, narrow room with moldy whitewashed walls. After clearing away the accumulated junk, the director realized the significance, of the room.

When the whitewash of the 33 x 9 foot cell had been removed, Michelangelo's sketches reappeared. It was among the century's greatest discoveries and one which was heralded throughout the art world. Subsequently it was decided to reproduce the Sotterraneo, at the Medici Chapel at Glendale, with photo murals of the art arranged identically as in Florence. The drawings were used in their entirety.

A pair of legs, for example, corresponds faithfully to those of a marble statue of Giuliano de Medici which Michelangelo finished three years later. Others of the figures and faces are identical to those subsequently executed in the Sistine Chapel.

When visitors step into the Sotterraneo, they behold the sketches exactly as they appear at Florence. One almost has the feeling of living with Michelangelo five centuries ago. Stone said that "It's a real miracle. Because you're looking at something absolutely authentic." He knew "the drawings are authentic because I've studied Michelangelo's work all my life. The Italian and German art critics agree."

SOUTHERN CROSS

A recent commentator on the Golden States publishing endeavors admits that "the life of a printer in early Southern California must not have been easy." Certainly it was not so for James H. Dougherty who founded the *Southern Cross* in April of 1912, as a non–official observer of Catholic activities. The small four–page paper originated at San Diego under the encouraging eye of Father Joseph Nunan, third pastor of Saint Joseph's Church.

Although at the time of its establishment the Diocese of Monterey–Los Angeles already had a Catholic newspaper, Dougherty felt that San Diego needed its own press for, as was later observed, the city "is a unit within itself, and this is particularly true of its Catholic religious life." Only the Churches of Saint Joseph and Our Lady of the Angels served San Diego in 1912. The Sisters of Saint Joseph of Carondelet operated a boarding school for girls and the Sisters of Mercy staffed a sanitarium on University Avenue. In such humble surroundings, it was indeed a heroic effort to launch a Catholic paper.

Nonetheless, as was subsequently pointed out editorially, the paper "surmounted obstacles which would have stopped forever the life of any other weekly newspaper in the city. It faced and overcame opposition which seemed more than once to be more direct and powerful than ever that which any other journal in San Diego had to meet."

In its early years, the *Southern Cross* served the Catholic population of San Diego County even "when economic conditions made such continuance a burden." The weekly publication held steadfastly to its original object, namely "the dissemination of accurate Catholic news to the people of San Diego." As its editor noted, "it made itself the servant of every parish in the county, it has opened its columns without question to every Catholic institution whose demands were legitimate; it has never hesitated to incur expense or to face trouble when called upon to do so for the advancement of Catholic interests, and it has been the most potent factor in the development of Catholic action and the furtherance of Catholic ideals."

Bishop John J. Cantwell observed in 1919, "The people of San Diego are very fortunate in having a Catholic paper to give expression to their beliefs, and to break down unreasonable prejudice." In later decades when certain policies of the *Southern Cross* conflicted with those of the Bishop of Monterey–LosAngeles, Cantwell offered to purchase the paper but its editor declined the overture maintaining that "no Catholic in San Diego believes that we can be served officially from 130 miles away!" For the next few years, *The Tidings* entered into active competition with the *Southern Cross* by issuing a special San Diego edition each week.

Shortly after the erection of an episcopal seat at San Diego, the weekly was purchased by the newly consecrated Bishop Charles Francis Buddy, and on August 18, 1937 it became the official publication of the San Diego jurisdiction.

Muir Dawson has observed that "the success of a printing office and newspaper depend to a large extent on local public support . . . . " That being the case, the Catholics of San Diego are to be congratulated, for they have supported the *Southern Cross* for over half a century in its noble efforts to further the apostolate.

SPANISH INFLUENZA

Those historians who regard 1918's so–called "Spanish Influenza" as "the most destructive in history," rank that world–wide epidemic with the Plague of Justinian and the Black Death, among the severest holocausts of disease ever encountered. Upwards of twenty million perished within a few months.

The wonders of modern medicine were unavailable in the later weeks of the year when the influenza spread through the populous areas of the Northern Hemisphere. According to one set of statistics, 548,000 deaths in the United States were attributed to the acute infectious respiratory disease and such subsequent complications as pneumonia and cardiac failure. Within California, upwards of 15,000 persons succumbed to the virus. The greater death toll was reported from the northern population centers of San Francisco, Sacramento and Stockton.

Quite naturally, priests were exposed to the influenza more frequently than others. In the Diocese of Monterey–Los Angeles, three clerics lost their lives ministering to the sick and dying and seven priests from the Archdiocese of San Francisco, six of them under the age of thirty–eight, died. From mid–October to December, schools, churches and all other places of assembly in the southland were closed. Instructions from the Los Angeles Health Department for treating the dreaded flu were printed in the diocesan newspaper and parochial bulletins.

In a number of parish Masses were offered in vestibules with the congregation standing outside, because of the widespread belief that infection spreads more easily indoors. In certain areas, people wore gauze masks when outside or in public gatherings since it was clearly recognized that infected persons tended to spread the flu by sneezing or coughing excretions from the respiratory tracts.

In the Diocese of Monterey–Los Angeles, Bishop John J. Cantwell directed that special prayers be recited after daily Mass for those struck down with the influenza. Among others was the following:

> O glorious Saint Camillus, special patron of the sick, who didst devote thyself for forty years to the relief of their spiritual and temporal necessities, be pleased to assist them now even more generously, since thou art blessed in heaven and they have been committed by Holy Church to thy powerful protection. Obtain for them from Almighty God the healing of all their maladies, or, at least, the spirit of Christian patience and resignation that may sanctify and comfort them in the hour of their passing to eternity; and, at the same time, obtain for us the precious grace of living and dying after thy example in the patience of divine love. Amen.

That the effects of more recent flu epidemics have been controlled by "wonder drugs" may well be an answer to the prayers uttered throughout California in 1918 by an earlier generation not so favorably blessed.

SPICES AND THEIR USE IN CALIFORNIA

Anyone who wants to understand history must know something about spices. Those prosaic little tins of powder on the shelves of modern supermarkets have played a remarkable role in the development of nations.

Interestingly enough, the flavors and aromas of spices are matched and maybe even surpassed by their preservative faculty. In fact, that aspect of spices helps to explain why spices were valued like gold—why peoples fought and died to obtain them in far distant lands.

Because of the uniquely wonderful properties of these plant products, great trade empires grew and flourished and struggling new nations were nourished into life. As Europeans entered the Middle Ages, their food was neither good nor enjoyable. There was no cattle fodder which could be stored, so beef was killed in the autumn and salted. There were no potatoes or lemons to prepare acid drinks. There was no corn, no sugar for sweetening, no teas, coffee or chocolate.

But a dash of pepper, a little cinnamon or ginger, mixed with the coarsest dishes, could make them palatable. Bits of bark or seeds or fruit could transform otherwise dull food into something desirable. They could also help preserve food in warm weather.

There is constant mention of spices in Holy Scripture. Some of the herbs and seeds known today as spices were cultivated in biblical times. Hundreds of years before Christ, the great monarchs of Babylonia, Egypt and Israel had gardens of thyme, saffron, dill, coriander, cardamom and caraway.

The tropical spices (cinnamon, pepper and ginger) had to be brought to the West from the Orient and, as a result, it was these that most influenced history. The Bible tells how King Solomon amassed considerable wealth from the traffic of the spice merchants. Recall how it was a slow–moving spice caravan from the East to which Joseph was sold by his jealous brothers.

In the 13th century, Marco Polo told of seeing spices growing at the court of Kubla Khan. Shrewd merchants realized that those who found a way to the East by ship would have a strangle hold on the future.

Portugal, Spain, England, Holland and France entered the spice trade. During the ensuing centuries the major western powers raced each other to the Orient, battling for control of the spice–producing lands. Spices lured the Europeans into a great new world. It was while carrying Spain's colors in the drive for spices that Christopher Columbus sailed west and discovered America!

The period that followed was one of almost constant warfare and piracy. Each of the powers succeeded in gaining a period of monopoly in the spice trade, but ruthless tactics and greed of each eventually brought about its downfall.

California and its Catholic colonizers also figured into the spice pattern, if perhaps peripherally. But here as elsewhere, herbs, aromatic seeds and seasoning salts played a vital part in the overall struggle of making local food products more palatable.

STAGECOACH INN

When the early bishops of California travelled overland between Los Angeles and San Francisco, they customarily stopped at James Hammel's Grand Union

Hotel in what is presently Newbury Park. Constructed of redwood lumber which was brought in by sea and then freighted up the steep Conejo grade by multiteam wagons, the hotel first opened its doors to visitors on July 4, 1876, the day of the nation's bicentennial.

Located on the *Rancho El Conejo* (later the *Rancho Nuestra Senora de Alta Gracia*), the hotel later came to be known as the Stagecoach Inn because it was a regular depot for the Coast Stage Line. In subsequent times, the Inn served other functions too. It was used as a church, school, military academy, tea room and gift shop.

Having stood undisturbed on the corner of what is now Highway 101 and Ventu Park Road for nearly ninety years, the Inn was faced with the threat of total destruction with the advent of the Ventura Freeway. In an heroic effort to preserve the historic landmark for future generations, a group of citizens banded together under the name of the Conejo Valley Historical Society.

With the financial backing of the Conejo Valley Chamber of Commerce and the moral support of the Conejo Recreation and Park District the society had the Inn declared California Registered Historical Landmark No. 659. Eventually, through special intervention at Sacramento, funds were obtained from the California Department of Highways to move the structure out of the freeway's path.

Mr. and Mrs. G. Allen Hayes, whose family had owned the Inn since 1885, deeded the building and five acres of land one half mile south of Ventu Park Road to the Recreation and Park District, with the stipulation that it should be maintained as a museum by the local historical society. For the next few years, the Inn was operated as a museum. Thousands of visitors came to Newbury Park hoping to catch a glimpse of Pierre, the legendary ghost who was murdered there by an unknown assailant in a small upstairs bedroom.

On April 25, 1970, the Stagecoach Inn was totally destroyed by fire. Despite the fact that the historic edifice was reduced to a rubble of ashes, about 400 artifacts were saved, cleaned and stored for future use. Reconstruction of the building, in its original 1876 Monterey style, was sponsored jointly by the Conejo Recreation and Park District and the City of Thousand Oaks. The historical society launched an appeal for funds with which to finish and furnish the interior of the building. Today, the Stagecoach Inn is completely restored. It has the unusual distinction of being among the few reconstructed buildings in California to be listed on the National Registry of Historic places.

Were the early visitors to once again make their way along *El Camino Real,* they would come upon the old Grand Union Hotel much the same as they saw it prior to the turn of the century.

RELIGION ON UNITED STATES STAMPS

During the many years that efforts were made to have a postage stamp issued for Fray Junípero Serra, the standard responses from the Stamp Advisory Council were couched in appeals to the First Amendment of the United States Constitution. Adopted in 1791, as part of the American Bill of Rights, that amendment reads thusly: "Congress shall make no laws respecting an establishment of religion, or prohibiting the free exercise thereof."

The Council members felt that portraying a priest on a stamp would somehow violate the Bill of Rights. Nor were they impressed when it was pointed out that priests had already appeared on United States stamps (no fewer than four times!) in 1898 (Jacques Marquette), in 1940 (Juan Padilla), in 1948 (John Washington) and 1968 (Jacques Marquette–again).

It took a Presidential nudge to finally get the stamp in 1985. And even then, Fray Junípero Serra's stamp was issued to honor an historical pioneer rather than a religious figure.

It is interesting to note that Christmas is the only legal Federal public holiday of a religious nature in the United States. Therefore, the only stamps with a religious theme are those featuring artistic renditions of the Nativity.

Between 1966 and 1980 ten stamps were issued depicting Mary and the Baby Jesus. Of these, only three also included Joseph, the husband of Mary. The other Christmas stamps issued in those years have non–religious themes. Mariologians can take satisfaction in knowing that, except for Mary, no other biblical personages or venerated religious figure has ever been portrayed on a United States postage stamp.

That Our Lady enjoys such a distinction is all the more significant inasmuch as women have appeared on U.S. stamps far less frequently than men. Only forty female individuals have been so honored. And those women, (8.62% of the 464 individual featured prior to 1980), appeared a total of fifty–nine times; thirty–five on one stamp and five on two or more.

No woman was honored on a stamp in the United States until Isabella (the Catholic!) was portrayed on seven stamps in 1893. Between then and 1933, only three other women were so honored, namely Martha Washington, Pocahontas and Molly Pitcher.

More than half of all females who have been on United States stamps appeared in the years between 1960 and 1980, but not even during those decades did the percentage of women reach 10% of the identifiable persons honored. One statistician noted that there are

1108 ENCYCLOPEDIA OF CALIFORNIA'S CATHOLIC HERITAGE

fewer stamps depicting females than there are featuring trees, headgear or flags.

Although many stamps depict persons of non–Christian religions, only five contain religious elements unrelated to Christianity. Listed below are the headings of stamps with related religious themes:

Christmas	37
Churches	16
Angels and cherubim	16
Crosses	11
Biblical personages	10
God	7
Gods and goddesses	5
Clergy and missionaries	4
Halos	4
Missions	4
Bible	3
Christmas trees	3
Freedom of religion	3
Wreaths	3
Biblical quotations	2
Salvation Army	1
Temples	1

STRANGE AS IT SEEMS

Some years ago, there was a newspaper column syndicated by King Features entitled "Truth is Stranger than Fiction." The following incidents in California's history are further confirmations of that old dictum.

In the pastoral times of California's history, when revolutions were almost as common as ember days, the Spanish–born friars often found it hard to reconcile their consciences with the demands of revolutionary leaders for pledges of loyalty. In 1836, for example, Governor Mariano Chico ordered the *comisario–prefecto* of the missions, Fray Narciso Duran, to offer a "Mass of allegiance" at Santa Barbara for the newly–proclaimed Mexican republic.

When Duran declined, the governor charged him with treason and ordered that he be brought to Monterey for deportation hearings. Soldiers were dispatched to place Duran in custody. However, when they arrived, the women of the *pueblo* surrounded Duran's carriage and threatened forcible resistance to his removal.

Faced with a possible uprising the governor relented. Not long afterwards, Chico was recalled to Mexico City. When he didn't return to his post, all the charges against Duran were dropped. To the end of his days, Duran remained one of the most popular and honored missionaries in California

And then there was the time, in December of 1841, when the inhabitants of San Diego were anxiously awaiting the arrival of California's first bishop, Fray Francisco Garcia Diego y Moreno. Long before his coming, the influence of his episcopal presence was felt. The *alcalde* had issued an order that cattle be kept out of the street as the bishop might arrive any day."

The letter written about the event by Mariano Guadalupe Vallejo could have appeared in the pages of the *National Catholic Reporter*:

> The coming of a bishop is going to cause much trouble. The priests are beside themselves with pride, and begin to fulminate sentences of excommunication, etc., relying on that prelate. Poor crazy fools, if they think they can browbeat the leading men in California. The age of theocratic domination is past. However, Californians who have never seen bishops will now know how they dress and observe their ceremonies. If they intended to plant new missions among the savages, some good might result; but nothing is farther from the minds of the priests.

Though Hispanic Californians held the Church in high esteem, there were pockets of anti–clericalism evident. An example would be Fray Francisco Gonzalez de Ibarra who had come to California in 1820 and served as a missionary at San Fernando. He was known to the natives as "Padre Napoleon," probably because of his efficient managerial style. He was also known for the trenchant manner in which he criticized civil authorities charged with secularization of the missions.

The traders called him "*El Cochino*," due to his insistence of storing hides until they brought the very highest prices. The Indians also called him "*Tequedeuma*," which meant a plain, modest, unassuming man. Likely, the natives' judgment was more nearly correct than that of their more civilized and critical neighbors.

Finally, there was the man who first proposed construction of a transcontinental railroad. He was formally accused of insanity for such rashness. His name was Colonel Low and he was a professor at Saint Joseph's College, Bardstown, Kentucky. It was in 1831 that he conceived the idea. He wrote a pamphlet and then decided to run for Congress. The trustees of his college, upon reading of his views, judged him insane and discharged him from his teaching position.

Yes, "truth is indeed stranger than fiction."

SUTRO COLLECTION

The celebrated Sutro Library has one of the finest and most extensive collections of religious publications in the world.

Adolph Sutro (1830– 1898) was an Alsatian Jewish immigrant and tobacconist in San Francisco who became a millionaire as a result of his designing the

Sutro Tunnel whereby the flooded silver mines of the Comstock Lode could be drained. Surely one of the most colorful and influential figures in California history, Sutro commenced the collection of a library with the hope of opening a great research center in his adopted city.

In the late 1880s, Sutro travelled to Mexico City, where he opened negotiations to purchase at auction the extensive holdings of Francisco Abadiano, an internationally–known bookdealer and publisher. The Abadiano firm had been extremely productive in earlier years, publishing several thousand titles. Highly conservative and religious, the Abadianos dealt mostly in books and pamphlets relative to the position of the Church in Mexico and the governmental confiscation of religious properties.

To avoid destruction, many of the books and manuscripts of the Franciscan houses in Mexico City, the oldest libraries in the Americas, had been transferred to the Abadianos by ecclesial authorities for safekeeping. Sutro's acquisition of the entire inventory of a century and a half of printing, bookselling and collecting in Mexico enabled him to obtain a unique collection of extraordinary value.

The most outstanding section of Sutro's Mexicana collection comprises 12,000 to 15,000 pamphlets printed between 1605 and 1888, the largest collection of its kind anywhere in the world. The pre–1810 titles are mostly religious in nature.

The Catholic Church is represented in the collection by hundreds of titles of theological studies, confessionaries, liturgical manuals and breviaries, catechisms, devotionaries and sermons. Of popular interest in this area is a very complete collection relative to Our Lady of Guadalupe, and religio–political sermons published during the Wars of Independence, 1810–1820.

The Mexican manuscript collection comprises a large number of seminary copybooks of the seventeenth and eighteenth centuries, military orders, sermons and documents relative to land holdings. Especially fascinating are manuscript copies of religious, historical and literary works submitted for publication to the Abadianos and their predecessors, and the records, inventories and correspondence of the family printing and publishing business from 1815 to 1884. Fortunately, most of the Mexican collection acquired by Sutro survived the great earthquake and fire of 1906. The public is welcome to use the collection which is now a branch of the California State Library, on the north campus of San Francisco State University.

Among the more notable treasures of the Sutro Library are such items as the 1754 printing of Miguel Venegas' biography of Father Juan Maria de Salvatierra, the only known copy of the corrected and augmented edition of Hispanic America's first novel (1825), a pamphlet eulogizing the great leader of Mexico's struggle for Independence (Jose Maria Morelos y Pavon) and the very first issue of the proto–newspaper published in Mexico (1722).

SYNOD OF 1927

As Bishop John J. Cantwell approached the end of his first decade as chief shepherd for the Church in California's southland, he announced the convocation of a synod, the fifth to be held in the area and the first in forty years.

The synod provided a superb opportunity for appraising the development of ecclesial growth in the Diocese of Los Angeles–San Diego. Cantwell made it clear that the purpose of the synod was "to build on what went before." An essay in *The Tidings* noted that "it would be unjust to discount the splendid work of the energetic and self–sacrificing pioneers, whose labors were nothing less than heroic."

While acknowledging that the "foundations of the missionary *padres* are well known" and "their fame has traveled the world over," the essay went on to say that "we must not forget the tremendous effort and untiring zeal of those who came after them. During what might be called the Spanish regime, when bishops and priests left their distant homes across the seas to come to California, the trying work was carried on amid the destruction wrought by the devastating hand of mission secularization." But then there dawned a brighter era.

As the Spanish–speaking clergy gradually gave way to their English–speaking counterparts "Spain gave fewer of her sons to the California church and Ireland, that great mother of priests, became a never falling source of recruits for the far western mission."

In his opening remarks to the priests attending the 1927 Synod, Bishop Cantwell could not say enough in praise of the area's "glorious pioneers." He pointed out that "it was upon the foundations they laid, in the midst of trials and difficulties, that . . . the mighty superstructure of the strong ecclesial establishment we know today has been built."

After enumerating the deeds and virtues of "a score of priests, many of whom were with us until recently and all of whom are still fresh in our memories," Cantwell said that "to these worthy pioneers and to all their collaborators our hearts turn with deep feelings of gratitude for the unceasing labors of themselves and their faithful people which prepared the way for the glories of today."

One era builds upon another. The growth of the Church in the southland after 1887 had been nothing short of phenomenal. A local newspaper reported that the increase of population brought "with it activity and expansion without parallel in Catholic annals. Increased material facilities, coupled with intense spiritual vigor have been achieved under the direction of a young and energetic shepherd whose capacity for leadership and untiring zeal are a source of wonderment to all."

In *The Tidings* for December 16, 1927, the statistics of ecclesial growth between 1887 and 1927 are carefully enumerated, along with the interesting observation that only one priest who attended the earlier convocation was still alive, the jovial Father Patrick Grogan, the patriarch and pastor of San Buenaventura Mission.

It is doubtful if Grogan or any other of the priests who processed into Saint Vibiana's Cathedral for the 1887 synod "dreamed in moments of wildest reverie what marvels the future held." The remarkable growth of the Church in Southern California had only just begun to show itself.

When the synod of 1887 was held, diocesan government in California was barely forty–seven years old. Yet, within less than a half century, the Church in that area had "come of age," ready to take its place within the family of American religious communities. In 1887, there were only thirty–two priests, secular and religious, laboring in sixteen parishes and looking after twenty–two mission stations scattered around the vast diocese.

When Cantwell came to the Diocese of Monterey–Los Angeles in 1917, there were 234 priests. The number of parishes had grown to ninety–three, with 109 mission stations. The next decade saw a further increase, with 405 priests (272 secular and 133 religious) working in 195 parishes.

The most striking increase had occurred within the area covered by the City of Los Angeles. The three parishes in 1887 had become twenty–five in 1917 and seventy by 1927

At the time of the earlier synod, there were only two religious orders of men and two of women working in the diocese. By 1927, there were sixteen orders of men and twenty–nine of women involved in parochial educational, charitable and social programs.

In the area of Catholic schools, the diocese had made remarkable strides in keeping pace with the growing population. The six parish schools of 1887 enrolled about a thousand youngsters. There were no high schools. Colleges, academics, orphanages and Indian schools numbered only four, with 735 pupils .

When John J. Cantwell arrived from San Francisco, he found thirty–four schools with 6,959 pupils. In all, 9,718 children were receiving some sort of instruction in the various institutions then serving the Catholic populace.

Things had improved noticeably by the synod of 1917. There were seventy–two parish schools with 16,483 pupils in attendance and eleven diocesan high schools, with 1,717 students. Colleges, academies, orphanages, etc. numbered twenty–three with 3,672 youngsters on the rolls. Statistics recorded the overall number of youngsters receiving Catholic instruction at 21,872.

During the forty years after 1887, according to *The Tidings*, "The Catholic population has grown by leaps and bounds." In 1887, the number of Catholics was 34,000. By 1927, that number had grown to 298,000 and the diocese had been divided into two jurisdictions by that time. In most cases, the growth in the decade preceding 1927 exceeded that of the thirty previous years.

Those who researched the figures used for an article appearing in *The Tidings* for December 16, 1927, were conservative about their prognostications for the future. Yet, experience had taught them "to accept willingly the predictions which in other places would be laughed to scorn." Hence, they confidently predicted that "we of the present generation expect even greater marvels of expansion to follow."

The report about the 1927 synod concluded with these words: "Who can measure the glories of the future or weigh the amount of material construction and spiritual vigor that will follow, when the solid foundations that are being laid today will have been built upon by the generations to come." Those statements proved modest indeed in the years that followed. By 1942, when the next synod occurred, Los Angeles had become an archdiocese and its statistics were "off the wall."

TAXATION OF CHURCHES IN CALIFORNIA

Traditionally, church property has been exempted from taxation for the same reasons that apply to governmental property, namely, that churches perform a public service in lieu of and in advance of taxation. The moral and cultural values afforded by religious influence have always been recognized as beneficial to the public, necessary to the advancement of civilization and conducive to the promotion of society's overall welfare.

Inasmuch as religious societies are deemed to be public benefactors, the practice of exempting church property from taxation is one which has become deeply imbedded in the fabric of this nation. Such an attitude rests on the immemorial custom which developed when the parish was as much a municipal corporation as towns, villages and cities are today. It continued after the reason for it had disappeared, and was then bolstered by statutory enactments, constitutional provisions, or by a combination of the two.

California's constitution of 1850, however,

absolutely prohibited the legislature from exempting any but public property from taxation: "Taxation shall be equal and uniform throughout the State. All property in this State shall be taxed in proportion to its value, to be ascertained as directed by law." The constitution further provided that assessments and collections should be made by local officers elected for that purpose in the districts, counties or towns where the property was situated. The fact that on the local level no real attempt was made to pressure the churches into paying taxes only confirms the generally held view about the crudities in the revenue system adopted.

The state's earliest lawmakers regarded "all property" as "all taxable property" and, in the Revenue Act of 1853, passed legislation whereby "churches, chapels and other public buildings used for religious worship, and lots of ground appurtenant thereto and used therewith, shall be exempt from taxation." The constitutionality of that action was sustained in 1854, when Chief Justice Hugh C. Murray ruled that "the power of the Legislature to exempt (from taxation) the property of religious and eleemosynary corporations has not been doubted." When the Revenue Act was amended in 1857, the clause exempting church property was continued. When that legislation was challenged six years later, Chief Justice Edward Norton agreed with the earlier interpretation and ruled that the failure to tax a portion of the land in the state did not thereby render the Revenue Act of 1857 void.

A complete reversal came in 1868, when Chief Justice Augustus L. Rhodes over–ruled the former decisions and directed that a tax be levied on all property, except that owned by the state or federal government. The jurist apparently acted with reluctance, however, noting that his decision would bring California's churches and charities under a burden not contemplated by the framers of the constitution. Between 1868 and 1879, the minimum of valuation was accessed against church property because of the general understanding that the churches had fallen victim to an unintentional injustice.

When the constitution for California was adopted in 1880, a considerable number of petitions were received asking that churches and schools be given explicit exemption. Unfortunately, however, the same spirit that called the convention controlled and adopted the new constitution and churches, along with colleges, asylums, charities, libraries, museums and even cemeteries failed to win exemption.

In 1885, Dr. C. C. Stratton, then President of the University of the Pacific, tried unsuccessfully to induce the legislature to submit an amendment for the relief of churches and schools from the tax rolls. Nine years later, however, an amendment did carry exempting free libraries and free museums from the tax rolls.

Early in 1896, the Reverend F. D. Bovard wrote an important article in the *Overland Monthly* in which he said that "the State by this unjust taxation has scoffingly demanded tribute of its benefactor." He called for removing the taxation of church property, arguing that (1) church property is unproductive, (2) that taxation is an unfair drain on the liberality of church membership, (3) that churches provide useful and important moral dimensions to society, (4) that churches are assisting the state by conducting orphanages, private schools and the like, (5) that church goers are effectively taxed an additional 4 to 6% for the privilege of worshipping God and (6) that taxation of churches is entirely foreign to the traditional spirit of California. He also contended that taxation had literally impoverished many church organizations, much to the detriment of the commonweal.

Bovard concluded his forceful appeal by suggesting that the State of California should acknowledge "in a delicate but substantial manner its obligation to (the Christian) religion by exempting from taxation the property dedicated to the worship of God."

The legislators paid attention to Bovard's pleas, as did many others among the general electorate. A further attempt to extend the 1894 provision was made three years later, but owing to the large number of amendments proposed and the lateness of the legislative session, no effectual action was taken at the time.

In 1898, the Presbyterian Synod of California took the initiative and organized a committee to work for tax relief of church property. Their work was rewarded on February 14, 1899, when both houses of the state legislature passed the following measure:

> All buildings and so much of the real property on which they are situated as may be required for the convenient use and occupation of said buildings, when the same are used solely and exclusively for religious worship, shall be free from taxation.

That legislation was approved by the voters of California on November 6, 1900.

TEATRO DE FRAY JUNÍPERO SERRA

According to the mandate given by Christ to the apostles, the office of teaching has precedence over the sacramental and liturgical ministries of the Church. "Go, teach all people my Gospel . . . '

Perhaps that explains why the apostles placed the work of teaching ahead of all their other activities. Saint Paul affirmed that practice when he said that "Christ did not send me to baptize, but to preach the Gospel."

The pre–eminence of the teaching ministry was underscored by then Archbishop John Krol of Philadelphia when he noted, in 1966, that "while the variety of social and charitable apostolates is vital, the apostolate of teaching the Gospel is not only vital but essential to the mission of Christ." Down through the centuries, the entire missionary apostolate of the Church has been a response to Our Lord's mandate of teaching all peoples. That was the primary and sustaining motivation that brought the friars to Alta California.

Most of the criticism directed against the friars and their work in California (and in other parts of the New World) is based upon a misreading or a misunderstanding about the Church's missionary goals and objectives. It was an endeavor to explain the concept of missionization that motivated the educational program developed over the past decade for visitors at San Fernando Mission.

In addition to the normal flow of tourists, upwards of 25,000 youngsters from the Los Angeles Unified School District, together with numerous students from private and religious schools, annually tour the facilities of San Fernando Mission as part of their courses on California history.

In addition to a detailed guide sheet, a sample questionnaire is sent to the teachers prior to their scheduled visit, along with a suggested procedure whereby students can utilize the visit for expanding their memory bank.

When possible, larger groups are assigned to one of the Mission Guides, a docent organization whose members are highly trained in the history of the seventeenth missionary foundations along California *El Camino Real*.

The latest feature at San Fernando is *El Teatro de Junípero Serra* which is located in the easternmost room of the convento building, This theatre has been outfitted with state–of–the–art electronic equipment through the generosity of the Fritz Burns Foundation. In *El Teatro de Junípero Serra*, with its seating capacity for fifty people, students and others will be able to choose between three filmed presentations, each lasting approximately thirty minutes.

The first of the films, which is narrated by Thomas Cassidy, a long–time and respected announcer at KFAC, is a descriptive overview of the California missions between 1769 and 1823. Then there is the Serra Commission's "Father of the American West" which tells about the Mallorcan friar and his collaborators who brought Christianity to the Pacific Slope. Finally, there is a shorter presentation, "Together for Mission," which tells about the Church in Southern California as it has evolved since the close of the mission era In 1840.

Bigotry and prejudice cannot flourish where there is understanding and knowledge. The educational program at San Fernando Mission is aimed at opening the channels of communication for peoples of all ages.

THANKSGIVING IN CALIFORNIA

Public acts of thanksgiving to Almighty God have a long and noble history in our country. In 1621, Governor William Bradford of the Plymouth Colony appointed a day for public prayer after the first harvest. Gradually the practice spread throughout the New England colonies. The Congregationalists, non–believers in the divinity of Christ, sought to substitute the observance for the Christian Feast of Christmas.

The first national recognition of Thanksgiving Day took place in 1789, when President George Washington recommended to Congress that the last Thursday in November, the 26th, be set aside as a day of public thanksgiving and prayer to be observed by acknowledging with grateful hearts the many and signal favors of Almighty God. Though, on the national level, Catholics have participated in Thanksgiving Day ceremonies only since the turn of the century, such was not the case in California, where the observance even pre–dates the Lincoln years when Thanksgiving Day became an established annual occurrence.

The first such day in California was proclaimed on October 24, 1849, when Governor Bennett Riley suggested such an observance in order that the people of California might make a general and public acknowledgement of their gratitude to the Supreme Ruler of the universe for His kind and fostering care during the past year and for the boundless blessings which they have enjoyed. A copy of the proclamation was sent by Secretary of State, Henry W. Halleck, to Father Gonzalez Rubio, Administrator of the Diocese of Both Californias. The Franciscan prelate wholeheartedly endorsed the proposal and promised that the designated day would be religiously observed throughout the vast territory comprising his jurisdiction.

Rubio immediately dispatched a circular letter to his priests, noting how appropriate it was that Catholics should carefully endeavor to cooperate in the execution of such pious designs of the government. The clergy were advised to direct their sermons on the following Sunday to an instruction "concerning the holy object and the purpose of this general solemnity, and to excite their piety in order that on the following Thursday, the 29th of this month, they may assist at Holy Mass, the *Te Deum*, and the public prayers which will be offered up with all the solemnity possible." That such a public observance was to have a permanent place was indicated by Rubio, who noted that "so rational and pious a custom is to continue in subsequent years."

THE TIDINGS

Pope Saint Pius X once said, "In vain you build new churches, give missions, found schools—all your work, all your efforts will be destroyed if you are not able to wield the defensive and offensive weapon of a loyal and sincere Catholic press."

Establishment of a Catholic newspaper in Southern California was occasioned by the religious bigotry of the American Protective Association. Fearful of losing its advertisers and readers, the southland's secular press of the 1890s maintained a policy of strict silence in face of the A.P.A.'s campaign to exclude Catholics from equal opportunities in the business world.

In 1890, the Right Reverend Francis Mora, Bishop of Monterey–Los Angeles, asked Joseph Mesmer to establish a diocesan paper and with assurances from local merchants, the *Cause* began publication on October 4th. Shortly thereafter, the name was changed to the *Voice* but before long that enterprise also failed and Southern California was still without a journal sympathetic to Catholic principles.

Four years later, the Junípero Serra Club of San Diego took steps to counteract the malicious public statements being made against the Church. Three of its members, Patrick W. Croake, James Connolly and Kate Murphy went to Los Angeles and there, on June 29, 1895, launched the *Catholic Tidings* from an office on the second floor of a building on New High Street. Founded on a capital of $400, the first issue had a circulation of fewer than 1,000 copies. The eight–page, four–column weekly was the product of "Irish working girls and working men who had nothing to lose and who gave willingly of the meager salaries to rally public support for the struggling journal."

In the initial editorial, the proprietors announced their purpose:

> The field which the *Catholic Tidings* will humbly aim to occupy is a wide fertile one. In territory, it includes the whole of Southern California, and in population more than sixty thousand Catholics . . . . In all matters pertaining to the best interests of the nation, state and city, the *Catholic Tidings* will be abreast of the most progressive.

Psychologically, the advent of the journal was well timed and "it was but a brief time before conditions commenced to improve" in the Church's relations with non–Catholics. There continued to be opposition to the journal, however. Several lay committees urged the editor to abandon the publication, claiming that "it caused the A.P.A. leaders to be more antagonistic than before." As a gesture to those outside the Church, the editor did agree to drop the word "Catholic" from the masthead on April 17, 1897. Though he had no financial investment in the paper, Bishop George T. Montgomery "did all in

his power to help it along." Together with Croake, the prelate organized a branch of the Catholic Truth Society for the southland. The lecture program of the new organization received unlimited publicity from *The Tidings* over the early years and by the time of William McKinley's election, "the small and ridiculous figure it [the A.P.A.] cut in the campaign was an eye opener even to the most stupid politicians."

Soon after the arrival in California of the Right Reverend Thomas J. Conaty, the new Bishop of Monterey–Los Angeles called a meeting of prominent Catholic businessmen at Cathedral Hall to consider a plan to acquire the paper as the official diocesan organ. The Tidings Publishing Company was subsequently formed and on October 7, 1904, *The Tidings* was purchased by the Church.

Subsequent decades have been no less challenging and while *The Tidings* has had its problems, it enjoys an enviable record in measuring up to John Steven McGroarty's ideal for the Catholic press which, he felt, must be "dignified, pure, and true, kindly and sweet, but above all, charitable."

TRE ORE SERVICES

The earliest authentic record of the public commemoration on Good Friday of the *Tre Ore*, the Three Hours' Agony of Our Lord, dates only from October 20, 1747. There is evidence, however, that the service was widespread even at the time among the Jesuits of Latin America. Though the practice had little or no appeal to the ritualistic instinct of Catholics, the edifying custom quickly spread to other countries where it was adopted as a recognized, if nonliturgical, part of the already lengthy ceremonies of Good Friday. Traces of the *Tre Ore* are discernible in Chili, Panama, Mexico, Spain and Italy at the close of the eighteenth century.

As one of the most searching and spiritual of religious practices, the *Tre Ore* is a series of reflections or meditations, interspersed with prayers and sacred canticles, each bearing upon some one of those seven utterances of Our Lord during the agony of His crucifixion. Like devotion to the Sacred Heart, to which it has always been allied in intention, if not in verbal form, the *Tre Ore* seeks to fix attention upon the fundamental facts of the atonement while simultaneously endeavoring to draw personal lessons from the life of Christ. Though of comparatively recent origin in its outward and mechanical format, the *Tre Ore* is as old and orthodox as the New Testament in its external preoccupation with the mysteries of the Cross.

This extra–liturgical manifestation of piety was introduced in California at the instigation of Stanislaus Riley, a member of The Young Men's Institute. It is recorded how, in 1908, he "conceived the idea of commemorating Good Friday by a three–hour recess from the business of this world, during which the public could attend suitable religious exercises."

The campaign was championed by The Young Men's Institute and publicized widely in and around the Bay Area. San Francisco's Archbishop Patrick W. Riordan endorsed the observance and called for a cooperative involvement by all Catholic organizations in the archdiocese. A Good Friday Committee was formed and the movement rapidly spread throughout California. Happily, though unexpectedly, a large segment of the Protestant community supported the various facets of the campaign.

By soliciting assistance from a wide range of societies and organizations, The Young Men's Institute made the *Tre Ore* one of the most appreciated devotions throughout the United States. In more recent times, the *Tre Ore* has lost favor among more liturgical–minded Catholics, despite its highly scriptural orientation. As a matter of fact, the practice has become significantly popular with our separated brethren and, by a paradoxical twist of values, there is far more likelihood of finding the Three Hours' Agony of Our Lord commemorated on Good Friday between noon and three o'clock in Protestant churches than there is in those where the practice originated.

TREASURE OF SIERRA MADRE

Bishop Thomas J. Conaty (1847–1915) was forever writing to his eastern friends about the lush flora and fauna of Southern California. He was especially enamored with the wisteria vine that blossomed every year in Sierra Madre.

Now designated by the *Guinness Book of World Records* as "the world's largest blossoming plant," the Chinese Lavender variety of wisteria "covers almost an acre, weighs 252 tons and has an estimated 1.5 million blossoms during its five–week blooming period."

When Marco Polo returned to Europe in the 13th century, he brought with him the best of what he had found in the great eastern civilizations. Among those treasures were seeds of the wisteria vine.

The ancient Chinese planted the spreading lavender–flowered vine to cover their magnificent outdoor pergolas at the royal palaces. Since then wisteria vines have been planted in attempts to shade patios the world over.

In 1894, Mrs. William F. Brugman drove her horse and buggy to Monrovia and there purchased a small Chinese Lavender wisteria from a local nursery. She planted the 75 cent vine by the front porch of her home at 201 West Carter. Within a few years, the vine had taken possession of the whole yard. In 1913, the property was sold to Mr. and Mrs. H. T. Fennell. The new owners built a frame on the east side of their house to support the massive spreading tendrils of the vine.

Each year, during the six week blooming period, the Fennells were inundated with visitors and sightseers who journeyed from Los Angeles and other areas of Southern California to see the giant canopy of flowers covering more than an acre of land.

After World War I, the Sierra Madre Chapter of the American Red Cross began sponsoring the Wisteria Festival of Sierra Madre as a benefit. The first year's event attracted 12,000 people! By 1931, the weight of the vine had collapsed the original Brugman house. By then, 30,000 visitors were coming annually to see the vine at *fiestas* presided over by a queen and princesses.

In 1937, the property was purchased by Mrs. Ida Lawless and she continued to improve the garden. Extensive arbors were erected to allow the vine to spread over a larger area. Succeeding owners were equally as solicitous for the now–famed wisteria. Around 1950, the property was sold again, this time to developers who subdivided the area into residential lots. For a while it looked as if the world's largest blooming plant was doomed. Happily provisions were made which allowed the wisteria to remain.

Sierra Madre's renowned vine evokes many memories to young and old. And though the vine has begun to age, each spring brings anew the fresh fragrant and colorful blossoms which still adorn the original location. Visitors from far and near come to remember or see what Bishop Thomas J. Conaty used to call "the Treasure of Sierra Madre."

TRIUMPH OF DAVID

Early in 1974, Sir Daniel Donohue presented a remarkably–preserved tapestry to the Archdiocese of Los Angeles. The historic work of art was subsequently hung in the Carrie Estelle Doheny Memorial Library, at Camarillo.

The magnificent wool and silk tapestry known to the artistic world as the "Triumph of David" measures 20' 4" wide by 12' 9 1/2" high. From the initials B.B., at the lower right hand corner, and the symbol of a warrior's hatchet on the opposite extreme, the tapestry can be identified as the work of Bernard Van Orley. The distinctive signature dates the tapestry as existing prior to the edict of King Charles V, in 1528, which directed

artists to incorporate into the galloon band at the lower right hand side of the tapestry, the coat–of–arms for the city in which it was woven.

A court–painter for Margaret of Parma, Bernard Van Orley inaugurated a new era of Flemish art by introducing into his native country the styles of the great contemporary Italian masters. The exceedingly–prominent weaver devised the cartoons for the "Seven Deadly Sins," three of which adorn Madrid's Del Prado Museum, "The Hunts of Maximilian," which is displayed at Fountainebleau and several additional series and single scenes featured in other noteworthy collections. Van Orley is also credited with the design for the Van Aelst tapestries, which were based on Raphael Santi's cartoonery.

The "Triumph of David" was initially owned by Eleanor, the grand–daughter of Maximilian, who married Francis I of France. Two of her aunts, Margaret of Parma and Mary of Hungary, had been among Van Orley's principal patrons. The exquisite tapestry remained in the French royal family until Louis XIII presented it and a host of others to Francesco Cardinal Barberini, who represented his uncle, Pope Urban VIII, at the court of France.

In 1889, the Van Orley masterpiece was among 135 tapestries acquired from the Barberini family by Charles M. Ffoulke of Washington. At the time of his death, the

Triumph of David

"Triumph of David," the gem of his vast collection, was valued at $100,000. The tapestry was displayed at Brussels, in 1905, in a famous exhibition of old and treasured masterpieces. The catalogue for that event described and illustrated the famous Van Orley tapestry with information from a manuscript by Luco Holstenio, written on October 25, 1695, and found among the Barberini family archives in Rome. The "Triumph of David" was subsequently purchased from the Ffoulke estate by the late Earle C. Anthony, in the 1930s After his death it was acquired by Mr. and Mrs. Daniel Donohue.

DESCRIPTION

The picturesque tapestry graphically illustrates the incidents related in I Samuel 18, 6–7. In the right foreground, the youthful David, with no apparent effort, carries the head of Goliath atop the decapitated giant's own sword. He is followed by King Saul, astride a richly–caparisoned horse. The king, wearing a wide–brimmed hat ornamented with tassels, holds a scepter in his left hand and gestures approval with his right one.

Included in the royal escort is Jonathan, carrying the baton of a commander. Numerous lesser armored officials follow, along with civilians wearing *toca* or caps. Two helmeted soldiers and two–bareheaded pages dressed in breeches and close coats with puffing sleeves, are also portrayed. The shoulder belts of the pages bear the imprint of a double eagle, symbolic for the House of Hapsburg, who ruled the Netherlands at the time the tapestry was woven.

Passing through the town gates, the crowd greets Saul and the victorious David. Young maidens are playing the harp, the hurdygurdy, the bagpipe and the tambourine. A youthful man manipulates the triangle, another the gongs and a third the ovular bells sewed into his clothing. While one of the musicians scrapes the marin trumpet, others play the flute, hautbois and drum.

In a panel, at the upper left, Saul is shown in front of his mountain tent, as Abner, the captain of the hosts, introduces David, who has brought him the head of Goliath. The other side depicts a turret in the foreground and, at a distance, the walls and towers of the Elkron Temple.

The rich and decorative border is enhanced by colorful flowers, fruit and vegetables, among which can be seen carnations, iris, lilies, apples, peaches, grapes, pumpkins and the like. The two gold shields on the upper border, with the silver *fleur–de–lis* in three horizontal rows, probably reproduces the coat–of–arms of the patron, whose munificence inspired the work.

EL TRIUNFO DE LA CRUZ

The first ship ever built in California was the work of Father Juan Ugarte. It was 1719, at the darkest period of the Jesuit colonization on the peninsula, and the missionaries found themselves obliged to rely on their own resources. The circumstances under which the ship was built, and the uses to which it was applied, render it one of the most interesting structures of which our early history treats.

Ugarte was one of those practical geniuses to whom all occupations seem subservient, and to whom nothing that seemed indispensible was impossible. Then working as a missionary in Loreto, on the Gulf shore of the peninsula, Father Ugarte found neither timber nor trees suitable for timber, nor iron, nor sails, nor tar, nor other necessary materials. To any other man, such obstacles would have proven insurmountable.

He was informed by the Indians that about two hundred miles to the northwest there were large and straight trees which might serve his purpose. Procuring a shipwright from across the Gulf, he set out over the mountains for the forests.

The enterprising Jesuit began felling trees, fashioning them into planks, and directing his followers how to help him and thereby hasten his labors. As soon as this part of his work was done, he began clearing out and constructing a road from the place to Santa Rosalia Mission, on the little river of Mulege.

From there he cleared out the channel of the stream so as to float down the remainder of the way to the Gulf shore. Oxen and mules were employed to help move the heavy planks in and out of the water.

He next procured from across the Gulf such materials as could not be supplied from his own establishments. Several carpenters were soon at work, with Father Ugarte superintending the entire work. Gradually he saw his new vessel grow up from keel to bulwarks and ready for the sea. In September of 1719, Ugarto, with his own hand, nailed the cross upon her bowsprit, launched her upon the brine, and christened the ship *El Triunfo de la Cruz.*

The finished ship, compared with the vessels then in use, was large and strong; and for beauty, as well as service, it was afterward, by competent judges of marine architecture, pronounced superior to anything of the kind that had ever sailed in those waters.

Ugarte's first voyage took place in November, 1720. It began at Loreto and ended at La Paz, a distance of about a hundred and fifty miles. In default of any other captain, Father Ugarte himself assumed command of the vessel and he showed that he was as good a navigator as he was a shipbuilder. For a number of years, *El Triunfo de la Cruz* continued to be the only ship in the service of the missionaries and there was always, as long as it lasted, employment for it.

What finally became of the ship, whether it sank, or was crushed upon the rocks, or beaten to pieces by the merciless waves, is uncertain. Surely it never lay idle or rotted by the wall. It answered well and faithfully the purposes of its construction.

El Triunfo de la Cruz, like the *Santa Maria* and the *Mayflower* ought also to be remembered and glorified in the histories of civilization yet to be written.

TWELVE STONES OF THE APOCALYPSE

The chalice used every Sunday at San Fernando Mission is a lesson in Holy Scripture. Designed by Donat Thomasson of Paris in 1932, its hemispherical bowl bears the inscription "*Rex Regum et Dominus Dominatium.*" Around the base is the crucified Christ and attending angels.

Besides its intriguing design, the chalice has a feature that is probably unique in all the world, adorned as it is with all the precious stones enumerated in the Book of Revelation (Apocalypse). In the 19th chapter of that book, the inspired writer describes how the foundations of the City Wall of Jerusalem were faced with a variety of precious stones. It then goes on to identify each by name.

The first is a *diamond* (or jasper), pre–eminent in the realm of gems and highly regarded by peoples everywhere. Also diamonds were among the gems associated with the breastplate of the high priest. The second was *lapis lazul*i (or sapphire), one of the most prized and sought–after stones of ancient times. Generally used for personal adornment, lapis has been suggested as the material on which were inscribed the tables of the law.

Third was *turquoise* (chalcedony). An ancient tradition suggests that Isaac, son of Abraham, was the first to open the turquoise mines in Persia. The fourth stone was the *emerald*, one of the rarest gems. Unrivaled because of its rich green color, many believed emeralds strengthened memory and enhanced eloquence. And the fifth was *agate* (Sardonyx), a stone highly favored by Biblical civilizations. Engraved amulets, carved seals and finger rings were typically fashioned from agate. The sixth was *ruby* (carnelian), among the most abundant elements in the earth's crust. It was equated with wisdom in certain versions of the Book of Proverbs.

The seventh of the stones was *gold quartz* (chrysolite). A truly royal mineral, gold was, even then, the most famous of the earth's elements. Esteemed highly by the Hebrews, it was plentiful in the reigns of David and Solomon and was used lavishly by them and others.

Eighth was *malachite* (beryl). Of all the minerals, none is more vivid and appealing to the eye than malachite. It was mined extensively in the time of King Solomon. The ninth was *topaz*, a very durable gem believed to bestow beauty, intelligence and long life. It occurs in well–formed brilliant crystals. Job described wisdom as the "topaz of Ethiopia."

And the tenth was *chrysoprase*, a gem admired and utilized by Biblical peoples. As a gem, chrysoprase has been exquisitely carved into cameos, It is a rather scarce, apple–green variety of chalcedony. The eleventh was *sapphire* (hyacinth). An age–old tradition, widely accepted by some Oriental peoples, maintained that the earth rests upon a gigantic blue sapphire, with the bowl of the sky mirroring its radiant blue.

Finally, there was *amethyst*, a stone that was scarce and greatly prized in ancient civilizations for its glowing color. Even today, it has been a traditional stone in rings of religious leaders.

History is where one finds it and surely this magnificent silver gilt French chalice is an example of that truism. It remains a monument to the liturgical ingenuity of the late Msgr. Robert E. Brennan (1908–1986) who commissioned and used it during years of his ministry in the Archdiocese of Los Angeles.

UNITED SERVICES ORGANIZATION (U.S.O.)

The United Services Organization or the USO was established in February of 1941, just prior to the entrance of the United States into World War II as a "federation of voluntary agencies through which the American people could assist in serving the spiritual, social, welfare, recreational and educational needs of men and women in the armed forces."

USO was envisioned as an agency that in peace and war would help to preserve and strengthen the ties between members of the armed forces and the civilian community. It was recognized as "home away from home" which would provide a welcome entertainment for military personnel everywhere.

The non–sectarian nature of the USO allowed it to offer comprehensive programs to Protestants, Catholics and Jews alike. Its member agencies were the YMCA, the YWCA, the National Catholic Community Services, National Jewish Welfare Board, the Salvation Army and National Travelers Aid.

During the Korean "peace action," Archbishop J. Francis A. McIntyre enlisted the local Catholic community in reactivating the USO, in Los Angeles. Of the 245 operations in the United States, none was more efficiently operated than the one opened in December of 1950 in quarters above Our Lady Chapel and the Catholic Information Center at 807 South Flower Street. Emergency financial support was allocated by the Saint Vincent de Paul Society and volunteer hostesses and canteen workers from Catholic parishes throughout the archdiocese answered the call to service. Estimates place the total number of people served during those years at over 500,000, with volunteers donating 750,000 hours of time, 1,110,000 units of food and 915,000 beverages. It was a totally awesome response to the cardinal's call.

McIntyre himself was a frequent visitor to the USO headquarters where he personally participated in all the programs underway for military people. He also enlisted members of the Hollywood entertainment community to assist in the USO's activities. The cardinal often recounted to visitors his experiences as military delegate in the Archdiocese of New York where he coordinated efforts to provide chaplains for United States forces during World War II.

Religious services were provided daily for visiting service men and women, and McIntyre scheduled himself for a monthly turn offering Mass and hearing confessions. He was the first to arrive and the last to leave. It was a ministry he thoroughly enjoyed. On one occasion, McIntyre read a letter from President Dwight Eisenhower which said that the President was aware of "the great number of young people in service who are enriched by your programs of recreation, friendliness and wholesome entertainment."

Of all the units of the USO in the United States, none received more accolades than the one in Los Angeles. After the war, retired soldiers and sailors would often drop into Our Lady Chapel with words of gratitude for what had been an enriching experience during the dark days of conflict.

McIntyre captured the ideals of USO when he observed that "wherever USO serves, it stands for home and for the generous impulse of civilization to guarantee that those in uniform remain in touch with the best features of our American way–of–life." Termed the "most truly American organization, exemplary in the democratic way–of–life," the USO forged Jews, Protestants and Catholics into a common effort of service on behalf of the armed forces.

UTAH — CATHOLIC CHURCH IN

A history of the Diocese of Salt Lake City has been published under the title: *Salt of the Earth*. It is available at the diocesan offices, 27C Street, Salt Lake City, 84103. Governor John Lee of Maryland uttered some very sage advice when he told historians to "gather up the letters of the past, gather up the traditions, gather up the pamphlets, gather up the records that are so essential for the fulness of our Catholic history, for surely our Catholic people have no reason to be ashamed but even reason to be proud of their glorious traditions." The Catholics of Utah, together with all people of good will, certainly can rejoice that Bernice Maher Mooney and Jerome C. Stoffel followed Lee's suggestions so faithfully.

In the noble pattern of W. R. Harris and Louis J. Fries, the compilers have assembled an encyclopedic treatise delineating the several beginnings of the Catholic Church in Utah—the missionary activities of Fray Francisco Silvestre Velez de Escalante (1776), the pioneering outreach of Bishop Joseph Machebeuf (1868) and the reerection of the Vicariate Apostolic and appointment of Lawrence J. Scanlan (1887). It was to commemorate the latter event that this volume was issued.

What a remarkable 226 years it has been, stretching from oxcarts to spaceships. Dominguez and Escalante, Scanlan, Glass, Mitty, Kearney, Hunt, Federal and Weigand—Niederauer—the Cathedral of the Madeleine—native vocations—lay organizations and associations—Vatican Council II—to mention but a scattering of the colorful threads woven into the fabric of Utah's Catholic heritage.

While they are indigenous to the area, Catholics have not been the dominant force in Utah, at least since the arrival of the Church of Jesus Christ of Latter-day Saints. Even today, Catholics account for only 4 to 5% of the nearly 1.7 million people residing in the 84,990 square mile state.

The major thrust of this book encompasses the years since 1868 and the establishment of the Vicariate Apostolic of Colorado and Utah. (Three years later, the vicariate was divided and the area of Utah reverted to the Metropolitan Province of San Francisco.) The modern era began on January 23, 1887, when the state of Utah and six counties of Nevada were formed into the Vicariate Apostolic of Utah. The region was advanced to diocesan status on January 27, 1891. The Nevada section was dismembered and made into the Diocese of Reno on March 22, 1931 and, two decades afterwards, the title of the original jurisdiction was changed to Salt Lake City.

Though the subtitle of this book indicates that it is a "history of the Catholic Diocese of Salt Lake City," it really is considerably more than that. Probably it could best be described as a "statistical abstract" of the area. There is very little of importance or significance that has happened in "Catholic" Utah that is not described or at least mentioned in this book. Indeed, there probably is a lot more recorded here than anyone (even historians) need or want to know. But that's not meant to be a put-down. If every diocese, institution and religious order had its development chronicled so carefully and accurately as does the Diocese of Salt Lake City, our regional and national ecclesial histories would be a lot more factual and considerably more interesting and relevant to the real world in which they subsist.

There are many facets of the Church's life in Utah that stand out in this book; one aspect that towers above the others is the depth of Catholic roots in the deserts and mountain ranges of the Old Utah Territory. If Utah is a great commonwealth today, a goodly portion of the credit goes to the Catholic pioneers and leaders who helped forge a particular spiritual dimension that will forever remain unique.

VATICAN COUNCIL I

Before his election as Pope Paul VI, Giovanni Battista Montini observed that the Vatican Council II was the first ecumenical gathering in history that has had "neither to surmount internal discord nor to solve problems of doctrine disputed within the Church."

Such was certainly not the case in December of 1869, when the world's hierarchy met in Rome for the First Vatican Council. The burning issue of the day was papal infallibility and so delicate were the implications involved that even the three bishops from California disagreed among themselves as to the expediency of its definition. The Right Reverend Thaddeus Amat, C.M., Bishop of Monterey–Los Angeles, described as "the shrewdest man in the council," belonged to that group which believed the doctrine could be defined in such a manner as to avoid completely the term "infallibility," a word with unfavorable connotation among many non–Catholics. Amat's position was based on his ever–present pastoral concern for the impact that such a definition might have in his own diocese where a strong

Vatican Council 1

current of anti–Catholic feeling existed even in those days.

Amat was not alone. Nearly half of the American bishops were opposed to the definition for one reason or another. Repeatedly, the Bishop of Monterey–Los Angeles pointed out that "the only question was whether it was expedient, prudent, seasonable and timely regard being had to the conditions of the world, of the nations of Europe, of the Christians in separation from the Church, to put this truth in the form of a definition." It was this concern that compelled Amat to joint a coalition of twenty–seven prelates from English–speaking countries, twenty of them Americans, in expressing disapproval of presenting the doctrine. Their petition was sent to the Holy Father, Pius IX, on January 15, 1870.

The Archbishop of San Francisco, Joseph Sadoc Alemany, O.P., on the other hand, made one of the most memorable addresses given at the council when, on May 14, 1870, he stated that while he did not personally regard the pope as wholly infallible, he wanted the doctrine proclaimed immediately. In the judgment of the California Dominican, his comments were not meant "to be profuse . . . but merely given lest the fear displayed by many about the definition of infallibility" be not sufficiently founded. Alemany gave as his reason the opinion that "at present this definition is necessary on account of the innumerable errors that daily gain ground and for the reason that once this Council is closed, it will be no easy task to assemble another."

When the balloting was concluded on July 13, 1870 at the last general congregation, Bishop Amat's vote was among the sixty–two cast *placet justa modum* (conditionally favorable) although the majority of the fathers favored the simple and more embracing *placet* (favorable). Seeing that his "expediency" plea had fallen on deaf ears, Amat professed his personal belief in the doctrine and at the final solemn session, July 18th, added his name to the 533 fathers giving assent to the papal definition of infallibility as we know it today.

On the following day, as if by Divine action, the Franco–Prussian War broke out and the council adjourned, never to meet again.

VATICAN MEMORIAL SERIES

Those interested in taking a vicarious journey to the Vatican were thrilled to see the forty water colors and pencil drawings on exhibit in the Forest Lawn Museum, Glendale, some years ago. The masterful renditions, owned by the University of San Diego, were on display for the first time in forty years. They were painted in 1932–1934 by Vernon Howe Bailey.

Bailey had studied at the Pennsylvania Museum of Art in Philadelphia, as well as the Pennsylvania Academy of Fine Arts. Shortly after the turn of the century, while Bailey was working as an illustrator for the Boston *Herald*, he was asked to cover the coronation of King Edward VII in London.

That commission resulted in others. Several nationwide magazines, including *Harper's*, *Collier's* and *McClures* entrusted assignments to him. A number of his works were subsequently on display at the Smithsonian Institution. In 1927, Bailey exhibited a series of lithographs of New York skyscrapers. Those works received worldwide acclaim, and resulted in the artist's being invited to join the prestigious Royal Academy of Fine Arts, the fourth American so honored.

During a reception in Rome, Bailey was asked by the Governor General of Vatican City if he would be interested in doing a series of sketches featuring the great halls and churches of the Eternal City.

Over the next few years, Vernon Howe Bailey was given access to each of the 11,000 rooms in the Vatican. It was an unforgettable opportunity and one which Bailey utilized to the fullest. The result was a remarkable series of glimpses in and around the Vatican. In addition to scenes inside Saint Peter's Basilica, viewers are able to see apartments, colorful galleries and historic hallways which are not accessible to most tourists.

The artwork was purchased and remained in private hands for a decade. It was last exhibited publicly in 1947, and then consigned to storage. Recently, after the paintings were willed to the University of San Diego, it was decided that the "Vatican Memorial Series" would travel to other parts of the nation.

This collection is a tribute to the remarkable talents of an artist who left behind the first intimate and comprehensive collection of art devoted to the architectural treasures of the Vatican. After viewing the collection, Msgr. Enrico Pucci, a secretary to Pope Plus XI, issued the following statement:

> It is to the genial brush of an outstanding American artist that we are indebted for this vivid, colorful presentation of the Vatican. For over a year, Bailey had lived in and absorbed the Vatican scene, and that elusive majesty, that old world atmosphere which no verbal virtuosity can ever hope to convey, he has with unerring felicity expressed in this series of paintings and drawings.

So it was possible, without ever leaving the confines of metropolitan Los Angeles, to visit the chapels, oratories, mausoleums and private chambers of the Vatican. Reproductions of the artwork of Michelangelo, Canova, Van Gogh, Picasso and others could be seen at Forest Lawn Museum in Glendale.

VEILING CEREMONY

The liturgical life of the neophytes attached to the California missions followed carefully structured patterns that allowed few exceptions. In a typical directive, dated October 1, 1806, the friars working in Alta California were exhorted to promote devotion among the faithful by holding "at all the missions, the blessing of ashes, candles and palms on the appropriate days."

The missionaries were reminded that "the instruction of the neophytes (in their religion) is the most important obligation" deriving from the ministerial office. For that reason, a "bell was to be rung every day in the morning, in the afternoon or at nightfall, to summon the neophytes to the church for reciting the catechism and the principal articles of our Holy Faith."

Among other devotions, the Franciscan crown rosary, honoring the seven joys of the Blessed Mother, was recommended for daily recitation. And, on festival days, there was to be an explanation of the doctrine or mystery being celebrated.

Many para–liturgical ceremonials found their way into the mission prayer–style, including such practices as the *velados* or "veiling" which even today is occasionally seen in certain areas of the Hispanic world. This practice was derived from a ritual which priests in the ancient See of Toledo used for the administration of the sacraments, the conferral of blessings, the conduct of processions and the performance of exorcisms.

The veiling was apparently a very important part of the ceremony because customarily the priest made a notation in the *Registro de Matrimonios* that he had not only witnessed the marriage but also had "veiled" the bride and groom.

The liturgical procedure in mission times directed that the priest receive the bridal party at the door of the church or chapel and there witness the exchange of marital vows with the usual questions, answers, vows and blessings. Then he opened the church door and led the wedded couple down the aisle to the sanctuary where they knelt before the altar for the celebration of Holy Mass.

During the Mass, after the recitation of the Lord's prayer, the priest turned to the married couple and, before giving them the nuptial blessing, placed a partly red and partly white veil over the head of the bride and the shoulders of the groom.

The veil over the head of the bride signified dedication to her spouse, while the one over the shoulders of the groom identified him as the breadwinner of the family. The color white emphasized conjugal fidelity and red indicated that blood passed from parents to children. This richly symbolical ceremonial is fully described in Antonio Lobera's *El Porque de Todas las Ceremonias de la Iglesia, y sus Mysterios* (Madrid, 1770).

When the Mass was finished, the priest, taking the bride by her right hand, gave her to her spouse saying: "I give you a companion, not a servant. Love her as Christ loved His Church."

VENUS AND ITS "TRANSIT"

Just a little more than a month before Fray Junípero Serra and his companions established the first of the California missions, San Diego de Alcala, another epochal event was occuring a few hundred miles away in Peninsular California. Scientists had determined that the "transit of Venus" would take place on June 3, 1769, an occurrence that happens twice every hundred years. It was felt that careful calculations of that event would enable experts to determine the distance between the earth and the sun.

Abbe Jean Baptiste Chappe d'Auteroche (1728–1769), a talented French astronomer, was one of those chosen to represent the French Royal Academy of Sciences in witnessing this astronomical phenomenon. (Born at Auvergne, Chappe studied with the Jesuits who early recognized his ability in drafting, mathematics and astronomy. Although Chappe received at least some of the minor orders, there is no evidence that he ever functioned as a cleric).

With the authorization of Spain's King Carlos III, Chappe was assigned to record the transit at a prime vantage point in Peninsular California on June 3, 1769, something that had been done earlier in Siberia. In addition to charting this scientific event, the small expedition accompanying Chappe was charged with reporting on the geography, physical and natural history of the region.

Chappe and his small party set out from Paris on October 18, 1768 for the long and treacherous journey to Vera Cruz. From there, they went on to Mexico City. After a brief respite, they set out again for Queretero, Guadalajara, Tepic and San Blas.

Leaving for San Blas on April 19th, Chappe and his contingency completed their long trek over the dangerous seas to Peninsular California, arriving at San Jose del Cabo Mission. Hurriedly Chappe removed the southeast part of the roof on a large stable and installed an awning which could be drawn or retracted. He carefully positioned his instruments and by June 3rd had everything in order.

Chappe d'Auteroche's documented account of the transit of Venus was made with utmost accuracy. His two Spanish assistants, Vicente de Doz and Salvador de Medina, were equally successful in their studies of the historical event. Unfortunately, there was an epidemic (possibly typhus, cholera or yellow fever) ravaging the area of San Jose del Cabo when Chappe's party arrived and most of them contracted the illness. The famed cleric died on August 1st and was buried in a Franciscan habit.

The artist, Alexander Jean Noel, recorded Chappe's funeral procession in a painting as it passed before the mission. He portrayed an officer wearing a blue uniform with red lapels following the litter.

Chappe's reports were taken back to Europe and deposited with the Royal Academcy of Sciences at Paris. They were first published in 1772. Later calculations confirmed that Chappe's recording of the transit of Venus were only forty seconds off absolute target, a remarkable feat in itself.

VIBIANA THE SAINT

Early in 1851, Pope Pius IX purchased a vineyard in Rome directly above a vast series of unexplored catacombs which had gone unknown and unused for almost a thousand years. Excavation of the area was entrusted by the Holy Father to the Pontifical Commission for Sacred Archeology, which at that time was under the direction of the famous Giovanni Battista de Rossi.

During the month of December 1853, an examination was made of that portion then known as San Sisto, later commonly referred to as *Pretestato* because of a picture of that saint visible therein. This cemetery was located to the left of the Appian Way in the locality called Bonfiglioli, about one mile from the *Porta di San Sebastano*. Excavations resulted in the discovery of an ancient entrance to the cemetery, one time probably well cared for, but now in almost complete ruin. On December 9, workmen came across a vault containing a number of vials of spices and quite a few marble tablets with epitaphs still remaining intact. Among the sepulchres remaining unbroken was that of a certain Vibiana. To the left and adjoining her tomb was a rose–colored crystal vase containing aromatic spices for the newly discovered martyr.

A marble tablet, seventy centimeters long and thirty wide, with an inscription attached, sealed the sepulchre. The tablet was unbroken, although cracked in several places. When the workmen attempted to remove the tablet, the arch, weakened by the excavations, collapsed and partially buried the tomb. After the debris was removed, the skeleton of a young woman, obviously put to death in a violent fashion, became visible. The date of the maiden's death, as well as other information about her person, is uncertain. From the inscriptions and other epitaphs in the area, it has been conjectured by archeologists that Vibiana lived in the third century. The

inscription on her tomb reads in English: "To the soul of the innocent and pure Vibiana, laid away the day before the Kalends of September [August 31st]."

At the end of the inscription is a garland of palm leaves, an emblem commonly used by early Christians to symbolize martyrdom. An investigation was ordered by Pius IX and after the authentic character of the relics had been officially established early in February of 1854, they were exposed for public veneration as "the precious relics of the illustrious Virgin and glorious Martyr, Vibiana."

Public enthusiasm for the newly discovered saint was manifested not only in the Eternal City itself but also in the surrounding areas. A number of prominent ecclasiastics petitioned the pope for the relics, all without success. It remained for the recently consecrated Bishop of Monterey, Thaddeus Amat, to win the privilege, almost without asking. When Bishop Amat was received by the Holy Father on March 18, 1854, the generous–minded pontiff conferred the widely sought relics on Monterey's new ordinary "with the express condition of building a Cathedral Church in honor of the saint."

Amat brought the relics with him on his long journey to California where he arrived in November of 1855. They were enshrined at Santa Barbara in the Church of Our Lady of Sorrows. When that edifice was leveled by fire, the untouched relics were moved to Los Angeles where they were housed for some years in the *Iglesia de Nuestra Senora de los Angeles*. The final disposition of the relics took place in 1876, when the cathedral dedicated to Vibiana's honor was solemnly consecrated by Archbishop Joseph Sadoc Alemany of San Francisco.

At the time of the golden jubilee of Saint Vibiana's Cathedral, one writer had this to say about the diocesan patroness:

> The body of the saint who is the patroness of the cathedral and the diocese was given to this far–distant part of the Lord's vineyard in the days before the church was built. It was reverently brought to these shores from its resting place in the darkness of the Roman Catacombs to be enshrined at last, here in our midst, with becoming pomp and ceremony. There, in the niche high above the main altar of the cathedral her relics have rested in peace for half a century, while from her heavenly home this gentle maiden has watched over the destinies of a now great diocese and lent a ready ear to those who have sought her intercession. It is much to be regretted that we have not developed a strong devotion to the sainted patroness of our diocese and its principal church. We can have no doubt that she will be anxious to intercede for us, her spiritual children, in a very special manner.

VIDA NUEVA

There is a long and rich historical precedent for *Vida Nueva*, the Spanish language newspaper inaugurated on April 10, 1991 by The Tidings Corporation for the Archdiocese of Los Angeles. Catholic journalistic influences stretch back to August of 1846, when the *Californian*, the first newspaper published in the state, was printed on a press "found in the cloisters of one of the missions."

Since that time, the Catholic press has consistently been an active force in California life. As early as 1850 the New York *Freeman's Journal and Catholic Register* carried a regular column from a Sacramento correspondent signed only as "Philos," probably the pen name for Dr. Gregory Phelan.

The first Catholic weekly newspaper published on the Pacific Coast originated at San Francisco under the auspices of Father Hugh Gallagher. The *Catholic Standard*, launched on May 6, 1854, advertised itself as "an organ of the Catholic Church."

Apart from the long list of English–speaking newspapers sponsored by the Church or issued "under Catholic auspices," *La Cronica* has the distinction of being the first published in California for the Hispanic community. Edited by E. F. Teodoli, *La Cronica* was described by a writer in the Los Angeles Star as "a substantial paper, published semi–weekly."

La Cronica appeared fairly consistently between 1872 and 1892 When the newspaper got into financial straits and ceased publication, it was succeeded by another Hispanic weekly known as *Las dos Republicas*.

A Portuguese newspaper was distributed in the Bay area under the masthead of *0 Vox Portuguesa* between 1884 and 1888 by Antonio Vicente. A second paper, begun in 1884 under the title *0 Progresso Californiense*, limped along for five years and was then made over to *A Unaio Portuguesa* by Manuel Trigueiro.

Der Californischen Volksfreund was a Catholic paper printed in the German language in San Francisco. Begun in 1885 by Carl Doeing and Frank Diepenbrock, the publication lasted until 1906. *0 Amigos dos Catolicos* originated at Irvington in 1888. The Portuguese publication was inaugurated by Fathers Manuel Francisco Fernandez and Jose Francisco Tavares. After a year the paper passed under lay control and moved to Pleasanton.

From 1892 to 1896 it was printed at Hayward. The name was changed to *0 Arauto* in 1896 and until 1917 it was published at Irvington under the editorship of Messrs. Lemos and Quaresma. In the latter year, Pedro L. C. Silveira purchased the paper and merged it with his *0 Jornal de Noticias*.

L'Imparziale was first published from San Francisco in 1891 by Joseph Morgana. The paper was inactive for some years but was revived between 1897 and 1909 as the *Impartial Californian* under the direction of P. S. Bergerot. In 1901 the Saint Louis *Review* called it "the only Italian Catholic paper in the United States."

Luigi Muzio edited a newspaper known as *La Verita* at San Francisco between 1893 and 1894. The venture started and finished as an Italian Catholic publication. "Devoted to the instruction in Catholic truth and doctrine" of the Spanish speaking people in Southern California was *La Actualidad*, printed from 1895 at San Bernardino under the direction of Father Juan Caballeria. The eight page weekly ceased publication about 1902. In 1897, Constantino Soares originated *0 Reporter* at Oakland. From 1910 to 1914 the weekly was owned and issued by the Reverend Jose Silva.

VOYAGE PITTORESQUE

Many of the most important illustrations of California scenes and incidents are preserved only through the painstaking sketches of early travelers or pioneer residents. This is especially true in regard to the missions. Before the days of photography, the most common representations of these old foundations were book illustrations made from sketches of visiting artists. The first of these were executed by John Sykes for George Vancouver's *A Voyage of Discovery*. Those volumes, published at London in 1798, contained carefully engraved plates.

In 1822, Ludovich Choris published his *Voyage Pittoresque* and seventeen years later Alexander Forbes' *California* was issued from London with ten plates, four of which related to the missions. Drawings from the latter book were done by Captain William Smith. There were three delicately executed plates on the missions in Eugene Duflot de Mofras' *Exploration* of 1844.

The illustrations of Edward Vischer occupy a category of their own for his sketches, done mostly in the 1860s are frequently the only contemporary representations of the missions. One early writer noted that Vischer's "works drawn with photographic detail, are our only source of pictorial data on the condition of the Mission establishments before the hand of neglect had crushed their roofs and left their walls to the mercy of winter rains."

In the early 1850s, the Daguerreotype was popular, especially for portraiture. Missions San Diego, San Jose and Santa Clara are examples of this medium in the work of Henry Chapman Ford. With the development, in 1851, of the dry collodion process by Scott Archer, photography came into its own and the number of mission portrayals increased rapidly. This new illustrative medium was first used in periodicals in the June, 1859 issue of *Hutchings California Magazine*.

Two woodcuts, one a view of Mission Dolores and the other representing "the old mission church and buildings built in 1776" were made from photographs taken by Hamilton and Company. Woodcut reproductions of the missions were utilized for the initial time in *Annals of San Francisco*, published at New York in 1885.

One authority said that "the first to photograph the Missions in any thorough manner was Carlton E. Watkins . . . whose superb work did more to make known our State's superior scenic attractions than all the other photographers combined." Watkins visited Southern California in 1876 and took pictures of Missions San Diego, San Luis Rey, San Juan Capistrano, San Gabriel, San Fernando, Santa Barbara, San Luis Obispo and others.

His likeness of Mission Dolores was copied from one already made by an English tourist. Watkins' version of San Jose was taken from Ford's daguerreotype. The negatives of Watkins were later acquired by the C.C. Pierce Company.

Herve Friend, characterized as "the father of artistic photographic work in Southern California," tried to do for that part of the state what Watkins did for the north. His collection subsequently came into the possession of George Wharton James.

The extensive and artistic collection of A. C. Vroman of Pasadena was started in 1897. The vast holdings of Charles F. Lummis were deeded, in 1910 to the Southwest Museum, where they are still available to researchers. Many of the Lummis photos appeared in the pages of *Land of Sunshine* and *Out West*.

WALK OF FAME FOR CATHOLICS

Nothing so personifies Hollywood as the "Walk of Fame" and the luminaries honored for their accomplishments in the entertainment capital of the world. At almost every hour of the day and night, visitors (and even local residents) can be seen "reading the stars" along Hollywood Boulevard.

It all began in 1955 when the Hollywood Chamber of Commerce implemented a suggestion of Harry Sugarman for preserving the memory of the multi–talented people who created and sustained the entertainment industry. The idea was to implant star landmarks in the sidewalks of Hollywood, featuring the historic figures and contemporary personalities responsible for putting the area on the map.

The stars were to be made of coral terrazzo, with the celebrity's name and the outlines of the stars in bronze, inset in three foot square black terrazzo blocks. A logo would indicate motion pictures, television, recording, radio or live theatre.

No fewer than 2,518 stars were imbedded into the five acres of sidewalk. The first dedication ceremony was held in 1958. Within sixteen months, over 1500 luminaries had been indelibly immortalized with hundreds of stars left blank for future dedications.

The walk begins at the famous Chinese Theatre and continues eastward to Vine Street. It lines both sides of Hollywood Boulevard, from Gower to Sycamore and both sides of Vine Street from Yucca to Sunset.

There are guide books available with listings of stars—whom they honor, where they are located and why they were included. Most people prefer to simply wander along and recall from memory the names imbedded on the pavement.

Catholics are extremely well represented along the Walk of Fame. Probably everyone's all–time Catholic favorite is Helen Hayes, the "First Lady of the American Stage," who won her initial Academy Award in 1931. Perry Como's star is located in front of 6631 Hollywood Boulevard. His velvety baritone voice, with its charismatic style, won Emmy's in 1954, 1955, 1957 and 1959. He remains one of the world's most successful crooners.

Gretchen Belzer is likely best known to her fans as Loretta Young, whose first Oscar came in 1947 for her role in "The Farmer's Daughter." Loretta's close friend, Jane Wyatt, is also included in the Walk of Fame, as is her brother–in–law, Ricardo Montalban. Band leader–accordionist Lawrence Welk and his champagne music charmed millions of Americans who listened faithfully to his television programs in the 1950s, 1960s and 1970s.

There's even a princess in the stars. Grace Kelly, the elegant, graceful blond beauty from Philadelphia appeared in "The Country Girl" in 1954, for which she was voted an Oscar for the year's best actress. Kate Smith (1909–1986) is remembered for many things, the greatest of which was her rendition of "God Bless America," first sung in 1938 and repeated hundreds of times during World War II. The "Songbird of the South" also had her own daytime and evening television show.

On and on the list could go. Next time visitors come from out–of–town, why not treat them to a stroll down memory lane, the Hollywood Walk of Fame. And watch the Catholics go by!

WARNER HOT SPRINGS — A CURSE

The story of the Indian "curse" on the Warner ranch is ghostly. According to the account by Gardner Bradford, it is the "southland's 'Evangeline'—an epic of travail and exile. It is a greater tale than Ramona because it is true." It all came about when the Cupeños faced eviction from lands they had occupied for centuries. A few members of the tribe reportedly forsook Christianity and placed a curse upon those who would supplant them.

The actual removal of the Indians took place in 1903. Charles Lummis told about that event in *Out West* magazine for June of that year: "The first installment of the Warner's ranch Indians were successfully moved to their new home at Pala in the second week of May and were at once set to work preparing their houses and lands."

Lummis paid scant attention to the curse. "All the hysteric talk about bloodshed, armed resistance, dying in their old homes and that sort of thing, reiterated until some of the Indians themselves echoed those foolish phrases, came to nothing. The people from the Hot Springs were transported by wagon without the slightest resistance." Thus even the usually understanding Lummis ignored the curse. The actual removal had been initiated and engineered by J. Downey Harvey, who went to court and eventually won a decision on patents issued by the United States government.

While the justice of the Indian claim to their land was generally conceded, a court decision upheld the claim of Harvey and others. It was clear that the Cupeños either had to fight or leave. They left, but not before leaving behind a "curse" on the land and its new inhabitants. It seems to have worked. Almost immediately, Harvey lost his wife. Financially, things went from bad to worse and Harvey died bankrupt. The new owner was nearly killed in an accident on the ranch. He was bitten by a gila monster in Arizona and finally perished in an electric car accident in Los Angeles. Another owner, a Mr. Gates, died suddenly during a hunting safari.

On and on the troubles went until the intervention of Colonel Ed Fletcher. He was genuinely sympathetic towards the Indians, allowing them to use the old bath house, to bury their dead in the ancient cemetery and to raise the funds for rebuilding their Church. Fletcher got permission from the new owner to let the Catholic Church hold services in the rebuilt quarters and shortly thereafter the Indians held their first *fiesta* in nearly thirty years at Warner's Hot Springs. It was during that *fiesta* that the Indians, to show their appreciation for Fletcher, held another ceremonial and removed the curse.

In later years, there were those who wondered if remnants of the curse remained. In an essay written for the Los Angeles *Times Sunday Magazine*, on January 26, 1936, a journalist noted that "populous cities have flourished on every spot selected by the *padres* except this one. At the Hot Springs, unexcelled by any in the land, time seems to be standing still."

Whether that situation was a curse or a blessing is open to discussion. In any event the story of the purported "curse" at Warner's Hot Springs is a favorite chapter in the folklore of the west.

WATTS TOWERS ON HERALDRY

Erected between 1921 and 1954, the Watts Towers were once described by Jack Smith as "the most remarkable work of open–air art in Southern California, perhaps the nation." The popular columnist went on to say that "Simon Rodia's towers are a wondrous poem, built in the sky by a man who was possessed by unquenchable urgings and fancies, as Columbus was possessed, and Mozart."

Rising like upside–down ice cream cones, the towers are located at 1765 East 107th Street, in that area of Los Angeles known as Watts. Today they attract thousands of tourists annually. The three distinctive towers are reminiscent of the work of Spain's Antonio Gaudi, whose churches, parks and apartments in Barcelona are decorated with colorful bits of tile.

Simon Rodia (1882–1965) built his towers from junk—broken tile, china, bottles, bits of wood and sea shells plastered on to a lacework of concrete reinforced by chicken wire. International attention was focused on the Watts Towers in 1959, when the Los Angeles City Building and Safety Department issued a report calling for their demolition as a safety hazard.

Art lovers vehemently responded and a campaign was mounted "to save" the towers. Stress tests were made to publicly demonstrate the stability of Rodia's whimsical construction.

Rodia was a tile setter by trade who early in life came to the United States from his native Italy. He once said that he built the towers "because there are nice people in this country." What better reason?

In 1959, the property on which the towers were located was sold to William Cartwright and Nicholas King. They formed a committee to repair, preserve and develop the Watts Towers as a public monument. Today the towers are owned by a non profit corporation. Nearby is the Watts Towers Community Art Center which holds classes in art, music and drama.

Father Joseph A. Francis, a priest attached to the Society of the Divine Word, came to Los Angeles in the early 1960s as the founding principal of Verbum Dei High School, an institution located only a few miles from the Watts Towers. When he was subsequently named Auxiliary Bishop of Newark, New Jersey, Francis decided to incorporate the Watts Towers into his episcopal coat–of–arms. This he did "because my presence in Watts was the most challenging and productive years of my life."

In an interview, the Louisiana–born prelate said that "those towers always facinated me. I've always found great inspiration from them every time I visit them." And so Simon Rodia's Watts Towers, an amateur artistic oddity that became a Los Angeles landmark, achieved an unusual (possibly even unique) recognition —portrayal on an episcopal shield.

One suspects that Simon Rodia would have been happy indeed that his "piece of folk art" had found its way into the heraldry books.

WELLS FARGO & COMPANY

The story of the Wells Fargo Express Company has aptly been described as one of the most thrilling and fascinating in the whole range of American history. On March 18, 1852, Henry Wells and William Fargo of New York, together with others closely connected with the earliest beginnings of the express business, formed a "joint stock association company."

By the following May 20th according to widely–distributed circulars, they were "ready to undertake the general forwarding agency and commission business; the purchase and sale of gold dust, bullion and specie, also packages, parcels, and freight of all descriptions in and between the City of New York and the City of San Francisco, and the principal cities and towns of California."

Though Wells Fargo hadn't planned on being mail carriers, the inefficiency of existing postal facilities caused miners and merchants to seek them out for that important service. When Wells Fargo established their office in San Francisco, there were many independent express companies already in business. Nonetheless, by the end of 1852, the industrious easterners had twelve branches in full operation.

Adopting as their creed "speed, safety and dependability," the shotgun messengers of Wells Fargo became a legend throughout the west. Rival concerns gradually closed down or were bought out by Wells Fargo. Due mainly to their capable management, Wells Fargo became the octopus of the express business in the west. The only real rival of any consequence in the mail service was the United States Government.

The little green Wells Fargo mailbox was as familiar as the red one used by the government. But that aspect of the Wells Fargo operation was forcibly changed in 1895, when a Federal statute was passed outlawing any but governmental handling of the mail. If, after forty years, the octopus had lost one of its tentacles, there were other areas in which the Wells Fargo Company continued to exercise their business acumen.

The freight and passenger business had thrived for some years. From the roadways between San Francisco–Marysville–Sacramento, the handsome Concord stages had expanded throughout most of the western states. In 1866, Wells Fargo became a transcontinental line. In 1905, the banking part of the Wells Fargo enter-

prise was merged with the Nevada Bank under the presidency of Isaiah W. Hellman, founder of the Union Trust Company. Today Wells Fargo continues to be one of the most prestigious names in banking.

Two historic safes, relics of the Wells Fargo era, painted with the familiar stagecoach logo, are still being used at San Buenaventura Mission as offering boxes for the poor. The presence of those two antiques of an earlier time testify to the place occupied by Wells Fargo in the building of the American West.

WOODBURY UNIVERSITY LIBRARY

King Louis XIV was once asked to enumerate his "favorite" rooms at Versailles. After mentioning the chapel, he said "my second most cherished room is the library, where I can read about all the mistakes made by my predecessors."

It isn't necessary to travel to Russia or Eastern Europe to find a library that formerly flourished as a church or chapel. There's one in Burbank on the campus of Woodbury University.

The story began early in this century, when Mother Frances Cabrini came to Southern California and opened a hospital for tubercular children, a kindergarten on Hill Street for working mothers and an orphanage known as Villa Cabrini Academy. The Villa was located on a parcel of land abounding in vineyards, at the foot of the Verdugo Hills, in the City of Burbank. The Villa evolved into a resident school for girls in 1938 and, five years later, a day school. Mother Cabrini's Missionary Sisters of the Sacred Heart worked there for over a half century.

In 1950, as part of the celebrations for the centennial of Mother Cabrini, a lovely chapel was built at Villa Cabrini. It was dedicated under the invocation of Mother Frances Cabrini on March 21 1950

The late Timothy Cardinal Manning told this writer that one of his "most unpleasant memories" involved the withdrawal of the Cabrini Sisters from Los Angeles. Without any prior hint, the community's provincial arrived one day from New Orleans for an interview with the cardinal. A few moments into the meeting, "she didn't ask, but told me that the Sisters were leaving the archdiocese. She handed me a relic of Mother Cabrini and abruptly left the office."

Appearing unmoved by the long and "precious association" with Los Angeles, the Sisters unceremoniously closed the door which Mother Cabrini herself had opened so many years earlier. It was, in the cardinal's words, "a very sad day for the Church in Southern California. "

Shortly after the Sisters closed Villa Cabrini, the

property was purchased by the Lutheran Church. Later it was acquired by Woodbury University, an educational institution established in 1884.

The twenty–two acre campus now housing the university is located behind huge wrought–iron double gates at 7500 Glenoaks Boulevard. Woodbury is an independent, non–profit, coeducational school of higher education specializing in business, architecture, internal design, graphic arts and marketing.

In 1987, as part of Woodbury's adaptation of Villa Cabrini, the chapel was converted into the Los Angeles Times Library. It presently houses 150,000 items and offers a diverse range of resources, including books, periodicals, annual reports, newspapers, trade journals, audio and video cassettes, compact discs, slides and other related materials.

Visitors to Woodbury University are invariably drawn to the attractive and functional library. The cross has been removed from the tower, but the building still looks very much like the chapel it once was.

YOUNG LADIES' INSTITUTE

The Young Ladies' Institute was founded at San Francisco by Annie Sweeney, Mary Richardson and Emily Coogan "as an organization of Catholic women with its first program a work of Christian charity." After discussing their plans with Archbishop Patrick W. Riordan and securing his approval, the ladies formulated a set of directives for their fraternal and benevolent organization. A constitution and by–laws were drawn up and on September 5, 1887, the Young Ladies' Institute was officially established with an initial roll call of 105 members.

Designed to encompass the age group between eighteen and forty, the San Francisco–based organization adopted as the core and center of the order and its members the motto, "May Christ Triumph." Though many helpful members contributed to the Y.L.I.'s success in the pioneering years, the name of Josephine Theresa Molloy stands out as the chief architect of the society in the early decades. As Grand Secretary for almost half a century, she took as her special field of endeavor in life the furtherance of the mental, moral and social life of Catholic women through the medium of the Young Ladies' Institute.

In the early years, the Institute adhered closely to its original social and benevolent blueprint, concentrating especially on the young women who were coming to the city as strangers. Gradually, however, the organization was drawn into other activities and before long had spread into numerous fields. Seminary burses and scholarships were founded, orphanages endowed, and any

number of charitable works undertaken for the Church's many relief programs. Members could be found "endeavoring to aid the sick and afflicted in hospitals, homes for the aged, veterans institutions, homes, and schools for underprivileged children."

Y.L.I. influence stretched in all directions, including the states of Washington, Oregon and Nevada. Even far–away Hawaii felt the friendly concern of the Institute. As introduced into California's southland at the turn of the century, the Y.L.I. took as its object the encouraging of "all young ladies of the Roman Catholic faith to become members, to promote the uniform administration of the privileges, honors and benefits of the Order; to provide for and comfort the sick and distressed members; also to improve the moral, mental and social conditions of the members." In the Bay area, Institute members supported the activities of Father Peter C. Yorke through their affiliation with the Women's Liberal League. This assistance was especially useful in the campaign against the American Protective Association.

During both the First and Second World Wars, members of the Y.L.I. volunteered their services to the Red Cross, the U.S.O., and other such agencies. Considerable effort was also expended sewing and mending hospital garments and providing delicacies and luxuries for wounded servicemen. Much of the relief work begun during war–time was carried on in subsequent years. Throughout its eighty year existence, the Young Ladies Institute has gained a reputation for its cultural and social programs. It has more than fulfilled the noble objects envisioned by its founders.

YOUNG MEN'S INSTITUTE

One of the earliest and most successful Catholic action organizations ever established in the United States was founded in the Bay City on March 4, 1883, under the title of the Young Men's Institute. The six founders of the Y.M.I., described as "men of earnest purpose, keen judgment and discernment," reportedly held their first meeting under a gas lamp–post in front of Saint Joseph's Church on Howard Street, near Tenth Street in San Francisco.

The movement was warmly applauded by Archbishop Joseph Sadoc Alemany and his successor, Patrick W. Riordan. The latter 'lavished time and thought and attention to it as though he himself were one of the voting founders." In later years, the prelate expressed his desire to see a council of the order organized in every parish of the Archdiocese of San Francisco

Inauspicious as was its founding, the Y.M.I. quickly

attracted a large membership and the first lodge became the nucleus of a beneficial society that grew to national stature, the only one of its kind originating in the west. According to one source, membership was restricted "to practical Catholics of good moral character."

Councils were even established outside the country in Canada, the Hawaiian and Philippine Islands and Mexico. The Young Men's Institute was subsequently endorsed and given papal approval by both Leo XIII and Pius X. In addition to offsetting the attractions offered Catholics by fraternal societies, the Y.M.I. served the very useful purpose of defending the Church against the social and political discrimination which had grown out of the vast immigration of Irishmen during the famine of 1846–48. As outlined by its founders, the central aim of the organization, limited to young men between eighteen and forty–five, was "mutual aid and development, the moral, social and intellectual improvement of its members, the upbuilding of sentiments of devotion toward the Catholic Church, and loyalty to the state."

Though its greatest success was in and around San Francisco, the Y.M.I. was strong in California's southland where it was introduced by W. B. Ward. Grand President Thomas P. White explained the organization's function when he noted, "The state today has need for religious men; men who are loyal to principle and appreciate the responsibility of citizenship. The Young Men's Institute takes the young man on the very threshold of life and inculcates within him a love of country."

These sentiments were echoed by the Right Reverend Thomas J. Conaty, Bishop of Monterey–Los Angeles, who remarked "The Y.M.I. has a noble mission to foster among our Catholic men, and that is—loyalty to their church, to their country and to one another. The intelligent Catholic young man has clearly defined ideas of life and its duties, and has within his reach those sacramental graces by which the church helps him to do his duty to his God and to his fellow men. Practical Catholicity sanctifies his whole life, not only while he is performing his religious duties, but also in his secular affairs. The man who is faithful to his God cannot be faithless to his fellowman."

Though time and circumstances have altered and redirected the activities of the Young Men's Institute, its motto, *Pro Deo, Pro Patria* (for God, for Country) continues to express the basic concept of the Y.M.I. in our days, namely, "to help men become better citizens, better fathers, better sons, better Catholics, better Americans."

Index

Moraga, Fr. Joaquin: 623

Moragues, Fr. Antonio Perello: 650

Moran, Bishop William Joseph: 217, 306–307

More, Dr. Warren D.: 927

Moreau, Fr. Basil Anthony: 707

Morelos y Pavon, Jose Maria: 1109

Moreno y Castañeda, Bishop Ramon María de San José: 884, 889

Moreno, Bishop Manuel D.: 212–13

Moreno, Fr. José Matias: 531

Moreno, Fr. Juan: 804

Moreno, Fr. Matías: 640

Moretti, Msgr. August: 331

Morgan, Fr. Henry Noel: 586–87

Morrell, Benjamin: 183

Morris, Fr. Edward: 803

Morris, Fr. Thomas: 242

Morrison, Fr. Harry B.: 257

Morrissey, Fr. James P.: 806

Mother Mary of the Incarnation: 725–26

Mother Teresa: 725

Mott, Thomas D.: 449–50

Moulton, Louis: 40

Mount Saint Mary's College: 804

Mugartegui, Fr. Pablo Jose de: 143, 651, 652

Muldoon, Bishop Peter J.: 217, 307

Mullane, Fr. William J.: 497–98, 568, 955

Mullins, Fr. Michael J.: 587, 941

Mundelein, George Cardinal: 358, 685, 770

Munoz, Fr. Pedro: 623

Murguia, Fr. Joseph Antonio de: 44

Muro, Fr. Miguel: 37

Murphy, Annie McGeoghegan: 450

Murphy, Daniel: 451

Murphy, Fr. Daniel W. J.: 587–88, 994

Murphy, Fr. Leo: 783

Murphy, Martin: 451–52

Mut y Rose, Jose: 588–89

Narjot de Franceville, Ernest Etienne: 452–53

Narvaez, Jose Maria: 453

Nash, Fr. James: 785

Nash, John Henry: 453–56, picture: 454

Navarette, Bishop Juan: 641

Navarro, Alex: 456

Neal, Thomas Atwill: 456–57

Neri, Fr. Joseph M.: 746–47

Nerincks, Fr. Charles: 995

Neuerburg, Dr. Norman: 30, 50, 88, 111, 120, 152, 169, 907, 934, 1063

Neumann, Bishop John: 230–31

Neve, Felipe de: 457–58

Nevin, Fr. James: 1047–48

Newcomb, Rexford: 150–51

Newman, John Henry Cardinal: 518, 581

Neylan, John Francis: 458

Nicholson, Bishop Lee: 599

Nixon, Richard M.: 458–59, 495, 875

Nobili, Fr. John: 44, 743, 803, 921, 1097

Noce, Angelo: 459

Noe, José: 34

Noonan, Fr. Hugh: 621

Norman, Jose: 459–60

North, Msgr. William: 581

Norton, Bishop John: 321

Norton, Joshua Abraham: 460–61

Nuestra Señora de San Juan de Lagos: 794–95

Nugent, Fr. John F.: 583

O'Boyle, Patrick Cardinal: 307–309

O'Brien, Fr. Cornelius: 863

O'Brien, Fr. Eric: 113, 668

O'Brien, Kenneth: 215

O'Connell, Bishop Denis J.: 212, 272, 309–10, 317

O'Connell, Bishop Eugene: 211, 238, 275, 277–78, 287, 297, 309, 310, 312, 413, 552, 559, 565, 595–96, 604, 749, 801, 844, 1003, 1038, 1048, picture: 311

O'Connell, Bishop William: 293

O'Connell, Fr. Joseph: 580, 592

O'Connor, Bishop John J.: 393

O'Connor, Fr. William: 589

O'Connor, John Cardinal: 534

O'Connor, Michael J.: 534

O'Connor, Myles P.: 461

O'Dea, Fr. Augustine: 74, 83, 148, 738

O'Donnell, Fr. Andrew: 842

O'Donnell, Fr. John: 783

O'Donnell, Fr. Terence: 929

O'Dowd, Fr. James T.: 217, 312–13, 827

O'Driscoll, Sister Mary Polycarp: 813

O'Dwyer, Msgr. Thomas J.: 241, 589–90

O'Farrell, Jaspar: 462

O'Flaherty, Msgr. Hugh: 590–91

O'Gorman, James A.: 534

O'Growney, Fr. Eugene: 591–92

O'Halloran, Fr. Michael: 592

O'Hara, Archbishop Edwin V.: 406, 513, 955

O'Hara, Cardinal John F.: 261

O'Hara, Fr. John: 765

O'Kane, Fr. Patrick: 276, 592–93

O'Kane, Fr. Thomas N.: 38

O'Keefe, Fr. Jeremiah Joseph: 92, 390, 747–48

O'Kelly, Fr. James J.: 593

O'Leary, Msgr. Lawrence: 827

O'Mahony, Fr. James: 532

O'Malley, Fr. Martin J.: 748

O'Malley, Thomas J.: 534